VOLUME

26

Master Fact-Index

Compton's Encyclopedia

and Fact-Index

1988 EDITION COMPTON'S ENCYCLOPEDIA

COPYRIGHT © 1988 by COMPTON'S LEARNING COMPANY
DIVISION OF ENCYCLOPAEDIA BRITANNICA, INC.

All rights reserved for all countries.
No part of this work may be reproduced or utilized in any form or by any means, electronic or mechanical, including photocopying, recording, or by any information storage and retrieval system, without permission in writing from the publisher.

COPYRIGHT © 1922, 1923, 1924, 1925, 1926, 1927, 1928, 1929, 1930, 1931, 1932, 1933, 1934, 1935, 1936, 1937, 1938, 1939, 1940, 1941, 1942, 1943, 1944, 1945, 1946, 1947, 1948, 1949, 1950, 1951, 1952, 1953, 1954, 1955, 1956, 1957, 1958, 1959, 1960, 1961, 1962, 1963, 1964, 1965, 1966, 1967, 1968, 1969, 1970, 1971, 1972, 1973, 1974, 1975, 1976, 1977, 1978, 1979, 1980, 1981, 1982, 1983, 1984, 1985, 1986, 1987, 1988
BY COMPTON'S LEARNING COMPANY, DIVISION OF ENCYCLOPAEDIA BRITANNICA, INC.

Library of Congress Catalog Card Number: 86-72756
International Standard Book Number: 0-85229-474-3
Printed in U.S.A.

THE UNIVERSITY OF CHICAGO
COMPTON'S ENCYCLOPEDIA IS PUBLISHED WITH THE EDITORIAL ADVICE
OF THE FACULTIES OF THE UNIVERSITY OF CHICAGO

"Let knowledge grow from more to more and thus be human life enriched"

EDITOR'S PREFACE

The Master Fact-Index volume contains, complete, the Fact-Index of Compton's Encyclopedia. It is a compilation of the 25 Fact-Index units from the other volumes of the encyclopedia. This inclusive index and the sectional index in all the other volumes thus offer two means of access to the main text.

This volume not only provides a supplementary source for reference and research but also serves as a mini-encyclopedia, with more than 30,000 short articles in all subject areas. It is packed with information and will appeal to the browser as well as the researcher.

Always start your search for information in the Fact-Index. Instructions for using the index are given on the following pages.

HOW TO USE THE FACT-INDEX

Always start your search for information in the Fact-Index. It locates specific facts, illustrations, maps, and study aids by the exact volume and page. In addition, the Fact-Index contains thousands of short articles that are also quick, simplified sources of facts. The many features of the Fact-Index are explained in this two-page section.

(1) At the head of each page of the Fact-Index are the guide words. The one on the left is the title of the first main entry to start on that page, and the one on the right is the title of the last main entry to start on that page. The guide words and the alphabetical arrangement of all main entries in the Fact-Index make it easy to find the entry you are looking for.

(2) The main entries in the Fact-Index all start with a **boldface title**. These titles form an alphabetical list of all the people, places, and things you may be looking for in your search for information. There are the following three types of main entries in the Fact-Index:

(2a) **Atheism** is a fact entry, a short encyclopedia article that is written in a compact, fact-filled style. It has one subentry, a reference into the main text of the encyclopedia. Other fact entries may have several such references or none at all.

(2b) **Astrolabe** is a text reference with a main entry and no subentries. **Astrology** is a text reference with a main entry plus two subentries. Text references lead you to all of the facts, illustrations, and study aids in the main text of Compton's that provide information on the topics you are looking up.

(2c) **Astoreth** is a cross-reference to another main entry **(Astarte)** that has the information you want.

(3) **Astronomy** is a text reference with a main entry and many subentries. There are almost 50 alphabetically arranged subentries, each of which is indented one space. Some of these *first-level* subentries are important enough to be divided into alphabetically arranged *second-level* subentries, each of which is indented another space.

Together these subentries provide a complete guide to all of the information in Compton's Encyclopedia that relates to the subject of astronomy. As you can see by the examples under the astronomy text reference, there are many articles that are important to this subject. Cross-references direct you to further information on some of these articles.

Note also that the many text references in this entry not only lead you to the exact volume and page on which the information is found but also specify whether that information is in the form of a chart, diagram, Fact Summary, graph, list, map, picture, or table. Each reference to a nontext form of information is identified in *italic type* to make it stand out. There are also cross-references to related main entries in the Fact-Index. These are given right after the page number on which the main article **Astronomy** begins.

Some of the main entries are accompanied by data-packed tables. For example, the main entry **Astrology** includes a cross-reference to the **Zodiac** table in the Fact-Index.

INDEX

The letter A

probably started as a picture sign of an oxhead, as in Egyptian hieroglyphic writing (1) and in a very early Semitic writing used about 1500 B.C. on the Sinai Peninsula (2). About 1000 B.C., in Byblos and other Phoenician and Canaanite centers, the sign was given a linear form (3), the source of all later forms. In the Semitic languages this sign was called *aleph,* meaning ''ox.''

The Greeks had no use for the *aleph* sound, the glottal stop, so they used the sign for the vowel ''a.'' They also changed its name to *alpha.* They used several forms of the sign, including the ancestor of the English capital A (4). The Romans took this sign over into Latin, and it is the source of the English form. The English small ''a'' first took shape in Greek handwriting in a form (5) similar to the present English capital letter. In about the 4th century A.D. this was given a circular shape with a projection (6). This shape was the parent of both the English handwritten character (7) and the printed small ''a'' (8).

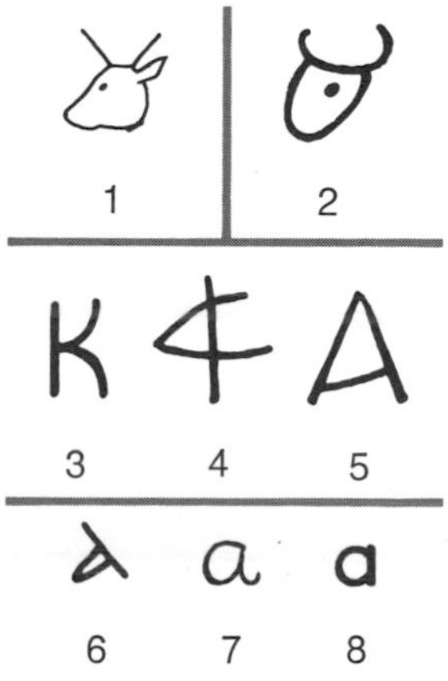

A

A-1, artificial satellite, *table* S-344

'A II', work by Moholy-Nagy M-518

A. & P. Company. *see in index* Great Atlantic and Pacific Tea Company, The

AA. *see in index* Alcoholics Anonymous

Aa, lava L-90

AAA. *see in index* Agricultural Adjustment Agency

AAC (Alaskan Air Command), U.S. Air Force A-164

Aachen (or Aix-la-Chapelle), West Germany, city near Belgian border; pop. 307,654 A-2
- Charlemagne C-274
- Germany, *maps* E-360, G-131
- World War II W-341

AAHPERD (American Alliance for Health, Physical Education, Recreation, and Dance), United States H-92

Aalborg, Denmark, chief port of n. Jutland; pop. 114,159, *map* E-360

Aalto, Alvar (1898–1976), Finnish architect A-2
- architecture A-568
- Finlandia Hall, *picture* F-91
- furniture F-462

AAP. *see in index* Association of American Publishers

Aardvark (or African ant bear, or ant bear, or earth pig), mammal *Orycteropusafer* of the family Orycteropodidae A-3, *picture* A-436

Aardwolf, hyena-like mammal A-3

Aare (or Aar), largest river (180 mi; 290 km) entirely within Switzerland B-174, *map* S-537

Aarhus, Denmark, seaport and 2nd largest city; pop. 181,518, *map* E-360
- Denmark D-97, *map* D-100

Aaron, first high priest of Israelites, brother of Moses; with Moses led Israelite exodus from Egypt
- breastpiece J-112

Aaron, Hank (Henry Louis Aaron) (born 1934), U.S. baseball outfielder, a right-handed hitter, born in Mobile, Ala.; with Milwaukee Braves 1954–65, Atlanta Braves 1966–74, and Milwaukee Brewers 1975–76; led in home runs in National League 1957, 1966, 1967, tied for lead 1963; on May 17, 1970, had 3,000th major-league hit (a single) and 570th home run; in April 1974 made 715th home run, breaking Babe Ruth's record B-95

AAU. *see in index* Amateur Athletic Union of the United States

AAVSO. *see in index* American Association of Variable Star Observers

ABA. *see in index* American Basketball Association

ABA (American Book Awards, formerly TABA), U.S. literary awards L-241

Abaca (or Manila hemp), natural fiber, *table* F-76
- Philippines P-256, 260
- rope R-291

Abacus, calculating device A-4
- arithmetic A-591

Abadan, Iran, city on island of same name in the Shatt-el-Arab; pop. 306,000 A-4
- Asia, *map* A-697
- Iran, *picture* I-307, *map* I-312

Abaft (or aft), direction aboard a boat, *diagram* B-326

ABAKO (Alliance des Ba-Kongo) Z-446

Abalone, shellfish, *picture* S-151

Abana. *see in index* Pharpar

Abbado, Claudio (born 1933), Italian conductor, *list* O-579

Abbai River. *see in index* Blue Nile River

'Abbas, al-, Islamic leader C-55

Abbas I the Great (1557–1628), ruler of Persia P-214

'Abbasid (750–1258), Islamic dynasty I-365
- caliphate C-55
- Middle East M-397

Abbe, Cleveland (1838–1916), U.S. meteorologist and astronomer, born in New York, N.Y. W-121

Abbe, Ernst (1840–1905), German physicist, born in Eisenach, Germany; partner with Carl Zeiss in the making of optical instruments Z-449

Abbeville, France, town on Somme, 12 mi (19 km) above English Channel; pop. 23,770, *map* F-369

Abbeville, La., town 65 mi (105 km) s.w. of Baton Rouge; pop. 12,391.

Abbevillian (or Chellean, or dawn man), prehistoric man M-84, *pictures* M-87, S-57c

Abbey, monastic house M-542

Abbey Theatre, on Abbey Street, Dublin, Ireland; center for Irish literary revival
- Irish literature I-327
- Yeats' contribution Y-412

Abbot, Anthony. *see in index* Oursler, Charles Fulton

'Abbot, The', historical novel by Scott S-74

Abbotsford, baronial home of Sir Walter Scott on Tweed River, Scotland S-73, *picture* S-74

Abbott, John (1821–93), Canadian jurist and statesman A-5

Abbreviation A-5

ABC. *see in index* American Bowling Congress

ABC. *see in index* American Broadcasting Company

ABC. *see in index* Audit Bureau of Circulation

'Abd ar-Rahman (fl. 750–788), Umayyad caliph of Spain C-55

Abdication, renunciation of an office, usually by a ruler. *see table* following

'Abd ol-Baha' (1844–1921), Baha'i leader B-19

Abdomen
- human body
  - muscles, *pictures* A-395
- insect I-217
  - mosquito M-596

'Abdor Rahman Khan (1880–1901), Afghan ruler
- Afghan Wars A-91
- history of Afghanistan A-91

'Abduction from the Seraglio, The', work by Mozart M-643
- opera O-565
- orchestra O-576

Abdülhamid II (1842–1918), sultan of Turkey; came to throne in 1876; deposed 1909 T-323
- Ottoman Empire O-618

Abdul-Jabbar, Kareem (born 1947), U.S. basketball player A-8

Abdullah (1882–1951), Jordanian leader J-142

Abdullah ibn-Hussein (1882–1951), king of Jordan 1946–51, born in Mecca, Saudi Arabia; 2nd son of Hussein ibn-Ali; assassinated July 1951, *list* A-704

Abe, Akira (born 1934), Japanese writer J-83

Abe, Kobo (born 1924), Japanese writer J-83

Abel, Niels Henrik (1802–29), Norwegian mathematician A-8
- mathematics M-216

Abel, Rudolf (1902–72), Soviet spy E-303

Abelard, Peter (1079–1142), French scholar and philosopher A-8
- educational contribution E-84
- Latin literature L-78
- philosophy P-265

Abelmosk (or musk mallow), plant H-149

Abelson, Philip Hauge (born 1913), U.S. physicist, born in Tacoma, Wash.; director of Geophysical Laboratory, Carnegie Institution of Washington, 1953–71, president 1971–78; with E. McMillan, discovered element neptunium 1940 P-394

Aberdare, Wales, urban district in s.e.; coal mining; refractories (firebrick), electric cable, television and radio sets, record players; pop. 38,210.

Aberdeen, Md., residential town 22 mi (35 km) n.e. of Overlea; Aberdeen Proving Grounds nearby; incorporated 1892; pop. 11,533, *map* M-182

Aberdeen, Scotland, city on e. coast; pop. 203,612 A-9, *maps* E-360, S-67

Aberdeen, S.D., city in n.e.; railroad center and wholesale distribution point; food processing, machinery; Northern State College; home of Fischer quintuplets; pop. 25,956, *maps* S-335, 323, N-350, U-40
- climate, *list* S-321

Aberdeen, Wash., port city on Grays Harbor, adjacent to Hoquiam and about 45 mi (70 km) w. of Olympia; lumber products; fishing; canneries; pop. 18,739, *map* U-40

Aberdeen, University of, Scotland A-9

Aberdeen Angus. *see in index* Angus

Aberdeen Proving Ground, Md.; U.S. reservation; for testing ordnance; pop. 7,403, *map* M-183

Aberdeenshire, county of n.e. Scotland; 1,971 sq mi (5,105 sq km); stock raising, agriculture, granite quarrying, fishing; pop. 321,783 A-9

Aberhart, William (1878–1943), Canadian political leader, born in Seaforth, Ont.; an organizer of Social Credit party in Alberta; premier of Alberta 1935–43 A-267

Aberration, in lenses
- chromatic and spherical S-371
- telescope T-66

Aberystwyth, Wales, municipal borough, resort on Cardigan Bay; seat of one of colleges of University of Wales and of National Library of Wales; pop. 10,420.

Abidjan, Ivory Coast, capital and port, on lagoon connected with Atlantic Ocean; pop. 685,800 A-9
- Africa, *maps* A-115, W-297
- Ivory Coast I-406, *picture* I-407

Abilene, Kan., city on Smoky Hill River about 85 mi (140 km) n. of Wichita; shipping point for farm produce; Old Abilene Town, restored village; pop. 6,572
- Eisenhower E-134

Abilene, Tex., city about 140 mi (225 km) s.w. of Fort Worth; trade and shipping center for farming and ranching region; petroleum products, packed meats, cottonseed products, clothing, candy, faucets, watches; Hardin-Simmons University, Abilene Christian University, McMurry College; military installations nearby; pop. 98,315, *maps* N-350, U-40

Abington, Mass., community 4 mi (6 km) n.e. of Brockton; settled 1668, incorporated 1713; pop. of township 12,334.

Abington, Pa., urban township n. of Philadelphia; chiefly residential; area turned over to William Penn 1683 by Tammany, Delaware chief; pop. 59,084, *map* P-185

Abiogenesis (or spontaneous generation), theory of evolution E-364

Abitibi, Lake, two lakes joined by narrows in Ontario and Quebec; total area 356 sq mi (922 sq km), most of it located in Ontario; source of Abitibi River, *maps* C-112, Q-9a

Abitibi River, river that flows 340 mi (550 km) n. from Lake Abitibi in e. Ontario to Moose River near James Bay; site of large hydroelectric power plant O-549, *map* C-112

Ablation, in aerospace, *table* A-70

Abnaki, North American people, *tables* I-136, 138
- Maine M-53
- mythology M-696
- New Hampshire N-177

Abnormal behavior M-301

Abnormal psychology P-522

Åbo, Finland. *see in index* Turku

Abolitionist movement, antislavery movement in United States A-9
- Allen A-308
- Brown B-465
- Civil War issue C-471
- Douglass D-234
- Dred Scott decision D-259
- Garrison G-36
- Greeley G-279
- Grimké sisters G-286
- Liberty and Free-Soil parties P-433, *table* P-495a
- Massachusetts M-196
- Phillips P-263
- Stevens S-445
- Sumner S-511
- Truth T-302
- Tubman T-303
- Whittier W-210
- Wilberforce W-202
- women's rights W-277
- Wright W-366

Abolition Society, in England A-10

Abominable snowman (or Yeti), legendary creature that is believed to inhabit the Himalayas
- apes and monkeys A-503
- Nepal N-116

Abominations, Tariff of A-37

Aborigines (or aboriginals), original, or earliest known, inhabitants of a country or area A-10. *see also in index* Pygmy
- Australia A-794, *pictures* A-795, 816
  - boomerang B-364
  - mythology M-697
  - Northwest Territory N-388
  - Western Australia W-153
- India
  - racial classification, *chart* R-26
- Malaysian Peninsula M-70

Abortion A-11
- adoption availability A-49
- bioethics B-214
- birth control B-284
- criminal law C-769
- spontaneous M-650
- United States Supreme Court decision U-196b
- women's rights W-273

Aboukir Bay (or Abukir Bay), on n. coast of Egypt, w. of Rosetta mouth of Nile; here Nelson destroyed French fleet (1798) N-154

Abraham, founder of Hebrew nation A-12

ABDICATIONS OF IMPORTANCE

(For biographical information, *see in index* names below)

Name	*Title*	*Country*	*Date*	*Cause*
Diocletian (245–313)	Emperor	Roman Empire	305	Wearied of rule
Romulus Augustulus (born 461?)	Emperor	Roman Empire	476	Revolt of German mercenary troops
Richard II (1367–1400)	King	England	1399	Insurrection
Charles V (1500–1558)	Emperor	Holy Roman Empire	1556	Wearied of rule
Mary Stuart (1542–87)	Queen	Scotland	1567	Insurrection
Christina (1626–89)	Queen	Sweden	1654	Distaste for rule
James II (1633–1701)	King	England	1688	Insurrection
Napoleon I (1769–1821)	Emperor	France	1814 1815	Defeat by foreign powers
Pedro II (1825–91)	Emperor	Brazil	1889	Revolution
Manuel II (1889–1932)	King	Portugal	1910	Revolution
Pu-yi (Hsuan T'ung) (1906–67)	Emperor	China	1912	Revolution
Nicholas II (1868–1918)	Czar	Russia	1917	Revolution
Ferdinand I (1861–1948)	Czar	Bulgaria	1918	Defeat in World War I
William II (1859–1941)	Emperor	Germany	1918	Revolution
Charles I (1887–1922)	Emperor	Austria-Hungary	1918	Revolution
Mohammed VI (1861–1926)	Sultan	Turkey	1922	Revolution
Edward VIII (1894–1972)	King	Great Britain	1936	Clash over marriage
Carol II (1893–1953)	King	Rumania	1940	Ousted by dictator
Victor Emmanuel III (1869–1947)	King	Italy	1946	Gave crown to son Humbert
Michael I (born 1921)	King	Rumania	1947	Communists dominated government
Wilhelmina (1880–1962)	Queen	Netherlands	1948	Gave crown to daughter Juliana
Leopold III (1901–83)	King	Belgium	1951	Gave crown to son Baudouin
Farouk I (1920–65)	King	Egypt	1952	Forced to abdicate
Charlotte (1896–1985)	Grand Duchess	Luxembourg	1964	Gave crown to son Jean
Juliana (born 1909)	Queen	Netherlands	1980	Gave crown to daughter Beatrix

ACE (Allied Command Europe), North Atlantic Treaty Organization N-352

Acesines River. *see in index* Chenab

Acetamide, organic compound, *diagram* O-603

Acetaminophen, drug A-387

Acetate, a salt of acetic acid; made by mixing acetic acid with a base; its many forms have a wide scope of industrial uses
  generic name F-103
  man-made fibers F-72
    rayon R-98

Acetic acid, an organic acid; gives vinegar its characteristic taste; important to industry in making of various acetates. *see also in index* Acetate
  organic chemistry O-604
  vinegar V-326
  white lead manufacture P-73

Acetobacter, genus of bacteria B-15

Acetone, an organic compound, $(CH_3)_2CO$, used as a solvent
  bacteria produce B-17
  gas G-38
  organic chemistry O-604, *diagram* O-603

Acetylcholine, substance in nervous system N-123

Acetylcholine esterase, enzyme, *table* E-290

Acetylene, unsaturated hydrocarbon used as illuminating gas
  cutting, *picture* S-9
  formula V-255
  neoprene P-228
  organic chemistry, *diagram* O-603
  synthetic rubber R-308
  welding, *picture* V-374

Acetylsalicylic acid. *see in index* Aspirin

Acevedo Díaz, Eduardo (1851–1924), Uruguayan novelist and political leader, born in Villa de la Union, present Montevideo; served as senator and minister to U.S., Argentina, Italy, and Brazil.

Achaea (ancient Greek Achaia), district on n. coast of Peloponnesus G-263

Achaemenian Dynasty (559–330 BC) I-308

'Acharnians, The', play by Aristophanes A-588

Achates, character in Virgil's 'Aeneid', Trojan hero noted for loyalty to Aeneas; hence phrase *fidus Achates,* "faithful Achates," for a faithful friend.

Achebe, Chinua (born 1930), Nigerian novelist A-18
  African literature A-123

Achene (or akene), a form of fruit F-219

Achernar, star S-414, *chart* S-417

Acheson, Edward Goodrich (1856–1931), U.S. inventor, born in Washington, Pa.; had little schooling and went to work when young; was assistant to Thomas Edison 1880–81; invented method of making artificial graphite S-195b

Acheulean industry, ancient toolmaking tradition; named for Saint-Acheul, France, where remains were found M-84

Achievement, heraldry H-135

Achievement test P-523
  educational use E-95

Achilles, Greek hero of Trojan War A-18
  Greek literature G-274
  Homeric legend H-221, *picture* H-222

Achilles tendon, tissue which connects the calf muscles to the heel bone T-80

Achinese, people of Sumatra I-160

Achmet I (or Ahmed I) (1590–1617), sultan of Turkey 1603–17; made peace with Austria in 1606, abolishing its payments to Turkey.

Achondroplastic dwarfism (or achondroplasia), genetic disorder D-294, G-48

Achroite, alkali of gem quality J-114

Acidophilus milk, dairy product, *list* D-6

Acid rain A-19
  aerosols A-66
  cities C-456
  Ontario O-553
  toxic waste W-75
  world W-301

Acid rock, type of music M-681

Acids, in chemistry A-19. *see also in index* Base; chief acids listed below
  acid rain A-19
  amino B-199
  electrochemistry E-170
  heat H-102
  normal and molar solutions S-256
  organic chemistry O-604, *diagram* O-603
  platinum P-384
  poisons P-410
  soapmaking S-229
  sulfuric S-510

ACLANT (Allied Command Atlantic), North Atlantic Treaty Organization N-352

A-class, type of model ship M-516

ACLU. *see in index* American Civil Liberties Union

Acne, a skin disease characterized by pimples, or papules; caused by inflammation of the sebaceous glands A-20
  adolescent occurrence A-47
  disease D-178

A.C. Nielsen Company, U.S. television ratings firm T-73

Aco (or Michel Accault) (fl. 1680–1702), French explorer, born in Poitiers; leader of party captured by Sioux near St. Anthony Falls, but freed by du Lhut; married daughter of chief of Kaskaskia Indians.

Acoma, pueblo 55 mi (90 km) s.w. of Albuquerque, N.M.; Acoma people belong to the Keresan language group of Pueblo Indians
  New Mexico N-214

Aconcagua, highest peak of Andes (22,834 ft; 6,959 m); also name of river and province in Chile
  Andes A-409
  Argentina A-575, *map* A-585
  comparative height. *see in index* Mountain, *table*
  South America, *diagram* S-295, *map* S-297

Aconitase, enzyme, *table* E-290

Aconite. *see in index* Monkshood

Aconitin, poisonous white crystalline alkaloid from aconite plants P-411

Acorn, oak O-452

Acorn worm, a wormlike marine animal of the genus *Balanoglossus*; possesses features of both invertebrates and vertebrates W-361

Acoustically navigated geophysical underwater survey (ANGUS), oceanic exploration O-463

Acoustic phonetics L-229

Acoustics A-21
  physics P-305

Acquired immune deficiency syndrome. *see in index* AIDS

Acquittal, in law, *table* L-92

Acre, Brazil, state situated in w. and bordered by nations Peru and Bolivia; 58,915 sq mi (152,589 sq km); cap. Rio Branco; pop. 306,893 B-307, *map* B-425

Acre (or Akko), Israel, port 10 mi (16 km) from Haifa across Bay of Acre; residence of Knights Hospitalers in 13th century; pop. 28,100
  Napoleon's defeat N-15

Acre, unit of land measure W-138, *table* W-140
  surveying S-520

Acrididae, an insect family consisting of true locusts, or short-horned grasshoppers; group includes both harmless nonmigratory insects and destructive swarming and migratory pests.

Acrilan, synthetic fiber P-228

Acrisius, in Greek mythology, king of Argos, grandfather of Perseus and father of Danae; story told by the Greek poet Simonides P-210

Acrocorinthus, citadel of Corinth, Greece G-264

Acromegaly, gigantism in some adults over 30 caused by excessive amounts of growth hormone D-294
  growth G-292
  hormones H-240

Acropolis, citadel of an ancient Greek city G-264, *picture* G-254
  Aegean civilization A-61, *picture* A-62
  Athens A-23, A-734

'Across the River and into the Trees', work by Hemingway N-409

Acrylic, fiber
  painting P-67h
    Lichtenstein, *picture* L-192
  plastics, *picture* P-381, *table* P-382
  synthetic fibers F-74, *table* F-72
  textile manufacture T-138

'Acta Diurna', in English 'Daily Events'; first newspaper dating from 59 BC in Rome N-235

ACTH. *see in index* Adrenocorticotropic hormone

Actia Nicopolis. *see in index* Nicopolis

Acting, dramatic art A-24
  director's role D-153
  mime M-422
  motion pictures M-607
  theater T-155

Actinide series, in chemistry
  periodic table, *table* P-207

Actinism, the property of radiant energy, particularly light, to produce chemical change
  photosynthesis. *see in index* Photosynthesis

Actinium (Ac), a radioactive chemical element, also a series of radioactive elements; from Greek *aktis* or *aktinos* meaning "ray"
  francium A-307
  periodic table, *table* P-207, *list* P-208
  radioactivity R-64

Actinometer, instrument used to measure light photons U-212

ACTION, U.S. agency A-28
  education E-105
  Peace Corps P-143

'Action Comics', comic books C-190

Action painting. *see in index* Abstract expressionism

Action potential (AP), in nervous system N-120, *diagram* N-122

Action verb, in grammar V-281, S-110

Actium, promontory and ancient town in n.w. Acarnania, in Greece; site of naval battle preceding Peloponnesian War 434 BC
  battle (31 BC), *list* W-14
  Antony A-496
  Augustus A-762

Activated carbon C-157

Activated-sludge method, sewage disposal S-119

Activation, chemical process
  charcoal C-272
  chemical analysis C-292

Active immunity, development of antibodies by one's own immune system D-168

Active transport, in biophysics B-237

Active voice, in grammar V-281

Act of Chapultepec (1945), Mexican history S-292

Act of Settlement (1701), in English history, an act that provided that the nearest Protestant descendant of the Stuarts should succeed to the English throne
  Church of England A-418
  Glorious Revolution G-169

Act of Supremacy (1534, 1559), English history C-782
  Henry VIII H-131

Act of Union
  Canada West and Canada East (1840) C-98, O-553
  Ireland and Great Britain (1801)
    Dublin D-282
    O'Connell O-490
  Scotland and England (1707) E-248, S-71
  South Africa (1909, effective 1910) S-267

Acton, Mass., 5 mi (8 km) w. of Concord; concrete, chemicals, motors; incorporated 1735; pop. of township 17,544.

Actor, performer in a dramatic work T-155
  ancient Greece A-87
  director D-153
  motion pictures M-607
  vocational opportunities V-365

Acts of the Apostles, 5th book of New Testament giving history of the Church from the ascension of Christ to the imprisonment of St. Paul in Rome; attributed to St. Luke B-183

Acts of Trade, British R-166

Actus, ancient Roman unit of measure, *table* W-141

Acuff, Roy (born 1903), U.S. country musician M-678

Acupuncture, Chinese surgical technique A-29
  anesthesia A-412
  folk medicine F-271
  holistic medicine H-203

Acute angle, in mathematics
  geometry G-73

Acute disease D-165

Acute-isosceles triangle, in mathematics G-74

Acute pulmonary edema, respiratory disease D-177

Acute triangle, in mathematics G-74

Ada, Okla., city 75 mi (120 km) s.e. of Oklahoma City; cement, glass, mobile homes, car components; oil fields; East Central State College; settled 1889, incorporated 1910; pop. 15,902, *map* U-41

Adagio, in music, term meaning slowly; in dancing, a slow duet by man and woman highlighting difficult maneuvers
  ballet B-35
  music, *list* M-670

Adam, James (1730–94), Scottish architect and furniture designer A-30

Adam, Robert (1728–92), Scottish architect and furniture designer A-30
  architecture A-568
  furniture F-460, *picture* F-457
  interior design contribution I-249, *pictures* I-243, 250

Adam, William (died 1748), Scottish architect A-30

Adam and Eve M-698, *picture* M-697
  Rodin's sculpture, *pictures* R-237

ADAMHA (Alcohol, Drug Abuse, and Mental Health Administration) H-90

Adams, Abigail Smith (1744–1818), wife of President John Adams A-32
  White House W-196

Adams, Alvin (1804–77), a U.S. pioneer expressman, born in Andover, Vt.; began route from Boston to New York 1840; carried huge volume of mail and parcels in Civil War E-382

Adams, Ansel (1902–84), U.S. photographer of the wilderness A-30

Adams, Charles Francis (1807–86) U.S. minister to Great Britain during Civil War A-38
  'Alabama' claims A-238

Adams, Charles Francis, Jr. (1835–1915), U.S. lawyer, historian, and railroad expert; born in Boston, Mass. A-38

Adams, Diana (born 1926), U.S. dancer B-37

Adams, Faye, U.S. gospel singer M-680

Adams, Henry (1838–1918), U.S. historian A-31
  Adams family A-38
  American literature A-353
  history writing H-173
  Saint-Gaudens memorial, *picture* S-17

Adams, Herbert Baxter (1850–1901), U.S. historian and educator; one of first to use seminar method in U.S. higher education; a founder of the American Historical Association H-173

Adams, John (1735–1826), 2nd president of the United States A-32
  Adams family A-38
  Alien and Sedition laws A-307
  constitutional law conflict C-686
  Declaration of Independence R-162
  Hall of Fame, *table* H-16
  Harrison H-49
  Jefferson J-93
  party split P-432
  Treaty of Paris R-174
  Virginia and Kentucky resolutions S-429d
  Washington W-42
  White House W-196
  XYZ affair X-406

Adams, John (assumed name of Alexander Smith) (1760?–1829), English seaman; one of the mutineers of the *Bounty* S-177c, P-15

Adams, John Couch (1819–92), English astronomer, born near Launceston, England; one of the discoverers of Neptune A-714, P-354

Adams, John Quincy (1767–1848), 6th president of the United States A-35
  Adams family A-38
  Clay C-487
  Hall of Fame, *table* H-16
  Monroe Doctrine M-549

Adams, John Quincy II (1833–94), U.S. lawyer; son of Charles Francis Adams A-38

Adams, Joseph Quincy (1881–1946), U.S. Shakespearean scholar, born in Greenville, S.C.; director Folger Shakespeare Library, Washington, D.C., after 1931 S-141

Adams, Louisa Johnson (1775–1852), wife of President John Quincy Adams A-35

Adams, Maude (stage name of Maude Kiskadden) (1872–1953), U.S. actress, born in Salt Lake City, Utah; on stage from childhood; especially noted for work in plays by Barrie, Rostand, and Shakespeare; first starred as Lady Babbie in Charles Frohman's production of 'The Little Minister' 1897; first appeared in 'Peter Pan' 1906; ceased acting 1918 except for appearances in 1931; professor of dramatics, Stephens College, Columbia, Mo., 1937–50, *picture* U-226

Adams, Samuel (1722–1803), American Revolutionary War patriot and statesman A-37
  Lexington and Concord battle L-144
  Statuary Hall, *table* S-437a

Adams, Thomas, U.S. inventor, noted for being a maker of chicle gum C-307

Adams, William Taylor. *see in index* Optic, Oliver

Adams, Mass., on Hoosic River near n.w. corner of state; lime quarries; paper mills, textile print works; birthplace of Susan B. Anthony; Mt. Greylock (3,491 ft; 1,064 m), highest point in state; incorporated 1776; pop. of township 10,381.

Adams, Mount, ancient volcanic peak of Cascade Range in s.w. Washington; 12,307 ft (3,751 m) high; located about 50 mi (80 km) s.e. of Mount Rainier W-48

Adam's apple, bulge of cartilage in front of neck; larger in men than in women V-377

Adams Express Company E-382

Adams-Onís Treaty (1819–21), *table* T-274
  Florida F-200
  Texas T-123

Adam's Peak, mountain in Sri Lanka; 7,679 ft (2,249 m); pilgrim resort of Buddhists, Hindus, Muslims; named for hollow on summit rock said to be footprint of Adam S-401

Adana, Turkey, city in s.e.; situated on old Roman road; once rival of Tarsus; has castle of Harun al-Rashid; pop. 574,515 T-320
  Asia, *map* A-697

Adapa, figure in Mesopotamian mythology B-7

Adaptation, in biology, fitness of organisms for their different lives; ability to change with environment A-39. *see also in index* Aestivation; Animal migration; Ecology; Hibernation; Protective coloration; Struggle for existence
  anthropology A-483
  humans M-86
  insects I-212
  living things L-267
  mammals M-80
  mimicry M-424
  prehistoric animals A-459

Adaptativ response, psychology S-488

Addams, Charles (Samuel) (born 1912), U.S. cartoonist, born in Westfield, N.J.; well known for his macabre style; contributor to *The New Yorker* since 1935

Addams, Jane (1860–1935), U.S. social reformer A-40
  Hall of Fame, *table* H-16
  women's rights W-277

Addax (or addas), an antelope of n. Africa and Arabian peninsula S-16

Adder, the common viper V-328

Adderley, Herbert (nickname Herb) (born 1939), U.S. football player, born in Philadelphia, Pa.; corner back; Green Bay Packers 1961–69, Dallas Cowboys 1970–72.

Adder's-tongue. *see in index* Dogtooth violet

Addiction, habitual or compulsive devotion to something H-2. *see also in index* Habit
  drug. *see in index* Drug abuse
  gambling G-9
  opium O-572

Addictive drug H-2

'Adding Machine, The', work by Rice A-356

Addis Ababa, Ethiopia, capital; pop. 1,277,159 A-40
  Africa, *map* A-115
  Ethiopia E-313, *picture* E-314
  world, *map* W-297

Addis Ababa, University College of, Addis Ababa; first university in Ethiopia; founded 1950; opened 1951, *picture* A-104

Addison, Joseph (1672–1719), English poet and essayist A-41
  literary contribution E-270
  Swift S-531

Addison, Ill., village 19 mi (31 km) w. of Chicago; foundries; industrial heating equipment; pop. 28,836, *map* I-52

Addison's disease, adrenal cortex deficiency H-242

Addition, in mathematics A-690
  fractions F-338
  numeration systems N-435

'Addition' ('Proslogium'), work by St. Anselm A-467

Additive color mixing, color process C-558

Additive inverse. *see in index* Negative numbers

Additives, chemical substances in foods F-274
  food processing F-281

Additive system, numeration N-435

Addo National Park, park in South Africa N-27

Address, forms of, in etiquette, *table* E-317

Adductors, muscles in a bivalve mollusk M-525

Adelaide, South Australia, capital and trade center; 7 mi (11 km) from sea on Torrens River; pop. 933,300 A-41
  Australia A-767, *map* A-819
  Pacific Ocean, *map* P-3
  world, *map* W-297

Adelard of Bath (fl. early 12th century), English scholastic philosopher
  translation of 'Elements' E-325

Adelboden, a picturesque valley and village in Switzerland, about 25 mi (40 km) from Lake of Thun; mineral springs; pop. 3,276.

Adélie penguin, bird P-162, *pictures* A-426, P-161

Adelphean, now **Alpha Delta Pi,** sorority F-389

Aden, People's Democratic Republic of Yemen, national capital in s.w., on Gulf of Aden; formerly in Aden Colony and Protectorate; pop. 343,000 A-42
  Asia, *map* A-697
  People's Democratic Republic of Yemen Y-413
  world, *map* W-297

Adenauer, Konrad (1876–1967), German political leader A-42
  Kennedy, *picture* K-202
  West Germany G-125

Adenine, a purine base that codes hereditary information in the genetic code in DNA and RNA G-56

Adenohypophysis. *see in index* Anterior pituitary lobe

Adenosine, in biochemistry P-273. *see also in index* Adenosine diphosphate; Adenosine triphosphate

Adenosine deaminase, enzyme, *table* E-290

Adenosine diphosphate (ADP), in biochemistry B-201
  metabolism M-306
  phosphorous P-273
  photosynthesis P-300

Adenosine triphosphate (ATP), in biochemistry B-200, *diagram* B-202
  biophysics B-238
  fatigue F-45
  metabolism M-306
  molecule M-522
  phosphorous P-273
  photosynthesis P-300

Ader, Clement F. (1841–1926), French aircraft designer; flew his airplanes secretly on grounds of Château d'Armainvillier, near Paris A-201

Adhesive A-43
  cement C-243
  gum G-318
  plastics P-381
  plywood P-397
  shoes S-181

Adige River, n. Italy, rises in Tyrolese Alps and empties into Gulf of Venice; about 230 mi (370 km) long; 170 mi (270 km) navigable; changed its course in AD 587 A-50, *map* I-404

Adirondack Forest Preserve, N.Y. A-44

Adirondack Mountains, in n.e. New York A-44
  New York N-245
  paleographic map, *map* E-25
  United States, *maps* U-36, 50

Adjective, a word, phrase, or clause that serves to modify, or make more exact, the meaning of a noun or pronoun; may be placed before the noun, after the noun, or after a linking verb; three degrees of comparison: the positive (tall), comparative (taller), and superlative (tallest)
  grammar G-209
  pronoun usage P-508

Adjustable-rate mortgage, home finance H-296

Adjustment disorders, a category of mental illnesses M-301

Adjutant General's Corps, U.S. Army
  insignia, *picture* U-10

Adjutant stork of Africa. *see in index* Marabou

Adjutant stork of India, large East Indian bird *Leptoptilus dubius* S-456

Adler, Alfred (1870–1937), Austrian psychologist A-45
  individual psychology P-519

Adler, Felix (died 1962), U.S. clown; wore white-face makeup (grotesque); noted for pantomime; performed until year he died C-437

Adler, Jacob P., Yiddish theater actor Y-419

Adler, Mortimer J. (born 1902), U.S. educator and author A-45
  Hutchins H-335

Adler Planetarium and Astronomical Museum, Chicago, Ill., in Grant Park; established 1930; given to city by Max Adler; noted for Zeiss optical projector and collection of astronomical instruments.

Ad libitum, in music, *list* M-670

Administration of Justice Act, in U.S. history C-692

Administrative law, in government A-46
  bureaucracy B-506

Administrator, in law, *table* L-92

Admiral, in U.S. Navy N-80. *see also in index* Fleet admiral
  insignia, *pictures* U-8

'Admiral Graf Spee', German armored cruiser
  Exeter, *picture* S-177
  World War II W-323

Admiralty Islands, group of small islands in Bismarck Archipelago; 800 sq mi (2,100 sq km); coconuts, pearls; pop. 15,765, *map* P-3

Adobe, sun-dried brick, or a clay for bricks A-46. *see also in index* Pueblo
  American Indians I-128, *pictures* A-600, I-113
  brick B-436
  San Antonio, *picture* S-35
  shelter S-159
  oven, *picture* S-338

Adolescence, transition period from childhood to adult life A-47
  acne A-20
  adopted children A-50
  anorexia nervosa A-467
  bibliography P-525
  bone injury B-342
  child abuse C-319
  juvenile delinquency J-162
  magazines and journals M-34
  Philippines P-254
  play P-385
  psychology P-522
  reproduction R-151c
  sexuality S-125
  26th Amendment U-154
  venereal disease V-274
  voice changes V-377
  youth organizations. *see in index* Youth organizations

'Adonais', elegy by Shelley on death of Keats S-154

Adonis, figure in Greek and Phoenician mythology A-49

Adonis, asteroid A-716

Adoption A-49
  family law F-21

'Adoration of the Magi', work by Memling M-294

'Adoration of the Shepherds, The', panel painting by Giorgione, *picture* G-146

Adoula, Cyrille (1921–78), Congolese public official, born in Léopoldville; premier of Democratic Republic of the Congo (now Zaire) 1961–64.

ADP. *see in index* Adenosine diphosphate

Adrenal cortex, adrenal gland that produces steroid hormones H-242, *table* H-241

Adrenal glands (or suprarenal glands), in anatomy G-153
  anatomy A-392
  hormones H-242, *table* H-241, *diagram* H-240

Adrenaline (or epinephrine), hormone H-243, *table* H-241
  stress S-488

Adrenal medulla, adrenal gland that produces two phenolic hormones H-243, *table* H-241

Adrenocorticotropic hormone (or ACTH), hormone that stimulates the production of steroids H-240, *table* H-241
  gland G-158

Adria, ancient town, Italy A-50, *map* I-401

Adrian IV (original name Nicholas Breakspear) (1100?–1159), only English pope; elected 1154; quarreled with Emperor Frederick Barbarossa, initiating long contest between papacy and house of Hohenstaufen P-445, *table* P-99

Adrian VI (1459–1523), pope 1522–23; born in Utrecht, The Netherlands; became pope through influence of his ex-pupil Emperor Charles V, *table* P-99
  Utrecht U-236

Adrian, Edgar Douglas (1889–1977), English physiologist, born in London; with Sir Charles Scott Sherrington discovered function of neuron; at Cambridge University after 1937, professor of physiology 1937–51, Master of Trinity College 1951–65. *see also in index* Nobel Prizewinners, *table*

Adrian, Gilbert (1903–59), U.S. dress designer, created glamorous images for movie stars D-271

Adrian, Mich., city on Raisin River 30 mi (50 km) n.w. of Toledo, Ohio; aluminum products, automobile parts and chrome plating, cable controls and linkage, laboratory and hospital furniture, concrete and metal products; Siena Heights College and Adrian College; pop. 21,186.

Adrianople (Turkish Edirne), Turkey, historic city on Maritsa River, 135 mi (220 km) n.w. of Istanbul; grapes, wine, silk, cotton; leather products; named Adrianople for Roman Emperor Hadrian; battle of Adrianople (378), in which Visigoths defeated Roman Emperor Valens, marked beginning of Rome's decline; city fell to Turks 1361 and for nearly a century was their capital, awarded to Greece 1920; regained by Turkey 1923; pop. 39,410, *map* E-360
  Ottoman Empire O-616
  treaty (1829), *table* T-274
  warfare, *list* W-14

Adriatic Sea, an arm of the Mediterranean, e. of Italy A-50. *see also in index* Ocean, *table*
  Europe, *maps* E-360, I-404
  Mediterranean Sea M-286

Adua. *see in index* Adwa

Adult Children of Alcoholics, support group for family members of alcoholics A-276

Adult education A-50
  population P-449
  United States U-113

Adult teeth, human. *see in index* Permanent teeth

Ad valorem duty, export tariff T-29

'Advancement of Learning, The', work by Bacon B-11

Advection fog F-246

Advent Christian Church, Adventist church organized in 1860 A-53

Adventists, various religious denominations believing in second coming of Christ A-53. *see also in index* Seventh-day Adventists

Adventitious cyst, type of cyst C-811

Ahaggar, mountain mass of Sahara S-15, A-94, *map* A-115
Ahasuerus, ancient king of Persia sometimes identified with Xerxes the Great; husband of Esther in Old Testament.
Aherne, James. *see in index* Herne, James A.
Ahimsa, doctrine of reverence for life
 Hinduism H-157
 Jainism J-14
  monks and monasticism M-541
Ahmad, Muhammad. *see in index* Mahdi, al-
Ahmadabad (or Ahmedabad), India, capital of Gujarat state; pop. 2,123,831 A-144
 Asia, *map* A-697
 India, *map* I-83
 world, *map* W-297
Ahmad Shah (1722?–1773), Afghan ruler A-91
Ahmad Shah I (reigned 1411–41), sultan of Gujarat A-144
Ahmed I, sultan of Turkey. *see in index* Achmet I
Ahmed III (1673–1736), sultan of the Ottoman Empire 1703–30, *picture* T-324
Ahmedabad, India. *see in index* Ahmadabad
Ahmed Bey Zogu. *see in index* Zog I
Ahnighito, meteor found in Cape York, Greenland M-315, *picture* M-314
'Ahram, Al', Egyptian newspaper E-120
Ahriman, the principle of evil in Zoroastrianism Z-471
 angels and demons A-414
Ahuacatl, fruit A-889
Ahura Mazda (or Ormazd, or Ormuzd), spirit of good in Zoroastrianism Z-471
 angels and demons A-414
Ahvaz, Iran, city in s.w., at head of navigation on Karun River; transshipping point; textiles; pop. 206,375, *map* A-697
Ahvenanmaa. *see in index* Aland Islands
'Ah, Wilderness!', work by O'Neill A-357
Ai, three-toed sloth S-218
AIA. *see in index* American Institute of Architects
AID. *see in index* Agency for International Development
'Aïda', opera by Verdi V-282
 arts, *picture* A-670
 opera O-567, *list* O-562
Aid Association for Lutherans F-387
Aide (formerly aide-de-camp), officer in confidential service of general; now also political rank
 insignia, *picture* U-10
AIDS (acquired immune deficiency syndrome), incurable disease caused by a virus that damages the human body's immune system; believed to be transmitted through sexual contacts, blood transfusions, or contaminated needles used for intravenous drug injections; often fatal; high percentage of victims are homosexuals or drug abusers
 disease, *table* D-171
 hospice care H-278
 immune system I-57
 sexuality S-126
'Aids to Reflection', book by Coleridge C-546
Aid to Families with Dependent Children (AFDC), United States U-164
Aiea, Hawaii, town on island of Oahu; pop. 32,879 H-70
Aigrette, a type of headdress H-141
Aigun, Treaty of (1858) A-382
Aiken, S.C., city 20 mi (30 km) n.e. of Augusta, Ga.; tourist and retirement center; textiles, fiberglass, lumber; kaolin mines, granite quarries; Savannah River plant of U.S. Department of Energy; site of Civil War battle 1865; pop. 13,436 S-316d, *map* S-318
Aikido, Japanese martial art J-57
Ailanthus, genus of trees belonging to the quassia family; one species *Ailanthus altissima* is called tree of heaven, or Chinese sumac; native to China, now common in e. North America
 seed dispersal S-106
Ailerons, airplane part A-189, *picture* A-190
Ailey, Alvin (born 1931), U.S. modern dancer and choreographer, born in Rogers, Tex.; founded own dance company 1958 D-24, *picture* D-27
AIM. *see in index* American Indian Movement
'Aims of Education, The', work by Whitehead W-195
Aintab, Turkey. *see in index* Gaziantep
Ainu, aboriginal people in n. islands of Japan A-11
 language distinction L-42
Air A-145
 airplane interaction A-179
  mechanics M-264
 ancient element A-273, U-198, P-304
 components
  nitrogen N-319
  oxygen O-622
 heating and ventilating H-107, 111
 humidity. *see in index* Humidity
 insulation material I-231
 internal combustion engine I-252
 ionized R-36, R-51
 jet propulsion J-106
 lungs L-336
 meteorology M-315
  fog F-246
  rain R-88
  snow S-227, *picture* S-228
  temperature I-6
  weather W-117
  wind W-220
 mountain M-633
 pollution P-441b, S-220, *picture* P-441. *see also in index* Smog
 pressure. *see also in index* Pressure, *subhead* atmospheric
  plumbing P-393
  pneumatic appliances. *see in index* Pneumatic appliances
  pump, *diagram* P-533
 sound waves S-258, *diagrams* S-259, *graph* S-260
 vacuum appliances V-254
 water cycle W-89
 wind tunnel W-234
Air age mapping
 Cassini's polar projection, *picture* R-127
Air bladder (or swim bladder), fish anatomy F-126
 sturgeon S-495a
Airborne troops (or paratroops) A-159, P-109
 Vietnam War, *picture* V-323
 World War II, *picture* P-325
Air brake B-405
 invention I-274, *table* I-273
 railroad R-79
 Westinghouse W-162
Air-breathing engine, jet propulsion J-106
Airbrush, in art P-399
Air Commerce Act (1926), United States A-215, A-880
Air conditioning A-149
 fan F-23
 heating and ventilating H-108
 home appliances H-212
Aircraft. *see also in index* Airplane; Airship; Balloon; Glider; Helicopter; Jet propulsion, *subhead* airplane; Sailplane
 aerial sports A-64
 armor A-631
 electronics E-180
 explosives E-381
 fire hazards and fire fighting F-105
 guided missile G-307
 machine gun M-13
 navy N-84, 87
 Tsiolkovsky's contributions T-303
 turbine T-316
 weapons history W-113
 wind tunnel W-234
Aircraft carrier, naval ship N-83, *picture* N-90
 air force history A-156
 John F. Kennedy, *picture* V-332
 United Kingdom, *picture* H-34
 United States, *picture* R-187
Air Defense Artillery, U.S. Army A-646
Airdrome, an airport, or flying field. *see in index* Airport
Airedale terrier, dog, *picture* D-203
Air embolism, physiological problem occurring in underwater diving; lungs overexpand to the point that air bubbles enter the blood stream D-188
Air-entraining cement, type of cement C-243
Air express E-385
Aire River, England, in w. Yorkshire; connects Leeds with sea; Airedale terrier dog breed originated in Airedale, valley of this river.
Aire River, France, rises about 10 mi (16 km) w. of Saint-Mihiel and flows n. along Argonne Forest between the Meuse and Aisne rivers, emptying into the Aisne.
Airfoil A-65
Airfoil centrifugal fan F-23
Air Force A-153. *see also in index* Royal Air Force; Royal Canadian Air Force; United States Air Force; and other Air Forces by name
 models M-517
Air Force, Department of the, United States U-160, *picture* U-159, *list* U-156
Air Force Academy, United States, *see in index* United States Air Force Academy
Air Force Communications Command (AFCC) A-164
Air Force Logistics Command (AFLC) A-164
Air Force Reserves (AFRES). *see in index* Reserves
Air Force Systems Command (AFSC) A-164
Air gun (or spray gun), tool P-399
Airlift
 Berlin G-124, R-357
 lifesaving, *picture* P-429
 Vietnam conflict, *picture* V-322
Airline A-165
 aviation A-876
 first scheduled airline S-24
 flight crew V-371
 helicopter H-121
 Korean jetliner shooting I-264
 Latin America L-66
 monopoly M-544
 U.S.S.R. R-330c, *picture* R-330b
 West Germany G-118
Airline Deregulation Act (1978) A-168, A-880
Air lines, railroad R-75
Airmail P-460a, P-463b, *pictures* P-458, 460
 airlines A-167
 helicopter H-121
 transportation T-264
Airman, U.S. Air Force
 uniform and insignia U-5
Air mass, air that has acquired a fairly uniform temperature and humidity over a large area of the earth's surface W-118, *table* W-126
Aïr Mountains, Niger, group of mountains rising sharply from the Sahara; several exceed 6,000 ft (1,800 m); highest is Mt. Gréboun N-308
Air National Guard. *see in index* Reserves
Airplane A-173. *see also in index* Airline; Airmail; Airport; Aviation
 aerospace industry A-67, *picture* A-73
 brakes B-405
 glider G-165
 helicopter H-121
 history
  flying machine, *picture* R-287
  Langley L-30
  Smith S-218
  Wright brothers W-368
 space travel S-341a
 hydraulics H-340
 jet propulsion. *see in index* Jet propulsion, *subhead* airplane
 mechanic V-372
 models M-515
 nationality marks, *chart* A-881
 parachute P-109
 pilot. *see in index* Pilot
 production
  Seattle plant, *picture* W-59
  Wichita factory, *picture* K-176
 radar R-32, *picture* R-29, *diagram* R-30
 rocket airplane. *see in index* Rocket airplane
 signaling S-195a, *diagram* S-194
 tachometer T-3
 uses
  aerial sports A-63
  ambulance A-326
  exploration E-377
  farming A-137
  forest fire fighting F-108
  police work P-430b
  transportation T-253, *picture* T-263, *chart* T-260
 travel T-269
 warfare W-19
Airplane tow, method of launching gliders G-166, *diagram* G-167
Air plants. *see in index* Epiphyte
Airport, place for landing, taking off, and servicing of airplanes A-209. *see also in index* Air traffic control
 aviation A-878
 fire fighting F-105
 radar R-32, *diagrams* R-31
 moving sidewalk E-187
 transportation T-256
 X rays X-404
Air purifier, appliance H-212
Air Quality Act (1967) P-441f
Air right, property right to the space at a specified distance above the ground, especially when owned separately from the ground right.
Air sacks. *see in index* Alveoli
Airship B-38. *see in also index* Balloon
 armor plate use A-631
 military use A-154
 World War I W-308, *picture* W-306
Airspeed, aviation A-70
 airplane indicator A-194
Air traffic control
 airline A-168
 automation A-839, *picture* A-840
 radar R-32, *diagrams* R-31
Air Training Command (ATC), U.S. Air Force A-164
Airway, designated air route between airports, particularly one equipped with navigational aids A-70
 transpacific P-16
Aisne River, n. France 175 mi (280 km), *map* F-372
 World War I W-310
Aitken, Robert Ingersoll (1878–1949), U.S. sculptor, born in San Francisco; monumental statues and portrait busts (McKinley monument in Golden Gate Park at San Francisco).
Aitken, William Maxwell. *see in index* Beaverbrook, William Maxwell Aitken, first Baron
Aix, France, historic city 18 mi (29 km) n. of Marseilles; former capital of Provence; hot springs; university (established 1409); pop. 74,948. *see also in index* Aquae Sextiae
Aix-la-Chapelle, French name of Aachen, West Germany. *see in index* Aachen
Aix-la-Chapelle, Treaties of (1668, 1748), *table* T-274
 Canada C-93
 Maria Theresa M-134
Aix-les-Bains (ancient Aquae Gratianae), France, famous resort in Savoy Alps; pop. 20,594, *map* F-369
Aiyar, Rajam (1872–98), Tamil author I-108
Ajaccio, Corsica, capital; seaport on w. coast; coral, sardines; birthplace of Napoleon; served as Allied naval base in World War I; pop. 38,776, *maps* E-360, F-369
Ajami, African poetry A-121
Ajanta, India, village in Maharashtra state; noted for fresco-decorated cave dwellings and halls, dating back to 200 BC; pop. 2,200 I-71, *map* I-83
Ajax, the name of two heroes of the Trojan War A-220
 wrestling W-366
Ajmer, former state in n.w. India; now part of Rajasthan state; area 3,283 sq mi (8,504 sq km); settled in 11th century; to British 1818; made state 1950; merged with Rajasthan 1956; pop. 1,431,609, *maps* A-697, I-83
Akademgorodok, U.S.S.R. N-415
Akam, literary theme in Indian literature I-106
Akamagaseki, Japan. *see in index* Shimonoseki
Akbar (1542–1605), greatest of Mughal emperors of India A-220
 Bangladesh B-62
 Mughal Empire M-645
Akbar Shah, diamond, *picture* D-129
AKC. *see in index* American Kennel Club
Akee, African tree *Blighia sapida*, grown in tropical and semitropical regions; 25 to 40 ft (8 to 12 m) high; leathery leaves; fruit splits into 3 parts, has 3 seeds having fleshy aril at base; in some Caribbean areas, arils are a staple food; in Florida chiefly ornamental P-408

Akeley, Carl Ethan (1864–1926), U.S. explorer, taxidermist, inventor, and sculptor, born in Orleans County, N.Y.; revolutionized taxidermy by representing animals as they appear in native haunts; died in Belgian Congo, now Zaire ('In Brightest Africa')
  Field Museum F-78
  taxidermy T-41

Akene (or achene), a form of fruit F-219

Akershus, Oslo, Norway; fortress O-610

Akhetaton. *see in index* Amarna, El

Akhtal, al- (640?–710?), Islamic poet I-365

Akiba Ben Joseph (c. 50–136?), Palestinian father of rabbinic Judaism A-221

Akihito (born 1933), crown prince of Japan; married commoner Michiko Shoda 1959; son Naruhito Hironomiya (born 1960); visited U.S. 1960, *picture* J-35

Akimiski Island, District of Keewatin, N.W.T., largest island in James Bay; measures 60 mi (96 km) long and 25 mi (40 km) wide; area 898 sq mi (2,326 sq km), *map* C-109

Akita, Japan, city on n.w. Honshu at mouth of Omono River; petroleum products, woodenware, silk textiles; university; pop. 235,873, *maps* A-697, J-75

Akkad, Mesopotamia M-305
  city-state C-461

Akko, Israel. *see in index* Acre

Aklavik, N.W.T., village on left bank of Mackenzie River; trading post in agricultural and cattle raising region; pop. 721, *maps* C-109, N-350

Akosombo Dam, dam, Ghana, on Volta River A-106, *picture* A-109
  Ghana G-139

Akritas, Digenis (died 700?), Byzantine author G-279

Akron, Ohio, city 35 mi (55 km) s.e. of Cleveland; pop. 237,177 A-221
  Ohio O-501, 512
  tire manufacture R-303
  United States, *map* U-41

'Akron', U.S. Navy airship B-43, *picture* B-40

Akron, University of, Akron, Ohio; founded in 1913 A-221

Ak-Sar-Ben, Omaha, Neb., community organization O-543

Akureyri, Iceland, town in n. on Eyja Fjord; good harbor; second town in importance and size; incorporated in 1786; pop. 9,943 I-11, *picture* I-13, *map* E-360

Akutagawa, Ryunosuke (1892–1927), Japanese writer J-82

ALA. *see in index* American Library Association

Alabama, Southern rock band M-679

Alabama, state, U.S.; 51,609 sq mi (133,615 sq km); cap. Montgomery; pop. 3,890,061 A-222
  cities. *see also in index* cities listed below and other cities by name
    Birmingham B-222
    Mobile M-512
    Montgomery M-569
  history
    Civil War C-472
    Confederate States of America C-642
    King K-244
  petroleum P-230
  state symbols
    flag, *picture* F-159
    tree P-328
  Statuary Hall, *table* S-437a
  taxation, *tables* T-37, 39
  Tennessee Valley Authority T-100, *map* T-101
  United States U-56, *maps* N-350, U-41, 58

'Alabama', music by Coltrane C-587

'Alabama', ship. *see in index* 'Alabama' claims

Alabama, University of, university, near Tuscaloosa, and at Birmingham and Huntsville, Ala.; state control; opened 1831; at University: arts and sciences, commerce and business administration, education, engineering, home economics, law, and social work; at Birmingham: general studies, dentistry, medicine, nursing, and optometry; at Huntsville: humanities, engineering, natural science and mathematics, and social and behavioral science; graduate studies at all three locations A-226

Alabama Agricultural and Mechanical University, university in Normal, Ala.; state control; opened 1875; arts and sciences, agriculture, applied science, business, education, home economics; graduate studies A-227

'Alabama' claims, dispute over British built steam cruiser in U.S. Civil War A-238
  Civil War C-477
  Confederate States C-643
  Grant G-218
  Russell R-319
  Treaty of Washington (1871) W-71

Alabama River, river, Alabama, 312 mi (502 km) long; navigable to Montgomery; used for shipment of sand, gravel, logs, pulpwood, cotton, gasoline U-58, *map* N-350

Alabaster A-238

Aladdin, character in 'Arabian Nights' A-525

Alameda, Calif., city on island in San Francisco Bay, nearly touching Oakland; shipbuilding; shipping terminals; U.S. naval air station; pop. 70,968, *maps* U-40

Alameda County State College. *see in index* California State University, Hayward

Alamein. *see in index* El Alamein

Alamo, fortified Franciscan mission in San Antonio, Tex. A-238
  Crockett's defense C-779
  flag F-154, *picture* F-155
  San Antonio S-35
  Texas T-119, 124, *picture* T-115
  western W-151

Alamo Canal. *see in index* Imperial Canal

Alamogordo, N.M., town 90 mi (145 km) s.w. of Roswell; diversified industry; farming, ranching, lumbering; lumber processing; state school for blind; nearby are Holloman Air Force Base, White Sands National Monument, Indian reservation, Lincoln National Forest; pop. 23,035, *map* N-228
  nuclear energy N-422

Alan Alexander Milne. *see in index* Milne, A.A.

Aland Islands (Finnish Ahvenanmaa), archipelago off Finland at Gulf of Bothnia; area 1,481 sq mi (572 sq km); ceded to Russia by Sweden (1809); awarded by League of Nations to Finland (1921); pop. 20,981 S-524

Alani (also called Alans), in ancient times, a nomadic pastoral people that occupied the steppe region n.e. of the Black Sea
  Huns H-330
  migration M-402

Al-Anon, support group for family and friends of alcoholics A-276

Alaric (370?–410), king of Visigoths (West Goths), born on island in Danube; under Theodosius, commanded Gothic auxiliaries 394; was elected king of Visigoths 395
  Goths G-197
  Middle Ages M-384

Alarm, stage of stress S-488

Alaska, state, U.S.; 586,412 sq mi (1,518,791 sq km); cap. Juneau; pop. 400,481 A-239
  cities. *see also in index* cities listed below and other cities by name
    Anchorage A-402
    Fairbanks F-11
    Juneau J-152
  conservation P-441e
  history
    boundary dispute. *see in index* Alaska Boundary Dispute
    Eisenhower E-141
    exploration A-339, *map* P-417
    Johnson J-128
    statehood S-429a
  North America, *picture* N-336, *map* N-350
  people
    American Indians I-156
    Eskimo E-301
  petroleum P-230, *pictures* P-234, U-196b
  physical geography
    Aleutian Islands A-278
    Arctic regions A-571
    glaciers, *picture* I-6
    mountains. *see also in index* Alaska Range
      Mount McKinley M-21
      Rockies R-234, *map* R-234a
    tundra, *picture* R-217
    Yukon River Y-439
  state symbols
    bird G-292
    tree S-398
  Statuary Hall, *table* S-437a
  taxation, *tables* T-37, 39
  transportation
    Alaska Highway. *see in index* Alaska Highway
    pipelines, *picture* T-265
  United States U-34, *pictures* U-38, 93, 95, *maps* U-39, 94, 117, 119
  world, *map* W-297

Alaska, Gulf of, along s. coast of Alaska between Alaska Peninsula and Alexander Archipelago
  United States U-94, *map* U-39
  world, *map* W-297

Alaska, University of, near Fairbanks, Alaska; state control; incorporated 1917, opened 1922; arts and letters, behavioral sciences and education, biological sciences and renewable resources; earth sciences and mineral industry, economics and government; engineering, physical sciences; graduate study; senior college campuses including graduate studies at Anchorage and Juneau; community colleges at Anchorage, Auke Bay (Juneau-Douglas), Bethel, Kenai, Ketchikan, Kodiak, Palmer, Sitka A-245, *picture* A-249

Alaska boundary dispute A-256
  Roosevelt R-286

Alaska cedar, evergreen tree *Chamaecyparis nootkatensis* of pine family, sometimes called yellow cedar or yellow cypress; average height 80 ft (20 m); tapering trunk, conical crown; lives over 500 years; wood clear yellow; also known in lumber trade as cedar Sitka cypress, yellow cypress, Nootka cypress and Alaska cypress, *table* W-282

Alaska Claims Settlement Act (1971) I-156

Alaska Federation of Natives (AFN) I-156

Alaska Highway, (first called Alaska-Canada Highway, or Alcan Highway) A-256
  Alaska A-244
  British Columbia B-455
  roads R-217
  Yukon Territory Y-440

Alaskan Air Command (AAC), U.S. Air Force A-164

Alaska Native Claims Settlement Act (1971) A-245

Alaskan Boundary Arbitration treaty (1903), *table* T-274

Alaskan brown bear B-116, *picture* B-117

Alaskan malamute, dog, *picture* D-200

Alaska Peninsula, s.w. extension of Alaska
  North America, *map* N-350
  United States, *map* U-39, 94
  world, *map* W-297

Alaska Purchase Treaty (1867), *table* T-274

Alaska Range, part of the coast range system, s. of the Yukon drainage system, Alaska; includes Mt. McKinley A-256
  Mount McKinley M-21
  United States, *maps* U-39, 94

Alaska seal, mammal S-100

Alaska time T-189, *map* U-40

Alateen, support group for teenage children of alcoholics A-276

Alava Cape, n.w. Wash., s. of Cape Flattery; westernmost point of United States, not including Alaska and Hawaii, *map* U-117

Alba, duke of. *see in index* Alva, duke of

'Albacore', U.S. submarine, *picture* S-496

Alba Longa, Italy, city of ancient Latium, birthplace of Romulus and Remus; founded, according to tradition, by Ascanius, son of Aeneas R-241, R-258

Albania, country along e. coast of Adriatic Sea; 11,100 sq mi (28,700 sq km); cap. Tiranë; pop. 2,800,000 A-257
  Balkan states B-25
  Church of Albania E-42
  Communism C-620, *map* C-619
  Europe, *map* E-360
  flag, *picture* F-161
  founding B-31
  national anthem, *table* N-64
  railroad mileage, *table* R-85
  Tiranë T-192
  totalitarianism T-234
  Warsaw Pact W-34
  World War I W-321

Albanians, people
  Yugoslavia Y-435

Albany, Australia, small town on the southern coast of Western Australia; important seaport; woollen mills, meat and fish canneries; pop. 15,222 W-153

Albany (formerly Ocean View), Calif., residential city on San Francisco Bay, 4 mi (6 km) n. of Oakland; U.S. Department of Agriculture Western Regional Laboratory; incorporated 1908 as Ocean View, present name 1909; pop. 15,130.

Albany, Ga., city on Flint River in s.w.; textile industries, meat-packing, peanut and pecan processing, lumber, farm implements; Albany State College; military installations and Radium Springs resort nearby; pop. 74,059.

Albany (originally Beverwyk), N.Y., capital of state, on Hudson River; pop. 101,727 A-259
  New York N-251, *pictures* N-261
  United States, *maps* N-350, U-41

Albany, Ore., city about 22 mi (35 km) s. of Salem, on Willamette River; farming, logging; lumber and paper products, metals; meat, poultry; vegetable processing; pop. 26,678 O-592, *map* U-40

Albany, State University at, Albany, N.Y., part of State University of New York; chartered 1844; arts and sciences, business, education, library science; graduate study.

Albany Congress, convention of North American colonists (1754) A-259
  American Revolution R-162

Albany-New York Highway (or Albany Post Road) R-220

Albany Regency, group of Democratic "bosses" who controlled state of New York under Van Buren's leadership (1820–54) V-261

Albany River, river, Ontario, 610 mi (880 km) long; rises in w. lake region and flows e. 400 mi (640 km) into James Bay at Fort Albany, *maps* C-112, N-350

Albatross, seabird A-260
  animal migration A-450
  Pacific Ocean, *picture* P-14

Albay, Philippines. *see in index* Legaspi

Albedo, in astronomy S-52

Albee, Edward (born 1928), U.S. playwright A-200
  American literature A-363
  drama D-249
  Woolf W-292

Albemarle, N.C., city about 38 mi (61 km) n.e. of Charlotte; grain, poultry products, textiles, hosiery, knit goods, furniture, brick and tile; aluminum plant in vicinity; Morrow Mountain State Park nearby; pop. 11,126.

Albemarle Island. *see in index* Isabela Island

Albemarle Sound, shallow inlet 60 mi (100 km) long indenting coast of North Carolina; just e. of the sound in Kitty Hawk, N.C., near the scene of Wright brothers' first airplane flight N-354

Albéniz, Isaac (1860–1909), Spanish pianist and composer, born in Camprodon, near Olot, Spain; child prodigy, later became court pianist to king of Spain; called first Spanish impressionist; operas and piano works M-674

Albert I (1255–1308), Holy Roman emperor and king of Germany B-344

Albert II (1397–1439), Holy Roman emperor; was duke of Austria as Albert V; also crowned king of Hungary and Bohemia A-828

Albert I (1875–1934), king of Belgium A-260
  Belgium B-149

Albert (1819–61), prince of Saxe-Coburg-Gotha, prince consort of Queen Victoria of

England; fostered interest in the arts and sciences; died of typhoid fever V-309
  United Kingdom E-253

Albert, Lake (or Albert Nyanza), situated in Zaire and Uganda; area 2,064 sq mi (5,346 sq km); named for British prince consort Albert, *map* A-115
  Stanley S-411
  Ubangi River U-1

Alberta, province in w. Canada; 255,285 sq mi (661,183 sq km); cap. Edmonton; pop. 1,627,874 A-261
  Canada C-75, 80, 102, *map* C-109
  cities. *see also in index* cities listed below and other cities by name
    Calgary C-30
    Edmonton E-76
  government agencies G-202
  national parks N-28
  North America, *map* N-350
  physical geography
    Peace River P-145
    Rockies R-234, *map* R-234a
  Trans-Canada Highway T-248

Alberta, University of, situated at Edmonton, Alta.; provincial control; opened 1908; arts and sciences, agriculture, commerce, dental hygiene, dentistry, education, engineering, home economics, law, medicine, nursing, pharmacy, physical and occupational therapy, physical education; graduate studies A-266, E-76, *picture* A-267

Alberta Game Farm, Canada Z-465

Albert Honoré Charles, (1848–1922), prince of Monaco, ruler of the principality of Monaco and oceanographer; succeeded his father, Charles III 1889.

Alberti, Leon Battista (1404–72), Florentine architect A-271
  architecture A-552

Albertite, asphalt A-702

Albert Lea, Minn., city about 90 mi (150 km) s. of St. Paul and near Iowa border; meat, poultry and dairy products, heating and cooling appliances, milking and other dairy equipment, laminated wood products; beams and rafters, clothing; pop. 19,418, *map* M-456

Albert Nyanza. *see in index* Albert, Lake

Alberto Azzo II. *see in index* Este, House of

Alberton, P.E.I., town on Gulf of St. Lawrence 33 mi (53 km) n.w. of Summerside; monument nearby commemorates beginning of silver fox industry; pop. 1,020 P-497f, *map* P-497h

Albertus Magnus, Saint (1193?–1280), German scholar, scientist, and Doctor of the Church; born in Swabia, Germany; joined Dominican Order 1223; teacher of Thomas Aquinas; wrote philosophical and scientific works, notably treatises on plants and animals; canonized 1931 A-520

Albigenses, heretical sect prominent in south of France in 12th and 13th centuries, named from city of Albi; styled themselves *Cathari* (the pure) P-252
  Dominic D-224
  Innocent III I-208

Albino, in biology A-271
  elephant E-184
  rat R-94

Albion, Mich., city 16 mi (26 km) w. of Jackson; iron, steel, and glass products; foundries; Albion College; pop. 12,112.

Albite, mineral containing aluminum and sodium silicates M-436

Albret, Jeanne d'. *see in index* Jeanne d'Albret

Albright-Knox Art Gallery, Buffalo, N.Y.; established 1862; noted for 18th- and 19th-century French and U.S. paintings, also contemporary arts B-361
  Miró's 'Harlequin's Carnival' P-60, *picture* P-59

Albula Pass, Switzerland, high pass in Alps, chief route from North to Upper Engadine; traversed by railway.

Albumen (also called egg white), egg E-113, *picture* E-110

Albumin, protein A-272
  serum albumin S-113

Albuquerque, N.M., largest city of state, about 60 mi (100 km) s.w. of Santa Fe; pop. 331,767 A-272
  New Mexico N-216, 224, *picture* N-221, *map* N-228
  United States, *maps* N-350, U-40

Alcalá de Henares, Spain, old town near Madrid; birthplace of Cervantes; pop. 20,572.

Alcalá Zamora y Torres, Niceto (1877–1949), Spanish lawyer and statesman, born in Córdoba, Spain; upon overthrow of monarchy became head of provisional government; after adoption of constitution was first president (1931–36), later lived in exile S-360

Alcan Highway. *see in index* Alaska Highway

Alcántara, Spain, ancient town on Tagus; owes name (Arabic "bridge") to bridge built by Trajan; about 1215 became stronghold of knightly Order of Alcántara organized for defense against Moors; pop. 3,564, *map* S-350

Alcatraz, rocky island in San Francisco Bay, Calif; formerly military prison; federal maximum-security prison 1934–63, *map* S-41b
  American Indians, *picture* I-154

Alcázar, name given to ancient Spanish or Moorish palace-fortresses; means "the castle," from the Arabic word *Al-Qasr* and the Latin word *Alces*
  Segovia, *picture* S-360
  Seville S-118
  Toledo T-212

Alcedinidae, family of large-headed, slender-billed birds; member of order of Coraciiformes; belted kingfisher most common American species. *see also in index* Coraciiformes; Kingfisher

Alchemy A-273
  chemistry C-300
  gold G-180
  mercury M-304
  metal and metallurgy M-309
  phosphorus P-271

Alcibiades (450?–404 BC), Greek leader A-273
  Peloponnesian War G-266
  Socrates S-246

Alcindor, Lew. *see in index* Abdul-Jabbar, Kareem

Alcmaeonidae, powerful family of ancient Athens, claiming descent from Alcmaeon, great-grandson of Nestor
  Pericles P-205

Alcmene, mythological figure, mother of Hercules H-138

Alcock, Sir John William (1892–1919), English aviator, born in Manchester, England; as World War I pilot was captured by Turks after bombing Constantinople A-204, 208, *picture* A-203

Alcohol A-274. *see also in index* Alcoholic beverages; Distillation; Fermentation
  carbon monoxide C-158
  fermentation F-55
  fuel F-442, *diagram* R-232
  methanol M-317
  organic chemistry O-603
  potato source P-466
  soapmaking S-231
  solubility S-256
  synthetic fibers F-72
  winemaking use W-236

Alcohol, Drug Abuse, and Mental Health Administration (ADAMHA) H-90

Alcoholic beverages A-275. *see also in index* Alcoholism; Prohibition; Temperance movement
  advertising restrictions A-59
  analgesic effect A-387
  beer B-132
  cancer cause C-132
  coma cause C-596
  criminal law C-775
  drugs D-276
  fermentation F-55
  grains G-206
  liquor industry L-234, *diagram* L-236
  traffic accidents A-862
  wine W-236
  yeast Y-411

Alcoholics Anonymous (AA), fellowship aiming to offer a spiritual program of living whereby an alcoholic can obtain sobriety, peace of mind, and happiness; founded 1935 in Akron, Ohio; groups in U.S., Canada, and 90 other countries; headquarters New York City A-276

Alcoholism, disease A-276
  adolescent social problem A-48
  alcoholic beverages A-275
  amnesia cause A-373
  criminal law C-775
  halfway house H-14
  hepatitis H-135
  liquor industry L-237
  liver disease L-261
  malnutrition M-77
  mental illness M-301
  temperance movement T-80

Alcor, star, *chart* S-422

Alcott, Amos Bronson (1799–1888), U.S. philosopher, educator, and writer, born in Wolcott, Conn.; father of Louisa May Alcott; wrote biography of Ralph Waldo Emerson A-277
  Concord, Mass. C-639

Alcott, Louisa May (1832–88), U.S. author A-277
  children's reading R-111c
  Concord, Mass. C-639

Alcuin, (735–804), English scholar and churchman; sponsored by Charlemagne he spread English learning in France; wrote texts on grammar, dialectics, and rhetoric; Biblical and theological works
  calligraphy C-58
  Latin script revival E-263

Ald, a signal or command given to a horse by a rider, *list* H-249

Aldanov, Mark, (pseudonym of Mark Aleksandrovich Landau) (1888–1957), Russian novelist, born in Kiev; to France 1919, to U.S. 1941 R-360a

Aldebaran, reddish star, the brightest in the constellation Taurus (Bull); in astrology a lucky star; classified as royal star by the Persians about 3000 BC S-414, *charts* S-415, 421

Aldehyde, a compound intermediate between a simple alcohol and an organic acid; obtained by taking two hydrogen atoms from alcohol O-603

Alden, John (1599?–1687), *Mayflower* Pilgrim, assistant to governor of Plymouth Colony A-277
  Longfellow's poem L-296
  Standish S-410

Alder, Kurt (1902–58), German chemist, born near present Katowice, Poland; worked on diene synthesis, method of making organic chemicals synthetically. *see also in index* Nobel Prizewinners, *table*

Alder, genus of shrubs or trees A-277

Alder fly, species of large net-veined insect peculiar to America; larvae (dobsons) used as bait for still-fishing; eggs laid on leaves or branches overhanging water, in which young live until maturity
  egg, *picture* E-111

Alderney, northernmost of Channel Islands 8 mi (13 km) across from Cape La Hague, France; 3 sq mi (8 sq km); farm products; pop. 1,686 C-270, *map* U-18a

Aldershot, England, a municipal borough 34 mi (55 km) s.w. of London; in military training area; printing; manufacture of cosmetics and briar pipes; pop. 38,120, *map* U-18a

Aldine Press. *see in index* Manutius

Aldiss, Brian (born 1925), science fiction writer, *list* S-62

Aldric (800?–856), bishop of Le Mans A-519

Aldrich, Nelson Wilmarth (1841–1915), U.S. politician, born in Foster, R.I.; father of Winthrop W. Aldrich; served in U.S. Senate, 1881–1911; authority on tariff and finance (Payne-Aldrich Tariff, Aldrich-Vreeland Currency Law) T-8

Aldrin, Edwin E., Jr. (born 1930), U.S. astronaut, born in Glen Ridge, N.J.; U.S. Air Force officer in NASA program 1963–71; commandant Aerospace Research Pilot School, Edwards Air Force Base, 1971–72 ('Return to Earth')
  Armstrong A-632
  exploration E-377
  moon landing M-576
  space travel S-341, 347, *table* S-348

Ale, alcoholic beverage B-134

Aleatory music (or chance music) M-676

Alegre, Caetano da Costa (1864–90), African poet A-122

Aleichem, Sholem. *see in index* Rabinowitz, Shalom

Aleijadinho (originally Antônio Francisco Lisboa) (1738?–1814), Brazilian sculptor B-418
  architecture A-703
  'Bom Jesus de Matozinhos', *picture* B-417

Aleixandre, Vicente (1898–1984), Spanish poet, born in Seville; belonged to "Generation of 1927" ('Espadas como labios'; 'Sombra de paraiso'; 'Historia del corazon'; 'Dialogos del concimiento') S-366. *see also in index* Nobel Prizewinners, *table*

Aleksandrovsky, Russia. *see in index* Novosibirsk

Alemán, Mateo (1547?–1614?), Spanish novelist, born in Seville; official in Spanish treasury for many years; later emigrated to Mexico S-366

Alemán, Miguel (born 1902), Mexican lawyer and statesman, born in Sayula, Veracruz; governor of state of Veracruz 1936–40, minister of government in Camacho's cabinet 1940–45; president of Mexico 1946–52 M-338

Alemanni (all-men), confederacy of German peoples; conquered 496 by Clovis; French call Germans "Allemands" and Germany "Allemagne"; descendants today in Switzerland, Alsace, and Swabia
  Germany G-121
  Switzerland S-544

Alembert, Jean le Rond d' (1717–83), French mathematician and philosopher, born in Paris; made important contributions to theories of mechanics
  Diderot D-138
  'Encyclopédie' R-124
  Laplace L-49

Alembic. *see in index* Retort

Alençon, France, city 107 mi (172 km) s.w. of Paris; manufacturing center; textiles; severely damaged in World War II, liberated by U.S. troops 1944; pop. 30,368, *map* F-369

Alençon lace L-16, *picture* L-15

Aleppo (or Haleb), Syria, city of n.w.; trade center; textiles, wool, hides, wheat, vegetable oils, sugar, soap, copper products; pop. 962,954 A-277
  Asia, *map* A-697
  Syria S-550

Alepoudhelis, Odysseus. *see in index* Elytis, Odysseus

Alessandria, Italy, city in Piedmont, 47 mi (76 km) n. of Genoa; railroad center; pop. 92,760, *map* I-401

Aleut, an Alaskan people A-242
  American Indians I-137, 156, *map* I-136, *table* I-138

Aleutian Islands, Alaska, chain of islands extending 1,100 mi (1,770 km) s.w. from Alaska Peninsula to Attu Island; area 6,821 sq mi (17,666 sq km); geologically, the Aleutian chain includes Commander (Komandorskiye) Islands, belonging to the U.S.S.R., and extends to Kamchatka Peninsula, a total of 1,500 mi (2,400 km); pop. 7,768 (Aleutian Islands census district) A-278
  Alaska A-240, *map* A-254
  world, *map* W-297
  World War II W-328, 346

Aleutian Range, mountains, Alaska A-242, *map* A-254

Alewife, fish *Alosa pseudoharengus* H-144

Alexander I, Saint, pope from 105 to 115; frequently identified with Alexander, a martyr, and represented with chest pierced with nails; festival May 3.

Alexander VI (originally called Rodrigo Borgia) (1431–1503), pope B-367, *table* P-99
  Julius II J-151
  Leo X L-131
  New World dispute settlement A-330
  Savonarola S-52d

Alexander I (1777–1825), emperor of Russia A-278
  Napoleon N-16
  Nicholas I N-306
  Russian history R-353

Alexander II (1818–81), emperor of Russia A-278

of potassium, sodium, magnesium, or calcium S-251
Alkaloids, nitrogen-containing organic compounds of plant origin; they are bases, that is, they react with acids to form salts; may occur oily or crystalline
antidotes P-411
caffeine P-248a
cocaine P-222
colchicine P-368
morphine B-298
opium O-572
quinine Q-18
strychnine S-493
tobacco T-198
Alkekengia. *see in index* Chinese lantern plant
Al-Khwarizmi (780?–840?), Arab astronomer and mathematician A-293
Alkyds, plastics P-228, *table* P-382
Alkylation, petroleum conversion process P-241a
Allah, Arabic proper name for God, in Islam I-359
Koran K-268
Mecca M-254
Allahabad (City of God), India, city at junction of Ganges and Jumna rivers; cotton, grain; University of Allahabad; pop. 490,622, *maps* I-83, A-697
Allama Iqbal Open University. *see in index* People's Open University
All-American Canal, in s.e. California
California C-36
Colorado River C-586
Imperial Valley I-59
irrigation I-356
Allantois, endodermal sac E-201
Allard, Harry Ardell (1880–1963), U.S. botanist, born in Oxford, Mass.; with Bureau of Plant Industry, U.S. Department of Agriculture, 1906–46 P-373
Allegheny Mountains, Appalachian system U-37, *maps* U-50, 59
Maryland M-167
Pennsylvania P-164, *map* P-165
Virginia, *maps* V-330, 348
West Virginia W-165
Allegheny Plateau, United States A-508
New York N-246
Allegheny River, rises in Potter County, n.-central Pennsylvania, *maps* P-165, 184, U-50
Pittsburgh P-345
Allegiance, Pledge of. *see in index* Pledge of Allegiance
Allegory, presentation of abstract thoughts or principles by means of stories, either in words or in pictures
Spenser's 'Faerie Queen' S-378
'Allegory of Love, The', work by Lewis L-141
Allegri, Antonio. *see in index* Correggio
Allegro, in music, means fast tempo M-691, *list* M-670
Allele, in genetics; an alternate form of gene located on a specific site on a chromosome G-53
evolution E-368
Allelopathy, in botany W-133
Allen, Ethan (1737?–89), American Revolutionary War leader A-308
flag F-154, *picture* F-155
folklore F-267
Statuary Hall, *table* S-437b
Vermont V-289, *picture* V-296
Allen, Eugene Thomas (1864–1964), U.S. geochemist, born in Athol, Mass.; research chemist Geophysical Laboratory, Carnegie Institution of Washington, 1907–32.
Allen, Harry Julian (born 1910), U.S. aeronautical engineer, born in Maywood, Ill.; on National Advisory Committee for Aeronautics 1936–58 A-79
Allen, Hervey (1889–1949), U.S. writer, born in Pittsburgh, Pa.; wrote poetry ('Earth Moods'), biography ('Israfel: the Life and Times of Edgar Allan Poe'), long picaresque novel ('Anthony Adverse'), other novels ('The Forest and the Fort', 'Bedford Village', 'Toward the Morning') A-358
Allen, Ira (1751–1814), American patriot, born in Cornwall, Conn.; brother of Ethan Allen; leader in establishing the statehood of Vermont V-289
Allen, Joseph (born 1937), U.S. astronaut, born in Crawfordsville, Ind., *table* S-348
Allen, Richard (1760–1831), U.S. abolitionist and minister A-308
black American history B-291
Methodism M-319
Allen, William (1803–79), U.S. statesman, born in Edenton, N.C.; prominent Democrat; U.S. senator 1837–49; governor of Ohio 1873–75; said to have originated slogan "Fifty-four forty or fight", *table* S-437b
Allen, Woody (born 1935), U.S. comedian, playwright, and filmmaker A-309
motion pictures M-627
Allenby, Edmund Henry Hynman Allenby, first Viscount (1861–1936), British field marshal, born in Southwell, near Newark, England; commander of Palestine expedition in World War I; high commissioner of Egypt 1919–25 W-305
Allende Gossens, Salvador (1908–73), Chilean physician and political leader, born in Valparaiso; helped found Chilean Socialist party 1933; senator 1945–70; president of Chile 1970–73 C-334
Allen Park, Mich., residential city 10 mi (16 km) s.w. of Detroit; U.S. veterans' hospital; settled 1860, incorporated as village 1927 and as city 1956; pop. 34,196.
Allenstein, Poland. *see in index* Olsztyn
Allentown, Pa., city on Lehigh River, 50 mi (80 km) n.w. of Philadelphia; pop. 103,758, *maps* P-185, 165, 174, U-41
Allergy, certain adverse reaction to foreign substances A-309
antibiotics A-490
antihistamine A-492
antitoxin sensitivity A-495
blood analysis B-314
first aid F-121
headache H-81
immune system I-57
medicine, *table* M-277
Alley, bowling B-385
All Fives, (or Muggins), form of dominoes D-228
All Hallow's Eve. *see in index* Halloween
Alliance, Ohio, city on Mahoning River, 50 mi (80 km) s.e. of Cleveland; in rich agricultural region; railroad center; machinery, traveling cranes, metal products, brick; Mount Union College; pop. 24,315.
Alliance des Ba-Kongo (ABAKO) Z-446
Alliance for Progress, development program for the OAS nations S-292, *picture* S-278
Kennedy proposal K-202
Allied Command Atlantic (ACLANT), North Atlantic Treaty Organization N-352
Allied Command Channel (ACCHAN), North Atlantic Treaty Organization N-352
Allied Command Europe (ACE), North Atlantic Treaty Organization N-352
Allied Expeditionary Forces, World War II
Eisenhower E-135
Germany G-124
Allied Powers (or Allies), international alliance among nations united against the Central European powers in World War I, or those united against the Axis powers in World War II
Germany G-123
World War I W-302
naval warfare N-84
World War II W-323, *map* W-335
Mussolini M-694
The Netherlands N-130
war crime definitions W-11
warfare W-21, 24
Allied War Crimes Commission W-11, W-358
Alligator, reptile A-310. *see also in index* Crocodile
brain B-401
crocodilians R-152
ecological role E-57, *picture* E-55
endangered species E-212
leather L-109
life expectancy, *chart* A-423
preservation C-676
Alligator gar, fish *Lepisosteus spatula* of the family Lepisosteidae; largest of the gars; can use its swim bladder as a lung; characterized by broad beak-like jaws; found in waters of s. United States G-16
Alligator lizard, reptile *Gerrhonotus liocephalus*, *picture* L-273
Alligator pear. *see in index* Avocado
Alligator snapping turtle, reptile T-329
Alligatorweed, plant W-133
Alliluieva, Svetlana (born 1926), Soviet writer, born in Moscow; daughter of Joseph Stalin; to U.S. 1967; returned to Soviet Union 1985; emigrated to U.K. 1986; author of 'Twenty Letters to a Friend', 'Only One Year' S-404
All in the Family, television program T-70
humor H-323
Allison, William Boyd (1829–1908), U.S. Republican party leader, finance expert, born in Perry, Ohio; member U.S. House of Representatives 1862–70; U.S. senator from Iowa 1872–1908.
Allison tuna, fish T-306
Alliteration, figure of speech F-81
Allogeneic antigen, in pathology I-57
Allograft (or homograft), tissue transplantation from one person to another T-250
Allosaurus, dinosaur R-155
Allotrope, a form of a chemical element or compound
iron I-329
phosphorus P-271
sulfur S-510
Allouez, Claude (1622–89), French Jesuit missionary, born in Saint-Didier, near Saint-Étienne; explored Lake Superior region and parts of Mississippi Valley; many years at Kaskaskia, Ill. W-253
Alloy A-312. *see also in index* alloys below and other alloys by name
aluminum A-321
brass B-410
bronze B-463
chromium C-408
cobalt C-530
coinage C-539, P-188
copper C-710
corrosion C-726
crystal structure S-254h
gold G-176
iron and steel I-333
lead L-99
magnesium M-41
manganese M-96
mercury M-305
metal and metallurgy M-307
mines and mining M-430
molybdenum M-527
nickel N-307
niobium N-318
platinum P-384
ruthenium R-366
silver S-204
solder S-204
tin T-190
'All Quiet on the Western Front', work by Remarque W-28
All Saints, Christian festival H-17
All Saints Church, London, built 1849–59, *picture* A-561
All Souls' Day, Nov. 2; Roman Catholicism; day for prayer and almsgiving in behalf of faithful departed A-402
All Souls Festival, in Buddhism B-483
Allspice (or Jamaica pepper), spice; flavor resembles combination of cloves, cinnamon, and nutmeg; sometimes called pimento P-197a
Allston, Washington (1779–1843), U.S. painter, born in Waccamaw, S.C. ('Belshazzar's Feast', portrait of Benjamin West), *picture* S-316
'All's Well That Ends Well', comedy by Shakespeare; plot based on story in Boccaccio's 'Decameron' from a 1566 translation by William Painter S-133, 139
'All the King's Men', book by Warren A-358
Allusion, literary device
folklore F-269
Alluvial mining M-426
Alluvial soil S-249, 253, *map* S-252
China C-341
Po River P-400
Alluvium, sedimentary material not hardened into rock M-437
India I-62
All-volunteer army A-648
Alma-Ata, U.S.S.R., capital of Kazakh Soviet Socialist Republic, in central Asia; center for an area growing wheat, sugar beets, tobacco, apples, grapes; manufactures machinery; pop. 851,000 K-194, *maps* R-322, 344
Asia, *map* A-697
Almadén, Spain, town 105 mi (65 mi) n. of Córdoba; rich mercury mines; area also produces sulfur and lead; known since Roman times; pop. 13,206 S-352
mercury M-304
'Almagest', work on astronomy by Ptolemy (Claudius Ptolemaeus); in 13 books; expounded theory that heavenly bodies revolve around earth; accepted as foundation of astronomy until time of Copernicus U-198
constellations C-680
Greek literature G-278
Almagro, Diego de (1475–1538), Spanish adventurer, born in near Ciudad Real; aided Pizarro in conquest of Peru; later led troops to conquer Chile P-349
Almanac, book or pamphlet containing a calendar and miscellaneous information; 17th- and 18th-century almanacs featured astrological forecasts; later editions dealt more with facts R-131, *picture* R-130
Aztecs A-891
earliest printed P-504
libraries L-162
'Poor Richard's Almanack' F-381, *picture* F-382
space almanac N-75
Almanac Singers, folk group organized by Pete Seeger G-320
'Almas de violeta', work by Jiménez J-118
Almería, Spain, seaport 60 mi (95 km) s.e. of Granada, capital of Almería Province; exports fruit; founded by Phoenicians; became flourishing port and pirate headquarters under Moors; pop. 76,643, *map* S-350
'Almira', work by Handel H-28
Almohads, Islamic people of Africa M-586
Almond, nut-bearing tree of the rose family A-314
Almoravids, an African people A-110
Morocco M-586
Alnico, alloy used to make permanent magnets for loudspeakers C-530, M-46
Aloe, American, plant. *see in index* American aloe
Aloes, bitter medicinal substance valued as a purgative, obtained by cutting leaves of various species of aloe and evaporating juice exuded; effective in healing of radiation burns; widely used in treatment of atomic bomb victims of World War II; the aloe is a genus of plants of the lily family; it does not include either American aloe or black aloe A-124
'Aloha Oe', song by Liliuokalani L-208
Aloha State. *see in index* Hawaii
Aloha Week, Hawaiian festival, *picture* H-69
Alonso, Alicia (born 1921), Cuban ballerina, born in Havana; joined Ballet Theatre 1940, ballerina 1946–50, prima ballerina 1950–55; founder (1948), director, and ballerina of Ballet Alicia Alonso, Havana, later called Ballet de Cuba; guest prima ballerina Ballet Russe de Monte Carlo 1955–57; danced at American Ballet Theater gala in New York City 1975 B-36
Alopecia. *see in index* Baldness
Alouettes, Canadian research satellites, *picture* S-348a, *table* S-344
Alpaca, South American animal *Lama pacos*, of the Camelidae family C-65, *picture* C-63
domestication, *picture* A-455
fur, *table* F-464
wool fiber, *table* F-105
Alpaca, originally the strong, lustrous cloth resembling mohair, made from the hair of the alpaca; today chiefly a rayon and cotton or rayon and

wool cloth, wiry and shiny; also silk alpaca, a dull, soft fabric which looks like wool.

Alpena, Mich., city on Thunder Bay, Lake Huron; limestone, cement, concrete blocks, paper, machinery, automotive equipment; hunting and fishing resorts nearby; pop. 12,214.

Alpenhorn (or alphorn), musical instrument A-319

Alphabet A-315. *see* story preceding Fact-Index in each volume
- African languages A-121
- ancient writing system A-404
- Braille B-396
- Cherokee O-523
- communication C-607
- Cyrillic S-215, R-359
  - Keller's popularization K-196
- Greek W-372
- Initial Teaching Alphabet. *see in index* Initial Teaching Alphabet
- Korean K-293, *chart* K-281
- phonics P-268a
  - movable alphabet, *picture* R-101c
- Russian R-359
- signaling, *pictures* S-194a, 195
- Slavonic B-535
- type and typography T-336, *picture*, T-337
  - lowercase letters, *picture* B-251
- writing W-373

Alpha Centauri, nearest visible fixed star S-413
- distance A-719
- earth E-9
- solar system S-254

Alpha Crucis, star S-414

Alpha Delta Pi (or Adelphean), sorority F-389

Alpha particles (or alpha rays) R-63, *picture* R-62, *chart* R-66
- emission process R-68
- nuclear physics N-431

Alpha waves, brain B-216

Alpheus, river-god in mythology. *see in index* Arethusa

Alpheus (modern Ruphia), river of Peloponnesus, Greece; drains part of Arcadia; enters Mediterranean Sea near Pyrgos; 100 mi (160 km) long
- Hercules H-138

Alphonso. *see in index* Alfonso

Alphonsus, crater on moon M-580

Alphorn (or alpenhorn), musical instrument A-319

Alpine house, folk art F-249

Alpine phlox, plant P-267

Alpine savory. *see in index* Calamintha

Alpine strawberry, plant *Fragaria vesca* of the family Rosaceae S-486

Alpine subrace, of Caucasoid race R-27, *chart* R-26

Alps, The, greatest mountain system of Europe A-318
- Apennines A-497
- Austria A-824
- continental development C-690
- Europe, *maps* E-329, 360, *pictures* E-328, 345
- France F-343
- Germany G-112
- glaciers G-150
- Italy I-381
- Matterhorn M-231
- skiing W-242
- Switzerland, *pictures* S-536, 538, *map* S-537

Al-Raschid, Harun. *see in index* Harun al-Raschid

Alsace-Lorraine, region in n.e. France; area 12,288,584 sq mi (31,827,300 sq km); taken by Germany in 1871, restored to France 1919 after World War I, taken by Germany 1940, by Allies 1944; pop. 3,872,900 A-320
- Bismarck G-122
- wine W-237
- World War I W-302

Alster River, in West Germany, flows into Elbe at Hamburg
- Hamburg H-20

Altadena, Calif., residential community just n. of Pasadena; in area growing citrus fruits and avocados; Christmas Tree Lane of giant cedars decorated with lights for holiday season; pop. 42,415.

Altaic language family L-42, *diagram* L-44

Altai Mountains. *see in index* Altay Mountains

Altair, star S-414, *charts* S-419, 422

Altamaha River, in Georgia, formed by confluence of Oconee and Okmulgee rivers; flows s.e. 155 mi (250 km) into Altamaha Sound; navigable all the way for boats drawing 5 ft (2 m) of water, *map* U-59

Altay Mountains (or Altai Mountains), between China and Mongolian People's Republic and between Kazakh Soviet Socialist Republic and Siberia; highest point Kuiten 15,266 ft (4,653 m); silver, lead, zinc, *map* A-697
- Mongolia M-535
- U.S.S.R., *maps* R-322, 344

Altdorf (or Altorf), Switzerland, capital of canton of Uri, on Lake Lucerne; site of Switzerland's oldest Capuchin monastery, built 1581; pop. 7,477.

Altenburg, East Germany, city 24 mi (40 km) s. of Leipzig; lignite and clay; textiles, machinery; old castle celebrated as scene of abduction (1455) of Saxon princes Albert and Ernest; pop. 46,905, *map* G-131

Alte Pinakothek, museum at Munich, West Germany; a major part of the Bavarian State Art Collection; established 1836; features the old masters M-663
- Dürer's 'Four Apostles', *picture* P-39

Alter, David (1807–81), U.S. physicist and physician, born in Freeport, Pa.; noted for pioneer work in spectral analysis S-58

Altered drug. *see in index* Analogue

Alternating current (AC), electric current that reverses its direction at regularly recurring intervals
- electricity E-158
- electric power E-165
- galvanometer G-7
- motor and engine M-631
- Tesla T-114
- Westinghouse W-162

Alternating gradient synchrotron (AGS), nuclear energy N-420

Alternation of generations, type of reproduction in which one generation reproduces sexually and the next asexually S-396
- jellyfish J-98
- moss M-599

Alternative school A-321

Alternator, electric generator furnishing alternating current
- automobile A-847
- electric power E-166

Altesch, Alpine glacier A-319

Altgeld, John Peter (1847–1902), U.S. politician, born in Nieder-Selters, Nassau, Germany; governor of Illinois 1893–97; pardoned Haymarket anarchists; furthered prison reform; friend of the "underdog" I-42

Althaea, shrubby. *see in index* Rose of Sharon

Althing, legislative body of Iceland; founded 930, has functioned almost continuously for more than 1,000 years.

Altimeter, airplane instrument A-194, B-82, *picture* A-195

Altimetry, measurement of altitude or elevation above sea level
- mountain M-633

Altiplano, plateau in South America, *pictures* S-269, 281c, *diagram* S-295
- Andes A-409
- Bolivia B-333

Altitude M-243. *see also in index* Azimuth
- aerospace hazards A-81
- airplane. *see in index* Airplane
- astronomy A-718
- climate control C-498
- latitude and longitude L-81
- mountain M-633
- ocean waves O-487

Altman, Robert (born 1925), U.S. motion picture director M-627

Altocumulus cloud, type of cloud C-517

Alton, Ill., manufacturing and railroad center 20 mi (30 km) n. of St. Louis, Mo., on Mississippi River; glass, oil, munitions, chemicals; the abolitionist Elijah Lovejoy was murdered here in 1837; pop. 34,171, *map* I-52

Altona, West Germany; industrial and commercial seaport on Elbe River; district of Hamburg; pop. 266,000, *map* G-131

'Alton Locke', novel by Kingsley K-247

Altoona, Pa., industrial city in s.-central part of state, about 85 mi (140 km) e. of Pittsburgh, near famous Horseshoe Curve; railroad shops; machinery and electrical products, clothing and shoes, bearings, garment patterns, food products, mobile and modular units; regional campus of Pennsylvania State University; pop. 57,078 P-182b, *maps* P-184, U-41

Alto-relievo. *see in index* High relief

Altorf, Switzerland. *see in index* Altdorf

Altostratus cloud, type of cloud C-517

Altruist (from Latin *alter,* "other"), one devoted to interests of others P-264

Altus, Okla., city in s.w. part of state; grain market; wheat, cotton, livestock; copper concentrates, wallboard; Altus Air Force Base; established 1891; pop. 23,101.

ALU. *see in index* Arithmetic and logic unit

Alum, chemical compound A-322

Alumina, aluminum oxide, most abundant of earths, and common constituent of silicate minerals forming basis of many rocks, clays, and soils A-322
- abrasive A-13
- watches and clocks W-79

'Aluminaut', research submarine S-500

Aluminum (or aluminium), very light metallic element A-321. *see also in index* Alumina
- alloys A-312
  - bronze B-463
- compounds
  - chloride S-256
  - silicates B-136b, P-73
- earth's crust, *table* E-11
- Hall H-15
- inventions I-275, *tables* I-273, 280
- manufacturing areas
  - Austria A-826
  - Canada Q-9e
  - Jamaica J-18
  - United States, *picture* U-89
- ore. *see in index* Bauxite
- periodic table, *table* P-207, *list* P-208
- radioactivity induced R-64
- tin T-190
- uranium U-212
- uses
  - brickmaking B-436
  - button, *picture* B-529
  - insulation I-232
  - money M-531
  - photolithographic plate P-277
  - wire W-245

Aluminum brass B-410

Aluminum bronze B-463

Aluminum oxide. *see in index* Corundum

Alum Rock, Calif., community 4 mi (6 km) e. of San Jose; nearby is Alum Rock Park, municipal playground, noted for scenic rock formations, mineral springs, pools, trails, and a junior museum; pop. 18,355.

Alunite, mineral M-435

Alur, African people Z-444

Alva, duke of (or duke of Alba) (1508–83), Spanish general, in war with The Netherlands
- William the Silent W-211

Alva B. Adams Tunnel, Colo. C-584

Alvarado, Pedro de (1485–1541), Spanish cavalier and explorer, born in Badajoz; companion of Cortez in the conquest of Mexico (1519)
- Latin America L-66
  - El Salvador E-196, S-33
  - Guatemala G-299
  - Honduras H-227
- Maya M-237

Alvarez, Luis Walter (born 1911), U.S. physicist A-323. *see also in index* Nobel Prizewinners, *table*

Álvarez Quintero, family name of two Spanish brothers, **Serafín** (1871–1938) and **Joaquín** (1873–1944), who together wrote comedies of manners and short musical dramas ('The Women Have Their Way'; 'A Sunny Morning'; 'One Hundred Years Old'; 'The Lady from Alfaqueque') S-365b

Alveoli (or air sacs), in anatomy
- birds B-245
- lung L-337
  - artificial B-211
  - disease D-177

Alvin, a submersible used for underwater research O-463, *picture* O-464

Alworth, Lance (born 1940), U.S. football player, born in Houston, Tex.; flanker; San Diego Chargers 1962–69, Dallas Cowboys 1971–72.

Alyssum. *see in index* Sweet alyssum

Alzheimer's disease, degenerative disease affecting nerve cells of the brain and leading to severe memory impairment and progressive loss of mental faculties; major cause of presenile dementia and largest single cause of senile dementia; causes unknown but associated with neuritic plaques, neurofibrillary tangles, and deficiency of neurotransmitter acetylcholine; evidence of genetic basis; no effective treatment known N-123
- memory M-295

A.M., abbreviation of Latin *ante meridiem,* "before noon."

AM. *see in index* Amplitude modulation

AMA. *see in index* American Medical Association

Amadeus, Lake, lake in Australia, *picture* A-775, *maps* A-819, P-3

Amadeus Basin, in central Australia, s.w. part of Northern Territory A-771

Amado, Jorge (born 1912), Brazilian writer, born in Ilhéus; works deal with life and social problems of his native land B-418, L-70

Amager, island, Denmark, off n.e. coast of Själland Island; 25 sq mi (65 sq km); most residents descendants of 16th-century Dutch settlers; pop. 178,184.

'Amahl and the Night Visitors', opera by Menotti M-299
- opera O-571

Amalfi, Italy, port 22 mi (35 km) s.e. of Naples; 13th-century cathedral and old Capuchin monastery; medieval rival of Genoa and Pisa; pop. 7,163, *picture* I-380, *map* I-401

Amalgam, alloy containing mercury M-305
- gold G-176, 179
- metal and metallurgy M-309

Amalgamated Clothing Workers of America, labor union formed 1915; merged with Textile Workers Union of America (founded 1939) in 1976 to form Amalgamated Clothing and Textile Workers Union; headquarters, New York, N.Y. G-35

Amami Islands, Japan, northern group in the Ryukyu Islands; area 438 sq mi (1,134 sq km); pop. 186,193, *maps* J-78, A-697

Amanah, river. *see in index* Pharpar

Amana Society, corporation since 1932, formerly a religious community incorporated in Iowa 1859; outgrowth of organization founded in Germany by Johann F. Rock and Eberhard Gruber 1714; community, n.w. of Iowa City, is made up of seven villages I-290, *picture* I-298
- commune C-605

Amanita, genus of poisonous fungi. *see in index* Deadly amanita

Amanollah Khan (1892–1960), king of Afghanistan; succeeded his father as amir 1919; took title of king 1926; tried to modernize Afghanistan; forced to abdicate 1929 A-91

Amanori culture, algae A-513

Amapala, Honduras, chief Pacific port, on Tigre Island, in Gulf of Fonseca; exports lumber, coffee, livestock; pop. 3,494.

Amaranthus albus, variety of tumbleweed T-306

'Amarcord', film by Fellini F-53

Amargosa River, in Nevada and California, flows into Death Valley and becomes a series of dry channels.

Amarillo, Tex., city in Panhandle, 65 mi (105 km) from w. border; pop. 149,230 A-323
- Texas T-120, *maps* N-350, U-40

Amarna, El (ancient Akhetaton, now called Tell el-Amarna), Egypt, site of city built by

THE AMERICA'S CUP COMPETITIONS

Year	Races	Winner	Loser
1851	1	*America* (United States)	Royal Yacht Squadron fleet (Great Britain)
1870	1	N.Y. Yacht Club (U.S.)	*Cambria* (Brit.)
1871	5	*Columbia, Sappho* (U.S.)	*Livonia* (Brit.)
1876	2	*Madeleine* (U.S.)	*Countess of Dufferin* (Canada)
1881	2	*Mischief* (U.S.)	*Atalanta* (Canada)
1885	2	*Puritan* (U.S.)	*Genesta* (Brit.)
1886	2	*Mayflower* (U.S.)	*Galatea* (Brit.)
1887	2	*Volunteer* (U.S.)	*Thistle* (Brit.)
1893	3	*Vigilant* (U.S.)	*Valkyrie II* (Brit.)
1895	3	*Defender* (U.S.)	*Valkyrie III* (Brit.)
1899	3	*Columbia* (U.S.)	*Shamrock* (Brit.)
1901	3	*Columbia* (U.S.)	*Shamrock II* (Brit.)
1903	3	*Reliance* (U.S.)	*Shamrock III* (Brit.)
1920	5	*Resolute* (U.S.)	*Shamrock IV* (Brit.)
1930	4	*Enterprise* (U.S.)	*Shamrock V* (Brit.)
1934	6	*Rainbow* (U.S.)	*Endeavour* (Brit.)
1937	4	*Ranger* (U.S.)	*Endeavour II* (Brit.)
1958	4	*Columbia* (U.S.)	*Sceptre* (Brit.)
1962	5	*Weatherly* (U.S.)	*Gretel* (Australia)
1964	4	*Constellation* (U.S.)	*Sovereign* (Brit.)
1967	4	*Intrepid* (U.S.)	*Dame Pattie* (Aust.)
1970	5	*Intrepid* (U.S.)	*Gretel II* (Aust.)
1974	4	*Courageous* (U.S.)	*Southern Cross* (Aust.)
1977	4	*Courageous* (U.S.)	*Australia* (Aust.)
1980	5	*Freedom* (U.S.)	*Australia* (Aust.)
1983	7	*Australia II* (Aust.)	*Liberty* (U.S.)
1987	4	*Stars and Stripes* (U.S.)	*Kookaburra III* (Aust.)

Amherst, N.S., manufacturing town near New Brunswick boundary, about 90 mi (145 km) n.w. of Halifax; agriculture; salt, coal, lumber; enamelware, aircraft, leather products, structural steel; pop. 9,684 N-404, *map* C-112

Amide, compound in which an organic acid radical takes the place of one or more of the hydrogen atoms in ammonia (NH_3); for example, acetamide (CH_3CONH_2), consisting of acetic acid radical (CH_3CO) plus NH_2 O-604, *diagram* O-603
- synthetic fibers F-72

Amidships, boat location, *diagram* B-326

Amiens, France, important manufacturing city; pop. 131,476 A-370
- France, *maps* F-369, E-360

Amiens, Treaty of (1802) A-370, T-274

Amin, Idi (full name Idi Amin Dada Oumee) (born 1925), Ugandan ruler A-370
- Nyerere N-450
- Obote O-455
- Uganda U-1

Amine, compound in which a hydrocarbon radical takes the place of one or more of the hydrogen atoms in ammonia (NH_3); for example, methylamine (CH_3NH_2), consisting of the methyl radical (CH_3) plus NH_2 O-604, *diagram* O-603
- synthetic fibers F-72
- vitamins V-354

Amino acids, group of organic acids containing amine radical NH_2; obtained by breakdown of protein in digestion, re-formed as proteins in body cells
- albumin composition A-272
- biochemistry B-199
- biophysics B-237
- disease D-167
- embryology E-202
- enzymes E-290
- evolution E-365
- health H-83
- Hopkins H-238
- hormones H-244
- immune system I-56
- liver L-261
- metabolism M-306
- milk M-414
- organic chemistry O-604
- protein P-514
- synthetic fibers F-72

Aminobenzene. *see in index* Aniline

Aminoglycoside, drug A-489

Amir (or emir), title used in Muslim countries, corresponding roughly to British title of lord; used to denote ruling power or distinct office; also title of honor given to descendants of Mohammed through his daughter Fatima
- Kuwait K-311

Amir Khosrow (1253–1325), Persian poet
- Indian literature I-107
- Islamic literature I-367

Amis, Kingsley (born 1922), British writer E-282, *picture* E-283

Amish, a branch of the Mennonite church, named from Jacob Ammon, or Amen, who founded it in Switzerland and s. Germany 1698, insisting on strict interpretation of Mennonite principles; many members migrated to Pennsylvania 1730–40, later to Ohio, Indiana, and other states
- family structure F-16
- health, *picture* H-86
- Mennonites M-299
- needlework N-112
- Pennsylvania, *picture* P-170

'Amistad', ship in slave revolt, *picture* B-290

Amistad Dam, dam, Rio Grande, between Tex. and state of Coahuila, Mexico M-338, R-209

Amitosis, in biology, direct cell division, in which the nucleus and the rest of the cell are squeezed into two parts by constriction.

Amman (Biblical Rabbath Ammon, ancient Philadelphia), modern capital of Jordan; pop. 648,587 A-370
- Asia, *map* A-697
- Jordan J-141

Ammann, Othmar Hermann (1879–1965), U.S. bridge designer, born in Schaffhausen, Switzerland; to U.S. 1904, became citizen 1924; chief engineer 1930–37, director of engineering 1937–39 of Port of New York Authority (now Port Authority of New York and New Jersey) B-447

Ammeter, instrument for measuring electric current in amperes G-7. *see also in index* Galvanometer

Ammonia
- calcium cyanamide C-19
- comets A-716
- nitric acid N-318
- nitrogen N-319
- uses
  - fertilizer F-32, F-58
  - inorganic chemistry solvent I-210
  - poisoning case stimulant P-411
  - refrigerating systems R-136

Ammonite, extinct type of mollusk belonging to the class Cephalopoda; had a flat spiral shell like the modern nautilus; a common fossil
- animal life record, *table* E-24
- prehistoric animals A-459, 461

Ammonium chloride (or sal ammoniac), chemical compound
- electric dry cell B-108
- Hutton H-336
- Solvay process S-247

Ammonium cyanate, chemical compound O-601

Ammonium diuranate, chemical compound N-427

Ammonium nitrate, chemical compound I-211

Ammons, A.R. (born 1926), U.S. poet A-364

Ammunition A-371. *see also in index* Shell
- artillery A-658
- firearms F-96
- Krupp family K-306
- machine gun M-12

Amnesia A-373
- memory M-295
- mental illness M-301

Amnesty, a pardon A-373
- criminals P-505b
- draft resisters P-144
  - Carter C-184
  - Ford F-303
- pirates P-342a

Amnesty and Reconstruction, Proclamation of (1863), Lincoln's offer of pardon to all citizens of the seceded states (except certain prominent leaders) who would lay down their arms and take an oath to support the Constitution R-114

Amnesty International, organization working to free prisoners jailed for political or religious reasons; founded 1961; members in 107 nations; chairman 1961–75, Sean MacBride A-374. *see also in index* Nobel Prizewinners, *table*

Amniocentesis, medical technique B-215
- genetic disorder detection G-48
- hospital H-280

Amnion, membrane forming a closed sac E-201

Amoeba, single-celled organism A-374
- breathing R-159
- cells C-238
- evolution E-366
- foot motion F-288
- living things L-265
- *Protozoa* classification P-515

Amoebic dysentery (or amebic dysentery), disease A-375, *picture* D-170

Amon, Egyptian sun-god. *see in index* Ra

'Amore dei Tre Re, L' ' (The Love of the Three Kings), opera by Italo Montemezzi; first produced at La Scala, Milan, Italy, in 1913.

Amorphous carbon C-157

Amorphous substances S-254g
- matter M-225

Amorphous sulfur S-510

Amos (8th century BC), Hebrew prophet P-508, *picture* P-509

Amount of substance, unit of measure, *table* W-141

Amoy. *see in index* Xiamen

Ampère, André Marie (1775–1836), French mathematician and physicist A-375
- electricity E-155, *picture* E-161

Ampere and amperage, electricity E-152, *table* W-141

Ampere meter. *see in index* Galvanometer

Ampère's law, in physics A-375

Amphetamines (street names: upper, pep, speed, bennies, whites), drug D-276
- analgesic A-387

Amphiarthrosis, type of joint J-136

Amphibian, class of vertebrate animals A-376. *see also in index* Frog; Salamander; Toad
- breathing R-159
  - gill slits V-304
- embryology E-200
- endangered species E-212
- evolution A-461, E-366, R-152
- first appearance P-487
- fish compared F-123
- heart R-152
- metamorphosis M-312
- migratory habits A-452

Amphibian plane, airplane, *picture* A-173

Amphibious Assault Ship (LPH), naval vessel N-86, *picture* N-90

Amphibious Cargo Ship (LKA), naval vessel N-86

Amphibious Command Ship (LCC), naval vessel N-86

Amphibious Transport Dock (LPD), naval vessel N-86

Amphibious vessel, in naval warfare N-85

Amphibole, mineral M-436

Amphibrach, poetic foot P-405

Amphimacer, poetic foot P-405

Amphineuran, class of mollusks M-525

Amphion, in Greek mythology, a son of Zeus; by playing a magic lyre which he had received from Hermes, Amphion charmed stones so that they built themselves into walls of the city Thebes.

Amphioxus (or lancelet), a fish-shaped sea animal; about 2 in. long; pinkish white; several species known; classed in the phylum Chordata, subphylum Leptocardia A-435, *picture* A-434
- invertebrate group I-286, *picture* I-285

Amphipoda, crustacean order C-790

Ampisbaenid, legless reptile group
- lizard comparison L-272

Amphitheater, building in which the spectators' seats surround the place used by the performers. *see also in index* Stadium
- Rome, Italy R-257, *pictures* R-256, 254, *map* R-250
- Verona, Italy, *picture* I-393

Amphora, a large, earthenware container used by ancient peoples to hold oil, honey, or wine and as an ornament; commonly had an oval body, narrow neck, and two handles
- glass decoration G-161

Amplification, electric circuits
- instrumentation I-228
- laser and maser L-54
- phonograph P-269, *diagram* P-268d
- photoelectric devices P-274
- radio R-60, *diagrams* R-46, 57
- transistor T-249

Amplitude, physics; measure of strength of a wave, similar to height from trough to crest of a water wave
- radio waves R-48
- sound waves S-260

Amplitude modulation (AM)
- radio R-46, *diagram* R-50

Amr Canal, built in early Christian era, still used to carry fresh water from the Nile River to the city of Suez, Egypt C-127

Amr ibn-al-As (or Amru) (AD 594?–664), Arab general and statesman, born in Mecca; opposed Mohammed until conversion in 629; known as conqueror of Egypt C-16

Amritsar, India, city in Punjab state; silks, shawls, carpets, chemicals; center of Sikh religion; pop. 407,628, *maps* I-83, A-697

Amsterdam, The Netherlands, capital, on Amstel River; pop. 712,294 A-381, N-126, *picture* N-127
- Europe, *map* E-360
- international trade I-271
- Rijksmuseum (State Museum). *see also in index* Rijksmuseum
- world, *map* W-297

Amsterdam, N.Y., city on Mohawk River and New York State Barge Canal, 30 mi (50 km) n.w. of Albany; carpet company headquarters; paper boxes, clothing, plastics, boats, fiber glass, electronics; pop. 21,872.

Amsterdam Concertgebouw, renowned orchestra of The Netherlands N-127

Amtrak (or National Railroad Passenger Corporation) R-87
- transportation T-255

products, sewing machines, glass fibers; pop. 27,313, *maps* S-318, U-41

Andersonville, Ga., village 52 mi (84 km) s.w. of Macon; Andersonville National Historic Park now on site of Civil War Confederate prison in which over 12,000 died; burial ground now a national cemetery; pop. 267.

Andes, mountains in w. South America; highest peak Mount Aconcagua 22,834 ft (6,960 m) A-409
 Aconcagua A-20
 Argentina A-575, *maps* A-585
 Bolivia B-333
 Chile C-329
 Colombia C-548
 Ecuador E-66
 Latin America L-58, *picture* L-57
 masks M-186
 mountain M-635
 Pacific plate O-466
 Peru P-221
 South America S-271, 279, *pictures* S-269, 274, 281b, 284, 287, 289, *map* S-297
 textiles T-142
 'The Christ of the Andes', *picture* A-474
 Venezuela V-275

Andesite, rock L-89
 Oceania O-466

Andhra Pradesh, state in s.e. India; area 110,250 sq mi (285,550 sq km); cap. Hyderabad; manganese, mica; timber; tobacco, cotton, rice; formed in 1956 from parts of former Madras and Hyderabad states; pop. 43,394,951, *map* I-83

Andizhan, U.S.S.R., city in e. Uzbek Soviet Socialist Republic; trade and railroad center; cotton ginning; dates from 9th century; frequently hit by earthquakes; pop. 188,000, *maps* R-345, A-697

Ando Hiroshige (or Ando Tokutaro). *see in index* Hiroshige

Andolu. *see in index* Asia Minor

Andorra, principality in valley of Pyrenees, between France and Spain; 175 sq mi (453 sq km); cap. Andorra la Vella; pop. 33,861 A-410
 Europe, *map* E-360
 flag, *picture* F-161
 Spain, *map* S-350

Andover, Mass., about 22 mi (35 km) n. of Boston; rubber products, woolens, plastics; electronics; Phillips Academy; incorporated 1646; pop. of township 26,370
 Ryder's 'Toilers of the Sea' P-54, *picture* P-55

Andrada e Silva, José Bonifácio de (1763–1838), Brazilian statesman, geologist, and author A-411

Andrade, Mario de (born 1928), African poet A-122

Andrade, Olegario Víctor (1841–82), Argentine poet, born in Gualeguaychú, near Paraná; career as journalist but famed for poems, *picture* L-71

Andrea del Sarto. *see in index* Sarto, Andrea del

Andreanof Islands, islands, Aleutian group, *map* U-39

Andrée, Salomon August (1854–97), Swedish scientist and aeronaut, born in Gränna, near Jönköping; made first attempt by air to explore the Arctic P-420, *picture* P-423

Andreev, Leonid (or Leonid Andreyev) (1871–1919), brilliant Russian writer, mystic, and fatalist, born in Orel; also lawyer, crime reporter, and editor; died in Finland in poverty R-361

Andrew, Saint, one of the Twelve Apostles; brother of Simon Peter; a fisherman from Capernaum; patron of Scotland and Russia; festival Nov. 30 A-506

Andrew, Prince (or Andrew Albert Christian Edward) (born 1960), son of Queen Elizabeth II of England.

Andrew Johnson National Historic Site, in Tennessee, *picture* J-126

Andrews, Roy Chapman (1884–1960), U.S. explorer and naturalist, born in Beloit, Wis.; director American Museum of Natural History, New York, N.Y., 1935–41; explored Alaska, East Indies, Korea, China, Mongolia, central Asia; discovered huge fossil fields in The Gobi; found first dinosaur eggs ever discovered, about 10,000,000 years old, and skeleton of largest land mammal (natural history: 'This Amazing Planet', 'Nature's Ways'; autobiography: 'An Explorer Comes Home'; for younger readers: 'Quest in the Desert', 'All About Dinosaurs', 'All About Whales', 'Quest of the Snow Leopard', 'In the Days of the Dinosaurs').

Andrews, Tex., city 40 mi (60 km) n.w. of Midland; trade and shipping center for oil-producing and cattle-raising region; cotton, sorghum; pop. 11,061.

Andreyev, Leonid. *see in index* Andreev, Leonid

Andrianov, Nikolai (born 1952), Soviet gymnast G-325

Andric, Ivo (1892–1975), Yugoslav diplomat and writer, born near Sarajevo, Bosnia, now Yugoslavia ('The Bridge on the Drina'; 'Devil's Yard'; 'The Woman from Sarajevo'). *see also in index* Nobel Prizewinners, *table*

Androgen, male hormone A-47
 sexuality S-124

Android, type of robot R-226

Andromeda, in Greek mythology; daughter of King Cepheus and Queen Cassiopeia of Ethiopia; offered to sea monster to appease Poseidon and sea nymphs, who had been angered by Cassiopeia's boasting of her own beauty
 Perseus P-210

Andromeda, constellation, *charts* S-415, 420, 423, C-681
 galaxy U-199, 201, *list* E-8

'Andromeda Strain, The', work by Crichton R-112e, *picture* R-111j

Andronicus III Palaeologus (1296–1341), Byzantine emperor B-536

Andropov, Yuri (1914–84), Soviet premier; former head of KGB A-411
 Russian history R-358

Andros, Sir Edmund (1637–1714), English colonial governor of New York 1674–81, New England 1686–89, and Virginia 1692–98, born in London; tyrannical and unpopular R-185
 flag F-153, *picture* F-155
 Mather M-221

Andros, Greece, fertile mountainous island in Cyclades group; in Aegean Sea; area 145 sq mi (380 sq km); important ancient naval base; pop. 10,457.

Androscoggin, river in New Hampshire and Maine; flows 180 mi (290 km) to Merrymeeting Bay; abrupt descent gives immense waterpower U-44, *map* N-191

Andros Island, largest island in Bahama archipelago, 125 mi (200 km) s.e. of Miami Beach, Fla.; area 1,600 sq mi (4,150 sq km); pine, mahogany, hardwood; fish, sponges; pineapples; oil wells; pop. 9,576 B-20, *map* N-350

'And They Shall Walk', work by Kenny K-207

'Andy and the Lion', work by James Henry Daugherty R-107

Anecdote, literary form
 folklore F-260

Anemia (or anaemia), term meaning "bloodless" for various forms of a blood disease B-316, B-224a
 food and nutrition F-279
 iron deficiency I-329
 sickle-cell B-237
 vitamins V-355

Anemometer, instrument used to measure surface wind speed M-317
 weather W-121
 wind tunnel W-235

Anemone, sea. *see in index* Sea anemone

Anemophilous flower, wind pollinated F-219

Aneroid barometer B-82
 mountain altitude M-633

Anesthesia, complete or partial loss of feeling A-412. *see also in index* Anesthetics
 body temperature B-207
 chloroform C-393
 hospital H-280
 Long's discovery L-295
 medicine M-285

Anesthesiologist, specialist in anesthesiology S-519b

Anesthesiology, science of anesthesia and anesthetics A-398, *table* M-277

Anesthetics, drugs able to cause complete or partial loss of feeling A-412. *see also in index* Anesthesia
 antihistamine uses A-492
 body temperature B-207
 chloroform C-393
 medicine M-285

Aneto, Pico de (French name Pic de Néthou), highest mountain 11,168 ft (3,404 m) of Pyrenees, in Spain, about 50 mi (80 km) w. of Andorra.

Aneurysm, localized abnormal dilation of an artery D-174

Anfa, Berber village on site of present-day Casablanca, Morocco C-194

Anfinsen, Christian Boehmer (born 1916), U.S. biochemist, born in Monessen, Pa.; laboratory chief National Institute of Arthritis and Metabolic Diseases from 1963. *see also in index* Nobel Prizewinners, *table*

ANG. *see in index* Reserves

Angara River, river in Siberia; outlet of Lake Baikal (Baykal); flows 1,150 mi (1,850 km) to Yenisey River; also called Upper Tunguska in lower course, *maps* R-345, A-697

Angel, James, U.S. adventurer A-415

Angel, John (1881–1960), U.S. sculptor, born in Newton Abbot, Devon, England; to U.S. 1925, became citizen 1936; known for religious figures and war memorials S-85, *picture* S-84

Angel, supernatural spirits of intermediary being between God and mankind A-414. *see also in index* Demon
 Bosch's 'Vision of Tondalys', *picture* P-33
 Cimabue's 'Madonna of the Angels', *picture* P-29
 El Greco's 'Assumption of the Virgin', *picture* P-40
 Giotto's 'Descent from the Cross', *picture* P-29
 'Jonah and the Whale' P-67e, *picture* P-67e
 Memling's 'Madonna and Child with Angels', *picture* P-32

Angel Falls, waterfall in Venezuela A-414
 Guiana Highlands G-302
 Orinoco River O-606
 Venezuela, *picture* V-276, *map* V-275
 waterfall W-95, *chart* W-98

Angelfish, popular name of several freshwater and saltwater fishes, including the scalare, a popular aquarium fish, silver with gray or black bars, under 6 in. (15 cm), native to the Amazon and Guiana; also some types of bright-colored coral-reef dwellers, especially the *Angelichthys,* edible fish weighing up to 4 lbs (2 kg) S-144. *see also in index* Spadefish

Angelico, Fra, title given to Giovanni da Fiesole (1387–1455), Italian religious painter A-415

Angel Island, largest island in San Francisco Bay; seat of U.S. immigration and quarantine stations; Fort McDowell military reservation, established 1865 as Camp Reynolds, abandoned by Army 1946; under Spanish occupation a rendezvous of pirates, *map* S-41b

Angell, James Rowland (1869–1949), U.S. educator, born in Burlington, Vt.; son of James Burrill Angell; professor of psychology and dean of faculty University of Chicago 1911–20; president of Yale University 1921–37 P-520

Angell, Sir Norman (or Ralph Norman Angell Lane) (1874–1967), English writer and lecturer, born in Holbeach; at various times resident of U.S.; in early career Paris correspondent for U.S. newspapers; general manager *Paris Daily Mail;* lecturer U.S. universities; ('The Great Illusion'; 'The Fruits of Victory'; 'Let the People Know'; 'After All', autobiography). *see also in index* Nobel Prizewinners, *table*

Angel Mounds, extensive group of prehistoric mounds near Evansville, Ind.

Angelo, Valenti (born 1897), U.S. artist and children's author, born in Massarosa, Tuscany, Italy; to U.S. 1905, became citizen 1923; wrote and illustrated 'Nino', 'Golden Gate', 'Paradise Valley', 'Hill of Little Miracles', 'Marble Fountain', 'Acorn Tree', and 'Honey Boat' R-111a

Angel shark (or monk fish), fish of the family Squatinidae S-144

Angel wings, mollusk shell *Barnea costata*, *picture* S-149

Anger, Kenneth, U.S. writer M-624

Anger, human emotion
 headache H-81

Angers, Félicité. *see in index* Conan, Laure

Angers, France, historic city on Mayenne River, 165 mi (270 km) s.w. of Paris; varied manufactures; slate quarry nearby; pop. 127,415, *maps* E-360, F-369

Angina pectoris, brief paroxysm of severe chest pain with feeling of suffocation D-173

Angiography, blood vessel X rays used in medical diagnosis D-127
 disease D-173
 heart H-100

Angiosperms (or angiospermae), class of flowering, vascular plants of the division Magnoliophyta having seeds in an enclosed ovary F-220
 plant classification P-371
 seeds, *picture* S-106
 trees T-282
 wood W-280

Angkor, group of ruins in Kampuchea built by a cultured ancient people called Khmers; most notable are the temple of Angkor and the old city of Angkor Thom; found in 1861 by the French A-415

Angkor Wat, Kampuchean shrine A-415
 architecture A-546
 stonecarvings, *picture* I-107

Angle
 mathematics
  geometry G-73
  trigonometry T-285, *table* T-287
 mechanical drawing M-256

Angle milling, a machine tool operation T-221

Angle of incidence, angle formed when light strikes a mirror M-464
 optics O-573

Angle of reflection, reflected beam M-464
 optics O-573

Angler fish, marine fishes of the order Lophiiformes with lure-like appendages for baiting prey
 deep-sea form D-60, *picture* D-59
 feeding behavior F-124
  mimicry M-423
 luminescence F-131

Angles, Teutonic people who invaded Britain E-238. *see also in index* Anglo-Saxon
 Middle Ages M-384

Anglesey (or Isle of Anglesey), Wales, island in Irish Sea, connected with mainland by two bridges; with nearby Holy Island, constitutes the county of Anglesey; area 276 sq mi (715 sq km); cattle, sheep, grain; megalithic remains; pop. 51,705 W-5

Angleworm. *see in index* Earthworm

Anglia, East. *see in index* East Anglia

Anglican Cathedral, Liverpool, England L-262

Anglican Church of Australia A-418

Anglican Church of Canada A-418

Anglican Communion, family of churches originating with the Church of England A-416. *see also in index* individual Anglican churches by name, such as Church of England
 canon law C-142
 monks and monasticism M-539
 women's organizations W-270

Anglican Consultive Council A-418

Anglo-Americans, a people of the United States
 Mexican Americans H-163
 North America N-337

Anglo-Egyptian Sudan. *see in index* Sudan, Democratic Republic of the

ARBOR DAY DATES IN THE UNITED STATES

Alabama. Usually first or second Friday in December.*
Alaska. No official date.
Arizona. In the northern part, Friday following April 1; in the southern part, Friday following February 1.
Arkansas. First Saturday in December.
California. March 7, Luther Burbank's birthday.
Colorado. Third Friday in April.
Connecticut. Last Friday in April.
Delaware. In April.*
District of Columbia. Third Friday in April.
Florida. First Friday in February.
Georgia. First Friday in December.
Hawaii. Last Friday in November.*
Idaho. In April. Fixed by school superintendents.
Illinois. Last Friday in April.
Indiana. Second Friday in April.
Iowa. Usually in April.*
Kansas. Last Friday in March.
Kentucky. In March.*
Louisiana. Usually in January.*
Maine. Last Friday in April.
Maryland. In April.*
Massachusetts. Last Friday in April.
Michigan. Usually last Friday in April.*
Minnesota. Early Friday in May.*
Mississippi. First Friday in February.
Missouri. First Friday after first Tuesday in April.
Montana. Second Tuesday in May.
Nebraska. April 22, J.S. Morton's birthday. Public holiday.
Nevada. Last Friday in April.
New Hampshire. Early May.*
New Jersey. Last Friday in April.
New Mexico. Second Friday in March.
New York. Proclamation by the Commissioner of Education; late in April or early in May.
North Carolina. First Friday after March 15.
North Dakota. First Friday in May.
Ohio. Fourth Friday in April.
Oklahoma.*
Oregon. Second Friday in February in west; second Friday in April in east.
Pennsylvania. In spring, in April; also in fall, in October.*
Rhode Island. Last Friday in April.
South Carolina. First Friday in December.
South Dakota. Last Friday in April.
Tennessee. First Friday in March.
Texas. Third Friday in January.
Utah. Last Friday in April.*
Vermont. Early in May.*
Virginia. Second Friday in March.
Washington. Late April or early May.*
West Virginia. Second Friday in April.
Wisconsin. Last Friday in April.*
Wyoming. In spring.*

*The date is set by governor's proclamation.

Army, Canadian. *see in index* Canadian Armed Forces

Army, Continental, United States Revolutionary War
  Washington W-41, *picture* W-39

Army, Department of the (until 1947 Department of War) A-634, U-159
  flags, *picture* F-158
  national cemetery supervision N-23
  secretary U-159

Army, United States. *see in index* United States Army

Army and Navy Union P-140

Army ant (or driver ant, or legionary ant), insect of the family Formicidae A-468

Army Corps of Engineers, United States. *see in index* United States Army Corps of Engineers

Army Forces Command, United States A-646

Army General Staff, United States A-645

'Army Goes Rolling Along, The', U.S. patriotic song N-65

Army Medical Department A-646

Army of the Potomac. *see in index* Potomac, Army of the

Army Reserve, United States. *see in index* Reserves

Army Signal Service, United States
  weather forecasts W-121

Army Special Staff, United States A-645

Armyworm, insect *Pseudaletia unipuncta*
  moth, *picture* B-523
  wheat W-188

Arnhem, The Netherlands, manufacturing city on Rhine River 50 mi (80 km) s.e. of Amsterdam; pop. 120,091.

Arnhem Land, aboriginal reservation on the n. coast of Australia, in Northern Territory A-771, *map* A-819
  Pacific Ocean, *map* P-3

Arnis (or arnis de mano, or kali), martial arts M-160
  Philippines P-255a

Arnold, Benedict (1741–1801), American Revolutionary War general and traitor A-648
  New London N-212
  Quebec campaign C-94, R-170
  Vermont troops V-289

Arnold, Bion Joseph (1861–1942), U.S. electrical engineer, born in Casnovia, Mich.; pioneer in electric traction; consulting engineer for building New York City subways and street railway systems of Chicago and other cities G-308

Arnold, Eddy (born 1918), U.S. country musician M-679

Arnold, Hap (in full Henry Harley Arnold) (1886–1950), U.S. Army officer, born in Gladwyne, Pa.; pioneer in military aviation; commanding general U.S. Army Air Forces 1942–46; retired 1946; received rank of general (5-star) of the Army 1944, general (5-star) of the Air Force 1949 A-208

Arnold, Matthew (1822–88), English poet, essayist, and critic A-649
  literary contribution E-276
  'Philomela' P-406
  Shelley S-154
  Wordsworth W-294

Arnold, Thurman Wesley (1891–1969), U.S. lawyer, public official, and writer; born in Laramie, Wyo.; assistant attorney general of U.S. 1938–43; associate justice, U.S. Court of Appeals for District of Columbia, 1943–45; 'Symbols of Government'; 'Folklore of Capitalism'; 'Fair Fights and Foul'.

Arnoldson, Klas Pontus (1844–1916), Swedish statesman and pacifist, born in Göteborg; wrote and lectured on peace and founded Swedish peace society. *see also in index* Nobel Prizewinners, *table*

Arnolfo di Cambio (1232?–1302?), Italian architect and sculptor of Gothic period, called greatest of his time; did much to beautify Florence
  Palazzo Vecchio, *picture* P-229a

Arno River, river in Italy, rises in Apennines, flows 150 mi (240 km) to Mediterranean, *map* I-402
  Florence, *pictures* F-191, E-352

Aroe Islands, Indonesia. *see in index* Aru Islands

Aromatic plants, those containing volatile oils of pleasant odor, used in perfumery and as flavors
  perfumes P-203
  spices S-379

Aromatic seeds, used in seasoning S-379. *see also in index* Herbs

Aromatic series (or benzene series), chemical compounds
  coal-tar products C-527
  organic chemistry O-602
  perfumes P-204
  petrochemicals P-228

Aroostook, county in Maine; famous for agricultural development; area 6,721 sq mi (17,407 sq km); county seat Houlton; pop. 94,078.

Aroostook River, n. Maine, flows 125 mi (200 km) to the St. John River, of which it is a tributary.

Aroostook War, boundary dispute between Maine and Canada
  Maine M-56
  New Brunswick N-157
  Scott S-75
  Van Buren V-261

Arouet, François Marie. *see in index* Voltaire

'Around the World in Eighty Days', work by Verne V-303

Arp, Bill. *see in index* Smith, Charles H.

Arpád (died 907), Magyar chief, a national hero of Hungary; in late 9th century led Magyars dwelling north of Caspian Sea over Carpathians into the Hungarian plain; founded Arpád Dynasty whose first crowned king was Saint Stephen (977?–1038); dynasty ended with Andrew III in 1301 H-329. *see also in index* Stephen, Saint

Arpeggio, in music, *list* M-670

Arraignment, legal term, *table* L-92

Arran, island off w. coast of Scotland, in Firth of Clyde; area about 166 sq mi (430 sq km); beautiful hills, lakes, and streams; visited by many tourists in summer; pop. 3,700, *map* A-586

'Arrangement in Grey and Black', work by Whistler W-194

Arras, town in France; pop. 48,494, *map* F-369
  lace L-16
  tapestry T-26

Array, aspect of memory in computers E-176

Arrhenius, Svante August (1859–1927), Swedish chemist and physicist, born in Wijk, near Uppsala; director Nobel Institute for Physical Chemistry 1905–27; advocate of theory that the energy of the world is self-renewing ('Worlds in the Making'). *see also in index* Nobel Prizewinners, *table*

Arrian (fl. 2 AD), Greek historian G-278

Arroba, Mexican unit of weight, *table* W-141

Arroba, Spanish unit of capacity, *table* W-141

Arrow, Kenneth Joseph (born 1921), U.S. economist, born in New York, N.Y.; professor Stanford University 1953–68, Harvard University 1968. *see also in index* Nobel Prizewinners, *table*

Arrow. *see in index* Bow and arrow

Arrow Dam, dam on Columbia River in British Columbia, *picture* B-453

Arrowhead, perennial plant of genus *Sagittaria* with leaves shaped like arrowheads; 6 to 72 in. (15 to 183 cm) tall; flowers white, 3-petaled; by changing shape of leaves adapts itself to life in water or on dry land, *pictures* A-516, P-360

Arrowhead, in archery A-649
  American Indian crafts, *diagram* I-114
  archery, *picture* A-539

Arrowhead country, region in the North Woods of Minnesota M-439, 443

Arrow Rock Tavern, historic shrine in Missouri, *picture* M-499

'Arrowsmith', work by Lewis L-142

Arrowworm (or glassworm), worm of the phylum Chaetognath W-362
  oceanography O-485

Arroya. *see in index* Wadi

Arsenate mineral, classification M-432, 435

Arsenic (As), highly poisonous semimetallic element A-649
  alchemists' discovery A-273
  antidote P-411
  minerals M-432
  periodic table, *table* P-207, *list* P-208
  semiconductor use C-799

Arsenic sulfide. *see in index* Realgar

Arsenopyrite. *see in index* Mispickel

Arson, the unlawful and voluntary burning of property
  crime C-771
  fire fighting F-110
  legal definition, *table* L-92
  police technicians, *picture* P-429

Arsonval, Jacques Arsène d' (1851–1940), French physicist and physician, born near Limoges; pioneer in therapeutic use of electricity, heat, and light.

Arsphenamine. *see in index* Salvarsan

'Ars Poetica', work by MacLeish M-21

Art. *see in index* Arts, the

Art and History Museum. *see in index* Kunsthistorisches Museum

Artaud, Antonin (1896–1948), French actor and director A-25

Artaxerxes III (died 338 BC), king of Persia, ruled 362–338 BC; cruel and despotic ruler; conquered Egypt on third attempt; also took part of Phoenicia P-212

Art Deco, style
  fashion F-42
  furniture F-461

Art director, in motion pictures M-607

Artemesium, battle of (480 BC) T-163
  warfare, *list* W-14

Artemis, in Greek mythology, daughter of Zeus and Leto, twin sister of Apollo; virgin huntress and moon goddess; Roman counterpart Diana M-700
  Homeric legend H-221
  Pleiades P-391
  statues, *picture* S-91
  temple at Ephesus S-115

Artemisia (4th century BC), queen of Halicarnassus, an ancient Greek city in Asia Minor; built famous tomb for her husband, Mausolus S-115, *picture* S-116

Art Ensemble of Chicago, jazz band, *picture* J-86

Arteriosclerosis (commonly called hardening of the arteries), condition in which artery walls thicken and lose elasticity H-98
  circulatory system disorder C-422
  diabetes D-126
  disease D-144
  food and nutrition F-279

Artery, blood vessel that carries blood from heart to body tissues B-313. *see also in index* Carotid artery
  circulatory system C-421
  silicone substitutes S-196

Artesia, Calif., city 4 mi (6 km) s. of Norwalk; feed mills, sheet metal works; pop. 14,301.

Artesia, N.M., city about 38 mi (61 km) s. of Roswell; oil fields; irrigation farming; beef cattle and sheep; oil refineries; potash mining; pop. 10,385, *map* N-228

Artesian Basin, Australia
  oasis O-454

Artesian well S-396
  oasis O-454
  water W-69

Art gallery. *see in index* Gallery

Arthritis, inflammation of joints and connective tissue; chronic stage often leads to deformity of joints A-650
  bone illnesses B-342
  disease D-163
  joints J-137

Arthropods, a phylum of animals comprising invertebrates with external skeleton, segmented body, and jointed appendages A-424. *see also in index* Insect
  body characteristics A-434
  invertebrate group I-284
  joint J-136
  jungle J-157
  prehistoric animals A-461

Arthur, legendary king of ancient Britons; founder of the Order of the Round Table A-655. *see also in index* Arthurian legend
  English literature E-265
  Order of the Round Table R-299a
  storytelling S-473

Arthur (1187–1203?), duke of Brittany J-124

Arthur, Chester Alan (1829–86), 21st president of the United States A-651
  Red Cross established R-117

Arthur, Ellen Herndon (1837–80), wife of U.S. President Arthur A-652

Arthurian legend A-655
  editions and translations S-481a, b, R-111b, 112d
  English literature E-265, 276
  Holy Grail H-207
  Parsifal, or Perceval. *see in index* Parsifal
  romance R-239
  Round Table R-299a
  storytelling S-473

Arthurs, Stanley Massey (1877–1950), U.S. artist, born in Kenton, Del.; painter of U.S. historical scenes, *picture* P-330

Arthus reaction, medical disorder I-57

Artibonite Valley, valley in Haiti H-11

Article, in grammar G-208

Articles of Confederation A-656
  Continental Congress C-692
  U.S. Constitution U-139, 141
  U.S. history U-172
  Washington W-41

Articulated truck, a basic type of truck T-291, *picture* T-292

Articulation, in anatomy, joint in skeleton of a vertebrate; union of bones or ligaments fixed to allow different degrees of motion of parts against each other
  human S-209
  ligaments B-242

Articulatory phonetics L-229

Artifact, term in archaeology for any object made by human agency (from Latin *ars,* "art"; *facere,* "to make") A-531
  hobby H-187
  prehistoric S-455

Artificial albatross, glider A-201

Artificial horizon (or gyro horizon), in flight instruments A-195

Artificial insemination, in animal breeding A-137, C-231

Artificial intelligence C-629

Artificial limb. *see in index* Bioengineering

Artificial organ, in bioengineering B-210, *picture* B-211
  surgery S-519d

Artificial respiration (or mouth-to-mouth resuscitation) R-160, B-511
  bioethical decisions B-214
  first aid F-115, *diagram* F-116

Artificial satellites. *see in index* Satellites, artificial

Artificial selection, in genetics H-140
  wheat W-189

Artigas, José Gervasio (1764–1850), Uruguayan soldier and political leader A-657

Artillery A-658. *see also in index* Antiaircraft artillery
  ammunition A-371
  armor plate protection A-631
  Krupp family K-307
  shells A-372
  warfare innovations A-641
  weapon W-111

Art Institute of Chicago, located in Grant Park, Chicago, Ill.; established 1879; noted for 19th- and 20th-century French paintings, Oriental arts, Thorne miniature rooms, and contemporary U.S. paintings, *picture* C-313
  El Greco's 'The Assumption of the Virgin' P-39, *picture* P-40
  quilts, *pictures* Q-17
  Rembrandt's 'Young Girl at an Open Half-Door' P-43
  Renoir's 'Two Little Circus Girls' P-23, *picture* P-22
  Rousseau's 'The Waterfall', *picture* R-299b
  Seurat's 'Sunday Afternoon on the Island of the Grand Jatte' P-53
  Shahn's 'Mine Disaster' P-62
  'The Priest Kōbō Daishi as a Child' P-67f
  Van Gogh's 'Bedroom at Arles' P-56, *picture* P-57

author of 'Mary Astor, A Life on Film', *picture* M-624

Astor, Nancy, Viscountess (or Nancy Witcher Langhorne) (1879–1964), American who became English political and social leader; born in Greenwood, Va.; member of Parliament 1919–45 A-707

Astor, Waldorf Astor, 2nd **Viscount** (1879–1952), English peer, born in New York City; great-great-grandson of John Jacob Astor; member of Parliament 1910–19; owner *London Observer* A-706

Astor, William (1830–1892) U.S. realtor and yacht builder A-706

Astor, William Backhouse (1792–1875) U.S. merchant and realtor A-706

Astor, William Vincent (1891–1959), U.S. realtor and philanthropist A-707

Astor, William Waldorf, first **Viscount** (1848–1919), financier and statesman, born in New York City; huge property holdings in New York City; U.S. ambassador to Italy 1882–85; became British subject and was made viscount 1917; owner of *Pall Mall Gazette* and *Pall Mall Magazine* A-706

Astoreth. *see in index* Astarte

Astoria, Ore., city at mouth of Columbia River; fishing, seafood packing and canning, machine shops, shipbuilding; lumber and wood products; on site of Fort Astoria; pop. 9,998 O-585, *map* U-40

Astoria Column, landmark in Astoria, Ore., *picture* O-585

'Astounding Stories', science fiction magazine S-62

Astrakhan', U.S.S.R., capital of Astrakhan' province and one of the chief ports on the Caspian Sea; pop. 465,000 A-707
- Europe, *map* E-360
- U.S.S.R., *maps* R-334, 344, 349, *graph* R-334
- world, *map* W-297

Astrobiology. *see in index* Exobiology

Astrocompass C-623

Astrodome (originally Harris County Domed Stadium), Houston, Tex. H-310, T-129

Astrogation, space navigation. *see in index* Space travel

Astrolabe, an astronomical instrument, forerunner of the sextant; used from 15th to early 18th century N-78, O-458

Astrology, originally study of the stars, forerunner of astronomy; term now used for practice of reading character and foretelling future events by positions of stars and other heavenly bodies A-707. *see also in index* Zodiac, *table*
- astronomy A-70, O-458
- education E-84
- totemism and taboo T-235

Astronaut S-343a, *pictures* S-346a, 341b, *table* S-348. *see also in index* Cosmonaut; Space travel, *subhead* manned flights
- gravitation G-240
- insignia, *pictures* U-6
- moon landings S-341, 347
  - stamp honors, *picture* S-405
- navy N-89

Astronautics , *list* S-341b. *see also in index* Space travel
- sciences S-64a

Astronomical observatory O-456

Astronomical tide, ocean waves O-489

Astronomical unit (A.U.), equal to the mean distance between the Earth and sun, about 93,000,000 mi (149,600,000 km); used for expressing distances within the solar system A-713
- planets P-351

Astronomy A-709. *see also in index* Earth; Light; Moon; Physics; Planet; Satellites; Star; Sun; *also* chief topics listed below
- asteroids A-705
- astrology A-707
- astrophysics S-412
- bibliography S-254e
- black hole search B-306
- calendar C-30
- comets C-596
- constellation C-680
- cosmology C-731
- distance measurement S-413
- dust-cloud hypothesis P-355
- eclipse E-48
- education E-84
- evolution E-365
- galaxy S-415, U-199, *pictures* S-412, U-203
- gaseous-tidal theory P-355
- history U-198, S-57g, *pictures* U-199
  - Adams P-354
  - Banneker B-74
  - Brahe K-45, A-661a
  - Bunsen S-371, B-374, P-303
  - Chaldeans B-9
  - Chamberlin P-355
  - Copernicus C-709, S-57g
  - Digges U-198, *picture* U-199
  - Einstein R-140, *diagrams* R-142
  - Galileo G-6, S-52, S-514, *pictures* S-57g, P-303
  - Galle P-354
  - Han Dynasty C-363
  - Herschel H-144, P-354
  - Janssen S-372
  - Jeans J-88, P-355
  - Jeffreys P-355
  - Kepler K-228, S-57g
  - Kirchhoff S-371, P-303
  - Kuiper P-355, S-254e, b
  - Laplace L-49, P-355
  - Leverrier P-354
  - Lockyer S-372
  - Maya M-237
  - Mitchell M-512
  - Newton P-302
  - Ptolemy U-198, S-57g
  - Stonehenge. *see in index* Stonehenge
  - Tombaugh P-355
  - Urey P-355
  - Weizsäcker P-355
- instruments
  - coronagraph S-512
  - interferometer S-414
  - spectrograph S-372, A-655
  - spectroheliograph S-513
  - spectroscope S-371, S-412, *diagram* S-372
- magnetism M-47
- mathematics M-214
- Milky Way U-198, S-412, S-254, *charts* S-415, 419
- motions of heavenly bodies U-198, *diagrams* S-254c
- planets P-350, S-254a, S-57g, *diagram* P-352, S-254c, *table* P-351
- stars S-254c, S-413, 653, 655, 659, *table* P-351
- navigation N-71, 74, *diagrams* N-76, 77
- nebular hypothesis P-355
- observatory O-456
- parallax S-413
- photography P-280
- physics P-301
- planetesimal theory P-355
- Ptolemaic system U-198, S-57g
- quasars Q-7, S-415
- relativity R-140
- sciences S-64a
- seasons S-101
- spectrum and spectrum analysis S-371
- speed of light L-198
- surveying S-520
- tides O-489
- time T-187
- universe U-198, *pictures* U-198, 202, *diagrams* U-200
- U.S. exploration A-329
- X rays X-404

'Astronomy', periodical A-731

Astronomy, amateur A-730

Astrophysics A-282, S-412
- sciences S-64a

Asturias, Miguel Angel (1899–1974), Guatemalan writer, born in city of Guatemala; ambassador to El Salvador 1953, to France 1966–70; won 1966 Lenin peace prize ('The President', novel) L-70, *picture* L-75. *see also in index* Nobel Prizewinners, *table*

Asturias, ancient province of n.w. Spain, nucleus of Spanish kingdom S-358

Astyages, last Median king, reigned 584–550 BC; captured by his own army when it mutinied M-273

Asunción, Paraguay, capital, on Paraguay River; pop. 513,300 A-731
- Panama P-111, *picture* P-112
- South America, *map* S-299
- world, *map* W-297

Aswan (ancient Syene), town and resort in Upper Egypt on Nile River; near ruins; pop. 117,490 E-114
- Africa A-94, *map* A-115
- ancient Egypt, *map* E-124
- Persian Empire, *map* P-212

Aswan High Dam, Egypt, on Nile River A-732
- Africa A-106, *map* A-115
- dam construction D-17
- Egypt E-114, *picture* E-116
- irrigation I-356
- Nasser N-21
- Nile N-317

Asymptomatic carrier D-166

'As You Like It', play by Shakespeare S-133, 139
- figures of speech F-81
  - world defined W-295

Asyut (or Asiut), Egypt, city near w. bank of Nile River, 200 mi (320 km) s. of Cairo; a Coptic center; pop. 246,796 E-119

Atabrine. *see in index* Quinacrine

Atacama Desert, Chile C-329

Atahualpa (died 1533), last Incan ruler of Peru P-349

Atamasco lily. *see in index* Zephyranthes

Atari, U.S. video game company I-194

Atatürk (full name Mustafa Kemal Atatürk) (1881–1938), president of Turkey A-732
- Turkey T-320, 323
  - Ottoman Empire O-618
- veils E-319

Atavism. *see in index* Reversion to type

Atbash, Hebrew cryptography C-420

ATC (Air Training Command), U.S. Air Force A-164

Atchafalaya River, river in Louisiana, outlet of Red and Mississippi rivers; flows s. about 220 mi (350 km) into Gulf of Mexico.

Atchison, Kan., city in n.e. part of state on Missouri River about 40 mi (60 km) n.w. of Kansas City, Kan.; railroad shops, steel foundry; flour, industrial alcohol; Benedictine College; pop. 11,407.

Atchison, Topeka and Santa Fe Railway, chartered 1859 as Atchison and Topeka Railroad Company by Cyrus Kurtz Holliday (1826–1900); built along old Santa Fe Trail 1868–80, later extended to operate from Chicago to w. coast; present name 1895 A-272

Ate, goddess in Greek mythology; impelled both gods and men to folly, reckless deeds, and crime; flung from Olympus by Zeus, her father; later believed to avenge sin.

A tempo, in music, *list* M-670

Aten. *see in index* Aton

Aterian, ancient toolmaking industry M-86

Atget, Eugène (1857–1927), French photographer A-733

Athabasca, Lake (or Lake Athabaska), lake in n. Alberta and Saskatchewan; area 3,120 sq mi (8,080 sq km)
- Alberta, *map* A-270
- Canada, *map* C-112
- Mackenzie River M-15
- North America, *map* N-350
- Saskatchewan S-49a, 49d, *list* S-49b
- world, *map* W-297

Athabasca, Mount, mountain in Banff National Park, Alberta; 11,452 ft (3,490 m), *map* C-109

Athabascan languages. *see in index* Athapaskan languages

Athabasca River, river in Alberta; flows 800 mi (1,290 km) n.e. to Lake Athabasca
- Alberta A-263, *map* A-270
- Canada, *map* C-109
- North America, *map* N-350

Athabasca University, Edmonton, Alta. A-266, E-76

Athanasius, Saint (296–373), bishop of Alexandria, chief defender of orthodox doctrine of Trinity against Arianism; festival May 2 B-185
- Constantine the Great C-680

Athapaskan Indians (or Athabascan Indians, or Athapascan Indians, or Dene Indians), linguistic stock of North American Indians centered about Yukon and Mackenzie rivers but extending into Alaska and s. to New Mexico, Arizona, and Texas A-242
- language, *tables* I-138, 139
- Northwest Territories N-388
- Yukon Territory Y-440

'Atharvavedat', canon of Hinduism I-105

Atheism, the belief that there is no Supreme Being or God; usually associated with materialism (the belief that matter is the sole guiding force of the universe); the term comes from the Greek word *atheos,* meaning "without God"
- Enlightenment E-289
- Eurocommunism E-355
- God G-173
- U.S.S.R. R-332e

Athena, in Greek mythology, goddess of wisdom A-733
- Acropolis A-23
- Greek mythology M-700, *picture* M-699
- Homeric legend H-221, *picture* H-222
- Perseus P-210
- temple. *see in index* Parthenon

'Athenaeum', magazine M-34

'Athenaeum', work by Stuart S-493

Athenagoras I (originally Aristocles Mathew Spyrou) (1886–1972), patriarch of Eastern Orthodox church, born near Ioannina, Greece, then part of Ottoman Empire; metropolitan of Corfu 1922–30; archbishop of North and South America 1930–48; archbishop of Constantinople, New Rome, and ecumenical patriarch 1948–72 P-142a

Athena Nike, Temple of. *see in index* Wingless Victory

Athena Parthenos, statue by Phidias A-733
- Acropolis A-23

Athens, Ala., city 14 mi (22 km) n. of Decatur in agricultural region; sawmills, cotton gins; Athens State College; incorporated 1818; occupied by Union troops 1862; pop. 14,558, *map* A-236

Athens, Ga., cotton trading city 60 mi (100 km) e. of Atlanta; textiles, clothing, wood products, electronic components, clocks, rubber products; U.S. Navy Supply Corps School; pop. 42,549, *map* U-41

Athens (or Athínai), Greece, capital; pop. 867,023, A-734
- Acropolis A-23. *see also in index* Acropolis; Parthenon
- ancient Greece G-265
- Aristophanes A-588
- Athena's worship A-733
- city-state C-461
- democracy D-92
- education E-78
- etiquette E-319
- Europe, *map* E-360
- Greece G-257
- Greek literature G-275
- hairdressing H-9
- international trade I-269
- jury system J-158
- navy T-163
- Peloponnesian War
  - Thebes T-162
  - Thucydides's account T-177
- Pericles P-205
- Persian Wars P-214
- Phidias P-249
- slave labor S-212
- Solon S-255
- Theseus myth T-168
- world, *map* W-297

Athens, Ohio, city on Hocking River 65 mi (105 km) s.e. of Columbus; meat and dairy products, business machinery, tire molds, tools; Ohio University; state mental hospital; pop. 19,743.

Athens, Tenn., city 28 mi (45 km) n.e. of Cleveland; diversified industry; Tennessee Wesleyan College; pop. 12,080.

Athens of the South. *see in index* Nashville

Atheroma, fatty deposit of cholesterol D-173

Atherosclerosis, type of arteriosclerosis. *see also in index* Arteriosclerosis
- aging A-126
- circulatory system disorder C-422
- disease D-174
- heart H-98
- transplantation of blood vessels T-251

Athlete's foot, fungus infection of the skin between the toes D-178

Athletic games A-737. *see also in index* Amateur athletics; Games; Physical education; Play; Sports
- black Americans B-300

Athlone, Ireland, town on Shannon River 70 mi (110 km) w. of Dublin; vital military point; taken by James II in 1690; pop. 9,623.

Athol, Mass., town on Millers River about 32 mi (52 km) n.w. of Worcester; tools and other metal products, shoes, paint, artificial leather, wood products; pop. of township 10,634.

Athos, one of the musketeers in Dumas's novel. *see in index* 'Three Musketeers, The'

Athos, peninsula in n.e. Greece; has Mt. Athos 6,670 ft (2,033 m) G-259, *picture* G-261

AUSTRALIA'S PRIME MINISTERS

Name	Term	Party
Sir Edmund Barton	1901–03	Liberal
Alfred Deakin	1903–04 1905–08 1909–10	Liberal
John C. Watson	1904	Labor
Sir George H. Reid	1904–05	Liberal Coalition
Andrew Fisher	1908–09 1910–13 1914–15	Labor
Sir Joseph Cook	1913–14	Liberal
William M. Hughes	1915–23	Labor to 1917, then Nationalist
Stanley M. Bruce	1923–29	Nationalist
James H. Scullin	1929–32	Labor
Joseph A. Lyons	1932–39	United
Sir Earle Page	1939	Country
Robert G. Menzies	1939–41	United
Arthur W. Fadden	1941	Country
John Curtin	1941–45	Labor
Francis M. Forde	1945	Labor
Joseph B. Chifley	1945–49	Labor
Robert G. Menzies	1949–66	Liberal-Country Coalition
Harold E. Holt	1966–67	Liberal
John G. Gorton	1968–71	Liberal
William McMahon	1971–72	Liberal
(Edward) Gough Whitlam	1972–75	Labor
Malcolm Fraser	1975–83	Liberal-Country Coalition
Robert Hawke	1983–	Labor

The letter B

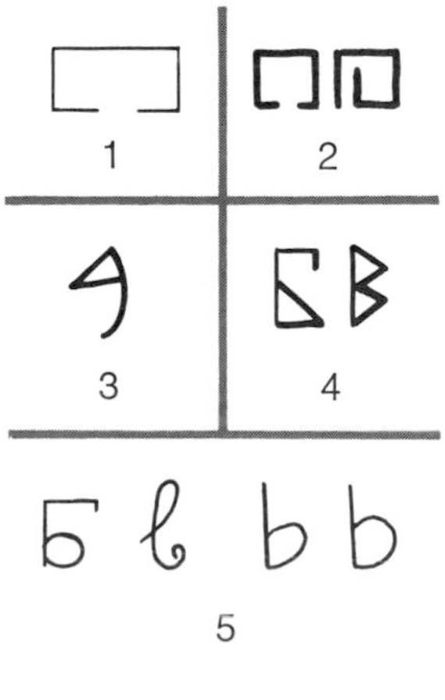

probably started as a picture sign of a house, as in Egyptian hieroglyphic writing (1) and in a very early Semitic writing used about 1500 B.C. on the Sinai Peninsula (2). About 1000 B.C., in Byblos and in other Phoenician and Canaanite centers, the sign was given a linear form (3), the source of all later forms. In the Semitic languages the sign was called *beth,* meaning "house."

The Greeks changed the Semitic name *beth* to *beta.* This word is found in the English word alpha*bet.* Later, when the Greeks began to write from left to right instead of from right to left, they turned the letter around (4). The Romans took this form almost unchanged into Latin, and from Latin it came down into English.

The present small "b" first took shape in later Roman times, when scribes fell into the practice of omitting the upper loop of the capital and making the sign long and thin (5). By the 9th century the letter had its present form.

B

B-17, U.S. military aircraft. *see in index* Flying Fortress
B-24, U.S. military aircraft. *see in index* Liberator
B-26 (or Marauder), U.S. military aircraft W-334
B-29, U.S. military aircraft. *see in index* Superfortress
B-52, U.S. military aircraft A-160, *picture* A-159
Baader-Meinhof Gang (or Red Army Faction), West German terrorists
  kidnapping K-234
  terrorism T-113
Baal, ancient Middle Eastern god B-2
Baalbek. *see in index* Heliopolis
Baalzebub. *see in index* Beelzebub
Ba'ath Party. *see in index* Ba'th Party
Bab, the (or Mirza 'Ali Mohammad) (1819–50), Persian religious leader B-19
Babakoto (or Indri), animal of the family Lemuroidea L-125
Babassu nut, hard-shelled Brazilian nut valued for its oil; obtained from a palm of the genus *Attalea*, related to coconut N-449
Babbage, Charles (1792–1871), English mathematician B-2
  computer's development C-628
  Jacquard J-12
Babbitt, Milton (born 1916), U.S. composer M-676
Babbitt, Nev., community sponsored by U.S. government, on s. shore of Walker Lake, 5 mi (8 km) n.w. of Hawthorne and 90 mi (140 km) s.e. of Reno; fishing, hunting, and boating; has homes of personnel of Naval Ammunition Depot, Hawthorne, Nev.; armed-forces headquarters; pop. 1,519.
'Babbitt', novel by Lewis A-359, L-142
Babbitt metal, a soft alloy of tin, copper, and antimony A-313
Babcock, Stephen Moulton (1843–1931), U.S. educator and agricultural chemist, born in Bridgewater, N.Y.; educated at Tufts College, Cornell University, and University of Göttingen, Germany; on faculty at Cornell and Wisconsin universities; did notable work in chemistry of milk; devised Babcock milk test, which he gave to the world, refusing to patent it for private gain D-3
  Wisconsin W-251, *picture* W-255
Babel, Isaac Emanuilovich (1894–1941), Russian short-story writer, born in Odessa of Jewish family; later works were written in secret and lost; arrested by political police 1939; death mysterious ('Stories of the Red Cavalry'; 'You Must Know Everything: Stories 1915–1937') R-360b, *list* R-361
Babel. *see in index* Babylon
Babel, Tower of, tower built by Noah's descendants as a monument that would reach to heaven; during construction occurred the 'confusion of tongues' (Bible, Gen. xi) in Babylon B-3
  Babylonian ziggurat B-4
Babenberg, House of, 1st Austrian dynasty (976–1246) A-828
Baber (or Babur) (1483–1530), founder of Mughal Empire in India B-2
  India I-76
  Timur Lenk T-190
Babe the Blue Ox, animal in Paul Bunyan tales
  folklore F-265
  statue, *picture* M-444
Bab-Ilu. *see in index* Babylon
Babington conspiracy (1585) M-165
Babirusa, pig P-321
Babism. *see in index* Baha'i faith
Babol (formerly Barfurush), Iran, trading and residential town about 15 mi (25 km) s. of Caspian Sea; cotton, rice, fish, citrus fruits, tobacco; airport to n.w., at nearby Babulsar; pop. 70,000
  Asia, *map* A-697
Baboon, monkey of the family Cercopithecidae
  animal colonies A-431
  characteristics A-502, *picture* A-500
  length of life, average, *chart* A-423
Babur. *see in index* Baber
Baby. *see also in index* Child; Pregnancy
  adoption A-50
  child development C-320
  hearing test, *picture* P-311
  incubator I-60
  newborn R-151c
  obstetrics H-280
  play P-386, *picture* P-389
Baby blue-eyes. *see in index* Nemophila
Baby bonnet, snail *Cypraecassis testiculus*
  shell, *picture* S-150
Babylon (Babylonian Bab-Ilu, Biblical Babel), ancient city, Babylonia B-3, *map* P-212. *see also in index* Babylonia and Assyria
  Alexander A-280
  archaeological excavation A-532
  Hanging Gardens B-9, S-114, *picture* S-116
  Mesopotamia M-305
  paved streets R-220
  Sennacherib S-108b
Babylon, N.Y., residential village 35 mi (60 km) e. of New York, N.Y., on s. shore of Long Island, on Great South Bay; popular summer resort; pop. 12,388.
Babylonia, ancient empire in the Tigris-Euphrates Valley B-3, *maps* A-280, P-212. *see also in index* Assyria; Chaldean Empire; Sumerians
  ancient civilizations A-404
  ancient writing A-537, W-371, *pictures* G-52, P-214
  architecture S-157
    brickmaking B-438
    bridge construction B-444
    Hanging Gardens of Babylon S-114, *picture* S-116
    ziggurat P-543
  army organization A-634
  arts
    enameling E-208
    pottery P-469
    sculpture S-82
  astronomical observation O-458
  banking B-72
  education E-78
  Egypt E-126
  Hammurabi's code H-23
    prohibition P-506
  Hebrews conquered J-146
  mathematics M-213
  medicine M-281
  Mesopotamia M-305
  religion and mythology A-199
  Sabbath S-1
  slavery S-212
  Tigris River T-184
  watches and clocks W-83
Babylonian captivity
  Judaism J-146
  Roman Catholic popes P-252
Babylonian Talmud, standard text of Judaic law and religion T-18
Bacchanalia, Roman festival celebrated in honor of Bacchus; brought to Rome from Greek settlements in s. Italy; originally secret ceremonies for women only D-147
Bacchus. *see in index* Dionysus
Bach, Carl Philipp Emanuel (1714–88), German musician, son of J.S. Bach B-10
Bach, Johann Christian (1735–82), German composer, youngest son of J.S. Bach B-10
  Mozart M-643
Bach, Johann Sebastian (1685–1750), German musician and composer B-10
  classical music M-668, *picture* M-669
  Mendelssohn M-297
  oratorio O-575
  orchestra O-576
Bach, Wilhelm Friedemann (1710–84), German composer, oldest son of J.S. Bach B-10
Bachelder, John (1817–1906), U.S. inventor, born in Weare, N.H.; made many improvements on sewing machine; substituted vertical needle for original horizontal type.
Bachelor, academic distinction given by a college or university, usually after four years' study as undergraduate; common form is B.A. or A.B. (Bachelor of Arts); also given in divinity, medicine, law, science, philosophy, literature U-204
  origin U-209
Bachelor's button (or cornflower, or bluebottle), name for several garden plants; *Centaurea cyanus* has blue, pink, purple, or white flowers, *picture* F-225. *see also in index* Globe amaranth
  growing conditions G-23
'Bachianas brasileiras', work by Villa-Lobos V-325
Bachmann, Ingeborg (1926–73), German novelist
  German literature G-108
Bachur, Elijah (pen name of Elijah Levita) (1469–1549), German-born Italian grammarian
  Yiddish literature Y-417
Bacillary dysentery (or Shigellosis), infectious disease, *table* D-171
Bacillus (plural bacilli), a genus of rod-shaped bacteria B-15, *picture* B-12
Backbone. *see in index* Spine
Backbone Mountain, highest point in Maryland, 3,360 ft (1,020 m) M-167, *map* M-183
Backgammon (or Tabula, or Tables, or Tric-Trac), game played by 2 persons, each with 15 pieces or "men," on a board divided into 4 "tables," the moves being determined by dice throws; probably of Oriental origin B-320
Background projection, motion pictures M-610
Backhand, tennis, *diagram* T-105
Backpacking, recreation and camping C-70
Backs, the, gardens, Cambridge, England C-60
Backstitch, sewing S-121
Backstroke, swimming, *pictures* S-534
Back swimmer, insect of the family Notonectidae W-94
Backus, Isaac (1724–1806), U.S. Baptist leader, *list* B-77
'Backwoodsman, The', work by Paulding W-151
Bacolod, Philippines, municipality on n.w. coast of island of Negros; sugar; university; pop. 146,800 P-253c, *map* P-262
  Asia, *map* A-697
Bacon, Francis (or Viscount St. Albans, or Baron Verulam) (1561–1626), English philosopher, statesman, and writer B-10
  Elizabeth I E-191
  empiricism P-266
  Enlightenment E-289
  essay E-306
  literary contribution E-268
  Shakespeare authorship controversy S-133
  zoology Z-470
Bacon, Henry (1866–1924), U.S. architect, born in Watseka, Ill. ('Court of Four Seasons', Panama-Pacific Exposition Building, and many other notable buildings and memorials in classic Greek style)
  Lincoln Memorial's design, *picture* L-224
Bacon, Nathaniel (1647–76), North American colonial leader of Bacon's Rebellion B-11
Bacon, Peggy (born 1895), U.S. artist and writer, born in Ridgefield, Conn.; author and illustrator of books for children ('Lion-Hearted Kitten, and Other Stories'; 'The Good American Witch') R-111
Bacon, Roger (1214?–94?), English monk, scientist, author B-11
  explosive E-379
  human flight A-200
  Latin literature L-78
Bacon's Rebellion (1676), uprising in colonial Virginia B-11, V-335
  Jamestown burned J-22
Bacteria, microscopic plants, some of which, popularly called "germs," cause sickness B-12. *see also in index* Pathogenic organism
  amoeba feeds A-375
  antibiotics' effects A-488
  antiseptics A-495, L-238
  antitoxins A-495
  arthritis A-650
  bioethical decision-making B-214
  bionic research B-234
  cells C-239, *picture* C-238
  cheese ripening C-288
  classification, *picture* P-370
  deep-sea forms D-60
  digestive system D-146, *diagram* D-143
  diseases D-165
    dental caries T-52
    venereal disease V-272, *picture* V-273
  fermentation F-55
  genetic engineering G-49
  invertebrate classification I-282
  Leeuwenhoek L-117
  leprosy L-136
  living things L-266, *picture* L-269
  luminescence P-270
  microbiology M-374
  nitrogen fixation N-318, P-363a
  photosynthesis P-300
  poisons generated P-411
  respiration R-159
  sewage disposal S-119
  soil making S-250
  supersonic waves S-260
  ultraviolet rays destroy U-3
  vaccines V-250
  vitamins V-355
Bacterial endocarditis, a type of heart disease H-98
Bacterial infection, disease D-178
Bacteriology B-12. *see also in index* Microbiology
  biological fields B-230
  Koch K-266
  Pasteur P-138
Bacteriophage, a bacteria-destroying virus B-13, V-352
  Burnet B-512

living things L-266
Bactra, district in Afghanistan. *see in index* Balkh
Bactria, ancient country (modern Balkh, Afghanistan) n. of Hindu Kush range; famous for horses and camels; one of earliest homes of Aryans; conquered by Cyrus the Great and Alexander; kingdom later extended to n. India.
Bactrian camel (or Asian camel), two humped camel *Camelus bactrianus* of the Camelidae family C-62, *picture* C-63
  zoo, *picture* Z-464
Badajoz, Spain, historic city on Guadiana River, 5 mi (8 km) from Portuguese frontier; taken by French (1811) and recaptured by British (1812); pop. 101,710, *map* P-455
'Bad Child's Book of Beasts, The', work by Belloc B-157
Bad Ems, West Germany, a health resort on Lahn River, 6 mi (10 km) e. of Coblenz; from here was sent famous Ems dispatch; pop. 9,700, *map* G-131
Baden, former state of s.w. Germany, former grand duchy; 5,819 sq mi (15,071 sq km); after World War II, n. part incorporated into Baden-Württemberg, s. part became South Baden (Südbaden), sometimes called simply Baden; now part of Baden-Württemberg.
Baden-Baden, West Germany, health resort in Baden-Württemberg, at edge of Black Forest; numerous mineral springs; pop. 44,300, *map* G-131
Baden-Powell, Agnes (1858–1945), national vice-president of Girl Guides for many years; author of 'Handbook'; important worker with British Red Cross Y-428
Baden-Powell, Robert (full name Robert Stephenson Smyth Baden-Powell) (1857–1941), British general B-16
  camping C-71
  Low L-325
  youth organizations Y-427
Baden-Württemberg, state in West Germany; formed from part of former states of Baden and Württemberg and from former states of South Baden and Württemberg-Hohenzollern; pop. 9,152,700, *map* G-131
Badger, a subfamily of the weasel family W-114
  fur, *table* F-464
  hibernation H-147
Badger State. *see in index* Wisconsin
Bad Kissingen, West Germany, famous spa in Bavaria, 63 mi (101 km) e. of Frankfurt; salt springs known from 9th century; pop. 12,439, *map* G-131
Badland, region marked by erosional sculpturing
  Alberta A-263
Bad Lands, areas in western United States where shale and sandstone surface has been eroded
  North Dakota N-373, *picture* N-380
  South Dakota S-322, 328
Badlands National Monument, S.D., *picture* S-330
Bad Langensalza, East Germany, town on Salza River 19 mi (30 km) n.w. of Erfurt; Hanoverians defeated Prussians in 1866, but surrendered on arrival of Prussian reinforcements; pop. 16,304, *map* G-131
Badminton, game similar to lawn tennis but played with shuttlecocks ('birds') instead of tennis balls; played both indoors and outdoors, either with two or four players; singles (two-player) court measures 44 by 17 ft (13 by 5 m), doubles (four-player) court 44 by 20 ft (13 by 6 m), net 5 ft (2 m) high at center; named for estate of duke of Beaufort, Gloucester, England; developed from game battledore and shuttlecock B-16. *see also in index* Battledore and shuttlecock
Bad Nauheim, West Germany, famous spa 17 mi (27 km) n.e. of Frankfurt; saline springs; pop. 14,242, *map* G-131
Badoglio, Pietro (1871–1956), Italian marshal in World War I; viceroy of Ethiopia 1936; chief of general staff 1940; retired after Greek campaign of 1940; succeeded Mussolini as premier in 1943; resigned in 1944
  World War II W-333
Baeck, Leo (1873–1956), Judaic theologian B-17
Baeda. *see in index* Bede, Saint
Baedeker, Karl (1801–59), German publisher B-17
Baekeland, Leo Hendrik (1863–1944), U.S. chemist and inventor, born in Ghent, Belgium; to U.S. 1889, became citizen 1897; invented Bakelite 1909
  Bakelite I-275, *table* I-273, P-383
Baer, Karl Ernst von (1792–1876), Russian zoologist, father of embryology, born in Estonia; named librarian Academy of Sciences, St. Petersburg, 1834
  embryological study E-203
Baer, Max (1909–59), U.S. boxer, born in Omaha, Neb.; began career 1929; lost last bout to Lou Nova 1941; entered U.S. Army 1942; elected to boxing's Hall of Fame 1969
  heavyweight champion B-391
Baeyer, Adolf von (1835–1917), German chemist, born in Berlin; synthesized indigo and formulated its structure; discovered phthalein dyes. *see also in index* Nobel Prizewinners, *table*
Baez, Joan (born 1941), U.S. musician F-273
  popular music M-681
Baffin Bay, large gulf of n.e. North America, on Atlantic Ocean between Greenland and Baffin Island; 800 by 280 mi (1,290 by 450 km); discovered by William Baffin 1616 B-17
  North America, *map* N-350
  world, *map* W-297
Baffin Island (or Baffin Land), island w. of Greenland, largest in Canadian Archipelago, 5th largest in world; 195,928 sq mi (507,451 sq km); populated chiefly by Eskimos, *maps* C-109, P-417, *picture* P-363e
  national park N-28
  North America, *map* N-350
  size, comparative. *see in index* Island, *table*
  world, *map* W-297
Baffin Island Current, cold ocean current flowing southward along e. coast of Baffin Island, Can.; carries polar ice that moves into Baffin Bay from channels to w. and n.; finally, with West Greenland Current, becomes Labrador Current.
Bag, container for air
  bagpipe W-228
Baganda, an African people U-2
  folktales S-478
Bagasse, sugarcane waste S-506
Baggataway. *see in index* Lacrosse
Baggins, Bilbo, character in 'The Hobbit', *picture* N-411
Baghdad (or Bagdad), Iraq, chief city and capital; pop. 3,205,600, with suburbs B-18
  Asia, *map* A-697
  caliphate C-56
  Iraq I-313, *map* I-312
  Mesopotamia M-305
  world, *map* W-297
  zoo history Z-466
Baghdad Pact (now Central Treaty Organization, or CENTO), mutual security agreement signed in 1955 which formed the Middle East Treaty Organization (METO) B-19
Bag model, theory in particle physics
  quark Q-5
Bagnell Dam, dam in Missouri, across Osage River in Ozark Mts., 120 mi (190 km) s.e. of Kansas City, Mo.; forms Lake of the Ozarks, one of largest artificial lakes in world; electric power generated delivered mostly to St. Louis M-489, *picture* M-493
  Ozark Mountains O-624
Bagnold, Enid (or Lady Jones) (1889–1981), British novelist, born in Rochester, England ('National Velvet', story about horses; 'The Loved and Envied', novel; 'The Chalk Garden', play), *list* H-274
Bagot, Sir Charles (1781–1843), British statesman, born in Rugely, Staffordshire, England; governor-general of British North America 1841–43; advocated 'responsible government'
  Rush-Bagot Agreement (1817) G-248
Bagpipe, wind instrument W-228, *picture* S-70
Baguio, Philippines, city on island of Luzon, 130 mi (210 km) n. of Manila; pop. 100,209, with suburbs, *map* P-262, *pictures* P-257b, 259b
  Asia, *map* A-697
Baguio, wind W-225. *see also in index* Typhoon
  Philippines P-259a
Bagworm moth, insect of family Psychidae B-526
Baha' Alla. *see in index* Mirza, Husayn 'Ali Nur
Baha'i faith (originally called Babism), a religious movement growing out of Babism; founded in Persia 1844 by Mirza 'Ali Mohammed, who took title of the Bab ('gate' or 'door') B-19
  Haifa H-6
  Iran M-459
  Islamic origins I-362
Bahamas, The (officially Commonwealth of the Bahamas), area 5,400 sq mi (13,900 sq km); pop. 209,600 B-20, *map* U-41
  Columbus, *picture* U-130
  Commonwealth membership C-602
  flag, *picture* F-162
  North America N-334, *map* N-350
  sponges S-394
  United Kingdom E-259
  West Indies 155, *map* W-159
  world, *map* W-297
  World War II W-325
Bahasa Indonesia, language
  Indonesia I-159
Baha' Ullah. *see in index* Mirza, Husayn 'Ali Nur
Bahia, city in Brazil. *see in index* Salvador
Bahia Blanca, Argentina, seaport and railroad center; exports wheat, wool; naval station; pop. 182,158 S-281, *maps* A-585, S-299
  world, *map* W-297
Bahrain, small Arab monarchy, area 260 sq mi (668 sq km); cap. Manama; pop. 358,857 B-20
  Arabia A-521, *map* A-522
  Asia, *map* A-697
  flag, *picture* F-162
  petroleum P-211
Bahr Yusef, river, Egypt, branch of the Nile River E-115
Bahutu. *see in index* Hutu
Baie d'Espoir Lowland, lowland in Newfoundland N-165
Baikal, Lake (or Lake Baykal), s. Siberia, U.S.S.R.; deepest freshwater lake in the world B-21, *map* R-322
  Asia, *map* A-697
  lakes L-24
  Trans-Siberian Railroad T-266
  world, *map* W-297
Bail. *see in index* Bailment
Bail. *see in index* Pick-up finger
Baile Atha Cliath, Ireland. *see in index* Dublin
Bailey (or Courtyard), enclosure C-199
Bailey, Carolyn Sherwin (1875–1961), U.S. writer of children's books, born in Hoosick Falls, N.Y.; married Eben Clayton Hill; ('Children of the Handcrafts'; 'Tops and Whistles'; 'Pioneer Art in America'; 'Miss Hickory', won 1947 Newbery medal; 'Finnegan II'; 'The Little Red Schoolhouse') R-111
Bailey, Hackaliah, U.S. farmer turned circus manager; brought one of the first elephants to U.S. C-427
Bailey, James Anthony (formerly James Anthony McGinness) (1847–1906), circus partner of P.T. Barnum, born in Detroit, Mich. C-429
Bailey, Mollie A. (or Maw Bailey), U.S. circus manager C-428
Bailey bridge, portable bridge B-444
Bailment (or bail), in law
  legal definition, *table* L-92
Baily's beads, circle of bright points seen around the moon during a solar eclipse M-580
Bain, Alexander (1818–1903), Scottish clock maker O-495
Bainbridge, William (1774–1833), U.S. Navy officer, born in Princeton, N.J.; in war with Tripoli commanded the *Philadelphia*, captured a Moorish frigate, but was himself taken prisoner with more than 300 men S-177g
  War of 1812 W-31
Bainbridge, Ga., city on Flint River, 34 mi (55 km) w. of Thomasville; residential and manufacturing center; pop. 10,553.
Baird, Bil (or William Britton Baird) (1904–87), puppeteer, born in Grand Island, Neb.; with wife, **Cora** (1912–67), gave puppet shows on stage, screen, and television; author of 'The Art of the Puppet'
  puppets P-535
Baird's sandpiper, bird of the family Scolopacidae S-40
Baireuth, West Germany. *see in index* Bayreuth
Bairiki, capital city of the republic of Kíribati K-250
Bait, something used in luring
  fishing F-140, *pictures* F-100, 141
  trapping T-267
Bait, tool used in glass manufacture G-158
Bait pricing, marketing M-143
Baiu (or tsuyu), June rainy season in Japan J-62
Baja California, peninsula of Mexico. *see in index* California, Lower
Baja California Norte, state of Mexico, occupying n. half of peninsula Lower California; 27,071 sq mi (69,984 sq km); cap. Mexicali; pop. 1,252,817 C-54
  Mexico, *map* M-341
Baja California Sur, state of Mexico, occupying s. half of peninsula Lower California; 28,447 sq mi (73,677 sq km); cap. La Paz; pop. 180,755 C-54
  Mexico, *map* M-341
Bajer, Fredrik (1837–1922), Danish pacifist and politician; a founder of International Peace Bureau at Bern, Switzerland, 1891. *see also in index* Nobel Prizewinners, *table*
Bakan, Japan. *see in index* Shimonoseki
Bake, in cooking C-700
Bakelite, industrial plastics P-383
  Baekeland I-275, *table* I-273
Baker, George. *see in index* Divine, Father
Baker, Janet (born 1933), British opera mezzo-soprano, *list* O-570
Baker, Josephine (1906–75), French entertainer, born in St. Louis, Mo.; to France 1925, became French citizen 1937; exotic performer on stage and off; worked with Free French in World War II; active in U.S. as civil rights demonstrator during 1960s B-301
Baker, Newton Diehl (1871–1937), U.S. lawyer and political leader, born in Martinsburg, W. Va.; city solicitor of Cleveland 1902–12; mayor of Cleveland 1912–16; U.S. secretary of war under President Wilson 1916–21; member Court of International Justice 1928; member Law Enforcement (Wickersham) Commission.
Baker, Mount, volcanic peak of Cascade Range in n.w. Washington; 10,750 ft (3,280 m); located in Mount Baker National Forest, 31 mi (50 km) e. of Bellingham W-48
Baker House, college dormitory, Cambridge, Mass.; designed by Alvar Aalto A-3
Baker Island, a tiny sand and coral island in mid-Pacific, colonized by the United States in 1935 for use as a way station for airplanes flying from Hawaii to Australia, *map* P-3
  world, *map* W-297
Baker's dozen, unit of measure, *table* W-140
Bakersfield, Calif., city 100 mi (160 km) n.w. of Los Angeles; fruit shipping; petroleum products, oil field machinery, electronic components, food products; California State College, Bakersfield; pop. 105,611, *map* U-40
  country music M-679

Baker vs. Carr, case in U.S. constitutional law C-686, *list* S-518b

Bakery B-429
- Pacific Islands, *picture* P-18
- Pompeii and Herculaneum P-443
- prison class, *picture* P-505d

Bakewell, Robert (1725–95), English farmer, established scientific stock breeding C-225

Bakhtiari, an Asian people
- Iran I-305

Baking. *see in index* Bread and baking

Baking powder, compound of sodium bicarbonate and an acid salt or an alum; chemical action causes pastry and quick breads to rise, or expand.

Baking soda, sodium bicarbonate S-247

Bakongo, a Central African people A-107

Bakr, Amad Hassan al- (l914-82), president of Iraq 1968–79
- Iraq I-315

Bakst, Leon Nikolaevich (1868–1924), Russian genre and portrait painter and decorative designer; noted for stage settings and costumes, especially for Diaghilev's Russian Ballet B-34

Baku, U.S.S.R., oil center and seaport, capital of Azerbaijan Soviet Socialist Republic, on w. coast of Caspian Sea; pop. 1,046,000 B-21, *maps* R-322, 344, 349
- world, *map* W-297

Bakufu, administrative organization of shogun in Japan J-63

Bakunin, Mikhail (full name Mikhail Aleksandrovich Bakunin) (1814–76), Russian anarchist and a founder of Nihilism B-22

Balaguer y Ricardo, Joaquín Vidella (born 1907), Dominican lawyer, writer, and diplomat; vice president of the Dominican Republic (1957–60); president (1960–62 and 1966–78); wrote numerous books on politics, history and literature ('Historia de la Literatura Dominica') D-228
- Caribbean literature C-166

Balakirev, Mili Alekseevich (1837–1910), Russian composer; a follower of Glinka, he became leader of Young Russian School of music with 'truth and nationalism' as battle cry; overtures, incidental music to 'King Lear', a piano fantasy 'Islamey', songs
- classical music M-674

Balaklava, port of the Crimea, 6 mi (10 km) from Sevastopol'; scene of battle of Oct. 25, 1854, during Crimean War, which was immortalized in Tennyson's poem 'The Charge of the Light Brigade', *map* R-349

Balalaika (or balalayka), Russian stringed musical instrument similar to a guitar; usually consists of triangular body with long neck R-331

Balance, accounting
- accounting records A-15
- bank account B-65

Balance, arts A-604
- design D-109

Balance, body. *see in index* Equilibrium

Balance, constellation. *see in index* Libra

Balance, weighing machine W-134

Balance Agriculture with Industry Act, United States Mississippi M-469, 472

Balance beam, gymnastics G-323

Balance of nature
- conservation C-669
- ecology E-50
- pollution damage P-441
- Saint Lawrence Seaway and Great Lakes H-144

Balance-of-payments, international finance I-258
- foreign exchange F-307

Balance of power, condition among nations in which none has sufficient power to endanger the independence of the others.

Balance of trade, international trade
- foreign exchange F-307
- mercantile theory R-166

Balance spring (or hairspring), watches and clocks W-78

Balanchine, George (formerly Georgy Melitonovich Balanchivadze) (1904–83), U.S. ballet dancer and choreographer B-22
- ballet B-32, D-29

Balante, a people of Africa
- Guinea-Bissau G-315

Balata (or gutta-balata), gum obtained from the tree *Manilkara bidentata* G-321

Balaton, Lake (German Plattensee), largest lake in Hungary, 60 mi (100 km) s.w. of Budapest; 50 mi (80 km) long, 6–10 mi (10–16 km) wide; rich with fish; popular resort H-326, *map* E-360

Balbo, Italo (1896–1940), Italian air marshal, governor of Libya; made head of Italian armed forces in North Africa 1937; killed in airplane crash in Libya
- transatlantic flight A-205

Balboa, Vasco Nuñez de (1475–1517), Spanish explorer B-23
- exploration E-373
  - America A-331
  - Latin America L-67

Balboa, Panama, port city, just w. of city of Panama; pop. 2568 P-85, P-89, 91, 94, *maps* P-90
- Sailfish Club S-16b

Balbriggan, Ireland, seaport about 20 mi (30 km) n.e. of Dublin; balbriggan hosiery and underwear made of fine unbleached cotton originated here; name balbriggan also given to a jersey cloth with mixed colors; pop. 3,248.

Balch, Emily Greene (1867–1961), U.S. economist and sociologist, born Jamaica Plain, Mass.; teacher Wellesley College 1896–1918; international secretary, Women's International League for Peace and Freedom 1919–22 (honorary president 1936). *see also in index* Nobel Prizewinners, *table*

Balcones Escarpment, part of Gulf Coastal Plain in Texas T-116

Bald cypress. *see in index* Southern cypress

Bald eagle, bird *Haliaelus leucocephalus* E-2
- predatory behavior B-278
- toxic waste W-76
- U.S. postal uniform P-458

Balder, character in Norse mythology, god of light and the most beloved god; son of Odin and Frigga; hated by Loki, who tricked another god, Hoder, into killing Balder with a twig of mistletoe M-703

Baldness (or alopecia) V-272
- hair H-8

Baldwin I (1172–1205), count of Flanders and emperor of Constantinople B-536

Baldwin, Frank Stephen, (1838–1925) U.S. inventor of rotary calculator C-20

Baldwin, James (1841–1925), U.S. author and compiler, born in Hamilton County, Ind.; edited schoolbooks and mythological and other classical stories for children ('Old Greek Stories'; 'Four Great Americans'; 'The Golden Fleece') S-466

Baldwin, James (full name James Arthur Baldwin) (born 1924), U.S. writer B-23
- American literature A-362
- 'Go Tell It on the Mountain' R-112c
- 'The Fire Next Time' R-111h

Baldwin, Robert (1804–58), Canadian statesman B-24, C-98

Baldwin, Stanley (first Earl Baldwin of Bewdley) (1867–1947), British statesman B-24
- United Kingdom E-256

Baldwin, N.Y., community 21 mi (34 km) e. of New York, N.Y.; on s. shore of Long Island; sport fishing and boating; light manufacturing; suburban community; pop. 34,525.

Baldwin, Pa., borough 3 mi (5 km) s.e. of Pittsburgh in industrial area on Monongahela River; pop. 24,598, *map* P-184

Baldwin Park, Calif., city 15 mi (25 km) e. of Los Angeles; concrete pipes, steel products, sand and gravel; machine shops; named for Elias J. (Lucky) Baldwin 1912; built on his former ranch; incorporated 1956; pop. 50,554.

Baldy Peak, peak in New Mexico, in Sangre de Cristo Range (12,623 ft; 3,847 m), about 14 mi (22 km) n.e. of Santa Fe; forms section of southernmost spur of Rocky Mountains.

Bâle. *see in index* Basel

Bale
- cotton C-739, R-115
- hay H-75
- rubber R-302, *picture* R-304
- silk, *picture* S-200
- sisal fiber, *picture* R-292

Balearic Islands (Spanish Baleares), province of Spain, in Mediterranean; 1,936 sq km (5,014 sq km); cap. Palma; pop. 658,319 B-24, *maps* E-360, S-350

Baleen whale (or whalebone) W-185
- animal A-429

Balenciaga, Cristóbal (1895–1972), Spanish fashion designer D-271

Baler, machine
- farm machinery F-35, *picture* F-36

Balestier, Charles Wolcott (1861–91), U.S. author and publisher, born in Rochester, N.Y. ('Life of James G. Blaine'; 'A Victorious Defeat').

Balfe, Michael William (1808–70), Irish composer, born in Dublin; studied on the continent; prolific composer; best-known work is light opera 'The Bohemian Girl'.

Balfour, Arthur James (1848–1930), British statesman B-24
- Zionism Z-455

Balfour Declaration, statement on Palestine mandate B-24
- Palestine P-80
- Weizmann W-143
- Zionism Z-455

Balgownie, Bridge of (or Auld Brig o'Don), bridge, Aberdeen, Scotland A-9

Bali, mountainous island of Indonesia, situated just east of Java; about 2,160 sq mi (3,480 sq km); people resemble Javanese; skillful at crafts; traces of ancient Hindu culture; old form of Brahmanism chief religion; exports rice, cacao, coffee; pop. 2,074,438 I-159, *map* I-166
- Asia, *map* A-697
- dance, *pictures* D-31
- rice fields, *picture* R-200

Baline, Israel. *see in index* Berlin, Irving

Baliol (or Balliol), name of a royal English family that emigrated to England with William the Conqueror; **Sir John de Baliol** (died 1269) married Scottish princess descended from King David I of Scotland and founded Balliol College; his son **John** (1249–1315) claimed Scottish throne and, as vassal to Edward I of England, ruled 1292–96; his grandson, **Edward,** ruled in 1332 S-70

Balkan Entente, formed by Yugoslavia, Romania, Greece, and Turkey 1934; collaborated in economic matters and communications; wrecked by Axis penetration in World War II.

Balkan League, alliance formed in 1911 between Serbia, Bulgaria, Greece, and Montenegro
- Balkan politics B-29
- Balkan Wars B-31

Balkan Mountains, mountains in Balkan Peninsula, an extension of the Carpathians; from Iron Gate of Danube, extend s. through Serbia, then turn e. to Black Sea; divide Danube and Maritsa watersheds
- Bulgaria, *picture* B-499

Balkan Peninsula, s.e. peninsula of Europe B-25

Balkans, the, countries of the s.e. peninsula of Europe, including Albania, Bulgaria, mainland Greece, European Turkey, and parts of Yugoslavia and Romania B-25, *map* E-360
- Albania A-257
- Berlin Congress partition B-172
- Crimean War C-774
- Hun wars A-758
- masks M-187
- Slavs S-214, *pictures* S-215
- World War I W-302, *map* W-304

Balkan Wars B-31
- Bulgaria B-500
- Macedonia M-8
- Romania R-318
- Serbia S-113, Y-437
- treaty B-29
- warfare, *list* W-13

Balkh, district of Afghanistan. *see in index* Bactria

Balkh (originally called Bactra, Turkish 'high town'), Afghanistan, chief city of district of Balkh; ancient city; early rival of Babylon and Nineveh; center of Zoroastrian religion; pop. 15,000 P-212

Balkhash, Lake, lake in Kazakh Soviet Socialist Republic, near Chinese border; 7,300 sq mi (18,600 sq km); w. section contains fresh water from Ili River, e. section is salt water B-31, R-323, *maps* R-322, R-344
- Asia, *map* A-697
- world, *map* W-297

Balk line, in billiards B-192

Ball, Doris Bell (or Josephine Bell) (born 1897), U.S. writer D-119

Ball, Mary. *see in index* Washington, Mary Ball

Ball T-241. *see also in index* Baseball; Basketball; Billiards; Bowling; Cricket; Football; Golf; Jai alai; Lacrosse; Polo; Soccer; Softball; Table tennis; Tennis

Ballad P-403, 407
- Australian literature A-797
- English literature E-265
- folk music F-272
- Library of Congress' collection S-477
- nursery rhymes N-442
- Robin Hood R-223
- Scott S-73

'Ballad of Baby Doe, The', opera by Moore O-571
- Tabor T-3

'Ballad of Cat Ballou, The', work by Chanslor W-151

'Ballad of Reading Gaol, The', work by Wilde W-203

'Ballad of the Sad Café, The', work by McCullers M-6

Ball and socket joint J-137

Ballarat, Australia, city of Victoria, 65 mi (105 km) n.w. of Melbourne; woolen mills; formerly gold-mining center; pop. 58,434, including suburban area, *maps* A-822, P-3

Ballast, heavy substance B-39

Ballast tank, tank in the hold of a ship S-497

Ball clay, type of clay C-488

Balleny Islands, group of five islands, in Antarctic Ocean, about 300 mi (480 km) s.w. of Victoria Land; volcanic origin; discovered 1839 by John Balleny, English shipmaster
- world, *map* W-297

Ballerina, female dancer B-32

Balleroy, French château designed by Mansart M-110

Ballesteros, Severiano (born 1957), Spanish golfer G-189, *picture* G-193

Ballet, a theatrical dance B-32
- 'A Midsummer Night's Dream', *picture* S-137
- artists
  - Balanchine B-22
  - Nureyev N-441
  - Pavlova P-142b
- Australia A-801
- dance D-26
- folk dance themes F-258
- literature L-244
- mime M-423
- music M-668, *list* M-670
- 'The Ballet Class' P-53, *picture* P-52
- U.S.S.R. R-332g, *picture* R-332f

'Ballet Class, The', painting by Degas P-53, *picture* P-52

Ballet Comique de la Reine, theatrical presentation of the late 16th century D-26

Ballet Folklorico, Mexican ballet company M-328, *picture* M-330

Ballet Russe de Monte Carlo, ballet company B-35

Ballets Russes, French ballet company B-22, B-34
- dance history D-28
- Fokine's choreography F-246

Ballet Theatre. *see in index* American Ballet Theatre

Ballinger, Richard Achilles (1858–1922), U.S. lawyer, born in Boonesboro, Iowa; secretary of the interior in Taft's administration T-9

Balliol. *see in index* Baliol

Ballista, war machine used in ancient times for hurling stones A-371, A-658

Ballistic missile, predirected missile that becomes a free-falling body in latter part of flight G-312, S-345
  Braun B-411
  ICBM space travel S-342b
  IRBM S-495b
  naval launchers N-85
  nuclear weapons N-434
  submarines S-497
  titanium T-193
Ballistic Missile Early Warning System (BMEWS) A-573
Ballistics (from *ballistas*, ancient machine for hurling stones), science dealing with impact, path, and velocity of projectiles; interior ballistics deals with motion of projectile in gun; exterior ballistics, of motion after leaving gun B-37
  police P-429
Ballistite, an explosive N-329
Ball mill, in manufacturing
  explosives E-380
  mining M-429
  paint P-75, *picture* P-73
Ballon, ballet skill B-35
Balloon B-38. *see also in index* Airship
  aerial sport A-64
  air experiments, *picture* A-145
  Andrée's balloon, *picture* P-423
  history A-200
  jet propulsion, *diagram* J-105
  military and naval use
    air force A-154
    signaling S-193
  Montgolfier's flight M-569
  Piccard family P-316
  scientific use
    cosmic ray research R-42
    Echo I S-195b
    meteorology, *picture* W-85d
    weather W-121
  stratosphere, *chart* S-327
Balloon, in cartoon dialogue C-186
Balloon, surgical device used in treatment of heart catheterization H-100
Balloon flower, a perennial plant
  flowering time G-25
Ballot, in elections E-147
Ballotade, in horse training E-295
Ball-peen hammer, a tool T-216
Ball-point pen P-157, *picture* P-156
Ball's Bluff, a bluff on the Potomac River in Virginia, about 33 mi (55 km) north of Washington; Confederate force under General Evans defeated Union force and killed its commander, Col. Edward D. Baker, Oct. 21, 1861.
Balltown, game F-295
Ballute, *picture* P-109
Bally Manufacturing Corporation, electronic games manufacturer E-173
Balmer, Johann Jakob (1825–98), Swiss physicist S-373
Balmoral Castle, in Aberdeenshire, Scotland; has been a British royal residence from the time Queen Victoria lived there.
Balmung, in Teutonic mythology, the powerful magic sword of Siegfried; called 'Gram' in Norse mythology, and 'Nothung' in Wagner's opera 'Siegfried'
  Siegfried legend S-192a
Balopticon S-444
Balsa (or corkwood tree), a tropical tree *Ochroma pyramidale* of the family Bombacaceae, found chiefly in Ecuador; wood is the lightest known, about half as heavy as cork, but strong and elastic; composed of minute cells in which air is confined; first used extensively in World War II; employed in life rafts and life preservers, airplanes, submarines, and dirigibles, and as soundproof and insulating material B-45
  models M-515
  wood W-280, 284
Balsam, garden, a succulent garden annual *Impatiens balsamina* of the touch-me-not family with low leafy stem and showy single or double irregular white, rose, red, or yellow flowers clustered in the axils of the leaves on short stalks; wild jewelweed close relative
  growing conditions G-23
Balsam family (or Balsaminaceae), a family of plants including the jewelweeds, or touch-me-nots, and garden balsam.
Balsam fir, tree F-92
Balsamo, Joseph. *see in index* Cagliostro, Alessandro, Count
Balsam of Peru (or Peruvian balsam), a product of the tree *Myroxylon pereirae* of the bean family; used in medicine, in perfumery, and as substitute for vanilla; obtained from El Salvador.
Balsam poplar. *see in index* Cottonwood
Balsas River (or Río Balsas), river in s. Mexico, flows 500 mi (800 km) w. to Pacific
  Mexico M-324, *map* M-341
Balthazar, one of the Biblical Wise Men. *see in index* Magi
Baltic languages L-41, *diagram* L-44
Baltic Sea B-45, *map* E-360. *see also in index* Ocean, *table*
  canals C-126, V-383
  Germany, *map* G-131
  Sweden S-522, 527, *map* S-524
  U.S.S.R. P-220
  world, *map* W-297
Baltic-White Sea Canal C-126
Baltimore, Cecil Calvert, 2nd Baron (or Cecilius Calvert, 2nd Baron Baltimore) (1605?–75), founder of Maryland B-46
  colonial history A-337
  Maryland M-171, 178
Baltimore, Charles Calvert, 3rd Baron (1667–1715), English governor of colony of Maryland B-46
Baltimore, David (born 1938), U.S. microbiologist, born in New York City; professor Massachusetts Institute of Technology. *see also in index* Nobel Prizewinners, *table*
Baltimore, George Calvert, 1st Baron (1580?–1632), English statesman B-46
  Maryland M-171
Baltimore, Md., largest city of state; pop. 786,785 B-47, *maps* N-350, U-41
  garbage and refuse disposal G-18
  mail delivery (1906), *picture* P-460d
  Maryland M-166, 170, *pictures* M-171, 175, 177, *map* M-182
  Peabody Institute P-143
  presidential conventions P-432
  War of 1812 W-32
Baltimore & Ohio Railroad R-73
  'Atlantic' locomotive, *picture* R-74
  Maryland M-170
Baltimore butterfly B-526
Baltimore clipper (or Chesapeake clipper), ship design, *picture* S-165
Baltimore oriole, *picture* B-251
  Maryland state bird, *picture* M-174
Baltimore-Washington International Airport, airport that serves both Baltimore and Washington, D.C. M-170
Baluchi, a member of the dominant group of Turko-Iranians of Baluchistan for whom region was named
  Iran I-305
Baluchi, language
  Indian literature influenced I-107
Baluchistan, large, historic region of Pakistan; cap. Quetta; mountainous, largely dry and barren; rich in minerals, including coal, gypsum, chromite, sulfur, lead, limestone, and brine salt; before 1947–48 administered by princely families and British India B-50
Baluchitherium, a genus of mammals E-27
Balzac, Honoré de (1799–1850), French novelist B-50
  French literature F-397, *picture* F-396
  realism N-413
Bamako, Mali, capital on navigable Niger River; terminus for railroad from Dakar, Senegal; formerly capital of French Sudan; pop. 419,239 B-50, *map* A-115
  Mali M-75
  world, *map* W-297
Bambara, a people of Africa
  animism, *picture* A-465
  Mali M-75
Bambara groundnut, plant
  legumes L-122
Bamberg, West Germany, Bavarian city 33 mi (53 km) n.w. of Nuremberg; has large breweries and cotton and woolen mills; 11th-century cathedral; pop. 70,581, *map* G-131
Bamberg Bible, printed in 1457 G-319
Bamboo, tree-like grass of the family Gramineae B-51, *picture* P-0
  Asia A-688
  grasses G-235
  uses
    basketry B-102
    houses P-253d
    papermaking P-100
Bamboo Curtain, hypothetical line restricting travel, trade, and communication between Communist-influenced Asia and the non-Communist world; less well defined than the Iron Curtain.
'Bamboo in the Wind', drawing by Wu Chên D-256
Banaba. *see in index* Ocean Island
Banana B-51, *chart* F-430, *picture* F-435
  berry's characteristics, *picture* B-177
  fruitgrowing F-436, F-439
  Latin America, *chart* S-293, *map* S-296
    Central America C-255, *picture* C-257
    Costa Rica C-734
    Guatemala G-297
    Panama P-85
    Ecuador E-67, *picture* E-68
Banana republic, term used to describe a small dependent country in which foreign investors, typically associated with American-owned fruit companies, attempt to control the internal affairs of the country
  Honduras H-226
'Bananas', film by Allen A-309
Banaras, India. *see in index* Varanasi
Banat, district chiefly in w. Romania; extends into Yugoslavia and Hungary [illegible]
Banbury, England, market town in Oxfordshire, 65 mi (105 km) n.w. of London; center of zealous Puritans in 17th century who destroyed ancient cross celebrated in rhyme 'Ride a cock horse to Banbury Cross'; pop. 27,900, *map* U-18a
Banco Amrosiano, Italian private banking group
  Italian banking scandal I-398
Banco de Rialto, bank in Venice, Italy B-72
Banco Giro, bank in Venice, Italy B-72
Bancroft, George (1800–1891), U.S. historian and statesman, born in Worcester, Mass.; as secretary of Navy to President Polk, planned Naval Academy at Annapolis ('History of the United States') M-411
  Hall of Fame, *table* H-16
  history writing H-173
Band, in music B-54
  jazz J-84
  musical instruments M-687
  popular music M-684
Banda, a people of Africa C-252
Banda Islands, islands in Indonesia, part of Molucca Archipelago, in Banda Sea, 60 mi (100 km) s. of Ceram; 20 sq mi (50 sq km); first visited by Europeans 1512, *map* I-166
  Asia, *map* A-697
Bandama River, river, Africa
  Ivory Coast I-406
Bandar, India. *see in index* Machilipatnam
Bandar 'Abbas, Iran, seaport on Strait of Hormuz, Persian Gulf; pop. 80,000
  Asia, *map* A-697
Bandaranaike, Sirimavo (full name Sirimavo Ratwatte Bandaranaike) (born 1916), prime minister of Sri Lanka B-58
  history S-402
  women's rights W-276
Bandaranaike, Solomon West Ridgeway Dias (1899–1959), prime minister of Ceylon
  assassination, *list* A-704
  Bandaranaike B-58
Bandar-e Anzali, Iran. *see in index* Pahlevi
Bandar Seri Begawan (formerly Brunei Town), Brunei, capital; port on Sungai River; pop. 63,868 B-469
  Asia, *map* A-697
Bandar Shah, Iran, strategic port on Caspian Sea; northern terminus of Trans-Iranian Railroad; pop. 13,000.
Bandar Shahpur, Iran, strategic port on Persian Gulf; southern terminus of Trans-Iranian Railroad; pop. 6,000.
Banda Sea, part of Pacific Ocean in East Malay Archipelago s. of Moluccas; greatest depth about 24,000 ft (7,300 m); about 625 mi (1,005 km) long, 275 mi (440 km) wide
  Asia, *map* A-697
Band brake, brake type B-404
Banded anteater (or numbat), marsupial mammal *Myrmecobius fasciatus* M-156
Bandeira, Pico da, highest mountain of Brazil 9,462 ft (2,884 m) B-428, *diagram* S-295, *map* B-425
Bandelier National Monument, park in north-central New Mexico, *picture* N-223
Banderillero, in bullfighting B-501
Bandicoot, any of several small burrowing animals of the marsupial family Peramelidae; found in Australasia M-156
Banding, in zoological research B-267, *picture* B-268
Bandjarmasin (or Bandjermasin), seaport, chief town in Indonesian Borneo; built mainly on piles; pop. 281,673.
Band machine, a machine tool T-223
Bandung (or Bandoeng), city in Java; airplanes, ammunition, quinine; former headquarters of Dutch East Indies; pop. 1,462,637 B-58, *map* I-166
  Asia, *map* A-697
Bandung Conference (1955), dealing with Third World issues
  Indonesia hosted I-163
Banff, Alta., health and pleasure resort in Bow River valley in Canadian Rockies; altitude 4,538 ft (1,383 m); ski lifts; pop. 4,208
  Alberta, *map* A-270
  Canada, *map* C-109
Banff National Park, park in Alberta N-25, 28, *map* N-29
  Alberta, *map* A-270
  Canada, *picture* C-72, *map* C-109
Banff School of Fine Arts and Centre for Continuing Education, school, Banff, Alberta A-261
Bangalore, India, city of Mysore state, in s. part of India; textiles, metal, tobacco; pop. 2,482,507 B-58, *map* I-83
  Asia, *map* A-697
Bangalore torpedo, weapon T-232
'Bang-e dara', poetry by Iqbal
  Indian literature I-108
Banger. *see in index* Banjo
Bangkok (Siamese Krung Thep), Thailand, capital; pop. 4,711,000 B-58
  Asia, *map* A-697
  Thailand T-148
  world, *map* W-297
Bangladesh (official name People's Republic of Bangladesh, formerly East Pakistan), a member of The Commonwealth; area 55,126 sq mi (142,776 sq km); pop. 87,052,000 B-60
  Asia, *map* A-697
  cities. *see also in index* Dacca and other cities by name
  flag, *picture* F-162
  flood, *table* F-181
  food supply F-286
  fourth world T-168
  genocide G-60
  India I-61, 80
  New Year's celebration N-243
  Pakistan P-77
  population P-449, *chart* P-447
  railroad mileage, *table* R-85
  world, *map* W-297
Bangladesh Biman, airline B-62
Bangor, Me., city on Penobscot River, 60 mi (100 km) from sea; paper, tools, food products; Husson College; airport, pop. 31,643
  Maine M-62
  North America, *map* N-350
Bangor, Wales, old cathedral city on coast; slate; University College of North Wales; seat of bishopric since 6th century, pop. 14,930.
Bangs, in hairdressing H-8
Bang's disease. *see in index* Brucellosis

Bar Harbor, Me., summer resort, headquarters of Acadia National Park; first settled permanently by English 1763; devastated by fire 1947; pop. of township 3,716 M-54

Bari (ancient Barium), Italy, seaport in s.e., on Adriatic; several old churches; extensive commerce and manufactures; pop. 311,268, *map* E-360

Bar-Ilan University, university, Tel Aviv, Israel T-55

Barisan Mountains, mountains in Sumatra S-510

Barite (or barytes), a heavy crystalline mineral (barium sulfate), white or of varying colors; used in barium chemicals, in manufacture of explosives, shade cloth, rubber tires, and in muds to facilitate drilling into sand and gravel A-276
  minerals M-435
  paint extender P-73

Baritone, in music, the male voice having a range higher than bass and lower than tenor.

Barium, Italy. *see in index* Bari

Barium (Ba), alkaline earth chemical element A-307
  nuclear fission N-427
  periodic table, *table* P-207, *list* P-208
  sulfate. *see in index* Barite
  X rays X-403

Bark, tough exterior covering of a woody root or stem. *see also in index* names of various trees
  beaver's diet B-121
  tree T-276, *diagram* T-277
  uses
    masks M-185
    quinine Q-18
    spices S-379
    tapa cloth P-13

Bark (or barque), a sailing vessel, *picture* S-165

Bark canoe C-141

Barkentine, a sailing vessel, *picture* S-166

Barker, Harley Granville. *see in index* Granville-Barker, Harley Granville

Barkerville Historic Park, park in British Columbia B-456

Barking and Dagenham, borough, London, England, *maps* L-287, U-18a

Barking deer. *see in index* Muntjac

Barking sands S-38

Barkla, Charles Glover (1877–1944), British scientist, born in Widnes, Lancashire, England, noted for his work on X-ray scattering. *see also in index* Nobel prizewinners, *table*

Barkly Tableland, region, n. Australia, n.e. part of Northern Territory A-771, *map* P-3

Bark painting A-796

Bar-le-Duc, France, a quaint old town 125 mi (200 km) e. of Paris; noted for currant jam; site of old Roman gate and 14th-century church; pop. 18,874, *map* F-369

Barley, grain G-206
  Bolivian field, *picture* P-193
  England E-235
  flour B-428, F-213
  harvesting, *picture* S-285
  hay H-75
  rusts and smuts R-363
  West Germany G-117

Barley sugar S-509

Barlow, Joel (1754–1812), U.S. poet and political leader, born in Redding, Conn.; chaplain during Revolutionary War; minister to France 1811; went to Poland for conference with Napoleon and died of exposure when caught in retreat of French army from Moscow; wrote epic 'The Vision of Columbus' ('The Columbiad'), 'Hasty Pudding' mock eulogy A-345

Bar mitzvah, ceremony in Judaism J-150

Barn, *pictures* S-68, U-48, V-295

Barnabas, in Bible, fellow laborer with the Apostle Paul; his epistle is one of the apocryphal books of the New Testament; commemorated as saint June 11 A-492, A-507

'Barnaby Rudge', novel by Dickens (1841), based on the Gordon riots of 1780 D-134

Barnack, Oskar (1879–1936), German inventor of the first miniature precision camera available commercially P-298

Barnacle, marine crustacean of the class Cirripedia C-789
  paints P-73
  whale barnacle, *picture* S-149

Barnard, Christiaan Neethling (born 1923), South African surgeon, born in Beaufort West, Cape of Good Hope Province; headed surgical team that achieved first human heart transplant, at Cape Town Dec. 3, 1967; author of 'Heart Attack: You Don't Have to Die' 'One Life' R-112e

Barnard, Henry (1811–1900), U.S. educator, born in Hartford, Conn.; founder and editor of *American Journal of Education*, and first U.S. commissioner of education.

Barnard's star P-355

Barn dance, country music radio show M-678

Barnet, borough, London, England, *maps* L-287, U-18a

Barnett, Ida Bell Wells (1862–1931), U.S. journalist and civil rights advocate, born in Holly Springs, Miss.; organized anti-lynching campaign of 1890s B-293

Barneveldt, Jan van Olden (1547–1619), Dutch statesman; secured Twelve Years' Truce with Spain 1609; unjustly beheaded on a charge of treason.

Barnhart Island, island, New York, in St. Lawrence River S-20, *picture* U-51

Barn owl, bird, *picture* B-269

Barn-raising bee, U.S. frontier custom
  farming F-27

Barnsley, England, a market and manufacturing town in Yorkshire, 12 mi (19 km) n. of Sheffield; coal, metal products, glass, textiles; pop. 74,880, *map* U-18a

Barnstable, Mass., on s. shore of Cape Cod Bay; summer resort; incorporated 1938; pop. of township 30,898.

Barn swallow, bird *Hirundo rustica* of the family Hirundinidae S-521
  captures insects A-428

Barnum, P.T. (full name Phineas Taylor Barnum) (1810–91), U.S. showman B-81
  Bridgeport B-448
  circus history C-428

Barnum and Bailey Circus
  Barnum B-81
  circus history C-429

Baroco. *see in index* Baroque

Baroda, India, trade and railroad center in Gujarat state, 250 mi (400 km) n. of Bombay; formerly capital of princely state of Baroda; pop. 467,422, *map* I-83
  Asia, *map* A-697

Barograph, instrument that registers atmospheric pressure continuously and graphically; used by aviators W-121

Baroja y Nessi, Pío (1872–1956), Spanish novelist, born in Sebastián; wrote vividly of his own Basque country ('Caesar or Nothing'; 'The Quest'; 'Weeds'; 'The Tree of Knowledge') S-366

Barometer, instrument used to measure atmospheric pressure B-81
  hobby H-189
  instrumentation I-229
  mathematics, *table* M-218
  mercury M-304
  meter M-317
  weather W-121

Barometric altimeter, flight instrument A-194

Baron, a title of nobility T-195

Baronet, an inheritable title in United Kingdom ranking next below that of baron; the highest degree of honor borne by commoners T-196

Barong, sacred Balinese dance, *picture* I-162

Barong tagalog, Philippine shirt P-253d

Barons' Wars, in English history, a rebellion of nobles against Henry III led by Simon de Montfort E-242
  Henry III H-129

Baroque (or baroco), the florid, ornate style characterizing fine arts in Europe from middle 16th to middle 18th centuries; developed into rococo style in France
  architecture A-555
    Borromini B-370
  dress D-263, *picture* D-264
  folk art F-251
  furniture F-458, *picture* F-452
  interior design I-248
  Italian literature I-376
  music
    Bach B-10
    classical M-668
    Haydn H-75
    wind instruments W-227
  sculpture S-87
    Bernini B-175

Baroque pearls, pearls of irregular shape P-149

Barque (or bark), a sailing vessel, *picture* S-165

Barra, island of Outer Hebrides; about 8 mi (13 km) long and 2 to 5 mi (3 to 8 km) wide; chief town Castlebay, a fishing center; pop. 1,369.

Barracan, fabric of the Levant; also a robe of this fabric S-16

Barrack emperors, in Roman history, name given by historians to the succession of Roman emperors placed in power by the army from reign of Septimius Severus to accession of Diocletian (AD 193–284) R-248

Barracuda, pike-shaped fish of the family Sphyraenidae B-83

Barrage, type of dam D-15
  Indus P-78
  irrigation systems I-354

Barrage balloon
  warfare B-39

Barranquilla, Colombia, seaport on Magdalena River, 7 mi (11 km) from mouth; exports coffee, hides; produces textiles, shoes, lumber, flour; pop. 1,053,000 C-551, *map* S-298

Barrault, Jean Louis (born 1910), French actor, director, and manager
  acting A-27
  mime M-422

Barre, Vt., city in n. center, 5 mi (8 km) s.e. of Montpelier; granite quarrying; agriculture; electronic goods; pop. 9,824 V-286, *map* V-301
  quarrying, *picture* V-294

Barre, in ballet B-35

Barred spiral galaxy, in astronomy A-723, *picture* A-724

Barrel, part of a gun H-332
  machine gun M-14

Barrel, unit of measure or weight; U.S. standard barrel for vegetables and fruits (except cranberries) holds 7,056 cu in. (115,627 cu cm), *table* W-140

Barrel cactus, plant *Echinocactus ingens* of the family Cactaceae, *picture* C-12

Barrel pen P-157

Barren ground caribou, a wild reindeer A-451

Barrès, Maurice (1862–1923), French author and political leader; developed from agnostic into strong nationalist and defender of Roman Catholicism.

Barrett, Elizabeth. *see in index* Browning, Elizabeth Barrett

Barrie, James M. (or James Matthew Barry) (1860–1937), Scottish novelist and dramatist B-83
  drama D-247
  literary contribution E-280

Barrie, Ont., city and summer resort on Lake Simcoe, 84 km (52 mi) n. of Toronto; leather and rubber products, textiles; pop. 27,676.

Barrier reef, coral formation C-715
  Great Barrier Reef G-241

Barringer. *see in index* Meteor Crater

Barrington, R.I., residential community 5 mi (8 km) n. of Bristol; shipbuilding; Barrington College; incorporated 1770; pop. of township 16,174.

Barrister, English lawyer L-97

Barro Colorado, island in Gatun Lake, Panama Canal Zone P-94, *map* P-90

Barron, James (1769–1851), U.S. commodore, born in Virginia; in command of *Chesapeake* when attacked by Britain's *Leopard*
  Decatur D-52

Barrow, Joseph Louis. *see in index* Louis, Joe

Barrow, Isaac (1630–77), English mathematician, *table* M-218

Barrow, Alaska, city on Arctic Ocean, just s. of Point Barrow; naval base nearby; 12 mi (19 km) s.w., monument marks site of 1935 plane crash fatal to Will Rogers and Wiley Post; pop. 2,207
  Alaska, *map* A-254
  climatic region, *map* U-119
  North America, *map* N-350
  world, *map* W-297

Barrow, male pig P-320

Barrow-in-Furness, England, seaport in Lancashire, 50 mi (80 km) n.w. of Liverpool; shipyards, steelworks; pop. 63,460, *map* U-18a

Barrow Island, island off n.w. coast of Australia A-776, *maps* A-822, P-3

Barrow River, 2nd largest river of Ireland, in s.e.; has its source in Slieve Bloom mountains; flows e. and s. 120 mi (190 km) to Atlantic, near Waterford.

Barry, Charles (1795–1860), British architect, born in London; King Edward's Grammar School, Birmingham, considered finest work L-292

Barry, James Matthew. *see in index* Barrie, James M.

Barry, John (1745?–1803), U.S. naval hero B-84
  Washington W-44

Barry, Philip (1896–1949), U.S. playwright, born in Rochester, N.Y.; well-constructed plays; clever dialogue ('White Wings'; 'Paris Bound'; 'Holiday'; 'Hotel Universe'; 'Tomorrow and Tomorrow').

Barry, St. Bernard dog that saved some 40 persons D-196

Barrymore, Ethel (1879–1959), U.S. actress (stage, screen, radio, and television), born in Philadelphia, Pa.; made debut in 1896 in company of her uncle John Drew (stage plays 'Captain Jinks', 'Alice-Sit-by-the-Fire', 'The Constant Wife', 'The Corn Is Green'; autobiography 'Memories') B-85

Barrymore, Georgiana Emma Drew (1856–93), U.S. actress, wife of Maurice Barrymore and mother of Lionel, Ethel, and John; appeared in plays with husband, also with Edwin Booth; ('The School for Scandal', 'L'Abbé Constantin', and 'The Wages of Sin') B-84

Barrymore, John (1882–1942), U.S. actor, born in Philadelphia, Pa.; brother of Ethel and Lionel; made debut in 1903 in 'Magda'; later appeared in 'The Fortune Hunter'; 'Are You a Mason?'; 'Peter Ibbetson'; 'Redemption'; 'The Jest'; 'Richard III'; 'Hamlet'; also famed motion-picture actor ('Don Juan'; 'Beau Brummel'; 'Svengali') B-85

Barrymore, Lionel (1878–1954), U.S. actor B-84

Barrymore, Maurice, (original name Herbert Blythe) (1847–1905), British actor B-84

Barstow, Mrs. Montagu. *see in index* Orczy, Emmuska, Baroness

Barstow, Calif., city 89 mi (143 km) n.e. of Los Angeles, in Mojave Desert; railroad shops, aircraft laboratories; U.S. Marine Corps depot and Goldstone tracking station nearby; busy mining town in frontier days; incorporated 1947; pop. 17,690.

Bar-sur-Seine, France, historic town on Seine River, 18 mi (29 km) s.e. of Troyes; devastated 1359 by English; pop. 2,408, *map* F-369

BART. *see in index* Bay Area Rapid Transit District

Barter, exchange of articles without use of money
  Aztec A-891
  fur trade F-470
  international trade I-269
  money M-530
  pioneer America P-332

Barth, Heinrich (1821–65), German explorer, born in Hamburg; published book on travels and discoveries in Africa.

Barth, John Simmons (born 1930), U.S. writer, born in Cambridge, Md. A-361

Barth, Karl (1886–1968), Swiss Protestant Reformed theologian B-85
  existentialism E-371

Barthelemy, Peter (11th century AD), Provençal priest; participated in siege of Antioch during First Crusade; supposedly discovered the Holy Lance which pierced Christ's side, inspiring crusaders to victory over Turks C-787

Barthelme, Donald (born 1931), U.S. writer A-367

Barthelmess, Richard (1897–1963), U.S. film actor and director, born in New York, N.Y., *picture* M-619

Bartholomew, Saint, one of Twelve Apostles; festival August 24 A-506

Bartholomew regional projection, maps, *picture* M-125

Bartlesville, Okla., city in n.e., in Mid-Continent oil field; office headquarters for oil firms, oil research laboratories; zinc processing; pumps; pop. 34,568 O-532, *picture* O-531

Bartlett, E.L. (full name Edward Lewis Bartlett, or Bob Bartlett) (1904–68), U.S. journalist and political leader, born in Seattle, Wash.; secretary of Alaska 1939–44; Alaskan delegate to U.S. Congress 1945–59; U.S. senator 1959–68; urged Alaskan statehood
  Statuary Hall, *table* S-437a

Bartlett, Josiah (1729–95), U.S. signer of Declaration of Independence, born in Amesbury, Mass.; president of New Hampshire 1790–93; elected governor 1793
  Declaration of Independence D-56

Bartlett, Paul Wayland (1865–1925), U.S. sculptor, born in New Haven, Conn.; first did animal sculpture; portrait statues of Lafayette and Franklin; six heroic figures for entrance New York Public Library; statues of Columbus and Michelangelo in Library of Congress S-91

Bartlett Dam, dam on Verde River, Arizona, *picture* D-12

Bartlett pear (or bon chrétien), fruit and tree belonging to the rose family P-147

Bartók, Béla (1881–1945), Hungarian composer B-85
  classical music M-675
  Hungary H-327
  opera O-569

Barton, Clara (1821–1912), 1st president American Red Cross B-86
  Hall of Fame, *table* H-16
  public school movement N-198

Barton, Derek Harold Richard (born 1918), British chemist, born in Gravesend; professor University of London 1953–55, 1957–, University of Glasgow 1955–57. *see also in index* Nobel prizewinners, *table*

Barton, Otis (born 1899?), U.S. oceanic explorer, born in New York, N.Y.; set deep-sea descent records 1934 and 1949; wrote 'The World Beneath the Sea' B-130
  exploration E-377

Bartonellosis. *see in index* Carrion's disease

Bartow, Fla., city 40 mi (60 km) e. of Tampa; phosphate, citrus fruit, livestock; settled 1851, first incorporation 1893, second 1905; pop. 14,780.

Bartram, John (1699–1777), U.S. botanist and ornithologist, born near Darby, Pa.; "father of American botany"; self-taught; served as honorary botanist to King George II of England B-379, P-251c
  horticulture F-222

Bartramian sandpiper (also called upland plover), bird of the family Scolopacidae S-40

Baruch, Bernard (1870–1965), U.S. financier B-86, *picture* S-316

Bary, Heinrich Anton de. *see in index* De Bary, Heinrich Anton

Barye, Antoine Louis (1796–1875), French sculptor, born in Paris; began by modeling relief maps while serving as topographical engineer in French army S-89

Baryon, class of elementary particles
  quark Q-5

Baryshnikov, Mikhail (born 1948), U.S. dancer B-36, *picture* B-32
  dance D-29

Barytes. *see in index* Barite

Barzani, Mustafa, Kurdish leader
  Kurd's revolt K-310

Barzini, Luigi (1908–84), Italian writer, born in Milan, Italy; founded newspaper *Il Globo* after World War II
  Italian literature I-379, *picture* I-378

Basal cell cancer, type of skin cancer C-134

Basal ganglia, anatomy B-401
  nervous system disorder N-123

Basal metabolic rate (or BMR), measurement of thyroid activity H-240

Basal metabolism. *see in index* Metabolism

Basal reader approach, reading R-103

Basalt, a fine-grained, heavy, igneous rock, often solidified into prismatic columns B-86
  coastal landforms B-112
  earth E-11, E-20, *diagram* E-12
  lava and magma types L-89
  minerals M-437
  Polynesian mountains, *picture* P-1
  prehistoric tools M-84
  rock cycle, *chart* R-229
  Syria, *picture* S-549b

Basalt ware, Wedgwood pottery P-475

Basanite. *see in index* Touchstone

Basava (fl. mid-12th century), Indian Hindu religious reformer, teacher, and theologian H-158

Bascule bridge type of bridge B-442, *picture* B-443

Base, chemistry A-19. *see also in index* Acids
  antidote P-410
  electrochemistry E-170
  heat H-102
  normal and molar solutions S-256

Base, geometry
  measurement M-243

Base, heraldry, *diagram* H-136

Baseball B-87
  batting average P-199
  black American athletes B-300
  cross-cultural transfer C-466
  Doubleday D-233
  franchises F-374
  softball's development S-248
  World Series R-365. *see table* following
  young players, *pictures* P-179, V-239

'Baseball Card Monthly', magazine H-183

Baseball cards, hobby H-183

Baseball Hall of Fame and Museum, National B-94. *see table* following
  Hall of Fame H-16

Base-five system, numeration N-435

Basel (or Basle, or Bâle), Switzerland, city on Rhine, near n. border; silks, chemicals; Gallic stronghold and then town of Romans; prominent in Reformation; university founded 1460; pop. 212,857 S-542, *maps* E-360, S-537
  harbor S-540, *picture* S-542

Base line, in surveying S-520

Base meridian. *see in index* Prime meridian

Basenji, dog, *picture* D-199

Base period, in statistics S-437

Base-sixty system (or sexagesimal system), numeration N-435
  mathematics M-213

Base-ten system. *see in index* Decimal system

Base-twelve system. *see in index* Duodecimal system

Base-twenty system, numeration N-435

Base-two system. *see in index* Binary system

Bashan, rich district in ancient Palestine, beyond the Jordan River; famed for cattle of great size (bulls of Bashan).

Basho (or Matsuo Basho) (1644–94), Japanese poet J-49, J-81

BASIC (or Beginner's All-purpose Symbolic Instruction Code), programming operation codes C-635, *picture* C-634

Basic Law (commonly known as Grundgesetz), constitution of West Germany G-120

Basic training, military, *picture* M-410

Basidiomycetes, class of fungi bearing basidia, special structures on which external spores are produced.

Basie, William (or Count Basie) (1904–84), U.S. jazz pianist, composer, and bandleader, born in Red Bank, N.J.; studied organ with 'Fats' Waller; transformed big-band jazz by simplicity of his arrangements ('One O'Clock Jump'; 'Basie Boogie')
  jazz contribution J-87

Basil I of Macedonia (died 886), Byzantine emperor B-535

Basil, herb *Ocimum basilicum* H-137, S-379

Basil, Wassily de (1888–1951), U.S. ballet impresario B-35

BASEBALL PENNANT AND WORLD SERIES WINNERS*

	National League	*American League*		*National League*	*American League*
1903	Pittsburgh (3)	**Boston** (5)	1946	**St. Louis** (4)	Boston (3)
1904†	New York	Boston	1947	Brooklyn (3)	**New York** (4)
1905	**New York** (4)	Philadelphia (1)	1948	Boston (2)	**Cleveland** (4)
1906	Chicago (2)	**Chicago** (4)	1949	Brooklyn (1)	**New York** (4)
1907	**Chicago** (4)	Detroit (0)	1950	Philadelphia (0)	**New York** (4)
1908	**Chicago** (4)	Detroit (1)	1951	New York (2)	**New York** (4)
1909	**Pittsburgh** (4)	Detroit (3)	1952	Brooklyn (3)	**New York** (4)
1910	Chicago (1)	**Philadelphia** (4)	1953	Brooklyn (2)	**New York** (4)
1911	New York (2)	**Philadelphia** (4)	1954	**New York** (4)	Cleveland (0)
1912	New York (3)	**Boston** (4)	1955	**Brooklyn** (4)	New York (3)
1913	New York (1)	**Philadelphia** (4)	1956	Brooklyn (3)	**New York** (4)
1914	**Boston** (4)	Philadelphia (0)	1957	**Milwaukee** (4)	New York (3)
1915	Philadelphia (1)	**Boston** (4)	1958	Milwaukee (3)	**New York** (4)
1916	Brooklyn (1)	**Boston** (4)	1959	**Los Angeles** (4)	Chicago (2)
1917	New York (2)	**Chicago** (4)	1960	**Pittsburgh** (4)	New York (3)
1918	Chicago (2)	**Boston** (4)	1961	Cincinnati (1)	**New York** (4)
1919	**Cincinnati** (5)	Chicago (3)	1962	San Francisco (3)	**New York** (4)
1920	Brooklyn (2)	**Cleveland** (5)	1963	**Los Angeles** (4)	New York (0)
1921	**New York** (5)	New York (3)	1964	**St. Louis** (4)	New York (3)
1922	**New York** (4)	New York (0)	1965	**Los Angeles** (4)	Minnesota (3)
1923	New York (2)	**New York** (4)	1966	Los Angeles (0)	**Baltimore** (4)
1924	New York (3)	**Washington** (4)	1967	**St. Louis** (4)	Boston (3)
1925	**Pittsburgh** (4)	Washington (3)	1968	St. Louis (3)	**Detroit** (4)
1926	**St. Louis** (4)	New York (3)	1969	**New York** (4)	Baltimore (1)
1927	Pittsburgh (0)	**New York** (4)	1970	Cincinnati (1)	**Baltimore** (4)
1928	St. Louis (0)	**New York** (4)	1971	**Pittsburgh** (4)	Baltimore (3)
1929	Chicago (1)	**Philadelphia** (4)	1972	Cincinnati (3)	**Oakland** (4)
1930	St. Louis (2)	**Philadelphia** (4)	1973	New York (3)	**Oakland** (4)
1931	**St. Louis** (4)	Philadelphia (3)	1974	Los Angeles (1)	**Oakland** (4)
1932	Chicago (0)	**New York** (4)	1975	**Cincinnati** (4)	Boston (3)
1933	**New York** (4)	Washington (1)	1976	**Cincinnati** (4)	New York (0)
1934	**St. Louis** (4)	Detroit (3)	1977	Los Angeles (2)	**New York** (4)
1935	Chicago (2)	**Detroit** (4)	1978	Los Angeles (2)	**New York** (4)
1936	New York (2)	**New York** (4)	1979	**Pittsburgh** (4)	Baltimore (3)
1937	New York (1)	**New York** (4)	1980	**Philadelphia** (4)	Kansas City (2)
1938	Chicago (0)	**New York** (4)	1981	**Los Angeles** (4)	New York (2)
1939	Cincinnati (0)	**New York** (4)	1982	**St. Louis** (4)	Milwaukee (3)
1940	**Cincinnati** (4)	Detroit (3)	1983	Philadelphia (1)	**Baltimore** (4)
1941	Brooklyn (1)	**New York** (4)	1984	San Diego (1)	**Detroit** (4)
1942	**St. Louis** (4)	New York (1)	1985	St. Louis (3)	**Kansas City** (4)
1943	St. Louis (1)	**New York** (4)	1986	**New York** (4)	Boston (3)
1944	**St. Louis** (4)	St. Louis (2)			
1945	Chicago (3)	**Detroit** (4)			

*World Series winner in boldface. World Series games won in parentheses. †New York refused to play Boston.

Basilan, Philippines, municipality including Basilan Island and nearby islets, off s.w. tip of island of Mindanao; area 530 sq mi (1,370 sq km); lumber, coconuts, rice, corn, rubber; pop. 171,266, *map* P-262

Basilan Island, province, Philippines; largest island in Basilan group; area 495 sq mi (1,282 sq km); cap. Isabela (pop. 12,879); mountainous; pop. 143,829, *map* P-262

Basile, Giambattista (or Giovanni Battista) (1575–1632), Italian writer and soldier, born in Naples; known for fairy tales L-245
  'The Pentamerone' S-474, 481b

Basilica (from Greek word meaning kingly), term now used for large rectangular church or for a church so designated by pope because of historical or religious associations; first basilicas were Greek, then later Roman, public halls
  Assumption, Baltimore B-47
  St. John Lateran, Rome R-256, *map* R-251, *picture* R-253
  St. Peter's, Vatican City V-268

Basilicata (or Lucania), region in s. Italy; area 3,856 sq mi (9,987 sq km); cap. Potenza; pop. 644,297, *map* I-401

Basilio, Norma Enriqueta, Mexican athlete, *picture* O-542

Basilisk (or cockatrice), fabled serpentlike monster A-457, *picture* A-458

Basil the Great, Saint (329–379), early father of Greek church, bishop of Caesarea in Cappadocia; opponent of Arian heresy; founder of Eastern monasticism; festival June 14 G-279, M-540

Basin, river R-210

Basin and Range Province, geologic province, *map* E-25
  Nevada N-133
  Texas T-116, *map* T-117

Baskerville, John (1706–75), English printer; printed beautiful editions of the Bible, Horace, Virgil, Milton, etc.
  style of type T-338, *picture* B-349

Basket. *see in index* Basketry

Basket ash. *see in index* Black ash

Basketball B-97
  Abdul-Jabbar A-8
  England E-233
  Erving E-298
  YMCA Y-425

Basket cloth, a textile in which two or more threads at a time are woven into the basket-weave pattern; most popular type a lightweight, soft cotton with a loose weave.

Basket flower. *see in index* Peruvian daffodil

Basket Makers, an early North American people
  Colorado C-571

'Basket of Apples, The', painting by Cézanne, *picture* C-262

Basketry, craft B-101
  American Indian I-122, 133, *picture* I-132

Basket weave. *see in index* Basket cloth

Basket willow (or common osier), tree *Salix viminalis* of Salicaceae family W-211

Basle, Switzerland. *see in index* Basel

Bas Mitzvah, ceremony in Judaism J-150

Basophil, one kind of white blood cell B-314, *table* B-317

Basotho, a people of Africa L-137

Basov, Nikolai Gennadievich (born 1922), Soviet physicist, born in Leningrad; at P.N. Lebedev Physical Institute since 1948, director since 1973. *see also in index* Nobel prizewinners, *table*

Basques, people of region of Pyrenees Mts. in n.e. Spain and s.w. France B-103
  jai alai J-13
  legend of Roland R-238
  Spain S-354, 361
  terrorism T-113, E-355

Basra (also called Bassora), Iraq, chief port on the Shatt-al-'Arab, 75 mi (120 km) from Persian Gulf; pop. 286,955
  Asia, *map* A-697
  Iraq I-314
  world, *map* W-297

Bas-relief (or low relief), sculpture S-80, *picture* P-264

Bas-Rhin, department of n.e. France, along the Rhine, in region called Alsace; area 1,848 sq mi (4,786 sq km); pop. 882,121, *map* F-369
  Strasbourg S-484

Bass, Sam (1851–78), U.S. outlaw O-619

Bass, Thomas Dwyer (born 1916), Australian sculptor A-802

Bass, a fish B-103
  fisheries, *table* F-136
  hibernation H-147

Bass, in music, the lowest part in a composition; also the lowest male voice and staff.

Bassae, a place in ancient Arcadia, Greece, near Phigalia. *see in index* Phigalia

Bassani, Giorgio (born 1916), Italian writer I-379

Bassarisk, animal
  fur, *table* F-464

Bass clarinet, wind instrument W-227
  orchestra O-576

Bass clef (or F clef), sign in music M-690

Bass drum, musical instrument O-576

Bassein, Burma, port on Bassein River, in the Irrawaddy delta, 80 mi (130 km) w. of Rangoon; trade center of rice-growing region; pop. 105,000, *map* I-83
  Asia, *map* A-697

Basse Terre, Guadeloupe, capital and port; situated on s.w. coast on island Basse Terre; rocky and mountainous; highest peak is volcano Soufrière 4,869 ft (1,484 m), which erupted in 1797, 1836, 1843, 1902, and 1980; pop. 16,000
  West Indies, *map* W-159

Basset horn, wind instrument W-227

Basset hound, dog, *picture* D-199

Bassett, Richard (1745–1815), U.S. Revolutionary War statesman, born in Cecil County, Md.; signed United States Constitution; U.S. senator 1789–93; governor of Del. 1799–1801.

Bassianus. *see in index* Caracalla

Bassoon, wind instrument W-227
  orchestra O-576

Bassora, Iraq. *see in index* Basra

Bass staff, musical notation M-690

Bass Strait, strait between Australia and Tasmania A-769, *maps* A-822, P-3
  Melbourne M-289
  world, *map* W-297

Bass viol. *see in index* Double bass

Basswood (or American linden), tree L-228
  tree, *picture* T-278
  wood, *table* W-283

Basswood family. *see in index* Linden family

Bastet (or Bast, or Pasht), cat-goddess of ancient Egypt M-700
  cat worship C-211

Bastia, Corsica, city and port on n.e. coast, stretching from mountains to Tyrrhenian Sea; exports wine, timber, fish, vegetables, and fruit; city affords fine view of islands Elba and Montecristo many miles away; formerly capital of Corsica; pop. 48,800, *picture* M-286, *map* F-369

Bastille, fort, Paris, France
  France, *picture* F-363
  French Revolution F-401, *picture* F-400

Bastille Day, holiday celebrated in France
  festivals and holidays F-60

Basting, in sewing S-121
  sewing machine attachment, *picture* S-126

Bastogne, Belgium, town situated on Wiltz River, in the Ardennes, 43 mi (69 km) s. of Liège; railroad and highway junction point; trade center for farm products; cattle and horse markets; pop. 6,151.

Bastrop, La., city 110 mi (180 km) n.e. of Shreveport; in farming and gas area; paper containers and products, chemicals; lumber and food processing; Chemin-à-Haut State Park nearby; pop. 15,527.

Basutoland. *see in index* Lesotho

Bat, a winged mammal B-104, *picture* A-436
  animal life record, *table* E-24
  book illustration, *picture* S-478
  flying fox, fox bat, or fruit bat P-10
  hand H-27, *picture* H-26
  hibernation H-147
  migration A-451

Bat, in bricklaying B-438

Bat, in pottery making, *picture* P-477

Bat, wooden implement used for hitting the ball in various games
  baseball B-90
  cricket C-764

Bataan, Philippines, peninsula on Luzon; province; area 530 sq mi (1,370 sq km); rocky jungle; pop. 216,210, *map* P-262

Bataan, battle of (1942), World War II, *list* W-14
  MacArthur M-3
  World War II W-344, *picture* W-345

Batak, people. *see in index* Battak

Batangas, Philippines, port of Luzon, about 60 mi (100 km) s. of Manila; cap. of Batangas province (pop. 926,308); trade center for farming area; pop. 125,304 P-257a, *map* P-262

Bâtard style, calligraphy C-59

Batavia, Indonesia. *see in index* Jakarta

Batavia, N.Y., city 36 mi (58 km) e. of Buffalo; television sets, shoes, metal and paper products; state school for blind; pop. 16,703.

Batch, glassmaking
  manufacture G-157

Batch method, heating of milk or a milk product D-4

Batch processing, method of processing data C-627

Bates, Henry Walter (1825–92), British naturalist and explorer
  mimicry M-423

Bates, Katharine Lee (1859–1929), U.S. writer and educator, born in Falmouth, Mass.; professor of English literature Wellesley College 1891–1925; author of collections of poetry, scholarly books on literature, and stories and poems for children
  'America the Beautiful' N-65

Bates College, Lewiston, Maine; opened in 1864; funded by a generous grant from businessman Benjamin Bates; coeducational M-55

Batesian mimicry, animals M-423

Bath, England, city, famous health resort 95 mi (150 km) w. of London, on Avon River; hot springs; abbey church; pop. 84,760, *map* U-18a
  Roman baths, *picture* E-239

Bath, Me., port city on Kennebec River, about 12 mi (19 km) from Atlantic Ocean and 29 mi (47 km) n.e. of Portland; shipbuilding; marine machinery; pop. 10,246, *picture* M-60

Bath, W. Va. *see in index* Berkeley Springs

Bath
  American Indians I-126
  babies B-2
  birds B-243, *picture* B-241
  health care H-88
  Japan J-28
  Pompeii P-443
  Rome R-255, *map* R-250, *picture* R-257

Bath, Order of the, order of knighthood, dated by legend to 1399; founded 1725 by George I; civil honors (highest in Britain) added 1847 K-259
  medals M-270

Ba'th Party(or Ba'ath Party), Arab political organization
  Iraq I-315
  Syria S-550

Bathsheba, wife of Uriah, later of King David D-41

Bathurst, N.B., town on Chaleurs Bay and Nepisiguit River; mining center; summer resort; lumber, pulp and paper; salmon fishing; pop. 15,705 N-156, *maps* C-109, N-350

Bathurst, The Gambia. *see in index* Banjul

Bathurst Island, island in Timor Sea, n. of Australia; part of Northern Territory, Australia; pop. 895, *maps* A-819, P-3
  world, *map* W-297

Bathypelagic zone, oceanography A-745

Bathyscaphe
  exploration E-377
  oceans O-463
  Piccard family P-316
  submarines S-500

Bathysphere, oceanography O-463

Bathythermograph, instrument to record water temperature O-464

Batik, dyeing process B-106
  dye D-295
  Indonesia I-160

Batina, region in Oman O-543

Batista, Fulgencio (1901–73), dictator of Cuba B-106
  Castro C-200
  Cuba C-802
  warfare W-17

Batlle y Ordóñez, José (1856–1929), Uruguayan statesman, born in Montevideo; president of Uruguay 1903, 1911–15 U-214

Batlle y Ordóñez Park, park in Montevideo, Uruguay M-568

Batman, John (1801–39), Australian settler, born in New South Wales
  Melbourne M-291

Batoche Battlefield National Historic Site, historical site in Saskatchewan S-49h
  national parks N-28, *map* N-29

Baton Rouge, La., state capital, railroad center, and port on Mississippi River; pop. 219,486 B-106, *map* N-350
  Louisiana, *pictures* L-317

Battak (or Batak), a people of Malayan stock traditionally inhabiting highlands surrounding Lake Toba in Sumatra; picturesque houses; after World War II many Battak migrated to lowland plantations on e. coast of Sumatra; not to be confused with **Batak,** a people on island of Palawan, Philippines.

Battalion, a military unit
  U.S. Army A-634

Batten, loom feature, *picture* S-391

Batten Pocket, boat feature, *diagram* B-326

Battering ram, war machine used in ancient and medieval times, consisting of a long beam of wood with heavy metal head.

Battery, unlawful use of physical force on another person. *see also in index* Assault
  crime C-770

Battery, the, chief arrival point for immigrants to the United States from Europe, *picture* M-300

Battery, electronics B-107. *see also in index* Electric battery; Electrochemical cell; Fuel cell; Solar battery and cell; Storage battery
  electric power E-169
  electronics E-180
  energy E-215
  lead L-99
  mercury M-304
  space travel S-343a
  submarines, *diagram* S-499

Batting, in needlework N-113

Battista, Giovanni. *see in index* Basile, Giambattista

Battle above the clouds. *see in index* Lookout Mountain, battle of

Battle Creek, Mich., city 38 mi (61 km) s.w. of Lansing, on Kalamazoo River; cereals, health foods, food packaging machinery, forklift trucks, paper and board, welded metal products, pumps, automotive valves; Fort Custer and Kellogg Bird Sanctuary nearby; pop. 35,724 M-358, *map* U-41

Battle cruiser, a large ship that carries guns of a contemporary battleship, but sacrifices armor protection for speed
  Hood S-177h

Battledore, type of book
  children's literature history L-245, *picture* L-246

Battledore and shuttlecock, game played by two persons with small parchment or stringed racket called a battledore, and a shuttlecock of cork stuck with feathers B-17

Battleford National Historic Park (or Fort Battleford National Historic Park), park in Saskatchewan S-49h
national parks N-29
'Battle Hymn of the Republic', U.S. patriotic song N-65
popular music M-684
Battle of . . . . *see in index* battles by name, such as Britain, battle of, except as below
'Battle of Anghiari', mural by Leonardo da Vinci L-132
'Battle of Bunker's Hill, The', painting by Trumbull P-49, *picture* P-48
'Battle of San Romano, The', painting by Uccello P-33, *picture* P-34
'Battle of the Books, The', satire by Swift S-531
Battles, Cliff (full name Clifford Battles) (1910–81), U.S. football halfback and coach, born in Akron, Ohio; played for Boston Braves 1932, Boston Redskins 1933–36, and Washington Redskins 1937; coach Brooklyn Dodgers 1946–47.
Battleship, game G-12
Battleship, warship of the largest and most heavily armed and armored class
Wisconsin, *picture* K-295
Batu, grandson of Genghis Khan M-534
Batumi (or Batum), U.S.S.R., port of Georgian Soviet Socialist Republic, on Black Sea; citrus fruits, tea, wood; pop. 101,000 G-102, *maps* R-344, 349
climatic region, *map* R-334
Europe, *map* E-360
oil pipeline R-330c
Batur, Lake, lake in Bali, *picture* I-158
Baucis and Philemon. *see in index* Philemon and Baucis
Baudelaire, Charles (full name Charles-Pierre Baudelaire) (1821–67), French poet B-110
French literature F-397
Baudot, Jean-Maurice-Émile (1845–1903), French engineer
telegraph code T-58
Baudouin I (born 1930), king of the Belgians B-110
Bauer, Georg. *see in index* Agricola, Georgius
Baugh, Samuel Adrian (nickname Sammy) (born 1914), U.S. football coach and quarterback, born in Temple, Tex.; quarterback Washington Redskins 1937–52; coach New York Jets 1960–61, Houston Oilers 1964.
Bauhaus, institution founded in Weimar, Germany, 1919 by a group of artists and architects with Walter Gropius as director; transferred to Dessau 1925; closed by Nazi regime 1933; New Bauhaus (later Institute of Design) opened in Chicago 1937 by Moholy-Nagy; chief aim was to combine practical manual training in workshops with theoretical instruction in design A-565, *picture* A-564
Breuer B-434
furniture F-462
Gropius G-289
industrial design I-171
interior design I-250
Kandinsky K-171
Klee K-254
metalworking M-311
Mies van der Rohe M-398
Moholy-Nagy M-518
Baule, a people of Africa
Ivory Coast I-407
Baum, L. Frank (full name Lyman Frank Baum) (1856–1919), U.S. author and journalist B-110
'The Wonderful Wizard of Oz' W-266
Baumé hydrometer H-341
Bausch, John Jacob (1830–1926), U.S. industrialist I-195
Bauxite, chief aluminum ore A-321
Asia A-689
Australia A-776, 810
Guinea G-314
Guyana G-322
ore, *table* O-600
Western Hemisphere U-106
Arkansas A-416
Jamaica J-18
Bavaria (German Bayern), West Germany, state in s.e.; pop. 10,928,151 B-111
Germany, *map* G-131
Munich M-652
World War I W-312
Bavarian Alps, mountains in West Germany G-111, *map* G-131
Tirol T-192
Bavarian Plateau, plateau region, West Germany G-111
Baxter State Park, park in Maine; largest recreation area; 200,000 acres M-54
Bay, Ohio. *see in index* Bay Village
Bayanihan Dance Company, group conceived in ancient spirit of bayanihan; as neighbors help each other with no desire for pay, this troupe works together with no individual stars, promoting Philippine culture P-258
Bayan Kara Shan, mountain range in Qinghai Province, China; spur of Kunlun Mountains.
Bay Area Rapid Transit District (BART), transit system in San Francisco, Calif. S-42
automated systems A-840
Oakland O-453
Baya weaver, bird *Ploceus philippinus* W-128
Baybars (1223–1277), Mamluk sultan of Egypt A-703
Bayberry (or myrtleberry), shrub of the family Myricaceae; greyish, waxy berries yield wax used in making bayberry candles
wax W-110
Bay cat (or Borneo Red cat), wild cat *Felis badia*, *table* C-215
Bay City, Mich., port city on Saginaw River, near mouth on Saginaw Bay, about 95 mi (150 km) n.w. of Detroit; Great Lakes and ocean shipping port; automobile parts, electrical transformers, cranes, hosiery; pop. 41,593, *map* U-41
Bay City, Tex., city 80 mi (130 km) s.w. of Houston, on Colorado River, in oil and gas producing region; petroleum refining; rice; chemicals, concrete products; incorporated 1902; pop. 17,837.
Bay Company. *see in index* Hudson's Bay Company
Bayer, Karl Joseph (1847–1904), Austrian chemist A-322
Bayern, West Germany. *see in index* Bavaria
Bayer process, for refining bauxite A-322
Bayeux, France, historic town in Normandy; famous for old cathedral and for Bayeux tapestry; pop. 11,190, *map* F-369
Bayeux tapestry, a seamless strip of linen, 230 ft (70 m) long and 20 in. (50 cm) wide, covered with 72 colored sketches in worsted embroidery; tells the story of the Norman Conquest A-716, H-272, T-25, *picture* E-240
Harold I H-43
Bayezid I (1360?–1403), Ottoman sultan O-616
Bayezid II (1448–1512), Ottoman sultan O-616, *picture* O-618
Bay Islands (or Islas de la Bahía), group of islands in the Caribbean Sea H-225
Baykal, Lake. *see in index* Baikal, Lake
Bay laurel (or sweet laurel), tree *Laurus nobilis* of the family Lauraceae
bay leaf S-379, L-88
herbs H-137
Bayle, Pierre (1647–1706), French philosopher and critic; was professor in Sedan and in Rotterdam; his writings, many of which subtly preach that religion and reason are opposed, greatly influenced skeptical philosophy of 18th century ('Historical and Critical Dictionary') B-223
Bay leaf, seasoning S-379
laurel L-88

MEMBERS OF BASEBALL'S NATIONAL HALL OF FAME

Name (Nickname)	Year Elected
Aaron, Henry Louis (Hank)	1982
Alexander, Grover Cleveland (Pete)	1938
Alston, Walter Emmons* (Smokey)	1983
Anson, Adrian Constantine* (Cap)	1939
Aparacio, Luis	1984
Appling, Lucius Benjamin (Luke)	1964
Averill, Howard Earl* (Rock)	1975
Baker, John Franklin* (Home Run)	1955
Bancroft, David James (Beauty)	1971
Banks, Ernest (Ernie)	1977
Barrow, Edward Grant* (Ed)	1953
Beckley, Jacob Peter (Eagle Eye)	1971
Bell, James† (Cool Papa)	1974
Bender, Charles Albert* (Chief)	1953
Berra, Lawrence Peter (Yogi)	1972
Bottomley, James Leroy* (Sunny Jim)	1974
Boudreau, Louis (Lou)	1970
Bresnahan, Roger Patrick* (Duke)	1945
Brock, Lou	1985
Brouthers, Dennis* (Dan)	1945
Brown, Mordecai Peter* (Three-fingered)	1949
Bulkeley, Morgan G.*	1937
Burkett, Jesse Cail* (Crab)	1946
Campanella, Roy (Campy)	1969
Carey, Max George*	1961
Cartwright, Alexander Joy*	1938
Chadwick, Henry*	1938
Chance, Frank Leroy* (Husk)	1946
Chandler, Albert B.* (Happy)	1982
Charleston, Oscar†	1976
Chesbro, John Dwight* (Happy Jack)	1946
Clarke, Frederick Clifford*	1945
Clarkson, John Gibson*	1963
Clemente, Roberto	1973
Cobb, Tyrus Raymond (Ty)	1936
Cochrane, Gordon Stanley (Mickey)	1947
Collins, Edward Trowbridge (Cocky)	1939
Collins, James J.* (Jimmy)	1945
Combs, Earle Bryan*	1970
Comiskey, Charles Albert* (The Old Roman)	1939
Conlan, John Bertrand* (Jocko)	1974
Connolly, Thomas Henry* (Tommy)	1953
Connor, Roger*	1976
Coveleski, Stanley Anthony* (Stan)	1969
Crawford, Samuel Earl* (Wahoo Sam)	1957
Cronin, Joseph Edward (Joe)	1956
Cummings, William Arthur* (Candy)	1939
Cuyler, Hazen Shirley* (Kiki)	1968

Name (Nickname)	Year Elected
Dean, Jay Hanna (Dizzy)	1953
Delahanty, Edward J.* (Big Ed)	1945
Dickey, William Malcolm (Bill)	1954
Dihigo, Martin†	1977
Di Maggio, Joseph Paul (Joe)	1955
Doerr, Bobby	1986
Drysdale, Donald Scott (Don)	1984
Duffy, Hugh*	1945
Evans, William George* (Billy)	1973
Evers, John Joseph* (Crab)	1946
Ewing, William Buckingham* (Buck)	1939
Faber, Urban Charles* (Red)	1964
Feller, Robert (Bob)	1962
Ferrell, Richard Benjamin (Rick)	1984
Flick, Elmer Harrison*	1963
Ford, Edward Charles (Whitey)	1974
Foster, George* (Rube)	1981
Foxx, James Emory (Jimmy)	1951
Frick, Ford Christopher*	1970
Frisch, Francis (The Fordham Flash)	1947
Galvin, James F.* (Pud)	1965
Gehrig, Henry Louis (The Iron Horse)	1939
Gehringer, Charles Leonard (The Mechanical Man)	1949
Gibson, Joshua† (Josh)	1972
Gibson, Robert (Bob)	1981
Giles, Warren Crandall	1979
Gomez, Vernon Louis* (Lefty)	1972
Goslin, Leon Allen* (Goose)	1968
Greenberg, Henry Benjamin (Hank)	1956
Griffith, Clark C.* (The Old Fox)	1946
Grimes, Burleigh Arland* (Ol' Stubblebeard)	1964
Grove, Robert Moses (Lefty)	1947
Hafey, Charles James (Chick)	1971
Haines, Jesse Joseph* (Pop)	1970
Hamilton, William Robert* (Sliding Billy)	1961
Harridge, William* (Will)	1972
Harris, Stanley Raymond* (Bucky)	1975
Hartnett, Charles Leo (Gabby)	1955
Heilmann, Harry Edwin	1952
Herman, William Jennings Bryan* (Billy)	1975
Hooper, Harry Bartholomew	1971
Hornsby, Rogers (The Rajah)	1942
Hoyt, Waite Charles* (Schoolboy)	1969
Hubbard, Robert* (Cal)	1976
Hubbell, Carl Owen (King Carl)	1947
Huggins, Miller James*	1964
Hunter, Jim (Catfish)	1987
Irvin, Monford (Monte)	1973
Jackson, Travis*	1982
Jennings, Hugh Ambrose* (Ee-yah)	1945

*Chosen by committee on baseball veterans. †Selected by committee on Negro leagues. All others elected by Baseball Writers Association of America.
(As of 1978 candidates from the Negro leagues and veterans categories were chosen by a single, reorganized committee on baseball veterans.)

Bayliss, William M. (1860–1920), British physiologist, co-discoverer of hormones
  medicine M-285
Bay lynx. *see in index* Bobcat
Bay of Pigs invasion, Cuba C-200
  Hispanic Americans H-166
Bayonet S-546
  gun, *picture* F-97
Bayonne, France, historic town and fortress 4 mi (6 km) from Bay of Biscay; manufacturing and export trade; petroleum and its by-products; 13th-century cathedral; gave name to bayonet, first made here; pop. 39,761, *maps* E-360, F-369, F-405
  banner, *picture* M-384
Bayonne, N.J., port city on peninsula just s. of Jersey City, between Newark Bay and Upper New York Bay; petroleum products, chemicals, metal products, clothing, food products; a military ocean terminal; pop. 72,743 N-195
  bridge B-446, *picture* B-440
'Bay Psalm Book' (or 'The Whole Booke of Psalmes Faithfully Translated into English Metre')
  American literature A-342
  popular music M-683
Bayreuth (or Baireuth), West Germany, city in Bavaria, 126 mi (203 km) n. of Munich; home of Wagner; pop. 64,536 B-111
  Germany, *map* G-131
  opera O-568
Bay State. *see in index* Massachusetts
Baytown, Tex., city 21 mi (34 km) e. of Houston, on Houston Ship Canal; petroleum products, synthetic rubber, carbon black, chemicals; rice, cattle; pop. 56,923.
Bay tree. *see in index* California laurel
Bay Village (sometimes called Bay), Ohio, city on Lake Erie, 10 mi (16 km) w. of Cleveland; Cahoon Park, 116 acres (47 hectares), within city; pop. 17,846.
Bay-winged bunting. *see in index* Vesper sparrow
Bazaar, Oriental marketplace
  Damascus D-18
Bazan, Don Alvaro de (1526–88), Spanish naval officer A-627
Bazeries cylinder, cipher device C-420
Bazooka (or rocket gun), U.S. Army's rocket antitank gun R-233
BBC. *see in index* British Broadcasting Corporation
BC (buoyancy compensator), a safety device used in underwater diving D-188
B cell (or B lymphocyte), white blood cell
  immune system I-55
  lymphatic system L-342
B-complex vitamin V-354, *table* V-355
  bread B-313
BCS theory, physics B-80
Beach, Sylvia (1887–1962), U.S. bookseller and publisher, born in Baltimore, Md.; settled in Paris 1919; her bookstore became a literary center; 'Shakespeare and Company', memoirs.
Beach and coast B-112
Beach Boys, The, California 'surfing' band M-681
Beachcomber, name applied to shiftless and drifting white population scattered over the Pacific P-15
Beachy Head, chalk cliff 532 ft (162 m) in Sussex, England, 3 mi (5 km) from Eastbourne; nearby, Dutch and English fleet defeated by French 1690.
Beacon, N.Y., city on Hudson River opposite Newburgh; petroleum research, printing; clothing, furniture; incline railway to Mt. Beacon; pop. 12,937.
Beacon, a guiding signal
  airport lighting A-212
  lighthouse. *see in index* Lighthouse
Beacon Hill, neighborhood, Boston, Mass. B-371, *picture* B-373
  Massachusetts, *picture* M-199
Beaconsfield, earl of. *see in index* Disraeli, Benjamin
Bead and beadwork B-113
  use as money S-153
Beaded lizard, poisonous reptile *Heloderma horridum*
  description L-272
Beadle, George Wells (born 1903), U.S. biologist, born near Wahoo, Neb.; professor and chairman of biology division California Institute of Technology 1946–60, acting dean of faculty 1960–61; president University of Chicago 1961–68; director Institute of Biomedical Research, AMA, 1968–70
  genetics G-54
Beadle, William Henry Harrison (1838–1915), U.S. pioneer and educator, born in Parke County, Ind.; brigadier general Civil War; president State Normal, Madison, S.D., 1889–1906
  North Dakota N-375
  South Dakota S-325, *picture* S-332
  Statuary Hall, *table* S-437b
Beagle, dog D-193, *picture* D-199
'Beagle', ship in which Darwin made voyage around world D-37
Beak (or bill)
  birds B-245, *pictures* B-243
Beaked whale, mammal of the family Ziphidae W-186
Beam, in architecture
  interior design I-244
  steel beam production, *picture* I-344
Beam, light L-54, L-204
Beam bridge, type of bridge B-441, *picture* B-440
Beamon, Bob (born 1946), U.S. athlete
  track and field T-246
Beam-rider, a missile guidance system G-312
Beam transmission, in radio R-53
Beam trawl, net F-134
Bean, Alan L. (born 1932), former U.S. astronaut, born in Wheeler, Tex.; U.S. Navy officer selected for NASA program 1963; member Skylab 2 in 1973; retired 1975 S-347, *table* S-348
Bean, Roy (1825?–1903), U.S. justice of the peace O-619
Bean, certain leguminous plants, especially of the genera *Phaseolus* and *Vicia* and their seed; name also applied to other bean-shaped seed and to the plants bearing them, such as the castor bean
  germination, growth, *diagram* P-374
  legumes L-120
  picking green beans, *picture*, U-54
  seed structure S-108, *diagram* S-106
  soybean S-340
Beanes, William, U.S. physician
  War of 1812 N-63
Bean family. *see in index* Legumes
Bear, animal of the family Ursidae B-116
  circus, *picture* C-431
  common family and group names, *table* A-427
  forest F-311
  furs, *table* F-464
  grizzly E-212
  hibernation H-147
  hunting, *picture* U-73
  lifespan, *chart* A-423
  polar A-572
  space research S-345
  symbol
    U.S.S.R. R-333
  zoo Z-462, *pictures* Z-463, 464
Bear, in finance S-453
Bearbaiting B-118

MEMBERS OF BASEBALL'S NATIONAL HALL OF FAME

Name (Nickname)	Year Elected	Name (Nickname)	Year Elected
Johnson, Byron Bancroft* (Ban)	1937	Plank, Edward S.*	1946
Johnson, Walter Perry (Barney)	1936	Radbourne, Charles* (Old Hoss)	1939
Johnson, William† (Judy)	1975	Reese, Harold Henry* (Pee Wee)	1984
Joss, Adrian* (Addie)	1978	Rice, Edgar Charles* (Sam)	1963
Kaline, Albert William* (Al)	1980	Rickey, Wesley Branch*	1967
Keefe, Timothy J.* (Tim)	1964	Rixey, Eppa*	1963
Keeler, William H. (Wee Willie)	1939	Roberts, Robin Evan	1976
Kell, George Clyde*	1983	Robinson, Brooks Calvert	1983
Kelley, Joseph James*	1971	Robinson, Frank	1982
Kelly, George Lange* (Highpockets)	1973	Robinson, Jack Roosevelt (Jackie)	1962
Kelly, Michael Joseph* (King)	1945	Robinson, Wilbert* (Uncle Robbie)	1945
Killebrew, Harmon	1984	Roush, Edd J.*	1962
Kiner, Ralph	1975	Ruffing, Charles Herbert (Red)	1967
Klein, Charles Herbert (Chuck)	1980	Rusie, Amos Wilson*	1977
Klem, William J.* (Bill)	1953	Ruth, George Herman (Babe)	1936
Koufax, Sanford (Sandy)	1972	Schalk, Raymond William* (Cracker)	1955
Lajoie, Napoleon (Larry)	1937	Sewell, Joseph Wheeler*	1977
Landis, Kenesaw Mountain*	1944	Simmons, Aloysius Harry (Bucketfoot Al)	1953
Lemon, Robert Granville (Bob)	1976	Sisler, George Harold (Gorgeous George)	1939
Leonard, Walter Fenner† (Buck)	1972	Slaughter, Enos* (Country)	1985
Lindstrom, Frederick Charles* (Fred)	1976	Snider, Edwin Donald* (Duke)	1980
Lloyd, John Henry† (Pop)	1977	Spahn, Warren Edward*	1973
Lombardi, Ernie	1986	Spalding, Albert Goodwill*	1939
Lopez, Alfonso Ramon* (Al)	1977	Speaker, Tristram E. (Tris)	1937
Lyons, Theodore Amar (Ted)	1955	Stengel, Charles Dillon* (Casey)	1966
McCarthy, Joseph Vincent* (Marsh Joe)	1957	Terry, William Harold (Bill)	1954
McCarthy, Thomas Francis*	1946	Thompson, Samuel L.* (Big Sam)	1974
McCovey, Willie	1986	Tinker, Joseph B.*	1946
McGinnity, Joseph Jerome* (Iron Man)	1946	Traynor, Harold Joseph (Pie)	1948
McGraw, John Joseph* (Little Napoleon)	1937	Vance, Arthur Charles (Dazzy)	1955
Mack, Connie*	1937	Vaughan, Floyd* (Arky)	1985
McKechnie, William Boyd* (Deacon Bill)	1962	Waddell, George Edward* (Rube)	1946
MacPhail, Leland Stanford* (Larry)	1978	Wagner, John Peter (Honus; Hans)	1936
Mantle, Mickey Charles	1974	Wallace, Roderick John* (Bobby)	1953
Manush, Henry Emmett* (Heinie)	1964	Walsh, Edward Augustin* (Big Ed)	1946
Maranville, Walter J. V. (Rabbit)	1954	Waner, Lloyd James* (Little Poison)	1967
Marichal, Juan Antonio (Sánchez)	1983	Waner, Paul Glee (Big Poison)	1952
Marquard, Richard William* (Rube)	1971	Ward, John Montgomery*	1964
Mathews, Edwin Lee, Jr. (Eddie)	1978	Weiss, George Martin*	1971
Mathewson, Christopher (Christy)	1936	Welch, Michael F.* (Smiling Mickey)	1973
Mays, Willie Howard	1979	Wheat, Zachariah Davis* (Zack)	1959
Medwick, Joseph Michael (Ducky)	1968	Wilhelm, Hoyt	1985
Mize, John Robert (Johnny)	1981	Williams, Billy	1987
Musial, Stanley Frank (Stan the Man)	1969	Williams, Theodore Samuel (Ted)	1966
Nichols, Charles A.* (Kid)	1949	Wilson, Lewis Robert* (Hack)	1979
O'Rourke, James Henry* (Orator Jim)	1945	Wright, George*	1937
Ott, Melvin Thomas	1951	Wright, William Henry* (Harry)	1953
Paige, Leroy Robert† (Satchel)	1971	Wynn, Early	1972
Pennock, Herbert Jeffries	1948	Yawkey, Thomas A. (Tom)	1980
		Young, Denton True (Cy)	1937
		Youngs, Ross Meddlebrook*	1972

*Chosen by committee on baseball veterans. †Selected by committee on Negro leagues. All others elected by Baseball Writers Association of America.
(As of 1978, candidates from the Negro leagues and veterans categories were chosen by a single, reorganized committee on baseball veterans.)

against Persians, Vandals, Ostrogoths, Goths, and Bulgars; late legend represents him blinded because of Justinian's jealousy, begging for alms in Constantinople
Vandals conquered V-265

Belize (formerly British Honduras), self-governing British colony in Central America; area 8,867 sq mi (22,965 sq km); cap. Belmopan; pop. 140,612 B-152
Central America C-253, *pictures* C-255, C-258
colonization A-333, 337
Commonwealth membership C-602
flag, *picture* F-162
North America, *map* N-350
West Indies W-155
world, *map* W-297
Yucatán Peninsula Y-432

Belize City, Belize, former capital of British Honduras (now Belize); mahogany and logwood used for dyes; chief port of area since early 18th century; pop. 42,184 B-152, *map* N-350

Bell, Acton. *see in index* Brontë, Anne

Bell, Alexander Graham (1847–1922), U.S. scientist and inventor B-153
electricity E-162
Hall of Fame, *table* H-16
Keller K-195
Nova Scotia museum N-28, N-402
telephone I-274, T-55, T-64

Bell, Alexander Melville (1819–1905), U.S. educator, born in Edinburgh, Scotland; father of A.G. Bell; invented 'visible speech,' a method of phonetic notation for deaf-mutes.

Bell, Currer. *see in index* Brontë, Charlotte

Bell, deBennville (nickname Bert) (1895–1959), U.S. football coach and founder of Philadelphia Eagles football team, born in Philadelphia, Pa.; NFL commissioner 1946–59.

Bell, Ellis. *see in index* Brontë, Emily

Bell, Gertrude Margaret Lowthian (1868–1926), British traveler and writer; authority on Orient, including archaeology and modern politics; aided British armies in Arabia during World War I through her knowledge of routes ('The Desert and the Sown'; 'Persian Pictures').

Bell, John (1797–1869), U.S. statesman, born in Nashville, Tenn.; speaker of the House of Representatives 1834–35; secretary of war in President William H. Harrison's Cabinet, later resigned; U.S. senator 1847–59; nominated for presidency 1860; supported Confederacy during Civil War
electoral vote, *chart* P-494

Bell, Josephine (or Doris Bell Ball) (born 1897), writer D-119

Bell, William H., U.S.-Soviet collaborator
espionage E-303

Bell, Calif., city 5 mi (8 km) s.e. of Los Angeles; chiefly residential; aircraft parts, other heavy industrial products; incorporated 1927; pop. 25,450.

Bell B-154. *see also in index* Bell tower
Big Ben L-292, *picture* P-131
bronze B-463
Liberty Bell D-55, U-115, *picture* P-178
Lutine Bell in Lloyd's of London. *see in index* Lutine Bell

Belladonna. *see in index* Deadly nightshade

Bellaire, Ohio, city on Ohio River, 4 mi (6 km) s.w. of Wheeling, W. Va.; in coal, clay, and salt region; glass and metal products, clothing; pop. 8,241.

Bellaire, Tex., residential city lying entirely within city of Houston; formerly a s.w. suburb, it was annexed in 1948.

Bellamy, Edward (1850–98), U.S. author and social reformer, born in Chicopee Falls, Mass. ('Looking Backward', depicts an imagined socialistic society) U-235, F-152

Bellamy, Francis (1855–1931), U.S. editor and preacher, born in Mount Morris, N.Y.; wrote pledge to the flag for first national Columbus Day celebration 1892.

Bellay, Jean du (1492–1560), French cardinal and diplomat; friend of Rabelais; appointed bishop of Bayonne 1526, of Paris 1533; created cardinal 1535.

Belleau Wood, France, battle in World War I, near Château-Thierry
World War I W-311, 314

Belleek ware, porcelain P-477

Bellefontaine, Ohio, city 48 mi (77 km) n.w. of Columbus, in farming district; electric motors and circuit breakers, power tools, auto bearings, food products; nearby, to the e., is Campbell Hill (1550 ft; 472 m), highest point of Ohio; Indian Lake State Park nearby; pop. 11,888.

Bellefontaine Neighbors, Mo., residential city just n. of St. Louis; named for a spring, 'La Belle Fontaine'; Fort Bellefontaine erected here in early 19th century, home of its commander, Gen. Daniel Bissel; pop. 14,084.

Belle Glade, Fla., city 38 mi (61 km) s.w. of West Palm Beach, on s.e. shore of Lake Okeechobee; sugar, livestock, vegetables; established 1925; leveled by hurricane 1928 and rebuilt; pop. 16,535.

'Belle Hélène, La', operetta by Offenbach O-572

Belle Isle, Strait of, channel between Labrador and island of Newfoundland, n. entrance to Gulf of St. Lawrence from Atlantic; 10 to 15 mi. wide; named from island at Atlantic end N-163, *map* C-109
North America, *map* N-350
world, *map* W-297

Bellenden Ker Range, Australian mountains A-771

Bellerophon, character in Greek myth, rider of Pegasus P-152
horse H-273

Belleville, Ill., city 14 mi (22 km) s.e. of St. Louis, Mo., in coal-mining region; stoves, furnaces, beer, shoes, clothing, meat products; Scott Air Force Base nearby; pop. 42,150
Illinois, *map* I-52

Belleville, N.J., residential town just n. of Newark, on Passaic River; wire products, fire extinguishers, cosmetics, water purifying equipment; pop. 35,367.

Belleville, Ont., port city on Bay of Quinte and Moira River, about 100 mi (160 km) e. of Toronto; cement works; electrical products, industrial alcohol, optical lenses; Albert College; pop. 35,128.

Bellevue, Neb., city 8 mi (13 km) s. of Omaha; farm area; oldest town in Nebraska, established as missionary station 1833, incorporated 1856; pop. 21,813 N-104

Bellevue, Pa., residential borough on Ohio River, 5 mi (8 km) n.w. of Pittsburgh; Bayne Memorial Park, famous for 350-year-old elm tree; settled 1802, incorporated 1867; pop. 11,586, *map* P-184

Bellevue, Wash., city 6 mi (10 km) e. of Seattle, across Lake Washington; light manufacturing; two floating bridges across lake; pop. 73,903 W-50, 60

Bellevue House National Historic Park, park in Ontario N-29

Bellflower, Calif., city 12 mi (19 km) s.e. of Los Angeles; truck and dairy farming, commercial flower growing; aircraft, missiles, space project systems, ordnance works; pop. 53,441.

Bellingham, Mass., 5 mi (8 km) s.e. of Milford; birthplace of Oliver Optic (William Taylor Adams); incorporated 1719; pop. of township 14,300.

Bellingham, Wash., port city 80 mi (130 km) n. of Seattle, on Bellingham Bay; fishing and lumbering center; pulp and paper mills; dairy products; aluminum, fiberglass boats; Western Washington State College; gateway to Mt. Baker National Forest; pop. 45,794 W-50, 60, *map* U-40

Bellingshausen, Fabian Gottlieb von (1778–1852), Russian Antarctic explorer and naval officer P-419, *table* P-422

Bellingshausen Sea, sea in South Pacific Ocean, off Antarctica, between Alexander I Island and Thurston Peninsula; named for Fabian G. von Bellingshausen, who led Russian Expedition of 1819–21.

Bellini, Gentile (1429–1507), Venetian painter, brother of Giovanni Bellini B-156

Bellini, Giovanni (1430?–1516), Venetian painter B-156
Mantegna M-111

Bellini, Vincenzo (1801–35), Italian composer, born in Catania, Sicily; so talented as a child that Sicilian nobleman paid for education at Naples conservatory; wrote operas with delightful melodies; arias exploit human voice, sung with success by Grisi, Patti, Lilli Lehmann, Callas ('La Sonnambula'; 'Norma'; 'I Puritani')
opera O-566
popular music M-683

Bellis. *see in index* English daisy

Bell Island, rocky island of s.e. Newfoundland, 12 mi (19 km) n.w. of St. John's; area 11 sq mi (28 sq km); named for bell-shaped rock off w. end.

Bell-lyra, lyre-shaped glockenspiel mounted on a rod, so that it is portable; used in bands.

Bellmawr (original name Heddings), N.J., borough 6 mi (10 km) s.e. of Camden; built on site of Bell Farm, famous for breeding of fine work horses; incorporated 1926; pop. 13,721.

Bello, Andrés (1781–1865), Latin American scholar, poet, and journalist, born in Caracas, Venezuela; to Chile 1829; there codified civil law; founded University of Chile 1842, rector 1843–65 L-68, 75, *picture* L-70

Belloc, Hilaire (1870–1953), British author B-157

Bello Horizonte, Brazil. *see in index* Belo Horizonte

Bellow, Saul (born 1915), U.S. novelist B-157
American literature A-362

Bellows, George (full name George Wesley Bellows) (1882–1925), U.S. painter B-158
'Lady Jean' P-61, *picture* P-60

Bell pepper, fruit P-197a, *picture* P-197b

Bell's palsy, muscular disease M-659

Bell tower (or belfry, or campanile)
belfry defined B-155
church bells B-154
Giotto's in Florence F-188, *picture* F-187, *map* F-189
Della Robbia sculpture, *picture* P-264
leaning tower of Pisa P-343
Parliament building, *pictures* P-131
Pennsylvania State University, *picture* P-171
St. Mark's V-277
Springfield, Mass. S-397

Bellwood, Ill., village 13 mi (21 km) w. of Chicago; wood products, metal products, electrical equipment; pop. 19,811
Illinois, *map* I-52

Belmont, Calif., city 3 mi (5 km) s.e. of San Mateo; electronic equipment; commercial flower growing; College of Notre Dame; incorporated 1926; pop. 24,505.

Belmont, Mass., residential town 7 mi (11 km) n.w. of Boston; includes village of Waverly; settlement dates from 1636; town incorporated 1859; pop. of township 13,067.

Belmonte (y García), Juan (1892–1962), Spanish matador B-501

Belmont Stakes, horse race H-275

Belmopan, Belize, capital, about 32 mi (51 km) s.w. of Belize City; founded 1970; named for Mayans who refused to surrender to Spanish; pop. 4,508 B-152, *map* N-350

Belo Horizonte (formerly Bello Horizonte), Brazil, capital of state of Minas Gerais, 215 mi (345 km) n.w. of Rio de Janeiro; mining, agriculture, diamond cutting; textiles; pop. 1,442,483 B-158
Brazil B-424, *map* B-425
South America S-277, *map* S-298
world, *map* W-297

Beloit, Wis., city on Rock River, near Ill. border, in rich agricultural region; diesel engines, electric motors, papermaking and woodworking machinery, refrigeration equipment, shoes, brakes and clutches; Beloit College; pop. 35,207, *map* U-41

Belorussian Soviet Socialist Republic, republic of the U.S.S.R.; 80,200 sq mi (207,600 sq km); cap. Minsk; pop. 9,452,000 B-159, *map* E-360
Minsk M-461
people R-325
U.S.S.R. U-15, *maps* R-325, 344, 348, U-14

Belshazzar, in Bible, Book of Daniel, last king of Babylon, son and successor of Nebuchadnezzar; warned of his doom by 'handwriting on the wall' B-11

Belted Kingfisher, bird *Megaceryle alcyon* of the family Alcedinidae K-246

Belter, John Henry (1804–63), U.S. cabinetmaker in New York; one of designers who revived rococo style in mid-19th century; known for chairs with pierced, carved backs
furniture F-462, *picture* F-459

Belt of calms. *see in index* Doldrums

Belt tunnel freezing
food processing F-283

Beluga. *see in index* White whale

Belvedere, a gallery in the Vatican which contains fine art treasures, including the 'Apollo Belvedere' and the 'Laocoön', *map* V-269

Belvidere, Ill., city 13 mi. e. of Rockford; truck and dairy farms; automobile assembly plant, food processing; metals; pop. 15,176
Illinois, *map* I-52

Bely, Andrei. *see in index* Bugaev, Boris Nikolaevich

Belyayev, Pavel Ivanovich (1925–70), Soviet cosmonaut; in Soviet air force 1945–70; piloted Voskhod II spaceship 1965, *table* S-348

Bemba, African people
Zaire Z-444

Bemidji, Minn., city and summer resort on Bemidji Lake, 140 mi. n.w. of Duluth; farming and lumbering region; dairy and wood products, brick, furs; Bemidji State University; Itasca State Park nearby; pop. 10,949.

Bemis Heights, battles of. *see in index* Saratoga, battles of

Benacerraf, Baruj (born 1920), U.S. physician and scientist. *see also in index* Nobel Prizewinners, *table*

Benalcazar, Sebastián de (1495?–1551), Spanish conqueror of Nicaragua, Ecuador, and southwestern Colombia
Ecuador E-68

Ben-Ami, Jacob, Jewish actor Y-419

'Ben and Me', work by Lawson R-108, *picture* R-111

Benares, India. *see in index* Varanasi

Benary-Isbert, Margot (1889–1979), U.S. author, born in Saarbrücken, Germany; to U.S. 1952, became citizen 1957; best known for stories for younger readers ('The Ark'; 'Rowan Farm'; 'The Wicked Enchantment'; 'Castle on the Border'; 'Dangerous Spring'; 'A Time to Love') R-111c

Benavente (y Martínez), Jacinto (1866–1954), Spanish dramatist, born in Madrid; influential in freeing modern Spanish stage from artificiality and melodrama ('The Bonds of Interest'; 'Smile of Mona Lisa') S-365b, *picture* S-365a

Benbecu'la, island of Hebrides; pop. 1,358.

Ben Bella, Ahmed (born 1918), Algerian political leader B-159
Algerian independence A-305

Bench-press, weight lifting W-137

Bench show, dog show D-210

Bench warrant, in law
legal definition, *table* L-92

Bencivieni di Pepo. *see in index* Cimabue, Giovanni

Bend, Ore., city in central part of state, about 90 mi (145 km) e. of Eugene, on Deschutes River; lumbering, agricultural, and tourist center; center of Deschutes National Forest Recreation Area; pop. 17,263, *map* U-40

Bend, knot K-262

Ben Day process, photoengraving P-275

Bend dexter, heraldry H-136

Bender Eregli, Turkey. *see in index* Eregli

Bending, in metalworking operation T-225

Bending. *see in index* Refraction

Bendire's thrasher, bird *Toxostoma bendirei* T-175

Bendjedid, Chadli (born 1929), president of Algeria 1979– A-305

Bends. *see in index* Decompression sickness

Bend sinister, heraldry H-136

Bénédette, Le. *see in index* Castiglione, Giovanni Benedetto

Benedict, popes, *table* P-99

Benedict, Ruth (or Ruth Fulton, pen name Anne Singleton) (1887–1948), U.S. author and anthropologist B-160
  anthropology A-486, *picture* A-485

Benedictine Rule, duty of prayer and work espoused by the Benedictines
  Middle Ages M-391

Benedictines, a monastic order sometimes called 'Black Monks'; also an order of nuns M-542

Benedict of Nursia, saint (480?–547?), Italian monk, founder of Benedictine Order; festival March 21 B-160
  bookmaking B-350
  Middle Ages M-391
  monks and monasticism M-541

Beneficiary
  trust T-301

Beneficiate, in metalworking I-336

Benefit of clergy, privilege claimed by medieval clergy of being tried in bishop's court instead of king's court under secular jurisdiction; finally abolished in England 1827
  Becket B-122

Benefits. *see also* Fact Summary with each state article
  labor movements L-10
  social security S-236

Benelux Economic Union, union of Belgium, The Netherlands, and Luxembourg formed during World War II to integrate the economies of the three participants E-338
  Belgium B-150
  Luxembourg L-341
  The Netherlands N-128

Benes, Eduard (1884–1948), president of Czechoslovakia 1935–38, 1945–48; foreign minister 1918–35; with Masaryk organized independence movement; helped found Little Entente; came to U.S., named to faculty of University of Chicago 1939; president of Czech government in exile after July 1941, returned to Czechoslovakia 1945; resigned as president 1948 rather than approve new constitution ('Democracy Today and Tomorrow').

Benét, Stephen Vincent (1898–1943), U.S. writer B-161
  American literature A-356
  children's literature R-111

Benevento (ancient Beneventum), Italy, city 32 mi (51 km) n.e. of Naples; pop. 55,381, *map* I-401
  battle of 275 BC P-544
  battle of 1266 [illegible]

Bengal, former British province in n.e. India; divided between India and Pakistan 1947; e. part is now Bangladesh (formerly East Pakistan); w. part is West Bengal B-62. *see also in index* Bangladesh; West Bengal
  Javan rhinoceros R-178

Bengal, Bay of, Indian Ocean I-62, *map* I-86
  Asia, *map* A-697
  Ganges River G-15
  world, *map* W-297

Bengal cat, hybrid cat; cross between a leopard cat and a domestic cat C-205

Bengali language, modern dialect of India, akin to Uriya, Assamese, Bihari, and Hindustani; word of English origin, derived from *Bengal* in which province it is spoken; makes free use of Sanskrit words; literature known in Western world through works of Tagore B-60, I-67, I-108
  Chatterjee's contribution C-282

Bengal tiger, animal, *picture* I-65

Benghazi (or Bengasi), Libya, seaport city in n.e.; founded by Greeks of Cyrenaica as Hesperides; renamed Berenice by Ptolemy III; pop. 131,970
  world, *map* W-297

Benguela Current (or Benguella Current), cold current in South Atlantic Ocean; moves northward along west coast of Africa A-745
  South Africa affected S-263

Ben-Gurion, David (originally David Gruen) (1886–1973), Israeli leader B-161
  Israel I-372

'Ben-Hur, a Tale of the Christ', a vivid story by Lew Wallace (1880); the hero, a noble young Jew, unjustly condemned to the galleys by the Romans, has many adventures and eventually becomes a Christian; subject of motion pictures, *picture* S-213

Benign neglect, form of child abuse C-319

Benign tumor C-812, D-175

Beni Hilal, a people of Africa
  Libya L-190

Benin, People's Republic of (formerly Dahomey), nation in n.w. Africa, on Gulf of Guinea; area 43,475 sq mi (112,600 sq km); cap. Porto-Novo; pop. 3,641,000 B-162, *map* A-115
  African political unit, *table* A-112
  communist world, *map* C-619
  flag, *picture* F-162
  folklore F-263
  Lagos' government L-22
  national anthem, *table* N-64
  railroad mileage, *table* R-85
  world, *map* W-297

Benioff linear strain seismograph, earthquake measurement E-38

Benioff zone, seismic belt E-39

Beni Salim, a people of Africa
  Libya L-190

Benjamin, Judah Philip (1811–84), U.S. lawyer, born on island of St. Thomas, present Virgin Islands; U.S. senator (Whig and Democrat) from state of Louisiana 1853–61; Confederate political leader, attorney general and secretary of war 1861, secretary of state 1862–65
  Confederacy C-644

Benjamin bush. *see in index* Spicebush

Benjamin Franklin Bridge, bridge over Delaware River P-251a, *picture* P-251

Ben Lomond, mountain (3,192 ft, 974 m) in Stirlingshire, Scotland, on shore of Loch Lomond S-67

Bennet, Elizabeth, sensible, charming heroine of Jane Austen's 'Pride and Prejudice'; Elizabeth is 'Prejudice' and Philip Darcy, whom she finally marries, is 'Pride'.

Bennett, Arnold (1867–1931), British writer B-163. *see also in index* Five Towns
  literary contribution E-279

Bennett, Floyd (1890–1928), U.S. aviator, born in Warrensburg, N.Y.; in aviation corps, U.S. Navy; awarded Congressional Medal of Honor; developed pneumonia in flight to aid German-Irish transatlantic fliers and was stranded near Quebec, where he died
  North Pole flight (1926) A-204, 208, *table* A-206

Bennett, James Gordon (1795–1872), U.S. journalist, born in Scotland; originated detailed reporting of public events, practice of interviewing, use of telegraph in reporting, and system of distribution by carriers; started the *New York Herald* 1835 N-236, *list* N-240

Bennett, James Gordon, Jr. (1841–1918), U.S. editor and proprietor *New York Herald*, born in New York, N.Y.; lived in Paris after 1877; started Paris edition of *Herald* 1877
  quoted R-281
  Stanley S-410

Bennett, Michael, (1943–87), U.S. choreographer and director, born in Buffalo, N.Y.; well-known choreographed works include 'A Chorus Line' (1975), 'Dreamgirls' (1981)
  opera O-560

Bennett, Richard Bedford Bennett, Viscount (1870–1947), Canadian statesman, born near Hopewell, N.B.; several years in Canadian House of Commons; served as minister of justice and attorney general and as minister of finance; as leader of Conservative party was prime minister of Canada 1930–35.

Ben Nevis, peak in western Scotland; highest point in British Isles (4,406 ft; 1,343 m) S-67

Bennington, Vt., 32 mi (51 km) w. of Brattleboro; textiles, plastics, paper, wood products, electronic equipment; Bennington College; pop. of township 15,815 V-286, *map* V-301
  monument, *picture* V-293
  Old First Church, *picture* V-289
  pottery P-477

Bennington, Battle of (1777) V-289
  celebrated F-94
  flag F-156, *picture* F-155
  monument, *picture* V-293

Bennington College, Bennington, Vt.; private control; coeducational, formerly for women; opened 1932; known for individually planned study programs; liberal arts; graduate studies V-300

Benny, Jack (formerly Benjamin Kubelsky) (1894–1974), U.S. motion-picture, radio, and television comedian B-163

Benoit, Joan (born 1957), U.S. athlete
  track and field T-245

Benozzo Gozzoli. *see in index* Gozzoli, Benozzo

Bensenville, Ill., village 17 mi (27 km) n.w. of Chicago; railroad yards; clothing, pipes; incorporated 1884; pop. 16,124
  Illinois, *map* I-52

Benson, Arthur Christopher (1862–1925), British essayist and literary critic; son of Edward W. Benson; meditative, refined, scholarly ('The Upton Letters'; 'From a College Window'; 'Walter Pater').

Bensurdatu, Italian folk hero, *picture* S-472

Benteen, Frederick W. (1834–98), U.S. soldier, born in Petersburg, Va.; in part of Little Bighorn expedition under Custer; rescued with troops two days after fatal battle; became colonel in Civil War C-808

Bentham, Jeremy (1748–1832), English philosopher and jurist B-164
  human rights H-320
  Mill M-416
  philosophy P-264

Benthic zone, in oceanography A-745

Benthos, oceanography O-483

Bentley, Wilson Alwyn (1865–1931), U.S. farmer and meteorologist, born in Jericho, Vt.; photographed snow crystals; in 1931 published 'Snow Crystals', book of 2,500 beautiful photomicrographs S-228

Benton, Thomas Hart (1782–1858), U.S. senator
  Missouri M-493, *picture* M-491
  Statuary Hall, *table* S-437b

Benton, Thomas Hart (1889–1975), U.S. painter B-164
  Pollock P-440
  'The Sources of Country Music', *picture* M-678

Benton, William (1900–1973), U.S. publisher, senator, and statesman B-164

Benton Harbor, Mich., city near s.w. corner of state, on Lake Michigan and on St. Joseph River, opposite St. Joseph; fruit market; industrial power lifting equipment, foundry products, machinery, record players; House of David, religious colony, founded 1903; pop. 14,707.

Bentonite, a claylike mineral B-165
  minerals M-437
  Wyoming W-388

Bent's Fort, famous trading post along Santa Fe Trail, on Arkansas River, near present La Junta, Colo.; built 1833–34 by Charles Bent (1799–1847), his brother William (1809–69), Cerán St. Vrain (1798–1870), and associates; in 1849 William, then sole owner, blew up fort after failing to sell it to U.S. for sufficient sum; he later built Bent's New Fort farther downstream and leased it to government 1859
  Colorado C-572, *map* C-583, *picture* C-573

Bentwood chair, furniture produced by Thonet F-462
  industrial design I-170

Benue River, river in West Africa; longest tributary of the Niger; 673 mi (1,083 km) long
  Niger N-314

Benz, Karl (1844–1929), German engineer and inventor, born in Karlsruhe; built two-stroke engine 1879; founded pioneer auto factory, Benz and Co., at Mannheim A-856, A-868, I-264

Benzene (often called benzol), compound of carbon and hydrogen (C_6H_6). *see also in index* Benzine
  organic chemistry O-602
  products P-228
  toxic waste W-75

Benzene series. *see in index* Aromatic series

Benzine, a mixture of paraffin hydrocarbons distilled from petroleum. *see also in index* Benzene

Benzodiazepine, narcotic drug N-19

Benzol. *see in index* Benzene

Benzoyl peroxide, bleaching agent B-310

Beograd, Yugoslavia, *see in index* Belgrade

Beothuk, a North American Indian tribe
  American Indians, *map* I-136, *table* I-138
  Newfoundland N-168

Beowulf, hero of Anglo-Saxon poem B-165
  mythology M-704
  storytelling S-472, 481
  Sweden S-527

'Beowulf', epic poem B-165
  Anglo-Saxon influence S-472
  English literature E-264

Bequest, in law, *table* L-92

Berain, Jean, the Elder (1637–1711), French designer and engraver
  furniture F-458

Berber, a people of n. Africa; includes Kabyle, Siwans, Tibu, and Tuareg; gave name to Barbary States
  Algeria A-303
  Atlas Mountains A-746
  Coleman C-545
  Mali M-75
  Moors M-581
  Morocco M-586
  Sahara S-16, *picture* S-15
  Tunisia T-308

Berceuse, in music, *list* M-670

Berchtesgaden, West Germany, village in s.e. Bavaria, in Salzburg Alps, 12 mi (19 km) s. of Salzburg, Austria; summer and winter resort, noted for scenic beauty; on the heights near Berchtesgaden were built Adolf Hitler's chalet, Berghof, and his retreat, Eagle's Nest; in 1945 the Berghof was shattered by bombs from British planes; in 1952 a German demolition firm salvaged some of the ruins of the Berghof and destroyed the rest with explosives; pop. 4,343, *map* G-131, *picture* G-113

Berdichev, Ukrainian Soviet Socialist Republic, market town 100 mi (160 km) s.w. of Kiev; famous fairs; scene of many conflicts between Poles and Russians; pop. 53,206, *maps* R-344, 349

Berea, Ky., town 35 mi (55 km) s.e. of Lexington, where Cumberland foothills meet Bluegrass region; seat of Berea College; pop. 8,226.

Berea, Ohio, city about 12 mi (19 km) s.w. of Cleveland; metal products; greenhouse for scientific cultivation of vegetables; Baldwin-Wallace College; settled 1809; pop. 22,396
  sandstone grit O-502

Beregovoy, Georgi Temogeyevich (born 1921),

Soviet cosmonaut and test pilot, born in Ukraine S-346f, *table* S-348
Berenice, wife of Ptolemy III, Euergetes; a myth says that her hair, which had been pledged to the gods for her husband's safe return from Syria, was carried to heaven from the Temple of Venus and became the constellation *Coma Berenices* ('Berenice's hair')
constellation, *charts* S-418, 422, C-681
Berenice, Libya. *see in index* Benghazi
Berenson, Bernhard (or Bernard Berenson) (1865–1959), U.S. art critic, born in Vilna, Lithuania, of U.S. parents; noted authority on Italian art ('Italian Painters of the Renaissance'; 'Rumor and Reflection', autobiography; 'Passionate Sightseer', diaries) F-188
Beret, hats and caps H-53
Berg, Alban (1885–1935), Austrian composer B-165
classical music M-675
opera O-569
Schönberg S-54
Berg, Patty (full name Patricia Jane Berg) (born 1918), U.S. golfer, born in Minneapolis, Minn.; at 20 had won all major amateur golf titles; turned professional 1940; in Associated Press poll was voted outstanding woman athlete of 1938, 1943, and 1955
golf G-189
Berg, Paul (born 1926), U.S. chemist. *see also in index* Nobel Prizewinners, *table*
Bergamo, Italy, picturesque city 30 mi (50 km) n.e. of Milan; silk and other textiles; notable old churches; pop. 114,907, *map* I-401
Bergamot, a kind of mint
explosive seed pods S-106
Bergelmer, frost giant in Norse mythology M-703
Bergelson, David, Yiddish writer Y-418
Bergen, Norway, chief port on s.w. coast; exports fish and fish products; shipbuilding; birthplace of Edvard Grieg and Ole Bull; settled about 1070 by Olav III; center of civil wars in Middle Ages; devastated by fires 1702, 1855, and 1916; bombed and occupied five years by Nazis in World War II; pop. 117,290, *map* E-360
Norway N-391, *picture* N-393
Bergenfield, N.J., borough 9 mi (14 km) e. of Paterson; textiles, machinery, clothing, metal and concrete products; pop. 25,568.
Bergen Theater, theater in Bergen, Norway
Bjørnson B-287
Berger, Victor Luitpold (1860–1929), U.S. Socialist political leader born in Nieder-Rehbach, Austria-Hungary; edited Socialist journals, Milwaukee; first Socialist ever elected to Congress (1910); because of pacifist preaching during World War I excluded from Congress and sentenced to 20 years' imprisonment; decision was reversed by Supreme Court, and he was seated 1923 S-235
Bergerac, Cyrano de. *see in index* Cyrano de Bergerac, Savinien
Bergh, Henry (1811–88), U.S. philanthropist, author, and humanitarian, born in New York, N.Y.; organized Society for Prevention of Cruelty to Children 1875
humane societies H-318
Bergius, Friedrich (1884–1949), German chemist; developed processes for converting coal into gasoline and oil, and wood into coal by high-temperature, high-pressure methods using hydrogen atmosphere; made edible sugar from wood.
Bergman, Ingmar (full name Ernst Ingmar Bergman) (born 1918), Swedish film writer and producer B-166
motion pictures M-623, *picture* M-610
Sweden S-526
Bergman, Ingrid (1915–82), U.S. Academy award-winning motion-picture actress, born in Stockholm, Sweden; stage, television, and international film star, lent intelligent charm and freshness to a variety of roles ('Casablanca', 'Gaslight', 'Anastasia', 'Murder on the Orient Express').
Bergson, Henri Louis (1859–1941), French philosopher; denied claim of science to explain universe on mechanical principles; regarded life not as something static but a matter of time and change, unending creation (creative evolution) ('Time and Free Will'; 'Matter and Memory'; 'Creative Evolution'; 'Laughter'; 'The Creative Mind') P-266
Beria, Lavrenti Pavlovich (1899–1953), Soviet political leader, born in Georgian Soviet Socialist Republic; elected to Central Committee of Communist party 1934; minister of internal affairs 1938–46, 1953; became alternate member of Politburo 1939, full member 1946; promoted to marshal in World War II; a deputy premier 1941–53, a first deputy premier 1953; convicted of treason and executed K-233, R-357
Beriberi, deficiency disease of the nerves V-355
food and nutrition F-279
Bering, Vitus (or Vitus Behring) (1680–1741), Danish navigator, commissioned by Peter the Great to explore n.e. Asiatic coasts for Russia A-245, A-339
Bering Sea B-166
Bering Sea, arm of North Pacific Ocean between Alaska and Siberia B-166. *see also in index* Ocean, *table*
Alaska A-240, *map* A-254
Asia, *map* A-697
North America, *map* N-350
seal fisheries S-99
world, *map* W-297
Bering Sea Arbitration Treaty (1891), *table* T-274
Thompson T-173
Bering Strait, channel separating Asia and North America and connecting North Pacific with Arctic Ocean B-166, *picture* U-95
Alaska A-240, *map* A-254
Asia, *map* A-697
human migration I-113, M-402
man M-83, 86
North America, *map* N-350
world, *map* W-297
Berkeley, George (1685–1753), Irish idealistic philosopher, political economist, writer, and Anglican bishop B-166
philosophy P-266
Berkeley, John, baron of Stratton (died 1678), grantee of New Jersey N-199
Berkeley, William (1606–77), tyrannical and extortionate English governor of Virginia, born in Bruton, Somersetshire; colony under his rule 1642–76 V-335
Bacon's Rebellion B-11
Berkeley, Calif., city on e. shore of San Francisco Bay, opposite the Golden Gate; pop. 103,328 B-167, *maps* C-50, U-40
botanical garden, *table* B-379
Berkeley, Mo., city on Coldwater River, 11 mi (18 km) n.w. of St. Louis; large aircraft corporation; parks; airport nearby; incorporated as city 1937; pop. 16,146.
Berkeley Heights, N.J., 7 mi (11 km) n.e. of Westfield; electronic measuring devices, chemicals, plastics; pop. of township 12,549.
Berkeley Springs (or Bath), W. Va., town and health resort 27 mi (43 km) w. of Hagerstown, Md.; glass-sand pits, hosiery, refrigerator parts, soft drinks; mineral springs; pop. 789
West Virginia W-167
Berkelium (Bk), chemical element
periodic table, *table* P-207, *list* P-208
Berkley, Mich., city 14 mi (22 km) n.w. of Detroit; residential suburb, part of greater Detroit area; incorporated as village 1925, as city 1932; pop. 21,879, *map* M-371
Berkshire (or Berks), agricultural county in England, s. of Thames River; 1,875 sq km (725 sq mi); county seat Reading; nuclear stations; pop. 504,154.
Berkshire, breed of pig P-320
Berkshire Hills, Mass. M-190
Berkshire Hills Region, geographical region in Massachusetts M-190
Berkshire Music Festival, Tanglewood (estate), Lenox, Mass.; originated at Interlaken, Mass., 1934, by Henry K. Hadley; taken over by Boston Symphony Orchestra at Tanglewood 1936; now six weeks of concerts July–Aug.
Koussevitzky K-302
Berle, Milton (born 1908), U.S. comedian
television T-69
Berlin, Irving (originally Israel Baline) (born 1888), U.S. popular songwriter, born in Russia; brought to U.S. 1893; wrote 'Remember', 'Always', 'Alexander's Ragtime Band', 'Easter Parade', 'White Christmas'; also wrote scores and lyrics for many musical plays and motion pictures; received gold medal 1954 authorized by Congress for his contribution to popular music 'God Bless America' N-65
musical comedy M-685
popular music M-684
Berlin, Conn., 3 mi (5 km) s. of New Britain; hardware, plastics, paper foam products, uniforms; incorporated 1785; pop. of township 15,121.
Berlin, Germany, largest city; divided into West Berlin and East Berlin; pop. 3,219,697 B-168. *see also in index* East Berlin; West Berlin
blockade and airlift B-312, R-357
warfare W-24
botanical garden, *table* B-379
Brandenburg Gate B-168, *map* B-170
Germany, *maps* E-360, G-131
international relations I-264, *picture* I-264
world, *map* W-297
World War I W-311
World War II W-343, 359
Berlin, N.H., city on Androscoggin River, at n. limits of White Mountains; waterpower; chemicals, textiles; winter sports; pop. 13,084 N-178, 186, *maps* N-190, U-41
Berlin, Ont. *see in index* Kitchener
Berlin, Congress of (1878), meeting of representatives of United Kingdom, Germany, France, Austria, Russia, Italy, and Turkey to revise Treaty of San Stefano B-172, *table* T-274
Armenia's partition A-628
Austria-Hungary A-831
Balkan states' independence B-29
Bulgaria's partition B-500
Disraeli D-185
Turkey T-323
Ottoman Empire O-618
United Kingdom E-254
Berlin, Treaty of (1885) Z-445
Berlin Act (1884–85), *table* T-274
Berlin Decree (1806), order issued by Napoleon, providing that all ports under his control be closed to British goods.
'Berlin Diary', work by Shirer M-658
Berliner Ensemble, German acting company A-28, B-434
Berlin-Rome Axis, in German history G-124
Berlin Wall, barrier in East Germany F-320, G-112, 127
Berlin work. *see in index* Needlepoint
Berlioz, Hector (full name Louis Hector Berlioz) (1803–69), French composer B-172
classical music M-673
opera O-566
Berm, land formation, *picture* B-112
Bermuda lawn, grass
growing conditions G-27
Bermuda-rig (or Marconi-rig, or jibheaded-rig) B-326
Bermudas, group of islands in Atlantic Ocean; 21 sq mi (54 sq km); chief island Bermuda; pop. 54,670 B-173
Commonwealth membership C-602
North America, *map* N-350
West Indies W-158, *picture* W-157, *map* W-159
world, *map* W-297
World War II W-325
Bermúdez, Juan de (died 1570), Spanish navigator; credited by Spanish navigator-historian Fernandez de Oviedo with exploration of Bermuda early in 16th century B-173
Bermudez Lake, asphalt lake in Venezuela A-702
Bern (also Berne), Switzerland, capital; pop. 145,254 B-174, S-542, *maps* S-537, *picture* S-544a
climate S-537, *graph* S-545
Europe, *map* E-360
Universal Postal Union P-463b, U-26
Bernadette, Saint (or Bernadette Soubirous, or Marie Bernard Soubirous) (1844–79), French saint L-325
Bernadotte (full name Jean-Baptiste Jules Bernadotte) (1763–1844), French general B-174
Sweden S-527
Bernadotte, Folke (1895–1948), Swedish count and diplomat; promoted Swedish-American relations; peace mediator in World War II; appointed United Nations mediator between Israel and Arabs 1948; assassinated in Jerusalem Sept. 1948
assassination, *list* A-704
Bernanos, Georges (1888–1948), French writer, born in Paris; began writing at 37; works deplored religious indifference; Roman Catholic viewpoint.
Bernard, Claude (1813–78), French physiologist B-174
animal experimentation A-449
Bernard, Henriette Rosine. *see in index* Bernhardt, Sarah
Bernardin de Saint-Pierre, Jacques Henri (1737–1814), French author; a friend of J. J. Rousseau and, like him, a champion of the return to nature; broke away from stilted vocabulary of French classical writing.
Bernard of Clairvaux, Saint (1090–1153), French monk, one of most eloquent preachers of Middle Ages; feast day Aug. 20 A-8
Berne, Switzerland. *see in index* Bern
Berne Convention (1886), international copyright agreement C-713
Bernese mountain dog, dog, *picture* D-201
Bernese Oberland (or Bernese Alps), range in Switzerland, *map* S-537
Bernhard of Lippe-Biesterfeld (born 1911), German prince, the prince of The Netherlands, consort of Queen Juliana.
Bernhardt, Sarah (formerly Henriette Rosine Bernard) (1844–1923), French actress B-175
'Camille' D-288
motion pictures M-618
Bernina, Piz, Alpine peak in s.e. Switzerland, near Italian border (13,295 ft; 4,052 m); highest peak in Bernina Alp group; first successful climb made 1850, *map* I-404
Bernini, Giovanni Lorenzo (1598–1680), Italian sculptor and architect B-175
baroque style A-556
metalworking M-311
Rome
colonnade, *picture* R-254
fountains F-334, R-255, *picture* R-254
St. Peter's Basilica V-268
'St. Teresa' S-88
Bernoulli, Daniel (1700–1782), Swiss mathematician and physicist, born in Basel; wrote on problems of acoustics; worked in differential equations (Bernoulli equation); most important publication, 'Hydrodynamica', advances the kinetic theory of gases and fluids
Bernoulli effect A-179, *diagram* A-180
hydraulics H-338
mathematics, *table* M-215
Bernoulli, Jakob (1654–1705), Swiss mathematician, *table* M-218
Bernoulli, Johann (1667–1748), Swiss mathematician, *table* M-218
Bernstein, Carl, news reporter who helped expose the Watergate scandal that forced President Nixon to resign N-239
Bernstein, Eduard (1850–1932), German moderate socialist and writer, born in Berlin; lived in England 1888–1901; associate of Friedrich Engels S-234
Bernstein, Leonard (born 1918), U.S. pianist, composer, and conductor B-176

classical music M-677
opera O-560
orchestra O-578

Berri, John, duke of (or John, duke of Berry) (1340–1416), 3rd son of John II (king of France); though cruel, vain, and unscrupulous, was patron of arts and letters.

Berry, Chuck (born 1926), U.S. rock-n-roll musician M-680

Berry, Martha McChesney (1866–1942), U.S. educator, born near Rome, Ga.; used her fortune to found schools for children of Georgia mountains.

Berry, Raymond Emmett (born 1933), U.S. football player, born in Corpus Christi, Tex.; offensive end with Baltimore Colts 1955–67; led league in receptions 3 seasons.

Berry, small fruit with seeds contained in pulp B-176
fruit F-436
mayapple M-237

Berryman, John (1914–72), U.S. poet, born in McAlester, Okla.; 1965 Pulitzer prize (poetry) for '77 Dream Songs'; National Book Award 1969 for 'His Toy, His Dream, His Rest' A-364

Bersimis River (or Betsiamites River), river in province of Quebec; tributary of the St. Lawrence Q-9e, *maps* C-112, Q-9a

Berson, Joseph Arthur Stanislaus (1859–1942), German meteorologist B-43

Berth, in harbor H-35

Berth, place to sleep
railroad car R-82, *pictures* R-80

Bertin, Rose (17th century), French dress designer D-268

Berto, Giuseppe (1914–78), Italian writer I-379

Bertoia, Harry (1915–78), U.S. sculptor in metal, born in San Lorenzo, Italy
furniture F-462

Bertoldo di Giovanni (1420–91), Italian Renaissance sculptor; student of Donatello and a teacher of Michelangelo
Michelangelo M-350

Berwick, Pa., borough on Susquehanna River, 23 mi (37 km) s.w. of Wilkes-Barre; clothing, food products, cigars, metal products; pop. 12,189, *map* P-185

Berwick-on-Tweed, England, frontier town at mouth of Tweed River, on Scottish border; prominent in border wars; pop. 11,530, *map* U-18a

Berwyn, Ill., residential and industrial city 10 mi (16 km) w. of Chicago; electrical equipment, machine tools, clay, leather, tobacco products; pop. 46,849
Illinois, *map* I-52

Beryl, mineral M-436
gem J-115

Beryllium (Be), chemical element A-307
industrial health hazards I-175
nuclear energy N-423
periodic table, *table* P-207, *list* P-208

Berzelius, Jöns Jakob, Baron (1779–1848), Swedish chemist; discovered silicon, zirconium, cerium, and thorium; invented chemical symbols
selenium discovery S-57j
television T-78

Bes, ancient Roman unit of weight, *table* W-141

Besançon, France, fortified city on Doubs River, 206 mi (332 km) s.e. of Paris; watches, clocks; Roman remains; birthplace of Victor Hugo; pop. 107,939, *maps* F-369, S-537
first rayon factory R-97

Besant, Annie (1847–1933), British social reformer and leader of Theosophical Society T-163

'Beside the Fire,' work by Hyde
Irish literature I-327

Beskow, Elsa (1874–1953), Swedish writer and illustrator of charming books for children; first picture book 'The Tale of the Wee Little Old Woman' (1897); also 'Aunt Green, Aunt Brown, and Aunt Lavender' 'Pelle's New Suit' R-105

Bessarabia, region that passed successively, during the 15th to 20th century, to Moldavia, the Ottoman Empire, Russia, Romania, and Soviet Union; acquired by Romania 1918; taken by Soviet Union in 1940, incorporated as Moldavian Soviet Socialist Republic; retaken by Germany and Romania 1941; seized finally by Soviet Union 1944; 17,146 sq mi (44,407 sq km) R-318. *see also in index* Moldavian Soviet Socialist Republic

Bessarion, Johannes, Cardinal (1395?–1472), Roman Catholic prelate and Greek scholar, born in Trabzon, Turkey; collected Greek manuscripts.

Bessel, Friedrich Wilhelm (1784–1846), German astronomer and mathematician, born in Minden; appointed director of observatory at Konigsberg 1810 S-413

Bessemer, Henry (1813–98), British inventor B-178
iron and steel I-351
metal and metallurgy M-309
Sheffield S-148

Bessemer, Ala., city 10 mi (16 km) s.w. of Birmingham, in great Alabama coal and iron-ore district; pop. 31,729; iron and steel industries; incorporated as town 1888, as city 1889
Alabama, *map* A-236

Bessemer converter B-178, I-340

Bessemer process, metalworking
iron production efficiency I-351
mining engineering E-226

'Bessie Bell and Mary Gray', nursery rhyme N-442

Bessy bug, beetle of the family Passalidae B-142

Best, Charles Herbert (1899–1978), Canadian physiologist, born in West Pembroke, Me.; joined Banting in insulin research 1922; appointed professor at Toronto 1929 B-75
medicine M-285

'Best Friend of Charleston', one of first locomotives built in America R-73, S-308, *picture*, S-311

Beta Centauri, a fixed star S-414

Beta hemolytic streptococcus, bacterium D-174

Betancourt, Rómulo (1908–81), Venezuelan political leader B-178, V-277

Betancur Cuartas, Belisario (born 1923), president of Colombia, born in Antioquia; elected president in 1982 C-554

Beta particles (or rays) R-63, *chart* R-66, *picture* R-62
emission process R-68
Fermi's theory F-56
matter M-229
nuclear radiation N-426

Beta Theta Pi, fraternity F-389

Betatron, electron (beta-ray) accelerator P-308

Betel, a palm, *picture* P-9
nut B-144, N-449

Betelgeuse, a fixed star S-414, A-718, *charts* S-415, 421, 423, *diagram* S-414
Michelson M-353

Bethany, (modern 'Eizariya), Israeli-occupied territory, village e. of Jerusalem; often mentioned in Gospels; home of Mary, Martha, Lazarus; pop. 3,560, *map* B-150

Bethany, Okla., city, adjoins n.w. Oklahoma City; in alfalfa, cotton, and wheat producing region; aircraft; Bethany Nazarene College; incorporated 1910; pop. 22,130.

Bethe, Hans Albrecht (born 1906), U.S. physicist, born in Strasbourg, Alsace-Lorraine; to U.S. 1935, became citizen 1941; professor of physics Cornell University after 1937; professor emeritus from 1975; head of theoretical physics division Los Alamos Scientific Laboratory 1943–46; won 1961 Enrico Fermi award.

Bethel, Palestine. ('house of God'), in Biblical times, village 10 mi (16 km) n. of Jerusalem (Bible, Gen. xii, 8: xxviii); here ark of covenant once rested and Jacob dreamed of ladder to heaven; excavated by archaeologists four times 1934–60; became site of Jordanian village of Beitin.

Bethel Park (formerly Bethel), Pa., borough 8 mi (13 km) s.w. of Pittsburgh; residential community with small industrial park; center of action in Whiskey Rebellion; incorporated 1950; named Bethel until 1961; pop. 34,755, *map* P-104

Bethesda, Md., community n.w. of Washington, D.C.; National Naval Medical Center; National Cancer Institute; pop. 62,736, *map* M-182

Bethlehem, Israeli-occupied territory, birthplace of Jesus; pop. 27,000 B-179
Christmas C-403
Jesus Christ J-103

Bethlehem, Pa., city about 50 mi (80 km) n. of Philadelphia, on Lehigh River; iron and steel mills; textiles, food products, electronic equipment, chemicals; Lehigh University; Moravian College; founded by Moravians; annual Bach Festival; Christmas City Program; pop. 70,419, *maps* P-174, 185

Bethmann-Hollweg, Theobald von (1856–1921), German chancellor from 1909 to 1917
World War I W-307

Bethogabris, Palestine. *see in index* Eleutheropolis

Beth-shan (or Beth-shean), Israel. *see in index* Beisan

Beth Sholom Synagogue, synagogue in Elkins Park, Pa. W-367

Bethune, David. *see in index* Beaton, David

Bethune, Mary McLeod (1875–1955), U.S. educator B-179
black Americans B-294
women's rights W-276

Bethune-Cookman College, Daytona Beach, Fla.; affiliated with United Methodist church; formed 1923 by a merger, present name after 1931, became senior college 1941; liberal arts, education B-179

Beti Mongo (pseudonym of Alexandre Biyidi) (born 1932), Cameroon writer A-122

Betjeman, John (1906–84), British poet and authority on architecture; born in London, England; his poetry has a light, nostalgic flavor
poet laureate P-402

'Betrothed, The', work by Manzoni
Italian literature I-376

Bet She'an, Israel. *see in index* Beisan

Betsiamites River. *see in index* Bersimis River

Betsileo, people of Madagascar M-23

Betsimisaraka, people of Madagascar M-23

Betsy McCall, U.S. magazine paper doll D-222

Betta. *see in index* Fighting fish

Bettelheim, Bruno (born 1903), U.S. psychologist B-179

Bettendorf, Iowa, city 5 mi (8 km) e. of Davenport, on Mississippi River; in farm area; foundry and aluminum products, oxygen gas, farm equipment; pop. 27,381
Iowa, *map* I-302

'Better Living', magazine M-34

Bettina. *see in index* Ehrlich, Bettina

Betting (or wagering), risking something, such as money, on an uncertain event
horse racing H-275

Between-lens shutter (or leaf shutter), camera P-285

'Between Rounds', painting by Eakins P-54, *picture* P-55

Bevel gear, mechanics M-268, *picture* M-269

Beverages. *see also in index* Alcoholic beverages; Coffee; Milk; Tea
food and drug laws F-274
plants provide P-376
soft drinks P-376

Beveridge, William Henry Beveridge, first **Baron** (1879–1963), British economist and sociologist, born in India; noted for plan for post-war social security, brought out in Dec. 1942, which would provide compulsory state insurance
social security program S-237
Wilson W-21

Beverly, Mass., city and summer resort on Atlantic Ocean, about 17 mi (27 km) n. of Boston; shoe machinery, machine tools, electronic and metal products, chemicals; first ship of U.S. Navy commissioned here 1775; pop. 37,665.

Beverly Hills, Calif., beautiful residential city, surrounded by city of Los Angeles; home of many motion-picture stars; pop. 32,367.

Beverwyck, N.Y. *see in index* Albany

Bevis, John (1695–1771), English scientist
electricity E-161

Bewick, Thomas (1753–1828), English wood engraver; illustrated many books on animals ('Quadrupeds'; 'British Birds'; 'Aesop's Fables')
'The Common Snipe', *picture* G-231

Bewick's wren, bird of the Troglodytidae family W-364

Bexley, borough, London, England, *maps* L-287, U-18a

Bexley, Ohio, residential city within e. Columbus; seat of Capital University (founded 1850); incorporated 1908; pop. 13,405.

Beyle, Marie Henri. *see in index* Stendhal

Beyrouth, Lebanon. *see in index* Beirut

Bezant, gold currency
international trade I-269

Béziers, France, cathedral town and trade center near s. coast, about 38 mi (61 km) s.w. of Montpellier; massacre of Albigenses in 1209; pop. 74,517, *map* F-369

Bezirke (or districts), political unit of East Germany G-120

'Bhagavadgita', Sanskrit narrative I-105
Hinduism H-157
India I-72

'Bhagavata-Purana', in Hinduism I-106

Bhagirathi, headwater of the Ganges River G-15

Bhakra Dam, dam on Sutlej River in India
irrigation I-356

Bhakti, Hindu devotional movement H-157
Indian literature I-106
yoga H-42

Bhaktivedanta (or Prabhupada) (1896–1977), Hindu mystic H-42

Bharat. *see in index* India

Bharatendu (or Harischandra) (850–85), Hindi poet
Indian literature I-108

Bhaskara II (1114–85), Indian mathematician M-214, *table* M-218

Bhopal, India, capital of Madhya Pradesh state; formerly a Moslem state; ruled 1844–1926 by women (begums, or princesses); Sultan Jahan Begum (1858–1930) did much to advance position of women, education, and medical aid; in 1926 abdicated in favor of son; state acceded to India 1947; disaster in 1985 caused by leak of deadly gas from Union Carbide Corp. plant; pop. 309,285 I-80, *map* I-83
Asia, *map* A-697

Bhubaneswar, India, capital of Orissa state, in e. India, 30 mi (50 km) n. of Puri; site of ancient temples; Ukal University, Rural University; pop. 38,211, *map* I-83

Bhumibol the Great (also called Bhumibol Adulyadej) (born 1927), king of Thailand T-149

Bhutan, country in e. Himalayas, between Tibet and India; area about 18,000 sq mi (46,500 sq km); cap. Thimphu; pop. 1,174,000 B-180
Asia, *map* A-697
flag, *picture* F-162
Himalayas H-152
India I-61
world, *map* W-297

Bhutto, Zulfikar Ali (1928–79), Pakistani lawyer and political leader, born in Larkana; foreign minister 1963–66; formed Pakistan People's Party 1966; president 1971–73; prime minister 1973–77; overthrown 1977; sentenced to death 1978; hanged 1979 P-79

BIA. *see in index* Indian Affairs, Bureau of

Biafra, Republic of, former African state; secession from Nigeria in 1967 brought on civil war; surrendered to Nigerian forces 1970.

BIRTHDAY CALENDAR

January

1 (1484) Ulrich Zwingli
1 (1735) Paul Revere
1 (1745) Anthony Wayne
1 (1752) Betsy Ross
1 (1834) Ludovic Halévy
1 (1895) J. Edgar Hoover
2 (1873) Saint Theresa of Lisieux
2 (1894) Artur Rodzinski
3 (106 B.C.) Cicero
3 (1793) Lucretia Mott
4 (1785) Jakob Grimm
5 (1779) Stephen Decatur
5 (1779) Zebulon Montgomery Pike
5 (1876) Konrad Adenauer
6 (1412) Joan of Arc
6 (1811) Charles Sumner
6 (1822) Heinrich Schliemann
6 (1878) Carl Sandburg
7 (1800) Millard Fillmore
8 (1792) Lowell Mason
9 (1859) Carrie Chapman Catt
9 (1904) George Balanchine
9 (1913) Richard M. Nixon
10 (1737?) Ethan Allen
11 (1807) Ezra Cornell
11 (1815) Sir John A. Macdonald
11 (1842) William James
11 (1856) Christian Sinding
12 (1588) John Winthrop
12 (1628) Charles Perrault
12? (1729) Edmund Burke
12? (1737) John Hancock
12 (1746) Johann Heinrich Pestalozzi
12 (1852) Joseph J. C. Joffre
12 (1856) John Singer Sargent
12 (1876) Jack London
12 (1890) Mordecai W. Johnson
14 (1741) Benedict Arnold
14 (1875) Albert Schweitzer
14 (1882) Hendrik Willem Van Loon
15 (1622*) Molière
15 (1832) Horatio Alger
15 (1908) Edward Teller
15 (1929) Martin Luther King, Jr.
17 (1504) Saint Pius V (pope)
17 (1706) Benjamin Franklin
17 (1860) Anton Chekhov
17 (1863) David Lloyd George
17 (1899) Robert Maynard Hutchins
18 (1782) Daniel Webster
18 (1882) A. A. Milne
19 (1736) James Watt
19 (1807) Robert E. Lee
19 (1809) Edgar Allan Poe
19 (1813) Sir Henry Bessemer
19 (1839) Paul Cézanne
19 (1887) Alexander Woollcott
20 (1876) Josef Hofmann
21 (1743) John Fitch
21 (1813) John C. Frémont
21 (1824) Thomas Jonathan (Stonewall) Jackson
22 (1561) Francis Bacon
22 (1729) Gotthold Ephraim Lessing
22 (1775) André Marie Ampère
22 (1788) George Gordon, Lord Byron
22 (1849) Johan August Strindberg
23 (1783) Stendhal
24 (1712) Frederick II, the Great, of Prussia
24 (1862) Edith Wharton
24 (1865) Paul Wayland Bartlett
25 (1627) Robert Boyle
25 (1759) Robert Burns
25 (1874) W. Somerset Maugham
26 (1763) Jean B. J. Bernadotte
26 (1831) Mary Mapes Dodge
26 (1880) Douglas MacArthur
26 (1884) Roy Chapman Andrews
27 (1756) Wolfgang Amadeus Mozart
27 (1832) Lewis Carroll
27 (1850) Samuel Gompers
27 (1859) William II of Germany
27 (1885) Jerome Kern
28 (1457) Henry VII of England
28 (1822) Alexander Mackenzie
28 (1833) Charles George (Chinese) Gordon
28 (1886) Artur Rubinstein
29 (1688) Emanuel Swedenborg
29 (1737) Thomas Paine
29 (1843) William McKinley
29 (1866) Romain Rolland
30 (1862) Walter Damrosch
30 (1882) Franklin D. Roosevelt
31 (1734) Robert Morris
31 (1752) Gouverneur Morris
31 (1797) Franz Schubert
31 (1848) Nathan Straus
31 (1881) Irving Langmuir
31 (1885) Anna Pavlova

February

1 (1859) Victor Herbert
1 (1882) Louis Stephen St. Laurent
1 (1902) Langston Hughes
2 (1875) Fritz Kreisler
2 (1901) Jascha Heifetz
2 (1754) Talleyrand
3 (1809) Felix Mendelssohn
3 (1811) Horace Greeley
3 (1842) Sidney Lanier
3 (1874) Gertrude Stein
3 (1894) Norman Rockwell
4 (1902) Charles A. Lindbergh
5 (1626) Madame de Sévigné
5 (1788) Sir Robert Peel
5 (1837) Dwight L. Moody
6 (1665) Anne, queen of England
6 (1756) Aaron Burr
6 (1833) James E. B. (Jeb) Stuart
6 (1838) Sir Henry Irving
6 (1895) Babe Ruth
7 (1478) Sir Thomas More
7 (1812) Charles Dickens
7 (1885) Sinclair Lewis
8 (1819) John Ruskin
8 (1820) William T. Sherman
8 (1828) Jules Verne
9 (1773) William Henry Harrison
9 (1853) Sir Leander Starr Jameson
10 (1775) Charles Lamb
10 (1868) William Allen White
10 (1893) William T. Tilden
10 (1927) Leontyne Price
11 (1847) Thomas A. Edison
11? (1873) Feodor Chaliapin
12 (1663) Cotton Mather
12 (1746) Thaddeus Kosciusko
12 (1809) Charles Darwin
12 (1809) Abraham Lincoln
12 (1828) George Meredith
12 (1880) John L. Lewis
12 (1893) Omar Bradley
13 (1892) Grant Wood
14 (1847) Anna Howard Shaw
15? (1564) Galileo
15 (1710) Louis XV of France
15 (1809) Cyrus Hall McCormick
15 (1820) Susan B. Anthony
15 (1845) Elihu Root
15 (1874) Sir Ernest Shackleton
15 (1882) John Barrymore
16 (1838) Henry Adams
16 (1898) Katharine Cornell
17 (1766) Thomas Robert Malthus
17 (1879) Dorothy Canfield Fisher
18 (1516) Mary I of England
18 (1745) Count Alessandro Volta
18 (1795) George Peabody
18 (1860) Anders Leonhard Zorn
18? (1896) Dmitri Mitropoulos
19 (1473) Nicolaus Copernicus
19 (1717) David Garrick
19 (1843) Adelina Patti
19 (1859) Svante August Arrhenius
19 (1865) Sven A. Hedin
20 (1874) Mary Garden
20 (1887) Vincent Massey
21 (1801) John Henry, Cardinal Newman
21 (1855) Alice Freeman Palmer
21 (1907) Wystan Hugh Auden
22 (1732) George Washington
22 (1788) Arthur Schopenhauer
22 (1810) Frédéric Chopin
22 (1819) James Russell Lowell
22 (1857) Robert, Lord Baden-Powell
22 (1857) Heinrich Rudolph Hertz
22 (1892) Edna St. Vincent Millay
23 (1633) Samuel Pepys
23 (1685) George Frederick Handel
23 (1817) George F. Watts
23 (1868) William E. B. Du Bois
24 (1500) Charles V, Holy Roman emperor
24 (1786) Wilhelm Karl Grimm
24 (1836) Winslow Homer
24 (1885) Chester W. Nimitz
25 (1778) José de San Martín
25 (1841) Pierre Auguste Renoir
25 (1866) Benedetto Croce
25 (1873) Enrico Caruso
25 (1890) Myra Hess
26 (1802) Victor Hugo
26 (1846) Buffalo Bill (William F. Cody)
27 (1807) Henry Wadsworth Longfellow
27 (1823) Ernest Renan
27 (1847) Ellen Terry
27 (1850) Henry E. Huntington
27 (1899) Charles Herbert Best
27 (1902) John Steinbeck
28 (1533) Montaigne
28 (1865) Sir Wilfred Grenfell
28 (1890) Vaslav Nijinsky
28 (1901) Linus Pauling
29 (1792) Gioacchino Antonio Rossini

March

1 (1837) William Dean Howells
1 (1848) Augustus Saint-Gaudens
1 (1924) Donald K. Slayton
2 (1545) Sir Thomas Bodley
2 (1769) De Witt Clinton
2 (1793) Sam Houston
2 (1824) Friedrich Smetana
2 (1829) Carl Schurz
2 (1876) Pius XII (pope)
2 (1890) Paul De Kruif
3 (1831) George Mortimer Pullman
3 (1847) Alexander Graham Bell
3 (1895) Matthew B. Ridgway
4 (1748) Casimir Pulaski
4 (1756) Sir Henry Raeburn
4 (1881) Thomas S. Stribling
4 (1888) Knute Rockne
5 (1512) Gerard Mercator
5 (1853) Howard Pyle
6 (1475) Michelangelo
6 (1806) Elizabeth Barrett Browning
6 (1831) Philip Henry Sheridan
6 (1834) George Du Maurier
6 (1872) Johan Bojer
6 (1885) Ring W. Lardner
6 (1927) Leroy G. Cooper, Jr.
7 (1841) William Rockhill Nelson
7 (1849) Luther Burbank
7 (1850) Thomas G. Masaryk

*Date of baptism.

BIRTHDAY CALENDAR—*Continued*

7 (1875) Maurice Ravel
8 (1841) Oliver Wendell Holmes (jurist)
8 (1858) Ruggiero Leoncavallo
9 (1824) Leland Stanford
9 (1902) Edward Durrell Stone
10 (1452) Ferdinand II of Aragon
10 (1867) Lillian D. Wald
11 (1544) Torquato Tasso
11 (1890) Vannevar Bush
11 (1899) Frederick IX of Denmark
12 (1685) George Berkeley
12 (1795) William Lyon Mackenzie
12 (1858) Adolph S. Ochs
12 (1863) Gabriele d'Annunzio
12 (1923) Walter M. Schirra
13 (1733) Joseph Priestley
13 (1872) Oswald Garrison Villard
14 (1782) Thomas Hart Benton (senator)
14 (1820) Victor Emmanuel II of Italy
14 (1837) Charles Ammi Cutter
14 (1854) Paul Ehrlich
14 (1868) Maksim Gorki
14 (1879) Albert Einstein
15 (1767) Andrew Jackson
15 (1858) Liberty Hyde Bailey
16 (1751) James Madison
16 (1787) Georg Simon Ohm
17 (1846) Kate Greenaway
17 (1902) Bobby Jones
18 (1782) John C. Calhoun
18 (1837) Grover Cleveland
18 (1844) Nikolai A. Rimski-Korsakov
18 (1858) Rudolf Diesel
19 (1813) David Livingstone
19 (1847) Albert P. Ryder
19 (1860) William Jennings Bryan
19 (1872) Sergei P. Diaghilev
19 (1891) Earl Warren
20 (1741) Jean Antoine Houdon
20 (1828) Henrik Ibsen
20 (1834) Charles William Eliot
20 (1890) Lauritz Melchior
21 (1685) Johann Sebastian Bach
21 (1806) Benito Juárez
22 (1599) Anthony Van Dyck
22 (1797) William I of Germany
22 (1846) Randolph Caldecott
22 (1868) Robert A. Millikan
22 (1884) Arthur H. Vandenberg
23 (1699) John Bartram
23 (1912) Wernher Von Braun
24 (1834) William Morris
24 (1855) Andrew W. Mellon
25 (1347) Saint Catherine of Siena
25 (1867) Gutzon Borglum
25 (1867) Arturo Toscanini
26 (1859) A. E. Housman
26 (1874) Robert Frost
27 (1813) Nathaniel Currier
27 (1845) Wilhelm Konrad Roentgen
27 (1886) Ludwig Mies van der Rohe
28 (1515) Saint Theresa of Avila
28 (1660) George I of England
28 (1749) Marquis de Laplace
28 (1888) James Francis Thorpe
28 (1903) Rudolf Serkin
29 (1790) John Tyler
30 (1746) Goya
30 (1853) Vincent van Gogh
30 (1883) Jo Davidson
31 (1596) René Descartes
31 (1732) Franz Joseph Haydn
31 (1809) Nikolai Gogol
31 (1811) Robert Wilhelm Bunsen

April

1 (1578) William Harvey
1 (1815) Otto von Bismarck
1 (1868) Edmond Rostand
2 (742?) Charlemagne
2 (1805) Hans Christian Andersen
2 (1834) Frédéric A. Bartholdi
2 (1840) Emile Zola
2 (1862) Nicholas Murray Butler
2 (1873) Sergei Rachmaninoff
2 (1914) Sir Alec Guinness
3 (1783) Washington Irving
3 (1822) Edward Everett Hale
3 (1837) John Burroughs
3 (1898) Henry R. Luce
3 (1926) Virgil Grissom
4 (1904) John Gielgud
5 (1648) Elihu Yale
5 (1827) Joseph, Lord Lister
5 (1837) Algernon C. Swinburne
5 (1856) Booker T. Washington
6? (1483) Raphael
6 (1874) Harry Houdini
7 (1506) Saint Francis Xavier
7 (1770) William Wordsworth
7 (1859) Walter Camp
7 (1873) John J. McGraw
8 (1875) Albert I of the Belgians
8 (1893) Mary Pickford
9 (1865) Charles Proteus Steinmetz
9 (1889) Efrem Zimbalist
10 (1583) Hugo Grotius
10 (1778) William Hazlitt
10 (1794) Matthew Calbraith Perry
10 (1829) William Booth
10 (1847) Joseph Pulitzer
11 (1862) Charles Evans Hughes
11 (1899) Percy Lavon Julian
12 (1777) Henry Clay
13 (1519) Catherine de' Medici
13 (1743) Thomas Jefferson
13 (1852) Frank Woolworth
14 (1629) Christian Huygens
15 (1843) Henry James
15 (1889) Thomas Hart Benton (artist)
15 (1889) Asa Philip Randolph
16 (1844) Anatole France
16 (1862) Amos Alonzo Stagg
16 (1867) Wilbur Wright
16 (1871) John M. Synge
17 (1837) J. Pierpont Morgan
17 (1870) Ray Stannard Baker
17 (1882) Artur Schnabel
17 (1894) Nikita Khrushchev
17 (1897) Thornton Wilder
17 (1903) Gregor Piatigorsky
18 (1887) Leopold Stokowski
19 (1912) Glenn T. Seaborg
20 (121) Marcus Aurelius Antoninus, emperor of Rome
20 (1586) Saint Rose of Lima
20 (1808) Napoleon III of France
20 (1850) Daniel Chester French
20 (1889) Adolf Hitler
21 (1782) Friedrich Wilhelm Froebel
21 (1816) Charlotte Brontë
21 (1828) Hippolyte Adolphe Taine
21 (1926) Elizabeth II of Great Britain
22 (1451) Isabella of Castile
22 (1707) Henry Fielding
22 (1724) Immanuel Kant
22 (1766) Madame de Staël
22 (1874) Ellen Glasgow
22 (1904) J. Robert Oppenheimer
22 (1916) Yehudi Menuhin
23? (1564) William Shakespeare
23 (1775) Joseph M. W. Turner
23 (1791) James Buchanan
23 (1813) Stephen A. Douglas
23 (1852) Edwin Markham
23 (1891) Sergei Prokofiev
24 (1576) Saint Vincent de Paul
24 (1743) Edmund Cartwright
24 (1815) Anthony Trollope
24 (1856) Henri Philippe Pétain
25 (1214) Louis IX of France
25 (1599) Oliver Cromwell
25 (1874) Guglielmo Marconi
26 (1711†) David Hume
26 (1785) John James Audubon
26 (1834) Artemus Ward
26 (1880) Michel Fokine
27 (1737) Edward Gibbon
27 (1791) Samuel F. B. Morse
27 (1822) Ulysses S. Grant
28 (1758) James Monroe
28 (1878) Lionel Barrymore
28 (1888) Henry D. G. Crerar
29? (1769) Duke of Wellington
29 (1818) Alexander II of Russia
29 (1860) Lorado Taft
29 (1863) William Randolph Hearst
29 (1879) Sir Thomas Beecham
29 (1893) Harold C. Urey
30 (1870) Franz Lehar
30 (1909) Juliana, queen of the Netherlands

May

1 (1218) Rudolph of Hapsburg, Holy Roman emperor
1 (1672) Joseph Addison
1 (1825) George Inness
1 (1925) M. Scott Carpenter
2 (1729) Catherine II, the Great, of Russia
3 (1849) Jacob A. Riis
4 (1796) Horace Mann
4 (1825) Thomas Henry Huxley
4 (1889) Francis J., Cardinal Spellman
5 (1818) Karl Marx
5 (1826) Eugénie, empress of the French
6 (1758) Maximilien Robespierre
6 (1856) Sigmund Freud
6 (1856) Robert E. Peary
6 (1861) Sir Rabindranath Tagore
7 (1812) Robert Browning
7 (1833) Johannes Brahms
7 (1840) Peter Ilich Tchaikovsky
7 (1892) Archibald MacLeish
8 (1884) Harry S. Truman
9 (1800) John Brown
9 (1860) Sir James M. Barrie
11 (1854) Ottmar Mergenthaler
11 (1888) Irving Berlin
11 (1904) Salvador Dali
12 (1496) Gustavus I Vasa of Sweden
12 (1804) Robert Baldwin
12 (1812) Edward Lear
12 (1820) Florence Nightingale
12 (1828) Dante Gabriel Rossetti
12 (1842) Jules Massenet
12 (1880) Lincoln Ellsworth
13 (1717) Maria Theresa of Austria
13 (1840) Alphonse Daudet
13 (1842) Sir Arthur Sullivan
13 (1907) Daphne Du Maurier
13 (1914) Joe Louis
14 (1686) Gabriel D. Fahrenheit
14 (1727*) Thomas Gainsborough
14 (1796) William Hickling Prescott
15 (1773) Prince Metternich
15 (1808) Michael Balfe
15 (1845) Elie Metchnikoff
15 (1859) Pierre Curie
16 (1801) William H. Seward
17 (1749) Edward Jenner
18 (1868) Nicholas II of Russia
18 (1872) Bertrand Russell
18 (1892) Ezio Pinza
18 (1919) Dame Margot Fonteyn

*Date of baptism.

†According to the Old Style Calendar.

19 (1762) Johann Gottlieb Fichte
19 (1795) Johns Hopkins
19 (1861?) Nellie Melba
19 (1864) Carl Ethan Akeley
20 (1768) Dolley Madison
20 (1799) Honoré de Balzac
20 (1806) John Stuart Mill
20 (1851) Emile Berliner
20 (1882) Sigrid Undset
21 (1471) Albrecht Dürer
21 (1527) Philip II of Spain
21 (1688) Alexander Pope
22 (1813) Richard Wagner
22 (1859) Sir Arthur Conan Doyle
22 (1907) Sir Laurence Olivier
23 (1707) Carl von Linné
24 (1819) Victoria, queen of Great Britain
24 (1863) George Grey Barnard
24 (1870) Jan Christiaan Smuts
24 (1878) Harry Emerson Fosdick
25 (1803) Edward George Bulwer-Lytton
25 (1803) Ralph Waldo Emerson
25 (1886) Philip Murray
25 (1897) Gene Tunney
25 (1899) Boris Artzybasheff
26 (1799†) Aleksander Pushkin
27 (1819) Julia Ward Howe
27 (1867) Arnold Bennett
27 (1871) George Rouault
27 (1878) Isadora Duncan
28 (1759) William Pitt, the Younger
28 (1779) Thomas Moore
28 (1807) Jean Louis Agassiz
28 (1884) Eduard Benes
29 (1736) Patrick Henry
29 (1874) G. K. Chesterton
29 (1917) John F. Kennedy
31 (1819) Walt Whitman

June

1 (1637) Father Marquette
1 (1801) Brigham Young
1 (1878) John Masefield
2 (1624) John Sobieski
2 (1773) John Randolph of Roanoke
2 (1835) Saint Pius X (pope)
2 (1840) Thomas Hardy
2 (1857) Sir Edward Elgar
3 (1808) Jefferson Davis
3 (1865) George V of England
4 (1738) George III of England
6 (1599*) Velasquez
6 (1606) Corneille
6 (1755) Nathan Hale
6 (1756) John Trumbull
6 (1804) Louis Antoine Godey
6 (1868) Robert Falcon Scott
6 (1875) Thomas Mann
6 (1892) Will James
6 (1901) Jan Struther
7 (1778) Beau Brummell
7 (1825) Richard Doddridge Blackmore
7 (1840) Carlota, empress of Mexico
8 (1810) Robert Schumann
8 (1814) Charles Reade
8 (1829) Sir John Everett Millais
8 (1869) Frank Lloyd Wright
9 (1672) Peter I, the Great, of Russia
9 (1781) George Stephenson
9 (1791) John Howard Payne
9 (1893) Cole Porter
11 (1776) John Constable
11 (1864) Richard Strauss
12 (1806) John Augustus Roebling
12 (1819) Charles Kingsley
12 (1864) Frank M. Chapman
12 (1897) Anthony Eden
13 (1786) Winfield Scott
13 (1795) Thomas Arnold
13 (1865) William Butler Yeats
13 (1894) Mark Van Doren
14 (1811) Harriet Beecher Stowe
14 (1884) John McCormack
15 (1843) Edvard Grieg
15 (1861) Ernestine Schumann-Heink
15 (1887) Malvina Hoffman
16? (1903) Helen Traubel
17 (1682) Charles XII of Sweden
17 (1818) Charles Gounod
17 (1914) John Hersey
18? (1239) Edward I of England
18 (1854) Edward Wyllis Scripps
18 (1868) Nicholas Horthy
18 (1896) Philip Barry
19 (1566) James I of England
19 (1623) Blaise Pascal
19 (1903) Lou Gehrig
21 (1882) Rockwell Kent
22? (1805) Giuseppe Mazzini
23 (1875) Carl Milles
23 (1876) Irvin S. Cobb
23 (1894) Edward, Duke of Windsor
24 (1650) Duke of Marlborough
24 (1813) Henry Ward Beecher
24 (1850) Earl Kitchener of Khartum
24 (1895) Jack Dempsey
26 (1824) William Thomson, Lord Kelvin
26 (1854) Sir Robert Laird Borden
26 (1892) Pearl Buck
27 (1846) Charles Stewart Parnell
27 (1850) Lafcadio Hearn
27 (1872) Paul Laurence Dunbar
27 (1880) Helen Keller
28 (1491) Henry VIII of England
28? (1577) Peter Paul Rubens
28 (1703) John Wesley
28 (1712) Jean Jacques Rousseau
28 (1858) Otis Skinner
28 (1867) Luigi Pirandello
28 (1873) Alexis Carrel
29 (1858) George W. Goethals
29 (1861) William James Mayo
29 (1865) William Edgar Borah
30 (1817) Sir Joseph Dalton Hooker

July

2 (1489) Thomas Cranmer
2 (1714) Christoph Willibald Gluck
2 (1821) Sir Charles Tupper
2 (1862) Sir William Henry Bragg
2 (1903) Sir Alexander F. Douglas-Home
4 (1804) Nathaniel Hawthorne
4 (1807) Giuseppe Garibaldi
4 (1826) Stephen Collins Foster
4 (1872) Calvin Coolidge
5 (1755) Sarah Siddons
5 (1801) David Glasgow Farragut
5 (1804) George Sand
5 (1810) P. T. Barnum
5 (1853) Cecil Rhodes
6 (1747) John Paul Jones
6 (1832) Maximilian, emperor of Mexico
6 (1865) Emile Jaques-Dalcroze
6 (1875) Roger Babson
8 (1621) Jean de La Fontaine
8 (1838) Count von Zeppelin
8? (1839) John D. Rockefeller
9 (1819) Elias Howe
9 (1856) Nikola Tesla
10 (1509) John Calvin
10 (1723) Sir William Blackstone
10 (1834) James A. McNeill Whistler
10 (1871) Marcel Proust
10? (1888) Toyohiko Kagawa
11 (1274) Robert Bruce, king of Scotland
11 (1767) John Quincy Adams
12 (102? B.C.) Julius Caesar
12 (1730) Josiah Wedgwood
12 (1817) Henry David Thoreau
12 (1849) Sir William Osler
12 (1854) George Eastman
12 (1884) Amedeo Modigliani
12 (1895) Kirsten Flagstad
12 (1895) Oscar Hammerstein II
14 (1602) Cardinal Mazarin
14 (1858) Emmeline Pankhurst
15 (1573) Inigo Jones
15 (1606) Rembrandt
15 (1808) Henry E., Cardinal Manning
16 (1723) Sir Joshua Reynolds
16 (1821) Mary Baker Eddy
16 (1872) Roald Amundsen
16 (1877) Bela Schick
17 (1674) Isaac Watts
17 (1763) John Jacob Astor
18 (1811) William Makepeace Thackeray
18 (1921) John H. Glenn, Jr.
19 (1834) Edgar H. G. Degas
19 (1865) Charles Horace Mayo
20 (1304) Petrarch
21 (1899) Ernest Hemingway
21 (1920) Isaac Stern
22 (1892) Haile Selassie I of Ethiopia
22 (1893) Karl Menninger
22 (1898) Stephen Vincent Benét
23 (1834) Cardinal Gibbons
24 (1783) Simón Bolívar
24 (1802) Alexandre Dumas, the Elder
24 (1898) Amelia Earhart
25 (1844) Thomas Eakins
25 (1848) Sir Arthur James Balfour
26 (1856) George Bernard Shaw
26 (1874) Serge Koussevitzky
27 (1824) Alexandre Dumas, the Younger
29 (1869) Booth Tarkington
29 (1877) Charles William Beebe
29 (1883) Benito Mussolini
29 (1887) Sigmund Romberg
30 (1863) Henry Ford
30 (1898) Henry Moore
31 (1803) John Ericsson

August

1 (1744) Jean Baptiste de Lamarck
1 (1815) Richard Henry Dana, Jr.
1 (1819) Herman Melville
2 (1754) Pierre Charles L'Enfant
2 (1820) John Tyndall
3 (1872) Haakon VII of Norway
3 (1887) Rupert Brooke
3 (1900) Ernie Pyle
4 (1792) Percy Bysshe Shelley
4 (1839) Walter Pater
4 (1859) Knut Hamsun
5 (1850) Guy de Maupassant
5 (1889) Conrad Aiken
6 (1809) Alfred, Lord Tennyson
6 (1820) Lord Strathcona
7 (1904) Ralph Bunche
8 (1819) Charles Anderson Dana
8 (1884) Sara Teasdale
8 (1901) Ernest O. Lawrence
9 (1593) Izaak Walton
9 (1631) John Dryden
9 (1776) Amadeo Avogadro
10 (1810) Count di Cavour
10 (1874) Herbert Hoover
11 (1833) Robert G. Ingersoll
12 (1774) Robert Southey
12 (1859) Katharine Lee Bates
12 (1862) Julius Rosenwald
12 (1880) Christy Mathewson
12 (1882) George W. Bellows
14 (1860) Ernest Thompson Seton
14 (1867) John Galsworthy
15 (1769) Napoleon Bonaparte

*Date of baptism.

†According to the Old Style Calendar.

BIRTHDAY CALENDAR—*Continued*

15 (1771) Sir Walter Scott
15 (1785) Thomas De Quincey
15 (1879) Ethel Barrymore
15 (1883) Ivan Mestrovic
15 (1887) Edna Ferber
15 (1888) T. E. Lawrence
17 (1786) David Crockett
18 (1774) Meriwether Lewis
18 (1830) Francis Joseph I of Austria
19 (1856) John Cotton Dana
19 (1870) Bernard Baruch
19 (1871) Orville Wright
19 (1878) Manuel Quezon
19 (1893) Alfred Lunt
19 (1902) Ogden Nash
20 (1778) Bernardo O'Higgins
20 (1818) Emily Brontë
20 (1833) Benjamin Harrison
20 (1873) Eliel Saarinen
20 (1910) Eero Saarinen
22 (1862) Claude Debussy
23 (1754) Louis XVI of France
24 (1591*) Robert Herrick
24 (1769) Georges Cuvier
25 (1530) Ivan IV, the Terrible, of Russia
25 (1836) Bret Harte
26 (1743) Antoine Lavoisier
26 (1873) Lee De Forest
27 (1770) Georg Hegel
27 (1871) Theodore Dreiser
27 (1908) Lyndon B. Johnson
28 (1749) Johann Wolfgang von Goethe
28 (1828†) Count Leo Tolstoi
28 (1833) Sir Edward Burne-Jones
29 (1632) John Locke
29 (1809) Oliver Wendell Holmes (author)
29 (1862) Maurice Maeterlinck
30 (1871) Ernest, Lord Rutherford
30 (1901) Roy Wilkins
31 (1811) Théophile Gautier
31 (1821) Hermann von Helmholtz
31 (1870) Maria Montessori
31 (1880) Wilhelmina, queen of the Netherlands
31 (1908) William Saroyan

September

1 (1795) James Gordon Bennett
1 (1877) Francis William Aston
2? (1850) Eugene Field
3 (1724) Guy Carleton
3 (1856) Louis H. Sullivan
4 (1802) Marcus Whitman
5 (1585) Cardinal Richelieu
5 (1791) Giacomo Meyerbeer
5 (1892) Joseph Szigeti
6 (1757) Marquis de Lafayette
6 (1766) John Dalton
6 (1860) Jane Addams
7 (1533) Elizabeth I of England
7 (1914) James A. Van Allen
7 (1930) Baudouin, king of Belgium
8 (1157) Richard I, the Lion-Hearted, of England
8 (1474) Ludovico Ariosto
8 (1841) Antonin Dvorak
8 (1889) Robert A. Taft
9 (1737) Luigi Galvani
10 (1885) Carl Van Doren
10 (1892) Arthur H. Compton
11 (1862) O. Henry
11 (1877) Sir James Hopwood Jeans
12 (1494) Francis I of France
12 (1880) H. L. Mencken
12 (1913) Jesse Owens
13 (1851) Walter Reed
13 (1860) John J. Pershing
13 (1874) Arnold Schönberg
13 (1876) Sherwood Anderson
14 (1769) Alexander von Humboldt
14 (1860) Hamlin Garland
14 (1867) Charles Dana Gibson
15 (1789) James Fenimore Cooper
15 (1857) William Howard Taft
15 (1876) Bruno Walter
15 (1889) Robert Benchley
16 (1638) Louis XIV of France
16 (1823) Francis Parkman
16 (1838) James J. Hill
16 (1880) Alfred Noyes
18 (1709) Samuel Johnson
18 (1819) Jean Foucault
20 (1878) Upton Sinclair
21 (1452) Savonarola
21 (1645) Louis Joliet
21 (1756) John Loudon MacAdam
21 (1866) H. G. Wells
21 (1867) Henry L. Stimson
22 (1694) Earl of Chesterfield
22 (1791) Michael Faraday
23 (63 B.C.) Augustus, emperor of Rome
24 (1717†) Horace Walpole
24 (1755) John Marshall
24 (1884) Ismet Inonu
25 (1844) Sarah Bernhardt
25 (1897) William Faulkner
25 (1906) Dmitri Shostakovich
26 (1870) Christian X of Denmark
26 (1888) T. S. Eliot
26 (1897) Paul VI (pope)
26 (1898) George Gershwin
27 (1722) Samuel Adams
27 (1840) Thomas Nast
27 (1862) Louis Botha
28 (1839) Frances E. Willard
28 (1841) Georges Clemenceau
28 (1863) Frederick MacMonnies
29 (1725) Robert, Lord Clive
29 (1758) Horatio, Lord Nelson
29 (1901) Enrico Fermi

October

1 (1781) James Lawrence
1 (1904) Vladimir Horowitz
2 (1452) Richard III of England
2 (1847) Paul von Hindenburg
2 (1851) Ferdinand Foch
2 (1869) Mohandas Gandhi
2 (1871) Cordell Hull
3 (1800) George Bancroft
3 (1854) William Crawford Gorgas
3 (1859) Eleanora Duse
3 (1900) Thomas Wolfe
4 (1814) Jean François Millet
4 (1822) Rutherford B. Hayes
4 (1858) Michael Pupin
5 (1703) Jonathan Edwards
5 (1713) Denis Diderot
5 (1829) Chester Alan Arthur
6 (1820) Jenny Lind
6 (1846) George Westinghouse
6 (1887) Le Corbusier
7 (1573) William Laud
7 (1786) Louis Papineau
7 (1849) James Whitcomb Riley
7 (1866) Martha McChesney Berry
7 (1885) Niels Bohr
8 (1838) John Hay
8 (1890) Eddie Rickenbacker
9 (1547*) Cervantes
9 (1835) Charles Camille Saint-Saëns
9 (1863) Edward William Bok
9 (1863) Gamaliel Bradford
10 (1684) Jean Watteau
10 (1731) Henry Cavendish
10 (1813) Giuseppe Verdi
10 (1825) Paul Kruger
10 (1861) Fridtjof Nansen
10 (1895) Lin Yutang
10 (1900) Helen Hayes
11 (1884) Eleanor Roosevelt
12 (1775) Lyman Beecher
13 (1821) Rudolf Virchow
14 (1644) William Penn
14 (1882) Eamon De Valera
14 (1888) Katherine Mansfield
14 (1890) Dwight D. Eisenhower
15 (70 B.C.) Vergil
15 (1844) Friedrich Wilhelm Nietzsche
15 (1858) John L. Sullivan
16 (1758) Noah Webster
16 (1888) Eugene O'Neill
17 (1760) Claude Henri, Comte de Saint-Simon
18 (1859) Henri Bergson
18 (1878) James Truslow Adams
19 (1784) Leigh Hunt
20 (1632) Sir Christopher Wren
20 (1859) John Dewey
21 (1772) Samuel Taylor Coleridge
21 (1833) Alfred Nobel
21 (1891) Ted Shawn
22 (1811) Franz Liszt
22 (1843) Stephen Moulton Babcock
23 (1844) Robert Bridges
23 (1844) Louis Riel
24 (1632) Anthony van Leeuwenhoek
25 (1800) Thomas Babington Macaulay
25 (1825) Johann Strauss, the Younger
25 (1838) Georges Bizet
25 (1881) Pablo Picasso
25 (1888) Richard Evelyn Byrd
26 (1800) Helmuth Karl, count von Moltke
27 (1782) Niccolo Paganini
27 (1858) Theodore Roosevelt
28 (1914) Jonas Salk
29 (1740) James Boswell
29? (1795) John Keats
30 (1735) John Adams
30 (1751) Richard Brinsley Sheridan
31 (1632*) Jan Vermeer
31 (1860) Juliette Gordon Low
31 (1887) Chiang Kai-shek

November

1 (1880) Shalom Asch
2? (1734) Daniel Boone
2 (1755) Marie Antoinette, of France
2 (1795) James K. Polk
2 (1865) Warren G. Harding
3? (1500) Benvenuto Cellini
3 (1794) William Cullen Bryant
3 (1879) Vilhjalmur Stefansson
4 (1879) Will Rogers
5 (1857) Ida M. Tarbell
6 (1854) John Philip Sousa
6 (1860) Ignace Jan Paderewski
7 (1867) Marie Curie
7 (1878) Lise Meitner
7 (1926) Joan Sutherland
9 (1818) Ivan Turgenev
9 (1841) Edward VII of England
10 (1483) Martin Luther
10 (1697) William Hogarth
10 (1728) Oliver Goldsmith
10 (1759) Friedrich Schiller
10 (1880) Sir Jacob Epstein
10 (1801) Samuel Gridley Howe
10 (1879) Vachel Lindsay
11 (1821) Fedor M. Dostoevski
11 (1872) Maude Adams
11 (1882) Gustavus VI Adolphus of Sweden

*Date of baptism.

†According to the Old Style Calendar.

13 (354) Saint Augustine of Hippo
13 (1831) James Clerk Maxwell
13 (1833) Edwin Booth
13 (1850) Robert Louis Stevenson
14 (1765) Robert Fulton
14 (1840) Claude Monet
14 (1863) Leo Hendrik Baekeland
14 (1889) Jawaharlal Nehru
14 (1891) Sir Frederick Banting
14 (1897) John Steuert Curry
14 (1948) Prince Charles of Great Britain
15 (1708) William Pitt, Earl of Chatham
15 (1738) Sir William Herschel
15 (1862) Gerhart Hauptmann
16 (1873) W. C. Handy
16 (1889) George S. Kaufman
17 (1878) Grace Abbott
17 (1887) Bernard Law Montgomery
18 (1786) Karl Maria von Weber
18 (1789) Louis Daguerre
18 (1836) Sir William S. Gilbert
18 (1899) Eugene Ormandy
18 (1923) Alan B. Shepard, Jr.
19 (1600) Charles I of England
19 (1752) George Rogers Clark
19 (1770) Bertel Thorvaldsen
19 (1805) Ferdinand de Lesseps
19 (1831) James A. Garfield
20 (1841) Sir Wilfrid Laurier
20 (1858) Selma Lagerlöf
20 (1871) William Heard Kilpatrick
21 (1694) Voltaire
22 (1643) Sieur de La Salle
22 (1819) George Eliot
22 (1869) André Gide
22 (1890) Charles de Gaulle
23 (1804) Franklin Pierce
23 (1862) Sir Gilbert Parker
24 (1632) Spinoza
24 (1713) Father Junípero Serra
24 (1713) Laurence Sterne
24 (1784) Zachary Taylor
25 (1562) Lope de Vega
25 (1835) Andrew Carnegie
25 (1881) John XXIII (pope)
27 (1874) Charles A. Beard
28 (1757) William Blake
28 (1829) Anton Rubinstein
28 (1835) Tzu Hsi
28 (1895) José Iturbi
29 (1607*) John Harvard
29 (1797) Gaetano Donizetti
29 (1832) Louisa May Alcott
30 (1554) Sir Philip Sidney
30 (1628*) John Bunyan
30 (1667) Jonathan Swift
30 (1819) Cyrus West Field
30 (1835) Mark Twain
30 (1874) Winston (L. S.) Churchill

December

2 (1825) Pedro II of Brazil
3 (1755) Gilbert Stuart
3 (1826) George Brinton McClellan
3 (1884) Rajendra Prasad
4 (1795) Thomas Carlyle
4 (1865) Edith Cavell
4 (1892) Francisco Franco
5 (1782) Martin Van Buren
5 (1830) Christina Rossetti
5 (1839) George Armstrong Custer
5 (1867) Josef Pilsudski
5 (1901) Walt Disney
6 (1732) Warren Hastings
6 (1857) Joseph Conrad
6 (1859) E. H. Sothern
6 (1863) Charles Martin Hall
6 (1886) Joyce Kilmer
6 (1887?) Lynn Fontanne
7 (1598) Giovanni Lorenzo Bernini
7 (1863) Pietro Mascagni
7 (1875) Willa Cather
7 (1879) Rudolf Friml
8 (65 B.C.) Horace
8 (1542) Mary Stuart, queen of Scots
8 (1765) Eli Whitney
8 (1832) Björnstjerne Björnson
8 (1865) Jean Julius Sibelius
9 (1594) Gustavus II Adolphus of Sweden
9 (1608) John Milton
9 (1848) Joel Chandler Harris
10 (1805) William Lloyd Garrison
10 (1822) César Franck
10 (1830) Emily Dickinson
10 (1837) Edward Eggleston
10 (1851) Melvil Dewey
11 (1803) Hector Berlioz
11 (1843) Robert Koch
12 (1745) John Jay
12 (1821) Gustave Flaubert
13 (1797) Heinrich Heine
13 (1835) Phillips Brooks
14 (1546) Tycho Brahe
14? (1553) Henry IV of France
14 (1895) George VI of England
15 (37) Nero
15 (1888) Maxwell Anderson
16 (1775) Jane Austen
16 (1863) George Santayana
16 (1899) Noel Coward
17 (1770*) Ludwig van Beethoven
17 (1778) Sir Humphry Davy
17 (1797) Joseph Henry
17 (1807) John Greenleaf Whittier
17 (1874) William Lyon Mackenzie King
17 (1908) W. F. Libby
18 (1856) Sir Joseph John Thomson
18 (1861) Edward A. MacDowell
18 (1886) Ty Cobb
19 (1814) Edwin M. Stanton
19 (1852) Albert Abraham Michelson
19 (1888) Fritz Reiner
20 (1868) Harvey S. Firestone
20 (1894) Sir Robert Gordon Menzies
21 (1639) Jean Baptiste Racine
21 (1804) Benjamin Disraeli
21 (1879) Joseph Stalin
22 (1696) James Oglethorpe
22 (1858) Giacomo Puccini
22 (1869) Edwin Arlington Robinson
22 (1885) Deems Taylor
23 (1732) Sir Richard Arkwright
23 (1777) Alexander I of Russia
23 (1804) Charles Augustin Sainte-Beuve
23 (1805) Joseph Smith
23? (1862) Connie Mack
24 (1491) Saint Ignatius of Loyola
24 (1809) Christopher (Kit) Carson
24 (1822) Matthew Arnold
25? (3 B.C. ?) Jesus Christ
25 (1642†) Sir Isaac Newton
25 (1821) Clara Barton
25 (1885) Paul Manship
26 (1716) Thomas Gray
26 (1837) George Dewey
27 (1571) Johannes Kepler
27 (1822) Louis Pasteur
28 (1856) Woodrow Wilson
29 (1800) Charles Goodyear
29 (1808) Andrew Johnson
29 (1809) William Gladstone
29 (1876) Pablo Casals
30 (1865) Rudyard Kipling
30 (1867) Simon Guggenheim
30 (1869) Stephen Butler Leacock
31 (1617) Murillo
31 (1738) Charles, Lord Cornwallis
31 (1869) Henri Matisse
31 (1880) George C. Marshall
31 (1904) Nathan Milstein

*Date of baptism.

†According to the Old Style Calendar.

Blackwood, Frederick Temple. *see in index* Dufferin and Ava, marquis of

Bladder, part of urinary system A-391
  bioengineering B-212

Blade, of plant
  leaf structure L-100, *picture* L-102
  palm P-81
  sundew S-517

Blade, device
  bulldozer B-500
  fan F-23
  helicopter H-118
  jet propulsion J-106, J-109
  lumbering P-397
  pump P-533, *diagram* P-532
  razor, *picture* S-222
  skate S-208
  sword S-546, S-192a

Bladensburg, Md., town 6 mi (10 km) e. of Washington, D.C.; U.S. troops defeated by British Aug. 1814; once noted dueling ground; pop. 7,488.

Blade tools, ancient tools M-85

Blagoevgrad, s.w. Bulgaria; chief town of Blagoevgrad province; wood, canning, textile, and craft industries; pop. 61,715 M-7

Blaik, Earl (born 1897), U.S. football coach F-297

Blaine, James Gillespie (1830–93), U.S. statesman
  Cleveland C-491
  Garfield G-30
  Harrison H-46
  Hayes H-78

Blaine, Minn., city 16 mi (26 km) n. of St. Paul; metal products, concrete; sod farms, landscape services; incorporated 1964; pop. 28,558.

Blaine resolution P-506

Blair, Eric Arthur. *see in index* Orwell, George

Blair, Francis Preston (1791–1876), U.S. editor and writer, born in Abington, Va.; friend of Jackson and Van Buren, active supporter of Abraham Lincoln; aided Union cause during Civil War.

Blair, Francis Preston, Jr. (1821–75), U.S. politician and soldier, born in Lexington, Ky.; prominent in Missouri politics, helped save state for Union; major general Union army; U.S. senator 1871–73
  Statuary Hall, *table* S-437b

Blair, Robert (1699–1746), English poet
  literary contribution E-271

Blair House (sometimes called Blair-Lee House), historic mansion in Washington, D.C.; built about 1824; purchased 1942 by federal government as guest house for distinguished visitors; joined to Lee Mansion.

Blake, Lyman Reed (1835–83), U.S. inventor, born in South Abington, Mass.; designer of the modern machine-sewn shoe and machinery to make it S-179

Blake, Nicholas. *see in index* Day-Lewis, C.

Blake, Robert (1599–1657), English admiral, naval commander of Oliver Cromwell's Commonwealth
  The Netherlands N-130

Blake, William (1757–1827), English poet, artist, and mystic B-310
  literary contribution E-270
  quoted P-407

Blakeslee, Albert Francis (1874–1954), U.S. botanist, born in Geneseo, N.Y.; director Carnegie Station for Experimental Evolution 1936–41; professor Smith College 1942–3; director of its Genetics Experiment Station 1943–54
  colchicine experiments P-368

Blakey, Art (born 1919), U.S. jazz musician J-87

Blakistone Island (originally St. Clements Island), island, Maryland, in Potomac River; landing place (March 25, 1634) of first settlers sent out by Lord Baltimore.

Blanc, Jean Joseph Charles Louis (1811–82), French socialist, born in Madrid, Spain; flourished 1848–49; pioneer of 'political,' or 'government-ownership,' socialism, chief outcome of which was gradual adoption in many lands of government ownership of railroads, telegraphs, telephones, water works S-234

Blanc, Mont (translation white mountain), highest peak (15,781 ft; 4,810 m) of Alps; 7 mi (11 km) inside French boundary; first climbed 1786; French observatory built on summit 1893 A-318, E-329, *maps* E-360, I-404
  France F-343, *map* F-372, *picture* F-347
  height, comparative. *see in index* Mountain, *table*
  mountain climbing M-637

Blanca Peak, peak in s.-central Colorado; highest peak (14,317 ft; 4,364 m) in Sangre de Cristo range.

Blanchard, Felix (nickname Doc) (born 1924), U.S. football fullback F-298

Blanche of Castile (1188–1252), Spanish princess, queen of Louis VIII of France; regent during minority of Louis IX L-304

Blanching F-281
  cooking C-700
  nuts N-448

Blanco-Fombona, Rufino (1874–1944), Venezuelan writer
  Latin American literature L-75

Blancos, political party of Uruguay U-214

Bland, Edith Nesbit (1858–1924), British author of children's books, born in London; stories of Bastable children based on own childhood ('Treasure Seekers'; 'Five Children and It'; 'Story of the Amulet') R-111b

Bland, James A. (1854–1911), U.S. minstrel and songwriter, born in Flushing, N.Y.; wrote words and music for over 500 songs ('Carry Me Back to Old Virginny'; 'In the Evening by the Moonlight'; 'Oh, Dem Golden Slippers') V-338
  popular music M-684

Bland-Allison Act (1878), United States H-80

Blankers-Koen, Francina Elsje (nickname Fanny) (born 1918?), Dutch track athlete A-471
  Olympics O-542

Blanket
  insulating materials I-232

Blank verse P-405
  Shakespeare S-138

Blanton, Jimmy (1921–42), U.S. musician J-87

Blantyre, Malawi, business and farm center and missionary headquarters; merged with Limbe to form present city in 1959; pop. 160,063 M-69, *map* A-115

Blarney, Ireland, village 5 mi (8 km) n.w. of Cork; castle built by Cormac McCarthy in 1446 contains Blarney Stone (block with Latin inscription including date and builder's name) said to transmit gift of eloquence to those who kiss it; pop. 932.

Blaschka, Leopold (died 1895), glass worker of Dresden, Germany, with his son Rudolph (1857–1939), fashioned many models of botanical specimens for the Botanical Museum at Harvard University
  glass rhododendron, *picture* R-197

Blasco Ibáñez, Vicente (1867–1928), Spanish novelist, born in Valencia; noted for realistic portrayal of provincial life; work also dealt with social revolution S-365b, *picture* S-365a

Blasis, Carlo (1797–1878), Italian choreographer and dancer, born in Naples; greatly influenced ballet until end of 19th century B-34, D-24

Blast chilling, in meat industry F-283

Blast furnace, in iron smelting, *pictures* F-451, U-69
  automated systems A-837
  iron I-336, *picture* I-338
  Ohio, *picture* O-501

Blasting (also called shooting)
  mining M-426
    coal C-519

Blasting cap (or detonator), device that initiates the detonation of a charge of high explosive by subjecting it to a shock wave
  explosive E-381
  mines and mining M-428
  Nobel N-329

Blasting gelatin, an explosive derived from cellulose nitrate
  Nobel N-329

Blasting powder, an explosive made of potassium nitrate and sodium nitrate E-379

Blast lamp, in glass manufacture G-159

Blastocoel, fluid-filled cavity, *diagram* E-200

Blastocyst, sexuality S-124

Blastoid, an echinoderm
  animal life record, *table* E-24

Blastula, spherical structure produced by cleavage of a fertilized ovum E-200

Blat, in Soviet industry R-330

Blaue Reiter, Der (or The Blue Rider), group of artists
  Kandinsky K-171
  Klee K-254

Blavatsky, Helena Petrovna (1831–91), Russian spiritualist, author, and co-founder of the Theosophical Society T-163

'Blazing Saddles', work by Bergman W-151

Blazing star. *see in index* Liatris

Blazon, heraldry H-136

Bleaching B-310
  chlorine C-393
  dry cleaning D-280
  furs F-466
  hair H-8
  lemon juice C-447

Bleak, small, silvery, European fish of the carp family, *picture* F-129
  artificial pearls P-149

'Bleak House', novel by Charles Dickens; plot built upon lengthy lawsuit of Jarndyce vs. Jarndyce, in court almost 50 years.

Bleb, abnormal blister D-177

Bleda (died 445), brother of Attila and co-ruler of the Huns A-758
  Huns H-330

Bledsoe, Tempestt (born 1973), U.S. actress
  'Cosby Show', *picture* T-71

Bleeding
  blood clotting B-315, S-113
    vitamin K V-357
  early medicine M-283
  first aid techniques F-118, *diagrams* F-117

Bleeding heart, a perennial flower
  flowering time G-25

'Bleeding Heart, The', work by French A-363

Bleeding tooth shell, mollusk shell *Nerita pelaronta*, *picture* S-152

Blend, in cooking C-700

Blended whiskey
  liquor production L-235

Blending, in phonics P-268c

Blenheim, West Germany, Bavarian village on Danube, 23 mi (37 km) n.w. of Augsburg; pop. 879

Blenheim, battle of (1704), in the War of Spanish Succession M-147
  warfare, *list* W-14

Blennerhassett Island, island, Ohio, in Ohio River, near Parkersburg, W. Va.; site of Aaron Burr's alleged treason plot B-513

Blenny, one of a genus *Blennius* of small spiny-rayed fishes whose skin is covered with slimy matter; frequents shallows along coasts, moving about among rocks and seaweeds.

Blériot, Louis (1872–1936), French pioneer in aviation, born in Cambrai; studied engineering and began experimenting with flying machines 1900; earliest successful flight in plane of his own design 1907 A-203, A-208, *picture* A-202
  famous flight A-154

'Blessing of the Bay', early ship S-174
  Massachusetts M-194

Blest Gana, Alberto (1831–1920), Chilean writer
  Latin American literature L-72

Bleve, type of fire
  fire fighting F-105

Blickling Homilies, *picture* B-361

Bligh, William (1754–1817), English admiral B-311
  Bounty S-177b, *picture* S-177c
  Christian's rebellion C-396
  Fiji F-83
  Macquarie M-22
  'Mutiny on the Bounty' R-112

Blimp, nonrigid dirigible A-156
  balloon B-38
  World War I, *picture* W-306

'Blind Colt, The', work by Rounds, *list* H-274

Blind eel. *see in index* Congo eel

Blinders (also called blinkers), eye pads to limit a horse's vision H-250

Blindfish, any of several species of small freshwater fish, family Amblyopsidae, in the dark waters of caves in central and s. U.S.; are sightless or nearly so; northern cave fish *Amblyopsis spelea* of Mammoth Cave, in Kentucky, is 5 in. (13 cm) long, whitish, and completely blind, feeling its way along with the help of touch-sensitive projections in rows on the head and body; many other sightless fishes also are called blindfish; they live in caves and ocean depths throughout the world.

Blind flying. *see in index* Instrument flying

Blind landing. *see in index* Ground controlled approach; Instrument Landing System

Blindman's Buff, game G-9

Blindness B-311
  Braille system B-396
  children V-273
  diabetes D-126
  eye E-390
  sensory aids D-212, D-166
  sun causes S-512
  talking books P-269

Blind stitch (or invisible stitch), in sewing S-122

Blinkers (also called blinders), eye pads to limit a horse's vision H-250

'Bliss and Other Stories', work by Mansfield M-110

Blister beetle, insect of the family Meloidae B-141, *picture* B-139

Blister copper C-712, *picture* C-710

Blister cress. *see in index* Erysimum

Blister pearl P-148

Blister rust, white pine R-363

'Blithedale Romance', work by Hawthorne H-74

Blitzkrieg, fierce, sudden warfare designed to bring quick surrender; especially an offensive combining bombardment from air with rapid invasion by mechanized ground forces; first notable use 1939 when Germans invaded Poland; name German for 'lightning war'
  World War II W-322
  warfare W-23

Blitzstein, Marc (1905–64), U.S. composer, born in Philadelphia, Pa.; influenced by Schönberg and other modernists; developed vigorous and original style ('The Cradle Will Rock', musical play; 'Percussion Music').

Blizzard (or buran, or norther), cold wind with driving snow W-225
  Siberia S-189

BLM. *see in index* Land Management, Bureau of

Bloch, Ernest (1880–1959), U.S. composer B-312

Bloch, Felix (1905–83), U.S. physicist and educator, born in Zurich, Switzerland; in physics department at Stanford University since 1934; war research Stanford University, Los Alamos, N.M., and Harvard University 1942–45.

Bloch, Konrad Emil (born 1912), U.S. biochemist, born in Neisse, Germany (now Poland); to U.S. 1936, citizen 1944; professor biochemistry Harvard 1954–.

Block, Adriaen (or Adrian Block) (fl. 1610–24), Dutch navigator who explored Long Island and Housatonic and Connecticut rivers 1614; Block Island, R.I., named for him; first to map s. coast of New England in detail L-297, R-183

Block, Herbert Lawrence (pseudonym Herblock) (born 1909), U.S. cartoonist, born in Chicago, Ill.; awarded Pulitzer prizes 1942, 1954, and 1979; editorial cartoonist *The Washington Post* 1946–.

Block, John R. (born 1935), U.S. public official, born in Galesburg, Ill.; director Illinois department of agriculture 1977–81; U.S. secretary of agriculture 1981–86.

Blockade B-312
  Berlin air lift G-124, R-357
    warfare W-24
  Civil War C-476
    navy N-91
  international law I-256
  'paper' blockade B-221
  World War I W-304, 312
  World War II B-221

Block-and-fault, geology U-83
Block anesthesia A-413
Blockhouse, a stronghold, built usually in two stories, of heavy logs banked with earth with loopholes for musketry in sides; used in wars with Indians and in Spanish-American and Boer wars.
Blocking, boxing B-390, *picture* B-389
Blocking, garment pressing G-33
Block Island, small island in the Atlantic Ocean, lying 10 mi (16 km) from the shore of Rhode Island; summer resort; pop. 489 R-183, *map* R-181
  climate R-180, *list* R-179
  Mohegan Bluffs, *picture* R-187
Block Island Sound, body of water between Block Island and mainland Rhode Island, *map* R-181
Block plane, a tool T-218
Block printing B-351
  computerized typesetting T-340
  folk art F-250
  Japan P-503
  textiles T-141
  wallpaper W-8
  Western art P-53
Block system, in railroads R-80
Block tin, tin refined by electrolysis T-191
Bloemfontein, South Africa, capital of Orange Free State; livestock trading center; University College of Orange Free State; site of Lamont Telescope; University of Michigan and Boyd Station (Harvard) observatories; pop. 145,273, with suburbs, *maps* A-115, S-264
Blois, France, town on Loire River, 100 mi (160 km) s.w. of Paris; splendid castle, once seat of counts of Blois; pop. 39,279, *map* F-369
Blois, French château designed by Mansart M-110
Blok, Aleksandr Aleksandrovich (1880–1921), Russian poet R-360a
Blommaert's Kill, Del. *see in index* Lewes
Blondel de Nesle (fl. 12th century), French minstrel, friend and attendant of Richard I R-202
'Blondie', comic strip, *picture* I-200
Blondin, Charles (original name Jean Francois Gravelet) (1824–97), French acrobat.
Blood B-313
  animal
    evolution A-462
    insect blood I-217
    mosquito's diet M-596
  circulation C-421
    Harvey H-51
  composition
    albumin A-272
    antitoxins A-495
    cells C-240, *picture* C-328
      Leeuwenhoek L-117
    serum S-114
  disease D-167
    metabolic D-180. *see also in index* Diabetes
  food and nutrition F-275
    vitamins V-356
  human anatomy A-391
  immune system I-55
  living things L-270
  lymphatic system L-343
  medicine M-282
    anesthetic A-412
    antibiotic A-488
    bioengineering B-206
    diagnosis D-127
    first aid techniques F-118, *diagrams* F-117
    tests, *picture* P-312
    transfusion T-251
    vaccines V-250
    venereal disease V-272
  organs
    heart H-97
    kidney K-235
    liver L-261
    lungs L-336
  pressure. *see in index* Blood pressure
  Red Cross donations R-119, *picture* R-118
  space travel affects S-346a
  typing
    physical anthropology A-483
    racial classification R-26
      Landsteiner's discovery L-27
Blood bank, place where blood is stored for future use B-316
Blood cells. *see in index* Blood, *subhead* cells
Bloodhound, dog, *picture* D-199
Blood knot, fisherman's knot, *picture* F-143
Bloodless Revolution, England. *see in index* Glorious Revolution
Bloodletting, early medical technique M-283
  barbers H-9
Blood line, ancient theory of lineage H-139
'Blood of a Poet, The' (1931), motion picture
  Cocteau C-533
Blood pressure
  bioengineering B-206
  circulatory system C-422
  heart H-97
Bloodroot, plant *Sanguinaria canadensis* B-318
  wildflower F-231, *picture* F-232
Bloodstone (or Heliotrope), semiprecious stone J-115
Blood vessel. *see also in index* Artery; Capillary; Circulatory system; Vein
  headache H-81
  transplantation T-251
Bloody Assizes, trials for rebellion against James II of England J-19
Bloody Mary. *see in index* Mary I
Bloom, in metalworking I-344
Bloomer, Amelia Jenks (1818–94), U.S. dress reformer and temperance lecturer, born in Homer, N.Y.; gave name to bloomers D-266
  women's rights W-275
Bloomfield, Leonard (born 1887), U.S. linguist B-318
Bloomfield, Conn., 5 mi (8 km) n.w. of Hartford; automotive and aircraft parts, machinery; printing; settled 1642, incorporated 1835; pop. of township 18,608.
Bloomfield, N.J., residential and industrial town just n.w. of Newark; electrical appliances, chemicals, pharmaceuticals, metal products, plastics; Bloomfield College; pop. 47,792.
Bloomington, Ill., city about 60 mi (100 km) n.e. of Springfield, in corn belt; seed corn; farm equipment, tires, vacuum cleaners, electrical components; Illinois Wesleyan University; annual American Passion Play; pop. 44,189
  Illinois, *map* I-52
Bloomington, Ind., city about 47 mi (76 km) s.w. of Indianapolis; center of limestone quarrying; electrical, electronic, and wood products; pop. 52,044
  circus history C-432
  Indiana, *map* I-102
Bloomington, Minn., city 10 mi (16 km) s. of Minneapolis; machinery and metal products; electronics; Metropolitan Stadium; pop. 81,831 M-442
Bloomsburg, Pa., town 57 mi (92 km) n.e. of Harrisburg; carpet mill, silk and rayon weaving, food processing; clothing, aluminum; Bloomsburg State College; pop. 11,717, *map* P-185
Bloomsbury, region in London, England L-293
Blotter, in police work P-425
Blouet, Paul. *see in index* O'Rell, Max
Blount, William (1749–1800), U.S. political leader, born in Bertie County, N.C.; appointed governor of the 'Territory South of the River Ohio' by President Washington 1790; signed United States Constitution for North Carolina; made his headquarters in Tennessee, elected to U.S. Senate; expelled from Senate because of his part in conspiracy to seize Spanish territory in North America for England; his was first impeachment trial ever brought before U.S. Senate.
Blount, Winton Malcolm (born 1921), U.S. public official, born in Union Springs, Ala.; headed construction company 1946–69, chairman of its executive committee 1973–; president Chamber of Commerce of the United States 1968–69; U.S. postmaster general 1969–71
  Nixon N-326
Blow, Susan Elizabeth (1843–1916), U.S. early kindergarten teacher, born in St. Louis, Mo.; established training school for kindergarten teachers 1874; wrote books on education.
Blower, fan F-23
  heating and ventilating H-112
Blowfly. *see in index* Flesh fly
Blowgun, a tube of wood or bamboo for blowing darts
  lizard-catching L-274
Blowhole, whale W-185
'Blowing Bubbles', painting by Chardin P-45
Blow molding, in plastics P-382
Blown glass G-158, *pictures* G-161, 162, V-340
  glass rhododendron, *picture* R-197
  glassware G-164
Blowpipe
  glassware G-164
Blubber, layer of fat beneath skin in certain animals
  whale W-185
Blücher, Gebhard Leberecht von, prince of Wahlstatt (1742–1819), Prussian field marshal, leader of patriot Prussian party during Napoleonic period W-100
Blue, color C-558
  pottery P-469
  wavelength S-372
'Blue', work by Darío D-35
'Blue, Black, Red', painting by Kelly P-67
Blue Andalusian, a breed of fowls P-482, *picture* P-481
Blueback salmon (or sockeye salmon, or red salmon), fish of the family Salmonidae S-28
Blue Beard, villain in French fairy tale (*'Barbe Bleue'*), by Charles Perrault; his wife, Fatima, disregards command not to open a certain door and discovers bodies of the six wives he had murdered; she is rescued just in time; similar stories exist in folklore of other countries
  folklore F-261, *picture* F-262
Blue beech. *see in index* Hornbeam
Bluebell, flower of the genus *Campanula* B-318
Bluebell of Scotland (or harebell), flower *Campanula rotundifolia* B-318, *pictures* F-235, P-359
Blueberry, fruit F-438
Bluebill, duck. *see in index* Scaup
Bluebird, a bird of the family Turdidae B-318
  egg, *picture* E-112
  habits B-241, *picture* B-264
  state bird
    Missouri, *picture* M-496
    New York, *picture* N-260
  thrush family T-177
'Blue Bird, The', fairy play by Maeterlinck, first produced in Belgium in 1909 M-31
Bluebonnet, blue flower of the lupine genus, *picture* S-427
Bluebottle. *see in index* Bachelor's button
Bluebottle fly. *see in index* Flesh fly
'Blue Boy, The', full-length portrait of Jonathan Buttall by Thomas Gainsborough; supposedly painted to disprove Sir Joshua Reynolds' statement that 'cold' color (such as blue) could not be used as the dominant color in a painting.
Blue bull. *see in index* Nilgai
Blue butterfly, a small azure butterfly of the family Lycaenidae
  egg, *picture* E-111
Blue cardinal flower (or great lobelia), *picture* F-235
Blue catfish, fish *Ictalurus furcatus* of the family Ictaluridae, *picture* C-220
Blue-collar worker M-460
Blue coral, type of coral, *picture* C-714
Blue crab, crustacean *Callinectes sapidus* C-792
  invertebrates, *picture* I-285
Blue Cross, health care insurance H-95, H-285
Bluecup. *see in index* Nierembergia
Blue daisy. *see in index* Heteropappus
Blue-eyed grass, perennial wild flower of iris family; common species *Sisrinchium angustifolium* 4–18 in. (10–46 cm) high, with long grasslike leaves; 6-petaled blue flowers, about 1/2 in. (1.3 cm) across, have yellow or white centers; Canada and n. states, May–July, *picture* F-234
Blue-eyed Mary. *see in index* Collinsia
Bluefield, W. Va., city in s.w. part of state; adjoins town of **Bluefield,** Va. (pop. 5,286), with which it forms economic unit; distributing center for Pocahontas coalfields; furniture, food products; Bluefield State College (W. Va.); pop. 16,060, *maps* V-348, U-41
Bluefields, Nicaragua, port on e. coast; pop. 12,293.
Bluefield State College, college in Bluefield, W. Va.; founded in 1895
  West Virginia W-168
Bluefin tuna, fish *Thunnus thynnus,* T-306, F-124
Blue fir. *see in index* White fir
Bluefish, *table* F-136
Blue-footed booby, a seabird *Sula nebouxii* of the family Sulidae G-16
Blue fox F-337, *table* F-464
Bluegill, freshwater fish *Lepomis macrochirus,* member of the sunfish family Centrarchidae; named from bluish color of cheeks and gill covers; general color greenish S-518
Blue globe thistle, plant T-171, *picture* T-170
Blue goose, bird of the family Anatidae D-285
  birds B-252
  migration B-252, *chart* A-451
Bluegrass, any of various species of the genus *Poa,* especially the Kentucky bluegrass; has many running rootstocks that form a dense sod, and grows from a few inches (centimeters) to 2 ft (61 cm) high; grows especially well in limestone regions of Kentucky and Tennessee
  Tennessee, *picture* T-86
Bluegrass, type of country music M-678
Bluegrass Plain. *see in index* Lexington Plain
Bluegrass State. *see in index* Kentucky
Blue-green algae A-284, L-270, *picture* F-450
Blue grosbeak, bird *Guiraca caerulea* of the family Fringillidae G-290
Blue ground. *see in index* Kimberlite
Blue hawk (or haggard), a falcon F-13
Blue hen chicken, game chicken P-483
  state bird of Delaware B-204
Blue Hills of Couteau, uplands in Newfoundland N-164
Blue Island, Ill., city just s. of Chicago; railroad shops and equipment, steel products, pop. 21,855
  Illinois, *map* I-52
Blue jay, bird *Cyanocitta cristata* C-784, *picture* C-785
Blue jeans, clothing C-466
Blue laceflower. *see in index* Trachymene
Blue laws, any laws designed to regulate the ordinary habits or morals of individuals; particularly, in Connecticut, the strict laws of Puritan days B-319, *table* L-92
Blue mold, fungus of the genus *Penicillium* M-519
Blue Mosque, mosque in Istanbul, Turkey I-375
Blue Mountain, ridge of the Appalachians in e. Pa., beginning in s.-central part of state and extending n.e. to Kittatinny Mountain, in n.w. N.J. P-164, *map* P-185
Blue Mountains, mountains in Australia, in Great Dividing Range A-771, *maps* A-819, P-3
Blue Mountains, mountains in Jamaica J-17
  West Indies, *map* W-159
Blue Mountains, mountains in n.e. Oregon and s.e. Washington; rise to some 9,000 ft (2,740 m); densely forested
  Oregon O-583
  Washington W-48, *map* W-49
Blue mud wasp, insect, *picture* W-72
Blue Network Company, Inc. *see in index* American Broadcasting Company
Blue Nile River (or Abbai River), river in Africa, rises in Ethiopia; unites with White Nile

near Khartoum S-501, *map* A-115
  Nile N-316

Blue Point, Long Island, New York L-297

'Blue Poles', painting by Pollock P-64, P-440

Blueprint B-319
  leaf collection L-103, *picture* L-102
  mechanical drawing M-262

Blue Rider, The. *see in index* Blaue Reiter, Der

Blue Ridge (or Blue Ridge Mountains), southeasternmost range of Appalachian Mts. B-319, *maps* U-36, 50, 59
  Appalachian geography A-508
  Maryland M-167, *maps* M-169, 183
  North Carolina N-354
  Pennsylvania P-164, *map* P-165
  South Carolina S-306, *map* S-307
  Tennessee T-82, *map* T-83
  Virginia V-330, *map* V-331, *picture* V-341
  West Virginia W-165
    Harpers Ferry H-43

Blue Ridge Parkway, road that joins Shenandoah and Great Smoky Mountains national parks R-222, *pictures* V-341
  North Carolina N-358

Blues, form of U.S. music originated by black Americans in the South
  black Americans B-300
  Handy H-30
  jazz J-84
  Joplin J-140
  popular music M-679

Blues and Royals, regiment of the English royal household cavalry
  uniform, *picture* U-12

Blue shark fish of the family Galeidae S-144, *picture* A-426

Blue sheep (or burrhel), animal of the family Bovidae S-148

Blue Shield, health insurance H-95

Blue spruce (or Colorado spruce), tree of the pine family S-398

Blue stellar object (BSO) S-415

Bluestone Dam, dam in West Virginia, on New River W-165, *picture* W-174

Bluet (or innocence), small wild flower *Houstonia caerulea* of the madder family, with delicate blue, violet, or nearly white flowers with yellow centers; native from Nova Scotia, to Georgia and Missouri, *picture* F-235

Blue-tailed skink, lizard
  superstitions L-274

Blue Tavernier, diamond, *picture* D-129

Blue vitriol. *see in index* Copper sulfate

Blueweed. *see in index* Viper's bugloss

Blue whale (or sulpher-bottom whale), mammal *Balaenoptera musculus* of the order Cetacea W-185
  animal A-422

Blue wildebeest, *picture* A-479

Bluford, Guion S., Jr. (born 1942), U.S. astronaut, first black American to fly in space; born in Philadelphia, Pa.; U.S. Air Force officer; selected as astronaut candidate by NASA in 1978; served as mission specialist for space shuttle *Challenger* in August 1983.

Blum, René (1884–1944), ballet impresario B-35

Blumberg, Baruch S. (born 1925), U.S. virologist and medical anthropologist, born in New York City; discovered Australian antigen, part of hepatitis B virus; associate director clinical research at Institute for Cancer Research, Philadelphia 1964–; professor of medicine and anthropology University of Pennsylvania.

Blume, Judy (born 1938), U.S. award-winning writer of juvenile and adult fiction, born in Elizabeth, N.J.; wrote frank children's stories dealing with problems of young adults; awards for 'Are You There God?, It's Me, Margaret' 1970, 'Tales of a Fourth Grade Nothing' 1972, 'Blubber' 1974, 'Otherwise Known as Sheila the Great' 1972, 'Superfudge' 1980, 'Tiger Eyes' 1981; founded KIDS Fund 1981.

Blumenbach, Johann Friedrich (1752–1840), German naturalist and anthropologist, born in Gotha; founded science of anthropology; placed comparative anatomy on scientific basis A-487, *picture* A-485
  human classifications C-232, R-25

Blunden, Edmund (1896–1974) British writer
  literary contribution E-280

Blunderbuss, gun F-100

Blunger, in pottery making P-477

Blunt, Anthony (1907–83), British art historian and spy
  espionage E-303

Blunt-nosed leopard lizard
  endangered species E-212

Bly, Nellie (pen name of Elizabeth Cochrane Seaman, or Elizabeth Cochrane, or Elizabeth Cochran) (1867–1922), U.S. journalist B-319

Bly, Robert (born 1926), U.S. poet A-364

B lymphocyte. *see in index* B cell

Blyth, Vernon. *see in index* Castle, Vernon

Blythe, Herbert. *see in index* Barrymore, Maurice

Blytheville, Ark., city about 55 mi (90 km) n. of Memphis; cotton and soybean growing; metal products, canned foods, caps and hats; Blytheville Air Force Base nearby; pop. 23,844, *maps* A-563, 551, U-41

BMEWS. *see in index* Ballistic Missile Early Warning System

BMR. *see in index* Basal metabolic rate

BMX, bicycle B-188

B'nai B'rith, Independent Order of, Jewish fraternal organization founded in New York, N.Y., 1843 for the moral improvement of its members and the furtherance of 'charity, benevolence, and brotherly love'; has branches throughout U.S. and Canada and in Europe and Near East; name means 'sons of the covenant.'

Boa constrictor, snake, *picture* S-226. *see also in index* Snake

Boadicea (or Bonduca, or Boudicca) (died 62 AD), queen of the Iceni, a people in ancient Britain; took poison after defeat of her army by Romans; subject of poems by Tennyson and Cowper and of tragedy, 'Bonduca', by Beaumont and Fletcher E-238

Boar, mature male hog, also the popular name for various wild hogs, particularly European and Indian wild hog
  Adonis myth A-37
  ancestor of domestic swine A-456
  pig P-320

Board foot, unit of measurement a foot long, a foot wide, and an inch thick; used for lumber and logs; volume equals 144 cu in. (2,360 cu cm); abbreviation, bd. ft. L-333, *table* W-140

Board games B-320

Boarding, warfare tactic M-136
  navy N-81

Board of Governors, in banking F-51

Board of Health .*see in index* Health agencies; Public health

Boas, Franz (1858–1942), U.S. anthropologist B-324
  anthropology A-485
  eugenics E-326

Boatbill, a bird of the heron family H-141

Boater (or sailor), type of hat H-54

Boating B-324. *see also in index* Canoeing; Motorboat; Navigation; Sailing craft; Shipbuilding; Ships; Steam craft
  America's Cup. *see table in index*
  basket boats B-102
  camping C-69
  coracle B-394
  early types S-163
  flatboat P-335, *picture* P-333
  gondola V-277, *picture* V-278
  houseboat, *picture* S-157
  hull P-383
  hydrofoil. *see in index* Hydrofoil boat
  Indian transportation I-122
  kayak, *picture* U-224
  models S-176b
  rowboat. *see in index* Rowboat
  safety, *picture* S-12
  sampan. *see in index* Sampan
  transportation T-255
  tugboat S-168, *pictures* P-87, R-177

Boat racing
  Campbell C-67
  rowing R-300
  yacht model S-177, *picture* S-176b

Boat rod, in fishing F-145

Boatswain, petty officer on merchant ship in charge of deck force, of boat crews, and of work parties maintaining hull, anchors, boats, and related equipment; in U.S. Navy, a warrant officer with like duties; orders given crew by shrill notes of boatswain's pipe
  insignia, *picture* U-10

Boat-tailed grackle, bird *Cassidix mexicanus major* of the family Icteridae B-305

Boaz, Biblical figure, 2nd husband of Ruth R-365

Bob, hairstyle H-10

Bobber, in fishing F-140

Bobbing wheel, for spinning S-390, *picture* S-389

Bobbin lace (or pillow lace), lace L-14, *pictures* L-15, 16

Bobby, British policeman P-430b, *picture* P-430a

Bobcat (or bay lynx, or red lynx), wild cat *Lynx rufus* L-344, *pictures* A-436, C-213, *table* C-216

Bobko, Karol (born 1937), U.S. astronaut, born in New York, N.Y., *table* S-348

Bob Marley & the Wailers, reggae group M-682

Bobo Dioulasso, Burkina Faso (formerly Upper Volta), town in s.w., on railway linking the capitals Ouagadougou, Burkina Faso, and Abidjan, Ivory Coast; pop. 174,000 B-508

Bobolink, bird *Dolichonyx oryzivorus* of the family Icteridae B-330, *chart* A-451
  birds B-249

Bobsled and bobsledding S-216, W-243

Bobwhite (sometimes called partridge), a North American quail *Colinus virginianus* B-259, *picture* B-246
  quail Q-3

Boca Raton, Fla., city 17 mi (27 km) n. of Fort Lauderdale; computers, hospital supplies; Florida Atlantic University; pop. 49,505.

Boccaccio, Giovanni (1313–75) B-330
  Italian literature I-376, 385
  Latin literature L-78
  Renaissance R-146

Boccaccio, word game
  charade form C-271

Boccie, an Italian form of lawn bowling, played on a sand or dirt alley about 75 ft by 8 ft (23 m by 2 m), enclosed with boarded ends and sides; players roll or throw wooden balls to a smaller wooden ball called the jack; rebounds from side walls are allowed B-387. *see also in index* Lawn bowling

Boccioni, Umberto (1882–1916), Italian futurist sculptor and painter, born in Reggio di Calabria S-93

Bocconia. *see in index* Plume poppy

Bochum, West Germany, industrial city 8 mi (13 km) e. of Essen; coal mines; metal and glass products; pop. 343,968, *map* G-131

Bock, Vera, U.S. artist, illustrator, and designer of books, born in St. Petersburg (now Leningrad), Russia, of American father and Russian mother; during Russian Revolution, she and her family fled to San Francisco, Calif. (illustrated for children 'The Oak Tree House', 'A Ring and a Riddle', 'Arabian Nights', 'King of the Cats'; for adults 'The Koran', 'Phantom Victory')
  'The Tale of Dick o' the Cow', *picture* S-482

Bock beer, a malt beverage B-134

Bocotia, region in central Greece T-162

Bode, Johann Elert (1747–1826), German astronomer, director of Berlin Observatory; Bode's Law named for him A-706

Bodensee. *see in index* Constance, Lake

Bodhisattva, Buddhist doctrine B-483, C-364

Bodhi tree. *see in index* Bo tree

Bodin, Jean (1530–1596), French political philosopher B-330

Bodleian Library, library at Oxford University, England L-173, S-140, *picture* L-176

Bodley, Sir Thomas (1545–1613), English scholar and diplomat, born in Exeter; sent by Queen Elizabeth I on diplomatic missions to Denmark, France, and Holland
  Bodleian Library S-140

Bodmer, Karl (1809–93), Swiss artist, born near Zurich
  Mandan lodge, *picture* I-124

Bodoni, Giambattista (1740–1813), Italian printer; superintendent of duke of Parma's private presses; printed beautiful editions of the classics
  type style T-338, *picture* B-349

Body, human. *see in index* Anatomy, human; Physiology; *also* parts of body by name

Bodybuilding, weight lifting W-136

Body cells. *see in index* Somatic cells

Body language L-36

Body lice (or sucking lice, or cooties), group of insects of the order Anoplura, family Haematopinidae; especially the hog louse *Haematopinus adventicius*, the largest species; 6 to 12 generations a year
  insect, *picture* I-214
  parasites P-114, *picture* P-115

Body signaling S-195a, *diagrams* S-194

Body temperature. *see in index* Temperature, body

Boehm, Theobald, German instrument maker
  wind instruments W-229

Boeing, William Edward (1881–1956), U.S. airplane manufacturer, born in Detroit, Mich.; instructed in flying by Glenn L. Martin; founded Boeing (Airplane) Company 1916 in Seattle, Wash.; Daniel Guggenheim medal 1934.

Boeing, airplane, *picture* A-165
  jet propulsion J-111, *pictures* J-105, 110

Boeotia, a district in Greece, n.w. of Attica; in ancient Greece, a state, chief city Thebes.

Boeroe, island, Indonesia. *see in index* Buru

Boers, Dutch farmers who settled in South Africa. *see also in index* Boer War
  British relations S-266
  World War I uprising S-220

Boer War (also called South African War) (1899–1902) B-330
  amnesty A-374
  Baden-Powell B-10
  Canada C-102
  Churchill C-412
  concentration camps C-638
  frontier movement F-426
  Johannesburg J-122
  leaders
    Kitchener K-251
    Kruger K-306
    Smuts S-220
  South Africa S-266
  United Kingdom E-254
  warfare, *list* W-13

Boethius, Roman statesman L-78

Bog, spongy, wet ground, usually composed of decaying vegetable matter and covered with coarse grass. *see also in index* Swamp
  flowers F-240
  peat bog P-151

Bogalusa, La., city near Pearl River, about 60 mi (100 km) n. of New Orleans; in managed forest area; paper products, lumber, tung oil; pop. 16,976, *map* U-41

Bogart, Humphrey (1899–1957), U.S. motion-picture actor, born in New York City; played 'tough guy' with a touch of idealism and gangster roles; a top box office attraction during the 1940s and 1950s ('The Maltese Falcon', 'Casablanca', 'The African Queen', 1951 Academy award for best actor; 'The Big Sleep'), *picture* M-624
  Hammett H-23

Bogaz Koi (or Boghaz Keui), Turkey, village 85 mi (135 km) e. of Ankara; near ancient ruins
  cuneiform tablets A-537

Bogey, in golf G-189

immune system I-55
transplantation T-251

Bone turquoise. *see in index* Odontolite

Bonfils, Frederick Gilmer (1860–1933), U.S. journalist, born near Troy, Mo.; with **Harry Heye Tammen** (1856–1924), born in Baltimore, Md., published *Denver Post* after 1895; made it huge success with sensationalism and bizarre features, as red headlines.

Bongo, an antelope A-478
zoo Z-466

Bonheur, Rosa (full name Marie-Rosalie Bonheur) (1822–99), French artist B-343

Bonhoeffer, Dietrich (1906–45), German Protestant theologian, born in Breslau, Germany G-107
martyr M-161

'Bonhomme Richard', ship of John Paul Jones J-139, *picture* R-172

Boniface (formerly Wynfrid) (675–755), English missionary and saint B-343

Boniface VIII (formerly Benedetto Caetini) (1235?–1303), pope B-344
Philip IV P-252
University of Rome R-253

Bonin Islands (Japanese Ogasawara Jima), Japanese island group in Pacific, 530 mi (850 km) s.e. of Yokohama; 30 sq mi (80 sq km); occupied by U.S. in 1945; returned to Japan 1968; pop. 782, *maps* J-78, P-3
Asia, *map* A-697
world, *map* W-297

Bonn, West Germany, capital of Federal Republic of Germany; pop. 288,100 B-344
Europe, *map* E-360
Germany G-112, *map* G-131, *picture* G-114
world, *map* W-297

Bonn, University of, university in Bonn, West Germany; founded in 1818 by Frederick William III of Prussia; faculties of law, medicine, philosophy, and Roman Catholic and Protestant theology B-344

Bonnard, Pierre (1867–1947), French painter, born in Paris; forceful but sensitive use of color; called a 'divergent impressionist,' also a 'perfectionist impressionist'.

Bonnet, Stede (died 1718), North American pirate, former English army officer and respected plantation owner in Barbados; bought sloop *Revenge* and became pirate; hunted prizes with notorious Edward Teach; pardoned by governor of North Carolina; sailed again, in *Royal James*, captured 1718, and hanged in Charleston, S.C. P-342a

Bonnet, hats and caps H-55, *picture* H-53

Bonnet rouge (or liberty cap), hats and caps H-53

Bonneville, Lake, extinct glacial lake in Utah L-24, U-216
Great Salt Lake G-251

Bonneville Dam, dam in Oregon and Washington, on Columbia River, *picture* U-91
Columbia River C-588
dam D-14
Oregon O-581, 586
Washington W-49

Bonneville Power Administration, United States C-588

Bonneville Salt Flats, barren salt flats in Utah U-221, G-251, *maps* U-217, 232, *picture* U-225

Bonney, William H. *see in index* Billy the Kid

'Bonnie and Clyde', motion picture by Penn M-627

Bonnie Blue flag, flag of Confederate States of America F-154, *picture* F-155

Bonnie Prince Charlie (popular name of Charles Edward Stuart) (1720–88), grandson of James II of England, born in Rome; also called Young Pretender P-496
English history E-248, N-65

Bono, lead singer of rock group U2, *picture* M-683

Bonpland, Aimé (Aimé Jacques Alexandre Bonpland) (1773–1858), French botanist H-321

Bonsai, dwarf trees or the art of training and growing them B-344, J-54
fruitgrowing F-436
houseplants H-288
Japan J-54

Bonspiel, curling tournament C-807

Bontemps, Arna Wendell (1902–73), U.S. poet and novelist, born in Alexandria, La. (books for adults, 'Drums at Dusk', 'Black Thunder', '100 Years of Negro Freedom'; for children, 'You Can't Pet a Possum', 'Sad-Faced Boy', 'The Story of the Negro', 'Chariot in the Sky', 'Famous Negro Athletes') R-111c

Bonus, something given in addition to what is strictly due, as a payment to employees above regular wages
U.S.S.R. R-330

Bonus Army, United States
Hoover H-236

Booby, a large seabird related to the gannet, so called because of its apparent stupidity and tameness when nesting G-16, *picture* G-4

Book and bookmaking B-345. *see also in index* Awards; Bibliography; Clay tablets; Illuminated manuscripts; Illustrated books; Literature; Literature for children; Manuscripts; Printing; Reference books; Storytelling; Textbooks; Type; *also* entries starting with Book
ancient, S-212
Mayan A-538
censorship C-246
children's literature L-245, 258, *pictures* L-246, 248
education E-82
etiquette E-316, 320, *picture* E-322
libraries L-149, *picture* L-175
Middle Ages M-391
paper P-100, *picture* P-101
paperback books W-152
preservation A-149
typography T-337

Bookbinding B-353, *picture* B-354
embossing E-198

Booker T. Washington National Monument, park in Virginia N-43, *map* N-40, V-348, *picture* V-341

Book hands, in calligraphy C-58

Bookkeeping A-15
machines C-20
vocational opportunities V-368, *picture* V-369

Bookmaking, gambling practice H-275

'Bookman's Manual'. *see in index* 'Reader's Adviser, The'

'Book of Animals', work by al-Jahiz
Islamic literature I-366

'Book of Beliefs and Opinions, The', by Saadia ben Joseph S-1

'Book of Changes'. *see in index* I Ching

'Book of Common Prayer'. *see in index* 'Prayer, Book of Common'

'Book of Concord', official teachings of the Lutheran churches L-339

'Book of Ephraim, The', work by Merrill A-364

'Book of Healing', work by Avicenna A-889

Book of Hours. *see in index* Limbourg

'Book of Kells'. *see in index* 'Kells, Book of'

'Book of Kings'. *see in index* 'Shah-nameh'

'Book of Kings', collection of Islamic mythology I-366

'Book of Misers', work by al-Jahiz
Islamic literature I-366

'Book of Mormon', sacred text of the Mormon faith M-583

'Book of the Dead', ancient Egyptian texts E-131

'Book of the Duchess, The', work by Chaucer C-285

'Book of the Dun Cow, The', Irish literature I-326

'Book of the Flower', work by Ibn Da'ud
Islamic literature I-365

'Book of the Novel and the Strange', work by al-Mu'tazz
Islamic literature I-365

Book of the Year for Children Award, Canadian literary award L-240

Bookplates B-362

Bookselling
Parisian bookstall, *picture* P-119

Book-wheel
library history, *picture* L-173

Boole, George (1815–64), English mathematician and logician B-364
algebra A-294

Boolean algebra, algebra of sets and of propositions in logic A-294, B-364
mathematics, *table* M-218

Boom, in sailboat, *diagram* B-326

Boom, motion pictures M-621

Boom, El, Latin American literary phenomenon L-70

Boomerang B-364
airplane A-200
Australia A-795

Boomers, name given to a group of men led by David L. Payne (1836–84), who agitated for the opening of the Indian Territory for settlement.

Boone, Daniel (1734–1820), North American pioneer B-365
autograph, *picture* A-832
folklore F-267
Hall of Fame, *table* H-16
Kentucky K-213
Missouri M-491
Tennessee T-87

Boone, Iowa, city about 35 mi (55 km) n.w. of Des Moines; extensive agricultural trade; railroad shops; pop. 12,468
Iowa, *map* I-302

Boonesboro (originally Boonesborough), Ky., village on Kentucky River, 16 mi (26 km) s.e. of Lexington K-213, *picture* K-212
Boone founds B-365

Boone's Trace. *see in index* Wilderness Road

Boot, footwear S-178. *see in also index* Sandal; Shoe
rubber R-304
St. Louis, Mo. production S-22
ski boots S-210b, *picture* S-210c

Boot (or kamik), sealskin boot worn by Eskimos, *picture* E-178

Boötes, northern constellation containing Arcturus; near Great Bear; name means 'herdsman', *charts* S-418, C-681

Booth, Ballington (1859–1940), U.S. religious leader, born in Brighouse, England; became U.S. citizen 1895; son of William Booth S-33
Volunteers of America S-34

Booth, Catherine Mumford (1829–90), British evangelist, born in Ashbourne, Derbyshire; known as 'Mother of the Salvation Army' S-33
women's rights W-275

Booth, Edwin Thomas (1833–93), U.S. actor, born in Bel Air, Md.; brother of John W. Booth; foremost U.S. tragedian of his day; won great fame also in England; played Shakespeare, notably Hamlet, King Lear, Othello, Richard III, Shylock, and Macbeth A-27
Hall of Fame, *table* H-16

Booth, John Wilkes (1838–65), U.S. actor, born in Hartford County, Md.; brother of Edwin Booth; assassinated President Lincoln April 14, 1865; escaped to Richard H. Garrett's barn, near Fredericksburg, Va.; fatally shot April 26 when soldiers and detectives set fire to barn and surrounded it; died same day; opinion divided whether Booth killed himself or was killed by a soldier's bullet despite order not to fire A-703, C-477, L-224
Confederacy C-644

Booth, William (1829–1912), English minister and founder of Salvation Army, born in Nottingham; father of William B., Ballington, and Evangeline Booth; author of 'In Darkest England and the Way Out', a work offering remedies for pauperism S-32

Boothe, Clare. *see in index* Luce, Clare Boothe

Boothia, Gulf of, inlet of Arctic Ocean in n. Can., *maps* N-350

Boothia Peninsula, northernmost peninsula of North American mainland, *maps* N-350, W-297

Bootle, England, at the mouth of the Mersey; great docks are part of dock system of Liverpool; pop. 79,950, *map* U-18a

Bop, a form of jazz J-86

Bophuthatswana, republic in s. Africa B-365, *map* A-115
African political unit, *table* A-112
flag, *picture* F-162
South Africa S-267, *map* S-264

Boquerón, volcano in El Salvador E-195

Boquerón, El, volcano in Mexico, *picture* V-380

Bor, Norse god M-697

Bora, northeast wind of the Adriatic A-50

Bora Bora, volcanic island of Leeward group of the Society Islands in s. Pacific; 15 sq mi (40 sq km); rises centrally in peaks of Pahia and Otemanu, the latter the island's highest point (2,385 ft; 725 m); harbor deep and sheltered; airport; pop. 2,196, *map* P-3

Boracic acid. *see in index* Boric acid

Borah, William Edgar (1865–1940), U.S. political leader, born in Fairfield, Ill.; U.S. senator from Idaho 1907–40; a Republican of independent views; brilliant debater; foe of monopoly; partly responsible for creation of Department of Labor; opposed League of Nations, World Court, Versailles Treaty; defended prohibition; as chairman Senate Foreign Relations Committee, championed Conference for Limitation of Armaments I-21
Insurgent leader T-9
Statuary Hall, *table* S-437a

Borah Peak, highest point in Idaho, 12,662 ft (3,859 m); in the Lost River Range in Lemhi National Forest, e.-central Idaho; named after William E. Borah, senator from Idaho
Idaho I-18, *map* I-30

Borate mineral, classification M-435

Borax, a salt (sodium borate, $Na_2B_4O_7$) of boric acid and sodium
fireproofing P-73
minerals M-435
Death Valley, Calif. D-50

Borchert, Wolfgang (1921–47), German dramatist and writer
German literature G-108

Bord-and-pillar system, mining. *see in index* Room-and-pillar system

Bordeaux, France, port near w. coast; pop. 223,131 B-366
France, *maps* E-360, F-369
wine w-237

Borden, Robert Laird (1854–1937), prime minister of Canada B-366
Canada C-102
Meighen M-287

Border collie, dog, *picture* D-207

Border terrier, dog, *picture* D-203

Bordet, Jules (1870–1961), Belgian bacteriologist, born near Brussels; with O. Gengou, found bacillus of whooping cough 1906 M-284

Boré, Étienne de (1741–1820), Franco-American sugar planter
sugar refining improvements L-310

Bore (or caliber), of firearms F-100

Bore, a wall of water O-490

Boreal, life region in North America
Canada C-75

Borer, parasitic fish. *see in index* Hagfish

Borg, Bjorn (born 1956), Swedish tennis player B-366
tennis T-104, *picture* T-108

Borgå, Finland. *see in index* Porvoo

Borger, Tex., city in the Panhandle about 40 mi (60 km) n.e. of Amarillo; oil refining; carbon black, synthetic rubber; pop. 15,837, *map* U-40

Borges, Jorge Luis (1899–1986), Argentinian poet and writer B-367
Latin America L-70

Borgese, Giuseppe Antonio (1882–1952), U.S. scholar, writer, born in Sicily; to U.S. 1931; professor Italian literature University of Chicago 1936–51; author of literary and political criticism and history, poetry, novels I-377

Borghese, Camillo. pope, *see in index* Paul V

Borgia, Alfonso. *see in index* Calixtus III

Borgia, Cesare (1476–1507), Italian military leader B-367
Leonardo da Vinci L-132

Borgia, Giovanni (1476–97), duke of Gandia B-367

Borgia, Lucrezia (1480–1519), duchess of Ferrara B-367
Borgia, Rodrigo. *see in index* Alexander VI
Borglum, Gutzon (1867–1941), U.S. sculptor
 Mount Rushmore memorial S-324, *picture* S-321
 sculpture S-91, *picture* S-79
Borgund, Norway, village 97 mi (156 km) n.e. of Bergen.
Boric acid (or boracic acid), a mild antiseptic (H_3BO_3) containing boron; found in nature and also prepared, as crystals; prepared as crystals by adding hydrochloric or sulfuric acid to a solution of borax A-495
Boring, a machine tool operation T-222
Boring animals
 hagfish P-114, F-132, A-435, *picture* A-434
 insects
  bee B-111
  deathwatch beetle B-118
Boring tool T-222, *picture* U-68
Boris I (died 907), king of Bulgaria (852–889); abdicated to become a monk; canonized by Orthodox Church; festival celebrated May 15 B-500
Boris III (1894–1943), king of Bulgaria B-500
Boris Feodorovich Godunov (1551?–1605), Russian czar; favorite of Ivan IV; while regent for Ivan's son Theodore, recolonized Siberia, regained land from Sweden; gained throne 1598; died in uprisings in favor of first false Dmitri; subject of play by Pushkin, opera by Musorgski
 Russian history R-352
'Boris Godunov' (1874), work by Musorgski M-693
 opera O-569, *list* O-562
Borlaug, Norman Ernest (born 1914), U.S. agronomist, born in Cresco, Iowa; director of Rockefeller Foundation wheat research, Mexico, 1944–; one of fathers of green revolution. *see also in index* Green revolution
Borman, Frank (born 1928), U.S. astronaut, born in Gary, Ind.; U.S. Air Force officer selected for NASA program 1962; NASA field director for space stations 1969–70; vice-president Eastern Air Lines 1970–75, president 1975– S-346f, *table* S-348
Born, Max (1882–1970), British physicist, born in Breslau, Germany; became British subject 1939; Tait professor of natural philosophy University of Edinburgh 1936–53; retired 1953 and moved to West Germany ('Principles of Optics').
Borneo, island in Malay Archipelago; about 290,000 sq mi (751,100 sq km); pop. 9,000,000 B-368
 Asia, *map* A-697
  East Indies E-45
  Indonesia I-158
  Malaysia M-70
 size, comparative, *see in index* Island, *table*
 world, *map* W-297
Borneo, Indonesian (Indonesian Kalimantan, formerly Dutch Borneo, or Netherlands Borneo), the w., s., and e. parts of the island of Borneo; 208,285 sq mi (539,456 sq km); pop. 6,723,000 B-369, *map* I-166
 East Indies E-45
Borneo Red cat (or Bay cat), wild cat *Felis badia*, *table* C-215
'Born Free', book by Adamson R-112
Bornholm, island of Denmark, in Baltic sea, about 25 mi (40 km) off s. coast of Sweden; 227 sq mi (588 sq km); pop. 48,217; Rönne (pop. 13,216), capital and chief port; tourist resort; barley, oats, wheat, cattle, pigs; fishing, smoking of herring, *maps* E-360, S-524
Bornite (or erubescite), a copper-iron sulfide, mined in British Isles and United States; iridescent color; chemical formula Cu_5FeS_4 M-432
Borodin, Aleksandr Porfirevich (1834–87), Russian composer, born in St. Petersburg; a chemist by profession, took up music as hobby (orchestral works, opera, songs, string quartets)
 classical music M-674
Boron (B), chemical element. *see also in index* Boric acid
 abrasives A-13
 aluminum alloys A-321
 glassmaking G-157
 periodic table, *table* P-207, *list* P-208
 semiconductor's use C-799
 Turkey's production T-319
Borotra, Jean (born 1898), French tennis player
 tennis T-107
Borough, a municipal corporation forming a separate village or town or a part of a large city
 New York City N-270
 United Kingdom U-18
Borovansky, Edouard (born 1902), Czech dancer A-801
Borromini, Francesco (or Francesco Castelli) (1599–1667), Italian architect and sculptor B-370
 Bernini's assistant A-557, *picture* A-558
 fountain F-334
 Rome R-255
Borron, Robert de (fl. 1200), French poet
 Holy Grail H-207
Borrowing, a means of obtaining revenue T-34
 national debt N-24
Bors, Sir, one of knights of Round Table R-299a
Borsch (or borscht), Russian soup R-330d
Borsippa (ancient city, now Birs-Nimrud), Iraq, 15 mi (25 km) s.w. of Babylon; sometimes called Babylon II; its patron deity was Nebo
 ziggurat P-543
'Borstal Boy', work by Behan I-328
Borthwick, Harry Alfred (1898–1974), U.S. botanist, born in Otsego, Minn.; with U.S. Department of Agriculture 1936–71; principal plant physiologist Agricultural Research Service 1951–68 P-374, *picture* P-372
Borzol, dog, *picture* D-199
Bosch, (Gaviño) Juan (born 1909), Dominican political leader and writer, born in La Vega; founded literary group 'Las Cuevas'; founded Dominican Revolutionary party 1939; president Feb.–Sept. 1963; lived in exile many years
 Caribbean literature C-166
Bosch, Hieronymus (1450?–1516), Dutch painter B-370
 The Netherlands N-126
 'Vision of Tondalys' P-31, *picture* P-33
Bose, Subhas Chandra (1897–1945), Indian patriot B-371
Bosnia and Herzegovina (or Bosnia and Hercegovina), part of Yugoslavia; nearly 20,000 sq mi (51,800 sq km); pop. 3,277,948
 Austria-Hungary annexes A-831
 Balkan wars B-31
 World War I W-302
 Yugoslavia Y-436
Boson (or vector meson), one of three main classes of subatomic particles A-750, *table* A-754
 matter M-230
 nuclear energy N-421
 nuclear physics N-432
 quark Q-5
Bosporus, strait 18 mi (29 km) long between Sea of Marmara and Black Sea B-371, *map* E-360
 bridge B-371
 Thrace T-175
 Turkey T-319
Bosporus University. *see in index* Robert College
Bossier City, La., city on Red River, opposite Shreveport; oil center; cotton, soybeans, cattle; chemicals, playground equipment; Barksdale Air Force Base; pop. 50,817.
Bossuet, Jacques-Bénigne (1627–1704), French preacher; bishop of Meaux and tutor to son of Louis XIV; considered one of world's greatest pulpit orators
 philosophy of history H-173
Boston, Mass., state capital and largest city of state; pop. 562,994 B-371, *maps* N-350, U-41
 Boston Braves B-89
 Boston Massacre R-167
 Boston Tea Party. *see in index* Boston Tea Party
 climatic region, *map* U-119
 firsts
  paint mill P-76
  privately owned waterworks W-92
 harbor
  tides O-488
 Massachusetts M-191, 202, *pictures* M-188, 199
 Museum of Fine Arts
  Bodhisattva
   Avalokiteshvara, *picture* S-78
  Copley's 'Paul Revere' P-49, *picture* P-48
 playgrounds P-125
 Revere's ride R-161
 Stamp Act, *picture* R-163
 Winthrop founds W-244
 wool W-291
 world, *map* W-297
Boston Bay, inlet of Massachusetts Bay M-189
Boston bluefish. *see in index* Pollack
Boston City Hall, in Boston, Mass.
 interior design I-246
Boston Common, park in Boston, Mass.; first city park in U.S. B-373, P-125
'Boston Gazette', early newspaper published by James Franklin N-236
Boston Globe-Horn Book, U.S. literary award L-240
'Bostonians, The', work by Henry James J-20
Boston ivy. *see in index* Japanese ivy
Boston Marathon, race M-131, T-244
Boston Massacre, riot caused by friction between British troops and North American patriots March 5, 1770; Crispus Attucks, an escaped slave, was the first man to be killed R-167
 Adams A-33
 Massachusetts M-195
Boston Mountains, a southern range of the Ozarks, in n.w. Arkansas O-624, *map* U-58
 Oklahoma O-522
Boston Naval Shipyard. *see in index* Charlestown Navy Yard
'Boston News-Letter', first regularly published North American newspaper N-236
Boston Pops Orchestra, U.S. musical group
 Fiedler F-77
Boston Port Bill, one of the Coercive Acts passed by British Parliament (1774) after Boston Tea Party; closed port, removed seat of government to Salem, and demanded reparation R-164
Boston Post Road, early highway between New York, N.Y., and Boston, Mass. R-221, *map* R-219
 Massachusetts M-192
Boston Public Latin School, in Boston, Mass.; first public school in U.S. B-374
Boston Public Library, in Boston, Mass.
 Sargent's paintings S-49, *picture* P-509
 storytelling S-461
Boston School Committee
 educational contribution E-90
Boston Tea Party R-164
 Continental Congress C-692
 Revere R-161
Boston terrier, dog, *picture* D-206
Boswell, James (1740–95), Scottish biographer and diarist B-376
 art of conversation C-695, *picture* C-694
 biography standards B-222
 Johnson J-136
 literary contribution E-272
Bosworth Field, Leicestershire, England, site of final battle of Wars of the Roses 1485 R-203
 English history E-243
 warfare, *list* W-14
Botanical garden and arboretum B-377
 museum M-661
Botany, the study of plant life B-379. *see also in index* Ecology; Plants; and chief subjects listed below
 biology B-230
 botanical garden staff B-378
 classification/taxonomy L-25, L-231, P-370
 flowerless plants P-370
 plants P-368
 research
  radioactive isotopes N-428
 roots R-290, *pictures* R-291
 sciences S-64a
 seaweed S-104
 seeds S-106
 spores S-395, *picture* S-396
 trees T-276
Botany Bay, inlet on e. coast of Australia, near Sydney; so named by Captain Cook (1770) because of richness of vegetation, *map* A-819
'Botchan' (1906), work by Natsume N-67
Botfly I-221, *picture* I-224
Botha, Louis (1862–1919), South African military leader and statesman, born near Greytown, Natal; became commander in chief of Boer forces in Boer War 1900; first prime minister of Transvaal 1907; first prime minister of Union of South Africa 1910–19; worked closely with Smuts S-220
 statue, *picture* S-267
Botha, P.W. (born 1916), South African political leader, born in Orange Free State; elected to parliament 1948; entered cabinet 1961; prime minister 1978–84; pushed through constitution admitting Asians and Coloureds to parliament 1984; president 1984– .
Bothnia, Gulf of, arm of Baltic Sea, between Finland and Sweden, *maps* E-360, S-524, W-297
Bothwell, James Hepburn, earl of (1536?–78), Scottish noble, powerful and dissolute; 3rd husband of Mary, Queen of Scots; escaped to Denmark, later was imprisoned there and died insane M-165
Botlek, shipping and industrial complex at Rotterdam R-299
 harbors and ports H-36
Bo tree (or bodhi tree), species of wild fig sacred to Buddhists
 Buddha B-480
 tree T-282
Botswana, Republic of (formerly Bechuanaland Protectorate), nation in s. Africa; 224,600 sq mi (581,700 sq km); cap. Gaberone; pop. 936,000 B-382, *maps* A-115, S-264
 African political unit, *table* A-112
 Commonwealth membership C-602
 flag, *picture* F-162
 world, *map* W-297
Botta, Paul Émile (1802–70), French archaeologist, born in Turin, Italy; physician to Mehemet Ali of Egypt; made notable archaeological discoveries in Assyria A-532
Botta's pocket gopher, rodent *Thomomys bottae*, *picture* G-194
Böttger, Johann Friedrich (or Johann Friedrich Böttiger) (1682–1719), German potter, born in Schleiz, near Plauen; made first European porcelain P-475, *picture* P-469
Botticelli, Sandro (originally Alessandro di Filipepi) (1444–1510), Florentine painter B-382
 'Abundance' D-252, *picture* D-253
 'Portrait of a Youth' P-23
 'Primavera', *picture* M-695
 'The Last Communion of St. Jerome', *picture* D-111
Botticelli, word game W-293
Bottineau, N.D., city near Canadian border, 57 mi (92 km) n.e. of Minot; resort; timber; wheat, corn, potatoes; pop. 2,760.
Bottle gentian (or closed gentian), plant *Gentiana andrewsii* of the family Gentianaceae.
Bottle gourd. *see in index* Calabash gourd
Bottle-nosed dolphin D-224
Bottle-nosed whale, mammal of the genus *Berardins* W-186
Bottles
 glass manufacture G-155, *picture* G-158
 plastics P-382
Bottle tree. *see in index* Sterculia family
Botulinum toxin, most poisonous substance P-411
Botulism, poisoning caused by food infected by *Clostridium botulinum*; affects central nervous system P-411
 antitoxin A-495
Botwood, Newf., town on Bay of Exploits, 160 mi (260 km) n.w. of St. John's; shipping port for newsprint from Grand Falls and for ore from Buchans; pop. 4,277.
Boucher, François (1703–70), painter and engraver, born in Paris
 Watteau W-110

HEAVYWEIGHT CHAMPIONS OF THE WORLD

Champion	Lost Title to
Sullivan, John L. (1882–92)	James J. Corbett
Corbett, James J. (1892–97)	Bob Fitzsimmons
Fitzsimmons, Bob (1897–99)	James J. Jeffries
Jeffries, James J. (1899–1905)	Resigned title
Burns, Tommy (1906–08)	Jack Johnson
Johnson, Jack (1908–15)	Jess Willard
Willard, Jess (1915–19)	Jack Dempsey
Dempsey, Jack (1919–26)	Gene Tunney
Tunney, Gene (1926–28)	Retired undefeated
Schmeling, Max (1930–32)	Jack Sharkey
Sharkey, Jack (1932–33)	Primo Carnera
Carnera, Primo (1933–34)	Max Baer
Baer, Max (1934–35)	James J. Braddock
Braddock, James J. (1935–37)	Joe Louis
Louis, Joe (1937–49)	Resigned title
Charles, Ezzard (1949–51)	Joe Walcott
Walcott, Joe (1951–52)	Rocky Marciano
Marciano, Rocky (1952–56)	Retired undefeated
Patterson, Floyd (1956–59)	Ingemar Johansson
Johansson, Ingemar (1959–60)	Floyd Patterson
Patterson, Floyd (1960–62)	Sonny Liston
Liston, Sonny (1962–64)	Cassius Clay
Clay, Cassius* (1964–67)	Title withdrawn
Ellis, Jimmy (1968–70)	Joe Frazier
Frazier, Joe (1970–73)	George Foreman
Foreman, George (1973–74)	Muhammad Ali (Cassius Clay)
Ali, Muhammad (1974–78)	Leon Spinks
Spinks, Leon† (1978)	Muhammad Ali
Norton, Ken‡ (1978)	Larry Holmes
Holmes, Larry‡ (1978–83)	Resigned title
Ali, Muhammad (1978–79)	Resigned title
Tate, John (1979–80)	Mike Weaver
Weaver, Mike (1980–82)	Michael Dokes
Dokes, Michael (1982–83)	Gerrie Coetzee
Coetzee, Gerrie (1983–84)	Greg Page
Holmes, Larry§ (1983–85)	Michael Spinks
Witherspoon, Tim‡ (1984)	Pinklon Thomas
Page, Greg (1984–85)	Tony Tubbs
Thomas, Pinklon‡ (1984–86)	Trevor Berbick
Tubbs, Tony (1985–86)	Tim Witherspoon
Tim Witherspoon (1986–)	
Spinks, Michael§ (1985–)	
Trevor Berbick‡ (1986–)	

*Title recognition withdrawn by WBA.
†Title recognition withdrawn by WBC.
‡WBC heavyweight titleholder.
§Designated IBF titleholder.

Massachusetts M-188
'Mayflower' M-239
writings A-341

Bradford, England, city in Yorkshire, 30 mi (50 km) n.e. of Manchester; coal and iron; center of worsted industry; hundreds of textile mills; wool buying from Australia and South America; 2,000 acres (800 hectares) of parks and open spaces; pop. 280,691 B-393, *map* U-18a

Bradford, Pa., industrial and railroad city near n. boundary of state, 75 mi (120 km) e. of Erie; in oil and natural-gas fields; oil production, electronics; steel products, resistors, cigarette lighters; pop. 11,211, *map* P-184

Bradley, Francis Herbert (1846–1924), British philosopher, born in London; made valuable contribution to absolute idealism ('Ethical Studies'; 'Appearance and Reality'; 'Collected Essays') P-266

Bradley, Omar Nelson (1893–1981), U.S. Army officer, born in Clark, Mo.; commanded victorious drive of U.S. 2nd Corps into Bizerte, Tunisia, 1943; senior commander U.S. ground forces in Europe 1944–45; administrator of veterans' affairs 1945–47; U.S. Army chief of staff 1948–49; chairman of the Joint Chiefs of Staff 1949–53; made general (5-star) of the Army 1950; retired 1953, *picture* E-136
Missouri M-494
World War II W-337, 340, *picture* W-334

Bradley, William Warren (nickname Bill) (born 1943), professional basketball player; U.S. senator from N.J. 1978– B-100

Bradman, Don (full name Donald George Bradman) (born 1908), Australian cricket player B-393

Brady, Diamond Jim (nickname of James Buchanan Brady) (1856–1917), U.S. railroad magnate B-393

Brady, Mathew (1823?–96), U.S. photographer B-394
Houston, *picture* H-308
photography P-297

Bradycardia, slow heartbeat H-99

Braford, breed of cattle C-230, *picture* C-228

Braga, Portugal, city, and ancient capital of Lusitania, about 30 mi (50 km) n.e. of Oporto; archbishop of Braga is Portuguese primate; thousands make annual pilgrimage to the Church of Bom Jesus do Monte; pop. 40,977, *maps* E-360, P-455

Bragg, Braxton (1817–76), general, Confederate States of America, born in Warren County, N.C.; brother of Thomas Bragg; served in Seminole and Mexican wars; defeated Rosecrans at Chickamauga; defeated by Grant at Chattanooga C-643
Civil War C-476, 483
Confederate States of America C-644

Bragg, William Henry (1862–1942), British scientist; director of Royal Institution and of Davy-Faraday research laboratory; researches on radioactivity.

Bragg, William Lawrence (1890–1971), British physicist, born in Australia; son of Sir William Henry Bragg; professor of physics, Victoria University, Manchester, 1919–37, experimental physics Cambridge University 1938–53, chemistry Royal Institution 1953–66, director 1954–66.

Brahe, Tycho (1546–1601), Danish astronomer; created new epoch in astronomy by improvements in astronomical observation A-728
Kepler K-228

Brahma, a Hindu god H-157

Brahma, a breed of poultry P-482, *picture* P-481

Brahmagupta (598–665), Indian astronomer
mathematics M-214

Brahman, a Hindu god H-155

Brahman (or Brahman cattle). *see in index* Zebu

Brahmanas, sacred writings of Hinduism H-157
Indian literature I-105

Brahmanism I-68

Brahmaputra River, river in southern Asia, 1,800 mi (2,900 km) long, rises in s.w. Tibet; flows e. across Tibet, at e. end of Himalayas, bends s. into Assam, flows s.w. across Assam, then flows s. in Bangladesh to Ganges delta B-394
Asia, *map* A-697
Bangladesh B-61, *picture* B-60
Ganges River G-15
India, *map* I-86

Brahmin, a Hindu caste M-539

Brahms, Johannes (1833–97), German pianist and composer B-394
classical music M-673, *picture* M-674
Dvořák D-294
oratorio O-575
orchestra O-578

Braid, James (1795?–1860), British surgeon, born in Scotland; made scientific investigations of mesmerism; wrote on hypnotism
hypnosis H-344

Braiding, method for interlacing yarns to create fabric; also used in hairstyles B-395
basketry B-103
hairdressing H-9
textiles T-139

Braila, Romania, city on Danube River, 105 mi (170 km) n.e. of Bucharest; grain-shipping port, railroad center; flour, furniture, textiles, metal products; important in conflicts of Turks and Russians; pop. 113,178. *map* E-360

Braille, Louis (1809?–52), French educator and organist B-396

Braille, system of writing by and for the blind B-396
Keller K-196
language L-36
new techniques B-312

Brain B-397
aging A-125
amnesia A-373
anatomy A-392
bioengineering B-204
biofeedback response B-216
damage and disorders. *see also in index* Cerebral palsy; Epilepsy; Mental illness; Multiple sclerosis; Stroke
coma C-595
paresis V-273
death D-49
electroencephalograph P-313
embryology E-200
eye E-389
blindness B-312
fish F-126
frog F-407
hand H-26
hormones H-244
learning L-105
habituation H-3
mammal M-79
memory M-294
nervous system N-118
pain pathway A-412
sleep and dreams S-216
surgery, *picture* S-519d
X rays X-403

Brain coral, type of coral C-714

Brainerd, Minn., city on Mississippi River, 110 mi (180 km) n.w. of St. Paul and near geographic center of state; trade center; railroad shops; iron mining nearby in Cuyuna Range; state hospital; gateway to lake and resort region; pop. 11,489, *map* U-41

Brain stem, anatomy B-398

Braintree, Mass., 10 mi (16 km) s. of Boston; electrical machinery, rubber, paper, and metal products, glass; settled 1634; pop. of township 36,337
Adams' home, *picture* A-34

Brainwashing, forcible method of indoctrination used to change social, political, or religious beliefs B-404

Braise, in cooking C-700

Braithwaite, E(dward) R(icardo) (born 1912), Guyanan diplomat, teacher, and writer, born in Georgetown; representative from Guyana to UN 1967–68; ambassador to Venezuela 1968–69 ('To Sir, With Love', won Anisfield-Wolf award 1961; 'A Kind of Homecoming'; 'Paid Servant'; 'Reluctant Neighbors') R-111h

Brake (or bracken), fern, *diagram* F-56

Brake B-404
automobile S-11, A-854
hydraulics H-340
bicycle B-188
elevator E-186
machine M-10
mechanics M-264
parachute P-109a
railway train R-79
Westinghouse W-162

Brakhage, Stan (born 1933), underground film-maker, born in Kansas City, Mo.M-625

Bramah, Joseph (1748–1814), British engineer, born in Stainborough, Yorkshire; invented Bramah lock 1784 and hydraulic press 1795.

Bramante, Donato (1444–1514), Italian architect B-405
Renaissance church A-553, *picture* A-556

Brampton, Ont., town 18 mi (29 km) w. of Toronto; flower growing; motor vehicles, footwear, paper products, furniture, optical goods; pop. 149,030, *map* C-112

Bran (or seed coat), husks of grain
corn C-722
flour and flour milling F-212
wheat W-192

Brancacci Chapel, part of the Church of the Carmine in Florence, Italy
frescoes M-184

Branch (or tributary), river system R-210

Branch operation (or subsidiary), retail trade F-373

Brancusi, Constantin (1876–1957), Romanian sculptor B-406
sculpture S-92

Brand, Hennig (or Hennig Brandt) (died 1692?), German alchemist, born in Hamburg; in 1669 discovered the element phosphorus, obtaining it by distilling urine; sold his secret to Johann Drafft of Dresden, who went to many countries and exhibited phosphorus, in 1677 performing experiments with it before the Royal Society in England P-271

Brand, Vance D. (born 1931), U.S. astronaut, born in Longmont, Colo.; test pilot for Lockheed; chosen for NASA program 1966, crew member Apollo-Soyuz project, *table* S-348

Brand, cattle ranching
cowboy C-751, *picture* C-754

'Brand', play by Ibsen I-5

Brandeis, Louis D. (full name Louis Dembitz Brandeis) (1856–1941), U.S. jurist B-406
Hall of Fame, *table* H-16

Brandenburg, former state in Soviet zone, Germany; 10,416 sq mi (26,977 sq km); included w. part of former Prussian province of Brandenburg (e. part of that province had gone to Poland 1945)
Berlin B-168
Germany, *map* G-131
Hohenzollern H-200
Prussia P-516

Brandenburg Gate, gate in East Berlin, East Germany B-168, *map* B-170

Brandes, Heinrich, German scientist
weather W-121

Brand manager, advertising A-60

Brand name, in marketing M-142

Brando, Marlon (born 1924), U.S. actor, born in Omaha, Neb. ('A Streetcar Named Desire', stage and screen versions; motion pictures: 'The Men', 'Julius Caesar', 'On the Waterfront', for which he won 1954 Academy award, 'Sayonara', 'Mutiny on the Bounty', 'The Night of the Following Day', 'The Godfather', for which he won 1972 Academy award but refused to accept as protest against plight of American Indians, 'Last Tango in Paris', 'Apocalypse Now') A-27, *pictures*, L-243, S-140

Brandon, Man., city on Assiniboine River, 125 mi (200 km) w. of Winnipeg; meat-packing plants, flour mills, oil refinery; metal products; Brandon University; annual agricultural exhibit; pop. 36,242 M-102, *maps* C-109, N-350

Brandon University, university, Winnipeg, Man. M-102

Brandt, Hennig. *see in index* Brand, Hennig

Brandt, Willy (formerly Herbert Ernst Karl Frahm) (born 1913), West German political leader B-407
West Germany G-126

Brandy, alcoholic beverage
alcohol distillation A-276
liquor production L-235

Brandywine, former village, now part of Wilmington, Del.

Brandywine River (or Brandywine Creek), tributary of Delaware River in Pa. and Del.; scene of battle in Revolutionary War (Sept. 11, 1777) in which Howe defeated Washington, leaving way open to Philadelphia D-78, *picture* D-80

Branford, Conn., 6 mi (10 km) s.e. of New Haven, on Long Island Sound; automotive products, wire, power fasteners; settled 1644; pop. of township 23,363.

Brangus, breed of cattle C-230, *picture* C-228

Brant, Joseph (or Thayendanegea) (1742–1807), Mohawk chief; educated Eleazar Wheelock's Indian school; lifelong member Episcopal church; translated English Prayer Book into Mohawk language; aided British in Revolutionary War (Cherry Valley Massacre) but after the war strove for peace between colonists and Indians.

Brant, a kind of goose D-285, *picture* D-287

Brantford, Ont., city 55 mi (90 km) s.w. of Toronto, on Grand River; machinery, textiles, electrical products, paints, roofing; named for Joseph Brant; here Alexander Graham Bell perfected telephone; pop. 74,315, *map* C-112

Branting, Karl Hjalmar (1860–1925), first Socialist prime minister of Sweden 1920, again 1921, born in Stockholm; leading advocate Wilson peace program and League of Nations.

Braque, Georges (1882–1963), French painter B-407
enameling E-208
'Interior with Table' P-26
Picasso P-314

Brasília, Brazil, capital, on plateau in interior; pop. of city 411,305; of Federal district 1,203,333 B-408
Brazil B-418, *maps* B-425, S-298
world, *map* W-297

Braşov (formerly Stalin), Romania, city 85 mi (140 km) n.w. of Bucharest; metal products, textiles; "Black Church" (14th century); pop. 129,615.

Brass, an alloy of copper and zinc B-410
ancient use P-327
Bessemer's pigment B-178
button type, *picture* B-529
copper C-710
furniture F-452
nonferrous alloys A-313
pins P-327
zinc Z-455

Brass, wind instruments M-687, W-229, *picture* M-688
orchestra O-576
trumpet S-193

Brassica chinensis. *see in index* Pak-choi

Brassica napobrassica. *see in index* Rutabaga

Brassica napus. *see in index* Rape plant

Brassica oleracea, cabbage group of plants, includes kale, collard, cauliflower, broccoli, head cabbage, brussel sprouts, and kohlrabi C-2

Brassica pekinensis. *see in index* Celery cabbage

Brassica rapa. *see in index* Turnip

Brasstown Bald Mountain, mountain in Georgia; highest point (4,784 ft; 1,458 m) in n.e. corner of the state B-319

Bratislava (formerly Pressburg), Czechoslovakia, trade and industrial city, on Danube River, 35 mi (55 km) e. of Vienna; capital of Hungary 1541–1784; pop. 401,383, *map* E-360
Czechoslovakia C-813, *map* C-814

Brattain, Walter Houser (born 1902), U.S. physicist, born in Amoy, China, of U.S. parents; research physicist Bell Telephone Laboratories 1929–41, 1943–67
electronics E-175

Brattleboro, Windham County, Vermont, on Connecticut River, 57 mi (92 km) s.e. of Rutland;

houses B-494, *picture* V-339
sand S-38

Brick Town, N.J., 6 mi (10 km) e. of Lakewood; concrete brick [illegible] township 35,057.

Bridal Cave, cave, Camdenton, Mo., *picture* C-233

Bridal Veil Falls (or Luna Falls), falls, Niagara Falls N-300

Bridalveil Fall, falls, Yosemite National Park, California, *pictures* C-46, W-95

Bridal wreath (spirea) S-392

'Bride of Lammermoor, The', novel by Sir Walter Scott, published 1819; heroine, Lucy Ashton, who loves the master of Ravenswood, is compelled to marry the laird of Bucklaw but becomes insane, stabs her husband on wedding night, and dies.

Bride of the Adriatic, Italy. *see in index* Venice

Bridewell, prison in London, England P-505c

Bridge B-439. *see also in index* types of bridges and names of various bridges
building S-254f
great bridges. *see table* following
mechanical drawing M-255

Bridge, card game. *see in index* Contract bridge

Bridge, raised transverse platform on a ship S-497, *diagram* S-499

'Bridge of San Luis Rey, The', novel by Wilder R-112d

Bridge of Sighs, covered bridge in Venice, Italy; so called because condemned prisoners formerly passed over it from the judgment hall to place of execution V-277, *picture* V-278

Bridgeport, Conn., largest city in state, on Long Island Sound; pop. 142,546 B-448
circus history C-432
Connecticut C-651, *maps* C-654, 662, *pictures* C-650, C-657
United States U-41

Bridger, Jim (or James Bridger) (1804–81), U.S. fur trapper and scout B-448
Great Salt Lake, *picture* U-221
Wyoming W-390

Bridges, Henry Styles (1898–1961), U.S. public official, born in West Pembroke, Me.; governor of New Hampshire 1935–37; U.S. senator 1937–61.

Bridges, Robert (1844–1930), British poet, poet laureate 1913–30; at 38 abandoned medicine for literature; verse scholarly and of high quality; 'The Testament of Beauty', his last work, published on 85th birthday, is a philosophical poem in 4 books ('Achilles in Scyros', 'The Christian Captives', poetic dramas; 'Milton's Prosody', criticism)
Hopkins H-238
literary contribution E-280
poet laureate P-402

Bridgeton, Mo., town situated 4 mi (6 km) s.e. of St. Charles, in St. Louis metropolitan area; pop. 18,445.

Bridgeton, N.J., city in s.w. part of state, on Cohansey River, near Delaware Bay; food processing; glass products, textiles, clothing, machinery; pop. 18,795.

Bridgetown, Barbados, capital; pop. 7,552 B-78
West Indies, *map* W-159

Bridgeview, Ill., residential village 13 mi (21 km) s.w. of Chicago; incorporated 1947; pop. 14,155
Illinois, *map* I-52

Bridgewater Canal, canal in England C-127

Bridgman, Percy Williams (1882–1961), U.S. physicist, born in Cambridge, Mass.; taught at Harvard University 1910–54.

Bridle, riding equipment H-264, *diagram* H-265

Brie, district of France between Seine and Marne rivers.

Brief, in law
legal definition, *table* L-92

Brienne-le-Château, France, town 23 mi (37 km) n.e. of Troyes, on Aube River; indecisive battle between Blücher and Napoleon 1814; Napoleon studied at military school (suppressed 1790) pop. 2,566.

Brienz, Lake, lake in Switzerland, in canton of Bern; expansion of Aare River; about 9 mi (15 km) long and 1½ mi (2½ km) wide, *map* S-537

Brig, in ship, *picture* S-166

Brigach River, a Danube headstream, 25 mi (40 km) long, in s. part of West Germany; rises in Black Forest, in state of Baden-Württemberg, flows past Villingen and joins Brege River near Donaueschingen to form Danube River D-33

Brigade, U.S. Army, formerly unit of 3,400 to 6,900 men; abolished with coming of triangular division after World War I; in World War II and Korean War, term applied to task force organized for special mission; revived in 1961 as tactical unit with headquarters, administrative, and combat support sections plus two to five combat battalions A-634

Brigadier general
U.S. Air Force, insignia, *picture* U-8
U.S. Army A-634, insignia, *picture* U-8
U.S. Marine Corps, insignia, *picture* U-8

Brigantine, a ship, *picture* S-166

Briggs, Clare (1875–1930), U.S. cartoonist, born in Reedsburg, Wis.; among his best-known series were 'Skin-nay', 'The Days of Real Sport', 'When a Feller Needs a Friend', 'Ain't It a Grand and Glorious Feeling', and 'Mr. and Mrs.'

Briggs, Henry (1561–1630), English mathematician, born in Warley Wood; proposed decimal logarithmic system in use today (Briggsian, or common, logarithms); calculated logarithmic tables ('Arithmetica Logarithmica'; 'Trigonometria Britannica') A-595

Brigham City (also Brigham, formerly Box Elder), Utah, city 20 mi (30 km) n. of Ogden; food processing; peaches, beet sugar; woolens, motor homes; nearby is U.S.-sponsored Bear River Migratory Bird Refuge; renamed 1856 to honor Brigham Young; pop. 15,596, *maps* U-232, U-40

Bright, Charles Tilston (1832–88), English engineer, born in London; chief of Atlantic Telegraphy Company, which laid first transatlantic cable
communication cables C-10

Bright, John (1811–89), English statesman and orator B-448

Brightener (or optical bleach), bleaching agent B-311

Bright line spectrum S-371, *diagram* S-372

Bright nebula, astronomy A-722

Brightness (or luminance), the quality or state of being luminous T-76

Brighton, bayside resort, Melbourne, Australia M-290

Brighton, England, popular seaside resort on English Channel, 50 mi (80 km) s. of London; emerged from obscurity as fishing village after visits by George IV (then Prince of Wales) made it popular as a resort; pop. 163,600 T-271, *map* U-18a

Brilliant (or rhinestone), imitation gem J-116

Brilliant cut, a gem cut D-130, *pictures* D-129, J-116

Brimstone, sulfur S-509

Brindisi (ancient Brundisium), Italy, chief Roman seaport on Adriatic; now a commune; pop. 70,657, *maps* E-360, I-401

Brine, sodium compound used for water softening W-91

Brinegar, Claude Stout (born 1926), Union oil executive, born in Rockport, Calif. N-327

Brine shrimp, crustacean of the class Branchiopoda C-789
Great Salt Lake G-251

Brink, Carol Ryrie (born 1895), U.S. author, born in Moscow, Idaho; won Newbery medal (1936) for 'Caddie Woodlawn' (books for children, 'Magical Melons', 'Family Grandstand', 'The Highly Trained Dogs of Professor Petit', 'Family Sabbatical'; for adults, 'The Headland', novel).

Brink's Inc., armored car service; founded 1859; serves United States, Canada, and other countries; headquarters, Chicago, Ill.; often robbed in mid-20th century.

Brisbane, Australia, capital of Queensland, on Brisbane River, 25 mi (40 km) above mouth; pop. 702,500 B-449
Australia A-767, *map* A-819, *picture* A-787
Pacific Ocean, *map* P-3
Queensland Q-16
world, *map* W-297

Brisé fan F-22

Bristlecone pine, a tree *Pinus aristata* of mountain regions from California to Colorado; bush-topped, to 50 ft (15 m) tall; sometimes shrublike, *pictures* L-101, T-277

Bristles
brushes B-464
pig P-320

Bristol, Conn., city about 15 mi (25 km) s.w. of Hartford; ball bearings, precision springs, metal products; famous as clock center since 18th century; pop. 57,370, *maps* C-654, 662
oldest U.S. amusement park A-385

Bristol, England, city 8 mi (13 km) from Bristol Channel, pop. 387,977 B-449, *maps* E-360, U-18a
trade center A-332

Bristol, Pa., borough on Delaware River, 20 mi (30 km) n.e. of Philadelphia; metal products, chemicals, textiles; pop. 10,867, *map* P-185

Bristol, R.I., on Narragansett Bay, 13 mi (21 km) s.e. of Providence; yachting center; fish and shellfish industries, yacht building; textiles; partly destroyed during Revolutionary War; site was once home of American Indian chief King Philip; pop. of township 20,128 [illegible]

Bristol, Tenn. and Va., two contiguous cities near n.e. corner of Tennessee; textiles; electronic equipment, calculating machines, chemicals, foods; King College (Tennessee); pop. (Tennessee) 23,986; (Virginia) 19,042, *maps* U-41, V-330, 348
Tennessee T-85, *map* T-97

Bristol Bay, inlet of Bering Sea n. of Alaska Peninsula, *maps* N-350, U-39, 94

Bristol Channel, arm of Atlantic between s. Wales and s.w. England.

Britain (Latin name Britannia), English form of ancient name of England, Scotland, and Wales, now sometimes applied to all of British Isles. *see in index* England; Great Britain; United Kingdom

Britain, battle of (1940), *list* W-14
United Kingdom E-257
World War II W-324, 339

Britannia Tubular Bridge, Menai Strait, Wales B-446

British Academy of Film and Television Arts, motion pictures M-627

British army. *see in index* Army, British

British Broadcasting Corporation (BBC) R-54
orchestra O-578
United Kingdom E-237
television T-73

British Cameroons. *see in index* Cameroons

British Columbia, westernmost province of Can.; 366,255 mi (948,596 sq km); cap. Victoria; pop. 2,687,000 B-450, C-81, *maps* C-109, N-350
cities. *see also in index* cities listed below and other cities by name
Vancouver V-263, *map* V-264
Victoria V-310
floral emblem B-329
history C-101
minerals V-265, C-80
mountains
Rockies R-234, *map* R-234a
Trans-Canada Highway T-248

British Columbia, University of, university in Vancouver, B.C.; provincial control; founded 1908, opened 1915; arts and science, agriculture, applied science, commerce, dentistry, education, forestry, law, medicine, pharmacy; graduate studies B-455, *map* V-264

British Commonwealth of Nations. *see in index* Commonwealth, The

British East India Company. *see in index* East India Company

British Empire, C-599, E-246, *map* C-600. *see also in index* England
colonialism and imperialism C-556
countries
Cameroon C-66
tea tradition T-45

British Empire, Order of the, order of knighthood founded by George V 1917; military and civil divisions created 1918; awards for men and women
medals M-270

British European Airways (BEA, now merged with BOAC as British Airways) A-170

British Guiana. *see in index* Guyana, Republic of

British Honduras. *see in index* Belize

British Imperial System (often called customary system), system of weights and measures [illegible], *diagram* W-139

British India. *see also in index* India

British Indian Ocean Territory, created 1965 from strategic islands scattered across w. Indian Ocean; consists of the islands of the Chagos Archipelago; included Aldabra Islands, Farquhar Islands, and Desroches Island until 1976
African political unit, *table* A-112
Asia, *map* A-697
Commonwealth membership C-602
world, *map* W-297

British Institute of Public Opinion G-6

British Isles, name popularly applied to United Kingdom, Channel Islands, Ireland, Isle of Man, Hebrides, Orkney Islands, Shetland Islands, and Isle of Wight B-460, *map* E-360. *see also in index* islands by name

British Museum, museum in London, England; established 1753 by government purchase of the collection and library of Sir Hans Sloane; noted for classical antiquities, medieval and oriental arts L-293, *map* L-289
archaeological work A-534
Egyptian collection, *picture* E-232
museum M-661, 663
Shakespeare collection S-140

British Nationality Act, law regarding British citizenship; first enacted in 1949, revised in 1983 C-442

British New Guinea. *see in index* Papua, Territory of

British North America Act (1867)
Canada C-77, 86, 100
Parliament P-132

British Open, golf tournament
golf G-191

British Open, tennis tournament
tennis T-108

British Somaliland. *see in index* Somaliland Protectorate

British South Africa Company
Zambia Z-448

British Tariff Act (1932) T-30

British thermal unit (BTU) F-441
heat H-104

British Union (or Union Flag, or Union Jack), flag of the United Kingdom.

Britons (or Brythons), people E-238

Brittany (French Bretagne), historic province of n.w. France
agriculture F-344, 353

Brittany spaniel, dog, *picture* D-198

Britten, Benjamin (1913–76), British composer B-462
music
band music B-55
classical M-675
opera O-569

Brittle stars, a type of starfish S-425

Brittle willow (or crack willow), tree *Salix fragilis* of Salicaceae family W-211

Brno, Czechoslovakia, city in Moravia, 70 mi (110 km) n. of Vienna; woolen manufactures; university; history dates back to 9th century; pop. 380,871, *map* E-360
Czechoslovakia C-813, *map* C-814

BRIDGES MOST NOTABLE IN THE WORLD

(Bridges are listed in order of length of main span. Total length includes causeways and/or approaches where applicable.)

SUSPENSION BRIDGES

Name	Location	Main Span Length (Feet)	Total Length (Feet)	Height above Water (Feet)	Traffic	Year Opened	Cost
Verrazano-Narrows	Narrows, Brooklyn—Staten Island, New York City	4,260	13,200	228	H	1964	$325,000,000
Golden Gate	Golden Gate (strait), San Francisco, Calif.	4,200	9,266	220	H	1937	35,000,000
Mackinac	Straits of Mackinac, St. Ignace—Mackinaw City, Mich.	3,800	26,444	148	H	1957	99,800,000
Bosporus	Bosporus Strait, Turkey	3,524	5,118	210	H	1973	33,400,000
George Washington	Hudson River, New York City—Fort Lee, N.J.	3,500	8,700	204	H	1931	60,000,000
Salazar	Tagus River, Lisbon, Portugal	3,323	10,575	246	H	1966	75,000,000
Firth of Forth	Firth of Forth, Scotland	3,300	8,244	150	H	1964	46,200,000
Severn	Severn River, Bristol, England	3,240	5,240	. . .	H	1966	16,800,000
Tacoma Narrows	Puget Sound, Tacoma, Wash.	2,800	5,450	184	H	1950	18,000,000
Kanmon	Kanmon Strait, Japan	2,350	3,525	201	H	UC	80,000,000
Angostura	Orinoco River, Venezuela	2,336	5,507	131	H	1967	18,500,000
San Francisco-Oakland Bay (Transbay)*	San Francisco Bay via Yerba Buena Island, San Francisco—Oakland, Calif.	2,310	43,560	214	H-RT	1936	77,200,000
Bronx-Whitestone	East River, Bronx—Queens, New York City	2,300	3,770	142	H	1939	18,000,000
Pierre-Laporte	St. Lawrence River, Quebec City, Canada	2,190	3,412	150	H	1970	35,000,000
Delaware Memorial	Delaware River, near New Castle, Del.—Deepwater, N.J., near Wilmington, Del.	2,150	10,765½	175	H	1951	43,900,000
Delaware Memorial†	Delaware River, near New Castle, Del.—Deepwater, N.J., near Wilmington, Del.	2,150	10,765½	175	H	1968	70,000,000
Seaway Skyway	St. Lawrence River, Ogdensburg, N.Y.—Johnstown, Ont.	2,150	13,510	124	H	1960	20,000,000
Tancarville	Seine River, Tancarville, France	2,000	4,592	168	H	1959	11,000,000
Walt Whitman	Delaware River, Philadelphia, Pa.—Gloucester City, N.J.	2,000	31,680	150	H	1957	90,000,000
Little Belt	Little Belt Channel, Denmark	1,968	3,542	. . .	H	1969	30,000,000
Ambassador	Detroit River, Detroit, Mich.—Windsor, Ont.	1,850	9,000	150	H	1929	22,500,000
Throgs Neck	East River, Bronx—Queens, New York City	1,800	12,310	142	H	1961	90,000,000
Benjamin Franklin	Delaware River, Philadelphia, Pa.—Camden, N.J.	1,750	9,620	135	H–ER	1926	41,987,886
Bear Mountain	Hudson River, near Peekskill, N.Y.	1,632	2,252	155	H	1924	6,000,000
Chesapeake Bay	Sandy Point—Kent Island, Md.	1,600	21,286	186½	H	1952	44,000,000
Newport	Narragansett Bay, Newport—Jamestown, R.I.	1,600	11,248	212	H	1969	61,000,000
Williamsburg	East River, Manhattan—Brooklyn, New York City	1,600	7,308	136	H–T–RT	1903	24,188,090
Brooklyn	East River, Manhattan—Brooklyn, New York City	1,595½	6,016	132	H	1883	25,094,577
Lions Gate	Burrard Inlet, Vancouver—North Vancouver, B.C.	1,550	2,778	200	H	1939	6,000,000
Vincent Thomas	Los Angeles Harbor, San Pedro—Terminal Island, Calif.	1,500	6,060	185	H	1963	21,000,000
Mid Hudson	Hudson River, Poughkeepsie, N.Y.	1,500	4,072	138	H	1930	6,000,000

CANTILEVER BRIDGES

Name	Location	Main Span Length (Feet)	Total Length (Feet)	Height above Water (Feet)	Traffic	Year Opened	Cost
Quebec	St. Lawrence River, Quebec, Que.	1,800	3,239	160	H–R	1917	25,000,000
Firth of Forth	New Edinburgh, Scotland	1,700	8,098	150	R	1889	16,000,000
Commodore John Berry	Delaware River, Chester, Pa.—Bridgeport, N.J.	1,644	12,418	192	H	UC	85,000,000
Greater New Orleans	Mississippi River, New Orleans, La.	1,575	12,144	150	H	1958	65,000,000
Howrah	Hooghly River, Calcutta, India	1,500	2,150	29	H–T	1942	8,500,000
San Francisco-Oakland Bay (Transbay)*	San Francisco Bay via Yerba Buena Island, San Francisco—Oakland, Calif.	1,400	43,560	185	H-RT	1936	77,200,000
Baton Rouge	Mississippi River, Baton Rouge, La.	1,235	4,550	135	H	1968	25,000,000
Tappan Zee	Tappan Zee, Tarrytown—Nyack, N.Y.	1,212	15,259	149	H	1955	65,000,000
Longview	Columbia River, Longview, Wash.—Rainier, Ore.	1,200	8,448	167	H	1930	7,200,000
Queensboro	East River, Manhattan—Queens, New York City	1,182	7,449	134	H	1909	17,591,762
Carquinez Strait	Crockett—Vallejo, Calif.	1,100	4,700	135	H	1927	8,000,000
Carquinez Strait†	Crockett—Vallejo, Calif.	1,100	4,700	135	H	1958	47,000,000
Second Narrows	Burrard Inlet, Vancouver, B.C.	1,100	4,240	—	H	1960	22,000,000
Jacques Cartier	St. Lawrence River, Montreal, Que.	1,097	8,670	150	H–R	1930	12,000,000
Richmond-San Rafael	San Francisco Bay, Richmond—San Rafael, Calif.	1,070	21,343	185	H	1956	68,000,000
World War II Memorial	Charleston, S.C.	1,050	14,374	150	H	1929	6,000,000

STEEL ARCH BRIDGES

Name	Location	Main Span Length (Feet)	Total Length (Feet)	Height above Water (Feet)	Traffic	Year Opened	Cost
Bayonne (Kill van Kull)	Kill van Kull, Staten Island, New York City—Bayonne, N.J.	1,652	8,100	150	H	1931	16,000,000
Sydney Harbor	Sydney—North Sydney, Australia	1,650	3,770	170	H–R	1932	25,000,000
Port Mann	Fraser River, near Vancouver, B.C.	1,200	6,900	. . .	H	1963	25,000,000
Thacher Ferry	Panama Canal, Balboa, Panama Canal Zone	1,128	5,425	201	H	1962	14,000,000
Widnes-Runcorn	Mersey River, Runcorn—Widnes, near Liverpool, England	1,082	1,582	. . .	H	1962	8,400,000
Birchenough	Sabi River, Rhodesia	1,080	1,080	280	H	1935	800,000
Nagasaki-Sasebo	Kyushu Island, Japan	1,042	. . .	. . .	H	1955	. . .
Glen Canyon	Colorado River, Arizona	1,028	1,271	700	H	1959	4,139,277
Lewiston-Queenston International	Niagara River, Lewiston, N.Y.—Queenston, Ont.	1,000	1,600	370	H	1962	6,850,000

*Suspension-cantilever bridge. †Second similar bridge paralleling first one. UC—Under construction. H—Highway. RT—Rapid transit. ER—Electric railway. T—Trolley. R—Railroad.

BRIDGES MOST NOTABLE IN THE WORLD

Name	Location	Main Span Length (Feet)	Total Length (Feet)	Height above Water (Feet)	Traffic	Year Opened	Cost
Hell Gate	East River, Queens—Bronx, New York City	977 ½	17,868	135	R	1917	$15,000,000
Rainbow	Niagara River, Niagara Falls, New York—Ontario	950	1,450	189	H	1941	4,000,000
Duisburg-Rheinhausen	Rhine River, West Germany	838	. . . .	. . .	H	1951	. . .
Volta River	Volta River, Adomi, Ghana	805	. . . .	200	H	1956	2,000,000
CONCRETE ARCH BRIDGES							
Gladesville	Parramatta River, Sydney Harbor, Australia	1,000	1,900	135	H	1964	5,600,000
Friendship	Paraná River, Brazil—Paraguay	952	1,812	250	H	1965	5,000,000
Arrábida	Douro River, Porto—Gaia, Portugal	886	1,617	. . .	H	1963	8,500,000
Sando	Angerman River, Sweden	866	9,840	144	H	1943	. . .
Van Staden's River	Van Staden's River, Port Elizabeth, South Africa	650	1,200	. . .	H	1971	1,800,000
Esla	Esla, Spain	645	. . .	. . .	R	1940	. . .
Antas River	Rio Grande do Sul, Brazil	612	856	92	H	1953	750,000
Plougastel (Albert Louppe)	Elorn River, Plougastel—Brest, France	612	2,952	. . .	H–R	1929	. . .
CONTINUOUS TRUSS BRIDGES							
Astoria	Columbia River, Astoria, Ore.—Megler, Wash.	1,232	21,769	205	H	1966	24,000,000
Tenmon-Kyo	Amakusa Archipelago, Japan	984	1,647	138	H	1966	1,772,120
Julien Dubuque	Mississippi River, Dubuque, Iowa—East Dubuque, Ill.	845	6,336	56	H	1943	3,250,000
Charles M. Braga	Taunton River, Fall River—Somerset, Mass.	830	5,780	135	H	1966	21,000,000
Earl C. Clements	Ohio River, Shawneetown, Ill.	825	. . .	. . .	H	1956	. . .
Kingston-Rhinecliff	Hudson River, Kingston—Rhinecliff, N.Y.	800	7,793	135	H	1957	19,000,000
Sciotoville	Ohio River, Sciotoville, Ohio—Kentucky	775	3,435	40	R	1917	1,366,000
SIMPLE TRUSS BRIDGES							
Metropolis	Ohio River, Metropolis, Ill.	720	. . .	53	R	1917	. . .
Paducah-Brookport (Irvin Cobb)	Ohio River, Paducah, Ky.—Brookport, Ill.	716	6,276	53	H	1929	1,566,000
Tanana River	Nenana, Alaska	700	. . .	45	R	1922	1,049,260
PLATE GIRDER BRIDGES							
Sava River	Sava River, Belgrade, Yugoslavia	856	1,318	. . .	H	1956	. . .
Zoo	Rhine River, Cologne, West Germany	850	4,600	123	H	1966	30,000,000
San Mateo-Hayward	San Francisco Bay, San Mateo—Hayward Calif.	750	5,500	135	H	1967	70,000,000
Düsseldorf-Neuss	Rhine River, West Germany	676	2,500	. . .	H	1951	. . .
Europabruecke	Sill River, Austria—Italy	649	2,296	623	H	1963	3,600,000
North Elbe Autobahn	Elbe River, near Hamburg, West Germany	565	1,350	. . .	H	1963	3,000,000
VERTICAL LIFT BRIDGES							
Arthur Kill (No. 212)	Arthur Kill, Richmond (Staten Island), N.Y.—New Jersey	558	1,645	135	R	1959	7,600,000
Cape Cod Canal	Buzzards Bay, Mass.	544	2,384	135	R	1935	1,800,000
Delair	Delaware River, Philadelphia-Camden area	542	4,397	135	R	1961	11,500,00
Marine Parkway	Rockaway Inlet, Brooklyn, New York City	540	4,022	150	H	1937	6,000,000
SWING SPAN BRIDGES							
El Ferdan	Suez Canal, Egypt	552	1,047	18	H–R	1965	2,811,956
Fort Madison (Santa Fe)	Mississippi River, Fort Madison, Iowa	525	3,330	7	R–H	1927	5,500,000
Willamette River	Portland, Ore.	521	. . .	144	R–H–T	1908	. . .
East Omaha	Missouri River, Omaha, Neb.—Council Bluffs, Iowa	519	1,608	12	R	1903	. . .
BASCULE BRIDGES							
Sault Ste. Marie	Sault Sainte Marie Canals, Sault Ste. Marie, Mich.	336	3,607	13	R	1941	. . .
Erie Avenue	Black River, Lorain, Ohio	333	1,430	33	H	1940	1,500,000
Chattanooga (Chief John Ross)	Tennessee River, Chattanooga, Tenn.	310	2,300	14	H	1917	1,050,000
PONTOON BRIDGES							
Hood Canal	Hood Canal, near Seattle, Wash.	600‡	7,131	. . .	H	1961	14,500,000
Kelowna	Okanagan Lake, Kelowna, B.C.	285	4,586	. . .	H	1958	. . .
Lake Washington Floating Bridge	Lake Washington, Seattle—Mercer Island, Wash.	202‡	6,561	. . .	H	1940	8,854,000
Evergreen Point	Lake Washington, Seattle—Bellevue, Wash.	200‡	7,518	. . .	H	1963	35,000,000
Hobart	Derwent River, Hobart, Tasmania, Australia	180	3,165	. . .	H	1944	1,100,000

‡Main Channel Opening. H—Highway. T—Trolley. R—Railroad.

Netherlands, and the United Kingdom N-352

Brusso, Noah. *see in index* Burns, Tommy

'Brut', metrical chronicle of Britain, one of monuments of early English language, written by the English poet and priest Layamon.

Bruttium, ancient name of Calabria, Italy. *see in index* Calabria

Brutus, Dennis (born 1924), U.S. teacher and poet; immigrated to U.S. from South Africa in 1966 A-123

Brutus, Lucius Junius, legendary Roman patriot; one of first two consuls of the republic (509 BC) R-241

Brutus, Marcus Junius (85?–42 BC), Roman republican, one of Caesar's assassins although he had been aided by Caesar; fled Rome and seized Macedonia; committed suicide when defeated at Philippi; character in Shakespeare's 'Julius Caesar' C-15

Bruxelles, Belgium. *see in index* Brussels

Bruyère, Jean de la. *see in index* La Bruyère, Jean de

Bryan, John Neely, U.S. pioneer, first white settler of Dallas, Tex.
  Dallas D-11

Bryan, William Jennings (1860–1925), U.S. political leader and editor B-472
  Cleveland C-493
  Lincoln, Neb. L-225
  McKinley M-19
  Statuary Hall, *table* S-437b

Bryan, Tex., city 80 mi (130 km) n.w. of Houston; agricultural and dairy market; aluminum, windows, furniture, business forms; Texas A & M University nearby; pop. 44,337 U-41

Bryant, Paul W. (nickname Bear) (1913–83), U.S. football coach F-296

Bryant, William Cullen (1794–1878), U.S. poet B-472
  Hall of Fame, *table* H-16
  writings A-345

Bryce, James (1838–1922), British statesman and historian B-473

Bryce Canyon National Park, park in Utah N-43, *maps* N-40, U-233, U-81, *picture* U-225

Bryn Mawr College, college in Bryn Mawr, Pa.; private control; primarily women; founded 1880, opened 1885; arts and sciences, education; graduate school coeducational P-251b

Bryology, branch of botany dealing with mosses. *see in index* Moss

Bryophyta (or bryophytes), phylum of the plant kingdom P-370

Bryozoa (or moss animals)

Brythonic languages, a group comprising Welsh, Cornish, and Breton, belonging to Celtic branch of Indo-European family.

Brythons (or Britons), people E-238

Bryusov, Valeri Yakovlevich (1873–1924), Russian writer, born in Moscow R-360a

B-scope, in radar R-32, *diagram* R-30

B.T.U. *see in index* British thermal unit

Buade, Louis de. *see in index* Frontenac, Louis de

Bubble cap, in petroleum refining P-239, *chart* P-241a

Bubble chamber, instrument for study of nuclear tracks A-323
  nuclear energy N-419

Bubble gum, a chewing gum C-307

Bubble tower, in petroleum refining P-239

Buber, Martin (1878–1965), Israeli philosopher and theologian B-473

Bubi, a people of Africa
  Equatorial Guinea E-294
  Malabo M-68

Bubka, Sergei (born 1963), Soviet athlete
  track and field T-245

Bubonic plague, infection caused by Pasteurella pestis bacteria B-473
  England E-242
  fleas F-177
  Hundred Years' War H-325
  Middle Ages M-393, *picture* M-392
  Norway N-394

Bucaramanga, Colombia, town in n., on Lebrija River; coffee, tobacco, cotton, gold, silver; pop. 491,000 C-551, *map* S-298

Bucare, tree. *see in index* Erythrina

Bucca, fairy F-12

Buccal mass (or visceral mass)
  mollusks M-523

Buccaneers, piratical adventurers of the 17th century who plundered Spaniards along coasts of West Indies and South America P-342. *see also in index* Pirates and piracy

Buccaning, method of sun-drying meat P-342

Buccinator, cheek muscle M-641

Bucephalus, favorite horse of Alexander the Great; city of Bucephala, on Hydaspes (now Jhelum) River in India, built by Alexander in his memory A-279
  famous horse, *list* H-249

Buchan, John, first **Baron Tweedsmuir** (1875–1940), Scottish writer and statesman, born in Perth; governor-general of Canada 1935–40 (novels, 'Prester John', 'The Thirty-Nine Steps', 'Greenmantle', 'Huntingtower', 'The Three Hostages', 'Mountain Meadow'; autobiography, 'Pilgrim's Way')
  literary contribution E-280
  Scott S-74

Buchanan, Cynthia (born 1937), U.S. writer
  literary contribution A-362

Buchanan, James (1791–1868), 15th president of the United States B-474
  Civil War views C-472
  Dred Scott decision D-259
  Pennsylvania, *picture* P-180
  secretary of state P-438
  United States U-179
  Young U-220

Bucharest (or Bucuresti), Romania, capital, 30 mi (50 km) n. of Danube River; pop. 1,988,610 B-477, *map* E-360
  world, *map* W-297

Bucharest, Treaty of (1913), *table* T-274
  Romania R-318
  Salonika S-29

Buchmanism. *see in index* Moral Re-Armament

Buchner, Eduard (1860–1917), German chemist, born in Munich; showed that alcoholic fermentation is caused by action of enzymes in yeast and not by yeast cells themselves.

Büchner, Georg (1813–37), German dramatist and poet, born in Goddelau, near Darmstadt; student of medicine and political revolutionary G-107

Buck, Pearl (full name Pearl Sydenstricker Buck) (1892–1973), U.S. writer B-478
  'My Several Worlds' R-111h
  'The Good Earth' R-112, A-359

Buck, male animal, especially a male deer, antelope or rabbit
  deer D-61
  rabbit and hare R-20

Bucket boot, *picture* S-178

Buckeye, a breed of poultry P-482

Buckeye and horse chestnut, tree B-478
  Ohio state tree, *picture* O-508

Buckeye butterfly, *picture* B-523

Buckeye State. *see in index* Ohio

Buckingham, Henry Stafford, 2nd **duke of** (Stafford line) (1454?–83), although initially one of the chief supporters of Richard III, led the revolt against him on behalf of the earl of Richmond (Henry VII) 1483 R-203

Buckingham (also Bucks, or Buckinghamshire), s. midland county, England; 749 sq mi (1,940 sq km); dairying; pop. 488,233, *map* U-18a

Buckingham Palace, home of British royalty, London L-292, *map* L-288, *picture* L-293

Buckner, Simon Bolivar (1823–1914), Confederate general and political leader, born near Munfordville, Ky.; father of Simon B. Buckner, Jr.; governor of Kentucky 1887–91
  surrender to Grant G-217

Buckner, Simon Bolivar, Jr. (1886–1945), U.S. Army officer, born near Munfordville, Ky.; son of Simon B. Buckner; infantryman and specialist in tanks; made commander Alaska Defense Force July 1940, commander 10th Army in Pacific theater 1944; killed by Japanese shell on Okinawa June 1945 W-349

Buck press, garment pressing machine G-33

'Buck Rogers', comic strip S-62

Bucks, England, *see in index* Buckingham

Buckskin, leather L-109

Bucktail, fly rod lure, *list* F-146, *picture* F-142

Buckthorn. *see in index* Ironwood

Buckwheat B-478
  flour F-213
  honey H-228

Bucovina (or Bukovina), region in n.e. Romania and w. Ukrainian Soviet Socialist Republic; 4,031 sq mi (10,440 sq km); chief city Chernovtsy, in Ukrainian Soviet Socialist Republic; cattle raising and farming; former crownland of Austria-Hungary R-318

Bucuresti, Romania. *see in index* Bucharest

Bucyrus, Ohio, city on Sandusky River, 65 mi (105 km) s.e. of Toledo; road construction machinery, rubber goods, metal products, fluorescent lamps, clothing; pop. 13,433.

Bud, an undeveloped shoot P-359, *diagram* P-363b
  adventitious R-291

Buda, part of Budapest, Hungary B-479

Budapest, Hungary, capital; pop. 2,060,644 B-479, *map* E-360
  Danube River D-33
  Hungary H-326
  world, *map* W-297

'Buddenbrooks', novel by Mann M-109

Buddha (originally Prince Siddhartha Gotama or Gautama) (563–483 BC), philosopher, founder of Buddhism B-480
  China C-363
  Indian literature I-106
  pacifism P-143b
  sacred mountain in Sri Lanka S-402
  statues, *picture* J-47
    Gupta Dynasty sculpture G-318
  stories S-467, 478
  women M-541
  Zen Z-450

Buddhism, religion B-480
  Asia A-684
    Bangladesh B-62
    Burma B-509, M-95, R-92
    China C-345, 363
      sculpture S-94
    India I-68
      literature I-106
    Japan J-33, 58, *picture* J-47
      Kobo Daishi K-226
      literature J-81
      Nichiren N-306
    Kampuchea K-169
    Korea K-284
    Laos L-47
    Nepal N-116
    Sri Lanka S-402
    Thailand T-147
    Tibet T-180
    Vietnam V-322
  Asoka A-701
  ethics and morality E-310
  folk art themes F-251
  God G-173
  hell H-124
  Hinduism H-157
  library development L-170, *picture* L-150
  monks and monasticism M-539, *pictures* M-541, 543
  mythology M-704
  teachings B-480
  Transcendental Meditation T-249
  Zen Z-450

Buddhist architecture
  Ho Chi Minh City, *picture* H-192
  Japan A-546

'Buddhist Temple in the Hills After Rain', painting by Li Ch'eng, *picture* C-369

Budding, bud grafting P-362
  rubber tree R-301

Budding (or gemmation), type of asexual reproduction
  coral C-714
  hydra H-338
  sea squirt A-425
  yeast Y-411

Budge, Don (born 1915), U.S. tennis player
  tennis T-107, *picture* T-106

Budgerigar. *see in index* Parakeet

Budget, a financial plan B-485
  money M-533

Budget, Bureau of the. *see in index* Management and Budget, Office of

Budgie. *see in index* Parakeet

Budweis, Czechoslovakia. *see in index* Ceske Budejovice

Buell, Don Carlos (1818–98), prominent in U.S. Army in Civil War, born near Marietta, Ohio; became major general of volunteers; after Tennessee and Kentucky campaign replaced by Rosecrans (1862)
  Civil War campaigns C-476

Buena Park, Calif., city 10 mi (16 km) n.w. of Santa Ana; tourist and commercial center; citrus, orchards, truck farms; dairying; warehouses; light industry; pop. 64,165.

Buenaventura, Colombia, important Pacific port at mouth of Dagua River; pop. 115,770, *map* S-298

Buena Vista, Battle of, Mexican War M-320

Buenos Aires, Argentina, capital; harbor on Río de la Plata, about 150 mi (240 km) from the sea; pop. 2,908,801 B-488, *maps* A-585, S-299, *picture* A-580
  Argentina A-578
  Río de la Plata P-384, *picture* S-281b
  world, *map* W-297

Buenos Aires Convention (or Pan American Convention) (1910), international copyright convention C-713

Buero Vallejo, Antonio (born 1916), Spanish novelist S-366, *picture* S-367

Buffalo, animal of the family Bovidae B-489
  American. *see in index* Bison
  water buffalo, or carabao. *see in index* Water buffalo

Buffalo, N.Y., at e. end of Lake Erie, 2nd largest city of state; pop. 357,870 B-490
  food source I-122, 125, *picture* I-112
  Lake Erie L-298
  museums. *see in index* Albright-Knox Art Gallery
  New York N-251, *maps* N-350, U-41

Buffalo Bayou, waterway in Houston, Tex. H-308

Buffalo Bill (full name William Frederick Cody) (1846–1917), U.S. frontiersman B-490
  frontier F-423
  marksmanship R-206
  western W-151
  Wild West Show C-433
    Hickok H-149
    Oakley O-453
  Wyoming, *picture* W-394

Buffalo Bill Dam, dam on Shoshone, in northwest Wyoming
  Wyoming W-387, 390, *picture* W-388

Buffalo gnat, an insect closely related to the northern black fly; torments horses and cattle.

Buffalo moth, larva of carpet beetle B-140

Buffalo Trace, historic road, U.S.
  Indiana settlement I-92

Buffering capacity, of environmental systems P-441a

Buffon, Georges Louis Leclerc, comte de (1707–88), French philosophic naturalist and writer ('Natural History') A-487
  Darwin D-38

Bug, an insect. *see also in index* Hemiptera; and names of individual bugs, except as listed below
  bedbug, *picture* P-115
  scale insects S-52e

Bug, a computer error C-627

Bug, an electronic eavesdropping device W-247

Bugaev, Boris Nikolaevich (pseudonym Andrei Bely) (880–1934), Russian poet and novelist R-360a

Bugaku, Japanese music and dance J-54

Buganda, semiautonomous kingdom in Uganda, n. and w. of Lake Victoria; 64,998 sq mi (25,096 sq mi), including water; largest city Kampala; pop. 1,881,149 U-2
  Obote O-455

Bugle, wind instrument W-230

Bugle call, military call or command W-230

Bug River, more than 450 mi (720 km) long, rises in w. Ukrainian Soviet Socialist Republic, flows n. along U.S.S.R.–Poland boundary, then turns n.w. and w. into Poland to Vistula River, *maps* P-414, R-349

Buhari, Mohammed (born 1942), Nigerian head of state 1983–.

Buick, David Dunbar (1855–1929), U.S. pioneer automobile manufacturer, born in Scotland; started Buick Manufacturing Company 1902; devised valve-in-head engine and windshield A-856, 859

Building and loan associations S-52c

Building code S-158
housing H-305

Building construction B-491. *see also in index* Architecture; Heating and ventilating
acoustics S-261
bridges. *see in index* Bridge
caissons C-18
carpentry C-173
census C-249
chimney S-158, S-483
drainage system P-393
economic geology G-72
fair and exposition F-9
fire hazards F-109
floors F-186
folk art F-249
foundations P-399
Fuller F-446
helicopters' use H-120
houses H-297, 301, 306. *see also in index* Housing; Shelter
industry I-186
insulation H-111
interior design I-244
inventors, *table* I-280
materials
adobe A-47, *picture* S-35
ancient and medieval S-157
brick B-436
insulation. *see in index* Insulation
paints P-72, *diagram* P-75, *pictures* P-76
stone Q-6
coquina S-16b
sandstone S-38
slate S-212
wood W-280
lumber L-333
plywood P-397
mechanical drawing M-255
mechanics M-263
model housing projects, *picture* R-266
plumbing P-392, *picture* P-393
prefabrication S-157, *picture* U-192
regulation S-158
signaling, *picture* S-195b
skyscraper. *see in index* Skyscraper

Buisson, Ferdinand (1841–1932), French statesman and educator, born in Paris; member Chamber of Deputies; professor of science of education at Sorbonne.

Bukhara (or Bokhara), former emirate and its capital in Asiatic U.S.S.R., n. of Afghanistan; following Russian Revolution, Bukhara became a soviet republic; later divided between Turkmen Soviet Socialist Republic and Uzbek Soviet Socialist Republic; city Bukhara (pop. 139,000) now in Uzbek Soviet Socialist Republic, *map* R-344
Asia, *map* A-697

Bukkenfjord, inlet of North Sea, Norway. *see in index* Boknfjord

Bukovina. *see in index* Bucovina

Bulawayo, Zimbabwe, most important city of Matabeleland; Cecil Rhodes buried nearby; pop. 308,000, with suburbs, *maps* A-115, S-264

Bulb. *see also in index* Corm; Rootstock; Tuber
garden G-20, 25
lily L-209
vegetative reproduction, *diagram* P-363a

Bulfinch, Charles (1763–1844), U.S. architect, born in Boston, Mass.; designed Beacon Hill monument, Boston, and built many public and private buildings in New England; appointed architect of Capitol at Washington, D.C., 1818 and designed west approaches and portico; his sincere, simple style greatly influenced U.S. architecture A-568
Massachusetts State House, *picture* M-199

Bulganin, Nikolai Aleksandrovich (1895–1975), Soviet government official and marshal, born in Nizhniy Novgorod (now Gorkiy); member Politburo 1948–52, Presidium 1952–58; minister of armed forces 1946–49; a deputy premier under Stalin; a first deputy premier and minister of defense 1953–55; premier 1955–58 R-357

Bulgaria (Bulgarian People's Republic), Balkan republic; 42,823 sq mi (110,921 sq km); cap. Sofia; pop. 9,059,000 B-498, *map* E-360
Balkan states B-25
Balkan wars (1912–13) B-31
cities. *see in index* Sofia and other cities by name
clothing, *picture* S-215
communist world, *map* C-619
flag, *picture* F-162
literature, folklore S-470, *list* S-481
Macedonia M-7
national anthem, *table* N-64
national park N-27
people, *picture* S-215
racial classification, *chart* R-26
railroad mileage, *table* R-85
sports
wrestling W-366
Thrace T-175
trade S-247
Warsaw Pact W-34
world, *map* W-297
World War I W-305, 311, 319
World War II W-326

Bulgaria, Church of, Eastern Orthodox church E-42

Bulgarian Macedonia, region of Bulgaria; area 2,506 sq mi (6,491 sq km); cap. Blagoevgrad M-7

Bulgars, people
Balkan rivalries B-31
Balkan states' settlement B-28
Basil II Bulgaroctonus B-535
Bulgaria B-500
racial classification, *chart* R-26

Bulge, battle of the, World War II W-335, 341
warfare, *list* W-14

Bulguksa Temple, temple in Kyongju, Korea, *picture* K-279

Bulimarexia (or bulimia), eating disorder A-467
weight control W-136

Bulk cargo, freight that is transported unpackaged, such as sugar, oil, wheat T-254
harbors and ports H-35

Bulkeley, Morgan G. (1837–1922), U.S. baseball organizer and first president of National League, born in East Haddam, Conn.; helped start N.L. 1876, *table* B-80

Bulkhead, of ships S-171, *diagram* S-172

Bull, Ole (1810–80), Norwegian violinist and composer, born in Bergen; composed fantasias on national themes, also concertos.

Bull, animal, the male of domestic cattle and many other animals, especially elk, moose, elephant, whale, seal
bullfighting B-501
cattle C-224
deer D-62
elephant, *picture* R-283
mythology
Egypt E-129
seal S-99

Bull, constellation. *see in index* Taurus

Bull, in financial market S-453

Bull, papal document P-100

Bull, Golden. *see in index* Golden Bull

Bullbat, bird. *see in index* Nighthawk

Bull bay (or great-flowered magnolia), tree *Magnolia grandiflora* of the Magnolia family M-47

Bull calf. *see in index* Calf

'Bull Dance of the Mandan Indians', painting by Catlin, *picture* A-465

Bulldog, dog, *picture* D-206

Bulldog ant, insect A-468

Bulldozer B-500
power shovel D-258

Bullet A-371
ballistics B-37
firearms F-98, *picture* F-99
heat H-101
warfare W 19

'Bulletin, The', Australian journal A-797

Bulletproof jacket, armor A-631

Bullfighting B-501. *see also in index* Toreador
Mexico City M-347
Portugal L-238, P-456
Spain S-355

Bullhead, catfish C-220, *picture* A-516

Bullins, Ed (born 1935), U.S. playwright A-363
drama D-249

Bull in the Ring, game G-10

Bullion, uncoined gold and silver in bars or ingots; bullion value of coins is determined by weight, proportion of precious metal to weight, and market price of metal
gold G-177, *picture* G-176

Bullmastiff, dog, *picture* D-201

Bull Moose party. *see in index* Progressive party

Bullock, William A. (1813–67), U.S. inventor, born in Greenville, N.Y.; made many improvements on newspaper presses; died of injuries incurred while testing one of his inventions P-504

Bull Run, battles of (also called battles of Manassas)
Civil War C-479, *map* C-475
first battle J-9
flag distinction problem F-154, *picture* F-155
McClellan M-4
Stuart S-494

Bull Shoals Dam, dam in n. Arkansas, on White River; completed 1951; forms Bull Shoals Lake in Arkansas and Missouri, *picture* A-621

Bull snake, *picture* S-224

Bull terrier, dog, *picture* D-203

Bull thistle, weed *Cirsium lanceolatum*, *picture* W-132

Bully (or face-off), begins play in field hockey H-193

Bülow, Hans Guido von (1830–94), German pianist, conductor, and profound student of music literature, born in Dresden; toured in U.S.
Brahms B-394
classical music M-673
orchestra O-578

Bulrush, any of several large rushlike or grasslike plants, especially the genus *Scirpus* of the sedge family; name sometimes given also to the cattail; the bulrush of the Bible was a species of papyrus S-106

Bulshaia. *see in index* McKinley, Mount

Bulwer, William Henry. *see in index* Dalling and Bulwer, William Henry Lytton Earle Bulwer, Baron

Bulwer-Lytton. *see in index* Lytton

Bumblebee (or humblebee), bee of the genus *Bombus* B-124, *picture* I-216
clover pollination
ecological importance E-51
protective coloration P-512

Bumper, device to absorb impact A-845

Bumper cars, amusement park ride A-384

Bumppo, Natty, frontiersman in Cooper's 'Leatherstocking Tales'; nicknames include Deerslayer, Hawkeye, the Pathfinder, Leatherstocking A-346

Buna, Papua-New Guinea, village on n. coast of Papua; Japanese established bases here and at Gona (15 mi; 25 km n.w.) July 1942; recaptured by Allies Dec. 1942.

Buna rubbers R-309

Bunau-Varilla, Philippe-Jean (1860–1940), French engineer and diplomat B-501
Roosevelt R-286

Bunchberry (or dwarf cornel), a red-berried herb *Cornus canadensis* of the dogwood family; flowers greenish white to creamy, sometimes pink-tipped, *picture* P-511

Bunche, Ralph Johnson (1904–71), U.S. educator and public official B-502

Buncombe, county in North Carolina; word "bunk" originated 1820 when Congressman Felix Walker made a lengthy speech on the Missouri Compromise, explaining that his district expected it, and he was "speaking for Buncombe"; pop. 145,056.

Bundesrat (or Federal Council), the senate of the former German Empire, appointed by and representing the federated states; had administrative, judicial, legislative powers; sessions not public; upper house of West German Parliament G-120

Bundestag (or Federal Diet), one of two legislative chambers of West Germany G-120

Bundle, unit of measure, *table* W-140

Bunin, Ivan Alekseevich (1870–1953), Soviet novelist and poet, born in Voronezh; known for translations of Longfellow's 'Hiawatha', and Byron's 'Manfred' and 'Cain' R-360a

Bunker, Chang (1811–1874), and **Eng** (1811–1874), Siamese twins who were joined at the chest; toured as a side-show attraction M-650

Bunker, in golf G-188

Bunker Hill, hill in Massachusetts M-189

Bunker Hill, battle of (1775) B-502, R-170
American Revolution R-170
Massachusetts monument, *picture* M-200
Trumbull's painting P-49, *picture* P-48
warfare, *list* W-14

Bunker Hill Mine, mine in Idaho, U.S., *picture* I-20

Bunraku, Japanese puppet drama J-49, 55
Osaka O-609

Bunsen, Robert Wilhelm (1811–99), German chemist B-503
spectroscopic studies S-371, P-303

Bunsen burner B-503

Bunting, bird common throughout most of Europe and North America; many are fine singers; valuable to farmers because they eat weed seeds; nests built from dried grasses and leaves on open fields or in low bushes B-503. *see also in index* Indigo bunting; Lazuli bunting; Painted bunting; Varied bunting

Bunting, colored cotton cloth of plain weave similar to cheesecloth, used for flags; also a material of worsted yarn similar to nun's veiling but narrower and coarser
United States flag F-152

Buntline, Ned. *see in index* Judson, Edward Zane Carroll

Buñuel, Luis (1900–83), Spanish filmmaker, born in Calanda; made films in Spain, France, U.S., and Mexico ('An Andalusian Dog'; 'The Golden Age'; 'Land Without Bread'; 'Viridiana'; 'Tristana')
Dali D-9
motion pictures M-623

Bunyan, John (1628–88), English Puritan leader and author B-503
literary contribution E-268

Bunyan, Paul (or Paul Bunyon), hero of lumber camp tales C-481d
Babe the Blue Ox, *picture* M-444
folklore F-265, *picture* F-266

Buonarroti. *see in index* Michelangelo

Buoy, a navigation aid
harbors and ports H-34
lighthouse L-205
navigation N-71
ocean measurements O-464

Buoyancy, ability to float; applied to supporting medium or the object floated
Archimedes' principle A-541
ships, *diagram* S-170
submarines S-497

Buoyancy compensator (BC), a safety device used in underwater diving D-188

Buraku, Japanese farming village J-27

Buran. *see in index* blizzard

Buranello, Il. *see in index* Galuppi, Baldassare

Burano, island, Italy L-16

Buraq, Islamic mythological animal, *picture* I-364

Burbage, James (or James Burbadge) (died 1597), English actor, theater manager; one of owners of Blackfriars Theatre S-130

Burbage, Richard (or Richard Burbadge) (1567?–1619), English actor A-27, S-130

Burbank, Luther (1849–1926), U.S. botanist B-505
berries R-94
Hall of Fame, *table* H-16

Burbank, Calif., city n.w. of Los Angeles; aircraft and aircraft components, motion pictures; pop. 84,625.

Burchell's zebra, hoofed mammal *Equus burchelli* Z-449

Burchfield, Charles Ephraim (1893–1967), U.S. artist, born in Ashtabula, Ohio; realistic paintings of 'the American scene'—street scenes, freight cars, drab houses, fields—also imaginative and mystical works
 'November Evening' P-24

Burden, Henry (1791–1871), U.S. inventor, born in Dunblane, Scotland; to U.S. 1819; patented first cultivator used in U.S. and machine for shoeing horses used by Union army in Civil War.

Burdigala. *see in index* Bordeaux

Burdock, a coarse biennial *Arctium* of the family Compositae, with large heart-shaped leaves and purple or pale violet flowers surrounded by stiff pointed bracts with hooked tips
 Arctium minus, picture W-132

Bure, Norse god M-697, 703

Bureau, in U.S. government. *see in index* bureaus by name, as Census, Bureau of the

Bureaucracy, a system of government the control of which is largely in the hands of officials organized into bureaus or departments B-505
 China's history C-361, 367
 cities C-458
 constitution C-683
 U.S.S.R. R-330a

Bureau International des Expositions (BIE) F-10

Bureau plat, French writing table F-459

Burgas, Bulgaria, port on Black Sea; flour and sugar mills, soap factories; emerged from obscurity after Bulgarian liberation 1878; grew rapidly with construction of railroad 1890 and new harbor 1904; pop. 131,700, *map* E-360

Burger, Warren Earl (born 1907), U.S. jurist, born in Saint Paul, Minn.; on faculty William Mitchell College of Law, Saint Paul, 1931–48; partner in law firms 1935–53; assistant U.S. attorney general 1953–56; judge U.S. Court of Appeals, District of Columbia, 1956–69; chief justice of the U.S. 1969–86, *pictures* S-518a
 Nixon N-326

Burger King, restaurant chain F-373

Burgess, Anthony (born 1917), British writer
 literary contribution E-283

Burgess, (Frank) Gelett (1866–1951), U.S. author, illustrator, and humorist, born in Boston, Mass. ('Goops and How to Be Them'; 'Are You a Bromide?'; 'Look Eleven Years Younger').

Burgesses, House of, first colonial North American representative legislative body, called in Jamestown, Va., 1619; moved to Williamsburg, Va., 1699 and to Richmond, Va., 1799; name continued until Revolution V-335
 first representative assembly, *pictures* V-337, U-130
 Henry, *picture* R-167
 Washington W-39

'Burghers of Calais, The', sculpture by Rodin R-238, S-76, *picture* S-77

Burghley, Baron. *see in index* Cecil, William

Burglar alarm
 photoelectric P-274

Burglary, the breaking and entering of a building with the intent to commit a theft or some other felony
 crime C-771

Burgos, Spain, former capital of old Castile, on Arlanzon River, 130 mi (210 km) n. of Madrid; well-known cathedral; capital of Franco government during Spanish Civil War (1936–39); pop. 79,810 S-356, *map* S-350

Burgoyne, John (1722–92), English general in American Revolution R-171, S-48

Burgundians, a Germanic people G-121

Burgundy (French Bourgogne), former kingdom and duchy in e.-central France, now included in four departments; world famous for its wine
 wine W-237

Burial and funeral customs D-50. *see also in index* Cremation; Tomb
 Aegean civilization A-61
 American Indians I-142
 catacombs C-218
 China P-470
 early Christian R-257, *picture* R-258
 Egypt. *see in index* Egypt, ancient, *subhead* burial and funeral customs
 folk art F-251, *picture* F-248
 India S-38
  Hinduism H-160
 masks M-186
 mummy M-651

'Burial of the Conde de Orgaz', painting by El Greco G-253

Burin, an engraving tool
 intaglio G-231
 man M-85

Burka, garment worn by orthodox Moslem women P-78

Burke, Edmund (1729–97), English statesman B-506
 architecture A-560
 conservatism C-679
 Hastings H-52
 human rights H-320

Burke, John (1859–1937), U.S. political leader, born in Sigourney, Iowa; first Democratic governor of North Dakota 1907–13; treasurer of the United States 1913–21; North Dakota supreme court justice 1925–37, chief justice 1935–37
 Statuary Hall, *table* S-437b

Burke, Martha Jane Canary. *see in index* Calamity Jane

Burke, Robert O'Hara (1820–61), Irish explorer B-506

Burke and Wills Expedition (or Great Northern Exploration Expedition) B-506

Burkina Faso. , n.w. Africa n. of Ghana; 105,900 sq mi (274,122 sq km); cap. Ouagadougou; pop. 8,126,000 B-507
 Africa, *map* A-118, *table* A-112
 arts
  dance D-31
  folktales, *list* S-482
 cities. *see in index* Ouagadougou and other cities by name
 flag, *picture* F-162
 illiteracy P-450
 national anthem, *table* N-64

Burl, in redwood S-112

Burlap, a coarse, plain-woven fabric made of jute, manila hemp, or flax; unfinished type used for bags and upholstery lining; colored or printed goods for draperies, slipcovers, and wall covering.

Burlesque, a comical, witty, or derisive imitation of some more serious work in literature or the drama (from Italian burla, mockery). *see also in index* Satire

Burley, Idaho, city 73 mi (117 km) s.w. of Pocatello, on Snake River; potatoes, sugar beets, wheat, barley, livestock; flour, dairy products; headquarters of Minidoka National Forest.; pop. 8,761
 Idaho, *map* I-30

Burling, in textile manufacture T-139

Burlingame, Calif., residential city on San Francisco Bay, 15 mi (25 km) s. of San Francisco; minor industries; Russell College; incorporated 1908; pop. 26,173.

Burlingame treaty (1868), *table* T-274

Burlington, Iowa, city in s.e., on Mississippi River; pop. 29,529
 Iowa, *map* I-302

Burlington, Mass., 5 mi (8 km) s.w. of Reading; truck and dairy farms; incorporated 1799; pop. of township 23,486.

Burlington, N.C., industrial city in farm region, about 50 mi (80 km) n.w. of Raleigh; weaving; hosiery, textiles, electronic products, furniture; Alamance Battleground State Historical Site nearby; pop. 37,266.

Burlington, N.J., city on Delaware River, 11 mi (18 km) s.e. of Trenton; shipping center for agricultural area; silk, typewriters, clothing, metal products; pop. 10,246.

Burlington, Ont., town on Lake Ontario, n. of Hamilton; steel products, furniture, chemicals, shoes; Burlington Bay Skyway; pop. 114,853.

Burlington, Vt., largest city of state, on Lake Champlain; pop. 37,712, *maps* V-301, 286, U-41, *picture* V-293
 climate, *list* V-284
 Shelburne Museum nearby, *pictures* V-295
 University of Vermont V-288, *picture* V-293

Burma (officially Socialist Republic of the Union of Burma), a republic in n.w. Indochina, on e. side of Bay of Bengal; 261,228 sq mi (677,577 sq km); cap. Rangoon; pop. 36,166,000 B-508
 Asia, *map* A-697
  India I-61
  Indochina I-157
 bells B-154
 cities. *see in index* cities listed below and other cities by name
  Mandalay M-95
  Rangoon R-92
 flag, *picture* F-163
 Irrawaddy River I-353
 language
  Judson's contribution J-151
 literature
  folktales S-468, *list* S-479, *pictures* S-463, 465
 national anthem, *table* N-64
 religion B-484, R-92
 transportation
  railroad mileage, *table* R-85
 United Kingdom E-258
 world, *map* W-297
 World War II W-328

Burma, battle of, World War II W-347

Burmans, a people of Burma B-509

Burma Road, 700 mi (1,150 km) long, from Lashio, Burma, to Kunming, China, finished 1939 to supply China while Japan occupied seacoast; important in World War II. *see also in index* Stilwell Road

Burn and scald B-511
 body B-51
 prevention F-113, S-7
 treatment S-348c
 tissue transplantation T-250

Burne-Jones, Edward Coley (1833–98), British Pre-Raphaelite painter, noted for highly decorative design, born in Birmingham
 illustration, *picture* B-351
 Morris M-588

Burner, lighting device
 Bunsen B-503
 gas, *picture* B-503

Burnet, Macfarlane (full name Frank Macfarlane Burnet) (1899–1985), Australian physician B-512

Burnett, Frances Eliza Hodgson (1849–1924), U.S. novelist, born in Manchester, England; wrote for both children and adults; stories are colorful and romantic ('Little Lord Fauntleroy'; 'The Secret Garden') R-111

Burnett, Whit (1899–1973), U.S. editor and writer, born in Salt Lake City, Utah; newspaperman in United States and Europe; worked for publishing houses in New York, N.Y.; founder (1931) and editor (until 1971, with some interruptions) of *Story* magazine; edited many anthologies, *picture* U-226

Burnett salmon. *see in index* Australian barramunda

Burnford, Sheila (born 1918), Canadian author, born in Scotland; 'The Incredible Journey', Canadian Books of the Year for Children Award 1963; memoirs, 'The Fields of Noon'
 'The Incredible Journey' R-112

Burnham, Daniel Hudson (1846–1912), U.S. architect and city planner, born in Henderson, N.Y.; planned Chicago's World's Fair of 1893 A-568
 city planning C-455
 Cleveland's design C-493

Burnham, Sherburne Wesley (1838–1921), U.S. astronomer, born in Thetford, Vt.; professor of astronomy University of Chicago; made important discoveries in double stars, *picture* V-296

Burning. *see in index* Combustion

Burning bush. *see in index* Spindle tree

Burning in, photographic technique P-295

Burning Index, measurement of the likelihood of a forest fire F-108

Burnley, England, city in Lancashire, 22 mi (35 km) n. of Manchester; cotton weaving; clothing, metal products; pop. 76,610, *map* U-18a

Burns, Robert (1759–96), Scotland's greatest poet B-512, *picture* L-149
 literary contribution E-273, *picture* E-274

Burns, Tex. *see in index* L'Amour, Louis

Burns, Tommy (formerly Noah Brusso) (1881–1955), Canadian boxer, born in Hanover, Ont. B-391

Burnside, Ambrose Everett (1824–81), U.S. Army general in Civil War, born in Liberty, Ind.; commanded McClellan's left wing at Antietam; succeeded McClellan in command of Army of Potomac, Nov. 7, 1862; removed after defeat at Fredericksburg but served as subordinate until end of war; governor of Rhode Island 1866–69; U.S. senator 1875–81; gave name to a style of side whiskers L-116, R-184, *picture* R-190
 Civil War C-475, 481

Burnsville, Minn., residential city 14 mi (22 km) s. of Minneapolis; lumber; grain processing; incorporated 1965; pop. 35,674.

Bur oak (or mossy cup oak), tree *Quercus macrocarpa* of the family Fagaceae O-452, *picture* L-101
 wood, *table* W-283

Burr, Aaron (1756–1836), 3rd vice-president of the U.S. B-513
 Hamilton H-22, E-321
 Jefferson J-93

Burrhel (or blue sheep), animal of the family Bovidae S-148

Burro, a small donkey A-702. *see also in index* Ass

Burroughs, Edgar Rice (1875–1950), U.S. novelist; creator of Tarzan stories S-62

Burroughs, John (1837–1921), U.S. naturalist and writer, *pictures* R-289

Burroughs, William Seward (1857–98), U.S. inventor, born in Rochester, N.Y.; designed first commercially successful adding machine, patented 1888 C-20

Burrow A-426
 beaver B-121
 bird
  owl B-256, P-486
  swallow S-521
 paca P-1
 prairie dog P-486
 trap-door spider S-382, *picture* S-388

Burrowing owl a small ground owl *Speotyto cunicularia* (9 in.; 23 cm long), often seen in daytime B-256, *picture* B-251

Burrows, Stephen (born 1943), U.S. dress designer D-271

Bursa (formerly Brusa), Turkey, historic city 15 mi (25 km) s. of Sea of Marmara; hot sulfur and iron springs; silk and carpet manufactures; pop. 445,113
 Asia, *map* A-697

Bursa of Fabricius, bird anatomy
 B cells' development L-342
 immune system I-55

Bursitis J-137

Burslem, England, famous pottery town in Staffordshire; birthplace of Josiah Wedgwood; became part of Stoke-on-Trent 1910.

Bursting powder, fireworks F-114

Burst of the monsoon, season India I-64

Burt, William Austin (1792–1858), U.S. inventor and surveyor, born in Petersham, Mass.; self-educated inventor of 'solar compass,' surveyor's instrument still in use; government surveyor in Michigan and discoverer of iron ore in Marquette County; active in politics.

Burton, Richard (full name Richard Francis Burton) (1821–90), British explorer and writer B-513
 'Arabian Nights' A-525

Burton, Robert (pen name Democritus Junior) (1577–1640), English author and clergyman, born in Lindley, Leicestershire; influenced style of later English writers. *see also in index* 'Anatomy of Melancholy, The'
 literary contribution E-268

Burton, Virginia Lee (1909–68), U.S. artist, illustrator, and author of children's books, born in Newton Center, Mass.; part of her childhood was spent in Carmel, Calif.; received Caldecott Medal in 1943 for 'The Little House'; other titles, 'Katy and the Big Snow', 'Mike Mulligan and His Steam Shovel', 'Maybelle the Cable Car', 'Life Story: a Play in Five Acts' R-105

Burton, William Meriam (1865–1954), U.S. chemist and executive, born in Cleveland, Ohio; president Standard Oil Company of Indiana 1918–27
oil cracking process I-276, *table* I-273

Burton upon Trent, England, county borough in Staffordshire, on River Trent and Trent and Mersey Canal; brewing industry dating from 1708, famous for stout and pale ale; pop. 50,850, *map* U-18a

Buru (or Boeroe), island of Molucca group, Indonesia, w. of Ceram; about 3,670 sq mi (9,505 sq km); exports sago, timber, cajuput oil; pop. 16,018, *map* I-166
Asia, *map* A-697

Burundi, country in e.-central Africa; area 10,747 sq mi (27,834 sq km); cap. Bujumbura; pop. 4,111,000 B-514, *map* A-115
African political unit, *table* A-112
flag, *picture* F-163
world, *map* W-297

Bury, England, town in Lancashire, 10 mi (16 km) n.w. of Manchester; cotton and woolen manufactures, machinery; pop. 67,070, *map* U-18a

Bury Saint Edmunds (or Saint Edmundsbury), England, town in West Suffolk, n.e. of London; named from Saxon King Edmund; ruins of old Benedictine abbey; pop. 25,140.

Bus B-515
omnibus, *picture* S-42
postal service, Australia, *picture* P-404
street railway S-487
transportation T-254, 256, *picture* T-263

Busch Memorial Stadium, stadium in St. Louis, Mo., *picture* M-499

Bush, George (Herbert Walker) (born 1924), U.S. public official, born in Wilton, Mass.; U.S. congressman (Republican) from Texas 1967–71; U.S. ambassador to the United Nations 1971–73; Republican National Committee chairman 1973–74; chief liaison officer People's Republic of China 1974–76; director Central Intelligence Agency 1976–77; vice-president of U.S. 1981– R-112j

Bush, remote, thinly settled interior of a country which has not been cleared for cultivation S-187

Bush. *see in index* Shrubs

Bush ballads, in Australian literature A-797

Bush bean, a vegetable plant
growing conditions G-26

Bush cricket. *see in index* Katydid

Bushel, unit of capacity, *table* W-140

Bushell, John (died 1761), North American pioneer printer and journalist; in Boston, Mass., 1742–49; in Halifax, N.S., after 1751.

'Bushido', code of conduct of the samurai Y-408

Bushmen. *see in index* Khoisan

Bushnell, David (1742–1824), U.S. inventor, born in Saybrook, Conn.; built man-propelled submarine; called "Father of the Submarine" S-495b

Bushnell's wasp, insect, *picture* W-72

Bush pig, pig *Potamochoerus porcus* of the family Suidae P-321

Bushranger, Australian outlaw
Kelly K-196

Bush squash, a vegetable plant
growing conditions G-26

Bush tit, bird *Psaltriparus minimus* T-197

Bushwhacking, boating
folklore F-265

Business. *see also in index* Accounting; Bank and banking; Capitalism; Cooperatives; Corporation; Credit; Economics; Industry; International trade; Manufactures; Market; Panics and depressions; Tariff; Taxation; Trade; Transportation; Trust; and chief industries by name
advertising A-59
age shift in population P-448
arbitration policy A-528
Astor family A-706
bankruptcy B-74
baseball leagues B-87
bookkeeping A-15
budget B-486
candy C-139
computers C-626
contracts C-693
copyright C-713
legal definition, *table* L-92
cosmetics C-730
dairying D-3
employment and unemployment E-205
estate and inheritance law E-307
football F-295
franchise F-373
industry I-183
insurance I-232
health insurance H-95
letter writing L-130
magazine and journal M-33
marketing M-140
monopolies M-543
percentage and interest P-198, *picture* P-200, *table* P-201
psychology in business P-524
shoes S-181
stocks and bonds S-450, *picture* S-451
trademark T-246
vocations
advertising A-41, V-365
clerical V-364, S-182, *table* V-363
sales V-369, *picture* V-370, *table* V-363

Business cycle, in economics B-517
economics E-63
employment and unemployment E-207
Great Depression G-242
inflation I-198
labor movements L-6
money M-531

Business interruption insurance I-232

Busing, U.S. governmental policy aimed at obtaining racial balance in school systems B-301
Nixon N-327

Busoni, Rafaello (1900–62), U.S. illustrator and writer, born in Berlin, Germany, of Italian father and Swedish mother; in U.S. after 1939; illustrated many children's books on geographical subjects; wrote and illustrated 'Somi Builds a Church' and 'Stanley's Africa'; biography, 'The Man Who Was Don Quixote' R-111d

Bustamante, Alexander, Jamaican political leader J-18

Bustard, bird A-521

Bustelli, Franz Anton (1723–63), Swiss potter, born in Locarno, Switzerland P-475

Bustle, pad or framework for a skirt D-266

Butadiene, in synthetic rubber P-228, R-309

Butane, hydrocarbon of paraffin series, found in petroleum P-228. *see also in index* Paraffin series
gas G-38
organic chemistry O-602
petrochemicals P-228
synthetic rubber R-309

Butcherbird (or Shrike) S-186

'Butcher's Dozen', work by Kinsella I-328

Butenandt, Adolf Friedrich Johann (born 1903), German chemist, born present Bremerhaven.

Butkus, Richard (nickname Dick) (born 1942), U.S. football player, born in Chicago, Ill.; middle linebacker for Chicago Bears 1965–73.

Butler, Andrew Pickens (1796–1857), U.S. senator from South Carolina, born in Edgefield, S.C.; supporter of John C. Calhoun; served in state legislature, circuit court, and court of appeals before election to Senate 1846
Sumner S-511

Butler, Benjamin F. (1818–93), U.S. major general in Union Army during Civil War; member of House of Representatives 1867–75, 1877–79; managed impeachment trial of President Andrew Johnson; governor of Massachusetts 1882 C-478

Butler, James Logan (1855–1923), U.S. miner and rancher, born in El Dorado County, Calif.; his discovery of Tonopah silver deposits in Nevada 1900 began new mining boom.

Butler, Nicholas Murray (1862–1947), U.S. educator and publicist, born in Elizabeth, N.J.; president of Columbia University 1902–45, then president emeritus; active in national and international affairs; president Carnegie Endowment for International Peace after 1925 ('The Meaning of Education'; 'The Faith of a Liberal'; 'Across the Busy Years').

Butler, Samuel (1835–1902), British satirical novelist and critic B-519
literary contribution E-278
'The Way of All Flesh' N-411
utopian theme U-235

Butler, Pa., city 30 mi (50 km) n. of Pittsburgh, in coal, limestone, natural gas, and oil region; iron and steel products, railroad cars, automobile parts, electronic controls, oil-well supplies, glass; pop. 17,026, *map* P-184

Butor, Michel (born 1926) French writer
avant-garde writing N-414
French literature F-398

Butt, archery target A-540

Butte, Mont., city 47 mi (76 km) s.w. of Helena; important copper mining and processing

BYZANTINE RULERS

Under Diocletian (AD 284), the Roman Empire was divided into the Eastern Empire and the Western Empire, but it was not until the death of Theodosius (AD 395) that the two were finally separated. The name "Byzantine" applies to the Eastern Roman Empire from that time on. For Eastern rulers preceding Arcadius, *see* Roman History, *table* Roman Emperors. In this table overlapping dates indicate corulers, except in the case of the Latin Emperors who, during the Crusades, were set up as rivals to the Nicaean Emperors.

395–408	Arcadius	1028–34	Romanus III, Argyropolus
408–450	Theodosius II	1034–41	Michael IV, the Paphlagonian
450–457	Marcianus	1041–42	Michael V, Palaphates
457–474	Leo I	1042–54	Constantine IX, Monomachus
474	Leo II	1054–56	Theodora
474–491	Zeno	1056–57	Michael VI, Stratioticus
491–518	Anastasius I	1057–59	Isaac I, Comnenus
518–527	Justin I	1059–67	Constantine X, Dukas
527–565	Justinian I	1067	Andronicus
565–578	Justin II	1067	Constantine XI
578–582	Tiberius, Constantinus	1067–71	Romanus IV, Diogenes
582–602	Mauricius	1071–78	Michael VII, Parapinakes
602–610	Phocas I	1078–81	Nicephorus III, Botaniates
610–641	Heraclius I	1081–1118	Alexius I, Comnenus
641	Constantine III	1118–43	John IV, Calus
641	Heracleon	1143–80	Manuel I
641–668	Constans II	1180–83	Alexius II
668–685	Constantine IV	1182–85	Andronicus I
685–695	Justinian II	1185–95	Isaac II, Angelus-Comnenus
695–698	Leontius II	1195–1203	Alexius III, Angelus
698–705	Tiberius III, Apsimar	1203–04	Alexius IV
705–711	Justinian II (restored)	1204	Alexius V, Dukas
711–713	Philippicus		
713–715	Anastasius II		***Latin Emperors***
715–717	Theodosius III	1204–05	Baldwin I
717–741	Leo III, the Isaurian	1205–16	Henry VI
741–775	Constantine V, Kopronymus	1216–17	Peter de Courtenay
775–780	Leo IV	1218–28	Robert de Courtenay
780–797	Constantine VI	1228–61	Baldwin II
797–802	Irene		
802–811	Nicephorus I		***Nicaean Emperors***
811	Stauracius	1206–22	Theodore I, Lascaris
811–813	Michael I, Rhangabé	1222–54	John Dukas Vatatzes
813–820	Leo V, the Armenian	1254–59	Theodore II, Lascaris
820–829	Michael II	1258–61	John IV, Lascaris
829–842	Theophilus II		
842–867	Michael III		***The Paleologi***
842–866	Bardas	1261–82	Michael VIII
867	Theophilus II	1282–1328	Andronicus II
867–886	Basil I, the Macedonian	1295–1320	Michael IX
886–912	Leo VI, the Wise	1328–41	Andronicus III
912–913	Alexander III	1341–47	John V
913–959	Constantine VII, Porphyrogenitus	1347–54	John VI, Cantacuzene
919–944	Romanus I, Lecapenus	1355–76	John V (restored)
959–963	Romanus II	1376–79	Andronicus IV
963–969	Nicephorus II, Phocas	1379–91	John V (restored)
969–976	John I, Tzimisces	1390	John VII
976–1025	Basil II, Bulgaroktonus	1391–1425	Manuel II
1025–28	Constantine VIII	1425–48	John VIII
1028–50	Zoë	1448–53	Constantine XI or XIII

center; zinc, manganese, and silver also produced; livestock marketing; phosphate chemicals; Montana College of Mineral Science and Technology; pop. (Butte–Silver Bow) 37,205 M-552, 560, *picture* M-558
United States, *maps* N-350, U-40

Butte, a hill
North Dakota N-373
Utah, *picture* U-216

Butter B-519
churn F-36
margarine M-134
milk M-415

Butter-and-eggs (or yellow toadflax), a wild flower *Linaria vulgaris* B-520, *picture* F-235

Buttercup, a breed of poultry P-482

Buttercup, a wildflower B-520
Illinois woodland, *picture* P-358

Butterfield, John (1801–69), U.S. pioneer expressman and financier, born in Berne, N.Y.; stagecoach driver, became stage line owner E-384

Butterfield, William (1814–1900), architect, born in London A-561
church of All Saints, Margaret Street, *picture* A-561

Butterfield and Wasson Express Company, an early U.S. express company; carried letters from St. Louis, Mo., to Calif. on southern route shortly before Civil War E-382

'Butterfield 8', novel by O'Hara O-496

Butterfly B-521. *see also in index* Caterpillar; Moth
anatomy
mouth A-428
eggs, *pictures* E-111
endangered species E-212
hibernation H-147
hobby H-186
insect I-222, *picture* I-215, 219
migration A-452
protective coloration P-509, *picture* P-510

Butterfly dog. *see in index* Papillon

Butterfly fish, fish of family Chaetodontidae; found in coastal waters and coral reefs of the East and West Indies.

Butterfly flower. *see in index* Schizanthus

Butterfly stroke, in swimming S-535, *picture* S-534
Australian swimming A-789

Butterfly weed, perennial *Asclepias tuberosa* M-416

Butterhead, lettuce L-140, *picture* L-141

Buttermilk B-519
milk M-415, *list* D-6

Butternut (or white walnut), tree *Juglans cinerea* B-528
walnut W-528

'Butterworth', British ship H-230

Button, Thomas (died 1634), English navigator; led an expedition in search of Northwest Passage 1612–13
Manitoba M-102

Button B-528
collecting B-398, *pictures* B-399
ivory's use I-406
mollusks M-525
nuts N-449

Button, mushroom part M-664

Button, Button, Who's Got the Button?, game G-12

Button shoe, *picture* S-178

Button snakeroot. *see in index* Liatris

Buttonwood, tree. *see in index* Sycamore

Butts, game D-37

Butyl alcohol, a compound (C_4H_9OH) of hydroxyl and butyl, *table* A-274

Butylene P-228

Butyl rubber R-309, P-228

Butyric acid F-55

Butz, Earl Lauer (born 1909), U.S. agricultural economist, born in Albion, Ind.; dean of agriculture Purdue University 1957–58, dean of continuing education and vice-president Purdue Research Foundation 1958–71; assistant secretary of agriculture 1954–57, secretary 1971–76
Nixon N-326

Buxton, Thomas Fowell (1786–1845), English politician A-10
Wilberforce W-203

Buyids, group of soldiers of fortune C-56

Buying. *see in index* Purchasing

Buzzard B-280
vulture V-388

Buzzards Bay, an inlet of the Atlantic, on the s. coast of Massachusetts M-189

Buzzati, Franz Dino (1906–72), Italian writer I-379

Buzz bomb. *see in index* V-1 missile

BWR. *see in index* Boiling water reactor

By, John (1781–1836), English military engineer, born in London; worked extensively in Canada
Ottawa O-615

Byblos (Biblical Gebal), ancient city on site of modern Jebeil in Lebanon, on Mediterranean coast, 25 mi (40 km) n.e. of Beirut; early center of Phoenician civilization; valuable remains of Egyptian occupation in 14th century BC; later chief fortress of Philistines until their defeat by Israelites
Phoenician writing A-317, *table* A-315

Bydgoszcz (German Bromberg), Poland, city on canal between Oder and Vistula rivers; trade center; formerly in province of Posen, Prussia; pop. 248,300, *map* E-360.

Bye-Lo Baby, doll that was introduced in the U.S. in 1924; gained instant popularity D-221

Byelorussia. *see in index* Belorussian Soviet Socialist Republic

Byerly Turk, horse, foundation sire of the Thoroughbred Horse H-249, 275

Bygdoy peninsula, peninsula near Oslo, Norway O-610

Bykovsky, Valery Fyodorovich (born 1934), Soviet cosmonaut, born in Pavlova-Posad, near Moscow; first cosmonaut to volunteer for training in isolation chamber and centrifuge, *picture* S-346b, *table* S-348
Tereshkova T-111

Bylaw, a rule or regulation made by a society or organization for its government P-132a

Bypass engine. *see in index* Turbofan engine

By-product, a product obtained as part of the manufacture of another product
agricultural P-379
sugar beet S-508
sugarcane S-508
fish U-105
fly ash. *see in index* Fly ash
gas G-38
lignin P-101
lumber P-380
meat industry, *table* M-249
paper-mill wastes P-107
petroleum, *chart* P-241
selenium S-108
silver S-204

Byrd, Harry Flood (1887–1966), U.S. political leader, born in Martinsburg, W. Va.; brother of Richard E. Byrd; governor of Virginia 1926–30; U.S. senator (Democrat) from Virginia 1933–65 V-387
U.S. presidential election V-387
electoral vote, *chart* P-495

Byrd, Richard E. (full name Richard Evelyn Byrd) (1888–1957), U.S. aviator and explorer B-531
Antarctic exploration A-204, A-477, P-423
North Pole exploration A-204, *picture* A-205, *map* P-417

Byrd, William (or William Birde) (1542?–1623), English organist and composer B-532

Byrd, William (1674–1744), U.S. lawyer, born in Westover, Va.; founder of Richmond and Petersburg, Va. R-204
writings A-341

Byrne, David, U.S. rock singer, *picture* M-683

Byrne, Jane (born 1934), U.S. public official, born in Chicago, Ill.; commissioner of Chicago department of consumer sales, weights, and measures; mayor of Chicago 1979–83
Chicago politics C-316
women's rights W-276

Byrnes, James Francis (1879–1972), U.S. lawyer and public official, born in Charleston, S.C.; Democratic representative from South Carolina 1911–25; United States senator 1931–41; associate justice U.S. Supreme Court 1941–42; director Office of Economic Stabilization 1942–43; director war mobilization 1943–45; secretary of state 1945–47; governor of South Carolina 1951–55; appointed member of U.S. delegation to United Nations Sept. 1953 ('Speaking Frankly'; 'All in One Lifetime'), *picture* S-316
post-World War II conference W-357

Byron, Lord (or George Gordon, Lord Byron) (1788–1824), English poet B-532
literary contribution E-274
quoted P-406

Byte, group of binary characters C-627
electronics E-176

Bytown, Can. *see in index* Ottawa

Byzantine architecture
castles C-198
Church of St. Basil the Blessed, *picture* R-332e
dome development A-549
St. Mark's Cathedral V-277

Byzantine art
Cimabue P-28, *picture* P-29

Byzantine Empire (or Eastern Empire, or Eastern Roman Empire, or Greek Empire) B-533
Ankara attack A-466
Attilla A-758
Constantine the Great C-680
Crusaders (1204) V-279
dress D-261, *picture* D-262
Egyptian conquest E-126
Europe E-347
exarchate of Ravenna R-97
furniture F-456
Greece G-267
literature G-279
Hun soldiers H-330
international trade I-269
Justinian I J-161
Vandal conquest V-265
Khosrow I and II K-232
Leo III L-130
library history L-171
military practices A-637
mosaic M-590
navigation N-78
rulers. *see table in index*
textiles T-144
silk industry S-202
Turkey T-323
Ottoman empire O-616
U.S.S.R.
Georgian Soviet Socialist Republic G-102
trade R-351
warfare W-20
warship N-81

'Byzantine History', work by Nicephorus Gregoras G-279

Byzantine rite, Eastern rite tradition E-44

Byzantium. *see in index* Istanbul

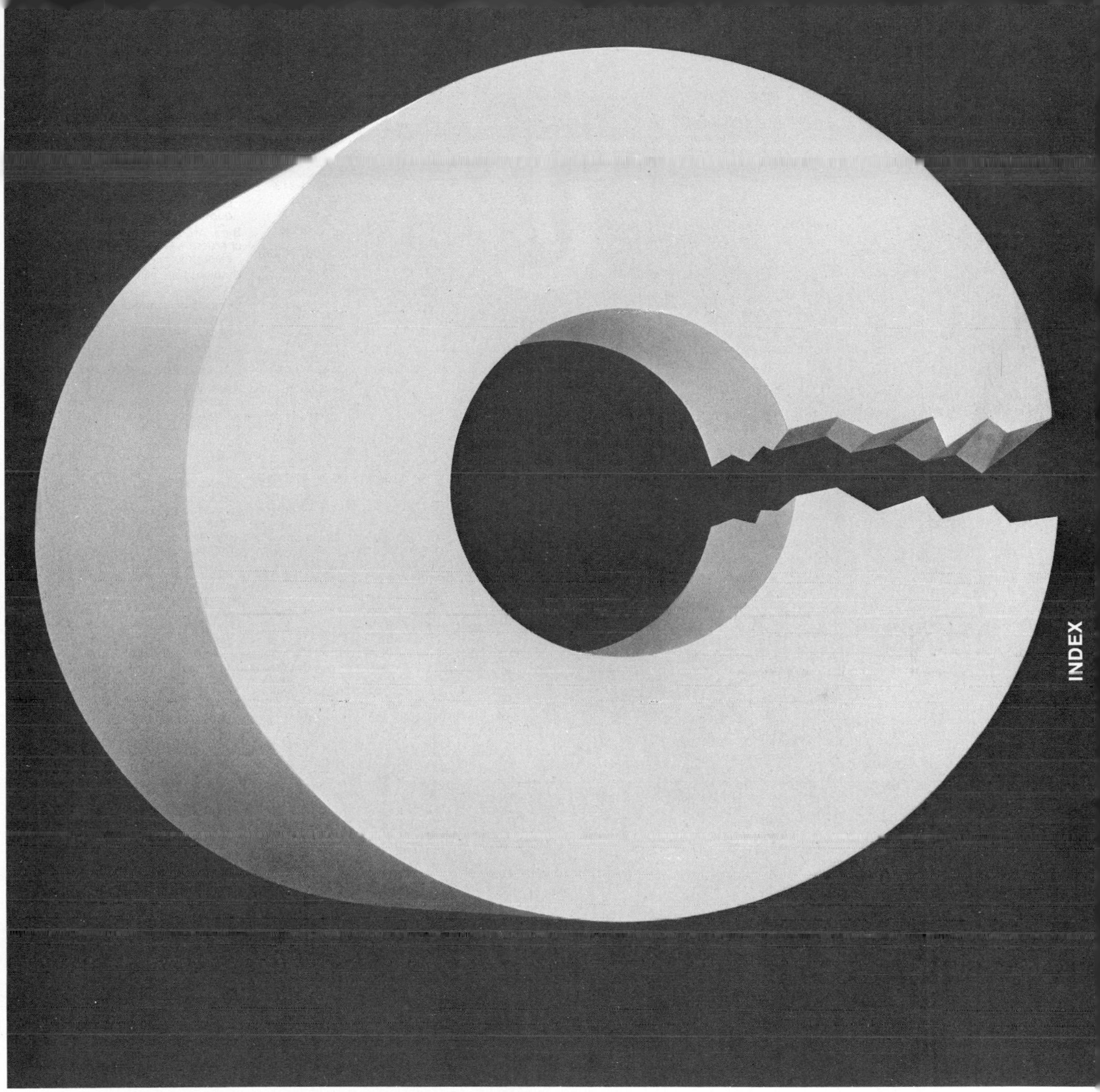

The letter C

may have started as a picture sign of a throwing stick, as in Egyptian hieroglyphic writing (1) and in a very early Semitic writing used about 1500 B.C. on the Sinai Peninsula (2). About 1000 B.C., in Byblos and other Phoenician and Canaanite centers, the sign was given a linear form (3), the source of all later forms. In the Semitic languages the sign was called *gimel* or *gaml,* meaning "throwing stick."

The Greeks changed the Semitic name to *gamma.* After the Greeks began to write from left to right, they reversed the letter (4). As among the Semites, the sign *gamma* was used for the sound "g."

The Romans took this sign over into Latin, but they rounded it (5). Originally they used the sign for the sounds "g" and "k." In time they differentiated the two sounds in writing. The original form of C was used for the sound "k," and a new form of G—C plus a bar—was used for the sound "g." The two sign forms passed unchanged into English.

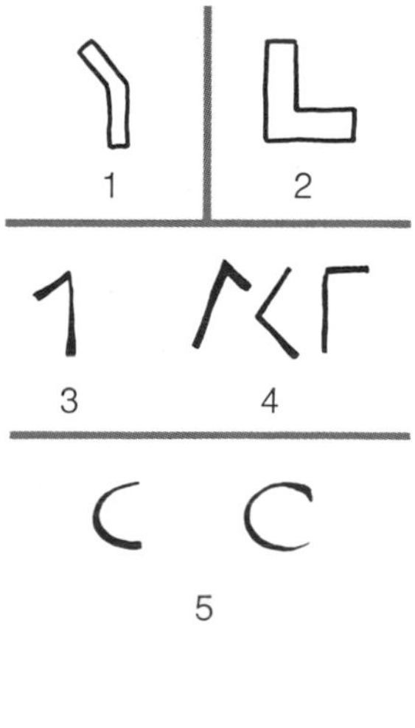

C

C, chemical element. *see in index* Carbon

C-12 (carbon-12), carbon atom C-157

C-13 (carbon-13), carbon isotope C-158

C-14, (carbon-14), carbon isotope. *see in index* Carbon-14

C-47, military air transport plane W-334

Ca, chemical element. *see in index* Calcium

Caaba. *see in index* Kaaba

Caatinga, forest in Brazil S-276, 287, *map* S-298

CAB. *see in index* Civil Aeronautics Board

Cabal C-2

Caballero, Fernán (pen name of Cecilia Böhl de Faber) (1796–1877), Spanish novelist, born in Switzerland ('The Sea-Gull') S-365b

Cabanel, Alexandre (1823–89), French painter, born in Montpellier, France; celebrated and highly popular in his time for portraits and historical paintings.

Cabbage, vegetable C-2, *picture* C-3
- Alaska, *picture* U-93
- sulfur S-509

Cabbage butterfly (or white butterfly), insect *Pieris rapae* of the order Lepidoptera, family Pieridae; its larva is a pest on cabbage and cauliflower B-528
- egg, *picture* E-111
- insect, *picture* I-215

Cabbage palm, name applied to certain palms, such as the coconut palm and royal palm, that bear large terminal buds that are eaten like cabbage, *picture* P-83
- root cap, *picture* P-363b

Cabbage palmetto P-84

Cabbage Patch Kids, dolls D-222

Cabbage rose R-294

'Cabbages and Kings', work by Henry H-133

Cabell, James Branch (1879–1958), U.S. novelist, born in Richmond, Va.; humorous fantasies (novels: 'The Cream of the Jest', 'Jurgen', 'Figures of Earth'; autobiography: 'As I Remember It'), *picture* V-342

Cabeza de Vaca, Álvar Núñez (1490–1557), Spanish soldier and explorer C-4
- Iguazu Falls I-32
- southwest explorations S-337
  - New Mexico N-217
  - Texas T-123
    - Houston H-311

Cabezone (or cabezon), fish *Scorpaenichthys marmoratus* of the Pacific coast; green in color, even to the flesh and bones; handsome and hardy in aquariums.

Cabildo, French Quarter, New Orleans, La.; erected 1795 as seat of governing body ("cabildo") for Spanish province of Louisiana; residence of Lafayette during visit 1825; now a museum of history and art
- Louisiana Purchase area, *picture* U-175

Cabin, house H-307

Cabin cruiser (or cruiser), pleasure boat, *picture* B-327

Cabinda (or Kabinda), exclave of Angola in Africa n. of mouth of Congo River; about 2,800 sq mi (7,250 sq km); pop. 46,238 A-419, *map* A-115
- world, *map* W-297

Cabinet government C-4
- Australia A-803
- democracy D-95
- constitution C-684
- Philippines P-255b, *chart* P-255c
- United Kingdom P-131b, U-17
- United States U-156, *table* U-155

Cabinet house, model M-517

Cabinetmaking, the art of making fine furniture C-175
- yew Y-416

'Cabinet of Dr. Caligari, The', motion picture M-626, *picture* M-621
- West Germany G-115

Cable, George Washington (1844–1925), U.S. novelist, born in New Orleans, La.; stories of Creole life and old plantation days in the South ('The Grandissimes'; 'Old Creole Days'; 'Strange True Stories of Louisiana')
- American literature A-351

Cable, in construction
- bridge construction B-441, *picture* B-440
- towing P-90
- wire W-245

Cable car (or cable railway), transportation T-264
- Pittsburgh P-345a
- San Francisco, *picture* S-44
- street railways S-486
- Switzerland, *picture* S-538
- Tennessee, *picture* T-85
- Wellington, New Zealand W-148

Cable length, unit of measure, *table* W-140

Cables, communication C-7
- Field's promotion F-77
- first transatlantic in Newfoundland N-167
- Hawaii H-62
- Kelvin's contribution K-196
- telephone T-64
- television C-451

Cable television, system that distributes television signals by means of transmission cables; originated in U.S. in 1950s; improves picture and sound quality in areas with poor reception; provides additional motion picture and sports channels to subscribers; a few systems allow viewers to call up various materials or participate in public opinion polls through two-way channels T-69, 77
- pornography C-451

Cable tool drill, oil well equipment P-235

Cabochon, method of gem cutting which gives jewels a domelike appearance; used for all stones until 14th century, when faceted cut became popular; still used for opaque and translucent stones and for carbuncles J-113, *picture* J-116

Caboose, railroad car at end of freight or construction trains; used for crew or workers, *picture* R-84

Cabora Bassa Dam, major development project of Mozambique M-642

Cabora Bassa reservoir, on the Zambezi River Z-447

Cabot, George (1752–1823), one of Federalist leaders in Massachusetts, born in Salem; president of Hartford Convention and member of Essex Junto.

Cabot, John (1450–99?), Italian explorer sailing under English flag C-11
- exploration E-373
  - Canada C-89
  - Newfoundland N-163, 166
  - North America A-332
- Henry VII H-130

Cabot, Richard Clarke (1868–1939), U.S. physician and writer, born in Brookline, Mass.; professor of medicine and of social ethics, Harvard University; author of books on medicine and on ethics.

Cabot, Sebastian (1476?–1557?), explorer, son of John Cabot C-11
- exploration E-373
- Paraguay P-112

Cabot Strait, between Newfoundland and n. Cape Breton Island, connects Gulf of St. Lawrence with Atlantic Ocean N-163, *maps* C-112, N-350

Cabot Tower, in Newfoundland N-163, 167

Cabra, Spain, city 35 mi (55 km) s.e. of Córdoba; cereals, fruit, wine, olive oil; captured from Moors 1240; recaptured by them 1331; finally gained by Christians in 15th century; pop. 15,688.

Cabral, Pedro Álvarez (1460?–1526), Portuguese navigator C-11
- Diaz D-133
- exploration E-373
  - Brazil B-423
  - South America A-330

Cabrera, one of Balearic Islands B-24

Cabrillo, Juan Rodríguez (died 1543), Portuguese navigator
- exploration E-373
  - California C-40, S-337
  - San Diego Bay S-40

Cabrini, Mother (1850–1917), Roman Catholic saint C-11

Cabrini College, Radnor, Pa.; Roman Catholic; founded 1957; conducted by the Missionary Sisters of the Sacred Heart of Jesus; liberal arts, education.

Cacalia. *see in index* Emilia

Cacao, tropical tree *Theobroma cacao*
- chocolate C-393
- Ghana G-139, *picture* G-140
- pod, *picture* P-244

Caccini, Giulio (1550?–1618?), Italian singer and composer, born in Rome; one of group of musicians who developed new style out of which opera grew O-561

Cachalot. *see in index* Sperm whale

Cachucha, Spanish dance with castanets, usually solo; music, in triple time, resembles bolero.

Cacomistle, animal. *see in index* Ringtail cat

Cactus, desert plant C-12
- endangered species E-209
- houseplants H-289
- state flower A-597, S-427

Cactus wren, bird of the Troglodytidae family W-364

CAD/CAM. *see in index* Computer-aided design/computer-aided manufacturing

Caddis fly, an order of insects, Trichoptera; found near streams, ponds, lakes; larvae, called caddis worms, are aquatic, *pictures* I-125, P-512

Caddo, American Indian tribe
- American Indians, *map* I-136, *table* I-138
- Arkansas A-614

Caddoan, linguistic group of American Indians comprising the Arikara in North Dakota, the Pawnee in Nebraska, and the Caddo and Wichita in n. Louisiana, Arkansas, Oklahoma, Texas.

Cade, Jack (or John Cade) (died 1450), English peasant leader of rebellion, born in Ireland; supposedly related to Duke of York; mentioned in Shakespeare's 'Henry VI'
- Henry VI H-130

Cadence, rhythm of a horse's gait, *list* H-249

Cadence, in music, *list* M-670

Cadet, military or naval student
- military education M-410
- United States, *pictures* S-177

Cadillac, Antoine de la Mothe (1656?–1730), French officer in North America C-13
- Bienville B-190
- Michigan M-361
  - Detroit D-122
- Missouri lead mine M-493

Cadillac, Mich., city 81 mi (130 km) n.e. of Muskegon, on Lakes Cadillac and Mitchell; year-round resort; metal and wood products, boats; Manistee National Forest nearby; pop. 10,199 C-13

Cadillac Mountain, Maine, 1,532 ft (467 m); highest point on the Atlantic coast of North America.

Cádiz, Spain, seaport and naval station on Bay of Cádiz 50 mi (80 km) n.w. of Strait of Gibraltar; pop. 117,871 S-356, *maps* E-360, S-350

Cadman, Charles Wakefield (1881–1946), U.S. composer, born in Johnstown, Pa.; studied American Indian music and wrote many American Indian songs and operas ('At Dawning'; 'From the Land of the Sky-Blue Water').

Cadman, Samuel Parkes (1864–1936), U.S. clergyman, born in England; pastor Central Congregational Church, Brooklyn, N.Y., 1901–36; president Federal Council of Churches of Christ in America 1924–28 ('Charles Darwin and Other English Thinkers'; 'Imagination and Religion').

Cadmium (Cd), metallic element C-13
- nuclear energy N-424
- periodic table, *table* P-207, *list* P-208

Cadmium bromide, chemical compound; used in photography and photoengraving C-13

Cadmium iodide, chemical compound; used in photography and photoengraving C-13

Cadmium oxide, chemical compound; used in batteries C-13

Cadmium sulfide, chemical compound; used in high-grade paints and artists' pigments C-13

Cadmus, brother of Europa in Greek mythology; sowed dragon's teeth which became men who helped him create city of Thebes.

Cadogan (or tie-wig), hairdressing H-10

Cadorna, Luigi, Count (1850–1928), Italian field marshal, chief of general staff 1914–17, commander in chief of Italian armies in field 1915–17; replaced by Diaz following defeat at Caporetto.

Caduceus, magic wand of Hermes; has two snakes twined around a staff topped by wings; associated with medicine because snakes symbolized wisdom
- U.S. military medical services, *picture* U-10

Caecilian, an order of wormlike amphibians J-157

Caedmon (7th century AD), earliest English Christian poet C-13
- literary contribution E-264

Caelian Hill, Rome, Italy R-254

Caelum, constellation, *chart* C-682

Caen, France, city of Normandy on Orne River near coast; iron, steel, lace, gloves; lost priceless architectural treasures in World War II; pop. 106,790, *map* F-369

Caerleon, England, town on Usk River near border of s. Wales; Roman antiquities; a traditional site of Camelot.

Caernarvon (or Carnarvon), Wales, town on Menai Strait;

of a witch and a devil, enslaved by Prospero.

Caliber, firearms. *see in index* Bore

Calibration, adjustment of different instruments, such as gauges or thermometers, to give identical readings under the same circumstances; also adjustment of the scale divisions on an instrument.

Calico, printed cotton cloth; originally white cotton cloth from Calicut, India, later printed or painted; made in England and France in 18th century.

Calico bass, fish. *see in index* Crappie

Calico bush. *see in index* Mountain laurel

Calico cat (or tricolor cat, or money cat) C-205

Calico scallop, clam shell *Pecten gibbus*, *picture* S-150

Calicut, India. *see in index* Kozhikode

Calif. *see in index* Caliph

Califano, Joseph A., Jr. (born 1931), U.S. lawyer and public official, born in Brooklyn; U.S. secretary of health, education, and welfare 1977–79.

California, (nickname Golden State), Pacific state of U. S.; 158,693 sq mi (411,013 sq km); cap. Sacramento; pop. 23,668,562 C-32, *maps* U-36, U-40, 81, 87
- agriculture
  - chilies, *picture* P-197a
  - citrus fruits C-446, U-88
  - grapes G-220
  - lettuce L-140, *picture* P-191
  - prunes P-516
- aqueduct A-520
- arts
  - folktales S-481d
- cities. *see also in index* cities listed below and other cities by name
  - Anaheim A-387
  - Berkeley B-167
  - Fresno F-404
  - Huntington Beach H-333
  - Los Angeles L-298
  - Oakland O-453
  - Pasadena P-135
  - Richmond R-204
  - Sacramento S-2
  - San Diego S-39
  - San Francisco S-41
  - San Jose S-44
- earthquake E-33
- Hispanic Americans H-163
- history S-337, U-178
  - Compromise of 1850 C-624
  - early settlement A-334
  - frontier movement F-422
  - gold rush G-183, S-2
- housing H-305
- initiative and Proposition 13 I-206
- Mexican War M-320
- migrants O-472
- mining
  - petroleum P-230
- mudslide, *picture* E-31
- name, *table* S-428
- North America N-338, *picture* N-336, *map* N-350
- physical geography, *map* S-528
  - mountains
    - Sierra Nevada S-192b
    - Sequoia N.P. S-112
- state symbols
  - flags F-154, *pictures* F-155, 159
  - flower P-446, *picture* S-427
  - tree S-112
- Statuary Hall, *table* S-437a
- taxation T-37, *table* T-39
- United States U-86
- waterpower W-106
  - dams D-17
- wine and winemaking W-237, *picture* W-236

'California', U.S. battleship, *picture* W-344

California, Gulf of, arm of Pacific 700 mi (1,150 km) long between Lower California and Mexican mainland; in 16th-century books and maps called Sea of Cortés after Hernando Cortez who explored it M-325, *maps* M-341, N-350. *see also in index* Ocean, *table*

California, Lower (or Baja California), peninsula of Mexico between Pacific and Gulf of California and Colorado River; 55,518 sq mi (143,791 sq km); pop. 1,446,825 C-54, *maps* M-344, N-350
- climate R-90
- history
  - Kino explores K-247
  - Spanish rule S-338
- Mexico M-323, 333, *picture* M-322
- pearl fisheries P-149

California, University of, California, educational complex including nine campuses and numerous research facilities; state control; chartered 1868; central office at Berkeley C-40

California, University of, Berkeley, part of University of California; opened 1873; letters and science, agricultural science, education, environmental design, forestry, law, librarianship, optometry, public affairs, public health, social welfare; graduate school B-167, *picture* C-45

California, University of, Davis, part of University of California; founded as University Farm School 1908; letters and science, agriculture, engineering, law, medicine, veterinary medicine; graduate division.

California, University of, Irvine, part of University of California; opened 1965; letters and science, education, medicine; interschool curricula.

California, University of, Los Angeles, part of University of California; founded 1919; letters and science, architecture, business, dentistry, education, engineering, fine arts, law, library science, medicine, nursing, public health, social welfare, urban planning; graduate study.

California, University of, San Diego, part of University of California; Scripps Institution of Oceanography founded 1912, undergraduate schools opened 1964; letters and science; Institute of Marine Resources.

California, University of, San Francisco, became part of University of California 1873; dentistry, medicine, nursing, pharmacy; university hospital and clinics; upper level and graduate studies only.

California, University of, Santa Barbara, became part of University of California 1944; present name 1958; letters and science, education; graduate study; College of Creative Studies.

California, University of, Santa Cruz, part of University of California; founded 1965; letters and science; environmental, community, and religious studies; Center for South Pacific Studies.

California and Intermountain Seed Gatherers, Indian culture group N-134

'California and the West', work by Weston W-163

California Baptist College, Riverside, Calif.; Southern Baptist; founded 1950; arts and sciences, teacher education.

California College of Arts and Crafts, Oakland, Calif.; private control; founded 1907; fine arts, design, humanities, sciences; graduate study.

California condor, bird
- endangered species E-212, B-271, B-280

California current, ocean current O-475

California Debris Commission F-183

California Fruit Growers Exchange (or Sunkist) C-707

California gull, bird *Larus californicus* G-317

California halibut. *see in index* Pacific halibut

California holly. *see in index* Christmasberry

California Institute of Technology, Pasadena, Calif.; private control; formerly for men, women admitted 1970; founded 1891 (as Throop Polytechnic Institute); civil, electrical, mechanical, chemical, and aeronautical engineering, and science; graduate school; administers Palomar Observatory jointly with Carnegie Institute.

California laurel (sometimes called Oregon myrtle, or bay tree, or pepperwood), an

A PERPETUAL CALENDAR

*This calendar gives the day of the week for any date from the beginning of the Christian Era to the year **2400**.*

CENTURY	Julian Calendar							Gregorian Calendar				
	0 / 700 / 1400	100 / 800 / 1500*	200 / 900	300 / 1000	400 / 1100	500 / 1200	600 / 1300	1500†	1600 / 2000	1700 / 2100	1800 / 2200	**1900** / 2300
YEAR	*Dominical Letters‡*											
0	DC	ED	FE	GF	AG	BA	CB	——	BA	C	E	G
1 29 57 85	B	C	D	E	F	G	A	F	G	B	D	F
2 30 58 86	A	B	C	D	E	F	G	E	F	A	C	E
3 31 59 87	G	A	B	C	D	E	F	D	E	G	B	D
4 32 60 88	FE	GF	AG	BA	CB	DC	ED	CB	DC	FE	AG	CB
5 33 **61** 89	D	E	F	G	A	B	C	A	B	D	F	**A**
6 34 62 90	C	D	E	F	G	A	B	G	A	C	E	G
7 35 63 91	B	C	D	E	F	G	A	F	G	B	D	F
8 36 64 92	AG	BA	CB	DC	ED	FE	GF	ED	FE	AG	CB	ED
9 37 65 93	F	G	A	B	C	D	E	C	D	F	A	C
10 38 66 94	E	F	G	A	B	C	D	B	C	E	G	B
11 39 67 95	D	E	F	G	A	B	C	A	B	D	F	A
12 40 68 96	CB	DC	ED	FE	GF	AG	BA	GF	AG	CB	ED	GF
13 41 69 97	A	B	C	D	E	F	G	E	F	A	C	E
14 42 70 98	G	A	B	C	D	E	F	D	E	G	B	D
15 43 71 99	F	G	A	B	C	D	E	C	D	F	A	C
16 44 72	ED	FE	GF	AG	BA	CB	DC	——	CB	ED	GF	BA
17 45 73	C	D	E	F	G	A	B	——	A	C	E	G
18 46 74	B	C	D	E	F	G	A	——	G	B	D	F
19 47 75	A	B	C	D	E	F	G	——	F	A	C	E
20 48 76	GF	AG	BA	CB	DC	ED	FE	——	ED	GF	BA	DC
21 49 77	E	F	G	A	B	C	D	——	C	E	G	B
22 50 78	D	E	F	G	A	B	C	——	B	D	F	A
23 51 79	C	D	E	F	G	A	B	——	A	C	E	G
24 52 80	BA	CB	DC	ED	FE	GF	AG	——	GF	BA	DC	FE
25 53 81	G	A	B	C	D	E	F	——	E	G	B	D
26 54 82	F	G	A	B	C	D	E	C	D	F	A	C
27 55 83	E	F	G	A	B	C	D	B	C	E	G	B
28 56 84	DC	ED	FE	GF	AG	BA	CB	AG	BA	DC	FE	AG

MONTH	*Dominical Letter*						
Jan., Oct.	A	B	C	D	E	F	G
Feb., March, Nov.	D	E	F	G	A	B	C
April, July	G	A	B	C	D	E	F
May	B	C	D	E	F	G	A
June	E	F	G	A	B	C	D
Aug.	C	D	E	F	G	A	B
Sept., **Dec.**	F	G	**A**	B	C	D	E

DAY							
1 8 15 22 29	Sun.	Sat.	Fri.	Thur.	Wed.	Tues.	Mon.
2 9 16 23 30	Mon.	Sun.	Sat.	Fri.	Thurs.	Wed.	Tues.
3 10 17 24 31	Tues.	Mon.	Sun.	Sat.	Fri.	Thur.	Wed.
4 11 18 **25**	Wed.	Tues.	**Mon.**	Sun.	Sat.	Fri.	Thur.
5 12 19 26	Thur.	Wed.	Tues.	Mon.	Sun.	Sat.	Fri.
6 13 20 27	Fri.	Thur.	Wed.	Tues.	Mon.	Sun.	Sat.
7 14 21 28	Sat.	Fri.	Thur.	Wed.	Tues.	Mon.	Sun.

*On and before 1582, Oct. 4 only.
†On and after 1582, Oct. 15 only.
‡Two letters are given for leap years; the first is for January and February, the second for the other months.

EXAMPLE: To find the day of the week for Christmas, **December 25, 1961:**
In the Century section, locate 1900.
In the Year section, follow down the column in which **1900** appears in the Century section to the line with 61. Note the dominical letter **A.**
In the Month section, locate **December** and follow its line to the dominical letter **A.**
In the Day section, locate **25** and follow its line to the column in which the dominical letter **A** appears for **December** in the Month section. The day of the week is **Monday.** Thus **December 25, 1961,** fell on a **Monday.**

evergreen tree *Umbellularia californica* native to Pacific coast of Oregon and California; grows to 80 ft (25 m), but is a shrub in dry locations; leaves oblong, glossy above, leathery, aromatic, dark green; flowers yellow green, tiny, in clusters; fruit oval, 1 in. (2.5 cm) long, purple when ripe. *see also in index* Myrtle burl

California Lutheran College, Thousand Oaks, Calif.; chartered 1959; opened 1961; liberal arts, education.

'Californian', ocean liner S-177d

California Polytechnic State University, San Luis Obispo, Calif.; founded 1901; arts and sciences, agriculture; education, engineering; graduate studies.

California poppy (or golden poppy), flowering annual P-446
growing conditions G-24
state flower, *picture* S-427

California privet, tree *Ligustrum ovalifolium* H-115

California quail, bird *Lophortyx californicus* Q-3
bird species B-259, *picture* B-270

California red fir. *see in index* Red fir

California rosebay. *see in index* West Coast rhododendron

California sea lion S-100

California State College, California, Pa.; founded 1852; liberal arts and education; graduate study.

California State College, Bakersfield, founded 1965; liberal arts, education, nursing; graduate studies.

California State College, Dominguez Hills, near Gardena, Calif.; founded 1960; humanities and fine arts, education; graduate studies.

California State College, San Bernardino, founded 1960; opened 1965; liberal arts, education; graduate studies.

California State College, Stanislaus (until 1972, Stanislaus State College), Turlock, Calif.; established 1957; liberal arts, teacher education; graduate studies.

California State Polytechnic University, Pomona, Calif.; founded 1938, separate state college 1966; agriculture, arts, business administration, education, engineering, science; graduate studies; Kellogg campus is main center; Voorhis campus, 5 mi (8 km) away, used for adult education in business and government.

California State University, Chico (until 1972, Chico State College), Chico, Calif.; chartered 1887; opened 1889; liberal arts, agriculture, education, engineering, nursing; graduate studies.

California State University, Fresno (formerly Fresno State College), Fresno, Calif.; founded 1911; arts and sciences, agriculture, business administration, education, engineering, and social work; graduate studies.

California State University, Fullerton (formerly called Orange State College), opened 1959; liberal arts, business administration, education; graduate studies.

California State University, Hayward (formerly called Alameda County State College), established 1957; liberal arts and sciences, education; graduate studies.

California State University, Long Beach (formerly called Long Beach State College), opened 1949; arts and sciences, business administration, education, engineering, home economics, industrial arts; graduate studies.

California State University, Los Angeles (formerly called Los Angeles State College of Applied Arts and Science), opened 1949; arts and sciences, business administration, education; graduate studies.

California State University, Northridge (until 1972, San Fernando Valley State College), Northridge, near Los Angeles, Calif.; founded 1958; arts and sciences, business administration; education, engineering; graduate studies.

California State University, Sacramento (until 1972, Sacramento State College), Sacramento, Calif.; opened 1947; arts and science, education; graduate school.

California sugar pine. *see in index* Sugar pine

California Trail, historic road in U.S. R-221, *map* R-219

California tree cricket, insect *Oecanthus californicus* of the family Gryllidae, *picture* C-768

Californium (Cf), chemical element
periodic table, *table* P-207, *list* P-208

Caligula ("Little Boot," nickname of Gaius Caesar) (AD 12–41); Roman emperor, succeeded AD 37; insanely cruel R-247

Caliph (or calif), formerly civil and religious head of an Islamic state
Africa A-110
Arabs A-527

Caliphate, ruling institution in Islam from 632 to 1517 C-54
Harun ar-Rashid H-51
international relations I-259
Islam I-361, I-363
Mongolian Empire M-535
Ottoman Empire O-617

Caliphate of Córdoba. *see in index* Córdoba, caliphate of

Calippus. *see in index* Callippus

Calixtus I, Saint (or Callistus I) (died 222), pope 217–22; martyr; feast Oct. 14; started ember days; eased severe penitential disciplines.

Calixtus II (or Callistus II) (died 1124), pope 1119–24; concluded Concordat of Worms with Henry V (1122) H-209

Calixtus III (originally Alfonso Borgia), pope
Borgia family B-367

Callaghan, James (born 1912), British political leader C-57
United Kingdom E-259

Callaghan, Morley (born 1903), Canadian writer, born in Toronto, Ont., of Irish parents; known for realism and treatment of moral problems (short stories: 'Now That April's Here, and Other Stories'; novels; memoirs: 'That Summer in Paris') C-122, 124, *picture* C-123

Calla lily, plant L-209

Callanan, Jeremiah Joseph (1795–1829), Irish author I-327

Callao, Peru, seaport forming a department; 14 sq mi (36 sq km); warehouse center; in mining and farming district, exports minerals, metals, wool, cottons, hides, and fish meal; pop. 296,220, *maps* P-224, S-298, W-297, *picture* P-221
Lima L-210

Callas, Maria (1923–77), U.S. operatic soprano C-57

Calles, Plutarco Elías (1877–1945), Mexican general and statesman, born in Guaymas, Sonora; president 1924–28; worked against Díaz, Huerta, and Villa; governor of Sonora 1917; in cabinets of Carranza and Obregón M-338

Callicrates (5th century BC), Greek architect and sculptor; designed Wingless Victory; with Ictinus designed the Parthenon, working under supervision of the sculptor Phidias A-547, *picture* A-546

Callière, Louis Hector de (1646–1703), French colonial official, born in Cherbourg; 1684–99 governor of Montreal; 1699–1703 governor-general of New France; known for his wise dealings with the Iroquois.

Calligraphy (from Greek for "beautiful writing"), art of fine handwriting C-57
China C-346, 386
handwriting H-29

Callimachus (5th century BC), Greek sculptor; credited with a group of dancing Laconian maidens and a gold lamp for the Erechtheum; said to be the originator of the Corinthian capital and the running drill for boring in marble.

Callimachus, Greek lyric poet of 3rd century BC, born in Cyrene; credited with some 800 works including 'Actia', a collection of legends; worked as schoolmaster and as chief of Alexandrian library G-277

Calliope, series of steam whistles arranged to give tunes when sounded by keyboard C-427

Calliopsis, flowering annual. *see also in index* Coreopsis
growing conditions G-24

Callippus (or Calippus) (4th century BC), Greek astronomer, born in Cyzicus, Asia Minor; instituted use of Callippic cycle, a period of 76 years (the equivalent of four Metonic cycles minus one day).

Callisto, in Greek mythology, attendant of Artemis and mother of Arcas; because of love affair with Zeus she was turned into a bear by Hera or Artemis; mistaken for an ordinary bear, was about to be slain when rescued by Zeus who placed her in the sky as the constellation Great Bear.

Callistus, name of several popes. *see in index* Calixtus

'Call of the Wild', work by London N-409

Callot, Jacques (1592–1635), French engraver, born in Nancy, France; master of art of design; famous for action pictures involving large groups.

Calloway, Cab (in full Cabell Calloway) (born 1907), U.S. orchestra leader, singer, and composer, born in Rochester, N.Y.; "King of Hi de Ho"; stage, screen, nightclubs, and radio M-684

Callus, skin, area thickened and hardened by prolonged rubbing or pressure; usually forms on feet or hands.

Calmar, Sweden. *see in index* Kalmar

Calms, belt of. *see in index* Doldrums

Calomel, Mercurous chloride M-305

Caloosahatchee River, s.w. Florida, 75 mi (120 km) long; main outlet of Lake Okeechobee; forms western arm of Cross-State Canal.

Calorie, unit of energy; used to measure heat; 1 gram calorie increases the temperature of 1 gram of water 1° C
food and nutrition F-275, *chart* F-276
heat H-104

Calorimeter, instrument for measuring quantity of heat
heat H-104
Montgolfiers invent M-569

Calosoma beetle, insect
gypsy moth eradication B-138

Calotype process, in photography P-296

Calpé, in ancient geography, one of the Pillars of Hercules; modern Gibraltar.

Calpurnia (died after 44 BC), Roman matron; became last wife of Julius Caesar in 59 BC; warned in a dream, she tried to keep him from going to the senate on the Ides of March; appears in Shakespeare's play 'Julius Caesar'.

Caltanissetta, city in Sicily; center of sulfur industry; ancient ruins nearby; annexed to Italy by Garibaldi 1860; suffered severe damage in World War II; pop. 63,027, *map* I-401

Calthrop, Samuel Robert (1829–1917), Unitarian minister, born in Lincolnshire, England; came to U.S. 1853; first U.S. patent for streamlined train 1865.

Caltrop family (or Zygophyllaceae), family of plants, shrubs, and trees, including the lignumvitae and the creosote bush.

Calumet, Mich., town on Upper Peninsula, about 68 mi (109 km) n.w. of Marquette; situated in Calumet township, center of copper-mining district; pop. 1,013, *map* U-41

Calumet (or ceremonial pipe), the "peace pipe" of North American Indians; tobacco pipe with stone bowl and reed stem ornamented with eagles' feathers
etiquette E-319

Calumet City, Ill., city just s. of Chicago, on Indiana line; chemicals, packinghouse products, pickles; pop. 39,673 I-87, *picture* I-98, *map* I-52

Calumet College, East Chicago, Ind.; Roman Catholic; established 1951 as branch of St. Joseph's College, Rensselaer; became separate institution 1963; arts and sciences, education.

Calusa, North American Indian tribe, *map* I-136, *table* I-138

Calutron process, uranium isotope separation U-211

Calvé, Emma (formerly Rosa Emma Calvet) (1858–1942), French opera soprano, *list* O-570

Calverley, Charles Stuart (1831–84), English poet, parodist, and barrister, born in Martley, Worcestershire ('Fly Leaves'; 'Theocritus, Translated into English Verse').

Calvert, Cecil. *see in index* Baltimore, Cecil Calvert, 2nd Baron

Calvert, Charles. *see in index* Baltimore, Charles Calvert, 3rd Baron

Calvert, George. *see in index* Baltimore, George Calvert, 1st Baron

Calvert, Leonard (1606–47), first colonial governor of Maryland, brother of Cecil, 2nd Lord Baltimore B-46, M-171

Calvert Cliffs, Maryland, on Chesapeake Bay, *picture* M-176

Calvet, Rosa Emma. *see in index* Calvé, Emma

Calvi, battle of (1794), named for small seaport in n.w. Corsica; naval battle between English and Corsicans in which Nelson lost his right eye.

Calvin, John (1509–64), French theologian and Protestant reformer C-60, *picture* R-134. *see also in index* Calvinism
French literature F-395
Geneva G-58
Puritans P-539
Reformation R-134

Calvin, Melvin (born 1911), U.S. organic chemist and educator, born in St. Paul, Minn.; with University of California at Berkeley since 1937, professor from 1947; associate director Lawrence Radiation Laboratory 1967–80.

Calvin College, Grand Rapids, Mich.; founded 1876 by Christian Reformed church; arts and sciences, teacher education.

Calvinism. *see also in index* Calvin, John
American religious literature A-342

Calvino, Italo (1923–85), Italian writer I-379

Calycanthus (popularly called Carolina allspice), genus of aromatic shrubs with opposite leaves and large brownish purple flowers; *Calycanthus floridus,* called the strawberry shrub because the crushed flowers yield the fragrance of strawberries, is a common garden shrub.

Calycanthus family (or Calycanthaceae), family of plants, native to North America and e. Asia, including Carolina allspice and the meratias.

Calydon, ancient city of Aetolia, Greece; scene of legendary hunt for the monstrous Calydonian boar which Artemis sent to ravage the country because she had been neglected in a sacrifice by the king of Calydon.

Calypso, in Greek mythology, nymph who detained Odysseus for seven years H-223

Calypso music, folk music of Trinidad; became popular as form of jazz music in U.S. 1938; simple, characteristic melodies; words often about persons prominent in current events.

Calyx, flower structure F-219

Cam, river in Cambridgeshire, England; 40 mi (65 km) long; rises near Ashwell, emptying into Ouse; navigable to Cambridge which is named for river C-61

Cam, machine M-10
automobile engine A-847
locks L-277
mechanics M-268, *picture* M-267

CAM (controlled automatic machining), aid to mass production M-209

Camaçho, Manuel Ávila. *see in index* Avila Camacho, Manuel

Camagüey, province, Cuba; sugarcane, cattle; pop. 683,889, *map* C-802

Camagüey, Cuba, largest inland city; in Camagüey Province, 170 mi (275 km) n.w. of Santiago de Cuba; cattle products; pop. 253,800, *maps* C-802, N-350

Camarasaurus supremus, dinosaur, *picture* F-322

Camargo, Marie Anne de Cupis de (1710–70), Belgian ballerina, born in Brussels, Belgium; made Paris debut 1726; The Camargo Society (founded London 1930 to sponsor ballet) named for her B-33, D-24

Camargue, delta region, France F-345

Camarillo, Calif., city e. of Oxnard in agricultural area; magnetic tape; site of St. John's College and state mental hospital; pop. 19,219.

Cambacérès, Jean Jacques Régis de, duke of Parma (1753–1824), French statesman, born in Montpellier, France; 2nd consul under Napoleon; played part in compiling Code Napoléon.

Camber, curvature of an airfoil A-166, G-167

Camberwell, area in Southwark borough, Greater London, England; Camberwell Green once celebrated for fairs.

Cambium, growth layer between bark and wood of trees P-360
  tree T-276, *diagram* T-277
  vacuole's development C-240

Cambodia. *see in index* Kampuchea

Cambodia tea plant, a variety of tea plant T-45

Cambon, Jules (1845–1935), French diplomat, born in Paris; brother of Pierre Cambon; governor-general of Algeria; French ambassador to U.S. 1897–1902, to Spain 1902–7, to Germany 1907–14; deputy prime minister 1917.

Cambon, Pierre Paul (1843–1924), French diplomat, born in Paris; brother of Jules Cambon; prefect departments of Aube, Doubs, Nord successively; minister Tunisia; ambassador to Spain 1886–90, to Turkey 1890–98, to England 1898–1920; instrumental in setting up the *entente cordiale.*

Cambrai, France, city 35 mi (55 km) s.e. of Lille; linen goods, especially cambric, to which it gave name; soap, flour, metal products; pop. 37,290, *map* F-369

Cambrai, League of (1508), alliance of Louis XII of France, Emperor Maximilian I, Ferdinand the Catholic of Spain, and Pope Julius II for partition of Venetian territories V-279, *table* T-274

Cambrai, Peace of (1529), *table* T-274

Cambrian Mountains, mountains, Wales W-5

Cambrian period, in geological time, *picture* P-487
  Earth E-23, *map* E-25, *table* E-24
  fossils F-323

Cambridge (or Cambridgeshire), former county in e. England; 867 sq mi (2,246 sq km); included administrative county, Isle of Ely (area 375 sq mi [971 sq km]; pop. 89,180); county seat Cambridge; pop. 279,564. *see also in index* Cambridgeshire

Cambridge (called in ancient times Granta, or Grantabridge, or Cantabridge), England, seat of Cambridge University, on Cam River 50 mi (80 km) n. of London; much of city built on reclaimed marshlands; Church of Holy Sepulchre built in Norman times; pop. 101,100 C-60, *map* U-18a

Cambridge, Md., city on Choptank River, 37 mi (60 km) s.e. of Annapolis; crab and oyster fishing; vegetable and seafood processing, corrugated boxes, printing, electronic equipment, metal products, boats; pop. 11,703 M-168, *map* M-182

Cambridge (originally called New Towne), Mass., suburb of Boston; pop. 95,322 C-61
  Massachusetts M-191, 202, *picture* M-192

Cambridge, Ohio, city 75 mi (120 km) e. of Columbus; in coal and clay area; electronic products, metal products, plastics, ceramics; pop. 13,573.

Cambridgeshire, county, England, formed in 1974 from county of Cambridge, administrative county of Isle of Ely, county of Huntingdon and Peterborough, and parts of West Sussex; 1,316 sq mi (3,409 sq km); pop. 570,200 C-60. *see also in index* Cambridge

Cambridge University, famous center of learning, Cambridge, England; established 12th century; given charter by Henry III (1231); 20 colleges, including three for women (women first given degrees 1923)
  Cambridge C-60
  England E-234

Cambunian Mountains, Greece, range in n. Thessaly intersecting the Pindus Mountains on west, culminating in Mount Olympus on east.

Cambuscan, king of Sarra in Tartary in Chaucer's 'Squire's Tale'; given magic horse, ring, mirror, and sword by king of Arabia and India.

Cambyses I (fl. 6th century BC), king of the Achaemenid dynasty of Persia; son of Cyrus I and father of Cyrus the Great; ruled Anshan.

Cambyses II (died 522 BC), king of Medes and Persians 530–522 BC; grandson of Cambyses I and son of Cyrus; conquered Egypt; reputation as inhuman and dissolute ruler.

Camcorder, in video recording V-313

Camden, Ark., industrial city on Ouachita River, in s. part of state, 27 mi (43 km) n.w. of El Dorado; paper products, furniture and wood products, pyrotechnics, telecommunication equipment; pop. 15,356, *map* A-562

Camden, England, borough of Greater London, *maps* L-287, U-18a

Camden, N.J., port and railroad center on Delaware River opposite Philadelphia, Pa.; electrical appliances, chemicals; food processing; incorporated as city 1828; pop. 84,910 N-195, *picture* P-168, *map* U-41

Camden, S.C., city 32 mi (51 km) n.e. of Columbia; textiles, synthetic fibers, lumber products; resort; scene of battle in American Revolution (1780); pop. 7,462, *map* S-319
  Gates' and De Kalb's defeat R-172
  second battle. *see in index* Hobkirk's Hill, battle of
  temperature record, *list* S-305

Camel, George Joseph. *see in index* Kamel, George Joseph

Camel, animal of the Camelidae family C-62
  Afghanistan A-90
  animal life record, *table* E-24
  caravan. *see in index* Caravan, *subhead* camel
  children's game, *picture* P-193
  express history E-384
  folktale illustration, *picture* S-476
  fur, *table* F-464
  wool W-288
  hoof H-231
  length of life, *chart* A-423
  Pakistan, *picture* P-77
  prehistoric A-462, *pictures* A-460, P-490
  riding, *picture* S-15
  ruminant R-318

Camel bird. *see in index* Ostrich

Camelidae, the camel family, including llamas, alpacas, guanacos, and vicuñas. *see also in index* Alpaca; Guanaco; Llama; Vicuña

Camellia, shrub, *picture* F-227

Camelopard, ancient name for giraffe. *see in index* Giraffe

Camelopardalis, constellation, *chart* C-681

Camelot, legendary seat of King Arthur's court; Caerleon, England, is a traditional site; others include Somersetshire and Camelford in Cornwall A-655

Camel Rock, geological feature, in Wyoming, *picture* W-395

Camel's-hair cloth, fabric made from camel's hair; often mixed with wool to add strength and shape; used for coats, jackets, suits, sweaters, blankets, and rugs.

'Camel with Driver', 16th-century Persian drawing D-250, *picture* D-251

Camembert, cheese C-288

Cameo S-151
  onyx O-559

Camera P-282, 285, 295
  automatic features A-836, *picture* A-835
  contribution of
    Eastman E-47
    Edison E-75, *picture* E-74
    Land L-26
  electron, *picture* P-307
  guided missiles G-311
  hobby H-188
  microfilm M-377
  motion pictures M-602, 607, *diagram* M-603
  optics O-574
  spectroscopic S-372
  stereo S-444
  television S-348, T-74, *picture* P-238
    color C-565, *picture* C-564
  video recording V-311

Camera crane, motion pictures M-609

Camera degli Sposi, room painted by Mantegna M-111

Cameraless abstraction, image produced directly on film P-299

Camera lucida, microscope attachment M-382

Camera obscura, photography P-295

Camerata, group of Italians, originators of opera O-561

Cameron, Sir David Young (1865–1945), British etcher and painter, born in Glasgow, Scotland; exhibited widely in Europe; received medal in Chicago 1893 ('The Clyde Set'; 'London Set').

Cameron, John Hillyard (1817–76), Canadian statesman, born near St. Omer, France; to Canada 1825; in Parliament 26 years; helped shape Conservative party.

Cameron, Julia Margaret (1815–79), British photographer; considered one of the greatest portraitists P-297

Cameron, Malcolm (1808–76), Canadian statesman, born in Trois-Rivières, Lower Canada; twice president of legislative council; minister of agriculture; postmaster general; advocate of prohibition.

Cameron, Simon (1799–1889), state "boss" in U.S. politics, born in Donegal, Pa.; senator; secretary of war under Lincoln 1861–62; minister to Russia; passed control of Republican party in Pennsylvania to his son, **James D. Cameron** (1833–1918) S-411

Cameron, La., village near s.w. corner of state, on Calcasieu River between Calcasieu Lake and Gulf of Mexico; fishing port; hunting grounds nearby; pop. 975.

Cameroon (officially United Republic of Cameroon), nation situated in w.-central Africa on the Gulf of Guinea; land area 183,377 sq mi (474,944 sq km); cap. Yaoundé; pop. 9,873,000 C-65, *maps* A-115, W-297. *see also in index* Cameroons
  African political unit, *table* A-112
  flag, *picture* F-163
  railroad mileage, *table* R-85

Cameroons (French Cameroun, German Kamerun), former German protectorate in w.-central Africa, extending from Gulf of Guinea to Lake Chad; became German protectorate 1884; in 1922 divided as mandates and in 1946 as trusteeships between United Kingdom and France; French Cameroons became independent under name Cameroon in 1960; British Cameroons (area 34,081 sq mi, 88,269 sq km) absorbed in 1961, n. part by Nigeria and s. part by Cameroon. *see also in index* Cameroon

'Camille', English title of play 'La Dame aux camélias' ('The Lady of the Camellias') by Dumas the Younger; an intense love story built around love of Camille (Marguerite Gauthier in original) for Armand Duval; favorite role of Sarah Bernhardt; furnished libretto for Verdi's 'La Traviata' D-288

Camillus, Marcus Furius (died 365 BC), Roman general, dictator in war against Veii 396 BC; defeated Gauls after siege of Rome by Brennus 390 BC.

Camino Real, El (or The King's Highway), chief highway of early California
  American Southwest S-337
  New Mexico N-216
  roads R-221, *map* R-219

Cammaerts, Émile (1878–1953), Belgian poet, born in Brussels; went to England to live; wrote in both French and English; won wide popularity for war poems ('Through the Iron Bars').

Camões, Luís de (1524–80), Portuguese poet C-67
  'The Lusiads' P-456

Camomile. *see in index* Chamomile

Camorra, Italian secret society organized in Naples about 1820 to aid prisoners of harsh Bourbon regime; soon degenerated into band devoted to robbery, blackmail, smuggling, and murder; crushed in 1912, when many Camorrists were imprisoned.

Camouflage, the art or science of disguising or concealing; many remarkable techniques were devised in World Wars I and II; ships, tanks, gun emplacements, etc., were camouflaged by deceptive painting, covering with netting, and similar devices. For camouflage in nature. *see in index* Protective coloration

Camp, Walter Chauncey (1859–1925), U.S. football authority, born in New Haven, Conn.; in 1889 originated annual practice of choosing "All-American Team" of football players ('American Football'; 'Football for the Spectator'; 'Training for Sports') F-296

Campagna di Roma, large plain around Rome, formerly made malarial by Tiber inundations and marshes R-249

Campagne, horse training E-295

Campanella, Roy (nickname Campy) (born 1921), U.S. baseball catcher, born in Philadelphia, Pa.; with Brooklyn, N.L., 1948–57; defensive star and power hitter; hit total of 242 home runs: 41 in 1953 when he batted in 142 runs and hit .312; career ended by auto accident 1958.

Campanella, Tommaso (1568–1639), Italian philosopher, born in Stilo, Calabria; entered Dominican Order at 15; imprisoned; persecuted as heretic during much of his life; finally found refuge in France under patronage of Louis XIII and Richelieu ('City of the Sun' depicts ideal commonwealth).

Campania, Italy, region on s.w. coast; 5,249 sq mi (13,595 sq km); charming climate and scenery; chief city, Naples; pop. 4,760,759, *map* I-401
  Vesuvius' eruption (AD 79) P-442

Campanile. *see in index* Bell tower

Campanula, genus of herbs including the bluebell or bellflower and the harebell B-318

Campbell, Alexander (1788–1866), Irish-American theologian; founder with his father, **Thomas** (1763–1854), of Disciples of Christ (Campbellites); also founder of Bethany College, W. Va.; prolific writer D-164

Campbell, Sir Alexander (1822–92), Canadian statesman; a leader in Confederation movement; first postmaster general of Dominion; leader of Conservative party for 20 years in senate
  Fathers of Canadian Confederation C-115, *picture* C-116

Campbell, Sir Colin (or Baron Colin Campbell Clyde) (1792–1863), British general, born in Glasgow, Scotland; served in Peninsular War, Crimean War, and Sepoy Mutiny.

Campbell, David (born 1915), Australian writer, *table* A-798

Campbell, Donald Malcolm (1921–67), English speedboat and auto racer, born in Povey Cross, Surrey; son of Sir Malcolm; in July 1955 became first person to exceed 200 mph (320 kph) on water and live when he set world speed record (202.32 mph; 325.60 kph) in jet-powered speedboat in England; died 1967 in attempt at new record.

Campbell, John (1653–1728), North American journalist, postmaster, and publisher of the first news weekly, the *Boston News-Letter* N-236

Campbell, John W., Jr. (1910–71), U.S. science fiction writer S-62

Campbell, Sir Malcolm (1885–1948), English auto, boat, and airplane racer C-67
Daytona Beach, Fla. D-45

Campbell, Mrs. Patrick (or Beatrice Stella Tanner) (1867–1940), English actress, born in London ('The Second Mrs. Tanqueray'; 'The Notorious Mrs. Ebbsmith'; 'Magda'; 'Pygmalion') A-27

Campbell, Robert, celebrated Scottish outlaw. *see in index* Rob Roy

Campbell, Robert (1804–79), U.S. fur trader and businessman; born in County Tyrone, Ireland; came to U.S. about 1824; joined Ashley's expedition to Rockies; soon led parties organized by the Sublettes and others; saved William Sublette's life in battle with Blackfeet at Pierre's Hole in 1832; settled in St. Louis in 1835; served as Indian commissioner W-390

Campbell, Robert (1808–94), Canadian fur trader and explorer, born in Glenlyon, Perthshire, Scotland; with Hudson's Bay Company 1832–71; explored Mackenzie River basin and the Yukon; 1848 explored Upper Yukon River.

Campbell, Thomas (1777–1844), Scottish poet, born in Glasgow; best known for his stirring lyrics ('Hohenlinden'; 'Ye Mariners of England'; 'Lord Ullin's Daughter'; 'The Battle of the Baltic'); buried in Westminster Abbey.

Campbell, Thomas (1790–1858), English sculptor of classical school, born in Edinburgh, Scotland ('Pauline Bonaparte', 'Duke of Wellington').

Campbell, Walter Stanley. *see in index* Vestal, Stanley

Campbell, William (1745–81), U.S. soldier, born in Augusta County, Va.; served with Patrick Henry's Virginia forces; in Virginia House of Delegates; brigadier general under Lafayette.

Campbell, William Edward March (pen name William March) (1894–1954), U.S. writer, born in Mobile, Ala. (novels: 'Company K', 'The Tallons', and 'The Bad Seed'; collected short stories: 'Trial Balance').

Campbell, William Wallace (1862–1938), U.S. astronomer, born in Hancock County, Ohio; director Lick Observatory 1901–30; president University of California, Berkeley, 1923–30; specialized in comets and orbits; pioneered in determination of radial motions of stars; estimated sun's speed and direction in galaxy.

Campbell, William Wilfrid (1861–1919), Canadian poet, born in Berlin (now Kitchener), Ont.; retired from Episcopal ministry ('Lake Lyrics'; 'Sagas of Vaster Britain').

Campbell, Calif., city 5 mi (8 km) s.w. of San Jose; electronics, prosthetics, metal products, furniture; fruit processing; founded 1885, incorporated 1952; pop. 27,067.

Campbell, Ohio, industrial and residential city on Mahoning River, suburb of Youngstown; pop. 11,619.

Campbell-Bannerman, Sir Henry (1836–1908), British Liberal leader, born in Glasgow; secretary for war 1886, 1892–95; premier 1905–8; noted for support of Irish home rule, liberal policy toward Boers, stand against House of Lords.

Campbell College, Buies Creek, N.C.; Southern Baptist; founded 1887, senior college 1963; liberal arts, education.

Campbell Island, island in Pacific Ocean s. of and belonging to New Zealand; area 44 sq mi (114 sq km); good harbors; discovered by Captain Hazelburgh, a whaler, in 1810; pop. 9.

Campbellites. *see in index* Disciples of Christ

Campbell Kids, dolls copied from characters used in advertising by a soup manufacturer; created by E.I. Horsman & Company D-221

Campbellsville College, Campbellsville, Ky.; Southern Baptist; opened 1907 as Russell Creek Academy; present name 1924; senior college 1963; liberal arts, education.

Campbellton, N.B., seaport city in n. on estuary of Restigouche River 14 mi (22 km) s.w. of Dalhousie; lumber products, pulp; vacation center; pop. 9,818 N-156, *map* C-109

Camp David Accords (1979), agreement for mutual recognition and peace between Egypt and Israel B-142
Carter C-184
Dayan D-44
diplomacy D-151
Egypt E-122
Hussein H-335

Campeador, el. *see in index* Cid, el

Campeche, Mexico, state on w. side of Yucatán peninsula; 20,013 sq mi (51,833 sq km); cap. Campeche; chicle, logwood, livestock, henequen; pop. 336,578
Mexico M-333, *map* M-341
Yucatán peninsula Y-432

Campeche, Mexico, capital of state of Campeche, on Gulf of Campeche; mahogany, logwood, sisal, chicle, and hides; pop. 43,874
Mexico, *map* M-341
Yucatán peninsula Y-433

Camp Fire, youth organization Y-428

Camp Gagetown, N.B., the largest army trading center in Canada N-152, 156

Camphene, volatile liquid used in dry cleaning D-280

Camphor, crystalline compound C-67

Camphor laurel, tree *Cinnamomum camphora* native to Taiwan; source of gum camphor C-67

Campin, Robert (1378–1444), Flemish painter W-183

Campinas, Brazil, city in s.e., 60 mi (95 km) n.w. of São Paulo; coffee production and trade; pop. 179,797, *maps* B-425, S-299

Camping C-68, V-237, *picture* V-244, *Reference-Outline* V-241
snakebite kit S-227
Soviet youth camps R-332

Camping Club of Great Britain and Ireland, founded 1907 C-71

Campion, Thomas (1567–1620), English poet and musician, born in London; composed words and music for many lyrics ('Four Books of Airs', 'Observations in the Art of English Poesie').

Campion. *see in index* Silene

Campobello, N.B., island at mouth of Bay of Fundy; 30 sq mi (80 sq km); pop. 1,208 N-154, *picture* N-157

Campoformido (formerly Campo Formio), Italy, village 60 mi (95 km) n.e. of Venice
treaty of Campo Formio (1797) N-14, *table* T-274

Campo Plaza, Sienna, Italy, *picture* I-387

Campos, the grassland regions (or savannas) of Brazil G-236, S-271, *map* S-298

Campo Santo, name meaning "holy field" applied to burial grounds in Italy; also proper name of cemetery in Pisa known for works of art; suffered severe damage in World War II.

Campus, *pictures* Q-9e, S-49f. *see* profile in each state article for picture of state university
University of Cape Town, *picture* S-266

Campus Life, U.S. youth organization Y-430

Campus Martius, large field on Tiber River near ancient Rome, used for military drills and popular assemblies R-257

Camrose, Alta., city 46 mi (74 km) s.e. of Edmonton; railroad and farm center; oil, gas; Scandinavian Lutheran College and provincial school; pop. 12,570 A-266, *map* C-109

Camus, Albert (1913–60), French writer C-71
French literature F-398, *picture* F-397
'The Plague' P-112c

Cana, Galilee, village in Palestine near Nazareth; scene of Christ's first miracle (Bible, John ii, 1–11), when water became wine at marriage feast.

Canaan, name of pre-Israelite Palestine, which was peopled by descendants of Canaan, son of Ham.

Canada, nation of North America; 3,851,809 sq mi (9,976,139 sq km); cap. Ottawa; pop. 24,343,181 C-72, *map* W-297
agriculture
bison interbreeding B-286
cooperatives S-49e, *picture* S-49d
International Wheat Agreement W-190
irrigation I-356
armed forces. *see in index* Canadian Armed Forces
arts
literature. *see in index* Canadian literature
music
bands B-55
bell change-ringing B-155
painting P-67a, *Reference-Outline* P-70
cities C-449. *see also in index* names of cities
Ottawa O-612, *picture* R-300a
Toronto T-228
Coast Guard C-529
coat of arms, *picture* P-132a
commerce
banks B-70
communications
microwave system S-195b
radio R-54
ham radio H-190
disease D-173
employment and unemployment E-206
engineering E-228
festivals and holidays F-61, 66
Thanksgiving T-150
fire fighting F-108
flag, *picture* F-163
foreign relations
Commonwealth membership C-602
United States U-128, *chart* U-120
government. *see also in index* Parliament, Canadian
aviation regulation A-881
citizenship C-442
courts of justice C-746
Fathers of Confederation. *see in index* Canada Confederation, Fathers of
government agencies G-202
governors-general and prime ministers. *see table* following
municipal government M-656
Supreme Court chief justices. *see table* following
harbors and ports H-37
history C-89. *see also in index* Canada Confederation, Fathers of; provinces by name
boundary dispute A-256, R-286
Canadian Pacific construction S-485
colonization A-338
frontier movement F-425
gold rush G-184
historical figures
Abbott A-5
Baldwin B-24
Borden B-366
Bourassa B-384
Champlain C-269
Clark C-485
Diefenbaker D-140
Fathers of Confederation C-113
Hughes H-316
Iberville I-3
Jolliet J-138
King K-243
Mulroney M-648
Papineau P-107
Pearson P-150
Thompson T-172
Trudeau T-293
Hudson's Bay Company H-314
military affairs
Queen Anne's War Q-15
Red River Rebellion R-120
War of 1812 W-30
World War I W-311
World War II W-322
North West Mounted Police R-300b
Treaty of Washington (1871) W-71
illiteracy P-450
industry I-196
furs F-471
garment industry G-35
synthetic rubber R-310
libraries L-185, *pictures* L-182, 183
magazine and journal M-33
medal M-272
medicine M-275, 280
mining
gold G-180
graphite C-157
iron I-331
ores O-601, *table* O-600
petroleum P-229, *map* P-230
platinum P-384
national anthem N-66
national parks N-25, 28, *map* N-29
North America N-334, *map* N-350
physical geography
Arctic regions A-571, *map* P-417
bays
Bay of Fundy F-447
Hudson Bay H-314
Great Plains G-249
lakes. *see also in index* names of lakes
Great Lakes G-243
Laurentian Plateau L-88
rivers
Peace P-145
Red River of the North R-120
St. Lawrence S-19
Yukon Y-439
Rockies R-234, *map* R-234a
size R-321, *charts* U-117
plants, *picture* P-363e
botanical gardens B-378
population, *chart* P-448
American Indians I-156, *tables* I-138
totemism and taboo T-236
census C-250
French Canadians
Quebec Q-9
Gypsies G-326
immigration
civil rights protest, *picture* C-468
migration of people M-403, 406
naturalization N-67
postal service P-463, *picture* P-463b
provinces and territories. *see also in index* provinces and territories below by name
Alberta A-261
British Columbia B-450
Manitoba M-98
New Brunswick N-152
Newfoundland N-163
Northwest Territories N-388
Nova Scotia N-397
Ontario O-546
Prince Edward Island P-497b
Quebec Q-9d
Saskatchewan S-49a
Yukon Territory Y-439
satellites, *picture* S-348a, *table* S-344
sports
curling C-807
ice hockey H-194
lacrosse L-18
skiing S-210a
taxation, *table* T-35
trade, *chart* R-335
transportation T-253
canals C-129

CANADA'S SUPREME COURT

	Born	Year Appointed
Robert George Brian Dickson	1916	1973*
Roland Almon Ritchie	1910	1959
Jean Beetz	1927	1974
Willard Z. Estey	1919	1977
William Rogers McIntyre	1918	1978
Julien Chouinard	1929	1979
Antonio Lamer	1933	1980
Bertha Wilson	1923	1982
Gerald LeDain	1924	1984

*Appointed Chief Justice 1984

CANADA'S GOVERNORS-GENERAL AND PRIME MINISTERS *

Governors-General

Charles Stanley, Viscount Monck	1867–68
John Young, Baron Lisgar	1869–72
Frederick Temple H.-T. Blackwood, marquis of Dufferin and Ava	1872–78
John Douglas Sutherland Campbell, duke of Argyll	1878–83
Henry Charles Keith Petty-Fitzmaurice, marquis of Lansdowne	1883–88
Frederick Arthur Stanley, earl of Derby	1888–93
John Campbell Gordon, marquis of Aberdeen and Temair	1893–98
Gilbert John Elliot-Murray-Kynynmond, earl of Minto	1898–1904
Albert Henry George Grey, Earl Grey	1904–11
Arthur, duke of Connaught	1911–16
Victor Christian William Cavendish, duke of Devonshire	1916–21
Julian Hedworth George Byng, Viscount Byng of Vimy	1921–26
Freeman Freeman-Thomas, marquis of Willingdon	1926–31
Vere Brabazon Ponsonby, earl of Bessborough	1931–35
John Buchan, Baron Tweedsmuir	1935–40
Alexander Cambridge, earl of Athlone	1940–46
Harold R.L.G. Alexander, Earl Alexander of Tunis	1946–52
Vincent Massey	1952–59
Georges Philias Vanier	1959–67
Daniel Roland Michener	1967–74
Jules Léger	1974–79
Edward Schreyer	1979–84
Jeanne Sauvé	1984–

Prime Ministers

Sir John Alexander Macdonald	1867–73	William Lyon Mackenzie King	1926–30
Alexander Mackenzie	1873–78	Richard Bedford Bennett, Viscount Bennett	1930–35
Sir John Alexander Macdonald	1878–91	William Lyon Mackenzie King	1935–48
Sir John Joseph Caldwell Abbott	1891–92	Louis Stephen St. Laurent	1948–57
Sir John Sparrow David Thompson	1892–94	John George Diefenbaker	1957–63
Sir Mackenzie Bowell	1894–96	Lester Bowles Pearson	1963–68
Sir Charles Tupper	1896	Pierre Elliott Trudeau	1968–79
Sir Wilfrid Laurier	1896–1911	Charles Joseph (Joe) Clark	1979–80
Sir Robert Laird Borden	1911–20	Pierre Elliott Trudeau	1980–84
Arthur Meighen	1920–21	John Turner	1984
William Lyon Mackenzie King	1921–26	Brian Mulroney	1984–
Arthur Meighen	1926		

*After Confederation

CANALS IMPORTANT FOR NAVIGATION

Name	Location	Length (Miles)	Depth (Feet)	Width (Feet)	Number of Locks	Year Opened
Albert	Belgium	80.6	16.5	80.5	6	1939
Amsterdam-North Sea	The Netherlands	15.6	49.2	492–885	3	1876
Amsterdam-Rhine	The Netherlands	45	13.8	170	4	1952
Baltic-White Sea	Soviet Union	141	. .	. . .	19	1933
Beaumont-Port Arthur (Sabine-Neches)	Texas	40	34	200	0	1916
Bruges-Zeebrugge	Belgium	6.8	26	72	2	1907
Brussels-Rupel	Belgium	20	21	66	4	1922
Calumet-Sag Channel	Illinois	16.2	9	60	1	1922
Cape Cod	Massachusetts	17.5*	32	540	0	1914
Chesapeake and Delaware	Delaware-Maryland	19	27	250	0	1829
Chicago Sanitary and Ship	Illinois	30	22	160	1	1900
Corinth	Greece	4	26	72	0	1893
Erie†	New York	339	12–14	45	35	1825
Ghent-Terneuzen	Belgium	21.5	28.5	166	5	1927
Göta	Sweden	119	10	47	58	1832
Houston Ship	Texas	50	36	300–400	0	1914
Inner Harbor Navigation (Industrial)	New Orleans, La.	5.5	12	150	1	1923
Jonglei	Egypt-Sudan	250	23	152	. .	1985
Juliana	The Netherlands	21	11.8	52.5	4	1935
Kiel	West Germany	61	37	144	4	1895
Kronstadt-Leningrad	Soviet Union	16	28	. . .	. .	1884
Lake Washington Ship	Washington	8	30–34	100–300	2	1917
Lindo	Sweden	2	32	147	0	1963
Manchester Ship	England	35.5	28	120	10	1894
Mississippi-Gulf Outlet	Louisiana	76	36	250	0	1963
Moscow (Moscow-Volga)	Soviet Union	80	18–20	100	11	1937
Moselle	France-Luxembourg-Germany	170	21–23	. . .	14	1964
Panama	Canal Zone	50.7	42	300	12	1914
Rhone-Marseilles	France	26	6.6	52	0	1929
Rhone-Rhine	France	201	6.6	17.2	158	1833
Rideau-Ottawa	Canada	126	. .	. . .	47	1833
Saimaa	Finland-Soviet Union	34	14	. . .	8	1968
St. Lawrence Seaway	Canada-New York	182‡	27	80	15	1959
Laprairie Basin	Canada	18	27	80	2	
Beauharnois	Canada	16	27	80	2	
Wiley-Dondero	New York	10	27	80	2	
Iroquois	Canada	1.5	27	80	1	
San Jeronimo	Argentina	4.5	12	165	0	1968
Sault Ste. Marie	Canada	1.4	18.3	60	1	1895
Sault Ste. Marie	Michigan	1.8	17–32	80–110	4	1855
Suez	Egypt	100	41	197	0	1869
Volga-Baltic	Soviet Union	223	. .	. . .	7	1964
Volga-Don	Soviet Union	63	. .	. . .	9	1952
Welland Ship	Canada	27.6	27	80	8	1932

*Including channel approaches. †Main section of the New York State Barge Canal. ‡Deep-draft (27 feet) ship channel includes section from Montreal to Lake Ontario and the Welland Ship Canal.

Canandaigua Lake, long, narrow lake of w. New York, 30 mi (50 km) s.e. of Rochester; one of famous Finger Lakes; length 15 mi (25 km).

Canarias, Islas, off n.w. coast of Africa. *see in index* Canary Islands

Canaris, Wilhelm (1887–1945), German admiral E-305

Canary, Martha Jane. *see in index* Calamity Jane

Canary, songbird *Serinus canaria* of the finch family C-130
  life expectancy, *chart* A-423
  pet care P-246

Canary-bird flower, annual twining climber *Tropaeolum peregrinum* of the nasturtium family; leaves 5-lobed, shield-shaped, light green; flowers yellow with green spur; native to Chile and Peru.

Canary Current, warm ocean current in Atlantic off n.w. Africa A-745

Canary grass, annual grass *Phalaris canariensis* native to the Mediterranean region; its seeds used as food for captive songbirds.

Canary Islands, group about 60 mi (95 km) off n.w. coast of Africa; 2,808 sq mi (7,273 sq km); pop. 1,444,626 C-130, *maps* A-115, S-350, W-297
  banana B-53
  canary C-130
  Columbus C-592

Canasta. *see in index* Rummy

Canaveral, Cape (called Cape Kennedy 1963–73), e. Florida, on Atlantic Ocean about 15 mi (25 km) n.e. of Cocoa S-342b, *maps* N-350, S-342a
  NASA N-22

Canberra, Australian Capital Territory, capital of Australia; pop. 219,331 C-130, *maps* P-3, W-297
  Australia A-767, *map* A-819
  space-tracking facilities S-343b

Canby, Edward Richard Sprigg (1817–73), U.S. general, born in Kentucky; served in Mexican and Civil wars; captured Mobile, 1865; slain by the Modocs.

Canby, Henry Seidel (1878–1961), U.S. literary critic and editor, born in Wilmington, Del.; editor *The Saturday Review of Literature* 1924–36; editor in chief Book-of-the-Month Club 1926–58 ('The Age of Confidence'; 'Alma Mater'; 'Thoreau'; 'Walt Whitman, an American').

Cancer (or Crab), constellation, *charts* C-681, S-418, S-421
  astrology, *chart* A-708

Cancer, disease C-131, D-175
  causes
    aerosols A-66
    pollution P-441b
    toxic waste W-76
  cyst, polyp, tumor C-811
  hospice care H-278
  liver H-134, L-261
  lymphatic system L-343
  therapy T-164
    analgesic effectiveness A-388
    radioactive materials R-62
      cobalt C-530
      radium R-70
  wart W-34
  X rays X-403

Cancer de Barbastro, Luis (fl. 1549), Roman Catholic prelate and Dominican missionary, born in Saragossa, Spain; about 1514 headed missionary work among American Indians of Vera Paz, Central America; killed while trying to found a mission at Tampa Bay, Florida.

Cancha, jai alai court J-13

Cancún, resort city in s.e Mexico, just off the n.e. coast of the Yucatán peninsula on an L-shaped island; service town specializing in tourism; pop. 50,000, *picture* H-287
  Mexico M-335
  Yucatán peninsula Y-433, *picture* Y-432

Candela (or candle), unit of luminous intensity L-192, *table* W-141

Candelilla, almost leafless shrub *Euphorbia antisyphilitica* of spurge family; grows in desert regions of Mexico and Texas; yields useful wax W-110

Candia, island in Mediterranean Sea. *see in index* Crete

Candia (or Herakleion), Crete, seaport, largest city, former capital, on n. shore; episcopal see; established by Saracens in 9th century AD; pop. 77,506.

'Candida', play by George Bernard Shaw; Candida Morell, the heroine, remains faithful to her husband against the entreaties of Marchbanks, a romantic young poet.

'Candide', philosophical novel by Voltaire, published 1759, recounting the adventures and misfortunes of Candide and satirizing optimism as expressed by his tutor Pangloss, who maintains that this is the best of all possible worlds.

C. and J.M. Studebaker. *see in index* Studebaker Brothers Manufacturing Company

Candle C-136
  energy radiation, *diagram* R-33
  fire and flame F-94
  lighting L-205
  wax W-110

Candle. *see in index* Candela

Candleberry tree. *see in index* Kukui

Candlefish (or oolakan), very oily smeltlike fish of n.w. coast of North America; used by American Indians as candle by stringing through it the pith of a rush or a strip of bark as wick; also used as food.

Candle flower. *see in index* Ocotillo

Candlemas, Christian festival, February 2; commemorates presentation of Jesus Christ in temple.

Candlenut. *see in index* Kukui

Candlepins B-386

Candle tree, tropical tree *Parmentiera cerifera* of

Canvas work. *see in index* Needlepoint
Canyon, deep gorge with precipitous sides C-145
  river creates, *diagram* R-210
  submarine O-460
  United States, *picture* U-84, *map* U-81
    Rio Grande R-209
    Snake River I-16
    Utah, *picture* U-225, *map* U-233
'Canyon de Chelly, Arizona', photograph by O'Sullivan, *picture* P-294
Canyon Diablo, gorge in n. Arizona about 30 mi (50 km) e. of Flagstaff; 225 ft (70 m) deep and 500 ft (150 m) wide; formed by Canyon Diablo River, a tributary of Little Colorado River.
Canyon Ferry Dam, on the Missouri River near Helena, Mont. M-508
Canyonlands National Park, Utah, *map* U-233, *picture* U-224
Canzona, a music form C-268
Canzonetta, in music, *list* M-670
Caoutchouc, rubber R-305. *see also in index* Rubber
Cap. *see in index* Hats and caps
Capa, Robert (or Andrei Friedmann) (1913–54), U.S. photographer C-146
Capablanca, José Raúl (1888–1942), Cuban diplomat and chess player, born in Havana; member Cuban state department 1913–42; child prodigy, played chess at 4; world chess champion 1921–27 ('My Chess Career'; 'Chess Fundamentals'; 'Primer of Chess').
Capacitance (or capacity), electricity
  radio R-57, *diagrams* R-58
Capacitive disc, type of videodisc V-314
Capacitive reactance R-58
Capacitor (or electrical condenser), device for storing electric charge
  electronics E-175
  radio R-57, *diagrams* R-56, R-58
  tantalum T-21
Capacity, unit of weight W-139, *table* W-140
Cap-de-la-Madeleine, Que., city on St. Maurice River opposite Trois-Rivières and on St. Lawrence River; newsprint, paper bags, textiles; Roman Catholic pilgrimage center; pop. 31,463 Q-9h, *map* Q-10
Cape, point of land jutting into sea or lake. *see in index* capes by name, as Hatteras, Cape
Cape aardvark, animal *Orycteropus capensis* A-3
Cape Alava, Washington W-48
Cape Breton Highlands, highlands, Nova Scotia N-399
Cape Breton Highlands National Park, park on Cape Breton Island, Nova Scotia N-399
  national parks N-29, *picture* N-30
  preservation C-146
Cape Breton Island (formerly Ile Royale), Nova Scotia; land area 3,970 sq mi (10,280 sq km); pop. 170,088 C-146, C-93, *maps* C-112, N-350
  Nova Scotia N-398, 401
Cape buffalo, animal of south and central Africa B-489
Cape Chincherinchee. *see in index* Ornithogalum
Cape Cod, Massachusetts, L-shaped peninsula between Nantucket Sound and Cape Cod Bay C-146, *maps* N-350, U-41
  Massachusetts M-189, 192, *pictures* M-200, 201
  'Mayflower' M-239
Cape Cod Canal, s.e. Massachusetts C-128, M-192
Cape Colony. *see in index* Cape of Good Hope
Cape Colored, name applied to a people of South Africa S-265
Cape Dutch, language. *see in index* Afrikaans
Cape Esperance, battle of, World War II W-345
Cape Fear, North Carolina N-354
Cape Fear River, in North Carolina, rises in n. cent. part and flows 200 mi (320 km) s.e. of Atlantic; formed by conjunction of Deep and Haw rivers; navigable to Fayetteville.
Cape fox, animal, *table* F-464
Cape Frontier Wars. *see in index* Kaffir Wars
Cape Girardeau, Mo., city on Mississippi River, in s. about 30 mi (50 km) n.w. of Cairo, Ill.; shoes, cement, electrical appliances, electronics, clothing; Southeast Missouri State University; pop. 34,361, *map* U-41
Cape Hatteras, North Carolina N-354, 358, *picture* N-359
Cape Horn, southernmost tip of the South American continent located on Isla Hornos C-147, *map* C-330
Cape jasmine, plant *Gardenia jasminoides* of the family Rubiaceae G-27
Čapek, Karel (1890–1938), Czech writer, born in Bohemia; wrote satirical and expressionistic dramas and short stories ('R.U.R.'; 'The Robber'; 'The World We Live In', with his brother Josef; 'War with the Newts')
  science fiction S-62
Capelin, small fish *Mallotus villosus* of smelt family in Arctic seas and in n. waters of Atlantic and Pacific; caught by commercial fishermen off Norway, Iceland, U.S.S.R., Canada, and Greenland.
Capella, Martianus (5th century AD), Latin writer of n. Africa; wrote 'Satyricon', encyclopedia greatly used in Middle Ages; his statement of heliocentric system may have influenced astronomer Copernicus.
Capella, fixed star, third brightest visible in Northern Hemisphere S-414, *charts* S-415, 418, 421
Cape Lookout, North Carolina N-354
Cape marigold. *see in index* Dimorphotheca
Cape May, N.J., resort at s. end of state; pop. 4,853 N-198
Cape of Good Hope (or Cape Province, formerly Cape Colony), largest province of South Africa; area (excluding Walvis Bay) 278,465 sq mi (720,444 sq km); cap. Cape Town; pop. 5,375,421 C-148, S-264, *map* A-115
  Diaz A-330
  Rhodes R-195
  stamp, *picture* S-409
Cape of Good Hope, southernmost tip of South Africa's Cape Peninsula C-147, *maps* A-117, S-264
  Diaz D-132
'Cape of Good Hope, The', book by Cocteau C-533
Caper, genus of plants *Capparis*; the spiny shrub *Capparis spinosa* has short-lived white flowers; flower buds used to make pickles.
Capercaillie (or capercailzie, or cock of the woods, or mountain cock), large European game bird *Tetrao urogallus* of the grouse family.
Capernaum (or Kefar Nahum), ancient town in Palestine, often visited by Jesus; location long disputed but now generally considered to have been at site of ruins of Tell Hum on n. coast of Sea of Galilee G-5
Cape Spear National Historic Site, historic site in Newfoundland N-29
Cape stock, annual plant of genus *Heliophila* of mustard family; native to s. Africa; flowers small, blue with white eye, in long clusters; stem hairy; some are perennial with yellow, white, or lilac flowers.
Capet, Hugh (939?–996), king of France 987–996; elected by nobles and prelates to succeed Louis V, last of the Carolingians; founded Capetian Dynasty C-147
Capetian Dynasty, reigning family of France from 987 to 1328; began with Hugh Capet and ended with Charles IV C-147. *see also in index* France subhead, kings, rulers, and leaders *table*
Cape Town, capital of Cape of Good Hope Province; legislative capital of South Africa; pop. 842,620 C-148, *maps* A-115, S-264, W-297
  botanical gardens, *table* B-379
Cape Town, University of, near Cape Town, South Africa R-195, *picture* S-266
Cape Verde, republic and archipelago in Atlantic Ocean 385 mi (620 km) w. Senegal; 1,557 sq mi (4,033 sq km); cap. Praia; pop. 291,000 C-149, *map* W-297
  African political unit, *table* A-112
  flag, *picture* F-163
Cape York Peninsula, n. Queensland, Australia, *maps* A-819, P-3
Cap-Haïtien (locally called Le Cap), seaport on n. coast of Haiti, West Indies; exports coffee, logwood, cacao, honey, sisal; called "Little Paris" before earthquake of 1842; pop. 46,217 H-11, *picture* H-12, *map* N-350
Capillary, minute blood vessel connecting veins and arteries of the body
  bioengineering B-206
  blood circulation B-313, C-421
  kidneys K-235
Capillary action, in soil S-250
Capistrano swallows. *see in index* San Juan Capistrano
Capital, in economics. *see also in index* Capitalism
  bank B-69
  foreign aid F-306
  foreign exchange F-307
  Industrial Revolution I-181
  industry I-193
  Marxism S-234
  stock S-450
Capital, in U.S. state government, *table* S-429. *see also in index* capitals by name
'Capital' (or 'Das Kapital'), work by Marx M-162
Capital, Operation, World War II campaign W-347
Capital gain, the increase in value of a capital asset T-35
Capitalism C-149, S-233. *see also in index* Communism; Laissez-faire; Socialism
  Asia A-690
  cities C-449
  economics E-61
  fascism F-37
  government G-199
  Industrial Revolution I-181
  industry I-196
  labor movements L-6
  Marx M-162
  social rights H-320
  trade I-267
    tariff T-28
  U.S.S.R. R-330
Capital letter
  early alphabet A-318
  early handwriting B-346
Capital punishment (or death penalty) P-506
  Hammurabi H-24
Capital University, Columbus, Ohio; affiliated with American Lutheran church; founded 1850; arts and sciences, education, law, music, nursing C-595
Capitanias, division of land in Portuguese colony in Brazil A-355
Capitation tax (or head tax), tax imposed on each individual in a society T-38
Capitol, in Washington, D.C. W-66, U-115, *picture* U-154
Capitol Hill, in Washington, D.C. W-67
Capitoline Hill, smallest but most famous of 7 hills of Rome; site of temple of Jupiter R-254
Capitol Reef National Monument, in Utah, *map* U-233
Capitulation, in international law I-255
Capo di Monte, porcelain factory in Italy P-476
Capone, Al (1899–1947) U.S. gangster C-153
Capon Springs, W. Va., resort in n.e.; pop. 260 W-167
Caporetto, battle of, World War I W-310
Capote, Truman (1924–84), U.S. writer C-153
  American literature A-361
Capp, Al (originally Alfred Gerald Caplin) (1909–79), U.S. cartoonist, born in New Haven, Conn.; creator of 'Li'l Abner' comic strip; comic strip for *Infantry Journal* and Treasury Dept. World War II; lost a leg in childhood; known for helping veteran amputees ('Life and Times of the Shmoo'; 'The Earliest Li'l Abner').
Cappadocia, ancient inland country in Asia Minor w. of Euphrates River; conquered by Persians and by Alexander the Great; reduced to Roman province by Tiberius AD 17, later passed into Turkish hands, *maps* P-212, R-242
Capper, Arthur (1865–1951), U.S. editor, publisher, Republican leader; born in Garnett, Kan.; publisher of many daily and weekly farm, news, and household papers; governor of Kansas 1915–19; U.S. senator 1919–48; active in interests of farmers.
Capper Agricultural Credits Act (1923), United States
  Harding H-40
Capra, Frank (born 1897), U.S. motion-picture director and producer, born in Palermo, Sicily; won Academy awards for 'It Happened One Night' (1934), 'Mr. Deeds Goes to Town' (1936), 'You Can't Take It with You' (1938); ('Lady for a Day'; 'Mr. Smith Goes to Washington'; 'Meet John Doe'); autobiography, 'The Name Above the Title' D-155, *picture* M-614
Caprera, Italian island near n.e. coast of Sardinia in Tyrrhenian Sea; about 4 mi (6 km) long; joined by causeway to island of Maddalena.
Capri, island s. of Bay of Naples, Italy; 5½ sq mi (14.2 sq km); resort of artists; vineyards, olive groves, wide variety of plants; favorite resting place for migratory birds, *map* I-404
'Caprichos', etching series by Goya G-203
Capricornus (or Goat), constellation, *charts* S-420, C-681
  astrology, *chart* A-708
Caprimulgidae, family of birds. *see in index* Nightjar
Caprimulgiformes, goatsucker order of birds, including the family Caprimulgidae (whippoorwill, chuck-will's-widow, poorwill, pauraque, nighthawk, and European goatsucker).
Capriole, horse training E-295
Caprivi, Count Georg Leo von (1831–99), German soldier and statesman; successor of Bismarck; chancellor 1890–94.
Cap rock fall, type of waterfall W-96
Caps. *see in index* Hats and caps
Capsicum, genus of peppers P-197a
Capstan drive system, a type of drive mechanism used in a tape recorder T-24
Captain
  aircraft A-197, S-203
  insignia, *picture* U-8
  U.S. Army A-634
Captain Kidd. *see in index* Kidd, Captain
'Captains Courageous', work by Kipling K-240
Capture-combination game, type of card game C-163
Capua, Italy, town 27 mi (17 km) n. of Naples, on site of ancient **Casilinum,** 8 mi (13 km) distant, which was luxurious city under Romans; pop. 18,242 S-370
Capuchin monkey (or sapajou monkey) A-503
Capuchins, branch of the Franciscan friars; vows of extreme poverty and much attention to learning; distinguished by beards and hooded cloaks; order founded in Italy 1525–28; known for missionary work, especially among early French-Canadians.
Capuchon (or cowl), head covering H-53
Capulet, noble family of Verona, Italy; feud with the Montagues forms basis for tragedy of Shakespeare's 'Romeo and Juliet' R-258
Capybara (also called water hog), largest living rodent *Hydrochoerus capibara*; about 4 ft (1 m) long; found in large lakes and rivers of S. America; feeds on reeds and water plants; color reddish-brown; flesh eaten by people; skin tans into thick, soft leather A-325
Caquetá River, in South America. *see in index* Japurá River
Carabao. *see in index* Water buffalo

Carabiner, mountain climbing equipment M-638
Carabinièri, the gendarmerie, or military police, of Italy, recruited from regular army for term of five years P-430, *picture* P-430a
Carabobo, Venezuela, plain in state of Carabobo near Valencia; victory of Bolívar over Spaniards (1821) established Colombian independence.
Caracal (or Persian lynx), species of lynx *Lynx caracal,* not to be confused with caracul, a breed of sheep; native to s.w. Asia and parts of Africa; slightly larger than a fox; coat reddish brown on top, whitish underneath; white spots above eyes, black-tufted ear tips; eats small animals and birds; trained as hunter in India, *picture* C-214
Caracalla (nickname of Bassianus) (188–217), Roman emperor; succeeded AD 211; recklessly extravagant; brutal in his fight for absolute power
  architecture A-549
  baths R-257, *map* R-250
Caracara, bird B-280
Caracas, Venezuela, capital; about 10 mi (16 km) by highway from seaport, La Guaira, on Caribbean Sea; pop. 2,064,033 with suburbs C-153, V-275, *maps* S-298, W-297
Caracci. *see in index* Carracci
Caracciola, Rudolph (1901–59), German auto racing driver, born in Remagen; raced 1922–52; European driving champion five times.
Caractacus (or Caratacus), king of Britain; defeated by Romans AD 51 after 8 years' war, imprisoned in Rome; Tacitus ('Annals', Book xii, chap. 37) quotes noble speech he made before Roman emperor.
'Caractères ou les moeurs de ce siècle, Les', work by La Bruyère L-12
Caracul. *see in index* Karakul
Caraffa, Giovanni Pietro, pope. *see in index* Paul IV
Caramanlis, Constantine. *see in index* Karamanlis, Konstantinos
Caramel, candy S-509
Carapace, shell covering the back of certain animals
  crustaceans C-790
Carat (or karat, abbreviation kt), (1) unit of weight for gems and precious metal, 200 mg; (2) unit of proportion for purity in alloys; name originally meant seed or bean used in weighing gold and precious stones
  gold G-176
  weights and measures W-138, *table* W-140
Caratacus. *see in index* Caractacus
Caravaggio (Michelangelo Amerighi da Caravaggio, or Michelangelo Merisi) (1569–1609), Italian painter C-154
Caravan, group of travelers
  camel
    ancient Egypt, *picture* S-381
    Baghdad B-18
    Ethiopia T-262
    Sahara S-16
  wagon P-336, *picture* P-335
Caravel, type of ship N-82
Caraway, Hattie Wyatt (1878–1950), U.S. public official, born in Bakerville, Tenn.; elected Democratic senator from Arkansas in 1932, to fill vacancy caused by death of husband, Thaddeus H. Caraway; reelected for terms expiring 1939 and 1945; became member U.S. Employees' Compensation Commission 1945
  women's rights W-275
Caraway, herb of parsley family S-379
Carbamide. *see in index* Urea
Carberry, John Joseph, Cardinal (born 1904), Roman Catholic prelate, born in Brooklyn, N.Y.; bishop of Lafayette, Ind., 1957–65, of Columbus, Ohio, 1965–68; archbishop of St. Louis from 1968; created cardinal 1969; retired 1979.
Carberry Hill, 7 mi (11 km) s.e. of Edinburgh, Scotland; 500 ft (150 m) high; here Mary Queen of Scots was taken prisoner in 1567 by Scottish nobles protesting her marriage to Bothwell.
Carbide, compound of carbon and a metallic element
  carbon compound C-157
  silicon carbide S-195b
Carbine, firearm, *picture* F-98
Carbinol. *see in index* Methanol
Carbohydrates C-155
  animals and plants A-421
  food and nutrition F-275
  metabolism M-306
  organic chemistry O-604
  sources
    peanut P-146
    sago S-14
  starch S-424
  sugars S-508
Carbolic acid (or phenol)
  hobby H-186
  Lister utilizes L-239
  organic chemistry O-602
Carboloy, alloy steel; one of the hardest of synthetic substances
  cobalt C-530
Carbon (C), chemical element C-156
  acid rain formation A-19
  aluminum production A-322
  atomic structure, *diagram* V-255
  carborundum S-195b
  charcoal C-271
  chemistry C-294
  fluorocarbon F-241
  Franklin's research F-385
  hydrogen H-341
  inorganic chemistry I-208
  isotopes N-416, *picture* N-417
  life L-268, P-373
  metal and metallurgy M-308
  minerals M-432
  organic chemistry O-601
  periodic table, *table* P-207, *list* P-208
  sewage disposal S-120
  soot S-220
  steel alloys A-312
  sun's atmosphere S-513
Carbon-13 (C-13), carbon isotope C-158
Carbon-14 (C-14), carbon isotope C-158, *picture* C-157
  American Indians I-143
  nuclear energy N-416, *picture* N-417
  radiocarbon dating A-535
    man M-82
Carbonari, secret society in Italy I-393
  Mazzini M-240
Carbonate, salt or ester of carbonic acid
  carbon dioxide C-158
  sal soda S-247
  shells S-148
  white lead P-73
Carbonated water, soft drinks P-376
Carbonate mineral, classification M-435
Carbon black, form of carbon C-157
  paint pigment P-73
  pencils P-158
  tire manufacture R-303
Carbon cycle C-156, S-514, *diagram* S-513
Carbondale, Ill., city 80 mi (130 km) s.e. of St. Louis, Mo., in fruit-growing and coal-mining region; varied industries; Southern Illinois University; pop. 27,194, *map* I-52
Carbondale, Pa., city 15 mi (25 km) n.e. of Scranton; anthracite region; textiles, metal products; railroad shops; resort area; pop. 11,255, *map* P-185
Carbon dioxide (CO_2) C-158, *diagram* V-255
  aerosol propellant A-66
  atmosphere A-145, *chart* A-119, *diagram* A-672
    cycle, *picture* A-748
  blood B-313
  chemical formula V-255
  dry ice R-137
  earth E-17, 31
  fire extinguisher F-101
  Mars A-717
  nuclear energy N-426
  photosynthesis P-300, P-372, *diagram* P-373
  pollution P-441e
  respiration R-159
  Solvay process S-247
  sublimation S-254f
  volcanic gases V-378
  wine W-237, 239
  yeast Y-411
Carbonear, Newf., town on Conception Bay 26 mi (42 km) n.w. of St. John's; commercial center; manufactures furniture and bedding; mineral water; pop. 4,584.
Carbonic acid A-19
  weathering E-31
Carbon fixation, chemical process
  photosynthesis P-300
Carboniferous period (or Coal Age) I-8
  animal evolution A-461
  coal formation C-518
  ferns F-56
  reptiles R-154
Carbonized fossil, *picture* F-324
Carbon microphone M-378
Carbon monoxide (CO), poisonous gas C-158
  poisonous effect P-411, S-8
Carbon paper O-495
Carbon tetrachloride, heavy, colorless, volatile liquid (CCl_4); vapor is nonflammable; dissolves fat, wax C-393
  dry cleaning D-280
  hobby H-186
  organic chemistry, *diagram* O-602
  structural formula V-255
  toxic waste W-75
Carbonyl chloride. *see in index* Phosgene
Carborundum, hard abrasive used in grinding S-195b
Carboxyhemoglobin, blood chemistry B-313
Carboxyl, group in chemistry O-604
  synthetic fibers F-72
Carbuncle, acute inflammation of tissue beneath the skin; resembles boil in early stages but much more painful and often accompanied by chills or fever.
Carbuncle, smooth-cut garnet J-115
Carburetor, in gasoline engine A-846, I-252
Carcassonne, France, city in south 53 mi (85 km) s.e. of Toulouse; wine market; on site of ancient city of **Carcaso** built in pre-Roman times; medieval fortress, wall; pop. 40,580, *picture* F-361, *map* F-369
Carchemish, ancient Hittite capital on upper Euphrates River; site excavated by D.G. Hogarth and T.E. Lawrence.
Carcinogen, cancer-causing substance C-131, D-176
Carcinoma, cancerous tumor C-133, C-812
Cardamom, spice S-379
Cardan, Jerome (or Hieronymus Cardanus, or Girolamo Cardano) (1501–76), Italian mathematician, physician, and astrologer; born in Pavia; credited with introducing imaginary numbers; published Tartaglia's solution of cubic equation as his own in 'Ars Magna'; indicated method of teaching blind by sense of touch and deaf by use of signs A-592, A-831
Cardboard P-103
Card-capturing game, type of card game C-159
Card-combination game, type of card game C-162
Cárdenas, García López de, (fl. 16th century AD) Spanish explorer, with Coronado in N. America 1540–42 C-586
Cárdenas, Lázaro (1895–1970), Mexican general and political leader, joined army in 1913; became governor of Michoacán, 1928; minister of interior and secretary of war before becoming president of Mexico in 1934; commander of Mexico's Pacific forces 1941, defense minister 1942 M-338
Cárdenas, Cuba, seaport on n.w. coast; exports sugar, tobacco; scene of battle during Spanish-American War of 1898; pop. 43,750, *map* W-159
Card games, entertainment C-159
  gambling G-9
Cardiac catheterization, medical procedure used to check heart functions D-173, H-100
Cardiac cycle, in heart's functioning H-97
Cardiac muscle M-658
Cardiff, Wales, seaport on Taff River just above Bristol Channel; iron and steel center; wire rope, guided-missile components, paper; Cardiff Castle; University College of South Wales and Monmouthshire; pop. 260,574 C-164, W-6, *map* E-360
Cardiff giant, crude statue of a man 10½ ft (3 m) tall, carved from gypsum; buried near Cardiff, N.Y., in 1868; "discovered" there in 1869; widely exhibited as "petrified man" until exposed as hoax.
Cardigan, James Thomas Brudenell, 7th **earl of** (1797–1868), general who led "charge of the Light Brigade" at Balaklava in the Crimea 1854, celebrated in Tennyson's poem.
Cardigan Bay, in Wales, *picture* W-7
Cardin, Pierre (born 1922), French dress designer, born in Venice; pioneer in men's high fashion; noted also for elegant women's designs D-268
Cardinal (or redbird), bird *Cardinalis cardinalis* C-165
  bird species B-261, *pictures* B-243, 248, F-86
  egg, *picture* E-112
  state bird
    North Carolina, *picture* N-362
    Ohio, *picture* O-508
    West Virginia, *picture* W-172
Cardinal flower, tall wild perennial *Lobelia cardinalis*; alternate, oblong, slightly toothed leaves; bright red irregular flowers clustered in leafy terminal spikes, *picture* F-234. *see also in index* Lobelia
Cardinal Glennon College, St. Louis, Mo.; Roman Catholic; for men; founded 1869; arts and sciences; contains St. Louis Archdiocesan Seminary.
Cardinal points, of compass C-622, D-158
Cardinals, Sacred College of, in Roman Catholicism C-165. *see table* following
  papal election P-445
  Pope Paul VI P-142a
Cardinal Stritch College, Milwaukee, Wis.; Roman Catholic; founded 1937 as St. Clare College; arts and sciences, education, home economics, music; graduate study in reading and special education.
Cardinal Virtues, Seven. *see in index* Seven Cardinal Virtues
Carding, process by which cotton, flax, and wool fibers are smoothed out and cleaned with the card, a wire-toothed device
  cotton C-740
  wool S-390, *picture* S-389
Cardiopulmonary resuscitation (CPR) B-511
  first aid F-116
Cardiovascular accident. *see in index* Stroke
Cardiovascular diseases D-173
  heart H-98
  jogging J-121
Cardoon, perennial plant *Cynara cardunculus* of the composite family; grown as vegetable for roots and leafstalks, which are blanched; developed from Globe artichoke; native to Mediterranean; now widely scattered on pampas of S. America.
Cardozo, Benjamin Nathan (1870–1938), U.S. jurist C-165
Cards, playing, small stiff rectangles usually of paper or paperboard; used in games; introduced into Europe from Asia in 14th century C-159
Cardston, Alta., town 38 mi (61 km) s.w. of Lethbridge; named for Charles Ora Card, Brigham Young's son-in-law, who settled group of Mormons here 1887; has Canada's chief Mormon temple, built 1913–23; pop. 3,267, *map* C-109
Carducci, Giosuè (1835–1907), Italian poet, born in Valdicastello, Tuscany, Italy; liberated Italian poetry from sentimental romanticism ('Hymn to Satan', 'Barbaric Odes') I-377. *see also in index* Nobel Prizewinners, *table*
CARE (Cooperative for American Relief Everywhere, Incorporated), nonprofit corporation through which Americans can send safely food and other relief packages to individuals and institutions in war-depleted lands; most packages $10 and $5; incorporated 1945 by 26 American welfare agencies; headquarters 660 First Ave., New York City F-329. *see also in index* MEDICO
Careers. *see in index* Vocations
Carew, Thomas (1595?–1639), English poet, probably born in London; earliest of "Cavalier poets"; known for love lyrics; follower of Ben Jonson.

CARDINALS OF THE UNITED STATES

	Appointed	*Archdiocese*
John McCloskey (1810–85)	1875	New York
James Gibbons (1834–1921)	1886	Baltimore
William H. O'Connell (1859–1944)	1911	Boston
John Farley (1842–1918)	1911	New York
Denis J. Dougherty (1865–1951)	1921	Philadelphia
Patrick J. Hayes (1867–1938)	1924	New York
George W. Mundelein (1872–1939)	1924	Chicago
John Glennon (1862–1946)	1946	St. Louis
Edward Mooney (1882–1958)	1946	Detroit
Francis J. Spellman (1889–1967)	1946	New York
Samuel A. Stritch (1887–1958)	1946	Chicago
James F. McIntyre (1886–1979)	1953	Los Angeles (retired 1970)
Richard J. Cushing (1895–1970)	1958	Boston
John F. O'Hara (1888–1960)	1958	Philadelphia
Albert G. Meyer (1903–65)	1959	Chicago
Aloisius J. Muench (1889–1962)	1959	(Archbishop ad personam)
Joseph E. Ritter (1892–1967)	1961	St. Louis
Lawrence J. Shehan (1898–1984)	1965	Baltimore (retired 1974)
Francis J. Brennan (1894–1968)	1967	(Roman Curial Official)
John P. Cody (1907–82)	1967	Chicago
John J. Krol (born 1910)	1967	Philadelphia
Patrick A. O'Boyle (born 1896)	1967	Washington (retired 1973)
John J. Carberry (born 1904)	1969	St. Louis (retired 1979)
Terence J. Cooke (1921–83)	1969	New York
John F. Dearden (born 1907)	1969	Detroit (retired 1980)
John J. Wright (1909–79)	1969	(Roman Curial Official)
Timothy Manning (born 1909)	1973	Los Angeles (retired 1985)
Humberto S. Medeiros (1915–83)	1973	Boston
William Wakefield Baum (born 1926)	1976	Washington (Roman Curial Official 1980)
Joseph L. Bernardin (born 1928)	1983	Chicago
John J. O'Connor (born 1920)	1985	New York
Bernard F. Law (born 1931)	1985	Boston

Carey, G.R., U.S. inventor
  television system T-78

Carey, Henry (1690?–1743), English poet and composer of musical farces and songs; best known for 'Sally in Our Alley'; also reputed author of 'God Save the King' N-65

Carey, Henry Charles (1793–1879), U.S. economist, born in Philadelphia, Pa.; advocate of protective tariff ('The Principles of Social Science'; 'The Unity of Law').

Carey, Max George (born Maximilian Carnarius) (1890–1970), U.S. baseball outfielder, born in Terre Haute, Ind.; with Pittsburgh, N.L., 1910–26, Brooklyn, N.L., 1926–29 (manager 1932–33); during career stole 738 bases, the modern record in N.L. until Lou Brock retired in 1979 with 938.

Carey, William (1761–1834), English Oriental scholar and first Baptist missionary to India, born in Northamptonshire; leader in 19th-century Protestant missionary movement; translated Bible into many Oriental languages
  English Baptist Missionary Society B-77

Cargo. *see in index* Transportation

Cargo ship S-168. *see also in index* Freighter; Tanker; Transportation
  fire hazards F-109

Caria, ancient country in s.w. Asia Minor; inhabitants Aegeans and Asians, except for Greeks in seacoast cities such as Miletus and Halicarnassus.

Carib, American Indian tribes inhabiting s. West Indies and n. coast of South America; drove out or absorbed the former inhabitants, the Arawak
  cannibalism C-139
  Dominica D-225
  Grenada G-284
  Martinique M-161
  North America N-339
  West Indies W-158

Caribbean. *see in index* West Indies

Caribbean Community and Common Market, North American international organization N-344

Caribbean literature C-166. *see also in index* Latin American literature

Caribbean Sea, arm of Atlantic between Central America, n. coast of South America, and West Indies C-100, *maps* N-350, W-297. *see also in index* Ocean, *table*
  folktales, *list* S-482, *picture* S-481c
  Grenada G-284
  Jamaica J-17
  sponge fisheries S-394
  West Indies W-155

Cariboo Mountains, in e. British Columbia; parallel with and w. of Fraser River and Rocky Mountains; 200 mi (320 km) long, highest point Mt. Titan, about 11,750 ft (3,580 m); in w. foothills is the Cariboo District, famous in gold rush of early 1860s B-450

Cariboo Road, in Canada; built between 1862 and 1865 C-99

Caribou, Me., town 17 mi (27 km) n. of Presque Isle on Aroostook River; potatoes, sugar beets; pop. 9,916.

Caribou, wild reindeer *Rangifer tarandus* of North America D-62, *table* D-63, R-139
  American Indians I-116
  Arctic regions A-572
  migration A-450

Caricature, art
  cartoon C-186
  Nast N-21
  drawing D-256

Caries, tooth decay D-101

Carillon, a set of tuned bells sounded by hammers controlled from a keyboard B-155

Carina, part of the constellation Argo; literally "the keel" C-682, *chart* S-417

Carinthia (or Kärnten), Austria, mining (especially lead) and manufacturing province in extreme south; area 3,681 sq mi (9,534 sq km); cap. Klagenfurt; pop. 495,226.

Carissimi, Giacomo (1604?–74), Italian composer of church music ('Jephthah' and other oratorios; masses and motets)
  classical music M-668
  oratorio O-575

Carleton, Guy (or Baron Dorchester) (1724–1808), British general and statesman, governor-general and commander of British forces in Canada at outbreak of American Revolution; commander in chief of British forces in North America 1782–83; governor of Quebec (then including Canada to Mississippi River) 1786–96; repulse of Arnold's attack on Canada (1776) probably saved British North America for Great Britain C-94

Carleton, William (1794–1869), Irish writer, born in Prillisk, County Tyrone, Ireland; gave realistic picture of Irish peasant life I-326

Carleton College, Northfield, Minn.; charter 1866, opened 1870; founded by Congregationalists, now nonsectarian; arts and sciences, education, music.

Carleton Martello Tower National Historic Site, historic site in New Brunswick N-29

Carleton University, Ottawa, Ont.; established 1942; arts and science, commerce, engineering, journalism, public administration; graduate studies O-552

Carlin, Nev., town 20 mi (30 km) s.w. of Elko on Humboldt River; altitude 4,897 ft (1,493 m); gold mining; settled 1868, incorporated 1927; pop. 1,232.

Carline thistle, genus *Carlina* of plants of the composite family; native to Europe; so named because supposed to have cured plague in army of Charlemagne.

Carlisle, England, city in n.w. on Eden River near Scottish border; textiles, metal products, bakery goods; castle where Mary, queen of Scots, was imprisoned; pop. 71,090, *maps* E-[illegible], U-18a

Carlisle, Pa., borough 18 mi (29 km) w. of Harrisburg; rugs and carpets, shoes, tires, electronics; Mt. Holly Springs, mountain resort, nearby; headquarters of Washington during Whiskey Rebellion of 1794; Dickinson College; Carlisle Barracks; pop. 18,314, *map* P-185

Carlisle Indian School, Carlisle, Pa., founded by Richard H. Pratt 1879; discontinued 1918.

Carloman (751–71), king of the Franks; ruled with his brother Charlemagne till death C-273

Carlo Maratta. *see in index* Maratti, Carlo

Carlos, kings of Spain. *see in index* Charles

Carlos I (1863–1908), king of Portugal, born in Lisbon; succeeded 1889; suspended constitution 1907; assassinated with son at Lisbon; grandson of Victor Emmanuel II of Italy.

Carlos, Don (1545–68), son of Philip II of Spain; vicious weakling about whose disappointment in love (his father married Carlos' fiancée, Elizabeth of France) and mysterious death Schiller and others have woven romances.

Carlos, Don (1716–88). *see in index* Charles III

Carlos, Don (1788–1855), uncle of Isabella II of Spain and first Carlist pretender to Spanish throne, called Charles V by followers.

Carlota (or Charlotte, in full Marie Charlotte Amélie) (1840–1927), daughter of Leopold I of Belgium and for three years empress of Mexico; accompanied her husband, Archduke Maximilian of Austria, to Mexico when empire was established; suffered a nervous breakdown after subsequent fall of the throne and execution of Maximilian; she lived secluded in Belgium for 60 years
  Mexico M-337

Carlow, agricultural county in Leinster Province, s.e. Ireland; 346 sq mi (896 sq km); pop. 33,593; also name of town in county (pop. 7,791).

Carlow College, Pittsburgh, Pa.; Roman Catholic; for women; founded 1929; arts and sciences, education, home economics, nursing, *map* P-345b

Carlowitz, Yugoslavia. *see in index* Karlowitz

Carlsbad, Calif., city 5 mi (8 km) s. of Oceanside; light industry; flowers, avocados; incorporated 1952; pop. 14,944, *map* C-51

Carlsbad, Czechoslovakia. *see in index* Karlovy Vary

Carlsbad, N.M., city in s.e. on Pecos River; just s. of lake and canal region formed by Avalon and McMillan dams; mineral springs; potash mining and refining, oil; pop. 25,496 N-216, *maps* N-228, U-40

Carlsbad Caverns National Park, in New Mexico N-217, *picture* N-222, *map* N-229

Carlscrona, Sweden. *see in index* Karlskrona

Carlsen, Henrik Kurt (born 1914?), U.S. sea captain, born in Denmark; as captain of the U.S. freighter *Flying Enterprise*, won world acclaim Jan. 1952 for heroic but futile effort to save his ship.

Carlson, Anton Julius (1875–1956), U.S. physiologist and educator, born in Sweden; moved to U.S. 1891; head of University of Chicago physiology department 1916–40; research on hunger, gastric secretion, heart and circulation, saliva, lymph, pancreas, thyroid and parathyroids, metabolism, immune bodies, and aging.

Carlson, Chester F. (1906–68), U.S. physicist O-495

Carlsruhe, West Germany. *see in index* Karlsruhe

Carlucci, Frank Charles, III (born 1930), U.S. diplomat and public official, born in Wilkes-Barre, Pa.; director of Office of Economic Opportunity 1971; undersecretary of health, education, and welfare 1973–75; national security adviser 1986– .

Carlyle, Thomas (1795–1881), Scottish essayist and historian C-169
  biography B-223
  economics E-60
  literary contribution E-275
  Shakespeare S-142

Carman, Bliss (1861–1929), Canadian poet, born in Fredericton, N.B.; lived most of life in U.S.; during 1890–1910 worked on editorial staffs of several journals including

Atlantic Monthly C-121, *picture* C-122
Carmana, Iran. *see in index* Kerman
Carmarthen, Wales, old town in s. on Towy River; seat of Dyfed county; pop. 12,820.
Carmel (officially Carmel-by-the-Sea), Calif. resort and residential city on Pacific Ocean 3 mi (5 km) s.w. of Monterey; founded in 1904 as colony for artists and writers; rustic forest setting; art and import shops; grave of Father Junipero Serra nearby at San Carlos Borromeo Mission which he established in 18th century; pop. 4,707, *map* C-51
Carmel, chewy candy C-138
Carmel, Mount, mountain range in n.w. Israel near Mediterranean, associated with Elijah and Elisha; Carmelite order founded there by hermits H-6
Carmelites, mendicant order of "Our Lady of Mount Carmel"; had early claimed the prophet Elias as its founder; modern historians set founding at middle of 12th century; called **White Friars** in England because of white mantle.
'Carmen' (1875), opera by Bizet B-287
  opera O-568, *list* O-562
Carmen Sylva (pen name of Elizabeth) (1843–1916), queen of Charles, first king of Romania; wrote and edited many works, some with Mite Kremnitz, her lady-in-waiting.
Carmer, Carl Lamson (1893–1976), U.S. writer and educator, born in Cortland, N.Y. (sketches and tales: 'Stars Fell on Alabama', 'Listen for a Lonesome Drum'; children's stories: 'Windfall Fiddle', 'A Flag for the Fort'; coeditor of 'The Rivers of America' series for which he wrote 'The Hudson' and 'The Susquehanna'; compiler of 'America Sings', songs and stories; editor of 'Cavalcade of America', 'Pets at the White House').
Carmichael, Hoagland (nickname Hoagy) (1899–1981), songwriter and actor, born in Bloomington, Ind.; studied law, turned to music ('Stardust', 'Georgia on my Mind', 'Rockin' Chair', 'Old Buttermilk Sky'); motion pictures: 'Best Years of Our Lives', 'To Have and Have Not', 'Young Man with a Horn'; autobiographies: 'Sometimes I Wonder', 'The Stardust Trail' M-684
Carmichael, Stokely (born 1941), U.S. civil rights leader, born in Trinidad, West Indies; militant in urging black people's efforts to improve status in society; chairman SNCC 1966–67; prime minister Black Panthers 1967–69; in Africa after 1969; coauthor of 'Black Power' B-297
Carmichael, Calif., community 12 mi (19 km) n.e. of Sacramento; mainly residential; nurseries; named for D.W. Carmichael, a developer who founded it as Carmichael Colony about 1910; pop. 37,625, *map* C-51
Carnac, France, Breton village famous for its museum of antiquities and for ancient stone monuments; pop. 1,044, *map* F-369
  archaeoastronomy A-729
  Stone Age S-456
Carnallite, mineral M-435
Carnarvon, George Edward Stanhope, Molyneux Herbert, 5th **earl of** (1866–1923), English Egyptologist; codiscoverer, with Howard Carter, of Tutankhamen's tomb. *see also in index* Carter, Howard
  Tutankhamen A-532
Carnarvon, Wales. *see in index* Caernarvon
Carnarvon basin, in Australia A-776
Carnatic, region in s.e. India between Eastern Ghats and Coromandel Coast; includes parts of Tamil Nadu state and Andhra Pradesh; originally an area in s.-central India including Karnataka state and parts of Andhra Pradesh.
Carnation (or clove pink), flower *Dianthus caryophyllus*; variety of pink C-169
  flowering time G-25
  gamma ray mutation, *picture* P-369
  Ohio state flower, *pictures* O-508, S-427
  pink variety P-329
Carnauba palm, tree *Copernicia cerifera* of the palm family, native to moist valleys of Brazil; grows 30 to 40 ft (9 to 12 m); crown fanlike with leaves 4 to 6 ft (1 to 2 m) long; flowers in clusters; wood used for building, roots in medicine, fruit as food, leaf fibers for cordage, pith as cork substitute, leaves for wax
  South America S-276
  wax W-110
Carnegie, Andrew (1835–1919), Scottish-U.S. philanthropist C-170, *picture* P-180
  Carnegie Trust Fund S-67
  Hall of Fame, *table* H-16
Carnegie, Dale (1888–1955), U.S. author, lecturer, and teacher of public speaking; born in Maryville, Mo.; "self-help" books ('How to Win Friends and Influence People').
Carnegie, Pa., borough 6 mi (10 km) s.w. of Pittsburgh; coal, steel, chemicals; named in honor of Andrew Carnegie; incorporated 1894; symphony orchestra; pop. 10,099, *map* P-184
Carnegie Corporation of New York, foundation established by Andrew Carnegie in 1911 C-170
  foundations and charities F-330, *table* F-332
  scholarship grant U-208
Carnegie Endowment for International Peace, fund created by Andrew Carnegie in 1910 with an endowment of $10,000,000, *table* C-170
Carnegie Foundation for the Advancement of Teaching, foundation created by Andrew Carnegie with original endowment of $10,000,000, increased by later gifts; makes surveys of educational work and provides pensions for retired teachers, *table* C-170
Carnegie Hero Fund Commission, Pittsburgh, Pa., foundation for the purpose of rewarding persons for heroic efforts to save human life; formed by Andrew Carnegie 1904 with grant of $5,000,000; similar funds were established in several other countries, making a total of more than $10,000,000 C-170
Carnegie Institute, Pittsburgh, Pa. P-345a, *map* P-345b, *table* C-170
Carnegie Institution of Washington, D.C., group of departments organized for the purpose of scientific research; founded 1902 by Andrew Carnegie, with $10,000,000 endowment, increased by later gifts to $22,000,000, *table* C-170
Carnegie libraries C-170, S-461
Carnegie medal, British book award, given annually since 1937 for the best children's book published in England; founded in memory of Andrew Carnegie; comparable to Newbery medal C-170, L-240
Carnegie medal, U.S. humanitarian award. *see in index* Carnegie Hero Fund Commission
Carnegie-Mellon Institute of Research. *see in index* Mellon Institute of Industrial Research
Carnegie-Mellon University, Pittsburgh, Pa.; private control; founded 1900 by Andrew Carnegie as Carnegie Technical Schools, became Carnegie Institute of Technology 1912; present name 1967 when Carnegie Institute of Technology and Mellon Institute of Research (founded 1913) merged; includes College of Fine Arts, Mellon Institute of Science, Carnegie Institute of Technology, College of Humanities and Social Sciences, School of Urban and Public Affairs; graduate studies; nuclear research center, Saxonburg, Pa., *map* P-345b
Carnelian (or sard), reddish translucent semiprecious stone found in India, Brazil, and Florida; color often improved with heat and dye J-115
  hobby H-187
Carner, JoAnne Gunderson (born 1939), U.S. golfer G-189
Carnera, Primo (1906–67), Italian boxer, born in Sequals; heavyweight champion 1933–34 B-391
Carney, Art, U.S. actor
  The Honeymooners, *picture* T-71
Carney, Robert Bostwick (born 1895), U.S. Navy officer, born in Vallejo, Calif.; became admiral in 1950; commander in chief of U.S. naval forces in e. Atlantic and Mediterranean 1950–52, of Allied forces in s. Europe 1951–53; chief of naval operations 1953–55.
Carniola, former province in s.w. Austria-Hungary; 3,856 sq mi (9,987 sq km); following World War I included in Yugoslavia except small strip to Italy.
Carnival C-170. *see also in index* Mardi Gras
  folk art tradition F-252
  masks M-187
  Tennessee T-85
Carnivora, the order of flesh-eating mammals, *table* M-80
  animal life record, *table* E-24
  digestive systems D-146
  dinosaurs A-462
Carnivorous plants (or flesh-eating plants) P-363
  pitcher plant P-344
  sundew S-517
  Venus's-flytrap V-280
Carnot, Lazare Nicolas Marguerite (1753–1823), French statesman, general, and mathematician; member of Committee of Public Safety and of Directory.
Carnot, Marie François Sadi (1837–94), 4th president of the Third Republic of France (1887–94), born in Limoges; assassinated by anarchist; grandson of L.N.M. Carnot A-703
Carnot, Nicolas Léonard Sadi (1796–1832), French physicist, formulator of "Carnot's principle," or the second law of thermodynamics; born in Paris; increased knowledge of conservation of energy; son of L.N.M. Carnot
  heat H-106
Carnotite, mineral
  ore, *table* O-600
  radium R-71
  uranium U-210
  vanadium V-258
Caro, Anthony (born 1924), British sculptor M-311
Carol, song C-406
Carol I, king of Romania. *see in index* Charles I, king of Romania
Carol II (1893–1953), king of Romania; abdicated 1940; marriage to Zizi Lambrino (1918) annulled 1920; married Princess Helen of Greece 1921, later divorced, then married Elena Lupescu R-318
Carol City, Fla., residential community 12 mi (19 km) n. of Miami; tourist attraction near Atlantic Ocean; pop. 27,361.
Carolina, North American colonial province S-309
Carolina allspice. *see in index* Calycanthus
Carolina chickadee, bird *Parus carolinensis* of the Paridae family C-318
Carolina hemlock, tree *Tsuga caroliniana* of the pine family H-127
Carolina parakeet P-135
  extinction E-210
Carolina wren, bird of the Troglodytidae family W-364
  state bird, *picture* S-312
'Caroline', U.S. vessel, destruction of which by Canadians during rebellion in Upper Canada (1837) threatened to bring on war between United Kingdom and United States.
Caroline Islands, 2,000-mi (3,200-km) chain of about 550 coral islets in Micronesia, Pacific Ocean, between Philippines and Marshall Islands; sold by Spain to Germany 1899; made Japanese mandate 1919; occupied by U.S. 1944–45; placed under U.S. trusteeship 1947; naval bases on Palau, Yap, Truk, and Ponape; copra, breadfruit, yams; bonito fisheries; pop. 62,731, *map* W-297
  Italik Island, *picture* O-471
  Pacific Ocean P-8, *map* P-3, *pictures* P-18
Caroline of Anspach (1683–1737), queen of George II of England.
Caroline of Brunswick (1768–1821), queen of George IV of England, who hated her, tried to divorce her, and excluded her from coronation G-81
Carolingian minuscule (or carolingian, or caroline), calligraphy B-346, C-58, *picture* B-349
Carolingian Renaissance, Latin literature L-78
Carolingians, Frankish rulers 751–987, descendants of Charles Martel F-361. *see also in index* France, *subhead* history, *table* of kings, rulers, and leaders
  Germany G-121
Carolus-Duran, A,E. (or Charles Auguste Émile Durand) (1837–1917), French portrait painter and art teacher, born in Lille, France.
Carom billiards (or French billiards) B-191
Caroni River, tributary of the Orinoco in Venezuela; flows n. 400 mi (650 km), *map* V-275
Carotene V-354
  butter B-520
  leaf product L-102
Carothers, Wallace Hume (1896–1937), U.S. chemist, born in Burlington, Iowa; his basic research led to development of several synthetic materials including nylon and neoprene H-450
Carotid artery, one of the two great arterial trunks of the neck that conveys blood to the head and brain.
Carp, freshwater fish *Cyprinus carpio* C-172
  fish culture F-132
  fisheries F-136
  goldfish G-183
  hibernation H-147
  length of life, *chart* A-423
Carpaccio, Vittorio (died 1522?), Venetian painter, among greatest of early Renaissance ('Life of St. Ursula' series; 'Story of Alcyone'; 'Burial of Christ'; 'St. Jerome in a Landscape').
Carpal bone, wrist bone H-27, S-210
'Carpathia', ocean liner S-177e
Carpathian Mountains, in central Europe C-173
  salt mines S-30
Carpatho-Ukraine, U.S.S.R. *see in index* Ruthenia
Carpeaux, Jean Baptiste (1827–75), French sculptor, noted also as painter, born in Valenciennes, France; among first to depart from academic in sculpture; sculptures include fountain, 'Four Quarters of the World'; 'The Dance'; and a monument to Watteau S-89
Carpel, the innermost structure of the flower, which contains the ovules.
Carpentaria, Gulf of, indentation in n. coast of Australia, extending into Northern Territory and Queensland with an average length and breadth of 350 mi (565 km); maximum depth 276 ft (84 m); visited 1627 by Dutchman named Carpenter A-769, *maps* A-819, P-3
Carpenter, Edward (1844–1929), English poet, philosopher, and socialist lecturer; born in Brighton; gave up fellowship at Cambridge and religious orders to live simple life; friend of Walt Whitman ('Towards Democracy'; 'Love's Coming of Age'; 'My Days and Dreams').
Carpenter, John Alden (1876–1951), U.S. composer, born in Park Ridge, Ill.; engaged in business and devoted leisure to music ('Adventures in a Perambulator', orchestral suite; 'The Birthday of the Infanta', ballet-pantomime; 'Skyscrapers').
Carpenter, Malcolm Scott (born 1925), U.S. astronaut and aquanaut, U.S. Navy, born in Boulder, Colo.; resigned 1969 to enter private business.
Carpenter C-173
Carpenter ant A-468, *picture* I-216
Carpenter bee, solitary bee B-124

Cartier-Brébeuf Park National Historic Site, park in Quebec N-29
Cartier-Bresson, Henri (born 1908), French photographer who helped establish photojournalism as an art form C-185
photography P-299
Cartilage, the gristle or white elastic tissue attached to the ends of bones or forming certain other parts of the skeleton B-342, S-209
joint J-137
throat V-377
Cartogram, maps M-122
Cartography. *see also in index* Globes; Maps
Cook's contributions C-696
geography G-68
Carton, Sydney, hero of Dickens' 'Tale of Two Cities'; lost Lucie Manette, whom he loved devotedly, to Charles Darnay, in whose stead he finally went to the guillotine.
Cartoon, drawing or sketch C-186
animation F-2
cartoonists
Cruikshank, *picture* S-531
Daumier D-40
Davenport, *picture* S-364
Disney D-185
Feiffer F-52
Goldberg G-182
Lichtenstein L-192
Nast N-21, *picture* P-431
drawing D-256
fables F-4
motion pictures M-622
tapestry T-25
Cartouche, term for oval ornaments and scrollwork used in art and architecture, especially applied to frame which enclosed names of Egyptian kings in hieroglyphs, *picture* W-369
Cartridge, charge for a firearm, or for blasting, in a case or shell of metal, paper, pasteboard, or cloth. *see also in index* Shell
ammunition development A-371
firearms F-99
machine gun M-13
mining M-428
Cartwright, Alexander Joy (1820–92), U.S. baseball pitcher, born in New York, N.Y.; "father of modern baseball"; organized Knickerbockers of New York City in 1845 and pitched for that team 1845–48; established many playing rules still in effect B-94
Cartwright, Edmund (1743–1823), English clergyman and inventor C-193
Hargreaves H-43
Industrial Revolution I-178
Cartwright, John Robert (born 1895), Canadian jurist, born in Toronto, Ont.; created king's counsel 1933; judge of the Supreme Court of Canada 1949–67, chief justice 1967–70.
Cartwright, Peter (1785–1872), U.S. clergyman of Methodist Episcopal church, born in Amherst County, Va.; became circuit rider in Kentucky, Tennessee, and later Illinois ('Fifty Years a Presiding Elder'; 'Autobiography of Peter Cartwright').
Cartwright, Sir Richard John (1835–1912), Canadian statesman and financier, born in Kingston, Ont., minister of finance; minister of trade and commerce; powerful influence in Parliament for years; first Conservative, then Liberal.
Caruso, Enrico (1873–1921), Italian dramatic tenor C-193
popular music M-684
Carver, George Washington (1860–1943), U.S. scientist and educator C-193
chemurgy P-379
Hall of Fame, *table* H-16
Missouri M-491
Carver, John (1575?–1621), one of the Pilgrim colonists, born in England; founder and first governor of Plymouth colony in North America P-395
Carver, Jonathan (1710–80), North American explorer, born in Weymouth, Mass.; sought northern route to the Pacific 1766–68; skirted shores of Lake Superior before return; wrote popular 'Travels to the Interior Part of North America'.
Carving S-80. *see also in index* Sculpture; Woodworking and wood carving
'Swords into plowshares', *picture* P-143d
Cary, Alice (1820–71) and **Phoebe** (1824–71), U.S. writers; sisters, born near Cincinnati, Ohio; largely self-taught; poems collected under title 'Poetical Works of Alice and Phoebe Cary'; Phoebe wrote 'One Sweetly Solemn Thought'; Alice, 'Pictures of Memory'.
Cary, Henry Francis (1772–1844), English writer and clergyman, born in Gibraltar; known for translation of Dante's 'Divine Comedy'.
Cary, Joyce (full name Arthur Joyce Lunel Cary) (1888–1957), Anglo-Irish novelist, born in Londonderry, Northern Ireland; with Sir Horace Plunkett, aided Irish farmers; entered Nigerian political service 1913 ('A House of Children', autobiographical; trilogy: 'Herself Surprised', 'To Be a Pilgrim', and 'The Horse's Mouth'; trilogy: 'Prisoner of Grace', 'Except the Lord', and 'Not Honour More'; 'The Captive and the Free'; 'Spring Song and Other Stories').
Cary, Phoebe. *see in index* Cary, Alice
Cary, Thomas. *see in index* Cary's Rebellion
Caryatid, in architecture, sculptured female figure used as a support (male figures in such use are called atlantes).
Caryophyllaceae. *see in index* Pink family
Cary's Rebellion, uprising in North Carolina (1711) caused by dissension over religious and political issues, chiefly franchise for Quakers and making Church of England established church of colony; rebellion followed refusal of Thomas Cary, deputy governor, to leave office when Quakers procured order to remove him.
Casa, Giovanni della (1503–56), Italian bishop, poet, and translator
'Galateo' E-320
Casaba, melon M-292
Casabianca, Louis (1755–98), French naval officer, commander of Napoleon's flagship which caught fire at Aboukir; his 10-year-old son (subject of Mrs. Hemans' poem 'Casabianca') refused to leave his father; both died when ship exploded.
Casablanca (or Dar el Beida), Morocco, port on Atlantic coast and economic capital; founded by Portuguese in 15th century on site of Berber village, Anfa; pop. 2,553,300 C-194, *map* A-116
harbor H-33, *picture* H-34
Morocco M-585
Casa de Contratación, Spanish body for regulating trade in colonies S-290
Casadesus, Robert (1899–1972), French pianist and composer, born in Paris; head, piano department, American Conservatory at Fontainebleau, France, 1935–49; U.S. debut 1935; lived in U.S. 1940–46.
Casa Giocosa (or Happy House), school formed in Renaissance Italy E-84
Casa Grande, Ariz., city 44 mi (71 km) s.e. of Phoenix; in valley irrigated by Coolidge Dam; Casa Grande Ruins National Monument nearby; pop. 14,971, *map* A-611
Casal, Julián del (1863–93), Cuban poet; leading inspiration for Modernist movement in Latin American literature ('Leaves in the Wind')
Caribbean literature C-167
Casals, Pablo (1876–1973), Spanish violoncellist, conductor, and composer C-194
Casanova (full name Giovanni Giacomo Casanova) (1725–98), Venetian churchman, musician, soldier, spy, diplomat, and writer C-195
Casas, Bartolomé de Las. *see in index* Las Casas, Bartolomé de
Casaubon, Isaac (1559–1614), French classical scholar, critic, and Protestant theologian, born in Geneva; librarian to Henry IV of France, then prebendary of Canterbury.
Casbah (or Kasbah), fortified area typical of many north African towns
Tangier, Morocco T-20
Cascade, waterfall of moderate volume, or series of small waterfalls. *see in index* Waterfalls
Cascade fir. *see in index* Silver fir
Cascade Range, in United States and Canada extending from n. California to British Columbia; highest peak Mt. Rainier (14,410 ft; 4,392 m) C-195, *maps* E-25, N-350, U-87, 90, *picture* U-91. *see also in index* Hood, Mount; Rainier, Mount; Shasta, Mount; Saint Helens, Mount
California C-34
Oregon O-582, *picture* O-583
Washington W-48, *map* W-49
Cascara, shrub or tree *Rhamnus purshiana* of the buckthorn family, native to Pacific coast of North America; grows 10 to 35 ft (3 to 11 m); leaves to 8 in (20 cm) long, oblong, dark green, slightly hairy; flowers tiny, greenish-white; fruit black, oval, berrylike.
Case, printing P-499, *picture* P-500
bookmaking B-360, *diagram* B-356, *pictures* B-359
Case, unit of measure, *table* W-140
Case dei Bambini, schools headed by Montessori E-90
Case history, record of medical data M-278
Casein, protein, of the class of albumins, existing in milk and separated from it by an acid; in pure form amorphous white solid, tasteless and odorless; commercial type yellowish with pleasing odor
adhesive A-43
dairy by-product D-7
industrial uses B-530, P-72
milk M-414
plastics P-383, *table* P-382
synthetic fibers F-71
Casella, Alfredo (1883–1947), Italian pianist and composer, born in Turin; instructor Santa Cecilia Conservatory, Rome, Italy 1915–23; compositions modern in style.
Casemaking clothes moth B-527, *picture* I-226
Casement, Sir Roger David (1864–1916), Irish Sinn Fein leader, born in Kingstown (now Dun Laoghaire), Ireland; knighted (1911) for investigations of Putumayo rubber atrocities; active in "Easter Rebellion" (1916).
Case-Western Reserve University, Cleveland, Ohio; private control; formed 1967 by merger of Western Reserve University and Case Institute of Technology; arts and sciences, engineering, applied social sciences, dentistry, education, law, library science, management, medicine, nursing; graduate schools; Cleveland College for part-time undergraduates C-494
Caseworker, social worker involved with the needs, problems and adjustments of a person or family V-366
Casey, Richard Gardiner, Baron (1890–1976), Australian statesman, born in Melbourne; minister to U.S. 1940–42; in Churchill's wartime cabinet; minister for external affairs, Australia, 1951–60; governor-general 1965–69.
Casey, William Joseph (1913–87), U.S. lawyer and public official, born in New York, N.Y.; member General Advisory Commission on Arms Control 1969–71; chairman Securities and Exchange Commission 1971–72; undersecretary of state for economic affairs 1972–74; president Export-Import Bank 1974–76; director of Central Intelligence Agency 1981–87.
'Casey Jones', title of song based on adventures and death in a collision of John Luther Jones, locomotive engineer. *see also in index* Jones, Casey
Casgrain, Henri Raymond (1831–1904), Canadian biographer and historian, born in Quebec; brother of P.B. Casgrain; ordained a priest; wrote, in French, historical studies of French Canada.
Casgrain, Marie Thérèse Forget (born 1896), Canadian feminist, born in Montreal, Que.; led fight to obtain full suffrage for women; president Quebec League for Women's Rights 1929–48; vice-chairwoman Cooperative Commonwealth Federation 1948.
Casgrain, Philippe Baby (1826–1917), Canadian lawyer and historian, born in Quebec City; brother of H.R. Casgrain; in Parliament a Liberal; wrote on French-Canadian history.
Cash, Johnny (born 1932), U.S. country and western singer and songwriter C-195
Cash, Chinese copper coin, historical value about one twentieth of a U.S. cent; name commonly used for ready money.
Cashew, species *Anacardium occidentale* of tropical tree with rose-tinted clusters of fragrant flowers; seed kernel is an edible nut and source of oil; fleshy receptacle of seed is a fruit and source of beverage; milky juice of tree is a gum used as basis of a varnish.
Cashew family (or Anacardiaceae), family of trees and shrubs including the sumac, varnish tree, smoke tree, kafir plum, mango, pistachio, pepper tree, and poison ivy
mango M-96
poisonous plants P-410
Cashmere, former name of Kashmir, state n. of Indian peninsula; gave name to Cashmere cloth, shawls, sweaters, rugs. *see also in index* Jammu and Kashmir
Cashmere goat G-171
wool W-288
Cash register, business machine that records sales; registers the amount of each sale, records total, and issues dated receipt for customer; invented by James Ritty 1879 C-20
Casilinum, Italy. *see in index* Capua
Casimir III (1310–70), king of Poland, called "The Great"; added Little Russia and Red Russia to Poland and founded University of Cracow
Jagiellon Dynasty J-12
Casimir IV (1427–92), grand duke of Lithuania and king of Poland C-196
Jagiellon Dynasty J-12
Casimir-Périer, Jean Paul Pierre (1847–1907), fifth president of the Third Republic of France (June 1894–Jan. 1895), born in Paris; resigned because of factional bickering and limitations on presidential power.
Casino, establishment for legalized gambling
Las Vegas L-56
'Casino Royale', work by Fleming F-178
Casinum, Italy. *see in index* Cassino
Casiquiare River, unique stream, a natural canal about 230 mi (370 km) long, in s. Venezuela, connecting Orinoco and Negro rivers; navigable; flows s.w. and w., its downward slope toward Negro River averaging only about 7 in per mi (11 cm per km); attains width of some 2,000 ft (600 m) as it enters Negro River, *map* V-275
Caskoden, Edwin. *see in index* Major, Charles
Caslavska, Vera (born 1942), Czechoslovakian gymnast G-325
Olympics O-542
Caslon, William (1692–1766), first of famous English family of type founders; name given to typefaces still much used
type T-337, *picture* B-349
Casona, Alejandro (born Alejandro Rodríguez Álvarez) (1903–65), Spanish playwright, born in Asturias S-366
Casper, Billy (or William Earl Casper, Jr.) (born 1931), golfer, born in San Diego, Calif.; professional since 1955; one of golf's top winners of prize money; won U.S. Open 1959 and 1966, Western Open 1965, 1966, and 1969, Canadian Open 1967, Masters 1970, and many other tournaments.
Casper, Wyo., largest city of state; on North Platte River in central part of state; oil, natural gas, uranium, wool, and livestock center; oil industries, electronic assembly; federal irrigation and reclamation projects; pop. 51,016 W-388,

396, *picture* W-393, *maps* N-350, U-40

Caspersson, Torbjörn Oskar (born 1910), Swedish biologist born near Linköping; noted for work on chemistry of the cell.

Caspian Sea, salt lake on borders of Europe and Asia; area 143,550 sq mi (371,795 sq km) C-196, *maps* E-360, R-344. *see also in index* Ocean, *table*
  Aral Sea A-527
  Asia, *map* A-697
  commercial port A-707
  lakes L-24
  world, *map* W-297

Cass, Lewis (1782–1866), U.S. statesman, born in Exeter, N.H.; governor of Michigan territory 1813–31; secretary of war 1831–36; U.S. senator 1845–48 and 1849–57; secretary of state 1857
  exploration M-445
  Michigan M-361
  Statuary Hall, *table* S-437a
  Taylor's campaign T-43

Cassander (358?–297 BC), son of Macedonian regent Antipater and king of Macedonia 305–297 M-7

Cassandra, daughter of Priam, king of Troy; prophetess of woe, doomed never to be believed; in vain warned against keeping Helen and admitting the wooden horse; Agamemnon's captive; slain with him by Clytemnestra
  Homeric legend H-221

Cassano, Italy, town 16 mi (26 km) e. of Milan; French defeated Imperialists 1705; Russians and Austrians defeated French 1799, *map* I-401

Cassatt, Mary (1845–1926), U.S. painter and etcher C-197

Cassava (or manioc), plant from which tapioca is obtained S-424, T-27
  bread, *picture* S-277

Cassel, West Germany. *see in index* Kassel

Cassena. *see in index* Yaupon

Cassette, a miniature reel-to-reel magnetic tape system T-24
  video recording V-311

Cassia, genus of the pea, or pulse, family; many species, most of them native to warm regions, include trees, shrubs, and wildflowers such as senna; most of them with showy clusters of golden or orange-yellow blossoms resembling the sweet pea in form, and with long beanlike seedpods and compound leaves of 6 to 20 leaflets.

Cassidy, Butch (or Robert Leroy Parker), U.S. outlaw O-619

Cassidy, Claudia (born 1899), music, dance, and drama critic, born in Shawneetown, Ill.; married to William John Crawford; known for column, "On the Aisle," in *Chicago Tribune* 1942–66.

Cassimere, plain woven or twilled wool fabric; has soft finish but no nap; used for men's clothing; also a similar fabric of wool mixed with cotton or rayon.

Cassin, René (1887–1976), French jurist, born in Bayonne; led in drafting Universal Declaration of Human Rights (UN); president European Court of Human Rights 1965–68.

Cassini, Gian Domenico (or Jean-Dominique Cassini) (1625–1712), French astronomer C-197
  polar-projection map, *picture* R-127

Cassini, Jacques (1677–1756), French astronomer, son of Gian Domenico Cassini; continued father's work C-197

Cassini de Thury, César-François (1714–84), French astronomer and director of Paris Observatory, born in Paris; grandson of G.D. Cassini; work continued by son, **Jacques-Dominique, comte de Cassini** (1748–1845) C-197

Cassini's division, Saturn P-354, *picture* P-350

Cassino (ancient Casinum), Italy, city, 75 mi (120 km) s.e. of Rome; Monte Cassino monastery nearby destroyed in World War II but was rebuilt; pop. 21,105, *map* I-401
  World War II W-340, *picture* W-342

Cassiodorus, Flavius Magnus Aurelius (490?–585?), Latin writer, statesman, and monk ('History of the Goths'; 'Variae', treats of Ostrogothic Kingdom in Italy) B-350
  library history L-171

Cassiopeia, in Greek mythology, Ethiopian queen, mother of Andromeda; wife of King Cepheus; taken into heavens as one of constellations.

Cassiopeia, constellation, *charts* C-681, S-415

Cassirer, Ernst (1874–1945), German philosopher, born in Breslau; left Germany 1933; at Yale 1941–44; influenced by Kant; held use of symbols basic to human culture ('The Philosophy of Symbolic Forms', condensed as 'An Essay on Man').

Cassiterite, chief ore of tin; ordinary massive variety called tinstone
  ore, *table* O-600
  tin T-190

Cassius Longinus, Caius (died 42 BC), Roman general, one of Caesar's murderers; commanded troops in Syria and Asia; committed suicide after defeat by Antony at Philippi.

Cassivellaunus, British king of Catuvellauni at Hertfordshire; was conquered by Julius Caesar (54 BC) after several encounters; identified by archaeological discoveries.

Cassone, Italian marriage chest F-457, *picture* F-456

Cassowary, flightless bird B-277

Castagno, Andrea del (1423–57), Italian realistic painter of early Florentine School, born near Florence; commissioned by Pope Nicholas V to decorate the Vatican 1454.

Castalia, Fountain of (now called Fountain of St. John), Delphi; sacred to Muses; waters supposed source of inspiration.

Castanheiro, tropical tree *Bertholletia excelsa* of lecythis family, native to S. America; grows to 100 ft (30 m); leaves to 2 ft (0.6 m) long, oblong, leathery, with wavy margins; flowers, white, in loose spikelike clusters; fruit is the Brazil nut
  nuts N-448

Caste, hereditary division of society according to family, religion, wealth, occupation, etc.
  Buddhism B-482
  Hare Krishna H-42
  Hinduism H-156
    monks and monasticism M-541
  India A-405, E-318, I-67, *pictures* [illegible]
    Maurya empire M-234
    mythology M-696
  Jainism rejects J-14
  minority group M-460

Castelar y Ripoll, Emilio (1832–99), Spanish Liberal statesman, orator, and writer; born in Cádiz; dictator of Spanish republic Sept.–Dec. 1873; author of histories, essays, novels, travel books.

Castel dell'Ovo, castle, Naples, Italy N-11

Castelli, Francesco. *see in index* Borromini, Francesco

Castellón de la Plana, Spain, industrial and trade city 40 mi (65 km) n.e. of Valencia, near Mediterranean; pop. 52,868.

Castelnau, Édouard de Curières de (1851–1944), French general; commanded in Lorraine 1914; organized emergency defense of Verdun 1916; on Eastern Front 1917–18.

Castel Nuovo, in Naples, Italy N-11

Castelnuovo-Tedesco, Mario (1895–1968), U.S. composer, born in Florence, Italy; to U.S. 1939, citizen 1946; wrote songs, choral music ('Three Chorales on Hebrew Melodies'), orchestral music, opera ('La Mandragola').

Castelo Branco, Humberto de Alencar (1900–67), Brazilian statesman, born in Fortaleza; career army officer; president 1964–67 B-310

Castel Sant' Angelo (or Hadrian's tomb), in Rome, Italy R-257, *map* R-250, *pictures* R-249, E-348

Castiglione, Baldassare (1478–1529), Italian prose writer and diplomat, employed on many important missions, born near Mantua, Italy; called "the perfect courtier"; wrote 'Il Cortegiano', famous treatise on what constitutes a courtier
  Italian literature I-376

Castiglione, Giovanni Benedetto (called Il Grechetto in Italy, Le Bénédette in France) (1616–70), Italian painter, etcher, born in Genoa; excelled in animal painting; also historical and mythological works; etchings noted for freedom in technique, skillful use of light and shade.

Castile (Spanish Castilla), region and former kingdom in central Spain. *see also in index* New Castile; Old Castile
  banner, *picture* M-384
  castle, *picture* S-360
  Ferdinand and Isabella F-54
  Moors S-358
  people S-353

Castile soap, soap originally made by saponifying olive oil with sodium carbonate; now peanut, coconut, and other oils are also used; named for Castile, Spain S-231

Castilian, standard dialect of Spanish language S-353, S-365

Castillo, El, or **Pyramid of Quetzalcoatl,** Mayan civilization M-236

Castilloa, genus of trees native to Central America and n. South America; secondary source of rubber, some trees produce caucho. *see also in index* Caucho

Castillo de San Marcos National Monument, in Florida S-16b, *picture* S-17

Castillon, France, town 26 mi (42 km) e. of Bordeaux; scene of French victory over English in 1453, last battle of Hundred Years' War; pop. 3,108

Castin (or St. Castin, Vincent, baron de) (1650–1722?), French trader, born in Oléron, France; arrived at Penobscot, Me., about 1667, adopted American Indian ways; married a native woman; took control of Fort Pentegoet 1676; grew rich on trade; returned to France 1701.

Casting, in drama D-153, T-153

Casting, in fishing F-145

Casting, in garment pressing G-33

Casting, making a mold or reproduction of something
  animal tracks A-463
  archaeological technique A-534
  bells B-154
  fossils, *picture* F-325
  iron and steel I-334, 337
  metal and metallurgy M-309
  metalworking M-311
  plastics P-382
  pottery P-478
  sculpture S-81

Cast iron I-334
  Bessemer process B-178
  design D-112
  furniture F-452
  plumbing pipes P-393
  tungsten used T-307
  vanadium used V-258

Castle, Irene (1893–1969), U.S. dancer, born in New Rochelle, N.Y., popularized slim figure and bobbed hair; with husband Vernon Castle, noted as exhibition ballroom dancer ('My Husband', life of Vernon Castle; 'Castles in the Air') D-21
  popular music M-684

Castle, Vernon (born Vernon Blyth) (1887–1918), English dancer and aviator, born in Norwich, England; husband of Irene Castle; to U.S. 1906; killed in airplane accident D-21
  popular music M-684

Castle C-198. *see also in index* Palace
  Aigle, Switzerland, *picture* S-538
  Alcazar of Segovia, *picture* C-360
  early cannon bombards, *picture* S-57f
  England S-158
  feudal social and political structure F-68, 70
  fort and fortification F-319
  Germany
    Rhine River castles R-178
  interior design I-247
  Middle Ages M-386
  shelter S-158
  Prague, Czechoslovakia, *picture* P-485
  Scotland, *pictures* S-70, 71

Castle, in chess C-306

'Castle, The', work by Kafka N-414

Castle Garden, New York, N.Y., *pictures* M-399

Castle Hill National Historic Park, park in Newfoundland N-29

'Castle of Otranto, The', work by Walpole E-273, W-11

'Castle Rackrent', work by Edgeworth
  Irish literature I-326

Castlereagh, Robert Stewart, Viscount (2nd marquis of Londonderry) (1769–1822), British statesman; secretary for Ireland (1798–1800); secretary for war (1805–6, 1807–9); foreign secretary (1812–22) V-316

Castle Shannon, Pa., residential borough just s. of Pittsburgh; cement; incorporated 1919; pop. 11,899, *map* P-184

Castle Square, in Warsaw, Poland W-33

Castleton Gardens, near Kingston, Jamaica, *picture* J-18

Castleton State College, Castleton, Vt.; founded 1787; present name 1962, senior college as Castleton Teachers College after 1947; liberal arts, education; graduate studies.

Castor and Pollux (also called the Dioscuri, "sons of Zeus"), in Greek and Roman mythology; twin sons of Zeus and Leda, a mortal; among the Argonauts who sailed with Jason; after death taken up to heaven to form constellation Gemini ("twins"); worshiped as protectors of seamen
  constellation. *see in index* Gemini

Castoreum, secretion of beaver, used in perfume B-121, P-205

Castor-oil plant, annual herb *Ricinus communis* of the spurge family; oil from seeds used in drugs and lubricants, and as drying agent in paints
  breeding experiment, *picture* P-366
  paints P-74

Castriota, George. *see in index* Scanderbeg

Castro, Cipriano (1858–1924), Venezuelan revolutionary leader and president, called "The Lion of the Andes"; dictator 1899–1908 V-277

Castro, Fidel (born 1927), Cuban revolutionary leader and president C-200
  Ben Bella B-160
  Cuba C-800
  Cuban Americans H-166
  Havana H-56
  Kennedy K-202
  Latin America L-66
  warfare W-17, *picture* W-19

Castro, Guillén de (1569–1631), Spanish dramatist, aristocrat and soldier; first to put Cid stories into play form; his 'Mocedades del Cid' was source for Corneille's 'The Cid'.

Castro, Raúl (born 1930), Cuban revolutionist, brother of Fidel Castro C-200

Castro, Rosalía de (1837–85), Spanish poet; little known while she lived, after death was considered one of great poets of her time; poetry simple and genuine ('Cantares gallegos'; 'En las orillas del Sar').

Castro Valley, Calif., unincorporated community 20 mi (30 km) s.e. of San Francisco; primarily residential; fruit, poultry; governed by Alameda County supervisor; pop. 44,760.

Cast steel
  Krupp family K-307

Casuariiformes, order of birds including the cassowary and emu. *see also in index* Cassowary; Birds, flightless

Caswell, Richard (1729–89), U.S. Revolutionary War soldier and political leader, born in Cecil County, Md.; member Continental Congress 1774–76; first governor of North Carolina 1776–80.

Cat C-201
  artistic portrayals
    book illustration, *picture* R-111e
    folk art motif F-252
    'Monkey and the Cat' fable F-3
  balance of nature E-50
  births M-649

disease V-251
domestication A-455
fur F-463, *table* F-465
length of life, *chart* A-423
pet care, *picture* P-242
receptors A-439
relatives
jaguar J-12
leopard L-135, *picture* P-513
lion L-231
puma P-531
saber-toothed tiger S-1
tiger T-183
vision C-563
weightlessness test, *picture* S-341a
whiskers H-7

Catabolism, destructive metabolism P-312
metabolism M-306

Catacomb, an underground cemetery C-218
Rome R-257, *picture* R-258, *map* R-251

Catadioptrics, lenses T-66

Catalan, language
Barcelona B-79

Catalana, breed of poultry P-482

Catalan furnace, Spanish industrial tool
early iron production I-350

Catalina Island. *see in index* Santa Catalina Island

Catalog (or catalogue)
mail-order U-110
stamp S-406

Catalonia (Spanish, Cataluña), region in n.e. Spain; 12,332 sq mi (31,940 sq km); former autonomous republic; pop. 3,925,779 S-352, 354
Barcelona B-79

Catalpa, pod-bearing tree *Catalpa bignonioides* or *Catalpa speciosa* of the Bignoniaceae family C-218
leaf P-358

Catalyst, in chemistry C-219
enzymes B-202, E-290
petroleum P-241, *chart* P-241b, *picture* P-240
platinum P-384
sulfuric acid manufacture S-510
vanadium V-258

Catalytic converter, in automobile A-848, A-867

Catalytic cracking (or cat cracking), of petroleum P-233, P-241, *chart* P-241b
gasoline production G-42

Catamaran B-325, *picture* B-326
oil-well drilling, *picture* P-239

Catamount ("cat of the mountain"). *see in index* Puma

Catana. *see in index* Catania

Catananche (also called Cupid's-dart), genus of annual or perennial plants of the composite family, native to Mediterranean region; flowers blue, white, or yellow, on long stems; used in ancient love philters.

Cat and Rat, game G-10

Catania (ancient Catana), Italy, seaport on e. coast of Sicily; textiles; chemicals, sulfur, cement, leather goods; established by Greeks 729 BC; frequent battle site from Athenian-Syracuse conflict 432 BC through World War II; pop. 361,466 S-192, *maps* E-360, I-401
Mount Etna E-323

Cataphract, heavy cavalry
Byzantine army A-637

Catapult, term for war machines of the crossbow type, much used in ancient and medieval warfare for hurling arrows, stones, etc.; modern slingshot works on same principle and is also called catapult; also device to launch aircraft from carriers
ammunition A-371
ancient and medieval use, *pictures* M-390, V-1
artillery A-658

Cataract, eye disorder E-390
blindness B-311

Cataract, waterfall of great volume. *see in index* Waterfalls

Catastrophes. *see in index* Disasters

Catawba, a North American Indian tribe, few in number now; live in South Carolina, *map* I-136, *table* I-138

Catawba College, Salisbury, N.C.; founded 1851; United Church of Christ; liberal arts, education.

Catawba grape G-220

Catawba rhododendron, flowering plant *Rhododendron catawbiense* R-196

Catawba River, in North Carolina, *picture* N-365

Catbird, songbird *Dumetella carolinensis* of Mimidae family C-219, *picture* B-257
egg, *picture* E-112
nest, *picture* B-182d
song pattern B-266

Catboat B-326, *pictures* B-230, V-238

Catch-as-catch-can, wrestling W-364

Catcher, in baseball B-89

'Catcher in the Rye', work by Salinger N-410

Catchfly. *see in index* Silene

Catch stitch, in sewing S-122

'Catch-22', work by Heller A-361
satire N-412

Catclaw (or Texas mimosa), tree *Acacia greggi* of pea family, native to desert regions from Texas to Mexico; 12 ft to 18 ft (4 m to 5.5 m) high; flowers yellow.

Cat cracking. *see in index* Catalytic cracking

Cat distemper (or cat typhoid, or panleucopenia, or viral enteritis), most widespread and serious infectious disease of cats C-210

Catechism, manual of instruction arranged in questions and answers; used especially by Jews and Christians in teaching religion; became widespread at time of Reformation; among U.S. Protestants supplanted by Bible study aids in 19th century; Roman Catholics' Baltimore Catechism used extensively from 1895 to 1960s
Philippines, *picture* P-255

Catechu (or cutch), substance obtained from acacia and certain other Asian and African plants; used in tanning and dyeing.

Categorical imperative, basic idea of Kant's philosophy K-190

Catering, in food industry C-699

Caterpillar, larval stage of moths and butterflies C-219, *pictures* A-430, P-511
butterflies and moths B-525, *picture* B-521
hibernation H-147
insects I-221
larva L-51
metamorphosis, *pictures* B-389
respiration A-425
silkworm S-197

Caterpillar Club P-109b

Catesby, Robert (1573–1605), English Roman Catholic conspirator, born in Lapworth; chief instigator of Gunpowder Plot (1605); also accused in Robert Devereux rebellion (1601) and plot against James I (1603)
Fawkes F-49

Cat Fanciers' Association, U.S. organization C-205

Catfish, fish; has a conspicuous set of feelers C-220
barbels A-430
egg hatching F-128
fish culture F-132
fisheries, *table* F-136
length of life, *chart* A-423

Catgut (presently gut), material used for strings on certain musical instruments S-490

Catharsis theory
drama D-241
play P-390b

Cathartidae, the Western Hemisphere's family of vultures B-280, V-388

Cathay, poetic name for China; originated with Marco Polo; used vaguely in Middle Ages for Far East. *see in index* China

Cathays Park, park in Cardiff, Wales, *picture* W-6

Cathedra, seat or throne (Greek); hence, *ex cathedra* (Latin), "spoken with authority"; infallible papal rulings are said to be made *ex cathedra.*

Cathedral (or ecclesia cathedralis), church containing the official throne of a bishop C-220
architecture A-666, *picture* P-457. *see also in index* Church architecture
Brazil B-408
Czechoslovakia, *picture* P-485
France F-350
Chartres S-85, *picture* S-84
Notre Dame. *see in index* Notre Dame
Reims R-138
Saint André B-366
interior design I-247
Italy
Florence B-470, D-88, S-86, *pictures* P-264, S-85
Pisa, *picture* P-343
St. John Lateran, *picture* R-253
Saint Mark's B-402, V-277
library history L-171
Middle Ages M-393
Peru, *picture* P-223
Philippines, *pictures* M-97, P-260
Portugal, *picture* P-457
Puerto Rico S-44a
Spain S-356, *picture* S-359
The Netherlands U-236
United Kingdom
Canterbury C-142, *picture* C-143
Saint Paul's. *see in index* St. Paul's Cathedral
Salisbury, *picture* P-46
United States
New York A-502, *picture* S-84
Santa Fe, *picture* S-46
U.S.S.R.
Kremlin K-304
Saint Isaac's, *picture* R-353

Cathedral bells. *see in index* Cobaea

Cather, Willa (1873–1947), U.S. novelist and short-story writer C-221
American literature A-358
'Death Comes for the Archbishop' R-112c

Catherine I (1683–1727), empress of Russia, wife of Peter the Great and empress after his death (1725); of humble birth, she became the wife of a Swedish dragoon and fell into Russian hands at the capture of Marienburg; though ignorant she had charm and practical intelligence, and exercised great influence over Peter A-830, P-226

Catherine II, the Great (1729–96), German princess who became empress of Russia C-222
Russia R-353
Russian literature R-359

Catherine de' Medici (or Catherine de Médicis) (1519–89), queen of Henry II of France M-273
Charles IX C-277
Coligny C-546
gloves G-169
Henry II H-131
lacemaking L-14

Catherine Howard. *see in index* Howard, Catherine

Catherine of Alexandria, Saint (4th century AD?), Christian virgin and martyr; tortured on a toothed or "Catherine" wheel; festival November 25.

Catherine of Aragon (1485–1536), daughter of Ferdinand and Isabella of Spain, and first queen of Henry VIII of England
Cranmer C-761
English history E-244
Henry VIII H-130

Catherine of Braganza (1638–1705), queen consort of Charles II of England, daughter of John IV of Portugal.

Catherine of Siena, Saint (1347–80), Italian ascetic and mystic, a dyer's daughter; born in Siena; persuaded Pope Gregory XI to return from Avignon to Rome; proclaimed doctor of the church by Pope Paul VI 1970; festival April 30.

Catherine of Valois (1401–37), daughter of Charles VI of France and queen of Henry V of England
Henry V H-129
House of Tudor T-304
Hundred Years' War H-325

Catherine Parr. *see in index* Parr, Catherine

Catherwood, Mary Hartwell (1847–1902), U.S. novelist, born in Luray, Ohio; successful writings include historical romances of French Canada and Great Lakes region ('The Romance of Dollard'; 'The Story of Tonty'; 'Old Kaskaskia'; 'The Days of Jeanne D'Arc').

'Cathleen ni Houlihan', work by Yeats Y-412

Cathode, negatively charged electrode in an electrolytic solution or ionized gas
battery B-107
electrochemistry E-170, *picture* E-171
phototube P-273, *diagram* P-274
X rays X-406

Cathode ray, stream of electrons emitted by cathode of vacuum tube
X rays X-406

Cathode ray oscilloscope, instrument I-230

Cathode ray tube (CRT), televisionlike device
computer C-627
electricity E-152
electronics E-177
mechanical drawing M-262
television T-77
typesetting T-340

Catholic Association, in Ireland O-490

Catholic church. *see in index* Roman Catholicism

Catholic Emancipation Act (1829), in England E-252
O'Connell O-490

Catholicity, principle of Eastern Orthodox churches E-42

Catholic League (1576). *see in index* Holy League

Catholic League (1609), led by Maximilian I, duke of Bavaria A-829

Catholic Library Association (CLA), founded 1921 to promote Roman Catholic literature and library work; publishes guides and indexes; headquarters Haverford, Pa. *see also in index* Regina Medal
literary awards L-240

Catholic University of America, Washington, D.C.; Roman Catholic; established by Pope Leo XIII, 1887; opened 1889; schools of sacred theology, canon law, philosophy; arts and sciences, education, engineering, law, nursing, social work; graduate school.

Catholic University of Louvain, Louvain, Belgium, founded 1425 by papal bull; leading scientific institution of medieval Europe, having 6,000 students in 16th century; famous department of Roman Catholic theology; active in Counter Reformation; suppressed during French Revolution, but reestablished 1816.

Catholic University of Puerto Rico, Ponce, P.R.; Roman Catholic; founded 1948; liberal arts and humanities, business administration, education, law, and sciences; graduate program.

Catholic Youth Organization (CYO), founded 1930 in Chicago, Ill., by Bishop Bernard J. Sheil; maintains program of religious, educational, recreational, and social service activities for boys and girls.

Catiline (or Lucius Sergius Catilina) (108?–62 BC), Roman conspirator C-413

Cation, positively-charged ion
analysis C-290
electrochemistry E-170

Cation-exchange process (or zeolite process), water softening W-91

Catkin (or ament), scaly spike of flowers on certain trees, *picture* T-282

Catlin, George (1796–1872), U.S. ethnologist, traveler, artist, and writer C-223

Catlinite, red pipestone of Pipestone County, Minnesota, quarried by American Indians for pipes and ornaments; hardens with age; named in English for George Catlin.

Cato, Marcus Porcius (234–149 BC), the Censor ("the Elder"), Roman statesman and orator; name a synonym for harsh morality and narrow patriotism L-76

Cato, Marcus Porcius (95–46 BC), of Utica ("the Younger"), Roman statesman and stoic philosopher, great-grandson of Cato the Elder; opponent of Caesar in war with Pompey; stabbed himself rather than live under the conqueror; hero of Addison's tragedy, 'Cato'.

'Cat on a Hot Tin Roof', play by Williams A-357

Catonephela numilia, butterfly, *picture* B-524

Catonsville, Md., unincorporated community; pop. 54,812, *map* M-182

Cato the Censor (234–149 BC). *see in index* Cato, Marcus Porcius

'Cats' (1982), musical by Webber M-686

Cats, Jakob (1577–1660), Dutch poet and humorist; twice sent as ambassador to England; his poems, simple and abounding in moral maxims, popular with the Dutch; called "Father Cats" ('Marriage'; 'Age and Country Life').
CAT scanner. *see in index* Computerized axial tomography scanner
Cat's-eye, chrysoberyl used as a gem, also a lustrous gray, brown, or green gem variety of quartz enclosing asbestos fibers, found in Sri Lanka J-115
Catskill Aqueduct system A-520
Catskill Mountains, picturesque range of low mountains in s.e. New York on west side of Hudson River; highest point, Slide Mt., 4,204 ft (1,281 m); famous as resort region, *map* U-50
Appalachian geography A-508
mountain M-634
New York N-246
Catt, Carrie Chapman (1859–1947), U.S. women's suffrage leader and peace advocate C-223
women's rights, *picture* W-276
Cattail, plant of the *Typha* species, *picture* P-360
seed dispersal S-106
water plant, *picture* W-101
Cattail moth, insect B-526
Cattalo, cattle and buffalo hybrid B-286
Cattaro, Yugoslavia. *see in index* Kotor
Cattegat, strait in Northern Europe. *see in index* Kattegat
Cattell, James McKeen (1860–1944), U.S. psychologist, writer, and editor; born in Easton, Pa.; professor psychology, University of Pennsylvania 1888–91; Columbia University 1891–1917; editor *Science, Scientific Monthly, American Men of Science, American Naturalist, School and Society, Leaders in Education.*
Cattermole, George (1800–68), English painter and illustrator; famed as a water-colorist, but painted also in oils; successful landscape and architectural paintings; illustrated many books including Sir Walter Scott's 'Waverley' novels.
Cattle C-224. *see also in index* Beef; Calf; Cattle ranching; Dairying industry; Ox; Steer; breeds by name, as Hereford; Longhorn cattle
anatomy
hoof H-231
skeleton, *diagram* S-209
stomach S-455
diseases
anthrax P-138, V-251
domestication A-456
farming F-25
machinery F-33
frontier F-423
length of life, *chart* A-423
meat M-246
industry M-250
plant poisoning P-408
producing regions
Africa A-808
Europe
Switzerland S-541
India I-65
Mexico M-332
New Zealand N-290
Queensland Q-16
South America S-275, *pictures* A-579, S-281b, 285
Colombia C-551
Uruguay U-213
Venezuela V-275
United States U-63, *map* U-73, *pictures* U-56, 77, 83
Arizona A-598, *picture* A-600
Great Plains G-249
Iowa I-290, *map* I-294
Kansas K-175, *map* K-178, *picture* K-176
Montana, *picture* M-550
Nebraska, *picture* N-96
New Mexico N-216, *map* N-218
North Dakota, *picture* N-381
Oklahoma O-525
South Dakota S-322, *map* S-326, *picture* S-330
Texas T-120, *picture* T-119
Washington, *picture* W-50
Wyoming W-385, 388, *map* W-390
ruminant R-318
Wichita W-201
Cattle egret (or cattle heron), bird *Bubulcus ibis* native to s. Spain, Africa, and Asia; appeared in South America about 1930, probably blown over the Atlantic by winds; spread rapidly over coast of South America; first observed in Massachusetts in 1952 and subsequently spread along Atlantic coast; believed to be only Old World bird in history to establish residence on mainland of the Americas without human aid; medium size (about 2–27 in.; 50–77 cm), breeding male white with yellowish-buff plumes on crown, back, and breast, yellow legs and bill B-257, *picture* B-244. *see also in index* Heron
Cattle ranching. *see also in index* Cattle trails; Cowboy; Ranch; Range
barbed wire W-247
cowboys C-750
outlaws O-619
rodeo R-236
roundup, *picture* U-77
Cattle tick S-387
Cattle trails
Chisholm Trail
Oklahoma O-525
Texas T-125
U.S. frontier F-423
Catton, Bruce (in full Charles Bruce Catton) (1899–1978), U.S. journalist and writer, born in Petoskey, Mich.; books about Civil War include trilogy ('Mr. Lincoln's Army'; 'Glory Road'; 'A Stillness at Appomattox', awarded 1954 Pulitzer prize for history); 'This Hallowed Ground'; 'Grant Moves South'; 'The Picture History of the Civil War'; 'The Centennial History of the Civil War'; editor *American Heritage* 1954–59, senior editor 1959–78
'A Stillness at Appomattox' R-111j
warfare W-27
Catty, Chinese unit of weight, *table* W-141
Cat typhoid (cat distemper, panleucopenia, or viral enteritis), most widespread and serious infectious disease of cats C-210
Catullus, Gaius Valerius (84–54 BC), Roman lyric poet C-232
Latin literature L-77
CATV (or community access television), television system T-77
Cat yawl, sailboat, *picture* B-327
Cauca, river in Colombia C-31
Caucasia, U.S.S.R. *see in index* Caucasus
Caucasoid race (or Caucasian race, or white race) R-25, *chart* R-26
Asian racial patterns A-682
Caucasus region C-232
numbers P-449
Caucasus (or Caucasia), region in U.S.S.R. divided by Caucasus Mts. into north Caucasus (part of R.S.F.S.R) and Transcaucasia (Armenia, Azerbaijan, and Georgian republics) C-232
folktales, *list* S-478
lingual diversity L-42, *table* L-44
rugmaking R-314
Caucasus Mountains, range in U.S.S.R., *maps* R-322, 344, 349, *picture* R-324. *see also in index* Caucasus
Europe E-329, *map* E-360
Caucho, rubber gum, product of the Mexican rubber tree *Castilla elastica* of the mulberry family. *see also in index* Castilloa
Cauchy, Augustin Louis (1789–1857), French mathematician, born in Paris; made important contributions to pure and applied mathematics; also wrote successful poetry
mathematics M-216, *table* M-218
Caucus, closed political meeting
early U.S. presidential elections P-432
primary elections' comparison P-496
Caudal fin, in anatomy of fish, *diagram* F-125
Caudata, order of the class Amphibia, most commonly salamanders A-376
Caudill, Rebecca (born 1899), U.S. writer, born in Cumberland, Ky.; taught in Rio de Janeiro, Brazil; books for older girls include 'Barrie & Daughter' and 'Tree of Freedom'; for younger children, she wrote a series of books based on her childhood in the mountains of Kentucky: 'Happy Little Family'; 'Schoolhouse in the Woods'; 'Up and Down the River'; 'Schoolroom in the Parlor'; 'Time for Lissa'; 'A Pocketful of Cricket'; 'The Far-Off Land'.
Caudillos, dictators in Spanish-speaking countries
Argentina A-583
Franco F-376
Latin America S-291
Caudine Forks, mountain pass in ancient Samnium, now Italy 25 mi (40 km) n.e. of Naples, where 40,000 Romans surrendered (321 BC) in 2nd Samnite War.
Cauliflower, vegetable C-2, *picture* C-3
Caulk
heating insulation H-112
ship planks S-164
Caura River, tributary of the Orinoco River in central Venezuela, in Guiana Highlands; flows n. 450 mi (725 km) through tropical forest regions; not navigable because of extensive rapids, *maps* S-298, V-275
Causalgia, in pathology
analgesics A-387
Cause and effect pattern, in reading R-103b
'Causes' (or 'Aetia'), elegy by Callimachus G-277
Causeway, raised road or walk across water or swampland
Alexandria, Egypt S-116
Singapore S-205
Caustic, substance which destroys living tissue; common caustics are household lye (sodium hydroxide), carbolic acid, chromic acid, arsenic, and silver nitrate.
Caustic potash (or potassium hydroxide), chemical compound, often called lye when dissolved in water P-465
soapmaking S-229
Caustic soda (or sodium hydroxide, often called soda lye) S-247
papermaking P-101
soapmaking S-229
Cauvery River, in India, flows 475 mi (765 km) through s. India and into Bay of Bengal
waterfalls, *table* W-98
Cavalier, hats and caps, *picture* H-53
Cavaliere, Emilio del (1550–1602), Italian composer, born in Rome O-575
Cavalieri, Francesco Bonaventura (1598–1647), Italian mathematician and astronomer; invented method of indivisibles, first published in 1635
mathematics, *table* M-218
Cavalier Parliament, in English history E-247
Cavalier poets, name applied to group of English lyric poets of 17th century among whom were Richard Lovelace, Sir John Suckling, Robert Herrick, and Thomas Carew; poems are courtly, light, and sophisticated E-269
Herrick H-143
Cavaliers, Royalists in English Civil War
Charles I C-275
England E-246
fashion F-41
'Cavalleria rusticana', opera by Mascagni M-184
opera O-568, *list* O-562
Cavalli, Francesco (or Pietro Francesco Caletti-Bruni) (1602–76), Italian composer of sacred and dramatic music, born in Crema, Italy.
Cavalry. *see also in index* Armor
Assyria A-635
Britain, *picture* U-12
sabers S-547
warfare W-20
weapons W-111
Cavan, inland agricultural and mining county in n. part of Ireland; 730 sq mi (1,890 sq km); name from Gaelic *an Chabhàin* ("the hollow place"); pop. 54,022.
Cavanna, Betty (or Mrs. Elizabeth Cavanna Headley) (born 1909), author, born in Camden, N.J.; engaged in newspaper work, advertising, and art; wrote short stories and books for teenage girls ('A Girl Can Dream'; 'Paintbox Summer'; 'Spring Comes Riding'; 'Lasso Your Heart'; 'Love, Laurie').
Cave, Edward, British editor
magazine and journal M-32
Cave C-233
United States
South Dakota, *map* S-334, *picture* S-330
Timpanogos Cave, *map* U-232
Cave bear, prehistoric animal, larger than polar bear; one of the fiercest enemies of cave dwellers; fossils found in caverns of Europe and Asia.
Cave dwellers C-234
art A-795, C-465, P-28
Cave of Altamira S-357
hairdressing H-8
horses H-272
classification, *chart* R-26
man M-91, *picture* M-87
weapons and tools S-455
Cavelier, René Robert. *see in index* La Salle, Sieur de
Cavell, Edith (1865–1915), English nurse, attached to hospital in Brussels; executed by German military government of Belgium in World War I for helping wounded Allied soldiers to escape.
Cavendish, Henry (1731–1810), English chemist and physicist, born in Nice, France; valuable discoveries in electricity; proved water a compound
chemistry C-301
electricity E-161
Cavendish, Spencer Compton. *see in index* Devonshire, 8th duke of
Cavendish, Thomas (1555?–92), English navigator, born in Suffolk; second Englishman to circumnavigate the globe (1586–88); died in shipwreck at Strait of Magellan during second attempt.
Cavendish, Victor Christian William. *see in index* Devonshire, 9th duke of
Cave of Altamira, in n. Spain S-357
'Cave of the Heart', dance by Graham, *picture* G-205
Cave of the Winds, Niagara Falls N-301
Cavern C-233
Caviar, salty relish made of the eggs of sturgeon or other fish, especially in U.S.S.R.
canning center A-707
Caspian Sea C-197
Volga River, *picture* E-341
sturgeon S-495a
Caving method, mines and mining M-428
Cavite, Philippines, residential city and seaport 8 mi (13 km) s.w. of Manila; chartered 1940; capital of Cavite Province until 1954; pop. 54,891 P-259c, *map* P-262
Cavour, Camillo (or Camillo Benso, count di Cavour) (1810–61), Italian statesman C-236
Italy I-393
Victor Emmanuel II V-308
Cavy. *see in index* Guinea pig
Cawein, Madison Julius (1865–1914), U.S. poet, born in Louisville, Ky. ('Kentucky Poems'; 'Blooms of the Berry'; 'Minions of the Moon').
Cawnpore, India. *see in index* Kanpur
Caxton, William (1422?–91), first English printer, born in Kent, England; called "Father of English Printing"
'Book of Courtesy' E-320
English history E-243
first English-language encyclopedia R-124
'Morte D'Arthur' E-266
typeface history T-337, *picture* B-349
Cayenne, French Guiana, capital and seaport, on island of Cayenne; gave name to Cayenne pepper; formerly French penal colony; pop. 19,668, *maps* S-298, W-297
French Guiana F-393
Cayenne pepper P-197b
Cayley, Sir George (1773–1857), English aeronautical engineer, born in Scarborough
aerospace research A-76, G-167
airplane history A-200
bionics B-233
helicopter H-122
Cayman Islands, West Indies, group n.w. of Jamaica, consisting of Grand Cayman, Little Cayman, and Cayman

Brac; the first is the largest, area 71 sq mi (184 sq km); the other two about 70 mi (115 km) n.e.; total area 100 sq mi (260 sq km); exports: mahogany logs, thatch rope, turtles, coconuts; pop. 7,622
  Commonwealth membership C-602
  West Indies W-158, *map* W-159

Cayuga, American Indians of the Iroquois group, originally living around Cayuga Lake, N.Y.; moved to Canada during the Revolutionary War I-142, *table* I-138

Cayuga Lake, in central New York, 35 mi (55 km) long; on it are Ithaca, Aurora, and Cayuga.

Cayuse, American Indians of the Waiilatpuan linguistic stock in Oregon and Washington; the cayuse pony, introduced by the Europeans, was named for them.

Cazin, Jean Charles (1841–91), French painter and designer of ceramics; noted for landscapes and for religious paintings.

CBC (or Canadian Broadcasting Corporation) R-54

CBs. *see in index* Seabees

CBS. *see in index* Columbia Broadcasting System

CCC. *see in index* Civilian Conservation Corps

CCC. *see in index* Commodity Credit Corporation

CCD. *see in index* Charge-coupled device

C.C.F. (or Co-operative Commonwealth Federation), Canadian political party S-49g

C clef, in music M-690

CCP. *see in index* Chinese Communist party

Cd, chemical element. *see in index* Cadmium

CD (or compact disc), high-quality audio disc T-76

CDU. *see in index* Christian Democratic Union

Ce, chemical element. *see in index* Cerium

Ceanannus Mór, Ireland. *see in index* Kells

Ceará, state of Brazil on n. seacoast; 57,102 sq mi (147,894 sq km); cap. Fortaleza; pop. 5,380,432, *map* B-425

Ceará, Brazil. *see in index* Fortaleza

Cease-fire. *see also in index* Armistice
  Kashmir dispute U-24
  Suez crises S-504
  Vietnam V-324

Ceausescu, Nicolae (born 1918), Romanian political leader, born in Scornicesti, near Bucharest; joined Communist party 1933; imprisoned 1936–39 for work with Communist underground; secretary-general of party 1965–; head of state 1967–; president of Romania 1974–.

Cebu, island of Philippines; 1,707 sq mi (4,421 sq km); farms, mines; cap. and chief seaport is city of Cebu (pop. 418,517) on e. coast; trade center; pop. 1,426,804 P-253c, *maps* A-697, P-262, *picture* P-257
  Magellan M-36

Cebuano, a Philippine people P-253b

Cecchetti, Enrico (1850–1928), Italian dancer and ballet teacher; at Russian Imperial School of Ballet 1890–1902; taught Pavlova, Nijinsky, Massine; instructor for Diaghilev ballet.

Cecil, great English family; most famous members, William Cecil, Lord Burghley, great minister of Queen Elizabeth I, and marquis of Salisbury, Victorian premier. *see below* and *also in index* Salisbury, Robert Arthur Talbot Gascoyne-Cecil, marquis of

Cecil, Edgar Algernon Robert (or first Viscount Cecil of Chelwood) (1864–1958), British statesman, son of marquis of Salisbury; entered Parliament 1906; filled various high offices; minister of blockade 1916; advocate of League of Nations; received first Woodrow Wilson peace prize 1924.

Cecil, Hugh Richard Heathcote (later first Baron Quickswood) (1869–1956), British political leader and soldier, brother of Robert; in House of Commons 1895–1906, 1910–36; Royal Flying Corps 1915.

Cecil, William (or first Baron Burghley) (1520–98), British statesman, principal adviser to Elizabeth I through most of her reign E-191

Cecilia, Saint, patroness of musicians and the blind; Roman noble who suffered martyrdom either in Sicily about AD 176 or in Rome about AD 230; festival November 22.

Cecropia moth, insect B-521

Cecrops, mythical founder of Athens; first king of Attica; represented as half human, half dragon; credited with inventing writing and establishing marriage and burial customs.

Cedar, name applied to many trees and to their woods, also to trees of the genus *Cedrus* C-236. *see also in index* Alaska cedar
  juniper J-157
  Northwest Indians' use I-134
  wood, *table* W-282

Cedar, Japanese. *see in index* Cryptomeria

Cedar bird. *see in index* Cedar waxwing

Cedar Breaks National Monument, in Utah, *map* U-233

Cedar City, Utah, town in s.w.; farm crops, livestock; iron mining; tourist center; Southern Utah State College; near Cedar Breaks National Park, and Bryce Canyon National Park; pop. 8,946 U-219, *maps* U-40, U-217, 233

Cedar Creek, small branch of Shenandoah River in Virginia
  Civil War battle S-161

Cedar Crest College, Allentown, Pa.; affiliated with United Church of Christ; for women; opened 1867; chartered 1868; arts and sciences, education.

Cedar elm, tree *Ulmus crassifolia* E-194

Cedar Falls, Iowa, city on Cedar River about 6 mi (10 km) n.w. of Waterloo; pumps, farm equipment, golf course equipment; University of Northern Iowa; pop. 36,322, *map* I-302

Cedar Grove, N.J., urban township 6 mi (10 km) s.w. of Paterson; plastics, paper, machinery, electronic research equipment; pop. 12,600.

Cedar of Lebanon, tree C-236
  ship S-164

Cedar Rapids, Iowa, 2nd city of state, on Cedar River about 65 mi (105 km) n.w. of Davenport; cereal and corn products, meat-packing, radio equipment, heavy machinery; Coe College, Mount Mercy College; pop. 110,243
  Iowa I-290, *map* I-302, *picture* I-297
  Wood's 'Woman with Plant' P-61, *picture* P-60

Cedar River, tributary of the Iowa River, in Minnesota and Iowa; about 330 mi (530 km); drops 740 ft (225 m) over course; not navigable; rises in s. Minnesota, flows s.e. across Iowa; source of hydroelectric power, *map* I-302

Cedar waxwing (or cedar bird), bird *Bombycilla cedrorum* of the family Bombycillidae W-110
  birds B-251, *pictures* B-241, 256

Cedarwood oil C-236

Cedric, of Rotherwood (or Cedric, the Saxon), character in Sir Walter Scott's 'Ivanhoe', guardian of Rowena and father of Ivanhoe.

Cedron, Valley of. *see in index* Kedron, Valley of

Cefotaxime sodium, antibiotic drug
  antibiotic therapy A-489

Ceiba, large tropical tree of silk-cotton family Bombacaceae; with showy bell-shaped flowers, and pods filled with seeds that yield the fiber kapok; sacred to Guatemalan Indians
  kapok K-190

Ceiba, La, n. Honduras, developed as a banana port; now also an industrial center; shoes, soap, furniture, plastics, and pharmaceuticals; pop. 61,900 H-226

Ceiling, base height of cloud layers
  aviation A-888
  weather W-121

Ceiling, in house, *picture* B-495
  interior design I-244

Ceiling balloon, balloon used to measure ceiling in daylight W-121

Ceiling fan F-23, *picture* F-24
  ventilation H-112

Ceiling light, beam used to measure ceiling at night W-121

Ceilometer, instrument that measures the ceiling W-121

Cela, Camilo José (born 1916), Spanish novelist, born in Pontivedra ('The Hive') S-366, *picture* S-367

Celadon (or sea green), pottery glaze P-470

Celandine, perennial herb *Chelidonium majus* of the poppy family, with clusters of yellow flowers; plant yields a saffron-colored juice used in medicine.

Celanese. *see in index* Acetate

Celastraceae. *see in index* Staff-tree family

Celebes (Indonesian Sulawesi), island in Indonesia; 72,986 sq mi (189,033 sq km); pop. 7,079,349 I-158, E-45, *maps* A-697, I-166, W-297

Celebes Sea, part of Pacific Ocean between Celebes, Borneo, and Mindanao; 420 by 500 mi (675 by 800 km); greatest depth 20,400 ft (6,200 m); connects with Java Sea by Makassar Strait, *maps* A-697, I-166, P-262

Celebrezze, Anthony Joseph (born 1910), U.S. government official, born in Anzi, Italy, of naturalized U.S. parents; mayor of Cleveland, Ohio, 1953–62; U.S. secretary of health, education, and welfare 1962–65; judge U.S. Court of Appeals (6th Circuit) 1965–.

Celery, plant with edible rootstalks S-379, *picture* F-28

Celery cabbage, Chinese cabbage *Brassica pekinensis* C-4

Celery salt S-379

Celesta, musical instrument containing steel plates backed by wooden resonators; keyboard operates hammers, as in a piano, and the instrument looks like a small piano M-687
  orchestra O-576

Celestial Empire, name given to the Chinese Empire from the beginning of the Chou Dynasty (1122 BC) C-360

Celestial equator (or equinoctial)
  astronomy A-718
  navigation N-71

Celestial globe, map M-115

Celestial mechanics S-64a

Celestial meridian N-72, *diagram* N-71

Celestial navigation (or nautical astronomy), navigation by observation of the sun, moon, stars, and planets N-68, 71
  sciences S-64a

Celestial poles. *see in index* Poles, celestial

Celestial sphere, in astronomy A-718
  maps M-116
  navigation N-71

Celestine (or Caelestinus), name of five popes, best known of whom is **Saint Celestine V** (1215–96), pope in 1294, a poor Benedictine monk devoted to monastic rigors; after 6 months abdicated as pope; returned to monastery; founded the Celestines, a strict congregation within the Benedictine Order; feast day May 19 B-343

Celestite (or celestine), colorless, white, or sky-blue mineral, strontium sulfate; resembles barite; source of strontium compounds including salts used in manufacturing of flares, fireworks, and fuses and in refining of beet sugar M-435

Cell, in biology, unit structure of living organisms C-236. *see also in index* Embryology; Ovum; Sperm cell
  aging A-125
  amoeba's reproduction A-375
  animals and plants A-421
    cork C-717
  bacteria B-13
  biochemistry B-198
  bioengineering A-206
  biophysics B-237
  blood B-313
  discovery B-229
  division. *see in index* Amitosis; Meiosis; Mitosis
  drug addiction H-3
  evolution E-365
  genetics G-52, *pictures* G-55, 57
  growth G-292
  heredity H-139
  living things L-266, *pictures* L-265, 267
  microbiology M-374
  mold M-519
  molecule M-522
  muscles M-658
  nerve N-118, *diagrams* N-121, 122
  organic chemistry O-605
  osmosis O-610
  pathology A-875
  protoplasm P-514
  virus damages V-352, *picture* D-166
  yeast Y-411

Cellini, Benvenuto (1500–71), Italian goldsmith and sculptor, born in Florence; brawling braggart, soldier of fortune, and mirror of his time C-242
  'Autobiography' A-831
  metalworking M-310
  sculpture S-87
    'Perseus', *picture* F-190

Cell membrane, thin band of protein and phospholipids C-236, *picture* C-237

Cello (or violoncello), stringed instrument S-491, V-327, *picture* V-365

Cellophane
  synthetic fibers F-72

Cell theory C-241

Cellular mobile telephone T-64

Celluloid, type of plastic P-383
  film M-616
  Hyatt invented N-150

Cellulose, a plant substance
  carbohydrate C-155
  cells C-240
  organic chemistry O-604
  plants A-421, L-266, P-373
  plastics P-383, *table* P-382
  sponges S-394
  synthetic fibers F-71
  termite food T-111
  wood W-284

Cellulose nitrate. *see in index* Nitrocellulose

Celosia. *see in index* Cockscomb

Celsius, Anders (1701–44), Swedish astronomer; professor at Uppsala; first to describe Celsius, or centigrade, thermometer (about 1742).

Celsius scale (or centigrade scale) H-103
  weights and measures, *table* W-140, *diagram* W-139

Celsus (2nd century AD), Platonist philosopher; in his 'The True Word', or 'The True Account', made first attack on Christianity.

Celtic languages and literature
  English E-261
  language classification L-41, *diagrams* L-40, L-44
  storytelling S-472, *lists* S-481a, S-481b
  Welsh W-6

Celtic ox, ancient forebear of European cattle *Bos longifrons* C-224

'Celtic Twilight, The', work by Yeats I-327

Celts, ancient European peoples C-242
  ancient Rome R-244
  classification, *chart* R-26
  fairy tales S-472
  legends A-655
  monks and monasticism M-540
  United Kingdom
    England E-237
    Northern Ireland I-324
    Scotland S-67

Cement C-243. *see also in index* Gypsum
  concrete C-640
  oil wells P-237
  paints P-72
  production regions
    Egypt E-118
    United States
      Tennessee T-85, *map* T-88
      Texas T-120
  spray-gun application P-399

Cement rock C-245

Cemetery D-50
  national and military N-23

Cemetery Ridge, in Pennsylvania, site of battle of Gettysburg G-137

Cenaculum (also Cenacle), in Jerusalem, alleged site of Last Supper which is believed to have taken place in upper room in home of Mary, mother of John Mark; present building a mosque
'Cendrillon', work by Perrault F-260
Cenobitic monasticism M-540
'Cenotaph', work by MacKennal A-802
Cenote, steep-sided sinkhole in limestone with a pool at the bottom
  Maya M-236
  Yucatán peninsula Y-432
Cenozoic era (or Age of Mammals), geological time
  bird fossils B-275
  British Isles B-460
  earth E-27, *table* E-24
Censor, Roman public official R-244
Censorship C-246
  British theater T-161
  criticism C-778
  East German literature G-115
  motion pictures M-629
  newspapers N-236
  pornography P-451
  radio R-55
  U.S.S.R. R-332f
Census C-247
  China C-364
Census, Bureau of the, United States C-247, U-162
  microfilm M-377
  questionnaire V-369, *pictures* S-430, V-370
Census Value Added, term employed in Canadian economic statistics; obtained by deducting the cost of intermediate materials from the gross value of shipments (not including sales taxes) or from accrued operating revenue; further adjustments are made for changes in the value of finished-products inventories and of goods in work.
Cent, coin P-188
Cental, British unit of weight, *table* W-141
Centaur, fabled monster half human, half horse
  horse H-270
  legendary animals A-456, *picture* A-458
Centaur, a U.S. two-stage liquid-fueled rocket used for launching spacecraft into orbit; consists of a modified Atlas lower stage and a liquid-hydrogen-fueled upper stage
  launch complex, *map* S-342a
'Centaur, The', one of two chief prose poems by Maurice de Guérin; first published 1840 with memoir by George Sand; book famous for its fine printing in Bruce Rogers' edition.
Centaur beetle, insect B-138
Centaurea, genus of plants of the family Compositae; includes bachelor's-button, star thistle, sweet sultan, knapweed, and dusty miller
  tumbleweed T-306
Centaurus, constellation; contains Alpha Centauri, the fixed star nearest Earth, *charts* C-682, S-417
Centavo, copper coin, historical value 1 cent or a fraction, used in South and Central America, Cuba, Mexico, Portugal, Philippines; circulates also in pieces of 5, 10 centavos, etc.
Centenary College of Louisiana (formerly Centenary College), Shreveport, La.; affiliated with United Methodist church; founded 1825; arts and sciences, teacher education; graduate studies.
Centennial (or centenary; Latin *centum*, "a hundred," plus *annus*, "year"), completion of 100 years; associated with 100th anniversary, *e.g.*, centennial celebration.
'Centennial', work by Michener A-361
Centennial Exhibition, international exhibition of manufactures, arts, agricultural and mineral products, held at Fairmount Park, Philadelphia, Pa. (1876), to celebrate the 100th anniversary of U.S. independence
  amusement park rides A-385
Centennial of Canadian Confederation. *see in index* Expo 67
Centennial Park, in Nashville, Tenn. N-20
Centennial state. *see in index* Colorado
Center, in European politics P-434
Center, in mathematics
  geometry G-76
Center base, in heraldry, *diagram* H-136
Centerboard B-328, *diagram* B-230
Center chief, heraldry, *diagram* H-136
Center Line, Mich., industrial city just n. of Detroit and surrounded by city of Warren; metalworking and tool plants; U.S. Army arsenal, settled in 1850s, chartered 1926; pop. 10,379.
Center line, in mechanical drawing M-261, *picture* M-260
Center of gravity. *see in index* Gravity, center of
Centers for Disease Control H-90
Centesimo, 100th part of the Italian lira, of the peso of Uruguay and Panama, basis of minor coins of small value.
Centigrade scale. *see in index* Celsius scale
Centigram, unit employed in the metric system (0.154 grains or .01 gram).
Centiliter, unit in metric system (0.338 fl oz or 10 cc).
Centime, copper coin, historical value 1/100 of a franc, or a small fraction of a cent; used in Belgium, Switzerland, Haiti; 5 centimes smallest French coin.
Centimeter, unit in metric system (0.3937 in or 0.01 m), *table* W-141, *diagram* W-139
Centimeter-gram-second system (cgs system), measurements of motions, forces, and work that use centimeters for distance, grams for mass, and seconds for time; yields measurements of force in dynes and of work in ergs.
Centimo, the 1/100 part of the Costa Rican colon, Venezuelan bolivar, Spanish peseta; a coin worth a fraction of a cent.
Centipede, type of many-legged arthropod C-251
  invertebrates, *pictures* A-433, I-285
Centlivre, Susannah (1667?–1723), English actress and dramatist (comedies: 'The Wonder! A Woman Keeps a Secret', one of David Garrick's successes, and 'A Bold Stroke for a Wife').
CENTO. *see in index* Baghdad Pact
Central African Federation, political union of Nyasaland, Northern Rhodesia, and Southern Rhodesia (1953–63)
  Zambia Z-448
Central African Republic (formerly Ubangi-Shari), directly s. of Chad; area 241,305 sq mi (624,975 sq km); cap. Bangui; pop. 2,305,000 C-252, *maps* A-115, W-297
  African political unit, *table* A-112
  Bangui B-63
  flag, *picture* F-163
  national anthem, *table* N-64
  transportation U-1
Central America, s. part of North America, extending from Mexico to Colombia; 220,000 sq mi (570,000 sq km); pop. over 14,600,000 C-253, *map* W-297. *see also in index* Latin America; names of separate countries
  Alliance for Progress S-292
  Columbus C-594
  international relations I-264
    Latin America L-57
    Reagan administration R-112j
  jungle J-157
  migration of people M-402
    Hispanic Americans H-168
  North America N-334, 339
  Panama Canal P-87
  Peace Corps P-143a
  turkey T-326
Central American Common Market (ODECA) C-256, L-65
Central American Federation, union of former Spanish provinces formed in 1823; dissolved in 1842; membership included Guatemala, El Salvador, Honduras, Nicaragua, and Costa Rica.
Central American tapir, mammal *Tapirus bairdii* T-28
Central Asia. *see in index* Turkestan
Central Australia, administrative division of Australia from 1926 to 1931 at which time it was reunited with North Australia to form once more the Northern Territory; its area was 236,400 sq mi (612,300 sq km).
Central bank, institution that provides services to a nation's private banks C-260
  money M-533
  national debt N-24
Central City, Colo., town 30 mi (50 km) w. of Denver; altitude, 8,560 ft (2,610 m); once a rich mining town; since 1932 noted for its summer opera and theater season, sponsored by University of Denver; pop. 329, *map* C-580
Central Committee, Communist party, U.S.S.R. R-327, R-334c
Central Connecticut State College (formerly called Teachers College of Connecticut), New Britain, Conn.; founded 1849; liberal arts, education; graduate study.
Central Falls, R.I., city on Blackstone River; adjacent to Pawtucket and about 4 mi (6 km) n. of Providence; textiles, machinery, wire, glass products, plastics; pop. 16,995.
Central Florida, University of (called Florida Technological University until 1979), Orlando, Fla.; state control; established 1963; arts and sciences, business, education, engineering, medical technology; graduate studies.
Central Hardwood Forest, forest area in United States F-310
Central Harlem, in New York City. *see in index* Harlem
Central heating system H-107
Central Highlands, in Florida F-194, *map* F-195
Centralia, Ill., city 58 mi (93 km) e. of St. Louis, Mo., oil center, coal mining; railroad shops, candy; established 1853, incorporated as city 1859; pop. 15,126, *map* I-52
Centralia, Wash., city 23 mi (37 km) s. of Olympia in timber region; founded by a former slave in the 1860s; pop. 10,809.
Central India, former collection of princely states in India; was supervised by Resident for Central India (with headquarters at Indore), assisted by political agents; now part of Madhya Pradesh state.
Central Intelligence Agency (CIA), United States I-237, U-156
  espionage E-302
  Ford administration F-304
  Kennedy administration K-202
Centralization, principle of government
  MacDonald M-6
Central Lowland
  Michigan M-355
  Minnesota M-440
  Missouri M-488
  Texas T-116
  Wisconsin W-249
Central Manufacturing District, industrial park in Chicago, Ill C-316
Central Methodist College, Fayette, Mo.; Methodist; established 1853; arts and sciences, education.
Central Michigan University, Mount Pleasant, Mich.; state control; opened 1892; liberal arts, business administration, education, fine and applied arts, health and physical education, and recreation; graduate studies.
Central Missouri State University, Warrensburg, Mo.; founded 1871; liberal arts, education, graduate studies.
Central nervous system. *see in index* Nervous system
Central Pacific Railroad, one of links in first transcontinental line in U.S.; completed in 1869 R-74, *pictures* U-131, U-181
Central Park, in New York City N-273, 279, *picture* N-276
  Dehn's 'Spring in Central Park' P-61, *picture* P-63
  Olmsted O-540
  parks and playgrounds P-125
  skating, *picture* S-207
  starlings S-426
  zoo, *picture* Z-457
Central Parkland, in Alberta A-263
Central Plains, in s. central United States
  Oklahoma O-522
Central Planning Committee, U.S.S.R. R-327
Central Plateau, in Brazil B-413
Central Powers. *see in index* Triple Alliance
Central processing unit (CPU), main portion of computer C-627, *pictures* C-630
  microprocessor M-379
Central Railway of Peru L-210
Central stage. *see in index* Theater-in-the-round
Central State University, Wilberforce, Ohio; founded 1887; present name 1951; arts and sciences, business administration, education, health and physical education, industrial and technical education, military science.
Central State University, Edmond, Okla.; founded 1890, opened 1891; arts and sciences, and teacher education; graduate program.
Central station, electric-power production, *picture* U-52
Central Statistical Board (CSB), U.S. R-265
Central tendency, in statistics S-434
Central time T-189, *map* U-40
Central Treaty Organization (CENTO), group of nations joined in a mutual security agreement in 1959 which had begun originally under the Baghdad Pact. *see also in index* Baghdad Pact
Central University of Iowa, Pella, Iowa; affiliated with Reformed Church in America; founded 1853; liberal arts, education.
Central Valley (or Great Valley, or Great Central Valley), in California C-34, U-86, *map* U-87
Central Valley Project, conservation program C-36, *picture* C-35
Central vent, in volcanic mountain M-634
Central Washington University (formerly Central Washington State College), Ellensburg, Wash.; established 1890; present name since 1977; arts and science, education, and music; graduate study.
Centrarchidae, sunfish family S-518
Centre College of Kentucky, Danville, Ky.; private control; founded 1819; in 1927 Kentucky College for Women merged with Centre; liberal arts, education.
Centre for Continuing Education, in Alberta A-261
Centreville, Ill., city just s. of East Saint Louis; chiefly residential; incorporated 1957; pop. 9,747, *map* I-52
Centrifugal compressor, jet engine component
  jet propulsion J-106
Centrifugal fan F-23
Centrifugal machinery, devices that employ centrifugal force
  glass manufacture G-159
  sugar-making S-506
  washing machine L-87
Centrifuge, centrifugal machine
  fans A-150
  human centrifuge S-346b
  vaccine preparation V-250
Centriole, part of centrosome C-239, *picture* C-237
Centripetal force, in mechanics M-264
Centromere, knot that holds chromosomes C-239
Centrosome, part of cell nucleus C-239, *picture* C-237
Centurion, in Roman army A-637
Century of Progress, world's fair of 1933 and 1934, in Chicago, Ill. A-385
Century plant. *see in index* American aloe
Century 21 Exposition, world's fair of 1962, Seattle, Wash. S-103a
Cephalic index (or cranial index), measurement used in racial classification R-25
Cephalonia. *see in index* Kephallenia
Cephalopod (or head-footed mollusk) M-523, 526

in Civil and Spanish-American wars; commanded expedition that relieved U.S. Legation at Peiping (Peking) in 1900.

Chaffee, Adna Romanza (1884–1941), U.S. Army officer, born in Junction City, Kan.; son of Adna R. Chaffee; strong advocate of mechanized army; major general 1939; chief of Armored Force of U.S. Army 1940.

Chaffee, Roger B. (1935–67), U.S. astronaut candidate, born in Grand Rapids, Mich.; U.S. Navy officer chosen for NASA program 1963; killed in fire during Apollo test
- NASA N-22
- U.S. space program S-347

Chaffinch, European bird of the finch family, sought as a cage bird because of its beauty of voice and its ability in learning to sing tunes
- cross-fostering experiment A-446

Chagall, Marc (1887–1985), Russian-born artist C-265
- 'I and My Village' P-60, *picture* P-58
- mosaic M-590

Chagas' disease (or American trypanosomiasis), parasitic disease prevalent in Central and South America; caused by protozoa which invade tissues, especially heart and brain cells; marked by fever, anemia, and heart disease symptoms; no known cure.

Chagatai, son of Genghis Khan M-534

Chagga, an African people
- Kilimanjaro K-237

Chagos Archipelago, coral atolls in Indian Ocean; only group remaining in British Indian Ocean Territory; area 18 sq mi (47 sq km); consists of 5 islands, largest Diego Garcia; coconut oil, copra; pop. 1,400, *maps* A-697, W-297

Chagres River, flows across Isthmus of Panama into Caribbean Sea P-91, *map* P-90

Chain, Sir Ernst Boris (1906–79), British biochemist, born in Berlin, Germany; university demonstrator and lecturer in chemical pathology Oxford University 1935–50; in Rome, Italy, 1950–61
- Fleming influences F-178

Chain, in chemistry M-521

Chain, unit of measure in surveying S-520, *table* W-140

Chained Rock, in Kentucky, *picture* K-211

Chain gang, system of handling prison labor, convicts working on public roads, bridges, etc., while chained together; practice now in disuse.

Chain mail, type of armor A-630
- clothing C-507
- dress D-262

Chain pickerel, fish P-326

Chain reaction, in nuclear fission N-422
- first achieved, *picture* U-131

Chain saw, tool
- lumber industry L-330

Chain-stitch machine, type of sewing machine S-122

Chain stores C-513, U-110

Chair F-453
- fashion, *picture* F-41
- industrial design I-170, *picture* I-173
- office equipment O-494
- wheelchair, *picture* S-348c

Chakri Dynasty, ruling house of Thailand T-149

Chalcedon, ancient seaport in Asia Minor on Bosporus, opposite Byzantium; Kadiköi now occupies site.

Chalcedon, Council of, ecumenical council A-[illegible]
- Leo I L-130

Chalcedony, variously colored quartz with waxy luster, probably containing opal; found in igneous rocks; commercial production largely in Brazil and s.w. Africa; many varieties used as gems J-112

Chalcidice (or Khalkidike), ancient name of peninsula in n.e. Greece with 3 smaller peninsulas projecting into Aegean Sea.

Chalcis, Greece. *see in index* Khalkis

Chalcocite (or copper glance, or cuprous sulfide), chief ore of copper M-432

Chalcopyrite, mineral M-432

Chaldea, name used in the Bible as an equivalent for Babylonia; derived from Chaldean people who overthrew Assyrian rule and set up the Second Babylonian Empire in the 7th century BC. *see also in index* Babylonia

Chaldean Empire (or New Babylonian Empire, or Second Babylonian Empire) (606–538 BC) B-9
- Mesopotamia M-305

Chaldean rite, Eastern rite tradition E-44

Chalet, Alpine cottage S-542

Chaleur Bay, Canada, inlet of Gulf of St. Lawrence 90 mi (145 km) long, between Quebec and New Brunswick; named (French *chaleur,* heat) by Cartier because of its warmth, *map* Q-10

Chalgrove Field, battle of, Oxfordshire, England, 1643; Royalists under Prince Rupert defeated Puritan army.

Chaliapin, Feodor Ivanovitch (1873–1938), Russian operatic singer, born in Kazan; grew up in poverty, working as shoemaker; porter; was choirboy and member of traveling opera company; possessed superb bass voice and had unusual dramatic power ('Mefistofele'; 'Boris Godunov'; 'Don Quixote'); author of 'Pages from My Life' and 'Man and Mask'
- opera, *list* O-570

Chalice (Latin *calix,* "cup"), drinking cup, usually gold or silver, used in Christian churches in Mass and Communion; in Roman Catholicism interior of cup is gilded; legendary Last Supper chalice called Holy Grail.

Chalice of Antioch, found 1910 near Antioch, Syria; possibly dates from 4th century AD; 7½ in. (19 cm) high; inner cup plain silver, outer cup open-work silver gilded and decorated with carved grapevines, birds, animals, and 12 male figures (two represent Christ, others have been identified as Apostles).

Chalk, soft limestone C-266
- brickmaking B-436
- cement C-243
- drawing D-251
- limestone L-210
- minerals M-435
- seabed formation O-459

Chalk Age. *see in index* Cretaceous period

Challener, Frederick Sproston (1869–1959), Canadian artist, born in England; landscapes and murals ('A Quiet Old Road'; murals in Royal Alexandra Theatre and King Edward Hotel, Toronto).

'Challenger', space shuttle
- NASA N-22
- space travel S-347

Challenger Deep, lowest explored point of the Mariana Trench in the Pacific Ocean O-461

'Challenger' Expedition, famous British expedition for study of deep sea (1872–76); results fill 50 volumes; scientists studied ocean temperatures, currents, and depths; explored contours of basins; made biological studies A-746
- oceanic exploration O-464

Challis (or challie), light soft wool fabric, generally printed; also a cotton fabric of similar texture; name was originally applied to a silk and worsted fabric.

Chalmers, Floyd Sherman (born 1898), Canadian publisher, born in Chicago, Ill.; editor *The Financial Post*, Toronto, 1925–42; vice-president Maclean-Hunter Publishing Company 1942–52, president 1952–64, chairman 1964–69.

Chalmers, Thomas (1780–1847), Scottish preacher and economist, one of chief promoters of Free Church of Scotland.

Châlons, battle of (AD 451), warfare, *list* W-14

Châlons-sur-Marne, France, city 95 mi (155 km) e. of Paris; exports champagne; taken by Germans in 1870, 1914, and 1940; gave name to battle of Châlons (AD 451); pop. 48,558, *map* F-369

Chalon-sur-Saône, France, city 73 mi (117 km) n. of Lyons on Saône River; copper and iron products; medieval cathedral; pop. 47,004, *map* F-369

Cham, a people of Indochina, chiefly in southern Vietnam V-318

Chamaeidae, family of birds, the wren tits; inhabit West coast; olive brown with curved beak and long tail; short, rounded wings.

Chamaeleon, constellation, *chart* C-682

Chamber acid S-510

Chambered nautilus, mollusk
- invertebrate group I-283

Chamberlain, Sir Austen (1863–1937), English statesman, born in Birmingham; son of Joseph Chamberlain C-266

Chamberlain, Clarence, aviator A-205, *picture* A-204

Chamberlain, Houston Stewart (1855–1927), English writer; wrote in German and French; settled in Bayreuth, Germany; married Richard Wagner's youngest daughter (biography of Richard Wagner; 'Foundations of the 19th Century').

Chamberlain, Joseph (1836–1914), British politician and statesman C-266

Chamberlain, Mellen (1821–1900), U.S. historian, born in Pembroke, N.H.; justice of Boston municipal court 1866–78; librarian of public library of Boston 1878–90 ('John Adams, the Statesman of the American Revolution, with Other Essays and Addresses, Historical and Literary').

Chamberlain, Neville (1869–1940), British statesman C-267
- Munich Pact M-653
- United Kingdom E-257
- World War II W-[illegible]

Chamberlain, Owen (born 1920), U.S. physicist, born in San Francisco, Calif.; on faculty University of California, Berkeley 1948–, professor 1958–. *see also in index* Nobel Prizewinners, *table*

Chamberlain, Samuel (1895–1975), U.S. photographer and etcher, born in Cresco, Iowa (collections of his photographs: 'Beyond New England Thresholds', 'Open House in New England', 'Soft Skies of France'; 'Italian Bouquet').

Chamberlain, Wilt (born 1936), U.S. basketball player C-267

Chamberlin, Guy (1894–1967), U.S. football end and coach, born in Blue Springs, Neb.; played for several teams, including Chicago Bears and Chicago Cardinals.

Chamberlin, Thomas Chrowder (1843–1928), U.S. scientist, famous as author of planetesimal theory, born in Mattoon, Ill.; president University of Wisconsin 1887–92; afterward professor of geology, University of Chicago; held state and federal positions as geologist ('The Geology of Wisconsin'; 'The Origin of the Earth'; 'The Two Solar Families')
- planetesimal theory P-355

Chamber music, music specially adapted for playing in private house or small hall, especially compositions in sonata form as for trios, quartets, and quintets C-268

'Chamber Music', poems by Joyce J-144

Chamber of Commerce, association of businessmen and women to promote the best interests of their city; the Chamber of Commerce of the United States, a federation of local groups, maintains a headquarters at Washington, D.C.

Chamber orchestra O-580

Chambers, Ephraim (1680?–1740), English encyclopedist; compiled a 2-vol. encyclopedia 1728 R-124

Chambers, Robert (1802–71), Scottish publisher and writer; joint editor *Chambers' Journal* ('Vestiges of the Natural History of Creation').

Chambers, Robert William (1865–1933), U.S. novelist and illustrator, born in Brooklyn, N.Y. (novels: 'Cardigan'; 'The Red Republic'; 'The Maid-at-Arms'; 'The Sun Hawk').

Chambers, Whittaker (1901–61), U.S. journalist, born in Philadelphia, Pa.; former Communist agent; 'Witness', book on Hiss trial, became a best-seller
- Nixon N-323

Chambers, Sir William (1726–96), English architect of classical practice, born in Stockholm, Sweden; works include grounds and buildings at Kew; architect to King George III; author of 'Treatise on the Decorative Part of Civil Architecture', a standard work.

Chambersburg, Pa., borough 46 mi (74 km) s.w. of Harrisburg, in Cumberland Valley; men's and women's clothing, steam and pneumatic hammers, power transmission apparatus; food processing, baby food, apples; Wilson College; burned by Confederate Army (1864); pop. 16,174, *map* P-184

Chamber sonata, music form C-268

Chambéry, France, historic city 55 mi (90 km) s.e. of Lyons; capital of Savoie; n.w. section modernized after World War II bombing; s.e. section dates from 15th–17th centuries; pop. 49,858, *map* F-369

Chambezi River, in Zambia, Africa; rises in n., flows s.w. forming multiple channels in swamp region emptying into Lake Bangweulu, from there becoming Luapula River.

Chambi, mountain in Tunisia; elevation 5,066 ft (1,544 m) T-308

Chambray, lightweight cotton cloth resembling gingham, usually having dyed warp and white filling; used in solid colors for play and work clothes.

Chambre Syndicale de la Couture Parisienne, French fashion trade association D-268

Chameleon, type of lizard
- lizard's ornamentation L-271
- mimicry M-423
- mythology M-698

Chaminade, Cécile Louise Stéphanie (1861–1944), French pianist and composer, born in Paris; for some time resident of England; composed orchestral music, songs, and ballets, but is best known for piano pieces ('The Flatterer'; 'Scarf Dance').

Chaminade University, Honolulu, Hawaii; Roman Catholic; founded 1955; arts and science, education H-63, H-230

Chamiso (or chamise), small evergreen shrub *Adenostoma fasciculatum* of the rose family with clusters of small white flowers; it covers large areas (chamisal zones) on foothills west of the Sierra Nevada.

Chamisso, Adelbert von (1781–1838), German naturalist and writer, born in Champagne, France; wrote popular lyrics and ballads ('Peter Schlemihl', prose tale).

Chamomile (or camomile), common name of group of herbs forming the genus *Anthemis* of the family Compositae. Garden chamomile *Anthemis nobilis* is cultivated for various medicinal uses; flowers and leaves have a sweet aromatic odor and bitter taste.

Chamonix, beautiful valley about 14 mi (22 km) long, 1–2½ mi (1.5–4 km) wide, and town (pop. 5,907) in s.e. France, at foot of Mont Blanc; winter sports center, mountain climbing
- Switzerland, *map* S-537

Chamorros, a people of Guam G-295

Champa, banana variety B-53

Champagne, former province in n.e. France; great fief in Middle Ages; chief city, Troyes; celebrated for wines
- fairs F-7
- wine W-237

Champagne, sparkling white wine; name from Champagne Province, France, its place of origin W-237

Champaign, Ill., city about 125 mi (200 km) s.w. of Chicago; adjacent to Urbana; agricultural center; metal products; contains part of University of Illinois; Chanute Air Force Base nearby; pop. 58,133, *map* I-52

Champ-de-Mars, park in Paris on Seine River; originally used for military drills P-121, *map* P-120

Champion, Gower (1921–80), U.S. dancer and choreographer, born in Geneva, Ill.; noted for musical comedies D-24

Champion, Richard (1743–91), potter of Bristol, England P-476

Champion's Cup, replaced the World Cup for international field hockey competition H-193

Champion's Hill, battle of, American Civil War; fought May 16, 1863, in Mississippi, e. of Vicksburg; Confederate Army defeated.

Champlain, Samuel de (1567–1635), French explorer C-269
- exploration E-373
  - Canada C-91
    - Montreal M-572
    - New Brunswick N-157
    - Nova Scotia N-403
  - Great Lakes G-249
  - Lake Champlain, *picture* V-291
  - New York N-256
- Henry IV H-132
- journal C-119
- North American colonization A-338
- sunflower S-518

Champlain, Lake, lake between Vermont and New York, discovered by Samuel de Champlain; length 110 mi (175 km); width ¼ to 13 mi (0.4 to 21 km)
- Canada C-91
- Champlain C-269
- New York N-246
- Vermont V-285, *maps* V-286, 301, U-50, *picture* V-293

Champlain Canal, part of New York State Barge Canal N-253, *map* C-126

Champlevé, enamel E-207, *picture* E-208

Champollion, Jean-François (1790–1832), French scholar and Egyptologist C-269
- archaeology A-536
- hieroglyphics H-150, E-131

Champs-Élysées, famous boulevard in Paris, France P-122, *maps* P-120, *picture* F-356

Ch'an. *see in index* Zen

Chance, Frank Leroy (nickname Husk) (1877–1924), U.S. baseball first baseman and manager, born in Fresno, Calif.; player for Chicago, N.L., 1898–1912, and New York, A.L., 1913–14; managed 4 pennant winners for Chicago, 1906–8, 1910; his 1906 team won 116 games, a record number B-93

Chancelade man, human ancestor M-90

Chancellor, Richard (died 1556), English navigator; explored White Sea, went overland to Moscow; trade negotiations with Russia forerunner of Muscovy Company, *table* P-422. *see also in index* Willoughby, Sir Hugh

Chancellor, term meant porter or doorkeeper in Roman times; used for various officers of government in modern times, *e.g.,* British lord high chancellor, the highest judicial officer of the crown; German chancellor, the premier; in U.S. sometimes president of a university.

Chancellor of the exchequer. *see in index* Exchequer, chancellor of the

Chancellorsville, battle of (May 1–4, 1863), American Civil War C-482, *maps* C-475, 483
- Lee L-116
- Stuart S-494

Chance music (or aleatory music) M-676

Chancery cursive (or italic), calligraphy C-59

Chanchan (or Gran Chimu), ruined city, n.w. Peru; was capital of the ancient Yuncas.

Chancre V-272

Chancroid, venereal disease V-273

Chandelier, lighting fixture
- Flemish home (15th century), *picture* P-30
- Marble House, Newport, *picture* R-189

Chandernagore (or Chandernagor), India, settlement on Hooghly River, 20 mi (30 km) n. of Calcutta; 4 sq mi (10 sq km); granted to France 1688; twice taken by British and twice restored to French; held by France 1816–1950; joined India 1950; pop. 75,238, *map* I-83

Chandigarh, India, joint capital of Punjab and Haryana states, about 160 mi (255 km) n. of New Delhi; totally planned by group of famous architects, notably Le Corbusier, of France; begun 1953; greenbelt, 400 ft (120 m) wide, between industries and city; large artificial lake to n.e.; Chandigarh territory created 1966; pop. 218,743, *map* I-83
- Le Corbusier L-114

Chandler, Albert Benjamin (nickname Happy) (born 1898), U.S. public official, born in Corydon, Ky.; governor of Kentucky 1935–39 and 1955–59; U.S. senator 1939–45; commissioner of baseball 1945–51.

Chandler, Edward Barron (1800–80), Canadian statesman; born in Amherst, N.S.; lieutenant governor of New Brunswick 1878–80
- Fathers of Canada Confederation C-115, *picture* C-116

Chandler, Raymond (1888–1959), writer D-119

Chandler, Zachariah (1813–79), U.S. political leader, born in Bedford, N.H.; foe of slavery; helped form Michigan Republican party; U.S. senator 1857–75; secretary of interior 1875–77; reelected to Senate 1879
- Statuary Hall, *table* S-437a

Chandler, Ariz., city 15 mi (25 km) s.e. of Phoenix; winter resort; cotton, grain, sugar beets, citrus fruits, cattle; electronic products, mobile homes; sugar refining; diamond cutting; Williams Air Force Base; pop. 23,889, *map* A-611

Chandni Chowk, commercial center, in Old Delhi, India D-86

'Chandos Anthems', work by Handel H-28

Chanel, Gabrielle (nickname Coco) (1883–1971), French dress designer, born near Issoire, France; made simplicity in women's apparel high fashion; manufactured perfumes, notably Chanel No. 5 D-271

Chaney, Lon (1883–1930), U.S. motion picture character actor C-270
- horror story H-246

Chang'an, capital city of China's T'ang Dynasty C-364

Chang and Eng. *see in index* Bunker, Chang and Eng

Changbai, mountain range on border between North Korea and n.e. China; highest point is Paektu (9,003 ft; 2,744 m) M-93

Changchun (formerly Hsinking), China, capital of Jilin Province; pop. 5,689,000, *maps* A-697, C-383, W-297

Change
- ancient Greek philosophy P-264
- civilization's development C-467

Changed plural (or mutated plural), in language E-260

Changeling, fairy child F-12

Change ringing, method of ringing church bells B-155

Changga (or pyolgok), Korean poetry form K-292

Chang Jiang. *see in index* Yangtze River

Chang Pai Shan. *see in index* Changbai

Changsha, China, capital of Hunan Province, port on Siang Kiang; trade in rice and tea; processing of antimony, lead, silver; metal and porcelain products, cloth, paper, embroidery; pop. 825,000, *maps* A-697, W-297

Chang Tso-lin (1873–1928), Chinese warlord, "magnificent" dictator of Manchuria; defeated by Nationalist forces in 1928; killed when bomb wrecked train in which he was fleeing M-94

Channel, in communications
- information theory I-201
- radio R-50

Channel, in river R-210
- flood control F-184
- Great Lakes G-245

Channel black. *see in index* Carbon black

Channel catfish, fish *Ictalurus punctatus* of the Ictaluridae family C-220

Channel Islands, British possession off coast of France; 75 sq mi (195 sq km); pop. 126,363 C-270, U-16, *maps* E-360, U-18a

Channel-Port aux Basques, Newf., town formed in 1961 by union of towns of Channel and Port aux Basques; in extreme s.w., island of Newfoundland, on Cabot Strait; railway terminal; port; pop. 5,988 N-169, *map* C-109

Channing, Carol (born 1923), U.S. singer, actress, and comedienne; born in Seattle, Wash.; musical comedies ('Gentlemen Prefer Blondes'; 1964 Tony award for 'Hello, Dolly!'); also in movies and television.

Channing, Edward (1856–1931), U.S. historian, born in Dorchester, Mass.; professor at Harvard; life work, history of U.S. from arrival of Norsemen to present; sixth volume won Pulitzer prize 1925.

Channing, William Ellery (1780–1842), U.S. Unitarian preacher, reformer, and writer; born in Newport, R.I.; opposed slavery but deprecated violence of abolitionists
- Hall of Fame, *table* H-16

Chanoyu, Japanese tea ceremony E-318, J-54, *picture* J-49

Chanson, four voices on a secular text C-268

'Chanson de Roland'. *see in index* 'Song of Roland'

Chansons de geste, "songs of great deeds," French chivalric epics written in verse and sung by minstrels; the best known one, 'Song of Roland', celebrating the hero of Charlemagne's army
- French literature F-394
- romance epics R-239
- 'Song of Roland' R-238

Chant, church music, a type of musical declamation, especially of the psalms and canticles; Gregorian chant in unison with free rhythm, Anglican chant harmonized and more metrical.

Chanter, tube used on a bagpipe W-228

Chanterelle, mushroom *Cantharellus cibarius* M-665

Chantilly, France, ancient town 23 mi (37 km) n. of Paris; splendid château; art collection; once noted for Chantilly lace; famous racetrack; pop. 10,156, *map* F-369
- lace L-16
- porcelain, *picture* P-469

Chantilly, Va., village 20 mi (30 km) w. of Washington; site of indecisive battle after 2nd battle of Bull Run (1862); generals Kearny and Stevens killed; also called battle of Ox Hill, *map* V-349

Chantrey, Sir Francis Legatt (1781–1841), English sculptor, born in Derbyshire, England; equestrian statues of duke of Wellington and George IV; also statues of George III and George Washington.

Chanukah. *see in index* Hanukka

Chanute, Octave (1832–1910), U.S. civil engineer and improver of glider design, born in Paris, France
- aviation A-201
- glider G-167
- Wright W-368

Chanute, Kan., city about 95 mi (155 km) s. of Topeka; electronic products, cement, petroleum, factory-built homes; railroad shops; pop. 10,506, *map* K-187

Chao Phraya, (in full Mae Nam Chao Phraya, often called simply Menam, or Mae Nam), chief river of Thailand; flows s. into Gulf of Thailand; 140 mi (225 km) long T-146
- Bangkok B-58

Chaos, in Greek mythology, most ancient of the gods; lord of disorder; with wife Nyx (Night) ruled formless Earth in its beginning; father of Erebus and Nox.

Chapais, Jean-Charles (1811–85), Canadian political leader, born in Rivière-Ouelle, Lower Canada
- Fathers of Canada Confederation C-115, *picture* C-116

Chapais, Sir Joseph Amable Thomas (1858–1946), Canadian historian, born in Quebec Province ('Jean Talon'; 'Le Marquis de Montcalm (1712–1759)'; 'Cours d'Histoire du Canada', 8 vols.).

Chapala, Lake, Mexico, 70 mi (115 km) long and 20 mi (30 km) wide, between states of Jalisco and Michoacan M-324, *picture* M-325, *map* M-341

Chaparral, thicket of dwarf oak, shrubs, etc., found in parts of Texas, New Mexico, Arizona, and Mexico.

Chaparral cock. *see in index* Roadrunner

Chapbook, small, illustrated book or pamphlet, sold by peddlers or "chapmen" to the common people of England in the 16th and later centuries, containing ballads, tracts, and old romances
- children's literature L-246

Chapel Hill, N.C., university town 25 mi (40 km) n.w. of Raleigh; in tobacco-raising and corn-growing area; founded 1792; incorporated 1851; pop. 32,421
- University of North Carolina N-355, *picture* N-363

Chaperon, hat worn in Middle Ages; a type of hood H-53

Chaplain, clergy
- insignia, *pictures* U-10
- U.S. Army A-646

Chaplin, Charlie (in full Sir Charles Spencer Chaplin) (1889–1977), English motion picture comedian and producer C-271
- mime M-422
- motion pictures A-27, M-619

Chapman, Frank Michler (1864–1945), U.S. ornithologist, born in Englewood, N.J.; important contributions to study of bird life ('Handbook of Birds of Eastern North America'; 'Bird Studies with a Camera'; 'The Distribution of Bird-Life in Ecuador').

Chapman, George (1559?–1634), English poet and dramatist; noted chiefly as earliest English translator of Homer and one of best (read Keats' sonnet 'On First Looking into Chapman's Homer').

Chapman, John. *see in index* Appleseed, Johnny

Chapman, Leonard Fielding, Jr. (born 1913), U.S. Marine Corps officer, born in Key West, Fla.; served in Pacific area World War II; assistant commandant 1967; 4-star general, commandant (member Joint Chiefs of Staff) 1968–71; commander Immigration and Naturalization Service 1973–77.

Chapman, Maristan (pseudonym of Mary Chapman) (born 1895 in Chattanooga, Tenn.) and **John Stanton Higham Chapman** (1891–1972) (born in London, England), wife and husband, U.S. coauthors of novels that depict with sympathy and penetration the mountaineers of the U.S. South ('The Happy Mountain'; 'Homeplace'; 'Rogue's March'; 'Tennessee Hazard'); also wrote books for boys and girls.

Chapman, Mark David, John Lennon's assassin A-703

Chapman, Oscar Littleton (1896–1978), U.S. public official, born in Omega, Va.; chief probation officer 1924–27 of Juvenile Court of Denver under Judge Benjamin B. Lindsey; assistant secretary of interior 1933–46; undersecretary of interior 1946–49; secretary of interior 1949–53.

Chapman, Philip Kenyon (born 1935), U.S. research scientist, born in Melbourne, Australia; came to U.S. 1961, naturalized 1967; instrumentation specialist and astronaut candidate 1967–73.

Chapman College, Orange, Calif.; private control; chartered 1861; liberal arts, education; graduate studies.

Chappe, Claude (1763–1805), French engineer and cleric T-57

Chaps, leggings worn by cowboys C-756, *picture* U-99

Charleston, Oscar (1886–1954), U.S. baseball player, born in Indianapolis, Ind.; outfielder Negro leagues 1915–44.

Charleston, Ill., city in e. center, about 48 mi (77 km) s.e. of Decatur; manufacturing and agricultural center; dairy products; Lincoln-Douglas debate, 1858; Eastern Illinois University; pop. 19,355, *map* I-52

Charleston, S.C., 2nd city of state, in s.e.; pop. 69,510 C-280, *map* N-350
 Pulaski defends P-531
 South Carolina S-308, *maps* S-307, U-41, *picture* S-315

Charleston, W. Va., state capital and 2nd city of state; river port on Kanawha and Elk rivers; pop. 63,968 C-281, *map* N-350
 West Virginia W-167, *picture* W-173, *map* U-41

Charleston, dance, *picture* D-23

Charleston, College of, Charleston, S.C.; state control; founded 1770; opened 1790; became first U.S. municipal college 1826; arts and sciences; marine biology laboratories in center at Fort Jackson, 8 mi (13 km) away; Air Force ROTC; graduate studies C-280, S-309

Charleston Confession of 1665, in Baptist faith B-76

Charleston Mountains, in Nevada, *picture* N-141

Charleston Museum, in Charleston, S.C. C-280

Charlestown, Mass., formerly separate city, now part of Boston; navy yard; battle of Bunker Hill; Massachusetts state prison B-376, *map* B-372
 Somerville S-257

Charlestown Navy Yard (until 1974 Boston Naval Shipyard), Boston, Mass.; established 1800; builds and repairs auxiliaries and destroyers, also repairs cruisers B-373

'Charles W. Morgan', wood whaling ship, *picture* C-653

Charlevoix, Pierre François Xavier de (1682–1761), French Jesuit missionary and historian, born in Saint-Quentin, France; explored Great Lakes and Mississippi River (1721).

Charlock, specifically wild mustard *Brassica kaber*, but name sometimes applied to any yellow-flowered weed of mustard family, *picture* W-133

Charlot, Jean (born 1898), U.S. artist, born in Paris, France; lived in Mexico 1921–29, a pioneer of Mexican mural movement; to U.S. 1929, became citizen 1939; well known for murals and color lithographs; illustrated children's books: 'Child's Good Night Book' and 'Two Little Trains' by Margaret Wise Brown; '...and now Miguel' (1954 Newbery Medal) by Joseph Krumgold; author of 'The Mexican Mural Renaissance'
 mural, *picture* A-664
 'Secret of the Andes' R-111
 'The Boy Who Could Do Anything' R-110, S-481c
 'Two Little Trains' R-105

Charlotte, empress of Mexico. *see in index* Carlota

Charlotte (1896–1985), grand duchess of Luxembourg, succeeded to throne 1919 at abdication of her elder sister; abdicated 1964.

Charlotte, N.C., largest city of state; pop. 314,447 C-281, *map* U-41
 North Carolina N-357, 366, *picture* N-363, *map* N-350

Charlotte Amalie (formerly St. Thomas), capital and chief port of Virgin Islands of the U.S., at head of St. Thomas Harbor, island of St. Thomas; pop. 12,220 V-352, *map* W-159

Charlottenburg, district of West Berlin on Spree River; independent city until 1920; site of 17th-century castle of Sophia Charlotte, queen of Frederick I of Prussia, *map* G-133

Charlottenburg Castle, in West Berlin, former royal residence.

Charlottesville, Va., city on Rivanna River, 67 mi (108 km) n.w. of Richmond; in apple-growing area; rayon, nylon textiles, woolen fabrics, pens, pencils, clothing; homes of Thomas Jefferson and James Monroe nearby; pop. 45,010, *maps* U-41, V-348

'Charlotte Temple', work by Rowson A-345

Charlottetown, P.E.I., provincial capital; fine harbor; Prince of Wales College; St. Dunstan's University; pop. 15,282 C-281, P-497, *maps* C-112, N-350

Charm, incantation or object believed to bring good luck.

Charmeuse, soft, lightweight satin of subdued luster; cotton charmeuse is a highly mercerized, light cotton of satin weave; also made of synthetics.

Charnisay, Charles de Menou, Seigneur d'Aulnay (died 1650), French governor of Acadia 1635–50; known for dispute over governorship with Charles de La Tour.

Charnock, Job (died 1693), English traveler; went to India about 1655; founded Calcutta; charnockite, a series of rocks first found in s. India, named for him C-26

Charolais, breed of cattle; named for Charolais, district in France; important in crossbreeding, as in **Charbray,** beef breed developed in s. U.S. by crossing with Brahman cattle C-230, *picture* C-228

Charon, in Greek mythology, ferryman of River Styx.

Charpentier, Gustave (1860–1956), French composer, born in Dieuze, near Nancy, France; studied composition under Massenet; won Prix de Rome 1887; wrote 'Louise', opera, and 'Impressions d'Italie', orchestral suite O-568

Charpentier, Marc-Antoine (1634–1704), French composer, born in Paris O-575

Charque, dried beef S-284

Chart. *see in index* Graph and chart

Chart, in navigation
 aviation A-884
 Maury M-234

Chart, in reading R-103, *picture* R-102

Charter, act of incorporation or a guarantee of privileges given by a sovereign power
 bank B-64, B-73
 Continental Congress C-692

Chartered accountant, one who has met the requirements of a chartered professional group in United Kingdom or the Commonwealth and has been given a certificate; corresponds to certified public accountant in U.S.

Charterhouse, Carthusian monastery in London, United Kingdom after 1611 used as a hospital for old men and a school for boys.

Charteris, Leslie (pen name of Leslie Charles Bowyer Yin) (born 1907), U.S. writer D-119

Charter Oak, historic tree at Hartford, Conn., blown down in 1856; site marked by "Charter Oak" monument H-51, T-282

Charter of Liberties, of Henry I of England H-128

Charter 77, Czech intellectual group opposed to governmental oppression C-816

Charters Towers, Australia, gold-mining town in Queensland, 60 mi (95 km) s.w. of Townsville on n.e. coast; pop. 7,518, *maps* A-819, P-3

Chartier, Alain (fl. early 15th century), French writer, born in Bayeux, France; secretary to Charles VI and Charles VII (poems: 'Le livre des quatre dames' and 'La belle dame sans merci'; political prose: 'Le quadrilogue invectif').

Chartism, radical movement in England, culminating between 1840 and 1848; sought reform in parliamentary representation and universal adult male suffrage E-253

Chartres, France, manufacturing city 49 mi (79 km) s.w. of Paris; occupied by Germans 1870 and 1940; pop. 34,128, *map* F-369
 cathedral sculpture S-85, *picture* S-84

Chartreuse, a liqueur L-235

Chartreuse, La Grande, original mother house of Carthusian monks, *picture* M-540

Charybdis, in Greek mythology, whirlpool in Straits of Messina H-223

Charyk, Joseph Vincent (born 1920), U.S. missile scientist, born in Canmore, Alta.; to U.S. 1942, citizen 1948; assistant Air Force secretary 1959, undersecretary 1960–63; president Communications Satellite Corporation 1963–.

Chase, Harry Woodburn (1883–1955), U.S. educator, born in Groveland, Mass.; professor of psychology and later president University of North Carolina; president University of Illinois 1930–33; chancellor New York University 1933–51.

Chase, Mary Ellen (1887–1973), U.S. author, born in Blue Hill, Me.; professor of English literature Smith College 1929–55 (novels: 'Mary Peters', 'Windswept', 'The Plum Tree', 'The Edge of Darkness', 'The Lovely Ambition', 'The Nunnery', 'A Journey to Boston'; Bible studies: 'The Bible and the Common Reader', 'Life and Language in the Old Testament', 'The Prophets for the Common Reader'; for younger readers: 'The Fishing Fleets of New England'; autobiographies: 'A Goodly Heritage', 'A Goodly Fellowship', 'The White Gate').

Chase, Richard (born 1904), U.S. folklorist and authority on English-American dances, born in Huntsville, Ala.; made home in Charlottesville, Va.; 'Grandfather Tales'; 'Hullabaloo and Other Singing Folk Games'; 'Wicked John and the Devil'
 'Jack Tales' R-111, S-481c

Chase, Salmon Portland (1808–73), U.S. statesman, born in Cornish, N.H.; leading Free-Soiler, early known as "attorney general of fugitive slaves"; secretary of treasury (under Lincoln); as chief justice of the U.S. (1864–73) presided at impeachment trial of President Johnson.

Chase, Samuel (1741–1811), U.S. jurist, born in Somerset County, Md.; signer of Declaration of Independence; associate justice U.S. Supreme Court; impeached for partisanship but not convicted; case important in history of U.S. judiciary S-518a

Chase, Stuart (born 1888), U.S. economist and writer, born in Somersworth, N.H.; on staff of Federal Trade Commission 1917–22; with Labor Bureau, Inc. 1922–39, TVA 1940–41 ('The Economy of Abundance'; 'Rich Land, Poor Land'; 'Tomorrow's Trade'; 'Money to Grow On'; 'The Most Probable World').

Chase, William Merritt (1849–1916), U.S. landscape, portrait, still life, genre painter, born in Williamsburg, Franklin County, Ind. ('Alice'; 'Flying Clouds'; portrait of James Abbott McNeill Whistler); successful teacher.

Chase, in printing. *see in index* Form

Chase, film genre M-618

Chase Hospital doll, watertight doll designed in 1910 by Martha Chase; used in hospitals to help train student nurses in handling babies D-215

Chasing, type of embossing process E-198, *picture* S-203

Chasins, Abram (1903–87), U.S. pianist and composer, born in New York, N.Y.; taught at Curtis Institute 1926–35; musical director of *The New York Times* radio station 1946–65; musician-in-residence University of Southern California 1972–77 ('Concerto in F Minor'; 'Parade'; 'Three Chinese Pieces').

'Chasse, La' (or 'The Hunt', or 'Symphony No. 73'), work by Haydn O-576

Chassis, in automobile A-853

Château, French term for castle, or manor house, or vineyard estate
 Grand and Petit Trianons V-303
 Mansart M-109, *picture* M-110
 wine W-237

Chateaubriand, François René, vicomte de (1768–1848), French author and statesman, born in Saint-Malo, France; ambassador to London, Berlin, Rome and foreign minister; opposed excesses of French Revolution; exquisite prose stylist
 French literature F-396

Château Chenonceaux, castle in Loire Valley, France, *picture* F-342

Château Clique, political clique in Canada C-97
 Papineau P-107

Château de Chambord, castle, France, *picture* F-351

Château de la Caze, castle, Tarn River Valley, France, *picture* F-351

Château d'If, fortress on islet of If near Marseilles, France, made famous by Dumas's 'The Count of Monte Cristo'.

Châteaudun, France, town on Loire River 70 mi (115 km) s.w. of Paris; old castle of counts of Dunois; burned by Germans in Franco-Prussian War 1870; pop. 13,715, *map* F-369

Château Gaillard, famous castle in Normandy, 50 mi (80 km) n.w. of Paris on Seine, now in ruins R-202

Château Laurier, hotel in Ottawa, Ont. O-612, *picture* O-613

Château-Thierry, France, town 47 mi (76 km) n.e. of Paris; pop. 10,858, *map* F-369
 World War I W-311, 314

Chatelaine, mistress of a castle M-387

Châtelet, Gabrielle-Émilie (1706–49), French scientist C-281

Chatelier, Henry Louis Le. *see in index* Le Chatelier, Henry Louis

Chatham, William Pitt, first **earl of** (1708–78), British statesman
 Great Britain E-248
 North American colonial policy R-167
 Seven Years' War S-117

Chatham, N.B., port town on Miramichi River 35 mi (55 km) n. of Gulf of St. Lawrence; lumber, fish; pop. 6,799, *map* C-109

Chatham, Ont., city on Thames River 43 mi (69 km) e. of Detroit, Mich.; motor trucks, containers, canned and frozen foods, beet sugar, flour, tobacco, fertilizers, textiles; pop. 40,952, *map* C-112

Chatham (or San Cristóbal), island, Galápagos Islands, Ecuador G-3

Chatham, England, seaport 25 mi (40 km) s.e. of London on Medway River, adjoining Rochester; naval dockyard; pop. 55,460.

Chatham College (chartered 1869 as Pennsylvania Female College), Pittsburgh, Pa.; present name 1955; private control; for women; liberal arts, education, *map* P-345b

Chatham Islands, group of islands 536 mi (863 km) e. of New Zealand to which they belong; 372 sq mi (963 sq km); sheep grazing; pop. 730, *maps* N-299, P-3, W-297

Châtillon-sur-Seine, France, town 125 mi (200 km) s.e. of Paris on Seine River; unsuccessful congress of Napoleon with Allies (1814); pop. 6,128.

Chatrian, Louis Gratien Charles Alexandre. *see in index* Erckmann-Chatrian

Chattahoochee River, 436 mi (702 km) long, rises in Blue Ridge Mountains of n.e. Georgia, flows s.w. to West Point, Ga., and then s., forming Georgia-Alabama and Georgia-Florida boundaries; at Chattahoochee, Fla., joins Flint River to form the Apalachicola; navigable from Columbus, Ga., to mouth; inspired Sidney Lanier's poem, 'The Song of the Chattahoochee', *map* U-58
 Columbus, Ga. C-594

Chattanooga, Tenn., railroad and industrial city in s.e. on Tennessee River; pop. 169,558 C-282, *maps* N-350, U-41
 Tennessee T-81, *map* T-97, *picture* T-85

Chattanooga, battle of (Nov. 24–25, 1863), in U.S. history
 Civil War C-483, *map* C-474

Grant G-217
Tennessee T-88

Chattel, in law, *table* L-92

Chatterjee, Bankim Chandra (1838–94), Bengali author C-282
Indian literature I-108

Chatterton, Thomas (1752–70), English poet and literary forger, precocious genius; wrote 'Rowley Poems', which he claimed were old manuscripts of 15th century; starving in a London garret, poisoned himself.

'Chatterton', work by Vigny V-325

Chaucer, Geoffrey (1340?–1400), English poet C-283
'Chanticleer and the Fox' R-107
Kelmscott Press edition, *picture* B-351
literary contribution E-265
poet laureate forerunner P-402
shield, *picture* H-136

Chaucer family
heraldic shield, *picture* H-136

Chauliac, Guy de (died 1380?), French surgeon; doctor to three popes at Avignon; his 'Great Surgery' was manual for physicians for three centuries.

Chaulmoogra oil, volatile oil obtained from the seeds of the chaulmoogra tree of the East Indies; formerly used in the treatment of leprosy.

Chaumonot, Pierre Joseph (1611–93), Jesuit missionary, born in France; labored among Hurons in Canada for 40 years (1639–79), with brief period among Iroquois in upper New York (1655–58).

Chaumont, France, manufacturing town 138 mi (222 km) s.e. of Paris; treaty of Allies against Napoleon 1814; general headquarters A.E.F. in World War I; pop. 25,602, *map* F-360

Chausson, Ernest (1855–99), U.S. composer, born in Paris, France; pupil of Massenet and César Franck ('Le Roi Arthur' and 'Hélène', operas; 'Poème', for violin and orchestra).

Chautauqua, N.Y., village on Lake Chautauqua, about 58 mi (93 km) s.w. of Buffalo; in fruitgrowing region; Chautauqua Institution; pop. 500.

Chautauqua Institution, established 1874 at Chautauqua, N.Y., to provide summer classes for Sunday-school teachers; later opened to public; program combines education with religious services, outdoor recreation, and entertainment; its success inspired nationwide Chautauqua movement which declined in 1920s A-51

Chautauqua Lake, in w. New York, 8 mi (13 km) from Lake Erie; 18 mi (29 km) long N-246

Chautauqua muskellunge P-326

Chautemps, Camille (1885–1963), French statesman, radical socialist leader, born in Paris, France; premier 1930, 1933–34, 1937–38; in U.S. after 1940.

Chauveau, Pierre Joseph Olivier (1820–90), Canadian statesman and lawyer, born in Quebec; prime minister of Quebec 1867–73; author of poems, novels, and essays.

Chauvin, Pierre (died 1602), French explorer and entrepreneur; obtained from King Henry IV a 10 years' monopoly of the fur trade in New France; established a short-lived settlement at Tadoussac, on the St. Lawrence River C-81

Chauvinism, exaggerated patriotism or "jingoism"; derived from name of a French soldier, Nicolas Chauvin, who was passionately devoted to Napoleon; also undue loyalty to specific group as "male chauvinist," phrase popularized by women's movement supporters.

Chaux-de-Fonds, La, Switzerland, town 30 mi (50 km) n.w. of Bern in Jura Valley; watches and clocks; pop. 41,200, *map* S-537

Chavannes, Puvis de, French painter, *see in index* Puvis de Chavannes

Chávez, Carlos (1899–1978), Mexican composer and conductor, first in his country to attain wide recognition; founder and director Symphony Orchestra of Mexico 1928–52; director National Conservatory of Music; a modernist, he expressed vital national spirit ('H.P.'; 'Sinfonia India'); author, 'Musical Thought'
classical music M-675

Chavez, César Estrada (born 1927), U.S. labor leader, born in Yuma, Ariz., organized migratory farm workers; in 1962 helped organize farm workers union, which merged with AFL-CIO group 1966 to form United Farm Workers Organizing Committee; president UFW since 1966
labor movements L-10
Mexican Americans H-165, *picture* H-164

Chavez, Dennis (1888–1962), U.S. political leader, born in Los Chavez, N.M.; Democratic representative from New Mexico 1931–35; U.S. senator 1935–62; won national prominence as vigorous supporter of fair employment practices
Statuary Hall, *table* S-437b

Chayefsky, Paddy (born Sidney Chayefsky) (1923–81), playwright, born in New York, N.Y., began career as writer of television drama 1952; work adapted for stage and screen ('Marty'; 'The Catered Affair'; 'The Hospital'; 1977 Oscar for 'Network').

Chayote (also called vegetable pear), vine belonging to the gourd and melon family; also its edible pear-shaped fruits, white or green in color, somewhat resembling the cucumber and the summer squash in flavor; introduced into U.S. from Mexico, Central America, and West Indies.

Cheaha Mountain, highest point in Alabama (2,407 ft; 734 m).

'Cheap Thrills', album recorded by Joplin J-140

Check (or cheque), in banking B-65, *picture* B-68
central bank C-260
money M-532

Check, in chess C-306

Checkerberry. *see in index* Spicy wintergreen

Checkerbloom. *see in index* Sidalcea

Checkers, Nixon family dog made famous in Nixon's nationally televised speech in defense of the sources of his senate campaign fund N-324

Checkers (or draughts), game
African version, *picture* P-193
board games B-321

Checkmate, in chess C-306

Cheddar, England, village in Somersetshire; located in Mendip Hills; numerous caverns, limestone cliffs; gives name to Cheddar cheese originally made here in 17th century.

Cheddar cheese C-288

Cheek, in anatomy M-641

Cheektowaga, N.Y., situated just e. of Buffalo; motors, aircraft parts, optical equipment; pop. of township 113,844.

Cheese C-287
bacteria B-14
bread and baking use B-429
food and nutrition F-278
goat G-171
milk M-415
mold M-519
processing D-7
Swiss S-539
Wisconsin, *picture* W-259

Cheesecloth, thin, loosely woven cotton material, originally used for wrapping cheese; lighter grades, known as gauze, used for bandages and surgical dressings.

Cheetah (or hunting leopard), wild cat *Acinonyx jubatus*, *pictures* A-455, C-215
fur, *table* F-464
leopard L-135
speed C-213

Cheever, John (1912–82), U.S. writer, born in Quincy, Mass.; 'The Wapshot Chronicle' won 1958 National Book Award; 'The Wapshot Scandal', 'Bullet Park'; short stories; 'The Way Some People Live', 'The Brigadier and the Golf Widow'
American literature A-360, 362
creative writing W-377

Cheffetz, Asa (1896–1965), U.S. wood engraver, born in Buffalo, N.Y.

Chefoo, China, port on n. coast of Shandong Province; fishing and silk center; pop. 180,000, *map* A-697

Cheiranthus, plant genus. *see in index* Wallflower

Cheju (or Quelpart), island of South Korea in East China Sea 60 mi (96 km) s. of mainland; 692 sq mi (1,792 sq km); has inactive volcano, Halla (6,398 ft; 1,950 m), highest point in South Korea; fisheries; cattle and grain; bamboo hats; chief city Cheju (pop. 106,456); pop. 365,522, *maps* A-697, K-290

Cheka, Soviet secret police R-355
intelligence agencies I-236

Chekhov, Anton (1860–1904), Russian dramatist and short-story writer C-290
creative writing W-380
drama D-246
Russian literature R-360a, *picture* R-360

Chekiang. *see in index* Zhejiang

Chelicera, clawlike fang of spider S-382, *picture* S-386

Cheliped, foot or appendage of crustaceans (as the lobster) furnished with claws, or chelae.

Chellean. *see in index* Abbevillian

Chelmsford, Frederick John Napier Thesiger, Viscount (1868–1933), British statesman; governor of Queensland, Australia, 1905–9; governor of New South Wales 1909–13; viceroy of India 1916–21; first lord of admiralty 1924.

Chelmsford, Mass, 5 mi (8 km) s.w. of Lowell; beverages, textiles; incorporated 1655; pop. of township 31,174.

Chelone (or turtlehead), genus of perennial plants of the figwort family, related to pentstemon (beardtongue); name from Greek for tortoise due to fancied resemblance of flowers to that reptile; flower spikes white or purple.

Chelonia, order of reptiles
turtle T-330

Chelsea, borough of London, United Kingdom L-293
potteries P-476, *pictures* P-469

Chelsea, Mass., city just n.e. of Boston; rubber and metal products, shoes, lithographing, fluorescent lamps, chemicals; naval hospital; pop. 25,431.

Chelsea, neighborhood in Manhattan, New York, N.Y. N-272

Cheltenham, England, resort town 90 mi (145 km) n.w. of London on Chelt River; medicinal springs; educational center; pop. 76,000, *map* U-18a

Cheltenham, Pa., urban township just n. of Philadelphia; includes 6 unincorporated communities; settled 1690, incorporated 1900; pop. 35,509, *map* P-185

Chelyabinsk, U.S.S.R., city in w. Siberia in e. foothills of s. Ural Mts. and on Trans-Siberian Railway; tractors, metal processing, cement, chemicals; pop. 874,000, *maps* A-697, R-322, 344, W-297

Chelyuskin, Cape, n. Siberia, U.S.S.R., *maps* A-697, R-345, W-297

Chemehuevi, Shoshonean tribe of American Indians living on Colorado River, Arizona; fragment of Paiutes; Uto-Aztecan language group; now nearly extinct.

Chemical analysis C-290
handwriting H-30
medicine M-278

Chemical and biological warfare C-292
Hahn H-6
warfare W-26
World War I W-305, 312

Chemical bond, sharing of electrons between atoms in a molecule
energy E-215
molecule M-521
organic chemistry O-602
valence V-255

Chemical change. *see in index* Reaction

Chemical compound
chemistry C-297
inorganic chemistry I-208
matter M-224
molecule M-522

Chemical Corps, U.S. Army A-646
insignia, *picture* U-10

Chemical differentiation, process of cell multiplication
embryology E-202

Chemical elements C-293
noble gases N-330

Chemical energy E-214
heat H-102

Chemical engineering
chemistry C-300
engineering E-222

Chemical mace. *see in index* Mace, chemical

Chemical machining (CHM), metalworking operation T-226

Chemical oceanography O-479

Chemical printing (or stone printing) L-258

Chemical retardant, in fireproofing F-113

Chemicals
East German economy G-119
transportation T-251
West German economy G-117

Chemical weathering, on earth E-31

Chemin des Dames ("Ladies' Road"), French road along ridge between Aisne and Ailette rivers; objective of "battles of Aisne," World War I.

Chemise, dress D-265

Chemistry C-296. *see also in index* chief topics listed below, *also* elements and important compounds
antiseptic A-495
battery and fuel cell B-107
cellulose R-97
elements, *tables* P-207, P-312
noble gases N-330
evolution E-365
history S-51i
alchemy A-273
atomic weights N-416
combustion and oxidation S-57i
Lavoisier L-90
Mendeleev M-297, S-58
radioactivity R-63
kinds
biochemistry B-198
chemurgy P-379
electrochemistry E-170
inorganic chemistry I-208
organic chemistry O-601
color C-561
dyes D-296
petrochemistry P-228
matter M-224
metabolism M-306
molecule M-521
Nobel prizes N-330
periodic table P-206, *tables* P-207, 208
physics P-301
proteins P-514
salts S-29
sciences S-64
soil S-250
solutions S-255
spectrum analysis S-37
synthetic fibers F-71
valence V-255
vocational opportunities V-367, *picture* V-368
wood pulping processes P-101
X-ray spectra S-374

Chemnitz, East Germany. *see in index* Karl-Marx-Stadt

Chemosynthetic bacteria, deep-sea organisms D-60
earth E-7

Chemotherapeutic agent, drug that destroys or slows the growth of disease-causing organisms D-274

Chemotherapy
cancer treatment C-135
medicine M-278
therapy T-165

Chemotropism
insects I-222
plants P-363

Chemulpo, South Korea. *see in index* Inchon

Chemurgy, branch of chemistry for developing new uses for farm products P-379
Carver C-193

Chenab (ancient Acesines), river of Kashmir and Punjab; 590 mi (950 km) long; flows s.w. into Sutlej River
India, *map* I-86

Chen Cheng (1897–1965), Chinese general and statesman, born in Chekiang; chief of staff 1946; governor of Taiwan 1948; premier of Taiwan 1950–54 and 1958–63, vice-president 1954–65.

Cheng. *see in index* Shih Huang Ti

Cheng Ch'eng-kung. *see in index* Koxinga
Chengchow. *see in index* Zengzhou
Chengde (formerly Jehol), China, city in Hebei Province 110 mi (175 km) n.e. of Peking; former summer residence of Manchu emperors; pop. 200,000.
Chengdu, China, capital of Szechwan Province, port on Min Kiang; educational and commercial center; pop. 3,950,000, *map* A-697
Cheng Ho (1371–1435), Chinese explorer and diplomat C-368
'Adventure to the Western Ocean' C-390
Chénier, André Marie de (1762–94), French poet, one of greatest of 18th century; born in Constantinople (now Istanbul), Turkey; guillotined during the Reign of Terror for opposing excesses of the Convention.
Chenille, soft, tufted or fluffy yarn of cotton, wool, silk, or worsted, made by weaving four warp threads or crossing three warp threads about soft filling threads that are afterwards cut; also cloth made with chenille yarn for filling; name from French for "caterpillar"
carpets R-313
Chennault, Claire Lee (1890–1958), U.S. aviator, born in Commerce, Tex.; became U.S. Army flier 1917, retired 1937 and went to China to plan aerial defense; commanded American Volunteer Group (Flying Tigers) 1941; chief of U.S. Air Force in China 1942–45; author of 'Way of a Fighter'
China C-356
World War II W-328, 337
Chen Ning-yang. *see in index* Yang, Chen Ning
Chenopodiaceae. *see in index* Goosefoot family
Cheops. *see in index* Khufu
Chephren. *see in index* Khafre
Cheque. *see in index* Check
Cher Ami, name of an U.S. homing pigeon in World War I P-324
Cherbourg, France, port situated on English Channel; immense breakwater; landing place for largest liners; naval station; shipbuilding, fishing; pop. 37,933, *maps* E-360, F-369
Cherenkov, Pavel A. (born 1904), Soviet physicist; discovered and interpreted the Cherenkov effect
speed of light, *picture* L-200
Chéret, Jules (1836–1932), French poster artist G-234
Cheribon, Indonesia. *see in index* Tjirebon
Cherimoya (or cherimoyer). *see in index* Custard apple
Chernenko, Konstantin (1911–85), Soviet leader C-303
Soviet Union R-358
Chernobyl, U.S.S.R., about 80 mi (128 km) northwest of Kiev; site of nuclear accident 1986 U-2
world W-301
Chernovtsy (German Czernowitz, Romanian Cernăuţi), U.S.S.R., industrial city on Prut River in s.w. Ukrainian Soviet Socialist Republic; formerly capital of Bucovina in n. Romania; ceded by Romania to Soviet Union, 1940; pop. 187,000, *maps* E-360, R-344
Chernozem, black soil G-237, S-253, *map* S-252, *picture* S-251
Argentina A-577
China C-341
U.S.S.R. R-324
Cherokee, American Indians of Iroquoian descent; originally lived in mountain region of Virginia, the Carolinas, Georgia, Alabama, and Tennessee I-149, *map* I-136, *table* I-138
Georgia G-90
Great Smoky Mountains G-251
North Carolina N-356, *picture* N-365
Oklahoma O-523
Tennessee T-84
Cherokee, Okla., city in agricultural region, 40 mi (65 km) n.w. of Enid; salt plains, now a federal wildlife refuge, nearby; pop. 2,105.
Cherokee rose R-296
Georgia's state flower, *pictures* G-92, S-427
Cherrapunji, India, village of Assam, in Khasi Hills; heavy rainfall, usually more than 400 in (10,200 mm) a year, sometimes 900 in (22,900 mm) R-89, *map* I-83
Himalayas H-153
Cher River, central France, tributary to Loire; 200 mi (320 km) long, *map* F-372
Cherry, Don (born 1936), U.S. jazz musician, born in Oklahoma City, Okla. J-188
Cherry, fruit belonging to the genus *Prunus* of the rose family C-303
fruit tree F-430, F-437
Michigan M-359, *picture* M-358
seed distribution S-107
Cherry birch. *see in index* Sweet birch
Cherry Hill (until 1961, Delaware), N.J., urban township e. of Camden; light industry, principally electronics; Garden State Race Track; first settled 1687; pop. 68,785.
Cherry laurel, ornamental evergreen shrub *Prunus laurocerasus* of the rose family; cherry-laurel water, of a flavor similar to bitter almonds, although poisonous, is used in medicine and flavoring.
Cherry Point, N.C., Marine Corps Air Station on Neuse River 35 mi (55 km) inland from Pamlico Sound; pop. 12,029.
Cherry Valley, N.Y., village 52 mi (84 km) w. of Albany; in farming and dairying area; massacre during Revolutionary War (Nov. 1778) by American Indians under Joseph Brant aided by Tories and English; pop. 684.
Chersonesus, Greek word for peninsula, applied especially to Thracian Chersonesus (modern Gallipoli), Tauric Chersonesus (Crimea), and Cimbrian Chersonesus (Jutland).
Cherub (also cherubim), Hebrew name for a winged creature attendant upon the deity; variously represented, in the vision of Ezekiel with four wings and four faces, those of a human, a lion, an ox, an eagle; the winged bulls of Babylonia are also called cherubim; in later Jewish and Christian literature the cherubim is an order of angels, next below the seraphim; often represented by painters as winged infants
angelic hierarchy A-414
Cherubini, Maria Luigi (1760–1842), Italian composer and author; "link between classic idealism and modern romanticism"; wrote operas, symphonies, requiems, marches, sonatas; his work on counterpoint still used
classical music M-672
opera O-565
Chervil, common name for two species of plants of the parsley family; salad chervil *Anthriscus cerefolium* has curled leaves used like parsley; turnip-rooted chervil *Chaerophyllum bulbosum* has root used like carrot
herbs H-137, S-379
Chesapeake, Va., city s. of Portsmouth and Norfolk; industrial, residential, and farming area; part of Dismal Swamp in w. and s.; Chesapeake formed 1963 by merger of Norfolk County and the city South Norfolk; pop. 114,486, *map* V-349
'Chesapeake', U.S. frigate in War of 1812 W-29
Adams A-36
Lawrence L-98
'Chesapeake', book by Michener A-361
Chesapeake and Delaware Canal, *map* C-126
Baltimore B-49
Chesapeake Bay C-304
Delaware D-73
Maryland M-169, *map* M-183, *picture* M-166
Chesapeake and Ohio Canal C-128, *map* C-126
Maryland M-169 *map*, M-183, *picture* M-176
Washington, D.C. W-67, 71
Chesapeake Bay, inlet on e. coast of United States C-304
Maryland M-166, 169, *maps* M-183, N-350, *pictures* M-176, 177
Chesapeake Bay Bridge, in Maryland C-304, M-170
Chesapeake Bay Bridge-Tunnel, in Virginia C-304
Chesapeake Bay retriever, dog, *picture* D-197
Chesapeake clipper (or Baltimore clipper), ship design, *picture* S-165
Chesbro, John Dwight (nickname Happy Jack) (1874–1931), U.S. baseball pitcher, born in North Adams, Mass.; with Pittsburgh, N.L., 1899–1902, and New York A.L., 1903; won 41 games in 1904.
Cheselden, William (1688–1752), prominent British surgeon and anatomist M-283
Cheshire, Conn., 8 mi (13 km) s.e. of Waterbury; machine tool accessories; incorporated 1780; pop. of township 21,788.
Cheshire, n.w. county of England bordering on n. Wales and Irish Sea; 1,015 sq mi (2,629 sq km); salt mining, dairying; county seat Chester; pop. 1,368,979.
Cheshire cat, grinning cat in 'Alice's Adventures in Wonderland'; when leaving Alice's view it disappeared so gradually that the grin was the last part to vanish; suggested to the author, Lewis Carroll, by the saying "to grin like a Cheshire cat," a saying of unknown origin C-202
Chesima, special form of China tea plant T-46
Chesnut, Mary Boykin (1823–86), aide to Jefferson Davis during Civil War; wrote daily journal valuable for its vivid description of problems caused by the war in the South ('Diary from Dixie') C-478
Chesnutt, Charles Waddell (1858–1932), U.S. writer, born in Cleveland, Ohio; first black American novelist ('The Conjure Woman', novel; 'Frederick Douglass', biography); won 1928 Spingarn medal B-293
Chess, game C-304
outdoor, *picture* P-125
Chest, anatomy. *see in index* Thorax
Chest, furniture
pirate, *picture* P-342
Chest compression (or external heart massage) F-117
Chester, George Randolph (1869–1924), U.S. author, born in Ohio; writer of stories that appeared in *Saturday Evening Post* ('Get-Rich-Quick Wallingford').
Chester, England, picturesque old city 16 mi (26 km) s.e. of Liverpool on Dee River; railroad center; cathedral; pop. 60,880, *map* U-18a
Chester, Pa., port city on Delaware River 14 mi (22 km) s.w. of Philadelphia; railroad shops; oil refineries; shipbuilding; steel, paper, helicopters; important shipbuilding center during World Wars I and II; Widener College; settled by Swedes 1643; pop. 45,794, *map* P-185
Chesterfield, Philip Dormer Stanhope, 4th **earl of** (1694–1773), English statesman, author, and patron of literature; ambassador to Holland, lord lieutenant of Ireland, secretary of state; name used as a synonym for courteous person
letters E-320, *picture* E-322
Chesterfield, England, town in Derbyshire; 22 mi (35 km) n.e. of Derby; iron and other metal products; George Stephenson buried in Trinity Church; pop. 70,420, *map* U-18a
Chesterton, G.K. (name in full Gilbert Keith Chesterton) (1874–1936), English novelist C-307
Belloc B-157
detective story D-119
Chester White, breed of pig P-320
Chestnut, tree in the family Fagaceae C-307, *picture* T-278. *see also in index* Horse chestnut
Chestnut blight, fungal disease C-307
Chestnut cowrie, Pacific Ocean mollusk *Zonaria spadicea*, *picture* S-151
Chestnut Hill College, Philadelphia, Pa.; Roman Catholic; for women; founded 1871; arts and sciences, music, and teacher education.
Chestnut oak (or yellow oak, or chinquapin oak), tree *Quercus muehlenbergii* or *Quercus acuminala* O-452
wood, *table* W-283
Chest of viols, group of instruments S-491
Chetumal, Mexico, capital of Quintana Roo state; chicle, lumber, plywood exports; pop. 56,709
Yucatán peninsula Y-433
Chetvert, Soviet unit of capacity, *table* W-141
Chevalier, Maurice Auguste (1888–1972), French actor and singer, born in Paris; bow tie, straw hat, jaunty style; starred in American-made motion pictures and on television; won special Oscar 1959 for contribution to entertainment; one-man show on Broadway 1963; author of 'I Remember It Well'.
Chevalier, Nicholas, Australian painter A-801
Cheviot, breed of sheep; also a rough-surfaced wool fabric similar to serge but heavier, so called because originally made of wool from Cheviot sheep; name now also given to a coarse cotton fabric S-147
Cheviot, Ohio, residential city 7 mi (11 km) n.w. of Cincinnati; incorporated as village 1901, as city 1932; pop. 11,135.
Cheviot Hills, range 35 mi (55 km) long, forming part of English-Scottish boundary; highest peak 2,658 ft (810 m); famous for sheep, *map* S-67
Chevreul, Michel Eugène (1786–1889), French chemist, born in Angers; noted for study of fats; director of natural history museum, Jardin des Plantes, 1864–79
soapmaking research S-229
Chevrolet, Louis (1879?–1941), U.S. motorcar designer, born in Switzerland; to U.S. about 1900; in first auto race, 1905, outdrove Barney Oldfield to set speed record of 68 mph A-856, 859
Chevron, in heraldry H-136
Chevrons, V-shaped devices, usually indicating rank, worn on sleeves by noncommissioned military officers U-6, *pictures* U-9
'Chevy Chase', English ballad celebrating battle of Otterburn (1388) when Scots led by James Douglas defeated English forces of Sir Henry Percy.
Chewa, people of central Malawi M-69
Chewing, digestive process H-84
Chewing gum, sweetened and flavored insoluble material C-307
Chewing tobacco T-200
Cheyenne, Algonquian group of Plains Indians originally living along Cheyenne River, *maps* I-136, 149, *table* I-138
tepees, *picture* S-154
Wyoming W-387
Cheyenne, Wyo., state capital and second largest city, in s.e. of state; pop. 47,283 C-308, *maps* N-350, U-40
Wyoming W-388, 396, *pictures* W-393
Cheyenne, television Western W-153
Cheyenne Mountain, in Colorado, just s.w. of Colorado Springs; height 9,565 ft (2,915 m); computerized Combat Operations Center of NORAD (completed 1966, expanded 1972); Will Rogers Shrine of the Sun, 100-ft (30-m) memorial tower of pink granite; has zoo on lower slopes.
Cheyenne River, about 525 mi (845 km) long, rises in Converse County, e. Wyoming, and flows generally e. into South Dakota and then n.e. in that state to Missouri River; the Cheyenne is sometimes considered to begin at junction of its South Fork and Beaver Creek in Fall River County, South Dakota, and to have length of only 290 mi (470 km), *maps* N-350, S-323, 334, U-70
Missouri River M-508
Cheyney State College, Cheyney, Pa.; established 1837; formerly a teachers college; arts and sciences, education; graduate studies.

Compton's Fact-Index
continues
on the next page

Latin American literature L-69, 75, *picture* L-73

Chock, section of a boat, *diagram* B-326

Chocolate C-393
candy C-137
Swiss, *picture* S-541

Chocolate drink, *list* D-6

Chocolate fudge, candy C-138

Chocolate liquor C-393

Chocolate milk, *list* D-6

Chocorua, Mount, mountain, New Hampshire, *picture* N-175

Choctaw, a North American tribe; formerly lived in southern Mississippi and Alabama; one of Five Civilized Tribes I-149, *map* I-136, *table* I-138
Mississippi M-468
Oklahoma O-521, 523

Ch'oe Ch'i-won (857–?), Korean writer
Korean literature K-292

Ch'oe Namson (1890–1957), Korean writer, born in Seoul; led movement to bring Western culture to Korea; introduced modern Korean poetry form (free verse style) K-294

'Choephoroi', part of trilogy 'Oresteia' by Aeschylus A-87

Choibalsan, Mongolian People's Republic, city about 350 mi (565 km) e. of Ulan Bator; center of rail lines to coal mines nearby; pop. about 14,000.

'Choir Invisible', love story by James Lane Allen; laid in Kentucky in pioneer days; the title is from a poem by George Eliot, 'Oh May I Join the Choir Invisible'.

Choka, Japanese poem J-79

Choke, in engine A-847

Choke, constriction of a gun barrel H-332

Chokeberry, name of several species of shrubs of rose family; oblong leaves; berries, which range from red through purple to black, have a puckery taste; found in e. U.S.

Chokeboring, in gun making F-100

Chokecherry, wild cherry *Prunus virginiana* having bitter dark red fruit in long clusters.

Chokedamp (or blackdamp), mine gas consisting largely of carbon dioxide; has killed many coal miners; smothers flames of lamps; preventive measure is ventilation of mine.

Choke pondweed. *see in index* Elodea

Choking, a medical emergency
first aid techniques F-119

Chokwe, people
Zaire Z-444

Cholera, acute infectious disease; now occurs endemically and epidemically in parts of Asia; transmitted through food and water contaminated by feces infected with cholera bacteria; prompt treatment withintravenous infusions and antibiotics usually successful; death rate in untreated cases 50 to 70 percent
Bangladesh flood, *table* F-181
infectious disease, *table* D-171
Koch's study K-267
vaccine V-249

Cholesterol, pearly, solid alcohol ($C_{27}H_{45}OH$) found in animal fats and oils, blood, bile, gall-stones, egg yolk, and nerve tissue; possible factor in arteriosclerosis V-356
egg E-113
exercise E-370
food and nutrition F-275
malnutrition M-77

Cholon ("great market"), industrial area of Saigon; absorbed by Saigon 1956 H-192, S-16a

Cholula (full name Cholula de Rivadavia), Mexico, city and tourist resort 6 mi (10 km) w. of Puebla; famous as site of giant Toltec pyramid and for many churches; as Aztec sacred city, dedicated to worship of Quetzalcoatl, was destroyed by Cortez; pop. 12,833, *map* M-341
pyramid P-543

Choluteca, s. Honduras on the Choluteca River; founded as a mining center; commercial and manufacturing city serving the agricultural hinterland; dairies, sawmills, and refineries; pop. 57,200 H-226

Chomolungma. *see in index* Everest, Mount

Chomsky, Noam (or Avram Noam Chomsky) (born 1928), U.S. linguist C-395
linguistics contribution L-230

Chomsongdae, observatory, Kyongju, Korea, *picture* K-279

Chondogyo (or Tonghak), Korean religion K-273

Chong Chiyong (born 1903), Korean writer K-294

Chong Ch'ol (1536-93), Korean poet K-293

Chongqing (or Chungking), China, port in Sichuan Province on Yangtze; steel, textiles, chemicals; capital of Nationalist China 1938–45; pop. 3,335,000 C-395, *maps* A-697, W-297

Chonjeyon Waterfall, Cheju Island, Korea, *picture* K-279

Chop, in cooking C-700

Chopin, Frédéric (1810–49), Polish pianist and composer C-395
classical music M-673
opera O-566

Chopin, Kate (1851–1904), U.S. writer, *list* W-275

Chopine (or Oriental clog), footwear S-179, *picture* S-178

Chopper. *see in index* Helicopter

Choppers and chopping tools, prehistoric tools M-84

Chopping, manual form of cultivating cotton C-737, *picture* C-736

Chopsticks, eating utensils, *picture* V-320
China E-319

Chop suey, dish of U.S. origin served with rice in Chinese restaurants in U.S.; bean sprouts, water chestnuts, bamboo shoots, mushrooms, and meat are typical ingredients.

Chorale prelude, in music M-669

'Choral Symphony', work by Beethoven. *see in index* 'Ninth Symphony'

Chorazin, ancient town in Palestine, denounced by Jesus (Bible, Matt. xi, 21); believed to have been located on site of ruins now called **Kerazeh,** 2 mi (3 km) n. of Lake Tiberias; ancient synagogue ruin.

Chord, in music M-666, 692, *list* M-670

Chordata (or chordates), all animals with spinal cords A-435, V-304

Chordophone. *see in index* Stringed instruments

Choreography, in dance
Astaire A-705
Diaghilev D-126
Nureyev N-441

Choriocarcinoma, type of malignant tumor C-812

Chorion, membrane
embryology E-201

Chorley, Henry Fothergill (1808–72), English author and musical critic; for many years on staff of London *Athenaeum* and for a time music critic of *Times* ('Modern German Music'; 'Thirty Years' Musical Recollections').

Choroid, middle coat of eyeball between sclera and retina; rich in blood vessels that nourish retina and lens; also serves to darken the eye E-387

Choron, Alexandre Étienne (1772–1834), French writer and musician, born in Caen; director of Grand Opera; established a conservatory of music, and was coauthor of a musical dictionary.

Choropleth map M-122

Chorus, Greek drama G-275
classical music M-667
opera O-560

'Chorus Line, A', musical M-686, *picture* D-28
opera O-560

Chose in action, law; a right to recover a chattel, a debt, a sum of money, or damages for breach of contract, which right cannot legally be enforced without bringing an action in a court of law; distinguished from a chattel (chose in possession).

Chosen. *see in index* Korea

Choson, historical state, Korea K-284

Chosroes I (died AD 579), king of Persia 531–79; warred against the Byzantines for twenty years (540–60); ruled with firmness, energy, and stern justice; encouraged agriculture, commerce, and science; introduced system of taxation.

Chosroes II (died AD 628), king of Persia 590–628; grandson of Chosroes I; with help of Mauricius, Byzantine emperor, gained throne; conquered Syria and Asia Minor and reached Chalcedon; defeated by Heraclius; murdered by eldest son, Sheroes.

Chota Nagpur Plateau, geographic area, India I-63

Chouans, nickname (corruption of French word for "screech owls") given to bands of peasants who during the French Revolution joined the royalist revolt in Vendée; story vividly told in Balzac's novel 'Les Chouans'.

Chou Dynasty, China (1124–256 BC) C-360
ancient civilization A-406
bronze casting S-93
'Lao-tzu' L-48

Chou En-lai. *see in index* Zhou Enlai

Chouinard, Julien (born 1929), Canadian jurist, born in Quebec City, Que.; judge court of appeal 1975–79; judge Supreme Court of Canada 1979–.

'Chou li', one of the Confucian Classics C-387

Chou Shu-jen. *see in index* Lu Xun

Chouteau family, American fur traders: **René Auguste** (1749–1829), commander of party that founded St. Louis, Mo., in winter of 1763–64, as a trading post; **Jean Pierre** (1758–1849), his half brother, one of founders of Missouri Fur Co.; by 1817 he had set up a trading post on site of Salina, Okla.; his sons were the following: **Auguste Pierre** (1786–1838), trader among Arkansas Osages, operator of trading post on Verdigris River, frontier baron; **Pierre** (1789–1865), head of Pierre Chouteau Jr. & Co., which bought out Astor's interests in American Fur Co., and **François** (1797–1838), who established a trading post on site of Kansas City, Mo., 1821.

Chow, animal feed Z-463

Chow chow, dog, *picture* D-206

Chrétien, Henri (1879–1956), French optical scientist, born in Paris; received 1954 Academy Award for developing anamorphic lens used in CinemaScope
French literature F-394
motion pictures M-623

Chrétien de Troyes (12th century), French writer of metrical romances: 'Erec'; 'Cligès'; 'Lancelot, ou Le Chevalier à la charette'; 'Yvain, ou Le Chevalier au lion'; 'Perceval, ou Le Conte du Graal'
Holy Grail H-207

Chrisman, Arthur Bowie (1889–1953), U.S. author, born near White Post, Va.; student in electrical engineering; lecturer, storyteller, and writer of Chinese folk tales and legends; awarded Newbery Medal for 'Shen of the Sea' (1926) S-478

Chrismation, sacrament of Eastern Orthodox churches E-43

Christ. *see in index* Jesus Christ

Christ, Order of, founded in 1318 by King Diniz of Portugal and by Pope John XXII; papal branch continues as the Supreme Order of Christ; the Portuguese branch was made distinct in 1522, secularized in 1789, and discontinued in 1910 when Portugal became a republic.

'Christabel', unfinished poem by Coleridge; heroine, the pious Christabel, encounters a wicked enchantress.

'Christ Before Pilate', engraving by Dürer, *picture* A-664

Christchurch, England, resort on s. coast, 30 mi (50 km) w. of Portsmouth, at confluence of Avon and Stour; great medieval church; pop. 31,780, *map* U-18a

Christchurch, New Zealand, city on South Island, 7 mi (11 km) from port Lyttelton, on e. coast; trade in timber, mutton, wool; pop. 328,000 C-396, *maps* N-299, P-3, W-297
New Zealand N-284, *picture* N-283

Christ Church, cathedral, Dublin, Ireland D-281

Christ Church, church, Coventry, England C-749

Christ Church, church, Philadelphia, Pa., *list* P-251d

Christ Church College, Oxford, England O-622, *pictures* E-336, O-621

Christian, hero of Bunyan's 'Pilgrim's Progress'; planned to show the experiences in the life of a Christian B-504

Christian II (1481–1559), king of Denmark and Norway; conquered Sweden 1520; deposed 1523 C-396
Sweden S-527

Christian IV (1577–1648), king of Denmark and Norway C-396
Thirty Years' War T-169

Christian VII (1749–1808), king of Denmark and Norway, born in Copenhagen; son of Frederick V, whom he succeeded in 1766; mentally weak, dominated by schemers.

Christian VIII (1786–1848), king of Denmark 1839–48; king of Norway in 1814; democratic views.

Christian IX (1818–1906), king of Denmark C-396

Christian X (1870–1947), king of Denmark C-396
Denmark D-100
German occupation resistance C-463

Christian, Fletcher (fl. 1789), British seaman C-396
Bligh B-311
famous ships S-177b

Christian, Henry Asbury (1876–1951), U.S. physician, born in Lynchburg, Va.; taught at Harvard Medical School 1903–39 and 1942–46; made important contributions to pathology and clinical medicine.

Christian and Missionary Alliance, holiness group H-202

Christian Brothers College, Memphis, Tenn.; Roman Catholic; founded 1854; arts and sciences, business administration, education, engineering, mathematics.

Christian Church, religious denomination. *see in index* Disciples of Christ

Christian Church (or General Convention of the Christian Church), religious denomination which grew out of three religious movements inaugurated soon after American Revolution, one in Virginia, one in Vermont, and one in Kentucky; holds Christian character only test of church fellowship and Bible only guide in faith; in 1931 united with Congregational churches as General Council of the Congregational and Christian Churches.

Christian Church (Disciples of Christ), one of three major bodies which split from the Disciples of Christ over doctrinal differences D-164

Christian Commercial Travelers Association of America. *see in index* Gideons

Christian Democratic Union (CDU), West German political party G-120, 125
Kiesinger K-236

Christian Endeavor, young people's movement, worldwide and interdenominational, to promote Christian life and service; organized 1881 in Portland, Me., by Francis E. Clark, Congregational minister.

Christian era, period of time from the birth of Jesus Christ to present; the practice of dating time from birth of Christ was begun in 6th century by monk Dionysius.

Christian flag, originated 1897 by Charles Carelton Overton; field, white with union of blue and cross emblazoned in red; intended for all Christian denominations but actual use confined to some of the Protestant churches.

Christian humanism H-319

Christiania, Norway. *see in index* Oslo

Christianity C-397. *see also in index* Jesus Christ
arts A-549
dance D-25
drama D-243, T-158
literature
Byzantine G-279

home economics, law, medicine, music, nursing and health, pharmacy; graduate school; quarter system; branches at Batavia and Blue Ash C-415, *picture* U-205

Cincinnati Zoo Z-466

Cincinnatus, Lucius Quinctius (519?–439? BC), dictator of Rome.

Cinclidae, family of birds including the dipper. *see in index* Dipper

Cinco de Mayo, a Mexican national holiday M-337

Cinderella, heroine who marries a prince in an old fairy tale of many lands; subject of Prokofiev children's ballet, Disney cartoon film 'Cinderella', and Rossini comic opera 'Cenerentola' S-469
  folklore F-260

'Cinemascope', motion picture innovation of the 1950s M-622

Cinématographe, early motion picture camera, printer, and projector M-617

Cinematography, motion pictures M-607

'Cinerama', motion picture innovation of the 1950s M-622

Cineraria, perennial plant of the genus *Senecio* of composite family, found throughout world; present plants largely work of horticulturists; flowers, daisy-like in brilliant colors; true cineraria is a related genus.

Cinna, Lucius Cornelius (died 84 BC), Roman noble, consul 87–84 BC; one of principal supporters of Marius against Sulla; his daughter Cornelia married Julius Caesar, but his son (L. Cornelius Cinna) sided with Caesar's murderers.

Cinnabar, ore from which mercury is obtained M-304
  minerals M-432
  ore, *table* O-600

Cinnamon, spice S-379, *picture* S-381
  ceremonial use P-136
  perfume, *picture* P-203

Cinnamon fern, plant, *diagram* F-56

Cinnamon vine (or Chinese yam), perennial twining plant *Dioscorea batatas* of yam family; native to Philippines, China; leaves heart-shaped; flowers cinnamon-scented, white; roots tubers, 2 to 3 ft (60 to 90 cm) long, used as food in tropics.

Cinque, Joseph (1811–52), chief of Mendi Africans, born in Caw-Mendi, Africa; in 1839 was sold to Cuban planters, revolted on slave ship *Amistad*; defended by John Quincy Adams, freed by U.S. Supreme Court, *picture* B-290

Cinquefoil (or five-fingers), herbs, or rarely shrubs, forming the genus *Potentilla* of the rose family; both English names refer to the compound leaves, cinquefoil being derived from the French *cinque feuilles,* meaning five leaves, *picture* F-234

Cinque Ports, five English Channel ports (Hastings, Sandwich, Dover, Romney, Hythe) granted charter by Edward I; had special privileges for defending coast; Winchelsea and Rye added later D-236

C.I.O. *see in index* Congress of Industrial Organizations

Cione, Andrea di. *see in index* Orcagna

Cipher C-416. *see also in index* Code
  information theory I-201

Cipher disk, cipher device C-420, *picture* C-416

Cipriani, Giovanni Battista (1727–85), Italian artist, born in Florence; lived in England 1755 until his death; noted for historical paintings and murals but chiefly for pen and ink drawings.

Circadian rhythm B-224, *diagram* B-227

Circassia, region of n.w. Caucasus; for many years independent but added to U.S.S.R. by treaty of Adrianople (1829).

Circassians, people C-232

Circe, in Greek mythology, sorceress who, by chants and magic potions, could turn men into beasts
  Homeric legend H-223

'Circe', ballet by Balthasar de Beaujoyeulx D-26

Circinus, constellation, *chart* C-682

Circle. *see also in index* Conic sections
  geometry G-76, *diagram* G-77
  mathematics M-213
  measurement M-243
  mechanical drawing M-257, *picture* M-258
  trigonometry T-285
  weights and measures, *table* W-140

Circle chart (or pie chart) G-223

Circle of equal altitude N-72

Circleville, Ohio, city on Scioto River, 25 mi (40 km) s. of Columbus; dairy cattle, livestock, grain, feed; fluorescent lamps, plastics; city laid out around prehistoric circular mound; annual pumpkin show; pop. 11,700.

Circuit court
  Henry II E-241
  judges' salaries, *table* U-155

Circuit rider, traveling clergyman in early North America P-332

Circular saw, tool T-223, *picture* T-216

Circular velocity S-342d, *diagram* S-343

Circulatory system, in animal
  invertebrate I-283

Circulatory system, in human C-421. *see also in index* Artery; Blood; Heart; Vein
  disease D-173
    cholesterol M-77
    diabetes D-126
  first aid techniques F-118, *diagram* F-117
  Harvey H-51
  nervous system N-119

Circumcision C-422

Circumference, distance around a circle
  measurement M-243
  weights and measures, *table* W-140

Circumferential Highway, Massachusetts M-191

Circus (from Latin word for "ring" or "circle"), form of entertainment C-423
  amateur, *picture* V-242
  Barnum and the Ringlings B-81
  museum, *picture* W-259
  horse, *pictures* H-258, 273

Circus Fans Association of America C-432

Circus Historical Society C-432

Circus Maximus (or Greatest Circus), huge U-shaped building in ancient Rome R-257, *map* R-250
  circus history C-423

Cirenaica, region of Libya. *see in index* Cyrenaica

Cirene. *see in index* Cyrene

Cire-perdue, process of casting bronze S-81

Cirque glacier G-150

Cirque Mountain, Canada N-165
  Laurentian Plateau L-88

Cirrhosis, chronic liver disease with formation of scar tissue resulting in atrophy; often a complication of alcoholism
  alcoholism A-276
  liver L-261

Cirrocumulus cloud C-515

Cirrostratus cloud C-517, *picture* C-516

Cirrus (Ci), cloud C-515, *picture* C-516
  ice crystals I-5
  weather W-120, *diagram* W-119

Cisalpine Gaul, portion of northern Italy; bounded on n. by Alps, on s. by Rubicon R-246

Cisalpine Republic, former state in n. Italy, including territory n. and s. of Po River with Milan as capital; created in 1797 by Napoleon N-14

Ciscoe (or lake herring), fish *Coregonus artedi* of the family Salmonidae W-195

Ciskei, African republic located south of the Great Kei River in southern Africa; declared a self-governing state in 1972; declared independent by itself and the Republic of South Africa in 1981; 2,079 sq mi (5,385 sq km); pop. 635,531 C-438, *map* A-115
  African political unit, *table* A-112
  flag, *picture* F-163
  independence S-267

Cispadane Republic, republic south of Po River, Italy (name comes from *cis,* meaning "this side of" and Padus, the ancient name of the Po); formed by Napoleon in 1796; became part of Cisalpine Republic in 1797.

Cistaceae. *see in index* Rockrose family

Cistercians (also called White Monks, or Gray Monks), Roman Catholic religious order patterned after Benedictines; best-known branch of the order is the Trappists M-542
  Middle Ages M-391

Citadel (or fortress), fort
  castle comparison C-198
  fort and fortifications F-320

Citadel Military College of South Carolina, Charleston, S.C.; state control; founded 1842; military training, arts and sciences, business administration, education, engineering; graduate studies.

CITES (Convention on International Trade in Endangered Species of Wild Fauna and Flora) E-209

Cithara, ancient musical instrument with a wooden sounding board, similar to the lyre, having from 4 to 20 strings; forerunner of modern guitar S-490
  classical music M-667

Citibank, New York, N.Y., second largest bank in U.S., with about 270 branch banks in New York City area; 840 banking offices in more than 90 countries overseas. Present name since 1976. Bank was founded 1812 as City Bank of New York; renamed National City Bank of New York (1865) and, after merger, First National City Bank of New York (1955). The holding company First National City Corporation (now Citicorp) created to take over ownership of bank (1967); acquired Carte Blanche (1978) and Diners Club (1981).

Cities of Refuge, six towns mentioned in Bible to which, under Mosaic law, one who had killed another by accident could flee and live without fear of any retaliation from victim's relatives, who would otherwise have right of "blood vengeance"; cities were Bezer, Ramoth, and Golan, east of the Jordan River; Kedesh, Shechem, and Hebron, west of the Jordan (Bible, Num. xxxv; Josh. xx).

Citium (Biblical Kittim), ancient Phoenician city, now in ruins, on s.e. coast of Cyprus; birthplace of Zeno of Citium; site of Citium lies partly within modern Larnaca, a seaport.

'Citizen Genet'. *see in index* Genet, Edmond Charles Edouard

'Citizen Kane' (1941), motion picture by Welles M-622

Citizen/Labor Energy Coalition
  lobbying L-276

Citizenship, membership in a state C-438. *see also in index* Americanization; Civil rights; Government; Women's rights
  ancient Rome R-245
  Australian Aborigine A-796
  civics C-462
  constitution C-683
  elections E-145
  naturalization N-67
  passport requirement P-137
  United States
    American Indians I-151
    education S-240
    14th Amendment U-152
    Hispanic Americans H-163
    rights. *see also in index* Bill of rights
      voting S-505, V-387, *pictures* V-386

Citizenship Act (1977), Canada N-67

Citlaltépetl, (or Mount Orizaba), highest peak in Mexico 18,000 ft (5,500 m); 175 mi (280 km) s.e. of Mexico City
  height, comparative. *see in index* Mountain, *table*
  Mexico M-322, *map* M-344

Citral, in perfume making P-204

Citrate, a salt of citric acid made by replacement of acidic hydrogens by metallic or organic radicals; used in medicines, plastics, blueprinting, and as resins.

Citric acid
  fermentation produces F-56

Citrin (or vitamin P) V-356

Citrine, gem materials J-115. *see also in index* Topaz

Citron, citrus fruit *Citrus medica* C-444, *picture* C-445

Citronella oil, insect repellent obtained from citronella grass *Cymbopogon nardus*, grown chiefly in East Indies and Sri Lanka and native in tropical America.

Citron melon, small variety of watermelon *Citrullus lanatus citroides* with hard, white flesh and a thick rind; used for preserves and jelly W-100

Citrus fruits C-444
  Florida F-196, *pictures* F-197, 204
  frost protection F-429
  fruitgrowing F-436
  perfumes P-203
  scale pests S-52e
  vitamins V-356

Cittern, stringed instrument, *picture* S-491

City C-448. *see also in index* City planning; City-states; Free city; Municipal government; Walled cities; *also* cities by name; *see table* following
  black Americans B-297
  civilization C-464
  colleges U-207
  crime C-772
  economics E-62
    employment and unemployment E-206
  elections E-146
  farm migration M-400, U-48, 102
  housing H-291, 298, 304
  Industrial Revolution I-180
  Mesopotamia B-4
  Middle Ages M-393
  pageant P-20

WORLD'S MOST POPULOUS CITIES AND METROPOLITAN AREAS*

Rank	*City*	*City Proper*	*Metropolitan Area*
1	Tokyo, Japan	8,353,674	29,002,000
2	New York, N.Y.	7,164,742	17,807,100
3	Mexico City, Mexico	9,931,413	17,321,800
4	Osaka, Japan	2,636,260	16,224,000
5	São Paulo, Brazil	10,099,086	15,280,375
6	Los Angeles, Calif.	3,096,721	12,372,600
7	London, England	6,767,500	12,231,200
8	Shanghai, China	6,725,700	12,050,000
9	Cairo, Egypt	6,205,000	12,001,000
10	Rhine-Ruhr, W. Ger.	*	10,984,000
11	Rio de Janeiro, Brazil	5,615,149	10,217,269
12	Paris, France	2,140,000	10,210,059
13	Buenos Aires, Arg.	2,924,000	9,677,200
14	Seoul, South Korea	*	9,645,932
15	Peking, China	4,983,000	9,470,000
16	Calcutta, India	3,305,006	9,194,018
17	Moscow, U.S.S.R.	8,408,000	8,642,000
18	Bombay, India	*	8,243,405
19	Chicago, Ill.	2,992,472	8,035,000
20	Tianjin, China	4,123,800	7,990,000
21	Nagoya, Japan	2,116,350	7,968,000
22	Jakarta, Indonesia	*	7,585,000
23	Manila, Philippines	1,725,500	6,914,581
24	Tehran, Iran	*	6,093,900
25	Istanbul, Turkey	5,494,916	5,858,558

*Cities ranked by metropolitan areas.

Rogers Memorial, dedicated 1938; pop. 12,085.

Clarence River, 245 mi (395 km) long, in n.e. New South Wales; [illegible] Great Dividing Range and flows generally s. and s.e. past Grafton and thence n.e. through an island-studded mouth into the Pacific, *map* A-819

Clarencetown, Equatorial Guinea. *see in index* Malabo

Clarendon, Constitutions of, England, document drawn up at a council at Clarendon in 1164; involved relations between church and state B-122

Clarendon, Edward Hyde, first **earl of** (1609–74), English historian and statesman, chancellor of Charles II, and grandfather of Mary II and Anne ('History of the Rebellion and Civil Wars').

Clare of Assisi, Saint, (1194–1253), Italian nun; festival August 12; follower of St. Francis and co-foundress of the Order of Poor Clares; proclaimed patron saint of television 1958.

Claricimbalum. *see in index* Harpsichord

Clarinet, wind instrument W-227, *picture* W-226
  opera O-565
  orchestra O-576
  reed R-121

Clarion State College, Clarion, Pa.; founded 1866; liberal arts, business administration, education; graduate studies; branch at Oil City.

Clark, Abraham (1726–94), U.S. signer of Declaration of Independence, born in Elizabeth, N.J.

Clark, Alvan Graham (1832–97), U.S. astronomer and astronomical instrument maker, born in Fall River, Mass.; won fame with 40 in. (100-cm) lenses of Yerkes telescope S-414

Clark, Ann Nolan (born 1898), U.S. author and teacher, born near Las Vegas, N.M.; author of children's books ('Looking-for-Something'; 'Blue Canyon Horse'; 'Santiago'; 'A Santo for Pasqualita'; 'World Song'; 'The Desert People'; 'Tia Maria's Garden'); awarded Regina Medal 1963, *list* R-105
  'Secret of the Andes' (Newbery Medal 1953) R-111

Clark, Catherine Anthony (born 1892), Canadian writer, born in London, England; known for children's books 'The Sun Horse' (Canadian Books of the Year for Children award for 1952) and 'The Golden Pine Cone'.

Clark, Champ (or James Beauchamp Clark) (1850–1921), U.S. congressman, born near Lawrenceburg, Ky.; Democratic representative from Missouri 1893–95, 1897–1921; speaker of House of Representatives 1911–19.

Clark, Charles Badger (1883–1957), U.S. poet, born in Iowa; known for cowboy ballads; named poet laureate of South Dakota 1937, *picture* S-332

Clark, Charles Joseph. *see in index* Clark, Joe

Clark, Earl (nickname Dutch) (born 1906), U.S. football quarterback and coach, born in Fowler, Colo.; quarterback Portsmouth (Ohio) Spartans 1931–33, Detroit Lions 1934–38; coach Cleveland Rams 1939–42.

Clark, Francis Edward (1851–1927), U.S. Congregational clergyman, born of New England parents at Aylmer, Que.; organized first Christian Endeavor society 1881. *see also in index* Christian Endeavor

Clark, George Rogers (1752–1818), American Revolutionary War soldier and frontiersman C-485, *picture* V-342
  Henry H-134
  Illinois I-41
  Indiana I-93, *picture* I-99
  Louisville L-324

Clark, James Beauchamp. *see in index* Clark, Champ

Clark, Jim (1936–68), Scottish auto racing driver, born in Dun; became youngest world champion driver 1963; killed in race at Hockenheim, Germany.

Clark, Joe (full name Charles Joseph Clark) (born 1939), Canadian political leader C-485
  Canada C-106

Clark, Kenneth Bancroft (born 1914), U.S. educator, born in Panama Canal Zone; with wife **Mamie Phipps Clark** (born 1917 in Hot Springs, Ark.), founded Northside Center for Child Development, New York, N.Y., 1946; professor of psychology at City College of the City University of New York 1960–75; won 1961 Spingarn medal ('Prejudice and Your Child'; 'Dark Ghetto'; 'A Relevant War Against Poverty'; 'The Pathos of Power').

Clark, Mark Wayne (1896–1984), U.S. Army officer, born in Madison Barracks, N.Y.; commanded U.S. 5th Army and Allied 15th Army group in Italy 1943–45; chief U.S. occupational forces in Austria 1945–47; chief of Army field forces 1949–52; UN commander in Korea and commander in chief of the U.S. armed forces in the Far East 1952–53 ('Calculated Risk'; 'From the Danube to the Yalu') W-337, 340

Clark, Ramsey (in full William Ramsey Clark) (born 1927), U.S. lawyer and public official, born in Dallas, Tex.; son of Thomas Campbell Clark; assistant U.S. attorney general 1961–65, deputy U.S. attorney general 1965–66, U.S. attorney general 1967–69; professor Howard University 1969–72, Brooklyn Law School 1973– ('Crime in America').

Clark, Thomas Campbell (1899–1977), U.S. lawyer and government official, born in Dallas, Tex.; attorney general of U.S. 1945–49; justice U.S. Supreme Court 1949–67; circuit judge U.S. court of appeals 1967–77.

Clark, Walter Van Tilburg (1909–71), U.S. writer and teacher, born in East Orland, Me.; to Reno, Nev., 1917 ('The Ox-Bow Incident', 'The Track of the Cat', novels).

Clark, William (1770–1838), U.S. Army officer and explorer C-485
  exploration E-376
    Lewis and Clark expedition L-142
    Montana M-554
    North Dakota N-376
    Oregon Trail O-598
  Fort Osage, Mo., *picture* M-498

Clark, N.J., urban township 6 mi (10 km) s.w. of Elizabeth and near Rahway River; residential and industrial community; machinery, roller bearings, electrical products, aircraft parts; pop. 18,829.

Clark College, Atlanta, Ga.; Methodist; founded 1869 as Clark University; arts and sciences, education. *see also in index* Atlanta University

Clarke, Arthur C. (in full Arthur Charles Clarke) (born 1917), English science writer and underwater explorer and photographer C-486
  young adult books R-112e

Clarke, Charles Cowden (1787–1877), English literary critic; authority on Shakespeare ('Tales from Chaucer'; 'Shakespeare's Characters'); his wife, **Mary Cowden Clarke** (1808–98), also known as a Shakespearean scholar.

Clarke, Elijah (1733–99), American Revolutionary War soldier; suspected of intriguing with Genêt, French minister; set up Trans Oconee state in Creek territory, capitulated to Georgia militia, was acquitted of treason without damage to his popularity.

Clarke, Frank Wigglesworth (1847–1931), U.S. geological chemist, born in Boston, Mass.; chief chemist U.S. Geological Survey 1883–1925 ('A Recalculation of Atomic Weights'; 'The Data of Geochemistry').

Clarke, Frederick Clifford (1872–1960), U.S. baseball outfielder, born in Winterset, Iowa; with Louisville, N.L., 1894–99 (manager last three years); managed Pittsburgh, N.L., 1900–15, winning pennant 4 times for Pirates.

Clarke, James Freeman (1810–88), U.S. Unitarian minister and author, born in Hanover, N.H.; pastor and one of founders of Church of the Disciples, Boston; friend of Emerson ('Ten Great Religions'; 'Orthodoxy'; 'Every-Day Religion').

Clarke, James Paul (1854–1916), U.S. politician, born in Yazoo City, Miss.; representative, senator, attorney general, and governor of Arkansas, later U.S. senator
  Statuary Hall, *table* S-437a

Clarke, Marcus (1846–81), Australian writer, *table* A-798

Clarke College, Dubuque, Iowa; Roman Catholic; for women; founded 1843; liberal arts and education; graduate studies.

Clark Fork River, rises in Silver Bow County, s.w. Montana, flows into Pend Oreille Lake, in Idaho; sometimes included with Pend Oreille River, which flows from the lake and through Idaho and Washington to Columbia River at British Columbia line; total length, including Pend Oreille River, 505 mi (815 km) C-588, *maps* C-589, I-17, 28, U-80

Clark Hill Dam, Georgia and South Carolina, on the Savannah River S-306, *maps* S-307, 318

Clarkia, small genus of annual plants of the evening primrose family; stem fleshy and red; flowers in clusters.

Clarksburg, W. Va., city in n. part of state, about 65 mi (105 km) e. of Parkersburg; coal, oil, gas center; glass, clay, carbon, wood, and metal products, chemicals, clothing; birthplace of Thomas Jonathan (Stonewall) Jackson; pop. 22,371 W-167, *map* U-41

Clarksdale, Miss., city 72 mi (116 km) s.w. of Memphis, Tenn.; agricultural area; food processing; lumber, cotton and cottonseed products; chemicals, builders' hardware, conveying equipment, mobile homes, rubber products; pop. 21,137, *map* U-41

Clark's nutcracker (or Clark's crow), bird of the crow family common in the w. U.S.; length about 12½ in. (32 cm); plumage whitish gray except for sooty brown wings and inner tail feathers.

Clarkson, John Gibson (1861–1909), U.S. baseball pitcher, born in Cambridge, Mass.; with Worcester, N.L., 1882, Chicago, N.L., 1884–87, Boston, N.L., 1888–92, Cleveland, N.L., 1892–94; in 1885 won 53 games, lost 16; won 36 in 1886, 38 in 1887, and 49 in 1889; during lifetime won 328, lost 176; pitched a no-hit game against Providence, July 27, 1885.

Clarkson, Thomas, U.S. abolitionist
  abolitionist movement A-10

Clarkson College of Technology, Potsdam, N.Y.; private control; chartered 1896; arts, engineering, industrial distribution, science and business administration; graduate school.

Clarksville, Ind., town on Ohio River, opposite Louisville, Ky.; trade center; first non-Indian settlement in Northwest Territory, 1784; pop. 15,164, *map* I-102

Clarksville, Tenn., city 40 mi (65 km) n.w. of Nashville; heating and air conditioning; shoes; tobacco markets and warehouses; rubber goods, clothing, snuff, cigars, food products; Austin Peay State University; pop. 54,777, *map* U-41

Clark University, Worcester, Mass.; private control; founded 1887, opened 1889; arts and sciences, business administration, education; graduate division; museum named for R.H. Goddard has rocket materials he used; pioneer in courses on anthropology and on international relations; first U.S. graduate school of geography W-292

Class, in biological classification A-432
  zoology Z-467

Class, in social structure
  Marx M-162, H-174
  minority group M-460

Classical age, in music M-669
  chamber music C-268
  wind instruments W-227

Classical art G-269

Classical genetics, the study of how traits are transmitted and expressed H-140

Classical literature (Greek and Latin). *see also in index* Greek literature; Latin literature; names of individual authors
  Renaissance literature R-145

Classical music M-667

Classical tragedy, dramatic action concerns a high and noble person who falls because of a 'tragic flaw' D-241

Classic architecture, term applied to Greek and Roman styles or those derived from them during the Renaissance. *see also in index* Greek art; Renaissance architecture; Roman art

Classicism, in literature
  French F-395
  German G-106

Classic Revival, U.S. architecture, *picture* S-159

Classification, in science
  animal A-432
    bird B-275
    insect I-223
  color C-560
  Cuvier's contribution C-808
  human R-25
  living things L-270, *picture* L-269
  minerals and rocks R-228
  plant B-378, P-370
  star S-414

Classified advertisement
  housing market H-294

Classroom E-99

Class struggle, in Marxist theory H-174, M-162
  Vico V-308

Clastic rock, rock composed of particles of varying size
  formation E-21
  oceanography O-486

Claude, Albert (1899–1983), U.S. biologist; born in Belgium; U.S. citizen 1941; discovered mitochondria; co-winner of 1974 Nobel prize for cell structure research; director of the Institut Jules Bordet, Brussels, 1948–72. *see also in index* Nobel Prizewinners, *table*

Claude, Georges (1870–1960), French chemist and physicist, born in Paris; invented process for liquefying air and other gases; made ammonia out of atmosphere; invented neon light; devised method of utilizing for power difference in temperature between the waters at the depths and the surface of tropical seas
  lighting innovations L-206

Claudel, Paul Louis Charles (1868–1955), French poet, dramatist, and diplomat; held diplomatic posts in China, Japan, Brazil, Germany, and Denmark; ambassador to United States 1927–33; writings mystical and religious
  French literature F-397

Claudius (or Tiberius Claudius Drusus Nero Germanicus) (10 BC–AD 54), Roman emperor C-486
  ancient Rome R-247
  Britain E-238

Claudius, Appius, Roman decemvir 451–449 BC, whose attempt to enslave Virginia, beautiful daughter of Virginius, a centurion, caused revolution and abolition of the decemvirate; Virginius killed daughter to prevent her fate; story told in Macaulay's 'Virginia' in the 'Lays of Ancient Rome'.

Claudius Caecus, Appius, Roman patrician chosen to censorship 312 BC, builder of Appian Way and aqueduct R-257

Claudius Galen. *see in index* Galen, Claudius

Claudius Ptolemaeus. *see in index* Ptolemy

Clause, in grammar S-110
  grammatical use G-211
  language construction L-33

Clausewitz, Karl von (1780–1831), Prussian general and military writer C-486
  warfare W-12, 17, 21

Clausius, Rudolf Julius Emanuel (1822–88), German physicist; one of founders of modern science of thermodynamics.

Clavarias, mushrooms M-665

Clavell, James du Maresq, writer A-360
Claverhouse, John Graham of, Viscount Dundee (1649?–89), persecutor of Scottish Covenanters and a Jacobite rebel; known as "bonny Dundee" among Jacobites and "bloody Claver'se" among Covenanters.
Clavichord, musical instrument, forerunner of piano M-687
Clavicle (or collarbone), bone which connects the breastbone and shoulder blade S-210
Claw, animal anatomy S-211
hand H-27
hoof H-231
Claw hammer, tool T-216
Clawson, Mich., city 14 mi (22 km) n.w. of Detroit; chiefly residential; manufactures tools, dies, and automobile parts; incorporated 1920 as village, 1940 as city; pop. 15,103.
Clay, Cassius Marcellus. *see in index* Ali, Muhammad
Clay, Henry (nickname Great Pacificator) (1777–1852), U.S. orator and political leader C-487
Adams J-8
Calhoun C-31
Compromise of 1850 C-624
Hall of Fame, *table* H-16
home, *picture* K-219
Missouri Compromise M-507
Senate address, *picture* F-85
Soo canal opposition G-249
Statuary Hall, *table* S-437a
Taylor's administration T-43
War of 1812 W-30
Clay, Lucius DuBignon (1897–1978), U.S. Army officer, born in Marietta, Ga.; made assistant chief of staff Material Service of Supply 1942; deputy to Dwight Eisenhower 1945; deputy U.S. military governor in Germany 1946; European theater commander of U.S. forces and U.S. military governor for Germany 1947–49; presidential representative in West Berlin 1961–62.
Clay C-488. *see also in index* Brick and tile; Porcelain and chinaware; Pottery; Tile; *also* kinds of clay by name
aluminum A-321
bentonite B-136b
cement C-243
glacial Ice Age deposits I-9
grain size, *table* S-36
rock cycle, *chart* R-229
soil G-21, S-253
uses
adobe A-47
bell casting B-154
brickmaking B-436
bridges B-439
building construction B-491
pencil making P-158, *picture* P-159
pottery P-477
Clayborne, William. *see in index* Claiborne, William
'Clayhanger', work by Bennett B-163
Claymore, two-edged broadsword formerly used by the Scottish Highlanders; name inaccurately used for single-edged, basket-hilted sword worn by Highland regiments of British army.
Claymore mine, weapon T-232
Clay prism, hollow polygon of clay with six, seven, or eight sides; used by Babylonians to record chief events.
Clay tablets, ancient writing B-5
Clayton, Henry de Lamar (1857–1929), U.S. jurist, born in Barbour County, Ala.; member of Congress 1897–1914; author Clayton Act.
Clayton, John Middleton (1796–1856), U.S. public official, born in Dagsboro, Del.; U.S. senator 1829–37, 1845–49, 1851–56; secretary of state under Taylor T-43. *see also in index* Clayton-Bulwer Treaty
Statuary Hall, *table* S-437a
Clayton, Mo., residential suburb of St. Louis, near Mississippi River; financial and commercial center; pop. 14,219.
Clayton Act (1914), United States
Wilson's administration W-217
Clayton-Bulwer Treaty (1850), between U.S. and United Kingdom P-92, *table* T-274
McKinley M-20
Taylor T-43
Clean and jerk, weight lifting W-137
Clean culture, method in agriculture
corn C-722
Cleaning equipment, appliances H-211
Cleanliness
surgery S-519
Clearfield, Utah, city 8 mi (13 km) s.w. of Ogden; in irrigated area; fruit and vegetable processing; Hill Air Force Base nearby; incorporated 1922; pop. 17,982, *map* U-232
Clearinghouse, in banking B-69, *diagram* B-65
Clearwater, Fla., city on Gulf of Mexico, 20 mi (30 km) w. of Tampa; tourist trade; citrus fruit packing and canning; cigars; electronics; incorporated in 1891; pop. 85,450
Tampa T-19
Clearwater River, Idaho, 200 mi (320 km) long; enters Snake River at Lewiston, *map* I-30
Cleary, Beverly (born 1916), U.S. children's author, born in McMinnville, Ore. (popular series about 'Henry Huggins', 'Ellen Tebbits', and others in small Oregon city; 'The Luckiest Girl'; 'The Mouse and the Motorcycle'); received Laura Ingalls Wilder Award 1975; awarded Regina Medal 1980
'Mitch and Amy' R-110
Cleary, Jon (born 1917), writer D-119
Cleat, *diagram* B-326
Cleavage, in embryo E-199, *diagram* E-200
egg E-110
Cleavage, in mineral M-431, R-229b
Cleaveland, Moses (1754–1806), U.S. pioneer and soldier, born in Canterbury, Conn.; left Yale to fight in Revolutionary War; practiced law and became director of Connecticut Land Company C-495
Cleaver, Eldridge (born 1935), former Black Panther Party leader, born in Little Rock, Ark.; fled U.S. 1968 after California parole-violation charges; settled in Algeria 1969; returned to U.S. 1975; broke with Black Panther Party and former associates and became Republican Party candidate for public office ('Soul on Ice').
Cleaver, Elizabeth, Canadian author and illustrator, born in Montreal, Que.; illustrated 'The Wind Has Wings', 'The Witch of the North', 'The Loon's Necklace' (awarded 1978 Canadian Library Association Award for illustration); wrote and illustrated 'The Miraculous Hind' (received 1974 Canadian Books of the Year for Children Award).
Cleburne, Patrick Ronayne (1828–64), U.S. general, born in Ireland; fought for Confederate States of America.
Cleburne, Tex., city 27 mi (43 km) s. of Fort Worth; dairying and farming center; railroad shops; limestone processing; clothing, furniture; pop. 19,218, *map* U-40
Clef, in music, sign used to indicate the pitch of notes represented on the staff; for voice, piano, and other instruments two clefs are used, the *G* to indicate the treble notes, the *F* for the bass; for viola and some other instruments the *C* clef is used M-689
Cleft palate, gap in the roof of the mouth resulting from a failure of the tissue to fuse in the fetus.
Cleisthenes. *see in index* Clisthenes
Clemenceau, Georges (1841–1929), French statesman C-489
Clemens, Samuel Langhorne. *see in index* Twain, Mark
Clement, name of 14 popes, *table* P-99. *see also in index below*
Clement I, Saint (known also as Clement of Rome, or Clemens Romanus), pope 88–97; best known for his epistle to the church of Corinth, dating from about AD 96; festival November 23.
Clement III (1025–1100), antipope from 1080–1100
Henry IV H-132
Clement IV (died 1268), elected pope 1265
Bacon B-11
Clement V (1264–1314), first Avignon pope (during Babylonian Captivity), elected 1305; abolished order of the Templars
Holy Roman Empire H-209
Clement VII (or Giulio de' Medici) (1478–1534), pope besieged in Castel Sant' Angelo during sack of Rome by Constable de Bourbon 1527; refused to divorce Henry VIII of England from Catherine of Aragon and thus caused separation of Church of England from Rome
Henry VIII H-131
Medici M-273
Clement VII (1342–94), first antipope of the Great Schism, born in Geneva, Switzerland; created cardinal 1371; chosen pope in election boycotted by Italian cardinals 1378 U-212
Clement VIII (1536–1605), pope 1592–1605; revised Vulgate; readmitted Henry IV of France to church; also **Aegidius Muñoz**, antipope 1424–29.
Clement XIV (1705–74), elected pope 1769, born near Rimini, Italy; suppressed the Jesuits in brief issued 1773; established Clementine Museum at the Vatican.
Clément, Béatrice (born 1905), French-Canadian author, born in Paris, France; won Canadian Books of the Year for Children Award 1958 for 'Le Chevalier du Roi'.
Clemente, Roberto Walker (1934–72), U.S. baseball outfielder, born in Carolina, near San Juan, Puerto Rico; with Pittsburgh, N.L., 1955–72; won 4 N.L. batting titles (hit .357 in 1967); had 3000th major-league hit in 1972; lifetime batting average of .317; died in crash of cargo plane laden with relief supplies he had led in collecting, meant for Nicaragua earthquake victims; chosen for Baseball Hall of Fame 1973 in special election.
Clementi, Muzio (1752–1832), Italian pianist, composer, teacher, born in Rome; first to write for piano in style distinguished from that of harpsichord.
Clement of Rome. *see in index* Clement I, Saint
Clemson, S.C., town in n.w.; textiles; Clemson University; pop. 5,578, *map* S-318
Clemson University, Clemson, S.C.; state control; founded 1889, opened 1893; on estate given by Thomas G. Clemson, son-in-law of John C. Calhoun; liberal arts, agriculture and biological sciences, architecture, education, engineering, industrial management and textile science, nursing, and physical and mathematical sciences; graduate school.
Cleobulus (fl. 6th century BC), one of Seven Wise Men of Greece, born in Lindus, Rhodes; reputed author of various riddles.
Cleome, genus of annual plants or shrubs of the caper family identified by spidery stamens of flowers; flowers white, yellow, or rosy purple G-23
Cleon (died 422 BC), Athenian political leader, opponent of Pericles, and leader of the democracy.
Cleopatra (or Cleopatra VII) (69–30 BC), queen of Egypt C-489
Antony A-496
Caesar C-15
Egypt E-126
name in hieroglyphics, *picture* W-369
Clepsydra (water clock) W-83
Clergy, in Christian church
French Revolution F-403
monks and monasticism M-539
Clerical occupations V-364, *table* V-363
typing and stenography S-182
women's rights W-274
Clerk, Sir Dugald (1854–1932), British engineer, born in Glasgow, Scotland; invented Clerk cycle gas engine; author of 'The Gas and Oil Engine'.
'Clermont', steamship built by Fulton F-447, *picture* F-446, S-165
Clermont-Ferrand, France, city 85 mi (135 km) w. of Lyons; formed by joining of Clermont and Montferrand 1731; birthplace of Pascal; pop. 145,856, *maps* E-360, F-369
Cleve, Per Theodor (1840–1905), Swedish chemist, born in Stockholm; discoverer of thulium and independent discoverer of holmium and helium.
Cleveite, mineral, oxide of uranium and lead; named for Per Theodor Cleve, a Swedish chemist; produces helium when heated with acid S-372
Cleveland, Grover (full name Stephen Grover Cleveland) (1837–1908), 22nd and 24th president of the United States C-490
Hall of Fame, *table* H-16
Liliuokalani L-209
Venezuelan dispute V-277
Cleveland Bay, horse, *picture* H-255, *table* H-254
Cleveland, Miss., city 30 mi (50 km) n.e. of Greenville; cotton, rice, soybeans; medical and drug supplies; Delta State University; pop. 14,524.
Cleveland, Ohio, on Lake Erie; largest city in Ohio; pop. 573,822 C-493, *maps* U-41, W-297
federal housing project, *picture* R-266
Lake Erie E-298
North America, *map* N-350
Ohio O-500, 512, *picture* O-510
public library S-461
social studies program, *chart* S-241a
Cleveland, Tenn., industrial city near s.e. corner of state, 12 mi (19 km) n. of Georgia border; stoves, textiles, furniture and wood products, chemicals; Lee College; headquarters Cherokee National forest; pop. 26,415.
Cleveland, Mount, loftiest peak (10,438 ft; 3,182 m) in Glacier National Park, in n.w. Montana; also highest point of Lewis Range, on e. front of Rocky Mountains.
Cleveland Heights, Ohio, city e. of Cleveland; residential suburb; Cain Park outdoor summer theater; Forest Hills Park; incorporated as village 1903, as city 1921; pop. 56,438.
Cleveland State University, Cleveland, Ohio; founded 1964 on nucleus of Fenn College (private control, founded 1923); arts and sciences, business administration, education, engineering, law; graduate studies C-495
Cleves, West Germany. *see in index* Kleve
Clew, section of sailing boat, *diagram* B-326
Clianthus, small genus of trailing plants of the pea family, native to Australia, New Zealand; flowers scarlet with black spot, crimson, or white, one petal long and beaklike; glory pea *C. dampieri*; parrots-bill or red Kowhai *C. puniceus*.
Cliché, in language L-34
Click beetle B-140
Clicking machine S-180
Cliff Dwellers, prehistoric people of s.w. U.S.
Colorado C-571
New Mexico N-215, *picture* N-223
Clifford, Clark McAdams (born 1906), government official and lawyer, born in Fort Scott, Kan.; adviser to Presidents Truman, Kennedy, and Johnson; member Foreign Intelligence Advisory Board 1961–68, chairman 1963–68; U.S. secretary of defense 1968–69; Medal of Freedom 1969.
Clifford, George, 3rd **earl of Cumberland.** *see in index* Cumberland, George Clifford, 3rd earl of
Clifford, Nathan (1803–81), U.S. jurist, born in Rumney, N.H.; attorney general in President Polk's Cabinet; negotiated treaty after Mexican War; associate justice U.S. Supreme Court after 1858; president Hayes-Tilden electoral commission 1877.
Cliffside Park, N.J., borough on Hudson River; residential suburb of New York, N.Y.; light

Clutha River, longest river of South Island, New Zealand; flows 210 mi (340 km) s.e. from Lake Wanaka to Pacific Ocean; provides hydroelectric power N-287, *map* N-299
Clyde, Colin Campbell, Baron. *see in index* Campbell, Sir Colin
Clyde, Firth of, in Scotland, estuary of Clyde River, which expands into bay 50 mi (80 km) long, 30 mi (50 km) wide; part of Greenock near head of the estuary; Ayr is on e. shore; islands of Arran, Bute, Great Cumbrae, Little Cumbrae.
Clyde River, in s.w. Scotland, flows n. and n.w. (106 mi; 171 km) to Firth of Clyde G-154
shipyard, *picture* S-69
Clydesdale, horse, *picture* H-255, *table* H-254
Clymene, in Greek mythology, mother of Phaethon P-248
Clymer, George (1739–1813), signer of Declaration of Independence, born in Philadelphia, Pa.; member Second Continental Congress; delegate Constitutional Convention 1787; signed U.S. Constitution.
Clytemnestra, in Greek mythology, sister of Helen and faithless wife of Agamemnon, whom she murdered; mother of Iphigenia, Electra, and Orestes.
Clytie, in Greek mythology, maiden beloved and deserted by Helios, the sun, at whom she gazed until the pitying gods changed her into a sunflower.
Cm, chemical element. *see in index* Curium
CMEA. *see in index* Council for Mutual Economic Assistance
Cnidus, ancient Greek city on promontory in Caria, Asia Minor; contained statue of Aphrodite by Praxiteles.
CNO (chief of naval operations), top military officer in the U.S. Navy N-88
Cnossus (called also Knossus), ancient capital of Crete; famed in Greek mythology. *see also in index* Aegean civilization
Minoan ruins A-61, 537, C-763
Cnut. *see in index* Canute the Great
CO, poisonous gas. *see in index* Carbon monoxide
Coacervate, colloidal droplet E-365
Coach, closed carriage. *see in index* Wagons, carriages, and carts
Coachella Canal, in s. California; supplies water to Coachella Valley C-586
Coachella Valley, in s. California, joins Imperial Valley to n.w.; date-growing region.
Coach-whip cactus. *see in index* Ocotillo
Coagulants, in waterworks, chemicals used to purify water; common ones are ferrous sulfate and lime, ferric chloride, ferric sulfate, aluminum sulfate, sodium aluminate and lime W-90
Coagulation, clotting or curdling
blood S-113
vitamin K V-357
Coahuila, Mexico, state in n., bordering on Texas; 58,522 sq mi (151,571 sq km); cap. Saltillo; cotton, corn, wheat, beans, sugar, and grapes; Parras district noted for wines and brandies; produces silver, lead, copper, coal, and iron; settled by Spanish 1575; part of Texas 1824–36; pop. 1,333,845, *picture* M-334, *map* M-341
Coal C-518. *see also in index* Cannel coal; Coke; Peat
acid rain A-19
ash use G-21
bituminous P-384
carbon C-156
conservation C-677
electric power E-165
fire F-94
formation P-151, S-516
gas G-38
heating H-108
mining M-425, *pictures* U-52, W-168
Industrial Revolution I-119
Molly Maguires M-526
Watt W-108
producing regions G-63
Antarctica A-474
Asia A-689
China C-338, 353
Japan J-39
Turkey T-319
Australia A-774
Chile C-330
Colombia C-552
Europe, *picture* E-333
Czechoslovakia C-813
France F-354
Poland, *picture* P-413
West Germany G-112
North America N-342
United Kingdom
England E-230, 234, N-162
Scotland S-68
Wales W-6
United States U-106, *charts* U-126, *map* U-53, *picture* U-52
Alabama A-226, *map* A-228
Alaska A-423
Appalachia A-507
Colorado, *picture* I-187
Great Lakes' transportation G-246
Great Plains G-249
Kentucky K-211, *picture* K-212
Ohio O-498
Pennsylvania P-168, *map* P-174, *picture* P-169
Texas T-120
Utah U-217, *map* U-220
Virginia V-333, *map* V-336
West Virginia W-167
Wyoming W-388, *map* W-390
U.S.S.R. R-324
uses
blacksmithing B-308
brickmaking B-436
dyes D-295
fuel F-441
furnaces and boilers F-451
locomotives L-279
ships S-170
Coal Age. *see in index* Carboniferous period
Coalescence word E-261
Coal gas, illuminating gas obtained by distilling coal
illuminating fixture, *picture* I-277
Coalition, union of several entities, especially a temporary combination of several political parties into one government or an alliance of various powers or states
Britain P-131b
cabinet government C-6
Canada P-132
Coal oil. *see in index* Kerosene
Coal sack, black spot in Milky Way caused by dust cloud, *chart* S-415
Coal-tar products C-527. *see also in index* Benzene
organic chemistry O-602
perfumes P-204
pitch T-28
saccharin S-509
Coaming, part of boat, *diagram* B-326
Coanda, Henri Marie (1885–1972), French aeronautics engineer and inventor, born in Bucharest, Romania; in 1910 designed and piloted a jet plane a short distance before it crashed; in 1930s demonstrated "flying saucer" type of aircraft.
Coast. *see in index* Beach and coast
Coastal breakwater harbor H-33
Coastal lake L-24
Coastal Plain. *see in index* Jackson Purchase
Coastal Plain, in United States
Maryland M-167, *map* M-169
Massachusetts M-189
New Jersey N-193
North Carolina N-354
United States U-35, *maps* E-25, U-36, 50, 59, 63
Coasters, U.S. singing group M-680
Coast Guard C-528
fire-fighting regulations F-109
flag F-158
ice patrol service I-10
Navy N-88
safety work S-5
ship model, *picture* S-177
uniforms and insignia U-6, *pictures* U-7
Coast Guard Academy, in New London, Conn. C-528
Coast Ranges, series of mountain ranges of western North America C-530, *map* N-350
Canada B-452, C-73, *map* C-109
United States U-38, 86, U-94, *maps* E-25, U-87
Alaska A-241
California C-34
Oregon O-582
Coast rhododendron. *see in index* West Coast rhododendron
Coast Salish, group of Indian tribes
Washington W-49
Coat, garment
fur F-467
Coates, Albert (1882–1953), English conductor and composer, born in St. Petersburg, Russia (now Leningrad) of English father and Russian mother; conductor Russian Imperial Opera, London Symphony Orchestra, and Royal Philharmonic Society; director Philharmonic Orchestra, Rochester, N.Y., 1923–25; exponent of Russian music ('Pickwick', 'Samuel Pepys', operas; 'Launcelot', a symphony).
Coates, Eric (1886–1957), English composer and viola player, born in Hucknall; known especially for light, lively orchestral suites ('Brighton'; 'London'; 'From Meadow to Mayfair'; 'London Again'); also composed ballets and numerous songs.
Coatesville, Pa., industrial city 39 mi (63 km) w. of Philadelphia; in rich agricultural and dairying district; extensive steelworks; textiles; veterans hospital; pop. 10,698, *map* P-185
Coati, fur-bearing animal of the genus *Nasua;* ranges from Mexico to Paraguay; long, upturned, white snout; long, soft, brown fur with reddish or gray tint; habits like those of small tree-climbing cats; eats birds, lizards, insects
fur, *table* F-464
Coating, protective or finishing layer
glass G-160
nickel N-307
plastic P-382
Coat of arms, in heraldry H-135, *picture* H-136
Shakespeare S-131
Coat-of-mail shell. *see in index* Chiton
Coats Land, Antarctica, extends w. from Queen Maud Land forming e. shore of Weddell Sea; discovered and named 1904 by 'Scotia' Expedition led by William Speirs Bruce, *map* W-297
Coatsworth, Elizabeth Jane (born 1893), U.S. poet and writer for children, born in Buffalo, N.Y.; travels in Europe, China, Japan, and Mexico gave rich background for her work (poems: 'Night and the Cat'; children's books: 'The Cat Who Went to Heaven', awarded Newbery Medal 1931, 'Door to the North', 'Hide and Seek', 'Lonely Maria', 'The Princess and the Lion', 'Jon, the Unlucky', 'Bess and the Sphinx'); married to Henry Beston R-110, S-478
Coatzacoalcos (or Puerto México), Mexico, petroleum-shipping port on Gulf of Mexico; terminus of railroad across Isthmus of Tehuantepec; pop. 69,753, *map* M-341
Coaxial cable
radio R-51
television T-76
Cob, male swan D-285
Cobaea (or cathedral bells), genus of annual vines of the phlox family, native to tropical America; leaves with climbing tendrils ending each leaf cluster; flowers bell-shaped, violet or yellow-green; grows to 20 ft (6 m).
Cobalt, Ont., town 235 mi (380 km) n.w. of Ottawa; minerals in vicinity include silver, cobalt, and nickel; pop. 2,197, *map* C-112
Cobalt (Co), metallic element C-530
Africa A-105
magnetism M-45
ore, *table* O-600
periodic table, *table* P-207, *list* P-208
radioactivity N-429
Cobaltite, commercial ore, *table* O-600
Cobalt-60, radioisotope C-530
Cobán, city in central Guatemala; trade in coffee, cacao, vanilla, tea, agave; founded about 1538 by a Dominican friar; Mayan burial mounds, 16th- and 17th-century churches; pop. 9,073.
Cobar, Australia A-774, *map* A-819
Cobb, Howell (1815–68), U.S. political leader, born in Cherry Hill, Ga.; governor of Georgia 1851–53; speaker of the House of Representatives 1849–51; secretary of treasury 1857–60; president of Confederate Congress 1861–62; Democrat, *picture* C-643
Cobb, Irvin Shrewsbury (1876–1944), U.S. short-story writer, humorist, and dramatist, born in Paducah, Ky.; began newspaper work when very young as reporter and contributor to comic weeklies; at 19 editor of *Paducah Daily News;* correspondent in Europe 1914–15, 1917–18; stories of Kentucky life; humorous treatment of foibles of the day ('Old Judge Priest'; 'Speaking of Operations—'; 'Ladies and Gentlemen'; 'Incredible Truth'; 'Exit Laughing', autobiography).
Cobb, John Rhodes (1899–1952), English fur broker and automobile racer, born in Esher; became first man to travel 400 mph (640 kph) on land, 1947; killed in jet-propelled hydroplane in attempt to break world motorboat record.
Cobb, Ty (1886–1961), U.S. baseball outfielder C-530
Cobbett, William (pseudonym Peter Porcupine) (1763–1835), English journalist and reformer C-531
Cobbler fish (or threadfish), fish *Alectis crinitus* whose dorsal and anal fins have some rays longer than the body when young, wearing shorter with age; range, West Indies n. to Cape Cod.
Cobden, Richard (1804–65), English Liberal statesman and economist, strong advocate of free trade, peace, arbitration, and disarmament; in Parliament 1846–57; leader in Anti-Corn-Law league in 1839 and worked against corn laws until their repeal in 1846; concluded commercial treaty with France 1860; author of political leaflets.
Cobden-Sanderson, Thomas J. (1840–1922), English bookbinding designer, born in Alnwick B-355
Cobequid Mountains, in Nova Scotia N-399
Cobh (formerly Queenstown), Ireland, seaport in s.; pop. 5,613, *map* E-360
Cobham, Sir Alan John (1894–1973), British aviator; air pilot in World War I; stimulated popular interest in aviation; round-trip flights London–Rangoon, London–Cape Town, England–Australia; author of 'Skyways' and 'My Flight to the Cape and Back'.
Cobia. *see in index* Sergeant fish
Coblenz (or Koblenz), West Germany, city at confluence of Rhine and Moselle rivers; Moselle wine; headquarters of Allies after World War I; pop. 119,434, *map* G-131
COBOL (COmmon Business Oriented Language), programming operation codes C-635
Cobourg, Ont., port town on Lake Ontario, 62 mi (100 km) e. of Toronto; resort; foods, textiles, chemicals, metal products; pop. 11,282, *map* C-112
Cobra, venomous snake of India and Africa, *pictures* S-226. *see also in index* Snakebite
viper comparison V-328
zoo Z-465
Cobre, Barranca del, canyon in Mexico M-322
Coburg (or Koburg), West Germany, industrial city in Bavaria; formerly one of capitals of duchy of Saxe-Coburg-Gotha; interesting old castle and other medieval ruins; pop. 42,619, *map* G-131
Cobweb S-383, *pictures* S-382
Coca, Imogene, U.S. actress
Your Show of Shows T-69
Coca, shrub of flax family, yields cocaine P-222
Coca-Cola, carbonated beverage A-742
nuts N-449

Cocaine, white, bitter alkaloid made from coca leaves
  drugs D-276
  narcotics N-19
  Peru P-222
  poisoning P-411

Coccus (plural cocci), sphere-shaped bacterium, *picture* B-12

Coccyx, small bone in the adult human skeleton forming the tip of the spinal column below the sacrum S-209, *diagram* S-210

Cochabamba, Bolivia, manufacturing city and trade center of rich grain district in w.; pop. 91,017, *map* S-298

Cochet, Henri (1901–87), French tennis player T-107

Cochin, breed of poultry P-482

Cochin, former princely state in s. India on Malabar Coast; now part of Kerala state; 1,493 sq mi (3,867 sq km); in forest region; commercial center for coconut products, *picture* I-69, *map* I-83

Cochinchina (or Cochin China, or Cochinchine), the southern region of Vietnam during the French colonial period H-192

Cochio, early coach W-2

Cochise (1815?–74), Apache (Chiricahua) chief C-531
  American Indian history I-145

Cochise culture, prehistoric North American culture; named for Cochise County, Ariz., which in turn was named for Cochise, the Apache chief.

Cochiti, pueblo 23 mi (37 km) s.w. of Santa Fe, N.M., on the Rio Grande; Cochiti people belong to the Keresan language group of Pueblo Indians.

Cochlea, part of the ear E-3
  deafness D-48

Cochlear implant, procedure to aid the profoundly deaf D-48

Cochran, Elizabeth (or Elizabeth Cochrane). *see in index* Bly, Nellie

Cochran, Jacqueline (1910–80), U.S. aviator and cosmetics manufacturer C-531

Cochrane, Gordon Stanley (nickname Mickey) (1903–62), U.S. baseball catcher and manager, born in Bridgewater, Mass.; catcher Philadelphia, A.L., 1925–33, Detroit, A.L., 1934–37; fiery catcher and good hitter; managed Detroit pennant-winning teams 1934–35 B-88

Cochrane, Thomas, 10th earl of Dundonald (1775–1860), British admiral, born in Annsfield, Lanarkshire, Scotland; commanded ship in Napoleonic wars; expelled from navy; led navies of Chile, Brazil, and Greece; reinstated in British navy.

Cock, pile of hay H-75

Cockade fan F-22

Cockaigne, Land of, imaginary land of luxury, joy, and delightful feasts; subject of a 13th-century satirical poem.

Cockatoo, crested, parrot-like bird P-135, *picture* P-134

Cockatrice. *see in index* Basilisk

Cockburn, James (1819–83), Canadian statesman, born in Berwick-on-Tweed, England
  Fathers of Canadian
    Confederation C-115, *picture* C-116

Cockcroft, Sir John Douglas (1897–1967), English physicist, born in Todmorden; professor at Cambridge University 1939–46; director, British Atomic Energy Research Establishment 1946–58; master, Churchill College, Cambridge University 1959–67; won Atoms for Peace Award 1961; see also in index Nobel Prizewinners, *table*

Cockerell, Douglas Bennett (1870–1945), British bookbinder and type designer; pupil of Cobden-Sanderson, after whose retirement Cockerell was generally recognized as leading English binder ('Bookbinding and the Care of Books').

Cocker spaniel, dog D-193, *picture* D-198

Cockle, bivalved mollusk, especially common in tropical waters; the European cockle *Cardium edule* is a valuable shellfish; related to the oyster
  mollusks M-525

Cocklebur, weed *Xanthium pensylvanicum* W-131
  plant improvement, *picture* P-368
  poisonous seedling P-408

Cockney, term of disputed origin; now applied to a dialect identified with the East End of London L-289

Cock of the rock, South American bird *Rupicola*, about the size of a pigeon; orange-colored plumage; prominent crest; orange-red flesh; males woo females by dances and antics.

Cock of the woods. *see in index* Capercaillie

Cockpit, section of airplane
  glider G-165

Cockpit Country, region in Jamaica J-17

Cockran, William Bourke (1854–1923), U.S. lawyer and political leader, born in Ireland; member of Congress; active in Democratic party politics; prominent orator.

Cockroach, insect C-531
  Carboniferous period A-461
  insects, *picture* I-213

Cockscomb, annual plant *Celosia* of the amaranth family; flower heads either plumy or crested, red, yellow, or purple; leaves sometimes colored.

Cocoa, Fla., city 65 mi (105 km) s.e. of Daytona Beach; aircraft; space technology center; satellite launching site nearby; pop. 16,110.

Cocoa, plant
  Abidjan A-9
  chocolate C-394
  Ghana G-139

Cocoa butter C-394

Cocoa powder C-394

Coconut palm P-81, *picture* P-82
  fruitgrowing F-436
  margarine M-134
  producing areas
    Kiribati K-250
    Oceania O-470, *pictures* O-472, P-12
    Philippines P-256
  seed, *pictures* P-8, 18, P-256
    dispersal S-106, *diagram* S-107

Cocoon, envelope, often largely of silk, which an insect larva forms around itself
  ant A-469
  caterpillar C-220
  metamorphosis M-312
  moth B-525, *pictures* B-522
  pupa P-534
  silkworm S-198
  spider S-383

Cocoon, of mudfish and lungfish M-644

Cocopa, American Indian people of the Yuman family living in the valley of the Rio Colorado in Lower California.

Cocos Island, Pacific Ocean, about 600 mi (950 km) s.w. of Panama Canal and 500 mi (800 km) n. of Galápagos Islands; 10 sq mi (17 sq km); belongs to Costa Rica; visited by expeditions in search of pirate treasure; airport, *map* W-297

Cocos Islands (or Keeling Islands), group of 27 small coral islands in Indian Ocean s.w. of Java; 5½ sq mi (14.2 sq km); incorporated with Singapore 1903; became territory of Australia 1955; merged with Australia 1984; air base; pop. 700 A-823, *maps* A-697, W-297
  Commonwealth membership C-602

Cocteau, Jean (1889–1963), French poet, essayist, novelist, and playwright C-532
  drama D-247

Cod, one of the world's most important food fishes C-533
  average life expectancy, *chart* A-423
  fisheries, *table* F-136
  Iceland I-11
  food cycle F-124, *picture* F-132
  haddock H-4
  pollack P-440

Coda, in music, *list* M-670

Coddington, William (1601–78), North American colonial governor, born in Lincolnshire, England; came to America 1630; first governor of Rhode Island 1640; founded Portsmouth and Newport, R.I. R-185

Code C-416. *see also in index* Cipher
  signaling S-194

Code, law. *see in index under* Law, *subhead* historic codes

Codeine, narcotic drug ($C_{18}H_{21}NO_3$) composed of morphine methyl ether and the equivalent of a molecule of water in chemical combination
  analgesia A-387
  narcotic N-19
  opium O-572
  poisoning P-411

Code Napoléon L-94

'Code of Hammurabi', collection of Babylonian laws developed during the reign of Hammurabi (1792–1750 BC) M-281

'Code of Justinian' (or 'Corpus Juris Civilis'), legal code J-161

'Code of Terpsichore', work by Blasis B-34, D-27

Codex, early form of book B-345
  Leonardo da Vinci L-134

Codex Alimentarius Commission, food quality control commission set up by United Nations
  food and drug laws F-274

'Codex Constitutionum', legal collection
  Justinian code J-161

Codex Juris Canonici, canon law C-142

Codex Sinaiticus B-350, *picture* B-183

Codicil, addition to a will
  legal definition, *table* L-92

Codification, in law
  international law I-257

Coding, task of writing computer instructions C-627

Codling moth (or codlin moth), insect parent of apple worm
  winter survival B-526

Codon, part of the genetic code G-56

C.O.D. system, type of delivery of merchandise E-382

Cody, John Patrick, Cardinal (1907–82), Roman Catholic prelate, born in St. Louis, Mo.; bishop of Kansas City-St. Joseph 1956–61; archbishop of New Orleans 1961–65, of Chicago 1965–82; created cardinal 1967; first American to serve in Vatican Prefecture of Economic Affairs, appointed 1972.

Cody, William Frederick. *see in index* Buffalo Bill

Cody, Wyo., city on Shoshone River, in n.w. part of state, about 50 mi (80 km) e. of Yellowstone National Park; in livestock area; oil refining; near Buffalo Bill Dam; pop. 6,790.

Coecke van Aelst, Pieter (1502–50), Flemish painter B-468

Coe College, Cedar Rapids, Iowa; incorporated 1851 as Cedar Rapids Collegiate Institute; private control; liberal arts and education.

Coefficient of linear expansion H-104

Coelacanth, fish F-132

Coelenterata (or coelenterates), animal phylum including coral, hydra, jellyfish, and sea anemone A-433
  frog anatomy F-406
  invertebrate group I-282

Coelom, mesodermally lined body cavity
  invertebrate anatomy I-283
    mollusks M-523
  vertebrates E-200, *chart* E-202, *diagram* E-202

Coenzyme, in biochemistry
  protein link E-290
  vitamins V-358

Coetzee, Gerri, holder of heavyweight boxing title 1983– B-392

Coeur d'Alene, Idaho, city on Coeur d'Alene Lake, 30 mi (50 km) e. of Spokane, Wash.; farming and livestock interest; lumber manufactures, aluminum products; resort for fishing, hunting, winter sports; pop. 20,054, *map* I-30

COFC (Container-on-flatcar), container cargo transportation T-255

Coffee C-533
  Bedouin Arab ritual E-318
  producing regions
    Central America C-255, *picture* C-257
      Costa Rica C-734, *picture* N-345
      El Salvador E-196, S-32
      Guatemala G-297, G-300
    Hawaii H-61, *map* H-64
    South America
      Brazil B-421
      Colombia C-551, *picture* C-553
      Venezuela V-275
  substitutes P-333

Coffeehouses C-537

Cofferdams, watertight enclosures D-15

Coffeyville, Kan., city in s.e. part of state, just n. of Oklahoma line; oil refineries, lead and zinc oxide smelters; foundries, oil-field equipment; pop. 15,185, *map* U-41

Coffin, Henry Sloane (1877–1954), U.S. clergyman, author, born in New York, N.Y.; pastor Madison Avenue Presbyterian Church, New York, N.Y., 1905–26; president Union Theological Seminary 1926–45; moderator Presbyterian Church in U.S. 1943–44.

Coffin, Lucretia. *see in index* Mott, Lucretia

Coffin, Robert Peter Tristram (1892–1955), U.S. writer, teacher, and lecturer, born in Brunswick, Me.; at Bowdoin College after 1934; Pulitzer prize (1936) for poetry, 'Strange Holiness' ('Primer for America', 'People Behave Like Ballads', poetry; 'Kennebec, Cradle of Americans' and 'Yankee Coast', books about Maine; 'Lost Paradise', autobiography).

Coffin texts, ancient Egyptian literature E-131

Cogeneration, simultaneous generation of electrical energy and low-grade heat from the same fuel E-169

Cognac, France, old town in s.w., famous for brandy which bears its name; on Charente River; pop. 21,137, *map* F-369

Cognac, brandy A-276, L-235

Cognitive learning L-106

Cognomen, a hereditary name N-6

Cogon, two tough coarse grasses of genus *Imperata*; used for thatching in Philippines; grown in some s. states, chiefly Florida.

Cogonales, cogon grasslands in Philippines P-259b

Cohan, George M. (1878–1942), U.S. actor, playwright, producer, and songwriter C-537, *picture* R-190
  creative writing W-382
  musical comedy M-685

Cohen, Judy. *see in index* Chicago, Judy

Cohen, Leonard Norman (born 1934), Canadian poet; also a novelist, musician, songwriter, and recording artist.

Cohen, Octavus Roy (1891–1959), U.S. writer, born in Charleston, S.C.; best known for stories of black Southerners ('Epic Peters, Pullman Porter'; 'Florian Slappey') and for detective fiction.

Cohen, Wilbur Joseph (1913–87), U.S. public official, born in Milwaukee, Wis.; helped draft Social Security Act of 1935 and enact medicare 1965; professor public welfare administration University of Michigan 1956–61, dean school of education 1969–; assistant U.S. secretary of health, education, and welfare 1961–65, undersecretary 1965–68, secretary 1968–69.

Cohesion, in physics, attraction between molecules.

Cohn, Edwin Joseph (1892–1953), U.S. biochemist, born in New York, N.Y.; joined faculty of Harvard University 1922, professor after 1935; conducted important researches in separation of blood fractions, notably the isolation of albumin.

Cohn, Ferdinand Julius (1828–98), German botanist, born in Breslau; often regarded as founder of bacteriology; showed how to study life histories of algae and fungi; proved that bacteria are plants.

Cohoba, form of snuff H-18

Cohoes, N.Y., manufacturing city 9 mi (14 km) n. of Albany, on Mohawk and Hudson rivers and on Erie Canal; abundant waterpower from Mohawk Falls; paper products, textiles and textile products; pop. 18,144.

Cohort, unit of Roman legion A-637

Coho salmon (or silver salmon), fish S-28

Cohune nut, fruit of a Central and South American palm N-449

chief, leader in raids (1835–63) on whites in Arizona, New Mexico, and w. Texas; was taken prisoner after battle of Apache Pass; killed by his guards.
Color Additives Amendment (1960), U.S. legislation F-274
Colorado, Rocky Mountain state of U.S.; 104,247 sq mi (269,998 sq km); cap. Denver; pop. 2,888,834 C-567, *maps* C-582, N-350, U-40, 80
Denver D-103
physical geography
Rio Grande R-209
Rockies R-234
rainfall R-89
statehood S-429c, *table* S-428
state symbols
flag, *picture* F-159
flower, *pictures* S-427, P-359
tree S-398
Statuary Hall, *table* S-437a
taxation, *tables* T-37, 39
Colorado, University of, in Boulder, Colorado Springs, and Denver, Colo.; state control; opened 1877; arts and sciences, architecture, business, dentistry, education, engineering, journalism, law, medicine, music, nursing, pharmacy; graduate school C-571, *picture* C-575
Denver D-103
Colorado-Big Thompson Project, water diversion project in Colorado C-569, C-584
Colorado Chiquito (or Little Colorado), river in Arizona, one of chief tributaries of Colorado River, *map* A-546
Colorado College, Colorado Springs, Colo.; private control; founded 1874; arts and sciences, education, fine arts, social sciences; graduate studies.
Colorado Desert, in s.e. California, extends into n. Lower California, Mexico
California C-35, *map* C-34
Colorado Plateau, tableland w. of the Rockies U-84, *map* E-25
Arizona A-597
Colorado C-568
New Mexico N-214
Utah U-216, *map* U-217
Colorado potato beetle. *see in index* potato bug
Colorado River, in Argentina, rises in e. slopes of Andes, flows s.e. 620 mi (1,000 km) into Atlantic A-576, *maps* A-585, S-297
Colorado River (sometimes called Eastern Colorado River), in Texas; flows 900 mi (1,450 km) s.e. into Gulf of Mexico through Matagorda Bay, *maps* M-341, N-350, U-40, 62
Colorado River, in western U.S.; flows 1,470 mi (2,365 km) through Colorado, Utah, Arizona, and Mexico C-584, *maps* C-583, 585, N-350, U-40, 81. *see also in index* Colorado-Big Thompson Project; Grand Canyon; Hoover Dam
Arizona's boundary A-596
California's water supply, *pictures* A-466
dam D-11
Grand Canyon E-16, G-212
hydroelectric power E-166
Imperial Valley's water source I-59
national parks and monuments U-224, *map* U-233
Nevada N-133, *picture* N-143
river system, *map* U-32
Colorado River Aqueduct, in s.w. United States
aqueducts A-520
Colorado River C-584
Colorados, political party in Uruguay U-214
Colorado School of Mines (formerly Jarvis College), in Golden, Colo.; state control; founded 1874; professional degrees in geological, geophysical, metallurgical, and mineral and petroleum engineering; graduate school C-571, D-103
Colorado Springs, Colo., 2nd city of state, at foot of Pikes Peak, about 65 mi (105 km) s. of Denver; altitude 6,000 ft (1,800 m); health and pleasure resort; airplane equipment, electronics, chemicals, tools and dies; Colorado College; branch of University of Colorado; Fort Carson and NORAD Command Operations Center; Garden of the Gods nearby; pop. 215,150 C-586, *map* N-350
Colorado C-570, *picture* C-568, *maps* C-583, U-40
Colorado spruce (or blue spruce), tree of the pine family S-398
Colorado State University, in Fort Collins, Colo.; founded 1870, opened 1879; arts and sciences, agriculture, education, engineering, forestry and range management, home economics, veterinary medicine; graduate school.
Colorado Women's College (formerly Temple Buell College), in Denver, Colo.; American Baptist Church; founded 1888; liberal arts, education D-103
Coloration, animal and plant. *see in index* Biological coloration
Coloratura, in vocal music
Lind L-226
Color blindness (or Daltonism), disorder of the eyes
abnormal color vision C-563
eye E-391
Color compensating filter, photographic equipment P-287
Color film, in photography P-290, 295
Color filter, transparent object C-559
photography P-287, 295, *picture* P-284
Colorimetry (or color measurement), study of color C-559
bioengineering B-210
Coloring, hair H-8
Coloring books R-101d
Color photography P-286, 295
Maxwell M-234
techniques C-565
Color printing. *see in index* Printing
Color television. *see in index* Television, *subhead* color
Colosimo, Jim, U.S. mobster C-153
Colosseum (or Coliseum, originally called Flavian Amphitheater), amphitheater in Rome, Italy, *pictures* E-347, I-386
acid rain corrosion A-19
Rome R-257, *pictures* R-254, 256, *map* R-250
Colossians, Epistle to the, 12th book of the Bible's New Testament, written by Paul to the Christians at Colossae, Asia Minor.
Colossi of Memnon E-126
'Colossus', work by Goya, *picture* G-203
Colossus of Rhodes, one of the Seven Wonders of the World R-196, S-115
Colostrum, thin fluid secreted from mother's breasts a few days before and after birth of child; has high content of lactalbumin (a protein found also in milk) M-414
Colt, Samuel (1814–62), U.S. firearms inventor C-587
firearms F-99, *picture* F-97
Hartford, Conn. H-51
machine gun M-12
warfare W-20
Colt, young male horse, *list* H-249
furs F-463
Colter, John (1775?–1813), U.S. explorer and trapper; member of Lewis and Clark Expedition (1803–6); joined Manuel Lisa's party and was sent (1807) as messenger to American Indians south of the Yellowstone
Wyoming W-390
Colton, Calif., city 3 mi (5 km) s.w. of San Bernardino; railroad yards; cement, metal products, plumbing fixtures; fruit packing and shipping; pop. 27,419.
Coltrane, John (1926–67), U.S. jazz saxophonist C-587
jazz J-88
Coltsfoot, small herb *Tussilago farfara* of the composite family used in medicine as remedy for coughs; has heads of yellow flowers, similar to dandelion.
Colum, Padraic (1881–1972), Irish writer, born in Longford, Ireland; associated with Irish Theater movement; his wife, **Mary Maguire Colum** (1887–1957), Irish literary critic and author of 'From These Roots'; in U.S. after 1914 ('Collected Poems'; books for children: 'The Children of Odin' and 'The Golden Fleece and the Heroes Who Lived Before Achilles'; editor of 'A Treasury of Irish Folklore'; 'The Flying Swans'); awarded Regina Medal 1961 R-111, S-479
Irish literature I-328, *picture* I-327
Columba, Saint (or Saint Colm, also called Columkille) (521–597), Irish missionary to Picts and Scots; called Columkille ("Colum of the churches") for great number of churches and monasteries he founded; festival June 9.
Columba, constellation, *charts* C-682, S-421
Columbia, Mo., city near center, in farming and coal area, 10 mi (16 km) n. of Missouri River; insurance; Stephens College; pop. 62,061 M-491, 500, *picture* M-497, *map* U-41
Columbia, Ohio. *see in index* Cincinnati
Columbia, Pa., borough about 26 mi (42 km) s.e. of Harrisburg, on Susquehanna River; metal products, silk, clothing, vending machines, tobacco products; founded by Quakers 1726; pop. 10,466, *map* P-185
Columbia, S.C., state capital and largest city of state, in center, on Congaree River; pop. 100,385 C-587, *pictures* S-313, *maps* N-350, S-307, 318, U-41
Columbia, Tenn., city on Duck River, 42 mi (68 km) s.w. of Nashville; agriculture, livestock markets; metal fabrication, phosphate mining and processing; apparel, electrodes; pop. 25,767, *map* U-41
Polk's family home, *picture* P-437
'Columbia', Apollo 11 spacecraft command module S-341
'Columbia', U.S. space shuttle S-347, *picture* E-227, *table* S-348
Columbia, Mount, in Jasper National Park, Alberta; second highest peak (12,294 ft; 3,747 m) in Canadian Rockies A-264
'Columbia, the Gem of the Ocean', U.S. patriotic song N-65
Columbia Basin, plateau in Oregon O-582
Columbia Basin Project, irrigation project on Columbia River G-213, W-49
Columbia Broadcasting System (CBS)
radio R-56
television T-69, 73
Columbia College, Columbia, S.C.; affiliated with United Methodist church; founded 1854; arts and sciences, education.
Columbia Heights, Minn., city on Mississippi River, just n. of Minneapolis; air compressors, hydraulic equipment; incorporated 1921; pop. 23,837.
Columbia Ice Field, in Alberta A-264, *picture* A-267
Columbia Institution for the Deaf. *see in index* Gallaudet College
Columbian College. *see in index* George Washington University
Columbian Exposition. *see in index* World's Columbian Exposition
Columbian Order. *see in index* Tammany Hall
Columbia Plateau, in North America, *map* E-25
Idaho I-18, *map* I-19
Nevada N-133
Washington W-48, *map* W-49
wheat production U-84, *picture* U-85
Columbia River (formerly Oregon River), one of largest rivers of North America; in British Columbia, Washington, Oregon C-588, *maps* C-109, N-350
Astoria Bridge, *table* B-324c
basalt deposits B-86
Cascade Range C-195
dams D-14
Grand Coulee Dam G-213, *picture* W-59
hydroelectric power E-166
waterpower W-106
explorations
Lewis and Clark L-143
Thompson T-172
Oregon O-582, *pictures* O-583, 584
salmon S-28
United States U-32, *map* U-90
Washington W-48, 51, *picture* W-58, *map* W-49
world, *map* W-297
Columbia River Treaty (1964), United States and Canada C-588
Columbia Union College, in Takoma Park, Md., Seventh-Day Adventist; founded 1904; arts and sciences, education, nursing; graduate studies; trimester system.
Columbia University (formerly King's College), in New York, N.Y.; private control; founded 1754; undergraduate courses in Columbia College (men) and School of General Studies (adult education); graduate and professional schools of architecture, business, dental and oral surgery, dramatic arts, engineering, international affairs, journalism, law, library service, medicine, nursing, painting and sculpture, public health, social work; nonprofessional graduate faculties of philosophy, political science, pure science; affiliated institutions: Barnard College (women), Teachers College, College of Pharmacy N-254, N-273, *picture* N-280
journalism school N-242
literary awards L-241
Columbiformes, order of small-headed, full-breasted birds, including the family Columbidae (doves and pigeons). *see also in index* Pigeons and doves
Columbine, dancing character in Italian comedy and pantomime; first appeared about 1560; daughter of Pantaloon; wife or sweetheart of Harlequin; later appeared in English pantomime
mime M-423
Columbine, flower of Ranunculaceae family, genus *Aquilegia* C-590, *picture* P-359
Colorado's state flower, *picture* S-427
flowering time G-25
Columbite, mineral ore of the element niobium; distinguished from the ore tantalite by containing more niobium than tantalum.
Columbium. *see in index* Niobium
Columbus, Bartholomew (1445?–1515?), Italian explorer and cartographer; brother of Christopher Columbus; sent to interest Henry VII of England in aiding Christopher but was captured by pirates; founded Santo Domingo 1496 C-590
Dominican Republic D-227
Columbus, Christopher (1451–1506), Italian explorer and navigator C-590
caravel ships N-82
diary L-68
exploration E-373
America A-330, *picture* A-327
Havana H-56
Hispaniola H-169
Honduras H-227
Latin America L-66
Puerto Rico P-530, *picture* P-530b
Trinidad and Tobago T-289
Virgin Islands V-351
West Indies W-155, *picture* U-130
Ferdinand and Isabella F-55
flag F-153, *picture* F-155
international trade I-270, E-47
migration of people M-403
navigation N-78
Polo's influence C-367
Seville, S-119
statue, *picture* N-149
wool W-287
Columbus, Diego (1480–1526), eldest son of Christopher Columbus, governor of Indies (original name of America) C-591
Columbus, Ferdinand (1488–1539), son of Christopher Columbus whom he accompanied on 4th voyage to Western Hemisphere in 1502; wrote biography of father.
Columbus, Ga., 2nd city of state, on w. border, at head of navigation on Chattahoochee River, opposite Phenix City, Ala.; immense waterpower; textile industries, food processing; Columbus College; Fort Benning nearby; pop. 169,441 C-594, G-87, *maps* N-350, U-41
Columbus, Ind., city on East Fork of White River, 42 mi (68 km) s. of Indianapolis;

diesel engines, automotive parts, electronic products, metal furniture, machinery control mechanisms; noted for outstanding modern architecture; pop. 30,292, *map* I-102

Columbus, Ky., town 17 mi (27 km) s. of Cairo, Ill., on Mississippi River; in farm area; Confederate stronghold in 1861; pop. 296.

Columbus, Miss., trade center for rich farming region and manufacturing city on Tombigbee River, 8 mi (13 km) w. of Alabama border; garments, furniture, automotive electrical motors, metal buildings; marble cutting; Mississippi University for Women; Columbus Air Force Base; pop. 27,383, *map* U-41

Columbus, Neb., city 75 mi (120 km) n.w. of Omaha, at junction of Loup and Platte rivers; livestock; grain and dairy farms; machine shops; surgical supplies; pop. 17,328 N-104

Columbus, Ohio, state capital and 2nd city of state, on Scioto River; pop. 564,871 C-594, *maps* N-350, U-41
Ohio O-500, 512, *pictures* O-502, 509

Columbus College, Columbus, Ga; state control; founded 1958; liberal arts, education; graduate study; off-campus center at Fort Benning C-594

Columkille. *see in index* Columba, Saint

Column, battle formation W-22

Column, vertical shaft, or pillar, used in building
Greek A-547
Roman A-492
Column of Trajan, *picture* G-273, *map* R-250
Marcus Aurelius' R-255, *picture* R-253

Column chromatography, chemical analysis C-202

Column diagram. *see in index* Histogram

Colvin, Sir Sidney (1845–1927), English critic; keeper of prints and drawings in British Museum 1884–1912; wrote lives of Walter Savage Landor and John Keats for 'English Men of Letters' series.

Colymbiformes, order of diving birds, including the grebes. *see in index* Grebe

Coma, head of a comet C-596, S-254c

Coma, physical disorder, deep state of unconsciousness C-595
diabetes D-180

Coma Berenices, constellation. *see in index* Berenice

Comanche, American Plains Indians of Shoshonean ancestry; formerly warlike and nomadic, traveling from Arkansas River to Mexico, *map* I-136, *table* I-138
Oklahoma O-525
Texas T-118

'Comanche Mounted War Party', painting by Catlin, *picture* C-223

Comaneci, Nadia (born 1962), Romanian athlete, born in Gheorghe Gheorghiu-Dej; won three gold medals for gymnastics in 1976 Olympic Games A-741, O-542
gymnastics G-323

Comayagua, Honduras, colonial capital; located in fertile valley; commercial center for w. Honduras; pop. 51,578 H-227

Comayagua Valley, Honduras H-225

Comb, in hairdressing H-8

Comb honey. *see in index* Honeycomb

Combat arms, U.S. Army A-646

Combat service support arms, U.S. Army A-646

Combat support arms, U.S. Army A-646

Combe Capelle man, human ancestor M-90

Comber test, soil acidity S-253

Combes, Justin Louis Émile (1835–1921), French statesman; as premier (1902–05) enforced law suppressing religious orders and took steps for church-state separation.

Comb honey, a honey product H-228

Combination, in business. *see in index* Monopoly; Trust, industrial

Combination lock (or dial lock) L-277

Combination square, tool T-218

Combine, in business. *see in index* Cartel

Combine, harvester and thresher, *pictures* P-191, S-269, S-324
farm machinery F-34, *picture* F-35
Illinois' harvest, *picture* I-33
wheat W-188

Combined command, U.S. Army A-644

Combing, fiber
flax fiber processing F-177

Comb jelly, jellyfishlike animal in the phylum Ctenophora
invertebrate group I-282

Combs, Earle Bryan (1899–1976), U.S. baseball outfielder, born in Pebworth, Ky.; with New York, A.L., 1924–35, lifetime batting average .325.

Combustion (or burning) F-93
Bunsen burner B-374, *picture* B-375
explosion E-378
heat H-102
Lavoisier S-57j
oxygen O-623
phlogiston theory S-57i
toxic waste W-76

Combustion boiler F-451

Combustion chamber, engine component
heating systems H-108
jet propulsion J-106

Comden, Betty (born 1919), musical comedy writer, born in Brooklyn, N.Y.; together with Adolf Green wrote librettos and scripts for many broadway shows and Hollywood film musicals, including 'Singin' in the Rain' (1952) M-685

Comecon. *see in index* Council for Mutual Economic Assistance

'Come Dance with Kitty Stobling', work by Kavanagh I-328

Comedy, type of drama A-26
Benny B-163
comedy of manners A-610, M-522
drama D-241
Greek literature G-276
Aristophanes A-588
Gwyn G-322
horror story H-246
humor H-323

'Comedy of Errors, The', play by Shakespeare; plot based on likeness between twin brothers and their two servants S-133

Comedy of manners (or artificial comedy), sophisticated subtle comedy D-242
Molière M-522

Comenius, John ([illegible] Jan Amos Komensky) (1592–1670), Moravian bishop and educator C-596
children's literature L-245
educational contribution E-85
'Orbis Pictus', *picture* R-124

Comet C-596. *see also in index* Comets by name; *see table* following
astronomy A-712
earth E-8
meteor M-315
origins P-355
solar system S-254, *pictures* S-254d, *diagram* S-254c

Comic book C-186

Comic opera, musical play with light subject matter and happy ending; dialogue is usually spoken rather than sung
classical music M-674
musical comedy M-685
opera O-560, 566

Comic strip
cartoons C-186
drawing D-256
fables F-4
Feiffer F-52

Comines, Philippe de (or Philippe de Commines, or Philippe de Commynes) (1445?–1511), French historian, born near Courtrai, Belgium F-394

Cominform. *see in index* Information Bureau of the Communist and Workers' Parties

'Coming of Age in Samoa', work by Mead M-241

Comino, island of Malta; 1 sq mi (2.6 sq km); pop. 30 M-78, *map* I-404

Cominotto, island of Malta M-78

Comintern, term popularly applied to the Third International (Communist). *see in index* Third International

Comiskey, Charles Albert (nickname Old Roman) (1859–1931), U.S. baseball first baseman and manager, born in Chicago, Ill.; with 6 teams 1882–94; pioneered modern first base defensive play away from the base; owner and president Chicago, A.L., 1900–31.

Comitia curiata, Roman assembly R-242
democracy D-92

Comitia tributa, Roman assembly R-244

Comma, punctuation mark P-534

Commager, Henry Steele (born 1902), U.S. historian, born in Pittsburgh, Pa.; professor at Columbia University 1939–56, at Amherst College 1956–; wrote history and biography (for younger readers: 'America's Robert E. Lee'; 'The First Book of American History'; 'The Great Declaration'; 'The Great Proclamation'; 'The Constitution'; 'Crusaders for Freedom'); inducted into American Academy of Arts and Letters 1970 H-174

Commander, U.S. Navy, *table* A-584
insignia, *picture* U-8

Commander Islands. *see in index* Komandorskiye Islands

Command fuze, weaponry B-338

Command module, in Apollo spacecraft S-346b, *diagrams* S-346c

Commando Brigade, principal operating unit of Great Britain's Royal Marines M-137

Commandos, Portuguese word meaning small bands of armed men, in Boer War guerrilla bands fighting against the English; in World War II bands of Allied volunteers specially trained to raid inside enemy territory; in Korean War and Suez crisis were used by British M-137

Commedia dell'arte A-26, T-159
masks M-187

Commelinaceae. *see in index* Spiderwort family

Commemorative stamp P-462b

Commencement, in education
college and university U-205

Commensal, living organism that forms partnership with another. *see in index* Symbiosis

'Commentaries', work by Blackstone L-94

'Commentaries on American Law', four volume work by Kent K-207

'Commentaries on the "Chun-ch'iu" ', Confucian classics in Chinese literature C-387

'Commentary on the Book of Habakkuk', Dead Sea scroll D-46

'Commentary on the Water Classic', book by Li Tao-yüan C-388

Commerce. *see in index* Trade

Commerce, Department of, United States R-285, U-162, *list* U-157. *see also in index* Census, Bureau of the; Standards, National Bureau of
international trade I-268
Maritime Administration S-176
Patent Office P-[illegible]

SOME HISTORIC COMETS

Name	*First Seen*	*Period of Orbit*
Halley	240 BC	76.09
Tycho Brahe	AD 1577	. . .
Lexell	1770	5.60
Biela	1772	6.62
Encke	1786	3.30
Pons-Winnecke	1819	6.34
Wolf	1884	8.43
Schwassmann-Wachmann I	1925	15.03
Arend-Roland	1957	. .
Ikeya-Seki	1965	879.88
Tago-Sato-Kosaka	1969	420,000
Bennett	1970	1,680
Kohoutek	1973	75,000
West	1976	500,000
IRAS-Araki-Alcott	1983	. . .

Commerce City (formerly Derby), Colo., community n. of Denver, on South Platte River; oil refining, steel manufacture, flour milling; incorporated as town 1952, city 1962; pop. 17,407.

Commercial, in advertising A-57
television T-73

Commercial art D-256

Commercial aviation A-877

Commercial credit C-761

Commercial law, rules and usages governing trade
contract C-693

Commercial port H-35

Commines, Philippe de. *see in index* Comines, Philippe de

Comminuted fracture, break in bone F-340

Commissioned officer, in military
United States
Army A-634
Navy N-80

Commission for Relief in Belgium H-233

Commission government, municipal government with commissioners elected at large, each heading a city department, enacting laws in common; deficiencies include lack of central control and lack of technical qualifications by commissioners C-459
municipal government M-655

Commission Internationale de l'Éclairage (CIE) C-561

Commission on Civil Rights, U.S. national government; created 1957 to examine complaints that persons have been denied civil rights; its members and staff director appointed by president with consent of Senate.

Committee
clubs and societies P-132a

Committee for Industrial Organization. *see in index* Congress of Industrial Organizations

Committee for the Abolition of the Slave Trade
Wilberforce W-203

Committee of Public Safety, French ruling body
French Revolution F-403
Robespierre R-223

Committee of State Security, U.S.S.R. *see in index* KGB

Committee on Space Research S-348a

Committees of Correspondence, committees spreading information in North American Colonies R-166

Commode, piece of furniture, *picture* F-457

Commodity Credit Corporation (CCC), U.S. A-142, R-265, U-162

Commodity exchange C-597
money M-531

Commodore, in U.S. Navy; rank used in wartime; equivalent to brigadier general; abolished 1899 but restored 1943, *picture* U-8

Commodus, Lucius Aelius Aurelius (AD 161–192), Roman emperor 180–192, son of Marcus Aurelius; a brutal tyrant; exhibited physical prowess in gladiatorial shows; assassinated.

self-help for black Americans B-296
Congress of Soviets, U.S.S.R. *see in index* Supreme Soviet
Congress of the United States, legislative branch of the government, composed of Senate and House of Representatives. *see also in index* Representatives, House of; Senate, U.S.; *see tables* following
Australian Parliament P-130
black members, *table* B-298
conscription C-668
constitution U-142
consumer protection C-687
government agencies G-200
law and legislation L-94
president P-493, U-154
veto power V-307
Washington, D.C. W-70
Congress of Vienna. *see in index* Vienna, Congress of
Congreve, William (1670–1729), English dramatist C-648
Congreve, Sir William (1772–1828), English artillerist
rocket R-232
Conicosia, perennial plant *Conicosia pugionformis* of the carpetweed family, native to s. Africa; leaves alternate, long, narrow, 3-sided, soft; flowers large, yellow, in clusters.
Conic projection, map M-123, *picture* 124
Conic sections, curves formed by the intersection of a right circular cone with a plane; an intersection parallel to the base of the cone gives a circle, an intersection parallel to a side of the cone gives a parabola, an intersection between these positions gives an ellipse; if the plane is parallel to the perpendicular from vertex to base but not through the vertex, the curve is a hyperbola; discovered by Menaechmus (4th century BC), properties elaborated by Apollonius and Archimedes. *see also in index* the curves named above
Apollonius A-506
geometry G-77
Hamilton H-22
mathematics M-214
Conifer (or coniferous tree), cone-bearing trees T-276
drugs P-377
forests F-309
juniper J-157
Conjugal family F-15
Conjunction, part of speech connecting word groups or words that are grammatically alike—*i.e.,* two adjectives; the most common are *and, but,* and *or*; the clauses they connect can be part of the same sentence or two separate sentences
part of speech G-210
Conjunctiva, part of the eye E-387
Conjunctivitis, disease of the eye E-390
Conjuring. *see in index* Magic
Conklin, Edwin Grant (1863–1952), U.S. biologist, born in Waldo, Ohio; professor biology Princeton University 1908–33; important work in embryology and cytology and in mechanism of heredity and evolution.
Conkling, Roscoe (1829–88), U.S. lawyer and political leader, born in Albany, N.Y.; member of House of Representatives 1859–63, 1865–67; U.S. senator 1867–81
Arthur A-652
Garfield G-30
Hayes H-79
Conlan, John Bertrand (nickname Jocko) (born 1899), U.S. baseball umpire, born in Chicago, Ill.; player Chicago A.L. 1934–35; N.L. umpire 1941–64; umpired six All-Star games, six World Series.
Conn, Bill (born 1917), U.S. boxer, *picture* L-307
Connally, John Bowden, Jr. (born 1917), U.S. lawyer, government official, born in Floresville, Tex.; naval officer World War II; managed Lyndon B. Johnson's campaigns for U.S. senator 1948 and for president of U.S. 1956 and 1960; secretary of the Navy 1961; governor of Texas 1963–69; secretary of the treasury 1971–72; switched from Democratic party to Republican 1973; special adviser to the president on domestic and foreign affairs 1973
Kennedy's assassination K-203, T-125
Nixon N-326
Connally, Tom (or Thomas Terry Connally) (1877–1963), U.S. political leader, born in McLennan County, Tex.; Democratic representative from Texas 1917–28; U.S. senator 1929–52; autobiography, 'My Name Is Tom Connally'.
Connaught, Arthur, duke of (1850–1942), British military officer, 3rd son of Queen Victoria; commander in chief in Ireland and in Mediterranean; governor-general of Canada 1911–16; father of Lady Patricia Ramsay ("Princess Pat").
Connaught (or Connacht), province of w. Ireland; area 6,611 sq mi (17,122 sq km); pop. 401,950.
Connaught Place, shopping center, in New Delhi, India D-86
Conneaut, Ohio, city in extreme n.e. part of state, on Lake Erie; iron ore and coal port; electronics, leather, machine tools, plastics; pop. 13,835.
Connecticut, southernmost of New England states; 5,009 sq mi (12,973 sq km); cap. Hartford; pop. 3,107,576 C-649, *map* N-350
aviation regulations A-881
cities. *see also in index* cities listed below and other cities by name
Bridgeport B-448
Hartford H-51
New London N-212
Stratford S-484a
Waterbury W-94
state symbols
bird R-223. *see also in index* Robin
flag, *picture* F-159
flower, *picture* S-427
Statuary Hall, *table* S-437a
taxation, *tables* T-37, 39
United States U-43, *maps* U-41, 44, *pictures* U-45, *Reference-Outline* U-132
Wyoming Valley dispute P-173
Connecticut, University of, Storrs, Conn.; state control; founded 1881; liberal arts and sciences, agriculture, business administration, dentistry, education, engineering, fine arts, home economics, insurance, law, medicine, nursing, pharmacy, physical education, physical therapy, social work; graduate school; branches at Groton, Hartford, Stamford, Torrington, and Waterbury C-653, *picture* C-657
Connecticut College, New London, Conn.; private control; chartered 1911, opened 1915; liberal arts, education; graduate school C-653, N-212
Connecticut Compromise, U.S. Constitutional Convention U-141
Connecticut River, largest stream in New England; rises in n. New Hampshire, flows s., forming boundary with Vermont, *map* U-44
Massachusetts M-190
Springfield S-397
New Hampshire N-176, *map* N-191
Vermont V-286
Connective tissue, tissue of mesodermal origin, *picture* C-238
meat M-246
skin S-210
Connector, in grammar P-491
Connellsville, Pa., city 36 mi (58 km) s.e. of Pittsburgh, on Youghiogheny River; coal and coke; railroad shops; glass and metal products, textiles; pop. 10,319, *map* P-184
Connelly, Marcus (1890–1980), U.S. dramatist, born in McKeesport, Pa.; began as reporter on *Pittsburgh Sun*; with George Kaufman wrote 'Dulcy', 'Beggar on Horseback'; Pulitzer prize (1930) for 'Green Pastures'; 'A Souvenir from Qam', novel; 'Voices Offstage', memoirs A-356
Connelly's Tavern, Natchez, Miss., *picture* M-471
Connemara, Ireland, coastal district of w. County Galway; mountains contain rich mineral deposits; famed for marble.
Connersville, Ind., city about 55 mi (90 km) e. of Indianapolis; kitchen equipment, fabricated metal products; pop. 17,023, *map* I-102
Conning tower, large housing on a submarine S-497
Connolly, Maureen Catherine (nickname Little Mo) (1934–69), U.S. tennis player, born in San Diego, Calif.; in 1951 at age of 16 won U.S. singles title; in 1953 became first woman to win all four of world's major championships in one year (U.S., Wimbledon, Australian, and French); injured on horseback ride 1954, retired from tournament play 1955; married Norman Brinker 1955 T-107, *picture* T-106
Connolly, Thomas Henry (nickname Tommy) (1870–1961), U.S. baseball umpire, born in Manchester, England; N.L. umpire 1898–1900; A.L. umpire 1901–31, umpire in chief, A.L., 1931–53.
Connor, George (born 1925), U.S. football player, born in Chicago, Ill.; tackle, linebacker; Chicago Bears 1948–55.
Connor, John Thomas (born 1914), U.S. lawyer and business executive, born in Syracuse, N.Y.; president Merck & Co. 1955–64; U.S. secretary of commerce 1965–67; president Allied Chemical Corp. 1967–69, chairman 1969–79.
Connor, Ralph (pen name of Charles William Gordon) (1860–1937), Canadian novelist, born in Indian Lands, Canada West C-121, *picture* C-122
Connor, Roger (1857–1931), U.S. baseball player, born in Waterbury, Conn.; first baseman N.L. and Players' League 1880–97.
Connors, Jimmy (born 1952), U.S. tennis player T-107, *picture* T-108
Connotation, in linguistics
language construction L-34
Connotative meaning, in writing W-375
Conowingo Dam, in Maryland, near the mouth of the Susquehanna River M-168, *map* M-183

PARTY STRENGTH IN UNITED STATES CONGRESS

	Senate		House	
	Dem.	Rep.	Dem.	Rep.
94th 1975–76	61	38	291	144
95th 1977–78	61	38	291	143
96th 1979–80	58	41	276	159
97th 1981–82	46	53	243	192
98th 1983–84	46	54	269	165
99th 1985–86	47	53	253	182
100th 1987–88	55	45	258	177

Note–Figures show each Congress as its first session began. Minor-party, vacant, and undetermined seats are omitted.

NUMBER OF UNITED STATES REPRESENTATIVES

Alabama	7	Montana	2
Alaska	1	Nebraska	3
Arizona	5	Nevada	2
Arkansas	4	New Hampshire	2
California	45	New Jersey	14
Colorado	6	New Mexico	3
Connecticut	6	New York	34
Delaware	1	North Carolina	11
Florida	19	North Dakota	1
Georgia	10	Ohio	21
Hawaii	2	Oklahoma	6
Idaho	2	Oregon	5
Illinois	22	Pennsylvania	23
Indiana	10	Rhode Island	2
Iowa	6	South Carolina	6
Kansas	5	South Dakota	1
Kentucky	7	Tennessee	9
Louisiana	8	Texas	27
Maine	2	Utah	3
Maryland	8	Vermont	1
Massachusetts	11	Virginia	10
Michigan	18	Washington	8
Minnesota	8	West Virginia	4
Mississippi	5	Wisconsin	9
Missouri	9	Wyoming	1
		Total	435

*Based on 1980 census. Not listed are nonvoting delegates from District of Columbia, U.S. Virgin Islands, and Guam, or resident commissioner of Commonwealth of Puerto Rico.

CONTINENT AREAS*

Name	Area sq mi	Area sq km
Africa	11,667,000	30,218,000
Antarctica	5,500,000	14,245,000
Asia	17,236,000	44,642,000
Australia	2,966,200	7,682,300
Europe	4,056,000	10,505,000
North America	9,355,000	24,230,000
South America	6,878,000	17,814,000

*Including islands off major landmass

Continental arctic air (cA), air mass W-118, *map* W-124

Continental Association, North American colonies R-166

Continental climate
France F-344
Great Plains G-249

Continental Congress, First, United States C-692, R-166
Carpenters' Hall P-251a
leaders
Franklin F-384
Washington W-41

Continental Congress, Second, United States, met in Philadelphia, Pa., May 10, 1775; for short period sat at York, Pa., and Baltimore; ended 1781 with organization of new government under Constitution A-595, C-692, P-168, U-171
Declaration of Independence D-53
Independence Hall P-251
leaders
Adams A-33
Franklin F-427
Hancock H-25
Washington W-41
veterans' benefits V-306

Continental Divide (or Great Divide), watershed in Rocky Mountain region between streams flowing toward Atlantic and those flowing toward Pacific R-234, U-34, *map* U-80
Canada C-74
Colorado C-568
Montana M-551
Wyoming W-386

Continental drift theory B-217
Atlantic Ocean origins A-743
continental development C-691
earth E-35
mountain M-635
oceanography O-486
Wegener W-134

Continental glacier G-150

Continental island I-368
continental development C-688
Oceania O-466

Continental margin, in geology C-688
oceanography O-485

Continental polar air (cP), air mass W-118

Continental rise, in geology C-688

Continental shelf
Atlantic Ocean A-743
continent C-688
navigation N-73
oceans O-460, *diagram* O-461
oceanography O-474, 485
petroleum supply P-230

Continental Shelf Station (or Conshelf), deep-sea station for oceanic exploration O-463

Continental shield C-690

Continental slope, in geology C-688
oceans O-460, *diagram* O-461
oceanography O-485

Continental system, blockade designed by Napoleon to defeat United Kingdom
War of 1812 W-29

Continental tropical air (cT), air mass, *map* W-118

Contino, Antonio (or Antonio Contini) (1566–1600), Italian architect; noted for bridges; designed Bridge of Sighs in Venice about 1595.

Continuo, in music, bass line with two players C-268
orchestra O-580

Continuous mining, underground mining M-427
coal C-522

Continuous spectrum, light S-371

Continuous tank, type of furnace used in glass manufacture G-157, *picture* G-156

Continuous voyage, in shipping I-257

'Continuum Hypothesis', work by Cantor M-220

Contorted willow (or dragon-claw willow), tree *Salix matsudana* 'Tortuosa' of the Salicaceae family W-211

Contour feather, bird B-242, F-50

Contouring, method of plowing for conservation of land and water C-674, *picture* C-669
water conservation W-93

Contour line, in maps M-120, *picture* M-121

Contraband
international law I-257

Contrabass. *see in index* Double bass

Contrabass clarinet, wind instrument W-227

Contrabassoon, wind instrument W-227

Contraceptives, drugs, chemicals, or devices used to prevent pregnancy.

Contract, in law C-693, *table* L-92
marriage M-150

Contract bridge, card game C-160

Contract carriers, transporters of people or goods by agreement with a limited number of shippers T-255

Contract design
interior design I-251

Contractile vacuole, in amoeba A-375
water regulation C-238
osmosis O-610

Contraction
heat H-104

Contrapuntal music (or polyphonic music) M-669

Contrast, photography P-293, *picture* P-291

Controlled automatic machining (CAM), aid to mass production M-209

Controlled Substances Act, law to regulate addictive drugs in the U.S. N-19

Control of Electromagnetic Radiation (CONELRAD), replaced by Emergency Broadcast System 1963 R-49

Control tower
railroad, *picture* R-79

Control unit, portion of central processing unit C-627, *diagram* C-632, *picture* C-631

Conundrum R-205
word games W-293

Convection
heat H-105
heating systems H-108
insulation I-231

Convective layer, sun, *diagram* S-512

Convector, in heating system H-108

Convenience products M-142

Convenience stores
franchises F-373

Convent, from Latin *conventus,* meaning "assembly", term for community of nuns and for buildings occupied by them.

Convention, in business
trade show industry F-8

Convention, in U.S. P-431, *pictures* P-432
elections E-146, *picture* E-145

Convention, National, French assembly (1792–95)
Louis XVI L-307
Napoleon N-14

Conventional mining, underground mining
coal C-521

Conventional system, measurements M-265

Convention center (or exhibition center), buildings or complexes of buildings used to host large gatherings H-286

Convention Concerning the Protection of the World Cultural and Natural Heritage (or World Heritage Convention), conservation agreement N-26

Convention of 1818, between the United Kingdom and the U.S., *table* T-274

Convention of Peking, Opium Wars O-573

Convention on Genocide, United Nations U-23
warfare W-26

Convention on International Trade in Endangered Species of Wild Fauna and Flora (CITES) E-209

Conversation C-694
reading readiness R-101b

'Conversation in a Park', painting by Gainsborough, *picture* D-265

Converse, Frederick S. (1871–1940), U.S. composer, born in Newton, Mass. ('The Pipe of Desire', opera).

Converse College, Spartanburg, S.C.; private control; for women; founded 1889; arts and sciences; graduate study; coeducational in music.

Conversion, football scoring method F-292

Conversion, in law, the unauthorized possession of personal property without the owner's consent C-770

Conversion process, petroleum refining P-241, *chart* P-241a

Convertaplane, aircraft H-122

Convertible, automobile A-844

Convex lens
optics O-574
spectacles S-370

Convex surface, in mathematics
measurement M-245

Conveyor belt R-301
cargo handling
harbors, *picture* V-276
coal mining C-520, *picture* C-524
food processing, *pictures* U-57, 98
machine M-10
mass production M-209
papermaking, *diagram* P-102, *picture* P-104

Convolvulaceae, large botanical family of chiefly twining or trailing herbs with large showy flowers; most abundant in tropics of Asia and America; several species, including morning-glory, cypress vine, and bindweed, are cultivated for ornamental purposes; another species, the sweet potato, is cultivated for edible roots.

Convoy, naval force protecting merchant ships on voyages in time of war.

Convulsions, violent, uncontrollable muscle spasms; in young children often caused by high fever or acute illness; symptom of epilepsy, uremia, tetanus, and other disorders
first aid F-119

Conway, Hugh. *see in index* Fargus, Frederick John

Conway, Patrick (1865–1929), U.S. band leader, born near Troy, N.Y.

Conway, Thomas (1735–1800), Revolutionary War general, born in Ireland; served in Continental army; intrigued against Washington, whom he considered less competent than Gates; wounded in duel, went to France; later became governor of French possessions in India.

Conway, Ark., city 25 mi (40 km) n.w. of Little Rock, in agricultural area; state colony for mentally retarded; State College of Arkansas, Hendrix College; Titan missile site.

Conway Cabal R-168

Conway of Allington, William Martin Conway, first **Baron** (1856–1937), English art critic, mountain climber, explorer; professor fine arts Cambridge University 1901–4; explored Himalayas, Spitsbergen, Bolivian Andes, Tierra del Fuego, Aconcagua; books on art, exploration.

Conwell, Russell Herman (1843–1925), Baptist clergyman, author, educator, lecturer, born in South Worthington, Mass.; pastor Baptist Temple, Philadelphia; founder and president Temple University ('Acres of Diamonds'; 'Woman and the Law').

Cony (or coney), name given to two different rabbitlike animals, the Old World hyrax and the pika; also, in the fur trade, name of rabbit skin or fur. *see also in index* Hyrax; Pika
fur, *table* F-464
hats and caps H-55

Conyne kite (or French military kite) K-252

Conzelman, James (nickname Jimmy) (1898–1970), U.S. football halfback and coach; coach world champion Providence Steam Rollers 1928 and world champion Chicago Cardinals 1947.

Cos, island. *see in index* Kos

Cook, Frederick Albert (1865–1940), U.S. Arctic explorer, born in Sullivan County, N.Y.; surgeon for Peary expedition 1891; said to have climbed Mount McKinley 1906
North Pole discovery claim P-151, P-420

Cook, George Cram (1878–1924), U.S. dramatist, born in Davenport, Iowa; with wife, **Susan Glaspell,** organized Provincetown Players in 1915; lived as shepherd in Greece after 1921 ('Suppressed Desires', with Susan Glaspell; 'The Athenian Women'; 'The Spring').

Cook, James (1728–79), English explorer C-696
Antarctic A-474
Australia A-815, S-549a
Great Barrier Reef G-241
kangaroo K-171
New South Wales N-234
Norfolk Island A-823
Canada C-95
British Columbia B-456
exploration E-373
Fiji F-83
Hawaii H-63
navigation N-78
New Zealand N-283, 295, *map* N-296

Cook, James Henry (1858–1942), U.S. naturalist and scout, born in Kalamazoo, Mich.; with U.S. cavalry in Geronimo Indian Campaign in 1885–86; wrote 'Fifty Years on the Old Frontier' and adventure stories.

Cook, Sir Joseph (1860–1947), Australian statesman, born in Silverdale, England; entered Parliament 1891; prime minister 1913–14.

Cook, Mount, Alps of South Island of New Zealand; highest peak in New Zealand (12,349 ft; 3,764 m) N-286, *picture* N-289, *maps* N-299, P-3

Cooke, Alistair (full name Alfred Alistair Cooke) (born 1908), U.S. journalist and essayist, born in Manchester, England; became U.S. citizen 1941; commentator on U.S. affairs, British Broadcasting Company 1938–; chief correspondent for *Manchester Guardian* in U.S. 1948–72; moderator 'America' series on television 1972–73; host 'Masterpiece Theatre' on television 1971–; author of 'A Generation on Trial: U.S.A. *v.* Alger Hiss', 'One Man's America', 'Alistair Cooke's America'.

Cooke, Jay (1821–1905), U.S. banker, born in Sandusky, Ohio; as chief financial agent for U.S. during Civil War floated over 2 billion dollars in bond issues; failure of his firm in 1873 hastened panic B-73

Cooke, John Esten (1830–86), U.S. novelist, born in Winchester, Va.; tales of South often based on Virginia history ('The Virginia Comedians'; 'Leather Stocking and Silk'; 'Virginia, a History of the People').

Cooke, Sam (1935–64), U.S. rock-n-roll singer M-681

Cooke, Terence James, Cardinal (1921–83), U.S. Roman Catholic prelate, born in New York, N.Y.; auxiliary bishop of New York 1965–68, archbishop 1968–83; created cardinal 1969.

Cooke, Sir William (1806–79), English electrical engineer, born in Ealing; built first telegraph line in United Kingdom.

Cookeville, Tenn., city 79 mi (127 km) n. of Chattanooga; trade center; apparel, machinery, furniture; incorporated as township 1903, as city 1962; pop. 20,350.

Cooking C-697. *see also in index* Food and nutrition
ancient Egypt E-127
ancient Rome, *picture* R-245
appliances H-210
butter B-519
herbs H-137
Pompeian and Herculanean bakeries P-443
prehistoric S-57c
silicone glazed pans S-196
stoves S-483
sugar S-509
vegetables F-314
vitamins V-357

Cook Inlet, s. Alaska A-242, *picture* A-250, *maps* U-39, 94

Cook Islands (or Hervey Archipelago), self-governing territory in free association with New Zealand, in Pacific Ocean, s.e. of Samoa; area of group 90 sq mi (230 sq km); cap. Avarua on chief island, Rarotonga (20 mi [30 km] in circumference); partly coral, remainder volcanic; citrus fruits, bananas, tomatoes, copra, handwork; pop. 18,125, *maps* P-3, W-297
Commonwealth membership C-602
New Zealand N-294
Oceania O-468

Cook Strait, in New Zealand; explored 1770 by Capt. James Cook N-281, *maps* N-299, P-3

Cooktown, Australia, port town in Queensland, on n.e. coast on Coral Sea; railroad terminus; founded 1873 when gold was discovered in area; pop. 593, *maps* A-819, P-3

Cookworthy, William (1705–80), English potter and chemist, born in Kingsbridge, Devon P-476

Coolant, liquid or gas used to cool a nuclear reactor N-423

Coolbrith, Ina Donna (1843–1928), U.S. poet, born in Springfield, Ill.; went as child to California and became librarian; poet laureate of California ('A Perfect Day and Other Poems'; 'The Singer of the Sea'; 'Songs from the Golden Gate'; 'Wings of Sunset').

Cooley, Charles Horton (1864–1929), U.S. sociologist, born in Ann Arbor, Mich.; on faculty of University of Michigan 1892–1929; known for theories of reciprocal influence of society and the individual ('Human Nature and the Social Order'; 'Social Organization'; 'Social Process').

Cooley, Denton Arthur (born 1920), U.S. heart surgeon, born in Houston, Tex.; famed for heart transplants and heart valve replacement surgery at Baylor College of Medicine, St. Luke's Episcopal, and Texas Children's hospitals, Houston; first to make long term use of implanted artificial heart 1969.

Cooley, Thomas McIntyre (1824–98), U.S. jurist and authority on constitutional law, born near Attica, N.Y.; chief justice of Michigan 1868–69; first chairman Interstate Commerce Commission 1887–91.

Coolgardie Aqueduct, in Western Australia A-520

Coolidge, Calvin (1872–1933), 30th president of the U.S. C-702
- Harding H-40
- homestead, *picture* V-294
- Hoover H-234
- strike S-489

Coolidge, Charles Allerton (1858–1936), U.S. architect, born in Boston, Mass.; eminent works include Stanford University, Public Library and Art Institute at Chicago, Rockefeller Institute in New York, N.Y.

Coolidge, Elizabeth Sprague (1864–1953), U.S. music patron, born in Chicago, Ill.; founder of Pittsfield, Mass., Music Festivals; endowed concert hall, Library of Congress; commissioned works by many contemporary composers.

Coolidge, Grace Goodhue (1879–1957), wife of President Coolidge C-703

Coolidge, William D. (1873–1975), U.S. physicist, born in Hudson, Mass.; with General Electric Company 1905–63, director of research laboratory 1932–40; invented and applied ductile tungsten for lamp filaments; developed cathode ray tube
- X rays X-406

Coolidge Dam, on Gila River in Arizona; irrigates 100,000 acres (40,500 hectares).

Coolidge tube (or hot cathode tube), X rays X-406

Coolie, name given to unskilled laborer in India and e. Asia
- North American colonies A-337

Cooling equipment, appliances H-212

Cool jazz, jazz form J-86

Coomaraswamy, Ananda Kentish (1877–1947), author and art historian, born in Colombo, Ceylon (now Sri Lanka); research fellow for Indian, Persian, and Islamic art in Boston Fine Arts Museum after 1917 ('The Dance of Siva'; 'Elements of Buddhist Iconography'; 'Am I My Brother's Keeper?').

Coomassie, Ghana. *see in index* Kumasi

Coon, Carleton Stevens (1904–81), U.S. anthropologist, born in Wakefield, Mass.; curator of ethnology University of Pennsylvania Museum 1948–63; author of 'Caravan: the Story of the Middle East', 'The Story of Man', 'The Seven Caves', 'The Origin of Races'.

Coon. *see in index* Raccoon

Cooney, Barbara (or Mrs. Guy Murchie) (born 1917), artist, born in Brooklyn, N.Y.; was a WAC in World War II; illustrated the following books for children: 'American Folk Songs for Children' and 'Animal Folk Songs for Children', by Ruth Seeger; 'Kildee House', by R. G. Montgomery; 'Where Have You Been', by M. W. Brown; 'Chanticleer and the Fox', awarded Caldecott Medal 1959; 'The American Speller'; 'The Little Juggler'; 'Cock Robin'; 'Ox-Cart Man', by Donald Hall, awarded Caldecott Medal 1980 R-107

Coon Rapids, Minn., residential city 13 mi (21 km) n. of Minneapolis; agricultural area; tool and die, pollution control industry; pop. 35,826.

Cooper, Anthony Ashley. *see in index* Shaftesbury, earl of

Cooper, Gary (formerly Frank James Cooper) (1901–61), U.S. motion-picture actor, born in Helena, Mont.; started career as cowboy extra; won Academy award (1941) for 'Sergeant York' and (1952) for 'High Noon', also special Academy award (1961) for many memorable performances ('Mr. Deeds Goes to Town'; 'Meet John Doe'; 'Pride of the Yankees').

Cooper, James Fenimore (1789–1851), U.S. novelist C-705. *see also in index* 'Leatherstocking Tales'
- American literature A-346
- Hall of Fame, *table* H-16
- western W-151

Cooper, Leon N. (born 1930), U.S. physicist, born in New York, N.Y.; associate professor Brown University 1958–62, professor after 1962.

Cooper, Leroy Gordon, Jr. (nickname Gordo) (born 1927), U.S. astronaut, born in Shawnee, Okla.; U.S. Air Force officer chosen for NASA program 1959, retired 1970 to enter private business, *table* S-348

Cooper, Peter (1791–1883), U.S. manufacturer, inventor, and philanthropist, born in New York, N.Y.; made fortune in the manufacture of glue and in iron and steel works; helped develop cable and telegraph companies
- Hall of Fame, *table* H-16
- industry I-195
- railroad inventor L-282

Cooper, Susan (born 1935), U.S. author, born in Burnham, England; came to U.S. 1963 ('Mandrake'; 'Over Sea, Under Stone'; 'Dawn of Fear'; 'The Dark is Rising'; 'Greenwitch'; 'The Grey King', awarded Newbery Medal 1976).

Cooper, Thomas (1759–1839), U.S. agitator, scientist, educator, and writer, born in Westminster, England; to U.S. 1794; practiced law and medicine; became president of South Carolina College (now University of South Carolina); wrote controversial pamphlets on politics.

Cooperation, in ecology E-53

Co-operative Commonwealth Federation (C.C.F.), Canadian political party S-49g

Cooperative extension service. *see in index* Federal Extension Service

Cooperative for American Relief Everywhere, Incorporated. *see in index* CARE

Cooperatives (or co-ops), associations of consumers or producers who band together for the group members' benefits C-706. *see also in index* Collective farm; Communal living
- agribusiness A-140, C-446
- banks S-52c
- Canada S-49e, *picture* S-49d
- China C-375
- credit unions B-64
- Cuba C-801
- Denmark D-98
- Elizabethan actors S-135
- housing H-297, 303
- Israel P-81
- Mexico M-332
- National Grange G-214
- origin S-233
- savings and loan associations S-52c
- Sweden S-524
- United States A-227
- U.S.S.R. R-325, 332, *picture* R-330d

Cooper-Hewitt Museum (also National Museum of Design and the Decorative Arts), New York, N.Y.; now part of Smithsonian Institution; housed in Andrew Carnegie's former mansion N-278

Cooper River, in South Carolina, stream 50 mi (80 km) long connected by canal with Santee River S-306, *maps* S-307, 319

Cooper's Creek (or Barcoo River), Australian stream rising in Queensland and flowing into Lake Eyre, in state of South Australia; during rainy season rises 20 ft (6 m) and widens to 2 mi (3 km); disappears in dry season B-507, *maps* A-822, P-3

Cooper Union, New York, N.Y.; private control; founded 1859 by Peter Cooper; tuition-free day and evening courses in humanities and social studies, art, architecture, engineering, and science; graduate studies; free adult evening courses; museum of the decorative arts; Abraham Lincoln gave famed address in Great Hall on Feb. 27, 1860, in which he upheld federal right to ban slavery in territories N-254

Co-ordinate, in mathematics C-21

Coordinate systems, in astronomy A-718, S-416

Coorg, former state in s.w. India; now s.w. part of Karnataka state; rainfall averages 120 in (3,050 mm) annually; agriculture; teak and sandalwood; prehistoric remains.

Coosa, river in n.w. Georgia and e. Alabama, 250 mi (400 km) long; formed at Rome, Ga., by junction of Etowah and Oostanaula rivers; joins Tallapoosa to form the Alabama.

Coos Bay, Ore., city 47 mi (76 km) n.w. of Roseburg, on inlet of Pacific Ocean; major lumber-shipping port; lumber by-products; commercial fishing; incorporated 1874 as Marshfield, name changed 1944; pop. 14,424.

Coot (or mud hen), water bird R-71

Coote, Sir Eyre (1726–83), British soldier; captain of 39th regiment, the first British regiment sent to India (1754); joined Clive (1756) as major in battle at Calcutta; made lieutenant colonel after battle of Plassy; later lieutenant general in India; died in Madras.

Cooties. *see in index* Body lice

Copa de Libertadores, soccer competition S-233

Copaiba (or Copaiva, sometimes called copaiba balsam), oleoresin obtained from tropical American trees of the genus *Copaifera*; transparent, yellow to gold in color; used in paints and varnish; in medicine, especially useful as a stimulant and as a disinfectant in various diseases of mucous membranes.

Copán, Honduras, name of a municipal district and of a village near Guatemalan border; monuments of Mayan civilization are nearby the village; pop. 2,190 H-227

COPD (chronic obstructive pulmonary disease), lung disorder L-337

Cope, Sir Arthur Stockdale (1857–1940), English painter; known chiefly for his portraits, which include King Edward VII, King George V, Archbishop of Canterbury, Lord Kitchener.

Cope, Edward Drinker (1840–97), U.S. naturalist and paleontologist, born in Philadelphia, Pa.; laid foundation for modern classification of fishes, amphibians, and reptiles; did early work on fossil remains of w. U.S.

Copeland, Charles Townsend (1860–1952), U.S. educator, born in Calais, Me.; taught English literature and rhetoric Harvard University 1893–1930; author 'Life of Edwin Booth'; editor 'The Copeland Reader'.

Copeland, Lammot du Pont (born 1905), U.S. industrialist, born in Wilmington, Del.; started with E. I. du Pont de Nemours & Company, Inc., 1929, director after 1942, secretary 1947–54, vice-president 1954–62, president 1962–67, chairman 1968–71.

Copenhagen, favorite horse of the Duke of Wellington, *list* H-249

Copenhagen (Danish København), capital of Denmark; pop. 641,904, metro. area 1,372,000 C-708, *maps* E-360, S-524
- Denmark D-98, *pictures* D-97, 99, *map* D-100
- porcelain P-476

Copenhagen, University of, Denmark D-99

Copepod, minute crustacean of the class Copepoda; found in fresh and salt water, *picture* F-124
- crustacean C-789
- oceanography O-484

Copernicus, Nicolaus (1473–1543), Polish astronomer C-709
- Galileo G-6
- planetary motion theories A-708, 719, 728, S-57g

Copernicus, U.S. scientific satellite S-343b, *table* S-344

Cophetua, legendary African king of great wealth who fell in love with the beautiful little beggar maid, Penelophon, and married her; story used by poets (Tennyson's 'The Beggar Maid').

Copiague, N.Y., unincorporated community 30 mi (50 km) s.e. of New York, N.Y., near s. shore of w. Long Island; electronics, machine shops; clothing; governed by Babylon Township; pop. 19,632.

Copilot (or first officer), in airplane A-197

Copland, Aaron (born 1900), U.S. composer C-709
- classical music M-677

Copley, John Singleton (1738–1815), U.S. painter C-709
- portraits
  - Adams, *picture* A-33
  - Revere P-49, *picture* P-48

Copolymer, in chemistry R-309

Coppard, Alfred Edgar (1878–1957), English short-story writer and poet, born in Folkestone, England; stories fanciful with lyrical quality ('Adam and Eve and Pinch Me' and 'Collected Tales', short stories; 'Collected Poems').

Coppée, François Édouard Joachim (1842–1908), French poet, dramatist, and novelist, born in Paris; called "poet of the humble"; wrote sympathetically of working people ('Le Reliquaire', a poem; 'Le Passant' and 'Les Jacobites', plays; 'Contes', stories; 'Toute une Jeunesse', autobiography).

Copper (Cu), metallic element C-710. *see also in index* Brass; Bronze
- alloys
  - aluminum A-321
  - brass B-410
  - bronze B-463
  - nickel N-307
  - nonferrous alloys A-313
- ancient use
  - Cypress C-810
  - Sumerians B-7
- corrosion C-726
- metal and metallurgy M-308
- metalworking M-311
- minerals M-432
- mines and mining M-430, *picture* M-425
- toxic waste W-76
- modern use
  - arts
    - engraving and etching P-276
  - battery and fuel cell B-108
  - communication cables C-7, *pictures* C-8
  - money M-531, P-188
  - petroleum refining P-241a
  - plumbing pipes P-393
  - shipbuilding S-165
  - voltaic electric cell B-92
  - wire A-282, W-245
- ore, *table* O-600, *map* O-600
- periodic table, *table* P-207, *list* P-208
- producing regions
  - Africa A-105
    - Zaire, *picture* Z-445
    - Zambia Z-447
  - Asia A-689
  - Australia A-774
  - South America P-222
    - Chile C-330
  - United States U-106, *charts* U-126

Cormorant, seabird of the family Phalacrocoracidae; found in Northern Hemisphere; color blackish, length about 3 ft (0.9 m); feeds upon fish; dives skillfully and uses both wings and feet in swimming underwater.

Corn (or maize), plant C-718. *see also in index* Cornstarch
farming F-28
farm machinery F-32
flour F-213
germination, *diagram* P-374
grains T-206
hybrid P-366
artificial selection H-140
liquor production L-234
malnutrition M-77
margarine M-134
Maya M-236, *picture* P-365
mythology M-696
pests and diseases
pesticides, *picture* F-60
smut R-364, *picture* R-363
pioneers P-333
plant structure
kernel S-108, *diagram* S-106
root, *picture* R-291
producing regions
France F-353
United States U-69, *map* U-72, *picture* U-34
Illinois I-37, *map* I-42
silage crop S-202
starch S-424
sugars S-508
water W-84, 89

Cornaceae. *see in index* Dogwood family

Corn belt, region in the U.S. C-718

Corn borer. *see in index* European corn borer

Corncob C-720

Cornea, part of the eye E-387
blindness B-310
transplantation T-251

Corn earworm (also called tomato fruitworm, or tobacco budworm, or cotton bollworm), larva of a moth *Heliothis armiger*; names vary depending on the various plants it infests; larvae on corn first eat the leaves, then the ears; pupation occurs in the ground; winter plowing in North kills many pupae
corn C-722

Corneille, Pierre (1606–84), French dramatist C-723
French literature F-395
Racine R-28

Cornelia (2nd century BC), Roman matron, daughter of Scipio Africanus, mother of the Gracchi; "these are my jewels," she said, showing her children to a friend who asked to see her ornaments.

Cornelius, Peter von (1783–1867), German painter; revived mural painting and founded Munich school of art ('Last Judgment').

Cornell, Ezra (1807–74), U.S. philanthropist, born in Westchester Landing, N.Y.; helped found Western Union Telegraph Co.; endowed Cornell University 1865.

Cornell, Katharine (1898–1974), U.S. actress, born in Berlin, Germany, of U.S. citizens; married Guthrie McClintic 1921; debut in New York, N.Y., 1917 ('Candida'; 'The Green Hat'; 'The Age of Innocence'; 'The Barretts of Wimpole Street'; 'Alien Corn'; 'Saint Joan'; 'The Wingless Victory'; 'Antony and Cleopatra'); last appearance 1960 A-27

Cornell College, Mount Vernon, Iowa; private control; chartered 1855 (founded 1853 by Methodists as Iowa Conference Seminary); liberal arts and education, *picture* U-205

Cornell University, Ithaca, N.Y.; private control; founded by Ezra Cornell; incorporated 1865; arts and sciences, architecture, business and public administration, education, hotel administration, law, nutrition, and aerospace, civil, chemical, electrical, mechanical, and metallurgical engineering; graduate school; colleges of agriculture and life science, human ecology, and veterinary medicine, and school of industrial and labor relations, which have been part of State University of New York since 1948; medicine and nursing at New York, N.Y. N-254, *picture* N-255

Cornemuse (or war bagpipe), wind instrument W-228

Corner Brook, Newf., city at mouth of Humber River, on w. coast of island; pulp and paper, cement, gypsum; pop. 24,339 N-164, 167, *map* C-109

Corner throw, in water polo W-102

Cornet, wind instrument W-229
Beiderbecke's style B-143

Cornet. *see in index* Trumpet

'Cornfield, The', painting by Constable, *picture* C-679

Cornflower. *see in index* Bachelor's button; Chicory

Cornflower aster. *see in index* Stokes' aster

Cornforth, John Warcup (born 1917) Australian biochemist, born in Sydney; noted for enzyme research; co-winner of 1975 Nobel prize for work in stereochemistry; Royal Society professor at University of Sussex. *see also in index* Nobel Prizewinners, *table*

'Cornhill Magazine', British periodical
Thackery's editorship T-145

Cornhusker state. *see in index* Nebraska

Corning, N.Y., industrial city 13 mi (21 km) n.w. of Elmira, on Chemung River; glass products, air compressors, fiber boxes; 200-in. (510-cm) reflector of Palomar Observatory was made here; pop. 12,953
Corning Glass Center, *picture* U-112

Cornish, Samuel (fl. 19th century), U.S. antislavery journalist and Presbyterian minister B-291

Cornish, breed of poultry P-482, *picture* P-481

Cornish language E-232

Corn laws, in England, series of laws extending from 1436 to 1846, regulating grain trade; also laws in Biblical Egypt (Bible, Gen. xii, 46–57), ancient China, Rome, and elsewhere C-723
international trade I-272
repeal E-253, P-152

Corn Laws (Frumentariae Leges), in Rome, laws by which the Roman government controlled the grain market and in times of scarcity bought grain in surrounding countries and sold it at a reasonable price to the people of Rome.

Corno, Mount, highest peak in the Apennine mountain range A-497, *map* I-404

Corn pone P-333

Corn poppy P-446

Corn-root aphis, insect pest *Aphis maidiradicis* A-455

Corn salad (or lamb's lettuce, or fetticus, or vetticost), annual plant of the valerian family grown as a vegetable for salad or as cooked green; common plant *Valerianella locusta*, variety *olitoria* native to Mediterranean.

Corn sheller, farm machinery F-36

Corn smut, fungus C-722, *picture* F-450

Corn snake (or red rat snake) S-226a, *pictures* S-223, 226d

Cornstalk (1720?–77), Shawnee chief; treacherously murdered by whites W-166

Cornstalk C-723

Cornstarch C-722, S-424

Corn syrup (or corn sugar). *see in index* Glucose

Corn thistle. *see in index* Canada thistle

Cornucopia, from Latin *cornu copiae*, meaning "horn of plenty," goat's curved horn brimming over with fruit and ears of grain; motif in art and architecture; since ancient times a symbol of abundance.

Cornwall, Barry. *see in index* Procter, Bryan Waller

Cornwall, county in extreme s.w. England; 1,357 sq mi (3,515 sq km); china clay, granite; mines formerly yielded much copper and tin; pop. 342,301 E-230
folktales S-472
shell sand S-36

Cornwall, Ont., port city on St. Lawrence River, 53 mi (85 km) s.e. of Ottawa; textiles, chemicals, pulp and paper, furniture; pop. 46,144, *map* C-112

Cornwallis, Charles, Marquis (1738–1805), British general whose surrender at Yorktown, Va., in 1781 ended American Revolution; later governor-general of India R-171
North Carolina N-360
surrender, *pictures* V-337, 340
Washington W-41

Cornwallis, Edward (1713–76), English soldier, born in London; in British army 1731–48; governor of Nova Scotia 1749–52; founded Halifax, N.S., 1749 N-402

Cornwell, David John Moore. *see in index* Le Carré, John

Cornwell, Dean (1892–1960), U.S. mural painter and illustrator, born in Louisville, Ky.; murals usually depict historical subjects; illustrations in popular magazines and books
painting, *picture* R-121

Corn whiskey, alcoholic beverage L-235

Coromandel Coast, e. coast of India extending n. from Point Calimere (opposite n. Sri Lanka) to mouth of Kistna River; includes the seaports Madras, Pondicherry, Cuddalore, and Nagapattinam.

Corona, Calif., city 38 mi (61 km) s.e. of Los Angeles; citrus processing; lemon by-products; orchard equipment, clay products, metals, mobile homes, plywood; pop. 37,791.

Corona, solar S-515
eclipse A-712, E-49
observatory O-457

Corona Austrina, constellation, *chart* C-682

Corona Borealis (or Northern Crown), constellation in the northern sky, *charts* S-419, 422

Coronado, Francisco (1510–54), Spanish explorer of s.w. North America C-724
exploration E-373, H-164
America A-331
Kansas K-177, *picture* K-179
Mexico L-66
New Mexico N-217
Oklahoma O-525
route, *map* U-176

Coronado, island in California, residential and resort city on San Diego Bay, opposite San Diego; U.S. Naval Amphibious Base, U.S. Naval Air Station; incorporated 1890; pop. 20,910.

Coronagraph S-512
eclipse E-48
observatory O-457

Coronary artery
disease D-173

Coronary bypass surgery
heart H-100

Coronary heart disease D-173

Coronary occlusion. *see in index* Heart attack

Coronation, act of crowning, as of a ruler or pope
Paul VI, *picture* P-142a
United Kingdom
coronation stone S-70

'Coronation of Poppea, The', opera by Monteverdi M-568

Coronationville, South Africa J-122

Coronel, Chile, seaport 17 mi (27 km) s. of Concepción; large coal mines; naval battle 40 mi (60 km) off coast, Nov. 1, 1914, in which British cruiser squadron under Admiral Cradock was defeated and sunk by Germans under Admiral von Spee; pop. 33,870.

Coroner, public officer whose principal duty is the investigation of cause and manner of any death which there is reason to suppose is not due to natural causes
juries J-160

Coronet, ceremonial headress worn by British peer or peeress, *picture* T-195

Corot, Jean Baptiste Camille (1796–1875), French painter C-724

Corozo nut. *see in index* Vegetable ivory

Corporal, military rank
United States insignia, *picture* U-9

Corporal punishment
education E-78, *pictures* E-82, 86

Corporate income tax, tax levied on corporations based on net profits T-36

Corporation, business form C-724. *see also in index* Government ownership; Government regulation of industry; Trusts
apprentice schools A-512
automotive industry A-865
banks B-64
capitalism C-151
estate and inheritance law E-307
franchises F-373
health and fitness programs H-93
Industrial Revolution I-182
international relations I-264
labor union contracts C-693
law L-97, *table* L-92
lobbying L-276
monopolies M-543
National Grange reforms G-214
Renaissance R-149
stocks and bonds S-450, *pictures* S-451
Third World T-169

Corporative state, form of economic organization in some fascist countries; production in each branch of industry and agriculture is regulated by a government-controlled "corporation," containing representatives of employers, labor, and the state; system originated in Italy.

Corps, in U.S. Army A-634

'Corps de Ballet', dance terminology B-32

Corpus callosum, in brain, *diagram* B-399

Corpus Christi, Tex., port and commercial center on Corpus Christi Bay; pop. 231,999 C-725, *maps* N-350, U-40
Texas T-119

Corpus Christi, Feast of, festival in Roman Catholicism on Thursday after Trinity Sunday.

Corpus Christi State University (formerly University of Corpus Christi), near Corpus Christi, Tex.; under state control since 1973, as Texas A & I University 1973–76; chartered 1947; liberal arts, business, education, marine science; graduate studies C-725

Corpuscle, blood cell. *see in index* Red cells; White cells

Corpuscular theory of light. *see in index* Particle theory of light

Corpus Juris Canonici, canon law B-343, C-142

Corpus Juris Civilis. *see in index* Code of Justinian

Corpus luteum, structure that produces progesterone H-243

Corral
cattle range, *picture* U-77
North Dakota, *picture* N-381
sheep, *picture* U-79

Correggio (or Antonio Allegri) (1494–1534), Italian painter C-726

Corregidor, Philippines, strategic fortified island in Manila Bay; pop. 91, *map* P-262

Correlation, in science, the comparison of two or more series of facts
statistics S-436

Correll, Charles James (1890–1972), U.S. radio writer and actor, born in Peoria, Ill.; with Freeman F. Gosden created radio serial 'Amos 'n' Andy' (entitled 'Sam 'n' Henry' 1925–27), and wrote script for the television serial; played character Andy.

'Correspondance Garnier', one of the first news-collecting services for the European press N-238

Correspondence
letter writing L-139

Corriedale, breed of sheep S-147

Corrie glacier (or glacieret, or niche glacier), very small glacier that occupies a cirque G-150

Corrientes, Argentina, city and river port on Paraná River, 500 mi (800 km) n. of Buenos Aires; commercial center; national college; pop. 136,924, *maps* A-585, S-297

'Corriere della Sera', Italian newspaper, *list* N-241

Corrigan, Mairead (born 1944), Irish secretary and peace movement leader; co-founder with Betty Williams of The Community of Peace People, movement to end violence in Northern Ireland. *see also in index* Nobel Prizewinners, *table*

Corrigan, Michael Augustine (1839–1902), U.S. Roman Catholic prelate and scholar, born in Newark, N.J.; president

Cotonou, Benin, port city on Gulf of Guinea; export center; sawmills; produces vegetable oil, soap, soda water, and shoes; pop. 178,000, *map* A-115

Cotopaxi, Mount, active volcanic peak of the Andes, in Ecuador; 19,498 ft (5,943 m), *maps* P-224, S-298

Cotswold, breed of sheep S-147

Cotswold Hills, range extending through middle of Gloucestershire, England; average height about 600 ft (180 m), highest point about 1,000 ft (300 m); named from sheep bred in this region in early times; famous for Cotswold games, which were founded by Robert Dover in 17th century E-230

Cottage cheese (or Dutch cheese, or pot cheese, or smearcase) C-289
  milk M-415

Cottage Grove, Minn., village situated 13 mi (21 km) s.e. of St. Paul; residential suburb; pop. 18,994.

Cottage industry I-177, *picture* I-178
  Afghanistan A-90
  Hargreaves H-43
  Switzerland S-541

'Cottage in Fife, In a', nursery rhyme N-444

Cottage tulip, flower T-305

Cotton, John (1585–1652), learned and popular Puritan preacher, born in Derby, England; pastor in Boston, England, until forced to flee to Boston, New England; became pastor of First Church of Boston; known as "patriarch of New England"; author of several religious books
  Hutchinson H-336

Cotton, Sir Robert Bruce (1571–1631), English antiquarian and writer; made wide collection of historical manuscripts, pamphlets, books, coins, etc.; founded Cottonian Library, which was moved to British Museum in 1753.

Cotton C-735. *see also in index* Cottonseed
  asbestos blends A-671
  bale, *picture* R-115
  Civil War issue C-470
  clothing C-507, *pictures* C-510, 511
  harvesting
    machine F-35
    manually, *pictures* I-69
  honey H-228
  improvement P-368
  Industrial Revolution I-179
  manufacturing
    early mill R-181, *picture* R-185
    spinning and weaving S-389
    textiles T-138
  natural fibers F-75
  plant, *picture* P-377
  producing and manufacturing regions
    Central America C-255, *picture* C-253
    Chad C-264
    Egypt E-117
    India I-74
    Mexico M-332
    Spain S-352
    Sudan S-502
    Turkey T-321, *picture* T-322
    United States U-60
      Alabama A-225, *map* A-228
      Arkansas A-612
      Georgia G-86
      Louisiana L-310
      Mississippi M-468, *pictures* M-466, 469
      New Mexico N-216, *map* N-218
      Oklahoma O-524
      South Carolina S-307
      Texas T-120, *picture* 122
    U.S.S.R., *pictures* R-324
  sound absorption S-259
  thread T-176
  water W-84
  Whitney W-200

Cotton belt, agricultural region in the United States C-735

Cotton boll, pod of cotton plant C-737, *picture* C-735

Cotton bollworm. *see in index* Corn earworm

Cotton Bowl, in Dallas, Tex. T-121, *picture* T-128
  football F-290

Cotton Club, nightclub in Harlem, New York, N.Y.
  Ellington E-193

Cotton gin, machine invented by Eli Whitney W-200
  clothing manufacture C-507
  cotton C-739
  farm machinery F-36
  Industrial Revolution I-179
  inventions I-273

Cotton grass S-106

Cotton gum. *see in index* Water tupelo

'Cotton Kingdom, The', work by Olmsted O-540

Cottonmouth, snake. *see in index* Moccasin snake

Cotton rat, rodent R-95

Cottonseed C-740
  linters R-99
  margarine M-134

Cottontail, type of rabbit R-20

Cotton thistle, plant *Onopordon acanthium* T-171

Cottonwood (also called balsam poplar), tree of the family Salicaceae P-445
  eastern cottonwood, *picture* T-281
  Wyoming state tree, *picture* W-392

Cotton worm, larva of the moth *Alabama argillacea* (family Noctuidae); eats leaves of cotton plants; can be destroyed by dusting with Paris green
  egg, *picture* E-111

Cottony-cushion scale S-52e

Cottony-maple scale S-52f

Cottrell, Frederick Gardner (1877–1948), U.S. chemist and inventor, born in Oakland, Calif.; invented Cottrell electrostatic precipitator.

Cottrell precipitator, device designed to reduce smoke pollution and recover industrial wastes; consists of an electrically charged pipe through which runs a wire of opposite charge; dust and particles in gases are deposited on walls of pipe.

Cotula, genus of low-growing annual or perennial plants of the composite family, suitable for rock gardens; flowers yellow, buttonlike, at end of stiff stems.

Coty, François (or Joseph Marie François Spoturno) (1874–1934), French perfume and cosmetics manufacturer C-742

Coty, René Jules Gustave (1882–1962), French political leader (Independent Republican) and lawyer, born in Le Havre; served as member of parliament 1923–53 except while France was occupied; president of France 1954–59
  De Gaulle D-66

Cotyledon, seed leaf S-108, *diagram* S-106

Cotylosaur, prehistoric reptile A-461, *picture* A-460, *table* E-24

Coubertin, Pierre, baron de (1863–1937), French educator and sportsman, born in Paris; organized modern Olympic Games; president international Olympic committee 1894–1925 A-740

Couch, furniture. *see in index* Sofa

Couchant position, in heraldry H-136

Coué, Philippe Émile (1857–1926), French psychotherapist; taught health could be maintained, disease overcome by autosuggestion; his formula "Every day in every way I am getting better and better" became famous.

Coues, Elliott (1842–99), U.S. naturalist, born in Portsmouth, N.H.; authority on birds ('Key to North American Birds'; 'Birds of the Northwest').

Cougar. *see in index* Puma

Coughing, explosive and noisy expulsion of air from the lungs through the mouth; caused by some irritation of the linings of the respiratory passages; cough is preceded by a short inspiration which closes the glottis; noise of cough caused by opening of the glottis
  lung cleansing L-337
  reflex action R-132

Coulee, gorge W-48

Coulee Dam, in Washington. *see in index* Grand Coulee Dam

Coulomb, Charles Augustin de (1736–1806), French physicist; founded mathematical theory of electric and magnetic action; practical unit of electric quantity named for him E-150

Coulomb, unit of electrical quantity E-150

Coulter, John Merle (1851–1928), U.S. botanist, born in Ningpo, China; son of missionaries; botanist with the U.S. Geological Survey in Rocky Mountains (1872–73) that resulted in development of Yellowstone National Park; taught in several colleges, including University of Chicago (1896–1925); was president of Lake Forest and Indiana universities; adviser Boyce Thompson Institute of Plant Research 1925–28; author of many textbooks.

Coumarin (or cumarin), crystalline substance, from sweet clover, tonka bean, and other plants; used in perfumes and flavors N-449

Council (or synod), in Christianity
  church councils C-410

Council Bluffs, Iowa, city on Missouri River, opposite Omaha, Neb.; railroad center, cattle center, food products; iron pipe, playground equipment, furniture; pop. 56,449, *map* I-302
  Lewis and Clark L-143

Council for Mutual Economic Assistance (CMEA, or Comecon), established Jan. 25, 1949, by Bulgaria, Czechoslovakia, Hungary, Poland, Romania, and U.S.S.R.; Albania joined in Feb., but withdrew in 1961; East Germany joined in 1950, Mongolia in 1962, Cuba in 1972; since 1965 Yugoslavia has participated but not joined; trade, credit, and technical assistance among members has included construction of several pipelines and creation in 1963 of International Bank for Economic Cooperation E-338, 346, R-317

Councillors, House of, Japanese government J-34

Council-manager government. *see in index* City-manager government

Council of Economic Advisers, United States, created by Employment Act of 1946; continually studies current economic situation; aids U.S. president in preparing biannual economic report to Congress U-156

Council of Europe, "parliament" for unification of w. Europe; consultative assembly made up of representatives of national parliaments; committee of ministers (executive body) made up of foreign ministers of member nations. *see also in index* European Organizations, *table*

Council of Ferrara-Florence (1439) E-44

Council of Foreign Ministers, formed by Potsdam agreement, 1945, to draft peace treaties; members include: China, France, United Kingdom, U.S.S.R., United States.

Council of Ministers, legislative cabinet
  India I-76

Council of Ministers, U.S.S.R. R-327, R-334c

Council of National Defense, United States
  Baruch B-86
  World War I W-312

Council of State, East German politics G-127

Council of Ten (1310–1797), tribunal of 10, afterward 17, which governed republic of Venice V-279

Council of Trent (1545–63), Roman Catholic ecumenical council
  canon law C-142
  church council history C-411
  Counter-Reformation C-744, R-135
  Pius IV and Pius V P-347
  surnames' adoption N-6

Council on Environmental Quality, United States U-156

Counseling. *see in index* Guidance

Counselor, guidance and vocational G-303

Count, title of nobility T-195

Countdown, space travel S-342c, *list* S-341b, *picture* R-231

Counterespionage E-304

Counterfeiting and forgery C-742
  handwriting H-30
  hobby H-183
  law, *table* L-92
  money M-531

Counterintelligence
  international agencies I-236

Counterpoint, in music M-669, *list* M-670

'Counterpoints', work by Stockhausen S-448

Counterpotent, heraldic fur, *picture* H-136

Counter-Reformation, Roman Catholic history C-744
  Loyola L-327
  Pius IV and Pius V P-347
  Reformation R-135

Countershading, protective coloration P-510

Countervair, heraldic fur, *picture* H-136

Countess, noble title; in British nobility, wife or widow of an earl, also a woman possessing an earldom; in European nobility, wife or widow of a count, also, in some countries, the daughter of a duke, a marquis, or a count.

'Countess's Morning Levée, The', painting by Hogarth, *picture* H-199

Counting, in arithmetic A-590
  mathematics M-212

Counting, units of measure, *table* W-140

Counting number. *see in index* Whole number

'Count of Monte Cristo, The', novel by Dumas; story of Edmond Dantès, sailor, who is imprisoned on false charge, escapes from prison, gains buried treasure, and returns as the mysterious count of Monte Cristo to dazzle Paris. *see also in index* Dantès, Edmond

Country music. *see in index* Music, Country

Counts, George Sylvester (1889–1974), U.S. educator, born near Baldwin City, Kan.; professor of education after 1927 and director of foundations of education division Teachers College, Columbia University, 1942–48.

County, political division. *see also* Fact Summary with each state article
  elections E-146
  England U-18
  parks and playgrounds P-125
  police P-430

County agricultural agent, trained agriculturist in the Cooperative extension service; works through educational programs for better farming methods; aids in soil conservation, insect control, and eradication of plant and animal diseases V-366. *see also in index* Federal Extension Service

County attorney. *see in index* State's attorney

County borough, in England U-18

Coup (in full, coup d'état), overthrow of government
  Africa A-108
    Sudan S-303
    Uganda U-1
  Vietnam V-322

Coupé (or coup), automobile A-844

Couperin, Armand-Louis (1727–89), French composer C-745

Couperin, Celeste (1793–1860), French musician C-745

Couperin, Charles (1638–79), French composer C-745

Couperin, François (1631–1701), French composer C-745

Couperin, Gervais-François (1759–1826) French musician C-745

Couperin, Louis (1626–61), French composer C-745

Couperin, Nicolas (1680–1748), French composer C-745

Couperin le Grand, François (1668–1733), French composer and court musician, born in Paris; famed not only as a composer for harpsichord but also as a performer on harpsichord and organ C-745

Couperus, Louis Marie Anne (1863–1923), Dutch novelist, whose stories of human tragedies have an Aeschylean inevitability ('The Book of the Small Souls').

Couplet, in poetry P-406
  heroic P-406
    Pope P-445
  Indian literature I-105

Islamic literature I-364

Coupling, of railroad cars R-78, *picture* R-77

Coupon, dated certificate, attached to bond or other commercial instrument; represents interest due; should be detached and presented independently for payment.

Courant, Richard (1888–1972), U.S. mathematician, born in Silesia (now Poland); U.S. citizen 1940; head Mathematics Institute, University of Göttingen, 1920–33; joined faculty New York University 1934, director Institute of Mathematical Sciences 1953–58; with **David Hilbert** laid base for use of computers by application of mathematics to physics problems and coauthored 'Methods of Mathematical Physics'.

Courante, court dance popular in 16th and 17th centuries; of French or Italian origin; name from French *courir* ("to run"); Italian type rapid with running steps, French slower with complex rhythms; in music, part of suite following allemande. *see also in index* Suite

Courbet, Gustave (1819–77), French painter C-745

Courbette, in horse training E-295, *picture* H-261

Coureurs de bois, French Canadians of early days who explored remote regions, engaged in hunting and trading with Indians, often lived and dressed like them
fur trade F-471

Courlander, Harold (born 1908), U.S. folklorist and author, born in Indiana; widely traveled; collected, in books for children, folktales of Ethiopia ('The Fire on the Mountain', with Wolf Leslau), of Indonesia ('Kantchil's Lime Pit'), of the Ashantis of w. Africa ('The Hat-Shaking Dance', with A.K. Prempeh), of Haiti ('The Piece of Fire'), and of the U.S. ('Terrapin's Pot of Sense'); author 'Negro Folk Music: U.S.A.' R-111g, S-479

Cournand, André Frédéric (born 1895), U.S. physician, born in Paris, France; in U.S. after 1930, became citizen 1941; joined faculty Columbia University 1934, professor of medicine 1951–64. *see also in index* Nobel Prizewinners, *table*

Courrèges, André (born 1923), French dress designer D-271

Course, in disease D-165

Course, in golf G-185, *diagram* G-188

Course, in knitting T-138

Course, in masonry B-438

Course made good (or track), navigation N-68

'Course of Popular Lectures', work by Wright W-366

'Courser', legendary ship F-266

Coursing, dog race D-214

Court, Margaret Smith (born 1942), Australian tennis player T-107

Court, law. *see in index* Courts of justice

Court, sports
badminton B-17, *diagram* B-16
basketball B-97, *picture* B-98
jai alai J-13
tennis T-104

Courtesan (or Hetaerae)
education E-82

Courtesy E-316
driving S-11

Courtesy book, etiquette E-320

Court fool. *see in index* Jester

Courthope, William John (1842–1917), English literary critic, born near Lewes; professor of poetry Oxford 1895–1901 ('Addison', for 'English Men of Letters' series; 'A History of English Poetry', 6 vols.).

'Courtier, The', work by Castiglione
Italian literature I-376

Courtly love, etiquette E-319

Court of Arbitration. *see in index* Permanent Court of Arbitration

Court of first instance (or trial court), in legal system C-746

Court of International Justice, Permanent. *see in index* Permanent Court of International Justice

Court of Justice, International. *see in index* International Court of Justice

Court of Lions, in Alhambra, Spain, *picture* S-358

Courtois, Bernard (1777–1838), French chemist, discoverer of iodine I-286

Courtrai (Flemish Kortrijk), Belgium, fortified town on Lys River, 45 mi (70 km) w. of Brussels; fine linen and lace; history dates from 7th century; battle of Spurs (1302), French conquered by Flemings; battle 1918; pop. 43,606.

Courtship, animal. *see in index* Animals, *subhead* courtship; Birds, *subhead* courtship and mating

'Courtship of Miles Standish, The', poem by Longfellow L-296
American literature A-348
Standish S-410

Courts-martial C-748

Courts of justice C-746
Australia A-805
England U-18
Star Chamber S-424
feudalism F-70
International Court of Justice U-21
jury system J-158
juvenile courts J-162
law L-95
administrative law A-46
criminal law C-775
United States
Constitution U-144, 150
frontier life F-424
pioneer days P-335b, *picture* P-334
state S-429. *see also* Fact Summary with each state article
Supreme Court. *see in index* Supreme Court of the United States
U.S.S.R. R-328

Courtyard (or bailey), enclosure C-199

Cousin, Jean, the Elder (1490?–1560?), French painter, wood engraver, and sculptor; said to have painted the glass windows in the Sainte Chapelle in Vincennes, France ('The Last Judgment').

Cousin, Jean, the Younger (1522?–94?), son of Jean, the Elder, designed glass windows in castle of Fleurigny in Sens, France; portraits and sculpture also ascribed to him.

Cousin, Victor (1792–1867), French philosopher, greater as expounder of historical systems than as original thinker, born in Paris; has been called greatest modern eclectic; important figure 1830–48 in reorganization of French public-school system.

Cousins, Samuel (1801–87), English mezzotint engraver, born in Exeter; used mixed method of engraving and etching; copied many paintings by Reynolds, Lawrence, Gainsborough.

Cousteau, Jacques-Yves (born 1910), French undersea explorer, writer, and photographer C-749
oceanic exploration O-463
'The Silent World' R-112e
underwater diving D-187

Cousy, Bob (or Robert Joseph Cousy) (born 1928), U.S. basketball player and coach, born in New York, N.Y.; star College of the Holy Cross; with Boston Celtics 1950–63; basketball coach Boston College 1963–69, Cincinnati Royals 1969–72, Kansas City-Omaha Kings 1972–73; elected to National Basketball Hall of Fame 1971 B-100

Couve de Murville, Maurice (born 1907), French diplomat, born in Reims; ambassador to Egypt 1950–54, to U.S. 1955–56; to West Germany 1956–58; foreign minister 1958–68; minister of finance 1968; premier 1968–69.

Covalence, in chemistry C-299, V-255

Covalent bonds (or electron-pair bonds, or homopolar bonds), in chemistry V-255
crystals C-796
inorganic chemistry I-209
molecule M-522
organic chemistry O-601

Covarrubias, Miguel (1904–57), Mexican painter, lithographer, stage scene designer, and illustrator, born in Mexico City; author and illustrator of 'Island of Bali', 'Mexico South', 'Indian Art of the Americas'.

Coveleski, Stanley Anthony (born 1890), U.S. baseball pitcher, born in Shamokin, Pa.; with Philadelphia, A.L., 1912, Cleveland, A.L., 1916–24, Washington, A.L., 1925–27, New York, A.L., 1928; won 215 games, lost 141; won 20 or more games in each of 5 seasons; won 3 games in 1920 World Series.

Covellite, mineral M-432

'Covenant', painting by Newman, *picture* N-212

'Covenant', work by Michener A-361

Covenant, Ark of the, sacred chest of acacia wood which Israelites took with them into Palestine; contained two stone tablets on which Ten Commandments were inscribed; placed by Solomon in temple at Jerusalem; similar chests now used in all synagogues to hold the Torah
Tabernacle T-2

Covenanters, in Scotland, the dissenters who bound themselves by oath or covenant to maintain Presbyterian forms and doctrines; first covenant signed 1557 at inspiration of John Knox; covenant of 1638 signed at Greyfriars' Church, Edinburgh, to resist introduction of Laud's prayerbook.

Covent Garden, in London, England L-288, T-160
Jones J-139

Coventry, England, city 18 mi (29 km) e. of Birmingham; pop. 335,650 C-749, *map* U-18a

Coventry, R.I., 2 mi (3 km) s.w. of West Warwick; millwork; knitting mills; set off from Warwick, incorporated 1741; pop. of township 27,065.

Cover crop, method of land conservation C-675

Coverdale, Miles (1488?–1569), Augustinian friar, bishop of Exeter, England, translator of first complete printed English Bible E-267

Coverdale, N.B. *see in index* Riverview

Covered bridge, *pictures* I-99, P-178, S-544, V-295

Covered wagon. *see in index* Conestoga wagon

Coverley, Sir Roger de, simple, kindly, whimsical country gentleman in *The Spectator* of Addison and Steele; also the country dance credited to his great grandfather.

Cover paper, paper stock used for folders and booklet covers P-103

Covert, medium-weight cloth of woolen, worsted, or cotton with warp of two-ply yarns, one of which is white, thus giving a mixed effect.

Covina, Calif., city situated at base of San Gabriel Mountains, 8 mi (13 km) n.w. of Pomona; business and industrial community; pop. 33,751.

Covington, Ga., city 31 mi (50 km) s.e. of Atlanta; surgical supplies, clothing, textiles; incorporated 1822; pop. 10,586.

Covington, Ky., city on Ohio River, opposite Cincinnati; metal products, precision instruments, electrical and electronic equipment, paper products; pop. 49,563 K-211, *maps* K-210, U-41

Covington, Va., city 37 mi (60 km) n. of Roanoke; livestock and dairy products; paper, chemicals, rayon yarn, wrought iron; pop. 9,063, *map* V-348

Cow, the mature female of any animal the male of which is called bull. *see also in index* Cattle; Dairying
moose D-62
wool W-288

Cowans Ford Dam, in North Carolina, on the Catawba River, *picture* N-365

Coward, Noël (or Sir Noël Peirce Coward) (1899–1973), English playwright, actor, composer C-749
drama D-247

Cowberry. *see in index* Lingonberry

Cowbird B-305
feeding habit B-257, *picture* B-244

Cowboy (or cowpuncher), rider employed to handle cattle C-750. *see also in index* Rodeo
Chile, *picture* C-331
country music M-678
folklore F-266
frontier F-423, T-124
gaucho A-582, *picture* A-575
roundup, *picture* U-77
Montana, *picture* M-550
North Dakota, *picture* N-349
western's depiction W-151

Cowboy State. *see in index* Wyoming

Cowell, Henry Dixon (1897–1965), U.S. pianist and composer, born in Menlo Park, Calif.; known for tone clusters and experimental music; wrote over one thousand works in various forms I-405, M-677

Cowen, Sir Frederic Hymen (1852–1935), English conductor and composer of operas, oratorios, cantatas, and about 300 songs ('Sleeping Beauty'; 'St. John's Eve') A-800

Cowes, England, seaport on n. coast of the Isle of Wight, 10 mi (16 km) w. of Portsmouth; shipbuilding center; yachting resort; scene of Cowes Week, annual regatta; pop. 18,000 W-202, *map* U-18a

Cowfish, fish, *picture* F-130

Cowhide, leather L-108

Cowl, Jane (1884–1950), U.S. actress, born in Boston, Mass.; star in 'Within the Law', 'Lilac Time', 'Smilin' Through', 'Romeo and Juliet', 'First Lady'; coauthor 'Daybreak'.

Cowl (or capuchon), head covering H-53

Cowles, Gardner, Jr. (1903–85), U.S. publisher, born in Algona, Iowa M-35

Cowley, Abraham (1618–67), English poet and essayist, born in London; his sonorous lyric style was copied by Dryden and his successors of 18th century ('The Mistress', love verses; 'Davideis', a scriptural epic; 'Pindarique Odes') E-306

Cowley, Malcolm (born 1898), U.S. editor, writer, and translator, born in Belsano, Pa.; associate editor *New Republic*, 1929–44; contributor to *The New Yorker*, etc. (poems: 'The Dry Season', 'Blue Juniata'; criticism: 'The Litorary Situation').

Cow lily (or frog lily, or spatterdock, or yellow pond lily), plant *Nuphar advena* W-99

Cow parsnip, genus *Heracleum* of plants of parsley family; perennial or biennial; leaves large, lobed, and toothed, flowers white or purplish; grows 5 to 10 ft (1.5 to 3 m) high.

Cowpens, S.C., town in the Piedmont Region, 9 mi (15 km) n.e. of Spartanburg; former cattle-raising center; the Americans defeated the British n. of town 1781; pop. 2,023 R-172, *map* S-318

Cowpens National Battlefield Site, in South Carolina, *map* S-318

Cowper, William (1731–1800), English poet C-758
literary contribution E-271

Cowpox, mild form of smallpox V-250
Jenner's theories J-98

Cowpuncher. *see in index* Cowboy

Cowrie (or cowry, or Venus's-shell), genus of mollusks S-153, *picture* S-149

Cow trees, several South American trees T-282

Cox, David (1783–1859), English landscape painter proficient with both watercolors and oils; one of greatest English watercolorists; known for Welsh scenes.

Cox, Jacob Dolson (1828–1900), U.S. general and statesman, born in Montreal, Que.; major general in Civil War; wrote on Civil War.

Cox, James Middleton (1870–1957), U.S. political leader and journalist, born in Jacksonburg, Ohio; member of U.S. House of Representatives 1909–13; governor of Ohio 1913–15, 1917–21, *picture* R-263
Harding H-40

Cox, Kenyon (1856–1919), U.S. painter, born in Warren, Ohio; known chiefly for murals in public buildings; sought to uphold classic spirit; author of books on art subjects.

Cox, Richard (1500?–81), English Protestant reformer, helped compile Book of Common Prayer; was equally intolerant of Puritans and Catholics P-539

Coxey, Jacob Sechler (1854–1951) U.S. industrialist C-758

Coxey's Army, band of unemployed who marched to Washington, D.C., in the depression of 1894, under the leadership of Jacob Sechler Coxey, to urge the enactment of laws providing money without interest for public improvements so that unemployed might have work C-758
  Cleveland's presidency C-493

Coyote (or prairie wolf)
  domestication A-454
  fur, *table* F-464
  wolf W-267

Coypu, large rodent of South America *Myopotamus coypus*; makes its burrow in banks of lakes and rivers; eats leaves and roots of water plants; color brownish yellow with white chin; fur long and harsh, but undercoat makes valuable fur called nutria R-236
  fur F-463, *table* F-465

Cozumel, island in the Caribbean Sea, approximately 10 mi (16 km) off e. coast of Yucatán peninsula, Mexico; pop. 5,858 Y-433

Cozzens, James Gould (1903–78), U.S. novelist, born in Chicago, Ill. ('S.S. San Pedro', based on *Vestris* disaster; 'The Last Adam'; 'The Just and the Unjust'; awarded 1949 Pulitzer prize for 'Guard of Honor'; 'By Love Possessed').

CPA (certified public accountant) A-17

CPI. *see in index* Consumer Price Index

CPR. *see in index* Cardiopulmonary resuscitation

CPU. *see in index* Central processing unit

C.Q.D., former wireless code signal for ships in distress; replaced by SOS.

Cr. *see in index* Chromium

Crab, crustacean C-792
  deep-sea forms, *picture* D-60
  migrations A-453

Crab, constellation. *see in index* Cancer

Crab apple, fruit, any variety of the small Siberian crab *Pyrus baccata* A-509

Crabbe, George (1754–1832), English poet whose 'The Village', 'Tales in Verse', and 'Parish Register' with their realistic pictures of common life influenced Wordsworth and other poets E-271

Crabbing, process in textile manufacture T-140

Crabeater. *see in index* Sergeant fish

Crab louse, parasite of humans V-274, *picture* P-115

Crab spider S-385, *picture* A-433

Crabtree, Charlotte (nickname Lotta) (1847–1924), U.S. actress, born in New York, N.Y.; debut at age of six; notable work in 'Little Nell', 'Firefly', 'The Little Detective'; retired in 1891 with $2,000,000 fortune made by astute investments in real estate.

Cracidae, family of birds comprising the curassows and guans. *see in index* Curassow; Guan

Cracking process, in petroleum refining P-241, *chart* P-241b
  gasoline production G-42
  history P-233

Crackle (or craze), pottery glaze P-470

Crack willow (or brittle willow), tree *Salix fragilis* of Salicaceae family W-211

Cracow, Poland. *see in index* Krakow

Craddock, Charles Egbert. *see in index* Murfree, Mary Noailles

Cradle, baby's bed or cot
  pioneer P-333

Cradle (or rocker), device used in processing gold ore G-179

Cradle, device used for harvesting wheat W-188

Cradleboard, device for carrying babies I-120

Craft, any manual occupation requiring training and experience. *see in index* Arts and crafts

Craft guild G-313
  apprenticeship A-511
  labor movements L-6

Crafts, Wilbur Fisk (1850–1922), U.S. Presbyterian clergyman and reformer, born in Fryeburg, Me.; founder and superintendent of International Reform Bureau; editor *The Twentieth Century Quarterly* ('Dress Reform'; 'That Boy and Girl of Yours'; 'A History of National Prohibition').

Craig, Gordon (1872–1966), English actor C-758
  marionettes P-537

Craig, Sir James Henry (1748–1812), British soldier, born in Gibraltar; served in American Revolution; commanded division in India 1797–1802; governor-general of Canada 1807–11.

Craig, Alaska, city on Prince of Wales Island, in s.e. Alaska, about 60 mi (100 km) w. of Ketchikan; outfitting center for Alaska fishing fleets; salmon cannery; sawmill; customs office; pop. 527, *map* U-39

Craigavon, James Craig, first **Viscount** (1871–1940), Irish political leader; prime minister of Northern Ireland from 1921–1940; worked to keep Northern Ireland part of United Kingdom.

Craigie House, in Cambridge, Mass.
  Longfellow L-296

Craik, Dinah Maria (better known as Dinah Maria Mulock) (1826–87), English novelist and poet; 'John Halifax, Gentleman' was her most famous work; among the many books that she wrote for children are 'The Adventures of a Brownie' and 'The Little Lame Prince'.

Craik, James (1730–1814), U.S. physician, born in Scotland; came to America at age of 20; commissioned army surgeon, 1754; chief medical officer in Revolutionary War; intimate friend and physician of Washington; helped expose Conway Cabal.

Craiova, Romania, city 115 mi (185 km) s.w. of Bucharest; railroad junction; grain market; textiles, machinery, canned foods; archaeological collections; pop. 112,392, *map* E-360

Crakow (or poulaine), Renaissance shoe S-178

Cram, Ralph Adams (1863–1942), U.S. architect and writer, born in Hampton Falls, N.H.; college and church architect; consulting architect Cathedral of St. John the Divine in New York City ('The Gothic Quest'; 'My Life in Architecture').

Cramer, Richard (1889–1960), film actor, born in Bryan, Ohio, *picture* M-624

Cramp, painful involuntary contraction of one or more muscles, commonly in the limbs; also spasmodic intestinal pain; in gynecology, discomfort occurring during menstruation
  swimming hazard S-11

Crampon, mountain climbing equipment M-637

Cram school (or juku), school established in Japan T-208

Cranach, Lucas (or Lucas Kranach) (1472–1553), German painter C-758
  bookplate design B-362
  Luther's portrait, *picture* L-338

Cranberry B-177
  frost protection F-429
  Wisconsin bogs, *picture* W-258

Cranbrook Academy of Art, Bloomfield Hills, Mich.; founded in the 1920s by George G. Booth; art and design school, long directed by Finnish architect Eliel Saarinen D-122

Crandon Park, in Florida, *picture* F-193

Crane, Harold Hart (1899–1932), U.S. poet, born in Garrettsville, Ohio; poems modernistic and experimental; drowned in Caribbean Sea ('The Bridge'; 'White Buildings') A-356

Crane, Ichabod, character in Irving's 'The Legend of Sleepy Hollow', a lank grotesque country schoolmaster, suitor of Katrina Van Tassel, *picture* S-184

Crane, Nathalia (born 1913), U.S. poet, born in Brooklyn, N.Y. (verse: 'Janitor's Boy', 'Venus Invisible', 'Singing Crow'; novels: 'Sunken Garden', 'An Alien from Heaven').

Crane, Stephen (1871–1900), U.S. novelist, poet, short-story writer C-759
  creative writing W-380
  literary naturalism A-352
  realism N-413
  warfare W-28

Crane, Walter (1845–1915), English artist, craftsman, designer, social idealist, and writer, born in Liverpool; distinguished as an illustrator of children's books, especially fairy tales; associated with William Morris.

Crane, Winthrop Murray (1853–1920), U.S. manufacturer, born in Dalton, Mass.; worked in paper business founded by his grandfather and secured contract for paper used for government currency and bonds; governor of Massachusetts 1900–02; U.S. senator 1904–13; supporter of League of Nations.

Crane, bird C-759
  average life expectancy, *chart* A-423
  bird B-251, *picture* B-249, 272

Crane, hoisting machine, usually with extended, movable arm for horizontal or lateral motion C-760. *see also in index* Derrick
  gantry, *picture* R-231
  harbors and ports H-36

Cranesbill, type of wild geranium G-103, *pictures* F-234, P-358

Cranford, N.J., urban township, on Rahway River, 4 mi (6 km) w. of Elizabeth; chiefly residential; metal products, heaters, razor blades, cosmetics, and plastics; incorporated 1871; pop. 24,573.

Cranial index (or cephalic index), measurement used in racial classification R-25

Cranial nerve N-118, *table* N-119

Cranial nerve X. *see in index* Vagus nerve

Craniometry R-25

Cranium, portion of skull enclosing brain S-210, V-303
  nervous system N-119

Crank, mechanical device M-268, *picture* M-268

Crankshaft, in automobile M-10

Cranmer, Thomas (1489–1556), English church reformer, archbishop of Canterbury; chief author of Church of England prayer book still used A-417, C-761
  Henry VIII H-131

Cranston, R.I., city just s. of Providence; textile finishing, textile machinery, textiles, chemical products, brass tubing, plastics, rubber products, beer, ale; pop. 71,992 R-181

Crape, cloth. *see in index* Crepe

Crape myrtle, shrub *Lagerstroemia indica* of loosestrife family; native to China and grown in s. U.S.; has oblong leaves and pink, white, or purplish flowers, *picture* F-226

Crappie, either of two food fishes of sunfish family, abundant in Great Lakes region and Mississippi Valley; bodies short and compressed; white crappie *Pomoxis annularis*, mottled with silver and dark green, has five or six dorsal spines; black crappie, or calico bass *Pomoxis sparoides*, with olive-silver, dark green, and black markings, has seven to nine dorsal spines S-518

Craps, dice game D-133

Crapsey, Adelaide (1878–1914), U.S. poet, born in Rochester, N.Y.; poems have delicacy and subtle charm; originated "cinquains," five-line stanzas of strict poetic form.

Crary, Isaac Edwin (1804–54), U.S. educator and statesman, born in Preston, Conn.; settled in s. Michigan 1832; territorial delegate 1835, first representative 1837; one of founders of University of Michigan.

Crash, coarse fabric with rough texture, of linen or cotton, sometimes mixed with jute.

Crashaw, Richard (1612?–49), English metaphysical poet, born in London ('Steps to the Temple'; 'The Delights of the Muses').

Crassulaceae. *see in index* Orpine family

Crassus, Marcus Licinius (115?–53 BC), Roman general and statesman; called "the rich" because of great wealth; supported Sulla against Marius; suppressed Spartacan uprising; in battle for control of Parthia was murdered by Parthian general who poured molten gold down his throat P-444
  Caesar's alliance C-14

Crater, constellation, *charts* S-418, 422, C-682

Crater, in geology. *see also in index* Volcanoes
  lake formation L-24
  meteor M-315
  moon M-579, S-347

Crater Lake, in Oregon, deep lake within a huge volcanic caldera famous for its depth and blue color O-582, *picture* O-591

Craters of the Moon National Monument, in Idaho I-17, *picture* I-26, *map* I-30

Craton, in geology, relatively immobile area of the Earth's crust M-634
  continental structure C-689

Cravat, neckwear D-264

Cravenetting, process of rendering fabrics waterproof or moisture repellent; used especially for raincoats and topcoats; name from Craven, the inventor.

Craw, in bird S-455

Crawdad (or crawfish). *see in index* Crayfish

Crawford, Ethan, New Hampshire folk hero
  folklore F-268

Crawford, Francis Marion (1854–1909), U.S. novelist, born and lived much in Italy; 'Mr. Isaacs', his first novel, a story of Anglo-Indian life; his later novels, as 'Saracinesca' series, almost exclusively Italian in subject and setting.

Crawford, Isabella Valancy (1850–87), Canadian poet, born in Dublin, Ireland; to Canada 1858; wrote for Toronto newspapers and U.S. magazines.

Crawford, Joan (born Lucille Le Sueur) (1908–77), U.S. motion-picture actress, born in San Antonio, Tex.; began career as dancer; in first film 1925; won 1945 Academy award for 'Mildred Pierce' ('Our Dancing Daughters'; 'Susan and God'; 'A Woman's Face'; 'Sudden Fear'); autobiography, 'My Way of Life'.

Crawford, Samuel Earl (nickname Wahoo Sam) (1880–1968), U.S. baseball outfielder and first baseman, born in Wahoo, Neb.; outfielder Cincinnati, N.L., 1899–1902; outfielder and first baseman, Detroit, A.L., 1903–17; hit total of 312 triples to set major league record; total hits 2,964; lifetime batting average of .309.

Crawford, Thomas (1813?–57), U.S. sculptor, born in New York, N.Y.; followed classical tradition; (equestrian statue of Washington in Richmond, Va.) S-90

Crawford, William Harris (1772–1834), U.S. statesman, born in Amherst County, Va.; Democratic candidate for president of U.S. 1824 C-487

Crawford Notch, defile in White Mountains of New Hampshire, 3 mi (5 km) long; beautiful rock scenery; about 6,000 acres (2,430 hectares) set aside as state forest, *map* N-191

Crawfordsville, Ind., city in agricultural area, 43 mi (69 km) n.w. of Indianapolis; printing; wire, nails, and other metal products; Wabash College; pop. 13,325, *map* I-102

Crawl stroke, in swimming S-533, *pictures* S-534, V-240

Craxi, Bettino (born 1934), Italian politician, born in Milan, Italy I-398

'Cry, the Beloved Country', work by Paton R-112d
social issues N-412
CSB (Central Statistical Board), United States R-265
CSU. *see in index* Christian Socialists
Ctenophora. *see in index* Comb jelly
Ctesias (fl. late 5th century BC), Greek historian and physician, born in Cnidus, Caria; wrote history of Persia intended to discredit that of Herodotus A-458
Ctesibius of Alexandria (2nd century BC), Greek inventor; credited with invention of a water clock, a hydraulic organ, a force pump, and other devices
organ W-231
watches and clocks W-83
Ctesiphon, ancient city of Babylonia, on Tigris, 45 mi (70 km) n.e. of Babylon; capital of Parthian kingdom; declined after plundering by Arabs about 636, *map* P-212
CT scanner. *see in index* Computerized axial tomography scanner
Cu, chemical element. *see in index* Copper
Cuadrillan, in bullfighting B-501
Cuango River, river in Africa. *see in index* Kwango River
Cuauhnáhuac, Mexico. *see in index* Cuernavaca
Cuauhtemoc. *see in index* Guatemoc
Cuba, largest island of West Indies; 42,803 sq mi (110,860 sq km), including adjacent islands; cap. Havana; pop. 9,945,000 C-800, *maps* N-350, W-297
agriculture
land use reforms L-29
pineapples P-329
sponges S-394
cities. *see also in index* cities listed below and other cities by name
Havana H-56
classical music M-675
communism C-620, *map* C-619
Cuban Americans H-162, 166
flag, *picture* F-163
history. *see also in index* Cuban Missile Crisis
Batista's rule B-106
colonial times A-335
foreign affairs I-264
Angola L-327
Eisenhower E-143
embargo E-198
Grenada G-284
Kennedy U-195
Latin America L-66
McKinley M-20
Spanish-American War S-364
World War II W-328
literature
Caribbean literature C-167
Latin American literature L-68
national anthem, *table* N-64
OAS exclusion O-605
radio R-54
railroad mileage, *table* R-85
revolution W-17
terrorism T-113
West Indies W-155, *picture* W-158, *map* W-159
yellow fever epidemic M-598
Cuban Americans, Hispanic Americans H-162, 166, *pictures* H-167, 168
Cuban Missile Crisis
international relations I-264
Kennedy K-202
marines M-139
Cuban Refugee Act (1966), United States H-167
Cube, in mathematics
geometry G-79, *diagrams* G-78, 79
measurement M-244
Cube, power or root of a number P-484
Cubeb (or cubeb pepper), dried unripe berry of *Piper cubeba,* a climbing woody shrub native to Penang, Java, Sumatra; its volatile oil has medicinal uses.
Cuber, farm machine F-35
Cubic centimeter, unit of volume, *table* W-141
Cubic decimeter (or liter), unit of capacity W-139, *table* W-141
Cubic foot, unit of capacity, *table* W-140
Cubic inch, unit of capacity, *table* W-140
Cubicle, reading B-491
Cubic meter, unit of volume, *table* W-141
Cubic yard, unit of capacity, *table* W-140
'Cubi VII', sculpture by Smith, *picture* M-310
Cubism, in art
drawing
Léger D-250
metalworking M-311
painting P-26, 58, *picture* P-56
Braque B-407
Delaunay D-69
Léger L-118
Picasso P-314
sculpture S-92
Giacometti G-142
Lipchitz L-232
Cubit, early measurement W-138, *table* W-140
Cuboctahedron, in mathematics
geometry G-79
Cub Scout. *see in index* Boy Scouts
Cuchulain Cycle. *see in index* Red Branch Cycle
Cuchumatanes, mountain range in Central America G-296
Cuckoo, bird C-805
Cuckoo clock W-77, *picture* W-79
Cuckoo wasp, insect of the Chrysididae family W-75, *picture* W-72
Cucujo, tropical firefly F-113
Cuculidae, family of birds, including roadrunners, anis, and cuckoos C-805
Cuculiformes, order of long-tailed birds, including the family Cuculidae (cuckoos, road runners, and anis).
Cucumber, garden vegetable B-178
melons M-292
Cucumber tree, tree *Magnolia acuminata* of the Magnolia family M-47
Cucurbitaceae, the gourd family G-198
melons M-292
Cud, food brought up into the mouth by a ruminating animal R-318
cattle C-224
Cudahy, Michael (1841–1910), born in County Kilkenny, Ireland; president of Cudahy Packing Company (1890–1910).
Cudahy, Calif., city about 7 mi (11 km) s.e. of Los Angeles and just e. of Bell; incorporated 1960; pop. 17,984.
Cudahy, Wis., city on Lake Michigan, 7 mi (11 km) s. of Milwaukee; meat-packing; drop-forge products; pop. 19,547.
Cud-chewing animals. *see in index* Ruminants
Cudworth, Ralph (1617–88), English philosopher, one of Cambridge Platonists ('True Intellectual System of the Universe'; 'Treatise on Eternal and Immutable Mortality').
Cuenca, Ecuador, city in s.w.; manufacturing, trade center; Panama hats, flour, hides; pop. 104,667, *maps* P-224, S-298
Cuernavaca (formerly Cuauhnáhuac), Mexico, picturesque old city and health resort, capital of state of Morelos, 37 mi (60 km) s. of Mexico City; in ancient times an American Indian village; later became favorite residence of Cortez; pop. 295,000 C-805, *map* M-341
Cuffe, Paul (1759–1817), U.S. shipowner and colonizer; lived in New Bedford, Mass.; fought for the legal rights of black Americans and made possible their right to vote in Massachusetts B-291
Cugnot, Nicolas Joseph (1725–1803), French inventor; built first true automobile 1769, as agreed by British Royal Automobile club and Automobile-Club de France, *profile* A-856
transportation T-261
Cui, César Antonovich (1835–1918), Russian composer and military engineer; author of textbooks on fortification; in music, joined Young Russian movement ('Prisoner of Caucasus', 'Captain's Daughter', operas)
classical music M-674
Cuisine, manner of food preparation C-698
Cuitzeo, Lake, lake in Mexico, n. of Morelia; 160 sq mi (410 sq km); resort, *map* M-341
Cukor, George Dewey (1899–1983), U.S. motion-picture director, born in New York, N.Y. ('Little Women'; 'David Copperfield'; 'A Star is Born'; 'Philadelphia Story'; 'My Fair Lady').
Culbertson, Ely (1891–1955), U.S. bridge expert and writer, born in Romania of U.S. citizens; organized Culbertson bridge system; founded World Federation, Inc., 1943; which in 1946 became Citizens Committee for United Nations Reform, Inc.; elected to Bridge Hall of Fame 1964 ('Contract Bridge Complete'; 'The World Federation Plan'; 'Total Peace').
Cul de Sac, valley in Haiti H-11
Culebra Cut. *see in index* Gaillard Cut
Culion, Philippines, colony on island of same name in w. part of archipelago, where lepers are segregated and treated; established 1906; pop. of island 5,580, *map* P-262
Cullen, Countee (1903–46), U.S. poet, born in New York, N.Y.; wrote of comedy and tragedy in life of black Americans with lyric, wistful beauty ('Ballad of the Brown Girl'; 'Color'; 'Copper Sun'; 'On These I Stand'; 'The Lost Zoo') B-294
Cullet, in glass manufacture G-157
Cullinan, largest diamond ever found in Transvaal, South Africa; it was cut into 9 large and more than 90 small stones D-131, *picture* D-129
Tower of London T-237
Cullman, Ala., city 42 mi (68 km) n. of Birmingham; food cannery; poultry; corn; cigars, textiles, boxes; Southern Benedictine College; pop. 13,084.
Culloden Moor, battle of (1746), in Inverness-shire near Moray Firth, Scotland P-496
warfare, *list* W-15
Cullom, Shelby Moore (1829–1914), U.S. political leader, born in Wayne County, Ky.; governor of Illinois 1876–83; U.S. senator (Republican) 1883–1913; author of Interstate Commerce Law; a commissioner 1898 to establish government of Hawaii ('Fifty Years of Public Service').
Culottes, garment D-264
Culp, Oveta. *see in index* Hobby, Oveta Culp
Culper Ring, group that spied for George Washington E-303
Cultivation. *see in index* Agriculture; Farming; Garden and Gardening
Cultivator, farm machine F-33
Cult novel, work of fiction N-410
Culture, in biology A-491, B-15
microbiology M-375
Culture, human. *see in index* Civilization
Cultural anthropology, sciences S-65
Cultural Revolution (or Great Proletarian Cultural Revolution), period in China C-805
Chinese history C-345, 347, 375
Mao Zedong M-112
Culver City, Calif., city 9 mi (15 km) s.w. of Los Angeles; motion-picture studios; machine shops; aircraft and missile parts, plastics, chemicals; pop. 38,139.
Culverin, in warfare A-659
Culver Military Academy, Culver, Ind.; founded 1894; 8th grade and four years of college preparation with military and leadership training for boys; girls admitted 1971.
Culver-Stockton College, Canton, Mo.; founded 1853 by Christian church (Disciples of Christ); liberal arts, education, music.
Cumae, Italy, ancient city on west coast, 12 mi (19 km) west of Naples; oldest Greek colony in Italy; supposed home of Cumaean sibyl; remains of amphitheater, fortifications, and other ruins
Roman mythology M-702
Cumaean sibyl S-191
Cumarin. *see in index* Coumarin
Cumberland, Ernest August, duke of, 5th son of George III. *see in index* Ernest Augustus
Cumberland, George Clifford, 3rd **earl of** (1558–1605), English privateer; captured San Juan, Puerto Rico, 1598 but failed to capture fortress; sickness among his men forced him to give up city.
Cumberland, William Augustus, duke of. *see in index* William Augustus
Cumberland, extreme n.w. county of England; 1,520 sq mi (3,940 sq km); includes part of Lake District; coal, iron, lead; county seat, Carlisle; pop. 294,303
wrestling style W-366
Cumberland, Md., city in n.w., on Potomac River; ships coal, sand, clay; railroad shops; textiles, paper products; site of old Ft. Cumberland, built in 1754; pop. 25,933 M-168, 178, *maps* M-182, U-41
Cumberland Road R-221
Cumberland, R.I., town 4 mi (6 km) s.e. of Woonsocket; originally part of Massachusetts, annexed to Rhode Island 1746; pop. 27,069.
'Cumberland', Union warship in battle with *Merrimack* C-480
Cumberland College, Williamsburg, Ky.; Southern Baptist; founded 1889; liberal arts, education.
Cumberland Falls State Park, in Kentucky, *picture* K-218
Cumberland Gap, gorge through Cumberland Mountains where Kentucky, Virginia, and Tennessee meet; 500 ft (150 m) deep; used by Daniel Boone; strategic point in Civil War, *picture* K-217, *maps* U-59, V-348
Tennessee T-86, *picture* T-92, *maps* T-83, 97
Cumberland Lowland, region in Nova Scotia N-399
Cumberland Peninsula, peninsula of Baffin Island
national park N-28
Cumberland Plateau (or Cumberland Mountains), westernmost of three divisions of Appalachian system; reaches from n.e. Alabama to s.w. boundary of West Virginia, crossing Tennessee and s.e. edge of Kentucky A-508, *map* U-58
Georgia G-84
Kentucky K-209, *map* K-210
Tennessee T-82, *maps* T-83, 97
Cumberland River, tributary of the Ohio River, flowing through Kentucky and Tennessee, *map* U-58
Kentucky K-209, *maps* K-210, K-223
Tennessee T-83, *maps* T-82, 97
Cumberland Road (or National Pike), historic road in United States R-221, *map* R-219
Indiana I-92
Maryland M-169
Ohio O-503
transportation T-253
West Virginia W-167
Cumberland Sound, in s.e. Georgia; inlet of Atlantic Ocean on Georgia-Florida boundary; estuary of St. Mary's River.
Cumin, spice from a plant of the parsley family S-379
cummings, e. e. (originally Edward Estlin Cummings; 1894–1962), writer and painter C-805
American literature A-355
Cummings, Homer Stillé (1870–1956), U.S. lawyer and public official, born in Chicago, Ill.; attorney general in F. D. Roosevelt's Cabinet 1933–39, *picture* R-268
Cummings, William Arthur (nickname Candy) (1848–1924), U.S. baseball pitcher, born in Ware, Mass.; with 7 teams 1866–78; invented curve ball in 1867.
Cummins, Albert Baird (1850–1926), U.S. lawyer and statesman, born in Carmichaels, Pa.; governor of Iowa 1902–8; U.S. senator from 1908; joint author with J.J. Esch of Esch-Cummins Transportation Act (1920).
Cumulonimbus (Cb), cloud C-517, *picture* C-516, *diagram* W-119
Cumulus (Cu), cloud C-517, *picture* C-516
weather W-120, *diagram* W-119
Cunard, Samuel (1787–1865), English shipowner C-806
transportation T-261

Cunard Steam-ship Company Limited, name since 1950 of the steamship line started by Samuel Cunard; the Cunard Company merged 1934 with the White Star Line to form Cunard White Star Limited. *see also in index* 'Lusitania'

Cunaxa, town in Mesopotamia, on the Euphrates River, n. of Babylon; scene of defeat and death of Cyrus the Younger in battle against his brother Artaxerxes II 401 BC, *map* P-212

Cuneiform writing, ancient system of writing C-806
- ancient civilization A-404
- archaeology A-532
- Babylonia and Assyria B-5
- Hittites H-178
- Persian Behistun Rock, *picture* P-214
- writing W-370, *picture* W-372
  - communication W-373

Cuneo, Italy, city in Piedmont, 50 mi (80 km) s. of Turin; name ("wedge") from position between Stura and Gesso rivers; grain; silk, hemp, paper; pop. 46,065, *map* I-401

Cunner, small food fish *Tautogolabrus adspersus* often termed "bait-stealer" by fishermen on the Atlantic coast; greenish blue in color; flesh also blue.

Cunningham, Merce (born 1919), U.S. modern dancer and choreographer, born in Centralia, Wash.; soloist in Martha Graham's troupe before forming own company D-24, *picture* D-26

Cunningham, R. Walter (born 1932), U.S. astronaut, born in Creston, Iowa; physicist; worked as research scientist; in NASA program 1963–71 S-347, *table* S-348

Cunninghame Graham, Robert Bontine (1852–1936), Scottish writer and traveler, born in London, England; in House of Commons six years; ardent socialist; ('Mogreb-el-Acksa', 'The Conquest of New Granada'; 'Hernando de Soto').

Cunningham of Hyndhope, Andrew Browne Cunningham, first **Viscount** (1883–1963), British naval officer; commander of expeditionary force in French North Africa Nov. 1942; made commander of Allied Mediterranean fleet and admiral of the fleet 1943; first sea lord and chief of the naval staff 1943–46.

Cunobeline. *see in index* Cymbeline

Cup, in golf G-188

Cup, unit of measure, *table* W-140

Cupboard, furniture F-453

Cupellation, process in assaying ores or refining metals A-705

Cupertino, Calif., residential city 8 mi (13 km) w. of San Jose; research and development; incorporated 1955; pop. 25,770.

Cupflower. *see in index* Nierembergia

Cup fungus, *picture* F-448

Cuphea, genus of annual plants of the loosestrife family, mostly native to tropical America; leaves oval; flowers in loose clusters; Mexican cigar flower *C. platycentra* has solitary scarlet blossoms.

Cupid, in Roman mythology, god of love; same as Greek god Eros; son of Venus; pictured as blindfolded boy with bow and arrows. *see also in index* Psyche

Cupid's-dart, plant. *see in index* Catananche

'Cup of Coffee, The', work by Bonnard, *picture* D-212

Cupola, in architecture, dome resembling an inverted cup; term means "little cup" and is generally applied only to smaller domes. *see also in index* Dome

Cup plant, large coarse-leaved perennial herb *Silphium perfoliatum* of composite family; yellow flower heads.

Cuppy, William Jacob (or Will) (1884–1949), U.S. humorist and critic, born in Auburn, Ind. ('How to Be a Hermit'; 'How to Tell Your Friends from the Apes'; 'How to Become Extinct'; 'The Decline and Fall of Practically Everybody').

Cuprammonium process, in rayon making R-98

Cupric, term used in names of copper compounds
- oxide C-712

Cupric sulfate. *see in index* Copper sulfate

Cupronickel, alloy of copper and nickel
- coins C-539

Cuprous, term used in names of copper compounds
- oxide and chloride C-712
- sulfide. *see in index* Chalcocite

Curaçao, largest island in Netherlands Antilles, just n. of Venezuela; area 171 sq mi (443 sq km); chief city Willemstad, great oil-refining center, serves Venezuela as ocean port, transshipping oil and other products from mainland; Dutch liqueur curaçao originally made here from peel of special variety of oranges; until 1949, Curaçao was the official name for the political unit now called Netherlands Antilles; pop. 125,181, *maps* S-298, V-275, W-159, W-207. *see also in index* Netherlands Antilles
- American colonization A-330

Curaray River, river in n. Ecuador; rises in Andes, flows e. through forests into Napo River; 385 mi (620 km) long; navigability good on lower course.

Curassow, any member of a group of large fowllike game birds of the family Cracidae, with the exception of one species *Crax globicera*, which ranges as far n. as Mexico, they are found only in South America.

Curator, one that has care and superintendence of something
- zoo Z-461

Curb bit, steel part of a horse's bridle that fits in its mouth H-264

Curculionidae, large family of insects including typical snout beetles. *see in index* Snout beetles

Curd, coagulated part of milk C-287
- formation S-455
- milk M-415

Curel, François, vicomte de (1854–1928), French dramatist, born in Metz; plays written in a brilliant and vigorous style on abstract themes such as science, capital, and labor.

Curetes, Cretan priests R-176

Curia Regis (king's court), instituted by William the Conqueror as the supreme central judicial body of England; ceased to function in 1268
- Cabinet government C-4
- Henry II H-129

Curia Romana, collective body of administrative organizations which aid the pope in governing the Roman Catholic church P-100

Curie, Eve Denise (born 1904), French author, lecturer, and musician, born in Paris; made debut as concert pianist Paris 1925; worked for Free French in U.S. and covered battlefields as correspondent in World War II R-112e

Curie, Irène Joliot-. *see in index* Joliot-Curie, Irène

Curie, Marie (or Manya Skłodowska) (1867–1934), French physicist C-806, *picture* R-70
- "radioactivity" B-123
- radium R-63

Curie, Paul-Jacques (1855–1941), French physicist, born in Paris; worked with his brother Pierre in some early experiments on crystals.

Curie, Pierre (1859–1906), French physicist C-806, R-63, R-70

Curie, unit of radioactivity R-69

Curie family C-806. *see also in index* Curie, Marie; Curie, Pierre; Joliot-Curie, Irène; Joliot-Curie, Frédéric

Curing
- cancer cause C-132
- meat industry M-251
- plastics P-382
- tobacco T-199, *pictures* S-315, U-57

'Curiosa Americana', work by Mather M-221

Curiosity, in science S-59

Curitiba, Brazil, capital of state of Paraná in s.; railroad connection with port Paranagua, 68 mi (109 km) e.; exports corn, beef, tobacco, yerba maté; pop. 344,560 S-299, *map* B-425

Curium (Cm), chemical element
- periodic table, *table* P-207, *list* P-208

Curlew, large shorebird of family Scolopacidae, with long down-curved bill; long-billed curlew *Numenius americanus* ranges from Utah, Idaho, Nevada, Nebraska s. to Guatemala; 20–26 in. (51–66 cm) long, bill 6–7 in. (15–18 cm), buffy, bright cinnamon wing linings; Hudsonian curlew *Phaeopus hudsonicus*, 15–18 in. (38–46 cm), bill 2¾ in. (7 cm), smaller and browner than long-billed; nests in Arctic; winters, Central and South America; Eskimo curlew *Phaeopus borealis*, much smaller than Hudsonian, blacker above; nested in Arctic, formerly common migrant on Atlantic coast, now believed to be extinct B-271, *picture* P-14
- ibis I-4

'Curlew River', church parable by Britten B-462

Curling, game played on ice, *picture* W-244

Curling, in hairdressing H-9

Curly-coated retriever, dog, *picture* D-197

Curly parsley, type of parsley H-138

Curran, John Philpot (1750–1817), Irish lawyer, patriot, and orator; defended Wolfe Tone and other Irish rebels of insurrection of 1798; opposed union with Great Britain.

Curran, Joseph Edwin (born 1906), U.S. seaman and labor leader, born in New York, N.Y.; became a merchant seaman 1922; president of National Maritime Union (AFL-CIO) 1937–; vice-president AFL-CIO 1955–.

Currant, fruit B-177, *picture* F-433

Currency, money in circulation as a medium of exchange. *see in index* Coins and coinage; Devaluation of currency; Fractional currency; Money; Paper money

Currency Act, (1764) English legislation affecting her colonies of North America R-163

Currents of news (or corantos), early newspapers N-235

Curriculum, in education, *chart* E-80
- college U-207
- medicine M-275
- social studies S-239, *charts* S-241a
- U.S.S.R. R-332c

Currie, Sir Arthur William (1875–1933), Canadian soldier and educator, born in Napperton, Ont.; commanded 1st Canadian Division 1915–17; commander in chief Canadian forces in France 1917–19; principal of McGill University 1920–33.

Currier, Nathaniel (1813–88), U.S. publisher, introduced Currier & Ives prints, *picture* N-91. *see also in index* Ives, James M.

Curry, Jabez Lamar Monroe (1825–1903), U.S. educator, born in Lincoln County, Georgia; active in politics but chief work was in public education; agent of Peabody Fund for Southern Education, also of Slater Fund for Negro schools
- Statuary Hall, *table* S-437a

Curry, John Steuart (1897–1946), U.S. painter, born in Dunavant, Kan.; interpreter of rural U.S. life; painted murals for Departments of Justice and Interior buildings, Washington, D.C., 1934; artist-in-residence at University of Wisconsin after 1936 ('The Tornado'; 'Baptism in Kansas'; 'Circus Elephants').

Curry College, Milton, Mass.; private control; founded 1879; liberal arts.

Cursive writing B-346, C-59
- handwriting H-29

'Curtain of Green, A', collection of short stories by Welty W-149

Curtain wall, in skyscrapers B-497

Curtice, Harlow Herbert (1893–1962), U.S. industrialist, born near Eaton Rapids, Mich.; joined General Motors Corporation 1914, vice-president 1940–48, executive vice-president 1948–52, president and chief executive officer 1953–58.

Curtin, Andrew Gregg (1815?–94), U.S. public official, born in Bellefonte, Pa.; governor of Pennsylvania 1860–66; befriended Union soldiers; minister to Russia 1869–72; U.S. congressman as Democrat 1881–87.

Curtin, Jeremiah (1840?–1906), U.S. linguist and world-traveling folklorist, born in Greenfield, Wis.; with Bureau of American Ethnology 1883–91 ('Myths and Folk-Tales of the Russians, Western Slavs and Magyars'; 'Myths of the Modocs').

Curtin, John Joseph (1885–1945), Australian political leader, born in Creswick, Victoria; entered Parliament 1928; Labor party leader 1935–45; prime minister 1941–45.

Curtis, Charles (1860–1936), U.S. political leader, born in North Topeka, Kan.; had Indian ancesters on mother's side; congressman 1893–1907; U.S. senator 1907–13, 1915–29
- Hoover H-234

Curtis, Cyrus Herman Kotzschmar (1850–1933), U.S. newspaper and magazine publisher, born in Portland, Me.; controlled *Saturday Evening Post, Ladies' Home Journal, Country Gentleman, Philadelphia Public Ledger, New York Evening Post* M-34

Curtis, George Ticknor (1812–94), U.S. jurist and writer, born in Watertown, Mass.; had Dred Scott and other important cases ('Constitutional History of the United States from Their Declaration of Independence to the Close of Their Civil War'; 'Life of Daniel Webster').

Curtis, George William (1824–92), U.S. essayist and journalist, born in Providence, R.I.; many years editor of *Harper's Weekly*; strong advocate of civil service reform ('Nile Notes of a Howadji'; 'The Potiphar Papers'; 'Prue and I').

Curtis, Margaret (1883–1965), U.S. golfer G-189

Curtis Cup (officially Woman's International Cup), trophy awarded biennially in matches between women's amateur golf team of United Kingdom and that of U.S.; donated 1932 by Harriot S. and Margaret Curtis G-192

Curtis Institute of Music, Philadelphia, Pa.; founded with endowment by Mrs. Edward Bok 1924; students accepted on scholarship basis only after abolishment of tuition fees in 1928 P-251b

Curtis Publishing Company, U.S. company M-34

Curtiss, Glenn Hammond (1878–1930), U.S. pioneer aviator and inventor, born in Hammondsport, N.Y.; designed many flying craft; invented flying boat; developed seaplane; built many Army training planes; designed plane that won Guggenheim prize for safety A-203
- famous flights A-167, *picture* A-202

Curtius, Ernst (1814–96), German archaeologist, scholar, and historian; in charge of excavations at Olympia, Greece, 1875–81 ('History of Greece').

Curtius, Marcus, legendary Roman hero; an earthquake chasm in the Forum which soothsayers said would not close until it had received Rome's greatest treasure was closed when Curtius, declaring that Rome had no greater treasure than a brave citizen, rode his horse into it.

Curve, in mathematics
- geometry G-76

Curve-billed thrasher, bird *Toxostoma curvirostre* T-175

Curved line, in mechanical drawing M-257

Curved line graph G-225

Curved mirror M-465

Curwood, James Oliver (1878–1927), U.S. novelist, born in Owosso, Mich.; traveled extensively in Canadian Northwest; wrote stirring, adventurous romances of great popularity ('Flower of

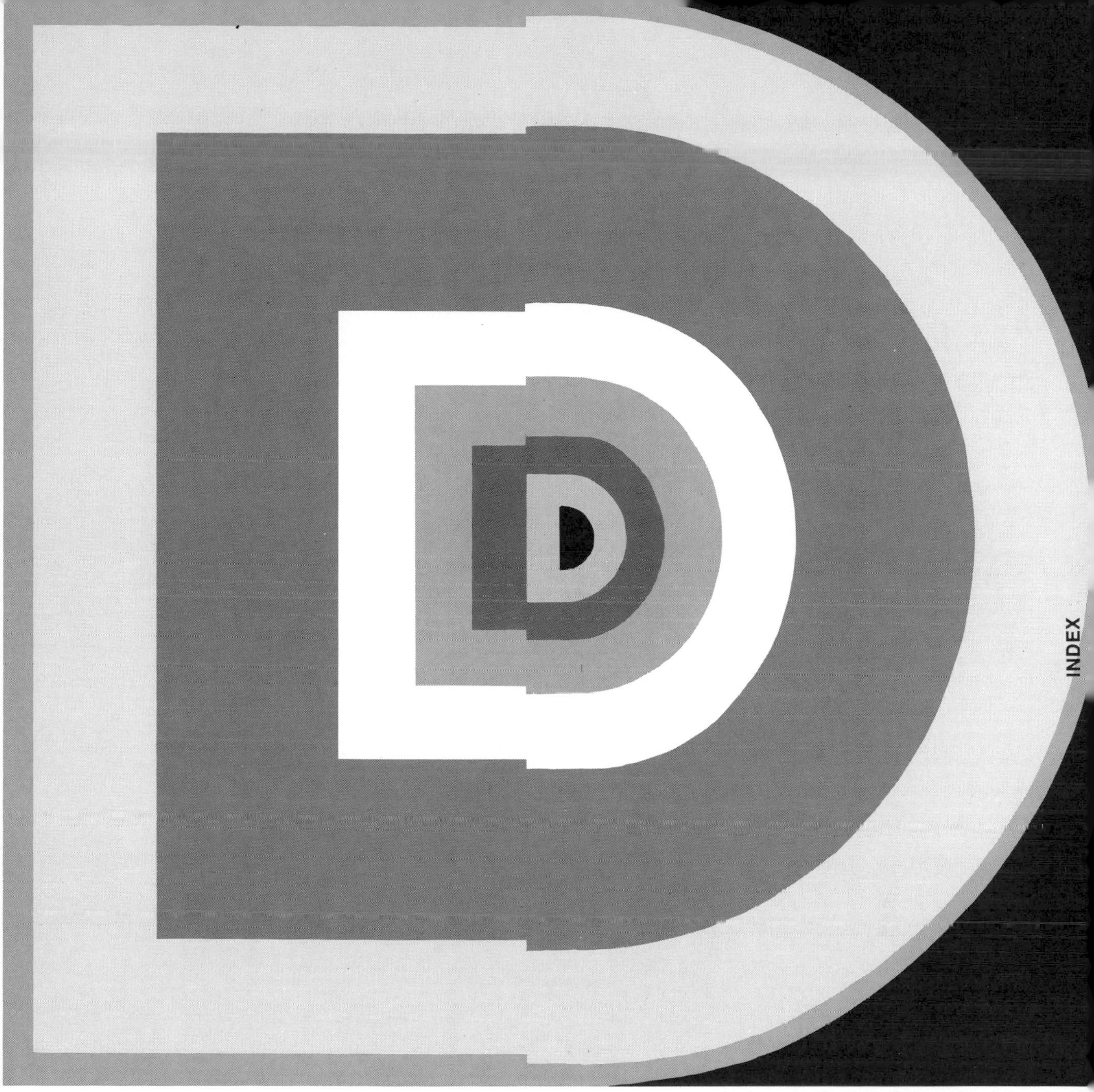

INDEX

The letter D

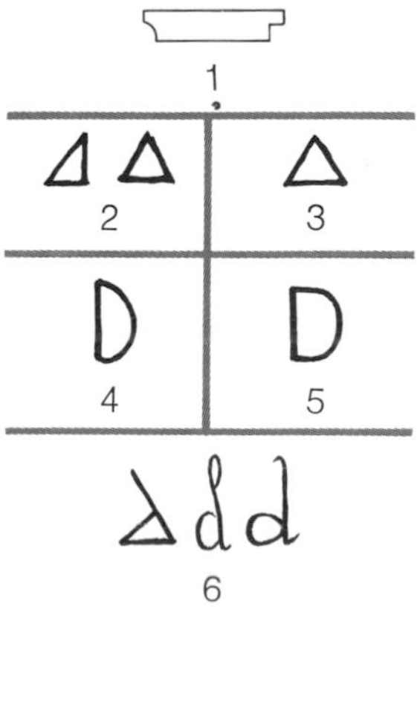

may have started as a picture sign of a door, as in Egyptian hieroglyphic writing (1). The earliest form of the sign in the Semitic writings is unknown. About 1000 B.C., in Byblos and in other Phoenician and Canaanite centers, the sign was given a linear form (2), the source of all later forms. In the Semitic languages the sign was called *daleth,* meaning "door."

The Greeks changed the Semitic name to *delta.* They retained the Phoenician form of the sign (3). In an Italian colony of Greeks from Khalkis (or Chalcis), the letter was made with a slight curve (4). This shape led to the rounded form found in the Latin writing (5). From Latin the capital letter came unchanged into English. In Greek handwriting the triangle of the capital letter was given a projection upward. During Roman times the triangle was gradually rounded (6).

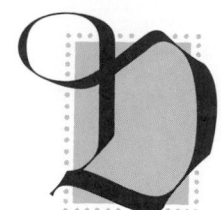

Dabaa, El, Egypt E-118
Dabbling duck, surface-feeding duck D-284
Daboia (or Russell's viper), snake V-328
Da capo, in music, *list* M-670
Dacca. *see in index* Dhaka
Dace, a freshwater fish of the family Cyprinidae D-2. *see also in index* Minnow
Dachau, West Germany, town 11 mi (18 km) n.w. of Munich; site of notorious Nazi concentration camp; pop. 32,349, *map* G-131
Dachshund, dog, *picture* D-199
Dacia, ancient country of central Europe; present Hungary and Romania
  Romania R-318, *map* R-242
  Transylvania T-267
Dacko, David, president of Central African Republic (1960–66, 1979–81) C-252
Dacron, a strong chemical fiber used to make knitting yarns, suitwear, and fabrics for men's and women's clothing; nonabsorbent, resists wrinkling, retains a crease well; is woollike in staple form F-73
  petrochemicals P-228
Dactyl, poetic foot, from Greek *daktylos,* "finger," because of fancied resemblance to three joints of finger, one long, two short P-405
Da Cunha, Euclydes (1866–1909), Brazilian writer L-69
Dadaism, a movement in art and literature based on deliberate irrationality and negation of traditional artistic values; began in 1916
  Duchamp's paintings D-283
  French literature F-397
  motion pictures M-621
Daddy longlegs (or harvestman), a spider with small body and unusually long legs S-387
Dadra and Nagar Haveli, union territory of India, near w. coast; area 189 sq mi (490 sq km); cap. Silvassa; formerly Portuguese possession; pop. 74,165, *map* I-83
Dadswell, Lyndon, Australian sculptor A-802
Daedalus, in Greek mythology D-2
  airplane history A-199
  Minoan culture A-62
Daemen College (until 1976 Rosary Hill College), in Amherst, N.Y., near Buffalo; Roman Catholic; founded 1947, opened 1948; liberal arts and science, art, music, medical records administration, and medical technology.
Daffodil (or lent lily, or trumpet narcissus), flower *Narcissus pseudonarcissus* N-18
  growing conditions G-25, *picture* G-23
  Netherlands, *picture* F-223
'Dafne', work by Rinuccini M-668, O-561
Da Gama, Vasco. *see in index* Gama, Vasco da
Dagger, a weapon S-546
Daggerboard, a sailboat B-328
Dagnan-Bouveret, Pascal-Adolphe-Jean (1852–1929), French painter, born in Paris; pupil of Gérôme; noted for pictures of peasants; an excellent colorist ('The Conscripts'; 'The Consecrated Bread').
Dagö, Estonian Soviet Socialist Republic. *see in index* Hiiumaa
Dagon, a Semitic god, worshiped by Philistines when they settled in Canaan; origin uncertain; little known of cult of the god.
Daguerre, Louis-Jacques-Mandé (1789–1851), French painter and physicist D-2
  photography P-295
Daguerreotypy, an early photographic process, using silver-coated copper plates D-2, P-296, *picture* P-293
Dagyr, John Adam (died 1806), Welsh shoemaker in North American Colonies, called the Father of American shoemaking S-179
Da Hingon. *see in index* Great Khingan Mountains
Dahl, Anders D. (1751–89), Swedish botanist and friend of Linné, under whom he studied; the dahlia is named for him.
Dahlgren, John Adolf (1809–70), U.S. admiral, born in Philadelphia, Pa.; blockaded Charleston during Civil War; inventor of smoothbore Dahlgren gun.
Dahlia, flower of the family Compositae D-3
  growing conditions G-23
Dahnā, ad-, Arabian desert, 30 by 400 mi (50 by 640 km) A-521, S-52b, *map* A-522
Dahomey. *see in index* Benin, People's Republic of
Dail Eireann, name formerly applied to Irish Republican Parliament, now to lower house (House of Representatives) of Ireland's legislature.
Dailies (or rushes), motion picture positive prints M-612
'Daily Freeman', Kingston, N.Y. newspaper H-182
'Daily Mirror', first tabloid newspaper N-242
'Daily News', newspaper founded by Dickens D-137
'Daily Racing Form', horse racing newspaper N-242
Daily tides, one complete tidal cycle per day O-488
Daimler, Gottlieb (1834–1900), German inventor and power automobile builder, born in Württemberg T-264
  gasoline automobile A-858, *table* A-856
  internal-combustion engine I-252
  motorcycle M-631
  trucking industry T-292
Daimler-Benz, West German manufacturer of Mercedes-Benz autos G-117
Daingerfield, Elliott (1859–1932), U.S. figure and landscape painter, born in Harpers Ferry, W. Va. ('Slumbering Fog', 'The Child of Mary'; mural paintings in Church of St. Mary the Virgin, New York, N.Y.).
Dairen (Chinese name Ta-lien), China, seaport in Liaoning Province; in municipality of Lüda with Port Arthur; pop. 3,086,000 L-328
Dairy farming
  geography G-65
  milk M-415
  Wisconsin W-249
Dairy industry D-3. *see also in index* Cattle; dairy products by name, such as Milk; and names of countries and states
  machinery F-35
  margarine M-134
  pasteurization P-138
Daisy, flower *Chrysanthemum leucanthemum* of Compositae family D-8
  oxeye, *picture* F-224
Dakar, Senegal, capital and port, on Atlantic Ocean, at tip of Cape Verde; pop. 798,800 D-8
  Africa, *map* A-115
  Senegal S-108b
  world, *map* W-297
Dakhla (formerly Villa Cisneros), Western Sahara, port on Rio de Oro Bay, the Atlantic coast; fisheries; pop. 6,532, *map* A-115
Dakhla, an oasis in Egypt O-454
Da Khure monastery (often called the green palace), Ulaanbaatar, Mongolia, *picture* M-536
Dakota, American Indian confederacy. *see in index* Sioux
Dakota River. *see in index* James River
Dakota State College (formerly General Beadle State College), in Madison, S.D.; chartered 1881; liberal arts, education.
Dakota Wesleyan University, in Mitchell, S.D.; affiliated with United Methodist church; established 1885; liberal arts, music, and teacher education.
Daladier, Édouard (1884–1970), French statesman, born in Carpentras, near Avignon; member Chamber of Deputies, elected by Radical Socialists, 1919–40; in cabinet most of this period; premier 1933, 1934, and from 1938 until invasion of France in 1940; imprisoned and tried by Vichy regime; interned in Germany 1943–45; member National Assembly 1946–58
  Munich Pact M-653
  World War II W-322
Dalai Lama, religious leader and temporal ruler of Tibet T-180, *picture* S-78
Dalcroze, Émile Jaques-. *see in index* Jaques-Dalcroze
Dale, Sir Henry Hallett (1875–1968), British physiologist, born in London. *see also in index* Nobel Prizewinners, *table*
Dale, Richard (1756–1826), U.S. naval officer, born in Norfolk County, Va.; brilliant service with John Paul Jones on the *Bonhomme Richard* and other ships; first to board the *Serapis*; in merchant service to East Indies 1783–94; captain in first U.S. Navy.
Dale, Samuel (1772–1841), U.S. pioneer and soldier, born in Rockbridge County, Virginia; frontier boyhood fitted "Big Sam" for job of government scout; fought in local American Indian outbreaks; elected to first General Assembly of Alabama 1817; state made him brigadier general and named Dale County for him.
Dalecarlia (the valleys), picturesque forested region in Sweden; iron ore, also copper, silver, lead.
D'Alembert, Jean le Rond. *see in index* Alembert, Jean le Rond d'
Dalén, Nils Gustaf (1869–1937), Swedish engineer, born in Stenstorp, near Skövde; noted for invention of automatic flasher and sun valve, used in Dalén light, and of safe method for bottling acetylene gas; Dalén light, automatically kindled at dusk and extinguished at sunrise, used in unmanned lighthouses and other beacons; was blinded by an explosion during an experiment in 1912 but continued active. *see also in index* Nobel Prizewinners, *table*
Daley, Richard J. (1902–76), mayor of Chicago D-8
  Chicago C-316
Dalgliesh, Alice (1893–1979), U.S. author and editor of children's books, born on island of Trinidad; to U.S. 1911, became citizen 1928 ('America Travels'; 'The Columbus Story'; 'The Fourth of July Story'; 'America Begins'; 'Adam and the Golden Cock') R-105
Dalhart, Vernon (original name Marion Slaughter) (1883–1948), U.S. musician M-678
Dalhousie, George Ramsay, 9th **earl of** (1770–1838), British soldier, one of Wellington's generals in Peninsular War and at Waterloo; lieutenant governor of Nova Scotia 1816–20; governor-general of Canada 1820–28; founded Dalhousie College.
Dalhousie, James Ramsay, 10th **earl** and first **marquis of** (1812–60), one of the builders of British Indian Empire; governor-general 1849–56; annexed Punjab and other native states; established imperial telegraph and postal systems; built first railroad, completed Ganges Canal, and many other public works.
Dalhousie, N.B., port town in n., at mouth of Restigouche River, 14 mi (22 km) n.e. of Campbellton; newsprint milling, lumbering, fishing, pop. 6,255.
Dalhousie University, in Halifax, N.S.; founded as Dalhousie College in 1818 by the 9th earl of Dalhousie, became a university 1841; arts and sciences (including commerce, education, engineering, music, nursing, pharmacy), dentistry, law, medicine; graduate studies H-15, N-402
Dali, Salvador (born 1904), Spanish painter D-9
  'The Persistence of Memory' P-60
Dalin, Olof von (1708–63), Swedish journalist, poet, and historian; tutor 1750–56 to crown prince (later Gustavus III); inspired by Addison, Swift, and Pope, introduced English influence into Swedish literature ('History of the Swedish Kingdom'; 'The Story of the Horse', satirical poem; 'Swedish Liberty', epic).
Dallapiccola, Luigi (1904–75), Italian composer M-676
Dallas, Alexander James (1759–1817), U.S government official, born on island of Jamaica; U.S. secretary of treasury 1814–16 under Madison; found government bankrupt, left surplus of $20,000,000; Henry Adams says he "fixed the financial system in a firm groove for twenty years."
Dallas, George Mifflin (1792–1864), U.S. statesman, son of Alexander J. Dallas, born in Philadelphia, Pa.; served as U.S. senator, attorney general of Pennsylvania, minister to Russia, minister to England 1856–61; Dallas, Tex., named for him P-438
Dallas, Tex., 2nd largest city of state; pop. 904,078 D-9
  North America, *map* N-350
  Southern Methodist University, *picture* U-204
  Texas T-119, *picture* T-128
  United States, *map* U-41
  world, *map* W-297
Dallas, television show D-11
Dallas, University of, in Irving, Tex.; Roman Catholic; opened 1956; liberal arts and teacher education; graduate program D-10
Dallas Baptist College, in Dallas, Tex.; chartered 1898; present name adopted 1965; liberal arts, education, nursing, theology D-10

Dallas-Fort Worth Airport, Texas, *picture* T-124

Dallas Market Center and World Trade Center, building complex, Dallas, Tex. D-10

Dalles (or dells), river rapids in a gorge or canyon; term used also for a rocky-walled gorge.

Dalles, The, Ore., port on Columbia River, 82 mi (132 km) e. of Portland; cherries, fruit and grain crops, livestock; fruit packing; aluminum; site of The Dalles Dam; pop. 10,820.

Dalles Dam, The, dam in Oregon and Washington, on Columbia River; built of concrete and earth; 300 ft (90 m) high; 8,875 ft (2,705 m) long.

Dallin, Cyrus Edwin (1861–1944), U.S. sculptor, born in Springville, Utah; known for monumental statues of American Indians with lean, starkly impressive figures ('Appeal to the Great Spirit'), *picture* U-226

Dalling and Bulwer, William Henry Lytton Earle Bulwer, Baron (better known as Sir Henry Lytton) (1801–72), British diplomat, born in London; served in Constantinople (now Istanbul), Turkey; Madrid, Spain; Florence, Italy; Washington, D.C; concluded Clayton-Bulwer Treaty with U.S.

Dallis grass (also called water grass, or paspalum, or water paspalum), a perennial grass *Paspalum dilatatum* used for pasture in southern U.S.; native to South America; grows on low ground, prairie or marsh; silky hairs on spikelets of the one-sided flower clusters.

Dall's porpoise, sea mammal *Phocoenoides dalli* D-224

Dalmatia, region in Yugoslavia bordering Adriatic Sea; 4,916 sq mi (12,732 sq km) Y-434

Dalmatian, dog, *picture* D-206

Dalmatians, a Slavic people S-214

Dalmatica, garment D-261

Dalou, Jules (1838–1902), French sculptor, born in Paris; during the Commune of Paris (1871), took refuge in England and was influential in development of English sculpture; monumental works, including 'The Triumph of the Republic' in the Place de la Nation, Paris.

Dalriada, name of two ancient Gaelic kingdoms, one in Northern Ireland (in County Antrim) and the other in Scotland (in Argyllshire); united with n. kingdom of Picts AD 843.

Dal River (Swedish Dalälven), river in central Sweden, rises on Norwegian frontier, flows s.e. and n.e. 250 mi (400 km); enters Gulf of Bothnia, *map* S-524

Dalton, John (1766–1844), British chemist and physicist, born in Eaglesfield, near Cockermouth; mathematics and physics teacher at Manchester 1793–99 C-301

Dalton, Ga., city 75 mi (120 km) n.w. of Atlanta; dairying, poultry, cotton, grain area; tufted carpets and other textiles, wood products; headquarters of Gen. Joseph E. Johnston, defending Atlanta 1863–64; pop. 20,743.

Dalton brothers, U.S. outlaws: **Grattan** (1861–92), **William** (1863–94), **Robert** (1870–92), and **Emmett** (1871–1937) O-619

Daltonism. *see in index* Color blindness

Daly, John Augustin (1838–99), U.S. dramatist and theatrical manager, born in Plymouth, N.C.; organized Shakespearean company headed by Ada Rehan; managed John Drew, Fanny Davenport, Maude Adams.

Daly, Marcus (1842–1900), U.S. miner, born in Ireland; came to New York about 1856; made fortune in West; called "copper king" M-554

Daly, Thomas Augustine (1871–1948), U.S. poet and journalist, born in Philadelphia, Pa.; associate editor *Philadelphia Record* 1918–29; columnist *Philadelphia Evening Bulletin* after 1929 ('McAroni Medleys').

Daly City, Calif., residential city just s. of San Francisco; dairy and truck farms, flowers; merged with old town of Colma 1936; pop. 78,519.

Dam, Carl Peter Henrik (1895–1976), Danish biochemist, born in Copenhagen; taught at University of Copenhagen 1923–41; discovered vitamin K (first announced 1935); lectured in U.S. and Canada 1940–41, 1949; did research in U.S. 1942–45; returned to Copenhagen 1946 to serve as professor of biochemistry and head of biology department (now department of biochemistry and nutrition) at Polytechnic Institute, emeritus 1965. *see also in index* Nobel Prizewinners, *table*

Dam, in zoology and animal husbandry, a mother animal; used particularly of mammals; in contrast to "sire," a father animal
- cattle C-224

Dam, in engineering D-11. *see table* following. *see also in index* Dike; Levee; Waterpower; and individual dams by name
- beaver B-121
- flooding
  - cause F-182, *table* F-181
  - control F-184
- hydraulics H-339
- irrigation dams I-354
- Pakistan P-78
- St. Lawrence Seaway S-20
- United States, *pictures* U-51, 91
  - Missouri River M-510
  - Tennessee Valley Authority T-100
- water W-90
- waterpower W-104
- waterway W-108

Daman, India. *see in index* Goa, Daman, and Diu

Damanhur (or Hermopolis Parva), Lower Egypt, railroad center 38 mi (61 km) s.e. of Alexandria; textiles; ancient Timenhor (town of Horus) pop. 126,100.

Damascening, type of inlay work M-310

Damascus (or ash-Sham), Syria, capital and chief city; pop. 1,202,000 D-18
- Asia, *map* A-697
- banner, *picture* M-384
- Middle East, *pictures* M-395, 396
- Syria, *picture* S-550
- world, *map* W-297
- World War I W-305, 319

Damask, a reversible, figured fabric, named for Damascus, Syria, where it was first woven in silk; now woven also in linen, rayon, cotton, wool, or combinations; flatter than brocade; table damask and drapery and upholstery damask are two types T-138
- Damascus D-18

Damask rose, a flowering plant of the family Rosaceae R-294

Damavand, Mount (or Qolleh-ye Damavand), highest point 18,934 ft (5,770 m) in Iran, in Elburz Range, n.e. of Tehran; permanently snow capped volcanic cone
- Asia, *map* A-697
- Middle East M-394

'Dame aux camélias, La'. *see in index* 'Camille'

Dame's violet. *see in index* Sweet rocket

Damien, Father Joseph de Veuster (1840–89), Belgian priest, born in Tremeloo, near Brussels; missionary to lepers of Molokai, Hawaiian Islands; organized sanitation, schools, industry, and worship; died of leprosy, *table* S-437a

Damietta, Egypt, port city, trade center on branch of Nile, 100 mi (160 km) n.e. of Cairo; ancient city bulwark of Egypt against Crusaders; pop. 77,200, *map* A-115

Dammar, resin R-158

Damocles (4th century BC), courtier of Dionysius, ruler of Syracuse (Sicily), who taught him the uncertainty of a king's life by seating him under a sword that hung by a single horsehair; hence the expression "sword of Damocles" to denote uncertainty and danger.

Damon and Pythias, characters in Greek legend of friendship D-19

Damper, device to regulate air flow H-108, 111

Damper, part of a piano M-688

Dampier, William (1652–1715), British adventurer and explorer, born in East Coker, near Yeovil; took part in buccaneering expeditions along coast of South and Central America (1679–81); commanded an expedition to the South Seas (1699–1701); discoveries include Dampier Archipelago and Dampier Strait
- Australia A-815
- Galápagos Islands G-4

Dampier Archipelago, group of high rocky islands off n.w. coast of Australia; chief islands include Enderby, Legendre, Dolphin, Rosmary, Lewis, and Delambre, *map* A-822

Damping-off, a fatal disease of young plants caused by parasitic fungi; controlled by sterilization of soil and plant seeds, and minimization of moisture.

Dampwood termite, insect of the order Isoptera T-112

Damrosch, Leopold (1832–85), U.S. musician, born in Germany; founder of German opera in New York, N.Y.; father of Walter Damrosch D-19

Damrosch, Walter (1862–1950), U.S. musician D-19

Damselfish, fish of the family Pomacentridae; found along coral reefs F-128

Damsel fly, insect of the family Odonata D-238

Damson plum, plant of the genus *Prunus* P-392

Dan, one of the 12 tribes of Israel, named for the first of two sons born to Jacob (also called Israel) and Bilhah (Bible, Gen. xxx, 6).

Dan, ancient town in n. Palestine, at head of the Jordan; settled by descendants of Dan; "from Dan to Beersheba," from one end of Palestine to the other.

Dana, Charles Anderson (1819–97), U.S. journalist, born in Hinsdale, N.H.; member of Brook Farm; associated with Greeley as editor of *New York Tribune*; assistant secretary of war during Civil War; later editor of *New York Sun*, on which he impressed his strong, concise style; an important influence in development of U.S. journalism.

Dana, Francis (1743–1811), U.S. jurist, born in Charlestown, Mass.; member Continental Congress 1776–78, 1784–85; chief justice Massachusetts Supreme Court 1791–1806 A-35

Dana, James Dwight (1813–95), U.S. geologist, mineralogist, and zoologist D-19

Dana, John Cotton (1856–1929), U.S. librarian, born in Woodstock, Vt.; introduced radical innovations in libraries; emphasized book service rather than storage; founded first business department and first picture collection; head Newark (N.J.) library 1902–29; founded Newark museum

Dana, Richard Henry, Jr. (1815–82), U.S. jurist and author, grandson of Francis Dana, born in Cambridge, Mass.; wrote 'Two Years Before the Mast', classic sea story; later distinguished as jurist and international lawyer; 'Autobiographical Sketch (1815–1842)' published 1953 G-217

Dana, William H. (born 1930), U.S. engineer and test pilot, born in Pasadena, Calif.; NASA research pilot in projects including X-15 and lifting body programs.

Dana College, in Blair, Neb.; affiliated with American Lutheran church; founded 1884; arts and sciences, business administration, music, and teacher education.

Danaë, in Greek mythology P-210

Danaides, in Greek mythology, the 50 daughters of Danaüs, king of Libya, doomed to fill sieves with water throughout eternity for killing their husbands at their father's command.

Danakil Depression, lowland in Ethiopia G-250

Da Nang (or Tourane), Vietnam, port city on South China Sea; air base; pop. 492,194 V-323, *map* A-697

Danbury, Conn., city 20 mi (30 km) n.w. of Bridgeport; diversified manufacture; Western Connecticut State College; Federal Correctional Institute; settled 1684; pop. 60,470.

Dance D-20. *see also in index* Ballet; Folk dance
- art forms A-661
- opera O-560
- suite C-268
- therapy T-167

Dance of death, medieval European rite D-26

'Dance of death, The', work by Holbein H-201

'Dancer with a Fan', painting by Degas, *picture* D-65

Dance Theatre of Harlem, first all-black American ballet company D-29

'Dance to the Music of Time, A', novel series by Powell E-282

Dancetty (or dancetté), heraldry H-136

Dancing dervish. *see in index* Dervish

'Dancing Master, The', work by Rameau D-27

Dandelion, flowering herb *Taraxacum officinale* of composite family D-32
- flower classification F-218
- weed W-131, *picture* W-132

Dandie Dinmont terrier, dog, *picture* D-203

Dandruff H-8

Dane, Clemence (pen name of Winifred Ashton) (1887?–1965), British writer; first novel, 'Regiment of Women', published 1917 (other novels: 'Broome Stages', 'The Flower Girls'; dramas: 'A Bill of Divorcement', inspired by English divorce law, and 'Will Shakespeare', in blank verse).

Danegeld, a tax levied in England 10th to 12th centuries; originated as a tribute to the Danes.

Danelaw (or Danelagh), territory in e. England ceded to Danes by Alfred the Great.

Danes, people of Denmark; also English name for the Northmen who invaded England. *see in index* Denmark; Vikings

Danger Cave culture, prehistoric people I-144

'Dangling Man', work by Bellow B-157

Daniel, Hebrew prophet, central figure of the Book of Daniel; explained Nebuchadnezzar's dreams; interpreted handwriting on the wall seen by Belshazzar P-508, *picture* P-509
- folklore F-263

Daniel, Saint Antoine (1601–48), Canadian Jesuit missionary, born in Dieppe, France; went to Canada with Samuel de Champlain 1633; worked among the Hurons and established school for American Indian boys; murdered by Iroquois.

Daniel, Samuel (1562–1619), English poet and historian, born near Taunton; his verse praised for grace and tender feeling (sonnet series to Della; 'Complaynt of Rosamond'; prose history of England.

'Daniel Deronda', George Eliot's last novel; story of a young Jew, reared a Christian, unaware of his Jewish ancestry, who returns to his own people.

Daniel Johnson Dam, dam on Manicouagan River in Quebec Q-9e

Daniell, John Frederick (1790–1845), English physicist born in London; inventor of a primary electric (Daniell) cell still in use, of a pyrometer, and other instruments B-108

Daniell cell, a cell for generating electric current B-108, *picture* B-107

Daniels, Jonathan Worth (born 1902), U.S. author, son of Josephus Daniels, born in Raleigh, N.C.; editor *Raleigh News and Observer*; administrative assistant to President Roosevelt 1943–45 ('A Southerner Discovers New England'; 'The Man of Independence', life of Harry

DAMS AND RESERVOIRS IMPORTANT IN THE WORLD

Name	Location	Type*	Purpose†	Year Completed‡	Height in Feet	Length in Feet	Material in Dam (Cubic Yards)	Reservoir Capacity (Billions of Gallons)
HIGHEST DAMS								
Rogunsky	Soviet Union	E	P-I	UC	1,066	2,506	81,096,000	3,091
Nurek	Soviet Union	E	P-I	UC	1,040	2,390	75,864,000	2,745
Grande Dixence	Switzerland	CG	P	1962	935	2,280	7,792,000	106
Inguri	Soviet Union	A	P-I-FC	UC	892	2,513	4,967,000	261
Vaiont	Italy	A	. . .	1961	858	624	460,000	. . .
Mica	Canada	ER	P-FC	1974	794	2,600	42,000,000	6,517
Sayano-Shushenskaya	Soviet Union	A	P-N	1980	794	3,504	11,916,000	8,261
Chicoasen	Mexico	ER	P	1981	787	1,568	15,700,000	439
Patia	Colombia	R	P-I-FC-WS	UC	787	1,804	30,869,000	4,993
Chivor	Colombia	ER	P	1977	778	919	14,126,000	215
Mauvoisin	Switzerland	CA	P	1957	777	1,706	2,655,000	48
Oroville	California	E	P-I-FC-WS	1968	770	6,920	78,008,000	1,153
Chirkeyskaya	Soviet Union	A	P-I-FC-WS	1975	764	1,109	1,602,000	734
Bhakra	India	CG	P-I	1963	742	1,700	5,400,000	2,607
Hoover (formerly Boulder)	Arizona-Nevada	CAG	P-I-FC-RR	1936	726	1,244	4,400,000	9,696
Contra	Switzerland	A	P	1965	722	1,246	861,000	23
Mratinje	Yugoslavia	A	P	1975	722	879	971,000	232
Dworshak	Idaho	G	P-FC-RP	1972	717	3,287	6,500,000	1,125
Glen Canyon	Arizona	CAG	P	1964	710	1,560	4,901,000	8,798
Toktogul	Soviet Union	A	P-I	1977	705	1,476	4,186,000	5,148
Daniel Johnson	Canada	CM	P	1968	703	4,311	2,950,000	37,473
Auburn	California	A	P-I	UC	700	4,000	6,000,000	758
Luzzone	Switzerland	CA	P	1963	682	1,738	1,739,000	23
Keban	Turkey	ERG	P	1974	679	3,881	20,900,000	8,182
Dez (formerly Mohammed-Reza Shah Pahlavi)	Iran	CA	P-I	1963	666	696	647,000	882
Almendra	Spain	AG	P	1970	662	1,860	2,188,000	700
Kölnbrein	Austria	A	P	1978	656	2,054	1,995,000	53
Karun (formerly Reza Shah Kabir)	Iran	A	P-I	1975	656	1,247	1,570,000	766
New Bullard's Bar	California	A	P-I-FC-RP	1970	637	2,200	2,700,000	557
New Melones	California	ER	P-I-FC-RP	1975	625	1,600	15,970,000	782
LARGEST DAMS								
New Cornelia Tailings	Arizona	E	M	1973	98	35,600	274,026,000	6
Tarbela	Pakistan	ER	P-I	1976	470	9,000	159,200,000	3,617
Fort Peck	Montana	H	P-I-FC-N	1940	250	21,026	125,612,000	6,234
Guri (final stage)	Venezuela	ERG	P	UC	531	30,853	101,819,000	36,720
Yacyreta-Apipe	Argentina and Paraguay	EG	P-I-WS-RP	UC	108	164,000	95,063,000	4,464
Oahe	South Dakota	E	P-I-FC-N	1963	245	9,300	92,008,000	7,687
Oosterschelde	The Netherlands	E	FC-WS	UC	148			
Mangla	Pakistan	E	P-I	1967	380	11,000	85,872,000	1,678
Gardiner	Canada	E	P-I-WS	1968	223	16,700	85,743,000	2,607
Afsluitdijk	The Netherlands	E	FC-WS	1932	62	10,500	82,927,000	1,585
Rogunsky	Soviet Union	E	P-I	UC	1,066	2,506	81,096,000	3,091
Oroville	California	E	P-I-FC-WS	1968	770	6,920	78,008,000	1,153
San Luis	California	E	P-I	1967	382	18,600	77,666,000	664
Nurek	Soviet Union	E	P-I	UC	1,040	2,390	75,864,000	2,745
Garrison	North Dakota	E	P-I-FC-N	1956	203	11,300	66,506,000	7,925
Cochiti	New Mexico	E	FC-RP	1975	253	26,891	64,631,000	167
Tabka	Syria	E	P-I-FC	1975	197	14,764	60,168,000	3,698
Kiev	Soviet Union	EG	P-N	1964	72	177,448	57,552,000	984
Aswan High	Egypt	ER	P-I-RP	1970	364	12,565	57,203,000	44,642
Bennett	Canada	E	P	1967	600	6,700	57,203,000	18,575
Tucurui	Brazil	EG	P-N-WS	1984	282	13,779	56,244,000	8,982
Mission Trailings #2	Arizona	E	. . .	1973	128	. . .	52,435	15
Fort Randall	South Dakota	E	P-I-FC-N	1956	165	10,700	50,205,000	1,858
Kaney	Soviet Union	E	P	1974	82	52,950	49,520,000	692
Itumbiara	Brazil	EG	. . .	1980	328	21,981	47,088,000	4,499
DAMS WITH GREATEST RESERVOIRS								
Owen Falls	Uganda	CG	P-I	1954	100	2,725	. . .	54,091
Bratsk	Soviet Union	ECG	P-N-WS	1964	410	16,864	18,283,000	44,713
Aswan High	Egypt	ER	P-I-RP	1970	364	12,565	57,203,000	44,642
Kariba Gorge	Zambia and Rhodesia	CA	P	1959	420	2,025	1,350,000	42,361
Akosombo	Ghana	R	P	1965	463	2,100	10,400,000	39,102
Daniel Johnson	Canada	CM	P	1968	703	4,311	2,950,000	37,473
Guri (final stage)	Venezuela	ERG	P	UC	531	30,853	101,819,000	36,720
Krasnoyarsk	Soviet Union	CG	P-FC-N	1972	407	3,493	5,685,000	19,364
Bennett	Canada	E	P	1967	600	6,700	57,203,000	18,575
Zeyskaya	Soviet Union	B	P-I-FC	1975	369	2,343	3,139,000	18,069

**A—Arch B—Slab and Buttress C—Concrete E—Rolled Earth Fill G—Gravity H—Hydraulic Earth Fill M—Multiple Arch R—Rock Fill S—Stone Masonry*
†FC—Flood Control I—Irrigation M—Mining N—Navigation P—Power RP—Recreation Purposes RR—River Regulation WS—Water Supply
‡UC—Under Construction

S. Truman; 'The End of Innocence', about Washington, D.C., during Woodrow Wilson's administration; 'Prince of Carpetbaggers', Civil War Reconstruction period; 'Stonewall Jackson').

Daniels, Josephus (1862–1948), U.S journalist and Democratic leader, born in Washington, N.C.; editor *Raleigh* (N.C.) *News and Observer* after 1894; secretary of navy 1913–21; ambassador to Mexico 1933–41 ('Our Navy at War'; 'Wilson Era'; 'Shirt-Sleeve Diplomat'), *picture* R-263

Danielsen, Karen. *see in index* Horney, Karen

Danielson, Mrs. Jacques S. *see in index* Hurst, Fannie

Danilova, Alexandra (born 1907), U.S. ballerina, born in Peterhov, Russia; in U.S. after 1934; member Russian State Ballet 1922–24, later with Diaghilev ballet, Col. de Basil's Ballet Russe, Ballet Russe de Monte Carlo.

Danio, any of several species of tropical fish belonging to family Cyprinidae.

Danish language and literature G-103. *see also in index* Scandinavian languages; Scandinavian literature

Danish modern, furniture style F-462

Dannay, Frederic. *see in index* Queen, Ellery

Dannecker, Johann Heinrich von (1758–1841), German sculptor, born in Württemberg; friend of Schiller; his work a constant struggle between classic and naturalistic schools S-89

D'Annunzio, Gabriele, prince of Montenevoso (1863–1938), Italian novelist, dramatist, and poet, born at Pescara, on Adriatic, of Dalmatian stock; given title of prince 1924 in recognition of patriotic services I-377
- Duse D-293
- Rijeka R-207

Dante (full name Dante Alighieri) (1265–1321), greatest Italian poet D-32
- angel and demon portrayal A-414
- hell and Hades H-123
- Italian literature I-376, I-385

Dantès, Edmond, hero of Alexandre Dumas's 'Count of Monte Cristo'; sailor who, condemned through conspiracy to life imprisonment, escapes, gains buried treasure, and returns to dazzle Paris as the fabulously wealthy count of Monte Cristo and to mete out special punishments to his foes.

Danton, Georges (full name Georges-Jacques Danton) (1759–94), French revolutionary leader D-33
- French Revolution F-403
- Jacobins J-11
- Robespierre R-223

Dantzig, Tobias (1884–1956), U.S. mathematician, born in Shavli, Russia; to U.S. 1910, citizen 1917; professor mathematics University of Maryland 1926–46 ('Number, the Language of Science').

Danube River (ancient Ister), 2nd longest river of Europe; measures 1,750 mi (2,820 km), from s.w. West Germany to the Black Sea
- Austria A-826
- Carpathian Mountains C-173
- Europe, *map* E-360
- Germany G-111, *map* G-131
- Hungary H-326
- Yugoslavia Y-434

Danube sheatfish (or wels), catfish *Silurus glanis* C-220

Danvers, Mass., about 4 mi (6 km) n.w. of Salem; baby shoes, leather, electronic, and plastic products; state mental hospital; birthplace of Israel Putnam; home of John Greenleaf Whittier; pop. of township 26,151.

Danville, Ill., city on Vermilion River, in e. part of state, about 75 mi (120 km) n. of Decatur; aerosol, metal, and electrical products; hydraulic-lift trucks, apparel; home of Joseph G. Cannon, long-time Republican leader; veterans hospital nearby; pop. 38,985, *map* I-302

Danville, Ky., city about 32 mi (52 km) s.w. of Lexington; tobacco and livestock center; clothing, shoes, glass products; Kentucky School for the Deaf; Centre College of Kentucky; pop. 12,942.

Danville, Va., city near s. boundary, on Dan River, 58 mi (93 km) s.e. of Roanoke; tobacco market; tobacco processing; textile products, hosiery; Stratford College; pop. 45,642, *maps* N-350, V-331, 348, U-41

'Danza de los arcos', Mexican folkdance, *picture* F-257

Danzig, Poland. *see in index* Gdańsk

Daphne, nymph in Greek mythology; pursued by Apollo, she prayed to be saved from his advances and was turned into a laurel tree L-88

Daphne, a genus of plants, chiefly shrubs, of the mezereum family, native to Eurasia; some are evergreen, with uncut leaves; fragrant white, lilac, or greenish tubular flowers in clusters; juice of some used in medicine.

'Daphnis and Chloe', Greek pastoral romance by Longus; Daphnis, a boy, and Chloe, a girl, found by shepherds, grow up together, come to love each other, and in the end are happily married; basis for ballet by Ravel

Dapsang. *see in index* K2

DAR. *see in index* Daughters of the American Revolution

Daras, battle of (528), Byzantine Empire defeats Persians B-534

Darby, Abraham, British engineer B-445

Darby, Pa., borough on Darby Creek, just w. of Philadelphia; textile mills; metal and wood products; one of oldest boroughs in state, settled 1660 pop. 13,729, *map* P-185

Darby and Joan, John Darby (died 1730) and his wife, Joan, originals of hero and heroine of Henry Woodfall's ballad 'Darby and Joan' or 'The Happy Old Couple'.

Dardanelles (or Hellespont), narrow strait separating Europe from Asia D-35
- Europe, *map* E-360
- Peloponnesian War G-267
- Turkey T-319
- World War I W-305

Dare, Virginia (born 1587), first child born of English parents in North America N-353, 359

Dar el Beida, Morocco. *see in index* Casablanca

Dar es Salaam, Tanzania, capital and seaport on Indian Ocean; pop. of city 900,000, region 1,394,000 D-35
- Africa, *map* A-115
- Tanzania T-23
- world, *map* W-297

Dargomyzhski, Aleksandr Sergeevich (1813–69), Russian composer, born in Tula, Russia; associated with Glinka as a leader of Russian national school; composed for orchestra and stage; influenced by Wagner ('Esmeralda'; 'The Stone Guest'; 'The Mermaid') M-674

Dari, Persian dialect A-89

Darien, Conn., residential community on Long Island Sound, in s.w. of state; incorporated 1820; pop. of township 20,411.

Darien, Gulf of, gulf of Caribbean Sea between Colombia and Republic of Panama.

Darien, Isthmus of, old name for Isthmus of Panama. *see in index* Panama, Isthmus of

Darien Scheme, unsuccessful attempt to establish Scottish colony on Isthmus of Panama (Darien) and attain a free trade route to the Pacific, headed by William Paterson; settlement begun 1698; Spanish opposition, starvation, and disease led to abandonment of project 1700.

Darío, Rubén (1867–1916), Nicaraguan poet D-35
- Jiménez J-118
- Latin America L-69, *picture* L-72

Darius I, the Great, surnamed Hystaspes (550–486 BC), king of Persia D-36
- audience hall, *picture* I-308
- Behistun Rock carvings A-537
- Persian history P-211, *picture* P-214

Darius II (died 404 BC), king of Persia, son of Artaxerxes I; ruled 423–404 BC; a weak ruler; many uprisings during his reign.

Darius III (380?–330 BC), last king of the ancient Persian Empire; ruled six years; brave and handsome A-279, P-212

Darjeeling, India, health resort in n. West Bengal state; produces quinine; famous for mountain scenery; sanatorium for British soldiers in 19th century; pop. 42,873 I-82, *picture* I-77, *map* I-83

Dark, Eleanor (born 1901), Australian novelist with flair for psychological analysis, born in Sydney (historical novels about Australia 'The Timeless Land' and 'Storm of Time'), *table* A-798

Dark Ages, European history. *see in index* Middle Ages

Dark chocolate, sweet made with cocoa butter, chocolate liquor and finely powdered sugar C-394

Dark horse, in U.S. politics, a term applied to a comparatively unknown man brought forward in a nominating convention as a compromise candidate; Presidents Polk, Pierce, Hayes, Garfield, and Harding were dark horses.

Dark-line S-371, *diagram* S-372

Darkling beetle, any beetle of the family Tenebrionidae, which includes meal worms, flour beetles, and many other species occurring under stones, in dead wood, fungi, and dry vegetable products; most species are black or brown.

Dark moon (or new moon) M-578

'Darkness at Noon', work by Koestler R-111i

Darkroom, in photography P-292, 295

Dark stars S-412

Darlan, (Jean-Louis-Xavier-) François (1881–1942), French naval officer and political leader, born in Nérac; commander in chief French naval forces 1939; vice-premier 1941–42; first in line of succession to chief of state of Vichy government; made head of land, sea, and air forces April 1942; deserted Vichy government to become chief of state for Allies in North Africa; assassinated W-324, 329

Darley, Felix Octavius Carr (1822–88), U.S. illustrator and historical painter, born in Philadelphia, Pa.; illustrated Irving's 'Sketch Book' and Lossing's 'History of the United States'; made notable banknote vignettes; published 'Sketches Abroad with Pen and Pencil'
- 'The Legend of Sleepy Hollow' A-346

Darley, George (1795–1846), Irish poet, born in Dublin; best known for fairy opera 'Sylvia' and for poem 'Nepenthe'.

Darley Arabian, horse H-275, *list* H-249

Darling, Esther Birdsall (1879–1965), U.S. author, born in Marietta, Ohio; lived in Nome, Alaska, 1907–17; bred Alaskan sled dogs ('Baldy of Nome'; 'Navarre of the North').

Darling, Grace Horsley (1815–42), British heroine, born in Bamborough, near Alnwick, daughter of a lighthouse keeper.

Darling, Jay Norwood (also known as J.N. Ding) (1876–1962), U.S. cartoonist, born in Norwood, Mich.; cartoonist *New York Tribune* (later *New York Herald Tribune*) 1917–49; won Pulitzer prize for cartoons 1923 and 1942.

Darling Range, low mountains in w. Australia, running parallel with s.w. coast for nearly 250 mi (400 km); highest peak Mount Cooke, 1,910 ft (580 m).

Darling River, river in Australia, rises in Queensland, flows s.w. through New South Wales, joins Murray; length 1,160 mi (1,870 km) A-769, *maps* A-819, P-3
- New South Wales N-234
- world, *map* W-297

Darlington, England, city 18 mi (29 km) s. of Durham; iron and steel manufactures and locomotive works; Stockton and Darlington Railway opened 1825; pop. 84,700, *map* U-18a

Darmstadt, West Germany, manufacturing and railroad city 20 mi (30 km) s. of Frankfurt; pop. 141,224, *map* G-131

Darnel. *see in index* Rye grass; Tare

Darnley, Henry Stuart, Lord (1545?–67), Scottish noble, 2nd husband of Mary, Queen of Scots, born in Temple Newsam, Yorkshire M-164

Darrow, Clarence (1857–1938), U.S. lawyer D-36. *see also in index* Scopes trial
- 'Clarence Darrow for the Defense' R-111j
- Roosevelt R-271

D'Arsonval, Jacques Arsène. *see in index* Arsonval, Jacques Arsène d'

D'Arsonval galvanometer G-7
- instrumentation I-230

Darter, group of small freshwater fishes of the perch family found only in America; brilliantly colored; has no air bladder.

Darter (also called snakebird, or water turkey), waterbird of the family Anhingidae found in Asia, Africa, Australia, and the s. U.S.; American species *Anhinga anhinga*; like cormorant in habits.

Dartford, England, picturesque market town of Kent, about 15 mi (25 km) s.e. of London; one of first paper mills in England (1590); traversed by Roman road, Watling Street; pop. 46,280, *map* U-18a

Dart leader, atmospheric discharge L-207, *diagram* L-208

Dartmoor, rugged tableland in s.w. Devon, England; 20 sq mi (50 sq km); height 2,039 ft (621 m) E-230, *map* B-341

Dartmoor Prison, near Princetown, in w. Dartmoor, England; built 1809 for French captives during Napoleonic Wars; U.S. prisoners of war also held here during War of 1812; at end of war delayed release of prisoners brought on rebellion (April 1815) in which several Americans were killed; later used for convicts and, in World War I, for conscientious objectors.

Dartmouth, England, seaport in Devon, near mouth of Dart River; here Crusaders embarked for Holy Land 1190; Britannia Royal Naval College; pop. 7,190, *map* U-18a

Dartmouth, Mass., 7 mi (11 km) s.w. of New Bedford; settled 1650, incorporated 1664; fisheries; pop. of township 23,966.

Dartmouth, N.S., industrial and residential city on Halifax Harbor, opposite city of Halifax; pop. 62,277 N-402, *map* O-112

Dartmouth College, in Hanover, N.H.; private control; formerly for men; chartered 1769; arts and sciences; graduate school of medicine, civil engineering, business administration; originated as American Indian school at Lebanon, Conn. U-207

Dartmouth College Case, famous case decided by U.S. Supreme Court 1819; legislature of New Hampshire tried to alter charter of Dartmouth College; decision was that charter was a contract which, according to Constitution, no state could alter, *list* S-518b
- Webster W-129

Darts, game D-37

Darwen, England, municipal borough 19 mi (31 km) n.w. of Manchester; cotton goods, paper, fireclay products; pop. 28,500, *map* U-18a

Darwin, Charles (1809–82), British biologist D-37. *see also in index* Darwinism
- animal experimentation A-449
- atoll's formation P-13
- biogeography B-217
- biological concepts B-229
- botany and evolution B-380
- civilization's progress C-467
- Darwin, Australia D-39
- earth E-36
- ecology E-50
- evolution E-366
- exploration E-373
- Galápagos Islands G-4
- Galton E-326
- genetics G-53
- heredity H-140
- Huxley H-336
- materialist philosophy M-210

Darwin, Erasmus (1731–1802), British physician, naturalist, poet; grandfather of Charles Darwin.

Darwin, Sir Francis (1848–1925), British botanist, born in Down, Kent; son of Charles Darwin; was assistant to his father; later became distinguished through his work in physiology of plants.

Darwin, Sir George Howard (1845–1912), British geologist and astronomer, born in Down, Kent; son of Charles Darwin.

Darwin, Sir Horace (1851–1928), British scientist and inventor, born in Down, Kent; son of Charles Darwin; designed instruments for recording earthquake shocks, and for measuring growth of small plants.

Darwin, Leonard (1850–1943), British economist, son of Charles Darwin; served in Royal Engineers 1871–90, winning rank of major; wrote on bimetallism and municipal trade.

Darwin, Australia, seaport, capital of Northern Territory; air and naval base; pop. 56,482 D-39
- Australia A-773, *map* A-819
- Northern Territory N-388
- Pacific Ocean, *map* P-3
- world, *map* W-297

Darwinism, natural selection theory of Charles Darwin. *see also in index* Darwin, Charles
- evolution E-366
- Lamarck's theories superseded L-25

Darwin tulip, flower T-305

Daryainoor, diamond, *picture* D-129

Das, Chitta Ranjan (1870–1925), Indian nationalist leader, born in Calcutta; active in Swaraj movement; first mayor of Calcutta 1924.

Dasanami, Hindu monastic order founded by Sankara M-541

Dasent, Sir George Webbe (1817–96), British author, born on island of St. Vincent, British West Indies; his translations of Scandinavian folklore especially appealing to children ('Gisli the Outlaw') S-472

Dash, punctuation mark P-534

Dash, running event T-243, *picture* T-244

Dashboard. *see in index* Instrument panel

Dasheen, broad-leaved plant of the arum family, a variety of Polynesian taro *Colocasia esculenta*; cultivated chiefly for its edible bulbs, which resemble the potato in food quality; introduced into the United States from Puerto Rico, grown commercially in the South.

Da Silva, Antonio José (1705–39), Brazilian writer L-72

Dasyure, marsupial, genus *Dasyurus,* found in Australia; lives in trees; carnivorous; size of small house cat, snout pointed, fur short and spotted, tail long and bushy; habits like those of weasel C-213

Data, factual information used as a basis for discussion, reasoning, or calculation
- computer C-627
- graph and chart G-221

Data bank (or data base), collection of information C-627

Data processing, operations involving computers and certain other devices whereby unorganized information is handled, organized according to preplanned procedure, stored, and presented for use C-627. *see also in index* Telemetry

Data transmission, in telecommunications T-56

Date line. *see in index* International date line

Date palm, plant of the family Palmaceae P-81, *picture* P-82

Dates, fruit of date palm F-430
- characteristics B-178
- Spain, *picture* E-340

Dating, social custom S-125

Datta, Michael Madhusudan (1824–73), British dramatist I-108

Datta, Narendranath. *see in index* Vivekananda

Datura, genus of annual or perennial plants, shrubs, and trees of the nightshade family, found in most parts of the world; includes jimsonweed, or thorn apple, and angel's trumpet; horn of plenty *D. metel* has large flowers, 7 in (8 cm) long, white within, violet outside, trumpet-shaped, fragrant, sometimes with several trumpets, one within another.

'Dauber', work by Masefield E-280

Daubigny, Charles François (1817–78), French landscape painter and etcher of Barbizon School, born in Paris; first pictures realistic landscapes; later work shows influence of impressionism.

Da'ud, Ibn (died 910), Islamic author I-365

Daudet, Alphonse (1840–97), French novelist D-40
- French literature F-397

Daudet, Léon (1867–1942), French literary critic, novelist, and polemical writer, born in Paris; son of Alphonse Daudet; a leader of Royalist party and one of founders of its organ, *Action Française*; most of his work reflects his vehement personality; his 'Souvenirs' depicts with gentle irony modern political and literary life.

Daugavpils (also called Dvinsk), Latvian Soviet Socialist Republic, city in s.e.; railroad center; linen and flax; sawmills; pop. 101,000, *maps* R-344, 348
- Europe, *map* E-360

Daugherty, Harry Micajah (1860–1941), U.S. lawyer, born in Washington Court House, Ohio; served as campaign manager for President Harding and as U.S. attorney general in his administration H-40

Daugherty, James Henry (1889–1974), U.S. illustrator and author, born in Asheville, N.C.; illustrated Washington Irving's 'Knickerbocker's History of New York' and other books; wrote and illustrated children's books ('Daniel Boone', awarded Newbery Medal 1940; 'Abraham Lincoln'; 'Of Courage Undaunted'; 'Marcus and Narcissa Whitman'; 'William Blake') R-107

Daughter cell, in genetics G-54

Daughters of the American Revolution (DAR), organization composed of female descendants of veterans of the American Revolution P-140
- women's organizations W-270

Daughters of the Founders and Patriots of America, U.S. patriotic society P-140

Daughters of the King, a religious organization of women and girls in the Anglican church corresponding to the Brotherhood of St. Andrew; senior and junior departments; founded 1885 in New York, N.Y.; chapters in England, Canada.

Daughters of the Revolution, U.S. patriotic society P-140

D'Aulnoy, Comtesse (or Comtesse d'Aunoy). *see in index* Aulnoy

Daumet, Pierre Jérôme Honoré (1826–1911), French architect, born in Paris; noted for restoring monuments of French architecture (Palais de Justice, Paris; Château de Chantilly).

Daumier, Honoré (1808–79), French caricaturist, painter, and sculptor D-40
- drawing D-254
- graphic arts G-233
- painting P-50

Dauphin, Man., town on Vermilion River, 145 mi (235 km) n.w. of Winnipeg; grain elevators, flour mills; just n. of Ridge Mountain National Park; pop. 8,971, *map* C-109

Dauphin, title of obscure origin; probably at first a proper name; borne first by Guigue IV (died 1142), dauphin of Viennois; the territory held by the Dauphin became known as Dauphiné; after 1364 title given to eldest son of French king, Dauphiné having become crown land
- Charles VII C-277

Dauphiné, former province in s.e. France; cap. Grenoble; site of Dauphiné Alps, range with greatest height (13,462 ft; 4,103 m).

'Dauphine, La', French ship N-256

Dausset, Jean (born 1916), French biologist. *see also in index* Nobel Prizewinners, *table*

Davao, Philippines, port city on Gulf of Davao, s.e. coast of Mindanao; capital of Davao province; trade in abaca and copra; pop. 278,600, with suburbs P-257a, *maps* P-253c, 262
- Asia, *map* A-697
- world, *map* W-297

Daveluy, Paule (born 1919), French-Canadian author, born in Ville-Marie, Que.; won Canadian Books of the Year for Children award 1960 for 'L'Été Enchanté' and 1963 for 'Drôle d'Automne'.

Davenant, Sir William (1606–68), English poet and playwright, born in Oxford, England; knighted 1643 by Charles I for fighting at siege of Gloucester; imprisoned, 1650–52; freed, it is said, through influence of Milton, whom he in turn helped after Restoration; buried in Westminster Abbey ('The Wits', comedy; 'Gondibert', epic poem) P-402

Davenport, Charles Benedict (1866–1944), U.S. biologist, born in Stamford, Conn.; after 1904 director Carnegie Institution laboratory for experimental evolution at Cold Spring Harbor, N.Y.; made important contributions to the study of genetics.

Davenport, Edward Loomis (1816–77), U.S. actor, born in Boston, Mass.; father of Fanny Davenport; known for characters from Shakespeare and Dickens (Brutus in 'Julius Caesar'; Bill Sikes in 'Oliver Twist').

Davenport, Fanny Lily Gypsy (1850–98), U.S. actress, born in London, England; starred in comic and tragic roles under management of Augustin Daly; greatest success in 'Fedora', 'Tosca', and 'Cleopatra'.

Davenport, Homer Calvin (1867–1912), U.S. caricaturist, born in Silverton, Ore.; remembered for his political cartoons; originated brutish giants to represent trusts and the dollar-marked suit of Mark Hanna
- McKinley cartoon, *picture* S-364

Davenport, John (1597–1670), Puritan divine, born in Coventry, England; left England after ecclesiastical disagreements; one of founders of New Haven, Conn., where he was minister for 30 years.

Davenport, Thomas (1802–51), U.S. inventor, born in Williamstown, Vt.; invented first commercially successful electric motor; exhibited the electric streetcar, *picture* V-291

Davenport, Iowa, city in e. part of state, on Mississippi River, opposite Rock Island, Ill. (these two cities, with neighboring Moline and East Moline, Ill., known together as the Quad Cities); farm machinery, aluminum rolling, electronic equipment, metal products; meat-packing; St. Ambrose College and Marycrest College; pop. 103,264 I-290, *map* I-302

Davey, John (1846–1923), U.S. tree surgeon, born in Somersetshire, England; known as Father of Tree Surgery; founded Davey Tree Expert Co.

David, Saint (544?–601?), patron saint of Wales, born probably in Cardiganshire; as primate of South Wales, moved seat of church government from Caerlon to Menevia; founded numerous churches.

David, king of Israel (about 1000 BC) D-40
- Bethlehem B-179
- Judaism J-149
- Ruth R-365

David I (1084–1153), king of Scotland 1123–53, son of Malcolm Canmore and Saint Margaret of England; called "Maker of Scotland"; reformed courts, established many towns; promoted trade, shipping, and manufactures.

David II (1324–71), king of Scotland, crowned 1331 at death of father, Robert Bruce; began to rule 1341; weak and inefficient.

David, Edgeworth (full name Tannatt William Edgeworth David) (1858–1934), Australian explorer, born near Cardiff, Wales; geology professor University of Sydney 1891–1924; one of two members of Shackleton's expedition 1907–09 who located south magnetic pole.

David, Edward Emil, Jr. (born 1925), U.S electrical engineer, born in Wilmington, N.C.; director of Office of Science and Technology 1971–.

David, Félicien César (1810–76), French composer, born in Cadenet, near Avignon; called "the musical Orientalist"; wandered for years in East; wrote vivid pieces, including symphonic ode, 'The Desert'; oratorio, 'Moses on Sinai'; operas, 'Herculaneum' and 'Lalla Rookh'.

David, Gerard (1460?–1523), Dutch painter who lived in Bruges, Flanders; last great Flemish primitive painter.

David, Jacques-Louis (1748–1825), French painter D-41
- sculptural history S-89

David, Pierre Jean (1788–1856), French sculptor; called David d'Angers from his birthplace of Angers, to distinguish him from the painter David; noted for naturalistic portrait busts and medallions (portraits of Washington, Lafayette, Jefferson, Goethe; medallion of Napoleon).

'David', statue by Donatello D-229

'David', statue by Michelangelo M-351

David, House of, dwindling communal religious colony in Benton Harbor, Mich.; founded 1903 by Benjamin Franklin Purnell (King Ben) (1861–1927); not associated with any other sect; in 1930 community split into House of David and Israelite City of David; members do not smoke, drink, or eat meat, and males wear beards.

'David Balfour', work by Stevenson, sequel to 'Kidnapped' S-446

'David Copperfield', novel by Dickens D-134, *picture* D-136
- novel N-410

'David Harum', novel by Edward Noyes Westcott (1847–98); hero a shrewd horse trader and humorous homely philosopher.

David Lipscomb College, in Nashville, Tenn.; affiliated with Church of Christ; founded 1891; liberal arts and teacher education; quarter system.

Davidson, Jo (1883–1952), U.S. sculptor, born in New York, N.Y.; known for his portraits of famous people (Pershing, Clemenceau, Will Rogers, F.D. Roosevelt, John D. Rockefeller, George Bernard Shaw).

Davidson, John (1857–1909), British poet, born in Barrhead, Scotland; deeply pessimistic, best known for ballads; wrote 'Bruce', 'Scaramouch in Naxos', fantastic plays; 'Fleet Street Eclogues'; 'Earl Lavender'.

Davidson, Randall Thomas, first baron of Lambeth (1848–1930), British divine, born in Edinburgh, Scotland; bishop of Rochester 1891–95; bishop of Winchester 1895–1903; archbishop of Canterbury 1903–28.

Davidson College, in Davidson, N.C.; affiliated with Presbyterian church, U.S.; founded 1837; liberal arts and sciences.

Davies, Arthur Bowen (1862–1928), U.S. artist of great versatility, born in Utica, N.Y.; best known as a painter; a sensitive dreamer and a mystic; for a time work showed influence of cubism; designed tapestries for Gobelin industry in France ('Maya, Mirror of Illusions'; 'Afterthoughts of Earth').

Davies, Sir John (1569–1626), English poet and statesman, born in Tisbury, near Shaftesbury; attorney general for Ireland 1609–19; speaker Irish Parliament 1613–19 (poems: 'Orchestra' and 'Nosce Teipsum').

Davies, Sir Louis Henry (1845–1924), Canadian statesman and jurist, born in Charlottetown, P.E.I.; premier Prince Edward Island 1876–82; Liberal in House of Commons 1882–1901, when he became judge of Supreme Court; minister of marine and fisheries 1896–1901.

Davies, Mary Carolyn, U.S. writer, born in Sprague, Wash.; best known for musical, wistful, sentimental verses ('Drums in Our Street', 'Youth Riding', 'Penny Show').

Davies, Peter Maxwell (born 1934), British composer M-676

Davies, Robertson (born 1913), Canadian novelist, playwright, and theater critic, born in Thamesville, Ont. ('Fifth Business', novel).

Davies, Rodger Paul (1921–74), U.S. ambassador to Cyprus A-704

Davies, William Henry (1871–1940), British poet, born in Newport, Monmouthshire, England, of Welsh parentage; was tramp and peddler in the U.S. and England for several years; published first book of verse at 34 ('The Soul's Destroyer'); 'The Autobiography of a Super-tramp' is account of early wanderings; in his 'Collected Poems' are lyrics of great simplicity and charm.

Dávila, Pedrarias (or Pedro Arias de Avila) (1440?–1530), Spanish governor in Central America, born in Segovia, Spain; governed Darien (Panama) and adjacent lands 1514–26; extended tyrannical rule by founding colonies; executed Balboa for insubordination; transferred to Nicaragua 1526
De Soto D-117
Panama P-86

Da Vinci, Leonardo. *see in index* Leonardo da Vinci

Davis, Arthur Hoey (pseudonym Steele Rudd) (1868–1935), Australian humorist, born in Drayton, near Toowoomba, Queensland (stories of rural life, 'On Our Selection') A-797, *table* A-798

Davis, Benjamin Oliver, Jr. (born 1912), U.S. Air Force officer, born in Washington, D.C.; father was first black general in U.S. Army; World War II combat pilot; became first black major general in Air Force 1959; director of air power and organization, Air Force, 1961–65; chief of staff U.S. and UN forces in Korea 1965–66; with U.S. Department of Transportation as director of civil aviation security 1970–71 and as assistant secretary for environment, safety, and consumer affairs 1971–75 B-295

Davis, Bette (full name Ruth Elizabeth Davis) (born 1908), U.S. actress, born in Lowell, Mass.; after short, successful career on stage, entered motion pictures 1931; twice won Academy award, for 'Dangerous' (1935) and 'Jezebel' (1938); also starred in 'Of Human Bondage', 'Now, Voyager', and 'All About Eve'; autobiographies, 'The Lonely Life', and 'This 'n That' with Michael Herskowitz.

Davis, Colin (born 1927), British conductor, *list* O-579

Davis, David (1815–86), U.S. jurist, born in Cecil County, Maryland; justice U.S. Supreme Court 1862–77; U.S. senator 1877–83.

Davis, Dorothy Salisbury (born 1916), detective story writer D-119

Davis, Dwight Filley (1879–1945), U.S. Republican statesman, born in St. Louis, Mo.; officer, World War I; secretary of war 1925–29; governor-general of Philippines 1929–32; established Davis Cup.

Davis, Elmer Holmes (1890–1958), U.S. writer, journalist, and news analyst (radio and television), born in Aurora, Ind.; on staff *New York Times* 1914–24; director Office of War Information 1942–45 (essays: 'But We Were Born Free'; novels and short stories) R-277

Davis, George (1820–96), U.S. lawyer and statesman, born in New Hanover County, North Carolina; attorney general Confederate States of America 1864–65.

Davis, Glenn (born 1924), U.S. football halfback F-298

Davis, Henry Winter (1817–65), U.S. statesman, born in Annapolis, Md.; as Whig member of Congress from Maryland 1855–61, 1863–65, opposed Lincoln's policies and urged stringent reconstruction.

Davis, James John (1873–1947), U.S. public official, born in Wales; came to U.S. 1881; worked in steel mills; secretary of labor under Harding, Coolidge, Hoover; U.S. senator from Pennsylvania 1930–44; director general Loyal Order of Moose 1906–47, founder of Mooseheart Home and School.

Davis, Jefferson (1808–89), president of the Confederate States of America D-42
Civil War C-473
Confederate States of America C-642
Davis, Varina D-43
Greeley G-280
Lee L-115
Memorial State Park, *picture* G-93
Mississippi homes, *pictures* M-476
North Carolina Tar Heels N-356
Statuary Hall, *table* S-437b
Stone Mountain, *picture* G-88
White Houses of the Confederacy R-205
Montgomery M-569

Davis, John (or John Davys) (1550?–1605), English navigator and Arctic explorer, born in Sandridge, near Dartmouth; explored Davis Strait 1587
America A-332
Falkland Islands F-14

Davis, John William (1873–1955), U.S. lawyer and diplomat, born in Clarksburg, W. Va.; member of Congress 1911–13; solicitor general U.S. 1913–18; ambassador to United Kingdom 1918–21; Democratic nominee for presidency 1924.

Davis, Marguerite (1887–1967), U.S. biochemist, born in Racine, Wis. V-357

Davis, Mary Gould (1882–1956), U.S. writer of children's stories, born in Bangor, Me.; supervisor of storytelling, New York Public Library, 1922–44; editor of Books for Young People *Saturday Review of Literature* (later *Saturday Review*) 1944–53 ('A Baker's Dozen'; 'The Truce of the Wolf'; 'Girl's Book of Verse') S-464, 481c

Davis, Miles (born 1926), U.S. trumpeter and composer D-43
Coltrane C-587
jazz J-86

Davis, Norman Hezekiah (1878–1944), U.S. statesman, born in Bedford County, Tennessee; financial adviser to government during and after World War I; assistant secretary of treasury 1919–20; undersecretary of state 1920–21; member League of Nations Financial Commission; national chairman of American Red Cross 1938–44; prominent Democrat.

Davis, Owen (1874–1956), U.S. playwright, born in Portland, Me.; nearly 200 plays; dramatized Edith Wharton's 'Ethan Frome' ('Nellie, the Beautiful Cloak Model'; 'Icebound', Pulitzer prize play 1923; 'The Nervous Wreck').

Davis, Richard Harding (1864–1916), U.S. novelist and journalist, born in Philadelphia, Pa.; war correspondent in Spanish-American, Boer, Russo-Japanese wars and World War I ('Soldiers of Fortune'; 'Van Bibber and Others'; 'The Bar Sinister').

Davis, Sam (1842–63), Confederate hero, born near Smyrna, Tenn.; hanged at Pulaski, Tenn., when captured inside Federal lines with military information; asked to betray source of information, he answered: "If I had a thousand lives to live I would lose them all before I would betray my friends or the confidence of my informer"; his statue on Capitol grounds, Nashville T-88, *picture* T-87

Davis, Sammy, Jr. (born 1925), U.S. singer, actor, and dancer; born in New York, N.Y.; star of theater, movies, and television; won 1968 Spingarn medal for civil rights work.

Davis, Stuart (1894–1964), U.S. painter, lithographer, and writer on art, born in Philadelphia, Pa.; influenced by modern art
'Summer Landscape' P-26, *picture* P-27

Davis, Thomas Osborne (1814–45), Irish author I-327

Davis, Varina Howell (1826–1906), first lady of the Confederate States of America D-43
Davis, Jefferson D-42

Davis, William Grenville (born 1929), Canadian public official, born in Brampton, Ont., n.w. of Toronto; elected premier of Ontario 1971; resigned 1984.

Davis, William Hammatt (1879–1964), U.S. lawyer and arbitrator, born in Bangor, Me.; administrator and national compliance director NRA 1933–34; chairman National Defense Mediation Board 1941–42; chairman National War Labor Board 1942–45; director Office of Economic Stabilization 1945; on patent advisory panel AEC 1947–57.

Davis, William Morris (1850–1934), U.S. geographer and geologist, born in Philadelphia, Pa.; on faculty Harvard University 1876–1912, became professor of geology ('The Coral Reef Problem').

Davis, Calif., city 15 mi (25 km) w. of Sacramento; in agricultural area; cannery; University of California at Davis; incorporated 1917; pop. 36,640.

Davis, Mount, in Pennsylvania. *see in index* Negro Mountain

Davis and Elkins College, Elkins, W. Va.; Protestant interdenominational; opened 1904; arts and sciences, teacher education W-169

Davis Cup, awarded annually to nation winning men's tennis team championship, cup donated 1900 by Dwight F. Davis, U.S. statesman B-366
tennis T-108

Davis Dam, dam in Nevada N-134

Davison, Frederic Ellis (born 1917), U.S. Army officer, born in Washington D.C.; commissioned 1941; served in all-black infantry unit in Italy, World War II; made brigadier general while on active duty in Vietnam 1968, third black man to hold rank of general.

Davisson, Clinton Joseph (1881–1958), U.S. physicist, born in Bloomington, Ill.; member of technical staff of Bell Telephone Laboratories P-307. *see also in index* Nobel Prizewinners, *table*

Davis Strait, strait between Greenland and Baffin Island; width 180 to 500 mi (290 to 800 km); ice blocks late fall and winter navigation; explored by John Davis 1587, *maps* N-350, W-297

Davitt, Michael (1846–1906), Irish political leader, of great force and bitter earnestness, born in Straide, County Mayo; had impoverished childhood; maimed in mill accident; jailed for helping arm Irish nationalists; helped found Irish Land League 1879; often member of Parliament; ardent "home ruler" but opposed Parnell.

Davos Platz, Switzerland, winter resort S-542, *map* S-537
winter sports W-242

Davout, Louis Nicolas, duke of Auerstädt and prince of Eckmühl (1770–1823), one of Napoleon's marshals, born in Annoux, n.-central France; won brilliant victories at Auerstädt and Eckmühl; turned tide at Wagram; minister of war during 100 days.

Davy, Humphry (1778–1829), English scientist D-43
chemical elements
magnesium M-41
potassium and sodium S-247
electricity E-161
electric light E-163
Faraday F-24
tanning materials L-110

Davy Jones, sailors' colloquial name for the spirit of the sea; "Davy Jones's locker" means the bottom of the sea; perhaps came from "duffy," meaning a ghost, and Jonah, who in the Bible story was swallowed by the whale.

Davys, John. *see in index* Davis, John

Dawes, Charles Gates (1865–1951), U.S. Republican statesman, born in Marietta, Ohio; U.S. comptroller of currency 1897–1901; organizer and official, trust companies and banks from 1902; U.S. brigadier general, on military board of allied supply 1918–19; first director U.S. Bureau of the Budget 1921–22; served as vice-president of U.S. 1925–29; ambassador to Britain 1929–32; president Reconstruction Finance Corporation 1932 ('The Banking System of the United States'). *see also in index* Nobel Prizewinners, *table*
World War I W-313, 321

Dawes, Henry Laurens (1816–1903), U.S. legislator, born in Cummington, Mass.; Republican representative from Massachusetts 1857–73; U.S. senator 1875–83; gave much attention to legislation for American Indians; chairman Dawes Commission to Five Civilized Tribes 1893–1903.

Dawes, William (1745–99), U.S. patriot, born in Boston, Mass.; ancestor of Charles Gates Dawes R-161
Lexington and Concord battle L-144

Dawes Plan, German reparations payments G-123
Weimar Republic W-142
World War I W-321

Dawn men. *see in index* Abbevillian

Dawson, George Mercer (1849–1901), Canadian geologist, born in Pictou, N.S.; son of Sir John William Dawson; director Geological Survey of Canada 1895–1901; Dawson, Y.T., named for him.

Dawson, Sir John William (1820–99), Canadian geologist, born in Pictou, N.S.; father of George Mercer Dawson; professor of geology and principal of McGill University 1855–93; his studies were largely responsible for development of Nova Scotia coal mines; opposed Darwinism.

Dawson, Simon James (1820–1902), Canadian civil engineer and statesman, born in Scotland; aided settlement of the Northwest by exploring country between Lake Superior and the Saskatchewan River; represented Ontario in Canadian House of Commons 1878–91.

Dawson, William Levi (1886–1970), U.S. public official and lawyer, born in Albany, Ga.; Chicago alderman 1933–39; U.S. congressman (Democrat) from Illinois 1943–70.

Dawson, Y.T., on Yukon River; center of Klondike region; capital of Yukon Territory 1898–1951; pop. at time of gold rush 20,000, now 762 Y-440, *picture* M-18, *map* C-112
North America, *map* N-350
world, *map* W-297
Yukon River Y-439

Dawson Creek, B.C., city 300 mi (480 km) n.w. of Edmonton, Alta.; oil refining and grain elevators; s. point of Alaska Highway; pop 11,373.

Day, Arthur Louis (1869–1960), U.S. physicist, born in Brookfield, Mass.; director Geophysical Laboratory, Carnegie Institution of Washington, 1907–36.

Day, Benjamin (1838–1916), U.S. printer; inventor about 1879 of process for shading plates for printing illustrations and maps, known as the Benday, or Ben Day, process.

Day, Clarence Shepard (1874–1935), U.S. writer, born in New York, N.Y.; refusing to enter father's brokerage business, joined Navy; contracted arthritis; after years of invalidism took up writing ('God and My Father'; 'The Best of Clarence Day')
'Life with Father' R-112a

Day, James Edward (1914–67), U.S. lawyer and government official, born in Jacksonville, Ill.; Illinois insurance commissioner 1950–53; joined Prudential Insurance Company of America 1953, vice-president 1957–61; U.S.

postmaster general 1961–63; Democrat.
Day, Sandra. *see in index* O'Connor, Sandra Day
Day, Stephen (or Stephen Daye) (1594?–1668), North American pioneer printer, born in London, England; set up first printing press in American Colonies 1639 at Cambridge, Mass.; printed 'Freeman's Oath', 'Psalms', almanacs, official documents; town granted him 300 acres (120 hectares) for "being the first that set upon printing."
Dayaks, a people of Borneo B-368
Dayan, Moshe (1915–81), Israeli general and statesman D-44
Day and night
calendar C-30
international date line I-253, *diagram* I-254
planetary motion A-710
polar regions A-572
Sabbath S-1
Day care, supervision of children to free mothers and fathers for work or other activities; establishment of adequate day-care centers is major issue with women's liberation groups and with the working poor D-44. *see also in index* Kindergarten and nursery school
Day-care center D-44, *picture* S-237
child abuse C-319
U.S.S.R. R-332c
Daydreaming
sexuality S-125
Daye, Stephen. *see in index* Day, Stephen
Day fly. *see in index* Mayfly
Day-Lewis, C. (1904–72), British poet and editor, born in Ballintogher, Ireland; professor of poetry Oxford University 1951–56; vice-president Royal Society of Literature 1958–72; poet laureate of England 1968–72 (poetry: 'Collected Poems', 'A Time to Dance', 'Poems, 1943–1947', 'An Italian Visit', 'Pegasus and Other Poems'; prose: 'Poetry for You' and 'The Poetic Image'); author of detective stories, under pen name Nicholas Blake E-281
poet laureate P-402
Daylight saving time T-189
Daylight tank, photographic darkroom equipment P-292
Day lily, showy garden perennial of genus *Hemerocallis* of the lily family, with loosely clustered, lilylike flowers on tall stalks; flowers in many colors last only a day L-209, *picture* F-224
flowering time G-25
Day nursery. *see in index* Day care; Day-care center; Kindergarten and nursery school
Day of Atonement. *see in index* Yom Kippur
'Day of Doom, The', work by Wigglesworth A-342
Days of grace, the days, usually three, added to the time stipulated, as for the payment of a promissory note; life-insurance companies may grant 30 days' grace.
Day tank, type of furnace used in glass manufacture G-157
Dayton, Jonathan (1760–1824), U.S. soldier and political leader, born in Elizabethtown, N.J.; with his father fought in Revolutionary War; youngest member of Federal Convention 1787; U.S. representative from New Jersey 1791–99, speaker of the House of Representatives 1795–99; senator 1799–1805; implicated in Burr's conspiracy 1805; Dayton, Ohio, named for him.
Dayton, Ohio, manufacturing city in s.w. part of state; pop. 203,588 D-45
city government C-459
municipal government M-655
North America, *map* N-350
Ohio O-501, 512, *picture* O-511
United States, *map* U-41
Dayton, University of, in Dayton, Ohio; Roman Catholic; founded 1850; arts and sciences, business administration, education, engineering, technology; graduate studies; trimesters.
Daytona Beach, Fla., city on Atlantic Ocean, about 90 mi (140 km) s.e. of Jacksonville; pop. 54,176 D-45
automobile racing S-38
United States, *map* U-41
Daytona 500, motorcycle race M-632
DBCP (dibromochloropropane), pesticide I-175
DC. *see in index* Direct current
DC motor M-631
D-Day, day set for opening of a military operation
amphibious vessels N-85
warfare W-21
World War II, *picture* R-267
DDE, insecticide metabolite E-57
DDT (or dichlorodiphenyl-trichloroethane), insecticide
ecological impact E-57
evolution E-365
pollution P-441d
toxic waste W-76
Deacon, an officer in the Christian church with duties varying in the different denominations.
Deaconess, one of an order of women in the early Christian church to whom various spiritual and charitable duties were assigned; in the 19th century various Protestant churches established deaconess homes, whose inmates devoted selves to ministering to sick and needy.
Deacons for Defense, organization of militant black Americans B-297
'Dead End', motion picture that introduced the "Dead End Kids" J-164
'Dead End', work by Kingsley A-356
Deadfall, type of trap T-267
Dead leaf butterfly. *see in index* Oriental leaf butterfly
Dead lift, weight lifting W-137
Deadly amanita (or death cup, or destroying angel), mushroom *Amanita phalloides* M-665, *picture* M-664
Deadly nightshade (or Belladonna), plant *Atropa belladonna* N-315
drug source D-273
poisonous plants P-411
Dead-mail office P-460a
Dead man's hand, the poker hand Wild Bill Hickok held when he was shot and killed H-149
Dead reckoning, method of navigation N-68, 71
Dead Sea, salt lake between Israel and Jordan; 405 sq mi (1,050 sq km) D-45
Bible B-184
industry P-81
Israel I-369, *picture* I-373
Jordan River J-143
lake L-24
Dead Sea Scrolls, famous collection of ancient documents D-46
archaeology A-531
'Dead Souls', novel by Gogol G-175, R-360
Dead stars, in astronomy S-412
'Dead Toreador, The', painting by Manet P-51
Deadweight tonnage, in shipping S-169
Deadwood, S.D., trade city and tourist center in Black Hills mining region, 34 mi (55 km) n.w. of Rapid City; lumbering and wood products; cattle raising; settled 1876 following gold discovery in Deadwood Gulch; pop. 2,035 S-323, *map* S-334
Deadwood Dick, romantic dime-novel hero of the wild West, created by Edward L. Wheeler in 1870s; later many self-styled prototypes adopted the name.
Deafness D-47. *see also in index* Ear
Bell B-130
hearing aids B-238, S-348
noise N-331
test, *picture* P-311
Deák, Ferencz Francis (1803–76), Hungarian statesman, one of ablest political leaders in Europe, born in Sojtor, Zala; chief organizer (1867) of Austro-Hungarian dual monarchy.
Deakin, Alfred (1856–1919), Australian statesman, born in Melbourne; prime minister 1903–4, 1905–8, 1909–10; brilliant orator; reconciling influence between Labor and Conservative parties.
Dean, Gordon Evans (1905–58), U.S. lawyer and government official, born in Seattle, Wash.; assistant to Robert H. Jackson, war crimes trials, Nuremberg, Germany; taught criminal law University of Southern California 1946–49; member U.S. Atomic Energy Commission 1949–53, chairman 1950–53; author of 'Report on the Atom'.
Dean, James (1931–55), U.S. stage and motion-picture actor, born in Marion, Ind.; portrayed restless, idealistic, lonely young men at odds with society; brief, spectacular film career ('East of Eden', 'Rebel Without a Cause', 'Giant'); sudden death in automobile accident contributed to his becoming a cult figure.
Dean, Jay Hanna (nickname Dizzy) (1911–74), U.S. baseball pitcher, born in Lucas, Ark.; with St. Louis, N.L., 1930–37, Chicago, N.L., 1938–41, and St. Louis, A.L., 1947; older half of colorful brother combination "Me and Paul," that pitched St. Louis Cardinals to 3 pennants and 2 world championships B-92
Dean, Jimmy (born 1928), U.S. country musician M-679
Dean, title given to certain college and high school officials; also to clergyman in charge of cathedral or a collegiate chapter U-205
Dean, Forest of, district (22,000 acres; 8,900 hectares) in w. Gloucestershire, England, between Severn and Wye rivers; ancient royal forest; iron mines.
Deane, Silas (1737–89), U.S. statesman and diplomat, born in Groton, Conn.; delegate to Continental Congress 1774–76; sent to France as semi-official financial and political agent 1776; made unauthorized promises to induce French officers to join American Revolutionary military and was recalled (1777) because of errors in his accounts; defended by John Jay and John Adams.
De Angeli, Marguerite Lofft (born 1889), U.S. illustrator and author of books for children, born in Lapeer, Mich.; works are rich in flavor and atmosphere of the past ('Henner's Lydia'; 'Copper-toed Boots'; 'Bright April'; 'The Door in the Wall', 1950 Newbery Medal; 'Book of Nursery and Mother Goose Rhymes'; 'Book of Favorite Hymns'); won Regina Medal 1968.
Dearborn, Henry (1751–1829), U.S. general for whom Fort Dearborn (now Chicago, Ill.) was named, born in Hampton, N.H.; served in Revolution and War of 1812; secretary of war under Jefferson; minister to Portugal 1822–24 ('Revolutionary War Journals').
Dearborn, Mich., city just w. of Detroit; pop. 90,660 M-358. *see also in index* Edison Institute; Greenfield Village
Dearborn Heights, Mich., city s.w. of Detroit; mainly residential; small-tool and die industry; incorporated 1962; pop. 80,069.
Dearden, John Francis, Cardinal (born 1907), Roman Catholic prelate, born in Valley Falls, R.I.; bishop of Pittsburgh 1950–58; archbishop of Detroit 1959–80; created cardinal 1969, retired 1980.
Death D-48. *see also in index* Assassination; Burial and funeral customs; Disasters; Suicide
autopsy A-875
beliefs
ancient Egyptian E-123
Christian R-257
hell and Hades H-123
Judaic J-148
mythology M-698
Pythagorean P-544
spiritualist S-392
bioethical issues B-215
causes
automobile accidents A-862
drugs P-411
execution P-506
famine R-355
poison P-410
pollution P-441b
estate and inheritance E-307
insurance S-236. *see also in index* Life insurance
'Death and Fire', painting by Klee K-255
'Death Be Not Proud', work by Gunther R-111g
'Death Comes for the Archbishop', novel by Cather R-112c
Death cup. *see in index* Deadly amanita
'Death in the Afternoon', work by Hemingway W-378
'Death in Venice', work by Mann M-109
Death mask M-186
'Death of Artemio Cruz, The', work by Fuentes L-71
'Death of a Salesman', play by Miller A-357, R-111g
'Death of Bessie Smith, The', work by Albee A-260
'Death of Marat, The', work by David, *picture* D-41
'Death of the Virgin', work by Joos van Cleve, *picture* M-163
'Death of the Virgin', work by Schongauer, *picture* G-232
Death penalty. *see in index* Capital punishment
Death rate. *see in index* Vital statistics
Death tax T-38
Death Valley, desert region of s. California D-50
California C-33
formation E-15
Mount Whitney W-201
Nevada N-136
North America, *picture* N-336
Deathwatch beetle, beetle of the family Anobiidae B-140
Deauville, France, fashionable resort on Normandy coast of English Channel, 10 mi (16 km) s. of Le Havre; famous racetrack; pop. 5,103, *map* F-369
De Bakey, Michael Ellis (born 1908), U.S. heart surgeon, born in Lake Charles, La.; professor and chairman department of surgery Baylor University after 1948; president Baylor College of Medicine 1969–; developed pump for heart-lung machine; Max Berg award, *picture* S-519b
De Bary, Heinrich Anton (1831–88), German physician and botanist, born in Frankfurt; professor of botany at universities of Freiburg and Halle; first rector of University of Strasbourg; notable research on fungi and bacteria.
Debate D-51
Lincoln and Douglas L-225
Webster and Hayne J-356
Debenture, credit instrument S-450
Debierne, André Louis (1874–1949), French chemist; discovered the radioactive element actinium in pitchblende
radium isolation R-70
Deborah, Hebrew heroine, prophetess, judge; helped deliver Israelites from Canaanites (Bible, Judges iv, v); her triumphal song known as most ancient piece of Hebrew literature.
Debré, Michel Jean Pierre (born 1912), French statesman and jurist, born in Paris; member French Resistance; senator 1948–58; as minister of justice, helped draft 1958 constitution; premier 1959–62.
Debrecen, Hungary, city 120 mi (190 km) e. of Budapest; tobacco processing; machinery, fertilizer, furniture; center of Hungarian Protestantism; here Kossuth (1849) proclaimed deposition of Hapsburgs, pop. 212,000 H-329, *map* E-360
Debs, Eugene V. (1855–1926), U.S. socialist and labor leader D-51
Darrow D-36
peace movement P-143b
socialism S-235
Debt. *see also in index* National debt
international relations I-264
Roman law R-244
slavery S-212
Debtor life insurance policy C-763
Debussy, Claude (1862–1918), French composer D-52
Ballets Russes B-34
classical music M-675
opera O-568
Debye, Peter Joseph Wilhelm (1884–1966), U.S. physicist, born in Maastricht, The Netherlands; research on molecular structure and physical chemistry; from 1936 director Max Planck Institute, Berlin, until forced out by Nazis in 1940; professor of chemistry

Cornell University 1940–52, head of department 1940–50; won National Medal of Science 1966
Decagon, in mathematics G-76, *diagram* G-75
Decalcomania (or transfer printing), process of transferring designs, pictures, or lettering from paper to china, glass, etc. P-476
'Decameron', one hundred stories by Boccacio; important source book for Elizabethan and French authors B-330, R-146
  Italian literature I-376
  novel N-408, 414
Decamps, Alexandre Gabriel (1803–60), French painter, born in Paris; excelled in painting landscape, genre, and Oriental subjects; noted as historical, scriptural, and animal painter ('Defeat of the Cimbri'; 'The Monkey Connoisseurs'; 'Joseph Sold by His Brethren').
Decathlon, athletic event T-246
  Olympics O-541
Decating, process in textile manufacture T-140
Decatur, Stephen (1779–1820), U.S. naval officer D-52
  War of 1812 W-31
Decatur, Ala., city on Tennessee River, 77 mi (124 km) n. of Birmingham; chemical fibers, tire fabrics, metal products, building materials; named for Stephen Decatur; pop. 42,002, *map* A-212
Decatur, Ga., city immediately e. of Atlanta, near Stone Mountain; metal products, foods, textiles; Agnes Scott College; named for Stephen Decatur; pop. 18,404.
Decatur, Ill., city about 37 mi (60 km) e. of Springfield; corn and soybean products, metal products, tires, glass; Millikin University; birthplace of Grand Army of the Republic; pop. 94,081 I-36, *map* I-52
Decay (or dental caries), tooth T-52
Decay (or rot, or putrefaction)
  atomic particles A-757
  bacteria cause B-13
  soil S-249
  wood W-285
Decay series, radioactivity R-64, *chart* R-66
Deccan (or Dekkan), the whole peninsula of India s. of the Narbada River
  agriculture, *picture* I-67
  India I-63, *map* I-86
Deceiver-scope (or phenakistoscope), optical toy M-615
Deceleration, in physics
  mechanics M-266
  space travel S-345
December, 12th month of the Gregorian calendar
  birthdays of famous persons. *see in index* Birthdays, *table*
Decembrist uprising, unsuccessful revolt of Russian revolutionaries Dec. 1825 against Nicholas I N-306
Decemvirs, Roman commission of ten men appointed 451 BC to draw up laws R-243
Decentralization of industry
  transportation T-257
  urban population U-108
  U.S.S.R. R-327
Deception Island, volcanic island in Antarctic Ocean, one of South Shetland Islands; deep lake and hot springs; base for Hearst-Wilkins expedition 1928–29.
Deception Pass, pass in Washington, *picture* W-58
Decibel, one tenth of a bel; unit of measure of loudness of sounds to normal human ears; because the power of the ear to distinguish differences in loudness decreases as volume increases, the bel scale is made logarithmic; each unit is 10 times the preceding one; thus a barely audible whisper measures one bel (10 decibels) and a speeding express train about 10 bels (100 decibels), though the train generates 10 billion times as much sound energy; in practice, measurements are made with a special sound meter (acoustimeter) containing numerous electrical circuits whose aggregate sensitivity to pitch and loudness corresponds to that of the human ear P-441e, S-260
  noise N-331
Deciduous forest, forest composed primarily of broad-leaved trees, *picture* E-51
Deciduous plants, those that shed their leaves periodically
  shrubs S-187
  trees T-276
Deciduous teeth, human. *see in index* Primary teeth
Decigram, metric unit of weight (1.543 grains).
Decimal system (or base-ten system), in numeration. *see also in index* Fractions, common and decimal
  abacus A-4
  arithmetic A-590
  Jefferson's adoption for coinage J-92
  mathematics M-213
  numeration systems N-435, *tables* N-438, N-439
  percentage equivalents P-198
  subtraction S-500
Decimeter, unit of metric system (3.937 in.; 10 cm), *diagram* W-139
Decimus Junius Juvenalis. *see in index* Juvenal
'Decisive Battles of the Western World, The', work by Fuller W-28
Decius (201–251), Roman emperor; cruelly persecuted Christians; killed in Thrace in battle against Goths C-401
Decius Mus, Publius, name of three Roman consuls who, according to legend, died for country—the father in the Samnite war (340 BC), his son in battle of Sentinum (295 BC), his grandson in battle of Ausculum (279 BC).
Decker, George Henry (born 1902), U.S. Army officer, born in Catskill, N.Y.; became 4-star general 1956; commander of UN forces in Korea 1957–59; Army vice-chief of staff 1959–60, chief of staff 1960–62.
Decker, Thomas. *see in index* Dekker, Thomas
Decker Slaney, Mary (born 1958), U.S. athlete
  track and field T-245
Declaration of Independence, United States D-53. *Reference-Outline* U-197a
  civil rights C-468, A-10
  Continental Congress C-692
  drafting committee, *picture* R-162
  Hancock H-25
  human rights H-319
  Jefferson J-89
  king's veto power V-307
  labor law's development L-4
  Locke L-278
  original draft, *picture* U-143
  signers A-38
  Statue of Liberty L-148
Declaration of London (1909), code of rules to govern naval warfare and blockade adopted by the London Naval Conference of 1908–9, in which United Kingdom, Germany, France, U.S., Austria-Hungary, Italy, Russia, Spain, The Netherlands, and Japan participated B-312
  warfare W-26
Declaration of Paris, agreement signed 1856 by France, United Kingdom, Austria, Prussia, Russia, Turkey, and Sardinia; result of dispute during Crimean War between France and England over treatment of property at sea B-312
Declaration of the Rights of Man and of the Citizen, (1789), France
  Bill of Rights B-195
  French Revolution F-402
  human rights H-320
Declaration of war W-26
Declination, in astronomy A-719, S-416
  navigation N-72, 75, *diagram* N-71
Declination (also called variation), of compass, error in magnetic compass due to irregularities in Earth's magnetic field C-622, D-161
'Decline and Fall of the Roman Empire', famous history by Gibbon, published 1776–88 G-143
'Decline of the West, The', work by Spengler S-377, C-467
Decoder. *see in index* Receiver
Decomposer, an inhabitant of an ecosystem E-55
Decompression, explosive S-346a
Decompression sickness (or aeroembolism), in aerospace medicine A-81
Decompression sickness (or bends, or caisson disease), physiological problem associated with underwater diving; results from differences in underwater pressure and air pressure D-188, C-18
  helium's use H-123
  underwater navigation N-73
Decoration Day. *see in index* Memorial Day
Decorations, of honor. *see in index* Medal
Decorative arts D-59. *see also in index* specific art forms, such as Fashion; Interior Design; Pottery
Decoupage, hobby H-181
De Coverley, Sir Roger. *see in index* Coverley, Sir Roger de
Decuma, in Roman mythology
  Fates F-44
Dedalus, Stephen, main character in 'A Portrait of the Artist as a Young Man' J-145, N-411
Dede Agach. *see in index* Alexandroúpolis
Dedekind, Richard (1831–1916), German mathematician M-216
Dedham, Mass., residential township 10 mi (16 km) s.w. of Boston, on Charles River; paper products; founded 1636, Fairbanks House, built 1636; pop. 25,298.
Deduction, in logic P-264
  paragraph pattern R-103d
Deductive reasoning, type of logic L-284
De Duve, Christian (born 1917), Belgian biochemist, born in Thames Ditton, near London, England; co-winner of 1974 Nobel prize for cell structure research; discovered lysosomes; professor University of Louvain 1951, Rockefeller University 1962 *see also in index* Nobel Prizewinners, *table*
Dee, river in Scotland famous for salmon and spectacular scenery; has source in Cairngorm Mountains, flows 87 mi (140 km) to North Sea at Aberdeen.
Dee, river in Wales and England, 70 mi (110 km) long; rises in n. Wales, flows n.e. past town of Chester into Irish Sea, *map* U-18a
Deed of Surrender, (1869), Canada; Northwest Territories purchased by Canada from the Hudson's Bay Company C-101
  Hudson's Bay Company H-315
Deeping, George Warwick (1877–1950), British novelist, born in Southend, Essex; gave up medicine for literature; work sympathetically portrays human character ('Sorrel and Son').
Deep mining. *see in index* Underground mining
Deeps, regions of an ocean floor that are below the mean depth of 12,000 feet O-461
Deep Sea Drilling Project
  frontier exploration F-427
Deep-sea life D-59
  fish F-128, *picture* F-131
  oceans O-461
    oceanography O-483
Deep Space Network (DSN), stations to track spacecraft S-343b
Deep-space probe. *see in index* Probe
Deep tillage (or stubble mulching), method of plowing to conserve the land C-674
  farm machinery F-32
Deepwater wave (or short wave), ocean wave O-487
Deer D-61
  buckskin L-109
  ecology E-58
  endangered species E-212
  fawn, *picture* P-511
  feeding in winter A-39
  hoof H-231
  Minnesota, *picture* M-450
  parasite, *picture* P-115
  ruminant R-318
  species
    reindeer R-139
  zoo Z-463
Deere, John (1804–86), U.S. inventor, born in Rutland, Vt.; after much experimenting, made first steel plowshare in his small shop in Illinois; became one of great plow manufacturers I-195, *picture* V-296
Deerfield, Ill., residential village 25 mi (40 km) n.w. of Chicago; incorporated 1903; Trinity College; pop. 17,430
  Illinois, *map* I-52
Deerfield, Mass., 33 mi (53 km) n. of Springfield, on Connecticut River; scene of Deerfield Massacre of 1704; pop. of township 4,517.
Deerfield Beach, Fla., town 12 mi (19 km) n. of Fort Lauderdale, on Atlantic Ocean; incorporated 1925; pop. 39,193.
Deerfly, insect related to but smaller than the horsefly; female inflicts painful bites on animals and humans in area of the forehead or in back of the neck.
Deergrass. *see in index* Meadow beauty
Deer Island, island in New Brunswick N-154
Deer Lake, Newf., town on Deer Lake and Humber River, 30 mi (47 km) n.e. of Corner Brook; supplies hydroelectric power for paper mills in area; pop. 4,289 N-164
Deer Park, N.Y., residential community 35 mi (55 km) e. of New York, N.Y., in Suffolk County; aircraft instruments laboratory; pop. 32,274.
Deer Park, Tex., city 30 mi (50 km) e. of Houston; chemicals; oil refining; annual rodeo; pop. 12,773.
'Deerslayer, The', novel by Cooper A-346
De facto, Latin term meaning "actual, based on fact," applied to a form of government that exercises governing power without internationally recognized legal authority; distinguished from *de jure* government, which exercises power by legal right in international law I-255
  legal definition, *table* L-92
Defarge, Madame Thérèse, character in 'A Tale of Two Cities', by Charles Dickens, an old woman, wife of a wine seller, who knits incessantly as she counts the heads that fall at the guillotine in the French Revolution.
'Defence of Fort M'Henry'. *see in index* 'Star-Spangled Banner'
Defendant, in law L-95
Defender of the Faith, title borne by English rulers
  Henry VIII H-131
Defender of the Holy Sepulcher, title borne by Godfrey of Bouillon during his rule of Jerusalem following the First Crusade C-787
Defenders of Wildlife, U.S. humane society H-318
Defense, warfare strategy and tactics W-23
Defense, Department of, United States U-159, *list* U-156. *see also in index* Air Force, Department of the; Army, Department of the; Navy, Department of the
  Eisenhower administration E-140
  guided missiles G-311
  navy N-87
  U.S. government U-159
  X rays X-406
Defense Advanced Research Projects Agency, United States A-77
Defense Intelligence Agency (DIA), United States I-237
Defense mechanism, in psychology, device used unconsciously to ward off problems one cannot resolve.
  repression P-519
Defense program, United States U-188
  guided missiles G-307
  World War II
    Roosevelt R-274
Defense Transportation, Office of (ODT), United States R-277
Defiance, Ohio, city on Maumee River, 50 mi (80 km) s.w. of Toledo; castings, screw machine products, radio and television parts, dairy products; Defiance College; Fort Defiance built here 1794 by Anthony Wayne; pop. 16,801.
Defiance College, Defiance, Ohio; private control, related to United Church of Christ; chartered 1850; arts and sciences, business administration, Christian

DENMARK'S RULERS SINCE THE UNION OF KALMAR

Denmark, Sweden, and Norway	
1397–1412	Margaret and Eric VII (Eric XIII of Sweden)
1412–1438	Eric VII (alone)
[1438–1440	Interregnum]
1440–1448	Christopher III
1448–1481	Christian I
1481–1513	John
1513–1523	Christian II (Sweden revolts and becomes independent, 1523)
Denmark and Norway	
1523–1533	Frederick I
1533–1559	Christian III
1559–1588	Frederick II
1588–1648	Christian IV
1648–1670	Frederick III
1670–1699	Christian V
1699–1730	Frederick IV
1730–1746	Christian VI
1746–1766	Frederick V
1766–1784	Christian VII
1808–1839	Frederick VI (regent 1784–1808) (Norway annexed to Sweden, 1814)
Denmark	
1839–1848	Christian VIII
1848–1863	Frederick VII
1863–1906	Christian IX
1906–1912	Frederick VIII
1912–1947	Christian X
1947–1972	Frederick IX
1972–	Margrethe II

Department of . . . , U.S. government. *see in index under* main word, *e.g.,* Agriculture, Department of, etc.

Department store, store made up of many departments, each of which is confined to one class of merchandise M-146
 clothing C-513
 franchise F-373
 Marshall Field's F-77
 Tokyo T-204
 United States U-110
 vocational opportunities V-370, *picture* V-369

De Paul University, in Chicago, Ill.; Roman Catholic; founded 1898; liberal arts and sciences, commerce, education, law, music; graduate school.

DePauw, Washington C. (1822–87), U.S. manufacturer and philanthropist, born in Salem, Ind.; made liberal gift to DePauw University, which was renamed for him.

DePauw University (formerly Indiana Asbury University), in Greencastle, Ind.; Methodist; founded 1837; became DePauw University in 1884; liberal arts, education, music, nursing; graduate studies.

Dependency, political unit. *see also in index* Mandates
 colonialism and imperialism C-556
 Commonwealth guidance C-603

Dependent clause, in grammar G-211, S-111

Dependent Pension Act (1890), money for disabled Civil War veterans
 Harrison H-47

De Pere, Wis., city on Fox River, 5 mi (8 km) s. of Green Bay; paper products, boats, plastics, feed; pop. 14,892.

Depew, Chauncey Mitchell (1834–1928), U.S. lawyer and Republican leader, born in Peekskill, N.Y.; U.S. senator from New York 1900–1911; noted for his brilliant wit as an after-dinner speaker.

Depew, N.Y., village e. of Buffalo; manufactures include textiles, paper bags, and steel products; printing; incorporated 1894; pop. 19,819.

De Peyster, Abraham (1657–1728), merchant, born in New Amsterdam; prominent as public official in New York; father of Arent de Peyster, Royalist officer in Revolution.

'De Pictura', work by Alberti A-271

Depletion allowance, a deduction used by corporations T-36

Depolarization, in biochemistry B-201
 nervous system N-120

Deportation
 citizenship C-441
 migration of people M-400

Deposit, money given as a pledge or down payment H-295

Deposition, the laying down of natural materials in a natural accumulation
 drift G-151
 geology G-72

Depreciation, in economics, decrease in the value of assets, due to wear and tear of equipment, to decline in market price, or to other causes; it is a loss recognized on a company's books while the assets are still retained
 taxation T-36

Deprès, Josquin (about 1450–1521), French composer of church music, one of greatest of his time; predecessor of Palestrina.

Depressants, narcotic and sedative drugs N-19

Depression. *see in index* Panics and depressions

Depression, a mental state B-400
 headache H-81
 malnutrition M-77
 mental illness M-301

De Priest, Oscar (1871–1951), U.S. political leader, born in Florence, Ala.; first black alderman in Chicago city council 1915–17; U.S. representative (Republican) from Illinois 1929–35.

'De Profundis' (out of the depths), the Bible's 130th Psalm, so called from the first words of the Latin translation; often used in funeral service of Roman Catholicism; title of a prose apologia by Oscar Wilde.

'De Propria Vita', work by Cardano A-831

Deptford, N.J., 3 mi (5 km) s.e. of Woodbury; agricultural region; established about 1796; pop. of township 23,473.

Depth finder (or depth recorder) N-70
 oceanic exploration O-464

Depth of field, in photography P-284, *picture* P-283

Depth psychology P-519

Dequello, Spanish bugle call A-238

De Quincey, Thomas (1785–1859), English essayist and critic D-103
 literary contribution E-275

Derain, André (1880–1954), French painter, born in Chatou; member of *Les Fauves*, later of cubist group; also studied classic and medieval art, and his colors show influence of the Italian primitives, especially of Giotto and Cimabue; later, he developed his own style, which shows rhythm and balance in design and variation in color tone.

Derby, Edward George Geoffrey Smith Stanley, 14th **earl of** (1799–1869), British statesman, born near Liverpool, England; ardent supporter of Reform Act of 1832; prime minister 1852, 1858–59, 1866–68; translated 'Iliad'.

Derby, Edward George Villiers Stanley, 17th **earl of** (1865–1948), British statesman, born in London; Conservative leader House of Commons 1892–1906; director general of recruiting 1915–16; secretary of state 1916–18, 1922–24; ambassador to France 1918–20.

Derby, Frederick Arthur Stanley, 16th **earl of** (or Baron Stanley of Preston) (1841–1908), British statesman and colonial administrator; held various offices in Disraeli and Salisbury cabinets; governor-general of Canada 1888–93 (as Baron Stanley of Preston).

Derby, Colo. *see in index* Commerce City

Derby, Conn., industrial city 8 mi (13 km) w. of New Haven on Housatonic and Naugatuck rivers; sugar mills; iron rolls and castings, textiles, pins, wire, rubber products; pop. 12,346.

Derby, county of England. *see in index* Derbyshire

Derby, England, county seat of Derbyshire, 120 mi (190 km) n.w. of London, on Derwent River; railway center; china, textiles, locomotives, aircraft engines, chemicals; pop. 221,240, *map* U-18a
 porcelain P-476, *picture* P-469

Derby, famous horse-racing event in England; held annually at Epsom Downs, 15 mi (25 km) s.w. of London; also, the chief horse-racing event in any other country H-275

Derby, hat modeled after English bowler; first manufactured by James Knapp at South Norwalk, Conn., in 1850; origin of name in dispute, either coming from England's earl of Derby, who popularized style, or from famous English horse race. *see also in index* Bowler
 hats and caps H-54

Derby Lane, dog-racing track in Saint Petersburg, Fla. D-214

Derbyshire (formerly Derby), n. midland county of England; 1,006 sq mi (2,606 sq km); manufacturing, mining, agriculture; pop. 877,620.

'De re aedificatoria'. *see in index* 'Ten Books on Architecture'

'De Remediis Utriusque Fortunae', work by Petrarch, *picture* L-77

Derennes, Charles (1882–1930), French writer, born in Villeneuve-sur-Lot, near Agen; noted for detailed descriptions of animal life ('Life of the Bat').

'De rerum natura', poem by Lucretius L-77

De Reszke, Édouard (originally Édouard Mieczislav) (1853–1917), Polish opera bass, *list* O-570

De Reszke, Jean (originally Jan Mieczislav) (1850–1925), Polish opera tenor, *list* O-570

Derivative, in mathematics C-24

Derived intelligence quotient
 intelligence tests I-241

Derleth, August (1909–71), U.S. writer, born in Sauk City, Wis.; famous for regional stories of Wisconsin (Sac Prairie Saga: 'Wisconsin Earth', 'Sac Prairie People', 'Place of Hawks', 'Walden West'); writer of mystery stories and editor of science-fiction anthologies.

Derma. *see in index* Dermis

Dermaptera, order of insects consisting of the earwigs.

Dermatitis. *see in index* Eczema

Dermatology, *table* M-277

Dermatome, lateral wall of each epimere E-200, *chart* E-202, *diagram* E-202

Dermatomyositis, muscular disease M-659

Dermis (or derma), inner layer of the skin S-210d, *diagram* S-211

Dermoid cyst, type of cyst C-811

Dermoptera, order of mammals, *table* M-80

Dermot MacMurrough (1110?–71), Irish ruler, king of Leinster, pivot of first English intervention in Ireland (1135–71); dethroned because he had carried off another chieftain's wife; sought aid of Henry II; compiled 'Book of Leinster'.

Dern, George Henry (1872–1936), U.S. public official, born in Dodge County, Nebraska; governor of Utah 1925–32; secretary of war 1933–36; prominent Democrat, *picture* R-268

Derne (or Derna), Libya, Mediterranean coast city and resort; products include honey, bananas, wool, corn, soap, and flour; pop. 15,218, *picture* L-188

Derome, Nicolas-Denis (also called Derome the Younger) (1731–91), most important of French family of bookbinders; his work was uneven, but best is highly prized by collectors; developed dentelle (lacework style of gilding); his nephew Alexis Pierre Bradel, called Bradel-Derome the Elder, succeeded him.

Derozio, Henry (1809-31), British author
 Indian literature I-108

Derrick, a boom or frame rigged with pulleys for lifting heavy weights. *see also in index* Crane
 machinery function C-760
 oil well P-235, *diagram* P-237
 sulfur field, *picture* S-509

Derringer, pistol of large bore with a short barrel.

Derry, N.H., 9 mi (15 km) s.e. of Manchester; shoes, books, wood products; set off from Londonderry 1827; pop. of township 18,875, *map* N-190

Derry, Northern Ireland. *see in index* Londonderry

Derthick, Lawrence Gridley (born 1905), U.S. educator and government official, born in Hazel Green, Ky.; superintendent of schools Chattanooga, Tenn., 1942–56; U.S. commissioner of education 1956–61.

Deruta, central Italy, small village near the Tiber River and 9 mi (15 km) s. of Perugia, famous for maiolica ware; also produces wrought-iron wares.

Dervish, a member of Muslim religious fraternity living in a monastery or wandering as a beggar; others include howling dervishes and whirling, or dancing, dervishes, *picture* T-321
 Jalal Ud-Din Rumi J-17

Derwent River, river in Cumberland, England, flows into Irish Sea; expands into Derwentwater, a small oval lake in s. Cumberland noted for its scenic charm, *map* U-18a

Derzhavin, Gavriil Romanovich (1743–1816), Russian poet, born near Kazan
 Russian literature R-359

De Sabata, Victor (1892–1967), Italian composer and conductor, born in Trieste; director La Scala Opera, Milan, Italy; guest conductor Pittsburgh Symphony 1948.

Desai, Morarji (born 1896), Indian political leader, born in Gujarat; prime minister 1977–79 I-80

Desalinization, removal of salt from water
 ocean O-460
 oceanography O-473
 solar energy S-516
 water W-90, 93

Desargues, Gérard (1593–1662), French mathematician, born in Lyons; helped found modern geometry; developed Desargues theorem of involutions and transversals.

Descant, a musically decorative treble part superimposed above the melody; usually sung by the sopranos while the tenors carry the melody.

Descartes, René (1596–1650), French philosopher and mathematician D-104
 air experiments A-148
 earth science E-35
 exponential notation A-595
 French literature F-395
 mathematics M-215
 world W-296

'Descent from the Cross, The', fresco by Giotto P-29

'Descent from the Cross, The', work by Weyden W-183

'Descent of Man, The', work by Darwin D-39

Deschanel, Paul-Eugène-Louis (1856–1922), French statesman, orator, and writer, born in Brussels, Belgium; Liberal leader; president of France 1920.

Deschutes River, river in Oregon, rises in Cascade Range; flows n. 250 mi (400 km) to Columbia River, *map* U-90

'Description de l'Égypte', work by Fourier F-336

'Description of Greece', work by Pausanias G-278

Desegregation, removal of barriers to access based on one's race
 schools B-301

Deseret, State of, name given by Mormons to their settlement in present Utah; one of nicknames of Utah U-219. *see also in index* Utah
 Mormons M-584
 Young Y-424

Desert D-104
 Africa, *map* S-15. *see also* Libyan Desert; Sahara
  Kalahari B-280, S-263, *map* S-264
  Niger N-308
 animals
  addax S-16
 Asia, *maps* A-618, 636, R-323. *see also in index* Gobi; Taklamakan
  Afghanistan A-89
  Iran I-305
  Pakistan P-77
  Saudi Arabia A-469, S-52b
  U.S.S.R. R-324, *map* R-344
 ecology, *picture* E-51
 Latin America L-60
 oasis. *see in index* Oasis
  United States U-84, *picture* U-31. *see also in index* Death Valley; Mojave Desert
  Great Salt Lake Desert U-216, *maps* U-80, U-217, 232
 plant adaptation P-363, *picture* P-362
  cactus C-12
  grassland G-236
  sagebrush S-14
  tumbleweed T-306
 soil S-253, *map* S-252
 South America S-272
 transportation, *picture* P-543

Desertas, a group of three uninhabited islands in the Madeiras (Chão, Bugio, and Deserta Grande); rabbits and wild goats, *maps* A-115, P-455
 Madeira M-24

Desert candle. *see in index* Eremurus

Desert flat. *see in index* Llano

Desert iguana, lizard *Dipsosaurus dorsalis*, *picture* L-273

'Déserts', work by Varèse M-676

De Seversky, Alexander Procofieff. *see in index* Seversky, Alexander Procofieff, de

De Sica, Vittorio (born 1901), Italian film director, born in Caserta, Italy; key director

in Italian neo-realist revival following World War II M-623
Desiderio da Settignano (1428–64), Italian sculptor in marble, wood, and terra-cotta; named for birthplace, Settignano, near Florence S-86
Desiderius, last king of the Lombards (ruled 756–774); hostile to Charlemagne when latter repudiated his wife, Desiderius' daughter; supported claims of Charlemagne's nephews to Frankish kingdom; attacked pope's territory and was captured by Charlemagne.
Design D-107. *see also in index* Architecture; Arts; Drawing; Carving; Enameling; Fashion; Furniture; Glass; Jewelry and gems; Metalwork; Painting; Porcelain and chinaware; Sculpture; Tapestry; Textiles; Woodworking and wood carving
  airplane, *diagram* S-168
  Breuer B-434
  decorative arts D-59
  dress design D-268
  Egyptian, *pictures* P-28, S-78
  Fuller F-446
  furniture F-452
  graphic arts G-230
  Greek and Roman, *picture* R-245
  illuminated manuscripts. *see in index* Illuminated manuscripts
  industrial design I-169
  interior design I-243
  knife, fork, and spoon K-257
  models M-517
  Oriental rugs R-314, *picture* R-312
  packaging M-141, *picture* M-142
  posters. *see in index* Posters
  quilts Q-17
  ship S-169, *picture* S-177
  stage setting T-155, *picture* T-157
  vocational opportunities V-365
Designer drug. *see in index* Analogue
Desires, conscious impulses toward objects or experiences that promise enjoyment or satisfaction in their attainment
  ethics and morality E-310
Desk, furniture F-457
  office equipment O-494
Deskey, Donald (born 1894), U.S. industrial designer I-174
Desman, name of two species of aquatic, insect-eating animals closely related to moles; one species, Russian desman, lives in s.e. Europe and w. Asia; head and body about 10 in. (25 cm) long, tail 7 in. (18 cm); fur reddish brown above, grayish white with silvery sheen below; tail laterally compressed almost entire length; scientific name *Desmana moschata;* the other species, Pyrenean desman, lives in Spain and France; about 10 in. (25 cm) long (half of this is tail); chestnut above, silver gray below, flanks brownish gray; last quarter of tail laterally compressed; scientific name *Galemys pyrenaicus*
  furs, *table* F-464
De Smet, Pierre Jean (1801–73), Jesuit missionary, born in Termonde, Belgium; came to U.S. 1821 and entered the Jesuit order at Baltimore, Md.; first mission 1838 at site of Council Bluffs, Iowa, among Potawatomi; began his work in the Far West 1840; known as Blackrobe among the American Indians, he made peace between tribes and between Indians and whites; mediated Mormon War and Yakima Indian War; in 1868 visited and pacified Sitting Bull, despite the latter's oath to kill the first white man to appear in his camp I-20
De Smet Range, mountain range of the Canadian Rockies, *picture* M-634
Desmid, a minute one-cell freshwater algae; bright green in color; divided into symmetrical halves; order Desmidiacead, *picture* L-269
Des Moines, Iowa, state capital and largest city; pop. 191,506 D-117
  Iowa I-290, *map* I-302, *picture* I-297
  North America, *map* N-350
Des Moines River, river that rises in s.w. Minnesota and flows 450 mi (720 km) s.e. through Iowa to Mississippi River; hydroelectric power source D-117
  Iowa, *map* I-302
Desmoulins, Camille (1760–94), French journalist, born in Guise, near Saint-Quentin; his crying "to arms" as the news of Necker's dismissal reached the Paris crowds (1789) initiated French Revolution; became alienated from Jacobins; guillotined; his wife, Lucile, guillotined a week later.
Desolation Island (Spanish Desolación), an island of Tierra del Fuego, belonging to Chile, near w. end of Strait of Magellan; name also of Kerguelen Island, *map* S-299
De Soto, Hernando (1500?–42), Spanish explorer of s.e. U.S. and Mississippi River D-117
  exploration E-373
    North America A-331
      Florida T-17, T-19, *picture* U-130
      Georgia G-89
      Mississippi M-471
      route, *map* U-176
      Tennessee T-87
Despenser, Hugh le (1262–1326), English peer; leader of Barons' party opposing Edward II; almost alone opposed execution of Piers Gaveston; later himself chief adviser and favorite of king; arrogance and rapacity of his son **Hugh the Younger** (died 1326) largely responsible for their fall and hanging.
Despiau, Charles (1874–1946), French sculptor, born in Mont-de-Marsan, near Bordeaux; portrait busts of women S-91
Des Plaines, Ill., city 17 mi (27 km) n.w. of Chicago, on Des Plaines River; electrical products; industrial research; Chicago-O'Hare International Airport nearby; pop. 53,568
  Illinois, *map* I-52
Des Plaines River, river in s.e. Wisconsin and n.e. Illinois; joins Kankakee to form Illinois River; length 150 mi (240 km); part of course used by Illinois Waterway
  Illinois, *map* I-52
Dessalines, Jean-Jacques (nickname The Tiger) (1758–1806), emperor of Haiti (1804–6), slave, insurrectionist general under Toussaint Louverture and tyrannical despot, born in Grande Rivière, near Cap-Haïtien, Haiti; assassinated
  Christophe C-407
  Haiti H-12
'De Stijl', European magazine of the arts M-529
Destin, Fla., community on Choctawhatchee Bay, 5 mi (8 km) e. of Fort Walton Beach; pop. 3,600.
Destinn, Emmy (or Ema Kittl) (1878–1930), Bohemian operatic soprano, born in Prague (now Czechoslovakia); debut 1898 at Berlin; gained world fame; created title role in Puccini's 'The Girl of the Golden West'
  opera, *list* O-570
Destroyer, naval vessel N-85, *picture* N-90
  Vietnam V-322
  World War I W-314, *picture* W-308
Destroyer tender, naval vessel, *picture* N-90
Destroying angel, poisonous mushroom. *see in index* Deadly amanita
Destructive distillation, chemical process
  coal-tar products C-527
Desyatina, Soviet unit of measure, *table* W-141
DET (diethyltryptamine), hallucinogenic drug H-18
Détaille, Édouard (1848–1912), French painter, born in Paris; renowned paintings of military subjects ('Defense of Campigny'; 'Movement of Troops').
Detection, in radio R-60
'Detective Comics', comic books C-190
Detectives, police division P-427
Detective story, in literature D-118
  Gothic fiction G-196
  Hammett H-23
  novel N-408
  Poe P-401
Detector, device for rectifying high-frequency currents in radio receivers R-47
Detent, watches and clocks W-78
Détente, normalization of relations between U.S. and U.S.S.R. B-435
  Kissinger K-251
  North Atlantic Treaty Organization N-352
Deterding, Sir Henri Wilhelm August (1866–1939), Dutch oil magnate, born in Amsterdam; supported the Nazi movement in Germany.
Detergent, cleansing agent S-231
  carpet cleaner H-211
  laundry L-84
Determinative, in hieroglyphics H-150
Determinative mineralogy G-71
Determiner, in grammar P-508
Determinism, the philosophical doctrine that ethical choices are determined, or prescribed, by mental, physical, and environmental causes; opposed to free will.
Detmold, West Germany, town at edge of Teutoburger Wald, 47 mi (76 km) s.w. of Hanover; nearby was erected a colossal statue of Hermann, or Arminius, who defeated Romans AD 9; pop. 63,266, *map* G-131
Detonation, type of explosion E-378
Detonator. *see in index* Blasting cap
Detroit, Mich., largest city of state, on Detroit River; automobile capital of the world; pop. 1,203,339 D-120, *map* U-41
  Ford F-305
  Lake Erie E-298
  Michigan M-354, 358, 361, 368, *pictures* M-360, 366
  museums and art galleries
    Flannagan's 'Frog' S-92
    Puppet Theater P-536
    Rivera's fresco P-67a, *picture* P-67b
  North America, *map* N-350
  popular music M-681
  War of 1812 W-31, C-96
  world, *map* W-297
  zoo Z-460
Detroit, University of, in Detroit, Mich.; Roman Catholic; founded by Jesuits 1877; arts and sciences, architecture, business administration, dentistry, education, engineering, general studies, law; graduate school D-122
Detroit Automobile Company, automobile industry corporation, Detroit, Mich.; organized 1899
  Ford's partnership F-305
Detroit Dam, dam in Oregon O-583, 586
Detroit Institute of Technology, in Detroit, Mich.; private control; established 1891; liberal arts, business administration, engineering.
Detroit Lakes, Minn., resort town, 48 mi (77 km) e. of Fargo, N.D., on Detroit Lake and near many lakes; pop. 7,106.
Detroit River, connecting Lake St. Clair and Lake Erie D-120
  Michigan M-358, *picture* M-360
Detroit-Windsor Tunnel, tunnel in Detroit, Mich., and Windsor, Ont.; 1 mi (1.6 km) long, 80 ft (24 m) beneath Detroit River; completed 1930.
Dett, Robert Nathaniel (1882–1943), U.S. pianist and composer, born in Drummondsville, Ont.; organized Hampton Institute Choir ('Magnolia Suite'; 'The Chariot Jubilee'; 'In the Bottoms'; 'America the Beautiful'); published 'Dett Collection of Negro Spirituals'.
Dettingen, West Germany, village of Bavaria, on Main River; decisive victory of Allies under George II of England over French under Duc de Noailles, June 27, 1743; pop. 3,619.
Deucalion, figure in Greek mythology who built an ark to survive a flood sent by Zeus; with wife Pyrrha, repopulated world by casting stones that turned into humans.
Deurne, Belgium, industrial and residential suburb just e. of Antwerp; parks; sports palace; pop. 68,703.
Deuterium, isotope of hydrogen H-341, *diagram* R-65
  matter M-224
  nuclear energy N-416
  nuclear weapons N-433
  plasma P-380
  water W-87
Deuterium oxide, heavy water W-87
Deuteronomy, the 5th book of the Bible; contains last injunction of Moses to the Hebrews and the account of his death
  Judaism's basic creed J-147
Deutsch, Babette (born 1895), U.S. writer, born in New York, N.Y.; married Avrahm Yarmolinsky, with whom she translated Russian and German poetry; her poems include 'Fire for the Night', 'Animal, Vegetable, Mineral', 'I Often Wish' ('Poetry in Our Time', criticism; 'Poetry Handbook'; for younger readers: 'Heroes of the Kalevala', 'Walt Whitman, Builder for America') R-111c, S-480
  'More Tales of Faraway Folk' S-480, *pictures* S-473
Deutsche mark. *see in index* Mark
Deutscher Werkbund, German association of craftsmen; founded in Munich 1907 A-565
'Deutschland, Deutschland über Alles', German national anthem N-66
'Deuxième Sexe, Le' (The Second Sex), work by Beauvoir, *list* W-275
De Valera, Eamon (1882-1975), Irish political leader D-124
  Ireland I-322
De Valois, Dame Ninette (originally Edris Stannus) (born 1898), Irish dancer, teacher, choreographer, and ballet director, born in Ireland; debut in London 1914, later soloist with Diaghilev ballet; her ballet school, established in London 1931, developed into the Royal Ballet ('Come Dance with Me', autobiography) D-24
Devaluation of currency, reduction of the legal value of a currency; usually by reducing the amount of gold represented by the monetary unit
  Great Depression G-242
  United States R-270
Devanagari script, in writing
  India I-67
Developer, in housing construction H-297
Developer, chemical solution used for processing film P-292
Developing, in photography P-292
Developing countries. *see in index* Third World
Developmental biology Z-469
Developmental psychology (or genetic psychology) P-522
Development banks
  international trade I-268
Development economics E-63
Deventer, The Netherlands, city on IJssel River; famous for Deventer koek, a honey cake; pop. 54,669.
DeVere, Aubrey Thomas (1814–1902), Irish poet, born in Curragh Chase, near Limerick; inspired by Greek spirit and by Irish legends ('Irish Odes'; 'Legends of St. Patrick'; 'Legends of the Saxon Saints').
Devereux, James Patrick Sinnott (born 1904), U.S. Marine Corps officer, born in Washington, D.C.; joined Marines as a private in 1923, retired 1948; congressman from Maryland 1951–59.
Devereux, Robert. *see in index* Essex, Robert Devereux, 3rd earl of
Devers, Jacob Loucks (1887–1979), U.S. Army officer, born in York, Pa.; graduated West Point; commander U.S. armored forces 1941–43; Allied deputy commander in Mediterranean theater 1943–44; chief of Allied forces invading s. France Aug. 1944–45; chief of U.S. Army field forces 1946–49.
Devi, in Hindu mythology, Siva's wife; dual nature, one gentle, one violent; when gentle, known as Devi, or Rhambha, Hindu Venus; when turbulent, as Durga or Kali, a goddess of murder, death, and plague.
Deviation, of compass C-622, D-161

Devil, in Christian and Jewish theology, a fallen angel or evil spirit, especially Lucifer or Satan, which represents absolute evil
  angel and demon beliefs A-414
  Faust legend F-49
  horror story H-245

Devilfish. *see in index* Giant squid; Manta ray; Octopus

Devil-in-a-bush. *see in index* Nigella

Deville, Henri Étienne Sainte-Claire. *see in index* Sainte-Claire Deville, Henri Étienne

Devil ray. *see in index* Manta ray

Devil's Advocate, popular name for Promoter of the Faith, an ecclesiastic of Roman Catholicism, who, during process of canonization, must offer all possible objections against the candidate for sainthood. *see also in index* Canonization

Devil's-darning-needle. *see in index* Dragonfly

Devil's Island, island in Atlantic Ocean, 8 mi (13 km) off coast of French Guiana A-337
  migration of people M-401

Devils Lake, N.D., city near lake of same name, 85 mi (140 km) w. of Grand Forks; farming and livestock center; resort; state school for deaf; Sully Hill National Game Preserve, pop. 7,442, *map* U-40

Devils Lake, salt lake in North Dakota N-373

Devil's-paintbrush. *see in index* Hawkweed

Devil's rearhorse. *see in index* Mantis

Devils Tower National Monument, national monument in Wyoming W-389

'Devil to Pay in the Backlands, The', work by Guimarães
  Latin American literature L-71

Devil worship (or satanism), devotion to Satan or the Devil, the personality regarded by the Judeo-Christian tradition as the absolute evil and completely opposite to God; centers around the Black Mass; is not to be confused with modern witchcraft or Neopaganism since these groups worship pre-Christian gods.

Devine, Edward Thomas (1867–1948), U.S. sociologist and educator, born in Union, Iowa; editor *Charities*, later *The Survey*, 1897–1912 ('The Normal Life'; 'Social Work').

De Vinne, Theodore Low (1828–1914), U.S. printer, born in Stamford, Conn.; fought for simplified typefaces; designed Renner type; helped design Century Roman; De Vinne type named for him; wrote 8 books on printing.

Devlin, Bernadette Josephine (born 1947), North Irish political leader, born in Cookstown, County Tyrone; led first great Catholic civil rights demonstration 1968; member of British Parliament from N. Ireland 1969–74; jailed four months for political activities 1970; author of 'The Price of My Soul'.

Devolution, War of (1667–68), waged by Louis XIV of France for possession of Franche-Comté and part of the Spanish Netherlands; he claimed territory in name of his wife, Maria Theresa, daughter of Philip IV of Spain, though she had renounced her rights at time of her marriage; Louis insisted that under the old law of Brabant, property of a deceased father devolves to the children of the first marriage, that is, to Maria Theresa rather than to Charles II of Spain; war halted by intervention of triple alliance of England, Sweden, and Holland; by the peace of Aix-la-Chapelle (1668), France retained captured towns of Charleroi and Lille but gave Franche-Comté back to Spain.

Devon, a breed of cattle; cows and bulls rather small; oxen grow to great size and are prized for work.

Devon (or Devonshire), county in s.w. peninsula of England; 2,612 sq mi (6,765 sq km); cap. Exeter; contains granite tableland of Dartmoor; dairying, agriculture, mining, fisheries; pop. 823,751
  shell sand S-36
  world, *map* W-297

Devonian period (or Age of Fishes), in geological time P-487, *picture* P-488
  animals, *picture* A-460
  Australia A-774
  British Isles B-460
  earth E-23, *table* E-24

Devonport, England, fortified port on promontory in s.w. Devon; part of Plymouth; military and naval station; large dockyard

Devonshire, Elizabeth, duchess of (1759–1824), one of the two beautiful duchesses of Devonshire painted by Gainsborough; Elizabeth's portrait was the famous Stolen Duchess, lost 25 years.

Devonshire, Spencer Compton Cavendish, 8th **duke of** (1833–1908), British statesman, prominent in Victorian era; a Liberal but opposed Gladstone's Home Rule policy; leader of Liberal Unionists.

Devonshire, Victor Christian William Cavendish, 9th **duke of** (1868–1938), nephew of 8th duke; was 17 years in House of Commons before succeeding to title; was treasurer of His Majesty's household, financial secretary to the treasury, and civil lord of the Admiralty; governor-general of Canada 1916–21; colonial secretary 1922–24.

Devonshire, county in England. *see in index* Devon

De Voto, Bernard Augustine (1897–1955), U.S. writer, born in Ogden, Utah; taught English at Northwestern University 1922–27 and Harvard 1929–36; editor 'The Easy Chair', *Harper's Magazine*, after 1935; editor *The Saturday Review of Literature* 1936–38 ('Mark Twain at Work'; trilogy on U.S. expansion: 'The Course of Empire', 'The Year of Decision: 1846', 'Across the Wide Missouri', 1947 Pulitzer prize; essays: 'The Easy Chair'), *picture* U-226
  creative writing W-382

De Vries, Hugo (1848–1935), Dutch botanist, born in Haarlem; professor University of Amsterdam; inaugurated plan for studying evolution.

De Vries, Peter (born 1910), U.S. writer and editor, born in Chicago, Ill.; with *Poetry* magazine 1938–44, *The New Yorker* after 1944; elected to National Institute of Arts and Letters 1969 (novels: 'The Tunnel of Love', 'The Blood of the Lamb', 'Cat's Pajamas & Witch's Milk').

Dew, moisture condensed from air W-120
  cloud C-515
  fog F-246

Dewar, Sir James (1842–1923), British physicist and chemist, born in Kincardine, Scotland; professor Cambridge University, and Royal Institution of London; joint inventor of cordite with Sir Frederick Abel; noted for work on liquefaction of gases and researches on temperatures near absolute zero; produced liquid oxygen in quantity; invented Dewar flask, original thermos bottle.

Dewberry
  hybrids R-94

Dewclaw, vestigial toe of a dog D-194, *picture* D-195

Dewdney, Edgar (1835–1916), Canadian civil engineer and statesman, born in Devonshire, England; came to British Columbia 1859 and became a surveyor; lieutenant governor of the Northwest Territories 1881; minister of the interior 1888–92; lieutenant governor of British Columbia 1892–97.

De Wet, Christiaan Rudolph (1854–1922), Boer general, born in Orange Free State, Union of South Africa; commander Orange Free State forces in Boer War 1899–1902; led rebellion against South African government at outbreak of war 1914; defeated, imprisoned for six months.

Dewey, Charles Melville (1849–1937), U.S. landscape painter, born in Lowville, N.Y.; favored early morning and evening effects.

Dewey, George (1837–1917), U.S. naval commander D-124, S-364, *picture* V-296

Dewey, John (1859–1952), U.S. philosopher, psychologist, and educator D-124, *picture* V-290
  civil rights C-468
  educational influence E-93, 97, S-240
  ethics and morality E-310
  functional psychology P-520

Dewey, Melvil (1851–1931), U.S. librarian, born in Adams Center, N.Y.; founder of the *Library Journal* and one of the founders of the American Library Association; inventor of decimal classification.

Dewey, Thomas Edmund (1902–71), U.S. lawyer, born in Owosso, Mich.; special prosecutor of racketeering gangs in New York, N.Y., 1935–37; district attorney of New York County 1937–42; governor of New York 1942–54; Republican presidential nominee 1944, 1948.

Dewey decimal classification
  library codes L-156

Dewing, Thomas Wilmer (1851–1938), U.S. figure and portrait painter, born in Boston, Mass.; paintings usually small, treatment refined, color delicate.

De Witt, Jan (1625–72), Dutch statesman, born in Dordrecht; grand pensionary for nearly 20 years; supported republicans against House of Orange; sought alliance with Louis XIV; lost influence when French designs against The Netherlands became apparent; killed by mob with his brother Cornelius N-130

'DeWitt Clinton', first locomotive operated in New York State; made initial run from Albany to Schenectady Aug. 9, 1831, over Mohawk and Hudson Railroad (now part of Penn-Central Railroad).

Dewlap, a hanging fold of skin under the neck
  lizard L-271

DEW line. *see in index* Distant Early Warning line

Dew point, temperature at which a vapor begins to form
  fog formation F-246
  weather W-120

Dew-point thermometer H-343

Dew retting, hemp processing H-127

Dewsbury, England, town in Yorkshire, 8 mi (13 km) s. of Leeds; carpets, blankets, worsteds; pop. 51,560, *map* U-18a

Dexter, Al (1905–84), U.S. country musician M-678

Dexter, Timothy (1747–1806), U.S. eccentric merchant, born in Malden, Mass.; set up shop as leather dresser in Newburyport 1770; bought up cheap Continental currency, which made him rich 1791; engaged in shipping and speculative enterprises, with enormous profit; bought mansion, where he lived as a self-styled lord (biography: 'Lord Timothy Dexter', by John P. Marquand).

Dexter base, in heraldry H-136

Dexter chief, in heraldry H-136

Dexter side, in heraldry H-136

Dextrin, adhesive gum A-43

Dextrose. *see in index* Glucose

Dezhnev, Cape, easternmost point of continent of Asia; in Siberia, on Bering Strait, *map* R-345
  world, *map* W-297

'D. Faustus, Tragicall History of'. *see in index* 'Tragicall History of D. Faustus'

Dhaka (or Dacca), Bangladesh, capital, on the Burhi Ganga River, pop. of greater city 3,160,200 D-125
  Asia, *map* A-697

'Dhammapada', work in Pali literature I-106

Dharma, religious obligations
  India I-67

Dharma Chakra (wheel of law), in Hinduism
  flag of India F-161

D'Harnoncourt, René (born 1901), U.S. museum official, born in Vienna, Austria, became citizen of U.S. 1939; director Museum of Modern Art, New York, N.Y., after 1949; authority on folk art of the Mexican Indian; author and illustrator ('Mexicana'; 'The Hole in the Wall')
  'The Painted Pig' R-108

Dhofar, region in Oman O-543

Dhole, wild dog of India *Cuon dukhunensis*, usually rusty red in color; differs from wolf in having hair between toes and in having shorter muzzle D-212

Dhoti, loincloth worn by some Hindu men.

DIA (Defense Intelligence Agency) I-237

Diabase (or greenstone), granular igneous rock with lime-soda feldspar and pyroxene (augite) as its essential minerals; generally crystalline; resembles basalt.

Diabetes, disease D-125
  coma C-596
  malnutrition M-77

Diabetes insipidus, disease D-125
  hormones H-240

Diabetes mellitus, disease D-125
  bioengineering B-206
  cause D-180
  coma C-596
  diagnosis D-127
    Fehling's solution. *see in index* Fehling's solution
  eye complications E-390
  food and nutrition F-279
    malnutrition M-77
  gland disorder G-153
  hormones H-242

Diacetylmorphine. *see in index* Heroin

Diacritic marks, in alphabet A-318

Diadromous, fish that lives part of its life in fresh water and part in the ocean O-485

Diaghilev, Sergei (1872–1929), Russian ballet and opera producer D-126
  ballet B-34, D-28
  Cocteau C-532
  Nijinsky N-315
  Picasso P-314

Diagnosis, the identification of the nature or cause of a condition or problem D-126
  bioengineering aids B-213
  diabetes D-126
  medicine M-278
  mental illness M-302
  reading problems R-103e
  surgery S-519b
  venereal disease V-272

'Diagnostic and Statistical Manual of Mental Disorders', book by American Psychiatric Association M-301

Dial, of watches and clocks S-60, W-78

'Dial, The', a periodical by the transcendentalists T-248
  Emerson E-204

Dialect, language L-37
  American Indian language I-135
  linguistics L-229
  reading problem R-103f

Dialectical materialism, philosophical approach to reality derived from the teachings of Karl Marx and Friedrich Engels C-619

Dialectics, philosophical concept of evolution applied to diverse fields
  Hegel H-115

Dialectology L-229

Dial lock (or combination lock) L-277

'Dialogue of Comfort Against Tribulation, A', work by More M-582

'Dialogue of Seven Wise Men' (Colloquium Heptaplomeres), work by Bodin B-330

'Dialogues', works by Plato P-384, G-276

'Dialogues', works by Pope Gregory I B-160

Dialysis, a separation of solutions through membranes B-210
  kidney therapy K-236

Diamagnetism, in magnetism M-45

Diameter, a line or the length of a line through or across the center of a plane or solid; from Greek words *dia* (through) and *metron* (measure)
  measurement M-243
  sun and planets, *tables* P-351, S-254a

Diamond, David Leo (born 1915), U.S. composer, born in Rochester, N.Y.; works vigorous with striking color changes; many awards include Prix de Rome for first symphony; orchestral works ('Psalm'; 'Rounds for Strings'), chamber music, works for solo instruments and orchestra, incidental music, choral works.

'Dies Irae' (day of wrath), name generally given to a 13th-century hymn on the Last Judgment; used in Roman Catholic liturgy.
Dieskau, Ludwig August, Baron (1701–67), German soldier, born in Saxony; joined French army and in 1755 sent to Canada as commander in chief of French colonial troops; defeated and taken prisoner by English at Lake George, N.Y.
Diesterweg, Friedrich Adolf Wilhelm (1790–1866), German educator and author, born in Siegen, Westphalia, Prussia; follower of Pestalozzi; stressed value of self-activity in education.
Diet, formal assembly or meeting; name often applied to legislative assemblies of central and n. European countries; also the formal meeting of councillors of Holy Roman Empire. *see also in index* Reichstag
  Japan J-34, T-205, *diagram* J-35, *picture* T-206
  Spires (1529) R-134
  West Germany G-120, 125
Diet, in nutrition F-275
  diabetes D-126
  health H-83
Dietetics F-278
  home economics H-216
  hospital care H-282
Diethyl ether, organic chemistry O-604, *diagram* O-603
Diethyltryptamine (DET), hallucinogenic drug H-18
Dietitian F-279
  home economics H-216, *picture* H-215
  zoo, *picture* Z-462
Dietrich, Marlene (born 1901), U.S. actress, born in Berlin, Germany; to U.S. 1930 (citizen 1939) after success in German motion picture 'Blue Angel' ('Shanghai Express'; 'Song of Songs'; 'Destry Rides Again'; 'A Foreign Affair').
Dietrich of Bern, name under which Theodoric the Great appears in the 'Nibelungenlied' and other heroic German legends. *see in index* Theodoric the Great
Diet therapy T-161
Dietzeite, a mineral M-435
Differential, a device that can produce multiple motions from one motion or combine several motions into one; permits automobile wheels to turn at different speeds
  automobile A-852
  machine M-10
Differential calculus (or fluxions), in mathematics C-22
  Fermat's invention F-55
  mathematics M-215
  sciences S-64
Differential geometry, in mathematics M-219
Differentiation, formation of different types of cells and tissues E-201
Diffraction, bending of radiant energy rays when passing an obstacle
  electrons P-307
  light structure L-200
  optics O-575
  X rays
    molecular biophysics B-237
    solar system S-254a
    spectrum S-374
Diffraction grating spectroscope S-372
Diffrient, Niels (born 1928), U.S. industrial designer
  functional design I-171, 174
Diffusion, in physical science
  cell process C-238
  osmosis O-610
  porometer, *picture* B-231
Digambara, sect of Jainism J-14
  monks and monasticism M-541
'Digest' (or 'Pandects'), in legal work J-161
Digest, magazine M-35
Digestif, after-dinner drink W-237
Digestive system D-142
  cattle R-318
  earthworm A-389
  frog F-407
  human A-391
    health H-84
    liver L-261
    metabolism M-306
    muscles M-658
    nutritive reflexes R-132
    stomach S-454
      pepsin P-197b
  organic chemistry O-604
Digestive tract. *see in index* Alimentary canal
Diggers, Indians who lived in the deserts of Western U.S.; they ate roots and lived in caves and grass huts.
Digger wasp, insect of the family Scoliidae W-74
Digit, single numerical figure N-435
  addition A-590
  mathematics M-213
Digital, type of electrical signal
  compact disc C-621
  electronics E-175
  video recording V-312
Digital calculator, device that performs arithmetic operations C-19
Digital circuitry, in technology T-78
Digital computer C-628
Digital-display watch W-79
Digital instruments I-230
Digitalis, drug. *see also in index* Foxglove
  heart disease treatment D-273
Digital X-ray imaging, in medical technology M-285
Digitus, ancient Roman unit of measure, *table* W-141
Dihigo, Martin (nickname El Maestro) (1905–71), U.S. baseball player, born in Matanzas, Cuba; pitcher, outfielder, infielder for Negro and Latin American leagues 1923–50.
Dijon, France, historic city in e., former capital of Burgundy; various manufactures; mustard, wine; university; fine churches; occupied by Germans in 1870 and in 1940; pop. 143,120, *maps* E-360, F-369
Dijon mustard M-694
Dika nut, a seed of the wild mango, of West Africa; source of oil; ground into an acidy paste and combined with spices for dika bread, a food staple of some Africans N-449
Dike, embankment, usually to protect lowlands from floods D-146. *see also in index* Levee
  dams D-15
  flooding F-182
  irrigation I-355
  levees R-211
Dilapidated housing unit H-294, *list* H-305
Dilaudid, alkaloid drug O-572
Diligenti quintuplets (born 1943), children of Franco and Ana María Diligenti, born July 15 in Buenos Aires, Argentina; combined weight at birth about 10 pounds (4.5 kilograms); two boys (Franco and Carlos Alberto) and three girls (María Ester, María Fernanda, and María Cristina).
Dill, a plant of parsley family S-379
Dillard University, New Orleans, La.; private control; formed 1930 by merger of New Orleans University (Methodist-related) and Straight College (Congregational), both founded 1869; liberal arts, education.
Dillenius, Johann Jakob (or Johann Jakob Dillen) (1687–1747), German botanist, born in Darmstadt; in 1728 became first professor of botany at Oxford University ('Historia Muscorum', book on mosses).
Dillon, Clarence Douglas (born 1909), U.S. government official and banker, born in Geneva, Switzerland, of U.S. parents; ambassador to France 1953–57; undersecretary of state for economic affairs 1958–61; secretary of the treasury 1961–65; chairman Rockefeller Foundation 1972.
Dillon, George (1906–68), U.S. poet, born in Jacksonville, Fla.; associate editor of *Poetry*, a magazine of verse, while student at University of Chicago; Pulitzer prize for poetry 1931; Guggenheim fellowship 1932–33; editor of *Poetry* 1937–49 ('Boy in the Wind'; 'The Flowering Stone').
Dillon, John (1851–1927), Irish Nationalist political leader, born in Dublin; worked to abolish British rule in Ireland; often in prison; member of Parliament more than 30 years.
Dillon, Leo (born 1933), U.S. artist, born in Brooklyn, N.Y. and **Diane Dillon** (or Claire Sorber) (born 1933), U.S. artist, born in Glendale, Calif.; illustrators of children's books; awarded Caldecott medals for 'Why Mosquitoes Buzz in People's Ears' (1976) and 'Ashanti to Zulu' (1977).
Dilwara Temple, Mount Abu, India, *picture* J-14
Di Maggio, Joseph Paul (nickname Joe) (born 1914), U.S. baseball outfielder, born in Martinez, Calif.; played for New York, A.L., 1936–42, 1946–51; led A.L. in batting 1939 and 1940; set major-league record 1941 by hitting safely in 56 consecutive games; hit 361 home runs; lifetime batting average of .325; played in 10 World Series, including 51 games; chosen A.L.'s most valuable player 1939, 1941, and 1947 B-93
Dime, U.S. coin worth 10 cents, or $1/10$ of a dollar; term once meant the tenth part, the tithe paid as church or state dues; Wycliffe's Bible translation reads, "He gave him dymes of alle thingis".
Dime novel (or pulp novel), a book printed on a cheap quality of paper W-151
Dimension line, in mechanical drawing M-261, *picture* M-260
Dimensions, size relations M-261, *picture* M-262
Dimeter, a line in poetry P-405
2,5-dimethoxy-4-methylamphetamine (DOM), a hallucinogenic drug H-18
Dimethyltryptamine (DMT), a hallucinogenic drug H-18
Diminuendo, in music, *list* M-670
Dimitrov, Georgi (1882–1949), Bulgarian Communist official; tried for complicity in setting fire to Reichstag 1933; defied Goering and found not guilty; secretary general of Communist International (Comintern) 1935–43; premier of Bulgaria 1946–49.
Dimity, a fine cotton fabric with corded stripes or bars; name first applied to heavy fabric of same type made in Spain for bed hangings.
Dimmer, a device for regulating the intensity of an electric lighting unit T-157
Dimnet, Ernest (1866–1954), French abbé, canon of Cambrai Cathedral, born in Trélon; popular in U.S. as lecturer ('The Brontë Sisters'; 'The Art of Thinking'; 'What We Live By'; 'My Old World', 'My New World', autobiography).
Dimond, Anthony Joseph (1881–1953), U.S. lawyer and political leader, born in Palatine Bridge, N.Y.; to Alaska as prospector 1904; delegate to U.S. Congress 1933–45; judge U.S. district court, Anchorage, after 1945; champion of Alaskan statehood.
Dimorphotheca, a genus of annual and perennial plants and shrubs of the composite family; native to s. Africa; flowers yellow, purple, or white rays with contrasting centers; they close toward sundown; also called Cape marigold or African daisy.
Dinan, city in France, pop. 13,303, *map* F-369, *picture* F-348
Dinant, town in Belgium on Meuse River, 48 mi (77 km) s.e. of Brussels; once noted for copperware; sacked by Burgundians 1466, by French 1554, 1675; captured and burned by Germans Aug. 23, 1914; pop. 6,851.
Dinar, a monetary unit of Algeria, Bahrain, Iraq, Jordan, Kuwait, Libya, People's Democratic Republic of Yemen, Tunisia, Yugoslavia; medieval gold coin of Arabia and other Muslim lands is worth about $4.50.
Dinaric Alps, mountains in w. Yugoslavia; highest point Dinara (6,008 ft; 1,831 m).
D'Indy, Vincent. *see in index* Indy, Vincent d'
Diners Club, credit card
  consumer credit C-762
Ding Dong School. *see in index* Horwich, Frances Rappaport
Dingley, Nelson, Jr. (1832–99), U.S. statesman and journalist, born in Durham, Me.; editor and publisher *Lewiston* (Me.) *Journal*; member of Congress (Republican) 1881–99; framed protective Dingley Tariff Act of 1897.
Dingley Tariff Act, in United States
  McKinley M-19
Dingo, an Australian wild dog A-781, D-212
  domestication A-454
Dinka, a group of people in the Sudan along the White Nile River; a tall people, with skins almost blue-black S-502
Dinkelsbühl, West Germany, town in Bavaria, on Wörnitz River, 44 mi (71 km) s.w. of Nuremberg; contains medieval walls and towers, also the German House, example of German Renaissance wooden architecture; founded 10th century; free imperial city 1351–1802; pop. 8,892, *map* G-131
'Dinner Party, The', exhibition by Chicago, *list* W-275
Dinoflagellates, algae C-715
  oceanography O-484
Dinosaur, extinct reptile
  earth E-26, *pictures* E-22, 23, *table* E-24
  evolution E-100
  fossils F-323
  Oklahoma O-528
  prehistoric animals A-461, P-488, *picture* P-487
Dinosaur National Monument, in Utah and Colorado, *maps* C-583, U-232, *picture* C-577
  fossil discovery, *picture* F-322
Dinwiddie, Robert (1693–1770), British colonial official, born near Glasgow, Scotland; lieutenant governor of Virginia 1752–58; supported French and Indian War W-39
Dio Cassius (150?–235), Roman historian H-172
Diocese, a district or churches presided over by a bishop; in Roman times was a civil division of territory, but as the early church developed along the same territorial divisions, the word gradually became ecclesiastical A-417
Diocletian (245–313), Roman emperor (284–305), able soldier and energetic ruler, under whom a memorable persecution of Christians took place R-248
  baths R-255, *map* R-251
  Christians C-401
  military reforms A-637
Diode (formerly called Fleming valve), a type of vacuum tube
  electronics E-180
  schematic diagram R-56
Diodorus Siculus (died about 20 BC), Greek historian of time of Julius Caesar and Augustus; of his 'Historical Library', history of world in 40 books, only parts remain G-278
Dioecious flower F-219
Diogenes (412–323 BC), a Greek Cynic philosopher D-147
Diogenes Laertius (fl. 3rd century), a Greek philosopher G-279
Diomedeidae, the albatross family of birds. *see in index* Albatross
Diomede Islands, two islands in Bering Strait, between Asia and N. America A-571, *maps* U-39, 94
Diomedes, mythological figure, king of Thrace; had flesh-eating wild mares H-138
  Homeric legend, *picture* H-222
Dionne quintuplets (born 1934), daughters of Oliva and Elzire Dionne, born May 28 in Callander, Ont.; combined weight at birth about 13 pounds (6 kilograms); names Annette, Cecile, Emilie (died 1954), Marie (died 1970), Yvonne; first known quints to live over one hour; Allan R. Dafoe (1883–1941) attending physician; made king's wards by Ontario government 1935, returned to father 1944 M-650, *picture* M-649
Dionysia, an ancient Greek religious festival A-87
Dionysius, the Elder (432?–367 BC), tyrant of Syracuse; cruel despot
  Damon and Pythias D-19
  Plato P-384
Dionysius of Halicarnassus (fl. 20? BC), Greek historian G-278
Dionysius Thrax (fl. 120? BC) Greek grammarian L-229
Dionysus, in Greek mythology D-147
  dance D-22
  drama D-242, G-275

Diskette, computer, office equipment O-494

Disk plow P-391

Dislocation, crystal imperfection S-254h

Dislocation, the displacement of a body part; usually pertains to a bone pulled from its place in a joint F-118
  fracture F-340
  joint injury J-137

Dismal Swamp, marsh 30 mi by 10 mi (50 km by 16 km) in s.e. Virginia, extending into North Carolina; partly reclaimed V-330, *map* V-331
  North Carolina N-354, 357
  peat bog P-151

Dismas, Saint, the "good thief," crucified alongside Christ; patron saint of the condemned; not mentioned by name in the Gospels, but the account of how his faith won Christ's promise of salvation is given in Bible, Luke xxiii, 32.

Disney, Walt (1901–66), U.S. animated-cartoon artist D-185
  amusement park A-386
  cartoons C-191
  fables F-4
  motion pictures M-622
  'Peter and the Wolf', *picture* L-249
  Walt Disney Productions L-310c

Disneyland, amusement park in Anaheim, Calif. A-385, D-185, *picture* C-47
  monorail M-545

Disney World. *see in index* Walt Disney World

Dispersed settlement, a rural settlement G-66

Dispersion, in light S-371
  diamonds D-128
  light L-197
  optics O-574
  spectroscope S-372

Dispersion, in statistics S-435

Displacement of water, Archimedes' principle A-541
  ship S-169

Displacement series (or electromotive series), in chemistry E-171

Disraeli, Benjamin, earl of Beaconsfield (1804–81), British statesman and novelist D-185
  Gladstone G-152
  Queen Victoria V-309
  United Kingdom E-254

Dissection, in medicine M-283

Dissenters (or Nonconformists), those who refused to comply with usages of Church of England P-539
  Defoe D-64
  English history E-247

Dissociation, in chemistry, the splitting of chemical molecules in solutions E-170

Dissociation, memory disorder. *see in index* Hysterical amnesia

Dissociative disorders, a category of mental illnesses M-301

Dissolve, motion-picture optical effect M-613

Dissonance, in music M-672

Distaff S-389

Distance
  astronomers measure A-720
  judging S-109
  mechanical drawing M-257

Distance race, a running event T-244

Distant Early Warning line (DEW line), a chain of radar bases built 1954–57 in North America
  Arctic regions A-573

Distemper, an infectious disease
  cat C-210
  dog D-209

Distillate, a light oil
  uses F-441

Distillation
  alcohol A-275
  liquor industry L-234, *diagram* L-236
  perfumes P-203, *picture* P-204
  petroleum P-239
  spices S-380
  water W-87, 93

Distilled spirits (commonly called hard liquor) T-80

Distortion, in art
  painting P-57
  sculpture S-80

Distributaries, of river, *diagram* R-210

Distribution, in economics
  civilization's development C-465
  fair and exposition F-6
  U.S. methods and costs U-110

Distribution, of plants and animals. *see in index* Ecology

Distribution center, type of warehouse M-144, *picture* M-143

Distributive education V-362

Distributive property (distributive law, or distributive principle), in mathematics
  algebra A-289, A-593

District attorney. *see in index* State's attorney

District courts, United States
  salaries of, *table* U-155

District of Columbia, federal district including Washington, capital of U.S., on e. bank of Potomac River, between Maryland and Virginia; area 69 sq mi (179 sq km); pop. 637,651, *map* N-350. *see also in index* Washington, D.C.
  Constitution U-149
  National Capital Parks V-346
  state symbols
    flag, *picture* F-159
    rose, *picture* S-427
  23rd Amendment (voting rights) U-146

Disulfide (or disulphide), compound of two sulfur atoms with another element or radical
  iron (iron pyrites) S-509

Ditcher (or ladder trencher), earth-moving machine D-269

Ditch weed. *see in index* Elodea

Dithyramb, a passionate hymn in honor of Dionysus, one of whose surnames was Dithyrambos; probably first sung at feasts for the god; given choral form by Arion T-158
  drama D-242

Ditmars, Raymond Lee (1876–1942), U.S. zoologist, born in Newark, N.J.; in charge of mammals and reptiles New York Zoological Park; self-educated ('The Reptile Book'; 'Snakes of the World'; 'Confessions of a Scientist'; children's books: 'Book of Prehistoric Animals', 'Book of Living Reptiles', 'Book of Insect Oddities').

Diu, India. *see in index* Goa, Daman, and Diu

Diula, an African people
  Ivory Coast I-407

Diuresis, condition that cause the kidneys to produce too much urine H-240

Diuretic, a drug that increases kidney output of urine; used to remove excessive fluids from the tissues or blood vessels
  caffeine C-535

Diurnal circle, in astronomy, the apparent circle around the Earth described by a celestial body as result of Earth's rotation.

Dive, flight maneuver A-191

Dives (Latin for "rich"), popular name of rich man in the Biblical parable of Lazarus and the rich man (Bible, Luke xvi, 19–31).

Divide, in physiography R-210. *see also in index* Continental Divide

Dividend, in economics
  industry I-189
  stocks S-450

Divider
  mechanical drawing M-257, *picture* M-259
  navigation N-69

Divi-divi, a tree native to South America but cultivated also in tropics of Asia and Africa; seedpods yield a fine tannin.

Divine, Father (or Rev. M.J. Divine, formerly George Baker) (1875?–1965), evangelist, born near Savannah, Ga.; founded Peace Mission sect, New York, N.Y.

'Divine Comedy, The', poem by Dante D-32
  angel and demon A-414
  Italian literature I-376, I-385

'Divine Poems', work by Donne D-230

Divine right of kings
  English history E-245
  James I J-19

Divine tree. *see in index* Deodar

Divine Word College, Epworth, Iowa; Roman Catholic; primarily men; founded, chartered 1912; liberal arts.

Diving, sport D-186
  plain diving S-535

Diving, underwater D-187
  inner space exploration N-73
  oceanic exploration O-463
  pearl divers, *picture* P-148
  police work, *picture* P-428
  U.S. Navy
    submarines. *see in index* Submarine

Diving bell, a diving apparatus open only at bottom; supplied with compressed air by hose; used for harbor and dock work
  development D-187

Diving birds, popular term for two orders of birds
  duck D-204
  loon L-298

'Diving Into the Wreck', work by Rich A-364

Divining rod, a forked twig of hazel, holly, beech, or other tree, or forked rod of metal held in the hand of dowsers, or water finders, as users of divining rods are called; the rod twists in the hand as the dowser crosses underground water or mineral; despite frequent uncanny success of dowsers, their art has been looked upon as fraud; some scientists have explained it as motor automatism.

Division, in mathematics A-593
  fractions F-338
  real numbers A-293
  slide rule S-217

Division, in military
  United States
    Air Force A-647
    Army A-634

Divisionism. *see in index* Pointillism

Division of labor (or specialization of labor) L-3
  assembly line. *see in index* Assembly line
  bureaucracy B-505
  foundation of society S-242
  industry I-190
  mass production M-208
  pioneer life P-332

'Division of Labor in Society, The', book by Durkheim D-292

Division of the North, a band of Mexican soldiers V-325

Division viol, stringed instrument S-491

Divorce, in marriage M-151
  family F-19
  law C-693, F-20

Diwali, one of the major religious festivals of Hinduism; marks the beginning of the new year according to the Vikrama calendar H-159

Dix, Dorothea (1802–87), U.S. reformer D-190
  women's rights W-277

Dix, John Adams (1798–1879), U.S. statesman and soldier, born in Boscawen, N.H.; secretary of treasury 1860; issued famous order: "If any one attempts to haul down the American flag, shoot him on the spot"; governor New York 1873–75.

'Dixie', Civil War patriotic song N-65
  popular music M-684

Dixiecrats, a group of Southern Democrats who broke away from party to form States' Rights Democratic party 1948; nominated J. Strom Thurmond for president and Fielding L. Wright for vice-president.

Dixie Highway, a popular name for two north-to-south highways beginning at Sault Ste. Marie, Mich., and terminating in Florida. The "east" route goes through Saginaw, Detroit (Mich.), Cincinnati (Ohio), Asheville (N.C.), Savannah (Ga.) to Miami (Fla.); the "west" route through St. Joseph (Mich.), Indianapolis (Ind.), Louisville (Ky.), Chattanooga (Tenn.) to Jacksonville (Fla.). The Dixie Bee Line Route goes from Chicago (Ill.) to Nashville (Tenn.), and the Dixie Overland Highway from San Diego (Calif.) to Savannah.

Dixieland Jass Band, jazz band J-85

Dixon, Charles Dean (1915–76), U.S. conductor, born in New York, N.Y.; first black conductor to conduct New York Philharmonic 1941; appeared with leading orchestras.

Dixon, Jeremiah (died 1777), British surveyor; helped fix boundary between Maryland and Pennsylvania

Dixon, Thomas (1864–1946), U.S. novelist and playwright, born in Shelby, N.C. ('The Clansman', filmed as 'Birth of a Nation').

Dixon, Ill., city on Rock River, about 95 mi (150 km) w. of Chicago; shoes, cable and metal products, cement; dairy products; flower growing; pop. 15,659
  Illinois, *map* I-52

Diyarbakir, Turkey, city on Tigris River; silk goods, gold and silver filigree work; pop. 169,535
  Asia, *map* A-697

Dizygotic twins (or fraternal twins) M-649

Dizziness, medical disorder F-120

Djajapura (or Jayapura, formerly Sukarnapura), Indonesia, city and port on n. coast of New Guinea; capital of Irian Jaya province; in World War II, when known as Hollandia, Netherlands New Guinea, it was Japanese air base; in 1944 taken by U.S. forces and made headquarters of Gen. Douglas MacArthur; pop. 45,786, *maps* I-166, P-3
  New Guinea N-174

Djakarta. *see in index* Jakarta

Djerba (or Jerba), island belonging to Tunisia, off e. coast, in Gulf of Gabes; about 16 mi long by 16 mi (26 km by 26 km) wide; olives; in Greek and Roman mythology, the lotus-eaters' island; pop. 62,445 T-308

Djibouti (officially Republic of Djibouti, formerly Afars and Issas; French Somaliland), nation in e. Africa on Gulf of Aden; formerly a French territory; independent 1977; 8,900 sq mi (23,050 sq km); cap. Djibouti; pop. 323,000 D-190, *map* A-115
  African political unit, *table* A-112
  flag, *picture* F-164
  world, *map* W-297

Djibouti, Republic of Djibouti, cap. and port; pop. 130,000 D-190, *map* A-115

Djilas, Milovan (born 1911), Yugoslav political leader, born in Montenegro; vice-president and head of parliament of Yugoslavia under Tito; left Communist party 1954; arrested for anti-Communist statements and writings; imprisoned 1956–61, 1962–67 ('The New Class'; 'Conversations with Stalin'; 'Montenegro').

Djokjakarta, Indonesia, city in s.-central Java; ancient temples of Borobudur and Prambanan; pop. 500,000.

Djoser (or Zoser) (2686?–2613? BC), king of Egypt E-125

Dmitri (or Demetrius), Russian pretender who appeared 1603 and took name of heir to the throne, who had been secretly killed by the usurping czar Boris Godunov; reigned ably until his murder 1606 R-352

DMT (dimethyltryptamine), hallucinogenic drug H-18

DNA (or deoxyribonucleic acid), found in cell nucleus B-199, C-239
  biophysics B-237
  embryology E-202
  Franklin's research F-005
  genetic engineering G-49, *picture* G-50
  genetics G-54, *pictures* G-55, 57
  heredity H-139
  mathematics, *picture* M-219
  microbiology M-377
  molecule M-522
  virus, *picture* D-166
  X rays X-404

Dnepr Dam, in U.S.S.R., on Dnieper River, 200 mi (320 km) from its mouth, at Zaporozh'ye, Ukrainian Soviet Socialist Republic; concrete dam with 3 locks; generates 660,000 kilowatts (900,000 horsepower); construction directed by U.S. engineers and cost about $110,000,000 D-191, K-231

Dnepropetrovsk, U.S.S.R, city in the Ukrainian Soviet Socialist Republic, 250 mi (400 km) n.e. of Odessa; iron and steel products; flour; timber depot; pop. 863,000, *maps* E-360, R-344

Dnepr River (or Dnieper River), river of s.w. U.S.S.R.; length 1,400 mi (2,250 km) D-190, *maps* E-360, R-322
  Russian history R-351

Dnestr River (or Dniester River), river of s.w. U.S.S.R; length 839 mi (1,350 km) D-191, *maps* E-360, R-322

Doan, Charles Austin (born 1896), U.S. physician, born in Nelsonville, Ohio; specialist in blood diseases; professor of medicine and director of medical research Ohio State University 1930–44, dean 1944–61.
Doane College, Crete, Neb.; affiliated with United Church of Christ; established 1872; liberal arts, teacher education.
Dobby, in weaving F-5
Dobell, Bertram (1842–1914), British bookseller and poet, born in Battle; arranged publication of James Thomson's 'The City of Dreadful Night'; identified and edited poetry of Thomas Traherne.
Döbereiner, Johann Wolfgang (1780–1849), German chemist, born near Hof, Bavaria; invented Döbereiner's lamp, ignited by action of hydrogen on platinum sponge and widely used before prevalence of sulfur match; discovered furfural; in chemistry, classified similar elements in groups of three (Döbereiner's triads).
Doberman pinscher, dog D-193, *picture* D-201
Dobie, James Frank (1888–1964), U.S. author and educator, born in Live Oak County, Tex.; professor of English at University of Texas 1933–47; popular, authoritative legends of Southwest ('Coronado's Children'; 'Tales of the Mustangs'; 'The Longhorns'; 'Cow People'); awarded Presidential Medal of Freedom 1964.
Dobrovolsky, Georgi T. (1928–71), Soviet cosmonaut, born in Odessa; chosen for space program 1963; flight commander Soyuz II, in which he and two others died as craft was reentering earth's atmosphere, *table* S-348
Dobruja, historic region in s.e. Europe, on Black Sea R-316
Dobrynin, Anatolii Fedorovich (born 1919?), Soviet diplomat, born in Ukraine; Soviet embassy staff to U.S. 1952–55; UN undersecretary 1957–60; ambassador to U.S. 1962–86; appointed to Communist Party Secretariat 1986.
Dobson, Henry Austin (1840–1921), British poet and essayist, born in Plymouth; graceful use of French verse forms ('At the Sign of the Lyre').
Dobsonian Telescope A-731
Dobzhansky, Theodosius (1900–75), U.S. scientist D-191
Dock, George (1860–1951), U.S. physician, born in Hopewell, Pa.; professor of medicine University of Michigan, Tulane and Washington universities; contributed to pathology of hookworm, malaria, and dysentery.
Dock, coarse weedy herbs of genus *Rumex* of buckwheat family; 2 to 4 ft (0.6 to 1.2 m) high; small greenish flowers in panicles; leaves long, lance-shaped.
Dock, a space for a ship between two adjoining piers or wharves; in U.S. often called a slip; also an enclosed place for ships, with gates to maintain desired water level regardless of tides. *see also in index* Port
  dry dock S-171, *picture* R-269
Docking. *see in index* Rendezvous and docking
Dock Landing Ship (LSD), amphibious naval vessel N-86, *picture* N-90
Dock Street Theater, in Charleston, S.C. C-280
Doctor, type of university degree U-204
Doctor, medical. *see in index* Medicine; Physician
Doctor bird, Jamaican name for hummingbird J-17
'Dr. Breen's Practice', work by Howells A-352
'Doctor Faustus', work by Marlowe. *see in index* 'Tragicall History of D. Faustus'
Doctorfish, a fish of the genus *Teuthis*, with knifelike movable spine on each side of tail; also known as surgeonfish, lancet, barberfish, or tang; lives in warm seas.
Doctor James's Fever Powder, patent medicine sold by Newbery N-151
Doctor of the short robe, barber of the Middle Ages who would also practice bloodletting and some dentistry H-9
Doctors' Commons, formerly a self-governing teaching body of practitioners of canon and civil law
  Dickens' position D-134
'Doctrine and Discipline of Divorce, The', pamphlet by Milton M-419
Doctrine of the Faith, Congregation for the, in Roman Catholicism P-100
Doctrine of the four humors, in ancient Greek medicine M-281
Documentary, M-622, 628
  acting history A-26
  Lange L-29
Documentation, assembling and coding of recorded information for maximum accessibility to users
  antiques A-494
  report writing R-151b
Documentation Center on the Fate of the Jews and Their Persecutors W-202
Dodd, William Edward (1869–1940), U.S. historian and diplomat, born near Clayton, N.C.; professor University of Chicago 1908–33; ambassador to Germany 1933–37 ('Woodrow Wilson and His Work').
Dodder, a leafless parasitic plant introduced into U.S. from Europe with clover seeds; now a rapidly growing pest P-114, *pictures* P-363a
Doddridge, Philip (1702–51), British nonconformist clergyman, born in London; wrote hymns; gave Bibles to poor.
Dodds, Johnny (1892–1940), U.S. jazz clarinetist, born in New Orleans, La.; self-taught; played with King Oliver; inspired other clarinetists.
Dodecagon, in mathematics geometry G-76, *diagram* G-75
Dodecanese, Greek island group chiefly in s.e. Aegean Sea, off Turkey; 1,035 sq mi (2,680 sq km); pop. 121,017
  Greece G-254, 260
Doderer, Heimito von (1896–1966), Austrian novelist, born in Weidlingau, Austria
  German literature G-108
Dodge, Grace Hoadley (1856–1914), U.S. social worker, born in New York, N.Y.; organized 1884 the Industrial Education Association to introduce industrial education into public schools; helped found Teachers College of Columbia University 1889.
Dodge, Grenville Mellen (1831–1916), U.S. civil engineer and Union general in Civil War, born in Danvers, Mass.; chief engineer Union Pacific Railroad 1866–70; Republican representative from Iowa 1867–69.
Dodge, John F. (1864–1920), and his brother **Horace E.** (1868–1920), early automobile manufacturers; after working as machinists and manufacturers of automobile parts, started their own automobile manufacturing company A-859
Dodge, Mary Elizabeth Mapes (1831–1905), U.S. editor and writer for children, born in New York, N.Y. ('Hans Brinker, or The Silver Skates'; 'The Land of Pluck').
DODGE, artificial satellite, *table* S-344
Dodge City, Kan., city on Arkansas River, about 150 mi (240 km) w. of Wichita; cattle market and wheat terminal; dairy and other food products; farm equipment; Saint Mary of the Plains College; annual rodeo; pop. 18,001 K-177
Dodg'em, amusement park ride A-384
Dodging, photographic technique P-295
Dodgson, Charles Lutwidge. *see in index* Carroll, Lewis
Dodo, an extinct bird B-276
Dodoma, Tanzania D-35, T-23, *map* A-115
Dodsley, Robert (1703–64), British author and publisher, birthplace probably Mansfield; suggested, published, and helped finance Johnson's 'Dictionary'.
'Dodsworth', work by Lewis L-142
Doe, John. *see in index* John Doe
Doe, a female, especially adult, of deer, antelope, hare, and most other mammals of which the male is known as a buck
  deer D-61
  rabbit and hare R-20
Doenitz, Karl (1891–1980), German submarine expert, born in Grünau, near Berlin; made commander in chief of German navy 1943; succeeding Hitler, was Führer May 1945; imprisoned for war crimes 1946–56; wrote 'Memoirs'.
Doering, William von Eggers (born 1917), U.S. chemist, born in Fort Worth, Tex.; first to synthesize quinine (1944), with R. B. Woodward; professor chemistry Yale University 1952–67, Harvard University from 1967.
Doe skin, a fabric W-291
Dog, animal belonging to the family Canidae D-192. *see also in index* dogs by name
  anatomy
    reflexes R-132
    senses S-218, S-260
  births M-649
  disease P-138, V-251
  domestication A-454, *picture* S-57d
  food and feeding, *picture* V-243
  fur, *tables* F-464, 465
  hunting dogs H-332
  lifespan A-126, *chart* A-423
  pet care P-243
  related species. *see in index* Coyote; Jackal; Wolf
  test of life L-264
  training, *picture* V-243
    police work, *picture* P-428
    space travel S-345
    whistle S-260
Dogbane, spreading, milky-juiced herb *Apocynum androsaemifolium* with erect branching stem; opposite, oval leaves; small bell-shaped flowers, white or pink; plant believed poisonous to dogs.
Dogbane family, a family of plants and trees, native chiefly to tropics, including the dogbane, oleander, crape jasmine, star jasmine, periwinkle, amsonia, and Indian hemp.
Dogberry, character in Shakespeare's 'Much Ado About Nothing', constable, type of official stupidity. *see also in index* 'Much Ado About Nothing'
Dogberry, tree. *see in index* American mountain ash
Doge, elective duke or chief magistrate of the city-republics of Venice and Genoa during Middle Ages V-278
Doge's Palace, Venice, Italy V-277
Dogfish (or grayfish), shark of the family Squalidae S-144
Dogie, a motherless calf in a range herd
  cowboys, *picture* C-753
Dog racing, sport D-214, *picture* D-207
Dogrib, American Indian tribe of the Northwest Territories, *map* I-136, *table* I-138
Dog salmon. *see in index* Chum salmon
Dogsled E-299
Dog Star. *see in index* Sirius
Dog tooth. *see in index* Cuspid
Dogtooth violet (also called adder's-tongue, or trout lily, or fawn lily) F-240, *picture* F-232
Dogwood, shrub or tree
  state flowers, *picture* S-427
    North Carolina, *picture* N-362
Dogwood family (or Cornaceae), a family of shrubs and trees, including the dogwood, golddust tree, and cornelian cherry. *see also in index* Dogwood
Doha, Qatar, capital city and deepwater port on the Persian Gulf; pop. 190,000 Q-2
  Asia, *map* A-697
Dohnányi, Ernö (or Ernst von Dohnányi) (1877–1960), Hungarian composer, born in Pressburg, now Bratislava, Czechoslovakia; symphonies, piano pieces, string quartets, songs, and operas ('The Tenor').
Doisy, Edward Adelbert (1893–1986), U.S. biochemist, born in Hume, Ill.; professor of biochemistry St. Louis University School of Medicine 1923–65; isolated theelin, female sex hormone, 1929. *see also in index* Nobel Prizewinners, *table*
Dojo, martial arts training room M-159
Dokes, Michael, holder of heavyweight boxing title 1982–83 B-392
Dolbear, Amos Anderson (1837–1910), U.S. inventor and physicist, born in Norwich, Conn.; made valuable studies and inventions regarding the writing telegraph, electric gyroscope, magnetotelephone, wireless telegraphy, and electric waves as applied to photography; announced convertibility of sound into electricity 1873.
Dolce, in music, *list* M-670
'Dolce vita, La', motion picture F-53, M-623
Dolci, Carlo (1616–86), Italian painter, born in Florence; small religious paintings pleasing in color ('Christ Blessing the Bread and Wine'; 'St. Cecilia').
Doldrums (or belt of calms)
  daily thundershowers R-88
  wind W-221, *picture* W-222
Dole, Elizabeth (born 1936), U.S. public official, born in Salisbury, N.C.; secretary of transportation 1983–87
  women's rights W-276
Dole, James Drummond (1877–1958), U.S. industrialist, born in Boston, Mass.; to Hawaii 1900; organized Hawaiian Pineapple Co., Ltd. 1901 (now Dole Co., it is world's chief producer of pineapples); president and general manager 1901–32, chairman of board 1932–48.
Dole, Nathan Haskell (1852–1935), U.S. author, editor, and translator, born in Chelsea, Mass.; original works include 'Young Folks' History of Russia', 'Famous Composers', 'The Hawthorne Tree and Other Poems', 'Omar, the Tent Maker', 'The Pilgrims'; edited and translated many Russian, French, Italian, Spanish, German works.
Dole, Robert J. (born 1923), U.S. public official, born in Russell, Kan.; member (Republican) Kansas legislature 1951–53; U.S. representative from Kansas 1961–69; senator 1969–; chairman Republican National Committee 1971–72; vice-presidential candidate 1976
  Ford's 1976 candidacy F-305
Dole, Sanford Ballard (1844–1926), U.S. jurist and political leader D-214
  Hawaii H-64
  Liliuokalani L-209
Dolichocephaly, in ethnology, the condition of having a relatively long head R-25, *picture* R-27
Dolin, Anton (originally Patrick Healey-Kay) (born 1904), British dancer and choreographer, born in Sussex; with Diaghilev ballet 1923–25, 1928–29, later with Sadler's Wells Ballet (London), Markova-Dolin Ballet, and Ballet Theatre; ballets created include 'Bluebeard', 'Camille', 'Romantic Age'; author of 'Ballet Go Round', autobiography, and 'Alicia Markova, Her Life and Art'.
Doll D-215
  American Indian I-117
  puppets and marionettes. *see in index* Puppets and marionettes
  toys T-241
Dollar, monetary unit of nations; U.S. dollar equals 1/38 of troy oz (0.93 gram) of gold; besides U.S., nations on dollar system include Australia, Bahamas, Barbados, Belize, Canada, Fiji, Guyana, Jamaica, Liberia, Malaysia, New Zealand, Singapore, Trinidad and Tobago, and Zimbabwe
  foreign exchange F-307
  money M-533
  name's origin C-540
  United States R-270
    devaluation N-327
    American Revolution R-168
Dollar diplomacy, U.S. government's policy to promote U.S. citizens' commercial interests in foreign countries by peaceful means
  Wilson's administration W-217

Doll Collectors of America, U.S. organization founded in 1935 D-215

Dollfuss, Engelbert (1892–1934), Austrian statesman, born near Sankt Pölten of peasant stock; as chancellor 1932–34, defied Austrian Nazis; assassinated A-827, *list* A-704
aftermath of World War I W-321

Dollhouse D-222, *picture* D-215
models M-516

Dollond, John (1706–61), English optician, born in London; constructed achromatic lenses for telescopes by combining crown and flint glasses.

'Doll's House, A', a drama by Henrik Ibsen concerning Nora, a wife who demands a right to her own ideals and individuality; when first produced, in 1879, caused a stir.

Dolly, a platform on wheels for moving heavy materials, *picture* R-73

Dolly Varden trout, a fish of family Salmonidae T-291

Dolmen, Stone Age monument S-455

Dolmetsch, Arnold (1858–1940), French connoisseur and collector of musical instruments, born in Le Mans.

Dolomite (or calcium magnesium carbonate, or dolomitic limestone), a form of limestone; used as a building stone and for furnace linings, refractories, and in metallurgical processes M-41
minerals M-435
ore, *table* O-600

Dolomites (named from mineral dolomite), limestone mountains in e. Alps; highest peak, Marmolada (10,964 ft; 3,342 m), in n. Italy; tourists, mountain climbing T-192, *map* I-404
Italy, *picture* I-384

Dolophine. *see in index* Methadone

Dolores, Mission, in San Francisco, Calif.; founded 1776 by Father Junipero Serra; interior decorated with paintings done by Indians and a hand-carved altar covered with gold leaf, brought from Mexico 1870 K-247

Dolores Hidalgo, Mexico, city 25 mi (40 km) n.e. of Guanajuato; farming center; here in 1810 a Roman Catholic priest, Miguel Hidalgo y Costilla, began Mexico's revolt against Spain; pop. 12,311
Mexico M-336

Dolphin, a sea mammal related to whale D-223, *picture* A-426. *see also in index* Porpoise
whale W-185

Dolphin fish (coryphene, or dorado), an edible game fish D-224

Dolton, Ill., village 18 mi (29 km) s. of Chicago; glass and metal products; incorporated 1892; pop. 24,766
Illinois, *map* I-52

DOM (2,5-dimethoxy-4-methylamphetamine), hallucinogenic drug H-18

Dom, Portuguese equivalent of Spanish Don. *see in index* Don

Doma Cathedral, Riga, Latvian Soviet Socialist Republic, *picture* L-83

Domagk, Gerhard Johannes Paul (1895–1964), German physician and research chemist, born in Lagow, Brandenburg A-491

Domain, in magnetism M-46

Domain, in mathematics A-297

Domain, public. *see in index* Land, public

'Dombey and Son', novel by Dickens D-137, *picture* D-136

Dome, in architecture, cupped roof or ceiling, usually hemispherical B-497. *see also in index* Arch; Vault
Byzantine A-549, B-536
Dome of the Rock. *see in index* Dome of the Rock
Fuller F-446
geodesic. *see in index* Geodesic domes
St. Peter's V-268
U.S. Capitol, *picture* U-154

Dome mountain, in geology M-634

Domenichino, Zampiere (1581–1641), Italian painter, born in Bologna; pupil of the Carracci; excelled in religious frescoes; one of earliest landscape painters ('Communion of St. Jerome'; 'Scourging of St. Andrew'; 'The Guardian Angel').

Dome of the Rock (also called Mosque of Omar), in Jerusalem, built over rock supposed by Jews to be scene of the sacrifice of Isaac, and, by Muslims, of the Prophet's ascension J-100, *picture* J-99
Israel, *picture* I-370
mosaic M-590

Dome Rock, landmark in Nebraska, *picture* N-103

Domesday Book (or Doomsday Book), William I's statistical record of England W-206
English history E-240
Norman conquest N-333

Domestic animals. *see in index* Animals, domestic

Domestic goat, mammal *Capra hircus* G-171

Domestic guinea fowl, bird *Numida meleagris* G-315

Domestic science. *see in index* Home economics

Domestic tragedy, drama concerning the lives of ordinary people D-241

Domett, Alfred (1811–87), British poet and colonial statesman, born in London; prime minister of New Zealand 1862–71 ('Ranolf and Amohia').

Dominant, in music M-692, *list* M-670

Dominant trait, in heredity G-53

Domingo, Plácido (born 1941), Spanish opera tenor, *picture* O-566, *list* O-570

Domínguez, Francisco Atanasio, 18th-century Spanish missionary and explorer
explorations C-586, U-219, *map* U-176

Dominic (or Saint Dominic, full name Domingo de Guzmán) (1170?–1221), founder of Order of Friars Preachers, or Dominicans D-224

Dominica, island republic, West Indies; formerly British state; became independent 1978; 300 sq mi (780 sq km); cap. Roseau; limes, bananas, oranges, coconuts, cacao, vanilla; pop. 74,000 D-225, *map* N-350
Commonwealth membership C-602
flag, *picture* F-164
United Kingdom E-259
West Indies W-156, *map* W-159

Dominican College, in Houston, Tex.; Roman Catholic; for women; established 1946; closed 1974.

Dominican College of San Rafael, San Rafael, Calif.; Roman Catholic; chartered 1890; liberal arts, education; graduate school.

Dominican Republic (formerly Santo Domingo), the eastern two thirds of the island of Hispaniola; area 18,816 sq mi (48,733 sq km); cap. Santo Domingo; pop. 6,075,000 D-225
Caribbean literature C-166
Columbus C-594
first hospital H-279
flag, *picture* F-164
Hispaniola H-169
national anthem, *table* N-64
North America, *map* N-350
OAS O-606
railroad mileage, *table* R-85
United States R-286
Hispanic Americans H-162
West Indies W-155, *map* W-159
world, *map* W-297
World War II W-328

Dominicans (Black Friars, or Order of Friars Preachers), religious order of Roman Catholicism established in 1216 by Saint Dominic D-224
monks and monasticism M-541

Dominion Day, Canadian national holiday C-100

Dominions, in Britain's history
colonialism and imperialism C-556

Dominique, breed of poultry P-482

Domino, Fats (real name Antoino Domino) (born 1928), U.S. rock'n'roll musician M-680

Dominoes, U.S. music group M-580

Dominoes, a game D-228

Domitian (AD 51–96), Roman emperor (AD 81–96), murdered for his cruelties; the Apostle John was banished to Patmos probably during his reign R-247
Bible B-184
Christians persecuted C-401

Domitien, Elisabeth, Central African Republican political leader W-276

Domrémy-la-Pucelle France, village in n.e., on Meuse River; preserves house in which Joan of Arc was born; pop. 184, *map* F-369

Domus Aurea (or Golden House), Roman palace built by the emperor Nero A-548

Don, Spanish title of respect; derived from Latin *dominus,* "a lord"; name also applied to masters and fellows at English universities. For names preceded by Don, such as Don Carlos, *see in index* individual names, such as Carlos, Don
Oxford University O-622

Donaldson, Jesse Monroe (1885–1970), U.S. public official, born near Shelbyville, Ill.; from job as letter carrier in 1908, advanced to the position of U.S. postmaster general (1947–53).

Donatello (1386?–1466), Italian sculptor D-229
Alberti A-271
metalworking M-311
sculpture S-85, *picture* S-87
'Saint Peter', statue, *picture* P-225
singing gallery S-86

Donati's comet, discovered by Giovanni Donati 1858; 45,000,000 mi (72,000,000 km) long by 10,000,000 mi (16,000,000 km) wide; orbit about 2,040 years.

Donatus, Aelius (fl. mid-4th century), Roman grammarian L-230

Don Bosco College, in Newton, N.J.; Roman Catholic; for men; founded 1928; liberal arts, theology.

'Don Carlos', opera by Verdi O-567

Doncaster, England, city in Yorkshire, 30 mi (50 km) s. of York, between Don and Trent rivers; coal mining, locomotive works; Roman and Norman remains; pop. 84,050, *map* U-18a

Donck, Adriaen Van der. *see in index* Van der Donck

Donegal, Ireland, extreme n.w. county of island of Ireland; 1,865 sq mi (4,830 sq km); cap. Lifford; agriculture, fisheries, woolen manufactures; pop. 108,549, *map* E-360
fairy stories S-481b

Donetsk (formerly Stalino), U.S.S.R., city of e. Ukrainian Soviet Socialist Republic; industrial and educational center; pop. 879,000 U-2, *maps* R-344, 349
Europe, *map* E-360

Donets River, s.w. U.S.S.R.; flows s.e. 670 mi (1,080 km) to join Don River; navigable 255 km (140 mi) north of mouth, *maps* R-344, 349
basin K-230, U-2
Europe, *map* E-360

'Don Giovanni', Mozart's opera, of which Don Giovanni (Don Juan) is hero; first presented at Prague 1787 M-643
opera O-565, *picture* O-560, *list* O-562

Doniphan, Alexander William (1808–87), U.S. soldier, born in Mason County, Kentucky; led Missouri troops in the Mexican War M-494

Donizetti, Gaetano (1797–1848), Italian composer D-229
opera O-566

Donjon (or keep, or dungeon), a castle structure C-199

Don Juan legend (or Don Giovanni legend), Spanish legend of a libertine man; subject of many works D-229
Byron poem B-401
opera O-565
Spanish literature B-384, S-365a

Donkey. *see in index* Ass

Donleavy, James Patrick (born 1926), U.S. author, born in Brooklyn, N.Y. (novels: 'The Ginger Man', 'The Onion Eaters'; play: 'Fairy Tales of New York'; short stories: 'Meet My Maker the Mad Molecule').

Donnay, Charles Maurice (1859–1945), French dramatist and essayist, born in Paris; wrote of social problems; brilliant memoirs; elected to French Academy 1907.

Donne, John (1573–1631), English metaphysical poet D-230
literary contribution E-269

Donnelly, Ignatius (1831–1901), U.S. writer and political leader, born in Philadelphia, Pa.; U.S. Congressman from Minnesota 1863–69; wrote 'Great Cryptogram', trying to prove Bacon wrote Shakespeare's works.

Donner, Frederic Garrett (born 1902), U.S. business executive, born in Three Oaks, Mich.; joined financial staff of General Motors Corporation 1926, director 1942–, chairman of the board and chief executive officer 1958–67; director COMSAT 1968–.

Donner party, a party of immigrants to California led by George Donner; were trapped in snow in Sierras 1846–47 and underwent terrible suffering; three rescue parties were sent to their camp (on what is now Donner Lake)
cannibalism C-139

Donner Pass, a highway and railway pass, altitude 7,135 ft (2,175 m), just w. of Donner Lake, where tragedy befell Donner party, in Sierras of California, near Nevada border and n.w. of Lake Tahoe; U.S. Weather Bureau observatory.

Donnybrook, part of the city of Dublin, Ireland; known for its annual fair, started 1204 and abolished 1855 because of fights and debauchery.

Donora, Pa., borough on Monongahela River, about 20 mi (30 km) s. of Pittsburgh; in agricultural area; fiber partitions, chemicals; pipe fabrication; founded 1901; pop. 7,524, *map* P-184

Donoso, José (born 1924), Chilean writer
Latin American literature L-70

Donovan, Arthur (born 1925), U.S. football tackle, born in New York, N.Y.; played for Baltimore Colts 1950, 1953–61, New York Yanks 1951, and Dallas Texans 1952.

Donovan, Raymond J. (born 1930), U.S. businessman and public official, born in Bayonne, N.J.; executive of Schiavone Construction Co. 1959–81; U.S. secretary of labor 1981–85.

'Don Pasquale', opera by Donizetti O-566, *list* O-562

'Don Quixote de la Mancha', romance by Cervantes C-261
humor H-323
illustrations by Doré D-230
novel N-408
Spanish literature L-243, S-365a

Don River (or Dun River), in Yorkshire, England; rises on moor near Penistone; navigable for 39 mi (63 km) below Sheffield S-148

Don River, in s. U.S.S.R., rises in Lake Tura, flows s.e. and s.w. 1,325 mi (2,130 km) into Sea of Azov D-230, R-323, *maps* E-360, R-322
Volga-Don Canal V-383
world, *map* W-297

'Don't count your chickens before they're hatched', familiar saying F-4

Doodlebug, the larva of the ant lion A-495

Dooley, Thomas Anthony (1927–61), U.S. physician, born in St. Louis, Mo.; as U.S. Navy doctor, organized care of refugees from Communist Vietnam 1954; medical missionary in s.e. Asia 1956–60; described his experiences in 'Deliver Us from Evil', 'The Edge of Tomorrow', and 'The Night They Burned the Mountain'. *see also in index* MEDICO
'The Night They Burned the Mountain' R-111h

Dooley, Mr., a humorous Irish-American saloonkeeper, created by Finley Peter Dunne. *see also in index* Dunne, Finley Peter

Doolittle, Hilda (or H.D.) (1886–1961), U.S. poet, born in Bethlehem, Pa., one of best of imagist school; verses of clear, delicate beauty with classical atmosphere ('Sea Garden'; 'Walls Do Not Fall'; 'By Avon River'; 'Helen in Egypt').

Doolittle, Jimmy (in full James Harold Doolittle) (born 1896), U.S. aviator, born in Alameda, Calif.; U.S. Army 1917–30, 1940–45; led air forces in invasion of Tunisia; made commander of N.W. African Strategic Air Force Feb. 1943 and of 8th U.S. Air Force (Britain) Dec. 1943, transferred to Pacific 1945; a vice-president of Shell Oil Corp. 1946–58, a director 1946–67; chairman National Advisory Committee for Aeronautics 1956–58 A-205, 208
  World War II W-328

Doomsday Book. *see in index* Domesday Book

Doon, river of Ayrshire, Scotland, flowing n.w. 30 mi (50 km) into Firth of Clyde; immortalized by Burns ('The Banks o' Doon').

Door
  Ghiberti's bronze doors S-85, *picture* R-147
  lock and key L-277
  metalworking M-311
  painting tips, *picture* P-76

Doorn, The Netherlands, village near Utrecht; retreat of Kaiser William II of Germany after his abdication; pop. 7,148.

Doornik, Belgium. *see in index* Tournai

Door Peninsula, Wisconsin, bounded on n.w. by Green Bay.

Door-to-door selling, marketing technique M-146

Doo-wop, style of singing using nonsense syllables M-680

Dope, cellulose acetate solution
  models M-515
  synthetic fibers F-72

Doppler effect, law in physics discovered by Christian Doppler (1803–53); applied to sound, light, and radar from moving sources A-721, S-260, S-373, U-201, *diagram* S-261
  weather W-121

Doppler system, in radar R-32
  mines and mining M-425
  weather W-121

Dorado (or coryphene, or dolphin fish), an edible game fish D-224

Dorado, constellation, *chart* C-682

Dorado, El. *see in index* El Dorado

Dorati, Antal (born 1906), U.S. orchestral conductor, born in Budapest, Hungary; musical director Ballet Theatre 1941–45; conductor Dallas Symphony Orchestra 1945–49, Minneapolis Symphony Orchestra 1949–60.

Dorcas (or Tabitha), disciple of Jesus at Joppa, a woman "full of good works" (whence the "Dorcas societies" of the church); raised from the dead by Peter (Bible, Acts ix, 36–40).

Dorchester, Guy Carleton, Baron. *see in index* Carleton, Guy

Dorchester, England, capital of Dorsetshire; Roman remains; one of the towns on the circuit of Jeffreys' "Bloody Assizes" after the Monmouth Rebellion; 292 were sentenced to death here in 1685, pop. 13,660, *map* U-18a

Dordogne River, river in s.-central France; 305 mi (490 km) long; unites with Garonne to form Gironde, *maps* E-360, F-372

Dordrecht (or Dort), The Netherlands, port on island formed by Merwede and three other rivers, 12 mi (19 km) s.e. of Rotterdam; shipbuilding; heavy machinery, chemicals, food products; first assembly of independent states of Holland 1572; Synod of Dort (1618–19) upheld Calvinism pop. 80,714.

Dordt College, in Sioux Center, Iowa; Christian Reformed church; founded 1955; liberal arts, business, education.

Doré, Gustave (full name Paul-Gustave Doré) (1832–83), French painter and illustrator D-230
  folklore, *pictures* F-260, 262
  'Paradise Lost', *picture* E-263

Doria, Andrea (1468–1560), Genoese admiral and patriot, soldier of fortune under Francis I of France and Emperor Charles V; drove French from Genoa, set up republic, became perpetual censor.

Dorians, one of four great branches of Greek people; took name from Dorus, son of Hellen; came from n. or n.w. and invaded Corinth, then Crete; Spartans always regarded as representatives of unmixed Dorian ancestry A-62

Doric architecture A-546, *picture* A-547

Doric chiton, draped garment D-260

Dorion, Sir Antoine Aimé (1818–91), Canadian statesman and jurist, born near Trois-Rivières, Que.; held several Cabinet positions; one of leaders of French-Canadian Liberals during Confederation; chief justice of province of Quebec 1874–91.

Doris, a small state in n.-central part of ancient Greece, s. of Thessaly; reputedly cradle of Dorian branch of Greek people.

Dorking, a breed of poultry P-482, *picture* P-481

Dormant position, in heraldry H-136

Dormont, Pa., residential borough, s.w. suburb of Pittsburgh; settled about 1790, incorporated 1909, pop. 11,275, *map* P-184

Dormouse, a small Old World squirrellike rodent D-231

Doronicum (or leopard's-bane), a genus of perennial plants of the composite family, native to Eurasia; hairy leaves have long petioles (stems); flowers solitary, yellow, daisylike, borne high above foliage.

Dorothea, Saint, virgin supposedly martyred under Diocletian in Cappadocia; patroness of gardeners; festival Feb. 6.

Dorothea, heroine of Goethe's 'Hermann und Dorothea', a simple story of German small-town life (1798).

Dörpfeld, Wilhelm (1853–1940), German archaeologist, born in Barmen; aided Heinrich Schliemann in excavation of Troy.

Dorr, Rheta Childe (1872–1948), U.S. writer and suffragist, born in Omaha, Neb.; wrote 'What 8 Million Women Want' in behalf of women's rights; in 'Drink-Coercion or Control', she described Scandinavian liquor laws; also wrote a biography of Susan B. Anthony.

Dorr, Thomas Wilson (1805–54), U.S. lawyer and political reformer, born in Providence, R.I.; led action to widen suffrage in R.I. R-184, *picture* R-190

Dorsal fin, in fish anatomy, *diagram* F-125, *picture* F-126

D'Orsay, Alfred Guillaume Gabriel, Count (1801–52), French dandy and wit, born in Paris; friend of Byron and countess of Blessington; skillful amateur painter and sculptor.

Dorset, Thomas Sackville, first **earl of** (1536–1608), English statesman and poet, one of leading advisers of Queen Elizabeth I; carried death warrant to Mary, queen of Scots; author of 'Induction', introductory poem to 'Mirror for Magistrates', of which he was part author, probably most important work between Chaucer and Spenser; helped write 'Gorboduc', first English tragedy.

Dorset, a breed of sheep S-147

Dorset (or Dorsetshire), England, county on English Channel; 973 sq mi (2,520 sq km); cap. Dorchester; agriculture, stock raising; stone quarrying; pop. 313,460.

'Dorsetshire', British cruiser S-177h

Dorsey, George Amos (1868–1931), U.S. anthropologist, writer, and lecturer, born in Hebron, Ohio; curator of anthropology Field Museum of Natural History, Chicago, Ill., 1898–1915; professor of anthropology University of Chicago 1898–1915; made expeditions to many countries ('Why We Behave Like Human Beings').

Dorsey, Thomas Francis (nickname Tommy) (1905–56), trombonist and bandleader, born near Mahanoy City, Pa.; was coleader of orchestra with brother **James Francis** (nickname Jimmy) (1904–57), saxophonist, clarinetist, and bandleader, born in Shenandoah, Pa.; severed connections 1935, Jimmy kept their band, Tommy organized his own 1936, merged 1953
  popular music M-684

Dort, The Netherlands. *see in index* Dordrecht

Dortmund, West Germany, city 73 mi (119 km) n.e. of Cologne, in center of coal basin; first mentioned in 899; later a Hanseatic leader, pop. 648,883 D-231
  Europe, *map* E-360
  Germany G-112, *map* G-131

Dortmund-Ems Canal, canal in West Germany G-118

Dorus. *see in index* Dorians

Dory, fish. *see in index* John Dory

Dory, boat B-324

Doshisha University, in Kyoto, Japan K-312

Dos Passos, John (1896–1970), U.S. writer D-231
  expressionism N-414
  literary contribution A-359

Dost Mohammad (1826–1863), ruler of Afghanistan A-91

Dostoevski, Fedor (1821–81), Russian novelist D-232
  'Crime and Punishment' R-112c
  existentialism E-371
  psychological novels N-410
  Russian literature R-360, *picture* R-359

Dot, sign in musical notation M-690

Dothan, Ala., city near s.e. corner of state, 96 mi (154 km) s.e. of Montgomery; hosiery, lumber and wood products, clothing, wheel toys, peanut and cottonseed products; annual National Peanut Festival, pop. 48,750, *map* U-41

Dot map M-121, *picture* M-122

Dou, Gerard. *see in index* Douw, Gerard

Douai, France, manufacturing town 18 mi (29 km) s. of Lille; captured by Germans in 1914 and 1940; pop. 47,347, *map* F-369

Douala, city in Cameroon; pop. 636,980 D-233
  Africa, *map* A-115

Douaumont, fortified hill and village near Verdun, France V-282

Double agent (or mole), in espionage E-305

Double bass (or bass viol, or contrabass), musical instrument V-327
  Koussevitzky K-302
  orchestra O-576
  stringed instrument S-491

Double bassoon, musical instrument O-576

Double-crostic, word game W-292

Doubleday, Abner (1819–93), U.S. Army officer D-233
  baseball B-94, *picture* B-96

'Double Eagles', balloons B-44

Double flat, sign in musical notation M-690

'Double Helix, The', work by Watson R-112f

Double-housing planer, a tool T-220

Double jeopardy, a legal term; prosecution of an individual more than once for the same offense C-775

Double knit, a ribbed cloth with twice-knitted look obtained by knitting interlocking loops with two needles; usually made of acrylic or wool; used for clothing K-260

Double-reduced tin I-347

Double refraction, light by crystals, the breaking up of a beam of unpolarized light into two polarized beams
  cell analysis B-237

Double sharp, sign in musical notation M-690

Double stars. *see in index* Binary stars

Double step (or pace), Roman unit of measure W-138, *table* W-140

Double sugar. *see in index* Disaccharide

Doublet (or gipon), garment D-262

Doublet, imitation gem with a genuine top J-113

Double taxation, an issue in corporate taxes T-36

Double vision (or diplopia), disorder of the eyes E-391

Doubling (or duplation), multiplication technique A-593

Doubs River, river in w. Europe; 270 mi (430 km) long; in e. France, rises in Jura Mts., flows n.e. into Switzerland, loops w. into France, and finally flows s.w. into Saône River
  France, *map* F-372
  Switzerland, *map* S-537

Doubt, River of, Brazil. *see in index* Roosevelt River

Doubting Thomas A-507

Dough, bread B-429

Dougherty, Denis Joseph, Cardinal (1865–1951), Roman Catholic prelate, born in Ashland, Pa.; was first American bishop of Philippine Islands; archbishop of Philadelphia after 1918; created cardinal 1921.

Dougherty, Paul (1877–1947), U.S. painter, born in Brooklyn, N.Y., brother of Walter Hampden; known for marines that portray the sea in both calm and storm ('Land and Sea'; 'Sun and Mist'; 'Storm Quiet').

Dougherty, Walter Hampden. *see in index* Hampden, Walter

Doughty, Sir Arthur George (1860–1936), Canadian historian and archivist, born in Maidenhead, Berkshire, England; went to Canada 1886 ('Quebec of Yesteryear'; 'Canada and Its Provinces', edited with Adam Shortt).

Doughty, Charles Montagu (1843–1926), British traveler, poet, and scientist, born in Suffolk; lifelong student of geology, archaeology, and English of Chaucer and Spenser; lived for many years among Arabs ('Travels in Arabia Deserta'; 'Dawn in Britain', epic in 6 vols.).

Doughty, Thomas (1793–1856), pioneer in U.S. landscape painting, born in Philadelphia, Pa.; self-taught; works characterized by predominance of brown tones; member of Hudson River School.

Douglas, Scottish family famous in history, song, and legend; an earl of Douglas fell fighting against "Hotspur" Percy at Otterburn 1388; Douglas of Lochleven was jailer of Mary, queen of Scots 1567–68.

Douglas, David (1798–1834), botanist, born in Scone, Scotland; explored in California, Oregon, and British Columbia from 1823 to 1832; the Douglas fir and several plants named in his honor; killed in Hawaiian Islands.

Douglas, Donald Wills (1892–1981), U.S. engineer and aircraft manufacturer, born in Brooklyn, N.Y.; with Glenn L. Martin Co. 1915–20; in 1920 founded Douglas Co., incorporated as Douglas Aircraft Co. 1928.

Douglas, Sir James (1286–1330), noble of famous Scottish family; known as "the Good" and also as "Black Douglas" (because of his frequent raids on English border).

Douglas, Sir James (1803–77), Canadian statesman, born in British Guiana; governor Vancouver Island 1851–63, British Columbia 1858–64; founded in 1843, on present site of Victoria, B.C., the first Hudson's Bay Company post on Vancouver Island C-99

Douglas, James Henderson (born 1899), U.S. lawyer and government official, born in Cedar Rapids, Iowa; undersecretary of the air force 1953–57, secretary 1957–59; deputy secretary of defense 1959–61.

Douglas, John Sholto. *see in index* Queensberry, John Sholto Douglas, 8th marquis of

Douglas, Lloyd Cassel (1877–1951), U.S. author and clergyman, born in Columbia City, Ind.; ordained Lutheran minister 1903; began writing novels on spiritual regeneration in modern living 1929 ('Magnificent Obsession'; 'Green Light'; 'Disputed Passage'; 'The Robe'; 'Big Fisherman').

Douglas, Stephen (1813–61), U.S statesman D-233
Civil War C-472
Kansas-Nebraska Act K-189
Lincoln-Douglas debates L-219

Douglas, Thomas Clement (born 1904), Canadian political leader, born in Falkirk, Scotland; member of House of Commons 1935–44; premier of Saskatchewan 1944–61; head of New Democratic party 1961–71.

Douglas, William (1898–1980), U.S. jurist, born in Maine, Minn. D-234

Douglas, Ariz., city in s.e. corner, on Mexican border, just n. of Agua Prieta, Mexico; copper smelting; electronics; agriculture and cattle raising; pop. 13,058, *maps* N-350, U-40

Douglas, Ga., city 35 mi (55 km) n.w. of Waycross; farm and timber region; mobile homes and garment industries; poultry raising; incorporated 1858; pop. 10,980.

Douglas, Isle of Man, capital, on s.e. coast of island; seaport and resort area; automobile races; pop. 19,517, *map* U-18a

Douglas, Mount, peak in s. Montana, just n. of Yellowstone National Park; 11,300 ft (3,440 m).

Douglas fir, an evergreen tree *Pseudo-tsuga taxifolia* of pine family, sometimes called Douglas spruce; pyramid-shaped crown; leaves blue green, ¾ in. (2 cm) to 1½ in. (4 cm) long, two white bands on underside; cones, drooping with prominent bracts, grow to 3½ in. (9 cm); wood red brown to yellow brown; also known in lumber trade as larch, fir, Oregon pine; tree named for David Douglas
fir F-92
forest F-313
Oregon state tree, *picture* O-588
shipbuilding S-165
wood, *table* W-282

Douglas-Home, Sir Alec (born 1903), British political leader D-234
United Kingdom E-259

Douglass, Andrew Ellicott (1867–1962), U.S. climatologist and astronomer, born in Windsor, Vt.; professor after 1906 and director 1918–38 of Steward Observatory, University of Arizona; author of 'Climatic Cycles and Tree Growth'
tree-ring record A-536

Douglass, Frederick (1817–95), U.S. abolitionist and journalist D-234
black American history B-291, *list* B-299
Washington, D.C. W-71

Douglas spruce. *see in index* Douglas fir

Douhet, Giulio (1869–1930), Italian general, born in Caserta, near Naples; advocated "lightning war" with emphasis upon ruthless use of air power to crush resistance; author of 'Il Dominio dell'aria' (The Dominion of the Air) A-156

Doukhobors (or Dukhobors), a religious sect, founded in mid-18th century Russia ; emigrated to Canada in large numbers; name means "spirit wrestlers"; now call themselves "Christians of the Universal Brotherhood."

Doumer, Paul (1857–1932), 13th president of Third Republic of France, born in Aurillac; in French politics and statecraft from 1887; in Chamber of Deputies 26 years; finance minister under Briand; elected president 1931, assassinated by Russian fanatic May 1932.

Doumergue, Gaston (1863–1937), 12th president of Third Republic of France (1924–31), born in Aigues-Vives, near Nîmes; lawyer at age of 22; president French Senate 1923–24; retired 1931; reinstated as prime minister Feb. to Nov. 1934.

Doum palm, a tree *Hyphaene thebaica* of the palm family, native to Nile region; grows 20 to 30 ft (6 to 9 m); usually forked with leaves 25 to 30 in. (65 to 75 cm) long; fruit oval, yellow orange with fibrous center that tastes like gingerbread; common name is gingerbread tree.

Douro (Spanish Duero), river rising in n. Spain and flowing w. through Portugal to Atlantic Ocean; 485 mi (780 km) P-455, S-350, *maps* P-455, S-350
Europe, *map* E-360

Douw, Gerard (or Gerard Dou, or Gerard Dow) (1613–80), Dutch portrait and genre painter, pupil of Rembrandt; pictures done with utmost exactness ('Woman Sick of the Dropsy'; 'The Evening School'; 'Young Mother').

Dove, the name applied to various pigeons P-323. *see also in index* Pigeon; Rock dove
birds B-255, *picture* B-240

'Dove and the Ant, The', fable, *table* F-4

Dover, Robert (1575–1641), English captain and attorney; founded and directed the Cotswold games as a protest against the Puritanism of his day; games comprised wrestling, jumping, gymnastics, rural dances.

Dover, Del., state capital, 35 mi (55 km) s. of Wilmington; pop. 23,512 D-236
Delaware D-72, *picture* D-79
United States, *maps* N-350, U-41

Dover, England, port on English Channel; pop. 35,640 D-236
United Kingdom, *map* U-18a

Dover, N.H., city on Cocheco River, 6 mi (10 km) n.w. of Portsmouth; electronic devices, printing presses, business machines, molded plastic products, wood products, shoes; settled 1623; pop. 22,377 N-178, 186, *map* N-190

Dover, N.J., town 20 mi (30 km) w. of Paterson; knit goods, metal products, clothing; government munitions depot nearby; pop. 14,681.

Dover, Ohio, city 2 mi (3 km) n.w. of New Philadelphia, on the Tuscarawas River; products include steel, chemicals, bricks, tile, cheese, and cattle feed; pop. 11,516.

Dover, Strait of, channel connecting North Sea with English Channel and separating England and France; 20 to 27 mi (30 to 43 km) wide E-229

Dover, Treaty of, treaty between England and France (1670) C-2

Dover Castle, castle in Dover, England D-236, *picture* D-237

Dover sole, a flatfish *Solea solea* of the family Soleidae F-175

Doves Press, noted English printers T-338

Dovetailed line, in heraldry, *diagram* H-136

Dovetail joint, used in cabinetmaking C-175

Dow, Charles Henry. *see in index* Dow-Jones Average

Dow, Gerard. *see in index* Douw, Gerard

Dow, Lorenzo (1777–1831), U.S. evangelist M-318

Dow, Neal (1804–97), U.S. temperance orator, born in Portland, Me.; author of Maine prohibition law; Prohibition presidential nominee 1880.

Dowager, widow with a dower; especially designates widow of titled person to distinguish her from wife of her husband's heir who has same title, as queen dowager.

Dowden, Edward (1843–1913), Irish educator and literary critic, born in Cork; noted Shakespearean scholar; professor of English literature University of Dublin 1867 until death ('Shakespeare, His Mind and Art'; 'Poems'; 'Shakespeare Primer'; 'Life of Shelley').

Dowel, a pin of wood or metal for holding two parts together W-193

Dower, in law, *table* L-92

Dowie, John Alexander (1848–1907), U.S religious leader, born in Edinburgh, Scotland; self-styled "Elijah the Restorer"; preached "faith healing"; founded Christian Catholic church 1901 at Zion City, Ill.

Dowitcher, a shorebird of family Scolopacidae; the dowitcher *Limnodromus griseus* is about 10½ in. (27 cm) long; ranges from Arctic regions of North America to n. South America.

Dow-Jones Average, an index of relative prices of 30 selected industrial stocks, 20 railroad stocks, and 15 utility stocks; used to express general level of stock market prices; developed by Charles Henry Dow (1851–1902) and Edward D. Jones (1856–1920) S-452

Dow Jones News Services, collects and relays news about financial matters N-238

Dowland, John (1562?–1626), English composer and lutenist S-490b

Dowling College, in Oakdale, N.Y.; private control; founded 1959, chartered 1968; located on former William K. Vanderbilt estate; liberal arts; graduate study.

Down, county of Northern Ireland, in easternmost part of island of Ireland; land area 952 sq mi (2,466 sq km); pop. 286,631.

Down, direction D-157

Down, in football F-297

Down, plumage F-50, *picture* P-480
bird B-242
duck D-284
goose D-285

Downer, drug. *see in index* Barbiturate

Downers Grove, Ill., village 22 mi (35 km) s.w. of Chicago; bearings and other metal products, bakery products; Chicago College of Osteopathic Medicine; pop. 39,274, *map* I-52

Downes, Edwin Olin (1886–1955), U.S. music critic, born in Evanston, Ill.; on *Boston Post* 1906–24, afterwards on *New York Times*; lecturer and writer on musical theory, history, and appreciation ('Symphonic Masterpieces'; 'A Treasury of American Song', with Elie Siegmeister; 'Olin Downes on Music').

Downey, Stephen W. (1839–1902), U.S. public official, born in Westernport, Md.; to Territory of Wyoming 1869 as lawyer; member Wyoming territorial and state legislatures; Republican congressman 1879–81; in 1886 sponsored bill creating University of Wyoming (opened 1887).

Downey, Calif., city 9 mi (15 km) s.e. of Los Angeles; products include aircraft, missiles, electronics, metal goods, soap, chemicals, and plastics; pop. 82,602.

Downhaul Utility Capsule, in oceanic exploration O-463

Downhill skiing. *see in index* Skiing

Downing, Andrew Jackson (1815–52), U.S. landscape gardener, born in Newburgh, N.Y.; planned landscaping for U.S. Capitol and White House; wrote books on horticulture A-562

Downing Street, a popular name for the British government; so called because both Foreign Office and the official residence of the prime minister are there in London.

Down payment, in financing
consumer credit C-762
housing H-293, 297, *list* H-305

Downs, a system of chalk hills in s.e. England; North Downs in Surrey and Kent, South in Sussex; latter feeding ground for famous Southdown sheep E-230

Down's syndrome (or mongolism), a congenital condition with moderate to severe mental retardation; victims have broad flat faces, slanted eyes, small ears and noses; heart defects and other abnormalities frequent
genetic disorders G-48
genetics G-57
mental retardation M-303

Downstage, the part of a stage that is nearest the audience or camera T-153

Down under, term used to designate the Antipodes—Australia, New Zealand, and the like; for example, the woman from down under.

Downwelling, in oceanography O-484

Downy woodpecker, bird *Picoides pubescens* of the family Picidae W-286

Dowser. *see in index* Divining rod

Dowson, Ernest Christopher (1867–1900), British poet, born in Lee, near London; hypersensitive, ill with tuberculosis, and addicted to drugs and alcohol, lived lonely, unhappy life; best known for musical and delicate lyrics often colored with sadness; most famous poem popularly known as 'Cynara'.

Doyle, Conan (1859–1930), British novelist D-237
English literature D-118, S-184
Molly Maguires M-526

Dozen, unit of measure, *table* W-140

Dracaena, a genus of perennial plants of lily family, native to the tropics; used as foliage plants because of broad or sword-shaped, varicolored leaves; dragon tree *D. draco* of Canary Islands grows to 60 ft (20 m); its dried juice supposed to resemble dragon's blood.

Drachenfels, (dragon's rock), mountain in West Germany, 10 mi (16 km) s.e. of Bonn, on the Rhine River, 1,065 ft. high; medieval ruins on its crest.

Drachma, a monetary unit of Greece; historic value about 2 cents; coined in copper-nickel; in ancient Greece, silver coin worth 9 to 17 cents.

Drachmann, Holger Henrik Herholdt (1846–1908), Danish poet, dramatist, and short-story writer, born in Copenhagen ('Tendrils and Roses'; 'Once upon a Time' and 'Wayland the Smith', plays; 'The Sacred Five', autobiographical).

Draco (7th century BC), compiler of first written code of Athenian laws; penalties so harsh that any unduly severe laws are called "Draconian" G-265, L-91

Draco, a constellation, *charts* C-681, S-416, 418

'Dracula', novel by Stoker F-262
epistolary novel N-411
Gothic fiction G-197
horror story H-245
Transylvania T-266

Dracut, Mass., community situated 3 mi (5 km) n. of Lowell; incorporated 1702; pop. of township 21,249.

Draft, military conscription. *see in index* Conscription

Draft, ship, *diagram* S-176

Draft animals, animals used for drawing loads. *see in index* Transportation, *subhead* animal power

Drafting. *see in index* Mechanical drawing

Drafting board (or drawing board) M-255

Drafting machine M-258

Drag, in cattle driving C-754

Drag, in fishing, *list* F-146

Drag, of speeding object
airplane A-180
brake parachute P-109a
exterior ballistics B-37

Draga (in full Mme. Draga Mashin) (1867–1903), queen of King Alexander I (Obrenovich) of Serbia; formerly lady in waiting to his mother, Queen Natalie; assassinated with king by group that opposed the marriage.

Dragline, an earth-moving machine D-258

Dragon, a breed of pigeons P-324

Dragon, a mythological animal D-238
Chinese, *pictures* A-457
folklore F-260
Siegfried and Fafnir S-192a

Dragon Boat Festival, *list* F-66

Dragon-claw willow (or contorted willow), tree *Salix*

matsudana 'Tortuosa' of the Salicaceae family W-211

Dragonfly (or devil's-darning-needle, or horse stinger), insect of the Odonata family D-238
  fossil, *picture* E-23

Dragon Mountain Temple (or Lungshan Temple), temple at Taipei, Taiwan; noted for its architecture T-11

Dragon's blood, reddish-brown resin P-275

Dragon tree. *see in index* Dracaena

Dragoon bird. *see in index* Umbrella bird

Drag race A-874

Drainage, of land. *see in index* Irrigation and reclamation

Drainage, plumbing P-393

Drainage canal C-126

Drainage system (or drainage basin). *see also in index* rivers by name
  United States U-34, *map* U-32

Drake, Edwin Laurentine (1819–80), U.S. pioneer oil producer, born in Greenville, N.Y.; first to produce oil by drilling to its source P-232

Drake, Francis (1545–96), British explorer and privateer D-240
  Armada fleet raid A-627
  exploration E-373
    America A-332, *map* A-297
    California C-40
    St. Augustine, Florida S-16b
    San Juan, Puerto Rico P-530
  Hawkins H-74

Drake, Joseph Rodman (1795–1820), U.S. poet, born in New York, N.Y.; often used signature "Croaker" ('The Culprit Fay'; 'The American Flag'); subject of Fitz-Greene Halleck's eulogy
  Green be the turf above thee,
  Friend of my better days!
  None knew thee but to love thee,
  Nor named thee but to praise.

Drake, a male duck D-284

Drakensberg, mountain range in s.e. Africa S-263, *map* S-264
  Lesotho L-137

Drake University, Des Moines, Iowa; private control; opened 1881; liberal arts, business administration, education, fine arts, journalism, law, pharmacy; graduate division.

Dram, unit of weight, *table* W-140

Drama D-241. *see also in index* Motion pictures; Opera; Theater; chief dramatists by name; *also* by languages, such as German literature
  acting A-24
  arts A-662
  ballet B-32
  Greek drama G-275
    music M-667
  hobby H-182
  literature L-243
  medieval. *see in index* Miracle play; Mystery play
  pageant P-20
  puppets and marionettes P-535

Drama bharata natya, Indian dance D-30

Drama lyrique, type of French opera O-560

Dramamine, a proprietary name for Dimenhydrinate, an antihistamine drug used to relieve nausea and motion sickness.

Dramatic poetry P-407

Drammen, Norway, seaport at mouth of Drammen River, on arm of Oslofjord; pop. 31,312, *map* E-360

Draper, Henry (1837–82), U.S. scientist, born in Prince Edward County, Va.; son of John William Draper; known for proving presence of oxygen in sun and for spectral photography
  catalog of stars S-414

Draper, John William (1811–82), U.S. scientist, born near Liverpool, England; helped found medical school of New York University; renowned for researches in photochemistry, spectrum analysis, and radiant energy; made portrait photography possible through improvements on Daguerre's process; his sons **Henry** (1837–82) and **John Christopher** (1835–85) were also scientists of note.

Draper, Ruth (1884–1956), U.S. monologist, born in New York, N.Y., granddaughter of Charles A. Dana; international reputation for writing vivid character sketches.

Draught beer, alcoholic beverage B-132

Draughts. *see in index* Checkers

Drava River, (German Drau), rising in the Tyrol, flows s.e. between Hungary and Yugoslavia, joining Danube River after 450 mi (720 km), *map* E-360

Dravidian languages L-42, *diagram* L-44
  India I-67, I-106

Dravidians, a people of India
  Asian language patterns A-683
  classification, *chart* R-26

Drawbridge, a bridge that can be partly or wholly raised or lowered or moved to one side B-442

Drawers, in furniture F-453

Drawing D-250. *see also in index* Painting
  ink I-206
  mechanical drawing M-255
    vocation V-367, *pictures* V-362, 368
  pens P-157
  perspective P-220
  police sketches, *chart* P-428

Drawing, manufacturing process
  fibers F-74
    cotton manufacturing C-740
  glassmaking G-158, 163, *picture* G-157
  metalworking T-225

Drawing board (or drafting board) M-255

Draw loom S-392

Draw poker. *see in index* Poker

Drayton, Michael (1563–1631), British poet, born in Hartshill, near Nuneaton; work scholarly and varied ('Poly-Olbion'; 'The Ballad of Agincourt'; 'Nimphidia, the Court of Faery').

'Dreadnought', British battleship N-84

'Dream', drawing by Kuniyoshi D-256

Dream, illusion or hallucination of real experiences that occur during sleep D-257
  psychoanalysis P-518
  sexuality S-124
  sleep S-217

'Dream Keeper, The', work by Hughes H-316

Dreamland Park, in Coney Island, New York A-385

Dream Machine, video arcade in Massachusetts E-172

'Dream of Gerontius', work by Elgar O-575

'Dream of John Ball, The', work by Morris E-276

'Dream of the Red Chamber', novel by Ts'ao Chan C-390

'Dream Songs', work by Berryman A-364

Drebbel, Cornelis van (1572–1634), Dutch inventor, born in Alkmaar; some of his inventions so unusual he gained reputation as sorcerer; among them were new fabric dyeing processes and a compound microscope S-495b

Dredge, a machine for digging soil from bottoms of bodies of water D-257. *see also in index* Power shovel
  fishing F-134
  mining M-426
    ocean floor O-460
  Panama Canal dredge, *picture* P-87
  waterway W-108

Dredging spoil, a mixture of water and the material to be dredged D-258

Dred Scott decision (1857), United States Supreme Court decision D-259
  Buchanan's administration B-476
  Lincoln-Douglas debates L-226
  slavery territory issue B-291, C-472
  trial site, *picture* S-21
  U.S. Constitution U-147

Dreiser, Paul. *see in index* Dresser, Paul

Dreiser, Theodore (1871–1945), U.S. author D-259
  Anderson A-408
  literary contribution A-352
  realism N-413

Drepanum, Sicily. *see in index* Trapani

Dresden, East Germany, city of Saxony, on Elbe River; pop. 521,786 D-259
  Europe, *map* E-360
  Germany G-120, *picture* G-116, *map* G-131

Dresden china (or Dresden ware) P-475

Dresden Codex, astronomical records written by the Mayas A-729

Dresden Green, diamond, *picture* D-129

Dress D-260. *see also in index* Clothing; Garment industry; Sewing; Textiles
  dress design D-268
  fashion F-39

Dressage, in equestrian sports E-295, *list* H-249

Dress design D-268
  fashion F-39

Dresser, Paul (or Paul Dreiser) (1857–1911), U.S. songwriter, born in Terre Haute, Ind.; brother of Theodore Dreiser ('The Blue and the Gray'; 'On the Banks of the Wabash, Far Away', Indiana state song) M-684

Dressler, Marie (originally Leila Koerber) (1873–1934), Canadian actress, born in Cobourg, Ont.; joined Joe Weber as comedienne 1906; Academy award for 'Min and Bill' (1931); in many motion pictures, including 'Tugboat Annie'.

Dress rehearsal T-154

Dreux, France, town 35 mi (55 km) s.w. of Paris; Huguenots defeated here by Roman Catholics under duke of Guise 1562; taken by Germans 1870, 1940; pop. 28,156, *map* F-369

Drevet, Pierre (1663–1738), French engraver, born in Loire, near Vienne.

Drevet, Pierre Imbert (1697–1739), French engraver, born in Paris; son and pupil of Pierre Drevet; specialized in portrait engraving, often working on plates with his father.

Drew, Charles Richard (1904–50), U.S. medical scientist, surgeon, born in Washington, D.C.; head of surgery department Howard University 1941–50; blood-plasma authority; organized blood banks early World War II; Spingarn medal 1944.

Drew, Daniel (1797–1879), U.S. capitalist and stock speculator, born in Carmel, N.Y.; early associate of Jim Fisk and Jay Gould; founder of Drew Theological Seminary.

Drew, Georgiana. *see in index* Barrymore, Georgiana Emma Drew

Drew, John (1853–1927), U.S. actor, born in Philadelphia, Pa.; son of John Drew, Irish-American comedian; famed as Petruchio in 'The Taming of the Shrew' and Charles Surface in 'School for Scandal'.

Drew Ali (died 1929) U.S. religious leader B-307

Drew University, in Madison, New Jersey; independent control, affiliated with United Methodist church; founded 1866; liberal arts, theology; graduate school; offers special semester on United Nations.

Drexel, Anthony Joseph (1826–93), U.S. banker, born in Philadelphia, Pa.; founder of Drexel Institute of Art, Science, and Industry, Philadelphia; son of Francis M. Drexel, founder of Philadelphia banking house.

Drexel, Mary Katharine (1858?–1955), U.S. Roman Catholic nun, born in Philadelphia, Pa.; founded Sisters of the Blessed Sacrament for Indians and Colored People (1889).

Drexel University, in Philadelphia, Pa.; private control; founded 1891 as Drexel Institute of Art, Science, and Industry; humanities and social science, business administration, engineering, home economics, library science, and science; graduate studies; quarter system; off-campus center at Baltimore, Md. U-208, *map* P-251b

Dreyer, Carl (1889–1968), journalist, film director, born in Copenhagen, Denmark; best known for 'The Passion of Joan of Arc' (1928) M-602, *picture* M-622

Dreyfus, Alfred (1859–1935), French military officer, born in Mulhouse; center of case that convulsed French political life 1894–99; later cleared of treason charge, restored to his rank 1906, and promoted D-272. *see also in index* Dreyfus case
  France F-341
  Jaurès J-83
  Zola Z-456

Dreyfus case, (began Dec. 19, 1894), in France, trial of Alfred Dreyfus who was charged with passing military secrets to Germany; began wave of anti-Semitism D-272. *see also in index* Dreyfus, Alfred

Dreyfuss, Henry (1904–72), U.S. industrial designer I-169, 174

Dribble, in sports
  basketball B-97
  soccer S-232

Dried food. *see in index* Dehydrated food

Drift. *see in index* Ocean currents

Drift, glacial. *see in index* Glacial drift

Drift, type of mine tunnel M-427

Drifter, mine machine M-428

'Drifters' (1929), documentary by Grierson M-628

'Drifting Cloud, The'. *see in index* 'Ukigumo'

Drift mine M-427
  coal mining C-521, *diagram* C-520

Drill, a marine mollusk S-222

Drill (or drilling), a stout, twilled cotton material used for army uniforms, hunting and work clothes, pockets, shoe linings, and bookbinding; khaki-colored drill is called khaki.

Drill, a tool for boring holes T-218, 222, *picture* T-216
  bow, *picture* U-95
  oil well P-235, *picture* P-239, *diagram* P-237
  pneumatic P-398

Drill press, a tool T-222, *picture* T-218

Drill ship, vessel for marine research F-427

Drin, longest river in Albania A-257

Drinker's respirator. *see in index* Iron lung

Drinkwater, John (1882–1937), British poet, dramatist, and critic, born in Leytonstone, near London; was one of the promoters of the Pilgrim Players (later the Birmingham Repertory Theatre) and managed and produced for them ('Abraham Lincoln', 'Oliver Cromwell', plays; 'New Poems'; 'The Pilgrim of Eternity', life of Byron; 'Inheritance', autobiography).

Drip irrigation, *see in index* Trickle irrigation

Driscoll, John Leo (nickname Paddy) (1896–1968), U.S. football halfback and coach, born in Evanston, Ill.; halfback and coach 1919–31, 1941–64, Chicago Cardinals and Chicago Bears.

Driskill Mountain, mountain in n.w. Louisiana; highest point in state (535 ft; 165 m) L-309, *map* L-310

Driver ant (or army ant, or legionary ant), insect of the family Formicidae A-468

Driver's license S-5

Driver training, automobile A-863, S-5

Drive shaft, of automobile A-852, *picture* A-851

Droeshout, Martin (1601–1650?), English engraver, born in London; most active 1620–51; engraved portrait of Shakespeare appeared in 1623 S-132, *picture* S-135

Drogheda, Ireland, seaport on Boyne River, 27 mi (43 km) n. of Dublin; Poynings' Law, or Statute of Drogheda, which placed Irish legislature completely under England's control, was passed here in 1494; captured by Cromwell 1649; taken by William III 1690 after battle of the Boyne; pop. 17,908.

Drogue parachute S-346c

Dromedary (or Arabian camel), one-humped camel *Camelus dromedarius* of the Camelidae family C-62, *picture* C-63
Drome River, river in s.e. France; rises in Dauphiné Pre-Alps and flows into Rhône River 12 mi (19 km) s.w. of Valence; 75 mi (120 km) long, *map* F-372
Dromio, each of the twins in Shakespeare's 'Comedy of Errors'; slaves of two brothers, also twins, each named Antipholus.
Drone, tube used on a bagpipe W-228
Drone airplane, a pilotless plane A-160, *picture* A-163
  guided missile G-308
Drone bee, insect B-126
Dropmore, an attractive garden perennial *Anchusa italica* of the borage family, with blue flowers resembling forget-me-nots.
Drop-off, in fishing, *list* F-146
Dropper, in fishing, *list* F-146
Dropsie University, in Philadelphia, Pa.; nonsectarian; established 1907; Hebrew and Semitic studies, education; graduate study; Middle East institute.
Dropsy, a term sometimes used for edema, an abnormal accumulation of body fluids.
Drosophila, fruit fly I-227
Drought (or drouth), a long period of dryness, often in cycles; menaces crops, animals, and people; has driven starving peoples to attack and seize moist lands; combated by contour plowing and by planting drought-resistant crops D-272
  Brazil L-60
  Chad C-263
  Ethiopia E-311
  farming F-29
  flood control F-185
  Niger N 000
  Oklahoma O-526
  wheat production W-190
Drowned coasts and valleys, formed when coastline subsides below sea level, permitting sea to cover land; estuaries of rivers so flooded are called "drowned valleys," and a coastline is called a "drowned coast" I-5, R-211
Drowning F-119, S-535
Drug abuse
  alcoholism A-276
  crime C-771
  drug addiction D-275
  habit and addiction H-2
  halfway house H-14
  hallucinogens H-18
  health hazard H-86
  juvenile delinquency J-163
  narcotics N-19
Drug Abuse Control Amendments, penalties for illicit sale or possession of stimulants, sedatives, and hallucinogens D-277
Drug Enforcement Administration, United States U-160
Drug laws. *see in index* Food and drug laws
Drugs (or pharmaceuticals), special chemical compounds D-273
  advertising A-59
  animal experimentation A-448
  bioethical decisions B-214
  brain research B-400
  Food and Drug Administration F-274, P-538
  genetic disorders G-48
  homeopathy H-219
  industry P-248a
  organic chemistry O-605
  pharmacy P-248a
  popular music M-681
  smuggling H-165
  sources
    bionics B-234
    plants P-377
      herbs H-137
  types
    alcohol A-176
    anesthetics A-412. *see also in index* Anesthetics
    antidotes P-410
    antihistamine A-492
    caffeine C-535
    hallucinogen H-18
    immunosuppressive S-519c
    narcotics A-48. *see also in index* Narcotics
    opiates P-446
    opium O-572
Drugstore beetle, an insect of the family Anobiidae B-140
Drug therapy, treatment of disease D-169
  amnesia A-373
  arthritis A-650
  chemotherapy T-164
  fatigue F-46
  headache H-81
  heart disease H-100
  medicine M-278, 285
  mental illness M-302
  snakebite S-227
Druids, priestly class among ancient Celts
  Celts C-242
  Halloween H-17
Drum, any of a number of fishes belonging, with the croakers, to the family Sciaenidae; red drum *Sciaenops ocellata*, called channel bass on Middle Atlantic coast and redfish in Texas, reaches weight of 75 lbs (35 kg); only member found exclusively in fresh water is the freshwater drum *Aplodinotus grunniens*, also called gaspergou and sheepshead. *see also in index* Croaker
Drum (or membranophone), a musical instrument M-687
  bands B-55, *picture* B-57
  orchestra O-576
Drumcliff Churchyard, in County Sligo, Ireland, *picture* I-322
  Yeats Y-412
Drumheller, Alta., city on Red Deer River, 67 mi (108 km) n.e. of Calgary; coal mines, oil and gas fields in area; dinosaur bones found nearby, pop. 6,508.
Drumlin, an oval clay hill of glacial origin; common in w. New York, New England, and s. Wisconsin; Bunker Hill is a drumlin
  glacial dobric G-151
  Ice Age formation I-6
Drummond, Sir George Gordon (1772–1854), British soldier, born in Quebec; commanded British at Lundy's Lane, War of 1812; made general 1825.
Drummond, Henry (1851–97), Scottish religious writer and scientist, born in Stirling ('Natural Law in the Spiritual World'; 'The Ascent of Man').
Drummond, Sir Jack Cecil (1891–1952), British biochemist; professor of biochemistry University of London 1922–45; scientific adviser British ministry of food 1939–46.
Drummond, William (1585–1649), Scottish poet and historian, born near Edinburgh ('Flowers of Sion'; 'The Cypresse Grove').
Drummond, William Henry (1854–1907), Canadian poet D-278
Drummond, Lake, lake in s.e. Virginia, in center of Dismal Swamp; about 6 mi (10 km) in diameter; linked by Dismal Swamp Canal with Chesapeake Bay, *map* V-349
Drummond family, *picture* I-106
Drummond Island, island belonging to Michigan, in Lake Huron M-355
Drummond light (or calcium light, or limelight) L-210
'Drums along the Mohawk', work by Edmonds A-358
'Drum-Taps', work by Whitman W-200
  American literature A-350
Drupe, fleshy fruit containing a stony seed, such as a peach F-465
Drury, Allen Stuart (born 1918), U.S. author, born in Houston, Tex.; on staff *New York Times* 1954–59; Washington correspondent *Reader's Digest* 1959–63 ('Advise and Consent', awarded 1960 Pulitzer prize; 'A Shade of Difference'; 'Capable of Honor'; 'The Throne of Saturn').
Drury College, in Springfield, Mo.; founded 1873; private control; arts and sciences, art, music, and teacher education; graduate studies.
Drury Lane Theatre, in London, England L-288, T-160
Druze (or Druse), religious sect of Syria and Lebanon combining elements of Islam, Christianity, and Judaism, founded by Hakim, 6th Fatimite caliph in 11th century; teaches belief in one God, who has appeared many times on Earth, the last incarnation as Hakim D-278
  Hakim L-112, S-550
  Islam I-362
  Israel I-370
Dryad (or Hamadryad), in Greek mythology, a wood nymph F-12
Dryasdust, antiquary invented by Scott as figure in novels; the name, made more famous by Carlyle, is applied to a tiresome writer.
Dry brushing, painting technique T-156
Dry bulk, type of cargo T-254
Dry cell battery B-108. *see also in index* Electric battery
Dry cleaning D-278
  laundry L-85
Dry continental climate C-501
Dryden, Hugh Latimer (1898–1965), U.S. physicist, born in Pocomoke City, Md.; with National Bureau of Standards 1918–47, associate director 1946–47; director National Advisory Committee for Aeronautics 1949–58; deputy administrator NASA 1958–65; Presidential Certificate of Merit 1948 for developing missile used against Japanese in World War II; posthumously awarded National Medal of Science 1966.
Dryden, John (1631–1700), British poet, critic, essayist D-281
  literary contribution E-269
  poet laureate P-402
Dry dock S-171, *picture* R-269
  harbors and ports H-36
Dryer, for laundry L-84, *picture* L-87
  home appliances H-211
Dry farming
  Spain S-351
  United States U-77
Dry fly, fishing lure, *picture* F-142
Dry forest. *see in index* Tropical deciduous forest
Drygalski, Erich von (1865–1949), German polar explorer, geophysicist, and geographer, born in Königsberg, East Prussia, *table* P-422
Dry Ice, trade name for solidified carbon dioxide R-137
  matter M-226
  snow S-228
  sublimation S-254f
Drying (or firing), in tea processing T-46
Drying, in textile manufacturing T-140
Drying food. *see in index* Dehydrated food
Drying oils P-73
Dry milk, dairy product, *list* D-6
Dry mustard, spice M-694
Drypoint, engraving technique, *list* G-234
Dry subtropical climate C-500
Dry Tortugas, a group of 10 coral keys in Gulf of Mexico, 70 mi (110 km) w. of Key West; included in Florida; during Civil War, Fort Jefferson was Federal prison; Carnegie Institution set up marine biology laboratory 1904; nearby are commercially important shrimp beds, discovered 1949.
Dry wall (often called plasterboard) B-494
Drywood termite, insect of the order Isoptera T-112
DSB (or direct satellite broadcast), television T-77
DSN (or Deep Space Network), stations to track spacecraft S-343b
Dual Alliance of 1891, union formed between France and Russia by a secret treaty to offset Triple Alliance (Germany, Austria, Italy); with entrance of United Kingdom (1907) became Triple Entente.
Dualism, in philosophy, *list* P-265
  yin and yang Y-420
Dual Monarchy (Austria-Hungary). *see in index* Austria-Hungary
Dual-purpose cattle. *see in index* Cattle
Duane, William John (1780–1865), U.S. lawyer, born in County Tipperary, Ireland; came to Philadelphia when a child; appointed secretary of the treasury 1833 by President Jackson but replaced by Ralph B. Taney as result of quarrel over Bank of the United States; executor and director of Girard College 1831–65.
Duars plain, region in Bhutan B-180
Duarte, Calif., city 18 mi (29 km) n.e. of Los Angeles; electronic components, chemicals, wood products; pop. 16,766.
Duarte, Pico, mountain in Dominican Republic D-226, H-169
Dubai, United Arab Emirates, capital of the sheikhdom of Dubai and port, on Persian Gulf; commercial center and airport; pop. 55,000.
Du Barry, Marie Jeanne Bécu, Comtesse (1743–93), French adventuress, born in Vaucouleurs; followed Mme. de Pompadour as favorite of King Louis XV, over whom she had absolute influence; beheaded by revolutionists
  Petit Trianon V-303
Dubbing, in motion pictures M-610
Dubble Bubble, brand of chewing gum C-307
Dubček, Alexander (born 1921), Czech political leader, born in Uhrovec; joined Communist party 1939, first secretary 1968–69 C-816
Du Bellay, Jean. *see in index* Bellay, Jean du
Dubhe, star, *chart* S-422
Dubinsky, David (1892–1982), U.S. labor leader, born in Brest-Litovsk, Poland (now U.S.S.R.); an officer of International Ladies' Garment Workers' Union 1921–66, president 1932–66 L-10
'Du bist wie eine Blume' (Thou art like a flower), work by Heine H-116
Dublin, Ga., city 47 mi (76 km) s.e. of Macon, on Oconee River; farming and lumbering area; meat-packing; plywood, furniture, cottonseed and peanut oils, textiles; U.S. Navy hospital; pop. 16,083.
Dublin, county on e. coast of Ireland, in province of Leinster; area 356 sq mi (922 sq km); industries, farms, fisheries; pop. 795,047, *map* I-283
Dublin (Gaelic Baile Atha Cliath), Ireland, capital; pop. of greater city 650,153 D-281, *map* E-360
  Ireland I-317, *pictures* I-319, 321
  National Botanic Garden, *table* B-379
  world, *map* W-297
Dublin, University of (or Trinity College), founded 1591; arts and sciences, divinity, law, medicine, engineering; open to women; fine library and manuscripts I-321, U-209
Dublin Castle, castle in Dublin, Ireland D-281
'Dubliners', work by Joyce J-144
'Dublin University Magazine', Irish literary publication I-327
Dubois, Clément François Théodore (1837–1924), French organist and composer, born in Rosnay, near Argentan.
Dubois, Eugène (1858–1941), Dutch anatomist and surgeon; on Java discovered bones of *Pithecanthropus erectus.*
Du Bois, Guy Pène (1884–1958), U.S. artist and writer on art, born in Brooklyn, N.Y., of Creole ancestry; landscape and figure compositions; advocate of realism.
Dubois, Paul (1829–1905), French sculptor and painter; his greatest work, in Renaissance spirit, is tomb of General Lamoricière at Nantes; also noteworthy are statues of Joan of Arc at Reims and Montmorency at Chantilly; painted only portraits.
Du Bois, W.E.B. (full name William Edward Burghardt Du Bois) (1868–1963), U.S. social leader D-282
  NAACP B-293
  Washington W-35
Du Bois, William Pène (born 1916), U.S. author-illustrator of children's books, born in Nutley, N.J., son of Guy Pène du Bois ('Flying Locomotive', 'The Great Geppy', 'Lazy Tommy Pumpkinhead', 'The Horse in the Camel Suit', and the 'Otto' series; illustrated 'The Mousewife', by Rumer Godden).
Du Bois, Pa., industrial city 80 mi (130 km) n.e. of Pittsburgh;

in coal region; railroad shops; gas meters, metal products, electronic equipment; Gateway Fair; pop. 9,290, *map* P-184

Dubos, René Jules (1901–82), U.S. bacteriologist, born in France; professor Harvard Medical School 1942–44, The Rockefeller University 1957–71; 1969 Pulitzer prize in general nonfiction for 'So Human an Animal' shared with Norman Mailer.

DuBridge, Lee Alvin (born 1901), U.S. educator and physicist, born in Terre Haute, Ind.; director radiation laboratory Massachusetts Institute of Technology 1940–45; president California Institute of Technology 1946–69; science adviser to U.S. president 1969–70; wrote 'Introduction to Space'.

Dubrovnik (Italian Ragusa), Yugoslavia, Adriatic port of Dalmatia, 38 mi (61 km) n.w. of Kotor; center of Serbian culture 15th to 17th centuries; pop. 55,000 Y-436, *picture* E-339, *map* E-360

Dubuffet, Jean (1901–85), French painter and sculptor, born in Le Havre, France; best known for his development of art brut, showing childlike outlines moving across a surface textured with sand, gravel, glass.

Dubuque, Julien (1762–1810), Canadian trader, born in St. Pierre les Brecquets, Que.; first white settler of Iowa; in 1788 secured permission from Fox Indians to work lead mines on Iowa side of Mississippi River; put old Indian men and women to work in mines; died bankrupt; buried by Indians with the honors given a chief I-293, *picture* I-295

Dubuque, Iowa, city separated from Ill. and Wis. by Mississippi River; pin lead and zinc region; meat-packing, woodworking; construction and industrial equipment, furniture, farm machinery, plumbing supplies; Clarke College, Loras College, University of Dubuque; pop. 62,321, *map* I-302

Dubuque, University of, Dubuque, Iowa; affiliated with United Presbyterian Church in the U.S.A.; founded 1852; liberal arts, teacher education, and theology; graduate studies.

Ducat, gold coin formerly used in various countries of Europe; still used by The Netherlands and other countries for foreign trade; historic value about $3.90, silver ducat worth about half this; first coined by Roger II of Sicily about 1150; coined by Venice, where it became known as *zecchino* ("sequin").

Duccio di Buoninsegna (1260?–1320), Italian painter, born in Siena; founder of Sienese school of painting; influenced by Byzantine art; his great altarpiece painted for the Siena cathedral is still preserved.

Duce, Il. *see in index* Mussolini, Benito

Du Chaillu, Paul Belloni (1835–1903), U.S. explorer, born in France; first white man to make scientific study of gorillas and African Pygmies; wrote 'Explorations and Adventures in Equatorial Africa' and 'A Journey to Ashango-land'.

Duchamp, Marcel (1887–1968), U.S. painter D-283
  criticism C-778

Duchamp-Villon, Raymond (1876–1918), French architect and sculptor, born in Damville, near Evreux; brother of Marcel Duchamp; early work influenced by Rodin; later identified with cubists and futurists; killed by poison gas in World War I S-93

Duché, Andrew (1709?–62), North American potter, born in Philadelphia, Pa. P-477

Duchesne, Philippine Rose, Venerable (1769–1852), a nun of the Society of the Sacred Heart, born in Grenoble, France; came to U.S. 1818 and founded the first American house of the society, at St. Charles, Mo.; founded several other American houses.

Duchess, wife or widow of a duke, also a woman ruler of a duchy.

Duchesse lace L-17

Duck D-284
  antitoxin injection, *picture* U-161
  bird species B-242, *pictures* B-241
  eider duck I-11
  hunting, *picture* H-332
  mallard. *see in index* Mallard
  migration A-450
  pets P-244
  wood duck. *see in index* Wood duck
  wool W-288

Duck (also called sailcloth), a closely woven, stiff, durable cotton or sometimes linen fabric; for sails, casings, and clothing; in heavier weaves, called canvas.

Duckbill. *see in index* Platypus

Duckbill, a type of early shoe S-179, *picture* S-178

Duck-billed dinosaurs R-156, *picture* R-157

Duck hawk (or peregrine falcon), bird F-13
  flight B-252, *picture* B-246
  predation B-280

Ducking, in boxing B-390, *picture* B-389

Duckpins, bowling game B-386

Ducks Unlimited, a private, non-profit organization of U.S. and Canadian sportsmen whose objective is to increase the number of waterfowl D-288

Duckweed, water plant *Lemna minor* W-101, *picture* P-360
  wild flowers F-231

Ducommun, Élie (1833–1906), Swiss journalist and pacifist, born in Geneva; lectured, wrote, and worked untiringly for peace. *see also in index* Nobel Prizewinners, *table*

Duct, device
  fan F-24
  heating and ventilating H-108, 111

Ducted-fan engine. *see in index* Turbofan engine

Ducted gland. *see in index* Exocrine gland

Ductile cast iron (or nodular cast iron), metal I-335

Ductility, a capacity for being drawn thin, as in wire, without breaking or shortening
  iron I-333
  metal and metallurgy M-307
  platinum P-384
  silver S-203

Ductless fan F-23

Ductless gland. *see in index* Endocrine gland

Dudelange, Luxembourg L-340

Dude ranch C-757
  Arizona A-598, *picture* A-607

Dudevant, Baroness. *see in index* Sand, George

Dudley, Guildford (died 1554), husband of Lady Jane Grey; executed for part in plot against Queen Mary.

Dudley, John. *see in index* Northumberland, duke of

Dudley, Joseph (1647–1720), Massachusetts Bay Colony public official, born in Roxbury, Mass.; son of Thomas Dudley; president of Massachusetts council 1684–86; governor 1702–15.

Dudley, Robert. *see in index* Leicester, Robert Dudley, earl of

Dudley, Thomas (1576–1653), leader in Massachusetts Bay Colony, born in Northampton, England; father of Joseph Dudley; next to Winthrop was most influential in colony; between 1629 and 1653 was deputy governor for 14 years, governor for 4; one of founders of Cambridge, Mass.

Dudley, William (nickname Bill) (born 1921), U.S. football halfback, born in Bluefield, Va.; halfback Pittsburgh Steelers 1942 and 1945–46, Detroit Lions 1947–49, Washington Redskins 1950–53.

Dudley, England, city in Worcestershire, 8 mi (13 km) n.w. of Birmingham, in Black Country; pop. 181,380, *map* U-18a

Dudok, Willem Marinus (1884–1974), Dutch architect, powerful influence in development of modern architecture in The Netherlands; the severe geometrical units in his industrial and municipal buildings suggest cubistic principles.

Duel F-70, S-546
  etiquette E-321

Duero. *see in index* Douro

Du Fay, Charles François de Cisternay (1698–1739), French chemist, born in Paris; superintendent of royal gardens, Paris; discovered positive and negative electricity E-161

Dufay, Guillaume (1400?–74), Flemish composer, birthplace probably Chimay, near Mons, Belgium; regarded as one of the founders of artistic counterpoint.

Dufek, George John (1903–77), U.S. Navy officer, born in Rockford, Ill.; U.S. Antarctic leader, I.G.Y.; author, 'Through the Frozen Frontier' P-416

Duff, Alexander (1806–78), Scottish missionary, born in Perthshire; became first Church of Scotland missionary to India 1829; established 1830 at Calcutta a mission school that combined religion with Western learning; helped found University of Calcutta.

Duff, Sir Lyman Poore (1865–1955), Canadian jurist, born in Meaford, Ont.; judge Supreme Court of Canada 1906–33, chief justice 1933–44.

Dufferin and Ava, Frederick Temple Hamilton-Temple Blackwood, first marquis of (1826–1902), British diplomat, born in Florence, Italy; served as governor-general of Canada 1872–78, viceroy of India 1884–88, and British ambassador to Russia, Turkey, Italy, and France.

Duffy, Hugh (1866–1954), U.S. baseball outfielder, born in Cranston, R.I.; with Boston, N.L., 1892–1900; batted .438 in 1894, an all-time high.

Dufourspitze, peak in the Alps A-318

Dufy, Raoul (1877–1953), French artist, born in Le Havre; identified with the Fauvists; colorful and decorative landscapes; noted also for tapestry and fabric designs, ballet costumes, murals, and book illustrations.

Du Gard, Roger Martin. *see in index* Martin du Gard, Roger

Dugesia, freshwater planarian, type of flatworm A-434, *picture* A-433

Duggar, Benjamin Minge (1872–1956), U.S. botanist, born in Gallion, Ala.; professor plant physiology and economic botany University of Wisconsin 1927–43; research consultant Lederle Laboratories, Pearl River, N.Y., 1944–56; noted as discoverer of aureomycin, *picture* A-488

Dugong, an aquatic, herbivorous mammal related to the manatee.

Dugout, primitive canoe S-163

Du Guesclin, Bertrand (1320?–80), French general under Charles V; constable of France; called "Eagle of Brittany"; spent a decade fighting the English.

Duhamel, Georges (1884–1966), French novelist, poet, and essayist, born in Paris; studied medicine and served as surgeon in World War I; wrote 'Scenes from the Life of the Future' after visit to U.S. ('La Vie des martyrs' and 'Civilisation', war books).

Duiker, antelope species A-478

Duisburg, West Germany, city on Rhine River, north of Düsseldorf; important German river port; export and import trade, manufacturing, coal mining; pop. 454,839, *map* G-131

Dujardin, Félix (1801–60), French zoologist, born in Tours; in 1835 distinguished protoplasm in animal cells, calling it sarcode ('Natural History of Infusoria').

Dukas, Paul Abraham (1865–1935), French composer, born in Paris; professor at the Paris Conservatory 1910–35; master of orchestration, one of leaders of modern French school; clever and witty ('L'Apprenti Sorcier', orchestral work; 'Villanelle', for horn and piano; 'Ariane et Barbe-Bleue', opera based on text by Maeterlinck; 'La Péri', dance poem).

Duke, Charles M., Jr. (born 1935), U.S. astronaut, born in Charlotte, N.C.; U.S. Air Force officer chosen for NASA program 1966, *table* S-348

Duke, James Buchanan (1857–1925), U.S. tobacco manufacturer and philanthropist, born near Durham, N.C.; gave millions to charity.

Duke, title of nobility T-195

'Duke Bluebeard's Castle', opera by Bartók O-569, *list* O-562

Duke Endowment, established 1924, *table* F-362

Dukenfield, Claude William. *see in index* Fields, W.C.

Duke's Theatre, in London, England T-160

Duke University, Durham, N.C.; private control; for men and women (coordinate); founded 1924 by expansion of Trinity College (1838) as result of benefactions from James B. Duke; arts and sciences, business administration, divinity, education, engineering, forestry, law, nursing; graduate school N-357, *picture* N-359

Dukhobors. *see in index* Doukhobors

Dulac, Edmund (1882–1953), British artist, born in Toulouse, France; widely known as illustrator, also for portraits and designs for costumes and stage settings; books illustrated include 'The Arabian Nights', 'The Rubáiyát of Omar Khayyám', 'The Sleeping Beauty and Other Tales', and 'Tanglewood Tales'; designed 1937 coronation stamp.

Dulany, Daniel (1721–97), North American colonial lawyer, born in Annapolis, Md.; supported British rule but wrote pamphlet opposing Stamp Act (1765) R-163

Dulbecco, Renato (born 1914), U.S. biologist, born in Catanzaro, Italy; came to U.S. 1947, naturalized 1953; received 1975 Nobel prize for research in tumor viruses and cell genetics; assistant director research Imperial Cancer Research Fund Laboratory, London, England 1971. *see also in index* Nobel Prizewinners, *table*

Dulcimer, forerunner of the piano P-314
  musical instruments M-688

Dulcinea. *see in index* Toboso, Dulcinea del

Du Lhut, Daniel Greysolon, sieur (1636–1710), French explorer, born in Saint-Germain-en-Laye; set out from Montreal 1678 to explore Lake Superior and westward routes; made peace between Chippewa and Sioux in n. Minn.; built fort on n. shore of Lake Superior 1678; rescued Father Hennepin from Sioux 1680; friendliness with Indians made exploration safer and did much to establish French empire in Northwest D-288
  Minnesota M-445

Dulles, Allen Welsh (1893–1969), U.S. lawyer and government official, born in Watertown, N.Y.; brother of John Foster Dulles; in U.S. diplomatic service 1916–26; joined law firm of Sullivan and Cromwell, New York, N.Y., 1926; with Office of Strategic Services 1942–45; deputy director Central Intelligence Agency 1951–53, director 1953–61; author of 'The Craft of Intelligence' and 'The Secret Surrender'.

Dulles, John Foster (1888–1959), U.S. lawyer and diplomat, born in Washington, D.C.; grandson of John Watson Foster, brother of Allen Welsh Dulles; with law firm of Sullivan and Cromwell, New York, N.Y., 1911–49; acting chairman U.S. delegation to United Nations General Assembly 1948; interim U.S. senator (Republican) from New York 1949; special representative of president of U.S. to negotiate Japanese peace treaty 1950–51; U.S. secretary of state 1953–59; author of 'War or Peace'
  Eisenhower Administration E-141

Dulong, Pierre Louis (1785–1838), French physicist and chemist, born in Rouen; co-discoverer of Law of Dulong and Petit on atomic heats; discovered nitrogen trichloride 1811.

Dulong and Petit, Law of, in chemistry, the law that the atomic heat is about the same for the various elements in solid state

Dulse, red seaweed A-284

Duluth, Minn., important shipping center at head of Lake Superior; pop. 92,811 D-288
  Great Lakes G-243, *picture* G-244
  Minnesota M-439, 442, *picture* M-440
  North America, *map* N-350
  world, *map* W-297

Duma, former Russian national assembly R-353

Dumas, Alexandre (1802–70), French dramatist and novelist D-288
  creative writing W-382
  'The Three Musketeers'. *see in index* 'Three Musketeers, The'

Dumas, Alexandre, the Younger (1824–95), French dramatist and social novelist, author of 'Camille' D-288, F-397

Dumas, Jean-Baptiste-André (1800–84), French chemist, born in Alais; noted for research on atomic weights, laws of substitution, and theory of types; devised a way to determine vapor density.

Du Maurier, Dame Daphne (or Lady Browning) (born 1907), British novelist, born in London; granddaughter of George Du Maurier (novels: 'Jamaica Inn', 'The King's General', 'The Parasites', 'My Cousin Rachel', 'The Scapegoat'; stories: 'Kiss Me Again, Stranger', 'The Breaking Point', 'Frenchman's Creek')
  'Rebecca' R-112a
  romanticism N-413

Du Maurier, George Louis Palmella Busson (1834–96), British illustrator and novelist, born in Paris, France; drew lively pictorial satires on society, which were chiefly published in *Punch*; his novel of the Latin Quarter in Paris, 'Trilby', was amazingly successful (other novels: 'Peter Ibbetson'; 'The Martian').

Dumbarton Oaks peace conference R-279

Dum Dum, India, town in West Bengal state, 6 mi (10 km) n.e. of Calcutta; dumdum (expanding) bullets first made here; pop. 31,232.

Dumfries, Scotland, city on River Nith, 65 mi (105 km) s.w. of Edinburgh; hosiery, rubber goods, chemicals, milk products; burial place of Robert Burns, pop. 28,149.

Dummer, Jeremiah (1645–1718), New England silversmith and engraver, born in Newbury, Mass.; examples of work in colonial silver collections of Metropolitan Museum of Art, New York, N.Y., and Museum of Fine Arts, Boston, Mass.

Dumont, Gabriel (1838–1906), Canadian rebel, born in Assiniboia; took part in Northwest Rebellion of 1885 as adjutant general of rebel forces; escaped to United States.

Dumont, N.J., borough in Bergen County, 16 mi (26 km) n.e. of Jersey City; cement industry; clothing; pop. 18,334.

DuMont, television network T-69, 73

Dumont d'Urville, Jules-Sébastien-César (1790–1842), French navigator, born in Condé-sur-Noireau, near Saint-Lô; explored and charted in the South Atlantic, South Pacific, and Antarctic, *table* R-422

Dumouriez, Charles-François (1739–1823), French general, born in Cambrai; distinguished himself in French Revolution; had notable part in victories at Valmy, France, and at Jemappes, Belgium; suffered defeat at Neerwinden, Belgium, 1793, then denounced as traitor; died an exile in England.

Dun & Bradstreet, Inc. (formerly Mercantile Agency), credit agency supplying to subscribers reports on the antecedents, character, capacity, capital, and credit of people in business throughout the world; main office New York, N.Y.; grew from company formed 1841 by Louis Tappan; present name 1933 C-763

Dunant, Jean Henri (1828–1910), Swiss author and philanthropist, born in Geneva; founder of Red Cross Society R-117

Dunbar, Paul Laurence (1872–1906), U.S. writer, born in Dayton, Ohio; best known for poetry, much of it in dialect; home in Dayton has been made a public shrine ('Lyrics of Lowly Life'; 'Lyrics of the Hearthside'; 'Complete Poems') B-293, 301

Dunbar, William (1460?–1520?), Scottish poet; Sir Walter Scott said that he is "unrivaled by any which Scotland has produced"; disciple of Chaucer but with wider humor and less gentle satire ('Two Married Women and the Widow'; 'The Dance of the Seven Deadly Sins').

Dunbar, Scotland, resort town on Firth of Forth, 25 mi (40 km) e. of Edinburgh; historic old castle; Cromwell defeated Scottish Covenanters here 1650; pop. 4,460.

Dunbarton College of Holy Cross, in Washington, D.C.; Roman Catholic; for women; founded 1935; closed 1973.

Duncan (died 1040), Scottish king murdered by Macbeth; Shakespeare based his version of 'Macbeth' on Holinshed, who pictured Duncan as kind and honorable, but earlier historians disagree with this.

Duncan, Charles W. (born 1926), U.S. public official, born in Houston, Tex.; deputy secretary of defense 1977–79; secretary of energy 1979–81.

Duncan, Isadora (1877–1927), U.S. dancer D-289
  dance D-29
  Russian literature R-360a

Duncan, Okla., city 72 mi (116 km) s.w. of Oklahoma City; oil-field equipment, petroleum products; pop. 22,517.

Duncanville, Tex., town 11 mi (18 km) s.w. of Dallas; dairy farming; cotton; athletic equipment; pop. 27,781.

'Dunciad, The', satiric poem by Pope P-445
  English literature E-271

Dundalk, Md., urban community just s.e. of Baltimore; steel manufacturing; large marine terminal of the Port of Baltimore; pop. 71,293, *map* M-182

Dundee, Scotland, seaport on Firth of Tay, 36 mi (58 km) n.e. of Edinburgh; chief linen and jute manufactures in United Kingdom; shipbuilding; marmalade; three churches (Town Churches) under one roof; pop. 181,950, *maps* E-360, S-67

Dundonald, earl of. *see in index* Cochrane, Thomas

Dundreary, Lord, a caricature of a British nobleman in Tom Taylor's comedy 'Our American Cousin'; made famous by Edward A. Sothern; revived by his son Edward H. Sothern; at a performance of this play Lincoln was shot.

Dune. *see in index* Sand dune

Dunedin, New Zealand, important seaport on s.e. coast of South Island; woolen manufactures, gold mining; Otago University; pop. 105,600 D-289
  New Zealand N-284, *map* N-299
  Pacific Ocean, *map* P-3
  world, *map* W-297

Dunfermline, Scotland, in county of Fife, 16 mi (26 km) n.w. of Edinburgh; damask table linen; birthplace of Charles I and Andrew Carnegie; burial place of Robert Bruce; pop. 50,305.

Dung beetle (or tumblebug), insect B-140, *picture* B-138

Dungeon (or keep, or donjon), castle structure C-199

Dunguaire Castle, near Galway Bay, Ireland, *picture* I-317

Dunham, Bertha Mabel (1881–1957), Canadian author and librarian, born near Harriston, Ont.; won Canadian Book of the Year for Children award 1948 for 'Kristli's Trees'; books for adults include 'Toward Sodom', 'Trail of the King's Men', 'Grand River', 'Trail of the Conestoga'.

Dunham, Katherine (born 1910), U.S. dancer, choreographer, and anthropologist D-289

Dunkers (or Dunkards), name for German Baptist Brethren, the oldest body being Church of the Brethren (Conservative Dunkers); originated in Germany in early 18th century, but leaders soon moved to U.S.; practices similar to those of Quakers and Mennonites; advocate baptism by immersion, nonresistance, plain attire; refuse to take oaths
  Pennsylvania P-166, *picture* P-173

Dunkirk (French Dunkerque), France, seaport on the Strait of Dover; pop. 73,618 D-290
  France, *map* F-369
  United Kingdom E-257
  World War II W-324, 338, *pictures* W-325, 339

Dunkirk, N.Y., industrial city 37 mi (60 km) s.w. of Buffalo, on Lake Erie; in heart of grape belt; stainless steel, tool steel, foundry and metal products, textiles, grape juice and other food products; fine harbor; pop. 15,310.

Dun Laoghaire (formerly Kingstown), Ireland, seaport and resort on s. shore of Dublin Bay, 7 mi (11 km) s.e. of Dublin; pop. 51,772.

Dunlap, William (1766–1839), U.S. playwright, painter, and author, born in Perth Amboy, N.J.; first professional dramatist of U.S.; helped found National Academy of Design; wrote histories of theater and arts of design in U.S.

'Dunlap', U.S. Navy destroyer, *picture* N-85

Dunlin, a shorebird of family Scolopacidae; the dunlin *Erolia alpina* is 8–9 in. (20–23 cm) long, rusty red above, with black patch across belly in summer plumage; in winter, gray above, grayish breast; stout long bill, with downward droop at tip; bird known in U.S. as red-backed sandpiper; nests across n. part of world; winters along Gulf of Mexico, Africa, India.

Dunlop, John Boyd (1840–1921), Scottish inventor and veterinary surgeon, born in Dreghorn, near Irvine; invented pneumatic bicycle tire; wrote 'History of the Pneumatic Tyre'.

Dunlop, John T. (born 1914), U.S. educator, labor mediator, public official, born in Placerville, Calif.; professor Harvard University from 1950; director Cost of Living Council 1973–74; U.S. secretary of labor 1975–76.

Dunmore, John Murray, 4th earl of (1732–1809), British colonial administrator; governor of New York 1770; governor of Virginia 1771–76; governor of Bahamas 1787–96.

Dunmore, Pa., industrial borough 2 mi (3 km) e. of Scranton; in anthracite-mining district; brick, stone, apparel; pop. 16,781, *map* P-185

Dunne, Finley Peter (1867–1936), U.S. journalist and humorist, born in Chicago, Ill.; famous for creation of 'Mr. Dooley' ('Mr. Dooley in Peace and in War'; 'Mr. Dooley's Philosophy'; 'Mr. Dooley Remembers: the Informal Memoirs of Finley Peter Dunne', edited by Philip Dunne).

Dunning, John Ray (1907–75), U.S. nuclear physicist, born in Shelby, Neb.; with Columbia University from 1929 (professor from 1946, dean of engineering from 1950); pioneer in neutron research; a leader in developing atomic bomb, split uranium atom at Columbia University 1939; experimented with separation of U-235.

Dun River. *see in index* Don River

Dunsany, Edward John Moreton Drax Plunkett, 10th Baron (1878–1957), Irish story writer, dramatist, and poet, born in London, England; fantastic and imaginative work (plays: 'Plays of Gods and Men', 'Plays of Near and Far'; autobiography: 'Patches of Sunlight'; short stories: 'The Book of Wonder', 'The Sword of Welleran and Other Tales of Enchantment'; novel: 'Guerrilla') E-280

Dunsmore, John Ward (1856–1945), U.S. artist, born near Cincinnati, Ohio; known for historical subjects; work represented in National Academy of Design, New York, N.Y., and Art Museum, Cincinnati.

Dunsmuir, James (1851–1920), Canadian statesman and capitalist, born in Fort Vancouver, Wash., near Portland, Ore.; prime minister of British Columbia and president of the council 1900–2; lieutenant governor of British Columbia 1906–9.

Duns Scotus, John (also known as Doctor Subtilis) (1265?–1308), Scottish theologian and philosopher, born at Duns; one of the greatest of the scholastics; celebrated opponent of doctrines of Thomas Aquinas; the bigoted stand Duns Scotus' followers, Duns men, took against classicism of Renaissance gave rise to use of his name in form of "dunce" to mean pedant and later ignoramus D-266

Duns Scotus College, in Southfield, Mich.; Roman Catholic; for men; founded 1930; Franciscan Friars seminary.

Dunstable, John (1370?–1453), English musician, born in Dunstable; one of earliest composers to use counterpoint.

Dunstan, Saint (925?–988), abbot of Glastonbury, archbishop of Canterbury, and adviser to kings Edmund I and Edgar of England; first of a long line of English ecclesiastical statesmen; festival May 19 W-162

Duntroon (or Royal Military College), in Canberra, Australia M-412

Duodecimal system (or base-twelve system), of numeration N-435, *table* N-438

Duodenum, the first portion of the small intestine S-455, *diagram* S-454
  digestive system D-144, *diagram* D-143

Duomo, Italian word for cathedral. *see in index* Cathedral

Duotone, a special method of making printing reproductions from black and white photographs or drawings to add depth and interest by two-color printing; the dot pattern of the two printing plates, made much as in four-color printing, retains the same range of dark and light areas so that the darker areas take on more color and heighten contrasts.

Dupatta, Pakistani scarf P-78

Duplation. *see in index* Doubling

Dupleix, Joseph François, Marquis (1697–1763), greatest French governor in India, but failed to maintain French rule there; recalled to France 1754 and died in obscurity and want.

Duplessis, Joseph Sifrède, French artist, *picture* F-305

'Duplex, The', work by Bullins A-363

Duplex circuit, telegraph T-58

Duplicate bridge. *see in index* Contract bridge

Duplicating lathe (or automatic lathe), a tool T-220

Duplicating machine, appliance for making multiple copies of typewritten or handwritten pages D-290. *see also in index* Flexowriter; Mimeograph; Multigraph
  office equipment O-495
  printing P-503

Du Pont, Éleuthère Irénée (1771–1834), U.S. industrialist, born in Paris, France; younger son of Pierre Samuel du Pont de Nemours; learned gunpowder making from Antoine Lavoisier; in 1802 founded near Wilmington, Del., a powder plant that became great chemical corporation, E.I. du Pont de Nemours & Company, Inc.; the firm was continued by his descendants: **Alfred Victor du Pont** (1798–1856), senior partner 1834–50. **Henry du Pont** (1812–89), head of the firm 1850–89. **Thomas Coleman du Pont** (1863–1930), president of the company 1902–15; U.S. senator 1921–22 and 1925–28. **Pierre Samuel du**

Pont (1870–1954), president of the company 1915–19. **Irénée du Pont** (1876–1963), president of the company 1919–26. **Lammot du Pont** (1880–1952), president of the company 1926–40, chairman of the board 1940–48. Henry's son **Henry Algernon du Pont** (1838–1926), commanded Artillery in Civil War and was U.S. senator 1906–17. **Lammot du Pont Copeland** (born 1905), great-great-grandson of the founder, president of the company 1962–67, chairman 1968–71 D-291
Delaware D-76
Wilmington W-212

Du Pont, Samuel Francis (1803–65), U.S. Navy officer, born in Bergen Point, N.J.; served in Mexican War and as Union rear admiral in Civil War; his father, **Victor Marie** (1767–1827), was elder son of Pierre Samuel du Pont de Nemours.

Du Pont de Nemours, Pierre-Samuel (1739–1817), French statesman and political economist, born in Paris; imprisoned and property confiscated in French Revolution; emigrated to U.S. with family 1789; returned to France 1802, fled again to U.S. 1815; his sons Victor Marie and Eleuthère Irénée, founders of the two U.S. branches of the family, dropped the "de Nemours" D-291

Du Pont de Nemours, E.I., & Company, Inc., the world's largest maker of chemical products; headquarters, Wilmington, Del. D-291

Dupré, Jules (1812–89), French landscape painter, born in Nantes; member of the Barbizon School.

Dupré, Marcel (1886–1971), French organist, born in Rouen; brilliant record, Paris Conservatoire; phenomenal memory brought him wide acclaim; toured U.S. 1948.

Duquesne, Pa., iron and steel manufacturing city 10 mi (16 km) s.e. of Pittsburgh, on Monongahela River; pop. 10,094, *map* P-184

Duquesne University, in Pittsburgh, Pa.; Roman Catholic; founded 1878; arts and sciences, business administration, education, law, music, nursing, pharmacy; graduate school; Institute of African Affairs, *map* P-345b

Duquesnoy, François (1594?–1643), Flemish sculptor; skilled in portrayal of children in ivory, terra-cotta, bronze, and marble.

Duralumin, an alloy of aluminum with copper, magnesium, manganese, and trace quantities of iron and silicon; resistant to corrosion.

Dura mater, the outermost of three membranes, or meninges, which cover the brain and spinal cord; tough and fibrous; name from Latin, meaning "hard mother."

Durance River, river in France, rises in French Alps, flows 215 mi (345 km) to Rhone, *map* F-372

Durand, Mrs. Albert C. *see in index* Sawyer, Ruth

Durand, Asher Brown (1796–1886), U.S. portrait and landscape painter and engraver, born in South Orange, N.J.; one of the founders of the National Academy of Design.

Durand, Charles Auguste Émile. *see in index* Carolus-Duran, A.E.

Durang, John, U.S. dancer B-35

Durango, Colo., city and port in s.w., on Animas River, about 135 mi (215 km) s.e. of Grand Junction; pop. 11,426.

Durango, state in n. Mexico; 46,196 sq mi (119,647 sq km); cap. Durango; several mining districts; united with Chihuahua until 1823; pop. 1,121,925, *map* M-341

Durango, Mexico, capital of state of Durango; altitude 6,200 ft (1,890 m); center of agricultural, mining, and lumbering district; pop. 191,034, *map* M-341
North America, *map* N-350

Durant, William Crapo (1861–1947) organized General Motors Corporation in 1908, *list* A-856
Michigan auto industry M-358

Durant, William James (nickname Will) (1885–1981), U.S. historian and author, born in North Adams, Mass.; director Labor Temple School, New York, N.Y., 1914–27 ('The Story of Philosophy'); with his wife, **Ariel Durant** (full name Ida Kaufman Durant) (1898–1981), he wrote 'The Story of Civilization', the 10th volume 'Rousseau and Revolution' winning Pulitzer prize 1968, 11th and final volume 'The Age of Napoleon' 1975.

Durant, Okla., city 45 mi (70 km) s.e. of Ardmore; trade center of farming and livestock region; peanut processing; resort area; Southeastern State College; pop. 11,972, *map* U-41

Durante, Jimmy (full name James Francis Durante) (1893–1980), U.S. comedian, born in New York, N.Y.; called "Schnozzola" because of large nose; on stage, screen, radio, and television (plays: 'Strike Me Pink', 'Red, Hot and Blue', 'Stars in Your Eyes'; films: 'Get-Rich-Quick Wallingford', 'Music for Millions', 'Two Sisters from Boston').

Duranty, Walter (1884–1957), British journalist, born in Liverpool; in U.S. after 1949; best known for 'I Write as I Please', about his experiences as Moscow correspondent for *New York Times*; wrote other reports on U.S.S.R., including 'USSR: the Story of Soviet Russia' and 'Stalin & Co'.

Duration, in music M-690

Durazzo, Albania. *see in index* Durrës

Durban, South Africa, chief seaport of Natal Province, on Indian Ocean; resort area; automobile assembling; chemicals, textiles; pop. 960,792 D-291
world, *map* W-297

Durbar, historic British India, a court of Indian princes, held either for affairs of state or for receiving distinguished visitors.

Durendal, sword of Roland R-238

Dürer, Albrecht (1471–1528), German painter and engraver D-292
'Christ before Pilate', *picture* A-664
drawing D-253, *picture* D-254
engraving, *picture* H-272
'Four Apostles' P-38, *picture* P-39
graphic arts G-231, *picture* G-230

Durga. *see in index* Devi

'Durgesanandini', work by Chatterjee I-108

Durham, John George Lambton, first earl of (1792–1840), British statesman, born in London; governor-general of Canada 1838 C-98
Ontario O-553
Wakefield W-4

Durham, breed of cattle. *see in index* Milking Shorthorn; Shorthorn

Durham, maritime county of n.e. England; 1,015 sq mi (2,630 sq km); industries include shipbuilding, ironworking, coal; pottery, paper, and glass; pop. 1,515,643.

Durham, England, county seat of Durham County, in n.e., on Wear River; university; cathedral; castle built by William the Conqueror; pop. 25,780, *map* U-18a

Durham, N.H., 30 mi (50 km) e. of Concord; pop. of township 10,652, *map* N-190

Durham, N.C., city in n.-central part of state, 20 mi (30 km) n.w. of Raleigh; industrial, educational, medical center; North Carolina Central University, Duke University; pop. 100,538 N-357, 360, 366, *picture* N-359, *map* U-41

Durham report, Canadian history C-98. *see also in index* Durham, John George Lambton
Wakefield W-4

Durham Station, N.C., battleground of Civil War near Durham, scene of Johnston's surrender to Sherman April 26, 1865; end of the war.

Durian, tall forest tree *Durio zibethinus* resembling the elm; grown in East Indies.

Durkheim, Émile (1858–1917), French sociologist D-292

Durkin, Martin Patrick (1894–1955), U.S. labor official, born in Chicago, Ill.; Illinois state director of labor 1933–41; president United Association of Journeymen and Apprentices of the Plumbing and Pipe Fitting Industry of the United States and Canada (AFL) 1943–52 and after Sept. 1953; U.S. secretary of labor Jan.–Sept. 1953.

Duroc, breed of pig P-320

Duroc-Jersey, breed of pig, *picture* P-320

Durovernum, England. *see in index* Canterbury

Durra, a variety of grain sorghum native to Asia and n. Africa; introduced into U.S. as early as 1804; of slight economic importance.

Durrell, Lawrence George (born 1912), British novelist and poet, born in India; served in foreign press service in Athens, Greece, and in Cairo and Alexandria, Egypt (Alexandria Quartet: 'Justine', 'Balthazar', 'Mountolive', 'Clea').

Dürrenmatt, Friedrich (born 1921), Swiss author, born near Bern; novels and dramas significant in contemporary German literature G-108

Durrës (Italian Durazzo), Albania, seaport, formerly the capital; exports cheese, olive oil, cereal grains, tobacco; scene of important historical events since ancient times; pop. 39,946, *map* E-360

Dur Sharrukin (City of Sargon), Assyrian city near present village of Khorsabad, Iraq, close to modern Mosul; remains of Assyrian art found in 1843–55.

Durston, Hannah. *see in index* Dustin, Hannah

Durum wheat, plant *Triticum durum* W-188

Duruy, Victor (1811–94), French historian and educator, born in Paris; minister of education 1863–69; wrote histories of France, Rome, Greece.

Duryea, Charles Edgar (1861–1938), born near Canton, Ill., and brother **James Frank** (1869–1967), born in Washburn, Ill., automobile manufacturers T-264, *list* A-856

Du Sable, Jean Baptist Point, trader and first non-Indian settler on site of Chicago, Ill. D-293
Chicago C-317

Du Sable Museum of African-American History, in Chicago, Ill., *list* B-299

Duse, Eleonora (1859–1924), Italian actress D-293
acting A-27

Dushan, Stephen (or Stephen Nemanya IX) (1308?–55), ruler of Serbia S-113

Dushanbe (formerly Stalinabad), Tadzhik Soviet Socialist Republic, capital; textile center; Tadzhik State University; pop. 374,000 T-4, *maps* R-322, 344
Asia, *map* A-697

'Dusk', relief sculpture by Lachaise L-17

Dusky salamander, amphibian *Desmognathus fuscus* of the order Amphibia S-25

Düsseldorf, West Germany, industrial city and port on Rhine River, 22 mi (35 km) n.w. of Cologne; in Ruhr-Rhineland industrial area; banking center; art, music, and educational city; pop. 583,445 D-293
Europe, *map* E-360
Germany G-112, *map* G-131

Dust, fine, dry particles of matter
fog formation F-246
ice formation I-5
prevention S-6
solar system S-254d
Mars P-353
meteor M-314
nebula, *picture* U-202
volcanic V-378

Dust, grade of black tea T-45

Dust Bowl, United States D-272
Colorado C-568
documentary M-628
Oklahoma O-526
soil conservation C-673, U-77

Dust-cloud hypothesis, a theory of solar system's formation P-355

Duster, machine F-33

Dust explosion E-379

Dustin, Hannah (or Hannah Dustan, or Hannah Duston, or Hannah Durston) (born 1657), heroine, born in Haverhill, Mass.; captured in American Indian raid on Haverhill, March 1697; escaped after killing her captors with the aid of two other prisoners.

Dustpan dredge, a machine for digging soil from bottoms of bodies of water D-258

Dusty miller, common name for several plants, especially *Lychnis coronaria* and species of artemisia, cineraria, and centaurea; one plant *Centaurea cineraria* has yellow or purple flowers; plants named for white, flourlike appearance of leaves and stems.

Dutch art. *see in index* Netherlands, The

Dutch Borneo. *see in index* Borneo, Indonesian

Dutch cheese (or cottage cheese, or pot cheese, or smearcase) C-289

Dutch colonial architecture, *picture* S-266

Dutch East India Company (or United East India Company), a trading company established in 1602; had a monopoly of trade with East Indies I-271
American exploration A-333
Jakarta J-16
New York N-256
South Africa S-266

Dutch East Indies. *see in index* Indonesia

Dutch elm disease, fatal disease of elm trees, caused by fungus *Ceratostomella ulmi;* carried chiefly by European elm bark beetle; fungus spreads through the sapwood, destroying tree's circulatory system; diseased branches and trees must be removed and burned; first appeared in e. United States 1930 in a shipment of elm logs from The Netherlands; spread rapidly w., in many communities killing almost every elm; powerful new insecticides, injected into healthy trees, have been found effective in controlling the disease. *see also in index* Elm bark beetle
elm trees E-194
fungi F-450

Dutch Fresian, breed of horse H-277

Dutch Guiana. *see in index* Suriname

Dutch Harbor, Alaska, village on small island in Aleutians; U.S. naval base set up in World War II; pop. 5, *maps* U-39, W-297

Dutch Independence, War of (1568–1648), *list* W-13

Dutch language
Germanic languages G-103
linguistic analysis L-230

'Dutchman, The', work by Baraka A-363

Dutchman's-breeches, spring wildflower *Dicentra cucullaria* of the n. and e. U.S.; named from shape of cream-colored blossoms, which cluster from stalks growing directly from root F-231, *picture* F-233

Dutchman's log, early method of calculating ship speed L-283

Dutchman's-pipe (or pipe vine), climbing shrub *Aristolochia macrophylla* of birthwort family; alternate heart-shaped leaves and brownish purple, pipe-shaped flowers; vine may climb to height of 30 ft (9 m); native both in temperate and warm regions.

Dutch metal, malleable brass containing approximately 76 to 80 percent copper and 20 to 24 percent zinc; rolled into thin sheets and used as imitation gold leaf.

Dutch Reformed church. *see in index* Reformed churches

Dutch West India Company, established 1621 with monopoly of trade on American and African coasts
Aruba A-671
commercial traders A-335
Delaware D-75
Stuyvesant S-495a

Dutch West Indies. *see in index* Netherlands Antilles

Dutt, Romesh Chunder (1848–1909), British author I-108

The letter E

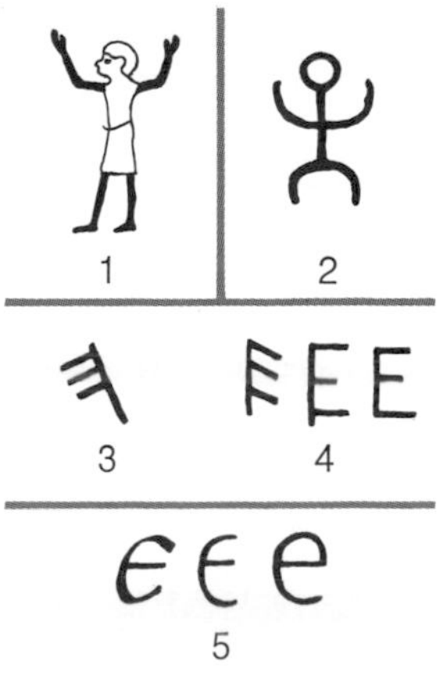

may have started as a picture sign of a man with arms upraised, as in Egyptian hieroglyphic writing (1) and in a very early Semitic writing used about 1500 B.C. on the Sinai Peninsula (2). The sign meant "joy" or "rejoice" to the Egyptians. About 1000 B.C., in Byblos and in other Phoenician and Canaanite centers, the sign was given a linear form (3), the source of all later forms. The sign was called *he* in the Semitic languages and stood for the sound "h" in English.

The Greeks reversed the sign for greater ease in writing from left to right (4). They rejected the Semitic value "h" and gave it the value of the vowel "e." They called the sign *epsilon,* which means "short e."

The Romans adopted this sign for the Latin capital E. From Latin this form came unchanged into English. The handwriting of Graeco-Roman times changed the letter to a more quickly written form (5). From this is derived the English handwritten and printed small "e."

E. *see in index* Eccentricity
E-3A Sentry, airplane, *picture* A-178
Ea, Sumerian deity B-7
Eads, James B. (full name James Buchanan Eads) (1820–87), U.S. engineer and inventor E-2
  Hall of Fame, *table* H-16
  Panama Canal P-92
  St. Louis bridge B-446, S-21
Eads Bridge, St. Louis, Mo. B-446, S-21
Eagle, bird E-2
  average length of life, *chart* A-423
  flight speed B-252, *picture* B-246
  predatory behavior B-28
  United States U-115
Eagle, in golf G-190
'Eagle', U.S. lunar landing vehicle S-341
Eagle, U.S. gold coin worth $10, first minted 1795; also, double eagle worth $20, first minted 1849; half eagle worth $5, first minted 1795; quarter eagle worth $2.50, first minted 1796; coinage of eagle, double eagle, and half eagle ceased in 1934 and quarter eagle in 1929.
Eagle Mountain, in Misquah Hills, n.e. Minnesota; highest point in state 2,301 ft (701 m); part of extension of Laurentian hills M-440
Eagle Pass, Tex., city on Rio Grande, opposite Piedras Negras, Mexico; agricultural center; mineral processing; apparel; pop. 21,407.
Eagles, Fraternal Order of, founded Seattle, Wash., 1898; pays sick and funeral benefits; has sponsored workmen's compensation, mothers' and old-age pensions, Mother's Day; subordinate bodies called Aeries F-387
Eaker, Ira Clarence (1896–1987), U.S. Army officer, born in Field Creek, Tex.; commander 8th U.S. bomber command in Britain 1942 and 8th U.S. Air Force there 1943; Allied air commander in Mediterranean theater 1943–45; deputy commander of Army Air Forces and chief of Air Staff 1945–47; retired 1947.
Eakins, Thomas (1844–1916), U.S. painter and sculptor E-2
  painting P-54, *picture* P-55
  Whitman, *picture* W-200
Ealing, England, borough in w. Greater London; interesting tombs in churches; birthplace of Thomas Huxley; pop. 297,910, *maps* L-287, U-18a
Eames, Charles (1907–78), U.S. architect, industrial designer, and toy designer, born in St. Louis, Mo.; worked with Eliel Saarinen at Cranbrook Academy of Art, Bloomfield Hills, Mich.
  furniture F-462, D-122
  industrial design I-170, 174
Eames, Emma (1865–1952), U.S. opera soprano, *list* O-570
Eanes, António Ramalho (born 1935), president of Portugal, born in Alcains, Portugal P-457a
Ear E-3. *see also in index* Deafness
  animal A-430
    bird B-246
    fish F-127
    frog F-407
    insect I-219
  audibility limits S-260
  biological models B-236
  electromagnetic radiation B-238
  health care H-88
  infant hearing test, *picture* P-311
  sound. *see in index* Sound
Ear canal (or external auditory meatus) E-3
Eardrum (or tympanic membrane) E-3
Earhart, Amelia (1897–1937), U.S. aviator E-5
  aviation A-205
Earl, title of nobility T-195
Earle, Ralph (1751–1801), U.S. painter, born in Shrewsbury, Mass.; paintings of battles at Lexington and Concord said to be first historical paintings done in North America.
Earley vs. DiCenso, law case
  education, *list* E-104
Earlham College, Richmond, Ind.; founded 1847 by Religious Society of Friends; became college 1859; arts and sciences, education, religion; biological field station on Dewart Lake; foreign study in Europe, Latin America, Japan; graduate school.
Early, Jubal Anderson (1816–94), Confederate general, born in Franklin County, Va.; opposed secession of Virginia but accepted Confederate States of America commission; won fame at Antietam, Fredericksburg, Chancellorsville; commanded division at Gettysburg
  Civil War C-476, 482
    Shenandoah Valley S-161
Early American style, style of furniture, architecture, or fabric. *see in index* Colonial architecture
'Early Bird', a communications satellite A-72, *table* S-344
Early chrysanthemum, a perennial flower
  flowering time G-25
Early summer phlox, a perennial plant
  flowering time G-25
Early-warning aircraft A-158, *picture* A-163
Earp, Wyatt (full name Wyatt Berry Stapp Earp) (1848–1929), U.S. frontiersman, well-known gunman E-5
  frontier F-424
  jail, *picture* K-181
  outlaws O-619
Earphone, headpiece for listening
  education use, *picture* P-268a
    spelling, *picture* S-375
  radio broadcasting, *picture* R-48
Earth E-6. *see also in index* Continent; Desert; Geology; Moon; World
  aluminum found A-321
  ancient element A-273, U-198, P-304
  astronomical observations A-710
    observatories O-456
  atmosphere A-747
  axis, *diagram* S-254c
  circular velocity S-342d
  climate. *see in index* Climate
  continental structure C-688
    temperature, *diagram* V-378
  earth sciences E-41
  eclipse E-48
  erosion. *see in index* Erosion
  evolution E-364
  geography G-62
  gravitation G-238
    mechanics M-266
  heat H-101
  hemisphere H-126
    equator E-293
  Kepler's theories K-228
  lakes L-24
  magnetism M-42
    field. *see in index* Magnetosphere
  minerals M-437
  oceans O-459, 464
    oceanography O-479
  ores O-600
  planets P-350, *table* P-351
  power source P-483
  rotation, *diagram* S-254c
    apparent position of stars S-413
    Foucault pendulum P-160
    seasons S-101
    time T-187
      international date line, *diagram* I-253
    winds, *picture* W-222
  shape
    Pythagorean teachings P-544
  sun S-512
  surveying S-520
  vegetation. *see in index* Vegetation
  water W-84, 87, *picture* W-88
  water cycle. *see in index* Water cycle
  waters. *see in index* Lake; Ocean; River
  weather W-117
  zodiac and, *picture* A-356
Earth almond (or chufa) S-106
Earth dam D-15, *picture* D-13
Earth Day P-441f
Earthenware, pottery P-469
'Earthly Paradise, The', work by Morris E-276
Earth-moving equipment, machinery
  dredge and power shovel D-258
Earthnut. *see in index* Peanut
Earth pig. *see in index* Aardvark
Earthquake (also called temblor) E-37
  continental structure C-688
  earth E-33
  Europe E-330
    Greece G-255
    Yugoslavia Y-434
  flood cause F-182, *table* F-181
  Japan J-60
  Latin America L-60
    Central America C-253
      El Salvador E-195
      Guatemala G-297, G-300
    Mexico M-322
      Mexico City M-347
    Peru P-225
    Venezuela V-277
  Oceania O-465
  oceanography O-485
  Turkey T-318
    Antioch A-492
  United States
    Los Angeles L-303
    San Francisco (1906) S-43
  volcanoes V-378
  waves O-487
Earth Resources Technology Satellite (ERTS), *table* S-344
Earthrise, *picture* S-342
Earth satellites. *see in index* Satellites, artificial
Earth sciences (or geosciences) E-41, S-64a. *see also in index* Earth; Geology; Meteorology; Oceanography
  earth E-35
Earthshine, sunlight reflected to the moon from the daylight region of the earth M-579
Earthstar, fungus-like organism F-449
Earthworm, (or angleworm) W-363, *picture* A-433
  breathing R-159
  digestive system A-389
  hibernation, *picture* H-148
  soil aeration S-250
Earwax. *see in index* Cerumen
Earwig, insect of the order Dermaptera, with pair of movable pincers at end of abdomen; named from erroneous notion that it creeps into ears of sleeping persons, *picture* I-213
Easement, in law
  legal definition, *table* L-92
Easley, S.C., city 13 mi (21 km) s.w. of Greenville, in agricultural area; clothing, textiles, pop. 14,264, *map* S-318
East, Edward Murray (1879–1938), U.S. biologist, born in Du Quoin, Ill.; professor Harvard University 1914–26 ('Heredity and Human Affairs').
East, direction D-157
East African Rift Valley. *see in index* Great Rift Valley
East Anglia, early kingdom in e. of Anglo-Saxon Britain, comprising present Norfolk and Suffolk E-230
East Aurora, N.Y., village 15 mi (25 km) s.e. of Buffalo; electronics; toys, wood products; pop. 6,803. *see also in index* Roycroft Shop
East Bengal. *see in index* Bangladesh
East Berlin, East Germany, capital; pop. 1,185,533 G-112. *see also in index* Berlin
  Berlin's division B-168, *map* B-170
Eastbourne, England, s. coast resort, between Brighton and Hastings; traces of Roman occupation exist; pop. 69,290, *map* U-18a
East Cape, at e. tip of North Island, New Zealand, *maps* N-299, P-3
East Carolina University, Greenville, N.C.; state control; opened 1909; arts and sciences, art, business, education, health and medicine, home economics, music, nursing; Air Force ROTC; graduate school.
East Central Oklahoma State University (formerly East Central State College), Ada, Okla.; established in 1909; liberal arts and sciences, and education; graduate school in education.
East Chicago, Ind., port city on Lake Michigan, 18 mi (29 km) s.e. of Chicago; extensive rail and lake shipping; petroleum refining; iron and steel products, railroad equipment, chemicals, building materials; port area named Indiana Harbor; pop. 39,786 I-91, *map* I-102, *picture* I-98
East China Sea, part of Pacific Ocean bounded by China, Korea, Japan, Ryukyu Islands, and Taiwan; includes Yellow Sea, *maps* A-697, J-78, W-297. *see also in index* Ocean, *table*
East Cleveland, Ohio, residential city 5 mi (8 km) e. of Cleveland; electrical research laboratory; incorporated as a city 1911; pop. 39,600.
East Detroit, Mich., city 10 mi (16 km) n.e. of Detroit; residential suburb; settled 1827, incorporated 1928; pop. 38,280.
Easter, Christian festival E-41
  calendar C-29
  festivals, *picture* F-61
  Hungary, *picture* H-275
  opera O-560
  Passover P-136
Easter eggs
  Fabergé eggs F-2
  folk art symbol F-251
Easter Island (locally called Rapa Nui), in s. Pacific; 50 sq mi (130 sq km); belongs to Chile; pop. 1,928 E-42, *map* W-297
  national park status N-27
  Pacific Ocean P-7, *picture* P-2, *map* P-3
  Oceania O-467
Eastern American mole, mammal *Scalopus aquaticus* M-521
Eastern arborvitae. *see in index* Northern white cedar
Eastern Catholics. *see in index* Eastern rite churches
Eastern Coal Field. *see in index* Appalachian Plateau
Eastern College (formerly Eastern Baptist College), St. Davids, Pa.; affiliated with the

American Baptist Convention; incorporated 1952; liberal arts and sciences.
Eastern Colorado River. *see in index* Colorado River
Eastern Connecticut State College, Willimantic, Conn.; established in 1889; arts and sciences, teacher education; graduate program.
Eastern cottonwood tree, a poplar *Populus deltoides* P-445, *picture* T-281
Nebraska's state tree, *picture* N-100
Eastern Empire. *see in index* Byzantine Empire
Eastern Front, World War I W-304
Eastern glossy ibis, bird I-4
Eastern goldfinch, bird
New Jersey's state bird, *picture* N-202
Eastern hare wallaby, animal A-779
Eastern hemisphere H-126
Eastern hemlock, tree
wood, *table* W-282
Eastern Highlands, Australia. *see in index* Great Dividing Range
Eastern Ice Yachting Association I-11
Eastern Illinois University, Charleston, Ill.; state control; opened 1899; letters and sciences, business, education, health and physical education, music; graduate study.
Eastern Kentucky University, Richmond, Ky.; state control; founded 1906; arts and technology, business, and education; graduate study.
Eastern kingbird, bird
flycatcher F-244
Eastern Mennonite College, Harrisonburg, Va.; established in 1917; liberal arts and teacher education; seminary.
Eastern Michigan University, Ypsilanti, Mich.; state control; founded 1849; arts and sciences, business administration, education, and international studies; graduate study.
Eastern Montana College, Billings, Mont., state control; founded 1925; arts and sciences, teacher education; graduate study.
Eastern Nazarene College, Quincy, Mass.; affiliated with Church of the Nazarene; chartered 1918; arts and sciences, education, and theology; graduate studies.
Eastern New Mexico University, Portales, N.M.; state control; opened 1934 as junior college, senior college 1940; general studies, liberal arts and sciences, business administration, education and psychology, music, speech and drama, technology; graduate school; branches at Clovis and Roswell N-217
Eastern Oregon State College (formerly Eastern Oregan College), La Grande, Ore.; state control; established in 1929; teacher education; graduate study.
Eastern Orthodox Churches (also called Eastern Orthodoxy, or Orthodox Catholic Church) E-42, R-143
Balkan conflict B-31
Byzantine period conflicts B-533
calendar C-28
canon law C-142
ecumenism E-69
Europe E-337
Fathers of the Church F-45
Leo IX L-130
monks and monasticism M-539, 543
Paul VI's diplomacy P-142a
Eastern Question, in European politics, the complicated problems arising out of European interference in affairs of Turkey and Balkan States formerly under Turkish rule.
Eastern red cedar, tree
juniper J-157
Eastern rite churches E-44
Eastern Roman Empire. *see in index* Byzantine Empire
Eastern Rumelia, Bulgaria. *see in index* Rumelia
Eastern Solomons, battle of, World War II W-345
Eastern spruce, a common name for red spruce, white spruce, and black spruce
wood, *table* W-282
Eastern Star, secret female order founded by Masons F-386
Eastern starfish, echinoderm, *picture* I-285
Eastern State Hospital, Williamsburg, Va. W-209
Eastern States, India, formerly an agency comprising 42 states in e. and n.e. Indian Empire; now part of Madhya Pradesh and Orissa states.
Eastern time T-189, *map* U-41
Eastern Washington University (formerly Eastern Washington State College), Cheney, Wash.; established in 1890; arts and sciences, teacher education; graduate studies.
Eastern white pine, evergreen tree *Pinus strobus*, of pine family; leaves to 5 in. (13 cm) long, grow in clusters of 5, blue green with white tinge; cones to 8 in. (20 cm) long, *table* W-282
Eastern yellow-shafted flicker (also called golden-winged woodpecker, or wake-up, or yellowhammer), bird F-178, *picture* F-179
Easter Revolt, abortive attempt of Irish to throw off British rule; much of Dublin seized Easter Monday (1916)
De Valera D-124
East European Plain, Belorussia B-159
East Florida, name given by English in 1763 to a part of Florida; n. boundary was from mouth of St. Mary's River to junction of Chattahoochee and Flint rivers, w. boundary Apalachicola River, and e. the Atlantic Ocean.
East Germany. *see in index* Germany, East
East Goths. *see in index* Ostrogoths
East Grand Rapids, Mich., residential city just s.e. of Grand Rapids in Kent County; first settled 1835, incorporated as city 1926; pop. 12,565.
East Greenland Current, cold ocean current of the Atlantic, along e. coast of Greenland; carries many icebergs.
East Gulf Coastal Plain, plain, United States
Louisiana L-309, *map* L-310
East Haddam, Conn., on Connecticut River, 13 mi (21 km) s.e. of Middletown; pop. of township 5,621.
Easthampton, Mass., just s. of Northampton and about 12 mi (19 km) n.w. of Springfield; textile industries; elastic webbing, metal products; pop. of township 15,580.
East Harlem (or Spanish Harlem), a neighborhood in Manhattan, New York, N.Y. N-273
Puerto Ricans H-165, *picture* H-166
East Hartford, Conn., urban town on Connecticut River, opposite Hartford; tobacco; aircraft engines, brushes, paper products, metal products; pop. 52,563.
East Haven, Conn., urban town just e. of New Haven; street lighting equipment; pop. 25,028.
East India companies, formed in 17th century for trade with East Indies; known as British, Dutch, French, Danish, Spanish, Portuguese, Swedish, Scottish, Austrian. *see in index* Dutch East India Company; East India Company (English)
East India Company, English E-44
American colonies R-164
England E-245, 254
India I-77
Bombay B-340
Clive C-504
Hastings H-52
Lucknow revolt L-328
international trade I-271
tea T-47
East Indians, people
Guyana G-321
West Indies W-157
East Indies (or Malay Archipelago) E-45. *see also in index* Borneo; Celebes; Indonesia; Java; Malaysia; New Guinea; Philippines; Sumatra
history
East India Company E-44
The Netherlands N-130
monsoons P-259a
products
sago S-14
spices S-379
reptiles D-238
East Islip, N.Y., residential village on Long Island, near s. shore; Heckscher State Park nearby; pop. 6,861.
East Kildonan, Man., residential city, part of metropolitan Winnipeg; in an area of small farms; supports light industry, pop. 30,152.
Eastlake, Sir Charles Lock (1793–1865), English painter and art critic, born in Plymouth, England; elected president of Royal Academy 1850 ('Pilgrims in Sight of Rome'; 'Christ Blessing Little Children').
Eastlake, Ohio, city located 7 mi (11 km) n.e. of Euclid, in Lake County; near Lake Erie; s.w. of Headland Beach State Park; pop. 22,104.
East Lansing, Mich., city just e. of Lansing; residential suburb; Michigan State University; settled 1850, incorporated as city 1907; pop. 48,309.
East Latvian Plains, geographic area, U.S.S.R. L-83
East Liverpool, Ohio, city on Ohio River, in e. part of state, 18 mi (29 km) n. of Steubenville; important ceramics center; brick, tile, steel products; pop. 16,687.
East Locris, district of ancient Greece. *see in index* Locris
East London, South Africa, seaport of Cape of Good Hope Province, on Indian Ocean; many industries; exports corn, wool, fruit, meat, dairy products; pop. 116,056, with suburbs, *maps* A-115, S-264
East Longmeadow, Mass., 4 mi (6 km) s.e. of Springfield; games, school equipment; incorporated 1894; pop. of township 12,905.
East Los Angeles, Calif., residential city just e. of Los Angeles; part of Los Angeles metropolitan area, in which major industries include aircraft, electronics, and petroleum refining; pop. 105,033.
Eastman, Charles Alexander (or Ohiyesa) (1858–1939), U.S. physician and writer, born in Redwood Falls, Minn.; son of Santee Sioux father and Anglo-Sioux mother; held U.S. government offices among Indians; authority on Indian life ('Indian Boyhood'; 'The Indian Today').
Eastman, Crystal (1881–1928), U.S. social worker, feminist, and pacifist, born in Marlborough, Mass., sister of Max Eastman; her treatise 'Work Accidents and the Law', 1910, did much to promote progress of workmen's compensation laws; active in Woman's Peace party; helped found London branch of National Woman's party
women's rights movement W-278
Eastman, George (1854–1932), U.S. pioneer in photographic industry E-47
flexible film P-299
motion pictures M-616
photography P-297
Eastman, Max Forrester (1883–1969), U.S. poet, essayist, born in Canandaigua, N.Y.; taught philosophy at Columbia University; editor *The Masses*, a socialistic periodical ('The Enjoyment of Poetry'; 'The Colors of Life', poems; 'The Enjoyment of Laughter').
Eastman Kodak Company (originally Eastman Dry Plate and Film Company), founded by George Eastman E-47
headquarters, *picture* N-250
East Massapequa, N.Y., community 30 mi (50 km) s.e. of New York, N.Y., on Long Island; pop. 15,926.
East Meadow, N.Y., residential community 23 mi (37 km) e. of New York, N.Y., in Nassau County, on Long Island; location of Nassau County Historical Museum; pop. 46,290.
East Moline, Ill., city in n.w. part of state, on Mississippi River, adjoining Moline (these two cities, with neighboring Rock Island, Ill., and Davenport, Iowa, known as the Quad Cities); farm equipment, scales, machinery; state hospital; pop. 20,907, *map* I-52
East North Central States, name used by the U.S. government for the geographic division including the states of Ohio, Indiana, Illinois, Michigan, and Wisconsin.
Easton, Mass., 8 mi (13 km) s. of Stockton; carbonated beverages; Stonehill College; incorporated 1725; pop. of township 16,623.
Easton, Pa., city on Delaware River, at mouth of Lehigh, opposite Phillipsburg, N.J.; steel and cement products, machinery; slate quarries nearby; Lafayette College; pop. 26,027 P-175, *map* P-174
East Orange, N.J., residential city n.w. of Newark and 12 mi (19 km) w. of New York, N.Y.; waterworks supplies; insurance center; Upsala College; pop. 77,878 N-206
East Pacific Rise, underwater mountain range O-461
East Pakistan. *see in index* Bangladesh
East Pass, jetty, Destin, Fla., *picture* J-111
East Paterson, N.J. *see in index* Elmwood Park
East Peoria, Ill., city opposite Peoria, on Illinois River; farm machinery, engines; incorporated 1919; pop. 22,385, *map* I-52
East Point, Ga., city 6 mi (10 km) s.w. of Atlanta; textiles, fertilizers, chemicals, machinery, auto batteries, paint; pop. 37,486.
East Providence, R.I., city on Seekonk River, opposite Providence; petroleum products, machinery, chemicals; pop. 50,980 R-183
East Prussia, formerly the easternmost province of Prussia, on Baltic Sea; 14,401 sq mi (37,298 sq km); cap. Königsberg; in 1945 n. part of East Prussia was included in U.S.S.R., s. part in Poland.
East Ridge, Tenn., residential town just s. of Chattanooga; in an area of food products, iron and steel, and textiles manufacturing; incorporated 1921; pop. 21,236.
East Riding, administrative district in York County, England.
East River, N.Y., strait separating Long Island from Manhattan Island; 15 mi (25 km) long
UN headquarters U-22, *picture* U-22
East Rockaway, N.Y., residential village on Long Island, 20 mi (30 km) s.e. of New York, N.Y.; instrument parts; pop. 10,917.
East Room, largest room in the White House where state receptions and balls are held W-199
East St. Louis, Ill., city on Mississippi River, opposite St. Louis, Mo.; railroad center; meat products, chemicals, alumina, metal products; pop. 55,200 I-36, *map* I-52
Eads Bridge S-21
East South Central States, name used by the U.S. government for the geographic division including the states of Kentucky, Tennessee, Alabama, and Mississippi.
East Stroudsburg State College, East Stroudsburg, Pa.; established in 1893; formerly a teachers' college; arts and sciences, education; graduate study.
East Tennessee State University, Johnson City, Tenn.; opened 1911; arts and sciences, business administration and economics, education, health, nursing; graduate studies; centers at Bristol, Greenville, and Kingsport.
East Texas Baptist College, Marshall, Tex.; affiliated with Southern Baptist convention; chartered 1912; liberal arts, humanities, natural sciences, social sciences, and teacher education.
East Texas oil field P-233
East Texas State University, Commerce, Tex.; founded 1889 as private school; arts and sciences, business administration, and education; graduate study.
East Tirol, region in Austria T-192
East-West Center, Honolulu, Hawaii H-63

Economic Regulatory Administration, United States Department of Energy U-165

Economics, science of the production, distribution, and consumption of wealth E-60. *see also in index* Bank and banking; Capitalism; Communism; Labor; Money; Panics and depressions; Socialism; *also* chief topics below
- Asian countries' diversity A-686
- black Americans B-301
- business cycle B-517
- census C-249
- central bank C-260
- city C-448
- civilization C-465
- colonialism and imperialism C-556
- commodity exchange C-597
- employment and unemployment E-205
- Enlightenment E-289
- franchise F-373
- government G-199
- gross national product G-290
- India's planning I-73
- Industrial Revolution system I-178
- industry I-184
- inflation I-198
- international relations basis I-259
- labor law's development L-5
- literacy and illiteracy L-239
- marketing M-140
- mercantile system R-166
- monopolies M-543
- national debt N-24
- Nobel prizes N-330
- population changes P-448
  - migration of people M-400
- Renaissance conditions R-149, *Reference-Outline* R-150
- Ricardo R-198
- sciences S-64b
- social sciences S-243
- social studies S-238
- taxation T-34
  - tariff T-30
- theories
  - Galbraith G-5
  - Marx S-234
- Third World T-169
- U.S. and U.S.S.R. comparison R-321, *table* R-336
- warfare W-18
- world W-301
- World Bank W-301
- World War I W-314

Economics, Statistics, and Cooperatives Service, United States Department of Agriculture U-162

Economic Stabilization, Office of (OES), United States, established 1942, terminated 1946 R-277

Economic zoology (or applied zoology) Z-470

'Economist, The', news magazine M-31

Economy, Pa., former communal village C-605

Ecorse, Mich., city situated on Detroit River, 8 mi (13 km) s.w. of Detroit; steel; pop. 14,447.

Ecosystem, a community and its environment E-54, *diagram* E-57
- world W-296

Ecotone, a transition area between two adjacent ecological communities; usually exhibits competition between the various organisms.

ECOWAS (Economic Community of West African States) A-109

ECSC (European Coal and Steel Community), founded on Aug. 10, 1952. *see in index* European Communities

ECT (or electroconvulsive treatment). *see also in index* Shock therapy
- mental illness M-302

Ectoderm, embryonic germ layer
- coelenterate A-433
- vertebrate E-200, *chart* E-202

Ecuador (full name Republic of Ecuador), South American republic, on Pacific coast; area estimated at 104,500 sq mi (270,600 sq km); cap. Quito; pop. 8,604,000 E-66, *Fact Summary* S-294, *picture* S-274, *maps* S-298, W-297
- boundary dispute P-225
- flag, *picture* F-164
- Galápagos Islands. *see in index* Galápagos Islands
- Guayaquil G-300
- literature L-73
- national anthem, *table* N-64
- railroad mileage, *table* R-85
- South America S-273, *picture* S-274

Ecumenical council, in Christianity E-69, C-410

Ecumenism (or ecumenical movement), movement toward worldwide Christian unity E-69, P-142a, *picture* V-270
- Methodism M-318
- Mott M-632

Eczema (or dermatitis), superficial inflammation of the skin D-178

'Edad de Oro, La,' Cuban children's magazine L-251

Edam, The Netherlands, town in n., 12 mi (19 km) n.e. of Amsterdam; cheese; ships, rope, leather; pop. 3,928.

EDC. *see in index* European Defense Community

Eddas, two collections of early Scandinavian literature S-52g, S-471

Eddington, Sir Arthur Stanley (1882–1944), British astronomer, born in Kendal; director observatory Cambridge ('The Mathematical Theory of Relativity'; 'Stars and Atoms'; 'The Nature of the Physical World').

Eddy, Mary Baker (1821–1910), U.S. religious leader; founder of Christian Science E-70
- Christian Science C-402

Eddy, Nelson (1901–67), U.S. baritone, born in Providence, R.I.; debut, Philadelphia, 1922; popular in opera, musical films, radio, concert.

Eddy, circulation of water in whirlpool fashion
- fishing, *list* F-146

Eddy currents, in electricity
- speedometer S-374

Eddy kite. *see in index* Bow kite

Eddystone lighthouse L-204

Edelinck, Gérard (1640–1707), Flemish engraver, born in Antwerp; with French school of portrait engraving.

Edelman, Gerald Maurice (born 1929), U.S. molecular biologist, born in New York, N.Y.; professor Rockefeller University. *see also in index* Nobel Prizewinners, *table*

Edelweiss, a small white velvety flower of the composite family, found in Alps S-538

Edema, an abnormal accumulation of fluid A-272
- lymphatic system L-343

Eden, Anthony (full name Robert Anthony Eden, earl of Avon) (1897–1977), British statesman E-70
- United Kingdom E-258

Eden, N.C., town 9 mi (15 km) n. of Reidsville; corn, wheat, tobacco; blankets, linens; pop. 15,672.

Eden, in Bible, garden of paradise
- Mesopotamia M-305

Edentata, an order of mammals comprising the sloths, armadillos, and anteaters; so called because members have few or no teeth, *table* M-80

Ederle, Gertrude (full name Gertrude Caroline Ederle) (born 1906), U.S. swimmer, first woman to swim English Channel E-70

Edessa, ancient city in Asia Minor; became great center of early Christianity and learning; modern **Urfa** in s.e. Turkey; pop. 59,863, *map* P-212

Edfu (or Idfu), Egypt, ancient town on Nile, 54 mi (87 km) s.e. of Thebes; favored by the falcon-headed god Horus.

Edgar (944–975), king of England; called the peaceful because of his quiet reign; supported monasteries, improved courts of law, and encouraged commerce.

Edge, Walter Evans (1873–1956), U.S. journalist and diplomat, born in Philadelphia, Pa.; proprietor *Atlantic Daily Press*, also *Evening Union*; governor New Jersey 1917–19, 1944–47; U.S. senator 1919–29; ambassador to France 1929–33; prominent Republican.

Edgecliff College, Cincinnati, Ohio; Roman Catholic; established 1935; arts and sciences and education C-415

Edge dislocation, in crystals C-799, S-254h

Edged-weapon warfare W-19

Edgehill, England, ridge 12 mi (19 km) s. of Warwick; first battle of Civil War, Oct. 1642, between Parliament forces under the earl of Essex and Royalists under Charles I.

Edgerton, Harold Eugene (born 1903), U.S. electrical engineer, born in Fremont, Neb.; professor Massachusetts Institute of Technology after 1932; invented stroboscopic high-speed photography apparatus.

Edgewood College, Madison, Wis.; Roman Catholic; established in 1927; arts and sciences, medical technology, and teacher education.

Edgeworth, Maria (1767–1849), British novelist, born in Oxfordshire; influenced Thackeray and Turgenev; her 'Belinda' introduced natural heroine, who failed to faint and blush constantly; work colored by life in Ireland, where she moved in 1782 with Irish father I-326

Edib, Halidé (also spelled Halidah Adib) (1885–1964), Turkish author and feminist, born in Constantinople (now Istanbul); leader in Turkish Nationalist movement; lectured in universities in U.S. and India ('Memoirs of Halidé Edib'; 'Turkey Faces West').

Edict of Restitution, act by Ferdinand II in Thirty Years' War T-169

'Edifying Monthly Discussions', magazine M-32

Edina, Minn., village 10 mi (16 km) s.w. of Minneapolis; home of several publications for banking, printing, and agricultural industries; pop. 46,073 M-442

Edinboro State College, Edinboro, Pa.; founded 1857; liberal arts, teacher education; graduate study; formerly a teachers' college; off-campus centers at Farrell and Warren.

Edinburg, Tex., city 50 mi (80 km) n.w. of Brownsville; natural gas and oil, citrus fruit and vegetable processing, cotton ginning; Pan American University; pop. 24,075.

Edinburgh, duke of. *see in index* Philip, Prince, duke of Edinburgh

Edinburgh, capital of Scotland; divided into Old Town and New Town; pop. 419,187 E-71, *map* E-360
- Royal Botanic Garden, *table* B-370
- Scotland S-68, *map* S-67

Edinburgh, University of, Edinburgh, Scotland; arts, medicine, law, theology, music E-71

Edinburgh Castle, Edinburgh, Scotland E-71, *picture* S-71

'Edinburgh Review', critical journal M-33
- Macaulay M-3

Edinburghshire, county of s.e. Scotland. *see in index* Midlothian

Edirne, Turkey. *see in index* Adrianople

Edison, Charles (1890–1969), U.S. political leader, born in West Orange, N.J.; son of Thomas A. Edison; secretary of navy 1939–40; governor of New Jersey 1941–44 E-74

Edison, Thomas Alva (1847–1931), U.S. inventor and manufacturer E-72
- doll D-156
- electricity E-162
- electric power E-165
- electronics E-180
- Hall of Fame, *table* H-16
- inventions I-274, *table* I-273
  - lighting contributions L-205
  - motion pictures M-616
  - phonograph P-268d
  - storage battery B-109
  - telegraph T-58
- laboratory, *picture* M-366
- Ohio O-500, *picture* O-510
- Roosevelt, *picture* R-263
- Tesla T-114

Edison, N.J., urban township 3 mi (5 km) n.e. of New Brunswick; building materials, chemical, electrical, and electronic equipment; pop. 70,193 N-206

Edison cell. *see in index* Nickel-iron cell

Edison effect, electronic emission from hot filaments; discovered by Edison R-57
- electronics E-180

Edison Institute, Dearborn, Mich.; consists of Greenfield Village, Edison Institute Museum, and Edison Institute schools
- Ford F-306
- quilts, *pictures* Q-17

Edisto River, s. and s.w. South Carolina; 150 mi (240 km) long, *maps* S-307, 318
- memorial gardens, *picture* S-315

Edith Cavell, Mount, in Jasper National Park, Alberta, height, 11,033 ft (3,363 m).

Edith Ronne Land, in Antarctica, extends s.e. from base of Antarctic Peninsula to Coats Land; discovered by Finn Ronne 1947–48 and named for his wife, who recorded expedition.

Editing (or cutting), in motion pictures M-612, *picture* M-611
- directing D-154

Editing, in publishing
- book publishing B-363

Editor N-239, 242

Editorial, an article in a newspaper or magazine with opinions of the editor or publisher; also a similar expression on radio or TV.

EDM (or electric-discharge machining), a metalworking operation T-226

Edman, Irwin (1896–1954), U.S. philosopher, born in New York, N.Y.; taught philosophy at Columbia University after 1918 (essays: 'Philosopher's Holiday', 'Philosopher's Quest', and 'Under Whatever Sky').

Edmond, Okla., city 12 mi (19 km) n. of Oklahoma City; hosiery, furniture; Central State University; incorporated 1890; pop. 34,637.

Edmonds, Walter Dumaux (born 1903), U.S. novelist, born in Boonville, N.Y.; author of historical fiction ('Wedding Journey'; 'In the Hands of the Senecas'; 'The Boyds of Black River') and children's books ('The Matchlock Gun', awarded Newbery medal 1942; 'Tom Whipple'; 'Two Logs Crossing')
- 'Drums Along the Mohawk' A-358, R-112

Edmonds, Wash., city just n. of Seattle; oil refining, fisheries; founded 1890; pop. 27,526.

Edmonton, Alta., capital of province; pop. 532,246 E-76, *maps* C-109, N-350, W-207
- Alberta A-261, *picture* A-267
- zoo Z-460

Edmund, Saint, king of East Anglia (840?–870), said to have been martyred by Danes for refusing to give up his faith or surrender his kingdom to heathen overlords; festival Nov. 20.

Edmund, Saint (full name Edmund Rich) (1175?–1240), English saint and archbishop of Canterbury, born in Abingdon; had long struggle with Henry III over latter's subservience to foreign favorites; festival Nov. 16.

Edmund (922–946), Saxon king of England, grandson of Alfred the Great and son of Edward the Elder; conquered Cumbria.

Edmund Ironside (981–1016), Saxon king of England, son of Ethelred the Unready; led Saxon armies against Canute, who defeated him and compelled division of England C-145

Edmunds, George Franklin (1828–1919), U.S. lawyer and Republican leader, born near Richmond, Vt.; U.S. senator from Vermont 1866–91; member of Hayes-Tilden Electoral Commission; author of Edmunds Act and Sherman Anti-Trust Act.

Edmundston, N.B., city in n.w., at confluence of Saint John and Madawaska rivers, opposite Madawaska, Me.; lumber, pulp and paper products; base for fishing and hunting; pop. 12,044 N-156, *map* C-109

Edo, Japan. *see in index* Tokyo

Edo Castle, castle and compound, Tokyo, Japan T-203, 210

Edom, ancient country, s.e. of Palestine, called Idumaea by Greeks and Romans; Edomites enemies of Israelites.

EDP. *see in index* Electronic Data Processing

Edred (died AD 955), Saxon king of England (946–955), youngest son of Edward the Elder; subdued Danes in Northumberland; guided chiefly by St. Dunstan; succeeded by his nephew Edwy.

Chicago C-311
transportation T-264

Elevation. *see in index* Altitude

Elevator (or lift) E-186
fire-fighting platforms F-104

Elevator, grain. *see in index* Grain elevator

Elf (plural elves), a supernatural being of Teutonic mythology; sometimes thought of as a mountain fay or, usually, as a small sprite; mischievous elves are thought to bring evil, especially bad dreams F-16

ELF (extremely-low-frequency communications system), underwater navigation N-73

El Faiyûm, Egypt. *see in index* Faiyûm, El

El Fasher, The Sudan, town in w., capital of Darfur Province; on route for motor trucks carrying tobacco, gum arabic, hides and skins, peanuts, and ostrich feathers; pop. 58,500.

Elfeld, West Germany. *see in index* Eltville

El Ferdan Bridge, over Suez Canal, Egypt, *map* S-504

El Ferrol del Caudillo (or El Ferrol), Spain, seaport and naval station of n.w.; shipbuilding, fishing; pop. 47,388, *map* E-360

Elfinwood (or Krummholz), stunted forest characteristic of mountainous regions M-636

Elf owl C-12

Elgar, Edward (1857–1934), English composer, born in Broadheath E-188, B-56
classical music M-675
Kreisler's performance K-303
oratorio O-575

Elgin, James Bruce, 8th **earl of** (1811–63), son of 7th earl, born in London; appointed governor of Jamaica at 30; governor-general of Canada 1846–54; viceroy of India (first appointed directly by the Crown) 1860 to his death C-98

Elgin, Thomas Bruce, 7th **earl of** (1766–1841), English diplomat and art collector; responsible for the acquisition of ancient Athenian pieces by the British Museum G-270

Elgin, Ill., city 36 mi (58 km) n.w. of Chicago, on Fox River; center of dairy region; watches, electrical appliances, metal products; state hospital for the mentally ill; pop. 63,798, *map* I-52

Elgin Marbles, remains of Parthenon sculptures, including the Parthenon frieze, transferred 1803–12 from the Acropolis to the British Museum G-270, L-293

Elgon, Mount, an extinct volcano in east Africa, on boundary between Uganda and Kenya; 14,178 ft (4,321m); 40 mi (60 km) in diameter (crater 5 mi; 8 km across), *map* A-115

El Greco. *see in index* Greco, El

Elhuyart, Fausto de (1755–1833) and **Juan José de** (died 1804), brothers, Spanish chemists who isolated tungsten (1783).

Eli, Hebrew priest and judge under whose care Samuel was brought up (Bible, I Sam.); his two sons were lascivious and greedy priests.

Elia. *see in index* Lamb, Charles

Eliacin. *see in index* Hervieu, Paul-Ernest

Elijah, Hebrew prophet; denounced Ahab, king of Israel, for idolatry; destroyed the 450 prophets of Baal; carried to heaven in chariot of fire (Bible, I Kings xvii; II Kings ii) P-508

'Elijah', work by Mendelssohn O-575

Elijah Muhammad. *see in index* Muhammad, Elijah

Elimination, expulsion of waste materials from the body. *see also in index* Excretion

Eliot, Charles W. (full name Charles William Eliot) (1834–1926), U.S. scholar, president of Harvard University 1869–1909 E-188

Eliot, George (pen name of Mary Ann Evans, Marian Evans, Mary Ann Cross, or Marian Cross) (1819–80), British novelist E-188
literary contribution E-277
novel N-410, 413

Eliot, George Fielding (1894–1971), U.S. military analyst and writer, born in Brooklyn, N.Y.; moved to Australia at age of 8; military and naval correspondent *New York Herald Tribune* 1939–46; military analyst Columbia Broadcasting System 1939–47, Mutual Broadcasting Company 1950–53 ('The Ramparts We Watch'; 'If Russia Strikes').

Eliot, Jared (1685–1763), U.S. clergyman and physician, born in Guilford, Conn.; wrote first U.S. work on agriculture.

Eliot, Sir John (1592–1632), English statesman, born in Port Eliot, Cornwall; Parliamentary leader with Pym and Hampden against Charles I's encroachments; advanced theory of a responsible ministry; imprisoned for 2 years and died in Tower of London.

Eliot, John (1604–90), colonial New England missionary, called apostle to the Indians, born in Hertford; came to Massachusetts 1631 and served as pastor and teacher at Roxbury, also worked among the Indians in New England; contributed to the 'Bay Psalm Book' and translated the Bible into Algonquian language.

Eliot, T.S. (full name Thomas Stearns Eliot) (1888–1965), British poet and critic E-189
creative writing W-379
drama D-247
literature
American A-355
English E-281
'Old Possum's Book of Practical Cats' C-201

Eliphaz, in Bible, one of Job's three friends and advisers; rebuked Job for his complaints against calamity; advice was displeasing to God, who commanded him to offer sacrifice.

Elis, district of ancient Greece, in w. Peloponnesus; cap. Elis; with Achaia forms nome, or department, of modern Greece
Olympic games O-542

Élisabeth, Madame (full name Élisabeth-Philippine-Marie-Hélène) (1764–94), devoted sister of Louis XVI of France; executed by Revolutionary Tribunal.

Elisabethville, Zaire. *see in index* Lubumbashi

Elisha, Hebrew prophet, on whom fell the mantle of Elijah, his master and predecessor in struggle against Baal worship (Bible, I Kings xix; II Kings xiii).

Elissa. *see in index* Dido

Elite Guard. *see in index* Schutzstaffel

Elixir, in modern medicine, term used for certain extracts or tinctures; name applied by alchemists to an imaginary substance of miraculous power.

Elizabeth, Saint (1207–31), Hungarian princess, wife of the landgrave of Thuringia; legend says, when her stern husband seized a basket she was carrying to the poor, the bread in it miraculously changed into roses; festival Nov. 19.

Elizabeth (1837–98), empress of Austria, wife of her cousin Emperor Francis Joseph I, born in Munich; assassinated at Geneva by an anarchist A-703

Elizabeth (1709–62), empress of Russia, daughter of Peter the Great and Catherine I; seized throne 1741; sided against Prussia in Seven Years' War
Catherine the Great C-222
Seven Years' War S-117

Elizabeth (1876–1965), queen of Albert I of Belgium.

Elizabeth (full name Elizabeth Stuart) (1596–1662), queen of Frederick V, winter king of Bohemia, and daughter of James I of England; ancestress through her daughter, electress Sophia, of Hanoverian kings of England.

Elizabeth (born 1900), queen of George VI of England, mother of Elizabeth II G-82

Elizabeth I (full name Elizabeth Tudor, or Good Queen Bess, or Virgin Queen) (1533–1603), queen of England E-190. *see also in index* Elizabethan Age
British Empire C-599
cosmetics C-729
Drake D-240
England E-244
espionage E-305
hairdressing H-9
Hakluyt H-13
Henry VIII H-131
James I J-19
knitting N-113
Mary, Queen of Scots M-164
Northwest Passage A-332
Raleigh R-90
controversy A-418
Royal Navy N-87
Scott S-74
symbol of the age S-135
Virginia V-330
wool W-287

Elizabeth, queen of Charles I of Romania. *see in index* Carmen Sylva

Elizabeth II (born 1926), queen of the United Kingdom E-192
Australia A-803
British Parliament duties, *picture* U-16
Commonwealth duties, *picture* C-601
United Kingdom E-258
visits
Canada C-99, 105, *picture* C-106
New Zealand, *picture* N-296
United States E-140

Elizabeth (pen name of Elizabeth Mary, Countess Russell, formerly Mary Annette Beauchamp) (1866–1941), British novelist, born Sydney, Australia; witty, charming style ('Elizabeth and Her German Garden'; 'The Enchanted April'; 'Mr. Skeffington').

Elizabeth, N.J., industrial and residential city and port on Newark Bay, 14 mi (22 km) s.w. of New York, N.Y.; pop. 107,455 E-193
container terminal, *picture* T-254
New Jersey N-195

Elizabethan Age, English literature
Shakespeare S-129

Elizabethan architecture, an English style derived from Gothic but passing first through the transitional style called Tudor.

Elizabethan theater T-159
acting A-26
Shakespeare S-136

Elizabeth City, N.C., commercial center of rich farming district in n.e. corner, on Pasquotank River; wood products, textiles; aircraft repairing; tourist resort; Elizabeth City State University; U.S. Coast Guard air base; pop. 13,784.

Elizabeth City State University, Elizabeth City, N.C.; chartered 1891; formerly a teachers' college; liberal arts and teacher education.

Elizabeth Islands, offshore Massachusetts M-189

Elizabeth Mary, Countess Russell. *see in index* Elizabeth

Elizabeth of York (1466–1503), queen of Henry VII of England H-130

Elizabethton, Tenn., industrial city on Watauga River, 100 mi (160 km) n.e. of Knoxville; rayon, polyester textiles, clothing, wire, aluminum, furniture; chemical research; home of Watauga Association; pop. 12,431.

Elizabethtown, Ky., city 39 mi (63 km) s. of Louisville; silicone products, magnetics, rubber; incorporated 1797; Sarah Bush Johnston born here; pop. 15,380.

Elizabethtown College, Elizabethtown, Pa.; founded by Church of the Brethren 1899, opened 1900; arts and sciences, business, education; University Center at Harrisburg.

Elizabeth Stuart. *see in index* Elizabeth (1596–1662)

Elizabeth Tudor. *see in index* Elizabeth I

Elizabeth Woodville (1437?–92), queen of Edward IV of England, mother of Edward V and Elizabeth, queen of Henry VII R-203
Edward IV E-107

El Jadida (or Mazagan), Morocco, seaport 55 mi (90 km) s.w. of Casablanca; farm products; pop. 102,000, *map* A-115

'El Jarabe Tapatio', Mexican hat dance F-256

El Juyo Cave, near Santander, Spain A-538

Elk, name given in North America to the wapiti and in Europe to the moose
deer D-62, *picture* D-61

El Karnak, Egypt. *see in index* Karnak, El

Elkhart, Ind., city on St. Joseph and Elkhart rivers, about 15 mi (25 km) e. of South Bend; railway division point; musical instruments, pharmaceuticals, mobile homes and recreational vehicles, radio and television parts, metal products, paper products; pop. 41,305, *maps* I-94, 102

Elkins Act (1903), United States R-285

Elk Island National Park, Alberta A-263, *map* C-109
national parks N-29

Elk Mountains, range of the Rocky Mountains in w. Colorado, just w. of Sawatch Range; several summits reach over 14,000 ft (4,270 m), including Snowmass Peak, Capitol Peak, Maroon Peak, and Mt. Carbon.

Elko, Nev., city in n.e., on Humboldt River, about 90 mi (140 km) from Utah border; ranching and mining; incorporated 1917; annual Silver State Stampede; pop. 8,758 N-134, 144, *maps* N-350, U-40

Elks, Benevolent and Protective Order of, a fraternal society, organized in New York, N.Y., in 1868 from an older society known as the Jolly Corks, and now having branches in practically all large cities of U.S. and its dependencies; in addition to assistance to members, known for response to outside requests.

Ell, obsolete measure of length, varies from 27 to 48 in. (68 to 102 cm) in different countries; English ell, 1¼ yards (1.1 meters), used primarily for measuring fabrics, *table* W-140

Ellensburg, Wash., city 27 mi (43 km) n. of Yakima; farm and timber region; Central Washington University; incorporated 1867; pop. 11,752.

Ellery, William (1727–1820), signer of Declaration of Independence, born Newport, R.I.; member of Continental Congress 1776–81, 1783–85; state chief justice 1785.

Ellesmere Island, Canada, n.w. of Greenland, from which it is separated by Smith Sound and Kennedy Channel; 82,119 sq mi (212,687 sq km); mountainous, almost covered by glacial ice caps; vegetation in ice-free areas, *maps* N-350, W-297
Arctic regions A-571
size, comparative. *see in index* Island, *table*

Ellice Islands. *see in index* Tuvalu

Ellington, Duke (full name Edward Kennedy Ellington) (1899–1974), U.S. pianist, conductor and composer E-193
jazz J-85
popular music M-684

Elliot, Robert Brown (1842–84), U.S. public official and lawyer, born in Boston, Mass.; South Carolina House of Representatives 1868–70, speaker 1874–76; U.S. House of Representatives 1871–74
political movement B-292

Elliot Bay, Seattle, Wash. S-102, *picture* W-57

Elliot family
heraldic shield, *picture* H-136

Elliotson, John (1791–1868), English physician, born in London; one of the first to urge clinical lectures as method of teaching medicine; physician to both Dickens and Thackeray; 'Pendennis' dedicated to him.

Ellipse, a closed curve, generated from two points called foci; the sum of the distances from any point on the curve to each of the foci is always the same for any given ellipse; can be drawn by placing a loop of string loosely over two pins stuck in a drawing board and passing a pencil around inside the loop; character of the ellipse will be determined by the length of the loop and the distance between the pins. *see also in index* Conic sections
Apollonius of Perga A-506
artificial satellites' orbits S-343
geometry G-76, *diagram* G-77
mathematics M-214
moon M-577

planets' orbits P-350, A-713, S-254a, *diagrams* S-254c
Kepler's laws S-57g

Ellipsoidal mirror M-464

Elliptical galaxy A-723, *picture* S-412

Ellis, Havelock (1859–1939), English psychologist and philosopher E-194

Ellis, Henry (1721–1806), English hydrographer and colonial official; elected fellow of Royal Society for book about voyage to Hudson Bay in search of northwest passage; as governor of Georgia (1757–60), provided for guarantee of titles to land; protected coast during French and Indian War.

Ellis, James (or Jimmy) (born 1940), U.S. boxer, born in Louisville, Ky. B-392

Ellis, Perry (1940–86), U.S. fashion designer, noted for sportswear D-271

Ellis Island, New York, N.Y. N-275

Ellison, Ralph Waldo (born 1914), U.S. writer, born in Oklahoma City, Okla. (novel: 'Invisible Man'; essays: 'Shadow and Act')
American fiction A-362
black Americans B-301

Ellmann, Richard (1918–87), U.S. writer and educator, born in Highland Park, Mich.; professor of English Northwestern University 1951–68, Yale 1968–70, Oxford 1970–84; books on famous writers; 1960 National Book Award for 'James Joyce', a biography.

Ellora, India, town in Maharashtra state; famous Buddhist, Hindu, and Jain rock-cut temples; one, the Kailasa temple, was cut downward from top of hill.

Ellsworth, Elmer Ephraim (1837–61), U.S. soldier, colonel of 'Ellsworth's Zouaves,' born near Saratoga Springs, N.Y.; shot at Alexandria, Va.; regarded in his day as first martyr to Union cause.

Ellsworth, Lincoln (1880–1951), U.S. explorer, born in Chicago, Ill.; with Amundsen in Arctic flights 1925, 1926; in 1935 raised U.S. flag over 300,000 sq mi (777,000 sq km) of unclaimed land in Antarctica; explorations in interior of Antarctica 1936, 1938, 1939 ("My Four Antarctic Expeditions", a magazine article; 'Exploring Today', a book)
polar explorations P-423, *table* P-422

Ellsworth, Oliver (1745–1807), U.S. statesman and jurist, born in Windsor, Conn.; U.S. senator from Connecticut 1789–96; drafted bill organizing federal courts; introduced Connecticut Compromise; chief justice of the U.S. 1796–99.

Ellsworth Highland, Antarctica; region extending s.w. from base of Antarctic Peninsula; discovered 1935 by Lincoln Ellsworth A-473
marble discovered, *table* P-422

Ellwood City, Pa., borough 33 mi (53 km) n.w. of Pittsburgh, in coal and limestone district; metal products, machinery, textiles; pop. 9,998, *map* P-184

Elm, tree E-194. *see also in index* Elm bark beetle
fungi F-450
leaf and bark P-358
Norse mythology M-697
wood, *table* W-283

Elman, Mischa (1891–1967), U.S. violinist, born in Russia, became citizen of U.S. 1923; pupil of Leopold Auer; made debut at age of 10; won international fame.

El Mansura, Egypt. *see in index* Mansura

Elm bark beetle, an insect of engraver beetle group (family Scolytidae); two species carry fungus of Dutch elm disease, the native *Hylurgopinus rufipes* and the European *Scolytus multistriatus*, which is more prevalent; adults feed in twig crotches of healthy trees, then fly to recently cut, dead, or dying elms, tunnel under bark and lay eggs; larvae tunnel as they feed; fungus grows in tunnels; adults emerging from tunnels carry fungus spores on their bodies and thus transfer spores to healthy trees. *see also in index* Dutch elm disease; Elm-leaf beetle.

Elmendorf, Theresa Hubbell West (1855–1932), U.S. librarian, born in Pardeeville, Wis.; became deputy librarian 1880, librarian 1892–96, Milwaukee (Wis.) Public Library; first woman president American Library Association 1911–12.

'Elmer Gantry', work by Lewis L-142

Elm family (or Ulmaceae), a family of shrubs and trees including the American elm, hackberry, sugarberry, English elm, Chinese elm, slippery elm, sawleaf zelkova, and the water elm.

Elmhurst, Ill., residential city about 15 mi (25 km) w. of Chicago; limestone quarry; Elmhurst College; settled in 1843; pop. 44,251, *map* I-52

Elmhurst College, Elmhurst, Ill.; founded 1871 by Evangelical and Reformed church, which became United Church of Christ; arts and sciences, teacher education.

Elmira, N.Y., manufacturing city on Chemung River, 7 mi (11 km) n. of Pennsylvania boundary; metal, glass, and electrical products, fire fighting equipment; food products; prefabricated homes; electronic tubes; Elmira College; pop. 39,945, *map* U-41
reformatory P-505d

Elmira College, Elmira, N.Y.; private control; chartered 1855 as the first college for women in the United States but now coeducational; arts and sciences, nursing and teacher education, secretarial studies; graduate study N-255

Elm-leaf beetle, a coleopterous insect *Galerucella luteola*, accidentally introduced into the U.S.; its larvae feed on the lower side of elm leaves. *see also in index* Elm bark beetle

Elmont, N.Y., residential community just e. of Queens, New York, N.Y., on Long Island; apparel; Belmont Park racetrack nearby; pop. 29,363.

El Monte, Calif., city 12 mi (19 km) e. of Los Angeles; electronics, aircraft, mobile homes; dairy products, poultry; truck farms; pop. 79,494.

El Morro National Monument, New Mexico, *map* N-229
'Inscription Rock', *picture* A-332

Elmwood Park, Ill., residential village adjacent to n.w. section of Chicago; metal products; incorporated 1914; pop. 26,160, *map* I-52

Elmwood Park, (formerly East Paterson until 1973), N.J., borough on Passaic River, opposite Paterson; paper products, television sets; electronics; pop. 18,377.

Elodea (also called water weed, or ditch moss, or choke pondweed), a water plant *Elodea canadensis*, loosely rooted or floating free entirely under water; solid beds of it fill many ponds and slow streams; branches crowded with dark green leaves arranged in circles of 3 or more leaves around the stem; flowers very small; snails feed on its leaves.

Elohim (often called El), name for God used in some Hebrew Scriptures; used in Old Testament for heathen gods also.

Elon College, Elon College, N.C.; affiliated with United Church of Christ; chartered 1889, opened 1890; arts and sciences, teacher education.

Elongation of a planet, in astronomy, the angular distance between a planet and the sun, as seen from the earth.

El Pao, mountain in n.e. Venezuela
iron mining V-276

El Paso, Tex., city on Rio Grande, in extreme w. part of state; pop. 425,259 E-194, T-119, *maps* N-350, U-40, W-297
Ciudad Juárez C-462
climatic region, *map* U-119
Mexico M-338

El Qahira, Egypt. *see in index* Cairo

El Qantara (or Kantara), Egypt, town on Suez Canal; Allied military base in World War I, *map* S-504

El Reno, Okla., city near North Canadian River, 25 mi (40 km) w. of Oklahoma City; wheat, livestock center; railroad shops; grain elevators; historic Fort Reno nearby; pop. 15,486.

El Salvador (or Republic of El Salvador), smallest of Central American republics; 8,164 sq mi (21,145 sq km); cap. San Salvador; pop. 5,235,700 E-195, S-32, *maps* N-350, 310, W-297. *see also in index* Central America
flag, *picture* F-164
Latin American conflicts L-66
literature L-73
name's origin S-33
national anthem, *table* N-64
railroad mileage, *table* R-85
San Salvador S-44b
World War II W-328

El Segundo, Calif., city 14 mi (22 km) s.w. of Los Angeles; oil refining; aircraft, electronic components; pop. 13,752.

Elsinore, Denmark. *see in index* Helsingör

Elssler, Fanny (1810–84), Austrian dancer, born in Vienna; debut at age of 6; U.S. debut 1840; remarkable for beauty and skill; most successful in ballet and in dances of Spain; often danced with sister Therese (1808–78) B-33, D-27

Elster (or White Elster), river of central Germany; rises on the East German-Czechoslovak border; flows n. and empties into Saale, 3 mi (5 km) s. of Halle; 115 mi (185 km) long, *map* G-131

Elston, Dorothy Andrews (married name Dorothy Andrews Kabis) (1917–71), U.S. public official, born in Wilkes-Barre, Pa.; president National Federation of Republican Women 1963–68; treasurer of the United States 1969–71.

Eltville (formerly Elfeld), West Germany; town on Rhine River, 6 mi (10 km) s.w. of Wiesbaden; printing press set up by Gutenberg in 1465; pop. 6,875.

Éluard, Paul (1895–1952), French poet, born in Saint-Denis; identified first with Dadaists, later with surrealist movement.

Eluviation zone, soil formation S-251

Elvehjem, Conrad Arnold (1901–62), U.S. biochemist, born in McFarland, Wis.; on faculty University of Wisconsin after 1925, became professor 1936, dean of graduate school 1946–58, president 1958–62; noted for researches on vitamin B complex.

Elver, stage in development of an eel E-109

Elves. *see in index* Elf

Elwood, Ind., city about 40 mi (60 km) n.e. of Indianapolis; tomato and other fruit and vegetable canning; metal products, hand-blown glass; annual glass festival; home of Wendell L. Willkie; pop. 10,867, *map* I-102

Ely, Richard Theodore (1854–1943), U.S. political economist, born in Ripley, N.Y.; professor University of Wisconsin 1892–1925, Northwestern University 1925–33 ('Outlines of Economics'; 'Studies in the Evolution of Industrial Society'; 'Hard Times—the Way In and the Way Out').

Ely, England, city 15 mi (25 km) n.e. of Cambridge, on Ouse River; beet-sugar refinery; leather products; cathedral part of 10th-century Benedictine monastery; pop. 10,020, *map* U-18a

Ely, Minn., city in n.e. part of state, in Superior National Forest, about 20 mi (30 km) s. of Canadian border; hunting, fishing; starting point for wilderness canoe trips; iron ore mining; pop. 4,904.

Ely, Nev., city in e. of state; copper mining and smelting center; farming, ranching; tourist area; pop. 4,882, *map* U-40

Elyot, Sir Thomas (1490?–1546), English diplomat and scholar; friend of Sir Thomas More; remembered for his books 'The Castle of Health', a popular treatise on medicine, and 'Book Named the Governor', a moral philosophy.

Elyria, Ohio, city on Black River, 24 mi (37 km) s.w. of Cleveland; auto accessories, electric motors, heating and air-conditioning equipment, metal products, chemicals, plastics, pipe tools, air brakes, golf balls; incorporated 1833; pop. 53,427.

'Élysée Montmartre Bal Masque', lithograph by Chéret, *picture* G-234

Élysée Palace, Paris, official residence of French presidents 1848–52, 1871–1940, and again since 1945; built in 1728 for a French count but made residence of Madame de Pompadour by Louis XV.

Elysium (or Elysian Fields), in Greek and Roman mythology H-124
mythology M-702

Elytis, Odysseus (originally Odysseus Alepoudhelis) (born 1911), Greek poet and essayist, born Hērákleion, Crete E-197. *see also in index* Nobel Prizewinners, table

Elytra, in zoology, a term for beetle wing covers B-137

Elzevir, family of 17th-century Dutch printers famous for beautiful types and choice grade of paper; **Louis** (1540–1617) began printing in 1583; his five sons carried on the work
type and typography T-337

Em, a type measure T-336

Emakimono, Japanese hand scroll J-50

Emanation. *see in index* Radon

Emancipation. *see in index* Slavery, *subhead* emancipation

Emancipation Act (1861), Russia R-353

Emancipation Proclamation (1863), statement by President Lincoln E-197, L-222, C-643
black Americans B-291
Civil War C-475, 481
Douglass D-236

Emancipists, in Australia
Maquarie M-22

Emanuel I, the Happy (1469–1521), king of Portugal in whose reign, called Portugal's golden age, Vasco da Gama opened sea route to India, Cabral took possession of Brazil, and Albuquerque established Portuguese rule in East Indies.

Emba, river in Kazakh Soviet Socialist Republic; flows s.w. 385 mi (620 km) to Caspian Sea; rich petroleum fields located along lower course.

Embalming, a procedure of using preservatives to keep a dead body intact for as long as possible D-50

Embankment, an artificial bank or dike to resist the encroachment of water. *see also in index* Breakwater, Dike, Jetty; Levee

Embargo, the holding, or detention, of ships or other property within a nation to prevent their departure to a foreign territory E-197

Embargo Act (1807), United States E-198
Jefferson's administration J-94
Massachusetts M-195
War of 1812 W-30

Embarras River, rises in s.e. Illinois and flows in a generally southerly direction, 185 mi (300 km) long; enters Wabash River 7 mi (11 km) w. of Vincennes, *map* I-53

Embassy D-150, F-339a

Embattled line (or crenellé), in heraldry H-136

Ember Days, fast days (12 in all) observed by Roman Catholic and Anglican churches at four seasons of the year; the Wednesday, Friday, and Saturday after December 13, after the first Sunday of Lent, after Whitsunday, and after September 14. On February 17, 1966, Pope Paul VI excluded the Ember Days as days of fast and abstinence for Roman Catholics.

Emberley, Edward Randolph (born 1931), U.S. illustrator and children's author, born in Malden, Mass.; illustrated books by himself ('The Wing on the Flea'; 'Punch and Judy'; series on drawing for children), by his wife, **Barbara Emberley** ('Paul Bunyan'; 'One Wide River to Cross'; 'Drummer

Hoff', awarded 1968 Caldecott Medal), and by other authors.
Embezzlement, the fraudulent appropriation of money, cargo, or other personal property by one entrusted with it; considered a felony C-771
Embioptera, an order of tiny silk-producing insects that inhabit silk-lined underground tunnels; found mostly in the tropics.
Emblems. *see also in index* Flags; Flags of the United States; Flags of the world
Canadian Mounties, *picture* R-300a
scallop shell S-52g
Embossing, producing raised figures upon various materials E-198
chasing, *picture* S-203
metalworking M-310
Embouchure, mouthpiece W-228
Embroidery S-122
antiques A-494
needlework N-110
Embryo, animal E-199, *pictures* E-199, 201
brain's development B-401, *diagram* B-402
egg E-110
Embryo, plant S-107, *diagram* P-374
nut N-448
wheat W-192
Embryogeny, all phases of embryonic development E-199
Embryology E-199. *see also in index* Cell; Embryo, animal; Embryo, plant; Fertilization; Metamorphosis; Ovum; Protoplasm; Reproduction; Sperm cell
biological fields B-231
evolution E-367
Fabricius F-5
sciences S-64b
zoology Z-469
Embryophyta, a subkingdom of plants P-370
Embryo transfer, fertilization technique C-231
Emden, West Germany, seaport in n.w., at mouth of Ems River; handles ore, grain, and wood imports; exports include coal, fish, and agricultural machinery; pop. 48,525, *map* G-131
Emek. *see in index* Esdraelon, Plain of
Emerald, precious stone
jewelry J-115, *pictures* J-113
minerals M-436
Emerald cut, gem cutting
diamond, *picture* J-116
Emergency Broadcast System, United States' nationwide radio warning system R-49
Emergency Home Finance Act (1970), United States, *list* H-304
Emergency Relief Act (1932), United States H-235
Emergency medicine, medical specialty M-280, *table* M-277
ambulance A-326
first aid procedures F-115
hospital H-282
Emeritus, term applied to an official who has resigned or been honorably retired from active duty because of long service, age, or illness (emeritus professor, emeritus pastor); originally applied to Roman soldier or official who received compensation and special privileges after honorable dismissal from service.
Emerson, Peter Henry (1856–1936), English photographer P-298
Emerson, Ralph Waldo (1803–82), U.S. philosopher, essayist, and poet E-203
American literature A-347
essay E-306
Concord, Mass. C-639
Hall of Fame, *table* H-16
transcendentalism T-248
Whitman W-200
Emerson, Roy (born 1936), Australian tennis player T-107
Emerson, William (1906–84), British poet and critic ('Collected Poems'; 'Some Versions of Pastoral').
Emerson College, Boston, Mass.; private control; founded 1880; liberal arts with specialization in broadcasting, drama, speech, and speech pathology and audiology; graduate studies.
Emery, powdered corundum M-435
abrasives A-13
Emesa, Syria. *see in index* Homs
Emett, Rowland (born 1906), British cartoonist, born near London; creator of famous character, Nellie, an old railroad engine; visited U.S. 1952 (author and illustrator of 'New World for Nellie'; collection of his cartoons from *Punch*, 'Emett's Domain').
EMG. *see in index* Electromyogram
Emigration, departure from one country to settle in another, *chart* U-120. *see also in index* Immigration
Cuba C-804
Mexico M-326, 338
migration of people M-399
steerage accommodations S-167
Emigrés, peoples in French Revolution F-402
'Émile', work by Rousseau L-246, R-300
Emilia (formerly called *Cacalia*), genus of annual and perennial plants of the composite family, the tassel flower *E. sagittata*, native to the tropics, has small heads of red or gold flowers and is called Flora's paintbrush.
'Emilia Galotti', drama by Lessing L-138
Emilia-Romagna, region of northern Italy, s. of the Po River and n. of Tuscany; 8,542 sq mi (22,124 sq km); cap. Bologna; pop. 3,666,680, *map* I-401
Eminescu, Michael (1849–89), Romanian poet; work marked by melancholy mysticism.
Emin Pasha (or Eduard Schnitzer) (1840–92), German explorer and administrator in Africa, born in Oppeln, near Breslau
Stanley S-411
Emir. *see in index* Amir
Emission spectrum, light S-371
Emma (1858–1934), queen of William III of The Netherlands, mother of Queen Wilhelmina, for whom she was regent 1890–98.
'Emma', work by Austen A-765
Emmanuel. *see in index* Immanuel
Emmanuel College, Boston, Mass.; Roman Catholic; for women; founded 1919; arts and sciences, teacher education; graduate studies.
Emmanuel Holiness church H-202
Emmaus, Pa., borough 4 mi (6 km) s. of Allentown; electrical products and acid-proof castings, textiles, foundry products; pop. 11,511, *map* P-185
Emma Willard School (formerly Middlebury Female Seminary), Troy, N.Y.; founded in 1814 W-204
Emmental, fertile valley in canton of Bern, Switzerland; 25 mi (40 km) long, 11 mi (18 km) wide.
Emmer wheat, plant *Triticum dicoccon* W-188
Emmet, Robert (1778–1803), Irish rebel, born in Dublin; led unsuccessful revolt against Dublin Castle; escaped but returned to his betrothed, Sarah Curran; was caught and hanged.
Emmett, Daniel Decatur (1815–1904), U.S. actor and songwriter, born in Mount Vernon, Ohio; composed 'Old Dan Tucker' at age of 16; originator of 'Negro minstrel' performances
patriotic song N-65
Emmons, Mount, Uinta Range, Utah; 13,428 ft (4,093 m), *map* U-232
Emmy, statuette presented annually by Academy of Television Arts and Sciences, Hollywood, Calif.; designed and sculptured by Louis McManus; first awarded 1949; name suggested by Harry R. Lubcke, Academy president 1949, from Immy, engineering term referring to Image Orthicon camera. *see also in index* Academy of Television Arts and Sciences
Emory and Henry College, Emory, Va.; affiliated with United Methodist church; established 1836, opened 1838; arts and sciences, teacher education.
Emory University, Atlanta, Ga.; Methodist; founded 1836; arts and sciences, business administration, dentistry, education, law, medicine, nursing, theology; graduate school; junior college at Oxford, Ga. A-742
Emotion E-204
arts A-663
automobile driving A-864
child
child abuse C-319
development and training C-323
communication C-609
headache H-81
memory M-294
play P-386, *pictures* P-387
polygraph, *picture* P-521
sleep S-217
smell S-218
Empathy, ability to see the world from another's point of view
communication C-610
Empedocles (490?–430 BC), great Greek philosopher, poet, statesman, superhuman character in legend; said to have cast self into crater of Mt. Etna (Matthew Arnold's 'Empedocles on Etna')
philosophy P-304
'Empedocles on Etna', work by Arnold E-276
Empennage, in airplane A-184
Emperor (derived from Latin *imperium*, power of a general to enforce his commands), head of empire; wife of emperor or woman ruling empire in own right is empress
abdications. *see in index* Abdications, *table*
China P-153, P-440
France. *see in index* Napoleon I; Napoleon III
Germany. *see in index* William I, first German emperor; William II
Holy Roman Empire. *see in index* Holy Roman Empire, *table*
India I-76
Rome, ancient R-246, *pictures* R-243, *table* R-247
Russia R-352, P-226, *picture* R-338
'Emperor', work by Beethoven B-136
'Emperor and Galilean', work by Ibsen I-5
Emperor grape G-220
Emperor penguin P-162
Antarctic habitat, *picture* A-474
Emphysema, respiratory disease D-177
lungs L-337
Empire, political unit I-259
colonialism and imperialism C-555
'Empire' (1964), underground motion picture by Warhol M-624
Empire Day. *see in index* Victoria Day
Empire State. *see in index* New York
Empire State Building, New York, N.Y. A-706
Empire State of the South. *see in index* Georgia
Empiricism, philosophy P-264
Berkeley B-166
Locke L-278
Employment E-205. *see also in index* Labor; Unemployment; Vocations; *see also* Fact Summary with each state article
apprenticeship training A-512
business cycle B-517
computer's influence C-626
employment agency E-205
etiquette E-316
Industrial Revolution I-180
labor movements L-6
men and women, *chart* U-103
paint industry P-76
petroleum industry P-230
population P-448
service C-316
20th-century
farm workers, *picture* V-359
women's rights W-275
workers, *chart* U-124
Employment agency E-205
Employment and Training Administration, United States U-163
Employment Retirement Income Security Act (ERISA) (1974), United States P-188
labor movements L-10
Employment Standards Administration, United States U-163
Emporia, Kan., city about 50 mi (80 km) s.w. of Topeka; food processing; Emporia Kansas State College; home of *Emporia Gazette*, William Allen White editor 1895–1944; pop. 25,287, *map* U-41
Emporia, College of, Emporia, Kan.; affiliated with Presbyterian Church, U.S.; established 1882; closed 1974.
Emporia Kansas State College (formerly Kansas State Teachers College), Emporia, Kan.; founded 1863; liberal arts; graduate studies.
Empress Eugénie, diamond, *picture* D-129
Empress Eugénie, hats and caps, *picture* H-53
Empson, William (1906–84), British poet and critic, born in Yorkshire; university professor at Tokyo, Peking, and Sheffield
literary contribution E-281
Ems, West Germany. *see in index* Bad Ems
EMS. *see in index* European Monetary System
Ems River, n.w. Germany; flows n.w. 200 mi (320 km) to North Sea; irrigates through canals, *map* G-131
Emu. *see in index* Birds, flightless
Emulsion, a liquid mixture in which a substance is suspended in minute globules
soap S-229
En, a type measure T-336
Enabling act (1933), Germany G-123
Enamel, a varnish V-267
Enamel, finely powdered glass used to coat a base that when heated forms a glaze E-207
glass G-160
Enargite, a blackish copper ore, copper sulfarsenate (Cu_3AsS_4) M-432
Encarnación, Paraguay, port in s.e., on Paraná River; lumber, yerba maté, cotton, tobacco, hides, wine; pop. 23,343, *map* S-299
Encaustic painting, method in which wax is combined with the colors; after the mixture has been applied, it is made permanent by being fused with a hot iron, *picture* P-28
Encephalic photoreception B-227
Encephalitis, nervous system disorder N-123
memory M-295
mosquito M-598
Enchanted Mesa, mesa in w.-central New Mexico, near Acoma Pueblo, 55 mi (90 km) s.w. of Albuquerque; called Katzimo (the Accursed) by Acoma Indians; according to tradition their ancestors, who had gone to their fields in the plains, were prevented from returning to their high mesa home by a terrific storm that destroyed their rock ladder, leaving 3 women above, 2 to die of starvation and 1 to commit suicide.
Encke, Johann Franz (1791–1865), German astronomer, born in Hamburg; determined orbit and period of recurrence (every 3.3 years) of comet first observed 1786, since called Encke's comet; measured distance between sun and earth.
Encke's comet, first observed 1786; period of orbit 3.3 years; named for German astronomer Johann Franz Encke, who charted its orbit.
Enclave, territory lying entirely or mostly inside the boundaries of a foreign nation or territory; Bangladesh, for example, is an enclave within India. *see also in index* Exclave
Encoder (or transmitter), in communications
Australia A-788
information theory analysis I-201, *picture* I-202
Encoding, in memory M-295
Encomienda (Spanish "to entrust"), land, including inhabitants, taken from Indians and granted to early colonists in the Western Hemisphere by Spanish crown S-290
American colonization A-335
Mexico M-336
'Encomium Moriae' (The Praise fo Folly), work by Erasmus
Holbein H-201
Encyclical, in modern usage a letter from the pope meant

for general circulation; most frequent means of papal instruction to Roman Catholics since reign of Pius IX (1846–78); addressed to bishops until John XXIII also included "all men of good will"; usually deals with dogma, social reform, general welfare, or condemnation of error; often prepared with help of experts; custom begun by Benedict XIV in 1740; famous labor encyclical by Leo XIII influenced 19th-century social movements
Paul VI P-142a
Pius XI P-347
Pius XII P-348

'Encyclopaedia Britannica' R-125
Adler A-45
Benton B-165

Encyclopedia, derived from ancient Greek word meaning whole circle of knowledge R-123
China's Sung Dynasty's creation C-366
'Compton's Encyclopedia'. *see in index* 'Compton's Encyclopedia'
libraries L-161
study S-495

'Encyclopédie', French encyclopedia F-396
Diderot D-138

Encyclopedists, writers of great French Encyclopedia, including Diderot and other distinguished thinkers of 18th century.

Endangered species, any plant or animal that is in danger of extinction E-209
hyena H-342
trapping T-268
whale W-186
zoo Z-460

Endangered Species Act (1973), United States E-209

Endangered Species Preservation Act (1966), United States, protection of wildlife C-678, E-209

Endecott, John (or John Endicott) (1588?–1665), English leader of Puritan band that settled (1628) at Numkeag, now Salem, Mass., born in Chagford, near Exeter, England; governor of Massachusetts Bay Colony for years; capable and zealous in public office, fanatical in religious matters M-194

Endemic disease, disease continually prevalent in a region D-165

Ender, Kornelia (born 1958), East German swimmer, born in Plausen, East Germany; won more Olympic gold medals (4) than any woman before her O-542

Enderbury Island, one of Phoenix Islands, s. Pacific. *see in index* Phoenix Islands

Enderby Land, region in Antarctica, between Ice Bay and Edward VIII Bay; discovered 1831 by John Biscoe, an Englishman, *map* W-297

Enders, John Franklin (1897–1985), U.S. bacteriologist, born in West Hartford, Conn.; on faculty Harvard University medical school after 1929, professor 1956–68; awarded Presidential Medal of Freedom 1963 M-284

Enders Reservoir, in Nebraska N-95

'Endgame', work by Beckett B-123

Endicott, John. *see in index* Endecott, John

Endicott, N.Y., industrial village on Susquehanna River, in s. part of state, 8 mi (13 km) w. of Binghamton; business machines, shoes, forgings; pop. 14,457.

Endicott Mountains, in Alaska, part of Brooks Range; name formerly applied to whole chain; some 150 mi (240 km) long; peaks rise to nearly 9,000 ft (2,740 m) high, *map* U-39

Endive, an annual or biennial plant *Cichorium endivia*; cultivated in Europe since 16th century; curled and narrow-leaved varieties used for salads; French endive produced by blanching is the Witloof variety.

Endlicher, Stephan Ladislaus (1809–49), Hungarian botanist and linguist, born in Pressburg, now Bratislava, Czechoslovakia; curator of botany Museum of Natural History, Vienna; professor of botany and director botanic garden University of Vienna; a founder of Vienna Academy of Sciences; made valuable contributions to study of Oriental languages and literature.

End milling, a machine tool operation T-221

Endocannibalism, ritual C-139

Endocarditis, bacterial infection of the heart D-174, H-98

Endocardium, part of the heart H-97

Endocrine gland (or ductless gland) G-153
hormones H-240
sexuality S-123

Endocrinology, in medicine, the science of internal secretions and the endocrine glands as related to one another and the organism as a whole.

Endoderm, embryonic germ layer
coelenterate A-433
vertebrate E-200, *chart* E-202

Endodontic treatment (or root canal), removal of the pulp from the tooth D-201

'End of St. Petersburg, The' (1927), motion picture by Eisenstein M-620

'End of the Trail', statue by James E. Fraser, depicting Indian rider bowed over in grief at fate of Indians; statue created 1915; original in San Francisco until 1919 and in Visalia, Calif., 1919–68; acquired 1968 by National Cowboy Hall of Fame, Oklahoma City; restored; enshrined 1970.

Endogamy, marriage within a specific group as required by law or custom
family F-17
marriage M-149

Endolymph, fluid that fills the otic labyrinth of the inner ear, including the semicircular canals important in equilibrium; produced by secretory cells in the inner ear.

Endometrium (or uterine lining), mucous coating of the uterus M-300

Endoplasmic reticulum, network of membranous tubes B-199, C-238, *diagram* B-198, *picture* C-237

Endor, Witch of, the sorceress at Endor, Palestine, to whom Saul appealed for aid against the Philistines (Bible, I Sam. xxviii).

End organ. *see in index* Sensory receptor

Endorphin, pleasure-producing chemical of the brain H-3

Endorsement (or indorsement), in law
definition, *table* L-92

Endoskeleton, an internal skeleton, as in humans, cats, frogs, etc. A-434

Endosperm, food material surrounding embryo in seed plants S-108
corn, *diagrams* P-374
flour milling F-212
wheat W-192

Endothermic reaction H-104

Endotherms. *see in index* Mammal

Endowments. *see in index* Foundations and charities

Endter, Michael, German illustrator of first children's picture book, 'Orbis Pictus'. *see also in index* 'Orbis Pictus'

Endymion, in Greek mythology, handsome young shepherd; Zeus bestowed on him immortality and everlasting sleep; the moon goddess, Selene, visited him nightly in his cave and caressed him without his knowledge.

'Endymion', work by Keats K-195
English literature E-275

'Enemies, a Love Story', work by Singer A-362

'Enemy of the People, An', work by Ibsen I-5

Energy E-213, *Reference-Outline* P-309. *see also in index* Force; Mechanics; Power
air conditioning A-151
Asian resources A-689
Austria's economy A-825
battery and fuel cell B-107
biology
animal behavior A-441
enzyme transfer B-200
fats and oils F-47
food and nutrition F-275, R-159
living things L-268
metabolism M-306
chemistry, *table* C-297
cryogenics C-793
Einstein's theory E-133, R-142
heat H-101
heating systems H-110
fuel. *see in index* Fuel
internal-combustion engine I-252
inventors, *table* I-281
light L-194
matter M-223
microwave oven H-210
motor and engine M-630
phosphorus P-273
physics P-308
atomic particle's system A-754
nuclear energy N-416
Bohr's theory B-332
nuclear weapons N-433
qualitative analysis Q-4
quantum theory S-254h
radiation R-33
radioactivity R-62
wave motion R-68
sciences S-64
sources P-380, P-483
oceans O-460
plants P-373
stars A-710
sun S-512
water W-86
spectrum S-374
storage release R-59
use, *chart* U-107
waterpower W-103
wind power W-232

Energy, Department of, United States U-165, U-197, *list* U-157
conservation measures C-678
wind power W-232

Energy efficiency ratio (EER), measurement in heating and cooling systems A-152

Energy Information Administration, United States U-165

Energy level, electrons N-418

Energy Reorganization Act (1974), United States N-430

Energy Research, Office of, United States U-165

Enesco, Georges (1881–1955), Romanian violinist and composer, born in Liveni, Moldavia; at 16 gave concert of his compositions; influenced by Wagner and Brahms ('Fantaisie pastorale'; 'Rhapsodies roumaines').

Enfant, Pierre Charles L' (1754–1825), French architect and engineer who planned Washington, D.C., born in Paris; came to fight in American Revolution before Lafayette; served as captain of engineers under Steuben and later was wounded in action at Savannah, Ga., and captured by British at Charleston, S.C. After war, worked as architect in New York City until called (1791) by President Washington to prepare plans for federal capital
Banneker's collaboration B-74
Washington, D.C. W-66, 71
White House W-196

Enfield, Conn., urban town 18 mi (29 km) n. of Hartford, on Connecticut River; center of extensive tobacco-growing region; textiles, plastics; pop. 42,695.

Enfield, borough, London, U.K., *maps* L-287, U-18a

Enfleurage, a perfume-making process P-204

Engadine, valley of Inn River, in e. Switzerland; 60 mi long (100 km); noted for picturesque scenery and health resorts.

Engelmann, George (1809–84), U.S. physician and botanist, born in Frankfurt, Germany; to U.S. 1832; first observer of immunity of American grapes to the Phylloxera; several plants named for him.

Engelmann spruce, evergreen tree *Picea engelmanni* of pine family, native to mountains from British Columbia to New Mexico; grows 70 to 120 ft (20 to 40 m) high; trunk slender, erect; crown narrow, cone-shaped; leaves 4-angled, to 1 in. (2.5 cm) long, blue-green, soft, aromatic; cones to 3 in. (8 cm) long.

Engels, Friedrich (1820–95), German socialist, born in Barmen, part of present Wuppertal, West Germany; coauthor with Marx of 'Communist Manifesto' C-619
Marx M-162

Engel vs. Vitale, case in U.S. constitutional law, *list* S-518b

Enghien, Louis Antoine Henri de Bourbon-Condé, duc d' (1772–1804), French émigré prince, last of the Condés, born in Chantilly; seized on neutral land as conspirator and executed by Napoleon's order though proved innocent; "It is more than a crime; it is a political fault" (this famous phrase is attributed to Fouché).

Engine, machine for creating or applying mechanical power M-630. *see also in index* Diesel engine; Internal combustion engine; Locomotive; Motor; Steam engine; Turbine
airplane A-185
automobile, *picture* A-845
efficiency ratio P-483
farm machinery F-30
jet propulsion. *see in index* Jet propulsion
motorboat. *see in index* Motorboat
nuclear S-342a
tachometer T-3
trucks T-291

Engineering E-222. *see also in index* Mechanics; Metallurgy
acoustics utilized A-21
aeronautical. *see in index* Aeronautical engineering
air conditioner A-152
bioengineering. *see in index* Bioengineering
bionic B-233
chemical engineering. *see in index* Chemical engineering
civil. *see in index* Civil engineering
computer C-636
economic geology G-72
fatigue F-46
fire protection F-112
Great Wall of China G-252
industrial. *see in index* Industrial engineering
instrument design I-228
machine M-0
marine. *see in index* Marine engineering
mechanical drawing M-255
mechanical engineering. *see in index* Mechanical engineering
mechanics M-263
microfilm M-377
petroleum mining P-231, P-235, *diagrams* P-237, 239, *pictures* P-236
profession V-364
Rome. *see in index* Rome, ancient, *subhead* engineering
safety S-6
science S-64
television T-77

Engine-pressure-ratio indicator (EPR)
airplane A-196

Engine room, area that houses the engine
submarine, *diagram* S-498

Engine room access trunk, submarine, *diagram* S-498

England, Anthony Wayne (born 1942), U.S. astronaut candidate, born in Indianapolis, Ind.; geophysicist chosen for NASA scientist-astronaut program 1967.

England, predominant country of the United Kingdom, located on s. part of the island of Great Britain; 50,871 sq mi (131,755 sq km); cap. London; pop. 46,102,300 E-229, *map* E-360. For history until 1801: *see below*; for current affairs and history after 1801: *see in index* United Kingdom. *see also in index* British Empire; Commonwealth, The; Ireland; Middle Ages; Scotland; Wales; and names of chief events and persons. For a list of the kings and queens of England: *see table* following
arts
architecture A-558
castles and palaces. *see in index* Castle; Palace
Gothic. *see in index* Gothic architecture
St. Paul's Cathedral. *see in index* St. Paul's Cathedral
beadwork B-114
classical music M-668
drama T-159
enameling E-208
furniture F-458, *picture* F-457
literature. *see in index* English literature
mime M-423
needlework N-111
lace L-13
opera O-561
oratorio O-575
pottery and porcelain P-476, *pictures* P-469
puppetry P-536
textiles T-144

ENGLAND'S KINGS AND QUEENS

(For biographical information, *see in index* names below)

Saxon	
802–839	Egbert
839–858	Ethelwulf
858–860	Ethelbald
860–865	Ethelbert
865–871	Ethelred
871–899	Alfred the Great
901–924	Edward the Elder
924–939	Athelstan
939–946	Edmund I
946–955	Edred
955–959	Edwy
959–975	Edgar
975–978	Edward the Martyr
978–1016	Ethelred "the Unready"
1016	Edmund II, Ironside
Danish	
1016–1035	Canute (Cnut)
1035–1040	Harold I
1040–1042	Harthacanute
Saxon	
1042–1066	Edward the Confessor
1066	Harold II
Norman	
1066–1087	William I, the Conqueror
1087–1100	William II
1100–1135	Henry I
1135–1154	Stephen
Plantagenet	
1154–1189	Henry II
1189–1199	Richard I
1199–1216	John
1216–1272	Henry III
1272–1307	Edward I
1307–1327	Edward II
1327–1377	Edward III
1377–1399	Richard II
Lancaster	
1399–1413	Henry IV
1413–1422	Henry V
1422–1461	Henry VI
York	
1461–1483	Edward IV
1483	Edward V
1483–1485	Richard III
Tudor	
1485–1509	Henry VII
1509–1547	Henry VIII
1547–1553	Edward VI
1553–1558	Mary I
1558–1603	Elizabeth I
Stuart	
1603–1625	James I
1625–1649	Charles I
[1649–1660	Commonwealth]
1660–1685	Charles II
1685–1688	James II
1689–1702	William III and Mary II (until her death in 1694)
1702–1714	Anne
Hanover	
1714–1727	George I
1727–1760	George II
1760–1820	George III
1820–1830	George IV
1830–1837	William IV
1837–1901	Victoria
Saxe-Coburg-Gotha (Windsor)	
1901–1910	Edward VII
1910–1936	George V
1936	Edward VIII
1936–1952	George VI
1952–	Elizabeth II

wool W-291
business and industry I-196
books and bookmaking B-351
coal mining C-525
gas distillation G-38
printing P-504
shipbuilding S-165
wire W-247
calendar C-28
dress D-264
Enlightenment E-289
foreign affairs
Canada C-76
New Brunswick N-152, 157
Newfoundland N-168
Nova Scotia N-403
East Indies E-47
France F-361
Wellington W-148
Gibraltar G-143
Holland N-130
India I-77
Mediterranean Sea M-286
North American exploration A-332, N-344, *map* A-329
Persian Gulf P-211
Sierra Leone S-192b
United States. *see also in index* America, Discovery and Colonization of
Detroit D-122
Florida F-199
New York N-256, N-280
New York City S-295a
Plymouth P-395, *picture* P-396
XYZ affair X-406
West Indies W-156
Glorious Revolution G-168
hairdressing H-9
insurance I-235
international trade I-270
East India Company E-44
fur trade F-469
legislation
corn laws C-723
Magna Carta M-41
habeas corpus H-2
Poor Law of 1601 W-145
Stamp Act S-409
magazine and journal M-32
marine corps M-136
Napoleon N-15
newspapers N-235
political parties P-434
postal system P-465
prehistoric times S-456
Renaissance R-149
royal houses
Stuart S-493
Tudor T-304
shoes S-178
slavery and serfdom S-213
sports
field hockey H-193
horse racing H-275
skating W-241
Star Chamber S-424
Stuart Pretenders P-496
tariff T-28
taxation T-35
technology T-49
titles of nobility T-195
Wallace W-7
wars
American Revolution R-162, W-41, *pictures* R-168, R-172
Declaration of Independence D-53
Civil War A-418
French and Indian War F-393
Montreal M-572
Hundred Years' War H-324
King George's War K-246
King William's War K-247
Norman Conquest N-333
battle of Hastings H-52
Roman conquest, *map* R-242
Seven Years' War S-117
Spanish Armada A-627
Hawkins H-74
Thirty Years' War T-169
War of the Roses R-296
War of the Spanish Succession A-829
weights and measures W-139, *table* W-140
England, Church of. *see in index* Church of England
Engle, Joe H. (born 1932), U.S. Air Force test pilot and astronaut, born in Chapman, Kan.; served in Air Force 1956–; X-15 research pilot 1963–66; chosen for NASA program 1966; Sperry Award for contribution to aeronautics 1967.
Engle, Madeleine, L' (born 1918), U.S. actress, teacher, and author; born in New York, N.Y.; awarded Newbery Medal 1963 for 'A Wrinkle in Time' ('The Young Unicorns'; 'The Journey with Jonah').
Engle, Paul Hamilton (born 1908), U.S. writer, born in Cedar Rapids, Iowa; professor of English University of Iowa 1937– (poetry: 'Corn', 'West of Midnight', 'American Child'; essays: 'Prairie Christmas'; poetry and essays: 'An Old Fashioned Christmas').
Englewood, Colo., city, suburb s. of Denver; farm region; carnation center; machinery; electronics; pop. 30,021.
Englewood, N.J., residential city on w. slope of Hudson Palisades, 13 mi (21 km) n. of Jersey City; manufactures include metal goods, electrical fixtures, and leather products; pop. 23,701.
English Channel, separates England from France; breadth 20 to 100 mi (30 to 160 km), length 350 mi (560 km); mean depth 175 ft (50 m) long; favored by endurance swimmers, *maps* E-360, F-372, U-18a, W-297. *see also in index* Ocean, *table*
Dover D-236
England E-229
English Classical School (or English High School), school founded in the United States
establishment E-90
English cocker spaniel, dog, *picture* D-198
English composition. *see in index* Report writing; Writing, Communication by; Writing, Creative
English cottage garden, *picture* F-221
English daisy, flower *Bellis perennis* of the Compositae family D-8, G-25
English Dresden, diamond, *picture* D-129
English elm, tree *Ulmus procera* E-194
English foxhound, dog, *picture* D-200
English High School (or English Classical School), school founded in the United States
establishment E-90
English holly (or European holly), plant *Ilex aquifolium* H-204
English horn (or cor anglais), wind instrument W-227
English ivy, plant *Hedera helix* of the family Araliaceae I-408
growing conditions G-27
English Justinian. *see in index* Edward I
English language E-260. *see also in index* Grammar; Report writing; Rhetoric; Spelling; Writing, Communication by; Writing, Creative
alphabet's development A-315
Asian language patterns A-683
Australian heritage A-785
dictionaries. *see in index* Dictionary
England E-232
Elizabethan Age S-134
Old English E-264
Germanic languages G-103
India I-72
language construction L-31, *diagrams* L-32
lingua franca A-119
linguistics L-229
slang S-212
Webster W-130
English literature E-263
Arthurian legends A-655. *see also in index* Arthurian legends
Australian heritage A-785
Chaucer C-283
children's literature L-246, 258, *lists* L-254
Caldecott C-26, *picture* C-27
Elizabethan Age A-26. *see also in index* Elizabethan Age
folklore F-261, S-472, *list* S-481a
genre
drama D-243, T-159
medieval romances R-239
poetry P-403
poet laureate P-402
short story S-184
Shakespeare S-129
English oak, tree *Quercus robur* O-452
English pheasant, bird P-249
English primrose, flower *Primula vulgaris* of the family Primulaceae P-496
English saddle (or flat saddle) H-264, *diagram* H-265
English setter, dog, *picture* D-198
English sparrow. *see in index* House sparrow
English springer spaniel, dog, *picture* D-198
English toy spaniel, dog, *picture* D-205
English walnut (or Persian walnut), tree *Juglans regia* known for the wood and the nuts that it produces W-10
English yew, tree *Taxus baccala* of the Taxaceae family Y-416
Engrailed line, in heraldry H-136
Engraver beetle, any of numerous beetles of family Scolytidae; most live under bark of trees and engrave the wood by burrowing. *see also in index* Elm bark beetle
Engraving and etching, *pictures* A-664
glass, *pictures* G-155, 161
graphic arts G-231
maps M-128
photoengraving P-275, *pictures* P-276
postage stamps S-405
wood. *see in index* Wood engraving
ENI (National Hydrocarbons Agency), Italian government agency I-388
ENIAC (or Electronic Numerical Integrator Calculator), first electronic computer C-629
Enid, Okla., city about 65 mi (105 km) n.w. of Oklahoma City; wheat, livestock, oil center; grain elevators, oil products, Phillips University; Vance Air Force Base; pop. 50,363 O-524, *map* U-40
'Enigma Variations', music by Elgar E-188
Eniwetok, Pacific Ocean, atoll at extreme w. end of Marshall Islands; measures 21 by 17 mi (34 by 27 km); air and sea base P-19, *map* P-3
Enkephalin, natural chemical produced by the body A-387
drug addiction H-3
Enlargement, photographic print P-293
Enlarger, in photography P-294, *picture* P-292
Enlightenment, European intellectual movement E-288
abolitionist movement A-10
civilization viewed C-467
English literature E-270
Gothic fiction G-196
eugenics E-326
history writing H-172
human rights H-320
Judaism J-150, H-113
labor law development L-4
Enlil, Sumerian god, creator of the universe B-6

Enlisted personnel, in armed forces
Canada, *pictures* U-13
United States
navy N-80
Uniforms and insignia U-5, *pictures* U-6
'Enneads', work by Plotinus T-163
Enneagon (sometimes called nonagon), in mathematics
geometry G-76, *diagram* G-75
Ennis, Tex., city 35 mi (55 km) s. of Dallas; cotton-growing area; business forms; incorporated 1872; pop. 12,110.
Enniskillen (or Inniskilling), Northern Ireland, market town; defeated James II's forces at battle of Crom 1689; famous cavalry regiment Inniskilling Dragoons formed by defenders; pop. 7,020.
Ennius, Quintus (239–169 BC), Latin epic poet, called father of Roman poetry; introduced the hexameter L-76
Enoch, Hebrew patriarch who "walked with God" and after 365 years "was not, for God took him" (Bible, Gen. v. 18–24).
'Enoch Arden', poem by Tennyson about Enoch Arden, a shipwrecked sailor who, returning years later, finds wife married again, leaves her untroubled, and conceals his identity until death.
'Enola Gay', United States' B-29 bomber from which atomic bomb was dropped on Japan in World War II W-349
Enology. *see in index* Winemaking
Enos, chimpanzee pioneer in space S-345
'Enquiry Concerning the Principles of Natural Knowledge', work by Whitehead W-195
'Enrico di Borgogna', opera by Donizetti D-229
Enrico Fermi award, cash award and medal presented by the Atomic Energy Commission for achievements in atomic energy; authorized by Congress 1954.
Enright, Elizabeth (1909–68), U.S. illustrator and author of children's books, born in Chicago, Ill. ('Kintu'; 'Thimble Summer', winner of 1939 Newbery medal; 'The Saturdays'; 'A Spiderweb for Two'; 'Gone-Away Lake'; 'Tatsinda'; 'Zeee'); writer of adult stories R-111a
Enrober, machine that coats candy C-138
Enschede, The Netherlands, city near e. border, on Twente Canal; cotton textiles; printing; rebuilt after being destroyed by fire in 1862; pop. 105,48.
'Enseigne de Gersaint', work by Watteau W-109
Ensemble, music for two or more parts O-576
Ensenada, Mexico, seaport in n. Lower California, 65 mi (105 km) s.e. of San Diego; tuna and shellfish; wheat and beans; iron ore nearby; pop. 45,561, *map* M-341
Ensi, ruler of a city-state B-4
Ensign, United States Navy officer N-80
insignia, *picture* U-8
Ensign, national flag flown by ships F-161, *list* F-149
Ensign wasp, insect *Evania appendigaster* W-74
Ensilage. *see in index* Silage
Ensor, James, Baron (1860–1949), Belgian painter of realistic interiors, panoramic scenes, mystical fantasies, burlesques; born in Ostend; called a father of expressionism and a presurrealist.
Entail, law restricting inheritance to a particular heir or class of heirs; an interference with the usual dispersal of inheritance J-91
Entamoeba, unicellular organism A-375
Entamoeba histolytica, parasite, *picture* D-170
Entasis, in architecture
illusions I-54
Entebbe, Uganda, former capital, situated on n.w. shore of Lake Victoria; extensive botanical gardens; famous for tropical plants; pop. 21,096, *map* A-115
Israeli hostage rescue I-373
Entelodont, prehistoric animal
animal evolution A-462
Entente cordiale, French for "cordial understanding"; in international politics, friendliness between nations
United Kingdom E-255
Enterprise, Ala., city in s.e., 28 mi (45 km) n.w. of Dothan; peanut butter, oil; electronics; food processing; textiles; pop. 18,033.
'Enterprise', U.S. Navy aircraft carrier N-88, *picture* N-89
Enterprise, deep-sea mining of International Seabed Authority I-258
Enterpriser (or entrepreneur), in economics
capitalism C-152
Enters, Angna (born 1907), U.S. dancer, born in New York, N.Y.; famous for cleverly patterned pantomime; also writer, painter, and sculptor; 'Artist's Life'.
Entertainment center, home appliance H-213
video recording V-311
Entomology, the scientific study of insects. *see in index* Insect
Entomophily, insect pollination F-218
Entr'acte, in music, *list* M-670
Entrance jetty (or training jetty) J-111
Entrenchment, military science A-643
Entrepreneur (or enterpriser), in economics
capitalism C-152
Entropy
mathematical calculation and communications I-202, 204
thermodynamics C-794, E-221, *picture* E-220
Entry, mining tunnel or shaft
coal mining C-521
Envelope
printing P-460b
stamps S-406
Enver Pasha (1881–1922), Turkish soldier; leader in Young Turk Movement; after Balkan War, 1912–13, shot Nazim Pasha and took his position as war minister; at outbreak of World War I took over government, making alliance with Germany; on collapse of Turkey fled to Germany, then U.S.S.R.; killed by Bolsheviks while leading revolt in Soviet Turkestan.
Environment. *see also in index* Ecology
aerosol pollution A-66
biogeography B-220
intelligence and intelligence tests I-238
people. *see also in index* Pollution, environmental
cities C-456
Conservation. *see in index* Conservation
endangered species E-209
environmental geology G-72
eugenics E-326
evolution E-366
growth G-293
health hazards H-87
life-support in space A-717
prehistoric changes A-459
transportation T-265
West Germany
Greens political party G-126
Environmental control, in space travel S-343a
Environmental geology G-72
Environmental pollution. *see in index* Pollution, environmental
Environmental Protection Agency (EPA), United States U-166
antipollution activity P-441f
establishment C-678
garbage and refuse disposal G-18
Environmental Science Services Administration, United States. *see also in index* Geodetic Surveying
Environmental Survey Satellite (ESSA), *picture* S-343
Enzymes E-290
bacteria B-13
biochemistry B-202, *diagrams* B-203
bioengineering B-207
bionic research B-234
catalyst C-219
cheese C-287
coenzymes V-358
digestion D-144, P-197b
disease prevention D-167
embryology E-202
energy regulation P-273
evolution E-365
fermentation F-55
genetic engineering G-49
genetics G-54
honey B-125
membrane enzymes B-199, *diagram* B-203
metabolism M-306
mold M-519
molecule M-522
pepsin P-197b
Eocene epoch, in geological time
earth, *map* E-25, *table* E-24
elephant E-185
horse evolution H-268
Eohippus, ancestor of the horse H-268
Eosinophil, type of white blood cell B-313
EPA. *see in index* Environmental Protection Agency
Epaminondas (418?–362 BC), Theban general and statesman; in 371 BC defeated superior Spartan force; supported Theban democracy G-267, T-163
Epaphus, in Greek mythology, son of Zeus and Io; king of Egypt and founder of Memphis; Libya is said to be named for his daughter, Libya.
Epcot Center (or Experimental Prototype Community of Tomorrow), amusement park, Lake Buena Vista, Fla., near Orlando; opened 1982 A-386, D-185
Orlando O-607
Epée, Charles Michel, Abbé de l' (1712–89), French priest noted for pioneer work in communication for deaf, born in Versailles; founded school for deaf-mutes, later taken over by government; developed finger alphabet, still used, to help his two deaf sisters.
Epée, fencing sword F-53
Ephedrine, an alkaloid drug frequently used as a nasal decongestant to alleviate hay fever and asthma and as a stimulant for the central nervous system.
Ephemera. *see in index* Mayfly
Ephesians, Epistle to the, 10th book of the Bible's New Testament; written by the Apostle Paul to the church at Ephesus about AD 61.
Ephesus, ancient Greek city, greatest of 12 on coast of Asia Minor; famous for Temple of Artemis (Diana); also seat of two notable church councils in 5th century; St. Paul labored there three years (Bible, Epistle to the Ephesians) C-461
temple S-115
Ephialtes, traitor at battle of Thermopylae T-168
Ephor, Spartan official S-369
Ephraim, Hebrew patriarch, younger son of Joseph; ancestor to tribe of Ephraim (Bible, Josh. xvi).
Ephraim, Mount, in Israeli-occupied territory, 25 mi (40 km) n. of Jerusalem; one of the many low peaks in the ridge extending s. from Lebanon Mountains.
Ephrata, communal colony in Pennsylvania; founded by Johann Conrad Beissel C-604
Ephthalites, a people of central Asia. *see in index* White Huns
Epic E-291
folk music F-273
Homeric legend H-220
novel N-414
painting P-67f
poetry P-407
'Aeneid' V-328
'Beowulf' B-165
Greek literature G-272, G-274
Indian literature I-105
Islamic literature I-364
'Kalevala' F-89
'Orlando Furioso' A-588
'Poem of the Cid' S-365
'Song of Roland' R-238
'Song of the Nibelungs' N-302
'The Lay of the Host of Igor' R-359
'The Lusiads' P-450
storytelling S-467, 470
'Epic of Gilgamesh', tale of great flood in Mesopotamia E-291, F-185
Epicenter, point on earth's surface above origin of earthquake E-37
Epictetus (AD 60?–130?), Greek Stoic philosopher E-291
Greek literature G-279
Epicureanism, philosophy E-291
philosophy P-264
Epicurus (341–270 BC), Greek philosopher who thought that the chief good of life is pleasure but that true pleasure comes from the practice of virtue E-291, P-265
Epidaurus, seaport city of ancient Greece, in n.e. Peloponnesus, s.w. across Saronic Gulf from Piraeus, port of Athens
theater T-158, *picture* T-156
Epidemic, disease widespread for a time in a certain region; opposed to endemic disease, one continually prevalent in a region
epidemiology E-292
flood F-182
health agencies H-89
Epidemic disease control, service performed by health agencies H-89
Epidemiology, study of the spread of disease E-292
disease D-165
Epidermis (or cuticle), in anatomy
human skin S-210d, *diagram* S-211
Epididymis, in sexual reproduction R-151c, *diagram* R-151d
Epiglottis, a lidlike structure of cartilage that covers the entrance to the windpipe during the act of swallowing
digestive system D-144, *diagram* D-143
throat T-176
Epigram, from the Greek words "on" and "to write"; originally applied to an inscription on a tomb or monument, next used for short pithy verse, and now used also for a concise pointed saying, as: "The greatest of faults, I should say, is to be conscious of none"—Carlyle
La Rochefoucauld L-51
Martial M-158
Epigyny, in botany F-218
Epilepsy, disease of the nervous system, frequently from subtle brain damage, less often from injury; characterized by sudden, recurrent seizures with loss of consciousness and severe convulsions (grand mal), or in mild form by brief blackouts and fainting spells (petit mal) D-179
cerebral cortex B-401
first aid F-119
nervous system N-123
Epimenides (fl. 6th or 7th century BC), poet and prophet of Greece, born in Crete; purified Athens from a pestilence; said to have slept 57 years and to have lived almost 300 years; among works attributed to him are an epic poem on Argonautic expedition, and a work on purifications and sacrifices.
Epimere, dorsal part of a mesodermic segment E-200, *chart* E-202
Epimetheus, in Greek mythology P-97
Epinephrine. *see in index* Adrenaline
Epiphany, festival of Christian church (Jan. 6) commemorating showing of Jesus to the Magi
Christmas C-403
Epiphyte, plant
fern F-57
orchid O-580
rain forest J-155
Spanish moss P-363, *picture* P-357
Epirus, region of n. Greece, on Ionian Sea
Greece G-254, 260
Pyrrhus P-544
Episcopal church, Protestant. *see in index* Protestant Episcopal church
Episcopal miter (or Bishop's miter), mollusk shell *Mitra episcopalis*; characterized by folds on inner lip of opening of shell, which is usually turreted, *picture* S-149
Epistemology, in philosophy P-264
Epistle, a written communication, more formal than a letter, which has literary merit, such as the epistles in the Bible and those of Plutarch and Seneca B-183, L-139. *see also in index* epistles by name, *e.g.,* Romans, Epistle to
'Epistle of Pardon', work by al-Ma'arri
Islamic literature I-366

'Epistle to the Romans', work by Barth B-85
Epistolary novel, novel that is written as an exchange of letters N-411
Epitaph, an inscription on a tomb or anything written for that use
Robin Hood R-224
Shakespeare S-132
Stevenson S-446
Epitaxy machine, electronics, *picture* M-11
Epithelium, the layer of essentially protective tissue that forms the outer body surface (epidermis) and lines body cavities; sometimes modified for a secretory role, as in intestinal epithelium S-210d
Epizootic, animal epidemic E-292
Epler, Stephen (born 1909), U.S. educator, born in Brooklyn, Iowa; originated six-man football in 1934 to make the sport as active but less injurious for younger players.
E Pluribus Unum (one out of many), Latin motto suggested by Franklin, Adams, and Jefferson, members of committee of Continental Congress appointed to design seal of U.S.
Great Seal F-156, *picture* F-157
Epoxy resin, a thermosetting plastic with high resistance to heat and chemicals; used as protective coating on casting tools and dies
Apollo spacecraft S-346c
insulating materials I-232
synthetic adhesives A-43
EPR (or engine-pressure-ratio), indicator
airplane A-196
Epsom and Ewell, England, municipal borough 15 mi (25 km) s.w. of London; the name Epsom salts comes from its mineral springs; famous horse races at Epsom Downs; pop. 72,190, *map* U-18a
Epsom salts (or magnesium sulfate), occurs naturally as the mineral epsomite M-41
minerals M-436
EPSPs (excitatory postsynaptic potentials), positive voltage changes in nerve cells N-122
Epstein, Jacob (1880–1959), British sculptor E-293
sculpture S-79, 91
Epworth, England, small town located in Lincolnshire, notable as the birthplace of John Wesley, the founder of Methodism.
Epworth League. *see in index* Methodist Youth Fellowship
Equal additions, method of subtraction S-497
Equal-arm balance, weighing machine W-134
Equal Employment Opportunity Act (1964), United States' legislation
labor movements L-10
Equality, condition necessary for people to have civil and human rights C-468
women's rights W-272
Equality State. *see in index* Wyoming
Equal Pay Act (1963), United States
labor movements L-10
women's rights W-272
Equal Rights Amendment (ERA), proposed 27th Amendment to the U.S. Constitution, stated that "Equality of rights under the law shall not be denied or abridged by the United States or by any state on account of sex" U-196a
Equation, in algebra A-285, *examples* A-286
Equation of time T-189
watch and clock W-83
Equator, in geography E-293
direction D-158
earth E-10
geography G-62
hemisphere H-126
Latin America L-60
latitude and longitude L-79, *picture* L-81
navigation N-71
weather W-117
climate S-270
rainfall R-88
Equatorial air (E), air mass W-118
Equatorial currents, warm surface ocean drift currents moving westward near the equator; North and South Equatorial currents separated by Equatorial Counter Current, which flows eastward.
Equatorial Guinea (formerly called Spanish Guinea), republic in w. Africa, including Bioko Island; 10,830 sq mi (28,050 sq km); cap. Malabo; pop. 325,000 E-294, *maps* A-115, W-297
African political unit, *table* A-112
flag, *picture* F-164
Malabo M-68
Equatorial rain forest. *see in index* Rain forest
Equator system, in astronomy A-718
Equestrian sports E-295
Equidae. *see in index* Horse family
Equilateral triangle, in mathematics
geometry G-74
Equilibrium, a state of balance S-109
brain's control B-401
inner ear B-204, E-3
mechanics M-264
space travel, *picture* S-346b
Equinoctial. *see in index* Celestial equator
Equinox, time of year when the sun is equidistant from both of Earths' poles
folk art traditions F-252
hemisphere H-126
Equinox, Mount, in Vermont V-285
Equinoxes, precession of, slow shift in time of year when poles are equidistant from the sun
gyroscope G-327
Equisetaceae. *see in index* Horsetail family
Equites, knights of ancient Rome; a privileged order of society; at first restricted to patricians serving as cavalry; later open to any favored person of wealth whether or not in military service.
Equity, in law, *table* L-92
English law U-18
women's rights W-272
housing, *list* H-305
Equivalent weight, in chemistry S-256
Equuleus, constellation, *chart* C-681
Equus, animal genus including the ass, horse, zebra. *see in index* Ass; Horse; Zebra
Er (Erbium), a rare chemical element of the rare earth group, *table* P-207
ERA. *see in index* Equal Rights Amendment
Era of Good Feeling, in U.S. history
Madison M-25, 28
Monroe M-548
Era of Reptiles. *see in index* Mesozoic era
Érard, Sébastien (1752–1831), French maker of musical instruments, born in Strasbourg; most famous instrument was a double-action harp S-490a
Eraser, pencil P-159
Erasistratus (3rd century BC), ancient Greek physician and anatomist; first to classify nerves into motor and sensory P-316
autopsy procedure A-875
Erasmo da Narni. *see in index* Gattamelata
Erasmus, Desiderius (also called Erasmus of Rotterdam) (1466–1536), Dutch scholar and theologian E-296
etiquette E-320
Holbein H-201
humanism H-319
Latin literature L-78
More M-582
Reformation R-134
Renaissance R-146, *picture* R-148
'The Cloister and the Hearth' E-278
The Netherlands N-127
Eratosthenes, of Alexandria (276?–194 BC), Greek scientist, chief librarian of Alexandrian Library G-268, G-278
earth science E-35
Homeric legend H-224
Erbil, Iraq. *see in index* Arbela
Erbium (Er), rare chemical element of the rare earth group
periodic table, *table* P-207, *list* P-208
Ercilla y Zuñiga, Alonso de (1533-94), Chilean poet L-68
Erckmann-Chatrian, signature of French literary collaborators **Emile Erckmann** (1822–99) and **Louis Gratien Charles Alexandre Chatrian** (1826–90); writers of novels, short stories, dramas ('Madame Thérèse'; 'L'Ami Fritz').
Erebus, a place of utter darkness between the earth and Hades; in Greek mythology, the son of Chaos and the brother of Nyx, with whom he ruled the gloomy regions.
Erebus, Mount, active volcano, highest point about 12,280 ft (3,930 m) on Ross Island, in Ross Sea, off Antarctica.
Erech, Iraq. *see in index* Uruk
Erechtheum, temple on Acropolis A-736, A-23
Eregli (or Bender Eregli, ancient Heraclea), Asiatic Turkey, town on Black Sea 130 mi (210 km) e. of Istanbul; coal mines, *map* P-212
Eremitic monasticism M-540
Eremurus (or desert candle), a genus of perennial plants of the lily family native to Asia; these desert plants grow to 8 ft (2.4 m); have long, narrow leaves and a long spike of rose, yellow, or white star-shaped flowers; also called foxtail lily.
Erevan, Armenian Soviet Socialist Republic. *see in index* Erivan
Erfurt, East Germany, city 70 mi (110 km) s.w. of Leipzig; flowers, vegetables, seeds; had famous university; pop. 195,994, *maps* E-360, G-131
Erg, desert formation D-105
Sahara S-15
Erg, in physics, work done when a force of one dyne acts through one centimeter of distance
quantum theory Q-5
Ergonomics E-223
machine M-9
Ergosterol, a substance isolated from vegetable fats (and also found in the body) from which vitamin D can be produced by irradiation with ultraviolet light
vitamin D V-356
Ergot, rye fungus F-450, R-366b
hallucinogen H-18
Erhard, Ludwig (1897–1977), German economist and political leader, chancellor of West Germany E-296
Germany G-126
Kiesinger K-236
'Erh ya', one of the Confucian Classics C-387
Ericaceae. *see in index* Heath
Ericson, Leif (or Leif Ericsson) (11th century), Norse mariner and adventurer E-297
Vinland A-328, C-89
Ericsson, John (1803–89), U.S. inventor and engineer E-297
Monitor C-480
navy N-83
Nobel N-329
Eric the Red (10th century), Norse navigator E-297
Greenland G-282
Eridanus, ancient name of river Po
Phaëthon myth P-248
Eridanus, constellation, *charts* S-417, 421, C-682
Eridu, ancient city of Mesopotamia (Iraq); originally built on Persian Gulf but now 120 mi (190 km) s.w. of Ur; famous archaeological excavations 1855 and 1918; most important finding, a brick stamp of 8th king of Larsa, Nur-Adab, which aided historical identification of city.
Erie, an Indian tribe of North America who formerly lived in New York, Pennsylvania, and Ohio; in war with the Iroquois, 1654–56, most of those not killed were absorbed by the Six Nations and the rest dispersed, *map* I-136, *table* I-138
Erie, Pa., lake port in extreme n.w.; pop. 119,123 E-298
North America, *map* N-350
Pennsylvania, *maps* P-165, 174, 184, U-41
Erie, Lake, shallowest and stormiest of the Great Lakes; area 9,910 sq mi (25,670 sq km) E-297
Great Lakes G-243, *maps* G-245, N-350
Michigan M-358
Detroit D-120
New York N-245
Pennsylvania P-167, *picture* P-168
pollution P-441c
Welland Ship Canal. *see in index* Welland Ship Canal
Erie Canal, N.Y., now included in New York State Barge Canal system G-247
canals C-128, *map* C-126
Cleveland C-495
Michigan M-357, 361
Detroit D-123
New York N-252
opening ceremony, *picture* U-175
transportation T-253, 261
Erie Railroad Company, United States
Gould G-197
Erie triangle, section of Pennsylvania claimed by New York and Massachusetts P-172
Erigena, Johannes Scotus (800?–877?), medieval Irish philosopher and theologian (later branded as heretic); head, under Charles the Bald, of the palace school founded by Charlemagne L-78
Erigeron, plant genus. *see in index* Fleabane
Eriha, Jordan. *see in index* Jericho
Erikson, Erik Homburg (born 1902), U.S. psychoanalyst and educator, born in Frankfurt, Germany; applied Freudian theory to child behavior; professor University of California 1939–51, Harvard University 1960–70 ('Childhood and Society'; 'Young Man Luther'; 'Identity: Youth and Crisis'; 'Life History and the Historical Moment').
Erin, ancient name for Ireland, now used poetically. *see in index* Ireland
Erinus, a perennial plant *Erinus alpinus* of figwort family, native to mountainous regions of Europe; grows 3 to 4 in. (8 to 10 cm) high; leaves spoon-shaped; flowers purple; used in rock gardens.
ERISA. *see in index* Employment Retirement Income Security Act
Eritrea, province of Ethiopia; 48,000 sq mi (124,000 sq km); former Italian colony, lost by Paris treaty 1947; pop. 1,889,700 E-315, *map* A-115
Erivan (also called Erevan), Armenian Soviet Socialist Republic, capital, 110 mi (180 km) s. of Tbilisi; connected with Tbilisi by railway; pop. 767,000, *maps* E-360, R-344, 349
Erlanger, Joseph (1874–1965), U.S. physiologist, author, born in San Francisco, Calif.; taught at Johns Hopkins University 1900–06, University of Wisconsin 1906–10, Washington University, St. Louis, 1910–46. *see also in index* Nobel Prizewinners, *table*
Erlanger, Ky., city 7 mi (11 km) s.w. of Covington, in n. of state; industrial controls, fabricated metal products; dairy products; pop. 14,433.
Erl-king (or Erlkönig), in Teutonic folklore, the king of the elves who was said to haunt the Black Forest and prepare mischief for children; subject of a poem by Goethe (set to music by Franz Schubert and translated by Sir Walter Scott) S-55
Ermine (or stoat), carnivorous mammal *Mustela erminea*; valued for winter fur; found in Europe, Asia, North America W-114
fur, *table* F-464
Ermine, heraldic fur, *picture* H-136
'Ernani', opera by Verdi V-282. *see also in index* 'Hernani'
Erne, name of river in Ireland and Northern Ireland; also name of two lakes (Upper Lough Erne and Lower Lough Erne) that are connected by the river.
Ernest Augustus (1771–1851), king of Hanover, duke of Cumberland, 5th son of George III of England, born in Kew, England; succeeded to Hanoverian throne 1837 instead of Queen Victoria (males alone being eligible), thus separating English and Hanoverian crowns after personal union of over 100 years; abolished Hanoverian

constitution; unpopular in both countries.

Ernst, Max (1891–1976), French painter, illustrator, and sculptor, born in Brühl, near Cologne, Germany; active in Dadaist movement; in Paris after 1922, where he was member of surrealist group; in United States 1941, became citizen 1948; citizen of France from 1958.

'Eroica', work by Beethoven M-672

Eros, Greek name for Cupid. *see in index* Cupid

Eros, asteroid A-706, 716

Erosion, gradual wearing away of land surfaces, *picture* S-250
- agriculture
  - conservation techniques C-673
- Bad Lands S-322, *picture* S-330
- canyon. *see in index* Canyon
- earth E-13, 31
- ecology, *picture* E-53
- food supply F-285
- forests F-315
- glacial G-151
- Mars P-353
- Niagra Falls N-302
- oceanography O-486
- rivers R-210
- sand S-249
- soil
  - Greece G-258
- valley V-256
- volcanic cones V-378
- willow W-211
- wind W-220

ERP. *see in index* European Recovery Program

Errol, Leon, U.S. comedian, *picture* F-80

Ersatz materials, substitutes for natural raw materials; term applied to many synthetic products, including foods, fuels, and textiles.

Erse (corruption of word Irish), name given to Scottish Highlanders and their language, also to Irish Gaelic.

Erskine, John (1879–1951), U.S. author, pianist, educator, born in New York, N.Y.; taught English literature at Amherst College and Columbia University; at Columbia established honors course that grew into Great Books program; later director Juilliard School of Music; satiric novels ('The Private Life of Helen of Troy'; 'Adam and Eve'); also poetry, essays, literary criticism, autobiography.

Erskine College, Due West, S.C.; affiliated with Associate Reformed Presbyterian church; established in 1839; arts and sciences; seminary for men only.

ERTS (or Earth Resources Technology Satellite), *table* S-344

Erubescite. *see in index* Bornite

Eruptions, volcanic. *see in index* Volcanoes

Ervin, Samuel James, Jr. (1896–1985), U.S. political leader, born in Morganton, N.C.; member North Carolina General Assembly 1923–27, 1931–33; judge Burke County Criminal Court 1935–37, North Carolina Superior Court 1937–43; U.S. representative 1946–47; associate justice North Carolina Supreme Court 1948–54; U.S. senator 1954–75; chairman Select Committee to Investigate 1972 Presidential Campaign Activities (Watergate case) 1973.

Ervine, St. John Greer (1883–1971), Irish writer, born in Belfast; manager of Abbey Theatre, Dublin, 1915 (plays: 'John Ferguson', 'The First Mrs. Fraser'; novels: 'Mrs. Martin's Man', 'The Wayward Man'; biographies: 'Parnell', 'Bernard Shaw').

Erving, Julius (full name Julius Winfield Erving, nickname Dr. J.) (born 1950), U.S. basketball player E-298

Erymanthian boar, mythological creature H-138

Eryngium, plant genus. *see in index* Sea holly

Erysimum (or blistercress), genus of annual and perennial plants of the mustard family, native to the north temperate zone; related to wallflowers and stocks; small orange, yellow, or purple fragrant flowers; coast wallflower *E. capitatum*; fairy wallflower *E. perofskianum*.

Erysipelas, streptococcal infection of the skin often characterized by red swellings on face and scalp; treated with antibiotics.

Erytheia, in Greek mythology, island beyond the Strait of Gibraltar; home of the monster Geryon H-138

Erythrina (or coral tree), genus of plants, shrubs, and trees of the pea family, native to tropics; all are thorny, with showy red or yellow flowers in clusters; seeds in twisted pods; cockspur coral tree *E. christa-galli*; bucare *E. poeppigiana*, which grows to 60 ft (18 m), used for shading coffee and cacao plantings; seeds of some used as medicines and poisons; flowers cooked and eaten.

Erythrocytes. *see in index* Red cells

Erzberger, Matthias (1875–1921), German political leader, born in Buttenhausen, s.w. Germany; leader of Democratic Catholic party in Reichstag; secretary of state without portfolio 1918; negotiated armistice and peace terms World War I; finance minister 1919; assassinated.

Erzerum. *see in index* Erzurum

Erzgebirge (or Ore Mountains), on border of East Germany and n.w. Czechoslovakia; range about 100 mi (160 km) long; heavily mined G-111, *map* G-131

'Erziehung des Menschengeschlechts, Die,' (translated 'The Education of the Human Race'), work by Lessing L-138

Erzurum (formerly Erzerum), Turkey, ancient city in Armenia; trade in barley, wheat, potatoes; capture by Russians in World War I (Feb. 1916) ended projected Turkish invasion of Egypt; pop. 90,069, *map* A-697

Es (or Einsteinium), chemical element, *tables* P-207

Esaki, Leo (born 1925), Japanese physicist, born in Osaka; while working for Sony Corporation developed tunnel diode that enables electric current to pass through electronic barriers; consultant to IBM's Thomas J. Watson Research Center in U.S. *see also in index* Nobel Prizewinners, *table*

Esarhaddon (died 668 BC), king of Assyria; son of Sennacherib and father of Assurbanipal; brought Egypt under Assyrian rule, rebuilt Babylon B-9

Esau, son of Isaac and Rebekah and elder twin brother of Jacob, sold his birthright to his brother for a mess of pottage and was cheated by Jacob (Bible, Gen. xxv, xxvii).

Esbjerg, Denmark, seaport on w. coast of Jutland; submarine cable connects with Calais; pop. 55,171 D-97, *maps* D-100, E-360

Escalante, Silvestre Vélez de, 18th-century Spanish Franciscan missionary and explorer; dispatched (1775) by governor of New Mexico to investigate Moqui (Hopi) tribes; traveled from Zuni to Grand Canyon; next year undertook to survey route between Santa Fe and Monterey, Calif.; went n.w. to Utah Lake, thence 200 mi (320 km) w. across desert; winter forced return by way of Zuni; diary and reports valued by historians
- explorations C-586, U-219, 221, *map* U-176

Escalator E-186

Escalibur (or Excalibur), King Arthur's sword A-655

Escanaba, Mich., city on Upper Peninsula, on inlet of Green Bay; lumber, veneers, paper, machinery, metal products; summer resort; good harbor; pop. 14,355, *picture* M-357

Escanaba River, Michigan, rises in n.w. part of Upper Peninsula and flows s.e. about 100 mi (160 km), emptying into Green Bay at Escanaba, Mich. M-355

Escapement, watches and clocks W-78, *picture* W-81

Escape velocity (or parabolic velocity) S-343, *list* S-341b

Escape wheel, watches and clocks W-78

Escarpment, in geology, steep face of cliff, usually caused by erosion or by prehistoric changes in the water line
- waterfall W-96

Escaut. *see in index* Scheldt

Eschenbach, Wolfram von. *see in index* Wolfram von Eschenbach

Escher, M.C. (1898–1971), Dutch graphic artist, *picture* M-216

Eschscholtzia californica, California poppy P-446

Esch-sur-Alzette, Luxembourg L-340

Escondido, Calif., city 28 mi (45 km) n.e. of San Diego; located in a farming valley; vineyards; produce includes avocados and citrus fruit; electronic equipment, chemicals; pop. 62,480.

Escorial, near Madrid, Spain, *picture* S-360

Escrow, in law
- definition, *table* L-92
- housing, *list* H-305

Escrow agent, in housing H-295

Escudo, monetary unit of Guinea-Bissau, Mozambique, and Portugal, historic value of Portuguese escudo $1.08.

Escutcheon, in heraldry H-135

Esdraelon, Plain of (also called Emek), Israel, the greatest plain in the country; fertile, level, bounded by Mt. Carmel on w., Mt. Gilboa on s.e., highlands of Galilee on n.; battlefield in all ages P-80

Esenin, Sergei Aleksandrovich (1895–1925), Soviet poet, born near Moscow; considered poet laureate of the Russian Revolution R-360a

Esfahan (or Isfahan, or Gabae), Iran; a major textile center; modern industries include steelmaking and petroleum refining; pop. 661,510 I-306, *maps* A-697, I-312

Eshkol, Levi (born Levi Shkolnik) (1895–1969), Israeli political leader, born in Oratova, Ukraine; settled in Palestine 1914; active in Zionist movement; minister of finance 1952–63; minister of defense 1963–67; prime minister 1963–69.

Esker, glacial mound I-6

Eskimo (or Inuit), people of the Arctic regions E-299, *picture* M-628
- Alaska A-572
- American Indians I-116, 137, 156, *map* I-136, *table* I-138
- bow drill, *picture* U-95
- Canada C-76
  - Newfoundland N-167
  - Northwest Territories N-388
- clothing C-506, *pictures* C-505, U-95
- folktales, *list* S-481d, *picture* S-479
- Greenland G-282
- hunting customs
  - seal S-98, *picture* S-99
- North America N-337, 344
- physical classification, *chart* R-26
- reindeer R-139
- shelter S-156, S-228, *pictures* S-155, U-95
- ventriloquism V-279

Eskimo curlew. *see in index* Curlew

Esmeralda, character in Victor Hugo's 'Notre Dame de Paris', a beautiful street dancer of Paris (supposedly a Gypsy) who is accused of witchcraft, is hidden from her accusers in the belfry of Notre Dame Cathedral by the hunchback bell ringer Quasimodo, but is finally executed, *picture* N-410

Esophageal speech V-377

Esophagus (or gullet), muscular tube from mouth to stomach S-454
- human digestive system D-144, *diagram* D-143
- pouter pigeon P-324
- throat T-176

ESP. *see in index* Extrasensory perception

Espartero, Baldomero (1792–1879), Spanish soldier and statesman, born in Granátula, near Ciudad Real; conspicuous for successes against Carlists 1836–40; then for three years regent for Isabella, child queen; retired from public life 1856; modest man of strongly liberal tendencies.

Esparto grass (or alfa plant), a fibrous grass, native to n. Africa and s. Spain; used for mats, baskets, rope, sandals, and in papermaking.

Espejo, Antonio de, 16th-century Spanish merchant-explorer; his journeys in n. Arizona (1582) and discovery of rich mines while searching for a lake of gold spurred prospectors and inspired Oñate's trip 20 years later.

Esperanto, international language L-39

Esperey, Louis Franchet d'. *see in index* Franchet d' Esperey

Espina de Serna, Concha (1877–1955), Spanish novelist, born in Santander ('Mariflor'; 'Altar Mayor'; 'The Woman and the Sea').

Espinel, Vicente (1550?–1624), Spanish writer and musician
- stringed instruments S-492

Espionage, the secret gathering of information about a rival E-302. *see also in index* Spy
- East Germany G-127
- Hitler H-175
- West Germany G-126

Espírito Santo, small state of Brazil, on s.e. coast; 15,281 sq mi (39,577 sq km); cap. Vitória; pop. 2,063,679, *map* B-425

'Espolio', painting by El Greco G-253

Esposito, Phil (full name Philip Anthony Esposito) (born 1942), Canadian ice-hockey player, born in Sault Ste. Marie, Ont.; center with Chicago Black Hawks 1963–67, Boston Bruins 1967–76, New York Rangers 1976–81; set scoring records; brother of Tony Esposito, *picture* H-195

Esposito, Tony (full name Anthony James Esposito) (born 1943), Canadian ice-hockey player, born in Sault Ste. Marie, Ont.; goalie with Montreal Canadiens 1968–69, Chicago Black Hawks 1969–84; trophy winner; brother of Phil Esposito.

Espresso, coffee C-537

'Esprit des lois, L' ', work by Montesquieu. *see in index* 'Spirit of Laws, The'

Espy, James Pollard (1785–1860), U.S. meteorologist, born in Westmoreland County, Pennsylvania; instituted telegraphic weather bulletins; appointed meteorologist to U.S. War Department 1842, later to Navy Department; laid foundation of present U.S. Weather Bureau; published 'Philosophy of Storms'.

Esquiline Hill, highest of the seven hills of Rome R-254

Esquire. *see in index* Squire

ESRO. *see in index* European Space Research Organization

ESSA (Environmental Survey Satellite), *picture* S-343

Essad Pasha, (1863–1920), Turkish soldier, bandit, and provisional president of Albania (1914); killed in Paris.

'Essais', work by Montaigne E-306

Essaouira (or Mogador), Morocco, seaport on Atlantic; fish processing, tanning, palm-fiber working; pop. 30,061, *map* A-115

Essay, form of writing E-306
- American A-345
- Lamb L-26
- Montaigne F-395, M-549

'Essay Concerning Human Understanding', work by Locke L-278

'Essay on Criticism', poem by Pope P-445

'Essay on Man', poem by Pope P-445

'Essay on Projects', work by Defoe D-64

'Essay on the Principle of Population', work by Malthus M-79
- Darwin D-38
- food supply F-286

'Essays, Moral and Political', work by Hume H-321

'Essays of Elia, The', collection of works by Lamb L-26
- essay E-306

Essen, West Germany, industrial center in Ruhr valley; pop. 628,800 E-306
Germany G-112, *maps* E-360, G-131
'Essence of the Novel, The' (or 'Shosetsu shinzui'), work by Shoyo Tsubouchi J-82
Essenes, Judaic religious sect A-531, D-46, P-143b
Essentialist. *see in index* Conservative
Essential oils, volatile, odoriferous oils F-48
perfumes P-203
spices S-380
'Essentials of the Three Treatises', work by Kobo Daishi K-266
Essequibo, largest river of Guyana, South America; about 600 mi (970 km) long; flows into Atlantic by estuary 20 mi (30 km) wide, *map* S-298
Essex, Robert Devereux, 2nd **earl of** (1566?–1601), English soldier and courtier, born in Netherwood, Herefordshire; favorite of Queen Elizabeth I; won distinction in war with Spain; later fell into disfavor, tried to incite insurrection, was executed for treason
Elizabeth I E-191
Essex, Robert Devereux, 3rd **earl of** (1591–1646), English general, born in London; son of 2nd earl; commander of Parliamentary forces 1642–45 in Civil War.
Essex, ancient kingdom of the East Saxons in England; conquered by Egbert, king of Wessex, and became part of Wessex.
Essex, maritime county in s.e. England; 1,528 sq mi (3,958 sq km); cap. Chelmsford; grazing, wheat, and barley; extensive manufactures; included in kingdom of East Saxons, pop. 2,288,058.
Essex, Md., community 7 mi (11 km) n.e. of Baltimore; clothing, tractors, pop. 39,614, *map* M-182
Essex, Vt., town 7 mi (11 km) n.e. of Winooski, includes industrial village of Essex Junction; town chartered 1763, pop. of township 14,392, *map* V-301
'Essex', U.S. frigate F-37, S-177g
Essex Junction, Vt., village on Winooski River, e. of Burlington; railroad center, pop. 6,511, *map* V-301
Essex Junto, U.S. group of Federalist leaders, including Timothy Pickering, Fisher Ames, George Cabot, and some of the Lowell family, living in Essex County, Mass.; accused by John Adams of being a British faction; opposed war with England in 1812.
Essling, Austria, former village on Danube River, 7 mi (11 km) e. of central Vienna; now part of Vienna.
Estaing, Jean Baptiste Charles Henri Hector, comte d' (1729–94), French admiral, born in Auvergne; served first in army, later in navy; aided U.S. against England in Revolutionary War; active in French Revolution; executed because of sympathy with Marie Antoinette.
Estancia, Spanish-American term for a cattle ranch S-286, *picture* S-281b
Argentina A-582
Estate, in law, a person's entire property, more particularly property left at death; an estate is said to be closed when the decedent's will has been carried out, or when, if no will was left, the estate has been divided in accordance with state laws E-307
definition, *table* L-92
taxation T-38
Estate law E-307
Estates-General, former representative assembly of France E-307
democracy D-93
French revolt F-401
Louis XVI L-306
Robespierre R-223
Este, House of, old and illustrious family of Italy, capital at Ferrara; famous for political importance and splendid court; encouraged poets, painters, and scholars; **Alberto Azzo II** (11th century) was common ancestor both of House of Este and of House of Guelf, to which the British royal House of Hanover belonged; **Alfonso d'Este** (1476–1534), duke of Ferrara, husband of Lucretia Borgia, was patron of Tasso A-368, A-588
Tasso T-33
Ester, one of a large group of liquid and solid compounds formed by reaction of an acid and an alcohol with elimination of water; for example, acetic acid (CH_3COOH) plus methyl alcohol (CH_3OH) gives the ester, methyl acetate ($CH_3CO_2CH_3$) plus water(H_2O); most oils, fats, and waxes are esters; so are many plastics F-47
fibers F-72
organic chemistry O-604, *diagram* O-603
wax W-110
Esterházy, noble Hungarian family of ancient origin, members of which have held prominent places in Hungarian history down to recent times; **Prince Nicholas Esterházy** (1765–1833), patron of the arts, friend of Haydn, refused Napoleon's offer of crown of Hungary
Haydn H-75
classical music M-669
Liszt L-239
Esterhazy, Ferdinand Walsin, (1847–1923), French army officer who was chief figure in the Dreyfus Case D-272
Esterhazy, Sask., town 42 mi (68 km) s.e. of Yorkton; established by Hungarians 1886; pop. 3,065, *map* S-491
potash mine S-49e
Estes, Eleanor (born 1906), U.S. writer of children's books, born in West Haven, Conn. ('The Moffats'; 'The Middle Moffat'; 'Rufus M'; 'The Hundred Dresses'; 'Ginger Pye', winner of Newbery Medal 1952; 'A Little Oven'; 'Pinky Pye'; 'The Witch Family'; 'The Alley'; 'Miranda the Great'; 'The Tunnel of Hugsy Goode')
'The Moffats' R-110a
Estes Park, Colo., town located in valley at e. entrance to Rocky Mountain National Park; tourist center and summer resort; pop. 2,703.
Estevan (also called Estevanico) (died 1539), African explorer; slave with ill-fated Narváez expedition reaching Florida 1528; worked way to n. Mexico by 1536; discovered Zuñi pueblo in New Mexico 1539 A-601, B-289
Estevan, Sask., city in s.e., near North Dakota border; petroleum and coal-mining center; meat and dairy products; pop. 9,523 S-49h, *maps* C-112, S-49l
Estevan Point, on Vancouver Island, British Columbia; situated in the Canadian Rockies; wettest point of Canada with more than 120 in (300 cm) of precipitation each year C-74
Estey, Willard Z. (born 1919), Canadian jurist, born in Saskatoon, Sask.; private law practice 1947–72; judge of court of appeals, and of high court of Ontario 1973–76; chief justice of Ontario 1976; judge of the Supreme Court of Canada 1977–.
Esther, heroine of the Bible's book of this name
folklore F-263
Purim J-150
Esthetics, branch of philosophy. *see in index* Aesthetics
'Esther', work by Handel H-28
Estienne, Henri (sometimes called Étienne, or Latin Stephanus) (1460?–1520), French printer, founder of the family that was supreme in printing for three generations; after his death his foreman, Simon de Colines, married his widow and continued the business T-337
Estienne, Henri (1528–98), French author, editor, and printer, son of Robert; compiled great Greek thesaurus, still used; wrote 'An Apology for Herodotus', bitter satire on contemporary life; his writings important in standardizing literary French.
Estienne, Robert (1503–59), French printer and scholar, son of the first Henri; noted for editions of Greek classics and for magnificent Greek New Testaments (1546 in 16mo, 1550 in folio) that remained the accepted text for three centuries.
Estigarribia, José Félix (1888–1940), Paraguayan general and statesman, born in Caraguatay, Paraguay; leader and hero of the Chaco War; minister to U.S. 1938–39; president of Paraguay 1939–40; self-proclaimed dictator 1940 C-263
Estivation. *see in index* Aestivation
Estonian Soviet Socialist Republic (formerly Estonia), U.S.S.R., on Baltic Sea; area 17,370 sq mi (44,990 sq km); cap. Tallinn; pop. 1,507,000 E-308, U-14, *maps* R-325, 344, 348, U-14
Europe, *map* E-360
folktales, *list* S-481
Estournelles de Constant de Rebecque, Paul Henri Benjamin Balluat, baron d' (1852–1924), French diplomat, born in La Flèche; founded French parliamentary group for voluntary arbitration. *see also in index* Nobel Prizewinners, *table*
Estremadura, province located on the coast of central Portugal; 2,062 sq mi (5,341 sq km); Lisbon capital of both province and nation; pop. 1,806,383.
Estremadura, region in w.-central Spain; about 16,000 sq mi (41,400 sq km); agriculture (livestock, olives, grapes, wheat, barley) and mining (phosphate, lead, iron, zinc, tin, copper).
Estrogen, hormone group that causes menstruation and controls development of secondary female characteristics; secreted primarily by ovaries; also made synthetically; used in treatment of prostate cancer and disorders of menstruation and menopause; ingredient in birth control pills; produces estrus in animals
adolescence growth rate A-47
bone injuries B-342
hormones H-243, *table* H-241, *diagram* H-242
menstruation M-300
Estrus (or heat), period when a female mammal is receptive to mating; prior changes in sex hormone concentration trigger growth of the egg-bearing follicles in the ovaries; during estrus, sexual intercourse ensues and eggs are released for fertilization.
Estuary, widened mouth of a river where it joins the sea; may be caused by the current of the stream and tidal action or may be a submerged section of a river valley R-211
delta D-90
Etah, Eskimo (Inuit) settlement on n.w. coast of Greenland, n. of Thule Air Base; known as base for Arctic expeditions.
Etchemin. *see in index* Malecite
Etching. *see in index* Engraving and etching
Eternal City. *see in index* Rome
Eternal Light, peace memorial at Gettysburg, Pa. G-137
Etesian wind (or meltemi) W-225
Greece G-255
'Ethan Allen', U.S. Polaris submarine, *picture* S-499
Ethane, colorless and odorless gaseous compound of hydrogen and carbon (C_2H_6); forms ethyl radical in chemical combinations. *see also in index* Paraffin series
alcohol A-275
natural gas G-38
organic chemistry, *diagrams* O-602, 603
petrochemicals P-228
'Ethan Frome', work by Wharton W-186
Ethanol. *see in index* Ethyl alcohol
Ethchlorvynol (or Placidyl), a sedative N-19
Ethelbald (or Aethelbald) (died 860), king of Wessex 858–60; eldest brother of Alfred the Great.
Ethelbert (or Aethelberht) (552?–616), king of Kent 560–616, bretwalda or overlord over all the English s. of the Humber, and author of the first written English laws
England E-238
St. Augustine A-761
Ethelbert (or Aethelberht) (died AD 866), king of Wessex 860–65; son of Ethelwulf and brother of Alfred the Great.
Etheldreda (also spelled Aethelthryth, or Saint Awdrey), daughter of king of East Anglia and wife of king of Northumbria; founded religious house at Ely AD 673; her festival became occasion for annual large fair at which cheap, trifling objects were sold, whence came the word tawdry, a contraction of St. Awdrey; festival observed in Roman Catholicism June 23, in Anglican Church Oct. 17.
Ethelfleda (or Aethelflaed) (died 917?), eldest daughter of Alfred the Great, wife of the earl of Mercia.
Ethelred (or Aethelred), king of Wessex and Kent 865–71, brother of Alfred the Great.
Ethelred the Unready (968?–1016), king of the English 978–1016; his marriage with Norman princess Emma opened distinct policy that led to the Norman conquest of England E-239
'Ethel Scull Thirty-six Times', painting by Warhol P-66, *picture* P-67
Ethelwulf (or Aethelwulf) (died 858), king of the West Saxons 839–58, father of Alfred the Great; successfully repulsed a Danish invasion.
Ether, any of the light, volatile, highly flammable liquids made by action of sulfuric acid on alcohol; used in industry as solvent for fats and oils
anesthetic A-413
hospital H-280
Long L-295
organic chemistry O-604, *diagram* O-603
Ether, in physics
Aristotle's view U-198
drift experiment R-140
Michelson-Morley experiment M-353
Etherege, Sir George (1635?–91), English dramatist, first important figure in Restoration comedy; originated comedy of intrigue ('The Comical Revenge: or, Love in a Tub'; 'She Wou'd, if She Cou'd'; 'The Man of Mode: or, Sir Fopling Flutter').
Ethical absolutism E-310
Ethical culture, movement inaugurated by the founding of New York Society for Ethical Culture by Felix Adler in 1876; two federations have been formed, the American Ethical Union, organized in 1886, composed of ethical societies in seven U.S. cities, and the International Ethical Union, organized in 1896; affirming the supremacy of moral law and seeking social reforms, the societies have pioneered in areas such as progressive education, settlement work, housing, etc.
Ethical relativity E-310
Ethics and morality E-309, P-263, 266
sociology S-243
sportsmanship. *see in index* Sportsmanship
Zoroastrianism and Parsiism Z-471
Ethiopia (full name Socialist Ethiopia, formerly Abyssinia), nation in n.e. Africa, formerly an empire; 457,267 sq mi (1,184,316 sq km); cap. Addis Ababa; pop. 42,019,418 E-311, *maps* A-115, W-297
African independence A-111, *table* A-112
cities. *see also in index* city listed below and other cities by names
Addis Ababa A-40
communist world, *map* C-619
education
illiteracy P-450
flag F-161, *picture* F-164
food supply F-285
fossil findings F-326
genealogy G-47
history
Africa's independence A-110
ancient Egypt E-126
Italy I-395
Mussolini W-321
Korean War losses, *table* K-296
Menelik II M-298
literature
folktales S-478
national anthem, *table* N-64
transportation

MEMBERSHIP IN PRINCIPAL EUROPEAN ORGANIZATIONS*

Austria	CE		EFTA			OECD	
Belgium	CE	EEC		NATO		OECD	
Bulgaria							WTO
Cyprus	CE	EEC†					
Czechoslovakia							WTO
Denmark	CE	EEC		NATO	NC	OECD	
Finland			EFTA†		NC	OECD	
France	CE	EEC		NATO		OECD	
Germany, East							WTO
Germany, West	CE	EEC		NATO		OECD	
Greece	CE	EEC		NATO		OECD	
Hungary							WTO
Iceland	CE		EFTA	NATO	NC	OECD	
Ireland	CE	EEC				OECD	
Italy	CE	EEC		NATO		OECD	
Liechtenstein	CE		EFTA‡				
Luxembourg	CE	EEC		NATO		OECD	
Malta	CE	EEC†					
Netherlands	CE	EEC		NATO		OECD	
Norway	CE		EFTA	NATO	NC	OECD	
Poland							WTO
Portugal	CE	EEC		NATO		OECD	
Romania							WTO
Soviet Union							WTO
Spain	CE	EEC		NATO		OECD	
Sweden	CE		EFTA		NC	OECD	
Switzerland	CE		EFTA			OECD	
Turkey	CE	EEC†		NATO		OECD	
United Kingdom	CE	EEC		NATO		OECD	
Yugoslavia						OECD‡	

KEY TO ORGANIZATIONS
CE—Council of Europe
EEC—European Economic Community (Common Market)
EFTA—European Free Trade Association
NATO—North Atlantic Treaty Organization
NC—Nordic Council
OECD—Organization for Economic Cooperation and Development
WTO—Warsaw Treaty Organization

*Only European members are listed
†Associate member
‡Special status

Eurypterids (also called sea scorpions), class of extinct arthropods, related to the scorpions; abundant during the Silurian period
earth E-23

Eurystheus, mythological figure; cousin of Hercules who made him perform the famed 12 labors H-138

Eusden, Laurence (1688–1730), English poet, born in Spofforth, near Leeds; chiefly remembered for Alexander Pope's satirical allusions to him; poet laureate 1718–30
poet laureate P-402

Eusebius of Caesarea (also called Pamphili) (260?–340?), Christian theologian, most learned man of his age; 'History of the Christian Church', most important ancient record of church; called Father of Church History; chief figure at Council of Nicaea B-185
Byzantine literature G-279
history writing H-172

Eusebius of Nicomedia (called the Great) (died AD 341?), leading defender of Arius, and after death of Arius leader of his party; a politician rather than a theologian; banished from his see; pardoned through sister of Constantine; promoted to bishop of Nicomedia and later of Constantinople.

Eustachi, Bartolomeo (died 1574), Italian anatomist, born near Ancona; described various structures in human body, including Eustachian tube, which was named for him.

Eustachian tube, connection between throat and middle ear E-4, T-176

Eutaw Springs, battle in Revolutionary War 1781, led British to abandon South Carolina; near Santee River, 60 mi (100 km) n.w. of Charleston; Americans led by Greene and Marion, British by Stuart
flag F-154, *picture* F-155

Euthanasia (or mercy killing), painless death, also painless killing, especially of a person or animal suffering from an incurable disease.

Eutrophication, process of aging and eventual drying up of a lake
pollution P-441c, *diagram* P-441d

Eva, character in 'Uncle Tom's Cabin' by Harriet Beecher Stowe, beautiful, affectionate, and exceedingly good child, daughter of Uncle Tom's master, Augustin St. Clare.

EVA. *see in index* Extravehicular activity

Evangel College, Springfield, Mo.; affiliated with Assemblies of God; opened 1955; arts and sciences, education, music.

Evangelical Adventists, religion A-53

Evangelical Alliance, association of members of Protestant churches organized in London 1846; extended to many other countries; U.S. branch organized 1867; purpose to strengthen Protestantism and to promote religious interest.

Evangelical and Reformed church, established 1934; formed by union of Evangelical Synod of North America (which originated with a synod organized at Gravois Settlement, Mo., 1840) and the Reformed church in the United States (established 1725 near Philadelphia, Pa.); accepts Bible as ultimate rule of life and faith; in 1957 united with the General Council of the Congregational and Christian churches to form the United Church of Christ.

Evangelical church, Christian religious body, formerly the Evangelical Association, founded among German-speaking people in Pennsylvania about 1800 by Jacob Albright, former Methodist; in 1946 united with United Brethren in Christ to become the Evangelical United Brethren church; in 1968 merged with Methodist church to form United Methodist church; until 1894 included Evangelical Congregational church, formerly United Evangelical church.
Methodism M-319

Evangelical United Brethren church. *see in index* Evangelical church; United Brethren in Christ

Evangeline, heroine of Longfellow's poem of that name
American verse A-348
deportation of Acadians A-14
Longfellow L-296
Nova Scotia N-397

Evangelists, writers of the Bible's New Testament Gospels of Matthew, Mark, Luke, and John.

Evans, Sir Arthur John (1851–1941), English archaeologist, born in Nash Mills, Hertfordshire; knighted 1911; noted for excavations on Aegean civilization ('Palace of Minos'; 'Scripta Minoa')
Aegean civilization A-61
Cretan excavations A-537, C-763
linear script's discovery A-62

Evans, Bergen Baldwin (1904–78), U.S. educator and author, born in Franklin, Ohio; on faculty at Northwestern University 1932–75, professor 1942–75; moderator of TV programs 'Down You Go' and 'The Last Word' ('The Natural History of Nonsense'; collected and arranged 'Dictionary of Quotations').

Evans, Chick (full name Charles Evans, Jr.) (1890–1979), U.S. golfer, born in Indianapolis, Ind.; founder of Evans Scholars Foundation 1930 G-189

Evans, Edward Ratcliffe Garth Russell, first Baron Mountevans (1881–1957), British naval officer and explorer, born in London; member of British Antarctic Expedition, assumed command after Robert Falcon Scott's death; served in World War I; author 'Keeping the Seas', 'South with Scott', and 'Man of the White South'.

Evans, Herbert McLean (1882–1971), U.S. anatomist and embryologist, born in Modesto, Calif.; discovered vitamin E; research in reproduction and in endocrinology.

Evans, James (1801–46), Canadian Methodist missionary, born in Kingston-upon-Hull, England; went to Canada in 1823; served among Indians on St. Clair River and Lake Superior; became general superintendent of Northwest Indian Missions 1840; invented syllabic character still used by Crees.

Evans, Mary Ann (or Marian Evans). *see in index* Eliot, George

Evans, Maurice (born 1901), U.S. actor, manager, born in Dorset, England; first appeared in United States 1935, became citizen 1941; best known for Shakespearean acting; won 1961 Emmy for 'Macbeth', *picture* S-140

Evans, Oliver (1755–1819), U.S. inventor, born in Newport, Del.; invented machine for making teeth for carding machines, machinery for flour mills, the first high-pressure steam engine, and a steam dredge I-182, R-73

Evans, Robley Dunglison (or Fighting Bob Evans) (1846–1912), U.S. Navy officer, born in Floyd Court House, Va.; ordered to Chile 1891, and with gunboat *Yorktown* defied Chilean navy; in 1898, at Santiago, his ship *Iowa* fired first gun at Cervera's fleet; rear admiral 1901; chosen commander in chief U.S. fleet 1907.

Evans, Ronald E. (born 1933), U.S. astronaut, born in St. Francis, Kan.; U.S. Navy officer chosen for NASA program 1966, *table* S-348

Evans, William George (or Billy) (1884–1956), U.S. baseball umpire and executive, born in Chicago, Ill.; umpire, A.L., 1906–27; general manager Cleveland, A.L., 1927–35; farm director Boston, A.L., 1936–40; president Southern Association 1942–46; vice-president and general manager Detroit, A.L., 1946–51; baseball columnist.

Evanston, Ill., residential city just n. of Chicago; electronic and photocopy equipment, hospital supplies; Northwestern University; National College of Education; world headquarters Rotary International; national headquarters Woman's Christian Temperance Union; pop. 73,706, *picture* L-176, *map* I-52

Evanston, Wyo., town near s.w. corner of state; railroad center in farm area; Wyoming State Mental Institution; pop. 6,421.

Evansville, Ind., city on Ohio River, in s.w. corner; pop. 130,496 E-363, I-91, *picture* I-90, *maps* I-102, N-350

Evansville, University of, Evansville, Ind.; Methodist; founded 1854 at Moores Hill, Ind.; moved to Evansville 1919; arts and sciences, business administration, education, engineering, fine arts, and nursing; graduate studies.

Evaporated milk M-415, *list* D-6

Evaporation
air conditioner A-150
conservation C-672
flood control F-184
ink I-207
rainfall R-88
salt S-30
solar energy S-516
water W-86, 89, *picture* W-88

Evaporator fan, of a refrigerator H-210

Evarts, William Maxwell (1818–1901), U.S. lawyer and statesman, born in Boston, Mass.; chief counsel for President Andrew Johnson in impeachment trial; U.S. attorney general 1868–69; U.S. senator from New York 1885–91.

Evatt, Herbert Vere (1894–1965), Australian government official, born in East Maitland, New South Wales; leader Labor party 1951–60; chief justice New South Wales 1960–62.

Eve. *see in index* Adam and Eve

Eve, Nicolas, and his son **Clovis** (16th and 17th centuries), French bookbinders, important in history of binding design; introduced fanfare style; patterns were originally geometrical but later filled in with decorations.

'Evelina', Fanny Burney's first and best novel; told in form of letters; early example (1778) of novel of domestic manners.

Evelyn, John (1620–1706), English diarist of the Commonwealth and Restoration, born in Wotton, near Dorking.

Evening grosbeak, bird *Coccothraustes vespertinus* of the family Fringillidae G-290

Evening primrose, flowering plant of genus *Oenothera*; flowers commonly yellow P-496, *picture* F-234

'Eve of St. Agnes, The', poem by Keats; Madeline, the heroine, believing in an old superstition, goes to bed supperless on St. Agnes' Eve that she may dream of her future husband; Porphyro, her lover, who has hidden in her bedchamber, arouses her with music and persuades her to flee with him W-379

Everest, Sir George (1790–1866), English surveyor and geographer, born in Wales; superintended first survey of India 1823–43; first fixed position and altitude of Mount Everest; height corrected to 29,028 ft (8,848 m) by survey of India 1952–54
Mount Everest E-363

Everest, Mount (or Chomolungma, or Sagarmatha; formerly known as Peak XV), in Himalayas 29,028 ft (8,848 m); loftiest mountain on earth E-363
Asia A-674, *map* A-697
earth E-10, 14
exploration E-377
Hillary H-152
mountain climbing M-637
height, comparative. *see in index* Mountain, *table*
Himalayas H-152
mountain M-633

Everett, Edward (1794–1865), U.S. statesman, clergyman, and orator, born in Dorchester, Mass.; Unitarian minister at 20; professor of Greek at Harvard at 21; member of House of Representatives 1825–35; governor of Massachusetts 1836–40; minister to England 1841–45; president of Harvard 1846–49; secretary of state 1852–53; U.S. senator 1853–54; fine example of the scholar in politics L-222

Everett, Mass., city 3 mi (5 km) n. of Boston; transportation equipment, chemicals, metal and leather products, pop. 37,195.

Everett, Wash., industrial city on Puget Sound, 27 mi (43 km) n. of Seattle, in rich agricultural and timber district; lumber; pulp and paper mills; dairying, food processing; steel products, machinery, pop. 54,413 W-50, 60, *map* U-40
aerospace plant B-491

Everglade kite, bird predatory feeding behavior B-278

Everglades, vast area of land and slowly moving river in s. Florida E-363, *map* U-59
ecology E-57, *picture* E-55

Everglades National Park, in Florida F-198, P-441f
hobby, *picture* H-185

Evergreen, tree or plant that retains its foliage all year or for several years, such as the pine, fir, laurel, and hemlock, in contrast to deciduous trees. *see also in index* Conifers
Christmas custom C-405
forests F-309
kinds
hemlock H-127
juniper J-157
pine P-327
sequoia and redwood S-112
spruce S-398
yew Y-416
shrubs S-187
trees T-276
wood W-280

Evergreen Park, Ill., residential village adjacent to s.w. Chicago; incorporated 1893, pop. 25,921, *map* I-52

Evergreen Point Floating Bridge, Washington, over Lake Washington S-103, *map* S-103b

Evergreen State. *see in index* Washington

Evergreen State College, Olympia, Wash.; established 1967; arts and sciences; innovative program of coordinated and contracted studies; quarter system.

Everlasting flower, common name given to several plants, especially species of helichrysum, or immortelle gomphrena, and sea lavender.

Everlasting League, Swiss history S-544

'Everlasting Mercy, The', work by Masefield E-280

Evers, James Charles (born 1922), U.S. civil rights leader, born in Decatur, Miss.; brother of Medgar; succeeded Medgar as Mississippi field secretary NAACP 1963; Democratic candidate for Congress from Mississippi 1968; member Democratic National Committee for Mississippi 1968–; mayor Fayette, Miss., 1969–.

Evers, John Joseph (nickname Crab) (1881–1947), U.S. baseball second baseman, born in Troy, N.Y.; player for Chicago, N.L., 1902–13, and Boston, N.L., 1914–17; member of famous Tinker to Evers to Chance double play combination of pennant-winning Chicago Cubs 1906–8, 1910; starred with Boston Braves miracle team of 1914 B-93

Evers, Medgar Wiley (1925–63), U.S. civil rights leader, born in Decatur, Miss.; brother of Charles; Mississippi field secretary NAACP 1954–63; killed in Jackson, Miss., by rifle bullet from ambush; buried in Arlington National Cemetery; posthumously awarded 1963 Spingarn medal A-704

Evert, Chris (or Christine Marie Evert, or Chris Evert Lloyd) (born 1954), U.S. tennis champion E-364, *picture* T-108

'Everyman', 15th-century English morality play; as Everyman (symbol of mankind) approaches Death he meets Worldly Goods, Beauty, and others but is accompanied to the end only by Good Deeds;

centennial of Canadian Confederation C-105
Montreal M-572
Expo '70 F-10, *picture* F-6
Exponent, in mathematics
algebra A-298
numeration systems N-435
powers and roots P-484
spectrum analysis S-372
Exponential numbers A-595
Export-Import Bank of the United States
international trade I-268
Exports and imports F-307. *see also in index* International trade; Trade
tariff T-28
Exposition. *see in index* Fair and exposition
Exposition (or summary), literary technique W-382
Exposition Internationale des Arts Décoratifs et Industriels Modernes (1925), Paris, France D-59
Expository method, in learning S-238
Ex post facto law, passed after an offense and providing penalty for it; U.S. Constitution (Art. 1, Sec. 9) forbids such laws
definition C-775, *table* L-92
Exposure
photography P-286, 289, *picture* P-207
Exposure meter. *see in index* Light meter
Express E-382
REA Express R-86
Expressionism, artistic style. *see also in index* artists by name, *e.g.,* De Kooning, Willem; Derain, André; Rouault, Georges; Tamayo, Rufino; Vlaminck, Maurice de
German literature G-107
motion pictures M-620, 625, *picture* M-621
novel N-414
painting P-64, *pictures* P-63
Expressway, highway R-214. *see also in index* Freeway; Toll road
cities C-455
Expropriation, government seizure
Latin America
El Salvador S-33
Peru P-225
Sri Lanka S-402
Extended family F-15
Extender pigments, paints P-73
Extension line, in mechanical drawing M-261
Extension service. *see in index* Federal Extension Service
Extensor, muscle used to straighten a part of the body, as the tongue, the head, or a limb; works opposite the flexor muscle.
Exterminator, The, video game, *picture* E-173
External auditory meatus (or ear canal) E-3
External-combustion engine M-630
External heart massage (or chest compression) F-117
External migration, people M-399
Extinct animal. *see in index* Animal, *subhead* extinct
Extirpative surgery, removal of diseased tissue or organs
therapy T-164
Extracranial headache, pain involving the head H-81
Extracted honey, a honey product H-228
Extradition, in law, the return of a fugitive by one government (state or national) to another I-256, U-150
definition, *table* L-92
Extrasensory perception (ESP), psychic experience or phenomena E-386
Extraterrestrial life E-386
microbiology M-375
Extraterritorial rights, in international law
diplomatic protection D-150
Extravaganza (or spectacle), musical comedy M-685
Extravehicular activity (EVA), in space travel S-346f, *table* S-348
moon landings, *see in index* Moon, *subhead* manned landings
Scott, *picture* S-341b
Extremely-low-frequency communications system (ELF), underwater navigation N-73
Extroversion, in psychology J-152
personality types P-216
Extrusion, in geology
earthquakes E-39
Extrusion, in industry
forging F-317
iron and steel production I-346
plastics P-382
Exudation cyst, type of cyst C-811
Ex-voto, small painting or sculpture F-251
Eyas (or Eyess), falcon F-13
Eyck, Jan and Hubert Van. *see in index* Van Eyck, Jan and Hubert
Eyde, Samuel (1866–1940), Norwegian chemist; invented a method of producing nitrogen fertilizer from the air.
Eye E-387
animal A-430
bird B-246
fish F-127
flatfish F-173, *picture* F-175
frog F-407
insect I-218
bee B-124
fly F-243
wasp W-73
invertebrate I-284
bioengineering studies B-204
binocular vision S-444
biological models B-236
care
antiseptic treatment A-495
first aid F-120
child development C-321
corrective measures
laser beam surgery L-54
space research by-products S-348b, *picture* S-348c
spectacles S-370
health care H-87
optometry O-575
illusions I-54, S-109
light L-195, *diagram* L-202
optics O-574
pathology
blindness B-311
strabismus A-272
sunlight damages A-730
syphilis V-272
physiology
brain B-401
color perception C-561
distance judging S-109
reflex reactions R-131
sensation and perception S-109
space hazards S-346a
vitamin A V-354
Eye-Bank for Sight Restoration, Inc., founded 1944 by R. Townley Paton assisted by Mrs. Aída de Acosta Breckinridge; headquarters, New York, N.Y.; receives eyes removed from donors shortly after death; eyes are distributed to eye specialists and are used generally within 24 to 72 hours after death of donor for corneal transplant, research in physiology of vision, or for sight-preserving work; eye banks in various parts of U.S.
Eyebar, in construction
bridges B-442
Eyed elater, click beetle, *picture* B-140
Eyed fish, *list* F-146
Eyeglasses E-392, E-390
safety, *picture* S-9
spectacles S-370
wheelchair guided, *picture* S-348c
Eyelid E-387
bird B-246
reflexes R-132
'Eye of the Story, The', work by Welty W-149
Eyepiece (or ocular), optical instruments M-381
Eye splice, knot K-264
Eyess (or Eyas), falcon F-13
'Eye Witness, The', weekly newspaper
Belloc B-157
Eyre, Edward John (1815–1901), English colonial governor, born in Hornsea; explored shores of Great Australian Bight for 1,200 mi (1,900 km) in 1840–41; served as lieutenant governor of New Zealand 1846–53; later governor of Jamaica; author of a book on his travels A-815, J-18
Eyre, Lake, shallow salt lake in South Australia; area about 3,700 sq mi (9,580 sq km); normally dry, but in 1950 heavy rainfall filled it; visited 1840 by Edward John Eyre A-769, *maps* A-822, P-3, W-297
Ezekiel (Hebrew "God will strengthen") (fl. about 592–570 BC), one of the major Hebrew prophets (author of 26th book of Bible's Old Testament); carried prisoner to Babylonia in 597 BC P-508, *picture* P-509
Babylonia and Assyria B-8
Ezra (translation "the Scribe"), Hebrew priest and reformer (Bible's books of Ezra and Nehemiah); sent to Palestine in 458 BC by Artaxerxes to investigate condition of Jews; brought back observance of Mosaic law B-182

The letter F

is a descendant of the letter V, which is discussed in the Fact-Index for Volume 24. Relatives of F are U, W, and Y.

The Greeks used the Semitic sign *waw* in two forms. One form (1), called *upsilon,* was for their vowel "u." The other form (2), called *digamma,* was for the sound "w." The latter sign disappeared in Greek, but it was preserved in the Latin writing because the Romans needed a sign for their consonant "f." Several forms of the new sign (3 and 4) were used in Italy. The latter form of this Latin capital came unchanged into English.

The English small handwritten "f" took shape in late Roman and early medieval times. Scribes in the 5th century began to use a continuous curving stroke, making the stroke at the top first, then the stroke down, and finally the lower side stroke (5). A carefully made 9th-century version (6) gave rise to the English printed small "f."

FAA. *see in index* Federal Aviation Administration
FAA (Federal Alcohol Administration), United States' New Deal agency R-265
Fabaceae. *see in index* Legume
Fabbrica Italiana Automobili Torina. *see in index* Fiat
Faber, Cecilia Böhl de. *see in index* Caballero, Fernán
Faber, Jacobus. *see in index* Lefèvre d'Étaples
Faber, Urban Charles (nickname Red) (1888–1976), U.S. baseball pitcher, born in Cascade, Iowa; with Chicago, A.L., 1914–33; won 253 games, lost 211; won over 20 games in each of 4 seasons; won 3 games in 1917 World Series.
Fabergé, Peter Carl (1846–1920), Russian artist F-2
enameling E-208
fan production F-23
Fabian, John (born 1939), U.S. astronaut, born in Goosecreek, Tex., *table* S-348
Fabian Society, English socialist organization F-2
Shaw S-145
Socialism S-235
United Kingdom E-255
Webbs W-128
Fabius (or Quintus Fabius Maximus) (died 203 BC), Roman general
Hannibal H-31
Fable F-3
Aesop A-87
Indian literature I-106
La Fontaine L-21
literature L-244
storytelling S-474, 481b, 480
'Fables', work by La Fontaine L-21
'Fables of Bidpai, The'. *see in index* 'Panchatantra'
'Fables of La Fontaine, The', translation by Moore M-581
Fabliau, medieval verse tale F-394
novel N-414
Fabre, Henri (1823–1915), French entomologist and author F-4
Fabricius, Hieronymus (1537–1619), Italian anatomist and surgeon F-5
Harvey H-51
Fabrics. *see in index* Cloth; Fibers, Man-made; Fibers, Natural; Spinning and weaving; Textile
Fabrikoid, trade name for pyroxylin-coated fabrics of leatherlike appearance, used for bookbindings, traveling bags, and upholstery.
Face, human, front part of the head; site of eyes, nose, and mouth. *see also in index* Eye; Nose; Teeth
bones S-210
diseases P-271
'Orbis Pictus', *picture* R-124
tissue transplantation T-250
Face, in geometry M-244
Face milling (or side milling), a machine tool operation T-221
'Face of Battle, The', work by Keegan W-28
Face-off (or bully), begins play in field hockey H-193
Facet, precious stone cut
jewelry and gems J-113
prehistoric tools M-84
'Face the Music' (1932), musical comedy by Berlin M-686
Face value (or par value), stocks and bonds S-451, P-200
Facing brick B-436
Facsimile, communications F-5
office equipment O-495
printer, *picture* R-45
news printing N-240
telecommunication T-55
Faction. *see in index* Special interest group
Factor and factoring
algebra A-299, A-594
Factory
Arkwright's factory A-626
cities' development C-452
India I-74
Industrial Revolution I-176
industry I-183
labor L-3
employment and unemployment E-206
machine M-11
manufacturing, *picture* O-500
monorail M-545
psychology P-524
smoke S-220
system's development C-151
women's rights W-274
Factory law. *see in index* Labor and industrial law
Factory ship (or mother ship), in fishing industry F-138
Fact Summary, 'Compton's Encyclopedia', provides detailed comparative statistics and factual information concerning certain geographical or political areas. It includes such subjects as population, occupations, sources of income, trade, government, and education presented by charts, maps, and text. The Fact Summary is found at the end of such articles as those on the 50 states, Canadian provinces, the United States, Canada, Australia, etc.
Factual memory, type of memory M-294
Faculae, bright patches on the sun S-515
'Facundo', work by Sarmiento L-68
Fadden, Sir Arthur William (1895–1973), Australian political leader, born in Ingham, Queensland; entered Parliament 1932; Country party leader 1942–58; prime minister 1941.
Fade, motion picture optical effect M-613
Fadeev, Aleksandr Aleksandrovich (1901–56), Soviet novelist; his childhood in Siberia later was background for some of his works; awarded Stalin prize R-360b
Fadiman, Clifton (born 1904), U.S. editor and literary critic, born in Brooklyn, N.Y.; master of ceremonies on former radio program Information Please and on television programs; book editor *The New Yorker* 1933–43 ('Party of One'; 'Any Number Can Play'; 'Enter, Conversing'; edited with Charles Van Doren: 'American Treasury'; for children, 'Wally the Wordworm')
'The Mathematical Magpie' R-112e
Faenza, Italy, city 19 mi (31 km) s.w. of Ravenna; 15th-century cathedral; faience pottery made here since 12th century; pop. 51,085, *map* I-401
ornamental tile B-438
'Faerie Queene, The', allegorical romance by Spenser S-378
English literature E-266
Faeroe Islands (or The Faeroes), known as Sheep Islands, Danish group in Atlantic Ocean between the Shetland Islands and Iceland; 540 sq mi (1,400 sq km); fishing, sheep raising; pop. 34,596 D-97, *map* E-360
world, *map* W-297
Faeroese language G-103
Fafnir, in Norse mythology, a dragon; guardian of the treasure later known as the Nibelung hoard
Siegfried S-192a
Fagan, Eleanor. *see in index* Holiday, Billie
Fagging, a custom in English public schools compelling younger boys to act as servants to older boys for set tasks, such as running errands; flourished in 19th century; by 1950s, abolished or reformed.
Fagin, character in Charles Dickens' 'Oliver Twist', head of a gang of thieves; tries to make Oliver a pickpocket. *see also in index* 'Oliver Twist'
Faguet, Emile (1847–1916), French critic and man of letters; elected to Academy 1901; professor of poetry at Sorbonne ('Notes sur le théâtre contemporain').
Fagunwa, Daniel O. (1910–63), Yoruba chief and popular Nigerian writer A-121
Fahrenheit, Gabriel (1686–1736), German physicist F-5
thermometer T-167
Fahrenheit scale
Fahrenheit F-5
heat H-103
weights and measures, *table* W-140, *diagram* W-139
Fahrney, Delmer Stater (born 1898), U.S. Navy officer, born in Grove, Indian Territory (now Oklahoma); pioneer in field of pilotless aircraft and guided missiles; director of Pilotless Aircraft Division, Bureau of Aeronautics, U.S. Navy 1945–49; retired as rear admiral 1950
guided missile G-308
Fa-hsien (fl. AD 399–414), Chinese Buddhist monk, *list* B-484
Faial, Azores. *see in index* Fayal
Faience (or Faïence), a variety of pottery P-474
beads B-114, *picture* B-115
brick and tile B-438
Faille, ribbed fabric of silk, cotton, synthetic fibers, or combinations of these; softer and with wider, flatter ribs than grosgrain.
Fainting, temporary loss of consciousness
first aid F-120
Fair and exposition F-6
amusement parks A-385
history
Middle Ages T-145, *picture* T-143
Renaissance R-149
Paris P-123
United States
Dallas, *picture* T-129
Knoxville K-266, *picture* K-265
Philadelphia P-252
Portland P-453
Rhode Island, *picture* R-188
St. Louis S-22
San Francisco S-44
Fairbairn, Sir William (1789–1874), Scottish engineer and inventor; a pioneer builder of iron ships in United Kingdom; with Robert Stephenson, built tubular bridge over Menai Strait.
Fairbanks, Charles Warren (1852–1918), U.S. lawyer and political leader, born in Union County, Ohio; U.S. senator from Indiana 1897–1905.
Fairbanks, Douglas (1883–1939), U.S. motion-picture actor and producer F-11, *picture* M-621. *see also in index* Pickford, Mary
Fairbanks, Douglas, Jr. (born 1909), U.S. motion-picture and television actor, producer, born in New York, N.Y.; in U.S. Navy in World War II ('The Prisoner of Zenda'; 'Gunga Din'; 'Sinbad the Sailor') F-11
Fairbanks, Thaddeus (1796–1886), U.S. manufacturer and inventor F-11
Fairbanks, Alaska, largest city in interior on Tanana River; pop. 22,645 F-11
Alaska A-242, *picture* A-251
Alaska Highway A-256
North America, *map* N-350
United States, *picture* U-96
world, *map* W-297
Fairborn, Ohio, city 9 mi (15 km) n.e. of Dayton; cement; Wright-Patterson Air Force Base nearby; pop. 29,702.
Fairburn, William Armstrong (1876–1947), U.S. inventor and industrialist, born in Bath, Me.; discovered (1910) a practical method of making nonpoisonous friction matches; developed spraying device to remove hazard of afterglow in wood matches; president Diamond Match Company 1915–47.
Fairchild, David Grandison (1869–1954), U.S. botanist and explorer, born in East Lansing, Mich.; with U.S. Dept. of Agriculture 1889–1935; introduced many plants into U.S.
horticulture contribution F-222
Miami M-348
Fairchild, Sherman Mills (1896–1971), U.S. inventor and manufacturer, born in Oneonta, N.Y.; inventor of cameras used in aerial mapping surveys and in studying flights of airplanes and missiles; builder of airplanes.
Fairchild Tropical Garden, Coconut Grove, Fla.; established 1938 through aid of Col. and Mrs. Robert H. Montgomery; named for David Fairchild; 83 acres (34 hectares) M-348
Fair Credit Reporting Act (1971) U.S. legislation C-763
Fair Deal, program of President Harry S. Truman U-192
Fair employment practices L-5
Fair Employment Practices Committee (FEPC), United States R-259
black Americans B-295
Fairfax, Thomas, Baron (1612–71), English general under Cromwell; victor at Naseby over Charles I (1645).
Fairfax, Thomas, Baron (1693–1781), North American colonist, born in England; owned "Northern Neck" and Shenandoah Valley of Virginia
Washington W-39
Fairfax, Va., city 14 mi (22 km) w. of Arlington; suburban community; commercial center; George Mason University; pop. 19,390, *map* V-349
Fairfield, Ala., industrial city adjacent to Birmingham; steel mills, coal and coal-tar products; Miles College; pop. 13,040.
Fairfield, Calif., city 35 mi (55 km) n.e. of San Francisco; canvas products, wine; Travis Air Force Base nearby; pop. 58,099.
Fairfield, Conn., urban town and summer resort on Long Island Sound, immediately s.w. of Bridgeport; metal products, chemicals; Fairfield University; founded 1639; burned by British forces 1779; pop. 54,849.
Fairfield, Ohio, city 3 mi (5 km) s. of Hamilton; residential with some industry; incorporated 1955; pop. 30,777.

Fairfield University, Fairfield, Conn.; Roman Catholic; founded 1942; arts and sciences, education; graduate study.

Fairhaven, Mass., opposite New Bedford on estuary of Acushnet River, at head of Buzzards Bay; boatyards; tacks, small hardware, marine machinery; set apart from New Bedford 1812; whaling once important industry; pop. of township 15,759.

Fair Housing and Equal Opportunity, U.S. Department of Housing and Urban Development U-165

Fair Labor Standards Act (1938, revised 1949), United States R-273, U-164

Fair Lawn, N.J., borough just n.e. of Paterson near the Passaic River; light industry; nurseries; incorporated 1924; pop. 36,421.

Fairleigh Dickinson University, Rutherford, Teaneck, and Madison, N.J.; private control; founded 1941, university 1956; liberal arts, business administration, dentistry, education, science and engineering; graduate school; two-year college at Hackensack; overseas campuses: Wroxton Abbey, England, for English literature and Virgin Islands for marine biology.

Fairmont, Minn., city 41 mi (66 km) s.w. of Mankato; railroad equipment; food processing; annual snowmobile derby; incorporated 1857; pop. 11,506.

Fairmont, W. Va., city on Monongahela River 18 mi (29 km) n.e. of Clarksburg; coal-mining region; glass products, fluorescent tubes, aluminum products, coal-mining machinery, steel products, cement products; Fairmont State College; pop. 23,863 W-167, *map* U-41

Fairmont State College, Fairmont, W. Va.; opened 1867; arts and sciences and teacher education W-168

Fairmount Park, Philadelphia, Pa. P-251c
  Japanese House, *picture* S-240
  Valley Green Inn, *map* P-251a

Fair Oaks, battle of (also called Seven Pines), a bloody engagement fought 7 mi (11 km) s.e. of Richmond, Va., May 31–June 1, 1862, between Unionists under George B. McClellan and Confederates under Joseph E. Johnston C-474, *map* C-475

Fair Packaging and Labeling Act (1966), United States F-284
  marketing M-141

Fair Rosamond, English legendary figure, beloved of King Henry II, hidden away by him in a bower at heart of a labyrinth in Woodstock; found by jealous Queen Eleanor and forced to drink poison.

Fair trade, maintenance of resale price on trademarked goods under contract between manufacturer and retailer for purpose of keeping large companies from selling goods cheaper than small companies could afford to sell them; effective 1976 federal law made fair-trade contracts illegal. *see also in index* Miller-Tydings Fair Trades Act

Fairview Park, Ohio, city on the Rocky River at w. border of Cleveland; residential suburb with extensive park and recreational facilities; incorporated 1910; pop. 19,311.

Fairwater free-flooding port, submarine, *diagram* S-498

Fairway, golf G-188

Fairweather, Mount, volcanic mountain of St. Elias Mountains on Alaska-British Columbia border; peak 15,300 ft (4,663 m) in British Columbia, *map* U-39

Fairy
  fairy tales F-12

Fairy lily. *see in index* Zephyranthes

Fairy ring, mushroom formation M-664

Fairy shrimp, crustaceans of the class Branchiopoda C-789, *picture* C-791

Fairy stone. *see in index* Staurolite

Fairy tale F-12
  Andersen A-407
  'Arabian Nights' A-524
  folklore F-260
  Indian literature I-106
  'Peter Pan' B-83
  storytelling S-461, 470, *list* S-481

'Fairy Tales for Children', work by Andersen A-407

Faisal (1905–75), king of Saudi Arabia; designated crown prince 1953; prime minister and commander in chief 1953–64; succeeded Saud Nov. 1964; assassinated by a nephew 1975 F-13
  assassination, *list* A-704
  Saudi Arabia S-52b

Faith, in religion R-143
  Christianity C-398
  Judaism J-147
  Reformation views R-134

Faith healer F-270

Faiyum, El (or Al Fayyum), Upper Egypt, province on w. side of Nile River; area 690 sq mi (1,790 sq km); pop. 839,000; cap. El Faiyûm (pop. 141,748) E-115
  ancient irrigation works E-125
  birthplace of Saadia S-1
  domesticated animals A-454

Falaise, France, town in n.w.; ruined castle, birthplace of William the Conqueror; pop. 6,977, *map* F-309

Falaise-Argentan Pocket, battle of, World War II W-340

Falange, Fascist party of Spain, founded 1933; became the only legal political party in Spain in 1939 after General Franco's victory in the civil war S-357, 360
  Franco F-376

Falasha, a Hamitic people of Ethiopia who profess the Jewish religion and claim descent from Jews who followed the queen of Sheba.

Falcon, bird
  falconry F-13
  predatory behavior B-280

'Falcon and the Snowman, The', motion picture E-303

Falconbridge, Sir William Glenholme (1846–1920), Canadian jurist, born in Drummondsville, Ont.; chief justice of Ontario 1900–16; knighted 1908.

Falcon Dam, dam in Texas and Mexico, on Rio Grande R-209, T-118, *picture* T-122

Falconer, Sir Robert Alexander (1867–1943), Canadian educator and clergyman, born in Charlottetown, P.E.I.; president of University of Toronto 1907–32 ('Idealism in National Character'; 'Citizenship in an Enlarging World'; 'Religion on My Life's Road').

Falconet, Étienne-Maurice (1716–91), French sculptor; best known for colossal equestrian statue of Peter the Great (in Leningrad) and the 'Bathing Girl' (in Louvre, Paris), *picture* R-352

Falconidae, a family of birds, including the falcons and the caracara. *see in index* Falcon

Falconiformes, an order of predatory birds, comprised of vultures, kites, eagles, hawks, ospreys, falcons B-278

Falconio, Diomede, Cardinal (1842–1917), U.S. Roman Catholic prelate; born in Italy; apostolic delegate to Canada 1899–1902, to U.S. 1902–11; made cardinal 1911.

Falcon Island, small volcanic island of the Tonga group in South Pacific; sighted as reef by British navy vessel *Falcon* in 1865; because of volcanic eruption emerged as island 1885; since then has been observed in cycle of disappearances and reappearances.

Falconry (or hawking) F-13
  knights' recreation K-258
  Middle Ages M-388, *picture* M-389
  predatory bird selection B-280

Falguière, Jean Alexandre Joseph (1831–1900), French sculptor and painter; sculptures are robust and realistic ('Diana'; monument to Lafayette; 'The Dance'); paintings show influence of Goya ('Wrestlers'; 'Spanish Dwarfs').

Faliero, Marino (or Marino Falier) (1278?–1355), doge of Venice (1354–55), conspired to make himself sovereign; executed; subject of dramas by Byron, Swinburne, and others.

Falkenhayn, Erich von (1861–1922), German general; served in China 1900–03; Prussian minister of war 1913; succeeded Von Moltke 1914 as chief of general staff of German army; failure of attacks on Verdun caused his retirement
  World War I W-307

Falkirk, Scotland, town 20 mi (30 km) n.e. of Glasgow; metal processing; famous "trysts of Falkirk" (stock fairs) were held here annually; pop. 38,625.

Falkirk, first battle of (1298), Wallace's forces were overcome by the army of Edward I W-7

Falkirk, second battle of (1746), Highlanders under Prince Charles defeated English under General Hawley.

Falkland, Samuel. *see in index* Heijermans, Herman

Falkland Current, cold current in South Atlantic Ocean; moves northward along east coast of South America.

Falkland Islands (or Malvinas), a British colony near tip of South America in South Atlantic Ocean; area (excluding dependencies) 4,618 sq mi (11,960 sq km); cap. Stanley; pop. 1,813 F-14
  Argentine-British dispute A-583, B-312, E-259
  Royal Navy N-79, 87
  Commonwealth membership C-602
  South America S-294, *map* S-299
  world, *map* W-297

Falkland Islands Dependencies, that part of Antarctic Continent between 20° and 80° w.; also adjacent and outlying islands.

Falköping, Sweden, town in s.; victory (1389) of Margrethe I, queen of Denmark and Norway, over king of Sweden, resulting in union of the three kingdoms; pop. 15,681.

Fall, Albert Bacon (1861–1944), U.S. legislator, born in Frankfort, Ky.; U.S. senator from New Mexico 1913–21, secretary of interior 1921–23
  Harding H-41
  oil scandal C-703

Fall. *see in index* Autumn

Fall, in wrestling W-364, *picture* W-365

Falla, Manuel de (1876–1946), Spanish impressionist composer, born in Cadiz; leader of modern Spanish composers (opera, 'La Vida Breve'; ballet, 'Three-Cornered Hat'; symphonic poem, 'Nights in the Gardens of Spain') M-674

Fallacy, a false idea; from the Latin *fallax*, "deceitful"; in logic, an error in reasoning, as in violating the rules of syllogism, used in stating a deductive argument.

Fall aster, a perennial flower G-25

Fall cankerworm moth, insect
  caterpillar and pupa, *picture* B-522

Fall Creek Falls State Park, park in Tennessee, *picture* T-93

Fallen Timbers, battle of, on Maumee River, 15 mi (25 km) from Toledo, Ohio; battle against American Indians won by U.S. forces under Wayne O-500, 505
  Washington W-43
  Wayne W-110

Fallersleben, Hoffmann von. *see in index* Hoffmann, August Heinrich

Fallières, Clément Armand (1841–1931), president of France 1906–13; previously was president of senate 7 years; interested in aiding working classes.

Falling star. *see in index* Meteor and meteorite

Fallingwater, house designed by Wright, *picture* W-367

Fall line, of rivers F-14
  Georgia G-84
  rivers R-210
  South Carolina S-306
  Virginia V-330

'Fall of the House of Usher, The', work by Poe P-402
  American literature A-348
  Gothic fiction G-197
  horror story H-245

Fallon, Nev., city 58 mi (93 km) n.e. of Carson City; stock-raising, farming center; Fallon Naval Air Station; Lahontan Reservoir nearby; pop. 4,262.

Fallopian tube, female reproductive tube extending from the ovary to the uterus M-300
  sexuality S-124

Fallopius (or Gabriel Fallopio) (1523–62), Italian anatomist; taught in Ferrara, Pisa, and Padua; made many discoveries ('Observationes Anatomicae') F-5

Fallout, nuclear weapons N-434

Fallow deer, deer *Dama dama*, woodland species; native of Europe D-62, *table* D-63

Fallow land, in agriculture
  ancient systems A-131

Fall River, Mass., city 49 mi (79 km) s. of Boston; pop. 92,574 M-191, 202, *map* U-41

Falls, Charles Buckles (1874–1960), U.S. artist, born Fort Wayne, Ind.; posters, fabric designs, stage sets and costumes, lithographs and etchings; wrote and illustrated: 'A B C Book', 'Modern A B C Book', and 'The First 3,000 Years'; illustrated: 'Great Heritage', by Katherine Shippen; 'Americans Before Columbus' and 'America Before Man', by Elizabeth Baity.

Falls. *see in index* Waterfall

Falls, The, former name of Trenton, N.J. *see in index* Trenton

Falls Church, Va., residential city 6 mi (10 km) n.w. of Arlington; business, research and development; on site of church built in 1734; pop. 9,515, *map* V-349

Falls of St. Anthony, Minneapolis, Minn. *see in index* St. Anthony Falls

Falmouth, England, seaport and winter resort in Cornwall at mouth of Fal River; fisheries, shipbuilding and ship repairing; Pendennis and St. Mawes castles, both from 16th century; pop. 17,350, *map* U-18a

Falmouth, Mass., 17 mi (27 km) e. of New Bedford near Buzzards Bay; residential and resort area; incorporated 1686; pop. 23,640.

FALN (Fuerzas Armadas de Liberación), group that seeks independence for Puerto Rico T-113

False crane fly, name for mosquito-like flies of family Anisopidae; adults of common genus *Anisopus*, with spotted wings, often seen on windows of houses; feed on sap of trees, nectar of flowers, and rotting fruit; larvae abound in decaying vegetable matter.

False dragonhead. *see in index* Physostegia

False face. *see in index* Mask

False imprisonment, unlawful restriction of a person's right of free location and movement, does not necessarily imply jailing.

False rib. *see in index* Rib

False Solomon's-seal, plant. *see in index* Solomon's-seal

False sunflower. *see in index* Heliopsis

Falsetto, extremely high singing voice M-680

Falsework, in bridge construction B-442, *picture* B-444

'Falstaff', opera by Verdi V-282, O-567

Falster, island of Denmark, in Baltic Sea, just s. of Zealand; area 198 sq mi (513 sq km); has Denmark's southernmost point, Gedser Odde; chief town Nykøbing; dairying; sugar beets; pop. 46,662 B-46, *map* D-100

Falwell, Jerry L. (born 1933), U.S. clergyman and political lobbyist, born in Lynchburg, Va.; founded Thomas Road Baptist Church in Lynchburg 1956; began religious television program, the Old-Time Gospel Hour, 1956; organized Lynchburg Baptist College (later known as Liberty Baptist College) 1971; founded fundamentalist group Moral Majority, Inc., 1979.

Federalist party, United States political party P-432
  Constitution U-142
  Hamilton H-22
  Louisiana Purchase L-324
  presidents, *table* P-495a
    Adams A-32
    Jackson J-6
    Jefferson J-93
    Madison M-26
Federal Law Enforcement Training Center (FLETC), United States U-159
Federal Loan Agency, United States R-265
Federal Maritime Commission, United States U-166
Federal Meat Inspection Act (1967), United States M-253
Federal Mediation and Conciliation Service, United States A-528
Federal National Mortgage Association (FNMA, or Fannie May), United States H-303, *list* H-304
Federal Open Market Committee, United States F-52
Federal Plant Quarantine Act (1912), United States I-226
Federal Power Commission, United States, since 1977 the Federal Energy Regulatory Commission U-165
  waterpower W-106
Federal Radio Commission, United States R-54
Federal Regulation of Lobbying Act (1946), United States L-276
Federal Republic of Germany. *see in index* Germany, West
Federal Reserve System, United States F-51
  business cycle B-518
  central bank C-260, B-69
  government agency G-201, U-166
  inflation regulation I-199
  money M-533
    coins C-538
  Wilson's administration W-217
Federal Safety Council, United States S-5
Federal Savings and Loan Insurance Corporation, United States S-52d, U-166, B-66
  housing H-302
Federal Security Agency (FSA), United States R-265, U-164
Federal-State Employment Security System, United States U-163
Federal Surplus Commodities Corporation (FSCC), United States R-265
Federal Trade Commission (FTC), United States U-166
  advertising regulation A-60
  Wilson's administration W-217
Federal Triangle, in Washington, D.C. W-67
Federal Works Agency (FWA), United States R-265
Federated Malay States. *see in index* Malay States, Federated
Federation, agreement between two or more parties or groups aimed at uniting them for common purpose; governments and professional societies often form federations to achieve joint action.
Federation Cup, trophy representing the women's amateur team-tennis championship of the world
  tennis T-108
Fédération Internationale de Camping et de Caravanning (FICC), international organization of camping clubs; founded 1932 C-68
Fédération Internationale de Football Association (FIFA), international governing body for soccer [illegible]
Fédération Internationale de Natation Amateur (FINA), international governing body for diving D-186
Fédération Internationale de Quilleurs (FIQ), bowling organization B-387
Federation Licensure Examination (or FLEX), United States M-277
Federation of American Motorcyclists M-632
Federation of European Meteor Astronomy A-730
Federation of Rhodesia and Nyasaland. *see in index* Malawi; Zambia; Zimbabwe
Fedin, Konstantin Aleksandrovich (1892–1977), Soviet novelist of the Revolution, born a peasant R-361
Fedor I Ivanovich (1557–98), czar of Russia (1584–98); last of Rurik rulers; reign dominated by brother-in-law Boris Godunov R-352
Fedora, type of hat H-54
Fedorenko, Nikolai Trofimovich (born 1912), Soviet diplomat and Oriental scholar, born in Pyatigorsk; in Soviet diplomatic service 1939–; deputy foreign minister 1955–58; ambassador to Japan 1958–62; permanent delegate to UN 1963–68.
Feedback
  automation A-833
  cybernetics C-809
  machine M-11
  robots R-225
  writing W-376
Feedback circuit (or regenerative circuit), in broadcasting A-632
Feeder, in glass manufacture G-157
Feedforward, machinery control system M-11
Feed grinder (or processing mill), farm machinery F-36
Feeding stuffs. *see in index* Forage crops
Fee-for-service, payment used in a private practice M-279
Feelers of animals. *see in index* Antennae
Feeling. *see in index* Emotion
Feeney, Charles S. (nickname Chub) (born 1921), U.S. baseball executive, born in Orange, N.J.; vice-president present San Francisco Giants 1946–70; president National League 1970–86.
Fee simple, estate in land with unrestricted rights for disposition; land inheritance not limited to any class of heirs.
Fehling, Hermann von (1812–85), German chemist, born in Lübeck, professor of chemistry at Polytechnic Institute, Stuttgart; did important work in industrial and analytical chemistry; introduced Fehling's solution.
Fehling's solution, a mixture of copper sulfate, potassium hydroxide, and potassium and sodium tartrate (Rochelle salt) in water; blue color changed by simple sugars (monosaccharides), by maltose and lactose, owing to formation of insoluble cuprous oxide, but not by cane sugar (sucrose); used to test for sugar in diabetes.
Fehmarn, or **Femern,** West German island in Baltic Sea, in Schleswig-Holstein; 72 sq mi (186 sq km); agriculture, stock raising, fishing; pop. 12,455, *map* G-131
Fehrbellin, East Germany, town 30 mi (50 km) n.w. of Berlin; defeat of Swedes under Wrangel by Frederick William, the Great Elector, 1675.
Feiffer, Jules (born 1929), U.S. cartoonist, born in New York, N.Y.; cartoons nationally syndicated; satirist of urban U.S. society F-52, A-363
Feininger, Lyonel (1871–1956), U.S. painter, born in New York City, lived in Germany 1887–1936; works show influence of cubism; often delicate, with fine line and color.
Feinstein, Dianne (born 1933), U.S. public official, born in San Francisco, Calif.; member San Francisco city and county board of supervisors 1969–78, president 1970–72, 1974–76, 1978; mayor of San Francisco 1978– W-276
Feint, feigned, or pretended, attack to mislead opponent by distracting attention from the main point of assault; used in boxing, fencing, and war B-390
Feldberg, highest point of Black Forest B-305, G-111, *map* G-131
Feldspar (or felspar), a silicate rock R-229, *picture* R-229a
  gemstones J-115
  granite G-214
  minerals M-436
Felicia, a genus of low-growing perennial plants of the composite family, native to Africa; sometimes called *Agathea;* flowers sky blue, asterlike; one species *F. amelloides* called blue daisy, blue marguerite.
Felidae. *see in index* Cat
Felis, the cat genus; flesh eaters (Carnivora), characterized by graceful, muscular bodies, claws and teeth equipped for hunting; ancestry, through fossils, dates back 40,000,000 years C-202
Felis minuta, extremely rare cat of the Philippines C-213
Felix I, Saint (died 274), pope 269–274; wrote encyclical on unity of Jesus Christ's person; martyred under Aurelian; commemorated as saint May 30.
Felix II (III), Saint (died 492), pope 483–492; excommunicated bishops of Eastern church; helped to restore African church; commemorated as saint March 1.
Felix III (IV), Saint (died 530), pope 526–530; strengthened custom of exempting clerics from lay jurisdiction; commemorated as saint Sept. 22.
Felix II (died 365), antipope 355–358, born in Rome; chosen by Arian party after Liberius had been banished; deposed when Liberius returned.
Felix V, (originally Amadeus) (1383–1451), antipope 1439–49, born in Chambéry, France; last of the antipopes; submitted to Nicholas V and was made cardinal.
Felix, Antonius, Roman procurator of Judea (AD 52–60), before whom the apostle Paul, arrested in Jerusalem, was sent to be judged.
Felix of Valois, Saint (1127–1212), French monk; cofounder of Trinitarian or Redemptionist Order for liberation of Christian captives from the Saracens; removed from sainthood by Pope Paul VI in 1969.
'Felix the Cat', cartoon strip series by Sullivan, *list* C-202
Feller, Robert (nickname Bob) (born 1918), U.S. baseball pitcher, born Van Meter, Iowa; player for Cleveland, A.L., 1936–41 and 1945–56; won 266 games, lost 162; won 20 or more games in each of 6 seasons (won 27 games in 1940); pitched 3 no-hit and 12 one-hit games; struck out 18 in 9-inning game and 348 in a season; lifetime earned-run average of 3.25 B-89
Fellies (or felloes), part of wheel rim W-193
Fellini, Federico (born 1920), Italian film director and writer F-53
  motion pictures M-623, *picture* M-626
'Fellini Satyricon', motion picture directed by Fellini F-53, *picture* M-626
Fellow, in university U-208
Fellowships
  literary awards L-241
  university U-208
Felony, in law
  crime C-770
  definition, *table* L-92
Fels Fund, Samuel S., incorporated in Pennsylvania 1936, providing grants to colleges and universities for projects in basic science, education, government, and medicine.
Felspar. *see in index* Feldspar
Fels Planetarium, in Philadelphia, Pa. P-251
Felt, Dorr Eugene (1862–1930), U.S. inventor and manufacturer, born in Beloit, Wis.; secured patent on first comptometer in 1887.
Felt, a fabric made by pressing fibers together into webs, steaming them under pressure, and pounding; wool, fur, and some hair make good felt T-100
  hats and caps H-54
  sound absorption S-259
Feltre, Vittorino da, Italian educator E-84
Felucca, Mediterranean vessel, usually undecked, with one or more lateen sails; oars used when there is no wind.
Female. *see in index* Reproduction, *subhead* sexual; Women
Female Medical College of Pennsylvania, est. 1850 W-273
'Female Spectator', magazine M-32
'Female Tatler', magazine M-32
Femern, island in Baltic Sea. *see in index* Fehmarn
'Feminine Mystique, The', work by Friedan W-279
Feminism. *see in index* Women's rights
Femur, long bone of upper part of leg S-210
  bone, *diagram* A-393, B-342, *picture* A-401
  frog F-406
Fence, a person who sells stolen goods C-771
Fence, an enclosure or barrier along boundary for confinement, protection, or ornamentation; wood, rock, and wire commonly used
  barbed wire W-247
Fence Cutters' War (1883), United States F-423
Fence lizard, reptile *Sceloporus undulatus* L-274, *picture* L-[illegible]
Fencing, sport F-53
  foil, *picture* S-546
  Japan J-57
  Philippines P-255a
Fénelon, François de Salignac de la Mothe (1651–1715), French churchman and author, archbishop of Cambrai and tutor to Louis XIV's eldest grandson, the duke of Burgundy; wrote 'Télémaque', famous didactic tale.
Fenestration, in architecture, the placement, proportion, and decoration of windows; in glass-encased buildings term refers also to size and proportion of panes and supports.
Feng Yu-hsiang (1880–1948), Chinese warlord, amassed large and well-disciplined army; joined Nationalist leaders in 1927 but broke with them in 1929.
Fenians, Irish revolutionary society that flourished about 1861–72; sought to end English rule in Ireland; active in the United States and made unsuccessful raids into Canada 1866–70; failure in direct results, but instrumental in convincing Gladstone and others of the need for reforms; name derived from Fianna, legendary band of heroes led by Finn MacCool
  Canada C-100
  Hughes H-316
Fennec, name of several species of small, foxlike animals characterized by large pointed ears A-430
Fennel, aromatic herb *Foeniculum vulgare* of the parsley family with large umbels of small yellow flowers; seeds used for seasoning, dried leaves for flavoring sauces S-379
Fennelflower. *see in index* Nigella
Fenner, James (1771–1846), U.S. political leader, born in Providence, R.I.; served as Democratic U.S. senator from R.I. 1805–7; governor of Rhode Island 1807–11, 1824–31, 1843–45.
Fenner, Phyllis Reid (born 1899), U.S. author, librarian, and teacher, born in Almond, N.Y.; became school librarian on Long Island, N.Y.; noted as compiler of short-story collections for younger readers ('Time to Laugh'; 'Dogs, Dogs, Dogs'; 'Heroes, Heroes, Heroes'; 'Brother Against Brother'; 'The Dark and Bloody Ground'); author of 'The Proof of the Pudding: What Children Read'; editor of 'Something Shared'.
Fennoscandian Shield, rock formation in Europe E-329, *map* 329, *picture* E-330
Fenrir (or Fenris the Wolf), in Scandinavian mythology, monster, child of the evil god Loki; kept chained by magic till Ragnarök (Judgment Day), when he is destined to break loose, spread his jaws to heaven and earth, and, breathing fire, devour Odin.
Fens, The, marshy low-lying area in e. England, in Lincoln, Huntingdon, Cambridge, and Norfolk counties E-230, *picture* E-231

Fenton, Roger (1819–69), English photographer P-297, *list* P-294

Feoktistov, Konstantin Petrovich (born 1926), Soviet cosmonaut and scientist, born Voronezh; spacecraft designer; first engineer to travel in space, *table* S-348

FEP. *see in index* Fair Employment Practices

FEPC. *see in index* Fair Employment Practices Committee

FERA. *see in index* Federal Emergency Relief Administration

Feral dog D-212

Ferber, Edna (1887–1968), U.S. novelist, dramatist, and short-story writer, born in Kalamazoo, Mich.; newspaper reporter in Appleton, Wis., when 17 years old; Pulitzer prize 1925 for 'So Big' (novels: 'Show Boat', 'Cimarron', 'Come and Get It', 'Giant', 'Ice Palace'; short stories: 'One Basket'; plays with George S. Kaufman: 'Dinner at Eight', 'The Royal Family', 'Stage Door'; autobiographies: 'A Peculiar Treasure', 'A Kind of Magic') A-368

FERC. *see in index* Federal Energy Regulatory Commission

Fer-de-lance, poisonous snake, *Bothrops atrox;* native to s. Mexico and tropical Central and South America; name means head of a lance and describes its pointed snout; length from 5 to 6 ft (1.5 to 2 m).

Ferdinand I (1793–1875), emperor of Austria; succeeded 1835; intermittently insane; informal regency headed by Metternich, governing in his name, provoked rebellion that led to abdication (1848), in favor of nephew Francis Joseph.

Ferdinand I (1503–64), Holy Roman emperor; succeeded his brother Charles V (1556); responsible for Peace of Augsburg; endeavored to establish religious harmony among Catholics and Protestants
- Austria-Hungary A-829
- Bohemia B-331

Ferdinand II (1578–1637), Holy Roman emperor, grandson of Ferdinand I; succeeded in 1619; hated Protestantism; Protestant estates deposed him in Bohemia, later he drove Protestantism from Bohemia
- Austria-Hungary A-829
- Thirty Years' War T-169
- Wallenstein W-10

Ferdinand III (1608–57), Holy Roman emperor, son of Ferdinand II, whom he succeeded 1637; active in terminating Thirty Years' War; distinguished for scholarship.

Ferdinand II (1452–1516), king of Aragon, (Ferdinand V, or Ferdinand the Catholic, Spanish king of Castile and León); first king of united Spain and patron of Columbus F-54
- Columbus C-592
- Spain S-358
- wool W-287

Ferdinand I (1861–1948), king of Bulgaria (1887–1918), "the old fox of the Balkans," prince of Saxe-Coburg when elected prince of Bulgaria in 1886; assumed title of king, or czar, 1908; fostered Balkan War 1912–13; entered World War I on side of Central Powers 1915; abdicated in favor of son, Boris, 1918 B-500

Ferdinand I (died 1065), first king of Castile and León, called "the Great"; reformed abuses of the church; victor over Muslims, beginning the reconquest by Spaniards.

Ferdinand V, king of Castile and León. *see in index* Ferdinand II, king of Aragon

Ferdinand I (1423–94), king of Naples, born in Valencia, Spain; reigned 1458–94; as a ruler he was able but tyrannical, cruel, and treacherous
- Medici M-273

Ferdinand I (1865–1927), king of Romania; succeeded his uncle Charles I (1914); joined Allies in World War I; established agrarian reforms and universal suffrage R-318

Ferdinand VII (1784–1833), king of Spain; succeeded on abdication of father, Charles IV, in 1808; deposed by Napoleon same year; restored in 1814; incompetent ruler under whom Spain lost American colonies on mainland S-358

Ferdinand I (1751–1825), king of the Two Sicilies (Ferdinand IV of Naples); succeeded 1759; son of Charles III of Spain; stupid, cruel, cowardly; twice dethroned as king of Naples; restored by the Congress of Vienna.

Ferdinand II (1810–59), king of the Two Sicilies; succeeded in 1830; cruel, treacherous tyrant; earned nickname King Bomba by bombarding rebellious cities.

Fergana Valley, in U.S.S.R. K-250

Fergus Falls, Minn., city in w.-central part of state, 170 mi (270 km) n.w. of Minneapolis; regional dairy, meat packing; wood products; state hospital; pop. 12,519.

Ferguson, George Howard (1870–1946), Canadian political leader, born in Kemptville, Ont.; minister of lands, forests, and mines, Ontario 1914–19; premier and minister of education, Ontario 1923–31.

Ferguson, Miriam Amanda (nickname Ma) (1875–1961), U.S. public official, governor of Texas 1925–27, 1933–35; second woman to be governor of a U.S. state; born in Bell County, Tex.; she claimed her election was vindication of her husband, James E. Ferguson, governor in 1917, who was impeached and removed from office W-276

Ferguson, Patrick (1744–80), British soldier; invented first breech-loading rifle used in British army; served with British at Brandywine; killed defending Kings Mountain, S.C.

Ferguson, Sir Samuel (1810–86), Irish poet and antiquary, president of Irish Academy 1882; his poetry deals with Gaelic traditions ('Lays of the Western Gael') I-326

Ferguson, Mo., city 9 mi (15 km) n.w. of St. Louis; residential; matchbook covers, motors; cheese products; pop. 24,740.

Ferland, Jean Baptiste Antoine (1805–65), French-Canadian priest and historian, born in Montreal, Que. ('Cours d'Histoire du Canada', 2 vols. of lectures delivered while professor of Canadian history Laval University).

Ferlinghetti, Lawrence (born 1919?), U.S. poet; a leader of the Beat movement in American literature K-229

Fermanagh, a county of Northern Ireland; area 653 sq mi (1,691 sq km); pop. 49,886; county town Enniskillen; scene of much fighting 1921–22.

Fermat, Pierre de (1601–65), French mathematician F-55
- mathematics M-214

Fermentation F-55
- alcohol A-275
  - beer and brewing B-132
  - liquor production L-235, *diagram* L-236
  - wines W-236, 239
- bacteria produce B-14
- food processing F-283
- Pasteur P-138
- silage S-202
- vinegar V-326
- yeast Y-411

Fermi, Enrico (1901–54), U.S. physicist F-56. *see also in index* Nobel Prizewinners, *table*
- Hahn H-6
- matter M-229
- nuclear weapons N-434

Fermi, Laura Capon (1907–77), U.S. writer, born in Rome, Italy; became U.S. citizen 1944 ('Atoms in the Family', life of husband, Enrico; 'Atoms for the World'; 'Mussolini'; 'Illustrious Immigrants').

Fermi Award. *see in index* Enrico Fermi Award

Fermi National Accelerator Laboratory (Fermilab), in Batavia, Ill.
- atomic particles, *picture* A-750
- nuclear energy N-421

Fermion, atomic particle, *table* A-755

Fermium (Fm), chemical element, *table* P-207, *list* P-208

Fermoy, Ireland, garrison town 18 mi (29 km) n.e. of Cork; market for farm produce; pop. 3,207.

Fern F-56
- classification P-371
- houseplants, *picture* H-289
- reproduction, *picture* S-396
- sensitive fern, *picture* P-358

Fernández, Juan (1536?–1602?), Spanish explorer and navigator; Juan Fernández Islands, which he explored, were named for him.

Fernández de Lizardi, José Joaquín (1776–1827), Mexican writer; often called 'The Mexican Thinker' L-68, 74

Fernando de Noronha, island about 200 mi (320 km) off n.e. coast of Brazil, to which it belongs; 7 sq mi (18 sq km); penal settlement; defense base; landing point for airplanes; with nearby islets (3 sq mi; 8 sq km in area) was made federal territory 1942; pop. 1,389.

Fernando Po, island, Equatorial Guinea. *see in index* Bioko Island

Fernão de Magalhães. *see in index* Magellan, Ferdinand

Ferndale, Mich., residential and industrial city adjoining Detroit on the north; steel tubing, forgings and castings; pop. 26,227.

Fernie, B.C., city in s.e. at base of Mt. Fernie on w. side of Rocky Mts.; coal mining, lumbering; pop. 5,444, *map* C-98

Ferozepore, India, town in Punjab state near Pakistan; trade in grain and cotton; military post nearby; center of operations in first Sikh War 1845; pop. 49,545.

Ferrara, Italy, city in Po Valley 30 mi (50 km) n.e. of Bologna; medieval seat of house of Este; 11th-century cathedral and massive campanile; 14th- to 15th-century school of painting; pop. 152,654, *maps* E-360, I-401

Ferrara, sword, *picture* S-546

Ferrari, Gaudenzio (1484?–1546), Italian painter, one of masters of Milan School; work uneven, but excels in heads and draperies; paintings usually dramatic ('Holy Family with Saints'; 'Life of Christ'; fresco of 'Crucifixion').

Ferraro, Geraldine (born 1935), U.S. public official F-58
- women's rights W-275

Ferreira, Antonio (1528–69), Portuguese poet, born in Lisbon; called "Portuguese Horace"; works include many poems ('Ines de Castro', a tragedy; 'Cioso', a comedy).

Ferrel, William (1817–91), U.S. meteorologist, born in Fulton County, Pennsylvania; study of how Earth's rotation affects winds and currents aided development of meteorology; with U.S. Coast and Geodetic Survey 1867–82 and Signal Service 1882–86.

Ferrelo (or Bartolomé Ferrer), Spanish explorer; explored coast of California 1542–43; perhaps first European to see coast of Oregon.

Ferrero, Guglielmo (1871–1942), Italian historian, disciple and son-in-law of Lombroso; brilliant rather than scholarly ('Greatness and Decline of Rome'; 'Ancient Rome and Modern America'; 'Four Years of Fascism').

Ferret, a carnivorous mammal of weasel family; an albino (yellowish-white) domesticated form of Old World polecat; head and body 14 in. (36 cm) long, tail 5½ in. (14 cm); in some countries, used for hunting rabbits; scientific name *Mustela furo.*

Ferret-badger. *see in index* Pahmi

Ferri, Antonio (1912–75), U.S. engineer, born near Spoleto, Italy; to U.S. 1944, naturalized 1952; professor of aerodynamics Polytechnic Institute of Brooklyn 1951–54, director aerodynamics laboratory 1954–63; at New York University after 1964, appointed chairman department of aerospace and astronautics 1972.

Ferri, Enrico (1856–1929), Italian criminologist, born near Mantua; a pioneer in scientific study of criminals and of crime prevention ('Criminal Sociology').

Ferric hydrate P-411

Ferric oxide, red oxide of iron (Fe_2O_3); chief ingredient of iron rust; hematite is mineral form; obtained in gray powder form by burning ferric compound in air; brown-red when finely ground; used to make Venetian red, a pigment.

Ferricyanic acid, compound of hydrogen, iron, and cyanogen, $H_3Fe(CN)_6$; salts used in blueprints and dyeing.

Ferris, George Washington, U.S. amusement park ride inventor A-383

Ferris, Jean Léron Gérome (1863–1930), U.S. painter, born in Philadelphia, Pa.; series of about 70 paintings covering period in U.S. history, 1492–1865, in Smithsonian Institution, Washington, D.C.

Ferris, Woodbridge Nathan (1853–1928), U.S. educator and political leader, born near Spencer, N.Y.; founder (1884) and thereafter president of Ferris Institute, Big Rapids, Mich.; governor of Michigan 1913–16; U.S. senator from Michigan 1923–28.

Ferris State College, Big Rapids, Mich.; established 1884; became Ferris Institute 1899; present name 1963; liberal arts, business, health sciences and arts, pharmacy, technology and applied arts, and teacher education; quarter system.

Ferris wheel, an amusement device invented by G.W.G. Ferris, Pittsburgh engineer; original weighed about 1,200 tons (1,100 metric tons)
- amusement park A-383
- carnivals C-172

Ferrite, magnetic ceramic M-46

Ferrocement, a dense concrete reinforced with steel mesh N-118

Ferrocyanic acid, compound of hydrogen, iron, and cyanogen, $H_4Fe(CN)_6$, a soluble, white nonvolatile solid substance used in dyeing.

Ferromagnesian minerals R-229

Ferromagnetism, magnetism M-45

Ferrous sulfate (or green vitriol, or copperas) S-510

Ferry, Elisha Peyre (1825–95), U.S. lawyer and public official, born in Monroe, Mich.; governor Washington Territory 1872–80; first governor of state of Washington 1889–93.

Ferry, Jules (1832–93), French statesman, opponent of the empire; premier 1880–81, 1883–85; promoted free, compulsory, nonclerical education; bitter against Jesuits; president of senate in 1893.

Ferry, means of conveyance across river or other narrow body of water; ferryboat carries passengers, freight, cars, etc., *picture* H-34

Ferryville. *see in index* Menzel-Bourguiba

Fertile Crescent, region in the Middle East and the Nile Valley of Egypt
- ancient civilization A-404
  - Babylonia and Assyria B-5, *map* B-4
  - Mesopotamia M-305
- Asia A-678
  - Middle East M-394
  - Syria S-549b
- Egypt, *map* E-124

Fertility drugs M-650

Fertilization, in biology. *see in index* Cell; Embryology; Ovum; Pollination; Reproduction; Seeds; Sperm cell; Spore

Fertilizer F-58. *see also in index* Guano
- agriculture A-137
- calcium C-19
- calcium phosphate P-273
- farm machinery F-32
- garden use G-21
- herbs H-138
- hops H-239
- houseplants H-289
- land conservation C-675
- nitrogen N-319
- phosphorus types P-271
- potassium types P-465
- production C-18
- Russia R-331
- saltpeter S-32
- sewage S-119
- soybean-oil meal S-340

Field, magnetic. *see in index* Magnet and magnetism, *subhead* magnetic field
Field Army, U.S. A-634
Field corn C-718
Field glasses and binoculars F-78
amateur astronomy A-730
bird-watching B-265
stereoscopic principle S-444
Field grade officer (or senior officer), in U.S. army A-634
Field hockey. *see in index* Hockey, field
Fielding, Henry (1707–54), English novelist F-79
literary contribution E-272
world W-296
Fielding, Sarah (1710–68), English writer, born in Dorsetshire; sister of Henry Fielding; author of 'The Adventures of David Simple in Search of a Faithful Friend' F-79
Fielding, William Stevens (1848–1929), Canadian statesman, born in Halifax, N.S.; premier Nova Scotia 1884–96; finance minister Canada 1896–1911 and 1921–25.
Field ion microscope M-383
crystallography C-798
Field marigold, flower *Calendula arvensis* M-135
Field Marshall, army rank A-634
Field mouse (or meadow mouse), rodent of the *Apodemus* species M-640
Field Museum of Natural History (formerly Chicago Natural History Museum), located in Grant Park, Chicago, Ill., a museum of anthropology, ethnology, geology, zoology, and botany, *picture* C-313
exhibits
plant life, *pictures* P-358–361
reptiles, *pictures* R-153–157
Field, Marshall F-78
Field of the Cloth of Gold, near Calais, France; meeting place (1520) of Henry VIII and Francis I
Field plotter, mapping device that uses electric currents to plot statistical gradients on isoline maps M-128
Fields, James Thomas (1817–81), U.S. publisher, author, and lecturer, born in Portsmouth, N.H.; editor of *Atlantic Monthly*, 1862–70 ('Underbrush'; 'Yesterdays with Authors').
Fields, W.C. (born Claude William Dukenfield) (1880–1946), U.S. comedian, born in Philadelphia, Pa.; started career as vaudeville juggler; appeared in 'Ziegfeld Follies' 1915–21; in 1925 entered motion pictures ('David Copperfield'; 'Alice in Wonderland'; 'Poppy'); author of 'Fields for President' F-80, *picture* M-624
Field spaniel, dog, *picture* D-198
Field trials, in dog show D-210
Field vole. *see in index* Meadow mouse
Fiesole, Giovanni da. *see in index* Angelico, Fra
Fiesole, Mino da. *see in index* Mino
Fiesole (ancient Faesulae), Italy, town 3 mi (5 km) n.e. of Florence; important Etruscan city; pop. 12,452, *map* I-401
Fiesta, a festival
Philippines P-253d
South America S-283, 285
FIFA (or Fédération Internationale de Football Association), international governing body for soccer S-232
Fife, a maritime county in e. Scotland, between Firth of Tay and Firth of Forth on North Sea; area 504 sq mi (1,305 sq km); pop. 320,692.
Fifi, hurricane that hit Honduras in 1974 H-225
Fifinella, female gremlin. *see in index* Gremlins
Fifteen Decisive Battles. *see in index* Creasy, Sir Edward S.
Fifteenth Amendment, United States Constitution U-153, S-505
Fifth Avenue, street in Manhattan, New York, N.Y. N-272, *picture* N-277
Fifth column, term for Nazis in Norway during World War II W-323, *picture* W-324
Fifth estate. *see in index* Fourth estate
Fifth Republic, in French history F-360
'Fifth Symphony', work by Beethoven
music M-666, 672
Fig, fruit F-80; *chart* F-430, *picture* F-435
fruitgrowing F-436
Figaro, roguish hero of Beaumarchais' 'The Barber of Seville' and 'The Marriage of Figaro'; Rossini and Mozart operas by same name based on these comedies; a brilliant periodical published in Paris was named for Figaro.
Figg, James (died 1734), English boxer, born in Oxfordshire; founded school for boxers; also fine swordsman and wrestler B-390
Fighter, plane A-175. *see also in index* Aviation, military and naval, *subhead* fighter
Fighting fish (or betta) F-128
Fighting French. *see in index* Free French
Fight or flight, defense mechanism S-488
Figuig, oasis O-454
'Figure a Poem Makes, The', work by Frost W-378
Figure eight halter hitch, knot K-264
Figurehead, ornament at prow of ship; usually a symbolic head, bust, or full-length figure; in early times, generally carved in wood.
Figure skating. *see in index* Skates and Skating
Figures of speech F-81
slang S-212
Fig wasp, insect *Blastophaga psenes* F-80, *picture* W-75
fruit pollination, *picture* F-435
Figwort family (or Scrophulariaceae), a family of plants, shrubs, and trees including snapdragon, foxglove, calceolaria, monkey flower, night phlox, pentstemon, veronica, and nemesia
butter-and-eggs flower B-520
snapdragon, *picture* F-225
Fiji, nation of Pacific composed of more than 300 islands; 7,055 sq mi (18,272 sq km); pop. 714,000 F-82
Commonwealth membership C-602
flag, *picture* F-164
marriage ceremony, *picture* M-150
money M-531
Oceania O-468, 472
Pacific Ocean, *map* P-3, *picture* P-7
United Kingdom E-259
world, *map* W-297
Filament, in electricity, a thin metal wire in bulb or vacuum tube used to give heat and light or to emit electrons
electron tube R-60
lighting and light bulb L-205, E-163
Filament, fibers
rayon R-98, 99, *picture* R-98
silk S-197, 201, *picture* S-200
Filament, flower structure F-218
Filament, sun S-515
Filaria, name for group of disease-causing, threadlike worms; embryonic forms enter bloodstream; transmitted by mosquito; *Filaria bancrofti* causes lesions which result in elephantiasis; found in s. United States, n. South America, East and West Indies, Africa, and Pacific islands.
Filariasis, disease caused by roundworms and transmitted by mosquitoes M-598
Filbert, nut. *see in index* Hazel
Filchner, Wilhelm (1877–1957), German explorer and geophysicist; led expeditions to China, Tibet, and Antarctica.
Filchner Ice Shelf, Antarctica, borders Edith Ronne Land, on Weddell Sea; discovered by Wilhelm Filchner, leader of German Expedition of 1911–12, *maps* A-475, W-297
Fildes, Sir Luke (1844–1927), English painter, born in Liverpool; best known for 'The Doctor', reproduced on U.S. postage stamp in 1947 to commemorate centennial of American Medical Association.
Filene, Edward Albert (1860–1937), U.S. merchant, born in Salem, Mass.; helped found U.S. Chamber of Commerce; experimenter in management-employee relations; supported consumer cooperatives and credit unions ('Model Stock Plan')
cooperatives C-708
Filet crochet, in needlework N-114
Filfa, island of Malta M-78
Filibuster, U.S. legislative obstruction F-83
Filicinae, class of plants made up of the true fern; characterized by true roots, leaves, and stems, absence of flowers, seeds, and fruit.
Filigree, ornamental metalwork J-112
Filipchenko, Anatoly V. (born 1928), Soviet cosmonaut, born in Davydovka, s. of Moscow; commander Soyuz 7, *table* S-348
Filipepi, Alessandro di. *see in index* Botticelli, Sandro
Filipinos, a people of the Philippines P-253b–260
Filippo Lippi. *see in index* Lippi, Fra Filippo
Filla-ma-loo bird, in folklore F-268
Filled energy bands, in quantum mechanics S-254h
Fillet, hats and caps H-53
Filling station. *see in index* Service station
Fillmore, Abigail Powers (1798–1853), wife of President Fillmore.
Fillmore, Millard (1800–74), 13th president of the United States F-84
presidential bid B-475
United States history U-176
Fillmore, Parker Hoysted (1878–1944), U.S. author, born in Cincinnati, Ohio; best known for books of folktales and fairy tales for children. 'Czechoslovak Fairy Tales', 'The Laughing Prince' (Yugoslav), and 'Mighty Mikko' (Finnish).
Fillmore, Utah, city in w.-central part of state; in livestock and farming area; capital of Utah Territory 1851–56; pop. 2,083, *map* U-233
Filly, female horse, *list* H-249
Film, photographic P-282, 286, 289
communication development C-617
Eastman E-47
holography H-206
motion pictures M-603, 607
directing D-152
Newark inventions N-150
newspaper printing N-240
Film advance, camera P-282
Film d'Art, early type of French motion picture that starred noted stage performers in famous roles M-618
Film gate, in typesetting T-339
Film matrix, in typesetting T-339
Filmsetting machine. *see in index* Photocomposition
Film speed, in photography P-286
'Fils Prodigue, Le' (The Prodigal Son), ballet by Prokofiev
Balanchine B-22
Filter, a device that allows solutions to drain, be drawn (vacuum type), or forced (pressure type) through specially prepared paper, diatomaceous earth, porcelain, or other absorbent material, to remove solid particles or coloring matter from the solution
air conditioner A-150
aquarium A-515
heating and ventilating H-112
Filter, in photography P-286, 295, *picture* P-284
sun photograph, *picture* S-254a
telescope A-730
Filter circuit, in electronics E-179
Filter factor, photography P-287
Filtration. *see in index* Filter
Fin, bomb stabilizer B-338, *picture* B-339
Fin, in zoology, external membrane used for propelling in water
evolution A-461
fish F-123, 126, 132, *diagram* F-125
flying fish F-245
mudfish and lungfish M-644
prehistoric reptiles R-154, *picture* R-153
FINA (or Fédération Internationale de Natation Amateur, international governing body for diving D-186
Final Act of the Conference on Security and Cooperation in Europe (or Helsinki Accords; 1975) B-197
Finale, in music, *list* M-670
Final solution, Nazi Germany H-205
Finance, the work of obtaining and using money and credit for the support of private and public enterprise. *see also in index* Bank and Banking; Capital; Capitalism; Credit; Money; National debt; Taxation; *also* Fact Summary with each state article
central bank C-260
financial planning B-485
housing H-295, 301, 306
industry I-189
percentage and interest P-198
stocks and bonds S-450–4
Finance Corps, U.S. Army insignia, *picture* U-10
'Financier, The', work by Dreiser A-352
Finback whale, mammal of the order Cetacea W-185
Finch, Francis Miles (1827–1907), U.S. poet and jurist, born in Ithaca, N.Y.; best known for lyrics 'Nathan Hale' and 'The Blue and the Gray'.
Finch, Robert Duer Claydon (born 1900), Canadian poet and professor at University of Toronto, born in Freeport, N.Y.
Finch, Robert Hutchison (born 1925), U.S. lawyer and public official, born in Tempe, Ariz.; manager 1960 and key adviser 1968 in presidential campaigns of Richard M. Nixon; lieutenant governor California 1967–69; U.S. secretary of health, education, and welfare 1969–70; counselor to President Nixon 1970–72
Nixon N-326
Finch, a large family of seed-eating birds F-86
zoo, *picture* Z-458
Finch College, in New York, N.Y.; private control; for women; founded 1900; liberal arts and sciences; closed 1975.
Finck, Henry Theophilus (1854–1926), U.S. music critic, born in Bethel, Mo.; on *New York Evening Post* for more than 40 years ('Wagner and His Works'; 'Songs and Song Writers'; 'Success in Music and How It Is Won').
'Finding of Christ in the Temple, The', painting by Hofmann, *picture* J-103
'Finding of Moses, The', painting by Veronese P-38, *picture* P-38
Findlay, Ohio, a manufacturing city 43 mi (69 km) s. of Toledo; petroleum products, rubber products, earth-handling machinery, radio and television parts, film processing; Findlay College; pop. 35,594.
Findlay College, in Findlay, Ohio; affiliated with Church of God; established 1882; humanities and science, business administration, education, fine arts.
Fine, Benjamin (1905–75), U.S. editor and writer, born in New York City; education reporter *The New York Times* 1937–41, education editor 1941–58 ('Our Children Are Cheated', 'American College Counselor and Guide', '1,000,000 Delinquents', 'The Modern Family Guide to Education', 'How to Be Accepted by the College of Your Choice').
Fine, payment, *table* L-92
Fine arts. *see in index* Architecture; Arts; Dance; Drama; Drawing; Literature; Music; Painting; Photography; Poetry; Sculpture; Theater; Writing, creative
Fineness, expression for purity of gold G-176
Finfish F-138
Fingal, name by which the legendary Celtic hero Finn MacCool was sometimes known in Scottish legend; popularized by Macpherson's epic 'Fingal'. *see also in index* Finn MacCool
Fingal's Cave, Scotland

Fitton, Mary (1578?–1647), maid of honor to Queen Elizabeth I; supposed by some to be the "dark lady" of Shakespeare's sonnets.

FitzGerald, Edward (1809–83), English poet whose famous translation, 'Rubáiyát of Omar Khayyám', is a very striking example of successful transplantation of a foreign poem E-276
  Omar Khayyám O-544

Fitzgerald, Ella (born 1918), U.S. jazz singer, born in Newport News, Va.; started career as band singer 1934; began recording 1935; foreign tours and nightclub appearances; numerous awards B-301
  jazz J-85

Fitzgerald, F. Scott (1896–1940), U.S. author F-147
  American literature A-359
  creative writing W-380
  'The Great Gatsby' R-112c

Fitzgerald, R.D. (born 1902), Australian poet A-797, *table* A-798

Fitzgibbon, James (1780–1863), British soldier, born in Ireland; served in Napoleonic Wars, in Canada in War of 1812 and in rebellion of 1837; became adjutant general.

Fitzpatrick, Sir Charles (1853–1942), Canadian jurist and statesman, born in Quebec, Que.; minister of justice for Canada 1902–06; chief justice of Supreme Court of Canada 1906–18; lieutenant governor of province of Quebec 1918–23.

Fitzpatrick, Daniel Robert (1891–1969), U.S. cartoonist, born in Superior, Wis.; editorial cartoonist *St. Louis Post-Dispatch* 1913–58; won Pulitzer Prize 1926 and 1955.

Fitzpatrick, Thomas (1799?–1854), U.S. fur trader and trapper, ranked with Carson and Bridger, born in County Cavan, Ireland; member of Ashley's expedition up the Missouri 1823; with Bridger and Milton Sublette, formed Rocky Mountain Fur Co., 1830; guide to De Smet, Frémont, and Kearny; became agent to American Indians U-177
  Oregon Trail O-598

Fitzroy River, one of the chief rivers of Western Australia; about 300 mi (480 km) long, navigable about 100 mi (160 km); has source in King Leopold Ranges; flows into Indian Ocean A-771, *map* A-819

Fitzsimmons, Robert Prometheus (nickname Bob) (1862–1917), Australian boxer, born in Helston, Cornwall, England B-391

Fitzsimmons, Thomas (1741–1811), U.S. political leader, businessman, born in Ireland; aided cause of Revolution; advocated Hamilton's policies as member of Federal Convention (1787); signed United States Constitution for Pennsylvania; congressman from Pennsylvania 1789–95; influential in founding Bank of North America and in obtaining protective tariff.

Fitzsimons General Hospital, 5 mi (8 km) e. of Denver, Colo., for military personnel and dependents; War Department granted authority to build 1918; named in honor of William Thomas Fitzsimons, first U.S. officer killed in World War I.

Fiume, Yugoslavia. *see in index* Rijeka

Five, The, group of Russian composers M-674, M-693

Five Civilized Tribes, group of American Indians I-149
  Oklahoma O-523
  Tennessee T-84

Five-day week, a week with five workdays, often totaling 40 hours of work. *see in index* Fair Labor Standards Act of 1938

Five-fingers, plant. *see in index* Cinquefoil

Five Forks, battle of, in U.S. Civil War fought April 1, 1865, 11 mi (18 km) s.w. of Petersburg, Va.
  Sheridan S-161

Five Intolerable Acts. *see in index* Intolerable Acts

Five-lined skink, lizard *Eumeces fasciatus*, *picture* L-273

Five Nations, confederacy of the Iroquois I-142. *see also in index* Iroquois

Fivepins, in bowling B-386

Five-Power Naval Limitation Treaty, international treaty signed in Washington, D.C. W-71

Five Satins, singing group M-680

Five-spot. *see in index* Nemophila

Five-star admiral. *see in index* Fleet admiral

Five-star general. *see in index* General of the Army

Five Towns, traditional name for Tunstall, Burslem, Hanley, Stoke-on-Trent, and Longton, since 1925 forming with Fenton the city of Stoke-on-Trent in n. Staffordshire, England; in Arnold Bennett's novels represented by Turnhill, Bursley, Hanbridge, Knype, and Longshaw.

'Five Women Who Loved Love' (or 'Koshoku gonin onna'), novel by Saikaku Ihara J-81

Five-year plan, in economics
  India I-79
  U.S.S.R. R-327, R-355
    Siberia S-191
    Stalin S-404

Fixed bridge B-439

Fixed condenser. *see in index* Capacitor

Fixed fan F-22

Fixed interest rate, in finance H-296

Fixed nitrogen. *see in index* Nitrogen, *subhead* fixation

Fixed round, artillery A-372

Fixed stars S-413, P-391

Fixer, in photographic developing P-292

'Fixer, The', work by Malamud A-362, M-68

Fixture, in law, *table* L-92

Fizeau, Armand Hippolyte Louis (1819–96), French physicist, born in Paris; in 1849 invented a reliable method of determining time that light takes to travel a distance on the earth P-306
  light experiment L-198

Fjord (or fiord), long, narrow, deep arm of sea running far inland with steep cliff on either side
  coastal regions B-112
  New Zealand N-286, *picture* N-289
  Norway N-389

Flaccus, Quintus Horatius. *see in index* Horace

Flack, Marjorie (1897–1958), U.S. author and illustrator of children's books; born in Greenport, L.I., N.Y.; married William Rose Benét 1941 ('Ask Mr. Bear'; 'Boats on the River') R-107

Flag F-148. *see also in index* Flags of the United States; Flags of the world; Pennant; Swallowtail
  pirates P-343, *picture* P-342b
  signaling S-194a, *pictures* S-194b, 195

Flag Day (June 14), United States, *list* F-63

Flagellants, a fanatic religious sect of medieval Europe; members scourged themselves, believing self-torture cleansed sins; rites still practiced by Penitentes, sect of Mexicans of New Mexico and s. Colorado

Flagellates, large group of organisms, usually one-celled, characterized by long whiplike extension, the flagellum.

Flagellum (plural flagella), a whiplike extension of certain protozoans P-515
  bacteria B-13
  collar flagellate A-428
  oceanography O-484

Flageolet, a musical instrument somewhat similar to the flute; tone more mellow; blown from end instead of side; invented at end of 16th century.

Flaget, Benedict Joseph (1763–1850), French missionary, born in Contournat, France; first Roman Catholic bishop of old Northwest Territory, with See at Bardstown, Ky.; ministered to Indians at Fort Vincennes 1792–95; professor at Georgetown University 1795–98, at St. Mary's, Baltimore, 1801–10; appointed bishop 1810.

Flag football. *see in index* Football

Flagg, Ernest (1857–1947), U.S. architect, born in Brooklyn, N.Y.; designed Singer Building, New York City, Corcoran Gallery of Art, Washington, D.C., and U.S. Naval Academy, Annapolis, Md.; author of 'Small Houses—Their Economic Design and Construction'.

Flagg, James Montgomery (1877–1960), U.S. author and illustrator, born in Pelham Manor, N.Y.; contributor to magazines; wrote and illustrated 'The Adventures of Kitty Cobb', 'The Mystery of the Hated Man'; patriotic war posters in World Wars I and II.

Flagler, Henry Morrison (1830–1913), U.S. capitalist, born in Hopewell, N.Y.; worked with John D. Rockefeller in developing the Standard Oil Company
  Florida's railroads F-198
  industry I-195
  Miami M-348

Flag officer, a navy officer who by rank is entitled to fly a special flag at the masthead of ships under his or her command; in the U.S. Navy, a fleet admiral, admiral, vice admiral, or rear admiral.

Flag of truce, a white banner hoisted during a conflict indicating a desire to communicate with the enemy; the bearers of the flag are respected and protected.

Flag signals. *see in index* Signaling

Flags of the United States F-150. *see also in index* Flag; Flags of the world
  moon landing, *picture* S-341
  Ross R-297

Flags of the world F-161. *see also in index* Flag; Flags of the United States
  Middle Ages M-384

Flagstad, Kirsten (1895–1962), Norwegian dramatic soprano, born in Hamar, Norway; noted for Wagnerian operatic roles with Metropolitan Opera in New York City 1935–41; acclaimed for acting ability and for the remarkable power and quality of her voice; returned to Norway 1941; retired from concert stage 1953
  opera, *list* O-570

Flagstaff, Ariz., health and tourist center, in n.-central part of state; lumber mills, ranching; Northern Arizona University; Navajo Ordnance Depot; All-Indian Pow-Wow in early July; pop. 34,641 A-533, *map* U-40

Flagstaff, a pole for displaying a flag, *list* F-149

Flaherty, Ray (born 1904), U.S. football player and coach, born in Spokane, Wash.; played end for Los Angeles Wildcats, New York Yankees, New York Giants; coached Boston Redskins 1936, Washington Redskins 1937–42, New York Yankees 1946–48, Chicago Hornets 1949.

Flaherty, Robert Joseph (1884–1951), U.S. explorer and pioneer documentary film producer, born in Iron Mountain, Mich.; explored n.e. subarctic Canada 1910–16; films: 'Nanook of the North', 'Man of Aran', 'The Louisiana Story'
  directing D-155
  motion pictures M-628

Flahiff, George Bernard, Cardinal (born 1905), Canadian prelate, born in Paris, Ont.; Superior General, Basilian Fathers, 1954–61; archbishop of Winnipeg 1961–; created cardinal 1969.

Flake, in toolmaking M-84

Flakeboard, a forest product F-316

Flake tools, ancient tools M-84, *picture* M-85

Flame
  acetylene, *picture* S-9
  fire F-94

Flame flower. *see in index* Kniphofia

Flame-fusion process (or Vernueil process), gem manufacture J-113

Flamenco, name applied to Andalusian gypsies of Spain, also to their lively and fiery dances; in recent times word sometimes applied to all nonformal Spanish dancing and music
  dance D-31

'Flame of Life, The', novel by D'Annunzio D-293, I-377

Flame reaction (or flame test), the identifying color an element gives to a flame; used as a test for the presence of a particular element.

Flame test, identification of chemical elements C-290

Flame tetra (or flame fish), tropical fish *Hyphessobrycon flammeus* of rivers of Brazil; aquarium fish; hardly two inches long (five centimeters); fore part is metallic green, latter part is red; fins deep red.

Flame Tokay grape G-220

Flame tree, evergreen tree *Brachychiton acerifolium* of sterculia family, native to Australia but widely grown in Calif.; 25 to 60 ft (8 to 18 m); leaves to 10 in. (25 cm) wide, maplelike, glossy; flowers scarlet, in large clusters; fruit black pod, to 4 in. (10 cm) long A-783, *picture* C-646

Flaming Gorge Dam, dam in Utah C-584, *map* C-585

Flamingo, bird F-173
  zoo Z-463

Flamingoes, singing group M-680

Flaminian Way (or Via Flaminia), road from ancient Rome to Ariminum (modern Rimini), constructed by censor Flaminius (220 BC) R-254

Flamininus, Titus Quintius (228?–174 BC), Roman general, victor of Cynoscephalae (197 BC) and "liberator of the Greeks."

Flaminius, Gaius (died 217? BC), Roman general and censor; built Circus Flaminius in Rome and the Flaminian Way; slain in battle with Hannibal.

Flammarion, Camille (1842–1925), French astronomer; wrote popular scientific books ('Marvels of the Atmosphere').

Flamme, Hélène (born 1935), Canadian author, born in Ottawa, Ont. ('Claude et Claudine'; 'Un Drôle de Petit Cheval', Canadian Book of the Year for Children award 1959).

Flamsteed, John (1646–1719), English astronomer; astronomer to Charles II; wrote 'Historia coelestis Britannica', a 3-volume work on his observations; 3rd volume catalogues about 3,000 stars.

Flanagan, Edward Joseph (or Father Flanagan) (1886–1948), U.S. Roman Catholic priest and founder of Boys Town, Neb., born in Roscommon, Ireland; came to U.S. 1904, became citizen 1919; founded Home for Homeless Boys in Omaha in 1917, later moved 10 miles w. of Omaha and established Boys Town. *see also in index* Boys Town
  Nebraska N-96
    Omaha O-543

Flanch, in heraldry H-136

Flanders, district in w. Europe B-116
  art. *see in index* Flemish art
  bell manufacturing B-155
  Brugge B-468
  World War II W-338
  Ypres Y-431

Flanders, battle of (1914), Ypres, Belgium, World War I Y-431

Flanders Field, a United States military cemetery at Waregem, Belgium; men buried there died in World War I.

Flandin, Pierre-Étienne (1889–1958), French political leader, born in Vichy, France; favored appeasement policy; prime minister 1934–35; foreign minister 1936 and in the Vichy government 1940–41.

Flank, in cattle driving
  cowboy teamwork C-754

Flank attack, in warfare W-23

Flannagan, John Bernard (1895–1942), U.S. sculptor, born in Fargo, N.D.; known for abstract sculptures of simplicity and originality, done chiefly in fieldstone S-92

Flannel, a loosely woven woolen fabric with soft surface, with or without nap; also soft napped cotton goods or a slightly napped rayon and acetate twill fabric
  wool W-288

Flannelbush, evergreen shrub or small tree *Fremontia*

californica of sterculia family, native to Calif.; leaves have 3 to 5 lobes; flowers large, yellow, with 5 petals.
Flap, in airplane A-180, 189, *diagram* A-192
Flare, in signaling S-194, 195a. *see also in index* Fireball
fireworks F-114
Flashback, drug H-18
Flashbulb, in photography P-291, 298
Flash cutting, movie editing technique M-613
Flash evaporation, method to remove salt from salt water W-93
Flash flood F-180
Flash point, of flammable liquids F-93
Flashpowder, in early photography P-298
Flash suppressor, machine gun M-15
Flat (or river raft), flat-bottomed boat N-357
Flat, in music M-690
Flat, in stage scenery T-156, *diagrams* T-154
Flat-bed press. *see in index* Cylinder press
Flatboat P-335, *picture* P-333
Louisiana L-311
transportation T-261, *picture* T-262
Flatbush, now part of borough of Brooklyn, New York City; Flatbush Pass, strategic point in American Revolution.
Flatcar, a platform car used on railroads to haul freight too bulky for a boxcar, as lumber, cars, etc.; widely used as "piggyback" carriers for truck trailers, *picture* R-83
transportation T-255
Flat-coated retriever, dog, *picture* D-197
Flat fell, a seam S-122
Flatfish F-173
fish F-126
Flat-headed cat, wild cat *Felis planiceps*, *picture* C-215
Flathead Indians. *see in index* Salish
Flathead Lake, lake in Montana, 40 mi (60 km) s. of Glacier National Park; 188 sq mi (487 sq km) M-551
Flathead River, river in Montana, issues from s. end of Flathead Lake and enters Clark Fork after course of 75 mi (120 km); fruit-growing region
Hungry Horse Dam D-17, *picture* D-13
Flat knit, in knitting K-260
Flat saddle. *see in index* English saddle
Flat slab dam, type of dam D-17, *picture* D-12
Flat stitches. *see in index* Crewelwork
Flattery, Cape, promontory, in n.w. Wash.; on U.S. side of entrance to Strait of Juan de Fuca; Makah Indian Reservation nearby; explored by Captain Cook 1778, *map* U-40
Flat-track racing, motorcycle M-632
Flatwork ironer, *picture* L-87
Flatworm, worm of the phylum Platyhelminthes W-361
animals A-434
invertebrate I-282
Flaubert, Gustave (1821–80), French novelist F-176
creative writing W-380
French literature F-397, *picture* F-395
Maupassant M-231
realism N-413
Flauto piccolo (or piccolo), wind instrument W-229
Flavian Amphitheater. *see in index* Colosseum
Flavor, fused sensation of taste, smell, and touch
atomic particles A-755
Flavors, the six types of quarks Q-5
Flax, plant cultivated for fiber, from which linen is made, and for its seed, called flaxseed or linseed F-176
cigarette paper P-379
linen L-229
natural fibers F-76
plant and flower P-377
poisonous seed P-408
production regions C-509
textiles T-142
Flax family (or Linaceae), a family of plants, including the flax and reinwardtias.
Flaxman, John (1755–1826), English sculptor and illustrator, born in York, England; designed decorations for Wedgwood pottery; illustrated Homer's 'Iliad' and 'Odyssey'; celebrated for memorial sculpture including Admiral Nelson's memorial at Westminster Abbey S-89
Flaxseed F-176
Flea F-177
bubonic plague B-473
champion jumper A-424
insect I-224, *picture* I-216
parasite, *picture* P-113
cats C-210
dogs D-209
Fleabane, common name for plants of genus *Erigeron*, having a peculiar aromatic odor, said to keep away fleas; native to U.S.; *E. canadensis* and *E. philadelphicus* are valued medicinally for their oil, which is a strong irritant.
Flea market, *picture* P-457
Flechette, ammunition A-372
Flecker, James Elroy (1884–1915), English poet and playwright; in British consular service at Constantinople (Istanbul), Smyrna (Izmir), and Beirut; wrote "with single intention of creating beauty" ('Bridge of Fire', 'Burial in England', poems; 'Don Juan', 'Hassan', plays).
Fleece, sheep W-288
hair H-7
Fleet, United States. *see in index* United States Navy
Fleet admiral, United States Navy, title created Dec. 1944; wears five stars; King, Halsey, Nimitz, and Leahy appointed N-80
insignia, *picture* U-8
Fleet Prison, jail that stood at Fleet rivulet in London; from 12th century the king's prison, it held many noted persons; prison for debtors from mid-17th century; secret marriages (Fleet marriages) performed there from 1600s to 1753; prison abolished 1842, torn down 1845–46.
Fleet Street, main thoroughfare in London, England L-289
Fleetwood, England, town at mouth of Wyre River 8 mi (13 km) n.e. of Blackpool; seaside resort and trading port; founded 1836; pop. 28,970, *map* U-18a
Fleetwood Mac, British rock group M-682
Fleming, Alexander (1881–1955), Scottish bacteriologist F-178. *see also in index* Nobel Prizewinners, *table*
applied biology B-232
medicine M-285
microbiology M-376
penicillin discovery A-491, M-519
Fleming, Ian (1908–64), English author and journalist F-178
Fleming, Sir John Ambrose (1849–1945), English physicist and electrical engineer, born in Lancaster; active in development of telephone, electric lighting
electronics E-180
Fleming valve R-57
Fleming, Peggy Gale (born 1948), U.S. ice skater, born in San Jose, Calif.; won U.S. figure-skating title 1964–68, world title 1966–68, Olympics gold medal 1968; turned professional in 1968; TV and ice-show star.
Fleming, Sir Sandford (1827–1915), Canadian engineer, born in Scotland; built Inter-colonial Railway; in charge of survey of main line of Canadian Pacific; pioneer in proposing worldwide system of standard time.
Fleming, Victor (died 1949), U.S. motion-picture director, born in Pasadena, Calif.; developed speed camera for analytical photography ('Gone with the Wind'; 'The Wizard of Oz'; 'Tortilla Flat').
Flemings, Flemish-speaking people of Belgium B-146
Hundred Years' War H-324
Fleming valve. *see in index* Diode
Flemish art
classical music M-668
motion pictures M-615
painting P-30, 41, *pictures* P-30–2, 42,
Rubens R-310
Van Dyck V-266
Flemish bond, in bricklaying, *diagram* B-438
Flemish language B-146
Germanic languages G-103
Flemming, Arthur Sherwood (born 1905), U.S. government official and educator, born in Kingston, N.Y.; director Office of Defense Mobilization 1953–57; U.S. secretary of health, education, and welfare 1958–61; president of University of Oregon 1961–68, of Macalester College 1968–71.
Flensburg, West Germany, seaport and manufacturing city in Schleswig-Holstein; pop. 95,476, *maps* E-131, E-360
Flesch, Karl (1873–1944), Hungarian violinist, noted as teacher and virtuoso; taught in Europe and at Curtis Institute, Philadelphia ('Art of Violin Playing').
Flesh, the soft tissue that covers the skeleton of a vertebrate animal; the part of the body made up mainly of fat and connective tissue.
Flesh fly (or blowfly), any one of several large, noisy blue or green flies that deposit their eggs or larvae in meat or other animal matter
animal behavior, *picture* A-440
egg, *picture* E-111
Fletcher, Charlie May (pen name Charlie May Simon) (1897–1977), U.S. author, born near Monticello, Ark; books for children: 'Popo's Miracle', 'Bright Morning', 'Lays of the New Land', 'Art in the New Land', 'A Seed Shall Serve', biography of Kagawa, 'The Sun and the Birch'; for adults: 'Straw in the Sun'.
Fletcher, Frank J. (in full Frank Jack Fletcher, nickname Black Jack) (1885–1973), U.S. naval officer; participated in both World Wars; Medal of Honor, 1914 W-344
Fletcher, Giles (1588?–1623), English poet and clergyman, born in London, England; gained fame as gifted preacher ('Christ's Victorie and Triumph').
Fletcher, Henry Prather (1873–1959), U.S. diplomat, born in Greencastle, Pa.; served with Rough Riders in Spanish-American War; undersecretary of state 1921–22; ambassador to Belgium 1922–24; ambassador to Italy 1924–29.
Fletcher, Horace (1849–1919), U.S. food expert, born in Lawrence, Mass.; emphasized importance of prolonged mastication of food, giving rise to the verb "fletcherize."
Fletcher, John (1579–1625), English dramatist, collaborator with Francis Beaumont, born in Rye, Sussex. *see also in index* Beaumont, Francis
Fletcher, John Gould (1886–1950), U.S. writer, born in Little Rock, Ark.; exponent of imagism ('Irradiations, Sand and Spray'; 'Goblins and Pagodas'; 'Selected Poems', awarded Pulitzer prize 1939); also wrote 'Life Is My Song', autobiography, and 'Arkansas', history.
Fletcher, Phineas (1582–1650), English poet, born in Cranbrook, Kent, England; brother of Giles Fletcher ('The Purple Island').
Fletcher vs. Peck U-147
Flettner, Anton (1885–1961), German engineer; inventor of the rotorship, which is propelled by wind blowing against revolving cylinders, said to be more efficient than sails.
Fleur-de-lis, an iris
flag F-153, *picture* F-155
heraldry, *picture* H-136
'Fleurs du Mal, Les', work by Baudelaire M-77
Fleurus, Belgium, town 7 mi (11 km) n.e. of Charleroi; scene of four important battles in Spanish and French wars; pop. 8,274.
Fleury, André Hercule de (1653–1743), French prelate and statesman, born in Lodève, France; became cardinal 1726; acted as prime minister 1726–43.
FLEX (Federation Licensure Examination), United States M-277
Flexibility, in physics, a property possessed by most materials, to a certain degree, which allows them to bend without breaking.
Flexner, Abraham (1866–1959), U.S. educator and author, brother of Simon, born in Louisville, Ky.; advanced views on education; director division of studies and medical education General Education Board 1925–28; director Institute for Advanced Study, Princeton, N.J., 1930–39.
Flexner, Simon (1863–1946), U.S. pathologist and bacteriologist, born in Louisville, Ky.; director of laboratories, Rockefeller Institute for Medical Research 1903–35; discovered serum for treatment of cerebrospinal meningitis.
Flexography, printing process I-207
Flexowriter, an automatic writing machine for producing individually typed documents; makes reproductions at speed of electric typing by means of a punched tape; used for letters, checks, menus, etc.
Flick, Elmer Harrison (1876–1971), U.S. baseball outfielder, born in Bedford, Ohio; with Philadelphia, N.L., 1898–1901, Cleveland, A.L., 1902–10; hit .344 in 1899, .378 in 1900, and .336 in 1901; had lifetime batting average of .315; tied with Samuel (Wahoo Sam) Crawford for major league record of leading league 3-base hits for 3 years in row.
Flicker, woodpecker F-178
birds B-254, *pictures* B-243, B-259
egg, *picture* E-112
protective coloration P-513
Flickertail State. *see in index* North Dakota
Flight, animal
bat B-104
birds B-244, 248, *pictures* B-246
Flight attendants A-198
Flight controls, in an airplane A-189
helicopter H-119
Flight engineer A-198
'Flight into Egypt, The', fresco by Giotto, *picture* G-146
Flinders, Matthew (1774–1814), English navigator and hydrographer F-179, A-815
Flinders bar, a piece of iron placed near a magnetic compass to decrease the deviation due to local influences; named for Matthew Flinders.
Flinders River, river in Queensland, Australia, flowing w. and n. into Gulf of Carpentaria; explored 1841 by J.L. Stokes who named it for Matthew Flinders, *maps* A-819, P-3
Flinders Street Railway Station, landmark in Melbourne, Australia M-289
Flin Flon, Man. and Sask., mining town on boundary of the two provinces; pop. 7,894 S-49a, *maps* C-109, S-491
Manitoba M-98, 101, *picture* M-99
Flint, Frank Stewart (1885–1960), English poet, one of leading imagists, born in London; wrote chiefly about London ('In the Net of the Stars'; 'Cadences'; 'Otherworld').
Flint, Mich., city on Flint River 58 mi (93 km) n.w. of Detroit; pop. 159,611 F-179, *maps* N-350, U-41
Michigan M-358, 368
Flint, a quartz F-220
abrasives A-13
firearms F-96
prehistoric man M-84
mines and mining M-430
tools S-455
Flint corn C-723, *picture* C-718
Flint glass (or crystal glass)
lead L-99
prism R-39
Flint head, bird. *see in index* Wood ibis
Flintlock, firearm F-96, *picture* F-97
Flintlock, Operation, World War II campaign W-346
Flint River, river in Georgia, rises near Atlanta and flows 350 mi (560 km) to s.w. corner of state where it joins Chattahoochee to form the

Follicle, small anatomical cavity
embryology E-199
hair H-7
hormones H-243
menstruation M-300

Follicle-stimulating hormone (or FSH), hormone that induces the gonads to produce sex hormones H-240, 243, *table* H-241, *diagram* H-242
menstruation M-300

Folsom, Marion Bayard (1893–1976), U.S. business executive and government official, born in McRae, Ga.; joined Eastman Kodak Company, Rochester, N.Y., 1914, treasurer 1935–53; undersecretary of treasury 1953–55; U.S. secretary of health, education, and welfare 1955–58.

Folsom Dam, dam in California C-36

Folsom points, remains of chipped flint tools and weapons found near Folsom, N.M., by J.D. Figgins' expedition
archaeology, *picture* A-530
man I-144

Fomalhaut, a bright star in the constellation Southern Fish S-414, *chart* S-420

Fonck, René (1894–1953), French aviator, born in Vosges department; shot down 75 planes during World War I; said to have become a monk.

Fonda, Henry (1905–82), U.S. actor, born in Grand Island, Neb.; played title role of 'Mr. Roberts' on stage and screen; movies include 'Young Mr. Lincoln', 'The Grapes of Wrath'; won 1981 Academy Award for 'On Golden Pond' D-36, *picture* M-614

Fonda, Jane (born 1937), U.S. actress; daughter of Henry Fonda ('A Walk on the Wild Side'; 'Period of Adjustment'; 'They Shoot Horses, Don't They?', 1969 New York Film Critics' Award; 'Klute', 1971 Academy Award), *picture* M-614

Fonda, Peter (born 1939), U.S. motion-picture actor and producer; son of Henry Fonda ('Easy Rider'), *picture* M-620

Fondant candy C-138

Fond du Lac, Wis., city at s. end of Lake Winnebago; in farming area; limestone quarries; railroad shops, machine tools, machinery, electrical products, outboard motors, snowmobiles, automotive parts, clothing, leather products, food processing; summer resort; Marian College; pop. 35,515, *map* U-41

'Fonetik', work by Jesperson J-102

Fong, Hiram L. (born 1907), U.S. political leader and businessman, born in Honolulu, Hawaii; Republican senator from Hawaii 1959–77; first U.S. senator of Asian ancestry; president and director of numerous business firms.

Fonseca, Manoel Deodoro da (1827–92), first president of Brazil (1891); dissolved Congress and declared himself dictator, but, finding himself unsupported by army and navy, resigned.

Fonseca, Gulf of, inlet of Pacific, bordering on San Salvador, Honduras, Nicaragua; fine natural harbor; U.S. naval base.

Font (from Latin *fons*, "spring of water"), receptacle for water in baptismal service; also container for holy water placed at doorway in Roman Catholic churches, institutions, and some homes.

Font, type T-336

Fontaine, Jean de la. *see in index* La Fontaine

Fontaine, Joan (originally Joan de Havilland) (born 1917), U.S. actress, born in Tokyo, Japan, of British parents, sister of Olivia de Havilland; in motion pictures since 1937; won Academy award for role in 'Suspicion' (1941); also starred in 'Rebecca', 'The Constant Nymph', 'Jane Eyre'.

Fontainebleau, France, forest-girdled town and resort 35 mi (55 km) s.e. of Paris, near Seine River; magnificent royal palace; revocation of Edict of Nantes (1685); abdication of Napoleon (1814); Barbizon, on n.w. edge of forest, made famous by painters; pop. 17,565, *map* F-369

Fontainebleau, Treaty of (1762) S-338

Fontainebleau State Park, in Louisiana, *picture* L-318

'Fontamara', novel by Silone I-378

Fontana, Domenico (1543–1607), Italian architect; papal architect under Pope Sixtus V; built Lateran palace and Vatican library at Rome and the royal palace at Naples; in 1586 erected in front of St. Peter's the great Egyptian obelisk brought to Rome during Caligula's reign.

Fontana, Nicola. *see in index* Tartaglia, Niccolo

Fontana, Calif., city 6 mi (10 km) w. of San Bernardino; steel and steel products; in region producing grapes, fruit, and poultry; incorporated 1952; pop. 37,109
steel mill, *picture* U-86

Fontana Dam, dam in North Carolina, on Little Tennessee River T-102, *picture* D-12
North Carolina N-353

Fontane, Theodor (1819–98), German novelist and poet, born in Neuruppin, Prussia; wrote books about wars, historical romances, novels of contemporary life ('Effi Briest'), and ballads.

Fontanne, Lynn (1887?–1983), U.S. actress, born in London; in U.S. after 1916; starred with husband, Alfred Lunt ('Elizabeth the Queen'; 'Strange Interlude'; 'Reunion in Vienna'; 'Design for Living'; 'The Taming of the Shrew'; 'There Shall Be No Night'; 'O Mistress Mine'; 'The Visit'); jointly awarded Presidential Medal of Freedom 1964 A-27. *see also in index* Lunt, Alfred

Fontarabia, Spain. *see in index* Fuenterrabia

Fontbonne College, in St. Louis, Mo.; for women; chartered 1917; opened 1923; Roman Catholic; liberal arts and teacher education.

Fontenelle, Bernard le Bovier de (1657–1757), French author, born in Rouen; nephew of Corneille; noted for poetry, drama, fiction, philosophy, and science ('Dialogues of the Dead'; 'Discourse on the Plurality of Worlds').

Fontenelle Forest, natural history landmark in Omaha, Nebraska O-543

Fontenoy, village in w. Belgium, 45 mi (70 km) s.w. of Brussels; Austria and allies defeated by the French (1745) in War of the Austrian Succession; pop. 657.

Fonteyn, Dame Margot (originally Margaret Hookham) (born 1919), English ballerina, born in Reigate, Surrey; spent part of childhood in U.S. and China; in 1934 joined Vic-Wells Ballet (named Royal Ballet after 1956), prima ballerina after 1940, partner of Rudolf Nureyev after 1962; U.S. debut 1949; president Royal Academy of Dancing after 1954; married Roberto Arias 1955 ('Swan Lake'; 'The Sleeping Beauty'; 'Firebird'; 'Ondine') B-36
Nureyev N-441

Fonvizin, Denis (1744–92), outstanding Russian playwright of 18th century, born in Moscow; best known for satirical comedies R-359, 361

Foochow. *see in index* Fuzhou

Food, Drug, and Cosmetic Act, Federal. *see in index* Federal Food, Drug, and Cosmetic Act

Food Additives Amendment (1958), United States F-274

Food Administration, organized during World War I to urge greater production of food W-314

Food adulteration
food and drug laws F-274
pure food laws P-538

Food and Agriculture Organization (FAO) agency of United Nations U-26
agribusiness A-140
International Institute of Agriculture R-254

Food and Drug Act (1955), England F-274

Food and Drug Administration (FDA), United States P-538, U-164
bread product regulations B-432
cosmetics C-730
drugs D-275
food processing rules F-284
health agencies H-90
laws F-274

Food and drug laws F-274
food processing rules F-284
pure food laws P-538

Food and Drugs Act (1920 and 1953), Canada F-274

Food and Drugs Act, Federal. *see in index* Federal Food and Drugs Act

Food and nutrition F-275. *see also in index* Cereal crops; Cold storage; Pure food laws; Refrigeration; also names of foods, as Bread; Milk; and topics beginning with Food
agriculture A-403
amoeba A-375
anorexia nervosa A-467
aquaculture A-513
bacteria and decay B-14
cancer C-132
carbohydrates C-155
starch S-424
sugar S-508
cooking C-697
earth E-16
eating customs P-190
American Indian I-121, 133, *map* I-147
etiquette E-316
knife, fork, and spoon K-255
Japan S-532, *picture* C-556
pioneer America P-333
Spain S-355, 352
totemism and taboo T-236
U.S.S.R. R-330d
Vietnam V-318, *picture* V-320
farming F-25
fast food F-43
fasting F-44
fats and oils F-47
fisheries, *chart* F-138
flour and flour milling F-213
flowers F-221
food and drug laws F-274
food processing F-280
food supply F-285
fruitgrowing F-436
health H-83
home economics H-214
Hopkins H-238
gelatin G-46
irradiation U-3, V-356, 357
legume L-119
malnutrition M-77
medicine M-285
metabolism M-306
minerals
calcium C-19
phosphorus P-271
physiology L-265, P-311, *pictures* L-266, 268
plants P-376
preservation
osmosis O-610
refrigeration R-135
proteins P-514
rationing and saving, *picture* W-313
salt S-30
teeth T-52
vitamins V-354
water W-84
weight control W-135
yoga Y-421
zoo Z-463, *picture* Z-462, *list* Z-461

Food and Nutrition Service, United States U-162

Food buying P-192

Food chain, sequences in which organisms within an ecosystem feed on one another
ecology E-55, *diagram* E-56
fish F-124
invertebrates' role I-284
pollution P-441d

Food energy, a form of chemical energy E-215, *picture* E-214

Food groups F-278

Food laws. *see in index* Pure food laws; Food and drug laws

Food processing F-280
borax S-247
canning. *see in index* Canning
concentrations V-254
cooking C-697
cryogenics C-794
farm machinery F-36
fisheries F-138
flour and flour milling F-215
food and drug laws F-274
freezing V-357
fruitgrowing F-439
inventions, *table* I-281
malnutrition M-77
meat industry M-251
pure food laws P-538
refrigeration R-135

Food Research Institute, established 1921 at Stanford University, Stanford, Calif.; objective to "promote understanding of food production, distribution, and consumption."

Food Safety and Quality Service, United States U-162

Food service manager H-216

Food stylist H-219, *picture* H-216

Food substitutes
margarine M-134
pure food laws P-538
vanilla substitutes V-266

Food supply F-285
agricultural surplus A-129
hydroponics H-342
Malthus M-79

Food values. *see in index* Food and nutrition

Food-waste disposer (or garbage grinder), home appliance H-210

Fool. *see in index* Jester

Fool hen. *see in index* Ruffed grouse

Fools, Feast of, festival popular in Europe in Middle Ages, in which the clergy and religious ritual were mimicked; donkey usually had a part.

Foolscap, sheets of writing paper, 33 x 40 centimeters (13 x 16 inches) in U.S.; name comes from early papermakers' custom of using a fool's cap as a watermark.

Fool's gold. *see in index* Iron pyrite

Foot, in anatomy F-288
animal tracks A-463
beaver B-120
birds, *picture* B-242
horse H-250, *diagram* H-251
bones S-210
mollusks M-523

Foot, a division of verse P-405

Foot, unit of measure W-138, *table* W-140, *diagram* W-139
drafting dimension M-261
nautical, *diagram* B-326

Foot-and-mouth disease (sometimes called hoof-and-mouth disease, or aftosa), an infectious disease of cloven-hoofed animals, particularly of cattle and hogs
cattle C-231
pig P-322

Football, sport F-289. For lists of college and pro champions, *see tables* following; *see also in index* Soccer
Australia A-709, M-291
Hutchins H-335
Lombardi L-285

Football Hall of Fame, in Canton, Ohio; honors outstanding players, coaches, and team founders; first members elected 1963, *picture* O-510
members. *see table* following Hall of Fame H-16

Foot-binding, old Chinese custom C-366, S-179, *picture* S-178

Footcandle, unit of illumination, the amount of direct light produced on one sq. ft. of surface by international candle one ft. away.

Foote, Andrew Hull (1806–63), U.S. rear admiral, born in New Haven, Conn.; commanded western flotilla in the Civil War, and captured Ft. Henry and Island No. 10.

Foote, Arthur William (1853–1937), U.S. composer, pianist, and organist; born in Salem, Mass.; for orchestra ('In the Mountains'); choral works based on Longfellow's poems ('The Skeleton in Armor', 'The Farewell of Hiawatha').

Footing, in building's foundation B-492

Footnote, a note appearing at the foot of a page
report writing R-151b

Foot-pound-second, a unit in a system of measurement simultaneously involving length, weight or mass, and time.

Foot soldier, in warfare W-19

Forage crops. *see also in index* chief topics below
farm machinery F-35
hay H-75
peanuts P-146
peas P-142b
rye R-366b
silage S-202
sorghum S-258
vetch V-305

Forage fish F-146

Forage harvester F-35, *picture* F-36

Forager, Operation, World War II campaign W-346

COLLEGE FOOTBALL'S MAJOR BOWL GAMES

ROSE BOWL

1902	Michigan	**49**	Stanford	**0**
1916	Washington State	**14**	Brown	**0**
1917	Oregon	**14**	Pennsylvania	**0**
1918	Mare Island	**19**	Camp Lewis	**7**
1919	Great Lakes	**17**	Mare Island	**0**
1920	Harvard	**7**	Oregon	**6**
1921	California	**28**	Ohio State	**0**
1922	California	**0**	Washington & Jefferson	**0**
1923	Southern California	**14**	Penn State	**3**
1924	Navy	**14**	Washington	**14**
1925	Notre Dame	**27**	Stanford	**10**
1926	Alabama	**20**	Washington	**19**
1927	Alabama	**7**	Stanford	**7**
1928	Stanford	**7**	Pittsburgh	**6**
1929	Georgia Tech	**8**	California	**7**
1930	Southern California	**47**	Pittsburgh	**14**
1931	Alabama	**24**	Washington State	**0**
1932	Southern California	**21**	Tulane	**12**
1933	Southern California	**35**	Pittsburgh	**0**
1934	Columbia	**7**	Stanford	**0**
1935	Alabama	**29**	Stanford	**13**
1936	Stanford	**7**	Southern Methodist	**0**
1937	Pittsburgh	**21**	Washington	**0**
1938	California	**13**	Alabama	**0**
1939	Southern California	**7**	Duke	**3**
1940	Southern California	**14**	Tennessee	**0**
1941	Stanford	**21**	Nebraska	**13**
1942	Oregon State	**20**	Duke	**16**
1943	Georgia	**9**	UCLA	**0**
1944	Southern California	**29**	Washington	**0**
1945	Southern California	**25**	Tennessee	**0**
1946	Alabama	**34**	Southern California	**14**
1947	Illinois	**45**	UCLA	**14**
1948	Michigan	**49**	Southern California	**0**
1949	Northwestern	**20**	California	**14**
1950	Ohio State	**17**	California	**14**
1951	Michigan	**14**	California	**6**
1952	Illinois	**40**	Stanford	**7**
1953	Southern California	**7**	Wisconsin	**0**
1954	Michigan State	**28**	UCLA	**20**
1955	Ohio State	**20**	Southern California	**7**
1956	Michigan State	**17**	UCLA	**14**
1957	Iowa	**35**	Oregon State	**19**
1958	Ohio State	**10**	Oregon	**7**
1959	Iowa	**38**	California	**12**
1960	Washington	**44**	Wisconsin	**8**
1961	Washington	**17**	Minnesota	**7**
1962	Minnesota	**21**	UCLA	**3**
1963	Southern California	**42**	Wisconsin	**37**
1964	Illinois	**17**	Washington	**7**
1965	Michigan	**34**	Oregon State	**7**
1966	UCLA	**14**	Michigan State	**12**
1967	Purdue	**14**	Southern California	**13**
1968	Southern California	**14**	Indiana	**3**
1969	Ohio State	**27**	Southern California	**16**
1970	Southern California	**10**	Michigan	**3**
1971	Stanford	**27**	Ohio State	**17**
1972	Stanford	**13**	Michigan	**12**
1973	Southern California	**42**	Ohio State	**17**
1974	Ohio State	**42**	Southern California	**21**
1975	Southern California	**18**	Ohio State	**17**
1976	UCLA	**23**	Ohio State	**10**
1977	Southern California	**14**	Michigan	**6**
1978	Washington	**27**	Michigan	**20**
1979	Southern California	**17**	Michigan	**10**
1980	Southern California	**17**	Ohio State	**16**
1981	Michigan	**23**	Washington	**6**
1982	Washington	**28**	Iowa	**0**
1983	UCLA	**24**	Michigan	**14**
1984	UCLA	**45**	Illinois	**9**
1985	Southern California	**20**	Ohio State	**17**
1986	UCLA	**45**	Iowa	**28**
1987	Arizona State	**22**	Michigan	**15**

ORANGE BOWL

1933	Miami	**7**	Manhattan	**0**
1934	Duquesne	**33**	Miami	**7**
1935	Bucknell	**26**	Miami	**0**
1936	Catholic University	**20**	Mississippi	**19**
1937	Duquesne	**13**	Mississippi State	**12**
1938	Auburn	**6**	Michigan State	**0**
1939	Tennessee	**17**	Oklahoma	**0**
1940	Georgia Tech	**21**	Missouri	**7**
1941	Mississippi State	**14**	Georgetown	**7**
1942	Georgia	**40**	Texas Christian	**26**
1943	Alabama	**37**	Boston College	**21**
1944	Louisiana State	**19**	Texas A & M	**14**
1945	Tulsa	**26**	Georgia Tech	**12**
1946	Miami	**13**	Holy Cross	**6**
1947	Rice	**8**	Tennessee	**0**
1948	Georgia Tech	**20**	Kansas	**14**
1949	Texas	**41**	Georgia	**28**
1950	Santa Clara	**21**	Kentucky	**13**
1951	Clemson	**15**	Miami	**14**
1952	Georgia Tech	**17**	Baylor	**14**
1953	Alabama	**61**	Syracuse	**6**
1954	Oklahoma	**7**	Maryland	**0**
1955	Duke	**34**	Nebraska	**7**
1956	Oklahoma	**20**	Maryland	**6**
1957	Colorado	**27**	Clemson	**21**
1958	Oklahoma	**48**	Duke	**21**
1959	Oklahoma	**21**	Syracuse	**6**
1960	Georgia	**14**	Missouri	**0**
1961	Missouri	**21**	Navy	**14**
1962	Louisiana State	**25**	Colorado	**7**
1963	Alabama	**17**	Oklahoma	**0**
1964	Nebraska	**13**	Auburn	**7**
1965	Texas	**21**	Alabama	**17**
1966	Alabama	**39**	Nebraska	**28**
1967	Florida	**27**	Georgia Tech	**12**
1968	Oklahoma	**26**	Tennessee	**24**
1969	Penn State	**15**	Kansas	**14**
1970	Penn State	**10**	Missouri	**3**
1971	Nebraska	**17**	Louisiana State	**12**
1972	Nebraska	**38**	Alabama	**6**
1973	Nebraska	**40**	Notre Dame	**6**
1974	Penn State	**16**	Louisiana State	**9**
1975	Notre Dame	**13**	Alabama	**11**
1976	Oklahoma	**14**	Michigan	**6**
1977	Ohio State	**27**	Colorado	**10**
1978	Arkansas	**31**	Oklahoma	**6**
1979	Oklahoma	**31**	Nebraska	**24**
1980	Oklahoma	**24**	Florida State	**7**
1981	Oklahoma	**18**	Florida State	**17**
1982	Clemson	**22**	Nebraska	**15**
1983	Nebraska	**21**	Louisiana State	**20**
1984	Miami	**31**	Nebraska	**30**
1985	Washington	**28**	Oklahoma	**17**
1986	Oklahoma	**25**	Penn State	**10**
1987	Oklahoma	**42**	Arkansas	**8**

SUGAR BOWL

1935	Tulane	20	Temple	14
1936	Texas Christian	3	Louisiana State	2
1937	Santa Clara	21	Louisiana State	14
1938	Santa Clara	6	Louisiana State	0
1939	Texas Christian	15	Carnegie Tech	7
1940	Texas A & M	14	Tulane	13
1941	Boston College	19	Tennessee	13
1942	Fordham	2	Missouri	0
1943	Tennessee	14	Tulsa	7
1944	Georgia Tech	20	Tulsa	18
1945	Duke	29	Alabama	26
1946	Oklahoma A & M	33	St. Mary's	13
1947	Georgia	20	North Carolina	10
1948	Texas	27	Alabama	7
1949	Oklahoma	14	North Carolina	6
1950	Oklahoma	35	Louisiana State	0
1951	Kentucky	13	Oklahoma	7
1952	Maryland	28	Tennessee	13
1953	Georgia Tech	24	Mississippi	7
1954	Georgia Tech	42	West Virginia	19
1955	Navy	21	Mississippi	0
1956	Georgia Tech	7	Pittsburgh	0
1957	Baylor	13	Tennessee	7
1958	Mississippi	39	Texas	7
1959	Louisiana State	7	Clemson	0
1960	Mississippi	21	Louisiana State	0
1961	Mississippi	14	Rice	6
1962	Alabama	10	Arkansas	3
1963	Mississippi	17	Arkansas	13
1964	Alabama	12	Mississippi	7
1965	Louisiana State	13	Syracuse	10
1966	Missouri	20	Florida	18
1967	Alabama	34	Nebraska	7
1968	Louisiana State	20	Wyoming	13
1969	Arkansas	16	Georgia	2
1970	Mississippi	27	Arkansas	22
1971	Tennessee	34	Air Force	13
1972	Oklahoma	40	Auburn	22
1973	Oklahoma	14	Penn State	0
1974	Notre Dame	24	Alabama	23
1975	Nebraska	13	Florida	10
1976	Alabama	13	Penn State	6
1977	Pittsburgh	27	Georgia	3
1978	Alabama	35	Ohio State	6
1979	Alabama	14	Penn State	7
1980	Alabama	24	Arkansas	9
1981	Georgia	17	Notre Dame	10
1982	Pittsburgh	24	Georgia	20
1983	Penn State	27	Georgia	23
1984	Auburn	9	Michigan	7
1985	Nebraska	28	Louisiana State	10
1986	Tennessee	35	Miami	7
1987	Nebraska	30	Lousiana State	15

COTTON BOWL

1937	Texas Christian	16	Marquette	6
1938	Rice	28	Colorado	14
1939	St. Mary's	20	Texas Tech	13
1940	Clemson	6	Boston College	3
1941	Texas A & M	13	Fordham	12
1942	Alabama	29	Texas A & M	21
1943	Texas	14	Georgia Tech	7
1944	Randolph Field	7	Texas	7
1945	Oklahoma A & M	34	Texas Christian	0
1946	Texas	40	Missouri	27
1947	Louisiana State	0	Arkansas	0
1948	Penn State	13	Southern Methodist	13
1949	Southern Methodist	21	Oregon	13
1950	Rice	27	North Carolina	13
1951	Tennessee	20	Texas	14
1952	Kentucky	20	Texas Christian	7
1953	Texas	16	Tennessee	0
1954	Rice	28	Alabama	6
1955	Georgia Tech	14	Arkansas	6
1956	Mississippi	14	Texas Christian	13
1957	Texas Christian	28	Syracuse	27
1958	Navy	20	Rice	7
1959	Air Force	0	Texas Christian	0
1960	Syracuse	23	Texas	14
1961	Duke	7	Arkansas	6
1962	Texas	12	Mississippi	7
1963	Louisiana State	13	Texas	0
1964	Texas	28	Navy	6
1965	Arkansas	10	Nebraska	7
1966	Louisiana State	14	Arkansas	7
1967	Georgia	24	Southern Methodist	9
1968	Texas A & M	20	Alabama	16
1969	Texas	36	Tennessee	13
1970	Texas	21	Notre Dame	17
1971	Notre Dame	24	Texas	11
1972	Penn State	30	Texas	6
1973	Texas	17	Alabama	13
1974	Nebraska	19	Texas	3
1975	Penn State	41	Baylor	20
1976	Arkansas	31	Georgia	10
1977	Houston	30	Maryland	21
1978	Notre Dame	38	Texas	10
1979	Notre Dame	35	Houston	34
1980	Houston	17	Nebraska	14
1981	Alabama	30	Baylor	2
1982	Texas	14	Alabama	12
1983	Southern Methodist	7	Pittsburgh	3
1984	Georgia	10	Texas	9
1985	Boston College	45	Houston	28
1986	Texas A & M	36	Auburn	16
1987	Ohio State	28	Texas A & M	12

GATOR BOWL

1946	Wake Forest	26	South Carolina	14
1947	Oklahoma	34	North Carolina State	13
1948	Clemson	24	Missouri	23
1949	Georgia	20	Maryland	20
1950	Maryland	20	Missouri	7
1951	Wyoming	20	Washington & Lee	7
1952	Miami	14	Clemson	0
1953	Florida	14	Tulsa	13
1954	Texas Tech	35	Auburn	13
1955	Auburn	33	Baylor	13
1956	Vanderbilt	25	Auburn	13
1957	Georgia Tech	21	Pittsburgh	14
1958	Tennessee	3	Texas A & M	0
1959	Mississippi	7	Florida	3
1960	Arkansas	14	Georgia Tech	7
1961	Florida	13	Baylor	12
1962	Penn State	30	Georgia Tech	15
1963	Florida	17	Penn State	7
1964	North Carolina	35	Air Force	0
1965	Florida State	36	Oklahoma	19
1966	Georgia Tech	31	Texas Tech	21
1967	Tennessee	18	Syracuse	12
1968	Florida State	17	Penn State	17
1969	Missouri	35	Alabama	10
1970	Florida	14	Tennessee	13
1971	Auburn	35	Mississippi	28
1972	Georgia	7	North Carolina	3
1973	Auburn	24	Colorado	3
1974	Texas Tech	28	Tennessee	19
1975	Auburn	27	Texas	3
1976	Maryland	13	Florida	0
1977	Notre Dame	20	Penn State	9
1978	Pittsburgh	17	Clemson	3
1979	Clemson	17	Ohio State	15
1980	North Carolina	17	Michigan	15
1981	Pittsburgh	37	South Carolina	9
1982	North Carolina	31	Arkansas	27
1983	Florida State	31	West Virginia	12
1984	Florida	14	Iowa	6
1985	Oklahoma State	21	South Carolina	14
1986	Florida State	34	Oklahoma State	23
1987	Clemson	27	Stanford	21

PRO FOOTBALL CHAMPIONS

NATIONAL FOOTBALL LEAGUE

1921	Chicago Bears	1954	Cleveland Browns
1922	Canton	1955	Cleveland Browns
1923	Canton	1956	New York Giants
1924	Cleveland	1957	Detroit
1925	Chicago Cardinals	1958	Baltimore
1926	Frankford (Phila.)	1959	Baltimore
1927	New York Giants	1960	Philadelphia
1928	Providence	1961	Green Bay
1929	Green Bay	1962	Green Bay
1930	Green Bay	1963	Chicago Bears
1931	Green Bay	1964	Cleveland Browns
1932	Chicago Bears	1965	Green Bay
1933*	Chicago Bears	1966	Green Bay†
1934	New York Giants	1967	Green Bay†
1935	Detroit	1968	Baltimore
1936	Green Bay	1969	Minnesota
1937	Washington	1970–71‡	Baltimore
1938	New York Giants	1972	Dallas
1939	Green Bay	1973	Miami
1940	Chicago Bears	1974	Miami
1941	Chicago Bears	1975	Pittsburgh
1942	Washington	1976	Pittsburgh
1943	Chicago Bears	1977	Oakland
1944	Green Bay	1978	Dallas
1945	Cleveland Rams	1979	Pittsburgh
1946	Chicago Bears	1980	Pittsburgh
1947	Chicago Cardinals	1981	Oakland
1948	Philadelphia	1982	San Francisco
1949	Philadelphia	1983	Washington
1950	Cleveland Browns	1984	Los Angeles
1951	Los Angeles	1985	San Francisco
1952	Detroit	1986	Chicago
1953	Detroit	1987	New York Giants

AMERICAN FOOTBALL LEAGUE

1960	Houston	1965	Buffalo
1961	Houston	1966	Kansas City
1962	Dallas	1967	Oakland
1963	San Diego	1968	New York†
1964	Buffalo	1969	Kansas City†

*Beginning 1933, championship decided by play-off between division leaders. †Winner of Super Bowl in January of succeeding year. ‡Leagues merged into single National Football League beginning with 1970 season; Super Bowl winner is league champion.

Forain, Jean Louis (1852–1931), French painter and etcher, best known for witty caricatures of Paris life; worked for a number of publications.

Foraker Act (1900), act of U.S. Congress under which Puerto Rico was governed from the time Spain ceded the island to the U.S. until 1917 P-530

Foramen magnum, an opening in the occipital bone for the passage of the spinal cord S-210

Foraminifera, an order of single-celled water-dwelling animals with limy outer coats, *pictures* A-432, C-238, C-266
 oceanography O-484

Forbes, Esther (1894?–1967), U.S. author, born in Westboro, Mass.; on staff of Houghton Mifflin publishers, Boston 1920–26. Received Pulitzer prize in history 1943 for 'Paul Revere and the World He Lived In'; books for children are 'Johnny Tremain' (Newbery Medal 1944) and 'America's Paul Revere', illustrated by Lynd Ward; novels for adults: 'The Running of the Tide' and 'Rainbow on the Road'
 'Johnny Tremain' R-111d

Forbes, Rosita (1893–1967), British traveler, author; expeditions to Libyan desert, Asir, and Abyssinia ('Secret of Sahara-Kufara'; 'Adventure').

Forbes-Robertson, Sir Johnston (1853–1937), British actor, born in London; remembered for 'As You Like It', 'Hamlet', 'Othello'.

Forbidden City, landmark area in Peking, China; contains palaces of imperial emperors F-298, C-368, *picture* C-372
 Peking P-153

Forbidden region, in quantum mechanics S-254h

Force, in physics, anything that tends to produce, stop, or change motion, if unopposed; may push or pull. *see also in index* Energy; Mechanics; Power
 atomic particles A-750, *diagram* A-757
 black hole B-306
 centrifugal C-200
 centripetal C-200
 measurement devices I-229

Force Act (1833), United States
 Ku Klux Klan K-309

Force balance, electronic scale mechanism W-134

Forced-air furnace F-451

Forced convection H-105

Forced labor. *see in index* Labor, *subhead* forced labor

Forced waves (or seas), ocean waves O-487

Force feed, a pressure system of lubricating an automobile power system A-849

Force pump P-532, *diagrams* P-533

Forchheim, West Germany, city in Bavaria, 14 mi (22 km) s.e. of Bamberg; dates from 8th century; pop. 22,009, *map* G-131

Ford, Betty (in full Elizabeth Bloomer Ford) (born 1918), wife of former President Ford and leader in anti-drug abuse campaign; born in Chicago, Ill. F-301

Ford, Edsel Bryant (1893–1943), U.S. automobile manufacturer, born in Bagley (now Detroit), Mich.; the only child of Henry Ford; president of Ford Motor Company 1919–43.

Ford, Edward Charles (nickname Whitey) (born 1928), U.S. baseball player, born in New York City; left-handed pitcher New York Yankees 1950–67; career total 236 wins, 106 losses; won the Cy Young award 1961.

Ford, Edward Onslow (1852–1901), English sculptor, born in London; noted for portrait busts and statues (Shelley memorial, Oxford University).

Ford, Ford Madox (or Ford Madox Hueffer) (1873–1939), British author; wrote postwar (World War I) novels ('A Man Could Stand Up', 'The Last Post'), historical romances ('The Fifth Queen'), critical studies ('Hans Holbein, the Younger', 'Portraits from Life') W-28

Ford, Gerald R. (born 1913), 38th president of the United States F-299
 amnesty A-373
 Grand Rapids, Mich. G-213
 Kissinger K-251
 Nixon N-327
 United States U-196b
 Warren Commission K-205

Ford, Guy Stanton (1873–1962), U.S. historian, educator, born in Salem, Wis.; professor of history, dean Graduate School, University of Minnesota 1913–38, president 1938–41; executive secretary, American Historical Association, managing editor, *American Historical Review* 1941–53; editor in chief, 'Compton's Encyclopedia' 1922–61.

Ford, Hannibal Choate (1877–1955), U.S. engineer and inventor, born in Dryden, N.Y.; patented first gunfire computers; helped Elmer A. Sperry develop gyroscope 1909.

Ford, Henry (1863–1947), U.S. manufacturer F-305
 automobile A-858
 automobile industry A-868
 Edison E-76
 Firestone F-113
 Industrial Revolution I-182
 industry I-191
 Michigan M-358, *picture* M-366
 Detroit D-123

Ford, Henry, II (born 1917), U.S. automobile manufacturer, born in Detroit, Mich.; son of Edsel Ford and grandson of Henry Ford; with Ford Motor Company since 1940, chairman and chief executive officer 1960–; won Presidential Medal of Freedom 1969
 Detroit D-123

Ford, John (1586–1640?), English dramatist, born in Ilsington; his work is characterized by its dramatic beauty and intensity of passion.

Ford, John (1895–1973), U.S. motion-picture director, born in Cape Elizabeth, Me.; won Academy awards for direction of 'The Informer' (1935), 'The Grapes of Wrath' (1940), 'How Green Was My Valley' (1941), and 'The Quiet Man' (1952) D-155

Ford, Leonard (nickname Len) (1926–72), U.S. football player, born in Washington, D.C.; defensive end; Los Angeles Dons 1948–49, Cleveland Browns 1950–57, Green Bay Packers 1958.

Ford, Paul Leicester (1865–1902), U.S. historian and novelist, born in Brooklyn, N.Y.; edited writings of Washington, John Dickinson; wrote lives of Washington and Franklin ('Honorable Peter Sterling'; 'Janice Meredith').

Ford City, Ont. *see in index* East Windsor

Forde, Francis Michael (1890–1983), Australian statesman, born in Mitchell, Queensland; member of Parliament 1917–46; prime minister 1945.

Ford Foundation, organized 1936 F-333, *table* F-332
 educational projects U-208
 Ford F-306
 Hutchins H-335

Fordham University, in New York, N.Y.; private control, Catholic-related; founded 1841; liberal arts, business administration, adult education, business, education, law, pharmacy, social service; graduate work N-254, N-279

Ford Motor Company A-868, *picture* A-865
 Canada, *picture* C-80
 Michigan M-362, *picture* M-354
 Detroit D-123
 Ford F-305
 mass production M-208
 West German plant G-117

Fordney-McCumber Act, United States
 Harding H-40

Fore-and-aft sails, in ship, *pictures* S-166

Forearm, part of arm between elbow and wrist
 bones S-210

Forebrain (or prosencephalon), *diagram* B-402

Forecasting weather. *see in index* Meteorology, *subhead* weather forecasting

Forecastle, in ship S-164

Foreclosure, in law
 definition, *table* L-92
 home mortgage H-296, 303

Forehand, in tennis, *diagram* T-105

Foreign Agricultural Service, United States government agency authorized by act of 1930; represents Department of Agriculture U-162

Foreign aid F-306
 food supply F-286
 international relations I-264
 Third World T-169

Foreign and Commonwealth Office, British administrative office for The Commonwealth C-603

Foreign Assistance Act (1948), United States U-192

Foreigner. *see in index* Alien; Immigration, *subhead* United States

Foreign exchange, in economics F-307
 International Monetary Fund I-258, U-26
 money M-531

Foreign language newspaper, provides news for immigrants and foreign-born people N-241

Foreign Legion, French military force F-308

Foreign missions C-337. *see also in index* Missions, Christian

Foreign office, a government department handling foreign affairs. *see also in index* State, Department of
 United Kingdom's diplomatic corps D-149

'Foreign Policy', journal M–31

Foreign policy, manner in which one country handles its dealings with another; involves official recognition of other countries, alliances, agreements, etc.
 diplomacy D-149
 international relations I-265
 U.S. government U-157

Foreign Policy Association (formerly League of Free Nations Association), nonpartisan educational organization aiming to improve citizen participation in foreign policy; headquarters New York, N.Y.; founded 1918; publishes *Headline Series* and *Great Decisions*.

Foreign relations. *see in index* International relations

Foreign Secretary, chief officer of Foreign Office D-149

Foreign Service, United States U-158
 Bureau of International Labor Affairs U-164
 diplomacy D-149
 salaries, *table* U-155

MEMBERS OF THE PRO FOOTBALL HALL OF FAME

elected in 1963
Baugh, Samuel Adrian (Sammy)
Bell, deBennville (Bert)
Carr, Joseph Francis (Joe)
Clark, Earl (Dutch)
Grange, Harold Edward (Red)
Halas, George Stanley (Papa Bear)
Hein, Melvin (Mel)
Henry, Wilbur Francis (Pete)
Hubbard, Robert Calvin (Cal)
Hutson, Donald (Don)
Lambeau, Earl Louis (Curly)
McNally, John Vincent (Blood)
Mara, Timothy James (Tim)
Marshall, George Preston
Nagurski, Bronko
Nevers, Ernest (Ernie)
Thorpe, James Francis (Jim)

elected in 1964
Conzelman, James (Jimmy)
Healey, Ed
Hinkle, Clarke
Lyman, Roy (Link)
Michalske, August (Mike)
Rooney, Arthur J.
Trafton, George

elected in 1965
Chamberlin, Guy
Driscoll, John Leo (Paddy)
Fortmann, Daniel F.
Graham, Otto
Luckman, Sidney (Sid)
Van Buren, Steve
Waterfield, Robert (Bob)

elected in 1966
Dudley, William (Bill)
Guyon, Joseph (Joe)
Herber, Arnold (Arnie)
Kiesling, Walter (Walt)
McAfee, George (Duke)
Owen, Stephen (Steve)
Ray, Hugh (Shorty)
Turner, Clyde (Bulldog)

elected in 1967
Bednarik, Charles (Chuck)
Bidwill, Charles W.
Brown, Paul
Layne, Robert (Bobby)
Reeves, Daniel F.
Strong, Kenneth (Ken)
Stydahar, Joseph (Joe)
Tunnell, Emlen

elected in 1968
Battles, Clifford (Cliff)
Donovan, Arthur (Art)
Hirsch, Elroy (Crazylegs)
Millner, Wayne
Motley, Marion
Trippi, Charles (Charlie)
Wojciechowicz, Alexander (Alex)

elected in 1969
Edwards, Albert Glen (Turk)
Neale, Earle (Greasy)
Nomellini, Leo
Perry, Fletcher (Joe)
Stautner, Ernest (Ernie)

elected in 1970
Christiansen, John LeRoy (Jack, or Chris
Fears, Thomas (Tom)
McElhenny, Hugh (The King)
Pihos, Peter Louis (Pete)

elected in 1971
Brown, James (Nathaniel (Jim)
Hewitt, William Ernest (Bill)
Kinard, Frank (Bruiser)
Lombardi, Vincent Thomas (Vince)
Robustelli, Andrew Richard (Andy)
Tittle, Yelberton Abraham (Y.A.)
Van Brocklin, Norman (Dutchman)

elected in 1972
Hunt, Lamar
Marchetti, Gino
Matson, Ollie
Parker, Clarence (Ace)

elected in 1973
Berry, Raymond (Ray)
Parker, James (Jim)
Schmidt, Joseph (Joe)

elected in 1974
Canadeo, Anthony (Gray Ghost)
George, William (Bill)
Groza, Louis (Lou, or The Toe)
Lane, Richard (Night Train)

elected in 1975
Brown, Roosevelt
Connor, George
Lavelli, Dante
Moore, Leonard (Lenny)

elected in 1976
Flaherty, Ray
Ford, Leonard (Len)
Taylor, James (Jim)

elected in 1977
Gifford, Francis (Frank)
Gregg, Alvin Forrest
Sayers, Gale
Starr, Bryan (Bart)
Willis, William (Bill)

elected in 1978
Alworth, Lance
Ewbank, Wilbur C. (Weeb)
Leemans, Alphonse (Tuffy)
Nitschke, Raymond (Ray)
Wilson, Lawrence (Larry)

elected in 1979
Butkus, Richard (Dick)
Lary, Robert Yale
Mix, Robald (Ron)
Unitas, John (Johnny)

elected in 1980
Adderley, Herbert (Herb)
Jones, David (Deacon)
Lilly, Robert (Bob)
Otto, James Edwin (Jim)

elected in 1981
Badgro, Morris (Red)
Blanda, George
Davis, Willie
Ringo, James (Jim)

elected in 1982
Atkins, Douglas (Doug)
Huff, Robert Lee (Sam)
Musso, George
Olsen, Merlin

elected in 1983
Bell, Robert Lee (Bobby)
Gillman, Sidney (Sid)
Jurgensen, Christian (Sonny)
Mitchell, Robert (Bobby)
Warfield, Paul

elected in 1984
Brown, William (Willie)
McCormack, Michael (Mike)
Taylor, Charles (Charley)
Weinmeister, Arnold (Arnie)

elected in 1985
Gatski, Frank
Namath, Joe (Boradway Joe)
Roselle, Alvin R. (Pete)
Simpson, O.J.
Staubach, Roger

elected in 1986
Hornung, Paul
Houston, Ken
Lanier, Willie
Tarkenton, Fran
Walker, Doak

elected in 1987
Csonka, Larry
Dawson, Len
Greene, Joe (Mean Joe)
Johnson, John Henry
Langer, Jim
Maynard, Don
Upshaw, Gene

Foreign Service, School of, first such school in United States, founded 1919; part of Georgetown University, Washington, D.C.
Foreign trade. *see in index* International trade; Trade; and *subhead* trade under names of countries
Foreign Wars of the U.S., Military Order of, patriotic and military organization founded 1894; membership limited to commissioned officers of U.S. Army who have served in wars against foreign powers and their descendants in direct male line; purpose, national defense against foreign aggression.
Foreman, George (born 1949), U.S. boxer, born in Marshall, Tex. B-392
  Ali match A-306
Forensics, art of argumentative exercise used in formal debates D-51
Foreordination. *see in index* Predestination
Foreshortening, an effect of visual perspective that causes an object to be apparently shortened in directions not lying in a plane perpendicular to the line of sight
  Correggio C-726
  Uccello P-34
Forest and forestry F-309. *see also in index* Lumber; Tree; Wood
  Africa A-94
    Congo C-513
    Sudan S-501
  agriculture A-132
  Asia A-688
    China C-340, 352
    Iran I-305
  climate C-395a
  conservation. *see in index* Conservation
  ecology E-51, *diagram* E-52
    endangered species E-209
  Europe E-342
    Alps A-320
    England E-231
    France F-345
    Norway N-392
    Spain S-351, 352
    Switzerland S-538
    West Germany G-112, 117
  fire fighting F-107. *see also in index* Forest fire
  flood control F-185
  forest products F-316
  industry I-185
  jungle J-153
  land use L-28
  Latin America L-60, 64
  lumber L-329
  mountain M-636
  North America N-343
    Canada C-82
    United States U-105, 129, *charts* U-124, *map* U-125, *picture* U-30
      Alaska A-243
      land used, *chart* U-118
      national forests U-162
      Roosevelt R-285
      sequoias and redwoods S-112
      Tennessee Valley Authority T-102
  petrified P-227. *see also in index* Petrified forests
  plantation farming A-133
  sciences S-64b
  soil S-251, 253, *map* S-252
  tree T-277
  wild flowers F-231
Forestay, part of a sailboat, *diagram* B-326
Forester, Cecil Scott (1899–1966), English journalist and novelist, born in Cairo, Egypt ('Payment Deferred', a murder story; a series of novels on Horatio Hornblower; 'The Age of Fighting Sail', naval history of War of 1812).
Foresters, Orders of, fraternal, beneficent, and benevolent orders first founded in England; written history dates from 1790 when order was known as Ancient Royal Order of Foresters; later superseded by Ancient Order of Foresters; introduced into U.S., 1832; Independent Order of Foresters founded at Newark, N.J., 1874, by seceding bodies; Ancient Order of Foresters of America founded 1889 by further seceders (name changed to Foresters of America 1895).
Forest fire F-314
  campfire C-68
  parachutes P-109a
  sequoia and redwood S-112
'Forest Hymn, A', work by Bryant A-345
Forest Lawn Memorial Park, in Glendale, Calif. G-165
Forest management F-311, 315
Forest Park, Ga., city just s.e. of Atlanta; railroad junction; metal, glass, and paper products; pop. 18,782.
Forest Park, Ill., residential village just w. of Chicago; formerly called Harlem; incorporated 1907; pop. 15,177.
Forest Park, Ohio, city 14 mi (22 km) n. of Cincinnati; chiefly residential; incorporated 1961; pop. 18,675.
Forest Park, park in St. Louis, Mo. S-22
Forest products F-316. *see also in index* Forest and forestry; Lumber; Rubber; Wood
  camphor C-67
  charcoal C-271
  resin R-158
  wood pulp P-101
Forest Reserve Act (1891), United States R-285
Forest reserves. *see also in index* Forest and forestry
Forest service. *see also in index* Forest and forestry
  lumber industry L-333
  United States U-162, P-109a
    fire fighting F-107
      helicopter H-120
    forest management F-315
'Forever Amber', work by Winsor N-409
Forfeiture, in law, term applied to loss of property, personal or real, because of misconduct, crime, or breach of promise.
Forgery. *see in index* Counterfeiting and forgery
Forgetting
  memory M-294
  repression P-519
Forging, metalworking operation F-317
  blacksmithing B-308

iron and steel industry I-348
press operator V-374
tools T-225

Forillon National Park, park in Quebec Q-9h
national parks N-29

Forint, monetary unit of Hungary, historic value about 9 cents.

Fork, utensil K-255. *see also in index* Knife; Spoon
etiquette E-319, *pictures* E-320, 321
garden use G-22

Forklift, a machine
crane and derrick C-761

Forlanini, Enrico (1848–1930), Italian pioneer of scientific aviation; built steam-engine driven helicopter model which rose 40 ft (12 m) from ground 1877; built new type of semirigid aircraft 1914; inventor of the hydrofoil boat B-329

Forli, Melozzo da. *see in index* Melozzo da Forli

Form, in music M-666, *list* M-670

Form (or chase), in printing P-500, P-501

Form, rabbit nest R-20, *picture* R-21

Formaldehyde, strongly antiseptic gas F-318
methanol M-317
organic chemistry O-603
petrochemicals P-228
vaccine manufacture V-252, *picture* V-253

Formalin, solution of formaldehyde in water used in embalming procedures D-50

Formalists, followers of David Hilbert's views of mathematics M-217

Formal operational stage, period of child development P-314

Forman, Milos (born 1932), film director, born in Cáslav, Czechoslovakia D-155

Formation, in warfare W-22

Formentera, one of the Balearic Islands B-24

Formic acid, organic chemistry, *diagram* O-603
formicines A-468

Formicary, ant nest. *see in index* Ant, *subhead* nest

Formicidae, ant family A-468. *see also in index* Ant

Formicines, subfamily of ants A-468

Forming roll, machine tool T-225

Formosa. *see in index* Taiwan

Formula
algebraic A-296

Formula fiction, term used to identify fiction that has similar story lines N-408

Formula Translating system. *see in index* FORTRAN

Form utility, factor in transportation T-252

Fornax, constellation, *chart* C-682

Forrest, Edwin (1806–72), U.S. tragedian, until the advent of Edwin Booth the most famous in U.S.; born in Philadelphia, Pa.; his best characters were Othello, Lear, Richard III A-27

Forrest, John, Baron (1847–1918), Australian statesman; first premier of Western Australia 1890–1901; introduced free homestead system; established Agricultural Land Bank; first Australian to receive peerage.

Forrest, Nathan Bedford (1821–77), Confederate general of cavalry, born in Bedford County, Tenn.; captured Fort Pillow 1864; distinguished service in several battles, including Chickamauga and Nashville, and in raids in Tennessee, Mississippi, and Alabama C-476

Forrestal, James Vincent (1892–1949), U.S. investment banker and public official, born in Beacon, N.Y.; aviator in World War I; undersecretary of the Navy 1940–44, secretary 1944–47; secretary of defense 1947–49; committed suicide, *picture* W-354

Forrest City, Ark., city 45 mi (70 km) s.w. of Memphis, Tenn., in agricultural area; metal products, clothing, electric motors; settled by Nathan Bedford Forrest; pop. 13,803, *map* A-625

Forssmann, Werner (1904–79), German physician, born in Berlin; early work on cardiac catheterization. *see also in index* Nobel Prizewinners, *table*

Forster, Edward Morgan (1879–1970), English novelist and critic F-318
literary contribution E-280

Forster, John (1812–76), English biographer and historian, born in Newcastle ('Life of Dickens'; 'Lives of the Statesmen of the Commonwealth').

Forster, William Edward (1818–86), English liberal, member of Commons 1861–86; secretary for Ireland 1880–82, before Phoenix Park plot.

Forster's tern, bird *Sterna forsteri* G-317

'Forsyte Saga, The', related novels by John Galsworthy, including 'The Man of Property', 'The Indian Summer of a Forsyte', 'In Chancery', 'Awakening', 'To Let'; a second series includes 'A Modern Comedy', 'The White Monkey', 'The Silver Spoon', 'Two Forsyte Interludes', 'Swan Song' G-7
English literature E-279

Forsyth, Alexander J. (1769–1843), Scottish clergyman and inventor, born in Aberdeenshire; developed percussion-firing device for firearms F-98, *picture* F-97

Forsyth Dam, (or Powersite Dam), dam in Missouri M-489

Forsythia (or golden bell), genus of Asiatic shrubs of olive family; cultivated in parks and gardens; small yellow bell-shaped flowers cover the bushes before the leaves appear; named in honor of William Forsyth, British botanist, *picture* F-226

Fort, Paul (1872–1960), French poet; in 1890 founded Théâtre des Arts; editor of *Vers et Prose* 1905–14; rhythmic verse printed like prose ('Ballades françaises').

Fort Abercrombie, in North Dakota, on the Red River N-376

Fort Abraham Lincoln, in North Dakota, on west side of Missouri River, south of Mandan; last headquarters of George Armstrong Custer; original fort called Fort McKeen, built 1872, later considered part of Fort Abraham Lincoln; abandoned 1895; became Fort Lincoln State Park 1908; new Fort Lincoln built south of Bismarck 1903
North Dakota, *picture* N-375

Fort Adams, fort on the Mississippi River near s.w. corner of Mississippi; earthworks, magazine, and barracks for defense against Spanish; built 1798–99 by Thomas Freeman; abandoned after U.S. acquisition of Florida.

Fortaleza (also Ceará), Brazil; pop. 529,933 F-318
Brazil, *maps* B-425, S-298
world, *map* W-297

Fortaleza, La, in San Juan, Puerto Rico S-44a

Fort Amador, U.S. Army, in former Canal Zone on Bay of Panama; area about 70 acres (28 hectares); post built 1914; named in honor of Manuel Amador Guerrero, first president of Republic of Panama.

Fort Amherst National Historic Park, park on Prince Edward Island P-497c
national parks N-29

Fort and fortifications F-319
castles C-198
Hadrian's Wall R-248
Kremlin K-304
Scotland S-69, *picture* S-71

Fort Anne, fort at Annapolis Royal, Nova Scotia N-401

Fort Anne National Historic Park, park in Nova Scotia N-29

Fortas, Abe (1910–82), U.S. lawyer, born in Memphis, Tenn.; undersecretary Department of the Interior 1942–46; practiced law Washington, D.C., 1946–65; associate justice U.S. Supreme Court 1965–69 S-518a

Fort Astoria, fur-trading post founded by employees of John Jacob Astor 1811, on site of present Astoria, Ore.
fur trade F-471, *picture* F-472

Fort Atkinson, in Iowa, *picture* I-299

Fort Atkinson (now Fort Calhoun), in Nebraska, first military post west of the Missouri River N-98

Fort Battleford National Historic Park. *see in index* Battleford National Historic Park

Fort Beauséjour National Historic Park, park in New Brunswick; established 1926; has historical museum N-156
national parks N-29

Fort Belvoir (formerly Fort Humphreys), U.S. Army post 14 mi (22 km) s.w. of Alexandria, Va.; pop. 14,591, *map* V-349

Fort Benjamin Harrison, U.S. army post near Indianapolis, Ind. I-104

Fort Benning, U.S. military reservation of about 182,000 acres (73,600 hectares), near Columbus, Ga.; pop. 27,495
infantrymen statue, *picture* G-94

Fort Benton, Mont., town on Missouri River at head of navigation; important early supply center for gold camps; pop. 1,693.

Fort Bliss, U.S. military post 5 mi (8 km) n.e. of El Paso, Tex.; once a cavalry post, now U.S. Army Air Defense Center, 3rd Armored Cavalry Regiment, service school; pop. 15,000.

Fort Bragg, U.S. Army post 10 mi (16 km) n.w. of Fayetteville, N.C.; established 1918, named for Gen. Braxton Bragg; 120,000 acres (49,000 hectares); pop. 36,500 N-353

Fort Bridger, fort, s.w. Wyoming; established in 1843 by Jim Bridger, *picture* O-599

Fort Brown, fort, established 1846 by Gen. Zachary Taylor; named for Jacob Brown, killed defending it against Mexicans 1846; present site of Brownsville, Tex.; taken from Confederates by Union forces 1865; U.S. Army post 1865–1946.

Fort Calhoun (formerly Fort Atkinson), in Nebraska, first military post west of the Missouri River N-98

Fort Campbell, U.S. Army post between Hopkinsville, Ky., and Clarksville, Tenn.; area 101,700 acres (41,200 hectares); founded 1942; home of 101st Airborne Division ("Screaming Eagles"); pop. 22,895.

Fort Carillon. *see in index* Fort Ticonderoga

Fort Caroline National Memorial, park in Jacksonville, Florida J-10

Fort Chambly National Historic Park, park in Quebec Q-9h
national parks N-29

Fort Charlotte, Mobile, Ala. *see in index* Fort Condé

Fort Chartres, in Illinois, French settlement on Mississippi River, n. of Kaskaskia; founded 1720; taken by British 1765; remains of fortress a state park.

Fort Christina, fort in Delaware D-75
Wilmington W-212

Fort Churchill, Canada. *see in index* Churchill

Fort Churchill Historic State Monument, in Nevada, *picture* N-142

Fort Clatsop National Memorial, in Oregon
Lewis and Clark L-144

Fort Collins, Colo., city on Cache la Poudre River about 60 mi (100 km) n. of Denver; in fertile irrigated district; beet sugar and food products, cement, machinery; headquarters, Roosevelt National Forest; Colorado State University; pop. 65,092 U-40

Fort Condé, in Mobile, Ala.; known as Fort Louis de la Mobile before 1720; built under Sieur de Bienville 1711; important French fort; transferred to British 1763 and called Fort Charlotte A-229

Fort Constitution, built 1775 on Martelaer's Rock (now Constitution Island) in middle of Hudson River, opposite West Point, N.Y.; ruins.

Fort D.A. Russell. *see in index* Francis E. Warren Air Force Base

Fort Dearborn, U.S. fort built in 1803 on site of Chicago, Ill.; destroyed 1812; rebuilt and used until 1837
Chicago C-317

Fort-de-France, capital of Martinique; port on w. coast; French military and naval station; hit by earthquake 1839 and by major fire 1890; pop. 100,000 M-160, *map* W-159

Fort Delaware, on Pea Patch Island, Delaware Bay; Civil War prison, *picture* D-81

Fort Devens, U.S. Army post 1 mi (1.6 km) s. of Ayer, Mass.; established 1917; home of U.S. Army Security Agency Training Center and School, 10th Special Forces Group (Airborne), 39th Engineer Battalion (Combat); pop. 12,951.

Fort Dilts, fort near Rhame, N.D., site where Captain James Fisk and his 80-wagon train band stopped to raise temporary defense 1864; sod wall around corral; historical site.

Fort Dix, U.S. Army post 17 mi (27 km) s.e. of Trenton, N.J.; next to McGuire Air Force Base; Walson Army Hospital; established as Camp Dix 1917; pop. 26,290.

Fort Dodge, Iowa, city on Des Moines River about 70 mi (110 km) n.w. of Des Moines; meat-packing; farm machinery, plaster, gypsum, clay products; pop. 29,423, *map* I-302

Fort Donelson, Confederate fortification on Cumberland River in Tennessee, 63 mi (101 km) n.w. of Nashville; national cemetery
Grant captures C-475, *map* C-474

Fort Douaumont, hill and village near Verdun, France V-282

Fort Douglas, now part of Winnipeg, Man.; scene of fur trade wars F-472

Fort Dummer, early settlement in Vermont V-289, *picture* V-291

Fort Duquesne, French fort on site of present city of Pittsburgh, Pa. P-345b
French and Indian War C-93
Washington W-39

Forte, in music, *list* M-670

Fort Edward, N.Y., village on Hudson River 40 mi (60 km) n. of Albany; fort built here 1755 was an important post during French and Indian War and the American Revolution; pop. 3,561.

Forten, James (1766–1842), U.S. businessman and inventor from Philadelphia, Pa.; promoted temperance, peace, women's rights.

Fort Erie, Ont., town on Lake Erie at head of Niagara River, opposite Buffalo, N.Y.; on site of old Ft. Erie; battle area during War of 1812; pop. 23,113.

Fort Eustis, U.S. Army post 18 mi (29 km) n.w. of Newport News, Va., a cantonment during World War I, later a transportation center.

Fort Fisher, Confederate earthworks in North Carolina defending entrance to port of Wilmington.

Fort Frederick, fort in Maryland, built during the French and Indian War, main attraction of Fort Frederick State Park, *picture* M-176

Fort Garry, in Manitoba, division of metropolitan Winnipeg
Red River Rebellion R-120, C-101

Fort George G. Meade, U.S. Army post in Maryland 18 mi (29 km) s.w. of city of Baltimore; established in 1917 as Camp Meade; renamed Fort Leonard Wood in 1928, present name 1929; pop. 16,699, *map* M-183

Fort George National Historic Site, historic site in Ontario N-30, *map* N-29

Fort George River, Quebec. *see in index* Grande-Rivière, La.

Fort Gordon, U.S. Army post in Georgia 12 mi (19 km) s.w. of Augusta; area 56,000 acres (23,000 hectares); established 1941; named in honor of John Brown Gordon.

Fort Greene, earthworks erected on Long Island during Revolutionary War; site now Ft. Greene Park in Brooklyn, New York City.

Forth, Firth of, estuary in Scotland, of Forth River on e. coast; 50 mi (80 km) long
bridges B-446

Fort Hall, Idaho, former fort on Snake River n. of Pocatello; built 1834; present village is headquarters for Fort Hall Indian Reservation O-598

Fort Hays State University, in Hays, Kan.; founded 1901; arts and sciences, fine and applied arts, and teacher education; graduate school.

Fort Henry, in n.w. Tennessee, 11 mi (18 km) w. of Ft. Donelson, on Tennessee River; site taken by Gen. Grant in 1862, *map* C-474

'For the Term of his Natural Life', work by Clarke A-797

'For the Time Being', work by Auden A-759

Fort Hill, historic home on campus of Clemson University, Clemson, S.C.; named to commemorate post built in 1776, *picture* S-209

Fort Hill, near Hillsboro, Ohio; 50-acre (20-hectare) site of prehistoric Mound Builders, enclosed by limestone wall 25 ft (8 m) thick; now 1,200-acre (500-hectare) park.

Fort Hood, U.S. Army post in Coryell and Bell counties, in Texas; area 158,000 acres (64,000 hectares); named in honor of John Bell Hood; pop. 32,597.

Fort Huachuca, Ariz., U.S. Army installation 25 mi (40 km) n.w. of Bisbee; pop. 6,659.

Fortifications. *see in index* Fort and fortifications

Fortified lowfat milk, dairy product, *list* D-6

Fortified wine, wine that receives an extra dosage of alcohol W-236

Fortin barometer B-82

Fortisan, trade name for an unusually strong cellulose yarn chemically similar to cotton; used to make sheer fabrics, raincoats, shower curtains, and conveyer belting; during World War II used for parachutes.

Fort Jackson, Confederate fort on Mississippi River 80 mi (130 km) south of New Orleans, La.; vainly besieged 6 days, April 1862, by Farragut's fleet.

Fort Jackson, U.S. Army post near Columbia, S.C.; established 1917; infantry training center, *map* S-319

Fort Jay, former U.S. Army post on Governors Island, New York; site acquired from state in 1800; named for John Jay. *see also in index* Governors Island

Fort Johnson, in Charleston, S.C.; named for Governor Nathaniel Johnson; built 1704–8 on James Island in harbor; protected against Spanish threat from Florida; aided in revolt against British tax stamps 1765.

Fort Kaministikwia, in Thunder Bay, Ont.; forts built 1678 and 1717; headquarters for North West Company after original site (Grand Portage) was found to be in United States 1801; became known as Fort William; site abandoned during Seven Years War.

Fort Kearney, Neb. *see in index* Kearney

Fort Knox, in Indiana. *see in index* Fort Sackville

Fort Knox, Ky., military reservation 30 mi (50 km) s. of Louisville; U.S. government gold depository built here (1936) as part of program to shift nation's gold reserve into interior; Armor School and Medical Field Research Laboratories; Patton Museum of Cavalry and Armor; pop. 31,055 C-538, *picture* K-213

Fort Krisholm (1647), Swedish colony in Delaware A-339

Fort-Lamy, Chad. *see in index* N'Djamena

Fort Langley National Historic Site, historical site in British Columbia N-30, *map* N-29

Fort Laramie, a fort built in 1834 in e. Wyoming at junction of North Platte and Laramie rivers, *picture* O-599

Fort Larned National Historic Site, in Kansas K-177

Fort Lauderdale, Fla., city on Atlantic Ocean; pop. 153,279 F-321

Fort Leavenworth, federal reservation on Missouri River, in n.e. Kansas, just n. of Leavenworth; area 7,000 acres (2,800 hectares); has Command and General Staff College for training officers of U.S. and allied countries; maintains U.S. Disciplinary Barracks for military prisoners; Fort Leavenworth was established 1827 to protect Santa Fe Trail; pop. 8,060.

Fort Lee, N.J., borough about 10 mi (16 km) n.e. of Jersey City, on Hudson River opposite New York City; pop. 32,449.

Fort Lennox National Historic Park, park in Quebec N-30, *map* N-29

Fort Leonard Wood, U.S. Army post s.e. of Waynesville, Mo.; center for engineer training; established 1941, became fort 1956; named for military surgeon who served as army chief of staff 1910–14; pop. 33,799. *see also in index* Wood, Leonard

Fort Lesley J. McNair, military post at Washington, D.C.; established 1797 as Washington Arsenal; site of U.S. penitentiary (1826–69) where Lincoln conspirators were tried and hanged, named Washington Barracks and made artillery post 1881; named Fort Humphreys 1935; given present name 1947.

Fort Lewis, U.S. Army post in Washington s.w. of Tacoma; area 76,000 acres (31,000 hectares); has varied types of terrain for military problems; named in honor of Meriwether Lewis.

Fort Lewis College, in Durango, Colo.; state control; founded 1910, senior college after 1962; liberal arts, education; trimester system.

Fort Lincoln State Park. *see in index* Fort Abraham Lincoln

Fort Loudoun Dam, TVA dam near Lenoir City, Tenn., on Tennessee River; gravity-type dam 122 ft (37 m) high and 4,190 ft (1,280 m) long; completed 1943; 282,000 acre-ft (347,842,000 cu m); power capacity 128,000 kilowatts.

Fort Louis de la Mobile, on Mobile River 20 mi. n. of present Mobile, Ala.; built 1702 by Jean Baptiste le Moyne, sieur de Bienville; capital moved to fort from Biloxi; moved to second Fort Louis de la Mobile 1711 (later Fort Condé). *see also in index* Fort Condé

Fort McClellan, U.S. Army post; just n.e. of Anniston, Ala.; pop. 5,334, *map* A-236

Fort McHenry, former U.S. military post in Baltimore, Md. harbor B-48
flag F-156, *picture* F-155
Key K-229, N-63
Maryland M-172, *picture* M-177, *map* M-183

Fort Mackinac, one of oldest fortifications in U.S., on Mackinac Island, Mich.; built by British; given to U.S. by treaty of Paris 1783; recaptured by British in War of 1812, *pictures* M-355, 367
Canada C-96

Fort McMurray, Alta., town on Athabasca River, about 230 mi (370 km) n.e. of Edmonton; fur-trading post; airport, railroad terminal; pop. 31,000.

Fort Macon State Park, park in North Carolina, *picture* N-364

Fort McPherson, U.S. Army post at Atlanta, Ga.; established 1889; named in honor of James Birdseye McPherson.

Fort Madison, Iowa, city on Mississippi River about 17 mi (27 km) s.w. of Burlington; pens and pencils, paints, paper products; fertilizers; railroad division point; state penitentiary; pop. 13,520, *map* I-302

Fort Malden National Historic Park, park in Ontario N-30, *map* N-29

Fort Mandan, now near Stanton, N.D.; built by Lewis and Clark L-143

Fort Mason, U.S. Army post at San Francisco, Calif., near Golden Gate Bridge; established 1863 as Point San José; redesignated 1882 as Fort Mason in honor of Richard Barnes Mason, military and civil governor of California 1847–49, *map* S-41b

Fort Meigs, former U.S. fort on Maumee River, n.w. Ohio; famous for defense against English and American Indians during War of 1812.

Fort Mims, old fort 35 mi (55 km) n. of Mobile, Ala.

Fort Monmouth, U.S. Army post near Oceanport, N.J.; area 444.5 acres (179.9 hectares); acquired by purchase 1919.

Fort Monroe, U.S. military post at Old Point Comfort, Va., commanding entrance to Hampton Roads, *map* V-349
Hampton H-24

Fort Moultrie (formerly called Fort Sullivan), fort on Sullivans Island at entrance to Charleston harbor, South Carolina; abandoned by Federals in Civil War and became one of strong Confederate defenses S-305. *see also in index* Moultrie, William
flag F-154, *picture* F-155

Fort Myer, U.S. Army post in Virginia, 4 mi (6 km) s.w. of Washington, D.C., on Potomac River; formerly Fort Whipple; renamed in 1881 for Brig. Gen. A.J. Myer, creator of Army Signal Corps, *map* V 349

Fort Myers, Fla., resort city in s.w. on Caloosahatchee River near Gulf of Mexico; flowers, citrus fruit, vegetables, fisheries, cattle; Thomas A. Edison's winter home, laboratory, and botanical gardens; Florida Marine Museum, noted for shell collection, nearby; location of fort during Seminole Wars; pop. 36,638, *map* U-41

Fort Nashborough, Tenn. *see in index* Nashville

Fort Necessity, stockade erected in 1754 on the Great Meadows, a level area 9 mi (15 km) s.e. of present Uniontown, s.w. Pennsylvania; fort surrendered by Major George Washington and his colonial troops July 3, 1754, in early battle of French and Indian War, *map* P-184

Fort Niagara, old fort at mouth of Niagara River in New York, overlooking Lake Ontario; strategic position at head of Great Lakes; first fort here built by La Salle in 1678, rebuilt by French in 1725 and 1756; captured by British in French and Indian War, 1759; surrendered to U.S. in 1796; recaptured by British in 1813, restored to U.S. in 1815 by Treaty of Ghent; rebuilt in 1934; use as fort discontinued Feb. 1946.

Fort of San Diego, in Acapulco, Mexico A-15

Fort Orange, early Dutch fort on site of Albany, N.Y. A-336
New York N-256

Fort Ord, U.S. Army post situated 10 mi n. of Monterey, Calif.; pop. 48,500.

Fort Peck Dam, dam in Montana, on Missouri River M-550, *picture* D-13
Missouri River M-509

Fort Peck Reservoir, in Montana M-508

Fort Phil Kearny, fort built 1866–67 on Piney Fork of Rock Creek at foot of Bighorn Mountains in Wyoming; abandoned 1868 after peace treaty with Sioux.

Fort Pierce, Fla., port city about 55 mi (90 km) n. of West Palm Beach, on Indian River and Atlantic; ranches in vicinity; fort built 1838 against American Indians; pop. 33,802.

Fort Pierre, military fort in Pierre, S.D. P-319

Fort Pillow, Confederate fort on Mississippi River, 40 mi (60 km) north of Memphis, Tenn.; occupied by Federals June 1862; recaptured April 1864.

Fort Pitt, English post on site of present Pittsburgh, Pa. P-345a, *map* P-345b

Fort Prince of Wales National Historic Park, park in Manitoba N-30, *map* N-29

Fort Prudhomme, French post built by La Salle in 1682 on present site of Memphis, Tenn.

Fort Pulaski National Monument, in Georgia, *picture* G-87

Fort Qu'Appelle, 35 mi (55 km) n.e. of Regina, Sask., built by North West Company about 1800 and discontinued 1880; temporary refuge for 1,200 Sioux under Sitting Bull 1881 S-49h

Fort Raleigh, reconstructed fort on Roanoke Island, North Carolina; site of "lost colony" of Sir Walter Raleigh; birthplace of Virginia Dare.

FORTRAN (FORmula TRANslating system), programming operation codes C-635

Fort Randall Dam, dam in South Dakota, on Missouri River S-323, *map* S-335
Missouri River, *picture* M-510

Fortress. *see in index* Citadel

Fortress of Louisbourg. *see in index* Louisbourg, Fortress of

Fort Rice, in North Dakota; established by Gen. Alfred Sully on Missouri River 1864; important military supply base; discontinued 1884; historical site.

Fort Richardson, Alaska, military post just n.w. of Anchorage; established 1941 as U.S. Army headquarters for Alaska; pop. 8,960.

Fort Riley, U.S. military post near Junction City, Kan. (about 58 mi [93 km] w. of Topeka); established 1853 to protect traffic on the Santa Fe Trail; pop. 14,779
monument, *picture* K-183

Fort Rodd Hill National Historic Park, park in British Columbia N-30, *map* N-29

Fort Ross (formerly Rossiya), Russian post in California, was built in 1812 on Bodega Bay and sold to John A. Sutter in 1841; in 1906 the state began restoration of buildings A-339, C-41

Fort Rucker, U.S. Army post in Alabama near Daleville; established 1942; named in honor of Edmund Winchester Rucker, Confederate general; pop. 14,242, *map* A-237

Fort Sackville, in Indiana, British fort taken by George Rogers Clark in 1779 and named Fort Patrick Henry; originally named Fort Knox; rebuilt and renamed Fort Knox 1788; later abandoned C-485

Fort St. Anthony *see in index* Fort Snelling

Fort St. Charles, on Magnussen Island, Minnesota, *picture* M-451

Fort Saint Elmo, fort on the island of Malta, *picture* M-79

Fort Ste-Marie, near Midland, Ont.; restored ruins of Jesuit mission built late 1630s from funds of Cardinal Richelieu; destroyed by Iroquois 1648.

Fort St. Joseph National Historic Site, historical site in Ontario N-30, *map* N-29

Fort Salisbury, Zimbabwe. *see in index* Harare

Fort Sam Houston, U.S. military post at San Antonio, Tex.; pop. 10,553 S-35

Fort Schuyler. *see in index* Fort Stanwix National Monument

Fort Scott, Kan., city in s.e. about 88 mi (142 km) s. of Kansas City, Kan.; dairy center; work clothing, metal products; pop. 8,893 U-41

Fort Shafter, U.S. military post on island of Oahu, Hawaii, just n.w. of Honolulu; area 1,344 acres (544 hectares); reserved for military purposes 1899; named in honor of William Rufus Shafter.

Fort Sheridan, U.S. Army post in Illinois on Lake Michigan 25 mi (40 km) n. of Chicago; established 1887 under name of Camp at Highwood; name changed 1888 to Fort Sheridan in honor of Gen. Philip H. Sheridan.

Fort Sill, U.S. Army post situated 4 mi (6 km) n. of Lawton, Okla.; founded 1868 as Camp Wichita; name changed 1869 by Gen. Philip H. Sheridan in honor of Gen. Joshua W. Sill; pop. 18,797 O-524, *picture* O-530

Fort Smith, Ark., 2nd city of state, on w. border at junction of Arkansas and Poteau rivers, in coal and gas region; furniture, electrical appliances; Fort Chaffee nearby; pop.

Rome R-255, *pictures* R-253, 254
Fountain grass, ornamental perennial plant *Pennisetum ruppelii* of the grass family, native to Africa; one foot (three-tenths of a meter) high, has narrow leaves and branching feathery clusters of flowers, pink or purple; used as a border plant.
'Fountain of the Nymphs', sculpture by Goujon, *picture* S-89
Fountain of Youth F-336, P-444
Fountain pen P-157
mechanical drawing M-257
ruthenium used R-366
Fountain Square, in Cincinnati, Ohio C-414, *picture* C-415
Fountain Valley, Calif., residential city 6 mi (10 km) s.w. of Santa Ana; mobile and modular homes; medical laboratory; incorporated 1957; pop. 55,080, *map* C-51
'Fount of Life', work by Ibn Gabirol I-4
Fouqué, Friedrich, baron de la Motte. *see in index* La Motte-Fouqué
Fouquet, Jean (or Jehan Fouquet) (1420?–80?), French artist, court painter to Charles VII and Louis XI, born in Tours; illuminator, miniaturist.
Fouquet, Nicolas (1615–80), French superintendent of finance, and procureur-général under Louis XIV, born in Paris; patron of arts; amassed great fortune and power; to prison for life 1664.
'Four Apostles', panels painted by Dürer P-38, *picture* P-39
Fourcault process, in glass manufacture G-163, *picture* G-157
Four-channel sound (or quadraphonic sound) P-269
Four Corners, meeting point of Arizona, Colorado, Utah, and New Mexico; marked by monument; surrounding region site of Anasazi culture U-216, *map* U-81.
Fourdrinier, Henry (1766–1854), and his brother **Sealy** (died 1847), English inventors; secured first patent for papermaking machine 1801 P-104
wallpaper W-9
Fourdrinier machine, device for making paper P-102, *pictures* P-103, 106
Four-eyed fish (or Anableps), river fish *Anableps anableps*; popeyed, with slender body; grows 30 to 36 centimeters (12 to 14 inches) long F-127, *picture* F-130
Four freedoms R-275
4-H Clubs Y-429
agriculture A-143
home economics H-219
Four-horned antelope, mammal A-478
Four Horsemen of Notre Dame, U.S. football players F-297
Four Horsemen of the Apocalypse, four beings symbolizing conquest, slaughter, famine, and death; from last book in New Testament (Bible, Rev. vi, 2–8).
'Four Horsemen of the Apocalypse, The', novel by Blasco Ibañez S-365b
'Four Horsemen of the Apocalypse, The', woodcut by Dürer, *picture* G-230
Fourier, François Marie Charles (1772–1837), French socialist and political economist, born in Besançon; originator of the cooperative community plan known as "Fourierism," tried unsuccessfully at Brook Farm, West Roxbury, Mass.
communal living C-605
utopian socialism S-233
Fourier, Joseph (1768–1830), French mathematician; accompanied Napoleon to Egypt; made governor of Lower Egypt F-336
Fourier series, in mathematics F-336
Four Modernizations, China's program of economic development C-377
Four Musketeers, team of French tennis players who won six consecutive Davis Cup victories (1927–32) T-107
Fourneyron, Benoît (1802–67), French engineer, born in St. Étienne, France; invented a hydraulic turbine 1827.
Fournier, Pierre Simon (1712–68), French type founder and writer on typography, born in Paris T-336
Four Noble Truths, essence of Buddhist doctrine B-480
Four-o'clock family (or Nyctaginaceae), family of plants, shrubs, trees, native chiefly to warm regions; includes bougainvilleas, sand verbena, umbrellawort, four o'clock, and pisonias
growing conditions G-24
Four-Power Pact, international treaty signed in Washington, D.C. W-71
'Four Quartets', work by Eliot A-355
Fourragère, military unit citation for distinguished service and gallantry on part of entire unit; awarded by France in World War I; by France, Belgium, and The Netherlands in World War II.
'Four Seasons', mosaic by Chagall M-590
Foursquare Gospel, International Church of the. *see in index* International Church of the Foursquare Gospel
Four-stroke cycle internal combustion engine, *diagram* A-847
Fourteen Points, terms of peace suggested by President Wilson in 1918, in an address to Congress W-218
Atlantic Charter R-275
Fourteenth Amendment, U.S. Constitution B-196, U-145, 152
Fourth dimension, in physics R-142
Fourth estate, term commonly applied to the public press; the traditional estates were the nobility, clergy, and townsmen, each with separate voice in government; representatives of the three met as the Estates-General in prerevolutionary France; the term **fifth estate** is sometimes used for some other influential group, such as scientists.
Fourth of July. *see in index* Independence Day
Fourth Republic, in French history F-365
Fourth world, a group of nations especially in Africa and Asia characterized by extremely low per capita income and an absence of valuable natural resources T-168
Four-wheel drive, machinery F-31
Fovea, in anatomy B-204
Fowke, Edith (born 1913), Canadian writer, born in Lumsden, Sask.; radio program, Folk Song Time, on Canadian network 1951–64; author of books on Canadian folk music; won Canadian Book of the Year for Children award 1970 for 'Sally Go 'Round the Sun'.
Fowl, domestic. *see in index* Poultry
Fowler, Henry Hamill (born 1908), U.S. lawyer, born in Roanoke, Va.; senior member Fowler, Leva, Hawes & Symington, Washington, D.C., 1946–51, 1953–61; administrator Defense Production Administration 1952–53; undersecretary of the treasury 1961–64, secretary 1965–68.
Fowler, Henry Watson (1858–1933), British lexicographer, born in Tonbridge, England; known for 'A Dictionary of Modern English Usage'.
Fowler, William Warde, British historian C-461
Fowles, John (born 1926), British novelist F-336
Fowliang, China. *see in index* Kingtehchen
Fox, North American Indian tribe, *maps* I-136, 149, *table* I-139
Illinois I-41
Iowa D-117
Fox, Charles James (1749–1806), British statesman and orator; one of Pitt's chief rivals and opponents; advocated religious freedom, abolition of slave trade, and electoral reform; foreign secretary 1782–83 and 1806; supported the cause of the North American colonists.
Fox, George (1624–91), English religious reformer F-337
Quakers Q-4
Fox, John, Jr. (1863–1919), U.S. novelist, born in Bourbon County, Kentucky; wrote 'Little Shepherd of Kingdom Come', 'Trail of the Lonesome Pine'.
Fox, Margaret (1833–93), U.S. spiritualist, born in Bath, near Kingston, Ont. S-392
Fox, Paula (born 1923), U.S. author and educator, born in New York City; married Martin Greenberg; adult novels; children's books ('How Many Miles to Babylon?'; 'Portrait of Ivan'; 'Blowfish Live in the Sea'; 'The Slave Dancer', awarded 1974 Newbery Medal) R-110a
Fox, William (1879–1952), movie producer, born in Tulchva, Hungary M-621
Fox F-337. *see also in index* by name, such as Red fox; Silver fox
animal, *picture* A-422, *table* A-427, *chart* A-423
folklore F-263
furs F-463, *table* F-464
social group, *picture* A-442
tracks, *picture* A-464
zoo Z-463
'Fox, The', opera by Stravinsky O-569
'Fox and the Crow, The', fable F-3
'Fox and the Grapes, The', fable, *table* F-4
'Fox and the Lion, The', fable, *table* F-4
'Fox and the Stork, The', fable F-3
Fox bat. *see in index* Flying fox
Foxberry. *see in index* Lingonberry
Foxboro, Mass., 11 mi (18 km) w. of Brockton; time recording and controlling devices; pop. of township 14,148.
Fox Broadcasting Company, fourth U.S. television network, organized by Rupert Murdoch 1985; combined Twentieth Century Fox Film Corporation with six television stations and new distribution company; major debut was late-night show starring comedienne Joan Rivers 1986.
Foxe, John (1516–87), English priest, author of 'Book of Martyrs'; born in Lincolnshire; ordained 1560.
Foxe Channel, arm of the ocean n. of Hudson Bay and w. of Baffin Island; named after **Luke Foxe** (1586–1635), who in 1631 explored the region, *maps* C-109, N-350
Fox fire, glowing light emitted by foxed or rotten wood due to the presence of luminescent fungi P-270
Foxglove, genus *Digitalis* of tall biennial or perennial plants of the figwort family; the large oval leaves yield the drug digitalis
flowering time G-25
Fox grape, a grape *Vitis labrusca* of the family Vitaceae G-220
wine W-236
Foxhole, in warfare F-319
Fox Islands, name given to easternmost group of the Aleutian Islands; discovered by Russians in mid-18th century; site of military bases in World War II.
Fox of Kinderhook, nickname of Martin Van Buren. *see in index* Van Buren, Martin
Fox River, river in Wisconsin; 175 mi (280 km) long; rises in s. center of state, flows s.w. to a point only 1 ½ mi (2.4 km) from Wisconsin River (the two rivers are linked here by Portage Canal), then flows generally n.e. through Lake Winnebago to Green Bay
paper mill, *picture* P-101
Fox shark (or thresher shark), fish S-144
Fox squirrel, mammal S-401
Fox tail lily. *see in index* Eremurus
Fox terrier, dog, *picture* D-203
Foxx, James Emory (nickname Jimmy) (1907–67), U.S. baseball player, born in Sudlersville, Md.; first baseman (also third baseman and catcher) Philadelphia, A.L., 1926–35, Boston, A.L., 1936–42, and Chicago, N.L., 1942–44; hit total of 534 home runs; was chosen for 7 All-Star games B-93
Foy, Eddie (originally Edwin Fitzgerald) (1856–1928), U.S. comedian, born in New York City; danced and sang in boomtowns of the West.
Foyer (from Latin *focarium,* "fireplace"), lobby of theater, hotel, or apartment house; hearth of home or other gathering place.
Foyt, Anthony Joseph, Jr. (born 1935), U.S. auto-racing driver, born in Houston, Tex.; winner of Indianapolis 500 four times; first driver to win racing's Triple Crown (the Indianapolis, Pocono, and California 500s).
Fra Angelico. *see in index* Angelico
Fractional currency (sometimes called shinplasters), small coins or paper money whose face value is a fraction of the standard monetary unit, specifically paper currency issued in United States between 1862 and 1876; term also applied to small denominations issued by private bankers after War of 1812 during a shortage of metal currency.
Fractional distillation (or fractionation), method for separating liquids
noble gases N-330
petroleum P-239
Fractional scale (or representative fraction), in mapping M-117
Fractions, common and decimal F-337
algebra A-289
arithmetic A-594
numeration systems N-436
percentages P-198
Fracture, bone injury F-340
fatigue F-46
first aid F-118, *diagrams* F-119
healing rate B-342
surgery S-519a
Fracture, in physics
iron and steel I-333
mineralogy R-229b
Fracture zone, in geology
ocean floor O-460
Fra Diavolo. *see in index* Diavolo
Fragmentation, method of plant reproduction
algae A-284
fungus F-448
Fragmentation bomb, weapon with thick metal walls formed around explosive filler; small pieces fly into air at high speeds when bomb bursts.
'Fragments of a Journal', book by Ionesco I-286
Fragonard, Jean-Honoré (1732–1806), French artist F-341
Watteau W-109
Fragrance. *see in index* perfumes
Fragrant water lily, plant *Nymphaea odorata* W-99
Frahm, Herbert *see in index* Brandt, Willy
Fraktur style, in calligraphy C-59
'Fram', Nansen's ship P-420
Amundsen A-382
Frame, Janet (or Janet Paterson Frame Clutha) (born 1924), New Zealand writer, born in Dunedin; numerous literary awards ('Owls Do Cry'; 'The Pocket Mirror: Poems').
Frame, inning in bowling B-385
Frame, reading aid R-103a
Frame, two fields together in a television T-74
Frame construction, in building B-493, S-157
carpentry C-173
Frame construction, in mechanics
automobile, *picture* A-843
bicycle design B-189
Framingham, Mass., 19 mi (31 km) s.w. of Boston; automobile assembling, paper and rubber products, carpets; Framingham State College; pop. of township 65,113.
Framingham State College, in Framingham, Mass.; coeducational, formerly for women; established 1839; education; graduate studies.
Frampton, Sir George James (1860–1928), English sculptor; excelled in use of bronze,

FRANCE—KINGS AND EMPERORS

Carolingian Line	
761–768	Pepin the Short
768–814	Charlemagne
814–840	Louis I, the Pious
843–877	Charles I, the Bald
877–879	Louis II
879–882	Louis III
879–884	Carloman
884–887	Charles II, the Fat
[888–898	Odo of Anjou]
893–923	Charles III, the Simple
[922–923	Robert I of Anjou]
[923–936	Rudolph of Burgundy]
936–954	Louis IV
954–986	Lothair
986–987	Louis V
Capetian Line	
987–996	Hugh Capet
996–1031	Robert I
1031–1060	Henry I
1060–1108	Philip I
1108–1137	Louis VI, the Fat
1137–1180	Louis VII
1180–1223	Philip II, Augustus
1223–1226	Louis VIII
1226–1270	Louis IX, the Saint
1270–1285	Philip III
1285–1314	Philip IV
1314–1316	Louis X
1316–1322	Philip V
1322–1328	Charles IV
Valois Line	
1328–1350	Philip VI
1350–1364	John II
1364–1380	Charles V
1380–1422	Charles VI
1422–1461	Charles VII
1461–1483	Louis XI
1483–1498	Charles VIII
1498–1515	Louis XII
1515–1547	Francis I
1547–1559	Henry II
1559–1560	Francis II
1560–1574	Charles IX
1574–1589	Henry III
Bourbon Line	
1589–1610	Henry IV
1610–1643	Louis XIII
1643–1715	Louis XIV
1715–1774	Louis XV
1774–1792	Louis XVI
[1792–1799	First Republic]
[1799–1804	Napoleon Bonaparte, First Consul]
The First Empire	
1804–1814	Napoleon I, Emperor
The Bourbon Restoration	
1814–1824	Louis XVIII
1824–1830	Charles X
1830–1848	Louis Philippe
[1848–1852	Second Republic]
The Second Empire	
1852–1870	Louis Napoleon reigns as Napoleon III
[1871	Third Republic established]

in 1921; commanded 5th Army in first battle of Marne; commander in chief at Salonika in 1918; overcame Bulgaria.

Franchise, privilege granted to an individual, group, or company F-373, U-110
  fast-food restaurants F-43

Francia (originally Francesco Raibolini) (1450?–1517), Italian painter and goldsmith; greatest of early Bolognese school; paintings show Raphael's influence.

Francia, José Gaspar Rodriguez (1766–1840), dictator of Paraguay 1814–40, austere, gloomy, ruthless despot, whose very name Paraguayans dared not pronounce (he was El Supremo during life and El Defunto when dead) and who for 26 years kept Paraguay a hermit nation, knowing neither want, wars, nor will of its own; described by Carlyle ('Dr. Francia') and by Edward L. White ('El Supremo') P-112

Francis I (1708–65), Holy Roman emperor, husband of Maria Theresa A-830

Francis II (1768–1835), Holy Roman emperor; later, as emperor of Austria, called himself Francis I A-830
  Holy Roman Empire H-209

Francis I (1494–1547), king of France F-374
  American exploration A-333
    Canada C-90
  button adornment B-528
  Charles V C-278
  France F-361
  Henry VIII H-131
  Leo X L-131
  Leonardo da Vinci L-133

Francis II (1544–60), king of France; ruled 1559–60; son of Catherine de Médicis; grandson of Francis I; first husband of Mary, Queen of Scots M-164

Francis, David Rowland (1850–1927), U.S. businessman and statesman, born in Richmond, Ky.; mayor of St. Louis, Mo., 1885–89; governor of Missouri 1889–93; U.S. secretary of interior 1896–97; ambassador to Russia during World War I.

Francis, Dick (Richard Stanley Francis) (born 1920), U.S. detective story writer D-119

Francis, James Bicheno (1815–92), U.S. hydraulic engineer, born in Southleigh, Oxfordshire, England; to U.S. 1833; invented mixed flow turbine 1849 W-103

Francis, Sir Philip (1740–1818), English political leader, born in Dublin; reputed author of the 'Letters of Junius', which attacked public figures of the day
  Hastings H-52

Franciscan nuns (or Poor Clares), Roman Catholic religious order F-375

Franciscans (sometimes called Gray Friars, or Minorites, or Begging Brothers), Roman Catholic religious order founded by St. Francis of Assisi
  Francis of Assisi F-375
  monks and monasticism M-540

Francisco, Peter (1761?–1831), American Revolutionary War hero, presumably of noble Portuguese parentage; put ashore near Hopewell, Va., at age of four, was cared for by Judge A. Winston; as a private 1776–81 performed incredible feats of strength and daring.

Francis E. Warren Air Force Base, in Cheyenne, Wyo., formerly **Fort D.A. Russell,** missile base; pop. 4,527 C-308

Francis Ferdinand (1863–1914), archduke of Austria, born in Graz; nephew of Emperor Francis Joseph; son of Archduke Charles Louis
  assassination A-703
  Austria-Hungary A-831
  Balkan history B-31
  Europe E-350
  World War I W-302, 307

Francis Joseph I (1830–1916), emperor of Austria and king of Hungary F-375
  Austria A-830

Francis of Assisi (1182–1226), Roman Catholic saint, founder of Franciscan order, patron saint of Italy; festival Oct. 4 F-375
  Christmas manger scenes C-406

Francis of Paola, Saint (1416?–1507), Italian saint, founder of Minims, mendicant order of Roman Catholicism; strictest of ascetics; festival April 2.

Francis turbine (or reaction turbine), waterpower W-103
  hydraulics H-340

Francis W. Parker School, in Chicago, Ill., a progressive school; opened in 1901, *picture* E-94

Francis Xavier, Saint. *see in index* Xavier, Francis

Francium (Fr), chemical element A-307
  periodic table, *table* P-207, *list* P-208

Franck, César (1822–90), French composer and organist F-376
  opera O-568

Franck, Harry Alverson (1881–1962), U.S. writer of travel books, born in Munger, Mich. ('A Vagabond Journey Around the World'; 'East of Siam'; 'Four Months Afoot in Spain'; 'The Lure of Alaska').

Franck, James (1882–1964), U.S. physicist, born in Hamburg, Germany; to U.S. 1935; taught at Johns Hopkins University 1935–38, later at Universities of Chicago and California; investigated the impact of electrons on atoms; also noted for work on photosynthesis. *see also in index* Nobel Prizewinners, *table*

Francke, August Hermann (1663–1727), German Protestant clergyman and philanthropist; professor of theology, University of Halle; institutions founded include a school for outcast children.

Franco, Francisco (1892–1975), dictator of Spain F-376
  Germany G-124
  Juan Carlos J-145, B-384
  Spain S-356, 360, *picture* S-357

Franco-German War. *see in index* Franco-Prussian War

François de Sales, Saint (1567–1622), French churchman, bishop of Geneva; his book 'Introduction to the Devout Life' has been translated into almost every language; patron of journalists; festival Jan. 29.

Francolin, name for birds of the genus *Francolinus,* allied to partridge; richly colored plumage; about 50 forms inhabit Asia and Africa; game birds, good for food.

Franconia ("land of the Franks"), medieval German duchy chiefly e. of Rhine in valley of Main.

Franconian Dynasty (or Salian Dynasty), German emperors (ruled 1024–1125). *see also in index* Holy Roman Empire, *table of rulers*
  Conrad II C-666
  Germany G-121

Franconian Jura, plateau region in West Germany G-111, *map* G-131

Franconia Notch, wooded gap in New Hampshire N-176

Franco-Prussian War (or Franco-German War) (1870–71) F-377
  Alsace-Lorraine A-320
  balloons B-42
  conscription C-667
  France F-362
  Garibaldi G-31
  Germany G-122
  Italian independence I-394
  Krupp family K-307
  Moltke M-527
  Napoleon III N-18
  Sedan S-105
  Versailles proclamation V-303
  warfare, *list* W-13
  William I W-205

Frangipani, fragrant flowering shrubs or trees (dogbane family Apocynaceae, genus *Plumeria*), native to tropical America, cultivated in all tropical countries; different species have red, pink, white, or yellow funnel-shaped flowers with five waxy, spreading petals; clusters of 20 or more blossoms; origin of name uncertain; may be from French *franchipanier* ("coagulated milk") referring to milky sap, or from Italian nobleman of that name who in the Middle Ages distilled a perfume called frangipani from red jasmine.

Frank, Anne (1929–45), victim of Nazis, born in Frankfurt, Germany; died in concentration camp after being captured by Nazis in Holland
  Amsterdam A-301
  'The Diary of a Young Girl' D-132, R-111d

Frank, Bruno (1887–1945), German writer and poet; left Germany 1933; with motion-picture companies in U.S. after 1937 ('Days of the King', 'Man Called Cervantes', historical novels; 'Storm in a Teacup', 'Young Madame Conti', plays).

Frank, Glenn (1887–1940), U.S. publicist and university president, born in Queen City, Mo.; editor of *Century Magazine*; president of University of Wisconsin 1925–37; editor of *Rural Progress*.

Frank, Ilya Mikhailovich (born 1908), Soviet physicist. *see also in index* Nobel Prizewinners, *table*

Frank, Waldo David (1889–1967), U.S. novelist and critic, born in Long Branch, N.J.; poetic in style ('The Unwelcome Man', novel; 'Virgin Spain', 'Bridgehead; the Drama of Israel', travel; 'America Hispaña', and 'Chart for Rough Water', essays).

Franke, William Birrell (1894–1979), U.S. accountant and government official, born in Troy, N.Y.; undersecretary of the Navy 1957–59, secretary of the Navy 1959–61.

Franken, Rose (born 1898), U.S. writer, born in Gainesville, Tex.; married William Brown Meloney; ('Claudia' novels, dramatized on stage, radio, screen, and television; plays: 'Another Language', 'Outrageous Fortune', and 'Soldier's Wife'; autobiography, 'When all Is Said and Done').

Frankenstein, student in Mary Shelley's novel 'Frankenstein', who fashions a soulless man monster, repulsive yet yearning for sympathy; lamenting its loneliness, it follows its creator everywhere and finally destroys him E-274
  Gothic fiction G-197
  horror story H-245
  science fiction S-61

Frankfort, Henri (1897–1954) U.S. archaeologist C-467

Frankfort, Ind., city in agricultural area 40 mi (60 km) n.w. of Indianapolis; railroad shops; electrical products, porcelain and enamelware, clothing, brass products; pop. 15,168, *map* I-102

Frankfort, Ky., state capital, on Kentucky River 50 mi (80 km) e. of Louisville; pop. 25,973 F-378, *map* U-41
  Capitol building, *picture* K-217
  North America, *map* N-350

Frankfort, Mich., city on n.w. shore of lower peninsula, 29 mi (47 km) n. of Manistee; food products, light industry; resort, fishing center; pop. 1,603.

Frankfurt (or Frankfurt-am-Main), West Germany, city in s. on Main River; pop. 629,375 F-378
  Europe, *map* E-360
  exposition grounds F-7
  Germany G-112, *picture* G-114, *map* G-131
  publishing B-350
  treaty (1871), *table* T-274

Frankfurt-an-der-Oder (Frankfort-on-the-Oder), East Germany, city on Oder River on border of Poland; shipping center; pop. 57,669, *map* G-131

Frankfurter, Felix (1882–1965), U.S. jurist and educator, born in Vienna, Austria; Harvard University law professor 1914–38; associate justice U.S. Supreme Court 1939–62; awarded Presidential Medal of Freedom 1963 ('The Public and Its Government'; 'Felix Frankfurter Reminisces').

Frankfurter. *see in index* Hot dog

'Frankfurter Allgemeine Zeitung', daily newspaper of Frankfurt, West Germany, *list* N-241

Frankincense (or olibanum), a fragrant gum resin from certain trees of the genus *Boswellia* found in East Africa, Arabia, China, India, etc.; used as incense; name also given to other tree gums
  Oman O-544

Franking privilege, mail benefit P-461, 462a, P-460b

Frankland, Sir Edward (1825–99), English chemist and physicist, formulator of the doctrine of chemical valence and discoverer (with Lockyer) of helium.

Frankland, State of. *see in index* Tennessee

Franklin, Aretha (born 1942), U.S. singer M-681

Franklin, Benjamin (1706–90), U.S. scientist, inventor, and statesman F-379
  Albany Congress R-162
  American literature A-343
  'Autobiography' A-831
  autograph, *picture* A-832
  'Ben and Me' R-108, *picture* R-111
  Declaration of Independence, *picture* R-162
  education E-88
  folklore F-261, 265
  foundations F-330
  grave, *map* P-251b
  Hall of Fame, *table* H-16
  Howe, *picture* R-174
  insurance history I-235
  inventions and experiments, *picture* I-274
    bifocal lenses S-370
    electricity E-161
    fireplace S-483
    kite K-254
    lightning L-207
    stove S-483
  magazines M-32
  magic M-37
  Pennsylvania, *picture* P-180
  'Poor Richard's Almanack'. *see in index* 'Poor Richard's Almanack'
  portraits
    Houdon busts S-88
    stamps, *pictures* P-439, S-408
  postal service P-460d
  Pulaski P-531
  Stamp Act S-409
  treaty R-173

Franklin, Edward Curtis (1862–1937), U.S. chemist, born in Geary City, Kan.; professor at Stanford University 1906–29; chief of division of chemistry, U.S. Public Health Service, 1911–18; chemist, Bureau of Standards, 1918.

Franklin, James (1697–1735), North American postmaster and newspaper publisher; brother of Benjamin Franklin N-236

Franklin, Sir John (1786–1847), British admiral and Arctic explorer; served in battle of Trafalgar; conducted several expeditions and wrote about them P-419, *maps* P-417
  Yukon Territory Y-440

Franklin, John Hope (born 1915), U.S. educator and author, born in Rentiesville, Okla.; history professor at University of Chicago after 1964 ('From Slavery to Freedom: A History of American Negroes') B-301

Franklin, Miles (pseudonym Brent of Bin Bin) (1879–1954), Australian writer, born in New South Wales (novel, 'All That Swagger'; with Kate Baker wrote biography, 'Joseph Furphy') A-797, *table* A-798

Franklin, Rosalind (1920–58), British biophysicist F-385

Franklin, William Suddards (1863–1930), U.S. physicist and electrical engineer, brother of Edward Curtis Franklin; born in Geary City, Kan.; professor of physics at Iowa State University, Lehigh University, and Massachusetts Institute of Technology.

Franklin, Mass., 7 mi (11 km) s.e. of Milford; foundry products, rubber goods, textiles; incorporated 1778; pop. of township 18,217.

Franklin, N.H., city 17 mi (27 km) n. of Concord; textiles, hosiery, machinery; Daniel Webster's birthplace here in area then part of Salisbury; pop. 7,901.

Franklin, N.J., community 10 mi (16 km) n.e. of Newton; source of zinc ores, franklinite, and willemite; pop. of township 12,396.

Franklin, Pa., city on Allegheny River, in n.w. part of State, 7 mi (11 km) s.w. of Oil City in dairying area; oil and natural gas, coal; petroleum products, oil-well equipment, metal products; pop. 8,146, *map* P-184

Franklin, Wis., city just s.w. of Milwaukee; metal work, woodworking; incorporated 1956; pop. 12,247.

Franklin, battle of, American Civil War; Federals under Schofield defeated Confederates under Hood near Franklin, town 17 mi (27 km) s. of Nashville (Nov. 30, 1864); one of bloodiest of the war, *map* C-474

Franklin, State of. *see in index* Tennessee

Franklin and Marshall College, in Lancaster, Pa.; private control, related to United Church of Christ; formed 1850 by union of Franklin College (founded 1787) and Marshall College (founded 1836); liberal arts; graduate studies.

Franklin College of Indiana, in Franklin, Ind.; established by Baptists in 1834; now nonsectarian, but Baptist related; liberal arts, teacher education.

Franklin District, in Canada, n. part of Northwest Territories; area 1,422,559 sq km (549,253 sq mi); pop. 7,167.

Franklin D. Roosevelt Lake, lake in n.e. Washington, at Grand Coulee Dam W-49, G-213
  Columbia River C-589

Franklin Institute, in Philadelphia, Pa.; founded 1824; workshops and seminars in mathematics and science; laboratories for research in physical sciences; Bartol Research Foundation and Biochemical Research Foundation affiliated; grants medals and certificates for scientific contributions P-251b
  foundations F-330
  Franklin statue, *picture* F-379

Franklin Institute of Boston, in Boston, Mass.; opened 1908; established by The Franklin Foundation with money left by Benjamin Franklin and endowed by Andrew Carnegie and J.J. Storrow; engineering and technical courses F-330

Franklinite, oxide of iron, zinc, and manganese; occurring as brittle blue or black crystals; valuable as ore of iron and zinc.

Franklin Lake, lake in n.e. Nevada; 35 mi (55 km) s.e. of Elko; area about 32 sq mi (83 sq km); shallow, slightly briny body of water with no outlet; federal game refuge.

Franklin Pierce College, in Rindge, N.H.; private control; founded 1962; liberal arts; marine biology laboratory in Puerto Rico.

Franklin's gull, bird *Larus pipixcan* G-317

Franklin Square, N.Y., community on Long Island 18 mi (29 km) e. of New York City; residential; pop. 32,156.

Franklin stove
  Franklin's invention F-382
  stoves and fireplaces S-483

Franks, warlike Germanic people who first settled along lower Rhine River as early as 3rd century AD; kingdom finally included greater portion of territory that now forms Belgium, France, The Netherlands, and West Germany G-121
  Belgium B-149
  Charlemagne C-272
  Charles Martel C-279
  Goths G-197
  Holy Roman Empire H-208
  Middle Ages M-384
  migration M-402
  The Netherlands N-126
  Treaty of Verdun (843) V-283
  Vandals V-265

Franz, Robert (1815–92), German composer; was director of music at University of Halle, but forced to give up because of deafness; best songs distinguished for tenderness and beauty, in the tradition of those of Schubert and Schumann ('Lullaby'; 'Stormy Night'; 'Dedication').

Franzen, Frans Michael (1772–1847), Swedish writer, clergyman, and educator, born in Finland; religious songs and biography; forerunner of Romanticism in Sweden.

Franz Josef Land (or Fridtjof Nansen land), archipelago in U.S.S.R. of some 191 islands in Arctic Ocean n. of Novaya Zemlya; area about 6,229 sq mi (16,134 sq km), *maps* R-322, 344, P-417
  world, *map* W-297

Frasch, Herman (1851–1914), U.S. chemist and inventor, born in Gaildorf, Württemberg, Germany; in U.S. 1868–85; inventions in petroleum products and oil refining S-509

Frasconi, Antonio (born 1919), Uruguayan artist and writer, born in Montevideo; to U.S. 1945; on art faculty New School for Social Research 1951–57; many awards; permanent art collections in U.S.; known also as author and illustrator of children's books R-107, *picture* R-110

Fraser, Dawn (born 1937), Australian swimmer F-386

Fraser, James Earle (1876–1953), U.S. sculptor, born in Winona, Minn. ('End of the Trail', a memorial to the North American Indian; busts of Theodore Roosevelt and Augustus Saint-Gaudens; Lincoln statue at Jersey City; John Ericsson Monument, Washington, D.C.; design for buffalo nickel). His wife, **Laura Gardin Fraser** (1889–1966), also a sculptor of note, born in Chicago, Ill.

Fraser, Malcolm (born 1930), Australian political leader F-386
  Australia A-816
  Hawke H-74

Fraser, Peter (1884–1950), prime minister of New Zealand F-386

Fraser, Simon (1776–1862), Canadian explorer, born in Bennington, Vt.; explored Fraser River, British Columbia (1808); leader of North West Company B-334b, C-96
  fur trade involvement F-471

Fraser, Mich., city 5 mi (8 km) e. of Warren in Detroit metropolitan area; incorporated 1895; pop. 14,560.

Fraser River, chief river of British Columbia; 1,370 km (850 mi) long; rises near Yellowhead Pass in Rocky Mts.; flows into Strait of Georgia s. of Vancouver B-456
  Canada C-74, 95, *map* C-109
  North America, *map* N-350

Fraternal insurance, provided by fraternal orders to members on a cooperative basis; usually nonprofit.

Fraternal societies, social groups organized as "lodges," primarily to provide sickness and life insurance; earlier societies were open only to men, later ones to both men and women F-386

Fraternal twins (or dizygotic twins) M-649

Fraternities and sororities (or Greek-letter societies) F-388
  universities U-206

Fraunces Tavern, in New York, N.Y., on Manhattan Island, built 1719 as residence by Étienne de Lancey; acquired by Samuel Fraunces and became Queen's Head Tavern 1762; headquarters for Sons of the Revolution in state of New York since 1805; scene of Washington's farewell address to officers of Continental Army 1783; now museum, *picture* N-257

Fraunhofer, Joseph von (1787–1826), German optician and physicist; worked to improve optical instruments; invented a heliometer and a micrometer
  spectrum and spectroscope S-371, S-512

Fraunhofer lines, dark lines that cross the spectrum
  physics P-303
  spectrum S-371
  sun S-512

Frazee, John (1790–1852), stone carver and sculptor, born in Rahway, N.J.; portrait busts of Daniel Webster and other noted contemporaries; said to have carved first marble bust in U.S. by a native artist.

Frazer, James (1854–1941), British anthropologist and classical scholar F-389
  anthropology A-485

Frazier, Edward Franklin (1894–1962), U.S. sociologist, author, born in Baltimore, Md.; professor and head of sociology department at Howard University, Washington, D.C., 1934–59 ('The Negro in the United States'; 'The Negro Church in America') B-301

Frazier, Joe (born 1944), U.S. boxer, born in Beaufort, S.C. A-306
  heavyweight champion B-392

Frazil, freezing water I-5

Fréchette, Louis Honoré (1839–1908), French-Canadian poet, born in Lévis, Que.; lyrics inspired by patriotism, nature, friendship, family ('Veronica', a tragedy; 'Papineau' and 'Felix Poutré', historical plays) C-120

Freckles, small, yellowish-brown spots on skin, especially on parts exposed to sun and wind; caused by uneven distribution of pigments; largely hereditary.

Frederic, Harold (1856–98), U.S. novelist, born in Utica, N.Y.; 'Damnation of Theron Ware', intensive study of middle-class U.S.; 'The Copperhead', a story of the Civil War.

Frederick III (1831–88), German emperor and king of Prussia (March 9 to June 15, 1888); commanded at Sedan and siege of Paris in Franco-Prussian War; liberal, cultured, friend of parliamentary government B-285, G-122

Frederick I (nickname Barbarossa) (1123?–90), Holy Roman emperor F-389
  Charlemagne's tomb A-2
  Germany G-121
  Holy Roman Empire H-209
  Italy I-391
  Third Crusade C-787
  University of Bologna U-209

Frederick II (1194–1250), Holy Roman emperor F-390
  Fifth Crusade C-788
  Germany G-121
  Gregory IX G-283
  Holy Roman Empire H-209

Frederick III (1415–93), Holy Roman emperor F-429, A-828
  William I W-205

Frederick IX (1899–1972), king of Denmark; encouraged resistance to Danish resistance movement against German occupation in World War II D-100

Frederick I (1657–1713), first king of Prussia (1701), previously Frederick III, elector of Brandenburg (1688–1701), and duke of Prussia; patron of learned men, but vain, extravagant; won title of king for aiding Leopold I in War of Spanish Succession P-517

Frederick II, king of Prussia. *see in index* Frederick the Great

Frederick I, the Victorious (1425–76), elector palatine 1451–76; tried to dethrone Emperor Frederick III; great military leader.

Frederick II, the Wise (1482–1556), elector palatine (succeeded 1544); commanded imperial army at siege of Vienna 1529; became Protestant through influence of Melanchthon.

Frederick III, the Pious (1515–76), elector palatine (succeeded 1559); laid foundation for systematic Calvinism; aided French Huguenots.

Frederick IV, the Upright (1574–1610), elector palatine (succeeded 1583); championed Protestantism; in 1608 promoted a short-lived league of Protestant princes.

Frederick V (1596–1632), elector palatine and "winter king" of Bohemia; through his marriage with Elizabeth, daughter of James I of England, ancestor of the Windsor (Hanover) line of English kings; king of Bohemia 1619–20; exiled.

Frederick III, the Wise (1463–1525), elector and duke of Saxony; refused imperial throne 1519 and suggested election of Charles V; friend of Luther and Melanchthon, whom he invited to teach at University of Wittenberg founded by him.

Frederick, Md., city 44 mi (71 km) n.w. of Baltimore; clothing, electronic products, brushes, iron and steel, kitchen utensils; Fort Detrick; Hood College and state school for deaf; scene of Whittier's 'Barbara Frietchie'; burial place of Francis Scott Key; Frederick Community College; pop. 28,086 M-178, *picture* M-176, *map* M-182

Frederick Henry (1584–1647), prince of Orange; youngest son of William the Silent and brother of Maurice of Nassau; ended the 80-year struggle with Spain by the treaty of Münster (1648), signed just after his death; his term as stadholder (1625–47) called golden age of Dutch Republic.

Fredericksburg, Va., city about 50 mi (80 km) n. of Richmond, on Rappahannock River at head of tidewater; plastics, men's clothing, shoes, dairy products; national and Confederate cemeteries; Mary Washington College; strategic point in Civil War; pop. 15,322, *map* V-349

Fredericksburg, battle of C-481, *map* C-475
  Hancock H-26

Frederick the Great (or Frederick II) (1712–86), king of Prussia F-390
  army innovations A-641
  Germany G-121, *picture* G-122
  Berlin B-171
  Maria Theresa M-134
  Mendelssohn M-298
  Poland P-414
    Wroclaw W-383
  Seven Years' War S-117
  Voltaire V-385
  War of the Austrian Succession A-829

Frederick William I (1688–1740), king of Prussia; came to throne 1713; the real founder of modern Prussia; left Prussia world's third military power and on sound financial basis F-390
  Germany G-121

Frederick William II (1744–97), king of Prussia, grandson of Frederick William I; came to throne 1786; with Austria, supported Louis XVI in French Revolution.

Frederick William III (1770–1840), king of Prussia; came to throne 1797; good, weak man under whom Prussia was almost effaced by Napoleon, but restored by Congress of Vienna and rehabilitated by the great ministers Stein and Hardenberg; member of Holy Alliance; his queen Louise, a heroine of modern Germany; founder of University of Bonn (1818)
  beet-sugar industry S-507

Frederick William IV (1795–1861), king of Prussia; came to throne 1840; reactionary idealist; reluctantly granted Prussian constitution following revolutionary uprisings of 1848; insane in later years; brother (later William I), regent
  William I W-204

Frederick William (1620–88), the "great elector" of Brandenburg and duke of Prussia; succeeded 1640; laid foundation for greatness of Prussia, previously ruined by Thirty Years' War P-517

Frederick William (1882–1951), crown prince of Prussia, renounced claim to throne in 1918; commander of Fifth German army in World War I V-282

Fredericton, N.B., capital of province, on Saint John River; food processing; boots and shoes, canoes, lumber and wood products; University of New Brunswick; pop. 43,388 F-391
  Canada, *maps* C-109, N-350
  New Brunswick N-152, 156, *pictures* N-155, 157

Frederik III (1609–70), king of Denmark; he transformed Denmark into an absolute monarchy and made crown hereditary; unsuccessful wars with Sweden 1657–60.

Frederik IV (1671–1730), king of Denmark and Norway from 1699–1730; son of Christian V; freed the serfs in 1702.

Frederik VI (1768–1839), king of Denmark and Norway; succeeded 1808 (previously regent); joined Armed Neutrality of North (1800) and was punished (1801) by destruction of fleet by English (read Campbell's 'Battle of the Baltic') and (1807) by bombardment of Copenhagen; formed alliance with Napoleon and was compelled (1814) to surrender Norway to Sweden as punishment.

Frederik VII (1808–63), king of Denmark, succeeded 1848; in his reign Schleswig-Holstein troubles grew ripe for Bismarck's intervention in next reign.

Frederik VIII (1843–1912), king of Denmark, succeeded father, Christian IX, in 1906; father of Haakon VII of Norway, brother of King George I of Greece and of Queen Alexandra of England.

Frederik IX (1899–1972), king of Denmark; first king of Denmark to be trained by nation's navy; his predecessors trained by army C-396

Frederik, Olav Alexander Edward Christian. *see in index* Olav

Frederiksberg, Denmark, municipality of Greater Copenhagen; established 1651 by Frederik III; pop. 113,127.

Frederikshavn, Denmark, seaport 36 mi (58 km) n.e. of Aalborg, on the Kattegat; pop. 22,522 D-97, *map* D-100

Frederiksted, Virgin Islands of the United States, port and commercial center on island of St. Croix; exports sugar; pop. 1,548.

Fredonia, N.Y., village near Lake Erie 40 mi (60 km) s.w. of Buffalo; grape-growing section; first to use natural gas for lighting (1821); College at Fredonia; pop. 11,126
- natural gas used G-38

Fredonia, College at, Fredonia, N.Y., part of State University of New York; chartered 1866; arts and sciences, and teacher education; graduate study.

Fredrikshald, Norway. *see in index* Halden

Fredrikstad, Norway, seaport and manufacturing town at mouth of river Glommen, 50 mi (80 km) s.e. of Oslo; export lumber trade; Hankö, most fashionable Norwegian resort, nearby; pop. 13,712, *map* E-360

Free association, in psychoanalysis P-518, P-523

Freeboard, height above watermark, *diagram* S-176

Free-charge separation, chemical process
- photosynthesis P-300

Free city, city with an independent government. *see also in index* City-states

Free Company, group of mercenaries hired out as units A-640

Free Democrats (FDP), West German political party G-120, 126

'Freelance Pallbearers, The', work by Reed A-362

Freedman, Marcia (born 1938), U.S. politician, *list* W-275

Freedmen's Bureau (in full U.S. Bureau of Refugees, Freedmen, and Abandoned Lands) established by U.S. Congress at close of Civil War to aid 4 million newly-freed black Americans
- blacks Americans B-292
- Johnson's opposition J-127
- Reconstruction R-114

Freedom. *see also in index* Bill of rights; Liberty; Slavery, *subheads* abolitionists and emancipation; and entries beginning with Freedom
- four freedoms R-275
- habeas corpus H-2
- Paine P-21
- underground railroad B-290

Freedom, Presidential Medal of. *see in index* Presidential Medal of Freedom

Freedom Day, National. *see in index* National Freedom Day

Freedom of assembly
- Bill of Rights B-196

Freedom of Information Act (1966), United States
- industrial espionage E-304

Freedom of speech
- U.S. Constitution's guarantee U-151
- Bill of Rights B-196

Freedom of the press
- Jefferson's support J-94
- newspaper N-235
- U.S. Constitution's guarantee U-151
- Bill of Rights B-196
- U.S.S.R. denies R-332e
- Zenger Z-450

Freedom of the seas, maritime law
- international law I-257

Freedom of worship. *see also in index* Religious liberty
- Bill of Rights B-196
- Maryland M-171

Freedom Pledge, pledge sometimes used in U.S. schools; appears in 'Education for Freedom', a bulletin of the U.S. Office of Education:
"I am an American. A free American.
Free to speak—without fear,
Free to worship God in my own way,
Free to stand for what I think right,
Free to oppose what I believe wrong,
Free to choose those who govern my country.
This heritage of Freedom I pledge to uphold
For myself and all mankind."

Freedom ride, in U.S. Civil Rights movement B-296

Freedoms Foundation at Valley Forge, U.S. nonprofit, nonpolitical, nonsectarian foundation chartered in 1949 with the aim of making awards to Americans for contributions to a better understanding of freedom by the things they write, do, or say; headquarters Valley Forge, Pa.

'Freedom's Journal', newspaper B-291

Freedom Trail, Boston, Mass. B-372

Freedom Train, red, white, and blue train for carrying and displaying U.S. historic documents and flags. (Documents date from 1493 to 1945 and include Jefferson's draft of Declaration of Independence.) Train began tour across nation 1947; in Philadelphia, Pa., was first opened to public (Sept. 17). Tour sponsored by Attorney General Tom C. Clark, endorsed by President Harry S. Truman, and directed by the American Heritage Foundation; tour ended January 1949 B-373

'Free Enquirer', U.S. publication, edited by Owen O-620

Free fall
- parachuting A-65
- space travel, *list* S-341b

Free French (or Fighting French)
- France F-364
- World War II W-324

Freehold, in law, *table* L-92

Freeholder, landowner in American Colonies who was given suffrage and officeholding rights; amount of land needed to qualify him for these rights varied.

Freeling, Nicholas (born 1927), writer
- detective story D-119

Freeman, Bud (or Lawrence Freeman) (born 1906), U.S. jazz musician, born in Chicago, Ill.

Freeman, Daniel (1826–1909), Union soldier who received first land grant under Homestead Act of 1862; received one-quarter section (near Beatrice, Neb.), now part of Homestead National Monument of America.

Freeman, Don (1908–78), U.S. illustrator and writer, born in San Diego, Calif.; illustrated William Saroyan's 'Human Comedy' and James Thurber's 'White Deer'; with wife **Lydia Freeman** (born 1907) wrote and illustrated 'Pet of the Met' and other children's books A-368

Freeman, Douglas Southall (1886–1953), U.S. editor and author, born in Lynchburg, Va.; editor *Richmond News Leader* 1915–49; professor of journalism Columbia University 1934–41; Pulitzer prize 1935 for biography 'R.E. Lee' and 1958 for 'George Washington' ('The Last Parade', 'The South to Posterity', 'Lee's Lieutenants').

Freeman, Edward Augustus (1823–92), English historian, born in Stafford, England; among his many historical works, the most famous is 'History of the Norman Conquest'.

Freeman, Mary Eleanor Wilkins (1852–1930), U.S. short-story writer and novelist, born in Randolph, Mass.; at her best in portraying repressed lives of New Englanders ('A New England Nun', short story; 'Jane Field' and 'Pembroke', novels; 'The Wind in the Rose-Bush', ghost story; 'The Long Arm', detective story) A-351

Freeman, Orville Lothrop (born 1918), U.S. public official, born in Minneapolis; secretary Minnesota Democratic-Farmer-Labor party 1946–48, chairman 1948–50; governor of Minnesota 1955–61; U.S. secretary of agriculture 1961–69.

Freeman
- black American B-292
- democracy D-91
- Greek G-212
- Reconstruction R-113
- Roman S-213

Freeman's Farm, battles of. *see in index* Saratoga, battles of

Freemasons (or Masons), secret fraternal society
- apprenticeship A-511
- fraternal societies F-386
- opera O-565

Free metal, metal, such as gold, found free in nature, not combined with other elements.

Free Methodist Church of North America, developed from the Methodist Episcopal church; organized 1860 at Pekin, N.Y., to bring about a return to Methodism as originated by Wesley; adopted doctrine of Methodist Episcopal church with added belief in entire sanctification (freedom from inward sin) and in a stricter view regarding general judgment and future reward and punishment H-202

Free-piston engine, in automobile A-846

Freeport, Ill., city in n.w. part of state, 26 mi (42 km) w. of Rockford; electrical switches and motors, batteries, drug products, toys; insurance center; pop. 26,406
- Illinois, *map* I-52

Freeport, N.Y., residential village 12 mi (19 km) e. of Jamaica on s. shore of Long Island; resort area, deep-sea fishing; pop. 38,272.

Freeport, Tex., city 45 mi (70 km) s.w. of Galveston on Gulf of Mexico; in farm area; oil and gas fields; chemicals, commercial fisheries; pop. 13,444.

Freeport doctrine
- Lincoln-Douglas debates L-226

Freer, Charles Lang (1856–1919), U.S. art collector and financier, born in Kingston, N.Y.; Freer Gallery of Art (gift to nation).

'Freeshooter, The' (German Der Freischütz) (1821), opera in three acts by Carl Maria von Weber; libretto by Friedrich Kind, based on story of "magic bullets" that never miss their target; produced in Berlin 1821 O-566, *list* O-562
- Lind's operatic debut L-226
- Weber W-128

Freesia, genus of plants of the iris family with narrow ribbonlike leaves and showy fragrant white, pale yellow, pink, or purplish flowers; native to s. Africa.

Free Soil party, minor U.S. political party, active 1848–56; fought extension of slavery, chiefly to block political power of slave states and black migration to the territories; slogan "Free soil, free speech, free labor, and free men" P-433
- Mann M-109
- presidential vote (1848 and 1852), *table* P-495a
- Taylor's campaign T-43

'Free Song, A', work by Schuman M-677

'Free Soul, A', work by Barrymore B-84

Free State. *see in index* Maryland

Free state, in United States' history, a state forbidding slavery U-174, 179

Freestone, fine-grained stone easily cut or sawed in any direction without splitting, especially certain sedimentary rock as limestone and sandstone.

Freethinker, person who forms opinions about religion independently of tradition; use of term dates back to early 18th century.

Free throw, in basketball B-98

Freetown, Sierra Leone, capital and port on Atlantic Ocean; one of Africa's best natural harbors; exports palm oil, nuts, piassava, cacao, ginger, iron ore, diamonds; pop. 314,340 F-391, *map* A-115
- Sierra Leone S-192a
- world, *map* W-297

Free trade, international commerce based on exchange of goods without restrictive tariffs designed to protect home industry I-267

Free Trade Hall, in Manchester, U.K. M-92

Free University of Brussels, in Brussels, Belgium B-148

Free verse (French *vers libre*), an unrhymed, unmetrical verse form; secures a variety of rhythmical effects by use of cadence; unit of rhythm is the stanza or strophe; form found in 'Psalms', 'Song of Solomon'; in poetry of Matthew Arnold, Walt Whitman, Amy Lowell, Carl Sandburg, and others A-354

Free waves (or swell), ocean waves O-487

Freeway, highway R-214. *see also in index* Expressway

Free will, an individual's power to act or choose consciously and independently in a way not determined by factors beyond his or her control.

Freeze-dried food F-283
- meat industry M-251
- water W-84

Freezer, home appliance H-210

Freezing
- cryogenics C-793
- food processing F-281
- refrigeration R-138
- solids S-254f
- water W-85

Freezing point, point at which a substance changes from a liquid to a solid M-225
- heat H-103
- water W-85

Frege, Gottlob (1848–1925), German mathematician F-392

Frei, Eduardo (in full Eduardo Frei Montalva) (1911–1982), Chilean lawyer and political leader, born in Santiago; president of Chile 1965–70
- Chile C-334

Freiberg, East Germany, mining town 20 mi (30 km) s.w. of Dresden; silver and lead smelting; optical instruments; pop. 47,671, *map* G-131

Freiburg, West Germany, city and tourist center in Black Forest; Gothic cathedral; university (founded 1457); called **Freiburg im Breisgau,** from old district of Breisgau of which it was capital; pop. 162,222, *map* G-131

Freighter, cargo ship S-168, 176a, *diagram* S-172–3,
- Michigan, *picture* M-357
- Philippines P-257a, *picture* P-257
- transportation T-254

Freight transportation. *see in index* Transportation

Freiligrath, Ferdinand (1810–76), German poet; wrote political and lyric verse; translated English, French, and U.S. classics into German.

'Freischütz, Der'. *see in index* Freeshooter, The'

FRELIMO (Front for the Liberation of Mozambique) M-642

Frelinghuysen, Theodore (1787–1862), U.S. lawyer, statesman, and educator, born in Millstone, N.J.; U.S. senator 1829–35; Whig vice-presidential candidate 1844.

Fremantle, Western Australia, port of Perth, 12 miles (19 kilometers) distant; at mouth of Swan River; railroad terminus; shipbuilding; manufactures of iron and steel, furniture, flour, soap; pop. 26,036, *maps* A-822, P-3
- world, *map* W-297

Frémiet, Emmanuel (1824–1910), French sculptor noted for equestrian statue of Joan of Arc at Paris and for animal studies.

Frémont, John Charles (1813–90), American Civil War general and explorer F-392
- Carson C-177
- exploration and conquests
  - California C-41, S-339
  - Oregon Trail O-598
- frontier movement F-422
- Kearny K-194
- Mexican War M-320
- Nevada exploration N-137
- presidential bid B-475

Fremont, Calif., city 29 mi (47 km) s.e. of San Francisco; automobiles, trailers; incorporated 1956 after merger of 5 communities; site of Mission San José de Guadalupe built 1797; pop. 131,945.

Fremont, Neb., city 30 mi (50 km) n.w. of Omaha; meat-packing, processing of agricultural products; metal products; mini-bikes; Midland Lutheran College; pop. 23,979 N-96, 104, *map* U-41

Fremont, Ohio, city 30 mi (50 km) s.e. of Toledo on Sandusky River; iron and steel products, cutlery, rubber goods, batteries, beet sugar; battle of Fort Stephenson 1813; pop. 17,834.

Fremont Peak, in the Wind River Mountains, Wyoming (13,730 ft; 4,180 m).

French, Allen (1870–1946), U.S. author, born in Boston, Mass.; writer of stories of history and mythology for young folks; especially noted for Revolutionary War stories ('Heroes of Iceland', 'The Story of Rolf and the Viking's Bow', 'The Siege of Boston').

French, Daniel Chester (1850–1931), U.S. sculptor
New Hampshire N-180
sculpture S-91
'Minute Man', *picture* C-639
'Seated Lincoln', *picture* L-224

French, Sir George Arthur (1841–1921), Canadian soldier, born in Roscommon, Ireland; 1873 organized North West Mounted Police, since 1920 Royal Canadian Mounted Police.

French, John Denton Pinkstone, first **earl of Ypres** (1852–1925), British field marshal; commander of British forces in Belgium and France 1914–15; commander in chief of forces in the United Kingdom 1915–18; lord lieutenant of Ireland 1918–21
World War I W-307

French, Marilyn (born 1929), U.S. author A-363

French Academy A-14, R-204

French Academy of Sciences
metric system development W-139

French-Alpine goat G-171

French and Indian War (1754–63), North American phase of Seven Years' War in Europe F-393
Acadia's role A-14, C-93
Albany Congress A-259
American Indians I-148
colonists lack unity R-162
effect on Spain S-338
first battle in Pennsylvania P-345b
Franklin F-383
Michigan M-357, 361
Minnesota M-445
Montcalm M-566
results A-338, R-163, S-338
Treaty of Paris S-118, U-169
Washington W-39
Wisconsin W-253

French billiards (or Carom billiards) B-191

French Broad River, river about 205 mi (330 km) long, rises in Blue Ridge of w. North Carolina and flows w. to the Holston River in Tennessee to form Tennessee River; French Broad River includes Douglas Reservoir e. of Knoxville.

French bulldog, dog, *picture* D-206

French Cameroons. *see in index* Cameroons

French chalk, variety of steatite talc; used by tailors to mark cloth and to remove perspiration from hands when working with fine fabrics.

French Colombard grape G-220

French curve, device used in mechanical drawing M-257

French Equatorial Africa, former French overseas territory in w.-central Africa. *see in index* Central African Republic; Chad; Congo, People's Republic of the; Gabon

French farthingale, skirt frame D-263

French Foreign Legion. *see in index* Foreign Legion

French Guiana, French overseas department on n.e. coast of South America; 35,135 sq mi (91,000 sq km); cap. Cayenne; pop. 73,022 F-393, *Fact Summary* S-295, *map* S-298
colonization A-337
migration of people M-401
South America S-275, *map* S-274
West Indies W-155
world, *map* W-297

French Guinea, Africa. *see in index* Guinea, Republic of

French horn, wind instrument W-230

French India. *see in index* French Settlements in India

French Indochina. *see also in index* Cochinchina; Laos; Tonkin; Vietnam; Vietnam, North; Vietnam, South
Ho Chi Minh City H-192
Indochina I-157
Kampuchea K-170
World War II W-327

French language L-37, 41, *diagram* L-40
Africa A-119
Burkina Faso B-507
Gabon G-2
Egypt E-116
Zaire Z-444
beginnings R-239
Belgium B-146
English
borrowings E-261
literature E-264
France F-348
Canada C-95, C-77
Montreal M-571
Quebec Q-9g
French literature F-394
Switzerland S-541

French Lick, Ind., resort town in s.w., about 65 mi (105 km) n.e. of Evansville; saline-sulfur springs; pop. 2,265, *map* I-102

'French Lieutenant's Woman', work by Fowles F-336

French literature F-394
Flaubert F-176
France F-349
romance tales R-239
'Song of Roland' R-238
storytelling S-475, 481b

Frenchman Creek, creek in Nebraska N-95

Frenchman Flat, desert basin in Nevada N-132

French marigold, flower *Tagetes patula* M-135

French military kite (or Conyne kite) K-252

French Morocco (or French zone of Morocco), former French protectorate comprising nearly all Morocco.

French Oceania. *see in index* French Polynesia

French Open, tennis tournament T-108, *picture* T-103

French Panama Canal Company P-92, R-286

French Polynesia (formerly French Settlements in Oceania), overseas territory of French Community, in s. Pacific Ocean; composed of Marquesas Islands, Tuamotu Archipelago, Gambier Islands, Society Islands (including Tahiti), and Tubuai Islands; total area 1,261 sq mi (3,266 sq km); cap. Papeete, on Tahiti; pop. 132,000, *map* P-3. *see also in index* island groups and islands by individual name
Oceania O-468

French poodle. *see in index* Poodle

French Prix de L'Arc de Triomphe, horse race H-275

French Protestants. *see in index* Huguenots

French Quarter (or Vieux Carré), in New Orleans, La. N-232, *picture* N-230
Louisiana, *picture* L-319

French Revolution (1789–95) F-400, E-348
abolitionist movement A-10
army A-642
Austria and Prussia A-830
bureaucratic history B-506
conservatism C-679
Corday C-715
Declaration of the Rights of Man B-195
democracy D-93
France F-349
French literature F-396
Great Britain E-250
English literature E-273
hair fashion H-10
international relations I-260
Jacobin J-11
labor law L-4
Lafayette L-20
Louis XVI L-306
Marat M-131
Marie Antoinette M-135
Mirabeau M-462
Napoleon N-13
Paine P-21
Robespierre R-222
Roland R-239
Rousseau R-299b
serfdom S-213
Seven Years' War S-118
Voltaire V-385
warfare W-13
weights and measures W-139
women's rights W-276
XYZ affair X-406

French rose R-294

French Settlements in India, former French territory on peninsula of India; consisted of five settlements; of these, Chandernagore merged with India in 1950, and Pondichéry, Karikal, Yanaon, and Mahé became part of India in 1954.

French Settlements in Oceania. *see in index* French Polynesia

French Somaliland. *see in index* Djibouti, Republic of

French Sudan, Africa. *see in index* Mali

French Togoland. *see in index* Togoland

Frenchtown, former village on site of present Monroe, Mich., on Raisin River 35 mi (55 km) s.w. of Detroit; Americans defeated by British and American Indians, 1813, followed by massacre of wounded Americans (Raisin River Massacre).

French West Africa, former French overseas territory in w. Sahara and adjacent coastal regions. *see in index* Burkina Faso; Guinea, Republic of; Ivory Coast; Mali; Mauritania; Niger; Senegal

French West Indies, collective name for French overseas departments of Guadeloupe and Martinique in West Indies. *see also in index* West Indies

Freneau, Philip (1752–1832), U.S. poet and journalist, born in New York City; edited anti-Federalist *National Gazette,* Philadelphia (1791–93) ('The British Prison Ship', 'Eutaw Springs', 'The Indian Burying-Ground') A-345

Frenssen, Gustav (1863–1945), German novelist; for several years was a village pastor; later devoted himself to writing; 'Jörn Uhl', novel of peasant life, made him famous.

Freon (CFC, or chlorofluorocarbon), chemical compound
fluorocarbon F-241
refrigerant R-137

Frequency, in biology B-224

Frequency, in physics, vibration rate
light waves L-200
noise N-331
radiation R-33, 36, *table* R-34
radio R-45, 50, *table* R-54
sound waves S-260, *diagram* S-262
star's electromagnetic radiation A-721

Frequency distribution, in statistics S-432, *table* S-433
graph and chart G-226

Frequency modulation (FM), in electronics
radio R-50

Frequency polygon, line graph G-227, S-433

Frere, Sir Henry Bartle (1815–84), English administrator, nephew of John Hookham Frere; governor of Bombay 1862–67; as special commissioner to East Africa influential in abolishing slave trade in Zanzibar; as governor of Cape Colony 1877–80 attempted confederation of South Africa.

Frere, John Hookham (1769–1846), English diplomat and author, uncle of Sir Henry B. Frere; minister to Portugal 1800–02, to Spain 1802–4 and 1808; his spirited verse translations of Aristophanes' plays have never been equaled.

Frere Hall, in Karachi, Pakistan K-191

Fresco, painting on fresh plaster P-67h. *see also in index* Mural painting
Bezzuoli, *picture* P-302
Giorgione G-145
Giotto G-146, *pictures* P-29
Masaccio P-32, *picture* P-33
Michelangelo M-351, *picture* M-350
Orozco, *picture* O-608
Raphael R-92
Rivera P-67a, *picture* P-67b
Sistine Chapel S-191, P-37

Frescobaldi, Girolamo (1583–1643), Italian composer and organist, born in Ferrara; organist at St. Peter's in Rome 30 years; composed for organ, also for voice.

Fresenius, Karl Remigius (1818–97), German chemist, born in Frankfurt; founder of chemical laboratory at Wiesbaden Agricultural Institution.

Freshwater dogfish (or common bowfin, or mudfish), fish *Amia calva* M-644

Freshwater eel, fish E-109

Freshwater polyp, hydra. *see in index* Hydra

Freshwater snail S-221

Fresnel, Augustin Jean (1788–1827), French physicist; demonstrated (after Young but independently) wave theory of light; established mathematical analysis of optical phenomena; contributed theory that light waves are transverse; changed entire world's lighthouse illumination ("Fresnel system") P-306
light experiments L-201

Fresno, Calif., city 162 mi (261 km) s.e. of San Francisco; pop. 217,289 F-404, *maps* N-350, U-40

Fresno Pacific College (until 1978 Pacific College), in Fresno, Calif.; affiliated with Mennonite Brethren church; founded 1944, senior college 1965; liberal arts and teacher education; graduate school.

Fresno State College. *see in index* California State University, Fresno

Freud, Anna (1895–1982), Austrian psychoanalyst, born in Vienna; daughter of Sigmund Freud; member London Institute of Psychoanalysis; director Hampstead Child Therapy Course and Clinic.

Freud, Sigmund (1856–1939), Austrian neurologist and psychiatrist F-404
Adler A-45
biographical writing B-223
cocaine D-276
dreams D-257
Ellis E-194
Fromm F-417
Horney H-244
hypnosis H-344
Jung J-152
literature L-242
medicine M-284
mental illness M-302
Oedipus complex O-493
psychoanalysis P-518, 521
totemism and taboo T-235
warfare essay W-28

Frey, in Norse mythology, god of peace, prosperity, and fruitfulness, brother of Freyja; according to old Danish legend he was reincarnated in the kings of Denmark M-703

Freyja (or Freyia, or Freya), in Norse mythology, goddess of love, sister of Frey, and in late German folklore wife of Odin; portrayed in chariot pulled by cats M-703

Freytag, Gustav (1816–95), German novelist and playwright; sturdy realism, with strong undercurrent of patriotism ('The Journalists', play; 'Debit and Credit', novel).

Friant Dam, dam in California C-36

Friar, member of a Roman Catholic religious order of mendicants
Aztecs' conversion attempts A-892
Middle Ages M-391
monks and monasticism M-541

Friars Minor, Order of, part of the First Order of St. Francis (Franciscans), established 1209; also part of the First Order are Friars Minor Conventuals and Friars Minor Capuchins.

Friars Preachers, Order of. *see in index* Dominicans

Friar Tuck. *see in index* Tuck, Friar

Frick, Ford Christopher (1894–1978), U.S. baseball executive, sportswriter, and sportscaster; born near Wawaka, Ind.; president of National League 1934–51; commissioner of baseball 1951–65; chairman board of directors National Baseball Hall of Fame and Museum 1966–78.

Frick, Henry Clay (1849–1919), U.S. capitalist and steel manufacturer, born in West Overton, Pa.; early obtained control of most of Connellsville

coal lands; entered Carnegie Steel Company (1882), becoming rival of Carnegie for control; left fortune of $100,000,000; donated Frick Museum to New York City
  industry I-195

Frick Museum, in New York, N.Y. N-278

Friction, in physics and mechanics
  brakes B-404
  energy E-220
  heat H-104, *picture* H-102
  lubricants L-327
  machine M-9
  mechanics M-264

Friday, in Defoe's 'Robinson Crusoe', a man rescued from cannibals by Crusoe.

Friday, day of the week
  Islam S-1

Fridley, Minn., city in Anoka County just n. of Minneapolis; chiefly residential; aluminum products, electronic components; ordnance; pop. 30,228.

Fridtjof Nansen Land, U.S.S.R. *see in index* Franz Josef Land

Fried, Alfred Hermann (1864–1921), Austrian journalist, born in Vienna; founded German pacifist periodical and wrote books on peace. *see also in index* Nobel Prizewinners, *table*

Friedan Betty (born 1921), U.S. author and feminist ('The Feminine Mystique') W-279

Friedland, U.S.S.R. *see in index* Pravdinsk

Friedman, Milton (born 1912), U.S. economist, born in Brooklyn, N.Y.; known for work in consumption analysis and monetary theory; advocate of laissez-faire principles; faculty of University of Chicago 1946–77, professor 1948–77; Hoover Institution 1977–. *see also in index* Nobel Prizewinners, *table*

Friedmann, Andrei. *see in index* Capa, Robert

Friedrich Schiller University, in Jena, East Germany; founded 1558; noted for eminent teachers including Schiller, Fichte, Hegel, and Schelling; identified with liberal movement in theology.

Friedrichshafen, West Germany, city on n.e. shore of Lake Constance; center of Zeppelin manufacture during and after World War I; fine harbor and bathing beach; pop. 43,140, *maps* G-131, S-537

Friends, Religious Society of. *see in index* Quakers

Friendship Bridge, bridge in Brazil and Paraguay, over Paraná River.

"Friendship" pipeline P-241c, R-330c

Friends' Public Grammar School, early Pennsylvania school P-171

Friends University, situated at Wichita, Kan.; affiliated with Religious Society of Friends (Quakers); opened 1898; arts and sciences, teacher education W-201

Fries, John (1750?–1818), U.S. insurgent, leader of Fries's Rebellion in Pennsylvania, 1799, revolt against a direct tax levied by Congress A-34

Frieseke, Frederick Carl (1874–1939), U.S. artist, born in Owosso, Mich.; an impressionist painter known chiefly for his portrayal of female figures in sunny outdoor settings or in colorful interiors.

Friesian Islands, North Sea. *see in index* Frisian Islands

Friesians. *see in index* Frisians

Friesland, province of n. The Netherlands; surface partly below sea level, protected by dikes; 1,249 sq mi (3,235 sq km); pop. 478,931 N-126
  folktales, *list* S-481c

Frietchie, Barbara (1766–1862), U.S. patriot
  replica of home
    Maryland, *picture* M-176
    Whittier's ballad A-348

Frieze, heavy woolen cloth having a nap on the surface; used chiefly for overcoats; lighter weights blended from rayon and wool; first frieze made in Friesland, Holland, in 13th century.

'Frieze of the Prophets', mural by Sargent, *picture* P-509

Frigate, name originally applied to merchant vessels propelled by sails or oars; later to full-rigged, fast war vessels, smaller than ships of the line; carried from 24 to 55 guns; in use from about 1650 to 1840; term now used in U.S. Navy for new, large destroyers; also a British escort vessel and an improved Canadian corvette are called frigates N-83, *picture* N-90
  Alabama R-319
  Essex S-177g
  Guerrière S-177f
  Java S-177g
  Serapis, *picture* R-172

Frigate bird (or man-o'-war), bird F-405, B-244

Frigga (or Frigg), in Norse mythology, wife of Odin and goddess of marriage and domestic life; Friday (day of week) named for her M-703

Frillback, pigeon P-324

Friml, Rudolf (1879–1972), U.S. pianist and composer, born in Prague, present Czechoslovakia; was accompanist to Jan Kubelik; settled in New York 1906; best known for operetta 'Rose Marie' M-685

Fringe benefits, in employment I-5

Fringed gentian, *picture* P-371
  wildflower, *picture* F-236

Fringe tree, small tree *Chionanthus virginica* of the olive family with fragrant fringelike white flowers in graceful drooping panicles.

Fringillidae, finch family, a large family of seed-eating birds including finches, sparrows, and buntings B-504

Fringing reef, coral formation C-715

Frio, Cape, point on the coast of Brazil, about 80 mi (130 km) e. of Rio de Janeiro; Spanish name, *frio*, means cold or icy, *map* S-299

Frisch, Frank Francis (nickname Fordham Flash) (1898–1973), U.S. baseball player, born in New York, N.Y.; second baseman New York, N.L., 1919–26, and St. Louis, N.L., 1927–37; went directly from college ranks to major leagues; outstanding infielder, base runner, and batter; played on 8 pennant-winning teams; managed St. Louis, N.L., 1933–38, B-93

Frisch, Karl von (1886–1982), Austrian zoologist, born in Vienna; professor of zoology at University of Munich 1925–46 and 1950–58; won Balzan Prize 1963 ('Bees: Their Vision, Chemical Senses, and Language', 'The Dancing Bees'). *see also in index* Nobel Prizewinners, *table*

Frisch, Max (born 1911), Swiss author and architect, born in Zürich; dramas and novels important in contemporary German literature G-108

Frisch, Ragnar (1895–1973), Norwegian economist, born in Oslo; professor at University of Oslo 1931–65; held in German concentration camp 1943–45. *see also in index* Nobel Prizewinners, *table*

Frisé, pile fabric used for upholstery; designs are produced by contrast of cut and uncut loops, by use of different colored yarns, or by surface printing; also rug or carpet with cut pile.

Frisian Islands (or Friesian Islands), chain in North Sea off Dutch, West German, and Danish coasts; from Zuider Zee e. and n. as far as Jutland; 400 sq mi (1,040 sq km) G-112, *map* E-360

Frisian language G-103
  English resemblance E-260
  The Netherlands N-126

Frisians (or Friesians), w. Germanic seafaring people who in 1st century AD were found by the Romans in occupation of the coastland from the Rhine to the Ems River; gradually conquered by the Franks and put under Frankish rule in 9th century, struggled for independence from 13th to 18th centuries, when part of Friesland went to The Netherlands, part to Prussia G-121
  The Netherlands N-126

Frissell, Mount, highest point in Connecticut (2,380 ft; 725 m) C-650

Frit, tiny fragments of glass
  enameling E-208
  pottery making P-475

Fritchie, Barbara Hauer, real name of Whittier's heroine. *see in index* Frietchie, Barbara

'Frithjof', 13th-century saga or myth of Icelandic hero Frithjof who married Ingeborg, daughter of petty king in Norway and widow of Hring; succeeded to Hring's dominion; poem by Esaias Tegnér based on this myth S-526

Fritillary, any plant of genus *Fritillaria* of lily family; characterized by spotted, bell-shaped, drooping flowers; found in warmer regions of temperate zone.

Fritz, John (1822–1913), U.S. ironworker and engineer, born in Chester County, Pennsylvania; chief engineer Bethlehem Iron Company 1860; introduced 3-high roller plant 1850's; one of first to apply Bessemer process to U.S. practice.

Froben, Johann (or Johannes Frobenius) (1460?–1527), Swiss printer and scholar; printed works of Erasmus, many editions of Latin Bible and other fine works.

Frobisher, Joseph (died 1810), Canadian fur trader, born in Halifax, England; came to Canada 1769; partner in North West Company; 1792–96 represented Montreal in Legislative Assembly of Lower Canada.

Frobisher, Sir Martin (1535?–94), British navigator and naval hero, first to seek the Northwest Passage A-332, *table* P-422
  exploration E-373
    Northwest Territories N-388

Frobisher Bay, inlet of Davis Strait opening westward at s. end of Baffin Island, Canada; explored by Sir Martin Frobisher, *map* C-109

Froebel, Friedrich (1782–1852), German educator F-405
  educational contribution E-89
  kindergarten K-241

Froehlke, Robert Frederick (born 1922), U.S. lawyer, born in Neenah, Wis.; with Sentry Insurance Company 1951–69; assistant secretary of defense 1969–71; secretary of the Army 1971–73.

Frog F-406
  amphibians A-376, *picture* A-378
  anatomy A-389
  animal A-431
    life record, *table* E-24
  eggs, *pictures* E-110, E-111
  embryology E-199
  heart R-152
  hibernation H-147
  migration A-452

Frog, device that allows railroad wheels to intersect the rails
  Westinghouse W-162

Frogfish F-128

Froghopper, leaping insect of the family Cercopidae; the young void a white frothy substance over themselves for protection; also called spittlebug and frothfly.

Frog lily (or yellow pond lily, or spatterdock, or cow lily), plant *Nuphar advena* W-99

Frogmen, underwater demolition teams of the U.S. Navy N-89

Frogner Park, park in Oslo, Norway N-391, *picture* N-392

'Frogs, The', work by
  Aristophanes A-588
  Euripides E-327

Frog shell, gastropod shell *Bursa perca*, *picture* S-149

Frohman, Charles (1860–1915), U.S. theatrical manager, born in Sandusky, Ohio, brother of Daniel Frohman; brought out Maude Adams, John Drew, Julia Marlowe; died on *Lusitania*

Frohman, Daniel (1851–1940), U.S. theatrical manager, brother of Charles Frohman, born in Sandusky, Ohio; author of 'Memories of a Manager' and 'Daniel Frohman Presents'.

Froissart, Jean (1333?–1400?), French chronicler and poet F-417
  French literature F-394
  Hundred Years' War H-324

'Frolic' and the 'Wasp', battle of, sea fight in War of 1812, between the sloops *Wasp* (U.S.) and *Frolic* (British), October 1812; marked by terrific fighting in high sea; *Wasp* took *Frolic* but was captured herself almost immediately by a British frigate.

Fromentin, Eugène (1820–76), French painter and author; best known for paintings of North Africa; wrote and illustrated book on Sahara; also wrote a novel ('Dominique') and a work on Dutch and Flemish painting.

Frome River, river in England, flowing 20 mi (30 km) into the Avon; Bristol is located at its junction with the Avon River; diverted in 13th century to improve Bristol harbor; section, with Avon, partly converted 1809 from tidal river to mark floating harbor.

'From Here to Eternity', work by Jones W-28

Fromm, Erich (1900–80), U.S. psychoanalyst F-417
  psychoanalysis P-519

'From the New World', symphony by Dvořák D-294

'From the Sea to a Youth', work by Namson K-294

Frond, shape of fern leaf F-56, *picture* F-57

Fronde, The, civil war in France during minority of Louis XIV (1648–52) and consequent war with Spain (1653–59), so called (*fronde*, "sling") from free use of slingshots by the Paris mob; its suppression contributed to the growth of absolutism under Louis XIV; also name of political party that opposed king.

Frondizi, Arturo (born 1908), Argentine lawyer, economist, and political leader; born in Paso de los Libres, Corrientes Province; member of House of Deputies 1946; president of Argentina 1958–62.

Front, transition zone between different air masses W-118, *table* W-126

Frontal attack, in warfare W-23

Frontal bone, bone forming the forehead, or front of the cranium S-210

Frontal cyclone. *see in index* Wave cyclone

Front de Libération Nationale. *see in index* National Liberation Front

Frontenac, Louis de (1622–98), governor of New France F-417
  Canada C-92
  Joliet J-138
  King William's War K-247
  La Salle L-52
  Ontario O-553

Frontenac Axis, rock belt of North America, most prominent in Ottawa-St. Lawrence lowlands C-73

Front for the Liberation of Mozambique (FRELIMO) M-462

Frontier F-418. *see also in index* Pioneer life in America; Southwest, American
  bibliography U-197e
  Buffalo Bill B-490
  fiction A-345
  Frémont F-392
  Kearny K-194
  outlaws O-619
  railroad development R-74
  settlement
    California S-2
    Nebraska O-543
    South Dakota S-326
  trails, *map* R-219
  Turner's theory T-327
  U.S. history U-176
  westerns W-151

Frontinus, Sextus Julius (1st century AD), Roman soldier and writer; governor of Britain 75–78; after becoming water commissioner of Rome, wrote 'De aquis urbis Romae' (On the Aqueducts of Rome).

Frontispiece, illustration facing title page of book, magazine, or a major division of a book; term also may refer to title page itself.

Front Range. *see in index* Canadian Rockies

Front Range, e. range of Rocky Mountains, in n.-central Colorado; contains Pikes Peak and Longs Peak R-234a, *map* U-80
  geologic history, *diagrams* R-235
  Rocky Mountain N.P., *pictures* R-234, 235

Front Royal, Va., town, 65 mi (105 km) w. of Washington,

D.C.; agricultural and tourist center; cattle and poultry raising; silk and rayon; "Stonewall" Jackson defeated Colonel Kenly in May 1862; pop. 11,126, *map* V-349

Frost, Arthur Burdett (1851–1928), U.S. illustrator and author, born in Philadelphia, Pa. ('Bull Calf and Other Tales', 'Carlo')
  Uncle Remus illustrations R-110a

Frost, Edwin Brant (1866–1935), U.S. astronomer, born in Brattleboro, Vt.; studied in Germany and United States; professor astronomy and director observatory, Dartmouth College; professor astrophysics at University of Chicago and director Yerkes Observatory; important work in stellar spectroscopy; became blind in later years but continued work ('Let's Look at the Stars').

Frost, Frances (1905–59), U.S. writer, born in St. Albans, Vt.; instructor creative writing at University of Vermont 1929–31 (poems: 'These Acres', 'Pool in the Meadow', 'Mid-Century'; novels: 'Innocent Summer', 'Yoke of Stars', 'Village of Glass'; books for children: 'Maple Sugar for Windy Foot', 'The Little Whistler', 'Rocket Away!').

Frost, Leslie Miscampbell (1895–1973), Canadian lawyer and political leader, born in Orillia, Ont.; member Ontario legislature 1937–61; leader of Ontario Progressive Conservative party after 1949; premier of Ontario 1949–61.

Frost, Robert (1874–1963), U.S. poet F-428
  American literature A-355
  creative writing W-377
  quotations P-406, A-664
  reading R-112a
  sculpture by Hancock S-80

Frost, frozen condensation F-429
  weather W-120

Frostbite
  first aid F-121

Frostburg State College, in Frostburg, Md.; established 1902; formerly a teachers college; arts and sciences, teacher education; graduate studies.

Frost-free refrigerator, home appliance H-210

Frost giants, in Norse mythology M-703

Frostgrape, *picture* L-101

Froth-flotation method, separation process for minerals
  coal cleaning C-524

Frothfly. *see in index* Froghopper

Froude, James Anthony (1818–94), English historian, often prejudiced but a master of style ('History of England from the Fall of Wolsey to the Defeat of the Spanish Armada'; biographies of Thomas Carlyle, Julius Caesar, Disraeli) B-223

Frozen Charlottes (or Frozen Charlies), littlest antique china dolls; origin in ballad, 'Fair Charlotte' D-221

Frozen food
  ice cream I-11
  refrigeration R-138
  vitamins V-357

Frozen milk concentrate, *list* D-6

Fructose (or levulose, or fruit sugar) simple monosaccharide sugar ($C_6H_{12}O_6$), one and three fourths times as sweet as cane sugar; found in sweet fruits and honey S-508
  carbohydrate C-155
  organic chemistry O-604

Fruit F-430. *see also in index* Fruitgrowing, *also* names of fruit, as Apple, Orange
  alcohol fermentation A-275
  cooking C-701
  diseases and pests
    fungus F-449
    scale insects S-52e
  flowers F-219
  food and nutrition F-278
  liquor production L-235
  organic chemistry O-604
  raisin R-90
  vitamins, *table* V-355
  water plants' reproduction W-101
  wine W-236

Fruit bat. *see in index* Flying fox

Fruit fly
  aging experiments A-127
  fly F-243
  insect I-226

Fruitgrowing F-436
  agriculture A-134, F-25
    citrus C-444
  titmouse T-196
  United States
    Florida F-197
    Great Lakes region G-246

Fruit sugar. *see in index* Fructose

'Fru Marie Grubbe', novel by Jacobsen J-11

Frumentariae Leges. *see in index* Corn Laws, Roman

Frumentius, Saint (died 380?), born in Tyre; founder and first bishop of Ethiopian church; known as Abba Salama (father of peace); feast day July 20 in Ethiopian church.

Frumenty, old English breakfast dish made by boiling wheat kernels with milk, spices, and sugar to which raisins sometimes were added.

Frunze, U.S.S.R., capital of Kirgiz Soviet Socialist Republic, 125 mi (200 km) s.w. of Alma-Ata; food processing; machinery, textiles; pop. 486,000, *map* R-344
  Asia, *map* A-697
  Kirgiz Soviet Socialist Republic K-250

Frustration, in psychology, either conscious or unconscious state of mind where person feels unable to satisfy certain impulses and desires; feelings of disappointment and defeat common.

Frustrum of a pyramid, in mathematics
  geometry G-79, *diagram* G-78

Fry, Christopher (born 1907), English dramatist F-440

Fry, Elizabeth (1780–1845), British prison reformer F-440

Fry, Roger Eliot (1866–1934), English painter and art critic; paintings show fine sense of form and design; published works include 'Vision and Design' and 'Architectural Heresies of a Painter'.

Fry, William Henry (1815–64), U.S. music critic and composer, born in Philadelphia, Pa.; critic for *New York Tribune;* symphonies included 'Childe Harolde'.

Fry, cooking process C-700

Frye, William Pierce (1831–1911), U.S. legislator, born in Lewiston, Me.; attorney general of Maine 1867–69; representative in Congress 1871–81; U.S. senator 1881 until death; member of Peace Commission at Paris, France, in 1898; as chairman of commerce committee influenced U.S. legislation.

FSA (Farm Security Administration), United States R-265

FSA. *see in index* Federal Security Agency

FSCC (Federal Surplus Commodities Corporation), United States R-265

FSH. *see in index* follicle-stimulating hormone

Fu, style of writing in Chinese literature C-386

Fuad I, Ahmed Ali Pasha (1868–1936), king of Egypt; became sultan 1917, proclaimed king 1922, upon removal of British protectorate
  Egypt E-121

Fuca, Juan de (originally Apostolos Valerianos) (died 1602), Greek navigator; served in Spanish navy; explored n.w. coast of North America.

Fuchs, Klaus Emil Julius (born 1911), German physicist (British citizen 1942–50); atomic scientist in United Kingdom and United States from 1942; sentenced to prison in England 1950 for having given atomic secrets to U.S.S.R.; freed in 1959 and went to East Germany.

Fuchs, Leonhard (1501–66), German botanist and physician, born in Bavaria; one of the fathers of science of botany; wrote 'De historia stirpium'; the fuchsia is named for him.

Fuchs, Sir Vivian Ernest (born 1908), English explorer and geologist, born in Surrey; led first overland crossing of Antarctica 1957–58; 'The Crossing of Antarctica', 'Antarctic Adventure' P-423

Fuchsia, flower F-440

Fuel F-441. *see also in index* principal topics listed below
  aerospace fuels A-73
  alcohol, *diagram* R-232
  automobile A-861
  bus B-516
  carbon C-156
  coal C-518
  conservation C-677
  energy crisis
    alternative power sources C-678
    Carter's programs C-183
    petroleum supplies and prices P-233
  furnaces F-451
  gas G-40
  geography G-63
  heat H-102
  heating and ventilating H-107
  internal-combustion engine I-252
  mines and mining M-424
  nuclear N-423
    uranium U-211
  peat P-151
  petroleum P-229, *charts* P-241–241b
  plants P-377
  pollution A-19
  smoke S-220
  space travel S-342a, R-232
  sugarcane stalks S-508
  United States
    electrical energy production, *chart* U-60
    supplies U-106
  wood W-280

Fuel Administration, organized during World War I; stimulated coal production and restricted its use W-314

Fuel cell B-107. *see also in index* Battery; Electric battery; Electrochemical cell; Solar battery and cell
  electric power E-169
  space travel S-346c

Fuel injection A-847
  diesel engine D-141

Fuel meter M-316

Fuel oil, certain petroleum products, *chart* P-241
  fuel F-441
  gas G-40
  heating systems H-108

Fuenterrabia (or Fontarabia), Spain, town on French frontier, on Bidassoa River; famous fortress destroyed by French 1794; Wellington crossed Bidassoa near here in 1813 in spite of French opposition.

Fuentes, Carlos (born 1928), Mexican author and editor, born in Mexico City; ('Aura', 'The Death of Artemio Cruz', 'Whither Latin America') L-71

Fuerte, river in w. Mexico; 180 mi (290 km) to Gulf of California, *map* M-341

Fuertes, Louis Agassiz (1874–1927), U.S. naturalist and illustrator, born in Ithaca, N.Y.; celebrated for his accurate and realistic paintings of birds.

Fuerzas Armadas de Liberación Nacional (FALN), group that seeks independence for Puerto Rico .

Fugger family, wealthy family of German merchants and bankers, famous in 16th century; founded by Johann Fugger, Bavarian weaver in 14th century F-444

Fugitive slave laws, U.S. laws, passed in 1793 and 1850, that provided for the return of escaped slaves from one state or territory to another state
  Buchanan B-476

Fugue, in psychiatry, term for episodes of nonremembered acts of considerable duration; hysterical symptom.

Fugue, in music M-669, *list* M-670

Führer, Der, German leader G-123

Fuji, Mount (or Fujiyama), sacred mountain of Japan, 70 mi (110 km) s.w. of Tokyo; 12,389 ft (3,776 m) high F-444
  height, comparative. *see in index* Mountain, *table*
  Japan J-60, *maps* J-59, 78, *pictures* J-23, 47

Fujian (or Fukien), province on coast of s.e. China; 46,000 sq mi (119,100 sq km); cap. Fuzhou; pop. 25,931,106 F-445
  porcelain making P-473

Fujianese (or Hokkien, or Fukienese), people T-13

Fuji-Hakone-Izu National Park, park in Japan N-27

Fujiwara family, powerful Japanese family founded by Fujiwara Kamatari (614–669); prominent in civil affairs until crushed by Minamoto Yoritomo in 1189 F-445
  Oda O-492

Fujiwara, Fuhito (659–720), Japanese statesman F-445

Fujiwara, Michinaga (966–1027), Japanese statesman F-445

Fujiwara, Mototsune (836–91), Japanese statesman F-445

Fujiwara, Teika (1162–1241), Japanese writer J-81

Fujiwara, Tokihira (871–909), Japanese statesman F-445

Fujiwara, Toshinari (1114–1204), Japanese poet J-81

Fujiwara, Yoshifusa (804–72), Japanese statesman F-445

Fukien. *see in index* Fujian

Fukienese (or Hokkien, or Fujianese), people T-13

Fukuda, Takeo (born 1905), Japanese political leader, born in Ashikado; member Japanese parliament 1952–; prime minister 1976–78 J-69

Fukui, Kenichi (born 1918), Japanese scientist, formulated the rules that predict chemical reactions on the basis of quantum mechanics. *see also in index* Nobel Prizewinners, *table*

Fukuoka, Japan, seaport of n. Kyushu; textiles, paper, metal goods, dolls; Kyushu University; pop. 1,039,286, *maps* A-697, J-75

Fula (or Fulah), numerous and powerful African people scattered over a wide area from near w. coast to Republic of the Sudan; have well-marked features and are light in color; probably Berber in origin with some Sub-Saharan African genetic heritage; chiefly a wandering pastoral people; religion, Islam.

Fulani, Fula people in and near n. Nigeria; also language of the Fula
  Guinea G-314
  Guinea-Bissau G-315
  Mauritania M-232
  Nigeria, *picture* N-310

Fulbright, James William (born 1905), U.S. political leader, born in Sumner, Mo.; president University of Arkansas 1939–41; U.S. representative from Arkansas 1943–45; U.S. senator 1945–74; chairman Senate banking subcommittee for investigating RFC 1950–51; chairman Senate foreign relations committee 1959–74; Democrat; author of 'Prospects for the West', 'Old Myths and New Realities', 'The Arrogance of Power'.

Fulcrum, fixed point about which lever turns M-266, *picture* M-267

Fulda, Ludwig (1862–1939), German dramatist; wrote 'The Talisman', 'The Lost Paradise'; translated works of Molière, Beaumarchais, and Rostand.

Fulgurites (from Latin *fulgur,* "lightning"), tubes in sand or rock made by lightning passing through these materials and fusing them; also rocks that have been fused on the surface by lightning.

Full cut crown, gem cut, *picture* J-116

Fuller, Alfred Carl (1885–1973), U.S. business and door-to-door-sales leader, born in Welsford, N.S.; established Fuller Brush Company at Somerville, Mass., 1906; rose from humble beginning as farmboy; 'A Foot in the Door', autobiography.

Fuller, Ben Hebard (1870–1937), U.S. major general, head of U.S. Marine Corps (appointed 1930), born in Big Rapids, Mich.; joined Marine Corps 1891, as second lieutenant, served in Spanish-American War; with Marines in Philippines 1899–1901, in Santo Domingo 1918–19, and in Haiti 1924–25.

Fuller, George (1822–84), U.S. figure and landscape painter, born in Deerfield, Mass. ('The Romany Girl', 'The Turkey Pasture', 'Quadroon', 'She Was a Witch').

Fuller, Henry Blake (1857–1929), U.S. novelist and literary critic, born in Chicago, Ill.; work shows charm and grace of style, good taste, and wide knowledge of literature; 'The Chevalier of Pensieri-Vani'

Furtwängler, Wilhelm (1886–1954), German conductor and composer F-472

Fury and Hecla Strait, n. Canada, narrow channel from Gulf of Boothia to Foxe Basin, between Melville Peninsula and n.w. Baffin Island, *map* C-109

Furze (or gorse, or whin), spiny shrubs comprising the genus *Ulex* of the pulse family native to Europe and n.w. Africa; used for fences, as winter food for livestock, and for fuel.

Fusan, South Korea. *see in index* Pusan

Fuse (or fuze), detonating device
 ammunition A-372
 bombs B-338

Fuse, electricity
 replacement S-8

Fused quartz (or fused silica)
 glassmaking G-156

Fusee, colored flare used on railroads to warn in emergency; term also used for a friction match with a large head intended to burn in the wind F-114

Fuselage, section of airplane A-183, P-383
 glider G-165

Fusel oil, poisonous liquid consisting mainly of amyl alcohols formed in fermentation; used in paints and varnishes.

Fushun, China, city in Liaoning Province, e. of Mukden; extensive coal mining began in early 20th century; pop. 1,019,000, *map* A-697

Fusible metal, any metal easily melted; for example, an alloy used for solder, fuses, or safety devices.

Fusing point. *see in index* Melting point

Fusion, nuclear N-416, 423
 nuclear weapons N-433
 plasma physics P-380
 sun S-514, *diagram* S-513

Füssen, West Germany, historic town 58 mi (93 km) s.w. of Munich; peace signed here between Elector Maximilian III, Joseph of Bavaria, and Maria Theresa, 1745; pop. 10,297, *map* G-131

Fust, Johann (died 1466?), German moneylender; associated with Gutenberg in printing firm P-504
 Gutenberg G-319

Fustanella, short, full, pleated white skirt of traditional Greek peasant costume; worn by evzones of Greek army.

Fustian, name given to various coarse cotton or cotton and linen fabrics, especially a corded cloth similar to corduroy.

Fusuma, sliding screens J-29

Futabatei, Shimei (1864–1909), Japanese writer
 Japanese literature J-82

Futhark. *see in index* Runes

Future Business Leaders of America, U.S. organization for high-school and college students interested in careers related to business; sponsored by United Business Education Association; founded 1942; headquarters, Washington, D.C. Y-431

Future Farmers of America (FFA), Y-429, *picture* A-143

Future Homemakers of America, U.S. organization of students taking home economics in junior and senior high schools. Home economics teachers and state supervisors of home economics education are advisers. Became national organization in 1945. Sponsored by U.S. Office of Education, Washington, D.C.; cosponsor, American Home Economics Association. Has chapters in all states of U.S., District of Columbia, Puerto Rico, and U.S. Army post schools overseas H-218

Future Scientists of America, U.S. organization created by National Science Teachers Association 1959; aimed to further interest in research, scientific investigation, and careers related to science among high-school students.

Futures trading, in commodity exchanges C-598

Future Teachers of America, U.S. organization for high-school students interested in teaching as a career; founded 1937 by Joy Elmer Morgan; after 1955 an integral part of National Commission on Teacher Education and Professional Standards, National Education Association; headquarters, Washington, D.C.

Futurism, movement, of Italian origin, in literature, painting, sculpture, and music; flourished 1911–15
 Russian literature R-360b
 sculpture S-92

Fuze. *see in index* Fuse

Fuzhou (or Foochow), China, seaport on Min Kiang; capital of Fujian Province; tea, timber, food products, chemicals, lacquerware; pop. 680,000
 Asia, *map* A-697
 Fujian F-445
 world, *map* W-297

FWA (or Federal Works Agency), United States R-265

Fyke net trap T-267

Fyleman, Rose (1877–1957), English writer of children's stories and poems, chiefly about fairies; also singer and lecturer; born in Nottingham (poems: 'Fairies and Chimneys', 'The Fairy Flute'; stories: 'Forty Good-Morning Tales'; plays: 'Eight Little Plays for Children').

Fyn (German Fünen), largest of Danish islands after Zealand; 1,149 sq mi (2,976 sq km); chief city Odense; pop. 376,872 D-97, *map* D-100

The letter G

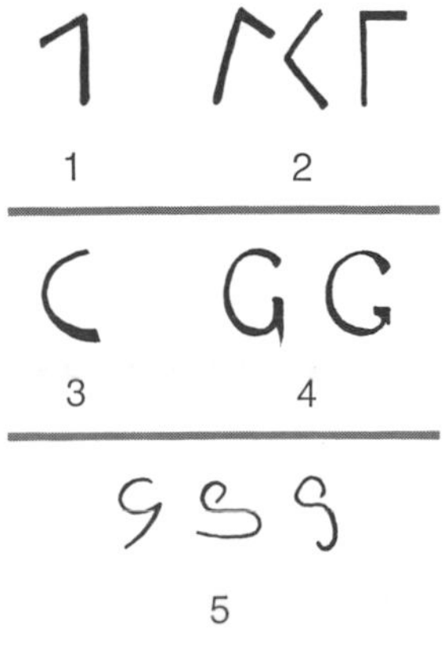

is a descendant of the letter C, which is discussed at the beginning of the Fact-Index for Volume 4. About 1000 B.C., in Byblos and in other Phoenician and Canaanite centers, the sign was given a linear form (1), the source of all later forms. In the Semitic languages the sign was called *gimel* or *gaml,* meaning "throwing stick." The Greeks changed the Semitic name to *gamma.* Later, when the Greeks began to write from left to right, they reversed the letter (2). As among the Semites, the sign *gamma* was used for the sound "g."

The Romans took this sign over into Latin, but they rounded it (3). Originally they used the sign for the sound "g." They also used it for the sound "k." In time they learned to differentiate the two sounds in writing. The original form of C was used for the sound "k," and a new form of G—C plus a bar (4)—was used for the sound "g." The two sign forms passed unchanged into English. The handwritten small "g" developed from the capital by using a loop at the bottom (5).

G

G (abbreviation for gravity), *list* S-341b. *see also in index* Gravitation; Weightlessness

Gabae, town in Persian Empire. *see in index* Esfahan

Gabardine, gown or cloak that Jews were compelled to wear in the Middle Ages in Europe; also a twilled cotton, worsted, silk, or rayon fabric having a raised cord on one side
- wool W-288

Gabars (Arabic infidel), term used in Iran until early 20th century to refer to Zoroastrians Z-471

Gabbro, an igneous rock
- earth E-20
- rock cycle, *chart* R-229

Gabelle, French history, a salt tax, abolished 1790.

Gaberones, Republic of Botswana. *see in index* Gaborone

Gabès (or Qabis), Tunisia; located on a Mediterranean oasis along the Gulf of Gabès; founded as the Roman city of Tacapa; pop. 40,585 T-309, *map* A-118
- oasis, *picture* O-454

Gabès, Gulf of (or Gulf of Qabis), inlet, east coast of Tunisia; contains oil and natural gas deposits T-308

Gable, Clark (1901–60), U.S. motion-picture actor, born in Cadiz, Ohio; won Academy award for performance in 'It Happened One Night' (1934); officer in U.S. Army Air Forces in World War II ('Mutiny on the Bounty'; 'Gone with the Wind'; 'Command Decision'; 'The Misfits'), *pictures* M-614, 625

Gable hood, hats and caps, *picture* W-53

Gabon, republic in w.-central Africa on Gulf of Guinea; area 103,089 sq mi (267,000 sq km); cap. Libreville; pop. 1,300,000 G-2, *map* A-115
- African political unit, *table* A-112
- flag F-161, *picture* F-164
- manganese M-96
- national anthem, *table* N-64
- world, *map* W-297

Gaboon viper, snake *Bitis gabonica*, *picture* S-226

Gabor, Dennis (1900–79), British physicist, born in Hungary; work in electron physics led to invention of holography. *see also in index* Nobel Prizewinners, *table*

Gaboriau, Émile (1835–73), French writer of detective stories, born in Saujon ('Monsieur Lecoq', 'The Slaves of Paris', 'Other People's Money', 'File No. 113')
- detective story D-118

Gaborone, (or Gaberones), Republic of Botswana, capital, located in s.e. near South African border; pop. 59,000, *map* A-115
- Botswana B-382, *map* S-264
- world, *map* W-297

Gabriel, Biblical archangel and heavenly messenger, sent to the Virgin Mary (Bible, Luke i, 19, 26), the prophet Daniel, and others; recognized by Muslims as well as Christians and Jews; commemorated as saint in Roman Catholicism March 24 K-268

Gabriel, Ange-Jacques (1698–1782), French architect
- contributions A-568

Gabrilowitsch, Ossip (1878–1936), U.S. pianist and conductor, born in St. Petersburg (now Leningrad), Russia; married Clara Clemens, daughter of Mark Twain; conductor Detroit Symphony Orchestra 1918–36.

Gad, Bible, son of Jacob, ancestor of Israelite tribe of Gad; also name of seer and chronicler of King David's reign.

Gaddi, family of Florentine artists of whom most important was the architect and painter **Taddeo** (1300?–66), pupil of Giotto; said to have continued Giotto's work on Florence campanile and to have planned the Ponte Vecchio.

Gade, Niels Wilhelm (1817–90), leading Danish Romanticist composer, born in Copenhagen; his music is lyrical and highly polished; wrote symphonies, overtures, suites, and songs ('Erl King's Daughter', 'The Springtide Phantasy', 'The Crusaders').

Gadfly. *see in index* Horsefly

Gadhafi, Muammar al. *see in index* Qaddafi, Muammar al

Gadolin, Johan (1760–1852), Finnish chemist, born in Turku; discoverer of yttrium; another element, gadolinium, named for him.

Gadolinium (Gd), chemical element
- periodic table, *table* P-207, *list* P-208

Gadsden, Christopher (1724–1805), a leader in American Revolution, born in Charleston, S.C.; delegate to Continental Congress 1774–76; brigadier general, Continental Army 1776–78; voted for ratification of U.S. Constitution 1788
- Hopkins flag F-154, *picture* F-155

Gadsden, James (1788–1858), U.S. diplomat, grandson of Christopher Gadsden, born in Charleston, S.C.; as minister to Mexico negotiated Gadsden Purchase (1853).

Gadsden, Ala., manufacturing city on Coosa River 56 mi (90 km) n.e. of Birmingham; farming and timber region; steel and fabricated metal products, tires, textiles, electrical equipment, plumbing supplies; pop. 47,565 U-41

Gadsden Purchase, territory s. of Gila River in Arizona and New Mexico, bought by U.S. from Mexico in 1853 A-601, T-304, U-178, *map* U-177, *table* T-274
- New Mexico N-218
- Pierce P-318

Gaea (or Ge), in Greek mythology, the ancient goddess 'Mother Earth'; corresponding Roman goddesses were Tellus and Terra M-700
- Rhea R-176

Gaelic, ancient language of Ireland and Scotland
- Ireland I-319

Gaels (also called Goidels), ancient Celtic peoples of Ireland and Scotland who spoke Gaelic language; might have arrived from Europe earlier than 500 BC
- England E-237

Gaer, Joseph (born 1897), U.S. author and mystic, born in Bessarabia, to U.S. 1917, became citizen 1926 ('The Lore of the Old Testament', 'The Lore of the New Testament') I-84, S-478

Gaeta, Italy, strongly fortified seaport 45 mi (70 km) n.w. of Naples; refuge of Pope Pius IX when he fled (1848–50) from Rome; Francis II of Naples surrendered to Garibaldi here in 1861 after long siege, *map* I-404

Gaff, in fishing, *list* F-146

Gaffing, cheating
- amusement park business A-384

Gaffney, S.C., city 20 mi (30 km) n.e. of Spartanburg; textiles, peaches, limestone, meat-packing, plastics, mobile homes; Limestone College; Cowpens National Battleground and King's Mountain National Battleground nearby; pop. 13,453, *map* S-318

Gaff-rigged, in boating B-326

Gafsa (or Qafsah), Tunisia; a noted fruit-growing oasis and a major shipping center for phosphates; pop. 42,225 T-309

Gág, Wanda (1893–1946), U.S. artist and author, born in New Ulm, Minn., of Bohemian parents; writer and illustrator of children's books ('Millions of Cats'; 'The A.B.C. Bunny'; 'Gone Is Gone'; 'Snippy and Snappy'; 'Tales from Grimm') R-106, 110a, S-481
- illustrations, *pictures* R-111e, S-462

Gagaku, Japanese music J-54

Gagarin, Yuri Alekseevich (1934–68), Soviet cosmonaut; made first successful space flight G-2, S-346f, *picture* S-346, *table* S-348

Gage, Lyman Judson (1836–1927), U.S. financier, born in De Ruyter, N.Y.; secretary of treasury 1897–1902; president U.S. Trust Co., N.Y., 1902–6; a leader of Middle West banking interests; president board of directors, World's Columbian Exposition, Chicago.

Gage, Thomas (1721–87), British general, born in Firle, Sussex; governor of Massachusetts and military commander in chief in North America at outbreak of American Revolution; entered army 1741; went to North America, under General Braddock, 1754; with Braddock when he was defeated by Indians, 1755; superseded by Howe after Bunker Hill L-144

Gage. *see in index* Gauge

Gage plum P-392

Gag panel, cartoons C-186, *picture* C-187

Gag resolution, rule adopted by U.S. Congress in 1836 that provided that all antislavery petitions submitted to Congress be disregarded.

Gag strip, cartoons C-186

Gahanna, Ohio, city 22 mi (35 km) s.e. of Delaware; chiefly residential; incorporated 1881; pop. 18,001.

Gaheris, Sir, knight of the Round Table R-299a

Gahn, Johan Gottlieb (1745–1818), Swedish chemist and mining engineer, born in Voxna, near Söderhamn, Sweden; first to isolate pure manganese.

Gaillard, David Du Bose (1859–1913), U.S. Army officer and engineer, born in Sumter County, S.C.; after 1908 in charge of construction of Panama Canal between Gatun and Pedro Miguel.

Gaillard Cut (formerly known as the Culebra Cut), section of Panama Canal P-90, 94, *pictures* P-87, 92
- Roosevelt, Theodore, *picture* R-289

Gaillardia, genus of annual and perennial herbs of the composite family; native to w. North America
- growing conditions G-24

Gaines' Mill, battle of, U.S. Civil War; McClellan's campaign 1862, on Chickahominy River 9 mi (15 km) n.e. of Richmond, Va.; second of Seven Days' battles.

Gainesville, Fla., city about 60 mi (100 km) s.w. of Jacksonville; pop. 81,371; wood products, agriculture, tung-oil processing, University of Florida, *map* U-41, *picture* F-203

Gainesville, Ga., city about 50 mi (80 km) n.e. of Atlanta; poultry center; textile and lumber products; Brenau College; pop. 15,280.

Gainesville, Tex., city about 60 mi (100 km) n.w. of Dallas; oil fields and oil refinery, farming, livestock, food processing; railroad shops; shoes, garments; Lake Texoma nearby; pop. 14,081.

Gainsborough, Thomas (1727–88), English painter G-3

Gainsborough, hats and caps H-55, *picture* H-53

Gairdner, Lake, lake in s. South Australia, *maps* A-771, 822, P-3

Gaiseric. *see in index* Genseric

Gait, sequence in which a horse places its feet H-262, *list* H-249
- horse racing H-277

Gaithersburg, Md., suburb of Washington, D.C.; research and development, technology; pop. 26,424 M-178, *map* M-182

Gaitskell, Hugh Todd Naylor (1906–63), British political leader and economist, born in London; became member of Parliament 1945; minister of fuel and power 1947–50; minister of state for economic affairs Feb.–Oct. 1950; chancellor of the exchequer Oct. 1950–51; leader of Labor party 1955–63.

Gaius Caesar. *see in index* Caligula

Gaius Julius Caesar Octavianus. *see in index* Augustus

Gajdusek, D. Carleton (born 1923), U.S. virologist and medical anthropologist, born in Yonkers, N.Y.; discovered cause of kuru disease among New Guinea aborigines; staff of U.S. National Institutes of Health. *see also in index* Nobel Prizewinners, *table*

Galactose, a simple (monosaccharide) sugar ($C_6H_{12}O_6$), occurring in the brain and nerves; not found in nature and obtained by reduction of milk sugar (lactose).

Galactosemia, a hereditary disease
- metabolic disease D-181

Galápagos hawk, bird, *picture* G-4

Galápagos Islands (or Archipiélago de Colón), group of islands belonging to Ecuador; area 3,000 sq mi (7,800 sq km); pop. 6,119 G-3
- Ecuador E-68
- iguana I-32
- national park status N-27
- tortoise A-127
- world, *map* W-297

Galapagos Rift, major rift in Earth's crust
- deep-sea life D-60

Galápagos tortoise, endangered reptile Z-460

Galatea, in mythology, statue made by the sculptor Pygmalion and endowed with life by Venus in answer to his prayer; also, nymph in various legends.

'Galateo', book by Giovanni della Casa E-320, *picture* E-322

Galati (or Galatz), Romania, port on lower Danube River 120 mi (190 km) n.e. of Bucharest; ships wheat, lumber; produces textiles, clay products, chemicals; refines petroleum; pop. 107,248 R-317, *map* E-360

Galatia, ancient country in central Asia Minor; settled by band of Celts during collapse of Empire of Alexander the Great, *map* R-242

Galatians, Epistle to the, 9th book of Bible's New Testament, written by Apostle Paul to Galatian churches.

Galaxy, in astronomy
- Andromeda, *charts* S-420
- astronomy A-723
- earth E-9
- intergalactic space S-341a
- magnetism M-47
- Milky Way. *see in index* Milky Way
- observatory O-456
- quasar Q-7
- stars S-412
- universe U-199

Galba, Servius Sulpicius (5 BC–AD 69), Roman emperor for seven months before his assassination; served in several civil offices, including consul.

Galbraith, John Kenneth (born 1908), U.S. economist G-5
- economics E-60
- Great Depression G-243

Galdhøpiggen, peak in s. Norway 8,103 ft (2,470 m) N-389

Gale, Henry Gordon (1874–1942), U.S. physicist and educator, born in Aurora, Ill.; with University of Chicago from 1899, dean of division of physical sciences 1931–40; author of 'Practical Physics'.

Gale, Zona (1874–1938), U.S. writer, born in Portage, Wis.; married William Llewelyn Breese; first wrote sentimental stories ('Loves of Pelleas and Etarre'; 'Friendship Village'); later, realistic novels ('Birth'; 'Faint Perfume'; 'Preface to a Life'); won 1921 Pulitzer prize for dramatization of her novel 'Miss Lulu Bett'.

Gale, a strong wind S-457
- warning signal, *picture* S-194b

Galen, Claudius (AD 130?–200?), Greek physician G-5,
- animal experimentation A-449
- drug innovations, *picture* I-276
- Greek literature G-278
- health education H-93
- medicine M-281

Galena, Ill., city in extreme n.w. of state; former lead- and zinc-mining center; numerous historic buildings; pop. 3,930
- Illinois I-41, *map* I-52

Galena, Kan., city in extreme s.e. Kansas; named for deposits of galena ore in vicinity; mining equipment; smelting; incorporated 1877; pop. 3,587.

Galena (or lead sulfide), a common ore of lead L-99, R-229b
- ore, *table* O-600

Galena Park, Tex., city located in Harris County just e. of Houston; steel, oil refining, chemicals; pop. 9,879.

Galerius (or Gaius Galerius Valerius Maximianus), Roman emperor 305–311; from common soldier became Diocletian's son-in-law and successor.

Galesburg, Ill., city about 45 mi (70 km) n.w. of Peoria; livestock market; railroad shops; home appliances, steel products, outboard motors, wood products; Knox College; birthplace of Carl Sandburg; pop. 35,305
- Illinois, *map* I-52

Galicia (Polish Galicja), former Austrian crownland, on n. slopes of Carpathians; now included in s.e. Poland and in w. Ukrainian Soviet Socialist Republic, U.S.S.R.; area, more than 30,000 sq mi (77,700 sq km); petroleum and natural gas in e.; timber; grains, potatoes; sugar beets; livestock
- Austrian possession A-830
- Maria Theresa M-135

Galicia, Spain, district in n.w. corner of peninsula; formerly independent kingdom; later under Castilian rule; dialect related to Portuguese S-352
- people S-354, 355

Galilean field glass, binocular F-78

Galilean satellites, of Jupiter S-52–52a

Galilee (Hebrew border, or ring), hilly region in n. Israel; in ancient times a Roman province in Palestine; land of Jesus' boyhood and chief center of his active work
- Israel I-369

Galilee, Sea of (also called Lake Kinneret, Lake of Gennesaret, and Sea of Tiberias), pear-shaped lake in n.e. Israel traversed by Jordan River; area 64 sq mi (166 sq km); frequented by Jesus and disciples G-5
- Israel I-371
- Jordan River J-143

Galilei, Vincenzo (1520–91), Italian lutist and composer, born in Santa Maria; member of the Camerata
- opera O-561

Galileo (1564–1642), Italian scientist G-6, *picture* S-57g
- astronomy A-728
- church law L-91
- discoveries
  - accelerated motion, *picture* P-302
  - gravitation G-238
  - Jupiter's satellites S-52
  - thermometer T-167
- Inquisition E-288
- Kepler K-228
- light theories L-197
- mathematics M-215
- mechanics M-269
- pendulum P-160
- physics P-304
- planetary motion A-708
- sun theory S-514
- telescope S-57g, T-68, *pictures* I-277, P-303
  - moon examined M-573
- watch and clock W-77

Galion, Ohio, city 15 mi (25 km) s.w. of Mansfield; electrical equipment, road-building machinery, communication equipment; pop. 12,391.

Gall (or Saint Gallus; died AD 640?), Irish monk and missionary to European continent; founded monastery of St. Gall, Switzerland.

Gall (Sioux name Pizi) (1840–94), chief of Hunkpapa Sioux, born in present S.D.; in 1868 refused to go to reservations, and 1876 was chief leader in battle of Little Bighorn when Custer was killed; after 1889 judge of Court of Indian Offenses at Standing Rock Agency in South Dakota.

Gall, Franz Joseph (1758–1828), German anatomist and founder of phrenology, born in Tiefenbrunn, near Pforzheim, Germany.

Gall (or gallnut), abnormal growth on leaves, stems, buds, flowers, or roots of plants caused by various parasites, especially insects and mites, and more rarely by nematodes, bacteria, fungi, slime molds, and algae; found on almost all forms of plant life, but especially common on oak trees, willows, roses, and goldenrod S-387
- oak O-453
- wasp W-74

Galland, Antoine (1646–1715), French orientalist, born in Rollot, near Amiens, France; first European translator of 'Arabian Nights'; professor of Arabic at Collège de France, Paris A-525

Galla Placidia, mausoleum of, mausoleum in Ravenna, Italy M-590

Gallatin, Albert (1761–1849), U.S. economist and statesman, born in Geneva, Switzerland, one of greatest of financiers; U.S. representative 1795–1801; as secretary of treasury under Jefferson and Madison systematized government's finances; led negotiations for Treaty of Ghent (1815); minister to France 1816–23; minister to England 1826; notable researches in life and history of American Indian; founded American Ethnological Society of New York 1842; helped found New York University
- canal proposal C-128

Gallatin, Tenn., city 26 mi (42 km) n.e. of Nashville; furniture, aluminum storm doors, shoes; incorporated 1802; pop. 17,191.

Gallatin River, river in Montana, flows n. 170 mi (270 km) from Yellowstone National Park, for 70 mi (110 km) through picturesque canyon to Missouri River.

Gallaudet, Edward Miner (1837–1917), U.S. educator, born in Hartford, Conn.; son of T.H. Gallaudet; teacher of the deaf; president Gallaudet College, Washington, D.C. 1864–1910.

Gallaudet, Thomas (1822–1902), U.S. missionary to the deaf, born in Hartford, Conn.; son of T.H. Gallaudet; established church for deaf-mutes in New York City, and missions in other cities.

Gallaudet, Thomas Hopkins (1787–1851), U.S. educator, born in Philadelphia, Pa.; founder of first deaf-mute institution in United States (at Hartford, Conn.); married Sophie Fowler, one of his pupils; sons, Thomas and Edward M. Gallaudet.

Gallaudet College (formerly Columbia Institution for the Deaf), in Washington, D.C.; private control; founded 1857 by Congress to carry on education of deaf; now includes Kendall School for children and a graduate department of education; supported by Congressional endowments, tuition; liberal arts, education, and professional courses
- Gallaudet statue, *picture* F-435

Gall bladder
- blood cell B-314
- digestive system D-145, *diagram* D-143
- liver L-261

Galle, Johann Gottfried (1812–1910), German astronomer, born near Bitterfeld, Germany; discovered three comets 1839–40; first to observe planet Neptune 1846 in position predicted by Le Verrier; director Breslau Observatory 1851–1910
- Neptune discovered A-714, P-354

Galle (formerly Point de Galle), Sri Lanka, port on s.w. coast; formerly chief port; trade center for products including rice, coconuts, and tea; pop. 72,720
- Asia, *map* A-697

Gallegos, Rómulo (1884–1969), Venezuelan writer L-75

Gallegos, inhabitants of the district of Galicia, Spain; frequently characterized as hardworking and shrewd; resemble Portuguese S-354

Galleon (derived from galley), a three- or four-decked sailing vessel of 15th to 17th century Europe, with lofty "castles" at bow and stern
- naval ships N-82
- Spain P-342, P-259c

Galleria Vittorio Emmanuele, arcade in Milan, Italy M-408

Gallerie dell'Accademia, museum in Venice, Italy M-663

Gallery, art M-660. *see also in index* Museum; and individual museums and galleries by name, such as Art Institute of Chicago
- Florence F-189
- Leningrad L-128
- Rodin museums R-238

Gallery woods G-236

Galley, in letterpress printing, an oblong steel tray for set type; the impressions taken from a filled galley (called galley proofs) are used in checking errors P-500

Galley, ship propelled wholly or partly by oars R-300
- Greek and Roman, *pictures* S-27, S-166, S-213
- Middle Ages S-166, *pictures* S-164
- naval ships N-80, 92
- Phoenician S-164

Galley, area in a ship used for cooking
- submarines, *diagram* S-499

Galley slaves, *pictures* S-164, 213

Gallfly I-225
- oak O-453

Gall gnat (or gall midge), fly of the order Diptera, family Cecidomyiidae, or Itonididae, *picture* I-216

Gallia. *see in index* Gaul

Galliard, lively 16th-century Italian court dance in triple time, popular especially in England; usually followed by the more formal pavane. *see also in index* Pavane

Gallico, Paul William (1897–1976), U.S. author, born in New York City; sports columnist, *New York Daily News*, 1926–36; war correspondent ('Farewell to Sport'; 'The Snow Goose'; 'The Small Miracle'; 'Snowflake'; 'Mrs. 'Arris Goes to Paris'; 'The Silent Miaow'; 'Matilda'; 'The Poseidon Adventure').

Galli-Curci, Amelita (1882–1963), U.S. coloratura soprano; born in Milan, Italy, of Italian-Spanish parentage; studied piano in Royal Conservatory, Milan, and taught there; was practically self-taught in voice; debut 1909 in Rome, Italy, as Gilda in 'Rigoletto'; sang with Chicago and Metropolitan opera companies; sang publicly only a few times after a throat operation in 1936; married Homer Samuels
- opera, *list* O-570

Gallieni, Joseph Simon (1849–1916), French general and colonial administrator, born in Saint-Béat, near Tarbes, France; conqueror of Madagascar (1896–1905), military governor of Paris (1914–15).

Galliformes, order of fowl-like, ground-dwelling birds, including curassows, guans, chachalacas, grouse, quails, partridges, pheasants, turkeys, and domestic chickens.

Gallinule, water bird resembling coot and rail in habits, and, like them, called mud hen R-71

Gallio, Lucius Junius Annaeus (1st century AD), Roman proconsul of Achaea (AD 53) who "cared for none of these things" when the Jews brought the Apostle Paul before him; "careless Gallio" has become a synonym for an indifferent person; older brother of Seneca.

Gallipoli (Turkish Gelibolu), Turkey, port on Gallipoli Peninsula; key to Dardanelles; first European possession of Turks, taken in 1353; pop. 12,945.

Gallipoli campaign, World War I W-305, *map* W-304
- Churchill C-412

Gallipoli Peninsula, separating the Dardanelles on e. from Gulf of Saros on w.; 55 mi (90 km) long, 4 to 13 mi (6 to 21 km) wide; seized by Ottoman Turks in 1353. *see also in index* Chersonesus

Gallipolis Dam, dam in Ohio and West Virginia, on Ohio River O-498

Gallitzin, Demetrius (1770–1840), U.S. Roman Catholic missionary, born in The Hague, The Netherlands; son of Russian prince; to U.S. 1792; ordained priest in Baltimore 1795; founded a colony at Loretto in s.w. Pa. (1799) and labored there 41 years, spending his fortune on the welfare of the settlement.

Gallium (Ga), chemical element
- metal and metallurgy M-307, *picture* M-309
- periodic table, *table* P-207, *list* P-208

Gällivare, Sweden, village n. of Arctic Circle; rail junction; iron ore mines; site of Old Lapp church; pop. 7,773.

Gall midge. *see in index* Gall gnat

Gall mite S-387

Gallnut. *see in index* Gall

Gallon, unit of capacity, *table* W-140

Gallop, a gait of a horse H-262, *diagram* H-266

Galloway, Joseph (1731–1803), British colonial lawyer, born in West River, Md.; tried to effect compromise between colonies and Great Britain; joined British army when war was declared R-167

Galloway, former division of s.w. Scotland, comprising counties of Kirkcudbright and Wigtown, famous for Galloway cattle; dairying chief industry.

Gallstones, insoluble stony masses formed in gallbladder or bile ducts; size, shape, and color vary; can block bile flow causing severe pain and jaundice; removal of gallbladder usually necessary; often associated with obesity and pregnancy.

Gallup, George Horace (1901–84), U.S. statistician G-6.

Gangplank, movable bridge used in boarding or leaving a ship N-81

Gang plow P-391, *picture* P-392

Gangrene, decomposition of dead tissue in a living body, resulting in foul-smelling gas and a toxic liquid that kills nearby healthy tissue
  antitoxin treatment A-495

Gangtok, India; situated in the Assam Himalayas; was capital of former monarchy of Sikkim; trade in corn, millet, rice, oranges; Namgyal Institute of Tibetology; Buddhist monastery nearby; pop. 15,000.

Gangue, mineral and rock that is waste
  gold G-178
  lead L-99
  metal and metallurgy M-308
  ore O-601

Gangway, part of a ship N-81

Ganivet, Angel (1865–98), Spanish writer, born in Granada; urged strengthening of national will power ('Idearium español'); also wrote philosophical novels ('La conquista del reino de Maya') S-367

Gannet, a seabird of the family Sulidae G-16

Gannett, Henry (1846–1914), U.S. geographer, born in Bath, Me.; called "father of American map-making"; chief geographer U.S. Geological Survey 1882–1914; a founder and chairman 1890–1910 U.S. Board of Geographic Names; president National Geographic Society 1910–14.

Gannett, Ruth Chrisman (born 1896), U.S. lithographer, born in Santa Ana, Calif.; illustrator of books for children: 'Miss Hickory', written by Carolyn Sherwin Bailey', which received Newbery medal 1947; 'My Father's Dragon', and 'Elmer and the Dragon', both by Ruth Stiles Gannett, stepdaughter of Ruth C. Gannett; 'My Mother Is the Most Beautiful Woman in the World', by Rebecca Reyher R-107, 111

Gannett Peak, highest point in Wyoming, in Wind River Range; just w. of Wind River Indian Reservation; 50 mi (80 km) n.w. of Lander; 13,804 ft (4,207 m), *map* U-80
  Wyoming W-386

Gannon College, college in Erie, Pa.; Roman Catholic; founded 1944; humanities, business administration, pure and applied sciences, and teacher education; graduate studies.

Ganoid, primitive fish M-644

Ganoid scale, a scale composed of bone G-16

Gansu (or Kansu), province in n. China; area 173,700 sq mi (449,900 sq km); cap. Lanchow; pop. 19,880,000 G-16
  Ningxia Huizu N-317

Gansu Corridor, area in Gansu province G-16

Ganswindt, Hermann (1856–1934), German inventor, born in Voigtshof, East Prussia; known as pioneer inventor of spaceship, published his first design 1891.

Gantrisin, type of sulfa drug A-489

Gantry, rail-mounted crane S-342c, *picture* R-231

Ganymede, in Greek mythology, a handsome prince carried off to be cupbearer to Zeus, succeeding Hebe.

Ganz, Rudolph (1877–1972), U.S. pianist and composer, born in Zurich, Switzerland; came to U.S. 1900; conductor of St. Louis Symphony Orchestra 1921–27; director Chicago Musical College 1928–33, president 1933–54.

Gap, a gorge or pass across ridge; carved by stream; called **water gap** if it still has stream, **wind gap** if stream has gone; examples in Appalachian Highlands are Delaware Water Gap and Cumberland Gap, the latter a wind gap. *see also in index* Cumberland Gap; Delaware Water Gap; Delaware Water Gap National Recreation Area

Gapeworm W-362

Gapon, Father Georgi (1870?–1906), Russian priest, revolutionary and government spy; led strikers' march to Winter Palace on Red Sunday (Jan. 22, 1905); believed murdered by revolutionaries he had betrayed.

Gar, fishes of the families Lepisosteidae and Belonidae G-16
  mudfish and lungfish M-644

G.A.R. *see in index* Grand Army of the Republic

Garage, a place for storing and caring for motor vehicles; word from French
  vertical parking garage, *picture* R-213

Garakonthie, Daniel (1600?–76), Onondaga Iroquois chief; friendly to French from time he lived with them as treaty hostage (1654); rescued 60 white captives from hostile Indians; converted to Catholicism 1669.

Garamantes, a people of Africa L-189

Garamond, Claude, French printer of 16th century, born in Paris; originated fine type designs; substituted then prevalent Gothic type with roman
  type and typography T-337

Garand, John Cantius (1888–1974), U.S. inventor of the Garand semiautomatic rifle adopted by U.S. Army in 1936; born in Saint Remi, near Montreal, Canada; became a U.S. citizen in 1920; a tool-maker, he entered U.S. government service in 1918; worked on small arms development at Springfield (Mass.) Arsenal 1919–53, *picture* F-99

Garay, Juan de (1527?–83?), Spanish conquistador B-489

Garbage disposal G-17. *see also in index* Waste, toxic
  fuel and power F-442
  health agencies H-89
  pollution P-441f, *pictures* P-441b
  toxic waste W-76
  waste removal W-91

Garbage grinder (or food-waste disposer), home appliance H-210

Garbo, Greta (formerly Greta Lovisa Gustafsson) (born 1905), U.S. motion-picture actress G-19

Garborg, Arne Evensen (1851–1924), Norwegian novelist and lyric poet, born in Time, near Stavanger; identified with movement for creating new literary language based upon peasant dialect derived from Old Norsk; novels show religious feeling ('Men'; 'Peace').

Garcés, Francisco (1738–81), Spanish missionary (Franciscan) and explorer, born in kingdom of Aragon; founded two missions on Colorado River and was killed by Yuma Indians
  trail in Southwest C-586, S-338

Garcia, Carlos P. (1896–1971), Philippine political leader, born in Talibon, Bohol; governor of Bohol 1933–41; Philippine vice-president 1953–57; president 1957–61.

García, Manuel Patricio Rodriguez (1805–1906), one of the most famous singing teachers of all time, born in Madrid; son of Manuel Vicente García; for almost 50 years professor in Royal Academy of Music at London; continued private teaching until his death; Jenny Lind was one of his pupils; he invented the laryngoscope.

García, Manuel Vicente (1775–1832), Spanish singer and teacher, born in Seville; father of Maria Malibran and Manuel García; theories laid groundwork of best modern teaching.

García, Michelle Ferdinande Pauline (known as Pauline Viardot) (1821–1910), French operatic mezzo-soprano, *list* O-570

García Gutiérrez, Antonio (1813–84), Spanish dramatist of romantic school, born in Chiclana de La Frontera, near Cádiz; play 'El Travador' adapted by Verdi in his opera 'Il Trovatore'.

García Iñiguez, Calixto (1836–98), Cuban patriot, born in Holguín, Cuba; twice imprisoned in Spain; the essay by Elbert Hubbard, 'A Message to Garcia', was inspired by the courage of Andrew S. Rowan in carrying message from United States to Garcia, then commander of the rebel army, at opening of Spanish-American War.

García Lorca, Federico (1898–1936), Spanish poet and dramatist G-19
  Spanish literature S-366

García Márquez, Gabriel (born 1928), Colombian writer G-19. *see also in index* Nobel Prizewinners, *table*
  Latin American literature L-70, *picture* L-68
  Colombia C-553
  novel N-412

García Monje, Joaquín (1881–1958), Costa Rican writer, professor, and literary critic, born in San Jose, *picture* L-74

García Sarmiento, Félix Rubén. *see in index* Dario, Ruben

Garcilaso de la Vega (1503–36), Spanish poet, courtier, and soldier; born in Toledo, Spain S-365a

Garcilaso de la Vega (nickname El Inca) (1540–1616), Peruvian historian, born in Cuzco L-68, 75

Gard, Roger Martin du. *see in index* Martin du Gard

Garda, Lake, largest lake in Italy, located in the n. extending from Lombard plain into Tyrolean Alps; 143 sq mi (370 sq km) area, *map* I-404

Garden, Alexander (1730?–91), naturalist and physician
  gardenia G-27

Garden, Mary (1874–1967), U.S. operatic soprano, born in Aberdeen, Scotland; first U.S. woman impressario; roles: Mélisande, Salome, Louise; director of Chicago Opera Company 1921–22
  opera, *list* O-570

Gardena, Calif., city 12 mi (19 km) s.w. of Los Angeles; aircraft and missile parts, electronic equipment, tools, chemicals; California State College nearby; pop. 45,165.

Garden and gardening G-20. *see also in index* Fruitgrowing; Insect; *also* individual names of flowers, fruits, and vegetables
  botanical garden and arboretum B-377
  disease. *see in index* Disease, plant
  flowers F-221, P-357, 363a
    wild flowers F-240
  hedges H-115
  hobby H-183, *picture* H-185
  hydroponics P-363d
  Iran I-306
  Japan J-29
  Rome R-252
  shrubs S-187

Garden City, Kan., city on Arkansas River about 48 mi (77 km) n.w. of Dodge City; cattle, irrigation farming; buffalo refuge nearby; pop. 18,256, *map* U-40

Garden City, Mich., city 15 mi (25 km) w. of Detroit; truck farming; automobile parts, paving equipment; pop. 35,640.

Garden City, N.Y., residential village on w. Long Island; publishing and printing center; Adelphi University; shopping center now on site of Roosevelt Field (closed 1951) where Charles Lindbergh began historic flight across Atlantic 1927; pop. 22,927.

Garden Grove, Calif., city 5 mi (8 km) n.w. of Santa Ana; citrus fruits, aluminum and plastic products, paper converting; pop. 123,307.

Gardenia, a tree or shrub of the family Rubiaceae; known for its fragrant flowers of white or yellow G-27

'Garden of Eden, The', work by Platt H-288

Garden of Gethsemane. *see in index* Gethsemane

'Garden of the Finzi-Continis, The,' novel by Bassani I-379

Garden of the Gods, red sandstone formations near Colorado Springs, Colo., *picture* C-576

Garden of the Gulf. *see in index* Prince Edward Island

Garden peppers. *see in index* Peppers, garden

Garden rhubarb (or pie plant), partly edible vegetable *Rheum rhabarbarum* R-198

Gardens, zoological. *see in index* Zoo

Garden spider S-382
  egg sac, *picture* S-383
  web S-383

Garden State. *see in index* New Jersey

Garden strawberry (or common cultivated strawberry), plant *Fragaria ananassa* of the family Rosaceae S-486

Garden zinnia. *see in index* Zinnia

Gardiner, Alan Henderson (1879–1963), British Egyptologist, born in London; authority on Egyptian language; worked on inscriptions found in Tutankhamen's tomb 1923; research professor University of Chicago 1924–34 ('Egyptian Grammar', 'The Theory of Speech and Language', 'Egypt of the Pharaohs').

Gardiner, Samuel Rawson (1829–1902), British historian, born in Ropley, near Winchester ('History of England', based on exhaustive study).

Gardiner, Stephen (1483?–1555), English bishop and statesman; succeeded Wolsey as bishop of Winchester; he was largely responsible for fall of Thomas Cromwell; lord chancellor 1553–55.

Gardner, Erle Stanley (1889–1970), U.S. novelist, born in Malden, Mass.; quit law practice to write; in 1933 originated mysteries starring attorney Perry Mason, series later adapted to radio and TV; prolific writer; noted for fast-paced style and authentic legal detail D-119

Gardner, John William (born 1912), U.S. psychologist, born in Los Angeles, Calif.; staff member Carnegie Corporation 1946–55, president 1955–67, chairman Urban Coalition 1968–70; U.S. secretary of health, education, and welfare 1965–68; chairman Common Cause 1970–77.

Gardner, Mass., city about 23 mi (37 km) n.w. of Worcester; furniture, baby carriages, time recorders; state mental hospital; pop. 17,900.

Gardner Island, *see in index* Phoenix Islands

'Gare Saint-Lazare', work by Manet, *picture* M-95

Gareth, Sir, knight of the Round Table R-299a

Garfield, James A. (1831–81), 20th president of the United States G-28
  assassination A-703
  civil service C-469
  Statuary Hall, *table* S-437b

Garfield, James Rudolph (1865–1950), U.S. lawyer, public official, born in Hiram, Ohio; son of President Garfield; secretary of interior 1907–9; lawyer in Cleveland, Ohio, after 1909 G-30

Garfield, Lucretia Rudolph (1833–1918), wife of President Garfield G-30

Garfield, N.J., city on Passaic River about 5 mi (8 km) s.e. of Paterson; chemicals, paper products, clothing; pop. 26,803.

Garfield Heights, Ohio, residential city about 8 mi (13 km) s.e. of Cleveland; established 1904; pop. 33,380.

Garfunkel, Art. *see in index* Simon, Paul

Gargano, mountainous peninsula of s. Italy extending about 30 mi (50 km) into Adriatic Sea; highest point 3,465 ft (1,060 m).

'Gargantua', work by Rabelais F-395

Gargarean, in Greek mythology A-323

Gargoyle, in architecture, ornate spout projected from cornice of building to funnel away rain water; term applied especially to weird bird, animal, and monster designs of Gothic period and classic lions' heads carvings of Greek and Roman era; made of stone, terra cotta, and lead.

Garibaldi, Giuseppe (1807–82), Italian national hero G-31
  Italian history I-394, *picture* I-396

Roman monument, *map* R-250
Victor Emmanuel II V-308
Garibaldi, a fish *Hypsypops rubicundus*, most frequently seen through the famous glass-bottomed boats at Catalina Island, Calif.; nearly a foot long; when fully grown is pure bright scarlet; abundant in the coral reefs of the tropics.
Garibaldi's snail shell, snail *Anixa garibaldiana*, *picture* S-149
Garland, Hamlin (1860–1940), U.S. writer, born in West Salem, Wis.; noted for vigorous portrayal of Midwestern life with strong local color ('Main-Travelled Roads', short stories; 'Son of the Middle Border', 'Daughter of the Middle Border', 'Back-Trailers from Middle Border').
Garland, Tex., industrial city about 12 mi (19 km) n.e. of Dallas; aircraft industries; food products, oil equipment, hats; pop. 138,857.
Garlic, onion-like plant of lily family G-31
garlic salt S-379
wheat crop damage W-189
Garment industry G-32. *see also in index* Clothing; Machinery; Textiles
fur coats F-467
Industrial Revolution, *picture* I-119
inventors, *table* I-279
Garmentworkers C-514
Garmo Peak. *see in index* Communism Peak
Garneau, François-Xavier (1809–66), French-Canadian historian and writer; born in Quebec; his 'Histoire du Canada', a standard historical work C-120
Garneau, Joseph Alfred (1836–1904), French-Canadian poet, born in Quebec City; son of François-Xavier Garneau; verses marked by sensitivity ('Poésies').
Garner, Erroll (1921–77), U.S. jazz pianist, born in Pittsburgh, Pa.; developed excellent technique without learning to read music; in 1950s achieved success by playing popular themes with pronounced jazz feeling; composed 'Misty', *picture* P-180
Garner, John Nance (1868–1967), U.S. political leader, born in Red River County, Tex.; congressman from Texas 1903–33; speaker of House 1931–33; vice-president of U.S. 1933–41 T-123, *picture* R-264
Hoover H-236
Roosevelt R-266
Garner, Wightman Wells (1875–1956), U.S. plant physiologist, born in Timmonsville, S.C.; with U.S. Department of Agriculture 1903–56; co-discoverer of photoperiodism P-373
Garnerin, André Jacques (1769–1823), French aeronaut, born in Paris, France; made first parachute jump from balloon 1797.
Garnet, Henry Highland (1815–82), U.S. abolitionist and clergyman, born in New Market, Md.; escaped slavery 1825; leader in anti-slavery movement B-291
Garnet, semiprecious stone J-115, *pictures* J-114, R-229a
abrasives A-13
Garnett, David (1892–1981), British author, born in Brighton; grandson of Richard Garnett ('Lady into Fox'; 'Go She Must'); also wrote 'War in the Air' and memoirs, 'The Golden Echo'.
Garnett, Edward (1868–1937), British author and critic, born in London; son of Richard Garnett; literary adviser to Conrad and Galsworthy; with his wife, Constance (1862–1946), translated many Russian works; wrote 'Tolstoy, His Life and Writings' and 'Turgenief, a Study'; edited 'Letters from Conrad' and 'Letters from John Galsworthy'.
Garnett, Richard (1835–1906), British librarian and author, keeper of the printed books in British Museum; born in Litchfield, England; wrote lives of Carlyle, Emerson, Milton; 'The Twilight of the Gods'; with Gosse wrote history of English literature.
Garnier, Saint Charles (1606–49), Canadian Jesuit missionary, born in Paris, France; went to Canada 1636; murdered by Iroquois.
Garnier, Charles (1825–98), French architect of the Beaux-Arts style
Paris Opera A-562
Garniertite, commercial ore, *table* O-600
Garnishment, in law, *table* L-92
Garonne River, chief river in s.w. France; rises in Spanish Pyrenees, flows n. into Bay of Biscay; length 357 mi (575 km) F-343, *maps* E-360, F-372
Gar pike, a river and lake fish; survivor of the primitive order Holostei G-16
Garrett, Patrick Floyd (1850–1908), U.S. frontiersman, born in Alabama; as sheriff of Lincoln County, New Mexico, shot and killed Billy the Kid at Fort Sumner 1881; wrote 'The Authentic Life of Billy, the Kid'.
Garrick, David (1717–79), British actor and manager G-36
theater T-160
Garrigue, group of low shrubs
France F-345
Garriott, Owen K. (born 1933), U.S. astronaut, born in Enid, Okla.; professor of physics Stanford University 1961–65; scientist-astronaut for NASA since 1965; crew member Skylab 1973; mission specialist Spacelab 1978–, *table* S-348
Garrison, William Lloyd (1805–79), U.S. editor and a leader of abolitionist movement G-36
abolitionist movement A-10
Douglass D-235
Liberator B-291
Phillips P-263
Garrison Dam, dam in North Dakota on the Missouri River, *picture* N-380
Missouri River M-508
Garros, Roland (died in World War I), French pilot A-203
Garter, Order of the (in full The Most Noble Order of The Garter), English order of knighthood established in 14th century; motto 'Honi soit qui mal y pense' (Evil to him who evil thinks) E-107
knighthood K-259
medals M-270
Garter snake S-226a, *picture* S-224
Garvey, Marcus (full name Marcus Moziah Garvey) (1887–1940), U.S. black nationalist leader G-37
black Americans B-294
DuBois D-283
Garvin, James Louis (1868–1947), British journalist and publicist, ardent imperialist, most powerful champion of Chamberlain's tariff reforms; editor of the *London Observer*, which he made a great organ of opinion, 1908–42.
Gary, Elbert Henry (1846–1927), U.S. financier and promoter, born in Wheaton, Ill.; chairman of finance committee and board of directors of U.S. Steel Corporation; Gary, Ind., named in his honor
industry I-195
Gary, Ind., one of world's greatest steel-producing centers; at southern edge of Lake Michigan, about 28 mi (45 km) from Chicago; pop. 143,096 G-37
Indiana I-90, *map* I-102
North America, *map* N-350
Gas, chemistry and physics
aerosol propellants A-66
air substance A-145
carbon dioxide C-158
carbon monoxide C-158
Earth's atmosphere A-747
electric light E-164
fire and explosion F-94
heat H-103
helium H-123
interstellar P-380, U-202
jet propulsion J-105
liquefaction C-793
matter M-223, *diagram* M-225
noble gases P-206, *table* P-207
plasma state P-380
poison gas P-411
sublimation S-254f
sun granulation S-514
water W-85
X rays X-406
Gas, natural and manufactured G-38
carbon C-156
conservation C-677
electric power E-165
fossil fuels F-441
furnaces F-451
heating systems H-108
household hazards S-8
oceanography O-474
petroleum by-product P-238, *charts* P-241, 241b
pipelines, *pictures* P-241c, T-265
microwave measuring S-195b
West Germany G-127
poisonous P-411
producing areas, *map* P-230
Algeria A-304
Atlantic Ocean A-746
Australia A-810
Canada C-83
Alberta A-261
China C-339
Egypt E-119
Europe E-342
Gulf of Mexico M-345
Indonesia I-162
Iran I-306
Ireland I-318
Latin America L-59
Mexico M-329, 334
North America N-341
United States U-106, P-230, *charts* U-126
Great Plains G-249
helium H-123
Oklahoma O-524
Texas T-120
Tulsa, Okla. T-305
Wyoming W-388, *map* W-390
refrigeration R-136, 138
regulation of companies P-526c
Gas bearing, used in machine lubrication L-328
Gas black, form of carbon, often called carbon black. *see also in index* Carbon black
Gas chromatography, chemical analysis C-292
Gascoigne, George (1525?–77), English writer, stepfather of Nicholas Breton; member of Parliament 1557–59 ('Supposes', earliest comedy in English prose, adapted from Ariosto; 'Certayne Notes of Instruction', considered first English critical essay; 'The Steel Glass', verse satire).
Gascoigne, William (1612?–44), English astronomer of Middleton, Yorkshire; invented micrometer 1636; also devised ways of grinding glasses.
Gasconade River, river in state of Missouri, rises in Ozark Mountains (Ozark Plateau) and flows n. 200 mi (320 km) to Missouri River.
Gascony (French Gascogne), former duchy in s.w. France; boundaries were Bay of Biscay, Garonne River, and the Pyrenees
Landes' redemption S-38
Gas-cooled reactor (GCR), type of nuclear reactor N-426
Gascoyne River, river in Western Australia; begins in Robinson Ranges and courses 475 mi (765 km) w. into Shark Bay of the Indian Ocean; flow varies, *maps* A-822, P-3
Gas dynamics, mechanics M-263
Gas engine. *see in index* Internal-combustion engine
Gas centrifugation, uranium enrichment U-211
Gaseous diffusion process, uranium enrichment U-211
Gaseous-tidal theory, origin of solar system P-355
Gas furnace, heating H-108
Gas grill, appliance H-211
Gasification, conversion of coal into gas G-41
Gaskell, Elizabeth Stevenson (1810–65), English novelist, born in London; many of her books deal with poor workmen in Manchester ('Cranford', a delightful sketch of village life; 'Life of Charlotte Brontë').
Gas meter M-316, *picture* M-317
Gasohol, fuel F-442
Brazilian research B-422
internal-combustion engine I-252
Gas oil, a medium-grade fraction of petroleum, *charts* P-241–241b
Gasoline, fuel liquid distilled from petroleum G-42
aerospace fuels A-73
asphalt A-702
automobile fuel A-842
cracking process P-241, *chart* P-241a
cobalt as catalyst C-530
farm machinery F-30
fire-fighting problems F-105
fuel F-441
gas G-40
internal-combustion engine I-252
mercury M-305
optics O-575
petroleum, *chart* P-241
refinery, *chart* P-241a. *see also in index* Petroleum technology, *subhead* refining
water W-85
service station, *pictures* S-16, P-229
storage, *picture* U-66
ultraformer, *picture* P-240
Gasoline engine. *see in index* Internal-combustion engine
Gaspar, one of Biblical Wise Men. *see in index* Magi
Gasparilla Pirate Invasion, annual festival in Tampa, Fla., commemorating the mythical invasion by the make-believe pirate José Gaspar and his men T-19
Gasparri, Pietro (1852–1934), Italian Roman Catholic cardinal, born in Ussita, central Italy; secretary of state under Benedict XV and Pius XI; played leading part in concordat between the papacy and Italy 1929.
Gaspé, Philippe Aubert de (1786–1871), Canadian novelist, born in Quebec; imprisoned over three years for debt; retired to family manor at Saint-Jean-Port-Joli, Que.; in his seventies, wrote classic 'Les Anciens Canadiens'.
Gaspé, a district and peninsula in s.e. Quebec, projecting into Gulf of St. Lawrence, and consisting of an elevated plateau traversed by Notre Dame Mountains, a continuation of the Appalachians of the U.S.; lumbering and fishing; visited by tourists because of scenery and picturesque villages; city of Gaspé (pop. 17,211) scene of Cartier's landing in 1534 Q-9a, *map*, Q-10, *picture* Q-9f
Canada C-73
'Gaspee', British vessel burned by Rhode Islanders in 1772 R-183, *picture* R-185
Gaspergou, fish. *see in index* Drum
Gasperi, Alcide de (1881–1954), Italian statesman, leader Christian Democrats, born in Trentino; organized anti-Fascist resistance; foreign minister 1944–46; prime minister 1945–53; spokesman for unification of Europe
Italian history I-397
Gasplant, an attractive perennial of genus *Dictamnus*, with large pinnate leaves and tall purple or white racemes; native to Eurasia.
Gas poisons P-411
Gassendi, Pierre (1592–1655), French philosopher and mathematician, born in Champtercier, near Digne, France; combined Epicurean philosophy with Catholic doctrine ('Syntagma philosophicum')
materialism M-210
Gasser, Herbert Spencer (1888–1963), U.S. physiologist, born in Platteville, Wis.; taught at Washington University, St. Louis, 1921–31, at Cornell University, Ithaca, N.Y., 1931–35; director Rockefeller Institute for Medical Research 1935–53. *see also in index* Nobel Prizewinners, *table*
Gaston, Lucy Page (1860–1924), U.S. reformer, born in Delaware, Ohio; founded Anti-Cigarette League, 1899, at Chicago; worked in U.S. and abroad for anti-cigarette legislation.
Gastonia, N.C., industrial city 20 mi (30 km) w. of Charlotte, in farming region; textiles, machinery, motor oil filters, chemicals, plastic; pop. 47,333 N-366, *map* U-41
Gastric balloon, for weight control W-136
Gastric juice S-454, P-197b
digestive system D-144, *diagram* D-142
Gastritis, inflammation of stomach lining; usually treated by diet, sedatives, and antispasmodics; may be acute or chronic.
Gastrointestinal tract, unit of digestive system consisting of stomach and intestines. *see in index* Stomach; Intestines

Gastropod, a class of mollusks including snails and slugs M-525
invertebrate groups I-283
snails and slugs S-221
Gastroscope, instrument used to examine stomach; introduced 1888; inserted through mouth; flexible, lighted shaft with lens and mirror system gives clear view of stomach wall; some types have tiny camera at tip.
Gastrovascular cavity, organ in worms W-361
Gastrula, stage of embryonic development, *diagram* E-200
Gas turbine T-315
automobile A-846
internal combustion engine I-252
jet aircraft engine J-106
locomotive L-280, R-78
motor and engine M-630
Gas warfare. *see in index* Chemical and biological warfare
Gat, Libya. *see in index* Ghat
Gateleg table, one with drop leaves held up by legs that fold to the frame when the leaves are lowered.
Gates, Arthur Irving (1890–1972), U.S. educator, born in Red Wing, Minn.; professor Columbia University Teachers' College 1924–56, supervisor of research Institute of Language Arts 1956–65; noted for work in remedial reading and educational psychology.
Gates, Doris (born 1901), U.S. author of children's books, born near San Jose, Calif.; as children's librarian in San Joaquin Valley, she worked among boys and girls in migrant camps, and as a result of this experience she wrote 'Blue Willow'; other books with a California setting are 'North Fork' and 'Little Vic' R-111a
Gates, Eleanor (1875–1951), U.S. novelist and playwright, born in Shakopee, Minn.; married Frederick F. Moore; ('The Biography of a Prairie Girl'; 'Cupid, the Cow-Punch'; 'The Poor Little Rich Girl', novel and play).
Gates, Horatio (1728–1806), U.S. general, born in England; served in British army in America, became a friend of George Washington; settled in Virginia as a planter in 1772; in Revolution, became a major general in Continental Army; in command at victorious Saratoga campaign and later at disastrous battle of Camden, S.C.; after Camden, Congress ordered an investigation of his conduct, but later repealed this order R-168
battles of Saratoga S-48, R-171
deserts De Kalb R-172
Gates, Thomas (1559?–1621?), first sole governor of Virginia colony (1611–14); born in Colyford, Devonshire; set sail from England 1609 in command of fleet carrying colonists to North America; his ship the *Sea Venture* was wrecked on Bermudas; two new vessels were built and reached Virginia 1610.
Gates, Thomas Sovereign, Jr. (born 1906), U.S. government official, born in Philadelphia, Pa.; in 1928 joined Drexel & Co., investment bankers, became partner 1940; Naval Reserve officer World War II; undersecretary of the Navy 1953–57, secretary of the Navy 1957–59; secretary of defense 1959–61.
Gateshead, England, county borough on Tyne River, opposite Newcastle-on-Tyne; steel products, safety glass, porcelain, flour; pop. 100,060, *map* U-18a
Gates Learjet 50, airplane A-176
Gates of Hell, cataracts on Congo River in Zaire Z-443
Gates of the Arctic National Park and Preserve, park in northern Alaska N-48, *map* N-40
Gateway Arch, arch in St. Louis, Mo. S-22, *pictures* M-497, S-21
Gateway National Recreation Area, recreational area in New York N-48
Gatineau, Que., located on the Ottawa River; pop. 74,988 Q-9h, *map* C-112
Gatineau River, river in Canada, flowing s. 240 mi (390 km) into Ottawa River near Ottawa; begins in Laurentian Mountains; powers hydroelectric turbines Q-9e, *maps* Q-9a, 10
Gatlin, Larry (born 1948), U.S. country musician M-679
Gatling, Richard Jordan (1818–1903), U.S. inventor, born in Hertford County, N.C.; invented the revolving battery gun.
Gatling gun, early machine gun M-12
Gato class, category of U.S. submarines, *pictures* S-496, 498
GATT. *see in index* General Agreement on Tariffs and Trade
Gattamelata (formerly Erasmo da Narni) (1370?–1442), celebrated Italian soldier; in service of popes Martin V and Eugenius IV; later in service of Venice against Milan 1434–41
Renaissance sculpture S-85, *picture* S-87
statue by Donatello D-229
Gattegno-Cuisenaire, a system of teaching arithmetic with colored wooden rods; named for its inventor, Georges Cuisenaire, Belgian kindergarten teacher, and its developer, Caleb Gattegno, British mathematics professor; introduced to U.S. 1958; related colors help child see numerical relations, thus 2-rod is red, 4-rod is maroon, and 8-rod is reddish brown.
Gatti-Casazza, Giulio (1869–1940), Italian operatic manager, born in Udine, Italy; director of La Scala, Milan 1898–1908; director of Metropolitan Opera Co., New York City, 1908–35.
Gatty, Harold Charles (1903–57), U.S. flier, born in Campbelltown, Tasmania; navigator for Wiley Post; taught navigation to Anne Morrow Lindbergh
round-the-world flight A-205
Gatun, town in Canal Zone; pop. 668; also name of dam and artificial lake in Panama Canal
dam P-91, 94, *map* P-90
locks P-89, 90, *picture* P-88
Gatun Lake, lake in Panama P-90, 91, *picture* P-88
Barro Colorado P-94
profile, *diagram* P-88
Gaucho, cowboy of the pampas A-575
South America S-281b
Gaucho novel, Latin American genre L-68, 71
Gauden, John (1605–62), English churchman, born in Mayland, near Maldon; claimed authorship of celebrated 'Eikon Basilike', a defense of Charles I purporting to have been written by the king; bishop of Exeter and of Worcester.
Gaudí, Antonio (1852–1926), Spanish architect G-42
architecture A-568
Barcelona B-79
Gaudier-Brzeska, Henri (1891–1915), French modernist sculptor, born in Saint-Jean-de-Braye, near Orléans; geometric, highly simplified style; known also for drawings; killed in World War I.
Gaugamela, battle of (331 BC) A-279
warfare, *list* W-14
Gauge (or gage), a standard measure; a device for testing standard measurements; also a measuring or recording instrument
firearms F-100
hunting H-332
hosiery yarn H-278
materials testing M-211
railroad track R-75
rain R-90
wire W-246
Gauguin, Paul (in full Eugène-Henri-Paul Gauguin) (1848–1903), French painter G-43
Maugham M-231
Gaul (Latin Gallia), name for districts occupied by Celtic peoples; (1) Cisalpine Gaul, now n. Italy; (2) Gaul proper or Transalpine Gaul, now modern France and Belgium with parts of Holland, Germany, and Switzerland, *map* R-242
Caesar's triumphs C-14
German history G-121
Goths G-197
Huns A-758
Roman conquest F-360
Vandals V-265
Gauleiter, German word, meaning district manager; under Nazis name of official appointed to manage a political district in Germany, or a foreign territory conquered or controlled by Germany.
Gaulle, Charles de. *see in index* De Gaulle, Charles
Gauls, an ancient people. *see in index* Celts
Gaultier, Pierre. *see in index* Vérendrye, Pierre Gaultier de Varennes, sieur de la
Gaunt, John of. *see in index* John of Gaunt
Gauntlet, metal-plated gloves introduced as part of armor of knights about 13th century; a gauntlet thrown down was a challenge to fight; term applied to any long, loose-cuffed glove.
Gaur, largest species of wild cattle, *picture* C-224
Gaura, a genus of annual and perennial plants of the evening primrose family, native to North America; large hairy leaves form rosette from which a tall stem grows; flowers white or rose in loose spikes at top of stem; fruit a 4-ribbed nutlike capsule.
Gauss, Carl Friedrich (1777–1855), German mathematician and physicist G-44
mathematics M-216
Gautama (or Gotama), family name of Buddha B-480
Gautier, Hubert (1660–1737), French engineer B-445
Gautier, Théophile (1811–72), French poet, novelist, and critic; born in Tarbes; his personal eccentricities have somewhat obscured his reputation as a literary craftsman of the first rank; wrote excellent travel accounts, theater and art criticism F-397
Gauvreau, Marcelle (born 1907), French-Canadian author, born in Rimouski, Que.; founder and director of natural history nursery school in Montreal; won 1961 Canadian Book of the Year for Children award for 'Plantes Vagabondes'.
Gauze, transparent, loosely woven fabric of many uses; bandages are made from cotton type, trimmings from rayon and silk; heavier cotton grades are classed as cheesecloth.
Gavarni (formerly Sulpice Guillaume Chevalier) (1804–66), French caricaturist and illustrator; born in Paris; critic of Parisian life, especially of the somewhat disreputable classes.
Gavarnie Falls, falls in the Pyrenees, s.w. France near Spanish border; outflow of glacier, beginning of the Gave de Pau; falls drop 1,385 ft (420 m)
waterfall, *table* W-98
Gave de Pau, stream in France L-325, *map* F-372
Gaveston, Piers, earl of Cornwall (died 1312), favorite of Edward II of England; served briefly as regent 1308; was banished three times because of greed and insolence, but returned and was beheaded by the barons.
Gavial, Indian or Malayan reptile of order Crocodilia; long, narrow, flat snout with lumpy tip.
Gaviidae, a family of birds, the loons. *see in index* Loon
Gaviiformes, an order of fish-eating water birds composed of the loons. *see also in index* Loon
Gavin, James Maurice (born 1907), U.S. Army officer and diplomat, born in New York, N.Y.; paratroop commander World War II; Army chief of research and development 1955–58; retired from Army 1958; ambassador to France 1961–62; author of 'War and Peace in the Space Age'.
Gavins Point Dam, dam in South Dakota, on the Missouri River S-323, *picture* S-330, *map* S-323
Nebraska, *picture* N-102
Gavotte, originally a French peasant dance, merry and light; after its introduction at court in 16th century became quieter and more dignified; popular as a theatrical dance; special music for it written by many composers, including Bach, Gluck, and Couperin
music, *list* M-670
Gawain, character in Arthurian legend, nephew of King Arthur and knight of the Round Table; called "the Courteous" R-299a
Arthurian legends A-655
Gay, John (1685–1732), English poet and dramatist, born in Barnstaple ('Polly', a play; 'Fables', didactic poems that went through about 350 editions). *see also in index* 'Beggar's Opera, The'
Gay, Walter (1856–1937), U.S. painter, born in Hingham, Mass.; studied and lived in Paris; noted for still lifes; commander Legion of Honor ('Benedicite'; 'Las Cigarreras').
Gay, Zhenya (born 1906), U.S. artist, illustrator, and author of children's books, born in Norwood, Mass.; noted for distinctive lithographs; animals favorite models ('Look!'; 'Wonderful Things'; 'Dear Friends'; 'I'm Tired of Lions').
Gayal, species of native cattle *Bos frontalis* domesticated in India for its flesh and hide; closely related to the gaur.
Gayfeather (also called Kansas grayfeather, or marsh blazing star, or liatrisa), perennial plant *Liatris spicata* of the composite family, grows wild from Mass. and Minn. to Mexico; has rough 6 ft (2 m) stem springing from cluster of grasslike leaves; flower spikes 4 to 15 in. (10 to 38 cm) long of rose-purple, rarely white, bundlelike heads; used in medicine.
Gayle, Crystal (born 1951), U.S. country musician M-679
Gayley, James (1855–1920), U.S. metallurgist, born in Lock Haven, Pa.; invented Gayley refrigerated dry-air blast in blast furnaces; first vice-president U.S. Steel Corp 1901–9.
Gay-Lussac, Joseph Louis (1778–1850), French chemist and physicist, born in St. Léonard; professor at École Polytechnique, the Sorbonne, and Jardin des Plantes; made an academician 1806; explained nature of prussic acid; discoverer of important law of gases; pioneer in scientific balloon observations; with Louis Thenard isolated boron
heat H-103
iodine identification I-286
Gay Nineties, term for turn of 19th century in U.S., an era of lavish display and social activity that resulted from accumulation of new wealth and growth of cities; whirl of amusements contrasted sharply with austere life of pioneer days A-353
Gaza, Palestine, ancient town 50 mi (80 km) s.w. of Jerusalem; most important of the five Philistine cities; it was taken by Alexander the Great, and later became a rival of Alexandria and Athens as a center of Hellenistic culture.
Gazania, a south African genus of perennial or annual plants of the composite family; some stemless, with leaves in cluster, others short stemmed, all with white, woolly hairs; flowers daisy-like, solitary, on long stems, white, orange, or scarlet; in some, base of rays spotted, hence name peacock gazania *G. pavonia*; flowers close at night and leaves turn upward.
Gazara, Canaan. *see in index* Gezer
Gaza Strip, rectangular area (about 5 by 25 miles; 8 by 40 kilometers), named for its town of Gaza, along Mediterranean, s.w. Israeli-occupied territory; occupied by Egypt after 1949 armistice between Egypt and Israel; occupied by Israel October 1956; evacuated by Israel March 1957 and occupied by United Nations Emergency Force; that same month, administration of Gaza Strip was taken over from the United Nations by Egypt, but the United Nations Emergency Force continued to police the border between Gaza Strip and Israel; retaken by Israel 1967 E-121

Gazetteer, a geographic encyclopedia L-162
selected list R-128
Gaziantep (formerly Aintab), Turkey, military post and trading center situated 60 mi (100 km) n. of Aleppo, Syria; textiles; pop. 374,290
Asia, *map* A-697
GCA. *see in index* Ground controlled approach
GCC. *see in index* Gulf Cooperation Council
G clef. *see in index* Treble clef
GCR. *see in index* Gas-cooled reactor
Gdańsk (or Danzig), Poland, a Baltic seaport on the Vistula River; pop. 464,600 G-45, *maps* E-360, P-414
Hitler's demands G-124
Gdynia, Poland, port on Baltic sea a few mi. n.w. of Gdańsk; exports coal, machinery, and foodstuffs; pop. 190,125, *map* E-360
Ge, in mythology. *see in index* Gaea
Gear, in mechanics, the moving parts or appliances by which motion is passed from one part of a machine to another M-268, *picture* M-269
automobile A-850
bicycle B-187
Geatland, homeland of 'Beowulf'; perhaps same as the region of Götaland in Sweden B-165
Geauga Lake Park, amusement park in Aurora Park, Ohio A-386
Geb (or Seb), deity in Egyptian mythology, identified by Greeks with Cronos; considered father of the gods; also god of Earth and underworld; father of Isis and Osiris M-700, *picture* M-699
Gebal, Lebanon. *see in index* Byblos
Geber ibn Hayyan. *see in index* Jabir ibn Hayyan, Abu Musa
Gecko, lizard
mobility L-272
Ged, William (1690–1749), Scottish goldsmith and printer, born in Edinburgh; inventor of a stereotyping process.
Geddes, Eric (1875–1937), British political leader, born in India; director general of military railways and inspector general of transportation (1916–17); first lord of the admiralty (1917–18).
Geddes, Norman Bel (1893–1958), U.S. artist, born in Adrian, Mich.; known for work in stage and industrial design; stage sets for 'The Miracle', 'Hamlet'; designs for automobiles, ships, airplanes; 'Miracle in the Evening', autobiography I-174
Geelong, Australia, seaport in Victoria 40 mi (60 km) s.w. of Melbourne; important woolen trade and manufactures; quarrying; pop. 137,173, with suburbs A-788, *maps* A-822, P-3
Gegenbaur, Karl (1826–1903), German comparative anatomist, born in Würzburg; first to study anatomy from evolutionary standpoint ('Comparative Anatomy of Vertebrates').
Gegenschein, a faint glowing area in the night sky always opposite the sun; believed to be the reflection of sunlight from particles in space beyond the earth's orbit.
Gehenna, place for wicked dead in Judaic theology H-124
Gehlen, Reinhard (1902–79), German spy
espionage E-303
Gehrig, Lou (full name Henry Louis Gehrig, nickname Iron Horse) (1903–41), U.S. baseball player G-45
baseball history B-93
Gehringer, Charles Leonard (nickname The Mechanical Man) (born 1903), U.S. baseball second baseman, born in Fowlerville, Mich.; player for Detroit, A.L., 1924–42; became vice-president of that team 1951; defensive star, lifetime batting average of .321; played in 6 All-Star games.
Geiger, Hans (1882–1945), German physicist, born in Neustadt, Rhineland-Palatinate, Germany; known for Geiger counter R-65
Geiger counter, instrument for detecting radioactivity R-65, *diagram* R-63, *pictures* R-63
cloud chamber R-42, *diagram* R-41
nuclear energy N-419
radiocarbon dating A-535
Geijer, Erik Gustaf (1783–1847), Swedish poet, composer, and historian; born in Ransater, near Karlstad, Sweden; professor of history University of Uppsala; wrote stirring music to his own verses.
Geikie, Archibald (1835–1924), Scottish geologist, born in Edinburgh; tried to determine earth's age from thickness of rocks that settled in lakes and ancient seas ('Story of a Boulder'; 'Class Book of Geology').
Geikie, James (1839–1915), Scottish geologist, born in Edinburgh; brother of Sir Archibald Geikie ('The Great Ice Age'; 'Prehistoric Europe'; 'Outlines of Geology').
Geisel, Theodor Seuss (pen name Dr. Seuss) (born 1904), U.S. author and illustrator, born in Springfield, Mass.; wrote script for motion picture, 'Gerald McBoing Boing' (children's books, 'And to Think That I Saw It on Mulberry Street'; 'Horton Hears a Who!'; 'The Cat in the Hat'; 'How the Grinch Stole Christmas'; 'Yertle the Turtle'; 'One Fish, Two Fish, Red Fish, Blue Fish'; 'Ten Apples Up on Top!'; 'Dr. Seuss's ABC'; 'The Lorax'); received Laura Ingalls Wilder Award 1980 R-108
Geisha, Japanese entertainers J-28
Geissler, Heinrich (1814–79), German maker of scientific instruments, born in Igelshieb; Geissler tubes named for him
X rays X-406
Geissler tube, a sealed glass vessel containing rarefied gas and electrodes between which high-voltage electricity is passed, causing the gas to glow brilliantly; used principally in spectroscopy.
Gelatin (or gelatine), a protein material obtained from connective tissues, bones and skins of food animals G-46
photoengraving processes P-276
photogravure process P-277
seaweed S-104
Gelation, drying method
ink I-207
Gelber, Jack (born 1932), U.S. playwright A-363
Gelbvieh, breed of cattle C-230, *picture* C-229
Gelding, horse, *list* H-249
Geldof, Bob (born 1951), Irish rock musician, born in Dun Laoghaire; member of Boomtown Rats rock group 1975–86; organized Band Aid recording and Live Aid concerts for relief of famine in Africa 1985; given honorary knighthood and nominated for Nobel peace prize for relief work 1986.
Gelée, Claude. *see in index* Lorrain, Claude
Gelibolu, Turkey. *see in index* Gallipoli
Gellért Hill, hill in Budapest, Hungary B-479
Gell-Mann, Murray (born 1929), U.S. theoretical physicist G-46. *see also in index* Nobel Prizewinners, *table*
electricity E-162
nuclear physics N-432
atomic particle A-752
quark Q-5
Gelon (died 478 BC?), Greek leader, succeeded Hippocrates as tyrant of Gela, Sicily (491 BC); Syracuse, of which he became tyrant about 485 BC, attained great power and riches under his rule; defeated Carthaginians 480 BC.
Gelsemium (or yellow jasmine, or yellow jessamine), a smooth twining shrub *Gelsemium sempervirens* of the logania family with opposite shining lance-shaped leaves and small fragrant funnel-shaped flowers in axillary clusters; rootstock yields drug gelsemium used in treating neuralgia, convulsions, and bronchitis
state flower of South Carolina, *pictures* S-312, S-427
Gelsenkirchen, West Germany, industrial town in Ruhr Valley, 8 mi (13 km) n.e. of Essen; coal mines, iron- and steel-works; pop. 348,292, *map* G-131
Gemara, part of the Talmud T-18
Gemayel, Amin (born 1942), Lebanese politician; elected member of Lebanese parliament in 1970; elected president in 1982, following the assassination of his brother, president-elect Bashir Gemayel.
Gemayel, Bashir (1947–82), Lebanese politician; president-elect of Lebanon; was assassinated ten days before he was to take office, *list* A-704
Gemini (or Heavenly Twins), constellation S-414, *charts* S-415, 418, 421, 423, C-681. *see also in index* Castor and Pollux
astrology, *chart* A-708
Gemini, Project. *see in index* Project Gemini
Gemma, an asexual reproductive body in mosses, liverworts, and some algae, fungi, and ferns L-262
Gemmation. *see in index* Budding
Gemmology, science of gems J-114
Gems. *see in index* Jewelry and gems
Gemsbok, antelope *Oryx gazella* of south and west Africa; about 4 ft (1.2 m) high; straight horns sometimes 3 ft (1 m) long; valued for its flesh and hide.
Gem State (or Gem of the Mountains). *see in index* Idaho
Gendarme, name of French police, employed in all departments and possessions P-430
Gender identity, in sexuality S-125
Gendron, Lionel (born 1924), Canadian physician and author, born in St. Antoine-sur-Richelieu, Que.; 1970 Canadian Books of the Year for Children award (French) for 'La Merveilleuse Histoire de la Naissance'; books on adolescence, marriage, and sex.
Genealogy, the study of human family's history G-46. *see also in index* Family tree
biological concept B-229
Gene frequency, in heredity H-140
Genera, plural of genus. *see in index* Genus
General, military M-21
General Accounting Office, United States G-202
General Agreement on Tariffs and Trade (GATT) U-26, T-30
international trade I-272
General Arab Women Federation, organization devoted to fostering solidarity among Islamic women W-270
General Arrangements to Borrow, in international finance I-258
General Assault Ship (or LHA), naval vessel N-86
General assembly, in U.S. state governments S-429. *see also* Fact Summary with each state article
General Assembly, United Nations U-20, *chart* U-21, *picture* U-22
General aviation, all flying except that of the air transport industry and military services A-876
General cargo, package freight T-254
harbors and ports H-35
General contractor, construction H-297
General Convention of the Christian Church. *see in index* Christian Church
General court, in U.S. state governments S-429
General delivery, postal service P-460b
General Education Board, an organization founded by John D. Rockefeller, Sr., 1902, to distribute his gifts for the promotion of education; chartered by Congress 1903 R-230
General Election Day V-387
General Electric Company, manufacturer of electrical equipment; established 1892 by merger of Thomson-Houston Electric and Edison General Electric companies; plants and offices throughout world
jet propulsion J-111
General Federation of Labour. *see in index* Histadrut
General Federation of Women's Clubs W-270
General Foods Corporation, U.S. company A-54
General Grant National Memorial, memorial in New York City N-48
'General History of Virginia' (1624), work by Smith A-340
Generalization, in algebra A-287
'General Magazine', magazine M-32
General Motors Corporation, Detroit, Mich., organized 1908 by William Crapo Durant (1861–1947) as General Motors Company of New Jersey, incorporated in Delaware as General Motors Corporation 1916; acquired and consolidated many automobile and accessory companies; makes Buick, Cadillac, Chevrolet, Oldsmobile, and Pontiac passenger cars, accessories, and trucks; Frigidaire appliances; worldwide operations S-452
automobile industry A-868
Michigan M-362
Detroit D-121
Nader N-2
West German plant G-117
General of the Air Force, top rank in the U.S. Air Force; created by Congress May 1949; wears five stars on uniform
insignia, *picture* U-8
General of the Armies of the United States, rank given Pershing P-210
General of the Army, top rank in the U.S. Army, created by Congress 1866 but lapsed until World War II after having been conferred on Grant, Sherman, and Sheridan; reestablished 1944; Marshall, Eisenhower, Arnold, MacArthur, and Bradley appointed A-634
insignia, *picture* U-8
General practice, in medicine M-280
General Pulaski Skyway, N.J. N-195
General-purpose map M-114
General Services Administration, United States U-166
General Sherman Tree, tree in Sequoia National Park, perhaps one of the oldest and largest in the world N-58, S-112
General Staff, body of officers helping commander in chief or chief executive to control air, land, or naval forces of nation; usually direct personnel, intelligence, training and combat operations, logistics
U.S. Army insignia, *picture* U-10
General store, type of store M-145
'General Theory of Employment, Interest and Money', work by Keynes K-230
General theory of relativity R-142
'General William Booth Enters into Heaven', poem by Lindsay A-354, L-228
Generation, period of computer development C-628
Generations, alternation of. *see in index* Alternation of generations
Generative grammar. *see in index* Transformational grammar
'Generative Painting: Black, Red and Orange', painting by MacEntyre P-67d
Generator, electric. *see in index* Electric generator
Genes, units of heredity H-139. *see also in index* Genetics
arthritis markers A-650
bioethical decisions B-215
cells C-239
embryology E-202
evolution E-368
immune system I-56
Mendel M-297
mutation. *see in index* Mutation
physical anthropology A-483
yeast Y-411
Genesee River, river in New York, rises in Pennsylvania; empties into Lake Ontario 7 mi (11 km) n. of Rochester; 135 mi (215 km) long

New York N-246, *picture* N-237
Rochester R-227

Geneseo, College at, Geneseo, N.Y., part of State University of New York; established 1867; liberal arts and sciences, education, library science; graduate studies at Geneseo and Buffalo.

Genesis (Greek coming into being), first book of Bible, called also Book of Creation; tells of creation of world and of founding of Israelite nation and its history to deaths of Jacob and Joseph
Abraham A-12
Doves Press Bible, *picture* B-352
flood legends F-185
Judaic interpretation J-148
mythology M-695, 697
storytelling S-460

Genessee Chief, case in U.S. constitutional law, *list* S-518b

Genet, Edmond Charles Edouard (or Citizen Genet) (1763–1834), French diplomat, born in Versailles; minister to U.S. (1793–94) at time of French Revolution, sent to induce U.S. to declare war on Great Britain; U.S. requested his recall for unneutral acts; married daughter of George Clinton, governor of New York; became U.S. citizen
Washington W-44

Genet, Jean (1910–86), French author, born in Paris; abandoned as infant, became beggar, thief, and homosexual prostitute; life sentence commuted after intervention by French intellectuals (novels: 'Our Lady of the Flowers', 'Funeral Rites'; plays: 'Deathwatch', 'The Maids', 'The Blacks', 'The Screens', 'The Balcony') F-398

Genet, any of six species of small carnivorous mammals allied to the civets; found chiefly in n. Africa, also s. Europe and Asia Minor; nocturnal; greyish fur spotted with black; long tail banded with black and white; fur used commercially; scientific name *Genetta genetta neumanni*.

Genetic code G-56
biophysical research B-238
heredity H-139

Genetic counseling D-184

Genetic disorders G-48
mental retardation M-303

Genetic engineering G-49
heredity H-139
human D-184
microbiology M-377
molecule M-522
plant F-28
wheat W-189

Genetic psychology (or developmental psychology) P-522

Genetics G-52. *see also in index* Cell; Genes; Heredity; Mutation
adolescent development A-47
aging cells A-125
albinism A-271
anthropology A-483
bioethical issues B-215
biological concepts B-229
cancer C-131
embryology E-202
eugenics E-326
evolution E-365
genetic engineering G-49
intelligence I-238
juvenile delinquency theories J-162
Mendel M-296
mental illness M-301
microbiology M-377
molecule M-522
multiple birth M-649
radiation genetics P-367, *picture* P-369
sciences S-64b
sexuality S-124
yeast studies Y-411
zoology Z-469

Geneva, N.Y., city on Seneca Lake 38 mi (61 km) s.e. of Rochester; canned and frozen foods; machine tools, optical goods, foundry products; nursery products; Hobart and William Smith Colleges; pop. 15,133.

Geneva, (or Genève), Switzerland, city on Lake Geneva; pop. 159,900 G-58
Botanic Garden, *table* B-379
Europe, *map* E-360
Red Cross R-117
Switzerland S-542, *map* S-537

Geneva, Lake (also Lac Léman), largest lake in Switzerland, in s.w. bordering on France; 224 sq mi (580 sq km), *maps* E-360, S-537
France, *map* F-372
Geneva G-58
vineyard nearby, *picture* S-538

Geneva Bible, published 1560 by English refugee reformers in Geneva, Switzerland; based on an existing English translation; quarto size, reasonable cost, and marginal commentary made it popular with Puritans.

Geneva College, Beaver Falls, Pa.; founded 1848 by Reformed Presbyterian church; liberal arts and sciences, teacher education.

Geneva Conference (1955) E-139

Geneva Convention (Red Cross Treaty) R-117
warfare W-26

Geneva Copyright Convention. *see in index* Universal Copyright Convention

Geneva Medical School, N.Y. B-309

Geneva Protocol (1925) G-293

Geneviève, Sainte (AD 422?–512), a patron saint of Paris, said to have saved Paris from Attila's Huns by her prayers; caused church to be built over tomb of St. Denis; festival Jan. 3

Genghis Khan (or Jenghiz Khan, or Jinghis Khan, or Temujin) (1162?–1227), conqueror who raised Mongols to power and swept over Asia G-58
army A-638
India I-76
migration of people M-402
Mongol empire M-534
Turkestan T-317, T-327

Genie (or jinn), supernatural being with magic powers; appears in Muslim writings and in folklore of Arabia.

Genital disorders D-182

Genius, according to the belief of the ancients a guardian spirit, good or bad, who presided over the birth of a child and had charge of its destiny; term has come to be applied to an extraordinary gift or aptitude, especially as displayed in creative work
Edison's definition E-74

'Genji monogatari'. *see in index* 'Tale of Genji, The'

Genlis, Stephanie, comtesse de (1746–1830), French author and educator, born near Autun, France; tutor to Philippe Egalité's children, including Louis Philippe; anticipated many modern methods of teaching.

Gennargentu, Mount, highest range on island of Sardinia; situated near center; highest point 6,017 ft (1,834 m), *map* I-404

Gennesaret, Lake of. *see in index* Galilee, Sea of

Genoa (Italian Genova), Italy, seaport on Mediterranean, gateway to n. Italy; pop. 746,785 G-59, *map* I-404
Europe, *map* E-360
Marco Polo A-329
Pisa P-343
Venice V-279

Genoa, Gulf of, large indentation of Mediterranean in n.w. Italy, with city of Genoa at its head; broad southern portion known as Ligurian Sea.

Genocide (from genos, meaning race, and cide, meaning killing) G-60
American Indians I-148
Armenians A-628
China C-373
colonialism and imperialism C-556
Hebrew literature H-113
minority groups M-461
Nazi Germany C-638
Holocaust H-205
human rights H-320
Jews J-151
Warsaw W-34
totalitarianism T-235
United Nations U-23
West Indies W-158
Arawak T-289

Genotype, genetic makeup that controls an individual's body form E-368
genetics G-53

Genova, Italy. *see in index* Genoa

Genro, Japanese government, the unofficial body made up of elder statesmen who formerly advised the emperor.

Genseric (or Gaiseric) (390?–477), Vandal king; conquered n. Africa including Carthage (429–439); plundered Rome (455) V-265

Gent, Belgium. *see in index* Ghent

Gentian, an autumn flower, *picture* P-371
fringed gentian, *picture* F-236

Gentian family (or Gentianaceae), a family of plants and shrubs including the gentians, exacum, buckbean, centaury, and water snowflake.

Gentile, Giovanni (1875–1944), Italian philosopher, born in Castelvetrano, Italy; minister of education under Mussolini; assassinated I-377

Gentileschi, Orazio (1565?–1647), Italian painter, born in Pisa; decorated interiors of several palaces in Rome; in 1626 settled in England where Van Dyck painted his portrait; paintings vivid in color but lack composition; his best works: 'Moses Saved from the Waters', 'Annunciation', 'Joseph and Potiphar's Wife'; daughter, **Artemisia Gentileschi** (1590–1642), born in Rome, became popular in England as a portrait painter and equaled her father in historical painting ('Judith and Holofernes'; 'Christ Among the Doctors').

Gentleman Adventurers. *see index* 'Governor and Company of Adventurers of England, trading into Hudson's Bay, The'.

'Gentleman and Cabinet-Maker's Director, The' (or 'The Director'), work by Chippendale C-391
furniture F-459

Gentlemen's agreement, an agreement binding only as a matter of honor and not legally enforceable, as between business rivals (to fix prices or standardize sales methods) or between nations.

'Gentleman's Magazine', magazine M-32

Gentofte, Denmark, n. suburb of Greater Copenhagen; has coast line of 4 mi (6 km) along the Öresund (sound); topographical museum; pop. 88,308.

Gentoo, species of penguin, *picture* P-421

Genus, a group of related species of plants or animals A-432
taxonomic classification B-231
zoology Z-467

Geocentric theory, theory that all the heavenly bodies revolve around earth; sometimes called Ptolemaic theory; disproved by Copernicus, Kepler, Galileo, James Bradley.

Geochemical balance, oceanography O-480

Geochemical prospecting (or exploration geochemistry) G-71

Geochemistry G-71, E-41

Geode, in geology R-229a

Geodesic dome, hemispheric structure for enclosing large space; "skin" often aluminum, plastic, or steel; economical, light, strong, wind resistant; easily built and transported; used commercially and as mobile military shelters, *picture* S-159
Fuller F-446

Geodetic surveying, surveying in which the curvature of the earth is taken into account S-520

Geoduck, a clam C-380

'Geoffrey Hamlyn', work by Kingsley A-797

Geoffrey of Monmouth (1100?–1154), Welsh historian, bishop of St. Asaph; his work greatly influenced later writers
Arthurian legends A-655
Latin literature L-78

Geoffrey Plantagenet (1113–51), count of Anjou, husband of Matilda (daughter of Henry I of England), and father of Henry II
Henry II H-128

Geoffrion, Bernard André (nickname Boom-Boom) (born 1911), Canadian ice-hockey player, born in Montreal, Que.; with Montreal Canadiens 1952–64; New York Rangers 1966–68, coach 1968–69, top scout 1969–72; coach, Atlanta Flames 1972–; fourth highest scorer in hockey history; All Star three seasons; elected to Hockey Hall of Fame.

Geoffroy Saint-Hilaire, Étienne (1772–1844), French naturalist, born in Étampes, near Paris; pre-Darwinian believer in mutability of species.

Geoffroy's cat, wild cat *Felis geoffroyi*, *picture* C-216

'Geographical Distribution of Animals', work by Wallace B-217

Geographical mile (or nautical mile), unit of measure, *table* W-140

'Geographical Sketches', work by Strabo G-278

Geographic center, the point on which a flat cutout map of a state, or other irregular geographic unit, balances. For geographic center of a state, *see* Fact Summary with each state article
United States U-116

Geographic Society, National. *see in index* National Geographic Society

Geographos, a minor planet discovered in 1951 by R. Minkowski and A.G. Wilson at Palomar observatory; named Geographos (Greek for "geographer") in 1956 in honor of National Geographic Society; approaches nearest to earth of all heavenly bodies with known orbit except the moon; its orbit around the sun cuts across the earth's orbit; length of year is about 17 months.

Geography G-61. *see also in index* Earth; World; the continents, countries, and chief regions by name; also topics below by name
al-Idrisi's contribution I-32
equator E-293
evolution E-367
Islamic literature I-366
latitude and longitude L-79
maps M-114
moon M-579, *picture* M-574
people P-446, *chart* P-447, *map* P-447
living conditions P-190, *Reference-Outline* P-195–6
racial classification R-27
rainfall R-88, *map* R-89
rivers R-210
rock and soil R-228, S-248, *chart* R-229, *map* S-252, *pictures* R-228, 229a, S-249, 253
sciences S-64b
social studies S-238, 241a

Geological engineering E-223

Geological oceanography O-485

Geological Survey, United States, a bureau (founded 1871) of Department of the Interior U-161
maps M-128

Geology, science of the Earth, its origin, evolution, materials, and physical structure G-70. *see also in index* Animals, Prehistoric; Earth; Fossils; and chief topics listed below
archaeology A-536, I-7
Australia A-769
British Isles' foundations B-460
carboniferous period, or Coal Age. *see in index* Carboniferous period
Earth E-22, 35
earthquakes E-39
earth sciences E-41
erosion. *see in index* Erosion
Great Rift Valley G-250
Hutton H-336
Ice Age I-6
land bridges between continents P-363e
Lyell L-342
magnetism M-47
man M-83
minerals M-431, 437
mountain M-633
Niagara Falls N-301
oceans O-459
petroleum deposits P-234, *diagrams* P-235
river R-210
rock R-228, *chart* R-229, *pictures* R-228, 229a
mines and mining M-424
sciences S-64a
soil S-248, *map* S-252, *pictures* S-249, 253
spring S-396
valley V-256
volcano V-378, *diagrams* V-378, *pictures* V-380
water W-85, 89

Geomagnetic field A-764

Geomagnetic poles, points at which the axis of the earth's magnetic field cuts the surface of the earth; the north geomagnetic pole is near Etah, Greenland (78.5° N. and 69° W.), the south geomagnetic

near Wittenberg; considered greatest of his time; best known for 'O Sacred Head, Now Wounded', which he translated from Latin to German; strong supporter of Lutheranism G-105

Geriatrics. *see in index* Senior citizens

Géricault, Jean Louis André Théodore (1791–1824), French painter, born in Rouen; leader of Realistic school and of revolt against David's classicism.

Gericke, William Frederick (born 1884), U.S. plant expert, born in Fremont, Neb.; known for work in hydroponics
- hydroponics H-342
- plants P-363d

Gérin-Lajoie, Antoine (1824–82), French-Canadian novelist and poet, born in Yamachiche, Que.; editor *La Minerve* (Montreal); one of founders and for several years president L'Institut Canadien ('Un Canadien', poem; 'Dix ans d'Histoire du Canada').

Gerizim, Mount, mount in Israeli-occupied territory about 2 mi (3 km) s.e. of Nablus (ancient Shechem); 2,890 ft (880 m); in historic area.

Germ. *see in index* Bacteria; Pathogenic organism;

Germ, part of seed of cereal grain; also the small mass of living substance capable of developing into an organism or one of its parts. *see also in index* Embryo; Embryology
- flour F-212
- wheat W-192

German, Edward (1862–1936), British composer, born in Whitchurch, near Shrewsbury; incidental music for several Shakespearean plays; comic operas ('Nell Gwyn' and 'Merrie England'), symphonies, suites, rhapsodies, songs.

German Baptist Brethren. *see in index* Dunkers

German carp. *see in index* Carp

German coach, horse, *picture* H-255, *list* H-253

German cockroach (or Croton bug), insect *Blattella germanica* of the family Blattidae C-532

German Confederation (1815–66) G-122

German Democratic Republic. *see in index* Germany, East

German General Staff, in military history A-634

'Germania', work by Tacitus S-527

Germanic languages (or Teutonic languages) G-103
- English borrowings E-261
- language classification L-40, *diagram* L-44

Germanic mythology M-697, 703

Germanic peoples (also called Teutonic peoples) G-121, E-347. *see also in index* groups by name
- education E-83
- languages and literature S-472
- Mediterranean Sea M-286
- Middle Ages M-384
  - Goths G-197
  - Vandals V-265, *picture* R-248
- Scandinavia S-52g
- Spain S-357

Germanicus Caesar (15 BC–AD 19), Roman general, nephew of Tiberius; had nearly conquered Germany when jealousy of Tiberius led to his recall and transfer to Syria; allegedly poisoned at instigation of emperor.

Germanium (Ge), metalloid
- crystals C-799, *diagram* C-798
- metal and metallurgy M-307
- periodic table, *table* P-207, *list* P-208

German language G-113
- alphabet A-319, *table* A-316
- France F-348
- Germanic languages G-104
- Grimm's contribution G-287
- linguistic analysis L-230
- Luther's influence L-338
- Switzerland S-541
- Yiddish literature Y-416

German literature G-105, G-114
- chief writers. *see in index* writers by name
- drama
  - theatrical principles T-161
- Faust legends F-49
- folklore and fairy tales F-260, S-470, *list* S-481
- opera O-567
- Song of the Nibelungs N-302

German measles (or rubella), contagious disease, *table* D-171
- immunization V-249, *picture* D-165

German New Guinea, former protectorate of Germany N-174

German Reformed church. *see in index* Reformed churches

'German Requiem, A', work by Brahms O-575

German Schlieffen Plan, a German military strategy of World War I; developed by Alfred von Schlieffen W-303

German shepherd (sometimes called police dog), dog D-193, *picture* D-201
- police work, *picture* P-428

German shorthaired pointer, dog, *picture* D-197

German silver, an alloy
- copper C-712
- nickel N-307

German Southwest Africa, former German colony. *see in index* Namibia

German-Soviet Non-Aggression Pact (1939) G-124, T-273

Germantown, Pa., former n.w. suburb, now district, of Philadelphia; scene of Revolutionary War battle (Oct. 4, 1777) where Washington's surprise attack against Howe failed P-166, 171
- historic buildings P-251b, *map* P-251a

German wirehaired pointer, dog, *picture* D-197

German Workers' party, nucleus of Nazi organization H-175

Germany, a land of central Europe; area 137,559 sq mi (356,276 sq km); divided into two countries, West Germany (Federal Republic of Germany) and East Germany (German Democratic Republic); historic capital, Berlin, also divided between East and West; pop. 78,251,583 G-110, *map* E-360. *see also in index* Germany, East; Germany, West
- architecture
  - Rhine River castles R-178
- arts
  - drawing D-253
  - folk art F-254
  - literature. *see in index* German literature
  - motion pictures M-620, 625
  - music
    - bands and musicians B-55
    - classical M-668
    - opera O-560, 566
    - oratorio O-575
  - painting P-38, *pictures* P-39
  - pottery and porcelain P-474, *picture* P-469
  - printmaking P-504. *see also in index* Gutenberg, Johann
  - puppets P-536
  - sculpture
    - neoclassicism S-89
  - textile design T-144
- customs and traditions
  - Christmas C-405
  - Renaissance dress D-263
- economics
  - cooperatives C-707
  - inflation I-198
  - money M-532
- education E-85, 88, 100, *picture* E-86
- government
  - constitution C-684
  - democracy D-94
  - rulers and heads of government. *see table* following
  - socialism S-234, S-370
- history before 1945 G-121. *see also in index* names of chief events, states, and historical characters. For lists of rulers, *see in index* Holy Roman Empire; Prussia
  - Alsace-Lorraine region A-320
  - Bavaria B-111
  - colonization
    - Africa A-111, R-366a, D-35
    - Cameroon C-66
    - Pacific islands P-15
    - Samoa S-34
    - Togo T-202
  - foreign affairs
    - Austria A-827
    - Crete C-763
    - Czechoslovakia C-815
    - England E-248
    - Estonia E-309
    - France F-363
    - Greece G-260
    - Iran I-309
    - Luxembourg L-341
    - Poland P-415
    - U.S.S.R. R-356
    - Venezuela V-277
  - Hague Peace Conferences H-5
  - Hanseatic league H-32
  - Holy Roman Empire H-208
  - Hungary H-330
  - influential families
    - Fugger family F-444
    - Guelfs and Ghibellines G-301
    - Krupp family K-306
  - Middle Ages M-384
  - Mussolini M-694
  - Reformation R-133, *pictures* R-134
  - Roman Empire R-246, *map* R-242
  - Third Reich (1934–45)
    - appeasement policy and Munich Pact C-267, M-653
    - concentration camps C-638
    - eugenics E-326
    - Fascism F-37
    - genocide G-60, M-461
    - Hitler Youth Y-431
    - Holocaust H-205
    - Rome-Berlin Axis I-395

GERMANY—RULERS AND HEADS OF GOVERNMENTS

Dates of Rule	Succession or Form of Government	Ruler or Chief Executive
800–1806	Holy Roman Empire	....
1701–1713	House of Hohenzollern—King of Prussia	Frederick I
1713–1740	House of Hohenzollern—King of Prussia	Frederick William I
1740–1786	House of Hohenzollern—King of Prussia	Frederick II, the Great
1786–1797	House of Hohenzollern—King of Prussia	Frederick William II
1797–1840	House of Hohenzollern—King of Prussia	Frederick William III
1806–1815	Confederation of the Rhine	....
1815–1866	German Confederation	....
1840–1861	House of Hohenzollern—King of Prussia	Frederick William IV
1861–1871	House of Hohenzollern—King of Prussia	William I
1867–1871	North German Confederation	....
1871–1888	House of Hohenzollern—Emperor of Germany	William I
1888–1888	House of Hohenzollern—Emperor of Germany	Frederick III
1888–1918	House of Hohenzollern—Emperor of Germany	William II
1919–1925	Weimar Republic—President	Friedrich Ebert
1925–1934	Weimar Republic—President	Paul von Hindenburg
1934–1945	Third Reich—Führer and Reich Chancellor	Adolf Hitler
1945–1949	Allied Military Government	....
	EAST GERMANY AND WEST GERMANY	
1949–	German Democratic Republic (East Germany)	
	Communist party chief (1949–1971)	Walter Ulbricht
	Communist party chief (1971–)	Erich Honecker
1949–	Federal Republic of Germany (West Germany)	
	Chancellor (1949–1963)	Konrad Adenauer
	Chancellor (1963–1966)	Ludwig Erhard
	Chancellor (1966–1969)	Kurt Georg Kiesinger
	Chancellor (1969–1974)	Willy Brandt
	Chancellor (1974–1982)	Helmut Schmidt
	Chancellor (1982–)	Helmut Kohl

Gigli, Beniamino (1890–1957), Italian dramatic tenor, born in Recanati, near Macerata; began as choirboy; sang in opera in Italy; with Metropolitan Opera Co., New York City, 1920–32; voice of beautiful quality
opera, *list* O-570

Gigue (or jig), a sprightly dance, probably of English origin, spreading to European continent in 17th century; rhythm typically a multiple of three; derivation thought to be from Italian giga (fiddle); jig also loosely applied to lively dance with no set pattern; in music, last movement of classical suite. *see also in index* Suite

G.I. Joe, doll of the 1960s; popular with boys; later replaced by Action Joe D-222

Gijón, Spain, port for rich mining district in center of n. coast on the Bay of Biscay; resort; pop. 84,057, *map* E-360

Gil, Emilio Portes. *see in index* Portes Gil, Emilio

Gila Cliff Dwellings National Monument, ruins in southwestern New Mexico N-40, *picture* N-50, *map* N-40

Gila monster, lizard
protective techniques L-272, *picture* L-273
zoo Z-463

Gila River, broad and shallow stream 630 mi (1,015 km) long; rises in Sierra Madre in s.w. New Mexico and crosses Arizona to Colorado River C-586, *maps* C-585, N-350, U-40, 81. *see also in index* Coolidge Dam
New Mexico, *map* N-229

Gilberd, William. *see in index* Gilbert, William

Gilbert, Alfred (1854–1934), British sculptor and goldsmith, born in London (statue of Queen Victoria for Winchester, England; memorial to duke of Clarence at Windsor Castle).

Gilbert, Cass (1859–1934), U.S. architect, born in Zanesville, Ohio; designer of many buildings, the Minnesota Capitol, the Woolworth Building and U.S. Custom House, New York City; planned University of Minnesota and University of Texas S-24
West Virginia State Capitol, *picture* W-173

Gilbert, Grove Karl (1843–1918), U.S. geologist, born in Rochester, N.Y.; joined U.S. Geological Survey 1879, chief geologist 1889–92; noted for studies of Lake Bonneville and Henry Mountains (Utah).

Gilbert, Henry Franklin Belknap (1868–1928), U.S. composer, born in Somerville, Mass.; one of the first to emphasize use of black Americans' musical idiom in his works.

Gilbert, Humphrey (1539?–83), English navigator, born in Compton, near Dartmouth; half-brother of Sir Walter Raleigh; seeking the Northwest Passage (1583), took possession of Newfoundland for Queen Elizabeth I, first English colony in North America (though it lasted but a short time); lost at sea on return voyage A-332
St. John's, Newf. N-167

Gilbert, John (1817–97), English painter and illustrator, born in Blackheath; famed for great historic themes of vigorous design and color.

Gilbert, Ronnie (born 1926), U.S. folksinger F-273

Gilbert, Seymour Parker (1892–1938), U.S. lawyer and financial expert; born in Bloomfield, N.J.; assistant secretary of treasury 1920–21; undersecretary of treasury 1921–23; agent general for reparations payments of Germany, 1924–30.

Gilbert, Walter (born 1932), U.S. chemist. *see also in index* Nobel Prizewinners, *table*

Gilbert, William (or William Gilberd) (1540–1603), English physician and physicist, born in Colchester; physician to Queen Elizabeth I; made important discoveries that laid foundation for later work in magnetism and electricity
electricity E-161
magnetism M-42

Gilbert, William Schwenck (1836–1911), English poet and dramatist G-144
classical music M-674
literary contribution E-278
operetta O-572
quoted P-404

Gilbert and Sullivan. *see in index* Gilbert, William Schwenck; Sullivan, Arthur Seymour

Gilbert Islands, group of coral islands on Equator in mid-Pacific; 102 sq mi (264 sq km); under British protection 1892–1979, as part of Gilbert and Ellice Islands dependency 1915–75; part of Kiribati since 1979; pop. 47,711
Kiribati K-250
Pacific Ocean P-8, *map* P-3, *picture* P-7
world, *map* W-297
World War II W-332, 346

Gilbert Peak, range in Uinta Mountains; runs from w. to e. from the Wasatch Range in n.e. Utah; peak located in Summit County 13,422 ft (4,091 m), *map* U-232

Gil Blas, the hero of a famous novel ('The Adventures of Gil Blas of Santillane') by Le Sage; serving 15 masters, he travels through Spain having many adventures; the book imitated the Spanish picaresque, or rogue, novel; published 1715–35.

Gilboa, settlement in Israel at s.e. end of Plain of Jezreel and at n.w. foot of Mt. Gilboa; in biblical history scene of Saul's defeat by Philistines.

Gilder, Richard Watson (1844–1909), U.S. poet and editor, born in Bordentown, N.J.; edited *The Century* 1881–1909; contributed to other magazines of the time
sonnet P-406

Gildersleeve, Virginia Crocheron (1877–1965), U.S. educator, born in New York City; professor of English at Barnard College 1900–1911 and dean 1911–47; known for work in broadening women's higher education; author of 'Many a Good Crusade; Memoirs'.

Gilding, art of covering a surface with gold or silver M-310

Gilds. *see in index* Guilds

Gilead, mountainous region in ancient Palestine, e. of Jordan River and s.e. of Sea of Galilee; spices, myrrh, and balm.

Gilels, Emil Grigoryevich (1916–85), Soviet pianist, born in Odessa; professor at Moscow University; U.S. debut 1955 at Philadelphia.

Giles, Saint (died 712?), patron saint of beggars and handicapped; hermit and Benedictine abbot of France; festival September 1.

Giles, Warren Crandall (1896–1979), U.S. baseball executive, born in Tiskilwa, Ill.; general manager of Cincinnati Reds 1936–48, president 1948–51; president of National League 1951–69.

'Giles Goat Boy', novel by Barth A-361

Gilgal, ancient city in Palestine in Jordan Valley between Jericho and river, where Israelites first encamped after crossing the Jordan (Bible, Josh. iv).

Gilgamesh, legendary king of Babylonia, hero of an epic poem written on clay tablets, found in the ruins of Nineveh; epic has affinities with Old Testament, contains story of the Flood B-7, S-469, 480, *picture* S-482
folklore F-263

Gilia, a genus of plants of phlox family, found in western N. America; leaves lance-shaped or finely cut; flowers funnel-shaped or saucer-shaped in thimblelike heads; thimble flower *G. capitata* has lavender blue heads; used as an everlasting; standing-cypress *G. rubra* grows to 6 ft (2 m), leaves needlelike; bird's-eye *G. tricolor*, flowers bell-shaped, violet, shading brownish-purple to yellow.

Gill, David (1843–1914), Scottish astronomer, born in Aberdeen; director of observatory, Cape of Good Hope 1879–1907; pioneer in using photography to catalog stars, particularly in vast survey of southern heavens 1885–1900.

Gill, Eric (1882–1940), English sculptor and stone carver, born in Brighton; work deeply religious; famous for carving of 'Stations of the Cross' in Westminster Cathedral; wrote on aesthetics ('Beauty Looks After Herself').

Gill, mushroom structure M-664

Gill, organ for breathing underwater
embryo vertebrates V-304
fish F-126, 132, R-159, *diagram* F-125
mollusk M-523

Gill, unit of measure, *table* W-140

Gillentine family
heraldic shield, *picture* H-136

Gillespie, John Birks (nickname Dizzy) (born 1917), U.S. jazz trumpet player; also bandleader and composer; born in Cheraw, S.C.; innovator in bop and progressive jazz J-87, *picture* J-85

Gillette, William (1855–1937), U.S. actor, stage manager, and playwright, born in Hartford, Conn.; most famous as actor in his own dramatization of 'Sherlock Holmes'; also wrote and acted in 'Held by the Enemy', 'Secret Service'
Gillette Castle, *picture* C-659

Gillette, Wyo., city 80 mi (130 km) s.e. of Sheridan; trade center in grain and livestock; oil, coal mining; pop. 12,134 W-396

Gilliflower. *see in index* Stock; Wallflower

Gill net, in fishing F-134, *picture* F-135

Gillot, Joseph (1799–1873), English pen manufacturer, born in Sheffield, England P-156

Gill raker, in fish F-126

Gillray, James (1757–1815) English cartoonist, born in Chelsea; lampooned British royal family, Napoleon and other leaders; caricatures done in etching with stipple hand-colored.

Gilman, Charlotte Perkins (1860–1935), U.S. writer and lecturer on labor and feminism ('Woman and Economics'; 'The Crux'; 'His Religion and Hers')
women's rights W-277

Gilman, Daniel Coit (1831–1908), U.S. scholar and educator, born in Norwich, Conn.; president of University of California and first president of Johns Hopkins University and of Carnegie Institution of Washington.

Gilman, George F. *see in index* Great Atlantic & Pacific Tea Company

Gilman, Lawrence (1878–1939), U.S. music critic and author, born in Flushing, N.Y.; on staff of *Harper's Weekly* 1901–13, *North American Review* 1915–23, *New York Herald Tribune* 1923–39.

Gilman, Nicholas (1755–1814), U.S. political leader, born in Exeter, N.H.; delegate to Congress from New Hampshire (1786–88); to Constitutional Convention (1787); signed Constitution of the U.S.; Federalist member of Congress (1789–97); Jeffersonian Republican senator (1804–14).

Gilmer-Aikin law (1949), in Texas T-121

Gilmore, Patrick Sarsfield (1829–92), U.S. bandmaster, born near Dublin, Ireland; leader of famous 22nd Regiment Band, New York City; sometimes wrote music under pen name Louis Lambert B-56
Civil War C-478

Gilpin, Charles Sidney (1878–1930), U.S. actor, born in Richmond, Va.; famed as Brutus Jones in 'Emperor Jones' 1920–24; Drama League award and Spingarn medal 1921.

Gilpin, John, character in Cowper's 'John Gilpin's Ride', a linen draper who has many ludicrous adventures on horseback.

Gilruth, Robert Rowe (born 1913), U.S. aeronautical engineer, born in Nashwauk, Minn.; National Advisory Committee for Aeronautics 1937–58; director Project Mercury, NASA 1958–61; director NASA-Manned Spacecraft Center, Houston, 1961–73; consultant to NASA after 1974.

Gilt, female pig P-320

Gimlet tower (or great screw shell), mollusk shell *Turritella terebra*, *picture* S-152

Gin, an alcoholic beverage A-276
liquor production L-235

Ginastera, Alberto (1916–83), Argentine composer
classical music M-676

Ginger, a spice S-379

Gingerbread tree. *see in index* Doum palm

Ginger family (or Zingiberaceae), a family of plants including the ginger, shellflower, spiral flag, curcuma, cardamon, and the ginger lily.

Gingham, a cotton fabric usually woven in checks, plaids, or stripes; carded ginghams used for dresses, aprons, and pajamas, finer combed ginghams for curtains and suits.

Gingivae. *see in index* Gums

Gingivitis, inflammation of the gums T-53
dentistry D-101

Gingivostomatitis, a mouth disease T-53

Ginkgo (also called maidenhair tree), tree *Ginkgo biloba* native to e. Asia, last surviving member of the family Ginkgoaceae G-144
tree T-282

Ginny May. *see in index* Government National Mortgage Association

Gin rummy. *see in index* Rummy

Ginsberg, Allen (born 1926), U.S. poet G-145
American literature A-363
Kerouac K-229

Ginseng, plant G-145

Ginseng family, family of plants, shrubs, and trees found throughout the world, including English ivy, ginseng, Hercules club and sarsaparilla.

Ginza, shopping district, Tokyo, Japan T-204, *pictures* C-455, J-46, T-206

'Gioconda, La', painting. *see in index* 'Mona Lisa'

Giolitti, Giovanni (1842–1928), Italian statesman, born in Mondovi, Italy; several times premier; opposed Italy's participation in World War I.

Giono, Jean (1895–1970), French novelist, born in Provence; known for stories of peasant life ('Harvest') F-398

Giordano, Luca (1632–1705), Italian painter, born in Naples; painted with astonishing speed; called Fa-Presto ('Christ Expelling the Traders'; 'Francis Xavier'; 'Judgment of Paris')
fresco, *picture* M-701

Giordano, Umberto (1867–1948), Italian composer, born in Foggia, Italy; pupil of Verdi ('Fedora'; 'Madame Sans Gene'; other operas).

Giorgione (possible former name Giorgio Barbarelli, also called Giorgio of Castelfranco) (1478?–1510), Italian painter G-145
Bellini B-156

Giotto (full name Giotto di Bondone) (1266?–1337), Italian painter, sculptor, and architect G-146
Florence F-188, *map* F-189, *picture* F-187
painting P-29

Giovanni, Don. *see in index* Don Juan

Giovanni de' Medici (1360–1429), Florentine merchant M-273

Giovanni de' Medici (1475–1521). *see in index* Leo X

Giovanni Pisano. *see in index* Pisano, Giovanni

Gipon. *see in index* doublet

Gipp, George (1895–1920), U.S. football player F-296

Gipsy. *see in index* Gypsy

Giraffe, animal *Giraffa camelopardalis* G-147
length of life, *chart* A-423

Girard, Jean Baptiste (nickname 'Le Père Girard') (1765–1850), Swiss educator; entered Franciscan Order; held that study should serve to stimulate the ability to think.

Girard, Stephen (1750–1831), U.S. merchant, banker, and philanthropist; born in

Bordeaux, France P-250, 251a. *see also in index* Girard College

Girard, Ohio, city 5 mi (8 km) n.w. of Youngstown, on Mahoning River; steel milling, leather goods, aluminum products; pop. 12,517.

Girard College, Philadelphia, Pa.; free boarding school for fatherless boys; gives primary, grammar, and high-school education preparing for college, business, and industry; established 1848 by will of Stephen Girard P-251b

Girardin, Émile de (1806–1881), French journalist N-236

Girardon, François (1628–1715), French sculptor, born in Troyes, France; notable sculptures include Cardinal Richelieu's tomb at the Sorbonne and equestrian statue of Louis XIV at Paris S-88

Girasol, a variety of opal with red play of color J-115

Giraud, Henri Honoré (1879–1949), French general, born in Paris; noted for military successes and escapes from German prisons in World Wars I and II; organized Fighting French forces in Algeria Nov. 1942, made high commissioner of French Africa Dec. 1942; cochairman with De Gaulle of French Committee of National Liberation June–Nov. 1943; commander in chief of French army Aug. 1943–April 1944.

Giraudoux, Jean (1882–1944), French writer and diplomat, born in Bellac, near Limoges, France; graceful, impressionistic, original style; best known for plays and novels.

Girder, in building construction, a supporting beam B-492, *picture* B-493

'Girdle of Gems' (or 'Manimekalai'), Tamil epic I-106

Girdle of Venus, long ribbonlike jellyfish of the Mediterranean; iridescent colors, luminescent at night.

Girga, Egypt, town and former capital of Upper Egypt, on Nile, 275 mi (445 km) s. of Cairo; Coptic center.

Girgenti, Sicily. *see in index* Agrigento

Girl Guides, British organization Y-428. *see also in index* Girl Scouts
  camping C-71
  Low L-325

'Girl in Pink', painting by Modigliani P-58, *picture* P-56

'Girl in White Boots', painting by Thiebaud, *picture* D-267

'Girl of the Golden West, The', opera by Puccini P-526d

Girls' clubs and organizations. *see in index* Youth organizations

Girls Clubs of America, Inc., founded 1945; national organization that sponsors an after school and early evening program for girls from 6 to 16 years of age.

Girl Scouts Y-428. *see also in index* Girl Guides
  Baden-Powell B-16
  Low L-325
  signaling S-195a

Girls' Friendly Society of the U.S.A., organization founded 1877; sponsored by Episcopal church; membership open to girls and women of all creeds.

Girls State, a project sponsored by state auxiliaries of the American Legion to give girls of advanced high-school age experience in operating the machinery of democratic government. Each Girls State aims to pattern its government as nearly as possible after that of its own state; the Illini Girls State, for example, follows the governmental pattern of Illinois. Sports and recreation programs teach principles of good sportsmanship. Girls States are held annually, usually at a college or a university. Two girls from each Girls State are selected to attend **Girls Nation,** held annually in Washington, D.C., to study federal government.

'Girl with a Ball', painting by Lichtenstein P-67, *picture* P-69

'Girl with a Maple Branch', work by Katsukawa Shunsho, *picture* J-50

Gironde, estuary in s.w. France, 45 mi. (72 km) long B-366, *map* F-372

Girondists, political party of French Revolution; advocated moderate republicanism; named for Gironde district; downfall 1793
  Corday C-715
  Roland R-239

Girth, a band or strap that encircles an animal's body to fasten something on its back H-264

Girty, Simon (1741–1818), North American soldier, known as "the Great Renegade," born near Harrisburg, Pa.; deserted Americans in Revolutionary War to lead British and Indians in raids.

Giscard d'Estaing, Valéry (born 1926), French political leader and economist G-148, *picture* G-149
  France F-366

Gish, Dorothy (1898–1968), U.S. actress G-149

Gish, Lillian (born 1896), U.S. actress G-149, *pictures* F-280, M-019

Gissing, George Robert (1857–1903), British novelist, born in Wakefield, England
  literary contribution E-278

Gist, Christopher (1706?–59), North American scout and soldier, born in Maryland; explored Ohio Valley 1749–52; he is said to have saved George Washington's life while crossing Allegheny River.

Gitana, name given to dance of gitanos (Gypsies) of Spain; vivacious, emotional, and most often improvised to fit the mood of the dancer.

'Gitanjali', work by Tagroe T-10

Gitano. *see in index* Gypsy

Gitschin, Bohemia. *see in index* Jicin

Giuliano de' Medici (1453–78), brother of Lorenzo de' Medici M-273

'Giulietta degli spiriti', film by Fellini F-53

Giulini, Carlo Maria (born 1914), Italian opera and orchestra conductor, born in Barletta, Italy; worked with Radio Milan and La Scala; U.S. debut led to appointment as principal guest conductor with Chicago Symphony; music director of Los Angeles Philharmonic 1978– .

'Guilio Cesare in Egitto', opera by Handel O-563, *list* O-562

Giulio de' Medici (1478–1534). *see in index* Clement VII

Giulio Romano (1499?–1546), Italian painter and architect; pupil, assistant, and successor of Raphael as head of Roman school of painting ('Dance of Apollo and the Muses') A-555, 568

Giza, (also called Gizeh), Egypt, town on w. bank of Nile River almost opposite Cairo; pop. 1,509,600 G-149, E-116
  pyramids P-542, *pictures* M-394, S-115
  Sphinx S-82, S-378

Gizzard, the more important of a bird's two stomachs; in seed-eating birds, has muscular walls and grinds food with aid of gravel; membranous sac in carnivorous birds; discharges prepared food into intestine B-245

Gjellerup, Karl (1857–1919), Danish poet and novelist, born in Roholte, Zealand; early disciple of Georg Brandes; wrote 'The Disciple of the Teutons', an antitheological work, under his influence; later works showed deep spiritual and ethical strain ('The Mill'). *see also in index* Nobel Prizewinners, *table*

'Gjöa', Amundsen's ship A-381, S-41a, *picture* A-382

Glace Bay, N.S., coal-mining town on e. coast of Cape Breton Island 11 mi (18 km) n.e. of Sydney; pop. 21,466 N-402, *map* C-112

Glacial acetic acid, acetic acid free from water, which forms icelike crystals at 17° C (62° F). *see also in index* Acetic acid

Glacial drift, a deposit
  glacier G-151
  Ice Age I-6
  iceberg I-10
  Michigan M-356

Glacial Drift Prairie, region in North Dakota N-373

Glacial flour E-33

Glacial period. *see in index* Pleistocene epoch

Glacial Plains, U.S.
  Kansas K-174
  Missouri M-400, *map* M-409

Glacial till, a claylike alluvium deposited by glaciers
  erosion G-151
  Ice Age I-6
  minerals M-437

Glaciation, action of glaciers upon surface over which they travel G-151
  Ice Age I-7

Glacier, a moving ice field G-150. *see also in index* Pleistocene epoch
  Alaska A-241, *picture* U-38
  Alps A-319, *pictures* E-328, 345
  animal migration A-453
  Antarctica A-472
  Arctic region A-574
  British Isles B-460
  Earth E-27, 32
  Himalayas H-153
  Ice Age I-6
  iceberg formation I-10
  Iceland I-13
  lake formation L-24
    Great Lakes G-248
  moraine I-4, *picture* U-38
  Mount Everest E-363
  New York N-245
  New Zealand N-286
  Norway N-389
  oceanography O-473
  parks and monuments. *see in index* Glacier Bay National Monument; Glacier National Park;
  sand formation S-36
  soil S-249, U-68
  source of river, *diagram* R-210
  water W-84
  waterfall W-98

Glacier Bay National Park and Preserve (formerly Glacier Bay National Monument), park in s.e. Alaska N-49, A-244, *maps* N-40, U-39, 94, *picture* I-6
  Alaska A-244
  Muir M-648

Glacieret (niche glacier, or cirque glacier), a very small glacier that occupies a cirque G-150

Glacier National Park, park in British Columbia N-30, *map* N-29

Glacier National Park, park in Montana N-49, *pictures* U-79, M-559, *map* N-40
  Montana M-550

Glacier Peak, mountain in n.-central Colorado; height 12,654 ft (3,857 m).

Glacier Peak, northern part of Cascade Range in Washington; 10,436 ft (3,181 m) W-48

Glackens, William James (1870–1938), U.S. impressionist painter, born in Philadelphia, Pa.; remarkable colorist, fine sense of form and composition; influenced by Renoir and Manet.

Gladden, Washington (1836–1918), U.S. clergyman, social reformer, and author, born in Pottsgrove, Pa.; directed attack on "tainted money"; urged personal responsibility of every citizen for good government.

Gladiator, professional fighter in ancient Rome G-152, S-213

Gladiolus (or sword lily), a flower of the Iris family G-152

Gladkov, Fedor Vasilievich (1883–1958), Soviet novelist whose 'Cement' (1925) served as a model for later industrial novels R-360b, 361, *picture* R-360b

Gladstone, William (1809–98), British statesman G-152
  Disraeli D-185
  Gordon G-195
  United Kingdom E-254
  U.S. Constitution U-144
  Victoria V-309

Gladstone, Mo., residential city 8 mi (13 km) n. of Kansas City; in Clay County; about 8 mi (13 km) s.e. of Midcontinent International Airport; pop. 24,990.

Glagolitic Alphabet, system used by some Slavic peoples related to the Cyrillic alphabet B-535

Glåma River, river in e.Norway; 380 m (612 km) long; rises in Dovrefjell plateau; flows s. into Skagerrak at Fredrikstad; longest river in Norway N-389

Glamorganshire, southernmost county of Wales; 813 sq mi (2,106 sq km); cap. Cardiff; great coal beds, iron, steel, tinplate, aluminum, and many other industries; livestock; pop. 1,229,728.

Gland, in animal
  antelope scent glands A-480
  bee B-127

Gland, in human G-153. *see also in index* Hormones
  anatomy A-391
  antihistamine action A-492
  brain regulates B-398, 401
  digestive system D-144, *picture* D-145
  exocrine (ducted)
    mammaries. *see in index* Mammary gland
    salivary R-131
    sebaceous (oil) S-211
    sweat S-211
  hormones H-240
  mouth M-641
  nose N-396
  reflex reactions R-131
  reproductive system R-151c

Glanders, an infectious disease, common among horses and asses, less frequently attacking cattle and other livestock; ulcers, pus discharge from lungs, and high temperature are characteristics.

Glandular fever. *see in index* Mononucleosis

Glarus, Switzerland, capital of canton of same name, 33 mi (53 km) s.e. of Zurich; cotton mills, breweries; pop. 5,852, *map* S-537

Glaser, Donald Arthur (born 1926), U.S. physicist, born in Cleveland, Ohio; professor University of California at Berkeley after 1960. *see also in index* Nobel Prizewinners, *table*

Glasgow, Ellen (1874–1945), U.S. novelist, born in Richmond, Va.; feminist; work shows fine characterization; keen wit; clear, forceful language ('The Romance of a Plain Man'; 'The Romantic Comedians'; 'In This Our Life', Pulitzer prize 1942; 'The Woman Within', autobiography) A-358, *picture* V-342

Glasgow, Ky., city 30 mi (50 km) e. of Bowling Green in dairying region; roller bearings, automobile parts, clothing; poultry processing; tobacco warehouses; pop. 12,958.

Glasgow, Mont., city in n.e. on Milk River, 55 mi (90 km) s. of Canadian border; center for shipping cattle, sheep, and grain; Glasgow Air Force Base; Fort Peck Dam nearby; pop. 4,455.

Glasgow, Scotland, largest city of country; on Clyde River; pop. 751,000 G-154, *map* E-360
  Scotland S-68, *map* S-67
  world, *map* W-297

Glasgow, University of, university in Glasgow, Scotland; founded 1451 by Bishop Turnbull; coeducational since 1893; retains many medieval customs, including student election of rector; faculties of arts, sciences, medicine, divinity, law G-154

Glasgow Cathedral, cathedral in Glasgow, Scotland, *picture* G-154

Glashow, Sheldon L. (born 1932), U.S. physicist, born in New York, N.Y.; on faculty of Stanford University 1961–62, of University of California, Berkeley, 1962–66; at Harvard University since 1966, professor 1967–; developed theory concerning fundamental interactions between particles A-757. *see also in index* Nobel Prizewinners, *table*

Glasnost, Russian word translated as "openness," used to describe the moderate democratizing of the U.S.S.R. under Mikhail Gorbachev in the late 1980s. The new policy resulted in some freedom to criticize government officials, greater freedom to publish, more freedom of information, and some democratizing of elections. Its greatest effect was the beginning of a radical reform in management of the economy.

Glaspell, Susan (1882–1948), U.S. novelist and dramatist, born in Davenport, Iowa; with her first husband, George Cram Cook, helped organize Provincetown Players; wrote for them popular plays, 'Suppressed Desires' and 'Trifles'; Pulitzer prize (1931) for 'Alison's House', play based on life of Emily Dickinson.

Glass, Carter (1858–1946), U.S. political leader, born in Lynchburg, Va.; member U.S. House of Representatives 1902–18; secretary of the treasury 1918–20; U.S. senator (Democrat) from Virginia 1920–46.
Glass, Montague (1877–1934), U.S. humorous author, born in Manchester, England ('Potash and Perlmutter' stories dealing with Jewish clothing merchants).
Glass, Philip (born 1937), U.S. composer M-676
Glass G-155
- antiques A-494
- beads B-113, *picture* B-115
- blown glass, *pictures* R-197, V-340
- building construction, *picture* U-23
  - greenhouse G-281
- buttons B-531, *picture* B-529
- crystal R-52, *diagram* R-56
- design D-112
- electric light E-163
- enamel E-207
- eyeglasses E-392
- inventors, *table* I-280
- lead L-99
- light refraction R-39
- manganese M-96
- materials used S-38, S-195b
- microscopic structure, *diagram* S-254f
- mirrors M-464
- plate glass, *picture* P-166

Glassboro, N.J., borough 17 mi (27 km) s. of Camden; glass products; agricultural trade center; settled 1775, incorporated 1920; pop. 14,574.
Glassboro State College (formerly New Jersey State Teachers College), college in Glassboro, N.J.; founded 1923; liberal arts and teacher education; graduate study.
Glass Capital. *see in index* Toledo, Ohio
Glasses, optical. *see in index* Eyeglasses
Glass fiber G-159
'Glass Menagerie, The', drama by Williams A-357, R-112b
- Williams W-209

Glass sponge, *picture* S-393
Glass-Steagall Banking Act, United States R-270
Glassware G-164
Glassworm. *see in index* Arrowworm
Glasswort, plant *Salicornia* H-19
Glastonbury, Conn., 5 mi (8 km) s.e. of Hartford; toiletries, aluminum wire; state correction camp; incorporated 1690; pop. of township 24,327.
Glastonbury, England, borough in Somerset, on Brue River, 22 mi (35 km) s. of Bristol; ruins of 12th-century abbey; "Glastonbury thorn," a variety that flowers twice a year, said to have sprung from a specimen planted by Joseph of Arimathea, who built here the first Christian church in England; pop. 6,310, *map* U-18a
Glauber, Johann Rudolf (1604–68), German chemist, born in Karlstadt, near Würzburg, Bavaria; discovered (1658) medicinal properties of Glauber's salt.
Glauber's salt, (or mirabilite), a natural sodium sulfate ($Na_2SO_4 \cdot 10H_2O$); found in Europe, Utah, Ariz., and Calif., in mineral springs, and in seawater; used medicinally as cathartic M-436
Glaucium (or horned-poppy), a genus of annual or perennial plants of the poppy family, native to Eurasia; several hybrid species were developed by Burbank; foliage blue-white, succulent, flowers yellow, red, or purple; also called sea poppy.
Glaucoma, eye disease E-390
- blindness B-311

Glauconite, a mineral containing iron and potassium silicate
- sand S-36

Glavnoye Razvedyvatelnoye Upravleniye (GRU), Soviet government I-236
Glaze, glassy coating on pottery P-479
- brick and tile B-436
- Chinese pottery P-470, 473, *picture* P-472
- Della Robbia D-89, P-474
- Moorish tile P-473
- underglaze and overglaze P-478

Glazunov, Aleksandr Konstantinovich (1865–1936), Soviet composer, born in St. Petersburg (Leningrad); studied under Rimski-Korsakov; director, Conservatory at Leningrad; wrote 8 symphonies, concertos, ballets, marches, piano and vocal works.
Gleaning, gathering of grain left in fields by reapers
- Ruth R-365

Gleason, Jackie (or Herbert John Gleason) (1916–87), U.S. comedian, musician, and television producer; born in Brooklyn, N.Y.; began career as master of ceremonies at nightclubs and theaters; musical comedies ('Follow the Girls'; 'Take Me Along'); entered television 1949 and became famous for humorous characterizations; orchestra leader for popular records, *picture* T-71
Gleiwitz, Poland. *see in index* Gliwice
Gleizes, Albert Léon (1881–1953), French artist, born in Paris; impressionist in early work; in 1911 became one of the first cubists.
Glen Burnie, Md., unincorporated suburb of Baltimore; chiefly residential; pop. 37,263, *map* M-182
Glen Canyon Dam, dam in Arizona, on the Colorado River A-598, *map* U-217, *picture* A-606
Glen Canyon National Recreation Area, park in Arizona and Utah N-49, *map* N-40
- Utah U-221, *map* U-233, *picture* U-224

Glencoe, Ill., residential village 20 mi (30 km) n. of the city of Chicago in Cook County; established 1836; pop. 9,200
- Illinois, *map* I-52

Glencoe, valley of Coe River in Scotland extending about 10 mi (16 km) from its mouth on Loch Leven; site of massacre of Macdonalds by Campbells and royal troops 1692.
Glen Cove, N.Y., residential suburb of New York City on n. shore of Long Island; carbon paper and ribbon, metal and electrical products; Webb Institute of Naval Architecture; pop. 24,618.
Glendale, Ariz., city 8 mi (13 km) n.w. of Phoenix; vegetables, cotton, textiles; diversified industry; Thunderbird Graduate School; Luke Air Force Base nearby; pop. 97,172 A-599
Glendale, Calif., city 7 mi (11 km) n. of Los Angeles; pop. 147,440 G-165, *maps* U-40
Glendale, Wis., city 6 mi (10 km) n. of Milwaukee; residential; light industry; incorporated 1956; pop. 13,882.
Glendive, Mont., city about 200 mi (320 km) n.e. of Billings, on Yellowstone River; poultry, stock, grain; oil and natural gas; Makoshika State Park nearby; pop. 5,978.
Glendora, Calif., city 21 mi (34 km) n. of Los Angeles; pumps, irrigating systems, dental products; electronics; founded 1887, incorporated 1911; pop. 38,654.
Glendower, Owen (1359?–1415?), Welsh chief, national hero; last independent prince of Wales and leader of last war for Welsh independence
- Henry IV H-129
- Wales W-7

Glen Ellyn, Ill., residential village in Du Page County, 22 mi (35 km) w. of Chicago; pop. 23,649
- Illinois, *map* I-52

Glenn, Hugh (1788–1833), U.S. trader and merchant, born in Berkeley County, Va. (now W. Va.); purveyor of supplies to frontier posts in Ohio Valley; led hunting and trading expedition (1821) from mouth of Verdigris River to Santa Fe.
Glenn, John Herschel, Jr. (born 1921), U.S. senator and former astronaut, born in Cambridge, Ohio; resigned from space program 1964, from U.S. Marine Corps 1965; elected to Senate from Ohio 1974
- space flight S-346f, *picture* S-346a, *table* S-348
- NASA N-22

Glennan, Thomas Keith (born 1905), U.S. educator, born in Enderlin, N.D.; president Case Institute of Technology 1947–65, on leave as AEC member 1950–52 and as head of National Aeronautics and Space Administration 1958–61.
Glennon, John Joseph, Cardinal (1862–1946), U.S. Roman Catholic prelate, born in Ireland, in U.S. after 1884; archbishop of St. Louis after 1903; died in Dublin, Ireland, on way home after being created cardinal.
Glen Rock, N.J., borough 4 mi (6 km) n.e. of Paterson; machinery, clothing, furniture, chemicals; settled 1710, incorporated 1896; pop. 11,497.
Glens Falls, N.Y., manufacturing city 47 mi (76 km) n. of Albany on Hudson River; paper products, electrical products, machinery, clothing; limestone quarries nearby; falls and famous cave described in Cooper's 'The Last of the Mohicans'; pop. 15,897.
Glenview, Ill., residential village 17 mi (27 km) n.w. of Chicago; nurseries; swimming pool supplies; dairy research laboratory; Glenview Naval Air Station; pop. 30,842
- Illinois, *map* I-52

Glenville State College, Glenville, W. Va.; established in 1872; liberal arts, music, teacher education, and vocational home economics
- West Virginia W-168

Glenwood Springs, Colo., resort city and ranching center 60 mi (95 km) n.w. of Leadville; mineral hot springs, lime products, cattle raising; pop. 4,637.
Glia, type of brain cells
- nervous system N-120

Glick, George Washington (1827–1911), U.S. statesman, born in Greencastle, Ohio; responsible for revised laws of Kansas (1868); made governor of Kansas 1882
- Statuary Hall, *table* S-437a

Glidden, Charles Jasper (1857–1927), U.S. businessman, born in Lowell, Mass.; pioneer in development of telephone, automobile, airplane; installed at Lowell (1879) one of first telephone multiple switchboards.
Glidden, Joseph Farwell (1813–1906), U.S. inventor, born in Charlestown, N.H.; patented barbed wire
- barbed wire W-247

Glider, a motorless aircraft G-165. *see also in index* Hang glider
- aerial sport advancements A-64, *picture* A-65
- airplane A-191
- guided missile G-308
- history and development A-201
- sailplane S-16b
- world records. *see table* following
- World War II W-334
- Wright brothers W-368

Glière, Reinhold (1875–1956), Soviet composer, born in Kiev; works classical in form but modern in harmony and use of orchestral color; wrote symphonies ('Ilya Murometz'), symphonic poems ('Cossacks of Zaporozh'), ballets ('Red Poppy'), also chamber music, operas, piano pieces, and songs.
Glinka, Mikhail Ivanovich (1804?–57), Russian composer, born near Smolensk, Russia; pioneer of modern Russian school of national music ('A Life for the Czar', 'Russlan and Ludmilla', operas; also songs, piano pieces, and orchestral music)
- classical music M-674

Glioma, type of tumor C-812
Glittertinden (formerly called Glittertind), peak in s. Norway, highest in Scandinavia 8,104 ft (2,470 m); in Norse legend part of the home of the giants or Jotun N-389
- Europe E-329

Gliwice (German Gleiwitz), Poland, former German city and mining center in Silesia; in Poland since 1945; metal goods, chemicals, glass, cement, paper; pop. 171,100.
Global Atmospheric Research Program (GARP), international program W-126
Global economy F-287
Globe, Ariz., city about 75 mi (120 km) e. of

WORLD SOARING RECORDS

Event	Single-Place Record		Year	Multiplace Record		Year
Distance						
In straight line	H.W. Grosse (W. Ger.)	907.70 mi.	1972	S.H. Georgeson (N.Z.)	617.49 mi.	1982
To goal	Group flight (N.Z.)	779.36 mi.	1978	S.H. Georgeson (N.Z.)	617.49 mi.	1982
To goal and back	T. Knauff (U.S.)	1,023.19 mi.	1983	T. Knauff (U.S.)	621.91 mi.	1981
Altitude						
Total gained	P.F. Bikle (U.S.)	42,303 ft.	1961	S. Jozefezak (Poland)	38,320 ft.	1966
Above sea level	P.F. Bikle (U.S.)	46,266 ft.	1961	L.E. Edgar (U.S.)	44,255 ft.	1952
Speed (Triangular Course)						
100 km. (62.14 mi.)	I. Renner (Aus.)	121.28 mph	1982	E. Müller (W. Ger.)	98.36 mph	1981
300 km. (186.41 mi.)	H.W. Grosse (W. Ger.)	98.59 mph	1980	E. Müller (W. Ger.)	87.29 mph	1979
500 km. (310.68 mi.)	H.W. Grosse (W. Ger.)	99.20 mph	1983	E. Müller (W. Ger.)	91.15 mph	1981

Phoenix; business center for copper-mining and cattle-raising area; tourist trade; pop. 6,708, *map* U-40

Globe, representation of the surface of Earth M-114. *see also in index* Map
  directions D-161
  hemisphere H-126
  latitude and longitude L-79, *picture* L-81

Globe amaranth, an annual plant *Gomphrena globosa* of the amaranth family, native to tropics; leaves soft, hairy; flowers clover-like, purple, orange, white, or variegated; used as everlastings; sometimes called bachelor's button. *see also in index* Bachelor's button

Globefish, oceanic fish with power of inflation when attacked; becomes like a football with tail and beak attached; species found on east U.S. coast *Spheroides maculatus*, called swelldoodle, puffer, eggfish; closely related to the porcupine fishes, which have the same power of inflation.

Globeflower. *see in index* Trollius

Globe section (or spherical map) M-116

Globe Theatre, old playhouse in London, U.K. S-132, T-160

Globe thistle, a genus *Echinops* of perennial plants of the composite family; tall, erect; leaves toothed, spiny at edges, often hairy on underside; flower heads steel-blue or white.

Globular projection, maps M-125

Globule, in astronomy A-716

Globulins, in blood plasma S-113
  gamma globulin S-113
    medical use S-114

Glockenspiel, a set of tuned steel bars or tubes; played with hammers; sometimes called carillon

Gloeocapsa, moneran, *picture* L-269

Glogg, a hot punch W-237

'Gloire', French warship N-83

'Glomar Challenger', deep-sea drilling ship A-746
  frontier exploration F-427

Glomerulonephritis (or nephritis), kidney disease K-235. *see also in index* Kidney diseases
  symptoms and cause D-182

Glomerulus, a tuft of capillary loops K-235
  kidney disease D-182

Glomma River, river in Norway, largest in Scandinavia; rises in Dovrefjeld tableland, flows s. 350 mi (550 km) into Skagerrak, 50 mi (80 km) s.e. of Oslo.

Gloria Dei (Old Swedes') Church National Historic Site, historical church in Philadelphia, Pa. N-49, P-251d, *map* P-251a

Gloriana, Spenser's 'Faerie Queene', the queen of Fairyland; personified glory and represented Elizabeth I as queen.

Glorious Revolution (Bloodless Revolution, or Revolution of 1688), in English history, overthrew James II G-168, E-247
  James II J-20

Glory hole, mining method M-426, *picture* M-427

'Glory of the Seas', clipper built by McKay, *picture* M-195

Glory pea. *see in index* Clianthus

'Glory Road', work by Catton W-27

Glost firing, in pottery making P-478

Gloucester, Humphrey, duke of (1391–1447), youngest son of Henry IV; protector of throne during youth of Henry VI; charged with treason at time of death.

Gloucester (or Gloucestershire), county in s.w. England at head of Severn estuary; 1,019 sq mi (2,639 sq km); dairying; many industries; cap. Gloucester; pop. 1,001,706.

Gloucester, England, city on Severn River, 95 mi (155 km) n.w. of London; capital of Gloucestershire; shipyards; varied industries; originally a Roman camp; Norman-Gothic cathedral; pop. 90,530, *map* U-18a
  Sunday school S-516

Gloucester, Mass., fishing port on Cape Ann, 27 mi (43 km) n.e. of Boston; fish processing; summer resort; artists' colony; pop. 27,768, *pictures* M-193, U-45

Gloucester City, N.J., city on Delaware River opposite Philadelphia; textiles, paper, lumber, chemicals, asbestos, cork; pop. 13,121
  Walt Whitman Bridge P-251d, *map* P-251a, *picture* P-251

Gloucestershire, county in England. *see in index* Gloucester

Glove G-169
  asbestos, *picture* P-271
  baseball B-90
  boxing B-388
  rubber R-304

Glover, John (1732–97), American Revolutionary War soldier, born in Salem, Mass.; rose from cobbler to brigadier general; in charge of retreat from Long Island and of boats in which Washington crossed Delaware; member of court that tried Major André.

Gloversville, N.Y., city in e.-central part of state, 40 mi (65 km) n.w. of Albany; tanneries, textile mills, woodenware factories, phonograph records; pop. 17,836.

Glove sponge S-394

Glow lamp
  sodium vapor lamps S-247

Glow plug, in-cylinder heat source D-142

Glowworm. *see in index* Firefly and glowworm

Gloxinia, a perennial plant of tropical America of the family Gesneriaceae; large bell-shaped flowers of velvety red, purple, white, or intermediate shades; garden plant known as gloxinia is of genus *Sinningia*.

Glucagon, hormone that raises the level of blood sugar H-242, *table* H-241
  hypoglycemia D-181

Gluck, Alma (1884–1938), U.S. dramatic soprano, born in Bucharest, Romania; attained operatic and concert success without European training; married Efrem Zimbalist.

Gluck, Christoph Willibald (1714–87), German composer G-169
  classical music M-669
  opera O-563

Glucocorticoid, steroid hormone H-242, *table* H-241

Glucose (or dextrose), simple (monosaccharide) sugar found in fruits and other foods and in the blood of animals; fuels the energy needs for most living organisms L-268
  bioengineering B-206
  carbohydrate C-155
  commercial S-508
  corn sugar C-722
  diabetes D-125
  fatigue F-45
  glycolysis B-202
  health H-83
  honey S-509
  hormones H-242
  liver L-261
  organic chemistry O-604
  plant chemistry P-372

Glue
  calcimine P-72
  potassium bichromate C-408

Glue sniffing, habit of inhaling glue fumes to produce false sense of well-being; prolonged use damages vital organs; concentrated dose may be fatal.

Glulam, wood product, *picture* W-285

Glume, part of a wheat plant W-192

Gluon, a subatomic particle A-754
  matter M-230
  nuclear energy N-421
  nuclear physics N-432
  quark Q-5

Glutamine synthetase, enzyme, *table* E-290

Glutamine transaminase, enzyme, *table* E-290

Glutathione, tripeptide (compound composed of three amino acids)
  Hopkins H-238

Gluten, a tough, elastic albuminous protein
  bread B-428
  flour F-213

Glycerin (or glycerol), syrupy liquid that occurs in combination with fatty acids; obtained as by-product in making soap from animal and vegetable fats and oils, also produced by fermenting sugar with special yeasts in certain salts and from propylene gas; has thousands of uses such as an ingredient in resins and gums for paints, toothpastes, cosmetics, explosives, and certain drugs, and as a solvent
  alcohols A-275, *table* A-274
  organic chemistry O-603
  soapmaking S-229

Glyceryl trinitrate. *see in index* Nitroglycerin

Glycine, amino acid O-604

Glycogen, animal starch L-268
  carbohydrate C-155
  liver L-261
  respiration R-160

Glycolysis, enzyme reaction which releases energy
  biochemistry B-201
  metabolism M-306

Glyptodont (Greek, "fluted tooth"), extinct armadillolike animal of South America; about size of ox; short broad feet, deeply grooved teeth.

GMT. *see in index* Greenwich mean time

Gnat, name generally applied to any very small two-winged insect. *see also in index* Buffalo gnat; Fungus gnat; Gall gnat.

Gnatcatcher. *see in index* Kinglet and gnatcatcher

Gneiss, rock R-229a, *chart* R-229
  minerals M-437

GNMA. *see in index* Government National Mortgage Association

Gnome, mischievous elf F-12

Gnomic projection, maps M-124

Gnosticism, movement in Christian church of 2nd and 3rd centuries G-170
  Bible B-184

GNP. *see in index* Gross national product

Gnu (or wildebeest), a member of the antelope family; found in Africa; both male and female have curved horns; head and neck resemble buffalo; has stiff mane and long, coarse tail; average height about 4 1/3 ft (1.3 m); sometimes called horned horse
  'Ape Riding a Gnu', *picture* S-89

Goa, Daman, and Diu (formerly Portuguese India), union territory of India, in w.; consists of the widely separated units Goa, Daman, and Diu; total area 1,537 sq mi (3,981 sq km); coconuts, copra, fish, spices, nuts, salt; Portuguese India seized by India 1961; pop. 857,180, *map* I-83

Goal, in sports
  field hockey H-193
  football goal posts F-291
  ice hockey H-194, *diagram* H-195
  water polo W-102

Goal judges, in water polo W-102

Goal throw, in water polo W-102

Goat G-170
  anatomy
    fur, *table* F-464
      wool W-288
    hoof H-231
    teeth R-318
  children's zoo, *picture* P-248
  domesticated animals, *picture* A-456
  ruminant R-318
  sheep S-148
  Spain S-351
  Turkey T-321, *picture* T-322

Goat, a constellation. *see in index* Capricornus

Goat, Rocky Mountain, an antelope G-171

Goat antelope. *see in index* Mountain goat

Goatfish (or surmullet), family of moderate-sized shore fish Mullidae, with flat, oblong body, large scales, and a pair of chin barbels for digging worms; inhabits warm seas; superior food fish; color, gold or red.

Goat Island, Calif., United States reservation. *see in index* Yerba Buena Island

Goat Island, island separating the two sides of Niagara Falls N-300

Goatsbeard, a biennial plant *Tragopogon pratensis* of composite family, native to Europe but common wildflower in North America; belongs to same genus as the vegetable salsify; grows to 3 ft (1 m); leaves gray-green, grasslike. Flower heads pale yellow, 2 1/2 in. (6.4 cm) across; seeds form a mass similar to dandelion; sometimes called meadow salsify.

Goatskin G-171
  leather L-108

Goatsucker. *see in index* Nightjar

Gobat, Charles Albert (1843–1914), Swiss statesman. *see also in index* Nobel Prizewinners, *table*

Gobbi, Tito (1915–84), Italian baritone, born near Vicenza; operatic debut in Rome 1938, Metropolitan Opera House 1956; extensive repertoire; movies.

Gobbing feeder, in glass manufacture G-158

Gobelin tapestries, famous French tapestries, made in Paris; so named from a family of dyers by name of Gobelin who owned building in which tapestry industry was established in 16th century; industry now maintained by French government T-27

Gobi, desert region of e.-central Asia, in Mongolian People's Republic and in Inner Mongolian Autonomous Region, China; area 500,000 sq mi (1,300,000 sq km); average elevation 3,000 to 5,000 ft (900 to 1,500 m) G-172
  Asia, *map* A-697
  Mongolia M-535, *picture* C-338
  world, *map* W-297

Gobineau, Joseph-Arthur de (1816–82), French writer and diplomat G-172

Goble, Paul (born 1933), British author, illustrator, and artist; born in Haslemere, Surrey; wrote and illustrated 'The Girl Who Loved Wild Horses', winner of 1979 Caldecott Medal; became interested in American Indians; lived South Dakota.

Goblins, in folklore, grotesque fairies similar to gnomes; sometimes evil, sometimes playful F-12, S-473

Goby any of numerous, widely distributed, spiny-finned fishes constituting family Gobiidae, having wide, flat head, large mouth, and ventral fins often united in funnel-shaped disk; small F-124, 131. *see also in index* Pandaka pygmaea and Mudskipper
  reproductive behavior A-442

God deity G-172. *see also in index* Religion; Theocracy; Theology
  American literature A-342
  atheism R-332e
  Aztec customs A-[illegible]
  Babylonia and Assyria B-6
  Baha'i faith B-19
  barber H-8
  Bible P-508
    Abraham A-12
    Paul P-141
    Peter P-225
    Tabernacle T-2
  Buber's I-Thou concept B-473
  Christianity
    Christian Science C-402
    Jehovah's Witnesses J-96
    Jesus Christ C-398
    Lutheranism L-338
    Roman Catholicism P-265
  evolution E-364
  Gnosticism G-170
  Hinduism S-93
  Islam I-359, K-268
  Judaism J-146
    Passover P-136
    Saadia S-1
  masks M-186
  mythology M-698
  philosophy P-265
  Sumerian culture A-404, B-6
  world W-295
  Zen Z-450
  Zoroastrianism P-211

God, church of H-202

Godard, Benjamin Louis Paul (1849–95), French composer, born in Paris; works for orchestra, violin, piano, songs, chamber music, operas ('Jocelyn').

Godard, Jean Luc (born 1930), French film director and actor, born in Paris; leader in French New Wave movement M-623

Godavari, large river in central India; rises n.e. of Bombay in Western Ghats, flows 900 mi (1,450 km) s.e., enters Bay of

Bengal by several mouths, *map* I-86
Asia, *map* A-697
'God Bless America', U.S. patriotic song N-65
Goddard, Calvin Hooker (1891–1955), U.S. ballistics expert, physician, and military historian, born in Baltimore, Md.; noted for devising method of identifying gun from which a given bullet has been fired (1925–29).
Goddard, Henry Herbert (1866–1957), U.S. psychologist, born in Vassalboro, Me.; authority on feeble-mindedness; researcher, lecturer, writer; most widely known study 'Kallikak Family'; professor of psychology Ohio State University 1922–38 I-239
Goddard, Robert H. (1882–1945), U.S. physicist and inventor G-173, S-341d, *picture* R-233
rockets, *picture* S-341c
Goddard College, Plainfield, Vt.; private control; incorporated 1938; liberal arts, education; adult degree program; leadership training for high-school students and music and art center in summer.
Goddard Space Flight Center, NASA N-22
Goddard-Townsend family, 18th-century U.S. furniture designers
furniture F-462, *picture* F-457
Godden, Rumer (born 1907), British author, playwright, and poet; born in Sussex, England; lived in India, then returned to England; for adults, novels, 'Black Narcissus', 'Kingfishers Catch Fire', 'China Court', 'The Battle of the Villa Fiorita'; for children, 'The Mousewife', 'The Fairy Doll', 'Mouse House', 'Mooltiki', 'Miss Happiness and Miss Flower', 'Home Is the Sailor' R-110a, 111d
Gödel, Kurt (1906–78), U.S. mathematician and logician G-174
mathematics M-217, 220
Godetia, a genus of ornamental herbs of the evening primrose family; chiefly hardy low-growing annuals, *Godetia grandiflora*; has numerous pink or crimson flowers; a common one, *Godetia amoena*, is called farewell-to-spring.
Godey, Louis Antoine (1804–78), U.S. publisher, born in New York City; known for publishing first woman's periodical in U.S., *Godey's Lady's Book*, Philadelphia, Pa.
'Godey's Lady's Book', U.S. periodical F-42
etiquette E-322
magazine and journal M-33
'Godfather, The', work by Puzo N-412
Godfrey, Arthur (1903–84), U.S. radio and television entertainer, born in New York City; began career as radio announcer in 1930.
Godfrey, Thomas (1736–63), U.S. dramatist and poet, born in Philadelphia, Pa.; died before his play 'The Prince of Parthia' was either staged or printed
drama D-247
Godfrey of Bouillon (1060?–1100), leader in First Crusade, and first Christian ruler of Jerusalem; hero of Tasso's 'Jerusalem Delivered' C-787
flag, *picture* F-148
Godhavn, settlement in w. Greenland; pop. 554, *maps* N-350, W-297
Godiva, Lady (died 1067), English heroine; subject of legend and poetry; supported and built monasteries C-749
Godkin, Edwin Lawrence (1831–1902), U.S. journalist and author, born in Moyne, near Carlow, Ireland; editor of *New York Evening Post* and *The Nation*; fought corruption.
Godley, John Robert, founder of Canterbury Association, 1848, which planned to establish English settlers in New Zealand C-396
Godman, John Davidson (1794–1830), U.S. physician, anatomist, and naturalist, born in Annapolis, Md.; one of the first in U.S. to prove that ether vapor has anesthetic power.
Godolphin Arabian (or Godolphin Barb), horse, *list* H-249
Godowsky, Leopold (1870–1938), U.S. pianist and composer, born in Vilna, Lithuania; made extensive concert tours; director piano department Chicago Conservatory, 1890–1900; director Master Piano School of Imperial Academy, Vienna, 1902–12; in U.S. after 1912; paraphrases of Bach, Chopin, Johann Strauss; many original compositions.
Godoy, Manuel de (1767–1851), Spanish duke of Alcudia and prince of the Peace, favorite of Charles IV and his queen; dominated Spain during the king's reign; born Badajoz, Spain.
Godoy Alcayaga, Lucila. *see in index* Mistral, Gabriela
Godparent, a sponsor of child Philippines P-253c
'God Save the King' (or God Save the Queen), British national anthem N-65
'God's Grace', work by Malamud A-362
Godthaab, Greenland, capital; on s.w. coast; fishing and sheep raising; first Danish settlement in Greenland; pop. 878, *maps* N-350, W-297
weather station, *picture* R-44
Godunov, Boris. *see in index* Boris Godunov
Godwin, Francis (1562–1633), English bishop, born in Hannington, Northamptonshire; author of 'Man in Moone'.
Godwin, Gail (born 1937), U.S. writer A-363
Godwin, Mary Wollstonecraft (1759–97), English writer and women's rights advocate; birthplace probably London; first novel, printed 1788, led to work for publisher; left London 1792 to witness French Revolution, returned 1795; in 1797 married William Godwin, who with Thomas Paine, William Blake, and others made up radical group on which she had great influence; died at birth of daughter, Mary, who became wife of Shelley
literary contribution E-273
women's rights W-276, *list* W-275
Godwin, Parke (1816–1904), U.S. journalist, essayist, and editor, born in Paterson, N.J., for years with *New York Evening Post*; compiled two biographical encyclopedias; wrote 'Out of the Past'; 'Vala'; 'Political Essays'.
Godwin, William (1756–1836), English political writer and novelist, born in Wisbeck, England; radical believer in freedom, power of reason ('Inquiry concerning Political Justice'); married Mary Wollstonecraft, 1797; inspired young writers, notably Bulwer-Lytton, and Shelley, who married Godwin's daughter, Mary; many financial difficulties (novels, 'St. Leon'; 'Adventures of Caleb Williams')
anarchism's roots A-388
literary contribution E-273
Godwin Austen, Mount, peak. *see in index* K2
Godwine, earl of Wessex (died 1053), most powerful man in Britain of his day; favorite of Canute; helped raise Edward the Confessor to English throne.
Godwit, shorebird of family Scolopacidae; the marbled godwit *Limosa fedoa* is about 18 in (46 cm) long; ranges from s. Alberta, s. Manitoba, and South Dakota to Ecuador and Peru; another species is the Hudsonian godwit *Limosa haemastica*; it grows to be 15 in (38 cm) long; ranges from Arctic regions of North America to Chile, Argentina, Patagonia, and the Falkland Islands.
Goebbels, Joseph Paul (1897–1945), German Nazi leader, born in Rheydt, near Düsseldorf; minister of propaganda after 1933; committed suicide G-123
Hitler H-177
Goering, Hermann Wilhelm (1893–1946), German Nazi leader, premier of Prussia, minister of aviation, president of Reichstag, chief of secret police, field marshal, marshal of the Reich; born Rosenheim, Bavaria; sentenced to death for war crimes Sept. 1946; committed suicide Oct. G-123, *picture* G-124
Hitler H-177, *picture* H-176
World War II W-324, 337
Goes, Hugo van der (1440?–82), Dutch painter of early Netherlands school; most important work Portinari altarpiece, now in the Uffizi Gallery, Florence, Italy.
Goethals, George Washington (1858–1928), U.S. Army officer and engineer of Panama Canal G-174
Panama Canal P-93
Goethe, Johann Wolfgang von (1749–1832), German author G-174
drama D-245
'Faust' F-49, P-537
German literature G-106, *picture* G-105
Schiller S-53
Vico V-308
'Wilhelm Meister's Apprenticeship' N-410
Goffe, William (1605?–79?), British military officer under Cromwell, one of judges who signed death warrant of Charles I of England, later fled to America and lived in New Haven, Conn., and Hadley, Mass.
Gog and Magog, in Bible, names of a king and his land (Ezek. xxxviii–xxxix), also of leaders in last battle against Christ's followers (Rev. xx); also names of two huge wooden statues in London Guildhall, which are more than 9 ft (3 m) high.
Gogebic Range, an iron region in Gogebic County, in upper peninsula of Michigan; extends into Wisconsin.
Gogh, Vincent Van (1853–90), Dutch artist P-54, 56
'Bedroom at Arles' P-56, *picture* P-57
book R-112
The Netherlands N-127
Gogol, Nikolai (1809–52), Russian novelist and dramatist G-175
drama D-246
Russian literature R-360, *picture* R-359
Goiás (or Goyaz), state in interior Brazil, chiefly forested highlands; 240,506 sq mi (622,907 sq km); cap. Goiânia (pop. 132,577); pop. 3,967,907 B-408, *map* B-425
Goidels. *see in index* Gaels
Goiter, an enlargement of the thyroid gland
food and nutrition F-279
malnutrition M-77
hormones, *diagram* H-243
iodized salt S-31
Golan Heights, strategic area in s.w. corner of Syria adjacent to Israel and Jordan S-550
Golconda, India, ruined city 5 mi (8 km) w. of city of Hyderabad; diamond-cutting center in 16th century; name hence used to mean a rich mine, *map* I-86
Gold (Au), metallic chemical element G-176. *see also in index* Gold rush; Gold standard
alchemy A-273
arthritis' treatment A-650
green gold. *see in index* Green gold
international trade I-271
metal and metallurgy M-309
metalworking M-310
Midas M-383
minerals M-432
money M-530, *picture* M-531
ore O-600
periodic table, *table* P-207, *list* P-208
silver by-product S-204
uses
beads and beadwork B-114
masks M-186
wire W-245
world distribution
Africa A-105
Central African Republic C-252
South Africa S-267
Zimbabwe Z-453
Australia A-774
Brazil B-413
Canada
Dominican Republic D-227
Philippines P-257
United States U-82, 85
Alaska A-246
Black Hills B-306
Colorado D-103, *picture* U-82
South Dakota S-324, *map* S-326, *pictures* S-325, 331
Goldberg, Arthur Joseph (1908–86), U.S. lawyer and government official, born in Chicago, Ill.; practiced law in Chicago 1929–61; general counsel Congress of Industrial Organizations 1948–55, United Steelworkers of America 1948–61; U.S. secretary of labor 1961–62; associate justice U.S. Supreme Court 1962–65; ambassador to United Nations 1965–68; chairman United Nations Association of U.S.A. 1968–70.
Goldberg, Bertrand (born 1913), U.S. architect, born in Chicago, Ill.; head Bertrand Goldberg Associates in Chicago 1937–
Marina City, *picture* R-213
construction signaling system, *picture* S-195b
Goldberg, Rube (1883–1970), U.S. cartoonist G-182
Goldberger, Joseph (1874–1929), U.S. public health official and medical research worker G-182
pellagra V-358
Gold Coast (now Southport), city in southern Australia; pop. 66,558 A-788, *map* A-819
Gold Coast, Colony of the. *see in index* Ghana
Gold Creek, Mont., gold rush town M-554
Gold-dust, a spring flowering perennial *Alyssum saxatile* of the mustard family, native to Europe; low growing; grayish leaves; flowers golden-yellow, in clusters; used in rock gardens; also called golden tuft, basket-of-gold, rock madwort.
Golden, Colo., city about 12 mi (19 km) w. of Denver; malt products, porcelains; Colorado School of Mines; pop. 12,237.
Golden Age, period of great happiness, prosperity and achievement
Athens P-205
Latin literature L-76
Persia P-214
Russia R-360
Spain S-365a
Golden apples, in classical mythology, guarded by the Hesperides H-138
'Golden Ass' (Latin 'De Asino Aureo'), satirical romance by Lucius Apuleius; concerns the adventures of one Lucius who is transformed into an ass; thus disguised he observes the preposterous behavior of humankind until, enlightened by his experiences, he emerges a new man; story includes the well-known fairy tale 'Cupid and Psyche'.
Golden bell. *see in index* Forsythia
'Golden Bough: a Study in Magic and Religion, The', work by Frazer F-389
'Golden Boy', statue in Winnipeg, Man. W-240
Golden brown (or golden algae), any of a major group (Chrysophyta) of algae, including diatoms, with yellowish green to golden brown pigments obscuring the chlorophyll A-284
Golden Bull, originally any charter with golden seal or bulla; especially edict issued 1356 by Emperor Charles IV F-378, G-121
Golden calf, image made by Israelites from their earrings at instigation of Aaron while Moses was absent on Mt. Sinai receiving the Ten Commandments (Bible, Exod. xxxii).
Goldenchain, a tree. *see in index* Laburnum
'Golden Dog, The' (or 'Le Chien d'or'), work by Kirby C-121
Golden eagle, bird *Aquila chrysaetos* E-2
characteristics B-278
Golden eardrops. *see in index* Dicentra
Goldeneye (or whistler), a diving duck; two species, the Barrows (*Glaucionetta islandica*) and the American (*Glaucionetta clangula*) with a large head; male has striking black and white markings D-285
Golden Fleece, sought by the Argonauts C-232
Golden Fleece, Order of the, order of knighthood in Austria and Spain; membership limited to 24 knights exclusive of sovereign; independent branches in Austria and Spain after 1700; Austrian order

WINNERS OF MAJOR GOLF TOURNAMENTS (1977–1987)

	U.S. Open	British Open	Canadian Open	U.S. Women's Open
1977	Hubert Green	Tom Watson	Lee Trevino	Hollis Stacy
1978	Andy North	Jack Nicklaus	Bruce Lietzke	Hollis Stacy
1979	Hale Irwin	Severiano Ballesteros	Lee Trevino	Jerilyn Britz
1980	Jack Nicklaus	Tom Watson	Bob Gilder	Amy Alcott
1981	David Graham	Bill Rogers	Peter Oosterhuis	Pat Bradley
1982	Tom Watson	Tom Watson	Bruce Lietzke	Janet Alex
1983	Larry Nelson	Tom Watson	John Cook	Jan Stephenson
1984	Fuzzy Zoeller	Severiano Ballesteros	Greg Norman	Hollis Stacy
1985	Andy North	Sandy Lyle	Curtis Strange	Kathy Baker
1986	Ray Floyd	Greg Norman	Bob Murphy	Jane Geddes
1987	Scott Simpson	Nick Faldo	Curtis Strange	Laura Davies
	Masters	**PGA**	**U.S. Amateur**	**LPGA**
1977	Tom Watson	Lanny Wadkins	John Fought	Chako Higuchi
1978	Gary Player	John Mahaffey	John Cook	Nancy Lopez
1979	Fuzzy Zoeller	David Graham	Mark O'Meara	Donna Caponi Young
1980	Severiano Ballesteros	Jack Nicklaus	Hal Sutton	Sally Little
1981	Tom Watson	Larry Nelson	Nathaniel Crosby	Donna Caponi
1982	Craig Stadler	Ray Floyd	Jay Sigel	Jan Stephenson
1983	Severiano Ballesteros	Hal Sutton	Jay Sigel	Patty Sheehan
1984	Ben Crenshaw	Lee Trevino	Scott Verplank	Patty Sheehan
1985	Bernhard Langer	Hubert Green	Sam Randolph	Nancy Lopez
1986	Jack Nicklaus	Bob Tway	Buddy Alexander	Pat Bradley
1987	Larry Mize	Larry Nelson	Bill Mayfair	Jane Geddes

Gomphrena. *see in index* Globe amaranth

Gomulka, Wladyslaw (1905–82), Polish political leader G-194, P-415

Gonad, sex organ R-151c
disorders D-182
hormones H-243

Goncharov, Ivan Alexandrovich (1812–91), Russian novelist, born in Simbirsk, now Ul'yanovsk, U.S.S.R.; wrote 'Oblomov', which gave Russia the term "Oblomovism" as a synonym for weak will and indolence R-360, 361

Goncourt, Edmond de (1822–96), French novelist and historian, born in Nancy; in collaboration with brother **Jules de** (1830–70), novelist, born in Paris, wrote valuable studies of French society; novels continued realistic method of Flaubert and influenced Zola ('Germinie Lacerteaux', called the clinic of love; 'Renée Mauperin', a story of young Parisian society girl; 'Madame Gervaisais', study of mysticism) F-397. *see also in index* Académie Goncourt

Gondar, religious center and former capital of Ethiopia, Africa, in the n., 250 mi (400 km) from Red Sea; pop. 30,734, *picture* E-313, *map* A-115

Gondola, long narrow Venetian boat V-277, *pictures* I-385, V-278

Gondola car, a railroad car, *picture* R-83

Gonds, an aboriginal people of India, who maintained independence until 18th century; Central Provinces corresponded roughly to their kingdom.

Gondwana (or Gondwanaland), prehistoric continent E-26
Africa A-94
Antarctica A-473
Latin America L-58

Goneril, one of Lear's two cruel daughters, in Shakespeare's tragedy 'King Lear'.

'Gone with the Wind', novel by Mitchell M-511
American literature A-358
historical novel N-409
motion picture M-622, *pictures* A-359, M-625
young adult reading R-112

Gong, a musical instrument
sound waves S-259

Góngora y Argote, Luis de (1561–1627), Spanish poet and priest, born in Córdoba; from comparatively simple ballads and satires he turned to elaborate and obscure poems S-365a

Goniometer, optical instrument for measuring angles; consists of telescope, light source, reflector crystal, and coordinate axes; for mineral identification.

Gonne, Maud (1865–1953), Irish patriot and actress, born in Aldershot, Surrey, England
Yeats Y-412

Gonorrhea, a disease V-273. *see also in index* Venereal disease
infectious disease D-182, *table* D-171

Gonyaulax, algae B-224, *picture* L-269

Gonzaga, Thomas Antonio (1744–1807), Brazilian writer L-72

Gonzaga University, university in Spokane, Wash.; Roman Catholic; opened 1889; arts and sciences, business administration, education, engineering, law; graduate studies W-52

Gonzales, Richard Alonzo (nickname Pancho) (born 1928), U.S. tennis player, born in Los Angeles, Calif.; U.S. singles champion 1948 and 1949; turned professional 1949, world champion 1953–61; author of 'Man with a Racket'
tennis T-107

Gonzalez, Henry Barbosa (born 1916), U.S. political leader, born in San Antonio, Tex.; city councilman, San Antonio, 1953–56, mayor pro-tem 1955–56; state senator 1956–61; U.S. congressman 1961–; first Texan of Mexican descent in Congress.

Gonzalez, Julio (1876–1942), Spanish sculptor and painter, born in Barcelona, Spain; taught metal techniques to Picasso S-93
metalworking M-311

González, Manuel (1833–93), Mexican general, born near Matamoros, Tamaulipas, Mexico; friend of Diaz, whom he aided in revolution of 1876; succeeded Diaz as president 1880–84.

Gonzalo de Córdoba, Hernández y Aguilar (1453?–1515), Spanish general, born in Montilla, near Córdoba, Spain; his many conquests made him famous throughout Europe.

Good, James William (1866–1929), U.S. secretary of war under President Hoover; born in Cedar Rapids, Iowa; Republican congressman from Iowa 1909–23.

Good, something conforming to the moral order of the universe
ethics and morality E-309

'Good as Gold', work by Heller A-361

'Goodbye Columbus', work by Roth A-362

Good Counsel College, college in White Plains, N.Y.; private control; for women; established in 1923; arts and sciences, teacher education.

Good Country, region in Luxembourg L-340

Goode, George Brown (1851–96), U.S. naturalist, born in New Albany, Ind.; assistant secretary Smithsonian Institution 1887–96 ('American Fishes'; 'Oceanic Ichthyology', with T. H. Bean; 'Principles of Museum Administration').

'Good Earth, The', novel (1931) by Buck; won 1932 Pulitzer prize; dramatized on stage and screen R-112, A-359, B-478

Goode's projection, maps, *picture* M-125

Good Friday, the Friday before Easter observed in churches as the anniversary of the crucifixion of Christ; legal holiday in some states of the U.S. E-41
fasting F-44

Good Hope, Cape of, promontory near southern tip of Africa C-148, B-330, *maps* A-115, S-264, W-297

Goodhue, Bertram Grosvenor (1869–1924), U.S. architect, born in Pomfret Hill, Conn.; designed churches, cathedrals, and chapels in which Gothic was adapted to modern methods of construction (his last and probably greatest being the Rockefeller Chapel at the University of Chicago), used sculpture as integral part of building rather than surface ornament; for Nebraska State Capitol conceived design not only impressive but unique among buildings of this type.

Goodman, Benny (full name Benjamin David Goodman) (1909–86), clarinetist, orchestra conductor, born in Chicago, Ill.; remarkable for versatility, having won fame both as conductor of popular music and swing concerts and as clarinet soloist with symphony orchestras
Holiday H-202
popular music M-684

Good manners. *see in index* Etiquette

Good-neighbor policy, principles of friendship, cooperation, and noninterference in the internal affairs of another country R-273

Goodnow, Frank Johnson (1859–1939), U.S. educator and legal scholar, born in Brooklyn, N.Y.; on faculty at Columbia University 1883–1913; president Johns Hopkins University 1914–29; books include 'Social Reform and the Constitution' and 'Principles of Constitutional Government'.

Goodpaster, Andrew Jackson (born 1915), U.S. Army officer, born in Granite City, Ill.; aide to Presidents Eisenhower, Kennedy, Johnson, and Nixon; deputy commander U.S. forces in Vietnam 1968–69; supreme allied commander in Europe 1969–.

Good Queen Bess. *see in index* Elizabeth I

Goodrich, Benjamin Franklin (1841–88), U.S. physician and industrialist, born in Ripley, N.Y.; founded Akron, Ohio, rubber industry A-221

Goodrich, Samuel Griswold (pen name Peter Parley) (1793–1860), U.S. author, born in Ridgefield, Conn.; U.S. consul, Paris, France, 1851–53.

Goodspeed, Edgar Johnson (1871–1962), U.S. classical Greek and Biblical scholar, born in Quincy, Ill.; professor at University of Chicago 1898–1937; with J.M.P. Smith translated the Bible into modern English ('The Story of the Bible'; 'The Story of the Apocrypha'; 'How to Read the Bible'; 'A Life of Jesus'; 'As I Remember', autobiography; 'The Twelve, the Story of Christ's Apostles').

Good Templars, International Order of, society to promote worldwide prohibition of liquor and total abstinence for the individual; organized Syracuse, N.Y. 1851; prohibition party and Woman's Christian Temperance Union grew from it T-80

'Good Vibrations', song by The Beach Boys M-681

Goodwick, Wales. *see in index* Fishguard and Goodwick

Goodwill, the reputation, good standing, esteem, and public confidence in an organization, which in the transfer of a business can be sold like any other property.

Goodwill Industries, autonomous, non-profit workshops providing training, employment, and rehabilitation for disabled persons; founded by Edgar J. Helms in 1902 at Boston, then spread throughout world; main work is repair and resale of articles contributed by public; many programs subsidized by community charity funds.

Goodwin, Hannibal, U.S. amateur photographer; inventor of Celluloid film M-616
Newark, N.J. N-150

Goodwin Sands, range of dangerous shoals off s.e. coast of England, at n. entrance to Straits of Dover; scene of many wrecks.

Goodyear, Charles (1800–60), U.S. inventor, born in New Haven, Conn.; inventor of process of vulcanizing rubber R-306

rubber vulcanization I-274, *picture* I-275, *table* I-273

Goodyear, Charles, Jr. (1833–96), U.S. industrialist, born in Germantown, Pa.; promoted development of welt-shoe machinery S-179

Goodyear, Miles (1817–49), U.S. pioneer settler in Utah, born in New Haven, Conn.; worked his way west 1836 to Fort Hall, Idaho, with Marcus Whitman's party; as trapper and fur trader in Snake River region, he earned place as one of famed Mountain Men of the West; built Fort Buenaventura 1845 on site of present Ogden, Utah; sold it to Mormons 1847 and moved to California.

Goodyear welt, shoe construction method S-180, *picture* S-181

Googe, Barnabe (1540–94), English poet, born in Lincolnshire; his eclogues among earliest English pastoral poetry ('Eglogs, Epytaphes, and Sonettes').

Gooney bird (or black-footed albatross), a dusky ocean bird with whitish face; bill and feet dark; 7 ft (2.1 m) wingspread; nests on islands in central and w. Pacific; often collides with planes taking off or landing A-244

Goosander, a diving duck. *see in index* Merganser

Goose D-284
- Canadian D-285, *pictures* D-284, 287
- lifespan, *chart* A-423
- migration A-450
  - wild goose refuge, *picture* N-364
- Roman empire legend R-244
- wool W-288

Goose Airport, airport in Goose Bay, Newf. N-167

Goose barnacle, crustacean *Lepas fascicularis*, *picture* C-791

Goose Bay, Newf., home of Goose Airport, an important military and commercial airbase N-165, *map* C-109

Gooseberry, Mr. *see in index* Groseilliers, Médart Chouart, sieur de

Gooseberry. *see in index* Berry

Gooseflesh (or goose pimples), roughness of the skin produced by erection of its papillae usually from cold or fear S-211
- hair H-8

Goosefoot. *see in index* Lamb's quarters

Goosefoot family (or Chenopodiaceae), a family of plants and shrubs including saltbush, orach, quail bush, beet, mangel, wormseed, mock cypress, spinach, winter fat, and Russian thistle.

Goose Lake, lake on the boundary of California and Oregon; near Lakeview, Ore.; about 30 mi (50 km) long and 10 mi (16 km) wide.

Gooseneck die-casting (or piston die-casting) D-139

'Goose with the Golden Eggs, The', fable, *table* F-4

Goossens, Eugene (1893–1962), British musician, born in London; opera conductor in England; conductor Rochester, N.Y., Philharmonic Orchestra 1923–31, Cincinnati Symphony Orchestra 1931–47, Sydney, Australia, Symphony Orchestra 1947–56; composed 'Judith' and 'Don Juan', operas, also orchestral works.

G.O.P. *see in index* Grand Old Party; Republican party

Gopher (or pocket gopher), a rodent G-194
- food gathering A-429

Gopher State. *see in index* Minnesota

Gopher tortoise, reptile *Gopherus polyphemus* found in s.e. United States; lives in burrows in dry, sandy, barren regions T-330

Gorakhnath (fl. late 10th century?), Hindu master yogi Y-421

Gorbachev, Mikhail (born 1931), head of government of U.S.S.R. G-195, *picture* R-326
- Soviet history R-358

Gorbatko, Viktor V. (born 1934), Soviet cosmonaut, born in Kuban region in n. Caucasus; research engineer in Soyuz 7, *table* S-348

Gorboduc, mythical king of Britain; subject of first English tragedy. *see also in index* Dorset, Thomas Sackville, earl of.

Gordian knot, curious knot at Gordium, Asia Minor
- Alexander the Great A-279

Gordin, Jacob, Yiddish playwright Y-419

Gordium, ancient capital of Phrygia A-279

Gordon, Adam Lindsay (1833–70), one of most popular and distinctive of Australian poets, born in Fayal, island of Azores, *table* A-798

Gordon, Anna Adams (1853–1931), U.S. temperance worker, born in Boston, Mass.; secretary to Frances E. Willard 21 years; president International Woman's Christian Temperance Union ('Songs for Young Americans'; 'Life of Frances E. Willard'; 'Toots, and Other Stories', for children)
- Sudan S-503

Gordon, Charles Williams. *see in index* Connor, Ralph

Gordon, Chinese (or Charles George Gordon) (1833–85), British army officer G-195
- Kitchener avenges death K-251
- Mahdi M-48

Gordon, Lord George (1751–93), English agitator, born in London; headed anti-Catholic movement that resulted in Gordon riots of 1780.

Gordon, George Angier (1853–1929), U.S. Congregational minister, born in Aberdeenshire, Scotland; pastor, Old South Church, Boston, 1884–1929; university preacher to Harvard and Yale universities.

Gordon, John Brown (1832–1904), U.S. politician and Confederate general, later governor of and senator from Georgia; born in Upson County, Ga.; lecturer on Civil War; author of 'Reminiscences of the Civil War'.

Gordon, Judah Leob (1830–92), Russian-Jewish writer, born in Vilna, Lithuania; often called "poet laureate of the Haskalah" (movement for Jewish enlightenment); lyrics, satires.

Gordon, Juliette. *see in index* Low, Juliette

Gordon, Kermit (1916–76), U.S. government official, born in Philadelphia, Pa.; joined faculty Williams College 1946, professor of economics 1955–61; director Bureau of the Budget 1962–65; vice-president Brookings Institution 1965–67, president 1967–76.

Gordon, Mary (born 1845), U.S. author A-363

Gordon, Richard F., Jr. (born 1929), U.S. astronaut, born in Seattle, Wash.; U.S. Navy officer chosen for NASA program 1963 S-347, *table* S-348

Gordon College, college in Wenham, Mass.; private control; founded 1889; arts and sciences, education; graduate division in theology.

Gordone, Charles (born 1925), U.S. playwright, born in Cleveland, Ohio; his comedy 'No Place to Be Somebody' was first off-Broadway play to win Pulitzer prize (1970); acted in all-black production of 'Of Mice and Men'; also director and producer; National Institute of Arts and Letters Award (1971).

Gordon riots, London, England, on June 2, 1780, by a mob led by Lord George Gordon; caused by objections to repeal in 1778 of Catholic penal laws; Roman Catholic chapels and houses of magistrates were burned; Newgate prison wrecked and prisoners liberated.

Gordon setter, dog, *picture* D-198

Gordy, Wilbur Fisk (1854–1929), U.S. educator and historian, born near Salisbury, Md. ('A School History of the United States', 'Colonial Days'; 'Leaders in Making America').

Goren, Charles Henry (born 1901), U.S. bridge expert, born in Philadelphia; national bridge champion 21 times; books on bridge translated into many languages; daily column syndicated; elected to Bridge Hall of Fame 1964.

Gorgas, Josiah (1818–83), U.S. army officer who became a general in the army of the Confederate States of America; directed the production of armaments for the Confederacy during the U.S. Civil War G-195

Gorgas, William Crawford (1854–1920), U.S. Army officer and sanitary engineer G-195
- Hall of Fame, *table* H-16
- Panama Canal P-93

Gorge, a young valley in the geological sense; may be millions of years old; age detectable by steepness of sides, which level in time. *see also in index* Canyon

Gorges, Ferdinando, Sir (1566?–1647), English colonial proprietor in North America, born in Somersetshire, England; founder of Maine; called Father of English colonization in America
- Maine M-55
- New Hampshire N-179

Gorgias (485?–380? BC), Greek orator and sophist noted for florid eloquence, born in Sicily; one of Plato's dialogues is named for him.

Gorgons, in Greek mythology, three female monsters (Medusa, Stheno, and Euryale) P-210

Gorgonzola, Italy, town in Lombardy; 11 mi (18 km) n.e. of Milan; center of cheese-producing district.

Gorham, Jabez (1792–1869), U.S. silversmith, born in Providence, R.I.; founder of famous Gorham silverware company R-181, *picture* R-190

Gorham, Nathaniel (1738–96), U.S. businessman and statesman, born in Charlestown, Mass.; member of Continental Congress 1782, 1783, and 1785–87, president 1786; signed United States Constitution.

Gorilla, type of ape, *pictures* Z-461, 463, 465

Gorizia, Italy, 20 mi (30 km) n.w. of Trieste; capital of former Austrian crownland of Gorizia and Gradisca; ceded to Italy by Treaty of Rapallo (1920); pop. 42,187, *map* I-401

Gorki, Maksim (Aleksei Maksimovich Peshkov) (1868–1936), Russian revolutionist and writer G-196
- Gorki, U.S.S.R. G-196
- Russian literature L-128, N-411, R-360a

Gorky (or Gor'kiy, formerly [until 1932] Nizhniy Novgorod), U.S.S.R., trade center of e. on Volga River, 255 mi (410 km) s.e. of Moscow; pop. 1,382,000 G-196, *map* E-360, R-322
- world, *map* W-297

Görlitz, East Germany, city on Polish border, on Neisse River, 55 mi (90 km) e. of Dresden; lignite mining; textiles, metal and leather products; pop. 89,284, *map* G-131

Gorman, Willis Arnold (1816–76), U.S. lawyer, soldier, and 2nd territorial governor of Minnesota (1853–57); born near Flemingsburg, Ky., served in Civil War with distinction, became brigadier general.

Gorrie, John (1803–55), U.S. physician, born in Charleston, S.C.; settled in Apalachicola, Fla., 1833; invented mechanical refrigeration; obtained patent 1851; applied principle to cooling sickrooms and hospitals R-138
- Statuary Hall, *table* S-437a

Gorse. *see in index* Furze

Gorton, John Grey (born 1911), Australian government official, born in Melbourne; senator from Victoria Province 1950–68; held various government offices 1958–68; prime minister (Liberal) 1968–71; defense minister 1971.

Gorton, Samuel (1592?–1677), New England colonist, author, founder of 'Gortonites,' religious sect; born in Gorton, England; removed to Mass. 1637; after stormy years because of religious beliefs settled in Warwick, R.I., 1648; in Rhode Island legislature 1649–66 R-185

Gortyna, ancient town in central Crete, largest except for Cnossus; flourished under Romans; destroyed by Saracens in 8th century.

Gosbank, state bank, U.S.S.R. B-70

Goschen, William Edward (1847–1924), British diplomat; ambassador to Germany, 1908–14; also served in Yugoslavia, Denmark, and Austria-Hungary.

Gosden, Freeman Fisher (1899–1982), U.S. radio and television writer, also actor, born in Richmond, Va.; with Charles J. Correll created radio serial 'Amos 'n' Andy' and wrote script for TV serial; played character Amos.

Goshawk, hawk *Accipiter gentilis* of the northern parts of both Europe and the Western Hemisphere; larger than a crow, and has a white stripe above and behind the eye
- predatory characteristics B-278

Goshen, Bible's Old Testament name of region where Jacob and his sons settled in Egypt; probably w. of modern Suez Canal (Bible, Gen. xiv, 10).

Goshen, Ind., city in agricultural area 23 mi (37 km) s.e. of South Bend; automatic switches, rubber products, furniture, boats, mobile homes; Goshen College; pop. 19,665
- Indiana, *map* I-102

Goshen College, college in Goshen, Ind.; Mennonite; chartered 1894; arts and sciences, education, nursing, theology; graduate studies; trimester system.

Goslar, West Germany, city in Lower Saxony; Romanesque palace from the 11th century and several Romanesque and Gothic churches; tourist center for Harz Mountain trips; pop. 40,045, *map* G-131

Goslin, Leon Allen (nickname Goose) (1900–71), U.S. baseball outfielder, born in Salem, N.J.; player for Washington, A.L., 1921–30, 1933, 1938, St. Louis, A.L., 1930–32, Detroit, A.L., 1934–37; 6 straight hits in 1924 world series; batted .300 or better in 11 of 18 seasons (.379 in 1928); lifetime batting average .316.

Gosling, young goose D-285

Gosnold, Bartholomew (died 1607), English navigator and explorer, leading colonist of Jamestown, Va.; died there
- New England explorations A-332

Gospel music, religious music
- popular music M-679

Gospels, first four books of the Bible's New Testament (Matthew, Mark, Luke, and John) giving an account of the life and teachings of Jesus Christ A-507
- Bible B-183
- Jesus Christ J-103, C-398

Gossaert, Jan (or Jenni Gossart, or Mabuse) (1478?–1533), first of the "Italianized" Flemish painters; called Mabuse from his birthplace, Maubeuge, France.

Gossamer, filamentous substance spun by spiders S-383

Gosse, Edmund William (1849–1928), English poet and critic, born in London ('Aspects and Impressions', criticism; 'Father and Son', biography; with Richard Garnett 'English Literature; an Illustrated Record').

Gosse, Philip Henry (1810–88), British naturalist, born in Worcester, England ('The Ocean'; 'The Romance of Natural History')
- aquarium A-517

'Gösta Berling's Saga', story by Selma Lagerlöf based on legends and traditions about a romantic character who lived in a provincial part of southern Sweden during the first part of the 19th century.

Göta, Canal, canal in Sweden S-523, *map* S-524

Götaland, region s. part of Sweden S-523

Gotama. *see in index* Gautama

Gotch, Frank (1878–1917), U.S. wrestler W-366

Göteborg (or Gothenburg), Sweden, 2nd city, chief port, and a factory center, on s.w.

coast at mouth of Göta River; ships, furniture, textiles; pop. 451,079 S-523, *maps* S-524, P-417
  Europe, *map* E-360

'Go Tell It on the Mountain', novel by Baldwin A-362

Gotha, East Germany, city 14 mi (22 km) w. of Erfurt; publishing center; was joint capital with Coburg of Duchy of Saxe-Coburg-Gotha; Friedenstein Castle; pop. 56,334, *map* G-131

Gotha, German bomber A-156, *picture* A-155

Gotham, England, village in Nottinghamshire, inhabitants of which are said to have played the fool in order to dissuade King John from settling there and burdening them with expense of royal residence; hence called Wise Men of Gotham; also nickname of New York City, first used by Washington Irving in 'Salmagundi' (1807).

Gothardt, Mathis. *see in index* Grünewald, Matthias

Gothenburg, Sweden. *see in index* Göteborg

Gothic, art P-28
  tapestry T-25

Gothic architecture A-551. *see also in index* Cathedral
  English
    cathedrals, *pictures* E-252
      Canterbury Cathedral, *picture* C-143
    Houses of Parliament, *pictures* P-131
    Tudor period T-304
  folk art comparison F-250
  French S-84
    Notre Dame Cathedral. *see in index* Notre Dame
  furniture F-456, *picture* F-455
  Middle Ages M-393
  sculpture S-84

Gothic dress D-262, *picture* D-263

Gothic fiction (or Gothic romance, or Gothic novel), style of literature that developed late in the 18th century G-196
  horror story H-245

Gothic Revival, 19th-century architectural style that evolved from the Gothic and Neoclassic styles; popular in United Kingdom and the U.S. A-560

Gothic school, artistic group in English literature, forerunner to Romantic movement; wrote horror tales and novels filled with the machinery of sensationalism, such as Mary Shelley's 'Frankenstein' E-273

Gothic type. *see in index* Black letter

Goths, a Germanic people composed of two branches, Visigoths and Ostrogoths, who lived in Europe about AD 100–700 G-197, G-121
  language L-230
  Middle Ages M-384
  Ostrogoths R-97
  Visigoths S-357

Gotland (or Gottland), largest island in Baltic Sea, e. of Sweden, to which it belongs; 1,159 sq mi (3,002 sq km); farming; pop. 53,053 S-525, *maps* E-360, S-524

Go-To-Ku-Ji, Buddhist temple in Tokyo, Japan; dedicated to cats C-212

'Götterdämmerung, Die' ('The Twilight of the Gods'), fourth opera in Wagner's series 'The Ring of the Nibelungs' ('Der Ring des Nibelungen') O-568

'Gott erhalte Franz den Kaiser', Austrian national anthem N-66

Gottfried von Strassburg (13th century), German writer G-105

Göttingen, West Germany, city 60 mi (95 km) s. of Hanover; University of Göttingen, founded 1737 by George II, had a noted library of modern literature; pop. 108,991, *map* G-131

Gottschalk, Louis Moreau (1829–69), U.S. pianist and composer, born in New Orleans, La.; played his own compositions throughout U.S. and Latin America; best known for piano pieces ('The Last Hope'; 'Le Bananier').

Gottsched, Johann Christoph (1700–66), German dramatist and critic G-106

Gouache, painting P-67h
  Graves's 'Bird Singing in the Moonlight' P-61, *picture* P-62

Goucher College, Towson, Md.; private control; for women; founded 1885 as Woman's College of Baltimore; opened 1888; changed name 1910; liberal arts, education; graduate study coeducational.

Goudge, Elizabeth (born 1900), English novelist, born in Wells, England; grew up in Wells and Ely, cathedral towns that form the background of 'A City of Bells'; other books 'Towers in the Mist'; 'Green Dolphin Street'; 'Pilgrim's Inn'; 'Gentian Hill'; 'Heart of the Family'; 'The Rosemary Tree'; 'The White Witch'; 'Dean's Watch'; 'My God and My All', life of St. Francis; for younger readers: 'Linnets and Valerians'; 'The Child from the Sea'; short stories; plays.

Goudy, Frederic William (1865–1947), U.S. type designer and printer, born in Bloomington, Ill.; created more than a hundred type faces; author of several books on lettering and type design; lecturer on type design and typography; founded Village Press (name given to his private press wherever he lived); his typographic style has been important in fixing contemporary trends
  type and typography T-338

Gouges, Olympe de (1748–93), French pioneer of feminism, guillotined for defending Louis XVI
  women's rights W-276

Gough, Hubert (1870–1963), British general, commanded Fifth Army during Germany's Somme offensive, March 1918; made scapegoat for failure of his superiors to give him adequate support.

Gough, John Bartholomew (1817–86), U.S. temperance lecturer, born in Sandgate, near Folkestone, England; popular for his earnest but amusing addresses.

Gouin, Lomer (1861–1929), Canadian lawyer and statesman, born in Grondines, near Quebec; Liberal leader; premier and attorney general of Quebec, 1905–20; Canadian minister of justice in King cabinet 1921–24; lieutenant governor of Quebec 1929.

Goujon, Jean (1515?–66?), French Renaissance sculptor and architect; skillful metalworker; assisted in work on the Louvre S-88
  fountains F-335

Goulart, João Belchior Marques (1918–76), Brazilian political leader, born in São Borja, Rio Grande do Sul State; vice-president of Brazil 1956–61, president 1961–64.

Goulburn River, river in Victoria, Australia, tributary of Murray; 330 mi (530 km) long; flows through Lake Eildon and past Shepparton.

Gould, George Jay (1864–1923), U.S. capitalist, born in New York City; eldest son of Jay Gould; controlled many railroads, including the Missouri-Pacific and the Wabash.

Gould, Helen Miller. *see in index* Shepard, Helen Miller Gould

Gould, Jay (or Jason Gould) (1836–92), U.S. capitalist G-197
  Black Friday panic G-218

Gould, Laurence McKinley (born 1896), U.S. geologist, born in Lacota, near Kalamazoo, Mich.; deputy commander Byrd Antarctic expedition 1928–30; professor geology and geography Carleton College, Northfield, Minn., 1932–45, president 1945–63; head of U.S. Antarctic program, International Geophysical Year, 1957–58; professor of geology University of Arizona 1963–.

Gould, Lois (born 1938), U.S. writer A-363

Gould, Morton (born 1913), U.S. pianist and composer, born in Richmond Hill, Long Island, N.Y.; used jazz rhythms in compositions ('American Symphonette'; 'Concertette').

Gounod, Charles (1818–93), French composer O-566

Goupil, Saint René (1607?–42), French missionary, born in Anjou, France; lay brother of Society of Jesus; captured by Iroquois on way to Huron mission and killed near what is now Auriesville, N.Y.; canonized 1930.

Gouraud, Henri Joseph Eugène (1867–1946), French general in World War I, born in Paris; high commissioner in Syria and commander in chief in the Levant 1919; military governor of Paris 1923–37.

Gourd family, varieties of the pumpkin and squash family Cucurbitaceae G-198
  watermelon W-100

Gourd head, bird. *see in index* Wood ibis

Gourlay, Robert Fleming (1778–1863), Canadian author and agitator, born in Fifeshire, Scotland; came to Canada 1817; criticized the poor laws and the 'Family Compact'; banished from Canada until 1842 ('Statistical Account of Upper Canada').

Gourmont, Rémy de (1858–1915), French critic and poet, born in Normandy; an authority on contemporary French literature; defender of naturalism of Huysmans and symbolism of Mallarmé ('A Night in the Luxembourg').

Gout, a metabolic disease D-181

Government G-198, *Reference-Outline* P-435. *see also in index* United States government; names of branches and functions of government; names of countries, provinces, and states, *subhead* government; *see also* Fact Summary with each state article
  African political systems A-99, A-108
  agriculture policy A-130
  American Indians I-142
  anarchy A-388
  bibliography P-436
  bureaucracy B-505
  census C-250
  central bank C-260
  church and state issue C-408
  citizenship C-438
  city C-449, 457
  city-state C-461
  civil disobedience C-463
  civil rights C-468
  constitution C-683
  county
    England U-18
  courts of justice C-746
  democracy D-91
  dictatorship. *see in index* Dictatorship
  economics E-61
    business cycle B-518
    employment and unemployment E-206
      employment agency E-205
    industry's regulation. *see in index* Government regulation of industry
    inflation I-98
    labor and industrial law L-4
    monopolies M-543
    national debt N-24
    taxation T-34
  elections E-145
  Enlightenment E-289
  ethics and morality E-309
  fascism F-37
  federal U-154
  feudalism F-68
  flag representation F-161
  food supply regulations F-287
  geography G-65
  health and medical care
    agencies H-89
    education H-91
    insurance H-95
  history H-170
  housing H-302, 306
  human rights H-319
  initiative, referendum, and recall I-205
  intelligence agencies I-236
  law and legal systems L-91
  liberalism L-146
  libraries L-151
  lobbying L-276
  Mesopotamia B-4
  minority groups M-460
  newspapers N-235
  parliament P-129. *see also in index* Parliaments by name, as Parliament, Australian
  political parties P-431
  political science S-239
  propaganda R-54
  socialism S-233
  state S-428. *see also in index* State government
  Switzerland S-543
  totalitarianism T-234
  warfare W-18
  welfare state W-145

Government agencies G-200. *see also in index* agencies by name, *e.g.,* Intelligence agencies

Government department, United Kingdom, an official establishment G-202

Government Ethics, Office of, U.S. C-469

Government National Mortgage Association (or GNMA, or Ginny May), United States H-304

Government of India Act (1935) I-78

Government of Ireland Act (1920), English legislation I-325

Government ownership, system in which the government controls the means of production G-199. *see also in index* Land, public; Municipal ownership
  Canada
    radio R-54
    Saskatchewan S-49g
  Hungary
    land use control L-29
  railroads. *see in index* Railroad, *subhead* government ownership
  Romania R-317
  Socialism S-233
  Spain S-352
  Sweden S-524
  Switzerland S-540
  totalitarianism T-234
  Uruguay U-214
  U.S.S.R. R-321
  Venezuela V-276

Government Printing Office, the official printing and publishing plant of the U.S. government, established 1860 by act of Congress; supplies all printing, publishing, and stationery needs of the federal government; office is under supervision of a Congressional committee and is managed by the Public Printer who is appointed by the president with the approval of the Senate; superintendent of documents has charge of the sale of government publications.

Government regulation of industry. *see also in index* Government ownership; Municipal ownership
  agriculture U-162
    Agricultural Adjustment Act R-269
  automobile safety A-866
  capitalism C-152
  drugs P-538
  employment and unemployment E-207
  food processing regulations F-284
  franchises F-373
  Italy S-235
  labor movements L-10
  liquor control P-506, A-274
  petroleum resources P-230
  public utilities P-526c, U-165
  pure food laws P-538
  radio R-53
  trade
    Interstate Commerce Commission R-87, R-285

Governor, in state governments in the United States. *see also* Fact Summary with each state article
  duties and powers S-429
  line-item veto V-307

Governor, in mechanics, feedback control mechanism A-833

'Governor and Company of Adventurers of England, trading into Hudson's Bay, The' (or Gentleman Adventurers), English traders F-469

Governor-general
  Australia P-131, A-803
  Canada C-86, P-132
    colonial era C-92

Governors Island, fortified island in New York City harbor at junction of Hudson and East rivers; area about 125 acres (50 hectares); called Nooten Island by Dutch colonists; received present name in late 17th century when colonial governors established a residence there; its Fort Jay a U.S. Army center from early 19th century until 1966, when island became U.S. Coast Guard facility.

Governor Thomas E. Dewey Thruway (formerly New York State Thruway), highway in New York N-253

Gower, John (1325?–1408), English poet, called by Chaucer "moral Gower" and by Lowell "undertaker of the fair medieval legend"; chief work, 'Confessio Amantis', includes many moral stories warning a lover against the vices of that day.

Gowland, Gibson (1872–1951), film actor, born in Spennymoor, England, *picture* M-621

Gown (or houppelande), garment D-262

Gowrie, John Ruthven, 3rd **earl of** (1577?–1600), Scottish nobleman killed, with his brother Alexander, in apparent attempt to assassinate King James VI of Scotland; some evidence that "Gowrie's Conspiracy" may have been a story contrived to hide the king's fault in a quarrel that led to violence.

Gowrie, William, first **earl of** (1541?–84), Scottish nobleman; concerned in murder of Rizzio in 1566; custodian of Mary, queen of Scots, at Lochleven; captured James VI of Scotland in 1582; executed for treason by order of James.

Goya, Francisco de (full name Francisco José de Goya y Lucientes) (1746–1828), Spanish portrait painter, lithographer, and etcher G-203
- 'Don Manuel Osorio de Zuñiga', *picture* C-212
- drawings D-254
- graphic arts G-232, *picture* G-233
- painting P-50
- Prado, *picture* M-30
- 'Señora Sabasa García', *picture* P-50

Goyathlay. *see in index* Geronimo

Goyaz, Brazil. *see in index* Goiás

Goyen, Jan Josephszoon van (1596–1656), Dutch landscape painter, born in Leiden, The Netherlands; depicted typical landscapes with naturalistic truth unmixed with sentiment; cool tints in the skies and scanty detail in foliage P-43

Gozo, island of Malta in Mediterranean 3 mi (5 km) n.w. of Malta; principal city Victoria; 26 sq mi (67 sq km); pop. 27,152, *map* I-404
- Malta M-78

Gozzi, Carlo (1720–1806), Italian dramatist, born in Venice; wrote plays, satirical dramas founded on fairy tales, and tragedies with a comic element; 'Turandot' best known.

Gozzoli, Benozzo (formerly Benozzo di Lese) (1420–98?), Florentine painter; worked first under Fra Angelico; excelled at richly decorative religious frescoes ('Madonna and Child with Saints'; 'Journey of the Magi to Bethlehem'; frescoes depicting lives of St. Francis and St. Augustine).

Grab, oceanography O-464

Graben, in geology M-634, *diagram* P-235

Grabhorn, Edwin (1879–1968) and **Robert Grabhorn,** brothers, contemporary U.S. printers, for many years working in San Francisco; known for skillful use of fine types and careful composition; leaders in group sometimes called California school of printers.

Grab Joint, amusement park concessions A-384

Gracchus, Gaius Sempronius (153–121 BC), Roman popular leader, son of Cornelia and brother of Tiberius Gracchus; as tribune of the people 123–121 BC carried out his brother's judicial and social reforms R-246

Gracchus, Tiberius Sempronius (163–133 BC), Roman tribune in 133 BC proposed agrarian laws and other reforms for relief of poor; murdered in riot caused by his attempt to secure reelection as tribune R-246

Grace (formerly Grace Kelly) (1929–82), princess of Monaco, born in Philadelphia, Pa.; was prominent screen star before marriage to Prince Rainier III in 1956; won 1954 Academy award for 'The Country Girl' and was chosen best actress of 1954 by New York Film Critics; niece of George Kelly
- Monaco M-528

Grace, Eugene Gifford (1876–1960), U.S. steel manufacturer, born in Goshen, N.J.; joined Bethlehem Steel Company as crane operator 1899, president of corporation 1916–46, chairman of board 1946–57.

Grace, in religion, the enjoyment of God's favor; spiritual gift of God by which people are able to choose the right and find salvation; in Roman Catholicism the state of grace is held to be obtained through the sacraments; the term grace is also used for a prayer before or after a meal, asking blessing or returning thanks.

Grace, days of. *see in index* Days of grace

Graceland, Elvis Presley's mansion and burial site in Memphis, Tenn. M-295

Graceland College, college in Lamoni, Iowa; affiliated with The Reorganized Church of Jesus Christ of the Latter-day Saints; incorporated 1895; liberal arts, teacher education.

Grace note, in music, *list* M-670

Graces, in Greek mythology, three daughters of Hera and Zeus: Euphrosyne (joyfulness), Aglaia (brightness), and Thalia (bloom), goddesses of grace and charm, *picture* M-695

Gracián, Baltasar (1601–58), Spanish writer and Jesuit, born in Belmonte, near Madrid; style concise and epigrammatic, but sometimes obscure; best known for philosophical novel 'El Criticón'.

Grackle, blackbird B-305

Grade, established set of standards
- education E-93
- meat industry M-253
- wool W-289

Graduate school U-204
- medicine M-275

Gradus, ancient unit of measure, *table* W-141

Grady, Henry Woodfin (1850–89), U.S. journalist and orator, born in Athens, Ga.; in 1879 he bought share in *Atlantic Constitution*, and as editor did much to restore friendly relations between North and South; lectured on 'The New South'.

Graeae, in Greek mythology, "the gray ones," three sisters, Dino, Enyo, and Pephredas, daughters of Ceto and Phorcys, grayhaired from birth
- Perseus P-210

Graetz, Heinrich (1817–91), German historian, born in province of Posen; professor University of Breslau 20 years; most noted for his scholarly history of the Jews, which has been translated into several languages.

Graffiti (singular graffito or sgraffito), sayings, drawings, verses, or figures found on rocks or walls; modern forms often in a humorous or political vein G-203
- juvenile delinquency J-163

Grafly, Charles (1862–1929), U.S. sculptor, born in Philadelphia, Pa.; noted for symbolical figures and groups and portrait busts; one of foremost U.S. portrait sculptors of day; instructor Pennsylvania Academy of Fine Arts and Boston Museum of Fine Arts.

'Graf Spee, Admiral', a German "pocket battleship"
- *Exeter* model, *picture* S-177

Graft, in plant P-362
- pecan P-151

Graft, in surgery, section of tissue that is removed from its original site and transferred to a new location on the same or different body T-250
- skin S-519c

Grafton, N.D., city in n.e. part of state, on Park River, about 40 mi (65 km) n.w. of Grand Forks; potatoes, grain, and livestock; shipping; state school for mentally retarded; pop. 5,293.

Graham, Billy (full name William Franklin Graham) (born 1918), U.S. evangelist G-204

Graham, Evarts Ambrose (1883–1957), U.S. surgeon, born in Chicago, Ill.; professor of surgery Washington University 1919–51; did pioneer work in lung surgery for cancer.

Graham, Gwethalyn (1913–65), Canadian novelist, born in Toronto, Ont.; books stress social problems ('Swiss Sonata'; 'Earth and High Heaven').

Graham, James, Viscount Dundee. *see in index* Claverhouse

Graham, Katherine (born 1917), U.S. newspaper publisher, *list* N-240

Graham, Martha (born 1893), U.S. dancer and choreographer G-204
- dance D-30, *picture* D-26

Graham, Otto (born 1921), U.S. football quarterback, coach, and general manager; born in Waukegan, Ill.; quarterback Cleveland Browns 1946–55; head coach United States Coast Guard Academy 1959–66; head coach Washington Redskins 1966–68, general manager 1966–69.

Graham, Robert Bontine Cunninghame. *see in index* Cunninghame Graham, Robert Bontine

Graham, Shirley (born 1906), U.S. writer and composer, born in Indianapolis, Ind.; wrote and composed music-drama 'Tom-Tom' (biographical works on Frederick Douglass, Benjamin Banneker, George Washington Carver, Paul Robeson, Phillis Wheatley, and Booker T. Washington).

Graham, Sylvester (1794–1851), U.S. reformer, born in Suffield, Conn.; advocated temperance, vegetarianism, use of whole wheat (graham) bread.

Graham, Thomas (1805–69), Scottish chemist, born in Glasgow; originated term "colloids," and discovered "Graham's law" that diffusion rate of gases varies inversely as square root of their densities
- osmosis O-611

Graham, William Alexander (1804–75); U.S. political leader, born in Lincoln County, N.C.; U.S. senator 1840–43; governor of North Carolina 1845–49; secretary of Navy 1850–52; opposed secession until outbreak of Civil War.

'Graham Children, The', painting by Hogarth P-47, *picture* P-46

Grahame, Kenneth (1859–1932), Scottish writer, born in Edinburgh G-205
- 'The Wind in the Willows' R-111a

Grahamstown, South Africa, town in Cape of Good Hope Province, 70 mi (115 km) n.e. of Port Elizabeth; college center; pop. 32,611, *map* A-115
- shantytown, *picture* S-265

Grahn, Lucile (1821?–1907), Danish ballerina, born in Copenhagen, Denmark; appeared successfully at Paris Opéra; popular in London, where she danced 'Pas de Quatre' (1845) with Taglioni, Grisi, and Cerrito B-33

Grail, Holy. *see in index* Holy Grail

Grain, crystals C-795

Grain, unit of weight, *table* W-140

Grain, grinding. *see in index* Flour and flour milling

Grain alcohol. *see in index* Ethyl alcohol

Grain drill (or seed drill), farm machinery F-32

Grain elevator, building to store grain, either country elevators, to which farmers bring produce, or large terminal elevators, to which the grain is then shipped F-36
- Saskatchewan, *picture* S-49b

Grain exchange. *see in index* Commodity exchange

Grainger, Percy Aldridge (1882–1961), U.S. pianist and composer, born in Melbourne, Australia; settled in U.S. 1915; influenced by friend Edvard Grieg; compositions based chiefly on folk music ('Molly on the Shore'; 'Shepherd's Hey'; 'Country Gardens').

Grainne, in Celtic mythology the Helen of the Fenian cycle of old Irish tales, beautiful young betrothed of the old Finn MacCool deserts him for Dermot, but weds him when Dermot dies.

'Grain of Wheat, A', work by Ngugi N-300

Grains, cereal G-206. *see also in index* Cereal crops

Gram, metric unit of weight W-139, *table* W-141

Gramatky, Hardie (1907–79), U.S. artist, illustrator, and author of children's books; born in Dallas, Tex.; grew up in Calif.; worked at Walt Disney's studio before going to live in New York City; children's books: 'Little Toot'; 'Loopy'; 'Hercules'; 'Creeper's Jeep'; 'Little Toot on the Thames' R-108

Grambling College, college in Grambling, La.; state control; chartered 1901; liberal arts, applied sciences and technology, education, and general studies.

Gramercy Park, a neighborhood in Manhattan, New York, N.Y. N-273

Gramineae. *see in index* Grass family

Grammar G-207
- auxiliary V-281
- connector P-491
- determiner P-508
- education E-82
- language construction L-33, 40, *diagram* L-35
- linguistics L-229
- preposition P-491
- pronoun P-507
- punctuation P-534
- sentence S-110
- verb V-281
- verbal V-282

'Grammar of the Spanish Language', work by Bello L-68

Grammy awards, presented annually by National Academy of Recording Arts and Sciences for best efforts in the recording field.

Grampian Mountains (or Grampian Hills), principal mountain mass in Scotland, really a series of spurs; 150 mi (240 km) long; rugged on n. side but good pastureland on s. S-67
- Ben Nevis. *see in index* Ben Nevis

Grampus. *see in index* killer whale

Granada, former Moorish kingdom in s. Spain; about 11,000 sq mi (28,500 sq km); divided into three modern provinces, of which Granada (4,838 sq mi; 12,530 sq km; pop. 769,408) is one
- history
  - banner, *picture* M-384
  - Ferdinand and Isabella F-55
  - Moors M-581

Granada, Nicaragua, one of chief cities and capital of Granada Department; located on Lake Nicaragua; a rail, commercial, and manufacturing center; founded 1524; pop. 36,037.

Granada, Spain, once capital of Moorish kingdom, now capital of province of the same name, 120 mi (195 km) n.e. of Gibraltar; university; pop. 150,186 S-358, *map* S-350
- Alhambra, *picture* S-358
- cathedral S-356
- Gypsy cave, *picture* S-354

Granadilla, fruit of a tropical passionflower F-436

Granados y Campina, Enrique (1867–1916), Spanish composer, born in Lérida, best known for Spanish dances and opera 'Goyescas'; died as passenger on *Sussex*, which was torpedoed during World War I.

Granahan, Kathryn O'Hay (1890?–1979), U.S. government official, born in Easton, Pa.; Democratic representative from Pennsylvania 1956–62; treasurer of the United States 1963–66.

Granby, Que., city on North Yamaska River 43 mi (69 km) s.e. of Montreal; rubber products, textiles, furniture, refrigerators, tobacco; pop. 34,385, *maps* C-112, Q-10

Granby, Lake, lake in Colorado, formed by Granby Dam on Colorado River C-584

Gran Chaco, South America. *see in index* Chaco

Gran Chimu, Peru. *see in index* Chanchan

Grand Alliance, league of European powers formed against Louis XIV of France in 1689 and renewed in 1701 A-829
- England E-248

Grand Alliance (1815) A-278

Grand Army of the Republic, society of Civil War veterans organized at Decatur, Ill., in 1866 P-140

Grand Bank, Newf., town on Fortune Bay 145 mi (235 km) s.w. of St. John's; base for Grand Banks fisheries; pop. 3,143.

Grand Banks (or Newfoundland Banks),

submarine plateau off island of Newfoundland; valued as fishing grounds A-746, G-212
Canada C-73
Newfoundland N-163, 166
Grand Canal, canal in China, extending from Hangzhou to Peking; oldest and longest canal in existence C-127, 364, *picture* C-357
Asia, *map* A-697
Hangzhou H-30
Grand Canal, canal in Venice, Italy V-277, *picture* I-385
Turner's painting P-47
Grand Canary (Spanish Gran Canaria), one of the Canary Islands; 592 sq mi (1,533 sq km); healthful climate; tourist trade; fishing; fruits, vegetables, sugar, tobacco; pop. 519,606, *map* A-115
Grand Canyon, canyon in n. Arizona, on Colorado River C-584, *picture* G-212
Arizona A-596, 604
ecological problem E-58
formation E-16
Grand Canyon N.P., *map* U-81
Grand Canyon College, Phoenix, Ariz.; affiliated with Southern Baptist Convention; opened 1949; liberal arts, education.
Grand Canyon National Park, park in Arizona N-49, *map* N-40
Grand Canyon G-212
Grand Canyon of the Snake River, long gorge in Snake River where it forms part of Idaho-Oregon boundary; deepest canyon in North America; averages 5,500 ft (1,700 m) depth for 40 miles (65 km); deepest point 7,900 ft (2,400 m) in southern part called Hells Canyon, or Seven Devils Canyon, or Box Canyon
Hells Canyon in Idaho I-17, *picture* I-18
Idaho, *map* I-30
Washington, *picture* W-51
Grand Canyon state. *see in index* Arizona
Grand Comoro, island. *see in index* Comoro Islands
Grand Coulee Dam, dam in Washington, on the Columbia River G-213, C-588
dams D-11
electric power E-166
pumps P-532
salmon industry S-29
Washington W-48, 54, *picture* W-59
waterpower W-106, *picture* W-104
Grande Chartreuse, Carthusian monastery near Grenoble, France M-542, *picture* M-540
Grande Dixence Dam, dam in Switzerland, on Dixence River D-17
Grandee, title of honor borne by highest class of Spanish and Portuguese nobility; from Latin *grandis.*
Grande Prairie, Alta., city 245 mi (395 km) n.w. of Edmonton and 70 mi (115 km) s.e. of Dawson Creek; farming; oil, gas; pop. 17,626, *map* C-109
St. Charles Mission A-250c
Grande-Rivière, La (or the Big River, or Fort George River), river in Canada; rises in Nichicun Lake, Quebec, and flows about 520 mi (835 km) into James Bay; consists largely of several uneven lakes strung together by rapids, *maps* C-112, N-350
Grandes Écoles, French educational system F-352
Grand Falls, Canada. *see in index* Churchill Falls
Grand Falls, N.B., town on Saint John River 90 mi (145 km) n.w. of Fredericton; hydroelectric power plant; potato products; pop. 4,158 N-154
Grand Falls, Newf., industrial center (officially Local Improvement District) on Exploits River about 165 mi (265 km) n.w. of St. John's; paper mill; pop. 8,765 N-165
Grandfather clause, provision formerly included in constitutions of several U.S. Southern states that excuses from other suffrage tests those who have served in any war and their descendants and those who were voters before Jan. 1, 1867, and their descendants; adopted as means of restricting suffrage to white voters; declared unconstitutional 1915 B-293
Grandfather clock W-78, *picture* W-80
Grandfather Mountain, mountain in Blue Ridge Mountains of n.w. North Carolina between Linville and Boone; 5,964 ft (1,818 m); profile resembles reclining giant.
Grand fir. *see in index* Giant fir
Grand Forks, N.D., 3rd city in state, on e. boundary, at junction of Red River of the North and Red Lake River; flour, meat products, potato products; beet sugar; Grand Forks Air Force Base; pop. 43,765 U-40
North Dakota N-374, 382, *picture* N-379
Grand Funk Railroad, heavy metal rock group M-682
Grand Haven, Mich., port and summer resort on Lake Michigan at mouth of Grand River 29 mi (47 km) w. of Grand Rapids; fishing center; metal products, automobile parts; Grand Haven State Park nearby; pop. 11,763.
Grandi, Dino (born 1895), Italian statesman, born in Mordano, near Bologna; identified with Fascist party from its beginning and played conspicuous part in Fascist march on Rome; minister of foreign affairs 1929–32; ambassador to England 1932–39; minister of justice 1939–43; sentenced to die 1944 for taking part in overthrow of Mussolini, escaped to Portugal.
Grand Island, Neb., city about 85 mi (135 km) w. of Lincoln; railroad shops; livestock marketing; food processing, mobile homes; army ordnance installation; State Soldiers and Sailors Home; U.S. Veterans Hospital; pop. 33,180 N-96, 104, *map* U-40
Grand Junction, Colo., agricultural, industrial, and mining center at junction of Colorado and Gunnison rivers, near Utah border; pop. 28,144 C-570, *maps* C-582, U-40
Grand Jury J-158
Henry II establishes E-241, H-129
legal definition, *table* L-92
Grand Lake, largest lake of island of Newfoundland; 15 mi (25 km) s.e. of Corner Brook; length 56 mi (90 km); area 192 sq mi (497 sq km).
Grand Lake (or Lake St. Marys, or Grand Lake St. Marys), largest man-made lake within Ohio; area 20 sq mi (51 sq km) O-498
Grand Lake Lowland, subdivision of a region in Newfoundland N-164
Grand mal, form of epileptic seizure D-179
Grandma Moses. *see in index* Moses, Anna Mary Robertson
Grand Manan Island, island located at mouth of Bay of Fundy in New Brunswick; 16 mi (26 km) long and 7 mi (11 km) wide; supports fisheries; a resort area; pop. 2,295 N-154, *picture* N-157
Grand Mère, Que., city on St. Maurice River, 20 mi (30 km) n.w. of Trois-Rivières; pulp, paper, textiles, clothing; pop. 17,137, *map* Q-10
Grand National, steeplechase horse race held in Lancashire, England H-277, *picture* H-276
Grand Ole Opry, music show in Nashville, Tenn. N-20
country music M-678
Grand Old Party, name given to U.S. Republican party by campaigners in 1880; since shortened to G.O.P. *see also in index* Republican party
Grand piano, musical instrument M-689, *picture* M-687
Grand Portage, nine-mile (fourteen-kilometer) overland carrying route in n.e. Minnesota between Lake Superior and Pigeon River; famous in North American fur trade and exploration history; trading post maintained here by North West Company
national monument, *picture* M-450
Grand Portage National Monument, monument in northeastern Minnesota N-49, *map* N-40
Grand Prairie, Tex., city 12 mi (19 km) s.w. of Dallas; aircraft industry; aluminum boats, concrete pipe, truck bodies; pop. 71,462.
Grand Pré, N.S., historic village about 50 mi (80 km) n.w. of Halifax, in farming and fruit-growing district; scene of Longfellow's 'Evangeline'; pop. 279
Acadia A-14
Nova Scotia N-397, 402, *picture* N-403
Grand Pré National Historic Park, park in Nova Scotia N-30, *map* N-29
Nova Scotia N-402, *picture* N-403
Grand Prix, automobile race A-874
Monaco M-528
Grand Prix de Rome. *see in index* Prix de Rome
Grand Rapids, Mich., 2nd city of state; "furniture capital of United States"; trade center; automobiles, appliances, and paper products; fruit-growing area; pop. 181,843 G-213, *map* U-41
Michigan M-358, 368, *map* N-350
Grand Remonstrance, protest against misgovernment presented to Charles I (1641) by English House of Commons; the king's impeachment of and attempt to arrest the 5 leaders responsible for the Remonstrance were causes of the English Civil War.
Grand River, river in Michigan, rises in Jackson County; flows 260 mi (420 km) n. and w. to Lake Michigan at Grand Haven M-355
Grand River, river in Oklahoma. *see in index* Neosho River
Grand River, river in South Dakota, rises in n.w.; flows nearly 210 mi (340 km) e. to Missouri River; Shadehill Dam located near n. and s. forks about 75 mi (120 km) n.w. of Mobridge built as part of Missouri River basin development, *maps* S-323, 334
Grand River Dam (or Pensacola Dam), dam in n.e. Oklahoma on Grand (Neosho) River; forms Lake of the Cherokees; construction finished 1940.
Grand Sable Dunes, sand dunes in Michigan, *picture* M-365
Grand Slam, in golf G-193
Grand Slam, in tennis T-108
'Grand Testament, Le', work by Villon V-326
Grand Teton National Park, park in Wyoming N-49, *map* N-40
Wyoming W-389
Grand Teton Peak, peak in n.w. Wyoming, in Teton range of Rocky Mountains; 17 mi (27 km) n. of Jackson, in Teton County (13,766 ft; 4,196 m) N-49.
Grand Turk Island, one of Turks and Caicos Islands in West Indies; seat of Grand Turk, chief town of that group; island about 7 mi (11 km) long, 2 mi (3 km) wide; pop. 2,346, *map* W-159
Grand Unified Theories, atomic particles A-757
Grand Valley State College, college in Allendale, near Grand Rapids, Mich.; founded 1960, opened 1963; liberal arts, economics and business administration, education; graduate studies; quarter system.
Grandview, Mo., city 8 mi (13 km) s. of Kansas City; farming, light industry; Richards-Gebaur Air Force Base; incorporated as village 1912, as city 1929; pop. 24,502.
Grange, National (full name National Grange of the Patrons of Husbandry), a major U.S. farm organization G-214
Minnesota M-446
railroad regulations R-87
Grange, Red (full name Harold Edward Grange) (born 1903), U.S. football halfback and sports commentator G-214
football F-297
Granicus, ancient name of small river in n.w. Asia Minor where Alexander the Great won first victory over Persians 334 BC A-279, *map* A-280
Granit, Ragnar (born 1900), Swedish neurophysiologist, born in Finland; professor Royal Caroline Institute 1946–67. *see also in index* Nobel Prizewinners, *table*
Granite G-214, *picture* R-229a
Aberdeen, Scotland A-9
Australia A-774
Earth E-11, E-20, *diagram* E-12
geologic formation R-229, *chart* R-229
minerals M-437
quarrying Q-6, *pictures* M-52, U-46
United States, *picture* U-46
Minnesota, *picture* M-443
Vermont V-287, *map* V-290, *picture* V-294
rock cycle, *chart* R-229
Granite City, Ill., manufacturing city near Mississippi River, just n.e. of St. Louis, Mo.; steel, lead, aluminum, and magnesium products; automobile frames, chemicals, graniteware, corn products, paper products; pop. 36,815
Illinois, *map* I-52
Granite moss (or rock moss), type of moss M-599
Granite Peak, peak in Rocky Mountains, highest point in Montana (12,799 ft; 3,901 m); in s. part of state, n.e. of Yellowstone National Park M-551
Granite State. *see in index* New Hampshire
Graniteware, type of enamelware E-208
Granny knot (or lubber's knot) K-262
Granny square, in needlework N-114
Gran Paradiso, Alpine peak in Italy, *map* I-404
Gran Sasso, mountain group in the Apennines in Italy A-497
Grant, Cary, (adopted name of Archibald Alexander Leach) (1904–86), U.S. motion-picture actor, born in Bristol, England; suave star of more than 70 films including comedies ('The Philadelphia Story'), thrillers ('North by Northwest'), and drama ('Penny Serenade'); Academy award for cumulative contribution to film 1970.
Grant, Duncan James Corrowr (1885–1978), British painter, born in Rothiemurchus, near Kingussie, Scotland; a modernist strongly influenced by Cézanne ('The Lemon Gatherers'; 'Tight-rope Walker').
Grant, Frederick Dent (1850–1912), U.S. general, born in St. Louis, Mo.; accompanied father, Gen. U.S. Grant, in many Civil War campaigns; graduated West Point 1871 but resigned from Army 1881; colonel of volunteers 1898, served in Cuba and Philippines, successively promoted until major general in Regular Army G-216
Grant, George Monro (1835–1902), Canadian clergyman and educator, born in Albion Mines, N.S.; known for his eloquence on political platform scarcely less than in pulpit; for 25 years principal of Queen's University; made it one of leading Canadian institutions.
Grant, Julia Dent (1826–1902), wife of President Grant G-215
Grant, Robert (1852–1940), U.S. judge and author, born in Boston ('Unleavened Bread'; 'The Chippendales'; 'Fourscore—An Autobiography').
Grant, Ulysses S. (1822–85), 18th president of the United States G-215, *picture* C-484
Arthur A-652
Civil War C-475, *pictures* C-484, C-644
Hancock H-26
Lee L-116, *picture* V-334
Sheridan S-161
Sherman S-161
Shiloh C-480
Vicksburg C-482
Gould G-197
Hall of Fame, *table* H-16
Illinois I-41
United States history U-181
Granta (or Grantabridge), England. *see in index* Cambridge
Grant-Kohrs Ranch National Historic Site, historical site in Montana N-50
Grant Land, n.w. part of Ellesmere Island in Canada,

Gray Monks. *see in index* Cistercians

Gray seal, animal S-100

Grays Harbor, inlet of the Pacific, w. coast of Washington; inlet some 15 mi (25 km) long; port city of Aberdeen and an adjacent city, Hoquiam, located on its n. shore.

Gray squirrel S-400, *pictures* S-399, 401
 tracks, *picture* A-464
 young S-401, *picture* S-401

Gray wolf (or timber wolf) W-267
 endangered species E-212

Graz (or Gratz), Austria, city 90 mi (145 km) s.w. of Vienna; iron and steel, machines, leather goods, paper; university and technical schools; medieval buildings; pop. 237,080 A-825, *maps* E-360, B-25

Graziani, Rodolfo (1882–1955), Italian marshal, born 50 mi (80 km) s.e. of Rome; viceroy of Ethiopia 1936–37; commander Italian forces in Africa and governor general Libya 1940–41; defense minister Mussolini's puppet regime 1943–45; found guilty of treason 1950, later released.

Grazing land, nonfarm area where animals feed on grass or other plants. *see also in index* Pastureland
 prairie dogs A-445

'Grease' (1972), musical by Jacobs and Casey M-686

Greasewood, spiny shrub *Sarcobatus vermiculatus* of the goosefoot family with fleshy leaves; common in Rocky Mt. region; grows in alkaline and saline soils; used as indicator of salty soil; farmers avoid land where it is abundant.

Great America, amusement park near Chicago, Ill. A-383

Great Appalachian Valley (or Great Valley), broad, fertile valley in the eastern U.S. A-508
 Maryland M-167
 United States U-36

Great Artesian Basin, largest area of artesian water in the world, primarily underlying Queensland, Australia A-775

Great Atlantic & Pacific Tea Company, The, U.S. retail food chain store company; established as tea stores by George F. Gilman (1826–1901), a hide and leather merchant, and George H. Hartford (1833–1917), an employee who conceived the profitable method of merchandising tea and became partner and manager 1878; Hartford's sons, George L. (1864–1957) and John A. (1872–1951), continued management of the business.

Great auk, extinct bird A-763

Great Awakening, powerful religious revival in the North American colonies from the 1720s to the 1740s; leaders included George Whitefield, Jonathan Edwards, and William and Gilbert Tennent; the revival caused serious divisions in several denominations; missions to American Indians were established; benefits included founding of such colleges as Brown, Rutgers, Princeton, and Dartmouth; another revival in the 1790s has been called the Second Great Awakening
 Edwards E-109
 Whitefield W-195

Great Barrier Reef, reef located off n.e. coast of Australia, longest coral reef in world (1,250 mi; 2,010 km); separated from mainland by channel 10–100 ft. wide G-241
 Australia A-771, *map* A-819
 coral C-714
 Pacific Ocean, *map* P-3

Great Barrier Reef Expedition (1928–29) G-231

Great Basin, region in w. U.S., about 200,000 sq mi (520,000 sq km) between Sierra Nevada and Wasatch Range U-83, *maps* U-32, 36
 California C-35, *map* C-34
 Idaho I-18, *map* I-19
 Nevada N-133
 Oregon O-583
 Utah U-216, *map* U-217

Great Basin National Park, park in east-central Nevada N-50, *map* N-40

Great Bear (or Big Bear, or Ursa Major), constellation containing the Big Dipper A-718, *charts* S-416, 418–19, 421–2, C-681. *see also in index* Big Dipper

Great Bear Lake, lake in Northwest Territories; 12,275 sq mi (31,792 sq km) G-242, *maps* C-109, N-350, W-297
 Mackenzie River M-15
 Northwest Territories N-388

Great Bear River, river in Northwest Territories; flows 70 mi (113 km) into Mackenzie River G-242

Great Belt, in Denmark, strait separating the islands of Fyn on the w., Langeland on the s., and Zealand on the e.; links the larger Kattegat Strait with the Baltic Sea B-46

Great Bend, Kan., city on Arkansas River, 92 mi (148 km) n.w. of Wichita; oil wells nearby; wheat shipping center; oil-field equipment, mobile homes; pop. 16,608.

Great Bermuda, largest island in the Bermudas B-173

Great bird of paradise, *picture* P-110

Great black-backed gull, bird *Larus marinus* G-317

Great blue heron, bird *Ardea herodias* H-142

Great Books Program, term applied to study by adults of present-day problems through reading and group discussion of classics of Western World; program organized by John Erskine for U.S. soldiers in Europe after World War I, later developed at Columbia University, University of Chicago, and St. John's College; great books programs for adults introduced in New York City, 1927, and Highland Park, Ill., 1930; Great Books Foundation, a nonprofit organization, was established at Chicago, Ill., in 1947, to form groups in United States A-45

Great Britain, largest island of the British Isles, separated from France by the English Channel and from Ireland by the Irish Sea; 88,756 sq mi (229,877 sq km); divided politically into England, Scotland, and Wales; term often used for United Kingdom of Great Britain and Northern Ireland; composed of England, Scotland, Wales, and Northern Ireland; 94,215 sq mi (244,016 sq km); pop. 55,533,540 G-242, *map* E-360. For climate and geology: *see in index* British Isles; for current affairs: *see in index* United Kingdom; for government: *see in index* Parliament, British, and United Kingdom; for history: *see in index* Commonwealth, The, and England; for comparative size: *see in index* Island, *table*

'Great Britain', early steamship B-470, S-167

Great Central Valley. *see in index* Central Valley

Great Charter. *see in index* Magna Carta

Great circle, in geography
 airways A-165
 navigation N-68, *diagram* N-69
 transportation T-257

Great circle, in mathematics
 geometry G-79

Great Coalition, in Canadian history C-113

Great comet of 1811, diameter of head about 1,225,000 mi (1,970,000 km), largest of any comet ever observed; length of tail 110,000,000 mi (177,000,000 km); period of orbit about 3,000 years.

Great Council, in English politics E-240, P-131b

'Great Crash, 1929, The', book by Galbraith G-243

Great Dane, dog, *picture* D-201

Great Depression G-242
 cosmetics C-729
 Germany G-123
  Hitler H-177
  Weimar Republic W-142
 Hoover H-235, U-187
 housing H-302
 inflation I-200
 money M-531
 North America N-345
 photography P-298
 Roosevelt R-268
 tariff T-29
 Wall Street, *picture* U-186
 World War I's influence W-321
 World War II W-17

Great Dismal Swamp. *see in index* Dismal Swamp

Great Divide. *see in index* Continental Divide

Great Dividing Range (or Eastern Highlands), in Australia, extends along Pacific Ocean from Cape York s. to Victoria and South Australia; highest peak Mount Kosciusko (7,316 ft; 2,230 m) A-771, *map* A-819
 New South Wales N-234

Great Dog, constellation. *see in index* Canis Major

'Great Eastern', British ship B-470
 transatlantic cables C-10

Great Egg Harbor River, river in s. New Jersey; rises s.e. of Camden, flows about 60 mi (105 km) to head of Great Egg Harbor Bay, inlet of Atlantic Ocean.

Great Elector. *see in index* Frederick William

Greater Antilles, western islands of West Indies (Cuba, Jamaica, Hispaniola, and Puerto Rico); 81,600 sq mi (211,300 sq km); pop. 25,600,000
 North America N-334, 339, *map* N-350
 West Indies W-155, *map* W-159

Greater East Asia, Japanese name for area of Far East that Japan tried to dominate P-18

Greater London, England; pop. 7,703,410 L-294, *map* L-287

Greater Paris, France P-118

Greater scaup, bird, *picture* D-286

Greater Sunda Islands. *see in index* Sunda Islands

Greater Vehicle, in Mahayana Buddhism B-482

Great Exhibition of Industry of All Nations (1851), English exposition F-9, *picture* F-8

'Great Expectations', novel by Charles Dickens; in which childhood Pip (Philip Pirrip), the hero, comes from a poor family but is educated as a gentleman of "great expectations"
 novel N-410

Great Exuma Island, island in The Bahamas; sheep, pigs, and goats raised; numerous harbors hug the island; communities include George Town and Moss Town; pop. 3,245, *map* N-350
 West Indies, *map* W-159

Great Falls, Mont., 2nd city of state, on Missouri River about 70 mi (115 km) n.e. of Helena; hydroelectric power; copper refining, copper and aluminum wire, railroad shops, flour, meat products, oil refining; College of Great Falls; Malmstrom Air Force Base adjacent; state fair; pop. 56,725 M-552, 560, *picture* M-559
 United States, *maps* N-350, U-40

Great Falls, College of, Great Falls, Mont.; Roman Catholic; founded 1932; arts and sciences, business administration and teacher education.

Great Falls of the Missouri, waterfalls of the Missouri River M-508

Great Falls of the Potomac, series of scenic falls and rapids of the Potomac P-468, *map* P-468

Great Fire, disastrous fire that destroyed one third of Chicago C-317

Great Fish River Canyon, canyon in Namibia, Africa, *picture* G-62

Great-flowered magnolia (or bull bay), tree *Magnolia grandiflora* of the Magnolia family M-47

'Great Gatsby, The', novel by Fitzgerald F-147, R-112c
 American novels A-359

'Great God Brown, The', work by O'Neill A-357

Great gray kangaroo, *picture* A-426

Great gray slug, land snail S-222

Great Grimsby, England. *see in index* Grimsby

Great gross, unit of measure, *table* W-140

Greathead, James Henry (1844–96), British civil engineer, born in Grahamstown, South Africa; improved tunneling shield
 tunnel T-310

Greatheart, character in Bunyan's 'Pilgrim's Progress', guide of Christiana and her children to the Celestial City.

Great Himalayas, Asian mountains
 Bhutan B-180
 Himalayas H-153
 India I-62

Great horned owl. *see in index* Horned owl

Great Horse, bred for size and strength during the Middle Ages H-253

Great Indian Desert. *see in index* Thar Desert

Great Interregnum, in German history, the interval (1254–73) between the fall of the Hohenstaufen emperors and the election of the first Hapsburg G-121

Great Khingan Mountains, mountains in n.e. part of China; extend n. and s. in Inner Mongolian Autonomous Region; highest point about 5,670 ft (1,730 m) M-93, *map* R-322
 Heilongjiang H-116

Great Lake, lake in Kampuchea. *see in index* Tonle Sap

Great Lakes, the five lakes (Superior, Michigan, Huron, Erie, and Ontario) lying on the borders of Canada and the U.S.; total area nearly 95,000 sq mi (246,000 sq km) G-243, *maps* U-41, W-297. *see also in index* individual lakes by name and *see table* following
 Canada C-75
  Ontario O-546
 canals C-128. *see also in index* New York State Barge Canal; Sault Sainte Marie canals; Welland Ship Canal
 fisheries S-518
 harbors and ports H-35
 lake L-24
 Michigan M-355
 Niagara Falls N-301
 pollution P-114
 profile, *diagram* S-19
 river system, *map* U-33
 trade, *picture* P-168
  iron and coal P-167
 transportation T-254
 waterway W-108

Great Lakes Naval Training Center, U.S. Naval center, in Ill. on Lake Michigan 35 mi (55 km) n. of Chicago; site purchased by Chicago merchants 1904; commissioned 1911; largest naval training center in world; covers 1,565 acres (635 hectares); headquarters of Ninth Naval District; other commands include Administrative, Recruit Training, Service School, Naval Examining Center, Naval Supply Depot, Marine Barracks, and Electronics Supply Office; Naval Hospital there
 Illinois, *map* I-53

Great Lakes-Saint Lawrence Lowlands, region in Canada C-73, 80

Great laurel rhododendron. *see in index* Rosebay rhododendron

Great Leap Forward, period in China C-350, 375
 Mao Zedong M-112

Great lobelia (or blue cardinal flower), *picture* F-235

Great Meadows, Pa. *see in index* Fort Necessity

Great Miami River. *see in index* Miami River

Great Mogul, diamond D-130, *picture* D-129

Great Mosque (or al-Haram) mosque in Mecca, Saudi Arabia I-360
 Mecca M-254
 mosaic M-590

Great National Pike. *see in index* Cumberland Road

Great Neck, N.Y., village 15 mi (25 km) n.e. of New York City on n. shore of w. Long Island; gyroscopes; incorporated 1921; pop. 9,168.

Great Northern Exploration Expedition. *see in index* Burke and Wills Expedition

Great Northern Railroad
 Roosevelt R-285

Great Ouse, river in s.e. England. *see in index* Ouse

Great Pacificator. *see in index* Clay, Henry

Great Palace, palace in Leningrad, U.S.S.R., *picture* L-127

Great Paul, bell B-154

Great Plague. *see in index* Bubonic plague

GREAT LAKES FACTS

Lake	Area sq mi	Area sq km	Length mi	Length km	Width mi	Width km	Shoreline mi	Shoreline km	Greatest Depth ft	Greatest Depth m
Superior	31,700	82,100	350	565	160	260	2,100	3,400	1,333	406
Huron	23,000	59,600	206	332	183	295	2,300	3,700	750	230
Michigan	22,300	57,800	307	494	118	190	1,300	2,100	923	281
Erie	9,910	25,667	241	388	57	92	800	1,300	210	64
Ontario	7,550	19,550	193	311	53	85	1,100	1,800	802	244

Green Mountain College, college in Poultney, Vt.; private; established 1834 as junior college for women; became 4-year coeducational institution 1975; liberal arts, education, recreation, business management.

Green Mountain Dam, dam in Colorado C-584

Green Mountains, range of Appalachian system extending through Vermont; highest peak, Mt. Mansfield (4,393 ft; 1,339 m) V-285, 289, A-508, *maps* V-286, 301, U-44, *pictures* V-287, 294
  Long Trail V-287

Green Mountain State. *see in index* Vermont

Greenock, Scotland, port 20 mi (30 km) n.w. of Glasgow; shipbuilding, sugar refinery, woolen milling; pop. 70,267.

Green onion (also called scallion, or table onion) O-545

Greenough, Horatio (1805–52), U.S. sculptor, born in Boston; designed Bunker Hill Monument and colossal statue of Washington in Washington, D.C. S-90

Green palace (or Da Khure monastery), Ulaanbaatar, Mongolia, *picture* M-536

Greenpeace Foundation, international organization for the protection of the environment C-678

Green pepper P-197a, *picture* P-197b

Green plover. *see in index* Lapwing

Green Revolution, spectacular world development, largely since World War II, in producing high-yielding strains of wheat, rice, corn, potatoes, and other crops. *see also in index* Borlaug, Norman Ernest
  India I-73
  wheat production W-189

Green River, river in Kentucky, 350 mi (565 km) long; flows through Mammoth Cave National Park; joins the Ohio River s.e. of Evansville, Ind.

Green River, river that rises in Wyoming; unites with the Colorado River in s.e. Utah; 730 mi (1,175 km) long C-584, *maps* U-217, 232, U-80–1, C-585

Greens (German Die Grünen), West German political party G-120, 126
  youth organization Y-431

Greensand, a clay or sand, colored green by glauconite P-466

Greensboro, N.C., 2nd city of state; 70 mi (115 km) n.w. of Raleigh; pop. 159,314 G-283
  North Carolina N-357, 366, *map* U-41

Greensboro College, college in Greensboro, N.C.; affiliated with United Methodist church; chartered 1838; opened 1846; arts and sciences, music, and teacher education G-283

Greensburg, Pa., city, center of natural-gas region, 26 mi (42 km) s.e. of Pittsburgh; diversified industry including metal and glass products, plumbing supplies, clothing; Seton Hill College; pop. 17,558, *map* P-184

Green snail (or green turban), mollusk S-151

Green snake S-226b, *picture* S-224

Green soap S-231

Greenspan, Alan (born 1926), U.S. economist, born in New York City; with Townsend-Greenspan economic consulting firm 1954–74 and 1977–87; member of *Time* magazine's board of economists 1971–74 and 1977– ; chairman Council of Economic Advisers 1974–77; chairman Commission on Social Security Reform 1981–83; chairman Federal Reserve Board 1987– .

Greenstick fracture
  diagnosis F-340

Greenstone. *see in index* Diabase

Greenstreet, Sidney (1879–1954), film actor, born in Sandwich, Kent, England, *picture* M-624

Green sunfish S-518

Green tea, a designation of tea T-45

Green tree snail, mollusk *Helicostyla viridostriata*, *picture* S-152

Green turban (or green snail), mollusk S-151

Green turtle, sea turtle *Chelonia mydas* T-330

Greenville, Miss., city, a port on Mississippi River about 95 mi (155 km) n.w. of Jackson; lumber, paper, concrete, and metal products, rugs, chemicals, cotton; pop. 40,613, *map* U-41

Greenville, N.C., city 73 mi (117 km) s.e. of Raleigh; tobacco market; tobacco processing, food products, textiles; founded 1786, named for Gen. Nathanael Greene; East Carolina University; pop. 35,740.

Greenville, Ohio, city in w., 34 mi (55 km) n.w. of Dayton; oil filters, glass, machinery, athletic clothing, dishwashers; pop. 12,999.

Greenville, S.C., city near extreme n.w.; textile-mill products, garments, metals, chemicals; dairy farming; Furman University; incorporated 1907; pop. 58,242 S-307, *maps* S-318, 310, U-41
  fur trade S-99
  shortwave station R-55

Greenville, Tex., trade center in agricultural region 50 mi (80 km) n.e. of Dallas; grain and cotton seed mills, cattle; aircraft industry; textiles; pop. 22,161, *map* U-41

Greenville, Treaty of (1795) O-505
  Wayne W-110

Greenville College, college in Greenville, Ill.; affiliated with Free Methodist church; established in 1855; arts and sciences, teacher education, and theology.

Green vitriol. *see in index* Ferrous sulfate

Greenwich, England, borough of London on Thames; hospital; naval college; lies on prime meridian; pop. 228,030 L-294, *maps* L-287, U-18a
  hemisphere H-126
  Royal Greenwich Observatory. *see in index* Royal Greenwich Observatory
  Wren W-363

Greenwich, Conn., urban town in s.w. part of state immediately w. of Stamford; printing and publishing, vacuum cleaners, research center; area purchased from American Indians in 1640; scene of battle in Revolutionary War; pop. 59,578, *map* C-532

Greenwich hour angle (GHA) N-72

Greenwich mean time (GMT) T-188
  navigation N-72

Greenwich Village (also called the Village), a neighborhood in Manhattan, New York, N.Y. N-272, *picture* N-276

Green-winged teal, duck, *picture* D-286

Greenwood, Arthur (1880–1954), British political leader, born in Hunslet, Leeds; member Parliament (Labor) 1922–54; deputy leader, Labor party 1942–54; lord privy seal 1945–47; paymaster general 1946–47.

Greenwood, Miss., city on Yazoo River 86 mi (138 km) n. of Jackson; cotton market; zippers, electronic equipment, metal products, pianos, organs; pop. 20,115.

Greenwood, S.C., city 67 mi (108 km) n.w. of Columbia; diversified industry including textiles, textile machinery, food products, flower seed, bulbs; Lander College; S.C. Festival of Flowers; pop. 21,613, *maps* S-318, 307, U-41

Greer, S.C., town 10 mi (16 km) n.e. of Greenville; textile mills; batteries, cotton yarn; pop. 10,525, *map* S-318

Greeting card
  comic strips adaptations, *picture* C-145e
  first Christmas card, *picture* C-333
  letter writing L-139
  valentine S-24

Gregg, Alvin Forrest (born 1933), U.S. football player, born in Birthright, Tex.; tackle and guard; Green Bay Packers 1956, 1958–70, Dallas Cowboys 1971.

Gregg, John Robert (1867–1948), U.S. educator, author, born in Ireland, emigrated to U.S. (1893); founder of Gregg system of shorthand; author of books on system S-182

Gregg, Norman McAlister (1892–1966), Australian doctor, born in Sydney; specialist in ophthalmology; first to associate German measles in early pregnancy with congenital birth defects.

Gregg shorthand S-182

Gregor, William (1761–1817), English clergyman and mineralogist, born in Trewarthenick, Cornwall; discoverer of titanium
  titanium T-193

Gregoras, Nicephorus (1295–1360), Byzantine scholar G-279

Gregorian calendar (or New Style calendar, or N.S. calendar) C-28

Gregorian chant (or modalchant, or plainchant), classical music; synthesized by Gregory I M-667
  music M-666

Gregory, the Illuminator, Saint (257?–337?), reputed founder and patron saint of Armenian church; festival October 1.

Gregory, popes G-283, *table* P-99

Gregory I (540?–604), pope; commemorated as saint March 12 G-283
  Augustine of Canterbury A-761
  English history E-238
  Gregorian chant M-667

Gregory II, Saint (died 731), pope 715–31, born in Rome; opposition to Byzantine Empire united Lombards and papacy; commemorated as saint February 11.

Gregory III (died 741), pope B-535

Gregory VII (originally called Hildebrand) (1025?–85), pope; commemorated as saint May 25 G-283
  Henry IV H-132
  excommunication M-389, *picture* M-390
  Holy Roman Empire H-209
  Investiture Conflict G-121

Gregory IX (originally called Ugo of Segni) (1170?–1241), pope G-283

Gregory X, Blessed (1210?–76), pope G-121

Gregory XIII (1502–85), pope 1572–85
  Villa Taverna, Rome R-252

Gregory, Cynthia (born 1946), U.S. ballet dancer, born in Los Angeles, Calif.; noted for impeccable technique, *picture* D-25

Gregory, Dick (born 1932), U.S. comedian, author, activist, born in St. Louis, Mo.; began career in Chicago nightclubs 1958; Carnegie Hall 1962; TV guest star; noted for satire on race relations; popular speaker on minority rights; autobiography, 'From the Back of the Bus'.

Gregory, Horace (1898–1982), U.S. poet and critic, born in Milwaukee, Wis.; lecturer, Sarah Lawrence College 1934–60 ('Poems, 1930–1940'; 'The Shield of Achilles: Essays on Beliefs in Poetry'; 'Collected Poems', Bollingen Prize 1965).

Gregory, Isabella Augusta (or Lady Gregory) (1852–1932), Irish dramatist and romance writer, born in Roxborough, County Galway; associated with Yeats in Irish literary revival ('Gods and Fighting Men'; 'Irish Folk History Plays') I-327, *picture* I-326
  Yeats Y-412

Gregory, James (1638–75), Scottish mathematician and astronomer, born in Drumoak, Aberdeen, Scotland
  telescope T-68

Gregory, St., Knights of. *see in index* Knights of St. Gregory

Gregory of Nazianzus, Saint (329?–389?), churchman whose writings contain best statement of doctrine of Trinity in Greek Orthodox theology; a graceful and powerful expounder but not an original thinker; festival May 9 G-279

Gregory of Nyssa, Saint (331?–396?), Greek churchman who anticipated transubstantiation doctrine; constructive thinker; festival March 9 G-279

Gremlins, in folklore, pixies that play tricks; may be devilish or good-humored and beneficent; young called widgets, females fifinellas; first reported by R.A.F. fliers in 1923; name said to be from obsolete English verb *greme*, "to vex."

Grenada, parliamentary state, includes island of Grenada, southernmost of Windward Islands, West Indies (120 sq mi; 310 sq km), and southern Grenadines (13 sq mi; 34 sq km); formerly British state; gained independence 1974; 133 sq mi (344 sq km); cap. St. George's (pop. 6,600); cacao, nutmegs, coconuts; pop. 96,000 G-284
  flag, *picture* F-165
  North America, *map* N-350
  United Kingdom E-259
  U.S. invasion R-112j
  West Indies W-155, *picture* W-156, *map* W-159
  world, *map* W-297

Grenade, from French *grenade* meaning "pomegranate," military weapon; made of steel, containing high explosives, sometimes gas- or flame-producing chemicals; made to be thrown by hand or rifle; used in 17th century; highly developed in World War I.

Grenadier, originally a soldier whose special duty was to throw hand grenades; as these were picked men, chosen for their boldness and strength, the term came to be applied to members of a special corps
  British guards U-12

Grenadine, a silk, cotton, or wool fabric similar to marquisette in weave; also a hard twist silk yarn used for lace and hosiery; in 18th century a black French lace.

Grenadine, a reddish syrup made from pomegranate juice; used in mixed drinks.

Grenadines, chain of 600 small islands of Windward Islands, West Indies, stretching 60 miles (95 kilometers) between Grenada and St. Vincent; northern islands part of St. Vincent and the Grenadines, southern islands belong to Grenada; pop. 12,400
  West Indies, *map* W-159

Grendel, monster slain by Beowulf B-165

Grenfell, Wilfred (full name Sir Wilfred Thomason Grenfell) (1865–1940), British medical missionary in Labrador G-284
  Labrador L-12

Grenfell Association, International. *see in index* International Grenfell Association

Grenoble, France, historic city of Isère River 60 mi (95 km) s.e. of Lyons; industrial center; university; pop. 161,230, *maps* E-360, F-369

Grenville, George (1712–70), English statesman; prime minister 1763; secured passage of American Stamp Act, one of causes of American Revolution R-163

Grenville, Richard (1541?–91), English naval hero; commanded fleet carrying colonists to Roanoke Island in 1585; killed when his ship *Revenge* tried to cut way through Spanish fleet (read Tennyson's 'Revenge') S-177f

Grenville, William Wyndham (1759–1834), English statesman, son of George Grenville; as premier (1807) secured abolition of English slave trade; advocated Catholic emancipation.

Gresham, Thomas (1519?–79), English merchant and royal financial agent, born in London; founder of Royal Exchange and Gresham College, London
  money M-531

Gresham, Walter Quintin (1832–95), U.S. jurist and statesman, born in Lanesville, Ind.; major general in Civil War; secretary of treasury 1884; secretary of state 1893; as postmaster general barred all lotteries from mails.

Gresham, Ore., suburb of Portland; pop. 33,005 O-592

Gresham's law, in economics, principle that "bad money drives out good"; tendency of money having less intrinsic

value to displace more valuable money from circulation
money M-531

Gretchaninoff, Aleksandr. *see in index* Grechaninov, Aleksandr

Gretna, La., industrial city on Mississippi River, southeast of New Orleans; oil refineries; chemical products; pop. 24,875.

Gretna Green, Scotland, village of Dumfriesshire in s. near English border; formerly scene of runaway marriages from England; pop. 1,930.

Gretzky, Wayne (nickname Great Gretzky) (born 1961), Canadian professional hockey player, born in Brantford, Ont.; set many records to become highest paid player in hockey; with Indianapolis Racers 1978; Edmonton Oilers 1978–; named World Hockey Association rookie of the year 1979; voted National Hockey League's most valuable player beginning 1980; youngest player named to league's All-Star team 1980.

Greuze, Jean Baptiste (1725–1805), French genre and portrait painter, born in Tournus, near Dijon; in painting, he represents a sentimental return to nature ('The Broken Pitcher'; 'Innocence').

Greville, Charles Cavendish Fulke (1794–1865), English public official and diarist whose journals (published 1875–87) contain rich historical material for first half of 19th century.

Grevillea (or silk-oak), a perennial *Grevillea robusta* of the protea family, native to Australia; used as house plant; erect, leaves fernlike; grows to 70 ft (21 m) in California and is used as shade tree; in Australia attains 150 ft (46 m); flowers orange, in clusters; lumber elastic, durable, used in furniture; gum resin derived from wood; over 200 species in genus, mostly Australian.

Grévy, Jules (1807–91), French statesman, born in Mont-sous-Vaudrey, near Dole; president of French Republic 1879–87; resigned owing to scandals involving his son-in-law in traffic in offices and decorations of honor.

Grevy's zebra, hoofed mammal *Equus grevyi* Z-449

Grew, Joseph Clark (1880–1965), U.S. diplomat, born in Boston; for many years in U.S. Foreign Service; ambassador to Japan 1932–41; undersecretary of state 1944–45 ('Ten Years in Japan'; 'The Turbulent Era'); retired 1945.

Grew, Nehemiah (1641–1712), English botanist, born in parish of Mancetter; worked on isolation of chlorophyll cell ('The Anatomy of Plants').

Grey, Albert Henry George Grey, 4th **Earl** (1851–1917), governor-general of Canada 1904–11, born in London; stimulated social and economic progress.

Grey, Charles Grey, 2nd **Earl** (1764–1845), English statesman, born in Fallodon, near Alnwick; premier 1830–34
Parliamentary Reform Bill R-319

Grey, Edward Grey, first **Viscount.** *see in index* Grey of Fallodon

Grey, George (1812–98), British colonial governor and explorer G-285
Burke and Wills expedition B-507
New Zealand N-292, 295

Grey, Jane (also called Lady Jane Grey) (1537–54), "nine-day queen" of England G-285
Cranmer C-761

Grey, Zane (1875–1939), U.S. novelist, born in Zanesville, Ohio; stories of life in western U.S. ('Desert Gold'; 'Riders of the Purple Sage'; 'Lone Star Ranger') W-152

Greyhound, dog, *pictures* D-200
dog racing D-214

Greyhound Derby, dog race D-214

Greylag goose, a European wild goose D-285, *picture* D-287

Greylock, Mount, highest peak in Massachusetts, in Berkshire County, near n.w. corner of state (3,491 ft; 1,064 m); lodge and war memorial on summit M-190, *picture* M-189

Greymouth, New Zealand, port on w. coast of South Island at mouth of Grey River; gold, coal, timber, lumber; pop. 7,750, *maps* N-299, P-3

Grey of Fallodon, Edward Grey, first **Viscount** (1862–1933), British Liberal statesman, born in London; foreign secretary 1905–16, with Edward VII arranged Triple Entente; in 1914 worked to prevent World War I W-307

Grey Owl (originally George Stansfele Belaney) (1888–1938), Canadian author and naturalist; claimed to be an Apache; built wildlife sanctuary, Prince Albert National Park ('Pilgrims of the Wild'; 'Sajo and the Beaver People').

Greysolon, Daniel, sieur du Lhut. *see in index* Du Lhut, Daniel Greysolon, sieur du

Greytown, Nicaragua. *see in index* San Juan del Norte

Griboedov, Aleksandr Sergeevich (1795–1829), Russian dramatic poet and statesman; sent to Persia as minister, where he was killed by a mob R-361

Grid, electron tube R-60
electric power transmission E-168

Grid, in mapping M-117, *map* L-79

Gridiron, a football field, so called from its shape.

Grieg, Edvard (full name Edvard Hagerup Grieg) (1843–1907), Norwegian composer G-285
classical music M-674
Norway N-391

Grierson, John (1898–1972), British documentary producer, born in Kilmarnock, Scotland M-628

Griffes, Charles Tomlinson (1884–1920), U.S. composer and pianist, born in Elmira, N.Y.; work impressionistic ('Pleasure Dome of Kubla Khan'; 'Four Roman Sketches')
classical music M-677

Griffin, Walter Burley (1876–1937), U.S. architect, born in Maywood, Ill.; lived in Australia 1914–35; designer of capital, Canberra C-130

Griffin, Ga., city 35 mi (55 km) s. of Atlanta; textiles, hosiery, apparel, towels, metal products; pimiento, fruit, and vegetable canning; Georgia Agricultural Experiment Station; pop. 20,728.

Griffin, a mythical creature, part eagle, part lion; the Arimaspians, a Scythian people, were always trying to steal gold from mines guarded by griffins A-457, *picture* A-458

'Griffin', La Salle's ship G-249

Griffith, Arthur (1872–1922), Irish statesman, born in Dublin; chief organizer of Sinn Fein; president of Irish Free State 1922.

Griffith, Clark C. (nickname Old Fox) (1869–1955), U.S. baseball pitcher and manager, born in Nevada, Mo.; player with 5 major league teams 1894–1914; manager of 4 teams 1901–20; president of Washington, A.L., after 1920.

Griffith, D.W. (in full David Lewelyn Wark Griffith) (1875–1948), motion-picture director and producer G-286
directing D-155
motion pictures M-618, *picture* M-607

Griffith, Ind., town 7 mi (11 km) s.w. of Gary; metal products, paperboard boxes; incorporated 1904; pop. 17,026
Indiana, *map* I-102

Grignard, Victor (1871–1935), French chemist, born in Cherbourg; discovered Grignard's reagent, used in synthesizing many organic compounds. *see also in index* Nobel Prizewinners, *table*

Grijalva, Juan de (1489?–1527), Spanish navigator, explorer of Mexico, born in Gueller, Old Castile; sailing from Cuba where his uncle, Diego Velásquez, was governor, explored Mexican coast as far as Veracruz; active in conquest of Nicaragua and slain there in battle with local inhabitants.

Grijalva River, river in states of Tabasco and Chiapas, in s.e. Mexico; called Chiapas in upper course; 350 mi (565 km) long, navigable for 90 mi (145 km); unites with Usumacinta
Mexico M-324, *map* M-341

Grill, appliance H-211

Grillparzer, Franz (1791–1872), Austrian dramatic poet, born in Vienna; works include classical dramas ('The Golden Fleece', a trilogy; 'Sappho'), historical tragedies, and romantic dramas G-109

Grimaldi, prehistoric Negroid race whose remains were discovered in s. France, associated with remains of the Cro-Magnon race
man M-90

Grimaldi, Joseph (nickname Joey) (1779–1837), famous English clown, born in London; Charles Dickens edited his 'Memoirs' C-436

Grimaldi family, rulers of the principality of Monaco since 1297 M-528

Grimes, Bryan (1828–80), Confederate soldier, born in Pitt County, N.C.; major of Fourth North Carolina Regiment in Civil War; made major general in 1865 and served in last battles of Lee's army.

Grimes, Burleigh Arland (1893–1985), U.S. baseball pitcher, born in Clear Lake, Wis.; player, for Pittsburgh, N.L., 1916–17, 1928–29, 1934, Brooklyn, N.L., 1918–26, New York, N.L., 1927, Boston, N.L., 1930, St. Louis, N.L., 1930–31, 1933–34, Chicago, N.L., 1932–33, New York, A.L., 1934; won over 20 games in each of 5 seasons.

Grimké, Angelina (1805–79) U.S. crusader for human rights G-286
women's rights W-277

Grimké, Archibald Henry (1849–1930), U.S. writer and lawyer, born near Charleston, S.C.; editor the *Hub*, a Boston newspaper, 1883–85; wrote biographies of William Lloyd Garrison and Charles Sumner; crusaded against racial discrimination; won 1919 Spingarn Medal.

Grimké, Sarah (1792–1873), U.S. pioneer civil rights worker G-286
women's rights W-277

Grimm, Jakob Ludwig Karl (1785–1863), German scholar, founder with his brother **Wilhelm Karl** (1786–1859) of science of folklore G-287
folklore F-260
German literature G-106
linguistics contribution L-230
stories S-470, *list* S-481, *picture* S-462
storytelling influence S-461
'The Sleeping Beauty' R-110a

Grimmelshausen, Hans Jacob Christoffel von (1625?–76), German writer and adventurer, born in Gelnhausen; wrote 'The Adventurous Simplicissimus' on own experiences in manner of picaresque novel G-105

Grimsby (or Great Grimsby), English seaport on n.e. coast near mouth of Humber River; immense fishing trade; timber, coal trade; shipbuilding; pop. 96,500, *map* U-18a

Grinding process T-224
abrasives and coolants A-13. *see also in index* Abrasives
paint making P-75, *picture* P-74

Grinnell, George Bird (1849–1938), U.S. writer, ethnologist, and ornithologist, born in Brooklyn; editor *Forest and Stream* 1876–1911; founded first Audubon society.

Grinnell, Henry (1799–1874), U.S. ship owner, born in New Bedford, Mass.; financed Franklin relief expeditions (1850 and 1853–55) and later Arctic explorations; Grinnell Land is named for him.

Grinnell, Josiah Bushnell (1821–91), U.S. clergyman, born in New Haven, Vt.; moved to Iowa where he established Congregational Church 1854; in U.S. Congress 1863–67; aided runaway slaves; promoted free state schools and railroad expansion; town of Grinnell and college there named for him.

Grinnell College, college in Grinnell, Iowa; nonsectarian, established by Congregationalists 1846, opened 1848 at Davenport as Iowa College; moved to Grinnell 1859, present name 1909; liberal arts, education.

Grinnell Land, central part of Ellesmere Island in Canada, n.w. of Greenland; explored 1850 by Grinnell expedition.

Grinoid, marine animal, *picture* F-326

Grip men, in motion pictures M-606

Gris, Juan (1887–1927), Spanish modernist painter and lithographer, born in Madrid; moved to Paris 1905 and became identified with cubist movement.

Griseofulvin, type of antifungal drug A-489

Grisi, Carlotta (1819?–99), Italian ballerina; began career as child; made Paris debut 1840; created role of Giselle in ballet 1841; popular in London in 'Pas de Quatre' with Taglioni, Cerito, and Grahn 1845 B-33

Gris-Nez, Cape, headland of France, point of French coast nearest Britain; on Strait of Dover, *map* F-372

Grison, a weasel-like carnivorous mammal of family Mustelidae found in Central and South America and Mexico; dark beneath, light above; emits disagreeable odor when annoyed; scientific name *Galictis*, or *Grison, vittata*.

Grisons, Swiss canton. *see in index* Graubünden

Grissom, Virgil Ivan (nickname Gus) (1926–67), U.S. astronaut, U.S. Air Force, born in Mitchell, Ind.; killed in launch-pad fire S-346f, *table* S-348
NASA N-22

Gristle. *see in index* Cartilage

Gristmill, mill to grind grain, *picture* V-294

Griswold, Rufus Wilmot (1815–57), U.S. editor and author, born in Benson, Vt.; in 1850 he helped to edit writings of Edgar Allan Poe, who had named him as his literary executor.

Grizzly bear (or silvertip) B-116
behavior studied, *picture* A-447
endangered species E-212

Grizzly Giant, big tree S-112

Groat, from Dutch *groot* meaning "big," name given to English silver fourpence, historical value about 8 cents; term once applied to any large, thick coin.

Grodno, U.S.S.R., former Polish city, on Niemen River, included in Russia since 1945; interesting old buildings; varied manufactures; trade in grain, timber; pop. 132,000, *maps* R-344, 349
Europe, *map* E-360

Grofé, Ferde (or Ferdinand Rudolph von Grofé) (1892–1972), U.S. composer, born in New York City; pianist and arranger for Paul Whiteman; exponent of "symphonic jazz" ('Mississippi Suite'; 'Grand Canyon Suite'; 'Symphony in Steel').

Grolier de Servières, Jean, vicomte d'Aguisy (1479–1565), French bibliophile and statesman, born in Lyons; ambassador to Rome and Milan and treasurer under Francis I; collected library of 3,000 beautifully bound books; Grolier Club, a club of book collectors in New York City, named for him B-354

Gromaire, Marcel (1892–1971), French expressionist painter, etcher, and designer of tapestries; born in department of Nord, France; pioneer in revival of tapestry.

Gromwell, a genus *Lithospermum* of hairy plants of the borage family found in n. hemisphere; low-growing, hardy; flowers white, yellow, or bluish, grow in leafy spikes; used in rock gardens; includes the puccoon.

Gromyko, Andrei (born 1909), Soviet statesman G-288, *picture* N-328

Groningen, The Netherlands, industrial and trade city of n.e.; cattle and grain market; sugar refineries; university (founded 1614); pop. 140,234 N-126

Gronouski, John Austin (born 1919), U.S. educator and government official, born in Dunbar, Wis.; professor at University of Maine 1948–50, Wayne State University 1957–59; Wisconsin tax commissioner 1960–63; U.S. postmaster general 1963–65; ambassador to Poland 1965–68; dean Lyndon B. Johnson School of Public Affairs, University of Texas, 1969–74.

Grooming
- horses H-267

Gropius, Walter (1883–1969), German architect G-289, *picture* A-564
- architecture A-568
- Bauhaus A-565, B-435
- industrial design I-171

Gropper, William (1897–1977), U.S. painter and illustrator, born in New York City; skillful as social satirist; depicts realistically current happenings, such as 'The Last Cow', a dust-bowl scene.

Gros, Antoine Jean (1771–1835), French historical painter, born in Paris; pupil of David; through Josephine was favored by Napoleon and is noted for scenes of Napoleonic Wars; at end of Napoleon's power turned to purely classical subjects; adverse criticism led to suicide.

Grosbeak, various stout-beaked birds of the finch family Fringillidae G-289
- bird species B-256, *picture* B-260

Groseilliers, Médart Chouart, sieur de (1621?–90?), intrepid French explorer and fur trader
- fur trade F-468
  - Hudson's Bay Company H-314
  - Minnesota exploration M-445

Grosgrain, a firm, stiff, closely woven, corded silk or rayon with cotton filling, sometimes made of all cotton; used for ribbons, ties, and trimmings.

Gros Michel, a variety of banana B-53, *picture* B-51

Gros Morne National Park, park in Newfoundland N-30, *map* N-29

Gros point (or cross stitch), needlework N-112

Gross, unit of measure, *table* W-140

'Gross Clinic', painting by Eakins, *picture* E-3

Grosse Pointe Farms, Mich., city on Lake St. Clair, just n.e. of Detroit; incorporated as village 1893, as city 1949; pop. 11,701.

Grosse Pointe Park, Mich., city adjoining Detroit on e.; residential suburb on Lake St. Clair; pop. 15,641.

Grosse Pointe Woods, Mich., city 11 mi (18 km) n.e. of Detroit; residential suburb; pop. 18,886; incorporated 1926 as Lochmoor, present name after 1939.

Gross Glockner, highest peak in Hohe Tauern, in Tirol region of Austria; 12,461 ft (3,798 m) A-824, T-192

Gross national product (GNP) G-290
- economics E-62
- industry I-184
- Philippines, *graphs* P-255d, 261b
- United States U-111
- U.S.S.R., *chart* R-336d

Gross tonnage, ship S-169

Grosvenor, Gilbert Hovey (1875–1966), U.S. geographer, born in Constantinople (now Istanbul), Turkey; father of Melville Bell Grosvenor; with *National Geographic Magazine* since 1899, editor in chief 1903–54; president National Geographic Society 1920–54, chairman of board 1954–66.

Grosvenor, Melville Bell (1901–82), U.S. editor, born in Washington, D.C.; son of Gilbert Hovey Grosvenor; with *National Geographic Magazine* 1924–, editor 1957–67, editor in chief 1967–77; president National Geographic Society 1957–67, chairman 1967–77.

Gros Ventres, people. *see in index* Hidatsa

Grosz, George (1893–1959), U.S. artist, born in Berlin, Germany; remarkable caricaturist; first noted as satirical painter, later as painter of nudes, still lifes, landscapes, and various birds.

Grote, George (1794–1871), English historian and banker, born in Clay Hill, near Beckenham; his 'History of Greece' is "one of the few great comprehensive histories."

Grotesque, type of clown C-435, *picture* C-434

Grotius, Hugo (1583–1645), Dutch statesman and jurist G-290
- international law I-255
- warfare W-26

Groton, Conn., city and town on Thames River opposite New London; submarines, pharmaceuticals; U.S. Navy submarine base nearby; site of historic Fort Griswold; pop. 41,062 C-654, *map* C-663, *picture* C-658

Grotowski, Jerzy (born 1933), Polish theater director A-24

Grouchy, Emmanuel, marquis de (1766–1847), French marshal, born in Paris; often blamed for Napoleon's defeat at Waterloo W-100

Groulx, Lionel Adolphe (1878–1967), Canadian historian, born near Montreal, Que.; ordained Roman Catholic priest 1903; professor University of Montreal 1915–48.

Ground (or field), flag, *list* F-149

Ground, in radio, *diagrams* R-46
- symbol, *diagram* R-56

Ground beetle, one of a group of the order Coleoptera, family Carabidae; especially the fiery searcher *Calosoma scrutator*, one of the largest beetles; if held carelessly will discharge quantities of "fiery" juice, *picture* I-216

Ground controlled approach (GCA) A-323, 886, R-32, *diagrams* R-31

Ground cover, plants
- growing conditions G-27

Ground cuckoo. *see in index* Roadrunner

Ground effect machine A-80

Ground fire F-314
- forest hazard C-676

Ground hemlock, shrub *Taxus canadensis* of the Taxaceae family Y-416

Groundhog (or woodchuck), a burrowing rodent
- hibernation H-147
- tracks, *picture* A-464

Ground ivy I-408

Ground laurel. *see in index* Trailing arbutus

Groundlings, in Elizabethan theater S-136

Ground-nesting termite, a termite *Reticulitermes flavipes* of the order Isoptera T-112

Groundnut. *see in index* Peanut

Ground Observer Corps (Operation Skywatch), a joint activity of U.S. Air Force and Civil Defense Administration; organized 1952 to detect low-flying intruder airplanes that cannot be picked up on radar; staffed by civilian volunteers (about 300,000 in 1954); silver wings and honor badges awarded for service; terminated 1959.

Ground pea. *see in index* Peanut

Ground pine. *see in index* Club mosses

Groundsel, a low-growing annual weed *Senecio vulgaris* of the family Compositae with leafy branching stem; leaves pinnate and toothed; flower heads yellow; also applied to entire genus *Senecio.*

Ground squirrel, name given to various squirrel-like rodents that live on the ground S-401

Ground state (or normal state), condition of minimum possible energy for an atom N-418

Groundwater, source of springs S-396, W-89, *picture* W-88
- earth E-13, *diagram* E-14
- irrigation methods I-355
- rivers R-210

Ground wave R-51

Groundwood pulp, papermaking P-101

'Group, The', work by McCarthy A-362

Group Areas Act (1950), South African legislation A-497

Grouper, name given to southern members of the sea bass group; among commonest are Nassau grouper, red grouper, or mero, yellow-fin grouper, jewfish, red hind, and rock hind
- Nassau grouper, *pictures* P-510

Group insurance I-234

Group life. *see in index* Sociology

Group marriage F-16

Group of Seven, movement in Canadian art P-67a
- Canada 79

'Group Portrait with Lady', (1977) by Böll B-337

Group practice, in medicine M-278

'Groups', work by Stockhausen S-448

Group Theater, U.S. acting group A-28

Grouse, bird G-290, B-247, *picture* B-271. *see also in index* Ptarmigan; Ruffed grouse
- hunting, *picture* H-332
- spruce grouse, *picture* P-511

Grout, a kind of concrete B-496
- cement C-640
- dam construction D-16

Grove, George (1820–1900), British engineer and writer, born in London; erected lighthouses in West Indies; director Royal College of Music from its foundation 1882 to 1894; editor in chief 'Dictionary of Music and Musicians'; author 'Beethoven and His Nine Symphonies'.

Grove, Robert Moses (nickname Lefty) (1900–75), U.S. baseball pitcher, born in Lonaconing, Md.; player for Philadelphia, A.L., 1925–33, and Boston, A.L., 1934–41; won 300 major league games B-92

Grove, William Robert (1811–96), British physicist and judge; born in Swansea, Wales; invented Grove battery; author of 'The Correlation of Physical Forces' B-109

Grove City, Ohio, village 9 mi (14 km) s.w. of Columbus in farming area; shoe soles and heels, adhesives; pop. 16,793.

Grove City College, Grove City, Pa.; private control, established in 1876; arts and sciences, business administration, music, and teacher education.

Groves, Leslie Richard (1896–1970), U.S. Army officer, born in Albany, N.Y.; military director Manhattan Project that developed atomic bomb; retired 1948; author of 'Now It Can Be Told: the Story of the Manhattan Project'.

Groves, Tex., suburban city just n.e. of Port Arthur; platted 1916 as Pecan Grove, renamed 1926, incorporated 1952; pop. 17,090.

Groveton, Va., unincorporated community in Fairfax County 4 mi (6 km) s. of Alexandria; pop. 11,750, *map* V-349

Grow, Galusha Aaron (1823–1907), U.S. political leader, born in Ashford, Conn.; U.S. congressman 1851–63; Speaker of House 1861–63; introduced first homestead bill.

Growing season S-101
- frost affects F-429
- United States U-30, 34, *map* U-31

'Growing up Absurd', work by Goodman, *list* A-388

Growth G-292
- animal
  - hydra H-337
- human P-313
  - child development C-321
  - embryology E-201
  - health H-83
  - life function L-265
  - sexuality S-124
  - stunted. *see in index* Cretinism

Growth hormone (or GH), hormone that affects the body's overall growth process H-240, *table* H-241

'Growth of the Soil', a simple, almost plotless novel by Knut Hamsun picturing Norwegian peasant life; awarded the 1920 Nobel prize in literature.

Growth regulators, in plants P-366, 375

Groza, Louis (nickname Lou) (born 1924), U.S. football player, born in Martins Ferry, Ohio; offensive tackle and placekicker; Cleveland Browns 1946–59, 1961–67.

Groznyy (or Grozny), U.S.S.R., city in n. Caucasus; site of valuable petroeum deposits; wells drilled since before Russian Revolution; pop. 341,000, *maps* E-360, R-344, 349

GR-S (or Government Rubber-Styrene) R-310, P-228

GRU (or Glavnoe Razvedyvatelnoe Upravlenie), Soviet government I-236

Grub, beetle larva L-51

Grubenmann, Hans Ulrich (1709–83), Swiss carpenter and bridge builder B-445

Grubenmann, Johannes (1707–71), Swiss carpenter and bridge builder B-445

Gruber, Franz Xaver (1787–1863), Austrian organist, born in Upper Austria; known as the composer of 'Stille Nacht, Heilige Nacht' (Silent Night, Holy Night).

Gruen, David. *see in index* Ben-Gurion, David

Gruenberg, Louis (1884–1964), U.S. composer, born in Brest-Litovsk, Russia; brought to United States in babyhood; developed from pianist into composer, chiefly of syncopated, impressionistic operas ('Emperor Jones'; 'Jack and the Beanstalk'; 'Enchanted Isle'; 'Jazz Suite').

Gruening, Ernest Henry (1887–1974), U.S. journalist and public official, born in New York City; governor of Alaska 1939–53; senatorial representative from Alaska 1957–59; U.S. senator 1959–68; Democrat; author of 'The State of Alaska', 'Vietnam Folly'.

Gruenther, Alfred Maximilian (1899–1983), U.S. Army general, born in Platte Center, Neb.; chief of staff to Mark W. Clark 1943–45, his deputy commander in Austria 1945–47; joint staff director for joint chiefs of staff 1947–49; deputy Army chief of staff for plans 1949–51; became 4-star general July 1951; chief of staff to Dwight D. Eisenhower then to Matthew B. Ridgway at SHAPE 1951–53; supreme Allied commander in Europe 1953–56; retired from Army 1956; president American National Red Cross 1957–64.

Grugru nut, edible fruit of the grugru palm of South America and the West Indies; source of valuable oil; sometimes used for beads N-449

Gruidae, the crane family of birds. *see in index* Crane

Gruiformes, an order of marsh birds; cranes and rails best known members; also includes limpkins, gallinules, coots, and trumpeters.

Grumman Aircraft Company, U.S. company C-140

Grundgesetz (or Basic Law), constitution of West Germany G-120

Grundtvig, Nikolai Frederik Severin (1783–1872), Danish poet, philologist, and theologian, born in Zealand; advocated religious and civic freedom; collected Danish folk songs ('Northern Mythology,' a study of Old Norse; 'The Decline of Heroic Life in the North', a long epic poem)
- Danish folk schools A-52, D-99

Grundy, Mrs., the personification of society's judgments; name originated in old play 'Speed the Plough', where a character asks continually, "What will Mrs. Grundy say?".

Grünewald, Matthias (formerly Mathis Gothardt) (died 1528), German painter of late Gothic period G-293

Grunion, small slender fish *Leuresthes tenuis* of silversides family, Atherinidae; thrives along sandy coasts from San Francisco to Lower California F-128

Grunt, a large family, Haemulidae, of food fishes of tropical seas; name comes from their ability to make a grunting noise
- oceanography, *picture* O-478

Grus, constellation, *charts* S-420, C-682

Gruyères, Switzerland, picturesque town perched on a high hill 16 mi (26 km) s.

of Fribourg; overlooks upper Saane valley; cheese; pop. 1,349.

Guad, prefix in names of Spanish rivers S-350

Guadalajara, Mexico, second city of nation, capital of Jalisco; 275 mi (445 km) n.w. of Mexico City; glass, pottery, textiles, flour, leather products; silver mining and farming region; health resort; severe earthquakes 1875 and 1912; city founded 1531; contains relics of Spanish colonial times; university and splendid cathedral; pop. 1,626,152 G-294
- Mexico M-328, *map* M-341
- North America, *map* N-350
- Orozco's murals O-608
- world, *map* W-297

Guadalaviar River, river, Spain. *see in index* Turia River

Guadalcanal, one of Solomon Islands; mountainous; area about 2,500 sq mi (6,500 sq km); World War II battleground; pop. 16,500, *map* P-3. *see also in index* Solomon Islands
- Oceania, *picture* O-470

Guadalcanal, battle of (1942–43), warfare, *list* W-15
- World War II W-329, 345, *picture* W-346

Guadalete, battle of (711) S-357

Guadalquivir (Arabic great river), river in Spain, 350 mi (565 km) long; rises in e. of province of Jaen; flows s.w. through Seville and Córdova into Atlantic Ocean, 20 mi (30 km) n. of Cádiz S-350, *map* S-350
- bridge at Córdoba, *picture* S-359
- Europe, *map* E-360

Guadalupe, Mexican island in Pacific Ocean, about 160 mi (260 km) off coast of Lower California (Baja California); an extinct volcano more than 4,000 ft. (1,200 m.) high; 15 mi (25 km) long
- Mexico, *map* M-341
- North America, *map* N-350
- sea elephants S-100
- world, *map* W-297

Guadalupe-Hidalgo, Mexico, town on n.e. edge of Mexico City, where treaty was signed 1848 ending Mexican War; renamed Gustavo A. Madero in 1931. *see also in index* Gustavo A. Madero
- treaty (1848) A-602, *table* T-274

Guadalupe-Hidalgo, Treaty of (1848), cession of California to the United States by Mexico
- California C-40
- Mexican Americans H-163
- Mexican War M-320
- New Mexico N-218
- Wyoming W-390

Guadalupe Mountains, range in New Mexico and Texas, between Rio Grande and Pecos River, *maps* N-229, U-81

Guadalupe Peak, highest point in Texas (8,751 ft; 2,667 m), in Guadalupe Mountains, *picture* T-116

Guadalupe River, river in Texas, rises in s.w. central part and flows s.e. to point about 20 mi (30 km) from Gulf of Mexico, where it divides, one branch uniting with San Antonio River, and other emptying directly into San Antonio Bay.

Guadeloupe, French overseas department in West Indies; total area, 687 sq mi (1,780 sq km); pop. 326,000 G-294, *map* N-350
- French colonies A-337
- West Indies W-155, *map* W-159

Guadiana, river of Spain and s.e. Portugal; about 500 mi (800 km) long, navigable for only 40 mi (65 km) from mouth; flows into Gulf of Cádiz S-350, P-455
- Europe, *map* E-360

Guaíra Falls (or Guayra Falls), falls at the head of navigation, Alto (Upper) Paraná River, between Brazil and Paraguay; the Paraná is about 3 mi (5 km) wide at crest of falls and pours over ledge in 18 separate cataracts (highest, 130 ft; 40 m); combined average flow of these cataracts is far greater than that of Niagara P-111
- waterfalls W-95, *chart* W-98

Guam, island possession of U.S. in w. Pacific; 212 sq mi (549 sq km); cap. Agana; pop. 109,000 G-294
- flag, *picture* F-160
- Pacific Ocean P-7, 15, *map* P-3
  - Oceania O-468, *picture* O-467
- world, *map* W-297
- World War II W-328

Guam, University of, (formerly College of Guam), Agana, Guam; territorial government control; founded 1952; arts and science, education; graduate program.

Guan, a turkeylike bird of Central and South America, belonging to same family (Cracidae) as the curassow; has dark green or black plumage, a long graceful tail, and a throat almost bare and usually with a pendent wattle; ranges n. through Texas.

Guanabacoa, Cuba, city 6 mi (10 km) e. of Havana; summer resort; near mineral springs; copper deposits, stone quarries; colonial city; pop. 32,490
- West Indies, *map* W-159

Guanabara, state of Brazil; created 1960 from former federal district of Rio de Janeiro; 524 sq mi (1,357 sq km); cap. Rio de Janeiro; pop. 3,307,163 B-307

Guanaco, South American ruminant *Lama guanico* of the Camelidae family C-64, *picture* C-63
- fur, *table* F-464

Guanajuato, state in central Mexico; rich in silver and other minerals; 11,810 sq mi (30,590 sq km); cap. Guanajuato; pop. 2,811,046
- Mexico, *map* M-341

Guanajuato, Mexico, historic city 165 mi (265 km) n.w. of Mexico City; capital of state of Guanajuato; gold and silver; first battle in Mexican war of independence fought here in 1810; pop. 28,212
- Mexico, *picture* M-330, *map* M-341

Guanajuato, Bajio of, agricultural region of Mexico M-322, 332

Guanche, people believed to be of Cro-Magnon origin who lived on Canary Islands; first encountered by conquering Spanish in 15th century; originally tall, blond, but later mixture with Arabs and Spanish changed these characteristics; by language allied to ancient Numidians.

Guangdong, former Japanese leased territory on s. tip of Liaotung Peninsula, China; area 1,337 sq mi (3,463 sq km); Kwantung was leased to Japan by China in 1905, but, after World War II, most was included in Port Arthur-Dairen administrative district.

Guangdong (or Kwangtung), province of s.e. China; 84,000 sq mi (218,000 sq km); cap. Canton; pop. 59,299,220 G-295

Guangxi Zhuangzu, autonomous region in s.e. China; 84,000 sq mi (218,000 sq km); cap. Nanning; pop. 36,840,000 G-295
- Zhuang population C-345

Guangzhou. *see in index* Canton, China

Guanine, a purine base that codes genetic information in DNA and RNA
- genetics G-56

Guanine, in fish anatomy F-128

Guano, a fertilizer formed by the excrement and carcasses of seabirds; composed of phosphoric acid, nitrogen, and potash; name also applied to other manures
- bat B-105
- Oceania O-472
- Pacific islands P-16
- Peruvian islands S-280

Guantánamo, province in Cuba, *map* C-802

Guantánamo, Cuba, city on Guaso River near head of Guantánamo Bay on s. coast; pop. 178,000, *map* C-802
- West Indies, *map* W-159

Guantánamo Bay, U.S. naval base in Cuba C-800
- West Indies, *map* W-159

Guaporé, territory of Brazil. *see in index* Rondônia

Guarani, group of South American Indians; their descendants form bulk of population of Paraguay and Uruguay, and are important element in Bolivia and Brazil A-577, P-112

Guarani Indian language
- Latin American literature L-75

Guarantee, in law
- definition, *table* L-93

Guarini, Guarino Camillo (1624–83), Italian architect A-557

'Guarani Indian, The', work by Martiniano de Alencar L-68

Guardafui, Cape, promontory of Somalia at entrance to Gulf of Aden; lies n.w. of Ras Hafun, the easternmost point of Africa
- world, *map* W-297

Guard hair, in mammals H-7

Guardi, Francesco (1712–93), Italian artist of late Venetian school; known for Venetian landscapes.

Guardian, in law, name generally given to one who has control of person and property of a minor; also to one who has control of person or property, or both, of one unable to care for himself or herself.

Guardian of Water, statue in Yokohama, Japan Y-422

Guarding the Treasure, game G-10

Guareschi, Giovanni (1908–68), Italian journalist and novelist, born Fontenelle di Parma, Italy; founded promonarchist paper 'Candido' 1945, and through works printed there was jailed 1954–55 for libel of government officials; 'Don Camillo' books, published 1951–57, became best sellers
- 'The Little World of Don Camillo' R-112a

Guarini, Giovanni Battista (1538–1612), Italian poet, born in Ferrara, Italy; wrote 'Il Pastor Fido'; like Tasso's 'Aminta', on which it is patterned, it is a lyric conception of the ideal life; 'Il Pastor Fido' and 'Aminta' are the finest pastoral poems in Italian literature.

Guarneri (or Guarnieri, or Guarnerius), famous family of Italian violin makers of Cremona, Italy: **Andrea** (1626?–98), pupil of Nicolo Amati; his sons **Pietro Giovanni** (1655–1720) and **Giuseppe** (1666–1740?); and Giuseppe's son **Giuseppe Antonio** (1698–1744), greatest craftsman of family.

Guatemala (or Republic of Guatemala), nation of Central America, s. of Mexico; area 42,042 sq mi (108,888 sq km); cap. Guatemala; pop. 7,915,164 G-296
- Central America C-253, *pictures* C-255, 258
  - Belize B-153
  - El Salvador E-195
- doll tradition D-216
- flag, *picture* F-165
- Guatemala (city) G-300
- literature L-73
  - folktales, *picture* S-481
- Maya M-235
  - ancient civilization A-538
  - corn god, *picture* P-365
  - limestone carvings at Piedras Negras S-82, *picture* S-82
- national anthem, *table* N-64
- national bird Q-16, B-240, F-51
- North America, *map* N-350
- railroad mileage, *table* R-85
- world, *map* W-297
- World War II W-328
- Yucatán Peninsula Y-432

Guatemala, capital city of Guatemala, railroad and commercial center; 50 mi (80 km) from Pacific coast; textiles; pottery; pop. 748,784 G-300, *map* N-350
- Guatemala G-296, *picture* G-299

Guatemoc (also called Guatemozin, or Cuauhtemoc) (1495?–1525), last Aztec emperor; nephew of Montezuma II; bravely resisted Spanish but was captured and executed for treason
- Cortez C-727

Guava, a fruit F-436

Guaviare River, river in Colombia, about 650 mi (1,045 km) long, rises in Andes, flows e. to Orinoco River; partly navigable, *map* S-298

Guayaquil, Ecuador, chief seaport; pop. 1,278,908 G-300, E-66, *maps* P-224, S-298
- world, *map* W-297

Guayaquil, Gulf of, large inlet of Pacific in Ecuador; over 100 mi (160 km) wide at its mouth; receives Guayas River, *maps* P-224, S-298

Guayas River, river in Ecuador; rises in w. Andes and flows s.w. into Gulf of Guayaquil; partly navigable.

Guaymas, Mexico, seaport on Gulf of California; resort; rail terminus; fishing; pop. 34,865
- Mexico, *map* M-341
- ski resort, *picture* T-271

Gubbio, Italy, town 18 mi (29 km) n.e. of Perugia; famous in Renaissance for maiolica ware still being made, *map* I-401

Gucci, retail store chain, *picture* M-140

Gudea (flourished 2400? BC), prince of Lagash and art patron; regarded as god after his death S-82, *picture* S-81

'Gudrun', a German epic poem of the Middle Ages, in three parts; Gudrun, a princess, is carried away by the king of Normandy and held prisoner for 14 years, when her brother and Herwig, her true lover, rescue her.

Guedalla, Philip (1889–1944), British biographer, historian, and lawyer; born in London; combined sparkling, witty style with sound scholarship ('The Second Empire'; 'Conquistador'; 'Gladstone and Palmerston'; 'Bonnet and Shawl'; 'The Hundred Years'; 'Mr. Churchill').

Guelf, House of. German ruling family. *see in index* Welf, House of

Guelfs and Ghibellines, political factions of medieval Germany and Italy G-301
- Florence F-192

Guelph, Ont., city on Speed River 43 mi (69 km) w. of Toronto; machinery and other metal products, electrical equipment, rubber and leather goods, clothing, food products; Ontario Agricultural College, Macdonald Institute, Ontario Veterinary College; pop. 71,207, *map* C-112

Guenon, an African monkey
- apes and monkeys A-503

Guéret, France, historic town 38 mi (61 km) n.e. of Limoges; market and transportation center; built 7th century around abbey; pop. 12,441, *map* F-369

Guereza a monkey A-503

Guericke, Otto von (1602–86), German physicist, born in Magdeburg, Germany; studied law and mathematics in Germany and Holland
- electricity E-161, S-57h

Guérin, Georges Maurice de (1810–39), French verse and prose writer, born near Albi, France; vivid, original style; works colored by intense love of nature.

Guerin, Jules (1866–1946), U.S. painter and illustrator, born in St. Louis, Mo.; executed the decorative work for Lincoln Memorial, Washington, D.C., and Pennsylvania Railroad station, New York, N.Y.

Guern Djediane, Ras, cape ("ras") on Mediterranean, in n. Tunisia, n.w. of Bizerte; northernmost point of continent of Africa (37° 20' 53" n. latitude).

'Guernica', painting by Picasso P-314

Guernsey, breed of cattle C-226, *picture* C-227

Guernsey, 2nd in size of Channel Islands; 25 sq mi (65 sq km); St. Peter Port and St. Sampson chief towns; pop. 51,346, *map* U-18a
- Channel Islands C-270

Guerrero, Vicente (1782–1831), Mexican revolutionary hero; president of Mexico 1829; when forced to retire put up armed resistance, but was finally captured and shot M-336

Guerrero, Mexico, state in s. on Pacific; 24,631 sq mi (63,794 sq km); cap. Chilpancingo (pop. 18,022); cotton, tobacco, coffee, grain, textile fibers, silver, mercury, gold, iron, lead; pop. 2,013,233
- Mexico, *map* M-341

'Guerrière', British frigate in War of 1812 S-177f, W-31, *picture* S-177g
- navy N-91, *picture* N-83

Guerrilla warfare G-301
- army A-645
- China C-373
- Guevara G-302
- Israel S-550

Lebanon L-113
Palestine D-44
Philippines, *picture* P-259d
Third World T-169
U.S.S.R. R-352
Vietnam V-321, 324
Western Sahara W-154

Guest, Edgar Albert (1881–1959), U.S. writer of verse, born in Birmingham, England; came to U.S. 1891; with *Detroit Free Press* 1895–1959; immensely popular for more serious verse dealing with everyday life, also for humorous verse and sketches ('Just Folks'; 'When Day Is Done'; 'All That Matters').

Guettard, Jean-Étienne (1715–86), French geologist L-90

Guevara, Che (1928–67), Argentinian revolutionary and guerrilla leader G-302
Cuba C-804
guerrilla warfare G-301

Gufa, a boat B-325

Guggenheim, Benjamin (1865–1912), son of Meyer Guggenheim, father of Peggy Guggenheim G-302

Guggenheim, Daniel (1856–1930), U.S. industrialist, eldest son of Meyer Guggenheim G-302

Guggenheim, Harry Frank (1890–1971), U.S. president aeronautics fund, ambassador to Cuba 1929–33.

Guggenheim, Meyer (1828–1905), Swiss capitalist, founder of Guggenheim family G-302
industry I-195

Guggenheim, Peggy (1898–1979), U.S. art collector, daughter of Benjamin Guggenheim G-302

Guggenheim, Simon (1867–1941), U.S. senator from Colorado (1907–13), who established scholarship fund for advanced study abroad in memory of son, John Simon G-302

Guggenheim, Solomon R. (1861–1949), U.S. philanthropist, son of Meyer Guggenheim G-302. *see also in index* Solomon R. Guggenheim Museum

Guggenheim foundations. *see in index* John Simon Guggenheim Memorial Fellowships

Guggenheim Museum. *see in index* Solomon R. Guggenheim Museum

Guglielmo Ebreo (or William the Jew), medieval ballet pioneer D-26

Guiana Highlands, region in n. South America G-302
South America S-275, 269, *map* S-274

Guianas, The, a region in n.e. South America, including Guyana, Suriname (formerly called Dutch Guiana), and French Guiana L-58, *map* S-298, *picture* S-277
Guiana Highlands G-302
Raleigh's expedition R-91

Guicciardini, Francesco (1483–1540), Italian statesman and historian H-172

Guidance, educational and vocational counseling G-303
disability D-163
leisure activities V-237
psychology P-523
personality tests P-218
social worker S-243
vocations V-359

Guided missile G-307
artillery's development A-660
bibliography S-348d
machine gun M-14
modern ammunition A-372
nuclear weapons N-434
rocket. *see in index* Rocket
titanium T-193

Guided Missile Cruiser, naval vessel, *picture* N-90

Guided Missile Destroyer, naval vessel, *picture* N-90

Guided Missile Frigate, naval vessel, *picture* N-90

'Guide of the Perplexed', work by Maimonides M-50

'Guide to Scandinavian Antiquities', work by Thomsen A-535

Guidi, Tommaso di Giovanni di Simone. *see in index* Masaccio

Guidon, flag used by military, *list* F-149

Guido of Arezzo (or Guido Aretinus) (995?–1050?), Benedictine monk; introduced modern system of music notation.

Guido Reni (1575–1642), Italian painter, born near Bologna, Italy; pupil of Calvaert and the Carracci; influenced by Caravaggio; religious paintings.

Guienne, France. *see in index* Guyenne

Guignol, name given by French to main character in a puppet show, also to a puppet or to a puppet theater.

Guilbert, Yvette (1869–1944), French singer, born in Paris; unsurpassed in her day for dramatic and humorous rendition of old ballads.

Guilder, monetary unit of The Netherlands. *see in index* Florin; Gulden

Guildhall, old council hall in Cheapside, London; severely damaged by bombs in World War II; many statues damaged and wooden figures of Gog and Magog destroyed; restoration completed 1954 L-290, *map* L-289

Guilds (or gilds) G-313
apprentice system A-511
foundations and charities F-328
franchises F-373
Industrial Revolution I-177
knitting N-113
labor L-2
Middle Ages M-303, R-148, *picture* M-392
economic minorities M-459
pinmakers P-327
shoemakers S-178
textiles T-143

Guild socialism, a kind of socialism developed in England in early 20th century, advocating control of industry by workers' guilds.

Guilford, Joy Paul (born 1897), U.S. psychologist I-242

Guilford College, Greensboro, N.C.; established in 1837 by Religious Society of Friends (Quakers); arts and sciences, education G-283

Guilford Courthouse, in North Carolina, site of battle March 1781, between Greene and Cornwallis, 5 mi (8 km) n.w. of Greensboro N-360
flag F-164, *pictures* 155

Guilford Courthouse National Military Park, park near Greensboro, N.C. N-50

Guillaume, Charles Edouard (1861–1938), French physicist, born in Fleurier, near Neuchâtel, Switzerland; inventor of invar. *see also in index* Nobel Prizewinners, *table*

Guillaume de Lorris (13th century), French writer F-394

Guillemin, Roger (born 1924), U.S. physiologist, born in Dijon, France; to U.S. 1953, naturalized 1965; professor Baylor College of Medicine, Houston, 1953–70; at Salk Institute and University of California, San Diego, 1970–; hormone research. *see also in index* Nobel Prizewinners, *table*

Guillemot, a bird of the auk family A-763
egg, *picture* E-111

Guillén, Jorge (1877–1984), Spanish author, born in Valladolid, Spain; first volume of poems 'Canticle' (1928) S-366

Guillotine, French instrument of execution F-403

Guilmant, Félix Alexandre (1837–1911), French organist and composer, born in Boulogne-sur-Mer, France; for more than 30 years, organist at church of the Trinity, in Paris; well known for compositions for organ.

Guimaraes Rosa, Joao (1908–67), Brazilian writer L-71

Guimaraes, Portugal, town 35 mi (55 km) n.e. of Oporto; birthplace of first king of Portugal; known also for historical buildings and fortifications, *map* P-455

Guinea (full name Republic of Guinea), nation in n.w. Africa on Atlantic Ocean; area 94,926 sq mi (245,857 sq km); cap. Conakry; pop. 5,579,000 G-314
African independence A-111, *table* A-112, *map* A-115
communist world, *map* C-619
flag, *picture* F-165
illiteracy P-450
railroad mileage, *table* R-85
world, *map* W-297

Guinea, a former English gold coin so named because gold of which it was coined came from Guinea Coast of w. Africa; term still used as money unit (21 shillings).

Guinea, Gulf of, gulf on w. coast of Africa, *map* A-115
Ghana G-139
world, *map* W-297

Guinea-Bissau (or Republic of Guinea-Bissau, formerly Portuguese Guinea), independent republic in w. Africa; area 13,948 sq mi (36,125 sq km); cap. Bissau; pop. 842,000 G-315, *map* A-115
African political unit, *table* A-112
communist world, *map* C-619
flag, *picture* F-165
world, *map* W-297

Guinea fowl, bird G-315

Guinea pig (or cavy), rodent *Cavia porcellus* G-316
pets P-244
research experiments V-357, *pictures* V-354
vision C-563

Guinea worm, nematode, *picture* I-285

Guinevere, character in Arthurian romance, Arthur's beautiful but unfaithful queen; had romance with Sir Lancelot A-655, R-299a

Guinness, Alec (born 1914), English actor G-316

Guinness, Benjamin Lee (1798–1868), Irish brewer and originator of 'The Guinness Book of World Records' and other sports record books G-316

Guinness Brewery, business in Dublin, Ireland D-282, G-316

Guion, David Wendel Fentress (born 1892), U.S. composer, born in Ballinger, Tex.; known for transcriptions of U.S. folk songs, including 'Home on the Range' and 'Turkey in the Straw'.

Güiraldes, Ricardo (1886–1927), Argentine writer L-70

Guiscard, Robert. *see in index* Robert Guiscard

Guise, French ducal family branch of house of Lorraine, whose heads led extreme Catholic party and aspired to snatch crown from house of Bourbon
Huguenots H-317

Guise, Henry, duke of (nickname Le Balafré, the Scarred) (1550–88); incited murder of Coligny and Massacre of St. Bartholomew; assassinated by order of Henry III of France.

Guise, Mary of. *see in index* Mary of Guise

Guise, France, historic town on Oise River, 90 mi (145 km) n.e. of Paris; industrial center; ruins of ancestral castle of House of Guise; pop. 6,732, *map* F-369

Guiser, person who dresses up in a mask
Halloween H-17

Guitar, stringed instrument S-492, *pictures* S-490a, 491
country music M-678

Guiteau, Charles Jules (or Charles Julius Guiteau) (1840?–82), U.S. lawyer, assassin of President Garfield; sought government post unsuccessfully A-703, G-29, *picture* G-31

Guiterman, Arthur (1871–1943), U.S. writer, born in Vienna of U.S. parents; to New York at age of 2; author of ballads, lyrics, humorous verse ('Chips of Jade'; 'I Sing the Pioneer'; 'Wildwood Fables'; 'Song and Laughter'); wrote libretto of opera 'Man Without a Country'.

Guitry, Lucien Germain (1860–1925), French actor, one of greatest French interpreters of modern realistic drama; his son **Sacha** (1885–1957) noted as writer of comedies, dramatic biographies, also as motion-picture actor and producer.

Guiyang (or Kweiyang), China, capital of Guizhou Province; coal mining; textiles and chemicals; seat of higher education; pop. 660,000.
Asia, *map* A-697

Guizhou (or Kweichow), province of s. China; 66,000 sq mi (171,000 sq km); cap. Guiyang; pop. 28,552,997.

Guizot, François (1787–1874), French statesman and historian, born in Nîmes; head of ministry under Louis Philippe ('History of Civilization in Europe').

Gujarat, state of w.-central and n.w. India, on Arabian Sea; area 72,137 sq mi (186,834 sq km); cap. Ahmadabad; salt, manganese; teak (Gir Forest the sanctuary of the only wild lions outside Africa); rice, millet, wheat, cotton; textiles; pop. 26,697,475 A-144, *map* I-83

Gujranwala, Pakistan, city 40 mi (65 km) n.w. of Lahore; center for wheat, rice, sugar, cotton, wool; textiles, metal products; pop. 196,154.

Gulbranssen, Trygve (1894–1962), Norwegian novelist; 'Beyond Sing the Woods' and 'The Wind from the Mountains', chronicles of life on a manor in forests of Norway R-112c

Gulden, monetary unit of the former free city of Danzig, equal to a 25th part of an English pound sterling, and nominally worth about 33 cents; also formerly used in Austria and Bavaria (worth when current about 48 and 41 cents, respectively); The Netherlands guilder is also called gulden.

Gules, in heraldry H-136

Gulf, a sea almost surrounded by land. For individual gulfs *see in index* name of gulf, as Aqaba, Gulf of

Gulf Coastal Plain, region in the United States U-37, 63, *maps* U-36, 58
Alabama A-223
Arkansas A-613
Mississippi M-467, *map* M-468
Oklahoma O-522
Texas T-116, *map* T-117

Gulf Cooperation Council (GCC), organization A-522, B-21

Gulf flounder, a flatfish F-174

Gulf Islands National Seashore, seashore of the Gulf of Florida and the Gulf of Mississippi N-50, *map* N-40

Gulf of Mexico. *see in index* Mexico, Gulf of

Gulf Oil Corporation, incorporated 1907 with A.W. Mellon as president; had origin in J.M. Guffey Petroleum Company and Gulf Refining Company of Texas, formed 1901 as outlet for oil from Spindletop field; operations throughout world; headquarters, Pittsburgh, Pa.

Gulfport, Miss., city on Mississippi Sound, Gulf of Mexico, 12 mi (19 km) w. of Biloxi; deepwater harbor; resort area; aluminum products, glass, creosoting, pharmaceuticals, fishery products, clothing, steel products; pop. 39,676, *map* U-41

Gulf Stream, a warm-water current flowing from the Florida Straits across the Atlantic to northern Europe
Atlantic Ocean A-745
Gulf of Mexico M-345
oceanography O-475
ocean waves and tides O-490
climate O-459

Gulfweed (or sargassum), a seaweed with air-bladder floats A-284, S-104

Gulick, Luther Halsey (1865–1918), U.S. educator and writer, born in Honolulu; organized physical education in YWCA and in New York City public schools; editor physical education magazines; with wife founded Camp Fire Girls Y-428

Gull, a long-winged water bird G-317, B-252, *picture* B-248
animal tracks A-463
California gull
Mormons' cricket plague U-220, *picture* U-221
Sea Gull Monument U-220, *picture* U-234
state bird, *picture* U-222
length of life, average, *chart* A-423

Gullet. *see in index* Esophagus

Gulliver, character in 'Gulliver's Travels', *picture* N-412

'Gulliver's Travels', satire by Swift, first published in 1726 S-530, R-111, *picture* S-532
English literature E-270
satire N-412
science fiction S-61

Gullstrand, Allvar (1862–1930), Swedish ophthalmologist and physicist; contributed to knowledge of the structure and function of the cornea; research on the eye as a light-refracting apparatus.

Gyges, character in Greek mythology, hundred-handed giant flung into Tartarus for warring on gods.

Gymkhana, automobile race A-875

Gymnasium, a place devoted to sports
  accident prevention S-8
  physical education H-94

Gymnastics G-323
  Greece, ancient S-368
    Sparta E-79
  physical education H-94

Gymnophiona, amphibian order. *see in index* Apoda

Gymnosperms (or Gymnospermae), a class of plants F-220, P-361, P-371, *picture* S-106
  trees T-282
  wood W-280

Gynecology, medical field H-280, *table* M-277

Györ (German Raab), Hungary, port on arm of Danube River 67 mi (108 km) n.w. of Budapest; steel; railroad cars, textiles, food products; pop. 129,000 H-329, *map* E-360

Gypsum, a soft mineral, usually white M-432, 435
  alabaster A-238
  building construction
    materials B-491
  cement C-243
  uses B-494, C-18

Gypsum Cave culture, prehistoric North Americans I-144

Gypsum Hills, cluster of eroded rocks in Kansas, *picture* K-183

Gypsy (or gipsy, or gitano, or tzigane) G-326
  caravans, *picture* S-156
  folktales S-470, *list* S-481
  Hungary H-327
  Nazi concentration camps
    C-638
  genocide G-60
  Holocaust H-205
  nomads N-332
  Spain, *picture* S-554

'Gypsy Girl, The', painting by Hals P-43

Gypsy moth, a moth of the silkworm family
  eradication B-138
  forest defoliation, *picture*
    F-312
  insect immigrants I-225
  winter survival B-526

Gyre, a complete twist in nucleotide chains in DNA
  genetics G-56

Gyrfalcon (or gerfalcon) F-13

Gyrocompass G-327
  magnetic compass C-622

Gyro flux gate compass C-623

Gyro horizon (or artificial horizon), flight instrument A-195

Gyroscope G-327
  airplane instruments A-194
  manufacturing laboratory
    M-445

Gyrosyn compass C-623

The letter H

may have started as a picture sign of a fence, as in very early Semitic writing used about 1500 B.C. on the Sinai Peninsula (1).

About 1000 B.C., in Byblos and other Phoenician and Canaanite centers, the sign was given a linear form (2), the source of all later forms. The sign was called *heth* in the Semitic languages, which may have meant "fence." The sound expressed by the *heth* sign stood for a pharyngeal sound which is not found in the English language.

The Greeks renamed the sign *eta* and used it in two functions—first for the consonant "h" and then for the long vowel "e" (3). The Romans took over the form H (4), with the sound value of the English "h." From Latin the capital letter came into English unchanged.

A small Greek *eta* with curves (5) was developed from the capital letter. By the 9th century the corresponding Latin letter acquired a shape (6) much like the English handwritten and printed small "h."

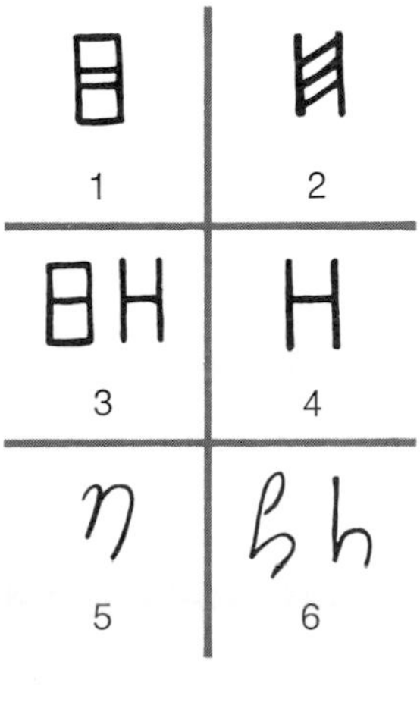

Haag, Den, The Netherlands. *see in index* Hague, The

Haakon I (born 920?), king of Norway; called "the Good" H-2

Haakon II (1147–62), king of Norway; called "the Broadshouldered" H-2

Haakon III Sverrson (died 1204), king of Norway H-2

Haakon IV Haakonsson (1204–63), king of Norway H-2
  Norway N-394

Haakon V Magnusson (1270–1319), king of Norway H-2

Haakon VI Magnusson (1339–80), king of Norway H-2

Haakon VII (1872–1957), king of Norway H-2
  Norway N-394
  Olav O-538
  World War II W-323

Ha'apai, a group of islands forming a division of Tonga T-214, *map* P-3

Haarlem, The Netherlands, cap. of North Holland province, on Sparne River; pop. 154,347; printing, shipbuilding, chocolate; flower fields; chartered 1245, *map* N-125

Haast, William E. (born 1910), U.S. herpetologist, born in Paterson, N.J.; as director of Miami Serpentarium 1948–, extracted snake venoms for research and medical treatment; bitten many times by deadly snakes, including king cobras; own blood supplied to treat snakebite victims.

Hába, Alois (1893–1973), Czech composer, born in Vizovice, near Zlín, Czechoslovakia; experimented with quarter, sixth, and twelfth tone music; influenced by ancient Slav and Greek music.

Habakkuk, a Hebrew minor prophet probably of 7th century BC; Book of Habakkuk, 8th of the Minor Prophets, deals with the wickedness of the nation, the rise of the Chaldeans, and the appearance of God in judgment.

Habana, Cuba. *see in index* Havana

Habeas corpus, a writ requiring a person in custody to be brought before a court H-2
  British civil rights C-442
  law, *table* L-93

Habeas Corpus Act (1679), England H-2

Haber, Fritz (1868–1934), German chemist, born in Breslau; professor Berlin University; specialized in electrochemical investigations; with Carl Bosch invented synthetic process of making ammonia.

Haber-Bosch process, nitrogen fixation N-319

Habib, Philip (born 1920), U.S. diplomat; sent by President Reagan in 1982 as special envoy to Middle East to conduct negotiations during Lebanon crisis D-152

Habichtsburg (or Hawk's Castle), seat of Hapsburgs H-32

Habima, Yiddish theater group Y-419

Habit H-2. *see also in index* Addiction
  alcoholism A-276
  automobile driving A-863
  opium O-572
  study S-495

Habitants, farm workers in feudal system of landholding adopted in New France, based on established practices in France; allegiance pledged to the seigneur, or noble C-92

Habitat, the natural location where plant or animal normally lives. *see also in index* Ecology
  birds B-252
  endangered species E-209
  evolution and accommodation A-461
  plants P-363f, *pictures* P-363e

Habitat box, hobby H-184

Habitation, settlement established by Champlain in western Nova Scotia C-91

Habit-forming drug H-2

Hablon, fabric produced in Filipino cottage industries; woven in combination of threads (rayon, cotton, silk, etc.) to reduce wrinkles and increase durability; made in bright colors.

Habsburg, ruling family. *see in index* Hapsburg

Habutai (or habutaye), a silk similar to China silk, but heavier; originally handwoven, now manufactured on power looms; name Japanese for soft as down.

Hachure, map making M-120, *picture* M-121

Hacienda, huge estate for farming or stock raising; name also applied to mining or manufacturing place; term used in nations where Spanish is or has been spoken, particularly in Latin America
  Mexico M-331, 336
  Philippines P-260
  South America S-286
    Peru, *pictures* P-223, S-269

Hackberry, tree *Celtis occidentalis* of the elm family, ranging over most of the U.S., resembling the elm in aspect, with ovate leaves and rough bark, and bearing small, round, purple-skinned fruit with sweet yellowish flesh; also called sugarberry and nettle tree.

Hackbut. *see in index* Harquebus

Hackensack, N.J., city 12 mi (19 km) n. of Jersey City on Hackensack River; clothing and footwear, paper products, chemicals; pop. 36,039.

Hackensack River, s. New York and n. New Jersey; empties into Newark Bay; 50 mi (80 km) long; dammed at Oradell, N.J.; navigable to New Milford, N.J. N-193

Hacker, computer hobbyist H-191

Hackett, Charles (1889–1942), U.S. operatic tenor, born in Worcester, Mass.; debut in 'Mignon', Genoa, Italy, 1915; later with Metropolitan (New York City) and Chicago Civic Opera companies.

Hackett, Francis (1883–1962), U.S. literary critic, biographer, and novelist, born in Kilkenny, Ireland ('Henry the Eighth', biography; 'Queen Anne Boleyn', novel).

Hackett, James Keteltas (1869–1926), U.S. actor and manager, born in Wolfe Island, s.e. Ontario ('The Prisoner of Zenda'; 'The Pride of Jennico'); son of **James Henry Hackett** (1800–71), who was one of the most noted comedians of his day.

Hackney, English horse breed, *pictures* H-254, 256, *list* H-254

Hackney, borough, London, *maps* L-287, U-18a

Hack saw, a tool T-218

Hadassah, the Women's Zionist Organization of America; founded 1912 by Henrietta Szold (1860–1945); devoted to health work in Palestine (now Israel); name is Hebrew form of Esther.

Hadden, Briton, publisher
  Time M-35

Haddock, bottom-dwelling codlike fish *Melanogrammus aeglefinus*, H-4, *table* F-136

Haddonfield, N.J., borough, residential suburb, about 5 mi (8 km) s.e. of Camden; first New Jersey state legislature met here 1777; pop. 12,337.

Haden, Sir Francis Seymour (1818–1910), British etcher and surgeon, born in London; in addition to distinguished career as surgeon, became foremost English etcher, causing revival of etching in England; brother-in-law of Whistler.

Hadendowa, Hamitic people of Sudan, Africa S-502

Hader, Elmer Stanley (1889–1973), U.S. artist and writer, born in Pajaro, Calif.; painted landscapes and portraits; collaborated with his wife, **Berta Hoerner Hader** (1891–1976), in writing and illustrating children's books ('Spunky'; 'Whiffy McMann'; 'The Big Snow', awarded Caldecott Medal 1949; 'Lost in the Zoo'; 'Wish on the Moon').

Hades, abode for the dead in various religious belief systems. *see in index* Hell and Hades

Hades (or Pluto), in Greek mythology, god of lower world, also name of lower world M-700. *see also in index* Pluto
  hell and Hades H-123
  Hercules H-138
  Homeric legend H-223
  Orpheus and Eurydice. *see in index* Orpheus
  Perseus P-210
  Rhea R-176
  Zeus Z-451

Hadfield, Sir Robert Abbot (1858–1940), British metallurgist, born in Sheffield ('Metallurgy and Its Influence on Modern Progress'; 'Faraday and His Metallurgical Researches').

Hadhramaut, a region of People's Democratic Republic of Yemen; port Mukalla, *map* A-697

Hadith, traditions of Islam I-365

Hadley, Arthur Twining (1856–1930), U.S. educator and political economist, born in New Haven, Conn.; associated with Yale University most of his life as student, teacher, and as president 1899–1921 ('Railway Transportation: Its History and Its Laws'; 'The Education of the American Citizen'; 'The Conflict between Liberty and Equality').

Hadley, Henry Kimball (1871–1937), U.S. composer, born in Somerville, Mass.; conducted orchestras of Seattle and San Francisco, also Manhattan Orchestra in New York; associate conductor New York Philharmonic Orchestra; composed operas ('Cleopatra's Night'), symphonies ('The Four Seasons'), cantatas, songs.

Hadley, John (1682–1744), English mathematician and physicist; invented sextant 1731; improved reflecting telescope
  navigation N-78

Hadrian (full name Publius Aelius Hadrianus) (AD 76–138), Roman emperor H-4
  Athens' reconstruction A-736
  Britain E-238, S-69, *picture* S-71
  bust, *picture* R-243
  empire, *map* R-242
  Roman history R-248
  villa, *pictures* I-382, 391

Hadrian's tomb. *see in index* Castel Sant' Angelo

Hadrian's Wall, ancient Roman wall, Britain F-319

Hadron, subatomic particle A-754
  quark Q-5

Haeckel, Ernst Heinrich (1834–1919), German zoologist, born in Potsdam; early advocate of Darwinism; professor at University of Jena 1865–1908
  biogenetic law E-203
  zoology Z-469

Haeckel's Law (or biogenetic law), biological theory Z-469

Haeinsa Temple, a Buddhist temple in Korea; built in the year 802; famous for 81,137 wooden printing blocks of the Buddhist canon T-5

Haematopodidae, a family of shorebirds, the oyster catchers. *see in index* Oyster catcher

Hafey, Charles James (nickname Chick) (1903–73), U.S. baseball outfielder, born in Berkeley, Calif.; with St. Louis, N.L., 1924–32, Cincinnati, N.L., 1932–37.

Hafiz (pen name of Shams ud-din Mohammed) (died 1388?), Persian lyric poet and philosopher; tomb near Shiraz, a place of pilgrimage.

Hafnium (Hf), chemical element
  periodic table, *table* P-207, *list* P-208

Hafstad, Lawrence Randolph (born 1904), U.S. physicist, born in Minneapolis, Minn.; first director reactor development division U.S. Atomic Energy Commission 1949–55; vice-president in charge of research General Motors Corporation 1955–69; chairman Committee on Undersea Warfare, National Academy of Sciences 1967–73.

Hafun, Ras, cape ("ras") of Somalia; easternmost point of continent of Africa; s.e. of Cape Guardafui, *map* A-118

Haganah, Zionist military organization representing the majority of the Jews in Palestine from 1920–48; engaged in terrorist acts and clashes with British forces D-44
  Haifa H-6

Hagar, Sarah's handmaid, mother of Abraham's son Ishmael (Bible, Gen. xvi, xxi).

Hagedorn, Hermann, (1882–1964), U.S. author, born in New York City; wrote poems, pageants, and plays; biographer of Theodore Roosevelt ('Boys' Life of Theodore Roosevelt'; 'Roosevelt in the Bad Lands'; 'The Rough Riders'; 'The Hyphenated Family', autobiographical).

Hageman, Richard (1882–1966), U.S. composer and conductor, born in The Netherlands; a conductor of Metropolitan (New York City), Chicago, and Los Angeles opera companies; composed many songs ('Do Not Go, My Love') and opera ('Caponsacchi').

Hagen, in 'Nibelungenlied', slayer of Siegfried S-192a

Hagen, John Peter (born 1908), U.S. astronomer, born in Amherst, N.S.; superintendent atmosphere and astrophysics division U.S. Naval Research Laboratory 1950–58, director Project Vanguard 1955–58; chief Vanguard division, NASA, 1958–62; professor of astronomy Pennsylvania State University 1962–76, head of department 1967–76.

Hagen, Walter (nickname The Haig) (1892–1969), U.S. golfer, born in Rochester, N.Y.;

retired from competition 1940; autobiography, 'The Walter Hagen Story' G-189, *picture* G-190

Hagen, West Germany, industrial city on Volme River about 31 mi (50 km) n.e. of Düsseldorf; important iron- and steelworks; pop. 200,909, *map* G-131

Hagenbeck, Karl (1844–1913), German animal dealer and showman; established zoo near Hamburg
  elephants E-185
  zoos Z-465

Hagenbeck zoo, Hamburg, West Germany H-20

Hagerstown, Md., city in center of rich farm section, 64 mi (103 km) n.w. of Baltimore; railroad shops; aircraft, engines and transmissions, textiles, sandblasting and dust-collecting equipment, shoes, pipe organs, furniture; refrigeration equipment; battlefields of Antietam and Gettysburg nearby; pop. 34,132 M-168, 178, *map* M-182

Hagerty, James Campbell (1909–81), U.S. government official and journalist, born in Plattsburgh, N.Y.; on staff *The New York Times* 1934–42; executive assistant 1943–50 and secretary 1950–52 to Gov. Thomas E. Dewey of New York; press secretary to Pres. Eisenhower 1953–61; a vice-president American Broadcasting Company 1961–75.

Hagfish (or borer), an eellike parasitic fish A-435, F-132, P-114, *picture* A-434

Haggadah, division of the Talmud T-18, P-136

Haggai, 10th book of the 12 Minor Prophets in the Old Testament; named for a Hebrew prophet (flourished 6th century BC) whose oracles the book contains.

Haggard, Sir Henry Rider (1856–1925), British novelist and writer on land economics, born in Norfolk, England; spent early life in S. Africa, scene of many of his best novels, including 'She', 'King Solomon's Mines', 'Allan Quatermain', 'Ayesha, or the Return of She' ('Days of My Life', autobiography).

Haggard, Merle (born 1937), U.S. country musician M-679

Haggard (or blue hawk), falcon F-13

Hagia Sophia. *see in index* Santa Sophia

Hagiographa (or Holy Writings), portion of the Old Testament and final third of Hebrew Scriptures P-509

Hagiwara, Sakutaro (1886–1942), Japanese poet
  literature J-82

Hague, The (or Gravenhage, or Den Haag), The Netherlands, governmental center; pop. 443,456 H-4, *map* E-360
  International Court of Justice U-21, *chart* U-21
  The Netherlands N-126
  world courts. *see in index* International Court of Justice; Permanent Court of Arbitration; Permanent Court of International Justice

Hague Court. *see in index* Permanent Court of Arbitration

Hague Peace Conferences H-5
  chemical warfare restrictions C-293
  disarmament D-164
  armament limitation fails P-143c
  Nicholas II N-306
  Roosevelt, Theodore R-286
  warfare W-26

Ha Ha, game G-13

Hahn, Otto (1879–1968), German physical chemist H-6
  Meitner M-287

Hahnemann, Christian Friedrich Samuel (1755–1843), German physician, born Meissen, Germany; known as founder of homeopathy H-219. *see also in index* Homeopathy

Hahnium (Ha), unofficial name of a chemical element
  periodic table, *table* P-207, *list* P-208

Haida, Indian tribe that lives in British Columbia and Alaska A-242, *map* I-136, *table* I-138

Haifa, Israel, seaport 70 mi (115 km) n.w. of Jerusalem built on Mt. Carmel; railway terminus; trade center; fine harbor; pop. 227,900 H-6
  Israel I-369
  Israel Institute of Technology, *picture* M-396

Haig, Alexander Meigs, Jr. (born 1924), U.S. army officer and public official, born in Bala-Cynwyd, Pa.; deputy assistant to President Nixon for national security affairs 1970–73; army vice chief of staff 1973; White House chief of staff 1973–74; supreme allied commander of NATO forces 1974–79; U.S. secretary of state 1981–82 R-112d

Haig, Douglas Haig, 1st **Earl** (1861–1928), British soldier, born in Edinburgh, Scotland; served under Kitchener in Nile campaign 1898; in World War I won fame as commander British 1st Army 1914–15 and commander in chief British expeditionary forces in France and Flanders 1915–19; made earl 1919
  World War I W-307

Haig-Brown, Roderick Langmere Haig (1908–76), Canadian writer, naturalist, and magistrate, born in Sussex, England; moved to British Columbia 1927; books for children: 'Starbuck Valley Winter' (Canadian Book of the Year for Children award 1947), 'Saltwater Summer', 'Mounted Police Patrol', and 'The Whale People' (Canadian Books of the Year for Children award 1964).

Hai Ho, river. *see in index* Pei Ho

Haiku, Japanese poetry J-49, J-81

Hail, precipitation of balls or pieces of ice, often during a thunderstorm; hailstones, 0.2 to 4 in (0.5 to 10 cm) in diameter, form when water freezes around an ice crystal held aloft by strong updrafts; hailstorms may damage crops and property W-120
  clouds C-517

Hailar, China, city in n.e. part of Inner Mongolian Autonomous Region, w. of Great Khingan Mountains; pop. 60,000.

'Hail Columbia', patriotic song of United States N-65

Haile Selassie (born Tafari Makonnen) (1892–1975), emperor of Ethiopia H-6
  Ethiopia E-314

Hainan, island of China, in South China Sea 15 mi (25 km) from mainland; 13,000 sq mi (34,000 sq km); jungle-covered mountains; rich valleys; sugarcane, *map* V-321
  Asia, *map* A-697
  world, *map* W-297

Haines, Jesse Joseph (nickname Pop) (1893–1978) U.S. baseball pitcher, born in Clayton, Ohio; player for Cincinnati, N.L., 1918, St. Louis, N.L., 1920–37; knuckleballer; won 210 games, lost 158; won 20 games in 1923 and 1928, 24 in 1927; pitched no-hit game against Boston, N.L., in 1924; in 4 world series, posted 3–1 record.

Hainisch, Michael (1858–1940) president of Austrian Republic 1920–28; noted Socialist writer; previously (1909) member of Austrian parliament; favored Germany's annexation of Austria.

Haiphong, port of Vietnam, in Red River delta about 60 mi (95 km) s.e. of Hanoi; shipping point for rice, corn, silk, cotton, tin, zinc; manufactures cement, glass, china; shipbuilding, tin smelting; pop. 276,300, *map* A-697, V-321
  United States' bombings V-324

'Hair' (1968), rock musical by Ragni, Rado, and MacDermot M-686

Hair, animal H-7. *see also in index* Furs; Wool
  beaver fur B-120
  leather L-107
  mammal M-79
  musk-ox M-693

Hair, human H-7
  braiding B-395
  brushes, *picture* P-382
  classification of humans R-25
  fashion F-40
  hair-erector muscle S-211
  health care H-88
    products C-728

Hair balls (or fur balls), cause of illness in cats C-210

Hairdressing, grooming H-8

Hair dryer, *picture* I-171

Hair frog, fishing term, *list* F-146

Hair seal S-100, *table* F-465

Hairspring (or balance spring), in watches and clocks W-78

Hairy hedgehog, mammal H-115

Hairy woodpecker, bird *Picoides villosus* W-286

Haise, Fred W., Jr. (born 1933), U.S. astronaut, born in Biloxi, Miss.; test pilot; chosen for NASA program 1966; Medal of Freedom for Apollo 13 flight 1970, *table* S-348

Haiti, republic in West Indies; 10,360 sq mi (26,833 sq km); cap. Port-au-Prince; pop. 5,251,500 H-11
  buccaneers P-342
  Christophe C-407
  Dominican Republic D-225
  flag, *picture* F-165
  fourth world T-168
  French colonies A-337
  hallucinogen use H-18
  Hispaniola H-169
  literature C-166
    folktales, *list* S-482, *picture* S-468
  national anthem, *table* N-64
  North America, *map* N-350
  Port-au-Prince P-451
  slavery
    abolished A-10
    introduced S-214
  sponges S-394
  West Indies W-155, *map* W-159
  world, *map* W-297
  World War II W-328

Haitink, Bernard (born 1929), Dutch conductor, *list* O-579

Hajji (or Hadji), title gained by pilgrim to Mecca.

'Hakai' (or 'The Broken Commandment'), novel by Toson Shimazaki J-82

Hake, fish of the hake family, Merlucciidae H-13

Hakka, people
  Taiwan T-13

Hakluyt, Richard (1552?–1616), English geographer H-13
  'Principall Navigations' C-119

Hakodate, Japan, seaport on a rocky promontory in s. Hokkaido; major industrial and fishing center; pop. 307,453, *map* J-75
  Asia, *map* A-697
  world, *map* W-297

Halaby, Najeeb Elias (born 1915), U.S. electronics executive, born in Dallas, Tex.; Army, Navy, and test pilot; practiced law in Los Angeles; administrator Federal Aviation Agency 1961–65; senior vice-president Pan American World Airways 1965–68, president 1968–73.

Halakah, division of the Talmud T-18

Halas, George Stanley (nickname Papa Bear) (1895–1984), U.S. football coach and owner of Chicago Bears, born in Chicago, Ill.; founded Chicago Bears 1920 as Decatur Staleys; coach 1920–29, 1933–42, 1946–55, 1958–68 F-298, *profile* F-296

Halcyon. *see in index* Kingfisher

Haldane, John Burdon Sanderson (1892–1964), English geneticist and writer, born in Oxford, England; son of John Scott Haldane; professor of genetics University of London 1933–37; professor of biometry University College, London, 1937–57.

Haldane, John Scott (1860–1936), British scientist and writer, born in Edinburgh, Scotland, father of J.B.S. Haldane and Naomi Mitchison; director, Mining Research Laboratory, Birmingham University; in charge of government inquiries on ventilation, respiration, and causes of death resulting from mine explosions and fires.

Haldane of Cloan, Richard Burdon Haldane, 1st **Viscount** (1856–1928), British statesman and philosopher, born in Scotland; wrote 'Life of Adam Smith', 'The Pathway to Reality', 'The Reign of Relativity', and 'The Philosophy of Humanism'; profound student of German philosophy, tried to avert World War I; sat in House of Commons 1885–1911; as secretary for war 1905–12, reorganized British army; lord chancellor 1912–15 and 1924.

Haldeman, Harry Robbins (nickname Bob) (born 1926), U.S. advertising executive, born in Los Angeles, Calif.; manager Los Angeles office of J. Walter Thompson Company 1960–69; chief of staff for Richard M. Nixon's presidential campaign 1968; assistant to the president 1969–73 ('The Ends of Power').

Halden (formerly Fredrikshald), Norway, fortified seaport on Idde Fjord; wood and paper products, footwear, textiles; Charles XII of Sweden was killed here in siege of 1718; pop. 9,967, *map* E-360

Haldimand, Sir Frederick (1718–91), British general and administrator, born in Switzerland; fought during French and Indian wars; governor of Canada 1778–84; sternly held down French sympathizers with American Revolution.

Hale, Barbara, U.S. actress
  'Perry Mason', *picture* T-69

Hale, Edward Everett (1822–1909), U.S. author and Unitarian minister H-14
  'The Brick Moon' S-341d

Hale, Enoch, U.S. engineer
  timber bridge B-445

Hale, George Ellery (1868–1938), U.S. astronomer, born in Chicago, Ill.; special research in solar and stellar spectroscopy; invented spectroheliograph; organizer of Yerkes Observatory (director 1895–1905), and of Mount Wilson Observatory (director 1904–23); his plans led to construction of a 200-in. (508-cm), reflecting telescope, completed 1948, for Palomar Observatory
  sunspot theory S-514

Hale, John Parker (1806–73), U.S. orator and statesman, born in Rochester, N.H.; long member of House of Representatives and, for 16 years, of Senate; antislavery advocate; nominated for president by Free-Soil Democrats in 1852; supported Lincoln throughout Civil War.

Hale, Lucretia Peabody (1820–1900), U.S. author and educator, born in Boston, Mass.; sister of Edward Everett Hale; children's books: 'The Peterkin Papers' and 'The Last of the Peterkins' R-111a

Hale, Nathan (1755–76), U.S. Revolutionary War soldier and patriot H-14

Hale, Sarah Josepha (1788–1879), U.S. editor and author, born in Newport, N.H.; editor Boston *Ladies' Magazine* and 'Godey's Lady's Book'; said to have suggested Thanksgiving Day as national holiday and to have worked for it from 1846 onward; 'Mary Had a Little Lamb' credited to her
  Thanksgiving T-150

Hale, William Jay (1876–1955), U.S. chemist, born in Ada, Ohio; director organic chemical research 1919–34, research consultant 1934–55, Dow Chemical Company, Midland, Mich.; patented processes for making aniline, phenol, and butadiene; called Father of Chemurgy P-379

Haleakala, crater on island of Maui in state of Hawaii H-58, *picture* U-99

Haleb, Syria. *see in index* Aleppo

Hales, Stephen (1677–1761), British physiologist and inventor, born in Bekesbourne; known for his 'Statical Essays', which describes experiments in plant physiology and in blood pressure and circulation M-283
  botany B-380

Hale telescope. *see in index* Hale, George Ellery

Halévy, Jacques Francois Fromental Elie (1799–1862), French composer, born in Paris; won Prix de Rome 1819; professor Paris conservatory after 1827, taught his future son-in-law, Georges Bizet, also Charles F. Gounod; known for 'La Juive', opera; member Legion of Honor.

Halevy, Judah. *see in index* Judah Halevy

Halévy, Ludovic (1834–1908), French dramatist and novelist, born in Paris; wrote 'L'Abbé Constantin', classic for French instruction; with H. Meilhac wrote libretto of 'Carmen' by Bizet and of operettas by Offenbach.

Haley, Alexander Palmer (nickname Alex) (born 1921), U.S. author, born in Ithaca, N.Y.; old family stories, museum research, and visits to Africa enabled him to trace his African ancestry; research resulted in 'Roots: the Saga of an American Family', which received Pulitzer prize in 1977; collaborator on 'Autobiography of Malcolm X'; Spingarn Medal 1977
 modern American literature A-361

Haley, Gail E. (born 1939), U.S. author and illustrator, born in Charlotte, N.C.; won 1971 Caldecott Medal for 'A Story—A Story'.

Half-and-half, dairy product, *list* D-6

Half hitch, knot K-264, *picture* K-263

Half-life, of a drug, refers to the time it takes for a drug to be removed from the bloodstream N-19

Half-life, the time in which half the quantity of an isotope undergoes fission R-67, *chart* R-66
 carbon-14 A-535
 radiometric dating E-22
 uranium U-210

'Half Moon', Hudson's ship N-256
 Hudson H-314
 models, *picture* M-516

Half-timber house S-158

Halftone engraving, in printing P-276, *pictures* P-277

Half uncial, in calligraphy C-58

Half-wave antenna, in radio R-53

Halfway house, residence for individuals who have been released from institutions H-14
 criminology C-777
 mental illness M-302

Haliburton, Thomas Chandler (pen name Sam Slick) (1796–1865), Canadian humorist, born in Windsor, N.S.; lawyer and judge in Nova Scotia; in England 1856–65 C-120, N-401

Halibut, fish, *chart* A-423, *table* F-136

Halicarnassus, ancient Greek city in Caria, Asia Minor
 Mausoleum S-115, *picture* S-116

Halictidae, family of small bees B-129

Halidah Adib. *see in index* Edib, Halidé

Halide mineral, classification M-435

Halides, binary compounds of the halogens. *see in index* Halogens

Halidon Hill, hill n.w. of Berwick-upon-Tweed, England, where English under Edward III defeated the Scots (1333).

Halifax, Charles Montague, earl of (1661–1715), English statesman; introduced into Great Britain national debt instead of annual taxation to meet expenses of war; carried out recoinage (1695); patron of Newton.

Halifax, Edward Frederick Lindley Wood, earl of (1881–1959), British statesman, born in Yorkshire; entered Parliament 1910 as Conservative; leader House of Lords; foreign secretary 1938–40; ambassador to United States 1940–46; 'Fullness of Days', autobiography.

Halifax, England, manufacturing city in n., 12 mi (19 km) s.w. of Leeds; woolens, carpets, machine tools and other metal products, confectionery; pop. 93,570, *map* U-18a

Halifax, N.C., n.e. corner on Roanoke River; settled 1723; designated a state historic site, 1965; pop. 253 N-360

Halifax, N.S., port, province capital; pop. 114,594 H-15, *map* C-112
 North America, *map* N-350
 Nova Scotia N-397, 402, *pictures* N-398
 world, *map* W-297

Halifax, British military aircraft W-333

Halite, sodium chloride in mineral form R-229b
 minerals M-435

Halitosis, dental disorder T-53

Hall, Asaph (1829–1907), U.S. astronomer, born in Goshen, Conn.; professor at Harvard University; discovered two moons of planet Mars.

Hall, Charles Francis (1821–71), U.S. explorer, born in Rochester, N.H.; searched for Franklin party 1860–69; died on North Pole expedition.

Hall, Charles Martin (1863–1914), U.S. inventor H-15
 aluminum A-323, I-275, *table* I-273

Hall, Chester Moor (1703–71), British lawyer, mathematician, and inventor, born in Leigh, Essex; first person to make an achromatic refracting telescope.

Hall, Emmett Matthew (born 1898), Canadian jurist, born in St-Columban, Que.; chief justice Court of Queen's Bench, Saskatchewan, 1957–61; chief justice Saskatchewan, 1961–62; justice Supreme Court of Canada 1962–73.

Hall, Glenn (born 1931), U.S. ice-hockey player, born in Humboldt, Sask.; goalie with Detroit Red Wings 1955–57, Chicago Black Hawks 1957–67, St. Louis Blues after 1967; won awards; named to many All-Star teams.

Hall, Granville Stanley (1844–1924), U.S. psychologist, educator, and editor; born near Ashfield, Mass.; president and professor of psychology Clark University, Worcester, Mass., 1888–1920 ('Adolescence').

Hall, James Norman (1887–1951), U.S. writer, born in Colfax, Iowa; lived many years in Tahiti; author of 'Doctor Dogbody's Leg', tales, and 'My Island Home', autobiography; with C.B. Nordhoff wrote 'Mutiny on the Bounty', 'Pitcairn's Island', 'The Hurricane', and 'The Dark River'.

Hall, Lyman (1724–90), American Revolutionary War leader, born in Wallingford, Conn.; signer of Declaration of Independence; governor of Georgia (1783–85).

Hall, Prince (1748–1807), U.S. champion of black peoples' rights, born in Barbados; Revolutionary War hero; founded first all-black Masonic lodge; worked for racial equality in education.

Halla, Mount, Korea K-282, *map* K-290

Hallam, Henry (1777–1859), English historian ('Europe During the Middle Ages'; 'Constitutional History of England'); father of **Arthur Henry Hallam** (1811–33), subject of Tennyson's 'In Memoriam'.

Hallandale, Fla., city 16 mi (26 km) n.e. of Miami; diversified industry; tourism; incorporated 1927; pop. 36,517.

Hallé, Sir Charles (1819–95), German-English pianist and conductor, born in Hagen, Westphalia; exerted important influence on musical education in England.

Halle, East Germany, city on the Saale River 20 mi (30 km) n.w. of Leipzig; saltworks; university founded in 1694 by Frederick III, elector of Brandenburg; pop. 257,300, *maps* G-131, E-360

Halleck, Charles Abraham (1900–86), U.S. political leader, born in Demotte, Ind.; U.S. Congressman (Republican) from Indiana 1935–69, majority leader 1947–49, 1953–55, minority leader 1959–65.

Halleck, Fitz-Greene (1790–1867), U.S. poet, born in Guilford, Conn.; remembered for 'Marco Bozzaris' and 'On the Death of Joseph Rodman Drake'.

Halleck, Henry Wager (1815–72), U.S. Civil War general, born in Westernville, N.Y.; succeeded McClellan in July 1862 as general in chief of all Union armies; superseded March 1864 by Grant
 Civil War C-474

Hallelujah, a Hebrew word meaning "praise ye the Lord".

Hallelujah Chorus, from Handel's 'Messiah' M-669

Haller, Albrecht von (1708–77), Swiss anatomist, physician, physiologist, botanist, and poet, born in Bern; particularly noted for doctrine of irritability of muscles ('Elementa Physiologiae Corporis Humani').

Halles, the (or Les Halles), Paris, France P-121

Halley, Edmond (1656–1742), English astronomer H-15
 comet observations C-596
 diving bells D-187

Halley's comet C-596, *pictures* A-716, C-597
 Halley H-15

Halliburton, Richard (1900–39), U.S. writer, lecturer, and traveler; born in Brownsville, Tenn.; wrote in youthful, vigorous style; lost in attempt to sail a Chinese junk across Pacific Ocean ('Royal Road to Romance'; 'Glorious Adventure').

Hallidie, Andrew Smith (1836–1900), Scottish-American civil engineer and inventor, born in London, England S-487

Hallmark, official stamp used by goldsmiths and silversmiths to indicate purity; originally used on gold and silver articles in Goldsmiths' Hall in London; used figuratively of persons or things showing signs of genuineness.

Hall of Fame H-16
 baseball. *see in index* Baseball Hall of Fame and Museum, National
 football. *see in index* Football Hall of Fame
 ice hockey H-198

Hall of Knights (or Ridderzaal), The Hague, The Netherlands H-4

Halloween (or All Hallow's Eve), evening of October 31 H-17
 folk art F-251
 science fiction S-61

Hallstatt, Austria, village on Lake Hallstatt 11 mi (18 km) s. of Bad Ischl; old and famous salt mines; ancient Celtic remains of Iron and Bronze ages.

Hallstein, Walter (1901–82), German government official, born in Mainz; professor of law at Rostock and Frankfurt universities; secretary of state foreign office, West Germany, 1951–58; president European Economic Community 1958–68.

Hallström, Per August Leonard (1866–1960), Swedish novelist, born in Stockholm; chairman of committee of Swedish Academy for Nobel awards ('Stray Birds'; 'An Old Tale').

Hallucination, perception of objects that have no reality
 dreams D-257

Hallucinogen H-18. *see also in index* types of hallucinogens by name, such as Marijuana
 drugs D-277
 narcotics N-19

Hallwachs, Wilhelm (1859–1922), German physicist, born in Darmstadt; professor of physics at Dresden technical institute and at Giessen; in 1888 discovered underlying principle, known as the Hallwachs effect, of the photoelectric cell.

Halmahera, island in Moluccas, Indonesia, w. of New Guinea; over 6,500 sq mi (16,800 sq km); mountainous, thick forests; sago palm, rice; pop. 97,133, *map* I-166
 Asia, *map* A-697
 world, *map* W-297

Halo, astronomy, luminous bands around the sun or moon caused by refraction and reflection of rays of light by the ice crystals in the atmosphere; in art, circle of light surrounding a head to denote divinity or saintliness
 astronomy A-725

Halogens, the four related chemical elements fluorine, chlorine, bromine, and iodine
 chlorine C-392
 periodic table, *table* P-207

Halogeton, a poisonous weed *Halogeton glomeratus* of the Chenopodiaceae family; several species in Mediterranean and central Asia regions; first found in U.S. in n.e. Nevada 1935; now in parts of Idaho, Utah, Oregon, Nevada; fatally poisons sheep and other animals P-409, W-131

Halophyte, a plant that lives in salty soil or water; structural adaptations enable it to save water and thus survive in a salty environment H-19
 weeds W-131

Halothane, anesthetic A-413, F-241

Halper, Albert (born 1904), U.S. writer, born in Chicago, Ill.; began writing in 1928; wrote his first novel, 'Union Square' (1933), while living in poverty ('The Foundry'; 'The Chute'; 'The Golden Watch').

Halpern, Bernard N. (1904–78), French immunologist, born in Russia; specialist on allergies; known for his discovery of antihistamine drugs and cancer cell properties.

Hals, Frans (1580?–1666), Dutch painter H-19
 Descartes' portrait, *picture* D-104
 'The Gypsy Girl' P-43
 The Netherlands N-127

Halsey, William Frederick, Jr. (nickname Bull) (1882–1959), U.S. Navy officer, born in Elizabeth, N.J.; led successful attacks on Gilbert, Marshall, Wake, and Marcus islands Feb. 1942; made head of naval forces in S. Pacific Oct. 1942, in command of Solomons campaign; commander of 3rd Pacific fleet 1944–45; appointed fleet admiral (5-star) 1945; retired 1947 W-332, 337

Hälsingborg (also Helsingborg), Sweden, seaport; in s. opposite Helsingör, Denmark; had important part in Scandinavian wars; pop. 82,432, *maps* E-360, S-524

Halsted, William Stewart (1852–1922), U.S. surgeon, born in New York, N.Y.; professor of surgery Johns Hopkins Hospital 1890–1922; introduced regional anesthesia by injecting cocaine into nerve.

Haltere, insect organ M-596

Halter hitch, knot K-264

Haltom City, Tex., village 6 mi (10 km) n.e. of Fort Worth; helicopters, corrugated boxes, electronics, refrigeration units; pop. 28,127.

Halutzim, Jewish pioneers in Palestine P-81

Halyard, apparatus for hoisting flag, *list* F-149

Halys River, Turkey. *see in index* Kizilirmak

Ham, son of Noah; Biblical ancestor of Hamites, who included the Cushites, the Phoenicians, and the Egyptians (Bible, Gen. vi, ix).

Ham. *see in index* Amateur radio operator

Hama (Biblical Hamath), Syria, city on Orontes River, 115 mi (185 km) n.e. of Damascus; remains of Hittites; trading center; pop. 110,809 S-550, *map* P-212

Hamadan, Iran, city 180 mi (290 km) s.w. of Tehran; leather products, copper work, rugs, wool, flour; pop. 150,000, *map* A-697. *see also in index* Ecbatana

Hamadhani, Badi' az-Zaman (969–1008), Arab author I-366

Hamadryad. *see in index* Dryad

Hamaguchi, Yuko (1870–1931), Japanese statesman, born on island of Shikoku; became premier 1929; called Warrior for Peace for support of London Naval Treaty 1930; assassinated.

Hamamelidaceae. *see in index* Witch hazel

'Haman and Mordecai', work by Handel H-28

Hamath, Syria. *see in index* Hama

Hambletonian, annual stake race for harness horses (3-year-old trotters); first held 1926 at Syracuse, N.Y.; held at Lexington, Ky., 1927; Syracuse, 1928; Lexington, 1929; Goshen, N.Y., 1930–42; Yonkers, N.Y., 1943; Goshen, 1944–56; Du Quoin, Ill., 1957–; named for Hambletonian (1849–76), a Standardbred stallion.

Hambletonian 10, stallion who sired 1,331 horses H-277

Hamblin, Jacob (1819–86), Mormon missionary to Indians, born in Salem, Ohio; converted to Mormonism 1842 and made elder; to Utah 1850; sent as missionary to southern Utah 1854; promoted peace between whites and Indians.

Hamburg, West Germany, state and city on Elbe River; pop. 1,580,000 H-20, *map* E-60
Germany G-112, *map* G-131
Hanseatic league H-32
harbor and port H-35

Hamden, Conn., urban town 6 mi (10 km) n. of New Haven; light industry; firearms, wire and concrete products, metal tools and products; Quinnipiac College; pop. 51,071.

Hameln (also Hamelin), West Germany, manufacturing city on Weser River 25 mi (40 km) s.w. of Hanover; scene of Pied Piper legend; pop. 47,414, *map* G-131. *see also in index* Pied Piper of Hamelin

Hamersley Range, mountains, Australia A-771, *map* A-822

'Ham Funeral, The', work by White A-799

Hamilcar Barca (270?–228 BC), Carthaginian general, father of Hannibal and Hasdrubal
Barcelona founded B-80
Hannibal H-31

Hamilton, Alexander (1712–56), Scottish physician and diarist, born in Edinburgh; practiced medicine Annapolis, Md., after 1739; known for 'Hamilton's Itinerarium', journal of his trip to Maine 1744, valuable as authoritative account of social life of period.

Hamilton, Alexander (1755?–1804), U.S. statesman H-21
Adams, John A-34
Bank of the United States B-72
Constitution U-140
constitutional law views C-685
duel with Burr B-513, E-321
essays A-345
Federalist papers F-51
Hall of Fame, *table* H-16
Jefferson J-93
Madison M-26
Paterson, N.J. N-194, P-139
Washington W-42, *picture* W-40
Washington, D.C. W-71

Hamilton, Andrew (original surname Trent) (1676?–1741), lawyer, born in Scotland; to North America 1679; practiced law in Philadelphia; known for successful defense of printer J.P. Zenger contributing to freedom of press in North America Z-450

Hamilton, Cosmo (original surname Gibbs) (1872–1942), English novelist and dramatist, brother of Arthur Hamilton Gibbs and Sir Philip Gibbs ('The Blindness of Virtue'; 'A Sense of Humour').

Hamilton, Edith (1867–1963), U.S. classicist, born in Dresden, Germany; headmistress Bryn Mawr College 1896–1922 ('The Greek Way'; 'The Roman Way'; 'Mythology'; 'Witness to the Truth'; 'Spokesman for God'; 'The Echo of Greece').

Hamilton, Emma, Lady (1765?–1815), wife of **Sir William Hamilton** (1730–1803), British envoy at Naples; active in social and political life of Naples, an intimate of Queen Maria Carolina; friend of Admiral Horatio Nelson; model for paintings by Romney.

Hamilton, Henry (died 1796), British soldier, governor of Detroit during Revolutionary War; incited Indian raids along frontier; later, governor of Canada and of Bermuda.

Hamilton, Sir Ian (1853–1947), British general, born in Corfu; with army 1873–1919; distinguished himself in South Africa and India; commanded Dardanelles expedition in World War I ('Gallipoli Diary'; 'Friends of England'; 'Soul and Body of an Army'; 'Jean', biography of wife)
World War I W-305

Hamilton, Virginia (born 1936), U.S. author, born in Yellow Springs, Ohio, married to Arnold Adoff, ('Zeely'; 'Time-Ago Tales of Jahdu'; 'Planet of Junior Brown'; 'M. C. Higgins, the Great', awarded 1975 Newbery Medal).

Hamilton, William Robert (nickname Sliding Billy) (1866–1940), U.S. baseball outfielder, born in Newark, N.J.; with Philadelphia, N.L., 1890–95, Boston, N.L., 1896–1901; stole 115 bases in 1891; during career, stole 797 bases, the N.L. all-time record.

Hamilton, William Rowan (1805–65), British mathematician H-22
mathematics M-216
mechanics M-269

Hamilton, Bermuda, capital and chief port of Bermuda Islands; pop. 2,763 B-173, *picture* W-157, *map* W-159

Hamilton, New Zealand, commercial and industrial city in n.-central North Island; dairy and meat processing, lumbering, and manufacturing; pop. 157,000 N-284, *maps* N-299, P-3

Hamilton, Ohio, city on Great Miami River, 20 mi (30 km) n. of Cincinnati; auto bodies, machinery, paper, safes, foundry products; named for Alexander Hamilton; pop. 63,189, *map* U-41

Hamilton, Ont., manufacturing city and port; pop. 306,434 H-22
Canada, *map* C-112
North America, *map* N-350
Ontario O-552, *picture* O-550

Hamilton, Mount, California, peak of the Coast Range, 25 mi (40 km) e. of San Jose.

Hamilton College, situated at Clinton, N.Y.; private control; for men; established in 1793 as academy, chartered as college 1812; liberal arts and sciences.

Hamilton River. *see in index* Churchill River

Hamites, a people of North Africa
Egypt E-116
Somalia S-257
Sudan S-501
Uganda U-1

'Hamlet', Shakespeare's greatest tragedy, based on story first told by Danish chronicler, Saxo Grammaticus
chronology of play S-133
English literature E-267
Gielgud's performance, *picture* S-140
Kronborg Castle, *picture* D-99
rank of play S-139

Hamlin, Hannibal (1809–91), U.S. antislavery statesman, born in Paris Hill, Me.; vice-president 1861–65; intimate friend and adviser of Lincoln, *table* S-437a
Maine M-55

Hamline University, St. Paul, Minn.; Methodist; founded 1854 at Red Wing, Minn.; transferred 1880 to Hamline (now Midway District of Minneapolis and St. Paul); arts and sciences, education.

Hamm, West Germany, city at junction of Ahse and Lippe rivers, in Ruhr Valley; railroad and trucking center; coal, steel, machinery; thermal baths; town founded 1226; joined Hanseatic League 1417; pop. 84,942, *map* G-131

Hammada, desert formation D-105
Sahara S-15

Hammarskjöld, Dag Hjalmar Agne Carl (1905–61), Swedish diplomat and financial expert, born in Jönköping, Sweden; son of Hjalmar Hammarskjöld; undersecretary Sweden's department of finance 1936–45; chairman of board Bank of Sweden 1941–48; deputy foreign minister 1951–53; secretary-general of the United Nations 1953–61; author 'Markings' U-24, *picture* U-25
Dag Hammarskjöld Library U-22

Hammarskjöld, Knut Hjalmar Leonard (1862–1953), Swedish statesman, born in Wederum, near Kalmar; father of Dag Hammarskjöld; prime minister 1914–17; member various international arbitration courts.

Hammer, a tool T-216, *picture* T-217
bell's sound production B-155
forging hammer F-317
magnetic S-348c
pneumatic P-398

Hammer, bone of the ear. *see in index* Malleus

Hammer, part of a piano M-688

Hammer and sickle, emblems in Soviet flag R-333

Hammerfest, Norway, port on island of Kvaloy on Arctic Ocean; northernmost town in Europe; ice-free harbor; pop. 5,862, *map* E-360

Hammerhead shark S-144

Hammerlock, wrestling hold W-364, *picture* W-365

Hammersmith, England, western borough of London; boat-building and other manufactures; home of William Morris; pop. 192,810, *maps* L-287, U-18a

Hammerstein, Oscar (1847–1919), U.S. opera and theater director, born in Germany; manager Manhattan Opera House, N.Y.; foremost in establishing French opera in U.S.

Hammerstein, Oscar, II (1895–1960), U.S. lyric writer and librettist, born in New York City, N.Y.; adapted 'Show Boat'; wrote book and lyrics for 'Rose Marie', 'Desert Song', 'Oklahoma!', 'Carousel', 'South Pacific', and lyrics for 'The Sound of Music' (for these last four, Richard Rodgers wrote the music); was co-producer with Rodgers of 'I Remember Mama' and 'Annie Get Your Gun'; with him and Joshua Logan received 1950 Pulitzer prize for 'South Pacific'
musical comedy M-685

Hammer throw, track and field sport T-245, *picture* T-246

'Hammer without a Master, The', (French 'Le Marteau sans maître'), work by Boulez B-383

Hammett, Dashiell (in full Samuel Dashiell Hammett) (1894–1961), U.S. author H-23
detective story D-119
Hellman H-124

Hammond, John Hays (1855–1936), U.S. mining engineer, born in San Francisco, Calif.; associated with Cecil Rhodes in South Africa; sentenced to death after Jameson raid, but was released by Boers upon payment of a $125,000 fine; after 1900 active in U.S. and Mexican mining development and in hydroelectric and irrigation projects.

Hammond, John Hays, Jr. (1888–1965), U.S. inventor, born in San Francisco, Calif.; inventor of radio-controlled torpedoes, radio system for controlling ships, a system of selective radio telegraphy.

Hammond, Laurens (1895–1973), U.S. inventor of Hammond electric organ, born in Evanston, Ill.; also invented Novachord and electric card-shuffling bridge table. *see also in index* Novachord

Hammond, Ind., city on Lake Michigan just s.e. of Chicago; steel and petroleum products, soap, railroad equipment, corn products, printing; pop. 93,714, *map* I-102

Hammond, La., city 43 mi (69 km) e. of Baton Rouge; strawberries, poultry; sawmills, steel foundry; Southeastern Louisiana University; state school for retarded children; pop. 15,043.

Hammonton, N.J., town 24 mi (39 km) s. of Mount Holly; furniture; fruit shipping and processing; pop. 12,298.

Hammurabi (ruled 1792–50? BC), king of Babylonia H-23
ancient civilization A-404
apprenticeship evolved A-511
code of laws B-7, P-506
beer regulations B-135
history writing H-170
Iraqi history I-314
law L-91, *picture* L-95

Hampden, John (1594–1643), English Puritan, patriot, and statesman H-24

Hampden, Walter (or Walter Hampden Dougherty) (1879–1955), U.S. actor, born in Brooklyn, N.Y.; debut in England 1901 with classical repertoire company; notable in 'Hamlet' and other Shakespearean plays, 'The Servant in the House', 'Cyrano de Bergerac', and 'The Patriots'.

Hampden-Sydney College, Hampden-Sydney, Va.; affiliated with Presbyterian Church, U.S.; for men; founded as Prince Edward Academy in 1776; arts and sciences.

Hampshire, breed of pig P-320

Hampshire, breed of sheep S-147

Hampshire, county of s. England; area 1,650 sq mi (4,275 sq km); includes administrative county Isle of Wight and the ports Southampton and Portsmouth; pop. 1,432,546.

Hampstead, district near heart of Greater London, England; formerly noted for mineral springs; residence of first earl of Chatham, John Constable, George Romney, Sir Richard Steele, John Keats, Leigh Hunt.

Hampton, Lionel (born 1913), U.S. bandleader M-684

Hampton, Wade (1818–1902), U.S. statesman and Confederate general, born in Charleston, S.C.; raised and equipped Hampton's legion; U.S. senator 1878–91; U.S. commissioner of Pacific railroads 1893–97, *picture* S-316, *table* S-347b

Hampton (formerly called Kecoughtan), Va., port city in s.e., situated on Hampton Roads and bordered by city of Newport News; pop. 125,300 H-24
Virginia V-334, 346, *map* V-349

Hampton Beach, beach in New Hampshire, *picture* N-177, *map* N-191

Hampton Court, England, palace on Thames River 10 mi. s.w. of London, *picture* E-244
Wren W-363

Hampton Institute, Hampton, Va.; private control; established in 1868; liberal arts, business, home economics, nursing, and teacher education; graduate study H-24

Hampton Roads, channel in which James, Nansemond, and Elizabeth rivers converge and flow into Chesapeake Bay, Virginia C-304
Civil War
battle of *Monitor* and *Merrimack* C-480
peace conference S-443
Norfolk N-332

Hamptons, The, Long Island, New York L-297

Ham radio, hobby H-190

Hamster, small rodent of the family Muridae H-24
pet P-244
fur, *table* F-464

Hamstring tendon, tendon of the thigh muscles T-80

Hamsun, Knut (pen name of Knut Pedersen) (1859–1952), Norwegian novelist H-25
see also in index Nobel Prizewinners, *table*
Norway N-391

Hamtramck, Mich., manufacturing city surrounded by Detroit; automobiles and accessories, metal products, paint, varnish, electrical supplies; pop. 27,245 D-120

Han, a people of China C-344, *picture* C-348

Han (translation the river), in South Korea rises 30 mi (50 km) from e. coast, cuts Korean peninsula nearly in half, and flows through Seoul and then into Yellow Sea; 292 mi (470 km) long; navigable for about 75 mi (120 km) for motor and sailing boats, *map* K-290
Hubei province H-313

Hanabusa, Itcho (1652–1724), Japanese painter, *picture* J-82

Hanalei Valley, valley, Kauai, Hawaii, *picture* G-63

Hanau, West Germany, city on Main River, 10 mi (16 km) e. of Frankfurt; machinery; Napoleon defeated Bavarians in 1813; pop. 55,379, *map* G-131

Hanby, Benjamin Russel (1833–67), U.S. songwriter, born in Rushville, Ohio; pastor United Brethren Church 1861–63 ('Darling Nelly Gray'; 'Little Tillie's Grave'; 'Ole Shady'; 'Up on the House-top'; 'Who Is He in Yonder Stall?').

Hancock, John (1737–93), U.S. patriot, first governor of Massachusetts H-25
Continental Congress, *picture* R-162
Lexington and Concord L-144

Hancock, Walker Kirtland (born 1901), U.S. sculptor, born in St. Louis, Mo.; won Prix de Rome 1925; served as head of sculpture department, Pennsylvania Academy of Fine Arts, Philadelphia; sculptor in charge of project on Stone Mountain, Georgia, from 1964 until its completion in 1970
Robert Frost bust, *picture* S-80

Zimbabwe Z-452, *picture* Z-453

Harbach, Otto Abels (1873–1963), U.S. lyricist and librettist, born in Salt Lake City, Utah; wrote lyrics for 'Rose Marie', 'The Desert Song', and 'Roberta', *picture* U-226

Harbin (or Pinkiang), China, capital of Heilongjiang Province, on Sungari River; pop. 2,550,000 H-33
- Asia, A-697
- Heilongkiang H-116
- Manchuria, *picture* M-93
- world, *map* W-297

Harbord, James Guthrie (1866–1947), U.S. Army officer, born in Bloomington, Ill.; entered Army 1889 as private; notable services in World War I, during which he attained rank of major general; chief of staff, A.E.F., 1917–18; commanded Marine brigade June–July, 1918; retired from Army 1922; president, later chairman of the board, Radio Corporation of America.

Harbor dolphin D-224

Harbors H-33. *see also in index* Ports

Harbor seal (or leopard seal) S-98

Harbour Grace, Newf., port town on Conception Bay 25 mi (40 km) n.w. of St. John's; cod-liver oil, fish, shoes and other leather products; starting point for early transatlantic flights; pop. 2,988, *map* C-109

Harcourt, Sir William Vernon (1827–1904), English statesman and debater; loyal lieutenant of Gladstone; home secretary 1880–85; as chancellor of exchequer 1892–95 introduced graduated income tax; after Gladstone's retirement 1894 he led Liberals in House of Commons, but disagreements with Rosebery led him to retire in 1898.

Hardanger work (sometimes called needle weaving), needlework N-111, *picture* N-112

Hardangerfjord, inlet 75 mi (120 km) long on w. coast of Norway, *map* E-360

Hard candy C-137

Hard coal. *see in index* Anthracite

Hardee, William Joseph (1815–73), U.S. soldier, born in Camden County, Georgia; graduated from U.S. Military Academy; served in Mexican War and fought skillfully as brigadier general in Confederate army.

Harden, Sir Arthur (1865–1940), English biochemist, born in Manchester. *see also in index* Nobel Prizewinners, *table*

Harden, Maximilian (1861–1927), German writer and editor, born in Berlin; was attacked and several times imprisoned for hostility toward Prussian imperialism.

Hardenberg, Friedrich Leopold Freiherr von (pen name Novalis) (1772–1801), German romantic poet and novelist, born in Oberwiederstedt, Prussian Saxony ('Hymns to Night') G-109

Hardenberg, Karl August, prince von (1750–1822), Prussian statesman, born near Brunswick, Germany; enforced and amplified Baron Heinrich Stein's reforms, including abolition of serfdom.

Hardening, in metals
- ruthenium R-366

Hardening of the arteries. *see in index* Arteriosclerosis

Hardhack, a species of spirea S-392

Hardhead sponge S-394

Hardicanute. *see in index* Harthacanute

Hardie, James Keir (1856–1915), British labor leader, born in Lanarkshire, Scotland; led the Scottish Labor party (1889) and the Independent Labor party (1893); after 1906 leader of Labor party in the House of Commons S-235

Hardin, Clifford Morris (born 1915), U.S. educator and public official, born in Knightstown, Ind.; dean school of agriculture of present Michigan State University 1953–54; chancellor University of Nebraska 1954–68; U.S. secretary of agriculture 1969–71; chairman of the board Ralston Purina of Canada Ltd. 1971–
- Nixon N-326

Harding, Chester (1792–1866), U.S. portrait painter, born in Conway, Mass.; was first an itinerant portrait painter; later in Boston and London became successful painter of prominent Americans and Englishmen; work clear and straightforward and full of character, though lacking in technique.

Harding, Florence Kling (1860–1924), wife of President Harding H-39

Harding, Warren G. (1865–1923), 29th president of United States H-38
- Coolidge C-702
- Hoover H-234
- Washington Conference P-18, P-143c
- World War I W-319

Harding College, Searcy, Ark.; affiliated with Church of Christ; opened 1922; arts and sciences, education; graduate school of religion.

Hardinge of Penshurst, Charles Hardinge, 1st **Baron** (1858–1944), viceroy of India 1910–16; put into effect Morley-Minto reforms; loyalty of India during World War I largely due to universal esteem for viceroy; moved capital to Delhi and held famous "durbar" 1911; his grandfather, **Henry Hardinge,** first **Viscount** (1785–1856), was governor general of India 1844–48.

Harding grass (also called Peruvian winter grass), a common name for the perennial grass *Phalaris stenoptera;* native home unknown but grown in California; used as forage plant, grows to one foot, with short branching rootstock, narrow leaves; lilac spikelike clusters.

Hardin-Simmons University, Abilene, Tex.; affiliated with Southern Baptist convention; founded 1891; arts and sciences, education, and music; graduate studies.

Hard liquor (or distilled spirits) T-80

Hard maple. *see in index* Sugar maple

Hardness, in physics
- abrasives A-13
- materials testing M-211
- minerals M-431
  - Mohs' scale, *pictures* R-229b

Hardouin-Mansart, Jules (1646–1708), French architect A-568
- interior design, *picture* I-248

Hard palate, human anatomy M-641

Hard soap S-229, 231

Hardtack, unsalted, unleavened hard bread, used by campers and soldiers.

'Hard Times', novel by Dickens N-411

Hardtop, car A-844

Hardwar, India, ancient town in Uttar Pradesh state, on right bank of Ganges River; Hindu place of pilgrimage; footprint of Hindu god Vishnu impressed on a stone in wall of bathing ghat; headworks of Ganges irrigation canal; pop. 77,940, *map* I-83

Hardware, computer equipment C-627

Hard water W-91
- soap S-231

Hardwicke, Sir Cedric Webster (1893–1964), British actor, born near Birmingham; began career in England, to U.S. 1935; knighted 1934 in recognition of his Shavian roles; showed versatility and skill in interpreting character parts.

Hardwood W-180, *table* W-283
- forest products F-316
- lumber L-334

Hardwood tar T-28

Hardy, Arthur Shorburne (1847–1930), U.S. mathematician and novelist, born in Andover, Mass.; professor of civil engineering at Dartmouth 1874–93; minister to Persia, Romania, Switzerland, Greece, and Spain ('But Yet a Woman'; 'Passe Rose'; 'His Daughter First').

Hardy, Oliver (1892–1957), film actor and director, born in Atlanta, Ga., *picture* M-619. *see also in index* Laurel, Stan

Hardy, Thomas (1840–1928), British novelist and poet H-41
- literary contribution E-277
- realism N-413

Hardy chrysanthemum, a perennial plant
- growing conditions G-24

Hardy River, lower course of Colorado River into Gulf of California C-586

Hare, Robert (1781–1858), U.S. chemist, born in Philadelphia; invented (1801) oxyhydrogen blowpipe (this could fuse refractory metals and therefore hastened founding of platinum industry); built electric furnace 1839.

Hare, William Hobart (1838–1909), U.S. Protestant Episcopal bishop, born in Princeton, N.J.; for 36 years Apostle to the Sioux in South Dakota; founded successful boarding schools for Indians, *picture* S-332

Hare, animal R-20, *pictures* A-436, R-21
- average lifespan, *chart* A-423
- folklore F-3
- fur F-463, *tables* F-464
- jumping, *picture* A-426
- speed, *picture* A-425

Hare, constellation. *see in index* Lepus

'Hare and the Tortoise, The', fable, *table* F-4

Harebell. *see in index* Bluebell of Scotland

Harefoot. *see in index* Harold I of England

Hare Krishna, religious group H-42

Harem, in Muslim countries, apartment of a house reserved for female members of family; also the women themselves; life in harem closely regulated by custom; usually under direction of chief wife.

Hare's-tail grass, a genus, *Lagurus,* with one species *L ovatus* of the grass family, native to Mediterranean; grows to one foot (0.3 m); used in bouquets.

Hare system (or single transferable vote), election system that gives minorities representation on elective bodies in proportion to votes received; voters indicate first, second, or other choices; a quota of votes necessary for election is fixed; if all seats are not filled, surplus votes of successful candidates and those of weakest candidates are distributed. *see also in index* Proportional representation; Preferential voting

Harfleur, France, town in n. on Seine River estuary 4 mi (6 km) e. of Le Havre; formerly important seaport; twice occupied by English in 15th century; pillaged by Huguenots in 1562; pop. 15,503, *map* F-369

Hargrave, Lawrence (1850–1915), Australian airplane and engine experimenter, born in England; invented the box kite 1893 A-201

Hargreaves, James (1730?–78), British inventor H-42
- Crompton's improvement C-781
- Industrial Revolution I-178
- spinning jenny I-276

Harijan (or untouchables), caste
- India I-68

Haringey, borough, London, *maps* L-287, U-18a

Hariri, al- (1054–1122), Arab scholar I-366

Harischandra (or Bharatendu) (850–85), Hindi poet I-108

Harkness, Stephen Vanderburg (1818–88), U.S. businessman, associated with John D. Rockefeller; members of family have been important philanthropists; his widow, **Anna M. Richardson Harkness** (1838–1926), established the Commonwealth Fund; his son, **Edward Stephen Harkness** (1874–1940), gave large sums to Harvard, Yale, Columbia, and the New York City Medical Center.

Harlan, James (1820–99), U.S. lawyer and legislator, born in Clark County, Ill.; Republican; U.S. senator from Iowa; appointed secretary of the interior in 1865 by President Lincoln, whose son Robert married Harlan's daughter, *table* S-437a

Harlan, John Marshall (1833–1911), U.S. jurist, born in Boyle County, Kentucky; associate justice of the U.S. Supreme Court from 1877 to his death; term of service exceeded only by Chief Justice Marshall; was a liberal constructionist of the Constitution and favored increase in federal power.

Harlan, John Marshall (1899–1971), U.S. jurist, born in Chicago, Ill.; grandson of John M. Harlan (1833–1911); chief counsel New York State Crime Commission 1951–53; judge U.S. court of appeals for second circuit 1954–55; associate justice U.S. Supreme Court 1955–71
- Eisenhower E-138
- Nixon N-326

Harlan County Reservoir, Nebraska N-95, 98

Harland, Henry (1861–1905), Anglo-American novelist, born in St. Petersburg (now Leningrad), Russia; educated in U.S., lived later years in London; 'The Cardinal's Snuffbox' his best and most popular novel; edited 'The Yellow Book'.

Harland, Marion. *see in index* Terhune, Mary Virginia

Harlech, Wales, seaside resort, in n.w.; ruins of Harlech Castle, captured by Yorkists 1468; pop. of parish 310
- castle, *picture* W-7

Harlem (or Central Harlem), neighborhood in Manhattan, New York City, N.Y.
- book R-111j

Harlem Renaissance (1920s), period of outstanding literary, musical, and artistic vigor and creativity in the U.S.; produced sophisticated explorations of black American life and culture that revealed and stimulated a new confidence and racial pride B-294
- Locke L-278

Harlem River, N.Y., n. boundary of Manhattan Island.

Harlequin, in pantomime, an amusing and good-natured character; wears tights and mask; lover of Columbine. *see also in index* Pierrot
- mime M-423

Harlequin bug. *see in index* Stinkbugs

'Harlequin's Carnival', painting by Miró P-60, *picture* P-59

Harley, Robert, earl of Oxford (1661–1724), British statesman, born in London; secretary of state (1704), lord treasurer (1711); the books and manuscripts collected by Harley and son Edward are known as the Harleian Collection.

Harlingen, Tex., city in agricultural area of lower Rio Grande Valley; port on channel to Gulf Intracoastal Waterway; apparel, aircraft engines, food packaging machinery; food and cotton processing; Padre Island National Seashore; pop. 43,543, *map* U-40

'Harlot's Progress, A', work by Hogarth H-199

Harlow, Bryce Nathaniel (1916–87), U.S. government official, born in Oklahoma City, Okla.; White House assistant 1953–61, his duties included the writing of President Eisenhower's speeches; assistant to the president 1969; counselor to the president 1969–70.

Harmar, Josiah (1753–1813), soldier, born in Philadelphia; served under Washington and Lee in Revolutionary War; unsuccessful in defeating Indians n. of Ohio River (1785–87, 1790); adjutant general of Pennsylvania (1793–99).

Harmattan, type of wind S-15, W-225

Harmodius. *see in index* Aristogiton

Harmon, Daniel Williams (1778–1845), Canadian fur trader and author, born in Vermont; joined North West Company in 1800 ('Journal of Voyages and Travels in the Interior of North America').

Harmon, Judson (1846–1927), U.S. lawyer and political leader, born in Newtown, Ohio; attorney general 1895–97; governor of Ohio 1909–13;

Democratic nominee for U.S. president 1912.

Harmonic, in music, an overtone S-260

Harmonica, small rectangular mouth organ with air channels; metal reeds in channels produce tones when air passes through them; usually consists of two parallel rows of wind channels with a range of two to four octaves that are sounded by inhaling and exhaling; player's tongue and lips cover unused channels.

Harmonic minor scale, in music M-691

Harmonium (or reed organ), wind instrument W-231

Harmony, Ind., communal village founded by George Rapp C-605, *map* I-102

Harmony, in music M-666, 692, *list* M-670

Harmsworth, Alfred. *see in index* Northcliffe, Viscount

Harnack, Adolf von (1851–1930), German Protestant theologian, born in Tartu, Estonia; an authority on early church history; sought to reconcile science and Bible ('History of the Christian Dogma'; 'What Is Christianity?').

Harnden, William Frederick (1812–45), U.S. pioneer expressman, born in Reading, Mass. E-382

Harness, parachute P-109a

Harness, in weaving S-391

Harness racing, sport H-275, *picture* H-258
  Missouri State Fair, *picture* M-499

Harney, William Selby (1800–89), U.S. general, born in Haysboro, near Nashville, Tenn.; won distinction fighting Indians in Florida Everglades and in battle of Cerro Gordo in Mexican War; later fought Indians in the West; recalled from command of Oregon Territory for seizing San Juan Island, claimed by British; Harney Peak, highest point in Black Hills, named for him.

Harney High Lava Plains
  Oregon O-583

Harney Peak, Black Hills, in s.w. South Dakota; highest point in state 7,242 ft (2,207 m) and in Black Hills B-306, *maps* S-323

Harnoncourt, René d'. *see in index* D'Harnoncourt

Harold I (nicknamed Harefoot) (died 1040), king of England H-43

Harold II (1022?–66), king of England H-43
  battle of Hastings H-52
  English history E-239
  Norman conquest N-333
  William I W-206

Harold, kings of Norway. *see in index* Harald

Harold Bluetooth (or Harald) (died 985?), king of Denmark (940?–985); son of Gorm; Christianized Denmark; killed in war against Sweyn, his son D-99

'Harold en Italie', composition by Berlioz B-172

Haro Strait, n.e. Pacific passage between Vancouver and Saturna islands of the province of British Columbia, and San Juan and Stuart islands in the state of Washington W-48

Haroun al-Raschid. *see in index* Harun ar-Rashid

Harp, constellation. *see in index* Lyra

Harp, stringed instrument S-490a, *picture* S-490b. *see also in index* Koto
  Middle Ages, *picture* P-32
  orchestra O-576

Harpastum, ancient Roman game S-232

Harpe brothers, U.S. outlaws; **Micajah,** and **Wiley** O-619

Harper, Theodore Acland (1871–1942), U.S. writer, born in Christchurch, New Zealand; mining engineer in Alaska, Siberia, and other parts of world; wrote adventure stories for boys, many with wife, **Winifred Mary Hunter-Brown Harper** (died 1933) ('Siberian Gold'; 'Kubick the Outlaw'; 'Mushroom Boy').

Harper, William Rainey (1856–1906), U.S. educator, scholar, and author; born in New Concord, Ohio; first president of University of Chicago, 1891–1906.

Harpers Ferry, W. Va., town at junction of Shenandoah and Potomac rivers; pop. 365 H-43
  Civil War battles C-474, *map* C-475
  Harpers Ferry N.H.P., *list* B-299

'Harper's Monthly' (formerly called 'Harper's New Monthly Magazine') magazine M-33
  Howells H-313

Harper Woods, Mich., residential city just n.e. of Detroit; incorporated 1951; pop. 20,186.

Harpies, in mythology, winged monsters with faces of old women, bear ears, and crooked talons; personification of storm winds; name means "robbers"; represented as carrying off persons to underworld or inflicting punishment, and snatching food from Phineus.

Harpoon, barbed spear
  Eskimo S-98, *picture* S-99

Harp seal (also called Greenland seal, or saddleback seal), a mammal *Phoca groenlandica* of the Phocidae family S-100
  Canada C-75

Harp shell gastropod shell *Harpa ventricosa*, *picture* S-149

Harpsichord (originally called claricimbalum, or keyed dulcimer), forerunner of piano
  chamber music C-268
  Landowska L-27
  musical instruments M-687

Harpur, Charles (1813–68), Australian poet, born in Windsor, near Sydney; first Australian poet of importance (poem, 'The Creek of the Four Graves').

Harpy eagle, bird of prey B-278

Harquebus (or hackbut), gun F-96
  weapons history W-112

Harraden, Beatrice (1864–1936), British novelist, born in Hampstead; achieved fame with her first novel, 'Ships that Pass in the Night', published 1893.

Harridge, William (1884–1971), U.S. baseball executive, born in Chicago, Ill.; president of American League 1931–59, longest major league presidency on record.

Harrier, dog, *picture* D-200

Harrier, hawk B-278

Harringyliet Dam, The Netherlands, *picture* N-126

Harriman, Edward Henry (1848–1909), U.S. capitalist, railway organizer, born in Hempstead, N.Y.; obtained control of and rehabilitated bankrupt Union Pacific 1898; failed in contest with J.J. Hill for control of Northern Pacific but finally dominated railroad world before his death
  Northern Securities case R-285
  stocks and bonds S-453

Harriman, Florence Jaffray (1870–1967), U.S. public official, born in New York City; manager New York State Reformatory for Women 1906–18; only woman member Federal Industrial Relations Commission 1913–16; minister to Norway 1937–41; wrote 'From Pinafores to Politics'.

Harriman, William Averell (1891–1986), U.S. financier and statesman, born in New York City, N.Y.; son of Edward Henry Harriman; ambassador to U.S.S.R. 1943–46, to United Kingdom 1946; secretary of commerce 1946–48; "roving ambassador" for ECA 1948–50; special assistant to President Truman 1950–51; governor of New York 1955–59; ambassador at large 1961, 1965–69, chief U.S. negotiator Vietnam peace talks in Paris 1968–69; assistant secretary of state 1961–63, undersecretary for political affairs 1963–65 ('Peace with Russia?').

Harriot, Thomas (1560–1621), British mathematician, born in Oxford; introduced some of the symbols and notations used in algebra today.

Harris, Abram Lincoln (1899–1963), U.S. economist, author, born in Richmond, Va.; professor and head of economics department Howard University, Washington, D.C., 1936–45; faculty University of Chicago 1948–63; with S.D. Spero wrote 'The Black Worker' ('The Negro As Capitalist').

Harris, Benjamin (fl. 1673–1716), British publisher; opened bookshop in Boston, Mass., 1686; in 1690 began publication of *Publick Occurrences*, first newspaper in North America; returned to London 1695. *see also in index* 'New England Primer'

Harris, Christie Lucy (born 1907) Canadian author, born in Newark, N.J. (books for younger readers: 'You Have to Draw the Line Somewhere'; 'Raven's Cry' awarded 1967 Canadian Book of the Year for Children award, 'Confessions of a Toe Hanger', 'Let X Be Excitement'; 'Mouse Woman and the Vanished Princesses', awarded 1977 Canadian Book of the Year for Children award S-481d

Harris, Frank (1856–1931), U.S. author and critic, born in Galway, Ireland; came to U.S. when 14; later lived chiefly in Europe; edited magazines in England and U.S.; many of his writings notorious for their frankness ('The Man Shakespeare'; 'Oscar Wilde'; 'My Life and Loves').

Harris, George Washington (1814–69), U.S. humorist, born in Allegheny City, Pa.; jewelry craftsman and steamboat captain in youth; wrote first sketch under pseudonym 'Sugartail'; stories told in mountaineer dialect with fresh, boisterous humor ('Sut Lovingood Yarns').

Harris, Joel Chandler (1848–1908), U.S. author H-44
  American literature A-351
  fable F-4
  folklore F-266, *picture* F-267
  reading R-110a

Harris, Julie (born 1925), U.S. actress of stage, motion pictures, and television; born in Grosse Pointe Park, Mich.; appearances include stage and film versions of 'The Member of the Wedding', the plays 'I Am a Camera', 'The Lark', 'Forty Carats', 'The Last of Mrs. Lincoln', 'The Belle of Amherst'; the TV plays 'Little Moon of Alban', 'Victoria Regina'; recipient of numerous awards.

Harris, Mary. *see in index* Jones, Mother

Harris, Patricia Roberts (1924–85), U.S. lawyer, educator, diplomat; born in Mattoon, Ill.; joined faculty Howard University 1961, professor of law 1967–69; co-chairman of National Committee for Civil Rights 1963–64; U.S. ambassador to Luxemburg 1965–67; practiced law Washington, D.C. 1970–77; U.S. secretary of housing and urban development 1977–79; U.S. secretary of health, education, and welfare (later renamed health and human services), 1979–81
  black Americans B-298
  Carter administration C-183
  women's rights W-276

Harris, Robert (1849–1919), Canadian painter, born in Conway, Wales; noted for portraits and genre; president Royal Canadian Academy 1893–1906.

Harris, Roy (1898–1979), U.S. composer, born in Lincoln County, Oklahoma; 'Third Symphony' (1939) recognized as distinctively American; works include symphonic, vocal, and chamber music ('Song for Occupations'; 'Folk-Song Symphony')
  classical music M-677

Harris, Seale (1870–1957), U.S. physician, born in Cedartown, Ga.; founded and directed Seale Harris Clinic, Birmingham, Ala., 1922–56; discovered hyperinsulinism 1923.

Harris, Stanley Raymond (nickname Bucky) (1896–1977), baseball player and manager, born in Port Jervis, N.Y.

Harris, Townsend (1804–78), U.S. merchant, political leader, diplomat; born in Sandy Hill, N.Y.; first U.S. consul general and first U.S. minister to Japan; negotiated commercial treaty (1858).

Harris, William Torrey (1835–1909), U.S. educator and philosopher, born in North Killingly, Conn.; U.S. commissioner of education 1889–1906; leading American expounder of Hegelian idealism.

Harrisburg, Ill., city in s. part of state 62 mi (100 km) n.e. of Cairo; coal mining, agriculture; dairy products, packing-house products, caps; headquarters for Shawnee National Forest; pop. 9,322, *map* I-52

Harrisburg, Pa. (originally called Harris's Ferry), state capital and manufacturing city; pop. 52,056 H-44
  Pennsylvania P-182b, *map*, P-185, *picture* P-177

Harris County Domed Stadium. *see in index* Astrodome

Harrison, Alexander (full name Thomas Alexander Harrison) (1853–1930), U.S. genre, landscape, and sea painter, born in Philadelphia, Pa.; lived most of life in Paris; brother of L. Birge Harrison; noted for luminous color and delicate line.

Harrison, Anna Symmes (1775–1864), wife of President William Henry Harrison H-49

Harrison, Benjamin (1726?–91), U.S. patriot, born in Charles City County, Virginia; father of William Henry Harrison; delegate to Congress 1774–78; governor of Virginia 1782–84.

Harrison, Benjamin (1833–1901), 23rd president of United States H-45
  electoral college E-148
  Memorial Home I-104

Harrison, Birge (full name Lovell Birge Harrison) (1854–1929), U.S. painter, born in Philadelphia, Pa.; brother of Alexander Harrison; best known for snow scenes and for paintings of city streets; especially skillful in depicting moonlight, twilight, and misty atmosphere; author of 'Landscape Painting'.

Harrison, Caroline Lavinia Scott (1832–92), first wife of President Benjamin Harrison H-45

Harrison, Frederic (1831–1923), English historian, jurist, literary critic, and positivist philosopher; born in London ('The Meaning of History'; 'Positive Evolution of Religion'; 'The Choice of Books'; 'Among My Books').

Harrison, George (born 1943), British rock musician
  Beatles B-119
  popular music M-682

Harrison, John (1693–1776), English inventor of devices for improving clocks and watches, born in Foulby, Yorkshire
  navigation N-78
  watches and clocks W-81

Harrison, Lou (born 1917), U.S. composer M-677

Harrison, Mary Scott Lord Dimmick (1858–1948), second wife of President Benjamin Harrison, born in Honesdale, Pa. H-47

Harrison, Rex Carey (born 1908), British actor, born near Liverpool; won 1957 Tony award; films: 'Blithe Spirit', 'Anna and the King of Siam', 'My Fair Lady' (Academy award 1964), 'The Agony and the Ecstasy', 'Staircase'; plays: 'Anne of the Thousand Days', 'The Cocktail Party', 'Bell, Book, and Candle'.

Harrison, Richard Berry (1864–1935), U.S. actor, born in London, Ont.; applauded as de Lawd in 'Green Pastures'; awarded Spingarn Medal 1931.

Harrison, Ross Granville (1870–1959), U.S. biologist and anatomist, born in Germantown, Pa.; on faculty Johns Hopkins University 1896–1907; managing editor *Journal of Experimental Zoology* 1904–46; professor Yale University 1907–38; chairman National Research Council 1938–46; noted for tissue-culture technique.

Harrison, Wallace Kirkman (1895–1981), U.S. architect, born in Worcester, Mass.; co-designer of Rockefeller Center, New York City, and of trylon and perisphere, theme structure of New York World's Fair (1939 and 1940); designer of Metropolitan Opera House, Lincoln Center, New York City
  United Nations buildings U-22, *pictures* A-666, U-23

Harrison, William Henry (nickname Old Tippecanoe) (1773–1841), 9th president of United States H-48
Harrison, Benjamin H-45
Tecumseh T-51
War of 1812 W-29

Harrison, N.J., industrial town on the Passaic River opposite Newark; steel, pumps, elevators, chemicals; pop. 11,811.

Harrisonburg, Va., city 24 mi (39 km) n.e. of Staunton; turkey center; poultry producing and processing; textiles, automotive parts, furniture; Madison College and Eastern Mennonite College; pop. 19,671, *map* V-348

Harrison Narcotics Act
drug-control law D-277

Harris's Ferry, Pa. *see in index* Harrisburg, Pa.

Harris-Stowe College, until 1977 Harris Teachers College, St. Louis, Mo.; city and state control; opened 1857; arts and sciences, education.

Harrod, James (1742–93?), U.S. pioneer and soldier, born in present Bedford County, Pennsylvania; opposed Richard Henderson and his Transylvania scheme; took active part in wars against Indians; elected to Virginia legislature 1779; mysterious disappearance from his home led to belief that he was murdered.

Harrodsburg, Ky., city situated 60 mi (95 km) s.e. of Louisville; glass products, clothing; first settlement (1774) in Kentucky; location of Fort Harrod; pop. 7,265.

Harrogate, England, municipal borough 15 mi (25 km) n. of Leeds; medicinal springs, produce market, candy manufacturing; pop. 62,680, *map* U-18a

Harrow, borough, London, *maps* L-287, U-18a

Harrow School, English school for boys at Harrow in Middlesex, 12 mi (19 km) n.w. of London, founded 1571 by John Lyon E-234

Harry Strunk Lake, Nebraska N-95

Hart, Albert Bushnell (1854–1943), U.S. historian and educator, born in Clarksville, Pa.; professor at Harvard 1883–1926 ('Formation of the Union'; 'Essentials of American History'; editor of 'American Nation' series, 'Epochs of American History').

Hart, Emma. *see in index* Willard, Emma

Hart, Gary (born 1936), U.S. politician, born in Ottawa, Kan.; national presidential campaign director for George McGovern 1970–72; U.S. senator from Colorado 1975–86; candidate for Democratic presidential nomination 1983–84 and 1987 until highly publicized charges of adultery forced him to end his campaign.

Hart, John (1711?–79), Revolutionary War leader, signer of Declaration of Independence; born in Stonington, Conn.

Hart, Lorenz (1895–1943), U.S. lyric writer for songs, musical shows; born in New York City; with Richard Rodgers, composer, produced popular shows. *see also in index* Rodgers, Richard
musical comedy M-685

Hart, Moss (1904–61), U.S. playwright, born in New York City, N.Y.; with George S. Kaufman wrote 'Merrily We Roll Along', about a writer's loss of ideals; 'You Can't Take It with You', comedy (Pulitzer prize 1937); 'I'd Rather Be Right', musical comedy about New Deal; 'The Man Who Came to Dinner', satire on celebrity worship; won Tony for direction of 'My Fair Lady' 1957; 'Act One', autobiography R-111g

Hart, Nancy, American heroine of Revolutionary War; among her many heroic deeds was the capture of six Tories who came to her cabin in Georgia and ordered her to prepare food; highway through Georgia to Florida named for her.

Hart, Sir Robert (1835–1911), British statesman, born in Portadown, County Armagh, present Northern Ireland; as inspector general of imperial Chinese customs, 1862–1907, placed Chinese national finance on solid footing.

Hart, William S. (1872–1946), U.S. actor, born in Newburgh, N.Y.; greatest of the early Western heroes on stage and screen M-619, *picture* M-620

Harte, Bret (pen name of Francis Brett Harte) (1836–1902), U.S. writer of Western stories H-50, A-351
western W-151

Hartebeest (or hartbeest), African antelope *Bubalis cama* about 4 ft (1.2 m) high, with long face and spreading horns curving back at tips; grayish-brown (some species reddish); valued for hide and flesh.

Hartford, George H. *see in index* Great Atlantic & Pacific Tea Company

Hartford, Conn., often called Insurance City, state capital and 2nd largest city; in central part of state on Connecticut River; pop. 135,200 H-51, *map* U-41
Beecher's female seminary B-131
Connecticut C-651, *picture* C-657, *maps* C-654, 663
North America, *map* N-350

Hartford, Vt., community situated 57 mi (92 km) n. of Brattleboro; settled 1765; pop. of township 7,963, *map* V-301

Hartford, University of, West Hartford, Conn.; private control; formed 1957 by merger of Hartford Art School, Hartt College of Music, and Hillyer College; arts and sciences, art, basic studies, business and public administration, education, engineering, and music; graduate studies C-653

Hartford Convention (1814), meeting of delegates from five New England states W-32
Madison M-27

Harthacanute (or Harthacnut) (1019–42), king of England, son of Canute; ruled over Denmark and West Saxons while his brother, Harold I, ruled in North; succeeded him in 1040
Harold I H-43

Hartigan, Grace (born 1922), U.S. abstract expressionist painter, born in Newark, N.J.; her bold strokes and vivid color depict the American scene.

Hartland bridge, New Brunswick, longest covered bridge in the world 1,282 ft (391 m) across Saint John River.

Hartlepool, England, seaport on n.e. coast; resort; exports coal and imports timber; shipbuilding; pop. 98,710, *map* U-18a

Hartley, David (1705–57), British philosopher; founded associationist school of psychology; believed mind is a blank until written upon by sensations, sensations being caused by vibration of the tiny particles of medullary substance of the nerves ('Observations on Man, His Frame, His Duty, and His Expectations').

Hartley, Fred Allan, Jr. (1903–69), U.S. representative from New Jersey, born in Harrison, N.J.; 11 consecutive terms in Congress; Republican; coauthor of Labor-Management Relations Act of 1947 (Taft-Hartley law).

Hartley, Marsden (1877–1943), U.S. artist and poet, born in Lewiston, Me.; known for landscapes, especially of Maine; paintings reflect experimental trends of 20th century
'Mt. Katahdin, Autumn, No. 1' P-26

Hartline, Haldan Keffer (1903–83), U.S. biophysicist, born in Bloomsburg, Pa.; professor at Rockefeller University 1953–74. *see also in index* Nobel Prizewinners, *table*

Hartman, Gertrude (1876–1955), U.S. teacher and author, born in Philadelphia, Pa.; writer of unusual factual books for children ('The World We Live In and How It Came to Be'; 'Medieval Days and Ways'; 'Making of a Democracy'; 'These United States and How They Came to Be').

Hartmann, Karl Robert Eduard von (1842–1906), German philosopher, born in Berlin; taught that existence is evil, and happiness an illusion ('Philosophy of the Unconscious').

Hartmann von Aue (1170?–1215?), German writer G-105

Hartnett, Charles Leo (nickname Gabby) (1900–72), baseball catcher and manager, born in Woonsocket, R.I.; catcher Chicago, N.L., 1922–40 (also manager 1938–40), New York, N.L., 1941; hit 236 home runs; caught 100 or more games in each of 12 seasons, led Chicago, N.L., to pennant, 1938.

Hartog, Jan de (born 1914), Dutch writer, born in Haarlem; known also under pseudonym F.R. Eckman; author of novels, plays, and film scripts that reflect social criticism
'The Hospital' R-111i

Hartsfield, Henry W. (born 1933), U.S. astronaut candidate, born in Birmingham, Ala.; U.S. Air Force officer chosen for NASA program 1969.

Hartsfield International Airport, Atlanta, Ga. G-88

Hartwick College, Oneonta, N.Y.; private control; established 1928 by Lutherans as outgrowth of Hartwick Seminary (opened 1797); arts and sciences, business administration, music and music education, nursing.

Harty, Sir Herbert Hamilton (1879–1941), U.S. conductor, composer, pianist, born in County Down, Ireland; conducted London Symphony and Manchester Hallé orchestras and after 1932 conducted in Australia and U.S. ('Ode to a Nightingale'; 'Irish Symphony').

Harun ar-Rashid (or Harun al-Raschid) (766–809), 'Abbasid caliph of Baghdad 786–809 H-51
'Arabian Nights' A-524
caliphate C-56
Iraq I-314

Harunobu Suzuki (1725–70), Japanese painter, born in Tokyo; one of the first great masters of the color print J-51

Harvard, John (1607–38), Puritan clergyman, born in London, England; to North America 1637; Harvard University named in his honor 1639 C-61

Harvard, Mass., town 8 mi (13 km) n.w. of Acton; apple orchards; remains of Shaker village nearby; incorporated 1732; pop. 12,170.

Harvard, Mount, one of the College peaks in central Colorado, 14,420 ft (4,395 m) high, 23 mi (37 km) s. of Leadville; third highest of United States Rocky Mountains.

'Harvard Classics', selection of books by Charles W. Eliot, president of Harvard University, who said they were "all the books needed for a real education" E-188

Harvard University, Cambridge, Mass.; oldest institution of higher learning in U.S.; private control; founded 1636, named for John Harvard 1639; arts and sciences, business administration, dentistry, design, divinity, education, law, medicine, public administration, public health; graduate studies; Radcliffe College, affiliated
Boston B-374, *picture* B-375
Cambridge C-61
chlorophyll synthesized P-372
education E-87
Eliot E-188
first gymnasium H-94
football origins F-296
hairdressing H-9
Massachusetts M-189, 193, *picture* M-192
museums. *see also in index* Fogg Art Museum; Peabody Museum
Botanical Museum, *picture* R-197
rowing R-300
social studies project S-241b

Harvard University Library, oldest library in U.S.; formed 1638; including college and departmental collections, is the third largest in U.S.; main collection housed in Widener Memorial Library, built 1914 in memory of Harry Elkins Widener, a young bibliophile and Harvard alumnus, who drowned in sinking of *Titanic*; collections include parts of libraries of Longfellow, James R. Lowell, and Amy Lowell; fine theater collection.

Harvester ant, insect A-468

'Harvesters, The', painting by Brueghel the Elder P-41, *picture* P-42

Harvest fly, insect
cicada C-413

Harvesting, agriculture A-136, F-27, *picture* F-26. *see also in index* crops by name as Wheat
banana B-52
combine. *see in index* Combine
Halloween H-17
pioneer American P-335
reaping machines R-113

Harvestman. *see in index* Daddy longlegs

Harvest mite S-388

Harvest moon, full moon nearest the autumnal equinox M-579

Harvest mouse, rodent M-640

Harvey, Charles T. (1829–1912) U.S. civil engineer; directed construction of the first Sault Sainte Marie canal, which was completed in 1855; built elevated railway line in New York city.

Harvey, Gabriel (1550?–1631), English poet, born in Saffron Walden; made literary attacks on Robert Greene and Thomas Nash; attempted to introduce classical meters into English poetry.

Harvey, George Brinton McClellan (1864–1928), U.S. editor and diplomat, born in Peacham, Vt.; editor *North American Review*, *Harper's Weekly*, *Harvey's Weekly*; ambassador to United Kingdom 1921–23.

Harvey, William (1578–1657), English anatomist and physician H-51
medicine M-283
blood circulation B-317

Harvey, Ill., industrial city 19 mi (30 km) s. of Chicago; diesel engines, foundry-plant equipment, metal products, cranes; oil research center; pop. 35,810, *map* I-52

Harvey Mudd College, Claremont, Calif.; private control; member of the Claremont Colleges; founded 1955, opened 1957; liberal arts; graduate study.

Harwich, England, port on e. coast, 65 mi (105 km) n.e. of London; fisheries, shipbuilding; naval station; pop. 14,870, *map* U-18a

Haryana, state in n.w. India; area 16,800 sq mi (43,500 sq km); cap. Chandigarh; dairy cattle, rice, sugarcane, cotton, corn, millet, wheat; textiles, bicycles; pop. 10,036,808, *map* I-83

Harz Mountains, range on border between East and West Germany; 60 mi (97 km) long; highest point Brocken (3,747 ft; 1,142 m), site of Walpurgis Night festival; local industries include tourism, quarrying, canary breeding, wood processing, w.-central Germany G-111, *map* G-132

Hasa, district in e. Arabia on Persian Gulf; many springs, hot and cold, used for irrigation of palm trees and other crops S-52b

Hasan and **Husein,** grandsons of Mohammed, sons of Fatima and Ali; killed AD 669 and 680 by adherents of the Ommiad caliphs and revered as martyr saints by the Shi'ites I-362

Hasbrouck Heights, N.J., borough 6 mi (10 km) s.e. of Paterson; settled 1685, incorporated 1894; pop. 12,166.

Hasdrubal (died 207 BC), Carthaginian general, son of Hamilcar Barca; brother of Hannibal; commanded army in Spain
Hannibal H-31

Hasenclever, Walter (1890–1940), German writer, born in Aachen ('The Son'; 'Beyond'; 'Marriages Are Made in Heaven').

Hashemite Kingdom of Jordan. *see in index* Jordan

Hashish, drug
assassination sect A-703
hallucinogen H-18
hemp H-127
narcotics N-19

Hashishins. *see in index* Assassins
Hash mark, in football F-291
Haskell Indian Junior College, until 1970 Haskell Institute, nonreservation boarding school for Indians, Lawrence, Kan.; founded 1884; maintained by U.S. government; post-high school training in 24 vocations, including commercial training, building trades, and mechanical trades.
Hasluck, Sir Paul Meernaa Caedwalla (born 1905), Australian statesman and historian, born in Fremantle; member of Parliament 1949–51; held various ministries 1951–69; governor-general 1969–74.
Hassam, Childe (1859–1935), U.S. impressionistic painter and etcher, born in Boston, Mass.; known for landscape, figure, and sea paintings; remarkable colorist and skillful luminist ('Summer Sea'; 'Lorelei'; 'The Church at Old Lyme').
Hassan II (born 1929), king of Morocco, born in Rabat; participated in independence negotiations with France 1953–55; wrote democratic constitution providing for elected parliament; mediator in Arab-Israeli conflicts of 1970s and 1980s; prime minister 1961–63, 1965–67; king 1961–.
  Morocco M-587
Hassel, Odd (1897–1981), Norwegian chemist, born in Oslo; professor of physical chemistry at University of Oslo 1934–64; prisoner in German concentration camp 1943–45.
Hassen Tower, Rabat, Morocco, *picture* R-20
Hassler, Hans Leo (1564–1612), German composer, born in Nuremberg; greatest of his age; pupil of Andrea Gabrieli.
Hassock fan F-23
Hastie, William Henry (1904–76), U.S. lawyer, educator, and public official, born in Memphis, Tenn.; dean of law Howard University 1939–46; governor Virgin Islands 1946–49; became first black judge U.S. Court of Appeals Oct. 1949, retired 1971; won 1943 Spingarn medal for jurisprudence B-294
Hastings, Sue, U.S. producer and director of marionette shows, trainer of marionette operators, born in Monticello, N.Y.
  marionettes, *picture* P-537
Hastings, Thomas (1860–1929), U.S. architect, born in New York City, N.Y., entered into partnership with John M. Carrère, 1885. *see also in index* Carrère, John M.
Hastings, Warren (1732–1818), first governor-general of India H-52
  Burke B-506
  East India Company E-44
  India I-77
Hastings, England, port and seaside resort in Sussex; one of Cinque Ports; fisheries; pop. 76,500
  battle of Hastings H-52
Hastings, Minn., city 20 mi (30 km) s.e. of St. Paul on Mississippi River; flour mills, coke refinery; incorporated 1857; pop. 12,827.
Hastings, Neb., city about 90 mi (145 km) w. of Lincoln; ammunition, farm implements, wheat, meat, dairy products, plastics, irrigation pipes, wood products; Hastings College; State Hospital; naval ammunition depot nearby; pop. 23,045 N-96, 104, *map* U-40
Hastings, battle of (1066) H-52
  England E-239, E-264
  warfare, *list* W-15
Hastings College, Hastings, Neb.; affiliated with Presbyterian Church, U.S.; opened in 1882; liberal arts, music, and teacher education.
Hatay, formerly the sanjak of Alexandretta, province of s. Turkey on Mediterranean; area 2,205 sq mi (5,710 sq km); includes cities Antioch (Antakya), the capital, and Alexandretta (Iskenderun); after World War I, under French mandate; in 1939 ceded by France to Turkey; pop. 441,209.
Hatch, fishing, *list* F-146
Hatch Act, "to prevent pernicious political activities" (passed 1939, amended 1940); includes rules such as: federal or state employees, who are paid in part from federal funds, are forbidden to take part in political campaigns and to join any party or organization that advocates overthrow of the constitutional form of government in United States; upheld by Supreme Court 1973 C-469, P-432
Hatchback, automobile style A-844
Hatcher, Richard Gordon (born 1933), U.S. public official and lawyer, born in Michigan City, Ind., mayor of Gary, Ind., 1967–87 B-301
Hatchery
  bird B-255
  fish F-132
  poultry P-482, V-371
Hatchet-footed mollusk. *see in index* Bivalve
Hatchett, Charles (1765–1847), British chemist, born in London; in 1801 discovered columbium (more commonly known as niobium).
Hatfield, Richard Bennett (born 1931), Canadian lawyer and political leader, born in Hartland, N.B.; premier of New Brunswick (Progressive Conservative) 1970–.
Hathaway, Anne (or Anne H. Shakespeare) (1556–1623), wife of William Shakespeare S-130
  burial place S-484b
  cottage, *picture* S-131
Hatha-yoga Y-421
Hathor, ancient Egyptian god E-128
Hathorne, William (1607?–81), Massachusetts colonial official and reformer, born in Binfield, England; lived in Salem from 1636 until his death; ancestor of Nathaniel Hawthorne.
Hatoyama, Ichiro (1883–1959), Japanese statesman, born in Tokyo; minister of education 1931–34; organized Liberal party 1946; prime minister 1954–56.
Hatpin, for hats and caps H-55
Hats and caps H-53
  Czechoslovakian, *picture* S-215
  dress D-262
  Dutch, *picture* P-43
  etiquette E-318
  Flemish, *picture* P-30
  hairdressing H-9
  helmet. *see in index* Helmet
  Panama E-67
  pioneer American P-333, *picture* P-330
  Quaker, *picture* P-162
  sombrero. *see in index* Sombrero
  tricorn, *pictures* R-163, 168
  U.S. armed forces U-5
Hatshepsut, queen of Egypt (reigned 1503–1482 BC), attained unprecedented power for a queen, adopting the full titles and regalia of a pharaoh E-126
  exploration E-372
Hatteras, Cape, easternmost island of North Carolina, separated from mainland by Pamlico Sound; many sailing ships wrecked in nearby waters, *map* U-41
  North America, *map* N-350
  world, *map* W-297
Hattiesburg, Miss., city 87 mi (140 km) s.e. of Jackson, in yellow pine belt; chemicals and explosives, naval stores, clothing, food processing; University of Southern Mississippi, William Carey College; pop. 40,829, *map* U-41
Hatto (died 970), archbishop of Mainz; according to legend, devoured by mice in Mouse Tower on Rhine, near Bingen.
Hau, a small tree *Hibiscus tiliaceus* of mallow family found in the tropics; wood used for boats; inner bark yields a rope fiber.
Hauberk, Byzantine body armor A-637
Hauck, Frederick (born 1941), U.S. astronaut, born in Long Beach, California, *table* S-348
Hauff, Wilhelm (1802–27), German novelist, short-story writer, and poet; born in Stuttgart ('Lichtenstein', historical novel).
Hauptmann, Gerhart (1862–1946), German dramatist, born in Lower Silesia H-55. *see also in index* Nobel Prizewinners, *table*
  drama D-245
  German literature G-106
Hauptwache, business center, Frankfurt, West Germany, *picture* G-114
Hauraki Gulf, New Zealand, large inlet of Pacific Ocean on north coast of North Island, *map* N-299
Hausa, a people of n. Nigeria and s. Niger; spread Hausa language while trading
  African folk tale A-121
  language A-119
  Nigeria N-311
Hauser, Jon William (born 1916), U.S. industrial designer I-174
Haushofer, Karl (1869–1946), German geographer, born in Munich; head of Geopolitical Institute at Munich; author of many works on geopolitics; influenced Hitler; committed suicide. *see also in index* Geopolitics
Hausmannite, an ore of manganese, found as an oxide in brownish-black tetragonal crystals; chemical formula Mn_3O_4.
Haussmann, Georges Eugène, Baron (1809–91), French official and city planner, born in Paris; prefect of Seine 1853–70 P-123
  architecture design A-563
Haus zum Römer, landmark, Frankfurt, West Germany, *picture* F-378
Hautbois strawberry, plant *Fragaria moschata* of the family Rosaceae S-486
Hautboy. *see in index* Oboe
Hautecloque. *see in index* Leclerc, Jacques Philippe
Haute couture, high fashion D-268
Haute École, in horse training, *list* H-249
  equestrian sports E-295
Haute-Savoie, department in e. France; 1,774 sq mi (4,595 sq km); cap. Annecy; once was part of the former duchy of Savoy; pop. 447,795. *see also in index* Savoie
Haut-Rhin, department of France in the region called Alsace; cereals and fruits grown; textile industries; area 1,354 sq mi (3,507 sq km); pop. 635,209, *map* F-369
Haüy, René (1743–1822), French mineralogist and a founder of the science of crystallography; studied pyroelectricity and piezoelectricity in crystals C-796
Haüy, Valentin (1745–1822), French professor, born near Beauvais; stirred by plight of the sightless who were illiterate and untrained, established a school for blind children where they were taught to read.
Havana, province, Cuba, *map* C-802
Havana (Spanish Habana), capital of Cuba; largest city in West Indies; pop. 1,924,900 H-56, C-800, *map* C-802
  Gorgas G-195
  North America, *map* N-350
  West Indies, *map* W-159
  world, *map* W-297
Havana, Act of (1940), *table* T-274
Havasu, Lake, on boundary between w. Arizona and s.e. California, formed by Parker Dam, *map* N-350
Havasupai, Yuman Indian tribe living in Cataract Canyon of the Colorado River in n.w. Arizona.
Havelok the Dane, hero of old Anglo-Danish romance, son of Birkabeyn (or Gunter), king of Denmark; set adrift on raft that bore him to Lincolnshire coast, England; rescued by Grim, a fisherman; married ward of king of Lincoln, and became king of Denmark and of part of England; Grim was rewarded and built Grimsby.
Havel River, n.-central Germany, a tributary of Elbe; rises in Mecklenburg and flows s.; about 220 mi (355 km) long; linked by canals with the Oder, Rhine, and Elbe rivers, *map* G-131
Haverford, Pa., urban township 6 mi (10 km) n.w. of Philadelphia; Haverford College founded 1833 by Quakers; pop. 52,349, *map* P-185
Haverford College, Haverford, Pa.; private control, Quaker related; founded 1833, became college 1856; arts and sciences; notable Quaker collection.
Havergal, Frances Ridley (1836–79), British hymn writer, born in Astley, near Worcester, England; daughter of clergyman; scribbled hymns at age of 7; simple expression of deep religious feeling ('Take My Life and Let It Be').
Haverhill, Mass., industrial city on Merrimack River, 30 mi (50 km) n. of Boston; shoes, machinery and machine tools, paper products, textiles, metal products, leather products; pop. 46,865.
Havering, borough, London, England, *maps* L-287, U-18a
Haviland, David (1814–79), U.S. china manufacturer, born in Westchester County, New York; in 1842 established pottery at Limoges, France, and produced fine porcelain primarily for export to U.S.; in 1864 admitted as partners his sons, **Charles Edward Miller Haviland** (1839–1922), born in Manhattan, N.Y., and **Theodore Haviland** (1842–1919), born in Limoges France; in 1892 Theodore withdrew and built at Limoges his own factory, which is still in operation; American line of Haviland china produced in U.S. since 1936.
Haviland, Thomas Heath (1822–95), Canadian political leader, born in Charlottetown, P.E.I.
  Fathers of Canadian Confederation C-115, *picture* C-116
Haviland, Virginia (born 1911), U.S. author, librarian, born in Rochester, N.Y.; awarded 1976 Regina Medal of the Catholic Library Association; author of 'William Penn, Founder and Friend', Favorite Fairy Tales series R-110a, S-479
Havilland, Olivia Mary de. *see in index* De Havilland, Olivia Mary
Havlícek, Karel (1821–56), Bohemian poet and political writer; editor of two Bohemian publications; imprisoned for liberal views, and died one year after release ('Tyrolese Elegies'; 'The Baptism of St. Vladimir').
Havre, Mont., city about 105 mi (170 km) n.e. of Great Falls, on Milk River; cattle and wheat; Northern Montana College; pop. 10,891 M-552, 560, *map* U-40
Havre, Le, France. *see in index* Le Havre
Hawaii, state of U.S., in n. Pacific Ocean; 6,450 sq mi (16,705 sq km); cap. Honolulu; pop. 964,691 H-57, *map* W-297. *see also in index* islands by name, as Maui
  agriculture
    pineapples P-329, *picture* P-191
    sugar, *picture* S-505
  algae diet A-284
  cities. *see also in index* Honolulu and other cities by name
  flag, *picture* F-159
  folktales, *list* S-479
  geography
    Oceania O-465, 472
    oceanography O-485
    Pacific Ocean, *map* P-3
    United States U-30, 97, *maps* U-100, 119, *pictures* U-98, 99
  history
    Cook's exploration C-696
    Kamehameha I K-167
    statehood S-429a, *table* S-428
      Eisenhower administration E-141
    U.S. territory
      Dole D-214
      Liliuokalani L-208
      McKinley administration M-20
    World War II W-328. *see also in index* Pearl Harbor
  sports S-519
  Statuary Hall, *table* S-437a
  taxation, *tables* T-37, 39
Hawaii, largest island of the state of Hawaii; 4,038 sq mi (10,458 sq km); pop. 92,053 H-58, *pictures* H-69, *maps* U-117, 98, W-297
  island formation I-368
  Pacific Ocean, *map* P-3
  Oceania O-465
'Hawaii', novel by Michener A-361

Hawaii, University of, Honolulu, Hawaii; state control; established 1907: arts and sciences, business administration, education, engineering, medicine, nursing, public health, social work, travel industry management, tropical agriculture; graduate school; East-West center; four-year campus at Hilo, also, community colleges at Honolulu, Kahului, Kaneohe, Lihue, and Pearl City H-62, H-230, *picture* H-67

Hawaiian, language H-61

Hawaiian goose, goose. *see in index* Nene

Hawaiian guitar, stringed musical instrument
country music M-678

Hawaii Loa College, Kaneohe, Hawaii; interdenominational Protestant; chartered 1963; liberal arts, Western-Asian studies H-63

Hawaii Pacific College, Honolulu, Hawaii; private; established 1965; arts and sciences H-63

Hawaii Volcanoes National Park H-62, N-50

Hawes, Charles Boardman (1889–1923), U.S. author, born in Clifton Springs, N.Y.; sea romances for young people; Newbery Medal for 'The Dark Frigate', 1924 ('The Mutineers'; 'Great Quest').

Hawes, Josiah Johnson (1808–1901), U.S. photographer famous for his portraiture, *list* P-294

Hawes, Stephen (1474?–1523?), English poet; birthplace probably Suffolk ('Passetyme of Pleasure' and 'Example of Virtue', allegorical poems).

Hawfinch, bird of the family Fringillidae G-290

Hawk, bird species B-246, *pictures* B-242, 243, 248. *see also in index* names of particular hawks, as Sparrow hawk
falconry F-13
nature study, *picture* V-244
osprey. *see in index* Osprey
predatory behavior B-278

Hawk, monoplane aircraft A-201

Hawk, U.S. guided missile, *picture* G-307

Hawkbill turtle (or hawksbill sea turtle), sea turtle *Eretmochelys imbricata* T-329

Hawke, Robert (full name Robert James Lee Hawke) (born 1929), Australian labor leader and prime minister H-74

Hawke of Towton, Edward Hawke, 1st Baron (1705–81), British naval commander, born in London; defeat of French fleet at Quiberon Bay 1759 decided naval outcome of Seven Years' War; first lord of the Admiralty 1766–71.

Hawker, Harry G. (1889–1921), Australian aviator, first to try Newfoundland-to-London flight (May 1919); forced to land in mid-ocean, rescued by Danish ship; killed in plane crash near London, July 1921.

Hawkeye. *see in index* Bumppo, Natty

Hawkeye State. *see in index* Iowa

Hawking. *see in index* Falconry

Hawkins, Sir Anthony Hope. *see in index* Hope, Anthony

Hawkins, Coleman (1904–69), U.S. jazz musician, born in St. Joseph, Mo.; created widely used hot jazz style of playing tenor saxophone.

Hawkins, John (also spelled Hawkyns) (1532–95), English adventurer and admiral H-74
Drake D-240
Royal Navy N-87
voyages to America A-332

Hawkins, Paula, U.S. senator from Florida W-276

Hawkins, Sir Richard (1562–1622), English admiral, son of Sir John; commanded vessel in attack on the Spanish Armada; commanded an expedition to South America 1583–97, but was captured by Spanish and imprisoned until 1602; later served in Parliament.

Hawk moth. *see in index* Sphinx moth

Hawks, Frank Monroe (1897–1938), U.S. aviator, born in Marshalltown, Iowa; in U.S. Army air service 1917–19; his numerous speed records include transcontinental nonstop records; killed in plane crash.

Hawks, Howard (1896–1977), U.S. film director ('Scarface: The Shame of a Nation'; 'Red River'; 'Gentlemen Prefer Blondes') D-155

Hawks-beard, plant. *see in index* Crepis

Hawksbill sea turtle (or hawkbill turtle), sea turtle *Eretmochelys imbricata* T-329

Hawksbill Head, Shenandoah National Park, Virginia, *picture* V-341

Hawk's Castle (or Habichtsburg), seat of Hapsburgs H-32

Hawksmoor, Nicholas (1661–1736), British architect, born in Nottinghamshire; worked so intimately with Christopher Wren that it is impossible to make exact division of credit for their work A-568
Westminster Abbey W-163

Hawkweed, a genus of perennial plants *Hieracium* of the family Compositae with loosely clustered yellow, orange, or white flower heads and oblong toothed leaves that grow from roots in rosette; troublesome weed in some places; an old superstition stated that hawks used the sap to sharpen their eyesight.

Hawley, James H. (or Grand Old Man of Idaho) (1847–1929), lawyer and political leader, born in Dubuque, Iowa; moved to Idaho 1862; mined in area 1862–71; began law practice 1871; mayor of Boise 1904–05; governor of Idaho 1911–13.

Hawley family
heraldic shield, *picture* H-136

Hawley-Smoot Tariff Act, introduced by Representative Willis C. Hawley (1864–1941), of Oregon, and Senator Reed Smoot (1862–1941), of Utah; passed in June 1930; greatly increased import duties on many products
Hoover H-235
international trade I-272
tariff T-30

Haworth, Sir Walter Norman (1883–1950), British biochemist, born in Chorley, Lancashire. *see also in index* Nobel Prizewinners, *table*

Haworth, England, former urban district (part of borough of Keighley since 1938); beautiful moorlands; famous as home and burial place of Charlotte and Emily Brontë; Brontë museum and library.

Hawthorn, any of a number of thorny shrubs or small trees of the genus *Crataegus*, in the rose family, Rosaceae; native to North Temperate Zone; many species grown as ornamentals
flower, *picture* S-427
Missouri state flower, *picture* M-496

Hawthorne, Charles Webster (1872–1930), U.S. painter, born in Lodi, Ill.; spent boyhood in Maine; well known for his figure paintings of Cape Cod and Provincetown fishermen.

Hawthorne, Hildegarde (1871–1952), U.S. poet and author, born in New York City, N.Y.; daughter of Julian and granddaughter of Nathaniel Hawthorne; books for children based on original sources and personal reminiscences of her father; 'Romantic Rebel, the Story of Nathaniel Hawthorne'; 'Youth's Captain, the Story of Ralph Waldo Emerson'; 'The Happy Autocrat, a Life of Oliver Wendell Holmes'; 'Concord's Happy Rebel, Henry David Thoreau'.

Hawthorne, Julian (1846–1934), U.S. civil engineer and author, born in Boston, Mass.; son of Nathaniel Hawthorne ('Garth', 'Sebastian Strome', novels; 'Hawthorne and His Circle').

Hawthorne, Nathaniel (1804–64), U.S. novelist H-74
American literature A-343
Hall of Fame, *table* H-16
Massachusetts home C-639, *picture* M-201
Longfellow L-296

Hawthorne, Calif., city 11 mi (18 km) s.w. of Los Angeles; aircraft and aircraft parts, electronic products, toys; pop. 56,447.

Hawthorne, Nev., unincorporated town 5 mi (8 km) s.e. of Babbitt and 95 mi (155 km) s.e. of Reno; trade center, mining, U.S. Naval Ammunition Depot, largest in world; Walker Lake vacation area nearby; pop. 5,166.

Hawthorne, N.J., a residential borough just n. of Paterson; textiles, chemicals, machinery, television tubes, cement blocks; pop. 18,200.

Hay, John Milton (1838–1905), U.S. statesman, diplomat, and writer, born in Salem, Ind.; U.S. secretary of state 1895–1905
McKinley M-20
open-door policy O-559

Hay, dried grass or other plants used as fodder H-74. *see also in index* Forage crops
Ireland, *picture* E-340
legume L-120
Minnesota, *picture* M-451
peanut P-146

Hayakawa, Samuel Ichiye (born 1906), U.S. educator and semantics expert, born in Vancouver, B.C.; to U.S. 1929; on faculty Armour Institute of Chicago (later Illinois Institute of Technology) 1939–47; lecturer at University of Chicago 1950–55; professor of language arts at San Francisco State College 1955–68, acting president 1968–69, president 1969–73; U.S. senator (Republican) from California 1977–83 ('Symbol, Status and Personality').

Ha-Yarden. *see in index* Jordan River

Hayden, Carl Trumbull (1877–1972), U.S. political leader, born in Hayden's Ferry (now Tempe), Ariz.; Democratic representative from Arizona 1912–27; U.S. senator 1927–69, president pro tempore of Senate 1957–69.

Hayden, Ferdinand Vandiveer (1829–87), U.S. geologist, born in Westfield, Mass.; professor, University of Pennsylvania; director of geological survey of Western territories.

Haydn, Joseph (in full Franz Joseph Haydn) (1732–1809), Austrian composer H-74
band compositions B-56
chamber music C-268
classical music M-669
German national anthem N-66
marionettes P-537
Mozart M-643
oratorio O-575
orchestra O-576

Hayes, Helen (born 1900), U.S. actress, born in Washington, D.C.; debut at age of six; early successes included 'Dear Brutus' with William Gillette; distinguished on stage, screen, radio, and television (stage plays: 'Bab'; 'Mary of Scotland'; 'Victoria Regina'; 'Time Remembered', for which she won 1958 Tony; films: 'The Sin of Madelon Claudet', 1932 Academy award; 'Arrowsmith'; 'Airport', 1970 Academy award); married Charles MacArthur 1928; professor of speech and theater University of Illinois, Chicago, 1969; memoirs, 'A Gift of Joy', 'On Reflection' A-27

Hayes, John Francis (born 1904), Canadian author, born in Ontario ('Buckskin Colonist'; 'A Land Divided'; 'Rebels Ride at Night'; 'The Dangerous Cove', Canadian Book of the Year for Children award 1959).

Hayes, Lucy Webb (1831–89), wife of President Hayes H-77

Hayes, Patrick Joseph, Cardinal (1867–1938), Roman Catholic prelate, born in New York City, N.Y.; president Cathedral College, New York City, 1903–14; appointed Catholic chaplain bishop for U.S. Army and Navy, 1917, and archbishop of New York, 1919; became cardinal, 1924.

Hayes, Roland (1887–1976), U.S. tenor, born in Curryville, Ga.; noted for singing of Negro spirituals; sang with Boston, New York, and other leading orchestras; Spingarn Medal 1924; author of 'My Songs'.

Hayes, Rutherford B. (1822–93), 19th president of United States H-76
Arthur's replacement A-653
electoral college E-148
McKinley M-17
presidency U-182

Hayes Mountains, mountains in Alaska A-257

Hayes River, river in Manitoba, rises near Lake Winnipeg and flows n.e. 300 mi (480 km) to Hudson Bay at village of York Factory M-100, *map* C-109

Hay fever, allergic disease A-309
antihistamine's function A-492

Hayflick phenomenon, in cell division
aging research A-127

Hayford, James H. (1828–1902), U.S. lawyer and journalist, born in Potsdam, N.Y.; publisher *Laramie Sentinel* 1869–1902; Wyoming Territorial Auditor 1870–75; Laramie postmaster eight years
Mother Jones J-140

Haym, Nicola, opera librettist O-563

Haymarket riot, Chicago, Ill. J-140

Haymow, pile of hay H-75

Hayne, Paul Hamilton (1830–86), U.S. poet, born in Charleston, S.C.; nephew of Robert Young Hayne; called the laureate of the South ('Legends and Lyrics'; 'The Mountain of the Lovers') A-350

Hayne, Robert Young (1791–1839), U.S. statesman, born in South Carolina; ardent nullification advocate; best remembered as having elicited, 1830, Webster's 'Reply to Hayne' S-310, *picture* S-316
Webster W-129

Hay-Pauncefote Treaty (1901), between United States and United Kingdom; instituted at desire of J.G. Blaine for modification or abolishment of Clayton-Bulwer Treaty, *table* T-274
McKinley M-20

Hays, Arthur Garfield (1881–1954), U.S. lawyer and writer, born in Rochester, N.Y.; began practice New York City 1905; in civil liberties cases, famous cases include Scopes and Sacco-Vanzetti ('Let Freedom Ring'; 'Democracy Works'; 'City Lawyer', autobiography).

Hays, Charles Melville (1856–1912), U.S. railroad official, born in Rock Island, Ill.; began railroading at 17; served with several companies, president Grand Trunk Railway Co. of Canada 1910; died in *Titanic* disaster.

Hays, Lee (1914–81), U.S. folk musician F-273

Hays, Will Harrison (1879–1954), U.S. lawyer, born in Sullivan, Ind.; U.S. postmaster general 1921–22; served as president Motion Picture Producers and Distributors of America 1922–45, adviser 1945–50 ('Memoirs').

Hays, Kan., city 85 mi (135 km) w. of Salina; wheat, oil, cattle, medical and surgical supplies, hydraulic cylinders; site of Fort Hays; Fort Hays State University; pop. 16,301.

Hayward, Calif., city 13 mi (21 km) s.e. of Oakland; nurseries; electronics, trucks, soft drinks, canned foods, glass and tin containers, steel products; California State University; pop. 94,167.

Haywood, Carolyn (born 1898), U.S. illustrator and author of children's books, born in Philadelphia, Pa.; noted for portraits of children; books: 'Betsy and Billy'; 'Here's a Penny'; 'Penny and Peter'; 'Little Eddie'; 'Eddie and Gardenia'; 'Betsy's Winterhouse'; 'Here Comes the Bus!'; 'Eddie's Green Thumb'.

Hazara, one of an Afghan people of Mongolian origin A-89

Hazard, Paul (1878–1944), French scholar and literary historian; born near Lille, France; author of numerous books, including study of children's literature 'Books, Children & Men'.

Hazaz, Hayyim (1898–1922), Israeli writer H-113

Haze, an atmospheric condition caused by suspension of fine particles in the air, making it less clear; unlike fog, which depends on moisture, haze is often present when atmosphere is dry F-245

Hazel (also called filbert), bushy shrub related to the birches H-80

insulating materials I-231
Pompeiian baths P-443
shelter S-156
stoves S-483

Heat of combustion. *see in index* Heat of reaction

Heat of reaction (or heat of combustion) H-104

Heatolator. *see in index* Duct

Heat pollution. *see in index* Thermal pollution

Heat pump, method of heating houses H-109, *picture* H-110
air conditioning A-151

Heat-resisting materials. *see in index* topics below
carborundum S-195b
platinum P-384

Heat-setting, process in textile manufacture T-140

Heat shield, in spacecraft S-346

Heatstroke, medical disorder
first aid F-121

Heat treatment (or hyperthermia), cancer treatment C-135

Heaven, in religion, the place or state of righteous souls after death
Hinduism H-157
Jainism J-14

Heavenly Blue, vine *Ipomoea tricolor*, variety of morning-glory M-584

Heavenly Twins. *see in index* Gemini

Heavenly Valley, ski area along the Nevada-California border, *picture* N-133

Heaviside, Oliver (1850–1925), British physicist, born in London; did foundation work for long-distance telephoning; suggested that there was an electrical ceiling, also called Heaviside layer.

Heaviside layer. *see in index* Kennelly-Heaviside layer

Heavy chemicals, in inorganic chemistry I-210

Heavy hydrogen, *diagrams* R-65

Heavy metal, type of music M-682

Heavy oil, coal-tar product C-527

Heavysege, Charles (1816–76), Canadian poet, born in Huddersfield, England; wrote 'Saul', a poetic drama original in conception and containing passages of great beauty.

Heavy soil, a clay soil G-21, S-250

Heavy water, water in which ordinary hydrogen is replaced by its deuterium isotope W-87
hydrogen H-341
nuclear energy N-423

Heavy water reactor (HWR), type of nuclear reactor N-426

Heavyweight, in boxing B-388, *table* B-391
Muhammad Ali A-306

Hebbel, Christian Friedrich (1813–63), German poet and dramatist, born in Wesselburen, near Rendsburg; one of greatest in 19th century; work shows skill in characterization and true feeling for dramatic situations, but is marred by occasional extravagances G-109

Hebe, in Greek mythology, cupbearer to gods; represented comely youth and joyousness; daughter of Zeus and Hera.

Hebei (or Hopei), province in n.e. China; area (excluding Peking) 78,260 sq mi (202,690 sq km); cap. Shijiazhuang; coal, iron ore; pop. 54,870,000 H-112

Hebei Plain, n. China H-112

Hebenstretia, a genus of south African perennial plants of the figwort family; one species *H. comosa* grown as annual; stems woody; flowers in 6-in. (15-cm) spikes, yellow or white, blotched orange-red; like mignonette; fragrant at night.

Heber, Reginald (1783–1826), British churchman and hymn writer, born in Malpas, Cheshire, England; bishop of Calcutta after 1823 ('From Greenland's Icy Mountains', music by Lowell Mason; 'Holy, Holy, Holy', music by J.B. Dykes).

Hébert, Jacques René (1755–94), French revolutionist and atheist, born in Alençon; published violent Republican papers
Robespierre R-223

Hébert, Louis (died 1627), Canadian colonist, born in Paris, France; apothecary at French court; emigrated to Acadia 1604, where he became first Canadian farmer; moved to Quebec 1617; many old French-Canadian families trace lineage to him.

Hébert, Louise Philippe (1850–1917), Canadian sculptor, born in Ste-Sophie d'Halifax, Lower Canada; noted for a monument to Queen Victoria at Ottawa and statues of prominent Canadians.

Hebrew Bible. *see in index* Old Testament

Hebrew College, Brookline, Mass.; private control; founded 1921; liberal arts, education, Hebraica; Ulpan Hebrew Language Institute; graduate studies; Hebrew used for instruction; nine off-campus centers.

Hebrew language
classification L-42
Hebrew literature H-113
Israel I-370, M-395
writing
alphabet, *table* A-316
calligraphy C-57
Yiddish literature Y-416

Hebrew literature H-113. *see also in index* Hebrew language
folklore F-263
history H-171
Judaism J-148
oldest dictionary S-1

Hebrews, people. *see also in index* Judaism
Moses M-595

Hebrews, Epistle to the, the 19th book of the Bible's New Testament, a letter addressed to Christians of Hebrew birth, probably those living in Rome, about AD 65. The authorship is unknown but frequently attributed to Paul B-183

Hebrew University, institution of higher learning in Jerusalem, founded mainly by the Zionist organization; opened 1925; science, Jewish and Oriental studies, humanities, medicine, law, and agriculture; instruction is in Hebrew, *picture* J-147

Hebrides (also Western Isles), islands off n.-w. coast of Scotland; 2,812 sq mi (7,283 sq km); potatoes; pop. 44,344, *maps* E-360, U-18b
world, *map* W-297

Hebron, Jordan, one of oldest towns of ancient Palestine, 18 mi (29 km) s.w. of Jerusalem; Abraham's tomb here; pop. 38,309.

Hecateus (fl. 6th–5th century BC) early Greek historian and geographer
history writing H-171
maps, *picture* M-126

Hecatomb, in modern usage, the destruction of a large number of things; originally, in ancient Greece, sacrifice of 100 oxen (from *hekaton*, Greek for "hundred"); later, sacrifice of any large number.

Heceta, Bruno (fl. 1775), Spanish explorer
Washington W-53

Hecht, Ben (1894–1964), U.S. author, born in New York City, N.Y. ('The Collected Stories of Ben Hecht'; 'Eric Dorn', novel; 'The Front Page', play, with Charles MacArthur; 'A Child of the Century', autobiography; 'Charlie', a tribute to MacArthur).

Hecker, Isaac Thomas (1819–88), U.S. Roman Catholic priest, born in New York City, N.Y.; member Brook Farm Experiment 1843; converted to Catholicism in 1844 and in 1858 founded Missionary Society of St. Paul the Apostle (Paulists).

Hecla, volcano in Iceland. *see in index* Hekla

Heckler, Margaret, (born 1932), U.S. secretary of Department of Health and Human Services 1983–85, ambassador to Ireland 1985–
women's rights W-276

Hectare (or hektare), unit of measure, *table* W-141

Hectograph. *see in index* Spirit Duplicator

Hector, character in Greek mythology, son of Priam H-114
Achilles' revenge A-19
Homeric legend H-221, *picture* H-222

Hector, Sir, knight in Arthurian legends A-655

Hector's dolphin D-224

Hecuba, in Greek mythology, wife of Priam, king of Troy; mother of Hector, Paris, and Cassandra; taken captive after fall of Troy.
Paris P-116

'Hedda Gabler', play by Ibsen I-5

Heddings, N.J. *see in index* Bellmawr

Heddle, in weaving S-391

Hedge, fence formed by living shrubs or trees H-115

Hedgehog, spiny animal H-115, *picture* A-427
hair H-7
mammal M-80

Hedgehog, military formation A-639

Hedge mustard, variety of tumbleweed *Sisymbrium altissimum* T-306

Hedge nettle. *see in index* Stachys

Hedgerows, battle of, World War II W-340, *picture* W-342

Hedges, Cornelius, early governor of Montana M-553

Hedging, in commodity exchange C-598

Hedin, Sven Anders (1865–1952), Swedish explorer H-115
exploration E-376

Hedley, William (1779–1843), railroad inventor L-281

Hedonism, in philosophy P-264, *list* P-265

Heel, in footwear S-179

Heep, Uriah, a character in Dickens' 'David Copperfield'; a designing hypocrite who pretends to be "very 'umble".

Heffelfinger, Pudge (William Walter Heffelfinger) (1867–1954), U.S. football player F-296

Hegel, Georg Wilhelm Friedrich (1770–1831), German philosopher H-115
Kierkegaard K-236
philosophy P-266
philosophy of history H-174

Hegemony, in international relations I-261

Hegenberger, Albert F. (born 1895), U.S. aviator, born in Boston, Mass. A-205

Heggen, Thomas Orlo (1919–49), U.S. author, born in Fort Dodge, Iowa; member editorial staff *Reader's Digest*; with U.S. Navy in South Pacific, World War II; 'Mister Roberts', his novel about life on a Navy supply ship, was basis of play 'Mister Roberts', of which he was coauthor with Joshua Logan.

Hegira, Muhammed's flight from Mecca (AD 622), from which Muslim dates are calculated M-646
Islam I-360

Heian-kyo, Japan, former name of Kyoto. *see also in index* Kyoto

Heiberg, Johan Ludvig (1791–1860), Danish poet and critic, born in Copenhagen, Denmark; edited *Flying Post*; championed Hegelian philosophy ('A Soul After Death'; 'The Newly Wedded'; 'The Nut-Cracker').

Heidegger, Martin (1889–1976), German philosopher H-116
existentialism E-371
philosophy P-267

Heidelberg, West Germany, university city on Neckar River in n. Baden-Württemberg; pop. 133,800; castle one of Europe's grandest; University of Heidelberg founded 1386, *map* G-133

Heidelberg College, Tiffin, Ohio; affiliated with United Church of Christ; established in 1850; arts and sciences, music, and teacher education.

Heidelberg School, in Australian art A-802

Heiden, Eric (born 1958), U.S. speed skater
Olympic achievement A-741, O-542, *picture* A-740

Heidenstam, Karl Gustaf Verner von (1859–1940), Swedish writer, born in Olshammer, near Orebro ('Hans Alienus', fanciful epic; 'Birth of God', 'The Soothsayer', dramas; 'The Charles Men', stories of Charles XII of Sweden and his wars; 'Nya Dikter', poems). *see also in index* Nobel Prizewinners, *table*

'Heidi', children's story by Spyri S-398

Heifer calf. *see in index* Calf

Heifetz, Jascha (born 1901), U.S. violinist H-116

Height. *see in index* Altitude; Azimuth

Heijermans, Herman (pen name Samuel Falkland) (1864–1924), Dutch writer of Jewish parentage, born in Rotterdam; first became known through sketches of Jewish family life under pen name ('The Good Hope'; 'Rising Sun'; 'The Ghetto'; 'Links'; 'A Case of Arson').

Heiji War, in Japanese history J-63, *picture* J-70

Heijo, North Korea. *see in index* Pyongyang

'Heike monogatari' (Tales of the Heike), Japanese literary work J-81

Heilbronn, West Germany, city on Neckar River, 25 mi (40 km) n. of Stuttgart; machinery, metal goods, chemicals, textiles, foods; fine Gothic church and Rathaus; pop. 101,660, *map* G-131

Heilmann, Harry Edwin (1894–1951), U.S. baseball outfielder, born in San Francisco, Calif.; with Detroit, A.L., 1916–29, and Cincinnati, N.L., 1930–32; had lifetime batting average of .342; led league in batting 1921, 1923, 1925, and 1927.

Heilongjiang (or Heilungkiang), province in n.e. part of China; 178,000 sq mi (460,000 sq km); cap. Harbin; pop. 32,950,000 H-116
Harbin H-33
Manchuria M-94

Heilprin, Angelo (1853–1907), U.S. naturalist and traveler, born in Hungary; professor invertebrate paleontology and geology, Academy of Natural Sciences, Philadelphia; made valuable investigations in Florida, Bermuda, Martinique; climbed crater of Mt. Pelée while volcano was erupting; chief editor *Lippincott's Pronouncing Gazetteer* (1905).

Heilsberg, Poland, former German (East Prussian) town about 80 mi (130 km) e. of Danzig; indecisive battle between French and allied Russians and Prussians 1807; included in Poland since 1945.

Heilungkiang. *see in index* Heilongjiang

'Heimat'. *see in index* 'Magda'

Heimdal, in Norse mythology, guardian of the rainbow bridge of the gods; can see perfectly day and night; can even hear grass grow; seldom sleeps M-703

Hein, Melvin (born 1909), U.S. football center, born in Redding, Calif.; played for New York Giants 1931–45.

Heine, Heinrich (1797–1856), German poet H-118
German literature G-106

Heinemann, Gustav Walter (1899–1976), West German political leader, born in Schwelm; minister of interior 1949–50; Bundestag representative 1957–66; minister of justice 1966–69; president Federal Republic of Germany 1969–74.

Heinkel, Ernst (1888–1958), German aircraft manufacturer, born in Württemberg; organized aircraft company 1922; produced first successful rocket-carrying airplane J-111

Heinlein, Robert Anson (born 1907), U.S. author and scientist H-117
reading R-112f
science fiction S-62

Heinz, Henry John (1844-1919), U.S. manufacturer I-195

Heir (or heiress), from Latin word *heres*, a person who is entitled to inherit
definition, *table* L-93

Heir apparent, in common law, one who will inherit property if he or she outlives the legal ancestor; one who will succeed to the position held by the ancestor.

Heir presumptive, one who will inherit property if no nearer heir is born to the ancestor;

one who will succeed to an ancestor's position if no nearer heir exists.

Heisenberg, Werner (1901–76), German physicist H-117. *see also in index* Nobel Prizewinners, *table*
  physics P-308

Heisman, John W. (1869-1936), U.S. football player F-296

Heisman Memorial Trophy, awarded to most valuable college football player of year; originated by Downtown Athletic Club of New York City in 1935 in honor of John W. Heisman, player and coach for 40 years.

Hejaz, part of Saudi Arabia, extending along coast of Red Sea; a separate kingdom from 1919 to 1925; area about 150,000 sq mi (388,500 sq km); pop. 1,250,000 S-52a
  Ottoman Arabia A-523

Hektare (or hectare), unit of measure, *table* W-141

Hektoen, Ludvig (1863–1951), U.S. pathologist and editor, born in present Westby, Wis.; professor Rush Medical College 1895–1933; head of department of pathology University of Chicago 1901–32.

Hektogram, unit in metric system (3.527 oz.).

Hektoliter, unit in metric system (26.42 gals.).

Hektometer, unit in metric system (328 ft. 1 in.).

Hel (or Hela), in Scandinavian mythology, goddess of death who ruled over the realm of the dead; daughter of Loki M-703

Hele, Peter (also known as Peter Henlein) (1480–1542), clockmaker of Nuremberg, Germany, credited with invention of first watch about 1500.

Helena, Saint (247?–327?), mother of Constantine the Great; legendary discoverer of the Holy Cross; festival August 18.

Helena, Ark., city on Mississippi River, about 55 mi (90 km) s.w. of Memphis, Tenn.; railroad center and river port; wood products, cottonseed products; scene of Federal victory in Civil War; pop. 9,598.

Helena, Mont., state capital, in w.-central part; pop. 24,643 H-117, *map* N-350
  Montana M-552, 560, *pictures* M-557, 559

Hélène, opera created by Saint-Saëns for Nellie Melba M-288

Helenium (or sneezeweed), a genus of plants of the composite family, native to North and South America; rough, erect plants; leaves dotted with tiny glands; flowers daisylike, yellow or brown ray florets notched at outer margins; plants have been used locally in medicinal preparations.

Helen of Troy, in Greek legend H-117
  Egyptian account S-469
  Homeric legend H-221

Helgoland (also spelled Heligoland, or Gibraltar of the North Sea), West German island in North Sea; 150 acres (60 hectares); pop. 3,184 G-112, *maps* E-360, G-131

Helianthemum (or sun rose), a genus of plants, chiefly shrubs of the rock-rose family, native to Mediterranean and North America; branching, with evergreen or half-evergreen foliage; flowers in clusters, white, yellow, or pink; used in rock gardens.

Helianthus, sunflower genus S-518

Helibus, aircraft H-120

Helical scanning, method of recording V-312

Helichrysum, a genus of annual and perennial plants of the composite family, native to Africa and Australia; one species *H. bracteatum* is grown as an everlasting; plants about 2 ft (60 cm) high; flower heads daisylike, white through purple, dry and stiff, hence called strawflowers.

Helicon, ancient name of a peak or mountain range in Boeotia, Greece; on the e. slope were a grove and temple sacred to the Muses.

Helicon, wind instrument W-230

Heliconius burneyi, *picture* B-524

Helicopter (nicknames chopper, copter, egg beater, flying windmill, whirlybird), type of aircraft H-118
  airplane A-173
  forest fire fighting F-108
  heliport. *see in index* Heliport
  history A-207
  Karman's contribution K-192
  Korean War use, *picture* K-300
  use
    lifesaving A-326, *pictures* P-429
      hospital, *picture* H-282
    military A-160, *pictures* V-322, A-52, A-157, A-581, R-187
      navy N-85
      warfare W-24
    police, *picture* P-429
    postal service P-460a
    prospecting, *picture* P-234
    ranching, *picture* U-83
    transportation, *picture* T-263
    weather forecasting, *picture* P-421

Helicopter minesweeper, naval aircraft N-85

Heligoland, West German island. *see in index* Helgoland

Heliocentric theory, theory that earth and other planets revolve around sun; believed in ancient times by Aristarchus; established by work of Copernicus, Kepler, Galileo, and James Bradley.

Heliogabalus (or Elagabalus) (AD 205–222), dissolute Roman emperor, proclaimed AD 218; introduced into Rome worship of Syrian sun-god, whose namesake and high priest he was; assassinated.

Heliograph, a sunlight reflector used in signaling.

Heliopolis, ancient city at head of Nile delta, Egypt; once seat of sun worship; also ancient name of Baalbek, Lebanon.

Heliopsis, a genus of sunflowerlike perennials of the composite family, native to North America; has become a weed in some places; leaves, stems usually rough; flowers showy, yellow. Rough oxeye is *H. scabra;* hardy sunflower, false sunflower, or oxeye is *H. helianthoides.*

Helios, in Greek mythology, sun-god P-248, S-514
  Colossus of Rhodes S-115
  Homeric legend H-223

Helios, space probe S-344

Heliosphere, an atmospheric layer of ionized helium A-748, *picture* A-749

Heliotrope, flowering plant H-123

Heliotrope (or bloodstone), semiprecious stone J-115

Heliotrope, garden. *see in index* Valerian

Heliotrope, winter. *see in index* Winter heliotrope

Heliotropism, tendency to turn toward or away from sunlight
  plants P-363

Heliox, mixture of helium and oxygen
  underwater diving D-189

Heliozoan, any protozoan of the order Heliozoa; often called sun animalcule; a single pseudopod may engulf food or several may work together A-428, *picture* A-410, L-267

Heliport A-209

Helipterum, genus of plants of the composite family, native to Australia and s. Africa; with the genus *Helichrysum*, this makes the largest group of everlasting flowers; includes the acroclinium and rhodanthe, or Swan River everlasting.

Helium (He), a gaseous element H-123
  air, *picture* A-145
  atom N-417
  balloons B-38
  cosmology C-731
  cryogenics C-794
  Landau L-27
  mass-unit value R-67
  natural gas G-38
  noble gases N-330
  nuclear binding energy, *diagram* E-218
    matter M-229
  nuclear energy N-426
  periodic table, *table* P-207, *list* P-208
  radioactivity R-64, *diagram* R-65
  spectroscope S-372
  sun's atmosphere S-513
  sun's thermonuclear process A-716

Hell and Hades, abodes for the dead in various religious belief systems H-123
  Hinduism H-157
  Jainism J-14

Hellas, originally a small district in Thessaly ruled by Peleus, father of Achilles; name Hellas later signified all of ancient Greece and remains today as the modern Greek name Ellas for the nation Greece. *see also in index* Greece; Greece, ancient

Hellbender, a salamander S-26, *picture* A-434

Hellebore, black. *see in index* Christmas rose

Hellebore, white. *see in index* White hellebore

Hellen, mythical founder of the Greeks, son of Deucalion and Pyrrha, father of Dorus (from whom came Dorians), and grandfather of Ion (Ionians) and Achaeus (Achaeans); myth probably arose about 8th century BC, when feeling of national unity developed among Greeks.

Hellenes, ancient Greeks G-263

Hellenistic Age G-267
  Alexandria A-280
  architecture A-547
  art G-272
  literature G-276

Heller, Joseph (born 1923), U.S. writer, born in Brooklyn, N.Y.; satirist and leading proponent of black humor style (novels, 'Catch 22', 'Something Happened'; play, 'We Bombed in New Haven') A-361, *picture* A-362

Heller, Walter Wolfgang (1915–87), U.S. educator and government official, born in Buffalo, N.Y.; fiscal economist U.S. treasury 1942–46; joined faculty University of Minnesota 1946, professor 1950–67; Regents professor of economics 1967–; on leave as chairman presidential Council of Economic Advisers 1961–64.

Hellerman, Fred (born 1927), U.S. folk musician F-273

Hellespont. *see in index* Dardanelles

Hell Gate, rocky narrow part of East River, New York City; spanned by noted steel-arch bridge, connecting Queens and Bronx, opened in 1917.

Hellman, Lillian (1905–84), U.S. playwright H-124
  drama D-248
  Hammett H-23

'Hello, Dolly!' (1964), musical by Herman M-686

Hellriegel, Hermann (1831–95), German agricultural chemist; in 1888 demonstrated the ability of leguminous plants to assimilate free nitrogen of the air.

Hells Canyon. *see in index* Grand Canyon of the Snake River

Helmand Valley project, Afghanistan A-89

Helmet
  armor A-631
  heraldry H-136, *picture* H-135

Helmet shell S-151

Helmholtz, Hermann von (1821–94), German physicist, physiologist, and mathematician H-124

Helmont, Jan Baptista van (1577–1644), Belgian chemist and physician, born in Brussels; supposedly first to use term "gas"; distinguished several kinds of gases; believed water the basic substance; also held many mystical beliefs (*'Ortus Medicinae'*)
  botany B-380

Helms, Richard McGarrah (born 1913), U.S. government official, born in St. David's, Pa.; with Central Intelligence Agency 1946–73, director 1966–73; U.S. ambassador to Iran 1973–1976.

Helms Athletic Trophies, awarded annually to outstanding athletes and teams; given by Helms Athletic Foundation of Los Angeles; established 1936 by Paul H. Helms, U.S. sportsman.

Helodermatidae, family of reptiles
  lizard classification L-274

Héloise (1101–64), talented French abbess, celebrated for her devotion to Peter Abelard, theologian and philosopher condemned for heresy A-8
  educational contribution E-84

Helot, Spartan serf S-369

Helotism, in botany, enslavement of one plant by another L-191

Helping verb, in grammar V-281

Helpmann, Sir Robert Murray (1909–86), British dancer, actor, and choreographer; born in Mount Gambier, Australia; solo debut 1923 in Adelaide; with Sadler's Wells Ballet 1933–50; joint artistic director Australian Ballet after 1965; choreographer and dancer in motion picture 'The Red Shoes'; created ballets 'Comus', 'Hamlet', 'The Birds'.

Helsingborg, Sweden. *see in index* Hälsingborg

Helsingör (or Elsinore), Denmark, seaport on n.e. coast of island Zealand; shipbuilding and commerce; scene of Shakespeare's 'Hamlet'; pop. 26,658.

Helsinki (Swedish Helsingfors), Finland, capital and largest city, on Gulf of Finland; protected by fortress of Sveaborg; paper, tobacco, carpets, machinery; publishing; pop. 486,111 H-125, *map* E-360
  Finland F-90
  world, *map* W-297

Helsinki Accords (or Final Act of the Conference on Security and Cooperation in Europe) B-197
  Kekkonen K-195

Helvetic Republic, Swiss history S-544a

Helvetii, Celtic people whose native home was the present s.w. Germany; later they inhabited what is now w. Switzerland; Caesar defeated them 58 BC.

Helvétius, Claude Adrien (1715–71), French encyclopedist and utilitarian philosopher, born in Paris; his most famous book, 'De L'esprit' ('Of the Spirit'), raised a storm, was condemned by the Sorbonne, and publicly burned.

Hemans, Felicia Dorothea (1793–1835), British poet, born in Liverpool; sentimental lyrics include 'The Landing of the Pilgrim Fathers', 'Casabianca', 'England's Dead', and 'The Graves of a Household'.

Hematite, most important iron ore (ferric oxide Fe_2O_3) I-329, J-115
  minerals M-432
  ore, *table* O-600

Hemerocallis. *see in index* Day lily

Hemicellulose, in biochemistry
  wood W-284

Hemichordata (or acorn worm), phylum of invertebrates I-286

Hemimetabolous metamorphosis, in insect development M-312

Hemimorphite (or calamine), mineral M–437

Hemingway, Ernest (1899–1961), U.S. author H-125. *see also in index* Nobel Prizewinners, *table*
  American literature A-359, *picture* A-360
  creative writing W-378
  novel N-409

Hemiptera, name of insect order, sometimes used to include all insects having sucking mouth parts, piercing beaks, and incomplete metamorphosis; these insects now usually classed in three orders: Hemiptera, the water bugs, chinch bugs, bedbugs, etc.; Homoptera, the cicadas, aphids, scale insects, etc.; and Anoplura or Siphunculata, the true lice. *see also in index* Bug

Hemis-Fair '68, international exposition held in San Antonio, Tex. T-125

Hemisphere, of brain B-398

Hemisphere, of earth, half of the globe, the earth being considered as divided at the equator into Northern and Southern hemispheres or at some point between Europe and America into Eastern and Western hemispheres H-126
  astronomy A-710
  latitude and longitude L-79

Hemlock, evergreen cone-bearing tree of the pine family with needles that are flat and blunt H-127

Henry, Cape, point of land in s.e. Virginia, 15 mi (25 km) e. of strategic seaport Norfolk, at entrance to Chesapeake Bay, *map* V-349

Henry, in electricity, the unit of inductance. One henry is equivalent to one volt divided by one ampere per second
  Henry H-133

'Henry Draper Catalogue, The' U.S. catalogue
  spectral classification C-140

Henry E. Huntington Library and Art Gallery, San Marino, Calif., given to the public by Henry E. Huntington in 1927; contains a fine collection of English 18th-century, early Italian, and Flemish paintings, and other objects of art; also rare books and manuscripts S-140
  'The Blue Boy'. *see in index* 'Blue Boy, The'

Henryetta, Okla., city 55 mi (90 km) s. of Tulsa in rich coal-mining district; abundance of fuel gas; zinc smelters; large glass factory; pop. 6,432.

Henry Fitz Henry (1155–83), second son of Henry II, and subsequently heir to English throne; intrigued against father and died warring against brother Richard.

Henry Ford Museum, Dearborn, Mich., exhibits all forms of transportation equipment; Henry Ford instrumental in founding D-122

Henry Francis du Pont Winterthur Museum, Winterthur, Del., about 5 mi (8 km) n.w. of Wilmington; noted for its collections of colonial American decorative arts D-74, *pictures* D-75, 81

'Henry Grace à Dieu', English warship N-82

Henry Hudson Bridge, New York, N.Y., *picture* B-444

Henry of Blois (1101–71), bishop of Winchester and papal legate, brother of King Stephen; quarreled with latter upon refusal of primacy and for a time supported Matilda's claims to throne.

Henry of Navarre. *see in index* Henry IV, king of France

Henry Street Settlement, social settlement in New York City; founded 1893 by Lillian D. Wald as a nursing service; aided immigrants
  women's rights W-277

Henry the Lion (1129–95), duke of Saxony and Bavaria, son of Henry, the Proud; son-in-law of Henry II of England; by series of wars extended power of his duchies in face of opposition of Hohenstaufen emperors.

Henry the Navigator (1394–1460), prince of Portugal H-134
  Age of Discovery R-150
  Portuguese empire extended P-457
  Western Hemisphere exploration A-330
  Columbus C-591

Henry the Proud (1108?–39), duke of Saxony and Bavaria; died fighting to hold his duchies against Conrad III, whose enmity he had earned by participating in a war against the Hohenstaufens.

Henschel, Sir George (1850–1934), British musical director, composer and singer, born in Breslau, Germany; first conductor of Boston Symphony Orchestra 1881–84; founder and conductor of London Symphony Orchestra 1884–95 ('Stabat Mater', an oratorio; 'Nubia', opera; 'A Sea Change', comic opera).

Henschke, Alfred. *see in index* Klabund

Henslowe, Philip (died 1616), English theatrical manager in whose theaters plays by Elizabethan dramatists were produced S-130

Henson, Josiah (1787–1883), U.S. clergyman, born in Charles County, Md.; his life furnished basis for 'Uncle Tom's Cabin'.

Henson, Matthew Alexander (1866–1955), U.S. explorer who accompanied Rear Admiral Peary to North Pole, born in Charles County, Md. P-150
  plaque, *list* B-299

Henson, William Samuel (1805–88), British engineer and lace manufacturer; patented monoplane 1842, containing all controls of modern airplane except ailerons
  airplane history A-200

Hentoff, Nathan Irving (nickname Nat) (born 1925), U.S. writer, born in Boston, Mass.; interested in writing about jazz and social problems; staff writer *The New Yorker* 1960–; contributor to numerous other magazines ('The New Equality'; 'Jazz Country'; 'Our Children Are Dying').

Henty, George Alfred (1832–1902), British author, soldier, and war correspondent; writer of adventure stories: 'In Freedom's Cause'; 'Under Drake's Flag'; 'In Times of Peril'; 'The Lion of the North'.

Henze, Hans Werner (born 1926), German composer M-676
  opera O-571

Hepatica (or liverleaf), plant of the family Ranunculaceae, with liver-shaped leaves H-134, *picture* F-232

Hepaticae, class of primitive plants, including liverworts.

Hepatic artery, in anatomy L-261

Hepatic vein, in anatomy
  digestive system, *diagram* D-143

Hepatitis, an inflammation of the liver; frequently produces yellow coloration of the skin called jaundice; may be acute or chronic; among its causes are organisms such as viruses and bacteria, toxins that may be present in drugs and other chemicals H-134
  blood disease B-317
  cancer cause C-132
  gamma globulin treatment S-114
  infectious disease, *table* D-171
  liver L-261

Hepburn, Audrey (born 1929), U.S. actress, born in Brussels, Belgium, of Dutch mother and English-Irish father; educated in England and The Netherlands; to U.S. 1951; starred in Broadway plays 'Gigi' and 'Ondine' and in U.S. motion pictures 'Roman Holiday' (for which she won 1953 Academy award), 'The Nun's Story', 'Breakfast at Tiffany's', 'My Fair Lady'.

Hepburn, James, earl of Bothwell. *see in index* Bothwell, James Hepburn, earl of

Hepburn, Katharine (born 1909), U.S. actress H-135, *picture* M-614
  acting A-27

Hepburn, William Peters (1833–1916), U.S. political leader, born in Wellsville, Ohio; served 11 terms as Republican congressman from Iowa; author of Hepburn law.

Hepburn Act (1906), United States R-285

Hephaestus, in Greek mythology, god of fire and the forge; called Vulcan by the Romans; son of Zeus and Hera; crippled by being hurled to Earth by Zeus; in some stories married Aphrodite M-698, 700

Hep Harmony, singing group style M-679

Hepplewhite, George (died 1786), British furniture maker, whose delicate, graceful chairs were lighter and smaller than Chippendale's and had typically straight slender legs; his pieces were characterized by simplicity and refined elegance F-460

Heptagon, in mathematics geometry G-76, *diagram* G-75

'Heptameron' (Greek 'Seven Days'), collection of short stories made by various writers at court of Marguerite of Valois (or Navarre); imitative of Boccaccio's 'Decameron'; important in history of French literature.

Heptathlon, in track and field T-246
  Olympics O-542

Heptane, fuel G-42

Heptarchy, Greek word meaning "seven kingdoms" applied to seven divisions of England under Angles and Saxons—Kent, Sussex, Wessex, Essex, Northumberland, East Anglia, and Mercia; term is misleading, as the number of kingdoms varied from time to time.

Heptateuch, the first seven books of the Old Testament; contains the five books of Moses called the Pentateuch.

Hepworth, Dame Barbara (1903–75), British sculptor, born in Wakefield; created abstract forms in wood, stone, and metal
  'Cosden Head', *picture* D-112

Hera, in Greek mythology, queen of the gods, wife of Zeus, identified with Roman goddess Juno M-700, *picture* M-699. *see also in index* Hera
  Hercules H-138
  Rhea R-176
  temple, *picture* G-266
  Zeus Z-451

Heraclea, ancient town in Asia Minor. *see in index* Eregli

Heraclea, battle of (280 BC), in Italy P-544

Heracles. *see in index* Hercules

Heraclides (or Ponticus Heracleides), Greek philosopher of 4th century AD, born Heraclea in Pontus; reputedly first to explain that the apparent rotation of the heavens is brought about by rotation of the earth on its axis rather than by the passage of stars around the earth.

Heraclitus (540?–475? BC), Greek philosopher, called founder of metaphysics; taught that constant change from being to not-being is fundamental principle of universe, and that all things are part of one primary substance, fire; sometimes called the Weeping Philosopher or Dark Philosopher P-264
  Fowles F-336

Heraclius (575–641), Byzantine emperor, son of one of Emperor Maurice's generals; killed Emperor Phocas to avenge death of Maurice and became emperor 610; saved empire from Persians, who had conquered Syria during reign of Phocas B-535

Herakleion, Crete. *see in index* Candia

Herakles. *see in index* Hercules

Herald, court chronicler of Middle Ages H-135

Heraldry H-135
  knots as badges K-262

Herat, Afghanistan, fortified city in n.w., capital of province of Herat, in strategic area; trade and agricultural center; once capital of Timur Leng's empire; pop. 100,000, *map* A-697

Herbal, Renaissance book about herbs H-137

Herbarium F-240
  botanical garden B-378

Herbart, Johann Friedrich (1776–1841), German philosopher, psychologist, and educator; born in Oldenburg, Germany; influenced by Fichte and Pestalozzi; occupied chair of philosophy in Königsberg 1809–33 ('Psychology as Knowledge'; 'Psychology')
  education E-89, 93

Herber, Arnold (nickname Arnie) (1910–69), U.S. football halfback, born in Green Bay, Wis.; played for Green Bay Packers 1930–39 and New York Giants 1944–45.

Herbert, George (1593–1633), English poet, born in Wales; saintly pastor of Bemerton, England, near Salisbury ('The Temple: Sacred Poems and Private Ejaculations'; 'A Priest to the Temple, or the Country Parson', prose) E-269

Herbert, Victor (1859–1924), Irish-American composer, born in Dublin; educated in Germany; lived in the U.S. after 1886; known for such popular operettas as 'Babes in Toyland'; 'The Red Mill'; 'Naughty Marietta', which included "Ah, Sweet Mystery of Life"; and 'Sweethearts'.
  classical music M-674
  musical comedy M-685

Herbert, Xavier (1901–84), Australian writer, *table* A-798

Herbert H. Lehman College, Bronx, N.Y., part of the City University of New York; municipal control; founded as Hunter College in the Bronx 1931, present name 1968; arts and sciences; graduate studies.

Herbert Hoover National Historic Site, Iowa, *map* I-302

Herbicide F-438
  endangered species E-209
  weed control W-133
    wheat crops W-189

Herbivorous animals, those that feed on plants
  antelope A-478
  digestive system D-146
    stomach R-318, S-455
  dinosaur A-462
  insect I-224

Herblock. *see in index* Block, Herbert Lawrence

Herbs, herbaceous plants used medicinally, as vegetables, or for flavoring H-137. *see also in index* Spices
  botanical gardens B-379
  flavoring herbs S-379
  folk medicine F-270

Herbs, plants without woody stems in which the stems and foliage die to the ground in winter P-357
  banana B-51

Herculaneum, ancient Roman city near Mt. Vesuvius, buried with Pompeii AD 79 P-442. *see also in index* Pompeii
  archaeological excavations A-531

Hercule Poirot. *see in index* Poirot, Hercule

Hercules (or Heracles), hero in Greek and Roman mythology H-138
  hairdressing H-9
  Olympic games O-542

Hercules, constellation, *charts* S-419, 423, C-681, *picture* U-203

Hercules, Pillars of. *see in index* Pillars of Hercules

Hercules beetle B-138

Herder, Johann Gottfried von (1744–1803), German critic, philosopher, and poet; born in Mohrungen, East Prussia G-106, *picture* G-105
  history writing H-173

Herd immunity, epidemiology E-292

'Here Comes the Bogie Man', etching by Goya, *picture* G-233

Heredia, José María (1803–39), Cuban poet, born in Santiago de Cuba, *picture* L-70
  Caribbean literature C-167

Heredity H-139. *see also in index* Genetics
  albinism A-271
  cancer tendencies C-133
  deafness D-47
  diseases. *see in index* Disease, *subhead* hereditary diseases
  DNA molecule B-199
  eugenics E-326
  eye E-390
  immune system I-56
  intelligence I-238
  Mendel's laws M-296
  multiple birth M-649
  natural selection B-229
  physical anthropology A-483
  play theory P-390b
  sociology links S-243
  zoology Z-469

Heredity-environment controversy (or nature-nurture controversy), regards the relative roles of heredity versus physical and social surroundings in the development of an individual H-140

Hereford (or Herefordshire), inland county in s.w. England on Wales border; cap. Hereford; pop. 130,928
  cave art A-538

Hereford, England, county town of Herefordshire, 120 mi (195 km) n.w. of London; pop. 47,170.

Hereford, Tex., city 40 mi (65 km) s.w. of Amarillo in farm area; feed lots, meat packing; Edgar D. Mitchell born here; incorporated 1898; pop. 15,853.

Hereford, breed of cattle C-230, *picture* C-229

Heresy, teaching opposed to established religion or religious authority. *see also in index* Arianism; Inquisition; Manichaeanism; Reformation
  Philip P-252
  Savonarola S-52d

Hereward (11th century), English patriot outlaw; led Saxon resistance until driven from Isle of Ely by William the Conqueror
  'Hereward the Wake' K-247

Herford, Oliver (1863–1935), U.S. humorist, artist, and playwright; born in Sheffield, England ('Kitten's Garden of

Verses', 'Child's Primer of Natural History'; 'The Florist Shop', play).

Hergesheimer, Joseph (1880–1954), U.S. novelist, born in Philadelphia, Pa. ('The Three Black Pennys'; 'Java Head'; 'Cytherea'; 'The Bright Shawl').

Hering, Ewald (1834–1918), German physiologist and psychologist, born in Alt-Gersdorf, Saxony; advanced theory of four colors occurring in pairs as opposed to three-color theory of Helmholtz C-562

Heritage, Conservation, and Recreation Service, United States U-161

Heritage Trust Programs, United States E-210

Herkimer, Nicholas (1728–77), American Revolutionary War general, born near present Herkimer, N.Y.; defeated British at Oriskany, N.Y., but was killed.

Her Majesty's Coastguard, United Kingdom C-529

Herman, Jerry (born 1933), U.S. composer-lyricist, born in New York, N.Y.; known for writing scores of outstanding musicals ('Milk and Honey'; 'Mame')
  musical comedy M-686

Herman, William Jennings Bryan (nickname Billy) (born 1909), U.S. baseball player, born in New Albany, Ind.; N.L. second baseman 1931–47.

Herman, Woodrow Wilson (nickname Woody) (born 1913), U.S. composer, clarinetist, saxophone player, and bandleader, born in Milwaukee, Wis.; led many big bands.

Hermaphroditism, existence in single plant or animal of both male and female reproductive organs R-151c
  hydra H-338

Hermas, Christian writer said to have lived in 2nd century; sometimes identified with the Hermas in Bible, Rom. xvi, 14; author of mystical allegory 'The Shepherd of Hermas'.

Hermes, in Greek mythology messenger of gods; Roman counterpart Mercury H-141
  astronomy A-716
  Greek mythology M-700
  Homeric legend H-223
  Perseus P-210
  Praxiteles' 'Hermes with the Infant Dionysus' S-83

'Hermes', British aircraft carrier N-84

Hermes Trismegistus (or Hermes the "thrice greatest"), Greek name of Egyptian god Thoth; reputed author of Hermetic Books, encyclopedic works on Egyptian religion, art, and science.

Hermeticism, in literature I-378

Hermit, one that retires from society and lives alone, especially for religious reasons M-540

Hermitage. *see in index* State Hermitage Museum

Hermitage, The, Nashville, Tenn., home of Andrew Jackson J-5, N-20, *pictures* J-7, T-93

Hermit crab, crustacean C-792, *picture* C-791

Hermit thrush, a bird *Hylocichla guttata* of the family Turdidae T-177
  state bird, *picture* V-292

Hermon, Mount, mountain on border between Syria and Lebanon, 30 mi (50 km) s.w. of Damascus; 9,232 ft (2,814 m); referred to in Bible.

Hermopolis Parva, Lower Egypt. *see in index* Damanhur

Hermosa Beach, Calif., residential city 15 mi (25 km) s.w. of Los Angeles, on Pacific; resort, textile printing; pop. 18,070.

Hermoupolis (or Hermopolis), Greece, city on e. coast of island of Syros; capital of Cyclades; shipbuilding and commercial center; exports tobacco; pop. 13,502.

Hernández, José (1834–86), Argentine poet, born near Buenos Aires A-580, L-63, 68

Hernández, Miguel (1910–42), Spanish poet and dramatist S-366

'Hernani', tragedy by Hugo; Count Hernani, to fulfill a pledge, ends life just as love, wealth, and high honors are his; Verdi's opera 'Ernani' founded on tragedy H-317. *see also in index* 'Ernani'

Herndon, William Henry (1818–91), U.S. lawyer, born in Greensburg, Ky.; mayor of Springfield, Ill.; law partner of Lincoln and author in collaboration with J.W. Weik of 'Herndon's Lincoln' and 'The True Story of a Great Life'.

Herne, James A. (originally James Ahern) (1839–1901), U.S. actor and dramatist, born in Cohoes, N.Y.; skillful in depiction of rural life and everyday types of character ('Shore Acres'; 'Margaret Fleming').

Hernia (or rupture), the protrusion of an organ or tissue from the cavity that normally contains it H-141

Hero (or Heron), of Alexandria (1st century AD), Greek scientist, mathematician, and writer; author of many works on physics and mechanics
  jet propulsion J-105, *diagram* J-106
  steam engine S-442

Hero and Leander, in Greek mythology, tragic love story of Hero, a priestess of Aphrodite in Sestos, and Leander, who swam across the Hellespont to visit her; a storm arose, blowing out the guiding torch; Leander drowned; Hero, finding Leander's body, drowned herself.

Herod I, the Great, king of Judea (37–4 BC) H-141, J-103

Herod Agrippa I (10? BC–AD 44), king of Judea; acquired territory equal in extent to that of his grandfather Herod the Great; favored Jews and persecuted Christians.

Herod Agrippa II (AD 27–100), son of Herod Agrippa I; last king of family of Herod the Great; St. Paul was tried before him at Caesarea.

Herod Antipas, tetrarch of Galilee (4 BC–AD 39) H-141

Herodas (fl. 3 BC), Greek poet G-278

Herodias, wife of Herod Antipas, mother of Salome, and instigator of the beheading of John the Baptist H-141

Herodotus (484?–425? BC), Greek historian H-141
  delta D-90
  ethnology A-486
  exploration E-373
  Greek literature G-276
    Homeric legend H-220
  history writing H-170
  maps, *picture* M-126
  Thermopylae T-168
  travels T-268

'Heroes, The', fairy tale by Kingsley K-247

Heroica Nogales, Mexico. *see in index* Nogales, Ariz.

Heroic couplet, a verse form P-406
  Dryden D-281
  Pope P-406, 445

Heroin (or diacetylmorphine), narcotic
  analgesic effect A-387
  drug addiction D-276
  narcotics and sedatives N-19
  opium O-572
  poisoning P-411

Hero myths M-699
  Arthurian legend A-655
  Beowulf B-165
  El Cid C-414
  folklore F-263
  Hercules H-138
  Robin Hood R-223
  Roland R-238

Heron, a group of wading birds H-141
  animal tracks A-463
  bird species B-251, *pictures* B-243, 245
  cattle heron. *see in index* Cattle egret
  crane C-760
  egret, *pictures* A-759, F-194
  length of life, average, *chart* A-423

Heron of Alexandria. *see in index* Hero

Heronry, nesting and breeding place of herons H-142

'Hero of Our Time, A' (Geroy nashego vremeni), novel by Lermontov L-136

Herophilus, (fl. 300 BC), Greek surgeon, born in Chalcedon in Bithynia; helped found school of anatomy, Alexandria; among first to carry on postmortem examinations; made important studies of nervous system
  autopsy developed A-875

Herostratus (4th century BC), Ephesian who set fire to temple of Artemis S-115

Héroult, Paul Louis Toussaint (1863–1914), French metallurgist, born in Thury-Harcourt, near Caen, France; discovered method of separating aluminum A-323, I-275
  Hall H-15

Herpes, group of viruses
  cancer cause C-132

Herpes simplex. *see in index* Cold sore

Herpes zoster. *see in index* Shingles

Herpetology. *see also in index* Reptiles
  lizard research techniques L-272

Herrera, Fernando de (1534–97), Spanish lyric and epic poet, born in Seville, Spain; foreign influence shown in his work; did much to enrich the language.

Herrera, Francisco de (1576–1656), called el Viejo (the old), Spanish painter, engraver, etcher, and architect, born in Seville; noted for genre and religious paintings ('Last Judgment' in church at Seville; 'St. Basil Dictating His Doctrine' in Louvre). His son, **Francisco,** called el Mozo (the young), was painter to King Philip IV, also noted as architect.

Herrera, Juan de (1530–97), Spanish architect who was influential on the contemporary style
  El Escorial design A-557, *picture* A-558

Herrera, Tomás (1804–54), Panamanian general and statesman; led uprising to free Panama from Colombia; became governor of Panama 1845, secretary of war and navy 1849, president 1853.

Herreshoff, John Brown (1841–1915), U.S. shipbuilder and yacht designer, born in Bristol, R.I.; member of a family of shipbuilders and founder of firm that designed yachts that defended America's Cup.

Herrick, Charles Judson (1868–1960), U.S. physiologist, born in Minneapolis, Minn.; professor of neurology University of Chicago 1907–34; editor *Journal of Comparative Neurology* 1894–1948.

Herrick, James Bryan (1861–1954), U.S. physician, born in Oak Park, Ill.; joined faculty Rush Medical College 1890, professor 1900–27; identified coronary thrombosis as cause of many heart attacks; discovered sickle-cell anemia.

Herrick, Myron Timothy (1854–1929), U.S. capitalist and diplomat, born in Huntington, Ohio; started rural credit movement in U.S.; governor of Ohio 1903–6; ambassador to France 1912–14, 1921–29.

Herrick, Robert (1591–1674), English lyric poet H-143
  literary contribution E-269

Herrick, Robert (1868–1938), U.S. novelist, born in Cambridge, Mass.; professor at University of Chicago 1895–1923; general secretary of Virgin Islands of the U.S. 1935–38; works deal with modern life; realist ('The Common Lot'; 'Together'; 'A Life for a Life'; 'The Conscript Mother'; 'Chimes'; 'The End of Desire').

Herrin, Ill., city in s. part of state, about 55 mi (90 km) n.e. of Cairo; washing machines, automobile equipment, dresses; coal mining; pop. 10,040, *map* I-52

Herring, a soft-finned food fish H-143, F-124, *picture* F-132
  Canada C-76
  fisheries, *table* F-136
  Hanseatic league H-32
  Michigan, *picture* M-358
  sardines S-48

Herringbone stitch, in needlework N-110

Herring family (or Clupeidae), family of soft-finned fishes with forked tails and narrow bodies, comprising the herring, alewife, shad, sardine or pilchard, and menhaden H-143. *see also in index* Herring; Menhaden; Pilchard; Sardine; Shad

Herring gull, bird *Larus argentatus* G-317

Herriot, Edouard (1872–1957), French statesman, born in Troyes; distinguished as scholar, man of letters, and radical political leader; premier and minister of foreign affairs 1924–25, 1926, and 1932; mayor of Lyons and president of the chamber of deputies; in German custody 1942–45 ('Life and Times of Beethoven'; 'United States of Europe').

Herrmann, Bernard (1911–75), U.S. composer and conductor, born in New York City; conducted various programs for Columbia Broadcasting System and served as chief conductor of CBS Symphony Orchestra; composed music for dramatic cantata, 'Moby Dick', and many works for radio and motion pictures ('Citizen Kane'; 'Psycho'; 'Taxi Driver'; 'Obsession').

Herschel, Caroline (1750–1848), British astronomer, born in Hanover, Germany; sister and assistant of William Herschel; discovered five comets.

Herschel, Sir John Frederick William (1792–1871), British astronomer, born in Slough; son of Sir William Herschel; discovered 525 star clusters and nebulae not recorded by his father; made first telescopic survey of southern heavens; invented a process of photography on sensitized paper; first to use terms positive and negative in photography
  blueprint process B-319
  Herschel, William H-144
  planetary studies A-714

Herschel, William (1738–1822), British astronomer and organist H-144
  discovers Uranus P-354
  light spectrum L-201

Herschel, William J. (1833–1917), British official, son of J.F.W. Herschel and grandson of William Herschel; inventor of system of fingerprint identification.

Herschel, Mount, in Antarctica
  Hillary H-152

Herschell, Farrer Herschell, first **Baron** (1837–99), lord chancellor of England in 1886 and again 1892–95; president of Anglo-American boundary commission 1898–99.

Hersey, John Richard (born 1914), U.S. writer, born in Tientsin, China; war correspondent in World War II (reporting—'Hiroshima'; 'The Algiers Motel Incident'; novels—'A Bell for Adano', 1945 Pulitzer prize winner, dramatized on stage and screen; 'The Wall', story of Jewish resistance in Warsaw 1939–43; 'The Child Buyer').

Hershey, Alfred Day (born 1908), U.S. scientist, born in Owosso, Mich.; director of genetics research unit Carnegie Institution of Washington, Cold Spring Harbor, N.Y., 1962–74. *see also in index* Nobel Prizewinners, *table*

Hershey, Lewis Blaine (1893–1977), U.S. Army officer, born in Steuben County, Ind.; War Department general staff 1936–40; director of Selective Service System 1941–46, 1948–70, director of Selective Service Records 1947–48, adviser to the president on personnel mobilization 1970–73.

Hershey, Milton Snavely (1857–1945), U.S. confectioner and philanthropist, born in Dauphin County, Pa.; built up huge chocolate industry; founded Milton Hershey School for orphan boys in Hershey, Pa., 1909; in 1918 transferred fortune estimated at $60,000,000 to school I-195

Hershey, Pa., unincorporated town 12 mi (19 km) e. of Harrisburg; chocolate; founded 1903 by Milton Snavely Hershey; national headquarters of Antique Automobile Club of America; pop. 7,407, *map* P-185
  amusement park A-385

Hershey Foods Corporation, U.S. company C-139

Herter, Albert (1871–1950), U.S. mural painter, born in New York City, N.Y.

Herter, Christian Archibald (1895–1966), U.S. government official, born in Paris, France, of American parents; to U.S. 1904; became member Mass. House of Representatives 1931, speaker 1939–43; U.S. Congressman (Rep.) from Mass. 1943–53; governor of Mass. 1953–57; U.S. undersecretary of state 1957–59, secretary of state 1959–61.

Hertford (or Hertfordshire), inland county in s.e. England; 632 sq. mi.; farming; many industries; cap. Hertford (pop. 15,737); pop. 832,901.

Hertogenbosch, 's, The Netherlands. *see in index* 's Hertogenbosch

Herty, Charles Holmes (1867–1938), U.S. chemist, born in Milledgeville, Ga.; professor of chemistry at University of North Carolina 1905–16; editor *Journal of Industrial and Engineering Chemistry* 1917–21; research in dye, turpentine, and paper industries P-105, P-328, P-379
  newsprint discovery G-85

Hertz, Alfred (1872–1942), German-American musician, born in Frankfurt; conducted Metropolitan Opera, New York City, 1902–15; directed first performance of Wagner's 'Parsifal' outside of Bayreuth; director San Francisco Symphony Orchestra 1915–30; inaugurated concerts in Hollywood Bowl, Los Angeles.

Hertz, Gustav (1887–1975), German physicist. *see also in index* Franck, James; Nobel Prizewinners, *table*

Hertz, Heinrich (1857–94), German physicist H-144
  electricity E-162
  electronics E-180
  light wave L-202
  Marconi M-132
  Maxwell M-234
  photoelectric effect P-307
  radio waves R-56

Hertz, Henrik (1798–1870), Danish poet and dramatist, born in Copenhagen; romantic feeling and graceful style ('King René's Daughter', 'Svend Dyrings Hus').

Hertz, John Daniel (1879–1961), U.S. transportation executive, born in Austria; founded Yellow Cab Company (Chicago), Chicago Motor Coach Company, developed Hertz Drive-Ur-Self Corporation; won Defense Department's highest civilian award for appropriating most of his fortune for U.S. defense (1958).

Hertz, a unit of frequency equal to one cycle per second
  electric power E-166
  noise N-331

Hertzberg, Harry, U.S. circus collector C-432

Hertzian waves, a term sometimes used for radio waves R-56. *see also in index* Radio, *subhead* waves.

Hertzog, James Barry Munnik (1866–1942), South African statesman and general, born in Wellington, near Cape Town; premier and minister for native affairs 1924–39; leader of old Republican Boers; after 1924 modified his anti-British policy; delegate to British Imperial Conference 1926 S-220

'Hervé Riel', poem by Robert Browning about a Breton sailor who piloted the French fleet safely into St.-Malo after its serious defeat by the English and Dutch off Cape La Hogue in English Channel (1692).

Hervey Archipelago, s. Pacific. *see in index* Cook Islands

Hervieu, Paul-Ernest (1857–1915), French playwright and novelist, born in Neuilly; first wrote under pseudonym Eliacin; noted for brilliantly constructed plays that exposed social evils and suggested remedies for them.

Herzberg, Gerhard (born 1904), Canadian chemist, born in Hamburg, Germany; professor Saskatchewan University 1935–45; member National Research Council, Ottawa, after 1948.

Herzegovina. *see in index* Bosnia and Herzegovina

Herzen, Aleksandr (1812–70), Russian author and publicist H-145
  Russian literature R-360

Herzl, Theodor (1860–1904), Hungarian Zionist leader and writer H-145
  Judaism J-151
  Palestine P-80
  Zionism Z-455

Herzog, Émile. *see in index* Maurois, André

Herzog, Maurice (born 1919), French mountain climber and engineer, born in Lyons, France; in 1950 led nine-man French expedition that scaled Annapurna in Himalayas; wrote of experiences in 'Annapurna'; on lecture tour in U.S. 1953. *see also in index* Annapurna
  'Annapurna' R-112a

'Herzog', novel by Bellow A-362, B-157

Hesiod (9th century BC), Greek didactic poet H-146
  Greek literature G-274
    Homeric legend H-224
  history writing H-171
  mythology M-696, 704

Hesper (or Hesperus), name given by Greeks to evening star; the son of Eos (Aurora) in Greek mythology; at first considered to be same as Phosphor, the morning star; later believed to be his brother.

Hesperia (The Western Land), name given to Italy by Greek poets in ancient times.

Hesperides, in Greek mythology, nymphs who guarded the golden apples of the Tree of Life, wedding gift to his bride, Hera, from Zeus
  Hercules H-138

'Hesperides', book of poetry by Herrick H-143

Hesperioidea, classification of butterflies B-528

Hesperis. *see in index* Sweet rocket

Hesperus. *see in index* Hesper

Hess, Alfred (1875–1933), U.S. pediatrician and pathologist; discovered treatment for rickets V-357

Hess, Dame Myra (1890–1965), British pianist, born in London; at age of 12 won scholarship to Royal Academy of Music; debut at Queen's Hall, London, 1907; appeared widely in Europe, and after 1922 also in U.S. and Canada; famed for rendition of Bach, Mozart, and Scarlatti.

Hess, Rudolf (1894–1987), German Nazi leader, born in Alexandria, Egypt; assisted Hitler in writing 'Mein Kampf'; became Hitler's deputy in Reichstag 1933; flew to Scotland May 1941, landed by parachute, surrendered to British; kept prisoner; his peace proposals revealed Sept. 1943; sentenced to life imprisonment for war crimes Sept. 1946
  Hitler H-177

Hess, Victor Francis (1883–1964), U.S. physicist, born in Waldstein, Austria; became U.S. citizen 1944; professor of physics Fordham University, New York, N.Y., 1938–56 R-42. *see also in index* Nobel Prizewinners, *table*

Hess, Walter Rudolf (1881–1973), Swiss physiologist, born in Frauenfeld, near Zürich; director physiological institute, University of Zürich. *see also in index* Nobel Prizewinners, *table*

Hesse, Hermann (1877–1962), German-Swiss novelist and poet H-146. *see also in index* Nobel Prizewinners, *table*
  German literature G-109
  novel N-410

Hesse (German Hessen), state in West Germany; former duchy in s.w. Germany; after World War II, state enlarged by addition of part of Hesse-Nassau; pop. 5,549,800, *map* G-131

Hesse-Cassel, former German electorate; joined Austria in Austro-Prussian War (1866); annexed by Prussia.

Hesse-Nassau, former province of Prussia, Germany; after World War II, incorporated into Hesse.

Hessian fly, a gall gnat, *picture* I-225
  wheat W-188

Hessians, German soldiers hired by England during American Revolution to fight against colonists; about half were from Hesse-Cassel and Hesse-Darmstadt
  battle of Trenton R-171

Hestia, in Greek mythology, goddess of hearth and home M-700
  Rhea R-176
  Vesta V-305

Heston, Charlton (born 1923), U.S. actor of screen, stage, and television; born in Evanston, Ill.; played Moses in movie 'The Ten Commandments'; Academy award for 'Ben-Hur' 1959; president Screen Actors Guild 1966.

Hesychasts, type of Eastern Christian religious zealots B-536

Hetaerae (or courtesan)
  education E-82

Hetch Hetchy Valley, California, a deep valley of the Sierra Nevada in Yosemite National Park.

Heterocera. *see in index* Moth

Heterogeneous catalyst. *see in index* catalyst

Heterograft (or xenograft), tissue transplantation from another animal to a person T-250

Heteropappus, genus of asterlike plants of the composite family; perennial, low-growing, with azure-blue flowers; native to Japan and China; also called blue daisy.

Heterosexuality S-125

Heterozygote, in genetics. *see also in index* Hybrid
  genetics G-53

Heuss, Theodor (1884–1963), German educator, author, and political leader; born in Brackenheim, Württemberg; book, 'Hitler's Way', condemned by Nazis; after World War II, became chairman of Free Democratic party; first president of Federal Republic of Germany 1949–59.

Hevea brasiliensis, a rubber tree R-301

Hevesy, George Charles de (1885–1966), Swedish chemist, born in Budapest; with D. Coster discovered hafnium (1923); won 1958 Atoms for Peace award for work with isotopes. *see also in index* Nobel Prizewinners, *table*

HEW. *see in index* Health, Education, and Welfare, Department of

Hewes, Agnes Danforth, U.S. author, born in Syria; children's books are historical in setting ('A Boy of the Lost Crusade'; 'Spice and the Devil's Cave'; 'Glory of the Seas'; 'Spice Ho!'; 'A Hundred Bridges to Go'; 'With the Will to Go').

Hewes, Joseph (1730–79), U.S. signer of Declaration of Independence; born in Kingston, N.J.; delegate from North Carolina to Continental Congress.

Hewins, Caroline Maria (1846–1926), U.S. librarian, born in Roxbury, Mass.; from 1875 librarian, Hartford, Conn., Public Library; one of earliest leaders in development of children's libraries.

Hewish, Antony (born 1924), British radio astronomer, born in Berkshire; pioneered in radio telescope use; discovered pulsars; professor Cambridge University 1971. *see also in index* Nobel Prizewinners, *table*

Hewitt, Abram Stevens (1822–1903), U.S. capitalist and political leader, born in Haverstraw, N.Y.; consistent advocate of good government; introduced into U.S. open-hearth process of making steel; Democratic representative in Congress 1875–79, 1881–86; mayor of New York City 1886–90.

Hewitt, Peter Cooper (1861–1921), U.S. inventor, born in New York City; son of Abram S. Hewitt and grandson of Peter Cooper; invented Cooper-Hewitt mercury vapor electric lamp and mercury vapor rectifier.

Hewlett, James Monroe (1868–1941), U.S. architect and mural painter, born in Lawrence, Long Island, N.Y.; designed Brooklyn Masonic Temple, Philadelphia War Memorial; murals in Carnegie Institute of Technology, Pittsburgh, and Columbia University Club, New York
  Fuller F-446

Hewlett, Maurice Henry (1861–1923), British romantic novelist ('The Forest Lovers'; 'The Queen's Quair'; 'Open Country')
  'The Life and Death of Richard Yea-and-Nay' R-202

Hexachlorophene, antiseptic A-495

Hexagon, in mathematics
  geometry G-76, *diagram* G-75

Hexahedron (plural hexahedra), in mathematics
  geometry G-78

Hexameter, in poetry P-405

Hexane, in chemistry. *see in index* Paraffin series

Hexaploid, species of wheat W-188

Hexapoda, former name for Insecta, the class of six-legged arthropods, or insects. *see in index* Insect

Hexateuch, name given to the first six books of the Bible's Old Testament—Genesis, Exodus, Leviticus, Numbers, Deuteronomy, and Joshua.

Hexham, England, market town in n. on Tyne River, 20 mi (30 km) w. of Newcastle; here Yorkists defeated Lancastrians in 1464; abbey church; pop. 9,930, *map* U-18a

Hexobarbital, anesthetic A-413

Heydrich, Reinhard (1904–42), German political leader, born in Halle, Germany; director of Gestapo; protector, Bohemia, 1941–42; assassinated in Prague
  Holocaust H-206

Heyerdahl, Thor (born 1914), Norwegian scientist and writer on travel H-146. *see also in index* 'Kon-Tiki'
  basketry ship construction B-102
  Easter Island E-42
  exploration E-377, *picture* E-373
    oceans O-459
  written work R-112a

Heyl, Paul Renno (1872–1961), U.S. physicist, born in Philadelphia, Pa.; with U.S. Bureau of Standards 1920–42; invented, with L.J. Briggs, earth induction compass.

Heymans, Corneille (1892–1968), Belgian physiologist, born in Ghent, Belgium. *see also in index* Nobel Prizewinners, *table*

Heyrovský, Jaroslav (1890–1967), Czech chemist, born in Prague. *see also in index* Nobel Prizewinners, *table*

Heyse, Paul (1830–1914), German poet, novelist, and short-story writer; born in Berlin; master of novelette ('Children of the World'). *see also in index* Nobel Prizewinners, *table*

Heyward, DuBose (1885–1940), U.S. writer and lecturer, born in Charleston, S.C.; wrote of black Americans' lives with understanding and realism ('Carolina Chansons', poems; 'Porgy' and 'Mamba's Daughters', novels, later dramatized; 'The Country Bunny and the Little Gold Shoes', child's story), *picture* S-316
  Gershwin G-135

Heyward, Thomas, Jr. (1746–1809), U.S. jurist, born in St. Luke's, S.C., a signer of Declaration of Independence; in Continental Congress 1775–78; taken prisoner by British in Revolution.

Heywood, John (1497?–1580?), English writer and entertainer at courts of Henry VIII and Mary I; wrote court interludes that introduced personal characters rather than abstractions, linking morality play with English comedy ('The Playe Called the Foure PP'); also wrote epigrams and proverbs.

Heywood, Thomas (died 1641?), English dramatist, born in Lincolnshire; claimed to have written in whole or part more than 200 plays; at his best in simple domestic drama.

Heyworth of Oxton, Geoffrey Heyworth, 1st Baron (1894–1975), English industrialist, born in Birkenhead, England; chairman 1942–60 of Unilever, Ltd., one of world's largest soap manufacturers.

Hezekiah (8th–7th century BC), king of Judah; leader in rebellion against Assyrian rule, which brought about an invasion of Judah by Sennacherib of Assyria in 701 BC; Assyrian troops withdrew after being struck by a plague, thus saving Judah.

Hg, chemical symbol. *see in index* Mercury

HGH (or human growth hormone), hormone that induces growth H-240

H.H. *see in index* Jackson, Helen Hunt

Hialeah, Fla., industrial city 7 mi (11 km) n.w. of Miami; horse racing; distribution center for food products and building materials; incorporated 1925; pop. 145,254.

Hiawatha, Mohawk chief H-146, *picture* I-142
'Tales of Nanabozho' S-481d

Hibben, John Grier (1861–1933), U.S. educator, born in Peoria, Ill.; Presbyterian pastor Chambersburg, Pa. 1887–91; taught logic and psychology at Princeton 1891–1912, president 1912–32; author of books on logic and philosophy.

Hibben, Paxton (1880–1928), U.S. journalist, born in Indianapolis, Ind.; diplomatic service in Russia, Mexico, Colombia, Holland ('The Famine in Russia'; 'Henry Ward Beecher').

Hibbing, Minn., village 60 mi (100 km) n.w. of Duluth in famous Mesabi iron-ore range; largest open-pit iron-ore mine in world; pop. 21,193 M-443, *picture* M-451, *map* U-41
bus B-386

Hibernation, dormancy of animals during the winter H-147. *see also in index* Aestivation
amphibian A-379
bear B-118
echidna A-781
fish F-131
hamster H-25
insects I-222
bee B-128
butterflies and moths B-526
wasp W-73
mammals' habitat A-431
prairie dog P-486
salamander S-25
skunk S-211
snail and slug S-222
snake S-223
spider S-385
thermoregulation B-207

Hibernia, ancient Latin and poetical name of Ireland. *see in index* Ireland

Hibernians, Ancient Order of, a fraternal society of Roman Catholic men of Irish birth or descent; history traced to 17th century or earlier in Ireland; American branch organized in New York City in 1836; aided Irish national movement; provides sick benefits, insurance, and help for members.

Hibiscus, a large genus of herbs and shrubs of the mallow family H-149, *picture* F-227
flowering time G-25
Hawaii's state flower, *picture* H-66

Hibiscus cannabinus, fibrous plant H-149

Hiccup (or hiccough), sharp sound caused by sudden arrest of breathing due to spasmodic contraction of the diaphragm and glottis.

Hichens, Robert Smythe (1864–1950), British novelist and playwright, born in Speldhurst, near Tunbridge Wells, England ('Green Carnation'; 'The Garden of Allah'; 'Bella Donna').

Hickel, Walter Joseph (born 1919), U.S. businessman and public official, born in Ellinwood, Kan.; to Alaska 1940; founded construction firm 1947; first Republican governor of state of Alaska 1966–69; U.S. secretary of the interior 1969–70; author of 'Who Owns America?'
Nixon N-326

Hickok, Wild Bill (born James Butler Hickok), U.S. frontiersman H-149, *picture* S-332
outlaws O-619

Hickory, N.C., city 45 mi (70 km) n.w. of Charlotte; hosiery, furniture, textiles, electronic products; Lenoir-Rhyne College; Lake Hickory nearby; pop. 20,757.

Hickory, North American tree of the walnut family H-149
wood, *table* W-283

Hickory horned devil, type of caterpillar B-526

Hickory poplar. *see in index* Tulip tree

Hickory Township, Mich. *see in index* Warren

Hicks, Edward (1780–1849), U.S. painter H-149, P-50, *picture* P-49

Hicks, Elias (1748–1830), U.S. minister of Society of Friends; born in Hempstead, Long Island; strong advocate of abolition; because of his liberal religious views, Society divided for years into Orthodox and Hicksite Friends.

Hicks, Granville (1901–82), U.S. author, born in Exeter, N.H.; editorial staff *New Masses Magazine* 1934–39; edited letters of Lincoln Steffens ('Great Tradition'; 'One of Us'; 'Small Town'; autobiography, 'Part of the Truth')

Hicks, Sir John Richard (born 1904), British economist, born in Warwick; professor Oxford University 1952–65, research fellow 1965. *see also in index* Nobel Prizewinners, *table*

Hicksites, group that separated from the Quakers in 1827 under leadership of Elias Hicks
Mott M-632
Quakers Q-4

Hicksville, N.Y., community on Long Island 23 mi (37 km) e. of New York City; aircraft, electrical products, cement, paper, drainpipes; pop. 49,820.

Hidalgo, Mexico, state in central part; 8,103 sq mi (20,987 sq km); cap. Pachuca; minerals, textiles; pop. 1,408,640, *map* M-341

Hidalgo y Costilla, Miguel (1753–1811), Mexican priest and patriot H-150
Latin America L-67
Mexico M-336

Hidatsa (or Gros Ventres, or Minitari), a group of Great Plains inhabitants of Siouxan heritage on upper Missouri River in North Dakota.

Hiddenite, a transparent green variety of spodumene, used as a gem; found in North Carolina M-436

Hidden line, in mechanical drawing M-261, *picture* M-260

Hide-behind, in folklore F-268

Hideweed, a seaweed, *picture* S-104

Hideyoshi, Toyotomi. *see in index* Toyotomi Hideyoshi

HID lamp (high intensity discharge lamp) L-206

Hiebert, Paul (born 1892), Canadian educator and author, born in Pilot Mound, Man.; professor at University of Manitoba ('Sarah Binks', a burlesque of popular criticism).

Hierarchy, a body of ecclesiastical rulers; especially applied to various Christian churches.

Hieratic writing, a running form of Egyptian hieroglyphic writing W-371
hieroglyphics H-150

Hieroglyphics, signs used in early writing H-150. *see also in index* Ideographic writing; Picture writing
ancient writing system A-403
Egyptian E-130
numeration systems N-435
Rosetta stone A-536, *picture* E-131
Champollion's translation C-269
Mayan M-237, *picture* S-82
Mycenaean A-62
writing W-370

Hieronymus. *see in index* Jerome, Saint

Hi-fi sound reproduction. *see in index* High fidelity

Higgins, Andrew Jackson (1886–1952), U.S. shipbuilder, born in Columbus, Neb.; in World War II at New Orleans developed assembly-line production of landing craft for armed forces.

Higgins, Edward John (1864–1947), British Salvation Army leader, born in Somerset; elected commanding general 1929; resigned 1934.

Higgins, Frederick Robert (1896–1941), Irish poet, born in Foxford, County Mayo, Ireland; visited U.S. in 1937 with Abbey Theatre players, for whom he was managing director; considered disciple of William Butler Yeats ('The Dark Breed'; 'Arable Holdings').

Higgins Flat, Pueblo, Ariz.
archeological digs, *picture* A-532

Higginson, Henry Lee (1834–1919), U.S. banker, born in New York City, N.Y.; major in Civil War; joined Lee, Higginson & Co., Boston bankers, 1868; founded Boston Symphony Orchestra, 1881.

Higginson, Thomas Wentworth (1823–1911), U.S. author and Civil War soldier, born in Cambridge, Mass.; colonel of first regiment of freed slaves ('Young Folks' History of the United States'; 'Cheerful Yesterdays').

High. *see in index* High-pressure center

High A-flat clarinet, wind instrument W-227

High-alloy cast iron, metal I-335

Highball, railroad term R-80

High blood pressure. *see in index* Hypertension

High-boiled candy C-137

High E-flat clarinet, wind instrument W-227

High-energy physics P-308
Alvarez' contribution A-323

Higher criticism, applied to the Bible, a detailed study of texts to determine their dates, authorship, and other features.

Higher education. *see in index* College; University

Higher Education Act (1965), United States
education, *list* E-104

'Higher Learning in America, The', work by Hutchins H-335

Highet, Gilbert Arthur (1906–78), U.S. classicist, born in Glasgow, Scotland, to U.S. 1937, citizen 1951; professor at Columbia University 1938–50, Anthon professor of Latin after 1950 ('The Art of Teaching'; 'People, Places, and Books'; 'Man's Unconquerable Mind'; 'Juvenal the Satirist, a Study'; 'Poets in a Landscape').

High fidelity (or hi fi), sound reproduction P-269
phonograph, *diagram* P-268d, *picture* P-269

High German, language G-113

High intensity discharge lamp (HID lamp) L-206

High jump, in track and field T-244, *picture* T-245

Highland, Ind., town 9 mi (15 km) s. of Whiting; dairy products, machinery; incorporated 1910; pop. 25,935, *map* I-102

Highland climates, in climate classification C-502

Highland fling, one of Scotland's animated national dances danced by three or four persons, so called because of unusual flinging action of steps, *picture* S-70

Highland Park, Ill., residential city on Lake Michigan 25 mi (40 km) n. of Chicago; Ravinia Park summer music center; Fort Sheridan nearby; pop. 30,611, *map* I-52

Highland Park, Mich., manufacturing city surrounded by Detroit; automobiles, milk packaging; pop. 27,909 D-120

Highland Park, N.J., borough just n. of New Brunswick; site of U.S. Bureau of Mines station; pop. 13,396.

Highland Park, Tex., residential suburb of Dallas; pop. 8,909.

Highlands, New Jersey N-193, *map* E-26

Highlands, part of Scotland n. of the Grampians S-67, *picture* S-66
clothing S-68, *pictures* S-70

'High Noon' (1952), motion picture by Zinnemann, *picture* M-625

High Plains, in Alberta A-262

High Plains, in Nebraska N-94

High Plains Border, plains region, U.S. K-174

High Plateau, land region in Algeria A-302

High Point, N.C., city in n.-central part of state, 14 mi (22 km) s.w. of Greensboro; furniture, hosiery, textiles, boats, machinery, glass, paints; High Point College; pop. 63,808 N-357, 366, *map* U-41

High Point, N.J., in Kittatinny Mountain N-193, *picture* N-195

High Point College, High Point, N.C.; affiliated with United Methodist church; established in 1924; liberal arts and teacher education.

High-pressure center (or high), region of high barometric pressure W-119, *table* W-126, *map* W-124

High-pressure ratio engine, turbojets J-107

'High Price of Bullion, The', work by Ricardo R-198

High priest, in Judaism, religious head of Hebrews, especially in Palestine at the time of the Temple of Solomon; guardian of the sanctuary. Aaron was regarded as first high priest; in postexilic times important political powers were exercised.

High relief (or alto-relievo), sculpture S-80

High resolution infrared radiometer (HRIR) W-123

High-rise, apartment buildings
fire fighting F-109
Paris, France P-123

High school. *see in index* Secondary school

High seas, all ocean waters not included within the jurisdiction or boundaries of any nation; open to all nations for navigation, fishing, and laying cables and pipelines.

High Tell, chain of mountains in Tunisia T-308

High-temperature, short-time method, (HTST method), in pasteurizing milk D-4

High-tension electric current, current under pressure of thousands of volts
insulation I-232

High tide, ocean tide O-488

High wave, *tables* R-34, R-50

Highwaymen, outlaws O-619

Highways. *see in index* Roads and streets

Highway Users Federation for Safety and Mobility S-5

Hiiumaa (or Dagö), island of Estonian Soviet Socialist Republic, in Baltic Sea, n. of Saaremaa; 373 sq mi (966 sq km); farming, fishing; settled by Teutonic Knights in 1200; taken by Sweden 1563, by Russia 1721; occupied by Germany 1917; given to Estonia 1918; leased by Estonia to U.S.S.R. for military base 1939, *maps* E-360, R-344, 348, S-524

Hijacking
terrorism T-113

Hiking H-151
forest recreation F-315
hobby, *picture* H-184
hostel H-285
mountain climbing M-637

Hilbert, David (1862–1943), German mathematician H-152. *see also in index* Courant, Richard
mathematics M-217

Hilda (or Saint Hild) (614–680), English abbess, princess of Northumbria; founded monastery of Whitby, in n. Yorkshire; feast day Nov. 17.

Hilda Baby, doll made by J.D. Kestner of Germany D-221

Hildebrand. *see in index* Gregory VII, Saint

Hildebrand, Adolf von (1847–1921), German sculptor, born in Marburg; combined naturalism with classic forms; famous for youthful male figures and portrait busts ('The Problem of Form') S-90

Hildesheim, West Germany, town 21 mi (34 km) s.e. of Hanover; seat of bishopric, prominent in Middle Ages; fine examples of Gothic and Romanesque architecture severely damaged in World War II; pop. 93,800, *map* G-131

Hill, Ambrose Powell (1825–65), U.S. soldier, born in Culpepper County, Va.; served in Mexican and Seminole wars; lieutenant general in Confederate army; led division during Seven Days', 2nd Bull Run, Antietam, and Fredericksburg battles; wounded at Chancellorsville; made commander of corps of Lee's army, which he led at Gettysburg and in Wilderness Campaign; killed at Petersburg
battle of Gettysburg G-136
Civil War C-475

painter, influenced by Van Ruisdael ('Avenue, Middelharnis'; 'Entrance to a Village') P-43
Hobbes, Thomas (1588–1679), British philosopher H-179
civilization C-465
materialism M-210
political science P-434
'Hobbit, The; or, There and Back Again', novel by Tolkien T-213
motion picture, *picture* N-411
Hobblebush. *see in index* Wayfaring tree
Hobbs, N.M., city situated in extreme s.e.; cattle, sheep, grain, cotton; petroleum industry, natural gas, carbon black, chemicals; pop. 29,153 N-216, 224, *maps* N-228, U-40
Hobby, Oveta Culp (born 1905), U.S. government official and publisher H-179
Eisenhower E-137
women's rights W-276
Hobby H-180.*see also in index* Collecting; Gardens and gardening; Leisure; Nature study
adult play P-385
antique collecting A-495
astronomy A-730
butterfly collecting B-527
button collecting B-530
candlemaking C-136
coins C-540
doll collecting D-215
flower pressing F-240
ham radio R-43, 55, *picture* R-52
handicrafts H-29
leisure time L-124
magic tricks, *Reference-Outline* V-242
models M-514
rockets S-348b, 342
painting P-67g
photography P-281, *Reference-Outline* V-244
plastics craftwork P-381
prisoner, *picture* P-505d
puppets P-535, 538
rugmaking R-314
sculpture S-94
Hobbyhorse, children's toy H-180
'Hobby Horse, The', magazine H-180
Hobhouse, Leonard Trelawney (1864–1929), British philosopher and first professor of sociology at London University; born in Saint Ives, Cornwall S-244
Hobkirk's Hill, battle of, British defeated Americans under Greene 1781, n. of Camden, S.C.; also called 2nd battle of Camden.
Hoboken, N.J., port of entry, railroad and industrial center opposite New York City on Hudson River; terminus of several important steamship lines; shipbuilding, coffee processing, marine equipment, leather, musical instruments; Stevens Institute of Technology; pop. 45,380.
Hobson, John Atkinson (1858–1940), British economist and writer, born in Derby; advocate of socialist economics ('The Evolution of Modern Capitalism').
Hobson, Laura Zametkin (1900–86), U.S. novelist, born in New York City ('Gentleman's Agreement'; 'First Papers'; 'Consenting Adult').
Hobson, Richmond Pearson (1870–1937), U.S. Navy hero, born in Greensboro, Ala.; in Spanish-American War sank collier *Merrimac* in attempt to close Santiago harbor; member of Congress from Alabama 1907–15 ('The Sinking of the Merrimac').
Hobson, William (1793–1842), British naval captain and governor of New Zealand, born in Waterford, Ireland; lieutenant governor of New Zealand and consul to Maori chiefs 1839–41; governor of New Zealand 1841–42
Auckland A-759
New Zealand N-283, 285, *picture* N-296
Hobson's choice, phrase meaning "this or nothing," originated from fact that Thomas Hobson (1544–1630), a stablekeeper of Cambridge, England, made each customer hire the horse nearest the door.
Hochelaga, Canada, early village at mouth of Ottawa River
Cartier's explorations C-90
Ho Chi Minh (originally Nguyen That Thanh) (1890–1969), Vietnamese leader H-191
Vietnam V-319
Ho Chi Minh City (formerly Saigon), Vietnam, port city; pop. 3,419,978 H-192, S-16a, *picture* S-16a
Asia, *map* A-697
Buddhist riots V-323
Vietnam V-319, *map* V-321
world, *map* W-297
Ho Chi Minh Trail, Viet Cong supply line V-322, *map* V-321
Laos protection L-48
Hochkirch, East Germany, village 35 mi (55 km) n.e. of Dresden; here Austrians defeated Prussians in Seven Years' War (1758); pop. 929.
Hochman, Sandra (born 1936), U.S. author
feminist literature A-362
Hockey, field H-193
Hockey, ice H-194. *see in index* table following
Ontario, *picture* O-553
play, *picture* P-388
skates W-241, *picture* S-208
Hockey Hall of Fame, Toronto, Ont. H-16
Hodag, in folklore F-268
Hodeida, Yemen Arab Republic, port on Red Sea; coffee trade; pop. 80,314.
Höd, in Norse mythology, blind god who slew Balder M-703. *see also in index* Balder
Hodge, cat that belonged to Samuel Johnson, *list* C-202
Hodgenville, Ky., city 45 mi (70 km) s. of Louisville; pop. 2,459.
Hodges, Courtney Hicks (1887–1966), U.S. Army officer, born in Perry, Ga.; from private in U.S. Army (1906) advanced to 4-star general (1945); commanded American 1st Army in World War II.
Hodges, Johnny (1906–70), U.S. alto and soprano saxophonist, born in Cambridge, Mass.; with Duke Ellington's orchestra for long periods after the 1920s.
Hodges, Luther Hartwell (1898–1974), U.S. business executive and public official, born in Pittsylvania County, Va.; joined Marshall Field & Company 1919, vice-president in charge of mills and sales 1943–50; lieutenant governor of North Carolina 1952–54, governor 1954–61; U.S. secretary of commerce 1961–65.
Hodgkin, Alan Lloyd (born 1914), British biophysicist, born in Danbury, Essex; professor Cambridge University 1952. *see also in index* Nobel Prizewinners, *table*
Hodgkin, Dorothy Crowfoot (born 1910), British chemist, born in Cairo, Egypt; research professor Oxford University 1960–; chancellor Bristol University 1970–; in 1969 with Oxford team revealed the structure of the hormone insulin used to treat diabetes. *see also in index* Nobel Prizewinners, *table*
Hodgkin's disease, disorder of lymphatic system, most common in young adults; signs include fever and progressive but painless enlargement of lymph nodes; treated with radiation, chemotherapy, and steroids; life expectancy varies; named for **Thomas Hodgkin** (1798–1866), British physician who described it in 1832.
Hodgson, James Day (born 1915), U.S. diplomat and labor-management executive, born in Dawson, Minn.; with Lockheed Aircraft Corporation, Burbank, Calif., 1941–69, senior vice-president for corporate relations 1973–74; U.S. undersecretary of labor 1969–70, secretary 1970–73; U.S. ambassador to Japan 1974–77; board chairman Uranium Mining Co. 1977–
Nixon N-326
Hodgson, Ralph (1871–1962), British poet, born in Yorkshire ('The Last Blackbird and Other Lines'; 'Eve and Other Poems'; 'The Skylark, and Other Poems').
Hodja, title given Muslim leader in folk tales S-469, 480
Hodler, Ferdinand (1853–1918), Swiss painter and lithographer, born in Bern; leader among Swiss moderns.
Hoe, Richard March (1812–86), U.S. manufacturer and inventor, born in New York City; with his brothers Peter S. and Robert contributed to development of printing press P-504
Hoecake, form of corn bread P-333
Hoegh, Leo Arthur (born 1908), U.S. lawyer, born in Audubon

ICE HOCKEY'S STANLEY CUP WINNERS*

Season	Team	Season	Team	Season	Team
1893–94	Montreal A.A.A.	1923–24	Montreal Canadiens	1954–55	Detroit Red Wings
1894–95	Montreal Victorias	1924–25	Victoria Cougars	1955–56	Detroit Red Wings
1895–96	Winnipeg Victorias	1925–26	Montreal Maroons	1956–57	Montreal Canadiens
1896–97	Montreal Victorias	1926–27	Ottawa Senators	1957–58	Montreal Canadiens
1897–98	Montreal Victorias	1927–28	New York Rangers	1958–59	Montreal Canadiens
1898–99	Montreal Victorias	1928–29	Boston Bruins	1959–60	Montreal Canadiens
1899–1900	Montreal Shamrocks	1929–30	Montreal Canadiens	1960–61	Chicago Black Hawks
1900–01	Winnipeg Victorias	1930–31	Montreal Canadiens	1961–62	Toronto Maple Leafs
1901–02	Montreal A.A.A.	1931–32	Toronto Maple Leafs	1962–63	Toronto Maple Leafs
1902–03	Ottawa Silver Seven	1932–33	New York Rangers	1963–64	Toronto Maple Leafs
1903–04	Ottawa Silver Seven	1933–34	Chicago Black Hawks	1964–65	Montreal Canadiens
1904–05	Ottawa Silver Seven	1934–35	Montreal Maroons	1965–66	Montreal Canadiens
1905–06	Montreal Wanderers	1935–36	Detroit Red Wings	1966–67	Toronto Maple Leafs
1906–07	Kenora Thistles†	1936–37	Detroit Red Wings	1967–68	Montreal Canadiens
1906–07	Montreal Wanderers‡	1937–38	Chicago Black Hawks	1968–69	Montreal Canadiens
1907–08	Montreal Wanderers	1938–39	Boston Bruins	1969–70	Boston Bruins
1908–09	Ottawa Senators	1939–40	New York Rangers	1970–71	Montreal Canadiens
1909–10	Ottawa Senators	1940–41	Boston Bruins	1971–72	Boston Bruins
1910–11	Ottawa Senators	1941–42	Toronto Maple Leafs	1972–73	Montreal Canadiens
1911–12	Quebec Bull Dogs	1942–43	Detroit Red Wings	1973–74	Philadelphia Flyers
1912–13	Quebec Bull Dogs	1943–44	Montreal Canadiens	1974–75	Philadelphia Flyers
1913–14	Toronto	1944–45	Toronto Maple Leafs	1975–76	Montreal Canadiens
1914–15	Vancouver Millionaires	1945–46	Montreal Canadiens	1976–77	Montreal Canadiens
1915–16	Montreal Canadiens	1946–47	Toronto Maple Leafs	1977–78	Montreal Canadiens
1916–17	Seattle Metropolitans	1947–48	Toronto Maple Leafs	1978–79	Montreal Canadiens
1917–18	Toronto Arenas	1948–49	Toronto Maple Leafs	1979–80	New York Islanders
1918–19	No winner§	1949–50	Detroit Red Wings	1980–81	New York Islanders
1919–20	Ottawa Senators	1950–51	Toronto Maple Leafs	1981–82	New York Islanders
1920–21	Ottawa Senators	1951–52	Detroit Red Wings	1982–83	New York Islanders
1921–22	Toronto St. Patricks	1952–53	Montreal Canadiens	1983–84	Edmonton Oilers
1922–23	Ottawa Senators	1953–54	Detroit Red Wings	1984–85	Edmonton Oilers
				1985–86	Montreal Canadiens
				1986–87	Edmonton Oilers

*National Hockey League took possession of Stanley Cup 1926–27.
†Thistles won in January.
‡Wanderers won in March.
§Finals between Montreal Canadiens and Seattle were halted because of influenza epidemic.
Source: Official National Hockey League records.

County, Iowa; governor of Iowa 1954–57; civil defense administrator 1957–58; director Office of Defense and Civilian Mobilization 1958–61.

Hoek van Holland. *see in index* Hook of Holland

Hoenir, in Norse mythology, god who with Odin and Loki created first man, Ask, and first woman, Embla, from trees in Midgard; from Odin they obtained life, from Hoenir, mind, and from Loki, the senses.

Hofburg, palace in Vienna, Austria V-314, *picture* V-315

Hofei, China, capital of Anhui Province; rice; food processing; textiles, metal products; pop. 360,000.

Hofer, Andreas (1767–1810), Tyrolese hero, born in St. Leonhard, Tyrol; leader of insurrection against Bavaria; betrayed, court-martialed, and shot.

Hofer, Karl (1878–1955), German artist, born in Karlsruhe, Germany; some works are in Flemish tradition, others suggestive of Cézanne or Picasso, and still others abstract and expressionistic.

Hoff, Jacobus Hendricus Van't. *see in index* Van't Hoff, Jacobus Hendricus

Hoffa, James R. (1913–75?), U.S. labor leader L-10

Höffding, Harald (1843–1931), Danish philosopher, born in Copenhagen ('History of Modern Philosophy'; 'Philosophy of Religion').

Hoffenstein, Samuel (1890–1947), U.S. poet and motion-picture writer, born in Lithuania; wrote light verse ('Poems in Praise of Practically Nothing').

Hoffman, Charles Fenno (1806–84), U.S. newspaper and magazine editor, novelist, poet, born in New York, N.Y. ('A Winter in the West'; 'Greyslaer, a Romance of the Mohawk').

Hoffman, Malvina (1887–1966), U.S. sculptor, born in New York, N.Y.; married Samuel B. Grimson; author 'Heads and Tales', an autobiography (portraits of Paderewski, Pavlova; groups and single figures illustrating racial types for Field Museum of Natural History), *picture* I-137

Hoffman, Paul Gray (1891–1974), U.S. business executive and public official, born in Chicago, Ill.; president Studebaker Corporation 1935–48; became chairman Committee for Economic Development 1942; head of Economic Coöperation Administration 1948–50; president of Ford Foundation 1950–53; board chairman of Studebaker Corporation 1953–54, of Studebaker-Packard Corporation 1954–56; administrator UN Development Program 1966–72; married Anna M. Rosenberg 1962.

Hoffman Estates, Ill., village n.w. of Chicago; primarily residential; incorporated 1959; pop. 22,238, *map* I-52

Hoffmann, August Heinrich (1798–1874), German poet and philologist, called Hoffmann von Fallersleben from birthplace, Fallersleben, near Brunswick, Germany
German national anthem N-66

Hoffmann, E.T.A. (or Ernst Theodor Amadeus Hoffmann) (1776–1822), German novelist and composer H-198
German literature G-109

Hoffmann, Ronald (born 1937), U.S. chemist. *see also in index* Nobel Prizewinners, *table*

Hoffmann von Fallersleben. *see in index* Hoffmann, August Heinrich

Hofmann, August Wilhelm von (1818–92), German chemist, born in Giessen, Germany; helped to found German coal-tar industry.

Hofmann, Hans (1880–1966), U.S. abstract expressionist painter H-199

Hofmann, Heinrich (1824–1911), German historical and portrait painter, born in Darmstadt, Germany; popular for ideal conceptions of life of Christ, also for paintings from mythology.
'The Finding of Christ in the Temple', *picture* J-103

Hofmann, Josef Casimir (1876–1957), U.S. pianist and composer, born in Cracow, Poland, became U.S. citizen 1926; child prodigy at 6; successful concert tour of Europe at 9; director Curtis Institute of Music, Philadelphia, 1926–38; compositions for piano and orchestra.

Hofmannsthal, Hugo von (1874–1929), Austrian neoromantic dramatist and poet, born in Vienna; dealt chiefly with imaginative world ('The Death of Titian', one of his best plays; 'Elektra' and 'Der Rosenkavalier' used as libretti for operas by R. Strauss)
German literature G-107

Hofmeister, Wilhelm (1824–77), German botanist, born in Leipzig; described fertilization and embryo formation in plants; discovered alternation of generations in life cycle of ferns, mosses, and other cryptogams.

Hofstadter, Robert (born 1915), U.S. physicist and educator, born in New York, N.Y.; with Stanford University since 1950, director high energy physics laboratory 1967. *see also in index* Nobel Prizewinners, *table*

Hofstra University, Hempstead, N.Y.; private control; founded 1935; granted absolute charter 1940; liberal arts and sciences, business administration, education, law; graduate study; center at Commack N-254

Hofuf, Saudi Arabia, city 40 mi (60 km) from Persian Gulf; commercial center in date-producing oasis; metalwork; pop. 100,000 S-52b

Hog. *see in index* Pig

Hogaku, Japanese superstition, *diagram* J-31

Hogan, Ben (born 1912), U.S. professional golfer, born in Stephenville, Tex.; in 1948 became first golfer to win the Professional Golfers' Association, U.S. Open, and Western Open tournaments in one season G-189

Hogarth, William (1697–1764), British painter and engraver H-199
cartoons C-187
painting P-47
'The Graham Children', *picture* P-46

Hogarth Act H-199

Hogben, Lancelot Thomas (1895–1975), British zoologist and writer, born in Southsea, England; professor of medical statistics University of Birmingham, England, 1947–61; vice-chancellor University of Guiana 1963–65; stressed practical and social significance of science in 'Mathematics for the Million', 'Science for the Citizen', and 'Mathematics in the Making'.

Hogchoker, freshwater flatfish F-173

Hog cholera, an infectious virus disease of swine P-322, V-352

Hogfish, Spanish. *see in index* Spanish hogfish

Hogg, James (or the Ettrick Shepherd) (1770–1835), Scottish peasant poet, born in Ettrick, near Moffat, Scotland ('Scottish Pastorals'; 'The Mountain Bard'; 'The Queen's Wake'; 'Pilgrims of the Sun'; 'The Poetic Mirror').

Hog Island, partly in Delaware County, Pennsylvania, and partly in s. Philadelphia, Pa.; municipal airport
World War I shipbuilding, *picture* W-312

Hog-nosed snake S-226c

Hogrogian, Nonny (born 1932), U.S. illustrator and book designer, born in New York, N.Y.; awarded Caldecott Medal 1966 for 'Always Room for One More' and 1972 for 'One Fine Day'; 'The Kitchen Knight' R-106, 111b, S-481
'The Fearsome Inn' R-110b

Hogshead, unit of measure, *table* W-140
tobacco barrels T-200, *picture* T-199

Hogue, La, battle of. *see in index* La Hogue

Hogweed. *see in index* Ragweed

Hohenfriedeberg, Poland, former German town in Silesia, 36 mi (58 km) s.w. of Breslau; victory of Frederick the Great over Austrians and Saxons 1745 in War of Austrian Succession; included in Poland since 1945.

Hohenheim, Theophrastus Bombastus von. *see in index* Paracelsus

Hohenlinden, West Germany, village in Bavaria, 19 mi (31 km) e. of Munich; French victory over Austrians in 1800; pop. 1,850.

Hohenstaufen, noble German family of Middle Ages H-200. For list of Hohenstaufen emperors, *see in index* Holy Roman Empire, *table*
Austrian reign ends A-828
foundation by Conrad III C-666
Frederick I F-389
Frederick II F-390
Germany G-121
Guelfs and Ghibellines G-301
Holy Roman Empire H-209

Hohenzollern, family of rulers that founded the German Empire in 1871 H-200
Berlin B-171
Germany G-121
growth of power P-516
William II W-205

Hohenzollern, former district of Prussia; 441 sq mi (1,142 sq km); after World War II became part of Württemberg-Hohenzollern.

Hohe Tauern, range of Eastern Alps; also, a summit 8,080 ft. (2,460 m) in this range; highest peak Gross Glockner 12,461 ft (3,798 m)
Tirol T-192

Hohokam culture, American Indians I-127, 145, *picture* I-143
irrigation systems I-357

Ho Hsiang-ning (1879–1972), Chinese politician, *list* W-275

Hoist, in engineering
bridge construction B-444, *picture* B-445

Hoist, in flag measurement, *list* F-149

Hojo, Tokimasa (1138–1215), Japanese warrior, born in Izu Province, Japan H-200

Hojo, Tokimune (1251–1284), Japanese regent, born in Kamakura, Japan H-200

Hojo, Takatoki (died 1333), Japanese regent H-200

Hojo family, governed Japan from 1199–1333 H-200

'Hojoki' (or 'The Ten Foot Square Hut'), essay by Chomei Kamo J-81

'Hokekyo Sutra', Japanese painted fan, *picture* J-50

Hokinson, Helen Elna (1893–1949), U.S. cartoonist, born in Mendota, Ill.; famous for caricatures of clubwomen in *The New Yorker* 1925–49.

Hokkaido, northernmost large island of Japan; forests, fisheries, coal, agriculture; 30,144 sq mi (78,073 sq km); pop. 5,184,287 J-27, *map* J-78
Ainu population A-11
Asia, *map* A-697
world, *map* W-297

Hokkien (or Fujianese, or Fukienese), people T-13

Hokusai, Katsushika (1760–1849), Japanese artist, born in Edo (present Tokyo), Japan; drawings and color prints ('Hundred Views of Mount Fuji') J-51

Ho Kyun (1569–1618), Korean writer K-294

Holabird, William (1854–1923), U.S. architect A-568

Holaday, William Marion (born 1901), U.S. government official and research engineer, born in New Vienna, Ohio; U.S. director of guided missiles 1957–59; chairman civilian-military space liaison committee 1958–60.

Holbach, Paul H.D., baron d' (1723–89), French philosopher M-210

Holbein, Hans, the Elder (1460–1524), German painter, born in Augsburg, Germany H-201
bookplate design B-362

Holbein, Hans, the Younger (1497–1543), German painter, son of Hans, the Elder H-201
painting P-39
portraits
Anne of Cleves P-39
Erasmus, *picture* R-148
Henry VIII, *picture* H-131
More, *picture* M-582
'The Ambassadors', *picture* D-264

Holberg, Ludvig, Baron (1684–1754), Norwegian-Danish dramatist, historian, and philosopher; born in Bergen, Norway; called the Molière of the North ('Subterranean Journey of Niels Klim'; 'Comedies')
Norway N-391

Holborn, district in central part of London, England; contains Lincoln's Inn and Gray's Inn.

HOLC (Home Owners' Loan Corporation), U.S. R-265

Holcomb, Thomas (1879–1965), U.S. Marine officer, born in New Castle, Del.; in World I; commandant U.S. Marine Corps 1936–43; became first Marine to attain 4-star rank 1943; U.S. minister to South Africa 1944–48; retired 1948.

Holden, Edward Singleton (1846–1914), U.S. astronomer, born in St. Louis, Mo.; president of University of California 1885–88; did most important work as director of Lick Observatory, California, 1888–98.

Holden, Mass., 8 mi (13 km) n.w. of Worcester; settled 1723, incorporated 1741; pop. of township 13,336.

Hölderlin, Johann Christian Friedrich (1770–1843), German poet, born in Lauffen, near Heilbronn H-201
German literature G-109

Holding, Thomas Hiram, father of modern camping C-71

Holding company
bank control B-69
monopoly M-544

Hole, crystal's defect C-799, *diagram* C-798

Holguín, Cuba; pop. 192,200, *maps* C-802, W-106
North America, *map* N-350

Holiday, Billie (born Eleanor Fagan, nickname Lady Day) (1915–59), U.S. jazz singer H-202
black Americans B-302
jazz J-85
Young Y-424

Holiday Inns, Incorporated, hotel and motel chain H-286

Holidays. *see in index* Festivals and holidays

Holiness movement, quest for individual perfection which arose in the 19th century H-202

Holinshed (or Raphael Hollingshead) (died 1580), English chronicler, compiler of 'Chronicles of England, Scotland and Ireland', source book of Elizabethan dramatists
Shakespeare S-136

Holistic medicine (or wholistic medicine), medicine based on a philosophy which treats the mind and body as a whole H-202
folk medicine F-271

Holladay, Utah, unincorporated community, 8 mi (13 km) s.e. of Salt Lake City; residential suburb of Salt Lake City; pop. 23,014, *map* U-232

Holland, Clifford Milburn (1883–1924), U.S. engineer, born in Somerset, Mass.; authority on underwater tunnels; assistant engineer in building East River tunnels, 1906–7; chief engineer New York-New Jersey vehicular tunnel under Hudson River which bears his name. *see also in index* Holland Tunnel

Holland, John Philip (1840–1914), U.S. inventor, born in Liscannor, near Ennistymon, Ireland; designed submarine *Holland*, purchased by U.S. government (1900)
submarine development P-139, S-495b

Holland, Josiah Gilbert (1819–81), U.S. editor and author, born in Belchertown, Mass. ('Bittersweet'; 'Sevenoaks').

Holland, a breed of poultry P-482

Holland. *see in index* Netherlands, The

Holland, Mich., city on Lake Macatawa 25 mi (40 km) s.w. of Grand Rapids; food processing; furnaces, air-conditioning equipment, pharmaceuticals; Hope College, Western Theological Seminary; pop. 26,281 M-359, *pictures* M-357, 366

HOLY ROMAN EMPERORS

Reign	
800–814	Charlemagne
814–840	Louis the Pious
840–911	Later Carolingians
919–936	Henry I, the Fowler
Saxon Line	
[911–918	Conrad I]
936–973	Otto I, the Great
973–983	Otto II
983–1002	Otto III
1002–1024	Henry II
Franconian Line	
1024–1039	Conrad II
1039–1056	Henry III
1056–1106	Henry IV
1106–1125	Henry V
[1125–1137	Lothair II of Saxony]
Hohenstaufen Line	
1138–1152	Conrad III
1152–1190	Frederick I (Barbarossa)
1190–1197	Henry VI
1198–1208	Philip of Swabia } rival claimants
1198–1214	Otto IV } rival claimants
1215–1250	Frederick II
1250–1254	Conrad IV
[1254–1273	Great Interregnum]
Rulers from Various Houses	
1273–1291	Rudolph of Hapsburg
1292–1298	Adolf of Nassau
1298–1308	Albert I of Hapsburg
1308–1313	Henry VII of Luxemburg
1314–1347	Louis IV of Bavaria } rival claimants
1314–1330	Frederick the Fair of Austria } rival claimants
Luxemburg Line	
1347–1378	Charles IV
1378–1400	Wenzel
[1400–1410	Rupert of the Palatinate]
1410–1437	Sigismund
Hapsburg Line	
1438–1439	Albert II
1440–1493	Frederick III
1493–1519	Maximilian I
1519–1556	Charles V
1556–1564	Ferdinand I
1564–1576	Maximilian II
1576–1612	Rudolph II
1612–1619	Matthias
1619–1637	Ferdinand II
1637–1657	Ferdinand III
1658–1705	Leopold I
1705–1711	Joseph I
1711–1740	Charles VI
[1742–1745	Charles VII of Bavaria]
1745–1765	Francis I
1765–1790	Joseph II
1790–1792	Leopold II
1792–1806	Francis II (after 1806 reigned as Francis I of Austria)

basswood L-228
bottling, *picture* S-49d
nectar B-106
sugars S-509

Honey ant, insect A-468

Honey badger, a subfamily *Mellivora capensis* of its own in the weasel family found in India and Africa; fur is ashy gray on top and black underneath; eats honey, rats, birds, frogs, and insects W-114

Honey bear (also known as Malayan bear, or sun bear), bear *Helarctos malayanus* of the family Ursidae B-116

Honey bear, small mammal of the racoon family. *see in index* Kinkajou

Honeybee, bee of the family Apidae B-124, *picture* I-227. *see also in index* Bee
animal navigation B-226
orienting behavior A-441
wax W-110

Honeycomb, a sponge S-395

Honeycomb, waxy many-celled structure made by bees for holding honey B-125, H-228

Honeydew, melon M-292

Honey guide, an African bird related to the woodpecker (family Indicatoridae of the order Piciformes); parasitic, lays eggs in the nests of woodpeckers and barbets; lives entirely on the larvae of bees and on honey and wax taken when the bees' nest is destroyed by other animals or humans; its call lead men and animals to the nest B-257
honey badger symbiosis W-116

Honey mesquite (or common mesquite), a plant *Prosopis juliflora* of the family Leguminosae, *picture* F-239

Honeysuckle, plant H-228

Honeysuckle family (or Caprifoliaceae), a family of plants and shrubs, native to north temperate regions and mountains of the tropics, including cranberry tree, snowball bush, the elders, twinflower, honeysuckles, and weigelas.

Hong, Lady (1735–1815), Korean princess of Hyegyong Palace K-294

Hong Kong, China, British colony, including Hong Kong, other islands, and areas on mainland; 398 sq mi (1,031 sq km); cap. Victoria; pop. 4,986,560 H-228, *map* W-297
Asia A-680, *picture* A-682, *map* A-697
escalator E-187
garment industry G-35
harbor H-33, *picture* H-34
housing H-293, 306
migration of people M-407
Opium Wars O-573
railroad mileage, *table* R-85
World War II W-328

Honing, grinding operation used to produce highly polished surfaces T-224

Honi soit qui mal y pense (translation, "Evil to him who evil thinks"), motto of the Order of the Garter. *see also in index* Garter, Order of the

Honiton lace L-17, *picture* L-16

Honolulu, Hawaii, state capital and largest city, on s.e. shore of island of Oahu; pop. 379,600 H-230, *map* W-297
Hawaii H-57, *map* H-58, *picture* H-67
Oceania O-469
Pacific Ocean, *map* P-3
United States U-100, *map* U-119

Honor, decorations of. *see in index* Medal

Honor, Legion of. *see in index* Legion of Honor

Honor, Order of, medals M-272

Honor, titles of. *see in index* Titles of nobility

Honorarium, gift
legal definition, *table* L-93

Honorius, Flavius (384–423), Roman emperor of the West, born in Constantinople; son of Theodosius the Great; vast decline of Roman power during his rule
Roman empire divided B-533

Honor point, in heraldry, *diagram* H-136

Honors course, in college curriculum U-207

Honor society F-389

Honshu (formerly Hondo), largest and most important island of Japan; 87,805 sq mi (227,415 sq km); pop. 90,873,000 J-24, 39, 61, *maps* J-59, 78
Asia, *map* A-697
cities. *see also in index* cities by name
Kyoto K-312
Nagoya N-3
Osaka O-608
Tokyo T-203
Yokohama Y-422
comparative size. *see in index* Island, *table*
flood, *table* F-181
Fuji F-444
world, *map* W-297

Honwana, Luis (born 1942), African writer A-122

Hooch, Pieter de (or Pieter de Hoogh) (1629–78?), Dutch artist, born in Rotterdam; best known as a genre painter; his interiors are illuminated with splashes of daylight or sunlight of varied intensities P-43

Hood, John Bell (1831–79), Confederate Civil War general, born in Owingsville, Ky.; commanded divisions at Gettysburg and Chickamauga; commander of Army of Tennessee, succeeding Johnston
Civil War C-476
Thomas T-172

Hood, Raymond Mathewson (1881–1934), U.S. architect, born in Pawtucket, R.I.; with John Mead Howells designed Tribune Tower, Chicago, and Daily News Building, New York City; collaborated on Rockefeller Center, New York City.

Hood, Robin. *see in index* Robin Hood

Hood, Samuel, Viscount (1724–1816), British naval commander in chief in America 1767–71; distinguished in battles 1780–83 with French fleet under De Grasse; in Mediterranean 1793.

Hood, Thomas (1799–1845), British poet and humorist, born in London ('The Song of the Shirt', 'The Bridge of Sighs', 'Miss Kilmansegg', and 'The Plea of the Midsummer Fairies').

'Hood', British battle cruiser S-177h

Hood, head covering H-53
dress D-262

Hood, Mount, highest point in Oregon 11,245 ft (3,425 m), in Cascade Range in n. part of state, 45 mi (70 km) s.e. of Portland P-453, *map* U-90

Hood College, Frederick, Md.; private control; primarily for women; founded 1893; arts and sciences, education, and home economics.

Hooded seal S-100

Hoodoo, a person or thing whose presence is thought to cause bad luck; associated with the practice of voodoo; of African origin.

Hoof, horny sheath encasing toes of many animals H-231
antelope A-478
hand H-27
horse H-250, *diagram* H-251

Hoof-and-mouth disease. *see in index* Foot-and-mouth disease

Hoof-pick, horse-grooming tool H-267

Hooft, Pieter Corneliszoon (1581–1647), Dutch poet, historian, and dramatist, born in Amsterdam; studied law and history at Leiden; translated Tacitus into Dutch and followed his style as historian; founded circle of intellectuals including poet Sir Constantijn Huygens (prose works: 'Henry IV of France', 'Dutch History'; poetry: 'Minneliederen', 'Baeto').

Hoogh, Pieter de. *see in index* Hooch, Pieter de

Hook, in boxing B-388, *picture* B-389

Hook, in fishing F-140, *pictures* F-141, 142

Hook cast, in fishing, *list* F-146

Hooke, Robert (1635–1703), British physicist, born Isle of Wight; made curator of experiments to the Royal Society 1662, and secretary 1677–82; first scientist to recognize principle of planetary motion; work basis for Newton's theories
botany B-380
cell studies B-229, C-240
synthetic fibers F-71
watch and clock W-78

Hooker, Joseph (nickname Fighting Joe) (1814–79), U.S. Civil War general, born in Hadley, Mass.; commanded Army of Potomac (1863) succeeding Burnside; resigned command after losing battle of Chancellorsville; later commanded Army of Cumberland
Civil War C-475, 481
Lee L-116

Hooker, Sir Joseph Dalton (1817–1911), British surgeon and naturalist, born in Halesworth, near Lowestoft; made important additions to botanical knowledge; expeditions to Antarctic regions, Australia, the Himalayas, and Syria; with George Bentham, wrote 'Genera Plantarum'.

Hooker, Richard (1554?–1600), English author, born in Heavitree, Exeter; wrote 'Laws of Ecclesiastical Polity', a masterly exposition of philosophical and political principles; it has been called the earliest English prose work "with enough of the preserving salt of excellence to adapt it to the mental palate of modern readers."

Hooker, Thomas (1586?–1647), Puritan clergyman, born in England; helped form (1643) New England Confederation
Connecticut colonies C-653
Massachusetts congregation M-194

Hook of Holland (Dutch Hoek van Holland), The Netherlands, port of North Sea at mouth of New Waterway, lying 15 mi (25 km) n.w. of Rotterdam and belonging to its vast complex of ports; has terminals for ferries connecting with England; pop. 5,114.

Hook shank, in fishing, *list* F-146

Hookworm, intestinal parasite W-362

Hoonah, Alaska, city on Chichagof Island, in s.e. Alaska, 50 mi (80 km) s.w. of Juneau; fish canneries; sawmill; pop. 680, *map* U-39

Hoop ash. *see in index* Black ash

Hooper, Harry Bartholomew (1887–1974), U.S. baseball outfielder, born in Bell Station, Calif.; with Boston Red Sox 1909–20, Chicago White Sox 1921–25; lifetime batting average .281.

Hooper, William (1742–90), signer of Declaration of Independence; born in Boston, Mass.; North Carolina's delegate to Continental Congress (1774–77) D-56

Hoopoe, any bird of the genus *Upupa,* native to warmer regions of Old World; common European hoopoe about size of blue jay; plumage black, white, and buff; long pointed bill; large erectile crest.

Hoop snake, a mythical reptile said to overtake victims by holding its tail in its mouth and rolling like a hoop; its tail said to have poisonous sting; story common in s.e. U.S.

Hoosac Range, a spur of the Green Mountains in n.w. Massachusetts (Spruce Hill, 2,588 ft; 789 m).

Hoosac Tunnel, n.w. Massachusetts, through Hoosac Range to North Adams.

Hoosic River, 90 mi. (140 km) long, rises in n.w. Massachusetts, flows n.w. across s.w. Vermont into New York, emptying into Hudson River, *map* V-301
Massachusetts M-190

'Hoosier Schoolmaster, The', (1871) novel by Eggleston A-351

Hoosier State. *see in index* Indiana

Hooton, Earnest Albert (1887–1954), U.S. anthropologist, born in Clemansville, Wis.; began teaching anthropology at Harvard University 1913, professor 1930–54 and curator of Peabody Museum 1914–54 ('Up from the Ape'; 'Why Men Behave Like Apes and Vice Versa').

Hoover, Herbert (in full Herbert Clark Hoover) (1874–1964), 31st president of the United States H-231
Great Depression G-242
Harding H-40
Roosevelt R-266
United States history U-187
World War I W-321

Hoover, Herbert Clark, Jr. (1903–69), U.S. government official and mining engineer, born in London, England; president United Geophysical Company, Pasadena, Calif., 1935–52, board chairman 1952–53; special adviser to state department in Iranian oil negotiations 1953–54, for this he won Medal of Freedom 1954; undersecretary of state 1954–57
Iowa I-194, *picture* I-299

Hoover, Ike (full name Irwin Hood Hoover) (1871–1933), U.S. chief usher at White House, born Washington, D.C.; author of 'Forty-Two Years in the White House'.

Hoover, J. Edgar (full name John Edgar Hoover) (1895–1972), U.S. lawyer and criminologist H-237

Hoover, Lou Henry (1875–1944), wife of President Hoover H-232, *picture* H-233

Hoover Dam (formerly Boulder Dam), in Arizona and Nevada, on Colorado River C-584, D-11, *picture* D-15
Arizona A-598
electric power E-166
irrigation I-355
Nevada N-134, *picture* N-143

Hoover Institution on War, Revolution, and Peace H-237

Hooverize, United States World War I term meaning 'to save' H-233

Hooverville, depression of 1929 G-242

'Hopalong Cassidy and the Rustlers of West Fork', novel by L'Amour L-26

Hopatcong, Lake, in New Jersey, 24 mi (39 km) w. of Paterson; about 8 mi (13 km) long; popular summer resort N-193

Hop clover S-143

Hope, A.D. (born 1907), Australian writer, *table* A-798

Hope, Anthony (pen name of Sir Anthony Hope Hawkins) (1863–1933), British novelist, born in London; 'The Prisoner of Zenda' and 'Rupert of Hentzau' set fashion for romantic comedies involving noblemen of ficticious principalities; later works deal with social and ethical problems.

Hope, Bob (full name Leslie Townes Hope) (born 1903), U.S. actor, radio and television entertainer H-237

Hope, John (1868–1936), U.S. educator, born in Augusta, Ga.; president Morehouse College 1906–31 and Atlanta University 1929–36; won 1936 Spingarn medal.

Hope (or Hope Blue), 44½-carat diamond of pronounced blue color, named for Henry T. Hope, London banker, who acquired it in the 1830s; purchased 1949 from Evalyn Walsh McLean estate by Harry Winston, New York City jeweler; given by him to Smithsonian Institution 1958; this diamond is believed to be part of a large stone that Tavernier sold to French Crown 1668, *picture* D-129

Hope, Point, Alaska, promontory on n.w. coast, *map* U-39

Hope College, Holland, Mich.; private control; established in 1866; arts and sciences, business administration, economics, music, and teacher education.

Hope Halls, U.S. halfway houses that were privately operated H-14

Hopei. *see in index* Hebei

Hopewell, Va., industrial city at confluence of Appomattox and James rivers 20 mi (30 km) s.e. of Richmond; cellulose products, chemicals, textiles, fiber containers; pop. 23,471, *map* V-349

Hopewell culture, American Indians I-145, *picture* I-143

Hophornbeam, a genus *Ostrya* of slender trees with very hard wood, brownish furrowed bark; often planted as ornamental tree.

Hopi, Indian tribe P-526d, A-598
American Indians, *pictures* I-113, 130, *table* I-139
braiding traditions B-395

Houghton, Mich., village opposite Hancock on Portage Lake, connected with Lake Superior by canal; shipping point for copper region; Michigan Technological University; pop. 7,512, *map* U-41

Houghton Lake, Michigan M-355

Houghton College, Houghton, N.Y.; established in 1883 by Wesleyan Methodist church; college level after 1899; arts and sciences, music, teacher education, and theology.

Houma, La., port city on Gulf Intracoastal Waterway about 45 mi (70 km) s.w. of New Orleans; oil, gas, sulfur; sugarcane, seafood, raw furs; shipbuilding; pop. 32,602.

Hound, hunting dog D-197. *see also in index* hounds by name

'Hound of Heaven,' religious poem by Thompson T-173

Hound's-tongue. *see in index* Chinese forget-me-not

Hounsfield, Godfrey Newbold (born 1919), British scientist, born in Newark, Nottinghamshire; at EMI, Ltd., since 1951, head of medical systems sections 1972–76, chief staff scientist 1976–77, senior staff scientist after 1977; research on radar and computer design led to his invention of a computerized axial tomography (CAT) scanner for X-ray examination. *see also in index* Nobel Prizewinners, *table*

Hounslow, borough, London, *maps* L-287, U-18a

Houppelande (or gown), garment D-262

Hour angle, in astronomy, the angular distance between the meridian of an observer and the hour circle through a celestial body at a given time.

Hour circles, in navigation N-72, *diagrams* N-71, 74

Hourglass, time-measuring device W-77, *picture* W-79
- British minute glass, *picture* P-129

Hours (or Horae), goddesses of law and order in mythology.

'Housatonic', U.S. corvette S-495b

Housatonic River, rises in Berkshires in w. Massachusetts, flows s. 155 mi (250 km) through Connecticut to Long Island Sound M-190

House, Edward Mandell (1858–1938), U.S. political leader, born in Houston, Tex.; confidential foreign agent of President Wilson; member American Peace Commission 1919.

House, in astrology A-708

Houseboat, covered flat-bottomed boat used as house or for cruising B-329, *picture* S-157

'House by the Medlar Tree, The', work by Verga I-377

House cricket, insect *Acheta domestica* of the family Gryllidae C-767

Housed joint, in cabinetmaking C-175

Housefly I-224, *picture* I-218
- egg, *picture* E-111
- parasite, *picture* P-115

Household H-290, *list* H-305

'Household Words', magazine founded by Dickens D-137

Houseleek. *see in index* Live-forever

House mouse, rodent *Mus musculus* M-640

House of . . . *see in index under* main word, *e.g.*, Commons, House of; Representatives, House of, except as below

'House of Mirth, The', work by Wharton W-186
- American literature A-358

'House of the Seven Gables, The', work by Hawthorne H-74
- house, *picture* M-192

House of Trade, Spanish organization to regulate commerce in the New World A-334

Houseplant, plant adapted for growing indoors H-288

Houses. *see also in index* Architecture; Building construction, *subhead* houses; Housing; Shelter
- models M-516

House snake. *see in index* Milk snake

House sparrow (or English sparrow), bird *Passer domesticus domesticus* of the family Ploceidae S-368, *picture* B-244
- egg, *picture* E-112
- feather wear B-244

House wren, bird *Troglodytes aedon* of the *Troglodytidae* family W-364

Housing H-290. *see also in index* Shelter
- ancient Near East A-500
  - Egypt E-127
- American Indian, *picture* O-530
- Australia A-785
- Aztecs A-891
- bibliography S-160
- census C-248
- construction B-101, B-492
- design D-114
- folk art F-249
- government aid U-165
- Korea K-272
- Middle Ages M-386, 393
- public housing, *picture* U-102
- rehabilitation, *picture* U-164
- savings and loan associations S-[illegible]
- slums
  - clearance, *picture* R-266
  - Puerto Rico P-528, *picture* P-529
  - Rome R-252
  - Soviet Union, *pictures* R-330, 332c
- zoning and building regulations S-158

Housing Acts, United States government, *list* H-304

Housing Administration, Federal, United States. *see in index* Federal Housing Administration

Housing Agency, National (NHA), United States R-265

Housing and Urban Development, Department of (HUD), United States U-164, *list* U-157
- building rehabilitation, *picture* U-164
- flood insurance F-182, I-233
- housing, *list* H-304
- Johnson administration J-134

Housing and Urban Development Acts, United States government H-303, *list* H-304

Housing Authority, United States (USHA), *picture* R-266

Housing code, *list* H-305

Housing unit H-290, *list* H-305

Housman, A.E. (full name Alfred Edward Housman) (1859–1936), British poet and scholar H-307
- creative writing W-381
- literary contribution E-280
- quoted P-405

Housman, Laurence (1865–1959), British writer and illustrator, born in Bromsgrove, near Worcester; brother of A.E. Housman; wrote children's stories ('What O'Clock Tales'), novels ('An Englishwoman's Love Letters'), plays ('Little Plays of St. Francis', 'Victoria Regina'), reminiscences ('The Unexpected Years'), and poetry ('Green Arras', 'Spikenard').

Houssay, Bernardo Alberto (1887–1971), Argentine physiologist, born in Buenos Aires; professor of physiology at University of Buenos Aires 1919–46.

Houston, Charles Hamilton (1895–1950), U.S. lawyer, born in Washington, D.C.; vice-dean, school of law, Howard University 1929–35; special counsel NAACP 1935–40, member national legal aid committee 1940–50; won 1950 Spingarn medal.

Houston, James (born 1921), Canadian artist and author, born in Toronto, Ont.; won Canadian Books of the Year for Children award for 'Tikta'liktak' (1966), for 'The White Archer: an Eskimo Legend' (1968), and for 'River Runners' (1980); also author and illustrator of 'Canadian Eskimo Arts' and 'Eagle Mask' R-111a

Houston, Sam (1793–1863), U.S. soldier and statesman H-307
- Austin's appointment A-765
- Statuary Hall, *table* S-437b
- Texas T-124, *picture* T-123
  - Houston H-311

Houston, Tex., largest city of state; pop. 1,746,375 H-308
- Astrodome T-129
- harbors and ports H-35
- Lyndon B. Johnson Spacecraft Center S-346b, *picture* S-342b
- North America, *map* N-350
- shopping center, *picture* U-109
- synthetic-rubber plants, *picture* [illegible]
- Texas T-119, *picture* T-121
- world, *map* W-297

Houston, University of, Houston, Tex.; state control; founded 1927, became university 1934; arts and sciences, architecture, business administration, education, engineering, law, optometry, pharmacy, social work, and technology; graduate school; ranches at Houston (Clear Lake City) and Victoria H-310

Houston Baptist University, Houston, Tex.; founded 1960, opened 1963; liberal arts, education.

Houston Ship Channel, Houston, Tex. H-309, *picture* H-311
- canals C-129
- Texas T-119, 121

Houston-Tillotson College, Austin, Tex. A-765

Houston toad, amphibian
- endangered species E-212

Houyhnhnms, creatures in 'Gulliver's Travels' S-532

Hove, England, town in Sussex adjoining Brighton; forms part of famous Brighton promenade; pop. 71,190, *map* U-18a

Hovenweep National Monument, in Utah and Colorado C-571, *maps* C-583, U-233

Hovhaness, Alan (born 1911), U.S. composer M-677

Howard, great English family, whose head is the duke of Norfolk, first duke and earl marshal of England, and whose branches hold many other peerages; rose to prominence in Tudor reigns.

Howard, Catherine (1520?–42), 5th queen of Henry VIII of England
- Henry VIII H-131

Howard, John (1726–90), British philanthropist and prison reformer H-312
- prisons P-505d

Howard, John Eager (1752–1827), American Revolutionary War officer, born in Baltimore County, Maryland; fought at Germantown, Monmouth, Cowpens, Eutaw Springs; governor of Maryland 1789–92.

Howard, Leland Ossian (1857–1950), U.S. entomologist, born in Rockford, Ill.; chief, Bureau of Entomology 1894–1927 ('Mosquitoes—How They Live'; 'The Insect Book'; 'The House-Fly—Disease Carrier'; 'Mosquitoes of North America').

Howard, Leslie (1893–1943), British actor, playwright, producer, born in London; stage successes: 'Her Cardboard Lover', 'Berkeley Square', 'Petrified Forest'; in motion pictures after 1930 ('Of Human Bondage', 'Petrified Forest', 'Pygmalion', 'Gone with the Wind').

Howard, Luke (1772–1864), British scientist; invented first generally accepted system of cloud nomenclature C-515

Howard, Oliver Otis (1830–1909), U.S. Civil War general, born in Leeds, Me.; commissioner of Freedmen's Bureau 1866–72; instrumental in establishing Howard University for black Americans, president 1869–73; founded Lincoln Memorial University at Cumberland Gap, Tenn.

Howard, Roy Wilson (1883–1964), U.S. newspaper publisher, born near Cincinnati, Ohio; became first president of United Press 1912; chairman of board, Scripps-Howard Newspapers 1921–36, president 1936–53, chairman executive committee 1953–64.

Howard, Sidney Coe (1891–1939), U.S. playwright, born in Oakland, Calif.; with Paul de Kruif wrote 'Yellow Jack', a play about the fight against yellow fever ('They Knew What They Wanted', won Pulitzer prize 1925; 'The Silver Cord'; 'Half Gods').

Howard of Effingham, Charles Howard, 2nd **baron** (1536–1624), created earl of Nottingham 1596; English lord high admiral; influential with Queen Elizabeth I.

Howard Payne University, until 1975 Howard Payne College, Brownwood, Tex.; affiliated with Southern Baptist convention; founded 1889; arts and sciences, education, music; graduate study.

Howard University, Washington, D.C.; private control; founded 1867; liberal arts, dentistry, education, engineering and architecture, fine arts, law, medicine, nursing, pharmacy, religion, social work; graduate school, *picture* U-208

Howe, Edgar Watson (1853–1937), U.S. author and editor, born in Treaty, Ind.; editor *Atchison* (Kan.) *Daily Globe* 1877–1911, *E.W. Howe's Monthly* after 1911 ('The Story of a Country Town'; 'Plain People').

Howe, Elias (1819–67), U.S. inventor H-312
- garment industry G-35
- Hall of Fame, *table* H-16
- invention I-274, *table* I-273
- Massachusetts M-196
- sewing machine S-123
- shoe industry S-179

Howe, George (1886–1955), U.S. architect, born in Worcester, Mass.; professor of architecture and chairman of department, Yale University 1950–55; modern designs.

Howe, Gordon (nickname Gordie) (born 1928), U.S. ice-hockey player, born in Floral, Sask.; with Detroit Red Wings 1946–71, Houston Aeros 1973–77, New England Whalers 1977–; six-time winner of Hart Trophy for most valuable player and of Art Ross Trophy for leading scorer; in 1977 scored 1000th goal; elected to Hockey Hall of Fame 1972.

Howe, Harold, II (born 1918), U.S. educator, born in Hartford, Conn.; executive director of Learning Institute of North Carolina 1964–65; U.S. commissioner of education 1966–68.

Howe, Joseph (1804–73), Canadian statesman and orator, born in Halifax, N.S.; son of John Howe; premier of Nova Scotia 1860–63; strong opponent of Confederation, but after it was secured accepted position 1867–73 in first Cabinet C-98

Howe, Julia Ward (1819–1910), U.S. writer and reformer, born in New York City; wife of Samuel Gridley Howe; pioneer in woman suffrage movement; first woman to be elected to American Academy of Arts and Letters 1908 ('Sex and Education'; 'Modern Society'; 'Margaret Fuller', biography)
- 'Battle Hymn of the Republic' N-65
- Civil War C-478

Howe, Richard, Earl (1726–99), British admiral, born in London; commanded British sea forces in American Revolution; relieved Gibraltar 1782; gained victory of "glorious first of June" 1794 over French off Ushant.

Howe, Samuel Gridley (1801–76), U.S. pioneer educator and reformer, born in Boston, Mass.; founder and first superintendent of the Perkins Institution for the Blind; founder of the first school in the U.S. for the mentally handicapped.

Howe, Sir William (1729–1814), British general, younger brother of Richard Howe; commander in chief of British land forces in North America 1775–78
- proposes peace, *picture* R-174
- Revolutionary War R-170

Howe, William Henry (1846–1929), U.S. animal painter, born in Ravenna, Ohio; known especially for his landscapes with cattle ('Return of the Herd'; 'Cattle at Rest').

Howell, Clark (1863–1936), U.S. journalist, born in Barnwell County, South Carolina; succeeded Henry W. Grady as managing editor 1889 (editor in chief after 1897) of the *Atlanta Constitution*, which he maintained as one of leading papers of the South; served several terms in Georgia legislature; member of Democratic National Committee 1892–1924, 1936.

Howell, N.J., community situated 5 mi (8 km) n. of Lakewood near w. edge of Monmouth County; pop. of township 25,065.

Howells, John Mead (1868–1959), U.S. architect, born in Cambridge, Mass.; son of William Dean Howells; designer of buildings for Columbia, Harvard, and Yale universities; in association with Raymond M. Hood designed Tribune Tower, Chicago.

Howells, William Dean (1837–1920), U.S. novelist, essayist, and critic H-312
American literature A-351
short story S-184

'How It Is', work by Beckett B-123

Howitt, William (1792–1879), British author, born in Heanor, near Derby; best known for prose and verse written in collaboration with wife, **Mary** (1799–1888), born in Coleford, near Monmouth, England
early Australian literature A-797

Howitzer, a piece of artillery firing at elevations higher than a field gun but lower than a mortar, *picture* A-659

'Howl', work by Ginsberg A-364, G-145

Howland, Sir William Pearce (1811–1907), Canadian politician and businessman; born in Pawling, N.Y.; lieutenant governor of Ontario 1867–73
Fathers of Canadian Confederation C-118, *picture* C-116

Howland Island, a tiny sand and coral island in the Pacific, about 1,900 mi (3,060 km) s.w. of Honolulu; colonized by the U.S. in 1935 as a way station for planes flying from Hawaii to Australia, *map* P-3
world, *map* W-297

Howler monkey
social behavior A-503

Howling dervish. *see in index* Dervish

Howrah, India, industrial city on Hooghly River opposite Calcutta; shipbuilding and repairing, jute milling, food processing; iron and steel products; botanic garden (founded 1786) famed for banyan tree; Bengal Engineering College; pop. 737,877, *map* I-83
Asia, *map* A-697

'How the Grinch Stole Christmas', work by Seuss C-406

'How to Read a Book', work by Adler A-45

Hoxha, Enver (1908–85), Albanian military and political leader, born in Gjinokastër; founded the Albanian Communist party in 1941.

Hoxie, Vinnie Ream (1847–1914), U.S. sculptor, born in Madison, Wis.; commissioned by Congress to make statues of Lincoln and Sequoya (in U.S. Capitol) and Farragut statue in Washington; first woman sculptor to receive a commission from U.S. government.

Hoy (Norse, "high island"), 2nd in size (53 sq mi; 137 sq km) of Orkney Islands; pop. 511.

Hoyle, Edmond (1672–1769), English author of rules of whist and other games; long regarded as authoritative, so that "according to Hoyle" has become a proverbial phrase.

Hoyt, Waite Charles (nickname Schoolboy) (1899–1984), U.S. baseball pitcher, born in Brooklyn, N.Y.; with New York, N.L., 1918, 1932, Boston, A.L., 1919–20, New York, A.L., 1921–30, Detroit, A.L., 1930–31, Philadelphia, A.L., 1931, Brooklyn, N.L., 1932, 1937–38, Pittsburgh, N.L., 1933–37; won 237 games, lost 182; won 23, lost 7 in 1928; in 7 World Series, posted 6–4 record.

Hradec Králové, (German Königgrätz), Czechoslovakia, city in province of Bohemia, 65 mi (105 km) e. of Prague; Sadowa, or Königgrätz, battlefield (1866) in Austro-Prussian War nearby; pop. 57,074.

Hrdlička, Aleš (1869–1943), U.S. anthropologist, born in Humpolec, s.e. Bohemia; authority on American Indians; curator U.S. National Museum; founder *American Journal of Physical Anthropology*.

HRIR (high-resolution infrared radiometer) W-123

Hrolf. *see in index* Rollo

Hrotsvit (or Roswitha) (935?–1000?), nun of the cloister of Gandersheim, first woman writer of German literature G-105

Hrozny, Friedrich (Czech Bedřich Hrozný) (1879–1952), Czech orientalist, born near Prague; placed Hittite language in Indo-European group
Hittites H-178

Hsia Dynasty, in China (2206–1766 BC) C-359

'Hsiao Ching', classic work in Chinese literature C-387

Hsiao Kung, Chinese duke C-385

Hsin Dynasty, in China (AD 9–23) C-362

Hsi-ning. *see in index* Xining

Hsinking, China. *see in index* Changchun

Hsiungnu. *see in index* Huns

Hsüan Tsung, (685–762), emperor of China's T'ang Dynasty C-365

Hsuan T'ung. *see in index* Pu-yi

Hsu Shih-chang (1853–1939), Chinese statesman, elected 1918 president of Chinese republic, resigned 1922.

HTLV (human T-lymphotropic retrovirus), virus
cancer cause C-132

HTST method (high-temperature, short-time method), in pasteurizing milk D-4

HUAC. *see in index* Un-American Activities, House Committee on

Hua Kuo-feng (born 1920?), Chinese political leader, born in Shaanxi Province; chairman Communist party 1976–81; premier 1976–80 J-67

Huambo (formerly Nova Lisboa), Angola, city on plateau 150 mi (240 km) s.e. of Lobito; railroad shops; trade center; pop. 61,885, *map* A-115
world, *map* W-297

Huang Ch'ao (died AD 884), Chinese rebel leader whose uprising so weakened the T'ang Dynasty that it collapsed a few years after the rebellion ended C-365

Huang He (or Hwang Ho, or Yellow River), 2nd longest (2,900 mi; 4,700 km) river in China H-313
Asia, *map* A-697
comparative length. *see in index* River, *table*
flood, *table* F-181
Henan H-127
world, *map* W-297

Huangpu Jiang (or Whang poo), tributary of the Yangtze River
Shanghai's location S-143

Huascarán, Andean mountain, w.-central Peru, highest in country; 22,205 ft (6,770 m), *diagram* S-295, *map* S-298

Huaso, Chilean cowboy, *picture* C-331

Huastec, Indians of s. Mexico along the Gulf of Mexico, said to be an offshoot of Mayan civilization
sculpture, *picture* I-145

Hub, central part of a wheel W-193

Hubay, Jeno (or Eugen Hubay) (1858–1937), Hungarian violinist and composer, born in Budapest; work includes operas ('The Violin Maker of Cremona'; 'Anna Karenina'), concertos, symphonies, songs.

Hubbard, Bernard Rosecrans (1888–1962), Jesuit scientist and lecturer, born in San Francisco, Calif.; professor of geology, University of Santa Clara 1926–62; noted for geological explorations in Alaska ('Mush, You Malamutes!').

Hubbard, Elbert Green (1856–1915), U.S. writer, born in Bloomington, Ill.; founded and edited *The Philistine*, "a magazine of protest"; founded Roycroft Shop, East Aurora, N.Y.; ('Little Journeys'; 'Message to Garcia').

Hubbard, Kin (full name Frank McKinney Hubbard) (1868–1930), U.S. caricaturist and humorous writer, born in Bellefontaine, Ohio; on *Indianapolis News* after 1891 ('Abe Martin's Sayings').

Hubbard, Leonidas, Jr. (1872–1903), U.S. journalist and explorer; with Dillon Wallace in 1903 journeyed 250 mi (400 km) farther in Labrador interior than former white explorers.

Hubbard, Robert Calvin (1900–77), U.S. football tackle and end, born in Keytesville, Mo.; with New York Giants 1927–28, 1936; Green Bay Packers 1929–35; also A.L. baseball umpire 1936–51.

Hubbard squash S-399

Hubbard's Trace, trail in Illinois I-39

Hubbell, Carl Owen (nickname King Carl) (born 1903), U.S. baseball pitcher, born in Carthage, Mo.; with New York, N.L., 1928–43; pitched 10 shutouts and 46 consecutive scoreless innings 1933; became director New York, N.L., farms system 1943 B-92

Hubble, Edwin Powell (1889–1953), U.S. astronomer, born in Marshfield, Mo.; at Mount Wilson Observatory 1919–53; at Mount Wilson and Palomar observatories 1948–53 ('Realm of the Nebulae') U-199, 201

Hubble's constant, in astrophysics C-733

Hubble time, in astrophysics C-733, *chart* C-731

Hubble Space Telescope, orbiting observatory O-458

Hubei (or Hupei, or Hupeh), inland province of China; 72,400 sq mi (187,500 sq km); cap. Wuhan; pop. 54,870,000 H-313

Hubel, David H. (born 1926), American who made discoveries concerning information processing in the visual system. *see in index* Nobel Prizewinners, *table*

Huber, François (1750–1831), Swiss naturalist, born in Geneva; first scientific research on bees.

Huberman, Bronisław (1882–1947), Polish violinist, born in Czestochowa; beginning 1892 had worldwide success as virtuoso; founded Palestine Symphony Orchestra 1935.

Hubert, Saint (died 727), apostle of the Ardennes; bishop of Maestricht and Liège; patron of huntsmen; festival November 3.

Hubertusburg, Peace of (or Peace of Hubertsburg), signed 1763 in château of Hubertusburg in Saxony, Germany, ending Seven Years' War, *table* T-274

Hubert Walter. *see in index* Walter, Hubert

Hucbald (or Hubaldus) (about 840–930), Benedictine monk, writer, and musician, born near Tournai; wrote lives of saints; best known for works on music.

Huch, Ricarda (1864–1947), German poet and novelist, born in Brunswick, Germany; opposed naturalism; ('Defeat', 'Victory', historical romances of Garibald; 'The Deruga Trial').

Huck (or huckaback), toweling of linen or cotton with small woven design; durable and absorbent; used in hotels, institutions, and schools.

'Huckleberry Finn, The Adventures of', Mark Twain's novel about Huckleberry Finn, a reckless boy who runs away from home with Jim, a runaway slave, the two becoming involved in a series of lively incidents connected with slavery troubles before the Civil War R-111e
American literature A-352
creative writing W-380
Twain T-332

HUD. *see in index* Housing and Urban Development, Department of

'Hud' (1963), motion picture, *picture* M-606

Huddersfield, England, manufacturing town 25 mi (40 km) n.e. of Manchester; milling center for wool, cotton, and silk; machinery, dyes, clothing; pop. 130,600, *map* U-18a

Hudibras, hero of mock epic poem ('Hudibras') by Samuel Butler; satire on hypocrisy and intolerance of Puritanism.

Hudson, Henry (1575?–1611), English navigator H-313
exploration E-373
Canada C-93
Hudson Bay H-314
Delaware Bay D-75, P-173
New Jersey N-199
New York N-156, N-279
Albany A-259
Long Island L-297
flag F-153, *picture* F-155
fur traders F-469
Hudson River H-314

Hudson, Manley Ottmer (1886–1960), U.S. jurist, born in St. Peters, Mo.; professor at Harvard University 1919–54; judge of Permanent Court of International Justice 1936–46.

Hudson, William Henry (1841–1922), British naturalist and writer, born in Quilmes, near Buenos Aires; ('The Purple Land', 'Green Mansions', romances; 'Tales of the Pampas', short stories; 'Far Away and Long Ago', autobiography; 'The Book of a Naturalist')
children's literature R-110a
literary contribution E-280

Hudson, Mass., industrial community 5 mi (8 km) n.e. of Marlborough; electronic devices, aircraft parts, footwear; incorporated 1866; pop. of township 16,408.

Hudson, N.H., 3 mi (5 km) n.e. of Nashua; electrical computers, fabrics; incorporated 1746; pop. of township 10,638, *map* N-191

Hudson, N.Y., industrial city on e. bank of Hudson River 28 mi (45 km) s. of Albany; refrigerators, cement, apparel, matches; once important whaling port; pop. 7,986.

Hudson & Manhattan Railroad. *see in index* Port Authority Trans Hudson

Hudson Bay, Canada, vast inland sea H-314. *see also in index* Ocean, *table*
Canada C-93, *map* C-112
Hudson H-314
Manitoba M-100, 103
North America, *map* N-350
river system C-74, *map* U-32
world, *map* W-297

Hudson Bay Lowlands, area bordering the Canadian Shield C-73

Hudsonian godwit, a shorebird. *see in index* Godwit

Hudson River, principal river of New York State, one of chief waterways in U.S. H-314
Albany A-259
basalt deposits B-86
heat pollution P-441d
highway to the west U-51
New Jersey N-193
New York N-246
United States, *map* U-50

Hudson River School, group of U.S. artists who painted romantic landscapes; flourished 1825–70; prominent members included Thomas Cole, Thomas Doughty, Asher B. Durand, and Albert Bierstadt; named for attraction to river area. *see also in index* artists by name

Hudson's Bay Company, trading company in Canada; under British charter 1670–1970; chartered in Canada 1970 C-93, H-314, I-270
British Columbia B-456
Fort Vancouver, *picture* W-53
fur trade F-470
Manitoba M-102
New World's development A-338
Northwest Territory N-388
Oregon country O-586
Idaho I-22
Thompson T-172
Yukon Territory Y-440

Hue, Vietnam, seaport city on Hue River near South China Sea; once capital city; Buddhist shrine dating from 17th century; pop. 209,043 V-323, *map* V-321
Asia, *map* A-697
climate V-318

Hue, color C-560
design D-108
dress design D-269
television T-76

Hue and cry, old English common-law practice of pursuing criminal with "horn and voice" ("hue" from old French verb *huer,* to cry or shout).

Huerta, Victoriano (1854–1916), Mexican general, born in Colotlán; overthrew Madero and made himself president 1913; resigned 1914
Carranza C-175

Mexico M-337
Villa V-325

Hueston Woods State Park, Ohio, *picture* O-511

Hufstedler, Shirley Mount (born 1925), U.S. judge and public official, born in Denver, Colo.; judge Los Angeles County Superior Court 1961–66; justice district court of appeals 1966–68; circuit judge U.S. Court of Appeals 1968–79; United States secretary of education 1979–81
women's rights W-276

Huggins, Charles Brenton (born 1901), U.S. scientist, born in Halifax, N.S.; professor of surgery University of Chicago after 1936, directed cancer research 1951–69.

Huggins, Miller James (1879–1929), U.S. baseball second baseman and manager, born in Cincinnati, Ohio; player with Cincinnati, N.L., 1904–9, St. Louis, N.L., 1910–16 (player-manager 1913–16, manager 1917); as manager New York, A.L., 1918–29, piloted team to 6 A.L. pennants and 3 world championships.

Huggins, Sir William (1824–1910), British astronomer, born in London; pioneer in spectroscopic astronomy ('Atlas of Representative Stellar Spectra').

Hugh, Saint (1024–1109), abbot of Cluny, born in Sémur, France; adviser of several popes; aided in reform of clergy; raised Abbey of Cluny to place of highest importance, amalgamating other monasteries; festival April 29.

Hugh Capet. *see in index* Capet, Hugh

Hughes, Charles Evans (1862–1948), chief justice of the U.S. H-316
Harding H-40
Roosevelt R-290
U.S. Supreme Court, *picture* S-518a

Hughes, David Edward (1831–1900), U.S. inventor, born in London, England; invented printing telegraph, microphone, and induction balance.

Hughes, Dorothy (born 1904), writer
detective story D-119

Hughes, Hatcher (1881–1945), U.S. playwright, born in Polkville, N.C.; long a teacher of English, Columbia University ('Hell-Bent fer Heaven', 1924 Pulitzer prizewinner, folk play of Carolina mountains).

Hughes, Howard (or Howard Robard Hughes) (1905–76), U.S. manufacturer, financier, aviator, and motion-picture producer H-315

Hughes, Hugh Price (1847–1902), U.S. clergyman M-318

Hughes, John Joseph (1797–1864), Roman Catholic prelate, born in County Tyrone, Ireland; bishop of New York 1842–51, archbishop 1851–64.

Hughes, Langston (full name James Langston Hughes) (1902–67), U.S. author H-316
black Americans B-294

Hughes, Richard Arthur Warren (1900–76), Welsh author, born in Surrey, England; ('A High Wind in Jamaica', also known as 'The Innocent Voyage').

Hughes, Rupert (1872–1956), U.S. editor and writer, born in Lancaster, Mo.; his 'George Washington' sought to strip the hero of myth and show him as a human being ('Stately Timber', novel; edited 'Music Lovers' Encyclopedia'); uncle of Howard Hughes.

Hughes, Samuel (1853–1921), Canadian soldier and political leader H-316

Hughes, Ted (full name Edward J. Hughes) (born 1930), English poet; born in Mytholmroyd, England; poet laureate 1984–
poet laureate P-402

Hughes, Thomas (1822–96), British author and social reformer, founder of an experimental cooperative colony at Rugby, Tenn.; born in Uffington, near Abingdon, England; his book 'Tom Brown's School Days' did much to fix ideals of English public schools; also author of 'Tom Brown at Oxford' and 'Life of Alfred the Great'
'Tom Brown's School Days' N-410

Hughes, William Morris (1864–1952), Australian labor and political leader, born in London, England; in Australia from 1884; prime minister 1915–23; government posts 1934–41; leader 1941–43 of United Australian party.

Hugh of Lincoln, Saint (1140?–1200), bishop of Lincoln; born in Avalon, France, of noble family; called to England by Henry II to establish English Carthusian monastery; festival November 17. Another St. Hugh of Lincoln was an English boy said to have been put to death by Jews at Lincoln in the 13th century; festival July 27.

Huginn, Odin's raven in Norse mythology M-704

Hugo, Joseph Léopold Sigisbert (1773–1828), French general, born in Nancy; father of Victor Hugo.

Hugo, Victor (or Victor Marie Hugo) (1802–85), French writer H-316
French literature F-396
Rodin's monument, *picture* R-237

Hugo award, science fiction award S-62

Huguenots, French Protestants of 16th and 17th centuries H-317
Coligny C-546
Florida F-199
Henry VIII H-131
Louis XIII L-305
North American Colonies A-333
oppression M-461
Orléans O-607
Richelieu R-204

'Huguenots, Les', opera by Meyerbeer H-317

Huhehot (or Huhehaote), China, capital of Inner Mongolian Autonomous Region; flour, wool textiles; pop. 320,000.

Hui, a Muslim people of China C-345

Huia bird, A-39

Hui-neng (638–713), sixth great patriarch of Zen Buddhism and founder of the Southern school, which became the dominant school of Zen, born in Guangdong Province, China Z-450

Hui Tsung (1082–1135), Chinese emperor of Sung Dynasty 1101–25; painter, patron of art.

Hukbalahaps (or Huks), Communist-directed members of a Philippine guerrilla army organized during Japanese occupation in World War II; after war kept arms and joined peasant political parties in demanding land; leader, Luis Taruc, surrendered 1954 P-261, 255c, *picture* P-259d

Hula, a Hawaiian art form H-61

Hula Basin, region, Israel
Jordan River J-143

Hülagü Khan (died 1265), Mongol leader, grandson of Genghis Khan, first independent ruler of Persia
conquers Assassin sect A-703
Mongol empire M-534

Hull, Bobby (or Robert Marvin Hull, nickname Golden Jet) Canadian ice-hockey player H-317, *picture* H-194

Hull, Cordell (1871–1955), U.S. statesman, born in Overton (now Pickett) County, Tennessee; member U.S. Congress 1907–21, 1923–31; U.S. senator 1931–33, secretary of state 1933–44; advocate of free trade, instrumental in organizing UN
Roosevelt R-266, *pictures* R-268, 272
World War II W-327

Hull, Isaac (1773–1843), U.S. commodore who gained first U.S. naval victory in War of 1812, born in Huntington (now Shelton), Mass.
commands *Constitution* S-177f, W-31

Hull, John (1624–83), silversmith and merchant; came to U.S. from England 1635, settled in Boston; took leading part in affairs of Massachusetts Bay Colony, became master of the mint 1652.

Hull, William (1753–1825), American Revolutionary War officer, born in Derby, Conn.; general in War of 1812; surrendered Detroit to British 1812; court-martialed and sentenced to be shot but pardoned by President Madison W-31

Hull (officially Kingston-upon-Hull), England, seaport in n.e. on Humber River; exports coal, metals, textiles; fisheries; pop. 292,600, *maps* E-360, U-18a

Hull, Que., industrial city in s.w., on Ottawa River opposite Ottawa, Ont.; pulp and paper, metal products, cement, meat-packing; pop. 63,580, *maps* C-112, Q-9a

Hull, body of a vessel S-170, P-383
boat manufacturing B-325, *diagram* B-327
early development S-164
submarines S-497

Hull House, famous social settlement in Chicago A-40, *picture* D-44
establishment C-318
playground P-125
women's rights W-277

Hull Island, Pacific. *see in index* Phoenix Islands

Human. *see in index* Man

Human behavior. *see in index* Behavior, human

Human body. *see in index* Anatomy, human; Physiology

'Human Comedy, The', name given to a series of novels by Balzac B-50

Human Development Services, Department of, United States U-164

Human engineering, in psychology P-524

Humane Slaughter Act (1958), United States M-253

Humane societies H-318

Human geography, study of Earth as the home of people S-243
sciences S-65

Human growth hormone (HGH), hormone that induces growth H-240

Humanism H-318
Boccaccio B-330
education E-84, 97
French literature F-395
Renaissance R-146

Humanist minuscule (or lettera antiqua), calligraphy C-59

Humanities, a group of disciplines or studies which concern human culture; generally includes the fine arts, philosophy, language, and literature.

Human leukocyte antigen (HLA) I-57

Human resources C-678

Human rights, those rights due all people H-319. *see also in index* Civil rights
citizenship C-438
Holocaust H-205

Human Rights Day U-23

Human society. *see in index* Sociology

Human T-lymphotropic retrovirus. *see in index* HTLV

Humason comet, discovered 1961 by Milton L. Humason at Palomar Observatory, Calif.; period of orbit about 3,000 years.

Humayun (1508–56), Mughal emperor A-220

Humber River, an estuary formed by Trent and Ouse rivers in n.e. England, *map* U-18a

Humber River, Newfoundland N-164

Humbert I (1844–1900), king of Italy, born in Turin; succeeded 1878; called Humbert the Good because of courage and generosity in plague and earthquake; fostered Triple Alliance, inaugurated colonial expansion policy
assassination A-703
Italy I-394

Humbert II (born 1904), king of Italy May 10–June 18, 1946, born in Racconigi, near Turin; son of Victor Emmanuel III, for whom he became regent 1944; left Italy 1946
Italy I-396

Humbert of Silva Candida, Cardinal (1000–61), papal legate and theologian B-536

Humblebee. *see in index* Bumblebee

Humboldt, Alexander von (or Friedrich Wilhelm Karl Heinrich Alexander von Humboldt) (1769–1859), German naturalist and explorer H-321
exploration E-373
geographical study G-69

Humboldt, Karl Wilhelm, baron von (1767–1835), German philologist, statesman, and writer; born in Potsdam; first to define philosophy of speech; brother of Alexander von Humboldt.

Humboldt, Tenn., city in agricultural area 15 mi (25 km) n. of Jackson; chemicals, shoes; incorporated 1866; pop. 10,209.

Humboldt Current. *see in index* Peru Current

Humboldt Lake (or Humboldt Sink), w. Nevada; 20 mi (30 km) long; receives Humboldt River; has no outlet; usually only a marsh N-133

Humboldt River, rises in n.e. Nevada, flows 375 mi (600 km) into Humboldt Lake N-133, *map* U-87

'Humboldt's Gift', novel by Bellow A-362

Humboldt State College, Arcata, Calif.; chartered as state normal school 1913; became state college 1935; arts and sciences, education; graduate study; quarter system.

Hume, David (1711–76), Scottish philosopher and historian H-321
Enlightenment E-289
God G-172
learning and knowledge L-105
philosophy P-266

Hume, Fergus, Australian writer
detective story D-118

Humerus, bone of the upper arm S-210
frog F-406

Humid continental climate, in climate classification C-500

Humidifier, appliance which puts moisture in the air H-212
heating systems H-111

Humidistat, device H-212

Humidity, moisture in air A-123
air conditioning A-150
climate C-496
fan F-23
heating H-111
hobby H-190
home appliances H-212
houseplants H-289
hygrometer H-342
jungle J-154
weather W-120, *table* W-126

Humid subtropical climate, in climate classification C-500

Hummingbird, bird H-322
bird species B-249, *pictures* B-245, 250
Jamaica J-17

Humor H-322. *see also in index* Comedy; Parody; Satire
nonsense rhymes and stories R-101b

Humor, one of the four fluids entering into the constitution of the body M-281

Hump, railway switching R-81, *pictures* R-79

Humpbacked fly, the name for tiny black flies (family Phoridae) with humped thorax and short abdomen; some larvae live as parasites inside wasps, bees, and other insects; some infest mushrooms.

Humpbacked salmon (or pink salmon) S-28

Humpback whale, mammal of the order Cetacea W-185

Humpback whitefish (or lake whitefish), fish *Coregonus clupeaformis* of the family Salmonidae W-195

Humped ox. *see in index* Zebu

Humperdinck, Engelbert (1854–1921), German composer, born in Siegburg, near Bonn, Germany; friend of Wagner, whom he assisted in producing 'Parsifal'; won fame with opera 'Hansel and Gretel'; exerted influence on opera of his time by reviving interest in folk themes; wrote incidental music for many stage productions of Max Reinhardt, including 'The Miracle'. *see also in index* 'Hansel and Gretel'.

Humphrey, Doris (1895–1958), U.S. modern dancer and choreographer, born in Oak Park, Ill.; studied with Ruth St. Denis and Ted Shawn; with Charles Weidman conducted school in New York City;

steel products, oil-field equipment; pop. 46,223.

Huntington's chorea, late-onset hereditary neurological disease arising from progressive degeneration of brain tissue; characterized by muscular spasms, mental deterioration, emotional disturbances; usually fatal; genetic test for detection developed 1983 N-123

Huntington Station, N.Y., community on Long Island, 30 mi (50 km) n.e. of New York City; automobile parts, aircraft instruments, tin containers, surgical supplies; pop. 28,817.

'Hunt of the Unicorn, The', series of tapestry designs T-26

Huntsman, Benjamin (1704–76), British inventor of cast steel and steel manufacturer, born in Lincolnshire S-148
  metal and metallurgy M-309

Huntsville, Ala., city 85 mi (140 km) n. of Birmingham; missile and space research center; farming and stock raising; rockets, missiles and components, textiles, shoes, heaters and stoves, farm implements, electronic equipment; branch of University of Alabama; Oakwood College; Alabama Agricultural and Mechanical College nearby; pop. 142,513 A-225, *map* U-41

Huntsville, Tex., city 70 mi (110 km) n. of Houston; cotton, lumber, and dairy products; state penitentiary; Sam Houston State University; historic home of Sam Houston; pop. 23,936.

Hunyadi, János (or János Hunyady) (1387?–1456), Hungarian hero, born in Transylvania; father of Matthias I, Hunyadi; by his defense of Belgrade against the Turks in 1456 made Hungary independent for 70 years H-329

Hunza, a feudal state in n.w. Kashmir (occupied by Pakistan); area about 3,900 sq mi (10,100 sq km); on old trade route into China.

Hupa, Indian tribe of Athapascan linguistic culture in n. California, noted for fine basketry and elaborate costumes, *picture* I-132
  mythology M-697

Hupeh, China. *see in index* Hubei

Hupei, China. *see in index* Hubei

Hura. *see in index* Sandbox tree

Hural, legislative body in Mongolia M-537

Hurd, Peter (1904–84), U.S. painter, born in Roswell, N.M.; studied with N.C. Wyeth and married his daughter Henriette, also a painter; especially noted for scenes of American Southwest.

Hurdles, in hurdling T-244

Hurdling, racing on foot over short distances in which ten hurdles, or light movable fences, have been placed; competitor disqualified if three or more hurdles are upset, or if he or she trails a leg or foot alongside any hurdle T-244

Hurley, Patrick Jay (1883–1963), U.S. lawyer, statesman, and U.S. Army officer; born in Choctaw Nation in present state of Oklahoma; son of Irish immigrant parents; attorney for Choctaw Nation 1912–17; served in World War I; helped organize U.S. Chamber of Commerce 1912; U.S. secretary of war 1929–33; first U.S. minister to New Zealand 1942–43; F.D. Roosevelt's representative in Middle East 1943, made ambassador to China Nov. 1944; resigned Nov. 1945.

Huron (or Wyandot), a tribe of Iroquoian Indians originally living in Ontario along Georgian Bay; driven into upper peninsula of Michigan; later into lower peninsula and Ohio; now live in Quebec, *map* I-136, *table* I-138
  Champlain C-91, C-269
  Montreal M-572
  Ontario O-553

Huron, S.D., city about 110 mi (180 km) e. of Pierre; distributing center for grain; stock-raising area; meat-packing; Huron College; state fair; pop. 13,000, *maps* S-335, 323, U-40

Huron, Lake, 2nd largest of the Great Lakes; area 23,000 sq mi (59,600 sq km) H-333
  canals
    Sault Sainte Marie. *see in index* Sault Sainte Marie canals
  Great Lakes G-243, *map* G-254
  Michigan M-354
  North America, *map* N-350
  size, comparative. *see in index* Lake, *table*

Huron College (originally Pierre University), Huron, S.D.; affiliated with United Presbyterian church in the U.S.A.; founded 1883 in Pierre; name and location changed 1898; arts and sciences, education, and music.

Hurrians, a people of Babylonia about 1500 BC B-8
  writing W-371

Hurricane (or tropical cyclone). *see also in index* Typhoon
  Atlantic Ocean A-744
  earth E-29
  flood cause F-180
  Gulf of Mexico M-345
  Latin America L-60
  storms S-457, *diagrams* S-458
  warning signal, *picture* S-194b
  weather W-121
  West Indies W-156
  wind W-225

Hurricane, British military aircraft W-333

Hurst, Fannie (or Mrs. Jacques S. Danielson) (1889–1968), U.S. author, born in Hamilton, Ohio; worked in New York as actress, shopgirl, waitress; first won success with short stories, particularly of Jewish life in America; later wrote novels ('Lummox'; 'A President Is Born'; 'Five and Ten'; 'Hands of Veronica') and plays ('Humoresque'; 'Land of the Free'); autobiography, 'Anatomy of Me'.

Hurst, Tex., city just n.e. of Fort Worth, close to Haltom City; aircraft, dress manufacturing, electronics; pop. 31,420.

Hurston, Zora Neale (1901–60), U.S. writer, born in Eatonville, Fla.; vivid stories of black American life ('Jonah's Gourd Vine'; 'Mules and Men'; 'Moses, Man of the Mountain'); studied voodoo rites in the West Indies, on Guggenheim Fellowship ('Tell My Horse'; 'Dust Tracks on a Road', autobiography).

Hus, Jan (1369?–1415), Bohemian religious reformer and martyr H-334
  Bohemian history B-331
  Czech history C-815
  Moravians M-581

Husák, Gustav, (born 1913), president of Czechoslovakia
  Czechoslovakia C-816

Husam ad-Din Chelebi, Islamic mystic
  Jalal ud-Din Rumi J-17

Husein. *see in index* Hasan and Husein

Hu Shih (1891–1962), Chinese philosopher and writer H-334
  Chinese literature C-390

Huskies, sled dogs of the North. *see in index* Siberian Husky

Husking bee
  pioneer life P-335a

Husky, Operation, World War II campaign W-339

Hussar, light-horse cavalryman; type originated in Hungary in 1458; from Magyar word *husz*, "twenty," because in levying troops one out of every 20 men was taken.

Hussein (in full Hussein ibn Talal) (born 1935), King of Jordan H-334

Hussein, Taha (1889–1973), Egyptian educator, scholar, and writer, born in Maghagha, Upper Egypt; blind from childhood; minister of education 1950–52; known as champion of free education for children of Egypt, autobiography, 'The Stream of Days'.

Hussein at-Takriti, Saddam (born 1937), Iraqi leader, born in Takrit, Iraq; president of Iraq 1979–
  Iraq I-316

Hussein ibn-Ali (1856–1931), first king of Hejaz and recognized by Muslims as descendant of Mohammed; for services with British during World War I, made king of Hejaz 1916; caliph 1924; six months later overthrown; retired to Cyprus; succeeded by his son **Ali ibn-Hussein** (1878–1935), who ruled until 1925. His second son, **Abdullah,** became king of Jordan and his third son, **Faisal,** king of Iraq. *see also in index* Abdullah ibn-Hussein; Faisal I

Husserl, Edmund (1859–1938), German philosopher, born in Prossnitz, Moravia; father of phenomenology; greatly influenced philosophy and psychology; professor University of Göttingen 1901–16, Freiburg in Breisgau 1916–28 ('Philosophy of Arithmetic'; 'Logical Investigations').

Hussey, Obed (1792–1860), U.S. inventor, born in Maine; sailor in early life; invented corn grinder, sugarcane crusher, and machine for making pins; rival of Cyrus H. McCormick as inventor and manufacturer of the reaper
  McCormick M-5

Husson College, Bangor, Me.; private control; founded 1898; liberal arts, business, education.

Huston, John (1906–87), U.S. film director, writer, and actor, born in Nevada, Mo.; with Warner Bros. and Metro-Goldwyn-Mayer (director: 'Key Largo'; 'The Treasure of Sierra Madre', won 1948 Academy award; 'Moby Dick'; 'The Night of the Iguana'; 'The African Queen'; 'Fat City'; 'Under the Volcano'; actor: 'The Cardinal', 'Chinatown').

Huston, Walter (1884–1950), U.S. actor, born in Toronto, Ont.; stage successes include 'Desire Under the Elms' and 'Dodsworth'; won 1948 Academy award for best supporting role in movie 'The Treasure of Sierra Madre' directed by his son John Huston.

Huston-Tillotson College, Austin, Tex.; interdenominational Protestant; formed 1952 by merger of Tillotson College (opened 1876) and Samuel Huston College (founded 1900); liberal arts, education.

Hut, in housing, *picture* O-470

Hutchins, Robert M. (in full Robert Maynard Hutchins) (1899–1977), U.S. educator H-335

Hutchinson, Anne (formerly Anne Marbury) (1591–1643), U.S. religious leader H-335
  Massachusetts' Puritans M-194

Hutchinson, Arthur Stuart-Menteth (1879–1971), British novelist, born in India ('Once Aboard the Lugger'; 'The Happy Warrior'; 'If Winter Comes'; 'This Freedom'; 'One Increasing Purpose').

Hutchinson, Thomas (1711–80), Tory governor of province of Massachusetts and historian, born in Boston, Mass. ('History of the Colony of Massachusetts Bay').

Hutchinson, Kan., city on Arkansas River about 40 mi (60 km) n.w. of Wichita; wheat, oil, salt, farm machinery, food and metal products, printing; state reformatory; Kansas State Fair; pop. 40,284, *map* U-40
  North America, *map* N-350

Hutchinson Family, early U.S. singing group M-683

Hutson, Donald (born 1913), U.S. football end, born in Pine Bluff, Ark.; played for Green Bay Packers 1935–45.

Hutson family
  heraldic shield, *picture* H-136

Hutten, Ulrich von (1488–1523), German humanist reformer, poet, and satirical writer; born near Fulda, Germany; author of notable Latin verse; member of Luther's party in Protestant Reformation.

Hutterian Brethren (or Hutterites), a Christian sect like the Mennonites except for their belief in the common ownership of things; name comes from Jacob Hutter, an Anabaptist minister who was burned at the stake in Innsbruck 1536; followers flourished in Moravia, fled to Russia 18th century, went to South Dakota 1874; use the German language, believe in nonviolence, live chiefly in rural areas
  communal living C-605
  Mennonites M-299

Hutton, James (1726–97), Scottish landowner and geologist H-336

Hutu (or Bahutu), a people of Africa R-366a

Huxley, Aldous Leonard (1894–1963), British writer, born in Godalming, England; grandson of Thomas H., brother of Julian, nephew of Mrs. Humphry Ward, grandnephew of Matthew Arnold; earlier works brilliantly satirical, later ones show mystical trend; wrote novels ('Antic Hay'; 'Point Counter Point'; 'Brave New World'; 'Eyeless in Gaza'; 'Time Must Have a Stop'; 'Brave New World Revisited'); essays ('On the Margin'; 'Jesting Pilate'; 'Themes and Variations'); and poems ('Leda'; 'Literature and Science'; in U.S. after 1937
  literary contribution E-281
  science fiction S-62
  utopia U-235
  young adult literature R-112c

Huxley, Andrew Fielding (born 1917), British physiologist, born in London; half brother of Aldous and Julian Huxley; professor of physiology University College, London, 1960.

Huxley, Sir Julian Sorell (1887–1975), British biologist and writer, born in London; brother of Aldous; director general UNESCO 1946–48 ('Evolution, the Modern Synthesis'; 'On Living in a Revolution'; 'UNESCO'; 'From an Antique Land'; 'The Wonderful World of Life'; 'The Humanist Frame').

Huxley, Thomas Henry (1825–95), British biologist and essayist H-336

Huygens, Christian (or Christiaan Huygens) (1629–95), Dutch mathematician, astronomer, and physicist H-336
  light theories L-199
  mathematics M-215
  pendulum clock P-160
  watch and clock W-78
  telescope T-68
  wave theory of light P-306

Huygens, Sir Constantijn (1596–1687), Dutch poet, one of ablest in Dutch language; born in The Hague; sent to Venice and twice to London on diplomatic missions; knighted by James I; father of Christian Huygens; friend of John Donne.

Huysmans, Joris Karl (1848–1907), French realistic novelist, born in Paris; a master of psychological analysis ('A rebours'; 'En route'; 'La Cathédrale'; 'En Ménage'; 'La-bas').

Huysum, Jan van (1682–1749), Dutch painter
  floral display, *picture* F-230

Hwang Chioi (1522–65), Korean poet K-293

Hwange National Park (formerly called Wankie National Park), Zimbabwe N-26, Z-452

Hwang Ho, river in China. *see in index* Huang He

HWR. *see in index* Heavy water reactor

Hyacinth (or jacinth), a gemstone J-115

Hyacinth, plant of the lily family with flowers clustered into spikes
  growing conditions G-25

Hyacinth bean, a stout twining annual garden plant *Dolichos lablab* of the family Leguminosae; large deltoid-ovate leaflets; profusion of purple flowers and pods.

Hyacinthe, Père. *see in index* Loyson, Charles

Hyacinthus, in Greek mythology, beautiful youth loved by Apollo; important Spartan festival of early summer, Hyacinthia, held in his honor.

Hyades, a V-shaped group of stars contained in the constellation Taurus; includes bright red star Aldebaran, *chart* S-423

Hyaline membrane disease, a disorder of some prematurely-born infants D-177

chewing and sucking; includes bees, wasps, ants, sawflies, and ichneumon flies
ants A-468
bees B-129
wasp, *picture* W-72

Hymettus, Mount, peak of Attica, bounding Athenian plain on s.e., about 3 mi (5 km) s. of Athens; 3,370 ft (1,030 m); marble quarries; famous for honey in ancient times.

Hymn, song of praise to God or gods
Hinduism H-156
spirituals F-266
Wesley W-149

'Hymns', work by Stockhausen S-448

Hyndman, Henry Mayers (1842–1921), British socialist, born in London; founded the Social Democratic Federation in United Kingdom; defended free institutions, particularly in Ireland and India.

Hyndman Peak, a mountain peak in s. Custer County, in s.-central Idaho (12,078 ft; 3,681 m); highest of Pioneer Mountains; n.e. of Sun Valley.

Hyogo, Japan
Kobe incorporation K-266

Hyogo Prefecture, Japan
Kobe K-266

Hyoid bone, a small U-shaped bone in the base of the tongue, attached by ligaments to temporal bone, and serves as attachment for muscles used in swallowing S-210

Hyoscine. *see in index* Scopolamine

Hypatia (AD 370?–415), Greek mathematician and philosopher famed for her beauty and wisdom; head of Neoplatonic school at Alexandria; murdered by Christian mob
'Hypatia' by Charles Kingsley K-247

Hyperbola, a plane curve so drawn that any point on it is distant from two fixed points, called foci, by a difference which is constant for all points. *see also in index* Conic sections
Apollonius of Perga A-506
geometry G-77
mathematics M-214

Hyperbole, in language F-81

Hyperbolic geometry. *see in index* Saddle geometry

Hyperboreans, in Greek mythology, a "blameless" people dwelling in a land beyond the north wind, a paradise of perpetual youth; connected with worship of Apollo.

Hypergolic ignition F-94

Hyperinflation I-198

Hyperinsulinism, pancreatic disorder H-242

Hyperion, in Greek mythology, a Titan, father of Helios the sun-god; later, sometimes the sun-god himself M-700

'Hyperion', work by Hölderlin H-201

Hypermetamorphosis, the type of development in some insects in which the larva undergoes more than one transformation before becoming a pupa
larva stages B-141

Hypermetropia. *see in index* Farsightedness

Hypermnesia, heightened memory M-295

Hyperon, atomic particle
nuclear physics N-432

Hyperplasia, mechanism by which animals adjust to loss of organ or tissue G-292

Hypertension (or high blood pressure), abnormal elevation of blood pressure D-174
circulatory system disorder C-422
health hazard H-86
heart H-98

Hyperthermia (or heat treatment), cancer treatment C-135

Hyperthyroidism, overactive thyroid gland H-242
metabolism M-306

Hypertonic, in osmosis O-610

Hypertrophy, increase in size of individual cells and fibers D-176, G-292

Hyphae, strings of filament M-519

Hyphasis, river in Punjab. *see in index* Beas

Hyphen, in punctuation P-534

Hypnos, in Greek mythology, god of sleep M-701

Hypnosis H-343
anesthetic use A-412
drugs N-19
memory M-295

Hypo. *see in index* Sodium thiosulfate

Hypocaust, furnace used by Romans S-483, S-157

Hypochondriasis, a mental illness M-301

Hypochondroplastic dwarfism D-294

Hypodermic needle N-19

Hypoglycemia, a condition caused by a low level of blood sugar D-180

Hypogynous flower F-218

Hypomere, lateral or lower mesodermal plate
embryology E-200, *chart* E-202, *diagram* E-202

Hypophysis. *see in index* Pituitary gland

Hyposulfite of sodium, a salt of sodium and hyposulfurous acid ($Na_2S_2O_4$); often confused with sodium thiosulfate, the photographer's hypo.

Hypothalamus, in brain's anatomy B-400, *diagram* B-399
glandular secretion G-153
hormones H-240, *diagram* H-243
thermoregulation B-207

Hypothermia, subnormal temperature of the body
first aid F-121

Hypothesis S-59c

Hypothyroidism, underactive thyroid gland H-242
metabolism M-306

Hypotonic, in osmosis O-610

Hypoxia, lack of oxygen A-81, S-346

Hypsometric map (or layer-tint map) M-120

Hyracoidea, the order of Hyraxes, or Old World conies, *table* M-80. *see also in index* Hyrax

Hyrax (or cony), a small rabbitlike mammal found in Africa and Near East; most of them live in rocky crevices, a few in trees; teeth and hooflike feet relate them to the elephant; comprise order Hyracoidea, *picture* A-436

Hyrcanus I, John (died 105? BC), high priest of Jews; under his rule Judea gained tremendously in power and independence, completing an advantageous alliance with Rome and conquering Syrians and Samaritans; was member of Maccabees, noted family of Jewish patriots.

Hyrcanus II (died 30 BC), high priest of Jews, grandson of John Hyrcanus I; ruled at intervals from 69 to 40 BC; incompetent ruler; finally put to death for treason.

Hyslop, James Hervey (1854–1920), U.S. psychologist and philosopher, born in Xenia, Ohio; professor of logic and ethics at Columbia University 1895–1902; editor, *Journal of American Society for Psychical Research*.

Hyson, a green tea T-45

Hyssop, a perennial garden herb *Hyssopus officinalis* of the mint family with spikes of small blue flowers; tea made from leaves formerly used in treatment of various pulmonary diseases. The hyssop referred to in the Bible, used for sprinkling purposes, is a different plant, probably a tropical member of pokeweed family.

Hysteria P-518

Hysterical amnesia (or dissociation), loss of memory from stress A-373
memory M-295

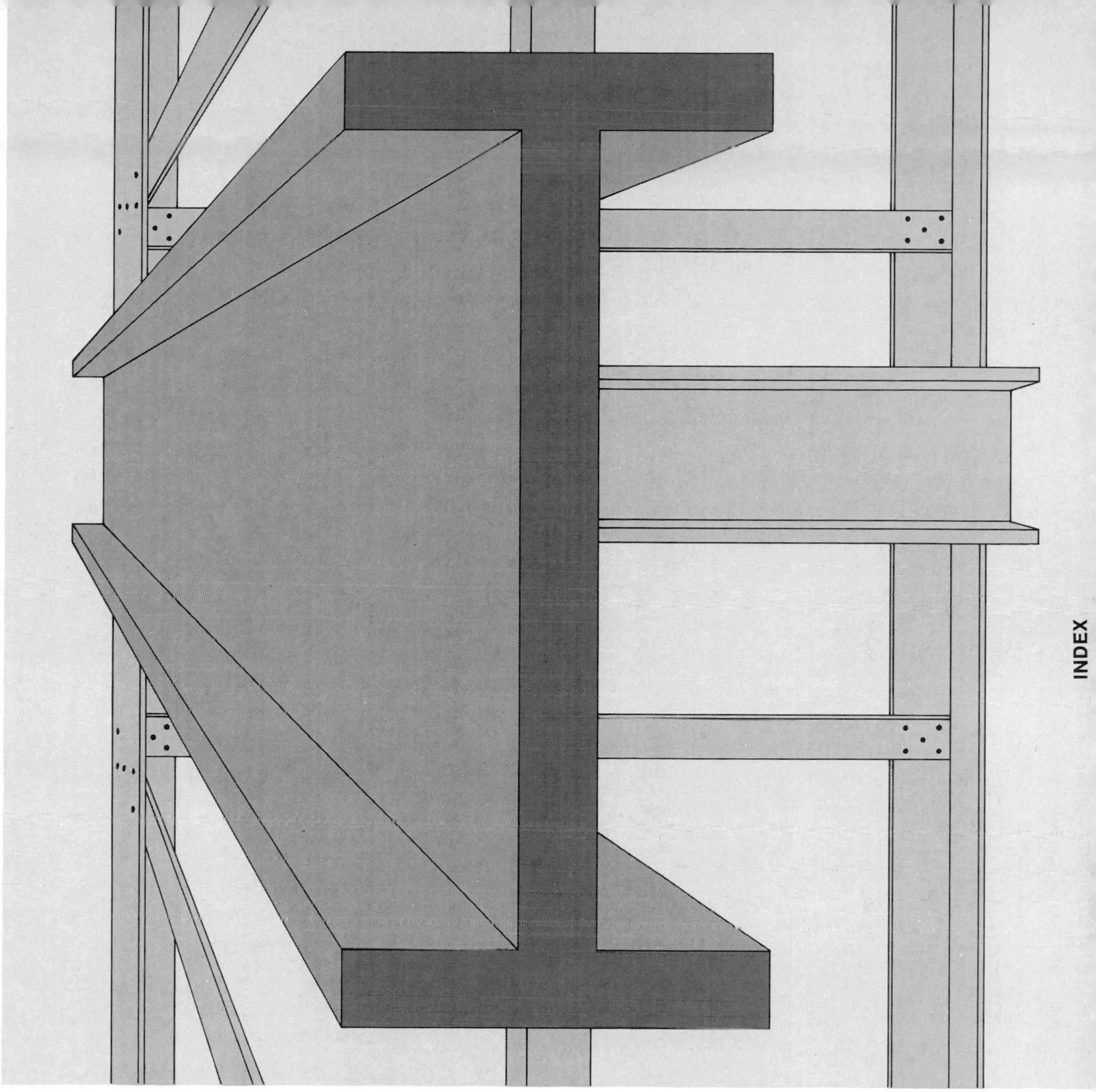

The letter I

probably started as a picture sign of a hand, as in Egyptian hieroglyphic writing (1) and in a very early Semitic writing used about 1500 B.C. on the Sinai Peninsula (2). About 1000 B.C., in Byblos and other Phoenician and Canaanite centers, the sign was given a linear form (3), the source of all later forms. In the Semitic languages the sign was called *yodh* or *yadh,* meaning "hand." It stood for the consonantal sound "y" (as in the English word "yes").

The Greeks renamed the sign *iota* and gave it the vocalic value of the English "i." They also simplified it into a single stroke (4).

The Romans took this sign over into Latin. From Latin the capital letter came into English unchanged.

The English small handwritten or printed "i" is the same sign as the capital except for a bottom curve and for a dot. The dot was added in medieval times to distinguish the letter from similar ones, such as a hastily written small "c."

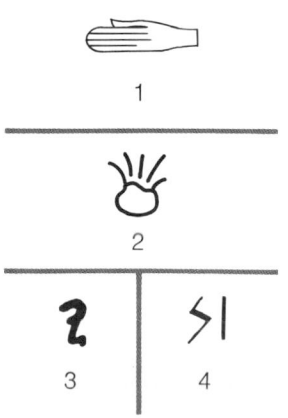

1

2

3

4

IAAF (International Amateur Athletic Federation)
athletic games' regulations A-739
Iacocca, Lee (born 1920), U.S. businessman A-856
IAEA. *see in index* International Atomic Energy Agency
'I am a Cat' (1906), work by Natsume N-67
Iambic meter, in poetry P-405
'I am Curious Yellow' (1969), motion picture by Sjöman M-629
'I and My Village', painting by Chagall P-60, *picture* P-58
'I and Thou' (or 'Ich und Du'), book by Buber B-473
IAPP (International Amateur/ Professional Photoelectric Photometry) A-731
Iasi (or Jassy), Romania, trade center for Iasi district; pop. 160,889, *map* E-360
IATA. *see in index* International Air Transport Association
IBA (Independent Broadcasting Company) E-237
Ibadan, Nigeria; pop. 2,500,000 I-2, *map* A-115
Ibadan, University of, in Ibadan, Nigeria I-2
Ibagué (or San Bonifacio de Ibagué), Colombia, city 75 mi (120 km) w. of Bogotá; coffee, yucca, sugar; founded in 1550; pop. 178,821, *map* S-298
Iberia, ancient district between Caucasus Mts. and Armenia, now part of Georgian Soviet Socialist Republic; also ancient name of Spain, *map* P-212
Iberian Peninsula, in s.w. Europe I-2
Portugal P-454
Spain S-349, *map* S-350
Iberians, ancient people S-353
Iberian Peninsula I-2
Ibert, Jacques (1890–1962), French composer, born in Paris; director French Academy in Rome 1937–61; known for colorful orchestral compositions.
Iberville, Pierre (1661–1706), French-Canadian explorer I-3
Bienville B-190
Canada C-93
Mississippi M-472
Ibex, Alpine goat *Capra ibex* A-319, G-171, *picture* G-170
IBF (International Boxing Federation) B-392
Ibis, a wading bird of the family Threskiornithidae I-3
hibiscus H-149
wood ibis S-456
Ibiza. *see in index* Iviza
IBM. *see in index* International Business Machines Corporation
Ibn Battutah (1304–68?), Arabian traveler and author I-4
Islamic literature I-366
travels T-268
Ibn Gabirol (full name Solomon ben Yehuda ibn Gabirol) (1021?–58?), Hebrew author and philosopher I-4
Ibn Khaldun (1332–1406), Arab historian and sociologist I-4
history writing H-172
Islamic literature I-367
Ibn Saud (1880?–1953), king of Saudi Arabia I-4
Arabian history A-523
conquest of Jiddah J-117
Kuwait K-311
Saudi Arabia S-52b
Ibn Sina. *see in index* Avicenna
Ibo, a people of w. Africa, along lower Niger River
Nigeria N-311
Ibo Ekpe, a people of Africa mask, *picture* M-186
Ibounzi, Mount, mountain in Gabon G-2
Ibrahim Pasha (1789–1848), Egyptian general and viceroy; commander (1826–28) in Greek war for independence.
Ibsen, Henrik (1828–1906), Norwegian dramatist I-5
drama D-245
folklore F-259, 262
influence on American drama A-356
Munch M-651
Norway N-391
ICAO. *see in index* International Civil Aviation Organization
Icaria, Greek island in Aegean Sea. *see in index* Ikaria
Icarus, son of Daedalus, *picture* A-199
astronomy A-716
Daedalus D-2
ICBM. *see in index* Intercontinental ballistic missile
Ice I-5. *see also in index* Snow
Antarctica A-472
Arctic Ocean A-570
clouds C-515
comets A-716, C-596
glacier formation G-150
refrigeration R-135
water W-84, *diagram* W-85
Ice Age. *see in index* Pleistocene epoch
Iceberg I-10
Antarctic A-472
Arctic A-570
Baffin Bay B-18
Titanic S-177d
Ice blink, peculiar whiteness of an iceberg at night I-10
Iceboating (or ice yachting) I-11, W-244
'Ice-Break, The', opera by Tippett O-569
Icebreaker, ship S-169
U.S.S.R. R-207, R-332, S-170
Ice cap. *see also in index* Ice sheet
Ice Age formation I-6, *map* I-8
Mars P-352
Ice cave, type of cave C-234
Ice cream I-11
milk M-415
Ice hockey. *see in index* Hockey, ice
Iceland, island republic of n. Atlantic; area 39,768 sq mi (103,000 sq km); cap., on s.w. coast, Reykjavík; pop. 235,000 I-13
Europe, *map* E-360
flag, *picture* F-165
illiteracy P-450
liquor laws P-507
national anthem, *table* N-64
polar exploration, *map* P-417
world, *map* W-297
World War II W-326
Iceland, University of, in Reykjavík I-15
Icelandic language I-14
Germanic languages G-103
Old English resemblance E-260
Icelandic literature I-15
Scandinavia S-52g
storytelling S-471, *list* S-481a
Iceland poppy, perennial plant *Papaver nudicaule* of the poppy family, native to Arctic regions; thick cluster of white, hairy leaves; flowers with yellow, white, orange, or scarlet petals.
Iceland spar. *see in index* Calcite
Ice milk
ice cream I-11
milk M-415
Ice plant, a flowering annual growing conditions G-24
Ice sculpture, *pictures* F-248, O-615
Ice sheet, a broad glacier of irregular shape G-150. *see also in index* Ice cap
Antarctica A-472
Ice Age I-6, *maps* I-7, 8
Ice skating. *see in index* Skates and skating, *subhead* ice skating
Ice slide, Soviet amusement A-383
Ice yachting. *see in index* Iceboating
'I Ching' (Book of Changes), book on divination and fortune-telling; one of Confucian Classics C-386
yin and yang Y-420
Ichneumon fly, insect I-16
Ichthyology. *see in index* Fish
Ichthyornis, prehistoric toothed, tern-sized seabird B-275
Ichthyosaur, prehistoric aquatic reptile R-155, *picture* R-154
animal life record, *table* E-24
evolution A-462
Ichthyosaur Paleontologic State Monument N-136
Ichthyostega, genus of extinct amphibian A-379
'Ich und Du' (or 'I and Thou'), book by Buber B-473
Icing, formation of ice on the wings of an aircraft A-888
Ickes, Harold Le Claire (1874–1952), U.S. lawyer and political leader, born in Blair County, Pa.; U.S. Secretary of the Interior 1933–46; administrator of public works 1933–39; ('The New Democracy'; 'Fightin' Oil'; 'Autobiography of a Curmudgeon'; 'The Secret Diary of Harold L. Ickes') R-268, *picture* R-272
Ickornshaw, viscount of. *see in index* Snowden, Philip
Icolmkill. *see in index* Iona
Icon (or ikon, or eikon), an image; in Eastern Orthodox church, a venerated mosaic or painting of sacred figures B-535
Moscow's Kremlin K-304
Russian folk art F-253
Iconium, Turkey. *see in index* Konya
Iconoscope, a camera tube T-79
Iconostasis, screen, or wall, in interiors of Eastern Orthodox churches E-43
ICSH. *see in index* Interstitial cell-stimulating hormone
Icteridae, family of birds, including blackbirds, orioles, meadowlarks, bobolinks, grackles, and cowbirds
bobolink B-330
Ictinus (5th century BC), Greek architect; with Callicrates, chief designer of the Parthenon at Athens A-547, *picture* A-546
ICU. *see in index* Intensive care unit
Ida, in Norse mythology M-703
IDA. *see in index* International Development Association
Idaho (nickname Gem State, or Gem of the Mountains), one of the n.w. states of U.S.; area 83,557 sq mi (216,412 sq km); cap. Boise; pop. 943,935 I-17
admission to Union S-429d
Boise B-332
flag, *picture* F-159
North America, *map* N-350
Rocky Mountains R-234, *picture* S-427
state flower S-550
Statuary Hall, *table* S-437a
taxation, *tables* T-37, 39
Idaho, The College of, in Caldwell, Idaho; affiliated with United Presbyterian Church in the U.S.A.; founded 1891; arts and sciences, education; graduate studies.
Idaho, University of, in Moscow, Idaho; state control; opened 1892; liberal arts and sciences, agriculture, business administration, education, engineering, forestry, law, mining; graduate school, *picture* I-25
Idaho Falls, Idaho, city on Snake River 48 mi (77 km) n.e. of Pocatello; market for grain, livestock; potato products, beet sugar, lumber products; pop. 39,590, *map* I-30
Idaho Springs, Colo., mining and resort city about 38 mi (61 km) w. of Denver; hot mineral springs; experimental mine of Colorado School of Mines; pop 2,077
gold mine, *picture* U-82
Idaho State University, in Pocatello, Idaho; established 1947 (founded as academy 1901); liberal arts, business administration, education, medical arts, pharmacy, trade and industrial education; graduate studies.
IDB. *see in index* Inter-American Development Bank
Idea, in psychology S-109
learning L-105
Idealism, in philosophy P-263, 266, *list* P-265
Ideal machines, law of, in mechanics M-267
'Idea of a University', work by Newman N-212
Idée fixe, in music M-673
Identical twins (or monozygotic twins) M-649
tissue compatibility S-519c
Identification of persons
fingerprints, *picture* P-429
handwriting H-30
passport requirement P-137
police P-427
Identity, in mathematics
trigonometry T-286
Ideography, picture writing in which pictures represent ideas W-370. *see also in index* Hieroglyphics; Picture writing
communication C-614
mechanical drawing M-262
Ideology, body of doctrine or pattern of related ideas typical of an individual or group, usually pertaining to a social or political program; in philosophy, the study of ideas
totalitarianism T-235
Ides, Roman calendar, name given to the 15th day of March, May, July, and October, and to the 13th day of all other months
Caesar C-15
Idfu, Egypt. *see in index* Edfu
Idiom, expression to which usage has given a special meaning as "catch cold"; also language identified with certain historic period, a specific region, or a class of people F-82
Idiophone. *see in index* Percussion instruments
'Idiot, The', novel (1868–69) by Dostoevski D-233, R-360a
'Idler', magazine M-32
'Idomeneo', opera by Mozart M-643
opera O-564
Idrisi, al- (1100–65?), Arabian geographer I-32
Islamic literature I-366
IDSA (Industrial Designers Society of America)
industrial design I-172
Idu, Korean writing K-292
Idumaea. *see in index* Edom
Iduna, apples of, in Norse mythology A-509
Idyll (or idyl), originally a short poem presenting simple scenes of pastoral or rustic life; extended to include any descriptive or narrative poem of elevated and artistic style.

'Idylls of the King', work by Tennyson T-109
  English literature E-275

IFAPA (International Federation of Airline Pilots' Associations) A-168

'If Beale Street Could Talk', work by Baldwin A-362

IFC. *see in index* International Finance Corporation

Ifni, former Spanish province on s.w. coast of Morocco; 579 sq mi (1,500 sq km); ceded to Morocco 1969; pop. 49,889 M-586

IFR. *see in index* Instrument Flight Rules

Ifriqiyah. *see in index* Tunisia

Ifugaos, a people of the Philippines P-257c, *picture* P-257b

'If We Must Die', poem by McKay B-294

Igloo, Eskimo dwelling E-300, S-156, S-228, *picture* S-155
  Arctic regions A-572

Ignatius, Saint, bishop of Antioch, Apostolic Father; legend says he was disciple of the Apostle John and was martyred in Rome; famed for epistles to various congregations (about 110–117); festival Feb. 1
  Xavier X-402

Ignatius, Paul Robert (born 1920), U.S. government official, born in Los Angeles, Calif.; secretary of the Navy 1967–69; president *Washington Post* 1969–71; president Air Transportation Association 1972–.

Ignatius of Loyola. *see in index* Loyola, Saint Ignatius of

Igneous rock R-228, *picture* R-229a, *chart* R-229. *see also in index* Basalt; Feldspar; Granite; Lava; Magma
  basalt B-86
  Canadian mining C-84
  clay C-488
  earth E-20, 33, *picture* E-21
  geology G-72
  minerals M-437
  moon M-576
  oceanography O-480

Ignition, of automobile engine A-847

Ignition point (or kindling point) F-93, F-102

Igorots, a people of the Philippines; term also used popularly to include all non-Christian tribes in n. Luzon P-253b

Iguaçu Falls. *see in index* Iguazu Falls

Iguaçu National Park, park in Brazil B-424

Iguaçu River, river in s. Brazil; rises near Atlantic, flows w. 800 mi (1,290 km) to Paraná River, *map* B-425

Iguana, reptile I-32
  Galápagos Islands G-4
  lizard L-272, *picture* L-273

Iguanidae, family of reptiles
  lizard classification L-274

Iguazu Falls (or Iguaçu Falls), waterfalls in South America I-32
  Argentina A-576, *picture* A-578, *map* A-585
  South America, *picture* S-281
  waterfall W-98

I.G.Y. *see in index* International Geophysical Year

Ihara, Saikaku (1642–93), Japanese writer J-49, J-81

'I Have a Dream', address by King K-245

I Ho Ch'uan (or Righteous and Harmonious Fists), Chinese rebels
  Boxer Rebellion B-387

IHS, symbol contracted from the Greek name for Jesus; often erroneously believed to stand for 'Iesus Hominum Salvator' ('Jesus, Saviour of men'), or for motto of Constantine I, 'In hoc signo vinces' ('in this sign thou shalt conquer').

IJmuiden, The Netherlands, seaport on w. coast at entrance to North Sea Canal leading to Amsterdam; fishing base; cement; paper mills and steel plant nearby; pop. 3,587.

IJsselmeer (or Zuider Zee), freshwater reservoir in The Netherlands N-124
  Amsterdam A-380

IJssel River, river in The Netherlands, n. branch of the Rhine; flows into the IJsselmeer N-125

Ikaría (or Icaria), Greek island in Aegean Sea 130 mi (210 km) s.e. of Athens; 99 sq mi (256 sq km); fruits, grain, and charcoal; taken from Turkey after Balkan wars 1912–13.

Ikebana, Japanese flower arrangement J-54

Ikeda, Hayato (1899–1965), Japanese political leader, born in Yoshina, Hiroshima Prefecture; minister of finance 1949–52, 1956–57, of trade and industry 1952–53, 1959–60; prime minister 1960–64.

Ikeya-Seki comet, discovered 1965 by two Japanese astronomers; orbit about 1,000 years; tail about 75,000,000 miles (121,000,000 kilometers) long; first comet visible by day since 1882, *picture* S-254d

Ikhnaton (or Amenhotep IV) (1370–1352 BC), king of Egypt I-32
  ancient Egypt E-126
  Nofretete S-82, *picture* S-78
  Tutankhamen T-331

Ikhwan, Islamic brotherhood I-5

Ikon. *see in index* Icon

Ilareta. *see in index* Yareta

Ile de France. *see in index* Mauritius

Ile de la Cité, small island in Seine River, the center of Paris P-117, 122, *picture* P-119, *map* P-120

Ile des Pins, island in Pacific, dependency of New Caledonia. *see in index* Pines, Isle of

Île-Jésus (or Jesus Island), coextensive with city of Laval, Que., in Saint Lawrence River just n.w. of Montreal; area 93 sq mi (241 sq km); pop. 228,010, *map* Q-11

Île Royale. *see in index* Cape Breton Island

Île St-John. *see in index* Prince Edward Island

Îles Loyauté. *see in index* Loyalty Islands

Ileum, lower part of small intestine; lies between jejunum and large intestine; with the rest of the small intestine absorbs products of digestion.

ILGWU. *see in index* International Ladies' Garment Worker's Union

'I li', one of the Confucian Classics C-387

'Iliad', epic poem by Homer on wrath of Achilles and the Trojan War G-274
  ancient Greece G-263
  archaeologists verify A-531
  educational use E-79
  Homeric legend H-220
  Jefferson inscription J-91
  mythology M-695, 704
  storytelling S-473, 481b
  Trojan War T-289
    Agamemnon A-124
    chariot race H-275
    Hector H-114
    Helen of Troy H-117
    Trojan horse, *list* H-249
  wrestling W-366

Iliamna, Lake, lake in Alaska, just n. of Alaska Peninsula; area 1,033 sq mi (2,675 sq km); second largest freshwater lake entirely within U.S.; rainbow trout, *maps* N-350, U-39

Ili crisis, (1879–81), dispute between Russian and China over the Chinese region of Ili C-370

I Like, game G-13

Ilion, N.Y., village in Herkimer County 12 mi (19 km) s.e. of Utica, on the Mohawk River; office machinery, guns; pop. 9,190.

Ilium. *see in index* Troy

Ilium, upper portion of hipbone S-210

Ilkhan, Mongol dynasty of Persia (1256–1353); established by Hugalu, grandson of Genghis Khan; overthrown by Timur Leng.

Illampu, Mount, Andean peak in Bolivia e. of Lake Titicaca; highest summit in the eastern Andes; 20,754 ft (6,362 m), *map* S-298, *diagram* S-295

'Illiac Suite', piece of music composed by a computer M-676

Illimani, volcanic mountain peak in the Andes in Bolivia, about 30 mi (50 km) s.e. of La Paz; 21,004 ft (6,402 m).

Illinois, a confederacy of American Indians, comprising the Cahokia, Kaskaskia, Michigamea, Moingwena, Peoria, and Tamaroa, formerly living in Wisconsin, Illinois, and parts of Iowa and Missouri; a few Kaskaskia and Peoria survive in Oklahoma; the name is French form of the native name illini (man), (plural iliniwek), *map* I-136, *table* I-138
  history I-35, 39
  La Salle L-53
  Marquette M-148

Illinois, central state of U.S.; 56,400 sq mi (146,100 sq km); cap. Springfield; pop. 11,418,461 I-33
  canals C-129
  Capitol S-397
  cities. *see also in index* cities listed below and other cities by name
    Chicago C-310
    Peoria P-197
    Rockford R-233
    Springfield S-397
  education U-206
  Hispanic Americans H-163
  Mormons M-584
  name, *table* S-428
  North America, *map* N-350
  parks and other areas
    New Salem State Park P-20
  places of interest S-397
  state symbols
    flag, *picture* F-159
    flower S-427
  Statuary Hall, *table* S-437a
  taxation, *tables* T-37, 39
  wild flowers, *pictures* P-358, 360

Illinois, University of, in Urbana and Chicago, Ill.; state control; founded 1867; opened 1868; in Urbana: liberal arts and sciences, agriculture, commerce and business administration, communications, education, engineering, fine and applied arts, law, library, physical education, social work, and veterinary medicine; in Chicago, liberal arts and sciences, architecture and art, associated medical sciences, business administration, dentistry, education, engineering, medicine, nursing, pharmacy, physical education, social work, and center for urban studies; graduate colleges, *picture* I-45
  Chicago Circle C-314
  football G-214
  universities, *picture* U-206

Illinoisan, glacial phase. *see in index* Riss

Illinois and Michigan Canal, canal in U.S. opened in 1848, *map* C-126
  Illinois I-38

Illinois and Mississippi Canal. *see in index* Hennepin Canal

Illinois Benedictine College (originally St. Procopius College), in Lisle, Ill.; Roman Catholic; established 1887; present name adopted 1971; arts and sciences, education; graduate studies.

Illinois College, in Jacksonville, Ill.; private control; established in 1829; liberal arts, teacher education; first college in state to graduate a class, *picture* I-39

Illinois Institute of Technology, in Chicago, Ill.; private control; established 1940 when Armour Institute of Technology (founded 1892) and Lewis Institute (founded 1896) were merged; Institute of Design (founded in Chicago 1937 as New Bauhaus) merged 1949; engineering and physical sciences, architecture, business, education, industrial arts, liberal arts, law; graduate school
  Mies van der Rohe M-398
  Moholy-Nagy M-518

Illinois River, chief river of Illinois; flows 433 mi (697 km) s.w. to Mississippi River U-71
  Illinois I-38, *picture* I-47, *map* I-53
  Peoria P-197

Illinois State Fair, *picture* F-7

Illinois State University, in Normal, Ill.; founded 1857; liberal arts and sciences, applied sciences, business, education, and fine arts; graduate school.

Illinois Waterway O-120
  Great Lakes G-247, *map* G-245
  Illinois I-38

Illinois Wesleyan University, in Bloomington, Ill.; Methodist; founded 1850; liberal arts, art, business administration, drama and speech, education, insurance, music, nursing; graduate study.

Illiteracy. *see in index* Literacy and illiteracy

Ill River, in Alsace-Lorraine, France; rises in Jura Mts. s.w. of Basel and flows n.w. parallel with Rhine, which it enters at Strasbourg; about 123 mi (198 km) long
  Strasbourg S-484

Illuminated manuscripts
  books B-349, *picture* B-348
  painting P-28, *picture* P-67e
  Persian, *picture* P-213

Illuminating gas. *see in index* Gas, natural and manufactured

Illumination L-195
  lighthouse L-204
  lighting L-205

Illusions I-54
  magic M-37
  motion pictures M-602
  op art P-61
  sensation and perception S-109

Illustrated books. *see also in index* Engraving and etching
  children's books, *pictures* R-105
  literary awards L-240
  Leonardo da Vinci L-134

Illustrative map G-68

Illyria (also Illyricum), ancient name of district bordering east coast of Adriatic Sea n. of Epirus; extended eastward perhaps as far as present Danube River, *map* R-242

Illyrians, ancestors of modern Albanians B-28

Ilmenite, mineral M-435
  ore, *table* O-600
  titanium T-193

ILO. *see in index* International Labor Organization

Iloilo, Philippines, seaport on Panay Island; actively hostile during annexation by United States in 1899; pop. 187,300, including suburbs P-253c, 257a, *map* P-262
  Asia, *map* A-697

'Il Penseroso' (translation 'the pensive man'), ode written by John Milton to 'divinest Melancholy', celebrating peace, leisure, and contemplation
  English literature E-269

ILS. *see in index* Instrument Landing System

Ilustrados, in Philippine history P-259c

Ilyushin IL-2 Shturmovik, Soviet fighter plane A-159, *picture* A-157

Imagawa family, Japanese ruling family
  Tokugawa Ieyasu T-202

Image, in psychology S-109

Image, mirage M-463

Image dissector, a tube
  television T-79

Images, in writing W-378

'Imaginary Invalid, The', work by Molière M-522

Imagination
  communication C-610
  play P-386, 390a, *pictures* P-388, 390
  science S-59

Imagism, movement in 20th-century poetry which aimed to present hard, clear-cut images and sense impressions instead of vague abstractions; influenced by Japanese poetry.

Imago, the final adult stage of an insect I-221
  mayfly M-239
  metamorphosis M-312

Imam, Muslim leader I-360

Imbecile, term no longer in use with reference to mental retardation.

Imbros (or Imroz), island in n.e. Aegean Sea n.w. of entrance to Dardanelles; 19 mi (31 km) long; greatest width, 8 mi (13 km); awarded to Turkey 1923 by Treaty of Lausanne.

IMCO. *see in index* Inter-Governmental Maritime Consultative Organization

IMF. *see in index* International Monetary Fund

Imhotep (2700 BC), Egyptian architect to Pharaoh Djoser; later became legendary; regarded as magician and astronomer; skilled in medicine E-125
  step pyramid, *picture* P-543

Imitation, in literature
  folklore F-269

Imitation, in music, *list* M-670

Immaculata College, in Immaculata, Pa.; Roman Catholic; for women; founded 1920; liberal arts, education, home economics, music.

WINNERS OF INDIANAPOLIS MOTOR SPEEDWAY 500-MILE RACE*

Year	Driver	Mph	Year	Driver	Mph
1911	Ray Harroun	74.59	1952	Troy Ruttman	128.922
1912	Joe Dawson	78.72	1953	Bill Vukovich	128.740
1913	Jules Goux	75.933	1954	Bill Vukovich	130.840
1914	Rene Thomas	82.47	1955	Bob Sweikert	128.209
1915	Ralph DePalma	89.84	1956	Pat Flaherty	128.490
1916	Dario Resta (300 miles only)	84.00	1957	Sam Hanks	135.601
1919	Howard Wilcox	88.05	1958	Jimmy Bryan	133.791
1920	Gaston Chevrolet	88.62	1959	Rodger Ward	135.857
1921	Tommy Milton	89.62	1960	Jim Rathmann	138.767
1922	Jimmy Murphy	94.48	1961	A.J. Foyt	139.130
1923	Tommy Milton	90.95	1962	Rodger Ward	140.292
1924	L.L. Corum; Joe Boyer	98.23	1963	Parnelli Jones	143.137
1925	Peter DePaolo	101.13	1964	A.J. Foyt	147.350
1926	Frank Lockhart (400 miles)†	95.904	1965	Jimmy Clark	150.686
1927	George Souders	97.545	1966	Graham Hill	144.317
1928	Louis Meyer	99.482	1967	A.J. Foyt	151.207
1929	Ray Keech	97.585	1968	Bobby Unser	152.882
1930	Billy Arnold	100.448	1969	Mario Andretti	156.867
1931	Louis Schneider	96.629	1970	Al Unser	155.749
1932	Fred Frame	104.144	1971	Al Unser	157.735
1933	Louis Meyer	104.162	1972	Mark Donohue	163.465
1934	Bill Cummings	104.863	1973	Gordon Johncock (333 miles)†	159.014
1935	Kelly Petillo	106.240	1974	Johnny Rutherford	158.589
1936	Louis Meyer	109.069	1975	Bobby Unser (435 miles)†	149.213
1937	Wilbur Shaw	113.580	1976	Johnny Rutherford (255 miles)†	148.725
1938	Floyd Roberts	117.200	1977	A.J. Foyt	161.331
1939	Wilbur Shaw	115.035	1978	Al Unser	161.363
1940	Wilbur Shaw	114.277	1979	Rick Mears	158.899
1941	Floyd Davis; Mauri Rose	115.117	1980	Johnny Rutherford	142.862
1946	George Robson	114.820	1981	Bobby Unser	139.085
1947	Mauri Rose	116.338	1982	Gordon Johncock	162.026
1948	Mauri Rose	119.814	1983	Tom Sneva	162.117
1949	Bill Holland	121.327	1984	Rick Mears	163.612
1950	Johnnie Parsons (345 miles)†	124.002	1985	Danny Sullivan	152.982
1951	Lee Wallard	126.244	1986	Bobby Rahal	170.722
			1987	Al Unser	162.175

*1917–18 and 1942–45 no race run. †Race stopped because of rain.

'In Memoriam', work by Tennyson T-109

Inn, river rising in e. Switzerland, one of chief tributaries of Danube; 320 mi (510 km) long; forms Austro-German border in lower course
- Germany, *map* G-131
- Switzerland, *map* S-537

Inn, establishment for lodging and entertaining travellers H-288

Inner Court (or Binnenhof), in The Hague, The Netherlands, quadrangle of government buildings H-5

Inner ear E-3
- brain B-401
- deafness D-47

Inner Mongolia (or Nei Moggol Zizhigu), autonomous region in n.e. China; area 450,000 sq mi (1,165,500 km); cap. Huhehot; pop. 19,274,279 I-207
- Asia, *map* A-697
- China C-345
- Gobi G-172
- Manchuria M-94
- Mongolia M-535

Inner planet S-254a, P-350, *diagram* S-254c

Inner tube R-304, 309

Innes, Hammond (born 1913), detective story writer D-119

Innes, Michael (or John Innes Mackintosh Stewart) (born 1906), detective story writer D-119

Inness, George (1825–94), U.S. landscape painter, born in Newburgh, N.Y.; distinguished for beautiful coloring and sensitive and poetic portrayal of nature; son **George** (1854–1926), born in Paris, also an artist.

Inning, in sports
- baseball B-92
- softball S-248

Innini, ancient Babylonian mother goddess B-8

Innis, Roy (born 1934), U.S. militant minority rights leader, born St. Croix, Virgin Islands; active in CORE 1963–, national director 1968–.

Inniskilling. *see in index* Enniskillen

Innocence, flower. *see in index* Bluet

'Innocence of Father Brown, The', work by Chesterton C-307

Innocent III (1160?–1216), pope I-208
- Fourth Crusade C-787
- Frederick II F-390
- John of England J-124

'Innocents Abroad, The', humorous travel book by Mark Twain (1869) written after his visit to the Mediterranean and the Holy Land A-351

Innocents' Day (or Childermas), December 28, festival in memory of the massacre of the children in Bethlehem by order of Herod the Great.

Innsbruck, Austria, historic and picturesque city on Inn River in Austrian Tyrol; university; cotton and wool weaving; glass and mosaic work; pop. 100,695, *map* E-360
- Austrian territory A-824
- Tirol T-192

Inns of Court, in London, headquarters of the legal profession in England; occupied by 4 legal societies which take their names from the original buildings in the groups—Lincoln's Inn, Gray's Inn, Inner Temple, and Middle Temple (the latter 2 known collectively as The Temple); seat of the Council of Legal Education, which superintends education and examination for the English bar L-289

Innuitian Mountains, in North America; located in the Arctic archipelago C-73

Inoculation, in medicine, injection of substance into body to communicate, cure, or prevent disease
- serum S-114
- vaccine V-249

Inönü, Ismet (1884–1973), Turkish statesman, born in Smyrna; surname was derived from field on which, as General Ismet Pasha, he defeated Greek army 1921; premier of Turkey almost continuously 1923–38; president 1938–50; leader of opposition in parliament 1950–61; premier 1961–65 T-324

Inorganic chemistry I-208
- chemistry C-300

Inositol, a B-complex vitamin V-356, 358

Inouye, Daniel Ken (born 1924), U.S. lawyer and political leader, born in Honolulu, Hawaii; Democratic representative from Hawaii 1959–63, first Japanese-American Congressman; U.S. senator 1963–; author of 'Journey to Washington'.

Inouye, Kaoru, Marquis (1835–1915), Japanese statesman, a leader in reform movement which culminated in Revolution of 1867; for 30 years a cabinet member.

I novel, Japanese literature J-82

Input, data C-627

Input arm (or effort arm), in mechanics M-267

Inquiline (from the Latin word inquilinus, meaning tenant), an insect or other animal form that lays eggs in or lives in the nest or abode of another species, thus existing as a parasite.

'Inquiry into the Nature and Causes of the Wealth of Nations'. *see in index* 'Wealth of Nations, The'

Inquiry method, in learning S-239

Inquisition, tribunal I-211
- Counter-Reformation C-744
- Enlightenment E-288
- Ferdinand and Isabella F-55
- Gregory IX G-284
- Innocent III I-208
- law L-91
- Philip II S-358, P-252

In Salah (or Aïn-Salah,) Algeria, oasis town in Sahara 230 mi (370 km) s. of El Goléa; airline and highway junction; gas pipelines; pop. 6,319.

Insanity, popular and legal term for mental disorder which renders patient unfit to manage own affairs or safely remain free. *see also in index* Mental illness
- criminal law defense C-775

Inscriptional letter, in calligraphy C-58

Insect, six-legged arthropod animal I-212. *see also in index* insects by name
- Africa A-96
- control
  - agriculture A-137
    - wheat W-188
  - trapping T-268
- disease carriers D-166
- double parasitism with fungus F-449
- ecology E-58
- endangered species E-212
- forests F-313
  - damage C-676
- hibernation H-147
- hobby H-186
- invertebrate group I-284
- jungle J-156
- luminous P-270
- metamorphosis M-312
  - egg E-110, *pictures* E-111
  - larva L-51
  - pupa P-534
- migration A-452
- navigational aid B-236
- parasites P-113
- prehistoric animals A-461
  - animal life record, *table* E-24
- protective coloration P-509, *pictures* P-510, 512
- scale insects S-52e
- silk S-197
- spiracles, *picture* R-159
- taxidermy T-40
- weed control W-133

Insect collecting T-268

Insecticide
- bird poisoning B-256
- camphor usage C-67
- ecological impact E-57
- endangered species E-209
- insect control I-225
  - flea F-178
  - fly F-242
  - mosquito M-598
- pollution P-441c
- World War II W-355

Insectivora, an order of insect-eating mammals
- animal life record, *table* E-24
- mammal, *table* M-80

Insect-trapping plants. *see in index* Carnivorous plants

Insei, in Japanese politics F-445

Inside Passage (or Inland Passage), a sheltered sea route extending about 1,000 miles from Seattle, Wash., to Skagway, Alaska; islands provide protection from winds and storms
- Alaska A-241, *picture* A-251
- British Columbia B-452

Insight P-521

Insignia, military U-5. *see also in index* Uniforms
- medals M-270
- World War II, *pictures* W-330, 331

Insolation, amount of heat received from the sun
- geography G-66

Insole, shoe part S-180

Insomnia, sleeplessness S-217

Inspectors General, Department of the U.S. Army
- insignia, *picture* U-10

Inspiration, in breathing R-159

Instamatic camera P-286

Instantaneous rate, in mathematics C-23

Instant film (or self-processing film), in photography P-286, 298

Instant tea (or powdered tea) T-46

Instinct, in psychology R-132

Instinct theory, of play P-390b

Institute for Comparative Biology Z-465

Institute for Defense Analyses, U.S. association for research, formed 1956 by Ford Foundation grant; makes studies for Department of Defense; research financed by government; membership consisted of universities but was changed 1968 to include individuals from public and academic life; headquarters, Washington, D.C.

Institute for Philosophical Research, in Chicago, Ill.
- Adler A-45

Institute of Design, in Chicago, Ill., an art school. *see in index* Illinois Institute of Technology

Institute of France, French academy A-14

Institute of Politics, a conference held annually at Williams College, Williamstown, Mass., to promote study of politics and international problems and relations; first session 1921; founded through generosity of Bernard M. Baruch.

Institute of Public Opinion, founded by George H. Gallup in 1935 to interview and record the votes of a small but representative cross section of public on a specific topic (called Gallup Poll); results published by newspaper syndicate.

'Institutes', textbook J-161

Institution, in sociology S-242
- marriage M-149

Institut National des Appellations d'Origine, French institute that regulates the wine industry W-237

Institutum Divi Thomae, U.S. research institute and graduate school of science under auspices of Cincinnati Catholic Archdiocese; founded 1935; marine laboratory at Palm Beach, Fla., affiliated laboratories in colleges and hospitals.

Instructional systems and technology (also called educational media), a special service in education E-103

'Instructions of Ptah-Hotep, The', oldest known book in the world C-694

Instrumental analysis, chemical analysis C-292

Instrumental music. *see in index* musical forms by name, as Quartet; Symphonic poem; Symphony; and composers by name

Instrumentation, machines that perform accurate measurements I-228
- tachometer T-3

Instrument Flight Rules (IFR) A-216, *table* A-71

Instrument flying (or blind flying) A-216, *table* A-70

Instrument Landing System A-219, A-886, *picture* A-218
- airplane A-194

Instrument panel (or dashboard)
- airplane A-193
- automobile A-845

Instruments, musical. *see in index* Musical instruments

Instruments, scientific I-228

Insular Cases, Supreme Court decision U-146

Insular letter, in calligraphy C-58

Insular Mountains, partially submerged ranges in Pacific off Canadian mainland; part of Coast Ranges; visible peaks form Vancouver Island and Queen Charlotte Islands; highest point Victoria Peak on Vancouver (7,484 ft; 2,281 m) B-452

Insulation I-231
- adobe A-47
- building construction B-494
- glass G-159
- heating and ventilation H-111
- wool W-287

Insulators, electric, substances that do not conduct electricity, or conduct it poorly
- insulation I-232
- quantum mechanics S-254h
- quartz Q-7

Insulin, hormone H-242, *table* H-241
- Banting and Best discover B-75
- bioengineering B-206
- deficiency D-180
- diabetes D-125, G-153
- genetic engineering G-50
- genetics G-54

Insull, Samuel (1859–1938), U.S. public utilities official, born in London, England; came to U.S. 1881 as secretary to Thomas A. Edison; president Commonwealth Edison Co., Chicago, Ill., after 1907; controlled public utilities in Middle West; bankrupted 1932; tried and acquitted on mail fraud charge.

Insurance I-232. *see also in index* Health insurance; Life insurance; Lloyd's of London
- banking B-64
- credit C-763
- farm crop U-162, R-265
- flood insurance F-182
- fraternal societies F-387
- hospitalization H-285, S-237
- housing H-295
- international trade I-270
- mail P-460b
- social security S-236
  - Israel I-370
  - pensions P-189
  - Roosevelt R-272

Insurance City, Conn. *see in index* Hartford

Intaglio, in printmaking P-277, P-501
- graphic arts G-231

Intarsia, inlay F-457

Integer. *see in index* Whole number

Integral calculus C-24
- Abel's research A-8
- mathematics M-215
- sciences S-64

Integrated circuit chip (IC, or integrated circuit), small piece of silicon C-627. *see also in index* Microchip
- electronics E-177
- microprocessor M-378
- X rays X-404

Integrated semiconductor circuit S-195b
- transistor T-250

Integration, in mathematics C-24

Integration, United States population
- constitutional amendments U-145, 152
- housing H-305

Intelligence, animal. *see in index* Behavior, animal

Intelligence, human
- Binet B-197
  - play P-390b
- educational development E-94
- heredity H-139
- mental retardation M-303
- tests I-238, *graph* I-239

Intelligence agencies, in government I-236
- Le Carré's fiction L-113

Intelligence and Security Command, U.S. Army A-646

Intelligence quotient (IQ)
- education E-95
- mental retardation M-303
- tests I-240

Intelligence tests I-238
- Binet and Simon B-197
- educational use E-95
- psychology P-523

'Intelligent Whale', U.S. submarine, *picture* S-495b

Intelsat (International communications satellite) F-427

INTELSAT (International Telecommunications Satellite Consortium) F-428

Intendant, appointed colonial government official in New France; established in 1665 C-92

Intensity
- light L-195
- sound S-260, P-441e

periodic table, *table* P-207, *list* P-208
radioactivity N-429
silver iodide S-204
Iodine deficiency D-180
Iodoform, in organic chemistry, *diagram* O-602
Iodopsin, eye chemical C-562
Iolani Palace, in Honolulu, Hawaii H-62, H-230
Ion, atom or group of atoms that carries a positive or negative electrical charge. *see also in index* Ionization
cell membrane B-237
chemistry C-299
electric cell B-107
electrochemistry E-170
geology G-72
matter M-224
metal and metallurgy M-307
neurons and nervous system N-120
plasma P-380
radioactivity, *picture* R-62
sulfuric acid S-510
true solutions S-256
Iona (or Icolmkill), island of Inner Hebrides, w. Scotland; 5 sq mi (13 sq km); center of Celtic Christianity; pop. 130.
Iona College, in New Rochelle, N.Y.; Roman Catholic; coeducational, formerly for men; founded 1940; arts and sciences, business administration, and education; graduate studies N-255
Ion drive, propulsion by an electrically charged jet of atoms or molecules.
Ion engine (or electrostatic engine) A-187
motor and engine M-631
Ionesco, Eugène (born 1912), French dramatist I-286
French literature F-398
Ion exchange, in uranium isotope separation U-212
Ion-exchange resins, in water softening H-213
Ionia, ancient geography, a district on the w. coast of Asia Minor and adjacent islands, settled by the Ionian Greeks
theory of universe U-198
Ionian Islands, islands in Greece G-254, *map* E-360
Ionian Sea, part of the Mediterranean Sea M-286
Ionic architecture A-546, *picture* A-547
Mausoleum at Halicarnassus S-115, *picture* S-116
Ionic bond, in chemistry M-522
Ionic chiton, draped garment D-260
Ionic compound. *see in index* Polar compound
Ionium, a radioactive isotope of thorium, mass number 230, *chart* R-66
Ionization, the process of ionizing. *see also in index* Ion
air conditioner A-150
chemistry C-299
detector H-213
electrochemistry E-171
molecule M-522
radioactivity R-65, *picture* R-62
sulfuric acid S-510
true solutions S-256
Ionization counter, X-ray detection device X-406
Ionization detector, appliance H-213
Ion of Chios (490?–421? BC), Greek writer in age of Pericles; knew Aeschylus and Sophocles; won prizes for his tragic and dithyrambic poetry.
Ionopsidium (or diamond flower, or violet cress), a perennial plant *I. acaule* of the mustard family, native to Portugal; low growing; leaves heart-shaped at base; flowers lilac; used in rock gardens.
Ionosphere, region of Earth's atmosphere A-749, *picture* A-748
earth E-19, *diagram* E-11
radiation R-36
radio waves R-51
world W-296
Iophon, Greek tragic poet, son of Sophocles, won second prize in 428 BC, Euripides being first; only fragments of works survived.
Ios. *see in index* Nio
IOTA (International Occultation Timing Association) A-731
IOU (I owe you), a paper given as acknowledgment of debt; it has on it the letters IOU, the sum owed, and the debtor's signature.
Iowa, North American people of Siouan stock, originally living in Minnesota; moved s. and later settled on Kansas and Oklahoma reservations, *map* I-149
Iowa, a n.-central state of U.S.; 56,290 sq mi (145,790 sq km); cap. Des Moines; pop. 2,913,387 I-287
North America, *map* N-350
state symbols
bird G-183
flag, *picture* F-159
flower R-294, *pictures* R-295, S-427
Statuary Hall, *table* S-437a
taxation, *tables* T-37, 39
United States U-68, *maps* U-41, 70
'Iowa', U.S. Navy battleship N-84
Iowa, University of, in Iowa City, Iowa; state control; founded 1847; liberal arts, business administration, creative writing, dentistry, education, engineering, law, medicine, nursing, pharmacy, religion, social work; graduate college I-292, *picture* I-297
Iowa City, Iowa, city on Iowa River about 24 mi (39 km) s. of Cedar Rapids; toiletries, food products; capital of Iowa Territory 1839–46; state capital 1846–57; pop. 50,508
Iowa I-292, *picture* I-297, *map* I-302
'Iowa Interiors', work by Suckow A-358
Iowa River, river in Iowa, flows 350 mi (560 km) s.e. to Mississippi River, *map* I-302
Iowa State University of Science and Technology, in Ames, Iowa; founded 1858; science and humanities, agriculture, education, engineering, home economics, veterinary medicine; graduate studies; quarter system.
Iowa Wesleyan College, in Mount Pleasant, Iowa; Methodist; founded 1842; liberal arts, economics and business administration, education, home economics, music, physical education.
Iphigenia, in Greek mythology, daughter of Agamemnon H-221
Ipomoea, genus including morning-glory and sweet potato. *see in index* Morning-glory; Sweet potato
Ipso facto, in law, *table* L-93
IPSPs (inhibitory postsynaptic potentials), negative voltage changes in nerve cells N-122
Ipswich, England, port and manufacturing town on Orwell estuary, 64 mi (103 km) n.e. of London; capital of Suffolk; pop. 122,050, *map* U-18a
geological deposits A-776
IQ. *see in index* Intelligence quotient
Iqbal, Muhammad (1877?–1938), Indian poet and philosopher I-304
Indian literature I-108
Iquique, Chile, one of leading ports, in extreme n.; average yearly rainfall only 0.05 in (1.27 mm); exports nitrate; pop. of greater city 64,900, *map* S-298
desert conditions D-104
world, *map* W-297
Iquitos, Peru, trade center in n.e. on Amazon River at head of navigation for ocean vessels, 2,300 mi (3,700 km) from mouth; pop. 111,327 P-224, *map* S-298
IRA (Individual Retirement Account) P-188
IRA. *see in index* Irish Republican Army
IRA Provos. *see in index* Irish Republican Army
Iran (or Islamic Republic, formerly Persia), a mountainous country of s.w. Asia; 636,294 sq mi (1,647,994 sq km); cap. Tehran; pop. 40,476,000 I-304. *see also in index* Persia
agriculture, *picture* A-688
Asia, *map* A-697
Behistun Rock, *picture* P-214
Caspian Sea C-196
child's game, *picture* P-193
church and state C-409
Elburz Mountains E-144
flag, *picture* F-166
folktales S-469, *list* S-480
history
foreign affairs
Iraq I-316
U.S. hostages C-184
Khomeini K-232
Medes M-273
Nader Shah N-3
World War II W-326
Kurds K-310
petroleum P-229
gas G-38
railroad mileage, *table* R-85
religion A-684
Baha'i faith B-10, M-469
Islam I-362
Zoroastrianism Z-471
rugs R-314, *picture* R-312
totalitarianism T-235
world, *map* W-297
Iran-Contra affair, in U.S. history H-112j
Iranian languages L-41
Iranians, an Indo-European people which migrated to the Iranian Plateau about 3,000 BC
classification, *chart* R-26
Persian Empire P-211–12
Iraq, Arab nation, including most of Mesopotamia; 171,600 sq mi (444,450 sq km); cap. Baghdad; pop. 14,014,000 I-312. *see also in index* Mesopotamia
Arab states A-521, *map* A-522
Asia, *map* A-697
Baghdad B-18
flag, *picture* F-166
history
Abadan's bombardment A-4
Iran war I-312
Israeli raid I-373
World War II W-326
irrigation E-327
Islamic literature I-365
Kurds K-310
palaces C-200
petroleum P-229
railroad mileage, *table* R-85
Tigris River T-184
world, *map* W-297
IRAS. *see in index* Infrared Astronomical Satellite
Irawadi River. *see in index* Irrawaddy River
Irazú, Mount, volcano in Costa Rica (11,260 ft [3,430 m]) C-733, S-44a
IRBM (intermediate-range ballistic missile), a type of trajectory missile G-312
Ireland, John (1838–1918), U.S. Roman Catholic prelate, born in Kilkenny County, Ireland; emigrated to St. Paul, Minn., at age of 11; ordained priest 1861; chaplain in Union army 1862–63; archbishop 1888–1918; advocated temperance, colonization of Northwest, organized labor, Catholic education.
Ireland (or Erin, or Éire, or Irish Free State, or Republic of Ireland), s. 5/6 of island of Ireland; 27,136 sq mi (70,282 sq km); capital is Dublin; pop. 3,443,405 I-317. *see also in index* Ireland, Northern
arts
bagpipes W-228
enameling E-208
literature. *see in index* Irish literature
cities. *see in index* cities by name
Europe, *map* E-360
history
America
crime C-772
Pennsylvania P-167
Virginia V-332
Belfast conflict B-144
Commonwealth membership C-602
England E-238
Home Rule
Gladstone G-152
O'Connell O-490
Parnell P-133
Peel P-152
St. Patrick P-139
industry
beer B-134
lace L-16
migration of people M-404, *picture* M-401
emigration, *chart* U-120
national symbols
flag, *picture* F-166
national anthem, *table* N-64
shamrock emblem S-143
railroad mileage, *table* R-85
sports
dog racing D-214
handball H-27
wrestling W-366
taxation, *table* T-35
temperance movement T-80
terrorism T-113
University of Dublin U-209
world, *map* W-297
Ireland, National University of, one of two universities of Republic of Ireland (the other, University of Dublin); founded 1908 in Dublin; governing senate largely Roman Catholic; 3 constituent university colleges at Dublin, Cork, Galway.
Ireland, Northern (or Ulster), a part of the United Kingdom with a parliament; 5,459 sq mi (14,139 sq km); cap. Belfast; pop. 1,490,288 I-324. *see also in index* Ireland; United Kingdom
assassination A-704
Belfast B-144
Belleek ware P-477
Europe, *map* E-360
government U-16
history. *see in index* Ireland, *subhead* history
literature. *see in index* Irish literature
Irenaeus, Saint (130–202), Greek church father and martyr, bishop of Lyons; born in Asia Minor.
Irene (752?–803), Byzantine empress, first woman to rule Eastern Empire; seized power in 780, on death of her husband Leo IV; planned to unite Eastern and Western Empires by marrying Charlemagne; blinded and later murdered her son Constantine VI; deposed (802) and exiled by Nicephorus, who was her successor B-535
IRI (Industrial Reconstruction Institute), Italian holding company I-387
Irian Jaya (formerly West Irian, or Netherlands New Guinea), w. half of New Guinea and adjacent islands; 162,928 sq mi (421,981 sq km); province of Indonesia since 1963; cap. Djajapura; pop. 1,025,300, *map* I-166
East Indies E-45
Indonesia I-158
New Guinea N-173
The Netherlands N-131
Iridium (Ir), silver-white metallic element, found chiefly in Ural Mts., *table* P-207, *list* P-208
platinum P-384
Irigoyen, Hipólito (1852–1933), president of Argentina (1916–22, 1928–30), born in Buenos Aires A-583
Irimoya, Japanese roof style, *diagram* J-31
Iris, in Greek mythology, rainbow goddess, carried messages for the gods, especially for Zeus and Hera, king and queen of the gods.
Iris (French fleur-de-lis), a flower
growing conditions G-24
rhizome, *diagram* P-363a
state flower of Tennessee, *pictures* T-90, S-427
Iris, a part of the eye E-387
bioengineering B-205
Iris family (or Iridaceae), family of plants including the crocus, gladiolus, freesia, iris, ixia, tigridia, blackberry lily, blue-eyed grass, and the tritonias.
Iris Fete. *see in index* Boys' Festival
Irish Free State. *see in index* Ireland, Republic of
Irish Guards, regiment formed 1900 by Queen Victoria in tribute to Irish troops in the Boer War U-12
Irish ivy, plant I-408
Irish Land Acts
Balfour B-24
Irish language. *see in index* Gaelic
Irish literary revival, literary movement
Yeats Y-412
Irish literature I-326
chief writers. *see in index* writers by name, such as Yeats, William Butler
folktales S-472, *list* S-481b
Ireland I-320
mermaid legend A-457
Irish moss (or carrageen), seaweed S-104, *picture* P-370
algae A-284
gelatin G-46
Irish potato. *see in index* Potato
Irish Republican Army (IRA), unofficial semi-military organization based in the Republic of Ireland; in 1969 divided into an official and a provisional wing; the latter, the Provos or IRA Provos, are committed to terrorist tactics to end British rule in Northern Ireland
terrorism T-113
assassination A-704, E-355
Irish Sea, body of water between Great Britain and Ireland, with North Channel at n. and St. George's Channel at s, *map* E-360. *see also in index* Ocean, *table*
Irish setter, breed of dog, *picture* D-198
Irish terrier, breed of dog, *picture* D-204

ISLANDS—LARGEST IN THE WORLD

	Area sq mi	Area sq km
Greenland	840,000	2,175,000
New Guinea	310,000	800,000
Borneo	290,000	751,000
Madagascar	226,658	587,041
Baffin	195,928	507,451
Sumatra	163,000	422,000
Honshu	89,212	231,058
Victoria	83,896	217,290
Great Britain	83,698	216,777
Ellesmere	75,767	196,236
Celebes	69,100	179,000
South Island, New Zealand	58,676	151,971
Java	49,000	126,900

The letter J

The history of the letter J is linked with the history of I. The Romans and their European successors used I both for the vocalic "i" and for the consonantal "y" (as in the English word "yet"). The English letter J did not come into existence until the end of medieval times, when scribes began to use a tailed form of "i," with or without the dot, next to the short form of "i" (1).

When printing was invented, the tailed form of "i" (2) was often used for an initial "i," which is usually consonantal. Not until the 17th century, however, was the distinction between J or j as a consonant and I or i as a vowel fully established.

1

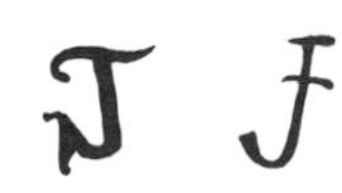

2

Jab, in boxing B-388, *picture* B-389

Jabalina (or collared peccary), mammal *Tayassu tajacu* of the family Tayassuidae P-152

Jabalpur, India. *see in index* Jubbulpore

Jabbok (modern Nahr ez Zerka), river in Jordan, flows 50 mi (80 km) w. to Jordan River n. of Dead Sea.

Jabir ibn Hayyan, Abu Musa (721?–813?), Arabic scientist; held sound views on chemical research; suggested geologic formation of metals.

Jabiru, the name of various large storks S-456

Jacana, small raillike bird with extremely long toes and claws which enable it to walk on the floating leaves of water plants, and with strong spurs at the bend of each wing; plumage black with usually bright chestnut back and parts of wings; two species in tropical America; one, the Mexican jacana, ranges n. to Texas.

Jacaranda, genus of tropical shrubs and trees *Jacaranda* of bignonia family; one species, green-ebony, grows 30 ft to 60 ft (9 m to 18 m); leaves fernlike; flowers blue, in loose clusters.

'J'Accuse', work by Zola Z-456
  Dreyfus case D-272
  France F-341

Jachymov (German Sankt Joachimsthal), Czechoslovakia, town in n.w. near Germany; silver mine discovered 1516; word dollar derived from Joachimsthaler, a coin minted in 1519; pop. 6,806.

Jacinth (or hyacinth), gemstone J-115

Jacinth, perennial plant of the lily family; three species are common garden flowers: Japanese jacinth *Scilla japonica*; Peruvian jacinth *Scilla peruviana*, also called Cuban lily; Spanish jacinth *Scilla hispanica*, called bell-flowered squill.

Jack, donkey. *see in index* Ass

Jack, a small flag flown from the prow of a ship, *list* F-149

Jack (or jak, or jaca, or jackfruit tree), East Indian tree of same genus as breadfruit; wood is hard, yellow, and used for almost every purpose; fruit weighs 5 to 50 lbs (2 to 23 kg).

Jack, part of a harpsichord M-688

Jackal, carnivore of the genus *Canis* of the family Canidae, *table* F-464

'Jack and Jill', nursery rhyme N-444

'Jack and the Beanstalk', fairy tale F-261

Jackass, donkey. *see in index* Ass

Jackdaw, bird of crow family B-258
  crow's relative C-784, *picture* C-785

Jackfish. *see in index* Northern pike

Jackfruit, tree. *see in index* Jack

Jackhammer P-398, *diagram* P-399
  mining M-428

Jack-in-the-pulpit (or India turnip), American perennial herb of family Araceae F-240, *picture* F-233

Jackleg, an air cylinder M-428

Jackling, Daniel Cowan (1869–1956), U.S. mining engineer and metallurgist, born near Appleton City, Mo.; began Utah's copper industry by utilizing low-grade ore, *picture* U-226

Jack London Square, waterfront area in Oakland, Calif. O-453

Jack mackerel, food fish caught in Pacific off California; iridescent green above and silvery on sides and belly; belongs to jack family Corangidae and has scientific name, *Trachurus symmetricus*, *table* F-136

Jack-o'-lantern, Halloween pumpkin H-17

Jack-o'-lantern, mushroom *Clitocybe illudens* M-665

Jack pine, first large tree *Pinus banksiana* to grow after a forest fire or lumbering; shelters trees that follow; grows in Canada and Great Lakes states; pulpwood, packing cases, posts. *see also in index* Lodgepole pine

Jack plane, a tool T-218

Jackrabbit R-20
  speed record, *picture* A-425

Jacks, Lawrence Pearsall (1860–1955), British philosopher; entered ministry as assistant to Stopford Brooke; professor of philosophy and principal, Manchester College, Oxford University, 1915–31; editor of *Hibbert Journal*, a Unitarian review ('Among the Idol-makers'; 'The Challenge of Life').

Jackson, Alexander Young (1882–1974), Canadian impressionist painter, born in Montreal; noted for rugged landscapes of Canada.

Jackson, Andrew (1767–1845), 7th president of the United States J-2
  Bank of the United States B-73
  Calhoun's opposition C-31
  Clay's objections C-487
  folklore F-268
  Hall of Fame, *table* H-16
  Indian policy I-149, P-341
    Houston H-307
  journalists N-236
  Polk's support P-437
  states' rights S-429d
  Statuary Hall, *table* S-437b
  Tennessee T-88, *picture* T-93
  United States' history U-175
  Van Buren V-261
  veto V-307
  War of 1812 W-32

Jackson, Charles Reginald (1903–68), U.S. novelist, born in Summit, N.J.; novels about psychologically abnormal individuals ('The Lost Weekend'—motion-picture version won Academy award 1945; 'The Fall of Valor'; 'The Outer Edges').

Jackson, Charles Thomas (1805–80), U.S. chemist and geologist, born in Plymouth, Mass.; discovered anesthetic property of ether independently of W.T.G. Morton.

Jackson, Chevalier (1865–1958), U.S. laryngologist, born in Pittsburgh, Pa.; perfected methods for oral removal of foreign bodies from lungs and throat; established the techniques of modern laryngeal surgery.

Jackson, Claiborne Fox (1807–62), U.S. political leader, born in Fleming County, Ky.; governor Missouri 1860–61; brigadier general in army of Confederate States of America
  Missouri M-494

Jackson, Helen Hunt (1830–85), U.S. poet and novelist, long known as H.H., born in Amherst, Mass.; her lyric 'Verses by H. H.' won praise from Emerson; her most famous novel, 'Ramona', was a plea for justice for American Indians.

Jackson, Henry. *see in index* Armstrong, Henry

Jackson, Henry Rootes (1820–98), U.S. diplomat and soldier, born in Athens, Ga.; U.S. minister to Austria 1854–58, to Mexico 1885–86; major general commanding all Georgia state troops at beginning of Civil War; later Confederate brigadier general.

Jackson, James Caleb (1811–95), U.S. physician and abolitionist, born in Manlius, N.Y.; operated spa in Danville, N.Y., 1858–79; author of 'How to Treat the Sick Without Medicine' B-432

Jackson, Jesse L. (born 1941), U.S. clergyman and civil rights leader, born in Greenville, S.C.; a founder and national director of Operation Breadbasket 1966–71; Midwest vice-president Southern Christian Leadership Conference 1970–71; founder and executive director of civil rights group PUSH (People United to Serve Humanity); leader of Rainbow Coalition who ran unsuccessfully as Democratic presidential candidate in 1984 B-302
  Cuban prisoners' release C-804

Jackson, Joseph Harrison, U.S. religious leader, born in Rudyard, Miss.; pastor of Olivet Baptist Church in Chicago, Ill.; president National Baptist Convention U.S.A.; vice-president Baptist World Alliance; observer at Second Ecumenical Council of the Vatican.

Jackson, Mahalia (1911–72), celebrated U.S. gospel singer, born in New Orleans, La.; concerts, radio, and television
  popular music M-680

Jackson, Michael (born 1958), U.S. pop entertainer, born in Gary, Ind.; lead singer with brothers in band, The Jackson 5 (1969–75), known later as The Jacksons; in 1972 began solo career that exploded with 1979 album, 'Off The Wall'; winner of unprecedented 8 Grammy awards for solo album 'Thriller'in 1983; top music videos included 'Thriller', 'Beat It', and 'Billy Jean'; his trademark, a single sequined glove, caused great sensation
  mime M-423
  popular music M-683

Jackson, Reggie (born 1946), U.S. baseball player, born in Wyncote, Pa.; played for Kansas City Royals 1967, Oakland Athletics 1968–75, Baltimore Orioles 1976, New York Yankees 1977–81, California Angels 1982– ; voted most valuable player in American League and World Series 1973; among all-time leaders in home runs, runs batted in, strikeouts.

Jackson, Robert Houghwout (1892–1954), U.S. judge, born in Spring Creek, Pa.; assistant attorney general of U.S. 1936–38; solicitor general 1938–39; attorney general 1940–41; appointed associate justice U.S. Supreme Court 1941; in 1945 appointed chief prosecutor, war crimes trials, Nuremberg, Germany; author of 'The Nürnberg Case' and 'The Supreme Court in the American System of Government'.

Jackson, Sheldon (1834–1909), U.S. Presbyterian missionary, born in Minaville, N.Y.; established many churches; Alaska's first superintendent of public instruction 1885–1909; imported reindeer to replace Eskimos' dwindling food supply.

Jackson, Shirley (1919–65), U.S. writer, born in San Francisco, Calif.; noted for macabre tales ('The Lottery'; 'The Haunting of Hill House'; 'We Have Always Lived in the Castle') R-112a

Jackson, Stonewall (full name Thomas Jonathan Jackson) (1824–63), general, army of Confederate States of America J-9
  Civil War C-474, 480, 643
    Lee L-116
    Stuart S-494
  Hall of Fame, *table* H-16
  Stone Mountain, *picture* G-88
  warfare W-21

Jackson, William Henry (1843–1942), U.S. photographer, best known for his Western landscapes and Indian portraiture P-297, *list* P-294

Jackson, Mich., manufacturing and railroad city on Grand River 70 mi (110 km) w. of Detroit; automobile and airplane parts, tires, metal products; state prison; pop. 39,739, *map* U-41
  convention of 1854 P-433

Jackson, Miss., capital and largest city of state; on Pearl River; pop. 202,895 J-10
  Mississippi M-469, *pictures* M-475, 477
  North America, *map* N-350

Jackson, N.J., 8 mi (13 km) n.w. of Lakewood; farming and fruit growing; pop. of township 25,644.

Jackson, Tenn., city about 75 mi (120 km) n.e. of Memphis; railroad center; textile products, wood products, aluminum foil, batteries, food products; Union University, Lambuth College, Lane College; Federal base in Civil War; pop. 49,131 T-85, *map* T-96

Jackson, Wyo., town on branch of Snake River, about 5 mi (8 km) s. of Grand Teton National Park; annual rodeo; pop. 4,511.

Jackson College, in Medford, Mass.; for women; chartered 1910; liberal arts. *see also in index* Tufts University

Jackson Five, U.S. music group; featured Michael Jackson M-683

Jackson Hole, region in Snake River valley, n.w. Wyo.; about 400 sq mi (1,040 sq km); named in 1829 for David E. Jackson, partner of William Sublette, the fur trader; became retreat of cattle thieves; now a hunting and fishing ground
  Wyoming, *picture* W-394

Jackson Lake, Wyo., near w. boundary; 8 mi (13 km) long; in Grand Teton National Park; its outlet feeds Snake River; waters irrigate Idaho.

Jackson Military Road, road in s. United States M-470

Jackson Purchase (or Coastal Plain, or Coastal Purchase)
  Kentucky K-209, *map* K-210
  Tennessee T-88

Jackson's chameleon, lizard, *picture* L-273

Jackson State University until 1974 Jackson State College, in Jackson, Miss.; established 1877 as Natchez Seminary, became state college 1956; liberal studies, education and technical studies; graduate program; quarter system.

Jacksonville, Ark., city 15 mi (25 km) n.e. of Little Rock; transportation center; metal products, lumber, shipbuilding, chemicals; Little Rock Air

Force Base nearby; pop. 27,589, *map* A-625

Jacksonville, Fla., inland port, railway center, tourist resort; pop. 540,898 J-10
  Florida F-196, *map* F-195
  North America, *map* N-350

Jacksonville, Ill., city 30 mi (50 km) w. of Springfield; vegetable products, clothing, bookbinding, polyethylene film and bags, ferris wheels; Illinois College, MacMurray College; state institutions for blind, deaf, and mentally ill; pop. 20,284, *map* I-52

Jacksonville, N.C., city on New River 46 mi (74 km) n.e. of Wilmington; wood products; Camp Lejeune (U.S. Marine Corps) nearby; pop. 17,056.

Jacksonville State University, in Jacksonville, Ala.; established in 1883; formerly a teachers college; arts and sciences, and teacher education; graduate division A-226

Jacksonville University, in Jacksonville, Fla.; private control; founded 1934; arts and sciences, music and fine arts, teacher education; graduate studies; trimester system.

'Jack Sprat', nursery rhyme N-442

Jack tales, U.S. folktales S-461, 481c

'Jack the Giant Killer', fairy tale F-262

Jack the Ripper, unknown murderer who killed at least seven women in London in 1888 J-11

Jacob, Hebrew patriarch, 2nd son of Isaac, supplanter of his brother Esau; husband of Leah and Rachel and progenitor of Israelites (Bible, Gen. xxv, 1) A-12

Jacob, François (born 1920), French biologist, born in Nancy; with Pasteur Institute 1950–, Collège de France 1964–
  genetics G-54

Jacobean lily. *see in index* Sprekelia

Jacobi, Abraham (1830–1919), U.S. physician, born in Hartum-in-Minden, Westphalia, Germany; called founder of American pediatrics; started clinics in New York City for children.

Jacobi, Frederick (1891–1952), U.S. composer, born in San Francisco, Calif.; assistant conductor, Metropolitan Opera Company, New York City, 1913–17; teacher of composition, Juilliard Graduate School; used Indian melodies; wrote music for Jewish religious service.

Jacobi, Karl Gustav Jakob (1804–51), German mathematician, brother of Moritz H. Jacobi; professor at Königsberg and lecturer at Berlin; contributed to higher mathematics
  mathematics M-216, *table* M-218

Jacobi, Moritz Hermann (1801–74), German physicist and architect, brother of Karl Gustav Jacobi; said to have constructed first electrically propelled boat.

Jacobins, in French history J-11
  French Revolution F-403
  Lafayette L-20
  Napoleon N-13
  Robespierre R-223

Jacobites, adherents of James II or the direct Stuart line after English Revolution of 1688; famous uprisings in 1715 and 1745 to restore Stuart pretenders P-496

Jacobs, Amos. *see in index* Thomas, Danny

Jacobs, Joseph (1854–1916), Jewish scholar and folklorist, born in Sydney, Australia; in U.S. after 1900 ('English Fairy Tales'; 'Celtic Fairy Tales') S-466, 478, 481b, R-110a

Jacobs, William Wymark (1863–1943), British humorist, born in London, England; wrote sea stories and horror tales ('Snug Harbour; Collected Stories').

Jacobsen, Jens Peter (1847–85), Danish novelist and poet J-11

Jacob's fan shell (or St. James's scallop shell), *Pecten jacobaeus*, *picture* S-149

Jacobs house, Usonian house in Madison, Wis. W-367

Jacob's staff. *see in index* Ocotillo

Jacobus Jonker (or Jonker), diamond D-131, *picture* D-129

Jacoby, Oswald (1902–84), U.S. bridge expert, born in Brooklyn, N.Y.; bridge player of the year 1959 and 1961–63; elected to Bridge Hall of Fame 1965; wrote syndicated column on bridge and numerous books on card games.

Jacquard, Joseph-Marie (1752–1834), French inventor, born in Lyon; known for inventing first loom for figured weaving (1800) J-12
  carpet loom R-312, *picture* R-315
  computer development C-628
  Industrial Revolution I-179
  lace machine L-13

Jacque, Charles Emile (1813–94), French etcher and genre painter of the Barbizon School; favored rural scenes and subjects ('Flock of Sheep', in the Louvre).

Jacques-Cartier, Que., former suburb of Montreal, *map* Q-11

Jacques-Cartier, Mount, peak of e. Quebec, on Gaspé Peninsula; highest point 4,160 ft (1,270 m) in Quebec Q-9b, *map* Q-9a

Jade, semiprecious stone ranging in color from white to nearly black, most valuable when emerald-green shade; old jade dug from tombs has often turned blue, yellow, red, or brown
  carving, *picture* A-685
  jewelry and gems J-112

Jadeite (sometimes called Chinese jade), a variety of jade, most treasured in emerald-green shade; occurs both in Burma and in Tibet; chemical formula $NaAl(SiO_3)_2$ M-436

Jade plant, houseplant H-289

Jaeger, seabird, belonging with the skuas to the family Stercorariidae; dark, falconlike birds that chase gulls and terns, forcing them to drop their catch of fish; flash of white across base of primary feathers, and long central tail feathers distinguish them; nest in Arctic regions, migrating across United States and Europe to winter in Southern Hemisphere; three species: pomarine jaeger *Stercorarius pomarinus*, parasitic *S. parasiticus*, long-tailed *S. longicaudus*.

Jael, Hebrew woman exalted in the 'Song of Deborah' as "blessed among women" because she killed Sisera, leader of the Canaanites (Bible, Judges iv).

Jaffa, Israel. *see in index* Tel Aviv-Yafo

Jagannath (or Juggernaut), title of Hindu god Vishnu; temple at Puri, India; at annual festival idol is drawn on enormous car under which some devotees have cast themselves.

Jagannath, India. *see in index* Puri

Jagger, Mick (born 1944), U.S. rock musician M-682

Jaggery, brown sugar obtained chiefly from the sap of East Indian jaggery palms; similar in appearance to cane sugar.

Jagiellon Dynasty, royal family J-12
  Casimir IV C-196

Jagiellonian University, in Krakow, Poland K-303

Jaguar, member of the cat family J-12
  fur, *table* F-464
  leopard L-135

Jaguarundi, wild cat *Felis yagouaroundi*, *picture* C-216

Jahan. *see in index* Shah Jahan

Jahangir (1569–1627), Mughal emperor of India S-127

Jahiz, al- (776–868), Muslim writer I-366

Jahn, Friedrich Ludwig (1778–1852), German educator; strove for the awakening of German national feeling by organizing youth of all classes into groups called Turnvereine (gymnastic societies).

Jai alai (or pelota vasca), game J-13
  Philippines P-255a

Jaimes Freyre, Ricardo (1870–1933), Bolivian writer L-69, 72

Jainism, religion J-14
  Hinduism H-157
  India I-68
  Mahavira M-48
  monks and monasticism M-539

Jaipur, former princely Rajputana state of India, now part of Rajasthan state; chiefly agricultural; some marble, copper, and cobalt, *map* A-607

Jaipur, capital of Rajasthan state, in n.w. India, 150 mi (240 km) s.w. of Delhi; famous for jewelry and other handicrafts; site of the pink palace and the Hall of the Winds; pop. 613,144, *picture* I-71, *map* I-83

Jaisalmer, city in n.w. India; pop. 20,355, *pictures* I-64, 69, *map* I-84

Jajce, Yugoslavia, town 65 mi (105 km) n.w. of Sarajevo; chief outpost of eastern Christendom from 1463 until it was captured by the Turks in 1528.

Jajmans, caste families I-70

Jakarta (or Djakarta, or Batavia), Republic of Indonesia, capital and largest city; pop. 6,556,000 J-15
  Asia, *map* A-697
  Indonesia I-160, *map* I-166
  world, *map* W-297

Jalal Ud-Din Rumi (1207–73), Persian poet J-17
  Iqbal I-304
  Islamic literature I-367

Jalan Thamrin, boulevard in Jakarta, Indonesia, *picture* J-15

Jalap, herbaceous climbing plant *Ipomoea purga* with alternate heart-shaped leaves and large purplish-pink flowers; grows in Mexico near the town of Xalapa, whence its name; large root tubers contain a resin used in cathartics.

Jalisco, Mexico, state on central w. coast; 30,941 sq mi (80,137 sq km); cap. Guadalajara; corn, wheat, cotton, tobacco; cattle; iron, silver, gold, lead, copper, zinc; one of wealthiest states; pop. 4,157,357, *map* M-341

Jaluit, atoll of Marshall Islands, in Pacific; measures 38 by 23 mi (61 by 37 km); chief island Jaluit; naval base; occupied by U.S. forces in 1945; pop. 925, *map* P-3

Jamahiriya, form of socialism L-190

Jamaica, island nation of the West Indies; 4,411 sq mi (11,424 sq km); cap. Kingston; pop. 2,222,000 J-17
  cities. *see in index* Kingston and other cities by name
  colonial history A-337
  Commonwealth membership C-602
  flag, *picture* F-166
  literature
   Caribbean C-167
   folktales, *list* S-482
  North America, *map* N-350
  Peace Corps, *picture* P-143
  railroad mileage, *table* R-85
  reggae M-682
  sponges S-394
  West Indies W-155, *picture* W-158, *map* W-159
  world, *map* W-297
  World War II W-325

Jamaican fruit bat, *picture* B-104

Jamaica pepper. *see in index* Allspice

Jamaica sorrel. *see in index* Roselle

James, called in Bible's New Testament the "brother of Jesus"; often identified with James the Less; traditional author of Epistle of James.

James I (or James VI) (1566–1625), king of England and Scotland J-19
  Acadia A-14
   Nova Scotia N-398, 403
  building code S-158
  England E-245
  Fawkes F-49
  Ireland I-322
  Mary, Queen of Scots M-164
  Puritans P-539
  Raleigh R-91
  Scotland S-71
  Shakespeare S-131
  Stuart S-493

James II (1633–1701), king of England J-19
  Anne's succession A-467
  England E-247
  Glorious Revolution G-168
  Gwyn G-322
  Ireland I-322
  Marlborough M-147
  New York N-256
  religious controversies A-418
  Stuart S-493
  William III W-207

James I (1394–1437), king of Scotland, poet and constitutional reformer; succeeded 1406 while captive in England; released 1424; murdered by rebel nobles.

James IV (1473–1513), king of Scotland; succeeded 1488; disputes with Henry VIII led to invasion of England; killed at Flodden S-70

James V (1512–42), king of Scotland; succeeded 1513; refused to become involved in policies of his uncle, Henry VIII of England, and failed to rout Henry's invading army at Solway Moss (1542) because of lack of support of Scottish nobles; died as result of this humiliation; succeeded by infant daughter, Mary, queen of Scots; appears in Sir Walter Scott's 'Lady of the Lake' S-70

James VI (1566–1625), king of Scotland. *see in index* James I, king of England

James, Daniel, Jr. (nickname Chappie) (1920–78), U.S. Air Force officer, born in Pensacola, Fla.; flew combat missions in Korean and Vietnam wars; became second black general in Air Force history 1970; assistant secretary of defense for public affairs 1970–73; principal deputy assistant secretary of defense for public affairs 1973–74 B-298

James, Edmund Janes (1855–1925), U.S. educator, born in Jacksonville, Ill.; president Northwestern University 1902–4; University of Illinois 1904–20; active also in civic affairs.

James, Frank (1843–1915), U.S. outlaw O-619

James, Harry (1916–83), U.S. composer, trumpeter, and bandleader; born in Albany, Ga.; at 15 won state championship as trumpeter; organized own orchestra 1939 M-684

James, Henry (1843–1916), U.S. novelist and essayist J-20
  American literature A-351
  creative writing W-377
  psychological novels N-410

James, Jesse (1847–82), notorious U.S. outlaw J-20
  folklore F-268
  Missouri history M-494
  outlaws O-619
  Younger brothers Y-425

James, Marquis (1891–1955), U.S. writer, born in Springfield, Mo.; began career as a news reporter in Enid, Okla., at age of 14 ('The Raven: a Biography of Sam Houston', Pulitzer prize 1930; 'Andrew Jackson', 2-vol. biography, Pulitzer prize 1938; 'The Cherokee Strip', story of Marquis James's boyhood).

James, Phyllis Dorothy (born 1920), writer, *list* D-119

James, Thomas (1782–1847), U.S. trader and trapper; with Missouri Fur Company's first expedition (1809) and later with Andrew Henry in Wyoming; made trading expedition to Santa Fe (1821) with John McKnight by way of Mississippi and Arkansas rivers; another expedition (1822) to perilous Comanche territory, now Oklahoma; member of Illinois legislature (1825–27).

James, William (1842–1910), U.S. philosopher and psychologist J-21
  psychology P-266, 520

James, William Roderick (1892–1942), U.S. writer and artist, born near Great Falls, Mont.; left an orphan and adopted by fur trader; ranch life and horses his specialty; illustrated his own books; awarded Newbery Medal for 'Smoky, the Cowhorse' 1927 ('Sand'; 'Cowboys North and South'; 'Horses I've Known'; 'American Cowboy'; 'Big Enough'; 'Lone Cowboy') R-111d
  'Smoky', *list* H-274

James, Epistle of, book of Bible's New Testament, addressed by James "the Lord's brother," from Jerusalem to 12 tribes of the Dispersion, inculcating practical morality.

James Bay, Canada, southern arm of Hudson Bay, about 300 mi (480 km) long and 160 mi (260 km) wide; named for Thomas James, English navigator who explored it in 1631–32, *maps* C-112, N-350

James-Lange theory, in psychology J-21

James Madison University (formerly Madison College), in Harrisonburg, Va.; state control; founded 1908; liberal arts, education, medical technology; graduate studies.

Jameson, Sir Leander Starr (1853–1917), South African statesman and physician, born in Edinburgh, Scotland; friend of Cecil Rhodes; leader of Jameson Raid on the Transvaal (1895); became leader of South African Progressive party and prime minister 1904–8 of Cape Colony
- raid B-331
- Rhodes R-195

Jameson, Margaret Storm (1891–1986), British novelist, born in Whitby, Yorkshire; married Guy Chapman; her 'Three Kingdoms' deals with the problem of marriage and a career for women; 'The Lovely Ship', 'The Voyage Home', and 'A Richer Dust' are related novels concerning the life of a Victorian woman; 'Europe to Let' and 'Cousin Honoré' treat Nazi domination of Europe.

James River (or Dakota River), river rising in e.-central North Dakota, flowing through South Dakota to Missouri River; length 500 mi (800 km), *maps* S-323, U-70
- North Dakota N-373

James River, river in Virginia, 340 mi (550 km); expands into broad estuary 50 mi (80 km) long flowing through Hampton Roads into Chesapeake Bay, *maps* V-331, U-59
- Richmond R-204

James River and Kanawha Canal, canal in Virginia, paralleled James River from Richmond to Buchanan, *map* C-126

James the Elder, Saint, also called the Greater; in Bible, son of Zebedee, one of the 12 apostles; festival July 25 A-506

James the Younger, Saint, also called the Less; in Bible, son of Alpheus, one of the 12 apostles; festival May 1 A-506

Jamestown, N.D., city on James River, 95 mi (150 km) w. of Fargo; trading center of agricultural and stock-raising region; Jamestown College; state mental hospital; incorporated 1883; pop. 16,280 N-382, *map* U-40

Jamestown, N.Y., manufacturing city on outlet of Chautauqua Lake, 58 mi (93 km) s.w. of Buffalo; wood and metal furniture, other metal products, wood products; Jamestown Community College; pop. 35,775, *map* U-41

Jamestown, Va., first permanent settlement made by English in North America J-21
- America, discovery and colonization A-336
- Chesapeake Bay C-304
- glassware industry G-164
- Smith S-219
- U.S. history U-168, *picture* U-169
- Virginia V-335, *pictures* V-340, *map* V-349
  - Williamsburg W-209

Jamestown College, in Jamestown, N.D.; affiliated with Presbyterian Church, U.S.; first organized 1883 but closed 1893; reopened 1909 ; arts and sciences, education N-375

Jamil (died 701), Islamic author I-365

Jam knot, in fishing, *picture* F-143

Jammu, Jammu and Kashmir, winter capital; silk, drugs, rubber goods, grain milling; pop. 155,249 J-22
- Asia, *map* A-697
- India, *map* I-83

Jammu and Kashmir, mountainous state n. of peninsula of India; 86,023 sq mi (222,798 sq km); pop. 5,981,600 J-22
- Himalayas H-154
- India I-79, *map* I-83
- K2, peak K-166
- Pakistan-India dispute P-79
- world, *map* W-297

Janácek, Leos (1854–1928), Czech composer, born in Moravia; choral works ('Our Father'; 'The Eternal Gospel') and operas ('Jenufa'; 'Katya Kabanova')
- opera O-569

Jane, Frederick Thomas (1870–1916), British naval officer; founded the annuals 'Jane's Fighting Ships', first published 1898, and 'All the World's Aircraft', first published 1910.

'Jane Eyre', novel by Brontë B-462
- English literature, *picture* E-276
- reading, R-111c, *picture* R-111f

Janesville, Wis., industrial city on Rock River, 72 mi (116 km) s.w. of Milwaukee in rich dairying and tobacco-growing region; fountain pens, automobile assembly, folding doors, dairy equipment; state school for visually handicapped; pop. 51,071, *map* U-41

Janis, Elsie (originally Elsie Janis Bierbower) (1889–1956), U.S. actress noted for clever impersonation; born in Columbus, Ohio; appeared in 'The Belle of New York' (1904), 'The Fortune Teller', 'Elsie Janis and Her Gang'.

Janissary music, style of band music B-55

Janizaries (or Janissaries), a powerful military force of the Ottoman Empire; suppressed 1826 by Mahmud II O-616

Jan Mayen Island, island between Iceland and Svalbard; incorporated in Norwegian state, 1929; discovered by Henry Hudson, 1607; rediscovered by Jan Mayen, Dutchman, a little later; 36 mi (58 km) long, 11½ mi (18 km) wide; radio station and weather bureau built 1921 by Norway; center of whaling and sealing expeditions; pop. 24, *map* E-360
- world, *map* W-297

Janney, Eli Hamilton (1831–1912), U.S. inventor, born in Loudoun County, Virginia R-79

Jannings, Emil (1886–1950), U.S. actor, born in Brooklyn, N.Y.; grew up in Europe; won fame on German stage and screen; made motion pictures in United States 1926–29; was first actor to win Academy award, 1928, for 'The Way of All Flesh'; returned to Europe 1929, *picture* M-621

Jansen, Cornelis (Latin Cornelius Jansenius) (1585–1638), Dutch theologian, bishop of Ypres, founder of Jansenism.

Jansenism, system of reformed belief in Roman Catholicism, named for Cornelis Jansen; some doctrines (predestination, loss of free will, irresistible grace) and religious austerity suggestive of Calvinism; disrupted France in 17th and 18th centuries; greatest center, abbey of Port-Royal-des-Champs, destroyed in 1710 by order of Louis XIV
- Pascal P-136
- Racine R-28

Jansky, Karl Guthe (1905–50), U.S. radio engineer, born in Norman, Okla.; Bell Telephone Laboratories scientist from 1928; direction finder research during World War II; founder of radio astronomy.

Janssen, Geraert. *see in index* Johnson, Garret

Janssen, Pierre Jules César (1824–1907), French astronomer, born in Paris; discoverer of helium in sun; founded and directed observatory on Mont Blanc 1893 S-372
- helium H-123

Janssen, Werner (born 1900), U.S. conductor and composer, born in New York City; conductor Portland Symphony Orchestra 1947–49, San Diego Philharmonic 1952–54, Toronto Philharmonic 1956–57.

Janssen, Zacharias (or Zacharias Jansen) (fl. 16th century), Dutch spectacle maker of Middelburg, s.w. Netherlands; believed to have invented use of two lenses as compound microscope about 1590 M-381

Jansson, Tove (born 1914), Finnish author and illustrator of children's books, born in Helsinki; best known for stories of imaginary troll-like creatures called Moomins; recipient of many literary prizes; won Hans Christian Andersen medal 1966.

Jansz, Willem (fl. 17th century), Dutch explorer A-815

Januarius, Saint San Gennaro (272?–305?), martyr and patron saint of Naples, Italy; bishop of Benevento; phials believed to contain blood of martyr are preserved in cathedral at Naples; reliquary shown several times during year when the blood is said to liquefy; commemorated September 19.

January, first month of the Gregorian calendar C-30
- birthdays of famous persons. *see in index* Birthdays, *table*

Janus, in Roman mythology, god of the door and good beginnings M-701, *picture* M-702

Janvier, Thomas Allibone (1849–1913), U.S. historical writer, born in Philadelphia, Pa.; years in Colorado and Mexico provided background for 'Aztec Treasure House', 'Stories of Old New Spain', 'In the Sargasso Sea', 'Santa Fé's Partner'; wrote also 'The Dutch Foundry of New York' and 'Henry Hudson'.

Japan, island nation of Asia; 145,785 sq mi (377,580 sq km); cap. Tokyo; pop. 118,460,000 J-23
- agriculture A-513
- amusements A-383
- arts
  - architecture
    - Buddhist influence A-546
    - homes S-155
  - bonsai B-344
  - calligraphy C-57
  - cats C-212
  - ceremonial dolls D-216
  - dance D-30
  - dragon legends D-238
  - drawing D-256
  - enameling E-208
  - folk art F-253
  - folk music F-273
  - furniture F-456
  - interior design I-246
  - literature. *see in index* Japanese literature
  - metalworking M-311
    - sword, *picture* S-546
  - mime M-423
  - motion pictures M-619, 622
  - painting P-67f
  - pottery and porcelain P-473
  - puppets P-536
  - witchcraft legend W-266
- Asia, *map* A-697
- chrysanthemums C-408
- cities C-453. *see also in index* cities listed below and other cities by name
  - Nagoya N-3
  - Okinawa O-520
  - Tokyo T-203
  - Yokohama Y-422
- climate A-675
- clothing C-507, *picture* C-506
- communications
  - postal service, *picture* P-464
  - satellite, *table* S-344
- conscription C-667
- customs
  - Christmas C-404
  - fan F-22
  - kite flying K-253, *picture* K-252
  - marriage M-151
  - New Year festivities N-243
  - tea ceremony E-318, T-45
- economics E-61
  - cartels M-544
  - employment and unemployment E-206
  - taxation, *table* T-35
- espionage E-304
- fire fighting F-111
- history
  - fascism F-38
  - Four-Power Pact W-71
  - Fujiwara period F-445
  - Hojo family H-200
  - Korean War K-296, *picture* K-288
  - occupation
    - East Indies E-47, N-130
    - Harbin H-33
    - Hebei H-112
    - Lüda L-328
    - Manchuria M-94
    - Taiwan T-13
  - peace movements P-143d
  - Perry's visits (1853–54) P-16
  - Russo-Japanese War R-362, *picture* R-287
  - Shanghai occupation S-143
    - air force A-159
    - India I-78
    - Singapore S-205
    - U.S. embargo E-198
  - World War I W-303, 319
  - World War II W-322, *map* W-329
    - Battle of Midway M-92
  - warfare W-17, 23
- housing H-293, 297, 302
- illiteracy P-450
- industry I-196
  - automobiles A-865
  - carpets R-316
  - fisheries F-138
  - garment industry G-35
  - pearls P-149, *picture* P-148
  - robot R-226
  - sake B-134
  - silk S-197, *picture* S-198
  - television T-78
- international relations I-260
  - Philippines P-257, *chart* P-257a
  - United Kingdom E-255
  - United States U-190, *chart* U-128
- land use reforms L-29
- language. *see in index* Japanese language
- man M-86
- martial arts M-159
- masks M-187, *picture* M-186
- Mount Fuji F-444
- mythology M-699, 704, *picture* M-696
- national parks N-27
- national symbols
  - flag, *picture* F-166
  - song, *table* N-64
- newspaper publishing N-240
- population, *charts* P-447
  - classification, *chart* R-26
  - migration of people M-400
  - multiple births M-649
- religion R-143
  - Buddhism B-483
  - Zen Z-450
- seal hunt S-100
- terrorism T-113
- transportation, *pictures* T-263
  - monorail M-545
  - railroad mileage, *table* R-85
  - ships S-176a
    - Maritime Service Agency C-529
- Wake Island W-4
- weights and measures, *table* W-141
- welfare programs W-146
- wrestling W-366
- world, *map* W-297
- Yellow Sea Y-412

Japan, Sea of, part of Pacific Ocean between Japan and Asia J-79, *map* J-78. *see also in index* Ocean, *table*
- Asia, *map* A-697
- Russo-Japanese War R-362
- warfare, *list* W-15
- world, *map* W-297

Japan Current (or Kuroshio), Japanese for black current; ocean current of n. Pacific
- Japanese climate J-60
- oceanography O-475
- ocean waves and tides O-490

Japanese Alps, mountain range extending n. to s. through central part of island of Honshu; formed by volcanic activity.

Japanese barberry, tree *Berberis Thunbergii* H-115

Japanese beetle, small metallic green and brown scarab beetle *Popillia japonica* B-140
- insects I-225, *picture* I-212

Japanese birch (or monarch birch), valuable timber tree *Betula maximo wicziana* in Japan B-239

Japanese chestnut, tree *Castanea crenata* of the Fagaceae family C-307

Japanese giant salamander, largest of all amphibians *Megalobatrachus japonicus*, *picture* A-377

Japanese honeysuckle, plant *Lonicera japonica*, *picture* F-237

Japanese hop, an ornamental twining herb *Humulus japonicus* of the mulberry family, usually with pretty 5-lobed leaves splashed and streaked with white; hardy annual.

Japanese iris, a perennial flower G-25

Japanese ivy (or Boston ivy), plant *Parthenocissus tricuspidata* of the Vitaceae family I-408

Japanese language L-33, *diagram* L-35
- Japanese literature J-79
- writing W-372

Japanese literature J-79
- children's L-252, *picture* L-245, *chart* L-257
- folktales S-467, *picture* S-481d , *list* S-478
- Kawabata K-193
- Natsume N-67

Japanese persimmon, Asian persimmon *Diospyros kaki* widely cultivated for its large edible fruit P-215

Japanese spaniel, dog, *picture* D-205

Japanese spider crab, crustacean *Macrocheira kaempferi* C-792

Japanese spurge (or *Pachysandra terminalis*), a ground cover
- growing conditions G-27

Japan National Railways (JNR) J-42
Japanned work, furniture F-458
Japan quince, shrub or small tree *Cydonia japonica* grown for the beauty of its spring flowers; green fruit is fragrant but inedible Q-18
Japan wax, vegetable wax obtained from the berries of several sumacs; used chiefly in polishes W-110
Japheth, in Bible, a son of Noah; according to tradition his descendants inhabited Europe and Asia Minor along the Mediterranean coast.
Japonisme, art style I-246
Japurá River (or Caquetá River, or Yapurá River), one of chief tributaries of Amazon, rising in Colombian Andes; 1,800 mi (2,900 km), *maps* B-425, S-298
Jaques-Dalcroze, Émile (1865–1950), Swiss composer, born in Vienna, Austria; originator of a system of eurythmics.
'Jarabe Tapatio, El', Mexican hat dance F-256
Jarana, Mexican folk dance, *picture* F-257
Jardin des Merveilles, children's zoo in Montreal, Que. Z-460
Jardin des Plantes, garden in Paris, France; 74 acres (30 hectares), *map* P-120
Jargon (or jargoon), name given to green, blue, and colorless varieties of zircon used as gems.
Jarir ibn 'Atiyah ibn al-Khatafa (650?–729?), Islamic poet I-365
Jarnac, France, town 60 mi (100 km) n.e. of Bordeaux; scene of duke of Anjou's victory over Huguenots in 1569; pop. 4,391 C-546
  France, *map* F-369
Järnefelt, Edvard Armas (1869–1958), Swedish conductor and composer, born in Viipuri, Finland (now Vyborg, U.S.S.R.); brother-in-law of J. Sibelius; wrote orchestral works, choral works, piano pieces, songs.
Jarrell, Randall (1914–65), U.S. poet and university professor, born in Nashville, Tenn. ('The Woman at the Washington Zoo' won 1960 National Book Award; for children: 'The Bat-Poet', 'The Gingerbread Rabbit'; 'The Complete Poems') R-111a
Jaruzelski, Wojciech (born 1923), Polish public official, born in Kurow, Poland; first secretary and premier 1981– P-415
Jarves, Deming (1790–1869), U.S. pioneer glass manufacturer in United States; founded glass works at Sandwich, Mass.
Jarvik heart, artificial mechanical heart powered by compressed air from external source and monitored by computer; success of most widely used model, Jarvik-7, as permanent replacement human heart was disputed; more commonly accepted as temporary replacement pending human heart transplant.
Jarvis, Anna M. (1864–1948), founder of Mother's Day, born Grafton, W.Va.
Jarvis, Gregory (1944–86), U.S. astronaut, born in Detroit, Michigan, killed in explosion of space shuttle *Challenger*.
Jarvis Christian College, in Hawkins, Tex.; affiliated with Disciples of Christ; chartered 1912; liberal arts.
Jarvis College. *see in index* Colorado School of Mines
Jarvis Island, tiny sand and coral island in Pacific, about 1,300 mi (2,090 km) s. of Honolulu; colonized by U.S. in 1935 as way station for flights from Hawaii to Australia, *maps* P-3, W-297
Jasione, genus of annual or perennial plants of the bellflower family, native to Europe; flowers blue or white, grow in heads united by whorl of tiny leaves (involucre). Shepherd's-scabious or sheep's-bit *J. perennis* has long-stalked globular heads of blue.
Jasmine, flower, *picture* F-227
Jasmine, Cape. *see in index* Cape jasmine
Jason, in Greek mythology, leader of Argonauts, *picture* M-698
  Homeric legend H-224
'Jason et Medée', work by Noverre B-33
Jasper, William (1750?–79), American Revolutionary War soldier; hero of many exploits, especially the rescue (1776) of the colors at Fort Moultrie; refused to accept commission because of lack of formal education.
Jasper, Ala., city 40 mi (60 km) n.w. of Birmingham; in agricultural and coal-mining area; lumber, cotton, building materials; pop. 11,894, *map* A-237
Jasper, gem material J-115
  hobby H-187
Jasper National Park, park in Alberta A-246, *picture* A-262
  Canada, *map* C-109
Jaspers, Karl (1883–1969), German philosopher, born in Oldenburg; professor of philosophy at universities of Heidelberg and Basel; developed his existentialism in 'Future of Mankind', 'Reason and Existence', and 'Philosophy' P-267
Jasperware, Wedgwood stoneware P-475, *picture* W-130
Jassy, Romania. *see in index* Iasi
Jastrow, Joseph (1863–1944), U.S. psychologist, born in Poland; professor of psychology, University of Wisconsin 1888–1927.
Jastrow, Robert (born 1925), U.S. physicist, born in New York, N.Y.; chief, Theoretical Division, Goddard Space Flight Center, NASA 1958–61, director Goddard Institute of Space Flight Studies 1961–; author of 'Exploration of Space'.
'Jatakas', Indian literature, tales of Buddha's several births in the form of animals S-467
  Indian literature I-106, *picture* I-107
Jati. *see in index* Caste
JATO (or jet-assisted take-off) F-126
Jaundice. *see also in index* Hepatitis
  liver diseases L-261
Jaunpur, India, city in Uttar Pradesh state on Gumti River 34 mi (55 km) n.w. of Benares; once a magnificent Mohammedan capital; pop. 80,737, *map* I-83
Jaurès, Jean (1859–1914), French socialist J-83
  peace movements P-143c
Java, island in Indonesia; 48,504 sq mi (125,625 sq km); chief city Jakarta; pop. (including island of Madura) 60,909,381 E-45
  Asia, *map* A-697
  batik B-106
  cities. *see in index* Jakarta and other cities by name
  fossils A-194
    man M-86
  Indonesia I-158, *map* I-166
  people, *picture* R-25
  products
    quinine Q-18
    rice, *pictures* R-199
  world, *map* W-297
'Java', British frigate S-177g
Java man (or Pithecanthropus erectus), human ancestor M-89
Javan rhinoceros R-178
Java Sea, part of Pacific n. of Java, s. of Borneo, *map* I-166
  Asia, *map* A-697
Java Trench, trench in Indonesia I-158
Javelin, track and field T-245
Javits, Jacob Koppel (1904–86), U.S. public official and lawyer, born in New York, N.Y.; attorney general of New York 1955–57; U.S. senator (Republican) 1957–80.
Jaw, in anatomy
  ant A-468
  fish A-461
  human S-210
    diseases
      phossy jaw P-271
      temperomandibular joint syndrome D-102
  mammal M-80
  rodents R-236
Jaw crusher, mining machine M-429, *picture* M-427
Jawless fish, prehistoric fish, *table* E-24
Jaxartes River. *see in index* Syr-Dar'ya
Jay, John (1745–1829), U.S. jurist and statesman J-83
  Constitution defense U-142
  Federalist papers F-51
  supreme court S-518a
  Washington W-42
  Wisconsin W-253
Jay, bird C-784, *table* A-427
Jaya, Puncak (or Mount Carstensz), volcanic peak on the island of New Guinea, Irian Jaya, Indonesia 16,503 ft (5,030 m) N-173
Jayapura, Indonesia. *see in index* Djadjapura
JAYCEES (or The United States Jaycees), organization for young men 21–35 interested in leadership training through civic improvement projects; founded 1920 by Henry Giessenbier; headquarters, Tulsa, Okla.
Jayewardene, Junius Richard (born 1906), Sri Lanka, political leader, born in Colombo; as finance minister developed Colombo Plan 1950; United National party leader since 1973; prime minister 1977–78; president 1978– S-402
Jayhawkers, guerrilla fighters; name applied especially to Kansans; used in Civil War for Unionist guerrilla fighters.
Jayhawker State, popular name sometimes applied to Kansas.
Jay's Treaty (1794), between U.S. and Great Britain
  arbitration A-529, *table* T-274
  Jay J-83
Jazz, music J-84
  Africa's contribution A-93
  bands B-54, *picture* B-57
  Chicago C-315
  music
    classical music M-677
    popular music M-679
  Newport, R.I., *picture* R-189
  people
    Armstrong A-632
    Beiderbecke B-143
    Coleman C-545
    Coltrane C-587
    Davis D-43
    Ellington E-193
    Gershwin brothers G-135
    Young Y-424
'Jazz, Plate XV', silk screen design by Matisse, *picture* G-233
Jazz Age, cultural period in U.S. history F-147
'Jazz Man, The', novel by Weik R-111e, *picture* R-107
'Jazz Singer, The' (1927), motion picture by Crosland M-621, *picture* M-623
J.C. Penney Company, Inc., chain of retail dry goods and clothing stores, started 1902 in Kemmerer, Wyo., by **James Cash Penney** (1875–1971), born in Hamilton, Mo.
Jean, grand duke of Luxembourg (born 1921), succeeded to throne 1964 upon abdication of his mother, Charlotte.
Jean, heavy twilled cotton fabric resembling drill but more closely woven and finer; woven in white, plain colors, or stripes; also called middy twill.
Jean de Meung (born Jean Chopinel) (1250–1305), French poet, born in Meung; known chiefly as author of second part of 'Romance of the Rose'; satirized women, clergy, and nobility F-394
Jeanes, Anna Thomas (1822–1907), U.S. philanthropist, born in Philadelphia, Pa.; Quaker; made significant donations to Philadelphia institutions. *see also in index* Negro Rural School Fund
Jean Jacques I. *see in index* Dessalines, Jean Jacques
Jeanne d'Albret (1528–72), queen of Navarre, mother of Henry IV of France
Jeanne d'Arc. *see in index* Joan of Arc
Jeanneret-Gris, Charles Edouard. *see in index* Le Corbusier
Jeannette, Pa., city 22 mi (35 km) s.e. of Pittsburgh; in agricultural, coal, and natural-gas region; glass, electrical machinery, foundry products, tires; pop. 13,106, *map* P-184
'Jeannette' Expedition, U.S. Arctic expedition 1879 under Lieut. Comdr. George W. De Long. Ice sank *Jeanette* n. of Siberia June 1881. De Long and most of crew reached shore, but some of these, including De Long, died of starvation Oct. 1881. Discovery 1884 of crew's possessions on s.w. coast of Greenland confirmed theory of continuous Arctic current.
Jeanron, Philippe Auguste (1808–77), French genre, landscape, and historical painter; expanded collection in Louvre while in charge of museum; founded Luxembourg Museum; art critic ('Isle of Calypso'; 'Mirabeau').
Jeans, James (1877–1946), British physicist, astronomer, mathematician, and author J-88
  gaseous-tidal theory P-355
Jebb, Sir Richard Claverhouse (1841–1905), Scottish classical scholar, born in Dundee; professor of Greek at University of Glasgow 1875–89, at Cambridge University 1889–1905; known for critical editions and translations of Greek writers.
Jebel-es-Sheikh, Syria. *see in index* Hermon, Mount
Jebel Jermaq (or Jermak), upper Galilean mountains; highest point in Palestine proper; 3,934 ft (1,199 m).
Jebel Neba, peak near Dead Sea (2,631 ft; 802 m), probably ancient Nebo, a mountain in Palestine from which Moses saw the Promised Land.
Jebel Toubkal, mountain. *see in index* Toubkal
Jecker, Jean Baptiste (1810–71), Swiss banker whose extensive holdings of land in Mexico involved France in quarrels with Mexico, and were a cause of intervention by Napoleon III.
Jeejeebhoy, Sir Jamsetjee (1783–1859), Indian merchant and philanthropist, born in Bombay of Parsee parents; famed for philanthropy among all sects and nationalities in India; given knighthood and baronetcy by England.
Jeep, U.S. Army, a midget ¼-ton (¼-metric ton) combat motor vehicle carrying 3 to 6 people, antitank guns, mortars, and machine guns up to 800 pounds (360 kilograms); its mobility and high speed have made it valuable in attack and reconnaissance work; name derived from g.p. (general purpose); also trade name for small civilian vehicle of similar type.
Jeepney, small bus used in the Philippines P-254
Jefferies, Richard (1848–87), English naturalist and writer born near Swindon, England; remembered for portrayal of English countryside ('The Gamekeeper at Home: Sketches of Natural History and Rural Life'; 'The Story of My Heart'; autobiography).
Jeffers, Robinson (1887–1962), U.S. poet, born in Pittsburgh, Pa.; work shows rugged strength, tragic, often violent intensity of passion ('Selected Poetry'; 'Be Angry at the Sun'; 'The Double Axe & Other Poems'; 'Hungerfield, and Other Poems') A-368
Jefferson, Joseph (1829–1905), U.S. actor, born in Philadelphia, Pa.; most famous role as title character in the popular play 'Rip Van Winkle' A-27
Jefferson, Thomas (1743–1826), 3rd president of the United States J-89
  architect A-572
  banjo S-492
  Bill of Rights B-196
  bioethics B-214
  constitutional amendment U-144
  constitutional law views C-685
  Declaration of Independence D-53
  Enlightenment E-289
  freedom of the press N-235
  Hall of Fame, *table* H-16
  human rights H-320
  Lewis and Clark Expedition L-143
    Missouri River M-510
  Louisiana Purchase L-324
    Minnesota M-445
    New Orleans N-233

memorials
Jefferson National Expansion Memorial N.H.S. S-22
Mount Rushmore N. Mem., *picture* S-321
Missouri Compromise M-507
people
Adams A-34
Burr treason trial B-513
Hamilton H-22
Jackson J-8
Madison M-26
Washington W-42
United States' history U-174
Virginia, *picture* V-342
Richmond R-205
War of 1812 W-29
Washington, D.C. W-71
writings A-344

Jefferson, Mount, peak in the Cascades of Oregon, in w. Jefferson County; 10,495 ft (3,200 m).

Jefferson City, Mo., state capital, on s. bank of Missouri River in center of state; pop. 33,619 J-96
Missouri M-491, 500, *picture* M-497
North America, *map* N-350

Jefferson Heights, La., unincorporated community just w. of New Orleans; pop. 16,489.

Jefferson Memorial, monument in Washington, D.C. W-67, *pictures* J-95, W-66

Jefferson National Expansion Memorial National Historic Site, site in St. Louis, Mo. S-22, *picture* S-21

Jefferson River, headstream of Missouri River in s.w. Montana; flows n.e. 140 mi (225 km).

Jeffersonville, Ind., port city on Ohio River opposite Louisville, Ky.; toiletries, chemicals, cement, boats, metal products; pop. 20,008, *map* I-102

Jeffrey pine, long-needle pine of w. North America, *picture* P-362

Jeffreys, George Jeffreys, first **Baron** (1648–89), English judge, chief justice, and later lord chancellor under James II; notorious for brutality in bloody assizes.

Jeffreys, Sir Harold (born 1891), British astronomer; theory of origin of solar system P-355

Jeffries, James J. (1875–1953), U.S. boxer, born in Carroll, Ohio B-391
Johnson J-128

Jehlam River. *see in index* Jhelum River

Jehoash, king of Israel. *see in index* Joash

Jehol, China. *see in index* Chengteh

Jehoshaphat (9th century BC), son of Asa and king of Judah; first king of Judah to maintain peace with kingdom of Israel.

Jehovah (or Yahweh), the Hebrew name for the God of Israel; means the self-existent or unchangeable One; in English generally rendered the Lord
Tabernacle T-2

Jehovah's Witnesses (or Russellites, or Millennial Dawnists, or International Bible Students), Christian society founded in 1872 by Charles Taze Russell J-96

Jehu, king of Israel; killed Jezebel and massacred house of Ahab (Bible, II Kings ix–x), enemy of Baal worshipers; furious driver, hence, nickname of coachman.

Jejunum, middle part of small intestine; lies between duodenum and ileum; attached to posterior wall of abdomen.

Jekyll, Dr., the kindly, reputable physician in Robert Louis Stevenson's 'The Strange Case of Dr. Jekyll and Mr. Hyde' who discovers a drug by which he can transform himself into criminal Mr. Hyde.

Jellicoe, John Rushworth Jellicoe, first **Earl** (1859–1935), British admiral, entered navy 1872; command of Grand Fleet in World War I, notable services at battle of Jutland; first sea lord, and chief of naval staff; admiral of the fleet, 1919; served as governor general of New Zealand, 1920–24 W-306

Jelliffe, Smith Ely (1866–1945), U.S. neurologist, born in New York City; managing editor of *Journal of Nervous and Mental Diseases* 1902–45 and *Psychoanalytic Review* 1913–45; pioneer in psychoanalysis in U.S.

Jellyfish, primitive coelenterate animal, *diagram* J-97
deep-sea forms D-60
invertebrate group I-282
oceanography O-485
prehistoric life A-459

Jelutong (or pontianak), name of a Malayan tree, also of its rubberlike juice

Jemappes, Belgium, village 3 mi (5 km) w. of Mons; decisive defeat of Austrians by French Revolutionary army 1792; pop. 13,092.

Jemez, pueblo about 45 mi (70 km) w. of Santa Fe, N.M.; on the Jemez River; Jemez Indians belong to the Tanoan language group of Pueblo Indians; pop. 1,197 P-526d
New Mexico, *map* N-229

Jemison, Mae C. (born 1956), U.S. astronaut, born in Decatur, Ala.; B.S., B.A., Stanford University 1977; M.D., Cornell University 1981; general practitioner, Glendale, Calif.; selected by NASA as mission specialist for space shuttle program 1987, thus becoming first black woman astronaut.

'Jemmy Green', work by Rashleigh A-799

Jena, East Germany, city on Saale River 45 mi (70 km) s.w. of Leipzig; optical instruments; university (founded 1558); pop. 82,113, *map* G-131

Jena, battle of (1806) G-122

Jenghiz Khan. *see in index* Genghis Khan

Jenifer, Daniel of St. Thomas (1723–90), U.S. statesman, born in Charles County, Maryland; member of Continental Congress 1778–82; favored permanent union of states and congressional power of taxation; delegate to Constitutional Convention 1787; signed United States Constitution.

Jenkins, Charles Francis (1867–1934), U.S. inventor, born near Dayton, Ohio; took out more than 400 patents, chiefly in the field of motion pictures and radio
motion pictures M-617

Jenkins, Charles Jones (1805–83), U.S. jurist, born in Beaufort district, S.C.; justice Georgia Supreme Court 1860–65; governor of Georgia 1865–68, removed by General Meade for opposing reconstruction acts.

Jenkins, Tom , U.S. wrestler W-366

Jenkins' Ear, War of, in English history, grew out of trade and colonial rivalry A-829
England E-248

Jenks, Jeremiah Whipple (1856–1929), U.S. economist and educator, born in St. Clair, Mich.; professor of political economy, Cornell University, 1891–1912; served U.S. and other governments in administrative and advisory positions ('The Trust Problem'; 'Principles of Politics'; 'The Immigration Problem').

Jenner, Edward (1749–1823), English physician J-98
medicine M-283
microbiology M-376
smallpox vaccine V-249

Jenner, Sir William (1815–98), British physician, born in Chatham, Kent; in 1847 began a study which established separate identities of typhoid fever and typhus; professor at University College, London, 1849–72; physician in ordinary to Queen Victoria 1862–90.

Jennet, name of small Spanish horse, also of female ass A-702

Jenney, William LeBaron (1832–1907), U.S. architect, born in Fairhaven, Mass.; engineer in Union Army in Civil War; noted for innovations in structure of office buildings
building construction B-496
steel-skeleton buildings A-568, *picture* A-563

'Jennie Gerhardt', novel by Dreiser D-259

Jennings, Herbert Spencer (1868–1947), U.S. naturalist, born in Tonica, Ill.; with Johns Hopkins University 1906–38; noted for research in animal behavior, physiology of microorganisms, and genetics ('The Universe and Life').

Jennings, Hugh Ambrose (nickname Ee-yah) (1870–1928), U.S. baseball shortstop, born in Pittston, Pa.; played chiefly for Baltimore, N.L., 1893–99; won 3 pennants as manager Detroit, A.L., 1907–20.

Jennings, Sarah. *see in index* Marlborough, Sarah Jennings Churchill, duchess of

Jennings, La., city in s.w., about 34 mi (55 km) e. of Lake Charles; trade center for agricultural area; flower growing; oil, fishing, timber; pop. 12,401.

Jennings, Mo., city 8 mi (13 km) n.w. of St. Louis; residential suburb; settled 1870; incorporated 1946; pop. 17,026.

Jenny, spinning. *see in index* Spinning jenny

Jensen, Alfred (1903–81), U.S. painter, *picture* M-212

Jensen, J. Hans D. (1907–73), West German physicist, born in Hamburg; professor of physics University of Heidelberg after 1949; lectured in U.S. 1951–53, 1961
nuclear physics N-432

Jensen, Johannes Vilhelm (1873–1950), Danish novelist and poet, born in North Jutland; noted for trilogy 'The Long Journey', consisting of 'Fire and Ice', 'The Cimbrians', and 'Christopher Columbus' S-52g

Jenson, Nicolas (1420–80), Italian printer, born in France; probably learned printing at Mainz from Gutenberg; printed at Venice ten years; his roman type used as model by Morris, Cobden-Sanderson, and Rogers
typeface, *picture* B-349

Jephthah, judge of Israel; in fulfillment of a rash vow, sacrificed to the Lord the first creature that met him on return from victory, his only daughter (Bible, Judges xi).

Jerba. *see in index* Djerba

Jeremiah (650?–570? BC), one of the major Hebrew prophets J-98
Michelangelo's fresco P-37
prophets P-508

'Jeremiah Symphony', work by Bernstein B-176

Jerez de la Frontera (or Jerez, or Xeres), Spain, city in s.w., 14 mi (22 km) n.e. of Cadiz; famous for sherry wine, to which it gave the name; pop. 96,209, *map* E-360
wine W-236

Jericho (or Eriha), Jordan, town 7 mi (11 km) n. of Dead Sea; important city of ancient Palestine; captured and destroyed by Joshua (Bible, Joshua vi, 20–4); later rebuilt and destroyed a number of times; pop. 5,312, *picture* P-80
archaeology A-529
fort and fortifications F-319

Jericho, N.Y., community 23 mi (37 km) n.e. of New York, N.Y.; residential suburb; agricultural region; pop. 14,010.

Jericho, rose of. *see in index* Rose of Jericho

Jeritza, Maria (stage name of Marie Jedlitzka) (1887–1982), Austrian operatic singer, born in Brünn, Austria, now Brno, Czechoslovakia; with Metropolitan Opera Company 1921–32; popular on concert stage.

Jermaq, Jebel, Galilean mountains. *see in index* Jebel Jermaq

Jernigan, Fla. *see in index* Orlando

Jeroboam I (died 912? BC), leader of revolting 10 tribes and first king of Israel (10th century BC) after separation from Judah (Bible, I Kings xii, 20).

Jeroboam II (died 744? BC), king of Israel, son of Joash, regained much territory previously lost (Bible, II Kings xiv, 23–9); Amos and Hosea preached during his reign.

Jerome, Saint (or Eusebius Hieronymus) (340?–420), most learned of early Fathers of Latin church; born in Strido, Dalmatia, of wealthy family; festival September 30
Bible translations B-184
Fathers of the Church F-45
Latin literature L-78
Middle Ages M-385
women's rights W-271

Jerome, Jerome Klapka (1859–1927), British humorist and dramatist ('Idle Thoughts of an Idle Fellow'; 'The Passing of the Third Floor Back'; 'Three Men in a Boat').

Jerome, Ariz., town near Verde River, 25 mi (40 km) n.e. of Prescott; formerly important copper camp; pop. 420.

Jerome brothers, French-Indian fur traders, *picture* F-468

Jerome of Prague (died 1416), learned and eloquent Bohemian religious reformer; studied in England; friend of Huss; condemned as heretic.

Jerrold, Douglas William (1803–57), British dramatist and humorist; contributed to *Punch* ('Black-Eyed Susan', 'Heart of Gold', plays; 'Chronicles of Clovernook', novel).

Jersey, breed of cattle C-226, *picture* C-227

Jersey, largest of Channel Islands, 20 mi (30 km) from Normandy coast of France; 45 sq mi (116 sq km); chief city St. Helier; resort; pop. 72,629, *map* U-18a
Channel Islands C-270

Jersey City, N.J., 2nd city of state, situated on Hudson River opposite New York City; pop. 223,532 J-99
New Jersey N-195

Jersey City State College, in Jersey City, N.J.; founded 1921; opened 1929; formerly a teachers college; arts and sciences, art, education, health education and nursing; graduate studies.

Jersey Giant, breed of poultry P-482

Jerusalem, city, in 1948 divided between Israel and Jordan, but in 1967 proclaimed by Israel as one city under Israeli rule; seat of government of Israel; pop. 415,000 J-99
Asia, *map* A-697
church history C-400
Crusades C-786
Middle Ages M-391, *pictures* M-384, 392
Saladin S-25
Solomon's temple S-255
Israel, *picture* I-370
Judaism J-147
Seljuks conquer T-323
World War I W-305

Jerusalem, Church of, Eastern Orthodox church E-42

Jerusalem artichoke, perennial American sunflower *Helianthus tuberosus* used as a vegetable, a livestock feed and levulose source P-379

Jerusalem cherry, perennial shrubby plant *Solanum pseudo-capsicum* of the nightshade family, native to Europe; leaves narrow, glossy on upper surface; flowers white; fruit globular, scarlet or yellow; a variant has pointed orange fruits.

Jerusalem Council, first known Christian convention C-410

Jerusalem cross (or scarlet lychnis), stout perennial garden herb *Lychnis chalcedonica* of the pink family with ovate leaves and clusters of scarlet flowers.

Jerusalem thorn (or horse bean), small tropical tree *Parkinsonia aculeata* of pea family, native to s. U.S. and Central America; grows 15 ft (4½ m) to 30 ft (9 m); thorny, with leaves divided into many small leaflets; flowers fragrant, yellow, in loose clusters; used as hedge plant.

Jervis Bay, inlet of Pacific, on coast, New South Wales, Australia; area of 28 sq mi (72 sq km), at the bay, included in Australian Capital Territory; summer resort.

Jespersen, Otto (1860–1943), Danish linguist J-102

Jessamine, yellow. *see in index* Gelsemium

Jesse, father of David; "the tree of Jesse," a favorite medieval church emblem, represents Jesse as the root and the Savior or Virgin and Child as the supreme flower (Bible, Isaiah xi, 1, 10).

Jessie M. Honeyman Memorial State Park, park in Oregon, *picture* O-591

Jessup, Walter Albert (1877–1944), U.S. educator, born in Richmond, Ind.; president, State University of Iowa 1916–34; made president Carnegie Foundation for Advancement of Teaching 1934.

Jester (or court fool), man kept in households of kings and other dignitaries to amuse; became prominent in Europe in the Middle Ages and was known by brightly colored costume with bells
- circus history C-435
- mime M-423

Jesuits (or Society of Jesus), religious order founded by St. Ignatius Loyola L-327
- American missionaries A-335, 577
  - Kino K-247
- Counter Reformation C-744
  - Reformation R-135
- Jansenists P-136
- Xavier X-402

Jesus Christ J-103. *see also in index* Christianity
- apostles A-506
- artistic representations
  - 'Christ the Redeemer', *picture* S-268
  - 'Madonna and Child Enthroned with Saints', by Raphael P-34, *picture* P-35
  - 'Madonna and Child with Angels', by Memling P-31, *picture* P-32
  - 'Madonna della Pietà', by Michelangelo V-268
  - 'The Descent from the Cross', by Giotto P-29
  - 'The Madonna of the Angels', by Cimabue P-28, *picture* P-29
  - 'The Resurrection', by Della Robbia, *picture* D-88
  - 'The Tribute Money', by Masaccio P-32, *picture* P-33
- birthplace B-179
- Christian Science C-402
- Christmas C-403
- Gnosticism G-170
- God G-173
- Herod H-141
- Jehovah's Witnesses J-96
- Lutheranism L-338
- Mary M-163
- Monophysitism B-533
- passion play O-455

'Jesus Christ Superstar' (1971), musical by Webber M-686

Jesus Island. *see in index* Ile-Jésus

Jet. *see in index* Jet propulsion; Turbojet engine

Jet, mineral J-112

Jet-assisted take-off. *see in index* JATO

Jeté, in ballet B-35

Jet engine A-175
- airplane usage A-187

Jet propulsion J-105
- airplane, *pictures* A-157, P-109a
  - commercial, *picture* S-289
  - height flown S-341a
- fireworks F-114
- guided missiles G-309
- motor and engine M-630
- octopus, cuttlefish, squid O-492
- Soviet railroad car, *picture* R-330b

Jet Propulsion Laboratory, research laboratory in California K-192
- NASA N-22

JETS. *see in index* Junior Engineering Technical Society

Jetsam, sunken cargo F-212

Jet stream, high-altitude wind W-225, *picture* W-223
- atmosphere, *picture* A-748
- weather W-119

Jetté, Sir Louis Amable (1836–1920), Canadian statesman and jurist, born in L'Assomption, near Montreal; lieutenant governor Quebec 1898–1908; chief justice province of Quebec 1909–11.

Jetty, an embankment J-111
- flood control F-184
- harbors and ports H-34

Jevons, William Stanley (1835–82), British economist and logician; brilliant writer of wide influence; developed marginal utility theory; simplified logic ('Treatise on Logic', 'Theory of Political Economy') B-517

Jewel Cave National Monument, monument in South Dakota, *map* S-334

Jeweled lacerta, lizard, *picture* L-273

Jeweler's putty P-540

Jeweler's rouge J-114

Jewel House, part of the Tower of London complex T-237

'Jewelled Anklet, The' (or 'Cilappatikaram'), Tamil epic I-106

Jewelry and gems J-112. *see also in index* gems by name, such as Diamond; Pearl
- ancient Egypt E-127
- chromium coloration C-408
- crystals C-795
  - quartz Q-7
- dress D-261
- hobby H-187
- onyx O-559
- platinum P-384, R-366
- silver S-203
- watches and clocks W-79

'Jewels of the Madonna, The', opera by Ermanno Wolf-Ferrari, his only tragic opera; libretto by E. Golisciani and C. Zangarini; first production in Berlin 1911.

Jewelweed, a common wild flower of the genus *Impatiens* of the balsam family; stems succulent; leaves usually alternate; flowers brownish-orange or yellow spotted, similar to snapdragon; explosive seedpods; found in moist places; also called touch-me-not.

Jewett, Charles Coffin (1816–68), U.S. librarian, born in Lebanon, Me.; librarian Smithsonian Institution 1848–54; superintendent Boston Public Library 1858–68.

Jewett, Frank Baldwin (1879–1949), U.S. electrical engineer, born in Pasadena, Calif.; president 1925–40 and chairman of board 1940–44 of Bell Telephone Laboratories, Inc.; president National Academy of Sciences from 1939; contributed to transcontinental and transoceanic telegraphy, radio, television, and aircraft communications.

Jewett, Sarah Orne (1849–1909), U.S. short-story writer and novelist, born in South Berwick, Me. ('Deephaven', 'A Country Doctor', 'The Country of the Pointed Firs', 'The Tory Lover') A-351

Jewfish, immense grouper reaching a length of 6 ft (2 m) or more and weighing 500 to 600 lbs (225 to 270 km), abundant in warm seas; among the most common are the California jewfish, the spotted jewfish of the West Indies, and the black jewfish of Florida; excellent food fish.

'Jewish Daily Forward', newspaper founded by Cahan C-15

Jewish Documentation Center, Vienna, Austria W-202

Jewish National Fund P-81

Jewish New Year's Day. *see in index* Rosh Hashana

Jewish War Veterans of the U.S.A., society of Americans of Jewish faith who served in wars of the United States; founded 1896; National Ladies Auxiliary founded 1928; headquarters for these organizations, Washington, D.C.

Jewish Welfare Board, national organization of Young Men's Hebrew Associations, Young Women's Hebrew Associations, and Jewish Community Centers; headquarters in New York City; founded 1917 to promote social, religious, and educational welfare of Jews in military service, it has since greatly extended its activities.

'Jew of Malta, The', tragedy by Christopher Marlowe; chief character, Barabas, is believed to have been pattern for Shakespeare's Shylock.

Jews. *see in index* Judaism

Jezebel, in Bible, wife of Ahab, cursed by Elijah for treachery to Naboth (I Kings xxi) and murdered by Jehu (II Kings ix, 30–7).

Jezreel, ancient city, now an agricultural settlement, n. Israel, in Plain of Jezreel, 55 mi (90 km) n. of Jerusalem; capital of Israel under Ahab; archaeological excavations in vicinity.

Jhelum River (or Jehlam River, ancient Hydaspes), flows s.w. from Himalayas into Chenab River in Punjab (450 mi; 725 km), *maps* I-86, P-212
- Alexander's battle A-280

Jiang Qing (born 1914?), most influential woman in China until her downfall in 1976 when husband Mao Zedong died; as member of Gang of Four was convicted in 1981 of counterrevolutionary crimes and imprisoned for life M-112
- China C-375, *picture* C-376

Jiangsu (or Kiangsu), province on e. coast of China; area (excluding Shanghai) 39,460 sq mi (102,200 sq km); cap. Nanjing; pop. 60,521,114 J-117
- Nanjing N-10

Jiangxi (or Kiangsi), an inland province of China; 67,000 sq mi (173,500 sq km); cap. Nanchang; pop. 33,184,827 J-117
- porcelain making P-470

Jib, sail B-328, *diagrams* B-326, S-166

Jíbaro (also spelled gibaro), Puerto Rican farmer P-527, *picture* P-528

Jibheaded-rig (or Marconi-rig, or Bermuda-rig) B-326

Jicarilla, an Apache people, formerly inhabiting large area; now on reservation in New Mexico; named by the Spaniards from little baskets they made.

Jicin (or Gitschin), Czechoslovakia, town in Bohemia, 48 mi (77 km) n.e. of Prague; Prussian victory over Austrians 1866; pop. 12,197.

Jiddah (or Jidda), Saudi Arabia, chief seaport of Hejaz, on Red Sea; principal income derived from pilgrims on way to Mecca; pop. 1,000,000 J-117
- Asia, *picture* A-691, *map* A-697

Jig, dance. *see in index* Gigue

Jig, type of gravity concentrator M-430

Jig borer, a machine tool I-222

Jigger. *see in index* Chigger

Jigger, pottery P-478

Jihad, Islamic holy war I-359

Jilin (or Kirin), province in n.e. part of China; area 73,000 sq mi (189,000 sq km); cap. Changchun; pop. 22,560,053 J-117
- Asia, *map* A-697
- Manchuria M-94

Jim, pressurized armored underwater diving suit D-189

Jim Crow, name given to former laws of Southern states of U.S. providing for separation of black and white people in streetcars, trains, schools, and theaters; Jim Crow is thought to be an old nickname for a black American, popularized in a song B-292

Jiménez, Juan Ramón (1881–1958), Spanish poet J-118
- Spanish literature S-365b, *picture* S-366

Jiménez de Cisneros, Cardinal Francisco. *see in index* Ximenes

Jiménez de Quesada, Gonzalo (1500?–1579), Spanish explorer; birthplace probably Granada, Spain; founded Bogotá 1538 C-553

Jiminez Aranda, Jose, Spanish painter
- 'Don Quixote' illustration, *picture* N-408

Jimmu (or Son of Heaven) (7th and 6th century BC), legendary founder of line of Japan's emperors and descendant of sun-goddess J-63

Jimson weed, plant *Datura stramonium*; annual with large, sweet-smelling, white, trumpet-shaped flowers; contains strong narcotics; named Jimson for Jamestown, Va. P-409, *picture* W-132

Jinan (or Tsinan), China, capital of Shandong Province near Yellow River about 220 mi (350 km) s. of Peking; pop. 1,100,000, *map* C-383
- Asia, *map* A-697

Jinghis Khan. *see in index* Genghis Khan

Jingo (2nd and 3rd centuries AD), legendary warlike empress of Japan, on whose alleged conquest of Korea Japan bases traditional claims of suzerainty over that country; mother of Ojin, deified as Hachiman, the god of war.

Jingoism, an aggressive, warlike policy in support of national ambition; derived possibly from the Persian *jang* (war), or from Jingo, legendary empress of Japan.

Jining (or Tsining), China, city of Inner Mongolian Autonomous Region; railroad center; pop. 100,000, *map* C-383

Jinmen (or Quemoy), island, Taiwan T-12

Jinn. *see in index* Genie

Jinnah, Mohammed Ali (1876–1948), leader of the Muslims in peninsula of India and its vicinity J-118
- India I-78
- Pakistan P-79

Jinrikisha (or ricksha), light man-drawn carriage said to have been invented in 1869 by an American Baptist missionary in Japan
- India, *picture* T-262

Jinsen, South Korea. *see in index* Inchon

Jipijapa, plant. *see in index* Toquilla

Jivaro, a people of Ecuador and n. Peru; noted for custom of preserving the heads of their enemies and their chiefs after removing the bones of the skull.

JNR (Japanese National Railways) J-42

Joab, ancient Israeli soldier, nephew of David D-41

Joachim, Joseph (1831–1907), Hungarian violinist and composer; first public appearance at the age of 7; concert master under Liszt ('Hungarian Concerto')
- Brahms B-395

Joachimsthal, Czechoslovakia. *see in index* Jachymov

Joad, Cyril Edwin Mitchinson (1891–1953), British philosopher, born in London; professor, University of London, 1930–53 ('Meaning of Life'; 'Guide to the Philosophy of Morals and Politics'; 'God and Evil').

Joan, mythical woman pope J-118

Joanna (1479–1555), queen of Castile, daughter of Ferdinand and Isabella, and mother of Emperor Charles V and Emperor Ferdinand I; did not actually rule because of mental deficiency A-828

Joannes, island, n.e. Brazil. *see in index* Marajó

Joan of Arc, Saint (French Jeanne d'Arc) (1412–31), called Maid of Orléans and Maid of France; festival May 30 J-119
- Charles VII C-277
- France F-361
- Henry V H-130
- Hundred Years' War H-325
- Orléans O-607
- Rossetti painting, *picture* R-298

João Pessoa, Brazil, capital of state of Paraíba on Paraíba River; cement, footwear; trade in sugar, cotton, manioc; pop. 203,935, *maps* B-425, S-298

Joash (or Jehoash), king of Israel, about 798–790 BC; expelled Syrians, captured Amaziah, king of Judah; plundered temple at Jerusalem (Bible, II Kings xiii–xiv).

Joash (or Jehoash), king of Judah, about 837–797 BC; slain by conspiracy of his servants (Bible, II Kings xi, xii; II Chronicles xxii–xxiv).

Job, long-suffering hero in the Book of Job in the Old Testament.

Job Corps, United States government U-196

Jobs. *see in index* Vocations

Job's Coffin, constellation. *see in index* Delphinus

Job's-tears, a tall grass *Coix lacryma-jobi* named from hard, white oval seedcases, used in making beads; cultivated for food in some countries and for its supposed medicinal properties in China.

Jocasta, in Greek mythology; mother of Oedipus O-493

Jochum, Eugen (1902–87), Bavarian conductor, *list* O-579

Jockey, in horse racing H-276, *picture* H-275

Jodhpur, India, city in Rajasthan state; was capital of princely state Jodhpur (Marwar); gave name to riding breeches; pop. 317,612, *maps* A-697, I-83

Jodl, Alfred (1890–1946), German general, born in Würzburg, Bavaria; signed World War II surrender May 7, 1945; executed as war criminal at Nuremberg 1946 W-336

Jodoshinsu (or True Pure Sect), largest Buddhist sect in Japan B-483

Joel (5th century BC), Hebrew minor prophet, author of the Book of Joel, the 29th book of the Old Testament; he prophesied the judgments that were to come to Israel, and urged the people to repent.

Joe-Pye weed, American perennial herb *Eupatorium purpureum* and *E. maculatum* with whorled leaves and end clusters of white, pink, or rose-purple flowers; often grows 12 ft (3½ m) high.

Joey, baby kangaroo K-172
Australia A-779

Joey, type of clown, also nickname for all clowns C-436

Joffre, Joseph-Jacques-Césaire (1852–1931), French general and marshal of France J-120

Joffrey, Robert (originally Abdullah Jaffa Bey Khan) (born 1930); choreographer and ballet dancer, born in Seattle; founded Joffrey Ballet D-24

Jogging, exercise J-121
weight control, *picture* W-136

Jogging shoe, footwear S-179

Jogues, Saint Isaac (1607–46), French Jesuit missionary, born in Orléans; captured by Mohawks, first time mutilated, 2nd time killed, at Ossernenon (a Mohawk village now a part of Auriesville, N.Y.), today a place of Roman Catholic pilgrimage; feast day March 16.

Johanan ben Zakkai (died AD 80?), Jewish scholar, pupil of Hillel; after destruction of Jerusalem by Romans founded school outside Jerusalem which preserved Jewish law and learning.

Johannesburg, South Africa, in s. Transvaal, largest city in southern Africa; center of goldfields; pop. 1,536,400 J-122
Africa, *maps* A-115, S-264
world, *map* W-297

Johanson, Donald C. (born 1943), U.S. anthropologist A-487, *picture* A-485

Johansson, Ingemar (born 1932), Swedish boxer, born in Göteborg B-392

John, saint, one of the Twelve Apostles, called the Evangelist; festival, Roman Catholicism, December 27, Anglican, May 6 A-506, *picture* P-39

John VIII, legendary pope J-118

John XXIII (1881–1963), pope J-123, C-165
Hus H-334

John XXIII (or Baldassare Cossa) (1370?–1419), antipope 1410–15; called Council of Constance by which he was deposed; imprisoned in Germany
John XXIII J-123

John V Palaeologus (1332–91), Byzantine emperor B-536

John VI Cantacuzenus (1292–1383), statesman, Byzantine emperor, and historian B-536

John VIII Palaeologus (1392–1448), Byzantine emperor; responsible for Council of Ferrara-Florence 1438 which effected reunion of Eastern and Western Church; repudiation of union soon after hastened downfall of Byzantine Empire.

John, king of England. *see in index* John of England

John (1319–64), king of France, called the Good; enthroned 1350 at Poitiers; English prisoner after defeat at Poitiers (1356); died in England, unable to obtain ransom
Hundred Years' War H-325

John I Albert, king of Poland; reigned 1492–1501 J-12

John III, king of Poland. *see in index* Sobieski, John

John I (1357–1433), king of Portugal, called the Great and father of his country, chosen king 1385; father of Henry the Navigator.

John II (1455–95), king of Portugal, called the Perfect; known as able political leader and patron of Renaissance art and learning; refused help to Columbus C-591
Diaz D-133

John VI (1769–1826), king of Portugal; came to throne 1816 (regent from 1799); accepted Portugal's constitution after insurrection (1821) and recognized independence of Brazil (1825) B-423
exile in Brazil P-457

John, Augustus Edwin (1878–1961), British painter, born in Wales; powerful draftsmanship; portraits of David Lloyd George and George Bernard Shaw; elected member of Royal Academy of Arts 1928.

John, Elton (born 1947), British musician, born in Middlesex, England; worked mainly with lyricist Bernie Taupin; first Western rock singer to perform in U.S.S.R.; received Gold Discs for 'Elton John', 'Goodbye Yellow Brick Road', 'Captain Fantastic and the Brown Dirt Cowboy'.

John, Epistles of, 23rd, 24th, and 25th books of Bible's New Testament, attributed to Apostle John; first book, exhortations to Christian faith; second and third are short notes; authorship disputed B-183

John, Gospel of, 4th book of Bible's New Testament, attributed to Apostle John; authorship disputed; purpose to present life and works of Jesus so as to arouse faith in readers B-183
Apostles A-507

John Birch Society, U.S. organization; anti-Communist, politically right-wing; founded 1958 by Robert H.W. Welch; named for Capt. John Birch, U.S. Army officer, killed 1945 by Chinese Communists; known for extremism.

'John Brown's Body', U.S. Civil War song by Benét A-356
Benét B-161
popular music M-683

John Brown University, in Siloam Springs, Ark; private control; established in 1919; arts and sciences, teacher education.

John Carroll University, in University Heights, near Cleveland, Ohio; Roman Catholic; established in 1886; arts and sciences, business, and education; graduate school C-495

John Carter Brown Library, in Providence, R.I. P-516

John Crerar Library, in Chicago, Ill.; scientific library established 1894 by John Crerar, Chicago railroad magnate; famous collections include works on medicine, international law, and aeronautics.

John Doe, fictitious name of plaintiff in action in which real plaintiff's name is withheld; a John Doe proceeding is a process to fix liability for a known wrong committed by an as yet unknown wrongdoer.

John Dory, gold or silvery food fish *Zeus faber* about 1 ft (30 cm) long, living in warm seas about Europe; legend says it is fish from which St. Peter took tribute money, dark spot on each side represents imprint of his thumb and finger.

John F. Kennedy Center for the Performing Arts, cultural center in Washington, D.C. W-69

John F. Kennedy Space Center. *see in index* Canaveral, Cape

John F. Slater Fund, established in 1882 by donation of $1,000,000 by John Fox Slater; for the education of Southern freedmen. *see also in index* Southern Education Foundation, Inc.

John Henry, legendary black hero of prodigious strength; worked himself to death trying to beat a machine, usually a rock drill, or, according to another version, a cotton-rolling machine; legend has been traced to drilling of Big Bend tunnel in Summers County, West Virginia, 1870–72 S-481d
folklore F-266

John Howard Association, prison reform H-312

John Mohegan. *see in index* Chingachgook

John Newbery Medal. *see in index* Newbery Medal

'Johnny I Hardly Knew You', work by O'Brien I-328

John of Austria (or Don Juan) (1545–78), son of the Emperor Charles V and half brother of Philip II of Spain; victor over Turks (1571) in famous naval battle of Lepanto.

John of England (nickname Lackland) (1167–1216), king of England J-124
democracy D-93
Eleanor of Aquitaine E-144
English history E-241
habeas corpus H-2
Henry II H-129
Magna Carta M-41
Richard I R-202
Shakespeare S-133, 139

John of Gaunt (1340–99), duke of Lancaster; 4th son of Edward III of England, ancestor of House of Lancaster and, through his daughters, of Tudor, Stuart, and Hanover-Windsor sovereigns of England
descendants, *table* R-297
Henry IV H-129

John of Leiden (1509?–36), Dutch religious (Anabaptist) fanatic and revolutionary; ruled Kingdom of Zion in Münster; executed after capture of city; central figure in Meyerbeer's opera, 'The Prophet', produced 1849.

John Paul I (1912–78), pope J-124

John Paul II (born 1920), pope J-124
assassination attempt I-398, E-355
liberation theology C-409

John Pennekamp Coral Reef State Park, park in Florida K-230

Johns, Jasper (born 1930), U.S. painter, born in Augusta, Ga.; moved to South Carolina in youth; exhibits in U.S. and Europe, *picture* S-316

John's Hill, hill in Budapest, Hungary B-479

Johns Hopkins Glacier, active glacier in Alaska, *picture* I-6

Johns Hopkins University, in Baltimore, Md.; private control; opened 1876; arts and sciences, education, hygiene and public health, medicine; graduate schools; advanced international studies at Washington, D.C.; research activities at Baltimore, Md., Washington, D.C., Silver Spring, Md.; technical publications B-49, M-170, *map* B-48

John Simon Guggenheim Memorial Foundation, founded in 1925 by Mr. and Mrs. Simon Guggenheim, in memory of their son, John Simon (died 1922) L-241

Johnson, Andrew (1808–75), 17th president of U.S. J-125
amnesty and pardon A-373
Grant G-218
impeachment I-58
Nebraska S-429d
Reconstruction policy R-114
Stevens S-445
Tennessee T-88

Johnson, Byron Bancroft (1864–1931), U.S. baseball organizer and first president (1901–27) of American League, born in Norwalk, Ohio B-96

Johnson, Charles Spurgeon (1893–1956), U.S. sociologist, born in Bristol, Va.; made head of Fisk University October 1946; wrote of black Americans' problems ('Ebony and Topaz'; 'Negro in American Civilization'; 'Black Man's Burden').

Johnson, Daniel (1915–68), Canadian political leader, born in Danville, Que.; leader Union Nationale party 1961–68; premier province of Quebec 1966–68.

Johnson, Edward (1881–1959), U.S. tenor, born in Guelph, Ont.; sang five seasons at La Scala in Milan, Italy; member Chicago and Metropolitan Opera companies; general manager Metropolitan Opera Assn., Inc., New York City, 1935–50.

Johnson, Emily Pauline (1861–1913), Canadian poet, born near Brantford, Ont.; daughter of Mohawk Indian chief and English mother ('Flint and Feather', collected poems; 'Legends of Vancouver', Indian tales) C-121

Johnson, Esther (nickname Stella) (1681–1728), friend of Jonathan Swift S-530

Johnson, Eyvind (1900–76), Swedish author, born in Svarbjörnsbyn; wrote more than 40 novels and short-story collections, including 'Olof' cycle of autobiographical novels; a fellow of the Swedish Academy.

Johnson, Garret (or Gerard Johnson, or Garratt Johnson, or Geraert Janssen) (fl. 1616), Dutch sculptor and tomb maker who lived in London
Shakespeare sculpture, *picture* S-129

Johnson, Harold Keith (1912–83), U.S. Army officer, born in Bowesmont, N.D.; commandant Command and General Staff College 1960–63; Army deputy chief of staff for operations 1963–64; chief of staff 1964–68.

Johnson, Hiram Warren (1866–1945), U.S. lawyer and political leader, born in Sacramento, Calif.; as prosecuting attorney convicted Ruef, chief of San Francisco boodlers; governor of California 1911–17; elected to U.S. senate 1917 R-289

Johnson, Hugh Samuel (1882–1942), U.S. soldier, lawyer, born in Ft. Scott, Kan.; in charge of U.S. draft 1917–18; NRA administrator 1933–34; editorial commentator for newspaper and radio after 1934 R-270

Johnson, Jack (nickname Li'l Artha) (1878–1946), U.S. boxer, born in Galveston, Tex. J-128
heavyweight champion B-391

Johnson, James P. (1891?–1955), U.S. jazz pianist, born in New Brunswick, N.J.; also songwriter J-87

Johnson, James Weldon (1871–1938), U.S. writer, educator, diplomat, born in Jacksonville, Fla.; professor Fisk University 1930–38; edited 'Book of Negro Spirituals'; wrote 'God's Trombones', poems; 'Along This Way', autobiography; won 1925 Spingarn medal for literature B-294, 299, 302

Johnson, Sir John (1742–1830), Loyalist, born near Johnstown, N.Y.; son of Sir William Johnson; kept the Six Nations on British side during Revolutionary War.

Johnson, John H. (born 1918), U.S. editor and publisher, born in Arkansas City, Ark.; president Johnson Publishing Company, publishers of *Ebony* 1945–, *Jet* 1951–, *Hue* 1953–59; won 1966 Spingarn medal.

Johnson, John Mercer (1818–68), Canadian politician and lawyer; born in Liverpool, England C-118, *picture* C-116

Johnson, Josephine Winslow (born 1910), U.S. novelist and poet, born in Kirkwood, Mo.; 1934 Pulitzer prize for first novel 'Now in November'; mature and subtle in portrayal of emotion; poetic and sensitive in style ('Winter Orchard'; 'Jordanstown'; 'Year's End'; 'The Dark Traveler').

Johnson, Lady Bird (or Claudia Alta Taylor) (born 1912), wife of President Lyndon B. Johnson J-130, *pictures* J-133
United States history U-196

Johnson, Louis Arthur (1891–1966), U.S. lawyer and government official, born in Roanoke, Va.; asst. secretary of war 1937–40; secretary of defense March 1949–Sept. 1950.

Johnson, Lyndon B. (1908–73), 36th president of U.S. J-129
human resource policies C-678
Kennedy's assassination K-203, T-123, *picture* K-201
Ku Klux Klan K-309
Texas ranch, *picture* T-130
U.S. history U-195, *picture* U-196
Vietnam War V-322

Johnson, Magic, (born Earvin Johnson) (born 1959), U.S. basketball player, born in Lansing, Mich.; attended Michigan State University 1977–79; played on NCAA championship team 1979; played for Los Angeles Lakers 1979– ; on NBA all-star team 1980, 1982–84; named league's most valuable player 1987.

Johnson, Martin Elmer (1884–1937), U.S. explorer and author, born in Rockford, Ill.; with his wife, Osa Johnson, made motion-picture records of expeditions to South Seas, Borneo, Australia, Africa; killed in plane accident; wrote, with his wife, 'Cannibal Land', 'Camera Trails in Africa', 'Safari', 'Lion'.

Johnson, Mordecai Wyatt (1890–1976), U.S. educator, born near Paris, Tenn.; became first black American to hold presidency of Howard University, president 1926–60; won 1929 Spingarn medal (education).

Johnson, Osa Helen (1894–1953), U.S. explorer, writer, and motion-picture producer; born in Chanute, Kan.; in 'Over African Jungles', 'I Married Adventure', she told of experiences with her husband, Martin Johnson.

Johnson, Owen McMahon (1878–1952), U.S. author, born in New York City; son of Robert Underwood Johnson; won popularity for his school and college stories ('The Varmint'; 'The Tennessee Shad'; 'Stover at Yale'); novels of contemporary social life ('The Salamander'; 'Sacrifice'); plays ('The Comet'; 'A Comedy for Wives')

Johnson, Philip Cortelyou (born 1906), U.S. architect, born in Cleveland, Ohio; director department of architecture and design Museum of Modern Art 1946–54; co-architect Seagram Building, New York, N.Y.; architect glass house, New Canaan, Conn.; Rappite shrine, New Harmony, Ind.; New York State Theater, Lincoln Center, New York, N.Y. A-566, 568
- interior design, *pictures* I-251

Johnson, Rafer Lewis (born 1935), U.S. track athlete, born in Hillsboro, Tex.; set world and Olympics records in decathlon 1960; won Sullivan Trophy 1960.

Johnson, Reverdy (1796–1876), U.S. political leader and jurist, born in Annapolis, Md.; U.S. senator; attorney general; minister to England; treaty he negotiated for adjustment of *Alabama* Claims rejected.

Johnson, Richard (fl. 18th century), Australian chaplain A-792

Johnson, Richard Mentor (1780–1850), U.S. statesman and soldier, born near Louisville, Ky.; 9th vice-president of U.S.; only vice-president ever elected by the Senate.

Johnson, Robert (1912–38), U.S. blues singer M-680

Johnson, Robert Underwood (1853–1937), U.S. editor, diplomat, and poet; born in Washington, D.C.; editor *Century* 1909–13; ambassador to Italy 1920–21 ('The Winter Hour'; 'Italian Rhapsody'; 'Remembered Yesterdays').

Johnson, Samuel (1709–84), British writer J-136
- art of conversation C-695, *picture* C-694
- Boswell B-376
- cat, *list* C-202
- 'Dictionary' R-126
- Garrick G-36
- literary contribution E-272
  - biography standards B-222
  - magazines M-32
  - novel N-408
- Milton M-419
- Newbery N-151

Johnson, Tom Loftin (1854–1911), U.S. municipal reformer and iron manufacturer, born in Georgetown, Ky.; mayor of Cleveland 1901–9; strenuous advocate of single tax, public ownership of utilities; called father of 3-cent streetcar fare C-495

Johnson, Uwe (1934–84), German novelist G-108

Johnson, Walter Perry (nickname Barney) (1887–1946), U.S. baseball pitcher, born in Humboldt, Kan.; with Washington, A.L., 1907–27; called the greatest fastball pitcher in baseball history; won 414 games (2nd highest total) for team that often finished in 2nd division; set many strike-out and shutout records B-92

Johnson, Sir William (1715–74), British colonial landowner and soldier; father of Sir John Johnson; superintendent of Indian affairs in North America; influence with Indians of Six Nations kept them neutral in French and Indian War.

Johnson, William (born 1899), U.S. baseball player, born in Snow Hill, Md.; third baseman, Negro leagues 1918–38.

Johnson, William Samuel (1727–1819), U.S. statesman, born in Stratford, Conn.; colonial agent in London for Connecticut (1767–71); his conservative attitude toward Revolutionary War cause changed to able work in Constitutional Convention; signed United States Constitution; president of Columbia College (now Columbia University) (1787–1800) S-484a

Johnson City, N.Y., industrial village 2 mi (3 km) w. of Binghamton; shoes, ordnance, reproduction machines, felt; pop. 17,126.

Johnson City, Tenn., city in resort area 92 mi (148 km) n.e. of Knoxville; textile products, hardwood flooring, furniture, tobacco, food products, brick; East Tennessee State University; Veterans Administration hospital; pop. 39,753 T-85, *map* T-97

Johnson City, Tex., town 44 mi (71 km) w. of Austin; early home of Lyndon B. Johnson; pop. 872.

Johnson County War, in Wyoming
- cowboy history C-753
- frontier F-423

Johnson C. Smith University, in Charlotte, N.C.; Presbyterian; founded 1867 as Biddle Memorial Institute; arts and sciences, education, theology.

Johnson of Boone, Benj. F. *see in index* Riley, James Whitcomb

Johnson-Sea-Link, submersible O-463

Johnson Shut-ins State Park, park in Missouri, *picture* M-498

Johnson Space Center, in Houston, Tex. H-311, *picture* H-310

Johnson State College, in Johnson, Vt.; established in 1867; formerly a teachers' college; liberal arts, teacher education; graduate studies.

Johnston, Albert Sidney (1803–62), U.S. soldier, born in Mason County, Ky.; one of ablest Confederate generals; leader in struggle for Texas' independence
- Shiloh C-480

Johnston, Alexander (1849–89), U.S. historian, born in Brooklyn, N.Y.; admitted to bar 1876; professor of jurisprudence and political economy at Princeton University after 1883 ('History of American Politics'; 'American Political History, 1763–1876'; 'History of Connecticut').

Johnston, Alvanley (1875–1951), U.S. labor leader, born in Seeley's Bay, near Kingston, Ont.; headed Brotherhood of Locomotive Engineers 1925–51.

Johnston, Edward (1872–1944) British teacher of calligraphy who had great influence on 20th century typography and calligraphy; called father of modern revival of lettering C-59

Johnston, Eric Allen (1896–1963), U.S. industrialist, born in Washington, D.C.; organizer and president, electric companies, Spokane, Wash.; president of U.S. Chamber of Commerce 1942–46, of Motion Picture Producers and Distributors of America 1945–63, took leave of absence to serve as administrator of Economic Stabilization Agency 1951; special representative of Presidents F.D. Roosevelt, Truman, and Eisenhower.

Johnston, Harriet Lane (1833–1903), niece and hostess of President Buchanan B-475

Johnston, Sir Harry Hamilton (1858–1927), British administrator, African explorer, zoologist, and author; originator of plan for British Cape-to-Cairo route; author of books on Africa as well as several novels; in 'The Gay-Dombeys' and 'The Veneerings' he follows the careers of supposed descendants of characters in novels by Charles Dickens.

Johnston, Joseph Eggleston (1807–91), U.S. soldier, born near Farmville, Va.; served in Black Hawk, Seminole, and Mexican wars with distinguished gallantry; became Confederate general 1861; commanded early operations against McClellan in Peninsular Campaign; Fabian tactics against Sherman in Georgia campaign won his opponent's praise as "the equal in all the elements of generalship to Lee"; elected to U.S. Congress in 1876
- Civil War C-473
  - First Bull Run C-480
  - surrender to Sherman N-360

Johnston, Mary (1870–1936), U.S. novelist, born in Buchanan, Va.; author of popular historical romances ('Prisoners of Hope'; 'To Have and to Hold'; 'Sir Mortimer').

Johnston, R.I., 5 mi (8 km) w. of Providence; granite quarries; once part of Providence, separate town 1759; pop. of township 24,907.

Johnston Atoll, U.S. naval base in the Pacific about 700 mi (1,150 km) s.w. of Honolulu; area less than 1/2 sq mi (1.3 sq km); taken over by U.S. in 1918; U.S. atomic-testing site 1958 and 1962; pop. 1,007 U-116, *map* P-3

Johnstown, N.Y., manufacturing city of historic interest, 40 mi (65 km) n.w. of Albany; leather, gloves, knit goods, gelatin, metal products; courthouse built in 1762 named national monument; city named for Sir William Johnson whose mansion, built in 1762, still stands; pop. 9,360.

Johnstown, Pa., city 58 mi (93 km) s.e. of Pittsburgh, on Conemaugh River, in soft-coal district; iron and steel mills; machine tools, textile products, food processing; Johnstown Center, branch of University of Pittsburgh; flood of 1889 took about 2,200 lives; pop. 35,496, *maps* P-184, 174, U-41

John the Baptist, saint, forerunner of Jesus Christ; commemorated as saint June 24 (nativity), August 29 (beheading)
- Herod H-141
- Jesus J-104

Johore, state in former Federation of Malaya; 7,321 sq mi (18,961 sq km); pineapples, iron ore, bauxite; became part of Malaysia 1963; pop. 1,273,990, *map* A-697. *see also in index* Malay States, Unfederated

Joined manuscript, type of handwriting H-29

Joint, in anatomy J-136
- arthritis, *picture* A-650
  - rheumatoid D-181
- hand H-27
- human anatomy A-390
- skeleton S-209

Joint, in carpentry C-174, *picture* F-453

Joint, in masonry B-438

Joint Chiefs of Staff, U.S. U-159
- chief of naval operations N-88

Joint Commission, International. *see in index* International Joint Commission

Joint tenancy, in law, *table* L-93

Joinville, Jean de (1224?–1317?), French historian, born in France; with Louis IX on crusade 1248–54 F-394

Joist, in building construction B-492, *picture* B-493

Jókai, Maurus (1825–1904), Hungarian novelist (the Magyar Dumas) and revolutionist of 1848 ('Timar's Two Worlds'; 'Black Diamonds').

Joke (or witticism) F-261
- humor H-323

Jol. *see in index* Yule

Joliet, Louis. *see in index* Jolliet, Louis

Joliet, Ill., city on Des Plaines River portion of Illinois Waterway about 30 mi (50 km) s.w. of Chicago; center for shipping by railroad, truck, and waterway; machinery, petroleum products, chemicals, food, apparel, metal products, printing specialties; College of St. Francis; pop. 77,956, *map* I-52
- prison, *picture* P-505c

Joliette, Que., city on L'Assomption River 35 mi (55 km) n.e. of Montreal; paper, cigarettes, steel products, textiles; pop. 20,127, *maps* C-112, Q-10

Joliot-Curie, Frédéric (1900–58), French physicist and chemist, born in Paris; professor at Radium Institute in Paris C-807
- radioactivity R-64

Joliot-Curie, Irène (1897–1956), French physicist, daughter of Pierre and Marie Curie, born in Paris; undersecretary of scientific research in French cabinet 1936 C-807
- radioactivity R-64

Jolliet, Louis (1645–1700), French-Canadian explorer J-138
- Illinois I-41
- Lake Erie E-298
- Marquette M-148
- Mississippi river M-484
- Missouri River M-493, 510
- United States route, *map* U-176
- Wisconsin W-253

Jolly, Philipp von (1809–84), German physicist; inventions include Jolly spring balance for determining specific gravity.

Jolly Roger, pirate's flag, *picture* P-342b

Jolo, Philippines, capital and chief port of Sulu province; on Jolo Island; pearl fishing; coconuts, hemp; pop. 46,586, *map* P-262

Jolo Island, chief island of Sulu Archipelago, Philippines; area 345 sq mi (895 sq km); 80 mi (130 km) s.w. of Zamboanga; mountainous, wooded; pop. 208,110, *map* P-262

Jolson, Al (originally Asa Yoelson) (1886–1950), U.S. actor and singer, born in Russia; starred in 'The Jazz Singer' (1927), first sound film with both music and dialogue M-621, *picture* M-623
- popular music M-684

Joly, John (1857–1933), Irish physicist and geologist, born in King's County, Ireland; professor of geology and mineralogy University of Dublin (Trinity College) 1897–1933; invented diffusion photometer; devised meldometer to determine melting point of minerals; saw importance of radioactivity in Earth history; estimated Earth's age by length of time for salt to accumulate in sea.

Jommelli, Niccolò (1714–74), Italian composer, born near Naples; welded German and Italian qualities; composed operas and church music ('Miserere').

Jomon, ancient Japanese pottery J-52

Jonah (8th century? BC), Hebrew minor prophet; as told in Bible's Book of Jonah, disobedient to divine summons, draws storm on ship in which he tries to escape; is thrown into sea and swallowed by a great fish; is saved by Jehovah; delivers divine message to Nineveh but resents city's preservation until taught compassion, *picture* C-218
- folklore F-263
- nursery rhymes N-443
- Persian painting P-67e

Jonathan, son of Saul and beloved friend of David (Bible, I Samuel xx; II Samuel i, 19–27) D-41

Jonathan, the Maccabean, leader of Jewish patriots (160–143 BC).

Jonathan, Leabua (born 1914), prime minister of Lesotho L-138

Jones, Absalom (1747–1818), Abolitionist and Episcopal minister; born in Sussex County, Delaware; co-founder with Richard Allen of Philadelphia's Free Africa Society 1787; first black minister ordained in U.S. 1794.

Jones, Anson (1798–1858), last president of Republic of Texas, born in Great Barrington, Mass.; practiced medicine, Brazoria, Tex., from

1833; in Texan army 1836; appointed Texas secretary of state 1841; president of Texas 1844–46.

Jones, Bobby (or Robert Tyre Jones, Jr.) (1902–71), U.S. golfer, born in Atlanta, Ga.; when 9, won his 1st golf championship, *picture* G-190

Jones, Casey (originally John Luther Jones) (1864–1900), U.S. locomotive engineer, born in Jordan, Fulton County, Kentucky; nickname from town, Cayce, Ky., where he was employed; with Illinois Central Railroad after 1888, became engineer 1890; made boast that he always brought his train in on time; killed in train wreck but kept train on tracks so all passengers were saved.

Jones, David (nickname Deacon) (born 1938), U.S. football player, born in Eatonville, Fla.; defensive end; with Los Angeles Rams 1961–71, San Diego Chargers 1972–73, Washington Redskins 1974.

Jones, Edith Newbold. *see in index* Wharton, Edith

Jones, Edward D. *see in index* Dow-Jones Average

Jones, Eli Stanley (1884–1973), U.S. missionary, born in Clarksville, Md.; to India as Methodist evangelist 1907; won fame with best seller 'The Christ of the Indian Road'.

Jones, Elizabeth Orton (born 1910), U.S. illustrator and author of children's books, born in Highland Park, Ill.; author and illustrator of 'Twig', 'Big Susan', and 'How Far Is It to Bethlehem?'; received Caldecott Medal 1945 for her illustrations in 'Prayer for a Child', written by Rachel Field; also illustrated 'This Is the Way', compiled by Jessie Mae Jones, and 'Song of the Sun', child's version of Saint Francis of Assisi's 'Canticle of the Sun'.

Jones, Everett Le Roi. *see in index* Baraka, Imamu

Jones, Henry Arthur (1851–1929), British dramatist; born on a farm; provided for self from age of 13 ('Saints and Sinners'; 'The Hypocrites'; 'The Lie'; 'Cock o' the Walk') E-278

Jones, Inigo (1573–1652), famous English architect, born in London; called the English Palladio J-138
  architecture A-568
  Banqueting House L-291
  stage design T-160

Jones, Jacob (1768–1850), U.S. Navy officer, born near Smyrna, Del.; commander of sloop-of-war *Wasp. see also in index* 'Frolic' and the 'Wasp', battle of

Jones, James (1921–77), U.S. novelist, born in Robinson, Ill. ('From Here to Eternity' won 1951 National Book Award; 'Some Came Running'; 'The Thin Red Line') A-368

Jones, Jesse Holman (1874–1956), U.S. public official, born in Robertson County, Tennessee; publisher *Houston Chronicle*; chairman of Reconstruction Finance Corporation 1933–39; administrator Federal Loan Agency 1939–42; secretary of commerce 1940–45 R-276, *picture* R-272

Jones, John Paul (1747–92), U.S. naval hero J-139
  Hall of Fame, *table* H-16
  taking the *Serapis*, *picture* R-172

Jones, John Percival (1829–1912), U.S. political leader, born in Herefordshire, England; to U.S. as infant; mined for gold in California; to Nevada 1867; Republican senator from Nevada 1873–1903.

Jones, Lady. *see in index* Bagnold, Enid

Jones, LeRoi. *see in index* Baraka, Imamu

Jones, Mary (or Mother Jones, or Mary Harris) (1830–1930), U.S. labor leader J-139

Jones, Robert Edmond (1887–1954), U.S. theatrical designer, born in Milton, N.H.; bold, original treatment; designs for 'Hamlet', 'Desire Under the Elms', 'Green Pastures', 'Lute Song', 'The Iceman Cometh'.

Jones, Rufus Matthew (1863–1948), U.S. educator, author, and humanitarian; born in South China, Me.; leading Quaker theologian; a founder of American Friends Service Committee; editor *Friends' Review* 1893.

Jones, Sir William (1746–94), English Orientalist and linguist; pioneer in study of Sanskrit; translated classic literature of India L-230

Jones Act, in Philippine history P-259d

Jonesboro, Ark., city in n.e. 62 mi (100 km) n.w. of Memphis, Tenn.; cotton, rice, soybeans, cattle; electric motors, shoes, brass fittings; Arkansas State University nearby; pop. 31,530, *map* U-41

Jonesboro, Ga., city 18 mi (29 km) s. of Atlanta; textiles, lumber; Federal victory under Gen. Oliver O. Howard, Aug. 1864, resulted in fall of Atlanta; pop. 4,132.

Jonestown, Guyana G-322

Jong, Erica (born 1942), U.S. writer A-363

Jonglei Canal, proposed canal to carry water 225 miles north from the White Nile river from Egypt to Sudan C-129

Jongleur, French name given, in Middle Ages, to strolling entertainers of lower class than troubadours
  classical music M-667
  French literature F-394

Jonker. *see in index* Jacobus Jonker

Jönköping, Sweden, city on s. shore of Vättern about 80 mi (130 km) e. of Göteborg; match industry; pop. 50,522, *maps* E-360, S-524

Jonquil, flower *Narcisscu jonquilla* N-18, *picture* F-223

Jonson, Ben (1573?–1637), English dramatist J-140
  court poet P-402
  literature E-267
    drama D-243
    theater T-160
  Shakespeare S-131

Jooss, Kurt (1901–79), German dancer, head of Jooss Ballet; born in Württemberg, Germany; founded school in Essen 1927, to England 1934; returned to Essen 1949; famous ballets: 'Green Table'; 'Big City'.

Joos van Cleve (1480?–1540), Flemish painter
  'Death of the Virgin', *picture* M-163

Joplin, Janis (1943–70), U.S. rock singer J-140
  popular music M-681

Joplin, Scott (1868–1917), U.S. musician J-141
  jazz J-84
  opera O-571
  popular music M-684

Joplin, Mo., city in s.w. near Kansas border, 10 mi (16 km) from Oklahoma; aircraft parts, zinc and lead processing, wood and paper products, machinery, clothing, chemicals, stockyards; Missouri Southern State College; pop. 39,023 M-491, 500, *map* U-41

Joppa, Palestine. *see in index* Jaffa

Jordaens, Jacob (1593–1678), Flemish historical, genre, and portrait painter; born in Antwerp; works characteristic of Flemish school; full, robust figures, broad humor, warm colors.

Jordan, David Starr (1851–1931), U.S. biologist, educator, and author; born in Gainesville, N.Y.; president of Indiana University, later of Stanford University; leading authority on fishes and prominent in world peace movement ('Evolution and Animal Life'; 'Fishes of North and Middle America'; 'War and Waste'; 'Days of a Man').

Jordan, James Edward (character Fibber McGee) (born 1896), U.S. radio entertainer, born in Peoria, Ill.; with wife and professional partner, **Marian Jordan** (character Molly) (1898–1961), born in Peoria, Ill.), began characters Fibber McGee and Molly in 1931 (on network 1935–56); also in motion pictures ('Look Who's Laughing'; 'Heavenly Days').

Jordan, June Meyer (born 1936), U.S. poet, teacher, and author of children's books, born in Harlem ('His Own Where'; 'Some Changes'), *list* R-111g

Jordan (or Hashemite Kingdom of Jordan, or Transjordan), Arab kingdom in s.w. Asia e. of Israel; 37,301 sq mi (96,609 sq km); cap. Amman; pop. 3,244,000 J-141
  Asia, *map* A-697
  canals C-129
  cities. *see also in index* cities listed below and other cities by name
    Amman A-370
    Bethlehem B-179
  flag, *picture* F-166
  Great Rift Valley G-250
  Israel I-372
  Jerusalem J-99
  Jordan River J-143
  railroad mileage, *table* R-85
  world, *map* W-297

Jordan River (Greek Aulon), river of Palestine; rises in n., flows 200 mi (320 km) s. in deep valley through lakes Merom (Huleh) and Tiberias (Galilee) into Dead Sea J-143
  Dead Sea D-45
  Israel I-369
  Jordan J-141
  Palestine P-81
  Sea of Galilee G-5

Jordan River, river in Utah, flows from n. end of Utah Lake into Great Salt Lake, *maps* U-232, 217

Jörmungand, evil serpent in Norse mythology M-703

Joseffy, Rafael (1852–1915), U.S. pianist and composer, born in Hungary; after 1880 lived in New York and was famous as teacher and concert virtuoso; author of 'School of Advanced Piano Playing'.

Joseph, saint, husband of Mary the mother of Jesus; patron of the workingman; festival March 19 J-103

Joseph I (1678–1711), Holy Roman emperor, succeeded to throne 1705; vigorously prosecuted wars against France and Hungary, and forced pope to acknowledge his brother Charles as king of Spain.

Joseph II (1741–90), Holy Roman emperor, son of Maria Theresa; benevolent despot; upset old customs and provoked discontent and revolt; died disillusioned and unhappy A-830
  Mozart M-643

Joseph, Hebrew patriarch, son of Jacob and Rachel; father of Ephraim and Manasseh (Bible, Gen. xxxvii) F-259

Joseph, Chief (1840?–1904), chief of Nez Percé J-143
  Montana M-551

'Joseph and His Brothers', novel by Mann M-109

'Joseph Andrews', novel by Fielding F-79
  English literature E-272

'Joseph and the Amazing Technicolor Dreamcoat', a Broadway production, *picture* F-259

Josephine (1763–1814), empress of France J-144
  Napoleon N-15

Joseph of Arimathea, rich Israelite who entombed the body of Jesus in his own sepulcher; commemorated as saint March 17.

Joseph's-coat, an annual plant *Amaranthus tricolor* of the amaranth family, native to tropical regions; leaves thin, oval, pointed; each leaf has several colors in it, giving a patched appearance.

Josephson, Brian D. (born 1940), British physicist, born in Cardiff, Wales; research in superconductivity and electron tunneling in solids; discovered Josephson effect used in measuring magnetic fields; professor of physics Cambridge University 1974–.

Josephson, Matthew (1899–1978), U.S. author, born in Brooklyn, N.Y. (biographies: 'Victor Hugo', 'Stendhal', 'Sidney Hillman', 'Edison'; U.S. economic and political studies: 'The Robber Barons' and 'The President Makers'; memoirs: 'Life Among the Surrealists', 'Infidel in the Temple').

Josephson junction, electronic device to provide superconductivity E-176

Josephus, Flavius (AD 37?–100), Jewish historian ('The Jewish War', 170 BC–AD 70; 'The Jewish Antiquities', from earliest time to reign of Nero) H-172
  educational views E-78
  Herod H-141

Joshua, sixth book of Bible's Old Testament, named for Joshua, successor to Moses; account of Israelites' settlement in Canaan
  espionage E-305

Joshua tree (or tree yucca), a species of yucca *Yucca brevifolia* native to w. and s.w. U.S.; also called Joshua yucca and yucca palm; clusters of stiff spikelike leaves.

Josiah (645?–608 BC), king of Judah; abolished idolatry and reestablished worship of Jehovah (Bible, II Kings xxii–xxiii)
  Jeremiah J-98

Joslin, Elliott Proctor (1869–1962), U.S. physician, born in Oxford, Mass.; joined faculty of Harvard Medical School 1898, clinical professor 1922–37; authority on diabetes.

Joslyn Art Museum, cultural center in Omaha, Neb. O-543

Josquin (1440?–1521), Flemish composer J-144

Joss, Adrian (nickname Addie) (1880–1911), U.S. baseball player, born in Juneau, Wis.; pitcher for Cleveland A.L. 1902–10; 45 shutouts in 160 career victories.

Joss flower (or Chinese sacred lily), type of narcissus N-18

Jostedalsbreen, glacier in Norway N-389

Jota, Spanish dance of exaggerated pattern and movement performed, usually by a couple, with castanets.

Jotunheim, in Norse mythology, land of frost giants M-703

Jotunheimen, mountain range in Norway N-389

Joubert, Joseph (1754–1824), French philosopher and writer, born in Montignac, near Périgueux, France; famed for brilliance of his conversation and correspondence.

Joubert, Petrus Jacobus (1834–1900), Boer general, commandant general in 1st and 2nd Boer wars; repelled Jameson Raid.

Jouffroy d'Abbans, Claude François Dorothée, marquis de (1751–1832), French inventor; pioneer in steam navigation; forerunner of Fulton.

Jouhaux, Léon (1879–1954), French labor leader, born in Paris; delegate to Versailles Peace Conference 1919 and League of Nations 1925–28; became head of General Confederation of Labor 1909, withdrew 1947 to found Workers' Force, anti-Communist labor union.

Joule, James Prescott (1818–89), British physicist, born in Salford, Lancashire; a large inheritance enabled him to devote his life to research; important work in subjects of heat, thermodynamics, electricity H-106

Joule, unit of energy equal to 10 million ergs; named for James Prescott Joule.

Journal M-31. *see also in index* Magazine
  indexes R-129
  scientific journals, *picture* S-59d

Journalism
  newspaper. *see in index* Newspaper
  Swift S-531

'Journal to Stella', work by Swift S-531

Journeyman, in medieval guild G-313
  apprenticeship A-511
  labor L-2
  labor movements L-6

'Journey to the Seven Streams, A', work by Kiely I-328

Joust (or just), knighthood combat K-258, *picture* K-259
  Middle Ages, *picture* M-389

Jouvenel, Henry de (1876–1935), French political leader and writer; editor *Le Matin* 1905–24; delegate League of Nations 1922 and 1924; minister public instruction 1924; high commissioner Syria 1925; wrote 'The Stormy Life of Mirabeau'; first wife was Mme. Colette, the French novelist.

Jovanovic, Jovan (1833–1904), Serbian poet and journalist; pen name Zmaj (the dragon) from one of two humorous periodicals he founded; educated in law and medicine; best known for his lyrics and humorous poems ('Saran', a play; 'Faded Roses', verse).

Jove, in Roman mythology. *see in index* Jupiter

Jove, planet. *see in index* Jupiter

Jovian planet P-350, S-254a

Jowett, Benjamin (1817–93), British scholar, theologian, and teacher; master of Balliol College, Oxford University; great influence on English life through eminent pupils; translated works of Plato, Aristotle, and Thucydides.

Joyce, James (1882–1941), Irish writer J-144
- literature L-243
  - 'A Portrait of the Artist as a Young Man' N-411, R-111g
  - English E-281
  - Irish I-328, *picture* I-327
- Svevo I-377
- Woolf W-292

Juan, Don. *see in index* Don Juan legend

Juan Carlos I (born 1938), king of Spain, born in Rome, Italy; designated in 1969 as eventual successor to Francisco Franco; became king after death of Franco 1975 J-145
- House of Bourbon B-384
- Spain S-354, 361

Juan de Fuca, Strait of, strait in the Pacific Ocean between Vancouver Island in Canada and Washington in the U.S. W-48, *maps* C-109, N-350, W-49

Juan Fernández, group of three small islands in South Pacific; Más a Tierra (Isla Róbinson Crusoe), which ranks as largest, Más Afuera (Isla Alejandro Selkirk), and Santa Clara; explored by Juan Fernández in 1574; owned by Chile; name formerly applied only to Más a Tierra; pop. 540, *maps* S-299, W-297
- national park status N-27

Juárez, Benito Pablo (1806–72), Mexican statesman, sometimes called the Mexican Washington; his reign as president was noted for liberal reforms J-145
- Mexico M-336

Juárez, Mexico. *see in index* Ciudad Juárez

Jubal, son of Lamech and Adah; called father of musicians (Bible, Gen. iv, 21); traditional inventor of musical instruments (harp and organ).

Juba River, river in Africa, rises in Ethiopia and flows s.e. to Indian Ocean.

Jubbulpore (or Jabalpur), India, manufacturing and trading city in Madhya Pradesh state; makes cotton goods, wire netting, statuary; once home of Thugs, society of religious assassins; pop. 426,224, *maps* A-697, I-83

Jubilee, diamond, *picture* D-129

Jubilee, Jewish history, every 50th year from entrance of Hebrews into Canaan to be set aside for rejoicing, Israelite slaves to be freed, alienated ancestral possessions to be restored, no sowing or reaping of land; term now applied to 50th anniversary of any event, or to a season of rejoicing.

Júcar River, river in e. Spain; about 310 mi (500 km) to the Mediterranean, *map* S-350

Juchi, son of Genghis Khan M-534

Judah, Hebrew patriarch, 4th son of Jacob and Leah, traditional ancestor of tribe of Judah, one of the 12 tribes of Israel.

Judah, s. kingdom of Palestine; remained faithful to house of David after break in kingdom of the Jews; cap. Jerusalem. *see also in index* Judea
- Jeremiah J-98

Judah Halevy (1085–1141?), Spanish poet, rabbi, and philosopher; born in Toledo; famed Hebrew writer; religious and secular poetry; prose work 'Sefer ha-Kuzari' declared superiority of faith over logic.

Judah ha-Nasi (AD 135?–220?), scholar and rabbi who collected Jewish Oral Law into the Mishna, the code of religious and civil laws governing society T-18

Judaism, in religion J-146
- ancestor veneration A-204
- Arab-Israeli conflicts H-6
- Asian religions A-683
- Baeck's contribution B-17
- bioethical issues B-214
- birth control views B-284
- calendar C-29
- Christianity C-397
- church and state history C-409
- circumcision C-422
- distribution R-143
- ethics and morality E-310
- fasting F-44
- God G-173
- history
  - Abraham A-12
  - Australia
    - Hobart H-179
  - Babylon B-3
  - Denmark C-463
  - education E-78
  - Egypt, ancient B-318
    - migration of people M-402
  - England E-106, E-233
  - Europe E-337
  - France F-349
  - Germany G-123
    - concentration camps C-638
    - genocide G-60
    - Hitler H-175
    - Holocaust H-205
    - Krupp family K-307
  - Israel made a state U-24
  - Jesus Christ J-103
  - monks and monasticism M-539, 542
  - Moses M-595
  - Palestine P-80
  - Poland P-415
    - Warsaw W-34
  - prophets P-508
  - Red Sea R-120
  - Solomon S-255
  - Spain S-353, 356, 358
  - surnames adopted N-7
  - The Netherlands A-381
  - United States
    - New York City N-272, 275
- holy days F-67
  - citron used C-447
  - Passover P-136
  - Sabbath S-1
- India I-69
- Islam I-359
  - Koran K-268
- Israel I-369, M-395, *pictures* I-370, 372, 373, *map* I-371
- language and literature. *see also in index* Hebrew language; Hebrew literature
  - Bible B-181
  - Dead Sea scrolls D-47
  - folklore F-263, S-470, *list* S-481
  - Josephus's works H-172
  - Saadia's works S-1
  - Talmud T-18
  - Torah T-227
  - Yiddish literature Y-416
- marriage M-151
- martyr M-161
- meat consumption M-247
  - industry M-253
- minority group M-461
- mythology M-698
- physical classification, *chart* R-26
- rainbow symbol R-88
- religion R-143
- world W-296
- Zionism Z-455
  - Herzl H-145
  - Palestine P-80
  - San'a S-34

Judas, Saint (also called Saint Jude, or Saint Thaddeus), one of the Twelve Apostles; said to have been martyred; festival October 28 A-506

Judas Iscariot, disciple who betrayed Jesus for 30 pieces of silver (Bible, Matthew xxvi, 14–16, 25, 47–50) A-506
- Jesus Christ J-104

Judas Maccabaeus. *see in index* Maccabees

Judas tree. *see in index* Redbud

Judd, Charles Hubbard (1873–1946), U.S. psychologist, born in Bareilly, India; professor at Yale University and University of Chicago; made many surveys of schools.

Jude, Saint. *see in index* Judas, Saint

'Jude, Der', journal edited by Buber B-473

Jude, Epistle of, twenty-sixth book of Bible's New Testament; doubtful authorship, often attributed to Judas Thaddeus (St. Jude); contains exhortation to constancy in Christian faith B-183

Judea (or Judaea, or Judah), a Greek and Roman name for s. Palestine; in time of Jesus part of province of Syria and also kingdom of the Herods; in Roman times southernmost division of Palestine
- Israel I-369

'Jude the Obscure', work by Hardy N-413

Judge, in law
- courts of justice C-746
- criminal law C-776
- jury system J-159
- law L-94
- state judges S-429

Judge advocate general, U.S. Air Force, Army, and Navy; has charge of legal matters arising in his or her respective department A-646
- insignia of U.S. Army, *picture* U-10

Judges, Book of, seventh book of the Bible's Old Testament; describes history of Israelites under the rule of the Judges
- hairdressing H-8

Judgment, in law, *table* L-93

Judicial review S-518b
- administrative law A-46
- bureaucratic limitation B-505
- constitutional law C-685

Judiciary. *see in index* Courts of justice

Judiciary Act (1789), United States court decision C-686

Judith, Jewish heroine, captivated Assyrian general Holofernes and killed him while he slept, thereby delivering the besieged Israelites; story told in book of Judith in the Apocrypha.

'Judith of Bethulia' (1913), early silent film spectacle by Griffith M-618

Judo W-366
- Japan J-57

Judson, Adoniram (1788–1850), missionary to India J-151, B-76

Judson, Clara Ingram (1879–1960), U.S. writer of children's books, born in Logansport, Ind. ('Mary Jane' series of stories; biographies: 'Soldier Doctor; the Story of William Gorgas', 'Abraham Lincoln, Friend of the People', 'George Washington, Leader of the People', 'Thomas Jefferson, Champion of the People', 'Benjamin Franklin'; Sault Sainte Marie Canal history: 'Mighty Soo'; 'St. Lawrence Seaway'); Laura Ingalls Wilder Award, 1960.

Judson, Edward Zane Carroll (pen-name Ned Buntline) (1823–86), U.S. author and adventurer; originator of the dime or pulp novel W-151

Judson, Harry Pratt (1849–1927), U.S. educator, born in Jamestown, N.Y.; educated Williams College; teacher and principal high school, Troy, N.Y.; professor history University of Minnesota; at University of Chicago after 1892, first as professor political science; as president 1907–23; writer on political science and history.

Judson, Wilfred (born 1902), Canadian jurist, born in Todmorden, England; to Canada 1923; admitted to Ontario bar 1932; justice of Supreme Court of Ontario 1951–58, Supreme Court of Canada 1958–77.

Judson College, in Elgin, Ill.; Baptist; founded 1963; liberal arts, education.

Judson College, in Marion, Ala.; affiliated with Southern Baptist Convention; for women; founded 1838; opened 1839; arts and sciences, teacher education.

Juggernaut. *see in index* Jagannath

Juglandaceae. *see in index* Walnut family

Jugoslavia. *see in index* Yugoslavia

Jugular vein, a large vein in the neck, *pictures* A-395-8

Jugurtha (died 104 BC), usurping king of Numidia; defied Roman power for several years, defeating and bribing opposing generals; captured by Marius.

Juhl, Finn (born 1912), Danish furniture designer and architect F-462

Juilliard, Augustus D. (1836–1919), U.S. businessman, born in Canton, Ohio; head of dry-goods commission house, New York; prominent in banking and insurance.

Juilliard School, The, in New York, N.Y.; private control; founded 1905; located at Lincoln Center after 1969; music, dance, drama; concurrent studies in humanities or liberal arts; graduate study N-254, N-273

Juilliard String Quartet, *picture* S-490

Juiz de Fora, Brazil, manufacturing city on Paraibuna River about 90 mi (145 km) n. of Rio de Janeiro; knitted goods; lumber, coffee, sugar, cotton; pop. 224,275, *maps* B-425, S-299

Jujitsu (or jujutsu) W-366
- Japan J-57

Jujube, a genus *Zizyphus* of shrubs and trees grown for foliage and small, brown, fleshy, oval fruits; used in candy or as preserved fruit; believed to have originated in Syria, carried by Romans to Europe, now found in all tropical regions; common, or Chinese, jujube grows to 40 ft (12 m); leaves oval, with 2 spines at base; flowers small, green or white, in clusters.

Jukes, fictitious name of a family in New York State investigated by R.L. Dugdale and known for large percentage of pauperism and criminality; records of 709 of 1,200 members show 280 paupers, 140 criminals, and large proportion of moral and physical deviates. *see also in index* Kallikak

Juku (or cram school), school established in Japan T-208

'Jules Feiffer's America', work by Feiffer F-52

Julia Augusta. *see in index* Livia Drusilla

Julian (or Flavius Claudius Julianus) (331–363), Roman emperor, called the Apostate; nephew of Constantine the Great; brought up as Christian, became philosophic pagan; proclaimed emperor by army 361; able ruler and last pagan emperor.

Julian, Percy Lavon (1899–1975), U.S. chemist, born in Montgomery, Ala.; known for fundamental organic researches and for researches made with soybeans; synthesized chemicals to combat glaucoma and arthritis; achieved first successful method for commercial isolation of soya sterols and bulk preparation of the hormones progesterone and testosterone from these sterols; won 1947 Spingarn medal for chemistry; studied and taught at DePauw University in Greencastle, Ind. B-260

Julian Alps, mountains in n.w. Yugoslavia, *maps* B-25, I-404

Julian calendar (or Old Style calendar, or O.S. calendar), C-28
- Caesar's institution C-15

Juliet, heroine of Shakespeare's tragedy 'Romeo and Juliet' R-258

Julius II (1443–1513), pope J-151
- Bologna B-337
- Swiss Guard P-100
- tomb sculpture, *picture* S-86

Julius Caesar. *see in index* Caesar, Gaius Julius

'Julius Caesar', tragedy by Shakespeare, written about 1599; relates story of death of Caesar, portraying characters of Brutus and Mark Antony; ends with Brutus' death
- Brando as Mark Antony S-133, 139, *picture* S-140
- funeral oration P-526a

Julius Rosenwald Fund, founded 1917 in Chicago, Ill., for (1) improving rural education, especially in the South; (2) developing leadership among black and white Southerners through fellowships; (3) facilitating advanced education and health among blacks F-333. *see also in index* Rosenwald, Julius

July, 7th month of the Gregorian calendar
- birthdays of famous persons. *see in index* Birthdays, *table*
- calendar C-30

July Fourteenth (or Bastille Day), national independence

festival of France, celebrating fall of Bastille F-66
July Revolution, in Paris, France. *see in index* Revolution of 1830
Jumbo, mine device M-428
Jumeau bisque, extremely fine type of porcelain made famous by the French Jumeau family; used in bisque dolls D-221
Jumna River. *see in index* Yamuna River
Jump band, small swing band M-679
Jump cutting, movie editing technique M-613
Jumping, in equestrian sports E-295
Jumping bean, triangular seeds of any of several Latin American swamp trees of the spurge family, containing the full-grown larva of a small gray moth; when a seedpod falls to ground the larva jumps and rolls, taking the bean with it; also called Mexican jumping bean and bronco bean.
Jumping event, in track and field T-244
Jumping mouse, North American mouse with very long hind legs; able to leap 9–15 ft (3–5 m) M-640
Jumping spider, small spider of family Attidae S-385
Jump River, river in n.-central Wisconsin, rises in Price County and flows 70 mi (115 km) s.w. to Holcombe Flowage at Chippewa River.
Junco, bird of the family Fringillidae, *picture* B-260
Junction City, Kan., city about 61 mi (98 km) w. of Topeka, at junction of Smoky Hill and Republican rivers; trade center for agricultural and livestock area, mobile homes, clothing; Fort Riley nearby; pop. 19,305.
June, 6th month of the Gregorian calendar
- birthdays of famous persons. *see in index* Birthdays, *table*
- calendar C-30

Juneau, Solomon Laurent (1793–1856), U.S. pioneer, born near Montreal, Que.; first mayor of Milwaukee, Wis. (1846) M-422
Juneau, Alaska, state capital, on inlet of Pacific 100 mi (160 km) n. of Sitka; pop. 19,528 J-152, *map* U-39, 94
- Alaska A-242, *picture* A-249
- North America, *map* N-350
- world, *map* W-297

'Juneau', U.S. naval ship W-345
Juneautown, town founded in 1835 by Solomon Juneau M-422
Juneberry. *see in index* Shadbush
June bug (or May beetle) B-140, *picture* B-137
- larva, *picture* L-51

Jung, Carl (1875–1961), Swiss analytical psychologist J-152
- psychology P-519

Jünger, Ernst (born 1895), German novelist, born in Heidelberg; realistic novels influenced by his experiences in World Wars I and II G-109
Jungfrau (translation maiden), Alpine peak 13, 667 ft (4,166 m) in Switzerland; scientific station for study of cosmos, human body at high altitudes, other phenomena, *map* S-537
Jungle J-153
- forest types F-309

'Jungle, The', novel of social criticism by Sinclair (1906); on Chicago Stockyards R-285
- food and drug laws F-274
- social criticism N-412

'Jungle Books, The', two collections of animal stories by Kipling; 'The Jungle Book' and 'The Second Jungle Book' R-111a
- Kipling K-249

Jungle cat (or swamp cat), wild cat *Felis chaus*, *picture* C-214
Jungle fowl P-480
'Jungle Peace', work by Beebe B-130
Juniata College, in Huntingdon, Pa.; private control; established in 1876; arts and sciences, teacher education.
Junior, Democritus. *see in index* Burton, Robert
Junior Achievement, Inc., U.S. organization founded 1919 in Springfield, Mass.; provides young people of high-school age with practical business experience by helping them to organize, finance, and operate miniature companies of their own under guidance of business-executive volunteers; offers scholarships, awards, trips for outstanding achievement; operates in United States and Canada; headquarters Stamford, Conn. Y-431
Junior Classical League, second largest youth organization in U.S.; membership open to junior high school and high school students studying Latin, Greek, or other classical subjects; promotes interest in culture of ancient Greece and Rome and its influence; founded 1936.
Junior Engineering Technical Society (JETS), a national high school organization which aims to stimulate interest in engineering and science; headquarters East Lansing, Mich., where first club was formed at Michigan State University in 1950; money, materials, and experts contributed by industries.
Junior Grange. *see in index* Grange, National
Junior high school. *see in index* Secondary school
Junior Leagues of America, The Association of, an organization to promote social welfare; made up (since 1921) of individual Junior Leagues, the first of which had been founded in 1900; branches in cities of U.S. and Canada, with main office in New York City W-270
Juniper, J-157, *picture* P-359
- liquor production L-235

Junípero Serra, Miguel José (1713–84), Spanish missionary to California, born in Majorca
- California C-41
- Southwest S-338
- Statuary Hall, *table* S-437a

Junius, pen name of author of a famous series of scorching English political letters attacking George III and his ministers 1769–72; real authorship never proved, attributed to more than 40 persons, but generally conceded to Sir Philip Francis; recent research names Laughlin Macleane, British army surgeon.
Junk, Chinese boat C-367, *pictures* C-373, T-263
- harbors and ports, *picture* H-34

Junkers, Prussian social class A-641
Junk food, *picture* H-83
Juno, in Roman mythology, goddess identified with Greek Hera, sometimes called Moneta M-701. *see also in index* Hera
- peacock P-146

Juno's volute (or junonia), snail *Scaphella junonia*
- shell, *picture* S-150

Junta (from Spanish word meaning joined), a group with political or administrative purposes; usually in control of government, often as a result of a seizure of power; frequently military; term generally used in Spanish and Latin American countries
- Peru P-225
- Sierra Leone S-192b
- Vietnam V-322

Junto Club, debating society formed by Benjamin Franklin in Philadelphia, Pa., in 1727; later developed into American Philosophical Society A-51
Jupiter (or Jove), in Roman mythology M-701. *see also in index* Zeus
Jupiter, planet P-353, *table* P-351, *diagram* P-352, *picture* P-354
- astronomy A-714, 717
- Cassini's study C-197
- earth E-8, *diagram* E-9
- eclipse E-48
- light's speed L-198
- probes, *table* S-344
- satellites S-52
  - Galileo's discovery G-6
- solar system S-254, *table* S-254b, *diagrams* S-254c, 254e

Jupiter C, rocket developed by U.S. Army, *picture* S-341d
Jura (translation deer island), 4th largest of Inner Hebrides, Scotland; 150 sq mi (390 sq km); pop. 249.
Jura Mountains, border of France and Switzerland
- France, *map* F-372
- Switzerland S-537, *picture* S-539

Jurassic period, in geological time A-775
- biogeographical changes B-218
- earth E-26, *table* E-24
- prehistoric animals R-155, *picture* R-153

Jurisdiction
- city government C-457
- law I-255

Juris Doctor, law degree L-97
Jurisprudence, science of the development and nature of law and the study and classification of laws. *see in index* Law
Juruá River, river about 1,200 mi (1,950 km) long, tributary of the Amazon in n.w. Brazil; rises in e. Peru; traverses rubber-growing region, *maps* B-425, S-298
Jury system J-158
- courts of justice C-746
- criminal law C-776
- feudal origins F-70
  - Henry II H-129
- trial U-150, 152

Jusserand, Jean Jules (1855–1932), French diplomat and scholar, ambassador to U.S. 1902–24; wrote works on English literature and life, notably 'Piers Plowman' and a 'Literary History of the English People'; awarded Pulitzer prize (1917) for 'With Americans of Past and Present'.
Jussieu, Adrien de (1797–1853), French botanist, member of family of distinguished doctors and botanists; wrote text on elementary botany that was widely translated.
Just, Ernest Everett (1883–1941), U.S. biologist, born in Charleston, S.C.; noted for studies in field of egg cells and fertilization; won 1915 Spingarn medal for research in biology.
Just. *see in index* Joust
Justice, U.S. Supreme Court S-518a. *see also in index* Supreme Court of the United States, *table*
Justice, the quality of being just, fair, and impartial
- civil rights C-468
- ethics and morality E-309
- warfare W-19

Justice, Court of, institution of the European Communities E-362
Justice, Department of, section of United States federal government U-160, *list* U-156
- Eisenhower E-139
- government agencies G-200
  - Bureau of Prisons P-505b
  - intelligence I-237

'Justice and Expediency', pamphlet by Whittier W-201
Justification, in printing T-337
Justin I (452–527), Byzantine emperor; a peasant, he rose to rank through army; administration aided by nephew and successor Justinian I.
Justinian I (483–565), Byzantine emperor J-161
- Byzantine Empire B-533
- Hagia Sophia E-43
- law L-91
- silk culture introduction S-202
- Vandals conquered V-265

Justinian Code, legal code
- Byzantine history B-534
- money B-72

Justin Martyr, Saint (100–165?), Church Father; adherent of Platonic system; one of foremost Christian apologists; born in Palestine of non-Christian parents; said to have been scourged and beheaded at Rome.
Justin Morgan, breed of horse, *list* H-249
'Just So Stories', work by Kipling R-110a, K-249
Jute, fiber J-161
- Bangladesh B-62
- harvesting, *picture* A-131
- India I-74
- textile manufacture T-138
- uses
  - communication cables C-7, *picture* C-8
  - paper P-101

Jutes, a Teutonic people related to the Angles and Saxons, generally believed to have come from Jutland E-238
Jutland (or Jylland), low flat peninsula of n. Europe forming largest part of Denmark D-97, *map* D-100
Jutland, battle of, in World War I W-306, *list* W-15
- naval warfare N-84, 87, 92
- Royal Marines M-137

Juvenal (or Decimus Junius Juvenalis) (55?–127?), Roman poet J-161
- Latin literature L-77

Juvenile (or ingenue), in theater, *list* T-155
Juvenile courts, in law J-162
- juvenile delinquency J-164

Juvenile delinquency J-162
- child abuse C-319
- juvenile courts J-162
- police prevention P-427
- rehabilitation P-505a

Juvenile organizations F-330
Juventud, Isla de la (formerly Isla de Pinos, or Isle of Pines, also called Isle of Youth), fertile island belonging to Cuba, about 40 mi (60 km) s. of western end of Cuba; 849 sq mi; chief town Nueva Gerona; pop. 10,105 C-800, *map* N-310
- West Indies, *map* W-159

Juyo Cave, El, religious shrine near Santander, Spain A-538
Jylland. *see in index* Jutland

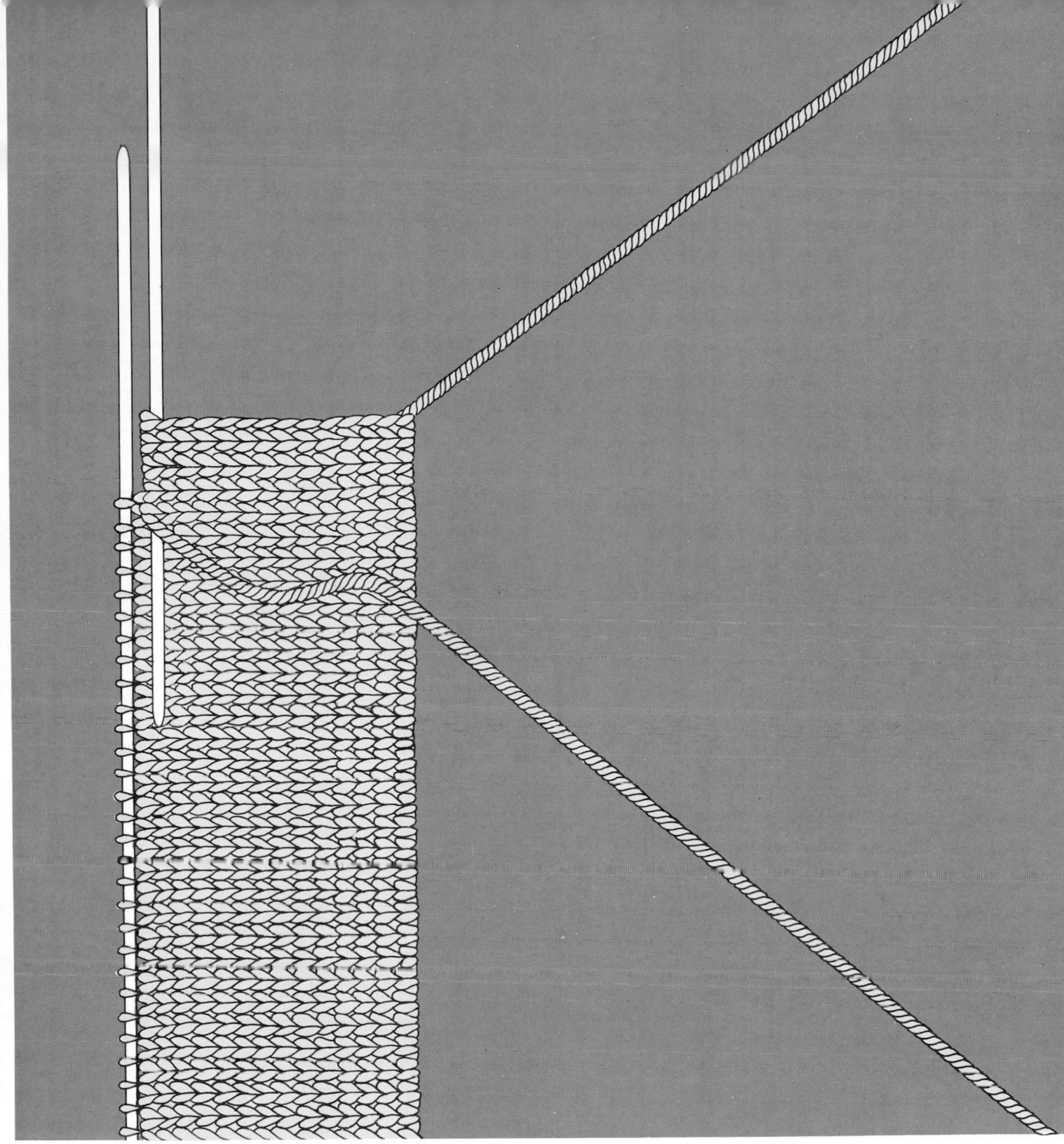

INDEX

The letter K

may have started as a picture sign of the palm of the hand, as in Egyptian hieroglyphic writing (1) and in a very early Semitic writing used about 1500 B.C. on the Sinai Peninsula (2). About 1000 B.C., in Byblos and other Phoenician and Canaanite centers, the sign was given a linear form (3), the source of all later forms. In the Semitic languages the sign was called *kaph,* meaning "palm."

The Greeks changed the Semitic name to *kappa.* They also turned the letter around to suit the left-to-right direction of their writing (4).

The Romans took the sign over into Latin, but they used it sparingly. From Latin the capital letter K came into English unchanged.

The English small handwritten "k" is simply a capital K with small, straight strokes, which were gradually rounded. The printed "k" is similar to the handwritten form.

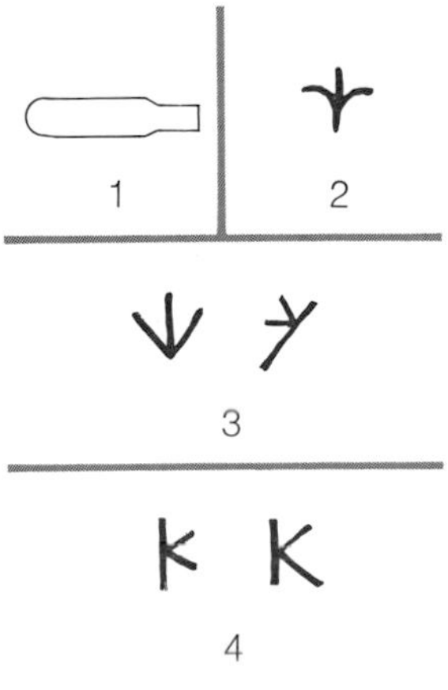

K

K2 (or Mount Godwin Austen, or Dapsang), peak in Karakoram Range, n. Kashmir; altitude 28,250 ft (8,610 m); 2nd highest mountain in world K-166
  Asia, *map* A-697
  height, comparative. *see in index* Mountain, *table*
  Karakoram Range K-192
Kaaba (or Caaba, or Kaabeh), Muslim shrine at Mecca
  Islamic pilgrimage I-360
  Mecca M-254
Kabah, Mayan pilgrimage center M-237
Kabak, Abraham (1883–1944), Israeli writer
  Hebrew literature H-113
Kabinda, Angola. *see in index* Cabinda
Kabir, (1440–1518), Indian mystic and poet who tried to bridge or unite Hindu and Islamic thought and preached the essential unity of all religions and the equality of all people H-158
Kabis, Dorothy Andrews. *see in index* Elston, Dorothy Andrews
Kabotie, Fred (born 1900), American Indian artist and author, born in Shungopavy, Ariz.; author of 'Designs from the Ancient Mimbrenos', *picture* I-130
Kabuki, Japanese dance drama
  Japanese culture J-49
  masks M-187
Kabuki Theater, theater in Tokyo, Japan T-207, *picture* T-210
Kabul, Afghanistan, capital, in province of Kabul; pop. 891,750 K-166, A-89
  Asia, *map* A-697
  world, *map* W-297
Kabul University, university in Kabul, Afghanistan A-90
Kachina, spirit of an ancestor, also a portrayal of the spirit
  doll D-215
  Indians, American I-117
Kachins, people of Indo-Chinese origin living along border of upper Burma.
Kádár, János (born 1912), Hungarian political leader, born in Kapoly, s. of Lake Balaton; active Communist 1932–; first secretary Hungarian Communist party 1956–; premier 1956–58, 1961–65 H-330
Kadiak Island. *see in index* Kodiak Island
Kaesong, North Korea, city 5 mi (8 km) n.w. of Panmunjom; commercial center; ginseng grown in area; fine porcelain ware; capital of Korea 915–1392; first city occupied by North Koreans in 1950 invasion; pop. 139,900 K-300, *map* K-290, *chart* K-299
Kaffir Wars (1779–1879), African history; sometimes called Cape Frontier Wars K-166
  frontier wars F-425
Kafir (or kafir corn) variety of sorghum introduced to U.S. from South Africa; grown in s.w. U.S.; grain used for livestock feed.
Kafka, Franz (1883–1924), Czech writer K-167
  expressionism N-414
  German literature G-107
Kagame, Abbe, Rwandan priest A-121
Kaganovich, Lazar Moiseevich (1893–1963?), Soviet government official, born in the Ukraine; joined Central Committee of Communist party 1924, Politburo 1926; as secretary of Ukrainian Central Committee 1925–28 built Dnieper Dam; as Communist party boss of Moscow 1930–35 reconstructed city and began subway; member of Presidium 1952–57; a first deputy premier 1953–57; expelled from Communist party in 1960s
Kagawa Toyohiko (1888–1960), Japanese preacher and social reformer, born in Kobe, Japan; converted to Christianity in his teens; author of poetry, essays, religious studies, stories for children, and novels.
Kagera River, river in e.-central Africa, flows into Lake Victoria; about 450 mi (725 km) long; courses through marshlands and lake regions; navigable in lower section; supplies hydroelectric power V-310
Kagoshima, Japan, one of chief cities of Kyushu Island; home of crackled Satsuma ware; space-industries center; pop. 1,729,150, *map* J-75
  Asia, *map* A-697
Kahanamoku, Duke (1890–1968), swimming champion, born in Honolulu, Hawaii; won 100-meter free-style race in 1912 and 1920 Olympics; revolutionized swimming by introducing flutter kick; called "greatest swimmer of his time."
Kahn, Louis (1901–74), U.S. architect A-566
  museum design M-663
Kahn, Otto Hermann (1867–1934), U.S. banker and patron of music and art, born in Mannheim, Germany; came to U.S. 1893; member firm Kuhn, Loeb & Co., New York City, after 1897 ('Of Many Things').
Kahn test, syphilis testing V-272
Kahoolawe, island of Hawaii; 45 sq mi (115 sq km) H-59, *maps* H-58, U-117
  Pacific Ocean, *map* P-3
Kahului, Hawaii, port town set in Iao Valley on n. coast of Maui; sugar, pineapples; Hawaii's first telephone line installed 1876 between Kahului and Wailuku; pop. 8,280.
Kaibab National Forest, forest in Arizona, adjoining Grand Canyon National Park; 1,780,475 acres (691,395 hectares); forest headquarters Williams, Ariz.
  ecological problem E-58
Kaieteur Falls, falls in central Guyana, *picture* S-276
  waterfall W-98, *picture* W-97
Kaifeng, China, city in Honan Province; flour, oilseed processing; pop. 318,000
  Asia, *map* A-697
Kailasa Temple, temple in Ellora, India I-71
Kailua, Hawaii, residential center on Kailua Bay on s.e. coast of island of Oahu; in livestock-raising region about 11 mi (18 km) n.e. of Honolulu; pop. 35,812 H-70
Kailua-Kona, Hawaii, resort area on the w.-central coast of Hawaii Island; Captain James Cook landed at Kailua in 1779; Kona district is center of the state's coffee industry
  Mokuaikaua church, *picture* H-69
Kailyard school (Kailyard meaning kitchen, or cabbage, garden), term applied to group of Scottish novelists who wrote of life of common people with copious use of dialect; best represented by Ian MacLaren and Sir James M. Barrie.
Kainite, mineral M-435
Kairouan (also spelled Kairwan), Tunisia, sacred city of Muslims; Ukbah mosque, rebuilt in 827; pop. 46,200 T-309
Kaisaria, Turkey. *see in index* Kayseri
Kaiser, Georg (1878–1945), German dramatist and critic, born in Magdeburg; a leader of expressionist school; his plays focus on various social problems G-107
Kaiser, Henry John (1882–1967), U.S. industrialist, born near Canajoharie, N.Y.; constructed piers for San Francisco-Oakland Bay Bridge; built Hoover, Bonneville, and Grand Coulee dams; shipbuilder, World War II; industries include cement, sand and gravel, aluminum, steel, chemicals, automobiles, electronics, aircraft components, real-estate development.
Kaiser, official title of German and Holy Roman emperors. *see also in index* Holy Roman Emperors, *table*
  Germany G-122. *see also in index* William I, first German emperor; William II, German emperor
Kaiser-Permanente plan, health-care system M-279
Kaiserslautern, West Germany, industrial city 35 mi (55 km) w. of Mannheim; Frederick Barbarossa built castle here about 1152; pop. 99,617, *map* G-131
Kaiser Wilhelm Memorial Church, church in West Berlin B-168, *map* B-170, *picture* B-169
Kajima Peace Award, gold medal and engraved certificate presented annually by Kajima Institute of International Peace, in Tokyo, "to the person or persons who have contributed toward peace in various fields of endeavor"; institute founded by Dr. Morinosuke Kajima, Japanese industrialist.
Kakemono, Japanese scroll painting J-50
Kakia, mythological figure; represents pleasure H-138
Kakinomoto Hitomaro (died 710), Japanese poet J-79
Kala azar, a fatal malarialike fever common in certain parts of India, transmitted by the bite of a sand fly.
Kalachi-Jo-goth. *see in index* Karachi
Kalah (or Nimrud), ancient Assyrian city, near Nineveh, built 1300 BC by Shalmaneser I; abandoned, then rebuilt as royal residence city about 880 BC
  archaeology A-532
Kalahari Desert, desert in s. Africa, lying chiefly in Botswana; about 240,000 sq mi (620,000 sq km) S-263, *maps* A-115, S-264
  Namibia N-9
Kalakaua, David (1836–91), king of Hawaii 1874–91; because of his extravagant and disorderly rule was forced to grant a new constitution (1887) that restricted royal power H-62
Kalakshetra, classical dance institute in Madras, India M-29
Kalamazoo, Mich., industrial city in s.w. on Kalamazoo River, about 40 mi (65 km) e. of Lake Michigan; celery and fruits; paper, pharmaceuticals, chemicals, metal products; Western Michigan University, Kalamazoo College, Nazareth College; pop. 79,722 M-359, U-41
Kalamazoo Case, The, in history of education; citizens of Kalamazoo, Mich., challenged (1872) collection of taxes for support of a public high school; the Michigan Supreme Court decided (1874) state had right to levy taxes for support of complete system of public education, including high schools and universities; case set a precedent for other states.
Kalamazoo College, college in Kalamazoo, Mich.; Baptist; chartered 1833 as Michigan and Huron Institute, as college 1855; arts and sciences, education; quarter system; programs in France, Spain, and West Germany.
Kalamazoo River, river in Michigan M-355
Kalanianaole, Prince Jonah Kuhio. *see in index* Kuhio, Prince
Kalantiaw, Code of, ancient Filipino legal code written by Lakan (Prince) Kalantiaw; admired by juridical scholars for its simple language, common sense, and clarity; consists of 18 orders.
Kalat, or **Khelat,** division of Baluchistan Province in Pakistan; formerly a princely state of India; joined Pakistan 1948
  Asia, *map* A-697
Kalatozov, Mikhail (born 1903), Soviet film director, born in Tiflis, now Tbilisi, U.S.S.R. M-623
Kale, vegetable C-2, *picture* C-3
Kaleidoscope, scientific toy invented by Sir David Brewster; tube that encloses angled mirrors and colored bits of glass between two flat plates.
'Kalevala', ancient Finnish epic S-470, 481
  Finland F-89
  folklore F-259
  Lönnrot L-297
  Sibelius S-187
KAL flight 007. *see in index* Korean Air Lines flight 007
Kalgan, China, city at gate in Great Wall, in Hopei Province, 100 mi. (160 km) n.w. of Peking; historic trade and transportation center; pop. 1,000,000
  Asia, *map* A-697
Kalgoorlie, mining town, Australia A-788, *maps* A-822, P-3, W-297
Kali. *see in index* Devi
Kali, martial arts. *see in index* Arnis
Kalidasa (5th century?), greatest dramatic and lyric poet of India; believed to have been court poet for rulers of Gupta dynasty, works translated into modern languages K-167
Kalimantan. *see in index* Borneo
Kalina, Zaire K-248
Kaline, Albert William (nickname Al) (born 1934), U.S. baseball player, born in Baltimore, Md.; outfielder with Detroit, A.L., 1953–74; career batting average .297.
Kalinin, Mikhail Ivanovich (1875–1946), Soviet statesman, born near Tver, later named Kalinin in his honor; a peasant himself, represented peasants in Soviet government in which he became president of central executive committee 1919, chairman 1923; chairman of Supreme Soviet of U.S.S.R. 1938–46.
Kalinin, formerly **Tver,** U.S.S.R., city on Volga River, 100 mi (160 km) n.w. of Moscow; capital of independent principality 13th

to 15th century; pop. 345,000, *maps* R-344, 348
Europe, *map* E-360
world, *map* W-297

Kaliningrad, (German **Königsberg**), U.S.S.R., fortified seaport, former capital of East Prussia, on Pregel River, 4 mi (6 km) from mouth; included in U.S.S.R. since 1945; university, castle; pop. 297,000, *maps* R-344, P-414
Europe, *map* E-360

Kalispell, Mont., city in Flathead Valley near Glacier National Park; pop. 10,648; tourist center in farm region; aluminum, lumber products; settled 1883 M-552, 560

Kalix River, river in Sweden, flows s.e. 335 km (208 mi) to Gulf of Bothnia, *map* S-524

Kallikak, fictitious name of a two-branch U.S. family dating from Revolutionary War days, investigated by H.H. Goddard in his studies of heredity; of 480 descendants of a feeble-minded mother and a sound father 282 were mental, moral, or physical defectives; all below normal in intelligence; of 496 descendants of same father and a mother of normal intelligence only 4 were defective; all were of sound mentality. *see also in index* Jukes

Kalm, Peter (or Per Kalm) (1715–79), Swedish botanist, born in Finland; visited North America to make survey of natural history 1748–51 ('Travels into North America') F-222

Kalmar, or **Calmar**, Sweden, port and cathedral town 320 km (200 mi) s. of Stockholm; historic castle dating from 12th century; pop. 34,918.

Kalmar Union (1397), in Scandinavian history S-52g, S-527, *table* T-274

Kalmia, genus of plants of heath family, best-known species being mountain laurel *Kalmia latifolia*. *see in index* Mountain laurel

Kalmus, Herbert Thomas (1881–1963), U.S. chemical engineer, born in Chelsea, Mass.; director Research Laboratory of Electrochemistry and Metallurgy, Canadian government 1913–15; invented Technicolor in motion pictures with wife, Natalie.

Kalthoeber, Charles, one of best of colony of German bookbinders who lived in London at end of 18th century; influenced by Roger Payne; style recognizable by ornaments in back panels.

Kamakura, Japan, seacoast city on Honshu s. of Yokohama; seat of shogunate 1192 to 1333; pop. 165,552, *map* J-75

'Kamalampal Carittiram', work by Aiyar I-108

Kama River, river in e. European Russia, largest tributary of Volga River; over 1,000 mi (1,600 km) long; timber trade, *maps* E-360, R-348

Kambalda, Western Australia A-814, *map* A-822

Kamchatka, peninsula of e. Siberia; 105,000 sq mi (270,000 sq km); pop. 280,000, *maps* R-322, 345
Asia, *map* A-697
world, *map* W-297

Kame, a hill of stratified drift G-151

Kamehameha I (1758?–1819), king of Hawaii (1795–1819) K-167
Hawaii H-63, *picture* H-67
Statuary Hall, *table* S-437a

Kamehameha III (1814–54), king of Hawaii (1825–54)
Hawaii H-61, 64

Kamehameha Day, holiday, *list* F-63

Kamel, George Joseph (or George Joseph Camel) (1661–1706), Moravian botanist, Jesuit missionary to Philippines; made study of plant and animal life and minerals on islands.

Kamerlingh Onnes, Heike (1853–1926), Dutch physicist, born in Groningen, The Netherlands; discovered method of liquefying helium; professor of physics, Leiden University in The Netherlands. *see also in index* Nobel Prizewinners, *table*

Kamerun. *see in index* Cameroons

Kami, entity in Shinto religion S-162

Kamik (or boot), sealskin boot worn by Eskimos, *picture* S-178

Kamikaze, Japanese for "divine wind"; applied to typhoon that swept away Kublai Khan's fleet during attempt to invade Japan 1281.

Kamikaze planes, term used for suicidal Japanese air force units in World War II
World War II A-159, W-336

Kamimura, Hikonojo, Baron (1850–1916), Japanese admiral; notable victory over Russian cruiser squadron off coast of Korea in Russo-Japanese War.

Kamloops, B.C., city at junction of North and South Thompson rivers 155 mi (250 km) n.e. of Vancouver; railway divisional point; oil refinery; lumber, cattle, fruit, vegetables; pop. 64,048, *maps* C-109, N-350

Kamo Chomei (1155–1216), Japanese priest and author J-81

'Kampaku', Japanese political office F-445

Kampala, Uganda, capital and chief commercial center; pop. 330,700 K-167, U-2, *map* A-115

Kampen, The Netherlands, city near mouth of IJssel River; formerly a Hanseatic town; 14th-century town hall, church; pop. 25,464.

Kampong, term applied to slums in s.e. Asia
Indonesia I-160

Kampuchea (formerly Cambodia), nation in s.w. Indochina on lower Mekong River; area 66,607 sq mi (172,511 sq km); cap. Phnom Penh; pop. 5,882,000 K-168
Asia, *map* A-697
China C-378
Indochina I-157
Thailand T-147
communist world, *map* C-619
flag, *picture* F-166
genocide G-60, M-461
Mekong River M-288
national anthem, *table* N-64
railroad mileage, *table* R-85
tea T-45
Vietnam conflict V-321
Ho Chi Minh City H-192
Nixon N-326
world, *map* W-297

Kana, Japanese language J-48
Japanese literature J-79

'Kanadehon Chushingura', play by Izumo Takeda J-56

Kanakas, Polynesians P-8, A-785, *picture* P-7

Kan-ami Kiyotsugu (1333–84), creator of drama A-27

Kananga (formerly Luluabourg), Zaire, city 500 mi (800 km) s.e. of Kinshasa; pop. 601,239 K-171, *map* A-115

Kanawha River, river in West Virginia; formed in w.-central part of state by junction of New and Gauley rivers; flows n.w. and joins Ohio River at Point Pleasant; length about 100 mi (160 km); Little Kanawha rises in central West Virginia and flows w. and n.w. about 100 mi (160 km) into Ohio River at Parkersburg
West Virginia M-165, *picture* W-173

Kanazawa, Japan, city on w. coast of Honshu Island; bronze and lacquer work, silk; fine public gardens; pop. 395,263, *map* J-75
Asia, *map* A-697

Kanban system, Japanese inventory control I-192

Kanchenjunga (or Kinchinjunga), 3rd highest mountain in world 28,146 ft (8,579 m); one of the e. Himalayas; on boundary between Nepal and India; first successfully climbed 1955, *map* I-86
Himalayas H-152

Kandahar (also Qandahar), Afghanistan, trade center in province of Kandahar, 300 mi (480 km) s.w. of Kabul; captured by Genghis Khan, Timur Lenk, and others; prominent in wars between British and Afghans; pop. 160,684
Asia, *map* A-700

Kandinsky, Wassily (1866–1944), Soviet painter, born in Moscow; identified with the German modern movement; one of leaders among nonobjective painters; splendid colorist; author of 'Upon the Spiritual in Art' K-171

Kändler, Johann Joachim (1706–75), German potter, born in Saxony P-475

Kandy, Sri Lanka, highland city in s.-central part of island on artificial lake; capital of former kingdom of Kandy; Buddhist and Brahman temples; pop. 93,602
Asia, *map* A-697

Kane, Elisha Kent (1820–57), U.S. Arctic explorer and scientist, born in Philadelphia, Pa.; accompanied Grinnell expeditions (commanded 2nd) searching for Sir John Franklin; attained Kane Basin (1853) and the then farthest north.

Kane, Harnett Thomas (born 1910), U.S. author, born in New Orleans, La. ('Queen New Orleans'; historical novels: 'Bride of Fortune' on Mrs. Jefferson Davis, 'The Lady of Arlington' on Mrs. Robert E. Lee, 'The Smiling Rebel' on Belle Boyd, Confederate spy; 'Gone Are the Days', pictorial history of the South).

Kane, Paul (1810–71), Canadian painter, born in Mallow, Ireland; large collections in Royal Ontario Museum, Toronto, and Parliament buildings, Ottawa.

Kaneohe, Hawaii, residential center on s.e. coast of island of Oahu; noted for coral gardens; Hawaii Loa College; missile-tracking station; pop. 29,919 H-70

Kanev Dam, dam in U.S.S.R., on Dneper River.

Kangaroo, marsupial animal of family Macropodidae K-171
Australia A-708
fur, *table* F-464
leather L-109
lifespan, *chart* A-423
mammal M-81
marsupials M-154, 157
Pacific Ocean, *map* P-3

Kangaroo paw, an Australian plant A-783

Kangaroo rat A-429, *picture* A-428

Kang Gang Su Wol Lae, Korean folk dance, *picture* K-281

K'ang Hsi, or **K'ang Hi** (1655–1722), Chinese emperor (1661–1722); encouraged arts and literature; consolidated empire C-368
Ch'ien-lung C-318
pottery P-473, *picture* P-472

K'ang te. *see in index* Pu-yi

Kania, Stanislaw, Polish political leader P-415

Kanji, Chinese characters adopted into Japanese language; each character stands for a word J-48. *see also in index* Kana

Kankakee, Ill., city about 50 mi (80 km) s. of Chicago; agricultural area; furniture and home appliances, farm implements, food processing; mental hospital; Olivet Nazarene College; pop. 30,141
Illinois, *map* I-52

Kankakee River, river that rises in n.w. Indiana and flows s.w. into Illinois; headstream of Illinois River
Illinois, *map* I-53
Indiana I-89, *map* I-102

Kannada, Dravidian language; spoken in s.w. India; official language of Karnataka state I-106

Kannapolis, N.C., community in Cabarrus and Rowan counties, 23 mi (37 km) n.e. of Charlotte; home of Cannon Mills, Inc., manufacturer of household textiles, including towels and bedsheets; mills established 1877, community founded 1905; pop. 36,293 N-357

Kano, Nigeria, industrial center and capital of Kano State, n. Nigeria on Jakara River; prehistoric tools found on site; largest mosque in Nigeria; pop. 487,100
Great Mosque, *picture* N-311

Kano Masanobu (1453–90), Japanese artist J-51

Kanpur, or **Cawnpore,** India, industrial city on Ganges River; pop. 1,154,388, *map* I-83
Asia, *map* A-697

Kansa, or **Kaw,** a Siouan people formerly living along Kansas River, now in Oklahoma, *map* I-149

Kansan. *see in index* Mindel

Kansas, a central state of U.S.; 82,264 sq mi (213,063 sq km); cap. Topeka; pop. 2,363,208 K-173, *maps* N-350, U-40
antiliquor efforts P-507
cities. *see also in index* cities by name
Kansas City K-188
Topeka T-227
Wichita W-201
geographic regions U-68, 75
Kansas-Nebraska Act K-189
state symbols
cottonwood P-446
flag, *picture* F-159
sunflower S-518, *picture* S-427
Statuary Hall, *table* S-437a
taxation, *tables* T-37, 39

Kansas, University of, university in Lawrence, Kan.; state control; founded 1865; liberal arts and sciences, architecture and urban design, business, education, engineering, fine arts, journalism, law, pharmacy, and social work; graduate school; medical school at Kansas City, *picture* K-181

Kansas City, Kan., 2nd city of state, on Kansas River; pop. 161,148 K-188, *maps* N-350, U-41

Kansas City, Mo., 2nd city of state, at confluence of Kansas and Missouri rivers; pop. 448,159 K-188, *maps* N-350, U-41
Missouri M-491, *picture* M-499, *map* M-500

Kansas grayfeather. *see in index* Gayfeather

Kansas-Nebraska Act (1854), United States K-189
Douglas D-233
Kansas K-175, 177
Lincoln L-219
Michigan M-361
Missouri M-494
Nebraska N-97
Pierce P-318
slavery territorial issue B-291
Sumner S-511

Kansas Newman College. *see in index* Sacred Heart College, Kansas

Kansas River, often called **Kaw River,** river in Kansas, formed by junction of Smoky Hill and Republican rivers, Geary County, Kan., flows 169 mi (272 km) across state to Missouri River, *maps* N-350, U-70
Missouri River M-509

Kansas State College at Pittsburg, college in Pittsburg, Kan.; founded 1903; formerly a teachers' college; arts and sciences, education, and technology; graduate studies.

Kansas State Teachers College. *see in index* Emporia Kansas State College

Kansas State University of Agriculture and Applied Science, university in Manhattan, Kan.; founded 1863; arts and sciences, agriculture, architecture, commerce, education, engineering, home economics, veterinary medicine; graduate school.

Kansas Wesleyan, university in Salina, Kan.; school affiliated with United Methodist church; established in 1886; liberal arts.

Kansu, province, China. *see in index* Gansu

Kant, Immanuel (1724–1804), German philosopher K-189
Enlightenment E-289
God G-173
Mendelssohn M-297
political theories P-434, C-463
citizenship C-438
philosophy P-266
views of universe U-199

Kantara, Egypt, *see in index* Qantara, El

Kanto Plain (or Kwanto Plain), lowland in Japan
Japan J-59
Tokyo T-210

Kantor, MacKinlay (1904–77), U.S. novelist, short-story writer, and poet, born in Webster City, Iowa; awarded 1956 Pulitzer prize for 'Andersonville', Civil War novel ('Turkey in the Straw', 'Glory for Me', poetry; 'Long Remember', 'God and My Country', 'Spirit Lake', novels; 'The Voice of Bugle Ann', 'The Daughter of Bugle Ann', dog stories).

Kantorovich, Leonid (1912–86), Soviet economist, born in Leningrad (then St. Petersburg); head of mathematical economics laboratory at Institute of Economic Management, Moscow. *see also in index* Nobel Prizewinners, *table*

Kantrowitz, Adrian (born 1918), U.S. heart surgeon, born in New York, N.Y.; director of surgery Maimonides Medical Center, Brooklyn, 1964–70; chairman department of surgery Sinai Hospital, Detroit 1970–; pioneer research in motion pictures inside the heart, pump oxygenators, and mechanical hearts; first permanent partial mechanical heart surgery 1966; first U.S. heart transplant 1967; Max Berg Award 1966.

Kantrowitz, Arthur Robert (born 1913), U.S. physicist, born in New York, N.Y.; collaborated with brother Adrian in heart research projects; professor Cornell University 1946–56; director Avco-Everett Research Laboratories 1955–72, chairman 1972–.

Kaohsiung (or Chi'i'hou), Taiwan, seaport of s. Taiwan; shipyards; refineries for petroleum and metals; food processing; pop. 1,242,400 K-190
 Asia, *map* A-697

Kao K'o-kung (fl. 13th century), Chinese painter, one of six great masters of Mongol period; took up painting after retiring from government service under Kublai Khan.

Kaolin (or China clay)
 clay C-488
 pottery P-470

Kaolinite, mineral M-437

Kaon, atomic particle N-432

Kapa cloth. *see in index* Tapa cloth

Kapidagi, peninsula of Turkey. *see in index* Cyzicus

'Kapital, Das' (Capital), work by Marx M-162

Kapitza, Peter Leonidovich (1894–1984), Soviet physicist, born in Kronshtadt, Russia; director Institute for Physical Problems, Moscow, 1935–46, 1955–84; noted for work with intense magnetic fields and low temperatures, also for atomic researches; a key figure in development of Sputniks. *see also in index* Nobel Prizewinners, *table*

Kaplan, Joseph (born 1902), U.S. physicist, born in Hungary; became U.S. citizen 1920; professor University of California at Los Angeles 1940–70; head of U.S. program, I.G.Y., 1957–58.

Kaplan turbine, hydraulics H-340

Kapok, fiber K-190
 milkweed M-415
 natural fibers F-76

Kapp, Wolfgang von (1858–1922), German monarchist, leader of revolt, March 1920, in which Berlin republican government was seized, but which failed because of a general strike; fled to Sweden; arrested for treason on return to Germany 1922; died before trial.

Kappa Alpha, U.S. fraternity F-388

Kappa Delta Pi, national college honor society in education, founded at University of Illinois, Urbana, 1909, for high-ranking junior, senior, and graduate students.

Kappel, Switzerland, village in canton of Zurich; pop. 648.

Kapteyn, Jacobus (1851–1922), Dutch astronomer; directed work of computing positions of stars on Sir David Gill's photographic plates of s. heavens; pioneered in modern study of Milky Way.

Karachi, or **Kalachi-Jo-goth,** Pakistan, capital of Sind Province; port on Arabian Sea; was also capital of province under Indian Empire; pop. 5,103,000 K-190, *pictures* P-77
 Asia, *map* A-697
 Indus River I-168
 laundry area, *picture* L-84
 policeman, *picture* P-430b
 silk mill, *picture* P-78
 world, *map* W-297

Karachi, University of, university in Pakistan K-191

Karafuto, U.S.S.R. *see in index* Sakhalin

Karaganda, U.S.S.R., city in e.-central Kazakh Soviet Socialist Republic; center of Karaganda coal basin; mining machinery, boots, candy, soft drinks; technical institutes, including medicine and mining; pop. 522,000, *map* R-344
 Asia, *map* A-697
 Kazakh Soviet Socialist Republic K-194

Karageorge (Black George) (1766?–1817), nickname given by Turks to George Petrovitch, or George Czerny, Serbian peasant, leader of first Serbian war of independence (1804–8) and founder of Karageorge dynasty S-113

Karaite sect, Judaism S-1

Karajan, Herbert von (born 1908), Austrian conductor, born in Salzburg; prominently associated with London Philharmonia, Berlin and Vienna Philharmonic, La Scala, and Vienna State Opera orchestras; won 1970 Grammy award for work with Berlin Philharmonic; toured widely K-191

Karajich, Vuk Stefanovich (1787–1864), Serbian writer, called father of modern Serbian literature; bent efforts toward adoption of Serbian mother tongue as literary language; wrote grammar and dictionary, published Serbian folk songs.

Karakoram Range, or **Karakorum Range,** system of mountains in n. Jammu and Kashmir; highest peak K2, or Mount Godwin Austen, 28,250 ft (8,610 m) K-192, *map* I-86
 Himalayas H-153
 K2 K-166

Karakorum, Mongolian People's Republic, ruined city 200 mi (320 km) s.w. of Ulan Bator; capital of Mongol Empire; established by Genghis Khan in early 13th century; capital moved to Peking by Kublai Khan in 1267
 Asia, *map* A-697
 Genghis Khan G-58

Karakul, also **Caracul,** a breed of sheep S-146
 furs F-463, *table* F-464
 Namibia N-9
 Turkmen Soviet Socialist Republic T-327

Kara-Kum (or Karakum), a desert in U.S.S.R., e. of Caspian Sea R-324, T-326, *map* R-344
 proposed canal construction C-129

Karamanlis, Konstantinos (or Constantine Caramanlis) (born 1907), Greek political leader, born near Serrai, Greece; member of Parliament 1935–55; prime minister 1955–63, 1974–80; president 1980–85 G-260

Karami, Rashid (1921–87), Lebanese politician, born in Miriata, Lebanon; served as prime minister on and off for over 30 years from 1955; was assassinated in 1987 L-113

Karamzin, Nikolai Mikhailovich (1765–1826), Russian historian, novelist, and critic; born in Mikhaylovka R-361

Karankawa, American Indian people who formerly lived in Texas, *map* I-136, *table* I-138
 Cabeza de Vaca's imprisonment C-4

Kara Sea (also called Karskoe More), arm of Arctic Ocean between Novaya Zemlya and n.w. coast of Siberia, *maps* R-322, R-344

Karat. *see in index* Carat

Karate, method of weaponless self-defense developed in the Orient in early times; hands, elbows, feet, and knees are used to strike various areas of the body; can maim or kill opponent
 Japan J-57
 martial arts M-159

Karawanken Tunnel, tunnel that crosses Austria-Yugoslavia border.

Karbala (or Kerbela), Iraq, town 60 mi (95 km) s.w. of Baghdad; sacred city and place of pilgrimage of Shi'ite Muslims; tomb of martyr Husein; pop. 211,214
 Asia, *map* A-697

Karelian Isthmus, land between Lake Ladoga and Gulf of Finland; in Russian Soviet Federated Socialist Republic F-91

Karens, an Asian people
 Thailand T-147

Kariba, Lake, lake on Zambezi River; 175 mi (282 km) long; formed by the Kariba Dam
 Zambia Z-447
 Zimbabwe Z-452

Kariba Dam, dam between Zambia and Zimbabwe, on Zambezi River
 Africa's natural resources A-106
 Zambezi River Z-447
 Zambia Z-448

Karikal, India, former French settlement in s.e. on Coromandel coast; 52 sq mi (135 sq km); became part of India in 1954; town of Karikal (pop. 26,080) in former settlement.

Karl August, duke of Saxe-Weimar. *see in index* Saxe-Weimar

Karlfeldt, Erik Axel (1864–1931), Swedish poet; wrote of life of peasants in Dalecarlia, his native region. *see also in index* Nobel Prizewinners, *table*

Karl Johansgate, street in Oslo, Norway O-610

Karl-Marx-Stadt (formerly Chemnitz), East Germany, city 38 mi (61 km) s.w. of Dresden; textiles, machinery, chemicals, food products; pop. 318,917, *maps* E-360, G-131

Karl Marx University (formerly University of Leipzig), university in Leipzig, East Germany; 3rd in size and 3rd in age of the universities of Germany; established 1409 by 400 teachers and students who seceded from University of Prague as result of Hussite agitations; medicine, law, theology, and liberal arts and sciences; renamed by government of East Germany in 1953.

Karloff, Boris (originally William Henry Pratt) (1887–1969), U.S. stage, motion-picture, and television actor; born in London, England; to U.S. 1909; in 'Frankenstein' (released 1931), began career as "menace" in horror films.

Karlovy Vary (or Karlsbad, or Carlsbad), Czechoslovakia, resort in Bohemia; ceded to Germany 1938, restored to Czechoslovakia 1945; Karlsbad decrees issued here at conference of German states (1819); pop. 43,091
 mineral waters S-31

Karlowitz (or Carlowitz, modern Sremski Karlovici), Yugoslavia, town on Danube River, 40 mi (65 km) n.w. of Belgrade; peace between Turkey, Austria, Poland, Venice, and Russia signed here (1699).

Karlsbad, Czechoslovakia. *see in index* Karlovy Vary

Karlskrona (or Carlscrona), Sweden, port on Baltic Sea, 238 mi (383 km) s.w. of Stockholm; Swedish naval headquarters; exports fish and lumber; pop. 33,010, *map* E-360

Karlsruhe, or **Carlsruhe,** West Germany, city 39 mi (63 km) n.w. of Stuttgart; mineral springs; pop. 249,528, *maps* E-360, G-131

Karma, or **karman,** religious belief
 Hinduism H-156
 India I-68

Karmal, Babrak (born 1929), Afghan politician, born near Kabul A-91

Kármán, Theodore von (1881–1963), U.S. aeronautical scientist K-192
 helicopter H-122

Karmaprabhrta, Jainist scripture J-14

Karnak, El, Egypt, town beside Nile River on n. part of site of ancient Thebes E-125, T-162, *picture* E-130
 sphinx S-379

Karnataka, formerly **Mysore,** state in s. India; area 74,122 sq mi (191,975 sq km); cap. Bangalore; gold, manganese, iron ore; coffee, tea, rice, cotton; early a Hindu kingdom; in mid-1700s taken by Muslim, Hyder Ali, and maintained as princely state until 1947; pop. 29,299,014 B-58, *map* I-86
 Asia, *map* A-700

Kärnten, Austria. *see in index* Carinthia

Karok, American Indian people who lived in Klamath River valley in n.w. California; a Quoratean division of Hokan language family
 mythology M-697

Károlyi, Mihály, Count (1875–1955), Hungarian statesman, born in Budapest; although from wealthy family was early influenced by Marxian socialism; president of Hungarian People's Republic 1918–19; resigned when Bolshevists seized government, lived in exile ('The Struggle for Peace'; 'Memoirs').

Kárpathos (Italian Scarpanto), island of Dodecanese in Aegean Sea; area 111 sq mi (287 sq km).

Karrer, Paul (1889–1971), Swiss chemist, born in Moscow, Russia; research on vitamins A and B_2, carotenids, and flavins. *see also in index* Nobel Prizewinners, *table*

Karroo, or **karoo,** barren tableland in South Africa S-263, 264
 Great Karroo, *map* S-264

Kars, Turkey, town 110 mi (175 km) n.e. of Erzurum; Muslim holy city, with 11th-century Cathedral of the 12 Apostles; capital of a medieval Armenian principality; pop. 32,141.

Karsavina, Tamara (1885–1978), Soviet dancer; ballerina of the Maryinsky Theater, the Russian Imperial theater, at St. Petersburg (now Leningrad), and of Diaghilev's company B-34, D-24

Karsh, Yousuf (born 1908), Canadian photographer, born in Armenia; to Canada 1924; known for sensitive portraits of the famous ('Faces of Destiny'; 'Portraits of Greatness'; autobiography, 'In Search of Greatness').

Karskoe More. *see in index* Kara Sea

Karstens, Harry, mountain climber M-21

Karun River, only navigable river in Iran; rises in western mountains and flows into the Shatt-al-'Arab; 400–500 mi (650–800 km) long I-305, *map* I-312

Kas, large cupboard F-459

Kasa, Korean poetry K-293

Kasack, Hermann (1896–1966), German author
 German literature G-107

Kasai River, river that rises in n.e. Angola and flows n.w. 1,000 mi (1,600 km) to Congo River; important for transportation; diamonds found in Tshikapa area, lower section known as Kwa River, *map* A-115

Kasavubu, Joseph (1910?–69), Congolese political leader, born near Léopoldville; president of Democratic Republic of the Congo (now Zaire) 1960–65
 Lumumba L-335
 Mobutu M-513
 Zaire Z-446

Kasayaprabhrta, Jainist scripture J-14

Kasbah. *see in index* Casbah

Kashgar (or Kashi, or Kaxgar), China, city in w. Sinkiang-Uigur Autonomous Region; trade in silk, cotton, sheepskins; pop. 175,000
 Asia, *map* A-697

Kashi holly, plant *Ilex chinensis* H-204

Kashmir. *see in index* Jammu and Kashmir

Kaskaskia, American Indian people of Algonquian family, one of leading peoples of Illinois confederacy; survivors removed to Indian Territory in 1867, *map* I-149. *see also in index* Illinois, a confederacy

Kaskaskia, Ill., village in s.w. part of state, on Kaskaskia Island in Mississippi River; site of French Jesuit mission (1703), later a trading post, nearby; Fort Kaskaskia built on bluffs (1733); capital of Illinois Territory (1809–18); old town destroyed and island of present village created by floods in late 1800s; pop. 33.

Kaskaskia River, river in s. Illinois; about 300 mi (480 km) long; rises in Champaign County; flowing s.w. enters the

Mississippi in Randolph County just n.w. of Chester.

Kassebaum, Nancy Landon (born 1932), U.S. political leader; daughter of 1936 presidential candidate and former Kansas governor Alf Landon; radio station executive 1975–76; U.S. senator (Republican) from Kansas 1979–
  women's rights W-276

Kassel, or **Cassel,** West Germany, city on Fulda River 90 mi (145 km) n.e. of Frankfurt; locomotives, machinery, scientific instruments; pop. 211,773, *maps* E-360, G-131

Kasserine Pass, battle of, World War II W-339

Kassites, Elamite people; overran Babylonia and founded dynasty (about 1600–1200 BC) B-8, *map* B-4
  Iraq's history I-314

Kastler, Alfred (1902–84), French physicist, born in Guebwiller; professor L'École Normale Supérieure, Paris. *see also in index* Nobel Prizewinners, *table*

Kästner, Erich (born 1899), German poet, journalist, and author, born in Dresden; children's book 'Emil and the Detectives' translated into many languages and used as text to teach German in various countries ('Lisa and Lottie'; 'Little Man'; 'Little Man and the Big Thief') R-111a

Kat, or **khat,** or **cafta,** evergreen shrub *Catha edulis* with clusters of small white flowers, native to Arabia and Egypt; leaves used to make stimulating beverage and are also chewed by many Arabs
  People's Democratic Republic of Yemen Y-413
  Yemen Arab Republic Y-414

Kataev, Valentin (1897–1986), Soviet novelist, short-story writer, and playwright, born in Odessa; won Stalin prize R-361

Katahdin, Mount (Indian for "big mountain"), bare granite peak in e. Piscataquis County, n.-central Maine, highest point in state 5,268 ft (1,606 m); situated in Baxter State Park M-52, *map* U-44
  painting by Marsden Hartley P-26, *picture* P-26

Katanga, now **Shaba,** former province in south of Zaire, about 192,000 sq mi (497,000 sq km); pop. 2,753,714, *map* A-115
  Tshombe T-302
  Zaire Z-444, *picture* Z-445

Katayama Tetsu (1887–1978), Japanese statesman, born near Wakayama; leader in labor groups; prime minister 1947–48.

Kate Greenaway Medal L-240

Kater, Henry (1777–1835), English physicist, born in Bristol; invented floating collimator; determined length of seconds pendulum; constructed standards of weights and measures for Russia.

Kathakali, Indian dance D-30

Katherina, Jebel (Mount Catherine), mountain in Egypt E-115

Katherine (or Katharina), daughter of Baptista of Padua in Shakespeare's 'Taming of the Shrew'; because of foul temper was called "the shrew."

Kathiawar Peninsula, peninsula in India I-63, *map* I-86

Kathmandu, Nepal, capital, situated near junction of Baghmati and Vishnumati rivers; noted for palaces and pagoda-shaped temples; pop. 235,211 K-192, N-116
  Asia, *map* A-697

Katipunan, nationalist organization in the Philippines; founded 1892 P-259d, A-144, R-211

Katmai, Mount, volcano of Aleutian Range, in Katmai National Monument, near head of Alaska Peninsula; height 7,000 ft (1,150 m) L-24
  national parks N-52

Katmai National Park and Preserve, park in s. Alaska N-52, *maps* N-40, U-39, 94, *picture* A-251

Kato Takaakira, Viscount (1859–1926), Japanese statesman, born in Nagoya; ambassador to United Kingdom 1894–99, 1908–13; four times foreign minister; leader of the Constitutionalist party.

Katowice (German Kattowitz), Poland, city, 165 mi (265 km) s.w. of Warsaw; ironworks, foundries; in zinc and coal area; pop. 282,500, *map* E-360

Katrine, Loch, lake near Glasgow, Scotland; 5 sq mi (13 sq km); its Ellen Isle immortalized by Scott in 'The Lady of the Lake'; furnishes water supply to city of Glasgow.

Katsukawa Shunsho (1726–92), Japanese artist, *picture* J-50

Katsura, Taro, Prince (1847–1913), Japanese statesman, governor of Taiwan, minister of war, then premier 1901–6; again premier 1908–11 and 1912–13; accomplished commercial and financial reforms, annexation of Korea

Katsura Imperial Villa, villa in Kyoto, Japan, *picture* K-312

Katsushika Hokusai. *see in index* Hokusai Katsushika

Kattegat (or Cattegat), strait between Denmark and Sweden, *maps* E-360, S-524
  Baltic Sea B-46
  North Sea N-388

Kattowitz. *see in index* Katowice

Katydid, or **long-horned grasshopper,** or **bush cricket** insect of the order Orthoptera C-766. *see also in index* cricket; grasshopper

Katyn, U.S.S.R., village 12 mi (19 km) s.w. of Smolensk; near Katyn Forest, scene of massacre of thousands of Polish officers captured by Soviets in 1939 invasion.

Katz, Sir Bernard (born 1911), British biophysicist, born in Leipzig, Germany; professor of biophysics University College, London, 1952–78. *see also in index* Nobel Prizewinners, *table*

Katzenbach, Nicholas deBelleville (born 1922), U.S. lawyer, born in Philadelphia, Pa.; associate professor of law Yale University 1952–56; professor University of Chicago 1956–60; deputy U.S. attorney general 1962–64, acting attorney general Sept. 1964–Jan. 1965, attorney general 1965–66; undersecretary of state 1966–69.

Katzimo, mesa. *see in index* Enchanted Mesa

Kauai, island of Hawaii; 553 sq mi (1,433 sq km); pop. 38,856 H-59, *maps* H-58, U-98, 117
  barking sands S-38
  Pacific Ocean, *map* P-3
    Oceania O-467

Kauffer, E. McKnight, English commercial artist, *picture* A-665

Kauffmann, Angelica (1741–1807), Swiss portrait painter, born in Chur; graceful but poorly drawn pictures; friend of Goethe and Reynolds.

Kaufman, George Simon (1889–1961), U.S. playwright, director, and producer, born in Pittsburgh, Pa.; began as newspaperman; with Marc Connelly wrote 'Dulcy', 'Merton of the Movies', 'Beggar on Horseback'; with Edna Ferber 'Royal Family', 'Dinner at Eight'; with Morris Ryskind 'Of Thee I Sing' (Pulitzer prize 1932); with Moss Hart 'You Can't Take It with You' (Pulitzer prize 1937), 'The Man Who Came to Dinner'; with Howard Teichmann 'The Solid Gold Cadillac' A-356

Kaufman, Sue (1926–77), U.S. author A-363

Kaufman, Mount. *see in index* Lenin Peak

Kaukauna, Wis., agricultural city 21 mi (34 km) e. of Appleton; paper, farm equipment; incorporated 1885; pop. 11,292.

Kaulbach, Wilhelm von (1805–74), German fresco and historical painter and book illustrator, first and most celebrated of a family of painters; born in Arolsen, Hesse-Nassau, w. Germany; illustrated 'Reynard the Fox'.

Kaunas, also **Kovno,** Lithuanian Soviet Socialist Republic, trade center on Niemen River; provisional capital of Lithuania 1918–40; pop. 306,000, *maps* E-360, R-344, 348
  world, *map* W-297

Kaunda, Kenneth (born 1924), president of Zambia K-193
  Zambia Z-448

Kaunitz, Prince Wenzel Anton von (1711–94), Austrian statesman, born in Vienna; minister of Maria Theresa S-117
  Maria Theresa M-134

Kauri gum G-318

Kauri pine, tree N-288

Kava, or **ava,** name of a shrub and of an intoxicating drink prepared from its root; plant belongs to pepper family; native to Pacific islands.

Kavanagh, Patrick (1904–66), Irish author I-328

'Kavirajamarga', Indian literature I-106

Kavya, Sanskrit court epic I-106

Kaw. *see in index* Kansa

Kawabata, Yasunari (1899–1972), Japanese novelist, born in Osaka ('Snow Country'; 'Thousand Cranes'; 'The Sound of the Mountain'; 'The Master of Go') K-193. *see also in index* Nobel Prizewinners, *table*
  Japanese literature J-82

Kawasaki, Japan, city on Tokyo Bay, island of Honshu; shipbuilding; textiles, machinery; pop. 1,032,852, *map* J-75

Kawm al Dikka, Roman amphitheater, Alexandria, Egypt A-281

Kaw River. *see in index* Kansas River

Kaxgar, China. *see in index* Kashgar

Kay, John (1704–64), English inventor, born near Bury; invented flying shuttle 1733; device considered a menace to labor; was mobbed by weavers and [illegible] destroyed; resumed work in France where he died in poverty I-178

Kay, Ulysses Simpson (born 1917), U.S. composer, born in Tucson, Ariz.; studied with Hindemith; composed suite for orchestra and music for film 'The Quiet One'; won many awards and prizes.

Kayak, Eskimo canoe C-69, E-299, *picture* U-224
  comparison to canoe C-140

Kayans, a people in Borneo, distinguished by industry, warlike qualities, and skill at handicrafts; live on riverbanks in long houses containing many apartments.

Kaye, Danny (originally David Daniel Kominski) (1913–87), U.S. comedian of stage, screen, radio, and television; born in Brooklyn, N.Y.; known for rapid patter songs and mimicry; much of his material written by wife, Sylvia Fine; starred in motion pictures: 'Up in Arms', 'The Secret Life of Walter Mitty', and 'Hans Christian Andersen'; named "Big Brother of 1956" by President Eisenhower for making world tour and motion picture for UNICEF.

Kaye, Nora (originally Nora Koreff) (1920–87), U.S. ballerina, born in New York, N.Y., of Russian parents; ballerina with Ballet Theatre and New York City Ballet ('Pillar of Fire'; 'Lilac Garden') B-36

Kaye-Smith, Sheila (1887–1956), British novelist, born in St. Leonards-on-Sea; married Theodore Penrose Fry; wrote chiefly of country life ('Sussex Gorse'; 'Joanna Godden'; 'Mrs. Galley'; 'The View from the Parsonage').

Kayseri, or **Kaisaria,** ancient **Caesarea Mazaca,** Turkey, city in Asia Minor, 160 mi (260 km) s.e. of Ankara; rugs, tile, meat; pop. 207,037.
  Asia, *map* A-697

Kaysville, Utah, city 14 mi (22 km) s. of Ogden; in agricultural region; food products; annual rodeo; pop. 9,811, *map* U-232

Kazakh, one of a Turkic people living in n.e. part of Aral-Caspian basin and related to the Kirghiz K-194
  nomads N-332
  Turkestan T-317
  Turkmen Soviet Socialist Republic T-327

Kazakh Soviet Socialist Republic, U.S.S.R., e. and n. of Caspian Sea and w. of China; area 1,067,950 sq mi (2,765,980 sq km); cap. Alma-Ata; pop. 14,684,000 K-193, U-14, *map* R-344
  agriculture, *picture* R-324
  Asia, *map* A-697
  folktales, *list* S-481
  people R-325
  Turkestan T-317
  Tyuratam S-342b

Kazan, Elia (originally Elia Kazanjoglous) (born 1909), U.S. theater and motion-picture director, born in Constantinople (now Istanbul), Turkey; directed stage plays ('Skin of Our Teeth', 'A Streetcar Named Desire', 'Tea and Sympathy', 'Cat on a Hot Tin Roof'); motion pictures ('A Streetcar Named Desire', 'East of Eden'); won Academy awards for 'Gentleman's Agreement' (1947), 'On the Waterfront' (1954); helped found Actors' Studio, a theater workshop; wrote novels ('America, America', 'The Arrangement', and 'The Assassins')
  directing D-155

Kazan', U.S.S.R., city 450 mi (725 km) e. of Moscow; industrial and cultural center; made capital of Tatar kingdom in 15th century; pop. 869,000, *maps* R-344, 348–9
  Europe, *map* E-360

Kazan passageway D-34

Kazantzakis, Nikos (1885–1957), Greek author and philosopher, born in Candia, Crete; director UNESCO translation bureau 1947–48 (novels: 'Zorba the Greek', 'The Greek Passion'; poem: 'The Odyssey'; autobiography: 'Report to Greco').

Kazbek, Mount, one of the highest peaks of the Caucasus Mountains (16,558 ft; 5,047 m); situated above Daryal Pass; noted in mythology as site of Prometheus' torture, *map* R-349

Kazvin, Iran, town 100 mi (160 km) n.w. of Tehran; rugs, cotton and wool weaving, flour; has suffered several earthquakes; pop. 110,000.

Kea, a sheep-killing parrot P-135

Kean, Charles John (1811–68), British actor, born in Waterford, Ireland; not as great as his father, Edmund Kean, but noted as actor in 'Hamlet' and other Shakespearean plays, and as theatrical manager; married Ellen Tree.

Kean, Edmund (1787–1833), English Shakespearean tragedian, born in London; father of Charles J. Kean; Coleridge said, "Seeing him act was like reading Shakespeare by flashes of lightning" ('Shylock'; 'Othello'; 'Richard III') K-194

Kean, Ellen Tree (1805–80), British actress, born in s. Ireland; played leads with husband, Charles J. Kean.

Kean College of New Jersey (until 1974 Newark State College), college in Union, N.J.; founded 1885; liberal arts and teacher education; graduate study.

Keane, John Joseph (1839–1918), U.S. Roman Catholic archbishop and educator, born in Ireland; founded churches and schools for black Americans in South; rector Catholic University of America 1886–97; archbishop Dubuque, Iowa, 1900–1911.

Kearney, Denis (1847–1907), U.S. labor organizer, born in County Cork, Ireland; in 1868 emigrated to San Francisco, Calif.; helped organize the Workingmen's party of California in 1877.

Kearney, Neb., city on Platte River, 125 mi (200 km) w. of Lincoln; livestock raising, metal products; Kearney State College, city was named for Fort Kearney (sometimes spelled Kearny), built nearby in 1848 to protect emigrants on Oregon Trail but abandoned in 1871; pop. 21,158 N-104, *map* U-40

Kearney State College, college in Kearney, Neb.; founded 1905; fine arts and humanities, business and technology, education, and natural and social sciences; graduate school.

Kearns, Utah, community s.w. of Salt Lake City; pop. 17,071, *map* U-232

Kearny, Philip (1814–62), U.S. brigadier general and cavalry leader, born in New York City; served in Mexican War, French cavalry, and Civil War; killed at Chantilly; nephew of Gen. S. W. Kearny
Statuary Hall, *table* S-437b

Kearny, Stephen Watts (1794–1848), U.S. major general, born in Newark, N.J.; served in War of 1812; in war with Mexico occupied New Mexico K-194
Carson C-177
frontier movement F-422
Mexican War M-320
New Mexico N-218

Kearny, N.J., town on Passaic River opposite Newark; shipyards, twine, plastics, linoleum, telephones, metal products; named for Gen. Philip Kearny; pop. 35,735.

Keating, Geoffrey (1569–1644), Irish author I-326

Keating, Kenneth B. (1900–75), U.S. public official, born in Lima, N.Y.; Republican congressman from New York 1946–58; senator from New York 1958–65; associate justice New York State Court of Appeals 1965–69; ambassador to India 1969–72.

Keaton, Buster (1895–1966), U.S. actor A-27

Keaton, Diane (originally Diane Hall) (born 1946), U.S. actress, born in Los Angeles ('Looking for Mr. Goodbar'; 'Shoot the Moon'; 'Reds'; 'Annie Hall') A-309

Keats, Ezra Jack (born 1916), U.S. author and illustrator, born in Brooklyn, N.Y.; awarded Caldecott Medal 1963 for 'The Snowy Day'; 'Whistle for Willie'; 'John Henry'; 'God Is in the Mountain' R-106

Keats, John (1795–1821), English poet K-195
creative writing W-379
literary contribution E-275
Roman memorial R-255
Shelley's elegy S-154

Keble, John (1792–1866), English poet and clergyman, born in Fairford, near Swindon; professor of poetry at Oxford University for 10 years; Keble College built as a memorial ('The Christian Year').

Kebnekaise, highest peak in Sweden, in Kjölen Mountains 6,965 ft (2,123 m); in n. 25 mi (40 km) from Norwegian border; glaciers, *map* S-524

Kecoughtan. *see in index* Hampton

Kecskemét, Hungary, city 50 mi (80 km) s.e. of Budapest; center of fruit, cattle, grain area; farm implements, chemicals, shoes, fruit preserves, wine, flour; pop. 68,327, *map* E-360

Kedah, state in former Federation of Malaya; 3,660 sq mi (9,480 sq km); rice, rubber, tapioca; tin, tungsten; became part of Malaysia 1963; pop. 955,374. *see also in index* Malay State, Unfederated

Keddah, corral for trapping elephants in s.e. Asia E-185, *picture* E-184

Kedron, Valley of (also Valley of Cedron, or Valley of Kidron), deep depression e. of Jerusalem where brook flowed in Biblical times, *map* J-101

Keefe, Tim (or Timothy J. Keefe) (1856–1933), U.S. baseball pitcher, born in Cambridge, Mass.; began career 1880, Troy, N.L., finished Philadelphia, N.L., 1893; won 346 games (19 in row 1888), lost 225.

Keel, in boat B-328, S-171, *diagram* B-326
development S-164

Keel, muscular structure in birds B-276

Keeler, William H. (nickname Wee Willie) (1872–1923), U.S. baseball outfielder, born in Brooklyn, N.Y.; outfielder with 3 N.L. teams and 1 A.L. team 1892–1910; famed for his batting philosophy "Hit 'em where they ain't!"; hit safely in 44 consecutive games 1897.

Keeley, Leslie E. (1832–1900), U.S. physician, born in Saint Lawrence County, N.Y.; originator of Keeley Cure, treatment for alcoholics and drug addicts; first sanitarium Dwight, Ill., 1879–1966; many branches.

Keeling Islands, Indian Ocean. *see in index* Cocos Islands

Keelung, Taiwan, seaport and naval base in n. Taiwan, 15 mi (25 km) n.e. of Taipei; shipbuilding; chemicals, food products; pop. 348,600.

Keen, William Williams (1837–1932), U.S. surgeon, born in Philadelphia, Pa.; professor of surgery Jefferson Medical College 1889–1907; pioneer work in delicate operations of brain and nervous system; wrote and edited books on surgery and anatomy.

Keene, Charles Samuel (1823–91), British pen-and-ink artist, born in Hornsey, England; for 40 years a contributor to *Punch*; foremost among English craftsmen in black and white; work unconventional.

Keene, Laura (1826?–73), U.S. actress and manager; her company was playing 'Our American Cousin' at Ford's Theater, Washington, D.C., when Lincoln was shot.

Keene, N.H., city on Ashuelot River, 42 mi (68 km) s.w. of Concord; ball bearings, machinery, textiles, furniture, leather products; Keene State College; pop. 21,449 N-186, *map* N-191

Keene State College, college in Keene, N.H.; part of University of New Hampshire; state control; founded 1909; liberal arts, teacher education, and vocational courses; graduate study.

Keep (or dungeon, or donjon), castle structure C-199

Keeshan, Bob, U.S. actor
'Captain Kangaroo', *picture* T-69

Keeshond, dog, *picture* D-206

Keewatin, District of, district in e. Canada, part of Northwest Territories in Canadian Shield; 228,160 sq mi (590,930 sq km); tundras; pop. 3,403.

Keewatin ice sheet I-7, *map* I-8

Kefar Nahum, Palestine. *see in index* Capernaum

Kefauver, Estes (1903–63), U.S. political leader, born near Madisonville, Tenn.; five terms in U.S. House of Representatives; U.S. senator 1948–63; chairman Senate Crime Investigating Committee 1950–51 ('Crime in America'); Democratic vice-presidential nominee 1956.

Keighley, England, town in Yorkshire, 55 mi (90 km) n.e. of Liverpool; Leeds-Liverpool Canal connects it with Hull; worsted, tools, machines, paper; pop. 55,400, *map* U-18a

Keihin, industrial zone, Japan J-40
Tokyo T-208
Yokohama Y-422

Keijo, South Korea. *see in index* Seoul

Keiser, Reinhard (1674–1739), German opera composer O-561

Keitel, Wilhelm (1882–1946), German army officer, born in Helmscherode, near Brunswick, Germany; made commander in chief of German armed forces 1938; signed World War II surrender 1945; hanged for war crimes 1946 W-336, *picture* W-326

Keith, Sir Arthur (1866–1955), British anthropologist and anatomist, born in Aberdeen, Scotland; a leading authority in study of human race and its antiquity and expert on reconstruction of prehistoric humans from fragments of fossil remains ('The Antiquity of Man'; 'A New Theory of Human Evolution'; 'An Autobiography').

Keith, Harold (born 1903), U.S. children's author, born in Watonga, Okla. ('Boy's Life of Will Rogers'; 'A Pair of Captains'; 'Sports and Games'; 'Rifles for Watie', awarded Newbery Medal 1958).

Keith, James Francis Edward (1696–1758), Scottish soldier, born near Peterhead; Jacobite adherent, field marshal under Frederick the Great in Seven Years' War.

Kékes Peak, peak in the Mátra Hills in Hungary; 3,330 ft (1,015 m) H-326

Kekkonen, Urho (in full Urho Kaleva Kekkonen) (1900–86), president of Finland K-195
Finland F-91

Kekulé, or **Kekulé von Stradonitz, Friedrich August** (1829–96), German chemist, born in Darmstadt; chemistry of explosives, dyestuffs, and coal-tar products based largely upon his researches.

Kelang River, river in Malaysia K-307

Kelantan, state in former Federation of Malaya; 5,746 sq mi (14,882 sq km); rice, coconuts, rubber; tin, iron ore, gold; pop. 680,626. *see also in index* Malay States, Unfederated

Kelland, Clarence Budington (1881–1964), U.S. writer of novels and short stories, born in Portland, Mich.; created fictional characters Mark Tidd and Scattergood Baines; story 'Opera Hat' basis for movie 'Mr. Deeds Goes to Town'.

Kellar, Harry (1849–1922), U.S. magician M-38

Keller, Friedrich Gottlob (1816–95), German weaver of Saxony, patented a machine to make wood pulp P-104

Keller, Gottfried (1819–90), German poet and novelist, born in Zurich, Switzerland; combined realism with imagination and sincerity G-106

Keller, Helen Adams (1880–1968), U.S. author who overcame blindness and deafness K-195

Kellermann, Bernhard (1879–1951), German novelist, born in Fürth; early novels subjective ('The Fool'); later work on social problems ('The Ninth November'; 'The Tunnel').

Kellermann, François-Christophe (1735–1820), French Revolutionary general, marshal of France, victor at Valmy (1792); father of François-Étienne Kellermann, one of Napoleon's ablest generals.

Keller milling machine, in industry
automobile manufacture A-872

Kelley, Florence (1859–1932), U.S. social worker, born in Philadelphia, Pa.; resident Hull House 1891–99, Henry Street Settlement 1899–1924; secretary National Consumers League 1899.

Kelley, Joseph James (1871–1943), U.S. baseball outfielder, born in Cambridge, Mass.; began career with Boston 1891, finished with Cincinnati 1906.

Kelley, Oliver Hudson (1826–1913), U.S. farmer and agrarian reformer, born in Boston, Mass.; founded National Grange of the Patrons of Husbandry 1867 G-214
Minnesota M-446

Kellgren, Johan Henrik (1751–95), Swedish poet and critic, born in Floby, near Falköping; cofounder and editor *Stockholmsposten*; librarian and private secretary to Gustavus III.

Kellogg, Frank Billings (1856–1937), U.S. lawyer and diplomat, born in Potsdam, N.Y.; U.S. senator from Minnesota 1917–23; ambassador to United Kingdom 1923–24; secretary of state 1925–29; coauthor of Kellogg-Briand Pact to outlaw war; elected to International Court of Justice 1930, resigned 1935
Minnesota M-445
World War I W-321

Kellogg, Vernon Lyman (1867–1937), U.S. zoologist, born in Emporia, Kan.; professor entomology, Stanford University, 1894–1920; secretary National Research Council 1919–31; wrote on zoology, entomology, heredity.

Kellogg, Will Keith (1860–1951), U.S. industrialist and philanthropist, born in Battle Creek, Mich.; in 1906 founded giant cereal industry
breakfast cereals B-433
industry I-195

Kellogg, Idaho, city 33 mi (53 km) s.e. of Coeur d'Alene; center for mining and smelting district producing lead, zinc, silver, cadmium, antimony; pop. 3,417, *map* I-30
mine nearby, *picture* I-18

Kellogg-Briand Pact (or Pact of Paris) (1928), *table* T-274
Coolidge administration C-704
post World War I W-321
war crime definitions W-11

Kells, or **Ceanannus Mór,** Ireland, market town of County Meath in e.; of ancient origin; pop. 2,274.

'Kells, Book of'. *see in index* 'Book of Kells'

Kelly, Colin Purdie, Jr. (1915–41), U.S. Army aviator ("America's first hero of World War II"), born in Madison, Fla.; in B-17 bomber, Dec. 10, 1941, he attacked Japanese heavy cruiser *Ashigara*; killed when his bomber crashed on Mt. Arayat on Luzon.

Kelly, Ellsworth (born 1923), U.S. artist, born in Newburgh, N.Y.; noted for bright geometrics on large canvas, also ink and pencil drawings, sculpture, and lithographs; numerous awards
'Blue, Black, Red' P-67

Kelly, Emmett (1898–1979), U.S. clown, born in Sedan, Kan.; famed for his "tramp" C-437
mime M-422

Kelly, Eric Philbrook (1884–1960), U.S. writer of children's books and educator, born in Amesbury, Mass.; lectured at University of Krakow (Poland) 1925–26 and wrote 'The Trumpeter of Krakow', awarded 1929 Newbery Medal; professor of journalism at Dartmouth College 1929–54 ('The Land of the Polish People'; 'In Clean Hay') R-111d

Kelly, George (1887–1974), U.S. playwright, born in Philadelphia, Pa.; uncle of Grace Kelly; author of penetrating plays tinged with satire ('Craig's Wife', won Pulitzer prize 1926; 'The Showoff').

Kelly, George Lange (nickname High Pockets) (born 1896), U.S. baseball player, born in San Francisco, Calif.; first baseman with New York, N.L., 1915–17, 1919–26, Pittsburgh, N.L., 1917, Cincinnati, N.L., 1927–30, Chicago, N.L., 1930, Brooklyn, N.L., 1932; batted .331 with Chicago 1930.

Kelly, Grace. *see in index* Grace

Kelly, John (1822–86), U.S. political leader, born in New York City; joined Tammany organization 1853; U.S. congressman 1855–59; sheriff of New York County 1859–61 and 1865–67; opposed "Tweed Ring" and controlled Tammany 1874–82.

Kelly, Michael Joseph (nickname King) (1857–94), U.S. baseball player, born in Troy, N.Y.; colorful catcher and outfielder with 4 N.L. teams 1878–93; batted .394 and stole 84 bases for Boston, 1887.

Kelly, Ned (1855–80), Australian criminal K-196

Kelly, Oakley, aviator A-204

Kelly, Walt (1913–73), U.S. cartoonist, born in Philadelphia, Pa.; animator Walt Disney Studio 1935–41; commercial artist New York, N.Y., 1941–48; political cartoonist *New York Star* 1948–49; creator of satirical comic strip "Pogo," *picture* C-190

Kelly, William (1811–88), U.S. inventor, born in Pittsburgh, Pa.; invented process for making steel now known as Bessemer process; designated (1857) by U.S. Patent Office as originator of the invention I-351

Kelmscott Press T-338

Kelowna, B.C., city on Okanagan Lake 165 mi (265 km) n.e. of Vancouver; center for growing and processing of fruits, vegetables; lumbering, resort; pop. 59,196, *map* C-109

Kelp, a large coarse seaweed S-104, *picture* P-361
algae A-283

Kelp crab, crustacean *Pugettia producta*, *picture* C-791

Kelpies, water fairies S-473
fairy tales F-12

Kelsey, Henry (1670?–1724?), English explorer, born in

London; with Hudson's Bay Company 1684–1722, led expedition to northern Saskatchewan 1690–92, governor of posts 1718–22
Canada C-95

Kelso, Wash., city on Cowlitz River at Oregon border, 74 mi (119 km) s.e. of Aberdeen; boat building; incorporated 1889; pop. 11,129.

Keltie, Sir John Scott (1840–1927), British geographer, born in Dundee, Scotland; editor *Statesman's Year Book* for 43 years ('History of the Scottish Highlands and Clans'; 'The Partition of Africa').

Kelts. *see in index* Celts

Kelvin, Lord (or William Thomson) (1824–1907), British scientist and inventor K-196
heat H-106
transatlantic communication cables C-10

Kelvin scale, temperature
cryogenics C-793
heat H-103
Kelvin devises K-196
sun temperature S-512
weights and measures, *table* W-141

Kemal, Yashar (born 1922), Turkish novelist and journalist; self-taught ('Memed, My Hawk'; 'The Wind from the Plain'; 'Anatolian Tales').

Kemal Atatürk. *see in index* Atatürk

Kemble, famous family of English actors (18th and 19th centuries); most celebrated members were Mrs. Sarah Siddons, her brothers John Philip and Charles, and her niece Fanny.

Kemble, Fanny (in full Frances Anne Kemble) (1809–93), English actress and author, born in London; daughter of Charles Kemble; married Pierce Butler, an American, and lived in U.S. 1834–48 ('Journals', interesting picture of U.S. life).

Kemerovo, U.S.S.R., city in s. Siberia, on Tom' River; coal mining; fertilizers, paint, plastics, pharmaceuticals, coke by-products, machinery, sawmilling; pop. 385,000, *map* R-344
Asia, *map* A-697

Kemmel, Mont, isolated rocky hill 6 mi (10 km) s.w. of Ypres, Belgium; overlooks Flanders plain to n.e. and s.e.; taken by Germans in World War I, 1918.

Kemmerer, Edwin Walter (1875–1945), U.S. economist, born in Scranton, Pa.; professor economics and finance, Cornell University, 1909–12, Princeton University 1912–43, professor emeritus after 1943; financial adviser to U.S. Philippine Commission, to Mexico, Guatemala, Colombia, South Africa, Chile, Poland, Ecuador, Bolivia, China; author of works on economics.

Kemp Coast, district in Antarctica between 56° and about 59°40' e.; discovered 1833 by Peter Kemp, a British sealing captain.

Kempis, Thomas à (1380?–1471), German monk and mystic, born in Kempen, near Krefeld; remembered for one book, 'Imitation of Christ', a classic of devotional literature.

Ken, Thomas (1637–1711), English bishop, born in Great or Little Berkhamstead, near St. Albans; one of seven imprisoned for refusing to read Declaration of Indulgences issued by James II; following the revolution, lost bishopric rather than transfer loyalty from James II to William of Orange; remembered today for his hymns ('Praise God from Whom All Blessings Flow'; 'Awake, My Soul, and with the Sun Arise').

Ken, Japanese unit of measure, *table* W-141

Kenaf, a fiber plant, botanically known as *Hibiscus cannabinus;* original home in India, grown now in Cuba and other Latin American countries, also in Florida; from 8 to 12 ft (2½ to 3½ m) high; fiber, which is in bark, used as substitute for jute.

Kenai Mountains, in Alaska A-242

Kenai Peninsula, s. Alaska; 150 mi (240 km) long; farmlands, coal deposits; includes city Kenai (pop. 4,324), on Cook Inlet, and ice-free seaports Seward and Whittier; severe earthquake 1964, *maps* U-94, 39

Kendall, Amos (1789–1869), U.S. newspaper editor and public official, born in Dunstable, Mass.; auditor in Treasury Department under Jackson 1829–35; postmaster general 1835–40; reorganized Post Office Department and paid off debt; S.F.B. Morse's agent in development of telegraph systems; helped found Columbia Institute for Deaf.

Kendall, Edward Calvin (1886–1972), U.S. biochemist, born in South Norwalk, Conn.; isolated thyroxin 1914; professor of physiological chemistry Mayo Foundation for Medical Education and Research, Rochester, Minn., 1914–51. *see also in index* Nobel Prizewinners, *table*

Kendall, Henry Clarence (1841–82), Australian poet, born in New South Wales; son of missionary; held government posts at Sydney; journalist at Melbourne 1869–73 A-797, *table* A-798

Kendo, martial art, *picture* M-160

Kendrew, John Cowdery (born 1917), English biochemist, born in Oxford; deputy chairman Medical Research Council Laboratory for Molecular Biology, Cavendish Laboratory, Cambridge 1946–75; director general European Molecular Biology Laboratory. *see also in index* Nobel Prizewinners, *table*
protein study B-237

Kendrick, John (1745?–1800), U.S. navigator, born in Boston, Mass., died in Hawaii; commanded privateer during Revolution; explored n.w. coast of North America and Pacific islands.

Kendrick, John Benjamin (1857–1933), U.S. cattleman and political leader, born in Cherokee County, Texas; governor of Wyoming 1915–17; U.S. senator (Democrat) 1917–33.

Kenilworth, England, town in Warwickshire; ruins of castle given by Queen Elizabeth I to earl of Leicester; scene of Sir Walter Scott's novel 'Kenilworth'; pop. 21,000, *map* U-18a

'Kenilworth', novel by Scott S-74

Kenilworth ivy, a creeping perennial plant *Cymbalaria muralis* of the figwort family, native to Europe; trailing stems root at nodes (joints); leaves lobed; flowers lilac with yellow throat, tiny.

Kenmore, N.Y., village 5 mi (8 km) n. of Buffalo; chemicals, machinery, silk, electrical appliances; incorporated 1899; pop. 18,474.

Kenna, John Edward (1848–93), U.S. statesman, born in Valcoulan, W. Va. (then Virginia); entered Confederate army at 16; admitted to bar 1870; served in House of Representatives and in U.S. Senate; Democrat, *table* S-437b

Kennan, George Frost (born 1904), U.S. diplomat, born in Milwaukee, Wis.; in foreign service 1926–53, ambassador to Soviet Union 1952–53; professor Institute for Advanced Study, Princeton University 1956–61, 1963–74; ambassador to Yugoslavia 1961–63; won two Pulitzer prizes, one in history 1956 for first volume of 'Soviet-American Relations, 1917–1920', the other in biography 1968 for 'Memoirs, 1925–1950'
Cold War C-545

Kennebec River, 2nd largest river of Maine; rises in Moosehead Lake, flows s. 190 mi (305 km) to Atlantic.

Kennedy, David Matthew (born 1905), U.S. public official, born in Randolph, Utah; president Continental Illinois National Bank and Trust Company of Chicago 1956–59, chairman 1959–69; special assistant to U.S. secretary of the treasury 1953–54, secretary 1969–71; ambassador at large, state department, 1971–72; ambassador to NATO 1972–73
Nixon N-325

Kennedy, Edward Moore (nickname Ted) (born 1932), U.S. political leader, born in Brookline, Mass., U.S. senator (Democrat) from Massachusetts 1962–; assistant majority leader (majority whip) 1969–70; campaigned unsuccessfully for the presidency in 1980
Kennedy, John F. K-201, *pictures* K-200, 203
Kennedy family K-206

Kennedy, Jacqueline Bouvier. *see in index* Onassis, Jacqueline Bouvier Kennedy

Kennedy, John E., U.S. advertiser A-59

Kennedy, John Fitzgerald (1917–63), 35th president of the United States K-197
Alliance for Progress S-292
assassination A-703
Dallas D-10, T-125
church and state issue C-408
Cuban missile crisis and embargo C-803
Eisenhower E-143
Johnson J-129
medals M-270
Nixon N-320
Peace Corps P-143
'Profiles in Courage' R-112
tariff T-31
United States history U-195
Vietnam War V-321

Kennedy, John Pendleton (pen name Mark Littleton) (1795–1870), U.S. author and statesman, born in Baltimore, Md.; fought in War of 1812; Whig representative from Maryland 1838, 1840, 1842; secretary of the navy 1852–53 A-346

Kennedy, Joseph Patrick (1888–1969), U.S. banker, business executive, and statesman, born in Boston, Mass.; father of John F., Robert, and Edward; chairman, Securities and Exchange Commission 1934–35; chairman, U.S. Maritime Commission 1937; ambassador to England 1937–40 K-206
Kennedy, John F. K-197

Kennedy, Margaret (1896–1967), English novelist, born in London; married David Davies.

Kennedy, Robert Francis (1925–68), U.S. lawyer and government official, born in Brookline, Mass.; brother of President John F. Kennedy; U.S. attorney general 1961–64; U.S. senator (Democratic) from New York 1965–68; author, 'Just Friends and Brave Enemies', 'Rights for Americans' U-196
assassination, *list* A-704
Kennedy administration K-200, 204, *picture* K-203
Kennedy family K-206

Kennedy, Rose Fitzgerald (born 1890), U.S. civic leader, born in Boston, Mass.; wife of Joseph P.; mother of John F., Robert F., and Edward
Kennedy, John F. K-197
Kennedy family K-206

Kennedy, Ted. *see in index* Kennedy, Edward Moore

Kennedy, Cape. *see in index* Canaveral, Cape

Kennedy, Mount, St. Elias Mountains, Yukon Territory; height about 14,000 ft (4,300 m); named by Canadian government in memory of President John F. Kennedy; Robert Kennedy first to climb.

Kennedy Round, in international trade T-31

Kennedy Space Center. *see in index* Canaveral, Cape

Kennelly, Arthur Edwin (1861–1939), U.S. electrical engineer, born in Bombay, India; principal electrical assistant to Thomas Edison 1887–94; professor at Harvard 1902–39.

Kennelly, Brendan (born 1936), Irish poet I-328

Kennelly-Heaviside layer, in upper atmosphere; suggested by Oliver Heaviside and A.E. Kennelly R-36

Kenner, La., city 9 mi (14 km) w. of New Orleans, on Mississippi River; trading and shipping center; sheet metal, concrete and wood products; pop. 66,382.

Kennesaw Mountain, a height 25 mi (40 km) n.w. of Atlanta, Ga., where Confederate troops repulsed Sherman's army inflicting heavy losses June 27, 1864.

Kenneth I, MacAlpine (died 860?), king of the Scots and conqueror of Picts, called first king of Scotland S-70

Kennett Square, in Pennsylvania; pop. 4,876, *table* B-379

Kennewick, Wash., city in s.e. part of state, on Columbia River opposite Pasco; river port; fruit and vegetable farming; chemicals, metals, cement; pop. 34,397 W-60

Kenney, George Churchill (1889–1977), U.S. Air Force officer, born in Yarmouth, N.S., to U.S. citizens; commander of Allied air forces in Southwest Pacific during World War II.

Kenny, Sister (1886–1952), Australian nurse who developed method for treating polio K-207

Kenny Institute, Minneapolis, Minn., medical therapy training school K-207

Kennywood Park, in Pittsburgh, Pa., amusement park A-386

Kenora, Ont., manufacturing town and summer resort on Lake of the Woods, 195 km (120 mi) e. of Winnipeg, Man.; flour, lumber, pulp and paper mills, boat factories, fisheries; gold, silver, copper, mica nearby; pop. 10,952, *map* C-112
North America, *map* N-350

Kenosha, Wis., manufacturing city and port on s.w. shore of Lake Michigan, 33 mi (53 km) s. of Milwaukee; automobiles, metal products, industrial tools, wire rope, cranberries; Carthage College, Gateway Technical Institute; pop. 77,685 W-260

Kensington, P.E.I., town 8 mi (13 km) n.e. of Summerside; near Malpeque Bay; agricultural market and shipping center; butter and cheese; pop. 1,143 P-497f, *map* P-497h

Kensington and Chelsea, borough in w.-central section of Greater London, England; Kensington district has Kensington Palace (birthplace of Queen Victoria) and Gardens; pop. 200,400, *map* U-18a
London L-293, *maps* L-287, 288

Kent, Edward Augustus, duke of (1767–1820), English prince, 4th son of George III; father of Queen Victoria; born in London
Prince Edward Island P-497e

Kent, James (1763–1847), U.S. jurist and author, born in Fredericksburg, Putnam County, N.Y.; his 'Commentaries upon American Law' is a legal classic K-207
Hall of Fame, *table* H-16
law L-94

Kent, Rockwell (1882–1971), U.S. artist K-207
Moby Dick, *picture* N-413
Paul Bunyan, *picture* F-266

Kent, William (1684–1748), English architect F-459

Kent, ancient kingdom of Anglo-Saxons in England; settled by Jutes; conquered by Egbert, king of Wessex, made part of Wessex.

Kent, county of s.e. England; 1,525 sq mi (3,950 sq km); pop. 1,388,820.

Kent, Ohio, city 11 mi (18 km) n.e. of Akron; electric motors, motor vehicles, machine parts, school blackboards, plastic products; Kent State University; pop. 26,164.

Kent, Wash., city 16 mi (26 km) s. of Seattle; aerospace research and products, fiberglass, telephone equipment; pop. 23,152.

Kente cloth, ritual garments in Africa A-101

Kenten-mon, Japanese gate, *diagram* J-31

Kent Island, largest island in Chesapeake Bay, Maryland, 7 mi (11 km) e. of Annapolis; oyster fisheries, *map* M-183

Kenton, Simon (1755–1836), U.S. frontiersman; birthplace probably Fauquier County, Virginia; scout for Daniel Boone 1775–78; with George Rogers Clark in capture of Kaskaskia and Vincennes; became brigadier general of militia 1805; in War of 1812.

Kenton, Stan (1912–79), U.S. bandleader, born in

Wichita, Kan.; band noted for progressive jazz; introduced new compositions and arrangements after mid-1940s.

Kent State University, Kent, Ohio; founded 1910; arts and sciences, business administration, education, fine and professional arts, library science, and nursing; graduate school; regional campuses at Ashtabula, East Liverpool, New Philadelphia, North Canton, Salem, and Warren C-495

Kentucky, an e.-central state of U.S.; 40,395 sq mi (104,625 sq km); cap. Frankfort; pop. 3,661,433 K-208, *maps* U-41, 58
- agriculture, *picture* U-56
- cities. *see also in index* cities by name
  - Frankfort F-378
  - Lexington-Fayette L-145
  - Louisville L-324
- geographic region U-56-67
- history
  - Boone B-365
  - Civil War 473
    - Confederate States of America C-642
    - states' rights conflict S-429d
  - pioneer life P-331-4
- North America, *map* N-350
- state symbols
  - flag, *picture* F-159
  - flower, *picture* S-427
- Statuary Hall, *table* S-437a
- taxation, *tables* T-37, 39
- Tennessee Valley Authority T-100, *map* T-101

Kentucky, University of, Lexington, Ky.; state control; founded 1865; arts and sciences, agriculture, allied health professions, architecture, business and economics, dentistry, education, engineering, home economics, law, library sciences, medicine, nursing, pharmacy, and social professions; graduate school; Lexington Technical Institute; 14 community colleges, *picture* K-217

Kentucky coffee tree, a medium-sized tree *Gymnocladus dioicus* of the pea, or pulse, family; so called because its seeds resemble coffee beans; grows w. of Appalachian Mountains to Great Plains; state tree of Kentucky.

Kentucky Dam, dam in Kentucky, on Tennessee River D-17

Kentucky Derby, in horse racing H-275
- Kentucky K-214, *picture* K-209
- Louisville L-324
- Shoemaker S-181

Kentucky Fried Chicken, fast-food chain F-43

Kentucky Lake, lake, United States, *picture* K-218

Kentucky Resolutions S-429d
- Jefferson's contribution J-93

Kentucky River, river in Kentucky, formed by several forks, rising in Cumberland Mts. of s.e.; flows 250 mi (400 km) n.w. to Ohio River.

Kentucky State University, Frankfort, Ky.; founded as normal school 1886; arts and sciences, applied sciences, and teacher education; graduate studies.

Kentucky Wesleyan College, Owensboro, Ky.; Methodist; founded 1858; opened 1866; arts and sciences, education.

Kentwood, Mich., city 5 mi (8 km) s.e. of Grand Rapids; pop. 30,438; residential; incorporated 1967.

Kenya, African nation on Indian Ocean s. of Ethiopia; area 224,960 sq mi (582,645 sq km); cap. Nairobi; pop. 17,142,000 K-224, *map* A-115
- Africanization A-105, *table* A-112
- Commonwealth membership C-602
- elephants, *picture* A-95
- flag, *picture* F-1166
- Great Rift Valley G-250
- Kenyatta's leadership K-228
- Lake Victoria V-310
- national anthem, *table* N-64
- national parks N-26
- Peace Corps aid, *picture* P-143a
- railroad mileage, *table* R-85
- world, *map* W-297

Kenya, Mount, volcanic peak (17,058 ft; 5,199 m) in central Kenya, Africa, near equator; discovered 1849; first ascended 1899 K-224, G-250, *map* A-115

Kenyahs, a people of Borneo; traditionally rice growers; entire village often lives in one huge communal house.

Kenyatta, Jomo (1894?–1978), African political leader, born near Nairobi, Kenya; imprisoned 1953–59 for Mau Mau leadership; prime minister of Kenya 1963–64, president from 1964–78 K-228
- Kenya K-227

Kenyon, Dame Kathleen Mary (1906–78), English archaeologist
- Jericho A-532

Kenyon College, Gambier, Ohio; Protestant Episcopal; founded 1824 (at Worthington, moved 1827 to Gambier); arts and sciences.

Kenzo (born 1939), Japanese dress designer D-271

Keogh, James (born 1916), U.S. journalist and government official, born in Platte County, Nebraska; on staff of *Time* 1951–68, assistant managing editor 1961–68, executive editor 1968; chief writer and researcher for Nixon for President campaign 1968; special presidential assistant 1969–70; director U.S. Information Agency 1973–76 ('This Is Nixon'; 'President Nixon and the Press').

Keogh plan individual retirement plan P-189

Keokuk ("one who moves alertly") (1780?–1848), member of the Fox clan; became leader of Sauks and Foxes and secured for them the territory of Iowa from the government; buried in Keokuk, Iowa, which was named for him; his son, **Moses Keokuk** (1818?–1903), was a famous orator.

Keokuk, Iowa, city on Mississippi and Des Moines rivers at s.e. corner of state; metal products, corn and cereal products, carbides; pop. 13,536 I-289
- Iowa, *map* I-302

Kephallenia (or Cephalonia), mountainous Greek island w. of mainland; largest of Ionian group; about 290 sq mi (750 sq km); currants and olives; pop. 31,787.

Kepler, Johannes (1571–1630), German astronomer K-228
- astronomy A-713
- Galileo G-6
- gravitation G-239
- mathematics M-214
- science S-57g
- story of trip to moon S-341d

Kepler's laws of planetary motion K-228, S-57g, A-713, G-239

Keppel, Frederick Paul (1875–1943), U.S. educator, born in Staten Island, N.Y.; assistant secretary of war 1918–19; president Carnegie Corporation 1923–41.

Kerala, state in s.w. India; area 14,980 sq mi (38,800 sq km); cap. Trivandrum; formed 1956 from parts of former Travancore-Cochin and Madras states; pop. 21,347,375, *map* I-83

Keratin (or horn), fibrous protein in hoof H-231

Kerazeh, Palestine. *see in index* Chorazin

Kerbela, Iraq. *see in index* Karbala

Kerch', U.S.S.R., port of Crimea, on Kerch' Peninsula; steel mills; pop. 128,000, *maps* E-360, R-349

Keren Hayesod, German Jewish organization B-17

Kerensky, Alexander Feodorovich (1881–1970), Soviet revolutionary statesman, born in Simbirsk (now Ulyanovsk); fled to Paris, France, when Bolsheviks overthrew his government Oct. 1917; moved to U.S. 1940; author of 'Russia and History's Turning Point' R-354
- World War I W-309

Keres (or Queres), a linguistic group of North American Indians living in pueblos on the Rio Grande and Rio Jemez and New Mexico.

Kerguelen Island, volcanic island 100 mi (160 km) long in s. Indian Ocean; French possession; whaling, seal-hunting base; discovered 1772 by Yves Joseph de Kerguélen-Trémarec, *map* W-297

Kerguélen-Trémarec, Yves-Joseph de (1734–97), French explorer, born in Quimper; discovered (1772) what he thought was rich continent in Antarctic and named it south France; realizing it was only a barren island, renamed it Isle of Desolation; later called Kerguelen Island.

Kérkyra, island. *see in index* Corfu

Kermadec Islands, group in Pacific about 600 mi (950 km) n.e. of New Zealand, to which it was annexed in 1887; total area, 13 sq mi (34 sq km); Raoul, or Sunday Island, largest; pop. 9, *map* P-3
- world, *map* W-297

Kerman (or Kirman, ancient Carmana), Iran, city in s.e.; capital of province of Kerman; Iran's chief rug exporter; 11th-century mosque, now restored; pop. 110,000, *map* P-212
- Asia, *map* A-697
- rugs, *picture* R-312

Kermanshah, Iran, city in w.; on road between Baghdad and Tehran; trade in grain, rugs; pop. 250,000
- Asia, *map* A-697

Kermit, Tex., city 40 mi (65 km) w. of Odessa; in area producing oil and natural gas; cattle ranching; incorporated 1938; pop. 8,015.

Kernel, fruit seed
- corn C-722
- nuts N-448

Kernel clause S-110

Kernite (or rasorite), mineral yielding borax M-435

Kern, Jerome (1885–1945), U.S. composer, born in New York City; with Oscar Hammerstein II wrote the musical comedy 'Show Boat' (1927) M-686
- popular music M-684

Kern River, stream rising in mountains of s.e. California; flows s.w. and n. to Lake Tulare.

Kerogen, a substance in oil shale P-230
- gas G-39

Kerosene (or kerosine, also coal oil), an oil distilled from petroleum; ending "ine" adopted 1957 by petroleum chemists because "ene" suggests falsely that oil consists of unsaturated compounds P-232, *charts* P-241–241b
- asphalt distilled A-702
- first used P-232
- fuel F-441
  - jet fuel A-74
  - rocket fuel S-342a, 346d
- lighting and lamps L-205
- soap S-231

Kerouac, Jack (1922–69), U.S. author, born in Lowell, Mass.; spokesman for the "beat generation" K-229
- Ginsberg G-145

Kerr, Jean Collins (born 1924), U.S. writer, born in Scranton, Pa.; married Walter F. Kerr 1943 ('Please Don't Eat the Daisies', 'The Snake Has All the Lines', humorous pieces; 'Mary, Mary', play and movie).

Kerr, Robert Samuel (1896–1963), U.S. lawyer, oil producer, and political leader; born in Ada, Okla.; governor of Oklahoma 1943–47; U.S. senator (Democrat) 1949–63.

Kerr, Walter Francis (born 1913), U.S. drama critic and playwright, born in Evanston, Ill.; on faculty Catholic University of America (drama department) 1938–49; drama critic *New York Herald Tribune* (1951–66), *The New York Times*; husband of Jean Kerr (play: 'Sing Out, Sweet Land'; criticism: 'How Not to Write a Play', 'The Theater in Spite of Itself', 'Tragedy and Comedy').

Kerrville, Tex., city 55 mi (90 km) n.w. of San Antonio, at mouth of Guadalupe River; wool processing, ranching, incorporated 1942; pop. 15,276.

Kerry, county of s.w. Ireland in province of Munster; 1,815 sq mi (4,700 sq km); beautiful mountain scenery; lakes of Killarney; pop. 112,785.

Kerry, Mountains of, in Ireland I-317

Kerry blue terrier, dog, *picture* D-204

Kersey, a thick, coarse woolen cloth used to make clothing; woven first in medieval England.

Kerst, Donald William (born 1911), U.S. physicist, born in Galena, Ill.; joined faculty of University of Illinois 1938, professor of physics 1943–57; invented betatron there.

Kerulen River, 780 mi (1,255 km) long, rises in n.e. Mongolian People's Republic, flows into Hulun Nor (lake) in China
- Asia, *map* A-697

Kerwin, Joseph P. (born 1932), U.S. astronaut, physician, born in Oak Park, Ill.; flight surgeon with U.S. Marine Corps 1956–58, with U.S. Navy 1958–; scientist-astronaut 1965–; member Skylab crew 1973, *table* S-348

Kerwin, Patrick (1889–1963), Canadian jurist, born in Sarnia, Ont.; created king's counsel 1928; appointed judge of the Supreme Court of Canada 1935, chief justice 1954–63.

Kesselring, Albert (1885–1960), German army officer; born in Marktstedt, Bavaria; led air attacks on Poland 1939, on The Netherlands, Belgium, Britain 1940, on U.S.S.R. 1941–42; became commander in Italy 1943, in West 1945; death sentence for war crimes in Italy commuted to life imprisonment, later to 21 years; freed by British 1952; wrote 'Kesselring: a Soldier's Record'.

Kestrel (or windhover), a bird of prey, one of smallest of true falcons *Falco tinnunculus* found throughout Old World; resembles common sparrow hawk of Americas, to which it is related; strong flier, hovers for minute or two in one spot.

Keswick Dam, dam in California C-36

Keta salmon. *see in index* Chum salmon

Ketch, sailing craft, *pictures* B-327, S-166

Ketchel, Stanley (originally Stanislaus Kiecal) (1887–1910), U.S. middleweight boxer, born in Grand Rapids, Mich.; scored 46 knockouts, 14 in succession; was shot to death.

Ketchikan, Alaska, city and port of entry in s.e. Alaska 235 mi (380 km) s.e. of Juneau; pulp mill; salmon canning, halibut processing, lumbering; totem pole collection; Ketchikan King Salmon Derby; pop. 7,198 A-242, *map* U-39
- North America, *map* N-350
- totem poles, *picture* T-235

Ketchwayo. *see in index* Cetewayo

'Keter Malkut', poem by Ibn Gabirol I-4

Ketoacidosis, life-threatening condition in diabetes D-125

Ketones, in chemistry O-603

Ket's Rebellion. *see in index* Kett's Rebellion

Kettering, Charles Franklin (1876–1958), U.S. engineer and inventor, born near Loudonville, Ohio; originated Delco electric power- and light-generating unit for farmhouses; president and general manager General Motors Research Corporation 1920–47, research consultant 1947–58; founded Charles F. Kettering Foundation 1927, board chairman 1927–58
- automobile history A-856, 859
- guided missile G-308

Kettering, Ohio, residential city just s.e. of Dayton; electric motors; Defense Electronics Center; incorporated 1955; pop. 61,186.

Kettledrum (or timpani), musical instrument O-576

Kettle Hill, Cuba. *see in index* San Juan Hill

Kett's Rebellion, or **Ket's Rebellion,** a revolt in Norfolk, England (1549), led by William and Robert Kett against the unlawful closing off from the people of common land; suppressed, at great loss to rebels, by forces under leadership of earl of Warwick; Kett brothers executed.

Keuka College, Keuka Park, N.Y.; private control; operated 1890–1915 as coeducational institution, reopened as college for women 1921; arts and sciences, education.

Kirchhoff, Gustav Robert (1824–87), German physicist, born in Königsberg, East Prussia (now Kaliningrad, U.S.S.R.); developed spectrum analysis and discovered cesium and rubidium (with Bunsen); explained the Fraunhofer lines; professor of physics at Heidelberg 1854–74, at Berlin 1874–87
spectroscopic discoveries P-303, S-371

Kirgiz, one of a nomadic people of central Asia, of Turko-Tataric (Mongolian) stock, ranging from borders of European U.S.S.R. to w. China
Asia, *picture* A-680
Kirgiz S.S.R. K-250
Turkestan T-317

Kirgizia, region, U.S.S.R. K-250

Kirgiz Soviet Socialist Republic, of U.S.S.R., in central Asia; area 76,450 sq mi (198,000 sq km); cap. Frunze; pop. 3,529,000 K-250, U-14, *maps* R-325, 344
Turkestan T-317

Kiribati, formerly Gilbert Islands, nation in Pacific; consists of Gilbert Islands, Ocean Island, Phoenix Islands, and eight of the Line Islands including Washington Island, Fanning Island, and Christmas Island; 275 sq mi (710 sq km); cap. Bairiki; most of area under British protection 1892–1979; self-governing since 1977; independent since 1979; pop. 58,500 K-250
Commonwealth membership C-602
flag, *picture* F-166
United Kingdom E-259

Kirin. *see in index* Jilin

Kirizuma, Japanese roof style, *diagram* J-31

Kirk, Grayson Louis (born 1903), educator, born near Jeffersonville, Ohio; joined faculty of Columbia University 1940, became professor of government 1943, provost 1949–53, vice-president 1950–53, acting head during Dwight D. Eisenhower's leave of absence 1951–53, president 1953–68.

Kirkland, Wash., city on inlet of Puget Sound 10 mi (16 km) n.e. of Seattle; furniture, paint, feed mill; pop. 18,779.

Kirklareli (or Kirk-kilissa), European Turkey, town; mosques and Greek churches; scene of first important Bulgarian victory over Turks in Balkan War of 1912; pop. 20,196.

Kirkpatrick, Jeane J. (born 1926), political scientist and diplomat, born in Duncan, Okla.; associate professor of political science Georgetown University 1967–73, professor after 1973; member Democratic National Committee after 1972; campaigned for Ronald Reagan in 1980 presidential race; chief U.S. delegate to UN 1981–85 R-112j
women's rights W-276

Kirkstall Abbey, in Leeds, England L-117

Kirksville, Mo., city about 75 mi (120 km) n.w. of Hannibal; shoes, gloves, dairy products, printing; Northeast Missouri State University; pop. 17,167.

Kirkuk, Iraq, city 150 mi (240 km) n. of Baghdad; oil center; in dry-farming region; distributing point for grains, fruit, cotton, wool, cattle, gallnuts, and tragacanth; pop. 187,509 I-313, *picture* I-315
Asia, *map* A-697

Kirkwall, Orkney Islands, capital; British base during World War I; fine Norman-Gothic cathedral begun in 1138; pop. 4,688 O-607, *map* E-360

Kirkwood, Samuel Jordan (1813–94), political leader, born in Harford County, Md.; Civil War governor of Iowa; U.S. senator; secretary of interior under President Garfield
Statuary Hall, *table* S-437a

Kirkwood, Mo., city 12 mi (19 km) w. of St. Louis; residential suburb with varied manufactures including cement and wood products; horticulture; founded 1853, incorporated 1865; pop. 27,987.

Kirman, Iran. *see in index* Kerman

Kirstein, Lincoln (born 1907), U.S. businessman and dance authority B-22

Kirsten, Dorothy (born 1917), concert and operatic soprano, born in Montclair, N.J.; United States debut 1940; member of Metropolitan Opera Co., New York City, from 1945.

Kiruna, Sweden, city n. of Arctic Circle; iron mining; pop. 23,279 S-523, *pictures* E-342, S-526, *map* S-524

Kisaeng, traditional Korean female singer and dancer at the feast; some famed for interest in poetry, calligraphy, and painting; originally a low caste serving ruling aristocracy.

Kisangani (formerly Stanleyville), Zaire, city on Congo River below Stanley Falls; railroad around falls; pop. 282,650 Z-443, *map* A-115

Kish, Mesopotamia (Iraq), ancient city near the Euphrates River, 8 mi (13 km) e. of Babylon K-251
Mesopotamia M-305

Kishinev (Romanian Chisinau), U.S.S.R., capital of Moldavian S.S.R., 95 mi (155 km) n.w. of Odessa; agricultural center; ceded by Russia to Romania after World War I; returned to Russia 1940; terrible pogroms (1903, 1905); pop. 605,000 M-520, *maps* E-360, R-344, 349

Kishi, Nobusuke (1896–1987), Japanese statesman, born in Yamaguchi, s.w. Honshu; prime minister 1957–60; president Liberal-Democratic party 1957–60; pro-Western.

Kiska Island, largest of Rat Islands in Aleutians, *map* U-39

Kislaya Guba station, hydroelectric power plant on the Barents Sea in the Soviet Union W-106

Kismayu (or Chisimaio), Somalia, port on Indian Ocean; fish, hides, livestock; pop. 17,872, *map* W-297

Kiss, heavy metal rock group M-682

Kiss, August (1802–65), German sculptor, born near present Katowice, Poland; well known for studies of animals ('Mounted Amazon Attacked by a Tiger').

Kissimmee River, river in Florida, rises in lake of same name; flows s.e. 90 mi (145 km) to Lake Okeechobee.

Kissing disease. *see in index* Mononucleosis

Kissingen, Bad, West Germany. *see in index* Bad Kissingen

Kissinger, Henry (born 1923), U.S. political scientist K-251. *see also in index* Nobel Prizewinners, *table*
diplomacy D-152, *picture* D-149
Ford F-304
international relations, *picture* I-260
Nixon N-327

Kissovo, Mount (ancient Ossa), in Thessaly. *see in index* Pelion, Mount

Kistiakowsky, George Bogdan (1900–1982), U.S. chemist, born in Kiev, Russia; to U.S. 1926, became citizen 1933; professor of chemistry Harvard University after 1937; presidential special assistant for science and technology 1959–61.

Kistna River (or Krishna River), in s. India, rises in Western Ghats and flows e. to Bay of Bengal; 800 mi (1300 km) long.
Asia, *map* A-697

Kisumu, Kenya, port on Lake Victoria, just s. of equator; terminus of railroad; commercial center; fisheries; processing of cotton, peanuts, coffee, and sesame; pop. 46,700, *map* A-115

Kiswahili, language T-22

Kit, young beaver B-121

Kitakyushu, Japan, seaport city on n. Kyushu; formed 1963 by merger of cities Yawata, Wakamatsu, Moji, Tobata, and Kokura; pop. 1,067,915 J-41, *map* J-75
Asia, *map* A-697

Kitazato, Shibasaburo (1852–1931), Japanese bacteriologist, born in Kumamoto; pupil of Robert Koch; isolated tetanus bacillus 1889; helped develop diphtheria antitoxin 1890; a discoverer of bubonic plague bacillus 1894.

Kit-Cat Club, famous 18th-century club in London including among members Addison, Steele, and other prominent writers and political leaders, all Whigs; named for tavern of Christopher Cat where meetings were held.

Kitchen S-160
cooking C-698
home appliances H-210
home economics H-216, *picture* H-214

Kitchen Cabinet, popular name applied to a group of friends and advisers who (though they held no important offices) influenced President Jackson.

Kitchener, Herbert (1850–1916), British general K-251
Boer War B-331
Sudan S-503

Kitchener (formerly Berlin), Ont., city 55 mi (90 km) s.w. of Toronto; meat-packing; furniture, electrical products, textiles, rubber products, shoes, machinery, chemicals; pop. 287,801, *map* C-112

Kitchen middens, refuse heaps of prehistoric settlements, containing bones, shells, debris, and relics of industry and art; valuable to archaeological studies.

Kite, bird of prey B-278

Kite, in mathematics G-74, *diagram* G-75

Kite flying K-252
Franklin's use F-382
safety in flying A-65, S-8
Thailand B-59, T-148
toys T-241

Kit fox, *table* F-464

Kitimat, B.C., city with deepwater harbor at head of inlet of the Pacific, 75 mi (120 km) s.e. of Prince Rupert; a thoroughly planned city (incorporated 1953) based on aluminum smelting; pop. 12,814, *map* C-109

Kitksan, a Tsimshian Indian tribe living on upper Skeena River in British Columbia; term also applied to individual members of the group and their dialect.

Kits, packaged materials and instructions for hobbyists H-181

Kitson, Henry Hudson (1863–1947), U.S. sculptor, born in Huddersfield, England; husband of sculptor **Theo Ruggles Kitson** (1871–1932); his many monuments to national and historic figures include 'The Pilgrim Maiden' at Plymouth, Mass., *picture* M-194

Ki, Tsurayuki (or Tsurayuki Ki-no) (884?–946), Japanese poet and government official at the old capital of Heian (now Kyoto); his literary criticism influenced court poetry for centuries
Japan J-49
literature J-79

Kittatinny Mountain, a ridge of the Appalachians, mainly in n.w. New Jersey along Delaware River; extends from Shawangunk Mountains in s.e. New York to Blue Mountain in e. Pennsylvania
Delaware Water Gap, *map* P-185
New Jersey N-193

Kitten ball S-248

Kittery, Me., community across bay from Portsmouth, N.H.; site of Portsmouth Navy Yard; incorporated 1647; pop. of township 11,028.

Kittim, Cyprus. *see in index* Citium

Kittinger, Joseph William, Jr. (born 1928), U.S. Air Force officer, born in Tampa, Fla.; broke many records as high altitude test parachutist P-109b
ballooning B-44

Kittiwake, a gull *Rissa tridactyla* that breeds in the Arctic regions and winters as far south as the Atlantic and Pacific coasts of the United States; about 46 centimeters (18 inches) long and has white plumage with a pale bluish-gray mantle; hind toe is entirely absent or rudimentary G-317

Kittl, Ema. *see in index* Destinn, Emmy

Kitt Peak National Observatory, 45 mi (72 km) s.w. of Tucson, Ariz., on Papago Indian reservation; dedicated 1960; maintained by National Science Foundation, coordinated with NASA astronomy in space program; world's largest solar telescope; 213-centimeter (84-inch) reflecting telescope O-457

Kittredge, George Lyman (1860–1941), U.S. educator and philologist, born in Boston, Mass.; professor of English at Harvard University 1894–1936; author of standard works on English grammar and philology; authority on Shakespeare.

Kittson, Norman Wolfred (1814–88), Canadian fur trader; born in Chambly, Lower Canada; joined American Fur Company 1830; ran trading post at Pembina on Red River and helped break Hudson Bay Company monopoly 1844–54.

Kitty Hawk, N.C., village in n.e. on strip of land between Albemarle Sound and Atlantic Ocean; Wright Brothers National Memorial nearby; pop. 600 N-353, *picture* N-364
first airplane flight A-202, *table* A-206
Wright W-368

Kiushu, Japan. *see in index* Kyushu

Kiva, North American Indian architecture I-128

Kivu, Lake, e.-central Africa on e. border of Zaire; 60 mi (95 km) long, 30 mi (50 km) wide; tourist center, *map* A-115
Great Rift Valley G-250

Kiwanis clubs, organizations of business, professional, and agricultural men for the rendering of civic and social service to their communities; the first Kiwanis club was formed in Detroit in 1915, and Kiwanis International was organized in 1917; clubs have two members of each business or profession in the community; motto, "We build"
fraternal societies F-387

Kiwi (or apteryx), a flightless bird native to New Zealand; about size of domestic fowl; nocturnal B-277
New Zealand N-288

Ki-Wives International, women's organization affiliated with the Kiwanis clubs W-270

Kizilirmak (ancient Halys), river in Turkey, rises near border of Armenia; flows n. and w. into Black Sea; 600 mi (950 km) long T-318, *map* P-212

Kjelgaard, James Arthur (1910–59), U.S. author of children's books, born in New York City; American history and the outdoors ('Big Red'; 'Snow Dog'; 'Explorations of Père Marquette'; 'Haunt Fox'; 'Desert Dog'; 'Rescue Dog of the High Pass'; 'The Black Faun'; 'Boomerang Hunter').

Kjölen Mountains, between Sweden and Norway E-329, S-523, *map* S-524
Europe, *map* E-360

Klabund (pen name of Alfred Henschke) (1890–1928), German author of lyrics, novels, and dramas; born in Crossen on the Oder; in his short life made important contribution to German literature; among his plays are 'Kirchblütenfest' with Japanese setting and Chinese play 'Kreidekreis'; novels, mainly historical, include 'Mohammed', 'Pjotr', and 'Borgia'.

Klagenfurt, Austria, city in s., capital of province of Carinthia; in manufacturing area; tourist center; pop. 69,218.

Klaipeda. *see in index* Memel

Klamath, a people of s. Oregon O-583. *see also in index* Modoc

Klamath Falls, Ore., city at s. tip of Upper Klamath Lake, about 15 mi (25 km) n. of California line; railroad and tourist center in lumbering, farming (barley, potatoes), and livestock-raising area; farm machinery; Kingsley Field; annual rodeo; pop. 16,661, *maps* N-350, U-40
Oregon O-585

Klamath Mountains, mountains that are a part of the Pacific Coast Ranges
California C-33, *map* C-34
Oregon O-582

Klamath River, 180 mi (290 km) long rising in Upper Klamath Lake in s. Oregon and flowing

Krebs, Sir Hans Adolf (1900–81), British scientist, born in Hildesheim, Germany; professor of biochemistry Oxford University 1954–67. *see also in index* Nobel Prizewinners, *table*
Krebs cycle B-202, *diagram* B-200

Krebs cycle, in biochemistry
cellular activity B-202, *diagram* B-200
metabolism M-306

Kredel, Fritz (1900–73), U.S. artist and illustrator, born in Michelstadt, Germany; taught art in Germany; to U.S. 1938; illustrated for children: Andersen's 'Fairy Tales'; Grimm's 'Fairy Tales'; 'Pinocchio', by Carlo Lorenzini.

Krefeld, West Germany, manufacturing town 50 km (30 mi) n.w. of Cologne; famous textile institute; pop. 216,871.

Krehbiel, Henry Edward (1854–1923), U.S. music critic and writer, born in Ann Arbor, Mich.; music critic *Cincinnati Gazette*, 1874–80, *New York Tribune*, 1880–1923; known as "dean of American critics" ('How to Listen to Music'; 'Chapters of Opera').

Kreisky, Bruno (born 1911), Austrian chancellor K-303

Kreisler, Fritz (1875–1962), U.S. violinist and composer K-303

Kremer, Gerhard. *see in index* Mercator Gerhardus

Kremlin, in Soviet architecture K-304
Kiev R-351
Moscow M-591, R-333, *picture* R-320

Krenek, Ernst (born 1900), U.S. composer, born in Vienna, Austria; to U.S. 1938, became citizen 1945; extreme modernist in style; won first widespread fame with 'Jonny spielt auf', jazz opera; other operas include 'The Life of Orestes'.

Kreps, Juanita M. (born 1921), U.S. educator and public official, born in Lynch, Ky.; member faculty Duke University 1955–77, professor 1968–77, vice-president 1973–77; U.S. secretary of commerce 1977–79
women's rights W-276

Kresge, Sebastian Spering (1867–1966), U.S. merchant and philanthropist, born in Bald Mount, Pa.; partner Kresge and Wilson, Detroit, 1907, incorporated as S.S. Kresge Company 1912.

Kress, Samuel Henry (1863–1955), U.S. merchant and art patron, born in Cherryville, Northampton County, Pa.; founded S.H. Kress & Co. (chain of 5-, 10-, and 25-cent stores) at Memphis, Tenn., 1896; established Samuel H. Kress Foundation 1929; donated many art treasures to National Gallery of Art and other leading museums.

Krete, island. *see in index* Crete

Kreuger, Ivar (1880–1932), Swedish "match king" and financial wizard, born in Kalmar; built a huge international match trust; committed suicide when faced with bankruptcy.

Kreutzer, Konradin (1780–1849), German pianist, conductor, and composer of operas, church music, and chamber music; born near Konstanz; among best-known works is light opera, 'Nachtlager von Granada'.

Kreutzer, Rodolphe (1766–1831), French violinist of German extraction, born in Versailles; wrote many operas and instrumental works; Beethoven dedicated to him the sonata for violin and piano known as the Kreutzer Sonata in A Major.

'Kreutzer' Sonata in A Major, work by Beethoven B-136

Kreuzotter, viper V-328

Krieghoff, Cornelius (1812–72), Canadian painter, born in Düsseldorf, Germany; with U.S. Army in Seminole Wars 1837–40; known for landscapes, portraits, and portrayals of early French-Canadian life.

Kriegsakademie, Berlin, Germany; founded in 1810
military education M-411

Kriemhild, wife of the hero Siegfried in the Nibelungenlied S-192a
'Song of the Nieblungs' N-303

Krill, animal
Antarctic food chain A-473

Krim, peninsula of s. U.S.S.R. *see in index* Crimea

Kris, Malay dagger, *picture* S-546

Krishna, a Hindu god H-157
painting P-67f
pearl myth P-149

Krishna Menon, Vengalil Krishnan (1897–1974), Indian diplomat, born in Calicut, now Kozhikode; worked for Indian independence; delegate to UN 1946–47, 1952–62; high commissioner of India in London 1947–52; minister for defense 1957–62.

Krishna River, India. *see in index* Kistna River

Kriss Kringle, German name for Santa Claus S-45

Kristallnacht, or **Night of Broken Glass,** Nov. 9–10, 1938, Germany
Holocaust H-205

Kristensen, Leonard, Norwegian whaling captain; member of small party of first persons to land on Antarctic Continent (1895), *table* P-422

Kristiansand, Norway, seaport on s. coast; exports wood pulp, lumber, nickel, fish; has 17th-century Gothic cathedral; founded 1641; pop. 50,217, *map* E-360

'Kristin Lavransdatter', trilogy by Undset U-4

Kríti, Greek island. *see in index* Crete

Krivoy Rog (or Krivoi Rog), U.S.S.R., city in s. Ukrainian Soviet Socialist Republic; pop. 573,000, *maps* E-360, R-344, 349

KRM. *see in index* Kurzweil Reading Machine

Kroeber, Alfred Louis (1876–1960), U.S. anthropologist, born in Hoboken, N.J.; taught anthropology at University of California 1901–46; expert on North American Indians and archaeology of Mexico and Peru; wrote textbook, 'Anthropology'.

Kroger, Bernard Henry (1860–1938), U.S. grocer, born in Cincinnati, Ohio; founded Kroger Grocery and Baking Co. (1882) which became a grocery chain.

Krogh, Schack August Steenberg (1874–1949), Danish physiologist, born in Grenaa; noted for experiments in respiration and for researches in capillaries and the blood. *see also in index* Nobel Prizewinners, *table*

Krohg, Christian (1852–1925), Norwegian painter and author, born in Oslo; depicted sea and seamen with realism and strength; wrote novels and books on art
painting, *picture* A-328

Krol, John Joseph, Cardinal (born 1910), U.S. Roman Catholic prelate, born in Cleveland, Ohio; auxiliary bishop of Cleveland 1953–61; archbishop of Philadelphia 1961–; created cardinal 1967; president National Conference of Catholic Bishops 1972–74.

Kroll, Leon (1884–1974), U.S. painter, born in New York City; simple, strong, and highly individual in landscape, still life, and figure work.

Kroll Process, titanium production T-193

Kronborg Castle, castle in Denmark, *picture* D-99

Kronshtadt, or **Kronstadt,** U.S.S.R., port and naval base on island of Kotlin in Gulf of Finland 20 mi (30 km) w. of Leningrad; founded 1710 by Peter the Great, *maps* P-348

Kroo, an African people. *see in index* Kru

Kropotkin, Peter (1842–1921), Russian geographer and anarchist K-306
anarchism A-388

Kru, or **Kroo,** or **Croo,** a people of Liberia and adjacent parts of w. Africa; famous as canoe men and sailors; tribal mark (black or blue line) tattooed on forehead.

Krueger, Karl (1894–1979), U.S. orchestral conductor, born in Atchison, Kan.; studied at Heidelberg, Germany, and Vienna, Austria; conductor Seattle Symphony Orchestra, Kansas City Philharmonic; Conductor Detroit Symphony Orchestra 1943–49.

Krueger, Walter (1881–1967), U.S. general, born in Flatow, Germany; participated in Spanish-American War; commanded Sixth Army in World War II W-346

Krug, Julius Albert (1907–70), U.S. public power expert and government official, born in Madison, Wis.; with Tennessee Valley Authority 1938–40, War Production Board 1942–45, chairman after Sept. 1944; U.S. secretary of the interior 1946–49.

Kruger, Paul (1825–1904), Boer patriot, known as "Oom Paul" (Uncle Paul) K-306
Rhodes R-195
Smuts S-220
South Africa S-267

Kruger National Park, park in South Africa S-264, *map* S-264

Kruglov, Sergei Nikiforovich (born 1900?), Soviet government official; deputy commissar for internal affairs during World War II; minister of internal affairs 1946–56.

Krumgold, Joseph (1908–80), U.S. author and motion-picture producer, born in Jersey City, N.J.; writer and producer for major motion-picture companies 1931–41, for Office of War Information during World War II, operated own company in Israel 1946–50 ('. . . and now Miguel', awarded 1954 Newbery Medal; 'Onion John', awarded 1960 Newbery Medal) R-111a

Krummholz (or elfinwood), stunned forest characteristic of mountainous regions M-636

Krung Thep, Thailand. *see in index* Bangkok

Krupa, Gene (1909–73), U.S. jazz drummer and bandleader, born in Chicago, Ill.; associated with Chicago style before becoming first drummer to win large public acclaim.

Krupp, Alfred (1812–87), German "cannon king," born in Essen; son of Friedrich and father of Friedrich Alfred Krupp; discoverer of method of casting steel in large pieces; made great guns used (1870–71) in the siege of Paris K-307
artillery A-660

Krupp, Alfried (1907–67), German industrialist; sentenced by U.S. tribunal at end of World War II, released from prison 1951; under his direction, the Krupp firm recovered spectacularly without making armaments K-307

Krupp, Arndt (died 1624) K-306

Krupp, Friedrich (1787–1826), German ironmaster, born in Essen; founder of house of Krupp and of great Krupp works at Essen; introduced manufacture of cast steel into Germany; died poor K-306

Krupp, Friedrich Alfred (1854–1902), German industrialist, born in Essen; son of Alfred and grandson of Friedrich Krupp; handed on the Krupp business to his daughter, Bertha K-307

Krupp von Bohlen und Halbach, Bertha (1886–1957), eldest daughter of Friedrich Alfred Krupp; brought up to manage Krupp works at Essen, which she inherited at 16; married **Baron Gustav von Bohlen und Halbach** (1870–1950), who added Krupp to his name and became chief director of works K-307

Krutch, Joseph Wood (1893–1970), U.S. critic and essayist, born in Knoxville, Tenn.; drama critic and associate editor *The Nation* 1924–32, literary editor 1933–37; professor of English 1937–43, of dramatic literature 1943–52, Columbia University ('Samuel Johnson'; 'The Twelve Seasons'; 'The Desert Year'; 'The Best of Two Worlds'; 'The Measure of Man'; 'The Great Chain of Life'; 'Human Nature and the Human Condition'; 'The Forgotten Peninsula'; 'If You Don't Mind My Saying So'; 'More Lives Than One', autobiography).

Krylov, Ivan Andreevich (1768–1844), noted Russian fabulist, born in Moscow; wrote fables largely in language of peasants, satirizing life of his time, often borrowed themes from Aesop and La Fontaine R-359

Krypton (Kr), colorless, odorless gas
air, *picture* A-145
noble gases N-330
periodic table, *table* P-207, *list* P-208

Kshatriya, Hindu of the soldier caste
India I-68

Kt. *see in index* Carat

KT (kiloton), unit of measure for the explosive force of a nuclear weapon N-434

Kuala Lumpur, Malaysia, capital, on Malay Peninsula near w. coast; pop. 937,900 K-307
Asia, *map* A-697
Islam, *picture* I-361
Malaysia M-70

Kuang-hsü (1871–1908), Chinese emperor during whose reign the empress dowager Tz'u-hsi dominated the government C-370

Kuang Wu Ti (ruled AD 25–57), emperor in China's Han Dynasty C-362

Kuan Han-ch'ing (1241?–1320?), Chinese playwright C-389

Kuban' River, n. Caucasus, rises on slopes of Mt. El'brus; flows about 585 mi (940 km) to Sea of Azov; rushing mountain river becomes sluggish stream lower C-232, *map* R-349

Kubasov, Valery N. (born 1935), Soviet cosmonaut, born in Vyazniki, n.e. of Moscow; flight engineer in Soyuz 6, *table* S-348

Kubelik, Jan (1880–1940), Bohemian violinist; father of Rafael Kubelik; popular and brilliant concert virtuoso.

Kubelík, Rafael (born 1914), Czechoslovak conductor and composer, born near Prague; made tour as conductor and piano accompanist for father, Jan Kubelik, 1934–35; chief conductor Czech Philharmonic Orchestra, Prague, 1942–48; musical director Chicago Symphony Orchestra 1950–53, Covent Garden Opera Company, London, 1955–58; chief conductor Bavarian Radio, Munich, 1961–; music director Metropolitan Opera, New York City 1972–74
orchestra, *list* O-579

Kubelka, Peter, motion pictures M-626

Kubelsky, Benjamin. *see in index* Benny, Jack

Kubik, Gail (born 1914), U.S. composer, born in South Coffeyville, Okla.; studied under Piston and Sowerby; chamber music, choral and orchestral works, film scores; won Pulitzer prize 1952.

Kubitschek, Juscelino de Oliveira (1902–76), Brazilian statesman, born in Diamantina in state of Minas Gerais; president of Brazil 1956–60 B-408

Kublai Khan (1215–94), one of greatest, most intelligent, and most cultured of Mongol rulers, grandson of Genghis Khan K-308, C-367
Marco Polo P-441g
Mongol Empire M-535
zoo history Z-466

Kuching, seaport, capital of Sarawak, Malaysia, on Borneo; Sarawak Museum, set in gardens; pop. 37,949
Asia, *map* A-697

Kuder General Interest Survey, guidance and vocational testing, *diagrams* G-304

Kudu, also **koodoo,** one of the largest of African antelopes; white stripe down the back and 8 or 10 vertical stripes descending from it down the sides A-478

Kudzu, or **kudzu vine,** a perennial climber *Pueraria thunbergiana* of the pea family, native to China and Japan; leaves in 3 parts, flowers in purple clusters; in Japan, roots used as starch source and inner bark in cloth; in s. United States, plant used as forage crop, to enrich worn-out land, and to protect against erosion
legume L-118

Kufra Oasis, group of oases in Sahara in s.e. Libya; camels; dates, barley, grapes, olives; caravan trade; pop. 9,530
  Oasis O-454

Kuhio, Prince, in full **Jonah Kuhio Kalanianaole** (1871–1922), Hawaiian statesman, born in Koloa on Kauai; descendant of last independent king of that island; Congressional delegate to U.S. 1903–22; obtained legislation for Hawaiian back-to-the-land movement.

Kuhlmann, Richard von (1873–1948), German diplomat, born in Constantinople; secretary of state for foreign affairs 1917–18, negotiating treaties with U.S.S.R. and Romania; opposition of army high command and Chancellor Hertling caused him to resign.

Kuhn, Bowie (born 1926), U.S. lawyer, born in Takoma Park, Md.; admitted to bar 1951; commissioner of baseball 1969–84.

Kuhn, Richard (1900–1967), Austrian chemist, born in Vienna; awarded 1938 Nobel prize in chemistry for work on carotenoids and vitamins, but declined because of a Nazi decree; received diploma and gold medal after World War II. *see also in index* Nobel Prizewinners, *table*

Kuhn, Walt (1877–1949), U.S. modernist painter, born in New York City; simple, positive design; brilliant often raw color; paintings of women of stage and circus, also of flowers.

Kuibyshev, or **Kuybyshev,** or **Samara,** U.S.S.R., port city on Volga and Samara rivers 525 mi (845 km) s.e. of Moscow; flour milling; large trade; capital of the Soviet Union in World War II; pop. 1,243,000 K-308, *maps* R-344, 349
  dam, *picture* V-383
  Europe, *map* E-360
  world, *map* W-297

Kuiper, Gerard Peter (1905–73), U.S. astronomer, born in The Netherlands; to U.S. 1933, became citizen 1937; with University of Chicago at Yerkes Observatory 1936–60, professor 1943–60, director of Yerkes and McDonald observatories 1947–49 and 1957–60; head Lunar and Planetary Laboratory, University of Arizona, 1960–73; author of books on astronomy P-355, S-254e, b, 254

Kukai. *see in index* Kobo Daishi

Ku K'ai-chih (350?–412), Chinese painter; remarkable expression with minimum detail; sure, rhythmic line; best known for a series of paintings on silk in British Museum, illustrating an essay 'The Admonition of the Instructress in the Palace'.

Kukla, Fran, and Ollie, puppet show on U.S. television, *picture* P-536

Ku Klux Klan, (or The Invisible Empire of the South), U.S. secret terrorist organization K-309
  Reconstruction R-116
  Tennessee T-88
  terror against blacks B-294
  United States U-187

Ku Klux Klan Act (1871), United States K-309

Kukri, a sword S-547, *picture* S-546

Kukui, also called **candle nut,** or **candleberry,** or **lumbang,** or **varnish tree,** tropical tree *Aleurites molluccana*, native to Malay region, found throughout tropics; state tree of Hawaii; fruit contains large seeds (candlenuts) useful in making candles, oil, dyes, paint, gum, food, and medicine
  Hawaii state tree, *picture* H-66
  nuts N-449

Kulaks, well-to-do Russian peasants S-404

Külek Bogazi. *see in index* Cilician Gates

Kumamoto, Japan, city on w. coast of Kyushu Island; textiles, tile; Kumamoto Medical University, school of pharmacy; pop. 488,166, *map* J-75
  Asia, *map* A-697

Kumar, Jainendra (born 1905), Hindu author I-108

Kumara Gupta (died 455? AD), ruler of India G-318

Kuma River, n. Caucasus, U.S.S.R.; flows e. until lost in swamps; reaches Caspian Sea in flood time only; about 360 mi (580 km) long, *maps* R-344, 349

Kumasi (formerly Coomassie), Ghana, city in w. Africa; pop. 260,286 G-139, *map* A-115

Kumina, Jamaican cult J-17

Kumkum, forehead decoration worn by Indian girls and women, except orthodox Hindu widows.

Kun, Béla (1886–1938?), Hungarian leader; captured by Russia in World War I, he became follower of Lenin; organized revolution in Hungary and set up a Soviet rule; overthrown; became member of executive committee, Communist International.

Kunersdorf, Poland, former Prussian village 4 mi (6 km) e. of Frankfurt-an-der-Oder; Prussians defeated by Russians and Austrians 1759 (Seven Years' War); included in Poland since 1945.

Kung, Hsiang-hsi (H.H. Kung) (1881–1967), Chinese leader, born in Shansi; governor, Central Bank of China, 1933–45; vice-president of executive department of national government 1933 and 1939; minister of finance 1933–44. *see also in index* Soong

!Kung, African language of the Khoisan language family A-119

Kung fu, martial art M-160

K'ung-fu-tzu. *see in index* Confucius

Kunin, Madeline, U.S. governor W-276

Kunitz, Stanley Jasspon (born 1905), U.S. poet, educator, and editor; born in Worcester, Mass.; editor of a biographical series on authors; lecturer Columbia University 1963–66, adjunct professor Graduate School of the Arts 1967–; won 1959 Pulitzer prize for 'Selected Poems, 1928–1958'.

Kuniyoshi, Yasuo (1893–1953), U.S. painter and lithographer, born in Okayama, Japan; identified with modernists; to U.S. 1906 D-256

Kunlun Mountains, mountains in China, along n. border of Tibet: highest peak Ulugh Muztagh; 25,340 ft (7,724 m) K-309, C-337
  Asia, *map* A-697
  India, *map* I-86

Kunming, China, capital of Yunnan Province; n.e. terminus Burma Road of World War II; pop. 1,100,000
  Asia, *map* A-697
  world, *map* W-297
  Yunnan Y-440

Kunsthalle, art gallery in Hamburg, West Germany H-20

Kunsthistorisches Museum, Vienna, Austria; established 1891; state control; noted for classical sculpture and antiquities, industrial arts M-663

Kunz, George Frederick (1856–1932), U.S. gem expert, born in New York City; research curator of gems, American Museum of Natural History; kunzite named for him.

Kunzite, a semiprecious stone found in California and Madagascar; phosphorescent after exposure to radium M-436

Kuomintang, Chinese Nationalist party, meaning "The People's Party," based on principles of Dr. Sun Yat-sen C-372
  Chiang Kai-shek C-309
  Hebei H-112
  Manchuria M-94
  Mao Zedong M-111
  Taiwan T-14

Kuprin, Aleksandr Ivanovich (1870–1938), Russian writer of novels, short stories, and sketches; born in Narovchat, near Nizhni Lomov; power undisciplined by formal literary education R-360a

Kura, principal river of Transcaucasus, flowing n.e. and then s.e. into Caspian Sea; 940 mi (1,515 km) long C-232, *maps* R-344, 349

Kurbash, or **courbash,** a whip of heavy hide; term also applied to forced labor under the lash which was outlawed in Egypt under British rule.

Kurdish language I-313, M-395

Kurdistan, mountainous region in s.e. Turkey, n. Iraq, n.w. Iran, and n.e. Syria K-310

Kurds, a Muslim people of Asia Minor K-310
  Iran I-305
  Iraq I-313, 316
  Lebanon L-112
  Turkey T-320, 325

Kure, Japan, naval port on Honshu Island and Inland Sea; shipbuilding; exporting; clothing and sake; pop. 242,655, *map* J-75

Kurelek, William (1927–77), Canadian author and illustrator, born in Whitford, Alta.; wrote and illustrated 'O Toronto', 'Some-one With Me' (autobiography), 'Lumberjack'; Canadian Book of the Year for Children awards for 'A Prairie Boy's Winter' (1974) and 'A Prairie Boy's Summer' (1976).

Kuria Muria Islands, group of five high, rocky islands off s. coast of Arabian Peninsula; area 28 sq mi (72 sq km); British ceded to Oman 1967; pop. about 70
  Asia, *map* A-697

Kuril Islands (or Kurile Islands, or Chishima), stretching n.e. from Hokkaido; 6,000 sq mi (15,500 sq km); name from Russian *kurit* ("to smoke") in allusion to volcanoes; owned by Japan 1875–1945; occupied and annexed by U.S.S.R.; pop. 15,000, *map* R-345
  Asia, *map* A-697
  seal herds S-99
  world, *map* W-297

Kuroki, Tamesada (or Count Tamemoto) (1844–1923), Japanese general and samurai, born in Kagoshima; distinguished in Sino-Japanese War of 1894–95; in Russo-Japanese War of 1904–5 commanded First Army, defeated Russians at Yalu River, and assisted Oyama at Mukden.

Kuropatkin, Alexei Nikolaievich (1848–1925), Russian general; in supreme command in East during Russo-Japanese War, until after battle of Mukden, in which he was defeated; again commanded an army 1916 in World War I; retired 1917.

Kurosawa, Akira (born 1910), Japanese film director ('Rashomon'; 'Kagemusha') D-155
  motion pictures M-623

Kuroshio. *see in index* Japan Current

Kurta, Pakistani shirt P-78

Kurtz, Efrem (born 1900), U.S. conductor, born in St. Petersburg (now Leningrad), Russia; musical director Ballet Russe de Monte Carlo; conductor Kansas City (Mo.) Philharmonic Orchestra 1943–48; became U.S. citizen 1944; conductor Houston (Tex.) Symphony Society 1948–54.

Kuru, disease D-170

Kurumba, a people of the Nilgiri Hills in s. India; live in mud and wattle huts; depend largely on jungle for food.

Kurusu, Saburo (1888?–1954), Japanese diplomat, born in Yokohama; began diplomatic career 1910; ambassador to Germany 1939–40, signed pact with Nazis W-327

Kurzweil Reading Machine (KRM) A-836

Kusch, Polykarp (born 1911), U.S. physicist, born in Blankenburg, Brunswick, Germany; to U.S. 1912, became citizen 1922; professor of physics Columbia University 1949–72, academic vice-president and provost 1969–72; professor University of Texas at Dallas from 1972. *see also in index* Nobel Prizewinners, *table*

Kushiro, Japan, seaport city on Pacific Ocean on s.e. Hokkaido 20 mi (30 km) s.w. of Akkeshi; exports sulfur and lumber; pop. 206,840, *map* J-75
  Asia, *map* A-697

Kuskokwim River, one of chief rivers of Alaska; 550 mi (885 km) to Bering Sea, *maps* N-350, U-94, 39

Kustenja, Romania. *see in index* Constanta

Kut, or **Kut al Imara,** Iraq, a city on Tigris River, 105 mi (170 km) s.e. of Baghdad; railroad terminus; pop. 71,360.

Kutaisi, or **Kutais,** U.S.S.R., city of Georgian Soviet Socialist Republic 120 mi (195 km) n.w. of Tbilisi; coal-mining equipment, chemicals, textiles, leather products; pop. 161,000, *maps* E-360, R-344, 349

Kutani ware, Japanese porcelain made originally from materials found near Kutani-mura, village near Kanazawa, Japan; oldest and best period (1664–1750) widely collected; ware ranges from stoneware to fine porcelain, glazes from green through Indian red and brown.

Kutaradja, or **Koetaradja,** Sumatra, city with seaport (Ule-Lue, or Ulee Lheue) on n.w. tip of island; pop. 53,668.

Kutb-ud-Din (died 1210), a Turki slave who became sultan of Delhi; appointed viceroy of India by Mohammed of Ghor 1192; founded Slave Dynasty in India (1206–88).

Kutch, or **Cutch,** former state in w. India; since 1948 part of Gujarat state; bleak, treeless region with rocky hills; ruled for centuries by independent dynasties that kept it in virtual isolation, *map* I-86. *see also in index* Rann of Kutch
  Asia, *map* A-697

Kutchin, Athabascan-speaking Indian tribe that lives in Yukon Territory, and Alaska, *map* I-136, *table* I-138

Kutchuk-Kainardji, Treaty of (1774), between Turkey and Russia, giving Russia strong position on Black Sea, *table* T-274

Kutenais, or **Kootenas,** two groups of Indians of Kitunahan stock, one living in Montana, the other in British Columbia.

Kuti, Fela Anikulapo, Nigerian singer M-682

Kutztown State College, Kutztown, Pa.; founded 1866; formerly a teachers' college; arts and sciences, education, fine arts; graduate study.

Kuvasz, dog, *picture* D-202

Kuwait, republic in n.e. Arabian Peninsula; area about 7,400 sq mi (19,000 sq km); cap. and seaport, Kuwait; pop. 1,668,400 K-310
  Arabian states A-521, *map* A-522
  Asia, *map* A-697
  first desalinization plant W-93
  flag, *picture* F-167
  petroleum P-229, *picture* M-396
  world, *map* W-297

Kuwait City, Kuwait K-310, *picture* K-311
  Asia, *map* A-697

Kuwait Oil Company K-311

Kuybyshev, U.S.S.R. *see in index* Kuibyshev

Kuybyshev Dam, dam in U.S.S.R., on Volga River, *picture* V-383

Kuznets, Simon (1901–85), U.S. economist, born in Kharkov, Russia; to U.S. 1921; professor University of Pennsylvania 1930–54, Johns Hopkins University 1954–60, Harvard University 1960–71. *see also in index* Nobel Prizewinners, *table*

Kuznetsk Basin, U.S.S.R., basin of Tom' River, Siberia; valuable mineral resources S-189

Kvutzoth, communal colonies in Palestine P-81

Kwajalein, largest atoll in Marshall Islands, in Ralik group; contains Kwajalein Island; occupied by U.S. 1944; pop. 5,469 O-466, *map* P-3. *see also in index* Marshall Islands

Kwakiutl, Indian tribe of Northwest Pacific Coast of North America; subsisted mainly on fishing, *map* I-136, *table* I-139

Kwammu, also **Kwammu Tenno** (738?–805), emperor of Japan 782–805; conquered Ainus; moved capital twice in effort to free government from Buddhist influence K-312

Kwan, Japanese unit of weight, *table* W-141

Kwangju, South Korea, city 40 mi (65 km) n.e. of Mokpo; railroad junction; textile center; Chonnam National University; radio station; historical site; pop. 607,058, *map* K-290
  Asia, *map* A-697

Kwango River, Portuguese **Cuango,** 700 mi (1,150 km) long, rises in Angola and flows n. into Zaire, forming part of border, *map* A-118

Kwangsi Chuang, China. *see in index* Guangxi Zhuangzu

Kwangtung, China. *see in index* Guangdong

Kwanto Plain, lowland in Japan. *see in index* Kanto Plain

Kwan-Yin. *see in index* Kuan Yin

Kwarizmi, al- (780?–850?), Islamic mathematician M-214, *table* M-218

Kwashiokor, disease caused by protein deficiency D-180

KwaZulu, South Africa, nonindependent state for black South Africans D-292

Kweichow. *see in index* Guizhou

Kweiyang. *see in index* Guiyang

Ky, Nguyen Cao. *see in index* Nguyen Cao Ky

Kyakhta, U.S.S.R., city on n. border of Mongolia, about 170 mi (275 km) n. of Ulan Bator; transit point for trade between U.S.S.R. and Mongolia; pop. 15,316, *map* R-345
  Asia, *map* A-697

Kyanite (or cyanite), aluminum silicate; colorless, or blue, white, gray, green, or brown; cut as gem.

Kyd, Thomas (1558–94), English dramatist, born in London; predecessor of Shakespeare
  literary contribution E-267

Kyne, Peter Bernard (1880–1957), U.S. novelist, born in San Francisco, Calif.; clerk general store, lumber broker, reporter; served in Spanish-American War and World War I ('Cappy Ricks', 'The Valley of the Giants', 'The Enchanted Hill').

Kyodo News Service, organization supplying news to Japanese press, radio, and television; founded 1945; headquarters, Tokyo.

Kyogen, Japanese drama J-55

Kyongbok Palace, in Seoul, Korea, *picture* K-279

Kyongju, South Korea, town 38 mi (61 km) e. of Taegu; rail junction; coal mining; tourism; 8th-century cave carvings; capital of Kingdom of Silla 57 BC–AD 935; pop. 108,447, *picture* K-279, *map* K-290

Kyongju temple, temple in Korea, *picture* K-293

Kyoto, or **Heian-kyo,** Japan, former capital; pop. 1,473,065 K-312
  Asia, *map* A-697
  Japan, *map* J-75

Kyprianou, Spyros, (born 1932), president of Cyprus 1977–
  Cyprus government C-634

Kyrie eleison, Greek words, meaning "Lord have mercy upon us," used as prayer in Greek and Roman Catholic churches, and also (translated) in Anglican church.

Kyser, Kay, U.S. bandleader M-684

Kythera, island in Ionian Sea. *see in index* Cerigo

Kyudo, in Japanese archery J-57

Kyushu (also spelled Kiushu), southernmost of four main islands of Japan; area 14,114 sq mi (36,555 sq km); mountainous and volcanic; extensive coal mines; pop. 12,666,000, *map* J-78
  Asia, *map* A-697
  folktale, *picture* S-418d
  world, *map* W-297

Kyzyl-Kum, desert in U.S.S.R. R-324, *maps* R-344

The letter L

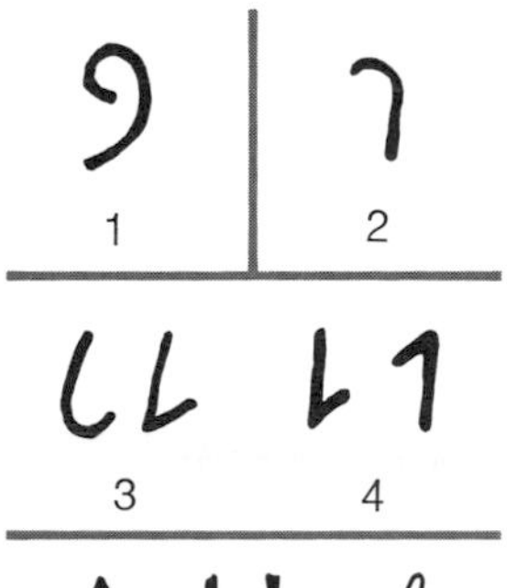

probably started as a picture sign of an oxgoad, as in a very early Semitic writing used about 1500 B.C. on the Sinai Peninsula (1). A similar sign (2), denoting a peasant's crook, is found in earlier Egyptian hieroglyphic writing. About 1000 B.C., in Byblos and other Phoenician and Canaanite centers, the sign was given a linear form (3), the source of all later forms. In the Semitic languages the sign was called *lamedh,* meaning "oxgoad."

The Greeks first gave the sign some unbalanced forms (4) and renamed it *lambda.* Later they formed their sign symmetrically (5). The Romans adopted the earlier Greek forms (6). From Latin the capital letter came unchanged into English.

In late Roman times the small handwritten "l" was developed from the capital by rounding the lines. Later a form with an open loop in the vertical stroke was developed (7).

L

Laaland, Danish island. *see in index* Lolland
Laban, Rudolf von (1879–1958), Hungarian dancer and teacher of dancing, born in Hungary; taught many years in Germany; originated a new system of dance and devised a method of dance notation called Labanotation D-24
Label, description
  clothing C-514
  consumer goods C-687. *see also in index* Packaging
  museums M-660
  zoo Z-461
Label, heraldry, *picture* H-136
Labellum, plant part O-580
Labia, part of the female genital organs S-123
Labná, ancient Mayan city M-235
La Boca, artists' district in Buenos Aires, Argentina A-580
Labor L-2. *see also in index* Industrial Revolution; countries by name; *also* topics beginning with Labor
  apprentice system A-510
  automobile industry D-123
  banks B-64
  business cycle affects B-518
  capitalism C-152
  child labor
    rugmaking R-313
  computer's influence C-626
  convict labor P-505
  division of labor W-200
  economics E-60
  employment. *see also in index* Employment
    East Germany G-119
    Poland P-415
    U.S.S.R. R-328
  employment agency E-205
  Haymarket Riot C-317
  Hispanic Americans H-164
  industry I-192
  inflation's role I-199
  labor and industrial law L-4
  labor movements L-6
    Gompers G-194
  Lassalle's views L-56
  leisure time L-123
  Middle Ages M-387, 393
  migrant labor M-398. *see also in index* Migrant labor
  Molly Maguires M-526
  money M-530
  railway workers R-75, 83, *picture* R-85
  safety S-4
  slavery and serfdom S-212
  Socialism S-234
  strike S-489
  unemployment. *see in index* Unemployment
  United States U-64, 103, U-179, 186, *chart* U-107
    age trends P-448
    Roosevelt, F. D. R-269
    Roosevelt, T. R-284
  vocations, *picture* V-364
  welfare programs W-145
    pensions P-188
    social security S-236
Labor, in childbirth R-151d
Labor, Department of, United States U-163, *list* U-157
Labor and industrial law L-4
  arbitration A-528
  contracts C-693
  industrial health hazards I-175
  labor L-3
  labor movements L-8, 10
  pensions P-188
  social security S-236
  Spain S-356
  United States U-164, 188, 191
    Kennedy K-202
    Roosevelt R-269
  women's rights W-272
Laboratory
  crime, *picture* P-429
  medical
    bioengineering B-210
Laboratory technology, disease diagnosis M-276
Labor Front, Nazi trade union organization in Germany G-123
Labor-Management Relations Act (1947) (or Taft-Hartley Act), United States
  arbitration A-528
  labor and industrial law L-5, 9
  U.S. history U-191
    Taft T-10
    Truman T-298
Labor-Management Services Administration, United States U-164
Labor movements L-6
  Industrial Revolution I-181
  Jones J-140
  labor and industrial law L-4
  Lewis L-142
  Solidarity W-7
Labor party, Great Britain, formed 1906 to represent organized labor and Socialists; cooperated with Liberals, later adopted socialistic program
  Attlee A-758
  Fabian Society F-2
  Socialism S-235
  United Kingdom E-255
  Webbs W-128
Labor Relations Act, National, United States. *see in index* National Labor Relations Act of 1935
Labor Relations Board, National, United States, U-166
Labor Statistics, Bureau of, United States U-164
  employment and unemployment E-207
  promotes safety S-6
Labor unions (or trade unions). *see also in index* Labor movements; *also* names of labor unions and labor leaders
  apprenticeships A-511
  arbitration A-528
  automobile workers D-123
  coal miners C-526
  contracts C-693
  economic minority group M-460
  garment industry G-35
  Industrial Revolution I-181
  labor and industrial law L-4
  lobbying L-276
  migrant workers H-165
  political activities P-434
  railway brotherhoods R-83
  socialism S-234
  Spain S-356
  strike S-489
  United Nations U-26
  United States U-164, U-191
    postal service P-460c
    Roosevelt, F.D. R-271
    Roosevelt, T. R-284
    U.S.S.R. R-330a, 332c
Labouchère, Henry du Pré (1831–1912), English journalist and radical political leader, editor of the weekly *Truth*, noted for exposure of public frauds.
Labouchère, Pierre Antoine (1807–73), French painter, born in Nantes, France; known for paintings of the Reformation
  painting of Calvin, *picture* R-134
Labour Party, Israel I-372
Labrador, a peninsula, most easterly part of the North American mainland; area 625,000 sq mi (1,620,000 sq km); e. triangle of Labrador Peninsula (area 112,826 sq mi; 292,218 sq km); together with Newfoundland Island, forms Province of Newfoundland; pop. 188,339 L-12
  Cabot C-11
  Canada, *map* C-109
  Newfoundland N-163, 167
  North America, *picture* N-350
  Quebec Q-9d
Labrador Current, or **Arctic Current,** cold ocean current along coast of Labrador; carries ice into important shipping lanes
  Canada C-73
Labrador duck, an extinct black-and-white sea duck closely allied to eider duck; ranged north Atlantic coast of North America as far south as Long Island, N.Y.; believed to have bred in Labrador B-271
Labrador ice cap, glacial formation I-7, *map* I-8
Labradorite, gem material J-116
Labrador retriever, dog, *pictures* D-197
Labrador tea, evergreen shrub *Ledum groenlandicum* of heath family; found in swamps of Greenland and Labrador; used for tea.
Labrouste, Henri (1801–75), French architect A-562
La Bruyère, Jean de (1645–96), French essayist, wit, and moralist L-12
  French literature F-395
Labuan, island off n. Borneo; formerly one of Straits Settlements; in 1946 became part of North Borneo (now Sabah), a part of Malaysia since 1963; 35 sq mi (90 sq km); pop. 14,904.
Laburnum (or golden chain), small tree of pea family native to s. Europe; cultivated for showy yellow flowers, glossy foliage; all parts poisonous.
Labyrinth, a name given by Greeks and Romans to buildings, entirely or partly underground, with intricate winding passages A-62
Labyrinthodont, prehistoric amphibian A-461, *picture* A-460
  animal life record, *table* E-24
'Labyrinth of Solitude, The', work by Paz L-71
Lacatan, banana variety B-53
Laccadive Islands, coral islands in Arabian Sea w. of s. India; part of union territory of India, known as Lakshadweep, formerly Laccadive, Minicoy, and Amindivi Islands; pop. 13,109, *map* I-86. *see also in index* Lakshadweep
  Asia, *map* A-697
  world, *map* W-297
Lace, textile L-13, T-139
  needlework N-111
Lace-bark tree, tree of the West Indies *Lagetta lintearia*; inner bark resembles coarse lace; used for collars, frills; also for making whips and rope.
Lacedaemon. *see in index* Laconia
La Ceiba, Honduras, Caribbean port city; ships bananas, hides, fruits; brewery; soap and vegetable oil factories; pop. 49,900, *map* N-350
Lacerta, constellation, *chart* C-681
Lacertilia (or Sauria), suborder of lizards L-274
Lace verbena. *see in index* Zaluzianskya
Lacewing fly. *see in index* Green lacewings
Lacey Act (1900), United States, on mongoose importation E-209
Lachaise, Gaston (1882–1935), U.S. sculptor L-17
  sculpture S-91
La Chaux de Fonds, Switzerland. *see in index* Chaux de Fonds, La
Lachesis, in Greek mythology, one of the three Fates F-44, M-701
Lachine, Que., manufacturing city and summer resort on Lake St. Louis connected with Montreal 6 mi (10 km) n.e. by Lachine Canal; structural steel and other metal products; burned and inhabitants killed by Indians 1689; pop. 44,423, *maps* C-112, Q-11
Lachine Canal, Montreal, Que., on the St. Lawrence River M-571
Lachine Rapids, St. Lawrence River S-20
Lachish, ancient city in s. Palestine, often mentioned in Tell el-Amarna tablets and in Bible; destroyed by Joshua (Bible, Josh. X, 31–3) and assigned to tribe of Judah (Bible, Josh. XV, 39).
Lachlan River, New South Wales, Australia; joins Murrumbidgee River near junction with Murray River; 700 mi (1,150 km) long, *map* A-819
Lachrymal gland, or **Lacrimal,** tear gland E-387, G-153
Lackawanna, N.Y., industrial and railroad city on Lake Erie just s. of Buffalo; pop. 22,701.
Lackland. *see in index* John of England
Laclede, Pierre, or **Pierre Laclede Liguest** (1724–78), North American fur trader and founder of St. Louis, Mo.; born in Lower Pyrenees, France; emigrated to New Orleans 1755 and established a fur trade with Indians of Missouri River area
  St. Louis S-21
  settlement founded M-493
Laclede's Village, old French town on site of St. Louis, Mo. S-22
Lacombe, Albert (1827–1916), Canadian Roman Catholic missionary, born in St. Sulpice, Lower Canada; one of first missionaries sent to Northwest Territories; author of grammar and dictionary of Cree language.
La Condamine, Charles Marie de. *see in index* Condamine, Charles Marie de la
Laconia, or **Lacedaemon,** ancient Greece, s.e. district of Peloponnesus of which Sparta was the capital S-369
Laconia, N.H., resort and industrial city on Winnipesaukee River 28 mi (45 km) n. of Concord in beautiful lake region; knitting machines, shoes, hosiery, needles, ball bearings, skis; pop. 15,575 N-186, *map* N-191
La Coruña, Spain, seaport on n.w. coast; sailing port of the Spanish Armada (1588); repulse of French by British under Sir John Moore in Peninsular War 1809; pop. 200,955, *maps* E-360, S-350
Lacoste, René (nickname the Crocodile) (born 1905), French tennis player and founder of sportswear company
  tennis T-107
Lacquer P-73
  varnish V-267
Lacquerwork, in decorative arts F-456
  China, *picture* C-356
Lacrimal gland. *see in index* Lachrymal gland
La Crosse, Wis., city on Mississippi River 120 mi (195 km) s.e. of St. Paul, Minn.; center of stock-raising and dairying region and tobacco market; heating and air-conditioning equipment, farm machinery, rubber footwear, beverage coolers, beer; University of Wisconsin–La Crosse; Viterbo College; pop. 48,347 W-250, *map* U-41
Lacrosse (or baggataway), sport L-17
Lacrosse, U.S. guided missile, *picture* G-307
Lacteal, any one of lymphatic vessels of intestinal canal.
Lactic acid, the acid formed in sour milk; $C_3H_6O_3$
  fatigue F-45
  fermentation F-55

muscle action R-160
Hopkins H-238
yogurt Y-421
Lactobacillus, a bacterium that makes lactic acid B-15
yogurt Y-421
Lactose (or milk sugar), double (disaccharide) sugar ($C_{12}H_{22}O_{11}$), reducible to galactose and glucose; differs from maltose and sucrose in structure of molecule S-508
carbohydrate C-155
dairy by-product D-7
milk M-414
Lacus Juturnae, fountain in Rome, Italy F-335
Ladanum (or labdanum), a resin obtained from the plants *Cistus ladaniferus* and *Cistus villosus;* used in the manufacture of heavy perfumes.
Ladd, Edwin Fremont (1859–1925), U.S. chemist, born in Starks, Me.; on faculty of North Dakota Agricultural College 1890–1920; U.S. senator 1921–25; pioneer in pure food legislation.
Ladd, George Trumbull (1842–1921), U.S. philosopher, born in Painesville, Ohio; one of first to introduce study of experimental psychology into U.S.; founded Yale University psychological laboratory (translation, Lotze's 'Outlines of Philosophy', 6 vols.).
Ladder
fire fighting F-104
safety measures S-7
spacecraft S-346d
Ladder dredge, machine for digging soil from bottoms of bodies of water D-258, *picture* D-257
Ladder trencher (or ditcher), earth-moving machine D-258
Ladd-Franklin, Christine (1847–1930), U.S. scientist, born in Windsor, Conn.; first woman student at Johns Hopkins University and at universities of Göttingen and Berlin in Germany; distinguished career in mathematics, physics, and psychology; famous for her theory of color perception.
'Ladies' Home Journal', U.S. periodical F-42
magazine and journal M-34
'Ladies' Mercury', magazine M-32
Ladies' sorrel. *see in index* Wood sorrel
Ladies tresses, a wild flower of the genus *Spiranthes* of the orchid family; the flowers are small, white, yellowish- or greenish-white, in twisted spikes
orchid O-580
Ladin. *see in index* Romansh
Ladino, Europeanized Central American person of predominantly Spanish origin. *see also in index* Mestizo
El Salvador E-195
Guatemala G-297
Ladislaus (or László I) (1040–95), saint and king of Hungary; obtained Croatia for Hungary and Christianized it; most beloved of Hungarian kings; canonized 1198; festival June 27 C-779
Ladoga, Lake, largest lake of Europe, in n.w. U.S.S.R.; area about 7,000 sq mi (18,000 sq km) L-19
Europe, *map* E-360
Russia, *maps* R-322, 344, 348
world, *map* W-297
Ladrone Islands. *see in index* Mariana Islands
'Lady Be Good', musical by Gershwin brothers G-135
'Ladybird, ladybird', nursery rhyme N-444
Ladybug (or ladybird, or lady beetle), a small spotted beetle B-138
hibernation H-147
insect, *picture* I-216
scale insects S-52f
citrus fruits C-444
'Lady Chatterly's Lover', work by Lawrence L-98
Ladycliff College, Highland Falls, near West Point, N.Y.; private control; primarily for women; founded 1933; liberal arts and sciences, teacher education.
Lady Day. *see in index* Holiday, Billie
'Lady Elizabeth Delmé and Her Children', painting by Reynolds P-47
Ladyfinger, banana B-53
'Lady Gone Astray, The'. *see in index* 'Traviata, La'
'Lady in the Dark' (1941), musical comedy by Weill M-686
'Lady Jean', painting by Bellows P-61, *picture* P-60
Lady Kim, Korean writer. *see in index* Uiyudang
Lady of the Lake, water fairy and enchantress of Arthurian legend; treacherously imprisoned Merlin in an enchanted tower in the forest of Bréceliande; reared Lancelot in her palace, situated in the middle of an imaginary lake
King Arthur's sword A-655
'Lady of the Lake, The', poem by Scott S-73
'Lady Sings the Blues', movie based on the autobiography of jazz singer Billie Holiday H-202
Ladysmith, South Africa, trade center, and railroad junction in n. Natal; besieged by Boers for 118 days (1899–1900) during Boer War; pop. 22,955, *maps* A-118, S-264
'Lady's Not for Burning, The', play by Fry F-440
Lady's-slipper, a plant of the orchid family
Minnesota's state flower, *pictures* M-448, S-427d
orchid O-580
Prince Edward Island's emblem, *picture* P-497
skin irritant P-409
'Lady with the Unicorn, The', medieval story A-458
Lae, New Guinea, port on e. coast; capital of Territory of New Guinea 1941–42; occupied by Japanese 1942–43; reoccupied by Allies Sept. 1943; pop. 4,146, *map* P-3
Laënnec, René (full name René Théophile Hyacinthe Laënnec) (1781–1826), French physician L-19
medicine M-284
Laertes, in Greek mythology, father of Odysseus H-224
Laestrygones, Greek mythology, cannibals H-223
La Farge, John (1835–1910), U.S. painter, mural decorator, and designer of first stained glass made in U.S.; born in New York City; grandfather of Oliver La Farge; exercised great influence on U.S. art (lunettes, Supreme Court room, Minnesota State Capitol; 'Battle Window', Memorial Hall, Harvard University).
La Farge, Oliver Hazard Perry (1901–63), U.S. writer, anthropologist; born in New York City, grandson of John La Farge; made archaeological and ethnological expeditions to Arizona for Harvard University and to Guatemala and Mexico for Tulane University; wrote with intimate knowledge and understanding of the Indians ('Laughing Boy', novel, won Pulitzer prize 1930; 'All the Young Men', 'A Pause in the Desert', short stories; 'Cochise of Arizona', biography; 'A Pictorial History of the American Indian'; 'Santa Fe', local history).
Lafayette (full name Marie-Joseph-Paul-Yves-Roch-Gilbert du Motier) (1757–1834), French general and patriot L-19
American Revolution R-173
De Kalb D-67
French Revolution F-401
Lafayette, George Washington Motier de (1779–1849), son of Lafayette; aide-de-camp to General Grouchy.
LaFayette, Marie Madeleine, comtesse de (1634–93), French novelist, born in Paris; her masterpiece, 'La Princesse de Clèves', is first modern novel of sentiment in which story's interest depends not on the incident but on the character of persons involved F-395
Lafayette, Calif., city 28 mi (45 km) n.e. of Berkeley; chiefly residential; settled 1834, incorporated 1968; pop. 20,879.
Lafayette, Ind., city on Wabash River about 60 mi (95 km) n.w. of Indianapolis; aluminum products, prefabricated houses, gears, sponge rubber, meters; railroad shops; Purdue University at West Lafayette; pop. 43,011, *map* I-102
Lafayette, La., city about 52 mi (84 km) s.w. of Baton Rouge; railroad division point; agricultural and oil center; food products, aluminum products; pop. 81,961.
'Lafayette', U.S. submarine, *picture* S-500
Lafayette class, category of U.S. submarines, *picture* S-496
Lafayette College, Easton, Pa.; Presbyterian; formerly for men, women admitted 1970; opened 1832 (chartered 1826); arts and sciences, education, engineering, international affairs.
Lafayette Escadrille, World War I French squadron made up of U.S. volunteers W-309
Lafayette Square, in Washington, D.C. public park north of the White House; contains statues of Generals Andrew Jackson, Lafayette, Kosciusko, and Steuben.
La Fère, France, town on Oise River, 15 mi (25 km) n.w. of Laon; scene of fighting in World Wars I and II; pop. 3,095.
Lafitte, Jean (1780?–1826?), U.S. pirate, slave trader, and smuggler L-20
Jackson J-7
La Follette, Philip Fox (1897–1965), U.S. lawyer and political leader, born in Madison, Wis.; son of Robert Marion La Follette; Progressive Republican; governor of Wisconsin 1931–33, 1935–39.
La Follette, Robert M. (1855–1925), U.S. political leader L-20
Insurgent leader T-9
Progressives P-434, *chart* P-494
Seamen's Act S-173
Statuary Hall, *table* S-437b
Wisconsin W-253
La Follette, Robert Marion, Jr. (1895–1953), political leader, born in Madison, Wis.; son of Robert Marion La Follette; Progressive Republican; U.S. senator from Wisconsin 1925–47; committed suicide W-254
La Fontaine, Henri (1854–1943), Belgian politician, born in Brussels; prolific writer on international arbitration.
La Fontaine, Jean de (1621–95), French storyteller L-21
fables F-3
Lafontaine, Sir Louis Hippolyte (1807–64), Canadian jurist and statesman, premier 1842–44 and 1848–51; chief justice of Lower Canada 1853–64 C-98
Baldwin B-24
Laforet, Carmen (born 1921), Spanish novelist, born in Barcelona S-366, *picture* S-367
Laforgue, Jules (1860–87), French symbolist poet, born in Montevideo, Uruguay; one of first to write modern free verse.
LAFTA (Latin American Free Trade Association), Latin American common market L-65
Lagado, capital of Balnibarbi in 'Gulliver's Travels'; here a celebrated Academy of Projectors engages in extracting sunbeams from cucumbers, in converting ice into gunpowder, and in similar ridiculous ventures.
Lagan, sunken cargo with buoy F-212
Lagash, ancient city-state in Babylonia, one of oldest centers of Sumerian civilization; on site of present Telloh, Iraq; reached peak about 3000 BC B-7, *map* B-4
Lager beer, alcoholic beverage B-132
Lagerkvist, Pär (1891–1974), Swedish poet, playwright, and novelist L-21
Lagerlöf, Selma (1858–1940), Swedish writer L-21. *see also in index* Nobel Prizewinners, *table*
storytelling S-472
'The Wonderful Adventures of Nils' R-111a
Lago Argentino, glacial valley, Argentina A-576
Lagomorpha, order of gnawing animals that differ from rodents in having 4 upper cutting teeth (incisors) instead of 2; includes hares, rabbits, and pikas.
mammal, *table* M-80
Lagoon, a pool or lake, especially one connected with the sea P-13
Lagos, a region (formerly province) of s. Nigeria; in w. Africa; 27,000 sq mi (70,000 sq km); low marshy coast, with countless lagoons; forested interior yields palm oil and kernels, mahogany, rubber; chief cities Ibadan (with surrounding suburban farm district; pop. 459,196) and Lagos, *map* A-118
Lagos, Nigeria, capital and chief port, in s.w.; pop. 1,404,000 L-22
Africa A-119
Nigeria N-310
world, *map* W-297
Lagrange, Joseph-Louis (1736–1813), French mathematician L-22
electricity E-161
mathematics M-215
mechanics M-269
La Grange, Ga., industrial city and trade center, 62 mi (100 km) s.w. of Atlanta; textiles, lumber products; La Grange College; pop. 24,204, *map* U-41
La Grange, Ill., village 14 mi (22 km) s.w. of Chicago, named for Lafayette's home in France; nearby are diesel locomotive plant, aluminum rolling mill, and factory making parts of automobile bodies; pop. 15,681, *map* I-52
La Grange College, La Grange, Ga.; Methodist; chartered 1831; opened 1832; arts and sciences, teacher education; graduate studies; quarter system.
La Grange Park, Ill., village 14 mi (22 km) s.w. of Chicago; electronic components, plastic products; pop. 13,359, *map* I-52
La Granja, Spain. *see in index* San Ildefonso
Lagting, part of the Norwegian parliament N-393
La Guaira, Venezuela, seaport for Caracas, on Caribbean Sea; artificial inner harbor; pop. 20,681 V-275, *map* S-298
La Guardia, Fiorello (full name Fiorello Henry La Guardia, nickname Little Flower) (1882–1947), U.S. politician L-22
New York City N-279
La Guma, Alex (1925–85), South African writer L-23
African literature A-123
Laguna (Spanish "lagoon"), pueblo 42 mi (68 km) w. of Albuquerque, N.M.; founded 1699; Laguna people belong to the Keresan language group of Pueblo Indians; pop. 4,233.
Laguna Beach, Calif., scenic city on Pacific Ocean about 45 mi (70 km) s.e. of Los Angeles; pop. 17,860, *picture* U-88
Laguna de Bay, largest lake in Philippines, s.e. of Manila; 344 sq mi (891 sq km) P-256, 259
Laguna Project, Mexico M-332
La Habra, Calif., city 17 mi (27 km) s.e. of Los Angeles; electronic components, metal products, processed foods, chemicals; pop. 45,232.
Lahaina, Hawaii, city on w. coast of Maui; exports sugar; first white settlement of Hawaii was here; capital 1810–45; pop. 3,718.
Lahn River, river in West Germany, after s.w. course of 135 mi (215 km) joins Rhine opposite Coblenz, *map* G-131
La Hogue, battle of, fought 1692 near n.e. extremity of peninsula of Cotentin, France; English and Dutch fleets under Admiral Russell defeated French fleet under Tourville.
Lahore, Pakistan, capital of Punjab Province, near Ravi River, about 270 mi (435 km) n.w. of New Delhi, India; transportation center; silk and cotton cloths, carpets, vegetable oils; Punjab University; pop. 2,922,000 L-23
Asia, *map* A-697
world, *map* W-297
Laibach, Yugoslavia. *see in index* Ljubljana
Laid paper, paper marked with parallel lines S-405
L'Aiglon, poetic name meaning "eaglet" given by Victor Hugo to duke of Reichstadt, son of Napoleon I and Marie Louise; subject of play by Rostand.
Laika, Soviet dog, first animal to orbit earth S-345, *table* S-344
dogs' history D-193

Laird, Melvin Robert (born 1922), U.S. public official, born in Omaha, Neb.; to Marshfield, Wis., at early age; member Wisconsin state Senate 1946–52; Republican congressman from Wisconsin 1953–69; U.S. secretary of defense 1969–73; chief adviser on domestic affairs 1973–74 N-326

Laissez-faire (let it be), the 18th-century (French) way of saying "less government in business"; in contemporary use means unrestricted industrial and commercial competition C-152. *see also in index* Capitalism
- Industrial Revolution I-181
- international trade I-271
- Socialism rejects S-233
- United Kingdom E-251

Laius, in Greek mythology; father of Oedipus O-493

Lajoie, Napoleon (nickname Larry) (1875–1959), U.S. baseball second baseman, born in Woonsocket, R.I.; second baseman chiefly Philadelphia, N.L., 1896–1900, and Cleveland, A.L., 1901–14; in 1901, batted .422, highest in A.L. history; lifetime average .339 B-93

La Jolla, Calif., community in city of San Diego; Scripps Institution of Oceanography; cliffs, caves, and scenic stretches of ocean beach attract many tourists.

La Jonquière, Jacques Pierre Taffanel, marquis de (1680–1753), French naval officer, born near Albi in s. France; fought numerous engagements against British; governor of New France (Canada) 1749–53.

La Junta, Colo., city on Arkansas River 60 mi (100 km) s.e. of Pueblo; railroad shops, food processing, livestock sales center; mobile homes; pop. 8,338, *picture* C-577, *map* C-582

Lake, Simon (1866–1945), U.S. naval architect and mechanical engineer, born in Pleasantville, N.J.; inventor of even-keel type of submarine S-495b

Lake L-24. For list of greatest lakes, *see table* following. *see also in index* names of individual lakes, as Erie, Lake
- acid rain pollution A-19
- pollution P-441c, *diagram* P-441d
- river R-210
- salt
  - potassium salts P-465
  - Tunisia T-308
- water W-89, 92

Lake, asphalt A-702

Lake Charles, La., port city in s.w. part of state, on Lake Charles, on direct channel to Gulf of Mexico; oil-refinery products, chemicals, synthetic rubber, wood products; meat-packing, rice milling; McNeese State University; pop. 75,226 L-310, *map* L-323

Lake Compounce, amusement park, Bristol, Conn. A-385

Lake District, n.w. England; has all principal English lakes E-229, *picture* E-231

Lake dwellers, Stone Age people who built huts on pile foundations along the shores of lakes S-544
- shelter S-157

Lake Erie, battle of (1813) W-31
- Currier depicts, *picture* N-91
- famous ships S-177h
- Perry P-209
- warfare, *list* W-15

Lake Erie College, Painesville, Ohio; private control; for women; chartered 1856; opened 1859; arts and sciences, fine arts; coeducational division Garfield Senior College offers liberal arts, business, education.

Lake Forest, Ill., residential city on Lake Michigan, 30 mi (50 km) n. of Chicago; Barat College; Lake Forest College; pop. 15,245, *map* I-52

Lake Forest College, Lake Forest, Ill.; private control, Presbyterian related; founded 1857; arts and sciences, teacher education; trimesters.

Lake Geneva, Wis., city in s.e. part of state, on Lake Geneva, 40 mi (65 km) s.w. of Milwaukee; resort; Yerkes Observatory of University of Chicago, 6 mi (10 km) w. of city; pop. 5,607.

Lake harbor (or canal harbor) H-34

Lake herring (or ciscoe), fish *Coregonus artedi* of the family Salmonidae W-195

Lakehurst, N.J., borough about 55 mi (90 km) s. of New York City; pop. 2,908.

Lake Jackson, Tex., city 50 mi (80 km) s. of Houston; metal products, store fixtures; dairy and fruit farms; pop. 19,102.

Lakeland, Fla., city about 30 mi (50 km) e. of Tampa; 12 lakes, resort center; citrus fruit, food-processing, machinery, tile products; phosphate mines; pop. 47,406, *map* U-41
- Florida Southern College, *picture* U-207

Lakeland College, near Sheboygan, Wis.; United Church of Christ; founded 1862; liberal arts, business administration, education, medical technology, music, science.

Lakeland terrier, dog, *picture* D-204

Lake Mead National Recreation Area, Ariz. and Nev. N-134, *picture* N-142
- Colorado C-585

Lake Nasser, reservoir, Egypt A-732

'Lake of Palms, The', work by Dutt I-108

Lake of the Woods, an island-dotted body of water of n. Minnesota and adjacent parts of Ontario; 1,485 sq mi (3,845 sq km); 105 mi (170 km) long, *map* U-70. *see also in index* Northwest Angle
- Minnesota M-440, *picture* M-451
- muskellunge fishing P-326

Lake Oswego, Ore., city 8 mi (13 km) s. of Portland; cement, infant's wear, wood products; incorporated 1918; pop. 14,573.

Lake Placid, N.Y., village at s. end of Lake Placid (about 4 mi [6 km] long and 1/2 mi [1 km] wide); a famous winter and summer resort in Adirondack Mts.; hosted 1980 winter Olympics; nearby is the grave of John Brown, the abolitionist; pop. 2,490
- Adirondack Mountains A-44
- bobsled run S-216
- New York N-245, *picture* N-262

Lake Plains, geographical region, U.S.
- Iowa I-88, *map* I-89
- Michigan M-355
- Wisconsin W-249

Lake Poets, Coleridge, Southey, and Wordsworth; lived in Lake District of England and expressed similar poetic ideals C-546

Lake Regillus, battle of (496 BC) R-242

Lake St. Marys (or Grand Lake), largest man-made lake within Ohio O-498

Lake Success, Long Island, N.Y.; pop. 3,254 U-22

Lake Superior State College, Sault Sainte Marie, Mich; founded 1946; arts and social sciences, science and technology; quarter system.

Lake trout, fish *Salvelinus namaycush* of the family Salmonidae T-291
- lamprey as enemy P-114

Lakeview, Mich., community 38 mi (61 km) n.e. of Grand Rapids; farm produce; pop. 1,139.

Lake Washington Floating Bridge, Wash. S-103, *map* S-103b

Lake Washington Ship Canal, Wash. S-103, *map* S-103b

Lake whitefish (or humpback whitefish), fish *Coregonus clupeaformis* of the family Salmonidae W-195

Lakewood, Calif., residential and commercial city 13 mi (21 km) s.e. of Los Angeles; incorporated 1954; annual Pan-American festival; pop. 74,654.

Lakewood, Colo., residential city w. of Denver; artificial kidneys, aerospace equipment; Camp George West Military Reservation; pop. 112,860.

Lakewood, N.J., community 19 mi (30 km) s.w. of Long Branch; plastics, cosmetics, woodwork; winter resort; pop. 17,874.

Lakewood, Ohio, city on Lake Erie, just w. of Cleveland; originally East Rockport, took present name 1889; pop. 61,963.

Lake Worth, Fla., city 9 mi (14 km) s. of Palm Beach, on Lake Worth, which opens into the Atlantic; resort; incorporated 1913; pop. 27,048.

Lakhemaa National Park, park in Soviet Union N-27

Lakshadweep (or Laccadive, Minicoy, and Amindivi Islands), union territory, India; islands and coral reefs; 11 sq mi (28 sq km); grain, bananas, copra, fisheries; pop. 31,810, *map* I-83

Lalande, Saint Jean de (died 1646), Roman Catholic martyr; missionary in Canada and New York; companion of Father Jogues; murdered by Mohawks at Ossernenon, N.Y.; canonized 1930; feasts celebrated Sept. 26 and March 16 (by Jesuits).

Lalande, Joseph Jérôme Le Français de (1732–1807), French astronomer, born in Bourg-en-Bresse, France; professor Collège de France, director Paris observatory; popularized astronomy; established annual Prix Lalande for most useful work on astronomy.

Lalemant, Gabriel (1610–49), Canadian saint and Jesuit missionary, born in Paris, France; came to Canada 1646; worked with Father Brébeuf among the Hurons and was killed by the Iroquois; canonized 1930.

Lalique, René (1860–1945), French jeweler, born in Ay,

LARGEST LAKES OF THE WORLD

Lake	Location	Area sq mi	Area sq km	Elevation Above Sea Level ft	Elevation Above Sea Level m	Maximum Depth ft	Maximum Depth m
Aral Sea	Soviet Union	25,000	64,700	174	53	226	69
Baikal	Soviet Union	12,160	31,494	1,486	453	5,315	1,620
Balkhash	Soviet Union	7,300	18,900	1,115	340	85	26
Caspian Sea	Soviet Union, Iran	143,000	370,000	−94	−29	3,360	1,024
Chad	Chad, Cameroon, Nigeria, Niger	9,950	25,770	922	281	23	7
Chelan	United States	55	142	1,096	334	1,605	489
Crater	United States	21	54	6,176	1,882	1,932	589
Dead Sea	Israel, Jordan	405	1,049	−1,316	−401	1,300	400
Erie	United States, Canada	9,910	25,670	570	174	210	64
Great Bear	Canada	12,275	31,792	512	156	1,356	413
Great Salt	United States	2,000	5,180	4,200	1,280	35	11
Great Slave	Canada	11,170	28,930	512	156	2,015	614
Huron	United States, Canada	23,100	59,830	579	176	750	229
Ladoga	Soviet Union	6,826	17,678	55	17	754	230
Michigan	United States	22,300	57,760	579	176	923	281
Nyasa	Malawi, Tanzania, Mozambique	11,430	29,604	1,550	472	2,310	704
Ontario	United States, Canada	7,550	19,550	245	75	802	244
Rudolph	Kenya, Ethiopia	2,473	6,405	1,230	375	240	73
Superior	United States, Canada	31,700	82,100	600	183	1,333	406
Tanganyika	Tanzania, Zambia, Zaire, Burundi	12,700	32,890	2,534	772	4,710	1,436
Titicaca	Peru, Bolivia	3,200	8,290	12,500	3,810	920	280
Victoria	Kenya, Uganda, Tanzania	26,828	69,484	3,720	1,134	270	82
Winnipeg	Canada	9,465	24,514	713	217	204	62

near Reims; famous for carving in jewels and glass E-208
'Lalla Rookh', Oriental poem by Thomas Moore; an Indian princess, on her way to Sultan Aliris, her betrothed, is entertained by a Persian poet, with whom she falls in love; is later overjoyed to find that the poet was her betrothed in disguise.
'L'Allegro', ("the happy man"), poem by John Milton; companion poem of 'Il Penseroso'; describes quiet pleasures of a contented man.
Lalo, Edouard (1823–92), French composer, born in Lille, France ('Le Roi d'Ys', opera; 'Symphonie Espagnole', 'Norwegian Rhapsody', orchestral works).
La Malbaie (also called Murray Bay), Que., town on St. Lawrence River at mouth of Malbaie River 77 mi (124 km) n.e. of Quebec (city); summer resort; pop. 4,307, *map* Q-11
La Mama Experimental Theatre Club, forum for creating and performing new plays A-363
Lamaism, religion of Tibet and Mongolia M-537
Lamanites, Mormon religious history M-583
Lamar, Lucius Quintus Cincinnatus (1825–93), U.S. jurist and statesman, born in Putnam County, Ga.; drafted Mississippi ordinance of secession; U.S. senator 1877–85; secretary of interior 1885–88; justice U.S. Supreme Court 1888–93; helped reconciliation between North and South after Civil War.
Lamar, Mirabeau Buonaparte (1798–1859), U.S. soldier, born in Louisville, Ga.; participated in Texas revolution and distinguished self at San Jacinto, president Texas Republic 1838–41; major general Mexican War; U.S. minister to Argentina, Nicaragua, Costa Rica.
Lamarck, Jean-Baptiste (full name Jean-Baptiste de Monet Lamarck) (1744–1829), French naturalist L-25
- Darwin D-38
- evolution E-366
- genetics G-52
- heredity H-140

La Marque, Tex., city s.w. of Texas City; chiefly residential; oil production and truck farming; established in 1860s, named 1890; pop. 15,372.
Lamartine, Alphonse de (1790–1869), French poet, historian, and statesman L-25
- French literature F-396

Lamar University, Beaumont, Tex.; established 1923 as junior college; became state-supported senior college 1951; liberal arts, business, education, engineering, fine and applied arts, sciences, vocational training; graduate school.
La Matanza, Argentina, suburb of Buenos Aires; pop. 402,642, *map* S-299
La Mauricie National Park, Que. Q-9h
Lamb, Charles (pseudonym Elia) (1775–1834), English essayist L-25
- book annotations B-362
- essay E-306
- literary contribution E-274
- Shakespeare S-140
- storytelling S-466

Lamb, Mary (1764–1847), English writer, sister of Charles Lamb L-26
- Shakespeare S-140

Lamb, William. *see in index* Melbourne, Viscount
Lamb, Willis Eugene, Jr. (born 1913), U.S. physicist, born in Los Angeles, Calif.; professor of physics Stanford University 1951–56, Oxford University 1956–62, and Yale University after 1962.
Lamb, a young sheep S-146
- farming F-29
- furs, *table* F-465
- meat M-246
  - industry M-250

Lamballe, Marie Thérèse de (1749–92), French princess, born in Turin, Italy; friend of Marie Antoinette; killed by revolutionists; her head carried past queen's prison windows.
Lambaréné, Gabon, town on Ogooué River 95 mi (155 km) s.e. of Libreville; Albert Schweitzer's medical center; pop. 3,750 G-2
- Africa, *map* A-118
- Schweitzer S-56

Lambeau, Earl Louis (nickname Curly) (1898–1965), U.S. football halfback and coach, born in Green Bay, Wis.; founded Green Bay Packers 1919, halfback and head coach 1919–49 F-298
Lambert, Johann Heinrich (1728–77), German physicist, mathematician, astronomer, and philosopher; born in Mulhouse, Alsace; made important contributions to mathematical theory; measured intensity and absorption of light (Lambert, unit of intensity, named for him).
Lambert, Louis. *see in index* Gilmore, Patrick S.
Lambert, Richard Stanton (born 1894), Canadian educator and writer, born in London, England; promoted educational and cultural films and radio broadcasts; books for children include 'Franklin of the Arctic' (Canadian Book of the Year for Children award 1950) and 'The Adventure of Canadian Painting'; also author of books for adults.
Lambert charts, navigation N-69
Lambeth, baron of. *see in index* Davidson, Randall Thomas; Fisher, Geoffrey Francis
Lambeth, borough of Greater London, England; pop. 325,070, *map* L-287
Lambeth Conference, Anglican Communion church council C-411
Lambeth Council (1888), defined essential positions of Anglican Church in hope of reconciliation with other Christian denominations A-417
Lambeth Palace, London, England; begun 1207; heavily damaged by bombing 1940–41 L-294
Lambing Flat, New South Wales, Australia A-785
Lambkill (or sheep laurel), evergreen shrub of heath family; grows to 3 ft (1 m); the flowers, which are purple or crimson, are arranged in flat-topped clusters P-409
- laurel L-88

Lambrequin. *see in index* Mantling
Lamb's-ears a perennial plant *Stachys lanata* of the mint family, native to w. Asia; grows to 18 in. (46 cm), entire plant white, woolly, with oblong leaves and spikes of tiny, tubular, purple flowers.
Lambskin L-108
- furs, *table* F-463

Lamb's lettuce. *see in index* Corn salad
Lamb's quarters (or goosefoot), an annual herb *Chenopodium album* of the goosefoot family with clusters of small greenish flowers and leaves shaped like the foot of a goose; although considered a pest, delicious greens may be made from it.
Lamb's wool W-288
Lambton, John George. *see in index* Durham, John George Lambton, first earl of
Lambuth College, Jackson, Tenn.; affiliated with United Methodist church; established 1843; arts and sciences and education.
Lamb vulture V-388
Lamé, a fabric made of any of various fibers combined with tinsel threads, often of silver or gold; most frequently used for evening wear; also trade name for metallic yarns.
'Lamech, Book of' (or 'Scroll of the Apocryphal Genesis'), Dead Sea scroll D-46
Lame Duck amendment, United States U-146, 153
'Lamentation', drawing by Dürer D-253, *picture* D-254
Lamentations, book of Bible's Old Testament traditionally ascribed to Jeremiah; comprises five dirges bewailing the destruction of Jerusalem B-182
Lamenting bird. *see in index* Limpkin
Lamer, Antonio (born 1933), Canadian jurist, born in Montreal, Que.; justice Superior Court of Quebec 1969–78, Quebec Court of Appeal 1978–80; justice Supreme Court of Canada 1980–.
La Mesa, Calif., residential city 8 mi (13 km) n.e. of San Diego; citrus fruit, avocados, poultry; incorporated 1912; pop. 50,342.
Lamesa, Tex., city 57 mi (92 km) s. of Lubbock; cotton and other farming, ranching; poultry; oil fields; cotton gins; garments; pop. 11,790.
Lamia, in Greek mythology, a beautiful vampire; in John Keats's poem 'Lamia', a serpent that assumes human form to win a man's love.
Laminar flow, air or liquid flowing in layers instead of dispersing
- hydraulics H-339

Laminar Flow Control (LFC), in aerodynamics A-80
- airplane A-180

Laminated fabric, material consisting of two or more layers of goods put together with adhesive plastic, rubber, or other joining substance; term also applies to fabric joined to plastic sheet, as goods bonded to synthetic foam; used for women's dresses and coats.
Laminating, arranging in thin layers (laminae)
- forest products F-316
- glass G-155
- lumber L-332, *picture* L-334
- plastics P-383
- plywood P-397

La Mirada, Calif., city located on freeway 17 mi (27 km) s.e. of Los Angeles; chiefly residential; Biola College; governed by city administrator system; pop. 40,986.
Lammergeier V-388
Lamming, George (born 1927), West Indian writer, born in Barbados; contributed to folk-dialect literature ('In the Castle of My Skin'; 'Natives of My Person') C-167
Lamoille River, rises in n. Vermont near Hardwick; cuts w. through Green Mts.; flows into Lake Champlain; dam forms Lake Lamoille at Morrisville, *maps* V-286, 301
Lamon, Ward Hill (1828–93), law partner, secretary, and biographer of Abraham Lincoln; born in Frederick County, Va.; served as marshal of District of Columbia 1861–65.
Lamona, a breed of poultry P-482
Lamont, Robert Patterson (1867–1948), U.S. secretary of commerce under President Hoover; born in Detroit, Mich.; engineer and manufacturer; president American Steel Foundries 1912–29.
La Motte-Fouqué, Friedrich Heinrich Karl, baron de (1777–1843), German romantic poet and novelist, born in Brandenburg; extremely popular in early 19th century G-109
Lamour, Dorothy (born 1914), U.S. actress H-237
L'Amour, Louis (originally Louis Dearborn LaMoore, also known as Tex Burns) (born 1908?), U.S. writer L-26
- western W-152

Lamp L-205. *see also in index* Lighting
- industrial design, *picture* I-174
- mercury vapor M-304
- oil P-232
- pottery as base, *picture* P-479
- signaling S-194
- sodium vapor lamps S-247
- stereopticon S-444
- tungsten T-307

Lampblack. *see in index* Carbon black
Lamp-eyed fish, a deep-sea fish having an organ below each eye in which bacteria live; the bacteria secrete a luminous chemical; the fish may draw a lid over the organ at will
Lampman, Archibald (1861–99), Canadian poet, born in Morpeth, Ont. C-121, *picture* C-122
Lamprey, fish L-26
- fish F-132
- Great Lakes G-248, P-114
- prehistoric animals A-461

Lampsacus, ancient Greek city of Mysia, Asia Minor, on Hellespont, opposite Gallipoli; settled by Ionian Greeks (654); known for its wines; center of worship of fertility god Priapus.
Lamp shell, bivalve S-151
Lampworker, glass manufacture G-159
Län, administrative district in Sweden S-526
Lana, Francesco de, Italian monk A-200
Lanai, island of Hawaii; 140 sq mi (361 sq km); 18 mi (29 km) long, 10 mi (16 km) wide; highest point 3,400 ft (1,035 m); pineapple plantations since 1922; previously pastureland; pop. 2,119 H-59, *map* H-58
- Pacific Ocean, *map* P-3

Lanao, Lake, second largest lake in Philippines, on island of Mindanao; 134 sq mi (347 sq km) P-259, 255d, 256
Lancashire (or Lancaster), county of n.w. England; 1,175 sq mi (3,043 sq km); cap. Lancaster; iron and coal mines; textiles, machinery; pop. 5,129,416, *map* U-18a
- Liverpool L-261
- Manchester M-92

Lancaster, John of Gaunt, duke of. *see in index* John of Gaunt
Lancaster, Calif., community 45 mi (72 km) n.e. of Los Angeles; in Antelope Valley region of Mojave Desert; cotton, citrus fruits, nuts; aircraft; pop. 48,027.
Lancaster, England, capital of Lancashire, on Lune River, 7 mi (11 km) from sea; pop. 48,170.
Lancaster, N.B. *see in index* Saint John
Lancaster, N.Y., village 11 mi (18 km) e. of Buffalo; in dairying area; stone quarries, glass products; settled 1810, incorporated 1849; pop. 13,056.
Lancaster, Ohio, city on Hocking River, 27 mi (43 km) s.e. of Columbus; glassware, machinery, boiler equipment, shoes, foundry products; birthplace of Gen. William Tecumseh Sherman; state industrial school for boys nearby; pop. 34,953.
Lancaster, Pa., city 34 mi (55 km) s.e. of Harrisburg; pop. 54,725 P-172
- Stevens S-445

'Lancaster', British military aircraft W-333
Lancaster, House of, famous English royal family, *table* R-297. *see also in index* Roses, Wars of the
- English history E-243
- Henry IV H-129
- rulers. *see in index* England, *table* of kings and queens
- Tudor, House of T-304

Lancaster Turnpike, historical road in United States
- Pennsylvania, *picture* P-175
- roads R-215, *map* R-219
- transportation T-261

Lance, in metalworking I-341
Lance corporal, U.S. military rank, *picture* U-9
Lancelet. *see in index* Amphioxus
Lancelot (or Lancelot of the Lake), Arthurian legend, bravest and most famous of the Knights of the Round Table; outstanding figure in Tennyson's 'Idylls of the King' R-299a
- Arthurian legend A-655

Lancers, dance, a type of quadrille; introduced in 19th century; danced by 8 or 16 couples; also its music.
Lancewood, name given to several trees of family *Annonaceae* native to West Indies and Guiana, and to their highly pliable and tough even-grained wood, which is used for fishing rods and for other articles requiring flexibility and strength.
Lanchow, China, capital of Kansu Province; petroleum refining; oil-field equipment, chemicals; pop. 732,000.
Lanciani, Rodolfo (1846–1929), Italian archaeologist, born in Rome; professor ancient topography University of Rome; made important discoveries at Ostia, Tivoli, Rome ('Ancient and Modern Rome').
Lancret, Nicolas (1690–1743), French painter, born in Paris; greatly influenced by Jean Antoine Watteau; portrayals of French society.

Land, Edwin H. (full name Edwin Herbert Land) (born 1909), U.S. inventor and corporation executive L-26
color experiments C-562
photography P-298
Land, Emory Scott (1879–1971), U.S. Navy officer, born in Canon City, Colo.; chairman U.S. Maritime Commission 1938–46; chief of War Shipping Administration 1942–46; president Air Transport Association of America 1946–53.
Land. *see also in index* Agriculture; Land grant; Land, public; Land tenure
ancient civilizations A-403
Aztec organization A-892
climate control C-497
earth E-16
oceanography O-486
world W-296
frontier movements F-418
homestead P-340
land use L-28
speculation P-335a
surveying S-520
U.S. farmlands U-104
Land, part of videodisc V-314
Land, public
ancient Rome R-244
government use L-29
pioneer movement P-340
railroad land grant R-74
Roosevelt R-285
surveying methods S-520
Taft T-8
Landau, Lev Davidovich (1908–68), Soviet physicist L-27
Landau, Mark Aleksandrovich. *see in index* Aldanov, Mark
Landau, type of carriage W-3
Land Between the Lakes, recreational site on Tennessee-Kentucky border T-102
Land breeze, winds W-220, *diagram* W-221
Lander, Richard Lemon (1804–34) and **John Lander** (1807–39), English explorers, were brothers born in Cornwall; determined course of Niger River 1830 and published journals.
Länder, political units or states in West Germany G-120
Lander, Wyo., town 120 mi (195 km) w. of Casper on Popo Agie River; dairy farming, timber, stock raising, oil and coal mining; popular resort; nearby Wind River Indian Reservation; incorporated 1890; pop. 9,126.
Lander College, Greenwood, S.C.; local control; coeducational, formerly for women; founded 1872; arts and sciences, education.
Landes, region of s.w. France, vast tract of sandy marshland bordered by dunes S-38
Landfill, in garbage and refuse disposal G-18
sewage disposal S-119
Landform G-62
climatic effects C-503
Land grant, in United States history
educational E-92
home economics H-215
South Dakota S-325
Vermont V-288
railroad R-74
Landing, airplane A-191
helicopter H-119
Landing gear, equipment of airplane A-184
glider G-166
helicopter H-119, *picture* H-118
Landing net, in fishing, *list* F-146
Landis, James McCauley (1899–1964), U.S. public official, born in Tokyo, Japan, of U.S. citizens, missionaries; taught law, Harvard University, 1926–34; chairman SEC 1935–37; dean Harvard Law School 1937–46; director Office of Civilian Defense 1942–43; director U.S. economic operations in Middle East 1943–45; chairman CAB 1946–47; special assistant to President John F. Kennedy 1961.
Landis, Kenesaw Mountain (1866–1944), U.S. jurist and baseball commissioner, born in Millville, Ohio; judge U.S. district court of n. Illinois 1905–22; tried Standard Oil rebate case in 1907 B-96, *list* B-95
Land Management, Bureau of (BLM), United States U-161
fire fighting F-107
Land mine, weapon T-232
Land of Enchantment. *see in index* New Mexico
Land of Nod, term used to designate the state of sleep; so called from the unknown land of "wandering," or Nod, to which Cain fled after the murder of Abel (Bible, Gen. iv).
Land of Opportunity. *see in index* Arkansas
Land of the Five Rivers. *see in index* Punjab
Land of the Long White Cloud. *see in index* New Zealand
Land of the Midnight Sun. *see in index* Alaska
Landon, Alfred Mossman (born 1887), U.S. political leader, born in West Middlesex, Pa.; governor of Kansas 1933–37; Republican candidate for presidency 1936 R-272
Kansas K-177
Landor, Walter Savage (1775–1864), English author, born in Warwick, England; a poet of distinction, also master of English prose style (poetry: 'Gebir', 'Rose Aylmer'; prose: 'Pericles and Aspasia').
Landowska, Wanda (full name Wanda Louise Landowska) (1879–1959), Polish-born musician, harpsichordist, and educator L-27
Landrace, breed of pig P-320
Land reform L-29
China C-374
Cuba C-801
Egypt L-29
Italy I-386
Mexico M-331, 338
Zapata Z-449
Landrieu, Moon (born 1930), U.S. lawyer and public official, born in New Orleans, La.; member Louisiana house of representatives 1960–65; councilman-at-large New Orleans 1966–70, mayor 1970–78; U.S. secretary of housing and urban development 1979–81.
Landrum-Griffin Act (1959), United States L-9
Landry, Tom (born 1924), U.S. football coach F-298
Lands, on compact disc C-621
Landsats, earth resource satellites, *table* S-344
Landscape B-377
'Landsdowne', work by Stuart S-493
Land's End, promontory of Cornwall, forming westernmost point of England E-229, *picture* E-231, *map* E-360
Landsgemeinde, Switzerland S-543, *picture* S-544a
Landshut, West Germany, city on Isar River in Bavaria, 35 mi (55 km) n.e. of Munich; 14th- and 15th-century gabled houses; Napoleon defeated Austrians (1809); pop. 52,417, *map* G-131
Landslide, in United States' politics
Eisenhower E-137
Nixon U-196a
Roosevelt R-272
Land snail S-221
Landsteiner, Karl (1868–1943), U.S. bacteriologist and pathologist L-27
blood research B-317
medicine M-285
physical anthropology A-483
Landsting (from Norse *land,* "land," and *ting,* or *thing,* "parliament"), certain legislative bodies in Scandinavian countries; in Sweden, county councils.
Land tenure. *see also in index* Land grant; Land, public
American pioneers P-340
ancient Greece S-369
ancient Rome R-244, 246
feudal system F-69
migration of people M-400
Peru P-222
Philippines P-261
Sicily S-192
Land use L-28
cities C-451
ecology, *picture* E-53
flood control F-185
food supply F-286
Philippines, *chart* P-255d
Portugal, *chart* P-457b
South America, *chart* S-296
Spain, *chart* S-362
Sweden, *chart* S-528
Switzerland, *chart* S-545
United States U-101, *chart* U-118
U.S.S.R., *charts* R-334, 336
Lane, Edward William (1801–76), English Arabic scholar, born in Hereford; spent many years between 1825 and 1849 in Egypt; published 'Account of the Manners and Customs of the Modern Egyptians' A-525
Lane, Joseph (1801–81), U.S. statesman, born in Buncombe County, N.C.; to Vanderburgh County, Ind., 1820; served as Indiana senator 1844–46; made major general for heroic action in Mexican War; governor of Territory of Oregon 1848–50; Oregon delegate to Congress 1850–58, U.S. senator 1859–61; candidate for vice-president on secession ticket 1860.
Lane, Ralph Norman Angell. *see in index* Angell, Sir Norman
Lane, Richard (nickname Night Train) (born 1928), U.S. football player, born in Austin, Tex.; defensive back; Los Angeles Rams 1952–53; Chicago Cardinals 1954–59, Detroit Lions 1960–65.
Lane, Sir William Arbuthnot (1856–1943), English physician, born in Ft. George, near Inverness, Scotland; consulting surgeon Guy's Hospital, Hospital for Sick Children, French Hospital, London; author books on operative treatment of fractures and of cleft palate.
Lane College, Jackson, Tenn.; Christian Methodist Episcopal church; founded 1882; liberal arts, teacher education.
Lane Theological Seminary, Cincinnati, Ohio B-131
Lanfranc (1005?–89), English prelate and scholar, born in Italy; archbishop of Canterbury 1070–89; as chief counselor of William the Conqueror played important part in fixing Norman rule upon English church and people.
Lang, Andrew (1844–1912), Scottish scholar, poet, and writer on many subjects; born in Selkirk, Scotland ('Ballads in Blue China'; 'Custom and Myth'; 'History of Scotland'; 'Blue', 'Red', 'Yellow', and other fairy books) S-465
reading R-111a
'The Arabian Nights' S-480
Lang, Cosmo Gordon (1864–1945), English divine, archbishop of Canterbury 1928–42; born in Aberdeenshire, Scotland; canon of St. Paul's 1901–08; archbishop of York 1908–28.
Lang, Fritz (1890–1976), Austrian film director ('Hangmen Also Die!'; 'M'; 'Metropolis'; 'While the City Sleeps') D-155
Lang Darma (died 842), Tibetan ruler T-181
Langdell, Christopher Columbus (1826–1906), U.S. lawyer and educator; born in New Boston, N.H.; after 1870 dean of Harvard University Law School; introduced "case system" of teaching, which revolutionized methods of law schools.
Langdon, John (1741–1819), U.S. merchant and political leader, born in Portsmouth, N.H.; an ardent supporter of the Revolution, he financed Stark's expedition against Burgoyne and built ships for Navy; signed United States Constitution; one of first senators from New Hampshire; governor of New Hampshire 1805–8, 1810–11.
Lange, Christian Louis (1869–1938), Norwegian pacifist and historian, born in Stavanger; represented Norway at Hague Peace Conference (1907) and League of Nations.
Lange, David (born 1942), prime minister of New Zealand; member of Parliament 1977–; deputy Labor Party leader 1979–83; headed Labor Party 1983–84; became country's youngest prime minister of the century 1984–.
Lange, Dorothea (1895–1965), U.S. photographer L-29
Langensalza, East Germany. *see in index* Bad Langensalza
Langer, William (1886–1959), U.S. attorney and senator, born in Everest, N.D.; governor of North Dakota 1933–34 and 1937–39; U.S. senator 1940–59; known for legislation for farmers; Republican.
Langerhans, islands of, part of the pancreas, discovered by Paul L. Langerhans, German pathologist (1849–88).
Langevin, Sir Hector-Louis (1826–1906), Canadian politician C-118, *picture* C-116
Langgässer, Elisabeth, (1889–1950), German novelist G-107
Langhanke, Lucile Vasconcellas. *see in index* Astor, Mary
Langland, William (1330?–1400?), English poet E-265
Langley, Samuel P. (1834–1906), U.S. physicist, astronomer, and inventor L-30
aerospace research A-77
flying machines A-201
Wright W-368
Langley Air Force Base, Hampton, Va. A-164, *map* V-349
Hampton H-24
Research Center N-22
Langley Park, Md., community situated 6 mi (10 km) n.e. of Washington, D.C.; pop. 11,564, *map* M-182
Langmuir, Irving (1881–1957), U.S. chemist, born in Brooklyn, N.Y.; engaged in research for General Electric Company 1909–50; invented gas-filled tungsten lamp and condensation vacuum pump; helped develop high-vacuum tube used in atomic hydrogen welding ('Atoms and Molecules')
Pupin P-535
Langres, France, ancient town in e. on Plateau of Langres; makes cutlery; famous strategic point since time of Roman empire; pop. 8,945, *map* F-369
Langshan, breed of poultry P-482, *picture* P-481
Langston, John Mercer (1829–97), U.S. public official, born in Louisa County, Va.; first black American elected to public office in United States 1855 (clerk Brownhelm Township, Ohio); elected 1888 for one term in U.S. Congress.
Langston University, Langston, Okla.; state control; founded 1897; arts and sciences, applied sciences, education, technical and vocational education.
Langton, Stephen (1150?–1228), English cardinal and archbishop of Canterbury, credited with being first to divide Bible into chapters; agitator for Magna Carta J-124
Langtry, Lily Emily (1852–1929), English actress, noted for her beauty, born on Island of Jersey and known as the "Jersey lily"; first great success in 'She Stoops to Conquer'.
Language L-31. *see also in index* Alphabet; Grammar; Rhetoric; Writing, Communication by; Writing, Creative; languages by name, *e.g.* English language; and language groups, *e.g.* Indo-European languages
American Indians I-135, 140, *table* I-138
art forms A-662
bilingual education B-191
brain's perception B-402
communication C-607
education E-83
Europe E-336
figures of speech F-81
information theory I-201
Jesperson J-102
Korzybski K-301
learning L-106
linguistics L-229
literature L-242
logic L-284
North America N-340
public speaking P-526b
Language arts. *see also in index* Reading for recreation; Spelling
reports R-151a, *list* R-151b
Language experience approach, reading method R-103
'Language: Its Nature, Development, and Origin', work by Jesperson J-102
Languedoc, former province in s. France; capital was Toulouse; wine producer.
Languedoc Canal. *see in index* Canal du Midi
Langur, monkey A-503, *picture* A-502
Lanham Act (l941–45), United States, *list* E-104

Lanier, Sidney (1842–81), U.S. lyric poet
 American literature A-350
 Hall of Fame, *table* H-16

Laniidae, shrike family of birds. *see in index* Shrike

Lanin, Sam, U.S. bandleader M-684

Lankester, Sir Edwin Ray (1847–1929), English biologist, born in London; widely known as a teacher and as a writer of popular works on science; director of Natural History Museum in London 1898–1907 ('Science from an Easy Chair'; 'Secrets of Earth and Sea').

Lanolin, purified form of wool wax used a base for ointments and salves W-110
 wool W-289

Lansdale, Pa., borough 9 mi (14 km) n.e. of Norristown; glue, building products, electronic components, tile, hosiery; pop. 16,526, *map* P-185

Lansdowne, Henry Charles Keith Petty-Fitzmaurice, 5th **marquis of** (1845–1927), British statesman, born in London; governor-general of Canada 1883–88; viceroy of India 1888–93; secretary of foreign affairs 1900–1906, during which time an alliance was made with Japan and friendship cemented with France; leader of Unionist party in House of Lords; favored a moderate peace after World War I.

Lansdowne, Henry Petty-Fitzmaurice, 3rd **marquis of** (1780–1863), English statesman, born in London; chancellor of the exchequer at 25, a Liberal leader and advocate of parliamentary reform and abolition of slavery.

Lansdowne, Md., community 5 mi (8 km) s.w. of Baltimore; metal products, transportation equipment, electronic components; pop. 17,770, *map* M-182

Lansdowne, Pa., borough, residential suburb about 5 mi (8 km) w. of Philadelphia; some small industries, council-manager government; incorporated 1893; pop. 11,891, *map,* P-185

Lansing, Robert (1864–1928), U.S. lawyer and authority on international law, born in Watertown, N.Y.; counsel for U.S. in Bering Sea and Alaska boundary arbitrations; secretary of state in President Wilson's Cabinet during World War I.

Lansing, Ill., village 24 mi (39 km) s. of Chicago; truck farms; aluminum windows and doors; founded in 1860s, incorporated in 1893; pop. 29,039, *map* I-53

Lansing, Mich., state capital, on Grand River 80 mi (130 km) n.w. of Detroit; pop. 130,414 L-45
 Michigan M-359, 368, *picture* M-365
 North America, *map* N-350

Lansknecht, German mercenary band A-640

Lanston, Tolbert (1844–1913), U.S. inventor, born in Troy, Ohio; patented Monotype in 1887, began production and marketing of machine 1897.

Lantern fish, found in almost all seas; some deep-sea and some not; has luminescent organs in groups; family Myctophidae F-131

Lanthanide series chemical series on the periodic table, *table* P-207

Lanthanum (La), rare earth metal, *table* P-207, *list* P-208

Lanuvium (or Lanuvio), Italy, city of Latium, 19 mi (30 km) s.e. of Rome; member Latin League; conquered by Rome 338 BC; temple of Juno, *map* I-401

Lan Xang, ancient kingdom, Indochina L-48

Lanzhou, China G-16
 Asia, *map* A-697

Lao, branch of T'ai people T-147

Laoag, Philippines, city, seaport on Laoag River near n.w. coast of Luzon; rice, indigo, sugar; pop. 61,727, *map* P-262

Lao Bridge, bridge in southern Italy A-447

Laocoön, in Greek mythology, Trojan priest of Apollo, warns countrymen against wooden horse H-221
 statue G-272

'Laocoon', book by Lessing (1766), in which the functions of poetry and painting are defined and distinguished; an important book in the history of art.

Laodamia, legendary Greek heroine, wife of Protesilaus; celebrated in William Wordsworth's 'Laodamia'. *see also in index* Protesilaus

Laodicea, name of several ancient Asiatic cities in realms extending from Aegean Sea to India; **Laodicea ad Lycum** (modern **Denizli,** Turkey, 120 mi (195 km) s.e. of Smyrna), once wealthy trade center; founded probably 3rd century BC; site of one of 7 early churches of Asia (Bible, Rev. i, 11); **Laodicea ad mare** (modern **Latakia,** Syria), pride of the Caesars, noted for ruins of triumphal arch built possibly by Septimius Severus.

Laoighis, Ireland. *see in index* Leix

Lao-Lu, people L-47

Laomedon, in Greek mythology, founder and king of Troy; father of Priam; lost Troy to Hercules and was killed by him for failure to deliver to Hercules the magic horses promised him.

Laon, France, city 80 mi (130 km) n.e. of Paris; fortified by Romans; Blücher defeated Napoleon 1814; captured by Germans 1870, 1914, and 1940; pop. 25,623, *map* F-369

Laos, republic in s.e. Asia; area 91,429 sq mi (236,800 sq km); cap. Vientiane; pop. 3,901,000 L-46
 Asia, *map* A-697
 cities. *see in index* Vientiane and other cities by name
 communist world, *map* C-619
 Indochina I-157
 national symbols
  flag, *picture* F-167
  song, *table* N-64
 neutrality V-321
 Vietnam conflict V-321
 world, *map* W-297

Lao-Soung, people L-47

Lao-Tai, people L-47

Lao-Theng (or Mon-Khmer), people L-47

Lao-tzu (or Lao-tse) (604?–531? BC), legendary founder of Taoism, to whom the 'Lao-Tzu', an important Taoist writing, was traditionally attributed L-48
 China C-346
 teachings R-143

'Lao-Tzu' (or 'Tao-te Ching'), sacred book of Taoism L-48
 Chinese literature C-388

Lap-and-lead lever, part of steam engine, *diagram* S-442

La Parida, Venezuela. *see in index* Cerro Bolívar

La Paz, Bolivia, largest city and seat of government; pop. 881,400 L-49
 Bolivia B-335
 South America, *picture* S-281a, *map* S-298
 world, *map* W-297

La Paz, Mexico, port in Lower California, on Bay of La Paz; capital of Baja California Sur; in agricultural area; pearl fishing center; silver mines; pop. 75,000 C-54
 Mexico, *map* M-341

Lap dissolve, motion picture optical effect M-613

La Peltrie, Marie Madeleine de (1603–71), French Roman Catholic nun, born in Alençon; founder of Ursuline convent at Que., 1639; conducted school for Indian and French girls until 1642, when she joined colonists under Maisonneuve and helped to found Montreal.

La Pérouse, Jean François de Galaup, count de (1741–88), French navigator, born near Albi; in war with England took British forts on Hudson Bay 1782; rounded Cape Horn, explored west coast of the Americas, discovered La Pérouse Strait between Hokushu and Sakhalin, Japan; lost at sea after reaching Australia, 1788; wreckage of his ships found 1826, on coral reef n. of New Hebrides.

Lapham, Silas. *see in index* 'Rise of Silas Lapham, The'

Lapidary, gem collector H-187

Lapido, Duro, African writer A-121

Lapis lazuli, semiprecious stone J-116
 Sumerian culture, *picture* B-6

Lapithae, in Greek mythology, people related to the centaurs, dwelling in Thessaly.

Lap joint, development of the wheel W-193

Laplace, Pierre-Simon (1749–1827), French mathematician and astronomer L-49
 mathematics M-215
 nebular hypothesis P-355

Lapland, region in extreme n. of Norway, Sweden, Finland, and U.S.S.R. L-49
 arctic regions A-571
 folk art F-254
 reindeer R-139
 Sweden S-523

La Plata, Argentina, city 35 mi (55 km) s.e. of Buenos Aires and 5 mi (8 km) inland from Ensenada, its port on Plata estuary; National University; meat-packing and petroleum refining; pop. 391,247, *map* A-585
 South America, *map* S-297
 world, *map* W-297

La Plata, Bolivia. *see in index* Sucre

La Plata, Río de, South America. *see in index* Plata, Río de la

La Plata, Viceroyalty of S-290

La Porte, Ind., city in lake area, 25 mi (40 km) w. of South Bend; farm machinery, airplane parts, heaters and radiators, furniture, wood products; pop. 21,796, *map* I-102

Lappet-faced vulture, bird B-280

Lapping, grinding operation used to produce highly polished surfaces T-224

Lapp language L-50

Lapps (or sabme, or Samis), people of Lapland L-50
 classification, *chart* R-26
 Europe E-336
  Finland F-89
  Norway N-391
 nomads N-332
 reindeer R-139

'La Prensa', newspaper, Argentina B-489

Laps, process in cotton manufacture C-740

La Puente, Calif., city 18 mi (29 km) e. of Los Angeles; air conditioners, heaters, trailers, chemicals; settled 1841, incorporated 1956; pop. 30,882.

Laputa, island visited by Gulliver in 'Gulliver's Travels'.

Lapwing (or green plover, or peewit), Old World plover *Vanellus vanellus* having iridescent bottle-green plumage on upperparts, crested head, and white underparts; noted for its wailing cry; its eggs are esteemed as a delicacy.

Laramide revolution, in geology R-235

Laramie, Jacques (1785?–1821), Canadian trapper; in Colo. foothills and s.e. Wyo. 1816–20; first explorer of upper Laramie River; killed by Indians.

Laramie, Wyo., city on Laramie River 43 mi (69 km) n.w. of Cheyenne; cattle and sheep; railroad shops, tie and timber treating plant; cement, brick; pop. 24,410 W-389, 396

Laramie Mountains, s.e. Wyo.; highest point 9,020 ft (2,750 m), *map* U-80

Larboard, old term for the left, or port, side of a boat; perhaps derived from Middle English "ladeborde," the loading side, "port" was substituted for larboard to avoid confusion with "starboard," the right side of a boat.

Larceny, taking of personal goods without the owner's consent, *table* L-93
 crime C-771

Larch, tree, *picture* F-310
 wood, *table* W-282

Larcom, Lucy (1824–93), U.S. poet, born in Beverly, Mass.; in her youth she was a factory worker, and some of her contributions to the factory magazine won praise of John Greenleaf Whittier, with whom she later compiled two books; editor *Our Young Folks;* outstanding for poems of life in New England ('Childhood Songs'; 'Wild Roses of Cape Ann and Other Poems').

Larder beetle B-140
 insects, *picture* I-226

Lardner, Ring (or Ringgold Wilmer Lardner) (1885–1933), U.S. writer of humorous stories showing keen insight and reproducing everyday conversation of ordinary persons; born in Niles, Mich.; sportswriter on newspapers ('You Know Me, Al'; 'Gullible's Travels'; 'How to Write Short Stories', which contains character sketch, 'The Champion'; 'Round Up'; 'First and Last'; 'The Portable Ring Lardner') A-360

Laredo, Tex., city in s. part of state on Rio Grande opposite Nuevo Laredo, Mexico; agriculture, stock raising, oil and gas; vegetable and fruit shipping; hats, garments, antimony smelting, brick; Laredo Air Force Base nearby; pop. 91,449, *map* N-350

Lares (singular Lar), deities in Roman mythology, protecting deities of the household, associated with the Penates M-702

Laretta, Enrique (1875–1961), Argentine writer and diplomat, born in Buenos Aires; minister to France 1910–16.

Large-scale integration (LSI), silicon chip C-629
 microprocessor M-379

Largetooth aspen (also called large poplar, popple, and large American aspen), tree *Populus grandidentata* of willow family, native from N.S. to N.C., westward to Man.; grows to 60 ft (18 m); wood is soft, weak, light, grayish-white; used for paper pulp, excelsior, matches.

Larghetto, direction in music meaning slow and broad but not quite so slow as largo; term also refers to a passage or movement within a musical composition.

Largo, Fla., town 5 mi (8 km) s. of Clearwater; tourist center; citrus groves; incorporated 1905; pop. 58,977.

Largo, in music M-691, *list* M-670

Largs, Scotland, yachting center and resort, on Firth of Clyde, 30 mi (50 km) s.w. of Glasgow; pop. 8,908.

'L'Arianna', opera by Monteverdi M-568

Lariat, cowboy's rope C-756

Laridae, bird family, including gulls and terns G-317

Lárisa (or Larissa), Greece, city in Thessaly on Salambria River; transit trade, textiles; important city in ancient times; pop. 72,336, *map* E-360

Lark, bird L-51

Larkin Building, Buffalo, N.Y. W-367

Lark sparrow (or lark finch), bird of middle and w. United States; abundant in Mississippi valley; head streaked chestnut and white; tail white-edged; good singer.

Larkspur (or delphinium), flower, *picture* F-224
 growing conditions G-23
 poison P-408

La Rocca, Dominick James (nickname Nick) (1889–1961), U.S. jazz cornetist, born in New Orleans, La.; formed Original Dixieland Jazz Band during World War I; credited with composing 'Tiger Rag'.

La Roche, Troilus de Mesgouez, marquis de, French fur trader who established a colony on Sable Island, near Nova Scotia in 1598 C-91

La Rochefoucauld, François de (1613–80), French courtier and writer L-51

La Rochelle, France, historic seaport of w.; once great maritime city and center of French Protestantism; pop. 72,075
 Europe, *map* E-360
 France, *map* F-369
 Richelieu besieges R-204

Larreta, Enrique (1875–1961), Argentine writer L-71, *picture* L-73

Larry P. vs. Riles, U.S. court case I-238

Larsa, ancient Sumerian city in s. Mesopotamia, on w. bank of old Euphrates River 15 mi (25 km) s.e. of ancient Erech;

temple libraries and important documents found in the ruins.
Larsen Ice Shelf, Antarctica, in n.w. Weddell Sea along e. coast of Antarctic Peninsula; named for Capt. C.A. Larsen, who sailed along edge of shelf in 1893.
Larson, Lewis Arthur (born 1910), U.S. government official and lawyer, born in Sioux Falls, S.D.; professor of law Cornell University 1948–53; dean University of Pittsburgh School of Law 1953–54; undersecretary of labor 1954–56; director U.S. Information Agency 1956–57; director Rule of Law Center, Duke University after 1958; author of 'A Republican Looks at His Party', 'Eisenhower: the President Nobody Knew'.
Larva, in zoology L-51
amphibians A-378
animal behavior experiment, *picture* A-440
flatfish F-174
insects I-220, *picture* I-215
ant A-469
bee B-125
beetle B-137, *picture* B-139
butterfly B-525, *pictures* B-521–23
flies F-242
mosquito M-597
wasp W-74
lamprey L-26
marine snail and slug S-222
metamorphosis M-312
Lary, Robert Yale (born 1930), U.S. football player, born in Fort Worth, Tex.; defensive back for Detroit Lions 1952–53, 1956–64.
Laryngeal pharynx, in anatomy T-176
Laryngitis V-377
Larynx (or voice box), organ of voice production V-377
anatomy A-391
throat T-176
La Salle, Sieur de (1643–87), French explorer L-52
explorations A-338, *map* U-176
Canada C-92
Great Lakes G-249
Indiana I-93
Louisiana N-233
Mississippi M-472
Mississippi river M-484
Ohio River O-519
Oklahoma O-525
Tennessee T-87
Texas T-123
Wisconsin W-253
Hennepin H-128
La Salle, Ill., city on Illinois River, adjacent to Peru and about 13 mi (21 km) w. of Ottawa; center of corn area: chemicals, electrical equipment, hydrotransmissions, zinc processing; Starved Rock State Park nearby; pop. 10,347, *map* I-53
La Salle, Que., residential city just s. of Montreal, at s. end of island of Montreal, overlooking Lachine Rapids in St. Lawrence River; named for La Salle, French explorer; pop. 76,299 Q-9h, *map* Q-11
La Salle College, Philadelphia, Pa.; Roman Catholic; chartered 1863; arts and sciences, business, education; graduate work in theology; Pennlyn Biostation.
Las Casas, Bartolomé de (1474–1566), Spanish missionary and theologian L-53
Latin American history L-66
Lascaux Cave, s. France; Stone Age cave drawings found here A-531, *picture* A-530
man, *picture* M-82
'The Stag Frieze' D-252
Las Cruces, N.M., city 40 mi (65 km) n.w. of El Paso, Tex., in livestock and agricultural region; pecans, alfalfa, vegetables; cotton ginning, cottonseed oil; New Mexico State University; White Sands Missile Range nearby; pop. 45,086, *map* U-40
New Mexico N-216, 224, *map* N-228
Laser and maser, instruments that produce an intense beam of light L-54
book production B-358
communication S-195b
compact disc C-621
electronics E-176
eye repair B-312
garment industry G-32
holography H-206
optics O-575
instrumentation I-229
laser-beam machining T-226
medical use S-519a
military use, *picture* M-12
platinum P-384
supermarkets' use A-834
reflector on moon M-576
video recording V-311
watches and clocks W-81
wind tunnel W-235
X rays X-405
Laser-beam machining (LBM), a metalworking operation T-226
Laser disc, technology used in home video games E-174
video recording V-311
Laser-doppler velocimeter, wind tunnel W-235
La Serena, Chile, iron-shipping center about 225 mi (360 km) n. of Valparaiso; historic cathedral, convents; founded in 1544, in 1552 declared a city; pop. 71,898, *map* S-299
Laser fusion, nuclear energy N-429
Lashio, Burma, town 125 mi (200 km) n.e. of Mandalay; s.w. terminus of Burma Road.
Lashkar, India. *see in index* Gwalior
Lashley, Karl Spencer (1890–1958), U.S. psychologist, born in Davis, W. Va.; professor of psychology University of Chicago 1929–35; professor of psychology Harvard University 1935–37, research professor of neuropsychology 1937–55.
Lasker, Albert (known as the father of modern advertising) (1880–1952), U.S. advertising executive A-59
Lasker, Eduard (1829–84), Prussian statesman, born in present Poznan, Poland; important service in civil consolidation of German empire.
Lasker, Emanuel (1868–1941), German chess master, born in Berlinchen, Germany (now Barlinek, Poland); world chess champion 1894–1921; wrote books on chess, philosophy, and mathematics.
Laski, Harold Joseph (1893–1950), British liberal writer, born in Manchester; professor political science (University of London after 1926); visiting lecturer in United States; author of many books, chiefly on contemporary political and social-political trends, also 'Letters, Correspondence, 1916–1935' with Oliver W. Holmes, U.S. jurist.
Laskin, Bora (1912–84), Canadian jurist, born in Fort Williamson, Ont.; professor University of Toronto 1949–65; judge Supreme Court of Ontario 1965–69; judge Supreme Court of Canada 1970–, chief justice 1973–.
Lasky, Jesse Louis (1880–1958), pioneer U.S. motion-picture producer, born in San Jose, Calif.; coproducer of Hollywood's first full-length motion picture, 'The Squaw Man'; produced over 1,000 motion pictures; specialized in biographical films ('I Blow My Own Horn', autobiography).
Las Palmas, Grand Canary Island, port on n.e. coast; largest city of Canary Islands; pop. 260,368 C-130
Africa, *map* A-118
La Spezia, Italy, city 50 mi (80 km) s.e. of Genoa, on Bay of Spezia; important naval harbor; shipbuilding; winter resort; pop. 121,923, *map* I-401
Europe, *map* E-360
Lassalle, Ferdinand (1825–64), German socialist L-55
Socialism S-234
Lassen Peak, volcanic peak in n. California; erupted 1914–21; vast lava beds; height 10,453 ft (3,186 m), *map* U-87
Cascade Range C-195
Lassie, a line of popular collie movie stars D-193
Lasso, Orlando di (1532?–94), celebrated composer, forerunner of Palestrina; born in Mons, Belgium, where he became choirboy; taken to Italy by patron, viceroy of Sicily; court musician to duke of Bavaria at Munich; composed more than 2,000 works.
Lasso, rope or a line of leather with a running noose used for catching horses and cattle.
Last, shoe part S-180, *picture* S-181
Last Chance Gulch, Helena, Mont. H-117
'Last Communion of St. Jerome, The', work by Botticelli, *picture* D-111
'Last Days of Pompeii, The', novel by Bulwer-Lytton giving detailed and vivid picture of life in Pompeii before city was destroyed by eruption of Mount Vesuvius (AD 79); realistic description of eruption.
Lastex, trade name for a rubber filament wrapped with cotton, silk, nylon, or rayon fibers; gives great stretch to fabrics woven from it; invented 1931.
'Last Judgment, The', fresco by Michelangelo M-351
'Last Laugh, The' (1925), motion picture by Murnau, *picture* M-621
'Last Leaf', work by Holmes A-347
'Last of the Mohicans, The', novel by Cooper, one of the 'Leatherstocking Tales'; thrilling story of frontier life; romantic idealization of the Uncas A-346
historical novel N-408, *picture* N-410
'Last Picture Show , The', novel by McMurtry W-152
Last quarter (or third quarter), moon phase M-579
Last Supper. *see in index* Lord's Supper
'Last Supper, The', painting by Leonardo da Vinci L-132
'Last Supper, The', painting by Tintoretto T-191
'Last Tycoon, The', novel by Fitzgerald F-147
Las Vegas, Nev., largest city of state, 23 mi (37 km) n.w. of Hoover Dam; in irrigated agricultural area; tourist center; legalized gambling; campus of University of Nevada; Nevada Test Site, Nellis Air Force Base, Lake Mead Base, Las Vegas Air Force Station nearby; pop. 164,674 L-56
Nebraska N-136, 144, *picture* N-141
Las Vegas, N.M., livestock center 42 mi (68 km) e. of Santa Fe; composed of modern city (pop. 14,322) and old town (pop. 6,307); livestock center; stone and wood products, garments; tourist trade; New Mexico Highlands University; established by Spanish about 1833 N-216, *map* N-228
Las Vegas Bombing and Gunnery Range, site for nuclear weapons tests in Nevada N-138
László. *see in index* Ladislaus
Latakia (or Lattaquié), Syria, Mediterranean port 115 mi (185 km) n. of Beirut; produces famous Latakia tobacco; ancient Laodicea; pop. 67,799, *map* A-697
Latchstring P-331
'Late George Apley, The', (1937) novel by Marquand; won 1938 Pulitzer prize A-359
Latent heat of fusion H-104
water W-86
Latent heat of vaporization H-104
water W-86
Late Period, period in Egyptian history, approximately 1090–332 BC E-126
Lateral line, in fish anatomy F-127, *diagram* F-125
Lateral surface, mathematics M-244
Lateran, basilica in Rome, Italy. *see in index* St. John Lateran
Lateran, The, palace in Rome, Italy; original building belonged to Lateranus family; taken from them by Nero; later given to pope by Constantine; used as residence by popes until 14th century; present palace, built in 16th century, now contains two museums.
Lateran Councils, series of ecumenical church councils held in the Lateran Palace and St. John Lateran at Rome from the 12th to the 16th centuries
Innocent III I-208
Leo X L-131
Lateran Treaty (or Concordat of 1929), between Italy and Vatican I-384
Pius XI P-347
treaty, *table* T-274
Vatican V-267
Laterite, soil S-253
China C-341
jungle J-155
Latex, milky juice secreted by various plants
chewing gum C-308
gutta-percha G-321
paints P-72, 76
rubber R-301, 305, 310, *picture* R-302
Latham, Hubert, U.S. pioneer in aviation A-203
Latham, Jean Lee (born 1902), U.S. writer, born in Buckhannon, W. Va.; editor-in-chief Dramatic Publishing Company, Chicago, 1930–36; author of plays presented on radio and television and of children's books ('Carry On, Mr. Bowditch', fictionalized biography awarded Newbery Medal 1956; 'This Dear-Bought Land'; 'On Stage, Mr. Jefferson'; 'Young Man in a Hurry'; 'Man of the Monitor'; 'Retreat to Glory: the Story of Sam Houston').
Lathen, Emma (pen name for Mary J. Latis and Martha Hennissart) D-119
Lathing, building material B-377
Lathrop, Dorothy Pulis (1891–1981), U.S. writer and illustrator of children's books, born in Albany, N.Y.; she illustrated 'Hitty', by Rachel Field, awarded Newbery Medal 1930; in 1938, Dorothy Lathrop's own book 'Animals of the Bible' was awarded the first Caldecott Medal ever given; among the books written and illustrated by her are: 'Who Goes There?'; 'Let Them Live'; 'The Littlest Mouse' R-111a
Field F-78
Lathrop, George Parsons (1851–98), U.S. journalist and poet, born in Oahu, Hawaii; married Rose, daughter of Nathaniel Hawthorne; associate editor *Atlantic Monthly*; editor *Boston Courier*; founder American Copyright League.
Lathrop, Julia Clifford (1858–1932), U.S. social worker, born in Rockford, Ill.; important work at Hull House, Chicago; chief 1912–21 U.S. Children's Bureau, first woman bureau chief; author of articles on child welfare, care of insane, and civil service.
Latifundios (or latifundia), large landed estates S-192
Latimer, Hugh (1485?–1555), English Protestant reformer and martyr
Latina (or Littoria), Italy, province on land reclaimed from Pontine Marshes s.e. of Rome; fertile farm lands; cap. Latina, *map* I-401
Latin America, collective name for the 20 independent nations of southern North America, Central America, South America, and the West Indies L-57. *see also in index* Central America; South America; and names of separate countries
arts
folk art F-254
literature. *see in index* Latin American literature
painting P-67a, *pictures* P-67b–d
bibliography S-302
Bolivar B-332
church and state issue C-409
genocide G-60
good-neighbor policy R-273
Alliance for Progress S-292
Peace Corps P-143a
illiteracy P-450
labor movements L-11
land use reforms L-29
languages L-61
nationalism N-66
national parks N-27
Third World T-168
Latin American Free Trade Association (LAFTA), Latin American common market L-65
Latin American literature L-68. *see also in index* Caribbean literature
children's literature L-251, *chart* L-254
folklore S-476, *list* S-481c
Latin America L-62
Latin grammar school
education E-84
Latin language L-37
alphabet A-315
influence on
education E-83
English
language E-261
literature E-264
Romance languages R-239
French F-349
Spanish S-353, S-365
Italy's literary heritage I-385
Latin literature L-76
linguistic analysis L-230

Middle Ages M-390
theater T-158
Latin League, confederation of cities of Latium in central Italy, existing from earliest historic times till 338 BC R-244
Latin literature L-76
children's literature L-245
epics E-291
German literature G-105
Greek literature G-277
Juvenal J-161
linguistics and grammar L-229
Livy L-270
Pliny the Elder R-124
Renaissance R-146
Roman history, *picture* R-241
Seneca S-108a
Virgil V-328
Latinos. *see in index* Hispanic Americans
Latin Quarter, in Paris, France P-122, *map* P-120
city C-452
Latins, inhabitants of Latium in ancient times; also modern Italians, French, and Spanish R-240, 244
Latinus, in Roman mythology, king of Latium and father of Lavinia, wife of Aeneas; name also given to one of the heroes in Torquato Tasso's 'Jerusalem Delivered'.
Latis, Mary J. *see in index* Lathen, Emma
Latitude and longitude L-79
climate control C-496, *chart* C-497
equator E-293
geography G-62
hemisphere H-126
maps M-117
navigation N-68, 71, 75, *pictures* N-69, 74
time T-188
watches and clocks W-80
Latium, ancient district in middle Italy, inhabited by Latins R-240, 241
Aeneas A-63
Latona. *see in index* Leto
La Tour, Charles Amador de (1596–1666), French governor of Acadia 1628–35; quarreled with Charnisay over governorship; regained post after death of Charnisay in 1650.
La Tour, Georges de (1593–1652), French painter; contemporary of Nicolas Poussin; painter to duke of Lorraine.
Latreille, Pierre André (1762–1833), French zoologist, born in Brives-la-Gaillarde, Corrèze; noted for his classifications of insects.
Latrobe, Benjamin Henry (1764–1820), U.S. architect and engineer, born in Fulneck, Yorkshire, England; to U.S. 1796; surveyor of public buildings, Washington, D.C., 1803; in charge of rebuilding burned Capitol A-568
Latrobe, Pa., borough 33 mi (53 km) s.e. of Pittsburgh in industrial district; iron and steel, metal products, building materials, ceramics, die castings, plastics, ingot molds; St. Vincent College; pop. 10,799, *map* P-184
Lattaquié, Syria. *see in index* Latakia
Latter-day Saints. *see in index* Mormons
Lattice, in basketry B-103
Lattimore, Eleanor Frances (born 1904), U.S. author and illustrator of children's books, born in Shanghai, China; married Robert Armstrong Andrews; works based on own experiences ('Little Pear' series; 'Peachblossom'; 'Bells for a Chinese Donkey'; 'The Monkey of Crofton'; 'The Journey of Ching Lai'; 'Fisherman's Son').
Lattimore, Owen (born 1900), U.S. author and educator, born in Washington, D.C.; director Walter Hines Page School of International Relations, Johns Hopkins University 1938–53; political adviser to Chiang Kai-shek 1941–42; deputy director Pacific operations Office of War Information 1942–44 ('High Tartary'; 'Solution in Asia'; 'Situation in Asia'; 'Ordeal by Slander'; 'Nomads and Commissars: Mongolia Revisited'; 'Studies in Frontier History').
La Tuque, Que., town and lumbering center on St. Maurice River 75 mi (120 km) n. of Trois-Rivières; pulp and paper, sashes and doors; pop. 13,099, *map* C-112
Quebec, *map* Q-10
'La Turista', work by Shepard A-363
Latvian Plains, geographic region, U.S.S.R. L-83
Latvians (or Letts), people L-83
Latvian Soviet Socialist Republic, U.S.S.R., on Baltic Sea; 24,710 sq mi (64,000 sq km); cap. Riga; pop. 2,521,000 L-83
Europe, *map* E-360
folktales, *list* S-480, *picture* S-471
Lithuanian Soviet Socialist Republic L-259
Riga R-207
Russia, *maps* R-325, 344, 348
Latynina, Larissa (born 1934), Soviet gymnast G-325
Lauan (or Philippine mahogany), wood of several species of trees of lauan family Dipterocarpaceae, native to Philippines, nearby islands, and s. Asia.
Laubach, Frank Charles (1884–1970), U.S. missionary and educator, born in Benton, Pa.; ordained Congregational minister 1914; began career as missionary in Philippine Islands 1915; known as founder of worldwide campaign for teaching illiterate peoples to read, using principle of "each one teach one;" author, 'Toward World Literacy'; autobiography, 'Thirty Years with the Silent Billion'.
Laud, William (1573–1645), English prelate, archbishop of Canterbury; born in Reading, England; tried to suppress dissent; beheaded on charge of treason I C-275
Laudanum, tincture of opium O-572
antidote P-411
Lauder, Sir Harry Maclennan (1870–1950), Scottish comedian, born in Portobello, Scotland; a great favorite for his Scottish songs composed by him and sung in character; knighted 1919.
Laudonnière, René Goulaine de (died 1566), French Huguenot noble; accompanied Jean Ribaut's expedition (1562) to what is now South Carolina; established Fort Caroline colony on St. John's River (1564), but governed badly; wounded in Menéndez' attack, escaped to Europe; wrote memoirs.
Laue, Max Theodor Felix von (1879–1960), German physicist, born in Pfaffendorf, near Coblenz; professor University of Berlin 1919–43; author of scientific books
crystallography C-798
solid state physics S-254h
Laugher pigeon P-324
Laughing gas. *see in index* Nitrous oxide
Laughing gull, bird *Larus atricilla* G-317
Laughing hyena (or spotted hyena), animal *Crocuta crocuta* of the family Hyaenidae, *picture* H-342
Laughing jackass (or kookaburra), Australian bird A-782
Laughing philosopher. *see in index* Democritus
Laughlin, James (1806–82), U.S. manufacturer and philanthropist, born in Ireland; one of group that developed Pittsburgh, Pa., as an iron center.
Laughlin, James Laurence (1850–1933), U.S. political economist, born in Deerfield, Ohio; head of department of political economy, University of Chicago, 1892–1916; prepared monetary reform scheme for Santo Domingo government, 1894–95; author of works on economics.
Laughter, reflex action stimulated by humor H-322
Laughton, Charles (1899–1962), U.S. actor, born in Scarborough, England; first appearance on New York stage 1931 ('Payment Deferred'); in motion pictures from 1932; won Academy award 1933 for his role in 'The Private Life of Henry VIII' ('The Barretts of Wimpole Street'; 'Mutiny on the Bounty'; 'Hunchback of Notre Dame'; 'Rembrandt'; 'The Beachcomber'); popular theatrical dramatic reader; compiler of 'Tell Me a Story' A-27
Benét B-161
Launceston, England, quaint old town in Cornwall 21 mi (34 km) n.w. of Plymouth; George Fox, the Quaker, imprisoned here (1655); pop. 4,700, *map* U-18a
Launceston, Tasmania, city in n.e. on Tamar River; wheat and potatoes grown in area; mining; trade with Victoria and South Australia; pop. 62,181, including suburbs T-32
Australia, *map* A-822
Launching, releasing or sending off an object
glider G-166, *diagram* G-167
ship S-172, *picture* S-171
Launch vehicles, in space travel S-342b, 346d, *diagram* S-346c, *pictures* S-242c, 341d, 348b
Laundromat L-84
Laundry L-84
appliances H-211
soap S-229
Laundry room, area used for the washing of clothes
submarine, *diagram* S-498
Launfal, Sir, knight of the Round Table and steward to King Arthur, in the Arthurian legends; hero of James Russell Lowell's 'Vision of Sir Launfal'.
La Unión, El Salvador, chief port, on gulf of Fonseca at e. end of El Salvador; port handles about half of country's foreign trade; railroad terminus; pop. 11,432.
Lauper, Cyndi (born 1953), U.S. pop singer, video performer, born in Queens, New York City; known for eclectic clothing, brightly dyed hair, and wacky persona; stresses individuality; sang with various bands during the 1970s; first solo album 1983; won Grammy award for best new artist 1985.
Laura (1308–48), woman loved by Petrarch and celebrated in his poems R-145
Lauraceae. *see in index* Laurel
Laura Ingalls Wilder Award, established 1954 by Children's Library Association; awarded to authors or illustrators whose books have made "a substantial and lasting contribution to children's literature" L-240
Laurana, Francesco da (1420?–1502), sculptor and medalist of Dalmatian origin; worked chiefly in Italy and France; stressed design rather than realism.
Laurasia, northern mass of Pangaea E-26
Laurel, Stan(1890–1965), film actor, producer, and director, born in Ulverston, England; partner in comedy team 'Laurel and Hardy' with Oliver Hardy; the pair won an Academy Award in 1933 for Best Short Subject for 'the Music Box', *picture* M-619
Laurel, Miss., city 76 mi (122 km) s.e. of Jackson, in yellow pine region; petroleum center; Masonite, lumber, garments, poultry, pop. 21,897 M-469
lignocellulose plant P-379
Laurel, common name for evergreen shrubs and small trees of the genus *Laurus* of the laurel family Lauraceae L-88
camphor C-67
poet laureate P-402
Laurelwood. *see in index* Madrona
Lauren, Ralph (born 1939), U.S. dress designer D-271
Laurencin, Marie (1885–1956), French painter, born in Paris; a modernist with highly individual style; known for female portraits done in soft, pale colors.
Laurens, Henri (1885–1954), French sculptor, born near Paris, France; identified with modernists who emphasized purely plastic forms S-92
Laurens, Henry (1724–92), U.S. statesman, born in Charleston, S.C.; father of John Laurens; president of Continental Congress 1777–78; one of commissioners to negotiate peace after Revolution R-173
Laurens, John (1754–82), U.S. soldier in Revolutionary War, born in Charleston, S.C.; son of Henry Laurens; confidential secretary to George Washington; called the "Bayard of the Revolution"; killed in a skirmish shortly before peace with England was concluded.
Laurens, S.C., city 22 mi (35 km) n. of Greenwood; glass, textiles, carpets; cotton and peaches; vermiculite mines; incorporated 1785; pop. 10,587, *map* S-318
Laurent, Robert (1890–1970), U.S. sculptor, born in Concarneau, near Quimper, France; achieved vital beauty in direct carvings in stone, marble, and wood; noted for figures in alabaster and plant forms in wood; elected to National Institute of Arts and Letters 1970.
Laurentian Library, Florence, Italy L-172, *picture* L-174
Laurentian Mountains (or Laurentides), Canada Q-9b
Laurentian Plateau (or Canadian Shield), highland area in Canada, extending into n.e. United States L-88
Canada C-73
Alberta A-263
Labrador L-12
Manitoba M-99
Newfoundland N-163
Northwest Territories N-388
Ontario O-548
Quebec Q-9b, *map* Q-9a
Saskatchewan S-49c
earth E-23, *map* E-25
North America N-337
United States, *map* U-36
Adirondacks A-44
Michigan M-355
Minnesota M-440
Wisconsin W-249
Laurentides Provincial Park, Que., about 30 mi (50 km) n. of Quebec City; 3,613 sq mi (9,358 sq km), 1,500 lakes; trout fishing, *map* Q-11
Laurentius, saint. *see in index* Lawrence
Laurier, Wilfrid (1841–1919), Canadian statesman L-89
Canada C-102
King K-243
Lauritsen, Charles Christian (1892–1968), U.S. physicist, born in Holstebro, Denmark; professor at California Institute of Technology 1935–62; research on nuclear physics.
Laurium (or Laurion), Greece, hill range 20 mi (30 km) below Athens; in ancient times known for silver mines worked until 400 BC, reopened by French 1864; remains of a Poseidon temple nearby.
Lausanne, Switzerland, historic city on n. shore of Lake Geneva; 13th-century cathedral; university; pop. 137,383 S-542, 544a, *map* S-537
Europe, *map* E-360
Lausanne, Treaty of (1912), closed Turko-Italian War; gave Tripoli to Italy; granted Italians right to occupy Dodecanese Islands and Rhodes; settlement made after Balkan states attacked Turkey, *table* T-274
Lausanne, Treaty of (1923), revised Treaty of Sèvres, extending Turkey's territory T-323, *table* T-274
Bosporus B-371
World War I W-319
Laut, Agnes Christina (1871–1936), Canadian author, born in Stanley, Ont.; authoritative historical books on early explorers and pioneer life in the Northwest ('The Conquest of the Western Empire'; 'Pathfinders of the West'; 'Vikings of the Pacific'; 'Life of Cadillac').
Lautarite, mineral M-435
Lauterbrunnen, Switzerland, village 34 mi (55 km) s.e. of Bern; lace manufactures; pop. 3,216.
Lautrec, Henri de Toulouse. *see in index* Toulouse-Lautrec
Lauzon, Que., city on St. Lawrence River opposite Quebec (city) and adjoining Lévis; shipbuilding center; pop. 12,809, *map* Q-11
Lava, molten rock discharged from volcanoes or intruded between rock strata under the ground L-89. *see also in index* Lava soil; Magma
basalt B-86
earth E-20, *pictures* E-21, 33
geology G-71
Iceland, *picture* I-16
igneous rocks R-228
granite G-214
island formation I-368
minerals M-437

beetles; larvae feed on animal substances, especially skins.

Leather carp, domesticated variety of carp; almost scaleless C-173

Leathernecks, nickname of United States Marines M-138

Leather splits. *see in index* Splits

'Leatherstocking Tales', series of five fast-paced adventure novels by Cooper starring Leatherstocking, the ideal North American frontiersman A-346
  Cooper C-705

Leavening B-428

Leavenworth, Henry (1783–1834), U.S. Army officer, born in New Haven, Conn.; built Army posts, later known as Ft. Snelling (1819) and Ft. Leavenworth (1827); stationed at Ft. Atkinson, Neb. (1821–24).

Leavenworth, Kan., city in n.e. on Missouri River; steel fabricating and products, paper products, plastics; nearby are state and U.S. penitentiaries and Veterans Administration Hospital; in early days outfitting point for cross-prairie wagon trains; pop. 33,656, *map* U-41

Leavenworth Prison P-505b

Leaves. *see in index* Leaf

'Leaves of Grass', poems by Whitman W-200
  American literature A-349

Leawood, Kan., residential city 15 mi (25 km) s. of Kansas City; incorporated in 1948; pop. 13,360.

Lebanon (from Arabic *laban,* "to be white"), republic on Mediterranean n. of Israel; cap. Beirut; area 4,015 sq mi (10,400 sq km); cedars of Lebanon supplied by Hiram of Tyre for Solomon's temple (Bible, I Kings v); pop. 3,316,000 L-111
  Asia, *map* A-700
  Israel I-373
  national symbols
    flag, *picture* F-167
    song, *table* N-64
  railroad mileage, *table* R-85
  soldiers, *pictures* I-263, M-397
  United States
    Eisenhower administration E-141
    marines' tragedy M-139
      Reagan R-112j
  world, *map* W-297

Lebanon, N.H., city 47 mi (76 km) n.w. of Concord; dairy products and poultry, textiles, wood products, machinery, leather goods; founded 1761; pop. 11,134, *map* N-191

Lebanon, Pa., industrial city 25 mi (50 km) n.e. of Harrisburg; in limestone and iron-mining district; chemicals, iron and steel products, textiles, food products, paper boxes, pharmaceuticals; pop. 25,711, *map* P-185

Lebanon, Tenn., city 30 mi (50 km) n.e. of Nashville; livestock, timber, Burley tobacco, and limestone; place where Sam Houston practiced law; pop. 11,872.

Lebanon, Cedar of L-111
  Beirut landmark B-144
  ships S-164

Lebanon Mountains, range in Lebanon close to the coastal plain; highest point 10,131 ft (3,088 m) L-111
  Beirut B-143

Lebanon Valley College, Annville, Pa.; United Methodist church; founded 1866; arts and sciences, education; member cooperative University Center at Harrisburg.

Lebedev, Pyotr N. (1866–1912), Russian physicist, born in Moscow E-162

Lebedev, Valentin (born 1942), Soviet cosmonaut, born in Moscow, U.S.S.R., *table* S-348

Le Bel, Joseph Achille (1847–1930), French chemist, born in Pechelbronn, Alsace; 1874 set forth concept of asymmetric carbon atom independently of his contemporary, Van't Hoff; experiments in organic chemistry.

Lebensraum, German word, meaning "living space," slogan of German imperialism; used by Adolf Hitler to express Germany's demand for new territories and economic self-sufficiency.

Leblanc, Maurice (1864–1941), French writer, born in Rouen; wrote stories about Arsène Lupin, gentleman-burglar who turned detective.

Leblanc, Nicolas (1742–1806), French chemist, born in Issoudun; in 1789 discovered method of making soda from common salt; lost both property and his patent rights in French Revolution.

Leblanc process, for making soda and by-products S-247

Le Blon, Jacques Christophe (1667–1741), French painter and engraver, born in Frankfurt, Germany; the father of modern color printing.

Le Bris, Jean Marie (died 1872), French sea captain and inventor; patterned first glider after albatross A-201
  glider G-167

Lebrun, Albert François (1871–1950), 14th president of France under the Third Republic, born in Mercy-le-Haut, n.e. France; president of the Senate 1931–32; president of France 1932–40.

Le Brun, Charles (1619–90), French artist and designer, born in Paris; as one of founders of the Royal Academy of Painting and Sculpture and director of Gobelin tapestry manufactory, he practically directed French art tendencies during his lifetime; court artist under Louis XIV F-458, 462

Lebrun, Elisabeth Vigée-. *see in index* Vigée-Lebrun

Le Cap, Haiti. *see in index* Cap-Haïtien

Le Caron, Joseph (1586–1632), French Roman Catholic missionary, born near Paris; pioneered among Hurons in Canada; compiler of first Huron dictionary; sent back to France (1629) by British after capture of Quebec.

Le Carré, John (formerly David John Moore Cornwell) (born 1913), British author L-113

Le Chatelier, Henry Louis (1850–1936), French chemist, born in Paris; known for law of chemical equilibrium.

Lechfeld, battle of (955), on plain of Lechfeld in Bavaria; Magyars defeated by Otto I, A-828

Lechon, Philippine food P-253d

Lech River, rapid and tortuous stream rising in Vorarlberg Alps at height of 6,120 ft (1,865 m); flows n. through Bavaria 180 mi (290 km), joining Danube below Donauwörth, *map* G-134

Lecithin, a fatty substance found in plant and animal cells S-340

Lecky, William Edward Hartpole (1838–1903), Irish historian and publicist, born in Newton Park, near Dublin ('A History of European Morals'; 'History of England in the Eighteenth Century').

Leclaire, Edmé Jean (1801–72), French social scientist; founded system of profit sharing at his interior decorating firm in Paris 1842.

Leclanché, Georges, French inventor B-108

Leclerc, Jacques Philippe (originally Jacques Leclerc de Hauteclocque) (1902–47), French army officer, born in Belloy-Saint-Léonard, n. France; prisoner of Germans 1940; escaped, joined Free French; led force across Sahara to meet General Montgomery 1943; led French into Paris Aug. 1944; signed for France at Japanese surrender on *U.S.S. Missouri* Sept. 2, 1945.

Lecocq, Alexandre Charles (1832–1918), French composer, born in Paris; produced many light operas, melodious, happy, and lively ('La Fille de Madame Angot'; 'Girofle-Girofla').

Lecompton, Kan., town on Kansas River, 15 mi (25 km) e. of Topeka; settled 1854 by proslavery men and was their headquarters during contest with free-state settlers for control of the state; pop. 576.

Lecompton Constitution, adopted by proslavery faction of Kansas in 1857 B-476

Le Conte, Joseph (1823–1901), U.S. scientist, born in Liberty County, Ga.; helped popularize geology ('Elements of Geology'; 'Religion and Science').

Leconte de Lisle, Charles Marie (1818–94), French poet, born on island of Bourbon (now Réunion); chief of modern Parnassian school ('Poèmes antiques').

LeConte's thrasher, bird *Toxostoma lecontei* T-175

Lecoq de Boisbaudran, Paul Emile (nickname François) (1838–1912), French chemist, discoverer of gallium, samarium, dysprosium, holmium.

Le Corbusier (or Charles-Édouard Jeanneret-Gris) (1887–1965), Swiss architect L-113
  architecture A-565, 568, *picture* A-564
  museum design M-663

Lecouvreur, Adrienne, French actress A-27

Le Creusot, France, town in e.-center, 75 mi (120 km) n.w. of Lyons; famous iron and armaments works; pop. 33,581, *map* F-369

Lecturer, college instructor U-206

'Lectures on Shakespeare', book by Coleridge C-546

Lecuona, Ernesto (1895–1963), Cuban composer, conductor, and pianist; born in Guanabacoa, Cuba; piano debut at 5; composed first work at 11 ('Malagueña'; 'Andalucía')
  classical music M-675

LED. *see in index* Light-emitting diode

Leda, in Greek and Roman mythology, a fair mortal wooed by Zeus (Jupiter) in guise of swan; mother of twins Castor and Pollux, of Helen, and of Clytemnestra.

Ledbetter, Huddie (or Leadbelly) (1888–1949), U.S. folksinger, born in Mooringsport, La. B-302
  folk music F-273

Lederberg, Joshua (born 1925), U.S. geneticist, born in Montclair, N.J.; professor University of Wisconsin 1954–59, Stanford University 1959–.

Ledger line, music notation M-690

Le Diable, a notorious French dog D-193

Lednik Fedchenko, glacier in U.S.S.R. T-5

Ledo Road. *see in index* Stilwell Road

Ledyard, John (1751–89), U.S. adventurer, born in Groton, Conn.; dreamed of opening up fur trade in Pacific Northwest, glimpsed on voyage (1776–80) with Captain Cook; enlisted interest of John Paul Jones, Thomas Jefferson, Sir Joseph Banks; failed in two attempts to cross Siberia on foot; died during expedition into Africa.

Ledyard, Conn., 7 mi (11 km) n.e. of New London in agricultural area; plastics; incorporated 1836; pop. of township 13,735.

Lee, Ann (or Mother Ann) (1736–84), U.S. religious leader; born in Manchester, England; to North America 1774; founder of the American Society of Shakers, set up first Shaker colony near Albany, N.Y., 1776 S-128

Lee, Arthur (1740–92), U.S. diplomat, born in Stratford, Va.; brother of Richard Henry Lee; served as American representative in various European countries during Revolutionary War.

Lee, Bruce (1940–73), Japanese martial arts star M-158

Lee, Charles (1731–82), American Revolutionary War general, born in Dernhall, Cheshire, England; dismissed for insubordination; involved in treasonable intrigues not discovered until after his death R-168, 172

Lee, Daulton, U.S.-born Soviet collaborator E-303

Lee, Dennis (born 1939), Canadian poet and author, born in Toronto (children's poetry: 'Wiggle to the Laundromat'; 'Alligator Pie', won Canadian Book of the Year for Children award 1975; 'Nicholas Knock and Other People'; 'Garbage Delight', won Canadian Book of the Year for Children award 1978).

Lee, Doris Emrick (born 1905), U.S. modernist painter, muralist, and book illustrator, born in Aledo, Mercer County, Ill.; married Arnold Blanch; known for rural scenes done with humor and charm; work represented in Metropolitan Museum of Art and major galleries ('Thanksgiving Dinner', 'Country Wedding').

Lee, Fitzhugh (1835–1905), Confederate Civil War general, born in Fairfax County, Va.; nephew of Robert E. Lee; military governor of Havana, Cuba, after Spanish-American War.

Lee, Francis Lightfoot (1734–97), signer of Declaration of Independence, born in Stratford, Va.; brother of Richard Henry Lee D-56

Lee, Harper (full name Nelle Harper Lee) (born 1926), U.S. novelist, born in Monroeville, Ala.; won 1960 Pulitzer prize for her first novel, 'To Kill a Mockingbird' R-111i

Lee, Jason (1803–45), U.S. Methodist missionary and Oregon pioneer, born in Stanstead, Que., then part of Vt.; went west with Wyeth's expedition (1834) to open mission among Flathead Indians; aided by Dr. McLoughlin in settling in Willamette Valley; established other missions in Clatsop region and at The Dalles
  Oregon establishment O-586
  Oregon Trail O-598
  Statuary Hall, *table* S-437b

Lee, Joseph (1862–1937), U.S. social worker, born in Brookline, Mass.; known as "father of American playground movement"; organized and was president of National Recreation Association from 1910; president War Camp Community Service during World War I ('Play in Education'); National Joseph Lee Day celebrated July 28.

Lee, Light-Horse Harry (or Henry Lee) (1756–1818), U.S. statesman and American Revolutionary War general L-114

Lee, Manfred B. *see in index* Queen, Ellery

Lee, Richard Henry (1732–94), American Revolutionary War leader L-114
  Declaration of Independence D-54

Lee, Robert E. (1807–70), general, Confederate States of America L-115
  Civil War C-474, 643, *picture* C-644
    Gettysburg G-136, *picture* P-178
    Grant G-217
    McClellan M-4
    Stuart S-494
  Hall of Fame, *table* H-16
  North Carolina Tar Heels N-356
  Statuary Hall, *table* S-437b
  Stone Mountain, *picture* G-88
  Virginia, *picture* V-342

Lee, Sir Sidney (1859–1926), English author and educator, born in London; editor 'Dictionary of National Biography'; works include 'Life of Shakespeare', 'Life of Queen Victoria' S-142

Lee, Tsung-Dao (or Tsung Dao-lee) (born 1926), Chinese physicist, born in Shanghai; professor Columbia University 1956–60, 1963–; professor Institute of Advanced Study 1960–63. *see also in index* Nobel Prizewinners, *table*
  Wu W-383

Lee, William (died 1610), English clergyman and inventor of the first knitting machine H-278
  needlework N-113

Leeboard, a slab of wood or metal hung over the leeward side of sailing canoes and other small craft to prevent drifting sideways.

Leech, John (1817–64), English caricaturist, whose *Punch* cartoons John Ruskin called "the finest definition and natural history of the classes of our society, the kindest and subtlest analysis of its foibles."

Leech, nautical, *diagram* B-326

Leech, worm W-363, *picture* W-361

Leechee. *see in index* Litchi

Leigh, England, town in Lancashire, 20 mi (30 km) n.e. of Liverpool; coal mining; textiles, electric cable; pop. 46,200, *map* U-18a

Leigh-Mallory, Sir Trafford Leigh (1892–1944), British air officer, born in Mobberley, near Manchester, England; headed Allied air forces for invasion of Europe 1944; lost in flight to command in s.e. Asia.

Leighton, Frederick, Baron Leighton of Stretton (1830–96), English painter and sculptor, born in Scarborough, England; best known for classical subjects S-90

Leighton, Margaret (born 1896), U.S. author, born in Oberlin, Ohio; daughter of Thomas Nixon Carver, professor of political economy at Harvard University for many years; books for children: 'The Singing Cave'; 'Judith of France'; 'The Sword and the Compass'; 'Journey for a Princess'.

Leinsdorf, Erich (born 1912), U.S. conductor, born in Vienna, Austria; to U.S. 1937, became citizen 1942; chief conductor of German opera Metropolitan Opera House, New York City, 1939–43; conductor Cleveland (Ohio) Orchestra 1943–44, 1945–47, Rochester (N.Y.) Philharmonic Orchestra 1947–56; musical director and conductor Boston Symphony Orchestra 1962–69
  orchestra, *list* O-579

Leinster, one of 4 provinces of Ireland, in middle and s.e. part s. of Ulster and s.e. of Munster provinces; bordered on e. by Irish Sea, on s.e. by St. George's Channel; 7,580 sq mi (19,630 sq km); pop. 1,414,415.

Leipzig, East Germany, city in Saxony, 70 mi (110 km) n.w. of Dresden; pop. 560,012 L-123
  bust of Bach, *picture* G-116
  Germany, *maps* E-360, G-134

Leipzig, battle of (1631), in Thirty Year's War, *list* W-15

Leipzig, battle of (1813), Napoleonic Wars, *list* W-15
  Napoleon N-17

Leipzig, University of. *see in index* Karl Marx University

Leipzig Trade Fair L-123

Leisler, Jacob (1640–91), popular leader in colonial New York, born in Frankfurt, Germany; executed for insurrection N-256

Leisure L-123. *see also in index* Hobby; Reading for recreation; Recreation; Sewing
  increase U-103
  industry I-184
  radio R-43, 48, 57
  television P-535

Leith, Scotland, seaport and shipbuilding center on s. shore of Firth of Forth; port for Edinburgh, with which it was incorporated 1920; pop. 51,378.

Leitmotiv, in music M-673
  opera O-568

Leitrim, county in Connaught province, Ireland; 589 sq mi (1,526 sq km); lost more by emigration than any other county; beautiful scenery, especially along River Shannon; organized as county 1583; pop. 30,572.

Leitzel, Lillian, circus performer C-432

Leix (or Laoighis, or Queen's), county in s.e. Ireland, in Leinster Province; 664 sq mi (1,720 sq km); farming, dairying, textile manufacturing; county town Port Laoighise (Maryborough); pop. 44,595.

Le Jeune, Paul (1591–1664), French Jesuit missionary, born in Châlons-sur-Marne; 1632–39 was in Quebec, as superior of Canadian missions.

Lek, river in w. Europe; part of the Rhine River N-125

Leland, Charles Godfrey (1824–1903), U.S. poet, ethnologist, traveler, and pioneer educator in art handicraft, born in Philadelphia, Pa. ('Hans Breitmann's Ballads', poems in Pennsylvania Dutch dialect).

Leland, Henry Martyn (1843–1932), U.S. pioneer automobile manufacturer; founder Cadillac Motor Car Company, Lincoln Motor Company A-858, *list* A-856

Leland Stanford Junior University. *see in index* Stanford University

Leloir, Luis Federico (born 1906), Argentine biochemist, born in Paris, France; director Institute of Biochemical Research, Buenos Aires, 1947–.

Lely, Sir Peter (originally Pieter van der Faes) (1618–80), English court painter, born in Westphalia, Germany, of Dutch family; portraits of beautiful women of court of Charles II.

Lem, Stanislaw, Polish science fiction writer S-61

Lemaître, Jules (1853–1914), French critic and dramatist, born in Vennecy, near Orléans, France ('Impressions of the Theatre' and 'Contemporaries', widely read critical essays; 'The Pardon', 'The Poor Little Thing', plays).

Léman, Lac. *see in index* Geneva, Lake

Le Mans, France, commercial and manufacturing city on Sarthe River, 115 mi (185 km) s.w. of Paris; French under General Chanzy defeated 1871 by Germans; again fell to Germans 1940; pop. 140,520, *map* F-369
  Grand Prix auto race A-874

Lemare, Edwin Henry (1866–1934), English organist and composer, born in Ventnor, Isle of Wight; organist in London, England, at Carnegie Institute, Pittsburgh, Pa., San Francisco, Calif., Portland, Me., and Chattanooga, Tenn.; composed organ and choral works, and made transcriptions of orchestral works for organ.

LeMay, Curtis Emerson (born 1906), U.S. Air Force officer, born in Columbus, Ohio; Air Force deputy chief of staff for research and development 1945–47; commanding general U.S. Air Forces in Europe 1947–48, Strategic Air Command 1948–57; became 4-star general 1951; Air Force vice-chief of staff 1957–61, chief of staff 1961–65; American Independent vice-presidential candidate 1968; author of 'America Is in Danger' A-159

Lemay, Léon-Pamphile (1837–1918), Canadian poet and novelist, born in Lotbinière, near Quebec; educated in theology and law; librarian to Quebec legislature 1867–92 ('Les Vengeances', 'Petits poèmes', 'Les Gouttelettes', 'Reflets d'antan', poetry; 'Le Pèlerin de Sainte Anne', 'L'Affaire Sougraine', fiction).

Lemay, Mo., residential city bordering St. Louis on south; stone quarries; pop. 40,516.

Lemberg, U.S.S.R. *see in index* L'vov

Lemke, William (1878–1950), U.S. political leader, born in Albany, Minn.; attorney general of North Dakota 1921–23; Republican representative from North Dakota 1933–50.

Lemmon slave case (1854) A-652

Lemnitzer, Lyman Louis (born 1899), U.S. Army officer, born in Honesdale, Pa.; commissioned 2nd lieutenant 1920, became 4-star general 1955; Army deputy chief of staff (plans and research) 1952–55; commander in chief of Far East command and of UN command 1955–57; Army vice-chief of staff 1957–59, chief of staff 1959–60; chairman Joint Chiefs of Staff 1960–62; supreme allied commander in Europe 1963–69; first person to receive distinguished service medals of Army, Navy, and Air Force at same time (July 1969).

Lemnos, island in n. Aegean; 150 sq mi (390 sq km); held in turn by ancient Greeks, Byzantine Empire, Italians, and Turks; Greek after World War I.

Lemon, Robert Granville (nickname Bob) (born 1920), U.S. baseball player, born in San Bernardino, Calif.; A.L. infielder-outfielder 1941–42, pitcher 1946–58.

Lemon, citrus fruit *Citrus limon* C-444, *picture* C-445
  cultivation B-178
  fruitgrowing F-438
  fruit production, *chart* F-430
  perfume making P-204
  pests and diseases S-52e
  vitamins V-356

Lemon Grove, Calif., community just s.e. of San Diego; chiefly residential; pop. 19,690.

Lemonnier, Pierre Charles (1715–99), French astronomer, born in Paris; made many observations of Uranus before its discovery as a planet; these led to the discovery of the planet Pluto.

Lemon verbena, a perennial plant *Lippia citriodora* related to lantana; flowers white or lilac in a 3-spike cluster; leaves lemon-scented, with glandular dots; native to South America.

Le Moyne, Charles (1626–85), French colonist in Canada; father of famous explorers and soldiers better known by territorial titles. *see also in index* Bienville; Iberville

Le Moyne, Jean Baptiste. *see in index* Bienville, sieur de

LeMoyne College, Syracuse, N.Y.; Roman Catholic; founded 1946; arts and sciences, business administration, and teacher education N-255

LeMoyne-Owen College, Memphis, Tenn.; affiliated with United Church of Christ and Tenn. Baptist Convention; founded 1870; liberal arts, education.

Lemur, a fox-faced monkey-like animal L-125
  Africa, *picture* A-98
  Madagascar M-23

Lena Basin, U.S.S.R. L-125

Lena delta, delta, U.S.S.R., *table* D-90

Le Nain, Antoine (1588–1648), **Louis Le Nain** (1593–1648), and **Mathieu Le Nain** (1607–77), French painters, brothers, born in Laon, France; depicted interiors; also portrayed scenes of everyday life of peasants; pictures grayish and dull in color.

Lenape. *see in index* Delaware

Lenard, Philipp (1862–1947), Hungarian physicist, born in present Bratislava, Czechoslovakia; head of radiological institute at Heidelberg, Germany.

Lena River, in n.e. Siberia; empties into Arctic, forming vast delta; length 2,860 mi (4,600 km) L-125
  Asia, *map* A-700
  comparative length. *see in index* River, *table*
  Russia, *map* R-322
  Siberia, *picture* S-190
  world, *map* W-297

Lenasia, town, South Africa J-122

Lenau, Nikolaus (pseudonym of Nikolaus Franz Edler von Niembsch von Strehlenau) (1802–50), Austrian poet, born in Hungary; intense melancholia gave his lyrics somber, pessimistic tone; died insane ('Faust'; 'Savonarola'; 'Die Albigenser').

Lenbach, Franz von (1836–1904), German portrait painter, born in Schrobenhausen, near Ingolstadt, Germany; called "greatest of his generation"; painted Emperor William I and Bismarck.

Lendl, Ivan (born 1960), Czech-U.S. tennis player, born in Ostrava, Czechoslovakia; became professional 1979; member Czech Davis Cup squad early 1980s; singles wins included French Open 1984, 1986, 1987; U.S. Open 1985, 1986; known for his powerful serve and physical fitness; defected to the United States 1986.

Lend-lease, U.S. program during World War II
  foreign aid F-307
  Roosevelt R-275
  World War II W-326, *table* W-333

Lenepveu, Jules Eugène (1819–98), French painter; best known for classical and historical paintings and for decorative frescoes in theaters, churches, and public buildings ('The Martyrs in the Catacombs').

Lenglen, Suzanne (1899–1938), French tennis player, born in Compiègne; six-time Wimbledon champion in women's singles, 1919–23 and 1925; also starred in doubles; professional 1926–27
  tennis T-107, *picture* T-106

Length, physics. *see in index* Measurement; Metric system; Relativity; Weights and measures

Lenin (or Vladimir Ilich Ulyanov, or N. Lenin, or V.I. Lenin) (1870–1924), Russian Bolshevist leader L-126,
  educational contribution E-101
  film M-620
  government G-199
    Communist theory C-619
  Khar'kov statue, *picture* K-231
  Moscow M-594
  portrait, *pictures* R-326, 328
  Russian history R-354, *pictures* R-355–57
  Socialism S-235
  Stalin S-403
  U.S.S.R., *picture* U-15

'Lenin', Soviet icebreaker S-170

Lenin, Order of, medals M-272

Leninakan, U.S.S.R., city in Armenian Soviet Socialist Republic; 85 mi (140 km) s.w. of Tbilisi; textile center; much destruction by earthquake 1926; pop. 164,000, *maps* R-344, 349
  Europe, *map* E-360

Leningrad (formerly St. Petersburg, or Petrograd), U.S.S.R., industrial and commercial city, former capital of Russia; pop. 4,719,000 L-127
  Europe, *map* E-360
  flood, *table* F-181
  Lenin L-126
  Moscow M-594
  Russia, *picture* R-354, *graph* R-334, *maps* R-322, 344, 348
  world, *map* W-297

Lenin Library, Moscow, U.S.S.R. M-593, *picture* M-594

Lenin Peak (formerly Mount Kaufman), U.S.S.R., mountain on border between Kirghiz Soviet Socialist Republic and Tadzhik Soviet Socialist Republic ; height 23,405 ft (7,134 m); highest point in Trans-Alai Range T-5

Lenin Square, Tashkent, U.S.S.R.

Lennep, Jacob van (1802–68), Dutch poet and novelist, born in Amsterdam; wrote patriotic songs and historical romances of which 'De Pleegzoon' (The Adopted Son) is most famous.

Lenni-Lenape. *see in index* Delaware

Lennon, John (1940–80), British singer B-119
  assassination A-703
  popular music M-682

Lennox, Calif., community 10 mi (16 km) s.w. of Los Angeles; industrial and farming area; pop. 16,121.

Lenoir, Jean Joseph Étienne (1822–1900), French inventor of practical gas engine, born in Mussy-la-Ville, Luxembourg A-856

Lenoir, William Benjamin (born 1939), U.S. astronaut candidate, born in Miami, Fla.; electrical engineer chosen for NASA scientist-astronaut program 1967, *table* S-348

Lenoir, N.C., town 62 mi (100 km) n.w. of Charlotte; resort, set in foothills of Blue Ridge Mountains; furniture, textiles, hosiery; incorporated 1851; pop. 13,748.

Lenoir-Rhyne College, Hickory, N.C.; affiliated with Lutheran Church in America; established in 1891; arts and sciences, nursing, and teacher education.

Lenormand, Henri René (1882–1951), French dramatist, born in Paris; plays deal with psychoanalytical and often abnormal themes ('The Failures'; 'Time Is a Dream').

Lenôtre, André (or André Le Nôtre) (1613–1700), French landscape architect, born in Paris; style formal, classical, symmetrical; designed Versailles, Fontainebleau, and other royal gardens for Louis XIV; also English gardens for Charles II F-335

Lenox, Walter Scott (1859–1920), U.S. potter, born in Trenton, N.J. P-477

Lenox porcelain P-477

Lenroot, Katharine Fredrica (born 1891), U.S. social worker, born in Superior, Wis.; served in Children's Bureau, U.S. Department of Labor, 1915–34, and was chief 1934–51.

Lens, France, coal-mining and iron-manufacturing city 17 mi (27 km) s.w. of Lille; victory of French under prince of Condé over Spaniards (1648); pop. 41,800.

Lens, freshwater that rests on heavier salt water O-468

Lens, part of the eye E-387

Lens, optics O-574
- camera P-283
  - motion pictures M-602
- eyeglasses E-392
  - spectacles S-370
- field glasses and binoculars F-78
- light refraction L-196
- microscope M-380
  - Leeuwenhoek L-117
- stereopticon S-443, *diagrams* S-444
- telescopic A-730
- Zeiss Z-449

Lens and turret system, printing T-339

Lenski, Lois (1893–1974), U.S. writer and illustrator of books for children, born in Springfield, Ohio; historical backgrounds are based on old records and diaries ('Bound Girl of Cobble Hill'; 'Ocean-Born Mary'; 'Indian Captive'); regional stories based on her experiences ('Strawberry Girl', winner of Newbery Medal in 1946; 'Prairie School'; 'San Francisco Boy'); picture books for small children ('Little Airplane'; 'Mr. and Mrs. Noah'; 'Cowboy Small'; 'Papa Small'); awarded Regina Medal 1969; autobiography, 'Journey into Childhood'.

Lent, Blair (born 1930), U.S. illustrator, born in Boston, Mass.; 1973 Caldecott winner for 'The Funny Little Woman' (author and illustrator 'Pistachio', 'John Tabor's Ride', 'Baba Yaga'; compiler and illustrator 'From King Boggen's Hall to Nothing-at-all'; illustrator 'The Wave') R-106

Lent, in Christianity
- calendar C-29
- Easter E-41
- fasting F-44

Lent lily. *see in index* Daffodil

Lento, in music, *list* M-670

Lenz's law, electromagnetic induction, *diagrams* R-59
- electricity E-159

Leo I (died 461), saint and pope, commemorated as saint April 11 L-130

Leo III (died 816), saint and pope, commemorated as saint June 12 L-130
- Charlemagne C-273
- Holy Roman Empire H-208

Leo IV (800?–855), saint and pope, commemorated as saint July 17.

Leo IX (1002–54), saint and pope, commemorated as saint April 19 L-130
- Great Schism B-536

Leo X (1475–1521), pope L-131
- Luther L-338
- Medici M-273

Leo XIII (1810–1903), pope L-131

Leo III, the Isaurian (680?–741), Byzantine emperor 717–41; in 718 saved empire from Saracens; freed serfs and reduced taxation
- campaign B-535

Leo VI, the Wise (866–912), Byzantine emperor 886–912; noted for legislative works ('Basilica', revision of Justinian laws; 'Book of Prefect', applied to guilds of Constantinople; 'Tactics', for the army and navy).

Leo (or Lion), constellation
- constellation, *chart* C-681
- Regulus, *charts* S-418, 422
- zodiac, *chart* A-708

Leofric, earl of Mercia (died 1057), husband of Lady Godiva; in 1051 acted as mediator between Edward the Confessor and Earl Godwin.

Leo Minor, constellation, *chart* C-681

Leominster, Mass., industrial city about 19 mi (31 km) n. of Worcester; plastic and paper products, clothing, furniture; pop. 34,508.

León, Mexico, city 200 mi (320 km) n.w. of Mexico City; center of agricultural and mining district; cereals, potatoes, fruit, livestock; shoes, textiles; pop. 209,870, *map* N-350
- Mexico, *map* M-341

León, Nicaragua, city 45 mi (70 km) n.w. of Managua; in fertile farming district; corn, coffee, sugarcane, cattle and dairy products; National University; cathedral (completed 1780); city founded 1524 on shore of Lake Managua; after destruction by earthquake, city was moved in 1610 to present site; former capital of Nicaragua; pop. 55,347, *map* N-350

León, Spain, ancient kingdom and modern province in n.w.; cap. León (pop. 73,483), *map* E-360
- early history S-358

Leonard, Benny, boxer B-392

Leonard, Sugar Ray, (real name Ray Charles Leonard) (born 1956), boxer, born in Wilmington, S.C.; Olympic gold medalist 1976; turned professional 1977; welterweight champion (WBA 1979, 1980–82; WBC 1980–82); retired 1982; made comeback in 1987 by winning middleweight title (WBC); retired 1987.

Leonard, Walter Fenner (nickname Buck) (born 1907) U.S. baseball first baseman, born in N.C.; famed as home run hitter for Homestead Grays; in Negro and Mexican leagues 1933–55

Leonard, William Ellery (1876–1944), U.S. poet and educator, born in Plainfield, N.J.; professor of English, University of Wisconsin ('Two Lives', 'A Son of Earth', poems; 'The Locomotive God', autobiography).

Leonardo da Vinci (1452–1519), Italian artist and inventor L-132
- anatomical drawings A-875
- automation A-833
- bicycle B-187
- flying machine A-200
- handwriting H-29
- history of biology B-228
- invention, *picture* I-277
  - diving helmet D-187
- medicine M-283
- 'Mona Lisa' P-37, *picture* P-36
- parachute idea P-109b
- weapons designs, *picture* W-112
- zoology Z-470

Leonardo of Pisa (1170?–1240), Italian mathematician, *table* M-218

Leoncavallo, Ruggero (1857–1919), Italian composer L-135
- opera O-568

Leonidas, king of Sparta, killed 480 BC at Thermopylae T-168
- Persian wars P-215
- warfare W-23

Léonin (12th century), French liturgical composer M-668

'Leonore', work by Beethoven B-136

Leonov, Aleksei Arkhipovich (born 1934), Soviet cosmonaut, born near Irkutsk; parachute instructor; copilot of Voskhod II spaceship; Soyuz commander of 1975 Apollo-Soyuz flight S-346f, *picture* U-196b, *table* S-348

Leonov, Leonid Maksimovich (born 1899), Russian novelist, born in Moscow R-360b, 361

Leontief, Wassily (born 1906), U.S. economist, born in Leningrad, Russia; came to U.S. 1931, naturalized citizen; did pioneer work in input-output analysis; professor Harvard University 1946–.

Leopard, animal of the cat family *Felis bengalensis* L-135
- cat, *picture* C-215
- endangered species E-212
- furs, *table* F-464
- protective coloration, *picture* P-513
- zoo Z-457

'Leopard', British warship W-29

'Leopard, The', work by Tomasi I-379

Leopardi, Giacomo, Count (1798–1837), Italian lyric poet, prose writer, and scholar; born in Recanati, near Macerata, Italy; master of finished style and slave of pessimism ('La Ginestra') I-377

Leopard's-bane. *see in index* Doronicum

Leopard seal. *see in index* Harbor seal

Leopold I (1790–1865), king of Belgium L-136
- Belgium B-149

Leopold II (1747–92), Holy Roman emperor A-830

Leopold II (1835–1909), king of Belgium L-136
- Belgium B-149
- Stanley S-410
- Zaire Z-443

Leopold III (1901–83), king of Belgium; abdicated 1951 L-136
- Belgium B-149
- Baudouin B-110
- World War II W-324

Leopold I (died 994), margrave of Austria A-828

Leopold V (1157–94), duke of Austria, succeeded 1177; went on Crusades 1182 and 1190; quarreled with Richard I in Palestine A-828
- Richard I R-202

Léopoldville, Republic of Zaire. *see in index* Kinshasa

Lepachys, annual or perennial plants of the composite family, native to North America; grow 2 to 5 ft (0.6 to 1.5 m); leaves finely cut; flowers solitary, on wiry stems, ray florets, 6 or 7, yellow or purple, droop from the cylindrical thimblelike center of disk florets that are first silver gray, later brown; called yellow, gray-headed, or longheaded coneflower.

Lepanto, battle of (Oct. 7, 1571), naval engagement between allied Christian forces and the Ottoman Turks during an Ottoman campaign to acquire the Venetian island of Cyprus
- navy N-92
- Ottoman Empire O-617
- warfare, *list* W-15

Lepaya, Latvian Soviet Socialist Republic. *see in index* Liepaja

Lepidolite, mineral M-436

Lepidoptera, the order of scaly-winged insects including butterflies, moths, and skippers B-521

Lepidus, Marcus Aemilius (died 13 BC), Roman consul and army commander; triumvir with Antony and Octavian (Augustus); his army betrayed him when he attempted a revolt against Octavian A-462, 496

Leporidae, a family of small, gnawing animals including hares and rabbits. *see in index* Rabbit and hare

Leprechaun, in Irish superstition, a pygmy sprite sometimes inhabiting wine cellars, sometimes farmhouses, and aiding in work; possesses treasure which human may get by keeping his eye fixed on sprite F-12

Le Prince de Beaumont, Jeanne Marie (1711–80), French writer, born in Rouen, France S-475

Lepromatous leprosy L-136

Leprosy (or Hansen's disease), chronic communicable disease of skin, mucous membranes, and peripheral nerves; known since ancient times; bacillus, discovered 1879 by G.H.A. Hansen (1841–1912) of Norway; treatment with sulfones, begun 1943, made possible cure or arrest of disease and eliminated need for traditional isolation of victims from society L-136
- infectious disease, *table* D-171
- nervous disorder N-123

Leptis Magna, Libya, ancient seaport 100 mi (160 km) e. of Tripoli; founded by Phoenicians; became splendid Roman city; birthplace of Emperor Septimius Severus; ruins of harbor, beautiful sculptures, and buildings have been uncovered.

Leptocephalus larva, stage in development of an eel E-109

Lepton (plural lepta), a minor coin of ancient times, worth about 1/10 cent; Jerusalem lepton famed in Bible as "widow's mite"; also a modern bronze Greek coin worth 1/100 drachma.

Lepton, one of three main classes of subatomic particles A-750
- big bang theory, *diagram* C-732
- matter M-230
- nuclear energy N-421
- quark Q-5

Leptospirosis, disease
- dog D-209
- pig P-322

Lepus (or Hare), constellation, *charts* S-421, C-682

Le Puy, France, city 140 mi (225 km) n.w. of Marseilles; 12th-century cathedral; lace, textiles, spirits; pop. 22,396, *map* F-369

Lerici, Carlo, Italian archaeologist A-533

Lérida, Spain, walled cathedral city 80 mi (130 km) w. of Barcelona; leather, glass, textiles; as a Celtiberian city, Ilerda, heroically resisted Romans; pop. 50,047.

Lérins, Monastery of, monastery on islet of Lérins group in Mediterranean off Cannes, France M-540

Lerma River (or Río Lerma), rises 18 mi (29 km) w. of Mexico City and flows 350 mi (560 km) w. to Lake Chapala, from which it emerges as Río Grande de Santiago and flows 250 mi (400 km) n.w. to Pacific Ocean; Santiago noted for scenic beauty of its canyon and, near Guadalajara, for the Juanacatlán Falls, which are 50 ft (15 m) high and 430 ft (130 m) wide
- Mexico M-324

Lermontov, Mikhail (full name Mikhail Yuryevich Lermontov) (1814–42), Russian poet and novelist L-136
- Russian literature R-360

Lerner, Alan Jay (1918–86), U.S. author and lyricist, born in New York City; collaborated with **Frederick Loewe** (born 1904), U.S. composer, born in Vienna ('Brigadoon', 'Camelot', musicals; 'An American in Paris', 'Gigi', films)
- musical comedy M-686

Lerwick, Scotland, capital and chief town of Shetland Islands, on s.e. coast of Mainland Island; pop. 5,919 S-162
- Europe, *map* E-360

Le Sage, Alain René (1668–1747), French novelist and dramatist, born in Sarzeau, near Vannes, France; a satiric realist ('Gil Blas', comic masterpiece of adventurous roguery).

Lesage, Jean (1912–80), Canadian political leader, born in Montreal, Que.; crown attorney 1939–44; member House of Commons 1945–58; delegate to UN 1950, 1952; leader Quebec Liberal party 1958–70; prime minister province of Quebec 1960–66.

Les Baux (or Les Beaux), France, village in s., near Arles; pop. 87.

Lesbos (modern Greek Mytilini), Greek island in Aegean Sea off coast of Asia Minor; about 650 sq mi (1,680 sq km); important naval and colonizing power in early history of Greece; famed for school of poets (7th century BC) and as birthplace of Sappho; passed to Turkey 1462, to Greece 1912; cap. Mytilene; olives, grapes, grain; pop. 114,797, *map* E-360
- ancient Greece G-264

Lescaze, William (1896–1969), U.S. architect, born in Geneva, Switzerland; came to U.S. 1920; leader in modernism.

Leschetizky, Theodor (1830–1915), Polish teacher of piano, born in Lancut, near Rzeszów, Poland; pupil of Czerny, he became eminent pianist; taught in St. Petersburg and Vienna; won chief fame as teacher of Paderewski; composed opera 'Die Erste Falte' and piano numbers.

Leskov, Nikolai Semenovich (1831–95), Russian author, born in St. Petersburg R-360a, 361

Leslie, Sir John (1766–1832), Scottish mathematician and physicist, born in Fife County, Scotland; inventor of a differential thermometer, photometer, and hygrometer; used air pump and sulfuric acid to freeze water and thus invented a process of artificial refrigeration.

Lesotho (or Basutoland), nation in s. Africa; 11,716 sq mi (30,344 sq km); cap. Maseru; pop. 1,499,600 L-137
- Africa, *map* A-118, *table* A-112
- Commonwealth membership C-602
- flag, *picture* F-167
- world, *map* W-297

Lespinasse, Julie Jeanne Eléonore de (1732–76), French

Daily Express; contributor *Daily Mail*; his studies and writings chiefly concerned with Middle Ages ('François Villon'; 'King Spider', on Louis XI of France; 'The World of Goya').
Lewis, Elizabeth Foreman (1892–1958), U.S. writer, born in Baltimore, Md.; missionary teacher in China; Newbery Medal (1933) for first book 'Young Fu of the Upper Yangtze' ('Ho-ming, Girl of New China'; 'To Beat a Tiger One Needs a Brother's Help').
Lewis, Francis (1713–1802), signer of Declaration of Independence as N.Y. delegate; born in Wales; a founder of Sons of Liberty.
Lewis, Gilbert Newton (1875–1946), U.S. chemist, born in Weymouth, Mass.; taught chemistry at Harvard University, Massachusetts Institute of Technology, and (after 1912) University of California; proposed (1916) his theory of atomic structure.
Lewis, Isaac Newton (1858–1931), U.S. Army officer and inventor, born in New Salem, Pa.; invented Lewis machine gun, which he manufactured in Belgium and supplied to the Allies in World War I.
Lewis, Jerry Lee (born 1935), U.S. rock'n'roll musician M-680
Lewis, John (born 1920), U.S. jazz innovator and pianist, born in La Grange, Ill.; was reared in Albuquerque, N.M.; leader of Modern Jazz Quartet.
Lewis, John L. (full name John Llewellyn Lewis) (1880–1969), U.S. labor leader L-142
labor movements L-8
Roosevelt R-271
Truman T-297
Lewis, Matthew Gregory (1775–1818), English romance writer and dramatist, born in London; nicknamed Monk after his most popular romance 'Ambrosio, or the Monk', which was suppressed; later reprinted in expurgated form E-274
Lewis, Meade Lux (1905–64), U.S. jazz pianist, born in Louisville, Ky.; popularized boogie-woogie upon emerging from obscurity several years after making a memorable record, 'Honky Tonk Train Blues' (1929).
Lewis, Meriwether (1774–1809), U.S. explorer L-142
Clark C-485
exploration E-376
Lewis and Clark Expedition L-143
Montana M-554
Oregon Trail O-598
Lewis, Sinclair (full name Harry Sinclair Lewis) (1885–1951), U.S. novelist L-142
American literature A-359
Minnesota M-444
Lewis, William Berkeley (1784–1866), U.S. political figure; friend, adviser, and campaign manager of Andrew Jackson and member of famous "Kitchen Cabinet."
Lewis, Wyndham (1884–1957), English author and artist, born in Maine; brought up in England; leader of vorticist painters ('Tarr', novel; 'Time and Western Man', philosophy; 'The Revenge for Love', a political satire; 'Rotting Hill', short stories).
Lewis and Clark Centennial Exposition (or American Pacific Exposition), held June 1 to Oct. 15, 1905, in Portland, Ore., to celebrate 100th anniversary of exploration of the Oregon country; cost about $7,000,000; attendance 2,545,509.
Lewis and Clark College, Portland, Ore.; private control; chartered 1867; opened as Albany College 1867; name changed 1942; arts and sciences, education, law; graduate studies; quarter system O-585
Lewis and Clark Expedition (1804–6), U.S. history L-143, *map* U-176
book about R-111c
Clark C-485
Columbia River C-590
frontier movements F-419
Idaho I-22, *picture* I-23
Lewis L-142
Missouri River M-510
Montana M-554
North Dakota N-376 Oregon O-585
Lewis and Clark Lake, on the Nebraska-South Dakota border, *picture* N-102
Lewis and Clark Trail, n.w. U S. M-553
Lewis College (or Lewis University), Romeoville, Ill.; private control; founded as technical school 1930, senior college 1950; liberal arts, aviation technology, education, and natural sciences; graduate studies.
Lewisham, borough, London, England, *maps* L-287, U-18a
Lewis Institute. *see in index* Illinois Institute of Technology
Lewisohn, Ludwig (1883–1955), U.S. writer, born in Berlin, Germany; to U.S. 1890; books show his attempted complete assimilation in Nordic civilization, his disappointment, and return to identification with Judaism (autobiography, 'Up Stream'; novel, 'The Island Within'; criticism, 'The Story of American Literature').
Lewisohn Stadium, New York City; belongs to and is on the campus of the City College of the City University of New York; site of summer concerts.
Lewisporte, Newf., port town on Notre Dame Bay 160 mi (260 km) n.w. of St. John's; former names include Big Burnt Bay and Marshallville; present name for English lumberman Lewis Miller who founded business here 1900; pop. 2,892.
Lewis Research Center, NASA N-22
Lewiston, Idaho, port city on Snake and Clearwater rivers, 90 mi (140 km) s.e. of Spokane, Wash.; wheat, livestock, fruit, vegetables; lumber, plywood, cartridges, paper; food processing; first capital of Idaho Territory 1863–64; annual Lewiston Roundup; pop. 27,986, *map* I-30
Lewiston, Me., 2nd city of state, on Androscoggin River opposite Auburn, 30 mi (50 km) n. of Portland; textiles, shoes, printing, wire goods, electronic tube and lighting equipment; Bates College; pop. 40,481
Maine M-54, 62
Lewistown, Mont., city at geographic center of state in farming, stock-raising, oil, and mining district; brick and tile, lumber, campers; honey, feed; pop. 7,104.
Lewistown, Pa., borough on Juniata River 43 mi (69 km) n.w. of Harrisburg; in farm and dairy area; iron and steel products, clothing; pop. 9,830, *map* P-184
Lewis-with-Harris, island, largest of Outer Hebrides; area 825 sq mi (2,135 sq km).
Lex Canuleia, Roman law R-243
Lex Hortensia, Roman law R-244
Lexington, Ky. *see in index* Lexington-Fayette
Lexington, Mass., 12 mi (19 km) n.w. of Boston; scene of first battle of Revolution (Lexington and Concord); pop. of township 29,479 M-189
Revere, *picture* R-161
Lexington, N.C., city 20 mi (30 km) s. of Winston-Salem; furniture, textiles, clothing, electronic and food products; pop. 15,711.
Lexington, Va., city in farming district 30 mi (50 km) n.w. of Lynchburg; Washington and Lee University, Virginia Military Institute; tombs of Stonewall Jackson and Robert E. Lee; pop. 7,292, *map* V-348
'Lexington', U.S. aircraft carrier W-344, *picture* W-345
Lexington and Concord, battle of L-144
American Revolution, *picture* R-168
Concord C-639
Revere's ride R-161
signaling S-193
Lexington-Fayette, Ky., city and county; in Bluegrass region, about 70 mi (110 km) e. of Louisville; horses, livestock, tobacco; machine products, tobacco processing, distilling, food products; Transylvania College; state and federal institutions; pop. 204,165 L-145
North America, *map* N-350
Lexington Plain (or Bluegrass Plain), area, Ky. K-209
Lex Valeria, Roman law R-242
Ley, Robert (1890–1945), German Nazi official, born in Niederbreidenbach, Rhine Province; committed suicide when captured at end of World War II G-123
Ley, Willy (1906–69), U.S. rocket authority and author, born in Berlin; to U.S. 1935, became citizen 1944; consultant office of technical services, U.S. Department of Commerce; wrote on space travel ('Conquest of Space'; 'Rockets, Missiles, and Men in Space'; 'The Exploration of Mars', with Wernher von Braun) and natural science ('Dragons in Amber'; 'Salamanders and Other Wonders'; 'Exotic Zoology'; 'Watchers of the Skies'; 'The Dawn of Zoology').
Leyden, Lucas van. *see in index* Lucas van Leyden
Leyden, The Netherlands. *see in index* Leiden
Leyden jar, electrical condenser
electricity E-161
lightning experiments L-207
Leyte, island of the Philippines; 2,786 sq mi (7,216 sq km); hemp, sugar, sulfur; cap. Tacloban (pop. of municipality, 53,551); pop. 1,223,667 P-255d, 256, 259, *maps* P-259a, 262
Asia, *map* A-700
World War II W-334, 348
Leyte Gulf, battle of, World War II W-348
navy N-92
LFC. *see in index* Laminar Flow Control
LHA (or General Assault Ship), naval vessel N-86
Lhasa, China, capital of Tibet; in s.e.; pop. 386,200 L-145
Asia, *map* A-700
Tibet T-180
world, *map* W-297
Lhasa apso, dog, *picture* D-206
Lhévinne, Josef (1874–1944), U.S. pianist, born in Russia; U.S. debut 1906; taught in Berlin, Germany, later in New York City.
Li, Chinese unit of measure, *table* W-141
Liability, in accounting A-15
Liability, in business C-150
Liability insurance I-233
malpractice M-78
Liakoura. *see in index* Parnassus, Mount
Liana, a climbing plant P-359
jungle plant life J-155
Liang Ch'i-ch'ao, (1873–1929) foremost intellectual leader of China in the first twenty years of the 20th century C-370
Liao, river in n.e. part of China; flows e. and s. to Gulf of Liaotung; 900 mi (1,450 km) long
Asia, *map* A-700
Manchuria M-93
Liaoning, (formerly Sheng-ching), province in n.e. part of China; area 56,000 sq mi (145,000 sq km); cap. Mukden; pop. 35,721,693 L-146
Lüda L-328
Manchuria M-94
Liaotung Peninsula, China, projects s.w. into Yellow Sea between gulfs of Liaotung and Korea; Port Arthur at tip. *see also in index* Dairen
Russo-Japanese War R-362
Liaoyang, China, city in Liaoning Province s.w. of Mukden; cotton milling, scene of Russian defeat in Russo-Japanese War; pop. 250,000 R-362
Liard River, Canada, 2nd largest tributary of Mackenzie River; rises in s. Yukon Territory and flows through n. British Columbia; enters Mackenzie at Fort Simpson, about 150 mi (240 km) west of Great Slave Lake, *map* O-100
North America, *map* N-350
Liatris (or blazing star, or button snakeroot, or liatrisa), a genus of perennial plants of the composite family, native to North America; tall wandlike flower spikes, purple or white, rise from clusters of narrow, ribbed leaves. *see also in index* Gayfeather
Libavius, Andreas, (1540–1616), born in Halle, Germany; chemist and physician; author of first modern chemistry textbook
crystallography C-796
Libby, Willard Frank (1908–80), U.S. chemist, born in Grand Valley, Colo.; professor of chemistry Institute for Nuclear Studies, University of Chicago, 1945–54; member of Atomic Energy Commission 1954–59; professor of chemistry University of California at Los Angeles 1959–80 A-535
man M-82
Libby Dam, Montana, on the Kootenai River M-554
Libby Prison, prison for captured Union officers at Richmond, Va., hastily established in Libby and Son's tobacco warehouse during Civil War; moved to Chicago 1889 and became the Libby Prison Museum; razed 1899; Libby Prison bricks used in North Wall of Civil War Room in Chicago Historical Society building.
Libel, in law, *table* L-93
Zenger Z-450
Liberace (1919–87) U.S. pianist and entertainer, born in West Allis, Wis.; known for flashy costumes and candelabra on piano; gave up serious career to achieve fame as flamboyant showman; had television show in 1950s; popular star in Las Vegas and on tour until his death.
Liberal, Kan., city in s.w. near Okla. boundary; trade center in agricultural region; oil, natural gas; food products, aircraft; incorporated 1888; International Pancake Race; pop. 13,789.
Liberal (or progressive), in education an individual that stresses the development of the "whole child"
education E-77, *chart* E-80
Liberal arts education E-83
history U-209
U.S.S.R. R-332d
Liberal-Country Coalition, political party, Australia A-816
Liberalism, political viewpoint L-146
Liberal party, Canada
King K-243
Pearson P-150
St. Laurent S-18
Liberal party (formerly Whig party), United Kingdom E-253. *see also in index* Whig party, England
Churchill C-412
conference, *picture* U-17
Gladstone G-134
Disraeli D-185
political parties P-434
Victoria V-309
Liberal Republican party, United States, formed 1872 by Republicans opposed to political abuses under President Grant, nominated candidates 1872 and 1876 G-218
Liberal Unionist party, United Kingdom, formed 1886 by Joseph Chamberlain C-266
Liberation theology, policy of Latin American Roman Catholic priests
church and state issue C-409
'Liberator', United States, abolitionist newspaper
Abolitionist movement A-10
Garrison G-36
Liberator (or B-24), U.S. military aircraft W-333, *picture* W-341
Liberec (or Reichenberg), Czechoslovakia, city in n. Bohemia; founded in 13th century; development began when first textile factory was established in 1823; pop. 66,365.
Liberia, republic on w. coast of Africa; 43,000 sq mi (111,400 sq km); cap. Monrovia; pop. 1,990,000 L-146
Africa A-111, *map* A-118, *table* A-112
anti-slavery movement A-10
Monrovia M-549
national symbols
flag, *picture* F-167
song, *table* N-64
Peace Corps, *picture* P-143a
political assassination A-704
railroad mileage, *table* R-85
ship tonnage, *table* S-176a
Libertinism, belief in doctrine of free will with behavior not restrained by conscience or conventions
Don Juan legend D-229
Liberty, Mo., city 13 mi (21 km) n.e. of Kansas City; corn,

mournful wail suggested its nicknames "the lamenting bird" and "mad widow."

Limpopo River, e. part of South Africa; forms n. boundary of Transvaal, then flows s.e. through Mozambique 1,000 mi (1,600 km) into Indian Ocean; scene of Kipling's 'Elephant's Child', *maps* A-118, S-264

Linaceae. *see in index* Flax family

Linacre, Thomas (1460?–1524), English humanist, physician, and divine; physician to Henry VII and Henry VIII; helped found College of Physicians, of which he was first president; but famed chiefly as classical scholar.

Linanthus, low-growing annual plants of the phlox family, native to western North America; leaves threadlike; flowers tiny starlike funnels or saucers, white through purple, completely cover plant in mass of bloom; used in rock gardens.

Linaria, genus of plants of the figwort family, including the toadflax, or butter-and-eggs, and Kenilworth ivy. *see also in index* Butter-and-eggs; Kenilworth ivy

Lin Biao (1907–71), Chinese Communist leader, born in Hupei Province; member politburo of Red China 1955–71; defense minister 1959–71; commander-in-chief of Red Guards 1966–71; Communist party vice-chairman 1969–71; named eventual successor to Mao Tse-tung 1969 C-375

Lincoln, Abraham (1809–65), 16th president of the United States L-211, *picture* C-472
- abolitionist movement A-10
- assassination A-703
- Cabinet
  - Seward S-121
  - Stanton S-411
- citizenship C-438
- Civil War C-472
  - Confederate States of America C-642
  - Emancipation Proclamation E-197
  - Gettysburg, Battle of G-137
- Douglas debates D-233, L-225
- government viewed G-198
- Hall of Fame, *table* H-16
- Illinois' history I-39, *pictures* I-46
- Johnson J-127
- memorials
  - Abraham Lincoln Birthplace N.H.S., *picture* K-213
  - Lincoln Boyhood N. Mem., *picture* I-99
  - Mount Rushmore N. Mem., *picture* S-321
  - Springfield, Ill. S-397
- political literature A-350
- Nast N-21
- Reconstruction views R-114
- slavery policy B-291
- statues
  - Saint-Gaudens, *picture* S-90
- Thanksgiving T-150

Lincoln, Benjamin (1733–1810), U.S. general, prominent in Revolutionary War, born in Hingham, Mass.; secretary of war 1781–84; commanded Massachusetts militia and suppressed Shays' Rebellion (1787) R-172

Lincoln, Mary Todd (1818–82), wife of President Lincoln L-217, *picture* L-220

Lincoln, Nancy Hanks (1784?–1818), mother of Abraham Lincoln, born in Virginia.

Lincoln, Robert Todd (1843–1926), U.S. lawyer, son of Abraham Lincoln; secretary of war 1881–89; minister to United Kingdom 1889–93
- Lincoln family, *picture* L-220

Lincoln, Thomas (1778–1851), U.S. pioneer; father of Abraham Lincoln L-211, 215

Lincoln (or Lincolnshire), agricultural county in e. England; 2,663 sq mi (6,897 sq km); divided into Parts of Holland, Parts of Kesteven, and Parts of Lindsey; cap. Lincoln; pop. 743,596.

Lincoln, England, capital of Lincoln County, on Witham River 125 mi (200 km) n. of London; metal products; Roman remains; pop. 75,770, *maps* B-341, U-18a
- Cathedral, *picture* E-252

Lincoln, Ill., city 28 mi (45 km) n.e. of Springfield in agricultural region; corrugated boxes, glass products; named for Abraham Lincoln when founded in 1853; pop. 16,327
- Illinois, *map* I-53

Lincoln, Neb., state capital, in s.e.; 2nd city of state; pop. 171,932 L-225, *maps* N-350, U-40. *see also in index* Nebraska at Lincoln, University of
- Nebraska N-96, 104, *picture* N-10

Lincoln, R.I., township 2 mi (3 km) n.e. of Pawtucket; composed of several villages including Lonsdale and Saylesville; limestone quarries; pop. 16,949.

Lincoln Boyhood National Memorial, Ind., *picture* I-99, *map* I-102

Lincoln Center for the Performing Arts, New York, N.Y. N-273, 278, *picture* N-280
- Rockefeller R-230

Lincoln-Douglas debates, U.S. history L-225
- Illinois I-41
- Lincoln L-219

Lincoln Highway, United States, a coast-to-coast national highway R-217

Lincoln Memorial, Washington, D.C. W-67
- design on $5 bill, *picture* L-224

Lincoln Memorial Garden, Springfield, Ill. S-397

Lincoln Memorial University, Harrogate, Tenn.; private control; chartered 1897; arts and sciences, education.

Lincoln Park, Mich., suburb of Detroit about 10 mi (16 km) s.; manufactures tools; incorporated as village 1921, as city 1925; pop. 45,105.

Lincoln Park Zoo, Chicago, Ill. Z-458, *pictures* Z-461, 463

Lincoln sheep S-147

Lincolnshire, county, England. *see in index* Lincoln

Lincoln's Inn Fields, square in London, England, laid out by Inigo Jones; named for Lincoln's Inn, on e. side, occupied by a guild of lawyers.

Lincoln University, Jefferson City, Mo.; state control; founded 1866; arts and sciences, journalism, music, and teacher education; graduate division J-96

Lincoln University, Lincoln University, Pa.; private control; established 1854; liberal arts.

Lincolnwood, Ill., village just n. of Chicago; photographic equipment and tape recorders; pop. 12,929
- Illinois, *map* I-53

Lind, Don L. (born 1930), U.S. astronaut candidate, born in Murray, Utah; physicist NASA Goddard Space Flight Center 1964–66; chosen for NASA program 1966.

Lind, James (1716–1794), British naval surgeon
- medicine M-283

Lind, Jenny (full name Johanna Maria Lind, nickname Swedish Nightingale) (1820–87), Swedish singer L-226

Lindbergh, Anne Spencer Morrow (born 1906), U.S. aviatrix and writer, born in Englewood, N.J.; wife of Charles A. Lindbergh; first woman to receive Hubbard gold medal of National Geographic Society 1934 for work as copilot and radio operator ('Bring Me a Unicorn', 'Hours of Gold, Hours of Lead', letters and diaries) L-227

Lindbergh, Charles Augustus (1859–1924), U.S. congressman, born in Stockholm, Sweden
- Minnesota M-445

Lindbergh, Charles A. (full name Charles Augustus Lindbergh) (1902–74), U.S. aviator L-226
- airline history A-170
- airplanes A-205, *picture* A-204
- archaeological survey A-532
- exploration E-377, *picture* E-376
- kidnapping of son K-234

Lindblad, Adolf (1801–78), Swedish composer, born near Stockholm; wrote many songs introduced by Jenny Lind, who was his pupil.

Lindblad, Otto (1809–64), Swedish composer, born in Karlstorp, s. Sweden; best known for quartets; wrote music for national song 'Ur svenska hjertans djup' ('From the Depth of Swedish Hearts').

Linde, Carl von (1842–1934), German engineer, born in Berndorf, near Baden, Austria; devised process of liquefying air 1895.

Linden, Guyana G-322

Linden, N.J., city about 3 mi (5 km) s.w. of Elizabeth; oil, gasoline; site purchased from American Indians 1664; pop. 41,409.

Linden, tree L-228

Linden family (or Tiliaceae), family of plants, shrubs, and trees; includes basswood, lindens, grewias, jute, Jewsmallow; often called basswood family.

Lindenhurst, N.Y., village 32 mi (52 km) s.e. of New York City; resort area; some manufacturing; settled 1869; pop. 26,919.

Lindenwold, N.J., borough 6 mi (10 km) s.e. of Haddonfield; mill work, plumbing fixtures; meat-packing; settled 1742, incorporated 1929; pop. 18,196.

Lindenwood Colleges, The, St. Charles, Mo.; affiliated with United Presbyterian Church in the U.S.A.; coordinate colleges for men and women; founded 1827; arts and sciences, teacher education.

Linderhof castle C-200, *picture* C-198

Lindgren, Astrid (born 1907), Swedish author of children's books, born in Vimmerby, 70 mi (110 km) s. of Norrköping; children's book editor, Raben and Sjögren Publishers, Stockholm 1946–70; many awards R-110a

'Lindisfarne Gospels' (about 700), England, example of calligraphy C-58

Lindsay, Howard (1889–1968), U.S. actor, director, author, and producer; born in Waterford, N.Y.; with Russel Crouse wrote and produced many plays ('Life with Father', in which he also acted; 'Arsenic and Old Lace'; 'State of the Union', awarded 1946 Pulitzer prize).

Lindsay, John Vliet (born 1921), U.S. public official, born in New York, N.Y.; U.S. congressman (Republican) from New York 1959–65; mayor of New York City 1965–73; joined Democratic Party 1971.

Lindsay, Vachel (full name Nicholas Vachel Lindsay) (1879–1931), U.S. poet and lecturer L-228
- American literature A-354
- figures of speech F-81

Lindsay, Ont., town on Scugog River 56 mi (90 km) n.e. of Toronto in fertile farming area and scenic lake region; flour, machinery, chemicals, lumber, meat and dairy products; pop. 13,596.

Lindsey, Benjamin Barr (1869–1943), U.S. judge and social reformer, born in Jackson, Tenn.; admitted to Colorado bar 1894; revolutionized methods of handling delinquent children ('Problems of the Children'; 'Revolt of Modern Youth'; 'House of Human Welfare'; 'Companionate Marriage') J-162

Lindstrom, Frederick Charles (nickname Fred) (born 1905), U.S. baseball player, born in Chicago, Ill.; N.L. third baseman 1924–36.

Line, art
- design D-108
- drawing D-250
- dress design D-270
- mechanical drawing M-256, 261, *picture* M-260
- optical illusions I-54

Line, battle formation W-22

Line, fishing F-143

Line, mathematics
- algebra A-295
- geometry G-73
- trigonometry T-285

Line ahead battle (or ship-of-the-line battle), naval tactic N-82, 87

Linear accelerator A-323
- nuclear energy N-421
- X rays X-405

Linear equation A-297

Linear function A-297
- Linear induction motor B-405

Linear measure M-242

Linear perspective P-220
- illusions I-54

Linear Scripts A and B A-61, A-537, *picture* A-531

Line drawing D-250
- mechanical drawing M-256

Line graph G-224

Line-item veto, in United States government V-307

Linen, fabric L-228
- Belfast's trade B-144
- flax F-176
- Northern Ireland I-324
- textile manufacture T-138

Linen supply, laundry L-86

Line of Demarcation, imaginary line from North Pole to South Pole.

Line officer, in the military
- army A-634
- navy N-80

Line of position, navigation N-70

Line printer, *picture* C-631

Liner. *see in index* Ocean liner

Line segment, in geometry G-74

Line spectrum, nuclear energy N-418

Linfield College, McMinnville, Ore.; affiliated with American Baptist Convention; founded 1849; arts and sciences, education; graduate study.

Ling, Per Henrik (1776–1839), Swedish playwright and poet, born in Ljunga, s. Sweden; created system of gymnastics used in therapeutics; founded Royal Gymnastic Central Institute at Stockholm 1813.

Ling, plant. *see in index* Heather

Lingala, language A-119

Lingonberry (or cowberry), a low-growing shrub *Vaccinium vitis-idaea* of heath family, native to n. Europe and Asia; creeping evergreen; leaves oblong; flowers white or pink in small clusters; fruit small, dark red, oblong, in clusters;. named "lingon" or "kroesa" in Denmark and Sweden; North American variety is smaller; native from Massachusetts to Alaska; also called mountain cranberry and foxberry.

Lingua franca, hybrid language A-119
- international communication L-39

Linguistic approach, reading R-103

Linguistics L-229, S-65
- anthropology A-481
- contributions
  - Bloomfield B-318
  - Grimm G-287
  - Jesperson J-102
  - Korzybski K-301
- etymology E-324
- language L-31

Linhai Industrial Park, Kaohsiung, Taiwan K-190

Link, Edwin (in full Edwin Albert Link) (1904–1981), U.S. aviator A-208

Link, unit of length in surveying S-520, *table* W-140

Linkage group, genes which tend to be inherited together H-140

Link Foundation, a fund established in 1953 by Edwin A. Link, who developed the Link trainer, to advance aviation education and training by grants in aid to other agencies engaged in such projects; a Link Foundation fellowship program has been started; headquarters, Smithsonian Institution, Washington, D.C.

Linking verb, in grammar V-281, S-110

Linlithgow, Victor Alexander John Hope, 2nd marquess of (1887–1952), English political leader, formerly a banker; viceroy and governor-general of India 1936–43.

Linnaea (or twinflower), delicate, creeping evergreen wild flower *Linnaea borealis* of honeysuckle family, with threadlike, upright flower stalks, each topped with two fragrant drooping, bell-shaped rose or white flowers; named after Linnaeus (Carl von Linné).

Linnaeus, Carolus (1707–78), Swedish botanist and naturalist L-231
- classification system B-229, 380
- clock garden B-224
- Lamarck L-25

Lithography L-258
graphic arts G-233
photography P-295
photolithography P-277, *pictures* P-278
printing P-500

Lithophyte, plant that grows on rocks O-580

Lithosphere, the solid body of the earth E-17, G-72, *picture* A-749
continental structure C-689
oceanography O-486

Lithuanian Soviet Socialist Republic, U.S.S.R., area 25,100 sq mi (65,000 sq km); cap. Vilna; pop. 3,398,000 L-259, U-14, *map* R-325
Europe, *map* E-360
Germany G-124
Polish history P-413
stamp, *picture* S-409

Li T'ieh-kuai, in Chinese mythology, one of the Eight Immortals, *picture* M-704

Litmus, purplish coloring matter; used as an acid-base indicator; turns red in acid, blue in alkali solution.

Litter, covered and curtained couch with shafts and used for carrying a single passenger wagon W-2

Litterae humaniores R-146

Little, Arthur Dehon (1863–1935), U.S. chemical engineer, born in Boston, Mass.; expert on papermaking.

Little, Malcolm. *see in index* Malcolm X

Little America, Admiral Byrd's base in Antarctica B-532, P-423, *picture* P-418

Little Bear (or Ursa Minor), constellation, *charts* S-416, 419, 422, C-681

Little Belt, strait between Fyn Island and mainland of Denmark
Baltic Sea B-46

Little Belt Mountains, range of Rocky Mountains, in Lewis and Clark National Forest, Montana

Little Bighorn, battle of (June 25, 1876), battle between the Plains Indian tribes, led by Sitting Bull, and the United States 7th Cavalry, led by General Custer
Montana, *picture* M-559

Little Bighorn River, river in s. Montana, flows n. across Crow Indian Reservation for 60 mi (100 km) to Bighorn River M-554

Little Black River Peak, Mauritius; 2,711 ft (826 m) M-233

Little blue heron, bird *Florida caerulea* H-142

'Little Brown Church in the Vale, The', hymn written 1857 by William S. Pitts, inspired by valley at Bradford, Iowa, *picture* I-293

Little Church Around the Corner (nickname of Church of the Transfiguration) Episcopal church in New York City on 29th St.; founded 1848 by George Hendric Houghton (1820–97), rector 1849–97; received nickname, 1870, when Joseph Jefferson, arranging funeral for an actor friend, was turned away from one church and advised, "There's a little church around the corner that might accommodate you"; nickname persisted and church remained a favorite with theatrical people.

Little Colorado (or Colorado Chiquito), river in Arizona, a tributary of Colorado River C-585, *map* U-81

Little Corporal. *see in index* Napoleon I

Little Diomede Island. *see in index* Diomede Islands

Little Dipper, seven stars corresponding to constellation Little Bear; tip of handle is North Star, *chart* C-681. *see also in index* Little Bear

Little Dog. *see in index* Canis Minor

'Little Dorrit', novel by Charles Dickens; Little Dorrit is born, brought up, and wed in the prison where her father was confined for debt.

Little Entente (1920), alliance between Czechoslovakia, Yugoslavia and Romania E-351, *table* T-274

Little Falls, Minn., city on Mississippi River 30 mi (50 km) n.w. of St. Cloud; paper, garments, boats; granite quarry nearby; pop. 7,250.

Little Falls, N.J., 5 mi (8 km) s.w. of Paterson on Passaic River; ornamental iron, carpets, scissors; pop. of township 11,496.

Little Falls, N.Y., manufacturing city on Mohawk River and Barge Canal 18 mi (29 km) e. of Utica; waterpower from cascades in river; food-processing equipment, food products, bicycles, footwear, textile products, paper; Gen. Nicholas Herkimer's grave nearby; pop. 6,156.

Littlefield, Catherine (1908–51), U.S. ballet dancer and choreographer, born in Philadelphia, Pa.; première danseuse Philadelphia Grand Opera Co. 1926–33; founded Littlefield Ballet 1935; created several ballets on U.S. themes: 'Barn Dance' and 'Terminal'; restaged 'The Fairy Doll', 'Daphnis and Chloe'.

Little Flower. *see in index* La Guardia, Fiorello

Little fox mitre, mollusk shell *Mitra vulpecula*, *picture* S-152

Little Havana, a neighborhood in Miami, Fla. H-168

Little Hunting Creek Plantation. *see in index* Mount Vernon

Little Italy, a neighborhood in Manhattan, New York, N.Y. N-272, *picture* N-275

'Little Jack Horner', nursery rhyme N-442

Little John, member of Robin Hood's band of outlaws R-224

Little Kanawha River, river in West Virginia. *see in index* Kanawha

Little Khingan Mountains, n.e. part of China; continuation of Great Khingan Mountains in Heilungkiang Province w. of Amur R.; highest point about 4,665 ft (1,422 m) M-93

Little League, baseball B-94, *picture* B-96
game, *pictures* P-179

'Little Lord Fauntleroy', story by Frances Hodgson Burnett of the seven-year-old Little Lord Fauntleroy whose curls and velvet suits set a fashion for small boys.

Little Maginot Line, wall, Czechoslovakia F-320

'Little Mermaid', statue by Edvard Eriksen set in Copenhagen Harbor, Denmark C-708, *picture* D-99

Little Miami River, Ohio, tributary of Ohio River; 140 mi (225 km) long.

'Little Minister, The', novel by Sir James Barrie; Babbie, daughter of a village squire, in the guise of a gypsy, wins the love of Gavin Dishart, the little minister; view of Scottish village life.

Little Missouri River, tributary of the Missouri, rising in Wyoming and flowing 450 mi (720 km) through Montana, North Dakota and South Dakota, *map* U-40

'Little Murders', work by Feiffer A-363

'Little Organum For the Theater, A', work by Brecht B-433

'Little Orphan Annie', comic strip C-189, *picture* C-187

Little Pee Dee River, tributary of Pee Dee in e. South Carolina, *map* S-319

Little people, people of abnormally small stature; the terms "dwarf" and "midget" have been used traditionally but are now considered insulting and little people is the preferred term D-294

'Little Pretty Pocket Book, A', work by Newbery N-151

'Little Red Lighthouse and the Great Grey Bridge, The', book by Swift L-204

Little Rhody. *see in index* Rhode Island

Little Richard (born 1935), U.S. rock'n'roll musician M-680

Little River Turnpike, historical road in United States R-221

Little Rock, Ark., state capital; largest city of state; on Arkansas River; pop. 158,461 L-260, *maps* N-350, U-41

LITERARY AWARDS
John Newbery Medal

Awarded	Author	Book
1922	Hendrik Willem Van Loon	The Story of Mankind
1923	Hugh Lofting	Voyages of Dr. Dolittle
1924	Charles B. Hawes	Dark Frigate
1925	Charles J. Finger	Tales from Silver Lands
1926	Arthur B. Chrisman	Shen of the Sea
1927	Will James	Smoky, the Cowhorse
1928	Dhan Gopal Mukerji	Gay-Neck
1929	Eric P. Kelly	The Trumpeter of Krakow
1930	Rachel Field	Hitty, Her First Hundred Years
1931	Elizabeth J. Coatsworth	The Cat Who Went to Heaven
1932	Laura A. Armer	Waterless Mountain
1933	Elizabeth F. Lewis	Young Fu of the Upper Yangtze
1934	Cornelia Meigs	Invincible Louisa
1935	Monica Shannon	Dobry
1936	Carol R. Brink	Caddie Woodlawn
1937	Ruth Sawyer	Roller Skates
1938	Kate Seredy	The White Stag
1939	Elizabeth Enright	Thimble Summer
1940	James Daugherty	Daniel Boone
1941	Armstrong Sperry	Call It Courage
1942	Walter D. Edmonds	The Matchlock Gun
1943	Elizabeth Janet Gray	Adam of the Road
1944	Esther Forbes	Johnny Tremain
1945	Robert Lawson	Rabbit Hill
1946	Lois Lenski	Strawberry Girl
1947	Carolyn S. Bailey	Miss Hickory
1948	William Pène Du Bois	The Twenty-One Balloons
1949	Marguerite Henry	King of the Wind
1950	Marguerite de Angeli	The Door in the Wall
1951	Elizabeth Yates	Amos Fortune: Free Man
1952	Eleanor Estes	Ginger Pye
1953	Ann Nolan Clark	Secret of the Andes
1954	Joseph Krumgold	. . . and now Miguel
1955	Meindert De Jong	The Wheel on the School
1956	Jean Lee Latham	Carry On, Mr. Bowditch
1957	Virginia Eggertsen Sorensen	Miracles on Maple Hill
1958	Harold Keith	Rifles for Watie
1959	Elizabeth George Speare	The Witch of Blackbird Pond
1960	Joseph Krumgold	Onion John
1961	Scott O'Dell	Island of the Blue Dolphins
1962	Elizabeth George Speare	The Bronze Bow
1963	Madeleine L'Engle	A Wrinkle in Time
1964	Emily Cheney Neville	It's Like This, Cat
1965	Maia Wojciechowska	Shadow of a Bull
1966	Elizabeth Borton de Treviño	I, Juan de Pareja
1967	Irene Hunt	Up a Road Slowly
1968	Elaine L. Konigsburg	From the Mixed-up Files of Mrs. Basil E. Frankweiler
1969	Lloyd Alexander	The High King
1970	William H. Armstrong	Sounder
1971	Betsy Byars	Summer of the Swans
1972	Robert C. O'Brien	Mrs. Frisby and the Rats of NIMH
1973	Jean C. George	Julie of the Wolves
1974	Paula Fox	The Slave Dancer
1975	Virginia Hamilton	M. C. Higgins, the Great
1976	Susan Cooper	The Grey King
1977	Mildred D. Taylor	Roll of Thunder, Hear My Cry
1978	Katherine Paterson	Bridge to Terabithia
1979	Ellen Raskin	The Westing Game
1980	Joan W. Blos	A Gathering of Days; a New England Girl's Journal, 1830–32
1981	Katherine Paterson	Jacob Have I Loved
1982	Nancy Willard	A Visit to William Blake's Inn
1983	Cynthia Boigt	Dicey's Song
1984	Beverly Cleary	Dear Mr. Henshaw
1985	Margaret Hodges	Saint George and the Dragon
1986	Patricia MacLachlan	Sarah, Plain and Tall
1987	Sid Fleischman	The Whipping Boy

LITERARY AWARDS

Caldecott Medal

Awarded	Artist	Book
1938	Dorothy P. Lathrop	Animals of the Bible (Text from King James Bible)
1939	Thomas Handforth	Mei Li
1940	Ingri M. and Edgar Parin d'Aulaire	Abraham Lincoln
1941	Robert Lawson	They Were Strong and Good
1942	Robert McCloskey	Make Way for Ducklings
1943	Vigìnia Lee Burton	The Little House
1944	Louis Slobodkin	Many Moons (Text by James Thurber)
1945	Elizabeth Orton Jones	Prayer for a Child (Text by Rachel Field)
1946	Maud and Miska Petersham	Rooster Crows
1947	Leonard Weisgard	The Little Island (Text by Golden MacDonald)
1948	Roger Duvoisin	White Snow, Bright Snow (Text by Alvin Tresselt)
1949	Berta and Elmer Hader	The Big Snow
1950	Leo Politi	Song of the Swallows
1951	Katherine Milhous	The Egg Tree
1952	Nicolas Mordvinoff	Finders Keepers (Text by William Lipkind)
1953	Lynd Ward	The Biggest Bear
1954	Ludwig Bemelmans	Madeline's Rescue
1955	Marcia Joan Brown	Cinderella
1956	Feodor Rojankovsky	Frog Went A-Courtin'
1957	Marc Simont	A Tree Is Nice
1958	Robert McCloskey	Time of Wonder
1959	Barbara Cooney	Chanticleer and the Fox
1960	Marie Hall Ets	Nine Days to Christmas
1961	Nicolas Sidjakov	Baboushka and the Three Kings
1962	Marcia Joan Brown	Once a Mouse
1963	Ezra Jack Keats	The Snowy Day
1964	Maurice Sendak	Where the Wild Things Are
1965	Beni Montresor	May I Bring a Friend?
1966	Nonny Hogrogian	Always Room for One More
1967	Evaline Ness	Sam, Bangs & Moonshine
1968	Ed Emberley	Drummer Hoff
1969	Uri Shulevitz	The Fool of the World and the Flying Ship
1970	William Steig	Sylvester and the Magic Pebble
1971	Gail E. Haley	A Story—A Story
1972	Nonny Hogrogian	One Fine Day
1973	Blair Lent	The Funny Little Woman
1974	Margot Zemach	Duffy and the Devil
1975	Gerald McDermott	Arrow to the Sun: a Pueblo Indian Tale
1976	Leo and Diane Dillon	Why Mosquitoes Buzz in People's Ears
1977	Leo and Diane Dillon	Ashanti to Zulu
1978	Peter Spier	Noah's Ark
1979	Paul Goble	The Girl Who Loved Wild Horses
1980	Barbara Cooney	Ox-Cart Man (Text by Donald Hall)
1981	Arnold Lobel	Fables
1982	Chris Van Allsburg	Jumanji
1983	Marcia Brown	Shadow
1984	Alice and Martin Provensen	The Glorious Flight
1985	Robin McKinley	The Hero and the Crown
1986	Chris Van Allsburg	The Polar Express
1987	Richard Egielski	Hay, Al

Regina Medal

1959	Eleanor Farjeon	1973	Frances Clarke Sayers
1960	Anne Carroll Moore	1974	Robert McCloskey
1961	Padraic Colum	1975	May McNeer and Lynd Ward
1962	Frederic Gershom Melcher	1976	Virginia Haviland
1963	Ann Nolan Clark	1977	Marcia Joan Brown
1964	May Hill Arbuthnot	1978	Scott O'Dell
1965	Ruth Sawyer	1979	Morton Schindel
1966	Leo Politi	1980	Beverly Cleary
1967	Bertha Mahony Miller	1981	Augusta Baker
1968	Marguerite de Angeli	1982	Theodor Seuss Geisel
1969	Lois Lenski	1983	Tonie De Paola
1970	Ingri and Edgar Parin d'Aulaire	1984	Madeleine L'Engle
1971	Tasha Tudor	1985	Jean Fritz
1972	Meindert De Jong	1986	Lloyd Alexander

Arkansas A-615, *picture* A-619
Eisenhower's administration E-140
Little St. Bernard Pass, Alpine pass (7,180 ft; 2,190 m) in Italy s. of Mont Blanc; connects valleys of Dora Baltea and Isère
France, *map* F-372
Switzerland, *map* S-537
Little Sisters of the Poor, founded in France 1840, extended to U.S. 1868; for relief and nursing.
'Little Spinner in a Carolina Cotton Mill', photograph by Hine, *picture* P-296
Little spotted cat, wild cat *Felis tigrina*, *table* C-216
Little Steel formula, system of U.S. wage increases in smaller steel plants to cover 15 percent rise in living costs between Jan. 1, 1941, and May 1, 1942; adopted by War Labor Board July 1942 to stabilize wages in World War II.
Little Tennessee River, river in North Carolina; rises in the Blue Ridge Mountains of Georgia and flows approximately 150 mi (240 km) n. and n.w.
Tennessee T-87, *map* T-97
Tennessee Valley Authority T-102
Fontana dam, *picture* D-12
Little theater, nonprofessional theatrical productions T-153
Little Tobago, island, Trinidad and Tobago T-288
Littleton, Sir Thomas (1422–81), English judge and writer on law; 'Treatise on Tenures', dealing with English land laws of his day, is still used as an authority.
Littleton, Colo., town 8 mi (13 km) s. of Denver on South Platte River; missiles, light industry; oil research center; pop. 26,466.
'Little Treatise on Strange and Suitable Feats', work by Meyer M-37
Little Trianon (or Petit Trianon), palace at Versailles, France V-303
Little Turtle (1752?–1812), chief of Miami Indians, born near Fort Wayne, Ind.; kept his people from joining Tecumseh's confederacy I-89
Little White School House, Ripon, Wis., place where the Republican party was organized in 1854, *picture* W-258
'Little Women', novel by Alcott A-277, C-639, R-111c
Littlewood, Joan (born 1914?), British director ('Oh, What a Lovely War!'; 'Sparrers Can't Sing').
Littoral nation, nation with shorelines I-256
Littoral zone. *see in index* Tidal zone
Littoria, Italy. *see in index* Latina
Liturgy (from Latin *liturgia*, meaning "a public service"), term applied to any or all of the services used in public worship; especially in Roman Catholic, Eastern Orthodox, and Episcopal churches
Eastern Orthodox churches E-43
Litvinov, Maxim Maximovich (1876–1951), Soviet statesman, born in Bialystok, Russia (now Poland); diplomatic agent in England after Bolshevik revolution; commissar for foreign affairs 1930–39; ambassador to the U.S. 1941–43; deputy commissar for foreign affairs March–Aug. 1946.
Li Tzu-cheng (or Li Tzu-ch'eng) (1605–45), Chinese rebel leader who dethroned last emperor of Ming Dynasty C-368
Liu An, (died 122 BC), Chinese nobleman and scholar; author 'The Master of Huai-nan' C-388
Liu Chih-Chi (661–721), Chinese historian H-171
Liu Hsieh (465–522), Chinese literary critic C-388
Liu Hui (fl. AD 250), Chinese mathematician M-218
Liukiu Islands. *see in index* Ryukyu
Liu Shaoqi (or Liu Shao-ch'i) (1898?–1974), Chinese Communist party theorist, born in Hunan Province, China; became chairman of China 1959; expelled from Chinese Communist party 1969 C-375
Live Aid concert (1985), rock music concert benefit for famine relief in Africa, *picture* M-679
Live-forever (or houseleek, or hen-and-chickens), perennial plants of the family Crassulaceae; thick, succulent leaves, often in rosettes close to the ground; white, green, rose, or yellow star-shaped flowers.
Live oak, evergreen oak *Quercus virginiana* O-452
state tree of Georgia G-92
Liver, human L-261
alcohol affects A-276
anatomy A-391
blood B-314
digestive system D-145, *diagrams* D-142, 143
gland G-153
hepatitis H-134
poisoning A-254
transplantation T-251
Liver fluke
invertebrate, *picture* I-285
Liverleaf. *see in index* Hepatica
Livermore, Mary Ashton Rice (1820–1905), U.S. reformer, early advocate of abolition of slavery, prohibition, and woman's suffrage; born in Boston, Mass.; won reputation in Civil War as worker for Sanitary Commission.
Livermore, Calif., city 35 mi (55 km) s.e. of San Francisco; wine; nuclear research center; annual rodeo; incorporated as town 1876; as city 1930; pop. 37,703.
Liverpool, England, seaport of United Kingdom; on estuary of Mersey River; pop. 677,450 L-261g, *maps* E-360, U-18a
England E-232
harbor H-34
Liverpool, N.S., port town 72 mi (116 km) s.w. of Halifax; fishing; papermaking, yeast manufacture; metal products; pop. 3,607.
Liverpool, University of, Liverpool, Eng. L-262
Liverpool and Manchester Railway, England, early railroad R-73
Stephenson S-443
Liverpool Sound (or Mersey Beat), in popular music L-262
Liverwort L-262
moss M-599
plants P-370, *picture* P-371
'Lives of the English Poets', biographies by Johnson B-222
Livestock. *see also in index* Animals, Domesticated; Breeding, animal; Dairy industry; Forage crops; Meat; Meat industry
alligators and crocodiles A-311
climate affects C-503
fair and exposition F-7
farm machinery F-33
Germany G-117, 119
improvements A-136
India I-74
injurious plants P-408
poultry P-480
reindeer R-139
sheep S-146, *picture* S-147
stock car, *pictures* R-82
Livia Drusilla (also called Julia Augusta) (58 BC–AD 29), Roman patrician
Tiberius T-179
Living costs
inflation I-198
statistics S-437, P-202
United States U-191
Livingston, Edward (1764–1836), U.S. lawyer and statesman, born in Clermont, N.Y.; brother of Robert R. Livingston; served as congressman, U.S. senator, secretary of state under President Jackson, and minister to France 1833–35.

LITERARY AWARDS

Canadian Library Association Awards

Awarded	Author or Artist	Book
1947	R.L.H. Haig-Brown	Starbuck Valley Winter
1948	Bertha Mabel Dunham	Kristli's Trees
1950	R.S. Lambert	Franklin of the Arctic (U.S. title, Adventure to the Polar Sea: the Story of Sir John Franklin)
1952	Catherine Anthony Clark	The Sun Horse
1954	Emile Gervais	Monseigneur de Laval (French)
1956	Margaret Louise Riley	Train for Tiger Lily
1957	Cyrus Macmillan	Glooskap's Country, and Other Indian Tales
1958	Farley Mowat	Lost in the Barrens
	Béatrice Clément	Le Chevalier Du Roi (French)
1959	John Francis Hayes	The Dangerous Cove
	Hélène Flamme	Un Drôle de Petit Cheval (French)
1960	Marius Barbeau	The Golden Phoenix
	Paule Daveluy	L'Été Enchanté (French)
1961	William Toye	The St. Lawrence
	Marcelle Gauvreau	Plantes Vagabondes (French)
1962	Claude B. Aubry	Les îles du Roi Maha Maha II (French)
1963	Sheila Burnford	The Incredible Journey
	Paule Daveluy	Drôle d'Automne (French)
1964	R.L.H. Haig-Brown	The Whale People
	Cécile Chabot	Férie (French)
1965	Dorothy M. Reid	Tales of Nanabozho
	Claude B. Aubry	Le Loup de Noël (French)
1966	James McNeill	The Double Knights
	James Houston	Tikta'liktak
	Monique Corriveau	Le Wapiti (French)
	Andrée Maillet	Le Chêne des Tempêtes (French)
1967	Christie Harris	Raven's Cry
1968	James Houston	The White Archer: an Eskimo Legend
	Claude Mélançon	Légendes Indiennes du Canada (French)
1969	Kay Hill	And Tomorrow the Stars
1970	Edith Fowke	Sally Go 'Round the Sun
	Lionel Gendron	La Merveilleuse Histoire de la Naissance (French)
1971	William Toye	Cartier Discovers the Saint Lawrence
	Henriette Major	La Surprise de Dame Chenille (French)
1972	Anne Blades	Mary of Mile 18
	S. Takashima	Child in Prison Camp (illustration)
1973	Ruth Nichols	The Marrow of the World
	Simone Bussières	Le Petit Sapin qui a Poussé sur une Étoile (French)
	Jacques de Roussan	Au delà du Soleil (illustration)
1974	Elizabeth Cleaver	The Miraculous Hind
	William Kurelek	A Prairie Boy's Winter (illustration)
1975	Dennis Lee	Alligator Pie
	Carlo Italiano	The Sleighs of My Childhood (illustration)
1976	Mordecai Richler	Jacob Two-Two Meets the Hooded Fang
	William Kurelek	A Prairie Boy's Summer (illustration)
1977	Christie Harris	Mouse Woman and the Vanished Princesses
	Pam Hall	Down by Jim Long's Stage (illustration)
1978	Dennis Lee	Garbage Delight
	Elizabeth Cleaver	The Loon's Necklace (illustration)
1979	Kevin Major	Hold Fast
	Ann Blades	A Salmon for Simon (illustration)
1980	James Houston	River Runners
	Laszlo Gal	The Twelve Dancing Princesses (illustration)
1981	Don Kushner	The Violin-Maker's Gift
	Douglas Tait	The Trouble with Princesses (illustration)
1982	Janet Lunn	The Root Cellar
	Heather Woodall	Ytek and the Arctic Orchid (illustration)
1983	Brian Doyle	Up to Low
	Lindee Climo	Chester's Barn (illustration)
1984	Jan Hudson	Sweetgrass
	Ken Nutt	Zoom at Sea (illustration)
1985	Jean Little	Mama's Gonna Buy You a Mockingbird
	Ian Wallace	Chin Chang and the Dragon's Dance (illustration)
1986	Cora Taylor	Julie
	Ken Nutt	Zoom Away (illustration)
1987	Janet Lunn	Shadow in Hawthorn Bay
	Marie Louise Gay	Moonbeam on a Cat's Ear (illustration)

Laura Ingalls Wilder Award

1954	Laura Ingalls Wilder	1975	Beverly Cleary
1960	Clara Ingram Judson	1980	Theodor Seuss Geisel
1965	Ruth Sawyer	1983	Maurice Sendak
1970	Elwyn Brooks White	1986	Jean Fritz

Livingston, Philip (1716–78), signer of Declaration of Independence, born in Albany, N.Y.
Declaration of Independence D-56

Livingston, Robert R. (1746–1813), U.S. statesman, jurist, and experimental farmer; born in New York City; brother of Edward Livingston; first chancellor New York State 1777–1801, secretary of foreign affairs 1781–83; minister to France 1801–5
Constitution U-142
Declaration of Independence, *picture* R-162
Fulton F-447
Statuary Hall, *picture* S-437b

Livingston, William (1723–90), U.S. lawyer, born in Albany, N.Y.; attacked English Parliament's interference in provincial matters and Anglican domination of King's College; representative from New Jersey to 1st and 2nd Continental Congress; signed United States Constitution; governor of New Jersey 1776–90 N-199

Livingston, Mont., city on Yellowstone River, 45 mi (70 km) n. of Yellowstone Park; hunting, fishing, resort area; livestock; timber; mobile homes; railroad shops; pop. 6,994, *map* U-40

Livingston, N.J., urban township 9 mi (15 km) n.w. of Newark; near Passaic River; beverages, poultry, dairy products; pop. 28,040.

Livingstone, David (1813–73), Scottish missionary explorer of Africa L-263
exploration E-376
Victoria Falls V-311
watermelon discovery W-100
Stanley S-410

Livingstone College, Salisbury, N.C.; affiliated with African Methodist Episcopal Zion church; chartered 1885; liberal arts, education and theology; graduate studies.

Livingstone Falls, on Congo River in Zaire Z-443

Livingstone Mountains, range in mainland Tanzania bordering n.e. shores of Lake Nyasa.

Livingston University, Livingston, Ala.; state control; incorporated as private academy 1840; arts and sciences, business education and administration, teacher education; graduate study.

Living theater A-363, T-152. *see also in index* Theater
directing D-154

Living things L-264. *see also in index* Biology; Embryology; Physiology; Plants; Reproduction
animals A-126
bioethical issues B-214
earth P-487
evolution E-364
groups S-242
human beings P-446
Mars P-352
trees T-276, *picture* T-277
water W-84

Living together, family lifestyle F-19

Living trust (also called inter vivos trust) T-301

Living will, legal document stating that the life of the testator or testatrix not be prolonged under specified circumstances D-49

Livius Andronicus, Lucius (284?–204? BC), first known Roman poet, a Greek; enslaved but later freed; became actor and teacher, introduced Greek literature to Rome.

Livonia, Mich., city 18 mi (29 km) n.w. of Detroit; automobile parts; automotive research laboratory; food processing; horse racing; Madonna College; pop. 104,814 M-368

Livonia, U.S.S.R., district in s. Estonian Soviet Socialist Republic and n. Latvian Soviet Socialist Republic; a former Baltic province of imperial Russia with capital at Riga; 17,574 sq mi (45,516 sq km) L-83

Livorno (or Leghorn), Italy, Tuscan port on w. coast; Leghorn straw hats; glass, metal products, chemicals; shipbuilding; pop. 161,077, *maps* E-360, I-401

Livre, old French silver coin worth about 19.3 cents, replaced by franc in 1795; originally equaled English pound in value (from *libra,* Latin for "pound").

Livy (anglicized name of Titus Livius) (59 BC–AD 17), Roman historian, great prose writer; 35 of the 142 books of his history of Rome still exist L-270
Latin literature L-77

Livyeres, people L-12

'Liza of Lambeth', novel by Maugham M-231

Lizard, The (or Lizard Head), a bold promontory of Cornwall; the most southerly point of United Kingdom; small bays and hazardous reefs line the coast.

Lizard canary, bird C-130

Lizards, largest living group of reptiles; more than 3,000 species L-271, R-152
animal life record, *table* E-24
embryo, *diagram* E-201
iguana I-32
legendary, *picture* S-481b
monitor, *picture* P-10
mythology M-698
prehistoric A-462, *picture* A-460
reproduction A-426
salamander S-25

Lizars, William Home (1788–1859), British artist, *picture* L-25

Ljubljana (or Laibach), Yugoslavia, Slovenian city 50 mi (80 km) n. of Fiume; old castle and cathedral; Congress of Laibach 1821, which emperors of Austria and Russia attended, restated basic principles of Holy Alliance; pop. 183,000, *picture* Y-436, *map* E-360

Ljusne River (or Ljusnan River), Sweden, rises in mountains on border of Norway; winds 320 mi (510 km) s.e. into Gulf of Bothnia; source of hydroelectric power; logging route; salmon, *map* S-524

LKA (Amphibious Cargo Ship), naval vessel N-86

Llama, South American animal *Lama glama* of Camelidae family C-64, *picture* C-63
domestication B-334
Indian herders, *picture* P-191
pack animal, *picture* S-289
ruminant R-318
wool W-288

Llaneros, cattlemen of Venezuela V-275

Llano (or desert flat) D-105, G-236

Llano culture (or Elephant Hunter culture), prehistoric lifestyle I-144

Llano Estacado (or Staked Plain), arid plateau in n.w. Texas and s.e. New Mexico; over 40,000 sq mi (103,600 sq km) U-62

Llanos, plains G-236
South America L-60, S-275
Colombia C-549
Venezuela V-275

Llanquihue, Lake, s. Chile; 240 sq mi (620 sq km); extends north of Puerto Montt, which is its outlet to the Pacific

Llewellyn, Richard (pen name of Richard David Vivian Llewellyn Lloyd) (1907?–83), Welsh writer (trilogy: 'How Green Was My Valley', 'Up, into the Singing Mountains', 'And I Shall Sleep . . . Down Where the Moon Is Small').

Lloyd, Harold Clayton (1894–1971), U.S. motion-picture actor, born in Burchard, Neb.; began as "extra" at 19; famous for comedy roles in which he wore horn-rimmed glasses; formed own company 1923 ('Safety Last'; 'The Freshman'; 'Harold Lloyd's World of Comedy').

Lloyd, John Henry (1884–1965), U.S. baseball player, born in Gainesville, Fla.; shortstop Negro leagues 1905–31.

Lloyd, John Selwyn Brooke (born 1904), English statesman, born in West Kirby, near Liverpool; Conservative member of Parliament 1945–; minister of state 1951–54, of supply 1954–55, of defense 1955; foreign secretary 1955–60; chancellor of the exchequer 1960–62; leader of House of Commons 1963–64, speaker 1971–.

Lloyd Barrage (also called Sukkur Barrage), in Indus River at Sukkur in Sind region, Pakistan; a dam 4,620 ft (1,410 m) long, completed in 1932; irrigates 5,300,000 acres (2,145,000 hectares).

Lloyd George, David (1863–1945), British statesman, Liberal prime minister (1916–22) L-275
- United Kingdom E-255
- Wales W-7
- World War I W-308

Lloydminster, Alta. and Sask., city on boundary of the two provinces, 140 mi (225 km) s.e. of Edmonton; petroleum and farm products; pop. Alberta 4,738, Saskatchewan 6,034 S-49e, *map* S-49k

Lloyd's of London, insurance organization I-235
- London L-289
- *Titanic* insurance S-177d

Lluchu, South American wool hat B-335

LNG (or liquefied natural gas), fuel F-441

Load, unit of measure, *table* W-140
- materials testing M-211

Loading, papermaking P-102

Loading coils, in telephone
- Pupin invents P-535

Load line, in ship, *diagram* S-176

Loalach (also called South American lungfish), fish *Lepidosiren paradoxa* M-644

Loam, a sand and clay soil G-21, S-250, 253

Loan, financial. *see also in index* Bond; Mortgage
- bank and banking B-64
  - central bank C-260
- Bank of United States B-73
- borrowing N-24
- contract C-693
- credit C-761
- housing H-293, 296, 301
- inflation I-198
- interest P-199
- international trade I-270
- savings and loans S-52c
- veteran V-306

Loan Agency, Federal. *see in index* Federal Loan Agency

Loanda, Angola. *see in index* Luanda

Lobachevski, Nikolai (full name Nikolai Ivanovich Lobachevski) (1793–1856), Russian mathematician L-275

Lobbying, practice of influencing legislators and other public officials L-276

Lobe, in anatomy
- liver L-261

Lobe-fin (or crossopterygian), primitive crawling fish A-461

Lobelia, genus of herbs of the family Campanulaceae with alternate leaves and white, blue, or red flowers; corolla very irregular; includes *Lobelia inflata*, Indian tobacco, used in medicine; *L. cardinalis*, cardinal flower. *see also in index* Cardinal flower

Lobengula (1833–94), king of the Matabele in Zimbabwe; ruled 1870–94; died in exile after 1893 attack on British settlers failed
- Rhodes R-195
- Zimbabwe Z-453

Lobito, Angola, one of best seaports on w. coast of Africa; terminus of Benguela railway; pop. 23,897, *map* A-115

Loblolly pine P-328

Lob Nor, China. *see in index* Lop Nor

Lobster, crustacean of family Homaridae C-790
- eggs A-426
- Maine, *picture* M-60
- prehistoric animals A-461

Lobster pot (or lobster trap)
- crustaceans C-790
- fisheries F-134
- trapping T-267

'Lobster Trap and Fish Tail', mobile by Calder, *pictures* C-27, S-93

Lobworm (also called lugworm and lugbait), marine annelid *Arenicola marina* about 8 in (20 cm) long, with bright red gills on its central segments, burrows in sandy shores between tide marks; used for bait.

Local apparent time T-188

Local cartage carrier, a motor freight transportation system I-291

Local government. *see in index* Municipal government

Local Government Act (1888), United Kingdom M-655

Local Government Act (1972), United Kingdom M-655

Local group, a cluster of galaxies E-9

Local option P-506

Locarno, Switzerland, town at n. end of Lake Maggiore; Madonna del Sasso sanctuary; Treaties of Locarno signed here; pop. 10,200 S-542, *map* S-537

Locarno, Treaties of (1925), *table* T-274
- Germany G-123
- World War I W-321

Location, a position or site
- geography G-62
- maps M-117, *picture* M-118

Loch, Scottish word for lake. *see in index* names of lakes, as Ness, Loch

Lochinvar, in Sir Walter Scott's 'Marmion', hero of ballad 'Lochinvar'.

Lochner, Stephan (born 1405–15, died 1451), German painter; birthplace probably Meersburg; his altarpiece is chief treasure of Cologne cathedral.

Loch Ness monster A-462

Loch Raven, Md., community at s.e. end of Loch Raven Reservoir; n.e. suburb of Baltimore; pop. 25,000, *map* M-183

Lock and key L-277

Locke, Alain (full name Alain LeRoy Locke) (1886–1954), U.S. author and historian L-278
- cultural involvement B-294

Locke, David Ross. *see in index* Nasby, Petroleum V.

Locke, John (1632–1704), English philosopher; father of English empiricism L-278
- bioethical bill of rights B-214
- Carolina constitution S-310
- Declaration of Independence D-54
- educational contribution E-85
- Enlightenment E-289
- political science P-434

Locke, William John (1863–1930), English novelist and playwright, born in Georgetown, British Guiana; first interest in architecture, secretary of Royal Institute of British Architects 1897–1907; a whimsical romanticist ('The Morals of Marcus Ordeyne'; 'The Beloved Vagabond'; 'Stella Maris'; 'Septimus').

Lockhart, John Gibson (1794–1854), Scottish writer and lawyer, born in Cambusnethan, near Glasgow; famous as biographer of his father-in-law, Sir Walter Scott; also wrote life of Burns and novels.

Lock Haven, Pa., city on West Branch of Susquehanna River about 25 mi (40 km) s.w. of Williamsport; paper, electronic equipment, aircraft, metal products, dyes, textiles; Lock Haven State College; pop. 9,617, *map* P-185

Lock Haven State College, Lock Haven, Pa.; established 1870; formerly a teachers' college; liberal arts, education.

Lockheed S-3A, Viking airplane, *picture* A-178

Lockjaw. *see in index* Tetanus

'Lock of Bernice', elegy by Callimachus G-277

Lockout, labor S-489

Lockport, N.Y., city on New York State Barge Canal, n.e. of Buffalo; named for two large locks situated there; grain and fruit; flour, textiles, wallboard, auto radiators and heaters, air conditioners, plastics, paper, steel products; pop. 25,399.

Locks, canal G-246
- canal construction C-126
- harbors and ports H-34
- Panama Canal, *pictures* P-89, 94, *diagram* P-88
- St. Lawrence Seaway S-20, *pictures* S-19, U-51
- Sault Sainte Marie Canal S-52b
- waterway W-108

Lock-stitch machine, type of sewing machine S-122

Lockwood, Belva Ann Bennett (1830–1917), U.S. lawyer, born in Royalton, N.Y.; first woman permitted to practice before U.S. Supreme Court; active in woman suffrage movements; nominated for president of U.S. 1884 and 1888 by Equal Rights party.

Lockyer, Sir Joseph Norman (1836–1920), English astronomer and physicist, born in Rugby, England; pioneer in application of spectroscope to sun and stars; explained sunspots; between 1870 and 1905 conducted eight British expeditions for observing total solar eclipses ('The Sun's Place in Nature'; 'Recent and Coming Eclipses'; 'The Chemistry of the Sun'; 'Inorganic Evolution')
- helium in sun H-123, S-372

Loco-foco, obsolete popular name for friction matches; also applied to a New York City faction of Democratic party, because a meeting at Tammany Hall (1835) was held by the light of candles and matches after a rival faction had turned off the lights.

Locomotive (or iron horse) L-279
- mining V-333
- motor and engine M-631
- Panama Canal P-90, *pictures* P-94
- pneumatic P-399
- railroads R-72, *pictures* R-74, 75
- steam engine S-438, *diagrams* S-439–441
- Stephenson S-443

Locoweed, plant *Oxytropis splendens*
- cattle C-231
- legume L-118
- poisonous plants P-408
- weed, *picture* W-133

Locris, name for two separate districts of ancient Greece: East Locris, on e. coast opposite Euboea; West Locris, on Gulf of Corinth, s. of Doris.

Locust, insect L-283
- animal migration A-452
- beetle's parasite B-141
- cricket C-768, *picture* C-766

Lod, Israel. *see in index* Lydda

Lodestone, mineral M-432
- compass C-621

Lodge, Henry Cabot (1850–1924), U.S. political leader and historian, born in Boston, Mass.; grandfather of Henry C. Lodge, Jr.; U.S. senator from Massachusetts 1893–1924; led Republican party in blocking U.S. entrance into League of Nations ('The Story of the Revolution'; 'Life of Alexander Hamilton'; 'Life of George Washington'; 'The Senate and the League of Nations')
- Wilson W-219

Lodge, Henry Cabot, Jr. (1902–85), U.S. political leader, born in Nahant, Mass.; grandson of Henry Cabot Lodge; U.S. senator (Republican) from Massachusetts 1937–53 (resigned 1944 to serve in World War II, reelected 1946); directed campaign that won Republican presidential nomination for Dwight D. Eisenhower 1952; chief U.S. delegate to the United Nations 1953–60; Republican vice-presidential nominee 1960; ambassador to South Vietnam 1963–64, 1965–67, to West Germany 1968–69; chief U.S. negotiator at Vietnam peace talks in Paris 1969; presidential emissary to Vatican 1970–75
- Kennedy K-200
- Nixon N-324

Lodge, Sir Oliver Joseph (1851–1940), English physicist, exponent of psychic research, and author; born in Penkhull, Staffordshire; did valuable foundation work in electricity and radio; principal of University of Birmingham 1900–19; in addition to autobiography and many scientific works, wrote 'Raymond, or Life and Death', and other books setting forth his belief in possibility of communication with the dead.

Lodge, Thomas (1558?–1625), English poet, dramatist, and writer of romances; his pastoral romance 'Rosalynde' gave plot to Shakespeare for 'As You Like It'.

Lodgepole pine, slender evergreen tree *Pinus contorta* of pine family; grows 30 to 80 ft (9 to 24 m); thin bark peels off in scales; leaves in twos, 2½ in (6⅖ cm) long; cones oval; sometimes called jack pine, spruce pine, blackjack, knotty pine, tamarack, scrub pine, and yellow pine, *table* W-282

Lodi, Calif., city 32 mi (52 km) s. of Sacramento; wines and brandies, food processing and canning, tire molds; grape festival and national wine show in September; pop. 35,221, *map* U-40

Lodi, Italy, town 18 mi (29 km) s.e. of Milan on right bank of Adda River; French victory over Austrians (1796); founded 5th century BC; destroyed in 12th-century wars; reestablished by Frederick I; pop. 38,158, *map* I-401

Lodi, N.J., borough on Saddle River just n.e. of Passaic; textile dyeing and finishing, chemicals, plastics; pop. 25,213.

Łódź, Poland, city 75 mi (120 km) s.w. of Warsaw; enormous recent growth due to large textile industry; battle of Łódź (1914); pop. 843,000 L-283, P-413, *map* E-360

Loeb, Jacques (1859–1924), U.S. biologist, born in Mayen, near Coblenz, Germany; in U.S. after 1891; fertilized sea-urchin eggs chemically ("artificial parthenogenesis"); developed theory that many so-called "intelligent" actions of animals are physical or chemical in nature ("tropism") A-127

Loeffler, Charles Martin (1861–1935), U.S. composer and violinist, born in Mulhouse, Alsace; with Boston Symphony Orchestra 1883–1903, wrote songs, orchestral and chamber music; impressionistic style ('The Death of Tintagiles'; 'La Bonne Chanson'; 'A Pagan Poem'; 'Canticle of the Sun').

Loening, Grover (1888–1976), U.S. aeronautical engineer, born in Bremen, Germany; invented first flying boat; designed Loening monoplane and seaplane.

Loess, type of soil S-249, *picture* S-250
- Argentina A-575
- China C-339, 341
- minerals M-437

Loesser, Frank (1910–69), U.S. songwriter and playwright, born in New York, N.Y.; won Academy award 1948 for song 'Baby, It's Cold Outside'; New York Drama Critics Circle Award 1950 for 'Guys and Dolls', 1956 for 'The Most Happy Fella', and 1961 for 'How to Succeed in Business Without Really Trying', which also won Pulitzer Prize for drama.

Loess Hills and Plains, natural region in Nebraska N-94

Loess Plateau, China C-339, 348, 351
- Huang He River H-313

Loewe, Frederick. *see in index* Lerner, Alan Jay

Loewe, Johann Karl Gottfried (1796–1869), German composer, born near Halle, Germany; cantor and teacher in Stettin; one of first to give artistic form to ballad.

Loewi, Otto (1873–1961), U.S. pharmacologist, born in

Frankfurt, Germany; worked with H.H. Dale on nerve impulses and their chemical transmission; to U.S. 1940, became citizen 1946.

Loewy, Raymond Fernand (1893–1986), U.S. industrial designer, born in Paris, France; in United States after 1919, became citizen in 1938; designed streamlined trains, ships, and automobiles, also buildings for New York World's Fair 1939–40; author 'The Locomotive—Its Esthetics'
industrial design I-169, 174

Löffler, Friedrich August Johannes (1852–1915), German bacteriologist, born in Frankfurt-an-der-Oder; discovered causative organism of glanders, of diphtheria (with E. Klebs), and of foot-and-mouth disease (with Paul Frosch).

Lofoten Islands (or Lofoden Islands), group of rocky islands off n.w. coast of Norway; 1,560 sq mi (4,040 sq km); pop. 28,980, *map* E-360
Norway N-389, *picture* N-392

Lofting, Hugh (1886–1947), U.S. writer and illustrator, born in Maidenhead, Berkshire, England; resident of U.S.; creator of character Doctor Dolittle and author of whimsical poetry and stories for young children; awarded Newbery Medal 1923 for 'Voyages of Doctor Dolittle' R-110a

Log, oil-well record P-236

Log, ship's, device for measuring speed; term also used for ship's record book L-283

Logan, George (1753–1821), U.S. statesman, born in Stenton, Pa. (now a part of Philadelphia); U.S. senator from Pennsylvania 1801–7; his attempt to settle difficulties between France and United States (1798) without authority from the government led Congress to pass Logan Act, forbidding such activities by nonaccredited persons.

Logan, James (1674–1751), North American colonial leader, born in Ireland; a Quaker and secretary to William Penn; chief justice Pennsylvania Supreme Court 1731–39 P-171

Logan, John (or James Logan) (1725?–80), English name of Cayuga chief **Tahgahjute;** birthplace probably Shamokin, Pa.; friend of the whites until the massacre of his family by the whites 1774; joined English and became a leader in Lord Dunmore's War.

Logan, John Alexander (1826–86), U.S. Civil War general and U.S. senator, born in Jackson County, Ill.; admitted to bar 1851; distinguished service in Civil War; except for 2-year interval was member of U.S. Senate 1871–86; candidate for presidential nomination on Republican ticket 1884.

Logan, Joshua (born 1908), U.S. producer and director, born in Texarkana, Tex.; plays: 'Mister Roberts', 'The Wisteria Trees', 'Picnic'; musical plays: 'South Pacific' (awarded 1950 Pulitzer prize), 'Fanny'; also motion-picture adaptations.

Logan, Rayford Whittingham (born 1897), U.S. educator and author, born in Washington, D.C.; professor of history Howard University, Washington, D.C., 1938–65, head of department 1942–64; edited 'What the Negro Wants'; author of 'The Negro and the Post-War World: a Primer' and 'The Negro in American Life and Thought'.

Logan, Stephen Trigg (1800–80), U.S. jurist, born in Franklin County, Ky.; judge of circuit court; delegate to Republican convention of 1860, which nominated Lincoln, his former law partner.

Logan, Sir William Edmond (1798–1875), Canadian geologist, born in Montreal; mapped coal basin in Wales; first director Geological Survey of Canada 1842–70.

Logan, Utah, city 67 mi (108 km) n. of Salt Lake City; dairy products; textiles, pianos, farm machinery; vegetable canning; Utah State University; pop. 26,844 U-218, *maps* U-217, 232, U-40

Logan, Mount, 2nd highest peak (19,524 ft; 5,951 m) of North America, situated in Saint Elias Mountains, s.w. Yukon Territory C-74, Y-439, *map* C-112
height, comparative. *see in index* Mountain, *table*

Logania family (or Loganiaceae), a family of plants, native chiefly to warm regions, including Carolina yellow jessamine, buddleia, pinkroot, ignatius bean, strychnine, natal orange, and summer lilac.

Logansport, Ind., city on Wabash and Eel rivers about 70 mi (110 km) n. of Indianapolis; railroad division point; electrical products, hydraulic machinery, springs; state mental hospital and Bunker Hill Air Force Base nearby; pop. 17,899
Indiana, *map* I-102

Logarithmic grid G-228

Logarithms, in mathematics A-595
information theory I-202, *table* I-204
slide rule S-217

Logbook L-283

Log cabin. *see in index* Shelter, *subhead* log cabin

Loggerhead shrike (or migrant shrike), S-186

Loggerhead turtle, sea turtle, genus *Caretta* T-330

Loggia dei Lanzi, art gallery of Florence F-189, *picture* F-190

Logging, in lumber industry L-331, 335
conservation C-676
geography G-65

Logic L-284
algebra A-294
Aristotle A-589
Boolean principles B-364
Frege F-392
mathematics M-213, 217, 220
philosophy P-264

Logic circuits, used in information processing
electronics E-175

Logic code, method of storing information in electronic systems
electronics E-175

Logistics, in military science; details of moving, quartering, and supplying troops W-24
navy N-80, 86

Logography, a system of writing in which individual signs stand for individual words W-370

Logo-syllabic writing. *see in index* word-syllabic writing

Logroño, Spain, ancient walled city in n., capital of province of same name; on Ebro River; wine trade; pop. 58,545.

'Lohengrin', opera by Wagner O-567

Loincloth (or schenti), garment D-260

Loire River, longest river in France (620 mi; 1,000 km) L-285
Europe, *map* E-361
France F-343, 350, *map* F-372
levees D-146

Loire Valley L-285
wine W-237

Loki, in Norse mythology, the trickster god M-703

Lok Sabha, Indian parliamentary chamber I-76

Lo Kuan-chung (1330–1400), Chinese novelist C-389

'Lolita', work by Nabokov N-2, A-361

Lolland (or Laaland), Danish island in Baltic Sea; 479 sq mi (1,241 sq km); sugar beets; pop. 83,170.

Lollards, name applied to followers of John Wycliffe in 14th century; originally a Dutch word meaning "mumbler".

Loma, Point, California, promontory at entrance to San Diego Bay S-39, *picture* S-40

Loma Linda University, Loma Linda and Riverside, Calif.; Seventh-day Adventist; founded 1905; arts and sciences, allied health professions, dentistry, education, medicine, nursing, and public health; graduate studies at Loma Linda.

Lomax, John Avery (1867–1948), born in Goodman, Miss. and his son, **Alan** (born 1915), born in Austin, Tex.; U.S. ballad, folk, and blues collectors ('American Ballads and Folk Songs'; 'Cowboy Songs and Other Frontier Ballads') S-477
folk music F-273

Lombard, Peter. *see in index* Peter Lombard

Lombard, Ill., residential village 21 mi (34 km) w. of Chicago; lilac nurseries; Morton Arboretum nearby; pop. 37,295
Illinois, *map* I-53

Lombard College, Galesburg, Ill.; founded 1851; merged with Knox College 1930.

Lombardi, Vince (full name Vincent Thomas Lombardi) (1913–70), U.S. football coach and administrator L-285
football F-298

Lombard League, medieval group of Northern Italian city-states
Frederick I F-390
Frederick II F-390
Holy Roman Empire H-208

Lombardo, Guy Albert (1902–77), U.S. orchestra leader, born in London, Ont.; became U.S. citizen 1937; orchestra (Royal Canadians) noted for "sweet" music; a national champion speedboat racer
popular music M-684

Lombards, medieval Germanic people who settled in n. Italy L-285
Middle Ages M-384

Lombard Street, San Francisco, Calif., *picture* C-37

Lombardy, region of n. Italy; area 9,191 sq mi (23,804 sq km); cap. Milan; pop. 7,406,152, *map* I-401
France N-14
Lombards L-285
Po River P-400

Lombardy poplar P-446

Lombino, Salvatore. *see in index* Hunter, Evan

Lombok, island of Indonesia, e. of Bali; about 1,810 sq mi (4,690 sq km); rice, coffee, indigo, sugar; pop. 1,581,193, *map* I-166
Asia, *map* A-700

Lombroso, Cesare (1836–1909), Italian criminologist, born in Verona; founded criminal anthropology; originated theory that there is a "criminal type" marked by physical signs ('The Criminal').

Lomé, Republic of Togo, capital and seaport, on Gulf of Guinea; pop. 148,443, *map* A-118

Lomita, Calif., residential community 13 mi (21 km) n.w. of Long Beach; Lomita Railroad Museum; pop. 17,191.

Lomond, Ben, Scotland. *see in index* Ben Lomond

Lomond, Loch, largest lake in Scotland, in counties of Stirling and Dumbarton; 27 sq mi (70 sq km); length 23 mi (37 km).

Lomonosov, Mikhail Vasilievich (1711–65), Russian poet and philologist; set up principle of latter-day Russian language; called Father of Russian Literature ('Ode on the Capture of Khotin') R-359

Lompoc, Calif., city near Pacific Ocean 48 mi (77 km) n.w. of Santa Barbara; oil, diatomite, missiles; Vandenberg Air Force Base nearby; est. 1874; pop. 26,267 S-342c

Londinium, ancient Roman city L-286

London, George (originally George Burnstein) (1920–85), U.S. bass baritone, born in Montreal, Que.; to U.S. 1935; with Metropolitan Opera Company 1951–68; artistic administrator John F. Kennedy Center for the Performing Arts 1968–71; director National Opera Institute 1971–77; director Opera Society of Washington from 1975; radio, television, and concert singer.

London, Jack (full name John Griffith London) (1876–1916), U.S. novelist and short-story writer L-285
U.S.S.R. R-332f

London, England, one of the largest cities in the world; capital of United Kingdom; pop. Greater London 6,713,165 L-286, *picture* E-354, *maps* E-361, U-18a
air pollution C-457
England E-231
history
Alfred the Great A-282
first waterworks W-92
missile attacks G-309
Pepys P-197b
housing, *picture* H-298
industry I-189
insurance I-235
police P-430, *picture* P-430a
postal service P-463
Palladium, *picture* C-454
street railway S-487
tea auctions T-47
Thames River T-150
Wren W-363
zoo Z-457

London, Ont., city on Thames River; pop. 254,280 L-295
Canada, *maps* C-112, N-350
Ontario O-552

London, Declaration of. *see in index* Declaration of London (1909)

London, Tower of. *see in index* Tower of London

London, Treaties of, *table* T-274
naval
1930 P-18
1936 P-143c
World War I W-305

London, University of, educational institution at London, England; grew out of University College, founded 1827; by royal charter of 1836 had been examining body only, for conferring degrees; reorganized 1900 to include teaching, research, and extension work L-294

London Agreement (1945) W-11

London Bridge, historic bridge over the Thames River, London, England; original, completed in early 13th century, bore rows of houses with chapel in center; second bridge, completed 1831, of granite, was 65 ft (20 m) wide with 5 arches of varying sizes; purchased 1968 by U.S. land developers and moved to Arizona desert, near Lake Havasu, as a tourist attraction; third bridge, 860 ft (262 m) long, opened 1973 L-286, B-445, *map* L-289
Shakespeare's time, *picture* S-134

'London Bridge', nursery rhyme N-443

London Company (or Virginia Company of London), organized 1606 by King James I of England to establish colonies in North America between 34th and 41st degrees of n. latitude; dissolved 1624; was the s. branch of a joint land stock company of which Virginia Company of Plymouth was n. branch. *see also in index* Plymouth Company
Jamestown J-21, V-335
'Mayflower' M-238

London Conference (1866), *table* S-495a
Fathers of Canadian Confederation C-113

London Conference on Naval Armament
Hoover H-236
1930 D-164
1936 P-143c, P-18

London Convention for the Protection of African Fauna and Flora (1933), treaty N-25

London Declaration (1919), division of Cameroon C-66

Londonderry, 2nd marquis of. *see in index* Castlereagh

Londonderry (or Derry), Northern Ireland, port on Foyle River about 65 mi (105 km) n.w. of Belfast; pop. 55,000; linen; besieged by James II in 1689; county borough and chief town of Londonderry County (land area 801 sq mi [2,074 sq km]); pop. 174,658, including county borough) I-324

London Prize Ring Rules, in boxing B-390

London School of Economics, London, England
Webbs W-128

'London Society', newspaper
Caldecott's contribution C-26

'London Spy, The', magazine M-32

'London symphonies' (or 'Salomon symphonies'), works by Haydn H-75

'Lonely House, The,' etching by Hopper, *picture* A-663

Lone Mountain College, San Francisco, Calif.; Roman Catholic; founded 1930 as San Francisco College for Women; arts and sciences; graduate school.

'Lone Ranger, The', radio and television show W-153

Lone Star State. *see in index* Texas

Long, Crawford W. (full name Crawford Williamson Long) (1815–78), U.S. surgeon L-295
ether A-413
medicine M-284
Statuary Hall, *table* S-437a

Long, Huey (full name Huey Pierce Long, nickname Kingfish) (1893–1935), U.S. politician L-295
assassination, *list* A-704
Louisiana politics L-314
New Orleans N-234
Statuary Hall, *table* S-437a

Long, John Davis (1838–1915), U.S. public official, born in Buckfield, Me.; governor of Massachusetts 1880–83; member of Congress 1883–89; secretary of navy 1897–1902, during Spanish-American War.

Long, John Luther (1861–1927), U.S. novelist and dramatist, born in Hanover, Pa. ('Madame Butterfly'; 'The Darling of the Gods').

Long, Russell Billiu (born 1918), U.S. political leader, born in Shreveport, La.; son of Huey Pierce Long; U.S. senator (Democratic) from Louisiana 1948–, assistant majority leader (majority whip) 1965–69.

Long, Stephen Harriman (1784–1864), U.S. Army surveyor and engineer, born in Hopkinton, N.H.; led exploring expedition to Rocky Mts. 1819–20; explored and named Long's Peak; authority on railroads
exploration
Minnesota M-445
Nebraska N-98
frontier F-419

Longabaugh, Harry (known as the Sundance Kid), U.S. outlaw O-619

Long Beach (or Wilmore City), Calif., city on s. coast about 20 mi (30 km) s. of Los Angeles; pop. 361,334 L-295, *maps* U-40
industry, *picture* I-186

Long Beach, N.Y., residential and resort city on island off s.w. shore of Long Island, 21 mi (34 km) s.e. of New York City; commercial fisheries, lobster beds; pop. 34,073.

Long Beach State College. *see in index* California State University, Long Beach

Long-billed curlew. *see in index* Curlew

Longbow, weapon A-639
battle of Agincourt, *picture* H-130

Long Branch, N.J., resort city on Atlantic coast about 6 mi (10 km) n. of Asbury Park; electronics, clothing, mill products; fishing pier and boardwalk; Monmouth College at West Long Branch; pop. 29,819.

Longchamps (or Longchamp), part of the Bois de Boulogne, w. of Paris, France; site of an abbey founded 1260 by Isabel, sister of St. Louis, and suppressed 1792; now a racecourse.

Longcloth, plain, lightweight, cotton fabric; soft, closely woven; used for children's clothes and underwear.

Long-eared sunfish S-518

Longfellow, Henry Wadsworth (1807–82), U.S. poet L-296
American literature A-348
'Evangeline' A-14
Nova Scotia N-397
'Song of Hiawatha' H-146
Minnesota M-444
'The Courtship of Miles Standish' S-410
'The Village Blacksmith' B-308
translation of 'Frithjof's Saga' S-526
creative writing W-381
Hall of Fame, *table* H-16
statue, *picture* M-60

Long-focus lens. *see in index* Telephoto lens

Longford, agricultural county in Leinster Province, e.-central Ireland; 403 sq mi (1,044 sq km); pop. 28,989; also name of town in county (pop. 3,454).

Long-haired cat C-205

Longhorn cattle, breed of cattle C-225
cowboys' history C-750, *picture* C-751
Nebraska, *picture* N-103

Long-horned beetle, beetle of the family Cerambycidae, *pictures* B-139, 141

Long-horned grasshopper. *see in index* Katydid

Long hundredweight, unit of weight, *table* W-140

Long Island, N.Y., island s. of Connecticut forming s.e. portion of New York State; 1,401 sq mi (3,628 sq km); pop. 6,728,074 L-297
national rifle matches R-206

Long Island, battle of (Aug. 27, 1776) L-297

Long Island Sound, arm of Atlantic Ocean between Long Island and mainland; 76 mi (122 km) long.

Long Island University, Greenvale, N.Y., and Brooklyn, N.Y.; private control; founded 1926; liberal arts, business administration, education, library science, and pharmacy; graduate study; centers at Greenvale and Southampton N-254

Longitude. *see in index* Latitude and Longitude

Long jump, in track and field T-244, *picture* T-245

Long Lake, N.Y., in Adirondack Mountains, 14 mi (22 km) long, 1 mi (1.6 km) wide.

Longleaf pine, *see in index* Southern yellow pine

Long lens, motion pictures M-603

Longman, Mary Evelyn Beatrice (1874–1954), sculptor, born in Winchester, Ohio; married Nathaniel Horton Batchelder; designed bronze doors for chapel of U.S. Naval Academy, Annapolis.

Long March (1934–35), historic 6,000 mile trek of more than 100,000 Chinese Communists C-373
Mao Zedong M-112

Longmeadow, Mass., 3 mi (5 km) s. of Springfield on Connecticut River; settled 1644, incorporated 1783; pop. of township 16,301.

Longmont, Colo., city 12 mi (19 km) n.e. of Boulder; in agricultural area; electronic equipment, trailers and campers; food processing; established about 1870, incorporated as town 1873, as city 1885; pop. 42,942.

Longnose gar (or billfish), a fish *Lepisosteus osseus* of the family Lepisosteidae G-16

Long Parliament, in British history E-246
Charles I C-275

Long Range Mountains, mountains in Newfoundland N-164

Long-range navigation. *see in index* Loran

Longshanks. *see in index* Edward I

Longshoreman (or stevedore), one who unloads cargo ships H-36

Long shot, motion pictures M-608, *picture* M-609

Long-snouted flounder, a shallow-water fish F-174

Longs Peak, Colorado, one of highest peaks of Rocky Mts. (14,256 ft; 4,345 m), Rocky Mountain National Park, 50 mi (80 km) n.w. of Denver, *maps* C-583, U-80, *picture* C-567
climatic region, *map* U-119

Longstreet, Augustus Baldwin (1790–1870), U.S. newspaper editor, educator, and Methodist minister; born in Augusta, Ga.; president Emory College, University of Mississippi, and University of South Carolina ('Georgia Scenes').

Longstreet, James (1821–1904), U.S. public official and Confederate Civil War general, born in Edgefield District, S.C.; distinguished himself at Bull Run, Fredericksburg, Chickamauga, and in battle of the Wilderness; U.S. minister to Turkey 1880–81; U.S. Railway Commissioner 1898–1904 R-115
Civil War C-474
Battle of Gettysburg G-136

Long-tailed shrew S-186

Long-tailed weasel (or common weasel), a carnivorous mammal *Mustela frenata* W-114

Long-term memory, level of memory M-294

Long-term potentiation (or LTP), electrical phenomenon in the brain involved in memory M-294

Long ton, unit of weight, *table* W-140

Longueuil, Que., suburb of Montreal; pop. 124,320 Q-9h, *map* C-112

Longview, Tex., city about 125 mi (200 km) e. of Dallas; oil production; earth-moving equipment, industrial machinery, oil field supplies, chemicals, LeTourneau College; pop. 62,762, *map* U-41

Longview, Wash., port city in s.w. part of state at confluence of Cowlitz and Columbia rivers; lumber, paper products, aluminum; incorporated 1924; pop. 31,052 W-51, *map* U-40

Longwall system, in mining coal mining C-523

Long wave (or shallow-water wave), ocean wave O-487

Longwood College, Farmville, Va.; state control; founded 1839; arts and sciences, education; graduate studies.

Longworth, Nicholas (1869–1931), U.S. political leader, born in Cincinnati, Ohio; Ohio Republican congressman 1903–13, 1915–31; speaker of House 1925–31.

Lon Nol (1913–85), premier of Kampuchea K-170

Lönnrot, Elias (1802–84), Finnish folklorist, philologist, and physician L-297
Finland F-89
folklore F-259
storytelling S-470

'Look', magazine M-35

'Look Back in Anger', play by Osborne E-282

'Look Homeward, Angel', autobiographical novel by Wolfe A-359, W-268

'Looking for Mr. Goodbar', novel by Rossner A-363

Lookout, Cape, North Carolina, 70 mi (110 km) s.w. of Cape Hatteras, *map* U-41

Lookout Mountain, ridge in n.w. Georgia extending into Tennessee and Alabama C-282, *map* A-223
Tennessee, *map* T-97, *picture* T-85

Lookout Mountain, battle of (often called 'battle above the clouds') C-484
Tennessee, *picture* T-92

Look-out Point Dam, Oregon O-583, 586

Loom, machine
Industrial Revolution I-178
Jacquard loom J-12
power loom
Cartwright C-193
rugs R-316, *picture* R-315
textiles T-142
weaving S-390, *pictures* S-391

Looming, a type of mirage M-463

Loon, a diving waterbird L-297, *picture* A-426
Minnesota state bird, *picture* M-448

Loop antenna, in radio, *picture* R-55

Looper. *see in index* Cankerworm

Looping pits, in metalworking I-346

Loop of Henle, in kidney K-235

Loos, Adolf (1870–1933), Austrian architect, *list* A-569

Loos, Anita (1893–1981), U.S. novelist, playwright, and motion-picture scenarist, born in Sisson, Calif. (novel, 'Gentlemen Prefer Blondes', later dramatized).

Loos-en-Gohelle (formerly Loos), town in n. France, about 3 mi (5 km) n.w. of Lens; scene of British offensive 1915; town captured but British lost about 70,000 men; pop. 3,918.

Loosestrife, leafy stemmed perennial herbs embracing the genus *Lysimachia* of the primrose family; common loosestrife is *L. vulgaris,* a tall coarse plant with large yellow flowers in terminal leafy panicles; *L. nummularia* (creeping Charlie, moneywort, or creeping jenny) is a trailing plant with large yellow flowers which are often used in rock gardens.

Loosestrife family (or Lythraceae), family of plants, shrubs, and trees, native chiefly to tropical America, including swamp loosestrife, loosestrife, henna, crepe myrtle, cigar flower, purple loosestrife, and blue waxweed.

Lope de Vega. *see in index* Vega Carpio

López, Alfonso Ramon (nickname Al) (born 1908), U.S. baseball catcher and manager, born in Tampa, Fla.; managed A.L. pennant winners, Cleveland Indians 1954, Chicago White Sox 1959.

López, Carlos Antonio (1790–1862), dictator of Paraguay, born near Asunción; teacher and lawyer; established country's first newspaper; rule marked by uneasy relations with U.S. and neighboring countries P-112

López, Francisco Solano (1826–70), dictator of Paraguay P-112

Lopez, Nancy (born 1957), U.S. golfer G-189, *picture* G-193

López de Legaspi, Miguel (1524–72), Spanish soldier, born in Zumarraga, near Tolosa, Spain; conquered Philippines and founded Manila P-259c

López de Segura, Ruy (fl. 1560), Spanish priest and chess writer C-304

López de Villalobos, Ruy (1500?–46), Spanish navigator; in 1542 attempted conquest of Philippines for Spain and named the islands "Las Filipinas."

López Mateos, Adolfo (1910–69), Mexican lawyer and statesman, born near Mexico City; minister of labor and social welfare 1952–57; president 1958–64.

López Portillo, José (born 1920), Mexican political leader, born in Mexico City; former professor of law National University of Mexico; finance minister 1973–75; president 1976–82 M-338

López y Fuentes, Gregorio (1897–1966), Mexican writer L-70

Lop Nor (or Lob Nor), marshy, salty depression in Sinkiang-Uigur Autonomous Region, China; receives Tarim River
Asia, *map* A-700

Loquat, small evergreen tree or shrub *Eriobotrya japonica* of the rose family and its fruit; originated in Asia; now widely cultivated in tropical and subtropical areas; fruit used for jellies, jams, and preserves.

Lorain, Ohio, port and industrial city on Lake Erie, 26 mi (42 km) w. of Cleveland; ships steel products, coal, iron ore; steel tubes and pipe, pumps, clothing, chemicals, communications and navigation equipment, toys, gypsum; pop. 75,416 O-512

Loran (or long-range navigation, or loran C), radar R-32
aviation A-[illegible]
fisheries F-134
navigation N-71, 78
signaling S-194
submarines S-498

Loras College, Dubuque, Iowa; Roman Catholic; est. in 1839; arts and sciences, and teacher education; graduate studies.

Lorca, Federico García. *see in index* García Lorca, Federico

Lorca, Spain, ancient city in s.e., on river Sangonera; trade center; many battles between Christians and Moors; pop. 19,854, *map* E-361

Lord, British title borne by bishops, marquises, earls, viscounts, and barons; also borne as courtesy title by eldest sons of dukes, marquises, and earls, and younger sons of dukes and marquises; title of office borne by lord chancellor.

Lord & Thomas, advertising agency A-58

Lord Dunmore's War (1774), named for John Murray, earl of Dunmore, governor of Virginia; expedition by colonists against American Indian coalition formed to check westward expansion of Virginia; ended at battle of Point Pleasant (now Tu-Endie-Wei Park, W. Va.).

Lord Howe Island, dependency of New South Wales, Australia, in Pacific 435 mi (700 km) n.e. of Sydney; resort; 5 sq mi (13 sq km); pop. 223, *map* P-3

'Lord Jim', work by Conrad E-280

Lord mayor, English magistrate L-289

aeronaut and inventor, born in Jefferson Mills, now Riverton, N.H.; as chief of aeronautic section of United States Army, used balloons for observation in Civil War.

Lowell, Abbott Lawrence (1856–1943), U.S. educator and political scientist L-326

Lowell, Amy (1874–1925), U.S. writer L-326

Lowell, Francis Cabot (1775–1817), U.S. merchant L-326
Industrial Revolution I-182

Lowell, James Russell (1819–91), U.S. poet, essayist, and critic L-326
American literature A-348
Hall of Fame, *table* H-16
Holmes H-204

Lowell, John (1743–1802), U.S. jurist, born in Newburyport, Mass.; said to have been author of clause in Massachusetts state constitution declaring "all men are born free and equal"; this clause was interpreted in 1783 by the Supreme Court of state to mean that slavery was abolished; father of Francis Cabot Lowell and grandfather of James Russell Lowell.

Lowell, Percival (1855–1916), U.S. astronomer L-326
astronomy A-714

Lowell, Robert (full name Robert Traill Spence Lowell, Jr.) (1917–77), U.S. poet L-326
American literature A-364

Lowell, Mass., one of the oldest industrial cities of the United States; pop. 92,418 M-191, 202, *map* U-41
carpet industry R-316

Lowell, University of, Lowell, Mass.; state control; est. 1975 by merger of Lowell State College and Lowell Technological Institute; arts and sciences, education, engineering and technology, music, nursing.

Lowell Observatory, Flagstaff, Ariz. A-601, 604, *picture* A-605
Saturn, *picture* S-52

Lowell State College, Lowell, Mass.; chartered 1894. *see also in index* Lowell, University of

Lowell Technological Institute, Lowell, Mass.; state control; est. 1895. *see also in index* Lowell, University of

Lower Austria, a province in n.e. Austria; area 7,402 sq mi (19,171 sq km); wooded hill country; capital Vienna; ruled by Hapsburgs until 1918; pop. 1,374,012.

Lower Burrell, Pa., city of Westmoreland county 16 mi (26 km) n.e. of Pittsburgh; in coal-mining area; incorporated 1958; pop. 13,200, *map* P-184

Lower California. *see in index* California, Lower

Lower Canada, name formerly given to province of Quebec C-95, Q-9g

Lowercase letters (or small letters) B-356, T-336, *picture* T-337

Lower East Side, a neighborhood in Manhattan, New York, N.Y. N-272

Lower Egypt, that part of Egypt north of 30° N. latitude.

Lower Falls, waterfall in Yellowstone National Park W-97

Lower house, in national legislatures P-130
Australia P-131
Canada P-132

Lower Merion, Pa., urban township on Schuylkill River just w. of Philadelphia; consists of 13 unincorporated communities; pop. 63,392.

Lower Mississippi Alluvial Plain, United States, *map* E-25

Lower Peninsula, southern section of Michigan M-354, 360

Lower Saxony (or Niedersachsen), state in West Germany, former state in British zone, Germany; pop. 7,230,050, *map* G-134
Hanover H-32

Lower Silesia. *see in index* Silesia

Lower Southampton, Pa., urban township situated in Bucks County just n.e. of Philadelphia; largely residential; pop. 17,578.

Lowes, John Livingston (1867–1945), U.S. educator and author, born in Decatur, Ind.; professor of English literature Harvard University 1918–39; noted for critical works on Chaucer, Shakespeare, Coleridge ('The Road to Xanadu'; 'Art of Geoffrey Chaucer'; 'Essays in Appreciation').

Lowestoft, England, seaport and resort of Suffolk, 110 mi (180 km) n.e. of London; fisheries; captured by Cromwell 1643; Dutch fleet defeated by duke of York 1665; pop. 50,730, *map* U-18a
porcelain P-476

Low-fat milk , *list* D-6
milk M-415

Low German, language G-114

Low-income families, housing H-298, 302

Lowland gorilla, *picture* Z-465

Lowlands, Canada
Alberta A-262
Manitoba M-100

Lowlands, central Scotland S-67, *picture* S-68

Lowlands, United States, *map* E-25

Lowland white fir. *see in index* Giant fir

Lownsbery, Eloise (1888–1967), U.S. writer, born in Pawpaw, Ill.; brought medieval history to life in her books for boys and girls ('Boy Knight of Reims'; 'Out of the Flame'; 'Marta the Doll').

Low-pressure center (or low), region of low barometric pressure W-118, *table* W-126, *map* W-124

Low relief, in sculpture. *see in index* Bas-relief

Lowry, Malcolm (1909–57), British writer
literary contribution E-282

Low tide, ocean tide O-488

Low wave, *tables* R-34, 50

Lox. *see in index* Liquid oxygen

Loyalist (or Tory), a person who remained loyal to England during the American Revolution P-432
Canada C-94
Revolution R-167, *pictures* R-166. *see also in index* United Empire Loyalists

Loyalists, United Empire. *see in index* United Empire Loyalists

Loyal Legion, Military Order of the, patriotic society founded 1865 at Philadelphia, Pa., on the day following Lincoln's assassination; organized by United States Army and Navy officers; membership limited to such officers and their direct male descendants; purposes: fellowship among and welfare of United States soldiers and sailors, care of widows and orphans of deceased members.

Loyal Order of Moose. *see in index* Moose, Loyal Order of

Loyalty Day (May 1), designated by Congress in 1958 to reaffirm loyalty to the United States and to acknowledge the heritage of freedom.

Loyalty Islands (French Îles Loyauté), Pacific group 60 mi (100 km) e. of New Caledonia, of which it is a dependency; 800 sq mi (2,072 sq km); copra, rubber; pop. 13,378, *map* P-3

Loyang, China, city in Honan Province 100 mi (160 km) w. of Kaifeng; farming, stock raising; trucks, cement, textiles; pop. 580,000.

Loyola, Ignatius of (1491?–1556), saint, founder of Jesuit Order; festival July 31 L-327
Counter Reformation R-135, C-744, *picture* R-134

Loyola College, Baltimore, Md.; Roman Catholic; established in 1852; arts and sciences, business administration, and teacher education; graduate division M-170

Loyola Marymount University, Los Angeles, Calif.; Roman Catholic; formed 1973 by merger of Marymount College (chartered 1948) and Loyola University of Los Angeles (established 1929); arts and sciences, business administration, education, and engineering; graduate division.

Loyola University in New Orleans, New Orleans, La.; Roman Catholic; established 1912; arts and sciences, business administration, dentistry, law, music, and teacher education; graduate studies N-231

Loyola University of Chicago, Chicago, Ill.; Roman Catholic; founded 1870; arts and sciences, business administration, education, law, nursing, social work; graduate school; Medical Center (medicine and dentistry) at Maywood; center for humanities at Rome, Italy.

Loyson, Charles (also called Père Hyacinthe) (1827–1912), French preacher, born in Orléans, France; eloquent speaker but his unorthodox beliefs caused his excommunication from the Roman Catholic church.

Lozeau, Albert (1878–1924), Canadian poet and journalist, born in Montreal; an invalid from youth; ranks high for sensitiveness and imagination.

LPD (Amphibious Transport Dock), naval vessel N-86

LP-Gas (or liquefied petroleum gas, or LPG), *chart* P-241a
farm machinery F-31

LPH. *see in index* Amphibious Assault Ship

LPH. *see in index* Lipotropic hormone

LRT (light rail transit), transportation S-486

LSD. *see in index* Dock Landing Ship

LSD (or lysergic acid diethylamide), a hallucinatory drug synthesized by Dr. Albert Hofmann, Basel, Switzerland, 1938; used to treat terminal cancer patients; nonmedical use considered dangerous D-277
hallucinogen H-18

LSI. *see in index* Large-scale integration

LST (or Tank Landing Ship), amphibious naval vessel N-85

LTP (or long-term potentiation), electrical phenomenon in the brain involved in memory M-294

Lualaba, river in Africa, *map* A-118
Congo River C-647

Luanda (or Loanda, or Sao Paulo de Loanda), Angola, capital and seaport; founded 1575; for about three centuries, a center of slave trade; pop. 480,613 L-327, A-419, *map* A-118

Luang Prabang. *see in index* Luoangphrabang

Luapula, river in Africa
Congo River C-647

Luau, Hawaiian feast H-61, *picture* H-59

Lubang Islands, small group off s.w. coast of Luzon, in the Philippines; largest island Lubang (74 sq mi; 192 sq km) commands entrance to Manila Bay; pop. 19,904, *map* P-262

Lubber grasshopper, insect *Brachystola magna* of the family Acridae C-768, *picture* C-767

Lubber's knot (or granny knot) K-262

Lubber's line, in navigation C-622

Lubbock, Tex., city about 110 mi (180 km) s. of Amarillo; oil wells in area; cotton and cotton products, packed meats, grain sorghums; Texas Tech University; Mackenzie State Park; Reese Air Force Base nearby; pop. 173,979 T-120, *map* U-40

Lübeck, West Germany, seaport on Trave River, 12 mi (19 km) from Baltic Sea; shipbuilding; machinery; pop. 239,339, *maps* E-361, G-134
Hanseatic league H-32, *picture* M-391

Lubin, David (1849–1919), U.S. agricultural organizer, born in Klodowa, Poland; brought to United States in 1855; founded dry-goods and mail-order business in California, 1874; devoted last part of his life to agricultural problems. *see also in index* International Institute of Agriculture

Lubitsch, Ernst (1892–1947), U.S. motion-picture director and producer, born in Berlin, Germany; to U.S. 1922; brilliant style and sophisticated humor ('Lady Windermere's Fan'; 'Merry Widow'; 'Ninotchka').

Lübke, Heinrich (1894–1972), West German political leader, born in Enkhausen, near Dortmund, Germany; minister of Food, Agriculture, and Forestry, Federal Republic of Germany, 1953–59, president 1959–69.

Lublin, Poland, city 95 mi (150 km) s.e. of Warsaw; flourished in 12th century; scene of Russian victory over Austrians in World War I; pop. 197,100, *maps* E-361, P-414

Lublin, Treaty of (1569), *table* T-274

Lubricant, oily or greasy substance used to diminish friction L-327
automobile, *picture* A-848
petroleum, *charts* P-241, 241b

Lubumbashi (formerly Elisabethville), Zaire, city in s.e.; copper and tin mining center; pop. 525,154, *map* A-118

Lucan (or Marcus Annaeus Lucanus) (AD 39–65), Roman poet, author of 'Pharsalia', epic on civil war between Caesar and Pompey.

Lucania, region in Italy. *see in index* Basilicata

Lucas, Anthony Francis (or Anthony Francis Luchich) (1855–1921), U.S. mining engineer and geologist, born in Dalmatia; to U.S. 1879, became citizen 1885
Texas oil industry T-125

Lucas, Edward Verrall (1868–1938), English essayist, novelist, and biographer; born in Eltham, Kent; "the modern Charles Lamb"; widely popular for his genial humor and broad sympathies ('The Open Road', anthology; 'The Life of Charles Lamb'; 'Over Bremerton's' and 'London Lavender', novels; 'Pleasure Trove', essays; 'A Wanderer in London' and 'A Wanderer in Paris', travel).

Lucas, Eliza. *see in index* Pinckney, Elizabeth

Lucas, Jerry (born 1940), U.S. basketball player, born in Middletown, Ohio; center, Ohio State University, selected as all-America player 1960, 1961, and 1962; with Cincinnati Royals 1963–69, Golden State Warriors 1969–71; New York Knickerbockers 1971–74.

Lucas, John Seymour (1849–1923), English historical and portrait painter, born in London
William I W-206

Lucas Van Leyden (1494?–1533), Dutch painter and engraver, born in Leiden, The Netherlands; superb technician; influenced by Albrecht Dürer, later by Marcantonio.

Lucca, Italy, old and picturesque city 12 mi (19 km) n.e. of Pisa; many antiquities; large trade; pop. 88,428, *map* I-401

Luce, Clare Boothe (born 1903), U.S. writer and diplomat, born in New York City; married Henry Robinson Luce; edited *Vogue* 1930, *Vanity Fair* 1931–34, then turned to writing plays ('The Women'; 'Kiss the Boys Goodbye'); later became a war correspondent; member U.S. Congress 1942–46; U.S. ambassador to Italy 1953–56.

Luce, Henry Robinson (1898–1967), U.S. editor and publisher, born in Shantung Province, China; son of American missionary; husband of Clare Boothe Luce; in 1923 became co-founder and editor in chief of Time, Inc., editorial chairman 1964–67 M-35

Lucerne (or Luzern), Switzerland, capital of canton of Lucerne at n.w. end of Lake Lucerne; tourist resort; pop. 69,879, *picture* S-544, *map* S-537

Lucerne. *see in index* Alfalfa

Lucerne, Lake, mountain-rimmed lake in central Switzerland; 24 mi (39 km) long, *map* S-537

Lu Chi (261–303), Chinese poet and literary critic C-388

Lucia, Santa. *see in index* Lucy, Saint

Lucia Day, in Sweden S-525

'Lucia di Lammermoor', opera by Donizetti D-229

Lucian (120?–180?), Greek satirist and humorist S-341c, 348d

moon M-580
Lundy, Benjamin (1789–1839), U.S. philanthropist, prominent in antislavery movement, born in Hardwick, N.J.; published antislavery magazine and lectured against slavery.
Lundy's Lane, battle of, in War of 1812, between British and U.S. forces near Niagara Falls on Canadian side W-32
Lüneburg, West Germany, city of Lower Saxony s.e. of Hamburg; was prominent in Hanseatic League; cement works, salt spring; pop. 60,900, *map* G-134
Lüneburger Heide, heath s.w. of Lüneburg, in Lower Saxony, West Germany, *map* G-134, *picture* G-113
Lunenburg, N.S., industrial and fishing town 40 mi (60 km) s.w. of Halifax; pop. 3,154 N-401, *map* C-112
Lunéville, France, town 18 mi (29 km) s.e. of Nancy; treaty between France and Austria in 1801; pop. 22,961
treaty, *table* T-274
Lung, Momsen, for submarine escape, *picture* S-495b
Lung abscess, an accumulation of a mass of pus D-177
Lung cancer C-134, L-337
Lungfish, a fish of the subclass Choanichthyes M-643. *see also in index* Mudfish
animal life record, *table* E-24
hibernation F-131
place in evolution A-461
Lungfish. *see in index* African mudfish
Lungs, organs of respiration in air-breathing animals L-336
evolution A-461
fish F-126
frog F-407
human A-391, R-159
artificial B-211
diseases D-177
pollution P-441b
exercise E-369
jogging J-121
heart H-97
transplantation T-251
Lungshan Temple (or Dragon Mountain Temple), temple at Taipei, Taiwan; noted for its architecture T-11
Lungworm W-362
Lungwort. *see in index* Virginia cowslip
Luniks, Soviet moon probes. *see in index* Luna, Russian spacecraft
Lunokhod, Soviet lunar landing vehicle, *table* S-344
Lunt, Alfred (1893–1977), U.S. actor and director, born in Milwaukee, Wis.; starred with wife, Lynn Fontanne, in numerous theater productions and motion-picture version of 'The Guardsman' A-27. *see also in index* Fontanne, Lynn
'Lun yü'. *see in index* 'Analects'
Luoangphrabang, formerly Luang Prabang, Laos, city in n., on Mekong River; historical residence; also name of former kingdom; pop. 44,244 L-47
Lupercalia, Roman festival in honor of ancient god Lupercus, protector of flocks against wolves, sometimes identified with Faunus.
Lupine, various plants of the bean family, with white, yellow, or blue flowers on a central spike; contain poison, *picture* N-287
growing conditions G-23
Lupus. *see in index* Systemic lupus erythematosis
Lupus, constellation, *charts* S-419, C-682
Luque, Hernando de, partner of Pizarro P-349
Lurçat, Jean (1892–1966), French modernist painter and tapestry designer, born in Bruyères, near Épinal, France; influenced revival of French tapestry-weaving industry
tapestry T-27
Lure, artificial, in fishing F-142, *pictures* F-141, 143
Luria, Salvador Edward (born 1912), U.S. biologist, born in Turin, Italy; to U.S. 1940, citizen 1947; professor Massachusetts Institute of Technology 1959–.
Lurs, a nomadic people of Iran, probably of Aryan origin I-305
Lusaka, Zambia, capital; pop. 538,469 L-337
Africa, *map* A-118
Zambia Z-447
Lü shih, Chinese verse form C-388
Lüshun, China. *see in index* Port Arthur
'Lusiads, The' (or 'The sons of Lusus', or 'The Portuguese'), one of greatest epic poems of world literature, by Camões P-456, C-67
Lusitania, ancient Roman province comprising most of modern Portugal and s.w. Spain; name comes from Lusitani, group of people who held off Roman domination until the death of their leader.
'Lusitania', ocean liner S-177e
Wilson W-218
World War I W-305
Lüta, China, municipality in Liaoning Province; made up of cities Port Arthur and Dairen and two counties; pop. 3,086,000. *see also in index* Dairen; Port Arthur
Lute, ancient pear-shaped stringed instrument of Arabian origin S-490a, *picture* S-491
Lutetia. *see in index* Paris
Lutetium (Lu), transitional chemical element
periodic table, *table* P-207, *list* P-208
Luther, Hans (1879–1962), German statesman, born in Berlin; in 1924 concluded Dawes loan for Germany; chancellor 1925–26; instituted taxation and tariff reform; president of Reichsbank 1930–33; ambassador to U.S. 1933–37.
Luther, Martin (1483–1546), German leader of Protestant Reformation L-337
Counter-Reformation C-744
Germany G-121
German literature G-105
Josquin J-144
Leo X L-131
Medici M-273
Lutheranism L-338
Reformation R-133
Zwingli Z-472
Lutheranism, religion L-338, G-121
Denmark D-99
early spread R-134
East Germany G-114
Finland F-89
Sweden S-524, 527
West Germany G-114
women's organizations W-270
Lutheran World Federation, international cooperative body of the Lutheran churches L-339
church councils C-411
Luther College, Decorah, Iowa; affiliated with American Lutheran church; established 1861; liberal arts and teacher education.
Luther League of America, an organization of several Lutheran Young People's Societies established 1895 at Pittsburgh, Pa.; originally nonsynodical; adopted by United Lutheran church in America, 1920.
Luthuli, Albert (1898–1967), South African liberation leader L-340
Lutine Bell, Lloyd's of London; from the frigate *La Lutine* which sank in 1799 with a cargo of gold; Lloyd's underwriters had insured the cargo and suffered heavy loss.
Luton, England, town 30 mi (50 km) n.w. of London; automobiles, ball bearings, hats, chemicals; pop. 156,690.
Lutoslawski, Witold (born 1913), Polish composer M-676
Luttrell Psalter, illuminated manuscript of 14th century, *pictures* E-242
Lutyens, Sir Edwin Landseer (1869–1944), British architect, born in London; designer of public buildings and homes; planned New Delhi, India; works include Government House, New Delhi, Whitehall Cenotaph, London, and British Embassy, Washington, D.C.; Royal Academy 1920, Order of Merit 1943.
Lutz, Frank Eugene (1879–1943), U.S. biologist, born in Bloomsburg, Pa.; with American Museum of Natural History, New York City, from 1909; curator of its Department of Insects and Spiders 1921–43 ('Field Book of Insects').
Lützen, East Germany, town 13 mi (21 km) s.w. of Leipzig; pop. 4,819
Thirty Years' War T-170
Gustavus Adolphus G-319
warfare, *list* W-15
Luvua, river in Africa
Congo River C-647
Luxembourg, country of n.w. Europe, surrounded by France, Germany, and Belgium; 998 sq mi (92,585 sq km); cap. Luxembourg; pop. 365,500 L-340, *map* E-361
furniture F-458
national symbols
flag, *picture* F-167
song, *table* N-64
railroad mileage, *table* R-85
taxation, *table* T-35
The Netherlands N-128
World War II W-323
Luxembourg, capital of grand duchy of Luxembourg; pop. 76,143 L-340, *picture* L-341
Luxemburg, Rosa (1871–1919), German socialist agitator L-341
Luxor, village in Upper Egypt on part of site of ancient Thebes, near El Karnak E-126, T-162, *map* A-118
"Avenue of Sphinxes" S-379
Lu Xun (or Chou Shu-jen, or Lu Hsün) (1881–1936), Chinese author L-341
Chinese literature C-346, C-390
Luzern, Switzerland. *see in index* Lucerne
Luzon, largest and most important island of Philippines; area 40,420 sq mi (104,690 sq km); contains Manila, largest city, and Quezon City, official capital of country; pop. 20,851,000
Philippines P-253, 257, *chart* P-253b, *maps* P-259a, 262, *pictures* P-259
World War II W-336, 348
L'vov (or Lwow, or Lemberg), U.S.S.R., former Polish fortified city 285 mi (460 km) s.w. of Kiev; capital of Austrian Galicia in 18th century; returned to Poland after World War I; included in Russia since 1945; pop. 553,000 P-412, U-2, *maps* R-344, 349
Europe, *map* E-361
L wave, type of seismic wave E-37
Lwoff, André (born 1902), French biologist, born in Allier Department; with Pasteur Institute in Paris; professor Sorbonne 1959–68.
LWR. *see in index* Light water reactor
Lyakhov, Vladimir (born 1941), Soviet cosmonaut, born in Antrasit, U.S.S.R., *table* S-348
Lyallpur, Pakistan, city 75 mi (120 km) s.w. of Lahore; railroad junction; wheat and cotton center; food products, farm implements, chemicals; pop. 425,248.
Lyase, enzyme E-290, *table* E-290
Lyautey, Louis Hubert (1854–1934), French marshal, born in Nancy; as resident general and high commissioner of Morocco (1912–25) put the government on a sound basis.
Lycabettus, Mount (or modern Mount St. George), hill n.e. of Athens 1,112 feet (339 meters) high; modern section of city spreads to its base; reservoir on its side built by Hadrian and Antoninus Pius still in use A-734, *picture* G-254
Lycaenidae, butterflies B-528
Lyceum, Aristotle's school in ancient Athens A-14
Aristotle's teaching A-589
Lyceum, United States A-51
Lychnis, scarlet. *see in index* Jerusalem cross
Lycia, ancient division of s.w. Asia Minor on Mediterranean, conquered by Persia 6th century BC, then subject in turn to Macedon, Egypt, Syria, and Rome, *maps* P-212
'Lycidas', poem by John Milton commemorating death of his friend Edward King, drowned at sea.
Lycoming College, Williamsport, Pa.; United Methodist; founded as Williamsport Academy 1812, as college 1947; arts and sciences, education.
Lycopodium, a genus of nonflowering mosslike plants of the club moss family Lycopodiaceae with trailing stems and numerous small evergreen leaves; the sulfur-yellow, highly inflammable powderlike spores produced by erect fruiting spikes are sometimes used in making fireworks.
Lycoris, a genus of perennial plants of the amaryllis family, native to eastern Asia; root a bulb; leaves long, narrow, disappearing before flowers develop; flowers yellow, red, or rose-lilac, fragrant, grow in cluster at top of tall stem, stamens project beyond flower tube; one species called golden spider lily.
Lycurgus (9th century BC), lawgiver of ancient Sparta L-342
ancient Greece G-265
legal codes L-91
Lydda (or Lod), Israel, ancient town 10 mi (16 km) s.e. of Tel Aviv-Jaffa; international airport; pop. 21,000.
Lydgate, John (1370?–1451?), English poet, scholar, and monk, born at Lydgate near Newmarket; contemporary of Geoffrey Chaucer and acknowledged him as his "master"; voluminous writer; style rough and verbose; founder of English literary school between Chaucer and Edmund Spenser.
Lydia, ancient kingdom in Asia Minor; early seat of Asiatic civilization with important influence on Greeks; later part of Roman province of Asia
coins C-537
money M-532
Croesus C-780
Lydian stone. *see in index* Touchstone
Lye, caustic compound. *see also in index* Caustic potash
soaps S-229
Lyell, Charles (or Sir Charles Lyell) (1797–1875), British geologist L-342
evolution E-366
Lyle, David Alexander (1845–1937), U.S. Army officer, born in Lancaster, Ohio; attained rank of colonel 1907; inventor of Lyle lifesaving gun.
Lyly, John (or John Lilly) (1554?–1606), English romancer and dramatist, born in The Weald; created euphuism, a writing style.
Lyman, Roy (nickname Link) (1898–1972), U.S. football tackle; with Canton Bulldogs 1922 and 1924, Cleveland Browns 1923, and Chicago Bears 1925–34.
Lyme grass (or wild rye), a coarse perennial grass of erect growth found in temperate climates.
Lyme Regis, England, seaside resort of Dorsetshire, 135 mi (217 km) s.w. of London; fine beach; pop. 3,310.
Lymph, a colorless liquid exuded through capillaries to nourish tissues of the body L-343
anatomy A-391
circulatory system's accessory C-422
disease prevention D-167
living things L-270
Lymphadenitis, inflammation of lymph nodes L-343
Lymphangiography, diagnostic procedure L-334
Lymphatic system, a system of vessels for collecting lymph and carrying it back into the blood L-342
blood B-314
immune system I-55
Lymphatic vessel, anatomy L-343
Lymph node, small glands scattered throughout lymphatic system, but especially in the neck, armpits, groin, thighs, and body organs; produce corpuscular elements of lymph L-342
Lymphocyte, one kind of white blood cell L-342
blood B-314, *table* B-317
immune system I-55
disease D-167, *picture* D-168
transplant surgery S-519c
Lymphogranuloma venereum, a venereal disease V-274
Lymphoid nodule (or lymphoid follicle), in anatomy L-342
Lymphokine, pathology I-56
Lymphoma, type of malignant tumor C-812
Lynbrook, N.Y., resort city on shore of Long Island, near New York City; chiefly residential; pop. 23,776, *map* A-260

Lynch, John Roy (1847–1939), U.S. political leader in Reconstruction period, born in Concordia Parish, La.; freed from slavery during Civil War; in U.S. Congress 1873–77, 1882–83; in army 1898–1911; active in Republican Party ('The Facts of Reconstruction') B-292

Lynch, Thomas, Jr. (1749–79), signer of Declaration of Independence, born in South Carolina S-310

Lynchburg, Va., industrial city on James River, about 95 mi (150 km) s.w. of Richmond; foundries, communications products, nuclear reactors; Randolph-Macon Woman's College, Lynchburg College; supply depot for Confederates during Civil War; pop. 66,743, *maps* N-351, V-348, 331, 336, U-41

Lynchburg College, Lynchburg, Va.; private control; opened 1903; arts and sciences, teacher education; graduate studies.

Lynd, Robert Staughton (1892–1970), U.S. sociologist, born in New Albany, Ind.; professor of sociology Columbia University 1931–60; with wife, **Helen Merrell Lynd** (1896–1982), wrote 'Middletown' and 'Middletown in Transition', studies of a Middle Western city (Muncie, Ind.).

Lyndhurst, N.J., urban township 6 mi (10 km) n.e. of Newark on the Passaic River; incorporated 1852; pop. 22,729.

Lyndhurst, Ohio, residential city 4 mi (6 km) n.e. of Cleveland Heights; incorporated 1917; pop. 18,092.

Lyndon B. Johnson National Historic Site, in Texas, *picture* J-131

Lyndon B. Johnson Space Center, near Houston, Tex. S-346b, *pictures* S-342b, T-129
  NASA N-22
  renamed in 1973 J-135

Lyndon State College, Lyndonville, Vt.; founded 1911; formerly a teachers' college; liberal arts, education; graduate studies.

Lynen, Feodor (1911–79), German biochemist, born in Munich; director Max Planck Institute for Cell Chemistry, University of Munich.

Lynn, James Thomas (born 1927), U.S. lawyer and government official, born in Cleveland, Ohio; general counsel Department of Commerce 1969–71, undersecretary 1971–73; secretary of housing and urban development 1973–75; director Office of Management and Budget 1975–77
  Nixon N-327

Lynn, Loretta (born 1935), U.S. country musician M-679

Lynn, Mass., a city near Boston; pop. 78,471 M-191

Lynnhaven Bay, on coast of Virginia e. of Norfolk.

Lynnwood, Wash., city 16 mi (26 km) n. of Seattle on Puget Sound; prefab homes and panels; pop. 21,937.

Lynwood, Calif., city 9 mi (15 km) s. of Los Angeles; metal products, chemicals; incorporated 1921; pop. 48,548.

Lynx, member of the cat family L-344, *picture* A-436
  furs, *tables* F-464, 465

Lynx, constellation, *chart* C-681

Lyon, Mary (1797–1849), U.S. pioneer in higher education for women, born near Buckland, Mass.; opened Mt. Holyoke Female Seminary (later Mt. Holyoke College) 1837
  Hall of Fame, *table* H-16

Lyon, Nathaniel (1818–61), U.S. soldier, prominent opponent of states' rights and slavery, born in Ashford, Conn.; organized Unionist troops in Missouri; killed at Wilson's Creek
  Missouri M-494

Lyon (or Lugdunum), France, city at junction of Rhone and Saône rivers; pop. 456,265 L-344, *map* E-361
  Botanic Garden, *table* B-379
  France, *map* F-372

Lyon, University of, France L-344

Lyonesse, fabled land in Arthurian legends, off s. coast of Cornwall, England; reputedly engulfed by sea.

Lyons, Joseph Aloysius (1879–1939), Australian political leader, born in Circular Head, Tasmania; premier, treasurer, and minister for railways 1923–28; prime minister 1932–39; founded United party 1931.

Lyons, Theodore Amar (nickname Ted) (1900–86), U.S. baseball pitcher and manager, born in Lake Charles, La.; pitcher Chicago, A.L., 1923–42, manager-pitcher 1946, manager 1947–48; won 260 games, lost 230; won over 20 games in each of 3 seasons; pitched no-hit game against Boston, Aug. 21, 1926.

Lyotropic liquid crystal L-234

Lyra (or Lyre), constellation across North Pole from Little Bear; represents lyre of Orpheus or of Mercury, *charts* S-419–20, 423, C-681

Lyra, stringed instrument S-490

Lyra viol, stringed instrument S-490

Lyre, stringed instrument S-490, *picture* S-490b

Lyrebird L-344, A-782, *picture* P-110

'Lyrical Ballads' (1798), book of poems by Wordsworth and Coleridge
  English literature E-274
  Wordsworth W-294

Lyric poetry P-407
  creative writing W-381
  Greek literature G-274

Lysander (died 395 BC), able unscrupulous Spartan admiral; defeated Athens at Aegospotami and ended Peloponnesian War.

Lysenko, Trofim Denisovich (1898–1976), Soviet biologist and agronomist
  evolution E-366

Lysergic acid diethylamide. *see in index* LSD

Lysias (459–380 BC), one of great Attic orators; originator of eloquent but plain style in Greek rhetoric.

Lysippus (4th century BC), Greek sculptor
  Greek art G-272

'Lysistrata', play by Aristophanes A-588, G-276

Lysosome, cell structure C-238, *picture* C-237
  immune system I-56

Lysozyme, germ-killing enzyme in most body fluids B-234, *table* E-290

Lys River, a tributary of the Scheldt; rises in extreme n. of France and flows n.e. 120 mi (190 km) joining Scheldt at Ghent; scene of terrific fighting in World War I.

Lyster, William, Australian opera director A-800

Lyte, Henry Francis (1793–1847), British divine and hymn writer, born near Kelso, Scotland; author of popular hymns 'Abide with Me', 'Jesus, I My Cross Have Taken'.

Lythraceae. *see in index* Loosestrife family

Lythrum (or purple loosestrife, or spiked loosestrife), perennial plant (*L. salicaria*) of the loosestrife family, found from New England to Utah; grows to 3 ft (1 m); leaves narrow, 4 in. (10 cm) long; flowers purple, in dense spikes.

Lyttelton, city, New Zealand C-396, *map* N-299

Lytton, Edward George Earle Bulwer-Lytton, first **Baron** (1803–73), English novelist, playwright, and political leader; born in London; member of Parliament 1831–41, 1852–66; made secretary for the colonies 1858; historical novels; known for 'Last Days of Pompeii.'

Lytton, Edward Robert Bulwer-Lytton, first **earl of** (pen name Owen Meredith) (1831–91), English statesman and poet, born in London; son of Baron Lytton; viceroy of India 1876–80 ('Lucile', novel).

Lytton, Sir Henry. *see in index* Dalling and Bulwer, William Henry Lytton Earle Bulwer, Baron

The letter M

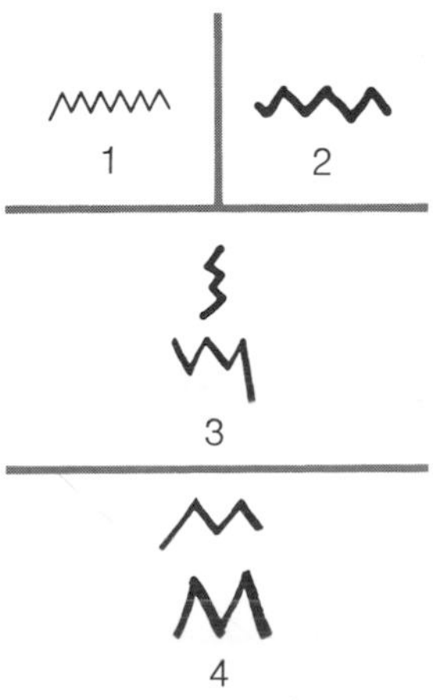

probably started as a picture sign of water, as in Egyptian hieroglyphic writing (1) and in a very early Semitic writing which was used about 1500 B.C. on the Sinai Peninsula (2). About 1000 B.C., in Byblos and other Phoenician and Canaanite centers, the sign was given a linear form with a tail (3), the source of all later forms. In the Semitic languages the sign was called *mem,* meaning "water."

The Greeks gave the sign a symmetrical, balanced form without the tail (4). They named it *mu.*

The Romans took the sign without change into Latin. From Latin the capital letter M came unchanged into English.

The English small handwritten "m" is simply a quickly made capital with curves instead of angles. The printed small "m" is similar to the handwritten one.

M

M1, money M-533

M-1 Abrams, battle tank, *picture* T-21

M2, money M-533

MA (mental age), intelligence test score I-239

Ma'arri, al- (973–1057), Syrian poet I-365

Maartens, Maarten (pen name of Joost Marius Willem van der Poorten-Schwartz) (1858–1915), Dutch novelist.

Maas, Nicolaes. *see in index* Maes, Nicolaes

Maasai. *see in index* Masai

Maas River, w. Europe; rises in France where it is called the Meuse, flows through Belgium and The Netherlands N-125. *see also in index* Meuse River
  Rotterdam R-299

Maastricht (or Maestricht), The Netherlands, city on Meuse River in s.e., on Belgian frontier; great sandstone quarries, worked since Roman times; beer, brandy, cigars, glass, earthenware; pop. 85,188.

Ma'at, Egyptian goddess M-700, *pictures* M-697, 699

Maazel, Lorin (born 1930), U.S. conductor, born in Neuilly, suburb of Paris, France, of U.S. parents; as a child prodigy conducted major orchestras of U.S.; went on to international fame; remarkable memory for musical scores.

Mab (or Queen Mab), in Celtic and English folklore, a fairy presiding over dreams; in Shakespeare's 'Romeo and Juliet', Act I, Scene iv; gives title to Shelley's 'Queen Mab'; originally a legendary queen, Maev of Connaught.

Mabie, Hamilton Wright (1845–1916), U.S. editor, critic, and essayist, born in Cold Spring, N.Y. ('My Study Fire'; 'Essays on Books and Culture').

Mabillon, Jean (1632–1707), French Benedictine scholar and historian; pioneered study of ancient handwriting; founded science of diplomatics, the critical study of the formal sources of history H-172

Mabinogion, collection of ancient Welsh bardic tales, particularly the collection of 12th-century knightly romances translated by Lady Charlotte Guest S-473
  'Taliesin' S-481b
  Wales W-6

Mabovitch, Goldie. *see in index* Meir, Golda

Mabuse. *see in index* Gossaert, Jan

MAC (Military Airlift Command), U.S. Air Force A-164

MacAdam, John Loudon (or John Loudon McAdam) (1756–1836), Scottish engineer, born in Ayr; inventor of macadam roads R-215, T-261
  Macadamia nut M-2

Macadamia nut, from the trees *Macadamia ternifolia* and *Macadamia integrifolia* of the protea family; has hard shell and is about 1 in. (2.5 cm) in diameter; kernel, solid and white, is edible and yields oil used in soap and in medicine; trees are native to Australia but cultivated in Hawaii, s. California, and s. Florida; first planted in Hawaii in 1892; average height 30 to 40 ft (9 to 12 m), trunk about 1 ft (0.3 m) in diameter; leaves dark green; flowers white, pink, or red M-2

Macadamized road B-449, R-215
  wagon W-3

McAdoo, William Gibbs (1863–1941), U.S. public official, born near Marietta, Ga.; practiced law 1885–1903; secretary of treasury 1913–18; director general of railroads 1917–19; U.S. senator from California 1933–39.

McAfee, George (nickname Duke) (born 1918), U.S. football halfback, born in Corbin, Ky.; played for Chicago Bears 1940–41, 1945–50.

McAfee, Mildred Helen (born 1900), U.S. educator, born in Parkville, Mo.; married Douglas Horton; president Wellesley College 1936–49; head of WAVES 1942–46.

Macagua Dam, dam in Venezuela, on Caroní River O-606

McAlester, Okla., city about 60 mi (100 km) s.w. of Muskogee; in coal and cattle area; ammunition, aerospace equipment, clothing, flotation materials; state prison; U.S. Naval Ammunition Depot nearby; pop. 17,255, *map* U-41

Macalester College, St. Paul, Minn.; Presbyterian; founded 1885; arts and sciences, business administration, education, music, religion; graduate study.

McAllen, Tex., city in Rio Grande valley about 50 mi (80 km) n.w. of Brownsville; processing of citrus fruits, vegetables; oil center; pop. 67,042, *map* U-40

MacAlpine, Kenneth. *see in index* Kenneth I, MacAlpine

Macao (or Macau, or Aomen), Portuguese settlement and seaport on Macao Island at mouth of Canton River 40 mi (60 km) w. of Hong Kong; settlement forms with neighboring islets the Portuguese overseas self-governing territory Macao; total area 6 sq mi (15.5 sq km); pop. 443,000
  Asia, *map* A-700

Macapagal, Diosdado (born 1910), Philippine political leader, born in Lubao, Pampanga Province, Luzon; professor of law University of Santo Tomas 1941–49; member House of Representatives 1949–57; vice-president 1957–61, president 1961–65.

Macaque, monkeys A-503, *picture* A-502

MacArthur, Arthur (1845–1912), U.S. general, born in Chicopee Falls, Mass.; father of Douglas MacArthur
  MacArthur M-2
  Taft T-8
  World War II W-328

MacArthur, Douglas (1880–1964), U.S. Army officer M-2
  Hoover H-236
  Korean War K-295, 298, *chart* K-299
  Roosevelt, *picture* R-274
  Truman T-299

MacArthur Lock, part of the Sault Sainte Marie Canal system, *picture* C-127

Macassar, Indonesia. *see in index* Udjung Pandang

Macassar Strait, Indonesia. *see in index* Makassar Strait

Macau. *see in index* Macao

Macaulay, Dame Rose (1881–1958), English author of novels, verse, essays; born in Cambridge, England; works have humorous, satirical touch ('Potterism'; 'Told by an Idiot'; 'Orphan Island'; 'Crewe Train'; 'Personal Pleasures'; 'John Milton'; 'The World My Wilderness').

Macaulay, Thomas (in full Thomas Babington Macaulay) (1800–1859), English essayist and historian M-3
  conversation C-695
  Hampden H-24
  history writing H-173
  literary contribution E-279

Macaulay, Zachary (1768–1838), English philanthropist; governor Sierra Leone 1793–99; organized antislavery society; father of Thomas Babington Macaulay
  Macaulay, Thomas M-3

McAuley, Catherine (1787–1841), Irish philanthropist, born near Dublin; founder of the Roman Catholic order of Sisters of Mercy.

McAuley, James (1917–76), Australian writer, *table* A-798

McAuliffe, Christa (formerly Sharon Christa Corrigan) (1948–86), U.S. school teacher-astronaut killed in the explosion of the space shuttle "Challenger" on Jan. 28, 1986; born in Boston, Mass.; graduated Framingham State College 1970; married Steven J. McAuliffe; two children, Scott and Caroline; high school social studies teacher in Concord, N.H., when she was picked on July 19, 1985, to be first teacher in space S-347
  NASA N-22

Macaw, South American parrot P-135, *picture* P-134

Maçayó, Brazil. *see in index* Maceió

McBain, Ed. *see in index* Hunter, Evan

Macbeth (died 1057), usurping king of Scotland, hero of Shakespeare's tragedy 'Macbeth'
  Shakespeare's play S-133, *picture* S-140

MacBride, Sean (born 1904), Irish diplomat, born in Paris, France; won fame as trial lawyer; founder (1946) and leader of Republican party; member Dail Eireann after 1947; foreign minister 1948–51; chairman of Amnesty International 1961–75. *see also in index* Nobel Prizewinners, *table*

McBurney, Charles (1845–1913), U.S. surgeon, born in Roxbury, Mass.; discoverer of McBurney's point (spot on abdomen where pressure reveals appendicitis) and pioneer in aseptic technique.

Maccabees, distinguished Jewish family dominant in Jerusalem in 2nd century BC, descendants of the brave priest Mattathias; chief member **Judas** (died 160 BC); story told in apocryphal Books of Maccabees.

Maccabees, The, fraternal society, organized 1878, London, Ont.; reorganized 1883; in 1926 Ladies of the Maccabees was merged with men's organization; local lodges called Tents (men), Hives (women), and Courts (juniors); has homes for aged at Alma, Mich., and Chatham, Pa.

McCandless, Bruce, II (born 1937), U.S. astronaut, born in Boston, Mass.; U.S. Navy officer chosen for NASA program 1966 S-347, *table* S-348

McCardell, Claire (1905–58), U.S. dress designer D-271

McCarran, Patrick A. (1876–1954), U.S. lawyer and political leader, born in Reno, Nev.; chief justice Nevada Supreme Court 1917–18; U.S. senator (Democrat) 1933–54
  Statuary Hall, *table* S-437b

McCarran-Walter Act. *see in index* Immigration and Nationality Act

McCartan, Edward (1879–1947), U.S. sculptor, born in Albany, N.Y. ('Eugene Field Memorial' in Chicago, and 'Diana' in Metropolitan Museum, New York City).

McCarthy, Denis Aloysius (1870–1931), U.S. poet and journalist, born in Ireland; to U.S. at 15; poetry musical, often patriotic ('The Sowers'; 'Songs of Sunrise'; 'The Harp of Life').

McCarthy, Eugene Joseph (born 1916), U.S. political leader, born in Watkins, Minn.; U.S. representative (Democrat) from Minnesota 1949–59; U.S. senator 1959–71; active candidate for presidential nomination 1968 U-196

McCarthy, Joseph R. (in full Joseph Raymond McCarthy) (1908–57), U.S. political leader M-3
  Benton B-165
  Eisenhower administration E-138
  Murrow M-658
  Oppenheimer O-573

McCarthy, Joseph Vincent (nickname Marse Joe) (1887–1978), U.S. baseball manager, born in Philadelphia, Pa.; with Chicago, N.L., 1926–30, New York, A.L., 1931–46, and Boston, A.L., 1948–50, won 9 pennants (Chicago, 1929, and New York, 1932, 1936–39, 1941–43) and 7 world championships (1932, 1936–39, 1941, 1943).

McCarthy, Justin (1830–1912), Irish historian, author, and nationalist leader, born near Cork; served in Parliament 1879–1900 ('Miss Misanthrope', novel; 'History of Our Own Times', story of reign of Queen Victoria; 'History of the Four Georges'). His son, **Justin Huntly McCarthy** (1860–1936), poet and dramatist ('If I Were King', novel adapted for stage).

McCarthy, Mary Therese (born 1912), U.S. editor and critic, born in Seattle, Wash.; editor *Partisan Review* 1937–38, drama critic 1937–48; noted for caustic style (novels, 'The Group', 'Birds of America')
  American literature A-362

McCarthy, Thomas Francis (1864–1922), U.S. baseball outfielder, born in South Boston, Mass.; with 5 teams 1884–96; stole 109 bases for St. Louis Browns 1889; made record number of 53 assists with Boston, N.L., 1893.

McCarthyism M-3

McCartney, Paul (born 1942), British musician-songwriter B-119
  popular music M-682, *picture* M-681

McClellan, George B. (in full George Brinton McClellan) (1826–85), U.S. general M-4
  Battle of Antietam C-480
  Civil War C-474
  Lee L-115
  Lincoln L-221

McClintic, Guthrie (1893–1961), U.S. theatrical producer and director, born in Seattle, Wash.; directed many plays for his wife, Katharine Cornell, including 'The Green Hat', 'The Barretts of Wimpole Street', 'St. Joan', 'Antony and Cleopatra'.

McClintock, Barbara (born 1902), U.S. botanist. *see also in index* Nobel Prizewinners, *table*

McClintock, Sir Francis Leopold (1819–1907), British admiral and Arctic explorer, born in Dundalk, Ireland; led 4 expeditions in search of Sir John Franklin's expedition.

McCloskey, John, Cardinal (1810–85), Roman Catholic prelate, born in Brooklyn, N.Y.; became bishop of Albany, N.Y. 1847, archbishop of New York 1864, and first U.S. cardinal 1875.

McCloskey, Robert (born 1914), U.S. artist, author and illustrator of children's books, born in Hamilton, Ohio; received Caldecott Medal 1942 for 'Make Way for Ducklings' and 1958 for 'Time of Wonder'; other books: 'Lentil'; 'Homer Price'; 'One Morning in Maine'; awarded Regina Medal of the Catholic Library Association 1974 R-106

McCloy, John Jay (born 1895), U.S. administrator, born in Philadelphia, Pa.; president, International Bank for Reconstruction and Development 1947–49; U.S. high commissioner for West Germany 1949–52; disarmament adviser to President Kennedy 1961; awarded Presidential Medal of Freedom 1963
  Krupp amnesty K-307

McClung, Nellie (or Helen Letitia Mooney) (1873–1951), Canadian novelist M-5

McClure, Sir Robert John LeMesurier (1807–73), Irish admiral and Arctic explorer, born in Wexford, Ireland; traversed Northwest Passage 1850–53 P-420, *map* P-417

McClure, Samuel Sidney (1857–1949), U.S. editor and publisher, born in County Antrim, Ireland; established McClure Syndicate 1884, first newspaper syndicate in U.S., *McClure's Magazine* 1893.

'McClure's Magazine', magazine M-33

McCollum, Elmer Vernor (1879–1967), U.S. biochemist; born in Fort Scott, Kan.; authority on relation of diet to growth and disease; identified vitamin A and other vitamins; professor University of Wisconsin and Johns Hopkins University V-337

McComb, Miss., city in farming and dairying section 60 mi (100 km) s.e. of Natchez; clothing, lumber products; rail center; pop. 12,331.

McConaughy, Lake, Nebraska N-95, 98

McCone, John Alex (born 1902), U.S. business executive, born in San Francisco; president Joshua Hendy Corporation (operates steamships), Los Angeles, 1945–58; undersecretary U.S. Air Force 1950–51; chairman U.S. Atomic Energy Commission 1958–61; director Central Intelligence Agency 1961–65.

McConnell, Francis John (1871–1953), U.S. Methodist bishop, born in Trinway, Ohio; president DePauw University, 1909–12; served as bishop number of years in Mexico and Pittsburgh dioceses; elected President Federal Council of Churches, 1928 ('Personal Christianity').

McConnell, John Paul (1908–86), U.S. Air Force officer, born in Booneville, Ark.; commander of Second Air Force 1957–61; Air Force chief of staff 1964–69.

MacCool, Finn. *see in index* Finn MacCool

McCord, David Thompson Watson (born 1897), U.S. author, born in New York City; known especially for children's poetry R-108, 111d

McCormack, James (1910–75), U.S. Air Force officer, born in Chatham, La.; retired 1955 as major general; vice-president Massachusetts Institute of Technology 1958–65; chairman and chief executive officer COMSAT 1965–70.

McCormack, John (1884–1945), U.S. tenor, born in Athlone, Ireland; London debut 1907 in 'Cavalleria Rusticana'; New York debut 1909 in 'La Traviata'; famous as a concert singer.

McCormack, John William (1891–1971), U.S. congressman and lawyer, born in Boston, Mass.; Democratic representative from Massachusetts 1928–70; majority leader of House of Representatives 1940–47, 1949–53, and 1955–62, minority whip 1947–49 and 1953–55, speaker 1962–70.

MacCormick, Austin Harbutt (1893–1979), U.S. penologist, born in Georgetown, near Toronto; commissioner of correction New York, N.Y., 1934–40; professor of criminology University of California 1951–60.

McCormick, Cyrus Hall (1809–84), U.S. industrialist and inventor M-5
  Industrial Revolution I-182
  invention I-274, *table* I-273
  reaper, *picture* V-337
  wheat W-188

McCormick, Joseph Medill (1877–1925), U.S. newspaper publisher and Progressive leader, born in Chicago; publisher *Chicago Tribune*, which his grandfather, Joseph Medill, had made famous; U.S. senator 1919–25.

McCormick, Robert R. (full name Robert Rutherford McCormick) (1880–1955), U.S. publisher M-5
  newspapers N-239

McCosh, James (1811–94), U.S. philosopher and educator, born in Ayrshire, Scotland; won distinction as preacher and as professor of logic and metaphysics, Queens University, Belfast; came to U.S. 1868 as president Princeton College ('Method of Divine Government, Physical and Moral').

McCoy, Elijah (1843–1929), U.S. inventor, born in Canada; devised automatic lubrication used in locomotives, steamships, and machinery.

McCracken, Harold (born 1894), U.S. explorer and author, born in Colorado Springs, Colo. ('The Biggest Bear on Earth'; 'Sentinel of the Snow Peaks'; 'Winning of the West').

MacCracken, Henry Noble (1880–1970), U.S. educator, born in Toledo, Ohio; president Vassar College 1915–46; authority on Shakespeare and Chaucer; author of texts on English composition.

McCracken, James Eugene (born 1926), U.S. tenor, born in Gary, Ind.; with Metropolitan Opera Co. 1953–57 and after 1963.

McCracken, Paul Winston (born 1915), U.S. economist, born in Richland, Iowa; professor University of Michigan, 1950; on U.S. president's Council of Economic Advisers 1956–59, chairman 1969–71.

McCrae, John (1872–1918), Canadian physician, soldier, and poet, born in Guelph, Ont.; served in Boer War and World War I ('In Flanders Fields') P-446

McCubbin, Frederick (1855–1917), Australian artist A-802

McCullers, Carson (born Lula Carson Smith) (1917–67), U.S. writer M-6
  American literature A-358

McCulloch, Hugh (1808–95), U.S. financier, born in Kennebunk, Me.; comptroller of the currency 1863–65, secretary of the treasury 1865–69, 1884–85.

McCulloch vs. Maryland, case in U.S. constitutional law U-147, *list* S-518b
  Marshall M-153

McCully, Jonathan (1809–77), Canadian legislator and jurist, born in Cumberland County, Nova Scotia
  Fathers of Canadian Confederation C-118, *picture* C-116

Maccumhail, Fionn. *see in index* Finn MacCool

McCutcheon, John Tinney (1870–1949), U.S. cartoonist and war correspondent, born near Lafayette, Ind.; president Chicago Zoological Society 1922–49; on staff *Chicago Tribune* from 1903; won Pulitzer prize for cartoons 1931
  cartoons, *pictures* R-288

McDermott, Gerald (born 1941), U.S. artist, born in Detroit, Mich.; author and illustrator of 'Arrow to the Sun' (winner of Caldecott Medal 1975), 'The Stonecutter', 'The Knight of the Lion'.

McDivitt, James Alton (born 1929), former U.S. astronaut, born in Chicago, Ill.; U.S. Air Force officer, NASA astronaut 1962–69; manager Apollo Spacecraft Program 1969–72; business executive since 1972, *table* S-348

Macdonald, Andrew Archibald (1829–1912), Canadian political leader, born in Three Rivers, P.E.I.
  Fathers of Canadian Confederation C-118, *picture* C-116

Macdonald, Flora (1722–90), Scottish Jacobite heroine P-496

MacDonald, George (1824–1905), Scottish novelist and poet, born in Huntly; studied for ministry; wrote chiefly of Scotland and its people ('David Elginbrod', 'Robert Falconer', novels) R-111b.

McDonald, Harl (1899–1955), U.S. composer and educator, born near Boulder, Colo.; composed symphonies, concertos, and choral works.

Macdonald, James Alexander (1862–1923), Canadian Presbyterian clergyman and editor; pastor Knox Church, St. Thomas, Ont., 1891–96; in 1896 founded *Westminster*, a religious journal; editor *Toronto Globe* 1902–16 ('Democracy and the Nations').

MacDonald, James Edward Hervey (1873–1932), Canadian painter and poet, born in Durham, England; principal Ottawa College of Art 1929–32
  'The Solemn Land' P-67a

MacDonald, Jeanette (1907–65), U.S. actress and singer, born in Philadelphia, Pa.; popular in musical films ('Naughty Marietta'; 'San Francisco'; 'The Firefly'; 'Rose Marie'; 'Maytime'; 'Sweethearts').

Macdonald, John A. (full name John Alexander Macdonald) (1815–91), Canadian statesman M-6
  Canada C-100
  Fathers of Canadian Confederation C-113, *pictures* C-115, C-116
  Thompson T-173

MacDonald, John D. (1916–86), U.S. writer D-119

Macdonald, John Sandfield (1812–72), Canadian statesman; prime minister of Canada 1862–64; first prime minister of Ontario 1867–71; helped settle relationship of provincial to federal government.

MacDonald, Malcolm (1901–81), statesman, born in Lossiemouth, Scotland; son of James Ramsay MacDonald; Dominion secretary 1935–39; minister of health 1940–41; high commissioner in Canada 1941–46; governor-general of Malaya and British Borneo 1946–48; chancellor of University of Malaya 1949–61.

MacDonald, Ramsay (in full James Ramsay MacDonald) (1866–1937), English statesman M-6
  Fabian Society S-235
  United Kingdom E-256

Macdonald, Ross (or Kenneth Millar) (1915–83), writer D-119

MacDonald, Wilson Pugsley (1880–1967), Canadian poet, born in Ontario Province; wrote melodious lyrics and nature poems ('A Song of the Prairie Land'; 'Miracle Songs of Jesus'; 'Out of the Wilderness')

Macdonald College, Ste-Anne-de-Bellevue, Que.; founded 1907; agriculture, household science, teachers' training; an incorporated college of McGill University.

McDonald Islands, 27 mi (43 km) west of Heard Island in the south Indian Ocean A-823
  Commonwealth membership C-602

McDonald Observatory, Mount Locke, near Ft. Davis, Tex.; completed 1939; joint enterprise of Universities of Chicago and Texas and affiliated with Yerkes Observatory, *picture* T-124

McDonald of Garth, John (1774?–1860), Canadian fur trader, born in Scotland; joined North West Company 1791; served in western Canada and in 1813 received surrender of Fort Astoria.

McDonald's, fast-food restaurant chain F-43

Macdonell, Alexander (1760–1840), Canadian Roman Catholic prelate, born in Glengarry, Scotland; emigrated to Canada with his kinsmen and formed a colony called Glengarry; made first bishop of Kingston, Ont., 1826.

Macdonnell Ranges, Northern Territory, Australia A-771, *map* P-3

McDonogh, John (1779–1850), U.S. merchant and philanthropist, born in Baltimore, Md.; moved to New Orleans 1800; amassed fortune; retired 1806; emancipated his slaves, sent them to Liberia; founded schools in New Orleans.

Macdonough, Thomas (1783–1825), U.S. commodore in War of 1812, born in Newcastle County, Delaware; often called the "hero of Lake Champlain".

McDougall, John Lorn (1838–1909), Canadian statesman, born in Renfrew, Upper Canada; member Canadian House of Commons 1869–72, 1874–78; auditor general 1878–1905.

McDougall, William (1822–1905), Canadian political leader, born in York, Upper Canada; minister of public works 1867–69
  Fathers of Canadian Confederation C-118, *picture* C-116

McDougall, William (1871–1938), U.S. psychologist, born in Lancashire, England; professor psychology Harvard University 1920–27, at Duke University after 1927; held that life is not merely response to stimuli but is purposeful striving ('An Introduction to Social Psychology'; 'Body and Mind'; 'Energies of Men').

MacDowell, Edward A. (1860–1908), U.S. composer, born in New York City; influenced by German romantic music; known for piano pieces 'Eroica', 'Fireside Tales', 'New England Idylls', 'Second Piano Concerto in D Minor', 'Woodland Sketches', which helped gain international recognition for American music; established music department at Columbia University 1896; MacDowell Colony in New Hampshire founded as a haven for writers and composers 1907
  Hall of Fame, *table* H-16

McDowell, Ephraim (1771–1830), U.S. surgeon, born in Rockbridge County, Virginia; practiced Danville, Ky.; performed first ovariotomy recorded in U.S. in 1809
  Statuary Hall, *table* S-107a

McDowell, Irvin (1818–85), U.S. general, born in Columbus, Ohio C-473
  battle of First Bull Run C-479

McDowell, Mary Eliza (1854–1936), U.S. social worker, born in Cincinnati, Ohio; director and head University of Chicago Settlement, in stockyards district 1893–1936; executive Chicago branch NAACP; director Chicago Immigrants' Protective League.

MacDowell, Patrick (1799–1870), British sculptor, born in Belfast (now Northern Ireland); distinguished for his statues of William Pitt, the earl of Chatham.

McDowell, William Fraser (1858–1937), U.S. Methodist bishop, born in Millersburg, Ohio; chancellor of University of Denver 1890–99; elected bishop 1904 ('A Man's Religion').

Mace, chemical stun spray used by police as anti-riot weapon; heavy, colorless liquid produces temporary blindness and immobility.

Mace, originally a weapon of offense; later a staff carried into battle by medieval bishops; now a symbol of ecclesiastical or civil authority, as in English House of Commons.

Mace, spice S-379

Macedonia, region of s.e. Europe, once seat of empire under Alexander the Great M-7
  ancient Greece G-267

Balkan wars B-29, B-31
Greece G-254, 260
international relations I-259
naval ships N-81
rise of empire A-279, *map* A-280
Salonika S-29

Maceió (or Maçayó), Brazil, important port and capital of state of Alagôas on Atlantic coast; about 125 mi (200 km) s.w. of Recife; pop. 153,305, *maps* B-425, S-298

McElhenny, Hugh Edward (nickname The King) (born 1928), U.S. football halfback and sportscaster, born in Los Angeles, Calif.; played for San Francisco 49ers 1952–60, Minnesota Vikings 1961–62, New York Giants 1963, Detroit Lions 1964; became sportscaster for San Francisco 49ers.

McElroy, Mary Arthur (1842–1917), sister of President Arthur; served as his White House hostess; revived pre-Civil War traditions of hospitality.

McElroy, Neil Hosler (1904–72), U.S. manufacturer, born in Berea, Ohio; joined Procter & Gamble Company 1925, president 1948–57, board chairman 1959–72; U.S. secretary of defense 1957–59.

McEnroe, John (born 1959), U.S. tennis player
tennis T-107

MacEntyre, Eduardo (born 1929), Argentinian painter, born in Buenos Aires; one-man shows 1960–; works exhibited U.S. and South America
'Generative Painting: Black, Red and Orange' P-67d

Maceo, Antonio (1848–96), Cuban patriot, born in Santiago de Cuba; one of leaders of the first Cuban insurrection in 1866; killed in battle of Punta Brava.

McFee, William (1881–1966), U.S. novelist, writer of sea stories, born on his father's square-rigger; came to U.S. 1911; in Mediterranean with British navy during most of World War I ('Casuals of the Sea'; 'Life of Sir Martin Frobisher'; 'North of Suez'; 'The Harbourmaster'; 'The Beachcomber'; 'Derelicts').

MacGahan, Januarius Aloysius (1844–78), U.S. journalist, born in New Lexington, Ohio; reported Franco-Prussian and Russo-Turkish wars, Paris Commune; assignments in Cuba and Arctic ('Campaigning on the Oxus'; 'Turkish Atrocities in Bulgaria'; 'Under the Northern Lights').

McGee, Fibber and Molly. *see in index* Jordan, James Edward

McGee, Thomas D'Arcy (1825–68), Canadian statesman, born in Ireland I-327
Fathers of Canadian Confederation C-114, *pictures* C-116, C-118

McGill, James (1744–1813), Canadian merchant and philanthropist, born in Glasgow, Scotland; became a partner of the North West Company; founded McGill University.

McGill, Ralph Emerson (1898–1969), U.S. publisher, born in Soddy, Tenn.; joined staff *Atlanta Constitution* 1929, editor 1942–60, publisher 1960–69; won Pulitzer prize for editorial writing 1958 ('The South and the Southerner').

McGill, Nev., unincorporated community in Schell Creek Range 13 mi (21 km) n.e. of Ely; copper smelting; pop. 2,164 N-135

McGillicuddy, Cornelius. *see in index* Mack, Connie

McGillivray, Alexander (1759?–93), Creek chief, born in Alabama; tried to form American Indian confederation; repudiated treaty he signed for Creeks with U.S.

McGillivray, Simon (fl. 1800–27), Canadian fur trader; joined North West Company 1810; in 1821 signed agreement merging it with Hudson's Bay Company
fur trade F-471

McGill University, Montreal, Que.; chartered 1821; arts and sciences, agriculture, architecture, commerce, dentistry, divinity, engineering, law, medicine, music; graduate courses; Royal Victoria College for women; agriculture, education, and household science at Macdonald College, Ste-Anne-de-Bellevue, *picture* Q-9e
football F-297
Montreal M-572

McGinley, Phyllis (1905–78), U.S. author, born in Ontario, Ore. (books for children: 'The Plain Princess', 'All Around the Town', 'The Most Wonderful Doll in the World', 'The Year Without a Santa Claus', 'Lucy McLockett'; poems for adults: 'Love Letters'; 'Times Three', awarded Pulitzer prize for poetry 1961; essays: 'The Province of the Heart'; 'Sixpence in Her Shoe') A-356

McGinness, James Anthony. *see in index* Bailey, James Anthony

McGinnity, Joseph Jerome (nickname Iron Man) (1871–1929), U.S. baseball pitcher, born in Rock Island, Ill.; with Baltimore, N.L., 1899, Brooklyn, N.L., 1900, Baltimore, A.L., 1901–2, and New York, N.L., 1902–8; 5 times he pitched 2 games in 1 day; pitched 434 innings 1903, a modern record.

McGovern, George Stanley (born 1922), U.S. political leader, born in Avon, S.D.; liberal; U.S. representative (South Dakota) 1956–60; U.S. senator 1962–81; Democratic candidate for president 1972 U-196a
Democratic party P-433
Nixon N-320
presidential vote, *chart* P-495, *table* P-495d

McGranery, James Patrick (1895–1962), U.S. jurist, born in Philadelphia, Pa.; U.S. representative from Pa. 1937–43; judge U.S. district court of e. Pennsylvania 1946–52; U.S. attorney general 1952–53.

McGrath, James Howard (1903–66), U.S. lawyer, businessman, born in Woonsocket, R.I.; governor of Rhode Island (Democrat) 1940–45; U.S. senator 1946–49; U.S. attorney general 1949–52.

McGraw, John Joseph (nickname Little Napoleon) (1873–1934), U.S. baseball third baseman and manager, born in Truxton, N.Y.; player with 4 teams 1891–1906; gained chief fame as manager New York, N.L., 1902–32; won 10 pennants and 3 world championships B-88, *profile* B-95

McGreal, Mrs. William. *see in index* Yates, Elizabeth

MacGregor, Ellen (1906–54), U.S. children's author and librarian, born in Baltimore, Md. ('Tommy and the Telephone'; 'Miss Pickerell' series; 'Theodore Turtle').

McGregor, James Drummond (1838–1918), Canadian statesman, born in New Glasgow, N.S.; member of Senate of Canada 1903–10; lieutenant governor Nova Scotia 1910–15.

MacGregor, John (pseudonym Rob Roy) (1825–92), Scottish traveler and writer ('A Thousand Miles in the Rob Roy Canoe')
canoeing C-141

MacGregor, Robert. *see in index* Rob Roy

McGuffey, William (in full William Holmes McGuffey) (1800–73), U.S. educator M-8

'McGuffey's Eclectic Readers', series of schoolbooks compiled by McGuffey M-8
educational use E-92, *picture* E-93

McGuigan, James Charles, Cardinal (1894–1974), Canadian churchman, born on Prince Edward Island; ordained priest 1918; archbishop of Regina 1930, of Toronto 1934–71; assistant at Pontifical Throne and papal count 1943; made cardinal 1946.

Mach, Ernst (1838–1916), Austrian physicist and psychologist M-8
aerospace A-77

Machado, Gerardo (1871–1939), president of Cuba 1925–33; second term marked by oppression; after downfall a fugitive until 1937 amnesty C-802

Machado de Assis, Joaquim Maria (1839–1908), Brazilian writer, born in Rio de Janeiro; wrote novels, short stories, poems, and plays B-418, L-68, 72

Machaut, Guillaume de (1300–77), French poet and musician
classical music M-668

'Mach-C', painting by Vasarely P-61

Machen, Arthur (1863–1947), English writer, born in Caerleon, England; known for fantasy ('The Hill of Dreams') and for bizarre tales ('Tales of Horror and the Supernatural'); autobiography, 'Things Near and Far'.

Mach number, wind tunnel W-234

McHenry, Donald F. (born 1936), U.S. diplomat, born in St. Louis, Mo.; with department of state 1963–73; project director Carnegie Endowment for International Peace 1973–77; U.S. deputy representative to UN Security Council 1977–79; ambassador to UN 1979–81.

McHenry, James (1753–1816), American Revolutionary War patriot, born in County Antrim, Ireland; served as surgeon, secretary to Washington, and aide to Lafayette; kept private record of Constitutional Convention, where he represented Maryland; signed U.S. Constitution; secretary of war in Washington's Cabinet.

Machete, large knife of the West Indies and Latin America; used to cut cane, to clear paths, and as a weapon, *picture* S-546

Machiavelli, Niccolò (1469–1527), Italian diplomat and writer M-9
Italian literature I-376
Maugham M-231
politics P-434
'The Prince' R-148

Machilipatnam (or Bandar), India, seaport in Andhra Pradesh state, on one of the mouths of Kistna River; weaving, bleaching, cloth printing, and rug making; pop. 112,612, *map* I-83

Machinability, in iron and steel I-334

Machine M-9. *see also in index* Machinery
die and diemaking D-139
efficiency ratio P-483
pendulum P-160
power P-483
world W-296

Machine, electrostatic, device for producing static electrification by friction
Von Guericke S-57h

Machine age. *see also in index* Industrial Revolution; Inventions
automation A-833
handicrafts H-29
modern age U-173
social aspects U-186–7
steam engine and S-438, 442

Machine gun M-12
military aviation A-155
World War I W-308, *picture* W-310
warfare W-20

Machine reamer, a machine tool T-222

Machinery. *see also in index* Inventions; Machine; Mechanics; Tools; and the names of various machines
accident prevention S-6, 10, *picture* S-12
agriculture A-135, F-30
automation A-833
building construction B-491
bulldozer B-500
clayworking
potter's wheel P-469, 478, *pictures* P-476–7
clothing and textiles
garment making G-32
knitting, *picture* R-329
pin making P-327
rope making and twine making R-291, *pictures* R-293
sewing S-121
shoemaking S-179, *picture* S-181
spinning and weaving. *see in index* Spinning and weaving
construction and engineering
pneumatic appliances P-398, *diagram* P-399
road making, *pictures* R-216
track laying, *pictures* R-76, 85
food processing
canning
pineapples, *picture* P-257
chocolate, *picture* S-541
dairying. *see in index* Dairying, *subhead* machinery
refrigerating R-135–8, *diagrams* R-136–7
sugar S-506, 507, *picture* 508
forging F-317
industrial design I-171
Industrial Revolution I-176
industry I-190
instrumentation I-229
lubricant use L-327
metals and mining M-425
coal mining C-519
iron and steel industry U-107
oil drills P-235–7, *diagram* P-237, *pictures* P-236, 239
motion pictures
paint making P-75, *pictures* P-72–4
papermaking P-102–3, *pictures* P-102–7
pencil making P-158, *picture* P-159
pen making, *pictures* P-157
phonograph P-268d–70, *pictures* P-269
plastic molding P-382–3
postal service P-460, *picture* P-460a
power
steam engine S-438–42
Watt W-108
printing and publishing
papermaking P-102–3
printing P-501, *diagrams* P-503, *pictures* P-499, 504
pumps P-532–3
vacuum V-254
rubber products R-303, *pictures* R-305
soapmaking, *pictures* S-230
ultrasonic stress tests A-22
vitamin processing, *pictures* V-356
voting, *picture* V-387

Machine Shop of America, The. *see in index* Milwaukee, Wis.

Machine tools. *see in index* Tools, *subhead* machine tools

Machmeter, airplane instrument A-194

Mach number, in physics
aerospace research A-77
airplane speed A-182
Mach M-8

Mach's bands, in optics M-8

Machu Picchu, Inca ruin in mountains in s.-central Peru; discovered in 1911, *pictures* I-60, S-290

Macías Nguema, Francisco (in full Francisco Macías Nguema Biyogo Negue Ndong) (1924–79), president of Equatorial Guinea E-294

Macías Nguema Biyogo, island, Equatorial Guinea. *see in index* Bioko Island

Maciejowice, battle of (October 10, 1794), final defeat of Polish forces under Thaddeus Kosciusko by an invading Russian army; prepared the way for the third and last of three 18th century partitions of Poland.

Macintosh, Charles (1766–1843), Scottish chemist, born in Glasgow; inventor of processes for making lead acetate, or sugar of lead, and bleaching powder
waterproof fabric R-305

MacIntosh, William (1775?–1825), Creek chief, born in Carroll County, Georgia; leader of Lower Creeks on U.S. side in War of 1812; brigadier general in U.S. Army during Seminole campaigns 1817–18; for signing treaty (1825) ceding lands to whites in defiance of tribal law, he was killed by Upper Creeks.

McIntyre, James Francis Aloysius, Cardinal (1886–1979), Roman Catholic prelate, born in New York, N.Y.; made auxiliary bishop New York 1940, coadjutor archbishop 1946; archbishop 1948–70; cardinal 1953.

McIntyre, William Rogers (born 1918), Canadian jurist, born in Lachine, Que.; justice of Supreme Court of British Columbia 1967–73, of Court of Appeal of British Columbia 1973–78; justice of Supreme Court of Canada 1978–.

MacIver, Loren (born 1909), U.S. painter and illustrator, born in New York, N.Y.; married Lloyd Frankenberg; one of Museum of Modern Art's group, Fourteen

Americans, exhibited 1946; works symbolic, imaginative, mysterious
  'Hopscotch' P-24

Mack, Connie (originally Cornelius McGillicuddy) (1862–1956), U.S. baseball catcher and manager, born in East Brookfield, Mass.; catcher 1886–96 but gained fame chiefly as manager Philadelphia, A.L., 1901–50; won 9 pennants and 5 world championships B-88, *profile* B-95

Mackail, John William (1859–1945), Scottish scholar and critic, born in Ascog, near Rothesay, Scotland; professor of poetry Oxford University 1906–11; translations of Greek and Latin literature
  Cicero L-76

McKay, Alexander (died 1811), Canadian fur trader of North West Company; murdered by Nootka Indians.

Mackay, Clarence Hungerford (1874–1938), U.S. capitalist, born in San Francisco, Calif.; son of John W. Mackay; president of several telegraph and cable companies; director Metropolitan Opera Company.

McKay, Claude (1890–1948), U.S. writer, born in Jamaica; to U.S. 1912 ('Songs of Jamaica', 'Harlem Shadows', poems; 'Home to Harlem', novel; 'A Long Way from Home', autobiography) B-294

McKay, Donald (1810–80), U.S. naval architect and shipbuilder, born in Nova Scotia; to U.S. 1827; 1850 built his first clipper ship, *Stag Hound* other famous clippers: *James Baines*, made Boston to Liverpool in 12 days, 6 hours; *Lightning* held record for greatest day's run under sail, 436 nautical miles (807 kilometers) S-175

McKay, Douglas (1893–1959), U.S. public official, born in Portland, Ore.; mayor of Salem, Ore., 1933–34; state senator 1935–37, 1939–41, 1943–45, 1947–49; governor 1949–52; U.S. secretary of interior 1953–56.

McKay, Gordon (1821–1903), U.S. inventor, born in Pittsfield, Mass.; known for inventions of boot and shoe machinery that revolutionized that industry.

McKay, John B. (1922–75), U.S. test pilot, born in Portsmouth, Va.; pilot NASA X-15 program 1954–71.

Mackay, John William (1831–1902), U.S. capitalist, born in Dublin, Ireland; one of discoverers of Bonanza mines of Comstock Lode in Nevada.

MacKay, Louis Alexander (pseudonym John Smalacombe) (born 1901), Canadian poet and educator, born in Hensall, near Stratford, Ont. ('The Ill-Tempered Lover, and Other Poems').

Mackay, Lake, central Australia, on the border between Northern Territory and Western Australia, *maps* A-819, P-3

MacKaye, Percy (1875–1956), U.S. dramatist and poet, born in New York City; writer of numerous community masques and poetic plays ('Jeanne d'Arc'; 'The Scarecrow'; 'Yankee Fantasies'; 'This Fine-Pretty World'); used Kentucky mountaineer folklore in 'The Gobbler of God', 'Kentucky Mountain Fantasies', and 'Weathergoose—Woo!'.

McKay effect, slowing aging by reducing caloric intake A-127

McKean, Thomas (1734–1817), signer of Declaration of Independence, born in New London, Pa.; member of Continental Congress 1774–83; governor of Pennsylvania 1799–1808.

McKean Island, Pacific Ocean. *see in index* Phoenix Islands

McKechnie, William Boyd (nickname Deacon Bill) (1887–1965), U.S. baseball infielder and manager, born in Wilkinsburg, Pa.; player with 7 major league teams 1907–20; manager Pittsburgh, N.L., 1922–26, St. Louis, N.L., 1928–29, Boston, N.L., 1930–37, and Cincinnati, N.L., 1938–46; won 4 pennants (Pittsburgh, 1925, St. Louis, 1928, and Cincinnati 1939, 1940) and 2 world championships (1925 and 1940).

McKee, William Fulton (born 1906), U.S. Air Force officer, born in Chilhowie, Va.; advanced to general 1961; vice chief of staff 1962–64; management expert for NASA 1964–65; administrator FAA 1965–68.

McKeesport, Pa., industrial city on Monongahela and Youghiogheny rivers about 10 mi (16 km) s.e. of Pittsburgh, in bituminous coal region; steel products, automobile bodies, meat-packing; pop. 31,012, *maps* U-41, P-184

McKees Rocks, Pa., industrial borough on Ohio River about 4 mi (6 km) n.w. of Pittsburgh; steel products; pop. 8,742, *map* P-184

McKendree College, Lebanon, Ill.; United Methodist; founded 1828; liberal arts, education.

McKenna, Joseph (1843–1926), U.S. jurist and statesman, born in Philadelphia, Pa.; congressman 1885–92; attorney general 1897–98; on U.S. Supreme Court 1898–1926; gained reputation for sound, conservative judgments.

McKenna, Reginald (1863–1943), English statesman, born in London; liberal member, House of Commons, 1895–1918; cabinet member; first lord of admiralty, home secretary, chancellor of exchequer; resigned when Lloyd George became prime minister; banker after 1919.

MacKennal, Edgar Bertram (1863–1931), Australian sculptor A-802

Mackensen, August von (1849–1945), German field marshal, born in Saxony; associate of Ludendorff and Hindenburg in World War I; led decisive offensives against Serbia and Romania; interned after Armistice; retired from army 1920.

Mackenzie, Sir Alexander (1755?–1820), Scottish explorer; birthplace probably Inverness; partner North West Company; first European to reach Pacific overland C-95
  exploration E-373
  fur trade F-471
  Mackenzie River M-16

Mackenzie, Alexander (1822–92), Canadian Liberal statesman, born in Scotland; premier 1873–78; administration introduced vote by ballot, created Supreme Court of Canada, organized territorial government of Northwest Territories.

Mackenzie, Sir Alexander Campbell (1847–1935), Scottish composer, born in Edinburgh; principal of the Royal Academy of Music 1888–1924 ('The Rose of Sharon' and 'Bethlehem', oratorios; 'His Majesty', comic opera).

Mackenzie, Sir Compton (1883–1972), English novelist, playwright, and poet; born in West Hartlepool, England; graceful style; literary critic London *Daily Mail* 1931–35; founder and editor *Gramaphone* magazine 1923–62.

MacKenzie, Kenneth (1797–1861), Scottish leader in fur trade; served as an officer in the British army in the War of 1812; in charge of Fort Union F-472

McKenzie, Robert Tait (1867–1938), Canadian sculptor and physical education director, born in Almonte, Ont.; best known for sculptures of athletes; professor and director of physical education, University of Pennsylvania 1904–30, research professor after 1931; wrote 'Exercise in Education and Medicine'.

McKenzie, Roderick (1761?–1844), Canadian fur trader, born in Scotland; emigrated to Canada 1784; built Fort Chipewyan on Lake Athabasca in 1788; his material for history of fur trade used by son-in-law L.R. Masson in 'Bourgeois de la Compagnie du Nord-ouest'; cousin of Sir Alexander Mackenzie.

Mackenzie, William Lyon (1795–1861), Canadian journalist and political agitator M-15
  Toronto T-231

Mackenzie, District of, in Canada, w. Northwest Territories; 527,490 sq mi (1,366,190 sq km); pop. 23,657.

Mackenzie River, in n.w. Canada; 2,635 mi (4,241 km) long M-15
  Canada C-71, *map* C-109
  comparative length. *see in index* River, *table*
  Great Bear Lake G-242
  North America, *map* N-351
  Northwest Territories N-388

Mackerel, North Atlantic food fish of the family Scombridae M-16
  animal, *picture* A-429
  fish F-125, *picture* F-132, *table* F-136

Mackerel family, large family Scombridae of spiny-finned, spindle-shaped fish; includes albacore, bonito, mackerel, tuna. *see also in index* Mackerel; Tuna

Mackerel shark S-144

McKim, Charles Follen (1847–1909), U.S. architect, born in Chester County, Pennsylvania; in partnership with W.R. Mead and Stanford White designed Public Library of Boston, *list* A-569

McKim, Isaac (1775–1838), U.S. merchant and political leader, born in Baltimore, Md.; served in War of 1812; Democratic representative from Maryland 1823–25 and 1833–38.

Mackinac, Straits of, 4 mi (6 km) wide, connecting Lakes Michigan and Huron M-355, 361, *picture* M-367

Mackinac Bridge, Michigan M-360, *picture* M-367
  bridges B-447, *pictures* B-439, I-336

Mackinac Island, Michigan, island at n.w. end of Lake Huron in Straits of Mackinac; pop. of city of Mackinac Island 517 M-360, *pictures* M-355, 367
  Cadillac's settlement C-13
  Great Lakes G-247, *picture* G-244

Mackinaw, heavy woolen fabric; sides may differ in color and design; has nap; often plaid; term also short for Mackinaw blanket, boat, and coat.

McKinley, Ida Saxton (1844–1907), wife of President McKinley M-18

McKinley, William (1843–1901), 25th president of the United States M-16
  assassination A-703
  Hanna H-31
  Spanish-American War S-364
  United States history U-183

McKinley, Mount (native name Denali, or Traleika, later called Densamores Peak), mountain in Alaska (20,320 ft; 6,194 m), highest mountain of North America M-21
  Alaska A-239
  Alaska Range A-256
  comparative height. *see in index* Mountain, *table*
  national park. *see in index* Mount McKinley National Park
  North America, *map* N-351

McKinley Tariff Act, United States H-47
  McKinley M-18

McKinney, Tex., city 30 mi (50 km) n.e. of Dallas; farming, livestock; clothing, furniture; pop. 16,249

MacKinstry, Elizabeth (died 1956), U.S. artist, illustrator of children's books; work imaginative and humorous ('Fairy Alphabet'; 'Fairy Tales', by Hans Christian Andersen).

Mackintosh, Charles Rennie (1868–1928), Scottish architect and designer A-569
  furniture F-462

Mackintosh, Elizabeth. *see in index* Tey, Josephine

Mackintosh, Sir James (1765–1832), Scottish scholar and philosopher, born in Aldourie, near Inverness; moved to London 1788, member of Parliament after 1813; author of historical and philosophical works.

McKissick, Floyd Bixler (born 1922), U.S. lawyer and organization executive, born in Asheville, N.C.; national chairman CORE 1963–66, national director 1966–68.

Mackmurdo, Arthur H. (1851–1942), British architect and designer; born in London
  wallpaper W-9

McLain, Dennis Dale (born 1944), U.S. baseball pitcher, born in Chicago, Ill.; with Detroit Tigers 1963–70, Washington Senators 1971; won 31 games in 1968 to break 34-year season win record; Ty Cobb and Most Valuable Player awards 1968.

MacLaren, Ian (pen name of Reverend John Watson) (1850–1907), Scottish clergyman and author, born in Manningtree, Essex ('Beside the Bonnie Briar Bush').

McLaughlin, James (1842–1923), U.S. government official, born in Avonmore, Ont.; U.S. Indian agent and inspector in North Dakota; noted for wide knowledge of American Indians.

Maclaurin, Colin (1698–1746), Scottish mathematician, born in Kilmodan, Argyllshire; a developer of calculus ('A Treatise of Fluxions').

'Maclean's Magazine', magazine M-35

MacLeish, Archibald (1892–1982), U.S. poet M-21
  American literature A-356

Macleod, Fiona. *see in index* Sharp, William

Macleod, Iain Norman (1913–70), British statesman, born in Yorkshire; member of Parliament 1950–70; leader House of Commons and chairman of Conservative party 1961–63; chancellor of the exchequer 1970.

McLeod, John (1788–1849), Canadian pioneer, born in Stornoway, Scotland; joined Hudson's Bay Company 1811 and conducted first group of colonists to Red River.

MacLeod, John James Rickard (1876–1935), Scottish physiologist, born near Perth, Scotland; professor University of Toronto 1918–28. *see also in index* Nobel Prizewinners *table*
  medicine M-285

McLoughlin, John (1784–1857), explorer, fur trader, and physician; born in Rivière-du-Loup, Que. C-99
  Oregon O-586
  Statuary Hall, *table* S-437b

McLoughlin, Mount, volcanic peak of Cascade Range, in Oregon; near Upper Klamath Lake; 9,497 ft (2,895 m).

McLucas, John Luther (born 1920), U.S. government official, born in Fayetteville, N.C.; assistant secretary general for scientific affairs NATO, Paris, 1964–66; undersecretary of the U.S. Air Force 1969–73, secretary 1973–75; administrator FAA 1975–77; executive COMSAT 1977–.

McLuhan, Marshall (1911–80), Canadian communications theorist and author M-21

Maclure, William (1763–1840), Father of American Geology, born in Ayr, Scotland; made first geological map of America 1809, revised 1817; used wealth in support of science.

MacMahon, Ed, U.S. television personality
  'Tonight Show', *picture* T-69

MacMahon, Marie Edmé Patrice Maurice de (1808–93), duke of Magenta and marshal of France; born in Sully, near Autun, France; crushingly defeated at Sedan 1870; president of the Third Republic of France 1873–79.

McMahon, William (born 1908), Australian politician and statesman, born in Sydney; prime minister (Liberal) 1971–72.

McManus, George (1884–1954), U.S. cartoonist, born in St. Louis, Mo.; on staff *St. Louis Republic*, *New York World*, *New York American*; created comic strips 'Let George Do It', 'Panhandle Pete', 'Snookums', and 'Bringing Up Father'

McMaster, John Bach (1852–1932), U.S. historian, born in Brooklyn, N.Y.; professor of American history University of Pennsylvania 1883–1932 ('History of the People of the United States'; 'Benjamin Franklin as a Man of Letters').

McMaster University, Hamilton, Ont.; chartered 1887 by Baptists, nonsectarian after 1957; arts and sciences, engineering, nursing, theology; graduate studies O-552

McMath, Virginia Katherine. *see* Rogers, Ginger

MacMechan, Archibald McKellar (1862–1933), Canadian writer and educator, born in Kitchener, Ont. (essays: 'The Life of a Little College, and Other Papers'; poems: 'Late Harvest'; stories of Nova Scotia: 'Sagas of the Sea', 'Old Province Tales').

McMeekin, Isabel McLennan (born 1895), U.S. author, born in Louisville, Ky.; books for children: 'Journey Cake'; 'Kentucky Derby Winner'; 'Robert E. Lee'.

Macmillan, Cyrus (1880–1953), Canadian educator and writer, born in Wood Island, P.E.I.; won Canadian Book of the Year for Children award 1957 for 'Glooskap's Country, and Other Indian Tales'.

MacMillan, Donald Baxter (1874–1970), U.S. explorer, born in Provincetown, Mass.; with Peary Arctic expedition 1908–9; led many expeditions to Arctic regions after 1913; author of 'Four Years in the White North' and 'How Peary Reached the Pole', *table* P-422

McMillan, Edwin Mattison (born 1907), U.S. physicist, born in Redondo Beach, Calif.; professor of physics at University of California at Berkeley after 1946, director radiation laboratory 1958–73; defense research at Massachusetts Institute of Technology Radiation Lab 1973–; helped discover element neptunium 1940; 1963 Atoms for Peace Award P-394. *see also in index* Nobel Prizewinners, *table*

MacMillan, Sir Ernest Campbell (1893–1973), Canadian organist, conductor, and composer; born in Mimico, Ont.; conductor, Toronto Symphony Orchestra 1931–56.

Macmillan, Harold (in full Maurice Harold Macmillan) (1894–1986), British statesman, prime minister 1957–63 M-22
United Kingdom E-258

MacMillan, Kirkpatrick (1810–78), Scottish blacksmith who contributed to the development of the bicycle B-187, *picture* B-188

McMinnville, Ore., city 20 mi (30 km) n.w. of Salem; mobile homes, steel; Linfield College; incorporated 1876; pop. 14,080.

McMinnville, Tenn., town 52 mi (84 km) n.w. of Chattanooga; wood products, clothing, marble quarries; pop. 10,683.

MacMonnies, Frederick (1863–1937), U.S. sculptor, born in Brooklyn; great fountain for Columbian Exposition in Chicago, Battle Monument at West Point S-91

MacMurray College, Jacksonville, Ill.; United Methodist; founded 1846; arts and sciences, business administration, education, and music.

MacMurrough, Dermot. *see in index* Dermot MacMurrough

McMurry College, Abilene, Tex.; United Methodist; founded 1923; liberal arts, teacher education.

McMurtry, Larry (born 1936), U.S. author A-362
western W-151

McNair, Lesley James (1883–1944), U.S. Army officer, born in Verndale, Minn.; formerly chief of staff of General U.S. Army Headquarters; commander U.S. Army Ground Forces 1942–44; killed in action in France.

McNair, Ronald (1950–86), U.S. astronaut, born in Lake City, N.C., killed in explosion of space shuttle "Challenger", *table* S-348

McNally, John Vincent (nickname Blood) (born 1904), U.S. football halfback, born in New Richmond, Wis.; player on professional teams 1925–39.

McNamara, Robert Strange (born 1916), U.S. government official and business executive, born in San Francisco, Calif.; U.S. secretary of defense 1961–67; president World Bank 1968–81.

McNarney, Joseph Taggart (1893–1972), U.S. Army officer, born in Emporium, Pa.; U.S. commander in Mediterranean area 1944, in Europe 1945; chief U.S. occupation zone in Germany 1945–47; chairman National Defense Management Committee 1949–52.

McNary, Charles L. (1874–1944), U.S. senator from Oregon after 1917; born in Salem, Ore.; Republican candidate for U.S. vice-president 1940; coauthor McNary-Haugen Farm Relief Bill.

McNary Dam, Oregon, on Columbia River O-581, 586

McNaughton, Andrew George Latta (1887–1966), Canadian army officer, born in Moosomin, Sask.; commander in chief of Canadian overseas force Dec. 1939–Dec. 1943; defense minister 1944–45; chairman Canadian section International Joint Commission 1950–62.

McNeer, May Yonge (or Mrs. Lynd Kendall Ward) (born 1902), U.S. children's book author, born in Tampa, Fla. (books illustrated by husband: 'The California Gold Rush', 'John Wesley', 'The Mexican Story', 'Martin Luther', 'The Alaska Goldrush'); received, with her husband, the Regina Medal of the Catholic Library Association 1975.

McNeese State University, Lake Charles, La.; became four-year college 1950; humanities, business, education, fine arts, and sciences and technology; graduate school.

MacNeice, Louis (1907–63), Irish poet and classical scholar, born in Belfast; writer and producer for British Broadcasting Corporation 1941–49 (poetry includes 'Agamemnon' of Aeschylus, translation in verse; 'Poems, 1925–1940'; 'Solstices'; 'The Burning Perch')
literary contribution E-281

MacNeil, Hermon Atkins (1866–1947), U.S. sculptor, born in Chelsea, Mass.; noted for American Indian subjects ('Coming of the White Man'; 'Primitive Chant'; 'The Moqui Prayer for Rain').

McNeill, James (born 1925), Canadian author, born in Edmonton, Alta. (books for younger readers: 'The Sunken City'; 'The Double Knights', won Canadian Book of the Year for Children award 1966).

McNutt, Paul Vories (1891–1955), U.S. political leader, born in Franklin, Ind.; governor of Indiana 1933–37; head of Federal Security Agency 1939–45, of War Manpower Commission 1942–45; U.S. high commissioner to Philippines 1937–39 and 1945–46, first U.S. ambassador to Philippines 1946–47.

Macomb, Alexander (1782–1841), U.S. soldier, born in Detroit, Mich.; distinguished himself in War of 1812 at Fort Niagara, Fort George, and Plattsburgh, N.Y.; commanding general U.S. Army, 1828.

Macomb, Ill., city 38 mi (61 km) s.w. of Galesburg; porcelain and pottery, roller bearings, mobile homes, camping equipment; Western Illinois University; named for Alexander Macomb; pop. 19,632
Illinois, *map* I-53

Macon, Ga., city in center of state, on Ocmulgee River; pop. 123,083 M-22, *map* N-351
Georgia G-87, *map* U-41

Macphail, Agnes Campbell (1890–1954), first woman member of Canadian Parliament; elected 1921; influential worker for disarmament and world peace.

MacPhail, Leland Stanford (nickname Larry) (1890–1975), U.S. baseball executive and manager, born in Cass City, Mich.; with Cincinnati Reds 1933–36, Brooklyn Dodgers 1939–42, New York Yankees 1945–47.

McPherson, Aimee Semple (1890–1944), U.S. evangelist, born near Ingersoll, Ont.; became evangelist at 17; drew huge crowds to Angelus Temple in Los Angeles. *see also in index* International Church of the Foursquare Gospel

McPherson, James (1736–96), Scottish writer, born in Kingussie
literary contribution E-273

McPherson, James Birdseye (1828–64), U.S. general, born in Sandusky, Ohio; commanded Army of Tennessee during Sherman's Atlanta campaign; killed in battle before Atlanta
Vicksburg campaign, *map* C-482

Macpherson, Jay (born 1931), Canadian poet ('Nineteen Poems'; 'O Earth Return'; 'The Boatman and Other Poems'; 'Four Ages of Man').

McPherson, Kan., industrial city 27 mi (43 km) n.e. of Hutchinson; oil refining, flour milling, insurance; McPherson College; incorporated 1894; pop. 11,753.

McPherson College, McPherson, Kan.; affiliated with Church of the Brethren; established in 1887; arts and sciences, and teacher education.

Macquarie, Lachlan (1761–1824), Scottish military officer M-22

Macquarie Island, more than 900 mi (1,450 km) s.e. of Tasmania, to which it belongs; 170 sq mi (440 sq km).

McRae, Milton Alexander (1858–1930), U.S. newspaper publisher, born in Detroit, Mich.; in 1889 with E.W. Scripps organized newspaper chain, 1897 organized press association that became United Press ('Forty Years in Newspaperdom').

Macramé (or macramé lace), coarse lace or fringe made by knotting thread or cord into geometrical patterns; used for hangings, bags, etc. L-17

Macready, William Charles (1793–1873), English tragic actor, born in London; Shakespearean roles; toured in U.S. 1826 and 1843–44.

Macro, Praetorian guard
Tiberius T-179

Mac-Robertson Coast, Antarctica, adjacent to Kemp Coast, on the Indian Ocean; named by Sir Douglas Mawson's expedition 1929–31.

Macroeconomics E-63
sciences S-64b

Macrolide, antibiotic A-489

Macromarketing, in economics M-140

Macromolecule, large molecule built up from smaller chemical structures M-522

Macronutrient F-58
hydroponics H-341

Macrophage, cell L-337, I-55

Macropodidae, kangaroo family A-778

MacSwiney, Terence (1879–1920), Irish leader; lord mayor of Cork; hunger striker against imprisonment for sedition; died of starvation in Brixton prison, London, after fasting 74 days.

Mactan Island, coral island, central Philippines
Magellan M-36

McTavish, John George (fl. 1808–19), Canadian fur trader of North West Company; represented the company when Astoria was acquired from the Pacific Fur Company; taken prisoner by Hudson's Bay Company 1819 and sent to England for trial
fur trade F-471

McTavish, Simon (1750–1804), Canadian fur trader, born in Scotland; one of the founders of the North West Company; interested in eliminating competition among fur traders.

Macular degeneration B-311

MacVeagh, Franklin (1837–1934), U.S. merchant and political leader, born near Phoenixville, Pa.; brother of Isaac MacVeagh; secretary of the treasury 1909–13.

MacVeagh, Isaac Wayne (1833–1917), U.S. lawyer and political leader, born near Phoenixville, Pa.; brother of Franklin MacVeagh; minister to Turkey 1870–71; U.S. attorney general 1881; ambassador to Italy 1893–97.

Macy, Anne Mansfield Sullivan. *see in index* Sullivan, Anne Mansfield

Madách, Imre (1823–64), Hungarian poet, wrote the ambitious drama 'The Tragedy of Man' H-327

Madagascar (in full Democratic Republic of Madagascar, formerly Malagasy Republic), island and nation in Indian Ocean, e. of Africa; 227,700 sq mi (589,740 sq km); cap. Antananarivo; pop. 10,012,000 M-23
Africa, *map* A-118
political unit, *table* A-112
Antananarivo A-471
flag, *picture* F-167
geologic history C-688
lemur L-125
national anthem, *table* N-64
products
graphite C-157
vanilla V-266
railroad mileage, *table* R-85
size, comparative. *see in index* Island, *table*

Madame Alexander dolls, creation of Beatrice Behrman; collected for their authentic costumes as well as their perfect faces D-222

'Madame Bovary', famous novel by Flaubert, published 1856; the heroine, Emma Bovary, is an irresponsible, selfish, extravagant young woman who, involved in debt and intrigue, poisons herself F-176

Mad Anthony Wayne. *see in index* Wayne, Anthony

Madariaga, Salvador de (1886–1978), Spanish writer and statesman, born in La Coruña; director Disarmament Section League of Nations (1922–27); ambassador to U.S. 1931, to France 1932–34 ('Shelley and Calderon'; 'The Heart of Jade', novel; 'Christopher Columbus', biography; 'Morning Without Noon', memoirs; 'Portrait of Europe', 'Spain, a Modern History', 'Latin America Between the Eagle and the Bear') S-365b, *picture* S-366

Madden Dam, Chagres River, Isthmus of Panama P-91, *map* P-90

Madder family (or Rubiaceae), family of plants, shrubs, and trees, including the woodruff, bouvardias, cinchonas, coffee, bedstraw, gardenias, and madder.

'Mad Dog Blues', work by Shepard A-363

Maddox, Richard L. (1816–1902), English physician and inventor
dry-plate photography P-297

'Maddox', U.S. Navy destroyer V-322

Madeira (formerly Purple Islands), island group off n.w. coast of Africa; owned and governed by Portugal; 306 sq mi (793 sq km); Madeira Island is largest of group; pop. 264,787 M-24
Africa, *map* A-118
canary C-130
Portugal, *map* P-455

Madeira, wine W-237

Madeira Autonomous Region of Portugal, M-24

Madeira River, largest tributary of Amazon; flows n.e. 900 mi (1,450 km) from frontier of Bolivia through w. Brazil
Amazon A-324
Brazil, *map* B-425
South America, *map* S-298

Madeira vine (also called mignonette vine), perennial twining vine *Boussingaultia baselloides* of the basella family, native to Ecuador but naturalized in s. U.S.; grows 10 to 20 ft (3 to 6 m); leaves fleshy, oval, pointed; flowers tiny, white, in long feathery clusters, fragrant.

Madeleine, church in Paris, France P-121, *map* P-120, *picture* P-122

Madera, Calif., city 20 mi (30 km) n.w. of Fresno; wine, olives, food products, lumber; chinchilla processing; pop. 21,732.

Madero, Francisco (1873–1913), president of Mexico 1911–13, *table* A-704
Carranza C-175
Mexico M-337
Villa V-325

Madhya Pradesh, state in central India; area 171,200 sq mi (443,400 sq km); cap. Bhopal; formed by merger of the following former units: Central Provinces (with Berar), Bhopal Agency, Gwalior, Indore, and many of the princely states of Eastern States Agency; pop. 41,654,119, *map* I-86

Madinat ash Sha'b (formerly Al Ittihad), People's Democratic Republic of Yemen, administrative center, just n. of Aden; pop. 29,987.

Madison, Dolley Payne Todd (also called Dolly Madison) (1768–1849), wife of President Madison M-27, *picture* M-26

Madison, James (1751–1836), 4th president of the United States, known as Father of the Constitution M-25
- Federalist papers F-51
- Hall of Fame, *table* H-16
- human rights H-320
- lobbying L-276
- United States Constitution U-139, 144
- Virginia, *picture* V-342
- War of 1812 W-30

Madison, Ind., city on Ohio River in s.e., 40 mi (60 km) n.e. of Louisville, Ky.; tobacco market, electric generating plant, shoes, organs, motors; Jefferson Proving Ground; annual regatta; pop. 12,472
- Indiana, *map* I-102

Madison, N.J., borough 11 mi (18 km) w. of Newark; Drew University and branch of Fairleigh Dickinson University; pop. 15,357.

Madison, S.D., city in lake area, 38 mi (61 km) n.w. of Sioux Falls; farming, meat-packing, food processing, light industry; Dakota State College; pop. 6,210, *map* S-335

Madison, Wis., state capital and 2nd city of state; summer resort in s. center, 75 mi (120 km) w. of Milwaukee; pop. 171,057 M-28, *map* N-351
- Wisconsin W-250, 260, *pictures* W-257
- United States, *map* U-41

Madison College. *see in index* James Madison University

Madison Heights, Mich., city 13 mi (21 km) n. of Detroit; rhubarb, mushrooms; metal products, electronic components; pop. 35,375.

Madison River, one of headstreams of the Missouri, 230 mi (370 km) long; rises in Rocky Mountains.

Madison Square Garden, New York, N.Y. N-279

Madisonville, Ky., city about 45 mi (70 km) s. of Evansville, Ind.; tobacco market; coal mining, textiles; named for James Madison; pop. 16,979.

Mädler, Johann Heinrich von (1794–1874), German astronomer, born in Berlin; with Wilhelm Beer made important map of moon 1834–36; also author of books on astronomy.

'Madman's Diary, A', work by Lu Xun L-341

Madoera, island, Indonesia. *see in index* Madura

Madog, ap Owen Gwynnedd (or ap Owen Gwynnedd Madoc) (1150?–80?), legendary Welsh prince; said to have discovered America on voyage in 1170; subject of poem 'Madoc', by Robert Southey.

Madonna, mother of Jesus. *see in index* Mary

Madonna (full name Madonna Louise Ciccone) (born 1958), U.S. singer, actress, pop icon, born in Bay City, Mich.; wrote catchy, often overtly sexual, rock songs popularized in albums including 'Like a Virgin'; had leading film roles in 'Desperately Seeking Susan', 'Shanghai Surprise', 'Who's That Girl' M-683

Madonna College, Livonia, Mich.; Roman Catholic; founded 1947; conducted by Felician Sisters; arts and sciences, nursing, and teacher education.

'Madonna Doni, The' (or 'The Holy Family'), painting by Michelangelo, *picture* M-352

Madonna lily
- Quebec, *picture* Q-8

Madras, India, former state. *see in index* Tamil Nadu

Madras, India, capital of Tamil Nadu state; pop. 3,276,622 M-28, *map* I-86
- Asia, *map* A-700

Madras, lightweight cotton fabric, usually with stripe effect; also a thin drapery fabric with design formed by floating weft; so named because first made near Madras, India.

Madras Snake Park and Conservation Center, Madras, India M-29

Madrid (called in ancient times Majrit), Spain, capital; transportation center; pop. 3,271,831 M-29
- climate, *graph* S-362
- Escorial nearby, *picture* S-360
- Europe, *map* E-361
- space-tracking facilities S-343b
- Spain S-360, *picture* S-357, *map* S-350

Madrid, University of, largest in Spain and one of the leading institutions of Europe prior to Spanish civil war (1936–39); founded 1508; became chief Spanish university in 1836, when University of Alcalá was moved to Madrid and combined with it; philosophy and letters, science, law, medicine, and pharmacy.

Madrid Hurtado, Miguel de la (born 1934), Mexican politician, born in Colima, Mexico; assistant director of finances at Pemex, the national petroleum monopoly 1970–72; deputy finance minister 1976–79; minister of planning and budget 1979–82; president of Mexico 1982–
- Mexico M-338

Madrigal, short lyric poem, generally on the subject of love, usually in 6 to 13 iambic lines, marked by terseness and quaintness of expression. In music the term is applied to a part song for several voices, simple in style with lively rhythms and free melodic lines that often reflect the words' meaning; composed 1400s to 1600s
- classical music M-668
- music, *list* M-670

Mad River, Ohio, 100 mi (160 km) long D-45

Madrona (or madrone, or laurelwood, or manzanita, or madrono), evergreen tree *Arbutus menziesii* of heath family, native to foothills of Pacific coast; grows 20 to 100 ft (6 to 30 m); bark rough, brown; shiny, leathery leaves; tiny white flowers in long, erect clusters; orange-red fruit; wood is light pink with deep red spots; used as veneer.

Mad tom, catfish F-128

Madura (or Madoera), island in Indonesia n. of e. Java; area 1,762 sq mi (4,564 sq km); pop. 1,509,774, *map* I-166
- Asia, *map* A-700

Madurai (or Madura), India, city in Tamil Nadu, 270 mi (430 km) s.w. of city of Madras; noted for its elaborate Hindu temple architecture; pop. 549,114, *picture* I-72, *map* I-86
- Asia, *map* A-700

Mad widow, bird. *see in index* Limpkin

Maeander River, Turkey. *see in index* Menderes River

Maecenas, Gaius (73?–8 BC), wealthy Roman patron of Horace and Virgil; name proverbial as that of liberal patron of letters; in Eugene Field's slang phrase, "Maecenas pays the freight"
- Virgil V-328, *picture* R-241

Maelstrom, term originally applied to the celebrated whirlpool or current off n.w. coast of Norway, between two of Lofoten Islands; term now used also for other whirlpools and for upheaval or turmoil.

Mae Nam Chao Phraya (in short Mae Nam). *see in index* Chao Phraya

Maerlant, Jacob van (1235?–1300?), Flemish poet, called Father of Dutch Literature; early work free translations of French romances; later wrote scientific and historical works.

Maes, Nicolaes (or Nicolaes Maas) (1632–93), Dutch portrait and genre painter; pupil of Rembrandt ('The Listener'; 'Old Woman at the Spinning Wheel'; 'Saying Grace').

Maestricht, The Netherlands. *see in index* Maastricht

Maeterlinck, Maurice (in full Maurice-Polydore-Marie-Bernard Maeterlinck) (1862–1949), Belgian dramatist and essayist. *see also in index* Nobel Prizewinners, *table*

Mafeking, South Africa, town in Cape of Good Hope Province; trade and business center for region of dairying and stock raising; founded 1885; pop. 8,362.

Mafia, organized crime group, predominant in Sicily S-192
- crime C-772

Magadi, Lake, s. Kenya near boundary of Tanzania; about 30 mi (50 km) long; valued for large deposits of soda (sodium carbonate).

Magallanes, Chile. *see in index* Punta Arenas

Magariya, Japanese farmhouse J-31, *diagram* J-30

Magazine (or periodical), publication M-31. *see also in index* Journal
- advertising A-57
- hobby H-181
- home economics H-219
- index R-128
- letters L-139
- libraries L-163
- printing, *pictures* P-499

Magazine Mountain, highest peak in Arkansas (2,823 ft; 860 m); 45 mi s.e. of Fort Smith A-613

'Magda', English title of Sudermann's play **'Heimat'** (Home); Magda, the heroine, rebels against the rigid tyranny of her father, leaves his house, and later returns an operatic singer.

Magdalena, river of Colombia; rises in Andes in s.w., flows n. 1,000 mi (1,600 km) to Caribbean at Barranquilla; chief route to interior, *map* S-298

Magdalena Bay, s.w. coast of Lower California, Mexico; tuna, mackerel, sardines C-54
- Mexico, *map* M-341

Magdalenian culture, named for La Madeleine, France, where remains were found
- caves C-235
- man M-85

Magdalen Islands, in Quebec, in Gulf of St. Lawrence n.e. of Prince Edward Island; lobster, cod, herring, seal; pop. 13,303 Q-9a, *map* C-112

Magdeburg, East Germany, port city on Elbe River, 75 mi (120 km) s.w. of Berlin; machinery, engines, chemicals, textiles; shipbuilding, sugar refining; pop. 289,075 G-120, *maps* E-361, G-134
- Gustavus Adolphus G-319

Magellan, Ferdinand (or Fernão de Magalhães) (1480?–1521), Portuguese navigator M-35
- exploration E-373
  - America A-331
  - Patagonia P-138
  - Philippines P-259c, *picture* P-261a
- navigation N-78

Magellan, Strait of (Spanish Estrecho de Magallanes), passage between mainland of South America and Tierra del Fuego; 360 mi (580 km) long, from 2 to 20 mi (3 to 30 km) wide M-35, *map* S-299

Magellanic Cloud, either of two veil-like appearances (Large Magellanic Cloud and Small Magellanic Cloud) in skies of Southern Hemisphere; composed, like Milky Way, of nebulae and star clusters, *chart* S-417

Magendie, François (1783–1855), early French experimenter in physiology, born in Bordeaux, France; distinguished sensory and motor roots of spinal nerves; studied veins and arteries; credited with introducing several drugs into medical practice B-174

Magenta, town in n. Italy 15 mi (25 km) w. of Milan, scene of battle (1859).

Magenta, color C-559

Mageroy, island of Norway off n. coast in Arctic Ocean; 111 sq mi (287 sq km); pop. 5,545. *see also in index* North Cape

'Maggie, A Girl of the Streets', work by Crane A-352, C-759

Maggiore, Lake, Switzerland and n. Italy, 83 sq mi (215 sq km); famous for scenery S-537, *map* I-404

Maggot, larva of an insect; term most often applied to larva that lives in decaying matter L-51
- fly F-242

Magi (English singular magus, often called the Three Kings of Cologne), from Persian magu, meaning "magician"; members of a priestly caste of ancient Medes and Persians; name is applied also to the "wise men" in the Bible (Matthew ii) who followed the star to Bethlehem; Bible story does not name them nor give their number, but Christian tradition (about 7th century) makes them three kings, Melchior, Gaspar, and Balthazar; their bodies are said to have been brought to Constantinople by Empress Helen, mother of Constantine, thence taken to Milan, and finally to Cologne in 1162 by Frederick Barbarossa
- Christmas C-403
- Jesus' birth J-103

Magic M-37
- folk medicine F-270
- Houdini H-288
- Pacific islands P-8
- superstition. *see in index* Superstition
- taboo P-8

Magical realism, in literature L-70

'Magic Flute, The' (1791), opera by Mozart; fantastic story contains allegorical allusions to politics, nationalism, and Freemasonry M-643
- opera O-565

'Magician of Lublin, The', work by Singer A-362

Magic lantern, early forerunner of the motion picture M-615

'Magic Mountain, The', novel by Mann M-109

Magic Skin Baby, doll introduced in 1946 with life-like skin D-222

Magic story, in literature F-260

Maginot, André (1877–1932), French statesman, born in Paris; minister of war 1922–24, 1926–31; firm advocate of military preparedness; Maginot Line named in his honor.

Maginot Line, French fortifications F-320
- World War II W-323, 338, *picture* W-339

Magion, Czechoslovakian satellite, *table* S-344

Magistrate court A-806

Magliabechi, Antonio (1633–1714), Italian bibliophile, born in Florence; became librarian to Cosimo III de' Medici 1673.

Magma, molten rock within the earth L-89. *see also in index* Lava
- earth E-20, 35, *picture* E-21
- minerals M-437
- rock R-228
- volcanoes, *diagram* V-378

Magna, Utah, community 13 mi (21 km) s.w. of Salt Lake City; copper mill; grain; sugar beets, and fruit grown in region; pop. 14,050, *map* U-232

Magna Carta (also called Great Charter), charter of English liberties M-41
- army innovations A-640
- bill of rights B-194, C-469
- English history E-241
- habeas corpus H-2
- Henry I H-128
- John J-124
- measurement standards W-138
- Rome conquers R-244

Magna Graecia (translated Great Greece), in ancient geography, name of Greek settlements in s. Italy and Sicily G-264
- Roman conquest R-244

'Magnalia Christi Americana', work by Mather A-342, M-221

Magnel, Gustave Paul Robert (1889–1955), Belgian civil engineer and educator, born in Essen, near Antwerp; invented Belgian system of prestressed concrete, widely used for bridges.

Magnesia, battle of (190 BC), decisive victory of Romans over Antiochus the Great of Syria at ancient town of Magnesia, Asia Minor, 20 mi (30 km) n.e. of Smyrna; brought w. Asia Minor under Roman control.

Magnesite (or magnesium carbonate), commercial ore M-41, *table* O-600
- minerals M-435

Magnesium (Mg), light, silver-white metallic element M-41
- alkaline A-308

of Scotland; area about 225 sq mi (580 sq km); capital and chief port Lerwick; pop. 13,495 S-162
Main River, river in West Germany formed by Red and White Main; has course w. for 310 mi (500 km), joining Rhine opposite Mainz
  Germany G-117, *map* G-134
Mainspring, in watches and clocks W-78, *picture* W-81
'Main Street', widely read novel by Sinclair Lewis published 1920, picturing the dullness and smugness of a small Midwestern town
  American literature A-359
  Lewis L-142
  Minnesota M-444
  novel of place N-409
'Main Traveled Roads', work by Garland N-409
Maintenon, Madame de (or Marquise de Maintenon, or Françoise d'Aubigné) (1635–1719), 2nd wife of Louis XIV M-68
Mainz (French Mayence), West Germany, commercial and manufacturing city on Rhine River opposite mouth of Main; 20 mi (30 km) s.w. of Frankfurt; head of league of Rhenish towns in 13th century; city greatly damaged in World War II; pop. 172,195, *maps* E-361, G-134
Maiolica (or majolica), ceramics B-438, P-474
Maipo (or Mipú), river of central Chile; rises in Andes, flows 155 mi (250 km) w. to Pacific; decisive battle of Chilean War for independence fought (1818) near its banks just s.w. of Santiago.
Mair, Charles (1838–1927), Canadian poet and journalist, born in Lanark, Upper Canada ('Tecumseh', poetic drama).
Mais, Roger (1905–55), Jamaican novelist ('The Hills Were Joyful Together')
  Caribbean literature C-167
Maisonneuve, Paul de Chomedy, sieur de (1612–76), founder of Montreal, and its governor for 22 years, born in Neuville-sur-Varnes, Aube, France; an able administrator, but removed because of governor-general's jealousy
  Canada C-91
  Montreal M-571
Maisons, French château designed by Mansart M-110
Maistre, Joseph de (1753–1821), French polemical author, born in Chambéry; exponent of conservative tradition C-679
Maitland, Frederic William (1850–1906), English jurist and historian, born in London ('History of English Law'; 'Canon Law in England').
Maitland, Lester James (born 1898), U.S. Army officer, born in Milwaukee, Wis.; Far East Air Forces 1941–42; 386th bomber group 1942–43; aeronautics research 1948–56; ordained Episcopal priest 1956
  famous flight A-205
Maitland, Sir Peregrine (1777–1854), English soldier, lieutenant governor of Upper Canada 1818–28 and of Nova Scotia 1828–32; born in Hampshire, England.
Maitre de Ballet, ballet master B-35
Maize. *see in index* Corn
Majapahit Kingdom, Indonesia I-164
Majesty, word used to express power and dignity of a sovereign; in Roman state signified supreme authority of ruler; "His or Her Majesty" now applied in Europe to any reigning king or queen, "His or Her Imperial Majesty" to any reigning emperor or empress.
Majolica. *see in index* Maiolica
Major, Charles (pen name Edwin Caskoden) (1856–1913), U.S. lawyer and writer of popular novels, born in Indianapolis, Ind. ('When Knighthood Was in Flower'; 'Dorothy Vernon of Haddon Hall').
Major, Henriette (born 1933), Canadian author; 1971 Canadian Book of the Year for Children award for 'La Surprise de Dame Chenille'.
Major, Kevin (born 1949), Canadian author and educator, born in Stephenville, Newf.; wrote children's books about Newfoundland ('Hold Fast', received 1979 Canadian Book of the Year for Children award; 'Too Far From Shore').
Major
  U.S. military insignia, *picture* U-8
Major (from the Greek Ionian mode), in music M-668, *list* M-670
Majorca (Spanish Mallorca), largest of Balearic Islands; 1,405 sq mi (3,640 sq km); cap. Palma; pop. 363,199 B-24, *maps* E-361, S-350
  folktales, *list* S-481c
  maiolica pottery P-474
  maiolica tile B-438
Major domus. *see in index* Mayor of the Palace
Major general
  U.S. military
    Army A-634, *table* insignia
    insignia, *picture* U-8
Majority, in election V-387
Major league, in baseball B-88
Major scale, in music M-691
Majrit. *see in index* Madrid
Majuscules, capital letters B-346, C-58
Makah, group of Nootka Indians living about Cape Flattery, Wash.; only members of Wakashan language family to inhabit U.S.
Makarios III, Archbishop (or Michael Christodoulos Mouskos) (1913–77), Eastern Orthodox prelate, Cypriot political leader, born on w. coast of Cyprus; archbishop and ethnarch of Cyprus 1950–77; exiled by British 1956–57 for promoting union with Greece; president of Cyprus 1960–77
  Turkey T-325
Makarova, Natalia (born 1940), Soviet ballerina B-36
Makassar, Indonesia. *see in index* Udjung Pandang
Makassar Strait, channel separating islands of Borneo and Celebes, uniting Java Sea and Celebes Sea, and making a celebrated biological division, *map* I-166. *see also in index* Wallace's line
  Asia, *map* A-700
Makatea, French island of Pacific about 150 mi (240 km) n.e. of Tahiti; 5 by 3 mi (8 by 5 km); phosphate; pop. 78, *map* P-3
Make-believe play P-386, 390a, *pictures* P-388, 390
Makemie, Francis (1658?–1708), U.S. clergyman, born near Ramelton, Donegal County, Ireland; to North America 1683; formed first U.S. presbytery at Philadelphia, Pa., in 1706.
Make-ready, in printing P-502
Makeup
  cosmetics C-728
  Federal Food, Drug, and Cosmetic Act P-538
  theater T-157
Makeup artist, in motion pictures M-607
Makhachkala, U.S.S.R., port on w. shore of Caspian Sea; center of petroleum, rice, cotton, and grain trade; pop. 186,000, *maps* E-361, R-344, 349
'Making a Photograph', work by Adams A-31
Makino, Nobuaki, Count (1861–1949), Japanese statesman and diplomat; represented Japan in the Versailles Peace Conference in 1919.
Makow, Henry (born 1949), Canadian writer, born in Zurich, Switzerland; began writing newspaper column at age 11; author of 'Ask Henry'.
'Makura-no-soshi' (or 'The Pillow Book of Sei Shonagon'), Japanese novel J-80
Malabar Coast, name often given to w. coast of India as far n. as Bombay; more strictly confined to s. part; includes most of Kerala state and coastal region of Karnataka state, *map* I-86
Malabo (or Clarencetown, or Port Clarence, or Santa Isabel), Equatorial Guinea, capital; commercial, financial, and export center; pop. 37,500 M-68, *map* A-118
  Equatorial Guinea E-294
Malacañang Palace, in Manila, Philippines M-97, *picture* P-255c
Malacca, Malaysia. *see in index* Melaka
Malacca, Strait of, channel about 500 mi (800 km) long between Sumatra and w. coast of Malay Peninsula
  Asia, *map* A-700
  Indonesia I-164, *map* I-166
Malacca cane, species of cane *Calamus scipionum* from Malacca (Melaka) and vicinity; of rich brown color.
Malachi, 39th book of the Bible's Old Testament and the last of the minor prophets, written between 464 and 424 BC; authorship disputed.
Malachite, bright green copper ore, commonly found massive though occasionally in stalactitic and other forms; chemical formula $Cu_2(OH)_2CO_3$; found in U.S., Cuba, Chile, Zimbabwe, Zambia, Australia, U.S.S.R.
  jewelry J-116
  minerals M-435
Málaga, Spain, manufacturing city and seaport on Mediterranean, 65 mi (105 km) n.e. of Gibraltar; ships, wine, grapes, raisins, olives; taken from Moors by Christians 1487; sacked by French 1810; pop. 330,000, *maps* E-361, S-350
Malaga, wine W-237
Malagasy, people of Madagascar M-23
Malagasy Republic. *see in index* Madagascar
Malamud, Bernard (1914–86), U.S. author and educator M-68
  American literature A-362
  young adult reading R-112c
Malan, Daniel François (1874–1959), South African statesman, born in Riebeek West, Cape of Good Hope Province; prime minister of Union of South Africa 1948–54.
Malang, industrial town in e. Java; trade center for agricultural area; pop. 422,428, *map* I-166
  Asia, *map* A-700
Malaprop, Mrs., character in Richard Brinsley Sheridan's play 'The Rivals' constantly using wrong word with sound resembling right one: name from *mal à propos* (inappropriate) E-273
Malar, cheek bone S-210
Mälaren, Lake, Sweden, extends inland from Baltic Sea at Stockholm; 450 sq mi (1,160 sq km); contains some 1,200 islands S-523, *map* S-524
Malaria, disease consisting usually of successive chill, fever, and "intermission" or period of normality
  Africa A-102
  campaign against, *picture* S-280
  Gorgas G-195
  infectious disease, *table* D-171
  Italy I-386
  mosquito M-598
  Panama P-93
  quinine Q-18
Malaspina Glacier, largest glacier in Alaska, w. of Yakutat Bay; covers 1,500 sq mi (3,880 sq km) and has front 70 mi (110 km) long A-241
Malatya (or Malatia), Turkey, regional trade center in e. Asia Minor; suffered earthquake 1893; massacre of Armenians 1895; pop. 83,692
  Asia, *map* A-700
'Malavika and Agnimitra', work by Kalidasa K-167
Malawi (formerly Nyasaland), nation in s.e. Africa; area 45,747 sq mi (118,484 sq km); cap. Lilongwe; pop. 7,279,800 M-68, *map* A-118
  African political unit, *table* A-110
  boundary dispute T-22
  Commonwealth membership C-602
  flag, *picture* F-167
  railroad mileage, *table* R-85
Malawi, Lake. *see in index* Nyasa, Lake
Malaya, Federation of, former sovereign state (cap. Kuala Lumpur) in the Commonwealth, nearly all on Malay Peninsula; included former Federated Malay States, former Unfederated Malay States, and two states (Malacca and Penang, the latter with Province Wellesley) of former Straits Settlements; became part of nation Malaysia 1963; 50,690 sq mi (131,290 sq km); cap. Kuala Lumpur; pop. 10,114,854 M-73
  Asia, *map* A-700
Malayan bear (or sun bear, or honey bear), bear *Helarctos malayanus* of the family Ursidae B-116
Malay Archipelago. *see in index* East Indies
'Malay Archipelago, The', work by Wallace B-217
Malay kite K-252
Malay language L-37, 42, *diagram* L-44
  East Indies E-45
  Malaysia M-71
Malayo-Polynesian languages. *see in index* Austronesian languages
Malay Peninsula, southernmost projection of Asia M-70
  Australian External Territories settlement A-823
  East Indies E-45
Malays, original people of Malay Peninsula and adjacent islands M-70
  Chamorros
    Borneo B-368
    Java J-423
    Sumatra S-511
  classification R-27, *chart* R-26
  East Indies E-45
  Filipinos P-253b, 259c. *see also in index* Filipinos
  Indonesia I-159
  kris, sword, *picture* S-546
  Singapore S-205
Malay Seas, part of Pacific Ocean including Arafura, Banda, Celebes, Flores, Java, Molucca, and Sulu seas, and Makassar Strait. *see also in index* Ocean, *table*
Malaysia, nation comprising Malaya (11 Malay states), Sarawak, and Sabah; area 127,578 sq mi (330,426 sq km); cap. Kuala Lumpur; pop. 16,090,000 M-70
  agriculture
    patchouli, *picture* P-203
    pepper, *chart* P-197a
  Asia, *map* A-700
  cities. *see also in index* cities listed below and other cities by name
    Kuala Lumpur K-307
  Commonwealth membership C-602
  flag, *picture* F-167
  East Indies E-45
  Indonesia I-159
  land reform L-29
  ores, *table* O-600
  people A-11
    Semang P-540
  products
    gutta-percha G-320
    rubber R-301
  railroad mileage, *table* R-85
  Sarawak. *see in index* Sarawak
  shelter S-156
  United Nations U-25
Malaysians. *see in index* Malays
Malay States, Federated, Malay Peninsula, the former collective name of the four states of Perak, Selangor, Negri Sembilan, and Pahang
Malay States, Unfederated, Malay Peninsula, the former collective name of the five states of Johore, Kedah, Perlis, Kelantan, and Trengganu.
Malay tapir, animal *Tapirus indicus* T-28
Malbaie, La, Que. *see in index* La Malbaie
Malbork (German Marienburg), Poland, former German (East Prussian) town on Nogat River 30 mi (50 km) s.e. of Danzig; included in Poland since 1945; machinery, cotton; old castle, founded in 13th century, seat of Teutonic Knights (1309–1457); historic 14th-century town hall; pop. 31,000.
Malcolmson, Anne Burnett (born 1910), U.S. author and teacher, born in St. Louis, Mo.; has adapted for children the stories of legendary heroes of America in 'Yankee Doodle's Cousins', and from old English ballads she derived 'Song of Robin Hood'; edited 'Miracle Plays' S-481d
Malcolm X (originally Malcolm Little, later el-Hajj Malik el-Shabazz) (1925–65), U.S. human and civil rights leader
  assassination, *list* A-704
  black American history B-297, 307
  'The Autobiography of Malcolm X' R-111j
Malcomia (or Malcolm stock, or Virginia stock), genus of annual and perennial plants

Minnesota man M-441
Neolithic Age. *see in index* Neolithic Age
plants P-364
Stone Age S-455
reproduction R-151c, *diagrams* R-151d
skull measurements R-25, *picture* R-27
water W-84

Man, human male
marriage M-149

Man, Isle of, island in Irish Sea; 227 sq mi (588 sq km); pop. 72,000 M-91, *map* U-18a
Europe, *map* E-361
United Kingdom U-16

Mana, power of supernatural spirits A-414

Management, in business and industry I-194
agriculture A-139
budget B-483
economics E-61
farming F-29
Industrial Revolution I-182
U.S.S.R. R-329
stockholders' voting rights S-451

Management and Budget, Office of B-486, U-156

Management engineering E-223

Management information system C-636

Managua, Nicaragua, capital, 30 mi (50 km) from Pacific coast, on Lake Managua; pop. 682,111 M-91, *map* N-351

Managua, Lake, lake in Nicaragua n.w. of Lake Nicaragua; area 390 sq mi (1,010 sq km).

Manama, Bahrain, capital and port, on n. end of the island Bahrain, in Persian Gulf; pop. 85,000 B-21

Man amplifier, bionic machine, *picture* B-235

'Man and Superman', play by George Bernard Shaw modernizing the Don Juan legend and based on the thesis that woman, not man, is the pursuer in love; first performed in 1905.

'Manasi', work by Tagore T-10
Indian literature I-108

Manassas, Va., town about 27 mi (43 km) s.w. of Washington; near the stream Bull Run; farming, timber, stock raising; steel fabricating, concrete blocks; pop. 15,438, *map* V-349
battles of Bull Run C-479
Lee L-116
Manassas N.B.P., *map* V-349

Manasseh, Hebrew tribe descended from Manasseh, the elder son of Joseph; occupied central Palestine e. and w. of the Jordan River; assimilated by other peoples after Assyrian conquest; one of the legendary Ten Lost Tribes of Israel.

Manatee (or sea cow) M-92, *picture* A-436
elephant relative E-185

Manaus (or Manáos), Brazil, capital of Amazonas, port in n.w., on Rio Negro 10 mi (16 km) from Amazon; commercial center; pop. 286,083
Brazil, *map* B-425
South America, *map* S-298, *picture* S-284

Mance, Jeanne (1606–73), French foundress (1644) of the Hôtel-Dieu, first hospital in Montreal, Que.
Canada C-91
Montreal M-571

Manchester, William (born 1922), U.S. author and journalist, born in Attleboro, Mass.; biographer of John F. Kennedy, H.L. Mencken, the Rockefellers, the Krupps, and Douglas MacArthur.

Manchester, Conn., manufacturing urban town 9 mi (15 km) e. of Hartford; electrical appliances, tools, textiles, paper products, clutches, heating equipment, machinery; pop. 49,761.

Manchester, England, seaport; pop. 593,770 M-92, *maps* E-361, U-18a
canals C-127
England E-232
harbors and ports H-35

Manchester, N.H., largest city in state, in s., on Merrimack River; manufacturing center; pop. 90,936 M-92, *map* U-41
New Hampshire N-178, 186, *picture* N-183, *map* N-191

Manchester, Vt., 22 mi (35 km) n.e. of Bennington; resort; pop. of township 3,261 V-285, *map* V-301

Manchester College, North Manchester, Ind.; established in 1889 by Church of the Brethren; arts and sciences, music, and teacher education; graduate studies.

Manchester Ship Canal, between Manchester and Liverpool M-92
canals C-127

Manchester terrier, dog, *picture* D-204

Manchu Dynasty. *see in index* Ch'ing Dynasty

Manchukuo (or Manchoukuo), former state composed of old Manchuria and adjacent regions; area about 502,000 sq mi (1,300,200 sq km); cap. was Hsinking (Changchun); pop. (1940) about 43,200,000 C-373, M-94
Harbin H-33

Manchuria, region in n.e. corner of China; 308,000 sq mi (797,700 sq km); pop. 51,500,000 M-93
Harbin H-33
history
China C-368
Russia, *map* R-322
Russo-Japanese War R-362
World War I W-321
World War II W-336
provinces
Heilungkiang H-116
Jilin J-117
Liaoning L-146

Manchus (or Manshous), nomadic Mongolo-Tatar people from Manchuria; invited to save the Ming Dynasty from rebels, they remained in China and ruled as the Ch'ing Dynasty for 267 years (1644–1912) C-368. *see also in index* Ch'ing Dynasty

Manco (1500?–1544), Inca leader, set up by Pizarro as sovereign of Peru P-349

Mandalay, Burma, on Irrawaddy River; pop. 532,895 M-95
Asia, *map* A-700

Mandan, group of Sioux Indians originally living along lower Missouri River; later driven n. to North Dakota.
American Indians, *picture* I-124, *map* I-136, *table* I-139

Mandan, N.D., city on Heart and Missouri rivers opposite Bismarck; oil industries, dairy products, flour; livestock market; railroad division point; lignite deposits; Fort Lincoln State Park nearby; pop. 15,513 N-374, 382, *map* U-40

Mandarin, a dialect of Chinese language C-345

Mandarin duck D-284, *picture* C-341

Mandarin orange C-444

Mandate (or mandated territory). *see also in index* Trusteeship Council; Trusteeships; British Empire
Namibia N-9

Mande, a people of West Africa
Guinea G-314

Mande-fu, a people of West Africa
Guinea G-314

Mandela, Nelson (born 1918), and **Winnie** (born 1936), South African anti-apartheid political activists, born in the Transkei territory; outspoken leaders of the African National Congress; Nelson was a lawyer and founder of the Congress Youth League; imprisoned 1962, serving life sentence for treason; his wife, Winnie, was a social worker and government critic; her quarter-century status as a "banned" person was lifted in 1986.

Mandeville, Sir John Jehan de Mandeville, reputed writer of a popular 14th-century book of Eastern travels, written in French; book is now thought to have been compiled from earlier works by Jean de Bourgogne A-457

Mandible, from Latin mandere, to chew; term applied to: (1) chewing jaws of insects and other arthropods; (2) the lower jawbone of mammals; (3) the upper or lower part of a bird's beak
bees B-124
lower jawbone S-210

Mandingo, large group of people dwelling in w. Africa from the Senegal River to Monrovia and numbering millions; they are predominantly Muslims influenced by Arab culture
The Gambia G-8

M&M/Mars, U.S. company C-139

Mandolin, stringed instrument, *picture* S-490a

Mandrake (or mandragora), plant of the nightshade family
mayapple M-237
poison P-409, *pictures* P-358

Mandrake, *see in index* Mayapple

Mandrel (or piercer), in metalworking I-348

Mandrell, Barbara (born 1950), U.S. country musician M-679

Mandrill, African baboon A-502

Mandyako, a people of Africa
Guinea-Bissau G-315

Man-eater shark (or great white shark) S-144

Man-eating tree, mythical tree frequently mentioned by writers of tall tales and located by them either in forests of Madagascar or the jungles of Mindanao Island in the Philippines; this tree is said to have a dark-grey smokestack-like trunk and green leaves at the ends of vinelike stems; with a crackling noise the entire tree is said to bend over and the leaves reach out to grasp the passerby.

Maneki-Neko, mythical Japanese cat C-212

Manes, name applied by ancient Romans to spirits of ancestors and friends in the underworld; also to deities of the lower regions.

Manet, Édouard (1832–83), French painter M-95
painting P-51
'Portrait of a Lady', *picture* C-272

Manetho, Egyptian historian of 3rd century BC; fragments of his work survive in Josephus; wrote his history in Greek; divided rulers of Egypt into 30 dynasties E-125

Maneuvering room, in submarine, *diagram* S-498

Mangabey, monkey A-503

Mangan, James Clarence (1803–49), Irish poet, born in Dublin; morbid genius who expressed the tragedy of Irish aspirations ('Romances and Ballads of Ireland'; 'The Nameless One', autobiographical ballad) I-326

Manganese (Mn), metallic chemical element M-96
Abidjan exports A-9
alloys B-463
oceanography O-474
ore, *map* O-600
periodic table, *table* P-207, *list* P-208
producing regions
Gabon G-2
Georgian Soviet Socialist Republic G-102
Ukrainian Soviet Socialist Republic U-2

Manganese brass B-301

Manganese carbonate (or rhodochrosite), mineral M-96, M-436, *picture* M-433

Manganese dioxide, compound (MnO_2) of manganese and oxygen; found in natural form as pyrolusite; also made synthetically M-96, *table* O-600
minerals M-432

Manganese spar, ore found in rhodonite. *see in index* Rhodonite

Mangbetu (or Mangbettu, or Mangbattu), people dwelling near the headwaters of the Uele River, Africa.

Mange, itching skin disease of domestic animals due to mites S-387

Manger scene (or crèche), miniature representation of the stable at Bethlehem used at Christmas
Christmas C-406
folk art F-250

Mangin, Charles Marie Emmanuel (1866–1925), French general, born in Sarrebourg, near Lunéville, France; corps commander at Verdun 1916; 6th Army commander in Aisne offensive 1917 ('Comment finit la Guerre', masterly review of World War I).

Mangla Dam, Pakistan, on Jhelum River
irrigation projects I-356

Mangling, garment pressing G-33

Mango, fruit *Mangifera indica* M-96

Mangosteen, fruit F-436

Mangravite, Peppino (born 1896), U.S. artist, born in Italy; teacher and writer on art and art education; in U.S. after 1915, became citizen 1924; works suggestive of Matisse.

Mangrove, tree M-96
halophyte H-19
Pacific Ocean, *picture* P-9
Philippines P-259b
tree T-277

Manhattan, Kan., city about 50 mi (80 km) w. of Topeka, on Kansas River near junction with Big Blue River; trade and insurance center for cattle-grazing and agricultural region; dress patterns, cereals; Kansas State University; pop. 32,644.

'Manhattan', Woody Allen film A-309

Manhattan, borough of New York, N.Y. (Manhattan and several small islands); pop. 1,427,533 N-270

Manhattan Beach, Calif., city 14 mi (22 km) s.w. of Los Angeles, on Pacific; aircraft and missile parts, electrical equipment; pop. 31,542.

Manhattan College, Bronx, New York City; private control, Catholic related; founded as an academy 1853; chartered as a college 1863; arts and sciences, business administration, education, engineering (chemical, civil, electrical, and mechanical); graduate division N-254

Manhattan District (popularly called Manhattan Project), engineering group formed by the Army Corps of Engineers in August 1942 to supervise development of the atom bomb; Brig. Gen. L.R. Groves was in charge; a plant was built at Oak Ridge, Tenn., to produce uranium; in 1946 the U.S. Atomic Energy Commission took over the project to develop peacetime uses of atomic energy, as well as weapons
Einstein's influence E-133
first atomic chain reaction, *picture* U-131

Manhattan Island, New York, N.Y.
early history A-355
island I-368
Minuit M-462
New York N-256

Manhattan Project, U.S. government research project (1942–45) that produced the first atomic bombs
Mayer M-238
nuclear weapons N-434
Oppenheimer O-573

Manhattans, members of Wappinger confederacy that occupied Manhattan Island, New York City.

'Manhattan Transfer', novel by Dos Passos D-231

Manhattanville College, Purchase, N.Y.; private control; founded 1841; arts and sciences, education, music; graduate studies.

Manichaeanism, religion founded in the 3rd century AD by Mani, a Persian philosopher, taught that the world was created by two principles, Good (the Kingdom of Light) and Evil (the Kingdom of Darkness), that the human's soul was good, the body evil; affected by Zoroastrianism and other Oriental religions as well as by Christianity. In the 4th and 5th centuries, the "Manichaean heresy" in n. Africa was a strong rival of Christianity; Saint Augustine was a Manichaean before conversion.

Manicouagane-Outardes rivers project, Quebec Q-9e
frontier movement F-419

Manifest destiny, term popular in 1840s and 1850s implying the inevitable expansion of United States territory U-175, P-16
warfare W-18

'Manifesto of the Communist Party'. *see in index* 'Communist Manifesto'

Manila, Philippines, chief city and capital; pop. 1,603,485 M-97
Asia, *map* A-700
Philippines P-254, *pictures* P-255, 255c, P-257b, P-260, *maps* P-253c, 262, *diagram* P-259b

Manila Bay, Philippines, inlet of China Sea in island of Luzon; fortified harbor P-256, 259d, *map* P-262
Manila Bay, battle of (1898) Spanish-American War S-364
warfare, *list* W-15
Manila hemp. *see in index* Abaca
Manilius, Gaius, Roman tribune of the people in 66 BC, whose proposal to give Pompey supreme command and unlimited power in the war against Mithridates was supported by Cicero in the famous oration 'Pro lege Manilia'.
'Manimekalai' (or 'Girdle of Gems'), Tamil epic I-106
Man in the Iron Mask. *see in index* Iron Mask, Man in the
Man in the Moon, the M-579
Manioc. *see in index* Cassava
Maniple, Roman Legion A-636
Manipulation, surgery S-519a
Manipur, state in n.e. India; area 8,628 sq mi (22,346 sq km); cap. Imphal; formerly an Assam state; pop. 1,069,555, *map* I-83
Manisa (or Manissa), Turkey, city 20 mi (30 km) n.e. of Izmir; ancient Magnesia, where Roman consul Scipio Asiaticus defeated Antiochus the Great 190 BC; pop. 59,675.
Manistee, Mich., shipping port on Manistee River and Lake Michigan, 95 mi (150 km) n.w. of Grand Rapids; salt; chemicals, paper, wood products, clothing, iron products; pop. 7,566 S-38, *map* U-41
Manistee River, Michigan M-355
Manistique River, Michigan M-355
Manitoba, Prairie Province of Canada; 250,947 sq mi; cap. Winnipeg; pop. 1,026,241 M-98
Canada C-80, *map* C-109
cities. *see in index* Winnipeg and other cities by name
history C-101
North America, *map* N-351
Red River of the North R-120
Trans-Canada Highway T-248
Manitoba, Lake, s.-central Manitoba; length 110 mi (180 km); drains into Lake Winnipeg through Dauphin River M-98, *map* C-109
North America, *map* N-351
Manitoba, University of, Winnipeg, Man.; provincial control; founded 1877; arts and sciences, agriculture, architecture, commerce, education, engineering, home economics, interior design, law, medical rehabilitation, medicine, music, nursing education, pharmacy, social work; graduate schools; several affiliated denominational colleges M-102
Manitoba Act of 1970, act designating Manitoba as a Canadian province C-101
Manitoba School Question, in Canadian history C-102
Manitou (or manito), American Indian name for certain unknown or mysterious powers.
Manitoulin, rugged island of Ontario, in Georgian Bay, Lake Huron; 80 mi (130 km) long; pulpwood; tourist trade; pop. 7,714, *map* C-112
Lake Huron H-334
Manitou Springs, Colo., health and pleasure resort at foot of Pikes Peak and about 5 mi (8 km) w. of Colorado Springs; nearby are Garden of the Gods and Cave of the Winds; mineral springs; pop. 4,475.
Manitowoc, Wis., port city on Lake Michigan, 75 mi (120 km) n. of Milwaukee; aluminumware, shipbuilding, bubble baths and soaps, cement, machinery, food processing, office furniture; Holy Family College; pop. 32,547.
Maniu, Juliu (1873–1951), Romanian statesman, born in Transylvania; organized revolts in Transylvania at close of World War I; elected head of local government of Transylvania after its union with Romania; leader of National Peasant party after 1926; premier 1928–30 and 1932–33; sentenced to prison for life by Communist-led Romanian government 1947.
Manizales, Colombia, city in Andes 107 mi (172 km) n.w. of Bogotá; coffee; mining; manufacturing; airport; mountain railroads; founded about 1846; pop. 199,904, *map* S-298
Manju-Patan. *see in index* Kathmandu
Mankato, Minn., city about 65 mi (105 km) s.w. of Minneapolis on Minnesota and Blue Earth rivers; center of farming, dairying, and stock-raising district; flour, food processing, cans, farm equipment, recreational vehicles and boats; limestone quarries nearby; threatened by Sioux uprising 1862; Mankato State University; pop. 28,651 M-442, *map* U-41
Mankato State College (since 1975 Mankato State University), Mankato, Minn.; founded 1867; arts and sciences, business, education, health and physical education, nursing; graduate studies; quarter system.
Manley, John (1733–93), U.S. Navy officer, born at Torquay, England; notable services in Revolutionary War when he commanded in turn the *Lee*, the *Hancock*, and the *Hague*.
Manlius Capitolinus, Marcus (died 384 BC), Roman patrician, consul 392 BC; aroused by cackling of sacred geese, he saved Capitol at Rome from the Gauls 390 BC; convicted of treason, sentenced to be thrown from Tarpeian Rock.
Manly, Charles Matthews (1876–1927), U.S. engineer, inventor, and airplane pioneer A-202
Mann, Erika (1905–69), U.S. author, born in Munich, Germany; daughter of Thomas Mann. *see also in index* Mann, Klaus
Mann, Heinrich (1871–1950), German novelist, born in Lübeck; brother of Thomas Mann; works show a feeling for beauty and power of satire; in U.S. after 1940 ('Mother Mary'; 'The Little Town'; 'The Patrioteer'; 'The Blue Angel'; 'Madame Legros') M-109
Mann, Horace (1796–1859), U.S. educator and publicist M-109
education E-77, 90
Hall of Fame, *table* H-16
Mann, Klaus (1906–49), U.S. author, born in Munich, Germany; to U.S. 1936, became citizen 1943; son of Thomas; with sister Erika wrote 'Escape to Life' and 'The Other Germany', books against Nazism.
Mann, Thomas (1875–1955), German novelist M-109. *see also in index* Nobel Prizewinners, *table*
Faust legend F-49
folklore F-269
German literature G-107
Manna, sweet substance exuded, after incision, from trunk of manna ash tree *Fraxinus ornus* and forming commercial product in Sicily; used in medicine; name manna also given to similar substances obtained from various plants and trees and also to a desert lichen *Lecanora esculenta*; manna referred to in the Bible (Exod. xvi) as food on which the Israelites lived in the wilderness is now believed to have been a secretion of the tamarisk tree caused by insect puncture.
Manned space flights. *see in index* Space travel, *subhead* manned flights
Mann-Elkins Act (1910), United States T-9
express history E-385
Mannerheim, Carl Gustaf Emil, baron von (1867–1951), commander in chief of Finnish army during World War II; president of Finland 1944–46.
Mannerheim Line, Finland, fortifications along Karelian Isthmus, between Gulf of Finland and Lake Ladoga; built by Carl Gustaf von Mannerheim
fort and fortification F-320
World War II W-323
Mannerism, art A-555
furniture F-457
interior design I-248
Manners. *see in index* Etiquette
Mannheim, West Germany, commercial city on Rhine River opposite Ludwigshafen; electrical products, chemicals, machinery; pop. 332,163, *maps* E-361, G-134
Manning, Ernest Charles (born 1908), Canadian political leader, born in Carnduff, Sask.; member Alberta legislature 1935–69, Social Credit party; premier of Alberta 1943–68; member Canadian Parliament 1970–.
Manning, Henry Edward, Cardinal (1808–92), English High Church leader, born in Totteridge, Hertfordshire; became Roman Catholic 1851, cardinal 1875; supported doctrine of papal infallibility.
Manning, Timothy, Cardinal (born 1909), U.S. Roman Catholic prelate, born in Balingeary, Cork, Ireland; auxiliary bishop of Los Angeles 1946–67; bishop of Fresno, Calif., 1967–69; coadjutor bishop of Los Angeles 1969–70, archbishop 1970–; created cardinal 1973.
Manning, William Thomas (1866–1949), U.S. Episcopal bishop, born in Northampton, England; rector Trinity Parish, New York City, 1908–21; bishop of New York 1921–46.
Mannyng, Robert (or Robert of Brunne) (fl. 1288–1338), English poet, born in Brunne (now Bourne) near Stamford, England; known for 'Handlyng Synne', adaptation in verse of William de Wadington's 'Le Manuel des Pechiez'.
Mano, handstone for grinding corn on metate; used by American Indians, especially the Anasazi.
Man-of-war, ship N-82
Man-of-war bird. *see in index* Frigate bird
Man-of-war fish, fish *Nomeus gronovii*, about 3 in. (76 mm), common in the Gulf of Mexico; seeks refuge among the poison tentacles of large jellyfish, particularly of Portuguese man-of-war.
Manometer, instrument for measuring pressure of air, gases, or vapors; barometer one type I-229
hydraulics H-338
'Manon Lescaut', work by Prévost N-410
Manor, in feudal times, estate of a lord F-69
interior design I-247
Middle Ages, *picture* M-386
Man o' War Bay, Trinidad and Tobago, *picture* T-288
Man-o'-war bird. *see in index* Frigate bird
'Man Pointing', sculpture by Giacometti G-142
Mansart, François (1598–1666), French architect M-109
Mansart, Jules-Hardouin (or Jules-Hardouin Mansard) (1646?–1708), French architect, born in Paris; works include the dome of the Invalides and the Place Vendôme, Paris; at Versailles, the palace (in large part), gardens, and Grand Trianon; he was a grand nephew of François Mansart for whom the Mansard roof was named A-558, *picture* A-559, *profile* A-569
'Man's Fate', novel by Malraux M-78
Mansfield, Katherine (or Kathleen Beauchamp Mansfield) (1888–1923), British writer M-110
New Zealand N-293
Mansfield, Michael Joseph (nickname Mike) (born 1903), U.S. statesman and educator, born in New York City; professor of history and political science Montana State University 1933–42; Democratic representative from Montana 1943–53; U.S. senator 1953–76, majority leader 1961–76 (retired).
Mansfield, Richard (1854–1907), U.S. actor, born in Berlin, Germany, while his mother, a singer, was on an opera tour; first roles were light opera in London; began stage career in U.S. 1878 ('Beau Brummel'; 'Dr. Jekyll and Mr. Hyde'; 'Peer Gynt'; 'Cyrano de Bergerac'; and Shakespearean roles); first to stage Shaw's plays in U.S.
Mansfield, Conn., community 11 mi (18 km) e. of Vernon on Willimantic River; incorporated 1703; pop. of township 19,994.
Mansfield, England, town in Nottinghamshire, 49 mi (79 km) s.e. of Manchester; center of coal-mining district; textiles, footwear; surrounded by remains of Sherwood Forest; pop. 56,210, *map* U-18a
Mansfield, Ohio, industrial city 65 mi (105 km) s.w. of Cleveland; site laid out in 1808; Louis Bromfield, born nearby, set several novels here; pop. 53,927, *map* U-41
Appleseed A-510
Mansfield, Mount, Green Mts., highest point in Vermont, 4,393 ft (1,339 m) V-285, *maps* V-286, 301, *picture* V-287
'Mansfield Park', work by Austen A-765
Mansfield State College, Mansfield, Pa.; opened 1857; formerly a teachers college; arts and sciences, education; graduate studies.
Manship, Paul (1885–1966), U.S. sculptor, born in St. Paul, Minn. ('Dancer and Gazelles'; 'Indian and Pronghorn Antelope'; portrait bust of John D. Rockefeller) S-92
'Diana' S-308, *picture* S-91
'Man's Hope', work by Malraux M-78
Mansion, structure in medieval theater T-159
Manslaughter, crime, *table* L-93
Manson, Sir Patrick (1844–1922), British physician, born in Aberdeen, Scotland; pioneer in tropical medicine; one of first to suggest that mosquito was active agent in spread of malaria.
Mansur, Abu al-Qasem. *see in index* Firdawsi
Mansur, al- (reigned 754–775), 'Abbasid caliph C-56
Mansura (also called El Mansura), Egypt, city on Nile River 70 mi (110 km) n. of Cairo; cotton; battle between Crusaders under Louis IX of France and Egyptians 1250; Louis imprisoned; pop. 146,700.
Manta ray (or devilfish, or devil ray, or sea devil), marine ray of the family Mobulidae S-206
Mantegna, Andrea (1431–1506), Italian painter M-110
Mantilla, headcovering H-54
Mantinea, battle of (362 BC) G-267
Thebes T-163
Mantis (often called praying mantis, popular name mule killer, or soothsayer, or devil's racehorse), insect of the order Orthoptera M-111
Mantis, deepsea diving device D-189
Mantis shrimp, crustacean *Squilla empusa*, *picture* C-791
Mantle, Mickey Charles (born 1931), U.S. outfielder, right- and left-handed batter, born in Spavinaw, Okla.; member New York Yankees 1951–68; American League home-run champion 1955–56, 1958, 1960; he hit total of 536 home runs; most valuable player 1956–57, 1962; author of 'The Quality of Courage' B-93, *picture* B-90
Mantle, outer fold of tissue that envelops the body and lines the shell of a mollusk; the shell is produced by secreting glands in the mantle
mollusk M-523
octopus, cuttlefish, and squid O-492
snail S-221
Mantle, layer between central core and crust on Earth E-11, 32, *diagrams* E-12
continent C-689
earthquakes E-39
Mantling (or lambrequin), heraldry H-136, *picture* H-135
Mantra, sacred word or phrase believed to have peculiar power for the one who uses it
Transcendental Meditation T-249
Mantua (Italian Mantova), Italy, city in n. part, 80 mi (130 km) s.w. of Venice; home of Virgil; held by French 1797–99, 1801–14, by Austria 1814–66; pop. 62,411, *map* I-401
Renaissance education E-84
seige (1796–97) N-14
Manu, "Adam" of Hindu mythology; also traditional

author of ancient Hindu lawbook compiled probably from 200 BC to AD 200; works formed basis for regulations set by India's first governor-general, Warren Hastings (1774).
Manua Islands, group of islands, Tau, Ofu, and Olosega, belonging to American Samoa; 22 sq mi (57 sq km); pop. 2,112, *map* P-3
Manual Alphabet, used in sign language, *picture* D-47
Manual arts. *see also in index* Handicraft; Home economics
'Manual of Discipline' (or 'Rule of the Community'), Dead Sea Scroll D-46
Manual processing, method of data processing C-626
Manuals and handbooks R-129
  selected list R-130
Manuel II (1889–1932), king of Portugal, 1908 to 1910, when Portugal became a republic; born in Lisbon P-457a
Manufactured gas. *see in index* Gas, natural and manufactured
Manufacturers' sales branches, merchandising M-144
Manufactures. *see also in index* Capitalism; Industry; Machine age; Mass production; *also* names of industries
  Africa A-105
  apprenticeship A-510
  Asia A-690
    China C-354
  automation A-836
  census C-249
  economics E-60
  employment and unemployment E-206
  Europe E-343
    West Germany G-117
  geography G-65
  industrial design I-169
    models M-517
  Industrial Revolution I-176, 182
  industry I-187
  labor L-3
  Latin America L-65
  materials handling M-211
  mechanical drawing M-255
  microprocessors M-380
  North America N-342
    United States U-107, *charts* U-124, U-127, *map* U-125. *see also* Fact Summary with each state article
    South U-66
  plant products used P-378
    chemurgic discoveries P-379
  quality control Q-4
Manul. *see in index* Pallas cat
Manure, fertilizer A-137
  farm machinery F-32
  fertilizer F-59
  herb cultivation H-138
Manuscript
  autograph A-382
  bookmaking B-351, *picture* B-349
  illuminated. *see in index* Illuminated manuscripts
  library L-171, *pictures* L-174
  papyrus P-249
  pen used P-156
Manuscript writing, type of handwriting H-29
Manush, Henry Emmett (nickname Heinie) (1901–71), U.S. baseball outfielder, born in Tuscumbia, Ala.; with Detroit, A.L., 1923–27, St. Louis, A.L., 1928–30, Washington, A.L., 1930–35, Boston, A.L., 1936, Brooklyn, N.L., 1937–38, Pittsburgh, N.L., 1938–39; hit .378 in 1926 and 1928; lifetime batting average, .330.
Manutius, Italian family famed as printers; most noted were the founder **Aldus,** his son **Paul** (1512–74), famous for his editions of Cicero, and his grandson **Aldus** (1547–97), *picture* B-349
  printing T-337
Manville, New Jersey, borough 9 mi (15 km) n.w. of New Brunswick; clothing; stone quarries; agricultural products; manufacturing; platted 1926, incorporated 1929; pop. 11,278.
'Man Without a Country, The', work by Hale H-14
'Man with the Hoe', work by Millet M-417
Manx, cat C-205, *picture* C-206
  Isle of Man M-91
Many bristled worm (or polychaete worm), segmented worm W-363
'Manyo-shu' (or 'Collection of Myriad Leaves'), Japanese anthology J-79
Manyplies, third stomach of ruminants. *see in index* Omasum
Manzala, El, lake, Egypt E-115
Manzanillo, Cuba, port city on Caribbean Sea; at e. end of Guacanayabo Gulf in mangrove-swamp region; sugar, tobacco; founded 1784; pop. 82,000, *map* C-802
  West Indies, *map* W-159
Manzanillo, Mexico, port on Pacific coast 40 mi (60 km) s.w. of Colima; shipping point for w. Mexico; resort; pop. 20,777
  Mexico, *map* M-341
  North America, *map* N-351
Manzanita, evergreen shrubs of genus *Arctostaphylos* of the heath family, especially common on Pacific coast of U.S.; 3 to 12 ft (1 to 3.5 m) high; dark-red, smooth bark; white or pink flowers; red berrylike fruit; ornamental uses.
Manzhous. *see in index* Manchus
Manzikert, battle of (1071), ancient Armenia, *list* W-15
Manzoni, Alessandro (1785–1873), Italian poet and novelist, born in Milan; 'I Promessi Sposi' (The Betrothed), called best historical novel ever written I-376
'Manzoni Requiem', work by Verdi V-282
Maoris, a people of New Zealand N-282, *pictures* N-292, 296
  Auckland A-759
  ventriloquism V-279
Mao Zedong (or Mao Tse-tung) (1893–1976), Chinese leader M-111
  China C-349, 357, 373, *pictures* C-375
  Chinese literature C-390
  Cultural Revolution C-805
  guerrilla warfare G-301
  Japanese culture J-66
  totalitarianism T-234
Map cowrie, mollusk shell *Cypraea mappa*, *picture* S-149
Maple, tree of the family *Aceraceae* M-112
  red, *picture* R-186
  seed dispersal S-106
  sugar maple. *see in index* Sugar maple
  wood, *table* W-283
Maple Heights, Ohio, city 9 mi (15 km) s.e. of Cleveland; chiefly residential; incorporated 1930; pop. 29,735.
'Maple Leaf Forever, The', Canadian patriotic song by Alexander Muir, a Toronto schoolteacher; written 1867; popular in English-speaking provinces; now superseded by 'O Canada'.
Maple Shade, N.J., urban township 7 mi (11 km) e. of Camden; truck gardens, orchards, dairy and poultry farms; paper goods, clothing, and radio parts factories; lumber mills; pop. 16,464.
Maple sugar M-113
  forest products F-316
Maple syrup M-113
  forest products F-316
  tapping trees, *picture* V-294
Maplewood, Minn., village just n.e. of St. Paul; pharmaceuticals; pop. 26,990.
Maplewood, Mo., residential suburb of St. Louis; pop. 10,960.
Maplewood, N.J., urban township w. of Newark; map publishing; light manufacturing; site of Timothy Ball House frequented by Washington during Revolutionary War; pop. 24,932.
Mapp vs. Ohio, case in U.S. constitutional law, *list* S-518b
Maps M-114. *see also in index* Globe
  atlas R-127
  Cassini's polar projection, *picture* R-127
  direction finding D-161
  geography G-68
  Geological Survey, U.S. U-161
  helicopters used H-121
  history, *picture* R-127
    Cook C-696
    Mercator M-304
  moon map M-574
  navigational, *pictures* N-71, 78
  surveying S-520
  weather W-122, *pictures* W-124, 125
Map turtle T-330
Maputo (formerly Lourenço Marques), Mozambique, capital; including suburbs; developed with opening of land around Delagoa Bay and coming of railroad (1895); pop. 882,800 M-130
  Africa, *maps* A-118, S-264
  Mozambique M-641, *picture* M-642
Maqamah, in poetry
  Islamic literature I-364
'Maqamat', work by al-Hariri, *picture* I-366
Maquis, guerrillas of French underground in World War II
  France F-364
Mara, Tim (in full Timothy James Mara) (1887–1959), founder of New York Giants football team, 1925.
Marabou (or adjutant stork of Africa), bird *Leptopilus crumeniferus* of the family Ciconiidae S-456
Maracaibo (formerly Nueva Zamora), Venezuela, one of chief ports; in n.w. on channel between Gulf of Venezuela and Lake Maracaibo; with suburbs; petroleum, coffee, cacao, hides; pop. 890,553 M-130
  South America S-274, *map* S-298
  Venezuela V-275
Maracaibo, Lake, n.w. Venezuela opening into Gulf of Venezuela; largest lake in South America; half of lake is fresh, but n. half, under tidal influence, is brackish M-130
  geography G-68
  oil field V-275
  Venezuela V-275
Maracanda, U.S.S.R. *see in index* Samarkand
Marais des Cygnes River, about 140 mi (225 km) long, rises n.e. of Emporia, Kansas, flows generally s.e. into state of Missouri and there joins Little Osage River to form Osage River.
Marajó (or Joannes), island formed by estuaries of Amazon and Pará rivers in n.e. Brazil; area about 18,500 sq mi (47,900 sq km); pop. 147,895 I-368, *map* S-298
Maranhão, state on n. coast of Brazil; 128,252 sq mi (332,171 sq km); cap. São Luís; settled by French 1594; part of Brazil 1823; pop. 4,097,231, *map* B-425
Marañon River, Peru, upper course of Amazon, *maps* P-224, S-298
Maranville, Walter James Vincent (nickname Rabbit) (1891–1954), U.S. baseball shortstop and second baseman, born in Springfield, Mass.; played 2670 games; player for Boston, N.L., 1912–20, Pittsburgh, N.L., 1921–24, Chicago, N.L., 1925, Brooklyn, N.L., 1926, St. Louis, N.L., 1927–28, Boston, N.L., 1929–35.
Marasmus, chronic severe wasting of the tissues of the body D-180
Marat, Jean-Paul (1743–93), French revolutionist M-131
  assassination A-703
  Corday C-715
  French Revolution F-403
  Robespierre R-223
Marathas, Hindu peoples in India. *see in index* Mahrattas
Marathi, Bombay's dominant language B-340
Marathon, Greece; a plain 25 mi (40 km) northeast of Athens M-131
Marathon, battle of (490 BC) M-131, P-214
  joint-command structure A-635
  Themistocles T-163
  Theseus T-168
  warfare W-23, *list* W-15
Marathon race, long distance race
  Marathon, Greece M-131
  Olympic games O-541
  track and field T-244
Maratti, Carlo (or Carlo Maratta) (1625–1713), Italian painter, born in Camerano, near Ancona, Italy; patronized by five popes; noted for Madonnas, Holy Families.
Marauder (B-26), U.S. military aircraft W-334
Maravi, a people of Africa M-69
Marble, Alice (born 1913), U.S. tennis player, born in Plumas County, Calif.; won national women's singles 1936, 1938, 1939, 1940; Wimbledon singles 1939; turned professional 1941; voted outstanding woman athlete in U.S. 1938.
Marble, rock M-131
  alabaster of the ancients A-238
  formation R-229a, *chart* R-229
  limestone L-210
  minerals M-435
  quarrying Q-6
  rock cycle, *chart* R-229
  sculpture A-667
    ancient Greek G-269
  United States
    Missouri, *picture* M-492
    Tennessee T-85, *map* T-88
    Vermont V-287, *map* V-290, *picture* V-291
Marbled cat, wild cat *Felis marmorata*, *picture* C-215
Marbled godwit, shorebird. *see in index* Godwit
Marblehead, Mass., on Atlantic coast, 15 mi (25 km) n.e. of Boston; yachting center; summer resort; settled by fishermen 1629, incorporated 1649; pop. of township 20,126.
Marblehead Peninsula, in Ohio, *picture* O-511
  Great Lakes G-248
Marbles, games M-132, *picture* G-10
Marburg, West Germany, city n. of Frankfurt; famous for university (founded 1527, first university established without papal privileges); 13th-century church containing tomb of St. Elizabeth of Hungary, and 13th-century castle; pop. 46,968, *map* G-134
Marbury, Anne. *see in index* Hutchinson, Anne
Marbury vs. Madison, case in United States constitutional law S-518b, U-146
  constitutional law C-686
  law L-95
  Marshall M-153
Marbut, Curtis Fletcher (1863–1935), U.S. geologist and soil chemist, born in Lawrence County, Missouri; director of Soils Survey, U.S. Department of Agriculture 1910–35 S-251
Marc, Franz (1880–1916), German expressionist painter, born in Munich, Germany; animals figure largely in his decorative paintings; killed in battle at Verdun ('Red Horses').
Marcantonio (1488?–1527?), foremost Italian engraver in the Renaissance, first to copy on copper the work of other artists (Dürer's 'Little Passion' and 'Life of the Virgin').
Marca-Relli, Conrad (born 1913), U.S. painter, born in Boston, Mass.; first one-man show New York, N.Y. 1947; known for collage P-65
  'The Blackboard', *picture* P-66
Marcasite, mineral used as a gem stone; mined in England, Czechoslovakia, France, Mexico, and in Illinois, Missouri, and Wisconsin
  jewelry J-116
  minerals M-432
Marceau, Marcel (born 1923), French pantomimist, born in Strasbourg; won world fame for stage and television shows; created character Bip, a white-faced clown, 1947; United States debut 1955
  mime M-422, *picture* M-423
Marcel, Gabriel Honoré (1889–1973), French philosopher, born in Paris; wrote books on philosophy and various plays P-267
Marcellus, Marcus Claudius (268?–208 BC), Roman general in 2nd Punic War, conqueror of Syracuse; five times consul; killed near Venusia.
Marcel wave, hairdressing H-10
March, Francis Andrew (1825–1911), U.S. philologist, born in Millbury, Mass.; professor at Lafayette College 1856–1906 ('Method of Philological Study of the English Language').
March, Peyton Conway (1864–1955), U.S. Army officer, born in Easton, Pa., son of Francis Andrew March; commanded Astor Battery, Spanish-American War; member Army General Staff 1903–7; artillery commander A.E.F. in France 1917; made

general and chief of Army General Staff May 1918.
March, William. *see in index* Campbell, William Edward March
March, regular measured stride or rhythmic step or music used in marching
marching bands B-54, *picture* B-55
popular music M-684
March, 3rd month of the Gregorian calendar
calendar C-30
naming M-152
Marches, The, region on e. coast of central Italy, formerly part of Papal States; area 3,742 sq mi (9,692 sq km); cap. Ancona; pop. 1,347,489, *map* I-401
Marchesi de Castrone, Mathilde (originally Mathilde Graumann) (1826–1913), German-French teacher of singing, born in Frankfurt; married Salvatore Marchesi, Italian baritone; pupils included Melba, Eames, Calvé
opera, *list* O-570
Marchetti, Gino (born 1927), U.S. football star, born in Antioch, Calif.; with Dallas Texans 1952; Baltimore Colts 1953–64, 1966.
March fly, name for stout-bodied flies of the family Bibionidae; common in early spring; adults black and red, sometimes yellow; larvae attack roots of grass.
March of Dimes. *see in index* National Foundation–March of Dimes
'March of Time, The' documentary news features begun in 1935 by Rochemont for Time, Inc. M-628
March on Washington (1963), organized, peaceful civil rights demonstration that helped secure passage of the Civil Rights Act of 1964, King's famous "I have a Dream" speech given.
Marciano, Rocky (originally Rocco Marchegiano) (1923–69), U.S. boxer, born in Brockton, Mass.; elected to Boxing Hall of Fame 1969
heavyweight champion B-392
Louis L-307
Marconi, Guglielmo (1874–1937), Italian electrical engineer and inventor M-132, *picture* M-133. *see also in index* Nobel Prizewinners, *table*
foundations for radar R-29
Tesla T-114
wireless radio system R-56
first signal in Newfoundland N-163, 167
Vatican station V-271
Marconi-rig (or Bermuda-rig, or jibheaded-rig) B-326
Marco Polo. *see in index* Polo, Marco
Marco Polo Bridge Incident, (1937), battle between Chinese and Japanese troops C-374
Marco Polo sheep S-148
Marcos, Ferdinand (born 1917), president of Philippines (1965–86); prime minister 1973–86 M-133
Aquino A-520
Philippines P-255b
Marcos de Niza (1495?–1558), Franciscan friar, chosen to explore region of fabled wealth n. of Sonora, Mexico; penetrated to Zuni, N.M. ("Seven Cities of Cibola") A-601
New Mexico N-217
Marcus, Siegfried (1831–99), Austrian mechanic and inventor, pioneer automobile builder A-858
Marcus Antonius. *see in index* Antony, Mark
Marcus Aurelius (AD 121–180), Roman emperor M-133
bust, *picture* R-243
Christians persecuted C-401
civilization's cycles C-467
five good emperors R-247
Galen G-5
Hadrian H-4
Rome R-255, *picture* R-253
world W-296
Marcuse, Herbert (1898–1979), U.S. political philosopher who was popular with student leftist radicals because of his support of radicalization, vociferous dissent and 'resistance to the point of subversion', though he did not applaud the campus demonstrations taking place; works include 'Eros and Civilization', 'Studies in Critical Philosophy'
terrorism T-114
Marcus Island, triangular island (each side about a mile [1½ kilometers] long) in Pacific 875 mi (1,410 km) n.w. of Wake Island; served as Japanese airfield and radio station in World War II; occupied by U.S. 1945; returned to Japan 1968, *map* P-3
Marcy, William Learned (1786–1857), U.S. statesman, born in Southbridge, Mass.; prominent in "Albany Regency"; author of phrase "To the victor belong the spoils"; secretary of state 1853–57 C-469
Jackson J-8
Marcy, Mount, in n.e. New York, highest peak of Adirondacks and highest point in state (5,344 ft; 1,629 m) A-44, *map* U-50
New York N-245
Mar del Plata, Argentina, city 230 mi (370 km) s.e. of Buenos Aires; settled in 1850s as meat-processing center; pop. 302,282, *maps* A-585, S-297
Mardi Gras (or Shrove Tuesday)
carnival C-171, F-61, *picture* F-62
Easter E-41
folk art F-252
New Orleans N-231
Mardikh, Tell, Syria, location of cuneiform tablets from the ancient Mesopotamian civilization of Elba A-538
Marduk, Babylonian god B-3, B-8
Mare, female horse more than three years old, *list* H-249
Mare clausum, in international law, sea or portion of sea under jurisdiction of one nation instead of open to all.
Mare Cognitum (or Sea of Knowledge), region on moon M-580
Mare Crisium (or Sea of Crises), region on moon M-579
Mare Imbrium (or Sea of Rains), region on moon S-347
moon M-579
Mare Island Navy Yard, California at e. end of San Pablo Bay, opposite Vallejo; on "island" (reached by causeway) more than 2,300 acres (930 hectares) in area; established 1854 by David Glasgow Farragut; in World War I, the yard broke many records for construction; in World War II, repaired 1,207 ships and built 391 new vessels; equipped to build all classes of naval vessels.
Marengo, favorite horse of Napoleon, *list* H-249
Marengo, battle of (1800), fought near village of this name in n. Italy 35 mi (55 km) n.w. of Genoa; took place between French and Austrian armies early in the Napoleonic Wars.
Mare Nostrum. *see in index* Mediterranean Sea
Mare Nubium (or Sea of Clouds), region on moon M-579
Mare Serenitatis (or Sea of Serenity), region on moon S-347
moon M-579
Mareshah. *see in index* Eleutheropolis
Mare Tranquillitatis (or Sea of Tranquillity), region on moon
moon M-576, *picture* M-573
U.S. astronauts S-341
Marey, Étienne Jules (1830–1904), French physiologist; devised camera for taking a series of pictures in rapid succession (called "photographic gun")
motion pictures M-616
Marfan's syndrome, genetic disorder G-48
Margaree Valley, Nova Scotia N-399
Margaret, Saint (1045?–93), queen of Malcolm III of Scotland and daughter of Edward the Exile of England; probably born in Hungary; canonized 1251 because of her benefactions; festival in Roman Catholicism June 10, in Anglican Communion July 20.
Margaret, Princess (born 1930), sister of Elizabeth II of United Kingdom E-192
Margaret of Anjou (1430–82), queen of Henry VI of England, born in Lorraine, France; with Andrew Docket founded Queen's College, Cambridge; died in exile
Henry VI H-130
Wars of the Roses R-296
Margaret of Valois (or Margaret of Angoulême) (1492–1549), queen of Henry d'Albret, king of Navarre, and sister of Francis I of France, joint author of the 'Heptameron' stories modeled on the 'Decameron' of Boccaccio; patroness of Marot and other literary men, and protector of Protestants; sometimes called **Margaret of Navarre** in order to avoid confusion with her grandniece, daughter of Henry II.
Margaret of Valois (1533–1615), daughter of Henry II of France and Catherine de Médicis, married to Henry of Navarre (afterward Henry IV of France) on eve of Massacre of St. Bartholomew
Henry IV H-132
'Margaret Ogilvy', work by Barrie B-83
Margarine (or oleomargarine) M-134
Margarita, Isla de, Venezuelan island in the Caribbean Sea; 444 sq mi (1,150 sq km); cap. La Asunción; pearl fisheries; discovered by Columbus 1498; pop. 85,296, *maps* V-275, S-298
West Indies, *map* W-159
Margate, England, popular summer resort on North Sea, 65 mi (105 km) e. of London; concert pavilions; winter gardens; light industry; church of St. John the Baptist built 1050; pop. 49,080, *map* U-18a
Margay, spotted cat *Felis wiedii* found from s.w. U.S. to Brazil; about size of large house cat; resembles ocelot, *table* C-216
fur, *table* F-464
Margerine (or oleomargerine) M-134
Marggraf, Andreas Sigismund (1709–82), German chemist, born in Berlin; discovered sugar in beetroot; valuable observations on phosphoric acid; introduced microscope in chemical research S-507
discovered chemical identity of aluminum A-322
Margherita, Mount, situated on boundary between Uganda and Zaire; highest point (16,795 ft; 5,120 m) of Ruwenzori mountain range U-1, *map* A-118
Margin, in speculation S-454
Marginal basin, in geology
continental structure C-690
Marginal belt, international boundary I-256
Margitszigit Island, part of Budapest, Hungary, located in the Danube between Buda and Pest B-479
Margrethe (or Semiramis of the North) (1353–1412), queen (governing as regent for nominal sovereigns) of Denmark, Norway, and Sweden
Denmark D-100
Sweden S-527
Margrethe II (born 1940), queen of Denmark, born in Copenhagen; crowned 1972 after death of her father, Frederik IX D-100
Marguerite, popular name of several flowers of the aster family, such as the China aster, the common garden daisy, and the oxeye daisy; also some cultivated species of chrysanthemum, which are sometimes called Paris daisies
chrysanthemum C-408
Margueritte, Paul (1860–1918) and **Victor** (1866–1942), French novelists, brothers, born in Algeria; wrote series of novels 'Une Epoque' (1898–1940); after World War I, Victor caused sensation with 'La Garçonne', 'Les Coupables', 'Appel aux Consciences'.
Maria, seas of moon M-573
Maria II, da Gloria (1819–53), queen of Portugal, born in Rio de Janeiro; succeeded 1827 on abdication of her father, Pedro I; reign troubled by rebellion of her uncle, Dom Miguel, and insurrections.
'Maria Chapdelaine', work by Hémon C-121
Maria Christina (1858–1929), queen mother of Spain, daughter of Archduke Karl Ferdinand of Austria; left convent, of which she was abbess, to marry Alfonso XII; ruled as queen regent from his death (1885) until Alfonso XIII became of age in 1902.
Mariana Islands (also called Marianas, formerly Ladrone Islands), group of 15 islands in Micronesia, Pacific Ocean, 1,500 mi (2,400 km) e. of Philippines; 450 sq mi (1,160 sq km); made Japanese mandate 1919 (except Guam, ceded to U.S. 1898); occupied by U.S. 1944; placed under U.S. trusteeship 1947; commonwealth status granted 1976; Saipan is naval base; sugar, copra, bonito fisheries; pop. 76,630, *map* P-3
World War II W-334, 346, *picture* W-347
Marianao, Cuba, resort city 5 mi (8 km) s.w. of Havana; breweries; pharmaceutical houses; paper, textile and tobacco factories; site of large military establishment, Camp Columbia; pop. 219,278
West Indies, *map* W-159
Mariana Trench, Pacific Ocean off Guam P-2, *diagram* E-10, *map* P-3
ocean deeps O-461
oceanography O-485
Marian College, Indianapolis, Ind.; Roman Catholic; founded 1851; present name 1937; liberal arts and sciences, art, business administration, education, medical technology, music.
Marian College of Fond du Lac, Fond du Lac, Wis.; Roman Catholic; founded 1936; arts and sciences, education, medical technology, nursing.
Marianna Lowlands, in Florida F-195
Marianske Lazne, Czechoslovakia. *see in index* Marienbad
'Maria Padilla', opera by Donizetti D-229
Maria Theresa (1717–80), archduchess of Austria and queen of Hungary and Bohemia M-134
Hungary H-329
Maintenon M-68
Seven Years' War S-117
War of the Austrian Succession A-829
Maria Theresa (1638–83), queen of Spain, queen of Louis XIV
portrait, *picture* D-264
wedding ceremonies V-272
Maria van Diemen, Cape, on n.w. tip of North Island, New Zealand, *map* N-299
Marib Dam, ancient dam in Yemen
irrigation projects I-356
Maricopa, Yuman tribe of American Indians affiliated with the Pima in s. Arizona; avid warriors established separate companies for bowmen and club fighters; ceremonies featured myth songs; dead cremated.
Mariculture, oceanography O-484
Marie (1875–1938), queen of Ferdinand I of Romania; born in England, granddaughter of Queen Victoria; married Prince Ferdinand, later king, 1893; active in Red Cross work in World War I ('The Lily of Life'; 'My Country'; 'Ilderim'); for many years strong influence in Romanian politics R-318
Marie Antoinette (1755–93), queen of France; wife of Louis XVI M-135
French Revolution F-402
Maria Theresa M-135
Mozart M-643
Petit Trianon at Versailles V-303
Robespierre R-223
Marie Byrd Land, Antarctica, discovered 1929 and named by Richard E. Byrd for his wife; in w. Antarctica, this area is largely an ice-covered archipelago.
Marie Charlotte Amélie. *see in index* Carlota
Marie de France, French poetess of 12th century; lived in England, for a time at court of Henry II; wrote narrative poems and fables.
Marie de l'Incarnation (1599–1672), French Roman Catholic nun, born in Tours; 1639 went to Canada with Madame de la Peltrie to found Ursuline convent in Quebec; first superior of convent; composed dictionary of French and Algonquian.

(born 1910), English ballerina, born in London; with Diaghilev Ballet 1925–29, later with Vic-Wells Ballet, London, Markova-Dolin Ballet, Ballet Russe de Monte Carlo, Ballet Theater; director Metropolitan Opera Ballet and Studio 1963–69 ('Giselle'; 'Les Sylphides'; 'Swan Lake'; 'Romeo and Juliet'); author, 'Giselle and I' B-36

Marks, Leonard Harold (born 1916), U.S. lawyer, born in Pittsburgh, Pa.; partner Cohn & Marks, Washington, D.C., 1946–65, 1969–; president Federal Communications Commission 1959–60; director U.S. Information Agency 1965–68; chairman U.S. delegation to International Telecommunications Satellite Consortium (Intelsat) 1968–69.

Marksmanship. *see in index* Riflery and marksmanship

Marks of cadency, in heraldry H-136

Mark Twain. *see in index* Twain, Mark

Marl, impure limestone P-230
  cement C-243
  minerals M-435

Marlboro College, Marlboro, Vt.; private control; chartered 1946; liberal arts; quarter system; home of Marlboro Summer Music School and Festival.

Marlborough, Duke of (or John Churchill) (1650–1722), English general and statesman M-147
  Anne A-467
  Swift S-531
  War of the Spanish Succession A-829

Marlborough, Sarah Jennings Churchill, duchess of (1660–1744), favorite of Queen Anne, born near St. Albans, England
  Anne A-467
  Marlborough M-147

Marlborough, Mass., city situated 26 mi (42 km) w. of Boston; shoes, paper products, sporting goods, matches, boxes, metal products; nearly destroyed by American Indians in 1676; pop. 30,617.

Marley, Bob (1945–81), Jamaican reggae singer and composer, born in St. Ann, Jamaica; introduced reggae music to an international audience with band, The Wailers; albums include 'Catch a Fire' and 'Exodus', *picture* M-683

Marlin, any of several saltwater fish related to sailfish and spearfish; family Istiophoridae, genus *Makaira;* game fish of Hawaii, Japan, California, Mexico, West Indies, and Florida north to Cape Cod; often taken with harpoon.

Marlin, Tex., health resort in agricultural area about 22 mi (35 km) s.e. of Waco; mineral-water wells; famous baths, clinics; pop. 7,099.

Marlinespike seamanship, in knot-making K-264

Marlowe, Christopher (1564–93), English poet and dramatist M-147
  drama D-243
  Faust legend F-49
  literary contribution E-266
  Shakespeare S-134

Marlowe, Julia (1866–1950), U.S. Shakespearean actress, born in Caldbeck, Cumberlandshire, England; starred with Edward Hugh Sothern, whom she married; retired 1924, *picture* S-140

Marmara, Sea of (or Sea of Marmora, in ancient times called Propontis), sea between European and Asiatic Turkey; connected with the Black and Aegean seas, *map* E-361. *see also in index* Ocean, *table*
  Turkey T-319

'Marmion: a Tale of Flodden Field', poem by Sir Walter Scott telling of the adventures and futile love for Lady Clare of Lord Marmion, leader of the Scots, who was slain at Flodden Field; contains the ballad of 'Young Lochinvar' S-73. *see also in index* Lochinvar

Mármol, José (1818–71), Argentine novelist, born in Buenos Aires; wrote plays, poetry, and historical novel 'La Amalia' (1855).

Marmolada, highest peak of the Dolomites, 10,964 ft (3,342 m), *map* I-404

Marmoset, small South American monkey of Hapalidae family A-503

Marmot, genus of rodents, belonging to the ground squirrel group
  Alpine habitat A-319
  fur, *table* F-465
  hibernation H-148

Marne, First Battle of the (1914), France during World War I W-303
  Joffre J-120
  warfare W-23, *list* W-15

Marne, Second Battle of the (1918), France during World War I W-311
  warfare W-23, *list* W-15

Marne River, n.e. France; scene of two decisive battles of World War I and of severe fighting in World War II, *maps* E-361, F-372. *see also in index* Château-Thierry

Maromokotro, Mount, in Madagascar (9,436 ft; 2,876 m) M-23

Maronite Church, Eastern-rite community in Roman Catholicism; origin traced to St. Maron, a Syrian hermit in the late 4th and early 5th centuries, and to St. John Maron, patriarch of Antioch in the 7th century; in coalition governments of Lebanon the president is always a Maronite.

Maronobu (1625–94), Japanese painter, noted chiefly for skillful and powerful paintings of actors and beautiful women; first Japanese painter to make designs for wood-block prints.

Marot, Clément (1495?–1544), French poet, born in Cahors, near Toulouse, France; introduced new grace and ease into stiff forms of French poetry.

Marot, Daniel (1661–1752), French émigré to Low Countries, architect and designer
  furniture design F-458

Marpessa, in Greek mythology, young maiden who was loved by Apollo but gave her affection to her human lover, Idas.

Marple, Pa., urban township w. of the city of Philadelphia in Delaware County; situated in an industrial and residential region; pop. 25,040.

Marquand, John Phillips (1893–1960), U.S. novelist, born in Wilmington, Del.; travels in China form the background of 'Ming Yellow' and the 'Mr. Moto' stories; 'The Late George Apley', Pulitzer prize novel (1938), 'Wickford Point', 'So Little Time', 'Point of No Return', 'Melville Goodwin, U.S.A.', 'Life at Happy Knoll', and 'Women and Thomas Harrow' are penetrating social satires ('The Late John Marquand: A Biography' by Stephen Birmingham) A-358
  detective story D-119

Marquard, Richard William (nickname Rube) (1898–1980), U.S. baseball pitcher, born in Cleveland, Ohio; played 1908–25; won 20 consecutive games 1912.

Marque, letters of. *see in index* Letters of marque

Marquesas Islands (French Iles Marquises), group of 11 volcanic islands in French Polynesia, s. Pacific Ocean; about 3,300 mi (5,300 km) s.w. of Los Angeles, Calif.; area 492 sq mi (1,274 sq km); pop. 4,837, *map* P-3

Marquess (or marquis), European noble next in rank below a duke; wife is called marchioness or marquise T-195

Marquetry. *see also in index* Inlay
  furniture decoration I-226, F-458

Marquette, Jacques (1637–75), French Jesuit missionary and explorer M-148
  Illinois I-41, *picture* I-43
  Jolliet J-138, *map* U-176
  Michigan M-361
    Sault Ste. Marie S-52c
  Mississippi River M-484
  Missouri River M-493, 510
  Statuary Hall, *table* S-437b
  Wisconsin W-253

Marquette, Mich., port city on Lake Superior about 57 mi (92 km) n.w. of Escanaba; shipping point for iron ore; resort center; mining machinery; iron ore pellets, lumber; fisheries; Northern Michigan University; pop. 23,288, *map* U-41
  North America, *map* N-351

Marquette University, Milwaukee, Wis.; Roman Catholic; founded 1864; organized as a college 1881, as a university 1907; colleges of liberal arts, business administration, dentistry, engineering, journalism, law, nursing, speech; courses in dental hygiene, medical technology, physical therapy; graduate school; Marquette School of Medicine became independent 1967, renamed Medical College of Wisconsin 1970; Jesuit College, for men, at St. Bonifacius, Minn.
  Milwaukee M-421

Marquis, Donald Robert Perry (1878–1937), U.S. writer of stories, plays, and verse, born in Walnut, Ill.; columnist *New York Evening Sun*; won wide audience for his humorous bits of wisdom ('The Old Soak'; 'Off the Arm') R-112b, *list* C-202

Marquise cut, in diamond cutting, *picture* J-116

Marquisette, fabric of open, loose weave, made of cotton, silk, rayon, or wool; used for curtains, mosquito netting, and dresses, also in millinery.

Marquis of Queensberry rules, in boxing B-390

Marrakech (or Marrakesh, formerly Morocco City), Morocco, city about 150 mi (240 km) s. of Casablanca; morocco leather manufactures; founded 1062; most prosperous about 1300, when population is said to have been approximately 700,000; pop. 439,728, M-585, *picture* M-586, *map* A-118

Marriage M-149. *see also in index* Family
  aborigine A-795
  Arabs A-526
  bioethical issues B-214
  clan C-485
  contract C-693
  family F-15, *diagram* F-18, *table* F-16
  family law F-20
  folk art celebrates F-251, *picture* S-470
  Hammurabi H-24
  Hinduism H-160
  India I-69, *picture* I-70
  Japan J-28
  park ceremony, *picture* P-126
  Philippines P-253d
  polygamy. *see in index* Polygamy
  rate by states. *see* Fact Summary with each state article
  sexuality S-125
  women's rights W-271

'Marriage à la Mode', work by Hogarth H-199

'Marriage of Figaro, The' ('Le Nozze de Figaro'), Italian opera buffa by Mozart, libretto by Lorenzo da Ponte, based on comedy by Beaumarchais; premiere at Vienna 1786 M-643
  French literature F-396
  opera O-565, *list* O-562

'Marriage of Giovanni Arnolfini and Giovanna Cenami, The', painting by Eyck P-30

Married print (or composite print), in motion pictures M-604

Marriner, Neville (born 1924), British conductor, *list* O-579

Marriott, Joyce Anne (or Mrs. Gerald J. McLellan) (born 1913), Canadian poet, born in Victoria, B.C. ('The Wind Our Enemy').

Marrow, in bone B-342
  blood cells B-314

Marryat, Frederick (1792–1848), English naval captain and novelist, born in London; own experiences formed background of his many famous sea stories ('Mr. Midshipman Easy'; 'Peter Simple'; 'Snarley-yow, or the Dog Fiend'; 'Masterman Ready' and other boys' stories).

Mars, Roman god of war, identified with Greek Ares M-152
  mythology M-696, 701

MARS (or Military Affiliate Radio System), volunteer organization of licensed amateur radio operators; networks organized 1948; under joint jurisdiction of the Air Force, Army, and Navy.

Mars, fourth planet from the sun P-352, *table* P-351, *diagram* S-254e
  astronomy A-714
  Kepler's observation K-228
  maps M-115
  meteor M-315
  naming M-152
    earth E-7, *diagram* E-9
  probes S-343b, *table* S-344
  satellites S-52

Mars, Soviet space probe, *table* S-344

Marsala, Sicily, ancient Lilybaeum, *map* I-401. *see also in index* Lilybaeum

Marsala, wine W-237

Marsalis, Wynton (born 1961), U.S. trumpet virtuoso; born in New Orleans; renowned for command of classical and jazz music; toured with Art Blakey, Herbie Hancock, and his own quintet late 1970s and 1980s; in 1984 became first to win Grammy awards in both jazz and classical areas; named Jazz Musician of the Year 1982, 1984–85.

Marschner, Heinrich (1795–1861), German composer O-566

'Marseillaise, La', French national anthem N-65

Marseilles (French Marseille; ancient Massalia), France, seaport on Mediterranean; 2nd city of France; pop. 880,527 M-152, *map* E-361
  France F-356, *map* F-372
  postal service P-463b
  soap S-229

Marsh, George Perkins (1801–82), U.S. diplomat, lawyer, and philologist, born in Woodstock, Vt.; U.S. minister to Turkey (Ottoman Empire) and to Italy ('Lectures on the English Language').

Marsh, Grant Prince (1834–1916), U.S. steamboat captain, pioneer pilot of the upper Missouri, born in Chautauqua County, New York; rendered invaluable assistance to armies of Sully, Forsyth, Custer, Terry, and Reno in wars with the Sioux (1864–76).

Marsh, Dame Ngaio (1899–1982), New Zealand author and theatrical producer, born in Christchurch; best known for detective novels ('Final Curtain', 'Death of a Fool', 'Hand in Glove', 'Killer Dolphin', 'Clutch of Constables', 'When in Rome').

Marsh, Othniel Charles (1831–99), U.S. paleontologist, born in Lockport, N.Y.; discovered many vertebrate fossils in w. U.S.; vertebrate paleontologist, U.S. Geological Survey from 1882.

Marsh, Reginald (1898–1954), U.S. painter M-152

Marsh, tract of low, wet land. *see in index* Swamp

Marshal, title derived from ancient title of masters of horse of Frankish kings; highest military officer in France called "marshal" since 13th century; German Feldmarschall and English Field Marshal derived from it; in U.S., ministerial officer of federal courts.

Marshall, Alfred (1842–1924), English economist, born in London; professor of political economy Cambridge University 1885–1908; known for neo-classical theories ('Principles of Economics')
  economics E-63

Marshall, Archibald (1866–1934), English novelist, born in London; pictured the English country gentleman and his family ('The Eldest Son'; 'The Old Order Changeth').

Marshall, Freddie Ray (born 1928), U.S. educator and public official, born in Oak Grove, La.; professor University of Texas 1962–67, 1969–77; chairman department of economics University of Kentucky 1967–69; U.S. secretary of labor 1977–81.

Marshall, George Catlett (1880–1959), U.S. Army officer M-152, *picture* P-180. *see also in index* Nobel Prizewinners, *table*
  China C-374
  Marshall Plan U-192
  World War II, *pictures* W-334, 354

Marshall, George Preston (1896–1969), founder and owner of Redskins, football team; born in Charleston, W. Va.

Marshall, James Wilson (1810–85), U.S. pioneer, born in Hunterdon County, N.J.; started on Oregon Trail 1844; took part in Bear Flag Revolt 1846 S-2
  gold rush G-183

Marshall, John (1755–1835), chief justice of the U.S. M-153, *pictures* S-518a, V-342
  constitution C-683
    constitutional law C-685
  Hall of Fame, *table* H-16
  Hamilton H-21
  important decisions U-146
  judicial review S-518b
  Washington's eulogy W-46
  XYZ affair X-406

Marshall, Peter (1902–49), U.S. clergyman, born in Coatbridge, Scotland; to U.S. 1927, citizen 1938; minister, Washington, D.C., 1937–49; chaplain of U.S. Senate 1947–49; subject of wife's book, 'A Man Called Peter'.

Marshall, Thomas Riley (1854–1925), U.S. statesman, born in North Manchester, Ind.; governor of Indiana 1909–13 ('Recollections: a Hoosier Salad').

Marshall, Thurgood (born 1908), U.S. lawyer, born in Baltimore, Md.; special counsel for NAACP 1938–61; judge U.S. court of appeals for second circuit 1962–65; U.S. solicitor general 1965–67; first black associate justice of U.S. Supreme Court 1967–; awarded 1946 Spingarn Medal B-302

Marshall, Mo., city 28 mi (45 km) n. of Sedalia; shoes, dairy products; Missouri Valley College; pop. 12,781.

Marshall, Tex., city 37 mi (60 km) w. of Shreveport, La.; livestock, farming, natural gas, oil, lignite in area; iron and steel products, lumber products, food products, clothing, bricks; East Texas Baptist College, Wiley College; pop. 24,921, *map* U-41

Marshall Apothecary, early U.S. drugstore P-249, *picture* P-248b

Marshall Field & Co., U.S. retail department store F-77, *picture* M-146

Marshall Islands, archipelago made up of Ralik group (11 main islands) and Ratak group (13 main islands) in Micronesia, Pacific Ocean, e. of Caroline Islands and n. of Gilbert Islands; about 160 sq mi (410 sq km); German rule 1885; Japanese mandate 1919; occupied by U.S. 1944; placed under U.S. trusteeship 1947; Jaluit was Japanese naval base; chief export copra; pop. 15,714 P-19, *map* P-3
  World War II W-334, 346

Marshall Plan. *see in index* European Recovery Program

Marshalltown, Iowa, city about 50 mi (80 km) n.e. of Des Moines; regulators, furnaces, metal products, power lawn mowers, fire apparatus, farm machinery; pop. 26,938
  Iowa, *map* I-302

Marshall University, Huntington, W. Va.; state control; founded 1837; arts and sciences, applied science, business, teacher education; graduate school
  West Virginia W-168

Marsh Arabs, a people of Iraq I-313

Marsh blazing star. *see in index* Gayfeather

Marsh blue violet, *picture* F-238

Marsh buggy. *see in index* Swamp buggy

'Marshes of Glynn, The', work by Lanier A-350

Marsh fiddler crab, crustacean *Uca pugnax*, *picture* C-791

Marshfield, Mass., residential town 11 mi (18 km) n. of Plymouth; summer resort; incorporated 1641; pop. of township 20,916.

Marshfield, Wis., city near center of state; doors, veneer panels, shoes, trailer homes, pumps and tanks, cheese; pop. 18,290.

Marsh gas. *see in index* Methane

Marsh hawk, *picture* B-278
  quail B-273

Mars Hill College, Mars Hill, N.C.; Southern Baptist; founded 1856; liberal arts, teacher education.

Marsh mallow, plant *Althaea officinalis* of the mallow family having large leaves and clusters of pink flowers; roots used for mucilage and in medicine; the whole plant may be eaten.

Marshmallow, candy C-138

Marsh rabbit. *see in index* Muskrat

Marsh shrew (or water shrew) S-186

Marsilius of Padua (1275–80?–1343), Italian scholar, born in Padua; rector University of Paris; with John of Jandun wrote 'Defensor pacis', a tract against the temporal power of the pope.

Marsiyeh, Persian laments I-107

Marston, John (1575?–1634), English dramatist, born of Italian mother, probably at Coventry, England (comedies: 'Eastward Hoe', with George Chapman and Ben Jonson, and 'The Dutch Courtezan'; tragicomedy: 'The Malcontent', with additions by John Webster).

Marston Moor, plain in Yorkshire, England, 8 mi (15 km) from York.

Marston Moor, battle of (1644), warfare, *list* W-15
  Cromwell C-275

Marsupial mouse (or planigale), small animal of the family *Dasyuridae* M-154, 157

Marsupial mole, burrowing animal of the family *Notoryctidae*, found in central and n.w. Australia; about 6 in. (13 cm) in length; blind, as eyes are beneath skin; lives on insects M-154

Marsupials, mammals of the order *Marsupialia* that carry their young in a pouch M-154
  animal life record, *table* E-24
  Australia A-778
  biogeography B-218
  cuscus, *picture* P-10
  mammal M-81, *table* M-80

Marsupium (or pouch), abdominal pouch that covers the nursing young of marsupials M-154
  kangaroo K-172

Marszalkowska Street, main thoroughfare in Warsaw, Poland W-33

Martaban, Gulf of, on coast of lower Burma, inlet of Bay of Bengal
  Asia, *map* A-700

'Marteau sans maitre, Le' (or 'The Hammer without a Master') (1954), work by Boulez B-383

Martel, Charles. *see in index* Charles Martel

Marten, a carnivorous mammal W-114
  fur F-463, *table* F-465

Martens, Conrad (1801–1878), Australian painter A-801

Martha, sister of Lazarus and Mary, and friend of Jesus (Bible, Luke x, 38), commemorated as saint July 29.

'Martha', light opera by Friedrich von Flotow; libretto by W. Friedrich; first presented at Vienna 1847; familiar melodies 'M'appari' and 'The Last Rose of Summer'.

Marthasville, early Georgia settlement A-742

Martha's Vineyard, summer resort island off s.e. coast of Massachusetts; 23 mi (37 km) long, 2 to 10 mi (3 to 16 km) wide; 4 mi (6 km) across Vineyard Sound from Cape Cod M-189, *picture* M-201, *map* U-41

Martí, José Julián (in full José Julián Martí Pérez) (1853–95), Cuban patriot and author M-158
  Cuba C-801
  Caribbean literature C-167

Martial (in full Marcus Valerius Martialis) (AD 40–104?), Roman poet M-158

Martial arts M-158
  Japan J-57
  wrestling W-366

Martial law, rule by military authorities
  constitution C-683
  Philippines M-133

Martin, Saint (316–400), bishop of Tours, born in Hungary; a patron saint of France and of cities of Mainz, Würzburg, and Buenos Aires; feast day November 11; founded monastery of Ligugé near Poitiers, France, in 360.

Martin, popes, *table* P-99

Martin, Abraham (1589–1664), Canadian settler, born in Scotland; emigrated to Canada 1614; member of Company of New France, he received grant of land on heights of Quebec, later known as Plains of Abraham.

Martin, Archer John Porter (born 1910), English biochemist, born in London. *see also in index* Nobel Prizewinners, *table*

Martin, Everett Dean (1880–1941), U.S. writer and lecturer on social philosophy and psychology, born in Jacksonville, Ill.; formerly Congregational minister; director of Peoples Institute and of Cooper Union Forum, New York; professor of social philosophy, Claremont Colleges in California, after 1936; did much to popularize study of psychology ('Psychology'; 'Meaning of a Liberal Education').

Martin, Felix (1804–86), French Jesuit priest, historian, born in Auray, France; sent by order to re-establish Jesuit order in Canada 1842–62; designed St. Patrick's church, Montreal; biographer of French explorers and missionaries; editor of 'Jesuit Relations'.

Martin, Glenn Luther (1886–1955), U.S. airplane manufacturer, born in Macksburg, Iowa; started building and flying airplanes 1907; founded Glenn L. Martin Co. 1911.

Martin, Gregory (died 1582), English scholar, born in Maxfield, England; translator of Douay, or Douai, version of Bible.

Martin, Helen Reimensnyder (1868–1939), U.S. novelist and short-story writer, born in Lancaster, Pa.; graphic stories of Pennsylvania Dutch life ('Tillie, a Mennonite Maid' and 'Barnabetta', both dramatized; 'For a Mess of Pottage').

Martin, Homer (1836–97), U.S. landscape painter, born in Albany, N.Y.; influenced first by U.S. Hudson River School, later by French Barbizon painters.

Martin, John Joseph (1893–1985), U.S. dance critic, born in Louisville, Ky.; dance critic *New York Times* 1927–62; called dean of U.S. dance critics ('World Book of Modern Ballet'; 'John Martin's Book of the Dance').

Martin, Joseph William, Jr. (1884–1968), U.S. political leader and newspaper publisher, born in North Attleboro, Mass.; served in Massachusetts state legislature 1912–14, in state senate 1914–17; U.S. representative from Massachusetts 1925–66; permanent chairman Republican national convention 1940, 1944, 1948, 1952, 1956; Republican minority leader House of Representatives 1939–47, 1949–53, 1955–59, speaker 1947–49, 1953–55; author, 'My First Fifty Years in Politics'.

Martin, Luther (1748?–1826), U.S. lawyer and political leader, born near New Brunswick, N.J.; delegate to the Constitutional Convention at Philadelphia in 1787, but opposed strong central government and did not sign the Constitution; first attorney general of Maryland, served 1778–1805 and 1818–22; defended Aaron Burr in trial for treason (1807).

Martin, Mary (or Mrs. Richard Halliday) (born 1913), U.S. actress and singer, born in Weatherford, Tex.; made Broadway debut 1938 singing 'My Heart Belongs to Daddy'; starred in musicals: 'Lute Song', 'South Pacific', 'Peter Pan' (awarded 1955 Emmy and Tony), 'The Sound of Music'; also motion pictures.

Martin, Paul Sidney (born 1898), U.S. anthropologist, born in Chicago, Ill.; chief curator of anthropology Field Museum of Natural History 1935–64; head of many expeditions to U.S. Southwest.

Martin, Pierre Emile (1824–1915), French engineer, born in Bourges; director of steel mill at Sireuil.

Martin, Richard (1754–1834), Irish member of British Parliament; birthplace probably Dublin; instigated laws against cruel treatment of animals 1822
  humane societies H-318

Martin, William McChesney, Jr. (born 1906), U.S. broker, born in St. Louis, Mo.; first salaried president New York Stock Exchange 1938–41; in World War II 1941–45; president and board chairman Export-Import Bank 1946–49; assistant secretary of treasury 1949–51; chairman Federal Reserve Board 1951–70.

Martin du Gard, Roger (1881–1958), French author, born in Neuilly, France. *see also in index* Nobel Prizewinners, *table*

Martineau, Harriet (1802–76), English writer, born in Norwich; popularized theological speculation of her day; from a Unitarian became an agnostic ('Eastern Life, Present and Past').

Martineau, James (1805–1900), English philosopher and Unitarian divine, born in Norwich; brother of Harriet Martineau; great influence as preacher in Liverpool and London; professor mental and moral philosophy at Manchester New College ('Endeavors After the Christian Life'; 'Types of Ethical Theory').

Martinelli, Giovanni (1885–1969), Italian operatic tenor, born in Montagnana, n.e. Italy; to U.S. 1913; a leading tenor with Metropolitan Opera Company, New York City, 1913–46.

Martinez, Calif., city on Suisan Bay 16 mi (26 km) n.e. of Oakland; oil refineries; cannery; veterans hospital; incorporated 1876; pop. 22,582.

Martínez Sierra, Gregorio (1881–1947), Spanish writer of plays, born in Madrid; collaborated with his wife, María de la O Lejárraga; helped replace old melodramas of Spanish stage with plays of delicacy ('The Cradle Song'; 'The Kingdom of God') S-365b

'Martín Fierro', poem by Hernández A-580

Martingale, horseback riding gear, *diagram* H-265

Martini, Giovanni Battista (1706–84), Italian musician, born in Bologna; teacher of composition, writer on theory of music; composed sacred music
  Mozart M-643

Martini, Simone (1285?–1344), Italian painter of Sienese school, pupil of Duccio; works highly decorative, influenced by Byzantine tradition; his exquisite surfaces, beautiful color, and sinuous line evident in subsequent Sienese painting; best known for frescoes for churches of Assisi, Siena, Naples, and Orvieto.

Martinique, island of West Indies; French overseas department; 421 sq mi (1,091 sq km); pop. 328,000 M-160
  French colonies A-337
  North America, *map* N-351
  West Indies W-155, *map* W-159

Martin of Troppau, Polish Dominican monk J-118

Martinon, Jean (1910–76), French composer and conductor, born in Lyons; toured world as guest conductor; director general of music Düsseldorf, West Germany, 1960–63; music director Chicago Symphony Orchestra 1963–68.

Martins, Peter (born 1946), ballet dancer and choreographer, born in Copenhagen, Denmark; became director of New York City Ballet in 1983 D-24

Martinsburg, W. Va., industrial city in n.e. part of state about 18 mi (29 km) s.w. of Hagerstown, Md.; hosiery, dresses, fruit products, limestone, cement, brick, explosives; veterans hospital nearby; strategic point in Civil War; pop. 13,063.

Martins Ferry, Ohio, industrial city on Ohio River almost opposite Wheeling, W. Va.; in coal region; steel products; birthplace of William Dean Howells; pop. 9,331.

Martinson, Harry (1904–78), Swedish author, born in Jämshög; over 20 volumes of poetry, stories, essays, and full-length fiction, including 'Aniara', an epic poem cycle; Swedish Academy 1949. *see also in index* Nobel Prizewinners, *table*

Martinsville, Va., city 40 mi (60 km) s. of Roanoke; in timber and farm area; tobacco market; furniture, knit goods, hosiery, nylon yarn, glass and mirrors, textiles, paper products; branch campus of University of Virginia; pop. 18,149, *map* V-348

Martin Vaz Rocks, group of three barren islets in South Atlantic Ocean.

Martin vs. Hunter's Lessee, case in U.S. constitutional law, *list* S-518b

Martiny, Philip (1858–1927), U.S. sculptor, born in Strasbourg, France; works include the sculpture for the grand staircase of the Congressional Library in Washington, D.C.; Soldiers and Sailors Monument in Jersey City, N.J.

Martland, Ronald (born 1907), Canadian jurist, born in Liverpool, England; created king's counsel 1943; judge of the Supreme Court of Canada 1958–82.

Martlet, in heraldry, *picture* H-136

Martyn, Edward (1859–1923), Irish playwright and critic, born in County Galway; a founder of Irish Literary Theatre 1899; president of Sinn Fein 1904–08 I-327

Martynia, plant. *see in index* Unicorn plant

Martynia family (or Martyniaceae), family of plants, native to the tropical regions, including proboscis flower, or unicorn plant, and South American vegetable escorzonera.

Martyr M-161. *see also in index* martyrs by name, as Christopher, Saint; Latimer, Hugh; Saints of North America

'Martyrdom of Isaiah, The', Jewish folktale F-263

'Martyrdom of Saint Maurice and the Theban Legion', painting by El Greco G-253

Martyrs' Day, annual commemoration of slaughter of Armenians by Turkish government that began April 24, 1915 G-60

Marvel, Ik (pen name of Donald G. Mitchell) (1822–1908), U.S. author, born in Norwich, Conn.; contributed to leading U.S. magazines from 1842 to 1897 ('Reveries of a Bachelor'; 'Dream Life').

Marvell, Andrew (1621–78), English poet and satirist M-161
- English literature E-269

Marvel of Peru. *see in index* Four-o'clock family

Marvin, Charles Frederick (1858–1943), U.S. meteorologist, born in Putnam, Ohio; chief, U.S. Weather Bureau 1913–34; invented a sunshine recorder and other weather instruments.

Marwar, India. *see in index* Jodhpur

Marx, Karl (1818–83), German philosopher M-162
- capitalism C-152
- civilization C-467
  - China 357
- cultural anthropology A-485
- government G-199
  - communism C-619
- Hegel H-115
  - totalitarianism T-235
- philosophy of history H-174
- religion R-332e
- socialism S-234
- Vico V-308

Marx, Wilhelm (1863–1946), German political leader, born in Cologne; entered Reichstag 1910; a leader of Center party, of which he became president 1921; chancellor of Reich 1923–24 and 1926–28.

Marx Brothers, comedians of vaudeville, films, Broadway musicals, and radio; **Chico** (Leonard, 1891–1961), **Harpo** (Adolph Arthur, 1893–1964), **Groucho** (Julius Henry, 1895–1977), **Gummo** (Milton, 1893–1977), and **Zeppo** (Herbert, 1901–79) M-162
- word games W-293

Marxism, philosophy developed by Karl Marx
- China's application C-349, 357
  - Mao Zedong M-111
- philosophy of history H-171

Marxism-Leninism-Mao Thought, Marxism as interpreted by Mao Zedong C-357

Mary, mother of Jesus; feast day May 31 (established 1955) M-163
- Della Robbia's 'Madonna and the Angels', *picture* P-474
- Jesus J-103
- Lippi L-233
- Michelangelo's 'Madonna della Pieta' V-268
- painting P-28, 67h, *pictures* P-29, 32, 40
- sculpture S-79

Mary (1867–1953), queen of George V of England; daughter of Francis, duke of Teck G-81
- Indian coronation, *picture* C-599

Mary, Queen of Scots (or Mary Stuart) (1542–87) M-164
- Elizabeth I E-190
- Knox K-265
- Scotland S-70
- Scott's portrayal S-74
- Stuart S-493

Mary I (also called Mary Tudor, nickname Bloody Mary) (1516–58), queen of England M-165
- Catholicism A-418
- Cranmer C-761
- Elizabeth I E-190
- England E-244
- House of Tudor T-304
- Lady Jane Grey G-285

Mary II (1662–94), queen of England; joint ruler with William III M-165. *see also in index* William III
- England E-247
- Glorious Revolution G-168
- Stuart S-493

Mary, sister of Martha and Lazarus (Bible, Luke x, 38–42; John xi, 1–46, and xii, 1–9); sometimes identified with St. Mary Magdalene.

Mary (formerly Merv), U.S.S.R., city in Turkmen S.S.R., in oasis on Murgab River 130 mi (210 km) n. of Afghan frontier; developed in 19th century as Merv w. of old Islamic city Merv; pop. 61,738
- Asia, *map* A-700

Mary Baldwin College, Staunton, Va.; Presbyterian; for women; founded 1842; arts and sciences, education; overseas junior program.

Maryborough, Queensland, Australia A-776, *maps* A-819, P-3

'Mary Celeste', mystery ship S-177a, *picture* S-177b
- Nova Scotia N-397

Mary College, Bismarck, N.D.; Roman Catholic; established 1955; liberal arts, teacher education.

Marycrest College, Davenport, Iowa; Roman Catholic; opened 1939 as women's division of St. Ambrose College, became independent 1954; liberal arts, nursing, and teacher education; graduate school.

Maryes' Height, low ridge behind Fredericksburg, Va.; position held by Confederates in battle of Fredericksburg.

Marygrove College, Detroit, Mich.; Roman Catholic; founded 1910; arts and sciences, education; graduate studies.

"Mary had a little lamb." *see in index* 'Mary's Lamb'

Mary Hardin-Baylor College, Belton, Tex.; Southern Baptist; coeducational, formerly for women; chartered 1845; arts and sciences, Bible and social science, biological and social sciences, education, language and literature, music.

Maryland, Middle Atlantic state of U.S.; 10,577 sq mi (27,394 sq km); cap. Annapolis; pop. 4,216,446 M-166, *maps* U-41, 50, 59
- Chesapeake Bay C-304
- cities. *see also in index* cities listed below and other cities by name
  - Baltimore B-47
- geographic regions, *maps* U-50, 58
  - Middle Atlantic U-49, *map* U-50, *picture* U-52, *Reference-Outline* U-133
  - South U-56, *map* U-58, *picture* U-57, *Reference-Outline* U-133
- history
  - Alexandria Conference U-139–40
  - Annapolis Convention U-140
  - Civil War C-473
  - colonial period A-337
  - *Peggy Stewart* burning, *picture* R-169
- North America, *map* N-351
- parks and other areas
  - national cemetery at Antietam N-23
- population density, *chart* P-261b
- Potomac River P-468
- state symbols
  - flag, *picture* F-159
  - flower, *picture* S-427
- Statuary Hall, *table* S-437a
- taxation, *tables* T-37, 39
- Washington, D.C. W-66

'Maryland, My Maryland', U.S. patriotic song M-172, N-65

Maryland, University of, College Park, Md.; state control; founded 1807; arts and sciences, agriculture, architecture, business and public administration, education, engineering, home economics, physical education, and recreation and health; graduate school; dentistry, law, medicine, nursing, pharmacy, social work, and graduate studies at Baltimore; branch campuses at Baltimore and Catonsville; University of Maryland Eastern Shore at Princess Anne; overseas program North Atlantic, Europe, Near and Far East B-49, *map* B-48
- Maryland M-170, *picture* M-175

Maryland Eastern Shore, University of, Princess Anne, Md.; division of University of Maryland; founded 1886; arts and sciences, agriculture, education, home economics, mechanic arts.

Maryland yellowthroat, bird. *see also in index* Yellowthroat

Marylhurst Education Center (formerly Marylhurst College), Marylhurst, Ore.; private control, Catholic related; founded 1930; arts and sciences, education, medical technology, music.

Mary Magdalene, Saint (or Mary of Magdala), devoted follower of Jesus (Bible, John xx); commemorated as saint July 22
- Jesus J-104

Mary Manse College, Toledo, Ohio; Roman Catholic; founded 1873 as Ursuline Convent of the Sacred Heart; became college 1922; closed 1974.

Marymount College, Los Angeles, Calif.; Roman Catholic; chartered 1948; arts and sciences; merged with Loyola University of Los Angeles 1973 to form Loyola Marymount University. *see also in index* Loyola Marymount University

Marymount College, Salina, Kan.; Roman Catholic; coeducational, formerly for women; founded 1922; arts and sciences, music, nursing, and teacher education.

Marymount College, Tarrytown, N.Y.; private control, Catholic related; for women; founded 1907; former branch in New York, N.Y., now Marymount Manhattan College; arts and sciences.

Marymount Manhattan College, New York, N.Y.; private control, Catholic related; for women; incorporated 1961; former branch of Marymount College, at Tarrytown; liberal arts.

Mary of Guise (or Mary of Lorraine) (1515–60), queen of James V of Scotland, later regent for her daughter, Mary, queen of Scots; arranged French alliance; used Scotland to aggrandize Guise family; opposed Protestant movement.

Mary of Modena (1658–1718), second wife of King James II of England J-19

Mary Queen of the World Cathedral-Basilica (formerly St. James Cathedral), Montreal, Que., scaled-down copy of St. Peter's in Rome, and Notre-Dame-de-Bon-Secours Chapel M-572, *picture* M-570

Mary's gold. *see in index* Marigold

'Mary's Lamb', familiar jingle by Sarah J. Hale, published 1830 in *Juvenile Miscellany*; known by first line, "Mary had a little lamb."

Mary Stuart. *see in index* Mary, Queen of Scots

Mary Tudor. *see in index* Mary I

Maryville, Tenn., city 14 mi (22 km) s. of Knoxville; aluminum, apparel, lumber, marble; pop. 17,480.

Maryville College, Maryville, Tenn.; Presbyterian; founded 1819; arts and sciences, business administration, education, fine arts, home economics, physical education.

Maryville College (formerly Maryville College of the Sacred Heart), St. Louis, Mo.; Roman Catholic; established in 1872; arts and sciences, art, education, music, and speech.

Mary Washington College of the University of Virginia, 1938–44 and since 1972 Mary Washington College, Fredericksburg, Va.; state control; chartered 1908 as normal school; independent of University of Virginia since 1974; liberal arts and sciences, education.

Marywood College, Scranton, Pa.; private control, Catholic related; coeducational, formerly for women; founded 1915; arts and sciences, education, social work; graduate division.

Marzipan, candy C-137

Masaccio (nickname of Tommaso di Giovanni di Simone Guidi) (1401–28?), Italian painter M-184
- 'The Tribute Money' P-32, *picture* P-33

Más Afuera, island in South Pacific. *see in index* Juan Fernández

Masai (or Maasai), African people speaking a Hamitic language and living in Kenya and Tanzania
- Kenya K-224
- nomads N-332

Masai-Amboseli Game Reserve, Kenya, *picture* K-224

Masaoka, Shiki (1867–1902), Japanese writer J-82

Masaryk, Jan Garrigue (1886–1948), Czechoslovakian statesman, born in Prague; minister to United Kingdom 1925–38; lectured in U.S. 1939–40; foreign minister, serving Czech government 1940–48; died of fall from his apartment window in Prague after Communists came to power; son of Thomas Masaryk.

Masaryk, Tomáš (also called Tomáš Garrigue Masaryk) (1850–1937), president of Czechoslovakia M-184
- Czechoslovakia C-815

Más a Tierra, island in South Pacific. *see in index* Juan Fernández

Masbate, island in central Philippines; area 1,262 sq mi (3,268 sq km); livestock; pop. 387,721 P-259b, *map* P-261d

Mascagni, Pietro (1863–1945), Italian composer M-184
- opera O-568

'Mascarades', Basque folk dance, *picture* F-256

Mascardi, Lake, Argentina; 10 mi (16 km) long, 2 mi (3 km) wide.

Mascon, concentration of mass on moon M-576

Mascouten, people of Algonquian family who lived in Wisconsin between Fox and Wisconsin rivers, in n. Illinois, in Indiana at mouth of Wabash River, and in lower Michigan peninsula; name means little prairie people.

Masculine gender
- pronouns P-508

Masefield, John (1878–1967), English poet, dramatist, and novelist M-185
- horse H-273
- literary contribution E-280
- poet laureate P-402

Maser (full name microwave amplification by stimulated emission of radiation). *see in index* Laser and maser

Maseru, Lesotho, capital, on Caledon River; pop. 29,049 L-137, *maps* A-118, S-264

Matthews, Brander (or James Brander Matthews) (1852–1929), U.S. writer, born in New Orleans, La.; professor at Columbia University 1892–1929; criticism, essays, plays ('Shakespeare as a Playwright'; 'Principles of Playmaking'; 'Molière: His Life and His Works').

Matthews, Francis Patrick (1887–1952), U.S. lawyer and businessman, born in Albion, Neb.; president of U.S. Chamber of Commerce, 1938–39, later a director; secretary of Navy 1949–51; U.S. ambassador to Ireland 1951–52.

Matthews, William (1822–96), U.S. bookbinder, born in Aberdeen, Scotland; to U.S. 1843; head of D. Appleton & Co. bindery 1854–90; wrote books on bookbinding.

Matthias, one of the apostles; commemorated as saint Feb. 25 A-506

Matthias I, Hunyadi (1440–90), king of Hungary, also called **Matthias Corvinus** from the raven (corvus) on his escutcheon; son of Janos Hunyadi; elected king 1458, repeatedly defeated Emperor Frederick III, Turks, Poles, and became most powerful ruler in central Europe; capable as soldier, administrator, orator, lawmaker H-329

Mattingly, Thomas K. (born 1936), U.S. astronaut, born in Chicago, Ill.; U.S. Navy officer chosen for NASA program 1966; assigned to space shuttle operations, *table* S-348

Matto de Turner, Clorinda (1852–1909), Peruvian writer L-70

Matto Grosso, state in Brazil. *see in index* Mato Grosso

Mattoon, Ill., city in agricultural and oil-drilling area about 40 mi (60 km) s.e. of Decatur; road machinery, flash bulbs, frozen foods, metal hose, springs; pop. 19,787
Illinois, *map* I-53

Matura diamond, colorless natural zircon or one that has been decolorized by heat; from Sri Lanka; used as a gem; nearly as brilliant as diamond.

Maturation, in child development
reading readiness R-101b

Maturity
emotional E-205
physical. *see in index* Child development

Matzeliger, Jan Ernst (1852–89), U.S. inventor, born in Surinam; to U.S. about 1872; in Lynn, Mass., invented machine, patented 1883, for shaping shoes over lasts
Lynn, Mass. statue B-299

Matzoth (or matzos), unleavened bread
ceremonial use P-136

Maubeuge, France, fortified town near Belgian border, 45 mi (70 km) s.e. of Lille; taken by Germans 1914 and 1940; pop. 31,992, *map* F-372

Maude, Sir Frederick Stanley (1864–1917), British general in World War I, born in Gibraltar; took part in Dardanelles and Kut-al-Amara relief expeditions.

Maudling, Reginald (1917–79), British statesman and lawyer, born in London; member of Parliament after 1950; deputy leader of Conservatives from 1965; chancellor of exchequer 1962–64; home secretary 1970–72.

Mau Escarpment, Kenya G-250

Maugham, Somerset (in full William Somerset Maugham) (1874–1965), English novelist, short-story writer, and dramatist M-231
drama D-247
literary contribution E-280, *picture* E-282
young adult literature R-111g

Maui, Hawaiian folk hero S-468

Maui, island of Hawaii; 728.8 sq mi (1,887.6 sq km); pop. 62,823 H-58
Pacific Ocean, *map* P-3
pineapple harvesting, *picture* P-191
United States, *maps* U-98, 117, *pictures* U-97, U-99

Mauldin, Bill (full name William Henry Mauldin) (born 1921), U.S. cartoonist, born in Mountain Park, N.M.; in U.S. Army 1940–45; on *45th Division News* and *Stars and Stripes*, Army publications; *St. Louis Post-Dispatch* 1958–62; awarded Pulitzer prizes 1945, 1959 for cartoons; *Chicago Sun-Times* after 1962 ('Mud, Mules and Mountains'; 'Up Front'; 'Back Home'; 'What's Got Your Back Up?').

Mau Mau, African guerrilla group K-227

Maumee, Ohio, city on Maumee River 8 mi (13 km) s.w. of Toledo; grain-handling port; road-building equipment, electronic products; pop. 15,747.

Maumee River, flows into Lake Erie near Toledo, Ohio, after course of 150 mi (240 km) through n.e. Indiana and n.w. Ohio.

Mauna Kea (Hawaiian, "white mountain"), extinct volcano on island of Hawaii; highest peak in state (13,796 ft; 4,205 m) H-58
comparative height. *see in index* Mountain, *table* ocean volcanic peaks O-401
Pacific Ocean, *map* P-3
Oceania O-467

Mauna Loa (Hawaiian, "great mountain"), active volcano on island of Hawaii, part of Hawaii Volcanoes National Park; 13,680 ft (4,170 m) H-58
basalt shield B-86
lava and magma L-89
mountain M-633
Oceania O-466

Maundy Thursday (or Holy Thursday) E-41

Maunoury, Michel Joseph (1847–1923), French general, born in Maintenon, near Chartres; recalled from retired list in 1914; commanded VI Army, which turned Von Kluck's left flank at first battle of Marne.

Maupassant, Guy de (in full Henri-René-Albert-Guy de Maupassant) (1850–93), French short-story writer and novelist M-231
creative writing W-380
Flaubert's tutoring F-176
French literature F-397, *picture* F-396

Maurandia, genus of perennial plants of figwort family, climbing by means of the leaf stems; native to Mexico and s.w. U.S.; related to snapdragon; leaves triangular; flowers irregular trumpet-shaped, white through blue.

Maurepas, Lake, s.e. Louisiana; 13 mi (21 km) long; connected with Lake Pontchartrain by 3 mi (5 km) channel.

Mauretania, ancient name for n.w. Africa, comprising modern Morocco and w. Algeria; in time of Augustus an independent kingdom; later was made two Roman provinces. *see also in index* Morocco

'Mauretania', ocean liner S-177f

Mauriac, Claude (born 1914), French writer F-398

Mauriac, François (1885–1970), French author, born in Bordeaux F-397

Maurice (539?–602), Byzantine emperor
Khosrow II K-232

'Maurice Guest', work by Richardson A-797

Maurice of Nassau (1567–1625), prince of Orange (son of William the Silent), Dutch general, one of ablest of his age, born in Dillenburg, Prussia; successfully resisted Spanish domination.

Maurice of Saxony (1521–53), duke and, by conquest of his cousin John Frederick, elector of Saxony, born in Freiberg, Saxony; one of foremost generals and most cunning diplomats of his day; extorted from Emperor Charles V, Treaty of Passau (1552), giving Protestants liberty of worship until Diet of Augsburg.

Maurice River, river in s. New Jersey; flows s. into Delaware Bay; navigable to Millville.

Mauritania (officially Islamic Republic of Mauritania), country in n.w. Africa on Atlantic Ocean; 397,700 sq mi (1,030,000 sq km); cap. Nouakchott; pop. 1,561,000 M-233
Africa, *map* A-118, *table* A-112
flag, *picture* F-167
Morocco M-587
railroad mileage, *table* R-85
Sahara S-14, *map* S-15
Western Sahara W-154

Mauritius (formerly Île de France), island in Indian Ocean; area 720 sq mi (1,860 sq km); pop. 881,100; with island dependencies, it forms the nation Mauritius: 788 sq mi (2,040 sq km); cap. Port Louis; pop. 993,700 M-233
African political unit, *table* A-112
Commonwealth membership C-602
flag, *picture* F-168
stamps, *picture* S-406
United Kingdom E-259

Mauritshuis, palace in The Netherlands; houses the royal art gallery H-5

Maurois, André (or Émile Herzog) (1885–1967), French writer, born in Elbeuf, near Rouen; liaison officer in British army in World War I, in French army in World War II; in U.S. much of time after 1940; popular for fictionalized biographies; 'Ariel' (Shelley); 'Disraeli'; 'I Remember, I Remember' (autobiography); 'Proust'; 'Lélia' (George Sand); 'Alexandre Dumas'; 'Olympio' (Victor Hugo) B-223

Maurras, Charles (1868–1952), French critic and journalist, born in Martigues, near Marseilles; a staunch nationalist; he preached discipline in art, politics, morality; influenced Italian Fascisti; imprisoned Feb. 1945 for collaboration with Germans ('Trois idées politiques'; 'Les amants de Venise'; 'Jean Moréas'; 'L'Étang de Berre').

Maury, Matthew Fontaine (1806–73), U.S. oceanographer and meteorologist M-234
Atlantic ocean A-746
Confederacy C-644
Hall of Fame, *table* H-16
navigation N-78

Maurya Empire, of ancient India M-234
Asoka A-701
India I-76

Mausoleum, large above-ground burial site D-50

Mausoleum at Halicarnassus S-115

Mausolus (4th century BC), king of Caria, whose wife Artemisia erected famous "mausoleum" at Halicarnassus to his memory S-115

Mauthe Doog (or Barghest, or Gwyllgi), legendary dog
folklore F-261

Mauve, Anton (1838–88), Dutch landscape and animal painter, chiefly self-taught; most celebrated for his quiet rural scenes of The Netherlands, which he interpreted with insight and feeling.

Mauve, delicate purple or lilac color; also a purple dye.

Mauveine, synthetic purple dye D-296

Mauvoisin Dam, in Switzerland, on Drance River D-17

Maverick, Samuel Augustus (1803–70), U.S. pioneer and lawyer, born in South Carolina; a founder of Republic of Texas
cattle ranching C-752

Maverick, in cattle ranching
cowboys C-752

Mavis (or song thrush), bird *Turdus ericetorum* of the family Turdidae T-177

Mavor, James (1854–1925), Canadian political economist, born in Stranraer, Scotland; professor of political economy, University of Toronto 1892–1923, author of government reports on immigration and on Canada's wheat-producing capacity.

Mawenzi, Mount, Tanzania K-237. *see also in index* Kilimanjaro

Mawson, Sir Douglas (1882–1958), Australian explorer and geologist, born in Bradford, England; one of two members of Shackleton's expedition who located south magnetic pole; commanded expeditions to Antarctic
Antarctic exploration, *table* P-422

Max, Adolphe (1869–1939), Belgian public official, born in Brussels; burgomaster of Brussels at beginning of World War I; for 3 months, until imprisoned in Germany, heroically resisted Germans who occupied city; afterward member Belgium Chamber of Representatives and minister of state.

Max Berg Award, annual $10,000 prize given by David and Minnie Berg Foundation for achievements in "prolonging or improving the quality of human life"; honors David's late brother, a lawyer noted for his philanthropy; first granted 1966 to Michael de Bakey and Adrian Kantrowitz.

Maxentius, Marcus Aurelius Valerius (died 312), elected Roman emperor in the West, AD 306; defeated and killed in battle against Constantine
Constantine the Great C-680

Maxilla. *see in index* Superior maxiilla

Maxim, Hiram Percy (1869–1936), U.S. inventor, born in Brooklyn, N.Y.; invented Maxim silencer for firearms, and applied principle to silencing other noises; founded (1914) the American Radio Relay League, president 1914–36; son of Sir Hiram Stevens Maxim and nephew of Hudson Maxim
machine gun M-13

Maxim, Sir Hiram Stevens (1840–1916), U.S. inventor, born in Sangerville, Me.; invented Maxim automatic machine gun; became British subject in 1900; brother of Hudson Maxim, *picture* R-263
aircraft A-201

Maxim, Hudson (1853–1927), U.S. inventor, born in Orneville, Me.; invented explosives and was first to make smokeless gunpowder in U.S.; brother of Sir Hiram Stevens Maxim.

Maxime, French form of epigram cultivated by La Rochefoucauld L-51

'Maximes' (or 'Réflexions ou sentences et maximes morales'), work by La Rochefoucauld L-51

Maximilian (1832–67), archduke of Austria and emperor of Mexico; younger brother of Emperor Francis Joseph; established on Mexican throne 1864 by France J-145
Mexico M-337

Maximilian I (1459–1519), Holy Roman emperor, born in Wiener Neustadt, near Vienna, Austria A-828
The Netherlands N-129

Maximilian I (1756–1825), first king of Bavaria, born in Schwetzingen, near Heidelberg, Germany; succeeded as elector 1799; aided Napoleon, received title of king as reward.

Maximilian I (also called Maximilian the Great) (1573–1651), elector and duke of Bavaria; formed Catholic League, which opposed Protestant Union in Thirty Years' War; party to Peace of Westphalia 1648; considered ablest Catholic ruler of his time.

Maximilian II (1811–64), king of Bavaria, monarch of liberal tendencies; succeeded to throne on abdication of his father 1848; opposed exclusion of Austria from German Confederation; father of the kings Ludwig II and Otto.

Maximilian, prince of Baden (or Max of Baden) (1867–1929), German soldier and statesman; as imperial chancellor (appointed Oct. 3, 1918), he began negotiations for armistice; forced Kaiser William II to abdicate; gave government control to Friedrich Ebert Nov. 1918.

Maximilian Alexander Philipp, prince of Wied-Neuwied (1782–1867), German soldier and traveler; general in Prussian army; explored Brazil; traveled in U.S. ('Travels in the Interior of North America').

Maxwell, James Clerk (1831–79), Scottish physicist M-234
atomic particles A-756
electrical theories E-158, P-307, S-58
light theory L-201, R-33
magnetism M-45
photography P-298

Maxwell Air Force Base, Montgomery, Ala. M-569
Maxwell's equations, in physics M-234
May, Cornelius. *see in index* Mey, Cornelius
May, Karl (1842–1912), German author of adventure and travel; stories often dealt with American Indians in the West W-151
May, Philip William (1864–1903), English black-and-white artist, skilled in using the fewest possible lines; chiefly depicted "low life" in London.
May, 5th month of the Gregorian calendar
birthdays of famous persons. *see in index* Birthdays, *table*
calendar C-30
Maya, people M-235
American Indians I-146, *picture* I-145
archaeologists study A-531
astronomy and archaeoastronomy A-728
Aztecs A-891
calendar C-29
Chichén Itzá A-533, *picture* A-537
civilization, *pictures* P-365, S-82
feathers' use F-51
Latin America L-61
Central America C-254
Guatemala G-296
Mexico M-325, 335
Yucatán peninsula Y-432
migration of people M-402
pyramids P-543
stele S-82, A-538, *pictures* S-82, P-365
temple, *pictures* A-531, 537, M-336
writing W-371, *picture* W-370
archeology A-486, *picture* S-82
Mayaguana, one of southernmost of Bahama Islands; area 96 sq mi (249 sq km); pop. 613
North America, *map* N-351
West Indies, *map* W-159
Mayagüez, Puerto Rico, city on w. coast; railway connection with interior; export trade; campus of University of Puerto Rico; pop. 82,968 P-529
West Indies, *map* W-159
Mayakovski, Vladimir Vladimirovich (1893–1930), Soviet poet and dramatist, born in Bagdadi (now Mayakovski), U.S.S.R. R-360a
Mayapán, ancient city of Yucatán s.e. of Mérida; Mayan ruins.
Mayapple, often erroneously called **Mandrake** in U.S., plant *Podophyllum pellatum* M-237
May beetle. *see in index* June Bug
May Day, festival
Robin Hood R-224
U.S.S.R., *picture* R-332b
Mayence, West Germany. *see in index* Mainz
Mayer, Julius Robert von (1814–78), German physician and physicist, born in Heilbronn, Württemberg; first to suggest theory of conservation of energy; applied mechanical theories to study of animal heat.
Mayer, Maria Goeppert (1906–72), U.S. physicist M-238
nuclear physics N-432
Mayer, René (1895–1972), French statesman and economist, born in Paris; minister of finance 1947–48 and 1951–52; minister of justice 1949–51; prime minister Jan.–May 1953; chairman High Authority of European Coal and Steel Community 1955–57.
Mayfair, district in London, U.K. L-293
Mayfield Heights, Ohio, residential city 12 mi (19 km) e. of Cleveland in Cuyahoga County; incorporated as a city in 1925; pop. 21,550.
Mayflower. *see in index* Trailing arbutus
'Mayflower', Pilgrims' ship M-238
landing C-147
Massachusetts M-194
'Mayflower II', copy of the original ship of Pilgrims; crossed Atlantic under Commander Alan Villiers 1957 P-395, *picture* P-396
Massachusetts, *picture* M-201
'Mayflower' M-239
Mayflower Compact, agreement written and signed by settlers to New England when they arrived at Plymouth aboard the 'Mayflower' M-239, A-341
Mayflower Descendants, Society of P-140
Mayfly (or day fly, or ephemera, or shad fly), insect M-239, *picture* I-215
May Fourth Movement, (1919–21) intellectual revolution and reform movement in China directed toward national independence, emancipation of the individual, and rebuilding society and culture C-372
Mao Zedong M-111
Mayhem, unlawful use of physical force on another person causing the crippling, mutilation, or disfigurement of part of the victim's body
crime C-770
Maykop (or Maikop), U.S.S.R., city in n.w. Caucasia 60 mi (100 km) s.e. of Krasnodar; oil fields; pop. 111,000, *maps* R-344, 349
Maynor, Dorothy (born 1910), U.S. soprano, born in Norfolk, Va.; debut in New York City 1939; appeared in recital and with leading symphony orchestras of U.S.; sympathetic interpretation of Negro spirituals; founder and director of Harlem School of the Arts.
Mayo, Charles William (1898–1968), U.S. surgeon, born in Rochester, Minn.; son of Charles Horace Mayo; surgeon Mayo Clinic 1931–63; taught surgery University of Minnesota; alternate delegate to UN 1953 M-240
Mayo, Henry Thomas (1856–1937), U.S. Navy officer, born in Burlington, Vt.; admiral and commander in chief Atlantic fleet 1916–19, of U.S. fleet 1919; reverted to rear admiral upon division of fleet; retired 1920.
Mayo, Robert Porter (born 1916), U.S. banker and public official, born in Seattle, Wash.; assistant to U.S. secretary of the treasury 1959–60; vice-president Continental Illinois National Bank and Trust Company of Chicago 1960–69; director U.S. Bureau of the Budget 1969–70; president Federal Reserve Bank of Chicago 1970–.
Mayo, William James (1861–1939), U.S. surgeon, and **Charles Horace Mayo** (1865–1939), U.S. surgeon, brothers who developed famous Mayo Clinic M-240. *see also in index* Mayo Clinic
Mayo, William Worrall (1819–1911), U.S. surgeon M-240. *see also in index* Mayo Clinic
Mayo, 3rd largest county in Ireland (2,084 sq mi; 5,398 sq km), in Connaught Province; bounded n. and w. by Atlantic; mountainous in w., flat in e.; cattle, salmon; linen; pop. 115,547.
Mayo Clinic, surgical and medical clinic at Rochester, Minn.; created through joint efforts of William W. Mayo and his sons, William J. and Charles H., who began practicing together in St. Mary's Hospital 1889; name in informal usage after 1905 when other doctors were added to staff; first Mayo Clinic building opened 1914
Mayo family M-240
Minnesota M-439
Mayo Clinic Museum, Rochester, Minn., *picture* M-450
Mayon, volcano in Philippines P-259, *maps* P-259a, 262, *picture* P-253
Mayonnaise, thick sauce made from egg yolks, vinegar or lemon juice, vegetable oil, and seasoning; used chiefly as salad dressing
colloid C-547
Mayor, chief executive of villages, towns and cities
municipal government M-654
United Kingdom U-18
Mayor-council government, oldest, most common form of municipal government with mayor executive to whom department heads (fire, police, etc.) are responsible; serves 2–4 years; single chamber council enacts laws, confirms or rejects mayor's appointments, may override his or her veto by 2/3 or 3/4 majority; members (councilmen or aldermen) elected by ward, at large, or in combination for 1–4 years C-458
municipal government M-654
Mayor of the Palace (or major domus), official in Frankish Kingdom under Merovingian rule
Charles Martel C-279
Mayotte, island off e. Africa, French dependency (special collectivity); formerly part of Comoros; 146 sq mi (378 sq km); cap. Dzaoudzi; pop. 46,500 C-620, *map* A-118
African political unit, *table* A-112
France F-366
Maypole S-525
dance, *picture* S-526
Mays, Benjamin Elijah (1895–1984), U.S. educator and minister, born in Epworth, S.C.; dean School of Religion, Howard University, 1934–40; president Morehouse College 1940–67; adviser to Martin Luther King, Jr.; president of Atlanta Board of Education from 1970.
Mays, Willie Howard (born 1931), U.S. baseball player, born in Westfield, Ala.; outfielder Giants 1951–72 (New York 1951–57, San Francisco 1958–72), New York Mets 1972–73; home-run champion of National League 1955, 1962, 1964, and 1965; in 1966 became second greatest home-run hitter of major leagues; in 1969 made 600th home run; in 1970 had 3,000th hit B-83, *pictures* B-90, *profile* B-95
Mays Island, in Cedar Rapids, Iowa, *picture* I-297
Maytag Zoo, Phoenix, Ariz. Z-460
Mayville State College, Mayville, N.D.; established in 1889; formerly a teachers college; liberal arts, education.
May wine, German punch W-237
Maywood, Calif., city 5 mi (8 km) s. of Los Angeles, on Los Angeles River; chiefly residential city for surrounding industrial area; pop. 21,810.
Maywood, Ill., village on Des Plaines River about 10 mi (16 km) w. of Chicago; soft drinks; food processing; Loyola University Medical Center; veterans hospital nearby; pop. 27,998
Illinois, *map* I-53
Maywood, N.J., borough 6 mi (10 km) s.e. of Paterson; chemicals, pharmaceuticals, malt products; pop. 9,895.
Mazagan, Morocco. *see in index* El Jadida
Mazarin, Jules (originally called Giulio Mazarini) (1602–61), French cardinal and statesman M-240
Colbert C-544
Mazarin Bible. *see in index* Gutenberg Bible
Mazar-i-Sharif (or Mazar-i-Sherif), Afghanistan, fortified city and important military post; its mosque is venerated as tomb of Ali, son-in-law of Mohammed; pop. 76,666.
Mazatlán, Mexico, port and resort on w. coast at entrance to Gulf of California; shrimp, fish; outlet for agricultural and mining region; pop. 154,140
North America, *map* N-351
Mazda, in Zoroastrianism. *see in index* Ahura Mazda
Mazeppa, Ivan (1644–1709), Cossack chief, powerful in Russia during reign of Peter the Great; deserted to Charles XII of Sweden; subject of a poem by Byron and of a symphonic poem by Liszt.
Mazovia, ancient principality and culture group of Slavic peoples
Warsaw W-34
Mazurka, national Polish dance in triple time with moderate tempo, danced by four or eight couples
Czechoslovakia, *picture* S-215
music, *list* M-670
Mazurov, Kyril Trofimovich (born 1918?), Soviet statesman; member Central Committee of Communist party 1956–; full member of Presidium 1965–66, Politburo 1966–78; a first deputy premier 1965–78.
Mazzini, Giuseppe (1805–72), Italian patriot M-240
Garibaldi G-31
Italian history I-393
papacy P-347
Mbabane, Swaziland; capital; pop. 22,000 S-522, *maps* A-118, S-264
Mbomu River, in Zaire, *see in index* Bomu River
Mbundu, people L-327
Mbuti, people. *see in index* Pygmy
MCAT (Medical College Admission Test) M-276
M-class, type of model ship M-516
MDA (3,4-methylenedioxy-amphetamine), hallucinogenic drug H-18
ME-109 (or Messerschmitt), German military aircraft W-333
Mead, George Herbert (1863–1931), U.S. philosopher, born in South Hadley, Mass.; professor of philosophy University of Chicago 1907–31.
Mead, Larkin Goldsmith (1835–1910), U.S. sculptor, born in Chesterfield, N.H. (Lincoln monument at Springfield, Ill.).
Mead, Margaret (1901–78), U.S. anthropologist M-241
Western Samoa W-154
Mead, William Rutherford (1846–1928), U.S. architect, born in Brattleboro, Vt., *profile* A-569. *see also in index* McKim, Charles Follen
Mead, Lake, in s.e. Nevada, at Hoover Dam (in Black Canyon of Colorado River), 115 mi (185 km) long, storage capacity 32,359,274 acre-ft (39,915,164,479 cu m); named for Dr. Elwood Mead, commissioner of reclamation while Hoover Dam was built, *map* U-87
Colorado C-584
electric power E-166
Nevada N-134, *picture* N-142
North America, *map* N-351
Meade, George G. (in full George Gordon Meade) (1815–72), U.S. Civil War general M-241
Gettysburg C-475, G-136
Meade, James Edward (born 1907), British economist; professor of commerce London School of Economics 1947–57, professor of political economy Cambridge University 1957–68; work centered on relationship between international trade and domestic economic policy. *see also in index* Nobel Prizewinners, *table*
Meader, Stephen Warren (born 1892), U.S. journalist and author of books of adventure, born in Providence, R.I.
Meade's Ranch, Kansas, surveying station S-520
Meadow beauty (or deergrass), genus of wild flowers *Rhexia* of the melastoma family, with square or round stems, opposite narrowly oval leaves and purple or yellow flowers with protruding stamens; found in bogs of North America.
Meadowcroft, Enid La Monte (1898–1966), U.S. teacher and author, born in Cranford, N.Y. ('Abe Lincoln and His Times'; 'On Indian Trails With Daniel Boone'; 'By Secret Railway'; 'Land of the Free').
Meadow fescue, perennial plant *Festuca elatior* of the grass family, native to Eurasia but naturalized in cooler parts of North America; tall with flat leaves; flower clusters, much-branched and nodding; used as hay and pasture crop.
Meadowlark, bird of the genus *Sturnella,* family Icteridae; sharp-billed, 8 to 11 in (20 to 28 cm) long; two North American species streaked brown above, with yellow breast crossed by black *V;* western meadowlark (*S. neglecta*) known for intricate fluting call
egg, *picture* E-112
song patterns A-447
Meadow mouse (or meadow vole, or field vole), mouse of the genus *Microtus*
ecological role E-51
Meadow rue (or Thalictrum), genus of perennial plants of the buttercup family, found chiefly in temperate regions; erect-growing with finely cut

respect; found especially in tribal cultures
American Indian I-141
Australian folktales, *picture* S-480
Medicine Mountain, in Wyoming, site of ancient stone patterns
archaeoastronomers A-729
Medicine Wheels, ancient stone patterns left by the Plains Indians A-729
MEDICO (or Medical International Cooperation Organization, Inc.), founded 1958 by Thomas Dooley and Peter Comanduras; nonprofit organization to provide medical facilities and aid to underdeveloped areas; joined with CARE 1962. *see also in index* CARE
Medieval period. *see in index* Middle Ages
Medill, Joseph (1823–99), U.S. journalist, born in New Brunswick; chief owner and editor, *Chicago Tribune*; ardent supporter of antislavery movement; mayor of Chicago 1871–73
newspaper publishers, *list* N-240
Medina, José Toribio (1852–1930), Chilean author and bibliographer, born in Santiago; wrote and edited books on Latin American history and geography L-72, *picture* L-71
Medina, Saudi Arabia, holy city in central Hejaz, 110 mi (180 km) e. of Red Sea; much visited by Muslim pilgrims; pop. 50,000
Asia, *map* A-700
Medina, in Tunis, Tunisia T-307
Medina Sidonia, Alonso Pérez de Guzmán, 7th duke of (1550–1615), Spanish admiral; made commander of the Spanish Armada by Philip II because of his noble rank; his lack of naval training and ability was a factor in bringing about defeat of Armada by English in 1588.
Mediolanum, ancient city in Italy, modern Milan M-408
Meditation, contemplation or reflection; focusing one's thoughts
Hinduism H-158
yoga Y-421
monks and monasticism M-540
Transcendental Meditation T-249
Zen Z-450
'Meditations', work by Marcus Aurelius M-133, C-467
Mediterranean climate
climate classification C-500
Europe E-331
France F-344
irrigation necessary I-353
United States U-86
Mediterranean fever (or Malta fever), fever of bacterial origin; occurs chiefly in Mediterranean region, occasionally in tropical America.
Mediterranean fruit fly (or medfly), destructive insect *Ceratitis capitata*; attacks fruit, nuts, and vegetables; yellow, black, and white markings, *picture* I-225
Mediterranean peoples
Mediterranean subrace R-27, *chart* R-26
Rome R-240
Western civilization B-3
Mediterranean Sea, between Europe and Africa M-286, *map* E-361. *see also in index* Ocean, *table*
Adriatic A-50
Aegean Sea A-63
Black Sea B-307
Beirut B-143
Egypt E-115, 119
France F-344, *map* F-372
Italy, *map* I-404
Phoenician trade P-267
Roman history R-242
sponge fishing S-395
Sumerian culture B-7, *map* B-4
Mediterranean subrace, Caucasoid race E-336, R-27, *chart* R-26
Medium, in spiritualism S-392
'Medium, The', opera by Menotti M-299
opera O-571
'Medium is the Massage, The', work by McLuhan M-22
Mediums. *see in index* Mass media
Medium wave, *tables* R-34, R-50
Medlar, tree *Mespilus germanica* of the rose family; a native of s. Europe and w. Asia; its fruit is good to eat only after it has begun to decay.
Medley relay, race T-244
Medulla oblongata, part of intracranial nervous system B-400, *diagram* B-399
breathing regulation R-132
Medusa, in Greek mythology, one of the Gorgons P-210
Pegasus P-152
Medusa, animal. *see in index* Jellyfish
Medusa, biological phase
invertebrate development I-282
Medway, navigable river in s.e. England, joining Thames at Sheerness near mouth; length 60 mi (100 km).
Medwick, Joseph Michael (nickname Ducky) (1911–75), U.S. baseball outfielder, born in Carteret, N.J.; with St. Louis, N.L., 1932–40, 1947–48, Brooklyn, N.L., 1940–43, 1946, New York, N.L., 1943–45, Boston, N.L., 1945; won N.L. triple crown in 1937 with .374 batting average, 154 runs driven in, and 31 home runs; lifetime batting average of .324.
Meehan family (or Meighan family)
heraldic shield, *picture* H-136
Meeker, Ezra (1830–1928), U.S. pioneer and author, born in Huntsville, Ohio; drove an ox team over Oregon Trail to Northwest 1852; returned by ox team at age of 76; for 50 years a farmer in Washington ('Ox-Team Days').
Meer, Jan van der. *see in index* Vermeer, Jan
Meerschaum (or sepiolite, sea foam), whitish claylike mineral that floats when dry; hydrous magnesium silicate; used mainly in tobacco pipes.
Meerut, India, city in Uttar Pradesh state, 35 mi (55 km) n.e. of Delhi; cotton trade; here Sepoy Rebellion first broke out (1857); pop. 270,993, *map* I-86
Asia, *map* A-700
Mees, Charles Edward Kenneth (1882–1960), U.S. chemist, born in Wellingborough, England; photograph researcher with Eastman Kodak Co. from 1912, vice-president in charge of research 1934–55 ('Photography of Colored Objects'; 'The Theory of the Photographic Process').
'Meet the Beatles' (1964), album by the Beatles M-682
Megachilidae, family of bees including leaf cutter bees, some sweat bees, and some parasitic bees B-129
Megacycle, million cycles
radio R-45, *tables* R-50, 54
television, *tables* R-54, R-34
Megali Idea, politics
Greece G-260
Megaliths, huge blocks of rough-hewn stone used by early peoples in building; associated with Neolithic culture around 3000 BC; examples at Avebury and Stonehenge
Stonehenge S-456
Megalopolis, ancient Greek walled city in Peloponnesus; founded by Epaminondas (370 BC) as capital of Arcadian confederacy; sacked by Spartans (222 BC).
Megalopolis (or interurbia), large urban cluster C-450, U-28
Japan J-27, 40
United States U-52
Megaphone S-261
Megara, in Greek mythology, first wife of Hercules, whom he gave to his friend Iolaus, when he wished to marry the daughter of King Eurytus.
Megaton (MT), unit of measure for the explosive force of a nuclear weapon N-434
Megawatt E-165
Mège-Mouries, Hippolyte, French chemist, inventor of oleomargarine M-134
Megged, Aharon (born 1920), Israeli writer
Hebrew literature H-114
Meghalaya, state in India, formerly part of Assam; area about 8,632 sq mi (22,357 sq km); cap. Shillong; pop. 1,011,699, *map* I-83
Meghna River, in East-Central Plain of Bangladesh B-61
Megiddo, ancient, fortified city in the Holy Land on border of Plain of Esdraelon; mentioned in Amarna letters and frequently in the Bible; said to be origin of word Armageddon; original walls built before 2000 BC.
Megiddo, battle of (1479 BC), warfare, *list* W-15
Mehari, riding breed of camel of the Camelidae family C-62
Meharry Medical College, Nashville, Tenn.; private control; established 1876; medicine, dentistry, medical technology, dental hygiene, X-ray technology; graduate school; only private predominantly black medical college in U.S.; has educated over half of all black physicians and dentists.
Mehemet Ali. *see in index* Muhammad 'Ali Pasha
Mehitabel, cat in novel by Marquis, *list* C-202
Mehta, Zubin (born 1936), Indian orchestral conductor, born in Bombay; conductor of Montreal Symphony 1961–67, Los Angeles Philharmonic 1962–78, New York Philharmonic 1978–
orchestra, *list* O-579
Méhul, Étienne-Nicolas (1763–1817), French composer O-565
Meighan family (or Meehan family)
heraldic shield, *picture* H-136
Meighen, Arthur (1874–1960), Canadian statesman M-287
Canada C-103
Meigs, Cornelia Lynde (1884–1973), U.S. author, born in Rock Island, Ill.; writer of historical adventure stories for young people ('Master Simon's Garden'; 'Covered Bridge'; 'The Wonderful Locomotive'; 'The Willow Whistle'); won 1934 Newbery Medal for 'Invincible Louisa', biography of Louisa May Alcott R-111d
Meiji (reign name of Mutsuhito) (1852–1912), emperor of Japan M-287
Ito I-405
Japan J-23, 28, 64, *picture* J-70
Meiklejohn, Alexander (1872–1964), U.S. educator, born in Rochdale, England; professor of philosophy and dean, Brown University 1901–12; president of Amherst College 1912–24; professor philosophy and director of experimental college, University of Wisconsin 1926–38; received 1963 Presidential Medal of Freedom.
Meilhac, Henri (1831–97), French dramatist, born in Paris; collaborated with Ludovic Halévy on operettas, farces, comedies about foibles of Parisian society; music for operettas was composed by Offenbach ('La Belle Hélène').
Meinesz, Felix Andries Vening. *see in index* Vening Meinesz, Felix Andries
'Mein Kampf', work by Adolf Hitler, first published 1925; several revised editions; translated into many languages, including Chinese; circulation in millions H-175
Meiosis, sex cell division
cell C-239, *diagram* C-241
embryology E-199
genetics G-54
yeast Y-411
Meir, Golda (adopted name of Goldie Mabovitch) (1898–1978), Israeli leader M-287
women's rights W-276
Meise, Belgium, site of National Botanic Garden, *table* B-379
Meissen, East Germany, town on Elbe River 15 mi (25 km) n.w. of Dresden; 13th-century cathedral; pop. 47,806, *map* G-134
Meissen ware P-475, *picture* P-469
Meissonier, Jean Louis Ernest (1815–91), French painter, born in Lyons; highly realistic historical, military, and genre subjects; one of best miniature painters in France.
'Meistersinger von Nurnberg, Die' ('The Mastersinger of Nuremberg'), opera by Wagner O-568
Meitner, Lise (1878–1968), Austrian physicist M-287
Meizhou Island. *see in index* Matsu Island
Meknès, Morocco, city in north on railway between Fez and Rabat; old city has mosques and sultan's summer palace; new city a trade center; pop. 403,000.
Mekong delta, delta of Mekong River, Vietnam D-90
Mekong River, in s.e. Asia; 2,600 mi (4,200 km) long; rises in Tsinghai Province, China, and flows generally s. to great delta, in Vietnam, on South China Sea M-288
Asia, *map* A-700
comparative length. *see in index* River, *table*
delta V-317, *map* V-321
Kampuchea K-168
Laos L-47
Vientiane V-316
Thailand T-146
Melaconite, blackish ore of copper occurring in Lake Superior district and Mississippi Valley; known chemically as cupric oxide.
Melaka (or Malacca), Malaysia, state on w. coast, on Strait of Malacca; 663 sq mi (1,717 sq km); cap. Melaka (pop. 86,357); pop. 403,722 M-72, *map* A-700
Melamine button, imitation pearl B-530
Melanchthon, Philipp (1497–1560), German religious reformer, friend and ally of Luther; born in Bretton, Baden; the peacemaker and scribe of the Reformation R-134
Lutheranism L-339
Mélançon, Claude (born 1895), Canadian author, born in Montreal, Que.; received 1968 Canadian Book of the Year for Children Award for 'Légendes Indiennes du Canada'.
Melanesia, division of Pacific islands; pop. 3,666,000 P-7, *map* P-3
folktales S-468
masks M-186, *picture* M-187
mythology M-699
Oceania O-465, 472
Melanesians, people P-7, *chart* R-26
New Guinea N-174
Melanin, dark pigment S-210d
hair H-7
Melanism, excess of the dark pigment melanin in the skin or in plumage or pelage; may be restricted to small areas or widespread throughout the body; opposite of albinism.
Melanocyte, cell that produces melanin
hair H-7
Melanocyte-stimulating hormone (or MSH), hormone that controls distribution of melanin H-240, *table* H-241
Melanoma, type of skin cancer C-134
Melba, Nellie (or Helen Porter Mitchell) (1861–1931), Australian singer and prima donna M-288
Australia A-801
Melbourne, William Lamb, Viscount (1779–1848), English statesman M-288
Victoria V-309
Melbourne, Australia, capital of Victoria; pop. 2,916,600 M-289
Australia A-767, 787, *map* A-822
Pacific Ocean, *map* P-3
population growth A-787
Royal Botanical Gardens and National Arboretum, *table* B-379
symphony A-800
theater company A-798
Victoria V-310
Melbourne, Fla., city in resort area 80 mi (130 km) s.e. of Daytona Beach; electronic and communications components, semiconductors; Florida Institute of Technology; pop. 40,236.
'Melbourne Punch', magazine M-33
Melbourne Cup, in Australian horseracing A-791, M-291
Melcher, Frederic Gershom (1879–1963), U.S. editor, born in Malden, Mass.; coeditor *Publisher's Weekly* 1918–58; president 1933–59, chairman 1959–63, R.R. Bowker Co.; awarded Regina Medal 1962
literary awards established L-240
Melchers, Gari (1860–1932), U.S. genre, mural, and portrait painter, born in Detroit; lived most of life in Europe; fine

interpreter of motherhood and of peasants
pioneer woman, *picture* P-331
Melchett, Alfred Moritz Mond, first Baron (1868–1930), British statesman, born in Farnworth, near Bolton, England; minister of health; chairman, Economic Board for Palestine.
Melchior, one of Biblical Wise Men. *see in index* Magi
Melchior, Johann Peter (1742–1825), German sculptor, art critic, and potter, born in Lintorf, Rhine Province, Germany P-475
Melchior, Lauritz (adopted name of Lebrecht Hommel) (1890–1973), Danish tenor, born in Copenhagen; debut with Copenhagen Royal Opera 1913; famous for his Wagnerian roles at Bayreuth Festival and with Metropolitan Opera, New York City
opera, *list* O-570
Melchizedek (or Melchisedec), biblical figure, king of Salem and priest of God, who blessed Abraham (Bible, Gen. xiv, 18). Jesus is called a priest "after the order of Melchisedec" (Bible, Heb. vii, 1–21).
Meleager, Greek writer and collector of epigrams; compiled, about 60 BC, a collection of his own and others' writings to form the first 'Greek Anthology'.
Meleager, in Greek mythology, a hero, son of Oeneus, the Calydonian king; took part in the expedition of the Argonauts; killed giant boar of Calydon.
Meleagrididae, family of birds, the turkeys. *see in index* Turkey
Mêlée, Middle Ages mock warfare M-388
Melegnano, Italy. *see in index* Marignano
Méliès, Georges (1861–1938), French film maker and magician of the Parisian theater; first to film fictional narratives; techniques included multiple exposure and other in-camera manipulations to achieve special effects
directing D-155
motion pictures M-617, 625, *picture* M-618
Melilla, Spanish possession, city, and enclave on n. coast of Morocco; port and military station; pop. 57,000, *maps* A-118, E-361
Melilotus, genus of herbs of family Leguminosae, the sweet clovers.
Melinite, high shell explosive, chiefly picric acid. *see in index* Picric acid
Mélisande. *see in index* 'Pelléas et Mélisande'
Melisma, classical music M-668
Melissa. *see in index* Balm
Mellette, Arthur Calvin (1842–96), U.S. political leader, born in Henry County, Ind.; as member Indiana state legislature, 1871, credited with laying foundations of township school system; last territorial governor of Dakota, appointed 1889; first governor of South Dakota, *picture* S-332
Mellon, Andrew William (1855–1937), U.S. financier, born in Pittsburgh, Pa.; prominent in industrial development of Pittsburgh; with brother founded Mellon Institute of Industrial Research; secretary of treasury under Presidents Harding, Coolidge, and Hoover; U.S. ambassador to England 1932–33; in 1937 presented $50,000,000 art collection to U.S., *picture* P-180. *see also in index* National Gallery of Art
Harding H-40
industry I-195
Melloni, Macedonio (1798–1854), Italian physicist, born in Parma, Italy; pointed out that heat, like light, is reflected, refracted, and polarized; studied transparency of substances to infrared radiation and coined word "diathermancy" to designate this property.
Mellon Institute of Industrial Research, founded at University of Pittsburgh by Andrew W. Mellon and his brother to make scientific research available to industry; now Carnegie-Mellon Institute of Research, a division of Carnegie-Mellon University P-345a, *map* P-345b
Melodeon (or reed organ), its reeds are sounded by an inward air current produced by exhaust bellows; about 1850 supplanted the English harmonium, whose reeds are sounded by an outward current from compression bellows W-231
Melodic minor scale, in music M 691
Melodrama, from two Greek words meaning song and drama; includes comic relief and has a happy ending D-242
Melody, in music M-666, *list* M-671
Melon-leaf nightshade, plant *Solanum citrullifolium* N-315
Melons M-292
fruitgrowing F-438
Melos (formerly Milo), mountainous Greek island 75 mi (120 km) e. of s. Greece; 52 sq mi (135 sq km); exports sulfur, manganese; 'Venus de Milo' found here in 1820.
Melozzo da Forli (1438–94), Italian artist of early Umbrian school; name from birthplace Forli, Italy; one of first to create illusion of unbounded space (vault of Santi Apostoli in Rome).
Melrose, Mass., residential suburb 7 mi (11 km) n. of Boston; radio, electronic, and laboratory equipment; settled about 1629; pop. 30,055.
Melrose Abbey, in Scotland, in town of Melrose, 32 mi (52 km) s.e. of Edinburgh S-69
Melrose Park, Ill., residential and industrial village 12 mi (19 km) w. of Chicago; heavy construction machinery, steel products, plastics, electrical products, cosmetics, radio and television parts, paint, bakery products; pop. 20,735
Illinois, *map* I-53
Meltemi. *see in index* Etesian wind
Melting point S-254f
liquid crystals L-234
'Melting Pot, The', work by Zangwill Y-418
Melton, James (1904–61), U.S. tenor (radio, opera, and television), born in Moultrie, Ga.; operatic debut, Cincinnati Zoo Opera, 1938; member of Metropolitan Opera Co., New York City, 1942–52.
Melton, thick, smooth, heavy woolen fabric used for overcoats; named from Melton Mowbray, a foxhunting resort in England.
Melt spinning, process that turns nylon into yarn N-450
Meltwater, water resulting from the melting of snow and ice G-151
Melun, France, historic town on island and on both banks of Seine River 28 mi (45 km) s.e. of Paris; pop. 33,345, *map* F-372
Melungeons (or Malungeons), people of mixed ancestry (American Indian and white, especially Portuguese, and sometimes black) living in remote mountain regions of n.e. Tennessee and w. Virginia; typically with dark skin, high cheekbones, and straight or curly black hair; uneducated, often illiterate; name probably derived from French mélange (translation mixture).
Melusina (or Mélusine), French legend, beautiful fairy who was changed every Saturday into a fish or serpent from the waist down; upon being observed in this form she disappeared and wandered thenceforward as a ghost.
Melville, George Wallace (1841–1912), U.S. admiral, scientist, and polar explorer, born in New York, N.Y.; member of *Jeanette* polar expedition (commanded by De Long) and commander of survivors; member of Greely relief expedition; engineer in chief of the Navy 1887–1903.
Melville, Herman (1819–91), U.S. writer M-293
creative writing W-381
Hawthorne H-75
whale W-186
works A-349, S-184. *see also in index* 'Moby-Dick'
Melville Island, in Australia, off n. shore; 2,400 sq mi (6,210 sq km); densely wooded, mostly with eucalyptus trees; pop. 154, *maps* A-819, P-3
Melville Island, uninhabited Canadian island of Arctic regions n. of Victoria Island; 16,141 sq mi (41,805 sq km); generally hilly; herds of musk oxen, *map* C-109
North America, *map* N-351
Melville Peninsula, in Canada, 400 mi (640 km) n. of Hudson Bay between Gulf of Boothia and Foxe Channel; 25,000 sq mi (65,000 sq km), *map* C-109
North America, *map* N-351
Melvindale, Mich., city 7 mi (11 km) s.w. of Detroit; metal products; settled 1870, incorporated as city 1932; pop. 13,862.
'Member of the Wedding, The', work by McCullers M-6
Membrane, covering, lining, or separating layer of tissue. Cell membrane separates cell protoplasm from surrounding medium or from other cells. In animal body, fibrous membrane, with parallel fibers, provides attachments or support. Serous membrane, with smooth surface, lines or covers organs to prevent binding and friction. Mucous membrane lines organs directly or indirectly open to the air; its glands and cells secrete a protective and lubrication fluid, the mucus
cell A-374, B-198
nerve N-120
living things L-266, *picture* L-265
Membranophone. *see in index* Drum
Memel River. *see in index* Niemen River
Memel Territory (or Klaipeda Territory), n.w. Lithuanian Soviet Socialist Republic along Niemen River to Baltic Sea; area 1,099 sq mi (2,846 sq km); chief city, Klaipeda (Memel), fortified Baltic port (pop. 140,000); territory taken from Germany by Peace Conference, 1919; given to Lithuania, 1924, as outlet to sea; ceded to Germany, 1939, with free port zone for Lithuania; to Lithuanian Soviet Socialist Republic in 1945, *maps* E-360, R-348
Germany G-124
Mementos (or memorabilia), in hobby H-183
Memling, Hans (or Hans Memlinc) (1430?–94), Flemish painter M-294
'Madonna and Child with Angels' P-31, *picture* P-32
'Tomasso Portiniari', *picture* A-662
Memminger, Christopher Gustavus (1803–88), U.S. lawyer and political leader, born in Württemberg, Germany; to U.S. as child; secretary of the treasury Confederate States of America 1861–64.
Memnon, in Greek mythology, son of Eos, goddess of the dawn; king of the Ethiopians; slain by Achilles in Trojan War; colossal statues in Egypt of King Amenhotep thought by Romans to be sacred to Memnon, *picture,* E-126
Memoir. *see in index* Autobiography A-831
'Memoirs of Field-Marshall Montgomery', work by Montgomery M-569
Memon Masjid, mosque, Karachi, Pakistan K-191
'Memorabilia' (or 'Recollections of Socrates'), work by Xenophon X-402
Memorabilia (or mementos), hobby H-183
Memorial Day (formerly Decoration Day)
flag etiquette F-151
holidays F-60, 63
national cemeteries N-24
Memorial rose R-296
Memorial University of Newfoundland. *see in index* Newfoundland, Memorial University of
Memorization, early teaching technique
education E-78
Memory M-294
aging affects A-125
amnesia A-373
brain B-400
child development C-324
learning L-106
memorizing S-495
Ebbinghaus E-47
speeches P-526c
Memory (or memory circuit), computer storage system C-627
electronics E-175
Memory B cell, type of white blood cell I-55
Memphis, early capital of Egypt at apex of Nile delta s. of Cairo, now in ruins E-125, *maps* E-124, P-212
Memphis, Tenn., largest city of state; pop. 648,399 M-295, *map* U-41
North America, *map* N-351
Tennessee T-81, *pictures* T-85, T-91, *map* 96
Memphis, Italian design group I-174
'Memphis Blues', song by Handy H-30
Memphis State University, Memphis, Tenn.; founded 1912; arts and science, business, education, engineering, law; graduate school M-295
Memphremagog, Lake, s. Quebec Province and n. Vermont; 1 to 4 mi (1.6 to 6 km) wide and 30 mi (50 km) long V-287, *maps* V-286, 301, Q-10
Menagerie, circus exhibit C-427
Menai Strait, narrow channel (spanned by bridge) separating island of Anglesey, Wales, from Caernarvon; near town of Menai Bridge.
Menam. *see in index* Chao Phraya
Menander (342–291?BC), Greek dramatist; known for his comedies; only one complete play still exists D-242
'Men and Machinery', fresco by Rivera P-67a, *picture* P-67b
Menangkabau, most advanced of Malay peoples, living in mountains of central Sumatra; believed to be first conquerors of island.
Menarche, first menstrual period A-47
Ménard, René (1605–61), Jesuit missionary in upper Great Lakes region, born in Paris, France; suffered brutal treatment by Iroquois and Ottawa; lost life when going to aid starving, fugitive Hurons in Wisconsin near Lake Superior border
Great Lakes exploration G-249
Menasha, Wis., twin city of Neenah, on n. end of Lake Winnebago, 32 mi (52 km) n. of Fond du Lac; paper and paper products, wood products; printing and publishing; pop. 14,728.
Mencius (or Meng-tse, or Meng-tzu) (372?–289? BC), Chinese philosopher and follower of Confucius M-296
China C-361, 387
Mencius (or Meng-tzu), book by Mencius C-387, M-296
Mencken, H.L. (full name Henry Louis Mencken) (1880–1956), U.S. editor, critic, and essayist M-296
Mendel, Gregor (born Johann Mendel) (1822–84), Austrian priest and biologist M-296
anthropology A-483
biological concepts B-229
botanical research B-380
evolution E-366
genetics G-53, *picture* G-54
heredity H-140
zoology Z-470
Mendeleev, Dmitri (born Dmitri Ivanovich Mendeleev) (1834–1907), Russian chemist M-297
atomic particle construction A-751
chemistry C-294, C-302
inorganic chemistry I-209
periodic table P-206, S-58
Mendele Mokher Sforim (Mendele the Itinerant Bookseller, pen name of Sholem Yakov Abramovitsch) (1835–1917), Jewish author, born in Kopyl, Russia
Yiddish literature Y-417
Mendelevium (Md), chemical element
periodic table, *table* P-207, *list* P-208
Mendelsohn, Eric (1887–1953), architect, born in Germany; became English citizen 1938; moved to U.S. 1941; identified with modern movement ('Architecture and the Changing Civilization') A-569

Mendelssohn, Felix (full name Jakob Ludwig Felix Mendelssohn-Bartholdy) (1809–47), German musician and composer M-297
classical music M-672
oratorio O-575
orchestra O-578

Mendelssohn, Moses (1729–86), German Judaic philosopher M-297
Hebrew literature H-113
Yiddish literature Y-417

Mendenhall Glacier, Alaska, *picture* A-250

Menderes River (or Maeander River, or Meander River), river in Turkey; famous for many windings, which made its name proverbial; 240 mi (390 km) to its mouth at (ancient) Miletus on the Aegean.

Mendès, Catulle (1841–1909), French poet and novelist, one of Parnassian group; a versatile and accomplished writer ('Philoméla', verse; 'Le roi vierge', novel).

Mendès-France, Pierre (1907–82), French political leader, born in Paris, France; admitted to bar at 21, elected deputy at 25; imprisoned by Vichy government 1940, escaped 1941 and served with Free French forces; minister of national economy 1944–45; on UN Economic and Social Council 1947–50; premier 1954–55; author of 'A Modern French Republic'.

Mendicant, monk dependant upon alms for support M-539, 541

Mending, textile manufacture T-140

'Mending Wall', work by Frost A-355

Mendip Hills, England, range 6 mi (10 km) wide and 30 km (20 mi) long in w. Somersetshire; highest point 1,067 ft (325 m); stalactite caves; Roman remains.

Mendive, Rafael (1821–86), Cuban writer; concerned with political justice
Caribbean literature C-167

Mendocino, Cape, most westerly point of California, *maps* N-351, U-40

Mendota, Lake, in Madison, Wis.; about 6 mi (10 km) long and 4 mi (6 km) wide.

Mendoza, Antonio de (1485–1552), Spanish administrator; first viceroy of New Spain, or Mexico; later viceroy of Peru A-334, S-337

Mendoza, Don Pedro de (1487?–1537), Spanish captain, colonizer of Río de la Plata region in Argentina; founded Buenos Aires 1536 A-582
Latin America L-67

Mendoza, Argentina, capital of province of Mendoza, at foot of Andes, 600 mi (960 km) n.w. of Buenos Aires; center for trade with Chile; grapes, fruit, wine; 10,000 killed in earthquake of 1861; pop. 118,568 S-281, *maps* A-585, S-300

Menehune, elf-like beings in Hawaiian folklore S-468

Menelaus, in Greek mythology, king of Sparta, brother of Agamemnon and husband of Helen
Helen of Troy H-117
Homeric legend H-221, *picture* H-222
Proteus P-514

Menelik II (born Sahle Miriam) (1844–1913), emperor of Ethiopia, 1889–1909 M-298
Ethiopia E-314
Addis Ababa A-40

Menéndez de Avilés, Pedro (1519–74), Spanish explorer M-298
St. Augustine S-16b

Menes, first of historical kings of Egypt; united Upper and Lower Egypt A-405, E-125

Mengelberg, Willem (1871–1951), Dutch orchestral conductor, born in Utrecht; conductor of Concertgebouw Orchestra, Amsterdam, and of New York Philharmonic Orchestra
orchestra O-578, *list* O-579

Meng-tzu. *see in index* Mencius

Menhaden (or pogy), oily fish of the herring family H-144
fisheries, *table* F-136
sardines S-48

Menhir, prehistoric monument S-455

Meninges, three layers of membrane that protect the brain and spinal cord.

Meningitis, inflammation of the meninges D-179
nervous system disorder N-123

Meniscus lens P-283

Menkaure (or Mycerinus), king of Egypt (2525 BC)
pyramid P-542

Menken, Adah Isaacs (1835–68), U.S. actress, born in New Orleans, La.; began career as ballet dancer; won fame as Mazeppa in play based on Byron's poem.

Menlo College, Menlo Park, Calif.; private control; founded 1915 as military academy, college since 1927; liberal arts and business administration.

Menlo Park, Calif., residential city 25 mi (40 km) s.e. of San Francisco; research center, publishing; Menlo College; first incorporated 1874; pop. 25,673.

Menlo Park, N.J., village 14 mi (22 km) s.w. of Newark; pop. 10,000 N-200, *picture* N-197
Edison E-73

Menninger, Charles Frederick (1862–1953), U.S. psychiatrist; father of William and Karl Menninger M-298

Menninger, Karl Augustus (born 1893), U.S. psychiatrist and author M-298

Menninger, William Claire (1899–1966), U.S. psychiatrist M-298

Mennonites, Protestant denomination growing out of Anabaptist movement in 16th century; opposed to oath-taking and military service; hold to simplicity of life and worship and often live in separate communities; named from Menno Simons, leader in The Netherlands M-299
abolitionist movement A-10
buttons forbidden B-528
Paraguay settlement P-112
Pennsylvania settlement P-166

Menno Simons (1496–1561), Dutch religious reformer, born near Harlingen, The Netherlands; founder of later school of Anabaptists in The Netherlands, from whom Mennonites took their name M-299

Meno, in music, *list* M-671

Menominee, American Indian group living in Michigan and Wisconsin; name means wild rice men, *picture* I-120, *map* I-149, *table* I-139

Menominee, Mich., port city situated on Green Bay, Lake Michigan, at mouth of Menominee River, opposite Marinette, Wis.; wood and metal products, paper, food products, helicopters; fisheries; resort area; pop. 10,099.

Menominee River, formed by union of Michigamie and Bois Brulé rivers on boundary between Wisconsin and upper Michigan; flows s.e. 125 mi (200 km) to Green Bay M-355

Menomonee Falls, Wis., village 15 mi (25 km) n.w. of Milwaukee; industrial area; metal fabrication; incorporated 1892; pop. 27,845.

Menomonie, Wis., city 20 mi (30 km) n.e. of Eau Claire; farm area; dried milk products; University of Wisconsin-Stout; incorporated 1882; pop. 14,728.

Meno mosso, in music, *list* M-671

Menopause, in human female, cessation of menstruation due to decline in ovarian function; occurs most frequently between ages 45 and 50; marks end of childbearing period M-300
sexuality S-123

Menorca, one of Balearic Islands. *see in index* Minorca

Menotti, Gian-Carlo (born 1911), Italian born U.S. composer M-299
opera O-571

Mensa, constellation, *chart* C-682

Mensaria Rumph, banana variety B-53

Mensheviks, minority of Russian Social Democrats, opposed to Bolsheviks C-619

Menstruation (or menstrual cycle, or period) M-300
hormones H-243, *diagram* H-242
sexuality S-123

Mensuration. *see in index* Measurement

Mental Age (MA), intelligence test score I-239

Mental deficiency. *see in index* Mental retardation

Mental health H-85
Dix's reforms D-190
mental illness M-301
play P-390b
space travel S-346a

Mental illness (or mental disorder) M-301
anorexia nervosa A-467
diagnosis P-523
syphilis causes V-273
treatment
psychoanalysis P-518
therapy T-164
Topeka T-227

Mental retardation M-303
disability D-163
education E-90
mental disorder M-301

Mental tests. *see in index* Intelligence tests

Mentha, plant genus including mint species
herbs H-138

Menthol (or mint camphor), crystalline substance obtained from essential oils of Japanese mint or peppermint; local applications used for relief of itching or pain.

Menton (Italian Mentone), France, town in s.e. on Mediterranean, about 14 mi (22 km) n.e. of Nice; protected on n. and w. by mountains; winter resort for invalids; pop. 23,401, *map* F-372

Mentor, in Greek mythology, friend of Odysseus and guardian of his son Telemachus; hence, a wise counselor.

Mentor, Ohio, residential and industrial city n.e. of Cleveland; large nurseries; diversified industry; founded 1799; pop. 42,065
Holden Arboretum, *table* B-397

Menu, in cooking C-701

Menuhin, Yehudi (born 1916), U.S. violinist and conductor, born in New York City; a child prodigy, made debut at 7 with San Francisco Orchestra: afterward studied in Paris with Enesco; at 11 played with Berlin Philharmonic Orchestra and since then appeared with leading orchestras of the world.

Menzel, Adolph von (1815–1905), German artist, born in Breslau; famous for series of pictures 'The Life of Frederick the Great', but best work found in many paintings of daily life; revived art of lithography and wood engraving.

Menzel-Bourguiba (formerly Ferryville), Tunisia, city on Mediterranean, 9 mi (15 km) s. of Bizerte; steel; made a military and naval base by the French; pop. 42,000.

Menzies, Robert G. (full name Robert Gordon Menzies) (1894–1978), Australian lawyer and statesman M-304

Meperidine (or Demerol), a narcotic drug N-19

Mephistopheles, evil spirit, personification of the devil in the Faust legends F-49

Meprobamate, a tranquilizer N-19

Mequon, Wis., city 13 mi (21 km) n. of Milwaukee; chiefly residential; incorporated as town 1846, as city 1957; pop. 16,193.

Meramec River, s.e. Missouri; flows n.e. to Mississippi near St. Louis.

Merano, Italy, town in Bolzano province, Italian Tyrol, formerly in Austria; noted as health resort; pop. 30,614, *map* I-401

Merauke, Indonesia, seaport on s. coast of New Guinea; pop. 21,366, *maps* I-166, P-3

Mercantile Agency. *see in index* Dun and Bradstreet

Mercantile system (or mercantile theory)
American Colonies R-166
international trade I-271
liberalism L-146

Mercator, Gerhardus (Latinized form of Gerhard Kremer) (1512–94), Flemish geographer and map maker M-304
atlas R-127

Mercator projection, in maps
aviation, *map* A-878
maps M-123, *pictures* 124, 126
Mercator M-304
navigation N-69, 77

Merced, Calif., city about 55 mi (90 km) n.w. of Fresno; agricultural and food processing center; aluminum products, doors, mobile homes; pop. 36,499.

Mercedes, Tex., city 30 mi (50 km) n.w. of Brownsville; citrus fruit and vegetable packing and processing; pop. 11,851.

Mercedes Benz, German automobile G-117

Merced River, rises in Sierra Nevada in e.-central California and flows 160 mi (260 km) s.w. to Joaquin River.

Mercenary, soldier hired into foreign service American Revolution. *see in index* Hessians
army and militia A-633
Foreign Legion F-308
Swiss pikemen S-544

Mercer, Johnny (1909–76), U.S. songwriter M-684

Mercer Island, Wash., city on Lake Washington e. of Seattle; 5 mi (8 km) long; connected to e. and w. shores by bridge; pop. 21,522.

Mercerizing, process that adds luster and strength to cotton thread or cloth by treating it under tension with caustic soda; John Mercer's invention T-176
textile T-140

Mercersburg, Pa., town in s.-central part of state; formerly seat of noted German Reformed church seminary; apparel; tannery; pop. 1,617, *map* P-184

Mercer University, Macon, Ga.; Southern Baptist; founded 1833; liberal arts, education, law, and theology; graduate studies; quarter system; has affiliate university, **Mercer University in Atlanta;** maintains Southern School of Pharmacy at Atlanta.

Merchandising M-144. *see also in index* Retailing; Wholesaling
capitalism C-151
mail-order store U-110
methods U-109
magazine and journal M-34

Merchant Adventurers, Company of R-149

Merchant builder (or speculative developer), housing construction H-297

Merchant flag F-161, *list* F-149

'Merchant George Gisze of Danzig, The', painting by Holbein the Younger, *picture* H-201

Merchant guild G-313

Merchant marine, commercial vessels as distinguished from the military marine, or navy S-173, 164, 167. *see also in index* Freighter; Ocean liner; Tanker, ship
England E-236
international law S-174
sailing vessels S-167, 174, *pictures* S-165
United States S-173
Maritime Administration U-163, S-176
percentage of world total, *chart* U-123
Seamen's Act S-173
world tonnage, *table* S-176a

Merchant Marine Academy, United States. *see in index* United States Merchant Marine Academy

Merchant Marine Act (1920) S-176

Merchant Marine Act (1936) S-176

'Merchant of Venice, The', comedy by Shakespeare featuring one of his best-known characters, the moneylender Shylock
Shakespeare S-133, S-139, *picture* S-138

Merchant ship S-169. *see also in index* Merchant marine
definition S-167

Merchants of the Staple R-149

Merchant wholesalers, in merchandising M-144

Mercia, Anglo-Saxon kingdom in central England, 6th to 9th centuries; in 8th century was most powerful of all the kingdoms.

Mercier, Désiré Joseph, Cardinal (1851–1926), Belgian prelate and patriot; while professor of philosophy at

University of Louvain, wrote important works on philosophy and psychology; appointed archbishop of Malines 1906; created cardinal 1907; called "Voice of Belgium" because of eloquence in opposing Germany's invasion of Belgium in World War I.

Mercier, Honoré (1840–94), Canadian lawyer and statesman, born in St. Athanase, Lower Canada; became leader of Liberal party 1883; premier and attorney general 1887; extremely popular in his native province of Quebec until 1891 when charges of corruption (of which he was acquitted) were brought against him in connection with railway subsidies.

'Mercure de France' (formerly 'Le Mercure galant'), magazine M-32

Mercuric chloride (or bichloride of mercury, or corrosive sublimate)
poisoning P-410

Mercurochrome, antiseptic made by combining fluorescein, an aniline dye of strong penetrating power, with mercury, which has great bactericidal properties
mercury M-305

Mercury (or Mercurius), in Roman mythology M-701, *picture* M-695. *see also in index* Hermes

Mercury, planet nearest sun P-351, S-254a, *diagram* S-254e
astronomy A-714
eclipse E-49
orbital shift R-142
earth E-8, *diagram* E-9

Mercury (or quicksilver; Latin hydrargyrum, hence chemical symbol Hg), fluid metallic element M-304
barometer B-82
bichloride poisoning P-410
electric lighting E-163
freezing point S-254f
gold G-179
industrial health hazards I-175
metal and metallurgy M-307
ore, *table* O-600, *map* O-600
periodic table, *table* P-207, *list* P-208
thermometer T-107

Mercury, Project. *see in index* Project Mercury

Mercury fulminate, explosive E-380
mercury M-305
Nobel N-329

Mercury Theater S-61

Mercy, Sisters of. *see in index* Sisters of Mercy

Mercy College, Dobbs Ferry, N.Y.; private control, Catholic related; opened 1950; liberal arts; education; program in criminal justice.

Mercy College of Detroit, Detroit, Mich.; Roman Catholic; coeducational, formerly for women; incorporated 1941; math and sciences, education, business, fine and performing arts, and health sciences.

Mercyhurst College, Erie, Pa.; Roman Catholic; coeducational, formerly for women; founded 1926; arts and sciences, teacher education; graduate studies.

Mer de Glace, glacier on Mont Blanc in the French Alps A-319

Meredith, George (1828–1909), English novelist and poet, born in Portsmouth, Hampshire; one of great masters of Victorian Age ('The Egoist', his masterpiece, analytical and subtle; 'The Ordeal of Richard Feverel', easier reading, containing some of his most beautiful passages; 'Diana of the Crossways', his greatest popular success; 'Adventures of Harry Richmond', a romantic novel) E-277

Meredith, James Howard (born 1933), U.S. lecturer and civil rights worker, born in Kosciusko, Miss.; active in voter registration drives.

Meredith, Owen. *see in index* Lytton, Edward Robert, earl of

Meredith, Sir William Ralph (1840–1923), Canadian statesman and jurist, born in Westminster, Upper Canada; did notable work as legislator, particularly on workingmen's laws; served as senator, chief justice of Ontario, chancellor of University of Toronto.

Meredith College, Raleigh, N.C.; affiliated with Southern Baptist Convention; for women; founded 1891; arts and sciences, music, and teacher education.

Meres, Francis (1565–1647), English author and clergyman, born in Lincolnshire; 1598 published 'Paladis Tamia: Wit's Treasury', a review of literary work from Chaucer to his own day
Shakespeare S-131

Merezhkovski, Dmitri Sergeevich (1865–1941), Soviet author of historical novels, born in St. Petersburg (now Leningrad) ('Romance of Leonardo da Vinci', one of a trilogy titled 'Christ and Antichrist', about struggle between Christianity and paganism) R-360a

Merganser (or saw-bill, or sheldrake, or goosander), duck; species include hooded *Lophodytes cucullatus*, American *Mergus americanus*, and red-breasted *Mergus serrator* D-285

Mergenthaler, Ottmar (1854–99), U.S. inventor of the Linotype, born in Hatchel, Württemberg, Germany; came to the U.S. 1872 I-275, *table* I-273
newspapers N-239

Mergenthaler Linotype, machine
die and diemaking D-139

Mérida, Carlos (born 1893), artist, born in Guatemala; moved to Mexico 1919 and became identified with Mexican modern art movement; called "representative of Mexican abstract painting."

Mérida, Mexico, capital of Yucatán, 23 mi (37 km) s. of its port, Progreso, on Gulf of Mexico; manufacture and export of henequen; pop. 400,142
Maya M-235
Mexico, *map* M-341
North America, *map* N-351
Yucatán peninsula Y-432

Mérida (ancient Augusta Emerita), Spain, city in s.w.; was occupied by Romans and Moors; ruins include a stone-arched bridge crossing the Guadiana, a wall, triumphal arch, and circus; pop. 28,791.

Mérida, Cordillera de. *see in index* Cordillera de Mérida

Meriden, Conn., city 17 mi (27 km) n. of New Haven; noted for silverware; telephone and signaling systems, machinery; pop. 57,118 C-651, *maps* C-654, 662

Meridian, Miss., city 90 mi (140 km) e. of Jackson in agricultural and industrial center; cotton products, lumber; pop. 46,577 M-469, *map* U-41
North America, *map* N-351

Meridian, imaginary line on the Earth's surface, connecting both geographic poles
equator E-293
hemisphere H-126
international date line I-254, *diagram* I-253
latitude and longitude L-80
maps M-117
navigation N-68, 71
time T-187

Mérimée, Prosper (1803–70), French novelist, historian, and critic, born in Paris; great master of style ('Chronique du règne de Charles IX'; 'Carmen'; 'Colomba'; 'Mateo Falcone'; 'Lettres à une inconnue')
French literature F-397

Merina, people of Madagascar M-23

Merino, breed of sheep S-147, A-808
fur F-463
wool W-288, *picture* W-287

Merion bluegrass
lawn use G-26

Merisi, Michelangelo. *see in index* Caravaggio

Meristem, growth area of plants G-292

Merit Systems Protection Board, United States U-166, C-469. *see also in index* Civil Service Commission

Merle d'Aubigné, Jean Henri (1794–1872), Swiss Protestant preacher, born in Eaux-Vives, near Geneva; known for his history of the Reformation.

Merlin, legendary bard, magician, and counselor in Arthurian romance; born of a human mother and a spirit father, from whom he inherited his supernatural abilities; aided kings of Britain, especially Arthur, by means of his magic art; through the treachery of Viviane, the Lady of the Lake, to whom he taught his magic, he disappeared and lived in an enchanted tower in the forest of Brécéliande A-655, R-299a

Merlin. *see in index* Pigeon hawk

Mermaid A-457
folklore F-260

Mermaids' purses, egg case of a skate or ray S-206

Mermaid Tavern, famous old London tavern S-131

Merman, in folklore F-260

Merocrine gland G-153

Merope, daughter of Atlas and wife of Sisyphus of Corinth; she is represented as the seventh and least visible of the stars of the Pleiades because she was ashamed of having married a mortal.

Merovingians, Frankish royal line, founded by Clovis (ruled AD 481–511); last of line was Childeric III (ruled 743–751)
France F-361

Merriam, Clinton Hart (1855–1942), U.S. naturalist, born in New York City; chief of United States Biological Survey 1885–1910; writer.

Merriam, John Campbell (1869–1945), U.S. paleontologist, born in Hopkinton, Iowa; president of Carnegie Institution of Washington 1920–38 ('The Living Past').

Merriam, Kan., industrial city 11 mi (18 km) s. of Kansas City; research center, electronics; incorporated 1864; pop. 10,794.

Merrick, Leonard (1864–1939), English writer, born in London; novels, short stories, plays ('Conrad in Quest of His Youth'; 'Cynthia'; 'The Actor-Manager').

Merrick, N.Y., community 26 mi (42 km) e. of New York City in Nassau County on Long Island; furniture, clothing, windows; pop. 25,904.

Merrifield, Robert Bruce (born 1921), U.S. biochemist, born in Fort Worth, Tex.; professor Rockefeller University 1966–; completed first total enzyme synthesis; studies on amino acids, vitamins B-233

Merrill, James (born 1926), U.S. poet A-364

Merrill, John O. (born 1896), U.S. architect A-569

Merrill, Robert (born 1919), U.S. singer, born in Brooklyn, N.Y.; with Metropolitan Opera Company in leading Italian and French baritone roles from 1945; also radio, television, and recording artist; autobiography, 'Once More from the Beginning'.

Merrill's Marauders, special combat team in World War II W-347

'Merrimack', Confederate ironclad warship in Civil War A-631
Hampton, Va. H-24
Monitor C-480, *picture* C-477
navy N-83, 91

Merrimack College, North Andover, Mass.; Roman Catholic; founded 1947; liberal arts and science, business administration, engineering, and teacher education.

Merrimack River, 110 mi (180 km) long, flows from s.-central New Hampshire through n.e. Massachusetts into Atlantic near Newburyport M-190, *map* N-191

Merrimack Valley, valley, New Hampshire; noted for manufacturing N-176, 178

Merritt, Wesley (1834–1910), U.S. Army officer, born in New York City; Union cavalry commander in Shenandoah Valley and in Richmond campaigns, and rose to major general of volunteers; May 1898 commanded U.S. troops in Philippines and was first military governor of the islands.

Merritt, William Hamilton (1793–1862), Canadian statesman, born in Bedford, N.Y.; founded St. Catharines, Ont., and promoted building of Welland Ship Canal; president of Executive Council of Canada.

Merritt, Lake, Calif., in the center of Oakland, and connected by narrow inlet with San Francisco Bay; resort
Oakland O-453

Merritt Island, e. Florida, between mainland and Cape Canaveral; causeway to mainland; orange groves, truck farms; pop. 29,233 S-342b, *map* S-342a
Vehicle Assembly Building, *picture* S-342c

Merry del Val, Rafael, Cardinal (1865–1930), Roman Catholic prelate, born in London, England, of Spanish parents; papal secretary of state under Pius X ('Truth of the Papal Claims').

Merry-go-round (French name carrousel) A-383
carnivals C-172

Merry Mount, settlement made by Thomas Morton and others within present Quincy, Mass. (1625); dispersed by Plymouth Puritans.

'Merry Wives of Windsor, The', rollicking farce by Shakespeare, written about 1600; Falstaff makes love to merry wives, Mrs. Ford and Mrs. Page, who make a dupe of him; secondary love plot that of Anne Page and Fenton S-133, 139

Mersen, Treaty of, agreement in which Charles the Bald of France and Louis of Germany divided Lotharingia, territory left by their nephew Lothair II (870).

Mersey, river in n.w. England; flows 70 mi (110 km) w. to Irish Sea; wide estuary forms Liverpool harbor L-261, *map* U-18a

Mersey beat (or Liverpool sound), popular music L-262

Mertensia, genus of smooth or fine-haired perennial herbs of borage family with veined pale-green leaves and purplish-blue flowers; a common species is the Virginia cowslip *Mertensia virginica*.

Merthiolate, antiseptic A-495

Merthyr Tydfil, Wales, city on Taff River 22 mi (35 km) n.w. of Cardiff; foundry products, clothing, washing machines, chemicals, aircraft controls; pop. 56,360.

Merton, Thomas (1915–68), U.S. Trappist monk, born in Prades, France; entered Abbey of Our Lady of Gethsemane in Kentucky 1941 and was ordained a priest in 1949 (autobiographical works: 'The Seven Storey Mountain', 'The Sign of Jonas'; religious writings: 'The Ascent to Truth', 'No Man Is an Island', 'The Silent Life', 'The Behavior of Titans', 'The New Man').

Merton, borough of Greater London, England, *maps* L-287, U-18a

Meru, Mount, mythical Hindu mountain where the gods dwell, symbolized in the ancient towers of Angkor Wat, Kampuchea A-416

Merv, U.S.S.R. *see in index* Mary

MERVAN (or mobile emergency room van), *picture* H-284

Merwin, W.S. (born 1927), U.S. poet A-364

Merychippus, ancestor of the horse H-269

Méryon, Charles (1821–68), French etcher, born in Paris; best known for his etchings of Paris.

Mesa, Ariz., city 13 mi (21 km) s.e. of Phoenix; tourist center in citrus fruit and irrigated agricultural area; electronic products; founded 1878 by Mormons; Mormon temple; pop. 152,453 A-599, *map* U-40

Mesa, flat-topped ridge
Mexico M-322
Pueblos P-526d

Mesabi Range, Minnesota, iron-mining region I-331
Minnesota M-439, 443, 446

Mesa Verde National Park, in w. Colorado; Mesa Verde means in Spanish green table C-571, *map* C-583, *picture* C-577

Mescal, liquor A-125, M-332

Mescaline, hallucinogenic drug H-18

Mesdag, Hendrik Willem (1831–1915), Dutch marine painter, born in Groningen; noted for studies of North Sea;

gave collection of modern paintings to The Hague.
Mesencephalon (or midbrain) B-400, *diagram* B-402
Meseta, plateau region of Spain S-350
Iberian peninsula I-2
Portugal P-454
Meseta Central, region of Costa Rica C-733
Meshed, Iran. *see in index* Mashhad
Mesmer, Friedrich Anton (or Franz Anton Mesmer) (1734–1815), Austrian physician, born near Konstanz, Germany; originator of theory of animal magnetism, or mesmerism
hypnosis H-344, *picture* H-343
Mesmerism (or animal magnetism), hypnosis H-344
Meso-American, ancient settlements of Mexico and Central America A-406
Mesocephaly (medium-headedness), in ethnology R-25, *picture* R-27
Mesoderm, embryonic germ layer A-434
vertebrates E-200, *chart* E-202, *diagram* E-200
Mesohippus, ancestor of the horse H-269, *picture* H-268
Mesolithic period (or Middle Stone Age) M-85
Mesolongion, Greece. *see in index* Missolonghi
Mesomere, muscle-plate region
embryology E-200, *chart* E-202, *diagram* E-202
Meson, particle composed of two quarks R-41
nuclear physics N-432
quark Q-5
Yukawa's theory Y-439
Mesopause, in atmosphere A-747, *diagram* E-19
Mesopelagic Zone, intermediate-depth layer of ocean A-745
Mesophytes, plants adapted to moderate conditions of dryness; intermediate between hydrophytes and xerophytes.
Mesopotamia, region, Argentina A-575
Mesopotamia, region in Asia between Tigris and Euphrates rivers (now included in Iraq) M-305. *see also in index* Assyria; Babylonia; Iraq; Sumerians
agricultural landmarks A-130
ancient civilization A-403
ancient Egypt E-125
archaeological excavations A-532
arts
glass G-161, G-164
literature
folklore F-263
Islamic I-365
mosaic M-589
temple architecture A-545
asphalt uses A-702
Babylonia and Assyria, *map* B-4
baking techniques B-430
city-state C-461
constellations C-680
Hammurabi H-23
Iraq I-314
irrigation E-327
maps M-125
Middle East M-396
New Year's festival N-243
numeration system N-435
Persia, *map* P-212
petroleum P-232
Rome, *map* R-242
shelter S-157
Tigris River T-184
wheel W-192
writing W-370
Mesopotamian architecture A-545. *see also in index* Babylonia, *subhead* architecture
Mesoscaphe, submarine O-463
Piccard P-316
Mesosphere, belt of air A-747
earth E-19, *diagram* E-11
Mesothorium, radioactive substance midway between radiothorium and thorium, resulting from the disintegration of thorium; used to make luminous paint, especially for clock dials.
Mesozoic era (or Age of Reptiles, or Era of Reptiles), geological time
Australia A-775
British Isles B-460
Canada C-73
earth E-26, *table* E-24
plant and animal life R-153, *picture* R-152
prehistoric animals P-488, 491, *picture* P-489
Mesquakie, people, *picture* I-298
Mesquite, Tex., city 11 mi (18 km) e. of Dallas; cotton, truck crops; sand and gravel; Mesquite Championship Rodeo; pop. 67,053.
Mesquite, any of small trees or spiny shrubs of genus *Prosopis,* in pea family, Fabaceae; found from South America through southwestern U.S.; long, pale-yellow beans are eaten by cattle.
Mesquite gum, G-318
Mess, place where meals are regularly served
submarines, *diagram* S-499
Messager, André Charles Prosper (1853–1929), French composer and conductor, born in Montluçon, France; director opera in Paris and London.
Messager, Charles. *see in index* Vildrac, Charles
Messalina, Valeria (died AD 48), profligate 3rd wife of Roman emperor Claudius; executed by him for contracting a new marriage.
Messana, Sicily. *see in index* Messina
Messenger, English Thoroughbred stallion imported to America in 1788; chief founder of the Standardbred Horse.
Messenger RNA (mRNA), carries hereditary information B-199
genetics G-56, *diagram* G-57
Messerschmitt (ME-109), German military aircraft W-333
Messerschmitt Me-262, jet airplane J-105, *picture* J-110
Messiaen, Olivier (full name Olivier-Eugène-Prosper-Charles Messiaen) (born 1908), French composer, organist and teacher M-306
Boulez B-383
classical music M-676
Messiah, means the Anointed; early Biblical history, one who had been anointed with holy oils and dedicated to some high service; name later used by Jews to signify the promised savior of the world; applied by Christians to Jesus; same as Greek word Christ C-397, J-149
'Messiah', work by Handel H-28, M-669
opera O-561
Messiah College, Grantham, Pa.; Brethren in Christ Church; opened as college 1951; liberal arts, nursing, theology.
Messina (ancient Zancle), Sicily, seaport in n.e. on Strait of Messina between Italy and Sicily; pop. 251,423 S-192, *map* I-404
Europe, *map* E-361
Fata Morgana mirage M-463
Mestiza, Philippine garment P-253d
Mestizo, person of European and American Indian ancestry in Spanish-speaking countries. *see also in index* individual countries
Central America C-253
Panama P-86
Mexico M-325
Philippines P-259c
South America S-282
Argentina A-578
Ecuador E-67
Peru P-224
Venezuela V-276
Meštrović, Ivan (1883–1962), U.S. sculptor, born in Croatia (now Yugoslavia); to U.S. 1947, became citizen 1954; professor fine arts Syracuse University 1947–55, University of Notre Dame 1955–62 (portraits of his mother and of President Masaryk; two equestrian statues of American Indians, in Grant Park, Chicago) S-91
Yugoslavia Y-435
Metabolic coma, type of coma C-596
Metabolism, M-306
basal metabolism test R-160
diseases D-180
homeostasis B-206
mammal M-80
physiology P-312
Metacarpal bone, any one of several bones between the wrist and the fingers S-210
hand H-27
Metacenter, *diagram* S-170
Metacomet. *see in index* Philip, King
Metairie, La., unincorporated residential suburb 8 mi (13 km) n.w. of New Orleans; pop. 164,160, *map* L-381
Metal M-307. *see also in index* principal metals by name, *e.g.,* Aluminum; metallurgy
acids and bases A-19
alkali types A-307
alloys A-312. *see also in index* Alloy
aluminum alloys A-321
assaying A-705
building construction materials B-491
button manufacturing B-531
casting methods S-81
coins. *see in index* Coins
corrosion C-726
crystalline structure C-796, S-254h
ductility. *see in index* Ductility
electrical conductivity S-254h
electrochemistry E-170
energy E-215
freezing point S-254f
geography G-63
insulation materials I-231
inventors, *table* I-280
metalworking M-310
mines and mining M-424
money M-532
ore O-600
periodic table, *table* P-207
ultrasonics detects impurities A-22
wind instruments W-226
wire W-245
Metal detector, security device used in airports A-213, *picture* A-214
'Metallica, De Re', work by Agricola M-309
Metallic cadmium, chemical element C-13
Metallic fiber, *table* F-72
Metallic paints P-73
Metallic soaps P-74
Metalloid (or semimetal) M-307
Metallurgical engineering E-223
Metallurgy, science of extracting metal from ore and refining M-307. *see also in index* Alloy; metal; and the principal metals by name, *e.g.* aluminum
assaying A-705
brass production B-410
bronze production B-463
electric furnace F-481
fireproofing F-113
Georgian Soviet Socialist Republic G-102
India I-75
microscope M-383
mines and mining M-424
ore O-601
sciences S-64a
weapons W-111
artillery improvement A-660
wire W-245
Metal tape rule, a tool T-218
Metalworking M-310
antiques A-494
automobile industry L-45
beads B-114
blacksmithing B-308
brass B-410
bronze B-463
Chinese ritual vessel S-93
Ghiberti's doors, *picture* R-147
Greek lamps, L-105
buttons B-531, *picture* B-529
embossing E-198
folk art F-250
forging F-317
iron I-329
lead L-99
Roman tools and utensils, *pictures* R-245
silversmithing, *pictures* S-203, 204
tools T-225
welding, brazing, and soldering W-143
wire W-245
Metalworking machinery tools T-225
Vermont plant, *picture* V-288
Metamorphic rock, derived from older rocks by heat, pressure, or chemical change R-229a
cycle, *chart* R-229
earth E-21, *diagram* E-20
geology G-72
minerals M-437
slate S-212
'Metamorphoses', poem by Ovid
Latin literature L-77
literature L-244
Ovid O-620
Metamorphosis (from Greek meaning change of form), in zoology M-312. *see also in index* Larva; Pupa
amphibians A-378
insects I-220, *picture* I-219
bee B-125
beetle B-137
butterflies and moths B-525, *picture* B-521
caterpillars C-220
mosquito M-596
larva L-51
'Metamorphosis, The', work by Kafka N-414
Metaphase, stage of cell division G-55, *diagram* C-240
Metaphor, figure of speech F-81
creative writing W-379
world W-295
Metaphysical poets, name applied to a group of English poets of the 17th century E-269
Metaphysics, branch of philosophy P-263
'Metaphysics', work by Aristotle G-276
Meta River, in Colombia, rises s. of Bogotá and flows into Orinoco River in n.e. Colombia; 600 mi (960 km) long, *map* S-298
Metastasio, Pietro (1698–1782), Italian poet and dramatist, born in Rome; court poet at Vienna 50 years; noted for lyric dramas
opera O-563
Metastasis, transfer of a causal agent of a disease D-175
cancer C-133
tumors C-812
Metatarsal bone, any of several bones between the ankle and the toes S-210
Metaurus, small river in central Italy, emptying into Adriatic Sea.
Metaxas, John (1871–1941), Greek political leader, born in Ithaca; chief of staff of army 1915; exiled for German sympathies when Greece joined Allies in World War I; led unsuccessful revolt against Venizelos in 1923; with support of king and army set up dictatorship 1936.
Metazoa, animal group A-433
Metcalf, Willard Leroy (1858–1925), U.S. landscape painter, born in Lowell, Mass.; painted outdoor light in all its varied gradations; quiet colors of exquisite tone.
Metcalfe, Charles Theophilus, Baron (1785–1846), British statesman, born in Calcutta, India; governor of Jamaica 1839–42; governor-general of Canada 1843–45.
Metchnikoff, Elie (or Ilya Mechnikov) (1845–1916), Russian bacteriologist, born in Ivanovka, near Khar'kov, Russia, naturalized in France; held that sour milk would lengthen life by checking intestinal bacteria M-285. *see also in index* Nobel Prizewinners, *table*
Metempsychosis. *see in index* Transmigration of the soul

Compton's Fact-Index
continues
on the next page

Meteor and meteorite (sometimes called shooting star, or falling star) M-313
astronomy A-712, A-730
Earth's atmosphere, *diagram* A-748
iron I-349
micrometeorite S-254d
Murchison meteorite E-365
Meteor Crater (or Barringer), Canyon Diablo region of Arizona; largest meteorite crater in the U.S. M-315, *picture* M-313
Meteoroid M-313
spacecraft hazard S-346a
Meteorite shower M-314
'Meteorologica', work by Aristotle M-316
Meteorological observatory O-456
Meteorological tide, ocean waves O-490
Meteorology, science of weather and climate M-315. *see also in index* chief topics listed below
aerospace research A-76
aviation A-887, *diagram* A-888
bibliography S-64e
earth sciences E-41
hobby H-189
hurricane S-457, *diagrams* S-458
instruments, *picture* A-747
balloons B-41
barometer B-81
rain gauge R-90
National Weather Service U-163
rainbow R-88
rainfall R-88, *map* R-89
sciences S-64a
snow S-227, *picture* S-228
solar radiation S-515
storms S-457, *diagram* S-458, *picture* S-459
thunderstorm S-457
tides O-490
tornado S-457, *picture* S-459
typhoon S-457
weather W-117, *table* W-126
Arctic weather, *picture* R-44
satellites S-343b, *picture* S-343, *table* S-344
wind W-220
World Meteorological Organization U-26, S-348a
Meteor shower M-315, *picture* M-313
Meter, in music M-666, 690, *list* M-671
Meter, in poetry P-405
Meter, instrument that measures the flow of liquids, gases, or electricity M-316. *see also in index* Electric watt-hour meter; Flowmeter
machine M-11
water W-90
Meter, metric measurement unit (39.37 in.) W-139, *table* W-141
Meter-kilogram-second system (or mks system), scientific and engineering system of measuring motions, forces, and work, using meters for distance, kilograms for mass, and seconds for time.
Methadone (also called Dolophine), synthetic narcotic ($C_{21}H_{27}NO$), pain reliever; now used as substitute for heroin and morphine in many addict-withdrawal programs N-19
opium O-572
Methane (or marsh gas), odorless hydrocarbon (CH_4), which forms a methyl radical in chemical combinations P-228. *see also in index* Firedamp; Paraffin series
chemical formula V-255
chemistry C-298
chloroform C-393
natural gas G-38
organic chemistry O-602, *diagram* O-603
outer space A-716
Methanol (or wood alcohol, or methyl alcohol, or carbinol, or wood spirit) M-317
alcohol A-275, *table* A-274
organic chemistry O-603, *diagram* O-602
petrochemicals P-228
Methaqualone (or Quāāludes, street names: sopers, or ludes, or pillows, or disco biscuits, or vitamin Q), drug D-277
narcotics and sedatives N-19
Method, The, acting technique A-24
Methodism, religious doctrines and practice of Methodists M-317
holiness movement M-202
Wesley M-149
Methodist church, Protestant organization formed by the union, in 1939, of the Methodist Episcopal church (organized in the U.S. in 1784), the Methodist Episcopal church, South (organized 1845), and the Methodist Protestant church (organized 1828); in 1968 merged with Evangelical United Brethren church to become United Methodist church M-319
England E-233
Tonga T-215
Methodist Church of Canada M-318
Methodist College, Fayetteville, N.C.; affiliated with United Methodist church; chartered 1956, opened 1960; liberal arts, teacher education.
Methodist Episcopal church H-202
Methodism M-319
Methodist Episcopal church, South M-319
Methodist Youth Fellowship, organization for young people; called Epworth League from its founding (in Cleveland, Ohio) in 1889 until 1941.
Methodius, Saint (826?–885), Greek missionary with his brother, Saint Cyril, to Slavs; archbishop of Moravia and Pannonia; festival July 5 B-535
Methoxyflurane, anesthetic A-413
3-methoxy-3,4-methylene-dioxyamphetamine (MMDA), hallucinogenic drug H-18
Methuen, Mass., in n.e. part of state, about 9 mi (15 km) n.e. of Lowell; woolen goods, yarns, shoes; pop. of township 35,456.
Methuen, Treaty of (1703), *table* T-274
Methuselah, son of Enoch and father of Lamech; Bible, Gen. v, 27 assigns him a lifetime of 969 years.
Methyl, chemical radical (CH_3) derived from methane existing in combinations; has never been isolated but is part of many compounds
organic chemistry O-603, *diagram* O-602
Methyl alcohol. *see in index* Methanol
Methyl amine, organic chemistry, *diagram* O-603
Methyl chloride, compound of methyl and chlorine (CH_3Cl), *diagram* O-602
Methylene chloride, compound of methane and chlorine (CH_3Cl_2) C-393
3,4-methylenedioxy-amphetamine (MDA), hallucinogenic drug H-18
Métis, Canadians of mixed American Indian and European ancestry S-49a, g, R-120
Manitoba rebellions M-103
Metlakatla, Alaska, American Indian cooperative village 15 mi (25 km) s. of Ketchikan; pop. 1,050, *map* U-39
Meton, Athenian astronomer, 5th century BC; instituted use of Metonic cycle, a period of 19 years, after which new and full moons fall on same days of year as they did when cycle started.
Metonymy, in rhetoric, figure of speech in which one word is used for another to which it bears some close relation, as "the kettle boils," instead of "the water boils." Synecdoche is a form of metonymy F-81
creative writing W-379
Metric Convention (1875), in France W-139
Metric system, a system of weights and measures W-139, *table* W-141
heat H-104
mechanics M-265
Metric ton, unit of measure, *table* W-141
Métro, subway
Montreal M-572
Paris P-120, *picture* P-121
Metronome, time-keeping device used in music M-691
Metroplex, metropolitan area in Texas, consisting of Dallas-Fort Worth; area 8,360 sq mi (21,652 sq km); pop. 2,974,878 D-11
Metropolitan, ecclesiastical title in the Christian church, almost equivalent to archbishop; holder has oversight over bishops of subordinate sees; title arose from old custom of giving precedence to bishop of metropolis.
Metropolitan area, term for area covered by a city or cities together with their suburbs and sometimes more remote districts; unit known as Standard Metropolitan Statistical Area is employed by Bureau of the Census in United States; this unit broken down into city or cities and area designated as "outside central city" C-450
housing H-291
Metropolitan Correctional Center, Chicago, Ill., *picture* C-243
Metropolitan Manila (or National Capital Region), Philippines; merger of Manila, Quezon City, Pasay, Caloocan, and 13 other municipalities; formed in 1975; pop. 5,925,884 M-97
Metropolitan Museum of Art, New York, N.Y. M-663, N-254, N-277
Houdon's Benjamin Franklin, *picture* S-88
paintings, *pictures* P-24, 37, 35, 42, 44, 45, 47, 51, 52, 63, 65, 67e, 67f
silks, *picture* S-201
Metropolitan Opera Company, term applied collectively to organizations that have presented operas at Metropolitan Opera House, New York City (in original structure 1883–1965, part of Lincoln Center 1966–); official name after 1932 Metropolitan Opera Association, Inc.; first performance Oct. 22, 1883 ('Faust'), first radio broadcast Christmas Eve, 1931 ('Hänsel und Gretel'), first telecast to theaters Dec. 11, 1952 ('Carmen')
Anderson A-407
opera house, *picture* N-280
productions A-670
Metropolitan State College, Denver, Colo.; founded 1963; liberal arts, business, education, engineering technology, experimental studies, science and mathematics, urban studies D-103
Metropolitan State University (formerly Minnesota Metropolitan State College), St. Paul, Minn.; established 1971; arts and sciences.
Metsu, Gabriel (1630–67), Dutch painter, born in Leiden; fair and market scenes; truthful representation of life in both low and high classes of society ('The Music Lesson'; 'Amsterdam Market').
Metternich, Prince of (in full Klemens Wenzel Nepomuk Metternich) (1773–1859), Austrian statesman M-319
Austria A-830
Congress of Vienna V-316
Mettur Dam, Tamil Nadu state, India, on the Cauvery; irrigates about 1,300,000 acres (526,000 hectares); hydroelectric power.
Metuchen, N.J., town 5 mi (8 km) n.e. of New Brunswick; aluminum products; oil refining; pop. 16,031.
Metz, France, cap. of Moselle department, in n.e.; pop. 113,236; transportation and manufacturing center of Lorraine region; Gothic cathedral of Saint-Étienne, promenades along Moselle River, ancient Roman aqueducts, *map* F-369
Alsace-Lorraine A-320
Meunier, Constantin (1831–1905), Belgian sculptor and painter, born in Etterbeek, suburb of Brussels; best known for sculptures portraying men and women at work ('The Hammerer', 'The Sower', 'Monument to Labor') S-90
Meurthe-et-Moselle, department of France in region called Lorraine; area, 2,038 sq mi (5,278 sq km); pop. 722,588, *map* F-369
Meuse, department of France in region called Lorraine; area, 2,408 sq mi (6,237 sq km); diversified industry and agriculture; pop. 203,904, *map* F-369
Meuse-Argonne, region in France between Verdun and Vouziers extending from Meuse River 25 mi (40 km) w. to Aisne River
warfare, *list* W-15
World War I W-314
Meuse River, river in w. Europe; 560 mi (900 km) long; flows through The Netherlands, where it is called the Maas, *map* F-372. *see also in index* Maas River
Liège, *picture* L-193
The Netherlands N-125
Mexicali, Mexico, capital of Baja California Norte; pop. 361,000 C-54
Mexico M-328, *map* M-341
Mexican Americans, Hispanic Americans H-162, *pictures* H-163, 164, 165
North America N-337
Mexican ash, tree A-671
Mexican blade apple, *picture* L-101
Mexican Farm Labor Supply Program (unofficially bracero program), arrangement to provide Mexican labor to the United States 1942–64 H-164
Mexican Independence Day M-336
Mexican jumping bean. *see in index* Jumping bean
Mexican Revolution (or Revolution of 1910)
Latin American literature L-69
Mexico M-331, 337
Mexican Riviera, coastal region of Mexico M-323
Mexican rubber tree. *see in index* Caucho
Mexican shell flower. *see in index* Tigridia
Mexican sunflower. *see in index* Tithonia
Mexican tulip poppy. *see in index* Hunnemannia
Mexican War (1846–48), between Mexico and United States M-319
American Indian displacement I-149
Davis D-42
frontier affected F-422
Grant G-215
Kearny K-194
Lee L-115
Mexican Americans M-162
Mexico M-336
Mexico City M-347
national cemeteries N-23
Polk P-438
Scott S-75
Taylor T-42
United States U-177
New Mexico A-272
Southwest S-339
veterans' benefits V-306
warfare, *list* W-13
Mexico (or Estados Unidos Mexicanos), republic of North America; 761,600 sq mi (1,972,500 sq km); cap. Mexico City; pop. 80,472,000 M-321. *see also in index* Latin America
archaeology A-532
Maya I-146
arts and crafts
classical music M-675
folk art F-254
literature S-476, *list* S-481c
Latin American literature L-68, 74
mosaic M-590
painting P-67a, *picture* P-67b
avocado A-889, A-100
birth and death rates, *chart* P-448
bullfighting B-501
cities. *see also in index* cities listed below and other cities by name
Acapulco A-15
Guadalajara G-294
Mexico City M-345
Monterrey M-567
Tijuana T-184
Veracruz V-280
clothing, *picture* P-67b
cowboy origins C-750
dams C-586, *map* C-585. *see also in index* Dam, *table*
flags F-154, *pictures* F-155, 168
Gulf of Mexico M-345
history. for a list of recent presidents, *see table* following
American Indian civilizations, *picture* A-890. *see also in index* Aztec; Huastec; Maya; Toltec; Zapotec
Díaz' rule D-133
exploration and conquest A-331
Cortez C-727
Gadsden Purchase U-178, *map* U-177
Juárez J-145
New Mexico N-218
Spain
Hidalgo H-150
Tampico incident V-281
Texas T-115
Alamo A-238
Austin A-765
Villa, *picture* V-325
war P-438. *see also in index* Mexican War
turkey T-326

MEXICO'S RECENT PRESIDENTS

(For biographical information, *see in index* names below)

Alvaro Obregón	1920–24
Plutarco Elías Calles	1924–28
Emilio Portes Gil*	1928–30
Pascual Ortiz Rubio	1930–32
Abelardo Lujan Rodríguez*	1932–34
Lázaro Cárdenas	1934–40
Manuel Avila Camacho	1940–46
Miguel Alemán	1946–52
Adolfo Ruiz Cortines	1952–58
Adolfo López Mateos	1958–64
Gustavo Díaz Ordaz	1964–70
Luis Echeverría Alvarez	1970–76
José López Portillo	1976–82
Miguel de la Madrid Hurtado	1982–

*Provisional

United States C-41, S-337, *chart* U-120
Wyoming W-390
irrigation I-356
land reform L-29
national anthem, *table* N-64
national parks N-27
North America N-334, 339, *pictures* N-336, 344, *map* N-351
ore O-601
postal service P-463b
radio R-54
Rio Grande R-209
rubber R-305
Third World T-168
transportation
railroad mileage, *table* R-85
Pan American Highway, *picture* R-218
volcanoes V-380, 383, *pictures* V-380, 381
weights and measures, *table* W-141
Yucatán peninsula. *see in index* Yucatán peninsula

México, state in s.-central Mexico; 8,286 sq mi (21,461 sq km); cap. Toluca, in great central plateau; includes most of Federal District; pop. 6,245,385
Mexico, *map* M-341

México, D.F., official name of Mexico City. *see in index* Mexico City

Mexico, Mo., city 100 mi (160 km) n.w. of St. Louis; farming area; saddle horses; firebrick, shoes, bags, plastics; soybean mill; pop. 12,176.

Mexico, Gulf of, arm of the Atlantic, almost enclosed by U.S., Mexico, and Cuba M-345. *see also in index* Ocean, *table*
Havana H-56
Louisiana L-309
drilling P-238, *picture* P-239
Mexico M-325, *map* M-341
North America, *map* N-351
oceans O-459
sponge fisheries S-394

Mexico, University of. *see in index* National Autonomous University

Mexico City (first called Tenochtitlán, later named Mexitli, officially called México, D.F.), capital of Mexico; city pop. 8,831,079, metro. area 15,668,800 M-345
Aztec city A-890, M-336
Montezuma II M-568
earthquake H-190
Gulf of Mexico M-345
Latin America L-66
Mexico M-321, 328, 334, *pictures* M-327, 337, *map* M-341
North America N-339, *picture* N-341, *map* N-351
Orozco's murals O-608
zoo Z-459

Mey, Cornelius (or Cornelius May) (fl. 1623), Dutch explorer of North America
New Jersey N-199

Meyer, Adolf (1866–1950), U.S. psychiatrist, born in Niederweningen, near Zurich, Switzerland; to U.S. 1892; became citizen 1901.

Meyer, Albert Gregory, Cardinal (1903–65), U.S. Roman Catholic prelate, born in Milwaukee, Wis.; bishop of Superior 1946–53; archbishop of Milwaukee 1953–58, of Chicago 1958–65; became cardinal 1959.

Meyer, Armin Henry (born 1914), U.S. diplomat, born in Fort Wayne, Ind.; ambassador to Lebanon 1961–65, to Iran 1965–69, to Japan 1969–72.

Meyer, Conrad Ferdinand (1825–98), Swiss poet and historical novelist, born in Zurich; clear, polished style; precursor of 20th-century psychological writing G-100

Meyer, Julius Lothar (1830–95), German chemist, born in Varel, Oldenburg; worked on physiology of blood; did independent research on periodic law.

Meyerbeer, Giacomo (originally Jakob Liebmann Beer) (1791–1864), German composer, born in Berlin; accomplished pianist at 9; studied piano with Clementi, counterpoint with Vogler; known for French operas, also wrote in German and Italian styles; collaborated with A.E. Scribe, librettist ('Robert le Diable'; 'Le Prophète'; 'L'Africaine')
Lind L-226
opera O-567

Meyerhof, Otto Fritz (1884–1951), German physiologist, born in Hanover. *see also in index* Nobel Prizewinners, *table*

Meyer zoysia (or Zoysia meyeri), tropical grass discovered in Korea about 1913 by Frank N. Meyer, U.S. Department of Agriculture plant explorer; further developed by plant scientists at the government's experimental farms, Beltsville, Md.; recommended for lawns and golf courses in warm sections of country
growing conditions G-27

Meynell, Alice (1847–1922), English poet and essayist, born in Barnes, Surrey; brought up in Italy ('Preludes', 'Renouncement', 'A Father of Women', 'The Rhythm of Life'); daughter **Viola Meynell** (born 1886) also an able poet and novelist
Thompson T-173

Meynell, Wilfred (1852–1948), British editor
Thompson T-173

Mezereum family (or Thymelaeaceae), family of plants, shrubs, and trees; includes spurge flax, leatherwood, rice flower, and the gnidias.

Mézières, France, town 125 mi (200 km) n.e. of Paris; resisted Allies for six weeks after Waterloo 1815; taken by Germans 1871, 1914, 1940; since 1966 one of twin towns, together known as Charleville-Mézières; pop. 25,214.

Mezokovesd, Hungary, town 72 mi (116 km) n.e. of Budapest; tobacco warehouses; embroideries; 14th-century church.

'Mezzetin', work by Watteau, *picture* W-109

Mezzo, in music, *list* M-671

Mezzo-soprano, music, female voice between soprano and contralto.

Mezzotint, engraving technique, *list* G-234

MHD. *see in index* Plasma engine

Miacis, prehistoric animal C-211
dogs' ancestor D-211

Miami, a North American Indian tribe that formerly lived in Midwest I-89, *maps* I-136, 149, *table* I-139

Miami, Ariz., town 7 mi (11 km) w. of Globe; copper mining and smelting; asbestos; pop. 2,716.

Miami, Fla., city in s.e. on Biscayne Bay; famous winter resort; pop. 380,446 M-348, F-196, *maps* F-195, U-41
climatic region, *map* U-119
Hispanic Americans H-163, 168, *picture* H-162
North America, *map* N-351
Seaquarium exhibit, *picture* S-187

Miami, Okla., city near n.e. corner of state, on Lake o' the Cherokees; lead and zinc mining; livestock raising, dairying; tires, clothing; Northeastern Oklahoma Agricultural and Mechanical College; pop. 14,237.

Miami, University of, Coral Gables, Fla.; private control; founded 1926; arts and sciences, business administration, education, engineering, law, medicine, music, nursing; graduate school; Institute of Marine Science.

Miami and Erie Canal, name given in 1849 to Miami Canal, Miami Extension Canal, and Wabash and Erie Canal; connected Cincinnati and Toledo, Ohio, *map* C-126

'Miami and the Siege of Chicago', work by Mailer M-50
American literature A-361

Miami Beach, Fla., island city off s.e. coast; popular winter resort; pop. 96,913 M-349, *pictures* F-203, U-67, *map* U-41

Miami Conservancy District F-185

Miami River (also called Great Miami River), rises in w. center of Ohio, flows s. to Ohio River; 160 mi (260 km) long.

Miamisburg, Ohio, industrial city 10 mi (16 km) s.w. of Dayton on Miami River; tobacco market; Miamisburg burial mound; pop. 15,304.

Miami Springs, Fla., town 5 mi (8 km) n.w. of Miami; chiefly residential; near Hialeah; pop. 12,350.

Miami University, Oxford, Ohio; state control; founded 1809; absorbed Western College 1974; arts and science, applied science, business administration, education, fine arts; graduate school; branches at Hamilton and Middletown; E.W. Scripps Foundation for Research in Population
honors courses U-207

Miantonomo (1565?–1643), Narraganset chief; condemned to death by whites for waging war against Uncas in spite of treaty; killed by brother of Uncas; monument near Norwich, Conn.

Miaskovsky, Nikolai Yakovlevich (1881–1950), Soviet composer, born in Novogeorgievski; pupil of Rimski-Korsakov; professor composition, Moscow Conservatory; wrote symphonies, string quartets, piano music, and songs.

Mica, any of several transparent silicate minerals that split into sheets M-349
black mica R-229
granite G-214, *picture* R-229a
minerals M-432, 436

Micah (about 757–700 BC), one of Hebrew minor prophets, contemporary of Isaiah; author of 33rd book of Bible's Old Testament.

Mica schist, metamorphic rock composed chiefly of mica and quartz; divides readily into slabs M-437

Micawber, Wilkins, chararacter in Charles Dickens' 'David Copperfield', an impractical optimist who is always waiting for "something to turn up."

Michael, Saint, archangel, leader of celestial armies (Bible, Rev. xii, 7), festival Sept. 29.

Michael (1596–1645), czar of Russia, first of Romanov line R-352

Michael (or Mihai) (born 1921), king of Romania, born in Sinaia, Romania; in 1927 succeeded his grandfather, Ferdinand I, his father, Carol II, having given up his rights to the throne; regency during reign, which lasted until father's return to throne in 1930; again king 1940 when his father abdicated; abdicated 1947 R-318

Michael III (called The Amorian, or The Phrygian, also called The Drunkard) (838–867), Byzantine emperor B-535

Michael VIII Palaeologus (1224?–82), Byzantine emperor 1261–82; recaptured Constantinople from the Latins 1261; recognized spiritual supremacy of popes at Council of Lyons 1274; responsible for cultural revival of empire.

Michael Cerularius (1000?–1059), patriarch of Constantinople B-536

Michaelmas, old English name for the feast of St. Michael, September 29; once popular celebration centering around Michaelmas goose meal.

Michael Obrenovitch III (1823–68), prince of Serbia, born in Kragujevac, Serbia; succeeded 1840, deposed 1842, restored 1860; secured withdrawal of Turkish troops from Serbia; assassinated by Karageorgevitch supporters.

Michalske, August (nickname Mike) (born 1903), U.S. football guard and coach, born in Cleveland, Ohio; player Green Bay Packers 1929–37.

Michaux, André (1746–1802), French botanist, born in Versailles; traveled widely in his work; in U.S. 1785–96
horticulture F-222

Michel, Claude (also called Clodion) (1738–1814), French sculptor, born in Nancy; favored by Louis XV; noted for nymphs, fauns, and bacchantes.

Michelangelo (1475–1564), Italian sculptor, painter, architect, and poet M-350
architecture A-554
book R-112
'Bound Slave', *picture* S-86
drawing D-251, *picture* D-253
Jeremiah's fresco, *picture* J-98
Julius II J-151
'Madonna della Pietà' V-268
Medici family M-273
'Moses' S-87, *picture* M-595
St. Peter's Church, *picture* A-556
Fates, *picture* F-44
sculpture S-87
Sistine Chapel P-37
sibyls S-191
'The Flood', *picture* F-186

Michelet, Jules (1798–1874), French historian M-352
history writing H-173

Michelin, André (1853–1931) French manufacturer M-353

Michelin, Édouard (1859–1940) French manufacturer M-353

Michelson, Albert A.(1852–1931), U.S. physicist M-353, *picture* P-308. *see also in index* Nobel Prizewinners, *table*
Hall of Fame, *table* H-16
speed of light L-198

Michelson-Morley experiment R-140
Michelson M-353
speed of light L-198

Michener, Daniel Roland (born 1900), Canadian statesman and lawyer, born in Lacombe, Alta.; member of Parliament 1953–62, speaker 1957–62; high commissioner to India 1964–67; governor-general of Canada 1967–74.

Michener, James Albert (born 1907), U.S. author and educator, born in New York City; served with U.S. Navy in South Pacific in World War II; his 'Tales of the South Pacific' won Pulitzer prize for fiction 1948 and was basis for musical play 'South Pacific', awarded Pulitzer prize 1950 ('The Bridges at Toko-ri', 'Sayonara', 'Caravans', 'Hawaii', 'The Source', and 'The Drifters', novels; 'The Floating World'; 'The Bridge at Andau'; 'Iberia: Spanish Travels and Reflections')
American literature A-361
novel of place N-409

Michigan, n.-central state of U.S.; 58,216 sq mi (150,779 sq km); cap. Lansing; pop. 9,258,344 M-354
cities. *see also in index* cities listed below and other cities by name
Detroit D-121
Saginaw S-14
Warren W-32
first mail train, *picture* P-460d
geographic region
North Central Plains U-68, *map* U-71, *picture* U-68, *Reference-Outline* U-135
Great Lakes G-247
Mackinac bridge, *picture* B-439
minerals S-518
name, *table* S-428

Milan (Milano), Italy, city; pop. 1,655,600 M-408
Europe, *map* E-361
Italy I-384, *picture* I-394, *map* I-401
policeman, *picture* P-430a
Sforza family S-127

Milan, Edict of (AD 313), by Constantine the Great; gave Christians the right to practice their religion openly C-680

Milan Obrenovitch IV (1854–1901), prince of Serbia; succeeded 1868; secured Serbian independence and became king 1882; abdicated 1889 in favor of his son, Alexander I.

Milanov, Zinka (born 1906), Yugoslavian opera soprano, *list* O-570

Milbank Memorial Fund, established 1905 by Elizabeth Milbank Anderson for advancement of health and social welfare.

Mildews and molds
paint mildewcides P-74

Mildred L. Batchelder Award, U.S. L-240

Mile, unit of measure, *table* W-140
railroad line R-74
track T-243

Miles, Nelson Appleton (1839–1925), U.S. soldier, born near Westminster, Mass.; fought at Antietam, Fredericksburg, Chancellorsville, the Wilderness, Spotsylvania, and Cold Harbor, and received Congressional Medal of Honor; captor of Apache chief Geronimo; commanded U.S. Army 1895–1903; lieutenant general by act of Congress (1900)
Montana history M-554

Miles City, Mont., city on Yellowstone River about 135 mi (215 km) n.e. of Billings; oil center; horse, cattle, and sheep district; railroad shops, stockyards, wool market; veterans' hospital; Fort Keogh Livestock Experiment Station; pop. 9,602 M-560
United States, *map* U-40

Miles College, Fairfield, Ala.; Christian Methodist Episcopal; founded 1907; liberal arts, education.

Miletus, great maritime city and republic on Aegean Sea in ancient Ionia, Asia Minor; center of learning; stormed and sacked by Persians 494 BC for leading Ionian revolt.

Milfoil (or yarrow), perennial herbs composing the genus *Achillea* of the composite family, with flower heads in flat, open clusters; among species that are cultivated are common yarrow or milfoil *Achillea millefolium* and fernleaf yarrow *Achillea filipendulina*.

Milfoil, water. *see in index* Myriophyllum

Milford, Conn., city on Long Island Sound at mouth of Wepawaug River, 9 mi (15 km) s.w. of New Haven; yachting center; machinery, hardware; pop. 49,101.

Milford, Del., city on Mispillion River 18 mi (29 km) s.e. of Dover; food processing, dental and pharmaceutical products; pop. 5,366.

Milford, Mass., on Charles River, 17 mi (27 km) s.e. of Worcester; textile machinery, shoes, hats, sportswear, tile products; near granite quarries; pop. of township 23,390.

Milford Sound, New Zealand, *picture* N-289

Milhaud, Darius (1892–1974), French composer, born in Aix-en-Provence, France; formerly member ultramodern group, Les Six; attaché French Legation, Brazil, 1917–18; autobiography, 'Notes Without Music'
classical music M-675

Milhous, Katherine (born 1894), U.S. author and illustrator of children's books, born in Philadelphia, Pa.; wrote and illustrated 'Lovina', 'Snow over Bethlehem', 'The Egg Tree' (won Caldecott Medal 1951), 'Patrick and the Golden Slippers', 'Appolonia's Valentine', 'Through These Arches'
children's books R-111c

Mililani Town, Hawaii, suburb of Honolulu, on island of Oahu; pop. 21,365 H-70

Military, a country's armed forces
hobby H-183

Military Academies M-409

Military Academy, United States. *see in index* United States Military Academy

Military Affiliate Radio System. *see in index* MARS

Military Airlift Command (MAC), U.S. Air Force A-164

Military art and science. *see in index* Warfare ; Weapon

Military attaché, representative of a country's army, navy, or air force D-149

Military cemeteries. *see in index* National cemeteries

Military District of Washington, D.C., U.S. Army A-646

Military education M-409

Military grid, maps M-118

Military-industrial complex W-22

Military insignia. *see in index* Insignia

Military intelligence, U.S. Army A-646

Military law C-748

Military Order of the Loyal Legion (1865) P-140

Military Park, park in Newark, N.J. N-149

Military Police Corps (MP), U.S. Army A-646
insignia, *picture* U-10

Military science. *see in index* Warfare; Weapon

Military service. *see in index* Army; Conscription; United States Army

Military Staff Committee, United Nations U-21, 22

Military strategy. *see in index* Strategy

Military tactics. *see in index* Tactics

Militia, United States, all able-bodied male citizens between 18 and 45, comprising National Guard, Naval Militia, and Unorganized Militia
American Revolution R-167, 170
conscription C-667
U.S. Congressional power U-149

Militia, state. *see in index* National Guard

Milk M-414. *see also in index* milk products by name, such as Cheese; and subjects beginning with Milk
composition, *table* C-230
sugar S-508
vitamins V-356, *table* V-355
dairy cows C-225
digestion H-84
farming F-25
food and nutrition F-278
goats G-171
immune system I-56
production and processing D-3
farm machinery F-35
malnutrition M-77
pasteurization P-138
vocation, *picture* V-371

Milk chocolate, sweet with milk added to cocoa butter and chocolate liquor C-394, *picture* S-541

Milk glass, popular name originally given to milk-white decorative glass and later also applied to colored opaque glass; may date from Egyptians, first made on wide scale in 18th-century Europe.

Milking Shorthorn, breed of cattle C-226, *picture* C-227

Milk of magnesia (or magnesium hydroxide) M-41

Milk River, Alberta, and Montana; tributary of the Missouri; 500 mi (800 km) long; not navigable A-263, *map* U-80
North America, *map* N-351

Milk sickness, virulent disease characterized by severe tremors of the body and disturbances in the alimentary tract; produced by consuming milk, dairy products, or meat from cattle poisoned by white snakeroot; common on the frontier but now rare.

Milk snake (or house snake), harmless common snake of North America about 4 ft (1.2 m) long or less; so named because of a misconception that it sucks milk from cows, although actually it seeks barns to feed on mice; strikingly colored; belongs to group of king snakes S-226b, *picture* S-225

Milk sugar. *see in index* Lactose

Milk teeth, animal
dog D-196

Milk teeth, human. *see in index* Primary teeth

Milkweed, perennial of genus *Asclepias* M-415
butterfly ecosystem B-527
kapok substitute K-190
plants, *picture* P-356
weed, *picture* W-132

Milkweed butterfly, popular name for the monarch. *see in index* Monarch butterfly

Milky Way, galaxy
astronomy A-710, 724, *chart* A-725
black holes B-306
earth E-9, 34
matter M-230
solar system S-254
stars S-412, *charts* S-415, 419
universe U-198

Mill, James (1773–1836), English philosopher and economist whose strong personality and brilliant conversation added to influence of his books ('History of British India'; 'Analysis of the Human Mind'); father of John Stuart Mill
Mill M-416

Mill, John Stuart (1806–73), English philosopher and economist M-416
Carlyle C-169
contributions
literature E-279
philosophy P-266

Mill
first U.S. mill R-181, *pictures* R-183, 185
flour and flour milling F-215, *picture* F-214
paint P-75, *picture* P-74
paper, *pictures* P-101, U-46
rubber R-303
steel. *see in index* Steel, *subhead* mill
sugar, *picture* S-506
textile *picture* S-315
silk, *picture* P-78
waterpower W-105, *picture* W-103

Mill, money of account in the United States, equal to a thousandth of a dollar; name derived from Latin mille (thousand); commonly used as rate of taxation (millage); has no equivalent coin.

Millais, Sir John Everett (1829–96), English painter M-416

Millar, Kenneth (or Ross Macdonald) (1915–83), writer D-119

Millay, Edna St. Vincent (1892–1950), U.S. poet M-417, A-356

Millbrae, Calif., city 13 mi (21 km) s. of San Francisco; chiefly residential; nurseries and growing of wholesale flowers; incorporated 1948; pop. 20,058.

Millburn, N.J., urban township in picturesque setting 8 mi (13 km) w. of Newark; impressive estates in Short Hills, a village included in Millburn; settled about 1725; incorporated 1857; pop. 19,543.

Millcreek, Pa., urban township adjacent to Erie and included in its metropolitan area; chiefly residential; manufactures variety of products; incorporated 1803; pop. 44,303.

Milledge, John (1757–1818), U.S. statesman and Revolutionary War patriot, born in Savannah, Ga.; governor of Georgia 1802–6; U.S. senator 1806–9; in 1800 presented more than 600 acres (243 hectares) of land to University of Georgia (chartered 1785); Milledgeville, Ga., named for him.

Milledgeville, Ga., city of historic interest, 29 mi (47 km) n.e. of Macon; textiles, lumber, medical supplies, mobile homes; Milledgeville State Hospital nearby; Georgia College; state capital 1807–68; pop. 12,176, *picture* G-87
secession convention S-443

Millefiori glass, type of mosaic glassware having a flowerlike pattern, *picture* E-208

Millefleur style, tapestry design T-26

Mille Lacs Lake, Minnesota M-445, *picture* M-439

Millennial Dawnists (or International Bible Students, or Jehovah's Witnesses, or Russellites), religious group J-96

Millennium, period of 1,000 years, especially the 1,000-year period referred to in the Bible (Rev. xx) as the coming kingdom of Christ on earth; also a period of happiness, righteousness, and prosperity M-698

Mille passus, Roman measurement W-138

Miller, Arthur (born 1915), U.S. playwright, born in New York City; married Marilyn Monroe, movie actress, 1956–61 ('All My Sons', 1947 New York Drama Critics Circle Award; 'After the Fall'; 'The Price') A-359
'Death of a Salesman' (Pulitzer prize 1949) R-111g, A-357
drama D-248

Miller, Bertha Mahony (1882–1969), U.S. editor and publisher, born in Rockport, Mass.; edited *The Horn Book Magazine* 1924–50; author of books on children's books; awarded Regina Medal 1967.

Miller, Dayton Clarence (1866–1941), U.S. physicist, born in Strongsville, Ohio; professor Case School of Applied Science; important experiments in sound, ether theory, and light.

Miller, George William (born 1925), U.S. public official, born in Sapulpa, Okla.; chairman Federal Reserve Board 1978–79; secretary of treasury 1979–81.

Miller, Glenn (1909–44), U.S. bandleader, born in Clarinda, Iowa; organized band that brought him fame 1938; entered U.S. Army Air Force 1942; lost on a flight between London and Paris
popular music M-684

Miller, Henry John (1860–1926), U.S. actor, born in London, England; starred in many plays, including 'Heartsease', 'The Only Way', 'The Great Divide', 'The Servant in the House'.

Miller, Hugh (1802–56), Scottish geologist and man of letters, born in Cromarty, Scotland; of great influence in establishment of free Scottish church; from work on Old Red Sandstone deposits decided that creation was perfected in six long periods.

Miller, Joaquin (pen name of Cincinnatus Hiner Miller) (1841?–1913), U.S. poet of the West, born in Liberty, Ind., taken as child to Oregon; was gold miner, soldier, journalist, lawyer, and judge at various times; verses colorful and vigorous though not great poetry ('Songs of the Sierras'; 'Songs of the Sunlands'; 'The Danites in the Sierras', novel, later a play).

Miller, John (1843–1908), U.S. grain merchant and political leader, born in Dryden, N.Y.; elected North Dakota's first governor 1889.

Miller, Kenneth Hayes (1876–1952), U.S. painter and etcher, born in Kenwood, N.Y.; instructor Art Students League, New York City, 1911–36; sculptural quality in compositions.

Miller, S.L., U.S. chemist; worked with Harold Urey E-386

Miller, Samuel Freeman (1816–90), U.S. jurist, born in Richmond, Ky.; practiced medicine 12 years; admitted to bar 1847; associate justice of U.S. Supreme Court 1862–90.

Miller, William (1782–1849), U.S. religious leader, born in Pittsfield, Mass.; captain in War of 1812; from study of Bible came to believe in second coming of Christ; founded Adventist movement in U.S. A-53

Miller, William Edward (born 1914), U.S. political leader and lawyer, born in Lockport, N.Y.; Republican representative from New York 1951–64; chairman of the Republican National Committee 1961–64; vice-presidential candidate 1964.

Miller, popular name for several kinds of moths, so called because the fine, dustlike scales on their wings and bodies reminded people of the men who work in flour mills.

Millerand, Alexandre (1859–1943), French statesman, born in Paris; French minister of war in first years of World War I; president of France 1920–24; senator after 1925; sponsored many social reforms; originally a Socialist, later a Liberal.

Millerite, commercial ore, *table* O-600

Miller's-thumb, small swift fish *Cottus* that lurks wherever salmon or trout are found, preying upon the eggs and fry of its neighbors; it is the only representative of the great sculpin family in North American fresh waters.

Millersville State College, Millersville, Pa; founded 1855; humanities, education, sciences, social sciences; graduate studies.

Miller-Tydings Fair Trades Act, amendment to Sherman Anti-Trust law; enacted 1937; validated contracts between wholesaler and retailer designating minimum resale prices for trade-marked commodities when state laws legalized such contracts.

Miller vs. California, case in U.S. constitutional law P-451

Milles, Carl (original name Carl Emil Wilhelm Anderson) (1875–1955), U.S. sculptor and art collector, born in Lagga, near Stockholm, Sweden; to U.S. 1929, became citizen 1945; professor of sculpture Cranbrook Academy of Art, Bloomfield Hills, Mich., 1929–51; returned to Europe 1951; received many awards ('Fountain of Diana'; 'Triton Fountain') F-335, S-91
designs
statue S-24
'The Meeting of the Waters' S-22, S-91
Wilmington monument W-212

Millet, Francis Davis (1846–1912), U.S. artist and author, born in Mattapoisett, Mass.; painted mural, 'Evolution of Navigation', in Custom House, Baltimore, Md.; wrote 'Capillary Crime and Other Stories'; 'The Danube'; 'The Expedition to the Philippines'; died in sinking of steamship *Titanic*.

Millet, Jean François (1814–75), French painter M-417

Millet, various cereal grasses with small grains in spikes or panicles G-206, *picture* P-191
flour F-213

Millett, Kate (born 1934), U.S. writer W-279

Mill Glacier, Antarctica, *picture* A-473

Milligan, ex parte, case in U.S. constitutional law, *list* S-518b

Milligan College, Milligan College, Tenn.; private control; founded 1881; arts and sciences, teacher education.

Milligram, unit in metric system (0.015 grain), *table* W-140

Millikan, Robert Andrews (1868–1953), U.S. physicist, born in Morrison, Ill.; department of physics University of Chicago 1896–1921; director Norman Bridge Laboratory of Physics, and chairman California Institute of Technology, Pasadena, Calif., 1921–45; especially known for isolating electron and for researches on cosmic rays and on radiating properties of light atoms
electricity E-162
oil-drop experiment P-303
Pupin's influence P-535

Millikin University, Decatur, Ill.; Presbyterian; founded 1901; arts and sciences, business and industrial management, education, music, and nursing.

Milliliter, unit in metric system (0.27052 fluid drams); one milliliter (ml) equals 1.000028 cubic centimeters (cc); used to measure volume or capacity.

Millimeter, unit in metric system (0.03937 in.).

Millimicron (mm), unit of wave length equal to one millionth of a millimeter or one thousandth of a micron; sometimes used in the measurement of light waves.

Millin, Sarah Gertrude (1889–1968), South African writer, born in Kimberley, South Africa, of Jewish parents; penetrating reporting on South African life ('God's Stepchildren'; 'What Hath a Man?'; 'The Dark River'; 'The People of South Africa'); also biographies ('Cecil Rhodes'; 'General Smuts').

Millinery, women's hats; originally a general term for all feminine finery; the word is probably derived from Milaner, an inhabitant of Milan, Italy, a city once famous as a trade center for women's wear
hats and caps H-55

Milling, cloth. *see in index* Fulling

Milling, flour. *see in index* Flour and flour milling

Milling machine, metal-cutting machine tool T-221, *pictures* U-68

'Millions of Cats', book by Gág R-106, *picture* R-111e

Million volt-amperes (MVA)
electric power E-166

Millipede, many-legged arthropod C-251. *see also in index* Centipede

Millis, Walter (1899–1968), U.S. journalist, born in Atlanta, Ga.; writer *New York Herald Tribune* 1924–54 ('The Road to War'; 'This Is Pearl!'; 'Arms and Men'; 'The Abolition of War'; 'An End to Arms'; edited 'The Forrestal Diaries').

Mill Mountain, park and mountain; 2,183 ft (665 m); Roanoke, Va. R-222

Millner, Wayne (1913–76), U.S. football end, born in Roxbury, Mass.; Boston Redskins 1936, Washington Redskins 1937–41, 1945; university and professional coach.

Millrace, part of a waterwheel W-103

Mills, Enos Abijah (1870–1922), U.S. naturalist, born in Kansas City, Kan.; author of articles urging protection of birds and wild flowers, and establishment of national parks ('Wild Life in the Rockies').

Mills, Florence (1895–1927), U.S. entertainer; starred in 'Blackbirds', revue; Duke Ellington wrote 'Black Beauty', a musical portrait of her.

Mills, Ogden Livingston (1884–1937), U.S. lawyer and political leader, born in Newport, R.I.; Republican; U.S. congressman 1921–27; undersecretary of treasury 1927–32; secretary of treasury 1932–33.

Mills, Robert (1781–1855), U.S. architect and engineer, born in Charleston, S.C.; studied with Thomas Jefferson; as architect of public buildings, designed the Treasury, Patent Office and old Post Office, Washington, D.C., *profile* A-569

Mills, Roger Quarles (1832–1911), U.S. Democratic leader, born in Todd County, Kentucky; member of Congress from Texas 1873–92; as chairman of Ways and Means Committee introduced Mills Bill 1888; U.S. senator 1892–99.

Millsaps College, Jackson, Miss.; United Methodist Church; established 1890 by Methodist Episcopal church, South; arts and sciences, education.

Mills bomb, hand grenade B-338

Mills Brothers, U.S. singing group M-679

Mills College, Oakland, Calif.; private control; founded 1852 in Benicia, Calif., moved to Oakland 1871; chartered as a college 1885; liberal arts, educational services, fine arts, natural sciences and mathematics, social sciences; graduate studies.

Millspaugh, Arthur Chester (1883–1955), U.S. political scientist, born in Augusta, Mich.; financial adviser to Iran (Persia) 1922–27, 1943–45 ('Public Welfare Organization' and 'Crime Control by the National Government').

Millstone, in flour milling F-215

Mill Valley, Calif., city 5 mi (8 km) s. of San Rafael; pop. 12,967.

Millville, N.J., manufacturing city about 40 mi (60 km) s. of Camden; agricultural area; glass products from glass sand obtained nearby; pop. 24,815.

Millwork, lumber industry
carpentry C-173

Milman, Henry Hart (1791–1868), English churchman, historian, and poet; dean of St. Paul's Cathedral, London ('History of Latin Christianity').

Milne, A.A. (full name Alan Alexander Milne) (1882–1956), English writer M-418
books R-108

Milne, John (1850–1913), English seismologist, born in Liverpool; professor geology and mining, Imperial University, Tokyo; helped to establish seismological stations throughout world.

Milner, Alfred, Viscount (1854–1925), British statesman and colonial administrator; won international fame as high commissioner for South Africa 1897–1905, period that laid foundations of British rule there; an Imperialist and Conservative, he opposed famous Lloyd George budget of 1909, but joined Coalition cabinet 1916 and except for Lloyd George took largest share in civilian war activities; secretary of state for colonies 1919.

Milnes, Sherrill (born 1935), U.S. opera baritone, *picture* O-566, *list* O-570

Milo (or Milon) (6th century BC), Greek athlete; crowned 6 times at Olympic Games and 6 times at Pythian Games for wrestling; bore ox through stadium A-741

Milo, Greek island. *see in index* Mēlos

Milo, variety of grain sorghum native to Africa; introduced into U.S. about 1880; grown over Great Plains.

Milosz, Czeslaw (born 1911), Polish-born U.S. poet M-418. *see also in index* Nobel Prizewinners, *table*

Milpa agriculture, type of subsistence farming C-256

Milpitas, Calif., city just s. of Palo Alto; automobiles, electronic components; pop. 27,149.

Milreis, former monetary unit of Brazil, worth at par about 55 cents; replaced as coinage unit by cruzeiro in 1926, but retained as basis of foreign exchange; historic value about 20 cents.

Milstein, Nathan (born 1904), U.S. violinist, born in Odessa, U.S.S.R.; studied with Auer and Ysaye; U.S. debut 1929; sensitive interpretations of Bach, Beethoven, and Tchaikovsky.

Milt, fish sperm F-128

Miltiades (died 488? BC), Athenian general; as commander of combined Athenian and Plataean troops won victory over Persians at Marathon (490 BC) P-214
warfare W-23

Milton, John (1608–74), English poet M-418, *picture* P-303
angel and demon themes A-414
censorship attacks C-247
folklore F-269
'Il Penseroso'. *see in index* 'Il Penseroso'
literary contribution E-269
'Lycidas'. *see in index* 'Lycidas'
'Paradise Lost'. *see in index* 'Paradise Lost'

Milton, Mass., 7 mi (11 km) s. of Boston, on Neponset River; settled in 1636; incorporated 1662; industrial center; chocolate, drugs, dyestuffs, pianos, artificial legs; Curry College; pop. of township 27,190.

Milton College, Milton, Wis.; private control; established 1844, chartered 1867; liberal arts and teacher education.

Milvian Bridge (or Mulvian Bridge), ancient bridge over Tiber River on Flaminian Way
battle, *list* W-15

Milwaukee (nicknamed the Machine Shop of America), Wis., largest city of state; pop. 1,380,188 M-421
meat industry, *picture* M-250
North America, *map* N-351
Wisconsin W-248, 260, *picture* W-257

Milwaukee Area Technical College, Milwaukee, Wis. M-421

Milwaukee School of Engineering, Milwaukee, Wis.; private control; founded 1903; engineering technology, electrical and mechanical engineering; graduate school M-421

Milwaukie, Ore., city on Willamette River 6 mi (10 km) s. of Portland; fruit farming; shingles, chain saws, tools, textiles, plywood, farm equipment; founded 1848, incorporated 1903; pop. 17,931.

Mime, form of popular comedy developed in 5th century BC in s. Italy; portrayed events of everyday life by means of dancing, gestures, and witty dialogue; barred from public stage by Christian church but kept alive by strolling players; preserved comic element in drama during Middle Ages and Renaissance as found in the mystery plays, interludes, and dumb shows; traces still evident in modern pantomime and vaudeville M-422. *see also in index* Pantomime
acting A-26
Greek literature G-277

Mimeograph (or stencil duplicator), machine for making multiple copies of documents; commonly but erroneously applied to stencil duplicating in general; consists of a stencil and a revolving, self-inking cylinder, turned by hand or by motor; paper fed at rate of several thousand sheets per hour; originated with Thomas A. Edison's electric pen in 1875 and Albert Blake Dick's "mimeograph" duplicator in 1884 D-290, P-502
office equipment O-495

Mimicry, among animals and plants, resemblance in physical structure or coloring to other animals, plants, or natural objects of their environment; provides protection or concealment M-423. *see also in index* Protective coloration
insects I-222
orchid O-580

Mimidae, family of perching birds embracing the mockingbirds, catbirds, and thrashers. *see in index* Catbird; Mockingbird

Mimir, in Norse mythology, giant who guarded the well of wisdom M-703

Mimnermus (fl.late 7th century BC), Greek poet, the first to make elegiac verse a vehicle for love poetry; only fragments of his works remain.

Mimosa, small tree *Mimosa nemu* with branched trunk, smooth gray bark, and feathery compound leaves, which fold up at night; small fragrant flowers with long pink stamens borne in dense spherical clusters that suggest powder puffs, native to Asia, bark used for tanning; few varieties of acacia called mimosa.

Mimosa, Texas. *see in index* Catclaw

Mimosoideae, acacia subfamily L-118

Mimulus (or monkey flower), genus of annual and perennial plants of the figwort family, found throughout world, often in moist places; leaves oblong or oval; stems square; flowers tubular, seeming like tiny monkey faces, yellow, spotted brown or white through red; Allegheny monkey flower *M. ringens*; common monkey flower *M. luteus*. *see also in index* Musk plant.

Min, Egyptian god M-700

Mina, standard weight for the ancient Sumerians B-6
mathematics M-213

Minakshi Temple, Madura, India I-71

Minamoto, Japanese warrior clan J-63
Taira family conflict T-11

Minamoto, Yoritomo (1147–99), Japanese soldier and statesman; shogun 1192–99. *see also in index* Fujiwara
Taira family defeat T-11

Minaret, slender tower of a mosque from which a muezzin calls Muslims to prayer
Islam, *picture* I-359

Minas de Ríotinto (also called Ríotinto), Spain, town 40 mi (60 km) n.w. of Seville; famed for extensive deposits of copper and for copper mines worked

Minneapolis M-438
St. Paul S-23, *picture* S-23
Mississippi M-466, *pictures* M-467, 476, 477
Vicksburg V-307
Missouri-Mississippi river system M-487, 492, *map* U-32
Missouri River M-509
North America, *map* N-351
St. Anthony Falls. *see in index* St. Anthony Falls
Tennessee T-82, *map* 96
Texas T-116
Twain's writings A-352
waterway W-108

Mississippi River Commission F-183

Mississippi River-Gulf Outlet, canal; 76 mi long; built in 1963 by the United States Army Corps of Engineers M-486

Mississippi State University, State College, Miss.; founded 1878; arts and sciences, agriculture, business and industry, education, engineering, forestry; graduate school.

Mississippi University for Women (formerly Mississippi State College for Women), Columbus, Miss.; established in 1884; became a university 1974; arts and sciences, fine arts, teacher education; graduate school.

Mississippi Valley State University, Itta Bena, Miss.; chartered 1946, founded 1950; arts and sciences, business, education, technical education; graduate studies.

Missolonghi (or Mesolongion), town in w. Greece on Gulf of Patras; defended against Turks in War of Liberation 1822–26; pop. 11,266.

Missoula, Mont., city on Clark Fork, 95 mi (150 km) n.w. of Helena; ranch and farm area; lumber and paper products, railroad shops, dairy products; pop. 33,388 M-552, 560
air pollution, *picture* P-441a
North America, *map* N-351
U.S., *map* U-40
University of Montana, *picture* U-204

Missouri (or Missouria), Siouan Indian tribe that left Wisconsin for Missouri and Nebraska; removed to Indian Territory (Oklahoma) in 1882, when only a few remained.

Missouri, n. central state of U.S.; 69,686 sq mi (180,486 sq km); cap. Jefferson City; pop. 4,917,444 M-487, *maps* U-41, 70–71
cities. *see also in index* cities listed below and other cities by name
Kansas City K-188
Jefferson City J-96
St. Louis S-21
geographic region
North America, *map* N-351
North Central Plains U-68, *map* U-70–71, *pictures* U-68–69, *Reference-Outline* U-135
history
Civil War C-473
Confederate States of America C-642
Missouri Compromise M-507
St. Louis founded S-21
St. Louis S-22
Jefferson National Expansion Memorial N.H.S. S-22, *picture* S-21
Radisson explores F-469
state symbols
flag, *picture* F-159
flower, *picture* S-427
tree F-277d
Statuary Hall, *table* S437b
taxation, *tables* T-37, 39

'Missouri', U.S. battleship W-336

Missouri, University of, Columbia, Mo.; state control; est. 1839; opened 1841; arts and sciences, agriculture, business and public administration, education, engineering, forestry, home economics, journalism, law, library and information science, medicine, nursing, social and community service, veterinary medicine; arts and sciences, dentistry, education, law, medicine, music, and pharmacy at Kansas City; liberal arts, engineering, mines and metallurgy, and science at Rolla; arts and sciences, business, and education at St. Louis; graduate studies M-492, *picture* M-497
journalism school N-242

Missouri Botanical Garden, St. Louis, Mo.; est. 1890 by Henry Shaw; 75 acres (30 hectares); owns an arboretum of 1,600 acres (647 hectares) at Gray Summit S-22

Missouri Compromise M-507
black Americans B-291
Civil War postponement C-472
Clay's role C-487
Dred Scott decision, *picture* S-21
Kansas-Nebraska Act K-189
Missouri M-493

Missouri Fur Company F-471

Missouri Plateau
Montana M-550
North Dakota N-373

Missouri River (nickname Big Muddy), chief tributary of Mississippi River; length of Missouri River proper, 2,316 mi (3,727 km) M-507, *maps* N-351. *see also in index* Fort Peck Dam
dams D-17
hydroelectric power generator, *picture* P-166
Iowa I-288
irrigation programs I-356
Lewis and Clark's exploration L-143
Missouri M-487, 492
Missouri-Mississippi river system, *map* U-32–33
Montana M-550
Nebraska N-94, 98, *picture* N-101
North Dakota N-373, *picture* N-380
South Dakota S-323, 328, *picture* S-330
trade K-188
United States, *maps* U-40, 70, 80

Missouri River Basin Program
farmers channel water, *picture* U-75
Missouri River M-510

Missouri Southern State College, Joplin, Mo.; opened as junior college 1937, present name 1965; liberal arts, education, sciences.

Missouri Valley College, Marshall, Mo.; Presbyterian; founded 1888; arts and sciences, education, human services, and music.

Missouri Western State College, St. Joseph, Mo.; state and district control; founded 1915 as junior college; liberal arts and sciences, applied science and technology, education and psychology.

'Miss Thompson', short story by Maugham M-231

Mist, fine particles of moisture in the air near the ground, not as dense as fog, but often with larger droplets that fall slowly
fog and F-245
Pacific Islands, *picture* P-1

Mistassini, lake in Quebec near the Height of Land; 120 mi (190 km) long, *maps* C-112, Q-9a
North America, *map* N-351

'Mr. Buchanan's Administration on the Eve of the Rebellion', work by Buchanan B-476

'Mr. Clutterbuck's Election', work by Belloc B-157

Mr. Pickwick, character developed by Dickens D-135

'Mr. Sammler's Planet', work by Bellow A-362, B-157

Misti, El, volcano of Andes e. of Arequipa, Peru; 19,199 ft (5,852 m); scenic snowcapped peak; prominent in Peruvian poetry and folklore, *map* S-298

Mistletoe, parasitic shrub M-510
adaptation A-39
Oklahoma's state flower, *pictures* O-528, S-427
seed dispersal S-107

Mistral, Frédéric (1830–1914), French poet, born near Arles; led Provencal literary revival ('Mireio'); Nobel prizewinner. *see also in index* Nobel Prizewinners, *table*

Mistral, Gabriela (pen name of Lucila Godoy Alcayaga) (1889–1957), Chilean writer, born in Vicuña, near La Serena, Chile
Latin American literature L-69, *picture* L-74

Mistral, wind W-225
Switzerland S-537

'Mistress Mary', nursery rhyme N-445

Misurata, Libya, city in oasis about 120 mi (190 km) e. of Tripoli; carpet industry; about 7 mi (11 km) to e. is port Misurata Marina, outlet to Mediterranean Sea; pop. 45,146, with suburbs.

Mitanni, ancient Indo-European empire in n. Mesopotamia
horse H-270

Mitchel, John (died 1768), English botanist and map maker
maps, *picture* M-127

Mitchell, Arthur (born 1934), U.S. ballet dancer and choreographer, born in New York City; co-founded Dance Theatre of Harlem D-24

Mitchell, Billy (or William Mitchell) (1879–1936), U.S. Army officer M-511
Air Force expansion A-157
Wisconsin W-254

Mitchell, Clarence M., Jr. (1911–84), U.S. civil rights leader, born in Baltimore, Md.; labor secretary NAACP 1945–50, director Washington, D.C., bureau 1950–78; worked for passage of Civil Rights acts; won 1969 Spingarn medal.

Mitchell, Donald G. *see in index* Marvel, Ik

Mitchell, Edgar D. (born 1930), U.S. astronaut, born in Hereford, Tex.; U.S. Navy officer chosen for NASA program 1966
moon landing S-347, *table* S-348

Mitchell, Helen Porter. *see in index* Melba, Nellie

Mitchell, James Paul (1902–64), U.S. public official and businessman, born in Elizabeth, N.J.; vice-president of Bloomingdale Brothers, New York City, 1947–53; assistant secretary of the Army 1953; U.S. secretary of labor 1953–61.

Mitchell, John (1870–1919), U.S. labor leader, born in Braidwood, Ill.; president, United Mine Workers of America; vice-president, American Federation of Labor; leader of anthracite strike 1901–2; on New York State Workmen's Compensation Board 1914 ('Organized Labor').

Mitchell, John Newton (born 1913), U.S. lawyer and public official, born in Detroit, Mich.; manager of Richard M. Nixon's presidential campaigns 1968 and early part of 1972; U.S. attorney general 1969–72; after conviction in Watergate case, disbarred 1975
Nixon N-326

Mitchell, Margaret (or Margaret Munnerlyn Mitchell) (1900–49), U.S. novelist M-511
'Gone with the Wind' A-358, R-112

Mitchell, Maria (1818–89), U.S. astronomer M-512
Hall of Fame, *table* H-16

Mitchell, Peter (1824–99), Canadian political leader, born in Newcastle, N.B.
Fathers of Canada Confederation C-118, *picture* C-116

Mitchell, Peter Dennis (born 1920), British biochemist, born in Mitcham, Surrey; at University of Edinburgh 1955–63; director of research, Glynn Research Institute since 1964; research on the action of adenosine triphosphate; Nobel prizewinner. *see also in index* Nobel Prizewinners, *table*

Mitchell, Silas Weir (1829–1914), U.S. neurologist and novelist, born in Philadelphia, Pa.; developed "rest cure" for diseases ('Hugh Wynne'; 'Dr. North and His Friends').

Mitchell, S.D., city 68 mi (109 km) n.w. of Sioux Falls; meat packing, sporting goods, farm machinery; Dakota Wesleyan University; famous Corn Palace (a building covered inside and out with corn); pop. 13,916, *maps* S-335, U-40

Mitchell, Mount, highest point (6,684 ft; 2,037 m) in Appalachian Mountains and in North Carolina, in w. part of state, n.e. of Asheville A-508, *map* U-59
comparative height. *see in index* Mountain, *table*
North Carolina N-354

Mitchell Caverns State Reserve, *picture* C-47

Mitchell Park Horticultural Conservatory, Milwaukee, Wis. M-421, *picture* M-422

Mitchill, Samuel Latham (1764–1831), U.S. physician, science promoter, legislator; born in North Hempstead, N.Y.; experiments helped to develop industrial chemistry; in U.S. Congress (Democrat) 1801–9, 1810–13
folklore F-264

Mite, tiny arachnid S-387
Antarctic fauna A-473
cat parasites C-210
ticks. *see in index* Tick

Mitford, Mary Russell (1787–1855), English novelist, born in Alresford, near Winchester, England; best known for 'Our Village', charming unpretentious sketches from life.

Mithradates I, king of Parthia, ruled 174–136 BC; founded the Parthian Empire; conquered Media Magna, Susiana, Persia, Babylonia, Assyria proper; took Greek kingdom of Bactria from Seleucids; allowed the subject kingdoms to rule themselves.

Mithradates VI Eupator (or Mithradates the Great) (132?–63 BC), king of Pontus; waged three wars against Rome in attempt to free Asia Minor from Roman rule; finally, defeated by Pompey, he took his own life; exalted in legend for his culture, courage, and physical strength.

Mithras, Persian god of sun and truth, whose worship was latest great Asian cult imported into Rome before establishment of Christianity; many resemblances to Christianity in doctrine and rites.

MITI. *see in index* Ministry of Industry and Trade

Mitochondrion (plural mitochondria), in cell structure B-200, C-238, *diagrams* B-198, *picture* C-237
nerve cell, *diagram* N-122

Mitosis, body cell's division
cell C-239, *diagram* C-240
genetics G-54
growth G-292
heredity H-139
yeast Y-411

Mitrailleuse, French breech-loading machine gun M-12

Mitral stenosis, heart blockage D-174

Mitre, Bartolomé (1821–1906), Argentine soldier and statesman, born in Buenos Aires; as president 1862–68 carried out constitutional reorganization and encouraged immigration A-583

Mitre Peak, New Zealand, *picture* N-289

Mitropoulos, Dimitri (1896–1960), Greek conductor, born in Athens; promoted 20th-century music including 12-tone style; directed Minneapolis Symphony 1937–49; musical director New York Philharmonic 1951–58; conducted Metropolitan Opera, New York City, and La Scala, Milan, Italy G-258

Mitscher, Marc Andrew (1887–1947), World War II naval commander, born in Hillsboro, Wis.; directed Task Force 58, the United States aerial assaults in the central Pacific
World War II W-346

Mitscherlich, Eilhardt (1794–1863), German chemist, born in Neuende near Jever, Oldenburg; in studying crystals, he discovered principle of isomorphism.

Mitsubishi A6M, Japanese fighter plane A-159, *picture* A-157

Mitsubishi Electric Corporation, Japanese corporation
industrial espionage E-304

Mitsubishi family, famous Japanese mercantile family owning banks, mines, manufacturing, insurance, and shipping companies; important since early 18th century.

Mitsui, Takatoshi (1622–94), Japanese businessman; started the businesses that made the Mitsui family powerful M-512

Mitsui family, famous Japanese mercantile family, controlling large holdings; important since late 17th century M-512

Mitsunarabe, Japanese farmhouse style J-31, *diagram* J-30

Mittelland Canal, canal, West Germany G-118

Mitten, covering for the hand and wrist having a separate section for the thumb only
glove G-169
Mitterrand, François (in full François Maurice Mitterrand) (born 1916), French political leader M-512
France F-366, *pictures* E-146, F-365
Giscard G-149
Miwok, American Indian tribe of California, *map* I-136, *table* I-139
Mix, Ron (born 1938), U.S. football player, born in Los Angeles, Calif.; offensive tackle, Los Angeles Chargers 1960, San Diego Chargers 1961–69, Oakland Raiders 1971.
Mix, in cooking C-700
Mixed economy C-152
Mixed fertilizer F-59
Mixed nerve N-118
Mixed number, whole number and a common fraction or a decimal fraction.
Mixed tide, type of tide O-488
Mixer, in motion pictures M-610, *picture* M-611
Mixtec, Indian tribe
Mexico M-325, 335
Mixture, in chemistry C-297
matter M-224
Miyajima Island, Japan, *picture* N-27
Miyun Dam, China I-356
Mizoram, union territory in India; area about 8,100 sq mi (21,000 sq km); created 1972 from Mizo Hills District of Assam; pop. 321,686, *map* I-83
Mizpah, name of several places in Israel; most important Mizpah of Gilead, where Jacob erected heap of stones and made covenant of peace with Laban: "The Lord watch between me and thee, when we are absent one from another" (Bible, Gen. xxxi, 49). So "Mizpah" is used as a parting salutation and inscription on jewelry.
Mjollnir, in Norse mythology, the hammer of Thor M-703
Mjøsa, Lake, largest lake in Norway, in s.e., 141 sq mi (365 sq km); 65 mi (105 km) long, 1 to 10 mi (1.6 to 16 km) wide, up to 1,473 ft (449 m) deep
Norway N-389
MKS. *see in index* Meter-kilogram-second system
Mmabatho, capital of Bophuthatswana B-366, *map* A-118
MMDA (3-methoxy-3,4-methylenedioxyamphetamine), hallucinogenic drug H-18
MMT. *see in index* Multiple Mirror Telescope
Mnemonics, techniques to improve memory M-295
Mnemosyne, in Greek mythology, goddess of memory; daughter of Uranus and Gaea, and mother of Muses M-700
Mnesicles, Greek architect; designed Propylaea of the Athenian Acropolis about 437 BC.
Moa, extinct bird B-276
New Zealand N-283, 288
Moab (or Moabites), Semitic people in ancient Palestine e. of Dead Sea and the Jordan River; often battled Israelites; conquered by David
Ruth R-365
Moabite stone, slab of black basalt, dating from 9th century BC, which bears ancient Semitic inscription describing victory of Mesha, Moabite king, over Israelites; negotiations for its purchase by the French led to quarrels among the Arabs and it was broken; fragments now in Louvre, Paris.
Moat, ditch, often filled with water
castle C-198
zoo Z-457
Mob, social group of marsupial mammals M-157
kangaroo K-172
Moberly, Walter (1832–1915), Canadian civil engineer, born in Oxfordshire, England; came to Canada when a child; 1859 made superintendent of public works in British Columbia; 1871 had charge of surveys for Canadian Pacific Railway.
Moberly, Mo., industrial city about 33 mi (53 km) n.w. of Columbia; in agricultural area; coal deposits nearby; railroad shops; shoes, wood and metal products, food processing; pop. 13,418, *map* U-41
Mobile, Ala., seaport and 2nd city of the state; pop. 206,505 M-512
Alabama A-225
North America, *maps* N-351, U-41
Mobile, art S-93
Calder's creations C-27
'Mobile', work by Butor N-414
Mobile Bay, Alabama, 27 mi (43 km) long, 8 mi (13 km) wide
DeSoto's exploration D-117
Farragut captures F-37
Mobile College, Mobile, Ala.; Southern Baptist; opened 1963; liberal arts and teacher education.
Mobile Command, Canadian Armed Forces U-12
Mobile emergency room van (or MERVAN), *picture* H-284
Mobile home, housing H-298, 303, 307, *list* H-305
shelter, *picture* S-157
Mobile telephone T-63
Möbius, August (1790–1868), German mathematician M-216
Möbius strip, mathematics M-216
Mobutu Sese Seko (or Joseph-Désiré Mobutu) (born 1930), Zairian military and political leader M-513
Zaire Z-446
Moby Dick, white whale in Melville's novel 'Moby Dick', *pictures* K-207, N-413
'Moby-Dick', romantic novel by Herman Melville telling the adventures of Captain Ahab, who, after losing a leg in first battle with Moby Dick, the white whale, swears revenge; the three days' fight with Moby Dick ends in death of Ahab and sinking of ship A-349, R-111d
creative writing W-381
Melville M-293
whale W-186
Moçambique, seaport in Mozambique; on narrow island of coral 3 mi (5 km) from coast; Arab town on site when Vasco da Gama visited it in 1498; pop. 21,906, *map* A-118
Moccasin, American Indian shoe, usually made of deerskin or other soft leather; often trimmed with beads or shells S-179, *picture* S-178
Moccasin flower. *see in index* Pink lady's slipper
Moccasin snake (or cottonmouth) V-328, *picture* S-226. *see also in index* Snake
average life expectancy, *chart* A-423
Mocha, Yemen Arab Republic, fortified seaport in s. Arabia, on Red Sea; 130 mi (210 km) w. of Aden; Mocha gloves and coffee named for.
Mockernut hickory, tree *Hicoria alba* of walnut family, native from Massachusetts to Florida and Texas H-149
Mockingbird M-513
bird, *picture* B-258
egg, *picture* E-112
state bird
Arkansas, *picture* A-618
Florida, *picture* F-202
Mississippi, *picture* M-474
Tennessee, *picture* T-90
Texas, *picture* T-127
Mock orange. *see in index* Syringa
Mock suns. *see in index* Sundogs
Moctezuma-Pánuco, Río, river system, Mexico M-324, *map* M-344
Modacrylic fiber F-74, *table* F-72
Modalchant. *see in index* Gregorian chant
Mode (or modal average), measure of average S-434
Mode, Greek musical scale M-667
Model, scale. *see in index* Scale model
Model A Ford A-860, *picture* A-859
Model Cities Program (1966), U.S., sought to improve the lives of slum dwellers H-305
Modeling, arts
sculpture S-80
Model Parliament E-106, P-131b
Models and model building M-514
airplanes. *see in index* Airplane models
automobiles A-866, *picture* A-871
hobby H-183
railroads, *picture* R-87
ships and boats S-176b, *picture* S-177
Model T Ford A-859, *picture* A-858
industry I-191, *picture* F-306
Modem, in computer communications I-203
hobby H-191
office equipment O-495
telecommunication T-56
wire W-247
Modena, Italy, city 100 mi (160 km) e. of Genoa; capital of Modena Province; Romanesque cathedral; university; pop. 139,183, *maps* E-361, I-401
Moderato, in music M-691, *list* M-671
Moderator, substance such as graphite, heavy water, or beryllium used to slow down neutrons in nuclear reactor
nuclear energy N-423
Modern art A-670
masks M-185
'Modern Chivalry', work by Brachenridge A-345
Modern dance D-29
Moderne. *see in index* Art Deco
Modern English
development E-262
'Modern Instance, A', work by Howells A-352
Modernism, artistic movement that emphasizes simplicity of design and suppresses incidental or merely decorative detail
architecture A-563. *see also in index* Architecture, *subhead* modern
bookbinding B-355
interior design I-250
literature
Latin American L-69
Darío D-35
U.S. A-353
sculpture S-92
Rodin S-91
'Modern Man in Search of a Soul', work by Jung J-152
'Modern Maturity', magazine M-34
Modern Woodmen of America, fraternal, beneficiary society, providing life insurance to members; founded at Lyons, Iowa, in 1883; the women's auxiliary is known as the Royal Neighbors of America.
Modesto, Calif., city about 70 mi (110 km) s.e. of Sacramento; frozen foods, canned and packed fruits and vegetables, dairy products, wine; pop. 275,741, *map* U-40
'Modest Proposal, A', satire by Swift S-531
English literature E-270
Modified Mercalli Intensity Scale, earthquake measurement E-38
Modifier, in grammar
adjective P-508
Modigliani, Amedeo (1884–1920), Italian painter M-517
'Girl in Pink' P-58, *picture* P-56
stone head S-82, *picture* S-81
Modjeska, Helena (1840–1909), U.S. tragic actress, born in Cracow, Poland; after successful career in Poland moved to U.S.; performed in English after 1877 (Shakespearean roles; 'Camille'; 'Mary Stuart') P-20
Modoc, small Indian tribe closely related to the Klamath, and originally living in n. California and s. Oregon; resistance to being moved to reservation led to Modoc War of 1872–73; later moved to Indian Territory (now Oklahoma) and to Klamath reservation in s. Oregon
Oregon O-583
Modred, Sir, King Arthur's nephew and one of knights of Round Table A-655, R-299a
Modular construction, type of building B-497
Modulation, in music M-692, *list* M-671
Modulation, in radio R-46, *diagrams* R-50
Moe, Jörgen Engebretsen (1813–82), Norwegian folklorist and poet, born in Hole, s.e. Norway; bishop of Kristiansand, collected folk tales in collaboration with Peter C. Asbjörnsen; wrote lyric poems of delicate charm ('In the Well and the Churn'; 'A Little Christmas Present') S-472
Möen, Danish island in the Baltic Sea between Zealand and Falster; 84 sq mi (218 sq km); fisheries; chalk cliffs; pop. 13,107.
Moesia, ancient Roman province s. of Danube River corresponding to modern Bulgaria and e. Yugoslavia; settled by Goths about AD 376, *map* R-242
Moffat, David Halliday (1839–1911), U.S. banker, born in Washingtonville, N.Y.; president First National Bank, Denver; promoted mining industry of Colorado.
Moffat, Robert (1795–1883), Scottish missionary in Africa, born in Ormiston, Scotland; father-in-law of David Livingstone; worked among Bechuana peoples 50 years and translated Bible into their language
Livingstone L-263
Moffat Tunnel, Denver and Salt Lake Railroad; named for David H. Moffat, builder of original railroad line C-569, *picture* C-573
Moffitt, Billie Jean. *see in index* King, Billie Jean
Mofolo, Thomas Mokapu (1876–1948), African novelist, wrote in his native Sotho language A-121
Mogadishu, Somalia, capital and seaport on Indian Ocean; old mosques and modern buildings; museum and library in palace built by sultan of Zanzibar in 19th century; pop. 500,000 M-518
Africa, *map* A-118
Somalia S-257
Mogador, Morocco. *see in index* Essaouira
'Mogens', work by Jacobsen J-11
Mogollan-Mimbres culture, prehistoric North American Indians I-145
archaeological dig, *pictures* A-532
Mogul, Great. *see in index* Mughal, Great
Mogul Empire. *see in index* Mughal Empire
Mohács, Hungary, port in s. on Danube River; coal and silk center; foundry products; pop. 18,100.
Mohács, battle of (1526), warfare, *list* W-15
Jagiellon dynasty J-12
Mohair, cloth G-172, T-321
wool W-288
Mohammad Zahir Shah (born 1914), king of Afghanistan; succeeded father Nadir Shah who was assassinated in 1933; deposed by military coup 1973 A-91
Mohammed. *see in index* Muhammad
Mohammed I (ruled 1413–21), Ottoman sultan O-616
Mohammed II (1430?–81), sultan of Turkey 1451–81; educated, ambitious, brave, but ruthless; overcame Serbia 1456–58; later subdued Trebizond, Greece, Crimea, and Albania T-323
Constantinople B-536
Ottoman Empire O-616
Mohammed V (1844–1918), sultan of Turkey 1909–18; succeeded to throne after brother, Abdul Hamid II, was deposed; during his rule Turkey suffered great loss of European territories.
Mohammed VI (1861–1926), sultan of Turkey, deposed 1922 by Nationalist Assembly T-323
Mohammed Daud Khan (1909–78), Afghanistan political and military leader, born in Kabul; prime minister 1953–63, president and premier 1973–78; assassinated in military coup.
Mohammed Murtala Ramat (1938–76), Nigerian military leader and president
assassination, *list* A-704
Mohammed Reza Pahlavi (or Mohammed Reza Pahlevi) (1919–80), shah of Iran 1941–79, born in Tehran, Iran; forced into exile 1979; son of Reza Shah Pahlavi; autobiography, 'Mission for My Country' I-307
Khomeini K-232
Tehran T-54

subclass of plants P-360, S-106
  orchid O-580
  trees T-282

Monocular microscope M-381

Monocular vision, in zoology
  birds B-246

Monocyte, type of white blood cell B-314, *table* B-317

Monod, Jacques (1910–76), French biologist, born in Paris; with Pasteur Institute from 1945, director from 1971; Nobel prizewinner. *see also in index* Nobel Prizewinners, *table*
  genetics G-54

Monoecious plant F-219

Monogamy
  animal behavior A-444
  family F-16

Monoline letter, in calligraphy C-58

'Monologium', work by St. Anselm A-467

Monologue, prolonged speech by one person; also a dramatic scene in which one actor speaks alone as a soliloquy or series of sketches; often used as opener by host on television talk shows.

Monomer, in chemistry F-72, *charts* F-73, 74

Monometallism, money system that has a single metal as standard; usually gold, but occasionally silver; opposed to bimetallism.

Monometer, line in poetry P-405

Monomotapa Empire, ancient African empire Z-453

Monona, Lake, Madison, Wis.; about 4 mi (6 km) long and 3 mi (5 km) wide.

Monongahela River, flows 125 mi (200 km) through West Virginia and Pennsylvania, joins Allegheny River at Pittsburgh to form Ohio River, *maps* P-165, 184, U-50
  Pittsburgh P-345, *pictures* P-169, U-53

Mononucleosis (or glandular fever, or kissing disease, or Mono), infectious virus disease marked by fatigue, sore throat, fever, and swollen lymph glands; symptoms may include rash, enlarged spleen, and involvement of liver and nervous system; diagnosed by blood test showing changes in white cells; most common in 10–35 age group; transmitted by infected persons; treated by bed rest; duration usually 1–2 weeks, longer in severe cases; second attacks rare, *table* D-171

Monophonic music (or one-voiced music) M-667

Monophysitism, belief that Christ had only one nature, divine and not human B-533
  Leo I L-130

Monoplacophora, class of mollusks M-525

Monopoly, board game B-322

Monopoly, control of a service or the supply of a commodity; usually includes the power to fix prices M-543. *see also in index* Competition; Government regulation of industry
  capitalism C-152
    corporation C-725
  early laws R-285
  patents P-139
  public utilities P-526c
  U.S. A-706
    AT&T divestiture T-56
    Northern Securities Case R-285
    Standard Oil Company R-230

Monorail, single-track electric railway M-545
  Japan T-263
  Seattle S-103a

Monorhyme, in poetry
  Islamic literature I-363

Monosaccharide, any of several simple sugars having the formula $C_6H_{12}O_6$ and differing in structure of molecule; none can be split, as can more complex sugars, into simpler sugars C-155, S-508

Monotheism, belief in one god
  ancient Egypt E-126
    Ikhnaton's reforms I-32
  Christianity C-399
  God G-173
  Judaism R-143
  mystery religions M-703

Monotremata (or Monotremes), order of primitive egg-laying mammals A-780
  Australia A-780
  mammal M-81, *table* M-80

Monotype, drawing technique G-234

Monotype, printing machine N-239
  typesetting T-337, T-341

Monozygotic twins. *see in index* Identical twins

Monro, Harold Edward (1879–1932), Scottish poet and critic, born in Brussels, Belgium; in 1912 founded Poetry Bookshop, London, famous meeting place of poets ('The Collected Poems of Harold Monro').

Monroe, Elizabeth Kortright (1768–1830), wife of President Monroe M-547

Monroe, Harriet (1860–1936), U.S. poet M-546
  American literature A-354

Monroe, James (1758–1831), 5th president of United States M-546
  Hall of Fame, *table* H-16
  Louisiana Purchase L-324
  Monroe Doctrine M-549
  Monrovia M-549
  U.S. history U-174
  Virginia, *picture* V-342
  White House W-196

Monroe, Marilyn (1926–62), U.S. actress M-548

Monroe, Paul (1869–1947), U.S. educator, born in North Madison, Ind.; professor of education, Teachers College, Columbia University; educational adviser for China; editor, 'Cyclopedia of Education' ('Text Book in the History of Education').

Monroe, La., city on Ouachita River about 95 mi (150 km) e. of Shreveport; farming, lumbering, natural-gas distribution; paper, chemical, carbon, and wood products; Northeast Louisiana University; pop. 57,597, *map* U-41
  North America, *map* N-351

Monroe, Mich., port city about 35 mi (55 km) s.w. of Detroit on Raisin River, near Lake Erie; agricultural region; auto parts, paper products, metal products; nurseries, fisheries, and limestone quarry; Raisin River Massacre (1813); pop. 23,531.

Monroe, N.C., city 24 mi (39 km) s.e. of Charlotte; commercial center for area producing cotton, grain, hay, cattle, and poultry; manufactures textiles, metal products, brick and tile; pop. 12,639.

Monroe Doctrine M-549
  America resists colonization A-335
  German-Venezuelan dispute V-277
  Latin American–U.S. relations L-66
  Haiti H-13
  Monroe M-546
  Roosevelt R-286

Monroeville, Pa., borough 8 mi (13 km) e. of Pittsburgh; steel; metal and chemical research laboratories; nuclear center; pop. 30,977, *map* P-184

Monrovia, Calif., city 15 mi (25 km) n.e. of Los Angeles in foothills of San Gabriel Mountains; electronics, paper products; health center; pop. 30,531.

Monrovia, Liberia, capital and seaport; pop. 243,243 M-549, *map* A-118

Mons, Belgium, mining and manufacturing city 35 mi (55 km) s.w. of Brussels; capital of Hainaut Province; important coal fields of Borinage are nearby; iron products, woolen and cotton goods, sugar; pop. 26,973
  World War I W-304

Monsanto Chemical Company, U.S. company
  industrial espionage E-304

Monsieur, meaning "my lord," French title of polite address to a man; equivalent to English "sir" in direct address and "Mr." as title; under First Republic term "Citoyen" (citizen) was substituted by decree.

'Monsieur Beaucaire', title and hero of romance by Tarkington; Frenchman of royalty who poses as a barber.

Monsoon, seasonal wind of Asia A-675
  Africa A-95
  Arabian Sea A-525
  Australian-Asian A-773
  Bangladesh B-61
  India I-64, W-127
  Indian Ocean I-109
  Indonesia I-159
  irrigation I-353
  jungle J-154
  Laos L-47
  Philippines P-259a
  Thailand T-147
  U.S.S.R. R-323
  wind W-225, *picture* W-224

Monsoon forest. *see in index* Tropical deciduous forest

Monster
  horror story H-245
  prehistoric reptiles R-153, *pictures* R-152
  Sphinx R-205, S-378

Montage, art, use of one or more mounted pictures as integral parts of a composition. *see also in index* Collage; Photomontage
  motion pictures M-613, 620, *pictures* M-612, 622, 626

Montagnais, group of American Indian tribes living in Quebec, *map* I-136, *table* I-139

Montagu, John. *see in index* Sandwich, earl of

Montagu, Lady Mary Wortley (1689–1762), English beauty, wit, letter writer, and eccentric; introduced smallpox inoculation into England.

Montague, Charles Edward (1867–1928), British journalist and novelist, born in Ealing, England; for years on staff of *Manchester Guardian*; noted for liberal views and trenchant style ('A Hind Let Loose'; 'Right off the Map', social and political fantasies; 'Dramatic Values', criticism).

Montague, P.E.I., town in e. near Gulf of St. Lawrence; agricultural market; museum; bird sanctuary nearby; pop. 1,957 P-497f, *map* P-497h

Montague family, in Shakespeare's 'Romeo and Juliet', Romeo's family, at feud with Capulets R-258

Montaigne, Michel de (1533–92), French essayist M-549
  dreams D-257
  essay E-306
  literary contribution F-395, *picture* F-394

Montale, Eugenio (1896–1981), Italian poet, born in Genoa; published five books of poems; translated writers such as T.S. Eliot and Shakespeare I-378. *see also in index* Nobel Prizewinners, *table*

Montalembert, Charles Forbes René de (1810–70), French publicist and historian; Roman Catholic Liberal leader ('St. Elizabeth of Hungary').

Montalte, Louis de. *see in index* Pascal, Blaise

Montalvo, García Ordóñez de, Spanish writer of early 16th century; translated romance of chivalry, 'Amadis of Gaul', from Portuguese original; his 'Deeds of Esplandián' influenced Spanish search for California.

Montana, state in n.w. U.S.; 147,138 sq mi (381,086 sq km); cap. Helena; pop. 786,690 M-550, *maps* U-40, 80
  agriculture, *picture* U-75
  air pollution, *picture* P-441a
  cities. *see also in index* Helena and other cities by name
  education, *picture* U-204
  geographic regions
    Great Plains U-75, *maps* U-36, 80, *pictures* U-75, U-77, *Reference-Outline* U-135
    North America, *map* N-351
    Rocky Mountains R-234, U-78, *maps* R-234a, U-80, *pictures* U-79, *Reference-Outline* U-136
  parks, monuments, and other areas
    Glacier N.P., *picture* U-79
  state symbols
    flag, picture F-159
    flower, *picture* S-427
    tree P-328
  Statuary Hall, *table* S-437b
  taxation, *tables* T-37, 39

Montana, University of, Missoula, Mont., part of Montana University System; state control; chartered 1893; arts and sciences, business administration, education, fine arts, forestry, journalism, law, pharmacy; graduate division; quarter system M-553, *pictures* M-557, U-204

Montana College of Mineral Science and Technology, Butte, Mont.; one of six units of the Montana University System; state control; founded 1893; liberal arts; geology, metallurgy, mineral dressing, mining, petroleum engineering; graduate studies.

Montana State University, Bozeman, Mont.; one of six units of the Montana University System; founded 1893; letters and science, agriculture, architecture, art, commerce, education, engineering, home economics, nursing; graduate division; quarter system M-553

Montana University System, operates as a single university with six units: Eastern Montana College, Montana College of Mineral Science and Technology, Montana State University, Northern Montana College, University of Montana, and Western Montana College M-553. *see also in index* schools by name

Montargis, France, town 63 mi (101 km) s.e. of Paris; famous for "dog of Montargis," said to have revealed master's murderer by constantly following him; Mirabeau born at the Château de Bignon nearby; pop. 18,087, *map* F-372

Montauk Point, Long Island, N.Y.; easternmost point of state, *picture* N-262

Mont Blanc. *see in index* Blanc, Mont

Montbretia, plant genus. *see in index* Tritonia

Montcalm, Louis-Joseph (full name Louis Joseph de Montcalm-Gozon, marquis de Saint-Véran) (1712–59), French general M-566
  Canada C-94
    Quebec monument Q-14
  Wolfe W-268

Montclair, Calif., city about 30 mi (50 km) e. of Los Angeles; chiefly residential; manufacture and retail sale of aircraft parts; incorporated 1956; pop. 22,628.

Montclair, N.J., residential town 6 mi (10 km) n. of Newark; on first range of Orange Mts.; Montclair State College nearby; pop. 38,321.

Montclair State College, Upper Montclair, N.J.; opened 1908; formerly a teachers' college; liberal arts and teacher education; graduate study.

Montebello, Calif., city 7 mi (11 km) s.e. of Los Angeles; oil wells, aircraft parts, steel products, nurseries; pop. 52,929.

Monte Carlo, town in principality of Monaco; pop. 13,154 M-566
  Monaco M-528

Montecristo, small barren Italian island in Mediterranean, about 25 mi (40 km) s. of Elba, *map* I-404. *see also in index* 'Count of Monte Cristo'

Montefiore, Sir Moses (1784–1885), Jewish philanthropist in England, born in Leghorn, Italy; amassed fortune on London stock exchange and after his 43rd year devoted all his time to improving condition of Jews, particularly in Russia and Turkey.

Montego Bay, town, Jamaica J-18
  West Indies, *map* W-159

Montelbaan Tower, Amsterdam, The Netherlands, *picture* A-380

Montelius, Oskar (1843–1921), Swedish archaeologist, born in Stockholm A-535

Montemezzi, Italo (1875–1952), Italian composer, born in Vigasio, near Verona, Italy; abandoned study of engineering for musical training at Milan conservatory; married U.S. pianist and lived several years in U.S.; operas characterized by rare melodic beauty and refinement.

Montenegrins, people
  Yugoslavia Y-435

Montenegro (black mountain), former kingdom of s. Europe on Balkan Peninsula n. of Albania; extends s.w. from Serbia to Adriatic Sea; mountainous, forested; became nation 1389; famed for never really yielding to Turkey; in 1918 became part of Kingdom of Serbs, Croats, and Slovenes (later Yugoslavia); overrun by Germany in World War II; in 1945 became a federal unit of Federal People's Republic of Yugoslavia; area 5,333 sq. mi.; cap. Titograd

(traditional cap. Cetinje); pop. 471,894
Balkan wars B-31
World War I W-305
Yugoslavia Y-436

Monterey, Calif., resort city and art colony on Monterey Bay, about 85 mi (140 km) s.e. of San Francisco; picturesque old Spanish buildings; capital of Alta California 1775; science research laboratories; Fort Ord; pop. 27,558, *map* U-40

Monterey cypress, tree *Cupressus macrocarpa* C-810

Monterey Institute of Foreign Studies, Monterey, Calif.; private control; founded 1955; liberal arts; graduate studies; majors in political science, international relations; Chinese, French, German, Russian, and Spanish.

Monterey International Pop Festival J-140

Monterey Park, Calif., city in the Monterey Hills 6 mi (10 km) e. of Los Angeles; chiefly residential; hardware, instruments, metal products; incorporated 1916; pop. 54,338.

Monterey pine, rare evergreen tree *Pinus radiata* of pine family, native to s. California coast region and Guadalupe Island, Mexico; grows 40 to 100 ft (12 to 30 m) high; rough dark brown bark; crown round-topped; leaves in threes, to 6 in. (15 cm) long, dark green; cones oval, slightly curved, to 7 in. (18 cm) long, remain on tree for several years.

Monte Rosa, Alpine peak (15,217 ft; 4,638 m) S-537

Monterrey, Mexico, railroad and manufacturing center; capital of Nuevo León state; pop. 1,090,009 M-567
Mexico M-328, *map* M-344
North America, *map* N-351

Montesquieu (or Charles-Louis de Secondat, baron of Montesquieu) (1689–1755), French political philosopher M-567
'Encyclopédie' R-124
French literature F-396
political theory P-434

Montessori, Maria (1870–1952), Italian educator and psychiatrist M-567
education E-90, 96
kindergarten and nursery school K-242
reading R-101a, *picture* R-101c

Monteux, Pierre (1875–1964), U.S. orchestra conductor, born in Paris, France; became U.S. citizen 1942; conductor of Diaghilev's Ballet Russe, of Boston Symphony Orchestra 1919–24, of Paris Symphony Orchestra 1930–38, of San Francisco Symphony Orchestra 1935–52, of London Symphony Orchestra 1961–64; made world tours as guest conductor
orchestra, *list* O-579

Montevallo, University of, Montevallo, Ala.; state control; founded 1896; liberal arts, teacher education, and vocational education; graduate study A-227

Monteverdi, Claudio (or Claudio Monteverde) (1567–1643), Italian composer M-568
classical music M-668
opera O-561

Montevideo, Uruguay, capital; pop. of metro. area 1,500,000 M-568, U-214, *map* S-299
Río de la Plata P-384

Montezuma I (1390?–1464?), Aztec chief, or "emperor," of Mexico 1436?–64?; warrior, law-giver, and patron of the arts; built temples and pyramids in Mexico City.

Montezuma II (1466–1520), Aztec chief, or "emperor," of Mexico M-568, A-890
Maya M-237

Montezuma Castle National Monument, Arizona, *picture* A-601

Montfort, Simon de, (1208?–65), English statesman and soldier M-569
democracy D-93
England E-242
Henry III H-129

Montgolfier, Joseph Michel (1740–1810) and **Jacques Étienne** (1745–99), brothers, French inventors of balloon M-569
airplane A-200
balloon B-38

Montgomery, Bernard Law, (1887–1976), British field marshal M-569
navy N-79
warfare W-12, 28
World War II W-329

Montgomery, James (1771–1854), British poet, born in Irvine, Scotland; Byron called his 'Wanderer in Switzerland' worth a thousand 'Lyrical Ballads'; humanitarian views; over 100 of his hymns in use.

Montgomery, John Joseph (1858–1911), U.S. glider pioneer, born in Yuba City, Calif.; professor at University of Santa Clara; tested his first *Gull Glider* 1884; his monoplane glider *Santa Clara* flew 8 mi (13 km) in 1905
glider A-201, G-167

Montgomery, Little Brother (born 1906), U.S. blues pianist M-680

Montgomery, Lucy Maud (or Mrs. Ewan Macdonald) (1874–1942), Canadian novelist, born on Prince Edward Island
Green Gables farmhouse P-497c

Montgomery, Richard (1738–75), U.S. soldier, born in Swords, County Dublin, Ireland; brigadier general in Continental army 1775, with Benedict Arnold led futile attack on Quebec Dec. 31, 1775; killed almost at first shot; Montgomery, Ala., named for him C-94, R-170

Montgomery, Robert (1904–81), U.S. motion-picture and television actor and director, born in Beacon, N.Y. (movies: 'Untamed', 'Night Must Fall', 'Here Comes Mr. Jordan'); helped develop Screen Actors Guild; television series Robert Montgomery Presents; Eisenhower's TV consultant.

Montgomery, Ala., state capital, near center of state on Alabama River; pop. 178,157 A-525, M-569, *map* U-41
civil rights B-296
Confederate States of America's capital C-642
King K-244
North America, *map* N-351

Montgomeryshire, county in n. Wales; 797 sq mi (2,064 sq km); county town Montgomery (pop. 972); soil fertile in valleys; pop. 44,165.

Montgomery Ward & Co., originally a mail-order house, founded in Chicago by Aaron Montgomery Ward and George R. Thorne 1872; retail store system added in mid-1920s.

Montherlant, Henry de (1896–1972), French writer ('Chaos and Night', novel) F-398

Montholon, Charles Tristan, marquis de (1783–1853), French soldier, born in Paris; accompanied Napoleon to exile at St. Helena; to him Napoleon dictated notes on his career.

Monti, Vincenzo (1754–1828), Italian poet and dramatist, born in Alfonsine, near Ravenna ('Aristodemo'; 'Bassevilliana').

Monticello, Thomas Jefferson's home in Virginia
$2 bill design, J-90, *pictures* J-91

Montini, Giovanni Battista. pope. *see in index* Paul VI

Montmartre, section of Paris, France P-117, *map* P-120
Utrillo's painting, *picture* U-236

Montmorency, famous French family of which most distinguished members were **Mathieu II** (1189–1230), called "the Great Constable," a successful warrior; **Anne de Montmorency** (1493–1567), distinguished in wars of Francis I; **Henry II, duc de Montmorency** (1595–1632), admiral of France and viceroy of Canada, successfully fought against Huguenots, but executed for treason through influence of Richelieu; two members of family fought in the American Revolution.

Montmorency Falls, Canada, beautiful cascade 274 ft (84 m) high in Montmorency River at confluence with St. Lawrence near Quebec Q-15

Montoya, Joseph M. (1915–78), U.S. public official, born in Pena Blanca, N.M.; New Mexico state representative 1937–40, state senator 1940–46, 1954–55, lieutenant governor 1947–51, 1955–57; U.S. senator (Democrat) 1965–77.

Montparnasse, section of Paris, France; has Dôme Café and other centers of artistic, literary, and Bohemian life, *map* P-120

Montpelier, Vt., state capital, on Winooski River; pop. 8,241 M-570, *maps* V-301, V-286, U-41
North America, *map* N-351
State Capitol, *picture* V-293

Montpelier, home of James Madison in Virginia, about 20 mi (30 km) n.e. of Charlottesville.

Montpellier, France, city 6 mi (10 km) from Mediterranean; noted university; large trade in wine, fruit, and silk; makes soap, candles, leather, and liquors; pop. 152,105, *maps* E-361, F-372

Montreal (formerly called Ville-Marie de Montréal), Que., city and inland seaport on St. Lawrence River; pop. 980,354 M-570, *map* Q-9a
Canada C-78, *picture* C-81, *map* C-112
history C-91
American Revolution R-170
Cartier's exploration C-185, C-90
McGill University, *picture* Q-9e
North America N-337, *map* N-351
Quebec Q-9i
tobogganing S-216
transportation *pictures* Q-9d
zoo Z-460

Montreal, University of (Université de Montréal), Montreal, Que.; Roman Catholic; founded 1876 as branch of Laval University; independent and present name 1919; arts and sciences, dental surgery, law, letters, medicine, optometry, pharmacy, philosophy, public health, theology; graduate school; affiliated schools; teaching in French; 32 affiliated junior colleges M-572

Montreal Botanical Garden, Montreal, Que.; established 1932 by city of Montreal; 260 acres (105 hectares) B-379

Montreal-Nord, Que., city, northern suburb of Montreal, situated on Rivière des Prairies (Des Prairies River); incorporated 1915 as town, 1959 as city; pop. 94,914 Q-9h, *map* Q-11

Montreal School, writing group formed in Canada in 1895 C-120

Montresor, Beni (born 1926), Italian designer, author, and illustrator, born in Verona; wrote and illustrated 'House of Flowers, House of Stars', 'The Witches of Venice', 'Cinderella'; illustrated 'May I Bring a Friend?', 1965 Caldecott medal, 'I Saw a Ship A-Sailing' S-481b

Montreux, Switzerland, resort on e. shore of Lake Geneva; formed by group of villages; Treaty of Montreux (1936) signed here; pop. 18,700, *map* S-537

Montreux, treaty of (or Montreux Convention) (1936), signed by the members of League of Nations authorizing Turkey to fortify the Dardanelles and to close them if Turkey should be at war; guaranteed free commerce through the Dardanelles in peace, and in war if authorized B-371
Turkey T-324

Montrose, James, duke of (died 1742), Scottish leader, favored union of Scotland and England; regent of kingdom on death of Queen Anne
Rob Roy R-227

Montrose, James Graham, marquis of (1612–50), Scottish Jacobite general; signed Covenant of 1637 but believed in subordination of church to state; joined Royalists 1640, and won many victories against Covenanters; hanged as a traitor by order of Scottish parliament; wrote many poems (celebrated lyric, 'My Dear and Only Love').

Mont-Royal, Que., town w. of Montreal near latter's famous height, Mount Royal; pop. 21,561, *map* Q-11

Monts, Pierre du Guast, comte de (1560?–1630?), French courtier, founder of Acadia, born in Saintonge Province, France; called the sieur de Monts; sent out expedition under Champlain that founded Quebec
Canada C-91
Nova Scotia N-403

Mont-Saint-Michel, rocky island of n.w. France a mile off coast of Normandy, with which it is connected by a causeway; famous for abbey-fortress, fine example of medieval Gothic architecture, *map* F-372, *picture* F-350

Montserrat, island, a colony, in Leeward Islands, in West Indies; 32 sq mi (83 sq km); Soufrière, an active volcano; cotton; pop. 12,108
Commonwealth membership C-602
West Indies W-157, *map* W-159

Montserrat, mountain 30 mi (50 km) n.w. of Barcelona, Spain; vast fissure, dividing it, said to have occurred at time of Crucifixion; Benedictine monastery, in medieval legend the castle of the Holy Grail.

Montsuki, Japanese coat J-29

Montt, Manuel (1809–80), Chilean statesman, born in Petorca, central Chile; president 1851–61; established modern communications, schools, and banks.

Montville, Conn., community 6 mi (10 km) n. of New London on Thames River; settled 1670, incorporated 1786; pop. of township 16,455.

'Monument of the Beast Standing' (or 'Monument à la Bête Debout', or 'The Beast'), sculpture by Dubuffet, *picture* C-315

Monuments, national, United States. *see in index* national monuments by name

Monument Valley, region in s.e. Utah and n.e. Arizona, *map* U-233, *pictures* U-216, 224

Monvel, Louis Maurice Boutet de. *see in index* Boutet de Monvel

Moodie, Susanna Strickland (1803–85), Canadian author, born in Bungay, England; wrote poems and novels of Canadian life C-120

Moody, Dwight L. (in full Dwight Lyman Moody) (1837–99), U.S. evangelist M-572

Moody, William Vaughn (1869–1910), U.S. poet and dramatist, born in Spencer, Ind.; taught English at University of Chicago; famous poems are 'Gloucester Moors' and 'Ode in Time of Hesitation' ('The Great Divide', play; 'The Masque of Judgment' and 'The Fire-Bringer', poetic dramas).

Moody Bible Institute, interdenominational evangelistic organization, founded in Chicago 1889; trains pastors, missionaries, other Christian workers; publishes *Moody Monthly*, evangelical books and pamphlets; produces gospel science films; operates radio station M-572

Moody's Investors Service, Inc., credit agency
credit rating C-763

Mooltan, Pakistan. *see in index* Multan

'Moominland Midwinter', work by Jansson, *picture* L-248

Moon, Sun Myung (born 1920), Korean head of controversial Unification church and self-ordained evangelist, born in North Pyongan Province; began preaching personal doctrines 1946; excommunicated by Presbyterian church 1948; fled to South Korea 1950; founded Unification church 1954; launched multimillion-dollar church-affiliated business empire in Japan and Korea; moved to U.S. 1971; claimed 3 million followers, called "Moonies," worldwide by 1983; imprisoned for income tax evasion 1984; released in 1985.

Moon, natural satellite of the earth M-573
astronomy A-710, 730
earth E-29
eclipse E-48
early observation O-458
solar S-514
exploration E-377

bodies and doglike mouths with highly developed teeth; found in all tropical seas; some are food fish, but others poisonous; greatly feared by divers E-109
fish F-124, *picture* F-126

Mordkin, Mikhail (1880–1944), ballet dancer and choreographer, born in Moscow, U.S.S.R.; entered Moscow Imperial Ballet School at 9; danced with Pavlova and was also a member of Diaghilev's ballet; came to U.S. 1922, appeared with own company B-35, D-24

Mordvinoff, Nicolas (pen name Nicolas) (1911–73), artist, born in St. Petersburg (now Leningrad), U.S.S.R.; escaped to Finland at age of 6; spent youth in Paris; lived 13 years in South Pacific; illustrated many children's books by other authors, including W. Lipkind's 'Finders Keepers' awarded 1952 Caldecott Medal; author and illustrator of 'Bear's Land'; 'Coral Island' R-108

More, Hannah (1745–1833), English writer of verse and of plays and books on moral and religious subjects, born in Stapleton, Gloucestershire; later years devoted to philanthropy and popular education ('Coelebs in Search of a Wife'; 'Practical Piety'; 'Moral Sketches').

More, Paul Elmer (1864–1937), U.S. essayist, critic, and editor, born in St. Louis, Mo.; associate in Sanskrit and classical literature, Bryn Mawr College 1895–97; literary editor, *Independent* and the *New York Evening Post*; editor, *Nation* 1909–14 ('Shelburne Essays'; 'Nietzsche'; 'Life of Benjamin Franklin'; 'The Religion of Plato').

More, Thomas (or St. Thomas More) (1478–1535), English statesman M-582
'Utopia' U-235

Morea. *see in index* Peloponnesus

Moreau, Jean Victor Marie (1763–1813), French Revolutionary general, born in Morlaix, France; victor of Hohenlinden 1800; exiled for alleged conspiracy against Napoleon; joined Allies against Napoleon 1813; killed on battlefield of Dresden.

Moreau River, South Dakota, tributary of the Missouri, 200 mi (320 km) long, *maps* S-323, 334

Morehead City, N.C., ocean port for worldwide commerce N-355, 358

Morehead State University, Morehead, Ky.; established 1922; opened 1923; humanities, sciences and mathematics, applied science and technology, education, social sciences; graduate program.

Morehouse College, Atlanta, Ga.; affiliated with Atlanta University as undergraduate college for men; private control; founded 1867; arts and sciences, education. *see also in index* Atlanta University

Morehouse comet, discovered 1908; moves in large parabolic path; famous for change in appearance of tail that seemed at times to break into fragments and separate from the head.

Morel, common name of genus *Morchella,* group of edible mushrooms M-665

Morelia, Mexico, city 130 mi (210 km) n.w. of Mexico City; capital of Michoacán; named for patriot Morelos; textiles, food products; cathedral; pop. 100,828
Mexico, *map* M-344
North America, *map* N-351

Morelos, Mexico, state in s. center; 1,908 sq mi (4,942 sq km); cap. Cuernavaca; overlooked on n.e. by Popocatépetl; conquered by Cortez; established as state 1869; pop. 866,376
Mexico, *map* M-344

Morelos Dam, Mexico C-586

Morelos y Pavón, José María (1765–1815), Mexican revolutionist and priest; city of Morelia and state of Morelos named for him
Mexico M-336

Morenci, Ariz., in s.e. part of state, about 110 mi (180 km) n.e. of Tucson; pop. 950
copper mine, *picture* A-599

Morendo, in music, *list* M-671

Moreno, Mario. *see in index* Cantinflas

Moreno, Lake, Argentina, *picture* A-577

Morés, Antoine Amédée Marie Vincent Manca de Vallombrosa, marquis de (1855–96), French adventurer, farmed in North Dakota; explored in Tibet; killed in Africa by Tuaregs.

Mores, values or customs of a group regarded as necessary for the welfare and preservation of that group.

Moresnet, small area 4 mi (6 km) s.w. of Aachen, near Eupen and Malmédy; neutral territory 1815–1919; ceded to Belgium 1919; taken by Germany 1940; restored to Belgium 1944.

Moretan Bay, *see in index* Brisbane, Australia

Morey, Samuel (1762–1843), U.S. inventor, born in Hebron, Conn.; lived chiefly in Vermont; an early inventor of the steamboat; failure of his capitalist backers halted his enterprises and prevented his receiving the honors that later went to Robert Fulton.

Morgagni, Giovanni Battista (1682–1771), Italian anatomist, born in Forlì in Romagna; regarded as founder of pathological anatomy A-875
medicine M-283

Morgan, Charles Langbridge (1894–1958), English novelist and critic, born in Kent, England; drama critic *The Times*, London, 1921–39 (novels: 'The Fountain', 'The Voyage', 'River Line', 'A Breeze of Morning', 'Challenge to Venus'; essays: 'Reflections in a Mirror'; play: 'The Burning Glass').

Morgan, Daniel (1736–1802), American Revolutionary War general, born in New Jersey; given command company of Virginia riflemen, 1775; distinguished himself in Arnold's expedition against Quebec, in battles of Saratoga, and at Cowpens
Cowpens R-172

Morgan, Edwin D. (1806–81), U.S. merchant, politician, philanthropist A-652

Morgan, Sir Henry (1635?–88), Welsh buccaneer; commissioned by the governor of Jamaica to take Spanish possessions, he ravaged the coast of Cuba and captured the city of Panama; was arrested and returned to England for fighting after peace had been arranged between Spain and England, but his immense stolen wealth gained his pardon, knighted and returned to Jamaica as lieutenant governor P-342a

Morgan, John (1735–89), U.S. physician, born in Philadelphia, Pa.; pioneer of U.S. medical education; surgeon general of the Continental armies during the U.S. War of Independence; founder of the first U.S. medical school M-284

Morgan, John Hunt (1825–64), Confederate general, daring and famous cavalry raider; born in Huntsville, Ala.
Civil War campaigns C-476

Morgan, J. Pierpont (in full John Pierpont Morgan) (1837–1913), U.S. banker, financier, and art collector M-582

Morgan, John Pierpont (1867–1943), U.S. banker and financier, born in Irvington, N.Y.; son of J.P. Morgan; succeeded to control of his father's banking business, which became incorporated state bank 1940; during World War I, British government's commercial agent in U.S.
library. *see in index* Pierpont Morgan Library

Morgan, John Tyler (1824–1907), U.S. senator from Alabama 1877 to his death, born in Athens, Tenn.; enlisted 1861 in Confederate army, brigadier general 1863; member of board (1892) to arbitrate Bering fisheries dispute and of commission (1898) to codify Hawaiian laws; Democrat.

Morgan, Junius Spencer (1813–90), U.S. financier and philanthropist, born in West Springfield, now Holyoke, Mass.; father of J.P. Morgan (1837–1913).

Morgan, Lewis Henry (1818–81), U.S. archaeologist and ethnologist, born near Aurora, N.Y. ('League of the Ho-dé-no-sau-nee, or Iroquois'; 'Ancient Society'); bequeathed fund to found women's college in University of Rochester A-484

Morgan, Thomas Hunt (1866–1945), U.S. zoologist, born in Lexington, Ky.; professor, Columbia University 1904–28; director of biological laboratories, California Institute of Technology; wrote books on embryology, evolution, and heredity. *see also in index* Nobel Prizewinners, *table*
genetics G-54
heredity H-139

Morganatic marriage, marriage of a member of a royal family to a woman of lesser rank; not unusual in European court circles; neither wife nor children receive royal rank and title.

Morgan City, La., port city on Grand Lake, a widening of Atchafalaya River, 67 mi (108 km) s.w. of New Orleans; offshore oil fields; shrimp fisheries; pop. 16,114.

Morgan Horse, horse breed developed in New England for general utility, *picture* H-257, *list* H-254

Morganite, gem material J-116

Morgan le Fay. *see in index* Fata Morgana

Morgan State College, Baltimore, Md.; interracial, founded as private college for black Americans 1867; joined state system with present name 1939; arts and sciences; graduate studies.

'Morgante Maggiore', poem by Pulci S-475

Morganton, N.C., city 15 mi (25 km) s.w. of Lenoir; furniture, textiles; Western Correctional Center; state facilities for deaf, retarded, and mental patients; incorporated 1839; pop. 13,763.

Morgantown, W. Va., city near n. boundary of state, on Monongahela River; coal, natural gas, glass-sand, and limestone in the area; coal mining; brass plumbing fixtures, glass products, chemicals, clothing; pop. 27,605
West Virginia W-167

Morgarten, hill in n. Switzerland, 18 mi (29 km) s. of Zurich, where Swiss mountaineers defeated Austrians (1315) S-544

Morgenthau, Henry (1856–1946), U.S. diplomat, born in Mannheim, Germany; ambassador to Turkey 1913–16; in charge of interests of Allies in Turkey during World War I; nominated ambassador to Mexico in 1920, but did not go on account of revolution.

Morgenthau, Henry, Jr. (1891–1967), U.S. public official, publisher, born in New York City; publisher of *American Agriculturist* 1922–33; governor Farm Credit Administration 1933; secretary of the treasury 1934–45, *picture* R-272

Morghen, Raffaello (1758–1833), Italian engraver; copied paintings by Leonardo da Vinci, Raphael, and others.

Mori, Arinori (1847–89), Japanese political leader J-65

Mori, Ogai (originally Rintaro Mori) (1862–1922), Japanese writer M-583
Japanese literature J-82

Mörike, Eduard (1804–75), German writer G-106

Morillo, Pablo (1777–1838), Spanish general
Colombia C-554

Morin, Paul (1889–1960), Canadian poet, born in Montreal; poems show Oriental influence.

Moriscos, a people of Spain, descended from the Moors M-581

Morison, Samuel Eliot (1887–1976), U.S. historian, born in Boston, Mass.; professor of history Harvard University 1925–55: won 1943 Pulitzer prize in biography for 'Admiral of the Ocean Sea', shortened and revised as 'Christopher Columbus, Mariner' ('History of United States Naval Operations in World War II', 15 vols.; 'The Story of the "Old Colony" of New Plymouth, 1620–1692'; 'John Paul Jones', 1960 Pulitzer prize in biography; 'The Caribbean as Columbus Saw It'; 'The European Discovery of America'); 1963 Balzan Prize; 1964 Presidential Medal of Freedom H-174

Morisot, Berthe (or Madame Eugène Manet) (1841–95), painter, great-granddaughter of Fragonard, and sister-in-law and pupil of Édouard Manet.

Morland, George (1763–1804), English painter of animals and rustic scenes; many of his best paintings are familiar through engraved copies.

Morley, Christopher Darlington (1890–1957), U.S. writer, born in Haverford, Pa.; charming informal essays ('Shandygaff'); verse, particularly in praise of domesticity ('Songs for a Little House'); novels of fantasy, satire, and whimsy ('Where the Blue Begins'; 'Thunder on the Left'); more realistic novels ('Parnassus on Wheels'; 'Haunted Bookshop'; 'Human Being'; 'Kitty Foyle'); conductor of column 'The Bowling Green'.

Morley, Edward Williams (1838–1923), U.S. chemist and writer on physics, born in Newark, N.J.; professor of chemistry Western Reserve University 1869–1906; noted for research on atomic weights of hydrogen and oxygen
Michelson M-353
Michelson-Morley experiment R-140
speed of light L-198

Morley, Henry (1822–94), English writer and educator, born in London; professor of English language and literature University College, London 1865–89; edited many classics and popularized good books ('English Writers', 10 vols.).

Morley, Thomas (1557–1603), English musician, one of greatest Elizabethan composers, organist at St. Paul's Cathedral; author of treatise on church music; composed madrigals, canzonets, ballets; wrote 'Plaine and Easie Introduction to Practicall Musicke', which remained an authority for more than a century.

Morley of Blackburn, John Morley, 1st Viscount (1838–1923), English statesman and writer, born in Blackburn, Lancashire; for 25 years a Liberal in House of Commons; secretary for Ireland under Gladstone and for India under Campbell-Bannerman and Asquith; wrote lives of Gladstone, Burke, Cobden, Cromwell, Voltaire, Rousseau, and his own 'Recollections'; general editor for 'English Men of Letters' series.

Mormon cricket (also called western cricket, or western grasshopper), insect *Anabrus simplex* of the order Orthoptera, family Tettigoniidae; body 1¼ in. (3⅕ cm) long; color green, black, red, or brown; migrates in groups, invades cultivated areas of w. U.S. and does great damage; methods of control: poisoning by use of arsenical dust and trapping by means of pits and barriers
Utah U-220, *picture* U-221

Mormons (or Latter-day Saints), religious group M-583
Arizona A-598, *picture* A-605
frontier movement F-422
Illinois I-41
Nevada N-147
Las Vegas L-56
North America N-338
Utah U-215, U-219, *pictures* U-223, 225, 234
Salt Lake City S-31, *picture* S-32
Young. *see in index* Young, Brigham

Mormon Trail, early overland route to Salt Lake City, Utah, *map* R-219
frontier F-422
Nebraska N-96
Oregon Trail O-599

Morning-glory, vine M-584
flower structure F-217, *picture* F-216

Morning-glory family. *see in index* Convolvulaceae

'Morning Hours, or Lectures on the Existence of God', work by Mendelssohn M-298
Morningside College, Sioux City, Iowa; Methodist; founded 1894; arts and sciences, education, music; graduate school.
Morningside Heights, a neighborhood in Manhattan, New York, N.Y. N-273, *picture* N-280
Moro, Aldo (1916–78), Italian statesman, premier, law professor
  assassination A-704
  Italy I-398
  kidnapping K-234
Morocco, kingdom in n.w. Africa; area 177,117 sq mi (458,730 sq km); cap. Rabat; pop. 22,455,000 M-585
  Africa, *map* A-118
  African political unit, *table* A-112
  Atlas Mountains A-746
  cities. *see also in index* cities listed below and other cities by name
    Casablanca C-194
    Tangier T-20
  flag, *picture* F-168
    Medieval banner, *picture* M-384
  OAS withdrawal O-605
  railroad mileage, *table* R-85
  Sahara S-14
  Spain S-361
  Western Sahara W-154
  World War II W-329
Moro-moro, Philippine folk drama P-258
Moron, archaic term used to describe a mentally deficient person who has a potential mental age of 8 to 12 years.
Moroni, Mormon religious figure M-583
Morot, Aimé Nicolas (1850–1913), French historical and portrait painter; portraits of members of fashionable and artistic world of Paris, battle scenes.
Morotai, mountainous island in the Moluccas, Indonesia, 12 mi (19 km) n.e. of Halmahera; 650 sq mi (1,683 sq km); air base; taken by American forces Sept. 1944; pop. 19,523, *map* I-166
  Asia, *map* A-700
Morpheme, in linguistics L-32, L-229
Morpheus, Greek and Roman mythology, dream god who calls human forms before the dreamer; son of Hypnos (Somnus), god of sleep; mentioned in Ovid
  Greek mythology M-701
  name for morphine N-19
Morphine, bitter crystalline narcotic alkaloid ($C_{17}H_{19}NO_3$), the active drug in opium and dangerously habit-forming A-387
  first aid P-411
  narcotics N-19
  opium O-572
Morpho Cypris, tropical butterfly native to Colombia, South America, *picture* B-524
Morphological differentiation, process of cell multiplication
  embryology E-201
Morphology, form and structure of the Earth's surface features viewed as a product of erosion, weathering, and glaciation
  geology G-72
Morphology, in linguistics L-229
Morphology, science dealing with the form and structure of living organisms B-231. *see also in index* Anatomy, human sciences S-64b
  zoology Z-467
Morrice, James Wilson (1864–1924), Canadian painter, born in Montreal; spent most of life in France; distinguished as colorist; works in Louvre, Tate Gallery, and National Gallery of Canada; 'The Ferry, Quebec' is typical of his Canadian winter scenes.
Morrice dance. *see in index* Morris dance
Morrill, Justin Smith (1810–98), U.S. legislator, born in Strafford, Vt.; member U.S. House of Representatives 1855–67; U.S. senator 1867–98; author of Morrill Act S-437b, *picture* V-296
Morrill Act (1862), United States U-207
  education, *list* E-104
  home economics H-215
Morris, Charles (1784–1856), U.S. Navy officer who commanded the *Constitution* in battle with *Guerrière*, born in Woodstock, Conn.; 1819 commander of South American squadron; later superintendent of Naval Academy.
Morris, Clara (1848–1925), U.S. emotional actress (Camille, Alixe, Lady Macbeth), born in Toronto; after retiring from stage wrote about stage life; author of novels.
Morris, Esther Hobart (1814–1902), U.S. woman suffrage leader, born near Spencer, N.Y.; active in woman suffrage movement in Wyoming; appointed world's first woman justice of the peace at South Pass City, Wyo., 1870
  Statuary Hall, *table* S-437b
Morris, Gouverneur (1752–1816), U.S. statesman, born in New York; aristocrat by training and temperament, but ardent supporter of Revolution because he believed in its justice; as assistant to Robert Morris 1781–85 proposed decimal system of coinage and words dollar and cent; member of Constitutional Convention 1787, where he advocated a strong national government; a signer of U.S. Constitution for Pennsylvania; much of later life spent abroad, two years as ambassador to France; U.S. senator from New York 1800–03; chairman of board 1810–16 that planned Erie Canal
  Constitution revised U-142
  Department of Commerce U-162
Morris, Gouverneur (1876–1953), U.S. writer of novels and short stories, born in New York City; great-grandson of Gouverneur Morris ('If You Touch Them They Vanish'; 'His Daughter'; 'Yellow Men and Gold').
Morris, Lewis (1726–98), signer of Declaration of Independence as New York delegate, born in Morrisiana, N.Y.; brother of Gouverneur Morris, the statesman
  Declaration of Independence D-56
Morris, Robert (1734–1806), financier of American Revolution M-587
  banking B-72
Morris, William (1834–96), English poet, artist, and social reformer M-587
  interior design contribution I-249, *picture* I-244
  wallpaper W-9
  literary contribution E-276
    'Volsunga Saga' translation S-471
  typography T-338, *picture* B-351
    Golden type, *picture* B-349
Morris, Wright (born 1910), U.S. novelist, born in Central City, Neb. ('My Uncle Dudley'; 'Man and Boy'; 'The Huge Season'; 'The Field of Vision', National Book Award 1957; 'Ceremony in Lone Tree'; 'One Day'; 'Fire Sermon').
Morris Brown College, Atlanta, Ga.; African Methodist Episcopal; founded 1881, first instruction 1885; arts and sciences, business, education, religion. *see also in index* Atlanta University
Morris Canal, N.J., abandoned canal; opened 1831; important waterway mid-19th century N-197, *map* C-126
Morris dance (or morrice dance), exhibition dance widely performed in England after 15th century; typically danced in traditional costumes by six men, a fool, a man with a cardboard hobbyhorse around his hips, and a boy dressed as Maid Marian; abolished by Puritans, revived 1899, *picture* F-256
Morris Harvey College, Charleston, W. Va.; private control; founded 1888; liberal arts, business administration, education.
Morrison, Herbert Stanley, Baron Morrison of Lambeth (1888–1965), British political leader, born near London; secretary London Labor party 1915–47; member of Parliament 1935–59; home secretary 1940–45; deputy prime minister, president of council, and leader of House of Commons July 1945–51; deputy prime minister and foreign minister 1951–52.
Morrison, Robert (1782–1834), English missionary to China, born in Morpeth, England; translated Bible into Chinese; compiled Chinese grammar and dictionary.
Morrison, Toni (born 1931) U.S. writer
  American literature A-362
Morrison, Mount. *see in index* Sinkao Shan
Morris plan bank, system of industrial banking founded by Arthur J. Morris in 1910; makes loans at reasonable rates of interest to responsible people of low income.
Morristown, N.J., residential town 17 mi (27 km) n.w. of Newark; food and paper products; pharmaceuticals, electronics, plastics; Morse and Vail worked on electric telegraph; Seeing Eye, Inc., nearby; incorporated 1865; pop. 16,614.
Morristown, Tenn., city 40 mi (60 km) n.e. of Knoxville; burley tobacco, dairying, and general farming; furniture, rayon textiles, chemicals, food products; pop. 19,683.
Morristown National Historical Park, New Jersey, *pictures* N-204
Morrisville, Pa., borough on Delaware River 30 mi (50 km) n.e. of Norristown; corn products, rubber, plastics, and tile industries; settled 1624, incorporated 1804; pop. 9,845, *map* P-185
Morro, El, fort at entrance to harbor of San Juan, P.R. S-44a, P-530, *picture* P-527
Morro Castle, fort at entrance to harbor of Havana, Cuba; built in late 16th century by Spanish colonists as a protection against French, English, and Dutch buccaneers; also used as a prison; guns last fired in Spanish-American War.
Morrow, Dwight Whitney (1873–1931), U.S. diplomat and statesman, born in Huntington, W. Va.; member J.P. Morgan & Co.; resigned 1927 to become ambassador to Mexico; elected U.S. senator (Republican) from New Jersey 1931; his daughter Anne married Charles A. Lindbergh.
Morrow, Elizabeth Reeve Cutter (1873–1955), U.S. author, born in Cleveland, Ohio; married Dwight Whitney Morrow; acting president of Smith College 1939–40; author of 'The Painted Pig', 'Beast, Bird and Fish', 'Quatrains for My Daughter', 'A Pint of Judgment' R-108
Morrow, Honoré Willsie McCue (1880–1940), U.S. writer, born in Ottumwa, Iowa; editor of *Delineator* 1914–19; known especially for historical novels ('Forever Free', 'With Malice Toward None', 'The Last Full Measure'—trilogy on Lincoln; 'Still Jim'; 'On to Oregon').
Morse. *see in index* Walrus
Morse, Samuel F.B. (full name Samuel Finley Breese Morse) (1791–1872), U.S. artist and inventor of the electric telegraph M-588
  Hall of Fame, *table* H-16
  Henry H-133
  New Jersey N-200
  portrait of Adams, *picture* A-34
  radio signals R-56
  telegraph T-58, I-274, *picture* I-275, *table* I-273
Morse, Wayne Lyman (1900–74), U.S. lawyer and political leader, born in Madison, Wis.; joined law faculty University of Oregon 1929, dean 1931–44; U.S. senator from Oregon 1945–69 (Republican 1945–52, independent 1952–55, Democrat 1955–69).
Morse code, telegraphy
  ham radio H-190
  language substitute L-36
  Morse M-588
  signaling S-194, *picture* S-195
Morta, in Roman mythology F-44
Mortality. *see in index* Vital statistics
Mortar, in masonry B-436
  lime L-210
  mosaic M-589
  production C-18
Mortar, short cannon A-659
Mortara, town in n. Italy 25 mi (40 km) s.w. of Milan; makes cheese and hats; Austrians defeated Sardinians 1849; pop. 14,383, *map* I-404
Mortar and pestle, tool of stone, wood, or metal for grinding or pulverizing; mortar is receptacle, pestle the sticklike crusher.
'Morte d'Arthur' (death of Arthur), work by Malory A-655
  English literature E-265
  Holy Grail H-207
  prose fiction L-243
Mortensen, Hans Christian (1856–1921), Danish ornithologist and teacher B-268
Mortenson, Ingri. *see in index* Aulaire, Edgar Parin d'
Mortgage B-69
  federal lending agencies U-165
  housing H-293, 296, 302
  legal definition, *table* L-93
  security for bonds S-450
Mortification, the subjection and denial of bodily passions and appetities by abstinence or self-inflicted pain or discomfort M-540
Mortimer's Cross, battle in Wars of Roses 1461, in w. England, 40 mi (60 km) s.w. of Birmingham; Edward, duke of York, defeated Lancastrians.
Mortise, cavity or opening cut in wood or masonry into which or through which some other part fits.
Mortise and tenon joint, in cabinetmaking C-175
Morton, Ferdinand (nickname Jelly Roll) (1885–1941), U.S. jazz musician, born in Gulfport, La.; pianist, bandleader, and composer ('Wolverine Blues'; 'King Porter Stomp'), *picture* J-84
Morton, John (1724–77), signer of Declaration of Independence; born in Ridley, Pa.
Morton, J. Sterling (full name Julius Sterling Morton) (1832–1902), U.S. journalist, born in Adams, N.Y.; U.S. secretary of agriculture 1893–97; estate in Nebraska City is a state park
  Nebraska N-95, *picture* N-102
  Statuary Hall, *table* S-437b
Morton, Levi Parsons (1824–1920), U.S. banker, born in Shoreham, Vt.; minister to France 1881–85; governor of New York 1895–97
  Harrison H-46
Morton, Oliver Perry (1823–77), U.S. statesman, born in Salisbury, Ind.; governor of Indiana 1861–67, and perhaps greatest of all war governors; U.S. senator 1867–77
  Statuary Hall, *table* S-437a
Morton, Rogers Clark Ballard (1914–79), U.S. public official, born in Louisville, Ky.; U.S. congressman (Republican) from Maryland 1963–71; chairman Republican National Committee 1969–71; U.S. secretary of the interior 1971–75; secretary of commerce April to Dec. 1975
  Nixon N-326
Morton, Thomas (1590?–1646), English adventurer, a Royalist rake who amused himself at expense of the "precise Separatists that lived at New Plymouth"; set up a Maypole, and sold rum and guns to the American Indians at Merry Mount, now Quincy, Mass.
Morton, William Thomas Green (1819–68), U.S. dentist, born in Charlton, Mass.; important work in discovery and use of anesthesia A-413, *picture* A-412
  Hall of Fame, *table* H-16
  medicine M-284
Morton Arboretum, near Lisle, Ill.; established 1922 by Joy Morton (1855–1934), son of J. Sterling Morton; 835 acres.
Morton Grove, Ill., village 15 mi (25 km) n.w. of Chicago; light industry; perfume, electronic components; pop. 23,747
  Illinois, *map* I-53
Mosaic M-589
  Byzantine A-549, B-534
  Italy, *picture* I-386
  Veracruz, Mexico, *picture* V-280
  Mexico City, Mexico, *picture* M-347
Mosaic, plate containing photoelectric cells
  television T-79
Mosaic disease, highly infectious virus disease affecting many plants including

cucumber, potato, tomato, bean, and turnip; dwarfs growth and mottles leaves V-350

Mosander, Carl Gustav (1797–1858), Swedish chemist and mineralogist, born in Kalmar, Sweden; discoverer of lanthanum, erbium, and terbium.

Mosasaur, prehistoric reptile R-156, *pictures* P-487, A-460
  animal life record, *table* E-24
  evolution A-462

Mosby, John Singleton (1833–1916), Confederate soldier, guerrilla raider, and commander of independent cavalry body called Mosby's Rangers, born in Edgemont, near Powhatan, Va.; particularly active in Virginia and Maryland 1863–64; said to have originated phrase "the solid South."

Moscheles, Ignaz (1794–1870), Bohemian pianist and composer, born in Prague; teacher and friend of Mendelssohn; compositions include piano concertos, sonatas, chamber music.

Moschus (2nd century BC), Greek pastoral poet of Syracuse; his poetry usually printed with works of Theocritus and Bion ('Europa', 'Love, the Runaway'; 'Bucolia').

Moscicki, Ignacy (1867–1946), Polish chemist, born near L'vov, U.S.S.R.; 3rd president of Poland, 1926–39; went to Switzerland 1939.

Mosconi, Willie (in full William Joseph Mosconi) (born 1913), U.S. championship billiards player B-193

Moscow, Idaho, city about 70 mi (110 km) s.e. of Spokane, Wash.; pea industry, wheat, lumbering, clay products; pop. 16,513, *map* I-30

Moscow (Russian Moskva), U.S.S.R., capital and largest city; pop. 8,703,000 M-591
  art theater company, *picture* A-251
  Botanical Garden, *table* B-379
  Church of St. Basil the Blessed, *picture* R-332e
  Europe, *map* E-361
  history R-351
  housing, *picture* H-296
  Kremlin K-304, R-333, *pictures* R-330a
  Lenin Stadium R-332b
  Lenin tomb, *pictures* R-356
  Moscow State University, *picture* E-336
  Napoleon N-17, *picture* N-14
  newspapers R-332e
  Pioneer Palace, *picture* R-332a
  Russia R-322, *picture* R-330b
  street railway S-487

Moscow Agreement, (1963), U.S., Soviet Union, and Britain agreed not to conduct atomic tests in the atmosphere, under water, or in outer space
  disarmament D-164

Moscow Art Theater, theater, Moscow, U.S.S.R.
  productions A-28

Moscow Canal (formerly Moscow-Volga Canal) R-323

Moscow M.V. Lomonosov State University, Moscow, U.S.S.R.; founded 1755, *picture* R-332c

Moseley, Henry Gwyn-Jeffreys (1887–1915), British physicist, born in Weymouth, England; gave his name to the Moseley number
  atomic number C-295
  X-ray spectra discoveries S-374

Moselle, department of n.e. France in region called Lorraine: 2,403 sq mi (6,224 sq km); iron and steel production; heavy chemical industries; coal and iron mining; farming; pop. 1,006,373, *map* F-369

Moselle River (German Mosel), n.e. France and s. Germany; flows 320 mi (510 km) n.e. to Rhine at Koblenz; valley noted for vineyards L-340
  France, *map* F-372
  German vineyards G-117, *map* G-134, *picture* G-118

Moses, Hebrew leader M-595
  art
    Michelangelo's statue M-351, S-87, *picture* M-595
    Veronese's painting P-38
  Bible B-181
  history writing H-171
  Judaism J-146
  Tabernacle T-2

Moses, Anna Mary Robertson (nickname Grandma Moses) (1860–1961), U.S. self-taught primitive artist, born in Washington County, New York
  hobby H-181

Moses, Phoebe Anne Oakley. *see in index* Oakley, Annie

'Moses', statue by Michelangelo M-351, *picture* M-595

'Moses and Aaron', opera by Schoenberg O-569

Moses ben Maimon. *see in index* Maimonides

Moses Lake, Wash., city on Moses Lake 68 mi (109 km) n.e. of Yakima; potatoes, sugar beets; food processing; pop. 10,629.

Moses of her people. *see in index* Tubman, Harriet

Moshav, cooperative system in Israel
  Israel I-370
  Palestine P-81

Moshava, private farmstead in Israel I-370

Moshesh, Basuto chief (died 1870), born near upper Caledon River; united African tribes and brought them into British Empire.

Moshi, Tanzania K-237

Moshoeshoe I (1786–1870), chief of the Sotho nation L-138

Moskva, U.S.S.R. *see in index* Moscow

Moskva River, U.S.S.R. M-591

Moslem, Muslim. *see in index* Islam

Moslem League. *see in index* Muslim League

Mosley, Sir Oswald Ernald, (1896–1980), British political figure, born in London; member of Parliament as Conservative, later as Labor; in 1931 headed "New Party" (Fascist), jailed 1941, freed 1943; later led Fascistlike Union Movement.

Mosque, building used for public worship by Muslims
  Alexandria A-281
  Damascus, *picture* M-395
  fountains F-335
  Islamic architecture A-550
  Islamic worship I-360
  minaret. *see in index* Minaret
  Santa Sophia. *see in index* Santa Sophia
  Senegal, *picture* S-108b
  Zamboanga, Philippines, *picture* P-257b

Mosquete. *see in index* Musket

Mosquitia, La. *see in index* Mosquito Coast

Mosquito, insect M-596
  egg, *picture* E-111
  evolution E-365
  insects I-224
  malaria M-284
  weed habitat W-131
  yellow-fever
    Panama P-93
    Reed's work R-121

Mosquito Bee B-125

Mosquito Coast (or La Mosquitia, or Costa de Mosquitos), strip of land occupied by Mosquito Indians on e. coast of Central America; British protectorate until 1860; now coastal part of both Nicaragua and Honduras; long source of diplomatic disputes between United Kingdom and U.S.
  Honduras H-225

Mosquito hawk, insect *Anax junius*, member of the Odonata family D-239

Mosquito netting (or mosquito bar), coarse, stiff net, plain or barred; used, especially in tropics, as canopy for beds and baby carriages; also for window screening; formerly made of cotton; nylon now used because resistant to mildew and bacteria.

Moss, Sanford Alexander (1872–1946), U.S. mechanical engineer, born in San Francisco, Calif.; pioneer in field of aircraft and car superchargers and compressors; joint winner of Collier Aviation Trophy 1941 J-111

Moss, Stirling (born 1929), British auto-racing driver, born in London; raced 1946–62; top international competitor until injury forced retirement; wrote books on racing; 'All But My Life', autobiography.

Moss, small, flowerless plant M-599
  classification P-370
  reproduction, *picture* S-396

Moss, club. *see in index* Club mosses

Moss, Irish. *see in index* Irish moss

Moss, Spanish. *see in index* Spanish moss

Mossadegh, Mohammed (1880?–1967), Iranian lawyer and statesman, born in Tehran, Iran; minister of justice 1920; finance 1921; foreign affairs 1922, member of parliament 1923–27, 1944–46; premier 1951–53; fought for oil nationalization, reforms to aid peasants; convicted of treason Dec. 1953; imprisoned 1953–56 I-309

Moss animals. *see in index* Bryozoa

Mössbauer, Rudolf Ludwig (born 1929), German physicist M-600

Mössbauer effect, in physics M-600

Moss campion. *see in index* Silene

'Mosses from an Old Manse', work by Hawthorn H-74

Mossi, a people of Burkina Faso B-507

Moss phlox, perennial flower
  flowering time G-25

Moss pink, phlox P-267

Moss Point, Miss., city 5 mi (8 km) n. of Pascagoula; paper and paper products, chemicals, shipbuilding; pop. 18,998.

Moss stonecrop. *see in index* Stonecrop

Mossy cup oak. *see in index* Bur Oak

Most, Johann (1846–1906), German publisher of socialist and anarchist newspapers A-388

Mostaganem, Algeria, seaport 45 mi (70 km) n.e. of Oran; exports wine, vegetables, citrus fruits, diatomaceous earth; modern section has large public garden; pop. 63,744.

Mostel, Zero (originally Samuel Joel Mostel) (1915–77), U.S. actor and painter, born in Brooklyn, N.Y.; Tony awards for 'Rhinoceros', 'A Funny Thing Happened on the Way to the Forum', and 'Fiddler on the Roof'; movies include 'The Producers', 'The Front' ('Zero by Mostel')
  Yiddish literature, *picture* Y-416

Most-favored-nation treatment, in international trade T-29

Mosul, Iraq, city on Tigris River 220 mi (350 km) n.w. of Baghdad; oil deposits; trade center; pop. 333,177
  Asia, *map* A-700

Moszkowski, Moritz (1854–1925), composer and pianist, born in Breslau, Germany, of Polish parents; works include an opera ('Boabdil'), a symphonic poem ('Jeanne d'Arc'), pieces for piano ('Spanish Dances').

Motacillidae, family of perching birds embracing the wagtails and pipits
  wagtail. *see in index* Wagtail

Motagua River, Guatemala G-296

Motel, business establishment that provides lodging for travelers H-286
  franchise F-373
  travel and tourism T-270

Motet, in music, *list* M-671
  classical music M-668

Moth, insect of the order Lepidoptera B-521. *see also in index* Butterfly; Caterpillar
  chrysalis P-534
  eggs, *pictures* E-111
  hibernation H-147
  hobby H-186
  insect I-224, *pictures* I-215, 219
  protective coloration P-509, *picture* P-510
  types
    bumblebee, *picture* P-512
    silkworm S-107
  wool W-288

'Mother and Child', work by Cassatt, *picture* C-197

'Mother and Child', work by Charlot, *picture* A-664

Mother Carey's chickens. *see in index* Petrel

Mother Goose, character in children's stories M-600
  children's literature L-246
  illustrated editions R-106
  Perrault tales S-475

Motherhood. *see in index* Baby; Pregnancy

Mother Jones. *see in index* Jones, Mary

Mother Lee. *see in index* Lee, Ann

Mother of God. *see in index* Mary

Mother of Michitsuna, anonymous Japanese writer J-80

Mother of Parliaments P-131

Mother-of-pearl (or nacre) S-150, P-148
  buttons, *picture* B-530
  Great Barrier Reef G-241
  mollusks M-524

Mothers Against Drunk Driving W-270

Mother's Day, U.S. holiday celebrated on second Sunday in May; children honor their mothers with cards, gifts, flowers; first observance in Philadelphia, Pa., 1907, based on suggestions by Julia Ward Howe in 1872 and Anne Jarvis in 1907; national observance dates from 1914, *list* F-63

Mother ship (or factory ship), in fishing industry F-138

Mother talk, reading foundation R-101b

Motherwell, Robert (born 1915), U.S. abstract painter, born in Aberdeen, Wash.; paintings exhibited internationally; served as editor *The Documents of Modern Art* 1944–52; associate professor Hunter College 1952–59; editor *Partisan Review* 1963–65; named to National Institute of Arts and Letters.

Motherwell, William (1797–1835), Scottish poet, born in Glasgow; 'Jeanie Morrison' and 'The Cavalier's Song' among best-known poems; made famous collection of ballads.

Motier, Marie-Joseph-Paul-Yves-Roch-Gilbert du. *see in index* Lafayette

Motif (or motive), in music M-666, *list* M-671

Motion, in parliamentary law P-132b

Motion, in physics
  astronomy A-720
  atmosphere A-747
  brake action B-404
  heat H-101
  mathematics M-215
  matter M-226
  mechanics M-264
  Muybridge's study M-694
  relativity R-140, *diagrams* R-141

Motion Picture Association of America (MPAA) (formerly Motion Picture Producers and Distributors of America) M-629

Motion Picture Patent Company, trust incorporated by ten motion picture companies on Sept. 9, 1908 to regulate all aspects of film production in the U.S. M-618

Motion pictures M-602. *see also in index* Photography; individual countries by name
  Academy award. *see in index table* following; *see also in index* Oscar
  art forms A-662
  contracts C-693
  director D-154
    Griffith G-286
    Hitchcock H-175
  driver training, *picture* S-5
  hair dressing H-10
  hobby H-189
  juvenile delinquency
    dramatization J-164
  made-for-television films T-73
  models M-516
  organized crime's depiction C-153
  technology
    Edison's contributions E-75
  photography P-297
    helicopter H-120
    three-dimensional S-444
  Western movies W-152

Motivation, learning L-106
  child development C-326
  education, *chart* E-80
  psychoanalysis P-519
  study S-495a

Motive (or motif), in music, *list* M-671

Motley, Constance Baker (born 1921), U.S. public official, born in New Haven, Conn.; New York state senator 1964–65; Manhattan borough president 1965–66; federal district judge in New York City 1966.

Motley, John Lothrop (1814–77), U.S. historian, born in Dorchester (now part

MAJOR MOTION PICTURE ACADEMY AWARDS

YEAR	BEST PICTURE	BEST ACTOR	BEST ACTRESS	BEST DIRECTOR
1927–28	'Wings'	Emil Jannings	Janet Gaynor	Frank Borzage
1928–29	'The Broadway Melody'	Warner Baxter	Mary Pickford	Frank Lloyd
1929–30	'All Quiet on the Western Front'	George Arliss	Norma Shearer	Lewis Milestone
1930–31	'Cimarron'	Lionel Barrymore	Marie Dressler	Norman Taurog
1931–32	'Grand Hotel'	Fredric March & Wallace Beery	Helen Hayes	Frank Borzage
1932–33	'Cavalcade'	Charles Laughton	Katharine Hepburn	Frank Lloyd
1934	'It Happened One Night'	Clark Gable	Claudette Colbert	Frank Capra
1935	'Mutiny on the Bounty'	Victor McLaglen	Bette Davis	John Ford
1936	'The Great Ziegfeld'	Paul Muni	Luise Rainer	Frank Capra
1937	'The Life of Emile Zola'	Spencer Tracy	Luise Rainer	Leo McCarey
1938	'You Can't Take It with You'	Spencer Tracy	Bette Davis	Frank Capra
1939	'Gone with the Wind'	Robert Donat	Vivien Leigh	Victor Fleming
1940	'Rebecca'	James Stewart	Ginger Rogers	John Ford
1941	'How Green Was My Valley'	Gary Cooper	Joan Fontaine	John Ford
1942	'Mrs. Miniver'	James Cagney	Greer Garson	William Wyler
1943	'Casablanca'	Paul Lukas	Jennifer Jones	Michael Curtiz
1944	'Going My Way'	Bing Crosby	Ingrid Bergman	Leo McCarey
1945	'The Lost Weekend'	Ray Milland	Joan Crawford	Billy Wilder
1946	'The Best Years of Our Lives'	Fredric March	Olivia de Havilland	William Wyler
1947	'Gentleman's Agreement'	Ronald Colman	Loretta Young	Elia Kazan
1948	'Hamlet'	Laurence Olivier	Jane Wyman	John Huston
1949	'All the King's Men'	Broderick Crawford	Olivia de Havilland	Joseph L. Mankiewicz
1950	'All About Eve'	José Ferrer	Judy Holliday	Joseph L. Mankiewicz
1951	'An American in Paris'	Humphrey Bogart	Vivien Leigh	George Stevens
1952	'The Greatest Show on Earth'	Gary Cooper	Shirley Booth	John Ford
1953	'From Here to Eternity'	William Holden	Audrey Hepburn	Fred Zinnemann
1954	'On the Waterfront'	Marlon Brando	Grace Kelly	Elia Kazan
1955	'Marty'	Ernest Borgnine	Anna Magnani	Delbert Mann
1956	'Around the World in 80 Days'	Yul Brynner	Ingrid Bergman	George Stevens
1957	'The Bridge on the River Kwai'	Alec Guinness	Joanne Woodward	David Lean
1958	'Gigi'	David Niven	Susan Hayward	Vincente Minnelli
1959	'Ben-Hur'	Charlton Heston	Simone Signoret	William Wyler
1960	'The Apartment'	Burt Lancaster	Elizabeth Taylor	Billy Wilder
1961	'West Side Story'	Maximilian Schell	Sophia Loren	Robert Wise & Jerome Robbins
1962	'Lawrence of Arabia'	Gregory Peck	Anne Bancroft	David Lean
1963	'Tom Jones'	Sidney Poitier	Patricia Neal	Tony Richardson
1964	'My Fair Lady'	Rex Harrison	Julie Andrews	George Cukor
1965	'The Sound of Music'	Lee Marvin	Julie Christie	Robert Wise
1966	'A Man for All Seasons'	Paul Scofield	Elizabeth Taylor	Fred Zinnemann
1967	'In the Heat of the Night'	Rod Steiger	Katharine Hepburn	Mike Nichols
1968	'Oliver!'	Cliff Robertson	Katharine Hepburn & Barbra Streisand	Sir Carol Reed
1969	'Midnight Cowboy'	John Wayne	Maggie Smith	John Schlesinger
1970	'Patton'	George C. Scott	Glenda Jackson	Franklin J. Schaffner
1971	'The French Connection'	Gene Hackman	Jane Fonda	William Friedkin
1972	'The Godfather'	Marlon Brando	Liza Minnelli	Robert Fosse
1973	'The Sting'	Jack Lemmon	Glenda Jackson	George Roy Hill
1974	'The Godfather Part II'	Art Carney	Ellen Burstyn	Francis Ford Coppola
1975	'One Flew over the Cuckoo's Nest'	Jack Nicholson	Louise Fletcher	Milos Forman
1976	'Rocky'	Peter Finch	Faye Dunaway	John G. Avildsen
1977	'Annie Hall'	Richard Dreyfuss	Diane Keaton	Woody Allen
1978	'The Deer Hunter'	Jon Voight	Jane Fonda	Michael Cimino
1979	'Kramer vs. Kramer'	Dustin Hoffman	Sally Field	Robert Benton
1980	'Ordinary People'	Robert De Niro	Sissy Spacek	Robert Redford
1981	'Chariots of Fire'	Henry Fonda	Katharine Hepburn	Warren Beatty
1982	'Gandhi'	Ben Kingsley	Meryl Streep	Richard Attenborough
1983	'Terms of Endearment'	Robert Duvall	Shirley MacLaine	James L. Brooks
1984	'Amadeus'	F. Murray Abraham	Sally Field	Milos Forman
1985	'Out of Africa'	William Hurt	Geraldine Page	Sydney Pollack
1986	'Platoon'	Paul Newman	Marlee Matlin	Oliver Stone

of Boston), Mass.; minister to Austria 1861–67 and to England 1869–70 ('The Rise of the Dutch Republic'; 'The History of the United Netherlands')
Hall of Fame, *table* H-16

Motley, Marion (born 1920), U.S. football fullback, born in Leesburg, Ga.; played for Cleveland Browns 1946–53, Pittsburgh Steelers 1955.

Motley, Willard (1912–65), U.S. novelist, born in Chicago, Ill.; a representative of naturalism in literature ('Knock on Any Door'; 'We Fished All Night'; 'Let No Man Write My Epitaph').

Motmot, tropical American bird of family Momotidae, about the size of a blue jay with brilliant blue and green plumage; middle feathers of its tail are longer than the others and have a peculiar racket shape because some barbs break off.

Motocross, motorcycle racing M-632

Motomachi, street, Kobe, Japan K-266

Moton, Robert Russa (1867–1940), U.S. educator, born in Amelia County, Va.; president of Tuskegee Institute 1915–35; won 1932 Spingarn Medal.

Motor M-630. *see also in index* Engine; Diesel engine; Internal-combustion engine; Steam engine
Davenport's invention, *picture* V-291
electricity E-157
machine M-10
motorboat. *see in index* Motorboat
rocket S-342a
submarine S-493

Motorboat B-328, *picture* B-231, *diagram* B-327
radio guidance, *picture* R-55
tachometer T-3

Motor Carrier Act (1935), United States T-292

Motorcycle M-631, *picture* I-170
police use P-424
safety S-11
transportation, *picture* T-263

Motor nerve, in human nervous system N-118, *diagram* N-121
brain B-398

Motor ship S-167, *diagrams* S-172

Motor-skill memory, type of memory M-294

Motown, record company founded in Detroit, Mich. M-681

Mott, John R. (in full John Raleigh Mott) (1865–1955), U.S. foreign mission and YMCA leader M-632. *see also in index* Nobel Prizewinners, *table*

Mott, Lucretia (formerly Lucretia Coffin) (1793–1880), U.S. Quaker abolitionist, women's-rights advocate M-632

Mott, Sir Nevill Francis (born 1905), British physicist, born in Leeds; professor University of Bristol 1933–54; at Cavendish Laboratory at Cambridge University 1954–71; research on wave mechanics and study of conduction. *see also in index* Nobel Prizewinners, *table*

Motta, José Vianna da. *see in index* Vianna da Motta, José

Motte-Fouqué, baron de la. *see in index* La Motte-Fouqué, Friedrich Heinrich Karl, baron de

Mottelson, Ben Roy (born 1926), Danish physicist, born in Chicago, Ill.; research in

atomic nuclear structure and motion; associate of Aage Bohr at Niels Bohr Institute in Copenhagen. *see also in index* Nobel Prizewinners, *table*
  nuclear physics N-432

Mottl, Felix (1856–1911), German conductor and composer, born near Vienna; gifted conductor of Wagner's music; general music director, Munich.

Motto, in heraldry H-136, *picture* H-135

Mouflon, wild sheep S-148

Mouillard, Louis Pierre (1834–97), French glider pioneer and writer; constructed numerous gliders patterned after birds A-201

Mould. *see in index* Mold

Moulins, France, town on Allier River about 90 mi (140 km) n.w. of Lyons; famous cathedral; pop. 25,778, *map* F-372

Moulmein, Burma, city and port on Salween River; exports teak and rice; industries include rice milling and sawmilling; pop. 108,020
  Asia, *map* A-700

Moulton, Forest Ray (1872–1952), U.S. astronomer, born in Le Roy, Mich.; University of Chicago 1898–1927; research associate Carnegie Institution 1908–23 ('Astronomy'; 'Consider the Heavens') P-355

Moultrie, William (1730–1805), general in Revolutionary War, born in Charleston, S.C.; built fort on Sullivan's Island to protect Charleston (later named Fort Moultrie), where he repelled a fierce British attack in 1776; held prisoner by British 1780–82; later governor of South Carolina S-310
  flag F-154, *picture* F-155

Moultrie, Ga., city 35 mi (55 km) s.e. of Albany; tobacco, cotton, peanut processing, meat-packing, garments, mobile homes; named for Gen. William Moultrie; incorporated 1895; pop. 15,708.

Mound, in archaeology A-530
  man M-83
  Sumerian villages B-4

Mound Bayou, Miss., founded 1887, incorporated 1898; 24 mi (39 km) s.w. of Clarksdale; farming; Tufts-Delta Health Center, under direction of Tufts University Medical School of Boston, Mass.; pop. 2,917.

Mound Builders, a prehistoric North American people
  culture I-142, *picture* I-119
  Illinois I-135
  Ohio O-499, *picture* O-504
  South Dakota S-323

Moundsville, W. Va., commercial city 10 mi (16 km) s. of Wheeling in farming and coal-mining area; enameled ware, toys, chemicals; zinc smelting; state penitentiary; named from relics of mound builders discovered there; pop. 12,419.

Mount, William Sidney (1807–68), U.S. artist, born in Long Island, N.Y.; portraits and American genre; after death sank into obscurity; later recognized as pioneer painter of everyday U.S. life.

Mount. *see in index* under specific names, as McKinley, Mount

Mountain M-633. *see also in index* names of chief mountains and mountain systems. For a list of the highest mountains. *see table* following
  civilization
    Spain S-349
    U.S. U-37
  continental development C-690
  earth E-14, *diagrams* E-15, 16
  Himalayas H-153
  lunar M-580
    exploration S-347
  petroleum source P-230
  Rockies R-235
  Venus P-352
  volcano V-378, *diagram* V-379, *pictures* V-380

Mountain ash, forest tree of North America M-636
  ash A-671

Mountain beaver (also called boomer, or whistler), rodent of the family Aplodontiidae, native only to the Pacific coast of North America; about 14 in. (36 cm) long, with a blunt head, small eyes and ears, and very short tail; lives in burrows in moist woods; not a true beaver.

Mountain belt, in geology
  continental development C-690
  under ocean O-460

Mountain bluebird, Nevada state bird, *picture* N-140

Mountain breeze, winds W-220, *diagram* W-221

Mountain Brook, Ala., city 5 mi (8 km) s.e. of Birmingham; residential suburb; incorporated 1942; pop. 17,400.

Mountain climbing M-637

Mountain cock. *see in index* Capercaillie

Mountain cranberry. *see in index* Lingonberry

Mountain dance, folk dance F-258

Mountain goat (or goat antelope), animal intermediate between goat and antelope; term often applied to any wild goat, such as ibex, living in mountains
  Sierra de Gredos, Spain S-351
  takin. *see in index* Takin

Mountain gorilla, endangered species of ape Z-460

Mountain hemlock, tree *Tsuga mertensiana* of the pine family H-127

Mountain Home, Idaho, city 43 mi (69 km) s.e. of Boise; timber, livestock, grain, sugar beets; mining; trailers; Mountain Home Air Force Base nearby; pop. 7,540, *map* I-30

Mountain laurel (or calico bush) L-88
  state flower S-426, *picture* S-427
    Connecticut, *picture* [illegible]
    Pennsylvania, *picture* P-176
  wild flowers, *picture* F-237

Mountain lion. *see in index* Puma

Mountain Men C-177, U-177

'Mountain Muse, The', work by Bryan W-151

Mountain music. *see in index* Music, Country

Mountain Nile. *see in index* Nile River

Mountain quail, bird *Oreortyx pictus* Q-3

Mountains of the Moon. *see in index* Ruwenzori Mountains

Mountain State. *see in index* West Virginia

Mountain States, name used by U.S. government for geographic division including states of Montana, Idaho, Wyoming, Colorado, New Mexico, Arizona, Utah, Nevada.

Mountain system, larger grouping of mountains E-14

Mountain tapir, mammal *Tapirus roulini* T-28

Mountain time T-189, *map* U-40

Mountain View, Calif., city 5 mi (8 km) s.e. of Palo Alto; electronic equipment, seeds, mill work; publishing; incorporated 1902; Moffett Naval Air Station nearby; St. Patrick's College; pop. 58,655.

Mountain zebra, hoofed mammal *Equus zebra* Z-449

Mount Allison University, Sackville, N.B.; United Church of Canada; chartered 1858; arts and sciences, commerce, applied science, engineering, fine arts, home economics, music N-157

Mount Angel College, Mount Angel, Ore.; private control, Catholic related; closed 1974.

Mountbatten, Louis (full name Louis Francis Albert Victor Nicholas, prince of Battenberg) (1900–79), British naval officer and statesman M-638
  assassination, *list* A-704

Mount Carmel, Pa., borough in anthracite-mining region, 45 mi (70 km) n.e. of Harrisburg; textiles, cigars, metal products, plastics; pop. 8,190, *map* P-185

Mount Clemens, Mich., city near Lake St. Clair, about 20 mi (30 km) n.e. of Detroit; health resort, with mineral water baths; automotive plastics, metal products, pottery; floral industry; Selfridge Air National Guard Base nearby; pop. 18,806.

Mount Desert Island, off coast of Maine; 100 sq mi (260 sq km) M-52

Mounted warrior, in warfare W-20

Mount Holly, N.J., urban township 18 mi (29 km) n.e. of Camden; temporary capital of New Jersey 1779; pop. 12,713.

Mount Holyoke College, South Hadley, Mass.; private control; for women; opened 1837 as seminary, college 1888; liberal arts, education, nursing, sciences; graduate studies, *picture* V-262

Mount Hood, mountain in Oregon O-582, *picture* O-581

Mount Hood National Park, Oregon
  forest, *picture* F-315

Mountie. *see in index* Royal Canadian Mounted Police

Mountlake Terrace, Wash., city 13 mi (21 km) n. of Seattle; residential, some industry; incorporated 1954; pop. 16,534.

Mount Lebanon, Pa., urban township s.w. of Pittsburgh and included in its metropolitan area; chiefly residential; incorporated 1912; pop. 34,414, *map* P-184

Mount McKinley National Park, s.-central Alaska A-20, *map* U-94
  Mount McKinley M-21

Mount Marty College, Yankton, S.D.; Roman Catholic; coeducational; formerly for women; became four-year college 1951; liberal arts, home economics, medical technology, music, teacher education.

Mount Mary College, Milwaukee, Wis.; Roman Catholic; for women; established in 1913; arts and sciences, teacher education.

Mount Mercy College, Cedar Rapids, Iowa; Roman Catholic; founded as junior college 1928, senior college after 1957; liberal arts, business, education, medical technology, social service.

Mount Palomar Observatory. *see in index* Palomar Observatory

Mount Pearl, Newf., town, U.S. suburb of St. John's; pop. 11,543 N-169

Mount Pleasant, Mich., city about 45 mi (70 km) n.w. of Saginaw, on Chippewa River; oil center; beet sugar and other food products; Central Michigan University; pop. 23,746.

Mount Prospect, Ill., residential village 20 mi (30 km) n.w. of Chicago; office machines, pharmaceuticals, cafeteria equipment, printing; pop. 52,534
  Illinois, *map* I-53

Mount Rainier. *see in index* Rainier, Mount

Mount Royal College, Alberta A-266

Mount Royal Park, park, Montreal, Que. M-571

Mount Rushmore National Memorial, South Dakota S-324, *map* S-334, *pictures* S-79, S-321

Mount Saint Helens National Volcanic Monument, Washington W-52

Mount St. Joseph-on-the-Ohio, College of, Mount St. Joseph, Ohio; Roman Catholic; for women; founded 1854; arts and sciences, nursing, and teacher education.

Mount St. Mary College, Hooksett, N.H.; private control, Roman Catholic related; for women; closed 1978.

Mount St. Mary College, Newburgh, N.Y.; Roman Catholic; coeducational, formerly for women; chartered 1959; liberal arts and teacher education.

Mount St. Mary's College, Los Angeles, Calif.; Roman Catholic; for women; founded 1925; arts and sciences, education, home economics; medical technology, nursing; music and graduate schools coeducational.

Mount St. Mary's College, Emmitsburg, Md.; Roman Catholic; founded 1808; arts and sciences, business administration, education, social science; graduate studies.

Mount St. Vincent, College of, New York, N.Y.; private control, Catholic related; coeducational, formerly for women; founded 1910; arts and sciences and teacher education.

Mount St. Vincent University, Halifax, N.S.; Roman Catholic; primarily for women; chartered 1925; arts and sciences, business studies, education, fine arts, home economics, nursing; graduate studies.

Mount Stephen, George Stephen, Baron (1829–1921), Canadian financier, born in Dufftown, Scotland; with Lord Strathcona responsible for completion of the Canadian Pacific Railway.

Mount Union College, Alliance, Ohio; United Methodist; founded 1846; arts and sciences, music, and teacher education; quarter system.

Mount Vernon, Ill., city 72 mi (116 km) s.e. of St. Louis in agricultural and oil section; shoes, clothing, electrical equipment, heaters, radiators, forest products, chemicals, food processing; pop. 16,995
  Illinois, *map* I-53

MOUNTAINS—HIGHEST IN VARIOUS PARTS OF THE WORLD

	Height ft	Height m
Aconcagua, Argentina (*highest in South America*)	22,831	6,959
Blanc, France (*highest in Alps*)	15,771	4,807
Citlaltépetl, Mexico (*highest in Mexico*)	18,406	5,610
Communism Peak, Soviet Union (*highest in Soviet Union*)	24,590	7,495
El'brus, Soviet Union (*highest in Europe*)	18,510	5,642
Etna, Sicily	10,705	3,265
Everest, Tibet-Nepal (*highest in world*)	29,028	8,848
Fuji, Japan	12,389	3,776
Jaya, Indonesia	16,500	5,030
K2, Kashmir (*2nd highest in world*)	28,250	8,611
Kilimanjaro, Tanzania (*highest in Africa*)	19,340	5,895
Kosciusko, Australia (*highest in Australia*)	7,310	2,228
Logan, Canada (*highest in Canada*)	19,524	5,951
McKinley, Alaska (*highest in North America*)	20,320	6,194
Mauna Kea, Hawaii	13,796	4,205
Mitchell, N.C. (*highest in Eastern U.S.*)	6,684	2,037
Vinson Massif (*highest in Antarctica*)	16,864	5,140
Washington, N.H. (*highest in Northeastern U.S.*)	6,288	1,917
Whitney, Calif. (*highest in U.S. mainland, excluding Alaska*)	14,495	4,418

Muhammad, Warith Deen (born 1933), U.S. religious leader, born in Detroit, Mich.; son of Elijah Muhammad; made hajj (pilgrimage to Mecca) 1967; advocate of orthodox Islam; leader of American Muslim Mission (formerly World Community of Islam in the West, or, popularly, Black Muslim movement) 1975–85 when it merged with the worldwide Islamic community. *see also in index* Black Muslims

Muhammad Ali. *see in index* Ali, Muhammad

Muhammad 'Ali Pasha (or Mehemet Ali) (1769–1849), Ottoman Empire's governor of Egypt M-646
Egypt E-121
Alexandria A-282
The Sudan S-503

Muhammad ibn Tughluq (1290?–1351), ruler of the Delhi sultanate M-647

Mühlberg, East Germany, town on Elbe River 35 mi (55 km) n.w. of Dresden; Emperor Charles V defeated Protestants under Elector of Saxony (1547).

Muhlenberg, Frederick Augustus Conrad (1750–1801), U.S. Lutheran clergyman, born in Trappe, Pa., member of Continental Congress and House of Representatives (speaker first and third Congresses) M-647

Muhlenberg, Gotthilf Henry Ernest (1753–1815), U.S. Lutheran clergyman and botanist M-647

Muhlenberg, Henry Melchior (1711–87), U.S. clergyman, born in Germany; emigrated to Philadelphia 1742 and organized first Lutheran synod in America 1748; real founder of American Lutheran church; father of John P.G., Frederick A.C., and Gotthilf H.E. M-647

Muhlenberg, John Peter Gabriel (1746–1807), "fighting parson" of the American Revolution M-647
Statuary Hall, *table* S-437b

Muhlenberg, William Augustus (1796–1877), U.S. Episcopal clergyman, born in Philadelphia, Pa., grandson of F.A.C. Muhlenberg; rector in New York, N.Y., 1846–58, founded St. Luke's Hospital there; wrote hymns.

Muhlenberg College, Allentown, Pa.; private control, Lutheran related; established in 1848; arts and sciences, teacher education.

Muir, Alexander (1830–1906), Canadian songwriter, born in Scotland; public-school teacher; wrote Canadian patriotic anthem 'The Maple Leaf Forever' 1867.

Muir, Edwin (1887–1959), Scottish poet and literary critic, born in Orkney Islands; he and wife, Willa, noted as translators from German, notably of Kafka.

Muir, John (1838–1914), U.S. naturalist, explorer, and writer M-648

Muir Glacier, large and picturesque ice sheet of s.e. Alaska; about 350 sq mi (910 sq km); explored by John Muir A-241

Muir Woods National Monument, California, *maps* C-53, *picture* C-47

Muisca. *see in index* Chibcha

Muizenberg, South Africa, resort suburb s. of Cape Town, *picture* S-263

Mujibur Rahman. *see in index* Rahman, Mujibur

Mujtahid, Islamic scholar I-361

Mukalla, al- seaport in Hadhramaut, People's Democratic Republic of Yemen; exports fish products, honey, tobacco; pop. 45,000 Y-413

Mukden. *see in index* Shen-yang

Mukden, battle of (1905), Japanese defeated the Russians, *list* W-15

Mukden Incident (1931), Mukden occupied by Japanese C-373

Mukerji, Dhan Gopal (1890–1936), Hindu (Brahmin) author, born in Calcutta, India; profound interpreter of Eastern civilization (for young people: 'Gay-Neck', awarded Newbery Medal 1928; 'Chief of the Herd'; for adults: 'Caste and Outcast'; 'Son of Mother India Answers').

Mukluk, knee-high fur boot worn by Eskimos; made of reindeer skins or sealskins trimmed with wool or grass; also boot, usually duck, with soft leather sole, worn with heavy socks.

'Muktibodh', work by Kumar I-108

Mulatas, Archipiélago de las, Panama. *see in index* San Blas Islands

'Mulatto', work by Hughes H-316

'Mulatto, The', novel by Azevedo L-68

Mulberry, any of several trees with black, white, or red fruit M-648, B-177, *picture* S-198
tapa cloth P-13

Mulberry family (or Moraceae), family of plants, shrubs, and trees including the osage orange, the mulberries, banyan, fig, bo tree, upas tree, breadfruit, jackfruit, breadnut, hemp, Mexican rubber tree, snakewood tree, fustic, and the hop.

Mulch, material such as manure, leaves, pulverized earth, placed on surface of soil to retain moisture and to protect plant roots from frost
fruitgrowing F-438
garden use G-22
land conservation C-675
weed control W-133

Muldoon, Robert (born 1921), New Zealand statesman M-648

Muldrow Glacier, Alaska A-244

Mule, hybrid animal A-702

Mule, device. *see in index* Spinning mule

Mule deer, deer *Odocoileus hemionus*, both sexes have large ears, and black-tipped tails; range in w. North America D-61, *picture* A-426, *table* D-63

Mule killer. *see in index* Mantis

Muleta, cape used by matadors B-501

Mulga, dwarf acacia tree of Australia A-783

Mulgara, crest-tailed marsupial mouse *Dasycercus cristacauda* M-156

Mulguf, ventilating device S-156, *picture* S-158

Mulhacén, highest summit in continental Spain, 11,417 ft (3,480 m); in Sierra Nevada, s.e. of Granada, *map* S-350

Mülheim-an-der-Ruhr, West Germany, city on Ruhr River just w. of Essen; coal mining; machinery, textiles, cement, food products; pop. 191,468

Mulholland, John (1898–1970), U.S. magician, writer, born in Chicago, Ill.; editor *The Sphinx*, for magicians ('Story of Magic').

Mulhouse (or Mülhausen), France, city in s. Alsace; textiles; under German rule 1871–1918; again occupied by Germany 1940–44; pop. 115,632 A-320, *maps* E-361, F-372

Mull, island off w. coast of Scotland, 2nd largest of Inner Hebrides; 367 sq mi (950 sq km); chief town Tobermory; pop. 2,149.

Mull, plainwoven, sheer fabric of cotton, silk, or a combination of these; in white or pastels; used for dresses and hats.

Mullah, complimentary title given to Muslim religious leader
Afghanistan A-91
folktale S-469, 480

Mulled wine, beverage W-237

Mullein, tall, woolly biennial herb *Verbascum thapsus* of the figwort family, with stout stem, large oblong leaves, and yellow flowers densely arranged on a long cylindrical spike
flower F-217
weed, *picture* W-133

Müller, Franz Joseph, (1740–1825), Austrian chemist, born in Sibiu, Romania; discoverer of tellurium (1782).

Müller, George Elias (1850–1934), German psychologist, known for work on memory and color perception; claimed a piece is memorized more quickly by reading whole than by learning bits.

Muller, Hermann Joseph (1890–1967), U.S. geneticist, born in New York City; taught at University of Texas, Rice Institute, Amherst College; became professor of zoology Indiana University 1945. *see also in index* Nobel Prizewinners, *table*

Müller, Johannes (1801–58), German physiologist, born in Coblenz, Germany; early student of comparative anatomy and nerves of animals; showed dependency of physiology on other sciences.

Müller, Lucas. *see in index* Cranach, Lucas

Müller, Max (full name Friedrich Max Müller) (1823–1900), Anglo-German Orientalist, Sanskrit scholar, and popularizer of comparative philology; born in Dessau, Germany; moved to England 1846; taught at Oxford University about 20 years.

Müller, Paul (1899–1965), U.S. chemist, born in Olten, Switzerland; in laboratories in Basel, discovered insect-killing powers of DDT. *see also in index* Nobel Prizewinners, *table*

Müllerian mimicry, animals M-423

Mullet, any of about 100 species, most of them tropical, of food fishes occurring in most seas; family Mugilidae; most abundant U.S. species is the striped, or jumping, mullet; stout-bodied; average weight 2 to 3 lbs (0.9 to 1.4 kg); silvery gray; scientific name *Mugil cephalus.* Mullets are the most important food fishes of the South Atlantic and Gulf states. The name mullet is given also to the goatfish, or surmullets, *table* F-136. *see also in index* Goatfish

Mullet (or molet), in heraldry H-136

Mulliken, Robert Sanderson (1896–1986), U.S. scientist born in Newburyport, Mass.; professor University of Chicago (physics 1931–61, also chemistry 1961); research professor chemical physics Florida State University 1965–71. *see also in index* Nobel Prizewinners, *table*

Mullins, Priscilla (or Priscilla Mullines), one of *Mayflower* Pilgrims
Alden A-277, S-410
'The Courtship of Miles Standish' L-296

Mulock, Dinah Maria. *see in index* Craik, Dinah Maria

Mulock, Sir William (1844–1944), Canadian statesman, born in Bondhead, near Toronto; postmaster general 1896–1905; first minister of labor 1900–05; chief justice of Ontario; chancellor University of Toronto; promoted penny postage within British Empire.

Mulready, William (1786–1863), Irish artist and illustrator, born in Ennis, Ireland; genre paintings resemble those of Dutch school
postage sheet design S-408

Mulroney, Brian, (born 1939), Canadian politician M-648
Canada C-106

Multan, (or Mooltan), Pakistan, city 190 mi (310 km) s.w. of Lahore; silk and cotton, carpets, shoes, pottery; captured by British in 1849; pop. 358,201
Asia, *map* A-700

Multicolor rotary press, in printing, *picture* P-502

Multigraph, duplicating machine for making facsimile copies of words, numerals, lines, pictures from individually prepared master; relief process, from master with raised surface, such as type, metal, or rubber plates; multilith, or offset process, from a plane surface using paper or metal masters P-503

Multilateral aid F-306

Multinational company I-102
corporation C-725
labor movements L-11
North America N-344

Multiple arch dam D-15, *picture* D-12

Multiple birth M-649

Multiple dome dam D-15

Multiple independently-targeted reentry vehicles (MIRVs), weapons N-434

Multiple Mirror Telescope (MMT), telescope T-67
observatory O-458

Multiple sclerosis (MS), chronic disease of the nervous system; cause unknown; leads to disturbances of vision, speech, coordination, and bodily functions D-179
nervous disorder N-123

Multiplexing
radio R-57

Multiplication, in mathematics
algebra A-286
arithmetic A-593
fractions F-338
numeration systems N-435, *table* N-438
slide rule S-217

Multiplier, in economics B-517

Multiplying lens, in motion pictures M-603

Multnomah Falls, beautiful cascade in the Columbia River, 30 mi (50 km) e. of Portland, Ore.; 850 ft (260 m) high including upper and lower falls; rises in short stream in Larch Mountains.

Mulvian Bridge, Tiber River. *see in index* Milvian Bridge

Mumford, Lawrence Quincy (1903–82), U.S. librarian, born in Ayden, N.C.; held executive positions at New York Public Library 1929–45 and Cleveland Public Library 1945–54; Librarian of Congress 1954–74; A.L.A. president 1954–55.

Mumford, Lewis (born 1895), U.S. author M-651

Mummenschantz, mime troupe M-423

Mummers (or maskers)
Philadelphia parade P-252

Mummy M-651
cloths T-142
Egypt E-123

Mumps, contagious disease characterized by inflammation and swelling of the parotid glands V-249
infectious disease, *table* D-172

Mumtaz Mahal (also called Arjumand Banu Begum), beloved wife of Shah Jahan; buried in the Taj Mahal T-16

'Mumyo sho', essay by Chōmei Kamo J-81

Munch, Charles (1891–1968), French orchestra conductor, born in Strasbourg, Alsace-Lorraine; debut as conductor 1932; exponent of modern music; conductor Boston Symphony Orchestra 1949–62; musical director and conductor Paris Symphony Orchestra 1963–68
orchestra O-578, *list* O-579

Munch, Edvard (1863–1944), Norwegian painter M-651
Norway N-391

München, West Germany. *see in index* Munich

Münchhausen, Baron von, the name given the pretended author of a book of tales and travels by **Rudolph Erich Raspe** (1737–94), a German scholar who had left his native Hanover for England. The real **Baron Karl Friedrich Hieronymus von Münchhausen** (1720–97) of Hanover had nothing to do with the book. In later editions other writers added "lies from all literature" to Raspe's original tales
folklore F-261

Muncie, Ind., city on West Fork of White River about 50 mi (80 km) n.e. of Indianapolis; automobile equipment, glass and metal products, meat-packing; Ball State University; pop. 77,216
Indiana I-91, *map* I-102

Munda, ancient town in s. Spain where Caesar defeated sons of Pompey (45 BC); location disputed, probably either near Ronda in Málaga Province or near Montilla in Córdoba Province.

Munda languages L-42, *diagram* L-44

Mundelein, George William, Cardinal (1872–1939), Roman Catholic prelate, born in New York City; archbishop of Chicago 1916–39; created cardinal 1924.

Mundelein, Ill., village 10 mi (16 km) s.w. of Waukegan; in district of lakes and dairy farms; varied industries; St. Mary of the Lake Seminary; village incorporated 1909 as Area, renamed 1925 for

Murray, George, British inventor
  telecommunication T-57

Murray, George Gilbert Aimé (1866–1957), British classical scholar, born in Sydney, Australia; best known for translations of plays of Euripides in English verse ('History of Ancient Greek Literature'; 'Rise of the Greek Epic'; 'An Unfinished Autobiography')
  'Antigone' R-112d

Murray, James (1721–94), British soldier and statesman, born in Ballencrief, Scotland; one of Wolfe's brigadiers in siege of Quebec in 1759; 1760 appointed military governor of Quebec; first civil governor of Quebec Province 1764–68.

Murray, Sir James Augustus Henry (1837–1915), British lexicographer, born in Denholm, Scotland; twice president of Philological Society of London, in connection with which he became editor, 1879, of the 'New English Dictionary' (Oxford English Dictionary).

Murray, James Stuart, earl of (or James Stuart, earl of Moray) (1531?–70), half brother of Mary, queen of Scots, and her protector and chief adviser on her return from France; her chief enemy after her open break with Protestantism, and regent for the infant James after Mary's abdication.

Murray, Sir John (1841–1914), British oceanographer, born in Cobourg, Ont.; edited reports of the *Challenger* expedition, wrote on scientific subjects
  atoll formation P-13

Murray, Lindley (1745–1826), U.S. grammarian, born in Dauphin County, Pennsylvania; his 'Grammar of the English Language' was standard in England and U.S. for 50 years.

Murray, Philip (1886–1952), U.S. labor leader, born in Blantyre, near Glasgow, Scotland; to U.S. 1902; coal miner in Pennsylvania; international vice-president United Mine Workers of America 1920–40; member National Industrial Recovery Board 1935; president C.I.O. 1940–52.

Murray, Ky., city 18 mi (29 km) s. of Benton; stoves, chemicals; Murray State University; Land Between the Lakes recreation area nearby; pop. 14,248.

Murray, Utah, city 7 mi (11 km) s. of Salt Lake City; trade center for irrigated farms nearby; vegetable and fruit canning; textiles, building materials; incorporated 1902; pop. 25,750 U-218, *maps* U-40, U-232

Murray Bay, Que. *see in index* La Malbaie

Murray River, chief river of Australia; drains, with Darling tributary, entire s.e. quarter; mouth on s. coast 40 mi (60 km) e. of Adelaide; total length of Murray-Darling system, 2,300 mi (3,700 km) M-657
  Australia A-769, *map* A-819
  Pacific Ocean, *map* P-6

Murray State University, Murray, Ky.; founded 1922; arts and sciences, applied science and technology, business, and education; graduate school.

Murre, sea bird of the auk family A-762

Murrow, Edward R. (full name Egbert Roscoe Murrow) (1908–65), radio and television news reporter M-658
  newspapers N-239

Murrumbidgee River, s.e. Australia; flows through New South Wales 1,350 mi (2,170 km) into Murray River; navigable between June and November for small boats as far inland as Hay A-769, *map* A-819

Murry, John Middleton (1889–1957), English editor and critic, born in London; husband of Katherine Mansfield; literary reviewer *London Times*; editor *Athenaeum, Adelphi*; critical studies include 'Shakespeare' and 'Keats'
  Mansfield M-110

Murut, a people of Borneo; farmers; moved villages from forest mountains to valleys; gradually abandoned communes for private homes; floors of dwellings often built over curved saplings to serve as springing dance floors.

Murviedro, Spain. *see in index* Sagunto

Murzuk, Libya, trade center in s.w. in an oasis of Fezzan; has ruins from early 14th century; formerly a major slave market of the Sahara; pop. 2,832.

Mus, Publius. *see in index* Decius Mus, Publius

Musa, Islamic imam I-362

Musa, genus of perennial herbs
  banana B-51

Musaceae, banana family consisting of two genera, *Musa* and *Ensete* B-51

Musa Mountains, Egypt E-115

Musca, insect genus. *see in index* Fly

Musca, constellation, *charts* S-415, 417, C-682

Muscadine grape, a grape *Vitis rotundifolia* of the family Vitaceae G-220
  wine W-236

Muscat (or Masqat), Oman, capital and seaport on Gulf of Oman in s.e. Arabia; natural harbor; adjacent to trade center Matrah; pop. 5,500 O-544
  Asia, *map* A-700

Muscat and Oman, former name of Oman. *see in index* Oman

Muscat grape (or muscatel grape), musk-flavored fruit, usually light colored; produce raisins of largest size; also used to make wine.

Muscatine, Iowa, city on Mississippi River about 25 mi (40 km) s.w. of Davenport; chemicals, food processing; wood products, plastics, metal and rubber products; pop. 23,467, *map* U-41

Musci, true mosses, one of two classes of phylum *Bryophyta*. *see in index* Moss

Muscles M-658
  anesthetic affects A-412
  arthritis A-650
  biophysics B-238
  birds F-51
  blood B-313
  bone B-342
  brain controls B-398
  cellular structure, *pictures* C-238, L-267
  chemical changes R-160
  child development C-331
  exercise E-369
  eye E-389
  fatigue F-45
  hair-erector S-211
  hand H-27
  health H-85
  hernia H-141
  Hopkins H-238
  human anatomy A-390
  joints J-137
  meat M-246
  nervous system N-110
  osteopathy O-611
  protein P-514
  reflexes R-131
    experiments, *pictures* P-524
  stomach S-454, *diagram* S-454
  weight control W-136

Muscle Shoals, Ala., town on Tennessee River opposite Florence; site of nitrate and munitions plants built under National Defense Act of 1916; fertilizers, chemical products; pop. 8,911
  Tennessee Valley Authority T-102

Muscovite, a form of mica M-349
  minerals M-436

Muscovy, until 1700s, name for European Russia, from city Moscow. *see in index* Russia

Muscular atrophy, medical disorder
  genetic disorders G-48

Muscular dystrophy, group of inherited diseases; gradual wasting away of certain limb and trunk muscles; marked by increasing limitation of normal motor activity
  genetic disorders G-48
  heredity H-139
  muscles M-659

Musée d'Orsay, Paris, France M-662

Museology, theory and practice of museum functioning M-660

Museo Pio-Clementino, Vatican museum M-663

Muses, in mythology, nine goddesses regarded as patrons of the arts and sciences M-701

Musette (or union bagpipe), wind instrument W-228

Museum, collection of articles arranged and classified for exhibition; also building for collections: "museum" in its Greek form meant temple sacred to Muses M-660. *see also in index* Gallery; and individual museums by name, such as British Museum
  Alexandria, Egypt A-281
  art. *see in index* Gallery
  diorama D-148
  photography P-281
  Rome, Italy R-256
  U.S. U-113, *picture* U-112. *see also* Fact Summary with each state article
  New York City N-277, *pictures* N-278, 280

Muséum National d'Histoire Naturelle, French scientific museum M-662

Museum of Modern Art, New York, N.Y. M-662
  Adams A-31
  paintings, *pictures* P-24, 25, 27, 59, 62, 65, 67c, 67d
  photography P-281
  sculpture S-91, *pictures* S-81, 90, 92, 93

Museum of Science and Industry, Chicago, Ill. M-662, *picture* I-45
  models M-514

Museum to the Muses (or Shrine to the Muses), founded by Ptolemy I G-277

Musgrave, Franklin Story (born 1935), U.S. astronaut candidate, born in Boston, Mass.; physician named 1967 to NASA scientist-astronaut program, *table* S-348

Musgrave Ranges, Australia, on the border of the Northern Territory and South Australia A-771, *maps* A-822, P-6

Mushih-ud-Din. *see in index* Sa'di

Mushrooms (also called toadstools), various types of fungi M-664
  classification P-370
  fungi F-447
  hallucinogen H-18
  spore formation, *picture* S-396

Musial, Stanley Frank (nickname The Man) (born 1920), U.S. baseball outfielder, first baseman, and executive; born in Donora, Pa.; player St. Louis, N.L., 1941–44, 1946–63, general manager 1967, senior vice-president 1967–; in 3,026 games; made 3,630 hits (total bases 6,134); lifetime batting average of .331 (hit .376 in 1948); won N.L. batting title 7 times; led league's outfielders in fielding in 1949, 1954, and 1961; director president's physical fitness program 1964–67 B-93, *profile* B-95

Music M-666. *see also in index* Leisure, *subhead* music; *also* entries starting with Music and Musical; musicians by name
  arts A-661
    dance D-20
      ballet B-32
    motion pictures M-611
    poetry P-403
  band. *see in index* Band
  forms
    chamber music C-268
    classical music. *see in index* Music, classical
    fiddle tunes P-335a, *pictures* P-337, 334
    folk songs F-272
    jazz J-84
    opera. *see in index* Opera
    oratorio. *see in index* Oratorio
    symphonic poem, or tone poem. *see in index* Symphonic poem
    symphony. *see in index* Symphony
  geographic locations
    Africa A-93, 101
    Australia A-800
    Germany G-115
    India I-72, *picture* I-70
    Latin America L-63
    Philippines P-258
    Russia. *see in index* Russia, *subhead* music
    Sparta S-369
  hobby H-182
  Middle Ages. *see in index* Minstrels; Musical instruments, *subhead* Middle Ages; Troubadours
  orchestra. *see in index* Orchestra
  people
    Bach B-10
    Beethoven B-136
    black Americans B-300
    Britten B-462
    Bruckner B-467
    Koussevitzky K-302
    Strauss S-485
    Toscanini T-233
  publishing B-532
  records. *see in index* Record, phonograph
  scales
    12-tone S-54
  sound S-259
    brain perceives B-402
    range of audible tones S-260
  uses
    advertising commercials A-57
    broadcasting R-48
    kindergarten and nursery school K-241
    therapy T-167
  vocational opportunities V-366, *picture* V-365

Music, classical M-667
  orchestra O-576

Music, country (originally known as hillbilly music, or mountain music) M-678

Music, popular M-679
  opera O-571

Musica da camera, music form that appeared in Italy in late 16th century O-200

Musical comedy M-685
  Astaire A-705
  dance D-30
  Gershwin G-135
  literature presentation L-244
  motion pictures M-622
  opera O-560
  operetta O-572
  popular music M-684
  Ziegfeld Z-451

Musical instruments M-687. *see also in index* Electronic instruments; Percussion instruments; Stringed instruments; Wind instruments.
  accordion R-121
  American Indian D-19, *picture* C-196
  ancient V-327
  Australian aborigine A-795
  bagpipe, *picture* S-70
  band B-54
  clarinet. *see in index* Clarinet
  classical music M-668
  drum. *see in index* Drum
  folk art F-250
  folk music F-272
  gong sound waves S-259
  harp. *see in index* Harp
  horn. *see in index* Horn, wind
  Middle Ages V-327
  orchestra O-576
  organ. *see in index* Organ
  piano. *see in index* Piano
  spruce wood used S-398
  tone S-260, *diagrams* S-262
  trumpet S-193
  violin V-326

Musical sands S-38

Music box, device to produce tune or tunes; origin probably Swiss, in late 1700s; uses principle of a rotating cylinder with protruding pegs that pluck the teeth of a steel comb.

Music festivals
  Berkshire Music Festival. *see in index* Berkshire Music Festival
  Edinburgh, Scotland E-71

Music synthesizer E-174

Music video, video version of a popular song, usually rock music; may be a "performance" video or a "concept" video, which includes graphic images and action sequences, or a combination of both, introduced in late 1970s; usually featured on television programs or in video bars; many song collections released on video cassettes.

Musil, Robert (1880–1942), Austrian writer
  German literature G-109

Musique concrète (or electronic music) M-676

Musi River, Sumatra, *picture* I-160

Musk, substance used in making perfume; obtained from glands of animals, especially musk deer P-205

Musk deer P-205

Muskego, Wis., city 8 mi (13 km) s.e. of Waukesha; farming, gravel pits; incorporated 1964; pop. 15,277.

Muskegon, Mich., port city on Lake Michigan at mouth of Muskegon River (here widening to form Muskegon Lake); about 35 mi (55 km) n.w. of Grand Rapids; automobile and marine engines, automotive parts, iron and steel castings, tools and dies, bearings, office furniture, bowling and billiard equipment, paper, chemicals; tourism; pop. 40,823 M-361, *map* U-41

Muskegon River, Michigan M-355

'Mystic Marriage of Saint Catherine, The', work by Memling, *picture* M-294

'Mystic Marriage of Saint Catherine of Alexandria, The', work by Correggio, *picture* C-726

Mystic River, outlet of Mystic Lakes (two connected lakes) in n.e. Massachusetts; enters Boston Harbor by wide estuary north of Charlestown area
  Somerville S-257

Mythological Cycle, Irish literature S-473

'Mythologiques', work by Lévi-Strauss L-141

Mythology M-695. *see also in index* Animal worship; Animals, legendary; Egyptian mythology; Folklore; Greek mythology; Magic; Nature worship; Roman mythology; Superstition
  Babylonia [illegible]
  Fates F-44
  health H-82
  India I-106
  legendary animals A-457, D-238
  opera O-568
  rainbow R-88
  Sumeria B-6, *picture* S-482

Mytilini, Greek island. *see in index* Lesbos

'My Turn at Bat', work by Williams W-209

Myvatn Lake, lake in Iceland, *picture* I-16

'My World Line', work by Gamow R-112e

Myxedema, disease characterized by the swelling of face and hands, caused by lack of thyroid secretion.

Myxomycetes, slime molds classed by botanists as plants S-218

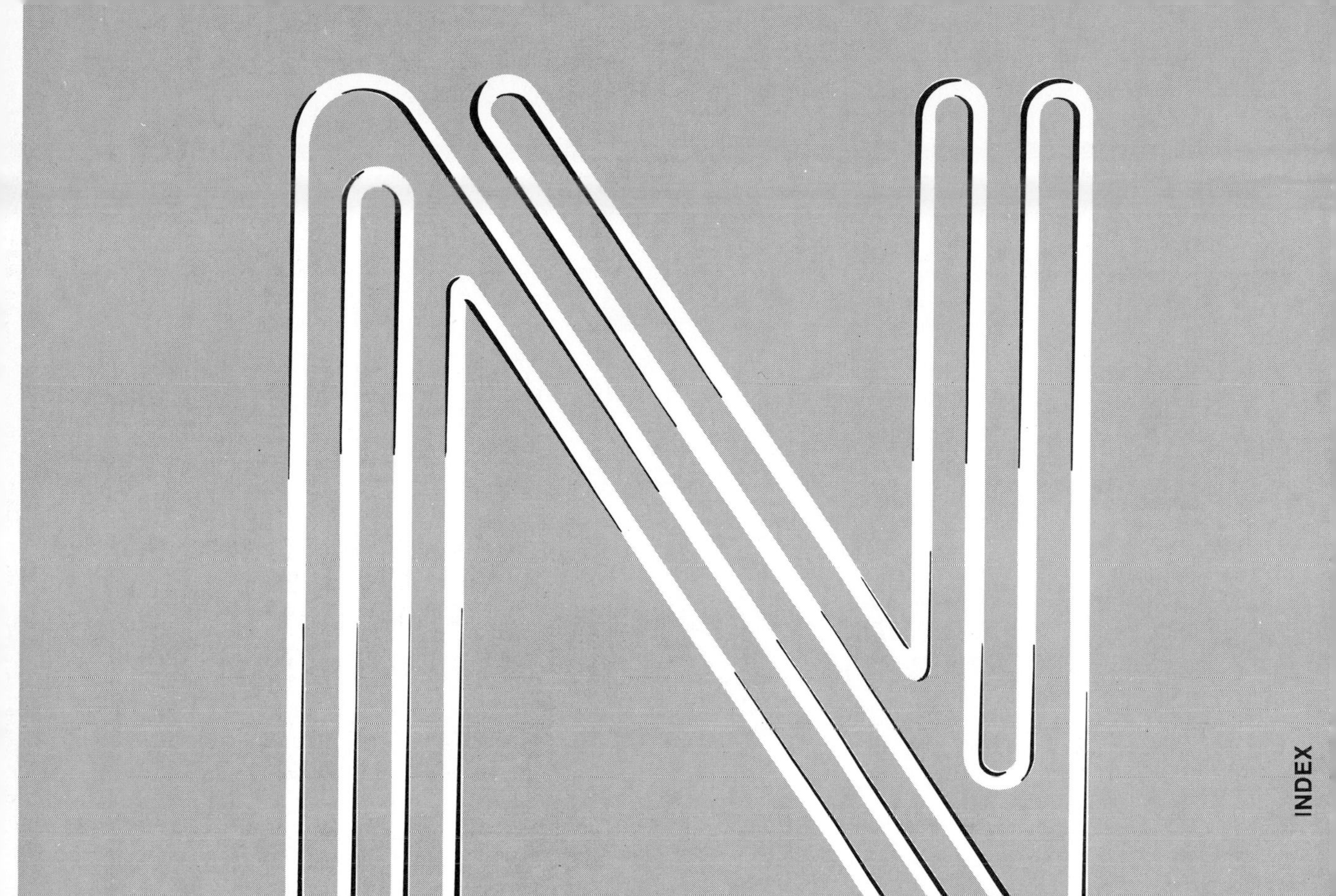

The letter N

probably started as a picture sign of a snake, as in Egyptian hieroglyphic writing (1) and in a very early Semitic writing which was used about 1500 B.C. on the Sinai Peninsula (2). About 1000 B.C., in Byblos and other Phoenician and Canaanite centers, the sign was given a linear form (3), the source of all later forms. In the Semitic languages the sign was called *nahas,* meaning "snake," or *nun,* meaning "fish."

The Greeks changed the Semitic name *nun* to *nu.* They also changed the direction of the sign to suit the left-to-right direction of their writing (4). Later they made the upright strokes of equal length (5).

The Romans took the sign without change into Latin (6). From Latin the capital letter N came into English.

The English small handwritten "n" is simply a quickly made capital N with curves instead of angles (7). The printed small "n" is similar to the handwritten form.

N

NAACP. *see in index* National Association for the Advancement of Colored People

NAB (National Association of Broadcasters), U.S. A-60

Naber, John, U.S. swimmer O-542

Nablus, Jordan. *see in index* Shechem

Nabokov, Vladimir (full name Vladimir Vladimirovich Nabokov) (1899–1977), Russian-U.S novelist N-2
American literature A-361
quoted R-111c
Russian literature R-360a

Nabonassar, king of Babylonia 747–734 BC; probably vassal of Tiglath-Pileser III, who invaded Babylonia but permitted Nabonassar to remain in nominal independence.

Nabonidus, last ruler of Chaldean Empire, and father of Belshazzar; succeeded to throne 556 BC, but gave more time to building temples than to preparing for Persians, who took him prisoner in 538 BC.

Nabopolassar, king of Babylonia 625–605 BC, founder of the Chaldean Empire; aided by Medes, he captured Nineveh in 606 BC; father of Nebuchadnezzar.

Nabrit, James Madison, Jr. (born 1900), U.S. educator, born in Atlanta, Ga.; faculty member Howard University 1936–69, dean of School of Law 1958–60, president 1961–69, on leave 1965 as U.S. delegate to UN Security Council.

'Nabucco', opera by Verdi O-567

NAC. *see in index* North Atlantic Council

Nacogdoches, Tex., city about 140 mi (225 km) n.e. of Houston; dairy and poultry area; lumber and sawmills, furniture, valves, dresses; Stephen F. Austin State University; in 18th century was Spanish mission; captured by U.S. in 1812; pop. 22,544.

Nacre. *see in index* Mother-of-pearl

Nacreous, inner surface of a shell M-524

Nader, Ralph (born 1934), U.S. author, lawyer and consumer advocate N-2
automobile industry A-867
consumerism C-687
lobbying L-276

Nader Shah (originally Nader Qoli Beg) (1688?–1747), ruler of Iran N-3
Persian history P-214

Nadir, in astronomy, the point in the celestial sphere opposite the zenith; that is, directly underfoot.

Nadir Shah (1880–1933), ruler of Afghanistan 1929–33; he had served as commander in chief of Afghan army 1919; minister to France 1924–26.

NADPH (nicotinamide adenine dinucleotide phosphate), chemical compound
photosynthesis P-300

Naevius, Gnaeus (3rd century BC), first Roman epic poet L-76

Näfels, Switzerland, village in canton of Glarus; at battle here in 1388 Swiss won independence from Austrians S-544

Nafūd, an-, desert in Arabia. *see in index* Nefud Desert

Nagai, Tatsuo (born 1904), Japanese writer J-83

Nagaland, state in n.e. India; 6,366 sq mi (16,488 sq km); cap. Kohima; Nagaland formerly part of state of Assam; pop. 516,449, *map* I-83

Nagana, Japan, seaport on w. coast of Kyushu; beautiful natural harbor; coal, cotton goods, rice exports; shipbuilding; pop. 450,194.

Nagana, disease transmitted by tsetse flies T-302

Nagasaki, Japan, port city on w. Kyushu; tourist center, pop. 449,382
Asia, *map* A-700
Japan, *map* J-75
World War II W-336, 349
atomic bomb N-434

Nag Hammadi, town in Egypt B-184

'Nag Hammadi Library, The', published English translation of Gnostic texts discovered in Egypt G-170

Nagoya, Japan, city; pop. 2,118,200 N-3
Asia, *map* A-700
Japan J-40, *map* J-75

Nagpur, India, city in Maharashtra state; railway center; cloth manufactures, manganese mines; pop. 866,076, *map* I-86
Asia, *map* A-700

Naguib, Mohammed (1901–84), Egyptian army officer and statesman, born in Khartoum, Anglo-Egyptian Sudan; served with distinction in Palestine war 1948; seized power after successful revolt against King Farouk 1952; premier and president of Republic of Egypt 1953–54
Nasser N-21

Nagurski, Bronko (born 1908), U.S. football fullback and tackle, born in Rainy River, Ont.; played for Chicago Bears 1930–37, 1943.

Nagy, Imre (1896–1958), Hungarian statesman, independent Communist, and premier of the 1956 revolutionary government whose attempt to establish Hungary's independence cost him his life H-330

Nagyszeben, Romania. *see in index* Sibiu

Naha, Japan, city on Okinawa; pop. 303,680 O-520
Asia, *map* A-700

Nahr an Nil. *see in index* Nile River

Nahr el 'Asi. *see in index* Orontes River

Nahua nations, inhabitants of Mexico in 15th century; allied with Aztecs A-892

Nahuatl language, or **Nahuan language** A-892

Nahuel Huapi National Park, park in Argentina N-27

Nahum (7th century BC), Hebrew minor prophet; his book, the 34th of the Old Testament, foretells the doom of Nineveh, *picture* P-509

NAIA. *see in index* National Association of Intercollegiate Athletics

Naiad, aquatic young of insects. *see also in index* Nymph
mayfly M-239

Naiads, in Greek mythology, nymphs attending Artemis M-700

Naidu, Sarojini (1879–1949), Hindu poet, reformer, and political leader; born in Hyderabad, India, of Brahman heritage; graduated University of Madras; studied at London and Cambridge universities, England; broke tradition, 1898, by marrying Dr. M. G. Naidu, medical officer, of lower caste than she; first Indian woman president of Indian National Congress 1925; jailed for Nationalist activities; wrote three books of poetry in English ('The Golden Threshold'; 'The Bird of Time'; 'The Broken Wing') I-108

Nail, in anatomy S-211
hoof H-231

Nail, in hardware N-4
wire W-245

Nail, unit of measure, *table* W-140

Nailor, Gerald, U.S. artist, *picture* I-127

Nainsook, fine, soft-finished white cotton fabric with lustrous finish on one side; similar to cambric and batiste; used for infants' wear and lingerie.

Naipaul, V.S. (full name Vidiadhar Surajprasad Naipaul) (born 1932), West Indian author and journalist N-5
Caribbean literature C-166

Nairne, Carolina Oliphant, Baroness (1766–1845), Scottish poet, born in Gask, near Perth; known for lyrics to traditional Scottish tunes ('The Land o' the Leal'; 'O, Charlie Is My Darling'; 'The Laird o' Cockpen'); poems ('Lays from Strathearn').

Nairobi, Kenya, capital, 85 mi (140 km) s.w. of Mount Kenya; foods, chemicals, sisal and paper products; outfitting point for safaris; pop. 1,162,200 N-5, *picture* A-101, *map* A-118
African languages A-119
Kenya K-226

Nairobi National Park, large scenic game preserve in Nairobi, Kenya N-5

Naismith, James (1861–1939), U.S. educator, born in Almonte, Ont.; professor of physical education University of Kansas, Lawrence, after 1898
basketball B-101

Naismith Basketball Hall of Fame, Springfield, Mass. H-16

Naiux, cave in s. France H-272

Naiveté, the quality of unaffected simplicity
acting A-24

Najaf, An, Iraq, town 90 mi (145 km) s. of Baghdad; Muslim pilgrimage center; founded by Harun al-Raschid 8th century AD; pop. 125,424.

Najran, oasis in s.w. Saudi Arabia O-454

Nakasone, Yasuhiro (born 1918), Japanese politician, born in Takasaki; member of lower house of parliament 1947–; chairman of Liberal Democratic party 1977–80; minister of state and director general of administrative management 1980–82; prime minister 1982– J-69

Nakatomi, Kamatari (614–669), Japanese imperial ruler F-445

'Naked and the Dead, The', work by Mailer M-50
American literature A-361
warfare W-28

Naked sole, fish *Gymnachirus williamsoni* of the order Pleuronectiformes, *picture* F-174

Naktong River, river in South Korea, flows from n. into Korea Strait near Pusan; 326 mi (525 km) long; navigable for 214 mi (344 km), *map* K-290

Nakuru, Lake, lake in Kenya, 90 mi (145 km) n.w. of Nairobi; saline lake known for the 2 million flamingos that feed on algae along the shore.

Namath, Joe (full name Joseph William Namath; nickname Broadway Joe) (born 1943) U.S. athlete N-5

Namatjira, Albert (1902–59), Australian artist N-5
aborigines A-796
subject matter A-783

Nambe, N.M., a pueblo about 10 mi (16 km) n. of Santa Fe; Nambe people belong to the Tanoan language group of Pueblo Indians.

Name N-6
Korean K-271
slave names replaced M-74
states, *table* S-428
trade P-383
Turkey T-324

Namib Desert, arid region along coast of s.w. Africa S-263, *maps* A-118, S-264
Namibia N-9

Namibia, formerly **South West Africa/Namibia,** before World War I it was **German Southwest Africa,** territory on w. coast of the South Africa region; area (excluding Walvis Bay) 318,099 sq mi (823,873 sq km); cap. Windhoek; pop. 1,097,000 N-9, *map* A-118
Africa A-97, *table* A-112
minerals S-265
South Africa S-267, *map* S-264
United Nations U-27

Namikara. *see in index* Persian lamb

Nammu, Sumerian mythological figure M-697

Nampa, Ida., city about 20 mi (30 km) w. of Boise; agricultural area; dairy products, beet sugar, food processing; mobile homes, railroad shops; Northwest Nazarene College; pop. 25,112 I-18, *map* I-30

Nampo, or **Chinnampo,** North Korea, port on w. coast; trade in cotton, silk, rice, timber; pop. 153,000, *map* K-290

Namur, Belgium, fortified industrial town 35 mi (55 km) s.e. of Brussels at junction of Sambre and Meuse rivers; repeatedly besieged; occupied by Germans 1914 and 1940; pop. 32,511 S-448

'Nana', novel by Émile Zola (1880) depicting the rise and fall of an untalented but beautiful actress at the time of the Second Empire in France.

Nanaimo, B.C., port city on Vancouver Island opposite Vancouver; shipyards; pulp mill; lumber products, fish; pop. 47,069 V-265, *maps* C-109, N-351

Nanak, (1469–1539), Indian spiritual leader; first guru of the Sikhs H-158

Nana Sahib (1825?–60?), Hindu prince, leader in the Indian Mutiny of 1857; directed slaughter of English forces, women, and children; forced to flee to Nepal 1859.

Nanchang, China, capital of Jiangxi Province; machinery, textiles, paper, pharmaceuticals; pop. 675,000
Asia, *map* A-700

Nancy, France, historic city 175 mi (280 km) e. of Paris; old capital of Lorraine; university, art and antiquity museums; pop. 121,910, *maps* E-361, F-372
Alsace-Lorraine A-320

Nanda Devi, peak in the Himalayas, in state of Uttar Pradesh, n. India 25,645 ft (7,815 m); first ascended 1936, *map* I-86

Nandaw, ruins of the royal palace in Burma M-95

Nandi, one of the Hindu god Shiva's chief attendants, *pictures* H-156, 158

Nandu, bird, popular name for rhea R-176

Nanga Parbat, mountain in w. Himalayas, n.w. Kashmir; 26,660 ft (8,130 m) summit reached July 4, 1953.

Nanjing, or **Nanking,** China, capital of Jiangsu Province; on Yangtze River; pop. 2,130,000 N-10
  Asia, *map* A-700
  Taiping Rebellion T-11
  treaty (1842), *table* T-274

Nanjing, Treaty of (1842), closing Opium War between China and United Kingdom C-369
  Opium Wars O-573

Nankeen, a cotton cloth first made at Nanking, China, from yellow cotton of that region; now made of ordinary cotton and dyed yellow or brownish yellow.

Nan Ling, mountain system in s.e. part of China C-337

Nanning, China, capital of Kwangsi Chuang Autonomous Region; sugar, dried fruit, leather, tobacco; pop. 550,000
  Asia, *map* A-700

'Nanook of the North' (1922), documentary by Flaherty M-628

Nansei-Shoto, or **Nansei Islands,** between Taiwan and Kyushu. *see in index* Ryukyu Islands

Nansen, Fridtjof (1861–1930), Norwegian scientist and explorer N-10. *see also in index* Nobel Prizewinners, *table*
  Arctic explorations P-420, *map* P-417
  biography review R-111d

Nansen bottles, in oceanography O-464

Nan Shan, mountain system in China; e. continuation of Altyn Tagh.

Nantes, France, port city on Loire River; shipbuilding; chemicals; food; university; pop. 237,789, *maps* E-358, F-370

Nantes, Edict of (1598), decree of Henry IV granting religious freedom to French Huguenots
  France F-349
  French literature F-395
  Henry IV H-132
  Huguenots H-317

Nanteuil, Robert (1630–78), French engraver and illustrator in court of Louis XIV; portraits show skillful composition, forceful modeling.

Nanticoke, Algonquian Indians
  Delaware D-72
  Maryland M-168

Nanticoke, Pa., city on Susquehanna River 7 mi (11 km) s.w. of Wilkes-Barre; anthracite mining center; silk and rayon yarns, clothing; veterans' hospital nearby; pop. 13,044, *map* P-185

Nantucket Island, island off s.e. coast of Massachusetts; about 15 mi (25 km) long; separated from Cape Cod by Nantucket Sound; resort; important historically as whaling center; Nantucket town (pop. 3,774) coextensive with Nantucket Island and adjacent islands; pop. of Nantucket village 2,461
  Massachusetts M-189

Naomi, biblical figure, mother-in-law of Ruth R-365

Nap, of cloth T-140

Napa, Calif., city 35 mi (55 km) n. of Oakland; grapes, wine, steel products, apparel, leather goods; state mental hospital; pop. 50,879, *map* U-40

Napalm, chemical warfare
  bomb use B-337

Naperville, Ill., city 22 mi (35 km) s.w. of Chicago; furniture, commercial bakery, research center; North Central College; settled 1831–2, incorporated 1857; pop. 42,330
  Illinois, *map* I-53

Naphtha, an oil distilled from petroleum, *charts* P-241–241b
  gasoline, *picture* P-240
  soap S-231
  solvent for rubber R-305

Naphthenes P-228

Napier, Sir Charles James (1782–1853), English general, born in London; fought in Napoleonic wars; in 1841 in India commanded army that conquered the Sind; for six years successfully governed territory he conquered.

Napier, John, or **John Neper** (1550–1617), Scottish mathematician, born in Merchiston
  exponential system A-595

Napier, Robert Cornelis, first **Baron Napier of Magdala** (1810–90), British field marshal, born in Colombo, Ceylon; took part in first and second Sikh wars, relief of Lucknow, and later Indian campaigns; commanded expeditions against Peiho ports in China 1860; captured Magdala, stronghold in Ethiopia, 1868.

Napier, New Zealand, port on e. coast of North Island; wool and meat exports; cathedral; pop. 38,309, with suburbs, *maps* N-299, P-6

Naples, Fla., resort city 37 mi (60 km) s. of Fort Myers on Gulf Coast; shrimp fisheries; pop. 17,481.

Naples (Italian Napoli), Italy, city in s., on Bay of Naples; pop. 1,208,545 N-10, *maps* E-361, I-404
  antiquities P-443
  Italy I-384, 392, 398
  medieval banner, *picture* M-384
  Mount Vesuvius V-305

Naples, Bay of, inlet of Mediterranean in s.w. Italy, *picture* I-382

Napo, river rising in Andes of Ecuador; flows 700 mi (1,130 km) s.e. to Amazon through tropical forests valued for timber, *maps* P-224, S-298

Napoleon I (nickname Little Corporal) (1769–1821), emperor of the French N-12. For military campaigns, *see in index* Napoleonic wars
  Alexander I A-278
  Alps A-320
  army reorganization and combat tactics A-642
  Austria A-830
  battle of Waterloo W-99
  Bernadotte B-174
  Bonaparte family B-341
  Duchy of Warsaw W-34
  Egypt E-121
    Alexandria A-282
    Cairo C-16
  French government F-362, 404
  Germany G-121
  Great Britain E-250
  hobby H-183
  Italy I-393, *picture* I-395
  Josephine J-144
  Louis XVIII L-307
  Louisiana Purchase L-324
  medals M-272
  New Orleans N-233
  Ney N-300
  Paris P-123
  Russian campaign, *picture* R-339
  slavery reestablished A-10
  sugar-beet industry S-507–8
  Talleyrand T-17
  The Netherlands N-130
  tomb P-122
  Volta, *picture* P-306
  warfare W-21
  War of 1812 W-29
  Wellington W-148

Napoleon II (1811–32), son of Napoleon I and Marie Louise
  Napoleon N-17

Napoleon III (or Charles-Louis-Napoleon Bonaparte) (1808–73), emperor of the French N-17
  aluminum production A-323
  Bavaria B-111
  France F-362
    Paris P-123
  Franco-Prussian War and surrender at Sedan F-377, S-105. *see also in index* Franco-Prussian War
  Germany G-121, *picture* G-122
  Italy I-393
  Mexican empire
    Monroe Doctrine M-549
  Sardinia-Piedmont V-311

'Napoleon', monumental historical motion picture, directed by Abel Gance; experimental techniques included superimposition, hand-colored film, and rapid cutting, emphasizing cinematic movement; precursor of Cinerama photography D-155

Napoleonic Code. *see in index* Code Napoléon

Napoleonic wars (1796–1815). *see also in index* Vienna, Congress of
  Bavaria B-111
  Hamburg H-21
  Holy Roman Empire H-209
  international relations I-260
  Jena, battle of P-517
  Nelson N-115
  Norway N-394
  Peninsular War S-359
  United States A-335
  warfare, *list* W-13

Napoli, Italy. *see in index* Naples

Napping, process in textile manufacture T-140

Naprapathy, therapy by manipulation of ligaments, particularly those of the spine.

Naqshbandiyah, mystic order in Islam M-542

Nara, Japan, city on Honshu, e. of Osaka; capital of Japan 710–84; ancient temples, shrines, giant Buddha image; pop. 208,266, *map* J-75

Narayan, Rasipuram Krishnaswamy (born 1906), Indian novelist, born in Madras; also noted for short stories (novels: 'Gods, Demons and Others', 'The Sweet-Vendor'; short stories: "An Astrologer's Day," "The Lawley Road") I-108

Narayanganj, Bangladesh, town on Meghna River complex just s.e. of Dhaka; river port; jute and cotton mills; leather goods, textiles, glass; pop. 389,000 D-125

Narbada River. *see in index* Narmada River

Narbonne, France, town 5 mi (8 km) from Mediterranean; wines; early Roman colony, Narbo Martius; pop. 35,236, *map* F-372

Narcissus, character in Greek mythology E-48, N-18

Narcissus, plant N-18, *picture* F-223
  bulb, *diagram* P-363a

Narcotic, drug N-19
  habit and addiction H-2
  nuts N-449
  opium. *see in index* Opium
  poisoning P-411
  prescription use P-248a

Narcotic Addict Rehabilitation Act (1966), U.S. drug law D-277

Nares Deep, a depression in floor of Atlantic Ocean, about 700 mi (1,130 km) n.e. of Puerto Rico; depth 22,950 ft (6,995 m); the most northerly and largest of the 3 deeps n.e. of Puerto Rico; named for George Strong Nares (1831–1915), British admiral.

Naris (or nostril), nose N-396

Narmada River, (also known as Narbada River), river that rises in n.-central India and flows 750 mi (1,210 km) to Gulf of Cambay; held sacred by Hindus, *map* I-86
  Asia, *map* A-700

Narodnaya, Mount, highest point in Ural Mountains 6,184 ft (1,885 m) U-211

Narraganset, an Algonquian Indian tribe; lived along w. side of Narragansett Bay, R.I., and controlled surrounding regions
  Great Swamp Fight, *picture* R-185
  King Philip's War K-246
  Plymouth P-395
  Williams W-208

Narragansett Bay, inlet of Atlantic, indenting coast of Rhode Island R-180, 182, *maps* R-181, 191
  Gaspee burned R-183, *picture* R-185

'Narrative of Riots at Alton', work by Beecher B-131

'Narrative of the Life of Frederick Douglass: an American Slave, The', autobiography by Douglass D-235

'Narrative of Travels', work by Mandeville A-457

Narrative poetry P-407

Narrows, The, passage in Newfoundland N-167

Narses (478?–573?), general of Byzantine Empire, grand chamberlain to Justinian.

Narva, Estonian Soviet Socialist Republic, city near Gulf of Finland; linen and cotton textiles; pop. 26,465, *maps* E-361, R-348

Narváez, Pánfilo de (1478?–1528), Spanish soldier and adventurer, born in Valladolid, Spain; one of earliest explorers of Florida F-199
  Tampa T-19

Narvik, Norway, port on w. coast; railway terminus; pop. 13,316 S-523, *map* E-361

Narwhal, mammal *Monodon monoceros* of the order Cetacea W-186

Naryn River, river in U.S.S.R. K-250, *map* E-361

NASA. *see in index* National Aeronautics and Space Administration

Nasal bone, one of the bones forming the arch of the nose S-210
  nose N-396

Nasal index, in ethnology R-26

Nasal septum, wall of cartilage that separates the nasal cavities N-396

Nasby, Petroleum V. (pen name of David Ross Locke) (1833–88), U.S. humorist, born in Vestal, N.Y.; in Ohio after 1852; his 'Nasby letters', in favor of Lincoln policy, appeared first in *Findlay Jeffersonian* and later in *Toledo Blade*
  Civil War C-478

Nascapee. *see in index* Naskapi

Naseberry. *see in index* Sapodilla

Naser od-Din (1831–96), shah of Iran (1848–96)
  Iran I-309

Nash, Charles Williams (1864–1948), U.S. automobile manufacturer, born in De Kalb County, Illinois; president of Buick Motor Company 1910–16; president of General Motors Corporation 1912–16, formed Nash Motors Company 1916 A-856

Nash, Francis (1742?–77), U.S. soldier, born in Prince Edward County, Va.; settled in Orange County, N.C.; member of assembly 1771, 1773–75, and captain in British army until 1775; twice delegate to provincial congress; advanced to brigadier general of First North Carolina Regiment; fatally wounded in battle of Germantown; monument at Guilford Courthouse, N.C.

Nash, John (1752–1835), English architect, birthplace probably London; laid out Regent's Park in London; improved London's streets
  architecture A-569

Nash, John Henry (1871–1947), U.S. printer, born in Woodbridge, Ont.; printer in San Francisco after 1895; folio edition of Dante probably his best work.

Nash, N. Richard (born 1915), U.S. playwright, born in Philadelphia, Pa.; plays for television adapted for stage and screen production ('The Rainmaker'; 'Girls of Summer').

Nash, Ogden (1902–71), U.S. humorist N-20
  American literature A-356

Nash, Richard (nickname Beau) (1674–1762), English society leader, born in Swansea, Wales; made Bath a fashionable resort, ruled it like a king.

Nash, Thomas, or **Thomas Nashe** (1567–1601), English dramatist and pamphleteer, born in Lowestoft; satirical, sometimes violent, tracts; pioneer in English novel of adventure ('The Unfortunate Traveller; or, The Life of Jacke Wilton').

Nashoba, socialist experimental community W-366

Nashua, N.H., 2nd city of state, on Merrimack and Nashua rivers, near Massachusetts boundary; shoes, cloth, paper and wood products, machinery, needles, radio and television parts; Rivier College; pop. 67,865 N-178, 186, *maps* N-191, U-41

Nashville, Tenn., state capital and 2nd city of state, on Cumberland River; pop. 462,450 N-20, *map* N-351
  country music M-679
  Peabody endowment P-143
  Tennessee T-81, *map* T-96, *pictures* T-91, 92, 93

Nashville, battle of, American Civil War (1864), *map* C-474

Nashville-Davidson, metropolitan area in Tennessee; pop. 948,200 N-20

Nashville sound, style of performing country music M-679

Nasir, an (died 1225), 'Abbasid caliph C-56

Naskapi, or **Nascapee,** a North American Indian tribe that lives in Quebec, *map* I-136, *table* I-139

Nasmyth, James (1808–90), Scottish engineer, inventor, and astronomer; born in Edinburgh; inventions include steam hammer and hydraulic punch.

Nasopharynx, upper part of the pharynx continuous to the nasal passages N-396

Nasr-ed-Din (1831–96), shah of Persia; succeeded 1848; introduced postal system; assassinated, succeeded by son Muzaffar-ed-Din.
Nassak, diamond, *picture* D-129
Nassau, former district in central Germany in Rhine basin, now included in state of Hesse, West Germany.
Nassau, capital and seaport of Commonwealth of the Bahamas; situated on New Providence Island, 200 mi (320 km) s.e. of Miami, Fla.; pop. 101,182, *maps* N-351, U-41
Bahamas territory B-20
West Indies, *map* W-159
Nassau grouper, a fish of the sea-bass family, *picture* P-510
Nasser, Gamal Abdel (1918–70), Egyptian president and statesman N-21
Egypt E-121
Suez Canal S-504
Tito T-197
Nasser, Lake, lake above 1st Cataract on Nile River; portion in Sudan also known as Lake Nubia E-114, *map* A-118
Nile N-317
Nasson College, Springvale, Me.; private control; founded 1912; liberal arts and teacher education.
Nast, Thomas (1840–1902), U.S. caricaturist N-21
Harper's Weekly, *picture* M-33
political cartoons C-188, *picture* P-431
Santa Claus picture S-45
Nastase, Ilie (born 1946), Romanian tennis player
tennis T-107
Nasturtium, any of various annual plants of genus *Tropaeolum*, family Tropaeolaceae; native to Mexico and Central and South America; introduced elsewhere as cultivated garden plants for bright yellow, orange, or red flowers; also genus of aquatic herbs of family Cruciferae.
Nasturtium officinale. *see in index* Watercress
Natal, province of South Africa; 33,578 sq mi (89,966 sq km); cap. Pietermaritzburg; pop. 4,315,847, *maps* A-118, S-264
Durban D-291
history S-266
Natal, Brazil, seaport and capital of state of Rio Grande do Norte, near n.e. extremity of South America; cotton textiles, salt refining; transatlantic airport; pop. 256,223, *maps* B-425, S-298
Natal Indian Congress, organization founded by Gandhi G-15
Natchez, American Indians who formerly lived in Mississippi, *picture* I-119, *table* I-139
Mississippi M-468
Natchez, formerly **Fort Rosalie,** Miss., port city on Mississippi River about 60 mi (100 km) s.w. of Vicksburg; farming, livestock, and oil area; tires and tubes, lumber products, rayon pulp, wallboard; pecan shelling; many historic homes; settled as Fort Rosalie by Bienville (1716); occupied by Federal troops in 1863; pop. 22,015 M-468, *map* U-41, *pictures* M-467, 471, 477
colonial mansions, *picture* U-61
'Natchez', steamboat S-177c–d, *picture* S-177d
Natchez Trace, road R-221, *map* R-219
Alabama A-226
Mississippi M-469
Tennessee T-86
Natchitoches, La., city 68 mi (109 km) s.e. of Shreveport; shipping and trading center for agricultural region; livestock, brick, paper and plywood; founded 1713–14 by French; Northwestern State University of Louisiana; pop. 16,664 S-338
Nathan, Hebrew prophet; counselor to King David whom he rebuked for treachery to Uriah and stealing of Bathsheba (Bible, II Sam. vii, xii); adviser to Solomon.
Nathan, George Jean (1882–1958), U.S. editor, author, dramatic critic, born in Fort Wayne, Ind.; onetime editor, with H.L. Mencken, of *The Smart Set* and *American Mercury* ('The Popular Theatre'; 'Comedians All'; 'Art of the Night'; 'Since Ibsen'; 'Autobiography of an Attitude'; 'The Theatre Book of the Year' series; 'The Magic Mirror').
Nathan, Robert (born 1894), U.S. writer, born in New York City ('A Winter Tide', 'The Green Leaf', poems; 'Portrait of Jennie', 'The River Journey', 'One More Spring', 'The Wilderness-Stone', 'The Devil with Love', 'The Fair', prose fantasies of beautiful style) R-112b
Nathans, Daniel (born 1928), U.S. microbiologist, born in Wilmington, Del.; professor at school of medicine of Johns Hopkins University since 1967, director of microbiology department since 1972; research on effect of restriction enzymes on DNA molecules. *see also in index* Nobel Prizewinners, *table*
genetic engineering G-49
Nathan's, refreshment stand at Coney Island, N.Y., *picture* A-384
'Nathan the Wise', or **'Nathan der Weise',** work by Lessing L-138
Mendelssohn M-298
Natick, Mass., 15 mi (25 km) s.w. of Boston; boots and shoes, baseballs, paper boxes, tools; founded 1650 by John Eliot for Indian converts to Christianity; pop. of township 29,461.
Nation, Carry Amelia (1846–1911), U.S. reformer, born in Garrard County, Ky. N-22
Kansas K-178, *picture* K-183
'Nation', Irish periodical I-327
'Nation, The', periodical edited by Thomas T-172
magazine and journal M-33
National Academy of Design, academy in New York, N.Y. A-14
Morse M-588
National Academy of Sciences, U.S. society incorporated 1863 for purpose of making investigations and reports, at call of U.S. government, on any subject of science or art; meetings held in Washington, D.C.
Henry H-133
National Advertising Review Board, U.S. agency A-60
National Aeronautics and Space Administration (NASA) N-22. *see also in index* projects by name, as Project Apollo
aerospace A-77
Eisenhower administration E-140
fire fighting F-106
Houston H-311
orbiting observatory O-458
space travel S-342b
U.S. government U-166
weather satellites W-123
wind tunnels W-235
X-15. *see in index* X-15
National Air and Space Museum, museum in Washington, D.C., *picture* M-660
National American Woman Suffrage Association (NAWSA) U.S. organization A-480, C-223
women's rights W-278
National Archaeological Museum, museum in Naples, Italy M-663
National Archery Association, U.S. organization A-541
National Archives, in Washington, D.C., created by act of Congress 1934 to inspect and preserve archives and records of the U.S. government, historical material, and motion pictures of historical activities; publishes the *Federal Register* which contains presidential proclamations, orders, and documents; work directed by archivist of the U.S. who is appointed by the president with the advice and consent of the Senate
building, *picture* U-145
United States documents, *picture* U-143
National Assembly, French parliament, *picture* F-395, *map* P-120
French Revolution F-401
Jacobins' rule J-11
National Assembly, Hungarian legislature H-328
National Assembly, Philippine legislature P-255b
National Association for the Advancement of Colored People (NAACP), organization founded 1909 by blacks and whites to safeguard civil, legal, economic, human, and political rights of black Americans; lobbies for legislation, sponsors educational programs, engages in protest actions against deprivation of rights; national headquarters Baltimore, Md. B-293
Spingarn Medal. *see in index* Spingarn Medal
National Association of Broadcasters (NAB), U.S. organization A-60
National Association of Colored Women (formerly National Federation of Afro-American Women), U.S. association, *list* W-275
National Association of Intercollegiate Athletics (NAIA), U.S. organization
football F-290
National Association of Manufacturers, U.S. organization founded 1895; composed of, and promotes interests of, individuals, firms, and corporations engaged in manufacturing.
National Association of Professional Baseball Leagues B-88
organized baseball B-96
National Association of Student Councils, founded 1931 by National Association of Secondary-School Principals (a department of National Education Association); aim, to foster in secondary schools through authorized student activities the spirit of responsibility, leadership, self-discipline, and citizenship and to promote a balanced school program and acceptable, integrated standards; headquarters, Reston, Va.
democratic principles C-462
public address training, *picture* P-526b
National Audubon Society. *see in index* Audubon Society, National
National Autonomous University (popularly called University of Mexico), in Mexico City, Mexico M-346
National Aviation Facilities Experimental Center (NAFEC), Atlantic City, N.J.; serves as Federal Aviation Administration's proving ground for new techniques and equipment. *see also in index* Federal Aviation Administration
National banks, United States B-64
supervision U-158
National Baseball Congress, U.S. organization B-94
National Baseball Hall of Fame and Museum. *see in index* Baseball Hall of Fame and Museum, National
National Basketball Association (NBA), U.S. organization B-99
game, *picture* B-85
National Battlefields Commission, Canadian organization N-28
National Battlefields Park National Historic Site, historic site in Quebec, Que. Q-9h
national parks N-28, 31, *map* N-29
National bibliography, type of bibliography B-186
National Board of Fire Underwriters, New York City; established 1866; protects interests of fire-insurance companies, establishes safety standards in building construction, represses incendiarism and arson; since 1964 part of the American Insurance Association.
National Board of Medical Examiners, created in 1915 as a voluntary organization to administer examinations acceptable to all state boards M-277
National Book Award, instituted in 1950 by its sponsors, American Book Publishers Council, Inc., American Booksellers Association, Inc., and Book Manufacturers' Institute, Inc.; presented annually to American writers for distinguished achievement in fiction, nonfiction, and poetry until 1980 L-241. *see also in index* American Book Awards
National Broadcasting Company (NBC), U.S. broadcasting firm
radio R-55
television T-69, 73
National Bureau of Standards. *see in index* Standards, National Bureau of
National Button Society, The, button collector's organization B-530
National Cancer Institute, institute in Bethesda, Md., created 1937 by act of Congress; conducts researches, investigations, experiments relating to the cause, prevention, diagnosis, and treatment of cancer; a division of the U.S. Public Health Service.
National Capital Commission (NCC), Canadian federal agency O-613
National Capital Region, in the Philippines. *see in index* Metropolitan Manila
National Catholic Welfare Conference. *see in index* United States Catholic Conference
National cemeteries, United States military cemeteries N-23
National Center for Disease Control, U.S. organization A-742
National Center for Service Learning (NCSL), U.S. program A-28
National City, Calif., residential and trading city on San Diego Bay, 5 mi (8 km) s. of San Diego; electronics, aircraft and missile parts, food processing; U.S. naval station; pop. 48,772.
National Civic Federation, an organization founded in 1901 for the study of social and industrial problems; executive committee comprises representatives of the public, employers, and wage earners.
National Civil Service Reform League, U.S. organization C-469
National Coal Board, British government corporation E-234
National College of Education, Evanston, Ill.; private control; founded 1886; liberal arts and teacher education; graduate study; quarter system; branch campus in Chicago has special programs in preschool education and for qualification of teachers from Latin America.
National Collegiate Athletic Association (NCAA), organized 1906 to maintain high standards in intercollegiate athletics; makes playing rules, conducts championships
boxing competition B-390
football F-290, 297
gymnastics G-325
wrestling W-364
National Commission on Safety Education, founded 1943, served as guide to National Education Association on education for safe living; headquarters Washington, D.C.
National Conference of Christians and Jews, Inc., The, an organization to promote justice, amity, understanding, and cooperation among Protestants, Catholics, and Jews; formed 1928; headquarters New York City.
National Conference of Safety Education, U.S. program A-863
National Conference on College Fraternities and Sororities, U.S. organization F-389
National Congress of American Indians (NCAI), American Indian political organization I-154
National Congress of Mothers, U.S. organization P-116
National Congress of Parents and Teachers, U.S. organization P-116
National Conservation Commission, U.S. organization R-286
establishment C-678
National Consumers' League, organized 1898 to regulate conditions of manufacture by helping to enforce labor laws, investigating conditions of labor, and awarding league's label to manufacturers conforming to its standards; state leagues in U.S. since 1891.
National convention. *see in index* Convention, in U.S. politics
National Cooperatives, Inc., U.S. wholesale co-op C-707

THE NATIONS OF THE WORLD

Nation	Location	Government	Capital	Area, Sq. Km.	Population
Afghanistan	Asia	Republic	Kabul	652,090	16,892,000
Albania	Europe	People's Republic	Tiranë	28,748	3,023,000
Algeria	Africa	Republic	Algiers	2,381,741	22,564,000
Andorra	Europe	Coprincipality	Andorra la Vella	464	46,000
Angola	Africa	People's Republic	Luanda	1,246,700	8,823,000
Antigua and Barbuda	West Indies	Parliamentary State	Saint John's	442	81,000
Argentina	South America	Federal Republic	Buenos Aires	2,758,829	31,030,000
Australia	Oceania	Federal Parliamentary State	Canberra	7,682,300	15,912,000
Austria	Europe	Federal Republic	Vienna	83,853	7,552,000
Bahamas, The	West Indies	Parliamentary State	Nassau	13,900	235,000
Bahrain	Asia	Monarchy	Manama	668	435,000
Bangladesh	Asia	Martial Law	Dhaka	143,998	103,084,000
Barbados	West Indies	Parliamentary State	Bridgetown	430	253,000
Belgium	Europe	Const. Monarchy	Brussels	30,521	9,856,000
Belize	Central America	Const. Monarchy	Belmopan	22,965	171,000
Benin	Africa	Republic	Porto-Novo	112,600	4,126,000
Bhutan	Asia	Monarchy	Thimphu	46,000	1,446,000
Bolivia	South America	Republic	La Paz, Sucre	1,098,581	6,611,000
Bophuthatswana	Africa	Republic	Mmabatho	40,430	1,564,000
Botswana	Africa	Republic	Gaborone	881,700	1,126,000
Brazil	South America	Federal Republic	Brasília	8,512,000	138,403,000
Brunei	Asia	Monarchy	Bandar Seri Begawan	5,765	233,000
Bulgaria	Europe	People's Republic	Sofia	110,912	8,979,000
Burkina Faso	Africa	Military Regime	Ouagadougou	274,200	8,126,000
Burma	Asia	Republic	Rangoon	676,577	38,493,000
Burundi	Africa	Republic	Bujumbura	27,834	4,830,000
Cameroon	Africa	Republic	Yaoundé	465,054	9,873,000
Canada	North America	Federal Parliamentary State	Ottawa	9,922,330	25,640,000
Cape Verde	Africa	Republic	Praia	4,033	342,000
Central African Republic	Africa	Military Dictatorship	Bangui	622,983	2,706,000
Chad	Africa	Military Regime	N'Djamena	1,284,000	5,139,000
Chile	South America	Military Regime	Santiago	756,626	12,278,000
China	Asia	People's Republic	Peking (Beijing)	9,561,000	1,053,703,000
Colombia	South America	Unitary Republic	Bogotá	1,138,914	28,231,000
Comoros	Africa	Republic	Moroni	1,862	409,000
Congo	Africa	People's Republic	Brazzaville	342,000	2,097,000
Costa Rica	Central America	Republic	San José	50,699	2,534,000
Cuba	West Indies	Socialist Republic	Havana	110,860	10,194,000
Cyprus	Asia	Republic	Nicosia	9,251	674,000
Czechoslovakia	Europe	Republic	Prague	127,899	15,552,000
Denmark	Europe	Const. Monarchy	Copenhagen	43,069	5,112,000
Djibouti	Africa	Republic	Djibouti	23,200	456,000
Dominica	West Indies	Republic	Roseau	750	86,000
Dominican Republic	West Indies	Republic	Santo Domingo	48,440	6,390,000
Ecuador	South America	Republic	Quito	281,335	9,651,000
Egypt	Africa	Republic	Cairo	1,011,500	48,007,000
El Salvador	Central America	Republic	San Salvador	21,041	5,461,000
Equatorial Guinea	Africa	Republic	Malabo	28,052	322,000
Ethiopia	Africa	Socialist State	Addis Ababa	1,223,510	48,850,000
Fiji	Oceania	Parliamentary State	Suva	18,272	710,000
Finland	Europe	Republic	Helsinki	337,033	4,927,000
France	Europe	Democratic Parliamentary Republic	Paris	543,965	55,427,000
Gabon	Africa	Republic	Libreville	267,667	1,187,000
Gambia, The	Africa	Republic	Banjul	10,403	765,000
German Democratic Republic (East Germany)	Europe	People's Republic	East Berlin	108,173*	16,636,000
Germany, Federal Republic of (West Germany)	Europe	Federal Republic	Bonn	248,543†	60,861,000
Ghana	Africa	Republic	Accra	238,900	13,144,000

*Excluding East Berlin. † Excluding West Berlin. Note: one square kilometer is equivalent to .3861 square mile.

National Republican party, U.S. political party P-432, 433, *table* P-495a

National Research Council, in Washington, D.C., established 1916 by National Academy of Sciences to solve military problems; now promotes mathematical, physical, and biological sciences and their application to engineering, agriculture, medicine; supported by Carnegie Corporation, Rockefeller Foundation, and other funds.

National Resident Matching Program, United States M-277

National Resources Planning Board (NRPB), United States R-265

National Rifle and Pistol Matches, United States R-206–7

National Rifle Association of America, U.S. organization R-206

Nationals, legal term for the citizens or subjects of a nation.

National Safety Council, U.S. association S-4

National School of Bridges and Highways, school founded in France in 1747 E-227

National Science Fair-International (NSF-I), an annual event to further the interests of students of science; each spring thousands of fairs are held in secondary schools, and the best exhibits are sent to regional or area fairs; top winners are sent to NSF-I; foreign countries also participate; headquarters in Washington, D.C.

National Science Foundation, established by Congress 1950 to foster basic research in mathematical, physical, medical, biological, engineering, and other sciences; consists of director and 24-man board appointed by president of U.S. and confirmed by Senate U-166
social studies S-241b

National Security Act (1947), United States I-237
Department of Defense N-87

National Security Agency, established by presidential directive 1952; part of Department of Defense
intelligence agencies I-237

National Security Council, United States U-156
intelligence agencies I-237

National Short Ballot Association, U.S city government organization M-655

National Shrine of the Immaculate Conception, church in Washington, D.C.; largest Roman Catholic church in U.S.; Romanesque-Byzantine architecture; built in form of cross; length 459 ft (140 m); no steel framework; foundation stone laid 1920; opened for worship 1926 W-69

National Soaring Contests, glider flying G-167

THE NATIONS OF THE WORLD

Nation	Location	Government	Capital	Area, Sq. Km.	Population
Greece	Europe	Republic	Athens	131,957	9,987,000
Grenada	West Indies	Parliamentary State	Saint George's	345	97,000
Guatemala	Central America	Republic	Guatemala City	108,888	8,191,000
Guinea	Africa	Military Regime	Conakry	246,000	6,225,000
Guinea-Bissau	Africa	Republic	Bissau	36,125	891,000
Guyana	South America	Republic	Georgetown	215,000	796,000
Haiti	West Indies	Republic	Port-au-Prince	27,748	5,427,200
Honduras	Central America	Republic	Tegucigalpa	112,088	3,938,000
Hungary	Europe	People's Republic	Budapest	93,033	10,624,000
Iceland	Europe	Republic	Reykjavík	103,000	246,000
India	Asia	Federal Republic	New Delhi	3,287,782	777,230,000
Indonesia	Asia	Republic	Jakarta	1,919,443	168,662,000
Iran	Asia	Republic	Tehran	1,648,000	46,097,000
Iraq	Asia	Republic	Baghdad	437,522	15,946,000
Ireland	Europe	Parliamentary Democracy	Dublin	70,285	3,547,000
Israel	Asia	Republic	Jerusalem	20,770	4,381,000
Italy	Europe	Democratic Parliamentary Republic	Rome	301,262	57,298,000
Ivory Coast	Africa	Republic	Abidjan	322,464	10,694,000
Jamaica	West Indies	Parliamentary State	Kingston	10,991	2,351,700
Japan	Asia	Const. Monarchy	Tokyo	377,728	121,470,000
Jordan	Asia	Const. Monarchy	Amman	94,946	2,749,000
Kampuchea	Asia	People's Republic	Phnom Penh	181,035	7,469,000
Kenya	Africa	Republic	Nairobi	580,367	21,148,000
Kiribati	Oceania	Republic	Dairiki	713	65,000
Korea, North	Asia	People's Republic	Pyongyang	121,929	20,543,000
Korea, South	Asia	Republic	Seoul	98,966	41,569,000
Kuwait	Asia	Const. Monarchy	Kuwait	17,818	1,791,000
Laos	Asia	People's Republic	Vientiane	236,800	3,703,000
Lebanon	Asia	Republic	Beirut	10,230	2,707,000
Lesotho	Africa	Const. Monarchy	Maseru	30,355	1,586,000
Liberia	Africa	Republic	Monrovia	111,400	2,303,000
Libya	Africa	Socialist State	Tripoli	1,749,000	3,953,000
Liechtenstein	Europe	Const. Monarchy	Vaduz	160	27,000
Luxembourg	Europe	Const. Monarchy	Luxembourg	2,586	367,000
Madagascar	Africa	Republic	Antananarivo	587,041	10,294,000
Malawi	Africa	Republic	Lilongwe	118,484	7,279,000
Malaysia	Asia	Const. Monarchy	Kuala Lumpur	330,434	16,090,000
Maldives	Asia	Republic	Male	298	189,000
Mali	Africa	Republic	Bamako	1,240,142	8,457,000
Malta	Europe	Republic	Valletta	316	336,000
Mauritania	Africa	Military Regime	Nouakchott	1,030,700	1,000,000
Mauritius	Africa	Parliamentary State	Port Louis	2,040	1,034,000
Mexico	North America	Republic	Mexico City	1,972,546	80,472,000
Mongolia	Asia	Republic	Ulaanbaatar	1,531,000	1,938,000
Morocco	Africa	Const. Monarchy	Rabat	458,730	22,455,000
Mozambique	Africa	People's Republic	Maputo	799,380	14,143,000
Nauru	Oceania	Republic	Yaren	21	8,000
Nepal	Asia	Const. Monarchy	Kathmandu	145,391	16,663,000
Netherlands, The	Europe	Const. Monarchy	Amsterdam	41,548	14,561,000
New Zealand	Oceania	Parliamentary State	Wellington	268,515	3,288,000
Nicaragua	Central America	Republic	Managua	148,000	3,384,000
Niger	Africa	Military Regime	Niamey	1,188,786	6,423,000
Nigeria	Africa	Republic	Lagos	923,768	98,112,000
Norway	Europe	Const. Monarchy	Oslo	323,895	4,166,000
Oman	Asia	Monarchy	Muscat	212,400	1,288,000
Pakistan	Asia	Republic	Islamabad	803,940	102,878,000
Panama	Central America	Republic	Panama	77,082	2,227,000
Papua New Guinea	Oceania	Parliamentary State	Port Moresby	461,690	3,400,000
Paraguay	South America	Republic	Asunción	406,752	3,531,000
Peru	South America	Republic	Lima	1,285,215	20,207,000
Philippines	Asia	Republic	Manila	300,000	56,004,000
Poland	Europe	People's Republic	Warsaw	312,683	37,456,000
Portugal	Europe	Republic	Lisbon	91,985	10,250,000
Qatar	Asia	Const. Monarchy	Doha	11,400	311,000
Romania	Europe	Socialist Republic	Bucharest	237,500	22,809,000

THE NATIONS OF THE WORLD

Nation	Location	Government	Capital	Area, Sq. Km.	Population
Rwanda	Africa	Republic	Kigali	26,338	6,336,000
St. Christopher and Nevis	West Indies	Federal Parliamentary State	Basseterre	267	46,000
St. Lucia	West Indies	Parliamentary State	Castries	620	140,000
St. Vincent and the Grenadines	West Indies	Parliamentary State	Kingstown	388	111,000
San Marino	Europe	Republic	San Marino	61	23,000
São Tomé and Príncipe	Africa	Republic	São Tomé	963	110,000
Saudi Arabia	Asia	Monarchy	Riyadh	2,240,000	11,670,000
Senegal	Africa	Republic	Dakar	196,722	6,699,000
Seychelles	Africa	Republic	Victoria	404	66,100
Sierra Leone	Africa	Republic	Freetown	71,740	3,733,000
Singapore	Asia	Republic	Singapore	616	2,588,000
Solomon Islands	Oceania	Parliamentary State	Honiara	28,896	277,000
Somalia	Africa	Republic	Mogadishu	638,000	5,992,000
South Africa	Africa	Republic	Pretoria	1,123,226	33,704,000
Spain	Europe	Const. Monarchy	Madrid	504,783	38,818,000
Sri Lanka	Asia	Republic	Colombo	65,610	16,087,000
Sudan	Africa	Republic	Khartoum	2,503,890	24,603,000
Suriname	South America	Military Dictatorship	Paramaribo	181,450	395,000
Swaziland	Africa	Monarchy	Mbabane	17,363	682,000
Sweden	Europe	Const. Monarchy	Stockholm	449,964	8,358,000
Switzerland	Europe	Federal Republic	Bern	41,293	6,556,000
Syria	Asia	Republic	Damascus	184,480	10,612,000
Taiwan	Asia	Republic	Taipei	36,002	19,439,000
Tanzania	Africa	Republic	Dar es Salaam	945,000	22,463,000
Thailand	Asia	Const. Monarchy	Bangkok	513,998	52,654,000
Togo	Africa	Republic	Lomé	57,000	3,072,000
Tonga	Oceania	Const. Monarchy	Nukualofa	746	98,000
Transkei	Africa	Republic	Umtata	41,620	2,755,000
Trinidad and Tobago	West Indies	Republic	Port of Spain	5,130	1,202,000
Tunisia	Africa	Republic	Tunis	163,610	7,327,000
Turkey	Europe-Asia	Republic	Ankara	780,570	52,419,000
Tuvalu	Oceania	Const. Monarchy	Funafuti Atoll	24	8,000
Uganda	Africa	Republic	Kampala	241,139	15,638,000
Union of Soviet Socialist Republics	Europe-Asia	Federal Socialist Republic	Moscow	22,402,200	280,038,000
United Arab Emirates	Asia	Monarchy	Abu Dhabi	83,600	1,700,000
United Kingdom	Europe	Const. Monarchy	London	244,100	56,679,000
United States	North America	Republic	Washington, D.C.	9,363,123	241,489,000
Uruguay	South America	Republic	Montevideo	186,925	3,035,000
Vanuatu	Oceania	Republic	Vila	11,900	137,000
Vatican City	Europe	Papal State	....	.44	1,000
Venda	Africa	Republic	Thohoyandou	6,340	448,000
Venezuela	South America	Republic	Caracas	912,046	17,791,000
Vietnam	Asia	Republic	Hanoi	329,465	61,218,000
Western Samoa	Oceania	Const. Monarchy	Apia	2,930	160,000
Yemen, People's Democratic Republic of	Asia	People's Republic	Aden	336,870	2,365,000
Yemen Arab Republic	Asia	Republic	San'a	135,230	7,046,000
Yugoslavia	Europe	Federal Socialist Republic	Belgrade	255,804	23,289,000
Zaire	Africa	Republic	Kinshasa	2,344,885	31,079,000
Zambia	Africa	Republic	Lusaka	752,164	6,896,000
Zimbabwe	Africa	Republic	Harare	390,270	8,553,000

of black Americans in cities; maintains liaison with white community leaders to seek solutions to such problems as unemployment, housing, and education B-293

'National Velvet', novel by Bagnold, *list* H-274

National Volunteer Week, U.S. observance A-28

National War Labor Board (NWLB) (1942), United States R-276, T-10

National Water Carrier, canal connected to Sea of Galilee G-5

National Weather Service (formerly called Weather Bureau), United States U-163
flood forecasting F-182
kite K-254
storm signals S-194b
weather W-121

National Wildlife Refuge System, United States E-209

National Woman's party (formerly the Congressional Union for Women's Suffrage), United States W-278

National Woman Suffrage Association (NWSA), U.S. organization W-278

National Women's Christian Temperance Union, U.S. organization devoted to stopping alcohol abuse W-270

National Women's Hall of Fame, museum in Seneca Falls, N.Y. W-279

National Women's Trade Union League, United States W-277

National Youth Administration (NYA), United States R-265, 272
education, *list* E-104
Roosevelt R-259

Nation and nationalism N-66
classical music M-673
Europe E-349
foreign aid F-306
frontier movements F-424
international relations I-259
literature
history writing H-173
Lessing L-138
new nations V-321
U.S. flag etiquette F-151
world W-301. *see table following*

Nation of Islam. *see in index* Black Muslims

Nations, Battle of the (also called battle of Leipzig) N-17

Nations, Law of. *see in index* International law; International relations

Native Americans. *see in index* Indians, American

Native cat, any of the marsupial mammals of the genus *Dasyurus* of the family Dasyuridae M-156

Native elements, mineral classification M-432

Native Land Trust Board, Fijian organization F-82

'Native Son', work by Wright W-368
novel N-412

NATO. *see in index* North Atlantic Treaty Organization

Natron, native sodium carbonate crystallized with water. *see also in index* Soda

Natsume, Soseki (pseudonym of Kinnosuke Natusume) (1867–1916), Japanese writer N-67
Japanese literature J-82

Natta, Giulio (1903–79), Italian chemist, born in Imperia, near Genoa; professor and director Institute of Industrial Chemistry, Milan Polytechnic institute, 1938–74. *see also in index* Nobel Prizewinners, *table*

Nattier, Jean Marc (1685–1766), French portrait painter, born in Paris; portraits of Peter the Great and noted ladies of Louis XV's court ('Magdalen' in Louvre).

Natural, in music, *list* M-671

'Natural, The', work by Malamud A-362, M-68

Natural bridge. *see also in index* Natural Bridge of Virginia
first bridges B-439
Natural Bridges N. Mon., Utah, *map* U-233

Natural Bridge of Virginia, on U.S. highway No. 11, 39 mi (63 km) n. of Roanoke; used as shot tower during Revolutionary War V-346
formation, *diagram* E-18

Natural Bridges National Monument, park in s.e. Utah N-54, *maps* N-40, U-233

Natural Bridge State Park, park in Kentucky, *picture* K-218

Natural coastal harbor H-33

Natural convection H-105

Natural fertilizer F-59

Natural gas. *see in index* Gas, natural

Natural history, the study of nature in general; forerunner of the sciences of biology and ecology. *see also in index* Nature study
ecology E-51

'Natural History', work by Buffon D-38

family includes members of genus *Parietaria,* source of niter used in drugs; also genus *Boehmeria,* source of China grass, or ramie, used in making textiles.

Nettle tree. *see in index* Hackberry

Networking, in computer use H-191

Networks, in broadcasting R-55

Neuberger, Maurine, U.S. legislator W-276

Neuberger, Richard Lewis (1912–60), U.S. writer and political leader, born in Portland, Ore.; Democratic senator from Oregon 1955–60.

Neuchâtel, Switzerland, city in w. on Lake Neuchâtel; watches and clocks; university; pop. 34,800, *map* S-537

Neuchâtel, lake in w. Switzerland, 18 mi (29 km) n. of Lake Geneva; 83 sq mi (218 sq km); greatest depth about 500 ft (150 m); traversed by Thièle River, *map* S-537
lake dwellers S-544

Neue Sachlichkeit, German literature. *see in index* New Objectivity

Neuilly, Treaty of (1919), between Allied Powers and Bulgaria, signed at Neuilly, France; Bulgaria lost conquests of Balkan War (1912–13) and World War I to Romania, Yugoslavia, and Greece, *table* T-274
World War I W-319

Neuilly-sur-Seine, or **Neuilly,** France, manufacturing and residential city, suburb of Paris, on Seine River; pop. 70,787, *map* F-372

Neumann, Balthasar (1687–1753), German architect A-558, 569, *picture* A-560

Neumann, John Nepomucene (1811–60), U.S. Roman Catholic prelate, born in Prachatitz, Bohemia; missionary worker in w. New York (1836–40), as far west as Ohio (1842–44); appointed vice-provincial of Redemptorist order 1847; bishop of Philadelphia, Pa. 1852; beatified 1963.

Neural crest, in embryos E-200, *chart* E-202

Neuralgia, severe, stabbing pain along course of nerve; not associated with nerve damage; attacks often triggered by infection, malnutrition, chilling, or fatigue; sometimes is symptom of organic disease; trigeminal neuralgia, popularly called tic douloureux, affects main sensory nerve of face and is treated by local anesthetic or cutting of nerve roots D-179

Neural tube, embryonic tube that differentiates into brain and spinal cord E-200, *chart* E-202, *diagram* E-202
genetic disorders G-48

Neuritis, disease of the nerves causing pain, abnormal circulation, and reflex action; differs from neuralgia because of inflammation; treatment includes heat, proper nutrition, physical therapy, and medication D-179

Neurohypophysis. *see in index* Posterior pituitary lobe

Neurological surgery, medical specialty, *table* M-277

Neurology, study of nervous disorders, *table* M-277
nervous system N-123

Neuromuscular disease (or neuromuscular disorder), disorder affecting voluntary muscles and resulting from damage to spinal cord or peripheral nerves which control their motion; may be inherited or caused by infection or injury to nerves or spinal cord; severe form produces inability to use muscles. *see also in index* Muscular dystrophy; Myasthenia gravis
nervous system N-123

Neuron, or **neurone,** or **nerve cell**
brain B-400
computer design B-236
drug addiction H-3
living things L-267
memory M-294
nervous system N-118

Neuropathy, an abnormal and usually degenerative state of the nervous system or nerves
diabetes D-126

Neurosecretion, in the brain B-400

Neurosis
blindness B-312
psychoanalysis P-518

'Neurotic Personality of Our Time, The', work by Horney H-244

Neurotoxicology, branch of medicine
industrial medicine I-175

Neurotoxin, nerve poison S-226c

Neusatz, Yugoslavia. *see in index* Novi Sad

Neuse, river in North Carolina, 300 mi (480 km) long.

Neutra, Richard Joseph (1892–1970), U.S. architect, born in Vienna, Austria; to U.S. 1923, citizen 1929; advocate of functionalism; housing, city planning ('Survival Through Design', 'Life and Human Habitat'; autobiography, 'Life and Shape') A-569

Neutral density filter, photographic equipment P-288

Neutrality, in international law I-256
Indochina V-321
League of Armed Neutrality (1780) R-169
Sweden S-522, 527
Switzerland S-544a

Neutral solution, in chemistry A-20

Neutral spirits, liquor L-234

Neutrino, particle of matter R-69, A-755
matter M-229
muon-type R-42

Neutrodyne circuit, radio R-57

Neutron, uncharged particle of an atom, *diagram* R-65
atomic particles A-752
quarks Q-5
chemistry C-295
energy E-216, *diagram* E-218
nuclear N-416, 422, 431
matter M-224
neutron bomb B-339
neutron-proton ratio R-66, *diagram* R-67
origin of universe U-203
radiometric dating E-22

Neutron star, star emitting intense X rays; mass about equal to sun, but diameter only about 10 mi (16 km) due to density, estimated at about 100 million tons per cu in. (5.5 million metric tons per cu cm); central temperature high as 10 billion degrees F (5.5 billion degrees C), and surface temperature 18 million degrees F (10 million degrees C); existence proposed in 1934 A-721, U-199
magnetism M-47
matter M-226
X rays X-404

Neutrophil, white blood cell. *see also in index* Granulocyte B-314
immune system I-55

Neuve-Chapelle, France, village, 19 mi (31 km) s. of Ypres; in battle March 10–12, 1915, British advanced a few miles; pop. 484.

Nevada, state in w. U.S.; 110,540 sq mi (286,300 sq km); cap. Carson City; pop. 799,184, *maps* N-351, U-40, 87
cities. *see also in index* cities listed below and other cities by name
Carson City C-178
Las Vegas L-56
Comstock Lode S-203
geographic regions
Lake Mead N.R.A. *see in index* Lake Mead National Recreation Area
Sierra Nevada S-192b
Western Basins and Plateaus U-83–5, *maps* U-36, 80–1, 87, *picture* U-83, *Reference-Outline* U-136
history
admission to Union S-429c
state symbols
flag, *picture* F-160
sagebrush S-14, *pictures* S-427, P-362
single-leaf piñon tree P-328
Statuary Hall, *table* S-437b
taxation, *tables* T-37, 39

Nevada, University of, in Reno and Las Vegas, Nev.; state control; founded at Elko 1874; opened at Reno 1886; at Reno: arts and sciences, agriculture, business administration, engineering, education, home economics, mining, nursing, vocational and technical institute, and graduate studies; at Las Vegas: humanities, business and economics, education, fine arts, general and technical studies, hotel administration, science and mathematics, social science, and graduate studies; two-year college at Elko N-136, *picture* N-141

Nevada City, Mont. M-553

Nevado del Ruiz, volcano in Colombia C-554

Neva River, river in n.w. U.S.S.R.; flows 46 mi (74 km) from Lake Ladoga to Gulf of Finland; connected by canal with Volga system L-19
Leningrad L-127

Nevelskoy, Gennadi (1814–76), Russian naval explorer A-382

'Never Give a Sucker an Even Break', film, *picture* F-80

Nevers, Ernest (nickname Ernie) (1903–76), U.S. football player, born in Willow Grove, Minn.; fullback Duluth Eskimos 1926, Chicago Cardinals 1927–37.

Nevers, France, manufacturing town on Loire River 130 mi (210 km) s.e. of Paris; cathedral; pop. 42,092, *map* F-372

Neville, great English family; famous member was Warwick (Richard Neville). *see also in index* Warwick

Neville, Emily Cheney (born 1919), U.S. journalist and author, born in Manchester, Conn.; first book, 'It's Like This, Cat', awarded Newbery Medal 1964; 'Berries Goodman'; 'Traveler from a Small Kingdom', autobiography.

Neville, Ralph, 1st earl of Westmorland (1364–1425), English noble; created earl by Richard II, but supported the usurpation of the crown by Henry IV
Henry IV H-129

Nevin, Arthur Finley (1871–1943), U.S. composer, born in Edgeworth, Pa.; brother of Ethelbert Nevin; lived for time among Blackfeet Indians and used Indian themes in his music ('Poia'; 'The Daughter of the Forest'; 'Lorna Doone').

Nevin, Ethelbert Woodbridge (1862–1901), U.S. composer, born in Edgeworth, Pa.; brother of Arthur F. Nevin; piano pieces and songs ('Narcissus'; 'The Rosary'; 'A Day in Venice'; 'Barchetta'; 'The Quest').

Nevins, Allan (1890–1971), U.S. educator and writer, born in Camp Point, Ill.; on editorial staff *The Nation* 1913–18, *New York Evening Post* 1913–23, and *World* 1925–31; professor of American history Columbia University 1931–58; Pulitzer prize 1933 for biography of Grover Cleveland and 1937 for biography of Hamilton Fish; posthumous National Book Award in history 1972 for 'The War for the Union'; 'A Study in Power'; 'Ordeal of the Union', 8 vols.; 'Ford', 3 vols.

Nevis, island of St. Christopher-Nevis, in the West Indies; area 50 sq mi (130 sq km); cotton, sugar, yams; birthplace of Alexander Hamilton; pop. 12,750, *map* W-159

Nevis, Ben, peak in Scotland. *see in index* Ben Nevis

New Albany, Ind., industrial and trade city opposite Louisville, Ky., on Ohio River; plywood, fertilizer, clothes, national cemetery; pop. 37,103
Indiana, *map* I-102

New Amsterdam. *see in index* New York, N.Y.

New Archangel, Alaska; Soviet commercial activity center A-339

Newark, Calif., city just s.e. of San Francisco; salt, trucks, light industry; incorporated 1956; pop. 32,126.

Newark, Del., 2nd city of state, 12 mi (19 km) s.w. of Wilmington; vulcanized fiber and paper, automobiles; pop. 25,247
Delaware D-72

Newark, or **Newark-on-Trent,** England, old town 65 mi (105 km) s.e. of Manchester; gave name to Newark, N.J.; pop. 24,580, *map* U-18a

Newark, N.J., largest city of state; pop. 316,356 N-149, *map* U-41
Elizabeth, N.J. E-193
New Jersey N-195, *pictures* N-203, 204
Pulaski Skyway, *picture* U-108

Newark, N.Y., village 27 mi (43 km) s.e. of Rochester; paper cartons, furniture, food processing, jewelry; state institution for mentally ill; pop. 10,017.

Newark, Ohio, industrial city 33 mi (53 km) e. of Columbus, on Licking River; in agricultural, gas and oil area; glass and aluminum products, electrical equipment, missile guidance systems, truck axles and transmissions, power lawnmowers, plastics; American Indian mounds; branch of Ohio State University; pop. 41,200.

Newark College of Engineering. *see in index* New Jersey Institute of Technology

Newark International Airport, airport in New Jersey, *pictures* N-196, 205

Newark Museum, museum in Newark, N.J. N-149

Newark State College. *see in index* Kean College of New Jersey

New Artists Association, founded in Munich, West Germany K-171

'New Astronomy, The', work by Kepler K-228

'New Atlantis, The', work by Bacon B-11

New Babylonian Empire. *see in index* Chaldean Empire

New Bauhaus. *see in index* Illinois Institute of Technology

New Bedford, Mass., city on Buzzards Bay; pop. 97,700 N-150, *map* U-41
Massachusetts M-191, 202
Ryder R-366b

New Berlin, Wis., city 11 mi (18 km) s.w. of Milwaukee; livestock, vegetables, dairy products; pop. 30,529.

New Bern, N.C., historic port city at confluence of Neuse and Trent rivers; tobacco area; food products, clothing, boats and marine products, lumber, fertilizer; pop. 14,660 N-358, *picture* N-365, *map* U-41

Newberry, Clare Turlay (1903–70), U.S. artist and writer, born in Enterprise, Ore.; famous for paintings of cats; author-illustrator of children's books: 'April's Kittens'; 'Mittens'; 'Smudge'; 'Frosty'.

Newberry, Walter Loomis (1804–68), U.S. philanthropist, born in East (now South) Windsor, Conn.; dry-goods merchant in Buffalo, N.Y. and Detroit, Mich.; made fortune buying land in Chicago, Ill.; founded Newberry Library.

Newberry College, in Newberry, S.C.; affiliated with Lutheran Church in America; founded 1856; liberal arts, teacher education.

Newberry Library, reference library in Chicago, Ill.; established by Walter L. Newberry 1887; significant collections in the humanities, printing arts, and history of the Americas.

Newbery, John (1713–67), English publisher N-151
children's literature L-246
'Circle of the Sciences' R-125
medal. *see in index* Newbery Medal

Newbery Medal, award for best children's book, established by Frederic G. Melcher L-240, N-151, *picture* L-241

Newbolt, Sir Henry John (1862–1938), British writer, born in Bilston, near Birmingham; lawyer 1887–99; professor poetry at Oxford University 1911–21; martial ballads 'Admirals All' (1897); knighted 1915.

New Braunfels, Tex., city about 30 mi (50 km) n.e. of San Antonio; textiles and clothing, flour, feed, hosiery, rock and lime products, precision metal products; site of Comal Springs; pop. 22,402.

New Brighton, Minn., village 7 mi (11 km) n.e. of Minneapolis; chiefly residential suburb of Minneapolis and St. Paul.

New Britain, formerly **New Pomerania,** largest island in Bismarck Archipelago, part of Papua New Guinea; 14,600 sq mi (37,800 sq km);

mountainous and volcanic; pop. 163,405, *map* P-6

New Britain, Conn., manufacturing city 9 mi (15 km) s.w. of Hartford; Central Connecticut State College; incorporated 1871; pop. 73,840 C-651, *maps* C-654, 663

New Britain Archipelago. *see in index* Bismarck Archipelago

New Brunswick, a province of Canada; 28,354 sq mi (73,436 sq km); cap. Fredericton; pop. 696,403 N-152, C-80, *maps* C-109, N-351
- Bay of Fundy S-18
- cities. *see also in index* Saint John and other cities by name
  - Fredericton F-391
- history C-95
- Nova Scotia N-403
- Trans-Canada Highway T-248

New Brunswick, N.J., manufacturing city on Raritan River about 23 mi (37 km) s.w. of Newark; surgical and medical supplies, clothing, rubber goods; occupied by British 1776–77; pop. 41,442.

New Brunswick, University of (formerly College of New Brunswick), in Fredericton, N.B.; non-sectarian; chartered 1800, became a university 1859; arts and sciences, business administration, education, engineering, forestry, law, nursing, physical education; graduate studies; campus at St. John N-157, U-211, *picture* N-155
- Fredericton F-391

New Brunswick Community College, in New Brunswick, Canada; main campus in Fredericton N-157

New Bullard's Bar Dam, dam in California, on North Yuba River

Newburgh, N.Y., port city on Hudson River 55 mi (90 km) n. of New York City; coated fabrics, furniture, floor tile, electronics, clothing, felt products, pocketbooks, candles, expansion bolts; Mount St. Mary College; Hasbrouck House was Washington's headquarters 1782–83; pop. 23,438, *map* U-41

Newburyport, Mass., city on Merrimack River 3 mi (5 km) from sea and 30 mi (50 km) n.e. of Boston; shoes, silverware, electrical goods; settled about 1635; built wooden sailing vessels; pop. 15,900.

New Byrd Station, Antarctica, *picture* P-420

New Caledonia, French **Nouvelle Calédonie,** overseas territory of French Community, in s.w. Pacific e. of Queensland, Australia; cap. Nouméa; consists of island New Caledonia and dependencies: Isle of Pines, Loyalty Islands, Chesterfield Islands, Huon Islands, Walpole Island and Belep Islands; area of New Caledonia, 7,366 sq mi (19,078 sq km), pop. 133,000; total area of dependencies, about 900 sq mi (2,300 sq km), pop. 149,400 N-162, *map* P-6, *picture* P-13
- migration of people M-401
- nickel P-13
- Oceania O-472

New Caledonia, fur-trading district in w. Canada belonging to Hudson's Bay Company in 19th century; mostly in British Columbia but extended s. of Canadian boundary.

New Canaan, Conn., summer resort 4 mi (6 km) n.w. of Norwalk; settled 1640, incorporated 1801; pop. of township 17,931.

New Carrollton, Md., suburban city 9 mi (15 km) n.e. of Washington, D.C.; incorporated 1953; pop. 12,632, *map* M-183

New Castile, the s. part of Castile, Spain, including the old Moorish kingdom of Toledo; chief cities are Madrid, Toledo
- colonizing the Americas A-334

Newcastle, Australia, port city in New South Wales, 100 mi (160 km) n. of Sydney; pop. 389,237 with suburbs, *maps* A-819, P-6

New Castle, Del., city on Delaware River 5 mi (8 km) s. of Wilmington; harbor; aircraft, nylon, metal products; Delaware's first permanent Dutch settlement 1651; landing place of William Penn 1682; pop. 4,814
- Delaware D-74, *picture* D-80
- replacement by Dover D-237
- Swedish colonization A-339

Newcastle, England, town 30 mi (50 km) s. of Manchester, bordered on three sides by city of Stoke-on-Trent; brick and tile; pop. 76,570, *map* U-18a

New Castle, Ind., city on Big Blue River 43 mi (69 km) n.e. of Indianapolis; automobile parts, steel products, machinery; state mental hospital; pop. 20,056
- Indiana, *map* I-102

Newcastle, N.B., port town in n.e. on Miramichi River 6 mi (10 km) s.w. of Chatham; lumber, wood pulp; pop. 6,284, *map* C-109

New Castle, Pa., industrial city on Shenango River 45 mi (70 km) n.w. of Pittsburgh; coal and farming region; limestone quarries; brass and bronze bearings, china dinnerware, radiators, mushrooms, grist mill products, truck axles, cold rolled strip steel; incorporated 1869; pop. 33,621, *maps* P-184, U-41

Newcastle upon Tyne, England, seaport on Tyne River; pop. 203,591 N-162, *map* U-18a

New China News Service, press outlet for the Communist party of China N-238

New City (or Nowe Miasto), section of Warsaw, Poland W-33

New College, in Sarasota, Fla.; chartered 1960, opened 1964; became part of University of South Florida 1975; liberal arts; 3-year degree program.

'New Colossus, The', work by Lazarus L-148

Newcomb, Simon (1835–1909), U.S. astronomer and mathematician N-162
- Hall of Fame, *table* H-16

Newcomb College, in New Orleans, La.; for women; founded 1886; liberal arts; fine arts; coordinate with Tulane University of Louisiana N-231

New comedy, Greek literary form G-276

Newcomen, Thomas (1663–1729), English inventor, born in Dartmouth; made first practical steam pumping engine, used in English mines until replaced by Watt's model
- engine S-57i, S-442
- Industrial Revolution I-178
- Watt W-108

New Communities, housing program H-305

New Community Development Corporation, United States U-165

New Connecticut, first name of Vermont V-285

New Cornelia Tailings Dam, dam in Arizona, on Ten Mile Wash River D-17

New Deal, depression recovery plan legislated under the administration of F.D. Roosevelt R-268, U-188. *see also in index* Roosevelt, Franklin Delano
- black Americans B-294
- Great Depression G-243
- labor movements L-8
- liberalism practiced L-146
- North America N-345

New Delhi, India, capital; pop. 301,801 I-76, *picture* I-78, *map* I-86. *see also in index* Delhi; Old Delhi
- Asia, *map* A-700
- flood, *table* F-181
- untouchable caste, *picture* M-460

New Democratic party, Canadian political party, founded 1961; advocates strong central government, national planning, socialistic reforms; headquarters Ottawa, Ont.

Newell, Homer E(dward) (1915–83), U.S. physicist, mathematician, and author; born in Holyoke, Mass.; with NASA from 1958, associate administrator for space sciences and applications 1963–67, associate administrator NASA 1967–74.

Newell, Peter (1862–1924), U.S. writer and illustrator of humorous books for children, born in McDonough County, Ill. ('Topsys and Turveys'; 'The Hole Book'; 'The Rocket Book').

New England, collective name for states of Maine, New Hampshire, Vermont, Massachusetts, Connecticut, and Rhode Island U-43–8, *map* U-44, *pictures* U-43, 45–8, *Reference-Outline* U-132–3. *see also in index* American Colonies; America, discovery and colonization of; United States, *subhead* geographic regions, New England; *also* names of states in New England
- abolitionist movement
  - Phillips P-263
  - Sumner S-511
- agriculture U-44
  - dairy farming and milk production U-44, *map* U-47
- American Revolution R-163, 164, 167, 170, 172, *pictures* R-163–4, 168, 174
- architecture, colonial S-159
- Boston B-371
- education
  - colonial U-43
  - historic colleges U-207
- fisheries U-45
- Industrial Revolution I-181
- industries U-46, *pictures* U-45–7
- King Philip's War S-398, *picture* R-185
- literature's beginning A-341
- mountains U-43
- name origin A-336, S-219
- North America N-337
- Pilgrims P-395
- slave trade P-515
- town government. *see in index* Town
- transcendentalism T-248
- village, *picture* U-48
- War of 1812 W-29
- waterpower U-46

New England, University of. *see in index* St. Francis College, Maine

New England aster, flower *Aster novae-angliae*, *picture* F-236

New England College, in Henniker, N.H.; private control; founded 1946; humanities, education, natural and social sciences.

New England Confederation (official name United Colonies of New England), formed in 1643, at Boston, by representatives from the colonies of Massachusetts, Plymouth, Connecticut, and New Haven, as a defense against Dutch and American Indians
- Winthrop W-244

'New England Courant, The', colonial newspaper F-379
- newspapers N-236

'New England Primer, The', schoolbook written and printed by Benjamin Harris, in Boston, Mass., about 1688; noted for alphabet rhymes and child's prayer, 'Now I lay me down to sleep'
- educational use E-87

New England Upland, geographical region
- Massachusetts M-189
- New Hampshire N-176

New Forest, wooded district in s.w. Hampshire, England; national park since 1877; 145 sq mi (375 sq km); about one fourth used by owners and tenants; includes several villages; created royal hunting ground by William I.

Newfoundland, island in Gulf of St. Lawrence; 43,359 sq mi (112,300 sq km); with Labrador forms province of Newfoundland, Canada; area 156,185 sq mi (404,517 sq km); cap. St. John's; pop. 567,681 N-163, C-80, *maps* C-109, N-351
- cities. *see in index* cities by name
- flags F-153, *pictures* F-155
- seals S-98
- Trans-Canada highway T-248
- Viking landings C-89

Newfoundland, dog, *picture* D-202

Newfoundland, Memorial University of, in St. John's, Newf.; provincial control; founded 1925; present name 1949; arts and sciences, agriculture, commerce, education, engineering, physical education; graduate studies N-168

Newfoundland Banks. *see in index* Grand Banks

Newfoundland Highlands, highland in Newfoundland N-164

New France, name for Canada under French rule C-91. *see also in index* Canada, *subhead* history; France, *subhead* history; Quebec
- French colonization A-337
- Frontenac F-417
- fur trade F-468

New Freedom, President Woodrow Wilson's philosophy of government W-217

New Georgia Islands, group in Solomons halfway between Bougainville and Guadalcanal; pop. 16,473, *map* P-6

New Glasgow, N.S., town on East River 80 mi (130 km) n.e. of Halifax; coal-mining center; steel products, building materials; pop. 10,464 N-404

New Granada, in full **Kingdom of New Granada,** in South American history
- Colombia C-553

New Granada, Viceroyalty of
- American colonization A-334
- South American history S-290, 291

Newgrange, site of Neolithic tomb in Ireland
- description A-729

New Guinea, largest island of Malay Archipelago; 310,000 sq mi (800,000 sq km) N-173, *map* P-6. *see also in index* Indonesia; Papua New Guinea
- Asia, *map* A-700
- birds of paradise, *picture* P-110
- East Indies E-45
- island I-368
- masks M-185, *picture* M-187
- Oceania O-467, 471
- shelter, *picture* S-158
- size. *see in index* Island, *table*
- tropical rain forest, *picture* F-311
- World War II W-328

New Guinea, Territory of, former trusteeship, now part of Papua New Guinea, including Northeastern New Guinea, Bismarck Archipelago, and part of Solomon Islands; total area 93,000 sq mi (241,000 sq km); former German New Guinea became in 1920 an Australian mandate under League of Nations; after World War II, became UN trusteeship administered by Australia. *see also in index* Papua New Guinea

Newham, borough of Greater London, England, *maps* L-287, U-18a

New Hampshire, breed of poultry P-482, *picture* P-481

New Hampshire (nickname Granite State), New England state of U.S.; 9,304 sq mi (24,097 sq km); cap. Concord; pop. 920,610 N-175, *maps* N-351, U-41, 44
- cities. *see in index* Manchester, N.H. and other cities by name
- geographic region
  - New England U-43, *map* U-44, *pictures* U-43, 45, *Reference-Outline* U-132
- history
  - Vermont boundary dispute V-289
- state symbols
  - flag, *picture* F-160
  - purple lilac, *picture* S-427
- Statuary Hall, *table* S-437b
- taxation, *tables* T-37, 39

New Hampshire, University of, in Durham, N.H.; state control; founded 1866 as New Hampshire College of Agriculture and Mechanic Arts; liberal arts (including education), agriculture, business, technology and engineering; graduate school; state colleges at Keene and Plymouth, *picture* N-183

New Hampshire College, in Manchester, N.H.; private control; founded 1932; business, education; off-campus centers at Laconia, Portsmouth, and Salem, N.H., at Brunswick and Winter Harbor, Me., and in Puerto Rico; graduate studies.

New Hampshire grants, land grants
- Allen A-308
- Vermont V-289

New Hanover, mountainous island in Bismarck Archipelago n.w. of New Ireland; part of Papua New Guinea; area 460 sq mi (1,190 sq km); pop. 7,829, *map* P-6

New Hanover, N.J., urban township in w.-central area of state, about 12 mi (19 km) s.e. of Trenton; pop. 27,410.

New Harmony, Ind., town 22 mi (35 km) n.w. of Evansville on Wabash River; settled 1814 by German Harmonists; property

administration, social work; graduate school; overseas program N-254, N-279
'New York Weekly Journal', political paper founded by those who were opposed to the policies of colonial governor William Cosby; first issue Nov. 5, 1733 Z-450
New York Woodwind Quintet, musical group, *picture* W-226
'New York World', newspaper N-236
New York World's Fair (1964–65), F-10
New York Zoological Society B-130
New Zealand (in full Dominion of New Zealand, Maori 'Aotearoa'), nation, group of islands in South Pacific Ocean, 103,675 sq mi (268,515 sq km); cap. Wellington; pop. 3,307,084 N-281, *map* N-299
  animals
    kea P-135
    tuatara R-153, *picture* R-152
  children's literature L-252, *chart* L-257
  cities C-449. *see also in index* Wellington and other cities by name
  Commonwealth membership C-602
  flag, *picture* F-168
  history
    ANZUS treaty A-497
    Cook C-696
    defense alliances U-193
    Fraser F-386
    Korean War, *table* K-296
    Western Samoa administered W-154
    World War II W-322
  Maoris
    genocide G-60
    ventriloquism V-279
  migration of people M-404
    Oceania O-468, 472
  national anthem, *table* N-64
  national parks N-27
  Pacific Ocean, *map* P-6
  taxation, *table* T-35
  transportation
    railroad mileage, *table* R-85
New Zealand Library Association, New Zealand L-241
Nexö, Martin Andersen (1869–1954), Danish novelist, born in Copenhagen; championed the working class ('Pelle the Conqueror'; 'Ditte', 5 vols.; 'In God's Land') S-52g
Ney, Michel (1769–1815), French marshal N-300
  Napoleon, *picture* N-14
  Wellington W-99
Nez Percé (pierced nose), American Indian tribe of North America I-149, *map* I-136, *table* I-139
  Chief Joseph J-143
  folktales, *list* S-481d
  Idaho I-19
  Montana M-551
  Oregon O-583
  Washington W-50
NFC. *see in index* National Football Conference
NFL. *see in index* National Football League
NFO. *see in index* National Farmers Organization
NFPA. *see in index* National Fire Protection Association
NFSHSA (National Federation of State High School Associations), U.S. organization
  gymnastics G-325
Ngo Dinh Diem (1906–63), South Vietnamese political leader, born in Hue; strong nationalist, anti-Communist; self-imposed exile 1950–54; premier South Vietnam 1954–55, president 1955–63; overthrown in military coup and killed 1963 V-320, 321
  assassination, *list* A-704
Ngouabi, Marien, president People's Republic of the Congo, *list* A-704
Ngugi Wa Thiong'o (in full James Thiong'o Ngugi) (born 1938), East African author N-300
Nguyen Cao Ky (born 1931), South Vietnamese political leader, born in Son Tay, North Vietnam; premier 1965–67, vice-president 1967–71; to U.S. 1975 V-320, 322
Nguyen That Thanh. *see in index* Ho Chi Minh
Nguyen Van Thieu (born 1923), South Vietnamese political leader, born in Phan Rang, Ninhthuan Province; military career from 1949; chief of state 1965–67, president 1967–75; in exile in England V-320
NHA. *see in index* National Housing Agency
NHL (National Hockey League), U.S. hockey league H-195
Niacin. *see in index* Nicotinic acid
'Niagara', U.S. warship in battle of Lake Erie P-209, S-177g
  transatlantic cables C-10
Niagara escarpment, cliff running from Rochester, N.Y. through Ontario N-302
Niagara Falls, N.Y., resort and industrial city on Niagara River; Niagara University nearby; pop. 71,384 N-264, *map* U-41
Niagara Falls, Ont., city opposite Niagara Falls, N.Y.; enormous hydroelectric plants; cereals and other food products, electrical equipment, fertilizers, chemicals, machinery, abrasives, silverware, sporting goods; railway center; pop. 70,960, *map* C-112
Niagara Falls, one of greatest waterfalls in world N-300
  Angel Falls compared A-414
  erosion, *picture* E-18
  Great Lakes G-245
  Horseshoe Falls, *picture* U-55
  hydroelectric turbine T-315
  New York N-251, *picture* N-263
  Ontario O-547
  waterfall W-96, *chart* W-98
Niagara grape G-220
Niagara Movement, civil rights movement for black Americans in early 1900s B-293
Niagara Reservation State Park, park in Niagara Falls, N.Y. N-301
Niagara River, outlet of Lake Erie flowing n. to Lake Ontario, 33 mi (53 km)
  Lake Ontario O-559
  New York N-246
Niagara University, in Niagara University, N.Y.; Roman Catholic; founded 1856; arts and sciences, business administration, education, nursing, transportation; graduate school N-255
Niamey, Niger, capital and port, on Niger River; commercial center at intersection of important land routes; airport; pop. 399,100 N-302
  Niger N-308, *picture* N-309
Niam-Niam, or **Azandeh,** or **Zandeh,** an important group of people in n.e. Congo basin; expert agriculturists, formerly warlike; name means "eaters"; so called because many practiced cannibalism.
Niantic, or **Nehantic,** Algonquian Indians, formerly occupying the coasts of Rhode Island and Connecticut; one became a part of the Narraganset, the other absorbed by the Mohegan after Pequot War.
Nias, island in Indonesia, w. of Sumatra; 1,569 sq mi (4,064 sq km); yams, rice, corn; gold and silver handicraft; pop. 372,483, *map* I-166
  Asia, *map* A-700
Niavaran Palace, villa in Tehran, Iran, *picture* T-54
'Nibelungs, Song of the' (or 'Nibelungenlied'), German epic of 13th century N-302
  mythology M-704
  origin S-471
  Siegfried legend S-192a
  Volsungs. *see in index* 'Volsunga Saga'; Volsungs
  Wagner W-2
'Nibelungs, The Ring of the' (German 'Der Ring des Nibelungen'), series of four operas by Wagner O-567
  folklore adaptation F-269
  'Song of the Nibelungs' N-302
Nibs, meat of cacao or cocoa bean; used in chocolate making C-393
Nicaea, or **Nice,** modern **Isnik,** Turkey, important ancient city of Bithynia, Asia Minor, on Lake Ascania 60 mi (100 km) s.e. of Constantinople; declined under Turkish rule (14th century)
  Anglican belief A-417
  council of AD 325 C-410
  Fathers of the Church F-45
Nicandra, or **apple of Peru,** annual plant *N. physalodes* of the nightshade family, native to Peru; grows to 4 ft (1.2 m); leaves oval, toothed; flowers blue, wheel-shaped, solitary.
Nicaragua, republic of Central America; area 57,143 sq mi (148,000 sq km); cap. Managua, on Lake Managua; pop. 3,384,000 N-303
  Central America C-253, *map* N-351, *picture* C-258. *see also in index* Central America
  cities. *see in index* Managua and other cities by name
  flag, *picture* F-168
  guerrilla warfare, *picture* G-302
  Latin American literature L-74
  national anthem, *table* N-64
  railroad mileage, *table* R-85
  sugarcane, *picture* N-343
  World War II W-328
Nicaragua, Lake, largest lake in Central America, in s.w. Nicaragua; 3,191 sq mi (8,265 sq km); drained by San Juan River, *map* N-351
Nicaraguan Canal Treaty (1884), *table* T-274
Niccoli, Niccolo de' (1363–1437), Italian humanist R-146
Niccolo Pisano. *see in index* Pisano, Niccolo
Nice, ancient city in Asia Minor. *see in index* Nicaea
Nice, France, resort on Riviera; pop. 331,165 N-305
  Europe, *map* E-361
  France, *map* F-372
  weather F-344
Nicene Creed, basic doctrine of most Christian churches
  Anglican beliefs A-417
  Constantine the Great C-680
Niche glacier, or **glacieret,** or **corrie glacier,** a very small glacier that occupies a cirque G-150
Nichiren, 13th century Buddhist monk in Japan N-306
  Buddhism B-485
Nicholas, Saint (4th century), bishop of Myra, Asia Minor; in many legends, patron of children; his feast day (December) was near Christmas, so he came to be the Christmas gift-bringer, St. Nick or Santa Claus; taken off Roman Catholic calendar 1969
  Christmas C-405, *picture* C-406
  Santa Claus S-46
Nicholas I (822?–867), pope 858–867; sometimes called the Great, uncompromising in upholding his claims to universal jurisdiction.
Nicholas II (died 1061), pope 1059–61; restricted election of popes to College of Cardinals; greatly influenced by Hildebrand (later Gregory VII).
Nicholas III (1216?–80), pope 1277–80; materially strengthened temporal power of the church; belonged to house of Orsini.
Nicholas IV (1227–92), pope 1288–92, first Franciscan monk to become pope; encouraged Crusades and sent missionaries to the East.
Nicholas V (1397–1455), pope 1447–55; founded valuable library and manuscript collection; extended wide patronage to classical scholars.
Nicholas I (1796–1855), emperor of Russia N-306
  Ottoman Empire O-618
  Russia R-353
Nicholas II (1868–1918), emperor of Russia N-306
  assassination A-704
  'Nicholas and Alexandra' R-112
  Russia R-353
Nicholas, or **Nikita** (1841–1921), hereditary prince of Montenegro; succeeded 1860; assumed title of king 1910; driven into exile by Germans during World War I; deposed 1918 when Montenegro became merged into Yugoslavia.
Nicholas, Grand Duke (1856–1929), grandson of Emperor Nicholas I; appointed commander in chief of Russian army 1914; later commander in chief in Caucasus; removed from command after emperor's abdication; died in Paris.
Nicholas, Louis Francis Albert Victor, prince of Battenberg. *see in index* Mountbatten, Louis
Nicholas, Samuel (1744–90), U.S. Marine Corps officer M-138
Nicholas II Land, Russia. *see in index* Severnaya Zemlya
'Nicholas Nickleby', novel by Dickens (1839), showing evils of English public school system; hero begins career at Squeers's school.
Nicholas of Pisa. *see in index* Pisano, Niccolo
Nicholls State University, in Thibodaux, La.; founded 1948; senior college after 1956; present name 1970; liberal arts, business administration, education, and sciences; graduate studies.
Nichols, Charles A. (nickname Kid) (1869–1953), U.S. baseball pitcher, born in Madison, Wis.; with Boston, N.L., 1890–1901; won 30 or more games in each season 1891–97; won 20 or more games in each season 1890–99; won total of 360 games.
Nichols, Edward Loring (nickname Red) (1905–65), U.S. jazz cornetist of the 1920s, born in Ogden, Utah; director of many fine players, notably in Five Pennies group.
Nichols, Mike (born 1931), U.S. film director ('The Odd Couple'; 'Plaza Suite'; 'The Graduate'; 'Silkwood') D-155
Nichols, Robert Malise Bowyer (1893–1944), British poet, born in Shanklin, Isle of Wight; wounded in World War I (poetry: 'Under the Yew', 'Aurelia'; drama: 'Wings over Europe', with Maurice Browne).
Nichols, Roy Franklin (1896–1973), U.S. historian and educator, born in Newark, N.J.; professor of history 1930–66 and dean of the graduate school 1952–66 at University of Pennsylvania; won 1949 Pulitzer prize for 'The Disruption of American Democracy'; also wrote 'The Stakes of Power'.
Nichols, Ruth (born 1948), Canadian author, born in Toronto ('A Walk Out of the World'; 'Ceremony of Innocence'; 'The Marrow of the World', awarded Canadian Book of the Year for Children award 1973).
Nichols College, in Dudley, Mass.; private control; founded 1815; liberal arts, business administration.
Nichols Field, former U.S. Army airfield, Luzon, Philippines, 6 mi (10 km) from Manila; attacked by Japanese December 1941.
Nicholson, Sir Francis (1655–1728), English colonial official, born near Richmond; lieutenant governor or governor of Virginia, Maryland, South Carolina, and Nova Scotia, Canada 1688–1725.
Nicholson, Meredith (1866–1947), U.S. novelist and essayist, born in Crawfordsville, Ind.; U.S. minister to Paraguay 1933–34, to Venezuela 1935–38, to Nicaragua after 1938 ('The House of a Thousand Candles'; 'A Hoosier Chronicle').
Nicholson, William (1753–1815), English writer and lecturer, born in London; edited *Journal of Natural Philosophy, Chemistry, and the Arts*, earliest work of the kind in England; wrote 'An Introduction to Natural Philosophy'; invented an aerometer and discovered a way of decomposing water by electric current.
Nicias (died 413 BC), Athenian statesman and general in Peloponnesian War; became leader of aristocrats on death of Pericles; arranged Peace of Nicias (421 BC) between Athens and Sparta.
Nickel (Ni), metallic element N-307
  alloys A-312, B-410, 463
    niobium N-318
  magnetism M-45
  ore, *table* O-600, *map* O-600
  periodic table, *table* P-207, *list* P-208
  producing regions
    Australia A-774, 810
    Canada C-84
      Ontario O-551
    New Caledonia N-162
  steel A-312
Nickel-cadmium battery, electricity B-109
Nickel-iron cell, or **Edison cell,** electricity B-109
Nickelodeon, history of motion pictures, place where nickel

shows were given; term later applied to automatic pianos and phonographs in public places
motion pictures M-618

Nicklaus, Jack (full name Jack William Nicklaus) (born 1940), U.S. golfer N-307
golf, *picture* G-191

Nickname, an informal, often descriptive, name
people N-8
U.S. states, *table* S-428

Nicobar Islands, in Bay of Bengal. *see in index* Andaman and Nicobar Islands

Nicodemus, figure in New Testament, a prominent Pharisee, who visited Jesus by night as an inquirer (John iii); helped bury Jesus.

Nicolas. *see in index* Mordvinoff, Nicolas

Nicolay, John George (1832–1901), U.S. author, secretary to Lincoln; born in Bavaria; joint author with John Hay of 'Abraham Lincoln: A History'.

Nicolet, Jean (1598–1642), early French explorer in North America (1634–35); born in Cherbourg, France
Great Lakes G-249
Michigan exploration M-361
Wisconsin W-253, *picture* W-255

Nicoll, Sir William Robertson (1851–1923), Scottish man of letters, born in Aberdeenshire; known as authority on the Brontë family ('Literary Anecdotes of the Nineteenth Century'; 'Life of Ian Maclaren'; 'Life of the Brontës').

Nicolle, Charles Jean Henri (1866–1936), French physician and bacteriologist, born in Rouen; discovered body louse transmits typhus. *see also in index* Nobel Prizewinners, *table*

Nicollet, Joseph Nicholas (1786–1843), French explorer and mathematician, born in Cluses, Savoy; to U.S. 1832; official surveyor of upper Mississippi and Missouri rivers 1836–39.

Nicollet Mall, in Minneapolis, Minn.; first downtown pedestrian mall built in the U.S. H-438

Nicolls, Sir Richard (1624–72), first English colonial governor of New York, born in Ampthill, near Bedford, England; sent to America to organize attack on New Netherland; firm executive; won respect of both Dutch and English.

Nicolson, Mrs. Harold. *see in index* Sackville-West, Victoria

Nicolson, Sir Harold (George) (1886–1968), British biographer and diplomat, born in Tehran, Iran; husband of Victoria Sackville-West; member of diplomatic service 1909–29; member of Parliament 1935–45; wrote biographies of Tennyson, Byron, and Swinburne.

Nicomedia, wealthy ancient city on e. arm of Sea of Marmara; capital of Bithynia; Hannibal committed suicide nearby (183 BC); Constantine the Great died here (AD 337); modern Izmit (also Ismid or Kocaeli) in Turkey; busy seaport; pop. 73,488.

Nicopolis, or **Actia Nicopolis,** ancient city of Epirus, in Greece near n.w. coast; now in ruins; founded 31 BC by Augustus to commemorate victory over Mark Antony at Actium.

Nicosia, capital of island nation Cyprus; rich in churches, public gardens; many light industries; woolens; pop. 45,629, *map* I-404
Asia, *map* A-700

Nicot, Jean (1530–1600), French diplomat, born in Nîmes; scientific name of tobacco given in his honor T-198

Nicotiana, genus of flowering annuals, includes tobacco
growing conditions G-23
tobacco T-198

Nicotinamide adenine dinucleotide phosphate (NADPH), chemical compound
photosynthesis P-300

Nicotine, chemical compound
tobacco T-198

Nicotinic acid, or **niacin,** a vitamin V-355, 358
effects of cooking V-357

Nictheroy, Brazil. *see in index* Niterói

Nictitating membrane, in anatomy B-246

Nidaros, Norway. *see in index* Trondheim

Niebuhr, Barthold Georg (1776–1831), German historian and classical scholar, born in Copenhagen, Denmark; pioneer in modern historical methods; his 'Roman History' regarded as epoch-making.

Niebuhr, Reinhold (1892–1971), U.S. theologian, born in Wright City, Mo.; widely known for forceful expression of neo-orthodox Protestant views and for his liberal social thought; professor, Union Theological Seminary, New York City 1930–60, dean of faculty 1950–55; vice-president 1955–60; Presidential Medal of Freedom 1964 ('Faith and History'; 'The Irony of American History'; 'Christian Realism and Political Problems'; 'The Self and the Dramas of History'; 'Man's Nature and His Communities'; 'Faith and Politics').

Niedersachsen, West Germany. *see in index* Lower Saxony

Niehaus, Charles Henry (1855–1935), U.S. sculptor, born in Cincinnati, Ohio; work outstanding for simplicity, excellent composition and classical line; did many public memorials (statues of Garfield, McKinley, Dr. Hahnemann, John Paul Jones, Lincoln).

Niello, mixture of silver, copper, and lead sulfides used in metalworking M-310

Nielsen, Kay (born 1886), U.S. artist and illustrator, born in Copenhagen, Denmark; moved to U.S.; work reveals rare imagination; illustrated 'Fairy Tales', by Hans Christian Andersen, and 'East of the Sun and West of the Moon', by Edgar Parin d'Aulaire.

'Niels Lyhne', novel by Jacobsen J-11

Niemen River (Russian Nemen, German Memel), river about 600 mi (970 km) long, rises in w. U.S.S.R. s. of Minsk, flows generally w. to Grodno, turns n. into Lithuanian S.S.R., then flows w. into Baltic Sea s. of Klaipeda (Memel) L-259, *maps* E-361, R-348

Niemeyer (Soares Filho), Oscar (born 1907), Brazilian architect, born in Rio de Janeiro; designed Brazilian Pavilion at 1939 New York World's Fair; bold, original designs
Brasília B-408, B-418
Hotel Guarani, Asunción A-731
Pampulha B-159

Nien Rebellion, (1854–64) major revolt in n. China C-370

Niepce, Joseph Nicéphore (1765–1833), French physicist, born in Chalon-sur-Saône, France; one of inventors of photography P-295, *picture* P-292
Daguerre D-2

Nierembergia, or cupflower, or bluecup, or whitecup, genus of dainty perennial plants with many bell-shaped flowers, violet or white; native to tropical America.

Nietzsche, Friedrich (full name Friedrich Wilhelm Nietzsche) (1844–1900), German philosopher N-307
fascism F-38
German literature G-109
philosophy P-266

Nieuwland, Julius Arthur (1878–1936), U.S. chemist, Roman Catholic priest, and educator; born in Hansbeke, Belgium; professor at Notre Dame University
rubber discoveries R-308

Nieuw Zeeland. *see in index* New Zealand

Nigella, or **fennelflower,** genus of annual plants of the buttercup family, native to Mediterranean and Turkestan; grows 1 to 2 ft (0.3 to 0.6 m); leaves threadlike; flowers with 5 petals, white, blue, or yellow; seed capsule a balloon enclosed in net of fine leaves; love-in-a-mist *N. damascena*, also called devil-in-a-bush.

Niger, or **Republic of Niger,** republic in Africa, n. of Nigeria; area 458,993 sq mi (1,188,786 sq km); cap. Niamey; pop. 6,423,000 N-308, *map* A-118
African political unit, *table* A-112
cities. *see in index* Niamey and other cities by name
flag, *picture* F-168
illiteracy P-450
Sahara S-14, *map* S-15, *pictures* S-16

Niger-Congo languages L-42, *diagram* L-43

Niger delta, delta in Nigeria, *table* D-90

Nigeria, nation in w. Africa on Gulf of Guinea; area 356,669 sq mi (923,768 sq km); cap. Lagos; pop. 93,600,000 N-310, *map* A-118
Africa A-93, 103, 108, *table* A-112
cities. *see also in index* cities listed below and other cities by name
Ibadan I-2
Lagos L-22
Commonwealth membership C-602
flag, *picture* F-168
literature
children's L-253, *chart* L-257
folklore, *list* S-482
population, *chart* P-447
multiple birth M-649
railroad mileage, *table* R-85

Niger River, 3rd largest river of Africa; 2,600 mi (4,200 km) long N-314
Africa, *map* A-118
Guinea G-314
Mali M-75, *picture* M-76
Niger N-308
Nigeria N-310
length, comparative. *see in index* River, *table*

'Nigger of the Narcissus, The', work by Conrad E-280

Night. *see in index* Day and night

Night, in mythology. *see in index* Nyx

'Night', work by Wiesel W-202

Night blindness (or nyctalopia), visual disorder E-388
malnutrition M-77

Night-blooming cereus, cactus C-12

Night crawler. *see in index* Fishworm

Nighthawk (also called bullbat), bird of the family Carpimulgidae N-314
food habits B-254, *pictures* B-242, 244

'Nighthawks', painting by Hopper H-238, *picture* H-239

Nightingale, Florence (1820–1910), British nurse N-314
Crimean War C-774
medicine M-284
nursing N-446
therapy T-164

Nightingale, songbird of the family Muscicapidae N-315
thrush family T-177

Nightjar (or goatsucker), a night-flying, insect-eating bird *Caprimulgus europaeus* related to American nighthawk and whippoorwill of the goatsucker family Caprimulgidae; nests in Europe, winters in Africa; so named from mistaken belief that it sucks the milk of goats.

Nightmare, frightening dream S-217

Night monkey. *see in index* Owl monkey

Night of Broken Glass (or Kristallnacht), Nov. 9–10, 1938, in German history
Holocaust H-205

Night phlox. *see in index* Zaluzianskya

Nightshade, group of poisonous plants of the family Solanaceae N-315
tobacco T-198

'Nightwalker', work by Kinsella I-328

'Night Watch, The', work by Rembrandt R-145

Nihilists, Russian revolutionists T-316

'Nihon shoki'. *see in index* 'Chronicles of Japan'

Niigata, Japan, port on Honshu Island 160 mi (260 km) n.w. of Tokyo; textiles, machinery, petroleum products; pop. 423,188, *map* J-75
Asia, *map* A-700

Niihau, a Hawaiian island; 73 sq mi (189 sq km); sheep; pop. 226 H-59, *maps* H-58, U-98, 117
Pacific Ocean, *map* P-6

Nijinska, Bronislava (1891–1972), Soviet choreographer, born in Warsaw; sister of Vaslav Nijinsky; dancer with Imperial Russian Ballet and Diaghilev's ballet; composed over 200 ballets ('Gypsy Dances'; 'Hundred Kisses'); to U.S. 1940 B-35

Nijinsky, Vaslav (1890–1950), Soviet ballet dancer N-315
ballet B-34, *picture* B-33

Nijmegen, also **Nimwegen,** The Netherlands, industrial center on Waal River; ancient Roman camp; pop. 127,172.

Nijmegen, Peace of (1678–79), *table* T-274

Nijmegen marches, physical fitness tests used in The Netherlands H-151

Nijubashi Bridge, bridge in Tokyo, Japan, *picture* T-204

Nika insurrection, revolt against the reign of Justinian and Theodora in Constantinople (AD 532) B-534

Nike, in Greek mythology, goddess of victory; daughter of the Titan Pallas and of Styx.

'Nike'. *see in index* 'Winged Victory'

Nike Apache, rocket S-342b

Nike Apteros. *see in index* Wingless Victory, Temple of

Nike-Hercules, U.S. guided missile, *picture* G-307

Nike-Zeus, U.S. guided missile, *picture* G-307

Nikisch, Arthur (1855–1922), Hungarian conductor; noted for Wagner; conductor of Boston Symphony Orchestra 1889–93; conductor of famous Leipzig Gewandhaus concerts 1895–1922
orchestra, *list* O-579

Nikita, king of Montenegro. *see in index* Nicholas

Nikko, mountainous region, containing town, Nikko (pop. 28,502) on island of Honshu, Japan, about 75 mi (120 km) n. of Tokyo; temples, tombs, sanctuaries, and a sacred bridge
national park, *map* J-78

Nikolayev, Andrian Grigorevich (born 1929), Soviet cosmonaut, born near Kazan'; in Soviet air force since 1954; married Valentina Tereshkova 1963, *picture* S-346f, *table* S-348

Nikolayev, also **Nikolaev,** U.S.S.R., port situated on the Bug River near Black Sea, 70 mi (110 km) n.e. of Odessa; shipbuilding; exports grain; pop. 331,000, *maps* E-361, R-344, 349

Nikolayevsk, U.S.S.R., seaport in e. Siberia near mouth of Amur River; hub for airlines; fishing, gold mining, fur collecting; shipyards, oil refineries; pop. 30,082, *maps* R-322, 345
Asia, *map* A-700

Nikopol', U.S.S.R., city in s. Ukraine on Dnieper River about 45 mi (70 km) s.w. of Zaporozh'ye; manganese; pop. 125,000 U-2, *map* R-349

Nile, battle of the (1798) E-121
warfare, *list* W-15

Nile basin, basin of the Nile River in Egypt N-316

Nile Delta, delta in Egypt D-90, E-115, E-124

Nile River (or Nahr an Nil), longest river of Africa 4,132 mi (6,650 km) N-316. *see also in index* Blue Nile; White Nile
Africa, *map* A-118
Egypt E-114, E-123, *picture* E-119
Aswan High Dam A-732
Cairo C-16
Lake Victoria V-311
Sudan S-501
canal C-127
earth E-32
irrigation S-502
Indus Valley comparison I-197
length, comparative. *see in index* River, *table*
Oasis O-454

Niles, John Jacob (1892–1980), U.S. folksinger F-273

Niles, Ill., village just n.w. of Chicago; office machines, electronics; incorporated 1899; pop. 31,432
Illinois, *map* I-53

Niles, Mich., city on St. Joseph River 47 mi (76 km) s.w. of Kalamazoo in rich dairy and fruitgrowing area; mushroom farms; dress patterns, metal and wood products, aircraft parts; air-movement equipment, wire; pop. 13,115.

Niles, Ohio, industrial city on Mahoning River 8 mi (13 km) n.w. of Youngstown; steel and metal products, prefabricated homes, road-building equipment; birthplace of William McKinley; pop. 23,088.

Nile Valley, valley of the Nile River in Egypt N-317

Nilgai, or **blue bull,** antelope *Boselaphus tragocamelus* of India; adult bulls are slate gray, with short horns.

Nilgiri Hills, plateau in s. India in Tamil Nadu state; some peaks over 8,000 ft (2,440 m); teak and bamboo; tea and coffee plantations.

'Nils, The Wonderful Adventures of', story by Lagerlöf S-472

Nilson, Lars Fredrik (1840–99), Swedish chemist, born in Östergötland; discovered the metallic element scandium.

Nilsson, Birgit (born 1918), Swedish dramatic soprano N-317

Nimble fly, name for certain long-legged bristly flies of family Tachinidae, remarkable for rapid movements; larvae inhabit and kill caterpillars, beetles, snails.

Nimbostratus cloud C-517

Nimbus, in art, the halo or disk of light surrounding head of a person to indicate holy or spiritual nature; sometimes shown as rays of light.

Nimbus III, satellite W-123

Nimes, France, city in s., 64 mi (103 km) n.w. of Marseilles; wine and brandy market; textiles, leather products; long noted for silk manufactures; pop. 115,561, *maps* E-361, F-372

Nimitz, Chester William (1885–1966), U.S. Navy officer, born in Fredericksburg, Tex.; commander in chief U.S. Pacific Fleet 1941–45; chief of naval operations 1945–47, *pictures* R-274
- World War II W-329, 337

'Nimitz', U.S. Navy aircraft carrier N-84, 88

Nimrod, a mighty hunter and founder of the Babylonian and Assyrian empires in Genesis x, 8–9; sometimes identified with Izdubar, hero of Babylonian Gilgamesh legend.

Nimrud, Iraq. *see in index* Kalah

Nimwegen, The Netherlands. *see in index* Nijmegen

Nin, Anaïs (1903–77), U.S. author, born in Neuilly, France (near Paris); came to U.S. 1914, lived in France during 1920s and 1930s, in U.S. again after 1939; U.S. citizen; influenced by surrealism and psychoanalytic theory; best known for diaries published in six volumes 1966–77 ('D.H. Lawrence: An Unprofessional Study'; fiction: 'Cities of the Interior', 'Collages', 'Winter of Artifice').

'Niña', one of the three ships of Columbus on his first voyage to America C-592

Ninebark, shrubs *Opulaster* or *Physocarpus* of the rose family with lobed heart-shaped leaves and white or pink flower clusters that resemble spirea; bark becomes loose and shredded when old, separating into many thin layers.

Ninepins, game B-386

Nine-Power Pact, international treaty signed in Washington, D.C. W-71

'Nineteen Eighty-four', novel by Orwell O-608, R-112d

'Nineteen Necromancers from Now', work by Reed A-362

Ninety-five theses, propositions for debate written by Luther, *picture* R-133

Nineveh, capital of ancient Assyria on the Tigris River; site of important archaeological discoveries A-532
- Assyrian revival B-9
- 'Epic of Gilgamesh' S-469, 480, *picture* S-482
- library L-229
- Medes siege M-273
- Mesopotamia M-305

Nine Worthies, The, heroes popular in medieval art and stories: three Christians—King Arthur, Charlemagne, Godfrey of Bouillon; three Jews—Joshua, David, Judas Maccabaeus; three paynims (or pagans)—Hector of Troy, Alexander the Great, Julius Caesar.

'Ninfeas', work by Jiménez J-118

Ningpo, China, city in n.e. Chekiang Province, near coast; fishing center; furniture, textiles; became treaty port 1842; pop. 280,000.

Ningxia Huizu (or Ningsia Hui), China s. of Inner Mongolian Autonomous Region; area 23,000 sq mi (60,000 sq km); cap. Yinchwan; pop. 3,930,000 N-317
- Hui population C-345

Ninja, member of a Japanese secret fighting society M-160

Ninjutsu, martial arts M-160

Ninon (sometimes called triple voile), a sheer, closely woven voile made of rayon or silk; used for dresses, glass curtains, and evening wear.

'Ninth Symphony' (or 'Choral'), work by Beethoven B-136
- classical music M-672

Ninus, legendary founder of ancient Assyrian city of Nineveh; husband of the great Assyrian queen, Semiramis.

Nio, modern name of ancient **Ios,** Greek island, one of Cyclades in Aegean Sea, 13 mi (21 km) s. of Naxos; about 45 sq mi (115 sq km); according to tradition Homer is buried there.

Niobe, in Greek mythology, daughter of Tantalus; she boasted that she and husband, Amphion, had many children while Leto had only two; as punishment Artemis and Apollo killed all the children and Zeus turned Niobe into a stone that wept continually.

Niobium (formerly columbium) (Nb), rare metallic element of silvery color, high melting point, and high resistance to acids; somewhat similar to tantalum; vital component in stainless steel and other alloy steels N-317
- periodic table, *table* P-207, *list* P-208

Niobrara River, river in Nebraska, rises in s.e. part of Wyoming and flows e. through n. Nebraska for 450 mi (720 km) into Missouri River, *map* U-70
- Nebraska N-94

Niort, France, city 32 mi (52 km) n.e. of La Rochelle; tanning, glovemaking; towers remain of fortress dating from 12th century; pop. 46,749, *map* F-372

NIOSH. *see in index* National Institute of Occupational Safety and Health

Nipa palm, native of East Indies and Australia; fruit edible; sugar and alcohol from juice; introduced into s. Florida
- Philippines P-259b
  - thatched roof, *picture* P-253b

Nipigon, Lake, lake in Ontario, 70 mi (110 km) long; discharges by Nipigon River into Lake Superior G-245, *maps* C-112, N-351

Nipissing, Lake, lake in Ontario, between Georgian Bay and Ottawa River; 55 mi (90 km) long; link in proposed Georgian Bay Canal.

Nipkow, Paul Gottlieb (1860–1940), German inventor, born in Lauenburg; pioneered in the development of television T-78

Nipmuc, the Algonquian Indians of central Massachusetts and extending into Connecticut and Rhode Island; they joined in King Philip's War in 1675 and at its close most of them fled to Canada or joined the Mahicans and other tribes on Hudson River K-246

Nippur, ancient city of Mesopotamia, 50 mi (80 km) s.e. of Babylon; flourished 4000 BC; 1952 excavations by Universities of Chicago and Pennsylvania found a temple and hundreds of Sumerian tablets.

NIRA. *see in index* National Industrial Recovery Act

Nirenberg, Marshall Warren (born 1927), U.S. biochemist, born in New York, N.Y.; director biochemical genetics National Heart, Lung, and Blood Institute 1962–; winner with two others of 1968 Nobel prize in medicine for research on genetics. *see also in index* Nobel Prizewinners, *table*

Nirvana, doctrine in Buddhism; objective of life; the condition of serenity of spirit B-481, C-364

Nis, also **Nish,** Yugoslavia, Serbian city 130 mi (210 km) s.e. of Belgrade; ancient Naissus, birthplace of Constantine the Great; held by Turks 1456–1878; pop. 150,400, *map* E-361

Nisei (second generation), name given in the U.S. and Canada to persons of Japanese parentage who were born and educated in America.

Nishapur, Iran, ancient town in n.e.; leather, carpets, pottery; birthplace of poet Omar Khayyám, his tomb nearby; pop. 33,482.

Niska, a Chimmesyan Indian tribe living on Nass River and its tributaries and on Nass Bay, B.C.; term also used for their language.

Niter. *see in index* Saltpeter

Niterói, formerly **Nictheroy,** Brazil, capital of state of Rio de Janeiro, across the bay from city of Rio de Janeiro; elegant suburban homes, fine bathing beaches; shipbuilding; steel products, textiles; pop. 228,826, *map* B-425

Niton, early name for radon. *see in index* Radon

Nitrate, a salt of nitric acid containing nitrate radical (NO_3)
- bacterial formation P-363a
- calcium S-32
- cellulose. *see in index* Nitrocellulose
- Chile C-330
- nitric acid N-318
- plants P-363
- potassium S-32
- saltpeter S-32
- silver. *see in index* Silver nitrate
- sodium S-32

Nitrate mineral, classification M-435

Nitric acid N-318. *see also in index* Nitrate
- acid rain A-19
- inorganic chemistry I-211
- nitrogen N-319
- platinum P-384

Nitric oxide, compound of nitrogen and oxygen (NO), a colorless, poisonous gas, discovered (1772) by Joseph Priestley; important in nitrogen fixation.

Nitrifying bacteria N-319

Nitriles, chemistry, cyanogen compounds with organic radicals; characterized by univalent group CN; usually liquid compounds with ethereal odor.

Nitrocellulose, or **cellulose nitrate**
- synthetic fibers F-71
  - rayon R-98

Nitrogen (N), gaseous element N-318. *see also in index* Nitrate; and headings beginning with Nitric and Nitro
- acid rain formation A-19
- aerosol propellant A-66
- air A-145, A-747, *picture* A-748
- explosive E-379
- fertilizers F-58
  - green manuring C-674
- inorganic chemistry I-211
- living things L-268
- periodic table, *table* P-207, *list* P-208
- plants P-363, P-378
- protein P-514
- sun's atmosphere S-513

Nitrogen cycle, in plant and animal life N-319, *picture* N-318
- plants P-373

Nitrogen fixation N-318
- legume L-118
- plants P-363a
- soil S-250

Nitrogen narcosis, or **raptures of the deep,** medical disorder
- underwater diving D-189

Nitroglycerin, or **glyceryl trinitrate,** an explosive
- energy release E-215
- explosive E-380
- inorganic chemistry I-211
- Nobel N-329

Nitrous oxide (or laughing gas) (N_2O), anesthetic A-413
- aerosol propellant A-66
- medicine M-284

Nitschke, Raymond (nickname Ray) (born 1936), U.S. football player, born in Elmwood Park, Ill.; middle linebacker; Green Bay Packers 1958–72.

Nitti, Francesco Saverio (1868–1953), Italian statesman and author, born in Melfi; professor economics, University of Naples; minister of agriculture, industry, trade, treasury; as premier distinguished himself in finance; opposed Fascism.

Nitze, Paul Henry (born 1907), U.S. government official, born in Amherst, Mass.; on research staff Washington Center for Foreign Policy 1953–60; assistant secretary of defense 1961–63, deputy secretary 1967–69; secretary of the Navy 1963–67.

Niu, Man Chiang, U.S. embryologist
- nucleic acid study E-203

Niue Island, or **Savage Island,** self-governing territory; in Pacific e. of Tonga Islands; 100 sq mi (260 sq km); chief town Alofi; copra; pop. 3,843, *map* P-6
- Commonwealth membership C-602
- New Zealand N-294
- Oceania O-467

Nivelle, Robert Georges (1856–1924), French World War I general, born in Tulle; rose from colonel in 1914 to commander in chief of French armies 1916–17 V-283
- World War I W-308

Nixies, water fairies F-12

Nixon, Pat (full name Thelma Catherine Patricia Ryan Nixon) (born 1912), wife of former President Nixon N-322, *picture* N-324

Nixon, Richard M. (full name Richard Milhous Nixon) (born 1913), 37th president of the United States N-320
- China visit C-355, 378
- conservation policies C-678
- Eisenhower E-134, *pictures* E-136, 139
- Ford F-299, 303, *picture* F-301
- impeachment proceedings I-58
- Kennedy K-197
- Kissinger K-251
- money M-533
- presidential vote, *chart* P-495, *table* P-395d
- U.S. history U-196a
- Vietnam War V-324

Niza, Marcos de. *see in index* Marcos de Niza

Nizam, diamond, *picture* D-129

Nizaris, branch of Muslim Isma'ili sect I-362

Nizhniy Novgorod, U.S.S.R. *see in index* Gorky

Nizhniy Tagil, or **Nizhni Tagil,** U.S.S.R., city in w. Siberia on e. slope of Ural Mountains 80 mi (130 km) n.w. of Sverdlovsk; deposits of iron, manganese, copper, gold nearby; chemicals; pop. 394,000, *maps* R-344
- Asia, *map* A-700

Compton's Fact-Index
continues
on the next page

Nkomo, Joshua (full name Joshua Mqabuko Nyongolo Nkomo) (born 1917), African revolutionary N-329
Zimbabwe Z-454
Nkrumah, Kwame (1909–72), Ghanaian political leader N-329
Ghana G-140
NKVD, former name of Soviet secret police R-328
N.L. *see in index* National League
NLF. *see in index* National Liberation Front
NLRB. *see in index* National Labor Relations Board
NLU. *see in index* National Labor Union
NMFS. *see in index* National Marine Fisheries Service
NMR. *see in index* Nuclear magnetic resonance
No, or **Noh,** form of Japanese drama J-49, 54, J-81, *picture* J-55
masks M-187, *picture* M-186
mime M-423
Zen Z-450
Noah, Biblical figure in Genesis vi–ix, builder of the Ark, in which he and his family and one pair of every kind of animal were saved from the Deluge; supposedly ancestor of various races through sons, Shem, Ham, Japheth
flood legends F-185
Mount Ararat A-528
mythology M-698
Nobel, Alfred (full name Alfred Bernhard Nobel) (1833–96), Swedish chemist and inventor N-329. *see also in index* Nobel Prizes
explosives E-380
literary awards L-241
Nobelium (No), chemical element
periodic table, *table* P-207, *list* P-208
Nobel prizes N-330
literature L-241
medals M-270
Oslo O-610
prizewinners. *see tables* following
Nobile, Umberto (1885–1978), Italian airship designer, aviator, and Arctic explorer; born in Lauro; designed dirigibles *Norge* and *Italia*; dean aeronautics, Lewis Holy Name School of Aeronautics, Lockport, Ill. 1939–42; returned to Italy 1943; author of 'My Polar Flights' P-421, A-382
Nobility titles. *see in index* Titles of nobility
Noble fir, evergreen tree *Abies nobilis* of pine family, native from Washington to California; grows 60 ft (18 m) to 200 ft (60 m) high; has rough red-brown bark, rounded crown; leaves rounded, gray-green, to 1½ in. (3.5 cm) long, with white lines on both sides; cones to 10 in. (25 cm) long; wood has reddish streaks; sometimes marketed as white fir and larch.
Noble gases, any of the six chemical elements that make up Group O on the periodic table N-330
periodic table P-206, *table* P-207
'Noble House', work by Clavell A-361
Noble metals, term applied to gold and platinum because their tendency to form compounds with other elements is extremely slight; also to palladium and rhodium
gold G-176
platinum P-384
Noble Order of the Knights of Labor, U.S. labor organization L-7
Nocera Inferiore, Italy, city 20 mi (30 km) s.e. of Naples; linen and woolen goods; pop. 43,050, *map* I-404
Noctiluca, marine organisms, *picture* L-269
Noctilucent cloud, faintly luminous, fast-moving cloud visible in summer twilight at high n. and s. latitudes; occurs at altitudes of about 50 mi (80 km); reflects sunlight which reaches it from below horizon; rocket experiments indicate composition of ice-covered extraterrestrial dust particles.
Nocturn, in music, *list* M-671
Nocturnal marsh deer, deer *Blastocerus dichotomus* native of wet lowlands of e. South America D-62
Noddack, Walter (1893–1960) and **Ida** (born 1896), German chemists; with O. Berg, codiscoverers of the elements masurium and rhenium.
Nodding lily. *see in index* Canada lily
Node, in astronomy, the two points where the orbit of a planet intersects the plane of the Earth's ecliptic; one is the ascending, the other the descending node
moon M-577
Node of Ranvier, in nerve fibers N-121
Nodular cast iron, or **ductile cast iron,** metal I-335
Noël, N.S. N-397
Noël, French name for Christmas. *see in index* Christmas
Noel-Baker, Baron (1889–1982), British statesman; helped found League of Nations and United Nations; member of Parliament 1929–70; ('The Arms Race; a Programme of World Disarmament'). *see also in index* Nobel Prizewinners, *table*
Nofretete, or **Nefretete,** Egyptian queen S-82, *picture* S-78
Ikhnaton I-32
Nogales, Ariz., city on Mexican border (pop. 8,946), adjoining the city of **Heroica Nogales,** Mexico (pop. 52,108); port of entry for w. coast of Mexico; shipping point for Mexican-grown vegetables to U.S. winter markets; cattle; silver, gold, copper, lead, zinc, and manganese, *map* U-40
Mexico, *map* M-260c
Nogi, Ki-Ten Marosuke, Count (1849–1912), Japanese general, born in Tokyo; victor of Port Arthur in Russo-Japanese War.
Noguchi, Hideyo (1876–1928), Japanese bacteriologist N-330
Noguchi, Isamu (born 1904), abstract sculptor, designer of stage sets and modern functional furniture, born in Los Angeles, Calif.; son of Japanese poet, Yone Noguchi; contributed bridge designs to Peace Park at Hiroshima: 'Isamu Noguchi: a Sculptor's World', autobiography.
Noh, form of Japanese drama. *see in index* No
Noise, loud or confused sound N-331
acoustics A-21
deafness D-48
ear E-5
fish F-127
information theory I-201, *picture* I-204
jet propulsion J-109
music comparison S-261
pollution A-219, P-441e
Noisemaker, submarine device S-497
Nola, Italy, city 16 mi (26 km) n.e. of Naples; prominent in Roman times; Augustus died there AD 14; pop. 24,623.
Nolan, Jeannette Covert (1896–1974), U.S. author, born in Evansville, Ind.; for children: 'The Young Douglas', 'Florence Nightingale', 'Story of Clara Barton', 'John Brown', 'George Rogers Clark, Soldier and Hero', 'Spy for the Confederacy', 'The Shot Heard Round the World', 'The Little Giant'.
Nolan, Philip, chief figure in E.E. Hale's 'The Man Without a Country'; a young U.S. Navy officer involved in Aaron Burr's conspiracy; because of a rash remark is sentenced to live at sea, never to hear of his country again.
Nolan, Sidney (born 1917), Australian artist, born in Carlton, Victoria; paintings based on Australian folklore and frontier legends, especially outlaw Ned Kelly and Burke and Wills expedition; designed stage sets in London; painting prize Venice Biennale 1954; knighted 1981; member Order of Merit 1983.
Nolde, Emil (1867–1956), German artist; early landscapes and flowers somber in color; later work robust and colorful; remarkable series of Biblical paintings.
Nolichucky River, river about 150 mi (240 km) long, rises in w. North Carolina, flows n.w. into French Broad River, e. Tennessee (Douglas Reservoir).
Nomad N-331
American Indians I-116, 127, 145
Asia A-688
Afghanistan A-89
China C-360
Huns H-330
Mesopotamia M-305
Mongol Empire M-534
grassland G-238
Lapps L-50
migration of people M-399
Sahara S-16, *pictures* S-15
water supply W-92
No-man's-land, unclaimed or disputed territory, particularly various borderlands.
Nombril, in heraldry, *diagram* H-136
Nom de plume. *see in index* Pseudonym
Nome, Alaska, city famed in history for gold mining, on s. coast of Seward Peninsula; pop. 2,301 (was about 20,000 during gold rush of 1899–1900) U-96, *maps* N-351, U-39
Nomellini, Leo (born 1924), U.S. football defensive tackle, born in Lucca, Italy; played for San Francisco 49ers 1950–63.
Nomenclature, a set of terms or symbols in a field of study, art, or science, especially the standardized classification system for animals and plants. *see in index* Classification
Nominalists, in philosophy P-265
Nominations, in politics
United States P-431, *pictures* P-432–3
U.S.S.R. R-328
Nona, in Roman mythology F-44
Nonagon. *see in index* Enneagon
Nonair-breathing engine. *see in index* Rocket engine
Non-A non-B hepatitis, liver disease H-134
Noncombatants, status in war time
international law I-256
Noncommissioned officers
British uniforms and insignia U-12
U.S. armed forces A-634
Air Force U-5–6, *pictures* U-5, 9–10
Army A-634, U-5, 9–10
Marine Corps U-6, *pictures* U-6, 9
Navy (petty officers) U-6, *pictures* U-5, 9, 11
Noncommunicable disease. *see in index* Disease, *subhead* noninfectious
Nonconformists. *see in index* Dissenters
'None but the Lonely Heart', work by Barrymore B-85
Nones, in the ancient Roman calendar the 9th day before the ides, falling in March, May, July, and October on the 7th of the month, in other months on the 5th.
Non-Euclidean geometry M-215, 219
Nonfiction. *see in index* Biography; Diary; Essay; Letter writing
Nonimportation agreements, in North American colonial history S-410
Nonindustrialized countries. *see in index* Third World
Noninfectious disease. *see in index* Disease, *subhead* noninfectious
Non-Intercourse Act (1809), United States W-30
Noninterlaced fabric, textiles T-139
Nonmetal, in chemistry
electrochemistry E-170
periodic table, *table* P-207
Nonni River, or **Nun Kiang,** river in n.e. China; principal tributary of Sungari River; 740 mi (1,190 km) long.
Nonobjective art P-25
Nonoloid, fiber classification
synthetic fibers, *table* F-72
Nonometer, line in poetry P-405
Nonpareil. *see in index* Painted bunting
Nonpartisan League, U.S. organization
Minnesota M-445
North Dakota history N-375
Nonproliferation, nuclear energy N-430
Nonsense rhymes and nonsense stories
Lear L-168
reading R-101b, c
Nonsporting dog, purebred not included in other categories D-197
Nonteaching hospital (often called community hospital) H-279
Non troppo, in music, *list* M-671
Nonverbal communication C-607
Nonviolent action, or **passive resistance** P-143d
civil disobedience C-463
King B-295, K-244
Thoreau A-347
Noon mark, in pioneer days, a line drawn on floor of cabin, marking an edge of a patch of sunlight when the sun was due south; it told the noon hour, and clocks were set by it.
Nooten Island. *see in index* Governors Island
Nootka, a group of American Indian tribes in British Columbia, *picture* I-133, *map* I-136, *table* I-139
fur trade F-471
Nootka cypress. *see in index* Alaska cedar
Nopal, a genus of the cactus family; resembles the prickly pear; grown as food for cochineal insects
fruit F-436
NORAD. *see in index* North American Air Defense Command
Noradrenaline. *see in index* Norepinephrine
Noranda, Que., city just n. of Rouyn and about 135 mi (215 km) n. of North Bay, Ont.; center for mining; pop. 10,741 Q-9d, *map* C-112
Norbert, Saint (died 1134), German ecclesiastic, archbishop of Magdeburg; founder of Premonstratensian monastic order M-542
Norco, Calif., community on Santa Ana River, 11 mi (18 km) s.w. of Riverside; agriculture; pop. 21,126.
Nordau, Max (1849–1923), Jewish author and philosopher, born in Pest, Hungary; Zionist leader ('Degeneration', criticism of modern civilization).
Norden, name for Northern Europe adopted by the people of that area; includes Denmark, Finland, Norway, Sweden, and Iceland E-333
Nordenskjöld, Nils Adolf Erik, Baron (1832–1901), Swedish Arctic explorer, born in Helsinki, Finland; first to traverse the Northeast Passage (1878–79)
Northeast Passage P-420, *map* P-417
Nordenskjöld, Nils Otto Gustaf (1869–1928), Swedish explorer, nephew of N.A.E. Nordenskjöld; after explorations in Patagonia, Alaska, and Greenland, led expedition to South Polar regions (1901–4); ship sank, he was rescued off Graham Land by Argentines.
Nordhoff, Charles Bernard (1887–1947), author, born of U.S. parents in London, England; in Tahiti several years; with James Hall wrote 'Lafayette Flying Corps', 'Mutiny on the Bounty', 'Men Against the Sea', 'Pitcairn's Island', 'The Hurricane' R-112
Nordica, Lillian (1859–1914), U.S. operatic soprano, born in Farmington, Me.; famous for Wagnerian roles; died in Java after exposure from shipwreck.
Nordic Council, an economic alliance created Feb. 12, 1953, in Copenhagen by Sweden, Norway, Denmark, and Iceland; Finland joined 1955. *see also in index* European Organizations, *table*
Nordic subrace, racial classification, subgroup of Caucasoid race R-26, E-336, *chart* R-26
Norway N-391
Nordkapp. *see in index* North Cape
Nordkyn, Cape, n.e. coast of Norway 95 mi (150 km) n.e. of Hammerfest; northernmost point of Europe's mainland (71° 7′ N. latitude).
Nördlingen, West Germany, town in Bavaria, 70 mi (110 km) n.w. of Munich; in Thirty Years' War, scene of Imperialist victory over Swedes (1634) and defeat by French (1645); pop. 14,692, *map* G-134

NOBEL PRIZEWINNERS*

Physics

1901	Wilhelm K. Roentgen	(1845–1923)	German	Discovery of X rays
1902	Hendrik A. Lorentz	(1853–1928)	Dutch	Influence of magnetism on radiation phenomena
	Pieter Zeeman	(1865–1943)	Dutch	
1903	Antoine H. Becquerel	(1852–1908)	French	Discovery of radioactivity in uranium
	Pierre Curie	(1859–1906)	French	Work on radioactivity based on Becquerel's discovery
	Marie Curie	(1867–1934)	French	
1904	John Strutt (Lord Rayleigh)	(1842–1919)	British	Studies on density of gases; discovery (with Sir William Ramsay) of argon
1905	Philipp Lenard	(1862–1947)	Hungarian	Work on cathode rays
1906	Sir Joseph J. Thomson	(1856–1940)	British	Conduction of electricity through gases
1907	Albert A. Michelson	(1852–1931)	American	Optical precision instruments and studies made with them
1908	Gabriel Lippmann	(1845–1921)	French	Color photography based on interference
1909	Guglielmo Marconi	(1874–1937)	Italian	Wireless telegraphy
	Karl F. Braun	(1850–1918)	German	
1910	Johannes D. van der Waals	(1837–1923)	Dutch	Laws and formulas for liquids and gases
1911	Wilhelm Wien	(1864–1928)	German	Discoveries in blackbody radiation
1912	Nils G. Dalén	(1869–1937)	Swedish	Automatic gas lighting
1913	Heike K. Onnes	(1853–1926)	Dutch	Method of liquefying helium
1914	Max von Laue	(1879–1960)	German	Diffraction of X rays by crystals
1915	Sir William H. Bragg	(1862–1942)	English	Work on crystal structure, using X-ray spectrometer they developed
	Sir William L. Bragg	(1890–1971)	English	
1917	Charles G. Barkla	(1877–1944)	English	Discovery of X-ray radiation of elements
1918	Max Planck	(1858–1947)	German	Quantum theory
1919	Johannes Stark	(1874–1957)	German	Discovery that spectral lines are distorted in an electrical field; Stark effect
1920	Charles E. Guillaume	(1861–1938)	French	Work on nickel-steel alloys; invented alloy invar
1921	Albert Einstein	(1879–1955)	American	Theory of relativity; photoelectric effect
1922	Niels Bohr	(1885–1962)	Danish	Studies in atomic structure and radiations
1923	Robert A. Millikan	(1868–1953)	American	Measurement of electron; photoelectric phenomena
1924	Karl M.G. Siegbahn	(1886–1978)	Swedish	Work in X-ray spectroscopy
1925	James Franck	(1882–1964)	American	Laws governing impact of electrons on atoms
	Gustav Hertz	(1887–1975)	German	
1926	Jean B. Perrin	(1870–1942)	French	Work on discontinuity of matter; studies on motion and distribution of particles suspended in liquid
1927	Arthur H. Compton	(1892–1962)	American	Discovery of Compton effect; shows that electromagnetic radiation behaves like a stream of particles
	Charles T.R. Wilson	(1869–1959)	Scottish	Wilson cloud chamber for study of ions
1928	Sir Owen W. Richardson	(1879–1959)	English	Law on emission of electrons
1929	Prince Louis Victor de Broglie	(1892–1987)	French	Wave character of electrons
1930	Sir Chandrasekhara V. Raman	(1888–1970)	Indian	Work on diffusion of light; Raman effect advanced study of molecular structure
1932	Werner K. Heisenberg	(1901–1976)	German	Creation of quantum mechanics
1933	Erwin Schrödinger	(1887–1961)	Austrian	New forms of atomic theory
	Paul A.M. Dirac	(1902–1984)	English	
1935	Sir James Chadwick	(1891–1974)	English	Discovery of the neutron
1936	Victor F. Hess	(1883–1964)	American	Discovery of cosmic rays
	Carl D. Anderson	(born 1905)	American	Discovery of the positron
1937	Clinton J. Davisson	(1881–1958)	American	Diffraction of electrons by crystals
	Sir George P. Thomson	(1892–1975)	English	
1938	Enrico Fermi	(1901–1954)	American	Discovery of radioactive elements
1939	Ernest O. Lawrence	(1901–1958)	American	Invention of cyclotron
1943	Otto Stern	(1888–1969)	American	For measuring the magnetic moment of a proton
1944	Isidor I. Rabi	(born 1898)	American	Resonance method of recording magnetic properties of atomic nuclei
1945	Wolfgang Pauli	(1900–1958)	Austrian	Exclusion principle of electrons
1946	Percy W. Bridgman	(1882–1961)	American	Discoveries in high-pressure physics
1947	Sir Edward Appleton	(1892–1965)	English	For studies of Earth's ionosphere and discovery of the Appleton layer
1948	Patrick M.S. Blackett	(1897–1974)	English	Cosmic-ray discoveries; improvement of Wilson cloud chamber
1949	Hideki Yukawa	(1907–1981)	Japanese	Prediction of existence of the meson
1950	Cecil F. Powell	(1903–1969)	English	Meson discoveries; method of photographing nuclear processes
1951	Sir John D. Cockcroft	(1897–1967)	English	Pioneer work in transmutation of atomic nuclei
	Ernest T.S. Walton	(born 1903)	Irish	
1952	Felix Bloch	(1905–1983)	American	Methods of measuring magnetic fields of atomic nuclei
	Edward M. Purcell	(born 1912)	American	
1953	Frits Zernike	(1888–1966)	Dutch	Phase-contrast microscope and method
1954	Max Born	(1882–1970)	British	Contributions to quantum mechanics
	Walter Bothe	(1891–1957)	German	Coincidence method of studying cosmic radiation
1955	Willis E. Lamb, Jr.	(born 1913)	American	Discoveries concerning structure of hydrogen spectrum
	Polykarp Kusch	(born 1911)	American	Determination of magnetic moment of the electron
1956	William Shockley	(born 1910)	American	Development of the transistor effect
	John Bardeen	(born 1908)	American	
	Walter H. Brattain	(born 1902)	American	
1957	Chen Ning Yang	(born 1922)	Chinese	Investigation of parity laws
	Tsung Dao-lee	(born 1926)	Chinese	
1958	Pavel A. Cherenkov	(born 1904)	Russian	Discovery and interpretation of Cherenkov radiation effect
	Ilya M. Frank	(born 1908)	Russian	
	Igor E. Tamm	(1895–1971)	Russian	
1959	Emilio Segrè	(born 1905)	American	Discovery of the antiproton
	Owen Chamberlain	(born 1920)	American	
1960	Donald A. Glaser	(born 1926)	American	Development of bubble chamber for photographing atomic particles
1961	Robert Hofstadter	(born 1915)	American	Studies in structure of proton and neutron
	Rudolph L. Mössbauer	(born 1929)	German	Work on resonance absorption of gamma rays

*No award for missing years.

1962	Lev D. Landau	(1908–1968)	Russian	Experiments with liquid helium
1963	Eugene P. Wigner	(born 1902)	American	Research on structure of the atom and its nucleus
	Maria G. Mayer	(1906–1972)	American	
	J. Hans D. Jensen	(1907–1973)	W. German	
1964	Charles H. Townes	(born 1915)	American	Research on laser and maser beams
	Nikolai G. Basov	(born 1922)	Russian	
	Aleksandr M. Prochorov	(born 1916)	Russian	
1965	Richard P. Feynman	(born 1918)	American	Work on defining basic theories of quantum electrodynamics
	Julian S. Schwinger	(born 1918)	American	
	Shin-Ichiro Tomonaga	(1906–1979)	Japanese	
1966	Alfred Kastler	(1902–1984)	French	Work on optical methods for studying Hertzian resonances in atoms
1967	Hans A. Bethe	(born 1906)	American	Studies in energy production of stars
1968	Luis W. Alvarez	(born 1911)	American	Study and detection of subatomic particles
1969	Murray Gell-Mann	(born 1929)	American	Discoveries regarding subatomic particles
1970	Hannes Alfvén	(born 1908)	Swedish	Studies of plasmas (gases) in magnetic fields
	Louis Néel	(born 1904)	French	Work on antiferromagnetism and ferromagnetism
1971	Dennis Gabor	(1900–1979)	English	Invention of holography
1972	John Bardeen	(born 1908)	American	Theory of superconductivity
	Leon N. Cooper	(born 1930)	American	
	John R. Schrieffer	(born 1931)	American	
1973	Leo Esaki	(born 1925)	Japanese	Theories on tunneling phenomena in solids, particularly in semiconductors and superconductors
	Ivar Giaever	(born 1929)	American	
	Brian D. Josephson	(born 1940)	British	
1974	Sir Martin Ryle	(1918–1984)	British	Pioneering research in radioastrophysics
	Anthony Hewish	(born 1924)	British	
1975	James Rainwater	(1917–1986)	American	Research on the inner structure of the atom
	Aage N. Bohr	(born 1922)	Danish	
	Ben Roy Mottelson	(born 1926)	Danish	
1976	Burton Richter	(born 1931)	American	Discovery of the subatomic J particle, which opened a new field of research
	Samuel Chao Chung Ting	(born 1936)	American	
1977	Philip W. Anderson	(born 1923)	American	Contributions to solid-state electronics
	Sir Nevill F. Mott	(born 1905)	British	
	John H. Van Vleck	(1899–1980)	American	
1978	Peter Leonidovich Kapitsa	(1894–1984)	Russian	Research on liquefaction of helium
	Arno Allan Penzias	(born 1933)	American	Discovery of electromagnetic radiation, supporting "big bang" theory
	Robert Woodrow Wilson	(born 1936)	American	
1979	Sheldon L. Glashow	(born 1932)	American	Contributions to theory of unified weak and electromagnetic interaction between elementary particles
	Abdus Salam	(born 1926)	Pakistani	
	Steven Weinberg	(born 1933)	American	
1980	James W. Cronin	(born 1931)	American	Discovery of Cronin-Fitch Effect in the behavior of subatomic particles
	Val L. Fitch	(born 1923)	American	
1981	Nicolaas Bloembergen	(born 1920)	American	Discoveries in electron spectroscopy
	Arthur L. Schawlow	(born 1921)	American	Pioneering work in the field of laser spectroscopy
	Kai M. Siegbahn	(born 1918)	Swedish	
1982	Kenneth G. Wilson	(born 1936)	American	Investigation of phase changes
1983	Subrahmanyan Chandrasekhar	(born 1910)	American	Pioneering work on the evolution of stars
	William A. Fowler	(born 1911)	American	
1984	Carlo Rubbia	(born 1934)	Italian	Discovery of W and Z field particles as proof of weak-force theory
	Simon van der Meer	(born 1925)	Dutch	Design of colliding-beam accelerator that led to discovery of W and Z field particles
1985	Klaus von Klitzing	(born 1943)	German	Application of quantum theory to commercial electronics
1986	Ernst Ruska	(born 1906)	German	Invention of the first working electron microscope
	Gerd Binnig	(born 1947)	German	Invention of the scanning tunneling microscope
	Heinrich Rohrer	(born 1933)	Swiss	

Chemistry

1901	Jacobus H. Van't Hoff	(1852–1911)	Dutch	Laws of chemical dynamics and osmotic pressure
1902	Emil Fischer	(1852–1919)	German	Syntheses of sugars and purines
1903	Svante A. Arrhenius	(1859–1927)	Swedish	Theory of electrolytic dissociation
1904	Sir William Ramsay	(1852–1916)	British	Discovery of inert gaseous elements
1905	Adolph von Baeyer	(1835–1917)	German	Work on dyes, notably synthesis of indigo
1906	Henri Moissan	(1852–1907)	French	Electric furnace; isolation of fluorine
1907	Eduard Buchner	(1860–1917)	German	Discovery of noncellular fermentation
1908	Ernest Rutherford	(1871–1937)	British	Decay of elements; chemistry of radioactive substances
1909	Wilhelm Ostwald	(1853–1932)	German	Work on catalysis, chemical equilibrium, rates of reaction
1910	Otto Wallach	(1847–1931)	German	Pioneer studies of alicyclic compounds
1911	Marie Curie	(1867–1934)	French	Discovery of radium and polonium; isolation of metallic radium
1912	Victor Grignard	(1871–1935)	French	Discovery of Grignard reagent
	Paul Sabatier	(1854–1941)	French	Hydrogenation of organic compounds
1913	Alfred Werner	(1866–1919)	Swiss	Coordination theory of valence; simplified classifying complex inorganic compounds
1914	Theodore W. Richards	(1868–1928)	American	Determination of many atomic weights
1915	Richard Willstätter	(1872–1942)	German	Work on coloring matter in plants
1918	Fritz Haber	(1868–1934)	German	Synthesis of ammonia
1920	Walther H. Nernst	(1864–1941)	German	Work in thermochemistry
1921	Frederick Soddy	(1877–1956)	English	Research on isotopes
1922	Francis W. Aston	(1877–1945)	English	Discovery of many isotopes, using mass spectrograph he invented; whole-number law
1923	Fritz Pregl	(1869–1930)	Austrian	Microanalysis of organic substances

1925	Richard Zsigmondy	(1865–1929)	German	Methods of studying colloid chemistry
1926	Theodor Svedberg	(1884–1966)	Swedish	Work on colloids and on disperse systems
1927	Heinrich O. Wieland	(1877–1957)	German	Research on bile acids
1928	Adolf Windaus	(1876–1959)	German	Discovery that ultraviolet rays change ergosterol to vitamin D
1929	Sir Arthur Harden	(1865–1940)	English	Studies in fermentation of sugar and [illegible]
	Hans von Euler-Chelpin	(1873–1964)	Swedish	
1930	Hans Fischer	(1881–1945)	German	Synthesis of hemin; study of chlorophyll
1931	Karl Bosch	(1874–1940)	German	High-pressure production of ammonia
	Friedrich Bergius	(1884–1949)	German	High-pressure method of converting coal into oil
1932	Irving Langmuir	(1881–1957)	American	Discoveries in surface chemistry
1934	Harold C. Urey	(1893–1981)	American	Discovery of heavy hydrogen (deuterium)
1935	Frédéric Joliot-Curie	(1900–1958)	French	Synthesis of radioactive elements
	Irène Joliot-Curie	(1897–1956)	French	
1936	Peter J.W. Debye	(1884–1966)	American	Work on molecular structure
1937	Sir Walter N. Haworth	(1883–1950)	English	Work on vitamin C and carbohydrates
	Paul Karrer	(1889–1971)	Swiss	Research on carotenoids, flavins, vitamins
1938	Richard Kuhn	(1900–1967)	Austrian	Isolation of vitamin B_2 and work on carotenoids (award declined)
1939	Adolph F.J. Butenandt	(born 1903)	German	Sex hormone discoveries (award declined)
	Leopold Ruzicka	(1887–1976)	Swiss	Work on polymethylenes and higher terpenes; synthesis of sex hormones
1943	George de Hevesy	(1885–1966)	Hungarian	Work with isotopes as tracers
1944	Otto Hahn	(1879–1968)	German	Nuclear fission
1945	Artturi I. Virtanen	(1895–1973)	Finnish	Method of preserving fodder
1946	James B. Sumner	(1887–1955)	American	Discovery that enzymes can be crystallized
	John H. Northrop	(1891–1987)	American	Preparation of enzymes and virus proteins in pure form
	Wendell M. Stanley	(1904–1971)	American	
1947	Sir Robert Robinson	(1886–1975)	English	Alkaloid studies
1948	Arne Tiselius	(1902–1971)	Swedish	Work on serum proteins
1949	William F. Giauque	(1895–1982)	American	Demagnetization method to produce temperatures approximating absolute zero
1950	Otto Diels	(1876–1954)	German	Diene synthesis, method of making organic chemicals synthetically
	Kurt Alder	(1902–1958)	German	
1951	Edwin M. McMillan	(born 1907)	American	Discovery of plutonium and other transuranium elements
	Glenn T. Seaborg	(born 1912)	American	
1952	A.J.P. Martin	(born 1910)	English	Development of chromatographic analysis of closely related compounds
	Richard L.M. Synge	(born 1914)	English	
1953	Hermann Staudinger	(1881–1965)	German	Work in macromolecular chemistry
1954	Linus C. Pauling	(born 1901)	American	Studies of molecular structure and the chemical bond
1955	Vincent du Vigneaud	(1901–1978)	American	Synthesis of pituitary hormones
1956	Sir Cyril Hinshelwood	(1897–1967)	English	Studies in chemical chain reactions
	Nikolai N. Semënov	(born 1896)	Russian	
1957	Sir Alexander Todd	(born 1907)	Scottish	Synthesizing nucleic acids
1958	Frederick Sanger	(born 1918)	English	Determining structure of insulin molecule
1959	Jaroslav Heyrovsky	(1890–1967)	Czech	Development of polarographic analysis
1960	Willard F. Libby	(1908–1980)	American	Technique of radiocarbon dating
1961	Melvin Calvin	(born 1911)	American	Sequence of chemical reactions in plants during photosynthesis
1962	Max F. Perutz	(born 1914)	British	Research on molecular structure of globular proteins
	John C. Kendrew	(born 1917)	English	
1963	Giulio Natta	(1903–1979)	Italian	Research in hydrocarbons leading to commercial products
	Karl Ziegler	(1898–1973)	German	
1964	Dorothy C. Hodgkin	(born 1910)	English	X-ray determination of structure of compounds that control pernicious anemia
1965	Robert B. Woodward	(1917–1979)	American	Contribution to art of organic synthesis
1966	Robert S. Mulliken	(1896–1986)	American	Work on structure of molecules
1967	Manfred Eigen	(born 1927)	German	Studies of extremely rapid chemical reactions
	Ronald G.W. Norrish	(1897–1978)	British	
	George Porter	(born 1920)	British	
1968	Lars Onsager	(1903–1976)	American	Work in science of thermodynamics
1969	Derek H.R. Barton	(born 1918)	English	Useful studies of conformation, or shape, of organic molecules
	Odd Hassel	(1897–1981)	Norwegian	
1970	Luis F. Leloir	(born 1906)	Argentine	Work on breakdown of sugars
1971	Gerhard Herzberg	(born 1904)	Canadian	Research on molecular structure
1972	Christian B. Anfinsen	(born 1916)	American	Fundamental contributions to enzyme chemistry
	Stanford Moore	(1913–1982)	American	
	William H. Stein	(1911–1980)	American	
1973	Ernst Otto Fischer	(born 1918)	German	Research on organometallic "sandwich compounds"
	Geoffrey Wilkinson	(born 1921)	British	
1974	Paul J. Flory	(1910–1985)	American	Research in physical chemistry of macromolecules
1975	John Warcup Cornforth	(born 1917)	Australian	Work on the stereochemistry of enzyme-catalyzed reactions and organic molecules
	Vladimir Prelog	(born 1906)	Swiss	
1976	William Nunn Lipscomb, Jr.	(born 1919)	American	Work with boranes; studies in the chemical bonding of one element to another
1977	Ilya Prigogine	(born 1917)	Belgian	Applications of thermodynamic theory
1978	Peter Dennis Mitchell	(born 1920)	British	Research concerning functions of cell membranes in metabolic processes
1979	Herbert Charles Brown	(born 1912)	American	Development of boron and phosphorus compounds as organic synthesizers; Wittig reaction
	Georg Wittig	(1897–1987)	German	
1980	Paul Berg	(born 1926)	American	Biochemical studies of nucleic acids
	Walter Gilbert	(born 1932)	American	
	Frederick Sanger	(born 1918)	English	
1981	Kenichi Fukui	(born 1918)	Japanese	Formulation of rules that predict chemical reactions on basis of quantum mechanics
	Roald Hoffman	(born 1937)	American	
1982	Aaron Klug	(born 1926)	South African	Biochemical studies of nucleic acids and proteins
1983	Henry Taube	(born 1915)	American	Research in oxydalin-reduction reaction

1984	Robert Bruce Merrifield	(born 1921)	American	Development of rapid automated procedure to produce peptides
1985	Herbert Hauptman	(born 1917)	American	Development of a mathematical method to determine the three-dimensional structure of molecules
	Jerome Karle	(born 1918)	American	
1986	Dudley Robert Herschbach	(born 1932)	American	Chemical reaction dynamics
	Yuan Tseh Lee	(born 1936)	American	
	John Charles Polanyi	(born 1929)	Canadian	

Physiology or Medicine

1901	Emil A. von Behring	(1854–1917)	German	Discovery of diphtheria antitoxin
1902	Sir Ronald Ross	(1857–1932)	British	Discovery of malaria parasite
1903	Niels R. Finsen	(1860–1904)	Danish	First use of ultraviolet rays to treat disease
1904	Ivan P. Pavlov	(1849–1936)	Russian	Physiology of digestion
1905	Robert Koch	(1843–1910)	German	Isolation of tubercle bacillus; development of tuberculin culture
1906	Camillo Golgi	(1844–1926)	Italian	Discoveries concerning anatomy of nervous system
	Santiago Ramón y Cajal	(1852–1934)	Spanish	
1907	Charles L.A. Laveran	(1845–1922)	French	Discovery of disease-causing protozoa
1908	Paul Ehrlich	(1854–1915)	German	Immunity studies
	Élie Metchnikoff	(1845–1916)	Russian	
1909	Emil T. Kocher	(1841–1917)	Swiss	Work on thyroid gland
1910	Albrecht Kossel	(1853–1927)	German	Studies of protein and cell chemistry
1911	Allvar Gullstrand	(1862–1930)	Swedish	Research in optics
1912	Alexis Carrel	(1873–1944)	American	Suture of blood vessels; transplant of organs
1913	Charles Richet	(1850–1935)	French	Body reactions to foreign proteins
1914	Robert Bárány	(1876–1936)	Austrian	Methods of diagnosing disorders of ear
1919	Jules Bordet	(1870–1961)	Belgian	Discoveries in immunity
1920	August Krogh	(1874–1949)	Danish	Work on function of capillaries
1922	Archibald V. Hill	(1886–1977)	English	Measurement of muscle-action heat
	Otto Meyerhof	(1884–1951)	German	Discoveries in muscle metabolism
1923	Sir Frederick G. Banting	(1891–1941)	Canadian	Discovery of insulin
	John J.R. MacLeod	(1876–1935)	Scottish	
1924	Willem Einthoven	(1860–1927)	Dutch	Invention of electrocardiograph
1926	Johannes Fibiger	(1867–1928)	Danish	Experimental cancer in rats
1927	Julius Wagner von Jauregg	(1857–1940)	Austrian	Fever therapy for paresis
1928	Charles Nicolle	(1866–1936)	French	Discoveries in epidemic typhus fever
1929	Christiaan Eijkman	(1858–1930)	Dutch	Discovery of vitamin B_1
	Sir Frederick G. Hopkins	(1861–1947)	English	Studies of growth-promoting vitamins
1930	Karl Landsteiner	(1868–1943)	American	Classification of human blood into groups
1931	Otto H. Warburg	(1883–1970)	German	Research on respiratory enzyme activity
1932	Sir Charles S. Sherrington	(1857–1952)	English	Neuron functions
	Edgar D. Adrian	(1889–1977)	English	
1933	Thomas H. Morgan	(1866–1945)	American	Role of heredity in genius
1934	George H. Whipple	(1878–1976)	American	Use of liver to treat anemia
	George R. Minot	(1885–1950)	American	
	William P. Murphy	(born 1892)	American	
1935	Hans Spemann	(1869–1941)	German	Cell differentiation in embryonic growth
1936	Sir Henry H. Dale	(1875–1968)	English	Chemical transmission of nerve impulses
	Otto Loewi	(1873–1961)	American	
1937	Albert Szent-Györgyi	(1893–1986)	American	Isolation of vitamin C (ascorbic acid); discoveries in biological combustion
1938	Corneille Heymans	(1892–1968)	Belgian	Roles of sinus and aorta in respiration
1939	Gerhard Domagk	(1895–1964)	German	First sulfa drug (accepted award 1947)
1943	Henrik Dam	(1895–1976)	Danish	Discovery of vitamin K
	Edward A. Doisy	(1893–1986)	American	Synthesis of vitamin K
1944	Joseph Erlanger	(1874–1965)	American	Studies of electric impulses carried by nerves
	Herbert S. Gasser	(1888–1963)	American	
1945	Sir Alexander Fleming	(1881–1955)	Scottish	Penicillin
	Ernst B. Chain	(1906–1979)	British	
	Baron Florey	(1898–1968)	British	
1946	Hermann J. Muller	(1890–1967)	American	Changes in genes by X rays
1947	Carl F. Cori	(1896–1984)	American	Process of converting starch into sugar and isolation of enzyme involved
	Gerty T. Cory	(1896–1957)	American	
	Bernardo A. Houssay	(1887–1971)	Argentine	Role of pituitary hormone
1948	Paul Müller	(1899–1965)	Swiss	Use of DDT as insecticide
1949	Walter R. Hess	(1881–1973)	Swiss	Discovery of control of organs by brain
	Egas Moniz	(1874–1955)	Portuguese	Prefrontal lobotomy, a brain operation
1950	Philip S. Hench	(1896–1965)	American	Application of cortisone to diseases
	Edward C. Kendall	(1886–1972)	American	Use of cortisone in clinical medicine
	Tadeus Reichstein	(born 1897)	Swiss	Synthesis of cortisone
1951	Max Theiler	(1899–1972)	South African	Yellow fever vaccine
1952	Selman A. Waksman	(1888–1973)	American	Discovery of streptomycin
1953	Sir Hans A. Krebs	(1900–1981)	British	Research in cell metabolism
	Fritz A. Lipmann	(1899–1986)	American	
1954	John F. Enders	(1897–1985)	American	Work on growth of polio virus for vaccine
	Thomas H. Weller	(born 1915)	American	
	Frederick C. Robbins	(born 1916)	American	
1955	Hugo Theorell	(1903–1982)	Swedish	Research on oxidation enzymes
1956	André F. Cournand	(born 1895)	American	Studies of the heart by catheterization
	Werner Forssmann	(1904–1979)	German	
	Dickinson W. Richards	(1895–1973)	American	

1957	Daniel Bovet	(born 1907)	Italian	Synthesis of curare; work in antihistamines
1958	George W. Beadle	(born 1903)	American	Studies in heredity
	Edward L. Tatum	(1909–1975)	American	
	Joshua Lederberg	(born 1925)	American	Research in bacterial genetics
1959	Severo Ochoa	(born 1905)	American	Syntheses of ribonucleic acid and deoxyribonucleic acid
	Arthur Kornberg	(born 1918)	American	(DNA)
1960	Sir Macfarlane Burnet	(1899–1985)	Australian	Theory of immunological tolerance of transplanted tissues
	Peter B. Medawar	(born 1915)	British	Proof of Burnet's theory
1961	Georg von Békésy	(1899–1972)	American	Research on mechanism of hearing
1962	Francis H.C. Crick	(born 1916)	British	Work on molecular structure of DNA
	James D. Watson	(born 1928)	American	
	Maurice H.F. Wilkins	(born 1916)	British	
1963	Sir John C. Eccles	(born 1903)	Australian	Research on functions of nervous system
	Alan L. Hodgkin	(born 1914)	English	
	Andrew F. Huxley	(born 1917)	English	
1964	Konrad E. Bloch	(born 1912)	American	Research on mechanism and regulation of cholesterol and
	Feodor Lynen	(1911–1979)	German	fatty acid metabolism
1965	François Jacob	(born 1920)	French	Discoveries in genetic control of enzyme and virus synthesis
	André Lwoff	(born 1902)	French	
	Jacques Monod	(1910–1976)	French	
1966	Charles B. Huggins	(born 1901)	American	Hormone treatment of prostate cancer
	Francis Peyton Rous	(1879–1970)	American	Discovery of tumor-inducing viruses
1967	Ragnar Granit	(born 1900)	Swedish	Discoveries concerning the eye's primary visual processes,
	Haldan K. Hartline	(1903–1983)	American	both chemical and physiological
	George Wald	(born 1906)	American	
1968	Robert W. Holley	(born 1922)	American	Explanation of heredity-controlling genetic code
	H. Gobind Khorana	(born 1922)	American	
	Marshall W. Nirenberg	(born 1927)	American	
1969	Max Delbrück	(1906–1981)	American	Discoveries regarding reproductive mechanism and genetic
	Alfred D. Hershey	(born 1908)	American	structure of viruses
	Salvador E. Luria	(born 1912)	American	
1970	Julius Axelrod	(born 1912)	American	Explorations of the chemistry of nerve impulse transmission
	Sir Bernard Katz	(born 1911)	English	
	Ulf von Euler	(1905–1983)	Swedish	
1971	Earl Sutherland, Jr.	(1916–1974)	American	Study of hormonal processes
1972	Gerald M. Edelman	(born 1929)	American	Separate studies on chemical structure of antibodies
	Rodney R. Porter	(1917–1985)	British	
1973	Karl von Frisch	(1886–1982)	Austrian	Studies of individual and social behavior patterns
	Konrad Zacharias Lorenz	(born 1903)	Austrian	
	Nikolaas (Niko) Tinbergen	(born 1907)	Dutch	
1974	Albert Claude	(1898–1983)	American	Discoveries in modern cell biology
	Christian de Duve	(born 1917)	Belgian	
	George Emil Palade	(born 1912)	American	
1975	David Baltimore	(born 1938)	American	Research into possible links between viruses and cancer
	Howard M. Temin	(born 1934)	American	
	Renato Dulbecco	(born 1914)	American	
1976	Baruch Samuel Blumberg	(born 1925)	American	Discoveries concerning new mechanisms for the origin and
	D. Carleton Gajdusek	(born 1923)	American	dissemination of infectious disease
1977	Roger Guillemin	(born 1924)	American	Research into role of the hypothalamus in regulation of the
	Andrew Schally	(born 1926)	American	endocrine system
	Rosalyn Sussman Yalow	(born 1921)	American	Work on radioimmunoassay development
1978	Werner Arber	(born 1929)	Swiss	Discovery of restriction enzymes and their application to
	Daniel Nathans	(born 1928)	American	problems of molecular genetics
	Hamilton O. Smith	(born 1931)	American	
1979	Allan MacLeod Cormack	(born 1924)	American	Development of computerized axial tomography (CAT)
	Godfrey Newbold Hounsfield	(born 1919)	British	scanner
1980	Baruj Benacerraf	(born 1920)	American	Work on genetically determined structures on the cell surface
	Jean Dausset	(born 1916)	French	that regulate immunological reactions
	George Snell	(born 1903)	American	
1981	Roger W. Sperry	(born 1913)	American	Studies of the functional specialization of the cerebral hemispheres
	David H. Hubel	(born 1926)	American	Discoveries concerning information processing in the visual
	Torsten N. Wiesel	(born 1924)	Swedish	system
1982	John R. Vane	(born 1927)	English	Research on prostaglandins
	Sune K. Bergström	(born 1916)	Swedish	
	Bengt I. Samuelsson	(born 1934)	Swedish	
1983	Barbara McClintock	(born 1902)	American	Discovery of mobile genetic elements ("jumping genes") in maize
1984	Niels Kaj Jerne	(born 1911)	British-Danish	Research on the development and control of the immune system
	Georges Köhler	(born 1946)	German	Research on immune system and production of monoclonal
	César Milstein	(born 1927)	Argentine	antibodies
1985	Michael Brown	(born 1941)	American	Research on cholesterol metabolism
	Joseph Goldstein	(born 1940)	American	
1986	Rita Levi-Montalcini	(born 1909)	American-Italian	Discovery and study of nerve growth factor
	Stanley Cohen	(born 1922)	American	

Literature

1901	Sully-Prudhomme	(1839–1907)	French	Poetry
1902	Theodor Mommsen	(1817–1903)	German	History, notably 'A History of Rome'
1903	Björnstjerne Björnson	(1832–1910)	Norwegian	Poetry
1904	Frédéric Mistral	(1830–1914)	French	Poetry, Provençal philology
	José Echegaray	(1832–1916)	Spanish	Dramas
1905	Henryk Sienkiewicz	(1846–1916)	Polish	Novels
1906	Giosuè Carducci	(1835–1907)	Italian	Poetry
1907	Rudyard Kipling	(1865–1936)	English	Poetry, novels, stories
1908	Rudolf C. Eucken	(1846–1926)	German	Philosophy
1909	Selma Lagerlöf	(1858–1940)	Swedish	Novels, tales
1910	Paul Heyse	(1830–1914)	German	Novels, short stories, dramas, poetry
1911	Maurice Maeterlinck	(1862–1949)	Belgian	Dramas
1912	Gerhart Hauptmann	(1862–1946)	German	Dramas
1913	Sir Rabindranath Tagore	(1861–1941)	Indian	Poetry
1915	Romain Rolland	(1866–1944)	French	Novels
1916	Verner von Heidenstam	(1859–1940)	Swedish	Poetry
1917	Karl Gjellerup	(1857–1919)	Danish	Poetry
	Henrik Pontoppidan	(1857–1943)	Danish	Novels
1919	Carl Spitteler	(1845–1924)	Swiss	'Olympian Spring', epic
1920	Knut Hamsun	(1859–1952)	Norwegian	'Growth of the Soil', novel
1921	Anatole France	(1844–1924)	French	Novels, short stories, essays
1922	Jacinto Benavente	(1866–1954)	Spanish	Dramas
1923	William Butler Yeats	(1865–1939)	Irish	Poetry
1924	Ladislas S. Reymont	(1868–1925)	Polish	'The Peasants', novel
1925	George Bernard Shaw	(1856–1950)	Irish	Dramas
1926	Grazia Deledda	(1875–1936)	Italian	Novels
1927	Henri Bergson	(1859–1941)	French	Philosophy
1928	Sigrid Undset	(1882–1949)	Norwegian	Novels
1929	Thomas Mann	(1875–1955)	German	'Buddenbrooks', novel
1930	Sinclair Lewis	(1885–1951)	American	Novels
1931	Erik A. Karlfeldt	(1864–1931)	Swedish	Poetry (posthumous award)
1932	John Galsworthy	(1867–1933)	English	Novels, notably 'The Forsyte Saga'
1933	Ivan A. Bunin	(1870–1953)	Russian	Novels, short stories
1934	Luigi Pirandello	(1867–1936)	Italian	Dramas
1936	Eugene O'Neill	(1888–1953)	American	Dramas
1937	Roger Martin du Gard	(1881–1958)	French	'Les Thibaults', novel-cycle
1938	Pearl S. Buck	(1892–1973)	American	Novels, biographies
1939	Frans E. Sillanpää	(1888–1964)	Finnish	Novels
1944	Johannes V. Jensen	(1873–1950)	Danish	Novels
1945	Gabriela Mistral	(1889–1957)	Chilean	Poetry
1946	Hermann Hesse	(1877–1962)	Swiss	Novels, poetry
1947	André Gide	(1869–1951)	French	Novels
1948	T. S. Eliot	(1888–1965)	British	Poetry
1949	William Faulkner	(1897–1962)	American	Novels
1950	Bertrand Russell	(1872–1970)	English	Philosophy
1951	Pär Fabian Lagerkvist	(1891–1974)	Swedish	Poetry
1952	François Mauriac	(1885–1970)	French	Novels
1953	Sir Winston Churchill	(1874–1965)	English	History and biography, speeches
1954	Ernest Hemingway	(1899–1961)	American	Novels, notably 'The Old Man and the Sea'
1955	Halldor Laxness	(born 1902)	Icelandic	Novels
1956	Juan Ramón Jiménez	(1881–1958)	Spanish	Poetry
1957	Albert Camus	(1913–1960)	French	Novels, dramas
1958	Boris Pasternak	(1890–1960)	Russian	Poetry, novels (award declined)
1959	Salvatore Quasimodo	(1901–1968)	Italian	Poetry
1960	Saint-John Perse	(1887–1975)	French	Poetry
1961	Ivo Andric	(1892–1975)	Yugoslavian	Novels, notably 'The Bridge on the Drina'
1962	John Steinbeck	(1902–1968)	American	Novels
1963	Giorgos S. Seferiades	(1900–1971)	Greek	Poetry
1964	Jean Paul Sartre	(1905–1980)	French	Philosophy, novels, dramas (award declined)
1965	Mikhail A. Sholokhov	(1905–1984)	Russian	Novels, notably 'And Quiet Flows the Don'
1966	Shmuel Yosef Agnon	(1888–1970)	Israeli	Novels, short stories
	Nelly Sachs	(1891–1970)	Swedish	Poetry, dramas
1967	Miguel Angel Asturias	(1899–1974)	Guatemalan	Novels, legends, poetry
1968	Yasunari Kawabata	(1899–1972)	Japanese	Novels
1969	Samuel Beckett	(born 1906)	Irish	Dramas, novels, poetry
1970	Alexander I. Solzhenitsyn	(born 1918)	Russian	Novels
1971	Pablo Neruda	(1904–1973)	Chilean	Poetry
1972	Heinrich T. Böll	(1917–1985)	German	Novels
1973	Patrick White	(born 1912)	Australian	Novels
1974	Eyvind Johnson	(1900–1976)	Swedish	Novels
	Harry Martinson	(1904–1978)	Swedish	Poetry, novels, essays
1975	Eugenio Montale	(1896–1981)	Italian	Poetry
1976	Saul Bellow	(born 1915)	American	Novels
1977	Vicente Aleixandre	(1898–1984)	Spanish	Poetry
1978	Isaac Bashevis Singer	(born 1904)	American	Novels, short stories, in Yiddish
1979	Odysseus Elytis	(born 1911)	Greek	Poetry
1980	Czeslaw Milosz	(born 1911)	American	Poetry, in Polish
1981	Elias Canetti	(born 1905)	British	Novel, plays, in German
1982	Gabriel García Marquez	(born 1928)	Colombian	'One Hundred Years of Solitude', novel
1983	William Golding	(born 1911)	English	Novels
1984	Jaroslav Seifert	(born 1901)	Czech	Poetry
1985	Claude Simon	(born 1913)	French	Novels
1986	Wole Soyinka	(born 1934)	African	Dramas, poetry

Peace

1901	Jean H. Dunant	(1828–1910)	Swiss	Founder, Red Cross
	Frédéric Passy	(1822–1912)	French	Founder, first French peace society
1902	Élie Ducommun	(1833–1906)	Swiss	Lectures and writings to promote peace
	Charles A. Gobat	(1843–1914)	Swiss	Activities in peace organizations
1903	Sir William R. Cremer	(1838–1908)	English	Founder, International Arbitration League
1904	Institute of International Law, Ghent	....	....	Studies on neutrality
1905	Baroness von Suttner	(1843–1914)	Austrian	'Lay Down Your Arms', novel
1906	Theodore Roosevelt	(1858–1919)	American	Negotiating peace in Russo-Japanese War
1907	Ernesto T. Moneta	(1833–1918)	Italian	President, Lombard League for Peace
	Louis Renault	(1843–1918)	French	Member, Hague Court
1908	Klas P. Arnoldson	(1844–1916)	Swedish	Founder, Swedish peace society
	Fredrik Bajer	(1837–1922)	Danish	President, Permanent International Peace Bureau
1909	Auguste M.F. Beernaert	(1829–1912)	Belgian	Member, Hague Court
	Baron d'Estournelles de Constant de Rebecque	(1852–1924)	French	Founder, peace groups
1910	Permanent International Peace Bureau, Berne	....	....	Efforts toward international arbitration
1911	Tobias M.C. Asser	(1838–1913)	Dutch	Originator, International Conferences of Private Law
	Alfred H. Fried	(1864–1921)	Austrian	Founder, German pacifist periodical
1912	Elihu Root	(1845–1937)	American	Settlement between U.S. and Japan over Japanese immigration to California
1913	Henri la Fontaine	(1854–1943)	Belgian	President, Permanent International Peace Bureau
1917	International Committee of the Red Cross, Geneva	....	....	World War I services
1919	Woodrow Wilson	(1856–1924)	American	Founder, League of Nations
1920	Léon V.A. Bourgeois	(1851–1925)	French	President, Council of League of Nations
1921	Karl H. Branting	(1860–1925)	Swedish	Work supporting Wilson peace program
	Christian L. Lange	(1869–1938)	Norwegian	Secretary-general, Inter-Parliamentary Union
1922	Fridtjof Nansen	(1861–1930)	Norwegian	Relief work for Russian refugees
1925	Sir Austen Chamberlain	(1863–1937)	British	Negotiating Locarno Pact
	Charles G. Dawes	(1865–1951)	American	Dawes Plan for payment of German reparations
1926	Aristide Briand	(1862–1932)	French	Chief architect, Locarno Pact and Kellogg-Briand Pact
	Gustav Stresemann	(1878–1929)	German	Achieving Germany's cooperation with reparations and peace effort
1927	Ferdinand Buisson	(1841–1932)	French	President, League of Human Rights
	Ludwig Quidde	(1858–1941)	German	Pacifist writings; founder, Munich peace society
1929	Frank B. Kellogg	(1856–1937)	American	Coauthor, Kellogg-Briand Pact
1930	Nathan Söderblom	(1866–1931)	Swedish	Efforts toward international peace and unification of churches
1931	Jane Addams	(1860–1935)	American	President, Women's International League for Peace and Freedom
	Nicholas Murray Butler	(1862–1947)	American	President, Carnegie Endowment for International Peace
1933	Sir Norman Angell	(1874–1967)	English	'The Great Illusion', on futility of war; work with various peace groups
1934	Arthur Henderson	(1863–1935)	British	President, World Disarmament Conference
1935	Carl von Ossietzky	(1889–1938)	German	Journalistic writings promoting peace
1936	Carlos Saavedra Lamas	(1878–1959)	Argentine	Mediation of Bolivia-Paraguay Chaco War
1937	Viscount Cecil of Chelwood	(1864–1958)	British	Coauthor, League of Nations Covenant; founder, International Peace Campaign
1938	Nansen International Office for Refugees, Geneva	....	....	Relief work for Russian, German refugees
1944	International Committee of the Red Cross, Geneva	....	....	World War II services
1945	Cordell Hull	(1871–1955)	American	Role in organizing UN
1946	Emily G. Balch	(1867–1961)	American	Work with Women's International League for Peace and Freedom
	John R. Mott	(1865–1955)	American	Organizing foreign YMCA and missionary groups
1947	The Friends Service Council, London; The American Friends Service Committee, Philadelphia	....	....	Relief activities
1949	Baron Boyd-Orr	(1880–1971)	Scottish	Recommending methods of abolishing food scarcities
1950	Ralph J. Bunche	(1904–1971)	American	Achieving armistice in Palestine conflict
1951	Léon Jouhaux	(1879–1954)	French	Working for peace through trade-union movement and international groups
1952	Albert Schweitzer	(1875–1965)	French	Founder, Lambaréné Hospital in Africa
1953	George C. Marshall	(1880–1959)	American	Marshall Plan for European recovery
1954	Office of UN High Commissioner for Refugees, Geneva	....	....	Emergency aid and protection to refugees
1957	Lester B. Pearson	(1897–1972)	Canadian	President, UN General Assembly; role in settling Suez crisis
1958	Georges Pire	(1910–1969)	Belgian	Organizing European refugee villages
1959	Philip J. Noel-Baker	(1889–1982)	British	A founder, League of Nations and UN
1960	Albert J. Luthuli	(1898–1967)	South African	Fight against racial discrimination
1961	Dag Hammarskjöld	(1905–1961)	Swedish	Secretary-general, UN (posthumous award)
1962	Linus C. Pauling	(born 1901)	American	Fight against atomic testing
1963	International Committee of the Red Cross and League of Red Cross Societies	....	....	Work to alleviate suffering throughout world

1964	Martin Luther King, Jr.	(1929–1968)	American	Nonviolent civil rights activities
1965	UNICEF	....	....	Worldwide help for children
1968	René Cassin	(1887–1976)	French	Defense of human rights
1969	International Labor Organization (ILO)	....	....	Service on international scale for 50 years
1970	Norman E. Borlaug	(born 1914)	American	Development of high-yield strains of cereal grains
1971	Willy Brandt	(born 1913)	German	Efforts toward normal relations between West Germany and Eastern Europe
1973	Henry A. Kissinger	(born 1923)	American	Negotiation of Vietnam cease-fire agreement (award declined by Tho)
	Le Duc Tho	(born 1911)	Vietnamese	
1974	Eisaku Sato	(1901–1975)	Japanese	Work toward nonproliferation of nuclear weapons
	Sean MacBride	(born 1904)	Irish	Work on behalf of human rights
1975	Andrei Sakharov	(born 1921)	Russian	Efforts against violence and brutality
1976	Mairead Corrigan	(born 1944)	Irish	Founders of movement to end violence in Northern Ireland (award conferred in 1977)
	Betty Williams	(born 1943)	Irish	
1977	Amnesty International	....	....	Work on behalf of political prisoners
1978	Menachem Begin	(born 1913)	Israeli	Efforts toward settlement of Arab-Israeli conflict
	Anwar el-Sadat	(1918–1981)	Egyptian	
1979	Mother Teresa	(born 1910)	Yugoslav	Work with the poor in India
1980	Adolfo Pérez Esquivel	(born 1931)	Argentine	Human-rights leadership of Service for Peace and Justice in Latin America
1981	Office of UN High Commissioner for Refugees, Geneva	....	....	Aid to refugees, including exiles, particularly in relations between nations
1982	Alva Myrdal	(1902–1986)	Swedish	Efforts toward disarmament
	García Robles	(born 1911)	Mexican	
1983	Lech Walesa	(born 1943)	Polish	Role in ensuring workers' right to establish their own organizations
1984	Desmond Tutu	(born 1931)	South African	Role in nonviolent struggle against apartheid in South Africa
1985	International Physicians for the Prevention of Nuclear War	....	....	Advocation of an unequivocal end to nuclear explosions
1986	Elie Wiesel	(born 1928)	American	Dedication to peace, atonement, and human dignity

Economic Sciences

1969	Ragnar Frisch	(1895–1973)	Norwegian	Work in econometrics, the use of mathematical models to analyze economic data
	Jan Tinbergen	(born 1903)	Dutch	
1970	Paul A. Samuelson	(born 1915)	American	Raising the level of scientific analysis in economic theory
1971	Simon Kuznets	(1901–1985)	American	Development of Gross National Product as measure of economic output
1972	Kenneth J. Arrow	(born 1921)	American	Contributions to general economic equilibrium theory and welfare theory
	John R. Hicks	(born 1904)	British	
1973	Wassily Leontief	(born 1906)	Russian	Development of input-output method of economic analysis
1974	Friedrich von Hayek	(born 1899)	Austrian	Pioneering analysis of the interdependence of economic, social, and institutional phenomena
	Gunnar Myrdal	(1898–1987)	Swedish	
1975	Tjalling C. Koopmans	(born 1910)	American	Contributions to the theory of optimum allocation of resources
	Leonid V. Kantorovich	(born 1912)	Russian	
1976	Milton Friedman	(born 1912)	American	Achievements in the fields of consumption analysis and monetary theory
1977	James Meade	(born 1907)	English	Pioneering contributions to international trade theory
	Bertil Ohlin	(1899–1979)	Swedish	
1978	Herbert A. Simon	(born 1916)	American	Pioneering research in the decision-making process within economic organizations
1979	Sir Arthur Lewis	(born 1915)	British	Work on the economic problems of developing nations
	Theodore Schultz	(born 1902)	American	
1980	Lawrence R. Klein	(born 1920)	American	Creation of econometric models and their application to the analysis of economic fluctuations and economic policies
1981	James Tobin	(born 1918)	American	Analysis of financial behavior
1982	George J. Stigler	(born 1911)	American	Analysis of government intervention in markets
1983	Gerard Debreu	(born 1921)	American	Research in how prices operate to balance supply with demand
1984	Sir Richard Stone	(born 1913)	English	Development of uniform system of national accounting
1985	Franco Modigliani	(born 1918)	American	Theories of savings and of corporate finance
1986	James M. Buchanan	(born 1919)	American	New methods for the analysis of economic and political decision making

cricket C-767
dragonfly D-239, *picture* D-238
metamorphosis M-312

Nymphaeaceae. *see in index* Water lily family

Nymphalidae, or **brush-footed butterfly,** family of butterflies B-528

Nyssaceae, plant family of trees and shrubs. *see in index* Tupelo

Nystad, Peace of (1721), treaty between Russia and Sweden, signed at Nystad, a small port on Gulf of Bothnia P-226, S-527, *table* T-274

Nystagmus, involuntary, rhythmical eye movement; sometimes congenital; causes include poor vision, ear disorders, brain lesions, and damage to the nerves that control eye muscles B-205

Nytril, fiber classification
synthetic fibers, *table* F-72

Nyx, in Greek mythology, goddess of night (Roman Nox), daughter of Chaos and mother of Charon.

The letter O

probably started as a picture sign of an eye, as in Egyptian hieroglyphic writing (1) and in a very early Semitic writing which was used about 1500 B.C. on the Sinai Peninsula (2). About 1000 B.C., in Byblos and other Phoenician and Canaanite centers, the sign was given a circular form (3), the source of all later forms. In the Semitic languages the sign was called *ayin,* meaning "eye." It had a pharyngeal sound which is not found in the English language.

The Greeks took over the form of the *ayin* sign (4). They had no use for the sound in their language, so they used it for the vowel "o." They changed the name to *omicron,* meaning "short o," as distinguished from the sign *omega* (5), meaning "long o," which they introduced into their writing and placed at the end of their alphabet.

The Romans made the form oval, which has come unchanged into English. The small "o" is distinguished from the capital O only by size (6).

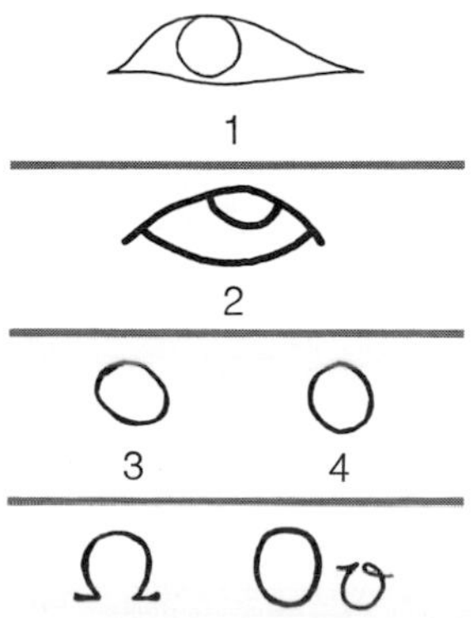

OAAU (Organization of Afro-American Unity) M-74
Oahe Dam, South Dakota, on Missouri River S-323, *maps* S-334, 323, *picture* S-322
Oahu, Hawaiian island; 608 sq mi (1,575 sq km); pop. 762,534 H-59, *maps* H-58, U-98, 117. *see also in index* Honolulu
  Pacific Ocean, *map* P-6
Oak, a hardwood tree of the Fagaceae family O-452
  leaf transpiration P-359
  wasp W-74
  water W-89
  wood, *table* W-283
Oak Creek, Nebraska N-95, 98
Oak Creek, Wis., city on Lake Michigan 11 mi (18 km) s. of Milwaukee; concrete and electronics products; truck farming; pop. 16,932.
Oak Creek Canyon, Arizona, *picture* U-84
  Chapel of the Rocks, *picture* A-607
Oak Forest, Ill., village 20 mi (30 km) s.w. of Chicago; chiefly residential, truck farms; pop. 26,096
  Illinois, *map* I-53
Oak Island, island, Nova Scotia N-397
Oakland, Calif., city on San Francisco Bay opposite San Francisco; pop. 351,898 O-453
  bridge to San Francisco B-324
  North America, *map* N-351
Oakland, N.J., residential borough 4 mi (6 km) n.w. of Wyckoff; nurseries, truck farms; pop. 13,443.
Oakland Park, Fla., city 4 mi (6 km) n. of Fort Lauderdale; residential; light industry; incorporated 1929; pop. 21,939.
Oak Lawn, Ill., residential village just s.w. of Chicago; incorporated 1909; pop. 60,590
  Illinois, *map* I-53
Oakley, Annie (born Phoebe Anne Oakley Moses) (1860–1926), U.S. sharpshooter O-453
Oakley, Slivers (or Frank Oakley), U.S. clown C-436
Oakley, Violet (1874–1961), U.S. painter, born in New York City; studied in U.S. and Paris, France; did murals for the State Capitol at Harrisburg, Pa.
Oak Park, Ill., village just w. of Chicago, incorporated 1902; some homes designed by Frank Lloyd Wright; birthplace of Ernest Hemingway; pop. 54,887, *map* I-53
Oak Park, Mich., city just n.w. of Detroit; automobile parts, tools and dies; pop. 31,537.
Oak Ridge, Tenn., city 17 mi (27 km) w. of Knoxville; created as federal area during World War II; war pop. reached 75,000; tool and die industry, electronic and nuclear instruments; Oak Ridge Operations Office, including National Laboratory, Institute of Nuclear Studies, and American Museum of Atomic Energy; branch of University of Tennessee; pop. 27,662, *map* U-41
  plutonium plant P-394
  Tennessee T-85, *picture* T-82, *map* T-97
Oak Ridge Boys, U.S. country music group M-679
Oak Ridge National Laboratory, energy research center, Knoxville, Tenn. K-265
Oakum, loosely twisted hemp or jute fiber impregnated with tar used in caulking seams and packing joints
  nuts N-449
Oakville, Ont., town on Lake Ontario 22 mi (35 km) s.w. of Toronto; automobiles; pop. 75,773.
Oakwood, Ohio, city just s. of Dayton; incorporated as village 1907, city 1930; pop. 9,372.
Oakwood College, Huntsville, Ala.; affiliated with Seventh-day Adventist church; founded 1896; liberal arts.
OAO (Orbiting Astronomical Observatory), U.S. scientific satellite, *table* S-344
Oar, instrument used for propelling or steering a boat R-300
  boating B-326
  naval galley ships N-80
  ships S-163
Oarfish, fish F-124
OAS. *see in index* Organization of American States
Oasis, fertile spot in a desert O-454
  desert D-106
  Egypt E-115
  Sahara S-14
  Saudi Arabia S-52b
  Syria, *picture* S-549b
Oastler, Richard (1789–1861), English reformer, born in Leeds; energetic advocate of the factory workers' cause.
Oates, Joyce Carol (born 1938), U.S. author, born in Lockport, N.Y.; professor of English at University of Detroit 1961–67, University of Windsor 1967–; writer-in-residence Princeton University, 1978–; O. Henry Prize Story Award 1967 for 'In the Region of Ice'; National Book Award 1970 for 'Them' ('Wonderland'; 'Do With Me What You Will'; 'The Assassins'; poems, essays, plays, short stories).
Oates, Lawrence Edward Grace (1880–1912), English army officer and polar explorer with Robert Falcon Scott, born in London S-72
Oates, Titus (1649–1705), English conspirator who falsely accused Roman Catholics of a Popish Plot (1678–80) to restore Catholicism; born in Oakham, England.
Oath (or pledge)
  feudalism F-69, *picture* F-68
  Freeman's Oath V-288
  Oath of the Tennis Court F-401
  United States' president P-492
Oatmeal, a cereal B-433
Oats
  flour B-428, F-213
  grains G-207
  grasses G-236
  harvesting, *picture* F-26
  hay H-75
  rusts and smuts R-363
  starch content S-424
OAU. *see in index* Organization of African Unity
Oaxaca, Mexico, state in s., on Pacific; 36,820 sq mi (95,360 sq km); cap. Oaxaca (de Juárez); gold, silver; corn, wheat, coffee, fruit; pop. 2,337,345
  Mexico M-323, *picture* M-329, *map* M-344
Oaxaca (de Juárez), Mexico, industrial city in beautiful Oaxaca Valley, 225 mi (360 km) s.e. of Mexico City; capital of Oaxaca state; formerly Huaxyacac, Aztec military post; pop. 72,370
  Mexico, *map* M-344
  North America, *map* N-351
Obadiah (6th century BC), Hebrew minor prophet, author of the 31st book of the Old Testament, which denounces Edomites.
Obaku, one of three Zen Buddhist sects in Japan; close to the Rinzai tradition except for its emphasis on invoking the name of Buddha Z-450
Obbligato, in music, *list* M-671
Obed, son of Ruth and Boaz in the Bible's Old Testament R-365
Obedience trials, dog show D-210
Obelisk, a four-sided tapering shaft with a pyramidal top; a favorite form of monument of the ancient Egyptians
  Obelisk of Luxor, Paris, France P-122
  Vatican City, *map* V-269
  Washington Monument. *see in index* Washington Monument
Oberammergau, West Germany, village 43 mi (69 km) s.w. of Munich; pop. 4,772 O-455, *map* G-134
  Passion Play B-111
  hobby H-182
Oberhausen, West Germany, city just w. of Essen; foundries, metal refineries; boilers, chemicals, glass; pop. 246,736, *map* G-134
Oberhoffer, Emil (1867–1933), U.S. musician, born in Munich, Germany; organizer and conductor (1903–22) of Minneapolis Symphony Orchestra.
Oberkampf, Christophe-Philippe (1738–1815), German textile printer, born in Bavaria; learned how to print cloth from carved rolls; 1768 started plant at Jouy, near Paris, France; plant destroyed in 1815
  wallpaper W-9
Oberlin, Johann Friedrich (1740–1826), Alsatian Lutheran clergyman, born in Strasbourg, France; improved industry, agriculture, education, roads; Oberlin, Ohio, named for him K-241
Oberlin College, Oberlin, Ohio; founded 1833; private control; first coeducational college in U.S.; arts and sciences, education, music, theology; graduate study O-504
  educational influence E-92
Oberon, character in English folklore, king of the fairies; Titania is his queen.
'Oberon', work by Weber W-129
Oberth, Hermann (born 1894), German mathematician and physicist, born present Sibiu, Romania; rocket expert for U.S. Army 1955–58; noted as Father of Astronautics; pioneer works are basis for most later books on rocket technique ('Man into Space') S-341d
Obesity, excessive bodily fat
  exercise E-371
  fatigue F-46
  food and nutrition F-279
    malnutrition M-77
  health H-84
  weight control W-135
Ob', Gulf of, estuary of Ob' River O-455
  Asia, *map* A-700
Object, in grammar S-110, P-507
Objective, in optics, the lens in an optical system nearest the object viewed O-381
Oblate, sphere which is slightly flattened at the poles
  hemisphere H-126
Oblate College, Washington, D.C.; Roman Catholic; for men; founded 1916; liberal arts, theology; graduate study.
Oblique triangle, in geometry G-74, *chart* G-74, *diagram* G-74
Oboe (or hautboy), woodwind musical instrument R-121
  orchestra O-576
  wind instruments W-226
Obolus, modern Greek unit of weight, equal to 1.54 grains or 0.1 gram (metric); in ancient times, equal to 11.0 grains or 0.71 gram, *table* W-141
OBO (oil-bulk-ore ship) T-254
Obote, Milton (full name Apollo Milton Obote) (born 1924), former president of Uganda O-455
  Amin A-370
  Nyerere N-450
  Uganda U-1
O'Boyle, Patrick Aloysius, Cardinal (1896–1987), U.S. Roman Catholic prelate, born in Scranton, Pa.; archbishop of Washington, D.C., 1948–73; became cardinal 1967.
Obregón, Alvaro (1880–1928), Mexican general and president of Mexico, born in Alamos, Sonora M-337, *picture* M-338
Obrenovitch (or Obrenović), ruling Serbian family; held power (not continuously) from accession of Milosh Obrenovitch (Miloş Obrenović) in 1813 to assassination of Alexander (1903) S-113
Obrenovitch, Milosh (or Milosch Obrenovitch, or Miloş Obrenović) (1780–1860), prince of Serbia, born a peasant; for services in freeing Serbia from Turkish rule called "father of his country" S-113
  Yugoslavia Y-437
O'Brien, Edna (born 1936), Irish author I-328
O'Brien, Edward Joseph Harrington (1890–1941), U.S. editor and anthologist, born in Boston, Mass.; editor of annual 'Best Short Stories' 1915–40 and 'Best British Short Stories' 1921–40.
O'Brien, Flann. *see in index* O'Nolan, Brian
O'Brien, Lawrence Francis (born 1917), U.S. government official, born in Springfield, Mass.; presidential special assistant for Congressional relations and personnel 1961–65; U.S. postmaster general 1965–68; head of Democratic National Committee 1968, 1970–72; managed presidential campaigns of John F. Kennedy, Lyndon B. Johnson, Hubert H. Humphrey, and George S. McGovern.
O'Brien, Robert Carroll (1922–73), U.S. author, born in New York, N.Y.; awarded 1972 John Newbery Medal for 'Mrs. Frisby and the Rats of NIMH' ('Silver Crown'; 'A Report from Group 17').
Ob' River, great navigable river of w. Siberia; 2,268 mi (3,650 km) long O-455, *map* R-346
  Asia, *map* A-700
  length, comparative. *see in index* River, *table*
'Obscene Bird of the Night, The', work by Donoso L-70
Obscenity P-451
'Observations', work by Moore M-581
Observatory O-456. *see also in index* Kitt Peak National Observatory; Mount Wilson Observatory; Palomar Observatory; Radio astronomy; Telescope
  Saturn photographed, *picture* S-52
'Observer, The', London newspaper A-707
Obsidian, a glasslike lava used as an ornamental stone, *picture* R-229a
  gem usage J-116
  minerals M-437
  prehistoric tools M-84
Obstetrics, medical specialty H-280, *table* M-277
  women's rights W-273

Obtuse angle, in mathematics
  geometry G-73, *diagram* G-73

Obtuse triangle, in
  mathematics
  geometry G-74, *chart* G-74

Ocala, Fla., city about 70 mi (110 km) s.w. of St. Augustine; citrus fruit, cattle industry; lumber products; limerock mining; horse and dog raising; pop. 37,170.

Ocampo, Victoria (1891–1979), Argentine writer, born in Buenos Aires; educated in France; founded literary review *Sur* 1931; known as Argentina's "queen of letters".

'O Canada', Canadian national anthem N-66

'O Canada, terre de nous aïeux', Canadian national anthem N-66

Ocarina (or sweet potato), simple wind instrument having finger holes and mouthpiece and made of terra cotta or metal; tones soft and hollow; name from *oca* (Italian for 'goose') because of similar shape.

O'Casey, Sean (original name John Casey) (1880–1964), Irish playwright, born in the slums of Dublin; a laborer, self-taught, he won wide praise for the theatrical skill, keen humor, and merciless realism of his plays; autobiography, 'Mirror in My House'; essays, 'Under a Colored Cap' I-328, *picture* I-326
  drama D-246

Occam, William of. *see in index* Ockham, William of

Occidental College, Los Angeles, Calif.; private control; founded 1887 by Presbyterians; now non-sectarian; liberal arts; graduate studies.

Occipital bone, in cranium S-210

Occluded front, cold front overtaking a warm front W-118, *map* W-124, *diagram* W-119

Occlusion, in dentistry T-52

Occultation, in astronomy A-731
  eclipse E-19
  natural satellites S-52

Occultism
  Yeats Y-412

Occupational Safety and Health Act (1970), U.S. legislation
  labor movements L-10

Occupational Safety and Health Administration (OSHA), U.S. Department of Labor U-164
  industrial hazard protection I-175
  labor and industrial law L-5

Occupational Safety and Health Review Commission, United States U-166

Occupational therapy T-165, V-366, *pictures* T-166, V-367
  hospital care H-282
  medicine M-276
  rehabilitation D-183
    disability D-163

Occupations. *see in index* Vocations

Ocean O-459. *see also in index* Oceanography. For list of oceans, *see table* following
  algae A-283
  atmosphere A-747
  continental structure C-691
  deep-sea life D-59
  earth E-13
  fish F-124
  frontiers F-427, *picture* F-424
  geography G-62
  inner space navigation N-73
  measurement
    hydrographic surveying S-520
    sound waves S-261
  mines and mining M-425
    petroleum P-230, P-238, *picture* P-239
  naval exploration N-89
  storms S-457
  water W-85
  waterpower W-104

Oceanarium. *see in index* Aquarium

Ocean basin (or ocean floor) O-460, *diagram* O-461

Ocean City, Md., city on the Atlantic seaboard; pop. 4,946 M-170

Ocean currents. *see also in index* currents by name, as Labrador Current; Peru Current
  Arabian Sea A-525
  Atlantic Ocean A-745
  atmosphere A-747
  Black Sea B-307
  climate control C-497
  oceanography O-475, *pictures* O-476, 477

Ocean Grove, N.J., village on Atlantic Ocean 6 mi (10 km) s. of Long Branch; controlled by Ocean Grove Camp Meeting Association (Methodist); pop. 7,000; summer pop. 20,000 to 30,000.

Oceania (or Oceanica), islands of Pacific Ocean; area 42,000 sq mi (109,000 sq km) O-465. *see also in index* chief islands and groups by name
  illiteracy P-450
  Pacific Ocean P-7

OCEANS AND OTHER BODIES OF WATER IN THE WORLD

	Area		*Mean Depth*		*Maximum Depth*		*Volume*	
I. Oceans	*sq mi*	*sq km*	*ft*	*m*	*ft*	*m*	*cu mi*	*cu km*
Pacific Ocean	63,801,600	165,245,400	14,052	4,283	35,800	10,900	169,749,500	707,549,900
Atlantic Ocean	31,830,700	82,441,100	12,874	3,924	27,498	8,381	77,609,600	323,492,300
Indian Ocean	28,356,200	73,442,200	13,002	3,963	26,400	8,050	69,821,000	291,027,900
Arctic Ocean	5,440,200	14,090,100	3,954	1,205	17,899	5,456	4,073,700	16,980,000
Total	129,428,700	335,218,800					321,253,800	1,339,050,100

The waters around the Antarctic Continent to the outer limit of icebergs, called by some geographers the Antarctic Ocean, are considered part of the Pacific, Atlantic, and Indian oceans, and add more than 24,000,000 square miles (62,000,000 square kilometers) to their total area. Greatest depth of these waters is 28,152 feet (8,581 meters).

II. Seas, Bays, Gulfs, and Channels	*sq mi*	*sq km*	*ft*	*m*	*ft*	*m*	*cu mi*	*cu km*
Malay Seas	2,248,600	5,823,800	3,401	1,037	13,422	4,091	1,440,000	6,030,100
Barents Sea	942,600	2,441,300	512	156	1,803	550	91,200	380,100
South China Sea	895,400	2,319,100	5,419	1,652	14,250	4,340	920,000	3,834,700
Bering Sea	878,000	2,274,000	4,716	1,437	13,260	4,040	784,100	3,268,300
Mediterranean Sea	843,000	2,183,400	5,383	1,641	15,240	4,640	859,000	3,580,500
Caribbean Sea	756,000	1,958,000	8,669	2,642	23,748	7,238	1,241,500	5,174,800
Gulf of Mexico	618,200	1,601,100	4,874	1,486	12,750	3,890	570,700	2,378,800
Sea of Okhotsk	589,800	1,527,600	2,748	838	11,154	3,400	306,800	1,278,800
East China Sea	482,300	1,249,200	618	188	14,250	4,340	56,400	235,100
Hudson Bay (greater)	475,800	1,232,300	420	128	2,886	880	37,900	158,000
Sea of Japan	389,100	1,007,800	4,428	1,350	12,180	3,710	326,500	1,360,900
Andaman Sea	308,000	797,700	2,856	871	14,445	4,400	166,500	694,000
Yucatán Channel and Gulf of Honduras	293,600	760,400	8,708	2,654	{ 6,857 16,259	2,090 4,956	484,400	2,019,100
North Sea	190,000	492,100	312	95	2,172	662	11,200	46,700
Red Sea	169,100	437,000	1,500	460	7,740	2,360	48,000	200,100
Baltic Sea (including Kattegat)	163,000	422,200	180	55	1,382	421	5,500	22,900
Black Sea	162,100	419,800	4,018	1,225	7,382	2,250	123,400	514,400
Caspian Sea	143,500	371,700	591	180	3,224	983	19,000	79,200
Persian Gulf	92,200	238,800	200	60	320	98	3,500	14,600
Gulf of St. Lawrence	91,800	237,800	420	128	1,770	540	7,200	30,000
Aegean Sea	69,100	179,000	1,912	583	7,370	2,250	25,100	104,600
Gulf of California	62,600	162,100	2,670	814	8,576	2,614	31,700	132,100
Adriatic Sea	51,000	132,100	794	242	5,200	1,600	7,700	32,100
Irish Sea	39,900	103,300	197	60	638	194	1,500	6,200
English Channel	29,000	75,100	177	54	566	172	900	3,800
Aral Sea	25,000	64,700	52	16	244	74	200	800
Sea of Azov	16,200	42,000	33	10	49	15	100	400
Sea of Marmara	3,200	8,300	1,027	313	4,258	1,298	600	2,500
Total	11,028,100	28,561,700					7,579,200	31,591,500
Total for the World	140,456,800	363,780,500					328,833,000	1,370,641,600

Note. The figures for each body of water exclude those of adjoining waters if the latter are named in the table. For example, the figures for the Mediterranean Sea do *not* include the Adriatic Sea or the Aegean Sea, but they *do* include the so-called Ionian Sea and Tyrrhenian Sea, which are not listed here. For the waters included in Malay Seas, *see in index* Malay Seas.

Oceanic bonito (or skipjack), variety of tuna *Thunnus pelamis* T-306
Oceanic climate (or maritime temperate), weather condition
France F-344
Oceanic island, in geology I-368
Oceania O-466
Ocean Island (or Banaba), island in Pacific Ocean, s. of equator, between Gilbert Islands and Nauru; belongs to Kiribati; phosphate deposits; area 2 sq mi (5 sq km); pop. 2,314, *map* P-6
Ocean liner S-168, *picture* S-303. *see also in index* Ships
Californian S-177d
Carpathia S-177e
France S-168
Lusitania. see in index 'Lusitania'
Mauretania S-177f
Queen Elizabeth 2 S-168
Titanic S-177d, I-8, *picture* S-177e
United States S-168, *diagram* S-169, *picture* S-169
Ocean marine insurance I-235
Ocean mining M-426
ocean O-460
Ocean of Storms. *see in index* Oceanus Procellarum
Oceanography (also called oceanology) O-473
Cousteau C-749
earth sciences E-41
exploration E-377
inner space navigation N-73
ocean O-460
research submarines S-500
U.S. Navy N-89
Ocean perch (or redfish, or rosefish, or Norway haddock), fish *Sevastes marinus* of the Scorpaenidae family O-486
fish, *picture* F-132, *table* F-137
Ocean routes (or sea routes) T-257, *map* T-259
Oceanside, Calif., city 35 mi (55 km) n.w. of San Diego; rubber products; truck farms; Camp Pendleton, Marine base, and San Luis Rey Mission nearby; pop. 76,698.
Oceanside, N.Y., residential community on Long Island 20 mi (30 km) s.e. of New York City; summer resort; nurseries; pop. 35,372.
Ocean Springs, Miss., resort on Gulf of Mexico, 3 mi (5 km) e. of Biloxi; dairy products; truck farms; pop. 14,504.
Ocean Thermal Energy Conversion (OTEC, or sea thermal power, or sea solar power), to measure and tap wave and current energy O-460
Oceanus, in Greek mythology, eldest of the Titans, personification of the all-encircling ocean; father of the Oceanides O-459
Greek mythology M-700
Oceanus Procellarum (or Ocean of Storms), region on moon M-576, 580
Ocean View, Calif. *see in index* Albany, Calif.
Ocean Wave, game G-10
Ocean waves O-487. *see also in index* Tides
beach and coast formation B-113, *picture* B-112
water, *picture* R-45
waterpower W-105
Ocelli (simple eyes)
insect I-218
Ocelot, animal *Felis pardalis* of the cat family found in western hemisphere from s.e. Texas to Paraguay L-135, *table* C-216
fur, *table* F-465
Ocher (or ochre), a natural earth or clay found in all parts of the world; color varies from pale to dark yellow, depending upon the amount of hydrated oxide of iron present.
Ocher cave, cave in Provence, France, *picture* F-352
Ochoa, Severo (born 1905), U.S. biochemist, born in Spain; to U.S. 1941, became citizen 1956; professor New York University 1946–74; member Roche Institute of Molecular Biology 1974–. *see also in index* Nobel Prizewinners, *table*
Ocho Rios, Jamaica J-18
Ochs, Adolph Simon (1858–1935), U.S. newspaper publisher; born in Cincinnati, Ohio; rose from newsboy to ownership at 20 of *Chattanooga Times*; acquired control of *New York Times* 1896; brought both papers from financial difficulties to great prosperity; his policy was to print sound news only; responsible for book review supplement and rotogravure picture printing; published 'The New York Times Index'; supported financially 'Dictionary of American Biography' 1925–35 N-237, *list* N-240
Ochtman, Leonard (1854–1934), U.S. painter, born in The Netherlands; largely self-taught; landscapes noted for atmospheric luminosity and lyrical quality ('Night on the Mianus River').
Ockenheim, Joannes. *see in index* Okeghem, Joannes
Ockham, William of (or William of Occam) (1280?–1349?), English philosopher O-490
philosophy P-265
Ockham's razor, principle stated by Ockham O-490
O class, category of submarines, *picture* S-497
O'Clery, Michael (1575–1643), Irish author I-326
Ocmulgee National Monument, Macon, Ga. M-22
Ocmulgee River, river rising in n.-central Georgia; flows 260 mi (420 km) s.e., joining Oconee River to form Altamaha River.
O Conaire, Padraic (1883–1928), Irish author I-327
O'Connell, Daniel (1775–1847), Irish lawyer and political leader O-490
Ireland's Home Rule I-322
O'Connell, William Henry, Cardinal (1859–1944), U.S. Roman Catholic prelate, born in Lowell, Mass.; archbishop of Boston after 1907, cardinal after 1911.
O'Connel Street, in Dublin, Ireland, *picture* I-319
O'Connor, Andrew (1874–1941), U.S. sculptor, born in Worcester, Mass.; statues and bas-reliefs in marble and bronze (porch of St. Bartholomew's Church, New York City; statue of Abraham Lincoln in Springfield, Ill.).
O'Connor, Flannery (1925–64), U.S. author, born in Savannah, Ga. (novel, 'Wise Blood'; stories, 'Everything That Rises Must Converge'; posthumous National Book Award in fiction 1972 for 'Complete Stories') A-362
O'Connor, Frank, (originally called Michael O'Donovan) (1903–66), Irish author, born in Cork; in U.S. after 1952; early work written in Gaelic; known for short stories ('Guests of the Nation'; 'The Mirror in the Roadway'; 'An Only Child') I-328
O'Connor, Sandra Day (born 1930), U.S. jurist O-490
women's rights W-276
U.S. history U-197
O'Connor, Thomas Power (or Tay Pay) (1848–1929), Irish political leader and journalist, born in Athlone; active in the cause of Irish nationalism; called "father of the House of Commons," of which he was a member for 49 years; founded and edited *T.P.'s Weekly*.
Ocotillo (or coach-whip cactus, or Jacob's staff, or candle flower), shrub *Fouquieria splendens* having numerous slender, spiny branches, scalelike leaves, and clusters of flame-red flowers; common in desert areas of s.w. United States and Mexico, *picture* P-362
OCR. *see in index* Optical character recognition
Octagon, in mathematics
geometry G-76, *diagram* G-75
Octane, hydrocarbon (C_8H_{18}). *see also in index* Paraffin series
aerospace fuels A-73
gasoline G-42
Octans, constellation, *chart* C-682
Octant, instrument to measure angles; like sextant, but with arc one eighth of circle; used in aircraft navigation; often popularly called sextant. *see also in index* Sextant
Octave, in music M-689, *list* M-671
Octavia (died 11 BC), sister of Roman emperor Augustus; wife of Mark Antony; deserted for Cleopatra
Cleopatra C-489
Octavia (AD 42–62), Roman empress, wife of Nero, who divorced her to marry Poppaea Sabina; banished on false charge of infidelity and killed.
Octavian, Octavianus (or Gaius Julius Caesar Octavius). *see in index* Augustus
October, 10th month of the Gregorian calendar
birthdays of famous persons. *see in index* Birthdays, *table*
October Revolution, Russia (1917) R-354
Octofoil (or quatrefoil, double), in heraldry, *picture* H-136
Octometer, line in poetry P-405
Octonagon River, U.S. river, flows into Lake Superior M-355
Octopus, mollusk of the order Octopoda O-490. *see also in index* cuttlefish; squid
body structure A-422
invertebrate I-283, *picture* I-285
mollusks M-526
'Octopus, The', work by Norris A-352
Ocular. *see in index* Eyepiece
Oda, Nobunaga (1534–82), Japanese leader O-492
Japan J-64
Tokugawa Ieyasu T-202
'Odd Couple, The', play by Simon A-363
drama D-249
Odd-even pricing, in marketing M-143
Odd Fellows, fraternal organization established in United Kingdom 1813, established in the U.S. 1819; society pays benefits to families of deceased members; organized under lodge system with auxiliary groups for women and young adults.
Ode, a form of stately and elaborate lyric poetry; originally a poem to be sung P-407
ODECA. *see in index* Central American Common Market
'Ode for the Queen's Birthday', work by Handel H-28
O'Dell, Scott (born 1898), U.S. author, born in Los Angeles, Calif. ('Country in the Sun'; 'Island of the Blue Dolphins', awarded 1961 Newbery Medal; 'The King's Fifth'); awarded Regina Medal 1978 R-111b
Odell, William Franklin (1774–1844), Canadian statesman, born in Burlington, N.J.; provincial secretary of New Brunswick 1812–44, succeeding father, Jonathan Odell, in office 1784–1812.
Odelsting, part of the Norwegian parliament N-393
Odenathus (died AD 267 or 271), general and ruler of Palmyra P-84
Odense, Denmark, city on island of Fyn at mouth of Odense River; named for Norse god Odin; splendid cathedral; industrial and commercial center; birthplace of Hans Christian Andersen; pop. 137,127, *map* E-361
Denmark D-98, *map* D-100
'Ode on a Distant Prospect of Eton College', poem by Gray G-241
'Ode on a Grecian Urn', poem by Keats K-195
Oder (ancient Viadua, Czech Odra), important river of Czechoslovakia, Poland, and East German border O-492
East Germany G-111, *map* G-134
Europe, *map* E-361
Odessa, U.S.S.R., seaport on Black Sea; pop. 1,126,000 O-493
Europe, *map* E-361
Russia, *maps* R-346, 350
Ukrainian Soviet Socialist Republic U-2
Odessa, Tex., city in w. part of state 120 mi (190 km) w. of San Angelo; oil and gas fields; oil-field supply center; petrochemical industry; sulfur; ranching; potash deposits in area; pop. 90,027.
Odessus, Bulgaria. *see in index* Varna
Odets, Clifford (1906–63), U.S. playwright, born in Philadelphia, Pa.; known for plays of social protest (plays: 'Awake and Sing', 'Paradise Lost', and 'The Flowering Peach' depict Jewish family life; 'Waiting for Lefty' is about taxi-drivers' strike; 'Golden Boy', a violinist turned prizefighter; 'The Country Girl', the long-suffering wife of a drunken actor).
Odetta (born 1930), U.S. musician F-273
Odeum, Roman theater A-736
Odin (or Woden, or Wotan), in Scandinavian mythology, father of the gods; ruled the heavens and Earth from the shining city of Asgard; traded an eye for a drink from the sacred fountain of wisdom; his messengers, the Valkyries, lead the souls of the hero dead to Valhalla M-697, 703
Odissi, ancient Indian dance, *picture* I-73
Odo (French Eudes) (died AD 898), king of the Franks, crowned 888 after deposition of Charles the Fat; son of Robert the Strong; fought Normans and his rival Charles III for throne.
Odoacer (433?–493), German warrior who became king of Italy in 476
Goths G-197
Middle Ages M-384
Odom, William (nickname Bill) (1920–1949), U.S. aviator, born in Columbus, Miss.; established round-the-world solo flight speed record Aug. 1947; set nonstop distance record for light aircraft March 1949; killed in air-race crash at Cleveland, Ohio.
Odometer, instrument for measuring distance traveled S-374
instrumentation I-229
O'Donnell, Peadar (born 1896), Irish novelist, born in County Donegal; tales of peasants; imprisoned for revolutionary activities ('Storm'; 'The Way It Was with Them'; 'There Will Be Fighting').
O'Donnell family, an ancient Irish family; **Hugh Roe O'Donnell** (1571?–1602), fought with Hugh O'Neill against British rule; with defeat in 1601 fled from the country; his brother **Rory O'Donnell** (1575–1608), 1st earl of Tyrconnel, fled in flight of the earls. *see also in index* O'Neill family
O'Donovan, Michael. *see in index* O'Connor, Frank
Odontoceti, suborder of whales comprising the toothed whales W-185
Odontoid process S-209
Odontolite, variety of fossil bone or tooth colored blue by iron phosphate, called fossil or bone turquoise; gem stone.
Odor, a scent S-218
O'Doul, Lefty (or Francis Joseph O'Doul) (1897–1969), U.S. outfielder, left-handed hitter, born in San Francisco, Calif.; lifetime batting average of .349; led National League with .398 for Philadelphia in 1929 and .368 for Brooklyn in 1932; on team tours through Japan, often demonstrated game; regarded as father of baseball in Japan.
O'Dowd, Bernard Patrick (1866–1953), Australian poet and lawyer, born in Beaufort, Victoria; strong national flavor to verse ('The Bush'; 'The Silent Land'; 'Dominion of the Boundary').
Odra River, river in central Europe. *see in index* Oder
Odysseus (Latin name Ulysses), in Greek mythology, king of Ithaca and Trojan War hero; appears in 'Iliad'; hero of 'Odyssey'; frequently portrayed in Western literature
'Adventures of Odysseus' R-111
Ajax A-220
wrestling W-366
Cyclops C-810
folklore F-262, G-274
Homeric legend H-221, *picture* H-222
'Odyssey', Greek epic poem relating adventures of Odysseus on return from Trojan War S-473, 481b. *see also in index* Homeric legend
ancient Greece G-263
educational use E-79
Greek literature G-274, *picture* G-275
folklore F-262
mythology M-704
Oea, ancient name of Tripoli. *see in index* Tripoli, Libya

'Oil Daily', newspaper for the petroleum industry N-242
Oildale, Calif., community on n.w. border of Bakersfield; oil refining; nursery; pop. 20,879.
Oiler, naval vessel, *picture* N-90
Oil glands. *see in index* Sebaceous glands
Oil industry. *see in index* Petroleum, *subhead* industry; Petroleum technology
Oiling, machinery. *see in index* Lubricant
Oil of vitriol S-510. *see also in index* Sulfuric acid
Oil painting P-67h. *see also in index* Painting
  early use of oil paints P-31
Oils F-47. *see also in index* Fats; Petroleum; and chief oils by name
  essential oils
    perfumes P-203
    spices S-380
  fire and spontaneous combustion F-94
  flaxseed oil F-176
  food and nutrition F-275
    margarine M-134
  lubricant L-327
  nuts N-449
  paints, varnishes P-73, V-267
  pine T-328
  soaps S-229
  soybean S-340
  water mixes poorly S-256
  wax W-110
Oil wells. *see in index* Petroleum technology, *subhead* wells
Oise River, river in n. France; rises in s.w. Belgium; flows s.w. receiving Aisne at Compiègne, and joins Seine 15 mi (25 km) n.w. of Paris; length 187 mi (301 km); strategic line in World Wars I and II, *map* F-372
Oisin. *see in index* Ossian
Oistrakh, David Fedorovich (1908–74), Soviet violinist, born in Odessa; on faculty Moscow Conservatory after 1937; awards include Stalin prize 1942; acclaimed on tours of Europe and U.S.
Oiticica oil P-74
Ojeda, Alonzo de (1465?–1515), Spanish explorer, born in Cuenca, e.-central Spain; accompanied Columbus on his second voyage, 1493; founded colony on Gulf of Darien, 1509
  Lake Maracaibo M-130
  Venezuela V-276
Ojibwa (or Chippewa), American Indians living in Minnesota, Wisconsin, Michigan, North Dakota, Montana, and in Ontario, *maps* I-136, 149, *table* I-139
  folktales, *list* S-481d
  Minnesota M-441, 445
  totemism T-235
Ojibwa River. *see in index* Chippewa River
Ojos del Salado, Andean peak on Argentina-Chile border; 2nd highest in Western Hemisphere (22,572 ft; 6,880 m), *maps* A-585, S-300
Okanogan Highlands, mountainous region between the Cascade Range and the Rocky Mountains W-48
Okanagan Lake, lake in s. British Columbia, 60 mi (100 km) long; city of Kelowna situated on e. shore, *map* C-109
Okanogan River (or Okanagan River), tributary of the Columbia in British Columbia, and Washington, rising in Lake Okawogus; 300 mi (480 km) long.
Okapi, animal *Okapia johnstoni*; relative of the giraffe G-148
  zoo Z-460
Oka River, navigable river in central U.S.S.R.; 1,000 mi (1,600 km); receives Moscow River s. of Moscow; joins Volga at Gor'kiy, *map* E-361
Okayama, Japan, port on s.w. Honshu Island on n. side of Inland Sea; textiles, flour, porcelain ware; pop. 513,471, *map* J-75
Okeechobee, Lake, lake in Florida, 40 mi (60 km) long, 25 mi (40 km) wide U-59
  Florida F-194, *map* F-195
    Everglades E-363
O'Keeffe, Georgia (or Mrs. Alfred Stieglitz) (1887–1986), U.S. painter O-520
Okefenokee Swamp, swamp in Georgia and Florida G-88, *picture* G-83, *map* U-59
Okeghem, Joannes (or Joannes Ockenheim) (1430?–95?), Flemish composer of church music, and a music teacher of great influence; his pupils were founders of schools of music in many parts of Europe.
O'Kelly, Sean Thomas (1882–1966), Irish newspaper publisher and statesman, born in Dublin; a founder of Sinn Fein; member of Dail Eireann 1918–45; president of Ireland 1945–59.
Okhotsk, Sea of, large inlet of Pacific indenting e. coast of Siberia, *maps* R-322, 345. *see in index* Ocean, *table*
  Asia, *map* A-700
  Japan, *map* J-78
  Robben Island fur seals S-99
Okhotsk Current (or Oyashio, Japanese for parent stream), a cold current that flows s. from Sea of Okhotsk dividing into two branches, one flowing toward mainland of Asia, the other along e. coast of Japan
  Japan's climate J-60
Okigbo, Christopher (1932–67), Nigerian poet O-520
Okinawa, Japan, largest island of Ryukyu chain about 60 mi (100 km) long, 2 to 20 mi (3 to 30 km) wide; strategic air and naval base; with nearby islets known as Okinawa Gunto (Okinawa "cluster of islands"); island pop. 924,563, prefecture pop. 1,179,000 O-520
  Asia, *map* A-700
  Japan, *map* J-78
  Pacific Ocean, *pictures* P-19
  World War II W-336, 349
Oklahoma, state of s. central U.S.; 69,919 sq mi (181,089 sq km); cap. Oklahoma City; pop. 3,025,266 O-521, *map* O-536
  cities. *see also in index* cities listed below and other cities by name
    Oklahoma City O-538
    Tulsa T-305
  liquor laws P-507
  North America, *map* N-351
  symbols
    flag, *picture* F-160
    flower, *picture* S-427. *see also in index* Mistletoe
    tree. *see in index* Redbud
  Statuary Hall, *table* S-437b
  taxation, *tables* T-37, 39
'Oklahoma!', musical comedy M-686
  dance D-30, *picture* D-28
  De Mille's contribution D-91
  motion picture M-623
'Oklahoma', U.S. battleship W-344
Oklahoma, University of, in Norman, Okla.; state control; founded 1892; arts and sciences, business administration, education, engineering, fine arts, law, nursing, pharmacy; graduate college; Health Sciences Center at Oklahoma City O-525
Oklahoma Baptist University, Shawnee, Okla.; affiliated with Southern Baptists; opened 1911; liberal arts, education, fine arts.
Oklahoma Christian College, Oklahoma City, Okla.; private control; founded 1950; has learning center with electronically equipped private carrels; liberal arts, education; trimester system.
Oklahoma City, Okla., state capital and largest city, on North Canadian River near geographic center of state; pop. 443,575 O-538
  North America, *map* N-351
  Oklahoma O-524, *pictures* O-529, 530
Oklahoma City University, Oklahoma City, Okla.; United Methodist; founded 1904; arts and sciences, business, education, law, music; graduate studies.
Oklahoma College of Liberal Arts. *see in index* Science and Arts of Oklahoma, University of
Oklahoma Panhandle State University (until 1974 Oklahoma Panhandle State College), Goodwell, Okla.; founded 1909; arts and sciences, business, education, home economics, industrial arts, and music.
Oklahoma State University, Stillwater, Okla.; founded 1891; arts and sciences, agriculture, business, education, engineering, home economics, veterinary medicine; graduate study; Oklahoma City branch.
Okmulgee, Okla., city 37 mi (60 km) s. of Tulsa, in coal, oil, and cotton region; glass products, oil refining, food processing; capital of Creek Nation 1868–1907; pop. 16,263, *map* U-41
Okoboji Lake, lake in Iowa, *picture* I-299, *map* I-302
Okoume (or Gabon mahogany), hardwood timber G-2
Okra, herbaceous, hairy, annual plant, *Abelmoschus esculentus*, of mallow family, Malvaceae; widely cultivated in tropics and subtropics; tender, unripe fruit, called gumbo, eaten as vegetable; related plant *Hibiscus esculentus*, cultivated in most warm regions, used for perfume and fiber H-149
Oktoberfest, German beer festival M-652
Okubo, Toshimichi (1830–78), one of Japanese leaders of Meiji Restoration; an advisor to emperor.
Okuma, Shigenobu, Marquis (1838–1922), Japanese statesman, early advocate of abolition of feudal system and advance reforms; founded schools; prime minister during first half of World War I.
Okun, Arthur Melvin (1928–80), U.S. economist, born in Jersey City, N.J.; professor at Yale 1963–67; on U.S. Council of Economic Advisers 1964–69, chairman 1968–69; with Brookings Institution after 1969.
Olaf V. *see in index* Olav
Oland, an island of Sweden, near its s.e. extremity, in the Baltic Sea, separated from the mainland by Kalmar Sound; 519 sq mi (1,344 sq km); cap. Borgholm; pop. 20,361 S-522, *maps* E-361, S-524
Olathe, Kan., city 20 mi (30 km) s.w. of Kansas City; batteries, electronics; state school for deaf; pop. 37,258.
Olav I (or Olaf I, or Olaf Tryggvessön) (969–1000), king of Norway; began Christianization of Norway; leaped into sea after defeat by Danes and Swedes; hero of Longfellow's 'Saga of King Olaf'.
Olav II, Saint (or St. Olaf II, or Olaf Haraldsson) (995–1030), king and patron saint of Norway, conquered throne 1016; unified kingdom and continued its Christianization
  Norway N-394
Olav (or Olaf V, in full Olav Alexander Edward Christian Frederik) (born 1903), king of Norway O-538
  Norway N-391
Olcott, Frances Jenkins (1873?–1963), U.S. librarian and writer, born in Paris, France ('The Children's Reading'; 'Tales of the Persian Genii').
Olcott, Henry Steel (1832–1907), U.S. philosopher and co-founder of Theosophical Society T-163
Old age. *see in index* Senior citizens
Old Bet, one of the first elephants brought to North America for exhibit C-427
Old Castile, Spain, n. part of Castile, an elevated plateau walled in by mountains; among the chief cities are Valladolid, Santander, and Burgos.
Old Catholic churches, religious bodies adhering to dogma and customs of Roman Catholicism but not accepting authority of its hierarchy; groups in U.S. are outgrowths of Old Catholic movement and churches of Europe.
'Old Christmas', book
  Caldecott's illustrations C-26
Old City (or Stare Miasto), Warsaw, Poland W-33
'Old Curiosity Shop', novel by Charles Dickens telling the story of an old curiosity-shop keeper and his sweet, unselfish granddaughter, Little Nell, who dies from weariness and privation
  landmark, *picture* D-135
Old Delhi, India, old capital of British India; pop. 4,865,077. *see also in index* Delhi; New Delhi
Old Deluder Satan Act, law enacted in 1647 in Massachusetts
  education E-87
Old Dominion. *see in index* Virginia
Old Dominion University, Norfolk, Va.; state control; founded 1930; arts and letters, business administration, education, engineering, sciences, technology; graduate studies N-333
Oldenburg, Claes (born 1929), Swedish born U.S. artist O-538
Oldenburg, former state of n.w. Germany on North Sea; 2,480 sq mi (6,420 sq km); after World War II in Lower Saxony; pop. 130,852 P-517, *map* G-134
Old English, style of type. *see in index* Black letter
Old English language (or Anglo-Saxon language)
  Alfred the Great A-282
  development E-262
Old English literature (or Anglo-Saxon literature) E-263
  'Beowulf' B-165, S-472
Old English sheepdog, dog, *picture* D-202
Old Faithful, geyser in Yellowstone National Park G-138, *picture* W-393
Oldfield, Barney (originally Berna Eli Oldfield) (1878–1946), U.S. automobile racer, born in Wauseon, Ohio; first to be clocked officially at a mile a minute, at Indianapolis in 1903.
'Old Folks at Home' (or 'Swanee River'), song by Foster F-327
Old Forge, Pa., borough on Lackawanna River, 5 mi (8 km) s.w. of Scranton; coal mining; clothing; incorporated 1895; pop. 9,304, *map* P-185
Old Germanic language L-230
Old Glory. *see in index* Flags of the United States
Old Guard, popular name of noted body of troops in army of Napoleon I; made last French charge at battle of Waterloo.
Oldham, England, important cotton manufacturing town in Lancashire 6 mi (10 km) n.e. of Manchester; coal; pop. 108,280, *map* U-18a
Old Harbor (French Vieux-Port), historic quarter in Marseilles M-152
Old High German, language
  German literature G-105
'Old Ironsides'. *see in index* 'Constitution'
'Old Ironsides', poem by Holmes A-347, H-204
  navy N-91
  quoted S-177f
'Old King Cole', nursery rhyme N-442
Old Kingdom, period in Egyptian history, approximately 2700–2200 BC E-125
Old Line State. *see in index* Maryland
Old Low German, language
  German literature G-105
'Old Maid and the Thief, The', opera by Menotti M-299
Old man. *see in index* Rosemary
'Old Man and the Sea, The', novel by Hemingway A-360
'Old Man Figuring', etching by Klee D-255
Old Man of the Mountains, cliff, New Hampshire, *picture* N-190
Old Man of the Sea, character in 'Arabian Nights', the little old man who begs Sinbad the Sailor to carry him across a brook and then will not be dislodged from his back; hence, a bore or burden.
Old Manse, Concord, Mass., home of Emerson and Hawthorne C-639
Old Mission Church, Los Angeles, Calif., *picture* L-302
Old Montreal, Montreal, Que., restored historic district M-571
Old moon (or waning crescent moon), moon phase M-579
'Old Mortality', novel by Sir Walter Scott telling of the struggles of the Scottish Covenanters with the royal forces under Claverhouse; title is taken from the nickname of old Robert Paterson, who kept the gravestones of the Covenanters in repair
  Buchan S-74
Old North Bridge, Concord, Mass. C-639, L-144
Old North Church, Boston, Mass., *picture* M-188
Old Point Comfort, Virginia, summer resort on n. shore

of Hampton Roads opposite Norfolk; Fort Monroe is here.

'Old Possum's Book of Practical Cats', work by Eliot E-189

Old regime, the despotic, oppressive government of France before the Revolution (1789).

Olds, Elizabeth (born 1897), U.S. artist and author, born in Minneapolis, Minn.; studied art in Paris; received Guggenheim Fellowship for her paintings of circus horses and trapeze artists; wrote and illustrated books for children ('Big Fire'; 'Riding the Rails').

Olds, Ransom Eli (1864–1950), U.S. pioneer automobile builder, born in Geneva, Ohio; built a 3-wheeled steam carriage 1887, a 4-wheeled steam car 1893, a gasoline car (Oldsmobile) 1896 A-858
automobile development A-856
Michigan M-358
Lansing L-45

Old Salem, restored community of Salem, N.C. N-357, *picture* N-365

Old Sarum, parish in Wiltshire, England, 2 mi (3 km) n. of Salisbury; former city, although almost entirely deserted by 16th century, sent members to Parliament until 1832.

Old Saybrook, Conn., town on Connecticut River near mouth; settled by English 1635; united with Connecticut 1644; early home of Yale University; resort; pop. of township 9,287.

Old Spanish Trail, in North America
Nevada N-136
New Mexico N-216
roads, *map* R-219
Utah U-219

Old State House, in Boston, Mass., *picture* B-374

Old Stone Age. *see in index* Paleolithic Age; Stone Age

Old Stormalong, legendary sailor
folklore F-266

Old Style calendar. *see in index* Julian calendar

Old Swedes' (Gloria Dei) Church National Historic Site, in Philadelphia, Pa. P-251d, *picture* P-251d

Old Testament, a division of the Bible B-181
Abraham A-12
angels and demons A-414
Dead Sea Scrolls D-46, A-531
dreams D-257
education E-78
folklore F-263
genealogy G-47
Hebrew literature H-113
hell and Hades H-124
history writing H-171
Hittites H-177
horror story H-245
human rights H-319
Judaism J-146, 150
legal codes L-91
literature L-243
Moses M-595
prophets P-508, *picture* P-509
riddles W-292
Ruth R-365
storytelling S-460
witchcraft W-266

'Oldtown Folks', work by Stowe
American literature A-351

Olduvai Gorge, in Tanzania T-23
Leakey's fossil discoveries L-104

Old Vic theatre, in London L-194

Old Winnemucca (born Poito) (died 1882), chief of northern Paiutes; signed one of first treaties with settlers in western Nevada; was chief at time of famous battle of Pyramid Lake (Nevada) 1860, though his nephew Numaga (Young Winnemucca) led American Indians at that battle.

Old wives' tale, odd tale, belief, or traditional superstition.

'Old Wives' Tale, The', work by Bennett, story of two sisters in the pottery-manufacturing section of Staffordshire, England; also title of comedy by George Peele B-163

Old World badger, a carnivorous mammal *Meles meles* W-114

Old World grape, a grape *Vitis vinifera* of the family Vitaceae G-220
wine W-236

Old World harvest mouse, rodent *Micromys minutus* M-640

Old World mole, mammal of the genus *Talpa* M-521

Old World monkey. *see in index* Apes and Monkeys

Oleaceae, the olive family, a group of trees and shrubs distributed over temperate and tropical regions; includes ash and olive trees, and lilac, fringe tree, privet, forsythia, and jasmine.

Olean, N.Y., industrial city on Allegheny River about 60 mi (100 km) s.e. of Buffalo; diesel engines and compressors, electronic components, tile, cutlery, electrical equipment, food, lumber, petroleum products, chemicals, plastics; pop. 18,207.

Oleander, any of ornamental evergreen shrubs of genus *Nerium,* dogbane family, Apocynaceae; native to warm regions from Mediterranean to Japan; contains poisonous milky juice.

Olefins (or polyolefins), fiber group F-74, P-228, *table* F-72

Oleg, early ruler of Russia R-351

Olein, compound found in fats and oils F-48

Ole Miss. *see in index* Mississippi, University of

Oleomargarine (or margarine) M-134

Oleomargarine Act of 1886, United States M-134

Oleoresin, a purified form of turpentine T-328

Oléron, Ile d', island of France off w. coast at mouth of Charente River; resort; pop. 16,355, *maps* E-361, F-372

Oleum (or fuming sulfuric acid), chemical compound S-510

Olfactory bulb, brain structure, *diagrams* B-401

Olfactory nerve, the nerve serving the sense of smell; branches are distributed to mucous membrane of nasal cavity S-218
nose N-396

Olibanum. *see in index* Frankincense

Olier de Verneuil, Jean Jacques (1608–57), French Roman Catholic prelate, born in Paris, France; helped establish Sulpician settlement at Montreal in 1640.

Oligarchy, form of government in which rule is by the few G-198
ancient Greece G-264
democracy D-91
Venice V-279

Oligocene epoch, in geological time
earth, *table* E-24
elephant E-185

Oligoclase, mineral M-180

Oligopoly, domination of a market by a small number of major manufacturers C-152, M-544

Oliphant, Laurence (1829–88), Scottish writer and mystic, born in Cape Town, South Africa; books reflect life of adventure and travel ('A Journey to Katmandu', travel; 'Piccadilly', novel; 'Episodes in a Life of Adventure', autobiography).

Oliphant, Margaret Wilson (1828–97), Scottish novelist, born in Wallyford, Midlothian ('Chronicles of Carringford'; 'Makers of Venice').

Olive, a small evergreen tree *Olea europaea* of the family Oleaceae O-539
Athena's symbol A-733
fruit production, *chart* F-430
Olympic games O-542
plants, *picture* P-377
Spain, *picture* S-352
stuffed olives P-197a

Olive family. *see in index* Oleaceae

Oliveira, Antonio Mariano Alberto de (1859–1937), Brazilian poet, born in Palmital de Saguarema L-72

Olive oil O-539
Tunisia T-308

Oliver, George. *see in index* Onions, Oliver

Oliver, James (1823–1908), U.S. inventor (1868) and manufacturer of chilled-steel plows; born in Scotland, to U.S. 1835.

Oliver, Joseph (nickname King) (1885–1938), U.S. early jazz cornetist, born in New Orleans, La.; formed King Oliver's Creole Jazz Band, *picture* J-84

Oliver Optic. *see in index* Optic

'Oliver Twist', novel by Charles Dickens; relates adventures of orphan who infringes workhouse etiquette by asking for more gruel; runs away and becomes innocent pupil of Fagin the pickpocket and tool of Bill Sikes the burglar, *pictures* D-137, E-277

Olives, Mount of, historic ridge e. of Jerusalem; favorite retreat of Jesus and Disciples; contains Hill of Offense, reputed scene of Solomon's idolatry; alluded to in Old and New Testaments.

Olive shell, a mollusk shell, *picture* S-150

Olivet College, Olivet, Mich.; private control, related to United Church of Christ; founded 1844; humanities and arts, education, natural sciences, social studies.

Olivet Nazarene College, Kankakee, Ill.; affiliated with Church of the Nazarene; founded 1907; liberal arts, teacher education; graduate studies.

Olivier, Laurence (in full Laurence Kerr Olivier) (born 1907), British actor, director, and producer O-539
acting A-27
Richard III, *picture* S-141

Olivier-Eugène-Prosper-Charles Messiaen. *see in index* Messiaen, Olivier

'Olivier Plantation, The', watercolor by Persac, *picture* L-313

Olivine (or chrysolite, or peridot), semiprecious stone J-115, *picture* J-114
rocks R-229
sand S-36

'Ollantay', Incan drama L-75

Ollivant, Alfred (1874–1927), English novelist, born in Manchester; known particularly for 'Bob, Son of Battle'.

Olmec, ancient Indians of Central America A-406
arts, *picture* I-146

Olmedo, José Joaquín (1780–1847), Ecuadoran political leader and poet O-540
Latin American literature L-68, 73, *picture* L-70

Olmsted, Frederick Law (1822–1903), U.S. pioneer landscape architect O-540
Central Park N-273
parks and playgrounds P-125

Olmsted vs. United States, 1928
wiretapping W-247

Olney, Richard (1835–1917), U.S. jurist and statesman, born in Oxford, Mass.; attorney general (1893–95) and secretary of state (1895–97) under President Cleveland; used injunction in railroad strike of 1894, first case of court injunction in strike.

Olomouc (German Olmütz), Czechoslovakia, town in Moravia on Morava River; coal mining; occupied by Swedes in Thirty Years' War; besieged by Frederick II of Prussia (1758); conference to settle Austro-Prussian conflict over German affairs (1850); pop. 71,175, *map* E-361

Olsen, Ib Spang (born 1921), Danish author and illustrator, born in Copenhagen ('The Marsh Crone's Brew', 'The Boy in the Moon', 'Smoke').

Olson, Charles (born 1934), U.S. poet A-364

Olsztyn (German Allenstein), Poland, former German (East Prussian) city in Masurian Lakes region; in Poland since 1945; pop. 72,300, *map* E-361

Olustee, Fla., village 46 mi (76 km) s.w. of Jacksonville; battle of Olustee or Ocean Pond (Feb. 20, 1864), one of the bloodiest battles of the Civil War, resulting in defeat for the Federal forces; pop. 400.

Olympia (modern Ruphia), Greece, plain in ancient Elis on Alpheus River; adorned by beautiful temples and statues; scene of Olympic Games A-739
temple and statue of Zeus S-115, *picture* S-116

Olympia (formerly Smithfield), Wash., state capital, at head of Puget Sound; pop. 27,447 O-540
North America, *map* N-351
Washington W-51, *picture* W-57

'Olympia', painting by Manet M-96

Olympiad, formerly the interval of four years between celebrations of Olympic Games; in modern usage, the Olympic Games A-737

Olympias (died 316 BC), fierce, ambitious Epirote princess, wife of Philip II of Macedon A-279

Olympic Games, ancient and modern athletic competitions O-540. *see also in index* Special Olympics
athletic games A-737
bobsledding S-216
boycott, 1980 C-184
cycling C-809
diving D-186
East Germany G-116
festivals and holidays F-61
field hockey H-193
Fraser F-386
gymnastics G-323
horse racing H-275
ice hockey H-198
illness and injury F-369
marathon race M-181
medals M-270
Melbourne M-289
Owens O-620
skiing S-210d, *picture* S-210a
Thorpe T-175
Tirol region T-192
Tokyo T-211
track and field T-243
water polo W-102
weight lifting W-137

Olympic Mountains, mountains in n.w. Washington, part of Coast Ranges, between Puget Sound and Pacific Ocean, *map* U-90
Washington W-48, *map* W-49

Olympus, mountain, highest point on island of Cyprus; height 6,406 ft (1,953 m) C-810

Olympus, Mount, mountain in n. Greece and Macedonia O-543
Greek mythology G-268, M-700, *picture* M-699
Italy, *map* I-149

Omaha, a Siouan Indian tribe formerly living between Platte and Niobrara rivers in Nebraska N-95, *picture* N-103

Omaha, Neb., largest city of state, on Missouri River; pop. 313,911 O-543
Nebraska N-96, 104, *picture* N-101
North America, *map* N-351
SAC headquarters. *see in index* Offutt Air Force Base

O'Mahoney, Joseph Christopher (1884–1962), U.S. lawyer, journalist, and political leader; born in Chelsea, Mass.; to Wyoming 1916; Democratic senator from Wyoming 1934–53 and 1954–60.

Oman, independent sultanate of s.e. Arabian Peninsula on Arabian Sea; 120,000 sq mi (310,000 sq km); cap. Muscat; pop. 1–1.5 million, chiefly Arabs O-543
Arabia A-521
Asia, *map* A-700
flag, *picture* F-168

Oman, Gulf of, arm of Arabian Sea s. of Iran; connected with Persian Gulf by Strait of Hormuz
Asia, *map* A-700

Omar (581?–644), 2nd Muslim caliph, organizer of Muslim power from warring sect to empire.

Omar, Mosque of. *see in index* Dome of the Rock

Omar Khayyám (1048–1122), Persian poet O-544
English literature E-276
Islamic literature I-367
Persia P-214

Omar Mukhtar, Libyan religious leader L-190

Omasum (or manyplies), third stomach of ruminants R-318

Omayyad Mosque, in Damascus, Syria
Damascus, *picture* D-18

Omayyads. *see in index* Umayyad

OMB. *see in index* Management and Budget, Office of

Ombu (or umbū, or bella sombra), evergreen tree *Phytolacca dioica* of pokeweed family, native to river courses of pampas of South America; grows to 60 ft (18 m); thick trunk; spreading, flat crown; leaves oval, smooth; flowers white, clustered.

Ombudsman, independent officer appointed by a government to receive and

investigate complaints from citizens and to suggest remedies for any governmental wrongdoings
Canada G-202
New Zealand N-294
Scandinavia C-684
Sweden S-526

Ombudsman, Office of the, Canada G-202

Omdurman, Sudan, city on Nile River opposite Khartoum; commerce in gum arabic, ivory, cotton goods; pop. 305,308 S-502, *map* A-118
Kitchener K-251

Omen, sign or indication of some future occurrence, favorable or unfavorable; some people believe flight and feeding of birds, action or sounds of animals or insects, and other natural phenomena and accidental happenings betoken future events. *see also in index* Augurs

Ommiads. *see in index* Umayyad

Omnibus, early bus B-516

Omnibus bill, in U.S., term applying to any bill carrying several separate and unrelated measures, but particularly used for Compromise of 1850; most states now require each statute to relate to one topic only.

'Omoo', novel by Melville A-349

Omphale, character in Greek mythology, queen of Lydia whom Hercules served for three years as a punishment for having slain Iphitus; to please her Hercules wore her garments and spun wool while she wore his lion skin.

Omphalodes. *see in index* Chinese forget-me-not

Omsk, U.S.S.R., city in w. Siberia on Irtysh River and Trans-Siberian Railroad 375 mi (600 km) w. of Novosibirsk; locomotive works; shipyards; farm machinery, flour; pop. 1,002,000 S-190, *maps* R-322, 344
Asia, *map* A-700

Onager, a wild ass A-702
zoo Z-460

'On Aggression', work by Lorenz L-298

Onagraceae, the evening primrose family, a botanical group of chiefly herbaceous plants containing about 40 genera and 500 species; most abundant in temperate America; familiar members are evening primrose, willow herb, fuchsia, and clarkia.

Onassis, Jacqueline Bouvier Kennedy (born 1929), U.S. editor, widow of President John F. Kennedy and Aristotle Onassis
Kennedy K-200, 204, *pictures* K-201, 203
White House refurnishing W-199

Oñate, Juan de (1550?–1624?), Spanish explorer and colonizer of New Mexico O-544
El Morro mesa, *picture* A-332
New Mexico N-217

'On Baile's Strand', work by Yeats I-327

Onça, leopard B-415

Oncken, Johann Gerhard (1800–84), Baptist missionary B-77

Oncogene, in genetics
cancer C-133
genetic engineering G-51

Ondol, Korean heating system K-272

O'Neal, Frederick (born 1905), U.S. actor and director, born in Brooksville, Miss.; noted for work in theater, films, and TV; won Drama Critics Award 1945 ('Anna Lucasta'); first black president of Actor's Equity, served 1964–73.

'One Day in the Life of Ivan Denisovich', novel by Solzhenitsyn R-112d
novel N-412

Onega, Lake (or Onejskoe-Ozero), lake in n.w. U.S.S.R.; 3,753 sq mi (9,720 sq km) O-544
Europe, *map* E-361
U.S.S.R., *maps* R-346, 350

100-meter dash, a running event T-243, *picture* T-244

'One Hundred Years of Solitude', novel by García Márquez L-71, G-19

Oneida, Iroquois Indian tribe formerly living near Lake Oneida, N.Y.
Iroquois Confederacy I-142, *table* I-138

Oneida, N.Y., city near geographic center of state, 25 mi (40 km) e. of Syracuse; near Lake Oneida; silverware, paper products, furniture, plastics; pop. 10,810.

Oneida Community, communal religious settlement founded by John H. Noyes 1838, and established near Oneida, N.Y., 1847–48; dissolved 1879, and reorganized as Oneida Community, Ltd., a joint stock company engaged in the manufacture of silverware, with plants at Oneida, N.Y., Northampton, Mass., Niagara Falls and Toronto, Ontario, and Sheffield, England; still operating C-605

Oneida Lake, lake in New York N-246

O'Neill, Eugene (1888–1953), U.S. dramatist O-545. *see also in index* Nobel Prizewinners, *table*
American literature A-357
drama D-248
folklore F-269

O'Neill, Rose Cecil (1874–1944), U.S. illustrator and writer, born in Wilkes-Barre, Pa.; married Harry Leon Wilson 1902, divorced; created the Kewpie doll 1909.

O'Neill, Thomas Philip, Jr. (nickname Tip) (born 1912), U.S. political leader, born in Cambridge, Mass.; U.S. congressman (Democrat) from Massachusetts 1952–; majority whip 1971–73, majority leader 1973–77; speaker of the House 1977–86.

O'Neill family, an Irish family long notable in fighting English rule; **Shane O'Neill** (1530?–67), fought and raided until defeated by O'Donnells; his nephew **Hugh O'Neill,** called the Great O'Neill (1540?–1616), 2nd earl of Tyrone, sought Spanish aid against England; though able and victorious for a time, was defeated 1601; made peace 1603; fled 1607. *see also in index* O'Donnell family

Onejskoe-Ozero. *see in index* Onega, Lake

Oneonta, N.Y., city on Susquehanna River about 65 mi (105 km) s.w. of Albany; railroad shops; cloth, trailer coaches and trucks, medical vans; Hartwick College; College at Oneonta; pop. 14,933.

Oneonta, College at, Oneonta, N.Y., part of State University of New York; established 1889; liberal studies, education, home economics; graduate studies.

One-part code, code system C-419

One-to-one correspondence, in mathematics A-589

'One Touch of Venus', work by Nash and Perelman N-20

One-voiced music (or monophonic music) M-667

'One Writer's Beginnings', work by Welty W-149

Onin War, in Japanese history (1467–77) J-63

Onion, a biennial bulb-bearing plant O-545
growing conditions G-26
producing hybrids, *picture* P-367

Onions, Oliver (legal name George Oliver) (1873–1961), English writer, born in Bradford, ('The Collected Ghost Stories of Oliver Onions'; 'Poor Man's Tapestry', awarded 1947 James Tait Black memorial prize).

Onion salt S-379

Onizuka, Ellison (1946–86), U.S. astronaut, born in Kealakekua, Hawaii, killed in explosion of space shuttle *Challenger*.

On-line processing, method of data processing C-627

'Only Child, An', work by O'Connor I-328

Onnagata, in Japanese theatre J-56

Onnes, Heike Kamerlingh. *see in index* Kamerlingh Onnes, Heike

O'Nolan, Brian (or Flann O'Brien, or Myles na O'Hpaleen) (1911–66), Irish author
literary contribution I-327

Onomastics, the study of names O-6

Onomatopoeia, formation of words in imitation of natural sound as "cuckoo," "hum"; in rhetoric, use of imitative and naturally suggestive words
creative writing W-379
figures of speech F-81

Onondaga, Indian tribe of the Iroquois group formerly living near Lake Onondaga, N.Y.
Iroquois Confederacy I-142, *table* I-138

Onsager, Lars (1903–76), U.S. chemist, born in Oslo, Norway; to U.S. 1928, became citizen 1945; professor of chemistry at Yale University 1945–72; professor University of Miami (Fla.) after 1972. *see also in index* Nobel Prizewinners, *table*

Onset, part of the cycle of a disease D-165

Ontake, peak in Japanese Alps on central Honshu about 65 mi (105 km) n.e. of Nagoya; 10,049 ft (3,063 m); climbed in summer by crowds of white-robed pilgrims who visit Shinto shrine on summit; ascent accompanied by tinkle of bells attached to sashes of pilgrims, *map* J-78

Ontario, Calif., city 32 mi. e. of Los Angeles; aircraft servicing and parts, electrical appliances, citrus-fruit products, apparel; Ontario Motor Speedway, a track 2½ miles (4 km) around, for auto racing, California '500'; settled 1882 by George and William Chaffey; pop. 64,118.

Ontario (formerly known as Upper Canada, or Canada West), central province of Canada; 412,582 sq mi (1,068,582 sq km); cap. Toronto; pop. 8,625,107 O-546
Canada C-80, *map* C-112
cities. *see also in index* cities listed below and other cities by name
Hamilton H-22
London L-295
Ottawa O-612
Stratford S-484a, *picture* S-484b
Toronto T-228
Windsor W-233
government agencies G-202
Lake Ontario O-559
North America N-337, *map* N-351
St. Lawrence river S-19
transportation
Sault Sainte Marie canal S-52b
Trans-Canada Highway T-248

Ontario, Lake O-559. *see also in index* Welland Ship Canal
Great Lakes G-243, *map* G-245
New York N-245
North America, *map* N-351

Ontario Agricultural College, Guelph, Ont.; founded 1874; agriculture, home economics, commercial baking; affiliated with University of Toronto.

'On the Art of War', work by Machiavelli M-9

'On the Law of Prize and Booty', work by Grotius G-290

'On the Law of War and Peace' (or 'De jure belli ac pacis'), work by Grotius G-290
international law I-255
warfare W-26

'On the Motion of the Heart and Blood in Animals', work by Harvey H-52

'On the Nature of Things', work by Lucretius
materialism M-210

'On the Origin of Species by Means of Natural Selection', work by Darwin D-39
biogeography B-217
botany and evolution B-380
evolution E-366
genetics G-53
zoology Z-470

'On the Road', book by Kerouac K-229

'On the Ultimate Origin of Things', work by Leibniz L-122

Ontogeny, growth and development of an individual organism Z-469

Ontonagon River, in Michigan M-355

'On War', work by Clausewitz C-486
warfare W-12

'On Your Toes' (1936), musical comedy by Rodgers and Hart M-686

Onyx, a form of quartz O-559
jewelry J-116

Ooka Shohei (born 1909), Japanese novelist, born in Tokyo; lecturer Meiji University 1952–55 ('Fires on the Plain'; 'Oxygene'; 'Shadow of Flowers').

Oolakan. *see in index* Candlefish

Oölitic limestone L-210

Oolong tea, a designation of tea T-45

Oort, Jan Hendrik (born 1900), Dutch astronomer, born in Franeker, Friesland Province, The Netherlands; on faculty Leiden University 1926–70, professor of astronomy 1945–70; director of Leiden observatory 1945–70; known for investigations proving rotation of Milky Way.

Oort Cloud, region surrounding solar system, contains comet nuclei C-597

Oostende, Belgium. *see in index* Ostend

OPA (Office of Price Administration), United States R-277

Opah. *see in index* Moonfish

Opal, a semiprecious stone O-559
Australia A-776
birthstone, *picture* J-114
minerals, *picture* M-434

Opaque substances
light affects L-196

Oparin, Aleksandr (1894–1980), Soviet biochemist noted for his studies on the origin of life from chemical matter
evolution E-365

Op art P-61, *picture* P-61

Opata, a group of American Indians of the Piman linguistic descent living in the valleys of the Río Sonora and its tributaries in Sonora, Mexico.

Op code (or operating code), in microprocessing M-380

OPEC. *see in index* Organization of Petroleum Exporting Countries

Opelika, Ala., city 57 mi (92 km) n.e. of Montgomery; farming and trade center, textiles, magnetic tape, auto tires; settled 1836, incorporated as town 1854, as city 1899; pop. 21,896.

Opelousas, La., city about 55 mi (90 km) w. of Baton Rouge; oil and gas field; sweet-potato canning, meat-packing, wood products; briefly capital of Louisiana in Civil War; pop. 18,903.

Open caisson, in construction C-18

Open-chain hydrocarbons. *see in index* Paraffin series

Open city, in wartime a city that belligerents agree to leave undefended, free from attack, and open to peaceful occupation by enemy troops, as Paris in World War II P-123

'Open city' (1945), motion picture by Rossellini, *picture* M-625

Open-cut mining. *see in index* Open-pit mining

Open-die forging, in metalwork F-317

Open-door policy, term used to designate equality of commercial opportunity to all nations O-559
McKinley M-20

Open-hearth furnace, in metalworking
iron and steel production I-340

Open-market operations, in banking F-51
central bank C-260

Open-pit mining (or opencut mining), type of surface mining M-425. *see also in index* Strip mining; Quarrying
coal C-519, *diagram* C-520
copper U-217, *pictures* U-218, 221

Open roadstead harbor H-34

Open school, a school building designed for the flexible use of space E-99

Open season, in game hunting H-333

Open sentence, in teaching A-285

Open society E-302

Open stage. *see in index* Thrust stage

Open-stope method, in mines and mining M-428

Open Theater, innovative theatrical creation of the

power; capital of the Minyae; superseded by Thebes.

Orczy, Emmuska, Baroness (or Mrs. Montagu Barstow) (1865–1947), Hungarian-English writer, born in Hungary; wrote 'Scarlet Pimpernel' novels about Englishman whose band helped aristocrats escape during French Revolution.

Order, in biological classification, a group of related families A-432
  zoology Z-467

Ordered pair, in mathematics A-297

Order in Council, United Kingdom; any order issued by the sovereign on advice of the Privy Council
  War of 1812 W-29

Order of. *see in index* order by name, as Garter, Order of the

Orders, two systems in Greek architecture A-546

Orders, religious. *see in index* Religious orders

Ordinance, law set forth by government, particularly by town body; also authoritative decree, as of God or fate.

Ordinance of 1785, United States, on Western lands U-172
  education, *list* E-104

Ordinance of 1787, United States. *see in index* Northwest Ordinance

Ordinary, an early type of bicycle B-187

Ordinary water reactor (or light water reactor), type of nuclear reactor N-426

Ordnance Corps, U.S. Army
  insignia, *picture* U-10

Ordóñez, José Batlle y. *see in index* Batlle y Ordóñez, José

Ordovician period, in geological time
  British Isles B-460
  earth E-23, *table* E-24

Ore, mineral. *see in index* Ores

Oreades. *see in index* Orkney Islands

Orebro, Sweden, manufacturing and trading town on Svarta River near w. end of Lake Hjälmaren; diet of 1540 declared crown hereditary; diet of 1810 made Bernadotte crown prince; 13th-century castle and church; pop. 92,250, *maps* E-361, S-524

Ore dressing, mining procedure M-429, O-601

Oregano, an herb *Origanum vulgare*; leaves used as seasoning H-138, S-379

Oregon (nickname Beaver State), n.w. state of U.S.; 96,981 sq mi (251,180 sq km); cap. Salem; pop. 2,632,663 O-581
  cities. *see also in index* cities listed below and other cities by name
    Salem S-26
  dams. *see in index* Bonneville Dam
  flag, *picture* F-160
  frontier movement F-421
  history
    boundary dispute P-438, *map* U-177
    Oregon Trail O-598
  impeachment stance I-58
  name, *table* S-428
  North America, *map* N-351
  redwoods S-112
  Statuary Hall, *table* S-437b
  taxation, *tables* T-37, 39
  United States U-89, *picture* U-92

Oregon, Ohio, city in n.w. part of state just e. of Toledo near Lake Erie; farming, oil refining; incorporated 1958; pop. 18,675.

'Oregon', United States battleship, built 1896; junked Aug. 1942 for metal
  Spanish-American War S-365

Oregon, University of, Eugene, Ore.; state control; chartered 1872; opened 1876; liberal arts, architecture and allied arts, business administration, community service and public affairs, education, health and physical education and recreation, journalism, law, librarianship, music; graduate school; dentistry, medicine, and nursing at Portland; quarter system O-584, *picture* O-589

Oregon ash (sometimes called water ash), tree *Fraxinus oregona* of the olive family, found in moist valleys from Washington to California; grows to 75 ft (23 m); wood used for tool handles, barrels, furniture, fuel.

Oregon Boundary Treaty (1846), between United States and United Kingdom settling w. Canadian boundary C-99, P-438, *table* T-274

Oregon cedar. *see in index* Port Orford cedar

Oregon College of Education, Monmouth, Ore.; state control; chartered 1856; arts and sciences and education; graduate study; quarter system.

Oregon country U-178
  Polk P-438, U-175

Oregon Emigration Society O-598

Oregon grape, shrub *Mahonia aquifolium* of barberry family; prickly evergreen leaves, dainty yellow flowers followed by clusters of acid blue berries that resemble small grapes
  Oregon O-588
  state flower of Oregon, *picture* S-427

Oregon myrtle. *see in index* California laurel

Oregon pine. *see in index* Douglas fir

Oregon question, dispute with United Kingdom. *see also in index* Oregon Boundary Treaty
  Polk P-438

Oregon State University, Corvallis, Ore.; chartered 1858; opened 1868; humanities and social sciences, agriculture, business and technology, education, engineering, forestry, home economics, pharmacy, and science; graduate school O-585

Oregon Territory U-175, *map* U-177
  Indians' removal I-149
  Oregon O-586
  Polk P-438, *map* P-439

Oregon Trail, emigrant route from Independence, Mo., to Fort Vancouver on the Columbia River O-598
  frontier F-421
  Idaho I-22
  Nebraska N-96
  Oregon O-586
  Parkman's book P-124
  roads, *map* R-219

O'Reilly, Alexander (full name Don Alexander O'Reilly) (1722–94), officer in Spanish army, born in Ireland; governor of Louisiana 1769; put down revolt against first governor, executed leaders, won nickname Bloody O'Reilly; his administrative policies followed to end of Spanish period; made count 1771 N-233

O'Reilly, John Boyle (1844–90), Irish poet, political leader, and journalist; born near Drogheda, e. Ireland; sent to penal colony in Australia because of revolutionary activities in Ireland; escaped and settled in Boston, Mass.; editor of *The Pilot*, Roman Catholic newspaper ('Songs of the Southern Seas'; 'Moondyne'; 'America').

O'Rell, Max (pen name of Paul Blouet) (1848–1903), French satirical writer, born in England; taught in St. Paul's School and in University of London; books written in French and translated into English ('John Bull and His Island'; 'A Frenchman in America'; 'John Bull and Co.').

Orellana, Francisco de (1490?–1549?), Spanish explorer, born in Trujillo, Spain; discovered course of Amazon River in 1541 S-290, A-325
  Latin America L-67
    Guayaquil, Ecuador G-300

Orem, Utah, city 7 mi (11 km) n.w. of Provo in agricultural area; truck gardening; tomato cannery; steel, electronics; pop. 52,399, *map* U-232

Ore mineral, profitable amount of mineral O-601

Ore Mountains. *see in index* Erzgebirge

Orenburg (or Chkalov), U.S.S.R., city on Ural River; locomotive repair shops; flour milling; meat and dairy products; aircraft and tractor parts; clothing; pop. 345,000, *maps* E-361, R-344, 349

Ores, natural combination of minerals O-600. *see also in index* individual metals by name, *e.g.* Iron; Lead
  inorganic chemistry I-210
  metal and metallurgy M-307
  minerals M-432
  mines and mining M-424

'Oresteia', Greek trilogy by Aeschylus G-275

Orestes, character in Greek myth, son of Agamemnon and Clytemnestra; killed mother because she had killed father
  Greek literature G-275
    Agamemnon A-124

Oresund, strait between Sweden and Danish island of Zealand *map* S-524
  Baltic Sea B-46

'Orfeo', opera by Monteverdi M-568
  classical music M-668
  opera O-561

'Orfeo ed Euridice', opera by Gluck M-669
  opera O-564, *list* O-562

Orford, earl of. *see in index* Walpole, Horace; Walpole, Robert

Organ, animal or plant L-267, P-311
  biophysics research B-238
  organic sensitivity S-109
  sensory B-397
  transplantation T-251, S-519c
  X rays X-403

Organ, wind instrument
  Bach B-10
  Bruckner B-467
  tone production S-262
  wind instruments W-226, 231

Organdy, a fine, sheer cotton fabric; smooth, crisp finish; also, similar silk and synthetic fabrics; household uses.

Organelle, part of a cell B-198

Organic acids, in chemistry
  amino P-514
  fatty S-229, 231

Organic chemistry, branch of chemistry dealing with compounds of carbon that are typically found in living organisms O-601
  biochemistry. *see in index* Biochemistry
  Bunsen B-503
  chemistry C-300
  Liebig L-192
  nitrogen compounds (proteins) P-514
  paint pigments P-73
  petrochemicals P-228
  plastics P-381
  silicones S-196

Organic compound, substance that contains carbon O-601

Organic Law of the Spanish State S-357

Organic mental disorders, a category of mental illnesses M-301

Organism L-266

Organization, a body of people working together for some specific purpose
  communication C-613

Organization for Economic Cooperation and Development (OECD), pact signed in Paris, France, Dec. 14, 1960 by Austria, Belgium, Britain, Canada, Denmark, France, Greece, Iceland, Ireland, Italy, Luxembourg, The Netherlands, Norway, Portugal, Spain, Sweden, Switzerland, Turkey, United States, West Germany; Japan became full member April 1964; aims to promote economic growth and financial stability, expand trade, and coordinate aid to underdeveloped nations; effective Sept. 30, 1961; replaced the 18-member OEEC, which did not include the United States and Canada. *see also in index* Organization for European Economic Cooperation; European Organizations, *table*

Organization for European Economic Cooperation (OEEC), organization of Western European nations formed in 1948 to coordinate their efforts under the European Recovery Program administered by the Economic Co-operation Administration of the United States; replaced by OECD. *see also in index* Organization for Economic Cooperation and Development
  foreign aid F-307
  international trade I-267

Organization of African Unity (OAU) O-605
  Africa A-108
  Nyerere N-450
  Transkei T-250

Organization of Afro-American Unity (OAAU) M-74

Organization of American States (OAS) O-605. *see also in index* Pan American Union
  agricultural aid A-141
  Alliance for Progress S-292, *picture* S-278
  Latin America L-66
  North America N-344

Organization of Petroleum Exporting Countries (OPEC) O-606
  Asian trade relations A-692
  fuel supply and costs F-443
  international banking B-71
  monopoly M-545
  price increases P-233
    inflation I-199
  Yamani's influence Y-409

Organized crime C-772

Organized labor. *see in index* Labor unions

Organized Marine Corps Reserve. *see also in index* Reserves

Organ of Corti, in human ear. *see in index* Corti, organ of

Organon, the Greek word for "instrument"; the title applied to Aristotle's treatises on logic, because logic is the tool of thought.

Organ-pipe cactus, plant *Lemaireocereus thurberi* of the family Cactaceae, *picture* C-12

Organ Pipe Cactus National Monument, Arizona C-12

Organ-pipe coral, type of coral C-714

Organum, in classical music M-667

Organzine, a silk thread S-200

Orgasm, in sexuality S-124

Orient, the East. *see in index* Asia

Oriental civet C-462

Oriental clog. *see in index* Chopine

Oriental fruit moth I-225

Oriental Institute, at University of Chicago, Chicago, Ill.
  history writing H-173, *picture* H-170

Oriental leaf butterfly (or dead leaf butterfly, or Indian leaf butterfly) P-509, *picture* P-510

Oriental poppy, perennial plant *Papaver orientale* of the poppy family; native to Mediterranean region and Iran; grows to about 4 ft (1.2 m); leaves lobed; flowers scarlet with black spot at base of each petal, or orange, pink, or white
  flowering time G-25

Oriental rugs R-313, 315, 316, *picture* R-312
  antique A-494
  Ardabil carpet R-315
  Turkey T-321, *picture* T-323

Oriental sculpture S-93, *picture* S-78, *Reference-Outline* S-95

Orientalwood (or Australian walnut, or Queensland walnut, or Australian laurel), veneer wood from huge laurel tree *Endiandra palmerstonii* of Queensland coastal regions.

Orientation, in maps M-118

Orientation course, in college U-207

Orifice flow meter M-317

Oriflamme (golden flame), royal standard of France in medieval times; originally the bright red three-tongued banner of the abbey of St. Denis.

Origami, Japanese paper folding J-53

Origen (185?–254?), early Christian theologian, native of Alexandria, Egypt; sought to reconcile Platonism and Christianity.

Original jurisdiction, in law S-518a, U-150

'Origin of Species by Means of Natural Selection, On the', book by Darwin. *see in index* 'On the Origin of Species by Means of Natural Selection'

Orillia, Ont., town on Lakes Couchiching and Simcoe 65 mi (105 km) n. of Toronto; summer resort; wood products, machinery, furnaces, textiles, boats; Stephen Leacock Memorial Home; pop. 24,040.

Orinoco delta, delta in Venezuela, *table* D-90

Orinoco River, river in South America O-606
  Columbus S-290
  ore barge, *picture* S-276
  Raleigh R-91
  South America S-275, *map* S-300
  Venezuela V-275

Oriole, any of two dozen species of birds of Old World genus *Oriolus,* family Oriolidae, or any of 30 species of New World genus *Icterus,* family Icteridae; 8 to 12 in (20 to 30 cm) long; black-and-yellow or black-and-orange, with some white; found chiefly in warm regions of the world
egg, *picture* E-112
migration A-450
nest B-254, *picture* B-251

Orion, in Greek mythology, a mighty hunter beloved by the goddess Artemis; tricked by her brother Apollo, Artemis shot him with an arrow; he was placed among the stars P-391

Orion, constellation, one of the brightest in the northern sky, *chart* C-682
Betelgeuse S-414, A-718, *charts* S-415, 421, 423, *diagram* S-414
nebula, *chart* S-415
Huygens H-337

Oriskany, N.Y., village 7 mi (11 km) n.w. of Utica; Revolutionary War battle between Americans (under General Herkimer) and British and American Indians (under St. Leger and Joseph Brant), Aug. 6, 1777; Herkimer was mortally wounded; pop. 1,680.

Orissa, state in e. India; area 60,178 sq mi (155,860 sq km); cap. Bhubaneswar; iron ore; rice, turmeric, fish; silver filigree work; pop. 26,272,054 I-63, *picture* I-73, *map* I-83

Orizaba, Mount. *see in index* Citlaltépetl

Orkhan (1288–1360), second ruler of the Ottoman dynasty T-323

Orkney Islands (or Oreades), off n.e. Scotland; 376 sq mi (974 sq km); pop. 19,351 O-607
Europe, *map* E-361

Orlando, Vittorio Emanuele (1860–1952), Italian statesman, born in Palermo, Sicily; favored intervention in World War I; prime minister 1917–19; one of leaders at Peace Conference; at first supported fascism but soon resigned from parliament in protest.

'Orlando', opera by Handel O-503

Orlando (formerly Jernigan), Fla.; pop. 142,025 O-607
North America, *map* N-351
Walt Disney World and Epcot Center D-185

'Orlando furioso', poem by Ariosto A-588, S-475
Italian literature I-376

'Orlando Innamorato', poem by Boiardo S-474

Orleanists, in French political history, supporters of House of Orléans.

Orléans, dukes of, heads of the junior branch of French royal house of Bourbon; descend from Philippe, brother of Louis XIV of France.

Orléans, Louis Philippe, duke of (nickname Philippe Égalité) (1747–93), the regent's great-grandson, born in Saint-Cloud, France; elected Paris deputy to Convention 1792; voted for death of Louis XVI; executed under the Reign of Terror; his son was Louis Philippe, king of the French.

Orléans, Maid of. *see in index* Joan of Arc

Orléans, Philip, duke of (1674–1723), regent of France during minority of Louis XV, born in Saint-Cloud, France; able but dissolute and corrupt; supported "Mississippi Bubble" scheme.

Orléans (formerly Aurelianum), France, historic city; pop. 81,615 O-607
Europe, *map* E-361
France, *map* F-372
Hundred Years' War H-325
Joan of Arc J-119
warfare, *list* W-15

Orloff, diamond D-131, *picture* D-129

Orlon, a synthetic substance P-228
synthetic fibers F-74

Orlov trotter, horse breed H-277

Orly International Airport, in Paris, France A-220, *picture* A-209

Ormandy, Eugene (1899–1985), U.S. conductor, born in Budapest, Hungary; to U.S. 1921, became citizen 1927; conductor Minneapolis Symphony Orchestra 1931–36; conductor and music director of Philadelphia Orchestra 1936; awarded Presidential Medal of Freedom 1970
orchestra O-578, *list* O-579

Ormazd, in Zoroastrianism. *see in index* Ahura Mazda

Ormond Beach, Fla., city on Atlantic Ocean 4 mi (6 km) n. of Daytona Beach; resort center; incorporated 1880; pop. 128,394, *map* F-208

Ormuz, Strait of (or Strait of Hormuz), between Iran and Arabian peninsula P-211

Ormuzd, in Zoroastrianism. *see in index* Ahura Mazda

Orne River, river in Normandy, France; flows n. 95 mi (150 km) to English Channel, *map* F-372

Ornithischia, order of dinosaurs R-158

Ornithogalum, genus of perennial plants of the lily family; native to the Eastern Hemisphere; the Cape Chincherinchee *O. thyrsoides* has a striking triangular cluster of white, apricot, or yellow flowers; Star-of-Bethlehem is *O. umbellatum.*

Ornithology. *see in index* Birds

Ornstein, Leo (born 1895), U.S. pianist and composer, born in Kremenchug, Russia; ultramodern in earlier compositions; declared he was "not concerned with form or with standards of any nature" ('Wild Man's Dance').

Orogeny, mountain formation M-635

Orographic effect, in weather M-633
Oceania O-467

Oromocto, N.B., town on Saint John River 11 mi (18 km) s.e. of Fredericton, capital of the province; pop. 9,064 N-156

Orontes River (Arabic Nahr el 'Asi), river in Lebanon, n.w. Syria, and s. Turkey; about 250 mi (400 km) long S-549b

'Oroonoko', title of a novel by Aphra Behn dealing with the tribulations of an African prince sold as a slave in Surinam (Dutch Guiana).

O'Rourke, James Henry (nickname Orator Jim) (1852–1919), U.S. baseball player; born in East Bridgeport, Conn.; outfielder, first baseman, third baseman, catcher for 5 teams 1876–1904; played in major leagues at age of 52.

Oroville Dam, in California, on Feather River D-17
California C-37

Oroya fever, stage of Carrion's disease characterized by acute febrile anemia, bone and joint pains, and a high mortality rate if untreated
Noguchi N-330

Orozco, José Clemente (1883–1949), Mexican artist O-607
Mexico M-328
'Zapatistas' P-67a, *picture* P-67b

Orpah, in Bible, sister-in-law of Ruth R-365

Orpen, Sir William (1878–1931), British painter, born in Dublin; his portraits show broad and free technique; official British artist during World War I; knighted 1918.

Orpheus, legendary poet and musician of ancient Greece; given lyre by Apollo and instructed by the Muses; enchanted men, beasts, and even trees; when his wife, Eurydice, died from snakebite he won her release from Hades by his music, but by violating the condition not to look back at her until they had left the lower world, he lost her; called "Father of Song"
mythology M-702

'Orpheus in the Underworld', operetta by Offenbach O-572

Orphic mysteries, ancient mystery religion M-702

Orphism, in modern art
Delaunay D-69

Orpine family (or Crassulaceae), family of plants and shrubs including the houseleek, the sedums, live-forever, the kalanchoes, and the echeverias.

Orpiment, mineral M-432

Orpington, breed of poultry P-482, *picture* P-481

Orr, Bobby (or Robert Orr) (born 1948), Canadian ice-hockey player, born in Parry Sound, Ont.; with Boston Bruins 1966–76, Chicago Black Hawks 1976–77; numerous awards; All-Star after 1967 *picture* H-196

Orr, John Boyd, first **Baron Boyd-Orr.** *see in index* Boyd-Orr, John Boyd Orr, first Baron

Orr, Kay, U.S. governor W-276

Orrisroot, fragrant rootstock used in perfumery
orchid O-580

'Or San Michele, Madonna of', famous painting by Bernardo Daddi in the Or San Michele, a building of the grain merchants, later converted into a church; this Madonna was declared on Aug. 13, 1365, by the Florentine Republic, to be the protectress of the Florentines; it is enshrined in a tabernacle of Florentine Gothic style by Orcagna.

Orsini, noble Roman family which first appears prominently in 12th century; conflict with Colonna, a rival family, kept Rome in a turmoil for centuries; three of its members became popes (Celestine III, Nicholas III, and Benedict XIII).

Orsted, Hans Christian. *see in index* Oersted, Hans Christian

Ortega Saavedra, Daniel leader of Nicaraguan government
Nicaragua N-305

Ortega y Gasset, José (1883–1955), Spanish philosopher, essayist, and statesman, born in Madrid, Spain; famed for humanistic approach to philosophy; helped set up Spanish republic 1931 ('The Revolt of the Masses') S-367

Orteig, Raymond (1870–1939), French restaurateur and patron of aviation, born in Louvie-Juzon; came to New York City as a boy; owner of Hotel Lafayette A-205

Ortelius, Abraham (1527–98), Flemish cartographer and dealer in maps, born in Antwerp; published first modern atlas in 1570
maps, *picture* M-127

Orthicon tube, a camera tube
television T-74, 79

Orthochromatic film, in photography P-286

Orthoclase, a glassy, variously colored silicate of potassium and aluminum M-432, 436

Orthodontia, treatment for misaligned teeth T-53
dentistry D-102

Orthodox Catholic Church. *see in index* Eastern Orthodox churches

Orthodox Judaism J-151

Orthographic projection, in maps M-125, *picture* M-124
mechanical drawing M-260, *picture* M-261

Orthography, study of correct or standard spelling; from Greek meaning "straight, or correct, writing." *see also in index* Spelling

Orthopedic surgery, medical specialty, *table* M-277

Orthopter, a flying machine A-200

Orthostatic fitness E-369

Orthotropic bridge
San Mateo-Hayward B-447

Ortiz Rubio, Pascual (1877–1963), Mexican political leader and diplomat, born in Morelia, s.w. Mexico; minister to Germany, ambassador to Brazil.

Ortler, peak of Ortler group, in n. Italy near border of Switzerland; highest point in Tirol and in eastern Alps (12,792 ft; 3,899 m) T-192

Orton, Helen Fuller (1872–1955), U.S. author of children's books, born in Niagara County, New York; first books, for small children, followed by historical stories and mysteries ('Twin Lambs'; 'Treasure in the Little Trunk'; 'Mystery of the Lost Letter').

Oruro, Bolivia, city in w.; altitude 12,160 ft (3,710 m); railroad and tin-mining center; museum of minerals; pop. 110,490, *map* S-298

Orvieto, Italy, town and episcopal see in Umbria, 80 mi (130 km) n.w. of Rome; built on a rock commanding fine views; numerous 13th-century houses and palaces; Gothic cathedral begun in 1290; pop. 25,088, *map* I-404

Orwell, George (pen name of Eric Arthur Blair) (1903–50), English writer O-608
'Animal Farm' N-411
literary contribution E-282
'Nineteen Eighty-Four' R-112d

Ory, Edward (nickname Kid) (1886–1973), U.S. musician and composer, born in Laplace, La.; jazz trombonist in early New Orleans style; leader of jazz bands until 1961 ('Muskrat Ramble'; 'Savoy Blues'; 'Creole Song').

Oryx, an animal A-521

Osage, Indian tribe A-614, *maps* I-136, 149, *table* I-139
Oklahoma O-527

Osage orange, North American tree *Maclura pomifera* with inedible fruit, resembling a large orange; wood bright yellow, fine grained, and very elastic
hedges H-115

Osage Plains, in United States
Kansas K-174
Missouri M-488, *map* M-489

Osage River, about 250 miles (400 kilometers) long, formed in Missouri by junction of Marais des Cygnes and Little Osage rivers, flows generally n.e. through Lake of the Ozarks to Missouri River at Osage City 10 mi (16 km) s. of Jefferson City, Mo. *see also in index* Bagnell Dam

Osaka, Japan, city on Osaka Bay; pop. 2,642,000 O-608
Asia, *map* A-700
Kobe K-266
Japan, *map* J-75

Osaka Castle, in Osaka, Japan O-609

Osawatomie, Kan., city about 45 mi (70 km) s.w. of Kansas City, Kan.; attack by proslavery men 1856 resisted by John Brown and followers; latter finally overpowered and town practically destroyed; pop. 4,459.

Osawatomie Brown, U.S. abolitionist. *see in index* Brown, John (1800–59)

Osborn, Chase Salmon (1860–1949), U.S. political leader, born in Huntington County, Indiana; newspaper publisher 1883–1912; governor of Michigan 1911–12; agitated for inclusion of Great Lakes water areas in official areas of adjoining states ('The Iron Hunter', 'The Earth Upsets').

Osborn, Henry Fairfield (1857–1935), U.S. paleontologist, born in Fairfield, Conn.; with American Museum of Natural History from 1891, president 1908–33; with U.S. Geological Survey from 1900; research professor zoology, Columbia University, from 1910 ('Men of the Old Stone Age'; 'Origin and Evolution of Life'; 'Impressions of Great Naturalists'; 'Creative Education').

Osborne, John James (born 1929), British dramatist and actor, born in London ('Look Back in Anger'; 'The Entertainer'; 'Epitaph for George Dillon'; 'Luther', 1963–64 Drama Critics Circle Award; 'Inadmissible Evidence'; 'Time Present'; 'West of Suez'; 'A Sense of Detachment')
literary contribution E-282

Osborne, Thomas Mott (1859–1926), U.S. prison reformer, born in Auburn, N.Y.; as warden of Sing Sing 1914–16 and of Portsmouth Naval Prison 1917–20 applied his Mutual Welfare League plan; wrote 'Society and Prisons', 'Prisons and Common Sense'.

Osborne, estate near East Cowes, Isle of Wight; convalescent home for army and navy officers; site of a Royal Naval College 1903–21.

Osbourne, Fanny de Grift (1840?–1914), wife of Robert Louis Stevenson S-446

Osbourne, Lloyd (1868–1947), U.S. author, born in San Francisco, Calif.; stepson of Robert Louis Stevenson ('Wild Justice') S-446

O.S. calendar. *see in index* Julian calendar

Oscar, statuette presented annually by Academy of Motion Picture Arts and Sciences; sketched by Cedric Gibbons,

plastics, brick and tile; site of first Lincoln-Douglas debate 1858; pop. 18,166
Illinois, *map* I-53

Ottawa, Kan., city 60 mi (80 km) s.w. of Kansas City, Kan.; metal products, clothing; Ottawa University; pop. 11,016.

Ottawa (formerly called Bytown), Ont., capital of Canada; pop. 302,341 O-612
Canada C-98, *map* C-112
canal C-129
North America, *map* N-351
Ontario O-552
Parliament, *pictures*, P-132, R-300a
Royal Canadian Mounted Police R-300a

Ottawa, University of, Ottawa, Ont.; Roman Catholic; founded 1848; charters in 1866 and 1889; arts and sciences, applied science, commerce, home economics, law, library science, medicine, music, nursing, philosophy, physical education, psychology and education, social science, theology; graduate school O-552

Ottawa River, river in Canada, chief tributary of St. Lawrence; rises in Quebec, flows w., and then s.e., forming boundary between Quebec and Ontario; length 696 mi (1,120 km)
Canada, *map* C-112
canal C-129
North America, *map* N-351
Ontario O-549
Ottawa O-612, 615
Quebec Q-9d, *picture* Q-9b, *maps* Q-9a, 10

Ottawa University, Ottawa, Kan.; affiliated with American Baptist Convention; founded 1865; arts and sciences, teacher education.

Otter, a subfamily of the weasel family W-114
fur, *table* F-465

Otterbein, Philip William (1726–1813), U.S. clergyman, born in Dillenburg, Prussia; founded United Brethren in Christ.

Otterbein College, Westerville, Ohio; affiliated with United Methodist church; founded 1847; arts and sciences, business administration, education, music C-595

Otterburn, England, village in n.e.; Scots under Douglas defeated English under Percy 1388; battle celebrated in ballad 'Chevy Chase'.

Otter civet, mammal C-462

Otter Creek, river in w. Vermont, about 110 mi (180 km) long, *map* V-301

Otter hound, dog, *picture* D-200

Otter shrew, aquatic mammal of Africa, related to shrews and moles; lives in Cameroun, Congo basin, and Angola; total length about 24 in. (61 cm) (half of this is tail); fur is brown above, whitish below; scientific name *Potamogale velox;* in fur trade sometimes called desman. *see also in index* Desman

Otter trawl, net F-134, *picture* F-135

Ottery St. Mary, England, village of Devonshire; birthplace of Samuel Taylor Coleridge; the Clavering of Thackeray's 'Pendennis'; pop. 5,770.

Otto I (or Otto the Great) (912–973), Holy Roman Emperor O-616
Austria-Hungary A-828
Germany G-121
Holy Roman Empire H-208

Otto II (or Otho II) (955–983), Holy Roman emperor H-209

Otto III (or Otho III) (980–1002), Holy Roman emperor H-209
Charlemagne's tomb A-2

Otto IV (or Otho IV) (1175?–1218), Holy Roman emperor.

Otto (1848–1916), king of Bavaria; insane throughout reign (1886–1913); his uncle, Prince Luitpold, regent until 1912; deposed.

Otto, James Edwin (nickname Jim) (born 1938), U.S. football player, born in Wausau, Wis.; center; Oakland Raiders (AFL) 1960–69, Oakland Raiders (NFL) 1970–74.

Otto, Nikolaus A. (1832–91), German inventor
four-stroke cycle gas engine A-858
internal-combustion engine I-252

Ottoboni, Pietro, Cardinal, Roman catholic cardinal
Corelli C-716

'Otto Hahn', West German freighter S-170

Ottokar II (or Ottakar II) (1230?–78), king of Bohemia; acquired Austria, Carinthia, Carniola, and Styria; later lost all except Bohemia and Moravia; famous for cleverness and valor.

Ottoman Empire O-616. *see also in index* Turkey
Algeria A-304
Arabia A-523
Arabs A-527
Asia Minor. *see in index* Asia Minor
Atatürk A-732
Balkan states B-29
Balkan wars B-31
battle of Lepanto N-92
Bulgaria B-500
Byzantine history B-533
international relations I-260
Iraq I-315
Islamic literature I-364
Istanbul I-375
Macedonia M-8
Mediterranean Sea M-286
Mesopotamia M-305
Middle Ages M-391
Middle East M-397
Transjordan J-142
Tripoli, Libya T-289
Tunisia T-309
Yugoslavia Y-435

Otto of Freising (1111?–58), German historian H-172

Ottumwa, Iowa, city on Des Moines River about 90 mi (145 km) s.e. of Des Moines; meat-packing; farm equipment, factory-built homes; pop. 27,381
Iowa, *map* I-302

Otway, Thomas (1652–85), English dramatist, born near Chichester; ('Don Carlos', in rhymed verse; 'The Orphan' and 'Venice Preserv'd', in blank verse).

Ouachita Baptist University, Arkadelphia, Ark.; Southern Baptist; founded 1885; opened 1886; arts and sciences, education; graduate studies.

Ouachita Mountains, outlying portion of main Ozark Plateau, s. of Arkansas River in Oklahoma and Arkansas; height 1,500 to 2,500 ft (460 to 760 m) A-613, *maps* U-36, 58
Oklahoma O-522

Ouachita National Forest, national forest preserve; comprises 2,129,270 acres (861,720 hectares) in w.-central Arkansas and 291,509 acres (117,974 hectares) in s.e. Oklahoma; mainly short-leaf pine and hardwoods.

Ouachita River, river that rises in w. Arkansas and flows s.e. across n. Louisiana to Red River near the latter's junction with the Mississippi River, *map* U-58

Ouagadougou (or Wagadugu), Burkina Faso (Upper Volta), capital; pop. 359,801 O-619
Africa, *map* A-118
Burkina Faso B-507

Ouargla (or Wargla), Algeria, town in Sahara about 200 mi (320 km) s. of Biskra; dates grown; pop. 19,451, *map* A-118
oasis O-454

Oubangui River. *see in index* Ubangi River

Oud, Jacobus Johannes Pieter (1890–1963), Dutch architect, born in Purmerend; aimed for purity of form, straightness of line, equilibrium of proportions; buildings in Amsterdam and Rotterdam.

Oudenaarde, Belgium, town on Scheldt River 16 mi (26 km) s. of Ghent; victory of Allies under Marlborough and Prince Eugene of Savoy over French under Vendôme (1708); pop. 6,923
battle (1708) M-147

Oudry, Jean Baptiste (1686–1755), French painter, born in Paris; known for studies of animals; official painter of royal hunts of Louis XV.

Ouedraogo, Jean-Baptiste, (born 1925), former ruler of Burkina Faso B-508

Ouida. *see in index* De la Ramée, Louisa

Ouimet, Francis (1893–1967), French golfer G-189

Oujda, Morocco, city in n.e. near Algerian border; trade and transportation center; founded during latter part of 10th century; pop. 349,400, *map* A-118

Ounce (or snow leopard), wild cat *Uncia uncia, table* C-215

Ounce, unit of measure, *table* W-140

'Our American Cousin', play by Tom Taylor; first produced 1858; at a performance of this play President Abraham Lincoln was assassinated.

Our Father Prayer. *see in index* Lord's Prayer, The

Ouricury (or licuri), name for useful wax secreted from leaves of licuri palm *Syagrus coronata* abundant in state of Bahia, Brazil.

Our Lady of Fatima. *see in index* Fatima, Our Lady of

Our Lady of the Elms, College of, Chicopee, Mass.; Roman Catholic; for women; founded 1928; arts and sciences, teacher education.

Our Lady of the Lake University of San Antonio (until 1975 Our Lady of the Lake College), San Antonio, Tex.; Roman Catholic; founded 1912; arts and sciences, business administration, education, home economics, library science, music, social service; graduate school.

'Our Magic', source book on the theory of magic published by John Nevil Maskelyne and David Devant M-38

'Our Mr. Wrenn', work by Lewis L-143

'Our Mutual Friend', novel by Dickens (1865); two plots are tied together by Mr. Boffin, the Golden Dustman, and his wife.

Oursler, Charles Fulton (1893–1952), U.S. writer and editor, born in Baltimore, Md.; editor *Liberty* magazine 1931–42; wrote popular books on religious themes ('The Greatest Story Ever Told'; 'The Greatest Book Ever Written'; 'The Greatest Faith Ever Known', with G.A.O. Armstrong); also mystery stories under pseudonym Anthony Abbot; autobiography, '1893–1952: Behold This Dreamer!'.

'Our Town', play by Wilder W-382

Ouse, river in Sussex, England; 30 mi (50 km) long; flows into English Channel at Newhaven; only lower part navigable, *map* U-18a

Ouse, river in Yorkshire, England; about 60 mi (100 km) long; flowing s.e., joins Trent River to form the Humber.

Ouse (or Great Ouse), river in s.e. England; about 160 mi (260 km) long; flows n.e. into The Wash; one of its tributaries is Little Ouse.

Outback, region in Australia
Burke and Wills expedition B-506
frontiers F-425, *picture* F-422

Outboard motorboat B-325

Outcault, Richard Felton (1863–1928), U.S. comic artist and advertising man, born in Lancaster, Ohio; created 'Hogan's Alley', 'Yellow Kid', 'Buster Brown'.

Outer ear, outer visible portion of the ear that collects and directs sound waves toward the eardrum by way of a canal which extends inward through the temporal bond D-48, E-3

Outer Mongolia. *see in index* Mongolian People's Republic

Outer planets S-254a, P-350, *diagram* S-254c

Outer Seven. *see in index* European Free Trade Association

Outer space, region beyond earth's atmosphere
travel. *see in index* Space travel

Outfielder, in baseball B-93

Outlanders. *see in index* Uitlanders

Outlaws O-610
folklore F-268

'Outline of History, The', work by Wells W-148

Out-of-court settlement, in law L-95

Output, in computer data C-627

Output arm (or resistance arm), in mechanics M-267

Outram, Sir James (1803–63), English general, born in Butterley Hall, Derbyshire; hero of Indian Mutiny; given title "the Bayard of India" by Sir Charles Napier, his superior, when he defended British residency at Hyderabad against 8,000 Baluchis 1843; helped to hold Lucknow against siege 1857.

Outremont, Que., residential city that adjoins Montreal; became city in 1915; pop. 28,552, *map* Q-11

Outrider, an attendant riding on a horse beside a carriage or on one of the horses drawing a carriage.

Outrigger, device attached to the side of certain boats of narrow beam to prevent capsizing B-325, S-163, *pictures* P-17, U-98
shell oars R-300

Outsole, shoe part S-180

Ouzel, water. *see in index* Dipper

Ouzo, type of liquor L-235

Ova, eggs S-123

Oval. *see in index* Ellipse

Ovary, female reproductive gland R-151c, *diagram* R-151d
birth control B-283
embryology E-199
gland G-153
hormones H-243, *table* H-241, *diagram* H-240
menstruation M-300
multiple birth M-649
sexuality S-123

Ovary, in flowering plants, the receptacle in which fertilized seed germs develop F-218
berries B-176

Oven
Pueblo, *picture* S-338
tunnel oven P-478

Ovenbird, a warbler
courtship B-250, *picture* B-251

Overburden, in coal mining C-519
dam construction D-16

Overcasting, in sewing S-122

Overcrowding, social condition
cities C-460
warfare W-18

Overcup oak, tree *Quercus lyrata* of beech family, grows to 100 ft (30 m); leaves to 8 in. (20 cm) long with large terminal lobe
wood, *table* W-203

Overdose, in drugs
antihistamines A-492

Overeaters Anonymous, for weight control W-136

Overhand knot (or thumb knot)
knot, hitch, and splice K-262

Overhand mining M-429

Overland, Mo., city 10 mi (16 km) n.w. of St. Louis; residential area; incorporated 1939; pop. 19,620.

'Overland Monthly', San Francisco newspaper
Harte H-50

Overland Park, Kan., city 10 mi (16 km) s. of Kansas City; chiefly residential; incorporated 1960; pop. 81,784 in metropolitan Kansas City area.

Overland Stage, historic road in U.S., *map* R-219

Overland trails, United States R-220, *map* R-219
Overland Trail R-221
Nebraska N-96
Oregon Trail O-599. *see also in index* Oregon Trail

Overlea, Md., community in Baltimore County in n. part of state just n.e. of Baltimore; pop. 13,086, *map* M-183

Overlord, Operation, World War II campaign W-340

Overmyer, Robert F. (born 1936), U.S. astronaut, born in Lorain, Ohio; U.S. Marine Corps officer chosen for NASA program 1969, *table* S-348

Overseas Highway, road, Florida F-198, K-230, *picture* F-194

Overshot wheel, type of waterwheel W-103

Overstreet, Harry Allen (1875–1970), U.S. psychologist, born in San Francisco, Calif.; head of philosophy department, College of City of New York 1911–39; later a conductor of radio program Town Meeting of the Air ('About Ourselves'; 'The Mature Mind'; 'The Great Enterprise'; with wife, Bonaro Wilkinson Overstreet: 'The Mind Alive', 'The Mind Goes Forth', 'What We Must Know About Communism', 'The

Strange Tactics of Extremism', and 'The FBI in Our Open Society').
Over-the-counter market S-452
financial page S-453
Over-the-road common carrier, a motor transportation system T-291
Over-the-road contract carrier, a motor transportation system T-291
'Over There', song by Cohan C-537
Overton, Anthony (1864–1946), U.S. manufacturer, banker, life-insurance executive, and publisher; born in Monroe, La.; to Chicago, Ill., 1910; awarded 1927 Spingarn Medal; Anthony Overton Elementary School, in Chicago, named in his honor.
Overtone, in music S-260, *diagram* S-262
Overture, in music, *list* M-671
Lully's French form L-328
Overweight. *see in index* Obesity
Ovid (or Publius Ovidius Naso) (43 BC–AD 17), Roman poet O-620
literature L-77, L-244
mythology M-704
Oviduct, in female reproductive system R-151c, d, *diagram* R-151d
embryology E-199
gonorrhea V-273
Oviedo, Spain, industrial city 16 mi (26 km) s. of Bay of Biscay; university; plundered by French in Peninsular War (1809 and 1810); pop. 66,234.
Oviparous animal, egg-laying animal
insects I-221, *picture* I-220
Ovipositor, egg-laying organ of insects
bee B-125
grasshopper C-768
dragonfly D-239
spider S-387
Ovists, group of biologists in 17th century Europe
genetics G-52
heredity H-139
Ovshinsky, Stanford Robert (born 1922), U.S. inventor, born in Akron, Ohio; devised semiconductor switches of amorphous, glassy materials instead of conventional crystalline substances; these switches, triggered by electricity or light or both, have shown potentialities for simplifying television sets, computers, and watches.
Ovulation, in female reproductive system
birth control B-283
menstruation M-300
sexuality S-123
Ovule, reproductive structure on megasporangium seed plants C-720
Ovum (or egg cell), female reproductive cell R-151c, d, *diagram* R-151d, *picture* R-151c. *see also in index* Egg
alcohol affects A-276
cell division C-239
embryology E-199, *diagram* E-200
evolution A-461
genetics G-54
hormones H-243
menstruation M-300
moss M-599
multiple birth M-649
Owatonna, Minn., city 62 mi (100 km) s. of St. Paul; diversified industrial and agricultural area: state school for disabled children; Pillsbury Military Academy; pop. 18,632.
Owen, Sir Richard (1804–92), English biologist, born in Lancaster, England; conservator of museum Royal College of Surgeons; superintendent natural history department British Museum ('Memoir on the Pearly Nautilus'; 'Odontography').
Owen, Robert (1771–1858), British reformer and utopian socialist O-620
commune C-605, 706
kindergarten and nursery school K-241
New Harmony, Ind. I-94, *picture* I-95
socialism S-233
Wright W-366
Owen, Robert Dale (1801–77), U.S. statesman and editor O-620
Owen, Ruth Bryan (1885–1954), U.S. political leader and lecturer, born in Jacksonville, Ill.; daughter of William Jennings Bryan; married to Boerge Rohde; lyceum and Chautauqua lecturer 1919–28; congresswoman from Florida 1929–33; minister to Denmark 1933–36 ('Leaves from a Greenland Diary'; 'The Castle in the Silver Wood').
Owen, Stephen (nickname Steve) (1898–1964), U.S. football tackle and coach, born in Indian Territory (now Oklahoma); tackle Kansas City Cowboys 1924–26, New York Giants 1926–30; player-coach 1931–32; head coach 1933–52.
Owen, Wilfred (1893–1918) British writer
literary contribution E-280
Owen Falls Dam, Uganda, on Victoria Nile River V-311
Nile N-317
Owens, Buck (born 1929), U.S. country musician M-679
Owens, Jesse (originally James Cleveland Owens) (1913–80), U.S. track athlete O-620
athletics A-741, *picture* A-739
Oylmpics O-542
track and field T-246
Owens, Michael Joseph (1859–1923), U.S. inventor and glass manufacturer, born in Mason County, Virginia (now W. Va.); held 45 patents; organized Owens Bottle Machine Co. 1903.
Owensboro, Ky., city on Ohio River about 29 mi (47 km) s.e. of Evansville, Ind.; oil, coal, and tobacco center; radio tubes, electric-light bulbs, metal and wood products; distilling, food processing; Brescia College and Kentucky Wesleyan College; pop. 54,450, *map* U-41
Owens Lake, lake in California, 12 mi (19 km) s.e. of Mt. Whitney; about 18 mi (29 km) long and 10 mi (16 km) wide; receives Owens River at n. end.
Owen Sound, Ont., city on Owen Sound, inlet of Georgian Bay, 98 mi (158 km) n.w. of Toronto; port for grain, oil, coal; livestock center; machinery, furniture, leather, textiles, meats, dairy products; pop. 19,883, *map* C-112
Owens River, river in s.e. California, flows s.e. and s. 175 mi (280 km) to Owens Lake.
Owen Stanley Range, range in s.e. New Guinea; scene of battle action 1942.
OWI (Office of War Information), United States R-277
Owings, Nathaniel (1903–84), U.S. architect, born in Indianapolis, Ind.; co-founded architectural firm of Skidmore and Owings (now Skidmore, Owings & Merrill) in 1936 A-569
Owl, any bird of prey, generally nocturnal, in order Strigiformes; characterized by forward oriented eyes, virtually noiseless flight, acute vision and hearing; commonly brown; species range from 5 to 28 in (13 to 70 cm) long; found worldwide except in Antarctica
barn owl, *picture* B-269
book illustration, *picture* R-111h
eyes B-246
great horned owl, *picture* B-251
parasites, *picture* P-115
prey B-281
screech owl, *picture* B-245, 269
snowy, *picture* B-269
Owl monkey (or night monkey) behavior and characteristics A-503
Owosso, Mich., city 75 mi (120 km) n.w. of Detroit on Shiawassee River; electric motors, abrasives, metal products, beet sugar; pop. 16,455.
Owyhee dam, on the Owyhee River in Oregon O-583
Ox (plural oxen). *see also in index* Oxcart
cattle C-224
Costa Rica, *picture* R-218
early use in North America, *picture* P-332
farming F-27
India, *picture* T-262
Latin America, *picture* L-131
rubber transportation in Far East, *picture* R-304
Venezuela, *picture* S-281c
wagon train O-599
Oxalic acid, poisonous crystalline compound ($C_2H_2O_4$) found in many plants (especially in wood sorrel or oxalis); artificially made by oxidizing sugar, starch, cellulose, etc., by nitric acid, or by fusing caustic alkalies with compounds having oxygen; used in bleaching and dyeing.
Oxalis, genus of plants with acid-tasting, cloverlike leaves; flowers red, violet, yellow, or white; both flowers and leaves fold, or "sleep," at night; wood sorrel a type in the United States.
Oxalis family (or Oxalidaceae, or wood-sorrel family), family of plants and trees including the violet wood sorrel, lady's-sorrel or sour grass, yellow wood sorrel, Bermuda buttercup, oca, bilimbi, and carambola.
Oxbow lake E-16, *diagram* E-17
formation R-210
Oxcart
India, *picture* T-262
Latin America, *picture* P-131
Philippines, *picture* P-256
Oxenstjerna, Axel Gustafsson, Count (1583–1654), noted Swedish statesman, born in Fåno, Uppland, Sweden; became chancellor 1616; showed great ability in directing foreign policy and home government of Sweden; held absolute control in central Germany during Thirty Years' War; guardian of Queen Christina, who opposed him S-527
Oxeye, type of sunflower. *see in index* Heliopsis
Oxford (or Oxfordshire), county of s.-central England; 749 sq mi (1,940 sq km); farming, manufacturing; county town, Oxford; pop. 309,452 O-621
Oxford, England, famous university town, 52 mi (84 km) n.w. of London; pop. 119,909 O-621, *map* U-18a. *see also in index* Oxford University
Oxford, Miss., city 60 mi (100 km) s.e. of Memphis, Tenn.; dairy, poultry, truck farms; lumber; University of Mississippi at nearby University; incorporated 1837; pop. 9,882.
Oxford, Ohio, residential village 19 mi (27 km) w. of Middletown; Miami University; pop. 17,655.
Oxford, type of sheep S-147
Oxford and Asquith, Herbert Henry Asquith, first **earl of** (1852–1928), English statesman, born in Morley, near Leeds; for many years leader of Liberal party; stood for many governmental reforms, one of which deprived the House of Lords of its veto power; sympathized with Irish struggle for home rule; opposed woman suffrage; as prime minister (1908–16) was criticized for his conduct of the government during World War I; became earl in 1925
Lloyd George L-321
United Kingdom E-255
Oxford and Asquith, Margot, countess of (1864–1945), English writer, wife of first earl of Oxford and Asquith; her autobiography made sensation in European society ('The Autobiography of Margot Asquith'; 'Places and Persons'; 'Octavia'; 'Myself When Young'; 'More Memories').
'Oxford Book of Modern Verse, The', work by Yeats Y-412
'Oxford Book of War Poetry', edited by Stalworthy W-27
'Oxford English Dictionary, The' R-126
Oxford Group. *see in index* Moral Re-Armament
Oxford Movement, a religious movement in Anglican church after 1832; aimed to restore to Church of England some of the doctrines and practices abandoned during the Reformation.
Oxfordshire, county in England. *see in index* Oxford
Oxford University, Oxford, England O-621
Bodleian Library S-140, *picture* L-176
England E-234
Rhodes scholarships R-195
Ox Hill, battle of. *see in index* Chantilly, Va.
Oxidation, chemical union of any substance with oxygen or other negative element or radical
biochemistry B-201
bleaching B-310
chemistry C-299
fire (rapid oxidation) F-93
food P-312
ink I-207
Lavoisier's discovery L-90
living things L-269
plants P-373, *diagram* P-373
platinum P-384
rust (slow oxidation) R-363
tea T-46
Oxidation-reduction reaction, reaction that involves a change in oxidation numbers C-299
Oxidative phosphorylation, in biochemistry B-201
Oxide, compound of oxygen with some other element
acid rain A-19
corrosion C-726
iron rust R-363
metal and metallurgy M-307
silicon S-195b
silver S-204
sulfur S-510
zinc P-73
Oxide mineral, classification M-432
Oxidoreductase, enzyme E-290, *table* E-290
Oxlip, flowering plant of primrose family, native to Europe and cultivated in gardens.
Oxnam, Garfield Bromley (1891–1963), U.S. clergyman, born in Sonora, Calif.; president DePauw University 1928–36; bishop of Methodist Episcopal church 1936–60; champion of liberal causes.
Oxnard, Calif., city 54 mi (87 km) w. of Los Angeles; frozen foods, citrus fruits, beet sugar, agricultural machinery, electronics; military installations nearby; pop. 108,195.
Oxus River. *see in index* Amu-Dar'ya
Oxyacetylene torch, *picture* S-9
Oxygen (O), gaseous element O-622. *see also in index* Oxidation; Oxides
aerospace hazards A-81
air A-145, 747
experiment, *picture* A-146, 748
algae produce A-283
atomic structure, *diagram* V-255
blood B-313
body's requirement R-159
aerospace hazards S-346
mammal M-80
chemical element C-294
corrosion C-726
cryogenics C-793
freezing point S-254f
earth's crust, *table* E-11
explosive E-379
fatigue F-45
fire F-93
fire-fighting F-102
fish P-441c, *diagram* P-441d
iron and steel industry I-339
liquid. *see in index* Liquid oxygen
living things L-268
lung exchange L-336
Martian atmosphere A-717
matter M-223
minerals M-436
periodic table, *table* P-207, *list* P-208
photosynthesis P-300
plants P-373, *diagram* P-373
rust R-363
sun's atmosphere S-513
water W-85, 91
Oxygen cycle, in biology O-623
Oxygen process, in steelmaking
efficiency I-339, *diagram* 340
Oxygen-16, an isotope of oxygen O-623
Oxyhemoglobin, combination of oxygen and hemoglobin found in arterial blood B-313
Oxytocin, hormone that initiates birth H-240, *table* H-241
Oyama Iwao, Prince (1842–1916), Japanese field marshal, born in Satsuma, s. Kyushu; captured Port Arthur in war with China; commander in chief in the Russo-Japanese War; defeated the Russians at Mukden, Manchuria.
Oyashio. *see in index* Okhotsk Current
Oyo, state in Nigeria
Ibadan I-2
slave trade A-110
Oyster O-623
anatomy A-422
cultured pearl industry P-149, *pictures* P-148
invertebrate group I-283
mollusk M-524

The letter P

is of uncertain origin. Picture signs of the human mouth are found in Egyptian hieroglyphic writing (1) and perhaps also in a very early Semitic writing used about 1500 B.C. on the Sinai Peninsula (2). They hardly resemble the form of the P sign which was developed about 1000 B.C. in Byblos and other Phoenician and Canaanite centers (3). From it all later forms are derived. In the Semitic languages the sign was called *pe,* meaning "mouth." The Greeks renamed the Semitic sign *pi* and turned the letter around to suit the left-to-right direction of their writing. They used both a curved and an angular form of the sign (4). Later the Greeks gave the angular sign more symmetry by lengthening the right-stroke tail (5).

The Romans closed the Greek curved form into a loop (6). From the Latin the shape of the capital letter P came unchanged into English.

The English small handwritten "p" is a copy of the capital.

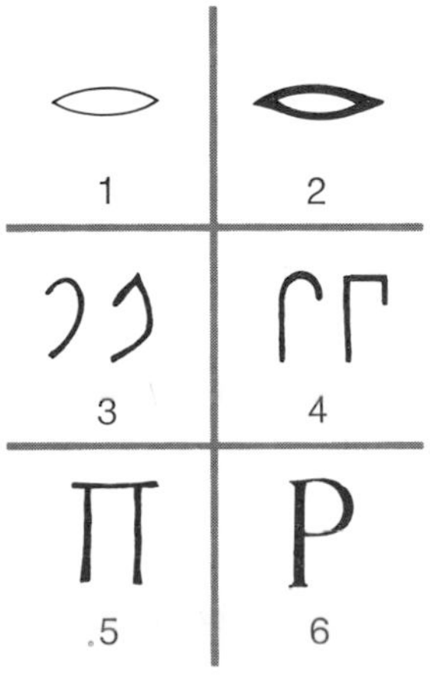

P

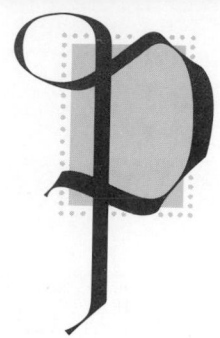

P-47 (or Thunderbolt), U.S. military aircraft W-333

P-51 (or Mustang), U.S. military aircraft W-333

PAC (political action committee) L-276

Paca, William (1740–99), signer of Declaration of Independence, born in Hartford County, Maryland; governor of Maryland 1782–86; U.S. district judge 1789–99
  Declaration of Independence D-56

Paca, ground-dwelling rodent *Coelogenys paca* P-1

PACAF (Pacific Air Forces), U.S. Air Force A-164

Paccard, Michel-Gabriel (1757–1827), French doctor who was the first person to climb Mont Blanc in the Alps M-637

Pace (or double step), Roman unit of measure W-138, *table* W-140

Pacemaker, electronic stimulator for body organs B-211
  heart B-161h, H-100

Pacer, a horse whose gait is the pace H-277

Pacer, reading aid, *picture* R-103a

Pace University (formerly Pace College), New York, N.Y.; private control; founded 1906; arts and sciences, business administration, education, law, nursing, graduate studies; campuses at Pleasantville and White Plains N-254

Pachomius, Saint (292?–346?), Egyptian monk; organized first monastery around 318 M-540

Pachuca, Mexico, city 55 mi (90 km) n.e. of Mexico City; altitude 8,000 ft (2,440 m); capital of state of Hidalgo; silver reduction plants; pop. 83,892 M-324, *map* M-344

Pachyderm, semiscientific term applied to the elephant, the rhinoceros, the hippopotamus, the tapir; from the Greek, meaning "thick-skinned"
  elephant E-184
  rhinoceros R-178
  tapir T-27

Pachysandra, genus of creeping plants of the box family, native to N. America and Japan; both evergreen and deciduous, with small flowers, white, greenish, or purple; one species called mountain spurge.

Pachysandra terminalis (or Japanese spurge), a ground cover
  growing conditions G-27

Pacific, University of the, Stockton, Calif.; private control, Methodist related; founded 1851; liberal arts, business administration, education, engineering, music, pharmacy; graduate studies; Elbert Covell College (Spanish speaking); law at Sacramento, dentistry at San Francisco.

Pacific, War of the (1879–88) P-224
  Bolivia B-336

Pacifica, Calif., city 12 mi (19 km) s.w. of San Francisco, on Pacific Ocean; chiefly residential; pop. 36,866.

Pacific Air Forces (PACAF), U.S. Air Force A-164

Pacification of 1917, Dutch political compromise during the reign of Queen Wilhelmina N-131

Pacific City. *see in index* Huntington Beach

Pacific College. *see in index* Fresno Pacific College

Pacific Equatorial Undercurrent (or Cromwell current), ocean current O-475

Pacific Fur Company F-471
  Oregon Trail O-598

Pacific Grove, Calif., city just n. of Monterey; chiefly residential; resorts; marine laboratory; pop. 15,755.

Pacific hake, fish *Merluccius productus* of the family Merlucciidae H-13

Pacific halibut (or California halibut), flatfish F-175

Pacific herring, fish *Clupea pallasi* H-143

Pacific hybrid, variety of flowering plant G-24

Pacific islands P-1
  sandalwood S-38
  Western Samoa W-154

Pacific Islands, Trust Territory of the, official name of former Japanese mandated islands (Marshall, Caroline, and Mariana islands except Guam) after transfer to strategic trusteeship of U.S. by agreement in 1947 with Security Council of United Nations; land area 687 sq mi (1,779 sq km), water area 7,797 sq mi (20,194 sq km); pop. 136,800, *maps* U-116, P-6

Pacific loon, bird L-289

Pacific Lutheran University, Tacoma, Wash.; founded 1890, present name 1960; arts and sciences, business administration, education, fine and applied arts, nursing; graduate studies T-4, W-52

Pacific mackerel, fish *Scomber japonicus* M-16

Pacific Northwest, geographical area of North America N-339

Pacific Oaks College, Pasadena, Calif.; private control; founded 1945; liberal arts, education; graduate study.

Pacific Ocean, largest of the oceans P-1. *see also in index* Ocean and Ocean, *table*; Pacific islands
  Balboa's exploration B-23
  communication cables C-10, *map* C-7
  fisheries
    salmon S-29
    seal S-98
  geography G-62
  Magellan M-36
  Peruvian currents P-221

Pacific Plate, in geology E-39
  Oceania O-465, 472

Pacific red cedar. *see in index* Western red cedar

Pacific region, in the United States. *see in index* United States, *subhead* geographic regions, North Pacific and South Pacific; *also* names of states in these regions

Pacific sailfish, fish S-16b

Pacific salmon, fish S-28

Pacific sardine, fish, *picture* F-132

Pacific Scandal, in Canadian history C-101

Pacific silver fir. *see in index* Silver fir

Pacific South Equatorial current, ocean current O-475

Pacific time T-189, *map* U-40

'Pacific 231', work by Honegger M-675

Pacific Union College, Angwin, Calif.; Seventh-day Adventist; chartered as Healdsburg College 1882, present name from 1909; arts and sciences, education; graduate studies; quarter system.

Pacific University, Forest Grove, Ore.; private control; founded 1849; arts and sciences, education, music, optometry; graduate school.

Pacific yew (or western yew), tree *Taxus brevifolia* of the Taxaceae family Y-416

Pacifism, opposition to war and violence P-143b
  Jainism J-14

Pacius, Fredrik (1809–91), Finnish violinist; composed music for Finland's national song, 'Our Land' ('Vårt Land' in Swedish, 'Maamme' in Finnish).

Pack, Charles Lathrop (1857–1937), U.S. banker and forester, born in Lexington, Mich.; aided in reforestations of Europe after World War I and established forestry foundations; started Cleveland Trust Co.; wrote 'Forests and Mankind' and 'Forest Facts for Schools'.

Packaging P-105
  adhesives used A-43
  cigar and cigarette T-200
  consumerism C-687
  food processing F-283
  industry I-188
  marketing M-141, *picture* M-142

Pack animals. *see in index* Transportation, *subhead* animal power

Packard, David (born 1912), U.S. businessman and government official, born in Pueblo, Colo.; cofounder of Hewlett-Packard Company, electronics concern, 1939; deputy secretary of defense 1969–71.

Packard, Frank Lucius (1877–1942), Canadian novelist, born in Montreal, Que., of U.S. parents ('The Miracle Man'; 'Greater Love Hath No Man'; 'The Night Operator'; 'Jimmie Dale' mystery stories).

Packers and Stockyards Act (1921), United States M-253

Packet, vessel carrying mail, cargo, and passengers on a regular schedule; originally the boat carrying official state packets of dispatches and letters S-167, 175, *picture* S-164

Pack ice A-572

Packing industry. *see in index* Meat industry

Pack rat. *see in index* Wood rat

Pack transportation. *see in index* Transportation, *subhead* animal power

Pact of Paris. *see in index* Kellogg-Briand Pact

Pactolus River, small stream in ancient Lydia, w. Asia Minor; gold found in its bed was ascribed in mythology to the bathing of Midas and contributed to the vast wealth of Croesus.

Pad, launching S-342c, *picture* R-231

Padang, Sumatra, seaport in center of w. coast; large trade in coffee, tobacco, copra; pop. 196,339 S-511, *map* I-166
  Asia, *map* A-700

Paddington, district in Westminster borough, London, England; at St. Mary's Hospital here, Sir Alexander Fleming discovered penicillin 1928.

Paddle, implement with broad flat blade S-163
  canoeing C-141

Paddlefish, also called **spoon-billed catfish,** a fish of the Mississippi River system; has long spadelike snout to stir up mud and get food; has scales only on part of its tail; member of family Polyodontidae; may grow 6 ft (1.8 m) long.

Paddle tennis, a game similar to tennis; played with laminated wooden paddles and a light sponge-rubber ball about $2\frac{5}{8}$ in. ($6\frac{7}{10}$ cm) in diameter on a court 44 by 20 ft (13.4 by 6.1 m); invented 1924 by Frank P. Beal, New York, N.Y.

Paddle wheel
  steamers S-165, 175
    Clermont F-447
    Fitch's experiments F-147
    Natchez and *Robert E. Lee* S-177c
  navy N-83

Paddock, place where horses are saddled H-276

Paddy, a term used to designate unhusked or unmilled rice, growing or cut; also the name for the field in which rice is grown A-134. *see also in index* Rice

Padeloup, family of French bookbinders, notably **Antoine** (died 1668), master binder, and grandson **Antoine Michel** (1685–1758), called the Younger; latter's work impeccable, binding solid yet supple, gilding in dentelle style, inlays in varicolored leathers unrivaled.

Paderewski, Ignace Jan (1860–1941), Polish musician and statesman P-20

Paderewski Fund, prize fund for U.S. composers P-20

Padilla, Ezequiel (1890–1971), Mexican lawyer and statesman; revolutionist under Pancho Villa 1914–16; exile in New York, N.Y., 5 years; as secretary of public education 1929–30, promoted Mexico's modern school system; minister to Italy and Hungary; foreign minister 1940–45.

Padilla, Juan de (1500?–1544?), Franciscan missionary, born in Andalusia, Spain; came to Mexico about 1528; built monasteries at Tuxpan, Zapotlán, and Tulancingo; accompanied Coronado's expedition (1540) north to Seven Cities; settled among Quivira Indians and established the first mission in what is now the s.w. U.S.; killed by Quiviras when he tried to convert nearby hostile tribes.

Padlock L-277

Padma River. *see in index* Ganges River

Padre Island, long reef off coast of Texas T-116, *map* U-41
  island I-368

Padua (Italian Padova), Italy, educational and art center and trade and manufacturing city on Bacchiglione River, 22 mi (35 km) w. of Venice; university, dating from 13th century, one of oldest in Europe; pop. 198,403, *maps* E-361, I-404
  Donatello's 'Gattamelata' S-85, *picture* S-87
  Giotto's frescoes, *picture* P-29

Paducah, Ky., city in w. part of state, on Ohio and Tennessee rivers; soybeans, tobacco; clothing, radio and automobile parts, industrial belting; railroad shops; popular vacation area; pop. 29,315, *map* U-41

Paedogenesis, reproduction in larval or pupal stages I-221

Paekche, former Korean Kingdom K-284

Paektu (also called Paektu san, Chinese Pai-t'ou Shan), highest peak of Korean Peninsula, in n.e., on border of Manchuria; 9,003 ft (2,744 m); has crater lake K-282, *map* K-290

Paer, Ferdinando (1771–1839), Italian composer O-565

Paestum (originally Poseidonia), Greek city on

w. coast of Italy, on Gulf of Salerno; founded 6th century BC; conquered by Romans 273 BC; destroyed by Saracens 9th century; ruins of 3 Doric temples.

Pagan, deserted city in Burma, *picture* B-508

Paganini, Niccolo (1782–1840), Italian violinist, born in Genoa; hailed as "greatest violinist of all time"; devised own technique of fingering and bowing; composed violin concertos.

Paganism F-251

Page, Sir Earle Christmas Grafton (1880–1961), Australian political leader, born in Grafton, New South Wales; Country party leader 1920–39; prime minister 1939.

Page, Greg, U.S. heavyweight boxer B-392

Page, Patricia Kathleen (born 1916), Canadian poet, born in England C-116

Page, Ruth (born 1905), U.S. ballet dancer and choreographer, born in Indianapolis; one of the first to create ballets on U.S. themes D-24

Page, Thomas Nelson (1853–1922), U.S. novelist, short-story writer, and diplomat, born in Hanover County, Va.; ambassador to Italy 1913–19 ('In Ole Virginia; or, Marse Chan, and Other Stories'; 'Two Little Confederates'; 'Red Rock: a Chronicle of Reconstruction').

Page, Walter Hines (1855–1918), U.S. editor and diplomat, born in Cary, N.C.; editor *Atlantic Monthly* 1896–99, *World's Work* 1900–13; ambassador to United Kingdom 1913–18.

Page, training for knighthood K-257
Middle Ages M-387

Pageant P-20
miracle play M-462

Pageboy, haircut H-9

Page makeup, in publishing N-239

'Pagliacci, I', opera by Leoncavallo L-105
opera O-568, *list* O-562

Pagoda, a sacred tower, several stories high, usually connected with a temple, in countries of the Far East. *see also in index* Temple
Burma M-95, R-92
Japan A-546

Pago Pago, capital of American Samoa, on island of Tutuila; pop. 2,491 S-33, *map* P-6

Pahang, state of former Federation of Malaya; 13,873 sq mi (35,931 sq km); farm products; tin, gold; became part of Malaysia 1963; pop. 503,131. *see also in index* Malay States, Federated

Pahlavi, or **Pahlevi.** *see in index* Mohammed Reza Pahlavi; Reza Shah Pahlavi

Pahlavi dynasty (1925–79), in Iranian history I-308

Pahlevi (officially Bandar-e Anzalī), Iran, port on s.w. coast of Caspian Sea; handles large part of waterborne trade between Iran and U.S.S.R.; pop. 41,785.

Pahmi (or ferret-badger), name for several species of Asiatic badger like animals of weasel family; scientific name *Helictis moschata*
fur, *table* F-465

Pahoehoe, lava L-90, *picture* L-89

Paideia, education designed to allow people to explore the whole range of knowledge in order to develop their full potential H-318

Paideia Group, educational reform group established by Mortimer Adler A-45

Paige, Satchel, or **Leroy Robert Paige** (1906–82), U.S. baseball pitcher, born in Mobile, Ala.; star 1927–48 in Negro leagues and in exhibitions; with Cleveland Indians 1948–49, St. Louis Browns 1951–53, Kansas City Athletics 1965 B-95

Paille-maille, game which developed into croquet C-783

Pain, sensation
acupuncture A-29
anesthetics A-142
brain processes B-397
child abuse C-319
labor pains R-151d
loud noise causes P-441e
narcotics and sedatives N-19

Paine, Albert Bigelow (1861–1937), U.S. biographer and writer of stories for children, born in New Bedford, Mass. ('Mark Twain, a Biography'; 'Joan of Arc: Maid of France'; 'Arkansaw Bear').

Paine, John Knowles (1839–1906), U.S. composer, born in Portland, Me.; professor Harvard University, occupying first chair of music in a U.S. university; compositions for orchestra ('Island Fantasy'; 'The Tempest'); chamber music; cantatas and songs.

Paine, Robert Treat (1731–1814), U.S. lawyer and statesman, born in Boston, Mass.; signer of Declaration of Independence; member Continental Congress 1774–78
Declaration of Independence D-56

Paine, Thomas (1737–1809), U.S. political writer and patriot P-21
'Common Sense' A-344
Declaration of Independence D-53
Hall of Fame, *table* H-16

Paine, Thomas Otten (born 1921), U.S. scientist, born in Berkeley, Calif.; with General Electric Company 1949–68, 1970–, vice-president 1970–; NASA administrator 1969–70.

Paine College, in Augusta, Ga.; affiliated with United Methodist and Christian Methodist Episcopal churches; authorized 1882, opened 1884; liberal arts, teacher education.

Painesville, Ohio, city on Grand River near mouth on Lake Erie, 27 mi (43 km) n.e. of Cleveland; nurseries; chemicals, plastics; Lake Erie College; pop. 16,391.

Painlevé, Paul (1863–1933), French statesman and scientist, born in Paris; active in politics, serving at various times as minister of public instruction and of inventions, minister of finance, minister of war, and premier; author of books on higher mathematics.

Paintbrush, plant. *see in index* Hawkweed; Indian paintbrush

'Painted Bird, The', work by Kosinski K-301

Painted bunting (or nonpareil), a small bird of the finch family; has bright red underparts, a dull red tail and rump, purple head and neck, and yellowish-green back B-375

Painted cup. *see in index* Indian paintbrush

Painted daisy, flower *Chrysanthemum coccineum* of Compositae family D-6

Painted Stoa (or Stoa Poikile), Athens A-538

Painted tongue. *see in index* Salpiglossis

Painted turtle (or painted terrapin), freshwater turtle of the genus *Chrysemys* T-330

Painter's colic, a severe stomach pain caused by lead absorption; sometimes experienced when the fumes of burning lead-based paint are breathed.

Painting P-22. *see also in index* Drawing; Fresco; Mural painting; also chief topics below and names of chief painters
abstract expressionism P-440
airbrush P-399
animals. *see in index* Animals in art, *subhead* paintings
Australian A-801
brushes B-464
design D-110
Egyptian. *see in index* Egyptian arts and architecture, ancient
finger painting F-87
folk art F-249
French F-50, 56, 356
German G-115
Greek G-269
hobby H-181
Indian I-71
mosaic M-589
perspective P-220
Philippine P-257d
Pre-Raphaelites R-298
primitive. *see in index* Primitive art, of self-taught artists, *subhead* painting
Renaissance R-146
Roman G-273
surrealism. *see in index* Surrealism
theater stages and settings T-156

Paints P-72, *diagram* P-75, *picture* P-76. *see also in index* Varnish
artists' paints P-67g
color C-559
formaldehyde P-228
gums and resins R-158
ingredients
cobalt C-530
lead L-99
oils F-47
nut N-449
soybean S-340
radium R-70
rubber R-305
spray guns P-399

Pair production, in physics M-230

Paisley, Scotland, burgh and river port 7 mi (11 km) w. of Glasgow; threadmaking; textiles, ships; Paisley shawls exhibited by museum; pop. 95,182.

Paisley shawls, formerly made in Paisley, Scotland, in imitation of those of Cashmere.

Paita, Peru, a seaport with fine harbor, in Piura district; ships cotton; pop. 9,615, *maps* P-224, S-298

Pai-t'ou Shan, peak in North Korea. *see in index* Paektu

Paiute, American Indian tribe that lives chiefly in Nevada and Utah, *map* I-136, *picture* I-114, *table* I-139
Oregon O-583
Utah U-217
Wovoka W-363

Pak-choi, Chinese cabbage *Brassica chinensis* C-4

Pakenham, Sir Edward Michael (1778–1815), British general, born in Ireland; veteran of Napoleonic campaigns; killed in battle of New Orleans.

Pakistan, independent nation now consisting of former West Pakistan Province area; established 1971 after civil war in which East Pakistan gained independence as Bangladesh; 310,403 sq mi (803,940 sq km); cap Islamabad; pop. 60,000,000 P-77, *map* A-700
agriculture
wheat W-189
cities. *see in index* cities listed below and other cities by name
Islamabad I-362
Lahore L-23
flag F-161, *picture* F-168
food supply F-286
Himalayas H-153
history
Bangladesh B-63
Commonwealth membership C-603
independent nation created
genocide G-60
post World War II W-358
Indus Valley civilization I-197
Jammu and Kashmir claim J-22
Jinnah's influence J-118
United Kingdom E-258
India I-61, 78
Indus River I-168
irrigation I-356
literature I-364
folktales, *list* S-479, *picture* S-465
Iqbal's contribution I-304
migration of people M-400
policeman, *picture* P-430b
population, *chart* P-447
railroad mileage, *table* R-85
religious problems A-684

Pakistan, East. *see in index* Bangladesh

Palace C-199. *see also in index* Castle
Austria, Schönbrunn. *see in index* Schönbrunn
China F-298
England
Buckingham Palace. *see in index* Buckingham Palace
France
Louvre P-121, *map* P-120
Rohan S-484a
Versailles V-303, P-123
India, *picture* I-61
Italy. *see in index* Italy, *subhead* architecture
Mexico
Aztec A-891
New Mexico S-46
Philippines, *picture* P-255c
Spain
Escorial, *picture* S-360
Moorish architecture, *picture* S-358
U.S.S.R.
Kremlin K-304
Leningrad R-354
Petrodvorets, *map* R-340

Palace, Mayor of the. *see in index* Mayor of the Palace

Palace Museum, in Peking, China F-298

Palace of Culture and Science, in Warsaw, Poland W-33

Palace of Justice, in Chandigarh, India
Le Corbusier's design, *picture* L-114

Palacio Valdés, Armando (1853–1938), Spanish novelist and critic ('The Marquis of Peñalta'; 'Sister Saint Sulpice'; 'Tristan'; 'José').

Palade, George E. (born 1912), U.S. biologist, born in Iasi, Romania; naturalized 1952; discovered ribosomes; director of cell biology studies Yale University Medical School 1972–. *see also in index* Nobel Prizewinners, *table*

'Pala d'Oro', altar screen in St. Mark's Basilica, Venice, Italy, *picture* E-208

Palais des Machines, in Paris, France, *picture* F-8

Palamon and Arcite, story of two Theban knights, prisoners of Theseus, king of Athens; they fall in love with Emelye, sister-in-law of the king, and compete for her in a tournament; Palamon is defeated, but Arcite, although victorious, is thrown from his horse and killed; after mourning him, Palamon and Emelye are united; early version of the story found in the 'Teseide' of Boccaccio, source of Chaucer's Knight's Tale.

Palance, Jack, U.S. actor
'Requiem for a Heavyweight', *picture* T-71

Palate, the roof of the mouth; consists of the hard palate in front and the soft palate behind; former has a bony framework, while latter is composed of muscular fibers enclosed by a movable fold of mucous membrane M-641

Palate bone. *see in index* Palatine bone

Palatinate (German Pfalz), two historically related regions in West Germany, Lower (or Rhine) Palatinate in the state of Rhineland-Palatinate and Upper Palatinate in Bavaria
counts and electors palatine. *see also in index* Frederick I, the Victorious; Frederick II, the Wise; Frederick III, the Pious; Frederick IV, the Upright; Frederick V
Louis XIV L-306

Palatinate, War of the (also called the War of the League of Augsburg, or Grand Alliance) (1689–97), North American phase known as King William's War.

Palatine, Ill., residential village 30 mi (50 km) n.w. of Chicago; incorporated 1869; pop. 32,166, *map* I-53

Palatine bone (or palate bone), L-shaped bone at the back of nasal cavity; forms a part of the wall of this cavity, the roof of the mouth, and the floor of the eye socket S-210

Palatine Hill, central and earliest settled of the 7 hills of Rome; its rectangular shape gave name *Roma quadrata* to primitive city founded, according to legend, by Romulus R-254
castle C-199

Palatka, Fla., city 46 mi (74 km) s. of Jacksonville; livestock; paper, wood products; pop. 9,444.

Palau Islands (or Pelew Islands), archipelago (26 main islands) in Pacific e. of Philippines, part of w. Caroline Islands; 175 sq mi (455 sq km); copra, sugar, breadfruit, bananas; bauxite, phosphates; discovered by Spanish 1543; sold to Germany 1899; made Japanese mandate 1919; became headquarters for entire Japanese South Seas government; naval and air base in World War II; occupied by U.S. 1944; made U.S. trusteeship 1947; pop. 12,673
Pacific Ocean, *map* P-6, *picture* P-18
World War II W-347

Palawan, westernmost of the larger islands of the Philippines; ranks 5th in size; 4,550 sq mi (11,784 sq km);

Los Angeles; in early 1930s developed as famous desert resort; pop. 32,271.

Palm Sunday, in Christianity E-41

Palmyra, Syria, capital of former kingdom; pop. 10,670 P-84

Palmyra Island, atoll consisting of 55 islets about 1,100 mi (1,770 km) s.w. of Honolulu; area 500 acres; taken over by U.S. 1898; administered from Hawaii; held by U.S. Navy as aviation station during World War II, *map* P-6

Palmyra palm, a magnificent and valuable palm *Borassus flabellifer*, common in India and nearby islands; named from the city of Palmyra.

Palo Alto, Calif., city 27 mi (43 km) s.e. of San Francisco; electronic products and research; Stanford University; pop. 55,225, *map* U-40

Palo Alto, plain in s. Texas, 8 mi (13 km) n.e. of Brownsville; Gen. Zachary Taylor defeated Mexicans in Mexican War battle (May 8, 1846).

Palolo worm, an annelid found in waters near Samoan and Fiji islands; swarms to surface in Oct., caught and eaten by the islanders; found also near Dry Tortugas and Puerto Rico, where it rises to surface in June or July; scientific name *Palolo* (*Eunice*) *viridis*.

Palomar Mountain, about 50 mi (80 km) n.e. of San Diego, Calif.; 6,126 ft (1,867 m) high; site of Palomar Observatory.

Palomar Observatory, n.e. of San Diego, Calif., on Palomar Mountain; administered jointly by California Institute of Technology and Carnegie Institute.

Palomino horse, a popular type (not a breed) of saddle horse characterized by color, which varies from orange-gold to ivory, and light-colored mane and tail, black hoofs and white "stockings" halfway to knee are considered ideal markings H-260, *picture* H-257, *list* H-254

Palos, Spain, Atlantic seaport on s. coast, 55 mi (90 km) s.w. of Seville; Columbus sailed from Palos Aug. 3, 1492; pop. 2,143 C-592, *map* S-350

Palouse district, in s.e. Washington; rolling plateaus U-84, *picture* U-85

Palouse River, rises in Idaho, flows w. into Washington and enters Snake River; 220 mi (350 km) long; lumbering and farming principal activities in its basin.

Paloverde tree, an intricately branched tree *Cercidium torreyanum* of the pea family; native to desert lands of California, Arizona, and Mexico; from 15 to 20 ft (4 to 6 m) high; has smooth, green bark, small leaves which soon fall, and showy clusters of yellow flowers that are followed by beanlike pods; also called green-barked acacia; state tree of Arizona.

Palpation, in medicine, feeling body tissue M-278

Palpus (plural palpi), jointed process attached to mouthparts of some insects, crustaceans, centipedes, spiders; sensory or feeding function.

Palsy, impaired muscular control; synonymous with paralysis. *see also in index* Cerebral palsy; Paralysis

Paludan-Müller, Frederik (1809–76), Danish poet ('Adam Homo', narrative epic in 3 vols.; 'The Dryad's Wedding' and 'The Death of Abel', idylls; 'Kalanus', poetic drama).

Paludrine, drug Q-18

PAM (plasma arc machining), metalworking operation T-226

'Pamela, or Virtue Rewarded', first modern novel, written by Samuel Richardson; story of a simple country girl whose master, failing to seduce her, marries her
English literature E-271
epistolary novel N-411
Fielding parodies F-79

Pamir (also called Pamirs), mountainous region in central Asia A-674, *map* A-700
Afghanistan A-88
sheep S-148
U.S.S.R. R-321

Pamlico Sound, in North Carolina, largest lagoon on Atlantic coast of U.S. N-354

Pampa (fl. 940), Kannada poet I-106

Pampa, Tex., city 55 mi (90 km) n.e. of Amarillo, in wheat and livestock district; oil and gas, carbon black, gasoline; oil-field supplies, heavy machinery; pop. 21,396, *map* U-40

Pampa, grassy plain G-237, S-281a, *map* S-274
Argentina A-575
Latin America L-59

Pampas cat, wild cat *Felis pajeros*, *table* C-216

Pampas deer, small, reddish-brown species of deer *Ozotoceros bezoarticus*; native of plains of Argentina and Brazil D-62

Pampas grass, perennial plant *Cortaderia selloana* of the grass family, native to plains of Brazil, Argentina, and Chile; grows to 7 ft (2 m), in clumps, with the narrow reedlike leaves and tall stems topped by plumelike clusters, silvery white to pink; used as an ornamental plant.

Pampero. *see in index* squall

Pamphili. *see in index* Eusebius of Caesarea

Pamphlet
health education, *picture* V-273
Paine P-21
Swift S-531
U.S.S.R. R-332f

Pamplona, Spain, city on Arga River, in foothills of w. Pyrenees, 20 mi (30 km) from France; agricultural and industrial center; cathedral; famous for Ernest Hemingway's 'The Sun Also Rises'; pop. 59,227
bulls, *picture* S-355

Pampulha, planned suburb of Belo Horizonte, Brazil B-159

Pan, in Greek mythology, god of flocks, fields, forests; portrayed with goat's horns, beard, and feet; symbolized paganism to early Christians M-701
Midas M-383

Pan, a device used in processing gold ore G-179

Panacea, goddess of all healing, daughter of Aesculapius.

Panacea, a remedy or medicine purporting to cure all diseases.

Pan-Africanism M-74

Panama, Republic of Panama, capital and chief Pacific port, on Gulf of Panama at s. terminus of Panama railroad; pop. 439,900 P-86, P-91
Central America C-253, *pictures* C-257, C-258
flag, *picture* F-169
national anthem, *table* N-64
North America, *map* N-351
World War II W-328

Panama, hat H-54
Ecuador E-67

Panama, Declaration of (1939), *table* T-274

Panama, Gulf of, *maps* N-351, S-298

Panama, Isthmus of, strip of land connecting North and South America; runs e. to w. in form of an S; usually regarded as coextensive with Republic of Panama; average width 70 mi (110 km); old name, Isthmus of Darien P-85, *map* P-90
Drake D-240
Pizarro P-349

Panama, Republic of, the southernmost of the Central American states; 28,753 sq mi (74,470 sq km); cap. Panama; pop. 1,825,900 P-85, *map* N-351
flag, *picture* F-169
history
Bunau-Varilla B-502
United States R-286
Johnson's foreign affairs J-133
treaties (1977) U-197
Latin American literature L-74
tagua nuts B-530
transportation
early railroads L-66
railroad mileage, *table* R-85
ship tonnage, *table* S-176a
whistle, *picture* S-78

Panama Canal P-87
Bunau-Varilla B-501
canal construction C-126
Carter's treaty C-184
Goethals G-174
Gorgas G-195
Lesseps L-138
Panama P-86
Roosevelt R-286
Suez Canal comparison S-504
Taft T-8

Panama Canal Commission P-95

Panama Canal Treaties P-86, 95
1903, *table* T-275
1977 U-197

Panama Canal Zone. *see in index* Canal Zone

Panama City, Fla., seaport and resort city in n.w., on Gulf of Mexico; paper products, chemicals; boat building, commercial fishing; oil terminals; pop. 33,346.

Panama disease, a fungus disease that attacks banana trees B-52

Panama-Pacific International Exposition, world's fair held in San Francisco, Calif., Feb. 20 to Dec. 4, 1915, to celebrate opening of Panama Canal; 36 foreign nations participated; area of grounds 635 acres (255 hectares); cost $50,000,000 F-10

Pan-American conferences, meetings of delegates from South, Central, and North America, and West Indies to consider various questions of mutual interest.

Pan American Convention. *see in index* Buenos Aires Convention

Pan American Convention on Nature Protection in the Western Hemisphere (1942), treaty N-25

Pan American Day, celebrated April 14, for on that day in 1890 the Pan American Union was formed; a legal holiday by presidential proclamation 1931.

Pan-American Exposition, held in Buffalo, N.Y., May 1 to Nov. 2, 1901, to illustrate progress of civilization in Western Hemisphere in 19th century; area of grounds 350 acres (142 hectares); attendance 8,179,674; cost $8,860,757; gate receipts $5,534,643; holding a reception in Temple of Music Sept. 6, President McKinley was fatally shot by Leon Czolgosz F-10
McKinley M-21

Pan American Foot-and-Mouth Disease Center, project of Pan American Health Organization; originally under Organization of American States; aims to eradicate foot-and-mouth disease from nations where it exists and to prevent its spread to nations now free of this disease; provides diagnostic and advisory services, training courses, research; headquarters, Rio de Janeiro.

Pan-American Games A-738
water polo, *picture* W-102

Pan American Health Organization (formerly International Sanitary Bureau), coordinates efforts among nations to combat disease H-90

Pan American Highway, system of highways proposed to connect capitals of all countries in North, Central, and South America from Alaska to Strait of Magellan R-218
Latin America L-66
Panama, *map* P-90
South America S-289

Pan-Americanism, movement for increased inter-American cooperation S-292

Pan American Union (PAU) P-143c. *see also in index* Organization of American States

Pan American University, in Edinburg, Tex., state control; founded 1927; social studies and humanities, business administration, education, science and mathematics; graduate studies.

Pan American World Airways A-170
jet airliner, *picture* S-289

Panamint Range, in California, n. and s. range, e.of Sierra Nevada, at foot of which lies Death Valley; Panamint Peak highest point (6,605 ft; 2,015 m).

Pan-Arabism, in Middle East M-397

Panathenaea, the oldest and most important of ancient Athenian festivals, in honor of Athena A-733

Panay, an island nearly in center of Philippines; 4,446 sq mi (11,515 sq km), 6th in size; Iloilo chief city, 250 mi (400 km) from Manila; fine grazing land; sugar, rice, copra; deer abound; pop. 2,010,297 P-256, 259, *maps* P-259a, 262
Asia, *map* A-700

'Panay', U.S. gunboat sunk by Japanese R-273

Pan Ch'ao (AD 32–102) Chinese general and colonial administrator of the Han Dynasty; reestablished Chinese control over Central Asia C-362

Pan Chao, (AD 45?–115?), famous Chinese scholar and lady-in-waiting to the empress C-363

'Panchatantra, The', an ancient collection of Sanskrit fables; originally designed for the moral and ethical instruction of princes; source of many European fables F-4
Indian literature I-106
storytelling S-461, 467, *list* S-478

Panchayat, village government in India I-70

Panchromatic film, in photography P-286

Pancreas, a gland in the abdomen G-153
anatomy A-392
Banting's and Best's experiments B-75
diabetes D-125
digestive system D-145, *diagram* D-143
hormones H-242, *table* H-241, *diagram* H-240

Pancreatic juice, fluid from the pancreas D-145

Pancreatin, a solution of digestive enzymes made from the pancreases of livestock; used to treat some digestive disorders.

Panda, the name that applies to two related mammals of the family Procynidae P-97
bear B-116

Pandaka pygmaea, fish of the Philippines, belonging to goby family; in lakes and streams; less than ½ in. (1¼ cm) long when full-grown; black-banded body, about size of rice grain; smallest fish and smallest vertebrate known in the world. *see also in index* Goby

Pandanus tree, tropical tree or shrub, also called screw pine because of spiral arrangement of leaves P-13, *picture* P-9. *see also in index* Screw-pine family
Kiribati K-250

Pandarus, in Greek legend, a Lycian, hero of Trojan War, distinguished as an archer; slain by Diomedes; in Shakespeare's 'Troilus and Cressida' acted as an intermediary in love, hence the word "pander."

'Pandects' (or 'Digest'), legal work J-161

Pandemic, widespread epidemic E-292

Pandit. *see in index* Nehru, Jawaharlal

Pandit, Vijaya Lakshmi (born 1900), Indian diplomat, born in Allahabad; with her brother Jawaharlal Nehru, active in Indian independence movement 1921–47; chief of Indian delegations to UN 1946–49, 1951–53, 1963–; ambassador to U.S.S.R. 1947–49, to U.S. 1949–51; first woman president UN General Assembly 1953–54; high commissioner in London 1954–61.

Pandora, in Greek mythology, first woman on Earth P-97
mythology M-698
women's rights W-271

'Pandora', British warship S-177c

Panegyric, formal eulogy
Islamic literature I-367

Panero, Leopoldo (1909–62), Spanish author ('Spanish to the Bones') S-367

Pan fish F-141

Pangaea, prehistoric supercontinent E-26
Atlantic Ocean's origin A-743
biogeography B-218
continental drift theory C-692
Wegener W-133

Pangalanes Canal, in Madagascar M-23

Pangalos, Theodore (1878–1952), Greek general and political leader; army chief of staff 1918–20; by coup d'etat established dictatorship 1925; ousted by General Kondylis 1926.

Pangborn, Clyde (1894–1958), U.S. aviator, born in Douglas County, Washington.

Pan-Germanism, a movement to unite Germans all over the world into groups for the promotion of German ideals and territorial expansion, organized 1891 and given name of Pan-German League 1894; later developed into movement for world domination.

Pangloss, character in Voltaire's 'Candide'. *see in index* 'Candide'

Pangolin (or scaly anteater), several species of toothless mammals of family Manidae, native to w. Africa and s.e. Asia; covered with horny scales; cannot fight but confuses enemies by rolling into a ball; captures ants with its long slender tongue; somewhat similar in structure to American anteater, *picture* A-436

Panhandle, of Alaska A-241

Panhandle, of Texas T-116

Panicle, a plant structure, *picture* F-127

Panics and depressions, in the economy. For a list of panics in the United States, *see table* following
- banking B-72
  - central bank C-260
- black Americans affected B-294
- book publishing history B-363
- business cycle B-517
- inflation I-199
- international relations I-263
- labor law development L-5
- labor movements L-8
- money M-531
- United States history
  - 1837 V-261
  - 1869
    - Grant G-218
  - 1873
    - Grant U-182
  - 1893
    - Harrison H-47
    - McKinley M-19
  - 1929. *see in index* Great Depression
- West Germany G-126

Panini (5th cent. BC), Indian grammarian L-229

Panizzi, Sir Anthony (1797–1879), British librarian, born in Italy; to England 1823, citizen 1832; chief librarian British Museum 1856–66.

Panjim (or Pangim), India, seaport 245 mi (395 km) s. of Bombay; formerly capital of Portuguese India, in Goa, seized by India 1961; pop. 34,837.

Pankhurst, Emmeline (1858–1928), British militant suffrage leader; founded National Women's Social and Political Union 1903; with daughters **Dame Christabel** (1880–1958) and **Estelle Sylvia** (1882–1960), led "militant suffragettes" W-278, *list* W-275

Pan Ku (fl. AD 32–92), Chinese poet, soldier, and historian C-363, 388

Panleucopenia (or cat distemper, or cat typhoid, or viral enteritis), most widespread and serious infectious disease of cats C-210

Panmunjom, South Korea, village 6 mi (10 km) s.e. of Kaesong; in Korean War, scene of series of truce negotiations, starting in Oct. 1951, of first exchange (April 1953) of sick and wounded prisoners between the United Nations forces and the Communists, and of armistice (July 27, 1953) and final exchange of war prisoners K-300, *chart* K-299, *map* K-290

Panned candy C-139

Panneton, Philippe. *see in index* Ringuet

Panning, in motion pictures M-609

Pannonia, province of the Roman Empire, lying s. and w. of the Danube River; the Illyrians probably were the original inhabitants.

Pannonian Plain (or Mid-Danube Plain), in Hungary H-326

Panorpa. *see in index* Scorpion fly

Pan-Slavism, movement toward political and cultural union of nations of Slavic descent; has played important part in politics of central Europe; movement is chiefly opposed to Magyar and German influence; congresses held 1848 at Prague, 1867 at Moscow, and 1908 at Prague B-29

Pan-Sori, Korean folk opera K-281, K-294

Panspermia, theory that living things on Earth developed from microorganisms which came from another planet E-364

Pansy, a flower of the family Violaceae P-98, *picture* F-225
- explosive seedpods S-106
- growing conditions G-23
- violet V-326

Pantagruel, giant in Rabelais's satire 'Gargantua and Pantagruel' R-23
- French literature F-395

Pantaloon, character in old Italian comedy representing San Pantaleone, portrayed as a foolish old man who wore spectacles and slippers and long trousers which ended in stockings; character later used in pantomime; term also applies to certain kind of trousers, whence "pants."

Pantaloons, garment D-264

Pantelleria, volcanic island in Mediterranean, 62 mi (100 km) s.w. of Sicily; belongs to province of Trapani, Sicily; 32 sq mi (83 sq km); chief town Pantelleria; pop. 9,601, *maps* E-361, I-404

Panthalassa, prehistoric superocean
- Wegener W-133

Pantheism, belief that the universe as a whole is God G-173

Panthéon, in Paris, France; formerly church of Ste. Geneviève, begun 1764; secularized during Revolution and dedicated to great men of nation; later again used as church but finally secularized by decree of 1885; burial place of many eminent men of France P-117, *map* P-120

Pantheon, in Rome, Italy R-257, *map* R-250

Panting, in mammals M-80

Pantograph, frame S-486

Pantographic punch cutter, in type and typography T-337

Pantomime (Greek all imitating), a play in which a story is told by gestures and dancing without words, often accompanied by music; of ancient origin M-422. *see also in index* Mime
- dance D-25
- Fields F-80

Pantothenic acid, vitamin V-356

Panty hose, hosiery H-277

Pánuco River, e.-central Mexico; flows into Gulf of Mexico at Tampico; about 240 mi (390 km) long, *map* M-344

Panurge, companion of Pantagruel in Rabelais's 'Gargantua and Pantagruel'; has wit and intelligence but is a coward with no moral principles.

Panza, Sancho, squire in Cervantes' 'Don Quixote', *picture* N-408

Panzer division, German term for armored division: army unit heavily equipped with tanks, mobile artillery, and motorized troop transport T-21
- World War II W-322

Panzini, Alfredo (1863–1939), Italian novelist; autobiographical novels and short stories; 'Il Mondo è Rotondo' (The World Is Round), 'Le Fiabe della Virtú' (The Fables of Virtue).

Paoli, Pasquale (1725–1807), Corsican general and patriot; a leader in rebellion against Genoese and French rule of Corsica; head of government 1757–68; increasing French control forced flight to England; during French Revolution returned as governor, remained until British occupied island.

Paolo di Dono. *see in index* Uccello, Paolo

Paolo Veronese. *see in index* Veronese

Paotow, China, city on Hwang Ho, in Inner Mongolian Autonomous Region; pop. 490,000.

Papacy P-98. *see also in index* Pope; Vatican City
- Babylonian captivity P-252
- Counter Reformation C-744, R-135
- encyclical. *see in index* Encyclical
- Frederick I and II F-390, F-395
- Great Schism. *see in index* Great Schism
- Italian history I-391
- Popes Pius P-347
- Reformation. *see in index* Reformation

Papadopoulos, Georgios, Greek prime minister G-261

Papago, American Indian tribe that lives in Arizona I-127, 145, *map* I-136, *table* I-139
- Arizona A-598

Papagos, Alexander (1883–1955), Greek statesman and field marshal, born in Athens; chief of Greek general staff 1936–40; as commander in chief of Greek forces, drove back Italian invaders 1940–41 and defeated Communist rebels 1949; head of Greek Rally party 1951–55; premier 1952–55.

Papal Infallibility, in Roman Catholic doctrine P-347
- Leo I L-130

Papaloápam River, river in Mexico, rises in mountains of Oaxaca; unites with San Juan and empties into Gulf of Mexico.

Papal States P-100. *see also in index* Papacy
- Bologna added B-337
- gift of Pepin R-97
  - Holy Roman Empire H-208
- Italian history I-394

Papandreou, Andreas (born 1919), Greek premier G-261

Papandreou, Georgios (1888–1968), Greek prime minister G-260

Papanicolaou's test. *see in index* Pap smear

Papaver, poppy genus P-446

Papaw (or pawpaw), a North American tree or shrub of custard apple family; has banana-shaped, edible pulpy fruit; grown in south, east, and middle U.S.; also name given to papaya F-430

Papaya (also called pawpaw), a tree with melonlike edible fruit, native to tropical America, now found in almost all tropical regions; fruit used for cosmetics and foods, bark for rope; juice of fruit a popular drink P-255d, *picture* P-11
- fruit F-430

Papeete, Tahiti, capital and seaport of French Polynesia; exports include copra, vanilla, sugar, and soap; pop. 23,496 T-10, *map* P-6

Papen, Franz von (1879–1969), German statesman; military attaché in U.S. 1914, expelled for espionage; chancellor of Germany 1932, vice-chancellor 1933–34; intrigues while envoy to Austria helped effect its fall; directed Nazi activities in Turkey while ambassador there 1939–44; tried for war crimes, acquitted 1946; sentenced by Bavarian denazification court to eight years in labor camp 1947, released 1949 ('Memoirs') W-143

Paper P-100
- bleaching B-310
- blueprint B-319
- bookmaking B-351
- dolls D-216, *picture* D-220
- drawing D-251
- embossing E-198
- envelope. *see in index* Envelope
- flax straw F-177
- forest products F-316
- mechanical drawing M-255, 262
- mill, *picture* U-46
  - Oregon, *picture* O-591
  - Tennessee, *picture* T-84
  - Wisconsin, *picture* W-259
- money M-532
- newsprint N-240
- photographic P-293, 296
- postage stamps S-405
- preservation A-149
- sources
  - papyrus P-108
  - pine P-328, P-379
  - spruce S-398
- wall covering W-8
- wood W-284

Paperback book B-363
- western W-152

Paper birch (or canoe birch) B-239
- wood, *table* W-283

Paperboard P-100, 105

'Paper Chase, The', motion picture, *picture* L-91

Paper chromatography C-292

Paper measure, a unit of measure, *table* W-140

Paper money M-532
- Continental Congress issues R-168
- greenbacks U-147
- inflation. *see in index* Inflation

Paper mulberry, tree M-648
- tapa cloth P-13

Paper nautilus. *see in index* Argonaut

Papershell pecan P-151

Paper wasp, insect *Polistes fuscatus* of the order Hymenoptera, family Vespidae W-74, *picture* W-72

Paper-white narcissus, flower *Narcissus tazetta* N-18

Paphlagonia, ancient country of Asia Minor, on Black Sea; subdued by Croesus; became part of Roman provinces of Galatia and Bithynia; made separate province by Constantine, *map* P-212

Paphos, name of two ancient cities on w. coast of island of Cyprus; Old Paphos, founded about 10th century BC, chief seat of worship of Aphrodite; New Paphos capital of island in Roman times.

Papiamento, creole language of the Caribbean region A-671

Papier-mâché, paper product resembling wood P-107
- buttons B-529
- folk art F-250
- masks M-185
- newspaper printing N-239

Papilionoideae, bean subfamily
- legume L-118

Papilla, in anatomy, minute conical elevation
- hair H-7
- hand H-27
- skin S-210d
- tongue T-215

Papillon (sometimes called butterfly dog), a tiny dog, *picture* D-205

Papin, Denis (1647–1712?), French physicist; improved air pump, conceived idea of pneumatic transmission of power, invented the digester; pioneer in steam navigation.

Papineau, Louis Joseph (1786–1871), leader of French Canadian rebellion of 1837; leader of Sons of Liberty P-107
- Canada C-97

Papini, Giovanni (1881–1956), Italian writer and editor P-108

Pappus (late 3rd century), Greek mathematician in Alexandria; his 'Collection' preserved ancient Greek mathematics.

Pappus, plant structure C-32

Paprika, a red pepper, much used in Hungary P-197a
- Hungary, *picture* E-340
- spices S-379
- vitamin P V-358

Pap smear (or Papanicolaou's test), test for cancer of the cervix D-127
- cancer D-176

Papua, battle of, World War II W-345, *picture* W-346

Papua, Territory of, s.e. New Guinea and neighboring islands; now part of Papua New Guinea; 90,600 sq mi (234,600 sq km); formerly administered by Australia; previously called British New Guinea; pop. 654,441 N-174
- Australian administration A-815

Papua New Guinea, parliamentary state, s.w. Pacific; includes former territories of Papua and New Guinea; total area 178,703 sq mi (462,840 sq km); cap. Port Moresby; self-governing 1973, independent 1975; pop. 3,345,000 P-19, *map* P-6
- Australian administration A-815
- Commonwealth membership C-602
- flag, *picture* F-169
- New Guinea N-173
- Oceania O-468, 472, *picture* O-470

Papyrus plant, a plant and the paper made from it P-108
- ancient Egypt E-128
- books B-345,
- library history L-170
- manuscripts P-249
- paper P-103

Par, in golf G-185

PANICS AND DEPRESSIONS IN THE UNITED STATES

Economists make a distinction between panics, crises, and depressions. An industrial or financial crisis reaches its peak in a panic, when commodity and security prices fall sharply. The panic is usually followed by a period of depressed activity and readjustment, until confidence is restored and business again reaches a normal level. Almost invariably a crisis is preceded by a period of abnormally high activity, when prosperity is accompanied by inflated prices of commodities, of securities, and of real estate. The earlier crises or panics were mostly the result of European difficulties, and were not so severe or widespread in the United States. In 1793 the unexpected declaration of war between France and England was followed by troubles for American shipping, and caused a period of decline. Again, after 1802, the peace of Amiens was followed by maritime prosperity, to be ended abruptly by the Embargo and Non-Importation troubles in 1807 and 1808. The War of 1812 brought industry in the United States to a low point, from which it recovered rapidly, for several years, only to suffer a slump in the years 1819–22. The first major panic and crisis came in 1837.

1837. The era of internal improvements, of building canals, railroads, and roads, involved excessive extension of credits by banks and unwarranted borrowings by the state governments. A crisis was precipitated by the refusal of Congress to renew the charter of the Bank of the United States. This was the signal for an outburst of fear; many banks closed, business firms failed, and industry was paralyzed. Some of the states repudiated bonds issued for the payment of improvements, and depression continued for seven or eight years.

1857. After the Mexican War and the discovery of gold in California, the United States went through a period of deflation, during which interest rates declined and speculation increased. Railroads were built on a scale far beyond the country's immediate need. Then came panic. Several large life insurance companies failed, and depression continued, with a short interruption during the war years, until the new industrial development in the late 1860s and early 1870s.

1869. The money panic of this year reached its climax on September 24, Black Friday, in the attempt of Jay Gould and Jim Fisk to corner the gold supply of the United States. At the peak, $1.63 in greenbacks was required to buy $1.00 in gold. The effects were limited to the financial centers, and there were no general disturbances throughout the country. At the same time, however, European markets were disrupted by the opening of the Suez Canal.

1873. A new period of inflation began about 1868. In the next five years over 30,000 miles of railroad were built. Joint stock companies were taking the place of old-fashioned partnerships. Industrial expansion was going on at a feverish rate. In Europe during the same years, following the Franco-Prussian War, there was great expansion in Germany and Austria culminating in the "Vienna crash" of 1873. The break in the United States was begun by the failure of Jay Cooke & Company. General business and financial deflation was followed by the worst depression the United States had yet seen. This low period continued for about six years, until a new burst of activity which followed the resumption of specie payments in 1879.

1884. The panic of 1884 was a money and bankers' panic, precipitated by the failure (May 8) of the firm of Grant and Ward, of which Gen. U.S. Grant was a partner. The resulting depression was not severe and lasted only about two years.

1890. This was another bankers' panic, brought on by the failure of Baring Brothers, the great London firm of international bankers, with very close connections in New York City and Boston. Baring Brothers failed November 10. The Bank of England and a strong private banking firm came to their rescue, and the effects of the crisis were slight.

1893. The panic or crisis of 1893 was caused by agricultural depression, by unsound railroad financing, and perhaps even more by uncertainty about the financial stability of the United States. The operation of the Sherman Silver Purchase Act was obviously endangering the gold reserves of the treasury. Many banks failed, 20,000 miles of railroad went into receivership, and the following economic depression was prolonged and severe, including grave labor disturbances in the East and Middle West. One of the consequences of this crisis was the formal adoption of the gold standard by the United States (March 4, 1900).

1901. Stock market panic, culminating May 9, as the result of a struggle between the Harriman-Kuhn-Loeb interests and the Morgan-James J. Hill group for the control of the Northern Pacific Railroad. The stock of this railroad was cornered, and the collapse of the corner was followed by a general collapse in security prices.

1907. The panic of this year was a money panic, sometimes called the Knickerbocker Trust panic, because the failure of that company (October 22) precipitated it. The financial difficulties of that company and of others that failed were caused chiefly by the efforts of the Heinze group to combine control of various banks, copper companies, and other interests.

1914. The outbreak of World War I was followed immediately by panic in all the financial centers of the world. Stock and grain exchanges were closed in New York, Chicago, and other cities. Clearinghouse certificates were used between banks in settling balances, and the treasury immediately made available, under the Aldrich-Vreeland Act of 1908, an ample supply of emergency bank notes, thus enabling the banks to meet the demand for cash while at the same time husbanding their gold reserves. Unlike most panics, this one was followed by a sharp expansion in business activity, made necessary by the Allied demand for supplies and munitions. This activity was greatly increased when the United States entered the war.

1921. The year 1921 marks a new crisis and the beginning of the "primary postwar depression." The end of the war found the United States with overexpanded facilities for production, and with an accumulation of food and material of all kinds which Europe could not use. One result of the situation was a sharp break in wholesale commodity prices, notably sugar. Readjustment and depression on a minor scale continued for several years until the turn which came with the "Coolidge prosperity" and reached its peak in the "bull market" of 1929.

1929. The years of the Coolidge administrations witnessed expansion and inflation on a scale hitherto unknown in any country in the world. Inflation in wages, real-estate values, and stock prices seemed to bring prosperity to everyone. While financial activity continued at an unprecedented rate through the summer of 1929, industrial activity was already slowing down. The collapse of the speculative mania in the stock market was slowly followed by a realization that in the United States as well as in other parts of the world many grave economic and financial problems had not been faced. These were now to cause the most serious disarrangement of economic structure that the world had yet known. Agricultural depression, the result of falling prices for farm products and for land, cost thousands of farmers their homes through foreclosure. Unemployment and bank failures were greater than ever before in American history. The domestic factors were complicated by foreign affairs, such as reparations and the questions of inter-Allied debts.

Marine Corps training center, *picture* S-314

Parrot, a tropical bird P-133, *picture* P-134
book illustration S-465
cockatoo P-135, *picture* P-134
length of life, *chart* A-423
macaw, *picture* P-134
pets P-245

Parrot fish, family of tropical food fishes Scaridae having semicircular rows of fused teeth forming a parrotlike beak, *picture* P-14

Parrots-bill, plant. *see in index* Clianthus

Parry, Sir Charles Hubert Hastings (1848–1918), British composer; noted for series of choral works with orchestra ('Blest Pair of Sirens'; 'Invocations to Music'); professor of music Oxford University 1900–1908; author of 'Studies of Great Composers' and 'Art of Music'.

Parry, Sir William Edward (1790–1855), British Arctic explorer; made three attempts to cross Northwest Passage; in 1827 tried to reach North Pole, attaining latitude 82° N', which remained for 49 years the "farthest north" reached by explorers, *table* P-422

Parry Sound, Ont., port town on inlet of Georgian Bay; summer resort, with numerous islands; lumber, wood products, boats; dairy products; pop. 6,124, *map* C-112

Parsa, ancient province on Persian Gulf. *see in index* Persis

Parsec, astronomical unit A-719

Parsifal (or Perceval), in Arthurian legend, innocent ignorant boy who becomes a knight-errant, withstands temptation, achieves the quest of the Holy Grail, thus delivering a stricken land and king; hero of Wagner's opera 'Parsifal' in King Arthur cycle R-299a
Holy Grail H-207

'Parsifal', opera by Wagner O-568, *picture* O-567

Parsiism. *see in index* Zoroastrianism and Parsiism

Parsippany, N.J., urban township 7 mi (11 km) n.e. of Morristown; light industry, stone quarries; pop. 49,868.

Parsis. *see in index* Zoroastrianism and Parsiism

Parsley, an herb *Petroselinum crispum*, the type plant of the parsley family H-138, *picture* H-137
spices S-379

Parsley family (or Umbelliferae), family of herbs with small flowers in umbrella-shaped clusters; includes carrot, celery, hemlock, parsley, and parsnip. *see also in index* plants by name

Parsnip, biennial plant *Pastinaca sativa* tapering white root eaten as vegetable in cultivated varieties; grown in Europe since Roman times P-409

Parsnip River, river in e.-central British Columbia; flows n. 145 mi (235 km) and joins Finlay River to form Peace River P-145

Parsons, Sir Charles Algernon (1854–1931), British engineer and inventor, born in London; inventions include Parsons compound steam turbine and a geared turbine: author of 'The Steam Engine' S-167, S-442

Parsons, James Benton (born 1911), U.S. federal jurist, born in Kansas City, Mo.; judge Cook County, Ill., court 1951–60; named to federal court of n. Illinois 1961, the first black American appointed for life term as U.S. district judge in continental U.S.

Parsons, Theophilus (1750–1813), U.S. jurist, born in Byfield, Mass.; chief justice Massachusetts Supreme Court 1806–13
Adams A-35

Parsons, William Barclay (1859–1932), U.S. engineer, born in New York, N.Y; designed first part of New York subway system; made surveys for Chinese railways; member of board of consulting engineers Panama Canal; chief engineer Cape Cod Canal; served in Spanish-American War and World War I.

Parsons, William Edward (1872–1939), U.S. architect and city planner, born in Akron, Ohio; consulting architect to the U.S. government in the Philippines 1905–14; made civic improvement plans and designs for Chicago, Ill., St. Paul, Minn., Washington, D.C., and other U.S. cities.

Parsons, Kan., city about 125 mi (200 km) s. of Kansas City; trade center of agricultural region; diversified industries; state hospital for retarded children; pop. 12,898, *map* U-41

Parson's Cause, law case H-133

Parsvantha, in Hinduism
Jainism J-14

Partch, Virgil Franklin, II (born 1916), U.S. cartoonist, born in Saint Paul Island, Alaska; contributor to magazines, *Look*, *True*, *The New Yorker*, and others; creator of comic strip 'Big George'.

Parthenogenesis, reproduction from unfertilized egg cells
insects I-221
lizards L-272
mollusks M-523

Parthenon, in Athens, Greece A-547, *pictures* A-531, A-546
Acropolis A-23
Athena A-733
Greece G-254
Greek art G-270, *pictures* G-269, G-272
horses H-272
illusionary qualities I-54
Phidias' work P-250
sculpture S-83

Parthenos, Athena, statue by Phidias A-23

Parthia, ancient country of Asia, s.e. of Caspian Sea; most extensive sway under Mithridates I, 174–136 BC P-212, *maps* P-212, R-242
Iran I-308

Parthian shot P-213, *picture* P-211

Partial lunar eclipse, in astronomy E-49

Partial solar eclipse, in astronomy E-48

Participle, in grammar G-209, V-281

Particle accelerator (or atom smasher)
betatron A-682
nuclear energy N-420, 432

Particle board F-452

Particle theory of light P-306
light structure L-199, L-203
Newton N-243
quantum theory Q-5
radiation R-37

Partido, jai alai game format J-13

Parties, political. *see in index* Political parties

Partington, Mrs., English anecdotal character, said to have tried to mop up a tidal wave; used as pen name by **Benjamin P. Shillaber** (1814–90), U.S. humorist. *see also in index* Smith, Sydney

Partisans, term applied to guerrilla fighters, particularly those organized by anti-Fascist leaders in the Spanish Civil War and in World War II W-324

Partition of Palestine P-81
Israel I-372
Zionism Z-456

Partition of Poland (1772, 1793, 1795), *table* T-275

Partnership, association of two or more persons in a business enterprise, sharing expenses, profits, and losses C-150

Partnership, in biology. *see in index* Symbiosis

Parton, Dolly (born 1946), U.S. country musician M-679

Partridge, Eric Honeywood (1894–1979), British lexicographer, born in New Zealand ('A Dictionary of Slang and Unconventional English'; 'A Dictionary of Clichés'; 'Usage and Abusage'; 'Origins', etymological dictionary).

Partridge, William Ordway (1861–1930), U.S. sculptor and author, born in Paris, France; noted for busts of poets Longfellow, Tennyson, Burns, Whittier, and for monumental statues (Shakespeare, Lincoln Park, Chicago, Ill.; equestrian statue of Grant, Brooklyn, N.Y.); author of 'Art for America'.

Partridge, name given various birds of the family Phasianinae Q-3. *see also in index* Bobwhite; Ruffed grouse

Partridgeberry (or twinberry, or squawberry), a small trailing evergreen plant *Mitchella repens* of the madder family, with shining dark green leaves, white pink-tinged fragrant flowers united in pairs, and scarlet berries in twos.

Parts of speech. *see in index* specific parts of speech, such as Adjective, etc.

Part-time work E-207

Par value. *see in index* Face value

Parvati, a Hindu deity H-159, *picture* H-156

Pas, dance, *table* B-35

Pasadena, Calif., city 10 mi (16 km) n.e. of Los Angeles; pop. 118,072 P-135, *map* U-40
Los Angeles L-301, *map* L-300
Mount Wilson Observatory. *see in index* Mount Wilson Observatory
Rose Bowl P-135
Tournament of Roses P-135, *picture* P-20

Pasadena, Tex., city 9 mi (15 km) e. of Houston, on Houston Ship Channel; petroleum refining; synthetic rubber, paper products, chemicals; pop. 112,560.

Pasadena College. *see in index* Point Loma College

Pasang, ancestor of domestic goats G-171

Pasargadae, ancient capital of Persia, said to have been built by Cyrus the Great on site of his great victory over Astyages (6th century BC); contained tomb of Cyrus, *map* P-212

Pasay, Philippines, city on Manila Bay, s. of Manila, in Rizal Province; trade in rice and fruit; pop. 163,000.

Pascagoula, Miss., city 32 mi (52 km) e. of Gulfport, on Mississippi Sound; shipbuilding, oil refining; clothing, chemicals; pop. 29,318 M-478

Pascagoula River, river in Mississippi, navigable stream 85 mi (140 km) long formed by junction of Chickasawhay and Leaf rivers.

Pascal, Blaise (1623–62), French scientist and religious philosopher P-135
computer development C-628
Fermat F-55
French literature F-395
hydraulics H-338

Pascal, Jean Louis (1837–1920), French architect, born in Paris; exercised wide influence; designed memorials to Hugo, Carnot, and Michelet, and many important public buildings and houses.

Pascin, Jules (1885–1930), U.S. artist, born in Bulgaria; depicted life of blacks of Cuba and southern United States; noted for figure studies and for satirical drawings of underworld.

Pasco, Wash., port city on Columbia River, about 37 mi (60 km) n.w. of Walla Walla; transportation, trade, and shipping center; nearby is Hanford Atomic Energy Reservation: name is acronym from term used on early shipping documents to inform railroad employees which rail cars were to be barged across Columbia River via the PAcific Steamship COmpany (via PASCO); pop. 17,944.

Pascoli, Giovanni (1855–1912), Italian poet and teacher, born near Rimini ('Selected Poems of Giovanni Pascoli').

Pas de deux, ballet B-32

Pase vs. Hannon (1980), U.S. court case
intelligence tests I-238

Pasha, former Turkish title of nobility, higher than bey; first given only to military officers, later also to civil officials or private citizens; abolished 1934 E-121

Pasha of Egypt, diamond, *picture* D-129

Pashitch, Nicholas (or Nicholas Pasic) (1845?–1926), Serbian statesman; founded Radical party 1878–81 and led it remainder of life; prime minister during World War I; largely responsible for establishment of kingdom of Yugoslavia.

Pasht (or Bast, or Bastet), cat-goddess of ancient Egypt C-211

Pashto, language spoken in Afghanistan A-89
Indian literature I-107

Pasig River, river in Philippines, short river in s. end of Luzon
Malacañang Palace, *picture* P-255c
Manila M-97

Paspalum. *see in index* Dallis grass

Pasqueflower, flower of the anemone family, *picture* P-359
state flower of South Dakota, *pictures* S-328, S-427

Passage, in horse training E-295

'Passage to India, A', work by Forster N-412, *picture* E-280

Passaic, N.J., manufacturing and residential city on Passaic River, about 4 mi (6 km) s. of Paterson; mechanical rubber goods, television, fire hose, plastics, clothing, cans, aircraft components; food processing, research center; several engagements in Revolutionary War; pop. 52,463.

Passaic River, river in n.e. New Jersey, flows into Newark Bay; immense waterpower; about 100 mi (160 km) long; navigable to rapids above Passaic, N.J. N-193
falls at Paterson P-139

Passamaquoddy, people, division of the Abnaki group, of Algonquian stock; lived in Canada and Maine M-53

Passamaquoddy Bay, inlet of the Bay of Fundy between New Brunswick and Maine
waterpower capabilities W-104

Passant position, in heraldry H-136

Passau, West Germany, old city of Bavaria, at junction of Danube, Inn, and Ilz, 90 mi (145 km) n.e. of Munich; Treaty of Passau (1552) granted religious freedom to Lutherans; pop. 30,700, *map* G-134

Passbook, in banking B-65

Passchendaele Ridge, in Belgium, 6 mi (10 km) n.e. of Ypres.

Pass Christian, Miss., city and resort on Gulf of Mexico, 10 mi (16 km) s.w. of Gulfport; pop. 5,014.

Passenger pigeon P-323
birds B-271
extinction E-210
Canada C-75

Passenger ship S-168. *see also in index* Ocean liner

Passenger transportation. *see in index* Transportation

Passfield, Baron. *see in index* Webb, Sidney

Passion (from Latin for suffer), sufferings of Christ from the Last Supper until His death; also oratorios based on the Gospel accounts.

Passionflower P-136

Passionflower family (or Passifloraceae), family of plants and woody vines, including the passionflower, maypop, granadillas, and Jamaica honeysuckle F-436

Passionists (in full Congregation of the Discalced Clerks of the Most Holy Cross and Passion of our Lord Jesus Christ), order founded in Italy 1720.

'Passion of Joan of Arc, The' (1928), motion picture by Dreyer M-620, *picture* M-622

Passion play, a dramatic representation of Christ's Passion
Islamic comparison I-362
miracle play M-462
Oberammergau O-455
Bavaria B-111
hobby H-182

Passive immunity, immunity acquired by transfer of antibodies D-168

Passive resistance. *see in index* Nonviolent action

Passive voice, in grammar V-281

Passos, John Dos. *see in index* Dos Passos, John

Passover, a Jewish festival in honor of the night when the Lord, smiting the firstborn of the Egyptians, "passed over" the houses in which the children of Israel lived P-136

kindergarten in Boston 1860 K-242

Peabody, George (1795–1869), U.S. banker and merchant [illegible]
- banking B-73
- Hall of Fame, *table* H-16
- Maryland M-172

Peabody, Mass., industrial city 2 mi (3 km) w. of Salem; leather, chemicals; made town as South Danvers 1855; name changed 1868 in honor of George Peabody; incorporated 1916; pop. 45,976 P-143

Peabody College. *see in index* George Peabody College for Teachers

Peabody Conservatory of Music. *see in index* Peabody Institute of the City of Baltimore

Peabody Fund, for education P-143

Peabody Institute of the City of Baltimore (or Peabody Institute of Baltimore, or Peabody Conservatory of Music), in Baltimore, Md.; private control; opened 1868; music; graduate studies P-143, B-49

Peabody Museum, in Cambridge, Mass.; established 1866; noted for comprehensive archaeological and ethnological collections, Mayan and American Indian collections particularly strong; control, Harvard University.

Peace, pact or agreement to end hostilities between hostile or warring nations W-27

'Peaceable Kingdom, The', painting by Hicks P-50, *picture* P-49
- Hicks H-149

Peace Bridge, bridge from Buffalo, N.Y., to Fort Erie, Ont. B-490

Peace Conference (1919). *see also in index* World War I, *subhead* Peace settlement and territorial changes
- Smuts S-220
- Versailles V-303

Peace Conferences, Hague. *see in index* Hague Peace Conferences

Peace Corps P-143
- Kennedy creates K-201
- Latin America P-143a

Peace Garden. *see in index* International Peace Garden

Peace movements P-143b, *picture* P-143d. *see also in index* Armaments, limitation of
- bibliography P-144
- Hague Peace Conferences. *see in index* Hague Peace Conferences
- League of Nations. *see in index* League of Nations
- Nobel prizes N-330
- societies P-143b
- United Nations U-20, *chart* U-21, *pictures* U-22, 27. *see also in index* United Nations
- Vietnam conflict
  - Nixon U-196a, V-324
  - protests C-668, U-196
- World Court. *see in index* International Court of Justice; Permanent Court of Arbitration; Permanent Court of International Justice

Peace Palace, The Hague, The Netherlands H-5

Peace pipe, American Indian. *see in index* Calumet

Peace Preservation Law (1925), Japanese legislation J-68

Peace River, river in Canada, important river of British Columbia and Alberta P-145
- British Columbia B-451
- North America, *maps* C-109, N-351

Peace River, Alta., town near confluence of Peace and Smoky rivers, about 240 mi (390 km) n.w. of Edmonton; pop. 5,907, *maps* C-109, N-351

Peace Tower, in Ottawa, Ont., *picture* P-132

Peach P-145
- blossom, state flower of Delaware, *picture* S-427
- fruit F-430, *picture* F-432
- fruitgrowing F-437, 439
- producing regions P-145

Peach Tree Creek, indecisive Civil War battle fought near Atlanta, Ga., July 20, 1864, between Federals under General Sherman and Confederates under General Hood.

Peacock, Thomas Love (1785–1866), English satirical novelist and poet, friend of Shelley ('Nightmare Abbey'; 'Crotchet Castle').

Peacock, bird of the pheasant family P-145, *picture* P-146
- feathers B-240
- Japan's wildlife, *picture* J-62
- myth P-146

Peacock, constellation. *see in index* Pavo

Peacock flounder, flatfish F-174

Peacock Revolution, 1960s men's clothing revolution D-267

Peacock throne, famous golden throne stolen from India by the Persians in 1739 N-3

Pea crab, crustacean of the family Pinnotheridae C-792

Pea family. *see in index* Legume

Peahen, a female peafowl P-145

Peak, a nautical description, the highest point of a fore-and-aft sail; the apex of a staysail; the aftermost corner of a spencer or spanker sail.

Peak. *see in index* Crest

Peak XV. *see in index* Everest, Mount

Peale, Charles Willson (1741–1827), U.S. portrait painter, one of the most eminent of colonial times, born in Queen Anne County, Maryland; father of Rembrandt Peale; captain in Revolutionary War; one of the Founders of the Pennsylvania Academy of Fine Arts; famous for portraits of George Washington (seven from life), Martha Washington, Franklin, Jefferson, Jackson, Clay, and others.

Peale, Norman Vincent (born 1898), U.S. clergyman and writer, born in Bowersville, Ohio; ordained 1922 in Methodist Episcopal church; minister of Marble Collegiate Reformed Church, New York, N.Y., after 1932; popular radio and television preacher; author of 'A Guide to Confident Living', 'The Art of Real Happiness' (with Smiley Blanton), and 'The Power of Positive Thinking'.

Peale, Rembrandt (1778–1860), U.S. portrait and historical painter, born in Bucks County, Pennsylvania; son of Charles W. Peale; portraits of Washington, Gilbert Stuart, Jefferson ('The Court of Death').

Peale Museum, in Philadelphia, Pa. M-662

Peale's dolphin D-224

Peanut (also called groundnut, or earthnut, or ground pea) P-146
- Africa A-103
  - [illegible]
  - Mali M-76
  - The Gambia G-8
- legume L-119
- products P-379
  - margarine M-134

Peanut butter P-147

'Peanuts', cartoon strip C-190

Peanut worm, worm of the phylum Sipuncula W-362

Pear, fruit P-147, F-430, *picture* F-431
- fruitgrowing F-437, 439

Pear, tree *Pyrus comunis* of the rose family P-147

Pea Ridge, Civil War battle fought at Pea Ridge (Ozark Mts.) in n.w. Arkansas, March 7–8, 1862; first major victory of Union troops; saved Missouri to Union cause.

Pearl, Raymond (1879–1940), U.S. biologist and statistician, born in Farmington, N.H.; connected with National Research Council 1916–35; chief of statistical division, U.S. Food Administration, 1917–19; at Johns Hopkins University—director Institute of Biological Research 1925–30, professor of biology 1930–40; research in questions of heredity, population, length of life.

Pearl, a gem P-148
- beadwork B-114, *picture* B-113
- buttons B-530, S-151
- jewelry J-112, *pictures* J-113, 114
- mollusks M-525
  - oyster O-623
- Sri Lanka fisheries S-402

Pearl, mother-of-. *see in index* Mother-of-pearl

Pearl City, Hawaii, town located on the island of Oahu; pop. 42,575 H-61

'Pearl Fishers, The', opera by Bizet O-566

Pearl Harbor, U.S. naval base in Hawaii H-64, *map* H-58, *picture* H-69
- Honolulu H-230
- warfare W-23
  - Japanese attack R-276, *picture* R-269, 267
  - MacArthur M-2
  - World War II W-327, 344
  - Yamamoto Y-409

Pearl Poet (14th century), English poet E-265

Pearl River, China. *see in index* Canton River

Pearl River, rises in e.-central Mississippi, flows 490 mi (790 km) s.w. and s. into the Gulf of Mexico; forms part of the boundary between Mississippi and Louisiana.

Pearl sago S-14

Pearly nautilus O-492

Pears, Peter (1910–86), British opera tenor, *list* O-570

Pearson, Karl (1857–1936), English mathematician; professor of eugenics University of London ('Chances of Death'; 'Grammar of Science'; 'Life and Letters of Francis Galton'; 'Tables for Statisticians'; editor of 'Biometrika' and of 'Annals of Eugenics') E-326

Pearson, Lester Bowles (1897–1972), Canadian statesman P-150. *see also in index* Nobel Prizewinners, *table*
- Canada C-106
- Diefenbaker D-140

Peary, Josephine Diebitsch (1863–1955), Arctic traveler and writer, born in Washington, D.C.; married Robert E. Peary 1888; interpreter of Arctic life for young children ('Snow Baby'; 'Children of the Arctic') P-150

Peary, Robert Edwin (1856–1920), U.S. Arctic explorer, discoverer of North Pole P-150
- polar exploration, *map* P-417

'Peasants, The', novel by Reymont R-174

Peasants' Revolt (or Wat Tyler's Rebellion) (1381), in English history
- Richard II R-202
- Tyler T-335
- Wycliffe W-384

Peasants' Revolt (1525), Germany R-134
- Zwingli Z-472

Pease, Elisha M. (1812–83), U.S. lawyer, born in Enfield, Conn.; settled in Texas to study law just before outbreak of revolt against Mexico; served Republic of Texas in many capacities; governor of state 1855–59, 1867–69.

Pease, Francis Gladheim (1881–1938), U.S. astronomer, born in Cambridge, Mass.; at Mt. Wilson Observatory 1904–38; helped design 100-in. (254-cm) telescope for Mt. Wilson, 200-in. (508-cm) telescope for Mt. Palomar, and 50-ft (15-m) interferometer; noted for measurements of distant stars, also for photographs of moon, stars, planets.

Pease, Howard (born 1894), U.S. author of sea stories for boys, born in Stockton, Calif. ('Tattooed Man'; 'Jinx Ship'; 'Long Wharf'; 'High Road to Adventure').

Peat, partly carbonized vegetable material P-151
- coal formation C-518
- fuel value F-441, P-151
- gas G-38
- Ireland I-317
- moss M-600

Peat moss, type of moss M-599
- garden use G-22

Peattie, Donald Culross (1898–1964), U.S. botanist and author, born in Chicago, Ill. ('An Almanac for Moderns', nature essays; 'Flowering Earth', botany; 'A Natural History of Trees of Eastern and Central North America'; 'A Natural History of Western Trees'; 'Singing in the Wilderness', life of Audubon; 'Green Laurels', great naturalists).

Peau de soie (skin of silk), a strong, firm fabric of silk or synthetic fiber; has satiny surface; used for dresses and trimmings.

Pebble mosaic M-589, *picture* M-590

Pecan, a nut-bearing tree P-151

Peccary (sometimes called muskhog), a small wild hog of North and South America P-152, *picture* A-436
- leather L-108

Pechenga (formerly Petsamo), U.S.S.R., town and district on Arctic Ocean, w. of Murmansk; nickel mining; ceded by U.S.S.R. to Finland 1920; was returned to U.S.S.R. 1944 R-332, *maps* R-344, 348
- Europe, *map* E-361

Pechora River, n. U.S.S.R., rising n. Ural Mts. and flowing 1,110 mi (1,790 km) to n. coast; petroleum, coal, and natural gas deposits in river basin, *maps* R-322, 344, 348
- Europe, *map* E-361

Pechorskaya Lavra, monastery, Kiev, U.S.S.R. K-237

Pechstein, Hermann Max (1881–1955), German expressionist painter, born in Zwickau; technique influenced by Matisse ('Drowned Fisherman'; 'Double Portrait').

Peck, Anne Merriman (born 1884), U.S. artist and author, born in Piermont, N.Y.; (for adults: 'Vagabond's Provence', 'France, Crossroads of Europe'; for children: 'Roundabout Europe', 'Young Mexico', 'Spain in Europe and America', 'Wings of an Eagle').

Peck, Samuel Minturn (1854–1938), U.S. writer, born in Tuscaloosa, Ala.; wrote chiefly about the South (poems: 'Rhymes and Roses', 'Rings and Loveknots', 'Fair Women of Today'; short stories: 'Alabama Sketches').

Peck, a unit of measure, *table* W-140

Pecos, Tex., city in Reeves County, 70 mi (110 km) s.w. of Odessa; shipping and commercial center; cotton, cantaloupes, cattle; oil; rodeo; pop. 12,855, *map* N-351.

Pecos Bill, legendary cowboy S-481c
- folklore F-266

Pecos River, chief tributary of Rio Grande; rises in New Mexico at base of Baldy Peak; flows s. and s.e. 800 mi (1,290 km), entering Rio Grande on Texas-Mexican border, *maps* R-209, U-62

Pécs (German Fünfkirchen), Hungary, city 105 mi (170 km) s.w. of Budapest; coal-mining center; champagne, ceramic products, leather goods, flour; university (founded 1367); pop. 177,000 H-329, *map* E-361

Pectin, the chemical substance in fleshy fruits and in some vegetable roots which causes them to jelly or solidify upon being boiled; commercial pectin produced from fruit juices with high pectin content.

Pectoral fin, in fish, *diagram* F-125, *picture* F-126

Pectoral sandpiper S-40

Pedagogy, the art or science of teaching. *see in index* Education; Teaching

Pedalfer, soil S-251, *map* S-252

Pedal steel guitar, stringed musical instrument M-678

Peddler doll D-215, *picture* D-217

Pedersen, Christiern (1480?–1554), "Father of Danish Literature"; his translation of the Bible, called 'Christian III's Bible', is landmark in Scandinavian literature.

Pedersen, Knut. *see in index* Hamsun, Knut

Pedestrian, in safety and accident prevention S-10

Pediatrics, medical specialty, *table* M-277
- hospital obstetrics H-282

Pedicab, small 3-wheeled passenger vehicle that is pedaled, *picture* T-263

Pedicel, in spider S-382

Pedicel, in plant F-216, *picture* F-217

Pedipalp, in spider S-382, *picture* S-386
- scorpion S-65

Pedocal, soil S-251, *map* S-252

Pedometer, a watch-shaped instrument worn on the body

and fitted with an oscillating weight which is affected by the motion of the body and thus records the number of steps taken; from this can be determined the distance covered.

Pedophile, person who desires to have sex with children S-126

Pedrero, early artillery piece A-659

Pedro I (1798–1834), emperor of Brazil, son of John VI of Portugal, crowned 1822; succeeded to Portuguese crown 1826; resigned it to daughter Maria da Gloria; abdicated Brazilian crown 1831; died after restoring his daughter to Portuguese throne B-423, S-291
Andrada e Silva A-411

Pedro II (1825–91), emperor of Brazil; succeeded under a regency 1831, proclaimed of age 1840, crowned 1841, compelled to abdicate 1889; reign notable for emancipation of slaves and a war with Paraguay 1864–70 B-423, *picture* S-292

Pedro III (1236–86), king of Aragon; called "the Great" because of success in conquering Sicily S-192

Pedro V (1837–61), king of Portugal; succeeded 1853; reign marked by freedom from civil strife and by economic improvement.

Pedro Miguel Locks, in Panama Canal P-90

Pedro the Cruel (1334–69), king of Castile and León; succeeded 1350; provoked rebellion of his brother Henry, by whom he was killed.

Pee Dee River, river in e. South Carolina, continuation of the Yadkin River of North Carolina; Little Pee Dee River is a tributary, *maps* S-307, 319, U-59

Peekskill, N.Y., city on Hudson River, 40 mi (60 km) n. of New York, N.Y.; clothing, yeast, leather goods, alcohol, food products; pop. 18,236.

Peel, Sir Robert (1788–1850), British statesman P-152
corn law's repeal C-723
police system P-430a
United Kingdom E-252

Peele, George (1558?–98?), English dramatist and poet; with Christopher Marlowe and Robert Greene influenced English literature through Shakespeare, who borrowed from them ('The Old Wives' Tale'; 'The Arraignment of Paris'; 'The Love of King David and Fair Bathsabe').

Peeler, nickname for policeman in Ireland P-152

Peenemünde, East Germany, village on island of Usedom in Baltic Sea, at mouth of Peene River; research and production center for V-type rockets in World War II, *map* G-134
guided missile G-308

Peerage, British titled nobility T-195
life peerages P-131a

Peerce, Jan (originally Jacob Pincus Perelmuth) (1904–84), U.S. tenor, born in New York, N.Y.; began musical career as violinist; soloist Radio City Music Hall 1933–41; opera debut 1938; with Metropolitan Opera Company, New York, N.Y. after 1941; opera festivals and concerts in Europe and Israel after 1968; also appeared on stage and screen.

'Peer Gynt', Henrik Ibsen's poetic drama; the hero, a character derived from Norwegian folklore, is a kind of Norse Faust; published 1867 I-3, 5

'Peer Gynt Suite', work by Grieg N-391

Peete, Calvin (born 1933), U.S. golfer; won more money and more PGA events than any other golfer (1982–); in 1984 won Vardon Trophy for lowest stroke average on the pro tour; won $162,000 Tournament Players Championship (1985) G-189

Peewit. *see in index* Lapwing

Pegasus, in Greek mythology, winged horse P-152
horse H-273, *list* H-294

Pegasus, constellation, *charts* S-420, 423, C-681

Peggotty, family in Charles Dickens' 'David Copperfield'; Clara Peggotty, David's nurse, marries Barkis, the shy carrier ("Barkis is willin' ").

Peggy's Cove, N.S., fishing village on Atlantic Ocean; pop. 60 N-399

'Peggy Stewart', ship, *picture* R-169
Maryland M-172

Pegler, Westbrook (1894–1969), U.S. journalist, born in Minneapolis, Minn.; European correspondent in World War I, then sportswriter; syndicated newspaper columnist 1933–62; noted for his attacks on corruption in politics and in labor unions; awarded Pulitzer prize 1941.

Pegmatite, rock veins rich in feldspar; a form of pegmatite is "graphic granite," in which the quartz crystals resemble cuneiform writing.

Péguy, Charles Pierre (1873–1914), French writer, born in Orléans ('The Mystery of the Charity of Joan of Arc', mystery play; 'Basic Verities; Prose and Poetry').

Pei, I.M. (born 1917), U.S. architect A-569
Washington, D.C. W-69, *picture* W-70

Pei Ho (literally White River), rises n. of Peking, flows s.e. 350 mi (560 km) to Gulf of Chihli; known as **Hai Ho** below Tianjin T-178

Peinture claire, painting technique developed by Manet M-95

Peiping, China. *see in index* Peking

Peipus, Lake, U.S.S.R.; 1,400 sq mi (3,600 sq km); fisheries, *maps* E-361, R-344, 348

Peiraievs, Greece. *see in index* Piraeus

Peirce, Benjamin (1809–80), U.S. mathematician and astronomer, born in Salem, Mass.; taught at Harvard University nearly 50 years.

Peirce, Charles Sanders (1839–1914), U.S. physicist and philosopher, born in Cambridge, Mass.; son of Benjamin Peirce; lectured on philosophy at Johns Hopkins University, Harvard University, and Lowell Institute; first to formulate doctrine of pragmatism, developed later by William James; wrote many treatises on logic, psychology, and scientific subjects P-266

Peirce, Waldo (1884–1970), U.S. artist, born in Bangor, Me.; best known for paintings of country life as lived by sophisticated city people ('Maine Trotting Race').

Peisistratos. *see in index* Pisistratus

Pejerrey, a fish *Atherinichthys bonariensis* found in lakes and rivers of South America; generally small with dry, delicate flesh; mouth small, teeth feeble; color translucent green with broad lateral band of silver; valued as food.

Pekan. *see in index* Fisher

Pekin, Ill., city on Illinois River, about 10 mi (16 km) s. of Peoria; agricultural and industrial area; corn products, chemicals, liquor, metal products, castings; birthplace of Everett Dirksen; pop. 33,967, *map* I-53

Pekinese, dog D-194, *picture* D-205

Peking (officially called Beijing, Westernization Peiping), China, capital; pop. 8,487,000 P-153
Asia, *map* A-697
China C-344, *picture* C-452
Boxer Rebellion B-387
Forbidden City F-298
Opera, *picture* C-350
Taiwan T-12

Peking, Peace of (1901), protocol which ended the Boxer Rebellion B-387

Peking man, extinct Pleistocene man *Sinanthropus pekinensis*
China C-359
Hebei H-112
man M-89

Pekoe, a grade of black tea T-45

PEL (also called picture element, or pixel) F-5

Pelage, mammal's coat of hair H-7

Pelagic sealing S-100

Pelargonium, genus of geraniums, developed for showy flowers G-103

Pelé (originally Edson Arantes do Nascimento) (born 1940), Brazilian soccer player, born in Tres Coraçoes; inside left forward of Santos Football Club 1956–74; won fame as world's greatest soccer player; scored 1,000th goal of career 1969, by far the highest total in professional soccer; came out of retirement to play for New York Cosmos 1975–77 S-232

Pelecanidae, family of gregarious birds in aquatic habitats that prey on fish; includes the white pelican and the brown pelican.

Pelecaniformes, order of short-legged water birds, comprising pelicans, tropic birds, boobies, gannets, cormorants, darters, man-of-war birds.

Pelecypod. *see in index* Bivalve

Pelée, Mont, volcano in Martinique V-380
Martinique M-161
West Indies W-155, *map* W-159

Pelee, Point, most southerly part of Canada C-73, *map* C-112

'Peleliu', U.S. Navy ship, *picture* N-86

Peleliu Island, one of Palau group, in Pacific, e. of Philippines; about 12 sq mi (31 sq km); guano; mangrove swamps; pop. 657, *map* P-6

Peleus, in Greek mythology, husband of Thetis and father of Achilles; legendary adventures include Argonauts' voyage and Calydonian boar hunt.

Pelew Islands. *see in index* Palau Islands

Pelham bit, part of a horse's bridle H-264, *diagram* H-265

Pelias, in Greek mythology, son of Poseidon and Tyro; king of Iolcus; sent Jason to seek Golden Fleece; destroyed by Medea.

Pelican, a water bird P-154, *pictures* P-155
brown P-156, P-441d
length of life, average, *chart* A-423
migration A-450
white P-156

Pelican Island, in Florida P-156

Pelican State. *see in index* Louisiana

Péligot, Eugène Melchior (1811–90), French chemist who isolated uranium.

Pelion, Mount, lofty mountain range in Thessaly, Greece, celebrated in mythology; had temple to Zeus and cave of Centaur Chiron; giants are said to have attempted to pile Ossa, a peak in Thessaly, upon Pelion to scale summit of Olympus; ship *Argo* built from wood on its slopes.

Pella, capital of Macedon under Philip II and Alexander the Great A-279, *map* A-280
mosaic M-589, *picture* M-590

Pellagra, a chronic nutritional disease, not contagious or hereditary, causing severe nervous and physical disturbances
Goldberger's work G-182
vitamins V-355, V-358

'Pelléas et Mélisande', play by Maurice Maeterlinck; forms libretto for opera by Claude Debussy M-31
Debussy D-52
opera O-568, *list* O-562

Pelly, river flowing w. across s. Yukon Territory, about 350 mi (560 km), *maps* C-112, N-351

Pelopidas (died 364 BC), Theban statesman and general, friend and associate of Epaminondas, whom he aided at Leuctra.

Peloponnesian War (431–404 BC) G-266
Alcibiades A-273
causes S-370
Euripides E-327
international relations I-259
Pericles P-205
Thebes T-162
warfare, *list* W-13

'Peloponnesian War, The', work by Thucydides W-27
Thucydides T-177

Peloponnesus (formerly Morea), s. extremity of Greek peninsula; probably named for Pelops, mythical founder of Pelopid dynasty at Mycenae G-254
Spartan control S-370

Pelops, in Greek mythology, son of Tantalus, king of Phrygia, and father of Atreus and Thyestes; Pelops' line was cursed by Myrtilus, the charioteer to whom he refused to pay a promised bribe; Peloponnesus ("Pelops' Island") named for him.

Pelorus, navigational instrument N-70

Pelotas, Brazil, seaport on s.e. coast; flour, soap, leather; exports include meat, wool; pop. 154,674, *maps* B-425, S-299

Pelota vasca. *see in index* Jai alai

Pelt, animal skin F-463, *picture* F-466
bear B-118

Peltast, ancient Greek soldier A-636

Peltier, Leslie Copus (born 1900), U.S. astronomer, born in Delphos, Ohio; draftsman, farmer; codiscoverer of comets, also of variable stars, novas, meteors.

Pelton wheel (or impulse turbine), waterpower W-103
hyrdraulics H-339

Pelusium, Egypt, ancient fortified city at n.e. extremity of Delta of Nile; gave name to e. mouth of Nile; important point in wars, *map* P-212

Pelvic fin. *see in index* Ventral fin

Pelvis, in human anatomy S-210

Pelycosaurs, prehistoric reptiles R-154

Pemaquid, peninsula, in s. Maine, including resort villages Pemaquid and Pemaquid Beach.

Pemba, island belonging to Tanzania, in Indian Ocean, off e. coast of Africa, n. of Zanzibar; 380 sq mi (980 sq km); pop. 164,321 T-21, *map* A-118

Pemberton, John Clifford (1814–81), U.S. general, born in Philadelphia, Pa.; served the Confederacy; surrendered Vicksburg C-482

Pembina, N.D., city in n.e. corner of state, at junction of Red and Pembina rivers; pop. 673 N-373, 376

Pembina Mountains, escarpment of wooded hills in s. Manitoba and n.e. North Dakota.

Pembina River, tributary of Red River, 150 mi (240 km) long; rises in Pembina Lake, Manitoba, and flows through n.e. corner of North Dakota.

Pembroke, Mary Herbert, countess of (1561–1621), born in Worcestershire, England; sister of Sir Philip Sidney, for whom he wrote 'The Countess of Pembroke's Arcadia'; subject of Ben Jonson's famous epitaph on "Sidney's sister, Pembroke's mother."

Pembroke, Richard de Clare, earl of. *see in index* Strongbow

Pembroke, William Herbert, 3rd earl of (1580–1630), English nobleman, born in Wilton, near Salisbury; son of Mary Herbert, countess of Pembroke; lord chamberlain at court of James I 1615–25; lord steward 1625–30; chancellor of Oxford University 1624, when Pembroke College was founded in his honor
Shakespeare's sonnets S-134

Pembroke, Ont., town on Ottawa River, 72 mi (116 km) n.w. of Ottawa; wood products, steel furniture, castings, textiles, leather products, flour; pop. 14,026, *map* C-112

Pembroke, Wales, municipal borough in s.w., on Milford Haven estuary; includes Pembroke Dock, center for ship repairing and light industries; ruined 11th-century castle, reputed birthplace of Henry VII; pop. 14,200.

Pembroke College, women's college in Brown University; founded 1891, present name adopted 1928; merged with Brown University in 1971. *see also in index* Brown University

Pembroke Pines, Fla., city 6 mi (10 km) w. of Hollywood; South Florida State Mental Hospital; incorporated 1960; pop. 35,776.

Pembroke State University, in Pembroke, N.C.; established 1887 as Cherokee Normal School, became Pembroke

State College 1949; liberal arts and teacher education N-358
PEMEX (Petroleos Mexicanos), semiautonomous Mexican government agency M-334
Pen, female swan D-285
Pen, instrument for writing or drawing P-156
  ball-point P-157, *picture* P-156
  calligraphy C-57
  drawing D-251
  fountain P-157
    point P-157, R-366
  ink I-206
  mechanical drawing M-255, 258
  quill and reed P-156, F-51
  steel P-156
Pen, internal shell of a squid M-526
Pena, Afonso Augusto Moreira (1847–1909), president of Brazil 1906–09 B-158
Peña, Roque Sáenz (1851–1914), president of Argentina 1910–13 A-583
Penal colony
  French Guiana F-393
Penalty, in sports
  football F-294
  ice hockey H-197
Penang, Malaysia. *see in index* Pinang
Penang Island, Malaysia. *see in index* Pinang Island
Penates, Roman gods of the storeroom; each family worshiped its own Penates M-702
Penaud, Alphonse (fl. 1870–1901), French aircraft designer; aided in development of helicopter
  Planaphore A-200
Pencil P-158. *see also in index* Stylus
  drawing D-251
  mechanical drawing M-255, 259
Penck, Albrecht (1858–1945), German geologist and geographer; with Eduard Brückner, produced standard study of glaciation in 'Alps During the Ice Age' 1901–08.
'Pendennis, The History of', novel by Thackeray, said to be largely autobiographical; first of three related contemporary novels written 1848–62.
Pendleton, George Hunt (1825–89), U.S. political leader, born in Cincinnati, Ohio; Democratic candidate for vice-president 1864; in U.S. House of Representatives 1857–65, in Senate 1879–85; sponsor of Pendleton Civil Service Act.
Pendleton, Ore., city on Umatilla River, 35 mi (55 km) s.w. of Walla Walla, Wash.; in wheat- and pea-growing region; lumber, woolen products; annual rodeo; pop. 14,521 O-585, *map* U-40
Pendleton Civil Service Act (1883), United States A-654
Pend Oreille Lake, lake in Idaho I-18, *map* I-30, *picture* I-27
Pend Oreille River, river in Idaho and Washington W-48, *map* I-30. *see also in index* Clark Fork River
Pendragon, title given to ancient British chiefs in times of danger when they had command over other chiefs or rulers; King Uther, father of Arthur, was called Pendragon.
Pendulum P-160
  energy E-214
  Galileo's experiments G-6
  mercury M-304
  student experiment, *picture* S-60
  torsion P-160
  watch and clock W-77
    Huygens H-337
Pénéiós (or Peneus), river in Greece. *see in index* Salamvria
'Penek', work by Bergelson Y-418
Penelope, character in 'Odyssey', wife of Odysseus; proverbial for patient faithfulness
  Homeric legend H-222, *picture* H-223
  loom S-391
Peneus River, in classical mythology; diverted by Hercules H-138
Penfeld River, short river in extreme w. France; divides Brest.
Penghu Islands. *see in index* Pescadores
Penguin, an Antarctic bird P-160, *pictures* P-161
  animals, *picture* A-426, 441
  Antarctica A-473
  birds B-240, *picture* B-249
  dictionary entry, *picture* R-126
  gentoo, *picture* P-421
  king P-160
  zoo Z-463
Penicillin, a drug A-445
  antibiotics A-489
  bacteria B-14
  bionic research B-234
  chloroform C-393
  disease treatment D-169
  fermentation produces F-56
  Fleming discovers F-178, B-232
  fungi beneficial uses F-450
  microbiology M-376
  mold M-519
  use in World War II, *picture* R-267
  venereal disease treatment V-273
Penicillium, genus of fungi M-519
Penikese Island, one of Elizabeth Islands, s.e. Massachusetts, at entrance to Buzzards Bay; 100 acres (40 hectares).
Peninsula, a body of land almost surrounded by water and joined to a larger body of land by a narrow body, or isthmus; also a body of land projecting into the water.
Peninsular Campaign, American Civil War C-474
  McClellan M-4
Peninsulares, officials sent from Spain to govern colonies S-291
Peninsular Ranges, mountains in California C-35, *maps* C-34, E-25
Peninsular War (1808–14), war fought in the Iberian Peninsula in which Britain helped Spain and Portugal oust French forces under Napoleon S-359
  Napoleon N-16
Penis, male sex organ R-151c, *diagrams* R-151
  sexuality S-123
Penitentes. *see in index* Flagellants
Penitentiary. *see in index* Prison
Penki, China, city in Liaoning Province, 35 mi (55 km) s.e. of Mukden; pop. 449,000.
Penknife, origin of name P-156
Pen lettering M-259
Penn, Arthur (born 1922), U.S. motion picture director M-627
Penn, John (1740–88), U.S. lawyer, North Carolina delegate to Continental Congress, signer of Declaration of Independence, born in Caroline County, Virginia.
Penn, Thomas (1702–75), English colonial proprietor, born in London; came to U.S. 1732 to manage proprietary interests in Pennsylvania which he inherited from his father, William Penn; returned to England 1741 P-166
Penn, Sir William (1621–70), English admiral, father of William Penn, the founder of Pennsylvania P-162
Penn, William (1644–1718), founder of Pennsylvania P-162, *picture* P-180
  Dover's establishment D-236
  Franklin's opposition to heirs F-383
  Hall of Fame, *table* H-16
  Hicks H-150
  museum, *pictures* P-177
  New Jersey N-199
  Pennsbury Manor, *picture* P-172
  Pennsylvania's foundation P-162, P-173, A-337
    Philadelphia P-250
  statue in Philadelphia P-251
  treaty with American Indians P-162, *picture* P-175
Pennacook, an Algonquian confederacy once living in Merrimack Valley and adjacent regions of New Hampshire, n.e. Massachusetts, and s. Maine M-92
Pen name. *see in index* Pseudonym
Pennant
  flag, *list* F-149
  signaling S-194a, *pictures* S-194b
  swallowtail. *see in index* Swallowtail
Penney, Sir William George (born 1909), English physicist, born in Gibraltar; helped U.S. produce first atomic bombs; chief of armament research in British ministry of supply 1946–52.
Penn Hills (formerly Penn), Pa., urban township on Allegheny River, just n.e. of city of Pittsburgh; pop. 57,632.
Pennine Alps, segment of the Central Alps along the Italian-Swiss border
  Matterhorn M-231
Pennines, range of low hills in England running n. and s. from Tyne River to Derbyshire; coal deposits E-230
Pennock, Herbert Jeffries (1894–1948), U.S. baseball pitcher, born in Kennett Square, Pa.; with Boston, A.L., 1916–22, and New York, A.L., 1923–33; won 241 games plus 5 (without a loss) in World Series play.
Pennsauken, N.J., urban township 3 mi (5 km) n.e. of Camden; pop. 33,775.
Pennsylvania, a Middle Atlantic state of U.S.; 45,333 sq mi (117,412 sq km); cap. Harrisburg; pop. 11,866,728 P-163
  cities
    Erie E-298
    Harrisburg H-44
    Philadelphia P-250, *maps* P-251a, *pictures* P-250, 251c
    Pittsburgh P-345, *map* P-345b
    Reading R-99
    Scranton S-75
    Valley Forge V-256
  floods F-180, *table* F-181
  geographic region, Middle Atlantic U-49, *map* U-50, *pictures* U-52, *Reference-Outline* U-133
  history
    Civil War C-474
    colonial period A-337
    Delaware control D-76
    founded by Penn P-162
  Constitutional Convention U-140, *pictures* U-139, 141
  first hospital H-279
  Revolutionary War R-171
    Continental Congress in Philadelphia R-166, 170, *picture* R-162
    Valley Forge V-256
  industries P-345
    carpets R-316
    iron and steel P-345, *pictures* P-345a, U-53
  libraries P-181
    Philadelphia P-251, *list* P-215d, *map* P-251b, *picture* R-131
    Pittsburgh S-461
  parks and other areas
    Gettysburg N. Mil. P., *picture* P-178
    Gloria Dei (Old Swedes') Church N.H.S. P-251d, *map* P-251a
    Valley Forge State Park V-257
  state symbols
    bird G-291
    flag, *picture* F-160
    flower, *pictures* L-88
  Statuary Hall, *table* S-437b
  taxation, *tables* T-37, 39
  transportation
    bridges, *pictures* P-251, 251c, P-345
'Pennsylvania', U.S. battleship, *picture* R-269
Pennsylvania, University of, in Philadelphia, Pa.; private control; established 1740 as charity school, made an academy in 1749 through the efforts of Benjamin Franklin, became a college 1755; arts and sciences, auxiliary medical services, communications, dentistry, education, engineering (chemical, civil and mechanical, electrical, and metallurgical), finance and commerce, fine arts, general studies, law, medicine, nursing, social work, veterinary medicine; graduate division P-251b, *maps* P-251a, *picture* P-177
  Franklin's influence F-381
  University Museum P-251c, *map* P-251b
    ancient and primitive sculptures, *pictures* S-78, 01
Pennsylvania Avenue, in Washington, D.C.
  White House W-196
  World War I parade, *picture* W-314
Pennsylvania Dutch (also called Pennsylvania Germans), descendants of early German settlers in Pennsylvania; their language, or dialect, also called Pennsylvania Dutch or Pennsylvania German P-166
  folk art F-254, *picture* F-250
  pottery P-477
    tulip ware, *picture* P-475
Pennsylvania Female College. *see in index* Chatham College
'Pennsylvania Gazette, The', U.S. newspaper
  Franklin's role F-380
Pennsylvania Main Line Canal, in Pennsylvania, *map* C-126
Pennsylvanian period, in geological time E-23, *table* E-24
  coal formation C-518
  reptiles R-154
Pennsylvania Railroad Company, The, chartered 1846 to extend service from Philadelphia and Harrisburg to Pittsburgh; later bought other railroads and linked e. coast to Chicago; figured prominently in Civil War by transporting troops and munitions; merged with New York Central 1968 to form Pennsylvania New York Central Transportation Company (Penn Central); became part of Consolidated Rail Corporation (ConRail) 1975
  ticker tape, *picture* S-453
Pennsylvania State University, The, in State College, Pa.; founded 1855; liberal arts, agriculture, arts and architecture, business administration, earth and mineral sciences, education, engineering, health and physical education, human development, medicine, science; graduate school; medical center at Hershey; graduate center at King of Prussia; 19 additional campuses, *picture* P-171
  Harrisburg H-44
Pennsylvania Turnpike P-170, *map* P-184
  roads R-215
Penny (plural pence), an English bronze coin, historic value 1/12 shilling, 1/240 pound sterling; in 1971 became 1/100 pound sterling; silver penny, early English coin, deeply indented with cross to permit breaking into two or four pieces, as half-pence and farthings were not coined until time of Edward I P-188. *see also in index* Denarius
Penny. *see in index* Cent
Penny black, stamps
  British Guiana, *picture* S-406
  United Kingdom, *picture* S-408
Pennyrile Plateau (or Pennyroyal Plateau), in Kentucky K-209
Pennyweight, unit of weight, *table* W-140
Penobscot River, chief river of Maine, rises in w. near Canadian boundary; flows to Penobscot Bay.
Penobscots, division of the Abnaki group, of Algonquian stock, occupied region on both sides of Penobscot Bay and River S-158
  Maine M-53
Penology, branch of criminology concerned with prison administration and treatment of offenders P-505a. *see also in index* Prison
Pen pals, individuals or groups, usually living in different countries, who exchange letters, stamps, souvenirs, etc.
Penrod, 12-year-old hero of Booth Tarkington's realistic and humorous novels 'Penrod' and 'Penrod and Sam'.
Penrose Laboratory Z-465
Pensacola, Fla., port city in extreme n.w., on Pensacola Bay, Gulf of Mexico; recreational area; paper, chemicals, wallboard, nylon yarn, seafood; Naval Air Training Station; founded 1698 by Spanish; figured in War of 1812 and Civil War; pop. 57,619, *maps* N-351, U-41
  Florida manufacturing center F-196
'Pensées', writings of Pascal P-135
'Penseroso, Il'. *see in index* 'Il Penseroso'
Pensions P-188, *picture* P-189
  old-age S-236
  poet laureate P-402
  veterans' V-306
  welfare programs W-146
'Pensive Man', photograph, *picture* P-295
Penstock, pipe that conveys water for hydraulic power D-11

Perennial plant P-357
  growth period and planting G-20, 24
  weeds W-131
  winter P-363b
Peres, Shimon (born 1923), Israeli politician, born in Wisniew, Poland; to Palestine 1934; director general of defense ministry 1952–59; member of Knesset (parliament) 1959–; deputy defense minister 1959–65; secretary general of Rafi party 1965; rejoined Labor party 1968; Labor party chairman 1977–; under power-sharing agreement, became prime minister 1984 I-374
Peretz, Isaac Leib (called the Father of Yiddishism) (1852?–1915), Polish writer Y-417, *picture* Y-418
Pérez, Antonio (1534?–1611), Spanish courtier; favorite and adviser of Philip II, who later prosecuted him; escaped from Spain; died poor in Paris; wrote 'Relaciones', an account of court life.
Pérez, José Julián Martí. *see in index* Martí, José Julián
Pérez, Juan (died 1513), Franciscan priest; influenced Queen Isabella to aid Columbus; accompanied second voyage.
Pérez de Ayala, Ramón (1880–1962), Spanish poet, critic, and novelist, born in Oviedo; ambassador to United Kingdom 1931–36; traveled widely and gained knowledge of foreign literatures ('El Sendero innumerable', poem; 'La Pata de la raposa', novel) S-365b
Pérez de Cuellar, Javier (born 1920), Peruvian diplomat; born in Lima, Peru; permanent representative to UN 1971–75, president of Security Council 1974, secretary-general 1982– U-27
Pérez Esquivel, Adolfo (born 1931), Argentine sculptor; secretary-general of Service for Peace and Justice in Latin America 1974–; imprisoned for 14 months 1977–78. *see also in index* Nobel Prizewinners, *table*
Pérez Galdós, Benito (1843–1920), Spanish novelist and playwright; wrote historical novels and stories of contemporary life; vigorous style ('Doña Perfecta'; 'La Corte de Carlos IV'; 'Zaragoza'; 'Electra', a play) S-365b
Perfumes P-203
  ambergris P-205
  attar of roses P-204
  civet C-462, P-205
  cosmetics C-728
  Coty's contribution C-742
  essential oils P-203
  musk P-205
  tuberose P-204
  vanilla V-266
Pergamum (or Pergamus), celebrated ancient city of n.w. Asia Minor, capital of Kingdom of Pergamum and later of Roman province of Asia; early center of Christianity; fine sculptures.
Pergolesi, Giovanni Battista (1710–36), Italian composer; although he lived only 26 years, composed many sacred works, of which the best known is 'Stabat Mater', and many operas.
Peri, Jacopo (1561–1633), Italian composer, born in Rome; one of founders of opera; wrote score of 'Euridice' for wedding of Henry IV and Marie de' Medici 1600 M-668, O-561
Periander (died about 585 BC), Greek sage and tyrant of Corinth; despotic but energetic ruler; patron of literature and music and known as one of the Seven Wise Men of Greece.
Pericarditis, inflammation of the outer lining of the heart D-174
Pericardium, outer lining of the heart H-97
Pericles (493?–429 BC), Athenian statesman P-205
  Alcibiades A-273
  beautifies Athens P-250, G-265
Pericles, Age of, in ancient Greece P-205
'Pericles and Aspasia', book by Walter Savage Landor, comprising imaginary letters, speeches, poems; "a kind of concentrated extract of the Periclean Age."
Peridot. *see in index* Olivine
Perigee S-343, *list* S-341b
  moon M-577
Perignon, Dom Pierre, Benedictine monk W-327
Périgordian, ancient toolmaking industry M-85
Perigynous flower F-218
Perihelion, point in orbit of planet or comet where it is nearest to the sun; from Greek words *peri* ("near") and *helios* ("sun") P-351, 355
  earth's orbit E-28
  solar system S-254a
Perilla oil, the product of seeds of certain Japanese and Chinese plants; supply for United States chiefly imported.
Perim, island at s. end of Red Sea; 5 sq mi (13 sq km); harbor on s.w. side; former coaling station, part of People's Democratic Republic of Yemen; pop. 360.
Perimeter, distance around an object M-242
Period, mark of punctuation P-534
Period. *see in index* Menstruation
Period, in ocean wave measurement O-487
Periodical. *see in index* Magazine
Periodic law, in chemistry C-294
  inorganic chemistry I-209
Periodic motion, in mathematics T-285
Periodic table, in chemistry P-206, *tables* P-207, 208
  chemical elements C-294
  Mendeleev M-297, A-751, S-58
  metal and metallurgy M-308
  noble gases N-330
  nuclear energy N-417
Periodontitis, bacterial inflammation at the base of the teeth D-101
Perioeci, free laborers of Sparta S-369
Periostracum, outer layer of a shell M-523
Peripatetic school A-588
Periperal Canal, proposed canal in California, rejected by voters in 1982 C-129
Periplus, in early navigation N-77
Periscope P-209
  submarines S-498, *picture* S-500, *diagram* S-499
Perisoreus canadensis. *see in index* Gray jay
Perissodactyla, order of mammals, *table* M-80
Peristalsis (or peristaltic motion) S-455, *diagram* S-454
  digestive system D-144, *diagram* D-143
Peristyle A-546
Peritoneum, the serous membrane that lines the walls of the abdominal cavity and covers the abdominal viscera.
Peritonitis, an inflammation of the peritoneum; marked by pain, vomiting, and fever.
Periwinkle, a gastropod mollusk; edible periwinkle *Littorina litoria*, shell rough, dark brown, yellowish, or reddish, with dark spiral bands; native to Europe and recently introduced on U.S. Atlantic coast as far s. as Delaware Bay S-222
Periwinkle, genus of plants of dogbane family with opposed evergreen leaves; some plants trailing, others erect G-23
Perjury, a crime, *table* L-93
Perkin, Sir William Henry (1838–1907), English chemist, born in London; first to synthesize an amino acid, glycine (with Duppa 1858); first to make artificial perfume (1868) D-296
Perkins, Anthony (born 1932), U.S. actor
  'The Trial', *picture* N-414
Perkins, Frances (or Mrs. Paul C. Wilson) (1882–1965), U.S. sociologist, born in Boston, Mass.; secretary of labor 1933–45; first woman member of a U.S. presidential Cabinet; civil service commissioner 1946–53; author of 'The Roosevelt I Knew' and books on labor problems E-137, R-268, *picture* R-272
  women's rights W-276
Perkins, Jacob (1766–1849), U.S. inventor, born in Newburyport, Mass.; devised steel plate for printing bank notes; printed first penny stamps at his factory in England 1840
  ice-making machine R-138
Perkins, Richard Marlin (1905–86), U.S. reptile expert, born in Carthage, Mo.; director Lincoln Park Zoo, Chicago, Ill., 1944–62; 'Zoo Parade' and 'Wild Kingdom', TV programs; director St. Louis (Mo.) Zoological Park 1962–70.
Perley, Sir George Halsey (1857–1938), Canadian public official, born in Lebanon, N.H.; Canadian high commissioner at London 1914–22; minister overseas forces of Canada 1916–17; member Dominion House of Commons 1904–13 and after 1925; minister without portfolio, Canada, 1930–35.
Perlis, state of former Federation of Malaya; 310 sq mi (800 sq km); rice; tin; became part of Malaysia 1963; pop. 121,062. *see also in index* Malay States, Unfederated
Perlman, Itzhak (born 1945), Israeli violinist, born in Tel Aviv; crippled by childhood polio; enrolled at Juilliard School, New York City, 1958; made professional debut at Carnegie Hall 1963; received Leventritt prize 1964; debut with New York Philharmonic 1965; European tours and performances with European orchestras from 1966.
Perm' (formerly Molotov), U.S.S.R., city on Kama River, about 300 km (185 mi) n.w. of Sverdlovsk; iron, machinery; copper refining; pop. 850,000, *maps* E-361, R-344, 348
Permafrost
  Arctic regions A-573
  pollution P-441e
Permalloy, a nickel-iron alloy, of high magnetic permeability
  communication cables C-7
Permanent Court of Arbitration (or Hague Court) H-5
  disputes
    German-Venezuelan R-286, 277
    U.S.-Canadian R-286
  international arbitration A-529
Permanent Court of International Justice (or World Court) H-5
  international arbitration P-143c
Permanent military cemetery N-23
Permanent press, the process of treating a fabric with a chemical and heat for setting the shape and for aiding wrinkle resistance T-141
Permanent teeth (or secondary teeth, or adult teeth), in humans T-51, *picture* T-52
Permanent wave machine, in hairdressing H-10
Permanent wave process, in hairdressing H-8
Permanganate, any salt of permanganic acid
  guided missiles G-310
Permian period, in geological time
  Australia A-774
  earth E-23, *map* E-26, *table* E-24
  prehistoric animals R-154, *picture* R-153
Permit class, category of U.S. submarines, *picture* S-496
Pernambuco, Brazil, state on central seacoast; 37,868 sq mi (98,078 sq km); cap. Recife; pop. 6,242,933, *map* B-425
Pernambuco, city in Brazil. *see in index* Recife
Pernicious anemia. *see in index* Anemia
Peroba, hardwood tree *Aspidosperma polyneuron* of dogbane family, native to S. America; red peroba belongs to same species as white quebracho; wood used for building and furniture; white peroba *Tecoma peroba* has yellow-brown wood and belongs to another species.
Perón, Juan Domingo (1895–1974), Argentine army officer and political leader P-209
  Argentina A-583
Perón, María Estela Martínez de Isabel (born 1931), Argentine leader, born in La Rioja; married Juan Perón 1961; elected vice-president 1973; became president of Argentina on the death of her husband 1974; removed from office in military coup 1976 P-209
  Argentina A-583
  women's rights W-276
Perón, Maria Eva Duarte de (1919–52), wife of Juan Perón after 1945, born in Los Todos, Argentina; tremendous social and political influence; inaugurated welfare programs for children, workers, and underprivileged P-209
  Argentina A-583
Perónista, in Argentine history P-209
Péronne, France, historic town on Somme River, 80 mi (130 km) n.e. of Paris; unsuccessfully besieged by Charles V in 1536; occupied by Wellington 1815, by Germans 1871, 1914, and 1940; pop. 6,877, *map* F-372
Perosi, Lorenzo (1872–1956), Italian priest and composer, born in Tortona, near Alessandria; music director Sistine Chapel, the Vatican, 1898–1915; noted especially for series of oratorios ('The Slaughter of the Innocents'; 'The Last Judgment').
Pérotin (died 1238?), French composer of polyphonic music M-668
Peroxide of sodium, a compound of sodium and oxygen (Na_2O_2), which liberates oxygen when mixed with water; used as bleaching agent.
Perpendicular, in geometry M-243
Perpetual check, in chess C-306
Perpetual motion, the movement of a hypothetical machine which would run forever without any outside supply of energy; for centuries men have tried in vain to build a device which would feed back its own output of energy to the input; such a device is mechanically impossible, because energy is lost due to friction; this energy must be replaced by an outside source.
Perpignan, France, city in s., on Tet River, 7 mi (11 km) from Mediterranean; 14th-century cathedral; citadel enclosing 13th-century castle; pop. 100,086, *map* F-372
Perrault, Charles (1628–1703), French author, born in Paris; collected fairy tales; noted in French Academy as defender of modernism, rebel against humanist tradition S-475
  folklore contribution F-260
  illustrations by Doré D-230
Perrin, Jean Baptiste (1870–1942), French physicist and chemist, born in Lille. *see also in index* Nobel Prizewinners, *table*
Perronet, Jean-Rodolphe (1708–94), French civil engineer, born in Suresnes, France; known for his stone-arch bridges, including Pont de la Concorde and Pont de Neuilly in Paris B-445
Perrot, François-Marie (fl. 1669–91), French soldier and governor of Montreal 1670–84; maintained trading post on Isle Perrot near Montreal, engaged in illegal trade with American Indians, exchanging brandy for furs; protected lawless *coureurs de bois;* arrested by Frontenac and sent to France but later regained governorship.
Perrot, Nicolas (1644?–1717), Canadian voyageur and fur trader, born in France; emigrated to Canada when a child; employed by Jesuits and Sulpicians; interpreter for Algonquins; persuaded western Indians to join in campaign against Iroquois 1684; discovered lead mines in Mississippi Valley 1693.
Perry, Antoinette. *see in index* Tony
Perry, Bliss (1860–1954), U.S. writer, editor, and educator, born in Williamstown, Mass.; professor of English at Williams College, Princeton University, and Harvard University; editor *Atlantic Monthly* 1899–1909 ('The Broughton House', fiction; 'The American Mind', essays; 'A Study of Prose Fiction', criticism; 'Walt Whitman', 'Whittier', biographies).
Perry, Fletcher (nickname Joe) (born 1927), U.S. football fullback and assistant coach,

born in Stephens, Ark.; fullback San Francisco 49ers (All America Football Conference 1948–49, National Football League 1950–60, 1963), Baltimore Colts 1961–62.

Perry, Fred (born 1909), British tennis player T-107

Perry, Matthew Calbraith (1794–1858), U.S. Navy officer, brother of O.H. Perry, born in Newport, R.I.; served in War of 1812; had command as captain of first steam vessel of U.S. Navy; later honorary commodore; in command of fleet in Gulf of Mexico during part of Mexican War
  Japanese persimmon introduced P-215
  Japan visit J-64, *picture* J-70
  marines M-139
  navy N-91

Perry, Oliver Hazard (1785–1819), U.S. Navy officer, hero of battle of Lake Erie P-209
  Rhode Island, *picture* R-190
  War of 1812 W-31
    flag F-154, *picture* F-155
    Lake Erie E-298
    Lawrence and *Niagara* S-177h
    Ohio naval victory O-505

Perry, Ralph Barton (1876–1957), U.S. philosopher, educator, born in Poultney, Vt.; professor of philosophy Harvard University 1913–46 ('The New Realism'; 'The Thought and Character of William James', Pulitzer prize for biography 1936; 'The Citizen Decides'; 'Realms of Value').

Perry's Treaty (1854), *table* T-275

Perryville, Ky., town about 38 mi (61 km) s. of Frankfort; pop. 841.

'Persai', play by Aeschylus G-275

Perse, St.-John. *see in index* Léger, Alexis Saint-Léger

Per se, in law, *table* L-93

Persea americana, avocado tree A-889

Persephone (or Proserpina), in Greek and Roman mythology, daughter of Demeter M-700
  Adonis A-49

Persepolis, ancient capital of Persian Empire, 30 mi (50 km) n.e. of modern Shiraz, Iran; probably became capital under Darius I; gradually declined after being sacked by Alexander 330 BC; another city, Istakhr, rose there about AD 200 and had several centuries of prosperity; ruins of colossal buildings and sculptured tombs, *map* P-212
  ceremonial stairway, *picture* P-213
  Iran I-306, *picture* I-308
  sculpture from treasury, *picture* P-213

Perseus, in Greek mythology, hero who slew Medusa P-210
  statue by Cellini S-87, *picture* F-190

Perseus, constellation S-414, *charts* S-415, 420, C-681

Perseus of Macedonia (212–161 BC), last king of Macedonia; defeated and captured by Romans under Aemilius Paulus 168 BC.

Pershing, General John Joseph (1860–1948), U.S. Army general P-210
  Marshall M-153
  Missouri M-494
  Philippines P-210
  Wilson W-218, *picture* W-217
  World War I U-185, W-313
    Saint-Mihiel S-22–3

Pershing, U.S. guided missile, *picture* G-307

Persia (officially Iran since 1935). *see also in index* Iran
  ancient religions A-537
  'Arabian Nights' origins A-524
  architecture, *picture* P-213
  art P-214, P-67e, *picture* P-213
    arts and crafts P-214, *pictures* P-213
    paint P-76
    Persian miniatures P-67e, *picture* P-213
    pottery P-469, *pictures* P-213
    rugmaking R-314, *picture* A-685, R-312
    silk S-202
  history P-211
    Alexander conquers A-279, P-212, *map* A-280
    Assassin sect A-703
    Behistun Rock, *picture* P-214
    Byzantium B-534
    conquest of Babylonia B-9
    Cyrus the Great P-211
    Darius I D-36
    Greek city-states G-265
    Medes M-273
    Medieval banner, *picture* M-384
    Mesopotamia M-305
    Middle East M-397
    Mongolia Empire M-535
    Persian Empire, extent, *map* P-212
    Persian Wars. *see in index* Persian Wars
    Turkmenia T-327
  Islamic literature I-364
  postal system P-464
  religion
    angels and demons A-414
    Zoroastrianism Z-471
  wind power W-232

Persian cat C-205, *picture* C-206

Persian Gulf, arm of Indian Ocean separating Iran from Arabia P-211. *see also in index* Ocean, *table*
  Iran I-307, *map* I-312
  pearls P-149

Persian Gulf War M-397

Persian knot, in rugmaking. *see in index* Sehna knot

Persian lamb, trade name for silky tightly curled fur of young Karakul lamb; primarily black in color S-146
  furs F-463, *table* F-465

Persian language
  Indian literature I-107
  Iran M-395

'Persian Letters' (or 'Lettres persanes'), work by Montesquieu F-396, M-567

Persian literature P-213
  folktales, *list* S-480, *picture* S-477
  Islamic literature I-364
  Jalal Ud-Din Rumi J-17

Persian lynx. *see in index* Caracal

Persian melon, fruit M-292

Persian miniature, painting P-67e, *pictures* P-213, B-350

Persian rugs R-314, *picture* R-312

Persian walnut (or English walnut), tree *Juglans regia* known for the wood and the nuts that it produces.

Persian Wars (499–479 BC) P-214
  Darius I D-36
  Marathon M-131
  Phoenician navy P-268
  Salamis S-26, *picture* S-27
  Themistocles T-163
  Thermopylae T-168
  warfare W-23, *list* W-13

Persimmon, a fruit tree P-215
  ebony E-48

Persinger, Louis (1887–1966), U.S. violinist and teacher, born in Rochester, Ill.; concertmaster and assistant conductor San Francisco Orchestra 1915; taught at Cleveland Institute of Music 1929–30, at Juilliard Graduate School, New York, N.Y., from 1930–66.

Persis (or Parsa), ancient province along n.e. coast of Persian Gulf; gave name to Persians, *map* P-212

'Persistence of Memory, The', painting by Dali D-9, P-60, *picture* P-59

Persistence of vision
  color C-561
  motion pictures M-602, 615

Perso-Arabic script, writing I-67

Person, in grammar P-507

Personal computer (PC), general-purpose microcomputer commonly used in offices and many homes; by 1980s increasingly popular for use in word processing, calculating, and processing data as well as for instruction and entertainment.

Personality P-216
  bibliography P-220
  juvenile delinquents J-162
  play P-386, 390b
  tests to measure P-218
    inkblot test P-523, S-110

Personal deduction, in taxation T-35

Personal exemption, in taxation T-35

Personality disorders, a category of mental illnesses M-301

Personal pronoun G-209, P-507

Personal property, in estate and inheritance law E-307

Personification, literary device F-81

Persons, Truman Streckfus. *see in index* Capote, Truman

Perspective P-220
  development in painting P-220
    Brunelleschi B-470
    foreshortening P-34
  eye E-389
    optical illusions I-54

Perspective drawing, in drafting M-260, *picture* M-261

Perspiration S-211

Per stirpes, legal term, *table* L-93

Perth, Australia, capital of Western Australia, in s.w. on Swan River, 12 mi (19 km) above port of Fremantle; furniture, clothing, automobiles, food products; University of Western Australia nearby; pop. with suburbs 898,918 P-6
  Australia A-767, *map* A-822
    Western Australia W-153

Perth, Scotland, capital of Perthshire, on River Tay, 32 mi (52 km) n.w. of Edinburgh; textiles, dyes, glass products; livestock market; scene of murder of James I of Scotland 1437; pop. 41,654.

Perth Amboy, N.J., port city on Arthur Kill, across from s. tip of Staten Island; copper refining; chemicals, petroleum products, wire cable, boats, ceramics, meat products, clothing; pop. 38,951.

Perturbation, in astronomy, the deviation of a celestial body from its exact elliptical orbit, caused by changing attraction of other celestial bodies M-577

Pertussis. *see in index* Whooping cough

Peru, republic on Pacific coast of South America; 496,223 sq mi (1,285,212 sq km); cap. Lima; pop. 12,011,500 P-221
  agriculture, *pictures* S-269, 281
  Andes A-409
  antiquities, *picture* S-293
    mask, *picture* M-186
    mosaic M-590
    pottery, *pictures* S-78
    ruin of Machu Picchu, *picture* S-290
  cities P-222. *see also in index* Lima and other cities by name
  flag, *picture* F-169
  geographic regions S-276, 279, *map* S-274
  history P-224, S-290
    Incas I-59, S-290
    Pizarro's conquest P-349, A-331
    San Martín aids liberation S-44b
    spinning S-389
  Latin America L-60, 64
    Ecuador E-66
  literature L-75
  minerals and mining, *picture* S-287
  national anthem, *table* N-64
  national parks N-25
  products
    drugs, *picture* S-288
    guano S-290
  railroad mileage, *table* R-85
  shelter S-155

Peru, Ill., city on Illinois River, adjacent to La Salle and about 15 mi (25 km) w. of Ottawa; clock center; polystyrene, metal products; Starved Rock State Park nearby; pop. 10,886, *map* I-53

Peru, Ind., city on Wabash River, about 70 mi (110 km) n. of Indianapolis; electrical products, heating apparatus, woodwork, furniture; railroad division point; pop. 13,764, *map* I-102
  circus history C-432

Peru, Viceroyalty of S-290

Peru Current (also called Humboldt Current), ocean current that flows from Antarctic regions n. along w. coast of South America; average temperature about 60° F (15° C)
  climatic influence on
    Chile C-329
    Lima L-210
    Peru P-221
  Humboldt H-321
  oceanography O-475

Perugia, Italy, historic city on Tiber River, 84 mi (135 km) n. of Rome; university (13th century); cathedral and other interesting buildings; Etruscan gateways, frescoes by Perugino; ancient Perugia one of 12 chief cities of Etruria; taken by Romans 310 BC; pop. 112,511, *maps* E-361, I-404

Perugino (easel name Pietro Vannucci) (1446–1524), Italian painter of Perugia; created classic type of Madonna and molded early style of Raphael R-92

Peru State College, Peru, Neb.; established in 1867, formerly a teachers' college, present name 1963; liberal arts, teacher education, and vocational courses.

Perutz, Max Ferdinand (born 1914), British biochemist, born in Vienna, Austria; director Medical Research Council Unit for Molecular Biology, Cavendish Laboratory, Cambridge, 1947–62; chairman Laboratory of Molecular Biology 1962–79 B-237. *see also in index* Nobel Prizewinners, *table*

Peruvian balsam. *see in index* Balsam fir

Peruvian bark, bark of the cinchona tree, source of quinine Q-18

Peruvian cotton, variety of cotton plant *Gossypium peruvianum*; mixes well with wool C-741

Peruvian daffodil (also called basket flower), a perennial plant of the amaryllis family, native to w. South America; sometimes classed as *Ismene calathina* but placed botanically as *Hymenocallis calathina* in the spider lily genus; leaves long, succulent; flowers, fragrant, white, tubular, with fringed edges produced by the partially attached stamens.

'Peruvian Traditions', work by Palma L-68, L-75

Peruvian winter grass. *see in index* Harding grass

Pervukhin, Mikhail Georgievich (1904–78), Soviet government official, engineer, and industrial expert, born in Yuryuzan, in Ural Mountains; a deputy premier 1950–55; full member Presidium of Central Committee of Communist party 1952–57; a first deputy premier 1955–57; ambassador to East Germany 1958–62.

Pesante, in music, *list* M-671

Pesaro, Italy, seaport on Adriatic, at mouth of Foglia River; silk, ships, ironware; palaces; founded by Romans as Pisaurum 184 BC; pop. 65,973, *map* I-404

Pescadores (also called Penghu Islands, translation fishers' islands), island group between Taiwan and mainland of China; about 50 sq mi (130 sq km); ceded by China to Japan 1895; with Taiwan, was returned to China 1945 T-12

Pescara, marchioness of. *see in index* Colonna, Vittoria

Peschanik, rodent, *table* F-465

Peseta, monetary unit of Spain; has been issued in gold, silver, brass, copper-aluminum, and other substances; historic value about 20 cents.

Peshawar, Pakistan, capital of Northwest Frontier Province, 10 mi (16 km) e. of Khyber Pass; center of trade with Afghanistan; long a British military post; pop. 268,366, *map* A-700

Peshkov, Aleksei. *see in index* Gorky, Maksim

Peso, monetary unit of Argentina, Bolivia, Chile, Colombia, Dominican Republic, Mexico, Philippines, and Uruguay
  Philippines, *list* P-253a

'Pessebre, El', oratorio by Casals C-194

Pest, Hungary, old town, now part of Budapest B-479

Pest (or varmint), in hunting H-331

Pestalozzi, Johann Heinrich (1746–1827), Swiss educational reformer, a founder of modern teaching methods E-89

Pestalozzi Children's Village, community for orphaned children of all nationalities at Trogen, in n.e. Switzerland; established 1946; funds raised by popular subscription in many countries; in each house children of one nationality live and study together according to customs of homeland; mixed groups share recreation; village named for J.H. Pestalozzi and follows his teaching.

pipelines P-241c, *pictures* P-241c, U-196b
microwave measuring S-195b
pumps P-241d, P-533
Rockefeller develops R-230
trans-Alaska A-570, B-464
U.S.S.R. R-330c
products P-229, *charts* P-241
asphalt A-702
coke. *see in index* Coke
fuel ships S-167
gasoline P-241
petrochemicals P-228
synthetic resins P-74
prospecting P-231, 234, *diagram* P-235
refining P-239, *chart* P-241a, *pictures* P-240, U-66, S-49d
automation A-836
New Jersey N-195
ultraformer, *picture* P-240
tanks for storage and transportation P-241d, *pictures* U-66, R-82
terms, *list* P-241d
transportation P-241c, *pictures* R-82, K-79
wells, *picture* F-441
drilling P-235, *diagram* P-237, *pictures* P-236, 239
first P-232
oil flow P-237

Petroleum V. Nasby. *see in index* Nasby, Petroleum V.

Petrology G-71

Petronius, Gaius (or Titus, also known as Petronius Arbiter) (died AD 66), Roman satirist; companion to Nero and director of his courtly pleasures; probably wrote 'Satyricon', a comic narrative of the age L-78, L-243

Petropavlovsk, U.S.S.R., city on Ishim River, in n. part of Kazakh Soviet Socialist Republic; agricultural and industrial center; pop. 173,000, *map* A-700

Petropavlovsk (or Petropavlovsk-Kamchatskiy), U.S.S.R., seaport and naval base in Siberia, on s.e. coast of Kamchatka peninsula; pop. 154,000, *maps* A-700, R-345

'Petrouchka', ballet by Stravinsky S-486

Petrovitch, George. *see in index* Karageorge

Petruchio, hero of Shakespeare's 'Taming of the Shrew,' who tames Katherine, "the shrew," into a model wife.

Petry, Ann Lane (born 1911), U.S. novelist, biographer, born in Old Saybrook, Conn.; known for books on black Americans' lives (novels: 'The Street', 'The Narrows', 'Tituba of Salem Village'; biography: 'Harriet Tubman') R-111d

Pets P-242
aquarium A-517
bibliography P-248
communication A-448
diseases and vaccines V-251
types
bird B-240
canary C-130
peacock, *picture* P-146
pigeon P-248, P-324
cat C-202, *picture* P-243
cricket P-247
dog D-192
gerbil G-103
guinea pig P-244
hamster H-24
lizard L-274
pony, *pictures* P-247
snake S-226c
squirrel S-401, P-247
turtle and tortoise P-247, *picture* P-245
zoo, *picture* P-248

Petsamo, U.S.S.R. *see in index* Pechenga

Pettie, John (1839–93), Scottish portrait, historical, and genre painter, born in Edinburgh; specially noted for paintings of 17th-century life in Scotland ('The Vigil'; 'Jacobites, 1745'; 'Distressed Cavaliers'; 'Bonnie Prince Charlie').

Pettigrew, James Johnson (1828–63), U.S. Confederate general, born in Tyrrell County, North Carolina; fought in Peninsular Campaign of 1862; led division and took part in Pickett's charge at Gettysburg; died of battle wounds.

Pettit, Robert (nickname Bob) (born 1932), U.S. basketball player, born in Baton Rouge, La.; formerly with Milwaukee (now Atlanta) Hawks; a leading scorer B-100

Petty, Sir William (1623–87), English economist and physician, born in Romsey, Hampshire; pioneered in comparative statistics; made surveyor general of Ireland by Charles II; an author of first book on vital statistics 1662; essays include 'Political Survey or Anatomy of Ireland' and 'Treatise of Taxes and Contributions'.

Petty jury. *see in index* Petit jury

Petty offense, in criminal law C-770

Petty officer, in U.S. Navy N-80
uniform and insignia U-6, *pictures* U-5, 9, 11

Petunia, small flower of nightshade family Solanaceae; trumpet-shaped blossoms range in color from white to purple G-24

Petuntse, Chinese name for variety of feldspar P-470

Pewter, alloy of tin and copper, lead, or antimony M-311

Peyote, a small cactus *Lophophora williamsii* grown in s.w. United States and Mexico; used by American Indians, who consider it of divine origin, to produce languor and visions in religious rites H-18

Pfalz, German name for Palatinate. *see in index* Palatinate

Pfeffer, Wilhelm (1845–1920), German botanist, born in Grebenstein, near Kassel; noted for research in plant physiology, particularly in osmotic pressure.

Pfeiffer College, Misenheimer, N.C.; affiliated with United Methodist Church; began as grammar school 1885, senior college after 1954; liberal arts and teacher education.

Pfennig, bronze coin, formerly a monetary unit of Free City of Danzig worth about 1/5 cent; German pfennig, called reichspfennig, historic value about 2/5 cent.

Pforzheim, West Germany, city in s.w., 15 mi (25 km) s.e. of Karlsruhe; watchmaking and jewelry center; pop. 90,338, *map* G-134

PGA (Professional Golfers' Association of America), golf G-189

pH, chemical symbol
acid rain measurement A-19

Phacelia (also called bee's friend), genus of plants, usually annuals, of the waterleaf family; tubular flowers, blue, purple, or white, in clusters; some have hairy, ill-smelling foliage.

Phaeacians, in Greek mythology, people who inhabited island of Scheria (probably Corfu).

Phaedo (early 4th century BC), Greek philosopher, born in Elis; founded Elian school; pupil of Socrates and said to have been present at his death; title of a dialogue by Plato which treats of immortality of the soul and the last hours and death of Socrates.

'Phaedo, or On the Immortality of the Soul', work by Mendelssohn M-298

Phaedra, in Greek mythology, the sister of Ariadne and wife of Theseus; fell in love with her stepson, Hippolytus, who spurned her; infuriated, she caused his death and in remorse committed suicide; story used by Euripides, Seneca, and Racine.

Phaedrus, Roman writer of fables copied after Aesop; lived in early days of Roman Empire; a freed slave.

Phaeozem, soil type A-577

Phaëthon, in Greek mythology P-248

Phaethontidae, family of seabirds. *see in index* Tropic bird

Phaeton, type of carriage W-3

Phagocyte. *see in index* Scavenger cell

Phagocytosis, process by which white blood cells engulf and destroy bacteria M-285

Phainopepla, a bird *Phainopepla nitens* of the silky flycatcher family Ptilogonatidae; male glossy black with slender crest, white wing patches; female dark gray with crest, no wing patches; nests in deserts of southwestern states.

Phalacrocoracidae, the cormorant family of birds. *see in index* Cormorant

Phalanger, any of the marsupial mammals of the family Phalangeridae M-156

Phalanges (plural of phalanx), scientific name for bones of toes or fingers, *diagram* S-210
hand H-27

Phalanstery, a communal group S-233

Phalanx, ancient battle array of heavily armed infantry A-635

Phalanx, Fourier's utopian social unit C-605

Phalarope, a shorebird with long slender neck and thin bill; when feeding in shallow pools, often spins around like a top, dabbing bill in water; nests in Arctic regions, winters in South America, s. Africa, Asia, and Pacific islands; seen in United States on coasts and inland lakes during migration; three species, red phalarope *Phalaropus fulicarius*, Wilson's *Steganopus tricolor*, and northern *Lobipes lobatus* B-243, *picture* B-265

Phalaropodidae, family of shorebirds, the phalaropes. *see in index* Phalarope

Phalerum, one of ancient harbors of Athens, chiefly used before Persian wars; superseded by port of Piraeus. *see also in index* Piraeus

Phanerozoic eon, the eon of visible light E-23, *table* E-24

Phantom, in gyrocompass G-328

'Phantom of the Opera' (1986), musical by Weber M-686

Phantom pain B-397

Pharaohs, kings of ancient Egypt E-125
ancient civilization A-405
sphinx S-378, S-82
tombs (pyramids) P-541, *pictures* P-542, S-115

Pharisees, most powerful and exclusive Jewish sect at the time of Jesus; especially exact in their observance of traditions and ceremonies
Dead Sea Scrolls D-46
Jesus' opposition J-104

Pharmaceuticals. *see in index* Drugs

Pharmacodynamic agents, drugs that stimulate or depress the normal way a cell or tissue acts D-274

Pharmacognosy, science of drugs P-248b

Pharmacology, science of how drugs act on body P-248b
animal experimentation A-448
drugs D-273

Pharmacy, compounding, preserving, and dispensing medicines P-248a

Pharos, peninsula of Alexandria, Egypt; formerly an island.

Pharos, famous lighthouse of Alexandria, one of the Seven Wonders of the World A-281, S-116
lighthouse L-204

Pharpar (or Abana, or Amanah, present names Awaj, or Barada), the two "rivers of Damascus" mentioned in the Bible (II Kings v, 12).

Pharr, Tex., city 10 mi (16 km) s. of Edinburg; truck and fruit farms; food processing and canning; natural gas; pop. 21,381.

Pharsalus, battle of (48 BC), warfare, *list* W-15

Pharynx, a part of the alimentary canal between the mouth and the esophagus; in humans a tube about 4½ in. (11½ cm) long T-176
worm W-361

Phase, in astronomy A-710
moon M-578, *diagram* M-579
Venus and Mercury P-350, *picture* P-353

Phase change. *see in index* Physical change

Phase shift, circadian rhythm B-225

Phasianidae, family of birds; includes the pheasant, quail, and partridge; often hunted as game; sometimes raised in captivity.

Pheasant, long-tailed bird P-249, *picture* B-259
hunting, *picture* S-330
ring-necked pheasant. *see in index* Ring-necked pheasant
ruffed grouse miscalled G-291

Pheasant's eye (or poet's narcissus), flower *Narcissus poeticus* N-18

Phelps, William Lyon (1865–1943), U.S. literary critic, born in New Haven, Conn.; professor of English Yale University 1901–33 ('Advance of the English Novel'; 'Essays on Modern Dramatists').

Phenacetin, a painkilling drug P-248a

Phenakistoscope (or deceiver-scope), optical toy M-615

Phencyclidine. *see in index* PCP

Phenix City, Ala., city in Russell County, on Chattahoochee River, opposite Columbus, Ga.; commercial center; products include bricks, paper, textiles, and lumber; pop. 26,928, *map* U-41

Phenobarbital, barbiturate drug N-19

Phenol. *see in index* Carbolic acid

Phenol, group in chemistry O-604
petrochemicals P-228

Phenomenal berry R-94

Phenomenology, philosophy
Heidegger H-116

Phenotypes, variations in body form sorted out by natural selection E-368
genetics G-53

Phenylamine. *see in index* Aniline

Phenylketonuria (PKU), an inherited metabolic disorder D-181
genetic disorder G-48
heredity H-139
mental retardation M-303

Pheromones, chemicals A-448
bees B-126

Phi Beta Kappa, honorary society U-206
fraternities and sororities F-388
medals M-270

Phi Delta Kappa, national college professional fraternity, founded at Indiana University, Bloomington, Ind., 1906 for graduate students, also juniors and seniors with high scholastic grades in education.

Phidias (500?–430? BC), Greek sculptor P-249
Greek art G-270
acropolis A-23
sculptures S-83, S-115, *picture* S-116
horses H-272
Zeus Z-451
Olympic games O-542

Phigalia, an ancient Greek city in Arcadia, among high mountains of the Peloponnesus; at Bassae, about 6 mi (10 km) away, are the ruins of a beautiful Doric temple of Apollo, designed by Ictinus, from which an almost perfect frieze (the Phigalian Marbles) has been removed to the British Museum.

Phi Kappa Phi, national college honor society, founded at the University of Maine, Orono, Me., 1897 for men and women in the top-ranking 10 percent of the senior class.

Philadelphia, Jordan. *see in index* Amman

Philadelphia, Pa., largest city of state, 4th city of U.S.; pop. 1,688,210 P-250, *map* N-351
captured by British (1777) R-171
Constitutional Convention, *picture* P-175
Continental Congress R-166
firsts
hospital H-279
penitentiary P-505d
harbor, *picture* H-35
Hog Island shipyard W-314, *picture* W-312
Independence Hall. *see in index* Independence Hall
Liberty Bell U-115, *picture* P-178
museums. *see in index* Academy of Natural Sciences; Philadelphia Museum of Art
newspapers P-171
Penn Center, *picture* P-177
Pennsylvania, University of. *see in index* Pennsylvania, University of
redevelopment plan M-517
United States Mint C-538
upholstery shop, Betsy Ross's R-297
waterfront, *picture* P-168

'Philadelphia', United States frigate captured by pirates, and held captive in Tripoli Harbor; daring attack by Stephen Decatur D-52
Philadelphia Confession (1742), Baptist confession of faith B-76
Philadelphia Museum of Art P-251, *map* P-251b, *picture* P-251c
Brancusi's 'Mlle Pogany', *picture* S-92
Degas' 'The Ballet Class' P-53, *picture* P-52
Eakins' 'Between Rounds', *picture* P-55
Lipchitz' 'Prometheus Strangling the Vulture', *picture* S-93
Picasso's 'Three Musicians', *picture* P-56
Rodin's 'Burghers of Calais' S-76, *picture* S-77
Philadelphia Navy Yard (or League Island), on Delaware River, established 1876; builds and repairs all types of naval vessels P-251d
Philadelphia Orchestra P-251c
orchestra O-578
Philadelphus Ptolemy II. *see in index* Ptolemy II, Philadelphus
Philander Smith College, in Little Rock, Ark.; affiliated with United Methodist Church; founded 1868, chartered 1883; arts and sciences, education
Philanthropy. *see also in index* Foundations and charities; Social service
foundations and charities F-328
Philatelic Sales Agency, of U.S. Postal Service P-462b
Philately, stamp collecting S-405
Philby, Harry St. John Bridger (1885–1960), British explorer, born in Ceylon; various political offices in Mesopotamia, Arabia, Jordan; author of 'Arabian Jubilee', life of Ibn Saud.
Philby, Kim (full name Harold Adrian Russell Philby) (born 1912), British spy, born in Ambala, India I-236
espionage E-303, *picture* E-304
Philemon, Epistle to, book of New Testament; written by Paul during first captivity at Rome, entreating the compassion of Philemon for his runaway slave whom Paul has converted to Christianity and is sending back to his master.
Philemon and Baucis, a mythical Phrygian man and wife, described by Ovid in his 'Metamorphoses', who befriended Jupiter and Mercury, in disguise, after all others had refused; in return they were saved from a flood which destroyed their village; their cottage was changed into a temple; Jupiter granted their wish that they might both die at the same time by turning them into trees—Baucis into a linden, Philemon into an oak.
Philip, one of Twelve Apostles; commemorated as saint May 1 A-506
Philip I (1052–1108), king of France P-252
Philip II, Augustus (1165–1223), king of France P-252
Capetian dynasty C-147
Henry II H-129
Paris P-122
Third Crusade C-787
Richard I R-201
Philip IV (1268–1314), king of France, called "the Fair" P-252
Boniface VIII seized B-343
Estates-General E-307
Knights Templars disbanded C-788
Philip VI (1293–1350), king of France P-252
Hundred Years' War H-324
Philip II (382–336 BC), king of Macedon, father of Alexander the Great and conqueror of Greece A-279, C-461
ancient Greece G-267
Thebes T-163
artillery development A-658
Macedonia M-7
uses phalanx in warfare A-636
Philip I (1478–1506), king of Spain; son of Maximilian I and Mary of Burgundy; right to Castile and Aragon through wife, Joanna, disputed by his father-in-law, Ferdinand; as father of Charles V, founded Hapsburg dynasty in Spain A-828
Elizabeth I E-190
Philip II (1527–98), king of Spain P-252
Armada defeated A-627
Austria-Hungary A-829
Henry IV H-132
Inquisition S-358
Mary I M-165
Menéndez M-298
Portuguese crown seized by P-457
Brazil controlled A-335
The Netherlands N-129
Philip III (1578–1621), king of Spain, a pious but feeble ruler S-359
Philip IV (1605–65), king of Spain; incapable administrator; reign marked decline of Spanish power and commerce; fought costly wars with France, Germany, and The Netherlands
Velasquez V-271
Philip V (1683–1746), king of Spain, grandson of Louis XIV, first of Bourbon dynasty P-252, A-829, B-384
Philip, King (or the chief Metacom, or Metacomet) (1639?–76), sachem of Wampanoag in Massachusetts; son of Massasoit; leader of King Philip's War (1676) against colonists K-246
Philip, Prince, duke of Edinburgh (born 1921), husband of Queen Elizabeth II of United Kingdom, born on Greek island of Corfu E-192
Royal Marines M-137
visit to U.S. C-140
Philip II, duke of Burgundy (or Philip the Bold) (1342–1404), son of the French king John II the Good N-129
Philip, the evangelist, one of the seven chosen deacons of the Jerusalem church (Acts vi, 5); sometimes confused with Philip the Apostle.
Philip of Swabia (1177?–1208), German king and duke of Swabia; youngest son of Frederick Barbarossa and member of house of Hohenstaufen; murdered while disputing with Otto IV his claims to Holy Roman Empire.
Philippe Egalité. *see in index* Orléans, Louis Philippe, duke of
Philippi, ancient city of n.e. Macedonia; named from Philip II of Macedon; Epistle to Philippians sent to city's Christians
battle (42 BC) A-496, A-762
Philippians, Epistle to, book of the New Testament; letter from Paul to Christians at Philippi reassuring them of his prospects of release and appealing for unity in their church; probably written at Rome shortly before his release AD 63.
Philippine Air Lines P-257a
Philippine Independent Church P-255a
Philippine mahogany P-257. *see also in index* Lauan
Philippines (or Republic of the Philippines), archipelago between China Sea and Pacific Ocean; 115,830 sq mi (300,000 sq km); official capital Quezon City; pop. 56,004,000 P-253
Asia, *map* A-700
cities. *see in index* city listed below and other cities by name
Manilla M-97
flag, *picture* F-169
geography
East Indies E-45
history
Aguinaldo A-144
Aquino A-520
Dewey and Spanish-American War S-364
Korean War losses, *table* K-296
Magellan M-35, A-331
McKinley M-20
Pershing P-210
Quezon Q-16
Taft T-7
World War II W-328
MacArthur M-3
naval warfare N-92
language and literature
folktales S-468, *list* S-479
literary awards L-241
children's L-310f
Rizal R-211
national anthem, *table* N-64
people
aboriginal A-11
railroad mileage, *table* R-85
religion A-684
Philippines, University of the, in Quezon City, Philippines P-253d, 258
Philippine Sea, battle of the, in World War II W-346, *picture* W-347
Philippine trench, in oceanography O-485
Philippolis, Bulgaria. *see in index* Plovdiv
Philips, Judson P. (or Hugh Pentecost) (born 1903), writer D-119
Philipse, Frederick (1626–1702), Dutch merchant in colonial New York, born in Friesland, The Netherlands; went to New Amsterdam 1647
Yonkers Y-423
Philipse Manor, museum, Yonkers, N.Y. Y-423
Philip the Good (1396–1467), duke of Burgundy; signed Treaty of Troyes for France; later aided English against France, gaining territory; patron of commerce B-469
Philistines, strongest people of Canaan when the Israelites entered this, the "Promised Land," which was to become Palestine; one of chief enemies of Israelites for many years; subjugated by David; slipped to minor role in history and yielded finally to conquerors who swept across Palestine—the Assyrians, Babylonians, Persians, Ptolemies of Egypt, Seleucids, and Romans; originally the Philistines may have come from some Minoan center of culture in Asia Minor, seafaring and land hungry; worshiped a god Dagon, part man, part fish; five cities—Gaza, Ascalon (Ashkelon), Ashdod, Gath, and Ekron, on the coastal plain of s. Canaan—formed the district Philistia, or Land of the Philistines (from this comes the name Palestine for the whole country); name Philistine used today for insensitive, materialistic persons M-699

Pine Bluffs, Wyo., town on Lodgepole Creek, at Nebraska boundary, about 40 mi (60 km) e. of Cheyenne; livestock and farm area, oil; pop. 1,077.

Pineda, Alonso Alvarez de, Spanish explorer; sailed along the n. shore of the Gulf of Mexico 1519.

Pine family (or Pinaceae), family of shrubs and trees, native chiefly to temperate regions, including the pines, firs, dammar pines, araucarias, cypress pine, cypress, cedars, China fir, junipers, larch, incense cedar, spruce, golden larch, Douglas fir, sequoia, arar tree, arborvitae, and hemlock A-529

Pine grosbeak, bird *Pinicola enucleator* of the family Fringillidae G-290

Pinehurst, N.C., resort in the sand hills, 62 mi (100 km) s.w. of Raleigh; recreational area; amateur golf tournaments; pop. 1,056.

Pinel, Philippe (1745–1826), French physician, born in St.-André, Tarn; pioneered in care of the insane by removing chains and advocating humane treatment; published work on classification of disease 1798 M-302

Pinellas Park, Fla., city n.w. of St. Petersburg; space equipment, electronic components; pop. 32,811.

Pinene, a product of turpentine used to make camphor C-67

Pine nut N-449

Pinero, Sir Arthur Wing (1855–1934), English playwright, born in London, of Jewish-Portuguese parents; skillful dramatic craftsman; acted on stage in youth; knighted 1909 ('Trelawney of the Wells'; 'The Gay Lord Quex'; 'Iris'; 'Letty') E-278

Pines, Isle of, Cuba. *see in index* Juventud, Isla de la

Pines, Isle of (French Île des Pins), small island in s. Pacific, 30 mi (50 km) s.e. of New Caledonia, of which it is dependency; 150 sq km (58 sq mi); pop. 978, *map* P-6

Pine siskin, a finch found mainly in the coniferous forests of North America; fairly inconspicuous due to small size, darkish coloration, and habitat in evergreens.

Pine snake, *picture* S-225

Pine strawberry. *see in index* Strawberry

Pine tree money, coined in Massachusetts 1652–82; had a pine tree on one side and the name New England with the date on the other; coined in values of shilling, sixpence, and threepence.

Pine Tree State, nickname for Maine. *see in index* Maine

Ping-Pong. *see in index* Table tennis

Pingyang, North Korea. *see in index* Pyongyang

Pinhole camera P-282

Pink, a flower P-329
- carnation. *see in index* Carnation

Pink bean B-96

Pink bollworm, larval stage of moth *Pectinophora obscura* of the family Gelechiidae.

Pinkerton, Allan (1819–84), U.S. detective, born in Glasgow, Scotland; organized federal secret service 1861 and founded a famous private detective agency; wrote 'Thirty Years a Detective'.

Pinkeye, a form of conjunctivitis resulting from a bacterial infection; highly contagious; most common in childhood.

Pink family (or Caryophyllaceae), family of plants, including the carnation, gypsophila, mouse-ear chickweed, sweet William, bouncing bet, starwort, and sandwort.

Pinkiang, China. *see in index* Harbin

Pink lady's-slipper, flower F-240, *picture* F-238
- Minnesota state flower, *picture* S-427

Pinkney, Edward Coote (1802–28), U.S. poet, born in London, England, son of William Pinkney ('Look Out upon the Stars, My Love'; 'Rodolph'; 'Poems').

Pinkney, William (1764–1822), U.S. lawyer, born in Annapolis, Md.; U.S. attorney general 1811–14; minister to Russia 1816–18.

Pinkroot (or worm grass), perennial herb *Spigelia marilandica* of the logania family, with opposite leaves and showy flowers, red outside and yellow inside, spiked in a one-sided cyme; root employed as vermifuge.

Pink salmon. *see in index* Humpbacked salmon

Pink scallop, clam *Chlamys hericus*
- shell, *picture* S-151

Pin money P-327

Pinna (or auricle), in ear E-3

Pinnated grouse. *see in index* Prairie chicken

Pinnate venation, vein system found in plants L-100

Pinnipedia, order of mammals, *table* M-80

Pin oak (or Spanish oak), tree *Quercus palustris* O-452
- wood, *table* W-283

'Pinocchio', a story of the adventures of a wooden puppet R-111. *see also in index* Collodi, C.

Pinochet, Augusto, (born 1915), president of Chile; born in Valparaíso, Chile; led military junta that overthrew the government of Salvador Allende in 1973 C-334

Pinochle, card game C-163

Pinocytosis, biological process C-238

Pinole, Calif., city 13 mi (21 km) n. of Oakland; farm and livestock area; chemicals; pop. 14,253.

Piñon, a nut pine of s.w. United States P-328
- New Mexico state tree, *picture* N-220
- nuts N-449

Pinos, Isla de, island off Cuba. *see in index* Juventud, Isla de la

Pinot Noir grape G-220

Pins, bowling equipment B-386

Pinsk, U.S.S.R., city 105 mi (170 km) e. of Brest, near Pripyat' River; former Polish city, included in U.S.S.R. since 1945; pop. 41,548, *maps* R-344, 349
- Europe, *map* E-361
- Poland, *map* P-414

Pint, unit of measure, *table* W-140

'Pinta', one of Columbus' vessels C-592

Pintail, duck D-284, *picture* D-286

Pintassilgo, Maria (born 1930), Portuguese political leader W-276

Pinter, Harold (born 1930), British playwright, born in London; repertory actor 1949–57 (stage plays: 'The Birthday Party', 'The Caretaker', 'Homecoming'; revues: 'One to Another', 'Pieces of Eight'; for TV and radio: 'A Slight Ache', 'Night School', 'The Lover') D-249

Pinto, Fernão Mendes (1509–83), Portuguese adventurer; companion of Francis Xavier on mission to Japan; his account of unknown Japan, long regarded as a sort of Munchausen yarn, is now conceded to contain much truth besides possessing literary value.

Pinto, a breed of horse H-260

Pin tumbler lock L-277

Pinturicchio (in Italian little painter, pseudonym of Bernardino di Betto) (1454–1513), Italian artist, one of the outstanding painters of Umbrian school; 'The Dispute of Saint Catherine' and the frescoes in the cathedral library at Siena are typical works.

Pinus, pine genus of trees P-329

Pin wheel
- jet propulsion, *diagram* J-106

Pinworm, a common human intestinal parasite; a roundworm up to 1/2 in. (1 1/4 cm) in length; egg deposits in anus cause severe itching; disease seldom serious.

Pinyin System, Chinese writing system C-336, 345

Pinza, Ezio (1892–1957), Italian basso, born in Rome; debut, Rome, 1919; U.S. debut 1926; with Metropolitan, Chicago, San Francisco, and St. Louis opera companies; on concert stage, in motion pictures, in musical plays 'South Pacific' and 'Fanny'; author of 'Ezio Pinza: an Autobiography', *list* O-570

Pinzón, family of Spanish navigators, three of whom, Martin Alonzo, Francisco, and Vicente Yañez (brothers), were companions of Columbus in discovery of America
- Vicente's exploration E-373

Piombo, Sebastiano del. *see in index* Sebastiano

Pion. *see in index* Pi-meson

Pion scattering, in nuclear physics N-432

Pioneer Day, celebration in Utah U-219, *picture* U-225

Pioneer life P-330
- Cather's depiction C-221
- farming F-27
- folk art F-254
- forests cleared U-54, 69
- frontier F-419
- geographic influences on settlement U-37
- gold rush of 1849 S-2
- houses S-159, *picture* U-178
- Lincoln L-211, 215
- Mississippi River route M-486
- needlework N-110
- roads R-221
- soapmaking S-229, 231
- South Dakota S-326
- Southwest, American. *see in index* Southwest, American
- trails, *maps* R-219, U-176. *see also in index* Oregon Trail

Pioneer Memorial State Park, park in Harrodsburg, Ky., *picture* K-219

Pioneer Organization of Lenin (or Pioneers), Soviet youth organization R-332

Pioneers, in botany W-131

Pioneers, U.S. interplanetary space probes V-259, *picture* S-254e, *table* S-344
- moon M-580

'Pioneer 10', U.S. space probe F-427, *picture* F-418

Pioneer Venuses, U.S. space probes, *table* S-344

Piozzi, Mrs. Hester Lynch Thrale. *see in index* Thrale

Pip, in radar R-31, *diagrams* R-30

Pipal tree. *see in index* Bo tree

Pipe, smoking
- peace pipe. *see in index* Calumet
- rocket material use S-348c
- tobacco T-200

Pipe, tube used in wind instruments W-231

Pipefish family (or Syngnathidae), includes pipefishes and sea horses, *pictures* F-127, S-97

Pipeline, cross-country pipe for transporting fluid or some solids, such as coal and ores, in a liquid suspension
- coal C-525
- Ecuador E-67, G-300
- Europe E-343
  - West Germany G-127
- gas G-38, A-810, *pictures* G-40, P-241c
- irrigation systems I-354
- Mexico M-334
- microwave measuring S-195b
- North America N-344
- petroleum. *see in index* Petroleum technology, *subhead* pipelines
- transportation T-254, 259, 265, *chart* T-260, *picture* T-265

Piperaceae. *see in index* Pepper family

Piperacillin, type of antibiotic drug A-489

Pipe vine. *see in index* Dutchman's pipe

Piping plover, a grayish-white shore bird *Charadrius melodus* with incomplete black ring around neck; nests from s. Canada to n.-central states, winters along Atlantic and Pacific coasts.

Pippa, character in Robert Browning's poem 'Pippa Passes', a little Italian mill girl whose songs on her one holiday of the year unconsciously influence several hearers to choose good instead of ill at momentous crises in their lives.

Pippin. *see in index* Pepin

Pippin, Horace (1888–1946), U.S. painter, born in West Chester, Pa.; because of injury in World War I, had to support right hand with left while painting; a self-taught primitive artist; work characterized by bold color effects; represented in leading art museums of U.S.

Piqua, Ohio, industrial city on Great Miami River, 27 mi (43 km) n. of Dayton; fans and propellers, fiber cans, funeral cars and ambulances, oil-mill machinery, paper products, prefabricated houses; historical restoration nearby; pop. 20,480.

Piqué, originally a heavy cotton cloth with corded surface; now also made of rayon; used for clothing and decorating fabrics; comes in a wide range of grades.

Piracy, act of reproducing copyright material without the permission of the owners C-713

Piraeus (Greek Peiraieus), Greece, seaport 5 mi (8 km) s.w. of Athens; pop. 196,389 A-734, *map* E-361
- Greek city-states G-265

Pirandello, Luigi (1867–1936), Italian dramatist and novelist P-341. *see also in index* Nobel Prizewinners, *table*
- drama D-245
- Italian literature I-378

Piranesi, Giovanni Battista (1720–78), Italian engraver; noted for engravings and etchings of ruins of Roman buildings and for his architectural creations—massive arches, great stairways, and columned structures dotted with shadowy figures A-559

Piranha, flesh-eating fish of the genus *Serrasalmo*; found in the rivers of South America; 10 1/2 in. (26.67 cm) long; triangular teeth; bold and savage F-128

Pirarucu (or arapaima), one of largest freshwater fishes *Arapaima gigas*; said to average 2.5 m (8 ft) in length; found in Brazil and Guiana; important food fish.

'Piratapamutaliyar Carittiram', work by Pillai I-108

Pirates and piracy P-342, *pictures* P-342b
- Barbary States
  - Cervantes captured C-261
  - Decatur attack D-52
- Caribbean Sea P-92
- flags P-343, *picture* P-342b
- folklore F-268
- Kidd, Captain K-234
- Lafitte L-20
- Pompey P-444
- privateering distinguished P-342
- Saxons S-52e
- Vandals V-265

'Pirates of Penzance, The', comic opera, words by W.S. Gilbert and music by Arthur Sullivan; scenes are set on coast of Cornwall, England.

Pire, Dominique Georges Henri (1910–69), Belgian Dominican priest, born in Dinant; founder of European organization for rehabilitation of refugees; autobiography, 'The Story of Father Dominique Pire'. *see also in index* Nobel Prizewinners, *table*

Pirene, in Greek mythology
- fountain dedication F-334

Pirna, East Germany, city on Elbe River, 10 mi (16 km) s.e. of Dresden; Prussians defeated Saxons in Seven Years' War Oct. 15, 1756; pop. 41,030, *map* G-134

Pirouette, in horse training E-295

Pisa, Italy, city in n.; famous for leaning tower; pop. 91,108 P-343, *picture* I-387, *map* I-404
- Baptistery pulpit S-85
- botanical gardens founded B-379
- Genoa G-59
- leaning tower P-343

Pisa, Council of (1409), church council that deposed rival popes Gregory XII and Benedict XIII; elected Alexander V.

Pisagua, Chile, seaport in n.; pop. of greater city 1,880.

Pisano, Andrea (or Andrew of Pisa) (1270?–1348?), Italian sculptor, pupil of Giovanni Pisano S-85

Pisano, Giovanni (or John of Pisa) (1247?–1314?), Italian sculptor, one of greatest of Renaissance, founder of Italian Gothic style; son of Niccolo Pisano S-85

Pogue, William R. (born 1930), former U.S. astronaut, born in Okemah, Okla.; U.S. Air Force officer in NASA program 1966–75; vice-president High Flight Foundation, Colorado Springs, after 1975, *table* S-348

Pogy. *see in index* Menhaden

Pohick Church, church in Virginia; where George Washington attended service, *picture* R-218

Poi, a food used in the Pacific islands P-13

'Poilen', work by Trunk Y-418

Poilu, a term meaning "hairy" or "bearded," applied during World War I, first to a French soldier who had served in trenches and become bearded, later to any French soldier.

Poincaré, Jules Henri (1854–1912), French mathematician, born in Nancy; cousin of Raymond Poincaré; professor University of Paris 1881–1912 M-216

Poincaré, Raymond (1860–1934), French statesman P-408

Poinciana, genus of tropical trees or shrubs of the pea family with showy orange-yellow or bright scarlet blossoms; grown for hedges.

Poinsettia, a slender shrub *Euphorbia pulcherrima* 2 to 10 ft (0.6 to 3 m) or more in height bearing small yellow terminal flowers surrounded by flaring scarlet bracts sometimes 9 in. (23 cm) long; native to Central America and Mexico; named for Joel Roberts Poinsett (1779–1851), who first brought it to the U.S. from Mexico P-369

Point, in cattle driving C-754

Point, in mathematics
- geometry G-73
- trigonometry T-285

Point, in measurements, *table* W-140
- type measurement T-336

Point Barrow, Alaska, northernmost point of the United States A-240, *maps* U-39, 94
- polar exploration, *map* P-417
- pollution P-441e

Point-count system, method of evaluation used in contract bridge that was originated by Charles H. Goren in the 1940s C-160

Point de Galle, Sri Lanka. *see in index* Galle

Pointe-a-Pitre, Guadeloupe, chief seaport; exports cacao, sugar, and vanilla; pop. 50,000, *map* W-159

Pointe-Noire, People's Republic of the Congo, seaport on Atlantic, 235 mi (380 km) s.w. of Brazzaville; ships palm products, hardwoods, livestock; pop. 141,700, *map* A-118

Pointer, dog, *picture* D-197

Point Four program, economic plan by President Harry S. Truman in his inaugural address on Jan. 20, 1949; points in U.S. foreign policy are: (1) support to the United Nations; (2) continuation of programs for world economic recovery; (3) defense agreements to strengthen freedom-loving nations against the dangers of aggression; (4) a new program for making the benefits of our scientific advances and industrial progress available for the improvement and growth of underdeveloped areas; program was directed by Foreign Operations Administration; a limited program administered by Department of State 1955–61 then transferred to Agency for International Development.

Pointillism (or Divisionism), impressionistic painting process; the chief exponents were French artists Georges Seurat and Paul Signac S-114
- color C-559
- painting P-52, *picture* P-53

Pointing, in fur processing F-466

Pointing, in sculpture S-80

Point lace. *see in index* Needlepoint lace

Point Lobos, point on the Monterey Peninsula, California, *picture* C-40

Point Loma College (until 1973 Pasadena College), San Diego, Calif.; Church of the Nazarene established 1902; arts and sciences, religion, and teacher education; graduate studies; quarter system; branch at Pasadena.

Point of departure, in navigation N-68, 71

Point Park College, Pittsburgh, Pa.; private control; founded 1960; liberal arts and sciences, business administration, engineering technology, information and computer science, journalism and communications, theater arts and dance.

Point Pelee National Park, in Ontario
- Great Lakes G-248

Point Pleasant, N.J., town near mouth of Manasquan River, 10 mi (16 km) s.w. of Asbury Park; resort; pop. 17,747.

Point Pleasant, W. Va., city on Ohio River at mouth of Kanawha, about 34 mi (55 km) n.e. of Huntington; shipbuilding; iron products, furniture. Virginians defeated American Indians Oct. 10, 1774, at present Tu-Endie Wei Park; treaty followed by which American Indians gave up extensive hunting rights s. of Ohio River; pop. 5,682 W-166

Points, on a magnetic compass C-622

Points of order, in parliamentary law P-132b

Poirot, Hercule, detective created by Agatha Christie C-402

Poison gas P-411. *see also in index* Gas, chemistry and physics; Gas, natural and manufactured
- protection against S-8
- World War I W-305

Poison hemlock, poisonous plant *Canium maculatum* with spotted stem and small white flowers H-127
- Socrates S-246

Poison ivy P-409, *picture* P-408
- ivy I-408
- poisoning
  - prevention P-410
  - treatment P-410
- weed, *picture* W-132

Poison oak P-410

Poisonous animals
- insects
  - ant A-468
  - black widow spider S-386, *picture* S-387
  - caterpillar B-526
  - scorpion S-65
  - wasp W-73
- invertebrate I-284
- lizard L-272
- sea anemone S-96, *picture* S-96
- snake S-226a, 226b, d, V-328, *pictures* S-223, 226 to 226b
  - bite treatment S-227
  - rattlesnake R-96

Poisonous plants P-408
- cattle C-231
- hemlock S-246
- ivy. *see in index* Poison ivy
- mushrooms M-665
- nightshade N-315
- rhubarb R-199
- strychnos tree (nux vomica) S-493
- upas tree T-258
- yew Y-416

Poisons P-410
- carbon monoxide C-158
- first aid techniques F-121
- industrial health hazards I-175
- mercury M-305
- methanol M-317
- narcotics. *see in index* Narcotics
- opium. *see in index* Opium
- phosphorus P-271
- protection S-8
- snake venom S-226c, R-96
  - treatment S-227
- strychnine S-493

Poison sumac (or swamp sumac) P-410

Poisson, Siméon Denis (1781–1840), French mathematician and physicist; did work in electrostatics and magnetism; wrote scientific memoirs ('Traité de mécanique') E-161

Poitier, Sidney (born 1927), U.S. actor, born in Miami, Fla. (stage plays: 'Anna Lucasta', 'A Raisin in the Sun'; movies: 'The Defiant Ones', New York Film Critics Award 1958, 'Lilies of the Field', 1963 Oscar) B-300

Poitiers, France, town 60 mi (100 km) s.w. of Tours; old churches, Roman remains; Charles Martel defeated Moors nearby AD 732; pop. 68,082, *map* F-372

Poitiers, battle of (1356), in the Hundred Years' War H-325
- warfare, *list* W-15

Poito. *see in index* Old Winnemucca

Poitou, old province of w. France; cap. Poitiers; governed by counts in Middle Ages; formed part of territory of Aquitaine; held by England 1152–1204 and for short time during Hundred Years' War.

Pojoaque, a pueblo about 16 mi (26 km) n.w. of Santa Fe, N.M.; people belong to the Tanoan language group of Pueblo Indians.

Poker, a card game C-162

Poker dice, a game D-133

Pokeweed (or pokeberry, or pigeon berry), tall perennial plant *Phytolacca americana* of the pokeweed family, with stout stem 6 to 10 ft (2 to 3 m) high; purple-tinged, large alternate veiny leaves; greenish-white flowers; bears purplish berries containing a dark red juice; young shoots are edible, but roots are poisonous P-408

Pokeweed family (or Phytolaccaceae), family of plants, shrubs, and trees, native chiefly to the tropics, including the pokeberry, agdestis, guinea-hen weed, and rouge plant.

Pola, Yugoslavia. *see in index* Pula

Poland, republic of central Europe; area 120,359 sq mi (311,728 sq km); cap. Warsaw; pop. 35,746,000 P-412, *map* E-361
- archery championship A-541
- cities P-412, 413. *see also in index* cities listed below and other cities by name
  - Gdańsk G-45
  - Warsaw W-33
  - Wrocław W-383
- communist world, *map* C-619
  - Warsaw Pact W-34
- cultural contributions P-413
- democracy D-94
- emigration to U.S., *chart* U-120
- flag, *picture* F-169
- fur industry F-463
- Galicia lost A-830
- government P-414, 415
- history P-413
  - boundary P-415, *map* P-414
  - food price revolt (1970) P-415
  - Krakow K-303
  - Łódź L-283
  - Moscow seized R-352
  - Paderewski P-20
  - Teutonic Knights P-413
  - three partitions (18th century) G-121
    - Maria Theresa M-135
  - World War I W-309, 320
    - peace settlement P-414
  - World War II W-322
    - genocide G-60
    - Holocaust H-205
- industries P-413
- international relations
  - West German agreement G-126
- labor movements L-11
- literature P-413
  - folktales S-470, *list* S-481
- Lithuania P-413, 414
- motion pictures M-624
- national anthem, *table* N-64
- people P-412, 413
  - minorities P-414
  - Slavs S-214, 215
- Polish Corridor. *see in index* Polish Corridor
- products P-412, 413
  - salt S-30
- railroad mileage, *table* R-85
- rivers P-412
  - Vistula V-353
- strike S-489
- underground newspapers N-242

Poland, battle of, World War II W-338

Polar air (P), air mass W-118

Polar bear, mammal B-116
- Arctic regions A-572
- zoo, *pictures* Z-463, 464

Polar case, map projection, *picture* R-127

Polar climates C-501

Polar easterlies, type of wind W-224, *picture* W-222
- weather W-117

Polar exploration P-416
- Amundsen A-381b
- Andrée P-420, *picture* P-423
- Antarctica A-474
- Arctic Ocean A-570
- Arctic regions A-572
- Byrd B-531
- exploration E-377, *picture* E-372
- Peary P-150–1
- Scott, Robert S-72

Polar front, in weather, *table* W-126

Polar ice cap, of Mars P-352, *picture* P-353

Polar ice cap climate C-502

Polaris, an intermediate range ballistic missile developed by the U.S. Navy, *picture* G-311
- submarines S-499

Polaris (also called North Star, or polestar, or Pole Star), star above North Pole S-414, *charts* S-415–16, 421–2
- constellations C-683
- direction-finding D-159
- early navigation N-77

Polariscope, an instrument for studying certain optical properties of substances, particularly sugars, by means of polarized light.

Polarity, the quality of being attracted to one magnetic pole, or one kind of electric charge and repelled from the opposite
- molecule M-522
- nervous system N-120

Polarization, in electric cells B-108, B-202
- air conditioners A-150

Polarization, in light
- qualitative analysis Q-6, *picture* Q-3

Polarizing filter, photographic equipment P-287

Polaroid Land camera P-298
- Land L-26

Polar-projection map, in aviation, *map* A-877

Polar regions. *see in index* Antarctica; Arctic regions; Polar exploration

Polar Star, diamond, *picture* D-129

Polar tundra climate C-501

Polasek, Albin (1879–1965), U.S. sculptor, born in Moravia; noted for vigorous portraits and strong monumental works; created statue of President Masaryk in Jackson Park, Chicago, Ill., which is among the largest equestrian statues in the world.

Polder, Dutch name for drained lowland N-124
- dikes D-147

Pole, Reginald (1500–58), English Roman Catholic cardinal and archbishop of Canterbury; opposed divorce of Henry VIII and compelled to leave England; leader in Council of Trent; returned to England on accession of Mary I.

Polecat, carnivorous mammal of weasel family, widely distributed in Europe; head and body about 17 in. (43 cm) long, tail 7 in. (18 cm); scientific name *Mustela putorius* C-213. *see also in index* Ferret; Fitch

Polemoniaceae. *see in index* Phlox family

Polenta, ancient noble family of Italy; ruled Ravenna; in last years Dante was a guest of Guido da Polenta R-97

Poles, celestial, the two opposite points on the celestial sphere, like the north and south poles on the earth, toward which the earth's axis is directed A-719, *chart* S-415

Poles, magnetic, of earth
- directions D-160
- magnet M-42
- magnetic compass C-622
- navigation N-68, *pictures* N-69, 71
- northern and southern lights, A-712

Polestar. *see in index* Polaris, star

Pole vault, in track and field T-244, *picture* T-245

Police P-424. *see also in index* Federal Bureau of Investigation
- armor A-631
- Canada. *see in index* Royal Canadian Mounted Police
- criminal investigation C-775
- dogs D-193
- fingerprint identification P-429
- helicopter H-120
- intelligence agencies I-236
- Peel P-152
- Roosevelt R-283, P-430b
- safety work S-5, *picture* S-10
- secret political. *see in index* Secret political police
- Secret Service U-158
- uniforms
  - Bolivia, *picture* P-430b
  - Canada R-300b, *pictures* R-300a

Portal vein, in anatomy
digestive system, *diagram* D-143
liver L-261

Port Angeles, Wash., seaport city in n.w. part of state, on Strait of Juan de Fuca; fisheries; lumber, paper, wood; dairy products; resort; headquarters Olympic National Park; pop. 17,311, *map* U-40

Port Arthur (Chinese Lüshun), China, naval base in Liaoning Province; in municipality of Lüda, *map* A-636
Lüda L-328
siege R-362

Port Arthur, Ont. *see in index* Thunder Bay

Port Arthur, Tex., trade center and seaport in extreme s.e. of state, on Sabine Lake, connected with Gulf of Mexico by Sabine-Neches Ship Canal; oil-refining center; chemicals; railroad shops, ironworks; pop. 61,195 B-119, *maps* B-99, U-41
oil refinery, *picture* P-241c

Port Augusta, South Australia, seaport, railway terminus, on Spencer Gulf; exports wool and wheat; pop. 13,092, *maps* A-822, P-6

Port-au-Prince, Haiti, capital and principal seaport, on w. coast; first laid out by the French 1749; pop. (including suburbs) 449,831 P-451, *map* N-351
Haiti H-11
West Indies, *map* W-159

Port authority, assigns berthing and anchorage space to ships in the U.S. H-36

Port Authority of New York and New Jersey (formerly Port of New York Authority)
harbors and ports H-36
New Jersey N-197, 200
New York City N-276

Port Authority Trans Hudson (PATH)
New Jersey N-197
Newark N-150

Port aux Basques, Newf. *see in index* Channel-Port aux Basques

Port Chester, N.Y., village on Long Island Sound, about 25 mi (40 km) n.e. of New York, N.Y., at Connecticut boundary; clothing, candy, metal, plastic, and wood products, brushes; pop. 23,565.

Port Clarence, Equatorial Guinea. *see in index* Malabo

Port Colborne, Ont., town and port on Lake Erie and Welland Ship Canal; nickel refinery, grain elevators, flour mills; pop. 19,225.

Portcullis, a sliding door C-198, *picture* C-199

Port Dalhousie, Ont., former town and port on Lake Ontario, near n. terminus of Welland Ship Canal; became part of St. Catharines in 1961.

Port Darwin, sheltered inlet forming the harbor of the city of Darwin, Northern Territory of Australia; naval base.

Port du Salut, a cheese. *see also in index* Trappist cheese

Porte, Sublime, name for government of Ottoman Empire; so called from guarded gate (porte) giving entrance to sultan's palace in Constantinople.

Port Elizabeth, South Africa, city and seaport in Cape of Good Hope Province, 400 mi (640 km) e. of Cape Town; large trade; pop. 468,797, *maps* A-118, S-264

Porteño, nineteenth century Argentines A-583

Porter, Cole (1893–1964), U.S. composer and lyricist, born in Peru, Ind.; wrote musical comedies: 'Fifty Million Frenchmen', 'The Gay Divorcee', 'Anything Goes', 'Kiss Me, Kate'; his hundreds of songs include 'Night and Day' and 'In the Still of the Night'; biography, 'The Cole Porter Story'
musical comedy M-685
popular music M-684

Porter, David (1780–1843), U.S. Navy officer in war with Tripoli 1801–03, War of 1812; commanded Mexican naval forces 1826–29; father of David Dixon Porter P-452
Essex S-177g

Porter, David Dixon (1813–91), U.S. Navy officer P-452

Porter, Edwin S. (1870–1941), U.S. inventor; worked with Edison in early development of motion-picture camera M-618
directing D-155

Porter, Eleanor Hodgman (1868–1920), U.S. author, born in Littleton, N.H. ('Pollyanna', one of most popular of the "glad books").

Porter, Fitz-John (1822–1901), Union general in American Civil War, born in Portsmouth, N.H.; blamed by General Pope for Union defeat in second battle of Bull Run 1862, court-martialed, cashiered 1863, vindicated 1879, reinstated and retired 1886 C-476

Porter, Gene Stratton (or Mrs. Charles Darwin Porter) (1863–1924), U.S. novelist and naturalist, born in Wabash County, Ind.; famous for novels of outdoor life ('Freckles'; 'A Girl of the Limberlost'; 'The Harvester').

Porter, Sir George (born 1920), British physical chemist, born in Stainforth, Yorkshire; professor at Royal Institution 1963–, director 1966. *see also in index* Nobel Prizewinners, *table*

Porter, Katherine Anne (1894–1980), U.S. writer, born in Indian Creek, Tex.; excellent stylist, combining insight with poetic power (short story collections: 'Flowering Judas', 'The Leaning Tower', 'Collected Stories', Pulitzer prize 1966; novelette: 'Pale Horse, Pale Rider'; novel, 'Ship of Fools') A-360

Porter, Noah (1811–92), U.S. educator; president Yale University 1871–76; editor of Webster's and other dictionaries ('The Human Intellect'; 'Books and Reading').

Porter, Pleasant (1840–1907), Creek Indian chief, born in Oklahoma; served South in Civil War; ably led his people through difficult period of readjustment.

Porter, Quincy (1897–1966), U.S. composer, born in New Haven, Conn.; professor of music Yale University 1946–65; known for chamber music and orchestral works; won 1954 Pulitzer prize in music.

Porter, Richard William (born 1913), U.S. electrical engineer, born in Salina, Kan.; expert on guided missiles; with General Electric Co. 1937–76; chairman U.S. earth satellite panel, I.G.Y.

Porter, Rodney Robert (1917–85), British biochemist and educator, born near Liverpool; professor of biochemistry Oxford University 1967–. *see also in index* Nobel Prizewinners, *table*

Porter, Sylvia Field (born 1919), U.S. journalist and author, born in Patchogue, N.Y.; known for her syndicated daily financial column ('How to Make Money in Government Bonds'; 'How to Live Within Your Income').

Porter, William Sydney. *see in index* Henry, O.

Porter, an alcoholic beverage B-134

Portes Gil, Emilio (born 1891), Mexican political leader; served as judge of lower and superior courts; deported to state of Chihuahua 1919 for activities in support of Obregón; as governor of Tamaulipas 1925–28, promoted interests of farmers and laborers; secretary of interior and head of cabinet 1928; provisional president 1928–30.

Port-Etienne, Mauritania. *see in index* Nouadhibou

Porthos, one of the musketeers in Alexandre Dumas's novel. *see in index* 'Three Musketeers, The'

Port Hudson, La., village 18 mi (29 km) above Baton Rouge, on Mississippi River; captured by Union forces under General Banks July 9, 1863; pop. 200 C-476, *map* C-474

Port Hueneme, Calif., city just s. of Oxnard; citrus fruit; port is part of U.S. Naval Construction Battalion Center; Port Hueneme lighthouse nearby; pop. 17,803.

Port Huron, Mich., port city on St. Clair and Black rivers, at foot of Lake Huron; extensive Canadian trade; salt, automobile parts, wire, paper, brass products, tools, textiles, paint; railroad shops; resort; connected with Sarnia, Ont., by railroad tunnel and Blue Water International Bridge; pop. 33,981, *map* U-41

Portico, in architecture
American colonial architecture, *picture* U-61
Mount Vernon, *picture* V-329
National Archives Building, *picture* U-145
Roman Forum, *picture* R-240
state capitols
South Carolina, *picture* S-313
Virginia, *picture* V-339
University of Utah, *picture* U-223
White House of South Africa, *picture* S-266

Portinari, Candido (1903–62), Brazilian painter, born in Brodowski, São Paulo; son of an Italian coffee worker; used ultramodern as well as classical styles; murals, portraits, and pictures of Brazilian life, especially life among blacks B-418
'Festival, St. John's Eve' P-67d, *picture* P-67c

Portland, Me., largest city and chief seaport in state; on Casco Bay 50 mi (80 km) s.w. of Augusta; food and fish processing; paper, furniture, and other wood products, textile products, tools, marine hardware; Westbrook College; burned by British 1775; pop. 61,572 M-53, 62, *picture* M-59
North America, *map* N-351

Portland, Ore., largest city of state; pop. 366,383 P-452, *map* N-351
Oregon O-584, 592, *picture* O-592
United States, *picture* U-92, *map* U-40

Portland, University of, Portland, Ore.; private control, Catholic related; founded 1901; arts and sciences, business administration, education, engineering, nursing; graduate school O-585

Portland cement C-243, 640

Portland Head Light, lighthouse on the coast of Maine built in 1791, *picture* M-51

Portland State University, Portland, Ore.; founded 1955; arts and letters, business administration, education, science, social work; graduate studies; quarter system O-585

Portland vase, beautiful dark blue glass urn decorated with white figures in relief; found in tomb near Rome; broken by a madman in 1845 but skillfully repaired; long exhibited in British Museum.

Port Louis, Mauritius, capital, on n.w. coast; seaport, center of sugar exporting; shipbuilding; cigarette factory; railroad; pop. 148,000
Mauritius M-233

Port Moresby, Papua New Guinea, seaport on s.e. coast of New Guinea; capital; pop. 117,000 N-174, *picture* N-173, *map* P-6

Port Nelson, Man., town at mouth of Nelson River on Hudson Bay.

Port Newark, part of Port Authority of New York and New Jersey N-149

Port Nicholson, seaport in New Zealand N-148

'Portnoy's Complaint', novel by Roth A-362

Porto, Portugal. *see in index* Oporto

Pôrto Alegre, Brazil, port and capital of state of Rio Grande do Sul, near n. extremity of Lake Patos, in agricultural and grazing country; educational center; pop. 869,795, *maps* B-425, S-299

Portobelo (or Portobello), Panama, port on Atlantic coast, 20 mi (30 km) n.e. of Colón; early shipping point; pop. 591 P-85, P-91

Port of call, a harbor or other haven at which ships stop during regular voyages to take on fuel, provisions, and water, and have repairs made.

Port of entry, any point, whether on the frontier or not, designated by the customs authorities as a place where merchandise or persons may fulfill the legal requirements for entering or departing from a country; need not be a nautical port.

Portofino, Italy, village 16 mi (26 km) s.e. of Genoa; resort; handmade lace industry; nearby is the monastery of Cervara, dating from the 14th century, *map* I-404

Port of Houston, port in Houston, Tex. H-310

Port of London, port in London, England L-294, H-37

Port of Melbourne, port in Melbourne, Australia M-290

Port of New York Authority. *see in index* Port Authority of New York and New Jersey

Port of Spain, Trinidad, capital of Trinidad and Tobago; harbor and commercial center; became capital 1783; pop. 60,400 T-288, *map* S-298
West Indies, *map* W-159

Porto Grande (or Mindelo), port in Cape Verde C-149

Portolá, Gaspar de, 18th-century Spanish explorer; governor of California 1769–71; discovered San Francisco Bay 1769 while searching for Monterey Bay after long, hunger-tortured march from Lower California; founded San Diego and Monterey missions and presidios S-338
California C-41

Portolano, a sailing chart
early navigation N-78
maps M-126

Porto-Novo, Benin, capital and port on lagoon connected with Gulf of Guinea; exports include kapok, cotton, and palm oil; produces soap; pop. 97,000, *map* A-118

Port Orford cedar, evergreen tree *Chamaecyparis lawsoniana* of pine family, sometimes called Lawson's cypress, Oregon cedar, and white cedar; many varieties used as ornamental trees; grows 125 to 200 ft (40 to 60 m); lives to 600 years; pyramid-shaped, with sharply drooping branches; wood pale brown, of moderate lightness; Oregon cedarwood oil used in insecticides, *table* W-282

Porto-Riche, Georges de (1849–1930), French dramatist, born in Bordeaux; his plays are studies of the emotions of men and women in love ('La Chance de Françoise'; 'Le Passé'; 'Le Marchand d'Estampes'; 'L'Infidèle'; 'Amoureuse').

Porto Rico, island of West Indies. *see in index* Puerto Rico

Porto Santo, a rugged island of Madeira group, 43 km (27 mi) n.e. of Madeira; 17 sq mi (44 sq km); grapes grown for wine; quarry; mineral springs; discovered by Portuguese 1418; pop. 3,927, *map* A-118, P-455
Madeira M-24

Port Phillip Bay, harbor in Australia M-289

Port Phillip District (1802–51), original name of the colony that became the state of Victoria, Australia A-815

Portrait d'apparat, roccoco device in painting portraying the subject with objects associated with his or her daily life
Copley C-710

'Portrait of a Lady', charcoal drawing by Manet, *picture* C-272

'Portrait of a Lady', painting by Rembrandt, *picture* R-144

'Portrait of a Lady', painting by Van der Weyden, *picture* P-31

'Portrait of a Lady, The', novel by James J-20, A-352

'Portrait of a Man', painting by Hals, *picture* H-19

'Portrait of a Youth', painting by Botticelli, *picture* P-23

'Portrait of Jean Cocteau', painting by Bérard, *picture* D-110

'Portrait of Louis Guillaume', painting by Cézanne P-56, *picture* P-56

'Portrait of Madame Matisse', painting by Matisse, *picture* D-266

'Portrait of the Artist as a Young Man, A', novel by Joyce J-145
novel N-411
young adult reading R-111g

Portraiture, in photography P-282, 296

Port Republic, Va., village on Shenandoah River, about 17 mi (27 km) n.e. of Staunton; here

Prickly ash, a shrub or small tree *Zanthoxylum americanum* of the rue family, so called because of its prickly leaves; one species, called toothache tree, has medicinal qualities in its bark.

Prickly pear, plant *Opuntia polyacantha* of the family Cactaceae, known also for its fruit C-12
- wild flowers, *picture* F-239

'Pride and Prejudice', novel by Jane Austen (1813); the quiet story of a middle-class English family, the Bennets, including charming Elizabeth Bennet, the heroine; marked by humor and keen observation of people and customs A-765, R-112c

Pride's Purge, in British history E-246
- Charles I C-275

Priene, ancient Greek city in w. Asia Minor; excavations have revealed a well-planned city, fine examples of Ionic architecture, and inscriptions and ancient objects.

Priest, Ivy Maude Baker (1905–75), U.S. government official, born in Kimberley, Utah; Republican national committeewoman for Utah 1944–52; treasurer of the United States 1953–61; autobiography, 'Green Grows Ivy', *picture* U-226

Priest, clergy. *see also in index* chief orders by name, as Dominicans
- Anglican A-418
- Counter-Reformation C-744
- Zoroastrianism and Parsiism Z-471

'Priest Kōbō Daishi as a Child, The', Japanese painting P-67f

Priestley, John Boynton (1894–1984), British novelist, essayist, and dramatist, born in Bradford (novels: 'The Good Companions', 'Angel Pavement'; plays: 'Dangerous Corner', 'An Inspector Calls'; travel: 'English Journey'; memoirs: 'Margin Released').

Priestley, Joseph (1733–1804), British chemist and nonconformist theologian; experiments important in development of chemistry; author of scientific, theological, and philosophical works; forced to leave England (for America) because of religious and political views
- botany B-380
- chemistry C-301
- oxygen O-623
- rubber R-305

Prigogine, Ilya (born 1917), Belgian physical chemist, born in Moscow, U.S.S.R.; to western Europe 1921, to Belgium 1929; professor, Free University of Brussels; director of Center for Statistical Mechanics and Thermodynamics at University of Texas, Austin; expanded applications of thermodynamic theory. *see also in index* Nobel Prizewinners, *table*

Prima Ballerina, in ballet terminology B-32

Primary colors C-558

Primary elections P-496. *see also* Fact Summary with each state article
- elections E-146
- voting V-387

Primary germ layers, layers developed early in embryonic life
- vertebrates E-200

Primary Health Care Services, United Kingdom H-90

Primary mental abilities, intelligence I-242

Primary succession, an ecological process E-54

Primary teeth (also called milk teeth, or temporary teeth, or deciduous teeth), in humans T-51, *picture* T-52

Primary wave (or P wave), type of seismic wave E-37

Primates, highest order of mammals, *table* M-80
- biological fields B-230
- color vision C-563
- hand H-27

Prime meridian (or base meridian), in geography G-62
- directions D-158
- hemisphere H-126
- latitude and longitude L-80, *picture* L-82
- time T-188

Prime minister (or premier), head of government and chief member of cabinet in some countries; makes government policy, appoints ministers, and distributes patronage of church and state; must resign if fails to win vote of confidence on important issues; in countries of Europe, he often has diplomatic duties similar to those of U.S. secretary of state P-129
- Australia A-803. *see also in index* Australian history, *table*
- cabinet government C-5
- Canada C-87
- democracy D-95
- government agencies G-200
- Philippines P-255b
- United Kingdom U-17

Prime mover, an original source of power or the machine for generating power from an original source; chief prime movers are animal muscles, wind, water, and heat engines P-483. *see also in index* Diesel engine; Internal-combustion engine; Motor; Steam engine; Turbine; Waterwheel; Windmill

Prime number, in mathematics M-220

Prime rate, in finance B-69

Primitive art, of early peoples
- animistic beliefs A-465
- cave dwellers P-28, S-357

Primitive art, of self-taught artists
- folk art comparison F-247
- painting P-50
  - Hicks P-50, *picture* P-49
  - Rousseau R-299a, *picture* R-299b

'Primitive Culture', work by Tylor A-465

Primo de Rivera, Miguel. *see in index* Rivera

Primogeniture, right of eldest son to inheritance
- estate and inheritance law E-307
- feudal times F-69
- Jefferson abolished J-91
- titles of nobility T-195

Primrose, Charles. *see in index* 'Vicar of Wakefield, The'

Primrose, a flowering plant P-496
- skin irritant P-409

Primrose, evening. *see in index* Evening primrose

Primrose family. *see in index* Primulaceae

Primrose League, Conservative political organization in England; founded 1883 in memory of Disraeli; name taken from his favorite flower; men and women members.

Primula, the primrose genus P-496

Primulaceae, the primrose family, a large group of herbs containing more than 25 genera and about 400 species of worldwide distribution but most abundant in temperate regions of the Northern Hemisphere; common members of the family are primrose, loosestrife, water pimpernel, American cowslip or shooting star, water violet, and cyclamen.

Primus, a hybrid berry R-94

Prince (born 1960), U.S. rock musician M-682

Prince, a title of power or rank, first applied to certain Roman senators; in Europe a male descendant of a royal house; in England confined to members of the royal family T-195

'Prince, The', political treatise by Machiavelli M-9
- Italian literature I-376
- Renaissance R-148

Prince Albert, Sask., distributing city for farming region on North Saskatchewan River, 82 mi (132 km) n.e. of Saskatoon; mineral, lumber, fishing, fur interests; meat, dairy products; federal penitentiary; pop. 31,380 S-49c, *maps* N-351, S-49k
- Canada, *maps* C-109, 112

Prince Albert fir. *see in index* Western hemlock

Prince Albert National Park, in Saskatchewan S-49c, *maps* C-112, S-49k

'Prince and the Pauper, The', book by Mark Twain; relates imaginary adventures of a beggar boy and prince of Wales (later Edward VI), who resemble each other and who change places temporarily R-111e
- American literature A-351

Prince consort, husband of a reigning queen, as Albert, prince consort of Victoria, and Philip, prince consort of Elizabeth II.

Prince Edward Island (formerly called Île St-Jean, nickname Garden of the Gulf), smallest Canadian province, in Gulf of St. Lawrence; 2,185 sq mi (5,656 sq km); cap. Charlottetown; pop. 122,506 P-497, *map* N-351
- Canada C-80, *map* C-112
- cities. *see in index* cities by name
- history C-101
- Nova Scotia N-403

Prince Edward Island, University of, Charlottetown, P.E.I.; province-supported; established 1969 by merger of Prince of Wales College and St. Dunstan's University; arts and sciences, education P-497d, *picture* P-497d

Prince Edward Island National Park, in Canada P-497b, *map* P-497h

Prince George, B.C., city at junction of Fraser and Nechako rivers, 320 mi (515 km) n. of Vancouver; transportation center; lumbering; Prince George College; pop. 67,559, *maps* C-109, N-351

Prince Harald Coast, Antarctica, portion of Queen Maud Land; discovered 1937 by Lars Christensen Expedition.

Prince of Wales, title in British royalty. *see in index* Charles, prince of Wales

Prince of Wales, Cape, in Alaska, westernmost point of North American mainland, on Bering Strait, *map* A-255
- United States U-39, 94, *picture* U-95

'Prince of Wales', British battleship S-177h

Prince of Wales College, Charlottetown, P.E.I. *see in index* Prince Edward Island, University of

Prince of Wales Island, Canadian island in Arctic Ocean; area 12,830 sq mi (33,230 sq km), *maps* C-109, N-351

Prince of Wales Island, largest island of Alexander Archipelago, Alaska; area about 2,220 sq mi (5,750 sq km), *map* A-255

Prince Patrick Island, Canadian island of Arctic region; area 6,081 sq mi (15,750 sq km), *map* N-351

Prince Rupert, B.C., seaport city and railroad terminus on Pacific coast, on an island about 32 mi (52 km) s.e. of Alaska boundary; ice-free harbor; fishing, fish processing, lumbering, mining; pulp mill nearby; pop. 15,747, *maps* C-109, N-351

Princes of the Church, metaphorical term for Roman Catholic cardinals; ranked after royal princes in succession to throne in some monarchies.

Princess Astrid Coast, Antarctica, portion of Queen Maud Land; discovered 1931 by H. Halvorsen.

'Princess Casamassima, The', work by James J-20

'Princesse Maleine, La', work by Maeterlinck M-31

Princess Martha Coast, Antarctica, portion of Queen Maud Land; discovered 1930 by Hjalmar Riiser-Larsen.

'Princess of Cleves, The', work by La Fayette N-410

Princess Pat. *see in index* Ramsay, Lady Patricia

Princess Ragnhild Coast, Antarctica, part of Queen Maud Land; visited 1931 by H. Halvorsen and Hjalmar Riiser-Larsen.

Princes Street Gardens, gardens in Edinburgh, Scotland E-71

Princeton, N.J., town 44 mi (71 km) s.w. of New York, N.Y.; educational and research center; Westminster Choir College; first state legislature of New Jersey met here Aug. 27, 1776; battle of Princeton; victory of Washington over British under Cornwallis Jan. 3, 1777; Continental Congress 1783; pop. 12,035. *see also in index* Institute for Advanced Study; Princeton University

'Princeton', naval steamer N-83

Princeton University (originally College of New Jersey), Princeton, N.J.; private control; traditionally for men but became coeducational 1969; chartered as College of New Jersey 1746, opened at Elizabeth 1747, moved to Newark 1748, to Princeton 1756; arts and sciences, architecture, aeronautical, basic, chemical, civil, electrical, geological, and mechanical engineering; school of public and international affairs; preceptorial plan of instruction; graduate school; James Forrestal Research Center N-198
- Elizabeth, N.J. E-193
- football F-295
- Newark N-150
- Wilson's presidency W-216

Princip, Gavrilo (1893?–1918), assassin of Archduke Francis Ferdinand
- assassination A-703
- World War I W-302

Principal, money upon which interest is paid P-200

Principe, island in Gulf of Guinea, w. Africa; area 42 sq mi (109 sq km); with island of São Tomé forms republic of São Tomé and Príncipe. *see also in index* São Tomé and Príncipe

'Principia' (or 'Mathematical Principles of Natural Philosophy') Latin 'Philosophiae Naturalis Principia Mathematica', treatise by Newton N-243, S-57h
- gravitation theory G-239

Principia College, Elsah, Ill.; affiliated with Christian Science church; established 1898, senior college 1932; liberal arts; quarter system.

'Principia Mathematica', work by Whitehead and Russell R-266
- mathematics M-217
- Whitehead H-195

'Principles and Practice of Medicine, The', textbook by Osler O-609

'Principles of Chemistry, The', work by Mendeleev M-297

'Principles of Mining', work by Hoover H-233

'Principles of Political Economy and Taxation', work by Ricardo R-198

'Principles of Psychology, The', work by James J-21

Pring, Martin (1580?–1626), British explorer, last of the Elizabethan seamen; commander of two ships that sighted Penobscot Bay 1603 and Casco Bay and landed at Plymouth; explored coast of Virginia 1606.

Print, in fossil discovery F-322

Printing P-499. *see also in index* Books and bookmaking; Printing press
- apprenticeship training A-512
- block printing. *see in index* Block printing
- Chinese invention C-365
- color printing C-564
- communication development C-615, S-57f
- folk art F-250
- drawing reproduction D-252
- facsimile F-5
- Franklin's contribution F-379, *picture* F-381
- graphic arts G-230
- Gutenberg G-319
- lithography L-258
- mechanical drawing M-259
- newspaper N-239
- paper P-100
- photoengraving and photolithography P-275, *pictures* P-276
- photography P-280, 293
- postage stamps S-405, *picture* P-462
- preventing paper shrinkage A-149
- type and typography T-336
- typesetting T-339
- vocations, *picture* V-362

Printing paper, in photography P-293, 296

Printing press P-501, *diagram* P-503
- die and diecasting D-139
- Gutenberg G-319
- literacy influenced by L-240
- magazine and journal M-32
- modern book production B-359
- typesetting T-339

Prints, in textiles T-141

Prints, in photography P-289, 293

Printz, Johan (1592–1663), Swedish colonial governor and soldier; founded early settlement in Pennsylvania.

'Prinz Eugen', German cruiser S-177h

inability to deal with reality; manifests in a variety of ways
mental illness M-301
psychoanalysis P-518

Psychosurgery, a treatment of mental illness M-302

Psychotherapeutic body work, practice of holistic medicine H-203

Psychotherapy, any form of treatment for psychological or emotional disorders T-166
Adler's advocation A-45
amnesia treatment A-373
hypnosis H-344, P-518
mental illness M-302
psychoanalysis P-518
weight control W-136

Psychotic disorders, a category of mental illnesses M-301

Psychrometer, type of hygrometer H-343
weather W-121

P.T.A. *see in index* Parent-teacher associations

Ptah, an Egyptian deity E-128, M-700

Ptarmigan (or snow grouse), bird of the order Galliformes G-291
Alpine animals A-319

Pteranodon, prehistoric reptile, *picture* R-155

Pteria, ancient capital of White Syrians (probably Hittites) of Cappadocia, Asia Minor; according to Herodotus, captured and ruined by Croesus of Lydia (6th century BC); ruins near Bogaz Koi.

Pterodactyl, member of a prehistoric order Pterosauria B-274

Pteropod, marine snail S-222

Pterosaur, member of a prehistoric order Pterosauria which included pterodactyl and other flying reptiles R-155, *pictures* R-153, P-487
animal life record, *table* E-24
birds B-274
evolution A-462, *picture* A-460

Ptilogonatidae, silky flycatcher family of birds, including the phainopepla of s.w. United States. *see also in index* Phainopepla

PTO (power takeoff), drive shaft F-30

Ptolemaic system, in astronomy U-198, S-57g

Ptolemy (or Claudius Ptolemaeus) (died 161?), Egyptian astronomer, geographer, mathematician; his greatest work, 'Almagest', expounded theory that heavenly bodies revolve around earth; work accepted until time of Copernicus G-268, G-278
astronomy A-728, U-198, S-57g
constellations C-680
maps M-125, *picture* 126
mathematics M-214

Ptolemy I (367?–283? BC), founder of line of Ptolemies; general of Alexander the Great; upon partition of empire became satrap of Egypt 323–306 BC; assumed title of king 305 BC; made Alexandria his capital; abdicated 285 BC in favor of son, Ptolemy II A-281, E-126

Ptolemy II, Philadelphus (309–247 BC), ruler of Egypt 285–247 BC; extended commerce and encouraged culture; made Alexandria center of Greek civilization; sent explorations to Ethiopia and s. Africa
Pharos of Alexandria S-116, A-280

Ptolemy III, Euergetes (known as Benefactor) (282?–222? BC), became ruler of Egypt on death of his father, Ptolemy II; his armies invaded Syria and India, and his fleets conquered shores of the Hellespont and Thracian coast; under him Ptolemaic Egypt attained greatest prosperity and widest dominion.

Ptolemy XII, Auletes (died 51 BC), father of Cleopatra and Ptolemy XIII, to whom he left Egypt; depended on Roman favor during his reign
Cleopatra C-489

Ptolemy XIII (died 47 BC), brother of and ruler with Cleopatra E-126
Cleopatra C-489

Ptolemy XIV (died 44 BC), youngest son of Ptolemy XII; ruled with Cleopatra until put to death to make way for her son Caesarion E-126
Cleopatra C-489

Ptolemy XV (or Caesarion) (47–30 BC), son of Julius Caesar and Cleopatra; with her, ruler of Egypt; put to death at orders of Augustus E-126
Cleopatra C-489

Ptolemys, line of Macedonian rulers of Egypt A-280, E-126

Ptomaine poisoning P-411

Puberty, in human development A-47
acne A-20
menstruation M-300
sexuality S-124

Pubis, part of the hipbone S-210

Publican, tax collector
franchises F-373

Publicani, tax farmers of ancient Rome R-246

Public assistance, welfare programs W-147. *see also in index* Relief measures

Public Broadcasting System (PBS) T-69

Public Citizen, Inc., citizen's group L-276

Public debt, debt incurred, usually by sale of bonds, by a government, such as a nation, state, county, or city. *see also in index* National debt

Public domain. *see in index* Copyright; Land, public; Patent

Public garden G-27

Public health H-82
bioethical issues B-215
bubonic plague B-473
garbage and refuse disposal G-17
health agencies H-89
health education H-91
venereal disease V-274
insects. *see also in index* Disease, *subhead* infectious diseases
New Zealand N-282
Panama P-85, 93
pesticide hazards P-441c
Philippines P-255a
plumbing P-392, *picture* P-393
pollution P-441b, *pictures* P-441
pure food laws P-538
radioactivity P-441e
rat menace R-94
Rockefeller R-230
Saskatchewan S-49f
sewage S-121
Social Security Act S-236
venereal disease V-274
World Health Organization U-26, S-348a
malaria, *picture* S-280

Public health nurse (or community nurse) N-447

Public Health Service (PHS), in United States U-164
air pollution hazard P-441c
flag F-158
health agencies H-90
smallpox vaccination V-249

Public housing H-302, *picture* U-102

Publicity. *see in index* Advertising; Propaganda

'Publick Occurrences Both Forreign and Domestick', first newspaper in British North America N-236

Public land. *see in index* Land, public

Public opinion. *see also in index* Censorship; Propaganda
advertising A-58
poll S-432
Gallup G-6
radio R-54

Public prosecutor. *see in index* State's attorney

Public relations
home economics H-219
hospital H-283

Public sanitation, service performed by health agencies H-89

Public school, in United States. *see in index* Education

Public speaking P-526. *see also in index* Debate; Rhetoric

Public utilities P-526c. *see also in index* Government ownership; Government regulation of industry; Municipal ownership; *also* names of public utilities
franchise F-373
industry I-188
monopoly M-544
power regulation U-165

Public Utility Regulatory Policies Act (PURPA), in United States W-106

Public Works Administration. *see in index* Federal Emergency Administration of Public Works

Publishing and publishers B-363. *see also in index* Books and bookmaking; Magazine; Newspapers; Reference books
awards, literary. *see in index* Awards
censorship C-246
children's literature N-151
copyright C-713
U.S.S.R. R-332f

Publius Cornelius Scipio. *see in index* Scipio Africanus

Puccini, Giacomo (1858–1924), Italian opera composer P-526d
opera O-568

Puccoon, several perennial plants of the gromwell genus; redroot or Indian paint *Lithospermum canescens* has orange-yellow, saucer-shaped flowers and is found from Ontario to Texas; roots are red, long, and deep; a Rocky Mountain species has pale-yellow flowers.

Puck (or Robin Goodfellow), character in 'Midsummer Night's Dream' by William Shakespeare.

'Puck of Pook's Hill', work by Kipling K-249

Pudding stone. *see in index* Conglomerate rock

Puddling, process of converting pig iron into wrought iron I-350
Industrial Revolution I-179

Pudu, smallest known deer *Pudu pudu* native of South America D-62

Puduchcheri, India. *see in index* Pondicherry

Puebla, state in s.-central Mexico; 13,096 sq mi (33,918 sq km); cap. Puebla; pop. 3,054,130, *map* M-344

Puebla, Mexico, manufacturing city and capital of state of Puebla, 65 mi (105 km) s.e. of Mexico City; agriculture, mining; textiles, glass, ceramics; fine cathedral; pop. 835,759, *map* N-351
Mexico M-328, *map* M-344
pyramids P-543

Pueblo, Colo., city on Arkansas River, 105 mi (170 km) s.e. of Denver; important center of industry, business, and agriculture; metal products, lumber, insulating materials, meat products; state hospital; University of Southern Colorado; Army ordnance depot; incorporated as town 1870, as city 1873; pop. 101,686 C-570, *map* C-583
North America, *map* N-351

Pueblo, name for American Indian village in s.w. United States P-526d, S-156
American Indians I-115, 128, 141, *map* I-136, *pictures* I-113, 137, *table* I-139
Colorado park, *picture* C-577
Hopi, *picture* P-526d
San Gerónimo de Taos, N.M., *picture* S-337

Pueblo Indians P-526d
houses S-156, *picture* S-337
marriage M-151
mosaic M-590
New Mexico N-215, *picture* N-222, *map* N-229
San Gerónimo de Taos, *picture* S-337

Puerperal fever (or childbed fever) S-108a

Puerta del Sol, plaza in Madrid, Spain M-30

Puerto Barrios, Guatemala, chief Atlantic port; terminus of transcontinental railroad; chief export bananas; pop. 22,929.

Puerto Cabello, Venezuela, city and port 75 mi (120 km) w. of Caracas; ships hides, coffee, cacao; dry dock and navy yard; pop. 111,559 (with suburbs) V-275, *maps* V-275, S-298

Puerto Cortés (formerly Puerto Caballos), Honduras; port on n.w. coast, on Gulf of Honduras; ships bananas; pop. 21,600 H-226

Puerto de Hierro, Venezuela, port on peninsula in n.e., on Gulf of Paria, w. of Port of Spain, Trinidad V-275, *picture* V-276

Puerto México, Mexico. *see in index* Coatzacoalcos

Puerto Montt, Chile, seaport about 600 mi (965 km) s. of Santiago; in timber and agricultural section; tourist center; pop. of greater city 86,750, *map* S-299
Chile C-332

Puerto Ricans, Hispanic Americans H-162, *pictures* H-166

Puerto Rico (formerly Porto Rico), island of West Indies, ceded to U.S. by Spain 1898; 3,435 sq mi (8,897 sq km) with nearby islets; cap. San Juan; pop. 3,196,520 P-527
cities. *see in index* San Juan and other cities by name
flag, *picture* F-160
literature
Caribbean literature C-167
folktales, *lists* S-481d
North America, *map* N-351
San Juan S-44a
United States S-365
Puerto Ricans H-162, 165
West Indies W-155, *map* W-159

Puerto Rico, University of, San Juan, Puerto Rico; commonwealth control; opened 1900, chartered 1903; humanities, architecture, business administration, dentistry, education, general studies, law, medicine, natural science, pharmacy, preventive medicine and public health, social science, arts and sciences, agriculture, engineering; graduate studies; campuses at Bayamon, Cayey, Humacao, and Mayaguez P-529, *picture* P-530

Puerto Rico Trench, deep-sea trench in the Atlantic Ocean A-669
oceans O-461

Puerto Williams, Chile, town and commune n. of Cape Horn; commune (pop. 949) includes the island Navarino.

Pueyrredón, Prilidiano (1823–70), Argentine artist A-580

Puff adder, poisonous snake V-328

Puffball, type of mushroom M-665
fungus F-447
plants P-370
spores scattering P-361, *picture* P-363a

Puffed Rice, breakfast cereal B-433

Puffer, marine fish of the family Tetradontidae; stomachs capable of enormous distension; when taken from water, they distend bodies with air until they resemble a ball
anesthetic research B-166b

Puffin (or sea parrot), bird of the auk family A-762

Puffing Billy, railroad invented by William Hedley L-281

Pug, type of dog D-194, *picture* D-205

Puget, Pierre (1622–94), French sculptor, painter, architect; best known for powerful sculptural works ('Milo of Crotona', 'Alexander and Diogenes' in Louvre; 'St. Sebastian' in church at Genoa) S-88

Puget Sound, large inlet of Pacific Ocean entering state of Washington at n.w. corner; extends from Strait of Juan de Fuca s. to Olympia, Wash. W-47, 51, *pictures* W-50, 58
Seattle S-102
United States, *map* U-90

Puget Sound, University of, in Tacoma, Wash.; Methodist; founded 1888; arts and sciences, business administration and economics, education, music, occupational therapy; graduate studies T-4
Washington W-52

Puget Sound Navy Yard. *see in index* Bremerton, Wash.

Puget Sound Trough, geographical region in Washington W-48, *map* W-49

Pugin, Augustus Welby Northmore (1812–52), British architect A-561

Pug mill, clay-mixing machine
bricks B-436
pottery making P-477

Pul (or Pulu). *see in index* Tiglath-Pileser III or IV

Pula (or Pola), Yugoslavia, Adriatic seaport on peninsula of Istria; many Roman ruins; formerly Austria-Hungary's chief naval station; ceded to Italy after World War I; ceded to Yugoslavia 1947; pop. 37,403.

Pulaski, Casimir (1748–79), Polish count and American Revolutionary War hero P-531

Pulaski, Va., town 50 mi (80 km) s.w. of Roanoke; cattle, sheep, alfalfa, grain; hosiery, chemicals, furniture; pop. 10,106, *map* V-348

Pulaski Skyway, a highway in New Jersey, *picture* U-108

Purple Islands. *see in index* Madeira

Purple loosestrife. *see in index* Lythrum

Purple martin, bird *Progne subis* of the family Hirundinidae S-521

Purple trillium, plant, *picture* F-232

Purple willow, tree, *Salix purpurea* of the family Salicaceae W-211

Purpure, in heraldry, *picture* H-136

Purring, sound produced by cats C-204

Purse seine, a net
fisheries F-134, *picture* F-135

Purslane (sometimes called pusley), annual herb *Portulaca oleracea* of the purslane family, with trailing stem, fleshy leaves, and small pale-yellow flowers; usually considered a weed, but leaves sometimes eaten as greens, particularly in Europe.

Purslane family (or Portulacacear), family of plants and small shrubs which includes portulaca (rose moss), red maids, spring beauty, bitterroot, winter purslane, and flameflower.

Purus River, one of chief southern tributaries of the Amazon; navigable for 800 mi (1,290 km) of its 1,850 mi course, *maps* B-425, S-298

Pus B-314

Pusan (or Fusan), South Korea, chief seaport, in s.e.; pop. 2,450,000, *map* A-700, K-290
Korean War K-296, *map* K-297, *chart* K-299

Pusey, Edward Bouverie (1800–1882), British theologian, a leader in the Oxford Movement; tried to unify churches but failed.

Push-drill screw driver (or ratchet screw driver), a tool T-218

Pusher propeller, of an airplane A-156

Pushkin, Aleksander Sergeevich (1799–1837), Russian poet, born in Moscow of noble family, his mother of Ethiopian descent; at first imitated Byron but in later poems was decidedly original; also dramatist, humorist, epigrammatist; many operas based on his works include Musorgski's 'Boris Godunov' and Rimski-Korsakov's 'The Golden Cockerel'; died in duel to defend wife's honor R-360, *picture* R-359
folktales S-469

Pushmataha (1764–1824), Choctaw Indian chief, born in Mississippi; friendly to whites; ceded lands in Alabama and Mississippi 1805 for $500 and small annuity, resisted Tecumseh's efforts toward a southern confederacy, fought on U.S. side in War of 1812 and Creek War.

Pusley (or pussly). *see in index* Purslane

Pussy willow, tree *Salix discolor* of the family Salicaceae W-211

P'u Sung-ling (1640–1715), Chinese writer C-390

Put-in-Bay, Ohio, harbor and village of South Bass Island, in Lake Erie, 15 mi (25 km) n.w. of Sandusky; resort; pop. 146, *picture* O-505

Putnam, George Haven (1844–1930), U.S. publisher, born in London, England, of U.S. parents; during Civil War became a major in Union army; became president 1872 of G.P. Putnam's Sons, the publishing firm founded by his father; largely responsible for copyright acts of 1891 and 1909 ('Question of Copyright'; 'Abraham Lincoln'; 'Memories of a Publisher').

Putnam, Herbert (1861–1955), U.S. librarian, born in New York, N.Y.; librarian Boston Public Library 1895–99; while librarian of Congress, Washington, D.C., 1899–1939, greatly expanded scope of institution; librarian emeritus of Congress after 1939.

Putnam, Israel (1718–90), American Revolutionary War soldier P-539

Putnam, Rufus (1738–1824), U.S. general, cousin of Israel Putnam; served in Revolutionary War in New England campaigns; one of organizers of Ohio Co. of Associates O-505

Putonghua, official spoken language of China C-345

Putrefaction. *see in index* Decay

Putter, golf club G-188, *diagram* G-186

Putting-out system. *see in index* Homework, industrial

Putty P-540

Putumayo River, river in South America, rises in Andes in s.w. Colombia, flows s.e. 800 mi (1,290 km) to Amazon, *map* S-298

Puuc style, in Mayan architecture M-235

Puvis de Chavannes, Pierre (1824–98), French painter; restored the purely decorative function of mural painting; (grand staircases of Boston Public Library, Paris City Hall).

Puyallup, Wash., city on Puyallup River, e. of Tacoma; lumbering and agriculture; light industry; Western Washington Fair; pop. 18,251.

Puy-de-Dôme, mountain in department of Puy de Dôme, France, in Auvergne chain; 4,806 ft (1,465 m); meteorological observatory on summit, *map* F-372

Puyi, Henry (1906–67), last emperor of China, succeeded 1908 as Emperor Hsuan T'ung, dethroned 1912 by revolution; temporary restoration 1917; title of emperor abolished 1924; named ruler of Manchukuo and enthroned as Emperor Kang Teh 1934; captured and interned by Soviets Aug. 1945–Dec. 1959 M-94

PVC. *see in index* Polyvinyl chloride

PWA. *see in index* Federal Emergency Administration of Public Works

PWR. *see in index* Pressurized water reactor

PX. *see in index* Post exchange

Pydna, Greek town in ancient Macedonia, on Thermaic Gulf; subdued by Macedonian kings; victory of Romans under Aemilius Paulus over Perseus, last king of Macedonia (164 BC).

Pye, Henry James (1745–1813), British noble, born in London; appointed poet laureate mainly for political reasons; member of Parliament; served also as police magistrate
poet laureate P-402

Pyelonephritis, bacterial infection of the inner portions of the kidneys and the urine D-182
kidney K-236

Pygmalion, in Greek legend, a sculptor who fell in love with an ivory statue he had made; Aphrodite granted life to the statue, so that Pygmalion might marry her; story told in Ovid's 'Metamorphoses', used in Gilbert's comedy 'Pygmalion and Galatea'.

Pygmy (or Pigmy) P-540
aborigines A-11
Africa R-366a
Cameroon C-66
Congo Basin C-648
Zaire Z-445
classification R-27, *chart* R-26

Pygmy chimpanzee, ape, *picture* Z-465

Pygmy elephant, elephant *Loxodonta africana* E-184

Pygmy hippopotamus, mammal *Choeropsis liberiensis* H-160

Pygmy nuthatch, bird *Sitta pygmaea* N-448

Pygmy right whale, mammal *Caperea marginala* of the order Cetacea W-185

Pyle, Ernie (full name Ernest Taylor Pyle) (1900–45), U.S. journalist and war correspondent, born in Dana, Ind.; roving reporter 1935–40; sympathetically depicted life of U.S. fighting men in World War II ('Here Is Your War'; 'Brave Men'; 'Last Chapter'); killed by Japanese machine-gun bullet on an island near Okinawa, April 18, 1945 N-238

Pyle, Howard (1853–1911), U.S. artist and author P-541
children's books
folk story contributions S-466
'The Merry Adventures of Robin Hood' R-111b, S-481a
'The Wonder Clock' R-110b, S-464

Pyle, Katharine (died 1938), U.S. author and artist, sister of Howard Pyle, born in Wilmington, Del.; wrote fanciful stories, poetry, and folktales for young children ('The Counterpane Fairy'; 'In the Green Forest'; 'Nancy Rutledge'; 'Lazy Matilda'; 'Fairy Tales from India').

Pylorus (or pyloric orifice), stomach valve S-455, *diagram* S-454

Pylos, city of ancient Greece 23 mi (37 km) s.w. of present Kalamai; seat of legendary counselor Nestor; declined after conquest of Messenia by Spartans A-61

Pym, John (1584–1643), Puritan statesman, parliamentary leader, conspicuous in struggle against Charles I
Hampden H-24

Pynchon, Thomas (born 1937), U.S. novelist, born in Glen Cove, N.Y.; satirist and writer of black humor ('V'; 'Crying of Lot 49') A-361

Pynchon, William (1590–1662), American colonial magistrate, born in Springfield, Essex, England; came to America 1630; settled site of Springfield, Mass., 1636 and named it for his English birthplace.

Pyolgok (or changga), Korean poetry form K-292

Pyongyang (or Heijo), capital of North Korea, on Taedong River, 40 mi (60 km) from w. coast; pop. of greater city 1,500,000, *map* A-700
Korea K-270, 278, 284, *map* K-272
Korean War K-296, *chart* K-299

Pyorrhea, a disease of the gums and other tissue surrounding the teeth; marked by inflammation, shrinking of the gums, resorption of bone, and loosening of the teeth T-53

Pyramid, in ecology E-55

Pyramid, in mathematics
geometry G-78, *diagram* G-78
measurement M-245

Pyramid Lake, lake in Nevada; 30 mi (50 km) long; at elevation of 3,880 ft (1,180 m) above sea; receives Truckee River from south; remnant of prehistoric Lake Lahontan; named for pyramid-shaped rock island N-133, *map* U-87

Pyramids P-541
Aztec A-890, M-328
Egypt E-125. *see also in index* Sphinx
civilization A-405
Giza G-149, *pictures* M-394, S-115, A-530
serfs S-213
symbolic architecture A-544
Maya M-236, *picture* M-237

Pyramids, battle of the (1798), victory gained near Egyptian pyramids by French under Napoleon over Mamelukes under Murad Bey E-121, N-15

Pyramid tent, a tent that is wide at the bottom and draws to a point at the top T-109

Pyramid Texts, ancient Egyptian literature E-131

Pyramus, hero of the classic story of Pyramus and Thisbe, parodied in the interlude of Shakespeare's 'Midsummer Night's Dream'.

Pyrenean desman, animal. *see in index* Desman

Pyrenees, mountain range between France and Spain; highest peak, Pico de Aneto, 11,168 ft (3,404 m) P-543, *map* E-360
Basques. *see in index* Basques
France F-343, *map* F-372
Iberian peninsula I-2
Spain, *map* S-350

Pyrenees, Peace of the (1659), *table* T-275

Pyrethrum, old genus of composite family which botanists now place in genus *Chrysanthemum*; most garden varieties were derived from *Chrysanthemum roseum*, or *Pyrethrum roseum*, a handsome perennial with finely dissected leaves and white to crimson and lilac flowers; the flowers of *Chrysanthemum cinerariaefolium*, used in insecticides, had important part in U.S. troops' fight against malaria-carrying mosquitoes in World War II C-408
daisy D-8

Pyridine, a toxic fluid
osmosis O-610

Pyridoxine (or vitamin B_6) V-356

Pyrites (also called iron pyrite, or fool's gold), any of several metallic sulfides; iron pyrites (FeS_2), is a hard, pale-yellow compound found in quartz and coal; valuable source of sulfur and sulfuric acid; copper pyrites, or chalcopyrite ($CuFeS_2$), is a brittle, yellow mineral; valuable source of copper
gem material J-116
minerals M-432
ore, *table* O-600
source of sulfur S-509
Tennessee production T-85, *map* T-88

Pyrolusite. *see in index* Manganese dioxide

Pyrolysis, in garbage and refuse disposal G-18

Pyrometallurgy M-308

Pyrometer, an instrument for measuring high temperatures P-543
thermometer T-167
volcano V-305

Pyrope, gem materials J-116

Pyrotechnics
fireworks F-114

Pyroxene, large group of silicate minerals; next to feldspars the most common rock-forming constituents; contain calcium and magnesium besides silica R-229
minerals M-436

Pyrrho (365?–275? BC), Greek philosopher, born in Elis; traveled with Alexander the Great to India, where he studied with Indian philosophers; came to believe that as thought and sensation often disagree, there is no actual way to determine truth; founded school of skepticism in Elis.

Pyrrhus, in Greek mythology. *see in index* Neoptolemus

Pyrrhus, King of Epirus (318?–272 BC) P-544
Roman history R-244, *picture* R-247

Pyrrhotite, a mineral M-432

Pythagoras (582?–500? BC), Greek philosopher and mathematician P-544
acoustics P-305
classical music M-667
mathematics M-213
view of universe U-198

Pythagorean theorem, method for calculating the sides of a right triangle M-213

Pytheas, Massilian navigator of 4th century BC
exploration E-373
polar P-418

Pythia, a Greek priestess D-89

Pythian Games, athletic festival in ancient Greece A-506

Pythias. *see in index* Damon and Pythias

Pythis (or Pythius), Greek architect and sculptor of 4th century BC, said to have sculpted part of the Mausoleum of Halicarnassus.

Python, serpent in Greek mythology, slain by Apollo A-506

Python, snake P-544. *see also in index* Snake
zoo Z-463

Pyxis, constellation, *chart* C-682

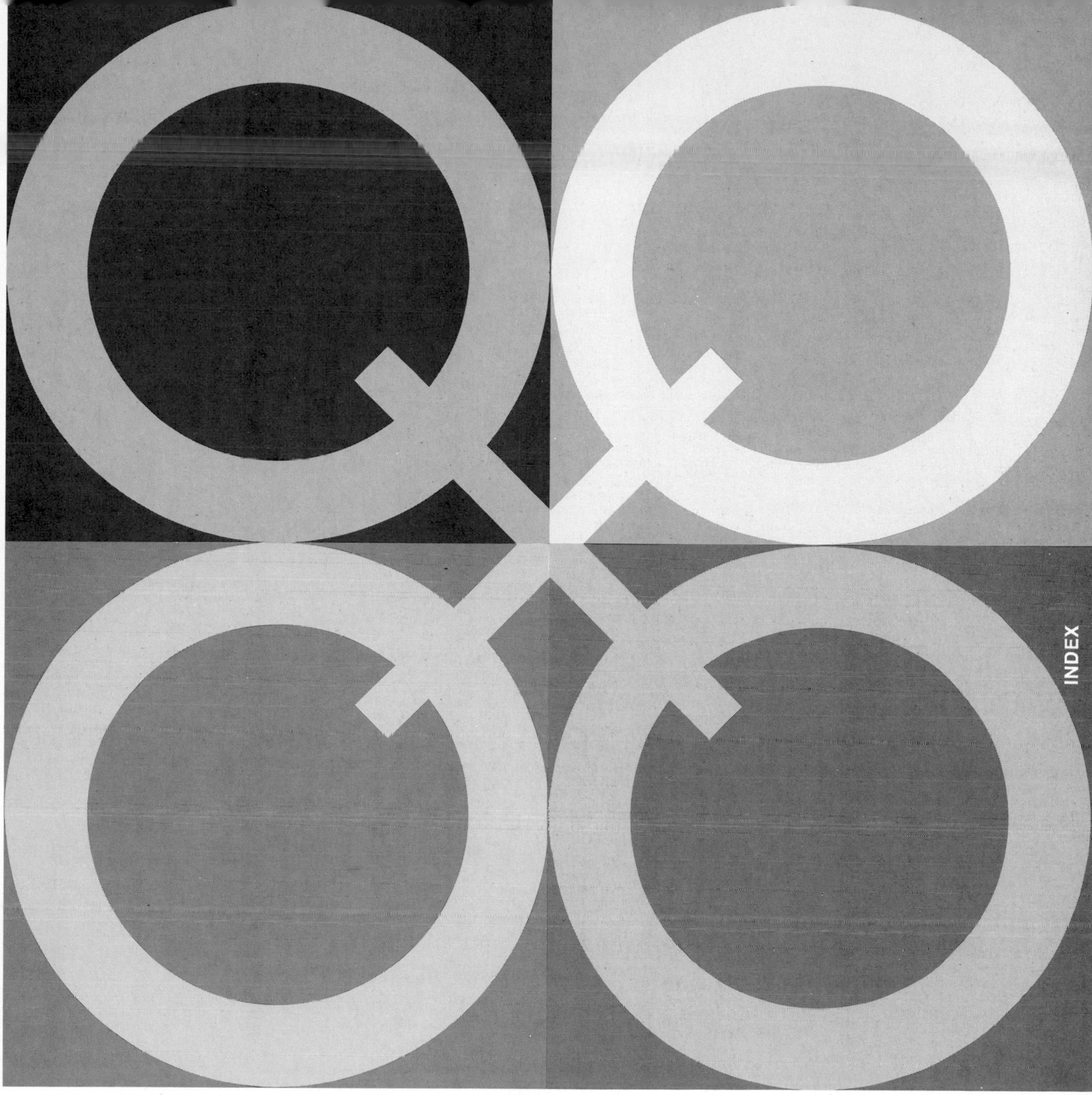

The letter Q

is of uncertain origin. There is a sign in Egyptian hieroglyphic writing which denotes a looped rope (1). Another sign in the shape of a doubled loop is found in a very early Semitic writing used about 1500 B.C. on the Sinai Peninsula (2). Both of these early signs have been compared by some scholars to the Q sign which was developed about 1000 B.C. in Byblos and other Phoenician and Canaanite centers (3). This is all doubtful. It is from the latter sign, called *qoph,* meaning "monkey" in the Semitic languages, that all later forms are derived. The Greeks renamed the sign *koppa* (4). It stood for exactly the same sound as their "k," or *kappa,* so they dropped *koppa* as useless. The Romans, however, had acquired the early Greek habit of using *koppa* for a "k" sound before "u" and gave the sign a round form with a curved tail (5). In this form the letter Q came from Latin into English. The English small handwritten "q" has the tail developed into a long vertical line (6).

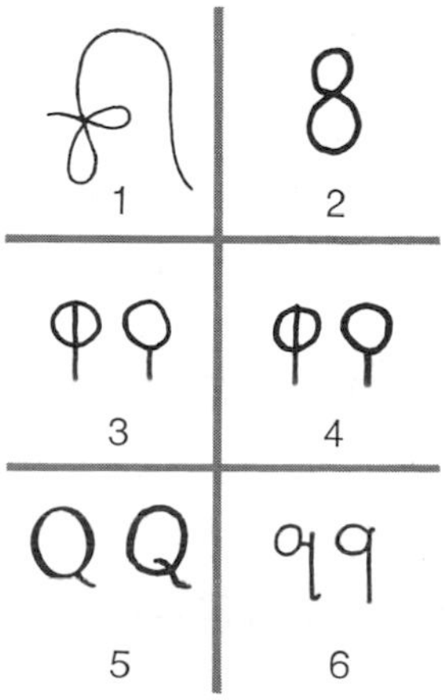

Qabis, Tunisia. *see in index* Gabès

Qabis, Gulf of. *see in index* Gabès, Gulf of

Qaddafi, Muammar al (or Muammar al Gadhafi, or Muammar al Khadafy, or Muammar al Qadhafi) (born 1942), Libyan head of state Q-2
  Libya L-190

Qafsah, Tunisia. *see in index* Gafsa

Qajar Dynasty (1799–1925) I-308

Qanaat, waterway A-518

Qandahar, Afghanistan. *see in index* Kandahar

Qantas Airways A-789

Qasidah, Indian poetic form I-107, 363

Qatar, monarchy and peninsula of Arabia on Persian Gulf; 8,500 sq mi (22,015 sq km); cap. Doha (pop. 55,000); pop. 276,000 Q-2
  Arabia A-521, *map* A-522
  Asia, *map* A-700
  flag, *picture* F-169

Qattara Depression, desert region, Egypt E-115

Q fever, disease B-512

Qingdao (or Tsingtao), China, port in Shantung Province on Kiaochow Bay of Yellow Sea; pop. 1,180,000, *map* A-700

Qinghai (or Tsinghai), province of China; 280,000 sq mi (725,200 sq km); cap. Sining; farm area; wool and hides; mineral resources; pop. 3,930,000.

Qinghai Hu. *see in index* Koko Nor

Quāāludes. *see in index* Methaqualone

Quabbin Reservoir, Massachusetts M-190

Quad Cities. *see in index* Davenport, Iowa ; East Moline, Ill.; Moline, Ill.; Rock Island, Ill.

Quadrant, in early navigation N-78

Quadraphonic sound (or four-channel sound) P-269

Quadratic equation, in algebra A-300

Quadratic function, in mathematics A-298

Quadrilateral, figure with four sides, as parallelogram, rectangle, square, trapezoid G-74, *diagram* G-75

Quadrille, square dance of French origin; name from Latin *quadrus* (square); popular in 18th and 19th centuries and in early years of 20th century; often danced as a group dance without regard to a "square" pattern on the floor; a strict square is used in American square dance. *see also in index* Lancers

Quadriplegia, paralysis from the neck down D-163

Quadrivium, an early division of the university E-83

Quadruplets, multiple birth M-649

Quadruplex system, of telegraph T-58

Quaestors, officials of ancient Rome, who controlled the finances of military and other organizations; financial assistants of the consuls R-243

Quagga, extinct species *Equus quagga* of zebra Z-449

Quahog, shell S-153

Quai d'Orsay, French foreign office, so named from the quay on the s. bank of the Seine River in Paris where its buildings stand, *picture* W-319

Quail, game bird of the family Phasianinae Q-3
  bird B-252, *pictures* B-241, 270
  ecology E-58

Quakers (or Society of Friends), religious organization Q-4
  abolitionist movement A-10
  England E-233
  Fox F-337
  Hicks H-150
  peace movement P-143c
  Penn P-162
  Pennsylvania P-163, P-173
  prison reforms P-505d
  Ross R-297

Quaking aspen (or trembling aspen), tree *Populus tremuloides* P-445

Quaking bog M-600

Qualitative and quantitative analysis, in chemistry C-290

Quality control, in manufacturing, the organized effort to keep a product to a set of standards by testing it at various points during production Q-4
  food and drug laws F-274
  industry I-192
  X rays X-404

Quality grade, determination of market price for beef cattle C-230

Quanah. *see in index* Parker, Quanah

Quantico, Va., town on Potomac River, about 30 mi (50 km) s.w. of Washington, D.C.; pop. 621, *map* V-349
  U.S. Marine Corps training and museum M-138

Quantifier, in logic A-288

Quantum, in physics P-305, S-254h. *see also in index* Quantum theory
  atomic particles A-754
  light theories L-202
  nuclear energy N-418
  photoelectric devices P-273

Quantum mechanics. *see in index* Wave mechanics

Quantum theory, that energy exists in "packets" called quanta or photons Q-5
  atomic particle A-752
  Bohr S-373, B-332
  energy E-221
    nuclear energy N-418
  light genesis L-202
  mechanics M-263, 269
  Planck P-305
  radiation applications R-37

Quapaws. *see in index* Arkansas

Qu'Appelle River (French, "who calls"), tributary of Assiniboine in s. Saskatchewan S-49c, *map* S-49k

Quarantine H-89

'Quare Fellow, The', work by Behan I-328

Quark, in physics Q-5
  atomic particles A-750, *picture* A-753
  big-bang theory, *diagram* C-732
  Gell-Mann G-46
  matter M-230
  nuclear energy N-421
  nuclear physics N-432

Quarles, Benjamin (born 1904), U.S. historian, born in Boston, Mass. ('The Negro in the Civil War'; 'The Negro in the Making of America'; 'The Negro American').

Quarles, Donald Aubrey (1894–1959), U.S. government official and electrical engineer, born in Van Buren, Ark.; vice-president Bell Telephone Laboratories 1948–52; assistant secretary of defense for research and development 1953–55; secretary of the air force 1955–57; deputy secretary of defense 1957–59.

Quarry, in hunting, the bird or animal hunted; the prey.

Quarrying, type of surface mining Q-6. *see also in index* Open-pit mining
  land use L-28
  mines and mining M-425
  tilemaking B-348

Quart, unit of capacity, *table* W-140, *diagram* W-139

Quarterback, football position
  football F-294, *picture* F-292, *diagram* F-290

Quarter Horse, a breed of horse, *picture* H-257, *list* H-254

Quarter-horse racing H-275

Quartering, maneuver in sailing B-328

Quartering Act (1765), in British history R-163, U-170

Quartermaster, U.S. Navy petty officer; duties include steering ship, signaling, and assisting in navigation
  insignia, *picture* U-11

Quartermaster Corps, U.S. Army A-646
  insignia, *picture* U-10

Quartersawn wood, lumber made by first sawing a log lengthwise into quarters by cuts passing through center or heart of log; boards are then cut alternately from the two flat faces of each quarter W-281

Quartet, a musical composition for four voices or instruments; also a group of four performers
  classical music, *list* M-671
  Schubert S-54
  string quartet, *picture* V-327

'Quartet for the End of Time', work by Messiaen M-306

Quartz, hard silica rock or sand Q-6
  abrasives A-13
  granite G-214, *picture* R-229a
  hobby H-187
  minerals M-432, 437
  onyx O-559
  prehistoric tools M-84
  rock crystal J-112
    radio R-52, *diagram* R-56
  sand S-36
  silicon S-195b
  solid structures S-254f
  ultraviolet rays U-3
  watches and clocks W-79

Quartz crystal. *see in index* Rock crystal

Quartzite, metamorphic rock
  prehistoric tools M-84
  quarrying Q-6
  rock cycle R-229a, *chart* R-229
  sand S-38

Quartz watch W-79, *picture* W-82

Quasar (or quasi-stellar radio source), the highly luminous cores of distant galaxies Q-7
  astronomy A-725
  star S-415

Quasimodo, hunchback character in Hugo's novel 'Notre Dame de Paris' H-316, *picture* N-410. *see also in index* 'Hunchback of Notre Dame, The'

Quasimodo, Salvatore (1901–68), Italian poet, born in Syracuse, Sicily ('The Selected Writings of Salvatore Quasimodo') I-379. *see also in index* Nobel Prizewinners, *table*

Quasi-stellar blue galaxies S-415

Quasi-stellar radio sources. *see in index* Quasar

Quaternary period, geological time E-27, *table* E-24

Quaternion, form of algebra M-216
  Hamilton H-22

Quatrain, rhyme scheme P-406

Quatre Bras, Belgium, village 19 mi (31 km) s.e. of Brussels.

Quatre Bras, battle of, indecisive battle between British and Germans under duke of Wellington and French under Marshal Ney, on June 16, 1815, 2 days before battle of Waterloo W-100

Quatrefoil, double (or octofoil), in heraldry, *picture* H-136

Quay, Matthew Stanley (1833–1904), U.S. senator from Pennsylvania 1887–1904; led Republican party in his state 35 years; from 1885 member of national committee.

Quay (or wharf), part of a harbor H-35

Quebec, oldest and largest of provinces of Canada; 594,860 sq mi (1,540,680 sq km); cap. Quebec; pop. 6,438,403 Q-8
  Canada C-80, 91, 105, *map* C-112
  cities. *see in index* Montreal and other cities by name
  fur trade F-468
  history
    exploration and colonization A-338
    French and Indian War F-393
      Wolfe W-268
  Labrador L-12
  North America N-337, *map* N-351
  St. Lawrence River S-19
  Trans-Canada Highway T-248

Quebec, Que., capital city of province; pop. 177,082 Q-13, *picture* Q-9d, *maps* Q-9a, 11
  American Revolution R-170
  Canada C-78, 94
  early higher education U-233
  literature C-120
  North America, *map* N-351

Quebec, battle of (1759) C-94, *list* W-15

Quebec Act (1774) C-94, R-164

Quebec Bridge, over the St. Lawrence River in Canada B-446

Quebec City Walls and Gate National Historic Site, Quebec, Que. Q-9h

Quebec Conference (1864) C-100
  Fathers of Canadian Confederation C-113

Quebec Zoological Society, Canada Z-459

Quebracho (from early Spanish word for "ax-breaker"), any one of several hardwood trees with hard, dense wood that contains tannin; quebracho blanco, or white quebracho *Aspidosperma quebracho blanco*, of dogbane family, is a tall tree with a white wood; quebracho colorado, or red quebracho *Schinopsis lorentzii*, is the chief source of the extract
  South America S-286
    Argentina A-579
    Paraguay P-112, *picture* P-111

Quechua, South American native tribes; formed greater part of ancient Inca Empire S-281d, *picture* S-281c. *see also in index* Incas

'Quedagh Merchant', pirate ship K-234

Queen, Ellery, pseudonym of Manfred B. Lee (1905–71), born in New York City, and his cousin, Frederic Dannay (1905–1982), born in New York City, writers of detective stories ('There Was an Old Woman'; 'Cat of Many Tails'); Ellery Queen is also name of fictional detective D-119

Queen, insect
  ant A-469
  bee B-126
  termite T-111

Queen, in chess C-305

Queen, title given to a woman sovereign of a state; queen regnant, queen in her own right; queen consort, wife of a king; queen dowager, widow of a king; queen mother, a queen dowager who is mother of a king or queen.

Queen Anne's lace (or wild carrot), weed *Daucus carota* Q-15
  flower, *picture* F-217
  weed, *picture* W-132

Queen Anne's War (1701–13), war between England and France over colonies in North America, a part of the War of the Spanish Succession Q-15
  America A-338
  Canada C-93
  England E-248
  King William's War K-247
  Treaty of Utrecht. *see in index* Utrecht, Treaty of
  War of the Spanish Succession A-829

Queen Charlotte Islands, Canada, 100 mi (160 km) off coast and 135 mi (215 km) above Vancouver Island; 3,970 sq mi (10,280 sq km); many American Indians; timber, fisheries; pop. 2,390 C-74, *maps* C-109, N-351

Queen Charlotte Islands, Melanesia. *see in index* Santa Cruz Islands

Queen City of the Adriatic, Italy. *see in index* Venice

'Queen Elizabeth', French film M-618

'Queen Elizabeth 2', ocean liner S-168

Queen Elizabeth Islands, collective name for all Arctic islands of Canada n. of Lancaster Sound and Viscount Melville Sound; this group includes Devon and many smaller islands; total area, about 160,000 sq mi (414,400 sq km), almost uninhabited; named in 1954 in honor of Elizabeth II, *map* N-351. *see also in index* Ellesmere Island; Melville Island

Queen Maud Land, Antarctica, between Coats Land and Enderby Land; first discovered by Hjalmar Riiser-Larsen 1930, *table* P-422

Queen Maud Range, Antarctica, extends from head of Ross Ice Shelf; discovered 1911 by Roald Amundsen.

Queen of Flowers, title first given by Greek poet Sappho for the rose. *see also in index* Rose

Queen of Sheba, ruler of the Kingdom of Sheba S-255

Queen of Spain butterfly, insect
  egg, *picture* E-111

Queen's, county in Ireland. *see in index* Leix

Queens, borough of New York, N.Y.; pop. 1,891,325 N-271, *picture* N-273
  Long Island L-297

Queensberry, John Sholto Douglas, 8th marquis of (1844–1900), British statesman and sportsman; represented Scotland in Parliament, 1872–80; patron of boxing; took part in formulating Queensberry rules for boxing B-388

Queens College, Flushing, Long Island, N.Y.; part of the City University of New York; municipal control; established 1937; arts and sciences, audiology and speech, library science, education; graduate divisions N-254

Queen's House, part of the Tower of London complex T-238

Queensland, state in n.e. Australia; 666,900 sq mi (1,727,300 sq km); cap. Brisbane; pop. 2,295,123 Q-16
  Australia A-767, *map* A-819
  Brisbane B-449
  oasis O-454
  Pacific Ocean, *map* P-6

Queensland walnut. *see in index* Orientalwood

Queen's Rangers. *see in index* Rogers, Robert

Queenston, Ont., hydroelectric center on Niagara River, 6 mi (10 km) n. of Niagara Falls; Ontario's first railroad, Queenston to Chippawa, 1839.

Queenston Heights, battle of, battle in War of 1812 at Queenston, Ont., where British, under General Brock, defeated Americans W-31

Queenstown, Ireland. *see in index* Cobh

Queen's University, Belfast, Northern Ireland; formed 1908 from Queen's College (founded 1845); arts and sciences and professional schools; college of technology allied with it B-144

Queen's University, Kingston, Ont.; founded by Presbyterians 1841, nonsectarian after 1912; arts and science, applied science, business, law, medicine, nursing, physical and health education, theology; graduate studies O-552

Queen's ware, Wedgwood pottery, named in compliment to Queen Charlotte, queen consort of George III of England P-475
  Wedgwood W-130

'Queen Victoria', biography by Strachey B-223

Queen Victoria Memorial, monuments, London, England L-292, *picture* L-293

Quelpart, island of South Korea. *see in index* Cheju

Quemoy (or Jinmen), island, Taiwan T-12

'Quem quaeritis', ceremonial chant of early Roman Catholic church that was dramatized in medieval times and developed into "liturgical drama" of the church; depicts incident of the Three Marys and the angel at tomb of Jesus D-243

Quenching, metalworking process I-334

'Quentin Durward', novel by Scott S-74
  Louis XI described L-305

Quercia, Jacopo della (1367?–1438), Italian sculptor, born near Siena, Italy; called "della Fonte" for his fountain (Fonte Gaia) in public square at Siena.

Queres. *see in index* Keres

Querétaro, state in central Mexico; 4,544 sq mi (11,769 sq km); cap. Querétaro; mountainous with fertile valleys; ore deposits; crops include wheat, legumes, corn, and cotton; pop. 617,059.

Querétaro, Mexico, capital of state of Querétaro, 110 mi (180 km) n.w. of Mexico City; cotton mills; Emperor Maximilian executed here in 1867, pop. 150,226, *map* N-351

Quesada, Elwood Richard (born 1904), U.S. government official, business executive, and former Air Force officer, born in Washington, D.C.; administrator of Federal Aviation Agency 1958–61.

Quesnay, François (1694–1774), French economist and founder of the school of physiocrats; became court physician in 1752.

Question mark P-534, S-110

Questionnaire
  personality tests P-218
  statistics S-432, *pictures* [illegible] 100

Quételet, Lambert Adolphe Jacques (1796–1874), Belgian astronomer, mathematician, and statistician; director Royal Observatory; published works on statistical research, astronomy, meteorology.

Quetico Provincial Park, Ontario, on the Minnesota border; 1,300 sq mi (3,370 sq km); Superior National Forest adjoins on s.; Quetico-Superior Foundation works to safeguard wilderness region by joining both areas in an international forest area.

Quetta, Pakistan, capital of Baluchistan Province, in elevated valley near Afghan border; was long a British army post; pop. 156,000 B-50
  Asia, *map* A-700

Quetzal, bright green-crested bird Q-16
  feathers B-240, F-51

Quetzal, monetary unit of Guatemala; historic value about $1.00.

Quetzalcoatl, Pyramid of (or El Castillo), Mayan civilization M-236

Queue (or pigtail), hairstyle B-395

Queuille, Henri (1884–1970), French statesman and physician, born in department of Corrèze, France; Radical Socialist member of Parliament 34 years; minister of agriculture, of health, of public works; with French Committee of National Liberation, World War II; premier 1948–49, 1951.

Quevedo y Villegas, Francisco Gómez de (1580–1645), Spanish writer, active in politics and diplomacy until imprisoned by Philip IV S-365a

Quezaltenango, Guatemala, 2nd largest city; industrial center for highlands; shoes, brooms, wool, flour, pop. 39,638
  Maya M-237

Quezon, Manuel (1878–1944), Filipino political leader Q-16
  Philippines P-261

Quezon City, Philippines, official capital 1948–76; pop. 501,800 P-253c

Quiberon, France, historic town on Quiberon Bay, on peninsula 22 mi (35 km) s.e. of Lorient; defeat of French Royalists by Republicans (1795); pop. 4,305, *map* F-372

Quiberon Bay, small arm of Bay of Biscay, e. of Quiberon; here British navy under Admiral Hawke defeated French under Conflans on Nov. 20, 1759 (Seven Years' War).

Quick, Herbert (1861–1925), U.S. novelist, born in Grundy County, Iowa; taught school; practiced law; edited *La Follette's Weekly, Farm and Fireside*; wrote on opening of Middle West ('Vandemark's Folly'; 'The Hawkeye'; 'One Man's Life', autobiography).

Quickbeam (or European mountain ash, or rowan), tree *Sorbus aucuparis* M-637

Quicklime. *see in index* Lime

Quickly, Mistress, character in three of Shakespeare's plays—in both parts of 'King Henry IV' and in 'King Henry V', hostess of a tavern; in 'The Merry Wives of Windsor', servant to Dr. Caius.

Quicksand Q-17
  hard wet sand S-38

Quicksilver. *see in index* Mercury

Quickswood, Baron. *see in index* Cecil, Hugh Richard Heathcote

Quidde, Ludwig (1858–1941), German historian, born in Bremen; criticized German militarism and was active in peace movement. *see also in index* Nobel Prizewinners, *table*

Quileute, an American Indian tribe of the Chimakuan stock living near Cape Flattery, coast of Washington.

Quill, anatomical projection. *see also in index* Spine
  hair H-7
  porcupine P-450, A-427

Quill, feather F-50
  used for writing P-156

Quillaia bark. *see in index* Soapbark

Quillay tree. *see in index* Soapbark

Quiller-Couch, Sir Arthur Thomas (1863–1944), British writer, known under pseudonym "Q"; professor of English literature at Cambridge University, England; edited 'The Oxford Book of English Verse', 'The Oxford Book of English Prose'; completed Robert Louis Stevenson's unfinished novel 'St. Ives'; also wrote historical novel, 'The Splendid Spur'; nonfiction, 'Studies in Literature'
  'Shakespeare's Christmas' S-140

Quill pen P-156

Quillworts, plant group F-58

Quilt Q-17
  folk art, *picture* F-248
  needlework N-112, *picture* N-110

Quilting stitch, needlework N-113, *picture* N-114

Quinacrine (or Atabrine), quinine substitute Q-18, B-234

Quince, fruit of the apple family Q-18
  fruits, *picture* F-431

Quincy, Josiah (1772–1864), U.S. statesman and author, born in Quincy, Mass.; member national House of Representatives and of Massachusetts state legislature; mayor of Boston; president of Harvard University 1829–45
  Louisiana purchase opposition L-324

Quincy, Ill., city on Mississippi River, about 95 mi (150 km) w. of Springfield; paper, pulp, and metal products, heating equipment, electronics; Quincy College, pop. 42,352, *map* I-53

Quincy, Mass., city on Quincy Bay, about 8 mi (13 km) s.e. of Boston; shipbuilding, granite quarrying; machine parts, electronic products, soap, gears; many historic associations; birthplace of John Hancock; pop. 84,743 M-191, 202
  Adams N.H.S., *picture* A-37

Quincy College, Quincy, Ill.; Roman Catholic; chartered 1873; arts and sciences, education.

Quincy Market, shopping center, Boston, Mass. B-373

Quinebaug River, stream 100 mi (160 km) long rising in Massachusetts and flowing s.e. into Connecticut, where it unites with Shetucket River to form Thames River.

Quinet, Edgar (1803–75), French author, professor of literature at the Collège de France; banished from France for agitation against Napoleon III, after whose fall he returned to Paris; wrote historical and philosophical works as well as poetry ('Ahasuerus', a prose poem).

Quiniela, jai alai game J-13

Quinine, drug from cinchona bark Q-18
  bionics B-234
  malaria M-598

Quinn, Anthony Rudolph Oaxaca (born 1916), U.S. actor, born in Chihuahua, Mexico; became citizen 1947; won Academy award for 'Viva Zapata' 1952 and 'Lust for Life' 1956 ('La Strada'; 'Zorba the Greek'; 'The Shoes of the Fisherman').

Quinnipiac College, New Haven, Conn.; private control; founded 1929; liberal arts, accounting, business administration, health sciences; graduate study.

Quinoa, annual plant *Chenopodium quinoa* of the goosefoot family, native to w. South America; grows to 5 ft (1.5 m); seeds large, red or white, according to variety; it is closely related to the common pigweed B-334

Quintal, British unit of weight, *table* W-141

Quintal, Spanish unit of weight, *table* W-141

Quintana Roo, state in e. Yucatán Peninsula, s.e. Mexico, on Caribbean Sea; 19,440 sq mi (50,350 sq km); cap. Chetumal; pop. 130,891 Y-432
  Mexico, *map* M-344

Quinte, Bay of, inlet of Lake Ontario on s.e. coast of Ontario; 60 mi (100 km) long; peninsula between it and the lake; receives the Trent River.

Quintero brothers. *see in index* Álvarez Quintero

Quintilian (full name Marcus Fabius Quintilianus) (AD 35?–95?), famous Roman teacher of oratory; wrote 'Institutio Oratoria', a complete treatment of the art of rhetoric L-78

Quintuplets, multiple birth M-649. *see in index* Diligenti quintuplets; Dionne quintuplets; Fischer quintuplets

Quintus Fabius Maximus. *see in index* Fabius

'Quintus Servinton', work by Savery A-797

Quipu, ancient Inca device for keeping records I-60
  communication development C-614

Quire, unit of measure, *table* W-140

Quirinale, palace in Rome, Italy R-251, *map* R-250

Quirinal Hill, Rome, Italy R-254

Quirino, Elpidio (1890–1956), Filipino political leader, born in Vigan on island of Luzon; vice-president and foreign secretary, Republic of the Philippines, under President Manuel Roxas 1946–48; president 1948–53.

Quirinus, name of Romulus after he became a divinity R-258

Quirites, name applied to citizens of ancient Rome in their civil or domestic capacity, *Romani* being reserved for military or foreign affairs.

Quiroga, Horacio (1879–1937), Uruguayan writer L-75

Quisling, term applied to a citizen who helps an enemy

power conquer his or her country; derived from name of **Vidkun Quisling** (1887–1945), who proclaimed himself premier of a Nazi-controlled government in Norway a few hours after the German invasion, April 1940; recognized as premier by Hitler 1942; shot as traitor 1945 W-323, 337
  Norway N-394

Quito, Ecuador, capital of republic, about 15 mi (25 km) s. of equator; the northern capital of Incas until taken by Spaniards in 1534, pop. 742,900 E-66
  South America, *maps* P-224, S-298

Quivira, settlement of reputed wealth and splendor sought by Coronado.

Quixote, Don, character in book by Cervantes S-365a, *picture* N-408

Quoits, game Q-18

Quonset hut, long steel building, semicylindrical in shape; named for Quonset Point, R.I., where it was first used by Navy during World War II; served as shelter and warehouses for armed forces; later used as residential, commercial, and industrial buildings.

Quonset Point, R.I., community on peninsula in w. Narraganset Bay, 16 mi (26 km) s. of Providence; site of naval air base 1941–74; pop. 1,200 R-184, *picture* R-187

Quorum, select group P-132b

Quota sampling, statistics S-431

Quotation mark, punctuation P-534

Quotations, famous
  reference book L-162

Quotations, stock and bond S-453, *picture* S-452. *see also in index* Ticker

'Quotations from Chairman Mao Tse-tung', work by Albee A-260, A-363

'Quotations from Chairman Mao Zedong', work by Mao C-376

Quotient, in mathematics N-440

'Quo Vadis?' (Latin, "Whither goest thou?"), historical novel of Rome in the time of Nero by Sienkiewicz; translated into more than 30 languages
  film M-618

Qur'an. *see in index* Koran

Quraysh, Islamic people C-54

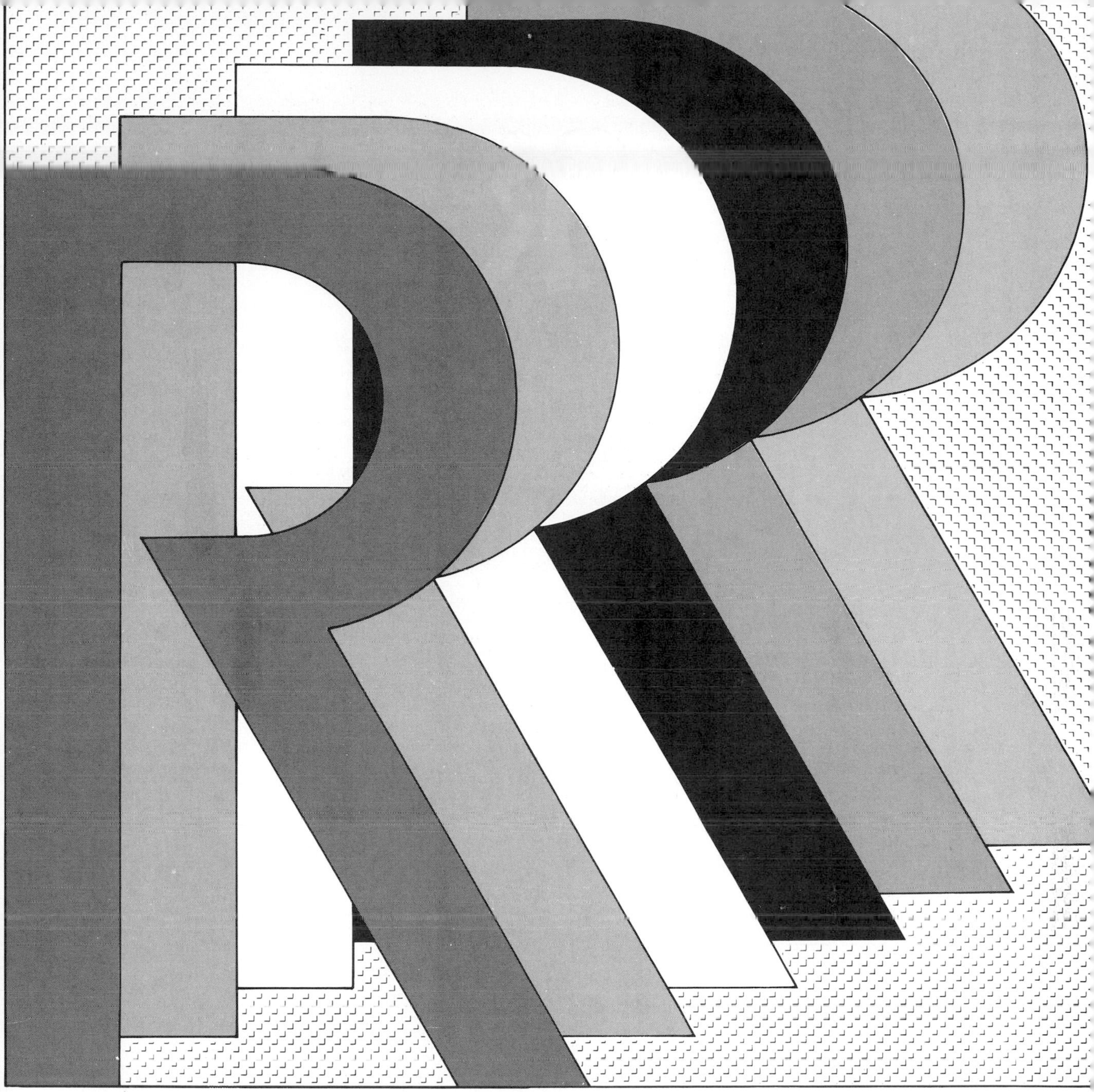

The letter R

probably started as a picture sign of a human head, as in Egyptian hieroglyphic writing (1) and in a very early Semitic writing used about 1500 B.C. on the Sinai Peninsula (2). About 1000 B.C., in Byblos and other Phoenician and Canaanite centers, the sign was given a linear form (3), the source of all later forms. In the Semitic languages the sign was called *resh,* meaning "head." The Greeks renamed the Semitic sign *rho.* They also turned the sign around to suit the left-to-right direction of their writing, changing its form slightly (4) and sometimes adding a slight tail (5). The Romans took the latter form, emphasizing the tail (6) to make a sharper distinction between it and their sign P. The Roman form of the capital letter R came unchanged into English.

The handwritten small "r" (7) started in medieval times when the curved stroke was made to the right to connect it to the next letter. It is also simplified into another handwritten form (8).

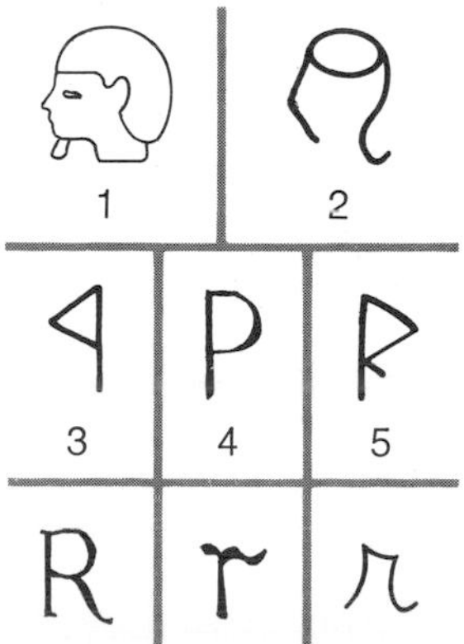

Ra (or Re, also called Amen, or Amon), Egyptian sun-god
sun worship S-514
temple at El Karnak E-125

RA (or rheumatoid arthritis), disease A-650

'Ra II', Thor Heyerdahl's reed boat H-146

Raab, Hungary. *see in index* Györ

Rabanne, Paco (born 1934), Spanish fashion designer D-271

Rabat, Morocco, capital, on Atlantic; pop. 596,600 R-20, *map* A-118
Morocco M-586

Rabaul, Papua New Guinea, until 1941 capital of Mandated Territory of New Guinea, on n.e. coast of New Britain Island; pop. 63,329 O-465, *map* P-6

Rabbath Ammon. *see in index* Amman

Rabbi, official title of Jewish clergy; a Hebrew word meaning "my master," originally applied to scholars and teachers of the law; used in New Testament as a title of respect in addressing Jesus J-149, *picture* J-146
educational contribution E-78
Saadia ben Joseph S-1

Rabbit R-20
Australian pest A-779
folklore F-2
fur F-463, *tables* F-464
wool W-288
pets P-243, *picture* P-247
tracks, *picture* A-464

Rabbit fever. *see in index* Tularemia

Rabbitfish F-124

'Rabbit Hill', children's story by Lawson R-110a

Rabbit Islands, group 3 mi (5 km) w. of coast of Asiatic Turkey and 7 mi (11 km) s. of Dardanelles; largest island 1 mi (1.6 km) long and 800 yds (732 m) wide; group awarded to Turkey 1923 by Treaty of Lausanne.

Rabe, David (born 1940), U.S. author A-363

Rabearivelo, Jean Joseph (1901–37), Francophone poet A-121

Rabelais, François (1493?–1553), French satirist and humorist R-23
French literature F-395, *picture* F-394
naturalism N-414

Rabi, Isidor Isaac (born 1898), Austrian-U.S. physicist; to U.S. in infancy; physics professor Columbia University 1937–67. *see also in index* Nobel Prizewinners, *table*

Rabi'ah, 'Umar ibn Abi (died 720?), Islamic poet
Islamic literature I-365

Rabies. *see in index* Hydrophobia

Rabin, Yitzhak (born 1922), Israeli political leader, born in Jerusalem; chief of staff Israel Defense Forces 1964–68; ambassador to U.S. 1968–73; member Israeli parliament since 1973; prime minister 1974–77.

Rabinowitz, Sholem (or Solomon Rabinowitz, pen name Sholem Aleichem) (1859–1916), U.S. humorist, born in Russia; spent last years in U.S.; sometimes called the Yiddish Mark Twain; tales: 'The Old Country', 'Tevye's Daughters'—basis for musical comedy 'Fiddler on the Roof', 'Old Country Tales'; autobiography, 'The Great Fair')
Yiddish literature Y-417

Raborn, William Francis, Jr. (born 1905), retired U.S. Navy officer, business executive, born in Decatur, Tex.; commissioned ensign 1928, retired as vice admiral 1963; developed Polaris missile system; chief of Central Intelligence Agency 1965–66.

Raccoon (or coon)
fur F-463, *tables* F-464, 465
lesser panda's resemblance, *picture* P-97
tracks, *picture* A-464
zoo Z-463

Raccoon Mountain. *see in index* Sand Mountain

Race, Cape, cape on extreme s.e. point of Newfoundland, off the tip of Avalon Peninsula; located 65 mi (105 km) s.w. of the capital, St. John's; famous lighthouse, *maps* C-109, N-351

Racer, black, snake, *picture* S-225

Race relations. *see also in index* Apartheid; Black Americans; Discrimination; Integration; Minority groups; Segregation
adoption problems A-49
American Indians U-102
anti-Semitism
Germany H-177
Warsaw W-34
Du Bois D-282
Gobineau G-172
Malcolm X M-74
Miami M-349
New Zealand N-283
North America N-339
Roosevelt R-259
South Africa T-234
Washington W-35
Zimbabwe M-645

Races of mankind, physical classification of humans R-25. *see also in index* races and peoples by name
Aborigine A-794
Gobineau G-172
man, *picture* S-57c
physical anthropology A-483
population distribution P-449
racial psychology P-523
sociological study S-243

Raceway, in leather production L-107

Rachel, in Bible, wife of Jacob, mother of Joseph and Benjamin; Jacob worked for her father a total of 14 years to win her in marriage.

Rachel (full name Élisa Rachel Félix) (1821–58), French actress; unequaled in such roles as Racine's 'Phèdre' A-27

Rachis, stem of bird feather F-50

Rachmaninoff, Sergei Wassilievitch (1873–1943), U.S. pianist, orchestral conductor, and composer, born in Novgorod Government, Russia; became U.S. citizen 1943; compositions include symphonies, a symphonic poem 'The Isle of Death', three operas ('Aleko', 'The Miserly Knight', 'Francesca da Rimini'), piano works
classical music M-675

Racial psychology P-523

Racine, Jean Baptiste (1639–99), French dramatist R-28, F-395, *picture* F-394

Racine, Wis., city and port on Lake Michigan, 60 mi (100 km) n. of Chicago, Ill.; pop. 85,725 R-28, *map* U-41
Wisconsin W-250, 260, *picture* W-259

Racing. *see also in index* Automobile racing and rallies; Boat racing; Horse racing
boating B-228
Campbell C-67
iceboating I-11
pigeon P-324
sailing B-229
skiing S-210d, *picture* S-210a
speed skating S-207

Racing Hall of Fame, in Saratoga Springs, N.Y. H-16

Rack, apparatus of torture that dislocates joints of victims; rectangular wooden frame with rollers at each end to which the arms and legs are fastened; used by Spanish Inquisition and in England (1400s to 1600s).

Rack, a gait of a horse H-263

Rack-and-pinion steering, in automobile, *picture* A-855

Racket (or racquet)
badminton B-16
tennis T-104

Rackham, Arthur (1867–1939), British illustrator of fairy tales, legends, folktales ('Peter Pan'; 'Alice in Wonderland'; Andersen's 'Fairy Tales') S-481a

Raclawice, battle of, fought at village of Raclawice, n. of Krakow, Poland, 1794; Russians defeated by Poles under Kosciusko.

Racon, radio and radar beacon
lighthouse L-205

Radar (or radio detecting and ranging) R-29
archaeology A-538
aviation A-886
air traffic control A-218, *picture* A-219
naval defense N-84
electronics E-177
guided missile G-312
loran R-32
iceberg location I-8
submarines S-498
microwave A-323
navigation N-68, 71, 78, *picture* N-69
weather W-121, 126

Radar altimetry, for measuring mountain altitudes M-633

Radar astronomy S-64a

Radar fire control, in warfare N-84

Radbourne, Charles (nickname Old Hoss) (1853–97), U.S. baseball pitcher, born in Rochester, N.Y.; with Providence, N.L., 1881–85, Boston, N.L., 1886–90, and Cincinnati, N.L., 1891; won 1884 pennant by pitching last 27 games of season, winning 26, for a total of 60, then won 3 straight in World Series; won total of 308 games.

Radcliffe, Ann (1764–1823), British novelist, born in London; excelled at romances of mystery ('The Sicilian Romance'; 'The Romance of the Forest'; 'The Mysteries of Udolpho') E-274

Radcliffe College, in Cambridge, Mass.; formerly for women, since 1975 coeducational with Harvard University; organized 1879; arts and sciences; has its own administration, but students receive degree from Harvard
Cambridge C-61

Raddall, Thomas Head (born 1903), Canadian writer, born in Hythe, England; moved to Nova Scotia 1913.

Radetzky, Joseph Wenzel, Count (1766–1858), Austrian field marshal, conspicuous at Wagram and Leipzig against Napoleon; crushed Italian uprising 1848–49; idolized by his armies.

Radford, Arthur William (1896–1973), U.S. Navy officer, born in Chicago, Ill.; in World Wars I and II; became admiral 1949; a leading figure in admirals' revolt against B-36 bomber 1949; commander in chief Pacific fleet 1949–53; chairman Joint Chiefs of Staff 1953–57.

Radford, Va., residential city 30 mi (50 km) s.w. of Roanoke; ammunition, iron products; Radford College; pop. 13,225, *map* V-348

Radford College, Radford, Va.; founded 1910; consolidated with Virginia Polytechnic Institute 1944–64 as woman's unit; state control; arts and sciences, education; graduate studies.

Radhakrishnan, Sir Sarvepalli (1888–1975), Indian statesman and philosopher, born in Tiruttani, s. India; lectured at universities in India, England, and U.S.; professor of eastern religions and ethics Oxford University 1936–52; leader Indian delegation to UNESCO 1946–52; ambassador to U.S.S.R. 1949–52; vice-president of India 1952–62, president 1962–67 ('Indian Philosophy'; 'An Idealistic View of Life').

Radial centrifugal fan F-23

Radial symmetry (or rotational symmetry) C-797
animal shapes A-422

Radiant energy. *see in index* Electromagnetic radiation

Radiation R-33. *see also in index* Radioactivity
beta particles F-56
biophysical research B-238
blackbodies U-201, 203
cancer C-132
hospital treatment H-282
cosmic rays A-282, *picture* A-749
cosmology C-732
earth O-456
electromagnetic spectrum, *table* R-34
gamma rays A-721, *diagram* L-202
garden flower breeding F-229
genetic disorders G-48
heat H-102, 105
heating systems H-109
insulation I-232
ionization detector H-213
light basis L-194, *picture* L-200
luminescence P-270
materials testing M-211
nuclear weapons N-434
optics O-573
origin of universe U-203
quantum theory. *see in index* Quantum theory
radio waves. *see in index* Radio, *subhead* waves
radium R-70
sciences S-64
space flight hazard S-343a, 346a
stars emit A-720
telescopes T-65
ultraviolet rays U-3
Van Allen belts V-259
wave and particle theory P-306
X rays X-403

Radiation curing, a drying method
ink I-207

Radiation fog F-246

Radiation genetics P-367, *picture* P-369

Radiation layer, of sun, *diagram* S-512

Radiation therapy (or radiotherapy), a treatment for disease T-165
cancer C-134, D-176
medicine M-278

Radiator, device for radiating heat H-107
internal-combustion engine I-252

Radiator, in radio antenna R-44, *diagrams* R-45

Radiator hydrometer H-341

Radical, in chemistry C-299
organic chemistry O-601

Radical mastectomy, surgery performed to remove breast cancer
therapy T-164

Radicle, embryo root S-108

Radio R-43
advertising A-57

airplane's usage A-195
announcer V-365, *picture* V-365
antenna. *see in index* Antenna
art forms A-662
Australia A-793
aviation navigation A-216, A-884
communication's development C-616
contributions by
De Forest D-64
Marconi M-132
Pupin P-535
Tesla T-114
country music M-678
electronics E-175
hobby H-190
International Telecommunication Union U-26
Kennelly-Heaviside layer R-36
microphone, *picture* V-365
models M-514
navigation N-68, 71
popular music M-680
pornography C-451
radar. *see in index* Radar
signaling. *see in index* Signaling, *subhead* radio
sports broadcasting B-87
telecommunication T-55
telemetry B-213. *see also in index* Telemetry
telephone T-64
two-way radio
police P-424, 426, *picture* P-429
railroad R-80
United States, *chart* U-123
Voice of America U-166
Murrow M-658
Vatican V-271, *map* V-269
walkie-talkie, *pictures* P-429, S-193
waves
atmospheric R-36
quasar Q-7
sun S-513, 515
western W-153

Radioactive isotope (or radioisotope, or tracer)
artificial heart B-211
cobalt C-530
nuclear energy N-425, 428
radioactivity R-62, 69
toxic waste W-76
uranium U-210
water W-87
X rays X-403

Radioactivity R-62. *see also in index* Radiation; Radium
Becquerel B-123
Curie, *picture* R-70
dating
radiocarbon A-535
man M-82
radiometric E-22
decay W-383
discovery S-58
disposal G-18
Fermi F-56
hazards of nuclear fission P-441e
safeguards, *picture* S-58
isotope. *see in index* Radioactive isotope
matter M-224
metal and metallurgy M-307
nuclear energy N-422
nuclear weapons N-434
uranium U-210
world W-301

Radio astronomy S-64a
observatory O-456
radio telescope R-43, S-513, *picture* W-174

Radiocarbon dating A-535
man M-82

Radio City Music Hall, in New York, N.Y. N-273

Radio Commission, Federal, in United States R-54

Radio compass C-623
aviation navigation A-886

Radio direction finder (RDF, or radiotheodolite), navigation device
Marconi M-132
weather W-121

Radio-frequency choke R-60

Radio-frequency heating, process used in cabinetmaking C-175

Radio galaxy A-723

Radiogram, message sent by commercial radio facilities
Marconi R-56

Radiograph (or roentgenogram), an X-ray photograph X-403, 406, *picture* X-404
disease diagnosis D-127

Radioisotope. *see in index* Radioactive isotope

Radiolaria, order of unicellular animals with silica spines, *pictures* A-432, C-238
oceanography O-484

Radiology, the medical specialty that deals with the use of such forms of radiant energy as X rays, radium, and radioisotopes in diagnosis and therapy, *table* M-277
hospital H-282

Radio Martí, United States government's radio transmission into Cuba; begun 1985 C-804

Radio mast, in submarine, *diagram* S-499

Radiometric dating, technique used to measure geologic time
earth E-22
physical anthropology A-484

Radio Moscow, communications station in U.S.S.R.
East German broadcast G-120

Radio navigation
aviation A-884
aids, *picture* R-55
field pattern R-53
air traffic control A-216
sea, *picture* R-55

Radio observatory, in astronomy O-456

Radiosonde, sounding balloon used in weather forecasting B-41
weather W-121, *picture* W-123

Radio telemetry B-213

Radiotelephone R-43
communication cables C-7

Radio telescope T-68
observatory O-456
radio R-43
radio wave detection E-216
sun studies S-513

Radiotheodolite. *see in index* Radio direction finder

Radiotherapy. *see in index* Radiation therapy

Radio waves, in Earth's atmosphere R-44, *picture* A-749
electronics E-175
Henry H-133
instrument amplification I-230
light waves L-202
Marconi M-132
navigation N-68, 71
observatory O-456
quasar Q-7

Radish
cabbage relative C-4
growing conditions G-26

Radishchev, Aleksandr Nikolaevich (1749–1802), Russian author, born near Saratov; criticized Russian institutions in 'Voyage from St. Petersburg to Moscow'; Siberian exile R-359, 361

Radisson, Pierre Esprit, sieur de (1636–1710?), French Canadian explorer and fur trader; Paris probable birthplace; wrote an account of his numerous expeditions
fur trade F-468
Hudson's Bay Company H-314
Minnesota M-445

Raditch, Stephan (or Stephan Radic) (1871–1928), Yugoslav statesman; leader of Croatian Peasant party; worked for Croatian autonomy; assassinated.

Radium (Ra), a metallic element R-70, *chart* R-66
alkaline earth metals A-308
discovery R-63
half-life R-67
lead R-64
periodic table, *table* P-207, *list* P-208
transmutation R-64

Radius, in mathematics
calculus C-21
geometry G-76
measurement M-243
trigonometry T-285

Radius, outer bone of forearm on side of thumb S-210

Radnor, Pa., urban township in Delaware County, w. of Philadelphia; in township are Cabrini College, at Radnor, and Villanova University, at Villanova pop. 27,676.

Radon (Rn, sometimes called emanation), gaseous radioactive element, discovered 1900 by Ernst Dorn; produced from the radioactive decay of radium R-64, 70, *chart* R-66
noble gases N-330
periodic table, *table* P-207, *list* P-208

Radula, tonguelike organ
mollusks M-524
octopus, cuttlefish, squid O-492
snails S-221, *picture* S-222

Raeburn, Henry (1756–1823), Scottish portrait painter, influenced by Sir Joshua Reynolds; produced virile, striking likenesses.

Raeder, Erich (1876–1960), commander-in-chief of German navy 1935–43, later naval adviser to Hitler and head of a naval service to combat Allied invasion; wrote books on naval warfare; sentenced to life imprisonment for war crimes 1946, released because of ill health 1955; autobiography, 'My Life'.

Raemakers, Louis (1869–1956), Dutch cartoonist; noted for his powerful anti-German cartoons during World War I; refugee in U.S. after June 1940.

RAF. *see in index* Royal Air Force

Raff, Joseph Joachim (1822–82), German composer; works for piano, violin ('Cavatina'), orchestra ('Im Walde'); operas; chamber music.

Raffia, a palm fiber P-84

Raffles, Sir Thomas Stamford (1781–1826), British colonial administrator, born at sea; colonial governor and official in Java and Sumatra; founded Singapore 1819; rafflesia named for him ('History of Java').

Rafflesia, leafless plant *Rafflesia arnoldii* of Malaya, parasitic on grapevine roots; its fleshy flower (largest flower in world), the only structure that appears above ground, is often 3 ft (1 m) across, weighs as much as 5 lbs (7 kg), and exudes an odor of decaying flesh that attracts carrion flies, the flower's pollinizing agents F-231
Sumatra S-511

Raft
life raft P-109a

Rag doll D-216, *picture* D-217

Ragged robin, common name applied to several attractive plants; usually used for the pink- or red-flowered perennial *Lychnis floscuculi*.

Raggedy Ann and Raggedy Andy, most enduring rag dolls of the century D-216

Ragnarök, in Norse mythology, time when world of gods was to be destroyed; a new world of good was to arise from the destruction; Wagner's opera 'Die Götterdämmerung' is based upon the myth M-703

Rags
paper P-101

Ragtime, music J-84
Joplin J-141
Handy H-30
popular music M-684

Ragusa, Yugoslavia. *see in index* Dubrovnik

Ragweed (or hogweed), a common weed of North America of the genus *Ambrosia;* grows 1 to 7 ft (0.3 to 2 m) high, with small green flowers; an annual; its pollen is extremely irritating to persons having hay fever W-131

Rahman, Mujibur (1920–75), Bangladeshi leader, born in Tungipara, India; cofounder of Awami League; led movement for independence of East Pakistan (now Bangladesh); prime minister 1972–75; president Jan.–Aug. 1975 when he was assassinated in army coup B-63, *list* A-704

Rahman, Ziaur (1936–81), Bangladeshi political and military leader, born in Bogra; chief of staff armed forces 1975–78; minister of information and broadcasting 1975–76, of commerce and foreign trade 1975–77, of finance and home affairs 1975–78; president 1977–81; assassinated 1981 B-63

Rahway, N.J., city on Rahway River, 6 mi (10 km) s.w. of Elizabeth; drugs and chemicals, vacuum cleaners, machinery, fiber drums and containers, books; scene of battle of Spanktown (1777) in American Revolution; pop. 26,723.

Raikes, Robert (1735–1811), British philanthropist S-516

Rail, waterbird R-71

Railroad R-72
amusement parks A-385
Brady B-398
Buffalo Bill B-490
cable railway
mountain P-345a, *picture* S-538
street S-44
development
Africa A-107
American Civil War C-473
Austria A-826
automated systems A-840
compressed air A-146
East Germany G-120
first transcontinental, *pictures* U-131, 181
France F-357
frontier movement F-423, *picture* F-420
India I-75
Indiana I-91
Kansas K-176
Pennsylvania P-170
South Carolina S-308, *picture* S-311
Stephenson S-443
West Germany G-118
Westinghouse W-162
electric S-524. *see also in index* Locomotive, *subhead* electric; Street railway; Subway
Europe E-345
featherbedding. *see in index* Featherbedding
first freight and passenger line M-170
freight trains, *pictures* B-51
funicular. *see in index* Funicular railway
gauge of track B-470
government ownership
Sweden S-524
Industrial revolution I-180
Interstate Commerce Commission R-285
iron and steel industry I-345
jet-powered car, *picture* R-330b
mediation J-474
Latin America L-66
locomotive L-279
models M-514
monorail
Seattle S-103a
Morgan M-583
National Grange reforms G-214
North America N-343
outlaws O-619
pensions and benefits for workers P-188, 189
postal service
first train to carry mail, *picture* P-460d
railway post office P-462
Canada P-463
United Kingdom P-463
rates
rebates R-230
refrigerator cars R-138, *picture* R-136
signals and safety devices S-195b
street railways. *see in index* Street railway
transcontinental
Asia
Trans-Siberian T-266, A-691, R-362, S-190, V-358, *maps* R-340, R-362
South America S-47
United States
first in United States U-218, *picture* U-181
Great Salt Lake G-251
transportation T-253, 264, *chart* T-260, *map* T-258, *pictures* T-255, 262, 263
coal C-524
travelers T-269
U.S. Supreme Court's regulation U-147
cable P-345a
warfare W-24

Railroad Retirement Act (1935), United States P-189

Railroads, Association of American. *see in index* Association of American Railroads

Railway, elevated. *see in index* Elevated railway

Railway, street. *see in index* Street railway

Railway brotherhoods, labor organizations among U.S. railway employees; the "Big Four," with dates of organization, were the Brotherhood of Locomotive Engineers (1863), the Order of Railroad Conductors and Brakemen (1868), the Brotherhood of Locomotive Firemen and Enginemen (1873), the Brotherhood of Railway Trainmen (1883); United Transportation Union formed 1969 by merger of last three plus the Switchmen's Union of North America (1894).

Railway Express Company, Inc. *see in index* REA Express

Railway Labor Act (1926, amended 1934), United States, first federal guarantee of right of employees (railway workers) to join trade unions; stipulated that agreements between unions and employers be in writing; established National Mediation Board, which reduced labor disputes in railway industry A-528

Railway post office P-462
Canada P-463
United Kingdom P-463

Rainbow R-88
Newton's explanation S-371
optics O-574

'Rainbow, The', work by Lawrence L-98

Rainbow Bridge National Monument, in Utah B-439, *map* U-233

Rain crow, name given to the yellow-billed or the black-billed cuckoo.

Rain dance
Australian folktales, *picture* S-480

Rainey, Joseph Hayne (1832–87), U.S. public official, born in Georgetown, S.C.; first black member of U.S. House of Representatives 1870–79.

Rainfall R-88. *see also in index* Storm
acidity A-19
Africa A-94, *map* A-95
cloud C-517
earth E-13, 31, *diagram* E-14
floods F-180
growing seasons, *map* U-31
jungle growth J-154
landforms affected R-120
plant life, *picture* P-9
soil affected S-251, U-76
solar energy S-516
South America S-270, *map* S-271
water W-89, *picture* W-88
weather W-120, 127

Rain forest (or tropical rain forest) F-309, *pictures* F-311, P-9
Africa A-94, S-501
biogeographical biomes B-219
India, *picture* I-64
jungle classification J-153
Mexico, *pictures* M-322, N-336
South America L-60, S-271, 274, 292
Amazon Basin P-363e, S-269, S-284
Brazil B-413

Rain gauge, instrument used to measure rainfall R-90
hobby H-190
weather W-121

Rainhill Trials, locomotive contest R-73

Rainier III (born 1923), prince of Monaco; succeeded grandfather, Prince Louis II, to throne of principality of Monaco 1949; married actress Grace Kelly 1956 M-528

Rainier, Mount, glacier-capped mountain in Cascade Range, Washington, 50 mi (80 km) s.e. of Tacoma; 14,410 ft (4,390 m); highest point in state, *maps* U-90, S-102
Cascade Range C-195
erosion V-378
Washington W-48, *picture* W-47

Rain-in-the-Face (1835?–1905), Sioux chief; in 1876 with Sitting Bull, led the Sioux who annihilated Gen. George A. Custer's forces in battle of Little Bighorn.

Rainis (pseudonym for Jan Plieksans) (1865–1929), poet, U.S.S.R. L-83

Rainwater, James (1917–86), U.S. physicist, born in Council, Idaho; research in atomic nuclear motion and structure; winner U.S. Atomic Energy Commission's E.O. Lawrence Memorial Award 1963; professor Columbia University 1952–. *see also in index* Nobel Prizewinners, *table*

Rainy Lake (originally called Reine des Lacs), a picturesque irregular lake nearly 50 mi (80 km) long forming part of the Canada-Minnesota boundary; drains through Rainy River into Lake of the Woods, *map* C-112

Rainy River, stream forming part of boundary between Minnesota and Ontario, connecting Rainy Lake and Lake of the Woods
Ontario O-549, *map* C-112

Rainy tropics (or tropical rain forest climate)
climate classification C-500

Raisa, Rosa (1893–1963), U.S. dramatic soprano, born in Bialystok, Russia; sang in Italy, England, South America, and with Chicago Civic Opera Company ('Aïda'; 'Tosca').

Raise, in mine shaft M-427

'Raisin in the Sun, A', play by Hansberry A-363, B-299, R-111i

Raisin River Massacre. *see in index* Frenchtown

Raisins, small, sweet grapes that are dried in the sun R-90
grape G-220

Raja, Indian title for a prince or chief; also assumed by others of rank; official title, maharaja (great prince), with its privileges and pensions, abolished 1971.

Rajah, silk S-201

Rajasthan, state in n.w. India; area 132,077 sq mi (342,078 sq km); cap. Jaipur; formed by the merger of former princely states in Rajputana; reorganized with addition of Ajmer, other areas, in 1956; pop. 25,724,142, *map* I-83

Raja-yoga Y-421

Rajputana, inland region in n.w. India; under empire was divided into Ajmer-Merwara Province and Rajputana Agency (the latter including 23 princely states, one estate, and one chiefship); now part of Rajasthan state.

'Raj Quartet', work by Scott N-412

Rajya Sabha, parliamentary chamber
India I-76

Rakata, Indonesian island where volcano Krakatoa is located K-302, *map* I-166

'Rake's Progress, A', work by Hogarth H-199

'Rake's Progress, The', opera by Stravinsky S-486
opera O-569, *list* O-563

Rákóczi, Ferenc (1676–1735), prince of Transylvania who headed an unsuccessful national rising of all Hungary against the Hapsburg Empire H-329

Rákosi, Mátyás (1892–1971), Hungarian Communist leader from 1945–56 H-330

Rakush, horse of the fictional character Rustam, *list* H-249

Râle, Sebastien (1654?–1724), French Jesuit missionary to Abnaki Indians on Kennebec River in Maine (1693–1724), author of Abnaki dictionary; beloved by Indians, hated by British, who blamed him for Indian raids, offered reward for his capture, burned his chapel, and finally shot him.

Raleigh, Sir Walter (1552–1618), English soldier, sailor, and historian; established first English colonies in North America R-90
Elizabeth I E-191
exploration and colonization E-373
Roanoke colony A-336
Mermaid Tavern Group S-131
North Carolina N-359
Spenser S-378

Raleigh, Sir Walter (1861–1922), British man of letters; professor of English literature at universities of Glasgow and Liverpool ('The English Novel'; 'Style'; 'Shakespeare'; 'Milton'; 'Six Essays on Johnson') I-352

Raleigh, N.C., state capital, a little n. of center of state; pop. 150,255 R-91, *maps* N-351, U-41
North Carolina N-357, 366, *picture* N-363

Rallentando, in music, *list* M-671

Rallidae, family of birds, including the rails, gallinules, and coots R-71

Ram. *see in index* Aries

RAM. *see in index* Random Access Memory

Ram, a male sheep or goat S-146, G-170

Ram, part of a galley ship N-81

Rama, one of incarnations of Vishnu in Hindu mythology; hero of Hindu epic 'Ramayana' H-157
Indian literature I-72, I-106

Ramadan, Islamic month of fasting I-306

Ramadier, Paul (1888–1961), French political leader, born in La Rochelle, France; active in resistance movement against German occupation of France in World War II; in Jan. 1947 became first premier of Fourth French Republic; resigned Nov. 1947; minister without portfolio July to Aug. 1948; minister of defense 1948–49.

Ramakrishna (1836–86), Hindu mystic, born near Calcutta, India; had little formal education but drew many adherents because of his great wisdom and saintliness; worshiped goddess Kali as mother of universe; believed all religions true, achieving same end.

Ramakrishna Mission, religious society seeking to spread the teachings of Vedanta; founded by Vivekananda in Calcutta, India, in 1897 H-159

Ramal, Walter. *see in index* De la Mare, Walter

Raman, Chandrasekhara Venkata (1888–1970), Indian physicist, born Trichinopoly, Madras Presidency, India R-41. *see also in index* Nobel Prizewinners, *table*

Raman effect R-41

Ramanuja (1017?–1137), Indian theologian and philosopher H-158, M-541

Rama Rau, Santha (born 1923), Indian author, born in Madras; to U.S. 1961 ('East of Home'; 'My Russian Journey'; 'Gifts of Passage'; 'Cooking of India').

'Ramayana', Hindu epic H-157, I-72
Indian stories I-106, S-467, 478
puppet plays P-536

Rambam. *see in index* Maimonides

Rambaud, Alfred Nicolas (1842–1905), French historian ('History of Russia'; 'History of French Civilization').

'Rambler', magazine M-32

Rambouillet, Catherine de Vivonne, marquise de (1588–1665), founder of first great French literary salon (satirized by Molière in 'Les précieuses ridicules').

Rambouillet, breed of sheep S-147, 148

Rameau, Jean Philippe (1683–1764), French composer; contributed to theory of musical harmony; wrote operas, the most famous of which is 'Castor and Pollux'
orchestra O-576

Ramée, Louisa de la. *see in index* De la Ramée

Rameses II. *see in index* Ramses II

Ramie. *see in index* China grass

Ramillies, Belgium, village 28 mi (45 km) s.e. of Brussels where Marlborough defeated French (1706) in War of the Spanish Succession; severe fighting in 1914
battle (1706) M-147

Ramjet engine, in aircraft A-80, J-109, *diagram* J-107
airplane usage A-187

Ramming, a warfare tactic M-136
navy N-81

'Ramona', novel by Jackson, published 1884, about an American Indian girl who preferred life among her own people to a great Spanish estate; contains fine descriptions of California scenery.

Ramón y Cajal, Santiago (1852–1934), Spanish histologist, born near Jaca, Spain. *see also in index* Nobel Prizewinners, *table*

Ramoth (or Ramoth-gilead), in Biblical times, city in Palestine e. of Jordan River; one of the six Cities of Refuge.

Rampal, Jean-Pierre (born 1922), French flutist, born in Marseilles, France; fine technique and clean tone brought new prominence to the flute; studied with father, then at Paris Conservatoire; principal flutist, Paris Opéra Orchestra; toured internationally, taught; edited 18th-century music.

Rampant position, in heraldry H-136

Rampolla, Mariano, marquis del Tindaro, Cardinal (1843–1913), as papal secretary of state 1887–1903, greatly extended political influence of the pope; popularly held responsible for the alliance of France and Russia; would have been pope succeeding Leo XIII but for Austrian and German opposition.

Ramsay, Allan (1686–1758), Scottish poet; started career as wigmaker, was later proprietor of a bookshop in Edinburgh; verse has fine poetic quality ('The Tea-Table Miscellany'; 'The Gentle Shepherd').

Ramsay, Lady Patricia (1886–1974), daughter of duke of Connaught and cousin of King George V; honorary colonel famous Princess Pat's Canadian regiment.

Ramsay, Sir William (1852–1916), British chemist, born in Glasgow, Scotland; brilliant teacher and investigator; discoverer of helium, neon, krypton, xenon; codiscoverer of argon; research in radioactivity led to new theory of transmutation of elements; knighted 1902. *see also in index* Nobel Prizewinners, *table*
discovers helium on earth S-372

Ramses II (or Rameses II), king of Egypt (1298–32 BC); known for great number of his statues and for having his name carved on monuments E-126
military strength A-635
Moses M-595
statues, *picture* S-79

Ramsey, Alexander (1815–1903), U.S. political leader, born near Harrisburg, Pa.; first territorial governor of Minnesota; U.S. senator and Cabinet officer under President Hayes.

Ramsey of Canterbury, Baron (Rt. Rev. and Rt. Hon. Arthur Michael Ramsey) (born 1904), British clergyman, born in Cambridge; professor of divinity Cambridge University 1950–52; bishop of Durham 1952–56; archbishop of York 1956–61; archbishop of Canterbury 1961–74.

Ramsey, N.J., residential borough 6 mi (10 km) n. of Ridgewood; electronic parts; dairy farms; settled 1846, incorporated 1873; pop. 12,899.

Ramsgate, England, seaside resort and yacht harbor 70 mi (110 km) s.e. of London; fishing trade; major lifeboat station; early home of Queen Victoria; pop. 39,140.

Rana dynasty, Nepalese family N-116

Rancagua, Chile, capital of O'Higgins Province, 50 mi (80 km) s. of Santiago; agricultural and mining center; pop. 95,030.

Rance River, river, rising in western France; flows for 60 mi (97 km) to form an estuary on the Brittany coast of the English Channel at Saint-Malo
hydroelectric power dam D-17
waterpower W-106

Ranch, an establishment for raising and grazing cattle, sheep, or horses; from the Spanish *rancho*, meaning "a meeting place for meals"; also a large farm. *see also in index* Cattle ranching; Cowboy
fur production F-463, *picture* F-467
Mexico M-332
United States
frontier life F-423
helicopters used H-121, *picture* U-83
Rocky Mountains U-79, 82
South Dakota S-322, 324, *picture* S-330

Rancho La Brea, in Hancock Park, Los Angeles, Calif.
fossils uncovered F-323

Rancho San Rafael, in California; first Spanish land grant in state G-165

Ranchos de Taos, in New Mexico. *see in index* Taos, Ranchos de

Rand, Ayn (1905–82), U.S. novelist, born in St. Petersburg (now Leningrad), Soviet Union; became U.S. citizen 1931 ('The Fountainhead'; 'Atlas Shrugged').

Rand, Paul (born 1914), U.S. graphic designer G-235

Rand, South Africa. *see in index* Witwatersrand

Rand, monetary unit of South Africa; introduced Feb. 14, 1961; name comes from the Witwatersrand, a gold-mining area which laid the economic basis of the nation; also monetary unit of Lesotho.

Randall, James Ryder (1839–1908), U.S. newspaperman and poet, born in Baltimore, Md.; descendant of Acadian exiles; sympathetic to Confederate cause M-172

Randalls Island, in East River, New York, N.Y.; part of Manhattan Borough; recreation park and municipal stadium; meeting place for three arms of Triborough Bridge; formerly site of children's corrective institution.

R and D (or Research and Development), in industry I-194

Randers, Denmark, city in n.e. Jutland, 23 mi (37 km) n. of Aarhus, at head of Randers Fjord; exports grain, dairy products, wool; pop. 42,238.

Randolph, Asa Philip (1889–1979), U.S. labor leader, born in Crescent City, Fla.; organized Brotherhood of Sleeping Car Porters (1925) and led fight for equality and fairness for black laborers; vice-president A.F.L.–C.I.O. 1957–77; president Negro-American Labor Council 1960–68; awarded Spingarn Medal 1942, Presidential Medal of Freedom 1964 B-295
  labor movements L-10

Randolph, Edmund (1753–1813), U.S. statesman, born in Williamsburg, Va.; governor of Virginia 1786–88; member Constitutional Convention (proposed "Virginia plan"); attorney general and secretary of state under Washington
  Washington W-42

Randolph, George Wythe (1818–67), U.S. lawyer and government official, born at Monticello (home of Thomas Jefferson, his maternal grandfather), near Charlottesville, Va.; brigadier general in Confederate army; secretary of war Confederate States of America March–Nov. 1862.

Randolph, Sir John (1693?–1737), North American colonial official, born in Henrico County, Virginia; son of William Randolph; king's attorney of Virginia 1727; on diplomatic missions to England 1728 and 1732; speaker of House of Burgesses 1734–37; only Virginia colonist to be knighted.

Randolph, John (1773–1833), "of Roanoke," U.S. statesman, born in Cawsons, Va.; eloquent, sarcastic, and eccentric representative and senator from Virginia between 1799 and 1827; defender of states' rights
  Clay C-487

Randolph, Peyton (1721?–75), North American statesman and patriot, born in Williamsburg, Va.; son of Sir John Randolph; king's attorney for Virginia 1748–66; member of House of Burgesses 1748–49, 1752–75, speaker of the House 1766 R-166

Randolph, William (1651?–1711), North American planter and colonial official, born in Warwickshire, England; first of a notable Virginia family; bought "Turkey Island" on James River 1684 and acquired other vast tracts; imported many slaves.

Randolph, Mass., 13 mi (21 km) s. of Boston in Norfolk County; rubber goods, paper boxes, business machines; settled about 1710; pop. of township 28,218.

Randolph-Macon College, in Ashland, Va.; Methodist; founded 1830 at Boydton, moved to Ashland 1868; arts and sciences.

Randolph-Macon Woman's College, in Lynchburg, Va.; Methodist; founded 1891, opened 1893; arts and sciences, education.

Random access memory (RAM), computer memory system C-627
  electronics E-176
  hobby H-191
  microprocessor M-379

'Random Record in the Midst of Leisure', work by Hong K-294

Random sampling, in statistics S-431

Randwick, N.S.W., Australia, on Pacific Ocean, 5 mi (8 km) s.e. of Sydney; in industrial area; pop. 123,865, *map* A-819

Range, in mathematics A-297

Range, in music, *diagram* M-688

Range, in statistics S-435

Range, in w. United States, applied to large tracts of land over which cattle graze. *see also in index* Cattle, *subhead* producing regions; Cowboy; Ranch

Range finder (or stadimeter), in navigation N-70

Rangefinder camera P-283

Rangeley Lakes, chain of six lakes in w. Maine and e. New Hampshire; fishing, hunting, and canoeing popular activities there; area the site of resorts, game preserve, and fish hatcheries.

Ranger, Tex., oil city in n. center of state, about 60 mi (100 km) e. of Abilene; oil field opened 1917, reached maximum production of 75,000 barrels a day 1919; population was about 50,000; pop. 3,142

Rangers, name given to commando-type U.S. fighters organized in World War II; named for Rogers' Rangers of colonial days. *see also in index* Rogers, Robert

Rangers, space probes, *table* S-344
  moon M-580

Rangoon, Burma, capital and port on Rangoon River, n.e. of the mouths of the Irrawaddy; pop. 1,700,000, with suburbs, *map* R-92
  Asia, *map* A-700
  Burma B-508
  1983 bombing K-287

Ranjit, Maharaja (1780–1839), Sikh prince ("lion of Punjab"); aided by French, built strong army; gained huge dominion in n. India.

Rank, Otto (1884–1939), U.S. psychoanalyst, born in Vienna; to U.S. 1935; student of Freud; developed new psychotherapeutic method; applied his principles to mythology, art, and literature.

Rank, placement within military organization
  Canadian armed forces, *picture* U-13
  U.S. Armed Forces insignia U-8

Ranke, Leopold von (1795–1886), German historian, professor University of Berlin 50 years; first to develop critical methods of historical study ('History of the Popes During the 16th and 17th Centuries')
  history writing H-173

Rankin, Jeannette (1880–1973), U.S. suffrage worker, born in Missoula, Mont.; first woman elected to U.S. Congress, served two terms, 1917–19, 1941–43; opposed entry of U.S. into World Wars P-143d
  Montana M-553
  women's rights W-275

Rankin, Louise Spiker (1897–1951), U.S. author, born in Baltimore, Md.; lived 12 years in India; for children, she wrote 'The Gentling of Jonathan' and 'Daughter of the Mountains' R-111b

Rankine, William John Macquorn (1820–72), Scottish civil engineer and physicist, born in Edinburgh; professor of engineering University of Glasgow 1855–72; noted for work on thermodynamics.

Rankine scale, named in honor of William J. M. Rankine C-793
  heat H-103

Rann of Kutch, vast salt flats, n.w. Indian peninsula, in s. Sind, Pakistan, and n. Gujarat state, India; scene of major India-Pakistan conflict 1965.

Ransom, John Crowe (1888–1974), U.S. poet and critic, born in Pulaski, Tenn.; leader of Southern agrarian group; English department, Vanderbilt University 1914–37, Kenyon College 1937–58; editor on periodicals, *The Fugitive* 1922–25 and *Kenyon Review* 1939–59 (verse: 'Poems About God', 'Two Gentlemen in Bonds', 'Selected Poems'; literary criticism: 'The New Criticism').

Ransom, payment demanded in kidnapping K-234

Ransome, Arthur (1884–1967), British journalist and author of children's books presenting a picture of outdoor life in England ('Swallows and Amazons'; 'Pigeon Post', awarded Carnegie Medal 1937; 'We Didn't Mean to Go to Sea') R-111e, S-481

'Ransom of Red Chief, The', short story by Henry H-133

Rantoul, Ill., village in Champaign County, 14 mi (22 km) n.e. of Champaign; modular homes; site of Chanute Air Force Base; incorporated 1869; pop. 20,161
  Illinois, *map* I-53

Ranunculaceae, the crowfoot family, a large botanical group consisting mainly of herbs with an acrid watery juice; well-known members are peony, clematis, larkspur, monkshood, columbine, anemone, marsh marigold, buttercup, meadow rue, and hepatica B-520
  columbine C-590

Ranunculus. *see in index* Buttercup

Rao, Raja (born 1909), British author in India I-108

Rapallo, Italy, port 15 mi (25 km) s.e. of Genoa, on Mediterranean Sea; olives, grapes; manufacturing; treaties of 1920 and 1922; pop. 28,318, *map* I-404

Rapallo, Treaty of (1920), *table* T-275

Rapallo, Treaty of (1922), between Germany and U.S.S.R.; annulled treaty of Brest-Litovsk and restored diplomatic relations; canceled all claims for reparations arising from World War I G-123

Rapa Nui. *see in index* Easter Island

Rape (Latin *rapum* meaning "turnip," also called coleseed), several plants of the cabbage family grown either as green crop or for the oil in the seeds; part of bird-seed mixtures
  England E-235

Rape, any sexual contact by force or threat of force by a male or female against a male or female of any age; such contact includes sexual penetration by body part or object into oral, anal, or vaginal orifice, as well as fondling
  crime C-771

'Rape of Lucrece, The', work by Shakespeare S-130, 134

'Rape of the Lock, The', poem by Pope P-445
  English literature E-271

Rape of the Sabine Women. *see in index* Sabines

Rape plant, plant *Brassica napus* C-4

Raphael, archangel commemorated as saint October 24
  statue in Spain, *picture* S-359

Raphael (full name Raffaello Sanzio, or Raffaello Santi) (1483–1520), Italian painter R-92
  burial place R-257
  Julius II J-151
  'Madonna and Child Enthroned with Saints' P-34, *picture* P-35
  mosaic M-590

Raphanus satinus. *see in index* Radish

Raphus cucullatus. *see in index* Dodo

Rapidan River, in n. Virginia, rises in the Blue Ridge and flows s. and e. to Rappahannock River north of Fredericksburg; about 90 mi (145 km) long, *map* V-348

Rapid City, S.D., 2nd city of state, about 40 mi (60 km) e. of Wyoming border; gateway to Black Hills; tourism; farming, mining, lumbering area; cement, lumber products, food products; granite quarries nearby; South Dakota School of Mines and Technology; about 240 lives lost in flood in June 1972; property damage $100,000,000; pop. 46,492 S-332d, *maps* S-323, 334, U-40
  climate, *list* S-321

Rapid Deployment Joint Task Force, in United States A-647

Rapid eye movement (REM), phase of sleep
  dreams D-257

Rapidograph, technical fountain pen used in mechanical drawing M-257, *picture* M-250

Rapids, place in river where water rushes over a rocky bed R-210
  St. Lawrence River S-20
  waterfall W-95

Rapid sand filter, in water purification W-91

Rapid transit, transportation S-487
  BART S-42
  subway. *see in index* Subway

Rapier, sword S-546

Rapotec, Stanislaus (born 1913), Australian painter A-802

Rapp, George (1757–1847), German Pietist linen weaver; born in Iptigen, Germany; emigrated to the U.S. and formed several communal communities: Economy and Community of Equality in Pennsylvania, and Harmony in Indiana C-605

Rappahannock River, in Virginia, flows s.e. from Blue Ridge Mts. 250 mi (400 km) to Chesapeake Bay, *maps* V-331, 349

Rappaport, Solomon Z. (pen name Sholem An-sky) (1863–1920), Russian Jewish playwright Y-419, *picture* Y-420

Rappeling M-638

Rapping (or rap music), style of popular music originating in the Bronx, New York City, in 1970s; characterized by rhythmic, rhyming, slang lyrics spoken or chanted forcefully over double-time, percussion instrumentation; elements made way into mainstream U.S. rock and roll M-683

Rappites, a communal religious group in Indiana I-94, *picture* I-93

Raptor, predatory bird. *see in index* Birds of prey, Falconiformes, Strigiformes

Raptures of the deep. *see in index* Nitrogen narcosis

Rare earth metals, similar metals (now called the lanthanide series) having atomic numbers from 57 to 71, *table* P-207

Rarefaction, in sound S-259

Raritan River, in New Jersey, formed by two branches in n. of state; 75 mi (120 km) to Raritan Bay; waterway for transport of various manufactured goods N-193

Raschel, a knitted fabric K-260

Rascoe, Arthur Burton (1892–1957), U.S. critic, editor, and journalist, born in Fulton, Ky.; rich, varied, and dynamic literary life ('Titans of Literature'; 'Before I Forget'; 'We Were Interrupted').

Ras Hafun, cape. *see in index* Hafun, Ras

Rashid, Egypt. *see in index* Rosetta

'Rashomon' (1950), Japanese motion picture directed by Akira Kurosawa J-57

Rask, Rasmus (1787–1832), Danish linguist L-230

Raskin, Ellen (born 1928), U.S. writer and artist, born in Milwaukee, Wis.; illustrator of many children's books by herself and others; wrote and illustrated 'Nothing Ever Happens on My Block', 'Ghost in a Four-Room Apartment', 'Twenty-two', 'Twenty-three', 'The Westing Game' (awarded 1979 Newbery Medal).

Rasminsky, Louis (born 1908), Canadian financier, born in Montreal, Que.; executive director International Monetary Fund 1946–62, of International Bank for Reconstruction and Development 1950–62, of International Finance Corporation 1957–62; deputy governor Bank of Canada 1955–61, governor 1961–73.

Rasmussen, Knud (1879–1933), Danish Arctic explorer, born in Greenland; explored Greenland, Arctic coast of North America, and Lapland; found evidence that Greenland Eskimos were descendants of American Indians ('Greenland by the Polar Sea', 'Eskimo Folk Tales', 'Across Arctic America', 'Beyond the High Hills').

Rasorite (or kernite), mineral yielding borax M-435

Raspberry B-176, F-438, R-94, *pictures* B-177, F-434

Raspe, Rudolph Erich. *see in index* Munchausen, Baron

Rasputin, Grigori Efimovich (1871–1916), Russian monk; peasant who deserted family for religious life 1904; vast influence through fanatical teachings and personal magnetism; interference in politics led to his murder by Russian nobles
  assassination, *list* A-704
  Nicholas II N-306

Rasselas, Prince of Abyssinia, in Samuel Johnson's philosophical romance of that name published 1759; seeker for happiness, at last disenchanted.

Ras Shamra, site in modern Syria on coast s.w. of Antioch; identified with ancient seaport of Ugarit and mentioned in Amarna letters.

Rastafari, a religious group of Jamaican origin J-17

Rastatt, West Germany, town near Rhine River, n.w. of Baden-Baden; rail center; manufacturing, printing; pop. 29,850, *map* G-134
treaty (1714), *table* T-275

Rat, animal R-94
aging A-127
environmental changes A-439
experimentation A-449
vitamins V-357
learning ability, *picture* P-523
length of life, average, *chart* A-423

Ratchet screw driver (or push-drill screw driver), a tool T-218

Ratel. *see in index* Honey badger

Ratemeter. *see in index* Flow meter

Rate-of-climb indicator (or vertical-speed indicator), airplane instrument A-194

Rate regulation, in railroads R-87

Rates, English tax system U-18

Rates of change, in mathematics C-22

Rat flea, *picture* F-177

Rathenau, Walther (1867–1922), German economist and industrialist; controller of raw materials in World War I; important in German postwar industrial reconstruction; foreign minister 1922; assassinated June 1922.

Ratiné, loosely woven fabric with rough surface effect produced by special yarns of nubby or knotty nature; usually cotton but also made of silk, wool, or rayon.

Rating, an estimate of the percentage of the public listening to or viewing a particular radio or television program
television T-73

Ratio, in mathematics F-377, R-95

Ratio chart G-228

Rationalism, in philosophy P-266, 264, *list* P-265
Saadia S-1

Rational number, in mathematics N-440

Ratisbon, West Germany. *see in index* Regensburg

Rat Islands, in Aleutian Islands, Alaska, *map* U-39

Ratites, bird classification B-276

Rat kangaroo A-779

Ratline hitch (or clove hitch), knot K-263

Raton, N.M., city about 115 mi (185 km) n.e. of Santa Fe and near Colorado border; railroad center in coal-mining and livestock region; ranching; electronics; tourist trade; steel windows and doors, lumber products; pop. 8,225, *maps* N-229, U-40

Ratoon, sucker or sprout developing on the roots of such plants as sugarcane or pineapple; new plants spring from it P-329

Ratsimandrava, Richard (1931–75), president of Madagascar
assassination, *list* A-704

Rattan palm (or cane palm), genus *Calamus* of palms, with flexible fibers that are used for canes, basketry, and furniture; resin from the fruit is used for coloring varnishes and in photoengraving P-84, *pictures* P-82, P-9

Rattigan, Terence Mervyn (1911–77), British playwright, born in London (plays and films; 'The Winslow Boy'; 'The Browning Version'; 'Separate Tables').

Rattle, toy or musical instrument
Northwest American Indians, *picture* S-78

Rattlesnake R-96, *picture* S-226. *see also in index* Snake bite
fangs, *picture* S-223
first aid S-227
striking, *picture* S-226a
tongue A-430
venom S-226c
head, *picture* S-226b
pit viper V-328
rattles, *picture* S-226b

Rattlesnake weed, *picture* P-363b

Ratzel, Friedrich (1844–1904), German geographer, born in Karlsruhe, Germany; instrumental in founding the study of anthropogeography.

Rau, Santha Rama (born 1923), British author from India I-108

Rauch, Christian Daniel (1777–1857), German sculptor, considered greatest historical sculptor of his time; monument to Queen Louise at Charlottenburg and bronze equestrian statue of Frederick the Great in Berlin.

Rauschenbusch, Walter (1861–1918), U.S. clergyman and leader of the Social Gospel movement
Baptist leadership B-76

Ravel, Maurice (1875–1937), French composer; his daring harmonies and complicated rhythms retain classical form; best known for piano pieces ('Valses nobles et sentimentales'); also chamber music, orchestral works ('Rapsodie espagnole'; 'Bolero'; 'Shéhérazade'); ballet ('Daphnis et Chloé'); opera ('L'Heure espagnole').

Raven, large crowlike bird of the family Corvidae R-97
crow relative C-784, *picture* C-785
mythology M-704
tool usage B-258

'Raven, The', poem by Poe A-348, R-97

Ravenala. *see in index* Traveler's tree

Ravenna, Italy, old city noted for its churches; 75 mi (120 km) s. of Venice; pop. 115,205 R-97, *map* I-404
Byzantine B-533
mosaic M-590

Ravenna, Ohio, city 17 mi (27 km) n.e. of Akron; industrial products include roadbuilding machinery, rubber goods, hardware, and textiles; settled 1799; pop. 11,987.

Ravenna, Battle of, victory of French over united Spanish and papal armies in 1512 R-97

Ravenscroft, George (1618–1681), English glassmaker; developer of flint glass G-162

Ravi (ancient Hydraotes), river of Punjab; 450 mi (725 km) long; rises in n.w. India and flows s.w. to Chenab River in Pakistan.

Ravielli, Anthony (born 1916), U.S. illustrator and author, born in New York, N.Y.; extensive commercial illustration; books for young people include 'Elephants' and 'From Fins to Hands'.

Rawalpindi, Pakistan, city 160 mi (260 km) n.w. of Lahore; hill resort; industrial and military center; polytechnic institute, pop. 340,175
Asia, *map* A-700

Rawinsonde, in weather observation W-121

Rawlings, Marjorie Kinnan (1896–1953), U.S. writer, born in Washington, D.C.; made her home in Florida 1928; married Norton Sanford Baskin; wrote novels ('South Moon Under'; 'Golden Apples'; 'The Yearling', won 1939 Pulitzer prize for fiction), stories for younger readers ('The Secret River'), and autobiography ('Cross Creek') R-111b, e

Rawlins, Wyo., city 150 mi (240 km) w. of Cheyenne; oil, uranium, and coal-mining area; sheep and cattle raising; railroad shops; tourist trade; pop. 11,547, *map* U-40
Wyoming W-396

Rawlinson, Henry Creswicke (1810–95), British Orientalist; first to decipher successfully Persian cuneiform inscriptions A-532
Behistun Rock, *picture* P-214

Rawls, Betsy (born 1928), U.S. golfer G-189

Raw materials I-192. *see also in index* names of raw materials such as Coal; Cotton; Iron
materials handling and testing M-211

Raw milk, *list* D-6

Raw silk S-198

Raw sugar S-506

Ray, Hugh (nickname Shorty) (1884–1956), U.S. adviser, born in Chicago, Ill.; National Football League technical adviser and officials' supervisor 1938–56.

Ray, John (1627–1705), taxonomist B-229
zoology Z-470

Ray, Man (1890–1976), U.S. photographer, artist, *list* P-294
Atget A-733

Ray, Rammohan (1772–1833), Indian author during culture revival H-159, I-108

Ray, Satyajit (born 1921), Indian film director ('Charulata'; 'Jana Aranya') D-155

Ray, fish. *see in index* Skates and rays

Ray, Cape, on s.w. point of Newfoundland, *map* C-109

Ray, in mathematics
geometry G-73

Ray, in light. *see in index* Light

Ray, in physics. *see in index* Radiation

Rayburn, Sam (1882–1961), U.S. congressman, born in Roane County, Tennessee; Democratic representative from Texas from 1913; speaker of the House of Representatives 1940–47, 1949–53, 1955–61 T-123, *picture* E-136

Rayleigh, John William Strutt, 3rd baron (1842–1919), British physicist; experimental work in electricity, light, sound; codiscoverer of argon. *see also in index* Nobel Prizewinners, *table*

Raymond, Henry Jarvis (1820–69), U.S. editor and political leader, born Lima, N.Y.; founder with George Jones of *New York Daily Times* (now *The New York Times*) 1851; remarkable for fairness in era of partisan editorship; leader in Republican party, member of House of Representatives 1864–68.

Raymond of Toulouse (died 1105), powerful count of Provence; a leader in First Crusade C-787

Raymond Orteig prize, monetary award for nonstop New York-to-Paris flight
Lindbergh L-227

Raynaud's phenomenon, a physical condition
biofeedback training B-216

Rayon (or Chardonnet silk), artificial silk R-97
clothing C-509
fibers F-72
forest products F-316
sources S-398
textile manufacture T-138

Raytown, Mo., city 9 mi (15 km) s.e. of Kansas City; meat-packing, railway communication, pipeline equipment; pop. 31,759.

Razor, instrument for removing hair
hairdressing H-10
snail climbs over blade, *picture* S-222

Razor-billed auk A-762

'Razor's Edge, The', novel by Maugham M-231

RCA Electronic Mail, *picture* T-56

RCAF. *see in index* Royal Canadian Air Force

RCC, Libya. *see in index* Revolutionary Command Council

RCMP. *see in index* Royal Canadian Mounted Police

RDF. *see in index* Radio direction finder

Re, Egyptian sun-god. *see in index* Ra

Ré, Île de, French island in Bay of Biscay; 33 sq mi (85 sq km); vegetables, wine, salt, oysters, pop. 9,967, *map* F-372

Reaching, sailing maneuver B-328

Reaction (or chemical change), process of combining elements C-297

Reaction engine, type of airplane or spacecraft engine A-187
jet propulsion J-105
rocket R-231, S-342a, *diagram* R-232

Reaction time, in driving A-864

Reaction turbine (or Francis turbine), waterpower W-103

Reactor, nuclear, device for controlling nuclear fission, *picture* R-332h
fuel F-442
uranium U-210
furnace F-451
fusion reactor P-380
heat, *picture* H-102
naval vessels N-84
submarines S-497, *diagram* S-498
niobium N-318
nuclear energy N-423, *picture* N-424
radiation hazards
safeguards S-58
water use W-87, 104
oceans O-460

Read, Gardner (born 1913), U.S. composer and conductor, born in Evanston, Ill.; his orchestral works were performed by symphony orchestras in U.S.; received many awards.

Read, George (1733–98), U.S. jurist and statesman, born in Cecil County, Maryland; signed Declaration of Independence; U.S. senator from Delaware 1789–93.

Read, Opie Percival (1852–1939), U.S. author, born in Nashville, Tenn.; edited the *Arkansas Traveler*; noted for truthful portrayal of local scenes, customs, characters ('A Kentucky Colonel'; 'A Tennessee Judge'; 'An Arkansas Planter'; 'Son of the Swordmaker').

Read, Thomas Buchanan (1822–72), U.S. poet and painter, born in Chester County, Pennsylvania ('Sheridan's Ride'; 'House by the Sea').

Reade, Charles (1814–84), British novelist and playwright R-99
literary contribution E-278
'The Cloister and the Hearth' R-146

Reader, a textbook R-103

'Reader's Adviser, The' (or 'Bookman's Manual'), work by R.R. Bowker Company B-186

'Reader's Digest', magazine M-35

'Readers' Guide to Periodical Literature' R-128, L-163, *chart* L-160, *picture* R-129
magazine and journal M-31

Reading, Rufus Isaacs, first marquis of (1860–1935), British jurist and political leader; Liberal member House of Commons 1904–13; first person of the Jewish faith to serve as lord chief justice 1913–21; special ambassador to U.S. 1918; viceroy of India 1921–26; foreign secretary in MacDonald's Cabinet 1931.

Reading, England, city 30 mi (50 km) w. of London, on Kennet River near junction with Thames; biscuits, flour, metal products; capital of Berkshire; pop. 127,530.

Reading, Mass., 11 mi (18 km) n. of Boston; textiles, metal products; settled in 1639, incorporated in 1644; Old South Church here is a reproduction of original one in Boston; pop. of township 22,678.

Reading, Ohio, city 12 mi (19 km) n.e. of Cincinnati; chemicals, paperboard, containers, grain products; incorporated as village 1851, as city 1930; pop. 12,879.

Reading, Pa., manufacturing city about 48 mi (77 km) n.w. of Philadelphia; pop. 78,686 R-99, P-182b, *maps* P-185, 165, 174, U-41

Reading, readiness for R-101b, P-268b, *picture* R-101d
kindergarten and nursery school K-241
literacy and illiteracy L-239

Reading, teaching of R-101a
communication skill C-618
old methods
'New England Primer'. *see in index* 'New England Primer'
phonics P-268a, *tables* P-268c
sensory aids B-212
spelling S-375

Reading for recreation R-104
list of recommended books S-464, 478
literature S-183
poetry P-407
storytelling S-460

Reading for young adults R-111f

Reading glass (or magnifying glass) M-380

Red Deer, Alta., city on Red Deer River, 90 mi (145 km) s. of Edmonton; pop. 46,393 A-263, *map* C-109

Redding, Calif., city about 145 mi (235 km) n.w. of Sacramento, on Sacramento River; pop. 41,995, *map* U-40

Reddish egret, bird *Dichromanassa rufescens* H-143

Red drum, fish. *see in index* Drum

Red Eagle (or William Weatherford) (1780?–1824), Creek chief, leader in Creek War (1812–14); massacred hundreds at Ft. Mims on Alabama River (1813); surrendered to General Jackson (1814), released.

Redeemer's Church, Jerusalem, *picture* J-99

Red elm. *see in index* Slippery elm

Redemptioner, an immigrant to North American colonies; without contract, sold to highest bidder for a certain amount of time A-336

Red Ensign, former flag of Canada; flag of Manitoba and Ontario.

Redeye, name given to several freshwater fish. *see in index* Rock bass

Red Eyebrows (or Shandong), Chinese rebel group who overthrew Emperor Wang Mang in AD 23 C-362

Red-eyed vireo (or preacher bird) V-328

Red-faced monkey, *picture* Z-462

Redfield, Edward Willis (1869–1965), U.S. painter, born in Bridgeville, Del.; his landscapes are glowing and realistic interpretations of nature ('Snowdrifts'; 'Brook in Winter').

Redfin pickerel, fish P-326

Red fir, evergreen tree *Abies magnifica* of pine family native to mountains of Oregon and California; grows 60–200 ft (18–60 m) high; branches short, forming triangular crown; bark deeply fissured, dark red; leaves 4-angled, gray-green with white lines, to 1½ in. (4 cm) long; cones to 9 in. (23 cm) long; sometimes called California red fir; wood similar to and sold as "white fir"; shasta red fir is a variety of this species; wood of Douglas fir often called red fir F-92

Redfish (or channel bass). *see in index* Drum

Redfish. *see in index* Ocean perch

Red-footed booby, seabird *Sula sula* of the family Sulidae G-16, *picture* G-4

Redford, Robert (full name Charles Robert Redford, Jr.) (born 1937), U.S. motion picture actor, director, born in Santa Monica, Calif.; films include 'War Hunt' (1962), 'Inside Daisy Clover' (1965), 'Barefoot in the Park' (1967); British Academy award (1970) for best actor for 'Tell Them Willie Boy Is Here' (1969) and 'Butch Cassidy and the Sundance Kid' (1969); 'All the President's Men' (1976); won U.S. Academy Award (best director) for 'Ordinary People' (1980), *picture* M-614

Red Fort, in Delhi, India D-79

Red fox F-337, *table* F-464
  tracks, *picture* A-464

Redgrave, Lynn Rachel (born 1943), British actress, born in London; daughter of Michael, sister of Vanessa; won New York Film Critics Award for 'Georgy Girl' (1966); play, 'Black Comedy'.

Redgrave, Sir Michael Scudamore (1908–85), British actor, born in Bristol; father of Vanessa and Lynn; stage roles: 'Hamlet', 'Macbeth', 'Uncle Vanya'; actor-director of 'Harry' and 'Jacobowsky and the Colonel'; films: 'Thunder Rock', 'Dead of Night', 'The Battle of Britain'.

Redgrave, Vanessa (born 1937), British actress, born in London; daughter of Michael, sister of Lynn; Cannes Film Festival awards for 'Morgan!' 1966 and 'The Loves of Isadora' 1969 (films: 'Blow-Up', 'Julia', 'Camelot'; plays: 'The Taming of the Shrew', 'The Sea Gull').

Red grouse (or moorfowl), game bird G-292

Red Guard, youth group during China's Cultural Revolution C-376

Red gum, common name of *Eucalyptus rostrata,* native of Australia; also name of the hardwood of the sweet gum tree. *see also in index* Sweet gum
  wood, *table* W-283

Red hake (or squirrel hake), fish *Urophycis chuss* of the family Merlucciidae H-13

Red-headed woodpecker, bird *Melanerpes erythrocephalus* W-286

Red Hills salamander
  endangered species E-212

Red hind. *see in index* Grouper

Redhorse, large group of fish with red fins and large, coarse scales; average length about 2 ft (0.6 m); abundant in n. United States and Canada.

Red-hot-poker plant. *see in index* Kniphofia

Redi, Francesco (1626–97), Italian physician and poet who demonstrated that the presence of maggots in rotting meat does not result from spontaneous generation but from eggs laid on the meat by flies
  evolution E-364

Rediscount, in banking, the selling of a discounted, or accepted, note in order to secure credit F-51

Red Jacket (1750?–1830), last great chief of Senecas; served with British in Revolutionary War, with U.S. in War of 1812.

Red kangaroo, mammal *Megaleia rufa* A-778
  marsupials M-154, *picture* M-156

Red Kowhai, plant. *see in index* Clianthus

Redlands, Calif., city 60 mi (100 km) e. of Los Angeles; one of largest orange-shipping centers of world; University of Redlands; pop. 43,619.

Redlands, University of, in Redlands, Calif.; American Baptist; founded 1907; arts and sciences, education, music; graduate studies.

Red lead (or minium), a red solid Pb_3O_4 formed by heating lead oxide at 752° F (400° C) for some time; used on iron structures to prevent rusting L-99, P-73

Red-lead putty P-540

Red-letter days, originally the chief festival days of the church indicated on the church calendar by red letters; an exceptionally happy or lucky day in one's life.

Red Lion and Sun, Iran's flag of the Geneva Convention.

Red lynx. *see in index* Bobcat

Red maple. *see in index* Swamp maple

Red meat M-246

Redmond, John Edward (1851–1918), Irish parliamentary leader, member British House of Commons 1881 to his death; friend and lieutenant of Parnell, whom he succeeded as leader of Irish members; as leader of reunited Irish nationalists after 1900 sought Home Rule by persistent but peaceable methods.

Redmond, Wash., city 11 mi (18 km) n.e. of Seattle; lumber mills, farming; ice cream; pop. 23,318.

Red mulberry, tree *Morus rubra* of the mulberry family M-648

Red newt S-25, *picture* S-26

Red oak, name *Quercus rubra* or *Quercus borealis* applied to the group of oaks with brown wood which has a red tint; includes the species northern red, southern red, swamp red, scarlet, black, blackjack, laurel, pin, shumard, water, and willow oaks O-452
  New Jersey's state tree, *picture* N-202
  wood, *table* W-283

Redon, Odilon (1840–1916), French painter, etcher, and lithographer; works are marked by imagination, keen vision, and mysticism; floral paintings.

Redondo Beach, Calif., city and beach resort on the Pacific, 16 mi (26 km) s.w. of Los Angeles; electronics; campers, clothing; pop. 57,102
  surfing S-519

Redoubt, a field fortification, an advance post defending a hilltop or other dangerous position.

Red oxide of zinc. *see in index* Zincite

Red pepper. *see in index* Chili

Red pine (or Norway pine) P-328, *picture* P-327
  Minnesota's state tree, *picture* M-448

Redpoll, finch F-86

'Red Pony, The', novel by Steinbeck, *list* H-274

Red quebracho, tree. *see in index* Quebracho

Red raspberry R-94, *picture* F-434

Red Riding Hood, Little, character in children's tale of same name; in original French version by Charles Perrault, she was eaten by a wolf disguised as her grandmother; in German and other variants, she was saved by a woodsman.

Red River (or Song Koi), river, about 700 mi (1,100 km) long; rises in Yünnan Province, China; flows s.e. into Vietnam and past city of Hanoi into Gulf of Tonkin V-317
  Asia, *map* A-700
  Hanoi H-31

Red River, southernmost of great tributaries of the Mississippi; rises in the Panhandle of Texas; 1,275 mi long S-185, *maps* N-351, U-58, 63
  Louisiana L-309, *maps* L-310, 323
  Oklahoma O-522
  Texas T-118

Red River of the North (or Red River), river, rises in Minnesota and flows 545 mi (875 km) n. to Lake Winnipeg in Manitoba R-120, *maps* N-351, U-70
  Manitoba M-100
  Minnesota M-440
  North Dakota N-373

Red River Rebellion C-101, R-120
  Strathcona S-484

Red River Settlement, colony established near present city of Winnipeg, Man., in 1811 by Lord Selkirk, member of Hudson's Bay Company; the colonists came from Scotland.

Red River Valley, in North Dakota N-373

Red Rock Park, amphitheater, w. of Denver, Colo., *picture* C-575

Red Rock River, headstream of the Missouri River, originates in the Rocky Mountains in s.w. Montana M-507

'Red Room, The' (or 'Röda Rummet'), work by Strindberg S-489

Redroot. *see in index* New Jersey tea

Red salmon (or blueback salmon, or sockeye salmon), fish of the family Salmonidae S-28

Red scale insect S-52f

Red Sea, arm of Indian Ocean between Arabian Peninsula and Africa connected with Mediterranean by Suez Canal; 1,200 mi (1,930 km) long R-120, *map* A-188. *see also in index* Ocean, *table*
  Asia, *map* A-700
  canals C-127
    Suez Canal S-503, *map* S-504
  Egypt E-115
  oceanic exploration O-464

Red shift, in astronomy
  cosmology C-731
  quasar Q-7
  relativity R-142

Red Shirts, terrorist group in the South during U.S. Reconstruction period R-116

Red sorrel. *see in index* Roselle

Red spider S-387

Red spruce, tree S-398

Red Square, square in Moscow, U.S.S.R. M-591, R-333, *pictures* M-592, 593, R-357
  Kremlin K-305
  May Day parade, *picture* R-332b

Red squirrel (or chickaree) S-401

Red Star, communist symbol R-333

Redstone, U.S. missile and rocket; replaced by Pershing missile
  space flights S-346f, *table* S-348
  launch complex, *map* S-342a

Red Sulphur Springs, W. Va., resort in Monroe County; pop. 75
  West Virginia W-167

Red suslik, animal. *see in index* Suslik

Red-tailed hawk
  falconry, *picture* F-13

Red-throated loon, bird L-298

Red tide, in oceanography O-484

Reduction, in chemistry
  bleaching process B-310

Reduction division, process in cell meiosis
  genetics G-55

Red viper, snake. *see in index* Copperhead

Red Wing, Minn., city on Mississippi River, 40 mi (60 km) s.e. of St. Paul; named for an American Indian chief; shoes and other leather products, industrial oil, scientific instruments, malt; pop. 5,210.

Red-winged blackbird (also called red-wing), bird *Agelaius phoeniceus* B-243, *picture* B-258
  blackbird family B-305
  egg, *picture* E-112
  song patterns A-447

Red wolf, wolf *Canis rufus* W-267

Redwood, sequoia tree S-112, *pictures* C-47, F-311, T-276
  wood, *table* W-282

Redwood City, Calif., city and port (connected by deepwater channel with San Francisco Bay) 23 mi (37 km) s.e. of San Francisco; electronics, food processing; wire and cable, cement, plastics; pop. 54,965.

Ree, a North American people. *see in index* Arikara

Reece Machinery Company, U.S. company
  garment industry G-35

Reed, Ezekiel (fl. 18th century), U.S. inventor of first nail-making machine N-4

Reed, Ishmael (born 1938), U.S. author
  American literature A-362

Reed, James Alexander (1861–1944), U.S. political leader and lawyer; born near Mansfield, Ohio; prosecuting attorney of Jackson County, Missouri, 1898–1900; mayor of Kansas City 1900–04; U.S. senator from Missouri 1911–29; opposed League of Nations; a prominent Democrat.

Reed, John (1887–1920), U.S. journalist and poet, born in Portland, Ore.; wrote eyewitness account of October (1917) Russian Revolution ('Ten Days That Shook the World'), also 'Tamburlaine and Other Poems'; his ashes buried in Kremlin.

Reed, Stanley Forman (1884–1980), U.S. jurist, born in Mason County, Kentucky; general counsel Reconstruction Finance Corp. 1932–35; solicitor general of U.S. 1935–38; associate justice U.S. Supreme Court 1938–57.

Reed, Thomas Brackett (1839–1902), U.S. statesman, born in Portland, Me., congressman from Maine 1876–99, Republican leader and speaker of House 1889–91 and 1895–99; called "Czar" Reed because of his stringent rulings (continued as permanent rules of procedure) to increase efficiency of House; able parliamentarian
  Harrison H-47

Reed, Walter (1851–1902), U.S. Army surgeon and bacteriologist R-121, *picture* V-342
  Hall of Fame, *table* H-16
  medicine M-284

Reed, William Maxwell (1871–1962), U.S. author of books of information, born in Bath, Me.; attended Harvard University; taught astronomy at Harvard and Princeton universities; later went into steel industry; his first book, 'The Earth for Sam', was written for his nephew; other books for children followed: 'The Sea for Sam'; 'Patterns in the Sky'.

Reedbird, bird. *see in index* Bobolink

Ireland; as leading lady for Augustin Daly and later as star won recognition in both high comedy and farce.
Rehearsal theory, psychological theory of play P-390b
directing D-153
theater T-153
Rehnquist, William Hubbs (born 1924), U.S. lawyer, born in Milwaukee, Wis.; assistant U.S. attorney general 1969–72; associate justice U.S. Supreme Court 1972–86; chief justice 1986–
Nixon N-326
Rehoboam (978?–920? BC), king of Israel, son of Solomon.
Rehoboth Beach, Del., resort city; pop. 1,730
Delaware D-72, *picture* D-81
Rehoboth Church, in West Virginia; oldest Methodist church building west of the Allegheny Mountains, *picture* W-175
Rei (plural reis), basis of coinage in Brazil under former system based on milreis; in 1942 cruzeiro replaced milreis as unit of currency.
Reich, Ferdinand (1799–1882), German metallurgist; discoverer, with H.T. Richter, of indium, an element used as a plating for bearings.
Reich, Steve (born 1936), U.S. composer M-676
Reich, Wilhelm (1897–1957), Austrian psychologist who developed a system of psychoanalysis that concentrated on the overall structure, rather than individual neuroses H-203
Reich, German noun meaning "realm," "empire"; genitive form *Reichs* used in many compound words, as *Reichskanzler,* "chancellor of the realm."
Reichenbach, Hans (1891–1953), German philosopher, born in Hamburg; professor University of California 1938–53; associated with logical positivism movement.
Reichenbach, Poland, former German town situated in Silesia, 30 mi (50 km) s.w. of Breslau; Prussian victory over Austrians 1762; place of convention 1790 guaranteeing integrity of Turkey; alliance against Napoleon 1813; included in Poland since 1945.
Reichenberg, Czechoslovakia. *see in index* Liberec
Reichsbank, former national bank of Germany with main office at Berlin; created 1875; a law in 1939 gave Hitler direct control of its policies; ceased to function 1945 in East Germany, liquidated 1947–48 in West Germany.
Reichsmark. *see in index* Mark
Reichspfennig. *see in index* Pfennig
Reichsrat, state council in legislative system of Germany made up of elected representatives from each state; established 1919; in 1934 legislative powers taken over by Reich cabinet W-142
Reichstag (German for "imperial diet"), in medieval times a meeting of emperor and vassals; evolved into German Imperial Diet; name given in 1871 to national parliament of Germany and retained as name of chief legislative body after fall of empire in 1918; members (one for every 60,000 voters) were elected for 4 years; under Nazis made advisory body; at end of World War II, Allies divided Germany into occupation zones, and in 1949 Reichstag was superseded in West Germany by Federal Diet, *Bundestag,* and in East Germany by People's Chamber, *picture* H-176
Weimar Republic W-142
Reichstein, Tadeus (born 1897), Swiss chemist, born in Wloclawek, Poland; became Swiss citizen 1914; synthesized vitamin C 1933; head of department of pharmacy 1938–46, of organic chemistry 1946–60, University of Basel. *see also in index* Nobel Prizewinners, *table*
Reid, George Agnew (1860–1947), Canadian painter, born in Wingham, Ont., known for genre, figure, landscape, and mural paintings; series of paintings in municipal buildings, Toronto; principal of Ontario College of Art, Toronto, 1912–29.
Reid, Sir George Houstoun (1845–1918), Australian political leader, born in Johnstone, Scotland; admitted to bar 1879; entered Parliament 1880; prime minister for Liberal Coalition government 1904–5.
Reid, Mayne (in full Thomas Mayne Reid) (1818–83), Irish writer of adventure tales and hunting romances; in U.S. 1840–49, traded with American Indians, fought in Mexican War ('Scalp Hunters'; 'White Chief'; 'The Rifle Rangers'; 'The Boy Tar'; 'Afloat in the Forest').
Reid, Ogden Mills (1882–1947), U.S. newspaperman, born in New York, N.Y.; son of Whitelaw Reid; editor *New York Herald Tribune* after 1913.
Reid, Robert (1862–1929), U.S. painter, born in Stockbridge, Mass.; influenced by impressionists; well known as mural painter (works in Library of Congress, Washington, D.C.; Massachusetts State House, Boston; Appellate Court House, New York, N.Y.); easel paintings are landscapes and figures.
Reid, Samuel Chester (1783–1861), U.S. Navy officer, born in Norwich, Conn.; commanded privateer *General Armstrong* in War of 1812; in repulsing a British attack at Fayal, 1814, he detained British ships on their way to New Orleans, La., thereby enabling Gen. Andrew Jackson to make adequate preparations to save the city; said to have designed present U.S. flag, with 13 stripes and the addition of a star for each new state.
Reid, Thomas (1710–96), Scottish philosopher and psychologist, who taught that common sense is enough to explain certain fundamental beliefs, such as the existence of material world; claimed that people have instinctive knowledge of first principles; foremost of the Scottish school of philosophers.
Reid, Whitelaw (1837–1912), U.S. journalist and diplomat, born in Xenia, Ohio; father of Ogden M. Reid; war correspondent and storywriter under pseudonym "Agate"; after 1872 editor and principal owner of *New York Tribune,* succeeding Horace Greeley; Republican nominee for vice-president 1892; ambassador to France 1889–92 and to United Kingdom 1905–12, where he became popular social figure as well as respected diplomat.
Reid Inlet, in Alaska, *picture* I-6
Reidsville, N.C., industrial city in n. part of state, about 20 mi (30 km) n.e. of Greensboro; tobacco, corn, grain region; cigarettes, textiles; pop. 13,636.
Reign of Terror, in French history
Danton D-33
French Revolution F-403
Jacobins J-11
Marat M-131
Marie Antoinette M-135
Robespierre R-223
Rochambeau R-227
Roland R-239
Reikjavik, Iceland. *see in index* Reykjavik
Reims (or Rheims), France, city in n.e. France, 100 mi (160 km) from Paris; pop. 151,988 R-138, *maps* E-361, F-372
Joan of Arc J-119
World War I bombing, *picture* W-318
Reincarnation, belief that souls of the dead return to earth in another form or body, especially in a new human body. *see also in index* Transmigration of the soul
Buddhism B-480
Hinduism H-155
India I-68
monks and monasticism M-540
theosophy T-163
Reindeer R-139, D-62, *picture* D-64
Arctic regions A-572
'A Visit from St. Nicholas' S-45
domesticated animals A-455
Europe E-332
Lapland L-50
length of life, average, *chart* A-423
Reindeer Lake, in Saskatchewan and Manitoba; 2,437 sq mi (6,312 km), *maps* C-112, N-351, S-49c, 491
Reindeer moss, lichen most abundant in Arctic and subarctic regions; large starch content D-64
reindeer food R-139
Reine des Lacs. *see in index* Rainy Lake
Reineke Fuchs. *see in index* Reynard the Fox
Reiner, Fritz (1888–1963), U.S. musical conductor, born Budapest, Hungary; conductor Cincinnati Symphony Orchestra 1922–31; became U.S. citizen 1928; conductor Pittsburgh Symphony Orchestra 1938–48; one of leading conductors Metropolitan Opera Company, New York City 1948–53; conductor and musical director Chicago Symphony Orchestra 1953–62
orchestra O-578, *list* O-579
Reinhardt, Django (1910–53), jazz guitarist, born in Belgium of Gypsy parentage J-87
Reinhardt, Max (1873–1943), Austrian theatrical director, producer of pantomime 'Sumurun', spectacle play 'The Miracle', Oscar Wilde's 'Salome', Shakespeare's 'Midsummer Night's Dream' (also in motion pictures); innovator in use of simple settings, symbolizing an emotion or a scene, lighting and mechanical devices to create illusion of simplicity and of bringing audience into the action of the play; moved to U.S. 1935.
Reins, in horseback riding H-265
Reizenstein, Elmer. *see in index* Rice, Elmer Lewis
Rejection, of organ and tissue transplants T-251, S-519c–d
Relative humidity, in meteorology W-120
heating systems H-111
Relative location, in geography G-62
Relative pronoun P-508
Relative weight. *see in index* Specific gravity
Relativity, in physics R-140, U-199
bibliography P-310
cosmology C-731
Einstein E-133
Mach M-8
mathematics M-217
matter M-227
mechanics M-263, 269
Newtonian views modified G-241, P-304
speed of light L-198
'Relativity' (1966), motion picture by Emshwiller, *picture* M-626
Relay
computer C-629
Relay, in communications satellite S-195b
television T-76
Relay race T-244
Relief, in geography
climate control C-498
Relief, in sculpture S-80
metalworking M-310
Relief Corps, Woman's, U.S. Civil War organization P-140
Relief map. *see in index* Topographic map
Relief measures S-237. *see also* Fact Summary with each state article
Red Cross R-117, *picture* R-117
Roosevelt R-265, 269
Salvation Army S-33
Relief model, in maps M-116, 121, *picture* M-120
Relief printing, in printmaking G-230
'Religio Medici' (religion of a physician), contemplative soliloquy and religious treatise written by Sir Thomas Browne.
Religion R-143. *see also in index* Animal worship; Animism; God; Nature worship; Sun worship; chief religions and religious organizations by name
American Indians I-114, 128, 140, 150
Maya M-236
American literature A-341
ancestor worship A-402
art influenced by F-251, P-28
astrology A-708
bioethics B-214
birth control B-283
church and state C-408
death D-49
denominations, or sects R-143
Africa A-100
Asia A-683
Europe E-337
India I-67
North America N-341
United States, *chart* U-120
ecumenism E-69
education E-83
Enlightenment E-288
ethics and morality E-310
sexuality S-124
evolution E-364
fasting F-44
folk medicine F-270
folktales incorporated S-470, 476
foundations and charities F-330
hell and Hades H-123
holiness movement H-202
magic M-37
marriage M-149
minority groups M-459
monks and monasticism M-539
mythology
Egypt E-128
Olympic games O-543
nationalism N-66
oldest known shrine A-538
philosophy P-265
philosophy of history H-173
popular music M-683
puppets P-536
rug design R-314
sculpture S-82, 84, 93, 94
televised broadcasts T-73
totalitarianism T-234
totemism and taboo T-235
warfare W-18
women's organizations W-270
yoga Y-421
youth organizations Y-430
Religious festivals
athletic games A-737
Religious liberty. *see also in index* Huguenots; Martyrs; Puritans; Quakers; Reformation
American Colonies
Mayflower M-238
Pennsylvania P-173
Rhode Island R-183
English Toleration Act P-539
Spain S-356
U.S. Constitution U-151
Bill of Rights B-196
U.S.S.R. R-332e
Religious music. *see in index* Hymn
Religious News Service, organization that collects and relays news of religious matters N-238
Religious order, in Christianity M-539. *see also in index* chief orders by name, as Franciscans, Jesuits
Religious Society of Friends. *see in index* Quakers
Religious vocation M-539
'Reliques of Ancient English Poetry', work by Percy E-273
'Reliques of Irish Poetry', work by Brooke I-326
Relocation, in housing, *list* H-305
REM (rapid eye movement), phase of sleep
dreams D-257
Remagen, West Germany; city on the Rhine; important crossing for Allies in World War II; produces Apollinaris mineral water; pop. 14,150, *map* G-134
World War II W-342
Remarque, Erich Maria (1898–1970), U.S. novelist, born in Osnabrück, Germany; joined German infantry at 18; injury to hand prevented career as pianist; finally turned to writing; to U.S. 1939, became citizen 1947 ('All Quiet on the Western Front', 'The Road Back', and 'Three Comrades' depict life during World War I and postwar period; 'Flotsam'; 'Arch of Triumph'; 'Spark of Life'; 'The Night in Lisbon') W-28
'All Quiet on the Western Front' R-112d
German literature G-107
Rembrandt (in full Rembrandt Harmenszoon van Rijn) (1606–69), Dutch painter R-143
drawings D-253, *picture* D-254
graphic arts G-232
Jesus, *picture* J-104
painting P-43
'Portrait of a Lady', *picture* R-144
self-portrait, *picture* R-143
The Netherlands N-127
'Young Girl at an Open Half-Door' P-43

Revelstoke, John Baring, Baron (1863–1929), British financier, member famous Baring banking firm; director Bank of England; receiver general of Duchy of Cornwall 1908–29; expert on German reparations after World War I.

Revelstoke, B.C., city on Columbia River, 92 mi (148 km) n.e. of Kamloops and just s.w. of Mount Revelstoke National Park; skiing center; pop. 5,544, *map* C-109

'Revenge', British battleship S-177f

Revenue, income of a government derived from taxes of various kinds T-34. *see in index* Tariff; Taxation

Revenue Service, Internal. *see in index* Internal Revenue Service

Revenue sharing, in U.S., federal grants to states and localities to fund educational, public aid, public housing, and health care programs N-327

Reverberatory furnace, furnace with vaulted ceiling that deflects flame and heat.

Revere, Paul (1735–1818), U.S. Revolutionary War leader R-161
apprenticeship institution A-511
Boston B-373, *pictures* B-374, 375, M-188
information theory I-201, *picture* I-202
Lexington and Concord L-144
portrait by Copley P-49, *picture* P-48

Revere, Mass., residential city just n.e. of Boston; beach resort; printing, food processing; paper, optical goods; settled 1630; incorporated 1914; pop. 42,423.

Reverse osmosis, a membrane process for desalting water W-93

Reversible ceiling fan, *picture* F-24

Reversing falls, in Saint John, N.B. S-18
New Brunswick N-154

Reversion to type (or atavism), traits or body characteristics of a domesticated animal or plant like those of an ancestral type; due to transmission of recessive genes or gene mutation.

Revetment, protective facing of a levee F-184

'Review, The', newspaper by Defoe D-64
English literature E-270
magazine and journal M-32

Revival of Learning. *see in index* Renaissance

'Revival of the Religious Sciences, The', work by al-Ghazali G-141
Islamic literature I-366

Revolution, of planet P-350, *table* P-351
celestial bodies A-718
earth E-28, *diagram* S-254c

Revolution, of spacecraft S-343

Revolution, the overthrow of a government by the governed
Fabian Society F-2
terrorism T-114
warfare W-17, 27

Revolution, American R-162, *Reference-Outline* U-197a–b. *see also in index* names of leaders, states, and events
Abolitionist movement A-9
American Indians I-149
black Americans B-289
Bunker Hill B-502
Declaration of Independence D-53
democracy D-93
Detroit D-123
flags F-153, *pictures* F-155
frontier movements F-419
Gaspee burned R-183, *picture* R-185
Great Britain E-249
Cornwallis, *picture* V-337
naval power N-79
Stamp Act S-409
uniforms, *picture* P-48
guerrilla warfare G-301, M-139
international relations I-260
King's Mountain S-118
labor law L-4
Lexington and Concord L-144
Loyalist emigration. *see also in index* United Empire Loyalists
navy N-89
New York City N-280
outlaws O-619
political parties P-432
Saratoga Springs S-48
Turtle S-493
Valley Forge V-256, *picture* W-40
veterans granted benefits V-306
warfare W-17, 27, *list* W-13
wool W-291
Yorktown Y-424

Revolution, Chinese C-336, 370
Chiang Kai-shek C-309
Mao Zedong M-111

Revolution, French. *see in index* French Revolution

Revolution, Islamic (1979)
Iran I-307

Revolution, Latin America L-67

Revolution, Mexican. *see in index* Mexican Revolution

Revolution, Puritan. *see in index* Civil War, England

Revolution, Russian (1917) R-354. *see also in index* Bolshevik Revolution; Russian history
Harbin H-33
Kropotkin K-306
Lenin L-126
World War I W-309

Revolutionary Action Movement, a militant black American organization B-297

Revolutionary Alliance Society, formed in China by Sun Yat-sen in 1905.

Revolutionary Command Council (RCC), Libyan military officers who overthrew the monarchy in 1969 L-190

Revolutionary Tribunal, powerful court established by the National Convention during French Revolution; sentenced numerous persons charged with political offenses to guillotine without fair trial; suppressed 1795.

Revolutionary War. *see in index* Revolution, American

'Revolution Betrayed', work by Trotsky T-291

Revolution Garden, in Tashkent, U.S.S.R. T-31

Revolution of 1688, England. *see in index* Glorious Revolution

Revolution of 1830, the July Revolution in Paris, France, which drove out the Bourbons and was followed by revolts throughout Europe
France F-362

Revolution of 1848, movement that spread from France throughout most of Europe
Lassalle L-56
Prussia P-517

Revolution of 1905, Russia R-353

Revolution of 1910. *see in index* Mexican Revolution

Revolution of rising expectations, the drive of underdeveloped nations for improved living standards, education, and economic and industrial expansion; phrase first used by Adlai E. Stevenson.

Revolver, small firearm with revolving chambered cylinder
Colt C-587
machine gun M-12
shooting matches F-100, R-207, *pictures* F-97, 98

Revolving turret, armored structure on a warship N-83

Revson, Charles (1906–75), U.S. businessman
cosmetics C-730

Revue, musical show burlesquing current events; features songs, chorus dances, comedy skits
musical comedy M-685

Revueltas, Silvestre (1899–1940), Mexican violinist and composer, born in Santiago Papasquiaro, Mexico; compositions have a nationalistic flavor
classical music M-675

'Rewards and Fairies', work by Kipling K-249

Rexburg, Idaho, city 25 mi (40 km) n.e. of Idaho Falls; lumber; dairy products, sugar beets, potatoes; settled 1883; pop. 11,559, *map* I-29

Rey, Hans Augusto (pen name Uncle Gus) (born 1898), U.S. illustrator and author of children's books, born in Hamburg, Germany; in Brazil 1924–36; in Paris 1936–40; to U.S. 1940, citizen 1946 ('Cecily G. and the 9 Monkeys'; 'Find the Constellations'; 'Curious George' series).

Rey, Jean Max Georges (1902–83), Belgian lawyer and public official, born in Liège; officer of European Economic Community (EEC) 1958–, president of EEC Commission 1967–70.

Reyes, Alfonso (1889–1959), Mexican writer and diplomat, born in Monterrey; an outstanding figure in contemporary Latin American letters; noted as critic, essayist, poet, and historian, *picture* L-74

Reyes Basoalto, Neftalí Ricardo. *see in index* Neruda, Pablo

Reye's syndrome, acute disease of children that may follow certain viral infections, most frequently influenza and chicken pox; in most serious form, may result in accumulation of fat in the liver and potentially fatal swelling of the brain; cause unknown, but use of aspirin during viral infection may be contributing factor; no specific cure.

Reykjavík (or Reikjavík), Iceland, capital and largest city, on s.w. coast; university; port ice-free in winter; pop. 79,202 I-13, *picture* I-15, *map* E-361
National Day celebration, *picture* I-14
temperature I-11
thermal springs, *picture* I-12
University of Iceland I-12

Reyles, Carlos (1868–1938), Uruguayan writer, born in Montevideo L-70

Reymond, Jean (16th century), French enamelist; member of Limoges family of enamelers.

Reymont, Ladislas (1868–1925), Polish writer R-174. *see also in index* Nobel Prizewinners, *table*

Reynard the Fox (German Reineke Fuchs), popular character depicted in medieval Beast Epic and in later fables and stories H-273, S-475

Reynaud, Paul (1878–1966), French statesman, born in Barcelonette, near Digne; member Chamber of Deputies 1919 and 1928–40; held various cabinet posts 1930–40; premier March to June 1940; interned by Vichy regime 1940–43 and by Germans 1943–45; minister of finance and economic affairs July to late Aug. 1948; author of 'In the Thick of the Fight, 1930–45', memoirs.

Reynolds, John (1713–88), British naval officer, first royal governor of Georgia (1754–56); called first legislative assembly, established courts, but soon became despotic; returned to navy after recall.

Reynolds, Sir Joshua (1723–92), British portrait painter R-175
painting P-47
West W-150

Reynolds, Sir Osborne (1842–1912), British physicist, born in Belfast, Northern Ireland; professor of engineering at Owens College, Manchester, 1868–1905 A-76
hydraulics H-339
Reynolds number A-77

Reynolds, Quentin James (1902–65), U.S. journalist and writer, born in New York, N.Y.; associate editor *Colliers'* magazine 1933–45; war correspondent World War II (books for adults: 'Courtroom, the Story of Samuel S. Liebowitz', 'Minister of Death: the Adolf Eichmann Story', 'By Quentin Reynolds', autobiography; for younger readers: 'Wright Brothers', 'Custer's Last Stand', 'Winston Churchill')
'They Fought for the Sky' R-112d

Reynoldsburg, Ohio, village 17 mi (27 km) e. of Columbus, in agricultural area; meat products; pop. 20,661.

Reynolds family
heraldic shield, *picture* H-136

Reynolds number, in aerospace industry A-76
wind tunnel W-234

Rezaieh (formerly Urmia), Iran, city in n.w., near Lake Urmia; fruit, grain, cotton, tobacco; traditional birthplace of Zoroaster; pop. 110,749.

Reza Shah Pahlavi (or Reza Shah Pahlevi) (1877–1944), shah of Iran 1925–41; peasant army leader; took part in revolution of 1921; premier in 1923; on conquering north Persia in 1925 elected to throne; dethroned by Allies in World War II I-307
Tehran T-54

Rezonville, France, village in n.e.; involved in battle of Gravelotte (1870); pop. 205.

RFC. *see in index* Reconstruction Finance Corporation

Rhadamanthus, in Greek mythology, son of Zeus and Europa; brother of Minos, king of Crete; made one of judges in underworld.

Rhaetians, people of Rhaetia, an ancient Roman province including modern Grison and part of Tyrol S-544

Rhambha. *see in index* Devi

Rhapsodists, in ancient Greece, a group of men who made a profession of wandering about and reciting epic poetry, sometimes their own but more often that of Homer and other poets.

Rhapsody, in music, *list* M-671

'Rhapsody in Blue', work by Gershwin G-135
classical music M-677

Rhazes (AD 841–926), Arabian physician, born in Persia; a great clinician; first to realize need for sanitation in hospitals; prolific author of medical works M-282

Rhea, in Greek mythology R-176
Greek mythology M-700
Zeus Z-451

Rhea, South American bird A-577, B-277, R-176, *pictures* B-277

Rhea, fiber. *see in index* China grass

Rhead, Louis John (1857–1926), U.S. artist and author of books on fishing, born in England; illustrated children's classics.

Rhea Silvia, in Roman mythology, a vestal, mother of Romulus and Remus R-258

Rhee, Syngman (1875–1965), South Korean political leader, born in Whanghai Province, Korea; an anti-Japanese nationalist, he lived in exile 1910–45; first president of Republic of Korea 1948–52 (he was elected by national assembly); first popularly elected president 1952–60 K-287, K-296, *chart* K-299, *picture* K-288

Rheims, France. *see in index* Reims

Rheinberger, Joseph Gabriel (1839–1901), German organist and composer; one of most noted theory and organ teachers of his time; sonatas for organ, operas, overtures, symphonies.

Rheinfels, old German castle and fortress on Rhine River, about 18 mi (29 km) s.e. of Coblenz; ruins overlook town of Sankt Goar; built 13th century; laid waste by French 1797.

'Rheingold, Das' ('The Rhine Gold'), first opera in Wagner's series 'The Ring of the Nibelungs' ('Der Ring des Nibelungen') O-568

Rheinland-Pfalz, West Germany. *see in index* Rhineland-Palatinate

Rhein River, w. Europe. *see in index* Rhine River

Rheinstein castle, on Rhine, 19 mi (31 km) w. of Mainz, West Germany; across from Assmannhausen; dates from 13th century; restored in early 19th century.

Rhenium (Re), chemical element, discovered 1925
periodic table, *table* P-207, *list* P-208

Rheostat (or variable resistor), device for introducing varying and known resistance into a circuit for controlling the amount of electric current.

'Rhesus', drama by Euripides G-275

Rhesus factor. *see in index* Rh factor

Rhesus monkey A-503, *picture* I-65

Rhetoric R-176
creative writing. *see in index* Writing, creative
debates D-51
education E-82
Gettysburg Address L-222
Islamic literature I-366

Sophists. *see in index* Sophists
'Rhetoric', work by Aristotle C-467
Rhett, William (fl. 1700), North American sailor S-310
Rheumatic fever, inflammatory disease probably caused by bacterial infection; damages connective tissue of the heart and joints
heart H-98
infectious disease D-173, *table* D-172
Rheumatic heart disease, damage to the muscle and valves of the heart resulting from rheumatic fever.
Rheumatoid arthritis (RA), chronic diseases of the connective tissue, causing painful sensations in joints and muscles A-650
cause D-168
metabolic disease D-181
Rh factor (or Rhesus factor), blood B-316, L-27
Landsteiner L-27
Rhine, Confederation of the, in German history G-122
'Rhine Gold, The' (German 'Das Rheingold'), first opera in Wagner's series 'The Ring of the Nibelungs' (Der Ring des Nibelungen') O-568
Rhine-Herne Canal R-177, *picture* C-128
Rhineland-Palatinate (German Rheinland-Pfalz), state in West Germany; pop. 3,665,800, *map* G-134
Rhine-Main-Danube Canal, canal, West Germany; scheduled for use by 1992 G-118
waterway W-108
Rhine River (German Rhein), w. Europe, rising in Swiss Alps and flowing 850 mi (1,370 km) n. to North Sea; one of best developed inland waterways in world R-177
Europe E-345, *map* E-361, *picture* E-346
France F-343, *map* F-372
Germany G-111, *map* G-134
Black Forest B-305
Bonn B-344
Cologne C-547
pesticide fish-kill, *picture* P-441c
Switzerland S-540, *map* S-537, *picture* S-542
The Netherlands N-125, 129
waterway W-108
Rhinestone. *see in index* Brilliant
Rhinitis, medical term applying to any inflammation of the mucous lining of the nose; "common cold" an acute form of rhinitis.
Rhinoceros R-178
animal life record, *table* E-24
hair H-7
hoof H-231
Indonesian species I-159
length of life, average, *chart* A-423
prehistoric ancestor A-462, *picture* A-460
Rhinoceros auklet, seabird A-763
Rhinoceros beetle B-138
Rhinoceros bird. *see in index* Tick bird
Rhinotracheitis, common upper respiratory infection in cats C-210
Rhizobia, bacteria of the genus *Rhizobium* B-13, L-118, *picture* B-14
nitric acid N-318
Rhizoid, rootlet in primitive plants
liverwort L-262
mold M-519
moss M-599
Rhizomes. *see in index* Rootstocks
Rhizopoda, class of Protozoa P-515
Rhodanthe, annual plant *Helipterum manglesii* of the composite family, native to Australia; grows to 18 in. (46 cm); hairy; flower heads are white to pink; used as everlastings; also called Swan River everlasting.
Rhode Island, New England state, smallest in U.S.; 1,214 sq mi (3,144 sq km); cap. Providence; pop. 947,154 R-179, *maps* N-351, U-41, 44
Brown University P-516
cities. *see in index* Providence and other cities by name
name, *table* S-428
New England U-43, *pictures* U-45, *Reference-Outline* U-133
population density, *chart* P-261b
slave trade P-515
state symbols
bird P-483, *picture* P-481
flags F-154, *pictures* F-155, 160
flower, *pictures* S-427, P-358
Statuary Hall S-437a, *table* S-437b
taxation, *tables* T-37, 39
Williams W-208
Rhode Island, University of, in Kingston, R.I.; state control; founded 1892; arts and sciences, agriculture, business administration, education, engineering, home economics, library science, nursing, oceanography, pharmacy; graduate school; off-campus center at Providence R-182, *picture* R-187
Rhode Island College, in Providence, R.I.; state control; founded 1854; liberal arts, education; graduate study R-182
Rhode Island Red, breed of fowl P-480, 482, R-186, *picture* P-481
state bird, *picture* R-186
Rhode Island School of Design, in Providence, R.I.; private control; established 1877; architecture, art, landscape architecture; graduate studies R-183
Rhodes, Cecil (in full Cecil John Rhodes) (1853–1902), British South African financier and statesman R-195
Boers' opposition S-267
home, *picture* S-266
Kruger K-306
Zambia Z-448
Zimbabwe Z-453
Rhodes, Eugene Manlove (1869–1934), U.S. writer, born in Tecumseh, Neb.; cowboy in New Mexico for 25 years; best known for Western stories ('Good Men and True'; 'Copper Streak Trail'; 'Once in the Saddle'; 'A Bar Cross Man', autobiography and writings).
Rhodes, James Ford (1848–1927), U.S. historian, born in Cleveland, Ohio ('History of the United States from the Compromise of 1850'; 'History of the Civil War, 1861–1865').
Rhodes, Zandra (born 1940), British fashion designer, exponent of punk D-271
Rhodes (Italian Rodi), easternmost of Aegean islands; principal island of the Dodecanese (Greece); area 542 sq mi (1,404 sq km); pop. 87,831 R-195
Europe, *map* E-361
Greece G-255
medieval banner, *picture* M-384
Rhodes, city on island of Rhodes R-196
Rhodesgrass, perennial plant *Chloris gayana* of the grass family, native to Africa but naturalized in s. U.S.; grows to 4 ft (1.2 m); leaves narrow, 12 in. (30 cm) long; flower clusters consist of many spikes at top of stem; used as hay.
Rhodesia. *see in index* Zimbabwe
Rhodesia, Northern. *see in index* Zambia
Rhodesia and Nyasaland, Federation of, former federation. *see in index* Malawi; Zambia
Rhodesian man, human ancestor M-89
Rhodesian ridgeback, dog, *picture* D-200
Rhodes scholars R-195
Rhodium (Rh), chemical element
periodic table, *table* P-207, *list* P-208
platinum P-384
Rhodochrosite. *see in index* Manganese carbonate
Rhododendron, flowering shrub R-196
state flower of Washington and West Virginia, *pictures* S-427, W-172
Rhodolite, rose red variety of pyrope garnet found in Macon County, Georgia; used as a gem J-116
Rhodonite, pale red triclinic mineral, essentially a manganese silicate, $MnSiO_3$, manganese spar; found in Harz Mountains of Germany, Urals of Russia, in Hungary, Italy, and Sweden; used for ornamental stone, especially in Russia.
Rhodope Mountains, mountain system of s. Bulgaria, extending into n.e. Greece; highest point 9,596 ft (2,925 m) B-498, *map* E-361
Rhodopsin. *see in index* Visual purple
Rhombic dodecahedron, in mathematics
geometry G-79
Rhombus, geometric figure that forms an equilateral parallelogram; distinguished from a trapezoid and a kite
geometry G-74, *diagram* G-75
Rhondda, Wales, city 17 mi (27 km) n.w. of Cardiff; coal mining; electronic equipment, clothing, furniture; pop. 94,300.
Rhône-Marseilles Canal, in France R-198
Rhône River, river of Europe rising in Swiss Alps and flowing through s.e. France 500 mi (800 km) to Mediterranean R-196
Europe, *map* E-361
France F-343, *map* F-372
Geneva G-58
Switzerland, *map* S-537
Rhubarb, plant R-198
Rhumb line, line on the surface of the earth that follows a single compass bearing and makes equal oblique angles with all meridians
navigation N-69
Rhyme, in poetry P-404
nursery rhymes. *see in index* Nursery rhymes
Rhymer's Club, literary club Y-412
Rhynchocephalia, order of lizard-like reptiles, extinct but for one species *Sphenodon punctatum*, commonly called the sphenodon or tuatara R-152
Rhyolite, picturesque Nevada ghost town, *picture* N-142
Rhyolite, lightweight lava L-89
earth E-20
minerals M-437
Rhys, Ernest (1859–1946), British author, born in London, of Welsh parents; edited 'Everyman's Library' 1906–16; wrote books on Welsh folklore, poetry ('Welsh Ballads'; 'The Leaf Burners').
Rhythm
design D-109
music M-666, 690, *list* M-671
poetry P-403
Rhythm and blues, style of popular music M-680
Rhythmic gymnastics G-323
Rhythmic progression, in mathematics
design D-109
Rhythm method, form of birth control B-283
menstruation M-300
Ri, a Japanese unit of measure, *table* W-141
Riad, El, Saudi Arabia. *see in index* Riyadh
Rialto, Calif., residential city 47 mi (76 km) n.e. of Los Angeles; in citrus area; asphalt; incorporated 1911; pop. 35,615.
Rialto, bridge in Venice, Italy V-277, B-445
Rib, in anatomy, a slender curved bone attached to the spine and forming part of the chest wall; of the 24 ribs, the upper 7 pairs are called true ribs because they are attached to the vertebrae and directly to the sternum; the lower 5 pairs are false ribs, so called because they are not directly attached to the sternum; any of the two lowest pairs, which are attached only to the vertebrae, are called floating ribs S-209, *diagram* S-210
lungs L-336
Ribaut, Jean (or Jean Ribault) (1520–65), French Huguenot navigator; as agent of Coligny established Protestant colony on Parris Island, near Port Royal, S.C. (1562) and later aided Fort Caroline settlement on St. Johns River, Florida; slaughtered, with most of his men, by Menéndez S-309
Ribbentrop, Joachim von (1893–1946), German foreign minister, born in Wesel (Rhineland); in business in Canada 1910–14; in German army 1914–20; made ambassador to England 1936; appointed foreign minister 1938; negotiated pact with Russia 1939; hanged for war crimes Oct. 1946
World War II, *picture* W-323
Ribbon Fall, highest uninterrupted waterfall in Yosemite National Park; 1,612 ft (491 m)
waterfall W-98
Ribbon microphone M-378
Ribbon seal S-100
Ribbon snake S-226c, *picture* S-225
Ribbon worm, worm of the Nemertea phylum W-361, *picture* W-362
Ribera, José (or Giuseppe Ribera, or Lo Spagnoletto meaning "little Spaniard") (1588–1656), Spanish painter; a leader of Neapolitan school in Italy.
Ribicoff, Abraham Alexander (born 1910), U.S. lawyer and public official, born in New Britain, Conn.; judge Hartford police court 1941–43 and 1945–47; U.S. congressman 1949–53; governor of Connecticut 1955–61; U.S. secretary of health, education, and welfare 1961–62; U.S. senator 1963–; author of 'Politics: the American Way', with Jon O. Newman.
Ribknit, a fabric K-260
Riboflavin, vitamin B_2 V-355, 358
Ribonuclease, enzyme, *table* E-290
Ribonucleic acid. *see in index* RNA
Ribosome, protein-assembling site in a cell C-238
embryology E-202
enzymes E-290
genetics G-56, *diagram* G-57
Ribot, Alexandre Félix Joseph (1842–1923), French statesman; minister of foreign affairs, of finance, premier; active in furthering Franco-Russian alliance.
Ribot, Théodule Armand (1839–1916), French psychologist; emphasized physical element of mental activity; founded and edited *Revue Philosophique*; enormously influenced other French psychologists.
Ribwort. *see in index* Plantain
Ricard, Jérôme Sixtus (1850–1930), Jesuit priest and astronomer, born in France; came to U.S. in 1873; taught at and became a trustee of University of Santa Clara, Calif.; believed that weather could be forecast long in advance by noting sunspots and was extremely successful in forecasting by this method.
Ricardo, David (1772–1823), British economist and financier R-198
Ricardo, Joaquín Vidella Balaguer y. *see in index* Balaguer y Ricardo, Joaquín Vidella
Ricci, Matteo (1552–1610), Italian Jesuit missionary and writer R-198
China C-368
Riccio, David. *see in index* Rizzio
Rice, Alexander Hamilton (1875–1956), U.S. geographer and physician, born in Boston, Mass.; professor Harvard University 1930–52.
Rice, Alice Hegan (or Mrs. Cale Young Rice) (1870–1942), U.S. novelist, born in Shelbyville, Ky. ('Mrs. Wiggs of the Cabbage Patch', tale of an optimist).
Rice, Dan (1823–1900), U.S. clown, possible inspiration for Uncle Sam cartoons C-428
Rice, Edgar Charles (nickname Sam) (1892–1974), U.S. baseball player, born in Morocco, Ind.; pitcher, Washington, A.L., 1915, but next an outfielder, Washington, A.L., 1916–33, Cleveland, A.L., 1934; hit .300 or better in each of 14 seasons (best was .350 in 1925); total hits 2,987; had lifetime batting average of .322; made 12 hits in World Series of 1925.
Rice, Elmer Lewis (formerly Elmer Reizenstein) (1892–1967), U.S. playwright, born in New York, N.Y.; graduate of New York Law School (plays: 'On Trial', 'American Landscape'; novel: 'The Show Must Go On'; essays: 'The Living Theatre'; autobiography: 'Minority Report') A-356
Rice, Henry Grantland (1880–1954), U.S. sportswriter,

born in Murfreesboro, Tenn.; best known for syndicated column, 'The Sportlight' (autobiography, 'The Tumult and the Shouting'; verse).

Rice, Henry Mower (1817–94), U.S. Democratic leader, born in Waitsfield, Vt.; influential with American Indians in territory of Minnesota; one of first two senators from new state
Statuary Hall, *table* S-437b

Rice, James (1843–82), British novelist; collaborated with Sir Walter Besant ('Ready-Money Mortiboy'; 'The Golden Butterfly'; 'The Seamy Side').

Rice, Luther (1783–1836), U.S. missionary to India and founder of *The Columbian Star* B-77

Rice, a cereal R-199
flour B-428, F-213
food value S-424
grains G-207
growing, *picture* A-133
producing regions
Burma I-353
Guyana G-321
Indochina V-318, *picture* V-317
Japan J-28, 37, *chart* J-38
Kampuchea K-169
Korea K-276, *tables* K-277, 289
Louisiana L-310
Philippines P-255d, *pictures* P-256, 257b
South Carolina S-311
Thailand T-146
starch S-424
vitamins V-355, 357
wine. *see in index* Sake

Ricebird, common name of a number of beautiful Oriental birds; including the Java sparrow, a cage bird, and other members of the Ploceidae family that feed on rice.

Rice rat R-95

Rice University (formerly Rice Institute), in Houston, Tex.; opened 1912; originally endowed by William Marsh Rice with his entire fortune of $10,000,000; arts and sciences, architecture, engineering, physical education; graduate studies H-310

Rich, Adrienne (born 1929), U.S. poet A-363

Rich, Buddy (died 1987), jazz drummer

Richard I (or Richard the Lion-Hearted, or Richard Coeur de Lion) (1157–99), king of England R-201
Austrian imprisonment A-828
Eleanor of Aquitaine E-144
England E-241
Henry II H-129
John of England J-124
Robin Hood legends R-224
Third Crusade C-787

Richard II (1367–1400), king of England R-202
Chaucer C-283
England E-243
Henry IV H-129, R-203
Shakespeare's play S-133, S-139
Tyler T-335

Richard III (1452–85), king of England R-203
Edward V E-107
England E-243
Shakespeare's play S-133, S-135
Tudor, House of T-304

Richard, brother of Edward V, *picture* E-245

Richard, Gabriel (1767–1832), French Roman Catholic missionary, Michigan pioneer; fled Revolution-torn France to labor first among French and American Indians in Illinois, then in Detroit province, including Michigan and Wisconsin territory; tried to restrain liquor traffic of trading posts, opened schools, imported first printing press and looms; delegate to Congress 1822–24
Michigan M-360

Richard of Wyche, Saint (1197?–1253), English saint and bishop of Chichester; festival April 3.

Richards, Dickinson Woodruff (1895–1973), U.S. physician, born in Orange, N.J.; on faculty Columbia University 1928–61; joined staff Presbyterian Hospital, New York, N.Y., 1928, attending physician 1945–61. *see also in index* Nobel Prizewinners, *table*

Richards, Ellen Henrietta (1842–1911), U.S. pioneer of home economics movement, born in Dunstable, Mass.; instructor at Massachusetts Institute of Technology ('Chemistry of Cooking and Cleaning'; 'The Cost of Living')
home economics H-215

Richards, Laura Elizabeth (1850–1943), U.S. author, born in Boston, Mass.; daughter of Julia Ward Howe; stories for children, girls' stories, and biographies of famous women ('Florence Nightingale'; 'Margaret Montfort'; 'Captain January'; 'Hildegarde' series).

Richards, Theodore William (1868–1928), U.S. physical chemist, born in Germantown, Pa.; taught at Harvard University from 1894. *see also in index* Nobel Prizewinners, *table*

Richards, Sir William Buell (1815–89), Canadian jurist, born in Brockville, Ont.; served on Court of Common Pleas 1853–75, chief justice 1863–75; first chief justice Canadian Supreme Court 1875–79.

Richardson, Dorothy M. (or Mrs. Alan Odle) (1882–1957), British novelist, born in Abingdon, England ('Pilgrimage', 12 novels).

Richardson, Elliot Lee (born 1920), U.S. lawyer and public official, born in Boston, Mass.; lieutenant governor Massachusetts 1965–67, attorney general 1967–69; U.S. undersecretary of state 1969–70; secretary HEW 1970–73; secretary of defense, U.S. attorney general 1973; ambassador to United Kingdom 1975; secretary of commerce 1975–77; ambassador at large 1977–
Nixon N-326

Richardson, Henry Handel (pen name of Ethel Florence Lindesay Richardson, or Henrietta Richardson, or Mrs. John C. Robertson) (1870–1946), Australian novelist, born in Melbourne; lived in London; famous for 'Ultima Thule' (1929), closing volume of a trilogy on Australian life entitled 'The Fortunes of Richard Mahoney' (first 2 vols.: 'Australia Felix' and 'The Way Home') A-797, *table* A-798

Richardson, Henry Hobson (1838–86), U.S. architect, born in St. James Parish, La.; revived Romanesque influence; also pioneered indigenous U.S. style B-562, 569

Richardson, John (1796–1852), Canadian writer, born in Queenston, Ont.; served in Canadian militia in War of 1812.

Richardson, Owen Willans (1879–1959), British physicist, born in Dewsbury, Yorkshire, England; professor Princeton University 1906–14, at King's College, London, 1914–44. *see also in index* Nobel Prizewinners, *table*

Richardson, Ralph David (1902–83), British actor of stage and screen, born in Cheltenham, England; knighted 1947; successful stage roles include Peer Gynt and Falstaff.

Richardson, Samuel (1689–1761), British novelist and printer, born in Derbyshire; known for character analysis ('Pamela'; 'Clarissa'; 'Sir Charles Grandison') E-271
epistolary novel N-411

Richardson, Tex., city 11 mi (18 km) n.e. of Dallas; electronic components; pop. 72,496.

Richardson Trophy, annual award by Golf Writers Association for the most important nonplaying contribution to golf.

Richberg, Donald Randall (1881–1960), U.S. lawyer and public official, born in Knoxville, Tenn.; defended labor against corporations; coauthor Railway Labor Act (1926) and NIRA (1933); general counsel NRA 1933–34; head of NRA policy committee 1934–35.

Richelieu, Cardinal (1585–1642), French churchman and statesman R-203
academy A-14
cat C-212, *list* C-202
literary works F-395
Louis XIII L-305
Thirty Years' War T-170
Gustavus Adolphus G-319

Richelieu River, in Quebec Province, outlet of Lake Champlain connecting with St. Lawrence River at Lake St. Peter; about 80 mi (130 km) long; explored by Champlain; route of early explorers.

Richepin, Jean (1849–1926), French poet, dramatist, novelist; vigorous, outspoken style (verse: 'Les Caresses, 'Les Blasphèmes'; novels: 'Grandes amoureuses', 'Flamboche'; plays: 'Nana Sahib', 'Le Chemineau', 'Don Quichotte').

Richet, Charles (1850–1935), French physiologist, born in Paris; professor of physiology University of Paris. *see also in index* Nobel Prizewinners, *table*

Richfield, Minn., village 6 mi (10 km) s. of Minneapolis; metal products; pop. 37,851 M-442

Richland, Wash., city 9 mi (15 km) n.w. of Pasco, on Columbia River; first incorporated as a town 1910, acquired by federal government 1942, expanded 1943–45 to house workers on Atomic Energy Commission project, returned to private control and incorporated as a city 1958; pop. 33,578 W-50, *maps* U-40

Richler, Mordecai (born 1931), Canadian author (adult novels: 'The Apprenticeship of Duddy Kravitz', 'Cocksure'; children's book: 'Jacob Two-Two Meets the Hooded Fang', winner of Canadian Books of the Year for Children award 1976) C-123

Richmond, Grace Smith (1866–1959), U.S. novelist and short-story writer, born in Pawtucket, R.I. ('Red Pepper Burns'; 'Red and Black'; 'The Listening Post').

Richmond, Calif., city on San Francisco Bay, 8 mi (13 km) n.e. of San Francisco; pop. 74,676 R-204

Richmond, Ind., city in agricultural area, 68 mi (109 km) e. of Indianapolis; farm machinery, machine tools, automotive equipment, lawn mowers, clothing; Earlham College; settled early 19th century by Friends; pop. 41,349
Indiana, *map* I-102

Richmond, Ky., city about 24 mi (39 km) s.e. of Lexington; tobacco and livestock market; ordnance, small light bulbs; Eastern Kentucky University; decisive victory of Confederates under Gen. E. Kirby Smith 1862; pop. 21,705.

Richmond, Va., state capital and 2nd largest city, situated on James River; pop. 219,214 R-204, *maps* I-94, N-351, V-349, 331, 336, U-41
Civil War C-474, *map* C-475
Confederate States of America C-642
Monument Avenue, *picture* V-332
Williamsburg W-209

Richmond, borough of New York, N.Y.; coextensive with Staten Island; pop. 352,121.

Richmond, University of, in Richmond, Va.; Baptist; Richmond College for men (founded as academy 1830, college 1840, present name 1920) and Westhampton College for women (opened 1914) are coordinate colleges; arts and sciences, business administration, law; coeducational in graduate and professional schools.

Richmond College, in New York, N.Y.; part of City University of New York; municipal control; founded 1965; liberal arts, education; graduate school.

Richmond Heights, Mo., residential city adjoining St. Louis on the west; on Daniel Boone Expressway; incorporated in 1913; pop. 5,449.

Richmond upon Thames, England, s.w. borough of Greater London; residential suburb; established 1965; pop. 170,000, *map* L-207

Richter, Burton (born 1931), U.S. physicist, born in New York City; Stanford University 1956–, professor 1967–; headed group at Stanford Linear Accelerator Center-Lawrence Berkeley Laboratory, which discovered the subatomic J (psi) particle. *see also in index* Nobel Prizewinners, *table*

Richter, Conrad (1890–1968), U.S. writer, born in Pine Grove, Pa.; known for novels of frontier life (trilogy: 'The Trees', 'The Fields', 'The Town', 1951 Pulitzer prize; 'The Lady'; 'A Simple Honorable Man'; 'A Country of Strangers')
'The Light in the Forest' R-112

Richter, Hans (1843–1916), Austrian musical conductor, born in Hungary; conducted in Vienna, Bayreuth, London, and other cities; closely associated with Richard Wagner and authority on his music.

Richter, Hieronymus Theodor (1824–98), German metallurgist; discoverer, with Ferdinand Reich, of indium.

Richter, Johann Paul Friedrich (pseudonym Jean Paul) (1763–1825), German novelist and humorist; quite popular in his own time but now little read because of his rather baffling style ('Quintus Fixlein'; 'Flegeljahre', translated as 'Wild Oats'; 'Titan').

Richter Magnitude Scale, instrument conceived by C. F. Richter in 1935
earthquake measurement E-38

Richthofen, Ferdinand, Baron von (1833–1905), German geographer, born in Karlsruhe; professor at universities of Bonn, Leipzig, and Berlin.

Richthofen, Manfred, Baron von (1892–1918), German fighter pilot, born in Breslau; known as the **Red Baron** after the color of his plane; shot down 80 Allied aircraft in World War I before being killed in aerial combat by Capt. Roy Brown of the Royal Air Force A-208

Rickard, George Lewis (nickname Tex) (1871–1929), U.S. prizefighter and promoter, born in Kansas City, Mo.; colorful early career as rancher and gambler in Texas, Alaska, and South America B-391

Rickenbacker, Eddie (in full Edward Vernon Rickenbacker) (1890–1973), U.S. aviator, born in Columbus, Ohio; noted as automobile racer; commander first U.S. aero unit to take active part in World War I; credited with 26 victories and recognized as U.S. leading ace in World War I; was awarded the Medal of Honor; head of Eastern Air Lines 1934–63; lost in s.w. Pacific for 3 weeks when plane was forced down Oct. 21, 1942, while he was on inspection trip of United States Air Forces in Pacific A-208

Ricker College, in Houlton, Me.; Baptist; founded 1848, senior college 1949; liberal arts.

Rickets, disease of childhood in which bones remain soft, producing deformities; caused by deficiency in diet B-342, F-279
vitamin D prevents V-354, 357

Ricketts, Charles (1866–1931), British painter, sculptor, stage designer, engraver, and printer, born in Geneva, Switzerland; coeditor *The Dial* 1889–97; designed types used by his private (Vale) press 1896–1904.

Ricketts, John William (died 1799), British circus manager, introduced the circus to the U.S. C-423

Rickettsia, a disease-producing microorganism
Burnett B-512
Rocky Mountain spotted fever. *see in index* Rocky Mountain spotted fever
typhus fever P-114
vaccine V-251

Rickey, Wesley Branch (1881–1965), U.S. baseball executive, born in Stockdale, Ohio; with St. Louis, N.L., 1917–42 (won 6 pennants, 4 world titles); president and general manager Brooklyn, N.L., 1942–50 (won 2 pennants); general manager Pittsburgh, N.L., 1950–55, board chairman 1955–59; founded farm system 1919; signed Jackie Robinson 1945, first black player in major leagues B-95

Rickover, Hyman George (1900–86), U.S. Navy officer, born in Makow, Russian Poland; to U.S. 1906; head of electrical section U.S. Bureau of Ships 1940–45; directed Navy project that developed

the *Nautilus* 1947–54; chief of Naval Reactors Branch of U.S. Atomic Energy Commission 1949–; retired as vice admiral 1964 but continued on active duty as assistant chief for nuclear propulsion; won Enrico Fermi Award 1964; author of 'American Education: a National Failure'
Carter C-180
nuclear energy N-425

Ricksha. *see in index* Jinrikisha

Ridderzaal (or Hall of Knights), in The Hague, The Netherlands H-4

Riddles R-205
African A-121
word games W-292

Ride, Sally Kristen (born 1951), first U.S. woman astronaut; born in Los Angeles, Calif.; selected as astronaut candidate by NASA in 1978; served as mission specialist on space shuttle *Challenger* in April 1983, S-347, *picture* F-107, *table* S-348
women's rights, *picture* W-271

Rideau Canal, in Canada C-129
Ottawa O-612, 615

Rideau Lake, in Ontario, at summit level of Rideau Canal; 21 mi (34 km) long; outlets in Ottawa River through Rideau River and in Lake Ontario through Cataraqui River.

Rideau River, river in Ontario, stream flowing n. to Ottawa River.

Rider, an addition to U.S. congressional bills V-307

Rider College, in suburban locality just n. of Trenton, N.J.; private control; founded 1865; liberal arts and sciences, business administration, education; graduate school.

'Riders of the Purple Sage', work by Grey W-152

'Riders to the Sea', work by Synge I-327

Ridge, Lola (1883–1941), U.S. poet, born in Dublin, Ireland; spent childhood in Australia and New Zealand; moved to U.S. 1907; verse shows intense sympathy for the laboring and oppressed classes ('The Ghetto'; 'Sun-Up'; 'Firehead'; 'Dance of Fire').

Ridge, Major (1771?–1839), Cherokee Indian, born in Tennessee; name derived from military rank in Creek War; farmer, trader, and leader of his people; in defiance of tribal law and probably with prospect of gain signed treaty (1835) ceding to U.S. all Cherokee lands e. of Mississippi; killed by opponents of treaty.

Ridge, a geologic structure M-634

Ridge-and-valley region, in Appalachian Highlands U-36
anthracite beds U-55
Appalachia A-508

Ridgefield, Conn., residential town and summer resort 16 mi (26 km) s. of Danbury; electronic equipment; scene of Revolutionary War battle 1777; pop. of township 20,120.

Ridgefield, N.J., borough 7 mi (11 km) e. of Passaic and n. of Jersey City; chemicals, food processing, metal products; pop. 10,294.

Ridgefield Park, N.J., village on Hackensack River, 5 mi (8 km) e. of Passaic and 8 mi (13 km) n. of Jersey City; paper products; pop. 12,738.

Ridgepole
log cabin P-331

Ridges, under ocean O-460, *picture* O-462

Ridge soaring, method of flying gliders G-166, *diagram* G-168

Ridgewood, N.J., residential village 5 mi (8 km) n.e. of Paterson; oil burners, diaphragm pumps, cement blocks; pop. 25,208.

Ridgway, Matthew Bunker (born 1895), U.S. Army general, born in Fort Monroe, Va.; prominent in airborne services World War II; commanded U.S. 8th Army in Korea Dec. 1950–April 1951, when he replaced Gen. Douglas MacArthur in all commands, including Allied occupation of Japan and UN operations in Korea; became 4-star general May 1951; commander North Atlantic Treaty Organization 1952–53; Army chief of staff 1953–55; retired 1955; author of 'Soldier', memoirs, and 'The Korean War' K-298, *chart* K-299
Truman T-299

Ridgway, Robert (1850–1929), U.S. ornithologist, born in Mt. Carmel, Ill.; curator division of birds, United States National Museum, Washington, D.C., 1880–1929 ('The Birds of North and Middle America').

Riding, Laura (born 1901), U.S. poet and critic, born in New York, N.Y.; experimental poetry ('Collected Poems'; 'A Survey of Modernist Poetry', with British poet Robert Graves; 'A Trojan Ending', novel).

Ridley, Nicholas (1500?–55), English Protestant reformer, bishop of Rochester; arrested upon Mary's accession to the throne; burned for heresy. *see also in index* Latimer, Hugh

Ridley, Pa., Delaware County, urban township 10 mi (16 km) s.w. of Philadelphia; main borough Ridley Park; chiefly residential; pop. 7,889.

Ridley turtle, a sea turtle T-330

Ridpath, John Clark (1840–1900), U.S. historian and educator, born in Putnam County, Indiana; wrote large number of histories, in popular style ('History of the United States'; 'Ridpath's History of the World').

Riebeeck, Jan Anthony van (1618–77), Dutch East India Company official; founded what became Cape Town, South Africa S-266

Riefenstahl, Leni (1902–), film actress, dancer, born in Berlin, Germany; best known for her Nazi documentaries which she made at the personal request of Hitler, including 'Olympiad', a film of the 1936 Olympic Games in Munich M-628

Riegger, Wallingford (1885–1961), U.S. composer, born in Albany, Ga.; early works conventional, later ones atonal; best known for 'With My Red Fires' and other music for modern dance; also choral works, orchestral works, and chamber music.

Riel, Louis (1844–85), French-Canadian leader of two rebellions in Canada; tried for treason and executed
Canada C-101
Manitoba M-103
Red River of the North R-120
Saskatchewan S-49a
Strathcona S-484b
Thompson T-173

Riemann, Georg Friedrich Bernhard (1826–66), German mathematician, born in Breselenz, Hanover; professor University of Göttingen (Germany) 1859–66.

Riemenschneider, Tilman (or Meister Dill, or Meister Till) (1465?–1531), German sculptor, one of the greatest of his day; as burgomaster of Würzburg worked for Reformation and political freedom; known for statues and wood carvings in churches of Bavaria.

Rienzi, Cola di (1313–54), Roman revolutionist; overthrew aristocracy and attempted to reestablish Roman republic and world rule; hero of Bulwer-Lytton's 'Rienzi, the Last of the Roman Tribunes'.

'Rienzi', opera by Wagner W-2
opera O-567

Riesenberg, Felix (1879–1939), U.S. writer, engineer, and nautical authority, born in Milwaukee, Wis.; sailor 1896–1907; degree in civil engineering Columbia University 1911; became lieutenant commander in World War I ('Standard Seamanship'; 'East Side, West Side'; 'Mother Sea'; 'The Pacific Ocean').

Riesengebirge. *see in index* Giant Mountains

Riesling grape G-220

Riesman, David (born 1909), U.S. sociologist and lawyer, born in Philadelphia, Pa.; professor of social science University of Chicago 1949–58, Harvard after 1958 ('The Lonely Crowd'; coauthor of 'The Academic Revolution').

Riessener, Jean-Henri (1734–1806), French furniture maker
furniture F-462

Rietschel, Ernst (1804–61), German sculptor of Dresden school; noted for portraits (Luther monument, Worms; Goethe-Schiller monument, Weimar) and gable groups for the University of Leipzig and the Berlin Opera House.

Rietveld, Gerrit (1888–1964), Dutch designer and architect
furniture, *list* F-462

Riff, Er, low mountain chain in n.e. Morocco near Mediterranean Sea; highest point Jebel Tidirhine, 8,058 ft (2,456 m); occupied by Riff Berbers or Riffians; name given to district.

Riffle, in fishing, *list* F-146

Rifle, a firearm F-98
jet propulsion, *diagram* J-106
National Rifle and Pistol Matches R-206
warfare W-20

Riflery and marksmanship R-206
hunting safety guidelines H-331
mirage M-464
Oakley O-453
police training, *picture* P-430
Canada, *picture* P-430a

Rift, a normal geological fault G-72
continental development C-690
Nicaragua N-303

Rig, arrangement of sails, masts, and lines of a sailing vessel B-230, *diagram* S-166, *pictures* S-165, 229
early development S-164

Riga, Latvian Soviet Socialist Republic, capital, Baltic port at mouth of Western Dvina River; pop. 732,500 R-207, *maps* R-344, 348
Europe, *map* E-361

Riga, Gulf of, inlet of Baltic Sea between Latvian and Estonian Soviet Socialist Republics; 100 by 60 mi (160 by 100 km); receives Western Dvina River; named for city of Riga, *maps* R-344, 348

Riga, Treaty of, treaty between Russia and Poland signed March 18, 1921; Poland gained about 44,000 sq mi (114,000 sq km) P-414, *table* T-275

Rigel, fixed star S-414, *charts* S-415, 421, 423

Riggs, Bobby (born 1918), U.S. tennis player
tennis T-107

Riggs, Kate Douglas. *see in index* Wiggin, Kate Douglas

Riggs, Lynn (1899–1954), U.S. playwright and poet, born near Claremore, Okla. (plays of Southwest: 'Green Grow the Lilacs', basis of musical comedy 'Oklahoma!', 'Russet Mantle', and 'The Cherokee Night'; poems: 'The Iron Dish').

Righi, Augusto (1850–1920), Italian physicist, professor at Bologna University; made original researches in magnetism, electricity, and light.

Right, direction D-156, *picture* D-157

Right, in European politics P-434

Right, in finance S-451

Right angle, in mathematics
geometry G-73, *diagram* G-73

Right ascension. *see in index* Ascension, right

Right face, military command W-22

'Right Royal', work by Masefield H-273

'Rights of Man', book by Paine P-21

'Right Stuff, The', work by Wolfe A-361

Right trapezoid, in mathematics
geometry G-76, *diagram* G-75

Right triangle, in mathematics
geometry G-74
trigonometry T-287, *diagram* T-285

Right whale, mammal *Balaena glacialis* of the order Cetacea W-185

Rigidity, in physics G-327

'Rigoletto', opera by Verdi V-282
opera O-567

Rig Veda, Hindu epic H-157
India A-405, I-76
Indian literature I-105

'Rihlah', work by Ibn Battutah I-4
Ibn Battutah's travels T-269
Islamic literature I-366

Riis, Jacob (1849–1914), U.S. social reformer, journalist, photojournalist, and author, born in Ribe, Denmark; to U.S. 1870; newspaper reporter in New York; worked for reforms in tenement-house conditions ('How the Other Half Lives'; 'The Making of an American', autobiography)
photography P-298, *list* P-294
playground movement P-125
Roosevelt R-283

Riiser-Larsen, Hjalmar (1890–1965), Norwegian polar explorer; in 1931 claimed Princess Ragnhild Coast and Princess Martha Coast in Antarctica for Norway; erroneously reported killed in German invasion of Norway in 1940; escaped to England; later active in Norwegian forces.

Rijeka (formerly Fiume), Yugoslavia, seaport near head of Adriatic Sea; pop. 141,700 R-207, *map* E-361
Yugoslavia Y-438

Rijksmuseum (translation, "state museum"), Amsterdam, The Netherlands; established 1808; noted for the national collection of paintings and the graphic arts A-381, M-663

Rijswijk, The Netherlands. *see in index* Ryswick

Rikers Island, East River, New York, N.Y.; part of Bronx Borough; occupied entirely by large, modern penitentiary.

Riksdag, Swedish parliament S-526, *picture* S-449
democracy D-93

Riley, James Whitcomb (or Benj. F. Johnson of Boone) (1849–1916), U.S. poet R-208
memorial home I-104

Riley, Margaret Louise (1904–57), Canadian librarian, born in Calgary, Alta.; children's librarian Calgary Public Library 1929–47, assistant librarian 1947–57; won Canadian Books of the Year for Children award 1956 for 'Train for Tiger Lily'.

Rilke, Rainer Maria (1875–1926), German author, born in Prague; lived in Vienna, Paris, Germany, and Switzerland; wrote melodious lyric poetry tinged with religious mysticism; also a book on Rodin G-107

Rill, small stream R-210

Rill erosion, small channels dug in soil C-674

Rillieux, Norbert (1806–94), U.S. scientist, born in New Orleans, La.; invented evaporating pan, introduced 1840, for sugar refining.

Rill mark, in maps M-120

Rim, wheel W-193

Rimbaud, Jean-Nicholas-Arthur (1854–91), French poet, identified with symbolist movement; associated with Verlaine; all his poetry written before age of 20; merchant in Abyssinia in later life.

'Rime of the Ancient Mariner, The', poem by Coleridge that tells story of the hero's suffering after killing an albatross with a crossbow; when love for his fellow creatures enters his heart, the mariner is set free but at certain times is driven to tell his story as a warning to others.

Rimini (ancient Ariminum), Italy, city on Adriatic Sea, 65 mi (105 km) s.e. of Bologna; resort; fisheries; triumphal arch of Augustus; pop. 92,912, *map* I-404

Rimski-Korsakov, Nikolai Andreevich (1844–1908), Russian composer; strove to express national spirit by use of folk tunes, developed with skillful orchestration; wrote first of three symphonies while midshipman in navy (symphonic suite, 'Scheherazade'; music for operas, 'Snow Maiden' and 'The Golden Cockerel'; chamber music, songs, piano pieces; author of 'Principles of Orchestration'; autobiography, 'My Musical Life') L-128
classical music M-674
Musorgski M-693

'Rinaldo', work by Handel H-28

Rinehart, Mary Roberts (1876–1958), U.S. novelist and playwright, born in Pittsburgh, Pa.; studied to be a nurse; married Dr. Stanley M. Rinehart, a surgeon; especially successful in detective and mystery stories ('The Circular Staircase'; 'The Door'); also 'Bab'; 'Tish'; and autobiography 'My Story'.

Rinfret, Thibaudeau (1879–1962), Canadian jurist, born in Montreal, Que.; judge of Supreme Court of Canada 1924–44, chief justice 1944–54.

Ring, jewelry
- Fisherman's ring of pope P-445

'Ring and the Book, The', poem by Browning B-446

Ring-billed gull, bird *Larus delawarensis* G-317

'Ring des Nibelungen, Der'. *see in index* 'Nibelungs, The Ring of the'

Ringed cowrie, shell used as money in some Pacific islands S-153

Ringed plover P-391

Ringed seal S-100

Ringed worms. *see in index* Segmented worm

Ringling, John (1866–1936), U.S. circus owner, born in Baraboo, Wis.; with brothers, founded Ringling Bros. Circus, which later merged with Barnum and Bailey, became its sole director 1930; established art museum Sarasota, Fla. C-430, *picture* F-204

Ringling brothers, founders of Ringling Brothers Circus
- circus history C-429
- first show, *picture* W-259

'Ringmaster, The', work by Toulouse-Lautrec, *picture* H-273

Ring-necked duck, *picture* D-286

Ring-necked pheasant P-249
- egg, *picture* E-112
- state bird, *picture* S-328

Ring of Fire, region around the Pacific Ocean A-673, O-465
- Mexico M-321

'Ring of the Dove, The', work by Ibn Hazm
- Islamic literature I-365

'Ring of the Nibelung, The'. *see in index* 'Nibelungs, The Ring of the'

Rings of Saturn P-354, *picture* P-350

Ringstrasse, boulevard in Vienna, Austria V-314

Ring structure, in organic chemistry O-602
- molecule M-521

Ringtail cat (or cacomistle), carnivorous mammal of Mexico and s.w. U.S.; related to and resembles raccoon; body 15 in. (38 cm) long, bushy tail of equal length.

Ring-tailed lemur L-125, *picture* A-428

Ringuet (pen name of Philippe Panneton) (1895–1960), French-Canadian writer and physician, born in Trois-Rivières, Que.

Ringworm, skin disease appearing in circular patches; caused by fungi
- cats' disease C-210

Rin Tin Tin, German shepherd movie star D-193

Rinuccini, Ottavio (1562–1621), Italian poet and librettist, born in Florence; wrote Italian melodrama 'Dafne' (1594)
- classical music M-668
- opera O-561

Rinzai, one of two major Zen Buddhist sects in Japan; stresses the abrupt awakening of transcendental wisdom, or Enlightenment Z-450

Rio Aguanaval, river in n.-central Mexico; 250 mi (400 km) long; flows into Laguna de Viesca, near Viesca; used for irrigation, *map* M-341

Rio Branco, Brazil, territory. *see in index* Roraima

Rio Bravo. *see in index* Rio Grande

Rio Catatumbo, river in South America; flows into Lake Maracaibo M-130

Rio Chama, river in Rio Arriba County, n. New Mexico, *map* N-229

Rio Coco, largest river in Central America H-225

Rio de Janeiro, state on s. coast of Brazil; area 16,443 sq mi (42,587 sq km); cap. Niterói; largest Brazilian steel mill at Volta Redonda; a principal producer of cane sugar; pop. 11,489,797, *map* B-425

Rio de Janeiro (or Rio), Brazil, capital of Guanabara; pop. 3,223,408 R-208
- Brazil, *map* B-425
- capitol relocation B-408
- South America, *map* S-299, *pictures* S-268, S-284

Rio de La Paz, river in Bolivia
- La Paz L-49

Río de la Plata, estuary. *see in index* Plata, Río de la

Río de Oro, region comprising southern and larger portion of Western Sahara; 71,043 sq mi (184,000 sq km); nearly all desert; livestock along coast where coarse grasses can be grown for feed; trawl fisheries offshore M-586
- Western Sahara W-154

Rio Grande (or Rio Bravo, or Río Bravo del Norte), river forming part of boundary between U.S. and Mexico; 1,800 mi (2,900 km) from source in Colorado to Gulf of Mexico R-209, *maps* N-351, U-81, 62
- Ciudad Juárez C-462
- dams D-17
  - Elephant Butte Dam. *see in index* Elephant Butte Dam
  - Falcon Dam. *see in index* Falcon Dam
- Mexican War M-319
- Mexico M-324, *map* M-344
- New Mexico N-214, *map* N-229
- Texas T-116, *maps* T-117, 135

Rio Grande College, in Rio Grande, Ohio; Baptist; founded 1876; liberal arts, medical technology.

Rio Grande de Santiago, Mexico. *see in index* Lerma River

Rio Grande do Norte, Brazil, state, on n.e. coast; 20,490 sq mi (53,070 sq km); cap. Natal; cotton the principal commercial crop; pop. 1,933,126, *map* B-425

Rio Grande do Sul, Brazil, southernmost state, on seacoast; 109,066 sq mi (282,480 sq km); cap. Pôrto Alegre; pop. 7,942,722, *map* B-425

Río Muni, territory in Equatorial Guinea, w. Africa on e. coast of Gulf of Guinea; area 10,045 sq mi (26,015 sq km); chief town Bata; pop.183,377 S-361

Rio Negro, river about 1,400 mi (2,250 km) long, one of chief tributaries of the Amazon; rises in Colombia; flows e. through n. Brazil, *map* S-300

Río Negro, river in central Argentina flowing e. 700 mi (1,130 km) to Atlantic Ocean, *maps* A-585, S-300

Río Negro, river in central Uruguay flowing w. 300 mi (480 km) to Uruguay River, *map* U-214

Riot
- Gordon. *see in index* Gordon riots
- race B-295
  - anti-Chinese S-103b
  - Detroit D-123
  - King's death U-196
  - Newark N-150
  - Watts U-196

Riot act, legislation passed by British Parliament 1714, commanding that a stern order to disband and go home be read by a justice, sheriff, mayor, or other authority wherever 12 or more persons are riotously assembled; origin of "to read the riot act."

Ríotinto, Spain. *see in index* Minas de Ríotinto

Riparian rights, in law
- legal definition, *table* L-93

Ripley, Aiden Lassell (1896–1969), U.S. painter, born in Wakefield, Mass.; murals; museum exhibits; one-man shows
- painting, *picture* R-161

Ripley, George (1802–80), essayist and critic, social reformer, born in Greenfield, Mass.; active in transcendental movement; a leader in Brook Farm experiment; editor 'New American Cyclopaedia'.

Ripley, Robert LeRoy (1893–1949), U.S. cartoonist, born in Santa Rosa, Calif.; 'Believe It or Not', his cartoon series of factual oddities, was syndicated in newspapers and published in book form.

Ripon, England, town in Yorkshire, 22 mi (35 km) n.w. of York and 24 mi (39 km) n. of Leeds; 12th-century cathedral; pop. 11,840.

Ripon, Wis., city 75 mi (120 km) n.w. of Milwaukee; Ripon College; home of the Wisconsin Phalanx, a communal experiment (1844–50); pop. 7,111
- Republican party P-433
- Wisconsin W-254, *picture* W-258

Ripon College, in Ripon, Wis.; founded 1853; private control; arts and sciences, education.

Ripuarians, division of the Franks; held land between Meuse and Rhine rivers at breakup of Roman Empire; subjugated by Salian Franks under Clovis early in 6th century.

'Rip Van Winkle', story in Washington Irving's 'Sketch Book' of a lovable good-for-naught, who, while hunting in the Catskills, drinks liquor offered him by Hendrik Hudson's legendary crew, falls asleep, and awakens 20 years later A-345, I-358
- folklore F-264
- Korean tales S-468, 479

'Rise of David Levinsky, The', work by Cahan N-412

'Rise of Silas Lapham, The', novel by William Dean Howells telling of a self-made businessman, his social life in Boston, his reverses and resultant gain in moral strength A-352

Rising sun, clam shell *Tellina radiata*, *picture* S-150

Rising Sun, Order of, Japanese order of knighthood established 1875; had eight classes; conferred upon men who rendered extraordinary services to the country.

Risorgimento, Italian political movement I-393

'Risorgimento, Il', Italian newspaper C-236

Riss (or Illinoisan), glacial phase I-5
- map M-83

Riss-Würm, interglacial period I-5

Ristori, Adelaide (1822–1906), Italian tragic actress, greatest of her generation ('Mary Stuart'; 'Queen Elizabeth'; 'Macbeth'); made three tours in U.S.; autobiography 'Memoirs and Artistic Studies'.

Rita Margarita de Cascia, Saint (1386–1456), Augustinian nun, born in Italy; entered convent after death of husband and two sons; revered by Spanish as "patroness of impossibilities"; feast day May 22.

Ritardando, in music M-691, *list* M-671

Ritchie, John William (1809–90), Canadian political leader and jurist, born in Annapolis, N.S.
- Fathers of Canadian Confederation C-118, *picture* C-116

Ritchie, Roland Almon (born 1910), Canadian jurist, born in Halifax, N.S.; admitted to bar of Nova Scotia 1934; lecturer Dalhousie University 1947–59; appointed king's counsel 1950; judge of Supreme Court of Canada 1959–.

'Rite of Spring, The', ballet by Stravinsky D-126, S-486
- classical music M-675

Rites and ceremonies
- American Indian I-118, 141, *picture* I-130
  - snake dance, *picture* W-259
- burial and funerals. *see in index* Burial and funeral customs
- Christmas. *see in index* Christmas
- circumcision. *see in index* Circumcision
- communication C-611
- coronation. *see in index* Coronation
- Easter. *see in index* Easter
- fan F-22
- Hinduism H-156, 160
- Judaism J-150
- knighthood K-258
- Lutheranism L-339
- marriage M-149
- masks M-185
- New Guinea
  - ritual clubhouse, *picture* S-158
- Oceania O-469
- Philippines P-253c
- sword ceremonies S-546
- vassal and lord, *picture* F-68
- Zoroastrianism and Parsiism Z-471

Rites Controversy, in Chinese history. *see in index* Chinese Rites Controversy

Rites of passage, events and rituals that people undergo at various stages of life
- circumcision C-422
- education E-78
- novel N-410
- Zoroastrianism and Parsiism Z-471

Ritschel, William (1864–1949), U.S. painter, born in Nuremberg, Bavaria; to U.S. 1895; paintings of the sea; cloud and light effects.

Ritt, Martin (born 1920), U.S. director, producer, and actor; born in New York, N.Y.; known especially for films ('Long Hot Summer'; 'The Sound and the Fury'; 'The Spy Who Came In from the Cold'; 'Hombre').

Rittenhouse, David (1732–96), U.S. astronomer, born in Philadelphia, Pa.; noted as maker of astronomical instruments; helped lay out boundaries of Pennsylvania.

Rittenhouse, Jessie Belle (1869–1948), U.S. author, born in Mt. Morris, N.Y. (criticism, 'Younger American Poets'; poetry, 'The Moving Tide'; autobiography, 'My House of Life').

Rittenhouse, William (1644–1708), manufacturer and Mennonite minister, born in Mülheim on the Ruhr, Germany; in 1688 moved to Germantown, Pa. P-104

Ritter, Johann Wilhelm (1776–1810), German physicist, born in Samitz, Silesia; did research work in electricity; discovered ultraviolet rays L-201
- ultraviolet radiation U-3

Ritter, Joseph Elmer, Cardinal (1892–1967), Roman Catholic prelate, born in New Albany, Ind.; bishop of Indianapolis 1934–44; archbishop of Indianapolis 1944–46, of St. Louis 1946–67; became cardinal 1961; authorized first mass in English in United States 1964.

Ritter, Karl (or Carl Ritter) (1779–1859), German geographer, founder of modern science of geography; showed its underlying principle to be relation of earth's surface to nature and to humans; influence as teacher, writer G-69

Ritter, Tex (in full Maurice Woodward Ritter) (1906–74), U.S. singer and actor, born in Nederland, Tex.; country-western star of radio (The Lone Ranger; Death Valley Days), movies, records ('Rock and Rye Rag'; 'High Noon'; 'I Dreamed of a Hillbilly Heaven'), and television; voted into Country Music Hall of Fame 1964 M-678

Ritty, James (1836–1918), U.S. restaurant owner, inventor, born in Cincinnati, Ohio; invented cash register 1879.

Ritz, César (1850–1918), founder of the Ritz Hotel in Paris, France; his name is now a synonym for luxury and elegance H-288

Ritz Hotel, Paris, France, *picture* H-287

'Rivals, The', comedy by Richard Brinsley Sheridan telling of the rivalry between Bob Acres and Captain Absolute ("Ensign Beverley") for the hand of Lydia Languish, niece of Mrs. Malaprop; first produced 1775 E-273

River R-210. *see also in index* Alluvial soil; Dam; Delta; Levee; and chief rivers by name. For a list of the longest rivers, *see table* following
- drainage basins. *see in index* Drainage systems
- earth E-16, 31
- fall line F-14
- flood F-180, 183, *picture* F-184
- irrigation systems I-354
- jetty controls J-111
- longest in world. *see table* following
- oceanography O-479
- pollution, *pictures* P-441c
  - acid rain A-19
  - thermal P-441d
- submerged channels N-73
- valley V-256
- water W-89, 92
- waterway W-108

'River, The' (1937), documentary by Lorentz M-628

Rivera, Diego (1886–1957), Mexican artist of modernist school; subjects are intensely

RIVERS—LONGEST IN THE WORLD

Name	Continent	Length* mi	Length* km
Nile	Africa	4,132	6,650
Amazon	South America	4,087	6,577
Mississippi-Missouri†	North America	3,710	5,971
Yangtze	Asia	3,400	5,500
Yenisey	Asia	3,400	5,500
Congo (Zaire)	Africa	2,900	4,700
Huang He (Yellow)	Asia	2,900	4,700
Lena	Asia	2,730	4,400
Mekong	Asia	2,700	4,350
Amur	Asia	2,700	4,300
Mackenzie	North America	2,635	4,241
Niger	Africa	2,600	4,200
Ob'	Asia	2,270	5,200
Volga	Europe	2,193	3,530

*Because of the problems in defining and measuring rivers, publications often differ in their figures for river lengths
†All the way from the Mississippi's Head of Passes to the Missouri system's Upper Red Rock Reservoir

nationalistic, especially murals in public buildings of Mexico City; great symmetry and rhythm in composition L-63
Mexico M-328
Mexico City M-346
mosaic M-590
murals P-67a, *pictures* M-347, P-67b

Rivera, José Eustasio (1889–1928), Colombian novelist, born in Neiva L-70

Rivera, Miguel Primo de, marqués de Estella (1870–1930), Spanish general and dictator; took part in Cuban, Philippine, and Moroccan campaigns S-359

River basin, geographic feature R-210

River basin harbor H-34

'River Between, The', work by Ngugi N-300

Riverdale, Ill., village 16 mi (26 km) s. of Chicago, on Little Calumet River; railroad center; pop. 13,233
Illinois, *map* I-53

River dolphin D-223

River Edge, N.J., borough on Hackensack River, 3 mi (5 km) n. of Hackensack; pop. 11,111.

River Forest, Ill., village 11 mi (18 km) w. of Chicago; residential; Concordia Teachers College, Rosary College; pop. 12,392
Illinois, *map* I-53

Riverfront Stadium, in Cincinnati, Ohio C-415

River horse. *see in index* Hippopotamus

River pirate, outlaw O-619

River raft (or flat), flat-bottomed boat N-357

River Rouge, Mich., industrial city 6 mi (10 km) s.w. of Detroit; oil refining; marine engines, machinery, chemicals, paper; pop. 12,912 M-359

Rivers, Sam (born 1930), U.S. avant-garde saxophonist, flutist, pianist, and composer J-87

Riverside, Calif., city about 50 mi (80 km) e. of Los Angeles; citrus packing; aircraft products, machinery, metal products; University of California at Riverside, Citrus Experiment Station of the University of California, California Baptist College, La Sierra campus of Loma Linda University, Sherman High School (for Indians); here navel orange tree was introduced in California (1873); military installations nearby; pop. 170,876, *map* U-40

Riverton, Wyo., city at junction of Wind and Popo Agie rivers in w.-central part of state; livestock feeding area; uranium; pop. 9,588 W-396

Riverview, Mich., city on Detroit River; 13 mi (21 km) s. of Detroit; steel, chemicals; incorporated 1959; pop. 14,569.

Riverview (formerly Coverdale), N.B., residential community amalgamated with Gunningsville, Riverview Heights, Coverdale, and parts of Coverdale Parish; pop. 14,907 N-158

Riverview Park, amusement park in Chicago, Ill. A-385

Riveting
shipbuilding S-167, 171

Riviera, picturesque district of Italy and France, on Mediterranean coast; extends from La Spezia, Italy, to Nice, France, or in broader sense, to Cannes, France; favorite winter resort
France F-357
Genoa G-59
Nice N-305

Riviera Beach, Fla., city just n. of West Palm Beach, on Atlantic Ocean; light industry, fishing; pop. 26,596.

Rivier College, in Nashua, N.H.; Roman Catholic; for women; founded 1933; arts and sciences, commerce, home economics; graduate division.

Rivière, Mademoiselle, portrait by Ingres, *picture* D-265

Rivière-du-Loup, Que., manufacturing city and summer resort on St. Lawrence, 105 mi (170 km) n.e. of Quebec; railroad shops; lumber, wood pulp, furniture, iron products; pop. 12,760 Q-9b, *maps* C-112, Q-11

Rivoli, duc de. *see in index* Masséna, André

Rivoli Veronese, Italy, village 75 mi (120 km) w. of Venice, and 15 mi (25 km) n.w. of Verona where Napoleon defeated Austrians 1797.

Rixey, Eppa (1891–1963), U.S. baseball pitcher, born in Culpeper, Va.; with Philadelphia, N.L., 1912–17, 1919–20; Cincinnati, N.L., 1921–33; went directly to Philadelphia, N.L., after graduation from University of Virginia; won 266 games, lost 251; won 20 or more games in each of 4 seasons (in 1922 won 25, lost 13).

Riyadh (or El Riad), Saudi Arabia, one of two capitals; oasis city in center of kingdom; pop. 150,000 S-52b
Asia, *map* A-700

Riyal, monetary unit of Saudi Arabia and Yemen Arab Republic.

Rizal, Jose (1861–96), Filipino patriot and writer R-211, P-257c
independence movement P-259c
monument, *pictures* P-257b
'My Last Farewell' P-257c

Rizzio, David (or David Riccio) (1533?–66), Italian secretary of Mary, Queen of Scots; entered her service as a musician M-164

Rjukan, Norway, town 75 mi (120 km) w. of Oslo; the factories nearby receive power from Rjukanfos, waterfall 350 ft. high; pop. 6,308.

R.L.S. *see in index* Stevenson, Robert Louis

RNA (or ribonucleic acid), found in cells C-238, B-199
embryology E-202
genetics G-55
molecule M-522

Roach, Max (born 1925), U.S. jazz musician, born in New York, N.Y., *picture* J-85

Roach. *see in index* Cockroach

Roach, carplike fish *Rutilus rutilus* with red fins; name sometimes given to shiner and some species of sunfishes, *picture* F-129

Roach Motel, device used to trap insects T-268

Road camp, system of punishment P-505c

Road map M-119, *diagram* M-115

'Road of Eloquence, The', collection of works
Islamic literature I-365

Road oils, asphalt A-702

Roadrunner, bird R-211, B-252, *pictures* B-242,
nest R-211
New Mexico's state bird, *picture* N-220

Roads and streets R-212. *see also in index* names of countries, provinces, and states, *subhead* transportation
Africa A-106
Appian Way. *see in index* Appian Way
automobiles A-863
bridges. *see in index* Bridge
cattle. *see in index* Cattle trails
explosive, *picture* E-381
jackhammer P-398, *diagrams* P-399
Latin America L-65
lighting
sodium vapor lamp S-247
lumber industry L-331
North America N-343
Pan American Highway. *see in index* Pan American Highway
paving materials
asphalt A-702
shells M-525
rubber, *picture* R-308
road to Jericho, *picture* P-80
safety S-4, 10
toll road or turnpike. *see in index* Toll road
traffic and traffic control T-247
Trans-Canada Highway T-248
transportation T-255, 259, 261, 264, *map* T-258, *pictures* T-262, 263
United States
Alaska Highway A-256
Dixie Highway. *see in index* Dixie Highway
Franklin's measurements F-381
Missouri M-487
oldest street P-251a, *picture* P-251d
percentage of world total, *chart* U-123
Pulaski Skyway, *picture* U-108
western, *maps* U-176. *see also in index* Oregon Trail
wagon W-3

'Road to Singapore, The' (1940), motion picture directed by Schertzinger; first of the many 'road' pictures starring Hope, Crosby, and Lamour
Hope H-237

Roanne, France, manufacturing and railroad center 40 mi (60 km) n.w. of Lyons; head of navigation on Loire River; textile manufactures; pop. 53,178, *map* F-372

Roanoke (originally called Big Lick), Va., city in s.w. on Roanoke River; pop. 100,220 R-222, *maps* V-348, 331, 336, U-41
climate, *list* V-329
factory, *picture* U-65

Roanoke College, in Salem, Va.; Lutheran Church in America; started 1842 as Virginia Institute, present name 1853; liberal arts and education.

Roanoke Island, island 12 mi by 3 mi (19 km by 5 km), off coast of n.e. North Carolina; pop. 1,750, *picture* N-364

Roanoke Rapids, N.C., city on Roanoke River, 36 mi (58 km) n.e. of Rocky Mount; cotton, peanuts, tobacco, lumber; textiles, paper, transformers; pop. 14,702.

Roanoke River, river that rises in Montgomery County, n.w. Virginia, flows s.e. into North Carolina and then into Atlantic Ocean; 380 mi (610 km) long V-331, *maps* V-331, 348, U-59

Roaring forties, region between 40th and 50th parallels in n. Atlantic Ocean; also zone of same latitude in Southern Hemisphere; both regions have strong westerly winds.

Roaring Twenties, period in U.S. history
portrayal in literature A-359

Roast, in cooking C-700

Roba'i, poetic type
Islamic literature I-364

Robalo, fish. *see in index* Snook

Robards, Jason Nelson, Jr. (born 1922), U.S. actor, born in Chicago, Ill.; star of 'The Iceman Cometh' and 'Long Day's Journey into Night' by O'Neill; 'The Disenchanted', 1959 Tony award; 'A Thousand Clowns' on stage and screen.

Robarts, John Parmenter (1917–82), Canadian political leader, born in Banff, Alta.; minister without portfolio of Ontario 1958–60, minister of education 1960–61, premier 1961–71.

Robbe-Grillet, Alain (born 1922), French author F-398

Robben Island, U.S.S.R., sealing island off s.e. coast Sakhalin Island S-99

Robbery P-424
banks L-95
crime C-771
suspect caught, *pictures* P-427

Robbins, Frederick Chapman (born 1916), U.S. pediatrician, born in Auburn, Ala.; professor of pediatrics present Case Western Reserve school of medicine, Cleveland, Ohio, 1952–, dean 1966–.

Robbins, Jerome (born 1918), U.S. dancer and choreographer, born in New York, N.Y.; co-winner of 1961 Oscar for direction of 'West Side Story'; 1965 Tony for direction and choreography of 'Fiddler on the Roof' B-36, D-29

Robbins, Margaret (1868–1945), U.S. reformer W-277

Robbinsdale, Minn., city 5 mi (8 km) n.w. of Minneapolis; dairy and farming area; metal products; pop. 14,422.

Robert I (865?–923), king of France, son of Robert the Strong and younger brother of Odo; permitted Charles III to succeed his brother but revolted 921 and was crowned king 922; his grandson was Hugh Capet.

Robert I, king of Scotland. *see in index* Bruce, Robert

Robert II (1316–90), king of Scotland, grandson of Robert Bruce; founder of Stuart line; succeeded to father's office as high steward 1326 S-493

Robert I, duke of Normandy (died 1035), called "the Devil"; father of William the Conqueror; his ferocity and strength subject of medieval legends; aided Edward the Confessor in exile; subject of opera by Meyerbeer ('Robert le Diable').

Robert II, duke of Normandy (1056?–1134), son of William I of England
England E-240
First Crusade C-787

Robert, Henry Martyn (1837–1923), U.S. Army officer and engineer, born in Robertsville, S.C.; authority on parliamentary law ('Rules of Order').

Robert, Nicholas-Louis (1761–1828), French inventor of a papermaking machine, born in Paris P-104

Robert, Shaaban (1909–62), Tanzanian author of prose and poetry, strongly supported movement to preserve African verse traditions of the past A-121

Robert College, in Istanbul, Turkey; nonsectarian; established 1863 by U.S. philanthropists under leadership of Christopher R. Robert (1802–78); in 1932 united with American College for Girls to form American Colleges in Istanbul; name changed to Bosporus University 1971 when it became a Turkish state university.

'Robert E. Lee', steamboat S-177c, *picture* S-177d

Robert-Fleury, Joseph Nicolas (1797–1890), French historical painter; father of Tony Robert-Fleury ('Scene of St. Bartholomew'; 'Triumphal Entry of Clovis at Tours'; 'Children of Louis XVI in the Temple').

Robert-Fleury, Tony (1837–1911), French painter, taught many of the best-known painters of 19th century; like his father, Joseph N. Robert-Fleury, excelled in historical paintings.

Robert Gordon Menzies. *see in index* Menzies, Robert G.

Robert Guiscard (nickname the Resourceful) (1015?–85), Norman soldier of fortune; began conquest of Sicily from the Saracens (completed by his brother Roger I and consolidated by his nephew Roger II); made duke of Apulia and Calabria by Pope Nicholas II in 1059.

Robert-Houdin, Jean-Eugéne (1805–71), French magician, born in Blois; sent by French government to Algeria to discredit native sorcerers; called Father of Modern Magic M-38

'Robert le Diable', opera by Meyerbeer
 Lind's role L-226

Robert Morris College, in Coraopolis, Pa.; private control; founded 1921; liberal arts, business administration; Pittsburgh Center at Pittsburgh, Pa.; graduate studies.

Robert of Molesme, Saint (1027?–1110), French Benedictine monk and abbot; founder of the Cistercian Order M-542

Roberts, Bartholomew (1682–1722), Welsh pirate, credited with capture of 400 ships and respected for strict discipline exercised over crew; died in battle off African coast
 flag, *picture* P-342b

Roberts, Charles George Douglas (1860–1943), Canadian poet and storywriter, born in New Brunswick; in New York 1897–1911, in England 1911–25 C-121, *picture* C-122

Roberts, Elizabeth Madox (1886–1941), U.S. poet and novelist, born near Springfield, Ky.; became prominent 1926 with first novel, 'The Time of Man', simple story of life in the Kentucky mountains ('My Heart and My Flesh'; 'The Great Meadow'; 'Under the Tree', poems).

Roberts, Frederick Sleigh, first Earl Roberts of Kandahar, Pretoria, and Waterford (1832–1914), British field marshal, born in Cawnpore, India; distinguished himself in Sepoy Mutiny 1857–58 and Afghan war 1878–80; commander in chief in India 1885–93, in South Africa 1899–1900, of British army 1900–04.

Roberts, Kenneth Lewis (1885–1957), U.S. novelist R-222, A-358

Roberts, Oral (full name Granville Oral Roberts) (born 1918), U.S. evangelist, born in Ada, Okla.; founder controversial television healing ministry based in Tulsa, Okla.; from 1947 founded Oral Roberts Evangelistic Association, Oral Roberts University, City of Faith Health Care Center; author of more than 50 books.

Roberts, Owen Josephus (1875–1955), U.S. jurist, born in Philadelphia, Pa.; professor of law University of Pennsylvania 1898–1918; corporation lawyer; associate justice U.S. Supreme Court 1930–45.

Roberts, Robin Evan (born 1926), U.S. baseball player, born in Springfield, Ill.; pitcher for Philadelphia, Houston, and Chicago, N.L., and for Baltimore, A.L., 1948–66 B-80a

Robertson, A.C. (1887–?), U.S. musician M-678

Robertson, Frederick William (1816–53), British preacher, famous as "Robertson of Brighton"; emphasized fundamental spiritual truths.

Robertson, James (1742–1814), U.S. pioneer, born in Brunswick County, Virginia; friend of Daniel Boone; one of founders of Nashville (1778); for ten years fought American Indians but later as Indian agent had great influence for peace.

Robertson, Oscar (born 1938), U.S. basketball player; graduate of the University of Cincinnati; with Cincinnati Royals 1960–70, Milwaukee Bucks 1970–74, All Star team 1961–74 B-100

Robertson, Pat (born Marion Gordon Robertson) (born 1930), U.S. religious broadcaster, born in Lexington, Va.; developed first Christian television station into cable network in Virginia Beach, Va.; founder-president Christian Broadcasting Network (CBN) 1960– , CBN University 1977– ; host '700 Club' talk show 1968–86; announced presidential candidacy 1986.

Robertson, William (1721–93), Scottish historian; with Edward Gibbon and David Hume formed great trio of his generation; his 'History of Scotland' and 'History of Reign of Charles V' set new standard in historical writing and research.

Robertson, William Robert (1860–1933), British field marshal who rose from the ranks; Gen. French's chief of staff 1915; chief of imperial general staff 1915–18.

Roberts Wesleyan College, in Rochester, N.Y.; Free Methodist; founded 1866; liberal arts, music, nursing.

Robert the Strong (died 866), count of Anjou and Blois; at first rebelled against Charles the Bald but later won king's confidence by defense of the Seine and Loire valleys against the Normans and Bretons; his two sons, Odo and Robert I, became kings of France.

Roberval, Gilles Personne de (1602–75), French mathematician, *table* M-218

Roberval, Jean-François de La Rocque, sieur de (1500?–60), French colonizer sent by Francis I to create a settlement on North American lands found earlier by Jacques Cartier C-90

Roberval balance, invented by Gilles Personne de Roberval; used in commercial weighing machines, *table* M-218

Robeson, Paul (1898–1976), U.S. actor and singer, born in Princeton, N.J.; won high scholastic and athletic honors at Rutgers College; graduated Columbia Law School; received the Spingarn medal in 1945 for singing and acting ('The Emperor Jones', 'All God's Chillun's Got Wings', 'The Hairy Ape', 'Show Boat', 'Porgy and Bess', 'Othello') A-27

Robespierre, Maximilien (1758–94), leader in French Revolution R-222, F-403, *picture* F-402
 Jacobins J-11
 Roland R-239

Robichaud, Louis Joseph (born 1925), Canadian political leader, born St. Anthony, N.B.; leader Liberal party of New Brunswick 1958–71, premier 1960–70; chairman Canadian section of International Joint Commission 1971; in Canadian Parliament 1973–.

Robidou brothers, U.S. trappers and fur traders: **Antoine** (1794–1860), "first fur trader out of old Taos," trapped in Nebraska, Utah; built Gunnison River post in Colorado (1828) and Fort Robidou in n.e. Utah (1832); **Joseph** (1783–1868) traded at Council Bluffs until American Fur Company intervened; began trading at Blacksnake Creek for American Fur Company 1812; by 1830 owned fort around which St. Joseph, Mo., grew up; **François, Louis,** and **Michel** are less known.

Robie House, in Chicago, Ill.; designed by Frank Lloyd Wright; built 1909; designated National Historic Landmark 1964
 design, *picture* D-114

Robin, a bird *Turdus migratorius* of the family Turdidae R-223
 bird B-275, *pictures* B-240, 245, 247
 egg, *picture* E-112
 endangerment E-58
 state bird
  Connecticut, *picture* C-656
  Michigan, *picture* M-364
  Wisconsin, *picture* W-256
 thrush family T-177

Robin Goodfellow. *see in index* Puck

Robin Hood, English outlaw R-223, R-111b, S-473, 481a, 460, *picture* P-541
 folklore F-262
 outlaw O-619
 Turkish tales related S-480

Robin Hood Dell, in Philadelphia, Pa.; natural amphitheater for summer music concerts; founded 1930, *map* P-251a

Robinson, Benjamin Lincoln (1864–1935), U.S. botanist, born in Bloomington, Ill.; curator Gray Herbarium 1892–1935 and professor systemic botany Harvard University 1899–1935.

Robinson, Bill Bojangles (originally Luther Robinson) (1878–1949), U.S. tap dancer, born in Richmond, Va.; danced in nightclubs, musicals, and movies ('Rebecca of Sunnybrook Farm'; 'Little Colonel') D-24

Robinson, Boardman (1876–1952), Canadian-American painter, illustrator, and cartoonist, born in Somerset, N.S.; murals in Rockefeller Center, New York City.

Robinson, Charles (1818–94), U.S. statesman, first governor of state of Kansas, born in Hardwick, Mass., emigrated west; did much to prevent California and Kansas from becoming slave states; as governor charged with treason but acquitted.

Robinson, Doane Jonah Leroy (1856–1946), U.S. lawyer, historian, and rancher, born in Sparta, Wis.; secretary and superintendent South Dakota Department of History 1901–26; conceived Mt. Rushmore National Memorial, *picture* S-332

Robinson, Edward G. (1893–1973), U.S. motion-picture actor, born in Bucharest; emigrated to New York City when he was 10; among his many pictures: 'Double Indemnity', 'The Ten Commandments', 'Little Caesar', 'Soylent Green', *picture* C-771

Robinson, Edwin Arlington (1869–1935), U.S. poet A-354

Robinson, Frank (born 1935), U.S. baseball player, born in Beaumont, Tex.; outfielder Cincinnati, N.L., 1956–65, Baltimore, A.L., 1966–71, Los Angeles, N.L., 1971–72, California Angels, A.L., 1972–74; first black manager in major leagues, of Cleveland Indians 1974–77; chosen most valuable player in National League 1961, in American League 1966; wrote 'My Life Is Baseball', autobiography.

Robinson, Henry Crabb (1775–1867), British journalist and diarist; friend of Lamb, Wordsworth, Coleridge, and Southey ('Reminiscences'; 'Diary'; 'Correspondence').

Robinson, Irene Bowen (born 1891), U.S. artist and illustrator, born in South Bend, Wash.; illustrated children's books written by her husband, **William Wilcox Robinson** (born 1891) ('Animals in the Sun'; 'Elephants'; 'On the Farm'; 'Picture Book of Animal Babies').

Robinson, Jackie (full name Jack Roosevelt Robinson) (1919–72), U.S. baseball player, born in Cairo, Ga.; chiefly 2nd baseman Brooklyn, N.L., 1947–56; set major league record in 1951 for least errors (7) by 2nd baseman in a season batting average .342 in 1949, lifetime .311; in 6 World Series; first black player in major leagues, first in Baseball Hall of Fame B-93, 300

Robinson, James Harvey (1863–1936), U.S. historian and educator, born in Bloomington, Ill. ('An Introduction to the History of Western Europe'; 'Medieval and Modern Times'; 'The Mind in the Making'; collaborated with James Henry Breasted, Charles Austin Beard, and others on 'History of Civilization').

Robinson, John (1575?–1625), English nonconformist, pastor of Leiden, The Netherlands, congregation of Pilgrim Fathers; organized Speedwell-Mayflower colony but died at Leiden.

Robinson, John Beverley (1791–1863), Canadian jurist and statesman, chief justice of Upper Canada 1829–63; opposed reforms of Baldwin and Lafontaine; was trusted guide of the "Family Compact."

Robinson, Joseph Taylor (1872–1937), U.S. political leader, born in Arkansas; U.S. congressman 1902–12; governor of Arkansas 1912; U.S. senator few weeks later; as Democratic floor leader in Senate showed great parliamentary ability; Democratic nominee for vice-president 1928.

Robinson, Lennox (1866–1958), Irish dramatist and novelist, born in Douglas, Cork; director Abbey Theatre, Dublin ('Harvest'; 'A Young Man from the South'; 'The White-headed Boy'; 'The White Blackbird') I-327

Robinson, Luther. *see in index* Robinson, Bill Bojangles

Robinson, Mabel Louise (1884?–1962), U.S. author of children's books, born in Waltham, Mass.; instructor in writing at Columbia University 1919–45 ('Bright Island'; 'Runner of the Mountain Tops'; 'All the Year Round').

Robinson, Robert (1886–1975), British chemist; professor of chemistry Oxford University 1930–55. *see also in index* Nobel Prizewinners, *table*

Robinson, Roscoe, Jr. (born 1928), U.S. Army four-star general, born in St. Louis, Mo., U.S. representative to NATO B-302

Robinson, Smokey (born 1940), U.S. singer M-681

Robinson, Sugar Ray (originally Walker Smith) (born 1921), U.S. boxer, born in Detroit, Mich.; welterweight champion 1946–51; middleweight champion five times 1951–59 ('Sugar Ray', autobiography, with Dave Anderson) B-392, *picture* B-388

Robinson, Theodore (1852–96), U.S. painter, born in Irasburg, Vt.; works are notable for skillful light effects; best known for landscapes and figures outdoors.

Robinson, Wilbert (nickname Uncle Robbie) (1864–1934), U.S. baseball catcher and manager, born in Hudson, Mass.; catcher chiefly Baltimore, N.L., 1892–99; made 7 consecutive hits in one game 1892; managed Brooklyn, N.L., 1914–31, *table* B-80a

Robinson, William (1840–1921), U.S. engineer and inventor, born in County Tyrone, Ireland; to U.S. as child
 railroad signaling system R-80

Robinson, William Wilcox. *see in index* Robinson, Irene Bowen

'Robinson Crusoe', novel by Defoe D-64, R-111c
 English literature E-270

Robinson Crusoe Island. *see in index* Tobago

Robinson-Patman Price Discrimination Act, amendment to Clayton Act of 1914; enacted 1936 to prevent price discrimination between buyers of same commodity; act protected independent merchants against quantity buying by chain stores.

Robot R-225, A-836
 bulldozer control B-500
 electronics E-179
 engineering E-227
 farming F-29
 industry, *pictures* I-191
 'I, Robot', book R-112d, *picture* R-111j
 machine M-9, *picture* M-10
 mass production M-209
 microprocessor M-380
 science fiction S-62
 ultrasonics A-22

Rob Roy (or Robert MacGregor, or Robert Campbell) (1671–1734), Scottish outlaw R-226

Rob Roy, Scottish writer. *see in index* MacGregor, John

Robsart, Amy (1532–60), wife of Lord Robert Dudley, afterward earl of Leicester, who was suspected of having caused her sudden death in order that he might be free to marry Queen Elizabeth I; story told in Scott's 'Kenilworth'.

Robson, Eleanor (or Mrs. August Belmont) (born 1879), U.S. actress, born in England; first appeared on U.S. stage 1897; starred in 'Merely Mary Ann', 'Salomy Jane', 'The Dawn of a Tomorrow' (her greatest success); retired 1910; active social worker ('The Fabric of Memory', autobiography).

Robson, Mount, in British Columbia, highest peak of Canadian Rocky Mountains (12,972 ft; 3,954 m) B-331, *map* C-109

Robstown, Tex., city 5 mi (8 km) w. of Corpus Christi; oil refineries, livestock, truck farms; pop. 12,100.

Robusti, Jacopo. *see in index* Tintoretto

Roc, monster bird in Arabic legend, said to have its home in Madagascar; so large that it could carry off elephants; Sinbad the Sailor tells of seeing its egg, which was "50 paces in circumference."

Roca, Julio Argentino (1843–1914), Argentine soldier and statesman; rose to general in war with Paraguay (1865–70); suppressed rebellion 1880 and elected president 1880–86, 1898–1904; greatly strengthened national administration and patriotic spirit A-583

Rochambeau, Jean Baptiste Donatien de Vimeur, comte de (1725–1807), French soldier R-227

Rochdale, England, manufacturing town 10 mi (16 km) n.e. of Manchester; cotton, wool, and rayon products; 'Rochdale Pioneers', 1844, first English cooperative society; pop. 86,600.

Rochdale Society of Equitable Pioneers, English cooperative society C-706

Roche, Arthur Somers (1883–1935), U.S. novelist, born in Somerville, Mass.; also magazine writer ('Ransom'; 'Uneasy Street'; 'Day of Faith'; 'What I Know about You'; 'The Sport of Kings').

Roche, Martin (1855–1927), U.S. architect A-568

Roche, Mazo de la. *see in index* De la Roche

Rochefort, Victor Henri, marquis de Rochefort-Luçay (1830–1913), French journalist and political leader; bitter opponent of Napoleon III; supporter of the Commune; several times exiled and imprisoned for his attacks on persons and projects he believed wrong.

Rochefort, France, seaport 78 mi (126 km) n. of Bordeaux and 18 mi (29 km) s.e. of La Rochelle, near mouth of Charente River; pop. 28,223, *map* F-372

Rochefoucauld, François, duc de la. *see in index* La Rochefoucauld, François de

Rochelle salt, double salt of tartaric acid (sodium potassium tartrate); produced in the action of cream-of-tartar baking powders.

Rochemont, Louis de (1899–), producer of newsreels and semi-documentaries, born in Boston, Mass.; films were based on genuine case histories, used on-the-spot locations and non-professional, real-life situations M-628

Rochester, England, port on Medway River, 26 mi (42 km) s.e. of London; noted cathedral, ruined castle; pop. 55,810.

Rochester, Minn., medical center and industrial city in s.e., 35 mi (55 km) n. of Iowa boundary; vegetable canning; dairy products, baked goods; electronic and metal equipment; pop. 57,890 M-439, 442, *picture* M-450, *map* U-41. *see also in index* Mayo Clinic

Rochester, N.H., city on Cocheco River, 34 mi (55 km) n.e. of Manchester, in industrial district; shoes, electrical components, wood products, textiles; pop. 21,560 N-186, *map* N-191

Rochester, N.Y., manufacturing city; pop. 241,741 R-227
  New York N-251, *maps* N-351, U-41, *picture* N-250

Rochester, University of, in Rochester, N.Y.; private control; founded 1850; arts and sciences, business administration, education, engineering, medicine, music; graduate studies N-254

Rochester Institute of Technology, in Rochester, N.Y.; private control; founded 1829 as Rochester Athenaeum; present name after 1944; applied science, business, fine and applied arts, general studies, graphic arts and photography; graduate study; National Technical Institute for the Deaf N-254

Rock, earth's crust R-228
  age U-202
  basalts B-86
  Bermuda's coral stone B-173
  bridges B-439
  collecting
    hobby H-187
  earth E-11, 20
  geography G-62
  geology G-70
  lava and magma L-89
  minerals M-437
  mines and mining M-424
    quarrying Q-6
  soil formation S-249
  sound transmission S-259, *graph* S-260
  stone money of Yap, *picture* P-18

Rock (or rock and roll, or rock 'n' roll), music
  Beatles B-119
  culture transfer C-466
  electronic instruments E-174
  Joplin J-140
  noise level P-441e
  popular music M-679

Rock, outer space
  moon M-576, S-347

Rockabilly, early form of rock 'n' roll music M-680

Rockall Islet, small rock peak in Atlantic Ocean; annexed by Britain 1955, *map* E-361

Rock and Roll Hall of Fame, in New York, N.Y. H-17

Rock asphalt A-702

Rock bass (sometimes called redeye), a fish found in streams and lakes in Mississippi Valley; often a foot long; olive green, with dark mottling B-89

Rock crab, crab *Cancer irroratus* frequenting rocky places, as along the New England coast; very secretive; unable to swim; sometimes substituted for blue crab as food.

Rock cress, genus of small plants; one species *Arabis alpine* has white flowers in flat-topped clusters; suited for rock gardens
  flowering time G-25

Rock crystal (or quartz crystal), pure quartz J-112
  quartz Q-6
  radio R-52

Rock dam D-16, *picture* D-13
  waterfall W-97

Rock dove, wild dove *Columba livia* native to s. Europe, the British Isles, n.w. Africa, Asia Minor; as the domestic pigeon it is raised throughout the U.S. P-324

Rockefeller, David (born 1915), U.S. banker, born in New York, N.Y.; son of John Davison Rockefeller, Jr.; joined Chase Manhattan Bank 1946, chairman and chief executive officer after 1969 R-230, B-73

Rockefeller, John Davison (1839–1937), U.S. capitalist, founder of Standard Oil Company R-230, *picture* R-230

Rockefeller, John Davison, Jr. (1874–1960), U.S. capitalist R-230
  New York City N-273, 278
  proxy fight, Standard Oil Co. (Ind.) S-451
  Reims cathedral R-138
  United Nations U-22
  Williamsburg W-209

Rockefeller, Laurance Spelman (born 1910), U.S. business executive and conservationist, born in New York, N.Y.; son of John Davison Rockefeller, Jr.; chairman Rockefeller Center Inc. 1953–56, 1958–66, later director R-230

Rockefeller, Nelson Aldrich (1908–79), U.S. financier and statesman, born in Bar Harbor, Me., son of John Davison Rockefeller, Jr.; chairman Rockefeller Center, New York, N.Y., 1945–53, 1956–58; coordinator of inter-American affairs 1940–44; assistant secretary of state (Latin America) 1944–45; undersecretary of Department of Health, Education, and Welfare 1953–54; White House administrative assistant on foreign affairs 1954–55; Republican governor of New York 1959–73; U.S. vice-president 1974–77 U-196b, S-292
  brothers R-230
  Nixon N-325
  U.S. vice-president F-302, *picture* F-303

Rockefeller, Winthrop (1912–73), U.S. business executive and political leader, born in New York, N.Y.; son of John Davison Rockefeller, Jr.; governor (Republican) of Arkansas 1967–71 R-230

Rockefeller Brothers Fund, established 1940 R-230

Rockefeller Center, in New York, N.Y. N-273, *picture* N-276
  "Swords into plowshares," carving, *picture* P-143d

Rockefeller Foundation, established 1913 by John D. Rockefeller R-230, U-208, F-333, *table* F-332

Rockefeller University, The (originally Rockefeller Institute for Medical Research), established in New York, N.Y., in 1901 by John D. Rockefeller; its first laboratory was opened in 1904; conducts research in many branches of science; graduate studies only R-230
  New York City N-279
  Osler's influence O-609

Rock elm (or cork elm), tree *Ulmus thomasi* E-194
  wood, *table* W-283

Rocker (or cradle), device used in processing gold ore G-179

Rocket R-231, *pictures* A-73, 747
  artillery A-660
  bibliography S-348d
  explosive E-381
  fire hazards F-106
  fireworks F-114
  fuel S-342a
  Goddard G-173
  gravitation G-240
  guided missile G-307
  jet propulsion, *diagram* J-106
  scientific use S-345, *pictures* S-57, 57b
  space travel. *see in index* Space travel, *subhead* rockets
  titanium T-193
  transportation T-266
  Tsiolkovsky T-302
  tungsten T-307
  Van Allen R-259
  warfare W-20
  weather W-121
  World War II W-355

'Rocket', early locomotive R-73, L-282, S-442, S-443, B-446

Rocket airplane S-346e–f, 341a, A-157. *see also in index* Jet propulsion

Rocket engine (or nonair-breathing engine) S-342a, 346c, d–e, *diagram* R-232
  airplane A-187
  jet propulsion J-106, 110
  motor and engine M-630

Rocket gun (or bazooka), U.S. Army's rocket antitank gun R-233

Rock Falls, Ill., city just s. of Sterling, on Rock River; in dairy and grain farming area; meat processing; builders' hardware, fertilizers; incorporated 1867; pop. 10,624
  Illinois, *map* I-53

Rockfish (or striped bass), fish, *table* F-136

Rockford, Ill., 2nd city of state, 75 mi (120 km) n.w. of Chicago, on Rock River; pop. 139,712 R-233
  Illinois I-36, *map* I-53

Rockford College, in Rockford, Ill.; private control; founded 1847; liberal arts, education; graduate studies R-233

Rockhampton, Australia, port in Queensland, on Fitzroy River, near e. coast; trade in gold, meat; pop. 51,500, *maps* A-819, P-6

Rock Hill, S.C., city 65 mi (105 km) n. of Columbia, in agricultural section; cattle raising, cotton, peaches; printing, finishing, and manufacturing of textiles; textile chemicals, hosiery; Winthrop College; large family amusement park nearby; pop. 35,344 S-361d, *maps* S-318, U-41

Rock hind, fish. *see in index* Grouper

Rockhurst College, Kansas City, Mo.; Roman Catholic; chartered 1910, opened 1917; arts and sciences, education; graduate studies.

Rockies. *see in index* Rocky Mountains

Rocking chair F-42

Rockingham, Charles Watson-Wentworth, 2nd marquis of (1730–82), British statesman; as prime minister 1765–66 tried to conciliate American Colonies by repealing Stamp Act; again prime minister for three months in 1782
  freedom for colonies R-170

Rockingham, Vt., town in Windham County, on Connecticut River, 20 mi (30 km) n. of Brattleboro; settled about 1753; pop. 5,538.

Rock Island, Ill., city in n.w. part of state, on Mississippi River, adjoining Moline (these two cities with neighboring East Moline, Ill., and Davenport, Iowa, known together as the Quad Cities); farm equipment, rubber footwear; railroad shops; U.S. arsenal on 990-acre (400-hectare) island (Rock Island) flanking the city; Augustana College; settled 1828, incorporated 1841; pop. 47,036
  Illinois, *map* I-53

Rockland, Mass., 6 mi (10 km) n.e. of Brockton; abrasives, fiberglass boats, shoes; incorporated 1874; pop. of township 15,695.

Rock madwort. *see in index* Golddust

Rock maple. *see in index* Sugar maple

Rock melon (or cantaloupe), type of European melon *Cucumis melo cantalupensis*; the true cantaloupe M-292

Rock moss (or granite moss), type of moss M-599

Rockne, Knute Kenneth (1888–1931), U.S. football coach, born in Voss, Norway; developed teams at University of Notre Dame, near South Bend, Ind.
  football F-297

Rock 'n' roll. *see in index* Rock

Rock of Gibraltar G-143

Rock of Monaco, Monaco, on the French Riviera M-528

Rock oil, petroleum. *see in index* Petroleum

Rock oyster, mollusk *Ostrea cucullata* O-623

Rockport, Ind., county seat of Spencer County, on Ohio River; Lincoln pioneer village dedicated here 1935; pop. 2,590
  Indiana, *map* I-102

Rockport, Mass., on Cape Ann, n.e. of Gloucester; artists' colony, summer resort, fishing center; granite quarries; pop. of township 5,636.

Rock River, tributary of the Mississippi, in s. Wisconsin and n. Illinois; 350 mi (560 km) long
  Illinois, *map* I-35
    Rockford R-233

Rockrose family (or Cistaceae), family of plants and shrubs including rockrose, helianthemum, and pinweed. *see also in index* Helianthemum

Rock salt S-29–31
  infrared detection R-38
  inorganic chemistry I-211

Rock soapwort, perennial plant *Saponaria ocymoides* of the pink family, native to central and s. Europe; trailing, branching, soft, hairy plants with oval leaves; flowers small, starlike, bright pink or white.

Rock spray, a ground cover *Coneaster horizontalis*
  growing conditions G-27

Rock Springs, Wyo., city in s.w. part of state; livestock, coal, oil and gas, soda ash; hunting and fishing; pop. 19,458, *maps* N-351, U-40
  Wyoming W-389, 396

Rock Venus clam *Prototheca staminea*
  shell, *picture* S-151

Rockville, Md., city in Montgomery County, 15 mi (25 km) n.w. of Washington, D.C.; technical research, printing; Montgomery College; pop. 43,811 M-168, 178, *map* M-183

Rockville Centre, N.Y., residential village near s. shore of Long Island, about 19 mi (31 km) s.e. of New York, N.Y.; Molloy Catholic College; pop. 25,405.

Rockweed, seaweed, *pictures* S-104, P-361
  used for clambake, *picture* R-189

Rockwell, Norman (1894–1978), U.S. illustrator, born New York, N.Y.; noted especially for cover designs and illustrations and portraits for popular magazines; author 'My Adventures as an Illustrator'.

Rock wren, bird of the Troglodytidae family W-364

Rocky Ford, Colo., city on Arkansas River, about 50

mi (80 km) s.e. of Pueblo; in irrigated farming region; beet sugar; pop. 4,804.

Rocky Mount, N.C., city 48 mi (77 km) n.e. of Raleigh; bright-leafed tobacco market; textiles, fertilizers, furniture, food products; North Carolina Wesleyan College; pop. 41,283, *map* U-41

Rocky Mountain bee plant. *see in index* Cleome

Rocky Mountain College, in Billings, Mont.; affiliated with Presbyterian and Methodist churches and United Church of Christ; founded 1883, present name 1947; arts and sciences, education.

Rocky Mountain goat, type of antelope G-171

Rocky Mountain Men, North American fur traders F-472

Rocky Mountain National Park, in Colorado, *maps* C-583, U-80-1, *pictures* C-567, R-234

Rocky Mountain region. *see in index* United States, *subhead* geographic regions, Rocky Mountain; also names of states in Rocky Mountain region

Rocky Mountains (or Rockies), a chain of ranges along east side of North American Cordilleras from Mexico to Alaska R-234, *maps* N-351, U-36, 80
Alaska Range A-241, 256
British Columbia B-451, *map* C-109
Brooks Range B-464
climate U-79
Colorado C-568, *picture* C-570
Colorado River C-584
early explorers
Lewis and Clark L-144
ecology E-52
forest F-311
Idaho I-18, *maps* I-19, I-31
Montana M-550
Nevada N-133
New Mexico N-214, *map* N-229
resources U-78, 82
Wyoming W-386

Rocky Mountain sheep. *see in index* Bighorn sheep

Rocky Mountain spotted fever, infectious disease first identified in Rocky Mts. region; has wide range over U.S.; marked by high fever and red, spotted eruption; caused by a blood parasite that is transmitted by a tick; preventive vaccine used S-388
tick T-182

Rocky River, Ohio, city on Lake Erie, just w. of Cleveland; residential; pop. 22,958.

Rococo style (or Louis XV style), in art
furniture F-459
interior design I-249, *picture* I-248

Rocroi, France, town near Belgian frontier, 50 mi (80 km) n. of Reims; French victory over Spaniards 1643 in Thirty Years' War; pop. 1,542.

Rod, fishing. *see in index* Fishing rod

Rod (also called rood), measurement W-138, *table* W-140

'Röda Rummet' (or 'The Red Room'), work by Strindberg S-489

Rodd, Mrs. L.C. *see in index* Tennant, Kylie

Rodeheaver, Homer Alvan (1880–1955), U.S. music director, writer of gospel songs, born Union Furnace, Ohio ('Song Stories of the Sawdust Trail'; '20 Years with Billy Sunday').

Rodents (or Rodentia), order of gnawing animals R-236
beavers B-120
bubonic plague carriers P-472
enemies
hawks and owls B-259
snakes S-226a, *picture* S-223
furs, *tables* F-464, 465
guinea pig G-316
hamster H-24
life span A-126
mammal, *table* M-80

Rodeo (from Spanish word meaning "going around"), annual roundup of cattle on ranches for counting and branding; also a form of entertainment built around activities of U.S. cowboy R-236, *picture* S-331
Iowa, *picture* I-298
Nebraska, *picture* N-103
Nevada, *picture* N-143

Roderick (or Roderic), last king of the Visigoths, reigning in Spain 710–11; overthrown by Moslem invasion, which was aided by his own Gothic enemies.

'Roderick Random', semiautobiographical novel by Tobias George Smollett (1748), named from the hero, a reckless young man who has adventures abroad, at sea, and in England E-272

Rodgers, Calbraith Perry (1879–1912), U.S. aviator, born in New York, N.Y.; made first successful transcontinental flight in United States in 1911 A-203

Rodgers, Jimmie (known as the Father of Country Music) (1897–1933), U. S. country musician M-678

Rodgers, John (1773–1838), U.S. Navy officer, born in Maryland; fought in naval war with France as first lieutenant of the *Constellation*; promoted captain 1799; fought against Barbary pirates (1802–6) and in War of 1812.

Rodgers, Richard (1902–79), U.S. composer, born in New York, N.Y., with Lorenz Hart and Oscar Hammerstein II, lyric writers, wrote over 1,000 songs and many musical shows; president and producing director of New York Music Theater, Lincoln Center, 1963– ('A Connecticut Yankee', 'I'd Rather Be Right', 'Pal Joey', 'South Pacific', 'No Strings'). *see also in index* Hammerstein, Oscar, II
musical comedy M-685

Rodi. *see in index* Rhodes

Rodin, François Auguste (1840–1917), French sculptor R-236, S-90
metalworking M-311
modern sculpture S-91
'The Burghers of Calais' S-76, *picture* S-77
'The Thinker', *picture* O-510

Rodman, Hugh (1859–1940), admiral, U.S. Navy, born in Frankfort, Ky.; commanded U.S. battleships with British Fleet in World War I; commanded Pacific Fleet 1919.

Rod mill, in mining M-429

Rodney, Caesar (1728–84), U.S. patriot, born in Dover, Del.; early advocate of independence and signer of the Declaration; general in Revolutionary War; president of Delaware 1778–82
Declaration of Independence D-56
Delaware D-76
Statuary Hall, *table* S-437a

Rodney, George Brydges, first **Baron Rodney** (1718–92), English admiral; defeated comte de Grasse of France off Dominica 1782, saving Jamaica for English and destroying French naval prestige

Rodó, José Enrique (1872–1917), Uruguayan writer L-69, *picture* L-73

Rodrigues (or Rodriguez), island in Indian Ocean, dependency of Mauritius; area 42 sq mi (109 sq km); pop. 18,300.
Mauritius M-233

Rodríguez, Abelardo Lujan (1889–1967), Mexican revolutionist and political leader; provisional president of Mexico 1932–34.

Rodríguez, Claudio (born 1934), Spanish poet S-366

Rodríguez Álvarez, Alejandro. *see in index* Casona, Alejandro

Rods, retinal structure E-388
color perception C-562

Rod weeder, farm machine F-32

Rodzinski, Artur (1894–1958), U.S. orchestra conductor, born in Dalmatia (now Yugoslavia); became U.S. citizen 1933; conductor Los Angeles Philharmonic Orchestra 1929–33, Cleveland Symphony 1933–43, New York Philharmonic Symphony 1943–47, Chicago Symphony 1947–48
orchestra, *list* O-579

Roe, Edward Payson (1838–88), U.S. novelist and Presbyterian minister; novels among best-sellers of their day ('Barriers Burned Away'; 'From Jest to Earnest').

Roe, fish eggs
sturgeon S-495a

Roebling, John Augustus (1806–69), U.S. engineer, born in Prussia; built the suspension bridge over Niagara River (1852) and designed Brooklyn Bridge, which was built by his son, **Washington Augustus Roebling** (1837–1926), engineer, born in Saxonburg, Pa.
Brooklyn Bridge B-446

Roe deer (also called roebuck), small deer *Capreolus caprea* of Europe and w. Asia; male has small erect antlers usually with three tines D-62, *table* D-63

Roehm, Ernest (or Ernst Röhm) (1887–1934), German army officer and Nazi official, born in Munich; charged with conspiracy to overthrow Adolf Hitler as chancellor; executed by his order
Hitler H-175

Roemer, Ole (or Olaus Römer) (1644–1710), Danish astronomer, born in Aarhus, Jutland; professor of astronomy University of Copenhagen 1681–1710 L-198

Roemmert, George (1892–1952), U.S. scientist and physician, born in Germany; came to U.S. 1929; gave lectures and instruction in Germany and the U.S. on the projection of microscope images; founded and conducted the first microvivarium at Chicago World's Fair 1932–34.

Roentgen, Wilhelm Konrad (or Wilhelm Konrad Röntgen) (1845–1923), German physicist, born in present Remscheid; professor at Strasbourg, Giessen, Würzburg, and Munich; discovered X rays 1895 R-63. *see also in index* Nobel Prizewinners, *table*
medicine M-284
X rays X-406

Roentgenogram. *see in index* Radiograph

Roentgen rays. *see in index* X rays

Roer (or Rur), river of West Germany and s. Netherlands; 125 mi (200 km) long; flows n.w. into Maas River in The Netherlands.

Roerich, Nicolas Constantinovich (1874–1947), Soviet painter, archaeologist, writer; earlier paintings realistic, later decorative, finally abstract and mystic; wrote libretto for Stravinsky's 'The Rite of Spring'.

Roethke, Theodore (1908–63), U.S. poet, born in Saginaw, Mich.; professor of English University of Washington 1948–63 ('Open House'; 'Praise to the End!'; 'The Waking', won 1954 Pulitzer prize for poetry; 'Words for the Wind'; 'I Am! Says the Lamb'; 'The Far Field').

Roe vs. Wade, case in U.S. constitutional law, *list* S-518b
criminal law C-769

Rogallo, Francis, U.S. space scientist A-65

Rogation Days, in Christianity, the three days before Ascension Day, observed in early church by fasting and chanting of litanies in public processions; introduced by French bishop in 5th century; still observed in minor degree by Episcopal and Roman Catholic churches.

Roger, pirate's flag. *see in index* Jolly Roger

Rogers, Bruce (1870–1957), U.S. typographer, born in Lafayette, Ind.; designed limited editions for Riverside Press 1895–1912; later consultant for publishers and for Oxford and Harvard university presses; designed Montaigne, Centaur, and other types; his masterpieces are Montaigne (folio), 'Pierrot of the Minute', and 'The Centaur'
typeface history, *picture* B-349

Rogers, Carl Ransom (1902–87), U.S. psychologist, born in Oak Park, Ill.; professor of clinical psychology at Ohio State University 1940–45; professor of psychology University of Chicago 1945–57, University of Wisconsin 1957–63; wrote 'Counseling with Returned Servicemen' (with J. L. Wallen) and 'Client-Centered Therapy' P-524

Rogers, Ginger (originally Virginia Katherine McMath) (born 1911), U.S. dancer and actress, born in Independence, Mo.; won Academy award (1940) for 'Kitty Foyle'; partner of Fred Astaire in movie musicals A-705

Rogers, Henry Huttleston (1840–1909), U.S capitalist, born in Fairhaven, Mass.; made vast fortune as vice-president and active head of Standard Oil Company; later influential in copper, steel, railroads, insurance, etc.

Rogers, John (1500?–55), English Protestant martyr, burned at stake for denying Christian character of Church of Rome.

Rogers, John (1829–1904), U.S. sculptor; popular, sentimental statuette groups ('Slave Auction'; 'One More Shot'; 'The Town Pump'; 'Rip van Winkle').

Rogers, Kenny (born 1941), U.S. country musician M-679

Rogers, Randolph (1825–92), U.S. sculptor, born in Waterloo, N.Y.; known for portrait statues and the bronze Columbus doors of the Capitol at Washington, D.C.

Rogers, Robert (1731–95), New England colonial soldier, born in Dunbarton, N.H.; 1755 formed company of scouts called Rogers' Rangers for service against the French in Seven Years' War; in American Revolution organized Queen's Rangers and, later, King's Rangers for British service; main character in Kenneth Roberts' 'Northwest Passage'.

Rogers, Roy (originally Leonard Slye) (born 1912), U.S. actor and singer, born in Cincinnati, Ohio; organized and appeared with musical group Sons of the Pioneers 1932–48; noted as cowboy star of motion pictures, radio, and television, often with wife, **Dale Evans Rogers** (born 1912), actress and singer, born in Uvalde, Tex.; author of 'Angel Unaware' and 'My Spiritual Diary' W-152
country music M-678

Rogers, Samuel (1763–1855), British banker, poet, art patron; published at his own expense several volumes of poems which, if not brilliant, showed care and taste ('Pleasures of Memory'); friend of William Wordsworth, Lord Byron, Thomas Moore; declined laureateship.

Rogers, Will (1879–1935), U.S. humorist and actor, born in Claremore, Okla.; appeared in vaudeville 1905; his shrewd, homely comments on people and affairs gave him wide popularity on stage, radio, in motion pictures, and as a writer for the newspapers; killed in Alaska in airplane crash. *see also in index* Cheyenne Mountain
stamp honoring, *picture* S-407
Statuary Hall, *table* S-437b

Rogers, William Pierce (born 1913), U.S. lawyer and government official, born in Norfolk, N.Y.; U.S. deputy attorney general 1953–57, attorney general 1957–61; secretary of state 1969–73
Nixon N-325

Rogers, Woodes (died 1732), English navigator P-432a

Rogers, Ark., city 21 mi (34 km) n. of Fayetteville; commercial center; food processing; plastics; incorporated 1881; pop. 17,429.

Rogers, Mount, highest point (5,720 ft; 1,740 m) in Virginia; in Grayson and Smyth counties, s.w. Virginia, in the Iron Mountains, 37 mi (60 km) e. of Bristol B-319, *maps* V-330, 348

Rogers' Rangers. *see in index* Rogers, Robert

Roget, Peter Mark (1779–1869), British physician; helped establish University of London ('Thesaurus of English Words and Phrases'; 'On Animal and Vegetable Physiology')
motion pictures M-615

Roggeveen, Jacob (1659–1729), Dutch explorer, born in Middelburg; carried out expeditions planned by his sailor father; imprisoned in Batavia, (1722) for trespass on rights of Dutch East India Company; later acquitted; accused by geographers of reporting under new names places previously visited by others

great-granduncle of Theodore Roosevelt; invented vertical paddle wheel for steamboats
  Mississippi River M-486
Roosevelt, Quentin (1897–1918), youngest son of President Theodore Roosevelt; killed in World War I R-290, *picture* R-285
Roosevelt, Theodore (1858–1919), 26th president of the United States R-281. *see also in index* Nobel Prizewinners, *table*
  cat, *list* C-202
  conservation C-678
  Hall of Fame, *table* H-16
  homes
    Long Island L-297, *picture* N-262
    North Dakota, *pictures* N-380
  McKinley M-20
  Minnesota M-444
  Monroe Doctrine M-549
  Mount Rushmore N. Mem., *picture* S-321
  Muir M-648
  Panama Canal P-93
  Russo-Japanese War mediation R-362
  Sims S-205
  Taft T-8
  U.S. history U-183
  U.S. Navy N-91
  Venezuelan policy V-277
  White House W-196
Roosevelt, Theodore, Jr. (1887–1944), eldest son of President Theodore Roosevelt, born in Oyster Bay, N.Y.; lieutenant colonel A.E.F. in World War I; assistant secretary of Navy 1921–24; governor of Puerto Rico 1929–32; governor-general of Philippines 1932–33; as brigadier general served in n. Africa and Sicily 1942–43; made chief liaison officer to French army under Gen. Dwight D. Eisenhower Nov. 1943; died of heart attack during invasion of Normandy July 1944, *picture* R-285
Roosevelt, N.Y.; community s.w. Long Island; pop. 15,008.
Roosevelt Dam. *see in index* Theodore Roosevelt Dam
Roosevelt Island (formerly Welfare Island, or Blackwells Island), island in N.Y., between Manhattan and Long Island in East River; city hospitals; crossed by Queensboro Bridge.
Roosevelt Island, island off Antarctica, in e. part of Ross Ice Shelf; about 90 by 40 nautical mi (170 by 75 km); discovered 1934 by Richard E. Byrd and named for Franklin D. Roosevelt.
Roosevelt Memorial Association, founded 1919 to perpetuate the memory of Theodore Roosevelt and to establish and maintain a national memorial at Washington, D.C., and a memorial park at Oyster Bay, N.Y.; Roosevelt medal established 1923, awarded annually for distinguished work associated with Theodore Roosevelt's career.
Roosevelt River, Brazil, a tributary of the Amazon explored by Theodore Roosevelt; previously called River of Doubt because so little was known about it R-290, *map* S-298
  Brazil, *map* B-425
Roosevelt Sanctuary, for birds, at Oyster Bay, Long Island B-273
Roosevelt University, in Chicago, Ill.; founded 1945; arts and sciences, commerce, music; graduate studies.
Root, Elihu (1845–1937), U.S. lawyer and statesman, born in Clinton, N.Y.; secretary of war, secretary of state, and U.S. senator from N.Y.; member Alaska boundary commission 1903; headed mission to U.S.S.R. 1917; member Washington limitation of armaments conference 1921–22; author of works on government, citizenship, international relations. *see also in index* Nobel Prizewinners, *table*
  secretary of state R-288
  Taft T-8
Root, George Frederick (1820–95), U.S. composer and teacher, born in Sheffield, Mass.; founded music teachers' training school (1853).
Root, of hair H-7
Root, of plant R-290, P-358, *diagram* P-363
  adaptations A-39
  cap, *picture* P-363b
  cellular structure, *picture* L-267
  cypress knees, *picture* P-357
  experiments, *diagram* P-363d
  gravity, *diagram* P-374
  mangrove M-96
  nitrogen-fixing bacteria P-363a
  osmosis P-359
  pressure S-250
    force, *picture* P-363b
  seed, *diagram* P-374
  tree T-277
Root, portion of the tongue that lies on the floor of the mouth T-215
Root, in music, the note that originates a chord M-692
Root canal (or endodontic treatment), removal of the pulp from the tooth D-102
Root crops, those grown for their edible roots or tubers
  potato P-466
  sweet potato S-530
Root meaning, in language S-376
Roots, in mathematics P-484
  quadratic equation A-300
  slide rule S-217
Rootstock (or rhizome), underground stem F-56
  banana B-51
  fern F-56
  vegetative reproduction, *diagram* P-363a
Rope-and-pulley system, in mechanics M-268
Rope and twine R-291
  hemp H-127
  henequen S-206
  knot, hitch, and splice K-262
  sisal fiber S-206, *picture* R-292
Roper, Daniel Calhoun (1867–1943), U.S. lawyer and political leader, born in Marlboro County, South Carolina; secretary of commerce in F.D. Roosevelt's Cabinet 1933–38, *picture* R-268
Rope skipping, game, *picture* G-13
Ropewalk, process in ropemaking R-291
Rops, Félicien (1833–98), Belgian lithographer, etcher, and painter of Hungarian descent; satirical, imaginative; illustrated Baudelaire's poems.
Roque, a form of croquet played on a hard-surfaced court with a raised border C-783
Roquefort, cheese C-288
Roquet, a play in croquet C-783
Roraima (formerly Rio Branco), Brazil, territory in extreme n.; 88,843 sq mi (230,102 sq km); cap. Bôa Vista; pop. 82,018, *map* B-425
Roraima, Mount, in South America, flat-topped mountain at boundary of Brazil, Guyana, and Venezuela; 9,219 ft (2,810 m); source of several rivers which fall from it in giant cascades G-321, *map* S-298
Rorem, Ned (born 1923), U.S. composer M-677
Rorqual, furrow whale W-185
Rorschach, Hermann (1884–1922), Swiss psychiatrist
  inkblot test P-523, S-110
Rosa, Salvator (1615–73), Italian painter, chief master of the Neapolitan school; excelled in landscapes, seascapes, and battle scenes; also famous as a poet.
Rosa, Monte, Alpine peak (15,217 ft; 4,638 m) S-537, *map* I-404
Rosa, the rose genus of plants. *see in index* Rose
Rosaceae, rose family of plants R-296
Rosario, Argentina, 2nd largest city, railroad center, and port, on Paraná River, 185 mi (300 km) n.w. of Buenos Aires; large foreign trade; pop. 750,455, *maps* A-585, S-300
Rosary, a form of Catholic prayer and the string of beads with which it is said; adopted by Eastern Christian monks in 3rd century.
Rosary College, in River Forest, Ill.; Roman Catholic; founded 1848; arts and sciences; foreign study at Fribourg, Switzerland, in junior year; graduate study in library science.
Rosary Hill College. *see in index* Daemen College
Rosas, Juan Manuel de (1793–1877), Argentine dictator 1835–52; absolute despot; overthrown by combination of foreign and domestic enemies A-583, U-214
Rosbaud, Hans (1895–1962), German conductor, born in Graz, Austria; music director Baden-Baden symphony orchestra 1948–62; American debut Chicago, Ill., 1959; many first performances of contemporary music.
Roscius, Quintus (died 62 BC), Roman actor, greatest comic actor of his time; among his patrons was Cicero, to whom he gave elocution lessons.
Roscoe, Henry Enfield (1833–1915), British chemist who isolated vanadium; worked with Bunsen in researches in photochemistry.
Roscommon, inland county in Connaught Province, Ireland, on the Shannon River; 951 sq mi (2,463 sq km); county town Roscommon (pop. 1,659); sheep and cattle; pop. 56,228.
Rose, Chauncey (1794–1887), U.S. businessman and philanthropist, born in Connecticut; endowed Rose Polytechnic Institute at Terre Haute, Ind.
Rose, Dorothy, U.S. state legislator, *picture* W-274
Rose, Mauri (1906–81), U.S. auto racing driver, born in Columbus, Ohio; raced 1927–51; three-time winner of the Indianapolis 500; national driving champion 1936.
Rose, Pete (born 1942), U.S. baseball player, born in Cincinnati, Ohio; with Cincinnati Reds 1963–78, Philadelphia Phillies 1979–83, Montreal Expos 1984, Cincinnati Reds 1985–; in national league named rookie of year 1963, most valuable player (MVP) 1973, MVP of World Series 1975; ball player of decade 1979; broke record held by Ty Cobb of 4,191 hits 1985.
Rose, Uriah Milton (1834–1913), U.S. lawyer, born in Marion County, Kentucky; jurist in Arkansas; delegate Hague Conference 1907
  Statuary Hall, *picture* S-437a
Rose, genus of flowering plants R-294
  District of Columbia's flower, *picture* S-427
  festivals
    Pasadena P-135, *pictures* P-20
    Portland P-453
  garden flower cultivation F-229, *picture* F-222
  heraldry, *picture* H-136
  New York state flower, *picture* N-260
  patented plant P-367
  perfume P-204
  wasp W-74
  wild. *see in index* Wild rose
Roseate spoonbill, bird *Ajaia ajaja* of the family Threskiornithidae I-2
Roseau, Dominica, capital and port city D-225
  West Indies, *map* W-159
Rosebay rhododendron (or great laurel rhododendron), flowering plant *Rhododendron maximum* R-196
Rosebery, Archibald Philip Primrose, earl of (1847–1929), British Liberal statesman, orator, and writer; prime minister 1894–95; later a political power without office; wrote on Pitt, Peel, Cromwell, Napoleon, and Lord Randolph Churchill.
Rose Bowl P-135
  football F-290
Rose-breasted grosbeak, bird *Pheucticus ludovicianus* of the family Fringillidae G-290
Roseburg, Ore., agricultural city 60 mi (100 km) s. of Eugene; lumbering; Veterans Administration Hospital; incorporated 1872; pop. 16,644.
Rose chafer, a fawn-colored beetle of the June-bug family; feeds on rose blossoms and grapes and other fruits; grows about ½ in (1¼ cm) long; does not thrive in cultivated groves.
Rosecrans, William Starke (1819–98), U.S. Civil War general, commander of Army of Cumberland from 1862 till after defeat 1863 at Chickamauga
  Civil War C-476, 478
  Thomas T-82
Rosefish. *see in index* Ocean perch
'Rose Garden, The', work by Sa'di
  Islamic literature I-367
Rosegger, Peter (1843–1918), Austrian poet and novelist; 'The Eternal Light' ('Das Ewige Licht'), one of the most popular German novels of 19th century.
Rose-Hulman Institute of Technology, in Terre Haute, Ind.; for men; incorporated 1874, first instruction 1883; endowed by Chauncey Rose; chemical, civil, electrical, and mechanical engineering; graduate studies.
Roselle, N.J., residential borough 2 mi (3 km) w. of Elizabeth, near the Garden State Parkway; furniture, machinery; pop. 20,641.
Roselle, an annual plant *Hibiscus sabdariffa* of the mallow family native to tropical or subtropical regions; grows to 7 ft (2 m); leaves divided; flower yellow with fleshy red calyx and collar of tiny leaves; before seed forms, calyx and leaves may be used to make jelly or beverage; also yields a fiber; sometimes called red, or Jamaica, sorrel H-149
Rosemaling (sometimes called rose painting), in Scandinavian art F-252
Rosemary (or old man), a low European shrub *Rosmarinus officinalis* of the mint family with opposite, pungent, evergreen leaves and bluish flowers; fragrant oil distilled from leaves H-138, S-379, *picture* H-137
Rosemary pine. *see in index* Shortleaf pine
Rosemead, Calif., city 9 mi (15 km) e. of Los Angeles; electronic equipment; pop. 42,604.
Rosemont College, in Rosemont, Pa.; Roman Catholic; for women; founded 1922; arts and sciences.
Rose moss. *see in index* Portulaca
Rosenau, Milton Joseph (1869–1946), U.S. physician, born in Philadelphia, Pa.; important work in preventive medicine, disinfectants, sanitation; developed serums for meningitis and diphtheria.
Rosenberg, Alfred (1893–1946), German political leader, educator of Nazi youth; urged revival of beliefs of early Teutonic peoples; directed "philosophical outlook for Reich"; made minister for East 1941; hanged for war crimes Oct. 1946
  Hitler H-177
Rosenberg, Anna Marie (1902–83), U.S. government official, born in Budapest, Hungary; became citizen 1919; regional director War Manpower Commission 1942–45; assistant secretary of defense 1950–53; married Paul Gray Hoffman 1962.
Rosenberg, Ethel Greenglass (1915–53) and her husband **Julius Rosenberg** (1918–53), first U.S. civilians to be sentenced and put to death for espionage, born in New York, N.Y.; sentenced to death 1951 after found guilty of charges they gave vital information on atomic bomb to U.S.S.R. 1944–45; electrocuted at Sing Sing Prison
  Douglas's stay of execution D-234
Rosenberg, Tex., city 34 mi (55 km) s.w. of Houston; farming and mining district; sugar refinery; oil, salt, and sulfur industries; state school for retarded; incorporated 1902; pop. 17,995.
'Rosenkavalier, Der', opera by Strauss S-485
Rosenthal, Moriz (1862–1946), U.S. pianist, born in Lemberg, Galicia (then in Austria); pupil of Liszt; brilliant virtuoso; wife, Hedwig Kanner, also a pianist.
Rosenwald, Julius (1862–1932), U.S. merchant and philanthropist, born in Springfield, Ill.; became head of Sears, Roebuck & Co.; gave immense sums to philanthropic projects, especially education of black Americans; founded Museum of Science and Industry, Chicago, Ill. F-333

Rose of Jericho (or resurrection plant), small desert annual *Anastatica hierochuntica* growing in Red Sea region; after leaves fall, branches curl about seedpods to form ball that rolls to moist spots and there opens to release seeds; grown as curiosity in warm locations.

Rose of Lima, Saint (1586–1617), first American saint, born Lima, Peru; patroness of Latin America and Philippines; feast day August 30.

Rose of Sharon (or shrubby althea), a lovely ornamental shrub *Hibiscus syriacus* with rose, violet, or white single or double flowers; leaves small and notched; belongs to mallow family; introduced into U.S. from Asia; name also applied to other plants; Biblical rose of Sharon was probably a kind of tulip
- hibiscus H-149

Rose painting. *see in index* Rosemaling

Roses, Wars of the, contest between rival houses of York and Lancaster for English throne R-296
- England E-243
  - Edward IV E-107
  - Henry VI H-130
  - Richard III R-203
  - Tudor, House of T-304
- warfare, *list* W-14

Rosetta (Arabic Rashid), Egypt, town on Rosetta mouth of Nile River; formerly of great commercial importance; Rosetta stone found nearby C-269

Rosetta stone, key to hieroglyphic inscriptions of ancient Egypt A-536, E-131
- Champollion's translation C-269
- hieroglyphics H-150

Roseville, Calif., city 15 mi (25 km) n.e. of Sacramento; freight yards; railroad car production and icing, cement and metal products; pop. 24,347.

Roseville, Mich., city 13 mi (21 km) n.e. of Detroit; residential suburb; pop. 54,311.

Roseville, Minn., village situated just n. of St. Paul; metal products, data-processing equipment; pop. 35,820.

Rosewall, Ken (born 1934), Australian tennis player
- tennis T-107

Rose window, a circular window decorated with tracery; developed to a degree of great beauty in Gothic architecture.

Rosewood, hard, close-grained, fragrant wood of Brazilian tree of the bean family; also wood of African tree prized in cabinetmaking
- legume L-122

Rosh Hashana, Jewish New Year's Day festival celebrated on the first or first and second days of Tishri (September or October) N-243
- Judaism J-150

Rosicrucian Order, international fraternity officially called the Ancient Mystic Order of Rosae Crucis (or AMORC); its emblem is a cross with a single rose in the center; existence traced back to 12th century in Europe and earlier in Orient; in America since 1694; operates on lodge system and teaches metaphysical-scientific philosophy of "practical arts and sciences"; U.S. headquarters, San Jose, Calif.

'Rosie O'Grady's', balloon which carried Joseph Kittinger on the first solo crossing of the Atlantic B-45

Rosin, a resin R-158. *see also in index* Resins
- forest products F-318
- laundry soap S-231
- paint P-73
- pine T-328
  - sap collection, *pictures* U-56

Rosinante, in Cervantes' 'Don Quixote', the hero's famous horse S-365a

Roskilde, Denmark, city 16 mi (26 km) w. of Copenhagen, on Zealand Island; capital until 1443; cathedral with tombs of Danish kings; pop. 31,928.

Roslyn, N.Y., village 6 mi (10 km) n. of Hempstead, on Long Island, at s. end of Hempstead Harbor; home and burial place of William Cullen Bryant; pop. 2,607.

'Rosmerholm', work by Ibsen I-5

Rospigliosi, noble Roman family; Pope Clement IX was its most famous member.

Ross, Alexander (1783–1856), Canadian fur trader, author, born in Scotland; emigrated to Canada 1805; joined Pacific Fur Company 1810 and helped to found Fort Astoria on Columbia River; joined Hudson's Bay Company; settled in Red River District 1825 ('The Fur Hunters of the Far West'; 'The Red River Settlement').

Ross, Betsy (1752–1836), traditional maker of first U.S. flag, the Stars and Stripes R-297
- Flag of June 14, 1777 F-156, *picture* F-155

Ross, Diana (born 1944), U.S. singer M-681

Ross, Edward Alsworth (1866–1951), U.S. sociologist, born in Virden, Ill.; professor University of Wisconsin 1906–37; author of many books on sociology.

Ross, George (1730–79), signer of Declaration of Independence as Pennsylvania delegate, born in Newcastle, Del.

Ross, Harold Wallace (1892–1951), U.S. editor, born in Aspen, Colo.; began career as reporter; editor *The Stars and Stripes* 1917–19, *The American Legion Weekly* 1921–23; a founder and first editor (1925–51) of *The New Yorker* M-35
- Thurber T-178

Ross, Harriet. *see in index* Tubman, Harriet

Ross, James Clark (1800–62), British admiral and polar explorer; determined approximate position of north magnetic pole 1831, while with his uncle Sir John Ross in his search for a Northwest Passage; in 1839–43 headed expedition to Antarctic, *table* P-422
- Ross Ice Shelf A-474
- Ross Sea P-421

Ross, John (1777–1856), British explorer, born in Scotland; explored Baffin Bay in 1818 when he commanded an expedition for discovery of Northwest Passage; 1829 made another attempt to find Northwest Passage but failed and was icebound four years.

Ross, John (1790–1866), Cherokee chief (Cherokee name Cooweescoowe), born in Georgia; Scottish father had him educated at home by tutor and at Kingston Academy; president of Cherokee National Council 1817–26; often delegate to Washington; opposed cession of land and migration west; chief of Cherokee nation from 1839 until death C-282

Ross, Leonard Q. *see in index* Rosten, Leo Calvin

Ross, Malcolm D. (born 1919), U.S. Naval Reserve officer and atmospheric physicist, born in Momence, Ill.; made valuable contributions to balloon research for Office of Naval Research B-44

Ross, Nellie Tayloe (1876–1977), first woman governor of a U.S. state; governor of Wyoming 1925–27, elected to fill unexpired term of her husband, William B. Ross; director of U.S. Mint 1933–53
- women's rights W-276
- Wyoming W-389

Ross, Robert (1766–1814), British major general; commander of British force that captured Washington, D.C., in the War of 1812.

Ross, Ronald (1857–1932), British physician, born in Almora, India; a medical officer Indian medical service 1881–99; professor of tropical medicine University of Liverpool 1902–12; discovered life history of malaria parasite P-93. *see also in index* Nobel Prizewinners, *table*

Ross, Pa., urban township just n.w. of the city Pittsburgh, in Allegheny County; communities in the township include Perrysville and West View; pop. 35,102.

Rossbach, battle of (1757), battle in which Frederick the Great defeated the French in the Seven Years' War; named for village 25 mi (40 km) w. of Leipzig, Germany.

Rossby, Carl-Gustaf Arvid (1898–1957), U.S. meteorologist, born in Stockholm, Sweden; to U.S. 1926, became citizen 1939; noted for pioneer work in long-range weather forecasts.

Ross Dependency, coasts of Ross Sea and adjacent islands in region; created dependency by United Kingdom 1923; under jurisdiction of New Zealand
- Commonwealth membership C-602
- New Zealand N-294

Rossel Island, in Louisiade Archipelago, s.e. of Papua New Guinea.

Rossellini, Roberto (1906–77), Italian motion picture director; part of Neorealist movement
- motion pictures M-623

Rossellino, Antonio (or Antonio Gambarelli) (1427–79), Italian sculptor; work influenced by Donatello.

Rossetti, Christina Georgina (1830–94), British poet R-298
- literary contribution E-276

Rossetti, Dante Gabriel (1828–82), British poet and painter R-298
- literary contribution E-276
- Morris M-588
- Swinburne S-535

Rossetti, Gabriele (1783–1854), Italian poet and critic; father of Christina, Dante Gabriel, and William M. Rossetti R-298

Rossetti, William Michael (1829–1919), British painter and poet, born in London; one of the founders of the Pre-Raphaelite school of painting R-298

Rossi, Bruno (born 1905), physicist, born in Venice, Italy; professor at Massachusetts Institute of Technology 1946–70; research in cosmic rays.

Ross Ice Shelf, in Antarctica, in Ross Sea A-472

Rossignol, Lake, in Nova Scotia, 16 mi (26 km) from Liverpool; named after French trader whose property was confiscated here 1604.

Rossini, Gioacchino Antonio (1792–1868), Italian composer, born in Pesaro; best known for 'Stabat Mater' and operas ('Otello'; 'Cenerentola', based on Cinderella; 'William Tell')
- opera O-566
- popular music M-683

Ross Island, in corner of Ross Sea, just off Victoria Land, Antarctica; 43 by 45 nautical mi (79 by 83 km); highest point is active volcano Mount Erebus (12,280 ft; 3,710 m) A-438

Rossiter, Thomas Prichard (1818–71), portrait, historical, and religious painter, born in New Haven, Conn. ('Washington and Lafayette at Mount Vernon, 1776'; 'The Prince of Wales and President Buchanan').

Ross Sea, large arm of South Pacific Ocean extending into Antarctica; named for Sir James Clark Ross
- Amundsen P-421
- Ross P-421

Rostand, Edmond (1868–1918), French dramatist; his play 'Cyrano de Bergerac' deals with real character of that name; 'L'Aiglon', with the young king of Rome, son of Napoleon I; 'Chantecler' is a satire in which the characters are barnyard fowls.

Rosten, Leo Calvin (pseudonym Leonard Q. Ross) (born 1908), U.S. author, born in Lodz, Poland ('Captain Newman, M.D.'; 'The Washington Correspondents'; 'Hollywood: the Movie Colony, the Movie Makers'; 'The Story Behind the Painting'; 'The Joys of Yiddish'; 'O Kaplan! My Kaplan')
- 'The Education of Hyman Kaplan' R-112b

Rostock, East Germany, Baltic seaport 95 mi (150 km) n.e. of Hamburg; university founded 1419; an old Hanse town; pop. 198,396 G-120, *maps* E-361, G-134

Rostov (also Rostov-on-Don), U.S.S.R., city on Don River, 25 mi (40 km) from Sea of Azov; transportation center; farm machinery, shoes, flour; pop. 789,000, *maps* E-361, R-344

Rostow, Walt Whitman (born 1916), U.S. economist, born in New York, N.Y.; professor economic history Massachusetts Institute of Technology 1950–61; state department policy planning council chairman 1961–66; special assistant to president for national security affairs 1966–69; professor of economics and history University of Texas 1969–; awarded Presidential Medal of Freedom 1969 I-190

Rostropovich, Mstislav (born 1927), Soviet-born conductor, cellist, and pianist, born in Baku; conducted National Symphony of Washington, D.C. 1977– ; won International Competition of Cellists in Prague 1950; Grammy awards 1970, 1977, 1980, 1984; Life in Music Prize 1984.

Roswell, N.M., city 177 mi (285 km) s.e. of Santa Fe; in cotton and cattle area; district offices of major oil companies; nearby is site of Walker Air Force Base, opened in 1941 and closed in 1967; leased by Air Force to city of Roswell, site is now used for industry, education, and airline-pilot training; pop. 39,676, *maps* N-229, 351, U-40
- New Mexico N-216, 224

Roswitha. *see in index* Hrotsvit

Rot. *see in index* Decay

Rot, name given to a number of plant diseases caused by parasitic fungi and bacteria; marked by breakdown of plant tissues
- retting uses F-176

Rotameter M-317

Rotary calculator C-20

Rotary drill P-236

Rotary engine (or rotating engine), automobile A-846
- internal-combustion engine E-252

Rotary International, organizations established for the purpose of making practical application of the ideal of service to business and professional life; first **Rotary Club** formed in Chicago, Ill., 1905 by Paul P. Harris; Rotary International, organized 1912, now includes clubs in many parts of the world; international headquarters in Evanston, Ill.; active membership limited to one representative of each business, profession, or institution in a community F-387

Rotary plow P-392

Rotary press, in printing P-501, *diagram* P-503, *picture* P-499
- newspapers N-240

Rotary steam engine W-162

Rotary wing. *see in index* Rotor, *subhead* helicopter

Rotating engine. *see in index* Rotary engine

Rotation, in physics
- gyroscopic principles G-327
- mechanics M-264

Rotation, of planets P-350, A-710, *tables* P-351, S-254b
- earth E-28. *see also in index* Earth, *subhead* rotation

Rotational speed (or angular velocity), in physics I-229
- mechanics M-266

Rotational symmetry. *see in index* Radial symmetry

ROTC. *see in index* Reserve Officers Training Corps

Rote learning, in psychology
- Ebbinghaus E-47

Roth, Frederick George Richard (1872–1944), U.S. sculptor, born in Brooklyn, N.Y.; noted for animal and for equestrian sculptures (bronze equestrian statue of General Washington in Morristown National Historical Park, at Morristown, N.J.).

Roth, Philip Milton (born 1933), U.S. writer, born in Newark, N.J.; named to National Institute of Arts and Letters 1970; (novels: 'Letting Go', 'When She Was Good', 'Portnoy's Complaint'; stories: 'Goodbye, Columbus', won 1960 National Book Award)
- American literature A-362

Rothamsted, scientific agricultural experiment station, founded 1843 by J.B. Lawes on his estate near Harpenden, England; research on plant and soil nutrition.

Rothenburg, West Germany, city in Bavaria on Tauber River, about 40 mi (60 km) w. of Nuremberg; pop. 11,662, *map* G-134, *pictures* E-339, 351

Rothenstein, William (1872–1945), British painter and author, known for portraits and illustrations ('Sir Rabindranath Tagore'; 'Augustus John'; 'Morning at Benares'); among his published works are 'Life of Goya', 'Twenty-four Portraits', and 'Men and Memories'.

Rotherham, England, manufacturing town 6 mi (10 km) n.e. of Sheffield, on Don River; iron and steel products, chemicals, glass; pop. 86,450.

Rothermere, Harold Sidney Harmsworth, first **viscount** (1868–1940), British newspaper proprietor and philanthropist; brother of Viscount Northcliffe, with whom he was associated; newspapers include *Daily Mail, Daily Mirror, London Evening News;* air minister 1917–18.

Rothschild family, European banking family of German origin; includes **Meyer Amschel,** or **Mayer Anselm** (1743–1812), **Amschel Meyer** (1773–1855), **Solomon** (1774–1855), **Nathan** (1777–1836), **Karl** (1788–1855), **Jacob,** or **James** (1792–1868), **Lionel** (1808–79), **Nathan Meyer** (1840–1915) R-299

Rothstein, Arnold (1882–1928), U.S. crime overlord, born in New York City; dreamed of making organized crime a national business C-772

Roth vs. United States, case in United States constitutional law P-451

Rotogravure, process of printing P-502. *see also in index* Gravure

Rotor
- gyrocompass G-327
- helicopter H-118
- hydrodynamic brakes B-405
- jet propulsion J-106
- motor and engine M-631

Rotorcraft, aircraft A-64

Rotor machine, cipher device C-420, *picture* C-419

Rotorship. *see in index* Flettner, Anton

Rotorua, New Zealand; district of n.-central North Island; hot springs, boiling mudpools, and spouting geysers; tourist and convention center, *map* N-299, *picture* N-289

Rototiller, farm machinery F-32

Rotterdam, The Netherlands, chief seaport and 2nd largest city; pop. 679,032 R-299, *map* E-361
- harbors and ports H-36, *picture* H-37
- The Netherlands N-126, 129

Rotterdam, N.Y., community just s.w. of Schenectady; aluminum and electrical products; nearby is Jan Mabie house, one of oldest in Mohawk Valley; pop. 29,451.

Rottweiler, dog, *picture* D-202

Rotunda style, calligraphy C-59

Rou. *see in index* Rollo

Rouault, Georges (1871–1958), French artist R-299
- enameling E-208
- expressionism P-68

Roubaix, France, manufacturing city in n., near Belgian border; textiles; occupied by Germans in World War I (1914) and again in World War II (1940); pop. 114,239, *map* F-372

Rouen, France, port city on Seine River; pop. 118,323 R-299a, *map* E-361
- France, *map* F-372
- Joan of Arc R-299a

Rouge, Canadian football F-292

Rouget de Lisle, Claude Joseph (1760–1836), French soldier and songwriter; composed the French national anthem 1792 while an officer of engineers N-65

Rough, in golf G-188

Rough fish, *list* F-146

'Roughing It', work by Twain A-351
- western W-151

Rough oxeye. *see in index* Heliopsis

Rough Riders, regiment of cavalry in Spanish-American War led by Theodore Roosevelt R-284, S-365

Rough-winged swallow S-521

Rougon-Macquart series, novels by Zola Z-456

Rouleau, Félix Raymond Marie, Cardinal (1866–1931), Canadian prelate, born near Rivière-du-Loup, in present Quebec Province; ordained Roman Catholic priest 1892; archbishop of Quebec 1926–31; cardinal from 1927.

Roumania. *see in index* Rumania

Round, music, a form of canon employing a complete melody rather than melodic phrases; various parts always enter on same note. *see also in index* Canon

'Rounders', novel by Evans W-151

Roundheads, nickname for Puritans, or Parliamentary party, in England in Civil War, because many wore their hair short in contrast to flowing locks of the Cavaliers F-41
- Charles I C-275
- English history E-246

Roundlet, a hat H-53

'Round Midnight', song by Monk M-538

Rounds, Glen (born 1906), writer, *list* H-274

Round ships, ancient commercial ships N-80

Round Table, Arthurian legends R-299a, A-655. *see also in index* Arthurian legends

Roundup, in cattle ranching, *pictures* U-77
- cowboy C-752

Roundworm, worm of the phylum Aschelminthes and the class Nematoda W-362, *picture* W-361
- invertebrate group I-283
- filariasis M-598

Rourke, Constance Mayfield (1885–1941), U.S. author of children's books, born in Cleveland Ohio; authority on North American folklore; work noted for careful research, vivid description, and fine prose ('Davy Crockett'; 'Audubon').

Rous, Francis Peyton (1879–1970), U.S. pathologist, born in Baltimore, Md.; with Rockefeller University (now The Rockefeller Institute) 1909–45. *see also in index* Nobel Prizewinners, *table*

Roush, Edd J. (born 1893), U.S. baseball player, born in Oakland City, Ind.; outfielder in N.L. 1916–29 and in 1931 (New York 1916, 1927–29, Cincinnati 1916–26, 1931); great hitter and center fielder; hit over .300 in each of 11 consecutive seasons, including mark of .352 in 1921; lifetime batting average of .323.

Rousseau, Henri Julien (1844–1910), French modernist painter R-299a-b
- 'The Waterfall', *picture* R-299b

Rousseau, Jean Jacques (1712–78), French philosopher R-299b
- autobiography A-831
- bioethics B-214
- children's literature L-246
- civilization C-467
- civil rights C-468
- contributor to 'Encyclopédie' R-124
- educational contribution E-86
- Enlightenment E-289
- French literature F-396, *picture* F-395
- optimism N-413
- philosophy P-266
- Robespierre R-223

Rousseau, Théodore (1812–67), French painter, one of the leaders of the Barbizon school; called "the epic poet of landscape art"; fine draftsmanship, harmony of color.

Roussel, Albert (1869–1937), French composer; original and strongly modern; was a naval officer 1889–94 ('Padmâvati' and 'Bacchus and Ariadné', ballets; 'Evocations', a symphony).

Roux, Pierre Paul Emile (1853–1933), French physician and bacteriologist; began working with Pasteur 1878 and became director of Pasteur Institute at Paris 1904; did valuable work in discovery of pneumonia microbe and in study of diphtheria and diphtheria toxin; elected to Academy of Medicine 1895 and Academy of Science 1899.

Roux, Wilhelm (1850–1924), German anatomist; founder of experimental embryology
- study E-203

Rouyn, Que., city just s. of Noranda and about 135 mi (215 km) n. of North Bay, Ont.; commercial and educational center in mining region; pop. 17,821 Q-9d, *map* c-112

ROV (remotely operated vehicle), oceanic exploration O-463

Roving, process in spinning F-4
- cotton, C-740

Rovuma River, in s.e. Africa. *see in index* Ruvuma River

Rowan, Andrew Summers (1857–1943) U.S. Army officer, born in Gap Mills, Va. (now in West Virginia); famous for carrying message to and from García, in Cuba, at opening of Spanish-American War; inspired Elbert Hubbard's essay 'A Message to Garcia'; awarded Distinguished Service Cross 1922.

Rowan, Carl Thomas (born 1925), U.S. columnist, born in Ravenscroft, Tenn.; staff writer *Minneapolis Tribune* 1950–61; deputy assistant secretary of state 1961–63; ambassador to Finland 1963–64; director U.S. Information Agency 1964–65; syndicated columnist 1965–.

Rowan (or European mountain ash, or quickbeam), tree *Sorbus aucuparis* M-637

Rowboat R-300, B-326
- Egypt, ancient R-300, S-163, *picture* S-164
- galleys. *see in index* Galley
- shell R-300

Rowe, Nicholas (1674–1718), British poet and dramatist; became poet laureate 1715 ('Tamerlane', 'The Fair Penitent', 'Jane Shore', and other plays; first important critical edition of Shakespeare 1709)
- poet laureate P-402

Rower, one who propels a boat with oars N-81

Row house H-292, *picture* H-299

Rowing, a water sport R-300
- Oxford University O-622

Rowland, Henry Augustus (1848–1901), U.S. physicist, born in Honesdale, Pa.; professor Johns Hopkins University 25 years; determined ohm and the mechanical equivalent of heat; discovered magnetic effect of electric convection
- diffraction grating S-372

Rowlandson, Thomas (1756–1827), British caricaturist, born in London; illustrated 'Tour of Dr. Syntax' (text by William Combe), also works by Oliver Goldsmith, Laurence Sterne, and Tobias Smollett
- cartoons C-187

Rowley, James Joseph (born 1908), U.S. government official, born in New York, N.Y.; in government service 1937–73; joined White House staff of Secret Service 1939, chief 1946–61, director of Secret Service 1963–73.

Rowlocks, brick masonry B-438

Rowson, Susanna Haswell (1762–1824), U.S. novelist, actress, and educator, born in Portsmouth, England; conducted school for girls at Boston, Mass., 1797–1822 ('Rebecca') A-345

Roxas y Acuña, Manuel (1892–1948), first president of Philippines 1946–48; brigadier general under Gen. Douglas MacArthur World War II; captured by Japanese, joined puppet government, but did espionage for U.S. P-261, *picture* P-261a

Roxbury, N.J., township 5 mi (8 km) s.w. of Dover; chiefly residential; dynamite, ceramics; incorporated 1742; pop. 18,878.

Roy, Camille (1870–1943), Canadian critic, literary historian, and Roman Catholic priest, born in Berthier-en-Bas, near Quebec, Que.

Roy, Gabrielle (or Mme. Marcel Carbotte) (1909–83), French-Canadian novelist, born St. Boniface, Man.

Roy, Maurice, Cardinal (1905–85), Canadian prelate, born in city of Quebec; ordained Roman Catholic priest 1926; chaplain Canadian armed forces 1939–45; archbishop of Quebec 1947–; became cardinal 1965.

Roy, Utah, city s.w. of Ogden; canning, salad dressing factories, slaughterhouse, machine shop, diversified farming; pop. 14,356, *map* V-232

Royal, Mount, on island of Montreal, Que., 763 ft (232 m) high M-570

Royal Academy, British A-14
- Gainsborough G-3
- Reynolds R-175

Royal Air Force (RAF), air arm of United Kingdom; formed 1918; absorbed Royal Flying Corps and Royal Naval Air Service
- uniform U-12
- World War I, *picture* W-306
- World War II W-324

Royal Air Force College, in United Kingdom M-411

Royal and Ancient Golf Club, in St. Andrews, Scotland G-193

Royal Architectural Institute of Canada, established 1907 as central organization of component societies to promote the architectural profession; headquarters Ottawa, Ont.

Royal Arch Masons, members of the Masonic order who have taken the Royal Arch degree.

Royal Ascot Gold Cup, horse race held in Ascot, England H-275

Royal Australian Air Force
- uniform, *picture* U-334

Royal Ballet D-29

Royal Botanical Gardens, in Hamilton, Ont. H-22

Royal Botanic Gardens. *see in index* Kew Gardens

Royal Botanic Gardens, gardens in Melbourne, Australia M-290

Royal Canadian Air Force (RCAF), former air force, merged into Canadian armed forces in 1968.

Royal Canadian Henley R-300

Royal Canadian Mounted Police (nickname Mounties, formerly North West Mounted Police) R-300a, *pictures* R-300b
- headquarters R-300a
- Saskatchewan S-49g
- training, *picture* P-430a

Royal Canadian Navy, former naval force, merged into Canadian armed forces in 1968.

Royal Dutch Airlines (KLM) A-170

Royale, Île, former French name of Cape Breton Island. *see in index* Cape Breton Island

Royal Exhibition Buildings, buildings in Melbourne, Australia M-290

Royal Festival Hall, in London, England, *picture* L-286

Royal Flying Doctor Service, in Australia A-326, A-788

Royal Fusiliers Museum, part of Tower of London complex T-237

Royal Geographical Society, a British society founded in 1930 G-69

Royal Gorge, canyon of Arkansas River, in s.-central Colorado A-626, *map* C-583, *picture* C-577

Royal Greenwich Observatory, in England, at Hurstmonceaux Castle, formerly at Greenwich O-458

Royal Institution, British scientific society for the promotion of research in experimental sciences; founded 1799; idea originated with Count Rumford; library and laboratories in headquarters in London, England.

Royalists (or Cavaliers), in English history, the partisans of Charles I and II
- American colonies A-341

Royal jelly, food of queen bees B-127

Royal lily. *see in index* Regal lily

Royal Marines, part of the Royal Navy of the United Kingdom M-136. *see also in index* Royal Navy

Royal Military Academy, in Sandhurst, England M-411

Northamptonshire, and Lincolnshire; 152 sq mi; pop. 23,504.

Rutland, Vt., 2nd city of state, near w. center, on Otter Creek, between Green Mountains on e. and Taconic Mountains on w.; marble quarrying and cutting, railroad shops; stone-working machinery, maple-sugaring equipment, scales, medical supplies, clothing; tourist center (winter and summer sports); pop. 18,436 V-286, *maps* V-301, 286, U-41

Rutledge, Ann (1816?–35), daughter of Abraham Lincoln's landlord, an innkeeper of New Salem, Ill.; Lincoln's fiancée; malaria victim L-217

Rutledge, Edward (1749–1800), U.S. statesman, born in Charleston, S.C.; brother of John Rutledge; signer of Declaration of Independence S-310
  Declaration of Independence D-56

Rutledge, John (1739–1800), U.S. patriot and jurist, born in Charleston, S.C.; brother of Edward Rutledge; member Stamp Act Congress; first state governor of South Carolina; helped frame United States Constitution and signed it; associate justice of U.S. Supreme Court; appointed chief justice but never confirmed because of loss of reason.

Rutledge, Wiley Blount, Jr. (1894–1949), U.S. educator and judge, born in Cloverport, Ky.; professor of law Washington University, St. Louis, Mo., 1926–35, University of Iowa 1935–39; associate justice U.S. Court of Appeals for District of Columbia 1939–43; associate justice U.S. Supreme Court 1943–49.

Ruvuma River (or Rovuma River), river, 450 mi (725 km) long, forms most of boundary between mainland Tanzania and Mozambique, *map* A-118

Ruwenzori Mountains (or Mountains of the Moon), mountain range in e.-central Africa R-366a
  minerals U-1
  Mount Margherita U-1

Ruysdael, Jacob van. *see in index* Ruisdael, Jacob van

Ruyter, Michael Adriaanszoon de (1607–76), Dutch admiral; fought under Admiral Martin Tromp in Anglo-Dutch War of 1652–54; commanded squadron in Baltic War of 1659; in wars of 1660s and 1670s with English and French captured English holdings on the Gold and Guinea coasts, burned English ships in the Medway, maneuvered the defeated Dutch fleet to safety, prevented bombardment of Dutch ports N-130

Ruzicka, Leopold (1887–1976), Swiss chemist, born in Vukovar, Serbia (now Yugoslavia). *see also in index* Nobel Prizewinners, *table*

Ruzicka, Rudolph (1883–1978), U.S. wood engraver, born in Bohemia; moved to U.S. at age 11; book designer and illustrator; type designer.

Ruzizi River, river along e. border of Zaire from Lake Kivu to Lake Tanganyika; 100 mi (160 km) long.

RV. *see in index* Recreational vehicle

Rwala, Arabian Bedouins N-332

Rwanda, republic in e.-central Africa; area 10,169 sq mi (26,338 sq km); cap. Kigali; pop. 4,321,000 R-366a, *map* A-118
  African political unit, *table* A-112
  flag, *picture* F-169

Ryan, Abram Joseph (or Father Ryan) (1838–86), U.S. Roman Catholic priest and poet, born in Hagerstown, Md.; chaplain in Confederate army during Civil War; noted for war poems ('The Conquered Banner').

Ryan, Aileen, U.S. legislator, *picture* W-274

Ryan, John Augustine (1869–1945), U.S. educator, ordained priest 1898; professor of sociology Catholic University of America; author of books on social welfare and labor questions.

Ryan, John Dale (born 1915), U.S. Air Force officer, born in Cherokee, La.; commander SAC 1964–67; commander in chief PACAF 1967–69; Air Force chief of staff 1969–73.

Rydberg, Johannes Robert (1854–1919), Swedish physicist; worked on the spectrum S-373

Ryder, Albert Pinkham (1847–1917), U.S. painter R-366b, *picture* R-366b
  'Toilers of the Sea' P-54, *picture* P-55

Ryder, Arthur William (1877–1938), U.S. Sanskrit scholar and translator, born in Oberlin, Ohio; professor University of California.

Ryder Cup, trophy awarded biennially in matches between men's professional golf team of United Kingdom and that of U.S.; donated 1927 by Samuel Ryder, British seed merchant
  golf G-191

Rye, N.Y., city 23 mi (37 km) n.e. of New York, N.Y.; residential; beach on Long Island Sound nearby; pop. 15,083.

Rye, a cereal grain R-366b
  East Germany G-119
  flour B-428, F-213
  grains G-207
  hay H-75
  liquor production L-235
  root P-359
  starch S-424

Rye grass, a common name for a genus *Lolium* of annual and perennial grasses native to Europe and Asia; naturalized in North America; English rye grass *L. perenne* and Italian rye grass *L. multiflorum* used for forage in Europe and U.S., also for lawns and in soil conservation; seeds of some, especially darnel, important food for wild birds; leaves flat, glossy dark-green when young; flowers in single spikes, flat, slender.

Rye House Plot, conspiracy (1683) of extreme opponents of English Catholic succession to assassinate Charles II and his brother, the duke of York, afterward James II; used as pretext for execution of innocent political opponents, including Algernon Sidney and Lord William Russell.

Rye Patch, irrigation project in Nevada N-134

Ryerson, Adolphus Egerton (1803–82), Canadian Methodist clergyman and educator, born in Victoria, Ont.; first editor *Christian Guardian* 1829; first principal Victoria University 1841; general superintendent of education for Upper Canada, later for Ontario; principles of Ontario school system which he established largely followed by other provinces.

Rye whiskey, alcoholic beverage A-275

Rykov, Aleksei Ivanovich (1881–1938), Soviet political leader, son of a peasant; imprisoned number of times for political activities; commissar for supplies during Revolution of 1917; president council of people's commissars of U.S.S.R. (equivalent to office of prime minister) 1924–30; expelled from office because of his opposition to the more drastic measures of Joseph Stalin; executed 1938.

Ryks Museum, Amsterdam, The Netherlands. *see in index* Rijksmuseum

Rylands, John (1801–88), British cotton and linen manufacturer and philanthropist; one of original financiers of Manchester Ship Canal; John Rylands Library, Manchester, founded by his widow, has famous collection of early printed books.

Ryle, Sir Martin (1918–84), British radio astronomer; born in London; pioneered in radio telescope use and development; invented aperture synthesis technique; professor Cambridge University from 1959; named astronomer royal 1972. *see also in index* Nobel Prizewinners, *table*

Rymer, Thomas (1641–1713), English historian; worked for years on the 'Foedera', a compilation in Latin of British treaties ('Foedera' issued in 20 vols. 1704–35, the last 5 of these vols. edited by his assistant Robert Sanderson); wrote poetry and dramatic criticism.

Rynchopidae, a family of birds, the skimmers. *see in index* Skimmer

Rynek, square in Krakow, Poland K-303

'Ryojin hisho', Japanese folk music J-80

Ryswick, Peace of (or Peace of Rijswijk, named from village in The Netherlands near The Hague), treaty signed 1697, which ended war begun in 1689 between France and England, Spain, The Netherlands, and the Holy Roman Empire, *table* T-275
  William III K-247

Ryti, Risto Heikki (1889–1956), president of Finland 1940–44, formerly prime minister; born in Huittinen, s.w. Finland; sentenced to 10 years' imprisonment in war guilt trials 1946; pardoned 1949.

Ryukyu Islands (or Nansei-Shoto, or Liukiu), island chain belonging to Japan and extending between Taiwan and Kyushu; sugarcane, sweet potatoes, rice; exports include sugar, fabrics, lacquer; islands included in Japanese empire 1879; occupied by U.S. 1945; under Japanese peace treaty with Allies, effective 1952, Ryukyus were to be administered by U.S. pending the placing of the islands under United Nations trusteeship, with U.S. as administering authority; in 1953, the Amami Islands were returned by U.S. to Japan; remainder of Ryukyus (pop. 934,176), including Okinawa, returned by U.S. to Japan 1972; under broader definition, including Osumi Islands just s. of Kyushu, the Ryukyu Islands have a total area of about 1,750 sq mi (4,530 sq km) and a population of 1,198,386, *map* J-78. *see also in index* Amami Islands; Okinawa
  Asia, *map* A-700

The letter S

may have started as a picture sign of a sandy hill country, as in Egyptian hieroglyphic writing (1), or of a "tooth" (peak) of a rock, such as is found in a very early Semitic writing which was used about 1500 B.C. on the Sinai Peninsula (2). About 1000 B.C., in Byblos and other Phoenician and Canaanite centers, the sign was given a linear form (3), from which all later forms are derived. In the Semitic languages the sign was called *shin* or *sin,* meaning "tooth."

The Greeks turned the Semitic sign sideways (4). Later they formed it more symmetrically (5). They renamed the sign *sigma,* confusing it with the Semitic sign *samekh,* the forerunner of the English X sign. The Romans took the Greek form of the sign into Latin but rounded it and left off the bottom stroke (6). From Latin the capital letter came into English unchanged. The small "s" has many forms, including a variant of the capital (7). Another form (8) was shaped to link easily with adjoining letters in handwriting.

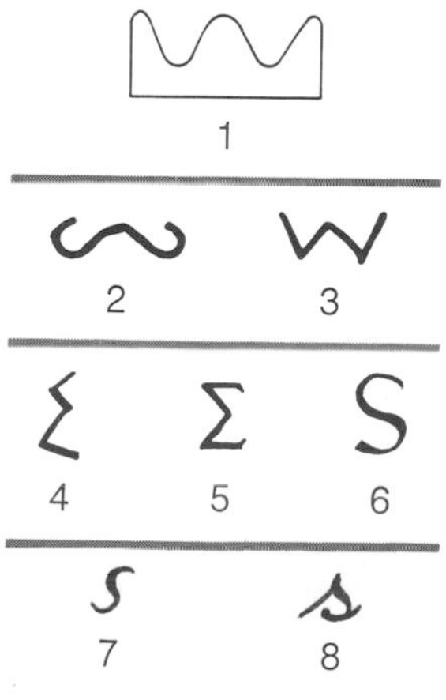

Saadi. *see in index* Sa'di

Saadia ben Joseph (882–942), Jewish scholar, born in Egypt S-1

Saale River, central Germany; flows n. 250 mi (400 km) to Elbe River, *map* G-134

Saanen goat, breed named for Saanen, town on Saane River in s.w. Switzerland; first imported into U.S. in 1904 G-171

Saar. *see in index* Saarland

Saarbrücken, West Germany, capital of Saarland, on Saar River, 38 mi (61 km) n.e. of Metz; coal-mining and industrial center; scene of early action in Franco-Prussian War; heavily damaged in World War II; pop. 127,989, *maps* E-361, G-134

Saaremaa (formerly Osel), largest island of Estonian Soviet Socialist Republic, in Baltic Sea, at mouth of Gulf of Riga; 1,046 sq mi (2,709 sq km); chief port Kuressaare; passed to Sweden 1645; to Russia 1721, to Estonia 1918, *maps* R-344, 348, S-524
  Europe, *map* E-361

Saarinen, Eero (1910–61), U.S. architect, born in Finland; came to U.S. 1923, became citizen 1940; associated with father, Eliel Saarinen, in designing many projects including opera shell at Berkshire Music Center, Lenox, Mass., and General Motors Technical Center near Detroit, Mich. A-569
  interior design I-246, 170
  St. Louis Gateway Arch S-22, *pictures* S-21, M-497
  University of Chicago law school building, *picture* U-206

Saarinen, Eliel (1873–1950), Finnish architect, born in Helsinki; father of Eero Saarinen; expert in city planning; director Cranbrook Academy of Art, Bloomfield Hills, Mich., 1925–50, also head of department of architecture there
  Detroit D-122

Saarland (or Saar), West Germany, state in Saar River basin and along boundary of France; held alternately by France and Germany since 17th century; after World War I, administered by League of Nations until 1935 when, by plebiscite, Saarland (area at that time 737 sq mi [1,909 sq km], pop. 865,000) reunited with Germany; occupied by U.S. forces May 1945; placed under French Military Government July 1945; frontier revised June 1947, making area 991 sq mi (2,567 sq km); a constitution went into effect Dec. 15, 1947, providing for representative government and for an economic union with France; 1952 parliamentary elections confirmed this status; independent status under Western European Union proposed in Paris pacts May 1955, rejected in elections; united with West Germany Jan. 1957 G-125

Saavedra Lamas, Carlos (1878–1959), Argentine lawyer and diplomat, born in Buenos Aires. *see also in index* Nobel Prizewinners, *table*

Saba, island in Netherlands Antilles, in n.w. Leeward Islands; 5 sq mi (13 sq km); the island is a volcanic cone, and the principal settlement, Bottom, lies in the extinct crater; fishing, boatbuilding, lacemaking; pop. 949 W-155, *map* W-159

Sabah, formerly North Borneo, includes island of Labuan; total area 29,388 sq mi (75,115 sq km); became part of Malaysia 1963; pop. 1,002,608 M-70
  Asia, *map* A-700
  Borneo B-369
  East Indies E-45

Sabatier, Paul (1854–1941), French chemist, born in Carcassonne. *see also in index* Nobel Prizewinners, *table*

Sabatini, Rafael (1875–1950), British novelist and dramatist, born in Jesi, Italy; proficient in many languages, preferred to write in English; colorful historical romances ('Scaramouche'; 'Captain Blood'; 'The Sea Hawk').

Sabbah, Hasan ibn al- (died 1124), Persian founder of sect of Assassins A-703

Sabbath S-1
  Judaism J-150

Sabbatical year, ancient Hebrew law, every seventh year during which fields were to lie fallow; term now applied to leave granted to teachers in some educational institutions every seven years.

Saber S-546
  fencing F-53

Saber-toothed tiger (or Smilodon), prehistoric cat S-1
  animal evolution A-462
  cat ancestor C-211
  prehistoric animals P-489, *picture* P-487

Sabin, Albert Bruce (born 1906), U.S. medical microbiologist, born in present Bialystok, Poland; associate professor of pediatrics University of Cincinnati College of Medicine 1939–46, professor research pediatrics 1946–60 V-253
  medicine M-284

Sabin, Florence Rena (1871–1953), U.S. anatomist, born in Central City, Colo.; professor of histology, Johns Hopkins University 1917–25; member Rockefeller Institute for Medical Research 1925–38; member emeritus after 1938; first woman elected to National Academy of Sciences
  Statuary Hall, *table* S-437a

Sabine Cross-Roads, place 3 mi (5 km) s.e. of Mansfield, La., where Confederates defeated Federal forces and stopped Red River expedition, April 8, 1864.

Sabine Lake, expansion of Sabine River in Louisiana and Texas 5 mi (8 km) above Gulf of Mexico; 18 mi (29 km) long, 9 mi (14 km) wide B-119

Sabine-Naches, industrial area, Beaumont, Tex. B-119

Sabine River, a stream flowing 400 mi (650 km) to Gulf of Mexico, forming part of boundary between Texas and Louisiana, *map* U-63
  Beaumont B-119
  Louisiana-Texas boundary L-310

Sabines, ancient people who lived northeast of Rome and became merged with Romans; according to legend, Romulus and his followers, wanting wives, seized the Sabine women at a festival; when Sabine warriors tried to free them, the women rushed between the two forces imploring them not to fight; story often painted by artists R-240

Sable, carnivorous mammal *Martes zibellina* W-114
  fur F-463, *table* F-465

Sable, in heraldry, *picture* H-136

Sable, Cape, Fla., southernmost point of United States mainland, *maps* U-41, 117

Sable antelope A-478

Sable Island, a narrow sandy island about 20 mi (30 km) long, situated in Atlantic Ocean about 95 mi (155 km) s.e. of Nova Scotia, to which it belongs; scene of many shipwrecks; noted for wild ponies C-91, *maps* C-112, N-351

Sabme. *see in index* Lapps

Sabot (or wooden shoe), name of wooden shoe worn by peasants in various European countries S-179, *picture* S-178

Sabotage, any obstruction of the processes of industry carried out with intent to hamper production; an ancient weapon of workers in labor disputes, though the term first came into general use about 1897; in time of war commonly committed by enemy saboteurs to weaken a country's military or economic power; word derived from French *sabot,* or wooden shoe; some authorities say it originated when a French workman threw his wooden shoe into the machinery of his employer; others say the term refers to the slow, clumsy movement of the *sabot,* hence meaning to work slowly or carelessly
  intelligence agencies I-236

Sabra, princess in the story of St. George and the Dragon D-238

Sabre-toothed blenny, fish M-423

Saburov, Maxim Zakharovich (born 1900?), Soviet government official; a deputy premier 1947–55; chairman of state planning commission 1949–March 1953 and Aug. 1953–Dec. 1956; member of Presidium of Central Committee of Communist party 1952–57; a first deputy premier 1955–57.

Sac, American Indian tribe. *see in index* Sauk

SAC. *see in index* Strategic Air Command

Sacagawea (or Sakakawea, or Bird Woman) (1788?–1812), Shoshone woman who acted as interpreter for Lewis and Clark Expedition; statues in her honor include one at Bismarck, N.D., one at Portland, Ore., and another on bank of Missouri River west of Mobridge, S.D.
  Lewis and Clark Expedition L-143
  North Dakota N-376

Saccadic movements, eye B-204

Saccharide, term used in scientific names of sugars, as monosaccharide or disaccharide; technical meaning, a carbohydrate having six or more carbon atoms.

Saccharin, a coal-tar sweetening substance, not a sugar S-509

Saccharomyces cerevisiae, species of yeast; commonly used for fermentation Y-411

Sacco-Vanzetti case, sensational murder case in Massachusetts 1920–27; Nicola Sacco and Bartolomeo Vanzetti, Italian immigrants, were convicted of murdering a paymaster and a guard on April 15, 1920; verdict protested by many individuals of varied political opinions in U.S. and abroad on ground defendants were not given fair trial because of their radical views; motions for new trial failed; defendants were executed Aug. 23, 1927
  Shahn paintings S-128

Saccule, part of the inner ear E-4

Sachs, Hans (1494–1576), German shoemaker-poet and dramatist; mastersinger; ardent adherent of Luther ('Shrovetide Plays') G-109

Sachs, Julius von (1832–97), German botanist; founder of modern science of experimental plant physiology; important researches in influence of light on plant assimilation.

Sachs, Nelly (1891–1970), Swedish poet, born in Berlin, Germany; to Sweden 1940; wrote of tragedy of Jews ('The Habitation of Death', 'O the Chimneys', collections of poems; 'Eli', poetic drama). *see also in index* Nobel Prizewinners, *table*

Sachsen-Anhalt, former state, Germany. *see in index* Saxony-Anhalt

Sackbut (presently trombone), wind instrument W-230

Sackets Harbor, N.Y., village on Lake Ontario, 11 mi (18 km) w. of Watertown; former naval station; unsuccessfully attacked by British in War of 1812; pop. 1,017.

Sackville, Thomas. *see in index* Dorset, Thomas Sackville, earl of

Sackville, N.B., industrial town in s.e., near head of Chignecto Bay; Mount Allison University; pop. 3,186.

Sackville-West, Victoria (or Mrs. Harold Nicolson) (1892–1962), English author, of noble family; influenced in literary style by Virginia Woolf, whose 'Orlando' is partly a portrait of her ('Knole and the Sackvilles'; 'The Edwardians').

Saco, Me., city at falls of Saco River opposite Biddeford and about 14 mi (22 km) s.w. of Portland; diversified industry including dairy and metal products; pop. 12,921.

Saco River, rapid stream in New Hampshire and s. Maine; flows 175 mi (280 km) to the Atlantic; abundant waterpower, *map* N-190

Sacrament, in religion
  Eastern Orthodox churches E-43
  Lord's Supper. *see in index* Lord's Supper
  Lutheranism L-338, R-134
  marriage M-150
  Zoroastrianism Z-471

Sacramento, Calif., state capital, on Sacramento River; 75 mi (120 km) n.e. of San Francisco; pop. 275,741 S-2
  California C-38, *maps* C-53, N-351, *picture* C-45
  United States, *map* U-40

Sacramento Mountains, range 50 mi (80 km) long, in s.-central New Mexico

Sacramento River, river in California, rises on Mt. Shasta in n.; flows 400 mi (650 km) s. through fertile valley between Sierra Nevada and Coast Ranges to Suisun Bay, 50 mi (80 km) above San Francisco S-2, *map* U-87

Sacramento State College. *see in index* California State University, Sacramento

Sacré-Coeur, church in Paris, France P-117
  Utrillo's painting, *picture* U-236

Sacred animals
  geese R-244
  Hinduism H-159
  ibis I-4

Sacred books
  Avesta Z-471
  Bible. *see in index* Bible
  Koran. *see in index* Koran

Fathers of the church; and names of individual saints, such as Paul, Saint; Peter, Saint
patron saint. *see in index* Patron saint
popes, *table* P-99
Zoroastrianism and Parsiism Z-471

Saint-Acheul, France, locality near Amiens S-257

St. Albans, Viscount. *see in index* Bacon, Francis

St. Albans, England, city n.w. of London; near old Roman Verulamium; Norman abbey church; pop. 52,680
battle (1455) R-296

Saint Albans, Vt., city in n.w., 3 mi (5 km) from Lake Champlain; vacation area; flashlight cases, paper containers, maple syrup products, food processing; Saint Albans Raid, New England's only Civil War action; pop. 7,308 V-286, *map* V-301
Confederate raid V-290

St. Albans, W. Va., city 12 mi (19 km) w. of Charleston, on Kanawha River; chiefly residential; incorporated 1917; pop. 12,402.

St. Alexander's Church, Warsaw, Poland; modeled after the Pantheon in Rome W-33

St. Ambrose College, Davenport, Iowa; Roman Catholic; founded 1882; arts and sciences.

St. Andrews, Scotland, port 12 mi (19 km) s.e. of Dundee; University of St. Andrews; golf supplies; ruins remain of cathedral founded 1160 and of castle begun 1200; pop. 10,890
golf G-193

St. Andrews, golf club in Yonkers, N.Y.; one of oldest golf courses in the U.S. G-193

St. Andrews, University of, oldest in Scotland, at St. Andrews; founded 1411; faculties of philosophy, law, medicine, theology.

St. Andrew's cross A-506

St. Andrews Presbyterian College, Laurinburg, N.C.; founded 1896; arts and sciences, music.

Saint Ann, Mo., city 13 mi (21 km) n.w. of St. Louis; pop. 15,523.

St. Anselm's College, Manchester, N.H.; Roman Catholic; founded 1889; arts and sciences, education.

St. Anthony Falls (or Falls of St. Anthony), on Mississippi River at Minneapolis M-438
Hennepin H-128
Minnesota M-442, 445
Mississippi River M-484

St. Augustine, Fla., oldest permanent European settlement in U.S.; pop. 11,985 S-16b
Caldecott's collections C-26
first settlement A-334
Menéndez de Avilés M-298
United States, *maps* N-351, U-41

Saint Augustine's College, Raleigh, N.C.; Protestant Episcopal; founded 1867; senior college after 1927; present name after 1931; liberal arts, education.

St. Bartholomew's Day, Massacre of (1572) C-546
Henry III H-132
Huguenots H-317
Medici M-273

Saint Basil the Blessed, Church of, Moscow, U.S.S.R. M-591, 594, *pictures* M-592, R-332e

Saint Benedict, College of, St. Joseph, Minn.; Roman Catholic; coordinate with St. John's University; founded 1913; arts and sciences, education.

Saint Bénézet's Bridge, bridge, Rhone River, at Avignon, France, *picture* F-347

St. Bernard, dog, *picture* D-202

St. Bernard College, St. Bernard, Ala.; Roman Catholic; founded 1892; merged with Cullman College 1976 to form Southern Benedictine College. *see also in index* Southern Benedictine College

St. Bernard Pass, Great. *see in index* Great St. Bernard Pass

St. Bernard Pass, Little. *see in index* Little St. Bernard Pass

St. Bonaventure University, St. Bonaventure, N.Y.; Roman Catholic; founded 1856; arts and sciences, business administration, education, theology; graduate school N-255

Saint Boniface, Man., city on Red River; part of metropolitan Winnipeg; railroad center; packed meats, flour, metal products, paint, soap; oil refineries; St. Boniface College; pop. 46,714 M-101

St. Castin, Vincent, baron de. *see in index* Castin

St. Catherine, College of, St. Paul, Minn.; for women; Roman Catholic; founded 1905; arts and sciences.

St. Catharines-Niagara Falls, Ont., industrial city on Welland Ship Canal, 10 mi (16 km) n.w. of Niagara Falls; wood, iron, and steel products, paper, electrical equipment; pop. 304,353, *map* C-112

St. Charles, Ill., city 37 mi (60 km) w. of Chicago on the Fox River; iron and steel products, kitchen equipment; pop. 12,928, *map* I-53

St. Charles, Mo., city on Missouri River, about 19 mi (30 km) n.w. of St. Louis; railway car, steel die, and foundry works; The Lindenwood Colleges; first state capital, 1821–26; pop. 37,379 M-493, 500

St. Charles River, Quebec, flows from Lake St. Charles to city of Quebec, 7 mi (11 km) s.e., and through it to St. Lawrence River Q-13

St. Christopher (or St. Kitts), island of the West Indies; with the neighboring island of Nevis, it composes a part of the Federation of St. Christopher and Nevis; 67 sq mi (174 sq km); sugar, cotton, coconuts; pop. 33,881, *map* N-351
West Indies W-156, *map* W-159

St. Christopher and Nevis (or St. Kitts-Nevis), sovereign state in West Indies; includes islands St. Christopher (St. Kitts) and Nevis; total area 103 sq mi (267 sq km); Anguilla was separated from St. Christopher-Nevis in 1980; pop. 43,309
Commonwealth membership, *table* C-602
flag, *picture* F-169
West Indies, *map* W-159

Saint Christopher's Hospice, England, first modern hospice H-278

St. Clair, Arthur (1736–1818), U.S. statesman, born in Scotland; major general in Revolutionary War; criticized for abandoning Fort Ticonderoga to British, but acquitted by court-martial; president Continental Congress 1787; first governor of Northwest Territory 1789–1802 M-361

St. Clair, Lake, Michigan-Ontario border, between Lake Huron and Lake Erie; 26 mi (42 km) wide; 460 sq mi (1,190 sq km); St. Clair River connects it to Lake Huron, Detroit River to Lake Erie G-245, *map* G-247
Detroit D-120
Michigan M-355

St. Clair River, outlet of Lake Huron, flowing 41 mi (66 km) s. on Michigan-Ontario border to Lake St. Clair; depth of 20 ft (6 m) maintained by dredging G-245, *map* G-247

St. Clair Shores, Mich., residential city on Lake St. Clair, 10 mi (16 km) n. of Detroit; boats; has 6½ mi (10½ km) of lake frontage; pop. 76,210.

St. Clement Danes, church in London, England, designed by Sir Christopher Wren; completed in 1682.

St. Clements Island, Md. *see in index* Blakistone Island

Saint-Cloud, France, s.w. suburb of Paris; pottery factories; château, burned in 1870, was residence of several kings and a seat of political activity in Napoleonic era; pop. 28,016 P-123, *map* F-372

St. Cloud, Minn., city on Mississippi River about 60 mi (95 km) n.w. of Minneapolis; granite processing, railroad repair shops, refrigerator units, gas turbine generators; St. Cloud State University; U.S. Veterans Administration Hospital; pop. 42,566 M-442, *map* U-41

St. Cloud State College, since 1975 **St. Cloud State University,** St. Cloud, Minn.; opened 1869; liberal arts, education; graduate studies.

St. Croix (or Santa Cruz), one of Virgin Islands of the United States; largest island 80 sq mi (205 sq km) of Virgin archipelago; chief city Christiansted (pop. 3,020), a port; raises sugarcane and cattle; commercial airport and U.S. air base; pop. 31,779 V-351
West Indies, *map* W-159

St. Croix River, a river in Wisconsin and Minnesota, tributary of the Mississippi; 164 mi (264 km) long M-440

St. Croix River, a stream, part of boundary between Maine and New Brunswick; 75 mi (120 km) long N-155

Saint-Cyr, Laurent Gouvion, marquis de (1764–1830), French marshal; served brilliantly as military leader in Italy, Germany, and Russia; ambassador to Spain 1801; minister of war 1815 and 1817–19.

St. Cyr. *see in index* École Spéciale Militaire

Saint-Cyr, French girls' school M-68

Saint-Cyr-l'École, France, town w. of Versailles; famous for military school established (1808) in convent that housed Marquise de Maintenon's girls' school (1686–1793); military school destroyed during World War II; pop. 9,002.

St. Denis, Louis Juchereau de (1676–1744), French explorer and trader; member of expedition that founded Louisiana (1698) and of expeditions into Natchitoches country, now Texas; built Fort St. Jean on Red River and opened trade with American Indians, arousing Spanish ire.

St. Denis, Ruth (original name Ruth Dennis) (1878–1968), U.S. dancer, choreographer, teacher, and lecturer; born in Newark, N.J.; a U.S. pioneer in freeing dance from rigid rules of traditional ballet; with husband, Ted Shawn, founded Denishawn School, Los Angeles; later cofounder of Authentic School of Oriental Dancing, called Natya, in New York City.

Saint-Denis, France, suburb of Paris on Seine River; abbey church (12th century); metallurgical and chemical industries; pop. 99,027, *map* F-372
abbey P-123

Saint Denis, Abbey of, north of Paris; first example of Gothic architecture M-393

St. Dunstan's University, Charlottetown, P.E.I.; Roman Catholic; founded 1855; merged with Prince of Wales College 1969 to form University of Prince Edward Island. *see also in index* Prince Edward Island, University of

Ste-Anne-de-Beaupré, Que., village and pilgrim resort on St. Lawrence River, 20 mi (30 km) below Quebec; world-famous shrine of Ste-Anne; church destroyed by fire in 1922 and since rebuilt; pop. 1,523 Q-9h, *map* Q-11

Sainte-Beuve, Charles Augustin (1804–69), French literary critic, perhaps best of the 19th century; showed fairness, sound judgment; had fine literary style; has been called the perfect critic ('Causeries du Lundi'; 'Port Royal'; 'Portraits of the Eighteenth Century').

Sainte Chapelle, church in Paris, France P-121, 122

Sainte-Claire Deville, Henri Étienne (1818–81), French chemist and educator, born in West Indies; known for theory of thermal dissociation of chemical compounds and for important research on preparation of metals, notably aluminum
sodium substitution A-322

St. Edmundsbury, England. *see in index* Bury Saint Edmunds

St. Edward's University, Austin, Tex.; Roman Catholic; founded 1881; liberal arts, business administration, education, humanities, physical and biological sciences, social sciences; graduate studies A-765

Ste-Foy, Que., suburb of Quebec; pop. 68,883 Q-9h

Sainte Genevieve, Mo., city on Mississippi River about 45 mi (70 km) s. of Saint Louis; lime products; city dates from French settlement about 1735; pop. 4,468.

St. Eleanor's, P.E.I., village 2 mi (3 km) n.w. of Summerside; historic site; pop. 2,716 P-497f, *map* P-497h

St. Elias, Mount, peak 18,008 ft (5,489 m) in St. Elias Mountains, on s.w. Yukon Territory and s.e. Alaska boundary near Pacific coast, *maps* C-112, U-94, 39

St. Elias Mountains, range in s.e. Alaska, s.w. Yukon Territory, and n.w. British Columbia A-241, *map* U-94
Canada C-74
Yukon Territory Y-439

Saint Elizabeth, College of, Convent Station, N.J.; for women; Roman Catholic; founded 1899; arts and sciences, education.

St. Elmo's fire, light appearing on ship masts, airplane wings, steeples, and other projecting objects; the light, frequently seen before and after storms, results from an electrical discharge; named for St. Erasmus, who was venerated under name Elmo as patron of the sailors.

Saint-Étienne, France, industrial city 32 mi (51 km) s.w. of Lyons; firearms, metal products, silks; pop. 212,843, *maps* E-361, F-372

St. Eustatius, volcanic island in Netherlands Antilles, n.w. Leeward Islands; area 8 sq mi (21 sq km); source of supplies for Continental army in Revolutionary War; captured by British fleet 1781; pop. 1,341, *map* W-159

Saint-Evremond, Charles de Marguetel de Saint Denis (1610–1703), French writer and soldier; political troubles caused him to flee to England, where he became a court favorite.

Saint-Exupéry, Antoine de (1900–44), French aviator and author; joined French Air Forces 1940, Free French Air Force in Africa 1943; lost in action R-111b

St. Fin Barr, cathedral, Cork, Ireland C-717, *picture* C-716

St. Francis, College of, Joliet, Ill.; Roman Catholic; coeducational, formerly for women; founded 1925; arts and sciences.

Saint Francis College, Fort Wayne, Ind.; Roman Catholic; founded 1890; liberal arts and sciences, education, medical technology; graduate school.

St. Francis College, since 1978 **University of New England,** Biddeford, Me.; chartered 1953; liberal arts, education; New England College of Osteopathic Medicine.

St. Francis College, Brooklyn, N.Y.; Roman Catholic; coeducational, formerly for men; chartered 1884; arts and sciences, business administration, education.

St. Francis College, Loretto, Pa.; Roman Catholic; founded 1847; arts and sciences, education; graduate studies.

Saint Francis de Sales College, Milwaukee, Wis.; Roman Catholic; primarily for men; liberal arts; founded 1856 as **Saint Francis Seminary,** oldest seminary in U.S. operated at one location.

St. Francis River, a tributary of the Mississippi in s.e. Missouri and n.e. Arkansas; 450 mi (725 km) long.

St. Francis Xavier University, Antigonish, N.S.; Roman Catholic; founded 1853; arts and science, commerce, engineering, home economics, music, nursing, social service, teacher training; graduate studies; College of Cape Breton at Sydney, N.S. affiliated; Coady International Institute.

St. François Mountains, mountain range in Missouri O-624

St. Gallen (French Saint-Gall, German Sankt Gallen), Switzerland, manufacturing town in n.e., 40 mi (65 km) e.

of Zurich; famous for textiles, embroideries, and laces; celebrated library; pop. 78,900 S-543, *map* S-537

Saint-Gaudens, Augustus (1848–1907), U.S. sculptor S-17, S-90
  Hall of Fame, *table* H-16
  New Hampshire N-180

Saint George, Utah, city in s.w. near Zion National Park; livestock, sugar beets, nuts; tents and sleeping bags; pop. 7,097, *picture* U-224, *map* U-233, *list* U-215

'Saint George', sculpture by Donatello D-229

St. George, Mount, Greece. *see in index* Lycabettus, Mount

St. George Leagues Club, Australia A-791

St. George's Channel, strait 100 mi (160 km) long and 60 to 100 mi (95 to 160 km) wide connecting Atlantic Ocean and Irish Sea and separating Ireland from Wales, *map* E-361

Saint George's Hall, Liverpool, England L-262

St. George's Island, one of the Bermuda Islands, 3½ mi (5½ km) long B-173
  West Indies, *map* W-159

St. George's Lowland, Newfoundland N-164

Saint-Germain, Treaty of, (1919) between Allies and Austria, *table* T-275
  World War I W-319

St. Germain des Prés, church in Paris, France P-122, *map* P-120

Saint-Germain-en-Laye, France, summer resort on Seine River, 11 mi (18 km) w. of Paris; treaty between Allies and Austria signed here in 1919 after World War I; pop. 36,251, *map* F-372

Saint-Gervais, church in France C-745

St. Gotthard (or Gothard), groups of Alps, Switzerland; highest points over 10,000 ft (3,000 m).

St. Gotthard Pass, Swiss-Italian Alps; long the chief route from n. Europe to Italy A-320, *map* S-537

St. Gregory the Great, Order of, papal order founded 1831 by Pope Gregory XVI; awarded for distinguished work for the church.

St. Helena, British volcanic island in Atlantic 1,200 mi (1,950 km) w. of Africa; 47 sq mi (122 sq km); cap. Jamestown; with Ascension Island and Tristan da Cunha forms British colony of St. Helena; pop. 5,300 C-602
  Africa, *map* A-118, *table* A-112
  Napoleon's exile N-17

St. Helens, England, town 10 mi (16 km) n.e. of Liverpool; plate glass, metal products, patent medicines; coal trade; pop. 102,770.

St. Helens, Mount, volcanic peak of Cascades in Washington, 60 mi (95 km) n.e. of Portland, Ore.; 9,677 ft (2,950 m); barren elevation with ice-capped peak; n. side overlooks Spirit Lake; erupted 1980
  Cascade Range C-195
  mountain M-634
  Washington, *picture* W-52

St. Helier, Channel Islands, capital of island of Jersey; resort, port; scene of battle against French 1781; church dates from 14th century; pop. 28,135.

St-Hubert, Que., town 8 mi (13 km) e. of Montreal; headquarters Mobile Command, Canadian Armed Forces; pop. 21,741, *map* Q-11

St-Hyacinthe, Que., city 30 mi (50 km) n.e. of Montreal on Yamaska River; textiles, organs, machinery, shoes, furniture; pop. 24,562, *map* Q-10

St. Ignace, Mich., summer resort on a bay of Lake Huron near Strait of Mackinac; pop. 2,892 M-361

Saint Isaac's Cathedral, Leningrad, U.S.S.R., *picture* R-353

St. Ives, England, seaport and winter resort in Cornwall, 57 mi (92 km) s.w. of Plymouth; famous market in 17th century; pop. 8,920.

St. James, district, London, England L-293

St. James-Assiniboia, Man., city s.w. of Winnipeg; part of metropolitan Winnipeg; pop. 71,431 M-102

St. James Cathedral, Montreal, Que. *see in index* Mary Queen of the World Cathedral-Basilica

St. James Palace, London, England; built by Henry VIII L-292, *map* L-288

St. James Park, London, England, was established by Charles II and improved by John Nash L-292, *map* L-288

St. James scallop shell. *see in index* Jacob's fan shell

St-Jean (or St. Johns), Que., port city on Richelieu River 22 mi (35 km) s.e. of Montreal; sewing machines, textiles, machinery, clay products, furniture, cables, rubber goods, food products; a British base in American Revolution; pop. 32,863 Q-9i, *map* C-112, Q-10

St-Jean, Île, former French name of Prince Edward Island. *see in index* Prince Edward Island

St-Jean, Lac, lake in s.e. Quebec; 414 sq mi (1,072 sq km); empties into Saguenay Q-9c, *maps* C-112, Q-9a, 11

St. Jean de Crèvecoeur, Michel Guillaume. *see in index* Crèvecoeur, Michel Guillaume St. Jean de

Saint Jean de Luz, city, in Bay of Biscay, France
  France, *picture* F-354, *map* F-372

St-Jérôme, Que., city on North River, 26 mi (42 km) n.w. of Montreal; textiles, rubber goods, paper, wood products; pop. 26,524, *map* Q-11

Saint John, N.B., port on Bay of Fundy; pop. 85,956 S-18, *maps* C-109, N-351
  New Brunswick N-152, 156, *picture* N-155

St. John, one of Virgin Islands of the United States; 20 sq mi (52 sq km); cattle; bay leaves produced for bay rum industry of nearby island St. Thomas; pop. 1,729 V-351
  West Indies, *map* W-159

St. John, fountain of. *see in index* Castalia, fountain of

St. John, Knights Hospitalers of. *see in index* Hospitalers

St. John Fisher College, Rochester, N.Y.; Roman Catholic; founded 1951; liberal arts and sciences, education.

St. John Lateran, basilica in Rome, Italy; the cathedral of Rome and first in rank of Catholic churches in the world; originally built in 4th century, probably as a chapel in Lateran Palace; rebuilt several times; last major restoration in 14th century V-268
  Rome R-256, *picture* R-253, *map* R-251

Saint John of Jerusalem, Order of the Hospital of. *see in index* Hospitalers

Saint John River, 550 mi (900 km) long; forms part of north boundary of Maine, then flows s.e. through New Brunswick to Bay of Fundy, *map* U-44
  New Brunswick N-152
  Reversing Falls S-18

St. John's, Newf., capital and seaport of province, lying near Cape Spear, easternmost point of Canada; fish processing and packing; machinery, textiles, wood products, confectionery; founded 1583; pop. 83,770, *maps* C-109, N-351
  Newfoundland N-163, 167

St. John's Bridge, Portland, Ore. B-442

St. Johnsbury, Vt., on Passumpsic River, 30 mi (50 km) n.e. of Montpelier; scales, maple products, feed, bowling pins; pop. of township 8,409 V-286, *map* V-301

Saint John's Cathedral, oldest church in Warsaw, Poland W-33

Saint John's College, Camarillo, Calif.; Roman Catholic; for men; opened 1961; liberal arts, theology; graduate school.

St. John's College, Annapolis, Md.; chartered 1784 (successor to King William's School, founded 1696); nonsectarian; liberal arts; graduate studies; affiliated college at Santa Fe, N.M. M-170
  New Mexico N-217
  Santa Fe S-46

St. Johns River, Fla., principal river of state; flows through many lakes; 300 mi (480 km) long F-195, *map* U-59

St. John's University, Collegeville, Minn.; Roman Catholic; coordinate with College of St. Benedict; chartered and opened 1857; arts and sciences, theology; graduate studies.

St. John's University, Jamaica, N.Y.; Roman Catholic; founded 1870; arts and sciences, commerce, education, law, nursing education, pharmacy; graduate school; branch campus on Staten Island
  New York City N-254, N-279

St.-John's-wort, genus of plants *Hypericum;* includes klamathweed or common St.-John's-wort *Hypericum perforatum*, native to Europe but now found in North America.

St. John the Divine, Cathedral of, New York, N.Y.; Episcopal; Gothic architecture; area 121,000 sq ft (11,240 sq m), length 601 ft (183 m); cornerstone laid 1892; crypt opened for worship 1899, nave 1941; not completed
  sculptures, *picture* S-84

St. Joseph, Mich., city near s.w. corner of state, on Lake Michigan and on St. Joseph River, opposite Benton Harbor; automotive parts, home appliances, plastics, rubber goods, paper products; pop. 9,622.

St. Joseph, Mo., city 50 mi (80 km) n.w. of Kansas City, on Missouri River; important livestock center; meat-packing, paper products, cereal manufacturing, clothing, batteries, cables; Missouri Western College; pop. 76,691 M-491, 500, *map* U-41

St. Joseph College, West Hartford, Conn.; Roman Catholic; for women; incorporated 1925, opened 1932; arts and sciences, education, nursing; graduate school coeducational.

St. Joseph College, Emmitsburg, Md.; Roman Catholic; for women; founded 1809; arts and sciences; closed 1973.

St. Joseph River, Michigan and n. Indiana; flows 200 mi (320 km) to Lake Michigan at St. Joseph M-355

Saint Joseph's College, Rensselaer, Ind.; Roman Catholic; founded 1889; opened 1891; arts and sciences, business administration, education; fine arts; graduate studies; former campus at East Chicago now Calumet College.

St. Joseph's College, Standish, Me.; Roman Catholic; chartered 1915; liberal arts, education.

St. Joseph's College, Brooklyn, N.Y.; Roman Catholic; founded 1916; arts and sciences.

St. Joseph's College, Philadelphia, Pa.; Roman Catholic; coeducational; founded 1851; arts and sciences, business administration, cooperative 4-year work-and-study program in electronics; graduate study in chemistry and education.

St. Joseph's Fountain, New Orleans, La. F-335

St. Joseph's Oratory, Montreal, Que., *picture* Q-9b

St. Joseph's University, Moncton, N.B.; Roman Catholic; founded 1864; present name 1928; Moncton site 1953; arts and sciences, civil engineering, commerce, education; graduate studies; junior college for men at St. Joseph.

Saint-Just, Louis Antoine Léon de (1767–94), French revolutionist, associate of Robespierre and Danton; one of organizers of Reign of Terror; member of Committee of Public Safety; arrested and guillotined with Robespierre.

St. Kilda, bayside resort, Melbourne, Australia M-290
  island of St. Christopher-Nevis. *see in index* St. Christopher

St. Kitts, island of St. Christopher-Nevis. *see in index* St. Christopher

St. Kitts-Nevis, West Indies. *see in index* St. Christopher-Nevis

St. Laurent, Louis Stephen (1882–1973), Canadian statesman S-18
  Canada C-104

Saint Laurent, Yves (born 1939), French dress designer D-268

St-Laurent, Que., city, suburb of Montreal; pop. 62,955, *map* Q-11

St. Lawrence, Gulf of, inlet of n. Atlantic at mouth of St. Lawrence River S-19, *map* N-351. *see also in index* Ocean, *table*
  New Brunswick N-155

St. Lawrence Island, Alaskan island in Bering Sea, s.w. of Nome; 88 mi (142 km) long and 20 mi (32 km) wide; inhabited chiefly by Eskimos; reindeer and foxes, *maps* N-351, U-94, 39

St. Lawrence Islands National Park, Ontario; has 13 of the Thousand Islands and a mainland area in Ontario; resort facilities.

Saint Lawrence River, one of chief rivers of North America, outlet of the Great Lakes; 740 mi (1,190 km) long, from Lake Ontario to Gulf of St. Lawrence S-19
  Canada C-75, 90, *map* C-112
    Ontario O-549
    Quebec, *picture* Q-9f
      Montreal M-572
  canals C-129
  early exploration A-333
    Cartier C-185
  French settlers A-14
  Great Lakes G-245
    Lake Michigan M-374
  New York N-245
  North America, *map* N-351
  river system, *map* U-33

St. Lawrence Seaway S-20, G-247, *diagrams* S-19
  Canada C-105
  canals C-129, S-20
  Eisenhower administration E-138
  harbors and ports H-35
  International Rapids section, *picture* U-51
  Lake Ontario O-559
  Michigan M-359
    Detroit D-120
  Minnesota M-443
    Duluth D-288
  models M-517
  Montreal M-571
  New York N-253
  Ohio O-506
    Toledo T-212
  Ontario O-549
  waterway W-108

St. Lawrence Seaway Development Corporation, United States S-20

St. Lawrence University, Canton, N.Y.; private control; chartered 1856; opened 1857; letters and science, theology; graduate studies N-255

St. Lawrence Valley, North America N-337

Saint Leger, Barry (1737–89), British soldier; fought under Wolfe at Quebec; during Revolutionary War commanded British at Fort Stanwix, which he failed to take R-171

Saint Leo College, Saint Leo, Fla.; private control, Catholic related; chartered 1889; liberal arts, education.

Saint-Léonard, Quebec, town on Montreal Island; pop. 79,429 Q-9h

St.-Lô, France, historic town 44 mi (71 km) s.e. of Cherbourg; textiles; pop. 17,347, *map* F-372
  World War II W-340, *picture* W-343

Saint Louis, Mo., largest city of state and chief market for central Mississippi Valley; pop. 453,085 S-21
  bridges S-21
  civic improvement plan S-22, *picture* S-21
  courthouse, *picture* S-21
  fur trade S-22
  housing project, *picture* U-102
  Louisiana Purchase Exposition S-22
  Milles' fountain S-91
  Missouri M-487, 490, 493, 500, *pictures* M-497, 499
  Missouri Botanical Garden S-22
  United States, *maps* N-351, U-41

Saint-Louis, Senegal, city on island in estuary of Senegal River; shipping center; founded about 1658 by French traders; pop. 88,404, *map* A-118

'St. Louis Blues', song by Handy H-30

St. Louis Cathedral, New Orleans, La., *picture* L-317

Saint Louis Park, Minn., city 5 mi (8 km) s.w. of Minneapolis; chiefly residential; hydraulic manufacturing, machine shops, sporting goods; incorporated as village 1886; pop. 42,931 M-442

'St. Louis Post-Dispatch', newspaper N-236

St. Louis River, flows through the Great Lakes into the Gulf of St. Lawrence M-440

St. Louis Trace (or Vincennes Trail), Illinois I-39

Saint Louis University, St. Louis, Mo.; Roman Catholic; founded 1818 (university since 1832); arts and sciences, aeronautical technology, commerce and finance, divinity, institute of technology, law, medicine, nursing, philosophy and letters; graduate school; branch at Cahokia, Ill. R-254

St. Louis Zoo, St. Louis, Mo. Z-460

St. Lucia, island nation in Windward Islands group, West Indies; 240 sq mi (620 sq km); cap. Castries; sugar, cacao, coconuts, limes, bay oil, cotton; pop. 118,000
- Caribbean literature C-167
- Commonwealth membership C-602
- flag, *picture* F-169
- North America, *map* N-351
- United Kingdom E-259
- West Indies W-157, *map* W-159
- World War II W-325

St. Lusson, Simon François Daumont, sieur de, 17th-century French soldier and explorer; headed expedition to upper Great Lakes (1670–71); before American Indians of 14 tribes at Sault Ste. Marie, claimed for Louis XIV territory "discovered and to be discovered"
- Great Lakes exploration G-249

Saint-Malo, France, fortified port, resort on English Channel; 40 mi (65 km) n.w. of Rennes; pop. 40,252, *map* F-372
- hydroelectric power dam D-17

'Saint Mark', sculpture by Donatello D-229

St. Mark's Cathedral (Italian San Marco), cathedral in Venice V-277, *picture* E-349
- mosaic M-590
- 'Palo d'Oro' screen, *picture* E-208
- piazza, *picture* V-279

St. Martin, an island in n.w. Leeward Islands, West Indies; the n. portion (20 sq mi [52 sq km]; pop. 5,062) belongs to French overseas department of Guadeloupe and the s. portion (13 sq mi [34 sq km]; pop. 7,435) to Netherlands Antilles, *map* W-159

St. Martin-in-the-Fields, Georgian church in London, England, built 1721–26 by James Gibbs.

St. Martin's College, Olympia, Wash.; Roman Catholic; founded 1895; arts and sciences, business and economics, civil engineering.

Saint Mary, College of, Omaha, Neb., Roman Catholic; for women; founded 1923; arts and sciences, education, health services.

Saint Mary College, Leavenworth, Kan.; Roman Catholic; for women; founded 1923; liberal arts, education.

St. Mary Dam, dam in Alberta, on the St. Mary River A-265

St. Mary-le-bow Church. *see in index* Bow Church

Saint Mary of the Plains College, Dodge City, Kan.; Roman Catholic; opened 1952; arts and sciences, education.

Saint Mary-of-the-Woods College, Saint Mary-of-the-Woods, Ind.; Roman Catholic; for women; founded 1840; arts and sciences, art, education, home economics, journalism, music, speech and drama.

St. Mary Redcliffe, famous old church in Bristol, England B-449

St. Marys City, Md., historic settlement and early capital of Maryland; on St. Marys River, 55 mi (90 km) s. of Annapolis; founded 1634; St. Mary's College of Maryland M-171, *map* M-183

Saint Mary's College, Notre Dame, Ind.; Roman Catholic; founded 1844; arts and sciences, business administration, education, fine arts.

St. Mary's College, Winona, Minn.; Roman Catholic; founded 1913; arts and sciences; graduate studies.

Saint Mary's College of California, near Oakland, Calif.; Roman Catholic; founded 1863; arts and letters, economics and business administration, science; graduate study.

Saint Mary's College of Maryland, St. Marys City, Md.; state control; founded 1839; liberal arts, education.

St. Mary's Dominican College, New Orleans, La.; Roman Catholic; for women; incorporated 1910; arts and sciences, business, education, home economics, medical technology, speech therapy.

St. Mary's Hall, Coventry, England C-749

St. Marys River (official name in Canada St. Mary River), channel linking Lakes Superior and Huron S-52b
- Great Lakes G-245, *diagram* G-247

St. Marys River, river in Georgia, rises in Okefenokee Swamp; forms part of boundary between Georgia and Florida; 175 mi (280 km) long.

St. Marys River, river in Maryland M-171, *map* M-183

St. Mary's Seminary and University, Baltimore, Md.; Roman Catholic; for men; established 1791; arts and sciences, theology; graduate study.

St. Mary's University, Halifax, N.S.; province-supported; founded 1802; present name 1952; arts and sciences, commerce, education, engineering, journalism, science; affiliated college at Guelph, Ont. H-15

St. Mary's University of San Antonio, San Antonio, Tex.; Roman Catholic; opened 1852; arts and sciences, business, law, music; graduate studies.

St. Matthews, Ky., city 6 mi (10 km) e. of Louisville; primarily a residential suburb; potatoes; pop. 13,354.

St. Maur, English family. *see in index* Seymour

St-Maurice River, Quebec, tributary of the St. Lawrence; 325 mi (525 km) long Q-9e, *maps* Q-9a, 10

Saint Meinrad College and **St. Meinrad School of Theology,** St. Meinrad, Ind.; Roman Catholic; for men; in complex of monastery founded 1854, schools incorporated 1890, became separate institutions 1959; liberal arts, education, theology; graduate school.

St. Michael, island of the Azores. *see in index* São Miguel

St. Michael and St. George, Order of, British order of knighthood founded in 1818 by George III; usually conferred on soldiers and diplomats.

St. Michael's Cathedral, Coventry, England C-749

St. Michael's College, Winooski, Vt., Roman Catholic; coeducational, formerly for men; founded 1904; arts and sciences; graduate study.

St-Michel, Que., former suburb of Montreal, on Montreal island; annexed 1968, *map* Q-11

Saint-Mihiel, France, town in n., 20 mi (30 km) s. of Verdun on Meuse River; pop. 5,262 S-22
- France, *map* F-372
- World War I W-311, 314

St. Moritz, Switzerland, loftiest village in Upper Engadine, on Lake Moritz; mineral springs; winter sports; pop. 3,751 S-542, *map* S-537
- bobsled developed S-216
- climate S-537
- skiing W-242
- ski resort, *picture* T-271

St.-Nazaire, France, port on w. coast at mouth of Loire River; shipbuilding yards; steelworks; pop. 60,696, *maps* E-361, F-372

St. Nick. *see in index* Nicholas, Saint

Saint-Nicolas, Belgium. *see in index* Sint-Niklaas

St. Norbert College, West De Pere, Wis.; Roman Catholic institution; founded 1898; arts and sciences, business administration, education.

'Saint of Bleecker Street, The', opera by Menotti M-299
- opera O-571

St. Olaf College, Northfield, Minn.; American Lutheran; founded 1874; college from 1886; arts and sciences, education, music, nursing.

Saint-Ouen, France, suburb n. of Paris on Seine River; river port and manufacturing center; pop. 48,304, *map* F-372

St. Patrick, Order of, Irish order of knighthood created by George III in 1783; meets in Dublin K-259

St. Patrick's, cathedral in Dublin, Ireland D-281

St. Patrick's Cathedral, Roman Catholic, one of the largest cathedrals in America, in New York City, on Fifth Avenue; begun 1858, completed 1879.

Saint Patrick's College, in Maynooth, Ireland I-321

St. Patrick's College, in Mountain View, Calif.; Roman Catholic; for men; opened 1898; arts and sciences, theology.

Saint Patrick's Day (March 17) P-139
- festival parade, *picture* F-65
- shamrock worn S-143

Saint Paul, Minn., state capital and 2nd city of state, on Mississippi River; pop. 270,230 S-23
- Minneapolis M-438
- Minnesota M-439, 442, *pictures* M-449, 450
- North America, *maps* N-351, U-41

Saintpaulia. *see in index* African violet

Saint Paul Rocks (or St. Peter and St. Paul Rocks), Brazilian islets in central Atlantic just n. of equator; group only about ¼ mi (0.4 km) long; uninhabited; age of rock in islets estimated at 4½ billion years.

St. Paul's Cathedral, in London, England L-286, *picture* L-290, *map* L-289
- architecture A-559
  - Wren W-363
- Jones J-139

St. Paul's Church, in Nova Scotia, oldest Protestant church in Canada N-402

Saint Paul's College, Lawrenceville, Va.; Protestant Episcopal; founded 1888; present name after 1957; liberal arts, education.

St. Paul's College, Washington, D.C.; Roman Catholic; founded 1889; closed 1974.

St. Paul's School, coed college preparatory school at Concord, N.H.; founded 1855; Protestant Episcopal.

St. Peter and St. Paul, Cathedral Church of (also called Washington Cathedral, or The National Cathedral), Washington, D.C., on Mt. St. Alban; Episcopal; Gothic architecture; area 75,000 sq ft (7,000 sq m); length 525 ft (160 m); cornerstone laid 1907; first portion, Bethlehem Chapel, opened for public worship 1912; not completed.

St. Peter and St. Paul Rocks. *see in index* Saint Paul Rocks

St. Peter's Anglican Church, Adelaide, Australia, *picture* A-41

St. Peter's Basilica, Rome, Italy R-256, *map* R-250, *pictures* R-249, 254, E-335
- Bernini B-175
- Bramante B-405
- Julius II J-151
- Michelangelo M-351, *picture* M-352
- mosaic M-590
- papal coronations P-445
- square, *picture* V-268

Saint Petersburg, Fla., city on Tampa Bay; pop. 238,647 F-196, S-24, U-41, *map* N-351
- Tampa T-19

St. Petersburg, Russia. *see in index* Leningrad

St. Peter's College, Jersey City, N.J.; Roman Catholic; founded 1872; arts and sciences, business administration.

Saint-Pierre, Bernardin de. *see in index* Bernardin de Saint-Pierre, Jacques Henri

Saint Pierre, formerly the chief town of Martinique; pop. 5,556
- Martinique M-161
- West Indies W-155, *map* W-159

St. Pierre and Miquelon, French overseas department consisting of several barren rocky islands 10 mi (16 km) off s. coast of Newfoundland; 93 sq mi (241 sq km); cod-fishing center seized by Free French December 1941; plebiscite voted fealty to Free French; pop. 6,000, *maps* C-109, N-351

Saint Pie X Church, in Lourdes, France L-325

Saint-Quentin, France, city in n. on Somme River, 82 mi (132 km) n.e. of Paris; textile center since Middle Ages; machinery, chemicals, sugar; notable 12th-century cathedral and many other buildings damaged in World War I; cathedral reopened 1920; city named for 3rd-century martyr; early seat of counts of Vermandois; captured by Spaniards 1557, by Germans 1871, 1914, and 1940; pop. 63,932, *map* F-372

Saint Rose, College of, in Albany, N.Y.; Roman Catholic; founded 1920; arts and sciences, business, education; graduate studies A-259

Saint Rufino in Assisi, Cathedral of, in Italy, *picture* I-382

Saint-Saëns, Charles Camille (1835–1921), French composer, pianist and organist; received first recognition with brilliant symphonic poems, 'Phaéton', 'La danse macabre', 'La jeunesse d'Hercule'; of his operas, 'Samson and Delilah' is most successful
- classical music M-674
- Melba M-288

Saintsbury, George Edward Bateman (1845–1933), English literary critic and historian ('A History of Criticism'; 'A History of English Prosody').

St. Scholastica, College of, Duluth, Minn.; Roman Catholic; founded 1912; arts and sciences, medical record science, music, nursing; graduate studies; quarter system.

Saints' Days F-67

Saint Sebastian basilica, on Appian Way near Rome C-218

Saint-Simon, Claude Henri de Rouvroy, comte de (1760–1825), French philosopher, born in Paris; founder of French Socialism; his social theories formed a system known to disciples as Saint-Simonianism S-233

Saint-Simon, Louis de Rouvroy, duc de (1675–1755), French writer, born in Paris; his 'Memoirs' important source of information on reign of Louis XIV.

St. Simons Island, part of Georgia, in St. Simons Sound, s. of entrance to Altamaha River; area, about 15,000 acres (6,070 hectares); ruins of Fort Frederica, lighthouse, Redfern air field, *pictures* G-84, 94

Saints of North America, Jesuit missionaries martyred in early 17th century while trying to convert American Indians; Fathers Isaac Jogues, Jean de Brébeuf, Noël Chabanel, Antoine Daniel, Charles Garnier, Gabriel Lalemant; Brothers Jean de Lalande and René Goupil; canonized June 29, 1930.

Saint Sophia, Cathedral of, in Kiev, U.S.S.R. K-237

Saint Stephen, Cathedral of, in Zagreb, Yugoslavia, *picture* Z-442

St. Stephen's, cathedral in Vienna, Austria; architecture largely Gothic; almost demolished in World War II; restoration begun in 1946, completed 1952 V-314, *picture* V-316

St. Stephen's College, in Alberta A-266

St-Sulpice Seminary, in Montreal, Que.; Roman Catholic theological school affiliated with University of Montreal; founded 1685; earliest school in Montreal.

St. Sylvester, Order of, papal order founded 1841 by Gregory XVI to absorb Order of the Golden Militia, or Golden Spur (founded 1559 by Paul IV); in 1905 divided into two orders, St. Sylvester and the Golden Militia.

Saint Teresa, College of, Winona, Minn., Roman Catholic; for women; founded 1907; arts and sciences; education; nursing.

St. Thomas, Ont., city 13 mi (21 km) s. of London and 8 mi (13 km) n. of Lake Erie; in fruit, farming, tobacco area; railroad center; metal products, vitrified clay, yarns, shoes, pharmaceuticals, food products, automobiles; pop. 25,545, *map* C-112

St. Thomas, Portuguese island. *see in index* São Tomé

St. Thomas, port of Virgin Islands. *see in index* Charlotte Amalie

St. Thomas, one of Virgin Islands of the United States; 32 sq mi (83 sq km); tourist trade; handicraft products, rum; College of the Virgin Islands; airport; submarine base; pop. 28,960 V-351
- Charlotte Amalie V-352
- West Indies, *map* W-159

St. Thomas, College of, St. Paul, Minn.; Roman Catholic; founded 1885; arts and sciences, business administration, education, fine arts, religion, social sciences; graduate studies.

St. Thomas, University of, Houston, Tex.; Roman Catholic; founded 1947; liberal arts, education, theology; graduate studies.

St. Thomas University, in New Brunswick N-157

Saint Valentine's Day S-24
- commemorative stamp P-462b
- festivals, *picture* F-63

St. Valentine's Day Massacre (1929), U.S. gangster killings C-153

Saint-Valéry-sur-Somme, France, port and resort at mouth of Somme River; pop. 3,225, *map* F-372

St. Vincent, one of Cape Verde Islands. *see in index* São Vicente

St. Vincent, one of Windward Islands, West Indies; 133 sq mi (344 sq km); with n. Grenadines 17 sq mi (44 sq km) it forms independent state of St. Vincent and the Grenadines; arrowroot, cotton, coconuts
- North America, *map* N-351
- West Indies, *map* W-159

St. Vincent, Cape (or São Vicente), promontory on s.w. tip of Portugal; British fleet under Jervis and Nelson defeated Spanish fleet 1797, *maps* E-361, P-455, S-350

St. Vincent and the Grenadines, nation consisting of the islands of St. Vincent and the northern Grenadines; 150 sq mi (390 sq km); cap. Kingstown; self-governing British state 1969–79; independent since 1979; pop. 118,000
- Commonwealth membership C-602
- flag, F-169
- United Kingdom E-259
- West Indies W-155

St. Vincent College, Latrobe, Pa.; Roman Catholic; for men; founded 1846; liberal arts, business; graduate school of theology.

St. Vincent de Paul, Society of, a Roman Catholic charitable society, founded by Antoine Frédéric Ozanam (1813–53), a French scholar; first established in U.S. in 1845, at St. Louis, Mo.

St. Vital, Man., residential city adjacent to s. St. Boniface, part of metropolitan Winnipeg; pop. 32,963 M-102

St. Xavier College, Chicago, Ill.; private control; founded 1846; arts and sciences, education, nursing; graduate studies.

Saionji, Kimmochi, Prince (1849–1940), Japanese statesman, born in Kyoto; minister to Austria 1885, to Germany 1888; minister of education 1892–96, 1898; premier 1905–7, 1910–12; president of the Seiyukai party 1903; adviser to emperor.

Saipan, second largest island of Mariana group in w. Pacific; 47 sq mi (122 sq km); in 1919 mandated to Japan, which used it as military outpost; conquered by U.S. forces July 1944; transformed into naval and air base; pop. 12,385, *map* P-6

Sair, a wild sheep S-148

Saito, Kiyoshi (born 1907), Japanese artist, born in Fukushima; exhibited throughout the world; famous for woodcut prints.

Sakakawea. *see in index* Sacagawea

Sakartvelo. *see in index* Georgian Soviet Socialist Republic

Sake, national drink of Japan made from rice; fermented with yeast cake called *koji;* yellowish; 12 to 15 percent alcohol J-29
- brewing process B-134

Sakhalin (formerly Saghalin), long, mountainous island of U.S.S.R. near e. coast of Siberia; 24,560 sq mi (63,610 sq km); s. part (Karafuto) ceded to Japan by Russia, 1905, after Russo-Japanese War; returned to U.S.S.R. after World War II; forests, fisheries, coal, oil; pop. 600,000, *maps* R-322, 345
- Asia, *map* A-700
- Korean jetliner shot down I-264

Sakharov, Andrei (born 1921), Soviet physicist, born in Moscow; worked on hydrogen bomb development; opposed plans for 100-megaton bomb testing 1961; published plea for nuclear arms reduction 1968; opposed political repression in U.S.S.R. *see also in index* Nobel Prizewinners, *table*

Saki. *see in index* Munro, Hector Hugh

Saktideva, legendary Indian hero F-263

'Sakuntala' (or 'Shakuntala'), Sanskrit drama by Kalidasa. Sakuntala is found in her forest home by King Dushyanta, who marries her and gives her a ring by which he is to recognize her when she joins him at his palace; the ring is lost and the king disowns her, but proclaims her his queen when the ring is found. Story used in Goldmark's opera K-167

Sal, one of Cape Verde Islands, in their extreme n.e.; 83 sq mi (215 sq km); beach for bathers; fishing; salt industry, with salt pans set in crater of extinct volcano; pop. 1,121.

Salad L-140

Salad garden, type of garden, *picture* G-26

Saladin (or Yusuf ibn Ayyub) (1138–93), chivalrous Muslim leader, sultan of Egypt and Syria S-25
- Cairo citadel C-16
- Crusades C-787
- Middle East M-397
- Richard I R-201
- Salado del Norte, *map* A-516
- Scott's 'The Talisman' S-25

Salajar, island, Indonesia. *see in index* Salayar

Salam, Abdus (born 1926), Pakistani physicist, born in Jhang Maghiana; at University of Cambridge, England 1954–56; professor of theoretical physics at Imperial College of Science and Technology, London, 1957–; director of International Centre for Theoretical Physics at Trieste, Italy, since 1964; developed theory concerning fundamental interactions of particles. *see also in index* Nobel Prizewinners, *table*
- electromagnetism theory A-757

Salamanca, Spain, city 110 mi (175 km) n.w. of Madrid; beautiful medieval buildings badly damaged in Spanish civil war; pop. 90,388, *maps* S-350, P-455
- Europe, *map* E-361
- university S-356

Salamanca, battle of (1812), *list* W-15

Salamander, an amphibian S-25
- amphibian species A-376
- animal life record, *table* E-24
- fairy tales F-12
- lizard comparison L-271

Salamaua, settlement on e. coast of Papua New Guinea s. of Lae.

Salambria, river in Greece. *see in index* Salamvria

Salamis, Greece, barren mountainous island in Gulf of Aegina, or Saronic Gulf; 36 sq mi (93 sq km); famous for defeat of Persian fleet by Greeks in strait between island and Attic coast (480 BC).

Salamis, battle of (480 BC) S-26, *picture* S-27
- Greece G-265
- Persian Wars P-215
- Themistocles T-163
- warfare, *list* W-15

'Salammbô', novel by Flaubert; heroine Salammbô is the daughter of Hamilcar Barca, Carthaginian general.

Sal ammoniac. *see in index* Ammonium chloride

Salamvria (also called Salambria, ancient Peneus, modern Greek Péneiós), chief river of Thessaly, Greece; 100 mi (160 km) long.

Salandra, Antonio (1853–1931), Italian statesman; as premier, responsible for Italy's early neutrality and later siding with Allies in World War I.

Salary, fixed pay. *see also in index* Income; Wages
- derivation of word S-30
- economics E-61
- Peace Corps P-143a
- U.S. federal officials, *table* U-155
- president P-493

Salary grab, popular term in U.S. history applied to an act to raise salaries of members of Congress, voted just before closing of Congress, 1873; so called because the incumbents whose terms were about to expire were benefited; called also "back pay grab."

Salayar (or Salajar), long, narrow island, generally mountainous, in Indonesia, s. of Celebes; 256 sq mi (663 sq km); copra, coconut oil, salt; pop. 87,278.

Salazar, Antonio de Oliveira (1889–1970), Portuguese statesman; dictator of Portugal P-457a
- Angolan independence A-420

Salazar Bridge, in Lisbon, Portugal, over Tagus River B-447

Salé (Roman Sala), Morocco R-20
- Morocco M-586

Sal effervescens. *see in index* Effervescent salt

Salem, Peter (1750?–1816), Revolutionary War hero from Framingham, Mass.; freed from slavery after fighting at Lexington and Concord; killed British commander Major John Pitcairn at Bunker Hill.

Salem, Mass., historic city on Atlantic Ocean about 14 mi (22 km) n.e. of Boston; electronic products, leather and shoes, paper and printing; Salem State College; Peabody Museum (marine collection); founded 1626; pop. 38,220 M-202, *picture* M-192
- Mather M-221

Salem, N.H., 14 mi (22 km) e. of Nashua; beverages, lumber, footwear; incorporated 1750; pop. of township 24,124, *map* N-191

Salem, Ohio, city about 18 mi (29 km) s.w. of Youngstown; coal-mining; farming, and stock-raising region; furnaces, pumps, machinery, kitchen cabinets, metal products, plastics; served as "underground railroad" station before Civil War; pop. 12,869.

Salem, Ore., state capital, 43 mi (69 km) s. of Portland on Willamette River; pop. 89,233 S-26, *maps* N-351, U-40
- Oregon O-584, 592, *pictures* O-589, 590

Salem, Va., city 8 mi (13 km) w. of Roanoke; elevators, bricks, leather; Roanoke College; pop. 23,958, *map* V-348

Salem College, in Salem, W. Va.; independent; founded 1888; liberal arts, teacher education; campus at Clarksburg.

Salem College, in Winston-Salem, N.C.; for women; founded 1772 by Moravian church; arts and sciences, music W-240

Salem State College, in Salem, Mass.; established 1854; liberal arts and education; graduate study.

Sale of Foods and Drugs Act (1875), England F-274

Salerno, Italy, port on Gulf of Salerno s.e. of Naples; textiles; famous medieval medical school; pop. 117,363, *map* I-404
- medical school H-93

Salerno, battle of (1943), World War II W-340, *pictures* I-380, W-341
- warfare, *list* W-15

Sales, Saint François de. *see in index* François de Sales, Saint

Sales, business technique C-687
- computers C-636

Sales contract C-693

Sales tax, a tax imposed on the sale of goods and services T-37

Salford, England, city on Manchester Ship Canal, just w. of Manchester; cotton imported; textiles; pop. 137,750.

Salian Dynasty, of German emperors. *see in index* Franconian Dynasty

Salians, division of Franks; pushed southward from homeland between Scheldt and Meuse as Roman power weakened; under Clovis (465–511) took all Gaul west of Loire.

Salicaceae. *see in index* Willow family

Salic law, an early medieval law (one of the Germanic laws) of the Salian Franks, an important Frankish people; used as early as time of Clovis; a penal code with some rules of civil law, which contain provisions against female inheritance of property; gave rise to so-called Salic law, enforced in France and various French and German kingdoms and duchies, which forbade succession to rule to females and to descendants through any female line.

Salicylic acid, a white crystalline substance ($C_6H_4 \cdot OH \cdot COOH$) used in medicines, flavoring agents, and dyes; chiefly used, millions of pounds annually, in preparation of aspirin. *see also in index* Aspirin
- beaver scent glands B-122
- organic chemistry O-602

Salientia. *see in index* Anura

Salina, Kan., city on Smoky Hill River about 80 mi (130 km) n. of Wichita; shipping center for wheat and livestock area; oil, natural gas, flour milling; diversified industry; Kansas Wesleyan, Marymount College; pop. 41,843 U-40–1

Salina, desert formation D-105

Salina Cruz, Mexico, Pacific port on Gulf of Tehuantepec; terminal of highway and railroad across Isthmus of Tehuantepec; pop. 22,004.

Salinas (y Serrano), Pedro (1891–1951), Spanish poet S-366

Salinas, Calif., city about 85 mi (135 km) s.e. of San Francisco; vegetables, beet sugar, fruits, dairy products; pop. 80,479, *map* U-40

Salination, accumulation of salts I-255

Salinger, J(erome) D(avid) (born 1919), U.S. novelist and short-story writer, born in New York, N.Y.; 'The Catcher in the Rye', 'Nine Stories', 'Franny and Zooey', 'Raise High the Roof Beam, Carpenters' and 'Seymour: an Introduction'
- American short story A-360
- 'Catcher in the Rye, The' N-410, R-111h

Salinger, Pierre (Emil George) (born 1925), U.S. government official, born in San Francisco, Calif.; child piano prodigy; special investigator U.S. Senate rackets committee 1957–59; press secretary to John F. Kennedy 1959–63, Lyndon B. Johnson 1963–64; interim appointment as Democratic senator from California 1964; author of 'With Kennedy', 'An Honorable Profession: a Tribute to Robert Kennedy', 'On Instructions of My Government'.

Salinity
- halophytes H-19
- oceanography O-480

Salisbury, Robert Arthur Talbot Gascoyne-Cecil, 3rd **marquis of** (1830–1903), British conservative statesman; imperialist, premier 1885–86, 1886–92, 1895–1902; chief political adviser, with Joseph Chamberlain, to Queen Victoria after death of Disraeli E-254
Salisbury, England, town on Avon River, 80 mi (130 km) s.w. of London; agricultural market; cathedral with tallest spire in England; pop. 36,440
cathedral, *pictures* A-667, P-46
Stonehenge S-456
Salisbury, Md., port city on Wicomico River, 83 mi (134 km) s.e. of Baltimore; textiles, food products, machinery, building materials; Salisbury State College; pop. 16,429, *map* M-183
Salisbury, N.C., city about 32 mi (51 km) s.w. of Winston-Salem; cotton textiles, lumber and wood products, food processing, granite products; Catawba College, Livingstone College; national cemetery; pop. 22,677.
Salisbury, Zimbabwe. *see in index* Harare
Salisbury Plain, high rolling plain in Wiltshire, England, n. of Salisbury
Stonehenge S-456
Salisbury State College, Salisbury, Md.; founded 1925; liberal arts, education; graduate studies.
Salish, a division of the Salishan linguistic stock of American Indians formerly living about Flathead Lake in w. Montana; known as Flatheads because they did not deform their heads into "pointed heads"
Oregon O-586
Saliva
human digestion D-142, H-84
hunger habituation H-3
tongue T-215
Salivary gland, a gland that secretes saliva R-131
digestive system, *diagram* D-143
gland G-153
mouth M-641
Salix, generic name of the willow family W-211
Salk, Jonas Edward (born 1914), U.S. physician, born in New York City; joined faculty University of Pittsburgh school of medicine 1947, professor 1949–63; director and fellow Salk Institute for Biological Studies 1963–; Congressional award 1955 for developing polio vaccine, *picture* V-249
medicine M-284
polio vaccine V-252, *pictures* V-251
Sallé, Marie (1701–56), French ballet dancer and choreographer; developed *ballet d'action*, or storytelling movements D-24
Sallust (or Gaius Sallustius Crispus) (86–34 BC), first Roman historian as distinguished from annalists; a student of human character and of the causes of events L-77
history writing H-172
'Salmagundi', name of a periodical published by Washington Irving and James K. Paulding in New York in 1807; depicted the customs of the day; named from salmagundi in cookery, a highly seasoned dish A-345
Salmon, a food fish F-125, 128, *picture* F-129
Alaska's production A-242
Canada C-75
British Columbia B-453
egg, *picture* E-111
fish culture F-132
fisheries, *table* F-137
migration A-450, S-29, *picture* S-28
Bonneville Dam C-588
mobility A-424
Pacific salmon. *see in index* Pacific salmon
related species S-28
speed, *picture* A-426
Salmonella, genus of rod-shaped bacteria consisting of more than 1,200 types; infects both man and animals; common diseases include paratyphoid, typhoid, food poisoning, and localized infections, *table* D-172
turtle T-330
Salmonidae, family of fishes including salmon and trout. *see in index* Salmon; Trout
Salmon River, river in Idaho, tributary of the Snake River; 450 mi (725 km) long, *map* U-30
Salmon River Mountains, mountains in Idaho; highest point, Hyndman Peak 12,078 ft (3,681 m), *map* I-30
Salome, daughter of Herodias, who bade her ask of Herod the head of John the Baptist (Bible, Matthew xiv); subject of play by Oscar Wilde that furnished libretto for opera by Richard Strauss
Herod H-141
'Salome', opera by Strauss S-485
opera O-569, *list* O-563
Salomon, Haym (or Haym Solomon) (1740?–85), U.S. patriot and financier, born in Lissa, Poland, of Jewish-Portuguese ancestry; to America 1772; opened commission merchant business in New York. Arrested by British for conspiracy, he escaped death 1778 by breaking jail; appealed in vain to Continental Congress for employment; became leading banker in Philadelphia, handling French and Dutch loans to colonies, advancing over $658,000 to finance American Revolution; after war suffered reverses.
'Salomon symphonies' (or 'London symphonies'), works by Haydn H-75
Salon, a kind of gathering of intellectuals and artists that flourished in Paris 17th, 18th, and 19th centuries; first held by Mme. de Rambouillet; other famous ones by Mme. de Scudéry, Mme. de Staël, Mme. Récamier.
Salonika (Greek Thessalonikē, ancient Thessalonica), Greece, chief port on n. Aegean; pop. 345,799 S-29, *map* E-361
Macedonia M-7
Saloon, place for retail sale of liquor P-506
Salpiglossis, also called **painted tongue,** an annual garden plant *Salpiglossis sinuata* of the nightshade family with large funnel-shaped, purple, blue, red, yellow, or white flowers that are beautifully penciled and veined with deeper colors; leaves notched, and have pungent odor; native to Chile.
Salsify (or oyster plant), a biennial of the chicory family cultivated for its long, cylindrical, white, delicately flavored roots.
Salsify, meadow. *see in index* Goatsbeard
Sal soda, sodium carbonate S-247
Salt, chemistry A-20, S-29, 31. For salts of the important elements, *see in index* element by name, as Aluminum
electrochemistry E-171
Great Salt Lake G-251
soap S-229
wood treatment W-285
Salt (or sodium chloride, or common salt, or table salt), mineral S-29, *picture* S-31, *charts* S-30. *see also in index* Halite
crystals C-795
Dead Sea P-81
earth E-13
fireworks F-114
food and nutrition F-279
malnutrition M-77
meat industry M-252
freezing point S-254f
inorganic chemistry I-210
irrigation and I-355
Leblanc soda process uses S-247
minerals M-435
mines and mining M-426
molecule M-522
money S-30
oceanography O-473
principal uses, *chart* S-30
producing regions S-30
Colombia, *picture* S-31
United States S-30, *chart* S-30
scarcity in pioneer days P-334
seasoning S-379
solubility S-256
transportation S-30, *pictures* S-29, 31
water W-85. *see also in index* Desalinization
SALT (Strategic Arms Limitation Talks) P-144, T-273, U-197
disarmament D-164
international relations I-265
Carter's contribution C-184
Kissinger's contribution K-251
nuclear energy N-430
Salta, Argentina, city 140 mi (225 km) n. of Tucumán; on railroad to Bolivia; commercial center; sugar mills, sawmills, rice cleaning; pop. 176,216 S-281, *maps* A-585, S-300
Salt cake S-247
Salt dome (or salt plug), geology
oil trap P-235
Salten, Felix (1869–1945), Austrian essayist, novelist, and dramatist; praised as stylist; gave sympathetic portrayal of animal characters ('Martin Overbeck'; 'Bambi', on which Walt Disney's motion picture 'Bambi' was based; and 'The Hound of Florence').
Salt gland, botanical structure H-19
Saltillo, Mexico, capital of Coahuila state; resort; industrial and educational center; textiles, flour; serapes made by American Indians nearby; pop. 211,129, *map* N-351
Mexico, *map* M-344
Saltire, in heraldry H-136
Salt Lake City, Utah, state capital and largest city of state, in n. of state near Great Salt Lake; pop. 163,697 S-31
Capitol, *picture* U-223
climate, *list* U-215
Mormons M-584
Pioneer Day marks founding U-219, *picture* U-225
Sea Gull Monument G-317, *picture* U-234
skiing nearby, *picture* U-225
Utah, *maps* N-351, U-232, U-217, 220, U-40, *pictures* U-215, 223
Young Y-424
Salt lakes. *see in index* Lake, *subhead* salt
Salt Lake State, popular name for Utah. *see in index* Utah
Salt marsh, area of ground flooded by salt water. *see also in index* Swamp
wildlife conservation C-676
Salt-marsh grass, plant *Spartina alterniflora* H-19
Salto, Uruguay, port on Uruguay River, 250 mi (400 km) n.w. of Montevideo; shipyards; meat-packing, flour milling; pharmaceuticals, chemicals; oranges, grapes; pop. 80,000, *maps* S-299, U-214
Salton Sea, lake in Imperial Valley in s. California I-59, *map* U-87
Saltpeter (or niter), potassium nitrate M-435. *see also in index* Chile saltpeter
explosive E-379
Salt Plains, two regions in Oklahoma covered by layers of salt varying in depth from a thin coating to about 6 in. (15 cm); Edith Plain, in n.w. on Cimarron River, covers 6,000 acres (2,400 hectares) and supports no life; Cherokee salt strip, about 40 mi (65 km) n.w. of Enid, covers about 28,000 acres (11,300 hectares) and supports only 4 forms of life, 2 species of beetles and 2 varieties of grasses; part of lake and dam built here is government owned and used as a game refuge chiefly for migratory waterbirds.
Salt plug (or salt dome), geology
oil trap P-235
Salt River, small tributary of the Gila River flowing through Arizona
Roosevelt Dam. *see in index* Theodore Roosevelt Dam
valley P-268
Salt sage, a desert plant S-14
Salt Springs Dam, in California, on North Fork of Mokelumne River, *picture* D-13
Salt-water fish F-124
Saltwort, plant *Batis* H-19
Saltykov, Mikhail Evgrafovich (1826–89), Russian satirical writer under pseudonym **Shchedrin;** exiled 1848 to Vyatka; editor ('A Complicated Affair'; 'Provincial Sketches'; 'The History of a Town') R-361
Saluda Dam, dam in South Carolina, on Saluda River S-311, *maps* S-307, 318
Saluda River, river in South Carolina, rises in Blue Ridge Mountains, unites with the Broad at Columbia to form the Congaree S-306, *maps* S-318, 307
Saluki, a hunting dog; sacred to ancient Egyptians, *picture* D-200
Salute F-152
Salvador (or São Salvador, also called Bahia), Brazil, seaport on All Saints Bay (Bahia de Todos los Santos), 775 mi (1,245 km) n.e. of Rio de Janeiro; capital of state of Bahia; pop. 1,506,602 S-32
Brazil, *maps* B-425, S-298
world, *map* W-297
Salvador, El. *see in index* El Salvador
Salvage, the saving of a ship or of its cargo, and the reward for such a service; also, less commonly, the saving of other forms of property (from Latin *salvus,* safe) F-212
Salvages, islands of the Madeira group M-24
Salvarsan, a drug
Ehrlich E-131
Salvatierra, Juan Maria (1648–1717), Italian Jesuit missionary, born in Milan; in 1697 founded mission on e. coast of Lower California.
Salvation Army S-32
England E-233
women's rights, *list* W-275
Salvemini, Gaetano (1873–1957), U.S. historian, born in Molfetta, Italy; professor of history University of Florence 1916–25 and after 1948; anti-Fascist, left Italy 1925, lived in England and U.S.; lecturer Harvard University 1934–48; became U.S. citizen 1940; returned to Italy 1948 ('Prelude to World War II', 'Mazzini').
Salve Regina–The Newport College, Newport, R.I.; Roman Catholic; chartered 1934; opened 1947; business and management, liberal arts, education, health professions; graduate studies.
Salverson, Laura Goodman (born 1890), Canadian writer, born in Winnipeg, Man.
Salvi, Niccolo (or Nicola Salvi) (1697–1751), Italian architect and sculptor, born in Rome; engaged in a variety of projects
Fountain of Trevi F-334, R-255, *picture* R-253
Salvia (or scarlet sage), genus of plants and shrubs of the mint family; includes about 500 species; flowers are tubular, scarlet, white, or blue
growing conditions G-23
Salvini, Tommaso (1829–1916), Italian actor; famous on Italian, English, and U.S. stages; chief successes in 'Oreste'; 'La Morte Civile'; 'Francesca da Rimini'; 'Othello' A-27
Salween River (or Salwin River), in southern Asia; rises in s.e. Tibet and flows 1,750 mi (2,800 km) s., principally through Burma, to Gulf of Martaban B-508
Asia, *map* A-700
Salyut, Soviet man-made satellite S-346f, *table* S-348
frontiers in space F-428
Salzburg, Austria, picturesque city in Salzburg Alps, 160 mi (260 km) s.w. of Vienna; capital of Salzburg Province (2,763 sq mi [7,156 sq km]; pop. 347,292); castle, cathedral; pop. 108,114, *map* E-361
Christianity A-828
Salzburgers, German Lutheran immigrants (about 135) to colony of Georgia (1734–35), seeking religious liberty; first settled near Springfield, moved to New Ebenezer; industrious, contributed to growth of silk-weaving industry.
Samanids, Iranian dynasty C-56
Samar, 3rd largest island of the Philippines; area 5,050 sq mi (13,080 sq km); principal crops are Manila hemp (abacá) and coconuts; pop. 861,765 P-259, 259b, 256, 257, *maps* P-259a, 261d
Asia, *map* A-700
Samara, U.S.S.R. *see in index* Kuibyshev
Samaria, ancient city of Palestine, 35 mi (55 km) n. of Jerusalem; became capital of Israel 9th century BC (name also applied to region of central Palestine occupied by Samaritans)
Israel I-369
Samaria, battle of, during World War I, at Samaria, Palestine, Sept. 19–22,

1918; British and Arabian troops under General Allenby defeated Turkish forces.

Samarium (Sm), chemical element
periodic table, *table* P-207, *list* P-208

Samarkand (also spelled Samarqand), U.S.S.R., city in Uzbek Soviet Socialist Republic, 150 mi (240 km) e. of Bukhara; ancient Maracanda; famous medieval center of learning; pop. 515,000 S-33, *maps* R-322, 344
Asia, *map* A-700
tomb of Timur Lenk T-190, *map* R-340, *picture* R-351

Samarra, Iraq, town on the Tigris n.w. of Baghdad; place of pilgrimage for Islamic Shi'ite sect; pop. 48,940.

'Samaveda' (or 'Veda of the Chants'), sacred Indian literature I-105

Sambain, Celtic festival H-17

Sambar, deer of Asia; brown color; weighs up to 700 lbs (320 kg); averages 4 ft (1.2 m) high at the shoulder; three-tined antlers; coarse hair.

Sambo, type of wrestling W-366

Sambre, river in n.e. France and Belgium; rises 120 mi (195 km) n.e. of Paris and flows 100 mi (160 km) n.e. to Meuse at Namur, *map* F-372

Sam Browne belt, leather belt held by strap over right shoulder; named for **Sir Samuel J. Browne** (1824–1901), British army officer.

Samford University, Birmingham, Ala.; Southern Baptist; founded 1842; arts and sciences, education, law, music, pharmacy; graduate study A-227

Sam Houston State University, Huntsville, Tex.; founded 1879; arts and sciences, education; graduate study.

Samian ware, Roman pottery P-470

Samil Independence Movement, Korean history K-287

Samis. *see in index* Lapps

Samisen, Japanese musical instrument J-55

Samnites, ancient peoples inhabiting mountainous portions of s. half of Italy R-244

Samoa (formerly called Navigators Islands), chain of islands in s. Pacific; more than 1,200 sq mi (3,100 sq km); divided into the sovereign state of Western Samoa with 1,093 sq mi (12,831 sq km), pop. 160,000 and American Samoa with 77 sq mi (199 sq km), pop. 36,000 S-33. *see also in index* Western Samoa
clothing, *picture* P-15–16
McKinley M-20
New Zealand N-294
Pacific Ocean P-17, *map* P-6
people, *pictures* P-7, 15, 16, R-25
shelter, *picture* P-16
Stevenson S-446

Samos, small Greek island in Aegean Sea near Asia Minor; area about 190 sq mi (490 sq km); flourishing Greek colony 6th century BC; famous temple of Hera; exports wine, raisins; pop. 41,124, *map* E-361

Samoset (died about 1653), American Indian chief, friend of Pilgrims at Plymouth P-395, *picture* U-169

Samothrace (Greek Samothrake), small Greek island in n. Aegean; 'Winged Victory' found here 1863 now in Louvre, museum in Paris, France.

Samothrace, Victory of. *see in index* Winged Victory

Samovar (translation self-boiler), a metal urn used to hold water for making tea; glowing charcoal, placed in a pipe through the center, heats the water
brass, *picture* B-411

Samoyed, a people living on Arctic coast between Pechora and Yenisey rivers; hunting, fishing; reindeer; stone huts; implements of bone and stone, *chart* R-26

Samoyed, a working dog, *picture* D-202

Sampan, a small flat-bottomed boat of Asian countries; used by Chinese as houseboats.

Sample, statistics S-431

Sampler, a decorative piece of embroidery, generally worked on canvas or on some other coarse material; usually square or rectangular A-494
needlework, *picture* N-111

Sample space, set of possible outcomes of a random event
mathematics M-220

Sampson, Edith S(purlock) (1901–79), U.S. lawyer, born in Pittsburgh, Pa.; in U.S. delegation to UN 1950, 1952; judge Circuit Court of Cook County (Ill.) 1964–78.

Sampson, William Thomas (1840–1902), U.S. rear admiral, born in Palmyra, N.Y.; served in Civil War; in Spanish-American War, led North Atlantic squadron and conducted the blockade of Santiago, Cuba; the battle of Santiago was fought according to his plans, while he was absent conferring with Army leaders S-365

Samsara, Buddhist doctrine of rebirth B-480

Samson, Hebrew judge and hero, celebrated for feats of strength. When Delilah had his hair shorn, his strength departed and he was enslaved and blinded by the Philistines. As his hair grew, his strength returned and he pulled down the house on his enemies' heads and on his own (Judg. xiii–xvi) F-263, M-699
hairdressing H-8

'Samson Agonistes', tragedy by Milton M-420
English literature E-269

'Samson et Dalila', opera by Saint-Saëns; libretto by Lemaire from the Biblical story.

Samsun, Turkey, port on s. coast of Black Sea about 200 mi (320 km) n.e. of Ankara; tobacco center; grain, beans, wool; location of ancient Greek city Amisus nearby; pop. 87,688
Asia, *map* A-700

Samudra Gupta (died AD 380?), ruler of India G-318

Samuel, last of Hebrew judges, anointed Saul and David (I Samuel); gave name to 9th and 10th books of Old Testament containing history of Israel from birth of Samuel to death of David.

Samuel, Herbert Louis Samuel, first **Viscount** (1870–1963), British Liberal political leader; high commissioner to Palestine 1920–25; home secretary 1916 and 1931–32.

Samuelson, Paul Anthony (born 1915), U.S. economist, born in Gary, Ind.; professor of economics Massachusetts Institute of Technology 1940–; adviser to U.S. government agencies; wrote 'Economics', a textbook that sold some 3 million copies. *see also in index* Nobel Prizewinners, *table*

Samurai, Japanese warriors S-34
Japan J-57, 63
martial arts M-159
Yamaga Y-408
Zen Z-450

San'a (or Sanaa), capital of Yemen Arab Republic; religious and educational center; pop. 277,818 S-34
Asia, *map* A-700
Yemen Arab Republic Y-414

Sananda, Papua New Guinea, strategic point in World War II on e. coast between Buna and Gona.

San Andreas Fault, geologic rift in California extending from Imperial Valley, just n. of Mexican border, n.w. through Coast Ranges to Golden Gate and thence out to sea; many earthquakes have occurred along this fault E-33, E-39, *picture* E-32

San Andres, University of, in La Paz, Bolivia L-49

San Angelo, Tex., city about 180 mi (290 km) n.w. of Austin; health resort; wool and mohair market, livestock and farming region; oil-distributing center; food products, leather and clay products; Angelo State College; Goodfellow Air Force Base nearby; pop. 73,240, *maps* N-351, U-40

San Anselmo, Calif., city 3 mi (5 km) w. of San Rafael; chiefly residential; San Francisco Theological Seminary; incorporated 1907; pop. 11,927.

San Antonio, Tex., city on San Antonio River; pop. 785,410 S-35, T-119, *maps* N-351, U-40
Alamo. *see in index* Alamo
Hertzberg circus collection C-432
zoo Z-458

San Antonio de Oriente, Honduras, village, *picture* H-225

San Augustin Church, in Lima, Peru L-209

San Benedicto, volcanic island of Mexico, in Pacific Ocean, *picture* V-380
Mexico, *map* M-344

San Benito, Tex., city near southernmost point of state, about 17 mi (27 km) n.w. of Brownsville; processing of vegetables and citrus fruits; pop. 17,988.

San Bernardino, Calif., city about 55 mi (90 km) e. of Los Angeles; railroad shops; steel products; California State College at San Bernardino; military base adjacent; annual National Orange Show; pop. 118,057, *maps* N-351, U-40

San Bernardino Mountains, range in s. Calif.; highest point 11,600 ft (3,535 m), *map* U-87

San Blas Islands (official name Archipiélago de las Mulatas), group of about 400 small islands on n. coast of Panama, extending s.e. from the Gulf of San Blas; inhabited by Cunas, also called Tules or San Blas.

San Bonifacio de Ibagué, Colombia. *see in index* Ibagué

San Bruno, Calif., city about 10 mi (16 km) s. of San Francisco; shortwave and electronic equipment; flower nurseries; divisional airlines offices; Western Regional Headquarters of U.S. Postal Service; pop. 35,417.

San Bruno elfin, butterfly
endangered species E-212

San Buenaventura, Calif. *see in index* Ventura

San Carlo, noted opera house in Naples, Italy, one of largest in Europe; founded 1737; rebuilt after destruction by fire in 1816.

San Carlos, Calif., city about 20 mi (32 km) s.e. of San Francisco; electronic center, machine shops; plastics; pop. 24,710.

San Carlos de Bariloche, ski resort in Argentina A-576, *map* A-585

San Carlos Valley, Costa Rica, *picture* J-153

Sánchez, Florencio (1875–1910), Uruguayan writer L-75

Sanchez, Phillip Victor (born 1929), U.S. public official, born in Pinedale, Calif.; director Office of Economic Opportunity 1971–73.

Sanchi, village in Madhya Pradesh state, India, 26 mi (42 km) n.e. of Bhopal; famous for topes, old Buddhist shrines.

Sancho Panza. *see in index* Panza, Sancho

San Clemente, Calif., city on Pacific 57 mi (92 km) s.e. of Los Angeles; estate of Richard M. Nixon, including Spanish-style home once called the Western White House; pop. 27,325.

San Cristóbal (or Chatham), island, Galápagos Islands, Ecuador G-3

San Cristóbal, Venezuela, a city in w. near border of Colombia; coffee, wheat, cattle, coal; pop. 98,777, *map* V-275

San Cristobal, volcano in Nicaragua N-304

Sancti Spíritus, Cuba, city 20 mi (30 km) from s. coast; livestock, dairy products, sugar, tobacco; founded 1514; pop. 37,741.

Sancy, diamond, *picture* D-129

Sand, George (pen name of Amandine-Aurore-Lucile Dupin, Baronne Dudevant) (1804–76), French novelist and feminist, born in Paris; early novels are of revolt of women against conventions; later stories of rural life are her greatest F-396
Chopin's friendship C-396

Sand S-36, *picture* S-37. *see also in index* Deserts; Sand dune
animal tracks A-463
brickmaking B-436
building material B-491
glassmaking G-156
musical sands S-38
quartz sand Q-6
quicksand Q-17
rock cycle, *chart* R-229
silicon S-195b
soil G-21, S-253

Sandae, Korean mask play K-281

Sandal, footwear S-178. *see also in index* Boot; Shoe

Sandalwood, a tree or its fragrant wood S-38

Sandarac, a resin of the pine tree of n. Africa and Australia, used in making lacquer.

Sanday, one of Orkney Islands; pop. 670.

Sandbar, in river R-210, *diagram* R-210

Sandblast S-38
pneumatic appliance P-399

'Sandbox, The', work by Albee A-260

Sandbox tree (or monkey dinner bell), tropical tree *Hura crepitans* native to Central and South America; grows to 100 ft (30 m); branches spiny; leaves oval, to 2 ft (60 cm) long; flowers red; secretes milky juice used by American Indians to poison darts; sometimes called assacu and dynamite tree; wood, pale yellow or brown, soft is used for furniture under name hura, or possumwood.

Sandburg, Carl (1878–1967), U.S. writer S-3, A-354
books A-356, R-107, 110b, 111e
children's S-464
Lincoln biography S-39
meat industry M-248
portrait, *picture* B-223

Sand cat, wild cat *Felis margarita*, *table* C-214

Sand dollar, a sea urchin S-425, 426

Sand dune S-36, *picture* S-37
desert D-105
Lake Superior, Mich., *picture* M-365
Sahara S-15

Sandeau, (Léonard Sylvain) Jules (1811–83), French novelist and dramatist; collaborated with George Sand on early works under pen name, Jules Sand; author of many romantic novels and plays ('Marianna'; 'Mlle. de la Seiglière'; 'Fernand').

Sander, a tool, *picture* T-216

Sanderling, shorebird S-39

Sand fly. *see in index* Stable fly

Sandglass. *see in index* Hourglass

Sandhill crane, bird *Grus canadensis* C-760

Sand Hills, natural region in Nebraska N-94, *picture* N-96

Sandia, a pueblo 12 mi (19 km) n. of Albuquerque, N.M., on the Rio Grande; Sandia people belong to the Tanoan language group of Pueblo Indians I-144, *map* N-229

San Diego, Calif., seaport in s.w. corner of state; pop. 875,504 S-39, *maps* C-53, N-351, U-40, *picture* S-40

San Diego, University of, Coordinate Colleges, in San Diego, Calif.; Roman Catholic; formed from merger of University of San Diego College for Men and College for Women 1971; arts and sciences, education; graduate study.

San Diego State College, in San Diego, Calif.; opened 1897; arts and sciences, business administration, education, engineering; graduate school; branch at El Centro.

San Diego Zoo, in Balboa Park, Calif. Z-458, *picture* Z-459

San Dimas, Calif., residential city n.w. of Pomona; pop. 15,692.

Sandinista, one of a Nicaraguan guerilla group that overthrew Anastasio Somoza Debayle in 1979; named for César Augusto Sandino, a hero of Nicaraguan resistance to U.S. military occupation (1927–33) N-304

Sandino, César Augusto (1893–1934), Nicaraguan leader and popular hero; gave his name to the Sandinistas, a revolutionary group that won control of the government in 1979 N-305

Sand launce, widely distributed family of shore fish

Ammodytidae, small, slender, silvery bodied, and with the habit of burying themselves in the sand.

Sand lily, a plant *Leucocrinum montanum* of the lily family; long narrow leaves tufted on rootstock and clusters of delicate white flowers; grows in Rocky Mountains region.

Sand martin, English term for bank swallow, also for rough-winged swallow S-521

Sand mold process, in casting metals S-81

Sand Mountain (or Raccoon Mountain), in n.e. Alabama; ridge of Appalachians; 1,800 ft (550 m), *map* A-236

Sando Bridge, in Sweden, *picture* B-446

San Domingo, name sometimes used for Santo Domingo, former name of Dominican Republic. *see in index* Dominican Republic

Sandow, Eugene (1867–1925), German strong man and physical culturist, born in Königsberg, Germany; noted for feats of strength; founded magazine 'Physical Culture'.

Sandoz, Mari Susette (1897?–1966), U.S. writer, born in Sheridan County, Neb.; won *Atlantic Monthly* prize 1935 for 'Old Jules', caustic biography of her Swiss immigrant father who settled in Nebraska 1884 ('Winter Thunder', 'Miss Morissa', 'The Cattlemen', 'Hostiles and Friendlies', 'These Were the Sioux'; for young people, 'The Horsecatcher').

Sand painting, *picture* I-140

Sandpaper, glue-coated paper sprinkled with sand; used in rubbing down paints, rough surfaces; comes in varying grades of abrasiveness A-13
- quartz Q-6

Sandpipers, shorebirds S-40
- animal tracks A-463
- flight, *picture* B-246
- nest B-253
- plover P-391
- spotted S-40

Sand rat. *see in index* Gerbil

Sand roller. *see in index* Perch trout

Sand shark, fish S-144

Sand skink, lizard, *picture* L-273

Sand Springs, Okla., industrial city 8 mi (13 km) s.w. of Tulsa on Arkansas River; textiles, glass; oil and gas wells; pop. 13,246.

Sandstone S-38, R-229a, *picture* R-229a
- minerals M-437
- quarrying Q-6
- quartz Q-6
- rock cycle, *chart* R-229
- sculpture use A-667
- uranium ore U-210

Sandusky, Ohio, industrial city on Sandusky Bay, Lake Erie, about 50 mi (80 km) w. of Cleveland; fishing port; large coal-loading docks; automobile parts; pop. 31,360, *picture* O-510, *map* U-41

Sand wasp, insect M-423

Sandwich, Edward Montagu, first **earl of** (1625–72) English admiral; assisted in restoration of Charles II; killed in naval action, buried in Westminster Abbey
- Pepys P-197b

Sandwich, John Montagu, 4th **earl of** (1718–92), English political leader, notorious for his personal and political vices; first lord of the admiralty 1771–82.

Sandwich, town in Kent, England, on Stour River near English Channel; one of Cinque Ports of Middle Ages; pop. 4,264.

Sandwich glass, term now used for pressed glass made in U.S. factories 1825–1900; formerly, glass made by Boston and Sandwich Glass Co., Sandwich, Mass.; made in raised patterns, such as the Hobnail, and in colors; name also given to a safety glass made with a layer of plastic between sheets of flat glass.

Sandwich Glass Museum, in Sandwich, Mass., *picture* M-200

Sandwich Islands, name given to Hawaiian Islands by Cook. *see in index* Hawaii, state

Sandworm, type of worm, *picture* W-362

Sandy City, Utah, city 13 mi (21 km) s. of Salt Lake City; center of irrigated agricultural area; pop. 50,546, *map* U-232

Sandy Hook, of New Jersey, slender peninsula of sand extending 6 mi (10 km) n. and partly enclosing New York Bay; lighthouse became National Historic Landmark on 200th anniversary, 1964.

Sandys, Sir Edwin (1561–1629), English statesman; member of Parliament; knighted when James I became king; treasurer of the Virginia Company; established first representative assembly in North American colonies.

Sandys, Frederick (1829?–1904), English painter of the Pre-Raphaelite group; highly skilled in drawing; favorite subjects from Norse mythology.

San Felipe (translation St. Philip), a pueblo 35 mi (55 km) s.w. of Santa Fe, N.M., on the Rio Grande; San Felipe people belong to the Keresan language group of Pueblo Indians; village pop. 1,187.

San Felipe de Austin, name of colony, founded 1823 by Stephen Fuller Austin, between lower Colorado and Brazos rivers in Texas; name later (1824–35) given to seat of government, near present town of San Felipe, Tex.

San Fernando, Calif., city 20 mi (30 km) n.w. of Los Angeles; textiles; electronic assembly, research development; Mission San Fernando nearby; pop. 17,731.

San Fernando Valley State College. *see in index* California State University, Northridge

Sanford, Fla., city on Lake Monroe, St. Johns River, about 20 mi (30 km) n.e. of Orlando; research and development, electronics; clothing, boats; pop. 23,176, *map* U-41

Sanford, Me., about 30 mi (50 km) s.w. of Portland; textiles, shoes, plastics, electronic components; Nasson College nearby; pop. of township, 18,020.

Sanford, N.C., town about 38 mi (61 km) s.w. of Raleigh; tobacco and general farming; brick, tile, pottery, textiles, textile machinery, cosmetics, electronic equipment, lumber products; pop. 14,773.

San Francisco, Calif., 2nd city of state; pop. 678,974 S-41
- bridges, *map* S-41b. *see also in index* Golden Gate, *subhead* bridge; San Francisco-Oakland Bay Bridge
- cable cars S-486, S-42, *picture* S-44
- California C-38, *map* C-53, *pictures* C-37
- Chinatown S-42, *map* S-41b
- conference, World War II U-20, U-190
- earthquake S-43, *picture* S-44
- fairs S-44. *see also in index* Panama-Pacific International Exposition
- museums S-43, *map* S-41b
- Oakland O-453
- parks, *picture* P-127–8
  - Golden Gate Park S-41a, *map* S-41a, *picture* P-128
- peace march, *picture* P-143b
- places of interest S-41a, *map* S-41a–b
- United States, *maps* N-351, U-40
- United States Mint C-538
- zoo Z-458

San Francisco, Church of, *picture* A-583

San Francisco, University of, in San Francisco, Calif.; Roman Catholic; founded 1855; arts and sciences, business administration; education, law, nursing; graduate studies.

San Francisco Bay, on coast of California at San Francisco; about 50 mi (80 km) long including n. part called San Pablo Bay; width from 3 to 12 mi (5 to 19 km); entrance to Pacific is by Golden Gate S-41, *map* S-41a, *picture* S-41
- bridges. *see also in index* Golden Gate, *subhead* bridge; San Francisco-Oakland Bay Bridge

San Francisco Conference, World War II U-20, U-190

San Francisco garter snake, reptile
- endangered species E-212

San Francisco Mountain (or San Francisco Peaks), Arizona, group of extinct volcanic cones n. of Flagstaff; Humphreys Peak, 12,655 ft (3,857 m), highest point in state V-378

San Francisco-Oakland Bay Bridge (or Transbay Bridge), in California B-447
- Oakland O-453
- San Francisco, *map* S-41b

San Francisco State College, since 1972 **San Francisco State University,** San Francisco, Calif.; opened 1899; arts and sciences, business, education, engineering, music, nursing, social work; graduate studies.

San Gabriel, Calif., residential city, 8 mi (13 km) e. of Los Angeles; electronic equipment; San Gabriel Mission; pop. 30,072.

San Gabriel Mission, early California mission in city of San Gabriel, 8 mi (13 km) e. of Los Angeles; present mission dates from 1794; original founding 1771; Mission Playhouse, in which mission plays were formerly produced, is now a motion-picture theater.

San Gabriel Mountains, range in California, n.e. of Los Angeles; contains nine peaks more than 8,000 ft (2,400 m) high; loftiest San Antonio peak, or Old Baldy (10,080 ft; 3,072 m), *picture* L-299

Sangallo, Antonio da, the Younger (1483–1546), Italian architect and military engineer, born near Florence.

Sangamon River, crooked stream flowing w. about 150 mi (240 km) across central Illinois to the Illinois River
- Springfield, Ill. S-397

Sanger, Frederick (1918–82), English biochemist; on staff British Medical Research Council 1951–82. *see also in index* Nobel Prizewinners, *table*

Sanger, Margaret (or Mrs. J. Noah Slee) (1883–1966), U.S. leader in birth control movement, born in Corning, N.Y.; 1917 founded American Birth Control League; established first permanent birth control clinic in New York City 1923 B-283
- women's rights W-277

Sangha, Buddhist monastic order B-482

Sangreal. *see in index* Holy Grail

Sangre de Cristo Range, of Rocky Mts., in s.-central Colorado and n. New Mexico R-234, *map* U-81
- ancient church, *picture* S-339

Sangria, wine W-237

Sangster, Charles (1822–93), Canadian poet, born in Kingston, Upper Canada C-120

Sanhedrin, the supreme judicial council of the ancient Jews under Roman rule.

San Ildefonso, a pueblo about 18 mi (29 km) n.w. of Santa Fe, N.M.; San Ildefonso people belong to Tanoan language group of Pueblo Indians; pop. 140.

San Ildefonso (also called La Granja), Spain, town 40 mi (65 km) n.w. of Madrid; palace built by Philip V; secret treaty between Napoleon and Spain (1800) ceding Louisiana to France was signed here; pop. 2,351.

Sanín Cano, Baldomero (1861–1957), Colombian writer, educator, and public official, born in Rionegro.

Sanitation. *see also in index* Public health; Sewage disposal
- garbage and refuse disposal G-17
- laundry L-85
- plumbing P-392–3, *picture* P-393

San Ivo della Sapienza, Baroque church designed by Borromini B-370

San Jacinto, battle of (1836), between Texans and Mexicans in Texan war for independence; anniversary celebrated April 21
- Houston H-307
- memorial, *picture* T-130

Sanjo II (11th century), Japanese emperor F-445

San Joaquin River, Calif., rises in Sierra Nevada near Yosemite National Park, flows w. and n. to meet the Sacramento River near its mouth, *map* U-87

San Jose, Calif., city 45 mi (70 km) s.e. of San Francisco near San Francisco Bay; pop. 636,550 S-44, *maps* N-351, U-40

San José, Costa Rica, capital and largest city; pop. 203,148 S-44a, C-733, *map* N-351

San José, Guatemala, port on Pacific coast; tourist resort; railroad terminus; ships coffee, sugar, forest products; pop. 5,771.

San José Mission National Historic Site, San Antonio, Tex., *picture* T-130

San José scale, an insect parasite of plants S-52f

San Jose State College, since 1974 **San Jose State University,** in San Jose, Calif.; opened 1857; under state control since 1862; arts and sciences, business, education, engineering, music, nursing; graduate studies.

San Juan, P.R., capital and chief port, on n. coast; pop. 432,973 S-44a, P-529, *map* N-351
- Capitol, *picture* P-530
- Puerto Rico, University of, *picture* P-530
- San Juan N.H.S. P-530, *picture* P-527
- West Indies, *map* W-106

San Juan Bautista, name given to Puerto Rico by Christopher Columbus. *see in index* Puerto Rico

San Juan Bautista, Cathedral of, in San Juan, Puerto Rico S-44a

San Juan Capistrano, Calif., city (pop. 3,781) and mission near Pacific Ocean, 20 mi (30 km) s.e. of Santa Ana; in mission's ruins, cliff swallows have built mud nests since days when Spain ruled here; these Capistrano swallows have been said to leave on every October 23 (Saint John's Day) and to return every March 19 (Saint Joseph's Day); actually, dates of arrival and departure vary with food supply and weather. *see also in index* Cliff swallow

San Juan del Norte (formerly Greytown), Nicaragua, port on Caribbean Sea at mouth of San Juan River, at extreme s.e. point of Nicaragua; once a major port; in California gold rush, it thrived as e. terminus of transisthmian transportation company; port identified with filibustering activity of William Walker; pop. 440.

San Juan Hill (or Kettle Hill), near Santiago, Cuba; capture by U.S. troops led to surrender of Santiago in Spanish-American War S-365, R-284

San Juan Islands, a group of islands off n.w. Washington; includes Orcas Island, San Juan Island, and Lopez Island W-54

San Juan Mountains, range in s.w. Colorado; highest peak over 14,000 ft (4,270 m), *map* U-81

San Juan Pueblo, N.M., situated about 25 mi (40 km) n.w. of Santa Fe; San Juan Indians belong to the Tanoan language group of the Pueblo Indians; pop. 900, *map* N-229

San Juan River, river in Nicaragua, flows e. from Lake Nicaragua 100 mi (160 km) to Caribbean Sea; forms part of Nicaragua and Costa Rica boundary.

San Juan River, tributary of the Colorado, in Colorado, New Mexico, and Utah; 360 mi (580 km) long C-584, *maps* C-585, U-81, U-217, 233

San Juan Teotihuacán (or Teotihuacán), archaeological area in Mexico, *picture* L-62
- Mexico M-328, 335, *map* M-344

Sanjurjo, José (1872–1936), general-in-chief of rebel forces during Spanish Civil War
- Franco succeeds F-376

Sankara (700?–750?), Indian philosopher and theologian, most renowned exponent of the Advaita Vedanta school of philosophy H-158
- monasticism M-541

Sankara, Thomas (born 1948?), head of state of Burkina Faso 1983– B-508

Sankey, Ira David (1840–1908), U.S. singer, hymn writer ('The Ninety and Nine'), and evangelist, born in Edinburgh, Pa.; associated with evangelist Dwight L. Moody.

Sankey, John, first **Viscount** (1866–1948), British statesman and lawyer; lord chancellor in both Labor and National governments of Ramsay MacDonald, 1929, 1931.

San-kin-kotai, Japanese governmental system T-210

Sankt Gallen, Switzerland. *see in index* St. Gallen

San Leandro, Calif., city immediately s. of Oakland; metal work, food and paper processing; floriculture; pop. 68,698.

San Lorenzo, Calif., community 11 mi (18 km) s.e. of Oakland; pop. 22,175.

San Luis, Colo., first permanent white settlement in Colo.; pop. 842 C-572, *map* C-583

San Luis Obispo, Calif., city in s. about 160 mi (260 km) n.w. of Los Angeles; California Polytechnic State University; pop. 28,036, *map* U-40

San Luis Potosí, Mexico, state in e. center; 24,266 sq mi (62,849 sq km); cap. San Luis Potosí; pop. 1,527,065, *map* M-344

San Luis Potosí, Mexico, commercial and railroad center, 225 mi (360 km) n.w. of Mexico City; capital of San Luis Potosí state; mining region; silver-, lead- and arsenic-processing; pop. 159,980 M-322, *map* M-344

San Marco, cathedral in Venice. *see in index* St. Mark's

San Marco, Italian artificial satellite, *table* S-344

San Marcos, Tex., city 30 mi (50 km) s.w. of Austin; agricultural and livestock region; cottonseed oil, woolens; Southwest Texas State University; huge springs of San Marcos River nearby; pop. 23,420.

San Marcos, University of, in Lima, Peru L-209

San Marino, small republic in n. part of Italian Peninsula, near Adriatic coast; 24 sq mi (62 sq km); cap. San Marino (pop. 2,621); pop. 17,000 S-44b, *maps* E-361, I-404
  flag, *picture* F-169

San Marino, Calif., residential city, suburb of Los Angeles; incorporated 1913; pop. 14,177
  Huntington Library. *see in index* Henry E. Huntington Library and Art Gallery

San Martín, José Francisco de (1778–1850), South American patriot, general, statesman S-44b
  Argentine history A-583
  Bolívar, *picture* S-291
  Latin America L-67
  statue, *picture* P-222

San Mateo, Calif., city 15 mi (25 km) s. of San Francisco; nurseries; food processing, printing; lumber products, wine, electronic equipment; pop. 77,561
  bridge B-447

San Men Dam, in China I-356

San Miguel, El Salvador, city about 70 mi (115 km) s.e. of San Salvador; coffee, henequen, cotton, cattle; pop. 40,432 E-196

San Miguel de Allende (or San Miguel), Mexico, city in Guanajuato state; flour, textiles; pop. 14,891.

S-A node. *see in index* Sinoatrial node

San Pablo, Calif., city 11 mi (18 km) n.w. of Oakland; heating and plumbing equipment; pop. 19,750.

San Pedro, Calif., seaport of Los Angeles, 20 mi (30 km) n.; annexed 1909; U.S. Navy fleet base.

San Pedro Sula, Honduras, industrial city in n.w.; chief distributing center; pop. 372,800 H-226

San Pietro in Vincoli (St. Peter in chains), church in Rome, Italy; part dates from 5th century or earlier
  Michelangelo's 'Moses' M-351, S-87, *picture* M-595

San Quentin Prison, California state prison in village of San Quentin on peninsula on San Francisco Bay; built 1852.

San Rafael, Calif., city about 15 mi (25 km) n. of San Francisco; yachting center; truck and dairy farms; aluminum products, plastics; Dominican College of San Rafael; pop. 44,700.

San Remo, Italy, famous winter resort on Riviera, 75 mi (120 km) s.w. of Genoa; conference of Supreme Council of Allied premiers (1920), which awarded Near East mandates; pop. 55,209, *map* I-404

San Salvador (or Watling Island), one of Bahamas; 60 sq mi (155 sq km); pop. 694
  Columbus' discovery B-20, C-593, *picture* U-130
  West Indies, *map* W-106

San Salvador, El Salvador, capital, 25 mi (40 km) from coast; pop. 255,744 S-44b, E-195, *map* N-351

San Salvador, volcano in El Salvador S-33

Sansanding, Mali, trading post on Niger River 25 mi (40 km) n.e. of Ségou; irrigation dam; pop. 5,366.

Sansculotte (without breeches), name applied to French revolutionary party; the upper classes in France wore knee breeches (culottes), while revolutionists wore long trousers D-265

San Sebastián, Spain, resort, industrial city near France on Bay of Biscay; pop. 98,603, *map* E-361

Sansevieria (or bowstring hemp), genus of herbaceous perennials of lily family; popular house plant because of stiff, erect leaves.

San Simeon, California estate of William Randolph Hearst
  Hearst H-96
  state historical monument, *picture* C-46

Sanskrit, ancient sacred and literary language of India, first found in Veda religious texts; Indo-Aryan language; because it is so regular, some think it was never a language of the common people
  Buddhist terminology B-480
  India I-67
  Indian literature I-105, S-461
  linguistic analysis L-230

Sansom, William (1912–76), British author, born in London ('The Loving Eye', 'The Cautious Heart', 'Good-bye', novels; 'A Touch of the Sun', 'The Stories of William Sansom', short stories; 'A Book of Christmas', essays).

Sansovino, Andrea (1460–1529), Florentine sculptor and architect; sculptor to King John of Portugal; designed royal palace in Portugal; executed notable sculptures for churches in Florence, Genoa, and Rome.

Sansovino, Jacopo (1486–1570), Florentine sculptor and architect, pupil of Andrea Sansovino, whose name he adopted; famous for beautiful Venetian buildings and for fine sculptural works.

San Stefano, European Turkey, port on Sea of Marmara; treaty ending Russo-Turkish War signed here in 1878
  treaty, *table* T-275

San Stefano, Treaty of, signed March 3, 1878, ended war between Russia and Turkey; revised at Congress of Berlin (1878) B-172
  Turkey T-323
  Ottoman Empire O-618

Santa Ana, Calif., city about 30 mi (50 km) s.e. of Los Angeles; vegetable and fruit processing; sugar-beet factories; woolen goods, glass products, farm implements, electronic equipment, missile parts; pop. 203,713, *map* U-40

Santa Ana, El Salvador, city, 40 mi (65 km) n.w. of San Salvador; in agricultural region producing grain and sugar; coffee processing; Spanish Gothic cathedral; pop. 72,839 S-33, E-196

Santa Ana (St. Ann), a pueblo on Rio Jemez, N.M.; Santa Ana people belong to the Keresan language group of Pueblo Indians.

Santa Ana. *see in index* Chinook wind

Santa Anna, Antonio Lopez de (1795–1876), Mexican general and intriguing political leader, alternately dictator and banished rebel; abolished Mexican constitution, causing Texas revolt
  chewing gum C-307
  Mexican War M-320
  Mexico M-336
  Texas revolt A-230, T-124
    Houston H-308

Santa Barbara, Calif., resort city on the Pacific, about 85 mi (135 km) n.w. of Los Angeles; in lemon and cattle-raising district; electronics, light industry; old mission (1786); Santa Barbara campus of University of California, Westmont College; pop. 74,542, *picture* H-163, *maps* N-351, U-40

Santa Barbara Islands, extending 150 mi (240 km) along coast of s. Calif., include San Miguel, Santa Rosa, Santa Cruz, Anacapa, San Nicolas, Santa Barbara, Santa Catalina, San Clemente, and many islets, *maps* N-351, U-40

Santa Barbara Mission, Calif., *picture* C-41

Santa Barbara poppy. *see in index* Hunnemannia

Santa Catalina Island (or Catalina Island), near Los Angeles, Calif.

Santa Catarina, Brazil, state on s.e. seacoast; area 36,602 sq mi (94,799 sq km); cap. Florianópolis (pop. 98,520); pop. 3,687,652, *map* B-425

Santa Clara, Calif., city immediately w. of San Jose; electronics, publishing, seeds, chemicals, food processing; Mission Santa Clara; University of Santa Clara; pop. 87,746.

Santa Clara, Cuba, city near center of island; asphalt, iron, manganese; center for sugarcane, coffee, tobacco, cattle; pop. 175,500, *maps* C-802, N-351
  West Indies, *map* W-106

Santa Clara, pueblo about 20 mi (30 km) n.w. of Santa Fe, N.M., on the Rio Grande; Santa Clara people belong to the Tanoan language group of Pueblo Indians.

Santa Clara, University of, in Santa Clara, Calif.; Roman Catholic; founded 1851; present name 1912; liberal arts, business administration, engineering, law, religion; graduate studies.

Santa Claus S-45. *see also in index* Nicholas, Saint
  Nast drawing N-21

Santa Claus, Ind., village 38 mi (61 km) n.e. of Evansville; pop. 63 S-46

Santa Cruz, Andrés (1792?–1865), Bolivian patriot, general in war of independence, president 1829–39; failed in forcible federation of Peru and Bolivia.

Santa Cruz, Argentina, seaport on Atlantic Ocean 115 mi (185 km) n.e. of Rio Gallegos; sheep raising, fishing; weather station.

Santa Cruz, Bolivia, town on e. slope of Andes about 170 mi (275 km) n.e. of Sucre; in sugar, coffee, and tobacco district; produces alcohol, petroleum, cigars, chocolate, and leather; pop. 149,230, *map* S-298

Santa Cruz, Calif., resort city on Monterey Bay about 60 mi (95 km) s. of San Francisco; electronics, frozen fruits and vegetables, tea processing, chewing gum, wire products, leather, cement; campus of University of California; pop. 41,483.

Santa Cruz, Virgin Islands of the United States. *see in index* St. Croix

Santa Cruz de Tenerife, port of Canary Islands on island of Tenerife; pop. 74,910.

Santa Cruz Islands (or Queen Charlotte Islands), group in independent portion of Solomon Islands, in Pacific Ocean; about 380 sq mi (985 sq km); discovered 1595; pop. 5,421, *maps* A-118, P-6
  World War II W-316

Santa Fé, Argentina, city on Paraná River near its junction with the Salado, 95 mi (155 km) n. of Rosario; trade in hides, timber; shipbuilding; university; pop. 244,655 S-281b, A-582, *maps* A-585, S-300

Santa Fe, N.M., capital and 2nd largest city of state, on Santa Fe River; pop. 48,953 S-46, *maps* N-351, U-40
  early history S-338, 339
  elevation M-636
  founding A-334
  New Mexico N-216, 224, *map* N-229

Santa Fe, College of, in Santa Fe, N.M.; Roman Catholic; founded 1947; liberal arts and education
  New Mexico N-217

Santa Fe Trail, early overland trade route to Santa Fe, N.M., part of modern Old Trails Road, *maps* U-176, R-219
  frontier F-422
  Missouri M-491
  New Mexico N-216

Santa Gertrudis, breed of cattle; cross between Brahman bull and Shorthorn cow C-230, *picture* C-229

Santa Isabel, Equatorial Guinea. *see in index* Malabo

Santa Maria, Azores Islands A-890

Santa Maria, Calif., city 56 mi (90 km) n.w. of Santa Barbara; petroleum products, beet sugar, food processing; pop. 39,685.

'Santa Maria', Columbus' flagship C-592

Santa Maria del Fiore Cathedral (or Cathedral of Florence), in Florence, Italy F-188, *pictures* F-187, E-352, *map* F-189
  sculptures S-86, *picture* S-85

Santa Maria della Salute, church in Venice, Italy, *picture* V-278

Santa Maria della Vittoria, church in Rome, Italy
  Bernini's chapel B-175
  sculpture, *picture* S-88

Santa Maria delle Grazie, Milan, Italy; former convent where Leonardo da Vinci's 'Last Supper' is painted on the refectory wall M-408

Santa Marta, Colombia, Caribbean port at mouth of Manzanares River; ships, bananas; pop. 102,484, *map* S-298

Sant' Ambrogio, in Milan, Italy M-408

Santa Monica, Calif., city and resort on Pacific 15 mi (25 km) w. of Los Angeles; aircraft, aircraft parts, electronic devices, ceramics; large airport; pop. 88,314, *map* U-40

Santana, Manuel (born 1938), Spanish tennis player
  tennis T-107

Santander, Francisco de Paula (1792–1840), Colombian statesman; twice elected vice-president of Colombia; governed country ably during Bolívar's many absences; president of New Granada 1832–36 C-554

Santander, Spain, important seaport on Bay of Biscay; fisheries, shipyards; fine harbor; iron ore, paper, wine; pop. 98,784, *maps* E-361, S-350

Sant' Angelo, Castel, Rome, Italy. *see in index* Castel Sant' Angelo

Santa Paula, Calif., city 51 mi (82 km) n.w. of Los Angeles; citrus fruit and avocado packing; petroleum products, cement products, building materials, paper cartons; pop. 20,552.

Santarém, Brazil, port in n.-center, on Tapajós River near junction with Amazon; handicrafts; trade in rubber, lumber, jute; group of Confederate veterans settled here after U.S. Civil War; pop. 52,665, *maps* B-425, S-298

Santa Rita, N.M., village 12 mi (19 km) n.e. of Silver City; copper-mining center, where steam shovels have unearthed many skeletons, perhaps of miners trapped by cave-ins long ago; pop. 600.

Santa Rosa, Calif., city about 50 mi (80 km) n. of San Francisco; trading center; electronics, wood products; Luther Burbank Memorial Gardens; pop. 83,205, *map* U-40

'Santa Rosa de Lima', painting by Botero P-67d, *picture* P-67c

Santa Sophia (Greek Hagia Sophia), meaning "holy wisdom," building at Istanbul, erected as Christian church in 6th century by Justinian I; became Muslim mosque in 1453; in 1935 was made a museum of Byzantine antiquities I-375
  architecture, *picture* A-550

Byzantine A-549, B-534
Eastern Orthodox E-43
Santa Trinita Bridge, over Arno at Florence, Italy B-445
'Santa Trinita Madonna', work by Cimabue, *picture* C-414
Santayana, George (1863–1952), Spanish philosopher and writer, born in Madrid, Spain; went to United States 1872; taught at Harvard 22 years; after 1912 lived in Europe; wrote many books on his system of materialistic philosophy ('The Sense of Beauty'; 'The Life of Reason'; 'The Realms of Being'); also wrote 'Poems'; 'The Last Puritan', novel; 'Persons and Places', autobiography L-242
Santee, a mixed Eastern Woodland-Plains Indian tribe, probably Siouan, formerly residing on middle Santee River in South Carolina, *table* I-138
Santee-Cooper Project, electric-power and navigation system in s.e. South Carolina between Charleston and Columbia; two dams, Santee on Santee River and Pinopolis on a tributary of the Cooper River; completed 1942 S-306, *map* S-319, *picture* S-311
Santee River, the chief river of South Carolina; formed by confluence of Congaree and Wateree rivers; flows s.e. into Atlantic; 143 mi (230 km) long, *maps* S-307, 319, U-59
dam S-306, *maps* S-307, 319
Santi, Raphael. *see in index* Raphael
Santiago, Spanish form of St. James, referring to St. James the Elder, patron saint of Spain. *see in index* James the Elder, Saint
Santiago, Cape Verde Islands. *see in index* São Tiago
Santiago, Chile, capital, on w. slope of Andes; pop. 2,596,929, with suburbs S-47, *map* S-299
Chile C-332
Santiago (or Santiago de Compostela), Spain, city in extreme n.w.; university; hospitals; 11th-century cathedral over shrine of Apostle St. James; pop. 37,916.
Santiago, battle of (1898), Cuba, *list* W-15
Santiago, Río Grande de, Mexico. *see in index* Lerma River
Santiago Bay, excellent landlocked harbor on s.e. coast of Cuba; Spanish fleet destroyed here in Spanish-American War.
Santiago de Cuba, port on s.e. coast of Cuba; good harbor; mining district; extensive export trade; founded by Spain (1514); stormed by United States (1898); pop. 353,400
naval battle (1898) S-364, *maps* C-802, N-351
West Indies, *map* W-106
Santiago de León de Caracas, Venezuela. *see in index* Caracas
Santiago del Estero, Argentina, city 90 mi (145 km) s.e. of Tucumán; pop. 60,039, *maps* A-585, S-300
Santo Domingo. *see in index* Dominican Republic
Santo Domingo. *see in index* Hispaniola
Santo Domingo (formerly Ciudad Trujillo), Dominican Republic, capital, on s. coast at mouth of Ozama River; pop. 671,402 D-227, *map* N-351
West Indies, *map* W-106
Santo Domingo Pueblo, about 24 mi (39 km) s.w. of Santa Fe, N.M., on the Rio Grande; Santo Domingo people belong to the Keresan language group of Pueblo Indians; pop. 1,662, *map* N-229
Santorin (corruption of St. Irene), volcanic island in Aegean Sea, southernmost of Cyclades, a Greek island group; area 27 sq mi (70 sq km); important remains of prehistoric Aegean civilization; ancient Thēra, powerful commercial state.
Santos, Brazil, city 33 mi (53 km) s.e. of São Paulo, whose seaport it is; coffee, bananas, citrus fruits, sugar, meat products; settled 1543–46; pop. 262,048 S-47
Brazil, *map* B-425
South America S-277, *map* S-299
Santos-Dumont, Alberto (1873–1932), French aeronaut, born in Brazil; built early dirigible propelled by gas engine, made first airplane flight in Europe A-203, *picture* A-202
Santo Tomas, University of, in Manila, Philippines; founded 1611; conducted by the Dominicans; theology, law, medicine, engineering, education, liberal arts P-253d, 255a
Manila M-97
Sanusiyah, mystic order in Islam M-542
San Vicente, El Salvador, city 30 mi (50 km) e. of San Salvador; on Acahuapa River; capital of republic 1839–40; pop. 203,713.
San Vitale, church of, in Ravenna, Italy M-590
San Xavier del Bac, mission near Tucson, Ariz. A-602, *picture* A-601
Kino K-247
São Francisco, river in e. Brazil; rises n.w. of Rio de Janeiro, flows 1,800 mi (2,900 km) n. and e. to Atlantic Ocean, *maps* B-425, S-298
São Luís (formerly São Luiz do Maranhao), Brazil, seaport, capital of Maranhão state, on island off n. coast; pop. 124,606, *maps* B-425, S-298
São Miguel (or St. Michael), largest of Azores; 288 sq mi (746 sq km); chief city Ponta Delgada A-890
Saône River, river in e. France, rises just w. of Vosges Mountains, flows 300 mi (480 km) s. to Rhône River; connected with Loire and Seine rivers by canals R-196, *map* F-372
São Paulo, seaboard state of s. Brazil; 95,452 sq mi (247,220 sq km); cap. São Paulo; textile industry; coffee, tobacco, and fruit; pop. 25,375,199 B-412, *map* B-425, *picture* B-413
São Paulo, Brazil, capital of state of São Paulo; 210 mi (340 km) s.w. of Rio de Janeiro; pop. 5,901,533 S-47
Brazil, *maps* B-425, S-279
São Paulo de Loanda, Angola. *see in index* Luanda
São Roque, Cape, cape on n.e. coast of Brazil 20 mi (30 km) n. of Natal; lighthouse; one of easternmost points of mainland of South America, *maps* B-425, S-298
São Salvador, Brazil. *see in index* Salvador
São Tiago (or Santiago), largest of Cape Verde Islands; 383 sq mi (992 sq km); pop. 88,940 C-149
West Indies, *map* W-106
São Tomé (also called São Thomé or St. Thomas), island in Gulf of Guinea, w. Africa; area 330 sq mi (855 sq km); with island of Príncipe forms republic of São Tomé and Príncipe, *map* A-118
São Tomé and Príncipe, republic in Gulf of Guinea, w. Africa; formerly Portuguese province; consists of islands of São Tomé, Príncipe, and several small islets; area 372 sq mi (963 sq km); cap. São Tomé (pop. 17,400); pop. 83,000
African political unit, *table* A-112
flag, *picture* F-170
São Vicente (or St. Vincent), one of Cape Verde Islands; strikingly rugged and picturesque; natural harbor; 88 sq mi (228 sq km); fishing; cable station; pop. 15,848 C-149
Sap, plant P-359
living things L-269
tree T-277
maple M-113, *picture* V-294
rubber R-301
Sapajou monkey (or capuchin monkey), mammal A-503
Sapodilla (or naseberry, or sapote), a tropical tree; source of chicle gum C-307
fruit F-436
Sapodilla family (or Sapotaceae), family of shrubs and trees, native chiefly to the tropics, including the canistel, sapote or marmalade plum, chittamwood of false buckthorn, star apple, the gutta-percha tree, and the sapodilla
gutta-percha G-320
Saponaria (or soapwort), genus of plants of the pink family; about 40 species; native to Mediterranean region; flowers red, pink, yellow, or white; used in rock gardens.
Saponification, the formation of soap S-229, 231, *picture* S-230
Sapote. *see in index* Sapodilla
Sapphire, precious stone J-112, *picture* J-114
synthetic C-796
watches and clocks W-79
Sapphire quartz. *see in index* Siderite
Sappho (7th–6th centuries BC), Greek poetess, born on island of Lesbos; called "flower of the Graces"; known today by fragments of exquisite verse; has been translated into English; legend says she flung herself from Leucadian rock for unrequited love G-274, *picture* G-275
Sapporo, Japan, city on Hokkaido Island; food products, rubber goods, textiles; Imperial University; site of 1972 winter Olympics; pop. 1,401,757 J-32, *picture* J-46, *map* J-78
Asia, *map* A-700
Saprophytes, plants that live on dead organic matter P-370
bacteria B-13
fungi F-447
mold M-519
mushrooms M-664
Sapucaya, tropical tree *Lecythis zabucajo* of lecythis family, native to South America; sapucaya nut, sometimes called cream nut, similar to Brazil nut.
Sapulpa, Okla., city in oil, farming, and ranching region 13 mi (21 km) s.w. of Tulsa; glass products, pottery, brick, meat-packing; pop. 15,853.
Sapwood, of trees T-277, W-281
Saqqara, Egyptian village near Nile River 15 mi (25 km) s.w. of Cairo E-125
step pyramid P-543
Sara, a people of Chad C-263
Saraband (or sarabande), a slow, stately dance introduced at European courts in 16th century; usually in 3/4 or 3/2 time; origin, probably Oriental or Spanish; also a basic movement in classical suite. *see also in index* Suite
Saracens, name for Muslims in Middle Ages. *see in index* Arabs; Islam; Moors
Saracoglu, Sukru (1887–1953), Turkish statesman; advocated Westernization of Turkey; justice minister 1932–38; foreign minister 1938–42 and 1944–46; prime minister 1942–46.
Saragossa (or Zaragoza), Spain, city in n.e., on Ebro River; transportation hub; taken by French after heroic resistance in Peninsular War (1808–9); pop. 414,000 S-356, *maps* E-361, S-350
Sarah, Biblical figure, wife of Abraham; mother of Isaac A-12
Sarah Lawrence College, Bronxville, N.Y.; opened 1928; arts and sciences, education; graduate studies N-255
Sarai, 13th-century Mongol capital in Russia R-351
Sarajevo (or Serajevo), Yugoslavia, formerly capital of Bosnia; 122 mi (196 km) s.w. of Belgrade (Beograd); iron mines; metal products; trade center; pop. 223,000, *map* E-361
Francis Ferdinand assassinated W-302
Saran, trade name for a synthetic resin fiber that is extruded into filaments and used to make window screening, automobile seat covers, draperies, and upholstery; resistant to fire, water, and chemicals; easy to clean; also plastic wrapping for food, *table* F-72
Saranac Lake, N.Y., village and health resort in Adirondack Mountains; summer and winter sports; pop. 6,086 N-245
Sarapis, Egyptian god
mystery religions M-703
Osiris I-358
Sarasate, Pablo de (1844–1908), distinguished violinist, born in Pamplona, Spain; began concert career at age of 15; composed pieces for violin ('Zigeunerweisen'; 'Nocturne-Sérénade'; 'Spanische Tänze').
Sarasota, Fla., resort city on Gulf of Mexico about 45 mi (70 km) s. of Tampa; fishing, vegetables, citrus fruit, cattle; electronics; Museum of the American Circus; New College of the University of South Florida; pop. 48,868
circus history C-432
Saratoga, Calif., residential city 10 mi (16 km) s.w. of San Jose; at foothills of Santa Cruz Mountains; fruit, wine; incorporated 1956; pop. 29,261.
Saratoga, N.Y. *see in index* Schuylerville
Saratoga, battles of (also called battles of Bemis Heights, or battles of Freeman's Farm) (1777) S-48
warfare, *list* W-15
Saratoga National Historical Park, in New York S-48
Saratoga Springs, N.Y., popular health resort 30 mi (50 km) n. of Albany; pop. 23,906 S-48
New York N-251, *picture* N-263
Saratov, U.S.S.R., city on Volga River, 450 mi (725 km) s.e. of Moscow; machinery, petroleum products, flour, textiles, chemicals; extensive river trade; pop. 758,000, *maps* E-361, R-344, 349
Saratsi, China, town in Inner Mongolian Autonomous Region near Hwang Ho 30 mi (50 km) e. of Paotow.
Sarawak, former British colony on Borneo; 47,500 sq mi (123,000 sq km); cap. Kuching; became part of Malaysia 1963; pop. 1,294,753 M-70
Asia, *map* A-700
Dyak long house, *picture* B-271
East Indies E-45
Malaysian Borneo B-369
pepper, *map* P-197a, *chart* P-197a
Sarazen, Gene (born 1902), U.S. professional golfer, born in Harrison, N.Y.; won many important tournaments G-189, *picture* G-190
Sarcee. *see in index* Sarsi
Sarcodina, subphylum of amoeba A-375
Sarcoma, cancerous tumor C-133, C-812, D-175
Sarcomere, muscles M-659
Sarcophagus, archaeological term, Greek and Roman name for a stone coffin; from Greek words *sarx* (flesh) *phagein* (to eat); term first commonly applied to big coffins in Roman imperial times.
Sard. *see in index* Carnelian
Sardana, Spanish dance B-79
Sardanapalus, Greek name of Assurbanipal, last great Assyrian king; subject of tragedy by Byron. *see also in index* Ashurbanipal
Sardes, Asia Minor. *see in index* Sardis
Sardine, a food fish S-48. *see also in index* Pilchard
herring family H-144
Sardines, game G-13
Sardinia, Italian island in Mediterranean w. of Italy; 9,299 sq mi (24,084 sq km); pop. 1,419,362 S-48, *map* R-242
Europe, *map* E-361
folk art F-253
Italy I-381, 392, *map* I-404
sardines S-48
sheep S-148
Tirso Dam, *picture* S-48
Sardinia, Kingdom of S-49
Italian history I-393
Napoleon N-14
Sardis (or Sardes), capital of ancient Lydia, Asia Minor; flourished under Croesus; destroyed by Timur (AD 1402); important recent excavations P-214, *map* P-212
Sardonyx, semiprecious stone J-116
Sardou, Victorien (1831–1908), French dramatist, dexterous and prolific ('Fédora'; 'Madame Sans-Gêne'; 'La Tosca').
Sarett, Lew (1888–1954), U.S. poet, born in Chicago, Ill.; woodsman, forest ranger, teacher at Northwestern University 1920–53; his poems ('Many, Many Moons'; 'Wings Against the Moon'; 'Slow Smoke') have tang of campfire and sagebrush.

Sarg, Tony (full name Anthony Frederick Sarg) (1882–1942), U.S. artist, born in Guatemala, son of German plantation owner and English mother; creator of "Tony Sarg's Marionettes," also illustrator, cartoonist, and mural artist; author of books for children P-537

Sargasso Sea (from the Portuguese word for gulfweed), region in the n. Atlantic S-104
  Atlantic Ocean A-746
  eels E-109
  weed fish, *picture* P-512

Sargassum. *see in index* Gulfweed

Sargassum fish (or mousefish), surface fish *Histrio pictus* inhabiting the Sargasso Sea; fantastic in shape; olive brown with black markings, *picture* F-130

Sargent, Charles Sprague (1841–1927), U.S. authority on trees, born in Boston, Mass.; professor of arboriculture at Harvard.

Sargent, Dudley Allen (1849–1924), U.S. specialist in physical education, born in Belfast, Me.; influential in the development of physical training in U.S. schools; 1881 organized Sanatory Gymnasium at Cambridge, Mass., later named Sargent School for Physical Education.

Sargent, John Singer (1856–1925), U.S. painter, born in Florence, Italy S-49
  'Frieze of the Prophets', *picture* P-509
  Henry James's portrait, *picture* J-20

Sargent, Malcolm (1895–1967), British conductor, *list* O-579

Sargeson, Frank (1903–82), New Zealand author of novels, plays, short stories, and memoirs, born in Hamilton; ('Conversation with My Uncle', 'A Man and His Wife', 'Joy of the Worm', 'Memoirs of a Peon', 'Sunset Village', 'Stories of Frank Sargeson') N-293

Sargo class, category of U.S. submarines, *picture* S-496

Sargon I (about 2350 BC), king of Babylonia, founded Akkad, Semitic dynasty, first great nation in w. Asia; legends later told of him B-7

Sargon II (reigned 722–705 BC), king of Assyria; usurped throne and took name of Sargon, the Babylonian king, from whom he claimed descent; built city of Dur Sharrukin, near village of Khorsabad B-8

Sari, garment worn by women of India B-62, P-78, *picture* I-67

Sarikol Range, mountains on e. edge of Great Pamir; rise but little above Pamir; form center from which great ranges of central Asia diverge.

Sark (French Sercq), one of the Channel Islands; 2 sq mi (5 sq km); famous cliffs, caves; pop. 590 C-270

Sarmiento, Domingo Faustino (1811–88), Argentine politician; president of Argentina 1868–74; ended war of Triple Alliance against Paraguay A-580, 583
  children's literature L-251
  Latin American literature L-68, *picture* L-70

Sarnia, Ont., port city on Lake Huron and St. Clair River; connected with Port Huron, Mich., by Blue Water International Bridge, railroad tunnel, and ferry service; grain elevators, saltworks, foundries; synthetic rubber, chemicals, petroleum products, automotive parts, structural steel, brass fittings, glass products; pop. 50,892 O-552, map C-112

Sarnoff, David (1891–1971), U.S. businessman, born in Russia; brought to U.S. when 9 years old; started working for Marconi Co. in 1906, for Radio Corporation of America (which absorbed Marconi Co.) in 1919; president of R.C.A. 1930–47, board chairman 1947–70.

Saronic Gulf (also called Gulf of Aegina, or Gulf of Egina), arm of Aegean Sea on e. coast of Greece.

Saros, The, interval of time, 18 years and 11.32 or 10.32 days (depending upon the number of leap years in the period), in which similar solar eclipses appear; discovered by the Chaldeans from their observations of eclipses; usually about 71 solar eclipses in the interval.

Saroyan, William (1908–81), U.S. author and playwright, born near Fresno, Calif., on grape ranch of his Armenian father; stories subjective, spontaneous, tender ('The Daring Young Man on the Flying Trapeze'; 'My Name Is Aram'; 'The Human Comedy'; 'Mama I Love You'); plays original in technique ('My Heart's in the Highlands'; declined 1940 Pulitzer prize for 'Time of Your Life'; 'Love's Old Sweet Song'; 'The Cave Dwellers'); autobiography, 'After Thirty Years' A-360

Sarpedon, legendary king of Lycia, son of Zeus and Europa; also name of his grandson, an ally of the Trojans in the Trojan War, who was slain by Patroclus.

Sarpi, Paolo (1552–1623), Venetian scholar and historian; entered Servite order at 13; close student of mathematics, Oriental languages, philosophy, theology, anatomy; made adviser (1606) to Venetian republic and led fight against Pope Paul V ('History of the Council of Trent').

Sarracenia, sidesaddle plant genus P-344

Sarsaparilla, extract from dried roots of several *Smilax* species; used to flavor soft drinks and as syrup medium in medicine.

Sarsat, artificial satellite, *table* S-344

Sarsi (or Sarcee), an American Indian tribe of n. Athapascan language family in n. Canada; hunting group; adapted easily to horse culture; ceded lands to dominion government 1877; placed on reservation 1880.

Sartain, John (1808–97), English engraver and editor, born in London; to America 1830 and introduced mezzotint engraving; daughter Emily and son Samuel became distinguished engravers.

Sarto, Andrea del (1486–1531), Italian painter, born near Florence, Italy; called "del Sarto" because father was a tailor; a superb colorist; known for frescoes (notably 'Nativity of the Virgin' at Florence) and oils ('Holy Family' and 'Charity' at Louvre in Paris).

Sarton, George (Alfred Leon) (1884–1956), U.S. scholar, born in Ghent, Belgium; to U.S. 1915, citizen 1924; lecturer history of science Harvard University 1916–18, 1920–40, professor 1940–51 ('Introduction to the History of Science', 3 vols.).

'Sartor Resartus', work by Carlyle C-169, E-275

Sartre, Jean Paul (1905–80), French writer, born in Paris; taught philosophy in lycées at Le Havre and Paris; leading existentialist; declined 1964 Nobel prize in literature; 'The Words', memoirs F-398, P-267. *see also in index* Nobel Prizewinners, *table*
  drama D-247
  existentialism E-371
  Giacometti G-142

Sarum, parish in England. *see in index* Old Sarum

Sarymsek Peninsula, in e. Kazakh Soviet Socialist Republic B-31

SAS (Scandinavian Airlines System), Norwegian airlines N-393

Sash, the frame holding the glass in a window
  painting P-76

Saskatchewan, a Prairie Province of Canada; 251,700 sq mi (651,900 sq km); cap. Regina; pop. 968,313 S-49a
  Canada C-80, 102, *maps* C-112, N-351
  cities. *see also in index* cities listed below and other cities by name
    Regina R-138
    Saskatoon S-51
  national parks N-28
  Trans-Canada Highway T-248

Saskatchewan, University of, in Saskatoon, Sask.; provincial control; founded 1907; arts and sciences, agriculture, commerce, education, engineering, home economics, law, medicine, nursing, pharmacy; graduate studies S-51, S-49f

Saskatchewan Plain, in Alberta A-263

Saskatchewan River, river in Canada, 340 mi (545 km) long, formed e. of Prince Albert, Sask., by junction of North Saskatchewan River (760 mi [1,225 km] long) and South Saskatchewan River (865 mi [1,390 km] long); flows e. to Lake Winnipeg
  Canada, *map* C-112
  Manitoba M-101
  name S-49b
  North America, *map* N-351
  Saskatchewan S-49c, *picture* S-49f, *maps* S-49c, 49k, 49l
  South Saskatchewan project S-49g

Saskatoon, Sask., city 82 mi (132 km) s. of Prince Albert; pop. 154,210 S-51
  Canada, *map* C-112
  climate, *list* S-49b
  education S-49h, *picture* S-49f
  North America, *map* N-351,
  Saskatchewan S-49g, *maps* S-49k, 49c

'Saskia with Her Child', drawing by Rembrandt D-253, *picture* D-254

Sassafras, a tree of the family Lauraceae S-51
  tree T-283

Sassafras Mountain, highest point in South Carolina, in n.w.; 3,560 ft (1,085 m) S-306, *maps* S-318, 307

Sassafras tea, an herbal tea T-47

Sassandra River, Ivory Coast, Africa; course runs s.-southeast; empties into Gulf of Guinea at Sassandra; area noted for timber, coffee, bananas, *map* I-406

Sassanid Dynasty, last native dynasty of ancient Persia (AD 226–637) P-213
  Iran I-308
  Iraq I-314
  Zoroastrianism Z-471

Sassari, Italy, province in Sardinia; also name of capital (pop. 89,482); latter has 18th-century town hall and cathedral, also university dating from 16th century, *maps* E-361, I-404

Sassetta, Stefano di Giovanni (1392–1450?), Italian painter, a Sienese master, noted for scenes from St. Francis legend
  Francis of Assisi, *picture* F-375

Sassoon, Siegfried Lorraine (1886–1967), English poet; served in World War I in France and Palestine, but hated the bloodshed and brutalities and threw his Military Cross into the sea as a protest against war; best known for bitter war poems ('Counter-Attack'; 'Satirical Poems'); also wrote prose ('Memoirs of an Infantry Officer'; 'The Old Century')
  literary contribution E-280

SAT. *see in index* Scholastic Aptitude Test

Satan. *see in index* Devil

Satanism. *see in index* Devil worship

Sateen (or satine), cotton fabric with lustrous surface resembling satin; carded type used for ticking, work clothes, and coated fabric base; combed type for dresses and coat linings.

Satellite dish, a round, concave dish-shaped antenna used in telecommunication systems and astronomy. An uplink antenna is used to send electronic signals to a communications satellite or other spacecraft; a downlink antenna is used to receive signals from such objects; in radio astronomy it is used for receiving radio waves emitted by celestial objects
  television T-77

Satellite infrared spectrometer (SIRS), remote sensor W-123

Satellites, artificial S-341b, *pictures* S-342d–3, 348a–b, *table* S-344
  aerospace industry A-72
  animal flights, *picture* P-273
  automated guidance systems A-839
  black hole discovery B-306
  earth's calculations E-10
  Eisenhower administration E-140
  frontiers in space F-427
  guided missiles G-312
  navy N-89
  oceanic exploration O-464
  photography P-280
  probe. *see in index* Probe
  solar studies S-513
  space navigation N-76
  types
    communications S-195b. *see also in index* Telstars
      ham radio H-190
      telecommunication T-55
      telegraph T-59
      telephone T-63
      television T-77
    scientific S-343b, 345, V-259. *see also in index* Explorers
    weather S-343b, W-123, *picture* S-343
      meteorological M-316
  Warsaw W-34

Satellites (or moons), of the planets S-52, *table* S-254b
  astronomy A-715
  earth. *see in index* Moon
  eclipse E-48
  Jupiter S-254c
  origin theory P-355, S-254e, *diagram* S-254d
  Saturn S-254b, *picture* S-52
  Uranus, *picture* P-355

Satellites, Soviet, countries dominated by U.S.S.R. R-357, chart R-355
  North Atlantic Treaty Organization N-352

Satelloid, aerospace term for a vehicle that revolves around the Earth, or other body at such altitudes as to require a sustaining thrust to balance drag; also a manned vehicle "half airplane and half satellite" designed to enter an orbit and return to Earth.

Satie, Erik (1866–1925), French composer of modernistic tendencies; influenced Debussy and Ravel; composed works as whimsical and eccentric as their titles ('Cold Pieces'; 'Pear-Shaped Pieces'; 'Vexations')
  ballet music B-34
  opera O-571

Satin, a glossy, closely woven fabric of silk, cotton and silk, or man-made fibers; used for evening wear, linings, bedspreads, sheets, upholstery, and draperies T-138

Satinflower. *see in index* Lunaria

Satin spar, name given to several fibrous minerals with silky luster used as ornamental stones or in cheap jewelry; commonest is a white gypsum (calcium sulfate), best from England, inferior from Niagara Falls; others are calcium carbonates.

Satin stitch, needlework, *picture* N-111

Satinwood, any of several trees yielding a hard, durable, golden-yellow wood with a satinlike sheen; used in fine cabinetmaking; *Euxylophora paraensis,* native to Brazil; *Chloroxylon swietenia,* native to s. India and Sri Lanka; *Zanthoxylum flavum* grown in West Indies.

Satire
  caricature and cartoon C-186
    Jackson, *picture* J-5
    Nash N-20
  humor H-323
  literature
    English literature
      Pope P-445
      Swift S-530, 531, 532, *picture* S-531
    French literature
      Rabelais F-394
    Juvenal J-161
    novel N-412
    Western W-151

Sato, Eisaku (1901–75), Japanese statesman, born near Kure; minister of finance 1958–60; director of Science and Technology Agency 1963–64; prime minister 1964–72 J-69. *see also in index* Nobel Prizewinners, *table*

Satrap, ancient Persian official P-211–12

Satsuma ware, a kind of earthenware made in Japan; named for Satsuma Peninsula of Kyushu P-473

Saturated fats and oils F-48
  margarine M-134
  meat M-247

Saturated solution S-256

Saturation, in chemistry O-602

Saturation, of color. *see also in index* Chroma
  design D-108
  dress design D-269

Saturation value, in magnetism M-45

Saxony, former province of Prussia, consisting partly of what had been n. half of kingdom of Saxony, [illegible] 1815; 9,760 sq mi (25,276 sq km); after World War II, incorporated into Saxony-Anhalt.

Saxony, Lower, state, West Germany. *see in index* Lower Saxony

Saxony-Anhalt (German Sachsen-Anhalt), former state in Russian zone, Germany; area, 9,525 sq mi (24,670 sq km).

Saxophone, wind instrument W-228

Saxton, Joseph (1799–1873), U.S. inventor, born in Huntingdon, Pa.; invented instruments used by the U.S. Coast Survey, including a deep-sea thermometer.

Say, Thomas (1787–1834), U.S. entomologist, born in Philadelphia; discovered many new species of insects; lived at Owen's Socialistic colony at New Harmony, Ind.

Sayan Mountains, moutains in central Asia, n.e. spur of the Altay range, extending from the Yenisey River to the s. shore of Lake Baikal (Baykal); general elevation 7,000 to 9,000 ft (2,100 to 2,700 m), with peaks rising 10,000 to 11,450 ft (3,000 to 3,500 m), *map* R-345

Sayano-Shushenskaya Dam, dam in U.S.S.R., on Yenisey River D-17

Sayao, Bidu (born 1908), Brazilian lyric soprano; sang at Opera-Comique, Paris, and La Scala, Milan; New York debut, 1930; member of Metropolitan Opera Co., New York City, from 1937.

Sayce, Archibald Henry (1845–1933), British Orientalist; professor Assyriology, Oxford, 1891–1919; traveled through East; valuable contributions to Oriental scholarship.

Sayers, Dorothy Leigh (1893–1957), English detective story writer, born in Oxford, England; created detective Lord Peter Wimsey ('Whose Body?'; 'The Nine Tailors'; 'In the Teeth of the Evidence'); also wrote essays, verse, plays.

Sayers, Frances Clarke (born 1897), U.S. author, librarian, and teacher; born in Topeka, Kan.; superintendent of work with children, New York Public Library 1941–52; lecturer, University of California, Los Angeles, 1954–65; children's books ('Bluebonnets for Lucinda'; 'Tag-Along Tooloo'; 'Sally Tait'; 'Ginny and Custard'); essays ('Summoned by Books'); compiler of 'A Bounty of Books'; awarded Regina Medal 1973 R-104, *pictures* R-109–11e

Sayers, Gale (born 1943), U.S. football player, born in Wichita, Kan.; halfback; Chicago Bears 1965–71.

Sayreville, N.J., borough 6 mi (10 km) s.w. of Perth Amboy, on Raritan River; manufactures chemicals, tile, and brick; incorporated 1919; pop. 29,969.

Sazhen, Soviet unit of measure, *table* W-141

SBS 1, artificial satellite, *table* S-344

Scab, nonunion worker hired to replace a union worker S-489

Scabies, a contagious skin disease caused by the itch mite, a parasite that burrows under the skin of humans and other animals; characterized by pimples and blisters S-387

Scabiosa (or mourning bride), genus of annual or perennial garden plants of the teasel family, often called pincushion flowers from the shape of the flower heads; branching stem, pinnately lobed leaves, and white, blue, dark purple, or pink flowers
- growing conditions G-24

Scaevola, Gaius Mucius, legendary Roman hero of 6th century BC; captured in attempt to murder Porsena who was besieging Rome; threatened with death if he would not reveal 300 comrades who also had sworn murder, he thrust his right hand into the fire and held it there until it burned away.

Scafell Pike, highest mountain in England 3,210 ft (978 m) E-229

Scala, La, opera house in Milan, Italy M-408

Scalawag, in U.S. Reconstruction period R-115

Scald (or skald), ancient Scandinavian minstrel-poet who sang of ancestors, great victories or great warriors; same as *bard* in Celtic history S-460, S-471

Scald, in cooking C-700

Scald and burn. *see in index* Burn

Scale, in maps M-116, *diagram* M-117

Scale, in mechanical drawing M-256
- micrometer M-378

Scale, in music M-666, 691, *list* M-671. *see also in index* Music, *subhead* scales

Scaled quail, bird *Callipepla squamata* Q-3

Scale insects, small bugs parasitic on trees and fruit S-52e
- citrus fruits C-444
- ladybugs S-52f

Scale model M-514
- motion pictures M-610, *picture* M-608
- Panama Canal, *picture* P-89

Scalene triangle, in mathematics G-74

Scales, constellation. *see in index* Libra

Scales, in weight measurement W-134
- Fairbanks' platform scale F-11
- instrumentation I-228

Scales, of animal, small plates forming a protective covering
- butterflies and moths B-521, *picture* B-526
- fish F-125
  - evolution A-461
  - mudfish and lungfish M-644
- snake S-223, *picture* S-223

Scali, John Alfred (born 1918), U.S. journalist, public official, born in Canton, Ohio; news correspondent ABC radio and television 1961–71; special assistant to President Nixon 1971–73; U.S. representative to United Nations 1973–75.

Scalia, Antonin (born 1936), U.S. jurist, born in Trenton, N.J.; assistant attorney general Office of Legal Counsel, U.S. Department of Justice 1974–77; professor University of Chicago Law School 1977–82; judge U.S. Court of Appeals 1982–86; associate justice U.S. Supreme Court 1986– .

Scaliger, Joseph Justus (1540–1609), French scholar, called Father of Chronological Science; established dates in Greek and Roman history; first to show that histories of various countries must be studied together; son of the philosopher **J.C. Scaliger** (1484–1558).

Scallion (also called green onion, or table onion) O-545

Scallop, a bivalve mollusk S-52f, *pictures* S-149–52
- body structure A-422
- mollusks M-525

Scalpel, surgical tool S-519a

Scaly anteater. *see in index* Pangolin

Scanderbeg (real name George Castriota) (1403–68), national hero of Albania; led struggle against Turks for Albanian independence.

Scandinavia, collective name applied to Denmark, Sweden, and Norway; term sometimes extended to include Iceland, Faroe, and adjacent islands S-52g. *see also in index* Scandinavian languages; Scandinavian literature; Denmark; Norway; Sweden
- braiding history B-395
- cooperative societies C-706
- folk art F-254
- folk music F-273
- garment industry G-35
- government G-199
- Iceland I-14
- needlework N-110
- ombudsman C-684
- racial classification R-27, *chart* R-26

Scandinavian Airlines System (SAS), Norwegian airlines N-393

Scandinavian languages S-52g
- linguistic analysis L-230

Scandinavian literature S-52g
- drama S-52g
- folktales F-262, S-471, *list* S-481a
- Jacobsen J-11

Scandinavian mythology S-52g

Scandinavian peninsula S-522, *map* S-524

Scandium (Sc), chemical element discovered 1879; belongs to cerium subgroup of rare earth metals; resembles boron; found in wolframite, *table* P-207, *list* P-208

Scanning, in poetry P-405

Scanning beam, television facsimile process F-5

Scanning disk, a round flat disk
- television T-78

Scanning electron microscope M-383, *picture* M-382
- microbiology M-375

Scanning tunneling microscope M-383

Scapa Flow, channel in Orkney Islands, important British naval base during World Wars I and II.

Scapegoat, in ancient Hebrew rites, the goat sent into wilderness on Day of Atonement after sins of people had been placed on his back by High Priest (Bible, Leviticus xvi, 8–10); in modern usage, a person made to bear blame.

Scaphopod, class of mollusks M-525

Scapula, the shoulder blade, a flat triangular bone S-210

Scarab, family of beetles B-140, *pictures* B-139

Scaramouche, French spelling of Scaramuccia, a boastful buffoon in old Italian farce constantly beaten by Harlequin.

Scarborough, England, popular seaside resort in Yorkshire, 37 mi (60 km) n.e. of York; ruins of Roman watchtower; fishing; pop. 42,500
- council meeting, *picture* U-18

Scarlatti, Alessandro (1660–1725), Italian composer, born in Palermo; composed more than 100 operas; shaped form of modern opera; his son **Giuseppe Domenico** (1685–1757), noted harpsichordist and composer O-563

Scarlet fever (or scarlatina), infectious disease, *table* D-172

Scarlet ibis, bird I-4
- zoo Z-463

'Scarlet Letter, The', novel by Hawthorne H-74
- American literature A-343

Scarlet lychnis. *see in index* Jerusalem cross

Scarlet maple. *see in index* Swamp maple

Scarlet sage. *see in index* Salvia

Scarlet tanager, bird
- egg, *picture* E-112

Scarpanto, island. *see in index* Kárpathos

Scarpe, small river in n.e. France; 60 mi (95 km) long.

Scarritt College, Nashville, Tenn.; United Methodist; founded 1892 at Kansas City, Mo.; present site 1924; liberal arts, religious education; graduate school.

Scarron, Paul (1610–60), French poet, novelist, and dramatist; born in Paris; first husband of Marquise de Maintenon ('Le Typhon'; 'Roman Comique').

Scarsdale, N.Y., residential city 19 mi (30 km) n. of New York City; once part of Manor of Scarsdale, est. 1701; pop. 17,650.

Scat, in jazz J-85

Scattergram (or scatter diagram) S-436, *diagram* S-436

Scattering, electromagnetic radiation R-34, *diagram* R-35

Scatter reflection and transmission, radio R-52, *diagram* R-51

Scaup (or bluebill), a diving duck; two species: greater scaup *Aythya narila* and lesser scaup *Aythya affinis*.

Scavenger cell (or phagocyte), cell that minimizes infections D-167

Scene, in art
- creative writing W-382
- motion pictures M-606

Scenery, stage T-155, *diagrams* T-154
- Elizabethan theater S-136

Scenic boulevard. *see in index* Parkway

Schacht, Horace Greeley Hjalmar (1877–1970), German financier; president Reichsbank, 1923–30, 1933–39; appointed economic adviser to Hitler 1939; indicted as war criminal 1945, acquitted in 1946 by International Military Tribunal at Nuremberg, in 1950 by a denazification court; after 1950 economic adviser to Egypt, Iran, and other nations (autobiography, 'Confessions of the Old Wizard').

Schadow, Johann Gottfried (1764–1850), German sculptor of neoclassical school; director Academy of Art, Berlin, 1816–50 S-89

Schaefer, Vincent Joseph (born 1906), U.S. research chemist and meteorologist, born in Schenectady, N.Y.; General Electric research associate 1938–54; from airplane over w. Massachusetts (1946) he seeded clouds with pellets of dry ice, producing snow.

Schaeffer, Pierre (born 1910), French composer M-676

Schäffer, Jacob Christian (1718–90), German minister in Regensburg; wrote a 6-volume treatise on vegetable fibers for papermaking P-104

Schaffhausen, Switzerland, capital of canton of same name, 24 mi (39 km) n. of Zurich; famous falls of Rhine River; pop. 32,900, *map* S-537

Schäffle, Albert Eberhard Friedrich (1831–1903), German sociologist and economist; professor at Tübingen and Vienna; influenced by Hegel, Darwin, and others; interested in socialism ('The Quintessence of Socialism').

Schalk, Raymond William (nickname Cracker) (1892–1970), U.S. baseball catcher, born in Harvey, Ill.; catcher Chicago, A.L., 1912–26, manager-catcher Chicago, A.L., 1927–28, catcher-coach New York, N.L., 1929; led A.L. catchers in fielding 8 times between 1913 and 1922; caught 100 or more games in each of 12 seasons.

Schally, Andrew Victor (born 1926), U.S. medical research scientist, born in Wilno, Poland (now Vilnius, Lithuanian S.S.R.); to England 1939; to U.S. 1957; at Baylor College of Medicine, Houston 1957–62; at Tulane University Medical School and Veterans Administration Hospital, New Orleans 1962–; hormone research. *see also in index* Nobel Prizewinners, *table*

Scharnhorst, Gerhard Johann David von (1755–1813), Prussian general, one of founders of Prussian military system (1809–13); fatally wounded at battle of Lützen.

Scharwenka, Franz Xaver (1850–1924), German composer, born in Samter, Posen; established conservatory in Berlin, where brother Philipp was associated with him; also conservatory in New York; compositions for orchestra and piano.

Scharwenka, Philipp (1847–1917), German composer, born in Samter, Posen; brother of Franz Xaver Scharwenka ('Sakuntala').

Schaumburg, Ill., residential village 24 mi (39 km) n.w. of Chicago; retail trade center; Agricultural Stabilization and Conservation Service installation; pop. 52,319, *map* I-53

Schaumburg-Lippe, former state in n. Germany, formerly principality; 131 sq mi (339 sq km); after World War II, incorporated into Lower Saxony.

Schawlow, Arthur L. (born 1921), U.S. physicist. *see also in index* Nobel Prizewinners, *table*

Scheduled caste, India's government I-68

Scheele, Karl Wilhelm (1742–86), Swedish chemist, born in Stralsund, Pomerania; discovered oxygen before Priestley, but failed to publish his work until after Priestley's announcement; discovered tungsten in the form of tungstic

acid, also molybdic and arsenic acids
oxygen O-623
tungsten T-307
Scheelite (or calcium tungstate), a tungsten ore T-307
minerals M-436
ore, *table* O-600
Scheer, Reinhard (1863–1928), German admiral in World War I; chief of admiralty staff 1918; advocated more extensive use of submarines W-306
Scheffel, Joseph Victor von (1826–86), German poet and novelist ('Der Trompeter von Säckingen'; 'Ekkehard').
Scheherazade, character in the 'Arabian Nights', wife of the sultan and narrator of the tales A-524, *picture* S-467
Scheidemann, Philipp (1865–1939), German Socialist leader, first chancellor of German republic (1919); exile after 1934 W-142
Scheldt River (also spelled Schelde, French Escaut), river of France, Belgium, and The Netherlands; flows 250 mi (400 km) to North Sea S-52h
Schelling, Ernest Henry (1876–1939), U.S. pianist, composer, and conductor, born in Belvidere, N.J.; conductor of children's concerts of New York Philharmonic-Symphony Orchestra ('Légendes Symphoniques'; 'Victory Ball').
Schelling, Friedrich Wilhelm Joseph von (1775–1854), German philosopher and professor, born near Stuttgart; spokesman for 19th-century romanticists P-266
Schenectady, N.Y., industrial city on Mohawk River and New York Barge Canal; pop. 67,972 S-52h
New York N-251, *map* U-41
Schenti. *see in index* Loincloth
Scherzo, in music, *list* M-671
Scheveningen, The Netherlands, fishing port and summer resort on North Sea, near The Hague; pop. 80,015 H-5
Schiacciato, type of sculpture invented by Donatello D-229
Schiaparelli, Elsa (1896–1973), Italian-French dress designer D-271
Schiaparelli, Giovanni Virginio (1835–1910), Italian astronomer, born in Savigliano; director Milan Observatory 1862–1900; discovered asteroid Hesperia 1861; detected peculiar markings ("canals") on Mars 1877.
Schick, Béla (1877–1967), U.S. pediatrician S-52h
Schick test, for diphtheria S-52h
Schiedam, The Netherlands, river port near mouth of the Maas just w. of Rotterdam; numerous canals; gin, ships, chemicals; pop. 75,421.
Schiff, Jacob Henry (1847–1920), U.S. financier and philanthropist, born in Germany; aided in reorganizing Union Pacific Railroad 1897 and in financing other railroads; founded Jewish Theological Seminary and the New York Semitic Museum at Harvard University.
Schikaneder, Emanuel (1751–1812), German actor, singer, playwright, and theater manager O-565
Schiller, Ferdinand Canning Scott (1864–1937), English philosopher; exponent of pragmatism; professor philosophy University of Southern California 1929–36 ('Humanism'; 'Eugenics and Politics'; 'Must Philosophers Disagree?').
Schiller, Friedrich (full name Johann Christoph Friedrich von Schiller) (1759–1805), German poet and dramatist S-53
German literature G-106
Schiller Park, Ill., village 14 mi (22 km) n.w. of Chicago; tool and die industry; vacuum cleaners, scientific instruments; pop. 12,712, *map* I-53
Schilling, Johannes (1828–1910), German sculptor; chief works include Schiller statue in Vienna; German national monument opposite Bingen; statues of Emperor William I and Bismarck at Wiesbaden.
Schinkel, Karl Friedrich von (1781–1841), German architect A-562
Schipa, Tito (1889–1965), Italian dramatic tenor, born in Lecce; favorite in Europe and U.S. ('Tosca', 'Traviata', 'Barber of Seville'); sang with Chicago and Metropolitan Opera companies.
Schipperke, dog, *picture* D-206
Schirra, Walter Marty, Jr. (born 1923), U.S. astronaut, U.S. Navy, born in Hackensack, N.J.; resigned from NASA program 1969: business executive 1969- S-346f, 347, *table* S-348
Schism. *see in index* Great Schism
Schist, rock formed by recrystallization of shale R-229a, *picture* R-229
minerals M-437
Schistosomiasis (or snail fever) P-114, S-222, A-102
invertebrate carriers I-283
mollusks M-525
Schizanthus (also butterfly flower, or poor man's orchid), small genus of annuals or biennials of the nightshade family, native to Chile; leaves finely cut; flowers orchidlike.
Schizomycetes, bacteria B-12
Schizophrenia, a mental illness M-301, P-518
Schlagzither, stringed instrument S-490a
Schlegel, August Wilhelm von (1767–1845), German critic, poet, and translator; his translations of Shakespeare one of the best, responsible for great popularity of Shakespeare in Germany.
Schlegel, Karl Wilhelm Friedrich von (1772–1829), German critic, scholar, poet; led romantic movement for complete individual freedom; brother of A. W. von Schlegel ('Lectures on Modern History'; 'Lectures on the History of Literature').
Schleiden, Matthias Jakob (1804–81), German botanist, born in Hamburg, Germany; taught at Jena and at Dorpat; helped establish that cell is the structural unit of plants and animals
cell theory C-241
Schleiermacher, Friedrich Ernst Daniel (1768–1834), German theologian and philosopher; combined emotional religion with a logical philosophy.
Schlesinger, Arthur Meier (1888–1965), U.S. historian and author, born in Xenia, Ohio; professor history, Harvard University 1924–54 ('New Viewpoints in American History'; 'Political and Social History of the United States, 1829–1925'; 'The Birth of a Nation'; coeditor, with D. R. Fox, 12-vol. 'History of American Life'; autobiography, 'In Retrospect').
Schlesinger, Arthur Meier, Jr. (born 1917), U.S. historian and author, born in Columbus, Ohio; presidential special assistant and speech writer 1961–64; professor of humanities City University of New York after 1966 ('The Age of Jackson', 1946 Pulitzer prize for history; 'The Age of Roosevelt', 3 vols.; 'A Thousand Days', 1965 National Book Award and 1966 Pulitzer prize for biography; 'The Imperial Presidency'; 'Robert F. Kennedy and His Times').
Schlesinger, Frank (1871–1943), U.S. astronomer, born in New York City; director Allegheny Observatory, University of Pittsburgh 1905–20; director Yale University Observatory 1920–41; developed photographic method for measuring stellar distances.
Schlesinger, James Rodney (born 1929), U.S. economist, born in New York, N.Y.; assistant director Office of Management and Budget 1969–71; chairman U.S. Atomic Energy Commission 1971–73; director Central Intelligence Agency 1973; secretary of defense 1973–75; secretary of energy 1977–79
Nixon N-327
Schleswig-Holstein, state in West Germany; former German province in Danish peninsula; state in British zone, Germany, after World War II; pop. 2,582,400
Germany G-122, *map* G-134
Prussia P-517
Schley, Winfield Scott (1839–1909), U.S. Navy officer, born in Frederick County, Md.; served in Civil War; commanded expedition that rescued explorer, Greely, in 1884; blockaded Spanish fleet in Spanish-American War until relieved by Admiral Sampson; in command at battle of Santiago July 3, 1898.
Schleyer, Hanns-Martin, (1915–77), German industrialist, born in Offenburg, Baden
kidnapping K-234
Schleyer, Johann Martin (1831–1912), German priest, inventor of Volapük L-39
Schlieffen, Alfred, count von (1833–1913), German soldier; chief of general staff 1891–1905, made field marshal 1911; master of military strategy, and author of books on the subject
World War I W-303, 307
Schliemann, Heinrich (1822–90), German archaeologist S-53, *picture* S-54
book R-111c
excavations A-61, A-531
Troy T-289
Homeric legend H-221
Schlieren system, optical device
aerospace A-79
wind tunnel W-235
Schmalkalden, East Germany, town and health resort 31 mi (50 km) s.w. of Erfurt; here Protestant princes of Germany formed Schmalkaldic League 1530 to resist efforts of Charles V to stamp out Protestantism; pop. 14,392, *map* G-134
Schmalkaldic War (also called Smalkaldic War) (1546–47) R-134
Schmeling, Max (born 1905), German boxer, born in Luckow B-391
Schmidt, Alexander (born 1930), U.S. physician and public official, born in Jamestown, N.D.; professor and dean University of Illinois medical school 1969–73; commissioner U.S. Food and Drug Administration 1973–76.
Schmidt, Helmut (born 1918), West German political leader, born in Hamburg; Social Democratic parliamentary floor leader 1967–69; defense minister 1969–72; finance minister 1972–74; chancellor 1974–82 G-126
Schmidt, Johannes (1877–1933), Danish biologist; worked on life story of eels for some 20 years.
Schmidt, Joseph Paul (nickname Joe) (born 1932), U.S. football player and coach, born in Pittsburgh, Pa.; linebacker with Detroit Lions 1953–65, linebacker coach 1966–67, head coach 1967–73.
Schmidt, Maarten (born 1929), U.S. astronomer whose identification of the wavelengths of the radiation emitted by quasars led to the theory that they may be among the most distant, and the oldest, objects ever observed by humans Q-7
Schmitt, Harrison H. (born 1935), U.S. senator and former astronaut, born in Santa Rita, N.M.; scientist-astronaut 1965–74, lunar module pilot Apollo 17, 1972; with NASA administration 1974–76; U.S. senator (Republican) from New Mexico 1977–83, *table* S-348
Schmitz, Ettore. *see in index* Svevo, Italo
Schnabel, Artur (1882–1951), Austrian pianist, born in Carinthia, Austria; pupil of Leschetizky; famous for his interpretation of Beethoven and Mozart; compositions include concertos, songs, sonatas.
Schnaps, liquor L-235
Schneckenburger, Max (1819–49), German poet; his best-known poem 'Die Wacht am Rhein' (The Watch on the Rhine) (1840) became famous after Franco-Prussian War.
Schneider, Leonard Alfred. *see in index* Bruce, Lenny
Schnitzer, Eduard. *see in index* Emin Pasha
Schnitzler, Arthur (1862–1931), Austrian dramatist and novelist; abandoned successful medical career for writing; famous for light, deft, psychological comedy and satire G-109
Schnorr von Karolsfeld, Julius (1794–1872), German Pre-Raphaelite painter; known for historical and religious works, including frescoes.
Schoeffer, Peter (died 1503?), German printer, associated with Gutenberg P-504
Gutenberg G-319
Schoenberg, Arnold. *see in index* Schönberg, Arnold
Schoenherr, Karl (1867–1943), Austrian dramatist ('Glaube und Heimat'; 'Vivat Academia'; 'Hungerblockade').
Schofield, Frank Herman (1869–1942), U.S. Navy officer, born in Jerusalem, N.Y.; head of War Plans Division 1926–29; commander in chief of U.S. Fleet 1931–32.
Schofield, John McAllister (1831–1906), U.S. Civil War general, born in Chautauqua County, N.Y.; graduated West Point 1853; commanded Army of the Ohio 1864; commanded 23rd corps in Sherman's Georgia campaign; superintendent U.S. Military Academy 1876–82; commanding general U.S. Army 1888–95.
Schofield, W(alter) Elmer (1867–1944), U.S. landscape painter, born in Philadelphia, Pa.; best known for snow scenes ('Sand Dunes Near Leland'; 'Midwinter Thaw').
Schofield Barracks, in Hawaii, military base on island of Oahu; pop. 18,851 H-70
Scholarship, colleges U-208
Rhodes R-195
Scholastic Aptitude Test (SAT), examination for U.S. high school students; consists of verbal and mathematical aptitude tests; administered nationwide; test results determine admission to many colleges as well as scholarship awards.
Scholastic philosophy P-265
Anselm of Canterbury A-467
Aquinas A-520
Scholastics. *see in index* Schoolmen
Schollander, Don(ald Arthur) (born 1946), U.S. swimmer, born in Charlotte, N.C.; won 4 gold medals in Olympic Games at Tokyo 1964; set world records.
Schönbein, Christian Friedrich (1799–1868), German chemist, born in Metzingen; professor at University of Basel; in 1839 he discovered ozone and in 1845, guncotton and collodion.
Schönberg, Arnold (1874–1951), Austrian composer S-54
classical music M-675
opera O-569
orchestra O-578
12-tone system S-54
Webern W-129
Schönbrunn, imperial palace near Vienna, Austria; reached greatest splendor under Maria Theresa; Napoleon's headquarters after battles of Austerlitz (1805) and Wagram (1809) V-315
Schönefeld, airport in East Germany G-120
Schongauer, Martin (1445?–91), German painter and engraver, who attained, especially in his engravings, unusual definiteness of line and precision of detail D-253
'Death of the Virgin', *picture* G-232
School (or shoal), group of fish F-127
School. *see in index* Education
'School and Society, The', book by Dewey D-125
Schoolcraft, Henry Rowe (1793–1864), U.S. explorer and ethnologist, born in Guilderland, N.Y.; U.S. agent in Lake Superior region for nearly 20 years; 'Indian Tribes of the United States', 6 volumes published by order of Congress, provided background for Longfellow's 'Hiawatha' S-477
Hiawatha H-146
Lake Itasca discovery M-445
Mississippi River M-484
School for Economic and Industrial Security, an organization in West Germany

than 300 plays; slight plots but bright dialogue, excellent technique, and understanding of popular taste made them successes; wrote librettos for operas 'Fra Diavolo' and 'Les Huguenots'.

Scribes, originally the learned Jewish group who copied the scriptures and who were authorities on the Torah, or law; Ezra the priest was a famous scribe; the later scribes were doctors of the law
  bookmaking contribution B-350

Scribing, in map making M-128

Scriblerus Club, an 18th-century London literary club S-531

Scrim, cotton or linen fabric of open weave, coarser than voile; used for curtains, summer apparel, and in needlework; term also applies to pressed, starched cheesecloth.

Scrimmage line, in football F-292, 297

Scrimshaw, hobby H-183

Scripps, Edward Wyllis (1854–1926), U.S. newspaper publisher, born in Rushville, Ill.; half brother of Ellen B. Scripps; controlled chain of 28 newspapers (headed by *Cleveland Press,* which he founded and edited), and United Press Association, supplying features to hundreds of newspapers; endowed Science Service for furnishing scientific news in popular form, *list* N-240

Scripps, Ellen Browning (1836–1932), U.S. newspaper woman and philanthropist, born in London, England; to U.S. 1844; half sister of Edward W. Scripps with whom she was associated.

Scripps College, in Claremont, Calif.; private control; for women; member of the Claremont Colleges; founded 1926 by Ellen B. Scripps; arts and sciences.

Scripps Institution of Oceanography, in San Diego, Calif., founded by Ellen B. and Edward W. Scripps for study of marine biology and ocean waves, tides, and currents; became part of University of California in 1912.

Script, written text of drama
  directing D-153
  motion pictures M-606

Script clerk, motion picture M-606

Scriptorium, writing room in medieval monastery M-391
  library L-171, *picture* L-174

Scrofula, term used for tuberculosis of lymphatic glands; in early times known as "king's evil," because of belief that it could be cured by touch of the sovereign (superstition prevalent in England in time of Edward the Confessor).

Scroll, a roll of papyrus, parchment, or paper B-181
  ancient books B-345. *see also in index* Dead Sea Scrolls
  Japanese P-67f

Scroll, in heraldry, *picture* H-135

'Scroll of the Apocryphal Genesis' (or 'Book of Lamech'), Dead Sea scroll D-46

Scrooby, England, village in Nottinghamshire, 20 mi (30 km) e. of Sheffield; English home of John Robinson, William Brewster, and other Pilgrims.

Scrooge, Ebenezer, chief character in Dickens' 'Christmas Carol', a miser who is reformed when the ghost of his old business partner comes to haunt his lonely house.

Scrophulariaceae. *see in index* Figwort family

Scrotum, part of male reproductive system R-151c, *diagram* R-151d

Scrub, type of cattle C-224

Scrubber, in industry
  coal-tar products C-527

Scrub forest G-236

Scrub jay, bird *Aphelocoma coerulescens* C-784, *picture* C-785

Scrub pine. *see in index* Lodgepole pine

Scruple, apothecaries' weight of 20 grains or 1/24 ounce, troy (from Latin *scrupulus,* "a little sharp stone"), *table* W-140

Scrupulum, ancient Roman unit of weight, *table* W-141

Scuba (self-contained underwater breathing apparatus) C-749
  inner space navigation N-73
  oceanic exploration O-463
  oceanography, *picture* O-475
  underwater diving D-187

Scudder, Horace Elisha (1838–1902), U.S. writer and editor, born in Boston, Mass.; noted for juvenile books ('Seven Little People and Their Friends'; 'The Bodley Books').

Scudder, Janet (1873–1940), U.S. sculptor, born in Terre Haute, Ind.; especially noted for fountains with playful childish figures ('Frog Fountain'; 'Fountain of Fighting Boys').

Scudéry, Madeleine de (1607–1701), French novelist, a leader of Mme. de Rambouillet's salon; 'Grand Cyrus', in 10 volumes, paints contemporary aristocracy in classic disguise.

Scullin, James Henry (1876–1953), Australian statesman, born in Trawalla, Victoria; Labor party leader 1928; prime minister 1929–32.

Sculling, in rowing R-300

Sculpins, grotesquely shaped fish with warted bodies, long spines, huge mouths; family Cottidae; inhabit rocky coasts of n. seas; also live in deep waters of these seas.

Sculptor, constellation, *charts* S-420, C-682

Sculpture S-76. *see also in index* names of famous sculptors
  animals. *see in index* Animal art, *subhead* sculpture
  art forms A-667
  Australia A-802
  baroque S-88, *picture* S-88
  design D-111
  Egyptian. *see in index* Egyptian art and architecture, ancient
  folk art F-250
  fountains F-334
  Greek G-269
  hobby H-182
  Italian, *pictures* R-147, 253, *Reference-Outline* S-95
  marble M-131
  metalworking M-311
  museums
    Rodin museums R-238
  Oriental S-93, *Reference-Outline* S-95
  Persian, *picture* P-213
  Philippine P-257d, *picture* P-257b
  plastics, *picture* P-381
    bibliography P-383
  pre-literate
    Easter Island E-42, P-7, *picture* P-2
  North American
    Aztec A-891
    Mayan, *pictures* P-365, S-82
  Renaissance R-146, *Reference-Outline* S-95
  Roman G-273
  snow, *picture* U-208
  United States S-90, *Reference-Outline* S-95
  wood. *see in index* Woodworking and wood carving

Scup, fish S-96

Scuppernong grape, a large yellowish variety of grape, grown chiefly in s.e. states; named for a river in North Carolina that empties into Albemarle Sound G-220

Scurvy, disease in which bloody spots appear under skin, gums bleed, and patient is prostrated by weakness
  Cook's discoveries C-696
  food and nutrition F-279
    citrus fruits C-444
    malnutrition M-77
    vitamin C V-354, *picture* V-354

Scutage (from Latin, *scutum,* shield), feudal tax paid in place of serving in the army
  Henry II H-129

Scutari, Albania. *see in index* Shkodër

Scutari, Turkey. *see in index* Uskudar

Scutching, in flax fiber processing F-177

Scute, large shieldlike plate forming part of the shell or skin of fishes, tortoises, armadillos, etc.; name is from the Latin, *scutum* (shield).

Scutum, constellation, *chart* C-682

Scylla, in Greek mythology, six-headed monster H-223

Scyros, island in Aegean Sea. *see in index* Skýros

Scytale, an ancient cipher device of Spartans C-419

Scythe, an agricultural implement consisting of a long curved blade and long bent handle R-113
  farm machinery replaces F-34

Scythia, name applied by ancient Greeks to steppes n. of Black Sea inhabited by nomads who disappeared from history about 2nd or 1st century BC; the name Scythia given also to lands reaching from Caspian Sea to region beyond the Jaxartes (modern Syr-Dar'ya) River; Romans gave name Scythia to n. Asia, *maps* P-212, R-242

SDECE (Service de Documentation Extérieure et de Contre-Espionnage, or Department for Foreign Information and Counterespionage), France I-237

SDI. *see in index* Strategic Defense Initiative

SDR (Special Drawing Right), in international finance I-258

Sea, general name for the body of salt water that covers the greater part of the surface of the globe; four largest sections are called oceans, and smaller landlocked bodies are called seas. *see also in index* Ocean, *table* Oceans and Other Bodies of Water in the World; and names of oceans and seas, such as Atlantic Ocean; Caspian Sea
  lakes L-24

Sea, god of, in Greek mythology. *see in index* Poseidon

Sea, air, and land teams (SEALS), special underwater teams of the U.S. Navy N-89

Sea anemone, a coelenterate animal S-96, *pictures* A-433, [illegible]
  conditioning experiment A-439
  fish symbiosis F-128

Sea arrow (or flying squid), type of squid O-491

Sea bass, name applied to group of food fishes, mostly found in warm seas; includes groupers and jewfishes Epinephelidae and black sea bass Serranidae.

Sea bear, seal-like mammal from which fur is obtained S-100

Seabees, Construction Battalions of U.S. Navy; motto: "Construmus Batuimus" ("We build, we fight") N-89

Seaboard Lowland, geographical region in North America
  Massachusetts M-189
  New Hampshire N-176

Seaborg, Glenn Theodore (born 1912), U.S. scientist, born in Ishpeming, Mich.; on staff University of California 1937–61, 1971–, professor 1945–61, 1971–, chancellor at Berkeley 1958–61; won Enrico Fermi Award 1959; chairman U.S. Atomic Energy Commission 1961–71 P-394. *see also in index* Nobel Prizewinners, *table*

Sea breeze, winds W-220, *diagram* W-221

Seabrook, William Buehler (1886–1945), U.S. writer, born in Westminster, Md.; wrote of travels and adventures in Arabia, Africa, and Haiti ('The Magic Island'; 'Jungle Ways'; 'Asylum'; 'Witchcraft, Its Power in the World Today').

Seabury, Samuel (1729–96), U.S. clergyman, born in Groton, Conn.; Loyalist in American Revolution; first bishop of Episcopal Church in America, consecrated in Scotland 1784.

Sea cave, type of cave C-234

Sea Convention, Law of the, approved by UN; established concept of archipelagic waters
  Indonesia I-158

Sea coots. *see in index* Scoters

Sea cow. *see in index* Manatee

Sea cucumber, marine animal of the class Holothurioidea S-96, S-425

Sea devil. *see in index* Devilfish

Sea dragon, fish, *picture* F-130

Sea elephant (also called elephant seal), mammal *Mirounga angustirostris* of the family Phocidae S-100, *picture* S-98

Sea fan, type of coral C-714

Seafloor E-7

Seaford, Del., city in s.w. on Nanticoke River; pop. 5,256 D-72, *picture* D-73

Seaford, N.Y., unincorporated urban community 27 mi (43 km) s.e. of New York City on s. shore of Long Island; boats; resort area; hamlet founded 1643; pop. 17,379.

Seager, Henry Rogers (1870–1930), U.S. economist, born in Lansing, Mich.; professor economics Columbia University; authority on labor and trust problems ('Principles of Economics').

Sea Girt, N.J., summer capital of state, on Atlantic coast 6 mi (10 km) s.w. of Asbury Park; state military encampment on shore of Stockton Lake; governor's residence (Little White House) near entrance to [illegible]

Sea gooseberry, a small jellylike marine animal; family Ctenophora, genus *Pleurobrachia*, *picture* A-433

Seagrave, Gordon S(tifier) (1897–1965), surgeon, born in Rangoon, Burma, of U.S. missionary parents; operated mission hospital Namhkam (also spelled Namkham), Burma, 1922–65; charged with treason by Burmese government 1951; acquitted same year ('Burma Surgeon'; 'Burma Surgeon Returns'; 'My Hospital in the Hills').

Sea green (or celadon), a pottery glaze P-470

Sea gull. *see in index* Gull

Sea Gull Monument, in Salt Lake City, Utah U-220, G-317, *picture* U-234

Sea holly, genus of plants *Eryngium* of parsley family; toothed, prickly leaves; blue or white bracted flowers.

Sea horse, fish F-128, S-97, *picture* F-130

Sea-island cotton, a long-staple variety *Gossypium barbadense* of cotton plant; native of tropical America C-741

Sea Islands, chain of low sandy or marshy islands in Atlantic Ocean along coast from South Carolina to Florida, *map* S-319

Seal, mammal S-98
  Alaska's fur production A-243
    Eskimos hunt, *picture* S-99
  Antarctic region A-473
  Bering Sea fisheries B-166
  furs F-463, *table* F-465
  life expectancy, *chart* A-423
  sea elephant S-100, *picture* S-98
  sea lion S-100
  zoo Z-462

Seal, impression in wax, paper, or metal, attached to a document as a mark of authenticity (from Latin *sigillum,* mark); originally used for signature when writing was uncommon; also the instrument for making the impression
  Sumerians B-6

Seal, Great, United States U-115
  custodian U-158
  flag symbols F-156, *picture* F-157

Seal, provincial, Canadian. *see in index* names of provinces, *subhead* seal

Seal, state. *see in index* names of states, *subhead* seal, state

Sealab
  ocean exploration O-463
    Atlantic A-746

Sea lamprey, fishlike vertebrate, *picture* L-26

Sea lavender. *see in index* Sea pink

Seal Beach, Calif., city 5 mi (8 km) s.e. of Long Beach; aerospace industry, foods; Naval Weapons Station, National Wildlife Refuge; incorporated 1915; pop. 25,975.

Sea lettuce, a seaweed, *pictures* S-104, P-361, 370
  living things L-267

Sea level (or surface level), level of the surface of oceans; varies throughout the world; *mean sea level* midway between mean high and low tides; used as standard of

Seitz, Frederick (born 1911), U.S. physicist, born in San Francisco, Calif.; professor of physics and chairman of department Carnegie Institute of Technology 1942–49; professor of physics University of Illinois 1949–57; chairman 1957–64; president National Academy of Sciences 1962–69; president Rockefeller University 1968–; helped develop atom bomb; important work on crystals.

Sei whale, a species of baleen whale; lives in oceans of temperate zone W-185

Seiyukai, Japanese political party I-405

Seizure, a medical disorder F-119

Sejanus, Lucius Aelius (died AD 31), Roman courtier, favorite of Tiberius; poisoned Drusus, son of Tiberius, and became virtually ruler of Rome; executed for plot to seize imperial power T-179

Sejong (1397–1450), Korean king of Yi dynasty; remembered for introducing in 1446 *hangul,* alphabet suited to the Korean language K-284, 293

Sekani, North American Indian tribe, *map* I-136, *table* I-139

Sekhet'enanach (fl. 2500? BC), Egyptian physician, *picture* M-282

Sekhmet, Egyptian goddess M-700

Sekia el Hamra, Spanish Sahara. *see in index* Saguia el Hamra

Selachii, order of scaleless fish with gristly skeletons; includes sharks, skates, and rays. *see also in index* Shark; Skates and rays

Selangor, state in former Federation of Malaya; 3,167 sq mi (8,202 sq km); cap. Kuala Lumpur; rice, tin, rubber; became part of Malaysia 1963; pop. 1,629,386. *see also in index* Malay States, Federated
  Kuala Lumpur K-307

Selden, George Baldwin (1846–1922), U.S. inventor, born in Clarkson, N.Y. A-858

Selden, John (1584–1654), English lawyer, scholar; politically active but chiefly noted for 'Table Talk', amusing miscellany in essay form.

Seldes, Gilbert (Vivian) (1893–1970), U.S. critic, born in Alliance, near Salem, N.J.; directed television programs Columbia Broadcasting System 1937–45; commentator of U.S. entertainment arts ('The Seven Lively Arts'; 'The Great Audience'; 'Writing for Television'; 'The Public Arts').

Selective breeding, breeding method C-225
  horse H-253

Selective permeability, in biophysics B-237

Selective service. *see in index* Conscription

Selective Service Act (1917), United States C-668
  World War I W-313

Selective Training and Service Act (1940), United States act calling for classification, drafting, and training of men for military and civilian emergency service A-648, U-188

Selene, Greek moon goddess, later identified with Artemis. *see in index* Artemis

Selenga River, important river in Mongolian People's Republic; formed by junction of Ider and Muren rivers; flows generally n.e. to Lake Baikal (Baykal), in U.S.S.R.; 600 mi (965 km) long, *map* R-345
  Asia, *map* A-700
  Yenisey River Y-415

Selenite, mineral M-435

Selenium (Se), nonmetallic chemical element S-108, *table* P-207
  duplicating machine D-290
  periodic table, *table* P-207, *list* P-208
  photoelectric devices P-273
  poisonous plants P-408
  television use T-78

Seleucia, ancient Greek cities named after Seleucus Nicator; most noted on Tigris River near Babylon, which it replaced as capital of Babylonia until destroyed by Romans 2nd century AD B-3, *map* P-212

Seleucid Dynasty, line of kings who ruled in w. Asia 312–64 BC; founded by Seleucus Nicator, general of Alexander, who conquered most of Alexander's empire; kingdom decayed under successors until taken by Romans A-280
  Babylonian civilization B-3
  Iraq I-314

Self-concept, in psychology
  Buddhist B-480

Self-contained underwater breathing apparatus. *see in index* Scuba

Self-defense
  martial arts M-159

Self-denying ordinance, a measure passed by English Parliament, 1645, denying members of that body any civil or military office; designed to remove inefficient officers from command of the army.

Self-determination, a term brought into current use by President Wilson during World War I to denote the right of a people to determine its form of government and political allegiance.

Self-healing, emphasizing an individual's own resources to promote health, prevent illness, and encourage healing H-203

Self-induction, in electric circuits. *see in index* Inductance

Self-launching glider (or powered glider) G-166

Self-pollination, the transfer of pollen from the stamen of a flower to the pistil of the same flower, as distinguished from cross-pollination F-219, P-440. *see also in index* Pollen and pollination
  fruitgrowing F-437

Self-processing film. *see in index* Instant film

'Self Reliance', work by Emerson A-347

Selfridge, Harry Gordon (1864–1947), British businessman, born in Ripon, Wis.; entered employ of Field, Leiter & Co., 1879, rising to become a partner in Marshall Field & Co., retired in 1904 and went to London in 1906, where he opened in 1909 Selfridge & Co., one of the largest department stores in Europe; became British subject in 1937.

Self-timed photography P-285

Selig, William (1864–1948), U.S. motion-picture pioneer, born in Chicago, Ill.; actor, theatrical manager 1888–99; improved early motion-picture camera; produced first long historical motion picture ('Coming of Columbus') M-618

Seligman, Edwin Robert Anderson (1861–1939), U.S. economist, born in New York City; professor Columbia University 1891–1931; editor 'Encyclopaedia of the Social Sciences'.

Selim I (1465–1520), Ottoman sultan; annexed Egypt and Syria; his conquests made him leader in Islamic world T-323
  Ottoman Empire O-616

Selim III (1762–1808), Ottoman sultan; administrative and military reformer; dethroned and killed by Janizaries O-618

Selima, Walpole's cat, *list* C-202

Seljuk Dynasty (also Seljukian Dynasty), ruled Turkey in 11th to 13th centuries; founded by Seljuk, a Turkish chieftain; capture of Jerusalem (1071) by Seljuk forces was the cause of the First Crusade
  caliphate C-56
  Iraq I-314
  Islamic literature, *picture* I-367
  Ottoman Empire O-616
  Turkey T-320, 323

Selkirk, Alexander (1676–1721), British sailor, the original of 'Robinson Crusoe'; born in Fifeshire, Scotland. *see also in index* 'Robinson Crusoe'
  Galápagos Islands G-4

Selkirk, Thomas Douglas, 5th **earl of** (1771–1820), Scottish nobleman interested in establishing colonial homes for evicted Scottish peasants P-497e
  Canada C-96
  fur trade F-472
  Manitoba M-103

Selkirk, Man., town and shipping point for Lake Winnipeg fishing industry on Red River 23 mi (37 km) n. of Winnipeg; government shipyards, cold-storage plants, steel and iron; pop. 10,037 M-102

Selkirk, county in s. Scotland; 267 sq mi (692 sq km); hilly country celebrated in literature; sheep raising; cap. Selkirk (pop. 5,634); pop. 21,052.

Selkirk Mountains, range in Canadian Rockies, British Columbia; highest peak, Sir Sandford (11,590 ft; 3,535 m).

'Selling of Joseph', work by Sewall A-342

Selly Oak colleges, in Birmingham, England B-282

Selma, Ala., city on Alabama River 40 mi (60 km) w. of Montgomery; cotton and livestock section; lumber products, hardware, machinery, cigars, cottonseed products, metal products; Cahaba State Capitol (1820–26) nearby; site of Confederate arsenal and shipyard; pop. 26,684, *maps* A-237, U-41
  civil rights march B-296, *picture* U-195
  storytelling S-462

Selous, Frederick Courteney (1851–1917), British writer and explorer of South Africa and daring big-game hunter; secured Mashonaland territory for Britain 1890; captain in World War I; killed in action ('A Hunter's Wanderings in Africa'; 'African Nature Notes and Reminiscences').

Selvon, Samuel (born 1923), author from Trinidad, presents a grim picture of native life ('A Brighter World'; 'An Island Is a World') C-167

Selye, Hans (Hugo Bruno) (1907–82), Canadian endocrinologist, born in Vienna, Austria; director and professor Institute of Experimental Medicine and Surgery, University of Montreal, 1945–76; known for researches on effect of stress in producing disease.

Selznick, David O(liver) (1902–65), U.S. motion-picture producer, born in Pittsburgh, Pa.; began career in his father's studio in 1921; headed Selznick International Pictures, Inc. 1935–40; won Academy awards for 'Gone with the Wind' (1939) and 'Rebecca' (1940) ('A Star Is Born', 'The Prisoner of Zenda', 'Intermezzo', 'Jane Eyre').

Semang, a people of Malaysia P-540

Semantics, the study of the exact meaning of words L-229
  Korzybski K-301
  sciences S-65

Semaphore, a visual signaling system T-57
  code L-36
  flags, *pictures* S-194b
  railroad signaling, *pictures* R-78

Semarang, Java, port on n. coast; pop. 756,100, *map* I-166
  Asia, *map* A-700

Sembène, Ousmane (born 1923), Senegalese filmmaker and author A-101

Sembrich, Marcella (stage name of Praxede Marcelline Kochanska) (1858–1935), Polish operatic soprano, noted for purity and brilliance of her voice.

Semele, in Greek mythology, daughter of Cadmus; mother of Dionysus by Zeus; when Zeus visited her, she was killed by lightning as schemed by jealous Hera D-147

Semen, in sexual reproduction R-151c
  sexuality S-124

Semënov, Nikolai Nikolaevich (born 1896), Soviet scientist, born in Saratov; professor at Moscow State University from 1944; director, Institute of Chemical Physics, U.S.S.R. Academy of Sciences. *see also in index* Nobel Prizewinners, *table*

Semeru, Mount (or Mount Semeroe), active volcano in e. Java; highest peak in Java, 12,060 ft (3,680 m), *map* I-166

Semiarid tropical climate (or tropical steppe climate), in climate classification C-500

Semiautomatic rifle, *pictures* F-98, 99

Semicircular canal, organ of equilibrium in inner ear E-4

Semicolon, in punctuation P-534

Semiconductor, an electronic device S-254g
  Bardeen's research B-80
  crystals C-799
  electronics E-175
  industry I-187
  integrated circuit S-195b
    microprocessor M-378
  transistor T-249

Semihydraulic fill dam, type of dam D-16

Semimetal (or metalloid) M-307

Seminal vesicle, in male reproductive system R-151c, *diagram* R-151d

Seminary Ridge, Pa., in battle of Gettysburg G-136

Seminole (runaway), a North American Indian tribe, one of "Five Civilized Tribes"; originally part of Creek I-149, *picture* I-121, *table* I-139
  Florida F-321, *picture* F-205
  Osceola O-609
  shelter S-156
  Van Buren administration V-261

Seminole, Okla., city about 50 mi (80 km) s.e. of Oklahoma City; oil field supply and service center; incorporated 1908 as town, 1926 as city; pop. 8,590.

Semipalmated plover, bird P-391

Semipalmated sandpiper, bird S-40

Semipermeable membrane, in osmosis O-610

Semiramis, legendary Assyrian queen, daughter of a Syrian goddess and a mortal; wife and successor of Ninus, founder of Nineveh; herself great ruler and conqueror, founder of Babylon; changed to dove; deified.

Semites, branch of Caucasoids originating in s.w. Asia, *chart* R-26
  Africa S-501
  alphabet use A-315
  Arabian origin A-523
  Mesopotamia M-305
  Phoenicians P-267
  Syrians S-550
  writing W-372

Semitic languages
  Babylon and Assyria B-6
  classification L-42, *diagram* L-44
  writing W-372
    alphabet A-317

Semitrailer, a vehicle that is attached to a truck tractor T-291

Semliki River, river in central Africa, outlet of Lake Edward into Lake Albert; about 125 mi (200 km) long; Henry Stanley arrived at river in 1888.

Semmelweis, Ignaz Philipp (1818–65), Hungarian physician S-108a
  medicine M-284

Semmering Pass, in Alps in e. Austria, 50 mi (80 km) s.w. of Vienna; altitude 3,215 ft (980 m); first great transalpine railroad built here 1854.

Semmes, Raphael (1809–77), U.S. Confederate admiral, born in Charles County, Md.; graduated Annapolis and served in U.S. Navy until 1861; commanded *Sumter* and Confederate destroyer, *Alabama*, sunk by *Kearsarge* off Cherbourg, France A-228

Semolina (or middlings), a hard wheat flour used for macaroni F-215

Sempach, Switzerland, town 10 mi (16 km) n.w. of Lucerne.

Sempach, battle of (1386), *list* W-15. *see also in index* Winkelried, Arnold von
  Switzerland S-544

Semper Fidelis (always faithful), motto of U.S. Marine Corps; also name of a march written for the Marine band by John Philip Sousa M-138

Semper paratus (always ready), motto of U.S. Coast Guard.

Sempervivum, the houseleek genus of plants of the orpine family, consisting of fleshy perennial plants; includes hen-and-chickens *S. tectorum*; cobweb houseleek *S. arachnoideum*; in all about 65 species.

Semple, Ellen Churchill (1863–1932), U.S. geographer, born in Louisville, Ky.; lecturer in anthropogeography at University of Chicago 1906–23 ('American History and Its Geographic Conditions').

Semple, Robert (1766–1816), Canadian traveler and

governor of Rupert's Land for the Hudson's Bay Company; killed in conflict with rival trading company

Senate, ancient Roman R-242, *picture* R-247
  Caesar's role C-14
  democracy D-92

Senate, Australian P-130, A-803

Senate, Canadian P-132

Senate, United States. *see also in index* Congress of the United States
  election E-146, E-148
  filibuster F-83
  Hall of Fame, *see table* following
  impeachment I-58
  lobbying L-276
  political appointments P-493
  Reconstruction, *picture* R-114
  salary U-155
  U.S. Constitution U-146
    election decisions V-388

Senate Permanent Subcommittee on Investigations M-4

Sendai, Japan, city near e. coast of Honshu Island 190 mi (305 km) n.e. of Tokyo; silk, lacquerware, food products; Tohoku Imperial University; pop. 545,065, *maps* J-78
  Asia, *map* A-700

Sendak, Maurice (born 1928), U.S. illustrator and children's author, born in Brooklyn, N.Y.; illustrated 'Little Bear', 'A Hole Is to Dig', and 'Hector Protector'; wrote and illustrated 'Nutshell Library' and 'Where the Wild Things Are', awarded 1964 Caldecott Medal; won Laura Ingalls Wilder Award 1983 R-108, *picture* R-110a

Sender, Ramón José (1902–82), Spanish-American writer, born in Huesca, Spain; to U.S. 1942, citizen 1946; professor of Spanish literature University of New Mexico 1947–63 ('The War in Spain'; 'Man's Place') S-365b, *picture* S-366

Seneca, Lucius Annaeus (4? BC–AD 65), Roman statesman, philosopher, and dramatist S-108a
  essay E-306
  humor H-322
  literary contribution L-77

Seneca, American Indian tribe of Iroquois confederacy; from Seneca Lake, N.Y., spread w. to Lake Erie and s. along Allegheny River I-142, *table* I-138, *map* I-149
  New York N-250

Seneca Lake, largest and deepest of Finger Lakes, in w.-central New York; area 67 sq mi (174 sq km); greatest depth 618 ft (188 m).

Seneca Oil Company P-232

Seneca Rocks, rock formation in Allegheny Mountains of e. West Virginia, *picture* W-165

Seneca snakeroot. *see in index* Snakeroot

Senecio (or groundsel), genus of plants of the composite family, probably the largest genus (over 1,200 species); includes florists' cineraria, German ivy, and tansy ragwort.

Senefelder, Aloys (1771–1834), German inventor of lithography
  graphic arts G-233
  lithography L-258

Senegal, republic in n.w. Africa, bordering Atlantic; area 76,124 sq mi (197,160 sq km); cap. Dakar; pop. 4,100,000 S-108a, *picture* S-108b
  Africa A-103, *map* A-118, *table* A-112
  flag, *picture* F-170
  Gambia, The G-8
  illiteracy P-450
  railroad mileage, *table* R-85

Senegal River, river in n.w. Africa; rises in Guinea, flows through w. Mali, forms Senegal-Mauritania boundary and flows into Atlantic; length 1,000 mi (1,600 km), *map* A-118
  Mali M-75

Senegambia. *see in index* Gambia, The; Senegal

Senfu-mon, Japanese gate, *diagram* J-31

Senghor, Léopold Sédar (born 1906), African poet, president of Senegal 1960–80 A-122

Senigallia, Italy, port on Adriatic n.w. of Ancona; ancient Roman city of Sena Gallica; pop. 35,337, *map* I-402

Senile dementia (or senility), brain impairment A-127
  memory M-295
  nervous disorders N-123
  nursing home N-447

Senior citizens
  African communities A-109
  aging study A-125
  bone disease B-342
  communal living C-606
  nursing home N-447
  economic and social aspects P-448
  housing H-301, 306
  Japan J-29
  leisure-time activities, *picture* P-125
  magazine and journal M-34
  welfare programs W-146
    Medicare S-237
    pensions P-188, S-236

Senior officer (or field grade officer), U.S. Army A-634

Senlis, France, town 25 mi (40 km) n.e. of Paris; Gallo-Roman walls, medieval cathedral; taken by Germans 1914 and 1940; pop. 10,111, *map* F-372

Senna, plants of the genus *Cassia,* in the pea, or pulse, family; many species in U.S. and tropical America. Common wild senna, *C. marilandica*, 3 to 8 ft (1 to 2.5 m) tall, leaves divided into 10 to 20 leaflets in pairs; showy yellow pealike flowers in axils of upper leaves.

Sennacherib (died 681 BC), Assyrian king, warrior, and builder S-108b, B-9

Sennar Dam, dam on the Blue Nile in Sudan; built of masonry, 129 ft (39 m) high and 9,900 ft (3,018 m) long; begun 1921, completed 1925 S-502

Sennett, Mack (real name Michael Sinnott) (1884–1960), motion-picture producer, born in Danville, Que.; started Keystone Studio 1912; famous for slapstick comedy of silent film era
  motion pictures M-619, *picture* M-620

Sens, France, industrial town on Yonne River, 65 mi (105 km) s.e. of Paris; Roman remains; cathedral of St. Étienne; pop. 22,658, *map* F-372

Sensation S-109
  anesthesia A-412
  nerves. *see in index* Sensory nerve

Sensationalism, journalistic strategy to attract readers N-236

'Sense and Sensibility', novel by Jane Austen contrasting the temperaments of two sisters.

Senses S-109
  anesthesia A-412
  animals A-421
  child development S-109
  illusions I-55
  learning L-105
  smell S-218

Sensitive plants, those with a quick response to certain stimuli, chemical, mechanical, or atmospheric; most familiar is the sensitive plant that droops its leaves with the slightest touch and folds its leaflets in pairs; this species *Mimosa pudica* of the pulse family Leguminosae P-363

Senso-ji Buddhist Temple, in Tokyo, Japan, *picture* T-209

Sensor, device that responds to electrical and other stimuli I-228

Sensorimotor stage, period of child development P-314

Sensorineural (or perception hearing loss), results from a loss of function of the sensory apparatus of the inner ear or its connecting nerve pathways to the cortex of the brain D-47

Sensory nerve, in human nervous system N-118, *diagram* N-121
  brain reception B-398

Sensory receptor (or end organ)
  brain regulation B-397
  nervous system N-118

Sentence, in grammar, group of words that form a complete thought with a subject and predicate S-110, L-31, *diagram* L-35
  grammar G-211
  linguistic analysis L-230

Sentimental comedy, dramatic work combining sentimental emotion with humor D-242

'Sentimental Journey, A', a narrative by Laurence Sterne of the reflections and adventures of a traveler in France and Italy E-272

Sentimental Tommy, hero of James M. Barrie's novel of same name, and of sequel 'Tommy and Grizel'.

Sentinel lily, plant, *picture* L-209

Sentinum, Italy, ancient city 37 mi (60 km) s.w. of Ancona; important battle (295 BC) R-244

Senussites, a fanatical ascetic sect centering in the oasis towns of the e. Sahara; founded 1837 by the Sheik es Senussi; has steadily resisted spread of European influence by force of arms; invaded w. Egypt 1915–16; defeated by Italian army 1928.

Senza, in music, *list* M-671

Seoul (Japanese Keijo), capital of Republic of Korea (South Korea), on Han River; pop. 5,536,377 S-111
  Asia, *map* A-700
  Korea K-270, *picture* K-269, *map* K-290
  Korean War K-295, *map* K-297, *chart* K-299
  marriage ceremony, *picture* M-151

Sepals, lower part of a flower F-217, *pictures* F-218

Separation, in law, when a husband and wife agree to stop living together M-151

Separation factor, uranium isotope separation U-212

Separation layer, of leaf L-102

Separatism
  Basques S-361
  Quebec Q-9g
  Switzerland S-544b

Separatist (or Independent), one who wished to form a separate denomination from the Church of England P-539. *see also in index* Pilgrims
  Brewster B-435
  Colonial American literature A-342
  'Mayflower' M-238

Sepia ink, drawing ink obtained form the ink sacs of the cuttlefish and squid O-491, M-525

Sepiolite, mineral known as meerschaum. *see in index* Meerschaum

Sepoy Rebellion. *see in index* Indian Mutiny

September, 9th month of the Gregorian calendar S-112
  birthdays of famous persons. *see in index* Birthdays, *table*

Septic tank S-119

Sept-Îles (or Seven Islands), Que., port town on n. shore of estuary of Saint Lawrence River; ships iron ore; pop. 24,320 Q-9d, *maps* C-112, U-061

Septimius Severus. *see in index* Severus, Lucius Septimius

Septuagint, a Greek version of Hebrew Bible, made, according to tradition, in 3rd century BC by about 70 translators (Latin *septuaginta,* "seventy") B-184
  Greek literature G-278

Septum, a dividing wall between two cavities
  heart D-174

Sequatchie River, river in s.e. Tenn., flows into Tennessee River, *map* T-97

Sequence, in motion pictures M-606

Sequoia, genus of giant evergreen trees S-112
  tree T-276

Sequoia National Park, in California
  General Sherman Tree S-112
  Muir M-648

Sequoyah (1770?–1843), Cherokee scholar, born in Loudon County, Tenn.; the sequoia tree was named in his honor; created the Cherokee alphabet
  Cherokee alphabet O-523
  Statuary Hall, *table* S-437b

Seraglio, formerly, a sultan's palace, especially the old palace of the sultan of Turkey at Constantinople (Istanbul); name also used as synonym for harem.

Seraing, Belgium, town on Meuse River 4 mi (6 km) s.w. of Liège; one of largest machinery factories in Europe; devastated during World War I; pop. 41,239.

Serajevo, Yugoslavia. *see in index* Sarajevo

Serao, Matilde (1856–1927), Italian novelist and journalist, born in Patras, Greece, of Italian and Greek parentage; noted for psychological novels that show sympathetic understanding of people with a tendency to sentimentality ('The Conquest of Rome'; 'The Land of Cockayne'; 'The Ballet Dancer').

Serapeum, special animal cemetery in ancient Egypt E-129

Seraphim (or seraphs), guardians of the threshold of the Most High (Bible, Isaiah vi, 2–6); in later Christian and Jewish lore, highest angelic order A-414

Serapis, Egyptian god worshiped in Greek-Roman towns of Egypt.

'Serapis', British warship, *picture* R-172
  John Paul Jones's battle J-139

Serbia (or Servia), formerly an independent Balkan state, now a constituent republic of Yugoslavia; 34,116 sq mi (88,361 sq km); pop. 7,642,227 S-113
  Belgrade B-151
  folktales, *picture* S-470, *list* S-481
  wars
    Balkan wars B-31
    World War I W-302, 305
  Yugoslavia Y-435

Serbia, Church of, Eastern Orthodox church E-42

Serbs, people Y-434

Serbs, Croats, and Slovenes, Kingdom of the, former name of Yugoslavia. *see in index* Yugoslavia

SENATE HALL OF FAME

(For additional biographical information, *see in index* senator by name)

The Senate Hall of Fame opened March 1959. It honors five "men whose statesmanship, transcending state and party lines, left a permanent mark on our nation's history." Clay, Calhoun, and Webster were chosen as outstanding spokesmen of the dominant forces of the 19th century; Taft and La Follette, as representatives of the conservative and progressive views of the 20th century. Each man's portrait has been painted on the wall of a public reception room near the Senate chamber.

Senator	*State*	*Term*
John C. Calhoun (1782–1850)	South Carolina	1832–43, 1845–50
Henry Clay (1777–1852)	Kentucky	1806–07, 1810–11, 1831–42, 1849–52
Robert M. La Follette (1855–1925)	Wisconsin	1906–25
Robert A. Taft (1889–1953)	Ohio	1939–53
Daniel Webster (1782–1852)	Massachusetts	1827–41, 1845–50

Sercq, one of Channel Islands. *see in index* Sark
Serdica, Roman city, now Sofia, Bulgaria. *see in index* Sofia
Seredy, Kate (1896–1975), U.S. illustrator and author of children's books; born in Budapest; to U.S. 1922, became citizen 1930; won Newbery medal 1938 for 'The White Stag'; known chiefly for stories about Hungary ('The Singing Tree'; 'The Chestry Oak'); 'Philomena'; 'The Tenement Tree' R-111b
'Serenade', ballet by George Balanchine B-32
Serengeti National Park, park in Tanzania N-26, *picture* N-25
Serengeti Plains, on plateau of Tanzania near Kenya border and s.e. of Lake Victoria, *picture* T-23
Serf (or villein), feudalism F-69
  England E-240
  Middle Ages M-386
Serfdom S-213. *see also in index* Peonage; Slavery
  ancient Sparta S-369
  England E-240
  labor L-2
  Middle Ages F-69, S-213
  Poland P-412
  Turgenev's description T-316
  U.S.S.R. R-352, 353
Serge, a firm twilled worsted fabric; also cotton or silk fabrics of similar weave; name originally from Latin *serica* (silk), later from Italian *sergea* (cloth of silk and wool).
Sergeant, military rank
  U.S. Air Force, uniform and insignia, *pictures* U-5
  U.S. Army, uniform and insignia, *pictures* U-9
  U.S. Marine Corps, insignia, *pictures* U-9
Sergeant, U.S. guided missile, *picture* G-307
Sergeant at arms, officer of legislative bodies appointed to enforce order at meetings; both houses of British, Canadian, and U.S. national legislatures have such officers.
Sergeant fish (or cobia, or crabeater), fish *Rachycentron canadus* with a black stripe along its side; maximum length five feet; commonly found along Atlantic coast.
Sergipe, state of Brazil, on e. coast; 8,505 sq mi (22,030 sq km); cap. Aracaju (pop. 112,516); agricultural regions produce rice, sugar, cotton, and livestock; pop. 1,156,642, *map* B-425
Serialism, in music M-676
Serial monogamy F-16
Sericin, secretion of silkworm S-199
Sericulture (or silk culture) S-197. *see also in index* Silk
Series connection, in electricity B-107
Serif, in calligraphy C-58
Serigraphy. *see in index* Silk-screen printing
Serkin, Rudolf (born 1903), U.S. pianist, born in Eger, Bohemia; prodigy at 4; concert tours in Europe and United States; concert debut in United States 1933; director Curtis Institute of Music, Philadelphia, 1968–76; awarded Presidential Medal of Freedom 1963.
Serling, Rod (1924–1975), U.S. playwright, born in Syracuse, N.Y.; network writer for radio 1946–48, television 1948–75; numerous awards include six Emmys (TV series: 'Twilight Zone'; TV plays: 'Patterns', 'Requiem for a Heavyweight', 'Tis the Season to Be Wary').
Sermo generalis. *see in index* Auto-da-fé
Sermon
  American literature A-342
Sermon at Benares, sermon by Buddha B-480
Sermon on the Mount, sermon by Jesus (Matthew v, vi, vii). Many of the same points are made in his **Sermon on the Plain** (Luke vi, 17–49).
Serous membrane, a membrane that secretes a liquid resembling serum, lines internal cavities of the body, and encases the internal organs
  tongue T-215
Serowe, Republic of Botswana, town in e.; pop. 15,723, *maps* A-118, S-264
Serpens, constellation, *charts* S-419, C-681
Serpent. *see in index* Sea serpent; Snake
Serpentes, old name of reptilian suborder comprising the snakes. *see in index* Snake
Serpentine, a mineral consisting of hydrated magnesium silicate ranging in color from green to brown and sometimes yellow, black, or red; often veined and mottled; it takes a high polish; with white calcite, magnesite, or dolomite it forms "verd antique," also called Connemara marble (in Ireland) or serpentine marble, much used for pillars and ornamental work M-436, *picture* R-229a
Serpukhov Institute for High Energy Physics N-421
Serpula, worm, *picture* W-362
Serra, Junípero. *see in index* Junípero Serra, Miguel José
Serra, Richard (born 1939), U.S. sculptor M-311
Serra da Estrela, highest mountain range in Portugal (6,532 ft; 1,991 m); forms sharp line dividing country and climate P-455
Serra do Espinhaço, mountain range in Brazil B-413
Serra do Mar, mountain range in Brazil B-412
Sérrai (or Serres), Greece, city 42 mi (68 km) n.e. of Salonika; produces cereals, tobacco, hides; occupied in World Wars I and II by Bulgarians; pop. 39,897.
Serum, in blood S-113
  antitoxin A-495
  blood B-315
  serum albumin S-113, A-272
Serum hepatitis. *see in index* Type-B hepatitis
Serum therapy S-113
  snakebite S-227
Serval, large, long-legged South African wildcat *Felis serval*; 3 ft (1 m) or more long, with yellow fur spotted and barred with black; the tail, 15 in. (38 cm) in length, is ringed with black, *table* C-214
Serve, tennis, *picture* T-105
Servetus, Michael (1511–53), Spanish physician and theologian; said to have discovered pulmonary circulation of blood; condemned by the Roman Catholic church and theologians of the Reformation for his teachings against the Trinity; burned at the stake in Geneva by Calvin's order.
Servia. *see in index* Serbia
Service, Robert William (1874–1958), Canadian poet, born in Preston, England; in Canada 1897–1912; called "Canadian Kipling"; spent later life in France and Monaco ('The Spell of the Yukon'; 'Rhymes of a Rolling Stone')
  Yukon home, *picture* C-121
Serviceberry. *see in index* Shadbush
Service clubs F-387
Service de Documentation Extérieure et de Contre-Espionnage (SDECE, or Department for Foreign Information and Counterespionage), French intelligence agency I-237
Service industry I-188
  capitalism C-151
  economics E-60
  employment and unemployment E-205
  Europe E-343
  labor movements L-9
  marketing M-140
Servicemen's Readjustment Act (or GI Bill of Rights) (1944), United States U-208, V-306
  education, *list* E-104
  housing, *list* H-304
Service module, of Apollo spacecraft S-346c, *diagrams* S-346b
Service scholarship U-208
Service station (or filling station), *pictures* P-229, S-16
  franchises F-374
Servitude, in international law I-256
Servius Tullius (ruled about 578–535 BC), 6th legendary king of Rome R-241
Servo motor, a power-driven mechanism that supplements a primary control operated by a comparatively feeble force
  typesetting T-339
Sesame (or sesamum), an herb (*Sesamum indicum*) widely cultivated in China, also grown in India, Africa, and Latin America; first commercial harvest in U.S. was in Texas, 1953; seeds yield oil (called sesame, gingili, benne, or teel oil) that does not turn rancid quickly, used in cooking and soapmaking, as a medicine, and as an adulterant for olive oil S-379
'Sesame and Lilies', by John Ruskin R-319
Sesame grass. *see in index* Gamagrass
Sesame Street, children's television program, *picture* R-101a
Sesostris, Greek name of legendary Egyptian king and world conqueror; deeds of several kings, including Ramses II, are attributed to him.
Sesotho language L-137
Sesquicentennial (Latin *sesqui*, "one half," plus *centennial*, "100 years"), pertaining to 150 years; a 150th anniversary.
Sesqui-Centennial International Exposition, a celebration held in Philadelphia, Pa., 1926, to commemorate the 150th anniversary of the signing of Declaration of Independence.
Sesshu (1420–1506), great painter of Japan, also a Buddhist priest; bold line, well-defined pattern; painted with ink; sometimes used impressionistic "ink splash" technique; his famous landscape scroll is in a collection in Tokyo J-51
Sessions, Roger (1896–1985), U.S. composer, born in Brooklyn, N.Y.; studied at Yale University with Horatio Parker and also with Ernest Bloch; taught at Smith College; founded, with Aaron Copland, Copland-Sessions Concerts; composed symphonies, violin concerto, string quartet, piano and organ music
  classical music M-677
  orchestra O-578
Set, in Egyptian mythology, god of evil; brother and murderer of Osiris I-358
Set, in mathematics
  algebra A-287
  Cantor's contribution C-145
  numeration systems N-440
Setae, worm W-363
Set designer, motion picture M-607
Sète (formerly Cette), France, Mediterranean seaport on s. coast; important trade in wine, petroleum; pop. 40,220, *map* F-372
Seth, Egyptian deity M-700
Seth, son of Adam and Eve, born after Abel's death; Book of Genesis says he lived 912 years and had many sons and daughters (Genesis iv, 25; Genesis v, 6–8).
Seti I (about 1315 BC), Egyptian pharaoh of XIXth dynasty; built much of Temple of Karnak; father of Ramses II, *picture* M-699
Seton, Anya (born 1916?), U.S. author, born in New York City; historical novels include: 'Dragonwyck', 'Katherine', 'The Winthrop Woman', 'Devil Water', and 'Avalon'
  'Katherine' R-112
Seton, Blessed (now Saint Elizabeth Ann Seton, formerly Elizabeth Ann Bayley, also called Mother Seton) (1774–1821), U.S. religious leader, born in New York, N.Y.; founder (1809) and first mother superior of Sisters of Charity in U.S., established at Emmitsburg, Md.; had became a Roman Catholic (1805) after her husband's death; first U.S.-born person beatified (1963); canonized 1975.
Seton, Ernest Thompson (1860–1946), U.S. naturalist, lecturer, and author and illustrator of animal books; born in South Shields, Durham, England; lived in Canadian backwoods 1866–70; founded Woodcraft Indians 1902; chief scout Boy Scouts, 1910–15 ('Wild Animals I Have Known'; 'Lives of the Hunted'; 'Animal Heroes') Y-427
Seto-Naikai National Park, park in Japan, *picture* N-27, *map* J-78
Seton Hall University, in South Orange, N.J.; Roman Catholic; founded 1856; arts and sciences, business administration, education, nursing, theology; graduate studies; law school at Newark
  Newark N-149
Seton Hill College, in Greensburg, Pa.; Roman Catholic; for women; founded 1918; arts and sciences, education, home economics, music.
Sets, small onions that did not reach full size G-26
Setter, a hunting dog, *pictures* D-198. *see also in index* setter by name, as English setter
Set theory, in mathematics M-216, 220
Settignano, Desiderio da. *see in index* Desiderio da Settignano
Settlement, in geography G-66
Settlement, Act of. *see in index* Act of Settlement
Settlements, social. *see in index* Social settlements
Settling basin (or sedimentation tank), for water purification W-91
Settlor, in trust law T-301
Setúbal, Portugal, seaport, 20 mi (30 km) s.e. of Lisbon; exports wine, fruit, salt, cork; pop. 44,435 P-455
Seurat, Georges (Pierre) (1859–91), French modernist painter S-114
  painting P-52, *picture* P-53
Seuss, Dr. *see in index* Geisel, Theodor Seuss
Sevareid, Arnold Eric (born 1912), U.S. newscaster, born in Velva, N.D.; reporter on *Minneapolis Star* 1936–37; correspondent for CBS 1939–77, consultant after 1977; author of 'Not So Wild a Dream' and 'In One Ear'.
'Sevasadan', novel by Prem Chand I-107
Sevastopol' (formerly Sebastopol'), U.S.S.R., naval station on Black Sea in s.w. Crimea; fell to Germans 1942, recaptured 1944, pop. 229,000, *maps* R-344, 349
  Crimean War C-774
  Europe, *map* E-361
Sevastyanov, Vitali Ivanovich (born 1935), Soviet engineer, born in Krasnoural'sk, U.S.S.R.; flight engineer on Soyuz 9 space flight, *picture* S-346f, *table* S-348
Seven, Group of, group of Canadian artists; formed in early 20th century C-79
'Seven Against Thebes', work by Aeschylus A-87
Seven Cardinal Virtues, in ancient and medieval literature and art, the seven principal virtues: faith, hope, charity, prudence, temperance, chastity, and fortitude.
Seven Champions of Christendom, in medieval literature, seven national saints: St. George of England, St. Denis of France, St. James of Spain, St. Anthony of Italy, St. Andrew of Scotland, St. Patrick of Ireland, St. David of Wales; celebrated in 'Famous Historie of the Seaven Champions of Christendom' by Richard Johnson (1573?–1659).
Seven Days' battles, U.S. Civil War (Mechanicsville, Gaines' Mill, Savage Station, Frazier's Farm, Malvern Hill) C-474, *map* C-475
  McClellan M-4
Seven Deadly Sins, in Roman Catholic doctrine—pride, avarice, lust, anger, gluttony, envy, and sloth; often personified in medieval literature.
Seven Devils Canyon. *see in index* Grand Canyon of the Snake River
Seven Golden Cities of Cibola, sought by explorer Coronado C-724
Seven Hills, Ohio, village situated 7 mi (11 km) s.e. of Parma Heights; residential suburb of Cleveland; pop. 13,650.
Seven Hills of Rome R-249, 254
Seven Islands, Quebec. *see in index* Sept-Iles
'Seven Lamps of Architecture, The', work by Ruskin A-561
Seven modern wonders of the world S-116

'Seven Pillars of Wisdom', work by Lawrence L-99

Seven Pines, battle of. *see in index* Fair Oaks, battle of

Seven Seas, The, name given to North and South Atlantic, North and South Pacific, Indian, Arctic, and Antarctic oceans; figuratively, all oceans of the world; title of a collection of poems by Kipling.

Seven Sleepers, in medieval legend, seven Christian youths of Ephesus who during persecution under Emperor Decius in 3rd century hid in cave and there fell into a miraculous sleep that lasted nearly 200 years.

17th Amendment, United States constitution L-276

Seventeen-year cicada (incorrectly called 17-year locust), insect C-413
  locust L-283

Seventh-day Adventists, Christian denomination believing in second coming of Christ, baptism by immersion, and observing the seventh day (Saturday) as Sabbath; originated about 1844; expenses of ministry met by tithing system; extensive foreign missions. For membership of Adventist bodies A-53. *see also in index* Adventists

Seventh Day Baptists, evangelical body, observing seventh day of the week as the Sabbath; first Seventh Day Baptist church in America was organized at Newport, R.I., on Dec. 23, 1671 (Old Style).

Seventh Day Baptists, outgrowth of German Baptist Brethren (Dunkers), founded 1728, near Ephrata, Pa. (near Lancaster), by John C. Beissel, of Germany; observe seventh day as Sabbath; emphasize Ten Commandments as rule of righteousness P-166, *picture* P-173

'Seventh Seal, The' (1956), motion picture B-166, *picture* M-610

'Seventh Symphony', work by Beethoven M-666

Seven Weeks' War (or Austro-Prussian War) (1866), between Austria and Prussia, *list* W-13
  Austria A-830
  Germany G-122
  Hanover H-32
  Moltke M-527

Seven Wise Men of Greece S-255

Seven Wonders of the World S-114. *see also in index* each of the seven by name

Seven Years' War (1756–63) S-117
  Frederick the Great F-390, A-830
  French and Indian War C-93, F-393
  Germany G-121
  Great Britain E-248
  India S-118
  Maria Theresa M-134
  New Orleans N-233
  Peace of Paris U-169
  warfare, *list* W-14

Severn, Joseph (1793–1879), English painter, friend of Keats, of whom he painted several portraits; noted work is 'Spectre Ship'.

Severnaya Zemlya, (also Northern Land, formerly Nicholas II Land), U.S.S.R., archipelago in Arctic Ocean, n. of central Siberia; discovered 1913, *maps* R-322, 345, P-417
  Asia, *map* A-700

Severn River, river traversing England and Wales; rises in Wales and flows 210 mi (340 km) to Bristol Channel
  England E-230
  Wales W-5

Severn River, river in n.w. Ontario; flows 350 mi (560 km) through Severn Lake to Hudson Bay, *maps* C-112, N-351

Seversky, Alexander Procofieff, de (1894–1974), U.S. airplane designer, born in Tbilisi, Russia; while aviator in World War I was shot down and lost right leg; returned to service and brought down 13 German planes; came to U.S. 1917, citizen 1927; designed speed, pursuit, and amphibian planes; advocate of supremacy of air power in war; author of 'Victory Through Air Power', 'Air Power: Key to Survival', and 'America: Too Young to Die!'.

Severus, Alexander. *see in index* Alexander Severus

Severus, Lucius Septimius (146–211), Roman soldier-emperor, raised to throne by provincial legions 193; spent reign chiefly in warfare; rebuilt Hadrian's wall in Britain. *see also in index* Leptis Magna

Sevier, John (1745–1815), U.S. frontiersman, first governor of Tennessee S-118
  Statuary Hall, *table* S-437b
  Tennessee T-87

Sevier Lake, salt lake in w. Utah, now dry for large part of year; fed by Sevier River, but has no outlet U-216, *maps* U-217, 233

Sevier River, river in w. Utah, flows n., then s.w. 200 mi (320 km) into Sevier Lake, *map* U-217

Sévigné, Madame de (1626–96), French letter writer S-118

Sevillana, Spanish dance in triple time; similar to seguidilla, which is called sevillana in Andalusia. *see also in index* Seguidilla

Seville (formerly Hispalis), Spain, an important seaport on the Guadalquivir River; pop. 598,000 S-118
  Europe, *map* E-361
  Spain S-355, *map* S-350

Sèvres, France, s.w. suburb of Paris on w. bank of Seine River; treaty between Allies and Turkey was signed here 1920; pop. 20,025, *map* F-372
  porcelain P-476

Sèvres, Treaty of (1920), *table* T-275
  Turkey T-323
  World War I W-319

Sewage disposal S-119
  bacteria used P-378
  disposal G-17
  gas G-38
  hydraulics H-339
  pollution P-441c
  water W-91

Sewall, Samuel (1652–1730), U.S. jurist, born in Hampshire, England; managed only licensed printing press in Boston A-342

Seward, Anna (pseudonym Swan of Lichfield) (1742–1809), English poet, born in Eyam; gave James Boswell information about Dr. Samuel Johnson; poems willed to Sir Walter Scott, who published them as 'The Poetical Works of Anna Seward'.

Seward, William Henry (1801–72), U.S. statesman S-121
  Alaska purchase A-245, A-339
  Johnson's administration J-109
  Pacific ocean P-16

Seward, Alaska, ice-free seaport on Kenai Peninsula; railroad terminus; shrimp, halibut, salmon processing; lumbering; hunting; August silver-salmon derby for fishermen; severely damaged by earthquake 1964; pop. 1,843, *maps* N-351, U-39

Seward Peninsula, in extreme w. of Alaska A-240, *maps* N-351, U-94, 39

Seward's Folly. *see in index* Alaska

Sewell, Anna (1820–78), English author, born in Yarmouth, England; permanently crippled in a childhood accident; in last years wrote 'Black Beauty' (published 1877), imaginary autobiography of a horse, *list* H-274

Sewell, Helen Moore (1896–1957), U.S. illustrator and author of children's books: born in Mare Island Navy Yard, Calif.; spent part of childhood on Guam; author of 'Blue Barns'; illustrator of 'First Bible' and books by many writers including Laura Wilder, Elizabeth Coatsworth, Frances Clarke Sayers, and Eleanor Farjeon R-107

Sewell, Joseph Wheeler (born 1898), U.S. baseball player, born in Titus, Ala.; shortstop Cleveland and New York, A.L., 1920–33; lifetime batting average .312.

Sewing S-121
  bookbinding B-353, *picture* B-355
  garment industry G-33
  needlework N-110
  quilts Q-17
    quilting bee Q-18

Sewing machine S-122
  clothing C-508
  garment industry G-33
  Industrial Revolution I-182, *picture* I-179
  inventions and inventors I-274, *table* I-273
    Howe H-312
  shoemaking S-179

Sex. *see also in index* Reproduction, *subhead* sexual; Sexuality
  adolescence A-48
  alcohol affects A-276
  bioethical issues B-214
  child abuse C-319
  education H-92
  Ellis' studies E-194
  family F-18
  Freud's theory P-519
  hypothalamus regulates B-400
  Kinsey's research K-248
  pornography P-451
  sex-linked genetic disorders G-48

'Sex', Broadway show by Mae West W-150

Sexagesimal system. *see in index* Base-sixty system

Sex cell. *see in index* Gamete

Sex Pistols, punk rock group M-682

Sextans, constellation, *chart* C-682

Sextant, instrument for measuring angles, especially to determine altitudes of celestial bodies above the horizon; uses arc of one sixth of a circle
  latitude and longitude L-80
  navigation N-72, 75

Sextilis, original name for the month of August. *see in index* August

Sexton, Anne Harvey (1928–74), U.S. author and poet, born in Newton, Mass.; won 1967 Pulitzer prize in poetry for 'Live or Die' A-364

Sexual abuse S-126

Sexual arousal S-124

'Sexual Behavior in the Human Female', work by Kinsey K-248

'Sexual Behavior in the Human Male', work by Kinsey K-248

Sexuality, the quality of being associated with sex or the sexes S-123
  marriage M-149

Sexually transmitted disease S-126

Sexual orientation S-125

'Sexual Politics', work by Millett W-279

Sexual reproduction. *see in index* Reproduction, subhead sexual

Seychelles, republic of some 90 islands and islets in Indian Ocean n. and n.e. of Madagascar; formerly British colony; independent 1976; 156 sq mi (404 sq km); cap. Victoria (pop. 14,500) on largest island Mahé (56 sq. mi.); pop. 62,000
  African political unit, *table* A-112
  Commonwealth membership C-602
  flag, *picture* F-170
  microcontinent development C-688
  United Kingdom E-259

Seymour (or St. Maur), noble English family; rose to power in Tudor times; heads became dukes of Somerset

Seymour, Charles (1885–1963), U.S. historian, educator, born in New Haven, Conn.; began teaching history at Yale 1911; to Paris Peace Conference 1919; provost Yale 1927–37, president 1937–50 ('Woodrow Wilson and the World War'; 'The Intimate Papers of Colonel House').

Seymour, Horatio (1810–86), U.S. statesman, born in Pompey, N.Y.; Civil War governor of New York State (draft riots); became Democratic candidate for presidency in 1868.

Seymour, Jane (1509?–37), 3rd queen of Henry VIII
  Henry VIII H-131

Seymour, Robert (1800?–1836), English caricaturist, first illustrator of 'The Pickwick Papers'; also known for 'Humorous Sketches' and 'The Book of Christmas'
  'Pickwick Papers', *picture* D-134

Seymour, Ind., city 18 mi (29 km) s. of Columbus; in agricultural area; automotive and plastics industries; settled 1850; pop. 15,050, *map* I-102

Seyss-Inquart, Arthur von (1892–1946), German political leader, born in Czechoslovakia; became a leader of Nazi movement in Austria; made governor of Austria after its seizure by Germany; deputy governor of German-occupied territory, Poland, 1939; Reich commissioner of Netherlands 1940–45; hanged as war criminal October 1946.

Sfax (or Safaqis), Tunisia, seaport at n. end of Gulf of Gabes; exporting; in region producing fine olives; phosphate; Sicilians occupied city in 12th century, Spaniards in 16th century; pop. 172,000 T-308, *map* A-118

Sforza, Carlo, Count (1873–1952), Italian statesman; foreign minister 1920–21; became anti-Fascist leader 1922; left Italy 1926; made head of the Italian National Committee in 1942; returned to Italy 1943; foreign minister 1947–51.

Sforza, Francesco (1401–66), Italian soldier of fortune, son of Muzio; conquered Milan and became first of Sforza dukes S-127

Sforza, Francesco (1495–1535), duke of Milan, son of Ludovico S-127

Sforza, Galeazzo Maria (1444–76), duke of Milan, son of Francesco S-127

Sforza, Gian Galeazzo (1469–94), duke of Milan, son of Galeazzo S-127

Sforza, Ludovico (or Ludovico il Moro Sforza) (1452–1508), duke of Milan, son of Francesco, regent for Gian Galeazzo S-127
  Leonardo da Vinci L-132

Sforza, Massimiliano (1492–1520), son of Ludovico S-127

Sforza, Muzio (originally called Muzio Attendolo) (1369–1424), Italian soldier of fortune, founder of Sforza dynasty S-127

Sforzando, in music, *list* M-671

SFPE (Society of Fire Protection Engineers), professional society F-112

S.F.S. Republic. *see in index* Russian Soviet Federated Socialist Republic

Sgambati, Giovanni (1843–1914), Italian pianist and composer, born in Rome; studied with Liszt; compositions strongly German in character; best known for piano pieces; also orchestral works.

Sgraffito, in art, a decoration produced by carving or scratching through a layer of overglaze, plaster, or paint to reveal the different undercolor
  pottery P-477

's Gravenhage, The Netherlands. *see in index* Hague, The

Sha (or urial), wild sheep found in n.w. India, Pakistan, Tibet, Afghanistan, Turkestan, and s. Iran; horns half-curved and flattened; color, reddish-brown and white.

SHA (sidereal hour angle) N-75

Shaanxi (or Shensi), province of China; 75,600 sq mi (195,800 sq km); cap. Xi'an; coal deposits; farmland produces fruit and cereals; pop. 29,660,000 S-127
  China C-373, *map* C-382–3

Shaba, former province, Zaire. *see in index* Katanga

Shabazz, el-Hajj Malik el-. *see in index* Malcolm X

Shack, type of house, *picture* H-302

Shackamaxon, Treaty of, agreement signed by William Penn and Delawares, June 23, 1683, at Shackamaxon, chief village of the Delawares, now part of Philadelphia; treaty granted Penn and his heirs land in s.e. Pennsylvania, *picture* P-175

Shackleton, Sir Ernest (1874–1922), British naval officer and Antarctic explorer; in 1909 reached point about 97 mi (156 km) from South Pole; sailed September 1921 on 3rd expedition but died on the way.

Shackleton Ice Shelf, Antarctica, borders Queen Mary Coast, on Indian Ocean; discovered and named for Sir Ernest Shackleton by Sir Douglas Mawson's expedition 1911–14.

Shad, an important food fish, lives in oceans, but goes up to coastal rivers to spawn; American, or common, shad weighs 3 to 6 pounds; roe is prized as food, *table* F-137
herring family H-144

Shadbush (or serviceberry, or Juneberry), shrubs or small slender trees composing the genus *Amelanchier* of the rose family with loose clusters of pretty white flowers followed by the sweet edible red or purple berrylike fruit.

Shaddock (or pummelo), citrus fruit *Citrus maxima* C-444, *picture* C-445

Shaded relief, in mapping M-121

Shad fly. *see in index* Mayfly

Shadoof, water-raising device, *picture* E-117

Shadow clock. *see in index* Sundial

Shadow Mountain National Recreation Area, in Colorado C-584

Shadow play P-538
motion pictures M-615

Shadows
eclipse. *see in index* Eclipse
signaling S-195a

Shadows, The, plantation home in Louisiana, *picture* L-317

'Shadows on the Pampas', work by Güiraldes L-70

Shadow stick, in direction finding D-159

Shadwell, Thomas (1642?–92), English poet and playwright, chiefly remembered for quarrel with Dryden, who satirized him in 'MacFlecknoe'; poet laureate 1688–92 P-402

Shaffer, John H(ixon) (born 1919), U.S. aviation executive, born in Everett, Pa.; vice-president of TRW, automotive-parts and aerospace firm, 1958–69; administrator FAA 1969–73.

Shaffer, Peter (born 1926), British playwright D-249

Shaft, feather F-50

Shaft, hair H-7

Shaft, machine M-10

Shafter, William Rufus (1835–1906), U.S. Army officer, born in Galesburg, Mich.; led volunteers in Civil War; in Spanish-American War commanded land forces in Cuba that took Santiago.

Shaftesbury, Anthony Ashley Cooper, first **earl of** (1621–83), English statesman; in Civil War in England fought first for king, then for Parliament; member of famous Cabal; lord chancellor
Carolina proprietorship S-309
Locke L-278

Shaftesbury, Anthony Ashley Cooper, 3rd **earl of** (1671–1713), celebrated moral philosopher, grandson of first earl ('Characteristics of Men, Manners, Opinions, and Times').

Shaftesbury, Anthony Ashley Cooper, 7th **earl of** (1801–85), Liberal Conservative political leader, philanthropist, and reformer, born in London; worked to improve conditions among poor; in 1842 effected passage of law forbidding employment of women and young children in coal mines.

Shaft mine M-427
coal mining C-521, *diagram* C-520

Shagari, Alhaji Shehu (born 1925), president of Nigeria (1979–83) N-313

Shagbark, hickory tree H-149

Shaggy-manes, mushroom *Coprinus comatus* M-665

Shagreen, variety of roughened, untanned, brightly dyed leather usually made from skin of ass, horse, or camel; also rough skin of shark or ray
sawfish S-52d
shark S-144

Shah Alam (1728–1806), Mughal emperor who had the protection of the British D-88

Shaham, Nathan (born 1925), Israeli writer H-114

Shahat, Libya. *See in index* Cyrene

Shah Jahan (formerly Prince Khurram) (1592–1666), Mughal emperor of India S-127
Delhi D-88
India I-71
Taj Mahal T-16

Shahn, Ben (1898–1969), U.S. artist S-128
'Handball', *picture* D-110
'Mine Disaster' P-62
'Ounce, Dice, Trice' R-111e, *picture* R-108

'Shah nameh' (or 'Shah namah', or 'Shahnama', or 'Book of Kings'), Persian epic I-367, S-469
Firdawsi's contribution F-92

Shah of Persia, diamond, *picture* D-129

Shahrashub, Persian verses I-107

Shahriyar, sultan in 'Arabian Nights' A-524

Shah Shoja (1780–1842), king of Afghanistan A-91

Shah Wali Allah (1702–62), Islamic theologian I-107

Shai, in Egyptian mythology F-44

Shairi, nonreligious poetry A-121

Shaka (1787?–1828), chieftain of Zulu empire S-128

Shaker Heights, Ohio, city 7 mi (11 km) e. of Cleveland; residential area; incorporated as village 1912, as city 1931; pop. 32,487.

Shakers (officially called United Society of Believers in Christ's Second Appearing), name given, originally in derision because of bodily movements during worship, to religious denomination (offshoot of English Quakers); founded by Ann Lee, who emigrated from England with followers in 1774; advocate celibacy and Christian communism S-128, *picture* N-184

Shakespeare, Frank J(oseph), Jr. (born 1925), U.S. communications executive, born in New York, N.Y.; executive vice-president CBS-TV 1965–69; chief TV adviser to Richard M. Nixon in presidential campaign 1968; director U.S. Information Agency 1969–72.

Shakespeare, John (died 1601), father of William Shakespeare S-129
coat of arms S-131
office and home, *picture* S-130

Shakespeare, Mary (Arden) (died 1608), mother of William Shakespeare S-129

Shakespeare, William (1564–1616), the greatest of English poets and dramatists S-129
chief plays
'Julius Caesar' P-526a
'Romeo and Juliet' R-112d, R-258
drama D-243, T-160
Elizabeth I E-191
English literature E-267
figures of speech F-81
Latin literature influences L-76
opera O-567
plots P-394
poetry H-247, 273
sonnets P-406
verse form P-405
puppets P-537
quotations P-406
Stratford-on-Avon S-484b
'Twisted Tales' R-112
world defined W-295

Shakespeare Memorial Theatre, in Stratford-on-Avon, England S-484b

Shakti, mother goddess in Hinduism H-157

Shaku, Japanese unit of measure, *table* W-141

'Shakuntala'. *see in index* 'Sakuntala'

Shale, stratified rock resembling slate S-212, R-229a
carbon C-156
clay. *see also in index* Clay
fuel source F-442
minerals M-437
oil-bearing shale P-230, U-216
quarrying Q-6
rock cycle, *chart* R-229

Shaler, Nathaniel Southgate (1841–1906), U.S. geologist, born in Newport, Ky.; professor at Harvard University 1868–87; dean of Scientific School 1891 ('First Book in Geology'; 'Man and the Earth').

Shaler, Pa., urban township situated just n. of Pittsburgh on Allegheny River; chiefly residential; pop. 33,369.

Shalimar Gardens, in Lahore, Pakistan L-23

Shallow-focus earthquake, type of earthquake E-38

Shallow-water wave (or long wave), type of ocean wave O-487

Shalmaneser II (or Shalmaneser III), king of Assyria, reigned 858–823 BC; reign marked by constant campaigns against eastern peoples; annals of reign engraved on black marble obelisk now in British Museum A-635

Sham, ash-, Syria. *see in index* Damascus

Shamanism, religion of the Ural-Altaic peoples living from Bering Strait to borders of Scandinavia; found in varied forms among Eskimos and American Indians; based on belief that good and evil come from ancestral spirits, gods, and demons that can be influenced by the priest or medicine man (shaman).

'Shame', film by Bergman B-166

'Shame of the Cities, The', work by Steffens M-654

Shamir, Moshe (born 1921), Israeli writer H-114

Shamir, Yitzhak (born 1915), Israeli politician, born in Yitzhak Jazernicki, Poland; a founder and leader of terrorist Stern Gang 1940–41; exiled from Israel 1946; given political asylum in France; returned to Israel 1948; speaker of Knesset 1977–80; minister of foreign affairs 1980–83; prime minister 1983–84, 1986–; deputy prime minister and foreign affairs minister 1984–86 I-374

Shamokin, Pa., city about 40 mi (60 km) n.e. of Harrisburg; anthracite mining, textile manufacturing, apparel, paper, furniture; pop. 10,357, *map* P-185

Shamoying, in leathermaking L-110

Shamrock, plant S-143

Shams ad-Din (13th century), Persian mystic J-17

Shandong (or Red Eyebrows), Chinese rebel group who overthrew Emperor Wang Mang in AD 23 C-362

'Shane', novel R-112, *picture* R-112b

Shang Dynasty (or Yin Dynasty), in Chinese history (1767–1123 BC) C-359
ancient civilization A-406
clothing C-507
pottery P-470

Shanghai, China, largest city and chief port, near mouth of Yangtze Kiang; pop. 11,859,748 S-143
Asia, *picture* A-682, *map* A-700
China, *pictures* C-344, 374, *map* C-383
warfare, *picture* W-20

Shanghaiing, form of kidnapping K-234

Shangri-La, mythical country created by James Hilton in his novel 'Lost Horizon'; name also given to place (later revealed as the aircraft carrier *Hornet*) from which James H. Doolittle led bombing raid on Tokyo April 1942; and to presidential retreat of F.D. Roosevelt.

Shang Yang, Chinese reformer C-385

Shannon, Monica (1898?–1965), poet and author of children's books, born in Belleville, Ont.; later made home in California; Newbery Medal (1935) for 'Dobry'.

'Shannon', British warship L-98

Shannon Airport, in Ireland I-321

Shannon River, river in Ireland, longest in British Isles; rises in Cavan County and flows 240 mi (390 km) s.w. to Atlantic, traversing series of lakes I-317

Shan Plateau, in e. Burma B-508

Shanti Nagar, a leper colony founded by the Order of the Missionaries of Charity T-110

Shantung (or Shandong), province on e. coast of China; 54,000 sq mi (140,000 sq km); cap. Tsinan; pop. 76,375,000, *map* C-383
World War I dispute W-319

Shantung, silk fabric with plain weave and a rough, uneven texture; originally hand-loomed in Shantung Province, China; now also made of silk and cotton or rayon blends S-201

Shanty, type of house H-301

'Shanty-man's Life, The', a lumberjack song F-265

Shanxi, province in n. China; 60,000 sq mi (155,400 sq km); cap. Taiyuan; sacred mountain in n.e. attracts pilgrims; pop. 22,451,000, *map* C-383
prehistoric human fossils C-359

SHAPE. *see in index* Supreme Headquarters, Allied Powers, Europe

Shaper, a tool T-220, *picture* T-218

Shapiro, Karl (Jay) (born 1913), U.S. poet, born in Baltimore, Md.; editor of *Poetry*, a magazine of verse, 1950–56; professor of English University of Nebraska 1956–66, University of Illinois 1966–68, University of California 1968– ('Person, Place and Thing'; 'V-Letter, and Other Poems', Pulitzer prize 1945; 'Essay on Rime'; 'Trial of a Poet'; 'Poems of a Jew'; 'The Bourgeois Poet'; 'Edsel', novel).

Shapley, Harlow (1885–1972), U.S. astronomer, born in Nashville, Mo.; director of observatory 1921–52 and professor of astronomy 1921–56 Harvard University; investigated brilliancy and composition of stars, measured spiral nebulae, and determined distances from earth of globular star clusters and Milky Way; wrote 'The View from a Distant Star'; main editor of 'The New Treasury of Science'.

Sharaku, Toshusai (1775?–1810?), Japanese color-print artist; started career as No dancer; noted for portraits, generally satiric, of dancers and theatrical idols of his day.

Sharecropping (or tenant farming), the operation of a farm in exchange for a share of the crop; in U.S. sharecropping arose after Civil War in cotton cultivation of the South
agriculture A-132
Brazil S-276, *picture* S-282
feudalism F-69
India I-69
Japan L-29
United States
cotton C-739
Douglass D-236
Reconstruction R-116

Shared electron pair V-255

Sharett, Moshe (named Moshe Shertok until 1949) (1894–1965), Israeli Zionist leader, born in Kherson, Russia; one of chief founders of state of Israel; foreign minister 1948–56; prime minister 1953–55; member of Knesset 1948–65.

Shariah, Islamic religious law
Iranian constitution I-307

Shari River, river flowing through Central African Republic and Chad; chief tributary of Lake Chad; about 900 mi (1,450 km) long; partly navigable, *map* A-118

Shark, fish S-144, *pictures* F-125, S-411
animal classification A-432
animal life record, *table* E-24
brain, *diagram* B-401
Devonian period A-461, *picture* A-460
egg, *picture* E-111
embryo, *diagram* E-201
fish F-124

Sharkey, Jack (born 1902), U.S. boxer, born in Binghamton, N.Y. B-391

Sharkskin, plain or basket weave fabric of dull filament rayon or of twilled worsted or woolen; feels very smooth and firm; a popular material for summer sportswear and suits.

Shark sucker (or remora), carnivorous fish, widely distributed in warm seas; family Echeneidae; first dorsal fin modified to a sucking disk, with which it attaches itself to sharks, barracudas, and other large fish, as well as to boats F-128

Sharman, Bill (born 1926), U.S. basketball player B-100

Sharon, Mass., town 9 mi (15 km) w. of Brockton; electronic pacemakers, wooden boxes; incorporated 1765; pop. 13,601.

Sharon, Pa., city on Shenango River at Ohio border near Youngstown, Ohio, and about 60 mi (100 km) n.w. of Pittsburgh, Pa.; steel and iron products, electrical equipment, railroad cars; pop. 19,057, *map* P-184

Sharon, Plain of, in w. Israel along Mediterranean between Tel Aviv-Jaffa and Haifa; region mentioned in Bible.

Sharon, Rose of. *see in index* Rose of Sharon

Sharp, Becky, heroine of Thackeray's 'Vanity Fair', clever, unscrupulous adventuress; from poverty-ridden background, which she sought to overcome at all costs.

Sharp, Cecil James (1859–1924), English musical scholar F-273

Sharp, Dallas Lore (1870–1929), U.S. author and educator, born in Haleyville, N.J.; Methodist minister 1895–99; professor English, Boston University; wrote delightful essays and books on nature.

Sharp, Margery (or Mrs. Geoffrey Castle) (born 1905), English novelist; known for clever plots and humor ('The Nutmeg Tree'; 'Cluny Brown'; 'Britannia Mews'; 'Lise Lillywhite'; 'Rosa'; for younger readers: 'The Rescuers', 'Miss Bianca').

Sharp, William (1856–1905), Scottish author; wrote poetry and criticism under own name; as Fiona Macleod did more famous work, largely tales of Celtic world in mystical, poetic prose and verse.

Sharp, sign in music M-690

Sharpsburg, battle of. *see in index* Antietam, battle of

Shasta, American Indian tribe that lives in California *map* I-136, *table* I-139

Shasta, Mount, peak near n. boundary of California; 14,162 ft (4,316 m) C-34, *map* U-87, *picture* C-35
- volcanic degradation V-378

Shasta daisy, a perennial plant
- flowering time G-25

Shasta Dam, dam in California, on Sacramento River C-36, *picture* C-35

Shastri, Lal Bahadur (1904–66), Indian political leader; transportation minister 1947–58 except 1951–52 when general secretary of Congress party; minister commerce and industry 1958–61, home affairs 1961–63; prime minister 1964–66.

Shatalov, Vladimir A. (born 1927), Soviet cosmonaut, born in North Kazakh region; piloted Soyuz 4 and Soyuz "troika" (6, 7, 8) in 1969, Soyuz 10 in 1971, *table* S-348

Shatt-al-'Arab (or Shatt-el-Arab), name of lower course of Tigris and Euphrates rivers after their junction 120 mi (190 km) from the Persian Gulf E-327, T-184
- Abadan A-4

Shaughnessy, Thomas George, first **Baron** (1853–1923), Canadian railroad executive, born in Milwaukee, Wis.; in 1882 entered employ of Canadian Pacific Railroad, became president 1898.

Shaving cream S-231

Shaw, Anna Howard (1847–1919), U.S. suffrage leader and first woman ordained by Methodists, born in England; credited with large share in passage of U.S. suffrage amendment; president 1904–15 National American Woman Suffrage Association, *picture* W-276

Shaw, Artie (real name Arthur Arshawsky) (born 1910), U.S. musician, born in New York, N.Y.; clarinetist, bandleader, and radio star; top recordings 'Begin the Beguine' and 'Frenesi'; compositions include 'Concerto for Clarinet' M-684

Shaw, George Bernard (1856–1950), Irish dramatist S-145. *see also in index* Nobel Prizewinners, *table*
- Belloc B-157
- drama D-246
- Fabian Society F-2, S-235
- Irish literature I-326
- literary contribution E-278
- puppets P-537

Shaw, Irwin (1913–84), U.S. writer, born in New York City ('Bury the Dead', play; 'Sailor Off the Bremen', 'Tip on a Dead Jockey', 'Love on a Dark Street', short stories; 'The Young Lions', 'Rich Man, Poor Man', novels) A-360
- drama D-248

Shaw, Lemuel (1781–1861), U.S. jurist, born in Barnstable, Mass.; admitted to bar 1804 and began practice of law in Boston, Mass.; drafted first charter of Boston 1822 (in effect until 1913); chief justice Massachusetts Supreme Court 1830–60
- photography, *picture* P-293

Shaw, Richard Norman (1831–1912), British architect, born in Edinburgh; although schooled in traditional forms, he developed a strikingly individual style; great influence; member of the Royal Academy.

Shaw, Robert Gould (1837–63), U.S. soldier, born in Boston, Mass.; led black regiment in Civil War; killed in attack on Fort Wagner.

Shaw, Robert Lawson (born 1916), U.S. musical conductor, born in Red Bluff, Calif.; director of Fred Waring Glee Club 1938–45; director of choral activities Juilliard School of Music 1946–49; founder (1948) and director (1948–66) of Robert Shaw Chorale; associate conductor Cleveland Orchestra 1956–66; conductor Atlanta Symphony Orchestra 1967–.

Shaw, Wilbur (1902–54), U.S. auto racing driver, born in Shelbyville, Ind.; raced 1921–41; president Indianapolis Speedway 1945–54.

'Shaw', U.S. naval destroyer, *picture* W-344

Shawangunk Mountains, mountains in New York N-246

Shawinigan, Que., city on St-Maurice River 20 mi (30 km) above Trois-Rivières; falls 150 ft (45 m) high furnish waterpower for manufacture of aluminum, pulp, paper, manganese, carbide; pop. 27,792, *maps* C-112, Q-10, 9c

Shawm, wind instrument W-226

Shawmut Peninsula, in Massachusetts B-371

Shawn, Ted (1891–1972), U.S. dancer, choreographer, and teacher; born in Kansas City, Mo.; in 1933 organized men's dance troupe that appeared in U.S. and England D-24

Shawnee, American Indian tribe that lives in Oklahoma P-166, *maps* I-136, 149, *table* I-139
- Boone's opposition B-365
- Harrison, *picture* H-49

Shawnee, Kansas, city 10 mi (16 km) s.w. of Kansas City, chiefly residential; animal biologicals, cookware; pop. 20,482.

Shawnee, Okla., city on North Canadian River 35 mi (55 km) s.e. of Oklahoma City, farm region; flour, feed, modular homes, pumps, glass, sausage; Oklahoma Baptist University; pop. 26,506, *map* U-41

Shawnee Lake, lake in Kansas, *picture* K-182

Shaw University, in Raleigh, N.C.; private control, Baptist affiliated; established 1865; present name 1875; liberal arts, education, religion.

Shayao Tower, in Tehran, Iran, *picture* I-305

Shayib, Jebel (or Mount Shayib), Egypt E-115

Shays, Daniel (1747?–1825), U.S. soldier, born in Hopkinton, Mass.; leader of Shays' Rebellion S-145
- Massachusetts M-195

Shays' Rebellion S-145

Shazar, Zalman (original name Shneor Zalman Rubashev) (1889–1974), Israeli political leader, born in Russia; to Palestine 1924; newspaper editor 1925–49; minister of education 1949–51; head of education department World Zionist Organization 1954–63; president of Israel 1963–73.

Shchedrin. *see in index* Saltykov, Mikhail Evgrafovich

Shea, Sir Ambrose (1815–1905), Canadian political leader, born in St. John's, Newf. C-118, *picture* C-116

Shear, in physics, breaking or deformation of a body by applied forces causing one portion to slide on another
- waves O-487

Shearing, metalworking operation I-346, T-225

Shearing, textile manufacturing process T-140

Shearling, type of fur F-463, *table* F-465

Shearwater, seabird belonging with petrel to family Procellariidae; in flight, skims surface of water; fat young birds considered delicacy, especially on Australian islands, where they are called muttonbirds.

Sheathbill, a white wading bird *Chionis* with horny sheath over nostrils; only land dweller in Antarctica; feeds on eggs of other birds.

Sheathing, in building construction B-493

Sheba, queen of, queen of great beauty, mentioned in Bible (I Kings, x); frequently regarded as ruler of Sabaeans in s. Arabia, the present Yemen Arab Republic
- ancient Arabia A-523
- Ethiopia E-314
- Solomon S-255

Sheba, kingdom that flourished around the 1st century BC in Yemen Y-415

Shebeli River. *see in index* Wabi Shebelle

Sheboygan, Wis., port city on Lake Michigan and Sheboygan River about 50 mi (80 km) n. of Milwaukee; dairying and cheesemaking in the area; plumbing supplies, enamelware, leather products, furniture, metal products, plastics, textiles; Lakeland College nearby; pop. 48,085, *map* U-41

Shechem, ancient city of Palestine, 30 mi (50 km) n. of Jerusalem; associated with Abraham, Jacob, and Joshua; made capital of kingdom of Israel by Jeroboam; later chief center of Samaritans; modern **Nablus,** Jordan; pop. 41,799.

Shed, in weaving S-391

Shedd Aquarium, in Chicago, Ill., *picture* A-517

Shedlock, Marie L., English storyteller ('The Art of the Storyteller'; 'Eastern Stories and Legends') S-461, 464

'She Done Him Wrong' (1933), motion picture by Sherman, *picture* M-624
- West W-150

Sheean, (James) Vincent (1899–1975), U.S. writer and foreign correspondent, born in Christian County, Ill. (political history of Europe 1938–39: 'Not Peace But a Sword'; autobiography: 'Personal History'; biography: 'The Indigo Bunting', on Edna St. Vincent Millay; 'Thomas Jefferson'; 'Mahatma Gandhi'; 'Orpheus at Eighty', on Giuseppe Verdi; 'Dorothy and Red', on Dorothy Thompson and Sinclair Lewis; and novels).

Sheeler, Charles (1883–1965), U.S. painter and photographer, born in Philadelphia, Pa.; his paintings of American scene are precisely painted in clear colors, with smooth surfaces, *picture* A-665

Sheen, Fulton J(ohn) (1895–1979), Roman Catholic bishop, born in El Paso, Ill.; professor of philosophy Catholic University of America 1927–50; bishop of Rochester, N.Y., 1966–69; noted radio and television preacher; won 1952 Emmy as most outstanding male personality on television ('Peace of Soul'; 'Lift Up Your Heart'; 'Three to Get Married'; 'Life Is Worth Living'; 'The Life of Christ').

Sheep S-146. *see also in index* Lamb; Wool
- anatomy
  - eye S-148
  - fur F-463, *tables* F-464, 465
  - hoof H-231
  - teeth R-318
- anthrax P-138, V-251
- breeding S-147
- corral, *picture* U-79
- domestication A-456
- fat-tailed S-148
- frontier F-423
- herding V-371, *picture* U-31
- Karakul S-146
- lifespan, *chart* A-423
- Lincoln S-147
- meat M-246. *see also in index* Mutton
- outlaws O-619
- producing regions
  - Australia A-807
    - Queensland Q-16
  - New Zealand N-290, *picture* N-291
  - Scotland S-69, *picture* S-68
  - South Africa S-265
  - South America S-281a
    - Uruguay U-213
  - Spain S-352, 362, *picture* S-353
  - United States, *picture* U-79
    - Great Plains G-249
    - New Mexico N-216, *map* N-218
    - Wyoming W-385, 388, *map* W-390, *picture* W-395
- Rambouillet S-147
- ruminant R-318
- Shropshire S-147
- wild S-148

Sheep, Rocky Mountain. *see in index* Bighorn

Sheep Islands, Danish group in Atlantic Ocean. *see in index* Faeroe Islands

Sheep laurel. *see in index* Lambkill

Sheep's-bit. *see in index* Jasione

Sheepshank, knot K-264

Sheepshead, most valuable food fish of porgy group; found along Atlantic and Gulf coasts; a favorite game fish; name also applied to the freshwater drum. *see also in index* Drum, fish

Sheepskin, kind of leather L-108

Sheep's-wool sponge (or wool sponge) S-394

Sheerness, England, seaport and naval station, with dockyard, on Isle of Sheppey at mouth of Thames River; in 1968 became part of municipal borough Queenborough-in-Sheppey; pop. 13,691.

Sheet, in boating, *diagram* B-326

Sheet, in metalwork I-346

Sheet, unit of measure, *table* W-140

Sheet bend (or weaver's knot), knot K-262

Sheet erosion, wasting away of level land in thin layers by water C-673

Sheet glass, type of glass G-158

Sheet-metal drafting M-262

Sheffield, Ala., city on Tennessee River, opposite Florence and near Wilson Dam; aluminum and aluminum products; pop. 13,115.

Sheffield, England, iron and steel manufacturing city of Yorkshire on Don River; pop. 528,860 S-148, *map* E-361

Sheffield steel S-148

Sheffield University, in Sheffield, England S-148

Shehan, Lawrence Joseph, Cardinal (1898–1984), Roman Catholic prelate, born in Baltimore, Md.; bishop of Bridgeport, Conn., 1953–61; archbishop of Baltimore 1961–74; became cardinal 1965.

Sheikh (or sheik), Arabian tribal leader A-526

Shekel, ancient unit of weight and coin of same weight, used by Babylonians, Phoenicians, and Jews; Hebrew gold shekel worth about $10, silver 75 cents.

Shelburne, N.S., seaport on s. coast 105 mi (170 km) s.w. of Halifax; shipbuilding, fish packing; pop. 2,654 N-401

Shelburne Museum, near Burlington, Vt., *pictures* V-295

Shelby, Isaac (1750–1826), U.S. soldier of Revolutionary War and War of 1812; first governor of Kentucky R-172

Shelby, N.C., city about 40 mi (60 km) w. of Charlotte; cotton, grain, poultry, cattle; textiles, hosiery, lumber products, food products; lithium and mica mined in vicinity; birthplace of Thomas Dixon; pop. 15,310.

Shelbyville, Ind., city on Big Blue River 27 mi (43 km) s.e. of Indianapolis; furniture, electrical equipment, paper and plastics, fiberglass, dresses, radio and television parts, heating equipment; pop. 14,989, *map* I-102

Shelbyville, Tenn., town on Duck River 50 mi (80 km) s.e. of Nashville; horse breeding; textiles, pencils, plastics,

Shire Plateau, plateau, Malawi M-68
Shirer, William L(awrence) (born 1904), U.S. reporter and foreign correspondent, born in Chicago, Ill. ('Berlin Diary'; 'Midcentury Journey', 'The Collapse of the Third Republic', 'Twentieth Century Journey', 'The Rise and Fall of the Third Reich'; for young people: 'The Rise and Fall of Adolf Hitler', 'The Sinking of the Bismarck') R-111j, D-272
Murrow M-658
newspapers N-239
Shire River, river transversing Malawi and Mozambique, flows from end of Lake Nyasa s. 370 mi (595 km) to Zambezi River; navigable from sea
Lake Nyasa N-449
Shirley, James (1596–1666), English dramatist, link between Elizabethan and Restoration periods ('The Traitor'; 'Hyde Park'; 'The Contention of Ajax and Ulysses').
Shirley, William (1694–1771), colonial governor of Massachusetts, born in Preston, England; organized expedition that took Fortress of Louisbourg (1745); succeeded Braddock as commander in chief of British forces in America.
Shirley Temple doll D-222, T-242
Shishak I. *see also in index* Sheshonk
Shite, Japanese drama J-54
Shiva, Hindu god. *see in index* Siva
Shivaism, worship of Hindu god Siva H-159
Shively, Ky., residential city just s.w. of Louisville; incorporated 1938; pop. 19,150.
Shizuoka, Japan, city on Honshu Island 55 mi (90 km) s.w. of Tokyo; textiles, metal products; pop. 446,952, *maps* J-78, A-700
Shkodër (or Scutari), Albania, city on Lake Scutari; taken by Austrians in World War I; pop. 43,234 A-258, *maps* B-27, E-358
Shkolnik, Levi. *see in index* Eshkol, Levi
Shoal (or school), group of fish F-127
Shoal Lake, lake in Canada, n.w. arm of Lake of the Woods, on border of Ontario and Manitoba 85 mi (140 km) s.e. of Winnipeg; area 114 sq mi (295 sq km); supplies water through aqueduct to Winnipeg.
Shoat, young pig P-320
Shochu, liquor L-235
Shock, medical disorder
blood replacement S-114
burn consequence B-511
first aid F-122
Shock absorber, automobile part A-854
Shockley, William (Bradford) (born 1910), U.S. physicist, born in London of U.S. parents; in U.S. after 1913; research physicist 1945–54; director transistor physics research Bell Telephone Laboratories 1954–55; Shockley Transistor Corp. president 1958–60, consultant 1960–65; Stanford University lecturer 1958–63, professor 1963–75. *see also in index* Nobel Prizewinners, *table*
electronics E-175
intelligence theories I-238
Shock therapy (or electroconvulsive therapy) T-167. *see also in index* Electroconvulsive treatment
medicine M-278
Shock wave (or seismic wave) P-235
nuclear weapons N-434
Shoe, footwear S-178. *see also in index* Boot; Sandal
jogging and running J-121
rubber R-304
St. Louis production S-22
shoe skates S-207, *pictures* S-208
Shoe brake B-404
Shoemaker, Bill (full name William Lee Shoemaker) (born 1931), U.S. jockey S-181
Shoen, Japanese medieval estate J-63
Shoe polish S-231
Shofar. *see in index* Shophar
Shogun, former commander in chief of Japanese armies and virtual ruler J-63
Hojo family H-200
Meiji M-287
Tokugawa family T-202
Tokyo T-210
'Shogun', work by Clavell
American literature A-361
historical novel N-409
Shoji, Japanese sliding doors J-29
Sholes, Christopher Latham (1819–90), U.S. inventor, printer, and newspaperman, born in Mooresburg, Pa.; state senator and editor of several newspapers in Wisconsin
invention I-274, *table* I-273
typewriter T-342
Wisconsin, *picture* W-255
Sholokhov, Mikhail Aleksandrovich (1905–84), Soviet writer, born in Veshenskaya on Don River; novels about Cossacks in Don River region; ('And Quiet Flows the Don'; 'The Don Flows Home to the Sea') R-360b. *see also in index* Nobel Prizewinners, *table*
Shona, group of culturally similar people of Africa
Mozambique M-641
Zimbabwe Z-452
Shonin, Georgi S. (born 1935), Soviet cosmonaut, born in Balta, near Odessa; commander Soyuz 6, *table* S-348
Shooting, in mining. *see in index* Blasting
Shooting script, motion picture M-606
Shooting star (or American cowslip), genus of perennial plants *Dodecatheon* of the primrose family, having white through rose-purple flowers with long, narrow petals bent back, exposing the yellow circle at the mouth of the corolla.
Shooting star. *see in index* Meteor and Meteorite
Shophar (or shofar), a trumpet made from a ram's horn; traditionally blown in the synagogue, at Rosh Hashana, the Jewish New Year festival.
Shopping center U-110, *pictures* U-109, 456
U.S.S.R., *pictures* R-332
Shopping goods M-142
'Shop Window: Tailor Dummies', photo by Atget, *picture* A-733
Shoran (or short-range navigation) N-71
Shore, Jane (died 1527), favorite of Edward IV of England; accused by Richard III of witchcraft; imprisoned.
Shorebird, popular term for a wading bird of seashore, mainly birds of order Charadriiformes; active and covered with down when newly hatched. *see also in index* Charadriiformes
Shoreditch, metropolitan borough of London, England
Shakespeare S-130
Shoreview, Minn., residential village and suburb in the Minneapolis-St. Paul metropolitan area; pop. 17,300.
Shorewood, Wis., residential village on Lake Michigan adjacent to n. Milwaukee; incorporated 1900 as **East Milwaukee** and renamed 1917; pop. 14,327.
Short, Walter C(ampbell) (1880–1949), U.S. Army officer, born in Fillmore, Ill.; commanding general of Hawaiian department of U.S. Army at time of Japanese attack on Pearl Harbor Dec. 7, 1941; relieved of command; found derelict of duty 1942 by presidential inquiry board, charges minimized to errors of judgment in 1946 Congressional investigation.
Short circuit, electricity S-8
Shortening, baking ingredient B-429
Shorter College, in Rome, Ga.; Southern Baptist; founded 1873; liberal arts, music, and education.
Short-haired cat, breed of cat C-205
Shorthand (or stenography) S-182
Pepys's diary P-198
vocational opportunities V-368, *picture* V-370
Shorthorn, breed of cattle C-226, C-230, *picture* C-229
Short-horned grasshopper, insect L-283
Short hundredweight, unit of weight, *table* W-140
Shortleaf pine, evergreen tree *Pinus echinata* of pine family; grows 80 to 100 ft (25 to 30 m) high; often lives 200 years; leaves in twos or threes to 5 in. (5 cm) long, blue green; cones oblong, to 2 in. (5 cm) long; heartwood light red or orange, surrounded by white sapwood.
Shortnose gar, a fish *Lepisosteus platostomus* of the family Lepisosteidae G-16
Short Parliament, in British history
Charles I C-274
Short-range navigation (or shoran) N-71
Short selling, stock market technique S-453
Short splice, knot K-264
Shortstop, position in baseball B-93
Short story L-244, S-183, *pictures* S-184. *see also in index* names of short-story writers
American literature A-360
China L-341
creative writing W-377, 382
novel N-408
Short-tailed opossum, marsupial M-157
Short-tailed shrew, mammal S-186
Short takeoff and landing (STOL) A-80
military aviation A-162, *picture* A-160
Short-term memory, level of memory M-294
Short ton, unit of weight, *table* W-140
Short-track racing, motorcycle M-632
Shortwave, radio
hobby H-190
Marconi M-132
world's largest station R-55
Short wave (or deepwater wave), type of ocean wave O-487
'Shosetsu shinzui' (or 'The Essence of the Novel'), work by Shoyo Tsubouchi J-82
Shoshone (or Snake), a North American Indian tribe that lives in Idaho, Nevada, Wyoming, and British Columbia, *map* I-136, *table* I-139
Idaho I-19
Lewis and Clark expedition L-144
Utah U-217
Wyoming W-387
Shoshone Falls, cataract in Snake River, in s. Idaho, *map* I-30, *picture* I-26
Shostakovich, Dimitri Dimitrievich (1906–75), Soviet composer S-185
classical music M-675
criticism C-778
Leningrad L-128
Shot, a ball used in track and field T-245, *picture* T-246
Shot (or take), in motion pictures M-606
Shotcreting, tunnel engineering T-313
Shotgun
firearms F-100, *picture* F-98
hunting safety guidelines H-331
trapshooting R-207
Shotgun formation, football strategy F-294
Shotoku, Prince (573–622), regent of Japan; important in development of Japanese civilization
Buddhism B-483
Shot tower, a high tower formerly used for making shot; melted shot metal poured in small streams from top of tower hardened into small round pellets as it fell; many towers preserved for historic interest in United States and Europe.
Shotwell, James Thomson (1874–1965), U.S. historian, born in Strathroy, Ont.; professor of history Columbia University 1908–42; director division economics and history Carnegie Endowment for International Peace 1924–48, president 1949–50; 'The Autobiography of James T. Shotwell'.
Shoulder, in anatomy
bones S-210
Shoulder Tap, game G-11
Shoup, David Monroe (1904–83), U.S. Marine Corps officer, born in Battle Ground, Ind.; commissioned 2nd lieutenant 1926; won Medal of Honor World War II; became 4-star general 1960; commandant U.S. Marine Corps 1960–63; retired 1963.
Shoup, George Laird (1836–1904), U.S. political leader and merchant, born in Kittanning, Pa.; colonel Union Army, in Civil War; first governor (Republican) of the state of Idaho (1890)
Statuary Hall, *table* S-437a
Shovelboard. *see in index* Shuffleboard
Shoveler, duck D-284
Showa constitution, in Japanese history J-34
'Show Boat' (1927), musical comedy by Kern and Hammerstein II M-686
Show Me State. *see in index* Missouri
Shrapnel, Henry (1761–1842), English soldier and inventor, born in Bradford-on-Avon, near Bath, England; invented the artillery shell bearing his name, first used in 1804 A-372
Shreve, Henry Miller (1785–1851), U.S. steamboat captain, born in Burlington County, N.J.; pioneer of steam navigation on Mississippi and tributaries; built the *President*, forerunner of shallow-draft Mississippi River steamboats; Shreveport, La., named for him S-185
Mississippi River M-486
Shreveport, La., 2nd city of state, on Red River; pop. 205,820 S-185, *maps* N-351, U-41
Louisiana's industry L-310
Shrew, insectivorous mammal S-185
lifespan, *chart* A-423
Shrew opossum, marsupial mammal M-156
Shrewsbury, England, old city, capital of Shropshire, on Severn River; famous school founded by Edward VI; Henry IV defeated and killed Hotspur (Sir Henry Percy) near here in 1403; pop. 54,190.
Shrewsbury, Mass., 5 mi (8 km) n.e. of Worcester; plastics, ball valves; biomedical research and development; incorporated 1727; pop. of township 22,674.
Shrike (or butcherbird), bird S-186
Shrimp, crustacean S-186, *picture* S-187
crustaceans C-790, *picture* C-791
fishing, *picture* G-95
Mississippi M-469
Shrimp fish, fish *picture* F-130
Shrine. *see also in index* Roman Catholicism
Buddhism R-92
Shrine, Masonic order, Ancient Arabic Order of Nobles of the Mystic Shrine, was founded in New York City 1872; more than 1 million members in 1980 F-387
Shrine of Remembrance, shrine in Melbourne, Australia M-290, *picture* M-291
Shrine to the Muses (or Museum to the Muses), founded by Ptolemy I G-277
Shrinkage, in textile manufacture T-141
Shrinkage stoping, mining method M-429
Shriver, Robert Sargent, Jr. (born 1915), U.S. business executive and lawyer, born in Westminster, Md.; assistant general manager Merchandise Mart, Chicago, 1948–61; director Peace Corps 1961–66; director Office of Economic Opportunity 1964–68; ambassador to France 1968–70; Democratic candidate for vice-president 1972; author of 'Point of the Lance'.
Shropshire, England, county on Welsh border; 1,347 sq mi (3,489 sq km); light industry; dairying; region noted for sheep; castle ruins and Roman ruins; pop. 297,466.
'Shropshire Lad, A', book of poems by Housman
creative writing W-381
English literature E-280
quoted P-405
Shropshire sheep, breed of sheep S-147
Shroud, of boat, *diagram* B-326
Shroud, of parachute P-109a, *diagram* P-109

art; university; pop. 61,453, *pictures* I-387, 393, *maps* E-361, I-404
Siena College, in Loudonville, N.Y.; Roman Catholic; opened 1937; chartered 1942; arts and sciences, business; graduate studies N-255
Siena College, in Memphis, Tenn.; Roman Catholic; founded 1922; closed 1972.
Siena Heights College, in Adrian, Mich.; Roman Catholic; incorporated 1919; liberal arts; graduate school.
Sienkiewicz, Henryk (1846–1916), Polish novelist ('Quo Vadis?', tale of Rome under Nero; 'With Fire and Sword', 'The Deluge', 'Pan Michael'—great historic trilogy of 17th-century Poland). *see also in index* Nobel Prizewinners, *table*; and 'Quo Vadis?'
Sienna, Italy. *see in index* Siena
Siepi, Cesare (born 1923), Italian operatic basso, born in Milan; member Metropolitan Opera Company 1950 and 1960s; active in concert, television, and radio, *list* O-570
Sierra Blanca, a mountain range in s. Colorado in Sangre de Cristo Mountains; Blanca Peak is highest summit (14,310 ft; 4,360 m).
Sierra de Gata, chain of mountains in Spain and Portugal separating the valleys of the Tagus and Douro rivers; 5,690 ft (1,735 m), *map* S-350
Sierra de Gredos, mountain range of central Spain; 8,730 ft (2,660 m) S-351, *map* S-350
Sierra de Guadalupe, mountain range in w. Spain; highest point, Cabeza del Moro, 5,110 ft (1,560 m), *map* S-350
Sierra de Guadarrama, mountain range of central Spain separating Old and New Castile; 7,900 ft (2,400 m), *map* S-350
  Civil War memorial, *picture* S-361
Sierra de Morena, low mountain range of s. Spain; rises slightly above Iberian plateau to the north and drops sharply on the south to valley of the Guadalquivir, *map* S-350
Sierra Leone, republic on w. coast of Africa north of Liberia; 27,925 sq mi (72,325 sq km); cap. Freetown; pop. 2,800,000 S-192a
  Africa, *map* A-118, *table* A-112
  Commonwealth membership C-602
  flag, *picture* F-170
  Freetown F-391
  illiteracy P-450
  railroad mileage, *table* R-85
Sierra Madre, name of the three mountain ranges in Mexico enclosing central plateau C-319, M-322
Sierra Nevada, loftiest mountain range in California S-192b, *maps* E-25, N-351, U-87
  California C-34
    Mount Whitney W-200
  formation E-15
  national parks
    Sequoia N.P. S-112
    Yosemite N.P. *see in index* Yosemite National Park
  Nevada N-133, *picture* N-132
Sierra Nevada (snowy range), loftiest mountain range in Spain; extends about 60 mi (100 km) e. and w. through Andalusia and Granada near Mediterranean coast; highest peak, Mulhacén, 11,411 ft (3,478 m); vineyards on s. slopes, *map* S-350
Sierra Nevada College, in Incline Village, Nev.; private control; established 1969; arts and sciences N-137
Sierra Vista, Ariz., city 24 mi (39 km) n.w. of Bisbee; ranching; electronic devices; incorporated 1956; pop. 25,968.
Sieyès, Emmanuel Joseph, Abbé (1748–1836), leader and pamphleteer in French Revolution; member of various revolutionary assemblies; published 1789 celebrated pamphlet beginning, "What is the Third Estate? Everything. What has it been? Nothing."
Sifton, Arthur Lewis (1858–1921), Canadian jurist and statesman; first chief justice of Alberta 1905–10; provincial premier 1910–17; Canadian delegate to peace conference at Versailles 1918; brother of Sir Clifford Sifton.
Sifton, Sir Clifford (1861–1929), Canadian statesman; prominent in Manitoba politics after 1888; Dominion minister of interior 1896–1905; chairman Dominion Conservation Commission 1909–18; in coalition cabinet 1917–21 and one of signers Treaty of Versailles.
Sigatoka, leaf spot disease banana B-52
Sigefroi (10th century), count of the Ardennes L-341
Sigel, Franz (1824–1902), U.S. soldier, born in Germany; major general in Civil War, active in keeping Missouri in Union and fought at Pea Ridge, 2nd battle of Bull Run, and Shenandoah Valley.
Sighs, Bridge of. *see in index* Bridge of Sighs
Sight. *see in index* Eye
Sigismund (1368–1437), Holy Roman emperor, succeeded 1410; caused convocation of Council of Constance, which ended the Great Schism 1417
  Hungary H-329
  Hus H-334
  Prussia P-516
Sigismund I (1467–1548), king of Poland J-12
Sigismund II Augustus (1520–72), king of Poland and Lithuania J-12
Sigismund III Vasa column, oldest monument in Warsaw, Poland W-33
Sigma Delta Chi, professional journalism fraternity; founded at DePauw University, Greencastle, Ind., 1909; honorary for college juniors and seniors; professional for men employed in the field, open to women since 1970; publishes *Quill*; headquarters Chicago, Ill.
Sigma Xi, national college honor society for scientific research, founded at Cornell University, Ithaca, N.Y., 1886.
Sign, in astrology A-707
Sign, element a physician can detect D-165
  medicine M-278
Signac, Paul (1863–1935), French painter; with Georges Seurat, developed neoimpressionism, also pointillism; influenced by Monet; noted for landscapes, street scenes, and marine subjects ('Venise', 'Pennoned Sailboats').
Signal Corps, U.S. Army A-646, S-193
  insignia S-193, *picture* U-10
  pigeons P-324
Signal Hill, in St. John's, Newf., where Marconi received the first transatlantic wireless message N-167
Signaling S-193, *Reference-Outline* V-243
  airplane S-195a. *see also in index* Airport
  bugle and trumpet S-193
  flags S-194a, *pictures* S-194b–5
  International Signal Code S-194a, 195a, *pictures* S-194b
  language substitute L-36
  lighthouses and light towers. *see in index* Lighthouse
  pigeons P-324
  radio S-194, 195a, *pictures* S-193, 195b
    microwave system S-195b, *picture* S-195a
    relay station, *picture* S-195a
  railroad R-80, *pictures* R-78, 84
  U.S. Army S-193
  U.S. Navy S-194, *pictures* S-193, 194a
  wigwag, *pictures* S-194b–195
Signatura, Apostolic, supreme Roman Catholic tribunal P-100
Signature, in printing, *picture* B-357
Signature (or autograph), in writing A-832
  book collecting B-262
  handwriting H-30
  letter writing L-139
  Shakespeare's signature, *picture* S-129
Signature, in music, *list* M-671
'Significance of the Frontier in American History, The', work by Turner T-327, F-424
'Significance of Sections in American History, The', work by Turner T-327
Sign language L-36
  American Indians I-135
  animal communication A-448
Signorelli, Luca (1441–1523), Italian painter, chiefly of religious subjects; finest works are frescoes; had deep knowledge of anatomy; forerunner of style of Michelangelo (frescoes in Orvieto Cathedral).
Signs, traffic
  international R-217
  traffic control T-247
Sigsbee, Charles Dwight (1845–1923), U.S. Navy officer, born in Albany, N.Y.; in command of battleship *Maine* when destroyed in Havana harbor (1898); commander of *St. Paul* in Spanish-American War; introduced numerous inventions in deep-sea exploration; retired 1907.
Sigsbee Deep, submarine plain in Gulf of Mexico
  Gulf of Mexico M-345
Sigurd, Norse hero of 'Volsunga Saga'; plays part taken by Siegfried in 'Song of the Nibelungs'; scholars dispute existence as historical figure H-273, S-471. *see also in index* Siegfried
Sigurdsson, Jon (1811–79), Icelandic statesman; waged a valiant fight for Icelandic home rule; chiefly responsible for obtaining constitution of 1874; made Reykjavik cultural as well as political capital of country.
Sihanouk, Norodom (born 1922), Kampuchean leader, born in Phnom Penh; king 1941–55; prime minister 1955–60; head of state 1960–70, 1975–76 K-170
Sijo, Korean poetry form K-280, K-293
Sikeston, Mo., city 30 mi (50 km) s. of Cape Girardeau; in farming area; flour, shoes, cottonseed oil, foundry and machine-shop products; pop. 17,431.
Sikhism, an Indian religion combining Islamic and Hindu elements, founded about 15th century; the Sikhs ruled Punjab from about mid-18th century until conquered by British (1849)
  Asia A-684
  England E-233
  Hinduism H-158
  India I-68, 80
  monks and monasticism M-542
Si Kiang (West River), largest stream in s. part of China; 1,250 mi (2,010 km) long; enters China Sea near Canton. *see also in index* Canton River
Sikkim, state in India in e. Himalayas, bounded by Nepal, Tibet, and Bhutan; 2,744 sq mi (7,107 sq km); cap. Gangtok; under treaty Dec. 5, 1950, Sikkim became a protectorate of India but retained internal autonomy; became a state of India 1975; pop. 209,843, *maps* I-79, 83
Sikorsky, Igor Ivan (1889–1972), U.S. airplane builder, born in Kiev, Russia; moved to U.S. 1919, became a citizen 1928; in 1912 constructed first successful multimotored airplane
  helicopter H-122
Sikorsky S-64 sky crane, helicopter H-123
Silage (or ensilage), a stored fodder S-202
  hay H-75
  legume L-120
Silas Lapham. *see in index* 'Rise of Silas Lapham, The'
Silbermann, Johann (1712–83), German builder of keyboard instruments M-689
'Silence, The', part of a film trilogy by Ingmar Bergman B-166
Silence Dogood, Mrs. *see in index* Franklin, Benjamin
Silene (popularly called catchfly, or campion), genus of annual or perennial herbs of the pink family with sticky stems; among the many species cultivated in gardens are *Silene armeria* (sweet William catchfly) with fragrant rose-colored flowers and *Silene acaulis* (moss campion), which forms a mosslike cushion and bears small pink or white flowers.
Silent cancer, small pockets of cancer cells D-176
Silent films, motion pictures M-617
'Silent Spring', work by Rachel Carson C-178
Silenus, Greek mythology, a satyr, pictured as old, fat, intoxicated; companion of Dionysus, whom he brought up; statue shows Silenus carrying infant Dionysus D-147
Silesia, central Europe, rich farm, factory, and mine (iron, zinc, coal) region divided into German (Upper and Lower) and Austrian Silesia before World War I; after this, Germany ceded 1,633 sq mi (4,229 sq km) of Upper Silesia to Poland following plebiscite, and Austrian Silesia became part of Czechoslovakia; Germany retained rest of Silesia (14,020 sq mi; 36,310 sq km) as a province of Prussia; in World War II, Germany regained all Silesia; after German defeat, Austrian Silesia was returned to Czechoslovakia, and nearly all of German Silesia was included in Poland. *see also in index* Silesian Wars
  history G-121
    Frederick the Great's conquest, *map* P-517
    Maria Theresa M-134
    Poland P-413
  products
    beet sugar S-507
    minerals P-413
Silesian Wars, three wars between Austria and Prussia over Silesia; the first (1740–42) and the second (1744–45) merged into the War of the Austrian Succession; the third (1756–63) is known as the Seven Years' War A-829. *see also in index* Austrian Succession, War of the; Seven Years' War
Silhouette, outline drawing, filled in with solid color, usually black; profile portraits cut from black paper and pasted on light mounting became popular about 1750; named from **Étienne de Silhouette** (1709–67), French minister of finance, whose drastic methods of economy made him a symbol for a figure reduced to lowest terms.
Silica, silicon dioxide S-195b
  dehumidifiers A-151
  glass G-156
  lava and magma L-89
  quartz. *see also in index* Quartz
  silica-alumina P-241a
Silica gel, a colloidal suspension of silicic acid made by dialysis from action of hydrochloric acid on water glass; when dried to 5% water, it resembles coarse sand and adsorbs gases strongly S-195b
Silicate, a salt of silicic acid S-195b
  brick B-436
  magnesium
  potassium P-465
Silicate mineral, classification M-436
Siliceous sinter (or geyserite), mineral M-432
  geyser G-138
Silicon (Si), metalloid S-195b. *see also in index* Silica; Silicate
  abrasive A-13
  bronze alloys B-463
  carbide S-195b
  Earth's crust, *table* E-11
  metal and metallurgy M-307
  microprocessor M-380
  minerals M-436
  periodic table, *table* P-207, *list* P-208
  properties, *table* S-195b
  semiconductors C-799
  solar battery, *picture* R-49
  structure, *diagram* S-254f
  transistor T-249
Silicon chip C-629
  electronics E-175
    calculators C-21
    transistor T-250
Silicone rubbers S-196
  insulating materials I-232
Silicones, plastic substances in which combinations of silicon and oxygen take the place of the usual carbon atoms S-196
  magnesium M-41
  uses, *table* P-382
Silicon steel S-195b
Silicon wafer, *picture* I-193
  electronics E-177
Silicosis, disease of the lungs, caused by inhaling tiny sharp particles of stone dust; fibrous tissue forming around particles causes cough, shortness of breath, and weakness D-177
  industrial health hazards I-175
  mine and mining M-431

Si Ling-chi, legendary Chinese empress, began silk culture S-201
Silk S-197. *see also in index* Silkworm
butterflies and moths B-525
button type B-531, *picture* B-529
clothing C-509
cocoon S-198
decorative arts
paintings P-67e, *picture* P-67f
tapestry T-25
fiber F-71, 76
manufacturing centers
Lyon L-344
Pakistan, *picture* P-78
manufacturing processes S-200
mulberry M-648, S-198
producing regions
China, *picture* C-356
Japan S-197, 202, *pictures* S-198
Spain V-256
reeling S-199
spider thread S-382
spun S-201
stringed instruments S-490
synthetic
rayon R-97, *picture* R-98
textiles T-138
wild silk S-201
Silk, threadlike filaments on corn plant C-719, *picture* C-720
Silk-cotton tree (or ceiba, or kapok), tropical tree belonging to family Bombacaceae; seeds of some species are covered with a cottony substance called silk cotton. *see also in index* Kapok
Silk-oak. *see in index* Grevillea
Silk-screen printing (or serigraphy), printmaking P-503
graphic arts G-233
Silkworm S-197, *picture* I-227
mulberry M-648
rayon process imitation R-97
scientific classification B-528
spiracle, or breathing hole, *picture* R-159
Silky terrier, dog, *picture* D-206
Sill, Edward Rowland (1841–87), U.S. poet and essayist, born in Windsor, Conn.; notable for choice diction and spiritual philosophy; 'Opportunity' and 'The Fool's Prayer' are among his best-known poems.
Sill, architecture B-492, *picture* B-493
Silla, former Korean kingdom K-281, 284
Sillanpää, Frans Eemil (1888–1964), Finnish writer, son of peasants in parish of Hameenkyrö; wrote realistically of simple people ('The Maid Silja', 'Meek Heritage'). *see also in index* Nobel Prizewinners, *table*
Silliman, Benjamin (1779–1864), U.S. chemist and geologist; professor at Yale University; founded and edited *American Journal of Science*; founder member of National Academy of Science.
Sillimanite, an aluminum silicate forming in slim white or colored crystals, sometimes cut as gems; called fibrolite when found in brown or gray masses.
Sillitoe, Alan (born 1928), English author and poet, born in Nottingham ('The Loneliness of the Long Distance Runner').
Sills, Beverly (originally Belle Miriam Silverman) (born 1929), U.S. operatic soprano, *list* O-570
Sills, Paul, U.S. theater director A-28
Silo, farm S-202
hay H-75
Silo, underground hardened missile storage and launching site, *picture* G-309
White Sands Missile Range, *picture* E-378
Siloam, pool in Jerusalem, forming part of ancient water supply; fed by tunnel from "fountain of the Virgin"; in wall is cut oldest known Hebrew inscription.
Silone, Ignazio (pseudonym of Secondo Tranquilli) (1900–78), Italian author, born near Arezzano; 'Bread and Wine' and 'Fontamara' are uncensored accounts of life in Italy under dictatorship; 'Emergency Exit', memoirs I-378, *picture* I-377
Silt (or suspended soil), earthy sediment carried and deposited by water. *see also in index* Alluvial soil
earth E-32
grain size, *table* S-36
lake bottoms, *diagram* P-441d
rivers convey R-210, 211
watershed mismanagement C-673
Silurian period, geological time
Australia A-774
British Isles B-460
Earth E-23, *table* E-24
Silva, José Asunción (1865–96), Colombian poet, born in Bogotá L 73
Silvanus, Latin mythology, the god of fields and forests; represented with young tree and pruning hook.
Silver (Ag), metallic element S-202. *see also in index* Colloidal silver; Silverware
alchemy A-273
assaying A-705
coins C-537
compounds S-204
design D-116
mercury M-305
metalworking M-310
minerals M-432
money M-530
McKinley administration M-19
ore O-600
periodic table, *table* P-207, *list* P-208
photographic film P-293, 296
producing regions
Mexico M-329, 333
United States U-85
Denver D-103
government depository U-158
Nevada N-135
properties, *table* S-202
solder S-204
sterling S-203
toxic waste W-76
trade
Argentine colonization A-582
Sumerian B-6
Silver Age, Latin literature L-77
Silver Belt, region of Mexico M-333
Silver City, N.M., health resort and mining center in s.w.; Western New Mexico University; founded 1870, incorporated 1878; pop. 9,887, *maps* N-229, U-40
Silver dollar. *see in index* Lunaria
Silver dollar, a coin C-539, *picture* C-543
Silver fir (or Cascade fir), evergreen tree *Abies amabilis* of pine family, native from British Columbia to Oregon; grows 60 to 200 ft (18 to 60 m) high; leaves flat, notched at tip, to 1 in. (2.5 cm) long, with 2 white bands on underside; cones to 6 in. (15 cm) long, purple; sometimes called lovely fir and Pacific silver fir; wood similar to and sold as "white fir"; a smaller tree *A. alba* but similar, native to central and s. Europe and cultivated in N. America, is also called silver fir F-92
Silverfish (or fish moth), an insect *Lepisma saccharina* of the order Thysanura, family Lepismatidae; common in the U.S. and much of the world, *picture* I-213
Silver fox F-337
farming P-497b
fur, *table* F-464, *picture* F-466
Silver gar, a fish *Strongylura marina* G-16
Silver hake. *see in index* Whiting
Silver halide, photography P-293
Silver lead. *see in index* Graphite
Silver leaf, metal S-203
Silverman, Belle Miriam (known as Beverly Sills) (born 1929), U.S. operatic soprano, *list* O-570
Silver maple, tree *A. saccharinum* M-112
Silver mirror M-465
Silver nitrate (or lunar caustic), a cauterizing antiseptic S-204, A-495
Silverplating K-257
electrolysis E-161
Silver poplar. *see in index* White poplar
Silver purchase acts, United States S-204
Silver salmon (or coho salmon), fish S-28
Silversides, small and silvery fish *Menidia* of family Atherinidae; carnivorous; inhabits fresh or brackish shallow water.
'Silversides', U.S. submarine, *picture* S-498
Silver-spotted skipper butterfly, *picture* B-523
Silver Spring, Md., community just n. of Washington, D.C.; pop. 72,893, *map* M-183
Silver Springs, limestone spring in Florida F-194
Silver state. *see in index* Nevada
Silver sulfide S-203
Silvertip. *see in index* Grizzly bear
Silverware
manufacture, *picture* S-204
craftsman, *picture* R-182
tableware K 257
tarnishing S-509
Silvester. *see in index* Sylvester
Sima, geochemistry C-689
Simcoe, John Graves (1752–1806), English soldier and first lieutenant governor of Upper Canada (1792–96); took active part in American Revolution
London, Ont. L-295
Ontario O-553
Simcoe, Lake, in Canada, 30 by 18 mi (50 by 29 km); 160 sq mi (415 sq km); empties into Lake Huron through Georgian Bay.
Simenon, Georges (Joseph Christian) (pseudonym Georges Sim) (born 1903), Belgian novelist, born in Liège; prolific writer with concise style; gained early fame with 'Maigret' mystery series; later psychological novels have tragic, often frightening twist ('The Train'; 'The Confessional')
detective story D-119
Simeon, figure in Old Testament, ancestor of tribe of Simeon; second son of Jacob and Leah (Gen. xxix, 33); with brother Levi killed the men of Shechem to avenge attack on their sister Dinah.
Simeon, devout man who saw the infant Jesus in his presentation at the temple and uttered the prophetic song called 'Nunc dimittis' (Luke ii, 25–35).
Simeon (or Symeon) (died AD 927), Bulgarian ruler B-500
Simeon Stylites, Saint (4th–5th century), Syrian monk, first and most famous of the "Pillar Saints," who lived on high pillars; festival Jan. 5 A-492
Simferopol', U.S.S.R., city on Crimean peninsula; famous for fruit; food processing; canning machinery; pop. 250,000, *maps* E-361, R-344, 349
Simile, a figure of speech F-81
creative writing W-379
Simi Valley, Calif., city 33 mi (53 km) n.w. of Los Angeles; nuclear generators, rocket engines, mobile homes; pop. 77,500.
Simla, India, former summer capital; now in Himachal Pradesh state in India, 170 mi (270 km) n. of Delhi; beautifully set in Himalayas, 7,000 ft (2,130 m) high; popular health resort; pop. 55,368, *map* I-86
Simmental, breed of cattle C-230, *picture* C-229
Simmer, in cooking C-700
Simmons, Aloysius Harry (real name Aloysius Harry Szymanski, nickname Bucketfoot) (1903–56), U.S. baseball player, born in Milwaukee, Wis.; outfielder chiefly Philadelphia, A.L., 1924–32, and Chicago, A.L., 1933–35; led league in batting 1930–31 and in runs batted in 1930.
Simmons, Jean, U.S. actress, *picture* L-243
Simmons College, in Boston, Mass.; private control; for women; founded 1899, opened 1902; liberal arts, business administration, education, home economics, library science, nursing, publication, retailing, science, social science, social work; coeducational in graduate work.
Simms, William Gilmore (1806–70), U.S. writer, born in Charleston, S.C.; prolific writer ('Atlantis', his strongest poem; 'Martin Faber', story of a criminal; 'The Yemassee', Indian tale of colonial Carolina; lives of Francis Marion, Nathanael Greene, Capt. John Smith) A-347, *picture* S-316
Simon, Charlie May. *see in index* Fletcher, Charlie May
Simon, Herbert A. (born 1916), U.S. social scientist, born in Milwaukee, Wis.; at Carnegie-Mellon University since 1949, professor of administration and psychology 1949–65, of computer science and psychology 1965–; work on analysis of decision-making process within organizations, later work on artificial intelligence and computers. *see also in index* Nobel Prizewinners, *table*
Simon, John Allsebrook, viscount of Stackpole Elidor (1873–1954), British Liberal statesman and lawyer, born in Manchester, England; chairman of Indian statutory commission 1927–30; foreign secretary 1931–35; home secretary 1915–16, 1935–37; chancellor of the exchequer 1937–40; lord chancellor of England 1940–45.
Simon, Neil (born 1927), U.S. playwright and television and motion picture writer, born in New York, N.Y. ('Barefoot in the Park'; 'Sweet Charity'; 'Promises, Promises'; 'The Odd Couple'; 'The Sunshine Boys')
modern drama A-363, D-249
Simon, Paul (born 1942), U.S. songwriter and performer, born in Newark, N.J.; collaborated with **Art Garfunkel** (born 1941), U.S. singer, born in Forest Hills, N.Y.; together they recorded seven best-selling albums 1964–70; 'Bridge Over Troubled Waters', their last album together, won six Grammy awards; composed and recorded the soundtrack for film 'The Graduate' 1968.
Simon, Théodore (1873–1961), French psychologist and physician; developed with Alfred Binet the Binet-Simon intelligence test B-197, I-239
Simon, William Edward (born 1927), U.S. government official, born in Paterson, N.J.; director Federal Energy Office 1973–74; secretary of the treasury 1974–77; newspaper executive after 1977.
'Simon Boccanegra', opera by Verdi O-567
Simon Commission, British government agency in India I-77
Simon Fraser University, in Brunaby, B.C.; provincial control; opened 1965; arts and sciences, education, *picture* B-354
Simonides (556–469 BC), Greek lyric poet, known as Simonides of Ceos from the island of his birth; a finished craftsman but not a great imaginative poet; celebrated the heroes of his own day in a great variety of verse.
Simon Magus, Samaritan sorcerer, converted to Christianity, who offered Peter and John money for the power of the Holy Ghost (Acts viii).
Simonov, Konstantin (1915–79), Soviet author and dramatist; graduate of Literature Institute of Union of Soviet Writers; winner of many literary awards R-360b, 362
Simon Peter. *see in index* Peter, Saint
Simons, David G(oodman) (born 1922), U.S. Air Force physician, born in Lancaster, Pa.; research in space biology.
Simons, Menno. *see in index* Menno
Simonsen Opera Company, Australia A-801
Simonson, Lee (1888–1967), U.S. scenic designer and art critic, born in New York City; designed scenery for 'Peer Gynt', 'Elizabeth the Queen', 'Jane Eyre'; author of 'The Stage Is Set' and 'Theatre Art'.
Simont, Marc (born 1915), U.S. illustrator, born in Paris, France; in U.S. after 1935; illustrated 'Good Luck Duck' by M. Dejong, 'Red Fairy Book' edited by A. Lang, 'The 13 Clocks' by J. Thurber, 'A Tree Is Nice' by J. Udry (1957 Caldecott Medal); wrote and illustrated 'Contest at Paca' R-108
Simony, purchase of spiritual benefit or church preferment, named from sin of Simon Magus, who attempted to buy the power of conferring gifts

engineer and business executive, born in New Haven, Conn.; president General Motors Corp. 1923–37, chairman board of directors 1937–56 (autobiographical works: 'Adventures of a White Collar Man', 'My Years with General Motors')
automobile development A-856

Sloan, John (1871–1951), U.S. painter, etcher, lithographer; born in Lock Haven, Pa.; instructor Art Students League, New York City 1914–30.

Sloane, Sir Hans (1660–1753), British collector and physician, born in Ireland, of Scottish parents; during his travels he collected plants and curiosities, which formed beginning of British Museum; first British physician to receive hereditary title.

Sloane, William Milligan (1850–1928), U.S. historian and educator, born in Richmond, Ohio; served 3 years in Germany as secretary to George Bancroft, U.S. minister to Germany; professor of history Princeton 1883–96 and at Columbia 1896–1916 ('Life of Napoleon Bonaparte').

Sloat, John Drake (1781–1867), U.S. Navy officer, born near Goshen, N.Y.; served in War of 1812; later against pirates in West Indies, and finally in war against Mexico
Mexican War M-320

Slobodkin, Louis (Julius) (1903–75), U.S. sculptor, illustrator, and author of children's books; born in Albany, N.Y.; received Caldecott Medal 1944 for illustrating 'Many Moons', by James Thurber; author and illustrator of 'Clear the Track for Michael's Magic Train', 'Dinny and Danny', 'Gogo: the French Sea Gull', 'The Polka-Dot Goat' R-110a

Slocum, Henry Warner (1827–94), general in Civil War, born in Delphi, N.Y.; fought in all the Virginia campaigns, and in battle of Chattanooga; commanded Atlanta garrison and took part with Sherman in march to sea; later a member of Congress.

Sloe (or blackthorn), a shrub *Prunus spinosa* of the rose family, closely related to the plum; fruit bitter; also the wild yellow plum and the black aloe.

Sloggett, Nellie. *see in index* Tregarthen, Enys

Sloid. *see in index* Sloyd

Sloop, sailing vessel, *picture* B-327

Sloop of War S-177g

Slope mine M-427
coal mining C-521, *diagram* C-520

Slosson, Edwin Emery (1865–1929), U.S. chemist, author and editor, born in Albany (now Sabetha), Kan.; professor of chemistry at the University of Wyoming; taught journalism at Columbia University; wrote on science in popular style ('Creative Chemistry'; 'Easy Lessons in Einstein'; 'Snapshots of Science'; 'Sermons of a Chemist').

Slot, airplane A-189

Slot-car racing, form of model-car racing on miniature track having metal-lined slots for guiding and electrically powering slot cars.

Sloth, tree-living mammal S-218, A-462
ground sloth, prehistoric, *picture* P-491

Sloth bear B-116

Slotter (or vertical shaper), a tool T-220

Sloughter, Henry (died 1691), colonial governor of New York N-256

Slovakia, former easternmost province, now region, of Czechoslovakia; 18,921 sq mi (49,005 sq km) C-812, *map* C-814

Slovaks, a Slavic people S-214
Czechoslovakia C-813

Slovenes, term for a Slavic people living chiefly in Yugoslavia B-31
Yugoslavia Y-435

Slovenia, a constituent republic of Yugoslavia; 7,819 sq mi (20,251 sq km); includes portions of former Austrian territory of Carniola, Carinthia, Styria, and Istria; pop. 1,591,523 B-31
folktales, *list* S-481
Yugoslavia Y-436

Slowdown, labor S-489

Sloyd (or sloid), a system of elementary manual training that originated in Sweden (from Swedish word meaning "skill").

Sludge, a product of garbage and refuse disposal G-18

Slue-foot Sue, legendary cowgirl F-266

Slug, gastropod mollusk S-221, *picture* S-222
mollusks M-525

Slug, in printing T-337, T-339

Slug, unit of mass S-342d

Sluice
dam construction D-11
gold ore processing G-179
mining M-426

Slums. *see in index* Housing, *subhead* slums

Slurry, fluid mixture
fire fighting F-108
nuclear energy N-427
transportation T-254
coal C-525

Sluys, battle of (1340), warfare, *list* W-15

Sly and the Family Stone, U.S. rock group M-682

Slye, Maud (1879–1954), U.S. pathologist, born in Minneapolis, Minn.; cancer research with mice at the University of Chicago 1911–54; author of many booklets on cancer.

Smackover, Ark., city 11 mi (18 km) n.w. of El Dorado; petroleum center; lumber and wood products; pop. 2,453.

Småland Highlands, in Sweden S-523

Smalkaldic War (also spelled Schmalkaldic War) (1546–47) R-134

Small Business Administration, U.S. U-166

Small Communities Air Service Program A-880

Smalley, Phillips, motion picture director, *picture* M-611

Small letters (or lowercase letters) B-356, T-336, *picture* T-337

Smallpox, communicable disease, *table* D-172
Australia
aborigines affected A-796
immigration policy A-785
vaccination, *pictures* V-249
Jenner J-98

Smalls, Robert (1839–1916), U.S. politician, born in Beaufort, S.C.; only black captain in Union Navy in Civil War; U.S. congressman from South Carolina 1875–79, 1881–87.

Smallwood, Joseph Roberts (born 1900), Canadian journalist and political leader, born in Gambo, Newf.; led movement to bring Newfoundland into union with Canada; Liberal party leader of Newfoundland and premier of Newfoundland 1949–72; author 'The Book of Newfoundland' (2 vols.).

Smaltite, commercial ore, *table* O-600

'Smart Set, The', literary magazine M-296

'Smart' terminal, office equipment O-495

Smartweed, annual plant (genus *Polygonum*) with glossy leaves and pink flower spikes; stem jointed; so called from acrid juice that will inflame tender skin
Polygonum hydropiper, picture W-132

Smearcase (or cottage cheese, or Dutch cheese, or pot cheese) C-289

Smeaton, John (1724–92), English civil engineer, born in Austhorpe, near Leeds
cement C-641
hydraulic cement C-245

Smell, sense of S-218
birds B-247
fish F-127
migratory techniques A-453
nose N-396

Smelling salts, aromatized ammonium carbonate; scented; stimulant and restorative; used as inhalant to revive persons suffering from fainting spells.

Smelt, a food fish
fisheries, *table* F-137

Smelting, extracting metal from ore by heating M-308
ancient origin S-57e, *picture* S-57d
copper C-712
iron and steel I-337

Smet, Pierre Jean de. *see in index* De Smet

Smetana, Bedrich (1824–84), Bohemian pianist, conductor, and composer; had piano school at Prague and was conductor at Bohemian Opera there; inspired many Czech musicians; tone poems, operas, chamber works
classical music M-673

Smetona, Antanas (1874–1944), Lithuanian statesman and journalist; editor of first Lithuanian daily; first president Lithuanian republic 1919–20, and again 1926–40; died in Cleveland, Ohio.

Smilanski, Moshe (1874–1950), Israeli writer
Hebrew literature H-113

Smilax, genus of woody or herbaceous climbing plants of lily family common in temperate and tropical regions of New and Old Worlds; greenbrier is a well-known American species.

Smiles, Samuel (1812–1904), Scottish biographer and didactic essayist ('Self-Help'; biographies of Watt, Stephenson, Wedgwood, and other industrial leaders).

'Smiles of a Summer Night', film by Bergman B-166

Smiley, George, fictional hero G-316
le Carré L-113

Smilodon. *see in index* Saber-toothed tiger

Smith, Adam (1723–90), Scottish economist, called "Father of Political Economy"; basing his conclusions on observation rather than theory, he laid foundations for modern science of economics; overthrew doctrines of Mercantilists and Physiocrats
city C-452
economics E-63
Enlightenment E-289
industry I-190
mass production M-208
international trade I-271
American Revolution R-170
liberalism L-146
sciences S-63
'The Wealth of Nations' C-150, E-205

Smith, Alexander (1865–1922), U.S. chemist, born in Edinburgh; professor at University of Chicago and Columbia University; a noted and much-loved teacher; author of many research papers and texts.

Smith, Alfred Emanuel (1873–1944), U.S. political leader, born in New York City; in New York Assembly 1903–15; sheriff of New York County 1915–17; governor of New York 1919–20, 1923–28; Democratic candidate for presidency 1928, *picture* R-264
Hoover H-234
Roosevelt, Eleanor R-259
Roosevelt, F.D. R-263

Smith, Arthur James Marshall (1902–80), Canadian poet and critic, born in Montreal, Que.; professor 1936–72.

Smith, Bessie (1894–1937), U.S. blues singer and recording artist, born in Chattanooga, Tenn.; greatly influenced jazz; performed with Louis Armstrong and other jazz artists.

Smith, Betty (1904–72), U.S. writer, born in Brooklyn, N.Y.; taught at University of North Carolina 1947–65; novel 'A Tree Grows in Brooklyn' dramatized for motion picture and for musical play; wrote many one-act plays
'A Tree Grows in Brooklyn' R-111h

Smith, Sir Charles Edward Kingsford (1897–1935), Australian aviator S-218

Smith, Charles Emory (1842–1908), U.S. journalist and political leader, born in Mansfield, Conn.; editor *Philadelphia Press;* U.S. minister to Russia, 1890–92; while U.S. postmaster general (1898–1902), established rural mail routes.

Smith, Charles H. (also known as Bill Arp) (1826–1903), U.S. lawyer, philosopher, and politician; born in Lawrenceville, Ga.; published satiric letters in Southern dialect against the North
Confederacy C-644

Smith, Cyrus Rowlett (born 1899), U.S. businessman and government official, born in Minerva, Tex., near Cameron; headed American Airlines 1934–42, 1946–68; secretary of commerce 1968–69.

Smith, David (1906–65), U.S. sculptor M-311, *picture* M-310

Smith, David Eugene (1860–1944), U.S. educator, born in Cortland, N.Y.; professor of mathematics at Teachers College, Columbia University 1901–26, later professor emeritus.

Smith, Donald Alexander. *see in index* Strathcona and Mount Royal, Baron

Smith, Edmund Kirby (1824–93), U.S. Confederate general and educator, born in St. Augustine, Fla.; last Confederate general to surrender; president University of Nashville (Tennessee) 1870–75
Statuary Hall, *table* S-437a

Smith, Elmer Boyd (1860–1943), Canadian author and illustrator, born in St. John, N.B.; noted for picture books depicting home and farm life ('Seashore Book'; 'Farm Book'; 'Chicken World'; 'The Story of Our Country') R-111e

Smith, Francis Hopkinson (1838–1915), U.S. civil engineer, artist, and novelist, born in Baltimore, Md.; wrote entertaining books of travel and novels ('Colonel Carter of Cartersville', portrait of an old-school Southern gentleman; 'Caleb West, Master Diver').

Smith, Sir Francis Pettit (1808–74), English inventor, born in Hythe; developed screw propeller; ship, *Archimedes*, built on his principle 1839 S-167
navy N-83

Smith, Frederick Madison (1874–1946), U.S. religious leader, born in Plano, Ill.; grandson of founder of Mormon religion; head of Reorganized church 1915–46 M-584

Smith, George Isaac (born 1909), Canadian political leader, born in Stewiacke, N.S.; member of Nova Scotia legislature 1949–67; premier of Nova Scotia 1967–70; member Canadian Parliament 1975–.

Smith, George Washington (1815–99), U.S. dancer B-35

Smith, Goldwin (1823–1910), Canadian scholar, historian, and journalist, born in Reading, England ('Irish History'; 'The United Kingdom'; 'Reminiscences').

Smith, Hamilton E., U.S. inventor
laundry industry L-87

Smith, Hamilton Lamphere (1818–1903), U.S. educator and scientist, born in New London, Conn.; wrote scientific books and papers
tintype P-207

Smith, Hamilton O. (born 1931), U.S. microbiologist, born in New York, N.Y.; with U.S. Public Health Service 1962–67; at School of Medicine of Johns Hopkins University 1967–, professor 1973–; research on effect of restriction enzymes on DNA molecules. *see also in index* Nobel Prizewinners, *table*
genetic engineering G-49

Smith, Hoke (1855–1931), U.S. lawyer and political leader, born in Newton, N.C.; published *Atlanta Journal*; secretary of interior, Cleveland's second Cabinet; governor of Georgia 1907–9, 1911; U.S. senator 1911–21.

Smith, Holland McTyeire (1882–1967), U.S. Marine Corps officer, born in Russell County, Ala.; father of modern U.S. amphibious warfare, in which he trained Marines and Army in and before World War II; commander Fleet Marine Force in the Pacific 1944–45; retired as 4-star general 1946.

Smith, Horace (1808–93), U.S. inventor and manufacturer of firearms, born in Cheshire, Mass. *see also in index* Wesson, Daniel Baird

Smith, Hyrum (died 1844), brother of Joseph Smith, Mormon prophet.

Smith, Ian Douglas (born 1919), Rhodesian political leader, born in Selukwe, Southern Rhodesia; member parliament 1953–61; founding member Rhodesian Front 1961; ministerial appointments 1962–64, prime minister 1964–79
  Zimbabwe Z-454

Smith, James (1720?–1806), signer of Declaration of Independence, born in Ireland; Revolutionary War general.

Smith, James L.B. (1897–1968), South African ichthyologist F-132

Smith, Jedediah Strong (1798–1831), explorer of Far West; first U.S. trapper to cross Sierras into California (1826); endured extreme hardships S-339, *map* U-176
  Nevada N-137

Smith, Jessie Willcox (1863–1935), U.S. artist, born in Philadelphia, Pa.; known for pictures of children and illustrations for juvenile books R-111

Smith, Captain John (1580–1631), North American colonial adventurer S-219
  American literature A-340
  Boston's mapping B-376
  Chesapeake Bay C-304
    Maryland M-171
  Jamestown, Va., J-22
  monument in Richmond, Va. R-205
  Northwest passage A-332
  Pocahontas P-400
  Potomac River W-70
  quoted on persimmon P-215

Smith, Joseph (1805–44), founder of Mormon religion, born in Sharon, Vt.; in 1830 published 'The Book of Mormon', foundation for the faith's doctrine, *picture* V-296
  Mormon history M-583
  Young Y-424

Smith, Joseph (1832–1914), U.S. religious leader, born in Kirtland, Ohio; son of founder of Mormon religion; head of Reorganized church 1860–1914 M-584

Smith, Kate (full name Kathryn Elizabeth Smith) (1909–86), U.S. radio and television singer, born in Greenville, Va.; famous for 'When the Moon Comes Over the Mountain' and 'God Bless America'; autobiography, 'Upon My Lips a Song'.

Smith, Keith (1890–1955), aviator A-204, *picture* A-203

Smith, Lula Carson. *see in index* McCullers, Carson

Smith, Margaret Chase (born 1897), U.S. political leader, born in Skowhegan, Me.; Republican representative from Maine 1940–49, succeeding husband, Clyde H. Smith; U.S. senator 1949–73; first Republican woman to seek nomination for president of U.S. (1964); author of 'Declaration of Conscience'
  Maine M-55
  women's rights W-276

Smith, Michael (1945–86), U.S. astronaut, born in Beaufort, N.C., killed in explosion of space shuttle *Challenger*.

Smith, Nora Archibald (1859–1934), U.S. writer, born in Philadelphia, Pa., associated with her sister, Kate Douglas Wiggin, in kindergarten work; author and compiler of poetry and folklore for children ('Action Poems and Plays for Children'; 'Twilight Stories'; with Kate Douglas Wiggin: 'The Story Hour', 'Posy Ring', 'Golden Numbers') S-480

Smith, Red (full name Walter Wellesley Smith) (1905–82), U.S. sportswriter, born in Green Bay, Wis.; columnist *New York Herald Tribune* 1945–66; syndicated with Publishers-Hall 1946–71, New York Times News Service 1971–82; author 'Out of Red', 'Views of Sport'.

Smith, Samuel Francis (1808–95), U.S. scholar and Baptist clergyman, born in Boston, Mass.; best known as author of 'America'; also wrote 'Poems of Home and Country'.

Smith, Stanley Edward (1775–1851), 13th earl of Derby L-104

Smith, Sydney (1771–1845), English clergyman and author; firm friend of religious toleration, and a famous wit; called Macaulay a "book in breeches," and compared House of Lords rejecting Reform Bill of 1831 to Mrs. Partington trying to mop up the Atlantic Ocean; a founder of the *Edinburgh Review*
  American literature criticism A-347

Smith, Sydney (1877–1935), U.S. comic artist, born in Bloomington, Ill.; created 'The Gumps', 'Old Doc Yak'; cartoonist for *Chicago Tribune* 1911–35.

Smith, Theobald (1859–1934), U.S. pathologist, born in Albany, N.Y.; professor of comparative pathology, Harvard University 1896–1915; director department of animal pathology, Rockefeller Institute for Medical Research 1915–29; important work on infectious and parasitic diseases.

Smith, W. Eugene (1918–78), U.S. photojournalist and war correspondent P-299, *list* P-294

Smith, Walter Bedell (1895–1961), U.S. Army officer and diplomat, born in Indianapolis, Ind.; chief of staff to Dwight D. Eisenhower 1942–45; ambassador to Soviet Union 1946–49; director of Central Intelligence Agency 1950–53; retired from Army as 4-star general to become under secretary of state 1953–54; author of 'My Three Years in Moscow' and 'Eisenhower's Six Great Decisions: Europe 1944–45'.

Smith, Willard John (born 1910), U.S. Coast Guard officer, born in Suttons Bay, Mich.; air, lake, and sea duty; superintendent Coast Guard Academy 1962–65; commandant, with rank of admiral, U.S. Coast Guard 1966–70.

Smith, William (1769–1839), English geologist; first to identify Earth's strata by their fossil content; made first geologic map of England and Wales ever published
  earth science E-36

Smith, William, English sea captain; discovered and named South Shetland Islands while rounding the Horn on a trading voyage 1819.

Smith, William French (born 1917), U.S. lawyer and public official, born in Wilton, N.H.; private law practice 1942–81; active in Republican politics in California; U.S. attorney general 1981–84.

Smith, Willoughby (1828–91), English telegraphic engineer; devised new methods of cable construction, engaged in manufacture and laying of cables.

Smith College, in Northampton, Mass.; for women; founded by Sophia Smith (1796–1870); chartered 1871; opened 1875; arts and sciences, art, music; graduate study.

Smithfield, England, district of London n. of St. Paul's; in medieval times fairs, markets, and executions held here; in recent times chief central meat market.

Smithfield, R.I., town 10 mi (16 km) n.w. of Providence; settled mainly by Quakers, incorporated 1731; pop. 16,886.

Smithfield, Wash. *see in index* Olympia, Wash.

Smith-Hughes Act (1917), United States A-143, V-363
  education, *list* E-104
  home economics H-215

Smithing. *see in index* Blacksmithing

Smith-Lever Act (1914), United States
  education, *list* E-104

Smith Rock State Park, in Oregon, *picture* O-591

Smiths Falls, Ont., town on Rideau River 38 mi (61 km) s.w. of Ottawa; resort; castings and other metal products, clothing; pop. 9,585.

Smithson, James (1765–1829), English scientist, born in France; discovered smithsonite; bequest created Smithsonian Institution.

Smithsonian Institution, Washington, D.C. W-69
  administration of Barro Colorado P-94
  American Indian folklore collection S-477
  Cooper-Hewitt Museum N-278
  Henry H-133
  Langley L-30
  museum M-661, *picture* M-660
  Owen O-620
  rocket work supported S-341d

Smocking, needlework N-111, *picture* N-112

Smog, combination of fog and smoke; common in industrial areas F-246, P-441b
  aerosol A-66
  cancer in zoo animals P-441b
  Los Angeles L-299

Smoke S-220
  aerosol A-66
  detection appliances H-213
  fire fighting F-102
    Pittsburgh P-346

Smoke detector H-213

Smoked haddock (or finnan haddie) H-4

Smoke jumper P-109a
  fire fighting F-108
  forest fires F-314, *picture* F-313

Smokeless powder, powder that produces little or no smoke
  camphor C-67
  explosive E-380
  rocket propulsion R-232

Smoker, underwater hot-water vents D-60

Smoke salt S-379

Smoke tree, shrub or small tree *Parosela spinosa* of pea family, native to deserts of the Southwest; grows 6 to 30 ft (2 to 9 m) high; spreading, nearly leafless, spiny branches covered with a gray, cottony fuzz; blooms in June; flowers purple, in short clusters.

Smoking. *see also in index* Tobacco
  cancer cause C-132
  health hazard H-86
  life span A-127
  lungs L-337
  North American Indians E-319

Smoking, meat-curing process M-252

'Smoky', novel by James, *list* H-274

Smoky Hill River, river, 540 mi (870 km) long, rises in e. Colorado, flows e. across Kansas to Junction City, and there joins Republican River to form Kansas River.

Smoky Mountains. *see in index* Great Smoky Mountains

Smoky quartz (or cairngorm, or Scotch topaz) J-115

Smolensk, U.S.S.R., one of oldest cities; on Dneper River, 225 mi (360 km) s.w. of Moscow; manufacturing and rail center; taken by French (1812), by Germans (1941); pop. 211,000, *maps* R-344, 349
  Europe, *map* E-361

Smollett, Tobias George (1721–71), British novelist called "founder of the satirical novel," born in Scotland; adopted medical career before devoting life to writing ('Humphry Clinker', in Thackeray's judgment "most laughable story ever written"; 'Roderick Random', first English sea novel) E-272

Smoot, Reed (1862–1941), U.S. political figure and Mormon leader, born in Salt Lake City, Utah; U.S. senator 1903–33; expert on tariff, taxation, and public finance, *picture* U-226. *see also in index* Hawley-Smoot Tariff Act

Smooth muscle M-658

Smooth tracking, eye movements B-205

Smooth turban, snail *Norrisia norrisii*
  shell, *picture* S-151

Smorgasbord, in Sweden, a table of delicacies eaten as appetizers before dinner; included are butter, several kinds of bread, pickled and smoked fish and meats, salads, and pickled vegetables; word means "bread-and-butter table"; in U.S. a buffet-style meal.

Smorzando, in music, *list* M-671

SMS (synchronous-orbit meteorological satellite), *table* S-344

Smuggling, illegal importation or exportation of goods or persons
  drugs H-165

Smuts, Jan Christiaan (1870–1950), South African soldier and statesman S-220, S-267
  holistic medicine H-202

Smuts, various fungi parasitic upon plants R-363

Smyrna, Del., town in Kent and New Castle counties near Smyrna River; agriculture, shipping, and light industry; pop. 4,750.

Smyrna, Ga., town 11 mi (18 km) n.w. of Atlanta; textiles, light industry; pop. 20,312.

Smyrna, Turkey. *see in index* Izmir

Smyrna fig F-80

Smyth, Dame Ethel Mary (1858–1944), English composer, born in London; studied Leipzig and Berlin; took prominent part in militant suffrage movement, for which she composed 'The March of the Women'; made Dame of British Empire because of eminence as composer; many orchestral, chamber, and choral works, and several operas ('Der Wald'; 'The Wreckers'; 'The Boatswain's Mate').

Smyth, Henry De Wolf (1898–1986), U.S. physicist, born in Clinton, N.Y.; at Princeton University 1924–66, professor 1936–66; member of Atomic Energy Commission 1949–54; U.S. representative to International Atomic Energy Agency 1961–70; corecipient 1968 Atoms for Peace Award; wrote official War Department report on atomic bomb, 'Atomic Energy for Military Purposes', commonly called the 'Smyth Report'; coauthor 'Matter, Motion and Electricity'.

Smyth, John (died 1612), founded Baptist churches in England B-77

Smyth sewing, bookmaking B-360, *picture* B-358

Snaffle bit, part of a horse's bridle H-264, *diagram* H-265

Snag, in fishing, *list* F-146

Snail, shelled gastropod mollusk S-221
  animal life record, *table* E-24
  body structure A-422
  egg, *picture* E-111
  fossils, *picture* F-325
  invertebrate animal group, I-283
  mollusks M-525
  pet, *picture* P-246
  shell S-150, *pictures* S-149

Snail fever. *see in index* Schistosomiasis

Snaith, John Collis (1876–1936), English novelist; great variety of stories from grim, realistic tales to light, whimsical comedies ('Broke of Covenden'; 'William Jordan, Junior'; 'The Sailor'; 'Indian Summer'; 'But Even So').

Snake. *see in index* Shoshone

Snake S-223, *picture* A-434
  Aesculapius A-87
  animal life record, *table* E-24
  cobra. *see in index* Cobra
  copperhead V-328, *picture* S-226
  crawling mechanism S-226a
  evolution R-152
  folk art motif F-252
  folktales, *pictures* S-472, 481d
  hibernation H-147
  legend and myth
    St. Patrick P-140
  lizard L-271
  milk snake. *see in index* Milk snake
  moccasin. *see in index* Moccasin snake
  mongoose M-538
  python P-544
  rattlesnakes R-96. *see also in index* Rattlesnake
  reproduction A-426
  scales S-223
  secretary bird S-105
  skeleton V-303
  vipers V-328, S-226b

Snakebird. *see in index* Darter

Snakebite S-227
  first aid F-122
  precautions against R-96

Snake caterpillar, insect M-423

Snake charmer, *picture* I-65

Snake flies, a group of the order Neuroptera, family Raphidiidae; especially the common raphidian *Agulla adnixa* that feeds on soft-bodied insects found on trees in dense forests w. of Continental Divide
  egg, *picture* E-111

Snake River, chief tributary of Columbia River; rises in Wyoming, s. of Yellowstone Park; flows through s. Idaho,

then n. along w. boundary and w. to Columbia in s. Washington; length 1,038 mi (1,670 km) C-588
basalt deposits B-90
Idaho I-17, *pictures* I-18, 26, *map* I-30
North America, *map* N-351
Oregon, *picture* O-583
Shoshone Falls, *map* U-80
Washington W-48, *picture* W-51

Snake River Gorge, canyon along Snake River in southern Idaho extending for about 350 mi (560 km) downstream from American Falls.

Snake River Plain, plateau in Idaho I-18, *map* I-30

Snakeroot, name given various plants that were supposed to cure snake bites; black snakeroot or cohosh (*Cimicifuga racemosa*), Seneca snakeroot (*Polygala senega*), and Virginia snakeroot or birthwort (*Aristolochia serpentaria*) are common in the U.S.; Canada snakeroot (*Asarum canadense*) is the wild ginger
white snakeroot P-409

Snapdragon, herbaceous plants composing the genus *Antirrhinum* of the figwort family with showy white, yellow, pink, or red flowers; lower lip of large tubular corolla snaps shut if opened; many beautiful garden varieties have been derived from *Antirrhinum majus*, *pictures* F-216, F-225
growing conditions G-23

Snappers, a number of carnivorous fishes *Lutianidae* of warm waters; gray and red snappers are excellent food.

Snapping turtle T-329
lifespan, *chart* A-423

Snare, type of trap T-267

Snatch, weight lifting W-137

SNCC. *see in index* Student National Coordinating Committee

Snead, Sam (in full Samuel Jackson Snead) (born 1912), U.S. golfer, born in Hot Springs, Va.; known as "Slammin' Sammy"; won various golf tournaments
golf G-189, *picture* G-191

Snedeker, Caroline Dale (1871–1956), U.S. writer, born in New Harmony, Ind.; author of historical stories for younger readers ('The Spartan'; 'Downright Dencey'; 'Luke's Quest'; 'Triumph for Flavius').

Sneeze, a respiratory reflex characterized by forceful, spasmodic, and audible expulsion of air through the nose and mouth.

Sneezeweed. *see in index* Helenium

Sneezewort, a perennial plant *Achillea ptarmica;* white flowers in loose clusters; leaves saw-toothed; its dry powdered leaves are used as snuff to produce sneezing.

Snell, George (born 1903), U.S. geneticist. *see in index* Nobel Prizewinners, *table*

Snelled fly, in fishing, *list* F-146

Snellius, Willebrordus (or Willebrord Snell) (1591–1626), Dutch mathematician, born in Leiden; discovered law of refraction of light
optics O-574

Snell's law, optics O-574

Snider, Edwin Donald (nickname Duke) (born 1926), U.S. baseball player, born in Los Angeles, Calif.; outfielder and outstanding slugger; Brooklyn Dodgers 1947–57, Los Angeles Dodgers 1958–62, New York Mets 1963, San Francisco Giants 1964.

Snipe, a large brown game bird with black stripes on back and crown; belongs to the family Scolopacidae; nests in marshy areas.

Snodgrass, W(illiam) D(eWitt) (born 1926), U.S. poet and educator, born in Wilkinsburg, Pa.; professor Syracuse University 1968– ('Heart's Needle' awarded Pulitzer prize for poetry 1960; 'After Experience', poems) A-364

Snook (or robalo), semitropical species of silvery pikelike fish *Centropomus undecimalis*, closely related to the bass; excellent food fish weighing 15 to 20 lbs (7 to 9 kg) and ranging as far north as Texas.

Snooker, billiards game B-193

Snoqualmie Pass, in Washington, route through the Cascade Range W-48

Snorkel, tube housing air intake and exhaust pipes S-498

Snorkeling, type of underwater diving D-188

Snorri Sturluson (1178–1241), Icelandic historian and official; author of 'Heimskringla' (sagas of Norwegian kings) and collector and editor of Younger or Prose Edda S-471
mythology M-704

Snout beetles, a group of the order Coleoptera, family Curculionidae; especially the low-tide billbug *Calendra aetigor*, which broods in Atlantic tidal lands, *picture* I-216. *see also in index* Weevil

Snow, C.P. *see in index* Snow of Leicester, Charles Percy Snow, Baron

Snow, Edgar Parks (1905–72), U.S. writer, born in Kansas City, Mo.; extensive travels in Asia, Africa, Europe as newspaper correspondent; associate editor *Saturday Evening Post* 1943–53; author of many magazine articles and books 'Red Star over China'; 'Stalin Must Have Peace'; 'Journey to the Beginning', 'The Other Side of the River: Red China Today').

Snow S-227. *see also in index* Ice
acid content A-19
animal tracks A-463
artificial S-210b
climate C-496
cloud C-517
colored S-228
earth E-13, *diagram* E-14
glacier formation G-150
remover H-212
sculpture, *picture* U-208
tires R-304
water W-89, *picture* W-88
weather W-120

'Snow and the Sun, The', book by Antonio Frasconi R-107, *picture* R-110

Snowball, any of several varieties of *Viburnum opulus;* a small tree or a shrub with compact clusters of small white flowers.

Snowberry, two ornamental shrubs with clustered white berries belonging to heath and madder families; term especially applied to North American variety with pink flower clusters.

'Snow-Bound', poem by Whittier W-201
American literature A-348

Snow bunting (or snowbird) B-244, *pictures* B-260, F-86

'Snow Country' (or 'Yukiguni'), novel by Kawabata
Japanese literature J-82
Kawabata K-193

Snow Cruiser, vehicle designed for use in 3rd Byrd Antarctic expedition 1939–41; named *Penguin I;* weight 37 tons (34 metric tons), length 55 ft (17 m), width 15 ft (4.6 m); crossed crevasses 15 ft (4.6 m) wide; speed up to 25 mph (40 kph); cost $150,000.

Snowden, Philip, viscount of Ickornshaw (1864–1937), English statesman; self-educated; overcame ill health and lameness to become noted lecturer, writer, and leader in English Labor party; became chancellor of exchequer in Labor government of 1924 and 1929; raised to the peerage 1931; lord privy seal 1931–32.

Snowdon, mountain in n. Wales (3,560 ft; 1,085 m); highest point in England and Wales; 5 peaks divided by passes; region famous for scenic beauty W-5

Snowdrop, a small low plant with bulbous roots, narrow leaves, and scapes bearing single white drooping flowers; there are many cultivated varieties of the genus *Galanthus*.

Snowfield, an area of snow that lasts from year to year G-150

Snowflake I-5, S-228

Snowflea. *see in index* Snow scorpion fly

Snow goose D-285
migration B-252

Snow grouse. *see in index* Ptarmigan

Snow leopard (or ounce), wild cat *Uncia uncia*, *table* C-215

Snow line S-227

Snow-making machine S-210b

Snowmobile, mechanized vehicle for recreational and business travel on snow; adapted from the armored tank; usually has tracks in rear, runners in front W-243, *picture* W-241
Eskimo E-301
use by Mounties, *picture* R-300b
Wisconsin marathon, *picture* W-258

Snow of Leicester, Charles Percy Snow, Baron (1905–80), English novelist and physicist, born in Leicester; fellow of Christ's College, Cambridge University, 1930–50; Civil Service Commissioner 1945–60; Parliamentary secretary, Ministry of Technology, 1964–66 ('Strangers and Brothers', series of 11 novels published 1940–70, beginning with title volume and ending with 'Last Things') E-282

Snow-on-the-mountain (sometimes called ghostweed), an annual plant *Euphorbia marginata* of the spurge family, found in e. North America; leaves shaded light green and white; flowers are the characteristic pistil and stamen flower arrangement of genus *Euphorbia;* P-409

Snow remover, appliance H-212

Snow scorpion fly (or snowflea), an insect *Boreus brumalis* of the order Mecoptera, family Boreidae; this is the smallest species of the genus; often found on the surface of snow.

Snowshoe, oval wooden frame strung with thongs and attached to the foot that enables a person to walk or run on snow without sinking W-241, *picture* W-242

Snowshoeing, winter sport W-241

Snowshoe rabbit (or varying hare) R-20, *picture* R-21

Snowstorm, weather condition W-120

'Snow Storm—Steam Boat off a Harbour's Mouth...', painting by Turner, *picture* T-328

'Snow White and the Seven Dwarfs', old fairy tale in Grimm brothers' collection, in which Princess Snow White, friend of the Seven Dwarfs, is awakened from sleeping death by the kiss of the prince
animated cartoons C-191
Disney D-185
motion pictures M-622
folklore F-260

Snowy egret, bird *Egretta thula* H-143, *picture* H-142

Snowy Mountains Hydro-electric Scheme, in Australia A-773

Snowy River, in Australia, *map* A-822
irrigation A-773

Snuff, pulverized tobacco used for inhaling or chewing; usually made from ground leaf and stem, fermented and fire cured; flavoring and salts sometimes added T-200

Snyder, John Wesley (born 1895), U.S. banker, public official, born in Jonesboro, Ark.; vice-president Defense Plant Corp., Washington, 1940–44; director war mobilization and reconversion 1945–46; secretary of treasury 1946–53.

Snyder, Simon (1759–1819), U.S. statesman, born in Lancaster, Pa.; pious Moravian and able representative of Germans and farmers of Pennsylvania in Constitutional Convention (1789–90); governor of Pennsylvania (1801–17); encouraged education and sought protection of common people.

Snyder, Tex., city about 205 mi (330 km) w. of Fort Worth; oil fields; cotton, cattle; petroleum products, clothing, magnesium; pop. 12,705.

Soaking pit, in metalworking
iron and steel production I-343

Soane, Sir John (1753–1837), English architect; designed Bank of England; Soane Museum in London (antiquarian collections) A-569

Soap S-229
bubbles, painting by Chardin, *picture* P-45
chemical nature S-229
cleansing properties S-229
composition S-229
cosmetics C-728
fats and oils use F-47
nuts N-449
laundering L-84
pioneer life, soapmaking S-229
sodium and potassium types S-247
substitutes S-229

Soap, metallic P-74

Soapbark (or quillay tree), evergreen tree *Quillaja saponaria* of rose family, native to w. South America but grown in s. U.S.; grows to 60 ft (18 m); leaves oval, to 2 in. (5 cm) long, glossy; flowers small, white, in clusters; inner bark (quillaia bark) yields a soap extract; exported for use by cloth dyers, in beverages, medicine, and soaps S-229

Soapberry, a tropical or subtropical tree of genus *Sapindus;* found in West Indies and India, also in s. Florida; the fruit (soap nut) used for washing and in ointments. *see also in index* Chinaberry

Soapless soaps S-231

Soap opera, television program T-71

Soap plants, name given to various plants used as soap, their bruised stems, bark, roots, leaves, or fruit forming a lather in water; includes bouncing bet or soapwort, soapberry, agave, star of Bethlehem or soaproot, sand lily, and yucca.

Soapstone (or steatite), mineral M-437

Soapwort. *see in index* Saponaria

Soares, Mário (born 1924), president of Portugal, born in Lisbon P-457a

Soaring, action of a flying glider, also sport of manipulating gliders G-165, *diagram* G-168

Soaring Society of America, organization of glider-flying enthusiasts G-167

Soback Mountains, in Korea K-282

Sobieski, John (1624–96), national hero and king of Poland (John III), elected 1674; many military victories over Turks stayed decline of Poland, and freed Hungary P-413

Sobolev, Arkadi Aleksandrovich (1903–64), Soviet diplomat; permanent representative to United Nations 1955–60; deputy foreign minister 1960–64.

Sobrero, Ascanio (1812–88), Italian chemist; developed nitroglycerin in 1847 by adding glycerin to concentrated mixture of nitric acid and sulfuric acid
explosive E-380

Soccer (or association football) S-232, *picture* V-239. *see also in index* Football
cross cultural transfer C-466
England E-233
football F-295
Mexico City M-347
West Germany G-116

Soccer War (1969), between Honduras and El Salvador E-197

Soche, China. *see in index* Yarkand

Sociable, type of carriage W-3

'Social Contract, The', work by Rousseau R-299b
Enlightenment E-289

Social dancing D-21

Social Democrats P-143c
East Germany G-127
United Kingdom E-259

Social geography G-68

Social insects, those living in communities and having differentiated forms or castes, as queens, workers, drones
ant A-468
bee B-126
jungle's fauna J-156
organization A-431
wasp W-73

Social insurance S-236

Socialism S-233. *see also in index* Capitalism; Communism
anarchism A-388
apprenticeship control A-511
Asian countries' industrialization A-690
Canada
Saskatchewan S-49g
Cuba C-804

cap. Mogadishu; republic proclaimed July 1, 1960, with uniting of Italian Somaliland and Somaliland Protectorate (British Somaliland); pop. 3,261,000 S-256, *map* A-118
Africa A-107, *table* A-112
Ethiopia E-315
flag, *picture* F-170
illiteracy P-450
Italian trusteeship I-396

Somaliland, easternmost projection of Africa between Gulf of Aden and Indian Ocean; comprises Somalia, Republic of Djibouti, and s.e. Ethiopia. *see also in index* Djibouti, Republic of; Somalia

Somaliland Protectorate (or British Somaliland), British protectorate (1884–1960) in e. Africa; area 68,000 sq mi. *see also in index* Somalia

Somali Republic. *see in index* Somalia

Somatic cells (or body cells), cells of the body that compose the tissues, organs, and parts of that individual other than the germ cells H-139
genetics G-53

Somatic ectoderm, embryology, *chart* E-202

Somatic mesoderm, external layer of the lateral mesoderm E-200, *chart* E-202

Somatoform disorders, a category of mental illnesses M-301

Sombrero, a hat, *picture* U-99
hats and caps H-54

'Some Prefer Nettles' (or 'Tade kuu mushi'), work by Jun-ichiro Tanizaki
Japanese literature J-82

Somers, Sir George (1554–1611), English navigator, born in Lyme Regis; landed first settlers in Bermuda; a founder of South Virginia Company B-173

Somerset, Edward Seymour, duke of (1506?–52), uncle of Edward VI and protector of England in early part of Edward's reign; important leader in English Reformation.

Somerset, county in s.w. England; 1,613 sq mi (4,178 sq km); county town, Taunton; dairying and fruit-growing; woolen industry; several famous churches; pop. 599,046.

Somerset, Mass., on Taunton River opposite Fall River; varnishes, paper products; resort; pop. of township 18,813.

Somerset case S-214

Somerset Island, large island of Canadian Arctic directly n. of Boothia peninsula; 9,370 sq mi (24,270 sq km), *maps* C-109, N-351

Somersworth, N.H., city on Salmon Falls River 5 mi (8 km) n. of Dover; electric meters, shoes, textiles; pop. 10,350, *map* N-191

Somervell, Brehon Burke (1892–1955), U.S. Army officer, born in Little Rock, Ark.; expert in army procurement and construction and former WPA administrator; commander of U.S. Army service forces 1942–46.

Somerville, Mass., city just n.w. of Boston; automobile assembling, meat-packing; food, metal, and paper products; pop. 77,372 S-257
Massachusetts M-191

Somerville, N.J., borough 26 mi (42 km) s.w. of Newark; chemical, pharmaceutical, asbestos products; electric fans and motors; foundries; pop. 11,973.

'Something Happened', work by Heller N-409

'Something of Myself', work by Kipling K-249

Somme, First Battle of the, (1916), France during World War I W-306, S-257
warfare, *list* W-15

Somme, Second Battle of the, (1918), France during World War I W-310, S-258

Somme River, river in n. France S-257
Amiens A-370
France, *map* F-372

Somnus, Roman mythology, god of sleep; son of Nox (Night); twin of Mors or Thanatos (Death); brothers traditionally portrayed together as sleeping youths; corresponds to Greek Hypnos.

Somoza Debayle, Anastasio (1925–80), Nicaraguan political leader, born in Leon; in Nicaraguan national Guard (army) 1941–79, commander 1967–79; president 1967–72, 1974–79
assassination, *list* A-704
Nicaragua N-305

Somoza Garcia, Anastasio (1896–1956), Nicaraguan president
assassination, *list* A-704

Sonar, supersonic device
camera automation A-836
orientation A-441
sound S-261
submarines S-498

Sonata, a musical composition of three or four individual movements so related as to form a unified whole, *list* M-671

Sonata-allegro form, in music M-669, *list* M-671

Sonata da camera. *see in index* Chamber sonata

Sonata da chiesa. *see in index* Church sonata

Sonatina, in music, *list* M-671

Sonderbund (German for "separate league"), a league of the seven Roman Catholic cantons of Switzerland (Lucerne, Fribourg, Valais, Uri, Schwyz, Unterwalden, Zug), formed 1845 for purpose of obtaining supremacy in Swiss Confederation; declared dissolved by federal diet of Switzerland July 1847, defeated by armed force Nov. 1847.

Sondheim, Stephen (born 1930), U.S. composer and lyricist, born New York City M-685
opera O-560

Songhai, people
Mali M-75

Songhua River, river in n. China H-116, M-93

'Song in Praise of Knight Kip'a', work by Ch'ungdam K-292

Song Koi. *see in index* Red River

Song-Nen River Plain, plain in n. China H-116

'Song of Death', work by Flaubert F-176

'Song of Eternity, The', poem by Muhammad Iqbal I-304

'Song of Hiawatha, The', poem by Longfellow H-146
American literature A-348
Longfellow L-296
Minnesota M-444

'Song of Life and Hope', work by Darío D-35

'Song of Myself', work by Walt Whitman
American literature A-350

'Song of Roland' (French 'Chanson de Roland')
French literature S-475
Roland R-238
storytelling S-481c

Song of Solomon (or Song of Songs), book of Old Testament; authorship ascribed to Solomon
Biblical literature B-182

'Song of Solomon' work by Morrison A-362

'Song of the Autumn Wind', poem by Shimazaki
Japanese literature J-82

Songs, in music
American Indians I-118
Beatles B-119
bird. *see in index* Animal communication
classical music M-667
folklore F-265
folk music F-272
hymns. *see in index* Hymn
Lieder. *see in index* Lied
nursery rhymes N-442
oral literature L-242
poetry P-403

'Songs of a Sentimental Bloke', work by C.M. Denis
Australian literature A-797

'Songs of Flying Dragons, The', Korean literary work
Korean literature K-293

'Songs of Innocence', by William Blake B-310
English literature E-274

Song sparrow, bird *Melospiza melodia* of the family Fringillidae S-368, *picture* F-86
egg, *picture* E-112

Song thrush (or mavis), a bird *Turdus ericetorum* of the family Turdidae T-177

Soniake, people
Mali M-75

Sonic boom, explosive noise resulting when aircraft exceeds speed of sound, generating shock waves on surface of aircraft, waves form trailing cone, normally extending to ground, making a boom
airplane A-182
noise pollution P-441e

'Sonnambula, La'. *see in index* 'Sleepwalker, The'

Sonneck, Oscar George Theodore (1873–1928), U.S. musicologist and librarian, born in Jersey City, N.J.; under his direction (1902–17) music section of Library of Congress became one of world's greatest; editor, *Musical Quarterly*.

Sonnet, poem of 14 lines P-406
Gilder P-406
Petrarch, or Italian P-406, R-145
Shakespeare S-133-4

'Sonnets from the Portuguese', work by Elizabeth Barrett Browning B-465
English literature E-276

Sonnino, Sidney, Baron (1847–1921), Italian statesman and financier; foreign minister during World War I.

'Son of a Servant, The', work by Strindberg S-489

Sonoma, Calif., city 35 mi (55 km) n. of San Francisco; food processing, wine; founded 1835; pop. 6,054.

Sonoma State University, in Rohnert Park, Calif.; opened 1961; arts and sciences, music, nursing, teacher education; graduate study.

Sonora, Mexico, state on Gulf of California bordering Arizona; 71,403 sq mi (184,933 sq km); cap. Hermosillo (pop. 95,978); pop. 1,414,872
Mexico, *map* M-344
missions S-338
Kino's contribution K-247

Sonora River, river in Mexico, flows 300 mi (480 km) to Gulf of California.

'Sons and Lovers', autobiographical novel (1913) by D.H. Lawrence; portrays mining life in late 19th-century England
Lawrence L-98

Sons of Confederate Veterans. *see in index* Confederate Veterans, United Sons of

Sons of Daniel Boone, youth organization Y-427

Sons of Heaven, name given to the rulers of China from the beginning of the Chou Dynasty (1122 BC)
China history C-360

Sons of Liberty, name given to the societies that sprang up in the various American Colonies in opposition to the Stamp Tax, and later promoted separation from England; died out after Revolution
Stamp Act opposition S-409

Sons of Norway, benefit society
fraternal societies F-387

Sons of the American Revolution
patriotic societies P-140

Sons of the Revolution
patriotic societies P-140

Sony Corporation
copyright lawsuit C-713

Soo, canals. *see in index* Sault Sainte Marie

Soochow, China, city in Kiangsu Province on Grand Canal 45 mi (70 km) w. of Shanghai; tea, rice; silk and cotton processing; one of oldest cities of China; pop. 730,000.

Sooner State. *see in index* Oklahoma

Soong (or Sung), name of famous Chinese family; **T.V. Soong** (1894–1971) set up budget for China; foreign minister 1941–45; became acting premier Dec. 1944 and was premier May 1945–Feb. 1947. His three sisters (educated in U.S.) have won fame in Chinese public and social life: **Ai-ling** (born 1888), widow of H.H. Kung, one of China's financial and political leaders; **Ching-ling** (1890–1981), widow of Sun Yat-sen; and **Mei-ling** (born 1897), wife of Chiang Kai-shek. *see also in index* Soong, Mei-ling; Soong, Ching-ling

Soong, Charles Jones, Chinese Christian missionary C-309

Soong Ching-ling (or Sun Ching-ling Soong) (1890–1981), Chinese political leader, born in Shanghai; married Sun Yat-sen 1915; served on Kuomintang Central Executive Committee and as a vice-chairman of Communist People's Republic at Peking
Chiang Kai-shek C-309

Soong Mei-ling (or Chiang Ching-kuo, or Madame Chiang Kai-shek) (born 1897), wife of Gen. Chiang Kai-shek
Chiang Kai-shek C-309

Soot, bits of partially burned carbon
smoke S-220

Soothsayer. *see in index* Mantis

Sooty tern, bird *Sterna fuscata* G-317

Sophia (1630–1714), electress of Hanover, granddaughter of James I of England and mother of George I G-81

Sophia, Bulgaria. *see in index* Sofia

Sophia Dorothea (1666–1726), wife of George I of England G-81

Sophists, a group of teachers of rhetoric and practical philosophy in ancient Greece (4th and 5th centuries BC), of whom the most famous was Protagoras
Academy's establishment A-14
philosophy P-264
Socrates S-246

Sophocles (496–406 BC), Greek tragic dramatist
'Antigone' R-112d
dance D-22
Greek literature G-275
drama D-242
Oedipus O-494

Soranzo Palace, Venice, built in 15th century for Soranzo family, patrons of literature, in style of Doge's Palace; restored 19th century.

Sora rail, wading bird
rail R-71

Sorbital, alcohol
production, *table* A-274

Sorbonne, college of University of Paris, seat of faculty of letters 1808– and faculty of science 1808–1961; founded by Robert de Sorbon 1257. *see also in index* Paris, University of
Paris, *map* P-120
university history U-209

Sorcery. *see also in index* Magic
witchcraft W-266

'Sordello', poem by Robert Browning B-466

Sorel, Agnes (1422?–50), favorite of King Charles VII of France; once reputed to have exercised powerful influence on French history, but now remembered chiefly for beauty and charm.

Sorel, Albert (1842–1906), French historian, born in France; member of French Academy ('L'Europe et la Révolution française'; 'Montesquieu'; 'Madame de Staël').

Sorel, George (Eugène) (1847–1922), social philosopher and author
anarchism A-388

Sorel, Que., port city on St. Lawrence and Richelieu rivers 42 mi (68 km) n.e. of Montreal; shipyards, ilmenite smelter, grain elevators; textiles, foundry products; pop. 19,347, *map* C-112
Quebec, *map* Q-10

Sorensen, Theodore Chaikin (born 1928), U.S. lawyer, born in Lincoln, Neb.; administrative assistant to John F. Kennedy 1953–61, presidential special counsel 1961–64; author of 'Kennedy'.

Sorensen, Virginia Eggertsen (born 1912), U.S. writer, born in Provo, Utah (Mormon novels: 'A Little Lower Than the Angels', 'Many Heavens'; books for children: 'Plain Girl', 'Miracles on Maple Hill', awarded Newbery Medal 1957, 'Lotte's Locket'; autobiographical stories: 'Where Nothing Is Long Ago').

Sorge, Richard (1895–1944), German national
espionage E-303, *picture* E-304

Sorghum S-258
flour F-213
pioneers use P-333
producing regions

Kansas K-175
Texas T-120, *picture* T-122

Sorgo (or sweet sorghum) S-258

Sorokin, Pitirim Aleksandrovich (1889–1968), U.S. professor, born in Russia; to U.S. 1923, became citizen 1930; professor sociology at University of Minnesota 1924–30, at Harvard 1930–55; author of many books on sociology; autobiographies: 'Leaves from a Russian Diary', 'A Long Journey'.

Sorolla y Bastida, Joaquín (1863–1923), Spanish impressionist painter; excelled in marine compositions involving brilliant sunlight effects.

Sorong, port city of Irian Barat, Indonesia; Japanese base 1942–46 N-174

Sororities. *see in index* Fraternities and sororities

Sorrel tree. *see in index* Sourwood

Sorrento (ancient Surrentum), Italy, resort on Bay of Naples; famous for wine; birthplace of Tasso; pop. 11,768, *map* I-404
Italy, *map* I-403

Sorus (plural sori), in ferns, one of the spore cases appearing as dots on the underside of fertile fronds or along the outer edges
fern F-57

SOS, wireless distress signal used at sea; adopted by International Radiotelegraphic Convention in 1912; the letters have no verbal significance, but are used because easily transmitted
Republic R-56

Sosigenes (1st century BC), Greek mathematician and astronomer; astronomical works lost except for fragments.

Sosnowiec, Poland, city in Upper Silesian coal field, 40 mi (60 km) n.w. of Cracow; textile center; pop. 144,700
Silesia P-413

Sosos, Greek mosaicist M-589

Sostenuto, in music, *list* M-671

Soter, famous dog of Greece; name in Greek means "savior" D-193

Sothern, Edward Hugh (1859–1933), U.S. actor, born in New Orleans, La.; in early years played romantic parts ('If I Were King'; 'The Three Musketeers'); later one of foremost Shakespearean actors (as Hamlet, Macbeth, Shylock, Petruchio); married (1911) Julia Marlowe; author of 'Julia Marlowe's Story' and autobiography.

Sothic cycle, Egyptian calendar, a cycle of 1,460 years of 365 days each; supposedly each year started on the day when the star Sirius (Sothis) rose with the sun, but the interval of 365 days was about 1/4 day short of being a full year; hence every four years the New Year started another day too soon, and the seasons moved "backward" (from March to February, January, etc.) through the year; once in 1,460 years, however, New Year's Day comes correctly with the proper rising of Sirius; this 1,460-year interval constitutes a Sothic cycle.

Soto, Hernando de (1500?–42), Spanish explorer
Florida history F-199
Mississippi river M-484

Soto, largest of the Zen Buddhist sects in Japan; practices method of quiet meditation (*zazen*) as a means of obtaining Enlightenment Z-450

Sottsass, Ettore, Italian designer
industrial design I-174

'Sot-Weed Factor, The', work by Barth
American literature A-361

Sou, old French coin of various metals and values; name applied to former French 5 centime piece; historical value about 1 cent.

Souari nut N-449

Soubirous, Bernadette (or Marie Bernard). *see in index* Bernadette, Saint

Souchong, a grade of black tea T-45

Soufflot, Jacques-Germain (1713–80), French architect [illegible]

Soul
alchemists' belief A-273
animism A-465
Jainism J-14
Judaism J-148
spiritualism S-392
theosophy T-163
transmigration P-544

Soulé, Pierre (1801–70), U.S. political leader, born in France; U.S. senator from Louisiana 1847–53; minister to Spain 1853–55
Ostend Manifesto B-475

Soul music, type of music inspired by gospel music M-681

Soul Stirrers, gospel singing group M-680

Sound S-258, P-305, *Reference-Outline* P-309
acoustics A-21
airplane high-speed flights A-181
amplification
microphone M-378
phonograph P-269, *diagram* P-268d
radio R-60, *diagram* R-46
animal communication A-448
language W-373
bell B-154
echo E-48
frequencies S-260, *diagram* S-262
intensity P-441e, S-260, *picture* P-441e
language basis L-31, 44, *picture* L-32, *diagram* L-33
linquistics L-229
motion pictures M-604
music M-689, S-259
noise. *see in index* Noise
oceans
oceanography O-482
navigation N-70
overtones S-260, *diagram* S-262
physics P-305
pitch S-259, *diagrams* S-261
radio transmission R-57, *diagrams* R-45, *pictures* R-52
field patterns R-53
reflection S-261
reproduction
phonograph P-268d, *pictures* P-269
tape recorder. *see in index* Tape recorder
sciences S-64
speed S-259, *graph* S-260
stereophonic radio R-50, *picture* R-49
supersonic S-260
sonar S-261
tone S-260, *diagrams* S-262
vacuum stops, *diagram* S-260
voice V-376, *diagrams* V-377
waves S-258, *diagrams* S-259, *graph* S-260
depth measurement S-261

Sound, in geography, a narrow strip of water joining two greater bodies of water, or lying between an island and the mainland; an arm or inlet of the sea.

'Sound and the Fury, The', work by Faulkner A-360

Soundboard, a part in some musical instruments
sound S-262

Sound channel, oceanography O-482

Sound effect, motion pictures M-611

Sounding, depth measurement
navigation N-68
oil P-235

Sounding rockets
space travel S-342a–b

'Sound of Music, The' (1965), motion picture by Wise, *picture* M-608

'Sound of the Mountain, The', work by Kawabata
Japanese literature K-193

Sound spectrogram (or voiceprint), a graphic representation of an individual's speech characteristics imprinted on paper, produced electronically on a spectrogram; each person's speech patterns are unique, *picture* L-31

Sound track, motion pictures M-604

Source, river, *diagram* R-210

'Sources of Country Music, The', work by Benton, *picture* M-678

Sour cream
dairy product, *list* D-6

Sourdough, a prospector or settler, particularly in Alaska and Canada; named from his practice of carrying a piece of sour dough, leaven saved while baking bread and used to raise the next dough.

Sourdough Rendezvous, festival in Whitehorse, Y.T. Y-440

Sour gum. *see in index* Black tupelo

Souris, P.E.I., town on Gulf of St. Lawrence 44 mi (71 km) n.e. of Charlottetown; fishing; pop. 1,413, *maps* C-109, 112
Prince Edward Island P-497f, *map* P-497h

Souris River (or Mouse River), rises in s. Saskatchewan, flows 500 mi (800 km) to Assiniboine River, making wide loop into North Dakota S-49c, *map* S-491
North Dakota N-373

Sour milk
dairy product, *list* D-6

Sourwood (or sorrel tree), a small tree of the heath family with clustered white flowers and acid-tasting leaves that turn red in autumn; common in Allegheny Mountains region.

Sousa, John Philip (1854–1932), U.S. composer and bandmaster, known as "the March King," born in Washington, D.C., of Portuguese ancestry; leader of famous Sousa's Band ('The Washington Post', 'Liberty Bell', 'Stars and Stripes Forever', and other marches, comic operas, and songs)
band B-57
Hall of Fame, *table* H-16
popular music M-684

Sousaphone, wind instrument W-230

Souslik. *see in index* Suslik

Sousse (or Susa), Tunisia, seaport in n.e.; cereals, olive oil; dates back to 9th century BC when it was founded by Phoenicians; pop. 69,500.

(39 km) e. of New York City; in Nassau County on Long Island; light manufacturing nearby; pop. 10,978.
Southwestern at Memphis, college in Tenn.; Presbyterian; founded 1848 at Clarksville, moved and changed name 1925; arts and sciences, education, music.
Southwestern College, in Winfield, Kan.; Methodist; founded 1885; arts and sciences, education, fine arts, social sciences.
Southwestern Louisiana, The University of, in Lafayette, La.; state control; founded 1898; arts and sciences, agriculture, business administration, education, engineering, nursing; graduate school.
Southwestern State College (since 1975 Southwestern Oklahoma State University), in Weatherford, Okla.; opened 1903; liberal arts, education, pharmacy; graduate studies.
Southwestern Union College (founded as Keene Academy 1893), in Keene, Tex.; Seventh-day Adventist; present name 1963; liberal arts, education.
Southwestern University, in Georgetown, Tex.; Methodist; founded 1840; arts and sciences, fine arts.
Southwest Missouri State College (since 1972 Southwest Missouri State University), in Springfield, Mo.; founded 1906; liberal arts, education; graduate studies.
Southwest State University, in Marshall, Minn.; established 1963; arts and sciences, education.
Southwest Texas State University, in San Marcos, Tex.; opened 1903; arts and sciences, business administration, education, home economics, industrial arts, music education; vocational agriculture; graduate school.
South Windsor, Conn., town 5 mi (8 km) n.e. of Hartford; farming and industrial area; trucking; aircraft, machinery; birthplace of John Fitch; incorporated 1845; pop. of township 17,198.
Southworth, Albert Sands (1811–94), U.S. photographer famous for his portraiture, *list* P-294
Southworth, George Clark (1890–1972), U.S. physicist, born in Little Cooley, Pa.; taught at Yale 1918–23; research engineer, Bell Telephone Laboratories 1923–55 ('Electric Waves and Their Application to Communication Problems') R-57
South Yemen. *see in index* Yemen, People's Democratic Republic of
Soutine, Chaim (1894–1944), painter, born in Vilna, Lithuania; moved to Paris 1913; works characterized by extreme simplification.
Souvanna Phouma (1901–84), premier of Laos, born in Luang Prabang, Laos; negotiated independence for Laos in 1953 L-48
Souvenir collecting, hobby H-183
Sovereign, a gold coin of United Kingdom, historic value 1 pound sterling; out of use since 1914.
Sovereignty, the supreme power of a state over its subjects, vested in the king in an absolute monarchy and in the people in a democracy; in a wider sense, the power of a state to declare war, negotiate treaties, administer its own internal laws.
Sovetsk (formerly Tilsit), U.S.S.R., former German commercial city on Niemen River about 60 mi (100 km) n.e. of Kaliningrad; captured by Russians in World Wars I and II; included in U.S.S.R. since 1945; pop. 31,941, *map* R-348
Soviet, government, governing body, or council of the U.S.S.R. C-459, R-354
- Supreme R-327, 334b

Soviet Federated Socialist Republic. *see in index* Russian Soviet Federated Socialist Republic
Soviet Socialist Republics. *see in index* Union of Soviet Socialist Republics
Soviet Union. *see in index* Russia; Union of Soviet Socialist Republics
Sovkhoz, Soviet state farm R-330c
Sovnarkhozy, Soviet regional economic councils R-327
Sow, female pig P-320
Sow bug, crustacean of the order Isopoda C-790, *picture* C-791
Sower, Christopher, (or Christopher Sauer) (1693–1758), U.S. printer, born in Germany; to America 1724; established first German print shop in U.S. P-171
'Sower, The', statue in Lincoln, Neb., L-225, *picture* N-101
'Sower, The', work by Millet, *picture* M-417
Sowerby, Leo (1895–1968), U.S. composer, born in Grand Rapids, Mich. ('Comes Autumn Time', 'From Northland', 'The Canticle of the Sun'); Pulitzer prize 1946.
Soweto (or South-Western Townships), in South Africa, an urban complex reserved for blacks A-497
- Johannesburg's segregation J-122

'Sowing Seeds in Danny', work by McClung M-5
Sow thistle, a leafy-stemmed weed *Sonchus oleraceus* of the composite family; 2 to 5 ft (0.6 to 1.5 m) high; prickly leaves; small yellow flower heads.
Soybean S-340
- farming F-28
- flour use B-428
- hay H-75
- Illinois I-36, *picture* I-33, *map* I-42
- legume L-119
- oil S-340
  - margarine M-134

Soyinka, Wole (born 1934), Nigerian author and dramatist, born in Isata; political satirist; manager and producer of theater group (plays: 'The Lion and the Jewel', 'Kongi's Harvest'; poetry; books: 'The Interpreters', 'The Man Died') A-123
Soyuz, Soviet spacecraft S-346f, *table* S-348
- Apollo-Soyuz project U-197, *picture* U-196b

Spa, Belgium, watering place 16 mi (26 km) s.e. of Liège; medicinal springs; German general headquarters in World War I and scene of William II's abdication; conference here between Germans and Allies 1920; pop. 9,055 S-397
- travel and tourism T-271

Spa, health resort T-271
Spaak, Paul Henri (1899–1972), Belgian statesman, born in Brussels; prime minister three times; first president UN General Assembly 1946; chairman council for European recovery 1948–50; president Consultative Assembly, Council of Europe, 1949–51; chairman International Council, European Movement, 1950–55; secretary-general NATO 1957–61; vice-premier and foreign minister of Belgium 1961–66 E-362
Spaatz, Carl (1891–1974), U.S. Air Force general, born in Boyertown, Pa.; chief of U.S. bombing forces against Germany 1944, Japan 1945; became general 1945; chief of staff U.S. Air Force 1947–48.
Space, extent in three dimensions
- cosmology C-731
- design D-108
- perceptions B-402, S-109

Space, universe beyond Earth's atmosphere S-341a. *see also in index* Universe
- aerospace A-67. *see also in index* entries beginning Aero
- almanac N-75
- black hole B-306
- Einstein's theories R-140
- exploration E-377
  - navigation N-73, 76
  - navy N-89
- microbiology M-375
- observatory O-458
- photography P-280
- radiation. *see in index* Radiation

U-195
Spacecraft S-343a, *diagram* S-343b, *list* S-341b, *tables* S-344. *see also in index* Satellites, artificial
- aerospace industry A-74, *picture* A-79
- Apollo S-346b, *diagrams* S-346c, *pictures* S-341d, *table* S-348
  - moon landings S-341, 347
- electronics E-175
- environmental control S-343a, 346
- flight paths S-342d, *diagram* S-343
- glass window construction G-155
- Goddard G-173
- launching S-342b, *pictures* S-341d, 342c, *map* S-342a
- reaction principle used S-342a
- United States U-194
- Von Braun's development B-411

Space Flight, Office of, NASA N-22
Space heater, appliance H-111, 212
Space Invaders, electronic game E-172
'Spacelab 1' space laboratory module S-347
Space navigation. *see in index* space travel
Space Needle, in Seattle, Wash., *picture* W-57
Space pilots. *see in index* Space travel, *subhead* manned flights
Space probe. *see in index* Probe
Space Science and Applications, Office of, NASA N-22
Space shuttle, U.S. A-835, F-428, *picture* F-426
- electronics E-180
- space travel, *picture* S-347
- wind tunnel W-235

Space-time continuum, Einstein's theory R-141
Space Tracking and Data Systems, Office of, NASA N-22, S-343b
Space travel S-341. *see also in index* Jet propulsion
- animal tests A-449
- automated systems use A-840
- chronology S-348d
- clothing S-346c
- countdown, *picture* R-231
- extraterrestrial life E-386
- fire hazards F-106
- food processing F-283
- frontiers F-427, *pictures* F-418, 426
- fuel R-233, *diagram* R-232
- Goddard G-173
- gravitation G-240
- guided missiles G-312
- hazards A-82, S-346
- hibernation research H-148
- history S-341c
  - Kennedy's contribution K-201, *table* K-197
  - Tsiolkovsky's contribution T-302
- instrumentation I-230, *picture* I-229
- insulating blanket I-232
- international cooperation S-348a
- manned flights S-346, *pictures* S-341b
  - Apollo-Soyuz project S-346f, U-197, *picture* U-196b
  - Gagarin G-2
  - moon, *pictures* S-341d, 342c
    - Armstrong A-632
    - landings S-341
    - stamp honors, *picture* S-405
  - procedure S-346b, *diagrams* S-346d, 346e
  - spacecraft components S-346b
    - altitude indicator, *picture* N-74
- moon M-576, S-343b, *table* S-344. *see also in index* Spacecraft, *subhead* Apollo
- NASA. *see in index* National Aeronautics and Space Administration
- navigation N-74, 77
- navy N-89
- petroleum products use P-241b
- photography P-280
- plants affected S-345
- private groups S-242, 348a
- probe. *see in index* Probe
- projects. *see in index* Project Apollo; Project Gemini; Project Mercury
- radio frequencies R-54
- reasons for S-341a
- rockets S-342a, 345, *pictures* S-341c, 341d
  - early efforts S-341d, *picture* R-233
  - Europas S-348a, *picture* S-348b
  - Saturn S-346d, 348c, *pictures* S-341d, 342c, *diagrams* S-346c to 346e
- satellites. *see in index* Satellites, artificial
- science fiction. *see in index* Science fiction
- spacecraft. *see in index* Spacecraft
- telemetry S-343a, 345, 346c, *pictures* R-231, S-342b, 343, *diagram* S-343b
- terms, *list* S-341b
- testing. *see in index* Testing, *subhead* space travel
- training procedures S-346b
- Van Allen belts V-259
- weightlessness. *see in index* Weightlessness

Space walk S-346f, *picture* S-341b, *table* S-348
- moon landings. *see in index* Moon, *subhead* manned landings

Spade, tool G-22
Spadefish (also called white angel), a good food fish *Chaetodipterus faber* of warm seas; allied to and resembles the angel fish; body is very deep, covered with roughish scales of varying color.
Spaeth, Sigmund (1885–1965), U.S. writer and lecturer on music, born in Philadelphia, Pa.; collected U.S. ballads and did much to promote appreciation of music.
Spaghetti western, type of movie W-151
Spagnoletto, Lo. *see in index* Ribera, José
Spahn, Warren (Edward) (born 1921), left-handed U.S. baseball pitcher, born in Buffalo, N.Y.; with Boston (later Milwaukee) Braves 1942 and 1946–64, New York Mets and San Francisco Giants 1965; set many pitching records B-92
Spaight, Richard Dobbs (1758–1802), U.S. statesman, born in New Bern, N.C.; signed United States Constitution; governor of North Carolina (1792–98); member of Congress (1798–1801); fatally wounded in duel.
Spain, a nation of s.w. Europe; 194,884 sq mi (504,747 sq km); cap. Madrid; pop. 36,229,900 S-349, *map* E-361
- agriculture
  - irrigation V-256
  - olives, *picture* G-65
- arts
  - architecture A-557. *see also in index* Mission architecture; Moorish architecture
  - classical music M-668
  - dance D-31
  - folk art F-253
  - motion pictures M-623
  - painting P-39, 60, *pictures* P-40, 59, *Reference-Outline* P-69
  - puppetry P-536
- bullfighting B-501
- Canary Islands C-130
- Christmas C-404
- cigarettes T-200
- cities. *see also in index* cities listed below and other cities by name
  - Barcelona B-79
  - Seville S-118
  - Toledo T-212
  - Valencia V-256
- flags F-153, *pictures* F-155, 170
- government F-419
  - Communist party C-619
  - elections S-357
  - taxation, *table* T-35
- history. *see in index* Spain, history of
- hydroelectric power P-543
- international trade I-270
- language and literature. *see in index* Spanish language; Spanish literature
- national anthem, *table* N-64
- people
  - Basques B-103
  - Moors and Moriscos M-581
  - racial classification R-27
- Pyrenees P-543
- space-tracking facilities S-343b
- stringed instruments S-492
- transportation
  - railroad mileage, *table* R-85
  - ship tonnage, *table* S-176a
- weights and measures, *table* W-141
- wine W-239

Spain, history of S-357, *Reference-Outline* S-363. *see also in index* South America, *subhead* history, exploration and conquest; and names of separate countries
- ancient S-357
  - Carthage S-357
  - Phoenicians P-267
- Byzantine capture B-535

Sputum, accumulation of saliva, mucus, and pus D-177

Spuyten Duyvil Creek, small stream that, with Harlem River, separates boroughs of Manhattan and the Bronx, New York City; now used as ship canal.

Spy, in military practice, anyone not wearing the uniform of his or her country and secretly or under false pretenses obtaining information in enemy territory with intent to communicate it to his or her own army I-326. *see also in index* Espionage
East Germany G-127
Korean jetliner incident I-264
U-2 incident E-142
West Germany G-126

'Spy, The', novel by James Fenimore Cooper, published 1821; hero is Harvey Birch, American spy in Revolutionary War; first American novel widely recognized.

Spy fiction L-113

Spyri, Johanna Heusser (1827–1901), Swiss writer S-398

Squab, young pigeon P-324

Squad car, police car P-424

Squadrol, police car P-424

Squadron, naval N-80

Squall (or pampero), abrupt change in wind direction with a drop in temperature W-225
Argentina A-576

Squamous cell cancer, type of skin cancer C-134

Squanto (or Tisquantum) (died 1622), American Indian chief, friend of English colonists P-395
Standish S-410

Square, device for measuring, drawing, or testing right angles; usually consists of two straight edges set perpendicularly; common types: try square, T square, and carpenter's square.

Square, in mathematics
algebraic formulas A-298
geometry G-74, *diagram* G-75
measurement M-242
powers and roots P-484

Square, public. *see in index* Plaza

Square capital, in calligraphy C-58

Square centimeter, unit of metric measure, *table* W-141

Square dance, folk dance F-257, *picture* P-337

Squared circle, in boxing B-388

Square Deal, policy of Theodore Roosevelt R-284, U-183

Square foot, unit of measure, *table* W-140

Square inch, unit of measure, *table* W-140

Square kilometer, unit of metric measure, *table* W-141

Square knot (also called reef knot, or sailor knot) K-262

Square meter, unit of metric measure, *table* W-141

Square mile, unit of measure, *table* W-140

Square-mouthed rhinoceros, mammal R-178

Square-rigged ship, *diagram* S-166, *picture* S-165

Square rod, unit of measure, *table* W-140

Square root, in mathematics P-484

Square yard, unit of measure, *table* W-140

Squash, vegetable S-399
gourds G-198

Squash rackets, game played in a covered or uncovered court with an India-rubber ball and rounded racket; players (two in singles, four in doubles) try alternately to hit ball against front wall of court within a certain marked space A-791

Squat, in weight lifting W-137

Squatter, one who settles on public land to obtain a title to it P-340

Squatter sovereignty. *see in index* Popular sovereignty

Squawberry. *see in index* Partridgeberry

Squawfish, large fish of the Cyprinidae, or minnow family, in the Pacific drainage region; the Colorado River squawfish is the largest American member of the Cyprinidae family, growing to 6 ft (2 m).

Squaw Valley, valley in Sierra Nevada of California, n.w. of Lake Tahoe; ski resort; ski trails on Squaw Peak; site of 1960 Winter Olympic Games.

Squeezebox extractor, in laundering, *picture* L-87

Squeeze cage, device used in veterinary medicine Z-464

Squeteague (or weakfish, or sea trout), famous sport and food fish *Cynoscion regalis* of the eastern seaboard; member of the croaker family; sold under name of sea trout.

Squid, ten-armed finned mollusk of the cuttlefish family O-490, S-399. *see also in index* Cuttlefish; Octopus
animal defense A-427
body structure A-422
deep-sea form, *picture* D-59
giant squid. *see in index* Giant squid
mollusks M-526

Squill, perennial plants *Scilla* of the lily family, native to Europe and Asia but widely cultivated spring flowers in North America; bulbs used in medicine.

Squire, Sir John Collings (1884–1958), English writer, born in Plymouth; editor *London Mercury* 1919–34; showed versatility in writing distinctive verse, witty parodies, brilliant criticism; founded *London Mercury* 1919 ('Steps to Parnassus', 'The Lily of Malud', 'Life at the Mermaid', 'Essays on Poetry').

Squire (or esquire), knight's attendant K-257, *picture* K-258
Middle Ages M-387

Squirrel S-399
bird feeder attack B-260
care P-247
flying squirrel S-401, *pictures* S-400
furs F-463, *table* F-465
habitat F-311
hibernation H-147
life expectancy, *chart* A-423
migration S-400

Squirrel corn, delicate plant *Dicentra canadensis* with grainlike tubers beneath ground that resemble grains of corn; belongs to same genus as Dutchman's breeches.

Squirrelfish, small bright red tropical fish allied to the groupers; inhabits rocks and reefs; nocturnal feeder with exceptionally large eyes.

Squirrel hake (or red hake), fish *Urophycis chuss* of the family Merlucciidae H-13

Squirrel-tail grass (also known as barley grass, or foxtail, or tickle grass), species of wild barley; has bushy spikes.

Squirting cucumber, weed *Ecballium elaterium* W-131

Sremski Karlovci, Yugoslavia. *see in index* Karlowitz

Sri Lanka (formerly Ceylon), island republic s.e. of India; 25,332 sq mi (65,610 sq km); cap. Colombo; pop. 14,300,000 S-401
animals and plants
cinnamon, *picture* P-203
coconut palm, *picture* P-82
Asia, *map* A-697
Bandaranaike B-58
Commonwealth membership C-602
flag, *picture* F-170
history
United Kingdom E-258
masks M-186
national anthem, *table* N-64
national park N-27
products
graphite C-157
pepper, *chart* P-197a
tea T-46
railroad mileage, *table* R-85
world, *map* W-300

Srinagar, Kashmir (Jammu and Kashmir), summer capital, situated on Jhelum River; paper, carpets, silver and copper ware, leather; pop. 403,413 J-22, *map* I-83

Srivijaya Kingdom, historical kingdom based in Palembang I-164

SS, Nazi military organization. *see in index* Schutzstaffel

SS 'Keno' National Historic Site, in Yukon Territory, Canada. *see in index* Palace Grand Theatre and SS 'Keno' National Historic Site

SST, supersonic transport A-207, P-441e

Ssu-ma Ch'ien (145–85 BC), Chinese astronomer, calendar expert, and first great historian of China C-363
history writing H-171
'Shih-chi' C-388

Ssu-ma Kuang (1019–1086), Chinese historian, statesman, and poet C-366
history writing H-171

Staatsrat (or Council of State), one of two legislative chambers of East Germany G-120

Stabat Mater ("the Mother was standing"), first words and title of a Latin hymn on the Crucifixion, ascribed to Jacopone, a Franciscan monk of 13th century; set to music by Palestrina, Haydn, Verdi, Rossini, Dvorak, and others
Verdi V-202

Stabile, in art S-93
Calder C-27

Stabilizer
glassmaking G-156
navigation
aviation A-181
ships G-328, S-170

Stable equilibrium. *see also in index* Equilibrium, in physics

Stable fly, bloodsucking fly of stables; often enters houses
egg, *picture* E-111

Stabroek, Guyana. *see in index* Georgetown

Staccato, in music, *list* M-671

Stachys, genus of tall annual or perennial plants of the mint family, native, chiefly, to the temperate regions; includes *S. sieboldii,* also called chorogi or knotroot, with edible tubers; hedge nettles or woundworts, once used in medicine. *see also in index* Lamb's-ears

Stack, Sir Lee (1868–1924), British statesman, entered army 1888; took post in Egypt 1889; made governor-general and sirdar of Sudan 1919; assassinated by a Wafdist.

Stadacona, Que., village near Quebec
Cartier C-185, C-90

Stadia, ancient Greek unit of measure, *table* W-141

Stadimeter (or range finder), in navigation N-70

Stadium, Greek measure of length (equal to about 606 ft; 184.7 m); term applied to racecourse at Olympia, which was exactly a stadium in length, and later to similar places for holding athletic contests
Cotton Bowl. *see in index* Cotton Bowl
John F. Kennedy Stadium, Philadelphia, Pa., *map* P-251a
Lenin Stadium, Moscow, U.S.S.R. R-332b
Orange Bowl. *see in index* Orange Bowl
Rose Bowl. *see in index* Rose Bowl

Staël, Madame de (or Anne Louise Germaine Necker, baronne de Staël-Holstein) (1766–1817), French novelist, born in Paris, France; daughter of financier Jacques Necker; her salon a center for intellectuals and political figures; banished by Napoleon ('Delphine', 'Corinne') G-58

Staff, compound consisting chiefly of plaster of Paris and cement mixed with water, dextrin, and tow, used for temporary buildings; first used at Paris Exposition 1878.

Staff, in music M-689, *list* M-671

Staff, U.S. Army. *see in index* General staff

Staffa, tiny island of Scotland off w. coast, 7 mi (11 km) from Mull.

Staff nurse N-446

Staff officer, U.S. Army A-634

Stafford, Henry. *see in index* Buckingham, Henry Stafford, duke of

Stafford, Thomas Patten (born 1930), U.S. astronaut, born in Weatherford, Okla.; U.S. Air Force officer; NASA astronaut 1962–75; chief, NASA astronaut office, 1969–75; commander Apollo/Soyuz Test Project 1975; commander test-pilot program Edwards Air Force Base, Calif., *picture* U-196b, *table* S-348

Stafford (or Staffordshire), midland county of England; 1,154 sq mi (2,989 sq km); coal, iron; iron-and-steel manufacture; shoes; pop. 1,733,519
potteries P-474

Staffordshire terrier, breed of dog, *picture* D-204

Staff-tree family (or Celastraceae), family of shrubs and trees, including the burning bush, khat or cafta, false bittersweet, false olive, and mayten.

Stag, male pig P-320

'Stag at Sharkey's', painting by Bellow B-158

Stag beetle B-138, *picture* B-140

Stage, of microscope M-381

Stage and staging T-152. *see also in index* Theater
acting A-24
motion picture comparison M-607
directing D-152
opera O-560
puppet P-536, *diagram* P-538, *picture* V-242
Shakespeare S-136

Stage carpenter, theater T-156

Stagecoach, game G-11

Stagecoach, horse-drawn vehicle, *picture* T-262
Concord N-178
early history R-220
express history E-384
outlaws O-619

'Stagecoach', motion picture depicting the wild West W-152

Stage fright, nervousness felt before an audience P-526c

Stage wagon W-2

Stagflation, in economics I-199

'Stag Frieze, The', cave painting at Lascaux D-252

Stagg, Amos Alonzo (1862–1965), U.S. football coach, born in West Orange, N.J.; football coach and director of athletics, University of Chicago, 1892–1933; football coach, College of the Pacific, 1933–46; cocoach Susquehanna University (with son Amos Alonzo, Jr.) 1947–52; advisory coach Stockton College 1953–60 F-296

Staghound, oversized foxhound bred in England and France for deer hunting; also saw service in England as war dog; now practically extinct.

Stagira, ancient town on coast of Chalcidice, Macedonia; birthplace of Aristotle, who was called "the Stagirite."

'Stag King, The', opera by Henze O-571

Stahl, Georg Ernst (1660–1734), German physician and chemist, born in Anspach; author of books on combustion, medicine, and chemistry S-57i
chemistry C-301

Stahlheim, Norway, *picture* N-389

Stahr, Elvis Jacob, Jr. (born 1916), U.S. lawyer, educator, and government official, born in Hickman, Ky.; president West Virginia University 1959–61; secretary of the army 1961–62; president Indiana University 1962–68; president National Audubon Society 1968–.

Stained-glass window A-552. *see also in index* Rose window
glass manufacture G-161, *picture* G-163
hobby, *picture* H-189
lead use L-99
Middle Ages M-393

Stainless steel. *see in index* Steel, *subhead* stainless

Stain removal, in dry cleaning D-279

Stair (or stairs), series of steps between two levels
accident prevention S-7
American pyramids P-543
ancient Egyptian house S-157
climbing energy P-483
escalator E-187
painting P-76
Paris store, *picture* P-121
Persepolis, *picture* P-213
Spanish Steps, Rome R-255, *map* R-250, *picture* R-252
theater, *picture* S-139

Staircase shell, mollusk shell of *Architectonica perspectiva*, *picture* S-152

Stairways, series of falls in Payette River, Idaho, *picture* I-27

Staked Plain. *see in index* Llano Estacado

Stalactites and stalagmites
cave C-233
limestone L-210
minerals M-435

Stalemate, chess move C-306

U.S. naval forces in Europe 1942–45; retired 1946.

Stark, Independence, U.S. businessman
laundry industry L-86

Stark, Johannes (1874–1957), German physicist, born in Schickenhof, near Regensburg, Germany; authority on radiation and atomic theory; discovered that spectral lines are distorted in an electrical field. *see also in index* Nobel Prizewinners, *table*

Stark, John (1728–1822), American Revolutionary War general, born in Londonderry, N.H.; fought at Bunker Hill, Trenton, and Princeton; won victory at Bennington, Vt., Aug. 16, 1777; later commander of Northern Department
Statuary Hall, *table* S-437b

Starkey, Richard. *see in index* Starr, Ringo

Starkville, Miss., city 23 mi (37 km) w. of Columbus; furniture, electric motors, metal buildings; incorporated 1831; pop. 15,169.

Starley, James (1830–81), designer of bicycle, *picture* B-188

'Starlight Express' (1985), work by Webber M-686

Starling, Ernest Henry (1866–1927), English physiologist, born in Bombay, India; discoverer, with William Maddock Bayliss, of hormone, secretin ('Principles of Human Physiology') M-285

Starling, bird of the family Sturnidae S-426
bird species B-246, *picture* B-244
egg, *picture* E-112
lifespan, *chart* A-423

Star-nosed mole, mammal *Condylura cristata* M-521

Star-of-Bethlehem, perennial plant *Ornithogalum umbellatum* of lily family; thin, grasslike fleshy leaves; clusters of green and white small starlike flowers.

Star of Este, diamond, *picture* D-129

Star of South Africa, diamond, *picture* D-129

Star of the South, Brazilian diamond found in 1853 by a female slave who was rewarded with freedom and pension for life; stone weighed 257½ carats in rough; cut into 125-carat brilliant that appears colorless from the top, but rose-tinted from the side, *picture* D-129

Starr, Belle (1848–89), U.S. outlaw O-619

Starr, Bryan (nickname Bart) (born 1934), U.S. football player, born in Montgomery, Ala.; quarterback, Green Bay Packers 1956–71; head coach 1975–83.

Starr, Ellen Gates (1859–1940), U.S. social worker, born in Laona, Ill.; helped found Hull House A-40

Starr, Ringo (or Richard Starkey) (born 1940), British rock musician
The Beatles B-119
popular music M-682

Star routes, routes marked in U.S. Postal Guide with star, over which mail was carried by horse or other means in absence of rail or steamboat facilities; term first used in report of postmaster general in 1859; conspiracy in President Hayes's administration to increase fees was exposed under President Garfield (Star route frauds); thousands of star routes in operation in U.S. today P-460a
Arthur A-654

Starry flounder, flatfish *Platichthys stellatus* of the family Pleuronectidae F-173

Stars and Stripes. *see in index* Flags of the United States

Star shell, snail *Astraea longispina*, *picture* S-150

'Star-Spangled Banner, The', the United States national anthem, composed by Francis Scott Key N-63
flag etiquette F-152, *picture* F-155
Key K-229
Maryland history M-172
popular music M-683
War of 1812 W-32

Star time. *see in index* Sidereal time

Starting powder, in fireworks F-114

Star Trek, science fiction television series S-62, *picture* S-61

Starved Rock, state park in Illinois I-39, *picture* I-47

'Starving Artist, The' (1907), early silent film, *picture* M-618

'Star Wars', trilogy of movies by George Lucas
folklore imitated F-270
'Return of the Jedi', *picture* F-269
science fiction S-62

Star Wars. *see in index* Strategic Defense Initiative

Stassen, Harold Edward (born 1907), U.S. lawyer, public official, born in West St. Paul, Minn.; when elected governor of Minnesota (1938) was youngest governor in U.S.; reelected 1940, 1942; resigned 1943 to join Navy; president University of Pennsylvania 1948–53; U.S. director of Foreign Operations Administration 1953–55; special assistant on disarmament problems 1955–58
Eisenhower administration E-138

Stassfurt, East Germany, town 18 mi (29 km) s. of Magdeburg; salt works; chemicals; engineering, radio, and scientific equipment plants; pop. 26,276, *map* G-134
minerals M-435

State, Papal secretary of P-100

State, of United States. *see also in index* states by name
area, *table* U-118
birds. *see in index* states by name, *subhead* bird, state
flags, *pictures* F-159
flowers S-426, *picture* S-427. *see also in index* states by name, *subhead* flower, state
forests. *see in index* states by name, *subhead* forests
governments. *see in index* State government
international relations I-259
jury system J-159
statehood S-429a, U-151, *pictures* S-429b
Statuary Hall S-437a
workmen's compensation insurance I-234

State, Department of, United States U-157, *list* U-156
Agency for International Development P-19
diplomacy D-149
Foreign Service U-158
passport P-137
secretary U-157

State banks, in United States B-64

State capitalism, system of government in which the means of production are controlled by the government G-199

State College, Pa., borough about 65 mi (105 km) n.w. of Harrisburg; near geographic center of state; metal products; limestone industry; research center; pop. 36,130, *map* P-184
Pennsylvania State University, *picture* P-171

State colleges and universities U-207. *see also in index* names of colleges and universities; *also* Fact Summary with each state article

State courts, in United States S-429. *see also* Fact Summary with each state article

State Fair Park, in Dallas, Tex., site of largest annual state fair in U.S. D-10

State fairs, in United States F-7, R-188

State farm. *see in index* Collective farm

State flowers S-426. *see also in index* states by name

State government, U.S. S-428. *see also* Fact Summary with each state article
Bill of Rights U-144
Civil War U-179
colleges and universities U-207
courts of justice C-748
elections E-146
electoral college E-148
employment agencies E-205
governors. *see in index* Governor
physician licensing M-277
police P-430, *pictures* P-429
prisons and punishments P-505, *pictures* P-506
public utilities P-526c
safety measures S-6
social insurance S-236, P-189
taxation T-37
voting V-386, *pictures* V-387

State governors, in United States. *see in index* Governor

State Hermitage Museum, in Leningrad L-128, M-663

State Historical Museum, in Moscow, U.S.S.R., *picture* K-305

Statehood S-429a, *map* S-429c, *pictures* S-429b. *see also in index* names of states, *subhead* history
Alaska A-246

Statehood Act, in U.S. A-244

Staten Island, in New York, an island forming Richmond Borough of New York City; pop. 352,121 N-270

Staten Island Ferry, of New York City N-271, *picture* N-272

State of the Union message, speech by the president of United States P-493, U-150, *picture* U-155

State ownership. *see in index* Government ownership

State parks P-126. *see also in index* states by name, *subhead* parks, monuments, and other areas

State Public Scientific and Technical Library of the Academy of Sciences of the U.S.S.R., copyright library, U.S.S.R. N-415

Stateroom, a private room
submarines, *diagram* S-499

State's attorney (also called county attorney, or district attorney, or prosecuting attorney, or public prosecutor) S-429

Statesboro, Ga., city 47 mi (76 km) n.w. of Savannah; iron castings, meters and measuring devices, textiles; Strategic Air Command unit; incorporated 1803; pop. 14,866.

States-General, France. *see in index* Estates-General

States-General, in The Netherlands, parliament N-129

State socialism S-234

States' rights, in United States history S-429d
Civil War C-470, U-144
Confederate States of America C-642
Calhoun C-31
Clay C-487
Constitutional amendments
Constitution limits U-149
10th U-152
11th U-144, 152
Jackson J-9
Jefferson J-93
Johnson, Andrew J-127
political parties P-432
Stephen S-443
Virginia and Kentucky Resolutions S-429d

States' Rights Democratic party. *see in index* Dixiecrats

State Street, in Chicago, Ill., shopping thoroughfare C-311

State succession. *see in index* Statehood

Statesville, N.C., city 38 mi (61 km) n. of Charlotte; dairy cattle, poultry; cotton, grain, tobacco; textiles, apparel, furniture, metal products, flour and other food; pop. 18,622.

State trees. *see in index* States by name

State universities U-207. *see also in index* universities by name; Fact Summary with each state article

State University of New York, established 1948 as part of The University of the State of New York; comprises the university centers at Albany, Binghamton, Buffalo, and Stony Brook; medical centers at Syracuse and Brooklyn; 15 four-year state colleges, including one at Cornell University and one at Alfred University; health science centers at Buffalo and Stony Brook; 3 specialized colleges; 29 community colleges; and 6 two-year agricultural and technical colleges N-254

Static, disturbing effects in radio receiver R-51

Statice, genus of plants. *see in index* Sea pink

Static electricity, electricity at rest E-149
Von Guericke, *picture* S-57h

Statics, field of mechanics that deals with bodies at rest or in motion with constant velocity M-263, 268
sciences S-64

Stationary front, boundary between two air masses W-118, *map* W-124

Stationer, medieval name for bookseller B-350

Stationery P-103

'Stations of the Cross', series of paintings by Newman N-212

Statism, supremacy of the state in all matters pertaining to its subjects
human rights H-319

Statistical forecasting, method of weather forecasting W-122

Statistical map G-229
maps M-121

Statistical surface, in maps M-122

Statistical table G-221, S-432, *tables* S-433

Statistics S-430
branches S-64
graph and chart G-221
index numbers P-202
mathematics M-220
sociology applications S-243
variability S-435
vital statistics. *see in index* Vital statistics

Stator
jet propulsion J-106
meter M-317
motor and engine M-631
torque converter A-815

Statoscope, in aviation, instrument for determining rate of descent or ascent of a balloon or airship.

Statuary. *see in index* Sculpture

Statuary Hall, U.S. Capitol, Washington, D.C. S-437a, *pictures* S-437b

Statue of Liberty. *see in index* Liberty, Statue of

Statues (also known as Red Light), game G-12

Status, social F-19

Statute law
law L-94, *table* L-93

Statute of Westminster (1931), English history E-257
Australia A-806
Canada C-103

Statutes of Limitations. *see in index* Limitations, Statutes of

Statutory days, legal holidays in Canada F-61

Statutory rape, sexual relations with a child, even with the child's consent
crime C-771

Staubbach, waterfall in Bernese Alps, Switzerland, s. of Lauterbrunnen; height 980 ft (300 m); part of stream of same name, branch of White Lutschine River.

Staudinger, Hermann (1881–1965), German chemist, born in Worms; pioneer in field of macromolecular chemistry. *see also in index* Nobel Prizewinners, *table*

Staunton, Howard (1810–74) British chess master, born in London; designed chess pieces C-306

Staunton, Va., city in Shenandoah Valley 32 mi (52 km) n.w. of Charlottesville; in fruit, farming, and dairying area; beef cattle, sheep; air conditioners, clothing, furniture; Mary Baldwin College; state school for deaf and blind; pop. 21,857 V-337, *map* V-348

Staupers, Mabel Keaton (born 1890), U.S. registered nurse, born on island of Barbados, West Indies; to U.S. 1903, became citizen 1917; fought effectively against racial discrimination both in the training and employment of nurses; won 1951 Spingarn Medal.

Staupitz, Johann von (1460?–1524), German Roman Catholic theologian; professor of theology at Wittenberg and vicar-general of the Augustinian Order in Germany; early friend and adviser of Luther.

Staurolite, cross-stone (or fairy stone), a reddish-brown iron aluminum silicate, often crystallizing in shape of cross; used as charms; legend says they fell from heaven.

Stautner, Ernest (born 1925), U.S. football player and assistant coach, born in state of Bavaria, Germany; defensive tackle Pittsburgh Steelers 1950–63; assistant coach Pittsburgh Steelers 1963–64,

corps in Mexican War and in coast survey office 1849–53; director of survey of northern railway route between St. Paul, Minn., and Puget Sound; criticized as governor for handling of American Indian affairs but later vindicated; territorial delegate (1857–59); major general of New York volunteers in Civil War; killed in battle of Chantilly.

Stevens, John (1749–1838), U.S. engineer and inventor, born in New York City; father of Robert L. Stevens; helped secure U.S. patent system; built *Phoenix*, a seagoing steamboat, 1807, that ran successfully on Delaware River
early railroads R-73

Stevens, John Paul (born 1920), U.S. jurist, born in Chicago, Ill.; private law practice 1948–70; U.S. circuit court judge 1970–75; justice U.S. Supreme Court 1975–.

Stevens, Risë (born 1913), U.S. mezzo-soprano, born in New York City; studied in Europe; debut in Prague 1936; with Metropolitan Opera, New York City, 1938–64; concert, radio, film, and television work, *list* O-570

Stevens, Robert Livingston (1787–1856), U.S. mechanical engineer, naval architect, and inventor, born in Hoboken, N.J.; son of John Stevens; in 1830 designed railway rail with flanged T-section still in use; also designed and built steamships and sailing vessels (*Maria*, fastest of its day) R-75

Stevens, Thaddeus (1792–1868), U.S. statesman and abolitionist S-445, R-116

Stevens, Wallace (1879–1955), U.S. poet and insurance executive, born in Reading, Pa.; poems have irony, wit, and polish ('Transport to Summer'; 'The Auroras of Autumn'; 'The Collected Poems of Wallace Stevens', 1955 Pulitzer prize) A-356

Stevens Institute of Technology, at Castle Point, Hoboken, N.J.; private control; founded for men 1870, now coed; engineering, science; graduate school.

Stevenson, Adlai Ewing (1835–1914), U.S. statesman, born in Christian County, Ky.; U.S. representative from Illinois 1875–77; assistant postmaster general 1885–89
Cleveland C-492
Eisenhower E-134

Stevenson, Adlai Ewing (1900–65), U.S. public official, born in Los Angeles, Calif.; special counsel, AAA 1933–34; special assistant to secretary of the Navy 1941–44 and to secretary of state 1945; worked in UN 1945–47; governor of Illinois 1949–53; Democratic presidential nominee 1952, 1956; ambassador to UN 1961–65 ('Major Campaign Speeches, 1952', 'What I Think', 'The New America', 'Friends and Enemies', 'Looking Outward') P-433
electoral vote, *chart* P-495

Stevenson, Fanny van de Grift Osbourne (1840–1914), wife of Robert Louis Stevenson, born in Indianapolis ('Our Samoan Adventure', with R.L. Stevenson) S-446

Stevenson, Robert (1772–1850), Scottish engineer, inventor of intermittent lights for lighthouses; built Bell Rock and many other lighthouses on Scottish coast; grandfather of Robert Louis Stevenson.

Stevenson, Robert Louis (1850–94), British story writer, poet, and essayist S-446. *see also in index* 'Kidnapped'
'A Child's Garden of Verses' R-111
horror story H-246
literary contribution E-278
'Treasure Island' R-111e
Western Samoa W-154

Stevens Point, Wis., city on Wisconsin River, 100 mi (160 km) n. of Madison; dairy farms, potatoes; paper, fishing tackle, lumber, and furniture; Wisconsin State University—Stevens Point; incorporated 1858; pop. 22,970.

Stevia, genus of perennial plants of the composite family, found from Texas to South America; leaves small, narrow; flowers small, purple through white, in terminal clusters; clusters of tiny, fragrant, white flowers of another perennial *Piqueria trinervia* are generally called stevia by gardeners.

Stevin, Simon (1548–1620), Dutch mathematician and inventor M-268

Stew, in cooking C-700

Steward, in horse racing H-276

Stewardship, in religion B-214

Stewart, royal family. *see in index* Stuart

Stewart, Alexander Turney (1803–76), U.S. merchant and philanthropist, born in Lisburn, County Antrim, Northern Ireland; his dry-goods store in New York City became one of largest in world, with branches in Europe; at death considered richest man in America.

Stewart, Douglas (born 1913), Australian writer A-799, *table* A-798

Stewart, Dugald (1753–1828), Scottish philosopher of the "common sense" school; immensely popular lecturer at University of Edinburgh.

Stewart, James Maitland (born 1908), U.S. actor, born in Indiana, Pa.; commanded bomber squadron in World War II; played awkward youth with hesitant drawl in early films ('Mr. Smith Goes to Washington'; 'The Philadelphia Story', 1940 Academy award); variety of mature roles after 1940s ('Anatomy of a Murder'); star television series 1972.

Stewart, John Innes Mackintosh (or Michael Innes) (born 1906), detective story writer D-119

Stewart, Mary (born 1916), British author, born in Sunderland; known for books for adults, young adults, and children ('The Moon-Spinners', made into motion picture; 'This Rough Magic'; 'The Hollow Hills'; 'The Last Enchantment'; for young children: 'The Little Broomstick', 'Ludo and the Star Horse'
'Crystal Cave, The' R-112
'Nine Coaches Waiting' R-112b

Stewart, Potter (1915–85), U.S. jurist, born in Jackson, Mich.; judge U.S. Sixth Circuit Court of Appeals 1954–58; justice U.S. Supreme Court 1958–81.

Stewart, Reginald (born 1900), Canadian pianist and conductor, born in Edinburgh, Scotland; director, Peabody Conservatory, Baltimore, Md.; conductor, Baltimore Symphony Orchestra 1942–52.

Stewart, Robert. *see in index* Castlereagh, Robert Stewart, viscount (2nd marquis of Londonderry)

Stewart, Robert L. (born 1942), U.S. astronaut, born in Washington, D.C. S-347, *table* S-348

Stewart, William H(uffman) (born 1921), U.S. physician, born in Minneapolis, Minn.; practiced pediatrics 1948–51; with Public Health Service 1951–69, surgeon general 1965–69.

Stewart, William Morris (1827–1909), U.S. lawyer and senator; developed famous Comstock Lode and made fortune in Nevada mines.

Stewart, diamond, *picture* D-129

Stewart Island, one of New Zealand group; 674 sq mi (1,746 sq km); volcanic; mountainous, highest point Mount Anglem, 3,200 ft (975 m); discovered 1808, purchased 1864 (from Maori) by British; pop. 513
New Zealand N-287, *map* N-299
Pacific Ocean, *map* P-6

Sthanekavasis, subsect of Jainism J-14

Stibnite (or antimony sufide), mineral M-432

Stick, printing, metal frame used in setting type by hand; holds about 15 lines of newspaper-size type P-499, *picture* P-500

Stick insect, various insects resembling branches and twigs of trees, *pictures* P-510, 512

Stickleback, fish S-447, *picture* P-447

Stickseed, hairy, grayish herbs comprising the genus *Lappula* of the borage family with small narrow gray-green leaves and racemes, or spikes, of small white to violet flowers; the burlike fruit is covered with barbed prickles.

Stiegel, Henry William (1729–85), U.S. glassmaker, born in Germany; founded Mannheim, Pa., in 1762, where he built a glass factory; produced valuable flint glass
design D-116
glass manufacture G-162

Stieglitz, Alfred (1864–1946), U.S. photographer and editor of photography magazines, born in Hoboken, N.J.; husband of Georgia O'Keeffe; founded galleries in New York City, where he exhibited photography "as a fine art," also works of French and U.S. modern painters
O'Keeffe O-520

Stieglitz, Mrs. Alfred. *see in index* O'Keeffe, Georgia

Stiff-mud process, in brickmaking B-436, *picture* B-437

Stigma, flower part F-218, *picture* F-219
corn plant C-720

Stigmata, in religion F-375

Stijl, De, group of Dutch artists in Amsterdam in 1917 F-462
The Netherlands N-127

Stikine River, river rising in n. British Columbia; flows 500 mi (800 km) to Alaska's coast; navigable about 130 mi (210 km); salmon, *map* C-109

Stikker, Dirk Uipko (1897–1979), Dutch statesman, born near Groningen; minister of foreign affairs 1948–52; ambassador to United Kingdom 1952–58; secretary-general NATO 1961–64.

Stilicho, Flavius (359?–408), Roman general and statesman of Vandal birth; as guardian of feeble Emperor Honorius was virtual ruler of Western Empire; put to death by order of Honorius.

Still, Andrew Taylor (1828–1917), U.S. physician, born in Jonesboro, Va.; founder of osteopathy O-611

Still, William Grant (born 1895), U.S. composer, born in Woodville, Miss.; won Guggenheim and Rosenwald fellowships; songs for musical shows, radio, and motion pictures, also ballets, and symphonic works.

Still fishing F-140

Still life, in painting P-25

'Still Life with Old Shoe', painting by Miró M-464

Stillman College, in Tuscaloosa, Ala.; Presbyterian; chartered 1876 as Tuscaloosa Institute; became senior college under present name 1948; liberal arts, education.

'Stillness at Appomattox, A', work by Catton W-27

Still rings, in gymnastics G-323, *diagram* G-324

Stillwater, Minn., city on St. Croix River, 15 mi (25 km) n.e. of St. Paul; milk products, shoes, garments, wood and metal products; formerly center of huge logging and lumber industry; pop. 12,290.

Stillwater, N.Y., village in e. of state on w. bank of Hudson River; near site of Revolutionary War battles; in dairy farm region; Saratoga National Historical Park nearby; pop. 1,572. *see also in index* Saratoga, battles of

Stillwater, Okla., city about 50 mi (80 km) n.e. of Oklahoma City; in gas and farm region; flour, feed, and milk products; meat packing; Oklahoma State University; Lake Carl Blackwell nearby; pop. 38,268 O-524

Stillwater River, river in Ohio, about 60 mi (100 km) long; rises near Indiana; parallels the Great Miami before joining it at Dayton D-45

Still wine. *see in index* Table wine

Stilt, long-legged shorebird; blacknecked stilt *Himantopus mexicanus* of the family Recurvirostridae; striking black and white pattern, extremely long red legs; nests from central Oregon and Nebraska to n. Lower California; winters across Southern states to South America.

Stilts, poles with footrests used for walking above the ground.

Stilwell, Joseph Warren (1883–1946), U.S. Army officer, born in Palatka, Fla., in service after 1904; chief of staff to the Chinese armies in Burma and India 1942, also commander of U.S. Army forces in China; recalled from China Oct. 1944; made head of U.S. Army ground forces Jan. 1945, of 10th Army in Pacific June 1945, and of 6th Army, headquarters San Francisco, March 1946 R-218, C-374
World War II W-337, 347

Stilwell Road (formerly called Ledo Road), 620-mi (998-km) highway from Ledo, Assam, to e. Burma where it joins Burma Road; opened Jan. 1945 R-218. *see also in index* Burma Road
World War II W-347

Stimson, Henry Lewis (1867–1950), U.S. lawyer and statesman, born in New York City; secretary of war 1911–13; governor-general of Philippines 1927–29; secretary of state 1929–33; secretary of war 1940–45, *picture* R-272
World War II, *picture* W-354

Stimulant, drug used medically for sleep disorders, appetite control, and overcoming depression F-46
coffee C-533
drugs D-276
narcotics N-19

Stimulated emission, light L-54

Stimulus, in learning L-106

Sting
ant A-469
bee B-125
first aid F-121
scorpion S-65
wasp W-73

Stingray, fish S-206

Stinkbugs, group of insects of the order Hemiptera, family Pentatiomidae, that discharge a disagreeable odor from glands at sides of the thorax; especially the harlequin bug *Murgantia histrionica*, a pest on radish, cabbage, and cultivated plants of mustard family, *picture* I-214

Stinnes, Hugo (1870–1924), German industrial manager and financier; leading figure in reconstruction after World War I; also owned several newspapers.

Stir, in cooking C-700

Stirling, Scotland, manufacturing town and port on Forth River, 30 mi (50 km) n.w. of Edinburgh; famous in wars of England and Scotland; pop. 28,786
Wallace W-7

Stirling Range, mountain range in Australia A-771

Stirrup, bone of the ear. *see in index* Stapes

Stirrup, of saddle
effect on warfare A-638

Stoa, Greek term for colonnade or portico; used both as a structural part of buildings and as an ornament of streets and open places A-736. *see also in index* Stoicism

Stoa Poikile (or Painted Stoa), building in Athens A-538

Stoat. *see in index* Ermine

Stock, Frederick August (1872–1942), U.S. conductor and composer, born in Jülich, West Germany; violinist with Cologne, Germany, orchestra 1891–95; joined Chicago Symphony Orchestra 1899 as first viola, became assistant conductor 1901, conductor from 1905 until his death; established Chicago Civic Orchestra 1919 as training ensemble for Chicago Symphony Orchestra.

Stock. *see in index* Livestock

Stock (or gilliflower), a flower of the genus *Mathiola* of the mustard family with stiff branching stem, alternate oblong leaves, and fragrant single or double, white, rose, crimson, or purple flowers in loose terminal clusters. The double-flowered varieties known as tenweeks stock are among the most attractive of garden annuals, blooming throughout summer.

Stock, capital represented by shares in a corporation S-450, *pictures* S-451–3
bank B-64
bibliography S-454

Stratford-on-Avon, England, town in Warwickshire; pop. 19,110 S-484b
  Shakespeare S-129, *pictures* S-130

Strathclyde, ancient British kingdom extending from Clyde to Derwent River; stronghold of original Celt inhabitants against invading Anglo-Saxons (7th–11th century).

Strathcona and Mount Royal, Donald Alexander Smith, first baron (1820–1914), Canadian railway builder S-484b, C-101

Stratified rocks. *see in index* Strata

Stratigraphic trap, a petroleum trap, *diagram* P-235

Stratigraphy, the study of the earth's strata G-72
  earth E-22

Stratocumulus cloud, type of cloud C-517

Straton, John Roach (1875–1929), Baptist clergyman, born in Evansville, Ind.; militant fundamentalist ('Our Relapse into Paganism').

Stratopause, layer of air A-747, *diagram* E-19

Stratoscope II, balloon B-45

Stratosphere, region of air A-747
  earth E-19, *diagram* E-11
  weather W-117

Stratton, Charles Sherwood. *see in index* Tom Thumb, General

Stratton, Dorothy Constance (1899–1980), U.S. commander of the SPARS 1942–46, born in Brookfield, Mo.; dean of women at Purdue University 1933–46, on leave 1942–46; national executive director of Girl Scouts 1951–60.

Stratus cloud, type of cloud C-517, *picture* C-516

Straus, Nathan (1848–1931), U.S. merchant and philanthropist, born in Bavaria; established distribution of coal and milk to New York poor and founded health centers in Palestine; brother of Oscar S. Straus.

Straus, Oscar (1870–1954), Austrian composer and musical conductor; noted for delightful light operas ('The Chocolate Soldier', 'The Waltz Dream').

Straus, Oscar Solomon (1850–1926), U.S. lawyer and diplomat, born in Bavaria; minister to Turkey 1887–89, 1898–1900 and ambassador 1909–10; secretary commerce and labor 1906–9.

Strauss, David Friedrich (1808–74), German theologian; his 'Life of Jesus' attempts to explain gospel stories as largely mythical.

Strauss, Johann (1804–49), Austrian composer and conductor, born in Vienna; wrote over 150 waltzes and many other dances and marches; 'Radetzky March' best known today S-485

Strauss, Johann, the Younger (1825–99), Austrian composer, called the "Waltz king" S-485
  operetta O-572

Strauss, Lewis L(ichtenstein) (1896–1974), U.S. government official, born in Charleston, W. Va.; a Wall Street banker 1919–46; member U.S. Atomic Energy Commission 1946–50, chairman 1953–58; recess appointee as U.S. secretary of commerce Nov. 1958–June 1959; memoirs, 'Men and Decisions'
  Eisenhower administration E-141

Strauss, Richard (1864–1949), German composer [illegible]
  classical music M-675
  opera O-569

Stravinsky, Igor (1882–1971), U.S. composer S-485
  Balanchine B-22
  ballet music B-34
  classical music M-675
  Diaghilev D-126
  opera O-569
  orchestra O-576

Straw, dried stems or stalk of plants
  flax F-177
  rye R-366b
  uses
    adobe A-46
    bricks B-436
    hats and caps H-54
    paper P-101
  wheat P-379

Strawberry (or pine strawberry), plant of the family Rosaceae S-486, *picture* F-434
  berry types B-176, *picture* B-177
  fruitgrowing F-438
  runner, *diagram* P-363a

Strawberry Hill, building in Twickenham, England W-11

Strawberry River, river in n.e. Utah; rises in Wasatch Range, flows e. about 70 mi (110 km); empties into Duchesne River U-216, *maps* U-232, 217

Strawberry Shortcake, doll D-222

Strawberry shrub. *see in index* Calycanthus

Strayer, George Drayton (1876–1962), U.S. educator, born in Wayne, Pa.; at Columbia University 1905–42; director educational surveys.

Strayer College, in Washington, D.C.; private control; opened 1904; business, education, hospital administration; quarter system.

Stream, a body of flowing water E-16, W-89, 92

Streamer, in fishing, *list* F-146

Streamer fly, fishing lure, *picture* F-142

Stream erosion, geological process R-210

'Streamers', work by Rabe A-363

Streamlining
  automobiles A-861
  trains, *pictures* R-72, 75, 87

Stream of consciousness, method in literature
  English literature E-281
  Joyce J-144, N-411
  Woolf W-292

Streamwood, Ill., village situated 7 mi (11 km) s.e. of Elgin; chiefly a residential suburb; pop. 23,456, *map* I-53

Streatfeild, Noel (1901–86), British actress and author, born in Sussex, England; books for adults: 'Mothering Sunday', 'Caroline England'; for children: 'Ballet Shoes', 'Circus Shoes' (Carnegie medal 1939), 'Theater Shoes', 'Skating Shoes', 'The First Book of the Ballet', and 'The First Book of England'; autobiographical story: 'A Vicarage Family'.

Streator, Ill., city on Vermilion River, about 80 mi (130 km) s.w. of Chicago; in coal and agricultural region; glass bottles, farm implements, food products, fertilizer; pop. 14,769, *map* I-53

Streep, Meryl (full name Mary Louise Streep) (born 1949), U.S. stage, film, and television actress, born in Summit, N.J.; professional debut Lincoln Center, New York City 1975; movie appearances include 'The Deer Hunter' (1978), 'Silkwood' (1983), 'Plenty' (1985); won Academy awards for best supporting actress (1980) in 'Kramer vs. Kramer' and for best actress (1983) in 'Sophie's Choice'; won 1978 Emmy award for 'Holocaust', *picture* M-614

Streetcar, transportation S-486, *picture* S-487

'Streetcar Named Desire, A', work by Williams A-357, W-209

Streeter, Ruth Cheney (born 1895), director of Women's Reserve, U.S. Marine Corps 1943–45, born in Brookline, Mass.; social worker; held commercial airplane pilot's license.

Street railway S-486. *see also in index* Subway
  cable cars, *picture* S-44
  regulation P-526c
  transportation T-264, *pictures* T-262, 263

Streets. *see in index* Roads and streets

'Street Scene', work by Rice A-356

'Street Scene', work by Weill M-686
  Hughes H-316

Street Which Is Called Straight, street in Damascus, Syria D-18

Streicher, Julius (1885–1946), Nazi political leader and editor of anti-Semitic newspaper; hanged for war crimes, particularly for persecution of Jews, Oct. 1946.

Streichzither, stringed instrument S-490a

Streisand, Barbra (or Barbara Streisand) (born 1942), U.S. singer and actress S-488

Streit, Clarence Kirshman (born 1896), U.S. journalist and author, born in California, Mo.; with A.E.F. in France 1917–18; correspondent in Rome 1921–23, Constantinople 1923–24; League of Nations correspondent 1929–39; with *New York Times* 1925–40; advocated plan ("Union Now") for British-U.S. union as a step toward world organization.

Strelitz. *see in index* Streltsi

Strelitzia (or bird-of-paradise flower), genus of perennial plants of the banana family native to S. Africa; leaves, large, with prominent midrib and long petiole (stem); flowers, in species *S. reginae,* yellow with dark-blue tongue, are set within a purplish, boatlike bract (modified leaf); other species are white, or orange and blue; tall, erect stem.

Streltsi (or Strelitz), household troops of the czars, instituted by Ivan the Terrible; backbone of Russian army in 16th and 17th centuries; frequent mutinies led to abolition by Peter I.

Strep throat, disease V-251

Streptococcus, bacterial group, *picture* D-170
  yogurt Y-421

Streptomyces, bacteria B-14

Streptomycin, an antibiotic drug A-489
  bubonic plague treatment B-473

Stresemann, Gustav (1878–1929), German statesman; staunch monarchist and militarist during World War I, gradually became republican after revolution; organized German People's party; foreign minister 1923–29 W-142. *see also in index* Nobel Prizewinners, *table*

Stress, an emotional state S-488
  arthritis A-650
  fatigue F-45
  headache H-81
  health H-86
  holistic medicine H-203
  hysterical amnesia A-373
  mental illness M-301

Stress, in language. *see in index* Accent

Stress, in physics
  acoustics test A-22
  machine M-10

Stressed-skin fuselage, in airplane construction A-183

Stretcher, device for carrying injured
  space-research by-product S-348c

Stretcher, in brick masonry B-438

Stria, glacial groove I-6

Striated muscle (or skeletal muscle) M-659

Stribling, Thomas Sigismund (1881–1965), U.S. novelist, born in Clifton, Tenn.; most of his novels deal with the South (trilogy: 'The Forge', 'The Store' (Pulitzer prize 1933), and 'Unfinished Cathedral'; Caribbean adventure stories: 'Strange Moon' and 'Clues of the Caribbees').

Strickland, Agnes (1796–1874), English historical writer; with her sister Elizabeth wrote 'Lives of the Queens of England'.

Strickland, William (1787?–1854), U.S. architect, engraver, and engineer, born in Philadelphia, Pa.; a leader in revival of Greek architecture; designed many public buildings in Philadelphia and restored steeple of Independence Hall.

Stridulation, shrill, croaking sounds produced by insects
  animal communication A-448
  cricket A-445

Strigidae, family of owls including all owls except barn owls. *see also in index* Owl

Strigiformes, order of nocturnal birds, comprising the owls B-278. *see also in index* Owl

Strijdom, Johannes Gerhardus (or Johannes Gerhardus Strydom) (1893–1958), South African statesman, born in Willowmore, Cape of Good Hope Province; member of Parliament (Nationalist party) 1929–58; minister of lands and irrigation 1948–54; prime minister of Union of South Africa 1954–58.

Strike, cessation of labor by employees to enforce their demands upon their employer, or to protest against his or her actions S-489
  East Germany G-127
  United Kingdom
    Baldwin B-24
  United States
    Idaho miners I-20
    immigration U-182
    post–World War II L-88
    Roosevelt R-284
    Truman T-297
  U.S.S.R. R-330a

Strike, in baseball B-91

Strike, in bowling B-385

Strike, in fishing, *list* F-146

'Strike Up the Band' (1930), musical comedy by Gershwin M-686

Strindberg, August (full name Johan August Strindberg) (1849–1912), Swedish novelist and dramatist S-490
  drama D-245
  Scandinavian literature S-52g

String bass, stringed musical instrument [illegible]
  country music M-678

Stringed instruments (or chordophones) S-490
  ancient V-327
  classical music M-668
  country music M-678
  harp. *see in index* Harp
  music M-687
  orchestra O-576, *picture* O-577
  piano and its ancestors. *see in index* Piano
  pitch S-262
  tone S-261, 262
  U.S. folk music P-335a, *pictures* P-334, 337
  violin family. *see in index* Violin

Stringer, Arthur (John Arbuthnott) (1874–1950), Canadian writer, born in Chatham, Ont.; lived in U.S.; wrote script for silent motion-picture serial, 'Perils of Pauline' ('Prairie Wife' and 'Prairie Mother', novels; 'Shadowed Victory', verse; 'Red Wine of Youth', life of Rupert Brooke).

Stringfellow, John (1799–1883), English engineer and lace manufacturer; built one of first model airplanes to fly under own power
  airplane A-200

String quartet, two violins, a viola, and a cello C-268

String quintet, string quartet with either a second viola or a second cello added C-268

Strip, in metalworking I-346

Strip-cropping, method of planting to conserve land and water C-674, *picture* C-669
  Quebec Q-9b

Striped bass (or rockfish), fish, *table* F-136

Striped burrfish, fish, *picture* F-130

Striped dace. *see in index* Black-nosed dace

Striped maple (or moosewood), a small tree *Acer pennsylvanicum* of maple family; range, n.e. U.S. and Canada; striped bark.

Striped skunk, a carnivorous mammal *Mephitis mephitis* W-116

Stripe rust, fungus
  wheat W-188

Strip mining type of surface mining M-425
  coal mining C-519
  Ohio reclamation law O-499
  Tennessee Valley Authority T-102

Stripper, type of tractor
  cotton harvesting C-738

Stripping, in coal mining C-519

Stripping crane, metalworking machine I-343

Stritch, Samuel Alphonsus, Cardinal (1887–1958), U.S. Roman Catholic prelate, born in Nashville, Tenn.; archbishop of Milwaukee 1930–39, of Chicago 1939–58; created cardinal 1946; named head of Roman Catholic missions 1958.

Stroboscope, device that makes a rotating or oscillating object appear stationary by providing a brief view each time the object reaches a given point I-229
  motion pictures M-615
  tachometer T-3

Stroessner, Alfredo (born 1912), president of Paraguay P-113

fermentation
liquor L-235
wine W-237
food and nutrition F-275
honey H-228
living things L-268
loaves S-507
maple M-113
metabolism M-306
organic chemistry O-604
photosynthesis P-300
producing areas
Central America C-255
colonial Brazil A-355
Cuba C-800
Guyana G-321
Latin America L-64
Philippines P-256
Puerto Rico P-527, *picture* P-528
South America, *picture* S-281
United States S-508, *map* U-100, *picture* S-505
Hawaii H-61
Nebraska, *picture* N-96
West Indies W-156, L-60
solubility S-255
starch S-424
tree
tapping trees, *picture* V-294

Sugar Act (1764), British R-163, U-170

Sugar beet, beet *Beta vulgaris* with high sugar content, *pictures* S-507
by-products S-508
factory S-506, *picture* S-508
farm machinery F-35
harvest, *picture* R-330d
industry S-506, *pictures* S-507, I-24
producing regions S-508
England E-235
East Germany G-119
Idaho, *map* I-22, *picture* I-26
South Dakota S-324

Sugarberry, tree. *see in index* Hackberry

Sugar Bowl, football F-290

Sugarcane, any of several plants genus *Saccharum* of the grass family that yield cane sugar S-505, *pictures* S-506. *see also in index* Sugar
breeding P-367
harvesting, *picture* P-528
farm machinery F-35
producing areas
Brazil B-422
Fiji F-82
Guatemala G-297, *picture* G-299
Hawaii H-61, *map* H-64
Louisiana L-310, *picture* L-311
Nicaragua, *picture* N-343
wax W-110

Sugar glider (or flying opossum), marsupial of the genus *Petaurus* and the family Petauridae, *picture* A-780

Sugar Loaf Peak, rock formation in Rio de Janeiro, Brazil R-208

Sugar maple (or rock maple), tree *Acer saccharum* M-112, *picture* M-113
New York state tree N-260
sap, *picture* V-294
seed dispersal S-106
tree, *picture* T-280
West Virginia state tree, *picture* W-172
Wisconsin state tree, *picture* W-256
wood, *table* W-283

Sugar pine (sometimes called California sugar pine, or white pine), evergreen tree *Pinus lambertiana* of pine family; largest of the pines, it may grow over 200 ft (60 m), but average height is 175 ft (55 m); trunk straight, free of branches on lower half; crown, flat-topped; leaves in fives, to 4 in. (10 cm) long, dark green with white line on underside; cones slender, drooping, to 20 in. (50 cm) long; wood odorless, light brown, tinged with red, shading to white, *table* W-282

Suggs, Louise (born 1923), U.S. golfer, born in Lithia Springs, Ga.; began to play golf at age of 12; turned professional 1948; won more than 60 amateur and professional tournaments; elected to Golf's Hall of Fame 1951.

Sugimoto, Etsu Inagaki (1874–1950), Japanese writer, born near Niigata, Honshu; lived in U.S.; she interpreted Japan's life for the western world ('A Daughter of the Samurai').

Suharto (born 1921), president of Indonesia, born in Sedaju-Godean, Java; commanded army units that destroyed attempted pro-Communist coup in 1965; army chief of staff 1965–; acting president 1967–68, president 1968– I-164

'Suicide', book by Durkheim D-292

Suicide, taking one's own life
Durkheim's study D-292
hara-kiri. *see in index* Hara-kiri
Seneca S-108a
Vietnamese Buddhists V-322

Sui Dynasty (581–618), China C-364, 388

Suite, in music M-669, *list* M-671
dance C-268

'Suite No. 2 in B Minor', work by Bach O-576

Sukarnapura, Indonesia. *see in index* Djajapura

Sukarno (1901–70), Indonesian political leader, born in Surabaja, Java; collaborated with Japan in World War II; proclaimed Republic of Indonesia and served as its first president, ousted 1967; autobiography, 'Sukarno' I-164

Sukkur Barrage, dam in Pakistan. *see in index* Lloyd Barrage

Sulaiman Mountains, range between Baluchistan and Punjab; peak (11,070 ft; 3,370 m) called Takht-i-Sulaiman ("throne of Solomon") is pilgrimage goal for Hindus and Muslims P-77

Sulawesi, island in Indonesia. *see in index* Celebes

Süleyman I, the Magnificent (or Solyman) (1494?–1566), greatest of Ottoman sultans; encouraged cultural endeavors and reformed administration of government T-323
Ottoman Empire O-616

Sulfa drugs (or sulfonamide compounds) A-489
antiseptics A-495
disease treatment D-169
leprosy treatment L-136
organic chemistry O-605

Sulfate (or sulphate), a salt of sulfuric acid
aluminum
fire extinguishers F-101
iron
green vitriol S-510
sodium S-29
Leblanc soda process S-247
papermaking P-101

Sulfate mineral, classification M-435

Sulfate pulp, in papermaking P-101

Sulfide (or sulphide), a compound of sulfur with metal without oxygen
iron S-509
metal and metallurgy M-307

Sulfide mineral, classification M-432

Sulfite (or sulphite), salt of sulfurous acid
lignin. *see in index* Lignin
papermaking P-101

Sulfonamide compounds. *see in index* Sulfa drugs

Sulfones, drugs L-136

Sulfosalt, any of an extensive group of minerals M-432

Sulfur (or sulphur) (S), nonmetallic chemical element S-509, *table* S-510. *see also in index* Disulfide; Sulfate; Sulfide; Sulfite; Sulfuric acid
acid rain A-19
Bessemer process B-178
crystals, *diagram* C-797, *picture* C-795
dioxide S-510
poisonous properties P-411
refrigeration R-137
smog P-441b
explosive E-379
hops H-239
inorganic chemistry I-210
lead processing L-99
minerals M-432, *picture* M-434
mining S-509
Frasch process S-509
periodic table, *table* P-207, *list* P-208
producing regions S-509
Asia A-689
Sicily S-192
properties, *table* S-510
rubber R-304
volcanic fumes V-378

Sulfuric acid (or sulphuric acid) S-510. *see also in index* Sulfate
acid rain A-19
aerosol pollution A-66
alchemists' discovery A-273
equivalent weight S-256
inorganic chemistry I-210
Leblanc soda process S-247
molecular weight S-256
organic chemistry O-604
platinum P-384
sodium sulfate formation S-29

Sulgrave Manor, home of George Washington's forebears in Northamptonshire, England; now maintained as museum.

Sulidae, family of birds, the boobies and gannets. *see in index* Booby; Gannet

Sulina, Romania, naval base and seaport in delta of Danube River, where grain and other cargoes are transferred to vessels of Black Sea; pop. about 8,000, *maps* E-361, R-349

Sulky, two-wheeled vehicle used for harness racing H-277

Sulky disk plow P-392

Sulky plow P-391

Sulla, Lucius Cornelius (138–78 BC), Roman general; conquered Mithradates (84 BC); as dictator noted for bloody proscriptions R-246

Sullivan, Anne Mansfield (or Mrs. John Albert Macy) (1866–1936), teacher of Helen Keller K-196

Sullivan, Arthur Seymour (1842–1900), English composer G-144
band compositions B-56
classical music M-674
literary contribution E-278
operetta O-572

Sullivan, Ed (full name Edward Vincent Sullivan) (1902–74), U.S. columnist and television emcee, born in New York, N.Y.; column, 'Little Old New York', in *New York Daily News* since 1932; show on television 1948–71.

Sullivan, Harry Stack (1892–1949), U.S. psychiatrist, born in Norwich, N.Y.; coeditor *Psychiatry,* professional journal, 1938–46, editor 1946–49; author of 'Conceptions of Modern Psychiatry'; made notable researches in schizophrenia P-519

Sullivan, John (1740–95), American Revolutionary War soldier, born in Somersworth, N.H.; became major general; distinguished himself at siege of Boston, was captured at Long Island, defeated English at Butt's Hill; led successful expedition to defeat the Six Nations in western New York; member Continental Congress; president (governor) state of New Hampshire.

Sullivan, John Lawrence (1858–1918), U.S. boxer, born in Boston, Mass.
heavyweight champion B-391

Sullivan, Kathryn (born 1951), U.S. geologist-oceanographer and first U.S. woman to walk in space, born in Paterson, N.J.; selected as astronaut candidate by NASA in 1978; during space walk from space shuttle *Challenger* in October 1984, practiced transferring fuel from one container to another to learn potential of refueling spacecraft.

Sullivan, Louis Henry (1856–1924), U.S. architect, born in Boston, Mass. A-569
examples of work, *pictures* A-565, D-114
interior design, *picture* I-244
Wright W-367

Sullivan, Mark (1874–1952), U.S. journalist, born in Avondale, Pa. ('Education of an American', autobiography; 'Our Times', a social history).

Sullivan, Thomas, U.S. merchant
tea innovation T-46

Sullivan Mine, in British Columbia B-454

Sullivans Island, entrance to Charleston harbor in South Carolina; site of Fort Moultrie and of town Sullivans Island (pop. 1,426), *map* S-319

Sullivan Trophy, awarded to outstanding amateur athlete each year; donated 1930 by Amateur Athletic Union to honor James E. Sullivan, early official of AAU.

Sully, Maximilien de Béthune, duc de (1560–1641), great French statesman and financier; trusted minister of Henry IV.

Sully, Thomas (1783–1872), U.S. portrait painter, born in Lincolnshire, England; work influenced by Gilbert Stuart ('Decatur', 'Lafayette', 'Jefferson', 'Fanny Kemble').

Sully-Prudhomme, René François Armand (1839–1907), French poet, born in Paris; trained for law, was a student of science and philosophy, preferred literature; his verse is ranked by some as greatest in French poetry since Victor Hugo ('La justice', 'Le bonheur', 'La vraie religion selon Pascal'). *see also in index* Nobel Prizewinners, *table*

Sulphur. *see in index* Sulfur

Sulphur, La., city 9 mi (15 km) w. of Lake Charles; in oil-producing and refining area, rice-growing region; pop. 19,709.

Sulphur, Okla., resort city with sulfur baths, about 75 mi (120 km) s.e. of Oklahoma City; Platt National Park adjacent; state school for deaf and state soldiers' hospital; pop. 5,516.

Sulphur, Mount, mountain in Alberta N-28

Sulphur-bottom whale. *see in index* Blue whale

Sulphur butterflies, numerous species of family Pieridae, abundant in North America; greenish-yellow with dark-bordered wings; black spot on fore wings, orange spot on hind wings; clouded sulphur and little sulphur butterflies are well-known types.

Sulphur Island, island in w. Pacific Ocean. *see in index* Iwo Jima

Sulphur polypore, mushroom *Polyporus sulphureus* M-665

Sul Ross State University, in Alpine, Tex.; opened 1920; arts and sciences, education, range animal husbandry; graduate study.

Sultan, favorite horse of Buffalo Bill, *list* H-249

Sultan, Muslim countries' title for ruler, applied especially to former ruler of Turkey T-323

Sultana raisins R-90, T-321

Sulte, Benjamin (1841–1923), French-Canadian historian and poet, born in Trois-Rivières, Que.; 'Histoire des Canadiens-Français' in 8 vols.; translated 'God Save the King' into French verse.

Sulu Archipelago, chain of islands in s.w. Philippines; 1,038 sq mi (2,688 sq km); formerly a province, now divided into Sulu province (618 sq mi [1,601 sq km]; pop. 240,001), cap. Jolo, and Tawi-Tawi province (420 sq mi [1,090 sq km]; pop. 143,487), cap. Bato-Bato (Balimbing); pop. 383,488 P-259, 259a, 259b, 255a, *maps* P-262
Asia, *map* A-700
pearl fisheries P-149

Sulu Sea, north of Sulu Archipelago, between the islands Mindanao and Palawan; width, 360 mi (580 km); greatest depth over 18,000 ft (5,500 m) P-256, *maps* P-259a, 262

Sulzberger, Arthur Hays (1891–1968), U.S. newspaper publisher, born in New York, N.Y.; started in newspaper business 1919; published *The New York Times* 1935–61, president 1935–57, chairman of board 1957–68.

Sumac (or sumach), shrubs and trees of genus *Rhus;* about 150 species native to temperate and subtropical regions
poison sumac P-410
wax W-110

Sumatra, Indonesia, 3rd largest island of Malay Archipelago; 163,000 sq mi (422,000 sq km); pop. 15,739,363 S-510, *map* I-166
animal life S-511
Asia, *map* A-700
Indonesia I-158
products S-511
size, comparative. *see in index* Island, *table*
transportation S-511

Sumatran rhinoceros R-178

Sumer, ancient name of s. Babylonia; inhabited by the Sumerians, who originated cuneiform writing; chief city was Ur A-404, *map* B-4
wagon W-2

Sumerians, predecessors of Babylonians in Tigris-Euphrates Valley B-3
alphabet history A-315
army organization A-634
calendar C-28
cuneiform writing W-373
geometry P-544
Kish K-251

Super Bowl, professional football's championship game
  medals M-270
Supercharger, airplane A-186
Supercold. *see in index* Cryogenics
Superconductivity, absence of all electrical resistance; property of certain metals, alloys, and compounds at very low temperatures; first discovered in 1911 by Heike Kamerlingh Onnes; in 1986 and 1987 discovered to be a property of certain rare-Earth-based oxide ceramics at temperatures approaching room temperature
  Bardeen B-80
  bioelectricity B-234
  cryogenics C-794
  electricity E-160
  electronics E-176
Superconductor E-176
Supercooling (or subcooling), in physics
  cryogenics C-793
  glass G-156
  water vapor I-5
Superdome, New Orleans, La., stadium; home to the New Orleans Saints professional football team N-231, *picture* N-232
Superenciphered code
  ciphers C-419
Superfluidity, in physics C-794
Superfortress (or B-29), U.S. military aircraft W-334, 346
Supergiant stars, in astronomy A-721
Superheating
  steam S-439
    Schmidt's development S-442
Superheavy water W-87
Superheterodyne, electronic circuit
  Armstrong A-632
Superhigh wave, *tables* R-34, R-50
Superhighway, road designed for high-speed traffic; may be within city or cross-country. *see also in index* Expressway; Freeway; Toll road
Super insulation
  spaceflight I-232
Superior, Wis., one of 2 most westerly ports of Great Lakes, at head of Lake Superior opposite Duluth, Minn.; railroad shops; shipbuilding; machinery, petroleum products; University of Wisconsin—Superior; pop. 29,571 W-250, *map* U-41
  Duluth, Minn. D-288
  Lake Superior S-518
Superior, Lake (or Gitche Gumee), most northern of Great Lakes; largest body of fresh water in the world; 31,700 sq mi (82,100 sq km) S-518, G-243, *maps* G-245, N-351
  lakes L-24
  Michigan M-354, *pictures* M-357, 365
  Minnesota M-439, 442, *picture* M-445
  Sault Sainte Marie canals. *see in index* Sault Sainte Marie canals
  size, comparative. *see in index* Lake, *table*
  trade S-518
  Wisconsin W-248
Superior maxillary (or maxilla), upper jawbone S-210
Superior mirage, atmospheric phenomenon M-463
Superior National Forest, in Minnesota M-443
Superior planets P-350, 351, S-254a
Superior Upland, geographical region
  Minnesota M-440
  Wisconsin W-249
Supermarket, retail grocery store M-146, *picture* P-192
  automated systems A-834
  franchises F-374
  social studies class, *picture* S-239
  United States U-110
Supernatural power M-37
Supernova, in astronomy S-424
  observatory O-456
Supernova 1987A, exploded star O-456
Superphosphate, an acid phosphate
  fertilizer F-59
    Oceania O-472
Superpolyamides. *see in index* Nylon
Supersaturated solution, in chemistry S-256
Supersaurus, prehistoric animal A-462
Supersonic aircraft
  aerospace research A-75, *picture* A-78
  military use A-161, *picture* A-160
  rocket plane S-346e, 341a
  transports A-199, P-441e
Supersonic speed
  aircraft A-182
  Mach M-8
Supersonic transport (SST), aircraft A-207
Supersonic wave (or ultrasonic wave) S-260
  acoustics A-21
Superstition, an irrational fear of the unknown; modern superstition is what remains of pagan magic. *see also in index* Fairy; Folklore; Magic; Mythology
  American Indians I-118
  dragons D-238
  gems J-112
    opals O-559
  Halloween H-17
  horror story H-245
  lizards L-274
  masks M-186
  Pacific islanders P-8
  petrel P-226
  rainbow R-88
  sacred ibis of Egypt I-3
  snakes S-223
  sociological aspects S-243
  stork S-456
Superstring theory (TOE, or theory of Everything), theory that attempts to unify theory of gravity and theories of other fundamental forces by interpreting subatomic phenomena as manifestations of vibrations of fundamental, one-dimensional strings; mathematics developed in 1960s; theory gained some support in 1980s; because of extremely small distances and high energies involved, the theory was criticized as untestable
  matter M-230
Suppé, Franz von (1820–95), Austrian composer of light operas, ballet music, symphonies, songs
  operetta O-572
'Supper at Emmaus', painting by Caravaggio, *picture* C-154
'Suppliants, The', work by Aeschylus A-87
  drama D-242
Supply, warfare logistics W-24
Supply and demand, economic theory that in general prices are determined by amount of a given commodity available for sale, relative to demand existing for it
  business cycle B-517
  capitalism C-149
  economics E-61
  employment and unemployment E-206
  food supply F-287
  inflation I-198
  money M-533
Supply fan F-24
Supporter, heraldry H-136, *picture* H-135
Support hose, stretch stockings H-278
Supporting player, in theater, *list* T-155
Suprarenal glands. *see in index* Adrenal gland
Supreme Court of Australia A-806
Supreme Court of Canada C-87
Supreme Court of the Soviet Union L-96
Supreme Court of the United States S-518a, C-748. For list of chief justices of the United States, *see table* following
  abortion decision U-196b
  American Indian relocation opposition I-149
  apportionment decision S-429
  black Americans B-295
  building, *picture* S-518a
  conscientious objectors P-144
  constitutional law C-685
  copyright decision C-713
  criminal law C-776
  Dred Scott decision D-259
  education, *lists* E-104, S-518b
    quota system decision U-197
  Eisenhower E-138
  gerrymander decision G-135
  government agencies G-201
  Jehovah's Witnesses J-97
  judicial review S-518b
  jurisdiction U-150, 146, S-518a
  law L-94
  Pentagon Papers U-196a
  pornography C-451
  Roosevelt, F.D. R-272, U-147
  salaries of justices, *table* U-155
  voting restrictions outlawed S-505
  Washington, D.C. W-67
  wiretapping W-247
Supreme Economic Council, following World War I
  Hoover H-234
Supreme Headquarters, Allied Powers, Europe (SHAPE), near Casteau, Belgium; until 1966, at Rocquencourt, near Paris, France; international military headquarters of NATO; authorized 1949; implemented by Gen. Eisenhower as first commander.
Supreme Order of Christ. *see in index* Christ, Order of
Supremes, singing group M-681
Supreme Soviet, U.S.S.R. R-327, R-334b
Suppressor cell, type of white blood cell. *see also in index* T cell
  immune system I-57
Sup'ung-nodongjagu, North Korea
  hydroelectric plant Y-408
Sur, Arabic name for **Tyre,** seaport of Lebanon; fishing and boats; was Phoenician city-state; pop. 16,483 P-268. *see also in index* Tyre
Surabaja (or Soerabaja), city, e. Java, one of chief ports and trading centers; naval and military base for Indonesia; center of sugar industry; pop. 2,040,800.
Surah, a soft, twilled fabric of silk or rayon; may be dyed or printed; sometimes plaid design; used for clothing.
Surakarta (or Soerakarta, or Solo), city of central Java and seat of former sultanate; rubber, rice, corn, cassava, sugar, indigo; batik industry; pop. 414,285, *maps* A-637, A-700, I-166
Surat, India, seaport on Tapti River in Gujarat state 150 mi (240 km) n. of Bombay; exports millet, cotton, rice, wheat; cloth, hats, paper, tiles, soap; great trade center 16th to 18th century; pop. 471,815, *map* I-86
  Asia, *map* A-700
Surcoat, in heraldry H-135
Surface level. *see in index* Sea level
Surface milling (or plain milling), a machine tool operation T-221
Surface mining M-425. *see also in index* Open-pit mining; Strip mining
  coal C-519, *diagram* C-520
  conservation measures, *picture* C-676
'Surface of the Earth, The', work by Price A-362
Surface runoff, water W-89, 93, *picture* W-88
Surface vessel, in marine exploration F-427
Surface water W-89, *picture* W-88
  irrigation I-355
Surface wave, class of seismic wave E-37
Surfbird, a wading bird *Aphriza virgata* of the family Charadriidae, the ploverlike birds; about 10 in. (25 cm) long; plumage dusky brown with white rump patch; frequents Pacific coast from Alaska to Chile, breeding on Alaskan tundra.
Surf casting, in fishing F-143, *pictures* F-139
Surfing S-519, *picture* B-326
  Australia A-789
  Hawaii H-61, *picture* H-59
  Huntington Beach, Calif. H-333
Surf scoter, duck, *picture* D-286
Surgeon general, title of chief medical officer of U.S. Army, U.S. Air Force, U.S. Navy, U.S. Public Health Service.
Surgery, medical specialty S-519a. *see also in index* Medicine
  anesthetics A-412
    Long L-295
  antiseptic methods A-495
    Lister L-238
    ultraviolet U-4
  arthritis A-650
  bioengineering developments B-207
  blood B-313
  cancer treatment C-134, D-176
  eye E-390
  heart defects H-100
  hospital H-280
  hypnosis H-344
  laser beams L-54
  mental illness M-302
  nursing, *picture* S-519b
  television S-348c
  therapy T-164
  transplantation of tissue T-250
  trauma center T-268
  vocational opportunities V-367, *picture* V-368
  weight control W-136
Suribachi, Mount, extinct volcano on island of Iwo Jima, Japan; height, 546 ft (166 m); site of famous U.S. Marine flag-raising at end of costly battle in World War II.
Suriname (formerly Dutch Guiana), republic on n.e. coast of South America; 70,060 sq mi (181,450 sq km); cap. Paramaribo; pop. 448,000, *Fact Summary* S-295, *map* S-298
  flag, *picture* F-170
  geographic regions S-275, *map* S-274
  The Netherlands N-126, 131
  West Indies W-155
Surmullet. *see in index* Goatfish
Surname (or family name) N-6
Surplus energy theory, in play P-390b
Surratt, Mary Eugenia Jenkins (1817–65), alleged conspirator in assassination of Abraham Lincoln; kept boardinghouse where John Wilkes Booth planned assassination; sentenced by military tribunal; hanged July 7, 1865; historians differ on question of her guilt C-478
Surrealism, modern movement, of French origin, in literature and art, aiming at unrestrained expression of subconscious thought; outgrowth of Freudian psychology
  Beckett B-123
  motion pictures M-621
  painting P-60, 67d, *pictures* P-59
    Miró M-464
  sculpture S-93
    Giacometti G-142
Surrentum, Italy. *see in index* Sorrento
Surrey, Henry Howard, earl of (1518?–47), English poet, soldier, and courtier who introduced blank verse and, with Wyatt, the sonnet

SUPREME COURT CHIEF JUSTICES

(For biographical information, *see in index* names below)

John Jay	1789–95
John Rutledge	1795
Oliver Ellsworth	1796–99
John Marshall	1801–35
Roger B. Taney	1836–64
Salmon P. Chase	1864–73
Morrison R. Waite	1874–88
Melville W. Fuller	1888–1910
Edward D. White	1910–21
William H. Taft	1921–30
Charles Evans Hughes	1930–41
Harlan Fiske Stone	1941–46
Frederick M. Vinson	1946–53
Earl Warren	1953–69
Warren E. Burger	1969–86
William Rehnquist	1986–

into England; beheaded on trumped-up charge of treason E-266

Surrey, county in s.e. England bordered on n. by Thames and adjoining London; 722 sq mi (1,870 sq km); many London businessmen have their homes here; pop. 1,731,042.

Surtees, Robert Smith (1803–64), English writer and lawyer, born near Newcastle-on-Tyne, England; best known for pioneer work in sports writing, chiefly on the English hunting scene ('Jorrocks' Jaunts and Jollities').

Surtsey, island off the s.w. coast of Iceland; created by a submarine volcanic eruption in 1963; colonized by various types of plant life I-13, *picture* E-33
- coastal landforms B-112
- island formation I-368
- lava and magma L-90
- ocean O-461

Surveying S-520
- geodetic S-520
- geological U-161
- hydrographic S-520
- maps M-128
- mathematics M-213
- plane S-520
- railroad routes R-75

Surveyors, space-moon probes S-348c, M-580, *table* S-344

Surveyors' measure, units of measure, *table* W-140

Survival of American Indian Association, U.S. political organization I-155

Susa (Biblical Shushan), ancient Persian city, capital of Elam; later capital of Persian Empire; in Iran about 150 mi (240 km) n. of Persian Gulf; ruins of palaces of Artaxerxes and Darius, *map* P-212
- Alexander A-280

Susa, Tunisia. *see in index* Sousse

'Susan Constant', name of one of ships in which first Jamestown colonists sailed to America
- replica, *picture* V-335

Susanna (or Susannah), heroine of apocryphal book, 'The History of Susanna'; was condemned to die on a false charge by two elders, but Daniel, the prophet, established her innocence by cross-examining her accusers who were then put to death; often portrayed in art.

'Susannah', opera by Floyd O-571

Susiana. *see in index* Elam

Suslik (or souslik), name of certain Old World ground squirrels; Caspian suslik, or peschanik, lives in s. U.S.S.R. around Caspian Sea; common suslik ranges from Altay Mts. through s. U.S.S.R. to Silesia and e. Erz Mts.; red suslik occurs w. of Ural Mts. from Kazan' to Chkalov; spotted suslik lives in s.e. Europe n. to the highlands of central Poland; all belong to squirrel family Sciuridae and to the genus *Citellus*
- fur, *table* F-465

Suslov, Mikhail (1902–82), Soviet theoretician; became candidate member of Central Committee of Communist party 1939, full member 1941; editor of *Pravda* 1949–51; member of secretariat 1952–82.

Suspect, in law, person under suspicion of a crime C-776

Suspended soil. *see in index* Silt

'Suspense' (1913), motion picture by Smalley, *picture* M-611

Suspension, automobile, *picture* A-853

Suspension bridge B-441, *picture* B-446
- Golden Gate S-42, *picture* S-41, *map* S-41b
- Mackinac, *pictures* B-439

Susquehanna (or Conestoga), American Indian tribe of Iroquoian lineage formerly living on Susquehanna River and its branches
- Maryland M-168

Susquehanna, river rising in Otsego Lake, N.Y., and flowing 420 mi (675 km) s. through Pennsylvania to Chesapeake Bay P-164, *maps* P-165, U-50
- Chesapeake Bay C-304
- Maryland M-168, *map* M-183

Susquehanna University, in Selinsgrove, Pa.; Lutheran; founded 1858; arts and sciences, business, education, music.

Sussex, breed of poultry P-482

Sussex, ancient kingdom of the South Saxons in England; conquered by Egbert, king of Wessex, and became part of Wessex.

Sussex, county in s.e. England on the Channel; 1,457 sq mi (3,774 sq km); divided into East and West Sussex; tourist resorts; sheep, cattle; pop. 1,077,517.

Sussex spaniel, breed of dog, *picture* D-198

Susu, a people of West Africa
- Guinea G-314

Sutcliff, Rosemary (born 1920), English author, born in Surrey; historical fiction for young: 'The Shield Ring', 'Warrior Scarlet', 'Brother Dusty-Feet', 'The Lantern Bearers', 'Knight's Fee', 'Dawn Wind', 'Sword at Sunset', 'The Hound of Ulster', 'The Mark of the Horse Lord' R-111e, S-481b

Sutherland, Earl Wilbur, Jr. (1915–74), U.S. physiologist, born in Burlingame, Kan.; director of medical department Western Reserve University 1950–63, professor Vanderbilt University 1963–74. *see also in index* Nobel Prizewinners, *table*

Sutherland, George (1862–1942), U.S. lawyer, jurist, and political leader; born in Buckinghamshire, England; Republican congressman from Utah 1901–3; U.S. senator 1905–17; appointed associate justice of U.S. Supreme Court 1922, *picture* U-226

Sutherland, Graham Vivian (1903–80), English artist, born in London; imaginative landscapes; expressionistic portraits; use of thorns typical; works in leading museums.

Sutherland, Joan (born 1926), Australian coloratura, born in Sydney; prima donna Covent Garden, London, 1952–; won great fame there as Lucia 1959; U.S. debut in Dallas, Tex., 1960; debut Metropolitan Opera House, New York City, and La Scala, Milan, 1961 A-801

Sutherland Falls, waterfall on South Island, New Zealand; waters fall in three leaps from a height of 1,904 ft (580 m) into Milford Sound on n.w. coast, *table* W-98

Sutlej, river of n.w. Indian peninsula; longest of five rivers that give name to Punjab; rises in Tibet and flows 850 mi (1,370 km) to Chenab River, *maps* I-86, A-700

Sutro, Adolph (1830–98), U.S. civil engineer, born in Prussia; to Nevada 1860; devised Sutro Tunnel to Comstock mines to drain water, reduce hazard of mine fires, and facilitate transport of ore.

Suttee, in Hinduism, the custom of a widow willingly being cremated on the funeral pyre of her husband as an indication of her devotion to him H-157

Sutter, John Augustus (1803–80), California pioneer on whose land gold was discovered in 1848 S-2
- California C-41
- gold rush G-183

Sutter's Fort, at Sacramento, Calif. S-2, *picture* C-41

Suttner, Bertha, baroness von (born Bertha Kinsky) (1843–1914), Austrian author and peace advocate, born in Prague. *see also in index* Nobel Prizewinners, *table*
- Nobel N-329

Sutton, Walter S. (1876–1916), U.S. geneticist and physician; noted for studies of chromosomes
- genetics G-54
- heredity H-140

Sutton, borough of Greater London, England, *map* L-287

Sutton Dam, dam in W. Va., on Elk river W-165

Sutton Hoo, in Suffolk, England A-534, *picture* A-531

Suture, in surgery S-519b

Suva, capital of Fiji, on island of Viti Levu; manufactures coconut oil and soap; site of a medical school; harbor; pop. 66,622 F-82, *map* P-6
- marriage ceremony, *picture* M-150
- Oceania, *picture* O-472

Suwannee River (or Swanee River, or Suwanee River), stream flowing from Okefenokee Swamp in s. Georgia 250 mi (400 km) through Florida to Gulf of Mexico.

Suzerain, superior feudal lord to whom fealty is due M-386

Suzor-Côté, Marc Aurèle de Foy (1869–1937), Canadian impressionist painter and sculptor, born in Athabaska, Que.; noted for Canadian genre scenes, also for bronze group, 'Caughnawaga Women'.

Suzuki, Zenko (born 1911), Japanese political leader, born in Yamada Town in Iwate Prefecture; member of Liberal-Democratic party; elected to Diet 12 times after 1947; chief cabinet secretary 1964; minister of health and welfare 1965–67, of agriculture, forestry, and fisheries 1976–77; prime minister 1980–82 J-69

Suzzallo, Henry (1875–1933), U.S. educator, born in San Jose, Calif.; president University of Washington 1915–26; made trustee of Carnegie Foundation for Advancement of Teaching 1919 and president 1930.

Svalbard, Norwegian possession in Arctic Ocean about 400 mi (645 km) n. of Norway, made up of Spitsbergen archipelago, east islands, and Bear Island (Bjørnøya); total area 23,958 sq mi (62,051 sq km); the Spitsbergen archipelago (area, 23,650 sq mi; 61,250 sq km) includes Spitsbergen, Northeast Land, Edge Island, and other islands; Svalbard was given its name by Vikings in 12th century; explored by Willem Barents in 1596; pop [illegible]; maps R-322, 344, P-417
- Arctic regions A-571
- Norway N-389, 394

Svealand, middle region of Sweden S-522

Svedberg, Theodor (1884–1971), Swedish chemist, director Gustaf Werner Institute for Nuclear Chemistry, Uppsala, also professor physical chemistry, University of Uppsala; studies of colloids of value to medicine. *see also in index* Nobel Prizewinners, *table*

Svendsen, Johan Severin (1840–1911), Norwegian violinist and composer, one of the most important Scandinavian masters ('Carnaval à Paris', 'Coronation March', 'A Minor String Quartet') N-391

Svengali, character in George Du Maurier's 'Trilby', hypnotist who makes Trilby a great singer.

Sverdlovsk (formerly Ekaterinburg), U.S.S.R., city in w. Siberia on Iset' River at s. end of middle Ural Mts.; railroad center; steel, heavy machinery, radio and television equipment, chemicals, paper, clothing, food products; educational center; gold, tungsten, copper, asbestos mined in area; pop. 1,171,000, *maps* R-322, 344
- Asia, *map* A-700
- Trans-Siberian Railroad T-266

Sverdrup, Otto (1855–1930), Norwegian Arctic explorer; crossed Greenland with Nansen 1888; commanded the *Fram* in Nansen's Arctic expedition 1893–96; led an expedition in the *Fram* 1898–1902, exploring wide territory and discovering Sverdrup Islands ('Arctic Adventures').

Svetambara, sect of Jainism J-14
- monks and monasticism M-541

Svevo, Italo (pen name of Ettore Schmitz) (1861–1928), Italian novelist; born in Trieste; almost unknown until near end of his life; deeply introspective ('Una Vita', 'La Coscienza di Zeno') I-377

Sviataslov, ruler of Russia AD 964–972 R-351

Svolvær, Norway, chief town and port of the Lofoten island group; economy almost entirely dependent on cod fisheries; pop. 3,942f, *picture* N-392

Swabia, medieval duchy of s.w. Germany; flourished under Hohenstaufens; disintegrated into small states 1268; great Swabian League for mutual protection (1488–1534); now district in Bavaria G-121
- Frederick I F-389

Swabian Jura, plateau region in West Germany G-111, *map* G-134

Swahili, an East African people of Bantu lineage with some Semitic ancestry; they are Muslims and are noted as traders; number about 1,000,000 A-97
- language A-119

Swains Island, island in American Samoa, n. of island of Tutuila; area 1 sq mi (2.6 sq km); U.S. territory after 1925; pop. 29, *map* P-6

Swakara. *see in index* Persian lamb

Swallow, Alan (1915–66), U.S. publisher and author, born in Powell, Wyo.; taught English at various universities 1940–54, owner of Alan Swallow, Publisher, Denver, Colorado, 1940–66; volumes of poetry include 'XI Poems', 'The Remembered Land', and 'The War Poems'.

Swallow, a long-winged bird S-521
- barn swallow. *see in index* Barn swallow
- Capistrano swallows. *see in index* San Juan Capistrano
- cliff swallow. *see in index* Cliff swallow
- daytime migrants A-450
- purple martin. *see in index* Purple martin
- swift S-532
- tree swallow S-521

'Swallow Barn', work by Kennedy A-346

Swallow float, in oceanography O-464

Swallow hole (or sinkhole) C-233

Swallowing, animal behavior
- birds B-255

Swallow pigeon, bird P-324

Swallowtail, flag, *list* F-149

Swallowtail butterfly, large butterfly recognized by tailliko extension on hind wings; about 20 species in North America n. of Mexico; black swallowtail *Papilio polyxenes,* wings black with yellow and orange spots; tiger swallowtail *Papilio glaucus,* wings yellow with black bars and yellow spots B-528

Swammerdam, Jan (1637–80), Dutch naturalist; trained in medicine but turned to zoology; discovered valves of the lymphatics; described red blood corpuscles; studied infections, movement of heart and lungs.

Swamp (or marsh), low, spongy, saturated land covered with vegetation. *see also in index* Bog; Dismal Swamp; Everglades; Okefenokee Swamp
- Arctic R-324
- blackbirds' habitat B-305
- coal formation P-151
- cypress, *pictures* P-357, S-305
- Louisiana, *picture* P-234
- water plants, *picture* P-360

Swamp ash. *see in index* Black ash

Swamp buggy (or marsh buggy), vehicle, *picture* P-234

Swamp cedar, a name sometimes used for both the northern white cedar and southern white cedar. *see in index* Northern white cedar; Southern white cedar

Swamp chestnut oak, tree *Quercus prinus* of beech family; leaves large and coarsely notched; acorn in thick, bowl-shaped cup; scaly bark mostly ashy gray tinged with red
- wood, *table* W-283

Swamp maple (or red maple, or scarlet maple), tree M-112, *picture* R-186

Swamp milkweed, perennial plant *Asclepias incarnata* M-416

Swamp pine. *see in index* Slash pine

Swamp red oak, tree
- wood, *table* W-283

Swamp rose mallow, a tall perennial herb *Hibiscus moscheutos* of the mallow family with pointed ovate

leaves and large, rose-colored flowers H-149
Swampscott, Mass., residential township and summer resort adjoining Lynn, on Nahant Bay; pop. 13,837.
Swamp sumac. *see in index* Poison sumac
Swamp tupelo (sometimes called water gum, or southern gum), a tree *Nyssa biflora* of the tupelo family, native to shallow swamps of coastal region from Virginia to Louisiana; tapering trunk has swollen base; grows 50 to 75 ft (15 to 25 m); leaves oblong, glossy, dark green; fruit round, dark blue; wood has twisted fibers.
Swamp white oak, tree *Quercus bicolor* of beech family; grows to 70 ft (20 m); leaves oval, to 6 in. (15 cm) long, with large lobes, dark green on upper side
wood, *table* W-283
Swan, John Macallan (1847–1910), English sculptor and painter; excelled in portraying wild animals ('The Jaguar'; 'Leopard Running', sculpture).
Swan, Sir Joseph Wilson (1828–1914), English physicist and electrician; in photography produced dry plates and first practical process of carbon printing; invented an incandescent electric lamp with carbon filaments L-205, E-163
Swan, bird D-284
animal migration A-451
Swan, constellation. *see in index* Cygnus
Swan dive, type of dive, *picture* S-533
'Swanee', song by Gershwin G-135
Swanee River. *see in index* Suwannee River
'Swanee River' (or 'Old Folks at Home'), song by Foster F-327
Swan Islands, two islands in Caribbean Sea about 110 mi (180 km) n. of Honduras; area 1 sq mi (2.6 sq km).
'Swan Lake', ballet to music by Tchaikovsky B-32
Nureyev's choreography, *picture* N-441
Swann vs. Charlotte-Mecklenburg Board of Education, U.S. law case, *list* E-104
Swan River, river in Western Australia, rising as the Avon; flows n.w. to Indian Ocean 12 mi (19 km) southwest of Perth; gave name to first colonial settlement in w. Australia, founded 1829 (Swan River colony).
Swansea, Mass., town 3 mi (5 km) n.w. of Fall River in agricultural area; settled 1632, incorporated 1668; pop. of township 15,461.
Swansea, Wales, seaport on Bristol Channel 34 mi (55 km) n.w. of Cardiff; refining of nickel, zinc, petroleum; large tinplate works at Trostre and Velindre, both n.w. of city; University College of Swansea; pop. 171,320 W-6, *map* E-361
Swanson, Claude Augustus (1862–1939), U.S. lawyer and political leader, born in Pittsylvania County, Va.; governor of Virginia 1906–10; U.S. senator 1910–33; secretary of navy in F.D. Roosevelt's Cabinet 1933–39, *picture* R-268
Swanson Reservoir, in Nebraska N-95
SWAPO (or South West Africa People's Organization), Namibian organization seeking independence of Namibia from the Republic of South Africa N-9
Swarm, insect
bees B-127
locusts L-283
Swarthmore College, in Swarthmore, Pa.; founded 1864 (opened 1869) by Friends; now nonsectarian; arts and sciences, engineering; graduate study P-251b
honors courses U-207
Swarthout, Gladys (or Mrs. Frank M. Chapman, Jr.) (1904–69), U.S. mezzo-soprano, born in Deepwater, Mo.; with Chicago and Metropolitan opera companies, and in motion pictures.
Swastika (Sanskrit "well-being"), ancient symbol widely used; adopted by Hitler as the emblem of the Nazi party in Germany
Hitler H-177
Swather. *see in index* Windrower
Swatow, China, seaport in Guangdong Province, on South China Sea; exports sugar, tropical fruit; pop. 400,000, *map* A-700
Swazi, an African people, chiefly of Swaziland S-522
Swaziland, nation in s.e. Africa; 6,704 sq mi (17,363 sq km); cap. Mbabane; pop. 496,835 S-522, *map* S-264
Africa, *map* A-118, *table* A-112
Commonwealth membership C-602
flag, *picture* F-170
railroad mileage, *table* R-85
United Kingdom E-259
Sweatbee, insect B-125
Sweat gland, either of two types of secretory skin glands S-211, G-153
Sweating, in mammal physiology M-80
Sweatshop, cramped and unsanitary place of work in which wages are inhumanly low and hours long; in advanced countries now largely abolished by labor and welfare legislation
garment industry G-35
King K-243
Kingsley K-247
Sweden, country of n. Europe, occupying the e. part of Scandinavian peninsula; 173,666 sq mi (449,793 sq km); cap. Stockholm; pop. 8,076,903 S-522
Arctic regions A-571
arts
folk art F-254
literature. *see also in index* Scandinavian literature
storytelling S-472, *list* S-481a
motion pictures M-620, 623, S-526
bank history B-72
bibliography S-529
church and state C-409
cities. *see also in index* cities listed below and other cities by name
Stockholm S-448
cooperative societies C-706
Europe, *map* E-361
flags F-153, *pictures* F-155, 170
medieval banner, *picture* M-384
history
Bernadotte B-174
Charles XII C-278, P-226
Finland F-91
North American settlements
Delaware A-336, D-75
Pennsylvania P-173
Norway N-394
Seven Years' War S-117
Thirty Years' War T-169
industries, *pictures* S-526, *table* S-528
automobile A-868
lumber and timber S-523
printing P-504
labor union growth, *table* L-8
language. *see in index* Swedish language
Lapland L-49
Lapp clothing, *picture* R-139
liquor laws P-507
military affairs
army innovations A-640
artillery development A-660
museum policy M-661
national anthem, *table* N-64
national fitness test H-151
natural features S-523, 522, *picture* S-526
newspapers N-235, *chart* J-416
people S-52g, S-524, *picture* R-25
children S-525
classification R-27, *chart* R-26
police, *picture* P-430b
sports S-525
skiing S-210d
taxation, *table* T-35
transportation
railroad mileage, *table* R-85
ship tonnage, *table* S-176a
Swedenborg, Emanuel (1688–1772), Swedish scientist, philosopher, and religious mystic; theological writings, expounding Bible and universe, form basis of doctrine of the Churches of the New Jerusalem, called Swedenborgian
Blake B-310
Swedish language. *see also in index* Scandinavian languages
Finland F-89
Germanic languages G-103
Sweden S-524
Swedish modern, architectural style
Stockholm S-448
Swedish nightingale. *see in index* Lind, Jenny
Swedish turnip. *see in index* Rutabaga
Sweet, Henry (1845–1912), English philologist, born in London; known as founder of modern phonetics ('New English Grammar', 'History of Language').
Sweet alyssum, genus of low spreading plants *Alyssum* of the mustard family, with small fragrant yellow, rose, or white flowers; used for garden borders
growing conditions G-23
Sweet bay, tree *Magnolia virginiana* of the Magnolia family M-47
Sweet birch (or black birch, or cherry birch), tree *Betula lenta* of the family Betulaceae B-239
wood, *table* W-283
Sweetbread, thymus gland of a young animal or the pancreas of a mature animal when prepared as a food; sometimes incorporated into meat pies and pastries.
Sweet Briar College, in Sweet Briar, Va.; private control; for women; established 1901; opened 1906; liberal arts; administers junior year programs in France, Rome, and Scotland.
Sweet cassava, South American plant *Manihot dulcis* of the spurge family T-27
Sweet cicely. *see in index* Cicely
Sweet coltsfoot. *see in index* Winter heliotrope
Sweet corn C-723, *picture* C-718
growing conditions G-25
Sweetened condensed milk, dairy product M-415, *list* D-6
Sweet flag. *see in index* Calamus
Sweet gale family (or Myricaceae), family of shrubs and trees, native to temperate regions, including the California wax myrtle or bayberry and sweet gale.
Sweet gum, a tree *Liquidambar styraciflua* of witch-hazel family; hardwood is called red gum, *picture* T-281
Sweet honeysuckle. *see in index* Italian woodbine
Sweet laurel. *see in index* Bay laurel
Sweet music, term for form of jazz in which improvising is less complex than in hot jazz, and brass instruments are often subordinated to the strings.
Sweet pea, a flowering plant *Lathyrus odoratus* of the family Leguminosae S-529
flower, *picture* F-216
growing conditions G-24
structure, *diagram* P-363
Sweet potato, tropical vine *Ipomoea batatas,* grown for edible root S-530
morning-glory M-584
Oceania O-471
textile starch P-379
Sweet potato, musical instrument. *see in index* Ocarina
Sweet potato squash, vegetable S-399
Sweet rocket (or dame's violet), tall perennial garden plant *Hesperis matronalis* of mustard family; lance-shaped leaves; purple or white flowers, fragrant at night.
Sweet-scented water lily. *see in index* American water lily
Sweet sorghum (or Sorgo) S-258
Sweet sultan, fragrant plant of the genus *Centaurea;* bears white, yellow, or purple flowers; an annual; stems grow about 2 ft (0.6 m) high.
Sweetwater, Tex., city about 40 mi (60 km) w. of Abilene; railroad shops; gypsum products, cement, petroleum products, cottonseed oil; pop. 12,242, *map* U-40
Sweetwater River, river crossing Rocky Mts. in s. center of Wyoming and enters n. fork of Platte River; 180 mi (290 km) long.
Sweet William, garden plant in the pink family P-329
flowering time G-25
Sweet William (or wild blue phlox), wild flower P-267, *pictures* F-217, F-233
Sweet William catchfly. *see in index* Silene
Swell (or free waves), ocean waves O-487
Sweyn I, Forkbeard (died 1014), king of Denmark 991–1014; ravaged England yearly after massacre of Danes in England in 1002; father of Canute the Great C-145
Swift, Gustavus Franklin (1839–1903), U.S. meat-packer, born near Sandwich, Mass.; established plant in Chicago 1875; developed refrigerator car; pioneer in production of packinghouse by-products such as oleomargarine, soap, glue, and preparations used in medicine.
Swift, Hildegarde Hoyt (1890–1977), U.S. writer, born in Clinton, N.Y.; active in work of Inter-Racial Fellowship of Greater New York; books for children: 'The Little Red Lighthouse', 'Railroad to Freedom', 'North Star Shining', 'The Edge of April', 'From the Eagle's Wing'.
Swift, Jonathan (1667–1745), British satirist S-530
conversation C-695
creative writing W-382
English literature E-270
'Gulliver's Travels' S-530, R-111, *picture* S-532
'Martin's Vagaries,' *pictures* S-531
science fiction S-61
word games W-293
Swift, a swallowlike bird S-532, B-249, *pictures* B-244, 250. *see also in index* Chimney swift
Swift Current, Sask., city on Swift Current Creek, 138 mi (222 km) w. of Regina; oil, natural gas; flour, meat; pop. 14,747 S-49h, *maps* C-112, S-49k
Swift River, river in Massachusetts M-190
Swigert, John L., Jr. (born 1931), former U.S. astronaut, born in Denver, Colo.; test pilot; with NASA 1966–73; executive director Committee on Science and Technology, U.S., House of Representatives 1973–77, *table* S-348
Swim bladder. *see in index* Air bladder
Swimmerets, small paddlelike limbs on segments of abdomen of some crustaceans C-789
Swimming S-533, *pictures* S-534
accident prevention S-11
Australia A-789
lifesaving S-535
Philippines, *picture* P-257b
pool, *pictures* P-127, V-240
strokes S-533, *pictures* S-534, V-240
'Swimmy', children's book R-106, *picture* R-111c
Swinburne, Algernon Charles (1837–1909), English poet S-535
literary contribution E-276
Swindon, England, market and railroad town 72 mi (116 km) w. of London; large locomotive and car works; old town is the Svindune of Domesday; pop. 98,290.
Swine. *see in index* Hog
Swing, form of jazz J-85, M-684
Swing, in cattle driving C-754
'Swing, The', painting by Fragonard F-341
Swinging (or schwingen), type of wrestling in Switzerland W-366
Swing span bridge, type of bridge B-442, *picture* B-443
Swinnerton, Frank Arthur (1884–1982), English novelist and critic, born in Wood Green, England; self-educated; critic on *Manchester Guardian;* works known for genial satire (novels: 'Nocturne', 'The Doctor's Wife Comes to Stay', 'A Month in Gordon Square', 'Death of a Highbrow', 'Quadrille'; criticism: 'The Georgian Literary Scene, 1910–1935'; autobiography).
Swinton, Sir Ernest Dunlop (1868–1951), English general; invented tank 1914; professor of military history Oxford University 1925–39.
Swinton, William (1833–92), U.S. educator, born in Salton,

Scotland; correspondent for *New York Times* during Civil War; professor of English, University of California; his textbooks popular in his day.

Swiss, a sheer, crisp cotton fabric, plain or embroidered in dots or figures; used for summer dresses and blouses, bedspreads, and curtains; originated in Switzerland.

Swiss Cantons, League of, in Swiss history, *table* T-275

Swiss cheese, a mild, sweet light-colored cheese full of holes, originally made in Switzerland, but now also produced in U.S. C-288, S-539

'Swiss Family Robinson, The', a novel by Johann Wyss describing the experiences of a shipwrecked family on a desert island in the Pacific Ocean; published in English 1820.

Swiss Guard, bodyguard of popes P-100
- barracks, *map* V-269

Swiss Guards, famous bodyguard of French kings after 1465 A-640

Swiss lake village, prehistoric settlement, *diagram* A-530

Swiss mondaine, pigeon, *picture* P-325

Swissvale, Pa., manufacturing borough on Monongahela River about 7 mi (11 km) e. of Pittsburgh; air brakes; pop. 11,345, *map* P-184

Switchboard of radio studio, *picture* R-47

Switch cane, bamboo *Arundinaria tecta* of the family Gramineae B-51

Switchyard, railroad R-80, *pictures* R-79
- engines R-77

Swithin, Saint (or Saint Swithun) (died AD 862), bishop of Winchester; when his body was about to be removed to Winchester cathedral in 971 after his canonization, violent rains fell delaying the removal for 40 days; hence the legend that if it rains on his feast day, July 15, it will rain thereafter for 40 days.

Switzerland, small mountainous country of Europe; area 15,941 sq mi (41,287 sq km); cap. Bern; pop. 6,269,783 S-536
- agriculture and dairying S-541, 545, 537, *picture* S-538
  - farm life S-541
  - food products S-539, 542
- cities S-542. *see also in index* cities listed below and other cities by name
  - Bern B-174
  - Geneva G-58
  - Zürich Z-472
- citizenship C-439
- climate S-537, *graph* S-545
- conscription C-667
- dams S-539
- education E-89, S-543
  - illiteracy P-450
- Europe, *map* E-361
- flag, *picture* F-171
- forests S-538, *chart* S-545
- government S-543
  - democracy D-95
  - initiative, referendum, and recall I-206
  - taxation, *table* T-35
- history S-544
  - Charles the Bold C-280
  - cooperatives C-707
  - lake dwellers S-157, S-544
  - neutrality S-544a
  - World Wars I and II S-554b
- industries S-539
  - printing P-504
  - tourism S-542
  - wine W-239
- international banking B-71
- land use, *chart* S-545
- languages S-541
- literature S-542
  - folktales, *list* S-481c
  - German literature G-106
  - Tell T-79
- masks M-187
- mountains M-636
- national park N-27
- people R-27
- rivers
  - Rhine R-177
  - Rhône River R-196
- sports
  - wrestling W-366
- transportation S-540, *pictures* S-538, 540, 542
  - bridges S-540, *picture* S-544
  - railroad mileage, *table* R-85
- waterpower S-538, *picture* S-539

Swivel, in fishing F-142

Sword S-546
- Damascus B-308, D-18
- fencing F-53
- metalworking M-311
- Perseus' P-210
- Roland's Durendal R-238
- Siegfried's Balmung S-192a
- Swiss, *picture* S-544a
- 'Swords into plowshares', *picture* P-143d

Sword dance, English folk dance F-255

Swordfish, long-snouted, mackerel-like fish S-547, *picture* A-408
- fisheries, *table* F-137
- mobility A-424, *picture* A-426
- sawfish S-52d

Sword lily. *see in index* Gladiolus

'Sword of Honor', work by Waugh W-28

'Swords into plowshares', carving by Lawrie, *picture* P-143d

Syagrius (died AD 487), Roman administrator of Gaul; ruled district n. of the Seine between the Marne and the Oise 457–486; defeated by Clovis at battle of Soissons (486).

Sybaris, ancient Greek city of s. Italy, proverbial for luxury (hence "sybarite"); destroyed 510 BC.

Sycamore, tree *Platanus occidentalis* S-548

Sycamore maple (or sycamore), tree *Acer pseudoplatanus* M-112

Sydenham, Charles Edward Poulett Thomson, first baron (1799–1841), British-Canadian statesman; Liberal member of Parliament; as governor-general of Canada, 1839–41, carried into effect union of Upper and Lower Canada.

Sydenham, Thomas (1624–89), English physician, born in Dorset, England; called the English Hippocrates and considered the founder of modern clinical medicine; known for his diagnosis of diseases, especially plague, malaria, smallpox, gout.

Sydney, New South Wales, Australia, largest city of nation; pop. 2,717,069, with suburbs S-548
- Australia A-767, 787, *map* A-819
- beach S-549
- climate S-548
- harbor bridges S-549, *map* S-549a
- history S-549a
  - Phillip S-549a
- industries S-549
- libraries S-549a, *map* S-549a
- New South Wales N-234
- Pacific Ocean, *map* P-6
- places of interest S-549a, *map* S-549a, *pictures* S-549
- population growth A-787

Sydney, N.S., city, chief port of Cape Breton Island; pop. 29,444 N-399, 402, *picture* N-401, *map* N-351
- Canada, *map* C-112
- shipping trade C-146

Sydney, University of, in Sydney, New South Wales, Australia S-549a

Sydney Basin, landform in Australia A-774

Sydney Cup, trophy for horseracing A-791

Sydney Harbor, in Australia A-801, B-446, *picture* I-330

Sydney-Hobart Yacht Race A-789

Sydney Island, in the Pacific. *see in index* Phoenix Islands

Sydney Mines, N.S., town, coal-mining center near mouth of Sydney Harbor, Cape Breton Island, near Sydney; pop. 8,501.

Sydney Opera House, in Sydney, Australia A-801

Syene. *see in index* Aswan

Syenite, a granite quarried in ancient Upper Egypt for obelisks; also an igneous rock similar to granite but containing no quartz, used in building; made up of an alkali feldspar and mica, hornblende, or augite.

Sykes, Bill, character in Dickens' 'Oliver Twist', brutal thief; kills Nancy, his mistress, and maltreats Oliver, *picture* D-137

Sykes-Picot Agreement (1916), between France and Britain; divided Transjordan between them J-142

Sylacauga, Ala., city 40 mi (60 km) s.e. of Birmingham; marble quarrying; textile products; dairying; near Talladega National Forest; pop. 12,708.

Syllabary, in writing W-371
- Semitic A-315

Syllable, in language L-31, 40
- alphabet A-315

Syllogism, in logic L-284

Sylt, West German island of Frisian group, in North Sea off Schleswig-Holstein coast; area 36 sq mi (93 sq km); resort; pop. 17,592 G-112, *map* G-134

Sylvania, Ohio, city 9 mi (15 km) n.w. of Toledo near Michigan border; cement, fertilizer; stone quarries; pop. 15,527.

Sylvan Lake, lake in South Dakota, *picture* S-331

Sylvester I (or Saint Silvester I) (died AD 335), pope 314–335; born in Rome; reorganized discipline of Roman Catholicism; commemorated as saint December 31.

Sylvester II (940?–1003), French monk named Gerbert, elected pope in 999; tutor to Otto III; scholar, mathematician, greatest private library collector of early Middle Ages.

Sylviidae (or silviidae), family of perching birds embracing the gnatcatchers, kinglets, and Old World warblers.

Sylvite (or potassium chloride), mineral M-435
- fertilizer F-59

Symbiosis, in biology, partnership between dissimilar plants or animals for mutual benefit
- crocodile and ziczac P-391
- fish F-128
- legumes and bacteria P-363a
- lichens L-191
- rhinoceros and tick bird, *picture* R-178
- termites and protozoa T-111

Symbol
- communication C-606
- exponent. *see in index* Exponent
- map M-116, *picture* M-119
- Roman numerals R-248, *table* R-248
- secret. *see in index* Ciphers and codes

Symbolic logic
- Boole B-364
- mathematics M-220

Symbolism, in art
- architecture A-544
- folk art F-252
- interior design I-246

Symbolism, in literature, tendency to suggest by various means more than the literal meaning; term applied especially to work and influence of group of late 19th-century French writers who suggested emotions and sensations through sound and rhythm imitating music
- creative writing W-381
- Darío D-35
- French literature F-397
  - Mallarmé M-77
- German literature G-107
- Russian literature R-360a

Syme, James (1799–1870), Scottish surgeon; professor of clinical surgery at universities of London and Edinburgh
- rubber experiments R-305

Syme, Ronald (born 1913), British author and world traveler, born in Napier, New Zealand; went to sea at age 16 (biographies for younger readers: 'Cortes of Mexico', 'Columbus', 'La Salle of the Mississippi', 'Magellan, First Around the World', 'John Smith of Virginia', 'Henry Hudson', 'Balboa, Finder of the Pacific', 'De Soto', 'On Foot to the Arctic', 'First Man to Cross America', 'Francisco Pizarro', 'Captain John Paul Jones', 'Garibaldi')

Symington, Stuart (full name William Stuart Symington) (born 1901), U.S. public official and industrialist, born in Amherst, Mass.; head of Surplus Property Administration 1945–46; assistant secretary of war for air 1946–47, secretary of the air force 1947–50; chairman National Security Resources Board 1950–51; RFC administrator 1951–52; U.S. senator (Democrat) from Missouri 1953–77.

Symington, William (1763–1831), Scottish engineer and inventor; built steamboat, *Charlotte Dundas,* which was operated on Clyde River 1802.

Symmetry, in design A-668

Symmetry, in mathematics
- atomic structure A-752
  - crystals C-797

Symonds, John Addington (1840–93), English critic, author of the monumental 'History of the Renaissance in Italy' and many other valuable works
- quoted R-146

Symons, Arthur (1865–1945), English critic and poet, born in Milford Haven, Wales; influenced by French literature, especially symbolist school ('The Symbolist Movement in Literature', 'Studies in Seven Arts').

Sympathetic nervous system, a double chain of ganglia along the spinal column and the nerves connected with them that supply the glands and involuntary muscles N-119

Sympetalous plants (or gamopetalous plants) F-217
- trees T-283

Symphonic poem (or tone poem), musical form M-673, *list* M-671
- Respighi R-255
- Sibelius S-187
- Strauss S-485, O-569

'Symphonic Variations', dance by Ashton B-32

'Symphonie Fantastique', symphony by Berlioz B-172
- classical music M-673

Symphony, musical composition, *list* M-671
- classical music M-669
- Schubert S-54, 55
- Schumann S-55
- Shostakovich S-185
- Sibelius S-187

'Symphony for One Man Only', work by Schaeffer M-676

'Symphony in Three Movements', work by Stravinsky O-576

'Symphony No. 2', work by Sessions O-578

'Symphony No. 40 in G Minor', work by Mozart O-576

'Symphony No. 73' (or 'La Chasse', or 'The Hunt'), work by Haydn O-576

'Symphony of a Thousand' (or 'Symphony No. 8'), work by Mahler M-49
- orchestra O-578

'Symphony of Three Orchestras', work by Carter M-677

'Symphony, Opus 21', work by Webern O-578

Symphony orchestra. *see in index* Orchestra

'Symposium', dialogue by Plato P-384

Symptom, in medicine M-278
- diseases D-165
- mental illness M-301

Synagogue, in Judaism, a congregation; a place of worship J-150, *pictures* J-147, 148
- Touro, *picture* R-188

Synapse, point at which a nervous impulse passes from one neuron to another N-120, *diagrams* N-121, 122
- genetics G-54

Synapsis, the mechanism for genetic crossing-over G-54

Synaptic cleft, of nerve N-121, *diagram* N-122

Synarthrosis, type of joint J-136

Synchrocyclotron, in nuclear energy N-420

Synchromesh, type of gear system A-850

Synchronous motor M-631

Synchronous orbit, artificial satellites S-343, *table* S-344

Synchronous sound, in motion pictures M-610

Synchrotron, in nuclear energy N-420

Syncline, a type of valley E-15

Syncoms, artificial satellites S-195b, *table* S-344

Syncopation, in music, *list* M-671

Syndicalism S-360
- anarchist associations A-388

Syndrome, in medicine, group of signs or symptoms that occur together and characterize a particular abnormality
- mental illness M-301

Synecdoche, figure of speech in which a part is used to signify the whole (as "hearth" for "home") or the whole to signify a part (as "army" for a "soldier") F-81

Synge, John Millington (1871–1909), Irish dramatist, born near Dublin; portrayed life of Arran Islanders; genius of Irish literary renaissance I-327
drama D-246
English literature E-280
Yeats Y-412
Synge, Richard Laurence Millington (born 1914), English biochemist, born in Liverpool, England; distant relative of John Millington Synge; researches on chromatography, facilitating the separation of closely related compounds. *see also in index* Nobel Prizewinners, *table*
'Synnove Solbakken', novel by Bjornson B-287
Synod, in Christianity C-410
Synodic month (or lunar month), time period between new moons M-578
Synodic period, of spacecraft S-343
Synod of Barmen, in German Protestant history C-411
Barth B-85
Synonym, name given to a word that means essentially the same as another word; such as, funny, amusing, laughable L-34
handbook R-127
'Synopsis of the Astronomy of Comets, A', work by Hall H-15
Synoptic chart, chart used in weather forecasting W-122, *table* W-126
Synoptic forecasting, method of weather forecasting W-122
Synoptic meteorology M-315
Synovial membrane, membrane that secretes a lubricating fluid called synovia and lines the interior of joints J-137, S-210
Synovium, lining of skeletal joints
arthritis A-650
Syntax, in grammar L-229
Synthesis, in Hegelian philosophy H-115
Synthesis gas P-228
Synthesizer, device that produces sounds M-676
popular music M-682
Synthetic chemistry, branch of chemistry dealing with building up of chemical compounds. *see in index* Synthetic products
Synthetic fiber. *see in index* Fibers, man-made
Synthetic philosophy
Spencer S-377
Synthetic products, those made by chemical or mechanical means to replace or improve upon natural products
camphor C-67
compost C-623
drugs D-274
quinine Q-18
dyes D-296
fake furs. *see in index* Fake furs
fibers. *see also in index* Fibers, man-made
rayon R-97–9, *picture* R-98
gems C-796, J-113, *picture* J-115
leather substitutes L-109
methanol M-317
neoprene P-228
organic chemistry O-605
paint pigments P-73
pearls P-149
perfumes P-204
plastics. *see in index* Plastics
resins. *see in index* Resins, *subhead* synthetic
rubber substitutes. *see in index* Rubber, synthetic
saccharin S-509
sponges S-394
vitamins V-354, 357, 358
wax W-110
Syphilis, a venereal disease V-272. *see also in index* Venereal disease
Ehrlich's treatment E-132
infectious disease, *table* D-172
mental illness M-302
nervous disorder N-123
Noguchi N-330
spirochete V-272, *picture* V-273
Syracuse (Italian Siracusa), Italy, city on s.e. coast of Sicily; founded by Corinthians 734 BC; powerful in ancient times; pop. 90,333 S-192, *maps* E-361, I-404, B-25
battle (413 BC), *list* W-15
Etruscans (474 BC) R-244
Pyrrhus P-544
Syracuse, N.Y., city at s. end of Lake Onondaga; pop. 170,105 S-549b
New York N-251, *map* U-41, *picture* U-54
Syracuse University, in Syracuse, N.Y.; private control; chartered 1870; liberal arts, architecture, art, business administration, education, engineering, home economics, journalism, law, library science, music, nursing, social work, speech and dramatic art; cooperative program with State University College of Environmental Science and Forestry at Syracuse; graduate school; branch campus at Utica N-254
social studies survey S-241
Syr-Dar'ya (ancient Jaxartes), river of Asia, flowing 1,300 mi (2,100 km) from Uzbek Soviet Socialist Republic to Aral Sea; used for irrigation A-527, *maps* R-322, 344
Syria, nation in w. Asia bordering on Mediterranean; area 71,228 sq mi (184,480 sq km); cap. Damascus; Syria historical name for all e. Mediterranean coast, including present Syria, Lebanon, Israel, and Jordan; pop. 8,328,000 S-549b, *maps* P-212, R-242
archaeological discoveries A-538, M-85
Asia, *map* A-700
cities S-550. *see also in index* cities listed below and other cities by name
Aleppo A-277
Damascus D-18
Palmyra P-84
flag, *picture* F-171
history S-550
Byzantine rule B-533
Crusades
Saladin S-25
Egypt E-121
Hittites H-177
horse H-270
Israel I-372
Jordan J-142
Lebanon L-112
Phoenicians P-267
World War I results W-319
national anthem, *table* N-64
people and language S-550
products S-550
railroad mileage, *table* R-85
rivers S-549b
Tigris River T-184
shelter, *pictures* S-549b–50
Syriac, eastern dialect of Aramaic, used by Christian writers in parts of Syria, Mesopotamia, and Persia from 4th to 13th century.
Syrian Desert, desert region in n. Arabia, s.e. Syria, w. Iraq, and n.e. Jordan.
Syrian hamster (or golden hamster), rodent *Mesocricetus auratus* H-25
Syringa (or mock orange), shrub of the saxifrage family S-550
Idaho state flower, *picture* S-427
Syrinx, vocal structure in singing birds B-247
Syros (or Syra), Greek island in the center of the Cyclades group in Aegean Sea; chief town is Hermopolis; trade center in 19th century.
Syrup (or sirup)
sorghum S-258
System, a group of interacting bodies under the influence of related forces E-213
Systematic botany L-231
Systematic geography G-67
Systematics, science of classifying species in terms of their natural evolutionary origins and relationships Z-467
Système International d'Unités, Le. *see in index* International System
Systemic circulation, general circulation in human body C-421
Systemic lupus erythematosus (SLE, or lupus), degenerative disease D-181
'System of Nature', work by Holbach M-210
Systems analyst C-636
Systems approach (or systems engineering) S-348c
Systole, period of contraction of heart H-97
Systolic blood pressure C-422
Szabadka, Yugoslavia. *see in index* Subotica
Szczecin (German Stettin), Poland, former German port on Oder River 17 mi (27 km) above mouth; included in Poland since 1945; pop. 299,200, *maps* E-361, P-414
Széchenyi, István, Count (1791–1860), Hungarian statesman; hero in Napoleonic Wars; improved navigation and introduced steamboats on the Danube and Theiss rivers; committed suicide when accused of sedition H-329
Szechwan (or Szechuan, or Sichuan), province of s.-central China; 210,000 sq mi (544,000 sq km); cap. Chengtu; pop. 97,705,000
flood, *table* F-181
Yangtze River Y-410
Szeged (German Szegedin), Hungary, city on Tisza River 100 mi (160 km) s.e. of Budapest; shipping center; pop. 183,000 H-329, *map* E-361
Szeklers, a Magyar people who form about a third of the population of what was e. Transylvania and is now in Romania.
Szell, George (1897–1970), U.S. conductor, pianist, and composer, born in Budapest, Hungary; debut with Vienna Symphony Orchestra at 11; turned to conducting at 17; came to U.S. 1939; became citizen 1946; conducted at Metropolitan Opera House 1942–45; musical director Cleveland Orchestra 1946–70, *list* O-579
Szent-Györgyi, Albert (1893–1986), U.S. physician and researchist, born in Budapest, Hungary; to U.S. 1947, citizen 1955; director of research at Institute for Muscle Research, Marine Biological Laboratory, Woods Hole, Mass., 1947–86; professor of biology Brandeis University 1966–86; work on vitamins V-357. *see also in index* Nobel Prizewinners, *table*
Szigeti, Joseph (1892–1973), U.S. violinist, born in Budapest, Hungary; U.S. citizen 1951; debut at age 13; autobiography, 'With Strings Attached'.
Szilard, Leo (1898–1964), U.S. physicist, born in Budapest, Hungary; with Enrico Fermi triggered world's first nuclear chain reaction at Chicago; first pointed out weapon potential to U.S.; later worked for peaceful uses of nuclear energy; won Atoms for Peace Award in 1959.
Szold, Henrietta (1860–1945), U.S. Jewish social service leader, born in Baltimore, Md.; founded Hadassah, the Women's Zionist Organization of America, 1912; lived many years in Palestine; director Youth Immigration from Europe to Palestine.
Szymanowski, Karol (1883–1937), Polish composer; operas ('Hagith', 'King Roger'); three symphonies; violin, piano, and choral works; his later music marked by atonality and postimpressionism.

The letter T

probably started as a sign for a mark or brand, as in Egyptian hieroglyphic writing (1) and in a very early Semitic writing used about 1500 B.C. on the Sinai Peninsula (2). About 1000 B.C., in Byblos and other Phoenician and Canaanite centers, both forms of this sign were used for the sound "t." They were given the name *taw,* meaning "mark" (3).

The Greeks named the sign *tau.* They also changed its form slightly by omitting the top of the upright stroke (4). The Romans took this sign into Latin. From Latin the form of the capital letter T came without change into English.

The English small handwritten "t" is simply the capital letter written quickly with curves (5). This form appeared in the handwriting of later Roman times. In English these curves connect the letter to its neighbors (6). One printed form of the small "t" omits the connecting lines but keeps the bottom curve.

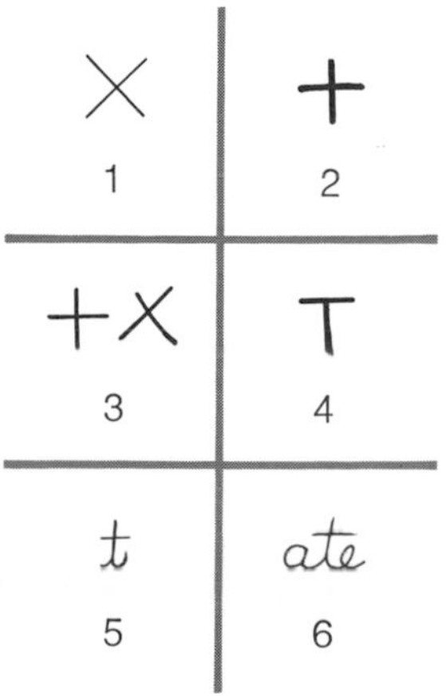

Ta, chemical element. *see in index* Tantalum

Taal, volcano on island in Lake Taal, Luzon Island, Philippines; crater over 7,000 ft (2,400 m) wide; erupted 1965, *picture* P-259

TABA (former name for American Book Awards, or ABA), U.S. literary awards L-241

Tabard Inn C-286

Tabari, at- (or Abu Ja'far Muhammad ibn Jarir at-Tabari) (839?–923), Islamic scholar T-2

Tabasco, Mexico, state in s.e., between the states Veracruz and Campeche, and on Gulf of Campeche; area 9,522 sq mi (24,662 sq km); cap. Villahermosa (pop. 52,262); pop. 1,053,363
  Mexico, *map* M-344

Tabasco pepper, variety of the genus *Capsicum* P-197b

Tabby cat (or tiger cat) C-205

Tabby weave (plain weave), a weave in which the threads interlace alternately T-138

Tabenna, island in Nile River, Egypt; site of early Christian monastery M-540

Tabernacle (Hebrew mishkan), portable sanctuary used by Israelites T-2
  Mormon S-31, *picture* S-32
  Solomon's Temple P-268, S-255

Tabitha. *see in index* Dorcas

Table, furniture F-453, *picture* F-459
  plastic tabletops P-383

Table Bay, harbor of Cape Town, Cape of Good Hope Province, South Africa C-148

Table cut, in gem cutting J-113

Tableland, geographic area
  India I-63

Table manners, in etiquette E-319

Table Mountain, just s. of Cape Town, South Africa, C-148, *picture* S-266

Table onion (also called scallion, or green onion) O-545

Table Rock Dam, in Missouri M-489

Tables. *see in index* Backgammon

Table salt. *see in index* Salt

Table setting and service, in etiquette E-319, *pictures* E-320, 321

Tablespoon, unit of measure, *table* W-140

Tablet, in writing
  bookmaking history B-345
  Mycenaean A-62

Table tennis (or Ping-Pong), indoor sport T-2

Table wine (German Tafewein, Italian vino da tavola, or still wine, or natural wine), wine made from the juice of the grape W-236, 239

Tabloid, type of newspaper N-242

Taboo, prohibition of certain acts or the use of certain things T-235
  Pacific Ocean P-8

Tabor, Horace (or Horace Austin Warner Tabor) (1830–99), U.S. silver baron and political leader T-3
  industry I-195

Tabor, Mount, famous mountain of Palestine, 8 mi (13 km) e. of Nazareth; height 1,840 ft (560 m); pilgrimage destination for ages.

Tabora, Tanzania, railroad town s. of Lake Victoria; agricultural products handled include corn, rice, and cotton; pop. 20,994, *map* A-118

Tabor College, Hillsboro, Kan.; Mennonite Brethren; founded 1908; liberal arts, education.

Tabouret, Jehan. *see in index* Arbeau, Thoinot

Tabriz, Iran, capital of Azerbaijan Province; in extreme n.w.; important commercial center; textiles, leather products, flour, soap, alcohol; repeatedly devastated by earthquakes; pop. 598,576 I-306

Tabula. *see in index* Backgammon

Tabula rasa, idea that the human mind is a blank tablet at birth
  education E-85

TAC (Tactical Air Command), U.S. Air Force A-164

Tacet, in music, *list* M-671

Taché, Alexandre Antonin (1823–94), Canadian Roman Catholic archbishop; worked as missionary among American Indians of Northwest for 40 years; founded several colleges, schools, convents; author of books on the Northwest C-101

Taché, Sir Étienne-Paschal (1795–1865), Canadian statesman, born in St. Thomas, Que.
  Fathers of Canadian Confederation C-118, *picture* C-116

Tachina fly, parasitic fly of family Tachinidae; larvae, parasitic especially in caterpillars, are valuable in controlling increase of insect pests.

Tachometer, device for measuring rates of revolution of machinery T-3
  instrumentation I-229
    airplane A-196
  meter M-317
  speedometer S-374

Tachycardia, extra heart beats D-173

Tachylyte (or tachylite), glassy black variety of basic igneous rock, as basalt or dolerite; forms the outer shell of some basalt masses.

Tacitus, Cornelius (AD 55?–120?), Roman historian T-4
  Latin literature L-77
  Swedes described S-527

Tack, horse's equipment for riding H-264, *list* H-249

Tack, in boating B-328, *diagram* B-326

Tacna, Peru, department in s.; area 5,701 sq mi (14,766 sq km); cap. Tacna (pop. 27,499); in desert region but contains fertile valley in which tobacco, fruits, sugar, and cotton are grown; seaport is Arica in Chile; pop. 78,400, *map* S-298
  Tacna-Arica treaty P-224, *table* T-275
  Hoover H-234

Tacoma, Wash., seaport situated on Puget Sound; pop. 158,501 T-4, *map* U-40
  North America, *map* N-351
  Seattle-Tacoma airport S-103, *map* S-103b
  Washington W-50, 60, *picture* W-48

Tacoma, Mount. *see in index* Rainier, Mount

Tacoma Narrows Bridge, Washington T-4, *picture* W-48
  suspension bridge B-447

Taconic Mountains, low range on borders of New York and Massachusetts; joins Green Mountains of Vermont with the Hudson Highlands; in Massachusetts called Berkshire Hills
  Appalachian geography A-508
  Massachusetts M-190
  New York N-246
  Vermont V-285, *maps* V-286, 301

Taconite, low-grade iron ores found in large deposits in ranges from Quebec to Lake Superior; rock matrix contains hematite and magnetite
  iron and steel I-331
  mines and mining M-424
  United States U-73

Tactical Air Command (TAC), U.S. Air Force A-164

Tactics, military art of maneuvering military forces in battle
  international regulation H-5
  machine gun M-12
  Miltiades at Marathon P-214
  Vietnam conflict V-321, 324, *picture* V-323
  warfare W-21

Tactile amnesia, loss of memory A-373

'Tade Kuu mushi' (or 'Some Prefer Nettles'), novel by Jun-ichiro Tanizaki J-82

Tadmor, Biblical name of Palmyra, Syria P-84, *map* P-212

Tadoussac, Que., village on St. Lawrence River at mouth of Saguenay River; museum, historic chapel; pop. 1,059, *maps* C-112, Q-11

Tadpole (or polliwog), larval amphibian
  development A-378
  larva L-51

Tadzhik (or Tadjik, or Tajik), people of Afghanistan; some scattered elsewhere.

Tadzhik Soviet Socialist Republic (also called Tadzhikistan), republic of the Soviet Union in central Asia; area 54,830 sq mi (142,010 sq km); cap. Dushanbe; pop. 4,239,000 T-4, *map* A-700
  bilingual education B-191
  U.S.S.R. U-15, *maps* R-325, 344, U-14

Taebaek Mountains, along e. coast of Korean peninsula; rise to 5,604 ft (1,708 m) at the mountain called Sorak K-282, *map* K-290

Taedong River, North Korea, flows from n. 245 mi mostly s.w. into Korea Bay of Yellow Sea; navigable to Pyongyang, *map* K-290

Taegu, South Korea, city 60 mi (100 km) n. of Pusan; trade and rail center; silk and cotton production; pop. 2,012,039 T-5, *maps* A-700, K-290

Tae kwon do, martial arts M-160

Tael, Chinese weight of silver used as a unit in keeping accounts and foreign trade, but represented by no actual coin; many different forms of tael; historical value of the Haikwan tael 37 to 75 cents, *table* W-141

TAF. *see in index* Tumor angiogenesis factor

Tafari Makonnen. *see in index* Haile Selassie

Taffeta, smooth fabric of plain, close weave; silk, cotton, wool, or synthetic fibers; term applied in the 16th century to a heavy costly dress fabric, later to a thinner silk.

Taffrail log. *see in index* Patent log

Tafilalt, oasis in Morocco O-454

Taft, Alphonso (1810–91), U.S. diplomat, born near Townshend, Vt.; father of William Howard Taft T-7

Taft, Helen Nellie Herron (1861–1943), wife of President Taft T-6, *picture* T-7

Taft, Lorado (1860–1936), U.S. sculptor, writer, and lecturer; born in Elmwood, Ill. ('Fountain of Time' on Chicago Midway); author of 'History of American Sculpture' and 'Modern Tendencies in Sculpture'
  'Black Hawk', *picture* I-46

Taft, Robert Alphonso (1889–1953), U.S. Republican leader, born in Cincinnati, Ohio, son of William Howard Taft; in Ohio legislature 1921–26, 1931–32; U.S. senator after 1939; coauthor of Taft-Hartley law T-10
  Ohio O-506

Taft, William Howard (1857–1930), 27th president of the United States T-6
  Arizona A-602
  flag dimensions F-150, 157
  McKinley M-20
  Roosevelt R-288
  United States U-183

Taft-Hartley act. *see in index* Labor-Management Relations Act of 1947.

Tagalog, a people of the Philippines, inhabiting chiefly central Luzon; they are Christians whose language, called Tagalog, is highly developed and widely used in the Philippines P-253b. *see also in index* Pilipino language and literature P-257c, *picture* P-255b

Taganrog, U.S.S.R., port on n.e. coast of Sea of Azov 37 mi (60 km) w. of Rostov; metallurgical works; pop. 254,000, *maps* R-344, 349
  Europe, *map* E-361

Taggard, Genevieve (1894–1948), U.S. poet, born in Waitsburg, Wash. ('For Eager Lovers'; 'Travelling Standing Still', poetry; 'The Life and Mind of Emily Dickinson', biography).

Tagish Lake, lake in Canada; source of Yukon River Y-439

Tagle Tower, Palace of the, in Lima, Peru L-209

Tagliacozzo, Italy, town 45 mi (70 km) n.e. of Rome; Charles of Anjou defeated Conradin, the last Hohenstaufen, 1268.

Taglioni, Maria (1804–84), ballet dancer, born in Stockholm, Sweden; daughter of an Italian ballet master; first appearance in Vienna 1822, in Paris 1827, in New York City 1838; invented new ballet steps
  ballet B-33, 36, D-27

Tagore, Rabindranath (1861–1941), Hindu poet and philosopher T-10. *see also in index* Nobel Prizewinners, *table*
  Indian literature I-108

Tagua nut. *see in index* Ivory nut palm

Tagus, largest river in Iberian peninsula, 550 mi (885 km) long; flows across Spain into Atlantic Ocean at Lisbon, Portugal S-350, *maps* E-361, P-455

Tahiti, largest of Society Islands; in s. Pacific; 33 mi (53 km) long and about 16 mi (26 km) wide; chief town Papeete; pop. 115,820 T-10, *map* P-6

Tahlequah, Okla., city in Cherokee County about 25 mi (40 km) n.e. of Muskogee; Northeastern State College; pop. 9,708.

Tahoe, Lake, largest lake in Sierra Nevada; on California-Nevada boundary; 20 by 10 mi (30 by 16 km); resort center
  Nevada N-133, *picture* N-132, *map* U-87
  Sierra Nevada S-192b

Tahquamenon Falls, on the Tahquamenon River, Upper Peninsula of Michigan 30 mi (50 km) n.e. of Newberry; Upper Falls drop 40 ft (12 m), Lower Falls drop 43 ft (13 m); associated with Longfellow's 'Hiawatha'; popular tourist attraction
  river M-355, 360

T'ai, group of people in s. China and Indochina; speak Siamese-Chinese languages. *see also in index* specific groups
  Laos L-47
  Thailand T-140

Tai, name for Japanese food fishes of genus *Pagrus* belonging to porgy family; red tai *P. major* is sacred and in pictures it is carried by the Japanese fish god.

Taichung, Taiwan, city in w.-central Taiwan; agricultural and commercial center; pop. 617,800, *map* A-700

Taiga. *see in index* Subarctic climate

Taiga, coniferous evergreen forests, south of the tundra P-363f
  Asia A-675
  biogeographical biome B-219, *picture* B-218
  Canada C-75

Tail, animal anatomy
  birds B-248
    lyrebird, *picture* P-110
    peacock P-145, *picture* P-146
  fish, *diagram* F-125
  lizard L-272
  monkey A-502
  sheep S-148
  whale W-185

Tail assembly (or empennage), airplane A-184

Tailings, mines and mining M-429

Taillefer, troubadour and soldier of the 11th century; first famous singer of the 'Song of Roland'; at the battle of Hastings led the Norman attack and was killed.

Tail-pipe burner, automobile engine part A-848

Tainan, Taiwan, city on s.w. Taiwan; food products; Anping, to w., is its port; pop. 605,900.

Taine, Hippolyte Adolphe (1828–93), French literary and art critic, philosopher, and historian; analyzed art and literature as products of race and environment F-397

Taino. *see in index* Arawak

Taipa. *see in index* Macao

'Tai-Pan', work by Clavell A-361

Taipei, Taiwan, capital; pop. 2,327,641 T-11, *map* A-700
  Taiwan T-14

Taiping Rebellion, in Chinese history T-11
  China C-369
  Gordon G-195
  warfare, *list* W-14

Taira, Japanese samurai warrior clan that dominated political life in the 12th century T-11
  Japan J-63

Taira Antoku (1178–85) final Taira leader; his death resulted in the loss of the great sword T-11

Taira Kiyomori (1118–81) first of the Japanese soldier-dictators T-11

Taira Masamori (fl. early 12th century), Japanese warrior responsible for the rise to power of the Taira clan in Japan T-11

Taira Tadamori (1096–1153), Japanese warrior whose military and diplomatic skills made the Taira clan the most powerful family in Japan T-11

Taira Takamune (fl. AD 825) Japanese prince; first to bear name of Taira T-11

Tai Shan, sacred mountain in Shantung, about 5,000 ft (1,500 m) high; near village where Confucius was born; pilgrim center.

Taisho. *see in index* Yoshihito

Taitu, founder of Addis Ababa A-40

T'ai Tsu (or Sung T'ai Tsu) (927–976), emperor of China and founder of Sung Dynasty C-365

T'ai Tsung (600–649), emperor of China and founder of T'ang Dynasty C-364

Taiwan (or Formosa, or Nationalist China, or Republic of China), country in e. Asia; area 13,885 sq mi (35,960 sq km); cap. Taipei; pop. 16,978,200 T-12, *map* A-700
  flag, *picture* F-171
  garment industry G-35
  history. *see also in index* China, *subhead* history
    Chiang Kai-skek C-309
    1912–1949 C-372
    United Nations C-336, U-27
    wars
      revolution A-693
  migration of people M-407
  national anthem, *table* N-64
  puppets P-536
  railroad mileage, *table* R-85
  United States relations C-309, 378

Taiwan (also called Formosa), island off coast of mainland China T-12
  Asia, *map* A-698
    China C-11
  world, *map* W-297

Taiyuan, China, capital of Shanxi Province, original site of Chin-yang; about 250 mi (400 km) s.w. of Peking; iron and steel, machinery, textiles; pop. 1,750,000 T-16, *map* A-700

Ta'izz, Yemen Arab Republic; twice capital of country; has several gates and mosques; pop. 78,642, *map* A-700

Taj Mahal, beautiful tomb near Delhi, India T-16
  India I-71, *picture* I-61
  Islamic architecture A-551
  Shah Jahan S-127

Tajumulco, volcano in Guatemala G-296

Takahe, bird
  New Zealand N-288

Takakkaw Falls, located in Yoho National Park, British Columbia; source is Daly Glacier; vertical plunge of 1,248 ft (380 km)
  waterfall, *table* W-98

Takamine, Jokichi (1854–1922), U.S. chemist, born in Takaoka, Japan; came to U.S. 1890; developed Takadiastase, an enzyme that digests starch; leader in isolating adrenalin in commercially important amounts.

Takashima, Shizuye (born 1928), Canadian artist and author, born in Vancouver, B.C.; won 1972 Canadian Book of the Year for Children Award for illustration of 'Child in Prison Camp', which she wrote as a reflection of her World War II internment in camp for Canadians of Japanese descent.

Take (or shot), in motion pictures M-606

Takeoff, flight maneuver A-190
  jet propulsion J-108

'Take the Money and Run', film by Allen A-309

Takin, rare mountain goat of Himalayas and w. China; heavily built, 3½ ft (1 m) tall at shoulder; hollow curved horns; shaggy coat reddish brown to yellow; resembles gnu; night grazer; agile climber; lives in brush; travels in small herds; hunted for meat.

Taklamakan, desert in Sinkiang-Uigur Autonomous Region, China; 260,000 sq mi (673,000 sq km); oases along its n. edge serve caravans, *map* A-700

Takoma Park, Md., town adjoining Washington, D.C., on n.; residential suburb; Columbia Union College; incorporated 1890; pop. 16,231 M-168, *map* M-183

Talal (1908–72), king of Jordan (1951–52), born in Mecca; came to throne after assassination of his father, Abdullah; deposed because of mental illness J-143
  Hussein H-334

Talara, Peru, port in n.w., on Pacific 35 mi (55 km) n.w. of Paita; petroleum refining center; in a desert area; receives water from the Chira River 25 mi (40 km) away; pop. 40,013.

Talavera de la Reina (Roman Caesobriga), Spain, town on Tagus River; victory of Wellington over French under Joseph Bonaparte, 1809; pop. 28,107.

Talbot, William Henry Fox (1800–77), English pioneer in photography; published 'The Pencil of Nature', first book illustrated with photographs S-58
  photography P-296

Talbot, Thomas (1771–1853), Canadian colonist, born in County Dublin, Ireland; in 1803 founded Talbot settlement at Port Talbot on Lake Erie in Upper Canada; ruled in patriarchal manner almost 50 years; land acquired by settlers in area
  Canada C-99
  Ontario O-553

Talbott, Harold Elstner (1888–1957), U.S. capitalist and public official, born in Dayton, Ohio; president Dayton Wright Airplane Company 1916–20; served as aviator in World War I; chairman of board North American Aviation Company 1931–32; director of aircraft production, war production board 1942–43; chairman Republican national finance committee 1948–49; secretary of the Air Force 1953–55.

Talbotype process, in photography P-296

Talc, mineral M-432, 437

Talca, Chile, capital of Talca Province on Rio Claro, 170 mi (270 km) s. of Valparaiso; matches, flour, shoes, furniture, paper, leather, metal products; pop. 115,130, *map* S-299

Talcahuano, Chile, seaport and naval station on Bay of Concepción, 8 mi (13 km) n.w. of Concepción; wheat-exporting point; ships lumber, hides, wool, vegetables, wine, coal; pop. 216,866, *map* S-299

Talent, ancient Greek unit of weight, *table* W-141

Talent, ancient weight and denomination of money; Attic talent equal to about $1,200; great Roman talent about $500, small Roman about $375; Hebraic, Assyrian, and Babylonian from $1,550 to $2,000, *table* W-141
  mathematics M-213

'Tale of a Tub, A', satire by Jonathan Swift (1704), directed mainly against hypocrisy in religion; harmed Swift's chances for high advancement in the church S-532, 531

'Tale of the Genji, The' (or 'Genji monogatari'), novel by Murasaki Shikibu J-40, J-80
  Fujiwara ruler F-445
  Murasaki M-656
  novel N-415

'Tale of Hong Kiltong, The', work by Hyo Kyun K-294

'Tale of Two Cities, A', novel of the French Revolution by Charles Dickens (1859); the two cities involved are Paris and London D-134

'Tales from Shakespeare', work by Charles and Mary Lamb L-26, S-140
  English literature E-274

'Tales of a Wayside Inn', collection of narrative poems by Henry Wadsworth Longfellow, founded largely on folk stories and legends and on events in U.S. history; each narrative written as though told by a different person.

'Tales of Hoffmann, The', opera by Offenbach
  Hoffmann's inspiration H-198

'Tales of the Colonies', work by Rowcroft A-797

'Tales of the Heike' (or 'Heike monogatari'), Japanese literary work J-81

'Tales of the Jazz Age', work by Fitzgerald A-359

'Tales of the South Pacific', work by Michener N-409

Talfourd, Sir Thomas Noon (1795–1854), English lawyer and author, to whom Dickens dedicated 'Pickwick Papers' in recognition of his labors for a copyright law; defended Moxon against charge of blasphemy for publishing Shelley's 'Queen Mab'; edited Lamb's letters.

Talgai skull
  Australian archaeological discoveries A-794

Taliesin, Frank L. Wright's home near Spring Green, Wis. W-367

Taliesin Fellowship, architectural school founded by Wright W-367

'Talisman, The', novel by Scott S-25

Talking books P-269

Talking Heads, U.S. rock band formed in Providence, R.I. in 1974; known for unconventional and imaginative approach to music; singer-songwriter-guitarist David Byrne, leader of band, became major figure in avant-garde music and film M-683

Talladega, Ala., city in agricultural and dairying region, 40 mi (60 km) e. of Birmingham; textiles; General Jackson defeated band of Creeks 1813; Talladega College and State Institute for Deaf and Blind; pop. 19,128.

Talladega College, Talladega, Ala.; Congregational-Christian; founded 1867; arts and sciences.

Tallahassee, Fla., state capital, 158 mi (254 km) w. of Jacksonville; pop. 112,258 T-17, *map* U-41
  Florida F-197, *map* F-195
  North America, *map* N-351

Tallahassee Hills F-194, *map* F-195

Tallapoosa River, flows into the Alabama; 250 mi (400 km) long; battle between troops under Andrew Jackson and Creeks fought at Horseshoe Bend of the Tallapoosa River.

Tallchief, Maria (born 1925), U.S. ballet dancer, born in Fairfax, Okla.; made debut with Ballet Russe de Monte Carlo 1942; with New York City Ballet 1947–65; artistic director Lyric Opera Ballet of Chicago 1975–80; founded Chicago City Ballet 1980.

Talleyrand (or Charles-Maurice de Talleyrand-Périgord) (1754–1838), French statesman T-17
  Congress of Vienna V-316
  warfare W-21

Tallien, Jean Lambert (1767–1820), French Revolutionist, leading Terrorist; he was chiefly responsible for fall and execution of Robespierre.

Tallinn (or Tallin, formerly called Reval), U.S.S.R., capital and chief seaport, on Gulf of Finland; pop. 363,000 E-308, *maps* R-344, 348
  Europe, *map* E-360

Tall iris, perennial plant
  flowering time G-25

Tallis, Thomas (1510–85), English organist and composer B-532

Tallmadge, James, Jr. (1778–1853), U.S. lawyer and leading Whig protectionist, born in Stanfordville, N.Y.; congressman 1817–19; lieutenant governor New York 1825–26; president New York University 1830–46
  Missouri Compromise M-507

Tallmadge, Ohio, city 4 mi (6 km) e. of Akron; metal and stone products, foodstuffs; settled 1808, incorporated 1936; pop. 15,269.

Tallow
  candles C-136
  fats and oils F-47

Tallow tree, tree of China, India, and other warm countries belonging to the spurge family and having seeds covered with greasy white substance used in making candles, soap; also butter or tallow tree of West Africa yielding yellow greasy juice.

Tall tale, literature
  folklore F-261

Talma, François Joseph (1763–1826), French tragedian; introduced practice of dressing in costume appropriate to time and country of play A-27

Talmage, Thomas De Witt (1832–1902), U.S. clergyman and pulpit orator, born in Bound Brook, N.J.; pastor of Brooklyn Tabernacle 1870–94; editor of *Christian Herald* after 1890; his sermons were published each week in hundreds of religious and secular papers.

Talmud, great collection of Judaic laws and commentaries T-18
  Haifa H-6
  Judaism J-148
  Karaite sect S-1

Talmudic Judaism, religion
  bioethical issues B-214

Talon, Jean Baptiste (1625–91), one of the French officials who governed New France C-92

Talus, heap of loose rock that accumulates at the foot of a cliff or mountain; caused by weathering.

Tamanend, American Indian chief. *see in index* Tammany

Tamaqua, Pa., borough on Little Schuylkill River, 32 mi (52 km) n. of Reading; agricultural area; coal mining; explosives and chemicals, tubing and

metals, garments; pop. 8,843, *map* P-185
Tamarisk family (or Tamaricaceae), family of shrubs and trees including the tamarisk, false tamarisk, and juniper tamarisk.
Tamatave, Madagascar, seaport on e. coast; meat-preserving plant; railroad to Antananarivo; pop. 59,060.
Tamaulipas, Mexico, state in n.e. on Gulf of Mexico; 30,822 sq mi (79,829 sq km); cap. Ciudad Victoria (pop. 50,797); pop. 1,901,040
  Mexico, *map* M-344
Tamayo, Rufino (born 1899), Mexican painter, born in Oaxaca; expressionist; taught in Mexico City public schools 1928–32, Dalton School, New York, N.Y., after 1938; frescoes in National Conservatory of Music and National Museum, Mexico City.
Tambov, U.S.S.R., grain center in farm area; 265 mi (425 km) s.e. of Moscow; university; founded 1636 as fortress to keep out Tatars; pop. 229,000, *maps* R-344, 349
  Europe, *map* E-361
'Tamburlaine the Great', work by Marlowe M-147
Tamerlane. *see in index* Timur Lenk
Tamil, language I-106
  Hinduism H-158
Tamil Nadu (formerly Madras), state in s. India; area 50,170 sq mi (129,940 sq km); cap. Madras; pop. 41,199,168, *map* I-83
  Madras M-28
  Shore Temple, *picture* H-158
Tamil New Year, religious celebration of India N-243
'Taming of the Shrew, The', one of the most popular of Shakespeare's comedies
  Shakespeare S-133, S-139
Tamm, Iigor Evgenievich (1895–1971), Soviet theoretical physicist, born in Vladivostok; head of Lebedev Physical Institute of U.S.S.R. Academy of Sciences 1934–71. *see also in index* Nobel Prizewinners, *table*
Tammany (also called Tamanend, or Tammanen) (died about 1740), Delaware chief, leading representative of Delawares at Treaty of Shackamaxon made in June 1683 with William Penn; famous for wisdom and leadership.
Tammany Hall, political organization of New York City T-18
  Nast N-21
  New York City N-279
  Roosevelt R-261
  Tweed T-333
'Tammany Tiger Loose, The', cartoon series by Nast N-22
Tammen, Harry Heye. *see in index* Bonfils, Frederick Gilmer
Tammerfors, Finland. *see in index* Tampere
Tammuz, Babylonian Adonis for whom women worshippers wept yearly (Bible, Ezek. viii, 14) B-8
Tammuz, Binyamin (born 1919), Israeli writer
  Hebrew literature H-114
'Tam o' Shanter', poem by Robert Burns about Tam o' Shanter, a drunken, good-natured farmer who, returning from a night of revelry, surprises some witches dancing and is pursued by them.
Tampa, Fla., commercial city, port, and winter resort; pop. 275,479 T-19, *map* U-41
  Florida F-196, *map* F-195
  Hispanic Americans H-167
  North America, *map* N-351
Tampa, University of, Tampa, Fla.; private control; founded 1931; liberal arts, education, music; graduate studies T-19
Tampa Bay, Florida, harbor 35 mi (55 km) long, inlet of Gulf of Mexico T-19
  DeSoto's landing D-117
Tampere (Swedish Tammerfors), Finland, city 100 mi (160 km) n.w. of Helsinki; waterpower from nearby falls; cotton, paper, sawmills, and iron mills; locomotive works and shipyards; pop. 127,260, *map* E-361
Tampico, Mexico, seaport of Panuco River near Gulf of Mexico; marshy, unhealthful small port until discovery of rich oil fields in early 20th century; now flourishing city with improved harbor and drained lands; exports petroleum, silver, copper, fiber, and farm products; pop. 222,188
  Mexico M-323, *map* M-344
  North America, *map* N-351
Tamping stick, in mines and mining M-428
Tamworth, breed of pig P-320
Tamworth, England, old town n.e. of Birmingham; on borders of Staffordshire and Warwickshire, on River Tame; interesting antiquities; pop. 37,360.
Tana, river of Kenya, rising on Mount Kenya; flows 500 mi (800 km) s.e. to Indian Ocean; partially navigable by small vessels, *maps* E-361, A-118
Tanagra, Greece, ancient town of Boeotia; 457 BC Spartans defeated Athenians; famous necropolis with terra-cotta statuettes
  figurines P-470
Tanaka, Kakuei (born 1918), Japanese public official, born in Niigata; member Japanese Parliament 1947; minister of finance 1962–64, of international trade and industry 1971–72; prime minister 1972–74 J-67, 69
Tanaka Giichi, Baron (1863–1929), Japanese statesman and general; son of servant; graduated from military school and rose high in army; minister of war in three cabinets; leader of Seiyukwai party 1926; prime minister 1927; bold policy; made many enemies.
Tanana, Alaska, city at confluence of Tanana and Yukon rivers; placer gold mining; mink and fox farms; pop. 388, *map* U-39
Tananarive, Madagascar. *see in index* Antananarivo
Tanana River, Alaska, stream flowing n.w. into Yukon River; navigable in summer for about 200 mi (320 km), *maps* U-39, 94
  Alaska A-242
  North America, *map* N-351
Tancred (died 1112), Norman-Sicilian hero of First Crusade, later prince of Antioch; nephew of Robert Guiscard, cousin and companion-in-arms of Bohemond; hero of Tasso's 'Jerusalem Delivered'.
Taney, Roger B. (1777–1864), chief justice of the U.S. Supreme Court T-19
  Dred Scott decision D-259
  Maryland M-170
  Supreme Court, *picture* S-518a
Tanga, Tanzania, port and railway terminus in Tanganyika on Indian Ocean, opposite the island of Pemba; pop. 61,058, *map* A-118
Tanganyika, mainland portion of Tanzania, in e. Africa; area 361,800 sq mi (937,100 sq km); cap. Dar es Salaam; pop. 11,958,654 T-21
Tanganyika, Lake (also called Lake Tanzania), Africa T-19, *map* A-118
  Burton B-513
  size, comparative. *see in index* Lake, *table*
  Tanzania T-21
Tanganyika and Zanzibar, United Republic of, former name of Tanzania. *see in index* Tanzania
T'ang Dynasty, China (618–907) C-364
  poetry C-388, L-232
  pottery P-470
  sculpture S-94
Tange Kenzo (born 1913), Japanese architect A-569
Tangelo, citrus fruit obtained by crossing the tangerine and the grapefruit; fruit is large and flavorful.
Tangent, in mathematics M-214
  calculus C-23
  trigonometry T-286, *table* T-287
Tangerine, mandarin orange *Citrus reticulata* C-446, *picture* C-445
  fruit production, *chart* F-430
Tangier, Morocco, on Strait of Gibraltar, one of chief seaports; pop. 266,346 T-20, *map* A-118
  Morocco M-586
'Tangled Hair' (or 'Midaregami'), collection of poetry by Akiko Yosano J-82
Tango, dance
  Argentina A-580
Tangshan, China, city in n.e. Hopei Province; steel, glass, cement; pop. 950,000, *map* A-700
Tangun, legendary ancestor-ruler of Korean people; reign began in 2333 BC; myth first recorded during Koryo dynasty K-292
Tanguy, Yves (1900–55), U.S. painter, born in Paris; leader of French surrealist movement in 1920s; settled in U.S. 1939, became citizen 1948 ('Black Landscape'; 'The Witness'; 'In Place of Fear').
Tanha, one of the four noble truths
  Buddhist doctrines B-480
Tanizaki, Jun-ichiro (1886–1965), Japanese writer T-20
  literary contribution J-82
Tanjore, India. *see in index* Thanjavur
Tank, armored motor vehicle T-20
  antitank weapons R-233
  armor plate protection A-631
  Spanish Civil War A-644
  Vietnam conflict, *picture* V-323
  World War I W-308, *pictures* W-304, W-309
Tanka, Japanese verse form J-49, J-79
Tank car, railroad
  fire fighting F-104
  gas G-38
  petroleum P-241d, *picture* R-82
  transportation T-254
Tanker, ship P-241d, S-168, 176a, *picture* P-241c
  building, *picture* S-69
  transportation T-254, *pictures* T-263, 265
  gas G-39
Tank Landing Ship (or LST), amphibious naval vessel N-85
Tank reactor, type of nuclear reactor N-424
Tank truck P-241d, T-254
Tankum, Korean sun god M-704
Tannenberg, Poland, former German (East Prussian) village about 80 mi (130 km) s.e. of Danzig; included in Poland since 1945.
Tannenberg, battle of (1914), in World War I W-304
  warfare, *list* W-16
Tanner, Henry Ossawa (1859–1937), U.S. painter, born in Pittsburgh, Pa.; noted for paintings of religious subjects; lived in Paris many years.
Tanner, Vaino Alfred (1881–1966), Finnish statesman, born in Helsinki; entered Parliament 1907; leader of Social Democratic party 1909–44; 1957–63; held numerous cabinet posts; premier 1926–27; imprisoned for war activities against the U.S.S.R. 1945–48.
Tannery, leather production L-107, *pictures* L-108–110
'Tannhäuser', opera by Wagner O-567
Tannin (or tannic acid), organic chemical compound used in tanning leather, dyeing fabric, making ink, and in various medical applications
  leather production L-107
    hemlock H-127
    oak O-452
  persimmon P-215
  pomegranate root P-442
Tanoak (or tanbark oak), evergreen tree *Lithocarpus densiflora* of beech family, native to the coastal region of Oregon and California, the only American member of a large genus native to Asia; grows 60 to 80 ft (20 to 25 m), rarely 150 ft (45 m); crown narrow, round-topped; leaves thick, oblong, to 5 in. (13 cm) long with toothed margins; acorn is set in a hairy cup; bark used in tanning leather.
Tanoan, linguistic stock of American Indians, consisting of the Tewa, Tigua, and Jemez groups; live in pueblos on Rio Grande and tributaries in Mexico.
Tansy, tall herb of the family Compositae with bitter aromatic flavor; used for garnishing and flavoring; native to Northern Hemisphere.
Tanta, Egypt, railroad town 60 mi (100 km) n. of Cairo; noted for fairs and Muslim festivals held every 3 years; pop. 184,299.
Tantalite, submetallic iron-black ore, ferrous tantalate, yielding the metal tantalum; the ore occurs in granite and pegmatite.
Tantalum (Ta), metallic element T-21
  periodic table, *table* P-207, *list* P-208
Tantalus, in Greek mythology, son of Zeus and father of Niobe and Pelops; because of sin he was punished in the lower world by eternally suffering hunger, thirst, and, by another story, fear; he stood in water up to his chin and fruit hung over his head; the water, or fruit, always receded when he reached for it; over his head a huge rock threatened to fall on him; from this story comes the word "tantalize," meaning to tease.
'Tantoli', Swedish folk dance, *picture* F-255
Tantra, any of numerous Hindu texts H-157
Tantramar Marshes, New Brunswick, fertile lowlands N-154
Tanwon (or Kim Hong-Do) (born 1745?), Korean painter K-238
Tanzania (officially United Republic of Tanzania), republic in e. Africa, formed by Tanganyika and Zanzibar; area 364,900 sq mi (945,100 sq km); cap. Dar es Salaam; pop. 21,730,000 T-21. *see also in index* Tanganyika; Zanzibar
  Africa A-105, *map* A-118, *table* A-112
  cities
    Dar es Salaam D-35
  Commonwealth membership C-602
  flag, *picture* F-171
  Kilimanjaro K-237
  Lake Victoria V-310
  national parks N-26
  railroad mileage, *table* R-85
  sisal shipment, *picture* R-292
Tanzania, Lake. *see in index* Tanganyika, Lake
Tao, unifying element of philosophical Taoism T-23
T'ao Ch'ien (365–427), Chinese poet C-388, *picture* C-389
Taoism, complex system of philosophical thought that emerged as a religion T-23
  China C-345, 361
    literature C-388
    religion R-143
  'Lao-tzu' L-48
  martial arts M-159
  Zen Z-450
Taormina, Sicily, winter resort on e. coast; has Greek, Roman, and medieval landmarks; named for Mt. Tauro; pop. 7,722 S-192, *map* I-404
Taos, a people in New Mexico; belong to Tanoan language group P-526d
Taos, N.M., village situated 50 mi (80 km) n.e. of Santa Fe; American Indian pueblos nearby; artists' colony; pop. 3,369, *map* N-229
Taos, Ranchos de, N.M., village about 3 mi (5 km) s. of Taos; mainly farming community; St. Francis of Assisi Church, built 1730–72, historic landmark; pop. 2,900.
Taos Pueblo, New Mexico, situated 2½ mi (4 km) n. of Taos; also known as the pueblo of San Geronimo; pop. 1,030, *map* N-229
'Tao-te Ching'. *see in index* 'Lao-Tzu'
Tapa cloth (or kapa cloth), fabric made from paper mulberry P-13
  Fijian design, *picture* F-83
Tapajós (or Tapajoz), river of n. Brazil, formed by junction of São Manuel and Juruena rivers, flows n.e. to the Amazon; length, about 500 mi (800 km); including the Arinos, its headstream, about 1,250 mi (2,000 km), *maps* B-425, S-298
Tap dance D-21
Tape, magnetic. *see in index* Magnetic tape
Tape, pressure-sensitive adhesive A-43
Tape grass. *see in index* Vallisneria
Tape recorder T-24

education, *picture* P-268a
electronics E-176
phonograph P-269
police P-426
radio R-49
video recording V-311

Tapestry
Arthurian legend, *picture* A-655
clothing C-597
horses H-272
Japanese, *picture* S-201
Vatican Museums, *picture* M-662

Tapestry moth, insect *Tricophaga tapetezella* B-527

Tapeworm W-361
invertebrate group I-283
parasite P-114

Taphrogeny, geologic process M-634

Tapioca, cereal T-27, *picture* P-11

Tapir, animal related to rhinoceros and horse T-27, *picture* S-273
hoof H-231

Tapiro, a people of New Guinea P-540

Tappan, Eva March (1854–1930), U.S. author, born in Blackstone, Mass.; wrote books of information, biography, history, science for young people ('American Hero Stories'; 'When Knights Were Bold').

Tappan Zee (formerly Tappan Sea), N.Y., expansion of the Hudson River, 12 mi (19 km) long and 3½ mi (5⅗ km) wide; Tarrytown and Ossining are on its shores H-314

Tapping machine, machine tool T-222

Taproot R-290, *picture* R-291
tree T-277

Taps, military signal for retiring, played in camp on bugle or drum.

Tar, dark oily liquid resulting from destructive distillation of wood, coal, or other organic matter; name is often applied to denser substance, pitch T-28. *see also in index* Coal-tar products
rope R-292

Tarabulus, Lebanon. *see in index* Tripoli

Tarahumare, a people of Piman stock living in the Sierra Madre in s. Chihuahua and Sonora, Mexico; some of them were Cliff Dwellers.

Tarakan Island, Indonesia, off n.e. coast of Indonesian Borneo (Kalimantan); 117 sq mi (303 sq km); oil fields, *maps* A-700, I-166

Taranapatha, subject of Jainism J-14

Tarantella, in music, *list* M-671

Tarantism S-386

Taranto (ancient Tarentum), Italy, seaport on Gulf of Taranto; oysters; varied manufactures; pop. 194,609, *maps* E-361, I-404

Tarantula, spider S-386

Tarascon, France, historic town on Rhone River; Roman ruins and medieval church and castle; pop. 8,842, *map* F-372

Tarascos (or Tarascans), a people of s. Mexico, chiefly in the state of Michoacán; formerly a powerful nation, considerably advanced in civilization at time of Spanish conquest.

Tarawa, atoll in the Gilbert Islands; site of major battle in World War II; shipping center for copra; pop. 17,129, *map* P-6

Tarawa, battle of (1943), World War II W-332, 346
warfare, *list* W-16

Tarbela Dam, Pakistan, on Indus River
irrigation projects I-356

Tarbell, Edmund Charles (1862–1938), U.S. painter, born in West Groton, Mass.; impressionist style; early works colorful ('The Venetian Blind'); later more somber ('Girl Crocheting'); also skilled as portrait painter ('Woodrow Wilson', 'Marshal Foch', 'Herbert Hoover').

Tarbell, Ida Minerva (1857–1944), U.S. author and magazine editor; best-known works are biographies (including several books on Lincoln) and 'History of the Standard Oil Company'; 'All in the Day's Work', autobiography R-285

Tarbes, France, town 75 mi (120 km) s.w. of Toulouse; trade center; English under Wellington defeated French 1814; birthplace of Marshal Foch; pop. 55,200, *map* F-372

Tarde, Gabriel de (1843–1904), French sociologist; developed theory that the many are imitators of the few.

Tardieu, André (1876–1945), French statesman; high commissioner to the United States 1917–19; plenipotentiary at Peace Conference 1919–20; premier 1929–30, and again, for a brief period, in 1932.

Tare, name applied to the common vetch *Vicia sativa*, a plant used as a cover crop in s. U.S. and as forage in Europe; the tares of the Bible may have been the rye grass called darnel *Lolium temulentum*.

Tarentum, chief ancient Greek city in s. Italy; modern Taranto. *see also in index* Taranto
war with Rome P-544

Target marketing M-143
international trade I-267

Targums, paraphrases of the Old Testament in Aramaic, the language that replaced Hebrew as everyday language of the Jews; designed for Jews who could no longer read and understand Hebrew.

Tar Heels, nickname of the people of North Carolina N-356

Tarheel State. *see in index* North Carolina

Tarifa, Spain, seaport on Strait of Gibraltar, southernmost town on mainland of Europe; anchovy and tuna fisheries; old Moorish walls; pop. 9,147.

Tariff (also called duty, or customs), tax on imports T-28
American Colonies R-163
Civil War issue C-472
European Communities E-362
farm price control A-130
international trade I-267
transportation T-265
U.S. law and legislation U-139, U-148
Arthur's administration A-654
Polk's tariff of 1846 P-438
Roosevelt's administration R-273
Taft's administration T-9
Tariff of Abominations (1828) A-37

Tariff Commission. *see in index* International Trade Commission

Tarik (also called Tarik ibn Ziyād) (died AD 720?), Islamic chief, leader of first Muslim invasion of Spain.

Tarim, chief river of Sinkiang-Uigur Autonomous Region, China; formed by junction of Yarkand and Khotan rivers; flows e. into Lop Nor; area of Tarim basin 350,000 sq mi (906,000 sq km), *map* A-700

Tarkio College, Tarkio, Mo.; United Presbyterian; founded 1883; arts and sciences, education.

Tarlatan, thin, heavily sized cotton fabric of open weave; usually dyed in plain colors; used chiefly for theatrical costumes and stage decorations.

Tarleton, Sir Banastre (1754–1833), English soldier; served in American Revolution under Cornwallis in southern campaigns; made general 1812 R-172
Marion M-139

Tarleton State University (formerly Tarleton State College), Stephenville, Tex.; opened 1899, senior college 1959; part of Texas A & M University system; arts and sciences, agriculture, education; graduate studies.

Tarn, lake formed by a glacier G-151

Tarnish, silver S-509

Tarnopol, U.S.S.R. *see in index* Ternopol'

Tarnow, Poland, city 45 mi (70 km) e. of Cracow; chemicals, fertilizer, machinery, ceramic products; pop. 85,700.

Taro, perennial plant *Colocasia esculenta* of the arum family with large fleshy underground tubers valued as food in many Pacific islands; a variety known as dasheen is grown in s. United States O-471, *picture* P-11. *see also in index* Dasheen

Tarot cards, picture cards from which modern playing cards evolved C-164

Tarpan, horse, *picture* H-253
animal domestication A-456

Tarpeian Rock, cliff of Capitoline Hill, Rome, from which condemned criminals were thrown; named for burial place of Tarpeia, daughter of Tarpeius, Roman governor in time of Romulus; she betrayed Rome to the Sabines by opening the city gates to them; as a reward, she demanded that they give her what they wore on their left arms, namely their bracelets; but the Sabines crushed her with the shields that they also wore on their left arms.

Tarpon (also called silver king), large herringlike fish
mobility A-424, *picture* A-426

Tarpon Springs, Fla., port, residential city, and resort situated on w. coast 22 mi (35 km) n.w. of Tampa; pop. 7,118
sponge fisheries S-395

Tarquinii, ancient Etruscan city 45 mi (70 km) n.w. of Rome; site near modern Corneto Tarquinia, marked by many remains, especially tombs
war with Rome R-242

Tarquinius Priscus, 5th legendary king of Rome R-241

Tarquinius Superbus 7th and last legendary king of Rome; by tradition a cruel tyrant; exiled from Rome R-241
Sibylline books S-191

Tarr, Curtis W. (born 1924), U.S. educator and government official, born in Stockton, Calif.; president Lawrence University 1963–69; assistant secretary of the Air Force for manpower 1969–70; director Selective Service System 1970–72.

Tarragon, herb *Artemisia dracuneulus*, variety of sage S-14
herb H-138, S-379

Tarragona, Spain, picturesque seaport town on Mediterranean at mouth of River Francoli about 50 mi (80 km) s.w. of Barcelona; exports wine, oil; ancient Tarraco, captured by Romans 218 BC in Second Punic War; pop. 35,689, *map* E-361

Tar River, North Carolina, rises in n. center, flows s.e. 215 mi (345 km), entering Pamlico Sound by Pamlico River.

Tarrytown, N.Y., village on Hudson River, 25 mi (40 km) n. of New York City; food research, precision instruments, concrete products; automobile assembling and battery manufacturing at North Tarrytown; Marymount College; home of Washington Irving nearby; pop. 11,115.

Tarsal bone, any of several bones of ankle S-210

Tar sand F-442

Tarshish, ancient country mentioned in Bible, usually identified with Spain; described as a rich, commercial country with an impressive fleet.

Tarsier, mammal
champion swimmer, *picture* A-426

Tarsus, Turkey, city in s. Asia Minor 20 mi (30 km) w. of Adana; in ancient times a splendid city, capital of Cilicia; birthplace of St. Paul (Bible, Acts xxii, 3); pop. 51,184 P-212

Tarsus (or ankle), joint between the foot and leg S-210

Tartaglia, Niccolo, (originally Nicola Fontana) (1500?–1557), Italian mathematician, born in Brescia; credited with discovering solution of cubic equation; applied mathematics to artillery; advocated method for raising sunken ships; claimed to have invented gunner's quadrant. *see also in index* Cardan, Jerome

Tartan, checkered cloth. *see in index* Plaid

Tartar (or dental calculi), calcareous deposits on teeth D-102

Tartarin, boastful quixotic hero of Alphonse Daudet's humorous masterpieces, 'Tartarin of Tarascon', 'Tartarin on the Alps', and 'Port-Tarascon'.

Tartars. *see in index* Tatars

'Tartar Steppe, The', work by Buzzati I-379

Tartarus, in Greek mythology, place of punishment H-123, M-700

Tartini, Giuseppe (1692–1770), Italian violinist and composer; discovered what is known as "Tartini's tone" or combinational tone, produced by two tones sounding together ('The Devil's Trill').

Tartu, U.S.S.R., city in e.; founded in 1030; member Hanseatic League; university chartered by Gustavus Adolphus (1632); pop. 74,263, *maps* E-361, R-344, 348

'Tartuffe, Le', comedy by Molière (1664); the main character, Tartuffe, a pious adventurer, is the most famous hypocrite in literature M-522

Tarzan, hero of novels by Edgar Rice Burroughs, created 1914; English baby raised by apes in African jungle; adventures later adapted for movies and comics
science fiction S-62

Tasaday, a people of the Philippines, found in Mindanao in 1971; cave dwellers, technology based on stone and wooden tools; diet consists of small animals and wild vegetation; clothing made of leaves P-253b

Taschengeige (or pochette), stringed instrument S-492

Taschereau, Elzéar Alexandre, Cardinal (1820–98), Canadian prelate, born near city of Quebec; ordained Roman Catholic priest 1842; archbishop of Quebec 1871–94; became first Canadian cardinal 1886.

Taschereau, Robert (1896–1970), Canadian jurist, born in Quebec, Que.; professor of criminal law Laval University 1929–40; created king's counsel 1930; judge of the Supreme Court of Canada 1940–63, chief justice 1963–67.

Tashkent, U.S.S.R., capital and largest city of Uzbek Soviet Socialist Republic; former capital of Soviet Turkestan; pop. 1,643,000 T-31, *maps* R-322, 344
Asia, *map* A-700
temperature and precipitation, *graph* R-334

Tashunca-uitco. *see in index* Crazy Horse

'Task, The', work by Cowper C-758

Task force, U.S. military N-88

Task Force on Racially Isolated Urban Indians, American Indian study group; sponsored by HEW I-155

'Tasma', novel by Couvreur A-797

Tasman, Abel (1603?–59?), Dutch explorer T-32
Australia A-815
Fiji F-82
New Zealand N-283, 295
South Pacific P-14
Tasmania T-32

Tasman Geosyncline
Australia's geological formations A-774

Tasmania (formerly called Van Diemen's Land), island state of the Commonwealth of Australia; 26,200 sq mi (67,900 sq km); cap. Hobart; pop. 432,600. *see also in index* Australia
aboriginal population A-12
Australia A-767, 815, *map* A-822
Hobart H-179
migration of people M-400
Pacific Ocean, *map* P-6
Tasman T-32

Tasmanian devil, marsupial *Sarcophilusharrisii* M-154, 157
Australian wildlife A-780
Tasmania T-32
mammal M-81

Tasmanian wolf, marsupial *Thylacinus cynocephalus* M-156

Tasman Sea, part of Pacific Ocean between Australia and New Zealand
Australia A-769, *map* A-822
New Zealand, *picture* N-289
Pacific Ocean, *map* P-6

TASS (Telegraph Agency of the Soviet Union), Soviet news agency R-332e
newspapers N-238

Tassel, top of corn plant C-719, *picture* C-720

Tassili n' Ajjer, plateau region of Sahara, in Algeria; n.e. extension of the Ahaggar.

Tasso, Torquato (1544–95), Italian poet T-33
  Italian literature I-376, I-385

Taste, sense
  smell confusion S-218

Taste bud, end organ found in the papillae of the tongue T-215

Taster
  coffee C-534
  tea T-47

Tata Iron and Steel Company I-75

Tatami, Japanese mats F-456, J-29

Tatar City, in Peking, China P-153

Tatarian honeysuckle, a bush plant *Lonicera tatarica* H-228

Tatars (sometimes called Tartars), group of central Asiatic people. *see also in index* Mongols
  Genghis Khan G-58
  Moscow M-594
  Russia R-351, R-359, *picture* R-338

Tate, Allen John Orley (1899–1979), U.S. writer, born in Winchester, Ky.; professor University of Minnesota 1951–68; president of National Institute of Arts and Letters 1968–69 ('Mr. Pope and Other Poems' and 'Selected Poems'; 'Jefferson Davis', biography; 'Reason in Madness', critical essays; 'The Fathers', novel).

Tate, John (born 1955), U.S. boxer
  heavyweight champions B-392

Tate, Nahum (1652–1715), English poet and playwright, born in Dublin; poet laureate (1692–1715); chiefly known for mangled versions of plays of Shakespeare, and for version of the Psalms in which he collaborated with Nicholas Brady
  poet laureate P-402

Tate Gallery, London, England L-293
  Hogarth's 'The Graham Children' P-47, *picture* P-46

'Tatler, The', periodical published by Steele E-270
  Addison A-41
  magazine and journal M-32

Tatra Mountains (also called Tatry), central and loftiest group of Carpathians, on Poland-Czechoslovakia border; highest point 8,737 ft (2,663 m).

Tatti, I, estate, Florence, Italy F-188

Tattler. *see in index* Wandering tattler

Tattoo T-33
  New Zealand N-293
  'The Illustrated Man', *picture* R-111g

Tatum, Arthur (1910–56), U.S. jazz pianist, born in Toledo, Ohio; was technically and harmonically advanced; acquired a world reputation for intricate solos; almost blind.

Tatum, Edward Lawrie (1909–75), U.S. biochemist, born in Boulder, Colo.; professor Yale University 1946–48, Stanford University 1948–57, and Rockefeller University 1957–75. *see also in index* Nobel Prizewinners, *table*
  genetics G-54

Tatum, Reece (nickname Goose, often known as Clown Prince of Basketball) (1921–67), U.S. basketball player, born in Calion, Ark.; with Harlem Globetrotters 1942–55; later had own team, Harlem Road Kings.

Tau, electric charge
  atomic particles' properties A-755
  matter M-230

Tau Beta Pi, engineering honor society F-389

Tauchnitz, Christian B. (1816–95), German publisher; in 1841 he began publication of a collection of British and U.S. authors, known everywhere as the "Tauchnitz edition."

Taufa'ahau (or George Tupou I), king of Tonga T-215

Tauler, Johann (1300?–61), German mystic R-134

Taum Sauk Mountain, Missouri, highest point (1,772 ft; 540 m) in state O-624

Taungya, shifting cultivation practiced in s.e. Asia
  Burma B-510

Taunsa Barrage, situated on Indus River, *picture* P-78

Taunton, England, county town of Somerset 38 mi (61 km) s.w. of Bristol; here Monmouth assumed title of king, and here Jeffreys held "bloody assizes"; taken by Robert Blake and the Parliamentarians in Civil War 1644–45; pop. 37,420.

Taunton, Mass., city on Taunton River about 14 mi (22 km) n. of Fall River; silverware and jewelry, leather products, textile products, plastics; pop. 45,001
  flag of 1774, F-153, *picture* F-155

Taunus, mountain range in West Germany between the Rhine and the Main rivers; average elevation 1,500 ft (460 m); Lorelei Rock on the Rhine is an abutment of the range, *map* G-134

Taupo, Lake, largest lake of New Zealand, on North Island; 234 sq mi (606 sq km); greatest depth 522 ft (159 m); celebrated for trout fishing.

Taurus (or Bull), constellation, *charts* C-681, S-415, 421, 423
  astrology, *chart* A-708
  Pleiades P-391
  zodiac. *see also in index* Zodiac, *table*

Taurus Mountains, series of ranges in Turkey, extending w. from Euphrates; highest peaks over 10,000 ft (3,000 m); n.e. extension is called Anti-Taurus
  Turkey T-318, *picture* T-320

Tausen, Hans (1494–1561), Danish religious reformer; follower of Luther; became a Protestant bishop and leader in Danish reformation.

Tausig, Carl (1841–71), German composer and pianist, born in Warsaw, Poland; possessed extraordinary technical skill; composed brilliant works for piano.

Taussig, Frank William (1859–1940), U.S. economist, born in St. Louis, Mo.; professor economics Harvard University 1882–1935; chairman U.S. Tariff Commission 1917–19; editor, *Quarterly Journal of Economics* 1896–1937 ('Tariff History of United States'; 'Principles of Economics'; 'International Trade').

Taussig, Helen Brooke (1898–1986), U.S. physician, born in Cambridge, Mass.; in 1944 with Alfred Blalock originated operation to help "blue babies"; associate professor of pediatrics 1946–59, professor 1959–63 Johns Hopkins University; won Presidential Medal of Freedom 1964; first woman president of American Heart Association 1965.

Tautog, food fish *Tautoga onitis* common along Atlantic coast of U.S.; deep, blunt body duskily mottled; jaws can crush hard shells of crabs and shellfish.

Taverna, Greek café G-257

Tawas Point State Park, Tawas City, Mich. G-247

Tawhidi, Abu Hayyan at- (died 1023), Arab stylist I-366

Tawi-Tawi, province, Philippines. *see in index* Sulu Archipelago

Tawney, Richard Henry (1880–1962), English economist, born in Calcutta, India; professor University of London; on important government boards and commissions ('The Acquisitive Society'; 'Religion and the Rise of Capitalism'; 'Land and Labor in China').

Taxaceae. *see in index* Yew family

Taxation T-34. *see also* Fact Summary with each state article
  alcoholic beverages A-276
  American Revolution R-165, 168
  automotive taxes R-216
  business regulation B-518
  cigarette T-200
  collection U-158
  economics E-61
  franchise rights F-373
  French Revolution F-400
  government budgeting B-486
  homeowners H-295
  inflation I-198
  Middle Ages R-149
  national debt N-24
  social security S-236
  tariff T-31
  underground economy E-207
  U.S. constitution U-146, 149, 153
  U.S. poll tax S-505
  welfare programs W-145
  World War I W-314
  World War II R-277

Taxation without representation R-165

Tax base, physical unit or the amount of money to which a tax rate is applied T-34

Taxco (officially Taxco de Alarcón), Mexico, town in Sierra Madre 70 mi (110 km) s.w. of Mexico City; pop. 27,089
  Mexico, *picture* M-329, *map* M-344

Taxi (or taxicab)
  airport traffic control A-211
  transportation T-256

Taxidermy T-40
  dioramas D-148
  Field Museum F-78

Taxis, in biology
  orienting behavior A-441

Taxodium distichum. *see in index* Southern cypress

Taxonomic character
  evolutionary relationships A-441

Taxonomy, process of assigning organisms scientific names. *see also in index* Classification
  biology B-229
  botanical garden B-378
  sciences S-64b
  zoology Z-467

Tax shifting T-36

Tay, largest river of Scotland; rises near borders of Perthshire and Argyllshire, flows e. 120 mi (190 km) to estuary, Firth of Tay
  Loch Tay, *picture* S-68

Taylor, A.J.P. (born 1906), English historian H-174

Taylor, Albert Hoyt (1879–1961), U.S. physicist, born in Chicago, Ill.; pioneer in development of radar (for this work he received U.S. Medal for Merit 1944); superintendent, radio division, U.S. naval research laboratory 1923–45.

Taylor, Ann (or Mrs. Josiah Gilbert) (1782–1866), and **Jane Taylor** (1783–1824), English writers of verse; 'Rhymes for the Nursery' contains Jane's "Twinkle, twinkle, little star."

Taylor, Bayard (in full James Bayard Taylor) (1825–78), U.S. translator, traveler, and poet, born in Kennett Square, Pa.; U.S. minister to Germany 1878 ('Poems of Home and Travel'; 'Views Afoot'; translation of 'Faust').

Taylor, Bert Leston (1866–1921), U.S. newspaperman, born in Goshen, Mass.; 'A Line o' Type or Two' in *Chicago Tribune*, signed "B.L.T.," made him nationally famous.

Taylor, Brook (1685–1731), English mathematician; noted for Taylor's theorem, basis of differential calculus, also for scientific work on linear perspective and mathematical study of vibration of strings.

Taylor, Cecil (born 1933), U.S. jazz musician, born in New York, N.Y.
  jazz J-88

Taylor, Deems (or Joseph Deems Taylor) (1885–1966), U.S. composer and music critic, born in New York City ('The Highwayman', cantata; 'Through the Looking Glass', suite for orchestra; 'The King's Henchman', 'Peter Ibbetson', and 'Ramuntcho', operas: 'Of Men and Music', 'The Well Tempered Listener', and 'Music to My Ears', books).

Taylor, Edward (1642–1729), North American poet and clergyman, born in England; came to Massachusetts 1668 ('God's Determinations'; 'Sacramental Meditations')
  Puritan verse A-343

Taylor, Frederick Winslow (1856–1915), U.S. efficiency engineer, born in Philadelphia, Pa.; worked as common laborer and machinist, and studied manufacturing conditions and methods; initiated scientific management in U.S. ('The Principles of Scientific Management') I-182
  mass production M-208

Taylor, George (1716–81), signer of Declaration of Independence for Pennsylvania; born probably in n. Ireland.

Taylor, Graham (1851–1938), U.S. clergyman, sociologist, born in Schenectady, N.Y.; founder, resident warden, Chicago Commons social settlement.

Taylor, Henry Osborn (1856–1941), U.S. author, born in New York City; wrote on law and history of thought ('Ancient Ideals'; 'The Mediaeval Mind'; 'Freedom of the Mind in History'; 'Human Values and Verities').

Taylor, James (nickname Jim) (born 1935), U.S. football player, born in Baton Rouge, La; fullback; Green Bay Packers 1958–66, New Orleans Saints 1967.

Taylor, Jeremy (1613–67), English clergyman and author
  literary contribution E-268

Taylor, Margaret Smith (1788–1852), wife of President Taylor T-42

Taylor, Maxwell Davenport (1901–87), U.S. army officer, born in Keytesville, Mo.; commander 101st Airborne Division in World War II; superintendent U.S. Military Academy 1945–49; U.S. commandant in Berlin 1949–51; deputy Army chief of staff 1951–53; became 4-star general June 1953; Eighth Army commander in Korea 1953–54; Army commander of Far East forces 1954–55; Army chief of staff 1955–59; chairman Joint Chiefs of Staff 1962–64; ambassador to South Vietnam 1964–65; author of 'Swords and Plowshares' V-321

Taylor, Mildred, U.S. author, born in Jackson, Miss.; moved to Toledo, Ohio, when 3 months old; worked with Peace Corps in Ethiopia and U.S.; influenced by father's storytelling; her books 'Song of the Trees' and 'Roll of Thunder, Hear My Cry' (awarded 1977 Newberry Medal) were basis for 1978 television drama.

Taylor, Paul (born 1930), U.S. modern dancer and choreographer, born in Allegheny County, Pennsylvania; danced in Martha Graham's company before forming the Paul Taylor Dancer Company D-24, *picture* D-20

Taylor, Richard (1826–79), U.S. Confederate general, born near Louisville, Ky.; only son of Zachary Taylor T-42, *picture* T-43

Taylor, Tom (1817–80), popular English dramatist, biographer, and editor of *Punch* ('Our American Cousin'; 'The Overland Route').

Taylor, Zachary (1784–1850), 12th president of the United States T-41
  Fillmore F-85
  Mexican War M-320

Taylor, Mich., suburban industrial city 4 mi (6 km) s. of Lincoln Park in Detroit metropolitan area; pop. 77,568.

Taylor University, Upland, Ind.; private control; chartered 1846; arts and sciences, education.

Tay Pay. *see in index* O'Connor, Thomas Power

Tay-Sachs disease, fatal, hereditary, enzyme deficiency; affects central nervous system; chiefly afflicts Jews G-48

Tazara Railway, Africa Z-448

Tb, chemical element. *see in index* Terbium

Tbilisi (or Tiflis), U.S.S.R., capital of Georgian Soviet Socialist Republic, at s. base of Caucasus Mts., midway between Black and Caspian seas; distributing and industrial center for Transcaucasian region; pop. 1,140,000 T-44, *maps* R-322, 349
  Europe, *map* E-361
  Georgian Soviet Socialist Republic G-102

T-bone steak, meat M-246

Tc, chemical element. *see in index* Technetium

T cell (or T lymphocyte), type of white blood cell
  immune system I-55
  lymphatic system L-342

Tchad, Africa. *see in index* Chad

Tchad, Lake. *see in index* Chad, Lake

Conn.; served throughout Civil War, and in 1876 commanded main column that drove Sitting Bull into Canada after Battle of Little Big Horn C-808
Terry, Dame Ellen Alice (1847–1928), English Shakespearean actress, born in Coventry; mother of Edward G. Craig; long associated with Sir Henry Irving; with grace and intellectual grasp, portrayed Portia, Lady Macbeth, Desdemona, and Cordelia A-27
Terry, Luther Leonidas (1911–85), U.S. physician, born in Red Level, Ala.; on faculty Johns Hopkins University 1944–61; U.S. surgeon general 1961–65; professor University of Pennsylvania 1965–75, vice-president 1965–71.
Terry, Megan (born 1932), U.S. playwright A-363
Terry, William Harold (nickname Bill) (born 1898), U.S. baseball player, born in Atlanta, Ga.; first baseman New York, N.L., 1923–36 (also manager 1932–36); nonplaying manager New York, N.L., 1937–41; batted .401 in 1930; lifetime batting average of .341 B-88, B-93
Terry cloth, cotton, sometimes linen or synthetic fiber, fabric with heavy loop pile on both sides; mainly used for Turkish towels, robes, and slippers.
Tertiary period, in geological time
  Australia's geological formation A-776
  earth E-27, *table* E-24
Tertry (formerly Testry), France, village near Somme River, n. of Soissons; site of battle in 687; pop. 166. *see also in index* Pepin II
Tertullian (AD 155?–222?), one of great Church Fathers; creator of Christian Latin literature and chief founder of Latin theology.
Teschemacher, Frank (1906–32), U.S. jazz clarinetist, born in Kansas City, Mo.; an imaginative soloist with an unorthodox tone; one of Austin High School "gang" of white musicians in Chicago.
Teschen (Polish Cieszyn, Czech Tesin), city and district in former Austrian Silesia; about 850 sq mi (2,200 sq km); important coal mines; road and railway center; after World War I, disputed by Poland and Czechoslovakia; in 1920, Conference of Ambassadors gave city and farm region to Poland, suburb and mine district to Czechoslovakia; Poles occupied Czech area 1938; annexed by Germany 1939; lost by Germany in World War II; back to 1920 status in 1945.
Teschen, Peace of M-135
Tesla, Nikola (1856–1943), U.S. inventor T-114
  electricity E-162
  electric power E-165
  induction motor I-274, *table* I-273
  Westinghouse W-162
Tesla, unit of magnetic flux density in the metric system; named in honor of Nikola Tesla T-114
Tesserae, mosaic tiles M-589
Test acts, legislation of English Parliament imposing religious tests on government officials; most celebrated are the Corporation Act 1661, and Test Act 1673
  1673 C-2, E-247
Testamentary trust, in trust law T-301
Testate succession, having a will by which property is disposed at the owner's death E-307
Testator, maker of a will W-203, *table* L-93
Test ban treaty (1963) P-144, *table* T-275
Testes. *see in index* Testis
Testis (plural testes), male reproductive gland R-151c, *diagram* R-151d
  hormones H-243, *table* H-241, *diagram* H-240
  sexuality S-123
Testosterone, hormone that plays a part in sperm formation H-243, *table* H-241
  sexuality S-124
Testry, France. *see in index* Tertry
Tests and measurements
  automobiles A-871, *picture* A-867
  Bureau of Standards U-163
  education and psychology. *see also in index* Intelligence tests
    aptitude tests, *picture* V-360
    Binet's experiments B-197
    personality tests P-218
    psychology tests P-523
    inkblot S-110
  health H-87
  instrumentation I-228
  petrochemicals, *picture* P-228
  space travel S-342c, S-345, S-346b, S-346f, *pictures* S-341a, S-341b, S-348b, *table* S-348
Tesuque, pueblo about 3 mi (5 km) n. of Santa Fe, N.M.; Tesuque Indians belong to the Tanoan language group of Pueblo peoples; pop. 800.
Tet, the Vietnamese New Year
  Viet Cong offensive (1968) V-324
Tetanus (or lockjaw), acute infectious disease caused by bacillus that produces deadly toxin; characterized by widespread convulsions and muscular rigidity; usually conveyed by animal bite, puncture, or crushing injury; treated with antitoxin, antibiotics, and sedatives A-495
  drug treatment D-273
  infectious disease, *table* D-172
  nervous disorder N-123
  vaccine V-250
Tetens, Johann Nicolas (1736–1807), German psychologist; based his system of psychology entirely on observation of experiences.
Tethys, in Greek mythology, daughter of Uranus and Gaea (Heaven and Earth); wife of Oceanus and mother of the Oceanides (river gods) M-700
Tethys, vast sea of Permian period in geology; covered s. Europe, central and s. Asia; Mediterranean Sea is chief remnant of this sea
  Alps A-318
Tethys Himalayas (or Tibetan Himalayas), Asia H-153
Teton, division of the Sioux, consisting of several groups living in North Dakota and South Dakota, with a few in Montana, *table* I-138
Teton Peak, in Wyoming. *see in index* Grand Teton Peak
Teton Range, in Rocky Mts., in n.w. Wyoming
  mountain M-635
  United States, *map* U-80
  Wyoming W-386, *picture* W-385
Tétouan, Morocco. *see in index* Tetuán
Tetra, popular name for a number of tropical fish; includes the German flag-fish.
Tetrachlorodioxin (or dioxin), chemical I-175
Tetracyclines, group of broad spectrum antibiotics A-489, V-273
  acne A-20
  bubonic plague B-473
Tetrad, group of four chromatids
  genetics G-54
Tetraethyl lead (TEL), colorless liquid Pb $(C_2H_5)_4$, formed by reaction of ethyl chloride and lead sodium amalgam; mixed with ethylene bromide, it is added to gasoline to produce "ethyl" motor fuel; because poisonous, fuels so treated are required by law to contain dye
  gasoline additive G-42
Tetrahedron (plural tetrahedra), in mathematics
  geometry G-78
Tetrahydrocannabinol (THC), hallucinogen H-18
Tetrameter, in poetry P-405
Tetraonidae, family of birds including the grouse and ptarmigans. *see in index* Grouse
Tetraploid, species of wheat W-188
Tetrarch, originally, among Greeks, the ruler of one of four divisions of a country; later, among Romans, a minor ruler under the emperor, as Herod Antipas.
Tetrazzini, Luisa (1871–1940), Italian coloratura soprano; famous for 'La Traviata'; 'Rigoletto'; 'Lucia di Lammermoor'; wrote 'My Life of Song'
  opera, *list* O-570
Tetrodotoxin
  bionic research B-234
Tetuán (or Tétouan), Morocco, city on Mediterranean 30 mi (50 km) s.e. of Tangier; railroad to Ceuta; pop. 104,455.
Tetzel, Johann (1465–1519), German Dominican friar; opposed by Luther for selling indulgences (forgiveness of sins)
  Reformation R-133
Teucer, in Greek mythology, the first king of Troy; also name of the best Greek archer in the Trojan War, half-brother of Ajax.
Teutoburger Wald, series of wooded hills in North Rhine-Westphalia, West Germany, extending 70 mi (110 km), *map* G-134
Teutoberger Wald, battle of (AD 9), warfare, *list* W-16
Teutone, German people who gave name to Teutonic peoples G-121
  Marius defeats R-246
Teutonic Knights, military and religious order that arose during the Crusades C-788
  knighthood K-259
  monks and monasticism M-540
  Poland P-413
  Prussia P-516
Teutonic languages. *see in index* Germanic languages
Teutonic peoples. *see in index* Germanic peoples
Tevere, river of Italy. *see in index* Tiber
Teverone River (ancient Anio), Italy, tributary of Tiber; 75 mi (120 km) long; has supplied Rome with water since ancient times.
'Tevya the Milkman', story by Aleichem Y-417
Tewa, division of the Tanoan linguistic stock of peoples living in several pueblos in Rio Grande Valley, New Mexico, and the pueblo of Hano, Arizona.
Tewkesbury, England, historic town in n. Gloucestershire on the Avon; remains of famous Benedictine abbey; Yorkists defeated Lancastrians 1471 in Wars of the Roses; pop. 8,810.
Tewksbury, Mass., s.e. of Lowell in Middlesex County; includes a portion of Silver Lake; pop. of township 24,635.
'Texaco Star Theater', television program T-69
Texarkana, Tex. and Ark., two cities about 28 mi (45 km) from n.w. corner of La., forming one community; cattle, poultry; ordnance, wood products, clay tile products, chemicals, cotton products; pop. (Texas) 31,271, (Arkansas) 21,459, *maps* N-351, U-41
Texas, state in s.w. U.S.; 267,338 sq mi (692,402 sq km); cap. Austin T-115; pop. 14,228,383, *map* U-40, 62
  cattle drives C-225
  cities. *see also in index* cities listed below and other cities by name
    Austin A-765
    Dallas D-9
    El Paso E-194
    Fort Worth F-321
    Houston H-308
    San Antonio S-35
  cowboy traditions C-750
  ecology E-56
  history S-35
    Alamo A-238
    Civil War C-472
      Confederate States C-642
    Mexican War M-319
    outlaws O-619
    Wyoming W-390
  Hispanic Americans H-162
  industries U-65
  minerals
    gas, *picture* G-40
    petroleum P-230
      offshore E-137
    sulfur S-509
  missions S-35, S-338
  name, *table* S-428
  North America, *map* N-351
  Rio Grande R-209
  state symbols
    bird M-513
    flags F-154, *pictures* F-155, 160
    flower S-427
    tree P-151
  Statuary Hall, *table* S-437b
  taxation, *tables* T-37, 39
  United States U-56, U-75, *picture* U-77, *maps* U-36, U-58, U-81
Texas, The University of, Austin; state control; opened 1883; arts and sciences, architecture, business administration, communication, education, engineering, fine arts, law, library science, pharmacy, social work; graduate school; health science centers at Dallas, Houston, and San Antonio; medical school at Galveston; public affairs and nursing school at Austin; campuses at Arlington, Dallas, El Paso, Odessa (Permian Basin), San Antonio, and Tyler A-765, T-121. *see also in index* Texas at Arlington, The University of; Texas at El Paso, The University of
  Botero's 'Santa Rosa de Lima' P-67d, *picture* P-67c
  Dallas campus D-10
Texas A & I University, Kingsville, Tex.; state control; founded 1925; arts and sciences, agriculture, business administration, engineering, teacher education; graduate school; campuses at Corpus Christi and Laredo. *see also in index* Corpus Christi, University of
Texas Agricultural and Mechanical University, The, College Station, Tex.; state control; opened 1876; arts and sciences, agriculture, engineering, military sciences, veterinary medicine; graduate school; system includes universities at Galveston, Prairie View, and Stephenville T-121. *see also in index* Prairie View Agricultural and Mechanical University; Tarleton State College
Texas at Arlington, The University of, Arlington, Tex.; part of University of Texas; founded 1895; liberal arts, business, engineering, science; graduate study.
Texas at El Paso, The University of, El Paso, Tex.; part of University of Texas; founded 1913; liberal arts, business, education, engineering, sciences; graduate study.
Texas Christian University, Fort Worth, Tex.; Disciples of Christ; founded 1873; arts and sciences, business, education, fine arts, nursing, theology; graduate school.
Texas City, Tex., seaport, across Galveston Bay from Galveston; chemical, oil-refining, and tin-smelting industries; boating and fishing; over 500 persons killed and most of city destroyed or damaged (April 1947) in chemical-plant and oil-refinery explosions set off when freighter in harbor caught fire and exploded; rebuilding of homes and industries was well under way six months later; pop. 41,403
  petrochemical plant, *picture* U-65
Texas College, Tyler, Tex.; Christian Methodist Episcopal; founded 1894; liberal arts, education.
Texas fever, cattle disease C-231
Texas longhorns. *see in index* Longhorn cattle
Texas Lutheran College, Seguin, Tex.; Lutheran; founded 1891; arts and sciences, education.
Texas Medical Center, Houston, Tex. H-310
Texas mimosa. *see in index* Catclaw
Texas Rangers, Texas state police T-124, *picture* T-123
Texas Southern University, Houston, Tex.; state control; founded 1947; arts and sciences, law, pharmacy, vocational and industrial education; graduate school H-310
Texas Tech University, Lubbock, Tex.; state control; founded 1923; arts and sciences, agriculture, business administration, engineering, home economics; graduate studies.
'Texasville', novel by McMurtry W-152
Texas Wesleyan College, Fort Worth, Tex.; United Methodist; founded 1891; arts and sciences, education.

Thor, in Norse mythology, god of thunder M-703
Thoracic duct, main duct of the lymphatic system that carries lymph upward through the thorax and discharges it into left subclavian vein L-343
Thoracic surgery, a medical specialty, *table* M-277
Thoracic vertebra S-209
Thorax (or chest)
butterflies and moths B-521
invertebrate characteristics I-284
Laënnec L-19
lungs L-336
mosquito M-596
respiration R-159
skeleton S-209
Thoreau, Henry David (1817–62), U.S. author and naturalist T-174
civil disobedience C-463
Concord, Mass. C-639
essay E-306
first editions B-361
government G-198
Hall of Fame, *table* H-16
literary contribution A-347
Thorium (Th), metallic chemical element, *chart* R-66
alloy products A-313
nuclear energy N-422
periodic table, *table* P-207, *list* P-208
radioactivity R-64, 68
Thorn, Poland. *see in index* Torun
Thorn, of plant
function P-363
Thorn, Second Peace of (1466), *table* T-275
Thorn apple (also known locally as thorn, or haw, or red haw or scarlet haw), common name applied to several members of the hawthorn genus *Crataegus* of the rose family; all species bear hard small fruits, usually bright red; thin outer pulp surrounds seeds.
Thorndike, Edward Lee (1874–1949), U.S. psychologist and educator, born in Williamsburg, Mass.; professor of education, Teachers College, Columbia University ('Elements of Psychology'; 'Animal Intelligence'; 'The Measurement of Intelligence'; 'The Psychology of Learning') P-521
education E-95
intelligence theories I-242
word list R-126
Thorne-Thomsen, Gudrun (1873–1956), U.S. storyteller and author, born in Trondheim, Norway ('East o' the Sun and West o' the Moon'; 'Sky Bed'; 'In Norway')
storytelling S-461-2
Thorn forest G-236
Thornthwaite, Charles Warren (1899–1963), U.S. climatologist and geographer; born in Bay City, Mich.; classified world climates
climate classification C-499
Thornton, Sir Henry Worth (1871–1933), Canadian railway executive, born in Logansport, Ind.; in charge British railways in France in World War I; knighted 1919; president of Canadian National Railways 1922–32.
Thornton, Matthew (1714–1803), signer of Declaration of Independence; born in Ireland; judge New Hampshire Supreme Court 1776–82
Declaration of Independence D-56
Thornton, William (1759–1828), U.S. architect and physician, born in Virgin Islands of English parents; designed Capitol building in Washington, D.C. W-69
Thornton, William Edgar (born 1929), U.S. astronaut candidate, born in Goldsboro, N.C.; physician chosen for NASA scientist-astronaut program 1967.
Thornton, Colo., residential city about 4 mi (6 km) n. of the city of Denver; in Adams County; w. of the South Platte River; fish hatchery nearby; pop. 40,343.
Thornycroft, Sir William Hamo (1850–1925), British sculptor; work shows influence of ancient Greek art ('Teucer', 'The Mower', and statue of Oliver Cromwell).
Thorold, Ont., town on Welland Ship Canal and on s.e. border of St. Catharines; paper mills; pop. 15,412.
Thoroughbred, distinct breed of running horses H-253, *picture* H-257
horse racing H-275
Kentucky K-211, *picture* K-208
Thoroughbred horse racing H-275
Thorpe, Jim (full name James Francis Thorpe) (1888–1953), U.S. athlete T-175
football F-297
Olympic achievements A-741, O-542
Thorpe, Thomas Bangs (1815–78), U.S. humorist and portrait painter, born in Westfield, Mass.; whimsical, exaggerated tales of backwoods life ('Big Bear of Arkansas').
Thorpe, Sir Thomas Edward (1845–1925), English chemist, born near Manchester; government chemist 1894–1909; noted for researches in inorganic chemistry ('Dictionary of Applied Chemistry').
Thorvaldsen, Bertel (1770–1844), Danish sculptor S-89
Thoth, Egyptian deity E-128, M-700
Thou, Jacques Auguste de (1553–1617), French historian and statesman; famous for his 'Historia sui Temporis' (in Latin), a history of his own times; collected large historical library.
'Thoughts for the Times on War and Death', work by Freud W-28
'Thousand and One Nights, The'. *see in index* 'Arabian Nights'
Thousand Islands, group of about 1,500 islands in St. Lawrence River, at outlet of Lake Ontario, near Kingston, Ont.; some belong to Canada, some to New York State; resort area S-20
Canada C-73
New York N-246, *pictures* N-254, 262
Thousand Islands International Bridge, across the St. Lawrence River S-20
Thousand Oaks, Calif., city 42 mi (68 km) w. of Los Angeles; electronic components, defense systems, plastic products; pop. 35,873.
Thrace (ancient Thracia, or Trakya), easternmost tip of Balkan peninsula T-175, *maps* P-212, R-242
Balkan Wars B-31
Greece G-254, 260
Turkey T-318
Thracians, people B-28
Thrale, Mrs. Hester Lynch (1741–1821), English woman, wife of Henry Thrale, a brewer; after his death married an Italian musician named Gabriel Piozzi; wrote delightful letters and was central figure of a charming literary and artistic circle.
Thrasher, bird of the family Mimidae T-175
Thraupidae, family of birds, the tanagers. *see in index* Tanager
Thread T-176
lacemaking L-13
sewing S-121
spinning process S-389-90
synthetic fibers, *pictures* F-71, 75
Thread-count embroidery, needlework N-110
Threadfish, fish *Polynemidae* allied to the mullet but distinguished by slender threadlike rays proceeding from the pectoral fin, and sometimes longer than the body; the name threadfish is also applied to the cobbler fish. *see also in index* Cobbler fish
Three Baskets, Pali canon B-487
Three-Chopped Way, road in s. United States
Mississippi M-470
'Three-Cornered World, The' (1906), work by Natsume N-67
Three-cornered trade. *see in index* Triangular trade
Three-cornered trophon, snail *Forreria catalinensis*
shell, *picture* S-151
Three Deep, game G-12
Three-dimensional drawing M-255, 260
Three-dimensional photography
holography H-206
motion pictures M-622, S-444
Three-dimensional sound. *see in index* Stereophonic sound
Threefold Refuge, belief by monks and devout laypeople of Buddhism that the Three Jewels of Buddhism - Buddha, his teachings, and the community of believers - shelter and protect them B-482
Three Gorges, canyons in China Y-410
Three Jewels, cornerstone of Buddhism, Buddha the teacher; Dharma, the teachings or law; and Sangha, the community of believers B-482
Three Kingdoms period, in Korea K-284
Three Kings of Cologne. *see also in index* Magi
Three little pigs, fable F-3
Three Lower Counties. *see in index* Delaware
Three Mile Island, nuclear plant near Harrisburg, Pa.; an accident on March 28, 1979 in which uranium in the reactor core was damaged cast doubt on nuclear power as a viable energy alternative N-430
'Three Musicians, The', painting by Picasso P-58, P-314, *picture* P-56
'Three Musketeers, The', novel by Alexandre Dumas that relates the fortunes of D'Artagnan, a Gascon soldier, and his three musketeer friends, Aramis, Porthos, and Athos D-288. *see also in index* Artagnan, Charles d'
'Threepenny Opera, The', opera by Brecht and Weill B-433
Three Petticoats, League of the S-117
Three Principles of the People (or Three Great Principles, or Three People's Principles), basis of political program of Chinese leader Sun Yat-sen; accepted by China and by the Nationalist regime on Taiwan C-372
Three-ring circus, *picture* C-424
Three Rivers, Que. *see in index* Trois-Rivières
Three stages, Law of the, sociological concept of Auguste Comte C-637
Three-sticker kite K-252
'Three Trees, The', etching by Rembrandt, *picture* G-232
Three Wise Men. *see in index* Magi
'Thresher', U.S. Navy nuclear-powered attack submarine; sank off Cape Cod in 1963.
Thresher shark. *see in index* Fox shark
Threshing
farm machinery F-34
Indonesia, *picture* F-26
primitive methods, *picture* S-285
rice R-199
Threskiornithidae, family of birds including the ibises and spoonbills.
Thrift, common name for 2 species of plants. *see in index* Sea pink
'Thriller', top-selling music album by Jackson M-683
Thrip, small insect of the order Thysanoptera, in some respects resembling aphids; feeds on plant juices; some species injurious, *picture* I-214
Throat T-176
larynx and vocal chords V-377
windpipe. *see in index* Trachea, *subhead* human
Throatwort, genus of perennials *Trachelium* of bellflower family, native to Mediterranean; grows to 3 ft (1 m); leaves oval; flowers blue, starlike, tubular, in clusters at ends of branches.
Thrombin, blood B-315
Thromboplastin, blood B-315
Thrombosis, formation of a blood clot. *see in index* Stroke
Thrombus, blood clot that remains attached to place of origin in blood vessel D-174
Throne chair F-455, *pictures* F-454
Throssell, Mrs. Hugo Vivian Hope. *see in index* Prichard, Katharine Susannah
Throop Polytechnic Institute. *see in index* California Institute of Technology
'Through a Glass Darkly', part of film triology by Bergman B-166
'Through the Looking Glass', work by Carroll
Throwing, in pottery making P-478
Throwing, in spinning
silk S-200
synthetic fibers F-74
Throwing event, in track and field T-245
Thrush, family of birds T-177
bird species B-247, *picture* B-255
nighttime migrants A-450
state bird, *picture* V-292
Thrush, fungus disease of babies that inflames the mouth and throat; in children and adults the disease is usually confined to the corners of the exterior mouth.
Thrust, force produced by a propeller, rotor blade, or jet or rocket engine to drive aircraft, missiles, or spacecraft J-106
airplane A-181
rocket S-342a, 346c
'Thrust', painting by Gottlieb P-65, *picture* P-65
Thrust brake (or thrust receiver), turbojet engineering
jet propulsion J-109
Thrust stage (often called open stage, or platform stage), theater system T-152, *diagram* T-153
Thruway, highway R-214. *see also in index* Expressway; Freeway; Toll road
Thucydides (460?–404? BC), Greek historian T-177
Greek literature G-276
history writing H-171
Pericles' funeral oration P-206
Peloponnesian War P-143b
warfare W-27
Thugs, organization of professional murderers in India who strangled their victims in honor of the goddess Kali, wife of Siva; killed 30,000 people a year; suppressed by British government 1840.
Thule. *see in index* Ultima Thule
Thule, Greenland, settlement on n.w. coast; on direct transpolar route between strategic areas in U.S. and U.S.S.R.; pop. 206
U.S. Air Base A-571
Thulium (Tm), chemical element
periodic table, *table* P-207, *list* P-208
Thumb, in anatomy H-27
apes and monkeys A-498
Thumb knot (or overhand knot)
knot, hitch, and splice K-262
Thun, Switzerland, town 17 mi (27 km) s.e. of Bern, near Lake of Thun; 12th-century feudal castle; military headquarters; popular tourist resort; pop. 31,300, *map* S-537
Thun, Lake of, lake in canton of Bern, Switzerland, w. of Interlaken, an expansion of Aare River, 10 by 2 mi (3 by 16 km), *map* S-537
Thunbergia, genus of perennial twining climbers of the acanthus family, found in tropical regions; leaves usually triangular; flowers funnel-shaped with 5 lobes, blue, purple, yellow, or white, solitary or in loose clusters; black-eyed Susan vine *T. alata* has creamy flowers, with dark purple throat, and is sometimes called clock vine.
Thunder
lightning L-208, S-259
Thunder Bay (formerly Fort William and Port Arthur), Ont., city and port on n. shore of Lake Superior; pop. 112,486 T-177
Canada, *map* C-112
North America, *map* N-351
Ontario O-549
Thunderbird, mythical eaglelike bird of North American Indian folklore, believed to produce thunder and lightning; term has been widely commercialized in recent times, *picture* S-479
Thunderbolt (or P-47), U.S. military aircraft W-333
Thundercloud, *diagram* S-457
Thunderstorm S-457
aviation hazard A-888, *diagram* A-887
lightning L-207
rainfall R-88
weather W-120

Thurber, James (1894–1961), U.S. writer and illustrator T-178
literary contribution A-360
storytelling S-464
young adult reading R-112b

Thuringia (German Thüringen), former state in central Germany formed 1919 by union of several small districts; after World War II, this area became new state, Thuringia, in Soviet zone; area 6,023 sq mi (16,000 sq km); new state dissolved 1952 G-121, *map* G-134

Thuringian, Germanic people who settled in central Germany G-121

Thuringian Forest (German Thüringer Wald), range of hills in East Germany from Werra River near Eisenach s.e. to Bavarian frontier; magnificent pine forest G-111, *map* G-134

Thurmond, James Strom (born 1902), U.S. lawyer and political leader, born in Edgefield, S.C.; governor South Carolina 1947–51; Dixiecrat candidate for president 1948; senator from South Carolina 1955–; Republican after 1964 V-387
electoral vote, *chart* P-495

Thurneysen, Eduard (born 1888), Swiss theologian
Barth B-85

Thursday, 5th day of week; named for Thunor (Anglo-Saxon), or Thor (Norse), god of thunder

Thursday Island, in Australia, in Torres Strait, off n. point of Queensland; fine harbor; pearl and trepang fishing; pop. 2,551, *map* A-819

Thurston, Howard (1869–1936), U.S. magician, born in Columbus, Ohio; invented and made much equipment in laboratory workshop M-38

Thurston, Lorrin Andrews (1858–1931), lawyer and statesman, born in Hawaii; son of U.S. missionaries; held various government positions in Hawaiian monarchy and republic, and was active in furthering annexation of Hawaiian Islands to United States.

Thurstone, Louis Leon (1887–1955), U.S. psychologist, born in Chicago, Ill.; professor of psychology University of Chicago 1924–52; with his wife **Thelma Gwinn Thurstone** (born 1897), devised intelligence tests I-242

Thutmose III (or Tuthmosis III), king of Egypt (1504–1450 BC); a great military leader; ruled jointly with Hatshepsut (his aunt and mother-in-law) until her death
New Kingdom E-126

Thwaites, Reuben Gold (1853–1913), U.S. historian, born in Dorchester, Mass.; managing editor *Wisconsin State Journal*; secretary and superintendent State Historical Society, Wisconsin; edited 'Jesuit Relations and Allied Documents', 73 volumes; author of historical books.

Thyme, herb *Thymus vulgaris* of the genus *Thymus* H-138, S-379, *picture* H-137

Thymelaeaceae. *see in index* Mezereum family

Thymine, pyrimidine base that codes genetic information in DNA
genetics G-56

Thymol, white, crystalline, aromatic, organic compound, $C_{10}H_{13}OH$; obtained by distillation of thyme oil; used as antiseptic.

Thymus, genus of woody perennial plants of the mint family native chiefly to the Mediterranean region; leaves small, sometimes gray and hairy; stem erect or creeping; flowers tiny, purple, rose, or white. *see also in index* Thyme

Thymus, organ located behind the breastbone and above the heart; participates in the production of white blood cells or lymphocytes; because it obtains maximum size at puberty and becomes smaller in adults, researchers feel it may be an endocrine gland that affects growth and sexual maturation
immune system I-55
disease D-168
lymphatic system L-342

Thyone, in Greek mythology. *see in index* Semele

Thyristor, electrical device E-169

Thyrocalcitonin, hormone that controls the body's calcium level H-242, *table* H-241

Thyroid cartilage, in throat V-377

Thyroid gland G-153
anatomy A-392
goiter. *see in index* Goiter
hormones H-242, *table* H-241, *diagrams* H-240, 243
metabolism M-306
respiration R-160
radioactive iodine N-429

Thyroid stimulating hormone (or TSH), hormone that stimulates production of thyroxine H-240, *table* H-241, *diagram* H-243

Thyrotropin-releasing factor (or TRF), hormone that is synthesized in the hypothalamus, *diagram* H-243

Thyroxine, amino acid derivative H-242, *table* H-241
metabolism M-306

Thyrsis, poetic name for a shepherd or rustic lad, first used by Theocritus; title of a poem by Matthew Arnold in memory of Arthur Hugh Clough.

Thyssen, August (1842–1926), German industrialist; had coal and iron mines, steel mills, railroads, and steamship lines all over world; called "king of Ruhr"; succeeded by son **Fritz** (1873–1951), who was convicted as minor Nazi offender 1948 for giving financial aid to early Nazi party.

Ti, chemical element. *see in index* Titanium

Tiahuanaco, Bolivia, village 38 mi (61 km) n.w. of La Paz
Lake Titicaca T-194

Tiamat, Sumerian mythological figure B-6

Tiananmen, square in Peking, China, *picture* C-346

Tian Chi (or Celestial Lake), in China, *picture* C-338

Tianjin (or Tientsin), China, capital of Hopei Province; seaport near Gulf of Chihli, arm of Yellow Sea; pop. 5,142,565 T-178, *map* A-700
China C-344

Tianjin, Treaty of (1858), China
Opium Wars O-573
trade opening T-178

Tianjin Massacre, violent outbreak against French in Tianjin, China (June 21, 1870) C-370

Tian Shan, mountain range in central Asia; divides Kirghiz Soviet Socialist Republic from Sinkiang-Uigur Autonomous Region, China; highest point Pobeda Peak (24,406 ft; 7,439 m) T-179
China C-337
U.S.S.R. R-323, *map* R-322

Tibbett, Lawrence (1896–1960), U.S. baritone, born in Bakersfield, Calif.; debut in concert 1917, in opera 1923; star in Metropolitan Opera, motion pictures, Broadway musicals, radio, and television
opera, *list* O-570

Tiber (Italian Tevere), famous river of central Italy, *maps* E-361, I-404
Rome R-240, R-249, *map* R-250

Tiberias, Israel, town on w. shore of Lake Tiberias n.e. of Nazareth; medicinal hot springs; 695 ft (210 m) below sea level; founded about 20 BC; pop. 22,300
Sea of Galilee G-5

Tiberias, Lake. *see in index* Galilee, Sea of

Tiberius (full name Tiberius Claudius Nero Caesar Augustus) (42 BC–AD 37), second Roman emperor T-179

Tiberius Claudius Drusus Nero Germanicus. *see in index* Claudius

Tiberius Claudius Nero, father of Tiberius
Caesar and Augustus T-179

Tiber River (or Father Tiber), second longest river in Italy T-179

Tibesti, highest mountain group of Sahara, *map* A-118
Africa A-94
Chad C-263
Sahara S-15

Tibet, plateau area in s.w. part of China; area about 470,000 sq mi (1,217,000 sq km); cap. Lhasa; pop. 1,270,000 T-180, *map* A-700
animals
pandas P-97
Buddhism B-481
China C-337
first European visitor H-115
Lhasa L-145
masks M-186
monks and monasticism M-540
Mount Everest E-363
mythology M-696
people. *see in index* Tibetans
United Nations U-25

Tibetan (or Zang), an Asian people
Bhutan B-180
China C-345
Jammu and Kashmir J-22
Karakorum range K-192
racial classification R-27
Tibet T-180

Tibetan Buddhism, religion T-180

Tibetan Himalayas (or Tethys Himalayas), Asia H-153

Tibeton-Qinghai plateau, Asia A-674, C-351

Tibia, inner bone of the leg below the knee S-210

Tibu (or Tibbu), one of a North African Berber people.

Tibullus, Albius (54?–19 BC), poet of ancient Rome; his poems deal mostly with love and with country life L-77

Tic, in physiology, usually a habitual muscle twitch T-182
disease D-179

Tic douloureux. *see in index* Neuralgia

Ticino, canton in s. Switzerland; 1,086 sq mi (2,813 sq km); wine, tobacco, textiles; abundant hydroelectric power; known for resorts Locarno and Lugano; pop. 203,700.

Ticino River, Switzerland and Italy, 150 mi (240 km) long; flows into Po; source in Swiss alps; provides hydroelectric power for Switzerland, *map* S-537

Ticinum, Italy. *see in index* Pavia

Tick, largest of the blood-sucking arachnid mites; term also applied to various parasitic insects T-182
first aid for bites F-122
parasite P-113, *picture* P-115
cattle C-231
dogs D-209
spider S-387

Tick bird (also called beefeater, or rhinoceros bird), bird that eats ticks infesting cattle and large wild animals; found in Africa
rhinoceros, *picture* R-178

Ticker, device for printing quotations and news on tape by telegraph; a modern ticker contains a rotating wheel and a moving tape, which is pressed by magnetic apparatus against any character desired on the wheel as incoming electric current impulses may direct; current impulses are controlled by apparatus similar to that for modern multiplex telegraphy; the earliest was invented (1867) by Edward A. Calahan; the present type is a combination of many ideas and inventions
Edison E-73
stock and bond quotations S-454, *pictures* S-452–3

Ticking, strong twilled cotton fabric with colored stripes; used as covering for pillows, mattresses, and box springs; most often made in blue and white.

Tickling, sensation
brain regulates B-398

Ticknor, George (1791–1871), U.S. critic and historian, born in Boston, Mass.; while professor of modern languages at Harvard University inaugurated present American University system, among first to propose elective system; his 'History of Spanish Literature' ranked as standard work even in Spanish countries.

Tickseed. *see in index* Coreopsis

Ticonderoga, N.Y., village on outlet from Lake George to Lake Champlain, 85 mi (140 km) n.e. of Albany; pop. 2,938 T-182. *see also in index* Fort Ticonderoga
Allen A-308

Tidal current, horizontal flow of water produced by tides O-488

Tidal cycle, tides O-488

Tidal range, amount of change in the water level during a tidal cycle O-488

Tidal trap (or weir), type of fish trap T-267

Tidal water mill, waterpower W-105

Tidal wave, term correctly applied to crest of tide in ocean or other large body of water due to gravitational pull of moon and sun; also popular name for destructive wave caused by high wind along shore; erroneous name for tsunami. *see also in index* Tsunami
floods F-182, *table* F-181

Tidal zone, area along the shore between the high-tide and low-tide levels O-460
Atlantic Ocean's marine life A-745

Tide gate harbor, harbor with locks to control water level H-34

Tidelands oil P-230, P-238, *picture* P-239
Eisenhower E-137

Tide predictor (or tide gauge) calculating device C-21
ocean waves O-490

Tides O-487. *see also in index* Ocean waves
Bay of Fundy F-447
New Brunswick N-154
Saint John S-18
earth E-30
floods F-182
harbors H-34
moon's influence M-573
Southampton S-303
waterpower W-105

Tidewater region
Virginia V-330

Tidore, Indonesia, small island in Molucca group, s. of Ternate; spices, copra; pop. 24,064.

Tie, sign in musical notation M-690

Tieck, Johann Ludwig (1773–1853), German writer, born in Berlin; a leader of romantic movement; many novels, short stories, plays, and poems
German literature G-109
Kirghiz terrain K-250

Tientsin. *see in index* Tianjin

Tiepolo, Giovanni Battista (1696–1770), Venetian artist T-182
drawing D-250

Tierra del Fuego, island group making up the s. tip of South America; divided between Chile and Argentina; land area about 28,473 sq mi (73,745 sq km); largest island Tierra del Fuego (area more than 18,000 sq mi; 46,600 sq km) T-183, *maps* A-585, S-300
Argentina A-575
people S-281d
shelter S-155

Tietjens, Eunice (1884–1944), U.S. author, born in Chicago, Ill. (for adults: 'Leaves in Windy Weather', poetry; 'World at My Shoulder', autobiography; for children: 'Boy of the Desert', 'Boy of the South Seas').

Tie-wig (or cadogan), hairdressing H-10

Tiffany, Charles Lewis (1812–1902), U.S. jewelry merchant, born in Killingly, Conn.; moved to New York City 1837, established fancy goods and stationery store with partner on borrowed capital of $1,000; gradually concentrated on jewelry, building up one of foremost houses in the world.

Tiffany, Gordon MacLean (born 1912), U.S. lawyer and public official, born in Port Chester, N.Y.; attorney general of New Hampshire 1950–53; staff director Commission on Civil Rights 1958–60.

Tiffany, Louis Comfort (1848–1933), U.S. painter and stained-glass artist, born in New York City; son of Charles Lewis Tiffany; invented Tiffany favrile glass; director Tiffany Studios, vice-president and trustee Tiffany & Co.

Tiffany Yellow, diamond, *picture* D-129

Tiffin, Ohio, industrial city on Sandusky River, 80 mi (130 km) n. of Columbus; heavy machinery, electrical products, pottery, glassware, blast furnace lining; Heidelberg College; pop. 19,549.

Tiflis, U.S.S.R.. *see in index* Tbilisi

Tift College, Forsyth, Ga.; Baptist; for women; chartered 1849; present name 1956;

North Carolina N-356, *pictures* N-357, 365, W-240
Tennessee T-85, *map* T-88, *picture* T-86
Virginia R-204, V-332, *map* V-336, *picture* V-341
Raleigh R-91

Tobacco, Indian. *see in index* Lobelia

Tobacco budworm. *see in index* Corn earworm

Tobacco worm, larva of a species of sphinx moth *Protoparce sexta*; color usually green; hornlike processes at hind end of body; feeds chiefly on leaves of tomato, tobacco, and potato plants.

Tobago (or Robinson Crusoe Island, or Tobaco), island in West Indies, part of republic of Trinidad and Tobago; 116 sq mi (300 sq km); pop. 39,280, *map* W-159. *see also in index* Trinidad and Tobago

Toba Sojo (1053–1140), Japanese artist
children's literature, *picture* L-245

Tobermory, cat, hero of a story by H.H. Munro (Saki), *list* C-202

Tobey, Mark (1890–1976), U.S. artist, born in Centerville, Wis.; known for "white writing" technique that he evolved after visiting the Orient in 1934; self-taught.

Tobias, Channing Heggie (1882–1961), U.S. social worker and civic leader, born in Augusta, Ga.; YMCA executive 1911–46; chairman board of directors NAACP 1953–59; won 1948 Spingarn Medal.

Tobin, Maurice Joseph (1901–53), U.S. political leader and lawyer, born in Roxbury, Mass.; mayor of Boston 1938–44; governor of Massachusetts 1945–46; U.S. secretary of labor 1948–53.

Toboggan W-243, *picture* W-242

Toboso, Dulcinea del, character in Cervantes' 'Don Quixote', name given to Aldonza Lorenzo, a country lass whom the hero makes the object of his knightly devotion.

'To Brooklyn Bridge', work by Crane A-356

Tobruk (or Tobruch), Libya, port on n. coast of Africa; protected harbor; naval base; scene of fighting by British and Axis in World War II; pop. 12,173, *map* A-118

Tocantins, river in e.-central and n.e. Brazil, flowing n. 1,700 mi (2,700 km) to Atlantic Ocean; Araguaia is its chief tributary, *maps* B-425, S-298

Toccata, in music, *list* M-671

Toch, Ernst (1887–1964), U.S. composer, born in Vienna, Austria; in U.S. after 1934, became citizen 1940; professor of composition University of Southern California 1940–47; composed music in almost all forms; works performed throughout the world; author of 'Shaping Forces in Music'; won 1956 Pulitzer prize in music for 'Symphony No. 3'.

Tocopherol, vitamin E V-356

Tocqueville, Alexis de (or Alexis-Charles-Henri-Maurice Clérel de Tocqueville) (1805–59), French statesman and political philosopher T-201

Tod, John (1791–1882), Canadian fur trader, born in Scotland; joined Hudson's Bay Company and for some time had charge of Thompson River district in British Columbia; member of first council of Vancouver Island.

Todai, University of. *see in index* Tokyo, University of

Todd, Alexander Robertus Todd, Baron, of Trumpington (born 1907), Scottish biochemist and educator, born in Glasgow; professor of organic chemistry University of Cambridge 1944–71; master, Christ's College 1963–78. *see also in index* Nobel Prizewinners, *table*

'Todd-AO', motion picture innovation of the 1950's M-623

Toddler, 1- to 3-year-old child C-323, *picture* C-324

TOE, in physics. *see in index* Superstring theory

TOFC (or Trailer-on-flatcar), container cargo transportation T-255

Toffee, candy C-138

Toga, garment D-261

Toggenburg goat, breed named for a district in n.e. Switzerland; imported into U.S. in 1893 G-171

Toggle joint, lever principle applied to jointed arms with power at knuckle to spread arms.

Togliatti, Palmiro (1893–1964), Italian Communist party leader and government official, born in Genoa; in exile from fascist Italy 1926–44; shot in assassination attempt 1948.

Togo, Heihachiro, Marquis (1847–1934), Japanese admiral, commander of navy in Russo-Japanese War.

Togo (formerly French Togoland), in w. Africa on Gulf of Guinea; 22,008 sq mi (57,000 sq km); cap. Lomé; pop. 2,947,000, *map* A-118. *see also in index* Togoland
African political unit, *table* A-112
flag, *picture* F-171
railroad mileage, *table* R-85

Togoland (or Togo), former German protectorate in w. Africa on Gulf of Guinea; became German protectorate 1884; divided between France and United Kingdom 1922 as mandates and then, in 1946, as trusteeships; British Togoland (13,041 sq mi; 33,776 km), producer of cattle, cocoa, coffee, palm oil, palm nuts, hardwood, rubber, rice, corn, and beans; joined Ghana 1957; French Togoland became independent Republic of Togo 1960. *see also in index* Togo, Republic of
Ghana G-140

Toile de Jouy, printed cotton cloth that originated in France in 18th century.

'Toilers of the Sea', painting by Ryder
painting P-54, *picture* P-55

Toilet S-158

Toiletries C-728

Toilet soaps S-231

Toilet water P-205

Tojo Hideki (1884–1948), Japanese political leader and general, of Samurai class; prime minister (1941–44), also minister of war and of education; hanged as war criminal Dec. 1948 J-68
World War II W-327

Tokaido Megalopolis, Japan J-27

Tokaj (English Tokay), Hungary, town 117 mi (188 km) n.e. of Budapest; famous for tokay wine from grapes grown in the region.

Tokay, lizard, *picture* L-273

Tokay grape, sweet, rich wine grape originally raised near Tokay, Hungary; flame Tokay raised on Pacific coast; ships and keeps well.

Tokelau (or Union Islands), group in Pacific n. of Samoa; about 4 sq mi (10 sq km); added to Western Samoa administration as dependency of New Zealand 1926; annexed to New Zealand 1949; pop. 1,625, *map* P-6
Commonwealth membership C-602
New Zealand N-294

Token money, coin the face value of which is more than its value as metal; examples in U.S. are quarters, dimes, nickels, and pennies.

Toklas, Alice Babette (1877–1967), secretary and companion to Gertrude Stein, born in San Francisco, Calif.; to France 1907 ('The Alice B. Toklas Cookbook', 'What Is Remembered', 'Staying on Alone: Letters of Alice B. Toklas').

Tokonoma, Japanese alcove J-29

Tokugawa administration, Japanese political power
Edo T-210
Yamaga Y-408
Yamagata Y-408

Tokugawa Hidetada (1579–1632), Japanese shogun T-202

Tokugawa Iemitsu (1604–51), Japanese shogun T-202

Tokugawa Ieyasu (1543–1616), Japanese shogun T-202
Japan J-64
Oda O-492

Tokugawa Nariaki (1800–60), Japanese ruler
Tokugawa family T-202

Tokugawa Yoshimune (1684–1751), Japanese shogun T-202

Tokugawa Yoshinobu (original name Tokugawa Keiki) (1837–1913), Japanese shogun and prince T-202

Tokyo (formerly Edo, or Ydo), Japan, capital and largest city; pop. 8,170,379 T-203, *pictures* C-455, 466, G-66
Asia, *map* A-700
Japan J-24, *map* J-78
noise meter, *picture* P-441e
smog problem P-411c

Tokyo, University of (or University of Todai), Tokyo, Japan; founded 1877; agriculture, economics, education, engineering, law, letters, medicine, science T-207

Tokyo Bay, inlet of Pacific, central Honshu, Japan; cities Tokyo, Kawasaki, and Yokohama on shore.

Tokyo Tower, tower in Tokyo, Japan, *picture* T-203

Tola, evergreen shrub *Lepidophyllum quadrangulore* native to the highland regions of w. South America.

Tolbert, William R. (1913–80), president of Liberia L-147
assassination A-704

Toledo (often called Glass Capital), Ohio, Great Lakes port, near mouth of Maumee River at w. end of Lake Erie; pop. 354,635 T-212, *map* U-41
Lake Erie E-298
North America, *map* N-351
Ohio O-501, 506, 512, *pictures* O-502, 510, 511

Toledo, Spain, former capital of kingdom, on Tagus River 45 mi (70 km) s.w. of Madrid; medieval Gothic art and architecture; pop. 61,813 T-212, *map* E-361
Spain, *picture* S-349, *map* S-350
swords S-358

Toledo, Mountains of (or Montes de Toledo), central Spain s. of the city of Toledo; highest point 4,750 ft (1,450 m).

Toledo, University of, Toledo, Ohio; state control; founded 1872; arts and sciences, business administration, education, engineering, law, pharmacy; graduate study; junior college division.

Toledo Bend Dam, in Louisiana L-310

Toledo War, Michigan and Ohio boundary dispute M-361

Toleration Act (1689), England G-169, P-539
Quakers Q-4

Toleration acts, American Colonies. *see in index* Religious liberty, *subhead* American Colonies

Tolima, Mount, in Colombia, inactive Andean volcano 100 mi (160 km) w. of Bogotá (18,438 ft; 5,620 m); erupted 1829; coffee grown on lower slopes, *map* S-298

'Tolkappiyam', Indian literature I-106

Tolkien, J.R.R. (full name John Ronald Reuel Tolkien) (1892–1973), English philologist and author of adult fairy tales T-213
books R-111e, R-112b
folklore F-269

Toll, tax or fee imposed for a privilege granted; common tolls during 19th century in the U.S. were on turnpikes where gates barred passage; tolls are still collected for passage on certain bridges, highways, and canals. *see also in index* Toll road
Panama Canal P-87

Toller, Ernst (1893–1939), German poet, dramatist, social revolutionary; active in experimental drama, had great influence on theater; exiled from Germany in 1933 G-107

Toll road (or turnpike) R-214
Lancaster Turnpike R-215, *pictures* P-175, *map* R-219
Little River Turnpike R-221
Maysville Turnpike, *picture* R-214
New Jersey Turnpike, *picture* R-214
Pennsylvania Turnpike P-170, R-215, *maps* P-184–5

Tolosa, France. *see in index* Toulouse

Tolosa, battle of (1212) S-358

Tol Saut. *see in index* Pol Pot

Tolstoi, Aleksei Konstantinovich, Count (1817–75), Russian author, distant relative of Count Leo Tolstoi; lyric poetry, a historical romance ('Prince Serebryany'), and a historical dramatic trilogy.

Tolstoi, Aleksei Nikolaevich, Count (1882–1945), Russian novelist, distant relative of Count Leo Tolstoi ('The Year 1918'; 'Peter the Great') R-360a, b, 362, *picture* R-360a

Tolstoi, Leo (or Leo Nikolaevich Tolstoi) (1828–1910), Russian writer and social reformer T-213
'Anna Karenina' R-112d
drama D-246
Russian literature R-360, 362
'War and Peace' N-409, R-112d, *picture* R-112f
warfare W-27

Toltec (or Tolteca), people inhabiting the central plateau of Mexico before coming of Aztecs; history bound up with legend and myth but they are generally believed to have reached height of development about 10th century, declining after that with invasions of other peoples
Maya M-236
Mexico M-335
pyramids P-543

Tolú, Colombia, seaport s. of Cartagena situated on the Gulf of Morrosquillo of the Caribbean Sea; shipping center for agricultural and forest products, particularly balsam; pop. 7,954.

Toluca, Mexico, capital of state of México; summer resort; agricultural center; textiles; foods; pop. 77,124
Mexico, *map* M-344
North America, *map* N-351

Toluene (commercial grade often called toluol), colorless liquid hydrocarbon ($C_6H_5CH_3$, methylbenzene)
organic chemistry O-602
petrochemicals P-228

Tom, Mount, hill in w. Massachusetts, n.w. of Holyoke (1214 ft; 370 m), *map* N-191

Tomahawk, U.S. guided missile G-312

Tomahawk, war implement of North American Indians; originally a club with head of bone, flint, or hard stone; later manufactured by white traders using European hatchet form with metal head; in colonial times a symbol of war, giving rise to phrase "bury the hatchet" for ending quarrels.

Tomarctus, prehistoric animal D-211

Tomasi, Giuseppe (1896–1957), prince of Lampedusa; Italian writer I-379

'Tomasso Portiniari', painting by Memling, *picture* A-662

Tomato, fruit *Lycopersicon lycopersicum* of the family Solanaceae T-214
berries B-178
farm machine harvests F-35
fruit F-430
growing conditions G-26
weed W-131

Tomato fruitworm. *see in index* Corn earworm

Tomato worm. *see in index* Sphinx moth

Tomb
ancient Rome R-257, *pictures* R-249, 258, *map* R-250–1
archaeoastronomy's evidence A-729
archaeology A-532
Egypt A-405, P-28, *pictures* E-128
inscription. *see in index* Epitaph
mastabas P-543
pyramids P-541, *pictures* P-542–3
France P-122

Tombaugh, Clyde William (born 1906), U.S. astronomer, born in Streator, Ill.; with Lowell Observatory, 1929–43; taught science at Arizona State College, 1943–45; astronomer with ballistics research laboratories White Sands Missile Range, Las Cruces, N.M., 1946–55; on faculty New Mexico State University, 1955–73, professor 1965–73 P-355

Tombigbee River, rises in n.e. Mississippi, crosses into Alabama w. of Carrollton and flows s. to join the Alabama River; 409 mi (658 km) long, *map* U-58

Town, medieval. *see in index* Middle Ages, *subhead* cities and towns
Town, in United States, political division of a state; in New England, unit of representation; in western states, subdivision of county, as a rule called township. *see also in index* City; Township
New England
elections E-146
Rhode Island R-183
Vermont V-288
'Town, The', work by Faulkner A-360
'Town and the City, The', novel by Kerouac K-229
Town crier, town official who makes proclamations and announces news.
Townes, Charles Hard (born 1915), U.S. physicist, born in Greenville, S.C.; professor of physics Columbia University 1950–61; provost Massachusetts Institute of Technology 1961–66; professor University of California at Berkeley 1967. *see also in index* Nobel Prizewinners, *table*
Townet, in oceanography O-464
Town gas, gas produced by the carbonization of coal
gas G-40
Town government. *see in index* Town
Town house, dwelling, *picture* H-294
Town meeting. *see in index* Town, *subhead* New England
Townsend, Francis Everett (1867–1960), U.S. physician, born in Fairbury, Ill.; author, in 1930s, of Townsend Plan for pensions of $200 a month for unemployed persons over 60.
Townshend, Charles (1725–67), English political leader; chancellor of the exchequer under Pitt; author of Townshend duties R-164
Townshend, Charles Townshend, 2nd **viscount** (1674–1738), English statesman; ambassador at The Hague 1709–11; secretary of state 1714–16, again 1721; devoted later life to agriculture; four-crop rotation plan credited to him.
Townshend duties, taxes levied on North American colonies R-164, U-170
Township
map grids M-118
Towson, Md., community 8 mi (13 km) n. of Baltimore; electric tools; scientific instruments; Goucher College; pop. 51,083, *map* M-183
Towson State College, Baltimore, Md.; founded 1866; arts and sciences, education; graduate studies.
Towton, England, village in Yorkshire, 11 mi (18 km) s.w. of York; Yorkists under Edward IV gained decisive victory over Lancastrians 1461 (Wars of the Roses).
Toxemia of pregnancy. *see in index* Preeclampsia
Toxic material, garbage and refuse disposal G-18
Toxic shock syndrome, infectious disease, *table* D-172
Toxin, poison P-411. *see also in index* Exotoxin
bacterial infections B-14
vaccine D-169, V-250
Toxoid, medicine V-250
immune system I-58
Toy dogs D-197. *see also in index* toy dogs by name
Toye, William (born 1926), Canadian author and children's book editor, born in Toronto; won Canadian Book of the Year for Children Award 1961 for 'The St. Lawrence' and 1971 for 'Cartier Discovers the Saint Lawrence'; coauthor 'A Picture History of Canada'.
Toynbee, Arnold (1852–83), English sociologist and economist, born in London, England; pioneer in social settlement movement S-237
civilization's cycles C-467
Toynbee, Arnold (or Arnold Joseph Toynbee) (1889–1975), English historian T-238
philosophy of history H-174
Toynbee Hall, first social settlement, London, England S-237
Hull House A-40
Toyohashi, Japan, city of s. Honshu on Atsumi Bay 37 mi (60 km) s.e. of Nagoya; textiles; pop. 284,585, *map* J-78
Toyon. *see in index* Christmasberry
Toyotomi Hideyoshi (1536–98), Japanese warrior and statesman; son of peasants, became dictator of Japan as regent (1586) C-368, J-64
Kyoto's rebuilding K-312
Osaka O-609
Tokugawa Ieyasu T-202
Toys T-239. *see also in index* Games; Hobby; Vacation activities
doll D-215
fashionable styles, *picture* F-41
models M-514
ship models S-176b
trains, *picture* R-87
play equipment P-390a, *pictures* P-125, P-387
puppets and marionettes P-537, *picture* P-536. *see also in index* Puppets and marionettes
Russian folk art F-253
spinning top G-327
sports equipment. *see in index* Sports
stilts S-447
vacation activities, *pictures* V-240, V-242
Toy soldiers, models M-516
TPA (Tournament Players Association Tour), in golf G-191
Trabert, Tony (born 1930), U.S. tennis player T-107
Trabzon (or Trebizond, ancient Trapezus), Turkey, seaport on Black Sea; formerly a center of trade between Europe and Persia; capital of empire of Trebizond 1204–1461; pop. 53,039, *maps* A-700, P-212
Trace element, in nutrition
fertilizer F-58
hydroponics H-341
manganese M-96
oceanography O-480
Tracer, in chemistry. *see in index* Radioactive isotope
'Tracer', painting by Rauschenberg P-66, *picture* P-67
Trachea (or windpipe)
human
digestive system, *diagram* D-143
voice V-377
lung system L-336
Tracheophyta, phylum of plants P-371
Tracheotomy, emergency operation in which windpipe is cut and tube inserted to permit breathing when air passage is obstructed.
Trachodon, duckbilled dinosaur, *picture* R-157
Trachoma (or granular conjunctivitis), contagious disease of eyeball covering, eyelid lining; associated with unsanitary conditions; sometimes causes blindness.
Trachymene (also called didiscus, or blue laceflower, or lavender laceflower), annual plant of the parsley family; leaves hairy, divided; globular flower heads blue or white; native to Australia.
Trachyte, finely-textured volcanic rock composed mainly of feldspar or of rock glass; once used as a general term for light-colored lavas and porphyries.
Tracing paper, in mechanical drawing M-255, 262
Track, in mechanics bulldozer B-500
Track (or course made good), in navigation N-68
Track and field T-243, *picture* A-737
world records. *see table* following
Tracker action, mechanism found in an organ W-231
Tracking and Data Relay Satellite System (TDRSS) S-343b
Trackless trolley, streetcar S-489
Tract, of brain B-400, *diagram* B-398
Tract, of feather F-51
Traction, a pulling force exerted on a skeletal structure
fracture treatment F-340
Tractor, farm vehicle
farming A-135, F-26, F-30
Illinois industry, *pictures* I-37
polar exploration, *picture* P-420
Puerto Rico, *picture* P-528
vocations V-371
Tractor, power unit on a truck T-291
Tracy, Alexandre de Prouville, sieur de (1603–70), French soldier, lieutenant general of French territories in North America 1663–67; made successful campaign against the Iroquois 1666; returned to France 1667.
Tracy, Spencer (1900–67), U.S. actor, born in Milwaukee, Wis.; in motion pictures 1930–67; won Academy award for 'Captains Courageous' (1937) and 'Boys' Town' (1938); named best U.S. actor, Cannes Film Festival 1955; 'The Last Hurrah', 'The Old Man and the Sea'
Hepburn H-135
Tracy, Calif., city 55 mi (90 km) e. of San Francisco; boating; dairy products, sugar beets, food packing; railroad shops; incorporated 1910; pop. 18,428.

SOME OFFICIAL WORLD RECORDS IN TRACK AND FIELD*

Event	*Record*	*Champion*	*Year*
100 meters	9.83 sec.	Ben Johnson, Canada	1987
200 meters	19.72 sec.	Pietro Mennea, Italy	1979
400 meters	43.86 sec.	Lee Evans, United States	1968
800 meters	1 min. 41.73 sec.	Sebastian Coe, United Kingdom	1981
1,000 meters	2 min. 12.18 sec.	Sebastian Coe, United Kingdom	1981
1,500 meters	3 min. 29.45 sec.	Said Aouita, Morocco	1985
1 mile	3 min. 46.31 sec.	Steve Cram, United Kingdom	1985
2,000 meters	4 min. 50.81 sec.	Said Aouita, Morocco	1987
3,000 meters	7 min. 32.1 sec.	Henry Rono, Kenya	1978
5,000 meters	12 min. 58.39 sec.	Said Aouita, Morocco	1987
10,000 meters	27 min. 13.81 sec.	Fernando Mamede, Portugal	1984
1 hour	20,944 m. (13.014 mi.)	Jos Hermens, The Netherlands	1976
110-meter hurdles	12.93 sec.	Renaldo Nehemiah, United States	1981
400-meter hurdles	47.02 sec.	Edwin Moses, United States	1983
3,000-meter steeplechase	8 min. 5.4 sec.	Henry Rono, Kenya	1978
400-meter relay	37.83 sec.	United States (Graddy, Brown, Smith, Lewis)	1984
800-meter relay	1 min. 20.26 sec.	United States (Andrews, Sanford, Mullins, Edwards)	1978
1,600-meter relay	2 min. 56.16 sec.	United States (Matthews, Freeman, James, Evans)	1968
20-kilometer walk	1 hr. 18 min. 39.9 sec.	Ernesto Canto, Mexico	1984
High jump	2.41 m. (7 ft. $10\frac{3}{4}$ in.)	Igor Paklin, Soviet Union	1985
Long jump	8.90 m. (29 ft. $2\frac{1}{2}$ in.)	Bob Beamon, United States	1968
Triple jump	17.97 m. (58 ft. $11\frac{1}{2}$ in.)	Willie Banks, United States	1985
Pole vault	6.013 m. (19 ft. $8\frac{1}{2}$ in.)	Sergei Bubka, Soviet Union	1986
Shot put	22.64 m. (74 ft. $3\frac{1}{2}$ in.)	Udo Beyer, East Germany	1986
Discus throw	74.08 m. (243 ft)	Jurgen Schult, East Germany	1986
Javelin throw	85.72 m. (281 ft. 3 in.)	Klaus Tafelmeier, West Germany	1986
Hammer throw	86.74 m. (284 ft. 7 in.)	Yuri Syedikh, Soviet Union	1986
Decathlon	8,847 points	Daley Thompson, United Kingdom	1984

*All track and field world records must be officially approved by the International Amateur Athletic Federation (IAAF). Standards of timing, wind velocity, and other conditions must be met. After all information on records equaling or surpassing current world marks has been collected by an IAAF member, it is submitted to the IAAF for consideration. In 1976 the IAAF voted to eliminate records for events run in yards, except for the mile, and to eliminate hand-timed records for distances up to and including 400 meters.

part of the Italian-Yugoslavian border until 1947 Y-434
Trigon, stringed instrument S-490a
Trigonometry, branch of mathematics T-285
mathematics M-214, 219
Tri-Hi-Y, girl's club Y-425
Triiodothyronine, hormone that controls iodine H-242, *table* H-241
'Trilby', novel by George du Maurier (1895), about artist life in Paris; heroine Trilby, beautiful artist's model, becomes a great singer through hypnotism by Svengali.
Trilling, Lionel (1905–75), U.S. writer, critic, and educator, born in New York City; joined faculty of Columbia University 1931, professor of English 1948–75 (novel: 'The Middle of the Journey'; critical biographies: 'Matthew Arnold', 'E.M. Forster'; essays in criticism: 'The Opposing Self').
Trilling nighthawk (or lesser nighthawk), bird *Chordeiles acutipennis* of the Carpimulgidae family N-314
Trillium, plant genus of lily family Liliaceae; native to North America and e. Asia; bears whorl of 3 leaves; also called **wake-robin** because of early blooming, *picture* P-358
Trilobite, extinct marine arthropod; thrived in Paleozoic Era; fossil remains common; remotely related to modern horseshoe crab P-487
earth E-23, *picture* E-26, *table* E-24
fossil remains, *picture* F-324
prehistoric animals A-459, *picture* A-460
Trilogy, group of three compositions about a single theme
Undset U-4
Trimeter, in poetry P-405
Trimming, submarine adjustment S-497
Trimountaine, Mass. *see in index* Boston
Trinacria, ancient poetic name for Sicily. *see in index* Sicily
Trinidad (or Trinidade), small volcanic island in South Atlantic more than 600 mi (970 km) e. of Brazil, to which it belongs.
Trinidad, Colo., city 78 mi (126 km) s. of Pueblo; in stock-raising, farming, and coal-mining district; trade and shipping center, brick and tile; annual rodeo; pop. 9,663, *map* U-40
Trinidad, Cuba, city 40 mi (60 km) s.e. of Cienfuegos and 5 mi. n. of its port, Casilda; sugar, coffee, tobacco; founded 1514; pop. 27,493
West Indies, *map* W-159
Trinidad, island in West Indies, part of republic of Trinidad and Tobago; 1,864 sq mi (4,827 sq km); pop. 892,317. *see also in index* Trinidad and Tobago
Caribbean literature C-167
Columbus C-594
West Indies W-156, *map* W-159
World War II W-325
Trinidad and Tobago, republic in West Indies; composed of islands Trinidad and Tobago; total area 1,980 sq mi (5,130 sq km); cap. Port of Spain; pop. 1,200,000 T-288
asphalt lake A-702
Commonwealth membership C-602
flag, *picture* F-171
North America, *map* N-351
West Indies W-157, *picture* W-158, *map* W-159
Trinità dei Monti, church, Rome, Italy R-255, *map* R-250, *picture* R-252
Trinitrotoluene (or trinitrotoluol, or TNT), explosive I-211
nuclear weapons N-434
Trinity, doctrine of, in Christianity, belief that there are three persons in God or the divine nature: the Father, the Son, and the Holy Ghost C-400
Trinity College, Burlington, Vt.; Roman Catholic; for women; arts and sciences, education.
Trinity College, Dublin, Ireland. *see in index* Dublin, University of
Trinity College, Hartford, Conn.; founded 1823 by Episcopalians for men of all faiths; now coed; arts and sciences; graduate studies.
Trinity College, Oxford, England O-622, *picture* O-621
Trinity College, Washington, D.C.; Roman Catholic; primarily for women; founded 1897; opened 1900; arts and sciences; graduate studies.
Trinity House, Corporation of, United Kingdom
lighthouse maintenance L-205
Trinity River, in Texas, flows 535 mi (860 km) s.e. entering Trinity Bay, a part of Galveston Bay, 40 mi n. of Galveston; navigable some 40 mi (60 km) from the bay, *map* U-63
Trinity Sunday, Christian church festival, designated the Sunday following Whitsunday; in honor of the Holy Trinity.
Trinity University, San Antonio, Tex.; Presbyterian; founded at Tehuacana 1869; moved to Waxahachie in 1902, to San Antonio in 1942; arts and sciences, education, engineering; graduate school.
Triode (or audion), electron tube R-56
De Forest D-64, I-275, *table* I-273
electronics E-180
Triolet, verse form derived from the French, consisting of eight lines, usually short, and containing only two rhymes; first line is repeated as fourth and seventh lines, second line as eighth line; rhyme scheme, abaaabab; example: Dobson's 'Rose-Leaves'.
Trio sonata, in music, two treble parts and a continuo C-268
Trip, railway car used in mining C-521, *picture* C-524
Tripartite Pact (1940), Europe
Japan J-68
Yamamoto's opposition Y-409
Tripartite Security Treaty. *see in index* Anzus Treaty
Triple (or three-bagger), in baseball B-90
Triple Alliance (also called Central Powers), formed 1882 between Germany, Austria-Hungary, and Italy, *table* T-275
William II W-205
World War I W-302, 305, 319
Italy I I-394
Triple Crown, horse-racing title representing the championship of three races: the Kentucky Derby, the Preakness Stakes, and the Belmont Stakes H-275
Triple Entente, agreement between France, Russia, and United Kingdom, formed 1907; inspired by mutual distrust of Germany, *table* T-275
Edward VII E-108
World War I W-302. *see also in index* Allied Powers
Triple-expansion engine S-442
Triple jump, in track and field T-244
Triplet, in music, *list* M-671
Triplets, multiple birth M-649
Trip lever, in mechanical drawing M-260, *picture* M-261
Triple voile. *see in index* Ninon
Trip odometer, *diagram* S-374
Tripoli (also called Tarabulus), Lebanon, city near coast, 45 mi (70 km) n.e. of Beirut; trade in tobacco, fruit, cotton; taken in 1109 by Crusaders after siege of 5 years; pop. 127,611, *picture* L-11
Tripoli (ancient name Oea), Libya, capital and largest city, seaport on Mediterranean; exports esparto grass, olive oil, petroleum, peanuts, fish, citrus fruits; pop. 858,500 T-289, *map* A-118
Libya L-188
Tripoli-Banghazi highway, Libya L-189
Tripolis (formerly Tripolitza), Greece, city in Peloponnesus; capital of Morea under Turks; taken 1821 by Greek insurgents; destroyed 1825 by Ibrahim Pasha; pop. 20,209.
Tripolitania, region of Libya, former ancient Phoenician, then Roman, colony in North Africa; pop. 1,559,071 T-289, *map* A-118
Tripolitan War (1801–05), conflict between the United States and Tripoli over the U.S. refusal to pay for immunity from attack on merchant vessels in the Mediterranean Sea
marines M-138
Tripolite. *see in index* Diatomite
Trippi, Charles (nickname Charlie) (born 1922), U.S. football player, born in Pittston, Pa; halfback-quarterback Chicago Cardinals 1947–55; later helped coach them L-188
Triptane, hydrocarbon (trimethylbutane) used to increase tremendously the antiknock properties of aviation fuels.
Triptolemus, in Greek mythology, an Eleusinian youth favored by Demeter, from whom he learned agriculture, which he taught humans; said to have invented plow.
'Trip to the Moon, A' (1902), early silent film by Méliès M-618
Triptych, art
Bellini's altarpiece B-156
motion pictures, *picture* M-611
Tripura, state in n.e. India; area 4,032 sq mi (10,433 sq km); cap. Agartala; formerly a princely state of Bengal States in Eastern States agency; pop. 1,556,342, *map* I-83
Triregnum, papal crown, *pictures* P-142a, P-444, R-255
Trireme, ancient galley S-164, *pictures* S-27, S-166, S-213
navy N-81
Tristan da Cunha, British island group in s. Atlantic, between Buenos Aires and Cape of Good Hope; area 81 sq mi (210 sq km); in 1961, volcanic eruptions on the chief island Tristan da Cunha (area 40 sq mi; 105 sq km) forced the evacuation of the more than 250 inhabitants; resettled near Southampton, England; many returned to island 1963; pop. 292. *see also in index* St. Helena
'Tristan und Isolde', opera by Wagner O-568, *list* O-563
Tri-State University, Angola, Ind.; private; founded 1884; liberal arts, business administration, drafting and design, engineering.
'Tristes tropiques', work by Lévi-Strauss L-141
'Tristram', work by Robinson A-355
Tristram of Lyonesse (or Tristan of Lyonesse), hero of Celtic legend, sent to bring Iseult (Isolde), bride of his uncle, king of Cornwall; drinks by mistake a love potion that makes him Iseult's lover
Arthurian legends A-655, R-299a, 300
'Tristram Shandy', (full title 'The Life and Opinions of Tristram Shandy, Gentleman'), novel by Laurence Sterne; has no plot, rambles in whimsical fashion; famous for wit, humor, human characters E-272
Tritheim, Johannes (1462–1516), German humanist, occultist, and abbot, born in Trittenheim, Germany; known as Father of Bibliography; pioneer in cryptography.
Tritium isotope of hydrogen P-380, *diagram* R-65
hydrogen H-341
matter M-224
nuclear energy N-416
nuclear weapons N-433
water W-87
Tritium oxide, superheavy water W-87
Tritoma, plant. *see in index* Kniphofia
Triton, in Greek mythology, son of Poseidon and Amphitrite, personification of roaring waters; blows a twisted seashell to calm or raise waves; tritons usually represented with torso of a man, tail of a dolphin, forefeet of a horse.
'Triton', U.S. submarine S-500, *picture* S-496
Tritonia (also called montbretia, or blazing star), genus of perennial South African plants of the iris family; grows to 3 ft (1 m); leaves narrow, swordlike; flowers brilliant orange, yellow, or scarlet, in erect spikes.
Tritylodon, mammal-like reptiles
fossil F-326
Triumphal arch, *picture* R-253. *see also in index* all entries beginning Arch of
'Triumph of Caesar', paintings by Mantegna M-111
Triumph tulip, flower T-305
Triumvirate, in Roman history
first P-444
second A-496
Trivandrum, India; seaport near the s. tip of India; capital of Kerala state; colleges, observatory, museum, and old temple; pop. 409,627, *maps* A-700, I-86
Trivium, early division of the university E-83
Trobriand Islands, group of coral islands about 100 mi (160 km) off s.e. New Guinea; part of Papua New Guinea; Kiriwini the chief island; pop. 11,728, *map* P-6
family structure F-17
Trocadéro (now known as Palais de Chaillot), building on right bank of Seine in Paris; first built (in Oriental style) for International Exposition 1878; new Trocadéro (modern architecture) replaced the first for 1937 exposition; art museum and theater in new building; an aquarium nearby retains name Trocadéro, *map* P-120
Trochee, metrical foot P-405
Trochilidae, hummingbird family. *see in index* Hummingbird
Trochophore, free swimming ciliate larvae typical of mollusks and worms M-523
Troezen, ancient city of Peloponnesus, Greece; prominent in Persian Wars, later ally of Sparta; ruins 30 mi (50 km) s.e. of Nauplia.
Troglodytes, name given by ancient Greek writers to various groups of cave-dwelling peoples; best known lived along Red Sea. *see also in index* Cave dwellers
Troglodytidae, wren family. *see in index* Wren
Trogon, tropical forest birds of the family Trogonidae, many of them gorgeously plumaged; 8 genera occur in South and Central America; coppery-tailed trogon *Trogon ambiguus*, 12 in. (30 cm) long, male bronze-green and red; female brown and pale geranium red; occurs in s. Arizona and s. Texas and is only trogon found n. of Mexico.
Troika, administrative or ruling body of three persons
United Nations U-25
Troika, sleigh drawn by a team of three horses; formerly a common method of travel in Russia; now troika races are sporting events.
Troilus, in Greek legend, son of Priam, king of Troy; in medieval legend, hero of the love story that forms basis of Shakespeare's tragedy 'Troilus and Cressida' and Chaucer's poem 'Troilus and Criseyde'
Shakespeare S-133
'Troilus and Criseyde', work by Chaucer C-285
Trois-Rivières (English Three Rivers), Que., city on St. Lawrence and St.-Maurice rivers; pop. 55,869, *maps* C-112, N-351, Q-10
Canada C-91
Trojan horse, in modern use, hostile device under friendly and attractive disguise; derived from story of wooden horse in Trojan War, *list* H-249
Homeric legend H-221, *picture* H-223
'Trojans, The' ('Les Troyens'), opera by Berlioz B-172, O-566, *list* O-563
Trojan War T-289. *see also in index* Homeric legend; Troy
Achilles A-18
Aegean civilization A-61
Aeneas A-63
Ajax A-220
archaeologists' proof A-531
Helen of Troy H-117
Paris P-116
warfare W-23, *list* W-14
Troll, Scandinavian fairy F-12, S-472
folklore F-262
Trolley bus (or trackless trolley), transportation
bus designs B-515
Trolley car, transportation S-487
Trolling, fishing technique F-145, *picture* F-139
Trollius (or globeflower), genus of perennials of the buttercup family, found in north temperate zone; leaves dark

green; flowers solitary, golden yellow, rarely white or purple, cuplike; common species is *T. europaeus.*
Trollope, Anthony (1815–82), British writer T-290
literary contribution E-277
Trollope, Frances Milton (1780–1863), British writer
literary contribution T-290
Tromba marina, stringed instrument, *picture* S-491
Trombone (originally called sackbut), wind instrument W-230
opera O-565
orchestra O-576
Tromp, Martin Harpertzoon (1597–1653), Dutch admiral; defeated Portuguese and Spanish fleets 1639; commander in several engagements with English fleet (1652–53) N-130
Trompe l'oeil, in art
interior design I-248, *picture* I-247
Tromso, Norway, far northern village on East Tromsoy island; fish processing; settled in 13th century; pop. 12,363, *map* E-361
'Tron', Walt Disney movie E-173
Trona, a mineral, hydrated sodium bicarbonate
Wyoming W-388
Trondheim (or Trondhjem, ancient Nidaros), Norway, seaport on west coast on Trondheimsfjorden; trade in timber, fish, copper, iron; pop. 134,406, *map* E-361
Trondheimsfjorden, Norway, on w. coast, 80 mi (130 km) long.
Troopers, state police P-430, *picture* P-429
Trooping the Color, traditional British military pageant performed in London by Brigade of Guards as part of sovereign's official birthday celebration; the color of a certain regiment is carried before the troops on Horse Guards Parade where sovereign takes the salute; name also applied to any ceremony of British army in which color is trooped.
Tropical air (T), air mass W-118
Tropical cyclone. *see in index* Hurricane and Typhoon
Tropical deciduous forest (also called monsoon forest, or dry forest), open woodland in tropical areas that have a long dry season followed by a season of heavy rainfall, *picture* E-50
Tropical desert climate (or arid tropical climate)
climate classification C-500
Tropical easterlies, winds
weather W-117
Tropical fish P-246
guppy G-318
zoo Z-465
Tropical fruit F-436
Tropical rain forest. *see in index* Rain forest
Tropical rain forest climate (or rainy tropics)
climate classification C-500
Tropical savanna climate (or wet-and-dry tropics)
climate classification C-500
Tropical steppe G-236
Tropical steppe climate (or semiarid tropical climate)
climate classification C-500
Tropical stingless bee, insect B-126
Tropic bird, any of several species of birds of family Phaethontidae, found in tropical and subtropical seas of both hemispheres.
Tropic of Cancer, line of latitude 23° 27' n. of equator; marks n. boundary of the tropics
equator E-294
latitude and longitude L-82
Tropic of Capricorn, line of latitude 23° 27' s. of equator; marks s. boundary of the tropics
equator E-294
latitude and longitude L-82
Tropics (also called tropical zone, or torrid zone, or low latitudes), region of greatest heat, bordering equator
climates C-500
Jamaica J-17
rainfall R-88
storms S-457, *diagrams* S-458
wind W-221
Tropism, involuntary turning of a cell or organism in response to a stimulus
insects I-222
orienting behavior A-441
plants P-363, P-375, *diagram* P-374
Tropopause, belt of air A-747, *diagram* E-19
Troposphere, region of air A-747
Arctic defenses A-573
earth E-19, *diagram* E-11
weather W-117
Tros, in Greek mythology, king of Phrygia in Asia Minor; gave name to city of Troy, which his son Ilus founded.
Trossachs, wooded glen in Perthshire, Scotland, between Lochs Achray and Katrine; Ben Venue and Ben A'an rise on either side; its beauty has been immortalized by Scott in 'The Lady of the Lake', 'Rob Roy'.
Trot, gait of a horse H-262, *picture* H-266
Trotsky, Leon (1879–1940), Russian revolutionary leader T-290
assassination A-704
Communism C-619
exile S-404
Lenin L-126
Russia R-355
Trotter, William Monroe (1872–1934), U.S. journalist and civil rights leader, born in Boston, Mass.; started *Boston Guardian* in 1901; outspoken critic of conciliatory position of Booker T. Washington B-293
Trotter, horse whose gait is the trot H-277
Troubadour (feminine trouvère), wandering singer R-239
classical music M-667
feudal culture, *picture* F-70
Middle Ages M-388
'Troubadour, The' (Italian 'Il Trouvatore'), opera by Verdi V-282
opera O-567
Troubetzkoy, Paul, Prince (1866–1938), Russian sculptor, born in Italy; influenced by Rodin; noted for portrait busts (of Rodin, Leo Tolstoi, Shaw, Anatole France) and for his many genre statuette groups.
Trough, lowest part of an ocean wave O-487, *diagram* O-488
Trough, in oceanography O-485
Trousers, garment D-265
Trout, food fish T-291
fisheries F-132, *picture* F-131, *table* F-137
Trout Lake, Wisconsin, *picture* W-248
Trout lily. *see in index* Dogtooth violet
Trouvère. *see in index* Troubadour
Trouville, France, fishing and fashionable resort town on English Channel near Deauville; pop. 5,718.
'Trovatore, Il'. *see in index* 'Troubadour, The'
Trowbridge, Alexander Buel (born 1929), U.S. public official, born in Englewood, N.J.; former president Esso Standard Oil Co. of Puerto Rico; assistant secretary of commerce 1965–67, secretary 1967–68.
Trowbridge, John Townsend (1827–1916), U.S. novelist and poet, born in Ogden, N.Y.; excelled in writing boys' stories ('Cudjo's Cave', Jack Hazard series, 'Neighbor Jackwood', novels; 'Darius Green and His Flying Machine', ballad).
Trowbridge, England, market and manufacturing town in Wiltshire; textiles; birthplace of Sir Isaac Pitman, inventor of shorthand method; pop. 17,940.
Troy, Ala., city in s.e., 43 mi (69 km) s.e. of Montgomery; cotton, wood products, textiles, fertilizers; Troy State University; pop. 12,587.
Troy (or Ilium), ancient city in n.w. Asia Minor famous in Greek legend; scene of Trojan War G-264. *see also in index* Trojan War
archaeologists find A-531
Schliemann S-53
fort and fortification F-319
Troy, Mich., residential city in Oakland County 20 mi (30 km) n.w. of Detroit; manufactures include machinery and metal products; pop. 67,102
first laundry L-86
Troy, Ohio, city 18 mi (29 km) n. of Dayton, on Great Miami River; farming; kitchen equipment, lawn furniture, paper products, meats, aircraft products; pop. 19,086.
'Troyens, Les'. *see in index* 'Trojans, The'
Troyes, France, town on Seine River, 90 mi (145 km) s.e. of Paris; hosiery; Renaissance churches; predates Roman era; pop. 74,409, *map* F-372
Hundred Years' War H-325
treaty (1420) C-276, *table* T-275
Troyon, Constant (1810–65), French painter of the Barbizon School; excellent animal painter; many of his landscapes include animals as an integral part ('Goose Girl'; 'Holland Cattle'; 'Return to the Farm'; 'Oxen'; 'Going to Work'; 'On the Road'; 'Going to Market').
Troy State University, Troy, Ala.; founded 1887; arts and sciences, education; graduate study; branches at Dothan (Dothan–Fort Rucker) and Montgomery.
Troy weight, unit of weight W-138, *table* W-140
gold G-177
Truce. *see in index* Armistice
Truce of God, Middle Ages, ban on warfare on certain days M-390
Trucial States (or Trucial Oman). *see in index* United Arab Emirates
Truck and Trucking T-291
cab, *picture* I-270
rental franchises F-373
Sahara, *picture* S-16
transportation T-253, *chart* T-260, *pictures* T-254, T-255, T-263
coal C-525
petroleum P-241d
piggyback transportation, *picture* R-83
types
armored, *picture* E-384
lift truck, *picture* R-73
sanitation, *picture* P-441b
Truckee-Carson Project (also Newlands Project), Nevada, first land reclamation project started by the federal government N-134
Truckee River, stream in California and Nevada that connects Lake Tahoe with Pyramid Lake; about 120 mi (190 km) long N-134
Truck farming, cultivation of garden products T-293. *see also in index* Gardens and gardening
United States, *map* U-54
New Jersey N-196, *picture* N-205
vocation, *picture* V-372
Truck garden, small, multicrop truck farm T-293
'Trud', Soviet newspaper R-332e
Trudeau, Edward Livingston (1848–1915), U.S. physician, born in New York City; afflicted by tuberculosis, went to Adirondack Mts.; founded, in 1884 at Saranac Lake, the Adirondack Cottage Sanatorium, (renamed Trudeau Sanatorium 1915–54), first U.S. institution for open-air treatment of tuberculosis; first president National Tuberculosis Association.
Trudeau, Garry B. (born 1948), U.S. cartoonist and writer, born in New York City; created satirical and controversial 'Doonesbury' comic strip, combining cast of fictional characters with social and political figures; based on 'Bull Tales' strip written while Yale undergraduate; 'Doonesbury' syndicated 1970–83; 1984–; book series 1972–; won 1974 Pulitzer prize for cartooning, first to be awarded to non-editorial page artist; 'Doonesbury' musical comedy 1983; married **Jane Pauley,** co-host of TV's Today show, 1980.
Trudeau, Pierre Elliott (in full Joseph Philippe Pierre Ives Elliott Trudeau) (born 1919), Canadian statesman T-293
Canada C-106
Trueblood, David Elton (born 1900), U.S. theologian and educator, born in Pleasantville, Iowa; professor Stanford University 1936–45, Earlham College 1946–66.
True course, in navigation A-885
'True Grit', novel by Portis R-112, *picture* R-112c
western W-151
True hickory, tree
wood, *table* W-283
True katydid, insect *Pterophylla camellifolia, picture* C-767
True moss, type of moss M-600
True Pure Land Sect (or Jodoshinsu), largest Buddhist sect in Japan B-483
'True Relation of Virginia, A', work by Smith A-340
True sonata, music form C-268
True weasel, a subfamily of the weasel family; includes minks, ferrets, martens, and wolverines W-114
True Word, Buddhist sect. *see in index* Shingon
Truffaut, François (1932–84) French film director; born in Paris; leading figure in the French *nouvelle vague* (New Wave) movement in film ('The 400 Blows'; 'Day for Night') D-155
motion pictures M-623
Truffle, mushroom of the class Ascomycetes F-449, M-665
Trujillo, n. Honduras on the Trujillo Bay; commercial center; exports bananas, coconuts, mohogany, and hides; tourism, fishing, and some industry; pop. 34,835 H-226
Trujillo Molina, Héctor Bienvenido (born 1908), president of Dominican Republic 1952–60; brother of Rafael Leonidas Trujillo Molina; born in San Cristóbal, Dominican Republic; professor American International Academy.
Trujillo Molina, Rafael (or Rafael Leonidas Trujillo) (1891–1961), dictator of Dominican Republic T-293
assassination, *list* A-704
Dominican Republic D-228
Truk Islands, group in e.-central Caroline Islands; about 50 sq mi (130 sq km); in World War II key to easternmost Japanese naval defenses in Pacific; occupied by U.S. in 1945; pop. 24,216, *map* P-6
Trullo, in architecture
folk art F-249
Truly, Richard H. (born 1937), U.S. astronaut candidate, born in Fayette, Miss.; U.S. Navy officer chosen for NASA program 1969.
Truman, Bess Wallace (1885–1982), wife of President Truman T-295, *pictures* T-299, U-196
Truman, Harry S. (1884–1972), 33rd president of the United States T-294
Benton B-165
mural for library, *picture* B-164
conservation policies C-678
Korean War K-295, *chart* K-299
MacArthur M-3
Israel's founding W-143
medals M-272
Missouri M-493, *picture* M-498
Potsdam conference R-356
United States history U-190, 193, *picture* U-196
World War II W-336, *pictures* 354, 357
Trumbauer, Frank (1900–56), U.S. jazz musician B-143
Trumbull, John (1750–1831), U.S. judge and political satirist, born in Watertown, Conn. ('Progress of Dullness', satire on college education) A-345
Trumbull, John (1756–1843), U.S. painter
Revolutionary War paintings
'Battle of Bunker's Hill' P-49–50, *picture* P-48
British surrender at Yorktown, *picture* R-173
Continental Congress, *picture* R-162
Trumbull, Jonathan (1710–85), North American colonial statesman, born in Lebanon, Conn.; provided supplies to Continental Army during Revolutionary War; became governor of Connecticut
Statuary Hall, *table* S-437a
Trumbull, Lyman (1813–96), U.S. jurist and legislator, born in Colchester, Conn.; justice Illinois Supreme Court 1848–54, senator 1855–73;

introduced resolution (1864) that became basis of 13th Amendment to the U.S. Constitution, and introduced the Civil Rights Bill.
Trumbull, Conn., town just n. of Bridgeport; chiefly residential; electronic components; incorporated 1797; pop. 31,394.
Trumpet (originally called cornet), wind instrument W-229
ancient S-193
band B-55
orchestra O-576
Trumpeter swan B-271, D-285, *picture* D-287
Trumpet fish, attenuated scaly fish of the family Aulostomidae, with a long snout bearing feeble jaws; species abundant in the West Indies, Polynesia, and Asia; used as food.
Trumpet honeysuckle, a climbing plant *Lonicera sempervirens* H-228
Trumpet narcissus. *see in index* Daffodil
Trumpet shell. *see in index* Triangular trumpet
Trumpet worm, *picture* W-362
Trump suit, winning value of cards D-159
card games C-160
Truncated prism, in mathematics
geometry G-79, *diagram* G-78
Truncated pyramid, in mathematics
geometry G-79, *diagram* G-78
Trung Sisters, Temple of the temple in Vietnam H-31
Trunk, Yehiel Yeshaia, Polish writer Y-418
Trunk, elongated flexible snout
elephant E-182
elephant seal S-100
Trunk, of tree T-277
Trunkfish, fish of family Ostraciidae, having body enclosed in a bony box leaving only jaws, fins, and tail free; it is slow, brilliantly colored, 4 to 12 in. (10 to 30 cm) long, common in waters of West Indies; members of group with two horns over eyes are known as cowfish.
Trunk hose, garment C-191
dress D-263
Trunnion, axle-like device on cannons
French artillery A-659
Truro, N.S., farming and dairying town on Salmon River, 2 mi (3 km) from head of Cobequid Bay, on Bay of Fundy; textiles, lumber, chemicals; pop. 12,552 N-404, *map* C-112
Truscott, Lucian K. (in full Lucian King Truscott, Jr.) (1895–1965), U.S. general; served in North Africa, Italy, and France during World War II W-340
Truss, in architecture and engineering
bridge B-441
building construction B-369, 493, *picture* B-494
mechanics M-263
Truss fuselage, body of airplane A-183
Trust, industrial, large business combinations, sometimes monopolistic. *see also in index* Government regulation of industry; Monopoly
history T-301
monopoly M-544
Roosevelt R-285
Standard Oil Co. R-230
Trust, in property law T-301, *table* L-93. *see also in index* Trust, industrial
bank and banking B-64
Trustee, person or persons to whom property management is legally entrusted; a country charged with supervising a trust territory T-301. *see also in index* Trust
college board U-205
foundations and charities F-330
Trusteeship Council, organization in the United Nations U-22, *chart* U-21
Trusteeships (or trust territories), non-self-governing territories supervised by United Nations Trusteeship Council; the areas placed under this trusteeship system in its opening year (1946) and in 1947 were formerly League of Nations mandates. For a list of trusteeships, *see table* following
Trustees of Dartmouth College vs. Woodward, case in U.S. constitutional law C-686
Trust Territory of the Pacific Islands. *see in index* Pacific Islands, Trust Territory of the
Truth, Sojourner (original name Isabella Van Wagener) (1797?–1883), U.S. abolitionist and feminist T-302
Truth P-264, 266, *list* P-265
Socrates S-246
Truth serum. *see in index* Pentothal sodium
Truxtun, Thomas (1755–1822), U.S. naval officer, born near Hempstead, N.Y.; privateersman during American Revolution; made captain in new American Navy 1794; captain of *Constellation* during naval war with France.
Tryggvessön, Olaf. *see in index* Olav I
Tryon, William (1729–88), colonial governor of North Carolina (1765–71); governor of New York (1771–78); born in Surrey, England
palace in North Carolina, *picture* N-365
Trypanosomes, various single-celled parasitic animals
Ehrlich E-132
tsetse fly T-302
Trypanosomiasis (or African sleeping sickness), disease transmitted by tsetse flies T-302. *see also in index* Chagas' disease

TRUSTEESHIPS OF THE UNITED NATIONS*

In 1946

1. British Cameroons (Britain)
2. French Cameroons (France)
3. Territory of New Guinea (Australia)
4. Ruanda-Urundi (Belgium)
5. Tanganyika Territory (Britain)
6. British Togoland (Britain)
7. French Togoland (France)
8. Western Samoa (New Zealand)

In 1947

9. The former Japanese mandated islands (United States). This strategic trusteeship includes the Marshall, Caroline, and Mariana islands except Guam. The trusteeship is known officially as Trust Territory of the Pacific Islands.
10. Nauru (Australia, New Zealand, and Britain)

In 1950

11. Italian Somaliland (Italy)

*All these trusteeships, except Trust Territory of the Pacific Islands, have been terminated, beginning 1957.

Trypsin, protein-digesting enzyme, *table* E-290
vaccine, *picture* V-252
Tryptophan, one of the several 'essential' amino acids; linked with the biosynthesis of niacin
Hopkins H-238
Tsamkong, China, port in s.w. Kwangtung Province on South China Sea; the area (325 sq mi; 840 sq km) now the municipality of Tsamkong was leased by China to France in 1898 and was organized as territory of Kwangchowan; returned to China 1945; pop. 220,000.
Ts'ao Chan (1715?–63), Chinese writer; 'Dream of the Red Chamber' C-390
Tsar. *see in index* Czar
Tsaratanana, mountain group in n. part of Madagascar; highest point (9,468 ft; 2,886 m) of island.
Tsaritsyn, Russia, former name of Stalingrad (now Volgograd); defended by Stalin against White Russians S-403, V-384
Tschaikovsky, Peter Ilich. *see in index* Tchaikovsky, Peter Ilich
Tschirnhaus, Ehrenfried Walter, count von (1651–1708), German mathematician and physicist, born in Kieslingswalde, near Görlitz, Germany; made discoveries in porcelain manufacture P-475
Tschumi, Jean (1904–62), Swiss architect; professor of architecture University of Lausanne; won design competition for headquarters of World Health Organization, Geneva, Switzerland, 1960.
Tsetse fly, a bloodsucking insect in tropical regions of Africa T-302
Africa A-96
insects I-224
TSH. *see in index* Thyroid stimulating hormone
Tshombe, Moise (full name Moise-Kapenda Tshombe) (1919–69), Congolese political leader T-302
Tsimlyansk Reservoir, reservoir of Don River, U.S.S.R. D-230, *map* E-361
Tsimshian, a people in British Columbia and s.e. Alaska; live by fishing, especially salmon, and hunting, *map* I-136, *table* I-139
Alaska A-242
Tsin Dynasty. *see in index* Ch'in Dynasty
Tsinghai, China. *see in index* Qinghai
Tsingtao, China. *see in index* Qingdao
Tsinling, mountain range of Shaanxi Province, China; highest peaks exceed 12,000 ft (3,700 m); range influences climate, forms natural defensive barrier.
Tsiolkovsky, Konstantin (1857–1935), Soviet research scientist in rocket and space studies T-302
Soviet history R-332g
space travel S-341d, 348d
Tsitsihar, China, city in Heilongjiang Province on Nonni River 170 mi (270 km) n.w. of Harbin; shipping center; grain and soybean products, machinery; pop. 760,000, *map* A-700
T-slot cutting, machine tool operation T-221
'Tso chuan', classic of Chinese literature C-387
Tsonga, a native people of South Africa found chiefly in Mozambique M-641
T-square, device used in mechanical drawing M-256
Tsubouchi Shoyo (1859–1935), Japanese writer J-82
Tsugaru Strait, Japan, separates islands of Honshu and Hokkaido; links Sea of Japan and Pacific Ocean; width 15 to 25 mi (25 to 40 km), *map* J-78
Tsunami (or seismic sea wave), wave caused by submarine earthquake
earthquakes E-37
Krakatoa's eruption K-302
Oceania O-465
waves O-487
Tsung Dao-lee. *see in index* Lee, Tsung-Dao
Tsunokakushi, Japanese hood J-29
Tsushima (or Tsu Islands), Japan, between Korea Strait and Tsushima Strait n.w. of Kyushu; made up of large island Tsushima, separated into n. and s. portions at high tide, and three small islands; total land area 269 sq mi (697 sq km); rocky and arid; fisheries; chief town Izuhara (21,989); battle of Sea of Japan fought n. of Tsushima 1905; pop. 52,472 R-362
Tsushima, battle of (1905), in the Russo-Japanese War N-91
Tsushima Current, Sea of Japan J-60
Tsuyu (or baiu), June rainy season in Japan J-62
Tswana (or Bechuana), an African people
Botswana B-382
Tsze Hsi. *see in index* Tzu Hsi
Tuamotu Archipelago (or Low Archipelago), 1,300-mi (2,100-km) chain of islands (nearly every one of them an atoll) in s. Pacific Ocean, included in French Polynesia, e. of Society Islands and s. of Marquesas; land area, 330 sq mi (855 sq km); copra, pearl shell; pop. 8,226, *map* P-6
Tuapse, U.S.S.R., port in n.w. Caucasia on Black Sea about 80 mi (130 km) s.e. of Novorossiysk; oil refineries; pop. 36,650, *maps* E-361, R-348
Tuareg, North African Berber people; men wear face veils; trace descent through the mother S-16
nomads, *picture* N-332
Tuat, oasis O-454
Tuatara (or tuatera, or sphenodon), reptile R-153, *picture* R-152
New Zealand N-288
'Tuatha Dè Danann', cycle of Irish folk tales S-473
Tuba, wind instrument W-230
Tubal ligation, means of birth control B-283
Tuba Mosque (or Masjid-i-Tuba), mosque, Karachi, *picture* K-191
Tubb, Ernest (born 1914), U.S. country musician M-678
Tubbs, Tony, boxer, heavyweight champion B-392
Tube, of radio. *see in index* Electron tube, *subhead* radio
Tube foot, in anatomy
invertebrate characteristics I-286
Tuber
legume L-121
potato P-467, *diagram* P-363a
sweet potato S-530
Tubercle bacillus, bacteria
Koch K-267
Tuberculin, used to detect tuberculosis
Koch K-267
Tuberculoid leprosy L-136
Tuberculosis, bacterial disease most frequently affecting lungs; associated with fever and loss of weight; commonly transmitted through the air ("droplet infection") but also from drinking unpasteurized milk obtained from infected cows
cattle C-231
infectious disease D-177, *table* D-172
Koch K-267
Tuberose, plant of amaryllis family; has tuberous root; cultivated for its fragrant white funnel-shaped flowers; used in perfume manufacture.
Tuberous rooted begonia, *picture* F-228
Tubeworm W-363
deep-sea form D-60
Tubiflorae, large order of plants with tubular corollas; includes the morning-glory family, borage family, nightshade family, vervain family, and bignonia family.
Tübingen, West Germany, city on Neckar River, 20 mi (30 km) s. of Stuttgart; seat of famous university, founded in 1477; pop. 54,892, *map* G-134
Tubman, Harriet (formerly Harriet Ross) (1820?–1913), U.S. abolitionist and feminist T-303
book about R-111d
underground railroad B-290, *list* B-299
Tubman, William Vacanarat Shadrach (1895–1971), Liberian political leader, born in Harper; associate justice Liberian Supreme Court 1937–43; president 1944–71 L-147
Tubuai Islands (or Austral Islands), group in s. part of French Polynesia, s. Pacific Ocean, s.e. of Cook Islands; area 115 sq mi (330 sq km); copra, coffee, cattle; pop. 5,079, *map* P-6
Tubule, in kidney K-235
Tubulidentata, order of mammals having teeth with

parallel vertical canals—the aardvarks, *table* M-80
Tucana (or Toucan), constellation, *charts* C-682, S-417
Tuchman, Barbara (born 1912), U.S. historian, born in New York City; worked as writer and correspondent for several publications; author of 'The Lost British Policy', 'The Zimmerman Telegram', 'The Guns of August' (1963 Pulitzer prize novel), 'Stilwell and the American Experience in China, 1911–1945' (1972 Pulitzer prize novel), 'The March of Folly: From Troy to Vietnam' 1984.
Tuck, Friar, vagabond friar in Robin Hood legends; appears in 'Ivanhoe' as the "holy clerk of Copmanhust" R-224, *picture* P-541
Tucker, Albert (born 1914), Australian artist A-802
Tucker, Richard (originally Reuben Ticker) (1913–75), U.S. singer, born in Brooklyn, N.Y.; famed as tenor with Metropolitan Opera Company, New York, N.Y.; cantor; radio, TV, concert, and recording star
  opera, *list* O-570
Tucson, Ariz., 2nd city of state, about 65 mi (105 km) n. of Mexican border, on Santa Cruz River; pop. 365,422 T-304, *map* U-40, *pictures* C-458
  Arizona A-599
  North America, *map* N-351
  Old Tucson, *picture* A-597
  San Xavier del Bac A-602, *picture* A-601
Tucumán, Argentina, capital of province of Tucumán, in n.; commercial and railroad center; university; declaration of independence from Spain signed by Plata provinces 1816; pop. 321,567 S-281, *maps* A-585, S-300
Tucumcari, N.M., city 130 mi (210 km) s.e. of Santa Fe; trade center and shipping point in farming and cattle-raising region; pop. 6,765, *maps* N-229, U-40
Tudor, Antony (1909–87), British choreographer, born in London; created major works for Ballet Rambert and Ballet Theatre B-36
Tudor, Frederic (1783–1864), U.S. merchant, born in Boston, Mass.; called the Ice King from his successful ice-exporting business R-137
Tudor, Owen (born 1461), handsome Welsh border lord, who gave name to house of Tudor T-304
Tudor, Tasha (born 1915), U.S. author and illustrator of children's books, born in Boston, Mass.; married Thomas Leighton McGready; subjects of books painted from life on old New Hampshire farm ('The White Goose'; 'The Dolls' Christmas'; 'A Is for Annabelle'); illustrated 'Mother Goose', R.L. Stevenson's 'A Child's Garden of Verses', J. Ewing's 'Jackanapes', 'The Tasha Tudor Book of Fairy Tales'; won Regina Medal 1971.
Tudor, House of, English royal family T-304
  book about R-111j
  England E-243
  Henry VII H-130
  rulers. *see in index* England, *table* kings and queens
Tudor style, architecture and decoration, transition between Gothic and Renaissance styles in England
  House of Tudor T-304
Tuesday, 3rd day of week; named for Tiw or Tyr, Teutonic god of war
  General Election Day V-387
  Mardi Gras, or Shrove Tuesday. *see in index* Mardi Gras
Tufa (or tuff), volcanic ash thrown out by erupting craters; often forms a soft rock when deposited in sea or saturated with water; used for building; covered Pompeii
  Roman catacombs R-252, R-257
Tuff, volcanic dust M-634
  minerals M-437
Tufted titmouse, bird *Parus bicolor* T-196
Tufting process, in carpet making R-311, 316, *diagram* R-313, *pictures* G-95, R-314
Tufts, James Hayden (1862–1942), U.S. philosopher, born in Monson, Mass.; professor University of Chicago 1892–1930 ('Ethics', with John Dewey; 'Our Democracy').
Tufts University, Medford, Mass.; founded 1852 (opened 1854) by Universalists; nonsectarian; engineering, international law and diplomacy, theology; graduate work; Jackson College, for women; medical and dental schools in Boston.
Tu Fu (712–770), Chinese poet T-305
  Chinese literature C-389
Tugboat (or towboat)
  Panama Canal, *pictures* P-87
  Rhine, *picture* R-177
  ship S-168
  transportation T-254, *chart* T-260, *picture* T-263
Tugela, river of Natal, South Africa; length 300 mi (480 km); over several falls, descends some 2,800 ft (850 m) from source to Indian Ocean
  waterfall, *table* W-98
Tuggurt. *see in index* Touggourt
Tug Hill Plateau, area in New York state N-246
Tugwell, Rexford Guy (1891–1979), U.S. economist, born in Sinclairville, N.Y.; professor economics, Columbia University; undersecretary agriculture 1934–36; coauthor Agricultural Adjustment Act; governor of Puerto Rico 1941–46; professor political science University of Chicago 1946–57 ('Industry's Coming of Age'; 'The Battle for Democracy'; 'Grover Cleveland'; autobiography, 'The Light of Other Days').
Tuileries, former royal palace in Paris on the Seine River; begun about 1564 by Catherine de Médicis; Marie Antoinette and Louis XVI besieged here before they were removed to prison and guillotined; destroyed by mob during Commune of Paris 1871; famous gardens are now a public park, *picture* E-353
  gardens, *map* P-120
Tula, Mexico, town 45 mi (70 km) n. of Mexico City
  Mexico M-335, *map* M-344
Tula, U.S.S.R., manufacturing city 110 mi (180 km) s. of Moscow; maker of firearms since 16th century; famous for samovars and other metalware; Leo Tolstoi born nearby at Yasnaya Polyana; pop. 462,000, *maps* E-361, R-344, 349
Tulagi Island. *see in index* Solomon Islands
Tulane University of Louisiana (formerly Medical College of Louisiana), New Orleans, La.; founded 1834; arts and sciences for men; coeducational in architecture, business administration, engineering, law, medicine, social work; graduate school; Middle American Research Institute; Center for Teacher Education N-231. *see also in index* Newcomb College
Tulare, Calif., city 45 mi (70 km) s.e. of Fresno; cotton and beef raising, dairying, farm machinery, food processing; pop. 22,475.
Tularemia (or rabbit fever), named for Tulare County, California, where it was discovered (1910) by U.S. Public Health Service; infectious disease of wild rabbits, quail, opossums, deer, and other wild game animals; recognized by whitish spots on liver and spleen on 3rd or 4th day of illness; usually transferred to humans by contact of liver or blood with open cut; symptoms similar to those of flu, and ulcerous sore; physicians recommend wearing rubber gloves for cleaning of game, liberal use of soap, water, and disinfectant, thorough cooking
  infectious disease, *table* D-172
  tick T-182
Tulip, a flower of lily family F-223, T-305
  garden, *picture* G-20
  The Netherlands, *picture* N-124
Tulip shell, mollusk shell *Fasciolaria tulipa*, *picture* S-152
Tulip tree (or hickory poplar, or tulip poplar, or white poplar, or whitewood, or yellow poplar), tree *Liriodendron tulipifera* of magnolia family P-446
  Tennessee state tree, *picture* T-90
  tree T-283, *picture* T-279
  wood, *table* W-283
Tulip ware, pottery, *picture* P-475
Tull, Jethro (1674–1741), English farmer and writer, born in Berkshire ('Horse-Hoeing Husbandry, or an Essay on the Principles of Tilling and Vegetation', published 1733).
Tullahoma, Tenn., city 32 mi (52 km) s.e. of Murfreesboro; lumber, sporting goods, whiskey, apparel; Arnold Engineering Development Center and University of Tennessee Space Institute; pop. 15,800.
Tulle, France, picturesque town 75 mi (120 km) s.w. of Clermont-Ferrand; firearms; cathedral dating from 12th century; pop. 17,640, *map* F-372
Tulle, fine net with softer finish than malines; made of silk, cotton, or synthetic fibers; manufacture dates from 18th century; named for Tulle, France L-17, T-139
Tullius, Servius. *see in index* Servius Tullius
Tullus Hostilius (ruled 673–642 BC), legendary third king of Rome R-241
Tulsa (originally called Tulsey Town), Okla., 2nd city of state, in n.e. on Arkansas River; pop. 360,919 T-305
  North America, *map* N-351
  Ohio, *map* U-41
  Oklahoma O-524, *pictures* O-521, 529
Tulsa, University of, Tulsa, Okla.; founded 1894; liberal arts, business administration, music, law, mineral and petroleum engineering; graduate school.
Tului, son of Genghis Khan M-534
Tumblebug. *see in index* Dung beetle
Tumbler, lock L-277
Tumbler pigeon P-324, *picture* P-325
Tumbleweed, any coarse annual weed in which the plant branches into a globular form that in the fall breaks off at the roots and rolls before the wind, dispersing its seeds as it travels; name is given to several species of tumbling plants T-306
  Russian thistle T-171
  seeds S-106
Tumen River, along n.e. boundary of North Korea; flows into Sea of Japan; about 325 mi (525 km) long, *map* A-700
  Korea K-282, *map* K-290
Tumor (or neoplasm), abnormal mass of cells C-811. *see also in index* Cyst; Polyp
  brain B-401
    amnesia A-373
  cancer C-131
  disease D-175
  eye E-390
  growth G-292
  wart W-34
  X rays X-403
Tumor angiogenesis factor (TAF), substance that causes rapid growth of tiny blood vessels C-812, D-176
Tumpline, strap placed across forehead or chest to aid in carrying or hauling heavy loads
  Amazon Basin, *picture* S-277
Tuna (or tunny), fish T-306, *picture* S-352
  Abidjan A-9
  fish F-124, *picture* F-132
  fisheries, *table* F-137
  oceanography O-485
Tunas, fruits from the nopal F-436
Tunbridge Wells, England, municipal borough, 30 mi (50 km) s.e. of London; mineral springs; trade in Tunbridge ware (wood products inlaid with mosaic); pop. 44,930.
Tundra, Arctic plain
  Arctic regions A-572
  Asia R-324, *maps* R-323, 334
  biogeographic biome B-219, *picture* B-217
  climate C-502
    U.S.S.R. R-324, *maps* R-323, 334
  fire hazards F-107
  North America N-336
    Alaska, *map* U-119
    Canada C-75
  oil drilling P-441e
  plants P-363f, *picture* P-363e
  soil S-251
Tundra swan, bird, *picture* D-287
Tung oil. *see in index* China wood oil
Tung nut, nuts N-449
Tungstate mineral, classification M-436
Tungsten (W, or wolfram), heavy metallic element T-307
  electric light E-164
  minerals M-436
  ore, *table* O-600, *map* O-600
  periodic table, *table* P-207, *list* P-208
  steel alloy A-313
Tungsten carbide, chemical compound T-307
Tungsten film (or Type B film), in photography P-286
Tungstic acid, yellow powder formed when sodium tungstate is broken down by hot sulfuric acid; used in textile and plastics manufacture
  tungsten T-307
Tung tree, tropical tree *Aleurites fordii* of spurge family, native to central Asia but cultivated in extreme s. U.S.; grows to 25 ft (8 m); crown spreading; leaves oval, sometimes have 3 lobes, to 5 in. (13 cm) long; flowers white, tinted with red, in loose flat clusters; fruit smooth, 2 to 3 in. (5 to 8 cm) across, yields tung oil, or China wood oil; trees begin to bear nuts when 3 to 6 yrs. old
  nut, *picture* P-377
  oil P-73
Tungus, Ural-Altaic people of eastern Siberia S-189
  classification, *chart* R-26
Tunic, part of the eye E-387
Tunic, garment D-261
Tunica, small genus of annual and perennial plants of the pink family, native to the Mediterranean region; low-growing with wiry stems and narrow, grass-like leaves; flowers small, in clusters similar to members of genus *Dianthus*, pink, lilac, or white; tunic flower or coat flower is *T. saxifraga*, used in rock gardens.
Tunicates, subphylum of marine animals; considered primitive chordates, precursors of the vertebrates, because of the presence of a notochord in the larvae and some adults.
Tuning fork
  timing device S-348c
Tuning fork watch W-79
Tunis, John Roberts (1889–1975), U.S. writer, born in Boston, Mass.; sports stories from unusual angles ('Iron Duke'; 'The Kid from Tompkinsville'; 'All-American'; 'Yea! Wildcats!'; 'Go, Team, Go!'; autobiography, 'A Measure of Independence').
Tunis, Tunisia, capital; pop. 596,654 T-307, *map* A-118
Tunis, breed of sheep S-148
Tunisia (or Tunisie, or Ifriqiyah, or Africa Minor), republic in North Africa, on Mediterranean coast, e. of Algeria; 63,379 sq mi (164,151 sq km); cap. Tunis; pop. 6,966,173 T-308, *map* A-118
  African political unit, *table* A-112
  archery A-539
  flag, *picture* F-171
  history
    Bourguiba B-384
    World War II W-339
      warfare, *list* W-16
  Islamic literature I-367
  national anthem, *table* N-64
  physical geography
    Atlas Mountains A-746
    Sahara S-14, *map* S-15, *picture* S-16
  railroad mileage, *table* R-85
  shelter S-156
  Tunis T-307
Tunnel T-310. *see also in index* Aqueduct; Subway
  Arctic P-420
  water W-92
Tunneling shield, in engineering T-310, *picture* T-311
  Brunel B-469
Tunnell, Emlen (1925–75), U.S. football halfback and coach, born in Bryn Mawr, Pa.; halfback New York Giants 1948–58; Green Bay Packers 1959–61; assistant coach Giants.
Tunney, Gene (originally James Joseph Tunney) (1897–1978), U.S. boxer,

born in New York City; retired from ring 1928; author of 'A Man Must Fight' and 'Arms for Living'; father of **John Varick Tunney** (born 1934), U.S. senator from California 1971–77
heavyweight champion B-391
Tunny, fish. *see in index* Tuna
Tuolumne River, in California, rises at base of Sierra Nevada, flows s.w. to join San Joaquin River 25 mi (40 km) s. of Stockton.
Tupelo, Miss., city 98 mi (158 km) s.e. of Memphis, Tenn.; farming area; garments and textiles, milk products, lighting fixtures, tools, machinery, wood products, furniture, foam rubber, meat processing; Tombigbee State Park nearby; pop. 23,905 M-478
Tupelo, tree T-313
Tupelo gum. *see in index* Water tupelo
Tupi, early group of people living in South America e. of Andes; language survives among peoples of Río de la Plata region.
Tupolev, Andrei Nikolaevich (1888–1972), Soviet engineer; established aerodynamics research center, Moscow, 1918; leading Soviet designer of heavy bombers and turboprop airliners.
Tupou, George, I (or Taufa'ahau), king of Tonga T-215
Tupper, Charles (1821–1915), Canadian statesman T-314
Fathers of Canadian Confederation C-115, *pictures* C-116, C-118
Tupper, Sir Charles Hibbert (1855–1927), Canadian statesman, born in Amherst, Nova Scotia; son of Sir Charles Tupper; British agent in Bering Sea dispute.
Tupper, Martin Farquhar (1810–89), English author, born in London; gained fame for 'Proverbial Philosophy', written in blank verse.
Tupperware, plastics company, *picture* M-146
'Turandot', opera by Puccini P-526d
Turban, head covering H-53
Turban shells S-151
Turbidity current, deep ocean current
earth E-13
oceanography O-486
Turbinate bones (or turbinals), bony projections into nasal cavity supporting the olfactory (smelling) nerves and the mucous membranes; consist in human beings of 3 pairs, superior, middle, and inferior turbinals S-210
Turbine T-315, *diagram* S-438
airplane T-254
first successful design S-442
gas turbine J-106
hydraulics H-339
locomotives R-78
machine M-11
motor and engine M-630
steamship engines S-169
steam turbine S-441, *diagram* S-438
submarines S-497
water turbine W-103
Turbine meter, device that measures rate of flow I-230
Turbit, breed of pigeons P-324
Turbocharger, engine part A-861
Turbofan engine (or bypass engine, or ducted-fan engine, or aft-fan engine)
airplane A-187
jet propulsion J-109, *diagrams* J-107, *picture* J-108
turbine T-316
Turbojet engine (or jet engine), *diagram* U-445
jet propulsion J-106, *diagram* J-107
turbine T-316
Turboprop engine (or prop-jet engine) A-175, 187
jet propulsion J-109, *diagram* J-107
Turbot, flatfish species F-175
Turbulence, departure in a fluid from a smooth flow
earth E-32
Turbulence, in meteorology A-82, A-888
radar finds, *picture* A-830
Turbulent flow, in hydraulics H-339
Turdidae, thrush family
bluebird B-318
Turenne, Henri de la Tour d'Auvergne, vicomte de (1611–75), marshal of France, one of great captains of history whose campaigns Napoleon advised soldiers to "read and reread."
Turgenev, Ivan (1818–83), Russian novelist T-316
drama D-246
Russian literature R-360
Turgor pressure, in cells
osmosis O-610
Turgot, Jacques (full name Anne-Robert-Jacques Turgot, baron de l'Aulne) (1727–81), French economist T-316
French Revolution F-401
Louis XVI L-306
Turia River (or Guadalaviar River), e. Spain; 150 mi (240 km) long; irrigates rich plain around city of Valencia and flows into Mediterranean V-256
Turin (Italian Torino, ancient Augusta Taurinorum), Italy, city; pop. 1,069,013 T-316, *maps* E-361, I-404
Turin, Treaty of (1860), *table* T-275
Turina, Joaquín (1882–1949), Spanish composer, born in Seville; pupil of d'Indy.
Turkana, Lake (or Lake Rudolf), lake, Kenya K-225, *map* A-118
Turkestan (or Turkistan, now called Central Asia), region in Asia between Caspian Sea on west and the Gobi on east T-317
classification, *chart* R-26
horse H-270
rugs R-314, 315
Samarkand S-33
Turkey (officially Republic of Turkey), country of Asia and Europe; 296,185 sq mi (767,115 sq km); cap. Ankara, lying in Asia; pop. 51,400,000 T-318
agriculture
hemp, *picture* R-292
tobacco T-198
arts
literature, *lists* S-469, 480
rug making R-314
Asia, *map* A-700
Balkan states B-25
cities. *see in index* cities listed below and other cities by name
Antalya, *picture* M-396
Istanbul I-375
Izmir I-408
Eastern Orthodox churches E-42
Europe, *map* E-361
history. For pre-13th century *see in index* Asia minor; for history from the 13th century to 1923 *see in index* Ottoman Empire
Balkan wars B-31
Dardanelles D-35
Korean War losses, *table* K-296
Thrace T-175
World War I W-302, 305, 309, 319, *map* W-304
Mount Ararat A-528
national symbols
flag, *picture* F-171
song, *table* N-64
population
classification of people, *chart* R-26
puppets P-536
railroad mileage, *table* R-85
Red Crescent Society R-117
rivers
Tigris River T-184
taxation, *table* T-35
women E-319
Turkey, fowl *Agriocharis ocellata* and *Meleagris galloparo* T-326
bird B-249, *pictures* B-271
domesticated fowl, *picture* A-456
National Turkey Improvement Plan P-482
Turkey cup, sponge S-395
Turkey Run State Park, in Indiana, *picture* I-97
Turkey toilet, sponge S-395
Turkey vulture (sometimes called turkey buzzard), bird V-388, *picture* B-280
Turkic language family
Islamic literature I-364
Turkish checkers, game B-322
Turkish Empire. *see in index* Ottoman Empire
Turkish knot, rug weaving. *see in index* Ghiordes knot
Turkish language, main language of Turkey M-395
Turkish rug R-314
Turkish towel. *see in index* Terry cloth
Turkistan. *see in index* Turkestan
Turkmen, Asian language A-89
Turkmen Soviet Socialist Republic (or Turkmenistan, or Turkmenia), in Asiatic U.S.S.R., e. of Caspian Sea; area 188,420 sq mi (488,005 sq km); cap. Ashkhabad; pop. 3,189,000 T-326, *map* A-700
Turkestan T-317
U.S.S.R. U-15, *maps* R-325, 344, U-14
Turkomen (or Turcomen, or Turkmen), one of a branch of the Turkish people in Turkmen Soviet Socialist Republic, Afghanistan, and Iran; chiefly nomads I-305
Turkestan T-317
Turkmen Soviet Socialist Republic T-327
Turks, a people of s.w. Asia
caliphate C-56
classification, *chart* R-26
Crusades C-786
Hungary H-329
Iraq I-315
West German emigration G-113
migration of people M-402
Turks and Caicos Islands, West Indies; area 166 sq mi (430 sq km); explored by Ponce de León 1512; salt, sponges, lobster; pop. 6,000
Commonwealth membership C-602
North America, *map* N-351
West Indies W-158, *map* W-106
Turk's-cap lily, plant, *picture* F-216
Turku (Swedish Åbo), Finland, Baltic port opposite Aland Islands; oldest city and former capital; shipbuilding; exports timber, dairy products; Swedish University; pop. 124,359, *maps* E-361, S-524
Turle knot, in fishing, *picture* F-143
Turmeric, plant S-379
Turn-and-bank indicator (or rate gyro), airplane instrument A-194, G-328
Turnbull, Julia (1822–87), U.S. ballerina B-35
Turner, Charles Yardley (1850–1918), U.S. landscape and figure painter, born in Baltimore, Md.; known for mural paintings, especially those in courthouses at Youngstown, Ohio, and Baltimore, Md.
Turner, Clyde (nickname Bulldog) (born 1919), U.S. football center, born in Sweetwater, Tex.; center Chicago Bears 1940–52.
Turner, Frederick Jackson (1861–1932), U.S. historian T-327
frontier theories F-424
history writing H-173
Turner, Henry MacNeal (1834–1915), U.S. civil rights leader and African Methodist Episcopal bishop, born in Newberry Court-House, South Carolina; Union chaplain for black American troops in Civil War; fought fierce battle for rights of blacks and poor whites during two terms in Georgia legislature; embittered by 1869 expulsion of blacks from political office, he promoted black nationalist movement, aiding freed slave expedition to Liberia in 1878 B-291
Turner, J.M.W. (full name Joseph Mallord William Turner) (1775–1851), English landscape painter
'Grand Canal, Venice', *picture* P-47
Turner, Joe (born 1911), U.S. blues musician M-679
Turner, John (born 1929), Canadian politician, born in Richmond, England; head of Liberal party in 1984, replacing Trudeau; prime minister June-Sept. 1984 C-106
Turner, Lana (born 1920), U.S. movie actress, born in Wallace, Idaho ('Dr. Jekyll and Mr. Hyde'; 'The Bad and the Beautiful'; 'The Postman Always Rings Twice'; 'Imitation of Life'; 'Madame X').
Turner, Nat (1800–31), U.S. slave leader T-328
black American history B-290
book about R-111j
Turner, Stansfield (born 1923), U.S. naval officer, born in Highland Park, Ill.; U.S. Navy 1946–; commander in chief NATO Forces, Southern Europe 1975–77; director of Central Intelligence Agency 1977–81.
Turner, Tina (original name Anna Mae Bullock) (born 1938), U.S. rock singer and actress, born in Nutbush, Tenn.; noted for energetic performances; recorded and toured with Ike Turner 1959–76, they later married and were divorced; solo album 'Private Dancer' led to major comeback 1984 M-683
Turner's syndrome, genetic disorder G-48
Turning basin, part of a harbor H-35
Turnip, vegetable *Brassica rapa* C-4, *picture* C-3
Turnpike. *see in index* Toll road
Turnstone, shorebird *Arenaria interpres* allied to plover, found in all parts of world; breeds in Arctic, migrates south; pied black and white.
Turntable, on phonograph P-269, *diagram* P-268d
Turnverein, German physical education society founded by Friedrich Ludwig Jahn, early 19th century; spread to United States.
Turpentine, pine sap or oil distilled from it T-328
sap collection, *pictures* U-56
tar T-28
paint P-74
synthetic camphor C-67
Turpin, Ben (1874–1940), U.S. actor, born in New Orleans, La.; vaudeville comedian who portrayed character Happy Hooligan; first slapstick comic in silent films; worked for Keystone Studio 1916–25, *picture* M-620
Turpin, Dick (1706–39), notorious English highwayman, born in Hempstead, Essex, England; legends of his courage and generosity are without foundation; executed as horse thief and murderer.
Turpin, Randy (born 1928), British boxer, *picture* B-388
Turquino, Pico, highest mountain in Cuba; in the Sierra Maestra, near s. coast.
Turquoise, precious stone J-116, *pictures* J-114
bead and beadwork B-114, *picture* B-115
minerals M-435, *picture* M-434
Turret lathe, tool T-220
Turtle T-329. *see also in index* Tortoise
animal life record, *table* E-24
Brazil's wildlife B-414
hibernation H-147
pet care P-247, *picture* P-245
reptile class R-152, *picture* R-155
'Turtle', North American colonial submarine S-495b
Turtle Creek, Pa., town 10 mi (16 km) s.e. of Pittsburgh; coal-mining center; electrical equipment; pop. 6,959, *map* P-184
Turtledove, European dove of genus *Streptopelia;* ringed turtle dove, *Streptopelia risoria,* introduced in North America; mourning dove sometimes called by this name.
Turtlehead. *see in index* Chelone
Turtle Mountains, plateau region in n.w. United States N-373
Turtle ship, historic Korean armored vessel K-284, *picture* K-288
Tuscaloosa, Ala., city on Black Warrior River about 50 mi (80 km) s.w. of Birmingham; cotton, corn, lumber, paper, rubber products, soil pipe, chemicals, coke; U.S. Veterans Hospital; two state mental hospitals; University of Alabama; Stillman College; was state capital 1826–46; pop. 75,143, *map* U-41
Tuscany (Italian Toscana), region in w. Italy, in valley of Arno corresponding roughly to ancient Etruria; area 8,876 sq mi (22,989 sq km); fertile, rich in minerals; cap. Florence; chief port Leghorn; pop. 3,286,160 I-327, *map* I-338, *picture* I-382. *see also in index* Florence
Italian language I-384
volcanic steam power V-383
Tuscarora, Sixth Nation of Iroquois; originally in Neuse River region of e. North Carolina
Iroquois Confederacy I-142, *table* I-138
North Carolina N-356

Tusculum, ancient city of Latium 15 mi (25 km) s.e. of Rome, Italy, near modern Frascati, a resort town; favorite residence of Cicero and other Romans.

Tusculum College, Greeneville, Tenn.; Presbyterian affiliation; established 1794; arts and sciences, business administration, education.

Tusi, at- (1201–74), Persian mathematician, *picture* M-213

Tusitala. *see in index* Stevenson, Robert Louis

Tusk, elongated tooth
  elephant E-183
  ivory I-406
  mammoth and mastodon M-81

Tuskegee, Ala., city in cotton and livestock area, 40 mi (60 km) e. of Montgomery; Tuskegee University nearby; veterans' hospital; pop. 11,028.

Tuskegee University (formerly Tuskegee Institute), Tuskegee, Ala.; founded 1881 by Booker T. Washington; arts and sciences, agriculture, education, engineering, home economics and food administration, mechanical industries, nursing, physical education, veterinary medicine; graduate school A-227
  Carver C-193

Tusk shell, mollusk M-525

Tussah silk S-201

Tussaud, Marie (1760–1850), wax modeler, born in Bern, Switzerland; first fame in Paris modeling leaders and victims of Revolution; established Madame Tussaud's waxworks in London 1802; later added Chamber of Horrors.

Tussock moth, insect, *pictures* C-220, I-215

Tustin, Calif., city 3 mi (5 km) s.e. of Santa Ana; Marine Corps Air Facility; incorporated 1927; pop. 32,073.

Tutankhamen (originally Tutankhaten) (ruled 1361–52 BC), boy-king of Egypt T-331
  ancient Egypt E-126, T-162
    Ikhnaton I-32
    tomb A-532
      gloves G-169
      mask, *picture* A-531
      perfume P-203

Tuthill, Richard Stanley (1841–1920), U.S. judge
  juvenile courts J-162

Tuthmosis III. *see in index* Thutmose III

Tutsi (or Watusi), a people of Africa
  Rwanda R-366a

Tuttlingen, West Germany, town on Danube River 60 mi (100 km) s.w. of Stuttgart; surgical tools; victory of Austrians and Bavarians over French 1643 (Thirty Years' War); pop. 26,353, *map* G-134

Tutu, Desmond (born 1931), South African Anglican bishop and outspoken social activist, born in Klerksdorp, Transvaal province, South Africa; became South Africa's first black Anglican dean 1975; appointed bishop of Lesotho 1976; general secretary of South African Council of Churches 1978–84; appointed first black Anglican bishop of Johannesburg 1984; winner Nobel Peace Prize 1984; appointed archbishop of Cape Town and head of the Anglican Church in southern Africa 1986. *see also in index* Nobel Prizewinners, *table*

Tutu, ballet costume B-35

Tutuila, largest island of American Samoa; 52 sq mi (135 sq km); exports copra; harbor at Pago Pago; pop. 25,548 S-34, *map* P-6

Tutuola, Amos (born 1920), Nigerian writer, born in Abeokuta; style influenced by oral tradition of myth and folktale and characterized by ungrammatical English A-123

Tuvalu (formerly Ellice Islands), nation made up of small coral islands in Pacific, n. of Fiji; 9¼ sq mi (24 sq km); cap. Funafuti; under British protection 1892–1978; included in Gilbert and Ellice Islands 1915–75; became separate colony 1975, self-governing since 1977; pop. 5,000 T-331
  Commonwealth membership C-602
  flag, *picture* F-171
  Pacific Ocean, *map* P-6
  people P-8
  United Kingdom E-259

Tuve, Merle Antony (born 1901), U.S. physicist, born in Canton, S.D.; studies of atmosphere helped develop radar; chief physicist (1938–46), director department of terrestrial magnetism (1946–66), Carnegie Institution.

Tuxpan (in full Tuxpan de Rodríguez Caño), Mexico, maritime city on Tuxpan River and linked with Gulf of Mexico; 145 mi (235 km) n.w. of Veracruz; export center; pop. 33,901
  Mexico, *map* M-344

TVA. *see in index* Tennessee Valley Authority

Tver, U.S.S.R.. *see in index* Kalinin

'TV Guide', magazine M-34

Twachtman, John Henry (1853–1902), U.S. landscape painter, born in Cincinnati, Ohio; impressionist; luminosity and subtle atmospheric effects.

Twain, Mark (pen name of Samuel Langhorne Clemens) (1835–1910), U.S. humorist and novelist T-331. *see also in index* 'Huckleberry Finn, The Adventures of'; 'Tom Sawyer, The Adventures of'
  American literature A-351
  boyhood home in Missouri, *picture* M-498
  creative writing W-378
  Grant G-219
  Hall of Fame, *table* H-16
  satire N-412
  'The Celebrated Jumping Frog of Calaveras County', *picture* S-184
  'The Prince and the Pauper' R-111e
  U.S.S.R. R-332f
  western W-151

Tweed, Boss (in full William Marcy Tweed) (1823–78), U.S. political leader T-332
  Gould G-198
  Nast N-21
  New York City N-279
  Tammany Hall T-18

Tweed, river, rises in Peeblesshire, s. Scotland, flows e. 97 mi (156 km) to Berwick; gives name to cloth S-67
  Tammany Hall T-18
  Tweed T-333

Tweed, woolen fabric W-288

Tweedsmuir, Lord. *see in index* Buchan, John

Tweedsmuir Provincial Park, British Columbia, in Coast Mts. w. of Prince George; 5,400 sq mi (14,000 sq km); established 1936.

Tweezers, tool, *picture* P-271

Twelfth Day. *see in index* Epiphany

'Twelfth Night; or, What You Will', comedy by Shakespeare, dealing with complications that arise when the shipwrecked Viola disguises herself as a boy, becomes the page of Duke Orsino, and is commissioned to win the Countess Olivia for him; subplot concerns practical joke played on Malvolio, Olivia's steward, by Sir Toby Belch, Sir Andrew Aguecheek, and Maria
  Shakespeare S-133, S-139

Twelve Apostles. *see in index* Apostles Island

Twelve labors of Hercules, in classical mythology H-138

Twelve Tables, Law of the, first written Roman law (451–450 BC) based on old custom; engraved on brass or wooden tablets, placed in Forum.

Twelve-tone system, in music S-54
  Boulez B-383
  classical music M-675
  scale M-692

'Twenty-One Balloons, The', children's book by Du Bois R-111

Twenty Questions, game G-13
  charade form C-271
  information theory I-203
  word games W-293

26th of July Movement, The, Castro's organization C-200

'Twenty Thousand Leagues Under the Sea', novel by Jules Verne (1870); highly imaginative and at time of its writing seemingly impossible, but convincingly told, story of adventures in a seagoing vessel similar to the modern submarine R-111e
  frontiers F-427

'Twice Told Tales', work by Hawthorne H-74

Twickenham, England, residential district situated on the Thames in s.w. Greater London; residence of Alexander Pope, Horace Walpole, and Louis Philippe.

'Twilight of the Gods, The' (German 'Die Götterdämmerung'), fourth opera in Wagner's series 'The Ring of the Nibelungs' ('Der Ring des Nibelungen') O-568. *see also in index* Ragnarök

Twilight sleep, semiconscious condition produced by scopolamine and other drugs; sometimes rendered during childbirth to reduce pain.

Twill, fabric in which the weft is carried over one and under two or more warp threads creating diagonal pattern; term refers to a variety of goods made of different fibers T-138

Twinberry. *see in index* Partridgeberry

Twin Cities, term popularly applied to St. Paul and Minneapolis, Minn. *see in index* Minneapolis; St. Paul

Twine. *see in index* Rope and twine

Twin Falls, Idaho, city in s., near Snake River, about 115 mi (185 km) s.e. of Boise; processing and shipping of farm products; beet sugar, beans, garden seeds, and potatoes; trout farming; Shoshone Falls nearby; pop. 26,209 I-18, *maps* I-30

Twinflower. *see in index* Linnaea

Twining, Nathan Farragut (1897–1982), U.S. Air Force general, born in Monroe, Wis.; became an infantry officer 1918, transferred to aviation 1924; in World War II commanded 13th Air Force in s. Pacific and 15th Air Force in Italy; became 4-star general 1950; vice-chief of staff of Air Force 1950–53, chief of staff of Air Force 1953–57; chairman Joint Chiefs of Staff 1957–60.

Twining
  basketry construction B-103

Twinleaf, perennial wildflower of barberry family; 12–18 in. (30–46 cm) high; leaves spring from root, are long-stalked, and part into two rounded leaflets; blossom white, about 1 in. (2.5 cm) across, with 8 flat, oblong petals; April–May, chiefly in n. states, *picture* F-232

Twin-lens reflex, in camera P-282

Twins, multiple birth M-649
  tissue compatibility S-519c

Twins, constellation. *see in index* Gemini

Twinspur. *see in index* Diascia

Twister. *see in index* Tornado

'Two Cultures and the Scientific Revolution, The', work by Snow E-282

Two-cycle engine I-252

2,4-D, weed killer P-369

'Two Gentlemen of Verona', comedy by Shakespeare concerning two friends, Valentine, who loves Silvia, and Proteus, sweetheart of Julia, who pursues Silvia to forest, where all four meet and make up
  Shakespeare S-133, S-139

'Two Little Circus Girls', painting by Renoir P-23, *picture* P-22

'Two Lovely Beasts and Other Stories', work by O'Flaherty I-328

Two-part code, code system C-419

Two Rivers, Wis., city on Lake Michigan 6 mi (10 km) n.e. of Manitowoc; commercial fisheries; aluminum products, bubble bath, electrical equipment, furniture, marine engines; pop. 13,354.

Two Sicilies, kingdom formed by union of Sicily and Naples (1130) and at times other parts of s. Italy
  House of Bourbon B-384

Two star theory, theory on the formation of earth E-34

'Two Trinities, The', work by Murillo, *picture* M-657

'Two Years Before the Mast', classic sea story by Richard Henry Dana, Jr. (1840), describing his voyage as a common seaman from Boston, Mass., around Cape Horn, to California and back.

Tyburn, chief place of execution in London, England, prior to 1783; near n.e. corner of Hyde Park; named for small tributary of Thames River.

Tycho Brahe. *see in index* Brahe

Tydings-McDuffie Act (1934), United States P-261

Tyee salmon (or Chinook salmon, or king salmon) S-28

Tygart Dam, West Virginia, on Tygart Valley River W-165

Tygart Valley River (formerly Tygart River), West Virginia, 160 mi (260 km) long, rises in Pocahontas County, flows n. to Fairmont W-165

Tyler, John (1790–1862), 10th president of the United States T-333
  Harrison H-50
  Virginia, *picture* V-342

Tyler, Julia Gardiner (1820–89), second wife of President Tyler T-335

Tyler, Letitia Christian (1790–1842), first wife of President Tyler T-334

Tyler, Moses Coit (1835–1900), U.S. literary historian, educator; born in Griswold, Conn.; professor at Cornell University and University of Michigan; broad scholarship ('History of American Literature During the Colonial Time').

Tyler, Ralph Winfred (born 1902), U.S. educator, born in Chicago, Ill.; professor of education University of Chicago after 1938, chairman of department 1938–48, dean division of social sciences 1948–53; director Center for Advanced Study in Behavioral Sciences (Ford Foundation) 1953–67.

Tyler, Royall (1757–1826), U.S. jurist, novelist, and playwright; born in Boston, Mass. ('The Contrast'; 'The Algerine Captive').

Tyler, Wat (or Walter Tyler) (died 1381), leader of Peasants' Revolt in England
  Richard II R-202

Tyler, Tex., city 95 mi (150 km) s.e. of Dallas; petroleum center; livestock and farm products, rose industry; cast-iron soil pipe, heating equipment; medical centers; pop. 70,508, *map* U-41

Tylor, Sir Edward Burnett (1832–1917), English anthropologist noted for Mexican research ('Primitive Culture'; 'Natural History of Religion')
  cultural anthropology A-484
    animism studies A-465
  Frazer F-389

Tympanic membrane. *see in index* Eardrum

Tyndale, William (1492?–1536), English clergyman and biblical scholar, born in Gloucestershire, England
  New Testament translation E-267

Tyndall, John (1820–93), British physicist, born in Leighlinbridge, near Carlow, Ireland; superintendent Royal Institution 1867–87; made important studies of motion of glaciers; his lectures and writings did much to popularize science.

Tyne, river of n. England, rising in Northumberland Hills, flowing e. through coal-mining and manufacturing region into North Sea.

Tynemouth, England, seaport and summer resort in Northumberland at mouth of River Tyne; export trade in coal and coke; fisheries, shipyards; ruins of 7th-century priory; pop. 72,390.

Type, in printing T-336. *see also in index* Printing
  bookmaking history B-346, *picture* B-349
  Gutenberg G-319
  newspapers N-239
  printing P-499, *picture* P-500

Type-A behavior, in psychology S-488

Type A film, in photography P-286

Type-A hepatitis (formerly called infectious hepatitis), liver disease H-134

Type-B behavior, in psychology S-488

Type B film (or tungsten film), in photography P-286

Type-B hepatitis (formerly called serum hepatitis), liver disease H-134

Type-C behavior, in psychology S-488

'Typee', work by Melville A-349

Typesetting T-339
by hand P-499, *picture* P-500
modern book production B-356
newspaper printing N-239
type and typography T-336

Typewriter T-342
invention I-274, *table* I-273
office equipment O-495
Okinawa, *picture* P-19
talking typewriter, *picture* R-103a
word processing W-293

Typhoid, cat (or cat distemper, or panleucopenia, or viral enteritis), most widespread and serious infectious disease of cats C-210

Typhoid fever, bacterial disease
infectious disease, *table* D-172
vaccine V-250

Typhoon, Asian name for tropical cyclone. *see also in index* Hurricane
China C-339
earth E-29
storms S-457
weather W-121

Typhus fever P-114
vaccine V-251

Typography T-336. *see also in index* Book and bookmaking; Printing; Type
newspaper publishing N-239

Typology, in archaeology A-531

Tyr (old English name Tiw), Nordic god of battles; lost his hand in struggle with the wolf Fenris; gave name to Tuesday M-703

Tyrannicide, killing a dictator or tyrant A-703

Tyrannosaurus, huge prehistoric reptile R-156
earth E-26

Tyranny, form of government G-198. *see also in index* Dictatorship
Greek city-states G-265

Tyrconnel, earl of. *see in index* O'Donnell family

Tyre, famous city of ancient Phoenicia on Mediterranean coast; modern Sur, Lebanon P-267, *map* P-212. *see also in index* Sur
Middle Ages, *picture* M-385

Tyrian purple, dye obtained from shellfish P-267

Tyrol. *see in index* Tirol

Tyrone, Earl of. *see in index* O'Neill family

Tyrone, inland county in Northern Ireland; land area 1,218 sq mi (3,155 sq km); coal mining; quarries; agriculture; pop. 136,040.

Tyrone Guthrie Theatre, Minneapolis, Minn. M-438, *picture* M-451

Tyrrell, James Williams (1863–1945), Canadian civil engineer, brother of Joseph Burr Tyrrell; participated in exploration and surveying expeditions to Hudson Bay and Canadian northwest ('Across the Sub-Arctics of Canada').

Tyrrell, Joseph Burr (1858–1957), Canadian engineer, explorer, and geologist; born in Weston, Ont.; brother of James Williams Tyrrell, with G.M. Dawson in Canadian Rockies explorations; conducted many exploring expeditions in n. and w. Canada; prolific writer and editor.

Tyrrhenians. *see in index* Etruscans

Tyrrhenian Sea (or Etruscan Sea), between west coast of Italy, and the islands of Sardinia and Corsica, *maps* E-361, I-404
Mediterranean Sea M-286

Tyrtaeus (7th century BC), Greek martial poet; legend says, a lame schoolmaster derisively sent by Athenians to Sparta in response to request for a general in 2nd Messenian War; his warlike songs inspired them to victory.

Tyson, Mike (born 1966), U.S. boxer, born in Brooklyn, N.Y.; youngest to win a heavyweight title; turned professional 1985; undefeated in climb toward concurrent heavyweight championships (WBC 1986–, WBA 1987–, IBF 1987–).

Tyumen', U.S.S.R., city on Tura River in w. Siberia 180 mi (290 km) e. of Sverdlovsk; shipbuilding, lumber products, woolen and felt goods, food processing; founded 1585; pop. 269,000, *maps* A-700, R-344

Tyuratam, U.S.S.R. S-342b

Tyutchev, Fedor Ivanovich (1803–73), celebrated Russian lyric poet and diplomat, born near Orel R-360

'Tzeno Ureno', work by Ashkenazi Y-417

Tz'u, Chinese verse style C-389

Tz'u-hsi (1835–1908), the Great Empress Dowager of China T-344
Boxer Rebellion B-387
China C-370

NO
U
TURN

The letter U

is a descendant of the letter V, which is discussed later in this volume. Relatives of U are F, W, and Y. The original forms of the sign in the Egyptian hieroglyphic, Phoenician, and Greek writings are shown in the illustrations numbered (1), (2), and (3) respectively.

For a time the Romans used one sign (4) for three sounds, namely "u," "v," and "w." For example, they wrote the name "Julius" as IVLIVS.

In late Roman times Latin scribes made the capital letter as V but rounded the small letter (5). People of the Middle Ages chose the pointed form for the consonantal "v" and the rounded form for the vocalic "u." To make the change complete, they added small "v" and capital U to their writing (6). This distinction of the four signs passed into English writing unchanged. The English small "u" is a copy of the capital, except that in handwriting it is connected to adjoining letters.

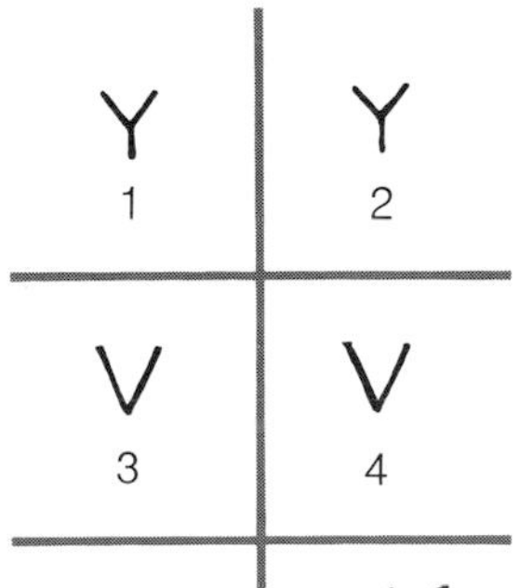
Y
1
Y
2
V
3
V
4
Vu
5
vU
6

U2, Irish rock group formed in Dublin 1976; music known for social conscience and religious overtones; performed in Live Aid (1985) and Amnesty International (1986) concerts; albums include 'Boy', 'War', and 'The Joshua Tree' M-683

U-2, U.S. observation plane E-142

U-235, U-238, U-239. *see in index* Uranium

Uakari, monkey A-504

UAW. *see in index* International Union, United Automobile, Aircraft & Agricultural Implement Workers of America

Ubangi River (French Oubangui), tributary of the Congo River U-1, C-645, *map* A-118
- Congo River C-647

Ubangi-Shari. *see in index* Central African Republic

Uber Cup, in badminton competition B-17

Ubico, Jorge (1878–1946), president of Guatemala 1931–44; made reputation as soldier and governor of various provinces; resigned presidency due to national strike.

U-boat (or Unterseeboot), popular name for German submarines during World War I S-495b

Ucayali River, river in Peru, one of main headstreams of Amazon; flows n. 1,000 mi (1,600 km) to join Marañon River, *maps* P-224, S-298

Uccello, Paolo (nickname of Paolo di Dono) (1397–1475), Italian portrait and fresco painter P-33

Uchatius, Franz von, Austrian inventor; developer of early motion picture projector M-615

'Ud, stringed instrument S-490a

Udaipur, former Rajputana princely state in India, now part of Rajasthan state; maharaja's palace dates from about 1570, *map* I-86

Udall, Nicholas (1505–56), English schoolmaster, author of earliest extant English comedy, 'Ralph Roister Doister'.

Udall, Stewart Lee (born 1920), U.S. public official and lawyer, born in St. Johns, Ariz.; U.S. congressman 1955–60; U.S. secretary of the interior 1961–69; chairman of conservation consulting firm 1969–; author of 'The Quiet Crisis' and '1976—Agenda for Tomorrow'.

Udasis, Sikh monastic order M-542

Udine, Italy, capital of Friuli-Venetia Julia Region, 63 mi (101 km) n.e. of Venice; makes silk, velvet; trades in flax and hemp; military base 1915–17; held by Austrians 1917; pop. 86,188, *map* I-404

Udjung Pandang (or Makassar, or Macassar), seaport and largest city of Celebes, Indonesia, on w. coast of s. peninsula of island; source of macassar oil, from seeds of the kusam tree *Schleichera trijuga*, so widely used as hair ointment in the 19th century that tidies to protect chair backs are called antimacassars; pop. 497,000, *maps* A-700, I-166

Udones, footwear worn by the Romans H-278

Ueberroth, Peter V. (born 1937), U.S. commissioner of baseball, born in Evanston, Ill.; founded travel agency, First Travel Corp., 1963; president of Los Angeles Olympic Organizing Committee 1979–84; elected baseball commissioner 1984–89; instituted changes in by-laws of position.

Uele River (or Welle River), one of the headstreams of the Ubangi River; flows through Zaire in w. Africa, navigable for long distances U-1, *map* A-118

Ueno Park, park in Tokyo, Japan T-207, *picture* T-210

Ufa, U.S.S.R., city 715 mi (1,150 km) e. of Moscow; capital of Bashkir Republic; river port, mining; airplanes, cables, typewriters, clothing, leather goods, food processing, clay refactory; Palace of Labor and Art, monument to Lenin; pop. 773,000, *maps* E-361, R-349

Uffizi Palace, palace in Florence, Italy (erected 1560–76); gallery famed for collection of Florentine Renaissance paintings F-190, *picture* F-192
- gallery M-661, 663
  - Michelangelo's 'The Holy Family', *picture* M-352

Uganda, country in e. Africa n. of Lake Victoria; 93,981 sq mi (243,410 sq km), including water; cap. Kampala; pop. 14,716,100 U-1
- Africa, *map* A-118, *table* A-112
- Amin A-370
- Commonwealth membership C-602
- flag, *picture* F-171
- Kampala K-167
- Lake Victoria V-310
- mountains U-366a
- Obote O-455
- railroad mileage, *table* R-85
- terrorism T-114
- white rhinoceros R-178

Ugo of Segni. *see in index* Gregory IX

Uhland, Johann Ludwig (1787–1862), German lyric poet, literary historian, and philologist; ballads ('The Luck of Edenhall').

UHT (ultra-high temperature method), process used in pasteurization of milk and cream D-4

Uinta Mountains, range of n.e. Utah U-216, *maps* U-217, 232, U-80

Uintatherium, a prehistoric mammal, *picture* P-490

Uitlanders (or outlanders), Boer name for foreign residents in South Africa S-267

Uiyudang (or Lady Kim), Korean writer K-294

Ujiji, Tanzania, former town, now part of Kigoma-Ujiji; in 1871 Stanley found Livingstone here S-411. *see also in index* Kigoma-Ujiji

'Ujishūi monogatari', Japanese anthology J-81

Ujjain, India, historic city of Gwalior (now in Madhya Pradesh state) on Sipra River; opium trade; one of 7 sacred cities of Hindus; pop. 209,118, *map* I-86

Ujvidek, Yugoslavia. *see in index* Novi Sad

Ukai Dam, dam in India, on Tapti River. *see in index* Dam, *table*

'Ukigumo' (or 'The Drifting Cloud'), novel by Shimei Futabatei J-82

Ukiyo-e, Japanese art style J-51

Ukrainian Soviet Socialist Republic (commonly known as the Ukraine), U.S.S.R.; area 233,100 sq mi (601,010 sq km); cap. Kiev; pop. 50,681,000 U-2, U-15, *maps* U-14, R-325, 344, 349
- cities. *see also in index* names of cities
  - Khar'kov K-230
  - Kiev K-236
- famine (1932) R-355
- folktales, *list* S-480
- people R-325, S-215

Ukrainian Soviet Socialist Republic Academy of Sciences, in Kiev K-237

Ukulele, small guitar-shaped musical instrument; used by Hawaiians; strummed; has four strings.

Ulaanbaatar (formerly Urga), Mongolian People's Republic, capital; pop. 488,200 U-3, *map* R-322
- Gandan Tekechiling monastery, *pictures* M-541, 543
- Mongolia M-535

'Ulalume', poem by Poe A-348

Ulanhot, China, city of Inner Mongolian Autonomous Region; pop. 51,400.

Ulanova, Galina (Sergeyevna) (born 1910), Soviet ballerina, born in St. Petersburg, now Leningrad; prima ballerina Bolshoi Theater, Moscow, 1944–61; appeared in United States 1959 ('Giselle'; 'Swan Lake'; 'Romeo and Juliet').

Ulan-Ude (formerly Verkhneudinsk), U.S.S.R., city in s.-central Siberia at junction of Uda and Selenga rivers e. of Lake Baykal; on Trans-Siberian Railroad; builds locomotives and railway cars; pop. 254,000, *maps* A-700, R-345

Ulbricht, Walter (1893–1973), East German political leader, born in Leipzig; in German Communist party after 1919; deputy premier of East Germany 1949–60, chairman Council of State 1960–73 G-127, *picture* G-128

Ulcer, a break in continuity of skin or mucous membrane; caused by death of large numbers of tissue cells; may result from injury, infection, or inadequate blood supply; peptic ulcer affects mucous lining of stomach or duodenum, causing abdominal pain and sometimes severe bleeding; varicose ulcer may form on skin of legs of person with varicose veins
- antiseptic treatment A-495
- therapy T-165

Ulfilas (311?–382?), bishop and missionary to the Goths who reputedly created the Gothic alphabet and wrote the earliest translation of the Bible into a Germanic language G-197

Ulloa, Antonio de (1716–95), Spanish mathematician and traveler; in 1748 identified platinum as an element N-233

Ulloa, Francisco de (died 1540?), Spanish conquistador sent by Cortez to explore the Gulf of California in 1539; established Lower California as a peninsula C-586

Ulm, West Germany, city and river port on Danube 43 mi (69 km) w. of Augsburg; varied manufactures; beautiful Gothic cathedral; pop. 92,943, *map* G-134

Ulmaceae. *see in index* Elm family

Ulna, inner bone of the forearm S-210

Ulnar nerve, nerve extending from the brachial plexus in the neck to various muscles of the forearm and fingers.

Ulothrix, plant, *picture* L-267

Ulsan, South Korea, seaport town near s.e. coast 33 mi (53 km) n.e. of Pusan; in industrial area; pop. 159,340, *map* K-290

Ulster, a former province of Ireland in n.e. corner of island; consisted of 9 counties; 6 of these now form Northern Ireland, while 3 form Ulster Province (area 3,393 sq mi [10,342 sq km]; pop. 208,303) in Republic of Ireland; name Ulster often used for Northern Ireland, *map* I-283. *see also in index* Ireland, Republic of; Ireland, Northern

Ultima Thule, name used in ancient times to denote the farthest (Latin *ultimus*), or most northerly known land; phrase now used for something far away or unattainable
- Shetland Islands S-162
- Thule P-418

Ultra-high temperature method (UHT), process used in pasteurization of milk and cream D-4

Ultralight glider. *see in index* Hang glider

Ultramarine, a permanent blue pigment originally obtained by powdering lapis lazuli; now made artificially; valued as oil and water color by artists; used in cloth and paper printing, dyeing, ink making P-73

Ultramicrofiche, type of microfilm M-377

Ultramicroscope, type of microscope M-382

Ultrasaurus, dinosaur A-462

Ultrashort wave. *see in index* Microwave

Ultrasonic machining (USM), a metalworking operation T-226

Ultrasonic wave. *see in index* Supersonic wave

Ultrasonography, technique for diagnosing disease and for determining size and position of fetus during pregnancy D-127
- genetic disorder detection G-48
- hospital H-282
- multiple birth M-650

Ultraviolet microscope, type of microscope M-383

Ultraviolet radiation, rays U-3
- bee vision B-124
- camera P-429
- cancer cause C-132
- cause R-39, *diagram* R-38
- health R-39, S-346a
- light L-194, 201, *diagram* L-202
- lighting types L-206
- photoelectric effect R-39
- photography P-281
- phototube P-274, 275
- plasma creation P-380
- vitamin production V-356, 357, U-3, 4
- wavelengths and frequencies, *table* R-34

Ulugh Muztagh, highest peak (25,340 ft; 7,720 m) of Kunlun Mountains; in area of n. border of Tibet K-309

Uluru National Park, park in Australia, *picture* N-26

Ulyanov, Vladimir Ilich. *see in index* Lenin

Ul'yanovsk, U.S.S.R., city on Volga River 430 mi (690 km) s.e. of Moscow; river trade; saw and flour mills, factories; pop. 351,000, *maps* E-361, R-344, 349

Ulysses. *see in index* Odysseus

'Ulysses', work by Joyce J-145, L-243
- English literature E-281
- naturalism N-414

'Umar I, patriarch of Islam C-54

Umatilla, a Shahaptian people in Oregon; lived along Columbia River; signed treaty with U.S. 1855; Umatilla Indian Reservation (pop. 1,800) just e. of Pendleton, Ore.

20TH-CENTURY PRIME MINISTERS OF THE UNITED KINGDOM

Name	Term	Party	Name	Term	Party
Marquis of Salisbury	1895–1902	Conservative	Winston Churchill	1940–45	National
Arthur James Balfour	1902–05	Conservative	Clement Attlee	1945–51	Labor
Henry Campbell-Bannerman	1905–08	Liberal	Winston Churchill	1951–55	Conservative
Herbert Henry Asquith	1908–15	Liberal	Anthony Eden	1955–57	Conservative
Herbert Henry Asquith	1915–16	Coalition	Harold Macmillan	1957–63	Conservative
David Lloyd George	1916–22	Coalition	Alexander Douglas-Home	1963–64	Conservative
Andrew Bonar Law	1922–23	Conservative	Harold Wilson	1964–70	Labor
Stanley Baldwin	1923–24	Conservative	Edward Heath	1970–74	Conservative
Ramsay MacDonald	1924	Labor	Harold Wilson	1974–76	Labor
Stanley Baldwin	1924–29	Conservative	James Callaghan	1976–79	Labor
Ramsay MacDonald	1929–31	Labor	Margaret Thatcher	1979–	Conservative
Ramsay MacDonald	1931–35	National			
Stanley Baldwin	1935–37	National			
Neville Chamberlain	1937–40	National			

UNITED STATES POPULATION GROWTH

Census	Population	Increase	Pct.
1980	226,504,825	23,202,794	11.4
1970	203,302,031	23,978,856	13.4
1960	179,323,175	27,997,377	18.5
1950	151,325,798*	19,656,523	14.9
1940	131,669,275	8,894,229	7.2
1930	122,775,046	17,064,426	16.1
1920	105,710,620	13,738,354	14.9
1910	91,972,266	15,977,691	21.0
1900	75,994,575	13,046,861	20.7
1890	62,947,714	12,791,931	25.5
1880	50,155,783	10,337,334	26.0
1870	39,818,449	8,375,128	26.6
1860	31,443,321	8,251,445	35.6
1850	23,191,876	6,122,423	35.9
1840	17,069,453	4,203,433	32.7
1830	12,866,020	3,227,567	33.5
1820	9,638,453	2,398,572	33.1
1810	7,239,881	1,931,398	36.4
1800	5,308,483	1,379,269	35.1
1790	3,929,214	....	...

*Includes populations of Alaska and Hawaii, though then not states

'Montmartre, Le Sacré Coeur', *picture* U-236

Uttar Pradesh, state in n. India; area 113,409 sq mi (293,728 sq km); cap. Lucknow; composed almost entirely of former United Provinces of Agra and Oudh; pop. 88,341,144, *map* I-83

Uvalde, Tex., city 82 mi (132 km) s.w. of San Antonio; agriculture, cotton, livestock, pecans, work clothes; pop. 14,178.

Uvula, a small, fleshy U-shaped mass hanging down from the soft palate of mouth above root of tongue.

Uxmal, Mexico, ancient ruined Maya city in Yucatán, 40 mi (60 km) s.w. of Mérida; one of continent's most remarkable archaeological sites
Maya M-235, *picture* M-237
Mexico, *map* M-344
Yucatán Peninsula Y-433

Uygurs, a people of China C-345, *picture* C-348
Kunlun Mountains K-309
Turkestan T-317

Uzbek, an individual, or the language, of a Turkic people; socially and politically rather than racially distinct, they were the dominant people in central Asia from the 13th century until the arrival of the Russians in the 19th century
Afghanistan A-89
Turkestan T-317
Turkmen Soviet Socialist Republic T-327

Uzbek Soviet Socialist Republic (also Uzbekistan), U.S.S.R.; 154,050 sq mi (398,990 sq km); cap. Tashkent; pop. 11,963,000 U-15, *maps* U-14, R-325, 344
Asia, *map* A-700
Samarkand S-33
tomb of Timur Leng, *map* R-340, *picture* R-351

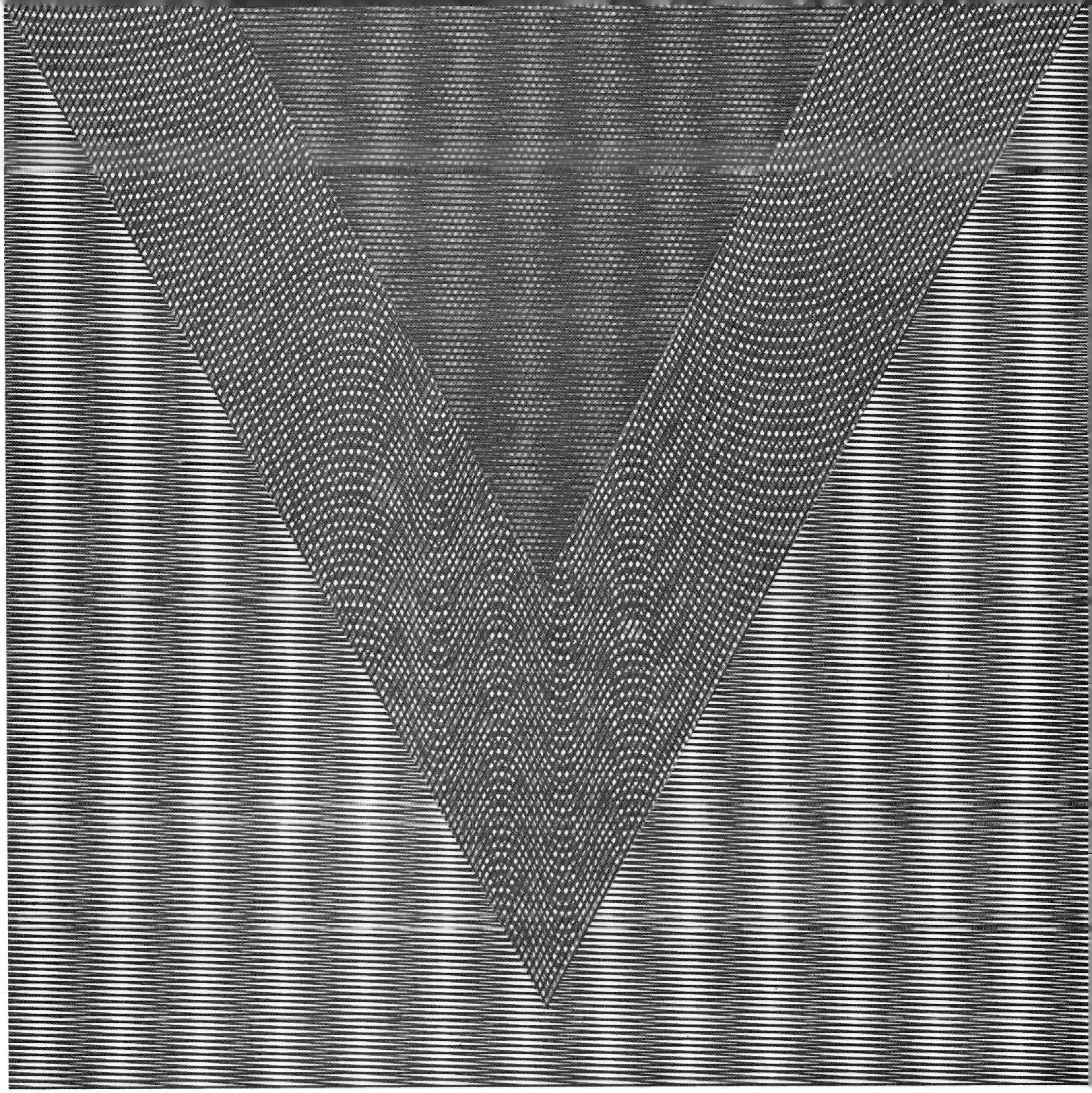

The letter V

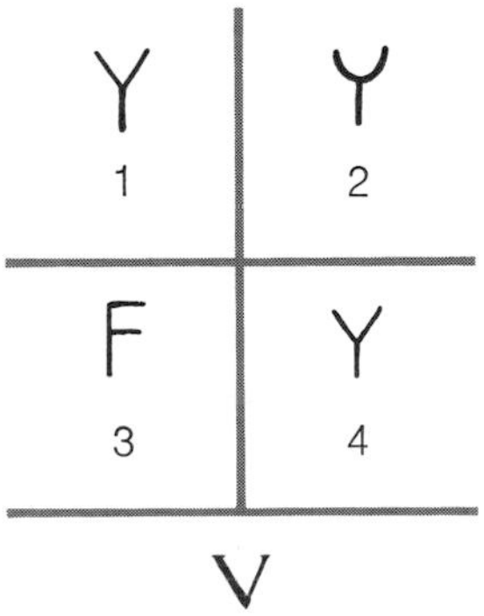

probably started as a picture sign for a branched supporting pole or prop, as in Egyptian hieroglyphic writing (1). Descendants of this letter are F, U, W, and Y. About 1000 B.C., in Byblos and in other Phoenician and Canaanite centers, the same sign was used, but its top part was rounded (2). In the Semitic languages the sign was called *waw,* meaning "prop." It had the sound of the "w" in "wine." The Greeks used the sign in two forms. One form (3) was called *digamma* for the consonantal "w," which disappeared in later Greek. This form led to the Latin sign F. Another form (4), called *upsilon,* meaning "bare u," was used for the vocalic "u."

The Romans eliminated the bottom tail (5) and used it for two sounds, consonantal "w" (later "v") and vocalic "u." Consonantal "v" passed into English writing. The English small "v" is a copy of the capital, except that in handwriting it is connected to adjoining letters.

V

V-1 and V-2, missiles developed by Nazi Germany S-342
guided missiles G-309
jet propulsion J-110
U.S. program S-345
World War II bombing B-339, W-335, 355

VA. *see in index* Veterans Administration

Vaal River (Dutch Yellow), river in South Africa, rises on w. slope of Drakensberg; flows w. 500 mi (800 km) to Orange River, *maps* A-118, S-264

Vaalserberg, mountain, highest point in The Netherlands N-125

Vaasa (Swedish Vasa), Finland, port on Gulf of Bothnia; timber, textiles, sugar, soap, machinery; pop. 42,701.

Vacana, Kannada prose poetry I-106

Vacancy, crystal defect C-798

Vacation activities V-237. *see also in index* Amusements; Camping; Games; Hobby; Reading for recreation; Recreation; Sports

Vacaville, Calif., city 34 mi (55 km) s.w. of Sacramento; in agricultural area; food processing; pop. 43,367.

Vaccination V-249
Jenner J-98
travel and tourism T-272

Vaccines V-249
bacteria B-14
disease prevention D-169
genetic engineering G-50
microbiology M-376
Pasteur P-138

Vacuole, cell structure C-238, *picture* C-237
feeding A-375, A-428
living things L-266, *picture* L-265

Vacuum V-254
air evacuation A-146, *picture* A-147
aneroid barometer B-82
black hole theory B-306
electric lamps V-254
food processing F-281
light L-197
microscope M-382
sound, *diagram* S-260

Vacuum appliances P-398. *see also in index* Pneumatic appliances

Vacuum aspiration, surgical technique A-11

Vacuum bottle V-254

Vacuum cleaner, appliance H-211
industrial design, *picture* I-171
pneumatic appliances P-398

Vacuum pump V-254
reciprocating P-533

Vacuum syringe B-315

Vacuum tube. *see in index* Electron tube

Vaduz, Liechtenstein, capital, near Rhine s. of Lake Constance; pop. 3,398, *map* S-537

Vaea, Mount, Samoa, burial place of Robert Louis Stevenson S-446

Vagina, structure in female reproductive system R-151c, *diagram* R-151d
sexuality S-123

Vaginissimus, a sexual dysfunction S-126

Vagrancy Act (1597), in England, authorized government to deport criminal and political offenders M-400

Vagus nerve (or cranial nerve X, or pneumogastric nerve, or tenth cranial nerve), mixed nerve descending from medulla oblongata through the carotid sheath and branching to the various internal organs N-119, *picture* A-384
therapy T-165

Vail, Alfred (1807–59), U.S. inventor, born in Morristown, N.J.; in 1837 lent money to Samuel F.B. Morse, and for several years worked with him in improving the telegraph
telegraph T-58

Vail, Theodore Newton (1845–1920), U.S. businessman, born in Carroll County, Ohio; president American Telephone and Telegraph Co.; did much to build up telephone industry.

Vailima, Robert Louis Stevenson's Samoan home S-446, S-34

Vaiont Dam, Italy, on Vaiont River; 858 ft (262 m) high, 624 ft (190 m) long; because of landslide overflowed and flooded surrounding country 1963; abandoned as source of electric power D-17

Vair, heraldic fur, *picture* H-136

Vaisnavism worship of the Hindu god Vishnu H-159

Vaisya, member of farmer caste among Hindus I-68

Vakhan Corridor, in Afghanistan A-88

Vakhtangov, Eugene, (1883–1922) Russian actor, director, and producer, born in Moscow; director of the Moscow Art Theatre A-27

Valais, canton of s.w. Switzerland, 2,021 sq mi (5,234 sq km); minerals and wines, but chiefly pastoral; Alpine peaks; summer and winter resorts; contains Great St. Bernard and Simplon passes; pop. 187,000 S-541
masks M-187

Valday Hills, in the U.S.S.R., groups of low hills and plateaus midway between Leningrad and Moscow; form divide for chief river systems of country; 600 to 1,200 ft (180 to 370 m) above sea level R-323
Volga River V-383

Valdemar, kings of Denmark D-99

Valdés, Juan de (1490?–1541), one of foremost Spanish writers of prose; dealt with problems of Biblical interpretation and their bearing on devout life S-368

Valdez, Pedro de, Spanish naval officer
Drake D-240

Valdez, Alaska, all-year-open port in s.e. on Prince William Sound; gold mining; severely damaged by earthquake 1964; rebuilt 5 mi (8 km) away; pop. 3,079, *map* U-39

Valdivia, Chile, port city on Valdivia River about 10 mi (16 km) from Pacific Ocean and 450 mi (725 km) s.w. of Santiago; distributing center for farm, livestock, and lumber district; metal, food, wood, and leather products; pop. 90,942, *maps* S-299, L-67
Chile C-332

Valdosta, Ga., city in s. center, near Florida line; tobacco, cotton, lumber, livestock center; naval stores, paper and paperboard, concrete pipe; Valdosta State College; pop. 37,596, *map* U-41

Valdosta State College, Valdosta, Ga.; founded 1906; arts and sciences, education; graduate studies.

Valdotains, a European people
Italy I-384

Valedictorian, student of highest rank in graduating class who delivers farewell address, *picture* P-526

Valence (Roman Valentia), France, historic town 57 mi (92 km) s. of Lyon on Rhone River; printed fabrics, flour, tinned foods; vineyards; pop. 60,662, *map* F-372

Valence (or valence number), combining capacity of a chemical element V-255
chemistry C-298
crystals C-796

Valencia, province of Spain, on e. coast; 4,155 sq mi (10,760 sq km); agriculture, fisheries, silk culture; cap. Valencia; pop. 1,429,708 S-351

Valencia, Spain, city; pop. 601,000 V-256, *maps* E-361, S-350

Valencia, Venezuela, city about 20 mi (30 km) s. of its seaport Puerto Cabello and 77 mi (124 km) s.w. of Caracas; with suburbs; trade in sugar, coffee, cacao, corn, tobacco, hides; cotton milling and many other industries S-274; pop. 224,552, *maps* V-275, S-298

Valencia orange, citrus fruit *Citrus sinensis valencia*, *picture* C-445

Valenciennes, France, industrial town 28 mi (45 km) s.e. of Lille on Scheldt River in coal district; pop. 46,237, *map* F-372
lace L-17, *picture* L-16

Valens (328?–378), Byzantine emperor, chosen AD 364 by his brother Valentinian I to rule East; warred with Persians and Goths; with his defeat by the Goths at Adrianople (AD 378) began the decline of the Roman Empire.

Valentia Island (or Valencia Island), off s.w. coast of Ireland; belongs to County Kerry, Ireland; 7 by 3 mi (11 by 5 km); terminus of cables between America and United Kingdom; pop. 847.

Valentine, Saint, Christian martyr of 3rd century; feast day February 14; dropped from Roman Catholic calendar in 1969 S-24

Valentine, a special person S-24

Valentine's Day. *see in index* Saint Valentine's Day

Valentinian I (321–375), Roman emperor, son of humble parents, who rose to high rank in army and was elected emperor AD 364; shared power with brother Valens, giving him eastern part of empire; a firm, impartial, tolerant ruler.

Valentinian II (372–392), son of Valentinian I, at age of four shared empire of the West with his half-brother, Gratian; driven out with his mother by Magnus Maximus, he was restored by Theodosius, emperor of the East; murdered in Gaul.

Valentinian III (419?–455), Roman emperor, succeeded AD 425; during his reign Africa, Sicily, Gaul, and Britain were lost; murdered Aetius, and was himself murdered the next year A-758

Valentino, Rudolph (original name Rodolfo d'Antonguolla) (1895–1926), U.S. motion-picture actor, born in Castellaneta, Italy; to U.S. 1913; with role of Julio in 'The Four Horsemen of the Apocalypse', became one of most popular of all romantic actors: starred in 'The Sheik', 'Blood and Sand', 'Monsieur Beaucaire'.

Valentinus (fl. 2nd century AD), Egyptian religious philosopher and teacher of Gnosticism, a system of belief in rival deities of good and evil
Gnosticism G-170

Valenzuela, Luisa (born 1938), Argentine writer L-71, *picture* L-75

Valera, Eamon de. *see in index* De Valera

Valera, Juan (1824–1905), Spanish statesman and eminent man of letters; his 'Pepita Jiménez' marked the renaissance of the Spanish novel.

Valerian (full name Publius Licinius Valerianus) (died AD 260), Roman emperor 253–260, elected by army when he was over 60; zealous worker but overwhelmed by constant fighting with barbarians and Persians; defeated by Persians AD 260 and held prisoner until his death
Christians persecuted C-401

Valerian, perennial herb with opposite leaves and small white or reddish flowers in rounded terminal clusters; thickened and strong-scented root of garden heliotrope, or common valerian *Valeriana officinalis* and of other species yields a volatile oil used in treating hysteria.

Valerian Way, a principal highway of ancient Italy; continued Tiburtina Way (Rome to Tivoli) n.e. to Adriatic.

Valéry, Paul (1871–1945), French poet and essayist; member of French Academy; writings of unusual beauty and form; a writer's poet, philosophical and difficult ('La Jeune Parque'; 'Odes'; 'Fragments du Narcisse', poetry; 'Variétés', essays).

Valhalla, in Norse mythology, hall of slain warriors in heaven M-703

Valium (or diazepam), a sedative N-19

Valjean, Jean, character in Hugo's 'Les Misérables' H-316

'Valkyrie, The' (German 'Die Walküre'), second opera in Wagner's series 'The Ring of the Nibelungs ('Der Ring des Nibelungen') O-568

Valkyries (or Valkyrs, or choosers of the slain), maidens in Norse mythology, sent by Odin to conduct souls of slain heroes to Valhalla M-704

Valladolid, Spain, former capital, 100 mi (160 km) n.w. of Madrid; Columbus died here; birthplace of Philip II; home of Cervantes; textiles, leather, ironware; university; pop. 133,486, *maps* E-361, S-350

Vallandigham, Clement Laird (1820–71), U.S. Civil War copperhead, born in New Lisbon, Ohio; Ohio congressman; convicted of sedition by military court 1863; sentence of imprisonment commuted by Lincoln to banishment to Confederate states; subsequently supreme commander Knights of the Golden Circle
Civil War C-478

Vallee, Rudy (original name Hubert Prior Vallee) (1901–86), U.S. bandleader, saxophonist, and singer; born in Iland Pond, Vt.; gained fame as first radio crooner; also on stage and screen.

Valle-Inclán, Ramón María del (1866–1936), Spanish writer; finely polished prose, also subtle, delicate verse ('Sonatas'; 'La Guerra carlista'; 'Cofre de sándalo'; 'Tirano Banderas', novels; 'Cara de plata', verse).

Vallejo, Mariano Guadalupe (1808–90), Spanish-American soldier, California pioneer; built Sonoma garrison on northern frontier; by 1835 had formed alliances with powerful American Indian tribes; backed rebellion of 1836 and commanded California troops 1838; after quarrel with governor was captured by Frémont's men (1846); member of constitutional convention (1849) and of first state senate; offered modern Vallejo as site of state capital.

Vallejo, Calif., city on arm of San Pablo Bay, about 25 mi (40 km) n.e. of San Francisco opposite Mare Island Navy Yard; in agricultural and industrial area; state capital 1851–53; pop. 80,188, *map* U-40

Valletta, Malta, capital and port; trade city and resort built to commemorate a victory in 1565 of the Knights of Malta over the Turks; became capital in 1570; pop. 14,100, *maps* E-361, I-404
  Malta M-78

Valley V-256, *diagram* R-210
  drowned. *see in index* Drowned coasts and valleys
  Earth E-15
  floods F-180
  Great Rift Valley G-250
  mountain M-634

Valley and Ridge, geographical region in e. United States
  Maryland M-167, *map* M-168

Valley breeze, winds W-220, *diagram* W-221

Valley Caviedes, Juan del (1652–92), Peruvian writer L-75

Valley City, N.D., city on Sheyenne River in s.e. part of state, 58 mi (93 km) w. of Fargo; grain, dairy products; Valley City State College; North Dakota winter show (livestock); pop. 7,774.

Valley City State College, Valley City, N.D.; founded 1889; arts and sciences, education; junior college affiliated; quarter system.

Valleyfield, Que., port city on St. Lawrence River at head of Beauharnois Canal, 35 mi (55 km) s.w. of Montreal; cotton textiles, chemicals, wood and metal products, canned goods; pop. 30,173, *maps* C-112, Q-10

Valley Forge, Pa., village on Schuylkill River 20 mi (30 km) n.w. of Philadelphia; winter quarters of Washington's army (1777–78); pop. 400 V-256, R-171, *map* P-185
  park V-257
  Washington W-41,R-171, *picture* W-40
    headquarters, *picture* P-172

Valley glacier, in geology G-150
  Ice Age I-6

'Valley of Fear, The', short story by Doyle M-526

Valley of Fire State Park, Nevada, *picture* N-142

Valley of Ten Thousand Smokes, volcanic area in Alaska created 1912; discovered by Robert F. Griggs, 1915–19; part of Katmai National Monument.

Valley of the Fallen, memorial to the Spanish Civil War dead, *picture* S-361

Valley of the Tombs of the Kings, in Egypt
  ancient Egypt E-126
  Tutankhamen T-331

Valley quail, bird *Lophortyx californicus* Q-3

Valley Station, Ky., community 11 mi (18 km) s.w. of Louisville; located near bank of Ohio River; mainly residential suburb of Louisville; pop. 24,471.

Valley Stream, N.Y., residential suburb of New York City on s. shore of Long Island; light industry; pop. 40,413.

Valley train, a long narrow body of outwash G-151

Vallisneria (also called eelgrass, or wild celery, or tape grass), a water plant *Vallisneria americana*; rooted in bottom of shallow ponds and streams; leaves may be 3 ft (1 m) or more long and scarcely ¼ in. (⅔ cm) wide; tiny greenish female flowers, borne singly at ends of long supple stems, float on surface of water; male flowers on short stems near base of plant in clusters of several hundred; as they mature, become detached and bubble of air carries each to the top where it opens and floats until it meets a female flower; masses of male flowers gather around the larger female flower to which the sticky pollen adheres; favorite food of waterbirds; as an aquarium plant grows easily and provides abundant oxygen for animal life W-101
  fish camouflage, *picture* F-127

Vallombrosa, Italy, summer resort in Apennines 20 mi (30 km) s.e. of Florence; Vallombrosian order of monks, founded 11th century, now extinct.

Valmy, France, village 40 mi (60 km) s.e. of Reims; pop. 267.

Valmy, battle of (1792), warfare, *list* W-16

Valois, Margaret of. *see in index* Margaret of Valois

Valois, old district of n. central France now in departments of Oise and Aisne; countship in Middle Ages; later united to crown; home of House of Valois.

Valois, House of, French royal dynasty, branch of Capetian family; reigned 1328–1589; name comes from historic region of France. For list, *see in index* France, history of, *table* of rulers
  Philip VI P-252

Valona (Albanian Vlorë, or Vlonë), Albania, port city 70 mi (110 km) s.-s.w. of Tiranë; olives, olive oil; held by Italy 1914–20; pop. 41,285.

Valour, Cross of, medal M-272

Valparaiso (Spanish Valparaíso), Chile, commercial and manufacturing city, chief U.S. Pacific port s. of Los Angeles; pop. 251,459 V-257, *map* S-299
  Chile C-332

Valparaiso, Ind., city 40 mi (60 km) s.e. of Chicago, Ill.; largely residential; electrical insulating materials, permanent magnets, ball and roller bearings; Valparaiso University; pop. 22,247, *map* I-102

Valparaiso University, Valparaiso, Ind.; Lutheran; founded 1859; arts and sciences, business administration, engineering, law, nursing; Christ College, an honors college; graduate studies.

'Valpinçon Bather', oil painting by Ingres, *picture* I-205

Valtellina, fertile valley of Adda River in n. Italy, fought over by ancient and medieval powers; wines and honey; mineral springs; ruled by Austria 1814–59.

Value, of color C-561
  design D-108
  dress design D-269

Value added by manufacture essentially, the difference between the value of a finished product and the value of the raw materials consumed in its manufacture; usually it is determined for industries as a whole, or for groups of industries within a geographic area; this figure is a means for measuring and comparing the economic importance of industries; it is found by subtracting from the value of finished products the cost of materials, supplies, fuel, and power used in their manufacture, as well as resale costs and miscellaneous receipts; it is also adjusted by the net change in finished-products and work-in-progress inventories between the beginning and end of the year.

Value-added tax, a form of sales tax T-37

Value concepts, in social studies S-241

Valve, a device that stops or regulates the flow of a liquid or gas V-258. *see also in index* Electron tube
  automobile engine A-847
  heart H-97, *pictures* H-98, 99
  pump P-533, *diagram* V-254
  steam engine S-439
  wind instruments W-230

Vampire, folklore legend F-262
  horror story H-245

Vampire bat B-105

Van, Turkey, town on s.e. shore of Lake Van; important city in Assyrian period; famous cuneiform inscriptions; pop. 22,043, *map* A-700

Van, motor vehicle A-844

Van, Lake, large salt lake in e. Turkey; about 1,400 sq mi (3,600 sq km); has no outlet; 5,400 ft (1,650 m) above sea level; communities along coast include Van T-318, *picture* T-320

Vanadate mineral, classification M-432, 435

Vanadinite, mineral, *picture* M-433

Vanadium (V), chemical element V-258
  ore, *table* O-600, *map* O-600
  periodic table, *table* P-207, *list* P-208

Van Allen, James Alfred (born 1914), U.S. physicist V-259

Van Allen belts, of radiation V-259

Van Alstyne, Frances Jane. *see in index* Crosby, Fanny

Van Biesbroeck, George (1880–1974), U.S. astronomer, born in Ghent, Belgium; authority on comets and double stars; became U.S. citizen 1922; professor Yerkes Observatory, Williams Bay, Wis., 1926–45; measured bending of starlight passing close to sun at times of eclipses, verifying Albert Einstein's predictions.

Van Brocklin, Norman (or the Dutchman) (1926–83), U.S. football quarterback, born in Eagle Butte, S.D.

Vanbrugh, Sir John (1664–1726), English dramatist and architect, one of leading wits of his day; designed Blenheim Palace and mansions for English nobility A-569

Van Buren, Hannah Hoes (1782–1819), wife of U.S. President Van Buren V-260

Van Buren, Martin (1782–1862), 8th president of United States V-260
  Harrison H-50
  Polk P-437

Van Buren, Steve (born 1920), U.S. football halfback and coach, born in Tecla, Honduras; played for Philadelphia Eagles 1944–51.

Vance, Arthur Charles (nickname Dazzy) (1891–1961), U.S. baseball pitcher, born in Orient, Iowa; with Pittsburgh, N.L., and New York, A.L., 1915, New York, A.L., 1918, Brooklyn, N.L., 1922–32, St. Louis, N.L., 1933, Cincinnati, N.L., and St. Louis, N.L., 1934, Brooklyn, N.L., 1935; won 197 games, lost 140; led N.L. in strikeouts 7 years in a row, 1922–28; had best earned-run average in N.L. 1924, 1928, and 1930; lifetime earned-run average of 3.54; won over 20 games in each of 3 major-league seasons; in 1924, best season, won 28, lost 6; pitched no-hit game against Philadelphia, Sept. 13, 1925.

Vance, Cyrus Roberts (born 1917), U.S. lawyer and government official, born in Clarksburg, W. Va.; general counsel U.S. Department of Defense 1961–62, secretary of the army 1962–64; deputy secretary of defense 1964–67; U.S. president's foreign and domestic troubleshooter 1967–68; deputy U.S. negotiator at Vietnam peace talks in Paris 1968–69; U.S. secretary of state 1977–80.

Vance, Zebulon Baird (1830–94), U.S. statesman, born near Asheville, N.C.; served North Carolina three times as governor and as U.S. senator (Democrat) from 1879 until his death
  Statuary Hall, *table* S-437b

Van Cliburn (or Harvey Lavan Cliburn, Jr.) (born 1934), U.S. pianist, born in Shreveport, La.; grew up in Texas; debut with Houston Symphony Orchestra 1947; won International Tchaikovsky Piano Competition at Moscow and every U.S. prize for pianistic ability; toured widely in U.S. and Europe.

Vancouver, George (1758?–98), English navigator, served under Capt. James Cook on 2nd and 3rd voyages; 1791–95 made explorations in Australia, New Zealand, Tahiti, Hawaiian Islands, Vancouver Island, and along n.w. coast of North America ('A Voyage of Discovery to the North Pacific Ocean and Round the World') C-95
  British Columbia B-456
  Washington W-53

Vancouver, B.C., city on west coast; pop. 410,188, with suburbs 1,166,348 V-263, C-78, *maps* C-109, V-264
  North America, *map* N-351

Vancouver, Wash., port on Columbia River opposite Portland, Ore.; lumber and wood products, aluminum, textiles, chemicals; food processing; veterans' hospital; incorporated 1857; pop. 42,834 W-50, 60, *map* U-40

Vancouver, Mount, peak in St. Elias Mountains in s.w. Yukon Territory, near Alaska border; on s.e. edge of Seward Glacier.

Vancouver Island, British Columbia, largest island off w. coast of the Americas; 12,408 sq mi (32,136 sq km); pop. 381,297 V-265, B-452, C-99. *see also in index* Victoria, B.C.
  Canada C-74, *map* C-109
  North America, *map* N-351
  Trans-Canada Highway T-248
  Victoria V-310

Vandalia, Ill., city on Kaskaskia River, about 65 mi (105 km) n.e. of St. Louis, Mo.; shoes, clothing; state capital 1820–37; pop. 5,338 I-41, *map* I-53

Vandals, a Germanic people V-265, G-121, *picture* R-248
  Andalusia S-357
  Byzantine Empire B-533
  Carthage C-185
  Leo I L-130
  Libya L-190
    Tripoli T-289
  Middle Ages M-384
  migration of people M-402

Van de Graaff, Robert Jemison (1901–67), U.S. scientist, born in Tuscaloosa, Ala.; associate professor of physics at Massachusetts Institute of Technology 1934–60.

Vandegrift, Alexander Archer (1887–1973), U.S. Marine Corps officer, born in Charlottesville, Va.; served in Nicaragua, Mexico, Haiti, China; commander of marines in Solomons 1942–43; commandant U.S. Marine Corps 1944–48 W-345

Vandenberg, Arthur Hendrick (1884–1951), U.S. political leader, born in Grand Rapids, Mich.; U.S. senator 1928–51; Republican leader in the Senate; author of 'The Private Papers of Senator Vandenberg' G-213

Vandenberg, Hoyt Sanford (1899–1954), U.S. Air Force general, born in Milwaukee, Wis.; commanded U.S. Ninth Air Force in Europe in World War II; head of Central Intelligence Agency 1946; deputy commander of U.S. Air Force 1947, chief of staff 1948–53.

Vandenberg Center, multimillion-dollar building complex in Grand Rapids, Mich. G-213

Vanderbilt, Amy (1908–74), U.S. authority on etiquette, born in Staten Island, N.Y.; newspaper column; radio and television programs ('Amy Vanderbilt's Complete Book of Etiquette'; 'Amy Vanderbilt's Complete Cook Book').

Vanderbilt, Cornelius (1794–1877), U.S. capitalist and financier, born in Staten Island, N.Y., founder of the Vanderbilt fortune; nicknamed Commodore for his early steamboat activities; acquired control of New York Central and other railroads; endowed Vanderbilt University with $1,000,000
  Nicaragua N-305
  Westinghouse W-162

Vanderbilt, Cornelius (1843–99), U.S. capitalist and philanthropist, born in Staten Island, N.Y.; son of William Henry Vanderbilt; trained in railway management by his grandfather Cornelius; directed family investments after father's death.

Vanderbilt, Cornelius (1873–1942), U.S. capitalist and inventor, born in New York, N.Y.; son of Cornelius Vanderbilt (1843–99); director of railroads and banks; patented many railroading devices.

Vanderbilt, Cornelius (1898–1974), U.S. journalist, author, and lecturer; born in New York, N.Y.; son of Cornelius Vanderbilt (1873–1942).

Vanderbilt, Harold Stirling (1884–1970), U.S. railroad official and sportsman, born in Oakdale, near Sayville,

N.Y.; son of William Kissam Vanderbilt; originated game of contract bridge, elected to Bridge Hall of Fame 1964; won America's Cup yacht races 1930, 1934, and 1937.

Vanderbilt, William Henry (1821–85), U.S. capitalist, born in New Brunswick, N.J.; built up railroad interests left by his father, Cornelius Vanderbilt (1794–1877); contributed freely to educational causes.

Vanderbilt, William Kissam (1849–1920), U.S. railroad official, philanthropist, and sportsman; born in Staten Island, N.Y.; son of William Henry Vanderbilt; Dowling College now located on Oakdale, N.Y., estate
Newport mansion, *picture* R-189

Vanderbilt University, Nashville, Tenn.; founded 1873 by Cornelius Vanderbilt; arts and sciences, divinity, engineering, law, medicine, nursing; graduate school.

Van der Donck, Adriaen (1620–55?), first lawyer of New Netherland and author of first book describing life in the colony; championed people's rights of self-government
Yonkers Y-423

Vandergrift, Pa., borough on Kiskiminetas River 27 mi (43 km) n.e. of Pittsburgh; steel foundry products; coal mining; pop. 6,823, *map* P-184

Vanderlip, Frank Arthur (1864–1937), U.S. banker, born in Aurora, Ill.; assistant secretary of treasury 1897–1901; chairman War Savings Committee during World War I; wrote on financial and economic subjects.

Vanderlyn, John (1775–1852), U.S. historical and portrait painter; an expert draftsman ('George Washington'; 'Marius Among the Ruins of Carthage'; 'Ariadne').

Van der Rohe, Ludwig Mies. *see in index* Mies van der Rohe, Ludwig

Vandervelde, Emile (1866–1938), Belgian Socialist statesman and orator; as foreign minister, influential in negotiations for Versailles Treaty and Locarno Pact.

Van der Waals, Johannes Diderik. *see in index* Waals, Johannes van der

Van der Waals force, in physics W-2

Van der Weyden, Rogier. *see in index* Weyden, Rogier van der

Van Devanter, Willis (1859–1941), U.S. jurist, born in Marion, Ind.; associate justice of U.S. Supreme Court 1910–37.

Van de Velde, Henri (1863–1957), Belgian architect A-569
furniture design F-462

Van Diemen's Land, former name of Tasmania. *see in index* Tasmania

Van Dine, S.S. *see in index* Wright, Willard Huntington

Van Doren, Carl Clinton (1885–1950), U.S. critic and biographer, born in Hope, Ill.; taught English, University of Illinois and Columbia University; former literary editor, *The Nation* and *Century*; author 'Three Worlds', autobiography; 'Benjamin Franklin', Pulitzer prize biography (1939); 'The Great Rehearsal', story of U.S. Constitution; with brother Mark Van Doren, 'American and British Literature Since 1890'.

Van Doren, Mark (1894–1972), U.S. writer and editor, born in Hope, Ill.; joined faculty Columbia University 1920, professor 1942–59; editor of 'Anthology of World Poetry', 'American Poets 1630–1930'; author of verse: 'Collected Poems, 1922–1938', awarded Pulitzer prize 1940, 'Selected Poems', 'That Shining Place'; biography: 'Nathaniel Hawthorne'; 'Autobiography'; drama: 'The Last Days of Lincoln'; 'Collected Stories'.

Van Dorn, Earl (1820–63), U.S. military leader, born near Port Gibson, Miss.; served in U.S. Army during Mexican War; captain Second Cavalry 1855–61; major general Mississippi militia and Confederate army 1861.

Van Druten, John William (1901–57), U.S. playwright, born in London, England, son of Dutch father and English mother; became U.S. citizen 1944 (plays: 'The Voice of the Turtle', 'I Remember Mama', 'Bell, Book, and Candle', 'I Am a Camera'; autobiographical: 'Playwright at Work', 'The Widening Circle').

Van Dyck, Sir Anthony (or Sir Anthony Vandyke) (1599–1641), great Flemish portrait painter V-266
Charles I, *picture* C-274

Van Dyke, Henry (1852–1933), U.S. Presbyterian clergyman and author, born in Germantown, Pa.; professor of English literature at Princeton University ('The Blue Flower', short stories; 'Fisherman's Luck', essays; 'The Builders, and Other Poems').

Van Dyke, John Charles (1856–1932), U.S. art critic; born in New Brunswick, N.J.; professor history of art, Rutgers College 1889–1932 ('New Guides to Old Masters'; 'Rembrandt and His School').

Vandyke print B-319

Vane, Sir Henry (1613–62), English Puritan statesman, friend of religious liberty; governor of Massachusetts 1636–37; returned to England; active Parliamentarian; imprisoned at Restoration and beheaded for treason
Hutchinson H-336

Vane (or web), a series of locked barbs on a feather F-50

Vane, blade of a waterwheel W-103

Vänern, Lake, Sweden, largest lake in Scandinavian peninsula and 3rd largest in Europe; 2,141 sq mi (5,545 sq km) S-523, *maps* E-361, S-524

Vanessa, poetical name given by Jonathan Swift to Esther Vanhomrigh (1692–1723) in his serious poem, 'Cadenus and Vanessa', Swift being Cadenus.

Van Eyck, Jan (1390?–1441) and **Hubert** (1366?–1426), Flemish artists and brothers; founders of the Flemish school of painting P-30

Van Fleet, James Alward (born 1892), U.S. Army officer, born in Coytesville, N.J.; served in World Wars I and II; headed U.S. military mission to Greece 1948–50; Eighth Army commander in Korea April 1951–Jan. 1953; promoted to four-star general July 1951; retired from active military service 1953
Korean War K-298, *chart* K-299

Van Gogh, Vincent. *see in index* Gogh, Vincent Van

Van Gulik, Robert (1910–67), writer D-119

Van Hise, Charles Richard (1857–1918), U.S. geologist and educator, born in Fulton, Wis.; president University of Wisconsin 1903–18; authority on geology of Lake Superior iron-bearing region.

Vanhomrigh, Esther. *see in index* Vanessa

Van Horne, Sir William Cornelius (1843–1915), Canadian railway executive, born in Illinois; after wide experience with U.S. railroads, superintended construction Canadian Pacific Railway, of which he was president 1888–99.

Vanhouttei, a species of spirea S-392

Vanier, Georges Philias (1888–1967), Canadian statesman, born in Montreal, Que.; eminent career as soldier and diplomat; ambassador to France 1944–54; governor-general of Canada 1959–67, *picture* P-132a

Vanilla, a flavoring substance V-266
Madagascar M-24
nuts N-449
orchid O-580

Vanillin, the active ingredient of vanilla V-266

Vanishing point, perspective P-220

'Vanity Fair', novel by Thackeray R-112d, T-145

Van Loon, Hendrik Willem (1882–1944), U.S. historian and illustrator, born in Rotterdam, The Netherlands ('R.v.R.', fictionized biography of Rembrandt; 'The Arts'; 'Van Loon's Geography'; 'Life and Times of Simon Bolivar' and 'Thomas Jefferson', biographies for young people)
'The Story of Mankind' R-111e

Vann, Robert L. (1887–1940), U.S. publisher, assistant attorney general in administration of Franklin Roosevelt B-294

Vannes, France, historic town 67 mi (108 km) n.w. of Nantes; fabrics, leather, iron; ancient capital of the Veneti, a seafaring people; museum containing prehistoric remains; pop. 36,380, *map* F-372

Vannucci, Pietro. *see in index* Perugino

Van Paassen, Pierre (1895–1968), U.S. journalist, writer, and Unitarian minister, born in Gorcum, The Netherlands; columnist for New York *Evening World* 1924–31; ordained Unitarian minister 1946; known as fighter against fascism and for Zionism (autobiography: 'Days of Our Years', 'A Pilgrim's Vow'; 'To Number Our Days'; 'Crown of Fire', biography of Savonarola).

Van Rensselaer, Kiliaen (1595–1644), first Dutch patroon of New York, one of founders of New York and Albany.

Van Rensselaer, Martha (1864–1932), U.S. expert in home economics, born in Randolph, N.Y.; at Cornell University from 1900, director of extension courses which developed into Home Economics College, of which she was head 1911–32.

Van Rensselaer, Stephen (1764–1839), U.S. political leader and soldier, last of Dutch patroons; ardent promoter of Erie Canal; founded Rensselaer Polytechnic Institute, Troy, N.Y.

Van Rijn, Rembrandt Harmenszoon. *see in index* Rembrandt Harmenszoon van Rijn

Van Stockum, Hilda (born 1908), U.S. portrait painter, illustrator, and author of children's books; born in Rotterdam, The Netherlands; spent part of her childhood in Ireland, and, after her marriage to Ervin Ross Marlin, lived in New York; became U.S. citizen 1935; later resided in Montreal with her large family of children; her books for children reflect her many homes ('Day on Skates'; 'Cottage at Bantry Bay'; 'Canadian Summer'; 'Patsy and the Pup').

Van't Hoff, Jacobus Hendricus (1852–1911), Dutch chemist and physicist, founder of stereochemistry and the first Nobel prize winner (1901) in chemistry. *see also in index* Nobel Prizewinners, *table*
osmosis O-611

Van Twiller, Wouter (1580?–1656?), governor of New Netherland, born in Nijkerk, The Netherlands; clerk Dutch West India Co. at Amsterdam; made governor 1633; inept government led to trouble with English and American Indians, as well as with own people; recalled 1637.

Vanua Levu, an island of Fiji; 2,130 sq mi (5,515 sq km); chief town, Lambasa; gold, sugar, rice, copra; pop. 84,892, *map* P-6

Vanuatu. *see in index* New Hebrides

Van Vactor, David (born 1906), U.S. composer and flutist, born in Plymouth, Ind.; professor in department of fine arts University of Tennessee 1947–76; conductor Knoxville Symphony Orchestra 1947–72; compositions include orchestral works, chamber music, and choral works.

Van Vechten, Carl (1880–1964), U.S. novelist, born in Cedar Rapids, Iowa; assistant music critic *New York Times*, later on *New York Press*; composed 'Five Old English Ditties'; a rebel against dullness and standardization ('Peter Whiffle'; 'The Blind Bow-Boy'; 'Spider Boy').

Van Vleck, John Hasbrouck (1899–1980), U.S. physicist, born in Middletown, Conn.; faculty of Harvard University 1922–23 and from 1934, professor 1935–69, professor emeritus 1969–80; study of sources of magnetism in atomic structure.

Van Wagener, Isabella. *see in index* Truth, Sojourner

Van Wert, Ohio, city 27 mi (43 km) n.w. of Lima; metal tool kits, fiberboard containers, oil seals, work clothes, cheese, electronic lighting equipment; pop. 11,035.

Vapor, gaseous form of a substance normally solid or liquid, *diagram* S-438. *see also in index* Evaporation
air A-145
petroleum refining P-239, *chart* P-241a
water W-84, 87
explosive power S-438
weather W-120

Vaporization, process whereby a substance changes from a liquid to a gas M-225

Vapor lamp S-247

Vapor tube, lighting L-206

Vara, Mexican unit of measure, *table* W-141

Varanasi (or Banaras, or Benares), India, city on Ganges River; pop. 704,772, *maps* A-700, I-86
Hinduism H-159

Varangians, Northmen from Sweden who settled in Russia R-351, *picture* R-338

Vardar River, river in the Balkan Peninsula; empties into Aegean Sea near Salonika, Greece.

Varden, Dolly, character in Charles Dickens' 'Barnaby Rudge' the locksmith's coquettish daughter whose dress of flowered dimity gave her name to fabric so figured.

Vardhamana. *see in index* Mahavira

Vardon, Harry (1870–1937), British golfer, born in Grouville on island of Jersey, Channel Islands; won British, U.S., and German open championships
golf G-189

Varennes, Pierre Gaultier de, sieur de la Vérendrye. *see in index* Vérendrye, Pierre Gaultier de Varennes, sieur de la

Varennes-en-Argonne, France, town 18 mi (29 km) n.w. of Verdun, on Aire River; taken by U.S. troops on first day of Meuse-Argonne offensive in World War I; pop. 643.

Varèse, Edgar (1883–1965), U.S. composer, born in Paris, France; to U.S. 1916, became citizen 1926; one of most radical of modern composers (chamber music: 'Hyperprism', 'Intégrales')
classical music M-676

Vargas, Getúlio Dornelles (1883–1954), president and dictator of Brazil, born in São Borja in the state of Rio Grande do Sul; governor of state 1928–30 B-423

Vargas, diamond D-131

Vargas Llosa, Mario (born 1936), Peruvian author L-71

Várhegy (or Castle Hill), central hill of Budapest, Hungary B-479

Variability, in statistics S-435

Variable, in mathematics M-214, 219
algebra A-263
calculus C-21

Variable air volume system (VAV), air-conditioning A-152

Variable resistor. *see in index* Rheostat

Variable star (or eclipsing binary) S-412

Variation, of compass. *see in index* Declination

'Variation of Animals and Plants under Domestication, The', work by Darwin D-39

Varicella. *see in index* Chicken pox

Varicose veins, bulging veins in the leg D-174

Varied bunting, a small bird of the finch family; has purple head and plum-red back and underparts.

'Varieties of Religious Experience, The', work by James J-21

'Variety', show business newspaper N-242

Variety store C-513

Varley, John (1778–1842), English landscape painter and art teacher whose instruction laid foundation of an English

Vermeer, Jan (also known as Jan van der Meer) (1632–75), Dutch painter V-283, P-44
  The Netherlands N-107
  'Young Woman with a Water Jug' P-44, *picture* P-44

Vermiculite, hydrous silicates usually derived from alteration of mica; so named because scales, when heated, open out in wormlike forms; used in insulation, fireproofing, and soundproofing materials.

Vermiform appendix. *see in index* Appendix, vermiform

Vermilion, a scarlet pigment used in paint; English vermilion, mercury sulfide, very opaque but not permanent in color; American vermilion, chromate of lead, has good color strength but is blackened by sulfides; because of high price, both the above have been extensively replaced by coal-tar dyes.

Vermilion Range, in Minnesota, underground iron-ore mine M-446

Vermillion, S.D., city on Vermillion River, near Missouri River, 33 mi (53 km) n.w. of Sioux City, Iowa; livestock; trade center for agricultural area; pop. 10,136, *maps* S-335, 323
  University of South Dakota, *picture* S-329

Vermont, a New England state of the U.S.; 9,609 sq mi (24,887 sq km); cap. Montpelier; pop. 511,456 V-284, *maps* U-41, 44
  Arthur's birthplace, *picture* A-654
  covered bridges, *picture* B-439
  geographic region
    New England U-43, *map* U-44, *picture* U-46, *Reference-Outline* U-132
    North America, *map* N-351
  Montpelier M-570
  quarrying, *picture* Q-6
  state symbols
    flag, *picture* F-160
    flower, *picture* S-427
    tree V-292. *see also in index* Sugar maple
  Statuary Hall, *table* S-437b
  taxation, *tables* T-37, 39

Vermont, University of, and State Agricultural College, Burlington, Vt.; founded 1791; arts and sciences, agriculture and home economics, education, medicine, technology; graduate studies V-288
  library, *picture* V-293

Vermouth, an aromatic wine W-237

Vernal equinox A-718

Verne, Jules (1828–1905), French author V-303. *see also in index* 'Twenty Thousand Leagues Under the Sea'
  'From the Earth to the Moon' S-341d, *pictures* S-341a
  frontiers F-427
  science fiction S-62

Verneuil process, in making jewels
  synthetic gems J-113
    sapphires and rubies C-796

Vernier, a scale invented by Vernier
  instrumentation I-229
  micrometer M-378

Vernis Martin (Martin varnish), a brilliant translucent lacquer developed in the 18th century by the Martin brothers; the secret of making it is now lost and articles decorated with it are in museums.

Vernon, Dorothy (16th century), daughter and heiress of Sir George Vernon; eloped with Sir John Manners and became ancestress of dukes of Rutland; heroine of Charles Major's novel, 'Dorothy Vernon of Haddon Hall'.

Vernon, Edward (1684–1757), English admiral; captured (1739) Porto Bello, Panama, with a fleet of 6 ships; Mount Vernon, Va., named for him M-639

Vernon, B.C., city near n. end of Okanagan Lake 27 mi (43 km) n.e. of Kelowna; fruit-growing and fruit processing; lumber, poultry, eggs; fishing, hunting; pop. 19,987, *map* C-109

Vernon, Conn., 11 mi (18 km) n.e. of Hartford; electronic components, chemicals; dairy and truck farms; pop. of township 27,974.

Veron, Tex., city in n. part of state, about 45 mi (70 km) n.w. of Wichita Falls; cotton, wheat, livestock; oil wells; meat-packing; clothing, feed; pop. 12,695.

Verona, Italy, fortified city 62 mi (100 km) w. of Venice on Adige River; noted art center in Middle Ages; famous art collections and Roman remains; Congress of great European powers 1822; bombarded by Austrian aviators in World War I; scene of 'Romeo and Juliet'; pop. 221,138, *maps* E-361, I-404
  amphitheater, *picture* I-393

Verona, N.J., borough 8 mi (13 km) n.w. of Newark, near Montclair; brushes, hardware; incorporated 1907; pop. 14,166.

Veronese, Paolo (originally Paolo Cagliari) (1528–88), great painter of Venetian school; all works outstanding for spectacular effects in color, pattern, and composition; magnificent mythological paintings in Doge's Palace, Venice, include 'Rape of Europa' P-38

Veronica, Saint, legendary woman of Jerusalem, on whose kerchief, used by Jesus to wipe the bloody sweat from his brow on way to Golgotha, his portrait was said to have been miraculously imprinted; festival July 12.

Veronica (popularly called speedwell), genus of plants and shrubs of the figwort family with blue, pink, or white flowers; well-known species is the long-leaved veronica *Veronica longifolia*, a tall garden perennial with small violet or blue flowers on erect spikes.

Verrazano-Narrows Bridge, in New York, links Brooklyn and Richmond N-271, *picture* N-263

Verrazzano, Giovanni da (1480–1528), Florentine explorer of North America for France
  Canada and Newfoundland C-90
  Long Island L-297
  New Jersey N-199
  New York N-256, N-279
  voyage A-333

Verres, Gaius, corrupt and rapacious Roman quaestor and propraetor (governor) of Sicily 73–71 BC; brought to trial by the people and prosecuted by Cicero; only two of the seven orations that Cicero wrote against him were delivered because Verres fled, knowing conviction was certain.

Verrill, Addison Emery (1839–1926), U.S. natural scientist, born in Greenwood, Me.; studied fauna of Atlantic and Pacific coasts and marine animals of Bermuda Islands.

Verrill, Alpheus Hyatt (1871–1954), U.S. naturalist and explorer, born in New Haven, Conn.; originator of autochrome process of color photography; explorer in Bermuda, West Indies, Panama ('Harper's Book for Young Naturalists'; 'Islands and Their Mysteries'; 'Old Civilizations of the New World').

Verrocchio, Andrea del (1435–88), Italian sculptor, goldsmith, and painter; one of greatest early Renaissance artists; painted famous 'Baptism of Christ'
  Leonardo da Vinci L-132
  statue of Colleoni H-272, S-86, *picture* S-87

Verruca. *see in index* wart

Verruga peruana, stage of Carrion's disease; skin eruption characterized by reddish papules and nodules
  Noguchi N-330

Versailles, France, suburb of Paris; pop. 89,035 V-303, *map* E-361
  court of Louis XIV E-320
  fountains F-335
  France, *picture* F-351, *map* F-372
  interior design I-248
  palace P-123, A-558, F-458, *picture* A-559
    imitations C-200

Versailles, Treaty of (1919), *table* T-275. *see also in index* Peace Conference of 1919
  China C-372
  France F-363
  Germany G-122
    gliders G-168
    Weimar Republic W-142
  United States U-185
    Wilson W-219
  warfare W-27
  World War I W-319

Verschaffelt, Pieter Anton (or Pietro Fiammingo, or Peter the Fleming) (1710–93), Flemish sculptor and architect of rococo style, born in Ghent; trained in Paris and Rome; became court sculptor in Germany.

Verse, a line of poetry; may mean more than one line, a "stanza," sometimes applied to poetry in general. *see also in index* Poetry
  forms P-406
  Indian literature I-105

Vers libre. *see in index* Free verse

Verst, Soviet measure of length or distance; equal to 0.6629 mi (about 2/3 mi), or 1.0684 km, *table* W-141

Vert, in heraldry, *picture* H-136

Vert, Cap. *see in index* Verde, Cape

Vertebra (plural vertebrae), any one of the segments of the spinal column S-209
  bird B-245
  development E-201
  human A-390

Vertebrates, animals having a spinal column V-303
  animal morphology A-422, *picture* A-423
  average length of life, *chart* A-423
  blood systems B-317
    reptiles R-152
  embryogeny E-200
  frog F-406
  hand H-27
  invertebrate comparison I-282
  joint J-136
  lungs L-336
  skeleton S-208

Verthandi (or Verdandi), in German and Norse mythology
  Fates F-44

Vertical boring mill, a machine tool T-222

Vertical draw, a glass manufacturing method G-163, *picture* G-157

Vertical file, for information storage
  libraries L-164

Vertical lift bridge B-442, *picture* B-443

Vertical shaper (or slotter), a tool T-220

Vertical-speed indicator. *see in index* Rate-of-climb indicator

Vertical takeoff and landing (VTOL), aircraft A-80, A-162, A-207
  helicopter H-118

Vertigo, a severe form of dizziness resulting from the inability of the body to adapt to abrupt or unexpected motion D-179

Vertumnus, in Roman mythology, a god who watched over plants in their change from blossom to fruit; husband of Pomona.

Verulam, Baron. *see in index* Bacon, Francis

Verulamium, Roman town in what is now Hertfordshire, England; archaeological excavations have revealed a high Roman culture.

Vervain family (or Verbenaceae), family of plants, shrubs, and trees including the hemp tree, verbenas, lantanas, golden dewdrop, lippias, and teak. *see also in index* Verbena

Verviers, Belgium, town 15 mi (25 km) s.e. of Liège; woolen goods, dyes, leather products; suffered severely during German occupation 1914–18; pop. 35,453.

Vervins, Treaty of (1598), *table* T-275

Verwoerd, Hendrik Frensch (1901–66), South African statesman, born in Amsterdam, The Netherlands; chief architect of apartheid; senator 1948–58, minister native affairs 1950–58, prime minister 1958–66
  assassination, *list* A-704

Very, Jones (1813–80), U.S. poet, born in Salem, Mass.; wrote religious sonnets and lyrics which he said were inspired directly by the Holy Ghost ('Essays and Poems').

Very, Very Tall, game G-13

Very-high wave, *tables* R-34, R-50

Very Large Array (VLA), telescope T-68, *picture* T-65

Very-large-scale integration (VLSI), microprocessor M-379

Very lights, signals of red, green, or white fire shot from a Very pistol; lights are fired in groups, thus indicating a code; used in Army and Navy; invented 1877 by Edward Wilson Very.

Very Long Baseline Interferometer (VLBI), in astronomical observation O-457

Very-low wave, *tables* R-34, R-50

Very pistol S-194

Verzuiling (or pillarization), long-entrenched system of religious and ideological strata of Dutch society N-131

Vesalius, Andreas (1514–64), Belgian anatomist
  medicine M-283
  science S-57f
  zoology Z-470

Vesey, Denmark (1767–1822), U.S. slave revolt leader, born in Africa; freed slave who organized an insurrection to take over Charleston, S.C., 1822; conspiracy betrayed and members executed B-290

Vesle, river of n.e. France; rises n. of Châlons-sur-Marne, flows 90 mi (145 km) past Reims to Aisne River 6 mi (10 km) e. of Soissons.

Vespasian (or Titus Flavius Vespasianus) (AD 9–79), Roman emperor AD 69–79, father of Titus and Domitian; in his reign Titus captured Jerusalem, the Colosseum was begun, and Agricola extended Roman sway in Britain
  Isle of Wight W-202

Vespers, Sicilian, massacre of French in Sicily (1282) S-192

Vesper sparrow (or bay-winged bunting), bird *Pooecetes gramineus* of the family Fringillidae S-368

Vespucius, Americus (1451 or 1454–1512), Florentine navigator for whom America was named V-304, A-330

Vessels. *see in index* Ships

Vesta, in Roman mythology, goddess of the hearth and home; Greek counterpart Hestia V-304
  Roman mythology M-701

Vesta, an asteroid A-706

Vesta, a type of match M-209

Vestal, Stanley (pseudonym of Walter Stanley Campbell) (1887–1957), U.S. author and educator, born near Severy, Kan.; professor and director of courses in professional writing University of Oklahoma after 1939; noted for carefully documented books on old West (biography; history; novels; ballads; literary manuals).

Vestal Virgins, priestesses in ancient Roman religion V-305, *picture* V-304
  Roman mythology M-702

Vestfjord (or West Fjord), Norway, arm of Atlantic Ocean between mainland and Lofoten Islands.

Vestris, Gaetano (1729–1808), ballet dancer and choreographer, born in Florence, Italy; ballet master of Paris Opéra and of King's Theatre, London D-24

Vestris, Madame (1797–1856), British actress and manager who inaugurated tasteful and beautiful stage decor, and set a standard in stage costumes
  directing D-154

Vestry, architecture, a room in a church where vestments are kept and where the clergy and choristers robe for services.

Vesuvius, Mount (Italian Vesuvio), volcano in Italy V-305, V-378, *maps* E-361, I-404, P-443
  archaeology A-531
  mountain, *picture* M-635
  Naples, *picture* N-11
  Pompeii and Herculaneum P-442

Vetch V-305
  milk vetch P-408

Veterans Administration (VA), United States
  expenditures, *table* U-114
  health agencies H-89
  housing H-303

Veterans' aid
  Civil War P-188
  GI Bill of Rights U-208
  pensions P-188

Veterans Committee. *see in index* American Veterans Committee

1940–53; elected to Presidium 1952, president 1953–60.

Vorster, Balthazar Johannes (born 1915), South African lawyer and political leader, born in Jamestown, South Africa; advocate of apartheid; right-wing extremist; minister of justice 1961–66; prime minister 1966–78.

'Vortex, The', work by Rivera L-70

Vorticella (popularly called bell animalcules), genus of bell-shaped Protozoa A-428, *picture* L-267

Vosges, department of France in region called Lorraine; agriculture and forestry; area, 2,279 sq mi; pop. 397,957, *map* F-372
  Alsace-Lorraine A-320

Vosges, mountains of e. France V-386
  France, *map* F-372

Voskhods, Soviet spacecraft S-346f, *table* S-348

Voss, Johann Heinrich (1751–1826), German poet, best known for translations of Homer, Virgil, Shakespeare, and Horace; in 'Luise', one of his famous 'Idylls' and his most famous poem, he expressed a German theme in classical style.

Vostoks, Soviet spacecraft S-346f, 342b, *table* S-348
  Gagarin G-2

Voting V-386, *pictures* V-386, *table* V-388. *see also in index* Elections; Suffrage
  Australian system A-803
  black Americans B-296
    King K-244
    Reconstruction era R-114, *picture* R-113
  caucus P-432
  citizenship C-440
  compulsory V-276
  franchise F-373
  Hispanic Americans H-164
  parliamentary law P-132a
  plebiscite. *see in index* Plebiscite
  president. *see in index* President, *subhead* election
  registration S-505

Voting machine E-148, *pictures* E-147, V-387

'Voting of the Greek Chiefs', *picture* D-252

Voting Rights Act (1965), United States B-297
  King K-245

Vowels, in alphabet P-268b
  early writing A-317
  language L-31, 40

'Voyager', experimental aircraft flown by Rutan and Yeager A-208

Voyagers, U.S. space probes, *table* S-344

Voyageur (French traveler), colonial French Canadian employed to carry men and goods, especially between the fur-trading posts F-471, *picture* F-469

Voyenkomat, Soviet military committee R-332a

Voysey, Charles (1857–1941), British furniture designer and architect F-462

Voyvodina, district in Yugoslavia, formerly part of Hungary; population a mixture of Slavs, Germans, Magyars, and Romanians.

Voznesensky, Andrei (born 1933), Soviet poet, born in Moscow; known for his experimental style and humanistic themes; traveled widely in Europe and U.S. ('Mozaika'; 'Parabola'; 'The Fifth Ace') R-360b

Vredeman de Vries, Hans (1527–1604?), Dutch architect and painter F-457

Vriesland, The Netherlands. *see in index* Friesland

VTOL. *see in index* Vertical takeoff and landing

VTR. *see in index* Videocassette recorder

Vuillard, Jean Edouard (1868–1940), French painter, lithographer; impressionistic, influenced by oriental prints; portraits, decorative interiors, still lifes.

Vulcan, in Roman mythology, god of fire and metalworking; identified with Greek Hephaestus M-701

Vulcanite, rubber hardened by combination with a large proportion of sulfur at high temperatures; used for combs, phonograph records, insulation.

Vulcanization of rubber R-304
  Goodyear R-306, I-274, *picture* I-275, *table* I-273

Vulgate, Latin Bible B-185, L-78

Vulpecula, constellation, *chart* C-681

Vulture, a carrion bird V-388, B-247, *picture* B-269
  predatory behavior B-280
  'Prometheus Strangling the Vulture', *picture* S-93

Vulturidae, vulture family V-388

Vyborg (Finnish Viipuri), U.S.S.R., city and seaport on Gulf of Finland; connected by canal with inland lakes; formerly Finnish, included in U.S.S.R. since 1944; pop. 51,088, *maps* E-361, R-344

Vyshinsky, Andrei Yanuarievich (or Andrei Yanuarievich Vishinsky) (1883–1954), Soviet diplomat and jurist, born in Odessa, U.S.S.R.; became chief state prosecutor 1935, conducted Moscow purge trials 1936–38; first deputy foreign minister 1940–49 and 1953–54, foreign minister 1949–53; head of Soviet delegation to UN General Assembly 1953–54.

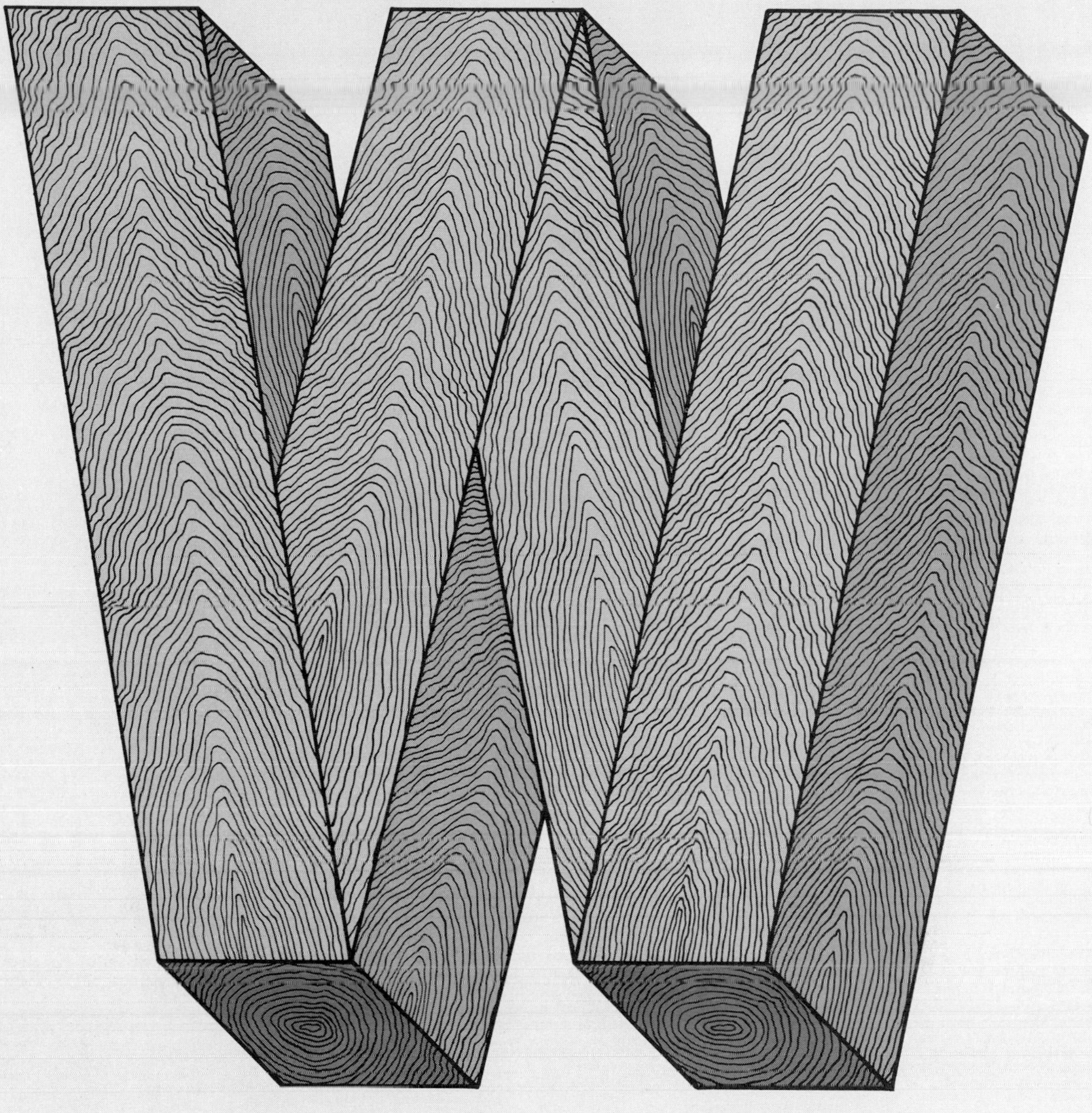

The letter W

is a descendant of the letter V, which is discussed in the Fact-Index for Volume 24. This letter did not come into existence until after the Norman Conquest of England in 1066. Until then, the Latin letter V, which was inherited from Greek and Phoenician writings (1), was used for both the sound "v" and the sound "w." The Anglo-Saxon runic writing developed a separate character (2) for the sound of "w," as in the English word "we." The Anglo-Saxons called the letter *wen.*

After the Normans conquered England, they needed a letter to take care of the sound "w" in Anglo-Saxon words. They developed the practice of using a double U for this sound (3). Gradually they linked together two of the old pointed capital letters for the new character (4). The present English name for this—"double U"—still indicates how the Normans invented the letter. The English small "w" is a copy of the capital, except that in handwriting it is connected to adjoining letters.

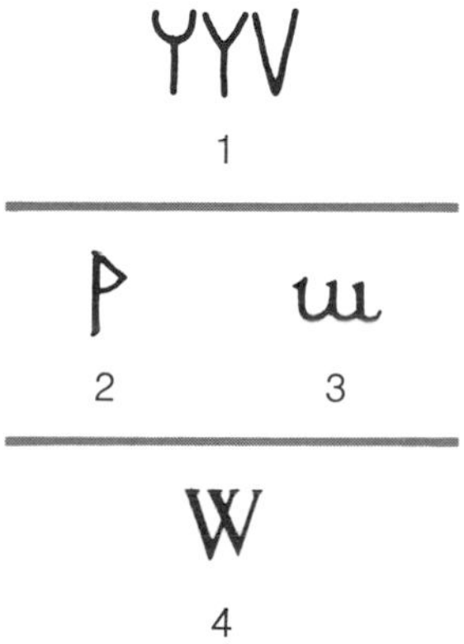

W, chemical element. *see in index* Tungsten
Waal River, river in w. Europe, branch of the Rhine River N-125
Waals, Johannes van der (full name Johannes Diderik van der Waals) (1837–1923), Dutch physicist W-2. *see also in index* Nobel Prizewinners, *table*
Wabana, Newf., town on Bell Island in Conception Bay 12 mi (19 km) n.w. of St. John's; iron mining; pop. 4,254 N-169
Wabash, Ind., city on Wabash River about 40 mi (60 km) s.w. of Fort Wayne; rubber products, temperature controls, insulating materials, paper products; pop. 12,985
  Indiana, *map* I-102
Wabash and Erie Canal, canal from Toledo, Ohio, to Evansville, Ind., *map* C-126
Wabash College, Crawfordsville, Ind.; private, for men; founded 1832; liberal arts.
Wabash River, Ohio River tributary rising in w. Ohio; forms part of the Illinois-Indiana boundary; 475 mi (765 km) long I-88, U-41, 71
Wabi Shebelle River, river in e. Africa, rises in Ethiopia and flows s.e. into Somalia then s.w. to the Juba River, *map* A-118
WAC. *see in index* Women's Army Corps
Waccamaw Lake, large natural lake in North Carolina N-354
Wac Corporal, U.S. rocket G-311
Wace, Alan John Bayard (1879–1957), British archaeologist; carried on excavations begun by Heinrich Schliemann at Mycenae, Greece; many publications A-61
'Wacht am Rhein, Die' (The Watch on the Rhine), German national song written by Max Schneckenburger (1819–49) when Rhine was imperiled by France in 1840; music by Karl Wilhelm (1815–73) N-66
Wachusett Mountain, in Massachusetts M-189
Wachusett Reservoir, in Massachusetts M-190
Waco, Tex., city on Brazos River in e.-central part of state about 85 mi (140 km) s. of Dallas; trade in cotton, corn, grain, livestock; textile products, tires and other rubber products, lumber products and furniture, glass; Baylor University; incorporated 1856; pop. 101,261 T-120, *map* U-40
  North America, *map* N-351
Waddell, George Edward (nickname Rube) (1876–1914), U.S. baseball pitcher, born in Bradford, Pa.; chiefly with Philadelphia, A.L., 1902–07; was noted for strike-out achievements and colorful conduct.
Wade, Benjamin Franklin (1800–78), U.S. statesman, born in West Springfield, Mass.; U.S. senator from Ohio 1851–69; bitter antislavery leader and critic of Lincoln's and Johnson's mild Reconstruction policies; as president pro tempore of Senate would have become president of United States if Johnson had been removed; a Republican.
Wade-Giles System, Chinese writing system C-336
Wadi (or wady, also called arroya in southwestern U.S.), desert gully or dry riverbed
  Libya L-188
  oasis O-454
  Sahara S-15
Wadsworth, Peleg (1748–1829), American Revolutionary War officer, born in Duxbury, Mass.; commanded eastern department (1780–81); member U.S. House of Representatives (1793–1807).
Wadsworth, Ohio, city located 12 mi (19 km) s.w. of Akron; metal processing, matches, coal, brick, tile, granite; dairy products; pop. 15,166.
Wafer tumbler lock (or disc tumbler lock) L-277
Wagadugu. *see in index* Ouagadougou
Wage, in economics. *see also in index* Income; Salary
  business cycle B-518
  economics E-61
  inflation I-198
  labor L-3, L-5
  minimum. *see in index* Minimum wage
  strike S-489
  United States U-112
  U.S.S.R. R-330a
  workmen's compensation insurance I-235
Wage and Hour Division, U.S. Department of Labor U-163–4
Wage and Price Stability, Council on, United States U-156–7
Wagenaar, Bernard (1894–1971), U.S. composer, born in Arnhem, The Netherlands; to U.S. 1920, citizen 1927; on faculty Juilliard School of Music, New York City, many years (chamber opera, 'Pieces of Eight'; symphonies; chamber music).
Wageni, people
  Zaire, *picture* Z-444
Wagering (or betting), risking something, such as money, on an uncertain event
  horse racing H-275
Wages and hours law, United States, popular name of Fair Labor Standards Act. *see in index* Fair Labor Standards Act of 1938
Wage Stabilization Board, created Sept. 1950 to administer wage stabilization under Defense Production Act of 1950; reconstituted July 1952; terminated 1953.
Wage Stabilization Board, National, created by President Truman Dec. 1945 to help settle wage labor disputes; assumed functions of National War Labor Board; functions transferred 1947 to Departments of Labor and Treasury.
Wagnalls, Adam Willis (1843–1924), U.S. Lutheran minister, publisher, born in Lithopolis, Ohio; one of founders of Funk and Wagnalls Co. *see also in index* Funk, Isaac K.
Wagner, Cosima (1837–1930), daughter of Franz Liszt; 2nd wife of Richard Wagner; created annual Wagnerian Festival at Bayreuth, Germany, and with son Siegfried directed it after Wagner's death W-2
Wagner, John Peter (nickname Honus, or Hans, often called The Flying Dutchman) (1874–1955), U.S. baseball shortstop, born in Carnegie, Pa.; played for Louisville, N.L., 1897–99 and for Pittsburgh, N.L., 1900–17; he was baseball's greatest shortstop; batted .300 or more for 17 consecutive seasons; played in 2,785 games; at bat 10,427 times; made 3,430 hits, including 2,426 singles, 651 doubles, and 252 triples B-93, *profile* B-95
Wagner, Otto (1841–1918), Austrian architect, *profile* A-569
Wagner, Richard (full name Wilhelm Richard Wagner) (1813–83), German composer W-2
  Bavarian music festivals B-111
  Bruckner B-467
  classical music M-673
  opera O-567
  'Parsifal' H-207
  'Siegfried' S-192a
  'Ring of the Nibelung' N-302
Wagner, Siegfried (1869–1930), German composer and conductor, son of Richard Wagner; directed Wagner Festival Playhouse at Bayreuth and put it on sound basis.
Wagner Act. *see in index* National Labor Relations Act of 1935
Wagner College, Staten Island, N.Y.; United Lutheran; founded 1883; arts and sciences; graduate study; program in Bregenz, Austria N-254
Wagner von Jauregg, Julius (1857–1940), Austrian physician, born in Vienna; noted for his treatment of goiter and cretinism. *see also in index* Nobel Prizewinners, *table*
Wagon W-2
  circus C-427
  development of wheel W-193
  frontier movement, *picture* F-420
  Gypsy caravans, *picture* S-156
  mail delivery, *picture* P-461
  oxcart. *see in index* Oxcart
  Pakistan, *picture* P-77
  stagecoach. *see in index* Stagecoach
  Studebaker S-494
  toy wagon, *picture* P-388
Wagoner, Porter (born 1930), U.S. country musician M-679
Wagon train, wagons used to travel overland O-599
Wagram, battle of (1809), warfare, *list* W-16
Wagtail, common name of a group of Old World passerine birds belonging with the pipits to the family Motacillidae; named from their habit of wagging the tail.
Wahhabi, Islamic sect in Saudi Arabia founded by Abd-al-Wahhab (1691–1787) S-52b, A-523
  Ibn Saud I-5
Wahiawa, Hawaii, city on central plateau of island of Oahu; pineapples, sugar; pop. 16,911 H-70
Wahlenbergia, genus of annual and perennial plants of the bellflower family; low-growing or creeping, with leaves small, narrow, sometimes clustered at base of plant; flowers bell-shaped or tubular, blue, usually solitary, nodding above the foliage.
Wahlöö, Per (1926–75) Swedish writer D-119
Wahoo, saltwater food fish *Acanthocybium solandri* found in waters of Florida and West Indies; family Scombridae; reaches 6 ft (2 m) in length.
Wahoo, name applied to several different trees including the winged elm, cascara, umbrella magnolia, white basswood and spindle tree.
Wahoo elm. *see in index* Winged elm
Wahpeton, division of the Dakota group of Sioux Indians; live in North Dakota and South Dakota N-383
Wahpeton, N.D., city in agricultural area on Red River near s.e. corner of state; farm machinery, metal culverts; North Dakota State School of Science, U.S. Indian school; pop. 9,064 N-382, *map* U-40
Waialeale, Mount, on Kauai, Hawaii; 5,080 ft (1,550 m); the wettest spot on Earth H-60
  rainfall R-89
Waiblingen, West Germany, town n.e. of Stuttgart; pop. 24,622. *see also in index* Guelfs and Ghibellines
Waikato River, in New Zealand N-286
Waikiki Beach, in Honolulu, Hawaii H-230, *map* H-58, *picture* H-57
Wailing Wall, in Jerusalem. *see in index* Western Wall
Wailuku, Hawaii, residential area on island of Maui, just w. of Kahului; sugar; pop. 7,979, *picture* U-97
Wainwright, Jonathan Mayhew (1883–1953), U.S. Army officer, born in Walla Walla, Wash.; succeeded General MacArthur as commander in Philippines March 1942 and refused to leave his men during siege of Corregidor; prisoner of Japanese 1942–45; head of 4th Army in San Antonio, Tex., 1946–47
  World War II W-328
Wainwright, Alta., town 120 mi (190 km) s.e. of Edmonton; railway divisional point; oil refining, flour milling; pop. 5,872.
Waipahu, Hawaii, residential city about 10 mi (16 km) n.w. of downtown Honolulu; on n.w. shore of Pearl Harbor; pop. 29,139 H-70
Wairakei, New Zealand township on North Island 193 mi (311 km) southeast of Auckland; tourist center with hot mineral baths; site of geothermal electrical generation plant; pop. 703 N-286
Waitaki River, river in New Zealand N-287
Waitangi, Treaty of, pact between United Kingdom and Maori people in New Zealand; signed 1840
  New Zealand N-283, 295
Waite, Morrison Remick (1816–88), U.S. jurist, born in Lyme, Conn.; chief justice of the U.S. 1874–88; in decisions growing out of Civil War and reconstruction, he opposed extension of federal powers.
'Waiting for Godot', play by Beckett B-123
Wakashan, linguistic family of North American peoples; consisting of the Kwakiutl and Nootka groups.
Wakato Bridge, Japan, bridge over Dokai Bay, Kyushu, *table* B-324b
Wakayama, Japan, city on s.w. Honshu near Osaka; textiles; 8th-century temple nearby; pop. 365,267, *maps* A-700, J-78
Wake, watch or vigil beside body of a dead person; sometimes accompanied by festivity; an ancient custom, it is found today among the Irish and many other peoples; church wakes, common in Middle Ages, were night vigils of meditation and prayer to celebrate the dedication of a church; suppressed when revelry supplanted prayer.
Wakefield, Edward Gibbon (1796–1862), colonization promoter, born in London W-4
Wakefield, England, manufacturing city of

Yorkshire, on Calder River 9 mi (15 km) s. of Leeds; buildings date from 1300s; pop. 59,630
  War of Roses R-290

Wakefield, Mass., town 10 mi (16 km) n. of Boston; electronics, shoes, knitwear, machinery, metal products; pop. of township 24,895.

Wakefield, Va., birthplace of George Washington, now George Washington Birthplace N.M. V-349, *picture* W-37

Wake Forest University, Winston-Salem, N.C.; Baptist; founded 1834 at Wake Forest, moved to present site 1956; arts and science, business administration, law, medicine; graduate studies N-358
  Winston-Salem W-240

Wake Island, coral island in Pacific; area 3 sq mi (8 sq km); pop. 302 W-4
  McKinley M-20
  Pacific Ocean, *map* P-6
  United States U-116
  World War II W-328, 344

Wake-robin. *see in index* Trillium

Wake-up. *see in index* Eastern yellow-shafted flicker

Waksman, Selman Abraham (1888–1973), U.S. microbiologist, born in Russia; to U.S. 1910, became citizen 1916; joined faculty Rutgers University 1918, professor 1930–58, director Institute of Microbiology 1949–58; discovered neomycin and was chief scientist in discovery of streptomycin; autobiography, 'My Life with the Microbes' M-285. *see also in index* Nobel Prizewinners, *table*

Walachia (or Wallachia), district including most of s. Romania R-316

Walapai, Yuman Indian tribe living in w. Arizona; inhabit an area from the Colorado River eastward.

Walburga, Saint. *see in index* Walpurgis

Walcheren, westernmost island of The Netherlands, in s.w. province of Zeeland; pop. 82,043.

Walcott, Derek (born 1930), St. Lucian poet and dramatist ('Twenty-Five Poems')
  Caribbean literature C-167, *picture* 166

Walcott, Joe (originally Arnold Raymond Cream, nickname Jersey Joe) (born 1914), U.S. boxer, born in Merchantville, N.J. B-392

Wald, George (born 1906), U.S. biologist, born in New York, N.Y.; professor Harvard 1948–; Max Berg Award 1969. *see also in index* Nobel Prizewinners, *table*

Wald, Lillian D. (1867–1940), U.S. social worker, born in Cincinnati, Ohio; founded Henry Street Settlement in New York City 1893; organized there the world's first public school nursing system 1902; obtained playgrounds in New York slums; author of 'The House on Henry Street' and 'Windows on Henry Street'
  Hall of Fame, *table* H-16
  women's rights W-277

Waldeck-Rousseau, Pierre Marie (1846–1904), French statesman, born in Nantes, France; defended De Lesseps in Panama Canal scandal; premier of France 1899–1902; paved way for pardon of Alfred Dreyfus.

'Walden', book by Thoreau A-347

Waldenses (or Vaudois), religious sect living in French and Italian Alps; founded 12th century by Peter Waldo, rich merchant of Lyons; massacred 1545
  Francis I F-374

Waldheim, Kurt (born 1918), Austrian diplomat and president 1986– W-4
  Austria A-827
  United Nations U-27, *picture* U-25

Waldo, Samuel (1695–1759), American merchant and general, born in Boston, Mass.; proprietor of land west of Penobscot River in Maine, known as Waldo patent; after 1733 invited settlers from Germany, Scotland, and Ireland; opened lime- and ironworks.

Waldseemüller, Martin (1470?–1518?), German geographer; named the Western Hemisphere "America" V-304, A-330

Waldwick, N.J., residential borough 7 mi (11 km) n.e. of Paterson; incorporated; pop. 10,802.

Wale, fabric texture in knitting T-138

Wales, principality of United Kingdom, occupying w.-central peninsula of island; 8,017 sq mi (20,764 sq km); pop. 2,724,540 W-5, *map* E-360. *see also in index* United Kingdom cities. *see also in index* names of cities
  emigration of Quakers P-166
  England E-230
  folktales S-472, *lists* S-481b
  government U-16, 18
  national parks N-27

Wales, prince of, usual title of the heir apparent to the British throne E-106

Walesa, Lech (born 1943), Polish labor leader W-6. *see also in index* Nobel Prizewinners, *table*
  labor movement L-10
  Poland P-415

Walgreen, Charles Rudolph (1873–1939), U.S. business executive, born near Galesburg, Ill.; founder of Walgreen Company, largest chain of drugstores in U.S.; opened first one in Chicago 1901.

Walhalla. *see in index* Valhalla

Walk, race T-244

Walker, Madame C.J. (1869–1919), U.S. businesswoman and philanthropist, born in Delta, La.; famous as manufacturer of cosmetics for black Americans.

Walker, David (1785–1830), U.S. abolitionist and pamphleteer, born in North Carolina; lecturer for abolitionist groups; his pamphlets considered insurrectionary B-291

Walker, Emery (1851–1933), English engraver and printer, born in London; with Morris founded Kelmscott Press; later associated with Cobden-Sanderson in Doves Press, and with Bruce Rogers
  typography T-338

Walker, Francis Amasa (1840–97), U.S. educator, political economist, born in Boston, Mass.; professor at Yale University 1873–81, president Massachusetts Institute of Technology 1881–97 ('The Wages Question').

Walker, Frank Comerford (1886–1959), U.S. lawyer and public official, born in Plymouth, Pa.; first director National Emergency Council 1933–35; postmaster general in F.D. Roosevelt's cabinet 1940–45, *picture* R-272

Walker, Henry Oliver (1843–1929), U.S. painter, born in Boston, Mass.; best known for idealized figure compositions ('Eros et Musa'; 'Morning Vision'; 'The Singers'), and for murals in Library of Congress and Massachusetts State House.

Walker, Horatio (1858–1938), Canadian artist, born in Listowel, Ont.; painter of rustic life ('Wood Cutters'; 'Shepherdess and Sheep').

Walker, John, Jr., U.S.-born Soviet collaborator
  spy ring E-303, *picture* E-305

Walker, Joseph A. (1921–66), U.S. test pilot, born in Washington, Pa.; chief research pilot, NASA; set many speed and altitude records in X-15; killed in midair collision.

Walker, Joseph Reddeford (1798–1876), U.S. trapper and guide; member of Bonneville and Frémont expeditions; Walker Pass and Walker Lake named for him
  Nevada N-137
  route, *map* U-176

Walker, Leroy Pope (1817–84), U.S. lawyer and political leader, born in Huntsville, Ala.; secretary of war, Confederate States of America 1861.

Walker, Mary Edwards (1832–1919), U.S. women's rights leader, born in Oswego, N.Y.; first woman assistant army surgeon (Civil War); practiced medicine in Washington, D.C., 1865–1919; worked for woman suffrage; wore men's clothing.

Walker, Mildred (born 1905), U.S. novelist, born in Philadelphia, Pa. ('Fireweed'; 'The Brewers' Big Horses'; 'The Southwest Corner')
  'Winter Wheat' R-112b

Walker, Robert John (1801–69), U.S. statesman, born in Northumberland, Pa.; secretary of treasury under Polk.

Walker, T-bone (born Aaron Walker) (1910–75), U.S. musician M-679

Walker, Thomas (1715–94), Virginia physician; led party through Cumberland Gap into region that is now Kentucky; gave name to Walker Mts. in s. Virginia.

Walker, William (1824–60), U.S. adventurer, born in Nashville, Tenn.; dominated in Nicaragua 1855–57; executed by Hondurans on his expedition there
  Nicaragua N-305

Walker, Mich., city 7 mi (11 km) n.w. of Grand Rapids; residential with some industry; incorporated 1962; pop. 15,088.

Walker Cup, trophy awarded biennially in matches between men's amateur golf team of United Kingdom and that of U.S.; donated 1921 by George H. Walker, former president of United States Golf Association; officially USGA International Trophy
  golf G-192
  Jones J-138

Walker Lake, in w. Nevada; receives Walker River; has no outlet; 125 sq mi (325 sq km).

Walker Pass, in s. California, across the Sierra Nevada, at altitude of about 5,250 ft (1,600 m), 60 mi (100 km) n.e. of Bakersfield.

Walker's Point, early Milwaukee settlement M-422

Walkerville, Ont., former municipality, now part of city of Windsor, opposite Detroit, Mich.; steel, automobiles, wire, and drugs.

Walkie-talkie, radio, *pictures* R-46, 49, P-429, S-193

Walking
  bionic studies B-236
  hiking H-151
  jogging J-121
  race T-244

Walking perch, fish F-126, 131

Walking stick, insect, *picture* P-510
  egg, *picture* E-111
  mimicry M-423

Walking the plank, fictional method used by mutineers and pirates to execute people; doomed person was made to walk blindfolded along a plank, laid over side of ship, until he fell into the sea; in Robert Louis Stevenson's 'Treasure Island' (1883) and William H. Smyth's 'Sailor's Wordbook' (1867).

'Walk in the Night, A', novel by La Guma L-23

Walk on, in theater, *list* T-155

Walkout, in labor S-489

'Walküre, Die' (The Valkyrie), second opera in Richard Wagner's series 'The Ring of the Nibelungs' ('Der Ring des Nibelungen') O-568

Wallaby, marsupial mammal M-154
  Australia A-779
  furs, *table* F-465
  kangaroo K-172
  mammal M-81

Wallace, Alfred Russel (1823–1913), English naturalist; spent 4 years exploring the Amazon and its tributaries, later publishing 'Travels on the Amazon and Rio Negro'; in 1854 went to Malay Archipelago for 8 years; while there evolved theory of natural selection in evolution, which Charles Darwin had discovered independently; wrote many scientific and philosophic works B-138, 217. *see also in index* Wallace's line
  Darwin D-39
  evolution E-366

Wallace, DeWitt (born 1889), U.S. editor and publisher, born in St. Paul, Minn.; founded *The Reader's Digest* 1921, editor and publisher 1921–65, cochairman with wife 1965–73; Medal of Freedom 1971 M-35

Wallace, Edgar (1875–1932), English writer; reporter in Boer War; mystery stories ('The Four Just Men', 'Sanders of the River', 'The Green Archer'); plays ('The Ringer', 'The Flying Squad').

Wallace, George Corley (born 1919), U.S. political leader, born in Clio, Ala.; assistant attorney general of Alabama 1946–47; state legislator 1947–53; judge 1953–58; governor of Alabama (Democrat) 1963–67, 1971–78, 1982–86; American Independent candidate for president 1968, Democratic primary candidate 1972 V-387
  electoral vote, *chart* P-495

Wallace, Henry Agard (1888–1965), U.S. editor and public official, born in Adair County, Iowa; son of Henry C. Wallace; editor *Wallace's Farmer* 1924–29, *Iowa Homestead and Wallace's Farmer* 1929–33; secretary of agriculture 1933–40; chairman Board of Economic Warfare 1941–43; vice-president of U.S. 1941–45; secretary of commerce 1945–46; Progressive party candidate for president 1948 R-268, 271, 276, P-434, *pictures* R-268, 272, 276

Wallace, Henry Cantwell (1866–1924), U.S. secretary of agriculture 1921–24, born in Rock Island, Ill.; father of Henry A. Wallace; published farm journals; contributed much to advancement of agriculture.

Wallace, Lewis (1827–1905), U.S. novelist, Civil War general, and statesman; born in Brookville, Ind.; governor New Mexico Territory 1878–81; minister to Turkey 1881–85 ('Ben-Hur', 'Fair God'). *see also in index* 'Ben-Hur, a Tale of the Christ'
  Statuary Hall, *table* S-437a

Wallace, Roderick John (nickname Bobby) (1874–1960), U.S. baseball player, born in Millvale, Pa.; chiefly a shortstop (also third baseman, outfielder, pitcher, second baseman); played in major leagues for 25 consecutive seasons (2,369 games); player for Cleveland, N.L., 1894–98, St. Louis, N.L., 1899–1901, St. Louis, A.L., 1902–16, St. Louis, N.L., 1917–18; manager Cincinnati, N.L., 1937.

Wallace, William (1270?–1305), Scottish hero W-7
  Edward I E-107
  Scotland S-70

Wallace's line, imaginary line dividing regions of Australian and Asiatic life first traced by A.R. Wallace A-416
  animals, *pictures* A-419

Wallach, Otto (1847–1931), German chemist, born in Königsberg, now Kaliningrad, U.S.S.R.; work on camphors, perfumes, and essential oils; stimulated perfume industry. *see also in index* Nobel Prizewinners, *table*

Wallachia, Romania. *see in index* Walachia

Wallack, James William (1795–1864), U.S. actor, born in London, England, founded and managed Wallack's Theatre with son **John Lester** (1820–88), a brilliant comedian, born in New York City.

Wallaroo, kangaroo *Macropus robustus* found in mountainous districts of Australia; large, heavy in body; color dark grayish-brown A-778, K-172

Wallasey, England, county borough on Mersey River, opposite Liverpool; docks built on Wallasey Pool, formerly a swampland; pop. 101,360.

Wallawalla, Shahaptian Indian tribe of Oregon and Washington; lived along Columbia and Snake rivers; Lewis and Clark visited 1850; name means "little river."

Walla Walla, Wash., city in s.e. part of state, near Oregon border; wheat, vegetable, fruit and livestock region; processing center for peas and other vegetables, fruits; flour, dairy products, lumber products, tin cans, fertilizer; Whitman College; Ft. Walla Walla; nearby are Walla Walla College and Whitman Mission National Historic Site; pop. 23,619 W-50, *map* U-40

Walla Walla College, College Place, near Walla Walla, Wash.; Seventh-day

Adventist; founded 1892; arts and sciences, education, engineering, nursing, theology; graduate studies; biological station at Anacortes.

Wallboard W-9

Wall covering W-8. *see also in index* Mural painting; Wallpaper
interior design I-244
paint P-72
tips, *picture* P-76

Walled cities C-449
China P-153
fortification F-319
Jerusalem J-100, *map* J-101
Mohenjo-daro I-197
Rome R-251, *map* R-250
San Juan S-44a

Wallenberg, Raoul (born 1912), Swedish businessman and diplomat W-10
Holocaust H-205

Wallenda family, troupe known as **Great Wallendas,** consisting chiefly of family members, founded by **Karl Wallenda** (1905–78), U.S. high-wire artist since 1921; performed with more than 40 circuses in North America and Europe, including Ringling Brothers 1928–38, 1942–46; created seven-person pyramid 1947 C-433, *picture* C-423

Wallenstein, Albrecht von (or Albrecht Wenzel Eusebius von Wallenstein) (1583–1634), German general W-10
Gustavus Adolphus G-319
Thirty Years' War T-169

Wallenstein, Alfred (born 1898), U.S. cellist and conductor, born in Chicago, Ill.; played cello in public at 9; conductor Los Angeles Philharmonic Orchestra 1943–56, also of Symphony for Youth concerts in Los Angeles.

Waller, Edmund (1606–87), English poet; took part in Royalist plot against Parliament, exiled 1643; wrote lyrics ('Go, Lovely Rose', 'On a Girdle').

Waller, Frederic (1886–1954), U.S. motion-picture producer and inventor, born in Brooklyn, N.Y.; inventions include gunnery trainer used in World War II and Cinerama
motion pictures M-622

Waller, Thomas (nickname Fats) (1904–43), U.S. jazz composer, vocalist, organist, pianist, and bandleader; born in New York City ('I've Got a Feelin' I'm Fallin'', 'Ain't Misbehavin'', 'Squeeze Me', 'Honeysuckle Rose').

Walleyed pike (or pike perch), food and game fish *Stizostedion vitreum*; found in U.S. throughout region east of Missouri River P-202, P-326

Walleye, eye disorder E-391

Wallflower, genus *Cheiranthus* of perennial plants of the mustard family; some species are climbers; flowers velvety orange, brown, purple, yellow, and fragrant; also called **gilliflower,** as is stock, to which it is related.

Wallingford, Conn., urban town on Quinnipiac River, 12 mi (19 km) n. of New Haven; silverware, plastics, steel products, clothing, electronics; pop. 37,274.

Wallis, John (1616–1703), English mathematician, born in Ashford, Kent; developed systematic use of algebraic formulas, studied quadratures, and introduced symbol ∞ for infinity.

Wallis, Samuel (1728–95), British navigator who explored Tahiti and other Pacific islands on voyage around the globe 1766–68 T-10

Wallis and Futuna Islands, French overseas territory in Pacific Ocean w. of Samoa; area 98 sq mi (254 sq km); pop. 9,000, *map* P-6

'Wall of Choices', outdoor mural in Chicago, Ill., *picture* A-661

Walloon, a people of Belgium B-146
New York colony N-256

Wallowa Mountains, in n.e. Oregon O-583

Wall painting. *see in index* Mural painting

Wallpaper P-383, W-8
interior design I-245, *picture* I-244

Wall pepper. *see in index* Stonecrop

Walls, historic. *see also in index* Walled cities
forts F-319
Great Wall of China, *map* R-322
Hadrian's Wall R-248, S-69, *picture* S-71
Kremlin, *pictures* R-320, 333
Wailing Wall P-81, J-101, *picture* J-100

Wall Street, in New York, N.Y., financial center of U.S. N-272
history A-336, *picture* U-186
stocks and bonds S-453

'Wall Street Journal, The', U.S. newspaper N-241
high-speed facsimile F-5
New York City N-278

Wall tent, basic wedge tent T-110

Waln, Nora (1895–1964), U.S. writer, born in Grampian Hills, Pa.; lived in China and in Germany; wrote 'The House of Exile', picture of life on a Chinese estate; 'Reaching for the Stars'.

Walnut, tree W-10
wood, *table* W-283

Walnut Creek, Calif., city 13 mi. n.e. of Oakland; area explored by Spanish 1772, settled 1849, incorporated 1914.

Walnut family (or Juglandaceae), family of shrubs and trees, native to north temperate region, including the butternut, black walnut, English walnut, pecan, bitternut hickory, shagbark hickory, mockernut hickory, pignut hickory, and the wing nuts
hickory H-149
walnut W-10

Walnut Lane Bridge, bridge, Philadelphia, Pa., *picture* C-640

Walpole, Horace, 4th **earl of Orford** (or Horatio Walpole) (1717–97), English author and wit W-11
cat, *list* C-202
English literature E-274
Gothic fiction G-196
Gray G-241

Walpole, Sir Hugh Seymour (1884–1941), English novelist, born in New Zealand; educated in England ('The Duchess of Wrexe', 'Portrait of a Man with Red Hair', 'Judith Paris', 'The Fortress', 'Vanessa', 'The Bright Pavilions').

Walpole, Robert, first **earl of Orford** (1676–1745), English prime minister W-11
Britain E-248
cabinet government C-4
George I G-81

Walpole, Mass., town 9 mi (15 km) s.w. of Dedham; textiles; state prison nearby; set off from Dedham 1724; pop. of township 18,149.

Walpurgis, Saint (or Saint Walburga) (754?–799?), English nun, missionary to Germany, regarded as protectress against witchcraft; hence May Day eve, the time of witches' carnival according to German legend, is called Walpurgis Night
Swedish festival S-525

Walrus (or morse), *Odobenus rosmarus;* large, heavy-bodied, seallike mammal; sole living member of family Odobenidae; up to 12 ft (3.7 m) long; grayish skin; long tusks used for digging and defense; found in Arctic seas of Eurasia and North America Z-463

Walsall, England, county borough 8 mi (13 km) n.w. of Birmingham; leather goods, machine tools, aircraft parts; pop. 184,260.

Walsenburg, Colo., city about 45 mi (70 km) s. of Pueblo; center for coal mining, agriculture, livestock, dairying; pop. 3,945.

Walser, Martin (born 1927), German novelist
German literature G-108

Walsh, Donald (born 1931), U.S. Navy officer, born in Berkeley, Calif.; copilot of bathyscaphe *Trieste* E-377
oceanic exploration O-463
Piccard P-316

Walsh, Edward Augustin (nickname Big Ed) (1881–1959), U.S. baseball pitcher, born in Plains, Pa.; pitcher Chicago, A.L., 1904–16, and Boston, N.L., 1917; pitched 3 complete games in succession, and total of 464 innings in 1908, a modern record; twice pitched and won 2 games in one day (1905, 1908).

Walsh, Raoul (born 1892), U.S. film director, born in New York, N.Y., *picture* M-621

Walsh, Thomas James (1859–1933), U.S. legislator, born in Two Rivers, Wis.; Democratic senator from Montana after 1913; investigated illegal leasing of government oil reserves in President Harding's administration; aided in drafting prohibition and woman suffrage amendments to U.S. Constitution.

Walsh College, Canton, Ohio; Roman Catholic; opened 1960; liberal arts, education.

Walsingham, Sir Francis (1532?–90), English statesman and diplomat, secretary of state under Queen Elizabeth I; exposed Babington plot to murder the queen and influenced Elizabeth to sign Mary Stuart's death warrant E-303

Waltari, Mika Toimi (1908–79), Finnish author, born in Helsinki (historical novels: 'The Egyptian', 'The Adventurer', 'The Wanderer', 'The Dark Angel', 'The Etruscan').

Walt Disney Productions C-191, C-713
Disney D-185

Walt Disney World, amusement park and vacation complex in Lake Buena Vista, Florida, near Orlando; opened 1971 A-386
monorail M-545
Orlando O-607

Walter, Bruno (originally Bruno Walter Schlesinger) (1876–1962), U.S. conductor, born in Berlin, Germany; to U.S. 1939, citizen 1946; conducted Metropolitan Opera orchestra; musical adviser, New York Philharmonic-Symphony Orchestra 1947–49; retired 1957; autobiographical, 'Theme and Variations', 'Of Music and Music Making'
orchestra, *list* O-579

Walter, Hubert (died 1205), English archbishop of Canterbury; went with Richard I on Third Crusade; justiciar 1193–98; instrumental in preventing John's revolt against Richard; virtual ruler of England in Richard's absence 1194; chancellor 1199–1205 E-241

Walter, John, III (1818–94), English newspaperman, pioneer of modern news printing N-240

Walter, Thomas Ustick (1804–87), U.S. architect, born in Philadelphia, Pa.; as architect of U.S. Capitol 1851–65 designed the present Senate and House wings and cast-iron dome.

Walter Dorwin Teague Associates (WDTA), U.S. industrial design firm I-169

Walter press, in newsprinting N-240

Walter the Penniless, French knight, leader of First Crusade C-786

Walthall, Henry Brazeal (1878–1936), U.S. motion-picture actor, born in Shelby County, Alabama; known for role of "Little Colonel" in 'The Birth of a Nation'.

Waltham, Mass., city about 9 mi (15 km) w. of Boston, on Charles River; electronic products, precision instruments, tools, clocks; Brandeis University, Bentley College; pop. 58,200.

Waltham Forest, borough, London, England, *map* L-287

Waltham Holy Cross (or Waltham Abbey), England, urban district, n.e. suburb of London; abbey, built 1030 to hold a famous cross, was enlarged 1060 by King Harold; pop. 13,670.

Walther von der Vogelweide (1170–1230), German minnesinger, one of greatest German lyric poets G-105

Walton, Ernest Thomas Sinton (born 1903), Irish physicist, born in County Waterford, Ireland. *see also in index* Nobel Prizewinners, *table*

Walton, George (1741–1804), signer of Declaration of Independence; born in Frederick County, Virginia; Georgia delegate to Continental Congress 1776–78, 1780–81; elected governor of Georgia 1779, 1789; U.S. senator 1795–96.

Walton, Izaak (1593–1683), English writer; after retiring about age of 50 from successful iron business, he wrote 'The Compleat Angler' (sometimes called 'The Bible of Fishermen'), a quaint delightful expression of the pleasures of outdoor life; also wrote biographies of John Donne, Sir Henry Wotton, Richard Hooker, George Herbert, Bishop Robert Sanderson
literary contribution E-268

Walton, Sir William Turner (born 1902), English composer, born in Oldham (oratorio, 'Belshazzar's Feast'; 'First Symphony'; 'Facade'; musical parodies for Edith Sitwell's satirical poems; violin concerto for Jascha Heifetz).

Walt Whitman Bridge, over Delaware River, between Philadelphia, Pa., and Gloucester City, N.J. P-251d, *map* P-251a, *picture* P-251

Waltz, dance in 3/4 time, probably evolved from German folk dances; became popular in 19th century; also music for the dance or in its rhythm D-21, *picture* D-23
Strauss S-485

Walvis Bay, name of territory, and also of its seaport and bay, on coast of Namibia; Walvis Bay territory (374 sq mi [969 sq km]; pop. 12,648) is an exclave of Cape of Good Hope Province, South Africa, *maps* A-118, S-264

Wampanoag, powerful Algonquian Indian tribe whose proper territory was the peninsula on the e. shore of Narragansett Bay, Rhode Island, and the adjacent parts of Massachusetts but whose chiefs ruled a much larger territory K-246
Massachusetts M-191
New Bedford N-150
treaty with Pilgrims P-395

Wampum, beads made of shells used in various ways by North American peoples S-153
money M-531

Wanamaker, John (1838–1922), U.S. merchant, born in Philadelphia, Pa.; built two of largest department stores in U.S., in New York City and in Philadelphia; U.S. postmaster general 1889–93; religious and philanthropic work.

Wandering Jew, any of several ornamental, trailing houseplants of family Commelinaceae, particularly certain spiderworts (genus *Tradescantia*), native to North and South America, and certain members of genus *Zebrina,* native to Mexico and Guatemala.

'Wanderings of the Oisin, The', work by Yeats I-327

Wandering tattler, shorebird of family Scolopacidae; the wandering tattler *Heteroscelus incanus* is a medium-sized (11 in.; 28 cm) bird of rocky ocean shores; grayish above, white underparts narrowly barred with black; nests in Alaska, Yukon, N. Siberia; migrates along Pacific coast to s. California, Ecuador; winters also in Pacific islands and Australia.

Wandervögel, German hiking society H-285

Wandsworth, borough, London, England, *map* L-287

Waner, Lloyd James (nickname Little Poison) (born 1906), U.S. baseball outfielder, born in Harrah, Okla.; brother of Paul Waner; with Pittsburgh, N.L., 1927–41, 1944–45, Boston, N.L., 1941, Cincinnati, N.L., 1941, Philadelphia, N.L., 1942, Brooklyn, N.L., 1944; lifetime batting average of .316.

Waner, Paul Glee (nickname Big Poison) (1903–65), U.S. baseball outfielder, born in Harrah, Okla.; outfielder chiefly with Pittsburgh 1926–40; made 200 hits in each of 8 seasons; made total of 3,150 hits; with younger brother Lloyd, or Little Poison, made brother combination of Pirates.

Waneta (1795?–1848), Sioux chief, born in South Dakota; fought on side of British in War of 1812 and was rewarded with captaincy and trip to England; favored U.S. after 1820 when attempt to destroy Fort Snelling was prevented; signed trade treaty at Fort Pierre (1855) and at Prairie du Chien (1848).

Wang Ching-wei (1885–1944), Chinese nationalist, born in Canton, Kwangtung; deputy leader of Nationalist (Kuomintang) party at outbreak of Sino-Japanese War 1937; made ruler of Japanese-sponsored Chinese National government 1940.

Wang Mang (ruled AD 9–23), emperor of China's Hsin Dynasty C-362

Wang Shih-fu (1250–1337?), Chinese playwright C-389

Wang Wei (699–759), Chinese painter and poet; especially celebrated for founding monochrome landscape tradition in Chinese painting; spent his later years in Buddhist monastery.

Wang Yang-ming (1472–1529), Chinese scholar-official whose Idealistic interpretation of Neo-Confucianism influenced thinking in East Asia for centuries C-368

Waning crescent moon (or old moon), moon phase M-579

Wankel, Felix (born 1902), German inventor of combustion engine I-252

Wankel engine, type of rotary engine A-846
  motor and engine M-630

Wankie National Park. *see in index* Hwange National Park

Wannsee Conference, in 1942, Berlin, Germany H-206

Wantagh, N.Y., residential community 28 mi (45 km) s.e. of New York City in Nassau County on Long Island; Jones Beach State Park nearby; pop. 21,873.

Wapiti (or American elk), *Cervus elaphus;* North American deer of family Cervidae; second largest living deer, with shoulder height up to 5 ft (1.5 m); light to dark brown with pale rump patch; male has large antlers D-62, *picture* D-63

Wappato (also wapato), bulblike root of a species of arrowhead *Sagittaria variabilis;* found in Northwest, eaten by American Indians; food of canvasback duck.

Wappinger, Algonquian Indian tribal confederacy, closely related to the Mahican and the Delaware, whose members occupied the e. bank of the Hudson River, from Poughkeepsie, N.Y., to Manhattan Island and the country e. of the Connecticut River.

'Wapshot Chronicle, The', work by Cheever A-362

'Wapshot Scandal, The', work by Cheever A-362

Wapsipinicon State Park, in Anamosa, Iowa, *picture* I-298

War. *see in index* Warfare

War, Department of, United States (1947–49 Department of the Army, since 1949 part of the Department of Defense) U-159. *see also in index* Army, Department of the; Defense, Department of

'War and Peace', novel by Leo Tolstoi; picture of Russian society during Napoleonic invasion T-213, R-122d, *picture* R-112f
  historical novel N-409
  motion picture M-624
  warfare W-27

'War and Rememberance', work by Wouk
  American literature A-361
  historical novel N-409
  warfare W-28

'Waratah', mystery ship S-177a

War bagpipe (or cornemuse), wind instrument W-228

Warbeck, Perkin (1474–99), English pretender, claimed to be Richard, younger of the two princes murdered by Richard III; started several revolts; captured and executed by order of Henry VII.

War Between the States. *see in index* Civil War, American

Warbler, any member of Old World songbird family Sylviidae and some American, Australasian, and African birds resembling silviids; small, active insect eaters, 3½ to 10 in (9 to 25 cm) long; generally drab; some species known for beautiful song
  blackpoll migration A-450
  songs B-266

Warburg, Otto Heinrich (1883–1970), German biochemist, born in Freiburg; discovered character and mode of action of respiratory ferment. *see also in index* Nobel Prizewinners, *table*

War crimes W-11
  Germany G-124
  Wiesenthal W-202

War Cross (French, Croix de Guerre), medal M-272

'War Cry, The', newspaper, *list* W-275

Ward, Artemas (1727–1800), American Revolutionary War general and jurist, born in Shrewsbury, Mass.; commanded army of Boston until Washington's arrival; later chief justice Court of Common Pleas at Worcester, Mass., president of Massachusetts executive council, member of legislature and of House of Representatives.

Ward, Artemus (pen name of Charles Farrar Browne) (1834–67), U.S. humorist, born in Waterford, Me. ('Artemus Ward: His Book', one of enormously popular series, which provoked laughter because of absurdity and misspelling).

Ward, Barbara Mary (1914–81), English journalist and lecturer, born in York; on staff of *The Economist* 1939–68; economics professor Columbia University 1968–73 ('The West at Bay', 'Faith and Freedom', 'The Interplay of East and West', 'The Rich Nations and the Poor Nations').

Ward, Christopher Longstreth (1868–1943), U.S. lawyer and writer, born in Wilmington, Del. ('New Sweden on the Delaware', 'The Delaware Continentals').

Ward, Frederick Townsend (1831–62), U.S. military adventurer, born in Salem, Mass; saved Shantung, China, from capture by Taiping rebels, became Chinese mandarin, and organized force that became the nucleus of Charles George Gordon's "Ever-Victorious Army."

Ward, Mrs. Humphry (or Mary Augusta Arnold) (1851–1920), English novelist, granddaughter of Thomas Arnold ('Robert Elsmere', problem novel of the battle of belief; became talk of the civilized world through review by William E. Gladstone; 'Marcella'; 'Lady Rose's Daughter').

Ward, James (1843–1925), English psychologist; a leading English representative of activist school; held mind is an entity in itself.

Ward, John Montgomery (1860–1925), U.S. baseball player, born in Bellefonte, Pa.; pitcher and other positions, Providence, N.L., 1878–82, New York, N.L., 1883–84, shortstop, New York, N.L., 1885–89; player-manager, Brooklyn, Players League, 1890, Brooklyn, N.L., 1891–92, New York, N.L., 1893–94; as pitcher, won 158 games, lost 102; pitched perfect game 1880.

Ward, John Quincy Adams (1830–1910), U.S. sculptor, born in Urbana, Ohio ('General Thomas', Washington, D.C.; 'Horace Greeley', New York City; Henry Ward Beecher monument, Brooklyn) S-90

Ward, Lester Frank (1841–1913), U.S. geologist, philosopher, and distinguished sociologist, born in Joliet, Ill.; opposed Herbert Spencer's laissez-faire individualism ('Dynamic Sociology').

Ward, Lynd Kendall (born 1905), U.S. artist and illustrator, born in Chicago, Ill.; author of children's books, also of a series of novels in woodcuts; received Caldecott Medal 1953 for 'The Biggest Bear'; with his wife, May Yonge McNeer, received the Regina Medal 1975 R-111d

Ward, Mrs. Lynd Kendall. *see in index* McNeer, May Yonge

Ward, Montgomery (or Aaron Montgomery Ward) (1843–1913), U.S. merchant, born in Chatham, N.J.; with George R. Thorne founded Montgomery Ward & Co. at Chicago in 1872.

Ward, Nathaniel (1578?–1652), North American essayist and clergyman, born in England; emigrated to Massachusetts Bay 1634; said to have composed legal code for Massachusetts; wrote 'The Simple Cobler of Aggawam'.

Ward, Rodger (born 1921), U.S. auto racing driver, born in Beloit, Kan.; began racing 1945, set many records; two-time winner of Indianapolis 500.

Ward, legal term applied to a minor, usually an orphan, who is under the care of a guardian until the minor reaches maturity.

Warden, in prison P-505d–6

Wardrobe supervisor, in motion pictures M-607

Wardroom, living quarters of commissioned officers
  submarines, *diagram* S-499

Wards. *see in index* Lists

Wards Island, island in East River, New York, N.Y.; part of Manhattan Borough; formerly site of Manhattan State Hospital for the Insane; now recreation area; crossed by Triborough Bridge.

Warehouse
  cold storage R-138
  marketing M-144

Warfare W-12. *see also in index* Air Force; Army; Aviation; Guerrilla warfare; Marines; Navy; Weapons; *also* chief wars by name, as World War II
  armistice. *see in index* Armistice
  bugle calls W-230
  conscription. *see in index* Conscription
  Foreign Legion F-308
  history
    Alexander the Great A-279
    ancient Greeks, *picture* S-27
    Krupp family K-307
    Napoleon N-16
    Parthians P-213, *picture* P-211
    samurai Y-408
  international law L-256, 259
  island societies O-471
  methods
    blockade. *see in index* Blockade
    Middle Ages M-389
    scorched earth policy R-356
  migration of people M-401
  parachute troops P-109
  Red Cross R-119
  technological developments
    armor. *see in index* Armor
    barbed wire W-247
    camouflage P-513
    castle C-198
    fort F-319
    inventors, *table* I-281
    masks M-186
    microbiology M-375
    pigeons P-324, *picture* P-325
    radar R-32
    signaling S-193

Warfield, David (1866–1951), U.S. actor, born in San Francisco, Calif. ('The Auctioneer', 'The Music Master'); starred by producer David Belasco.

Warfield, Wallis. *see in index* Windsor, Wallis Warfield, duchess of

Warfield, William Caesar (born 1920), U.S. baritone, born in West Helena, Ark.; concert singer after 1950; married Leontyne Price 1952, divorced 1972 ('Porgy and Bess', folk opera; 'Show Boat', movie; musicals and oratorios).

Wargla, Algeria. *see in index* Ouargla

War guilt. *see in index* War crimes trials

War Hawks, U.S. pro-war faction, War of 1812 W-30
  Calhoun C-31
  Clay C-487

Warhead
  nuclear weapons N-434
  rocket R-232

Warhol, Andy (1928–87), U.S. artist W-28
  motion pictures M-624

War Industries Board (1917), United States, B-86
  World War I W-314

War Information, Office of, United States R-277

Waring, Frederic Malcolm (1900–84), U.S. bandleader, born in Tyrone, Pa.; his band, Pennsylvanians, popular on radio, TV, and screen; glee club also featured on programs; organized workshop for choral groups at Shawnee-on-Delaware, Pa., 1948.

Warlock, name often given male witch W-266
  folklore F-262

Warlord, military commander exercising civil control by force
  Meiji M-287

War Manpower Commission, United States R-276

Warm-blooded animals. *see in index* Mammals

Warmerdam, Cornelius (born 1915), U.S. athlete, born in Long Beach, Calif.; in 1940 pole-vaulted 15 ft 1⅛ in., becoming first person to vault 15 ft; in 1942 set world record of 15 ft 7¾ in., broken by Bob Gutowski in 1957.

Warm front, trailing edge of a retreating cold air mass W-118, *table* W-126, *map* W-121, *diagram* W-119

Warminster, Pa., urban township 15 mi (25 km) n. of the city of Philadelphia in Bucks County; situated in a residential and farming region; pop. 35,543.

Warmouth, red-eyed sunfish of e. United States s. of the Great Lakes; resembles rock bass; grows 8 to 10 in. (20 to 25 cm) long; scientific name *Chaenobryttus gulosus.*

Warm Springs, Ga., a city located 65 mi (105 km) s.w. of Atlanta; was called **Bullochville** before its incorporation in 1924; famous health resort; pop. 425. *see also in index* Georgia Warm Springs Foundation

Warm Springs Foundation, Georgia. *see in index* Georgia Warm Springs Foundation

Warneke, Heinz (born 1895), U.S. sculptor, born in Bremen, Germany; to U.S. 1923, became citizen 1930; superb craftsman; portraits, reliefs, memorials.

Warner, Charles Dudley (1829–1900), U.S. essayist, humorist, and editor, born in Plainfield, Mass.; on editorial staff *Harper's Magazine* ('My Summer in a Garden'; 'Backlog Studies'; biography of Washington Irving).

Warner, Glenn Scobey (nickname Pop) (1871–1954), U.S. football coach, born in Springville, N.Y.; coached at University of Georgia 1895–96; Cornell University 1897–98, 1904–6; Carlisle (Pa.) Indian School 1899–1903, 1907–14; University of Pittsburgh 1915–23; Stanford University 1924–32; Temple University 1933–38; San Jose (Calif.) State College 1939, 1940
  football F-297, *profile* F-296

Warner, Malcolm-Jamal, U.S. actor
  'Cosby Show', *picture* T-71

Warner, Olin Levi (1844–96), U.S. sculptor, born in West Suffield, Conn. (bronze doors at front entrance of Library of Congress, Washington, D.C., symbolizing 'Tradition' containing two bas-reliefs, 'Memory' and 'Imagination'; portrait statues).

Warner, Seth (1743–84), American Revolutionary War soldier, born in Roxbury, Conn.; leader of Green Mountain Boys; captured Crown Point 1775 V-289, *picture* V-296

Warner, Sylvia Townsend (1893–1978), English writer, born in Harrow, England; books contain strong element of fantasy (novels: 'Lolly Willowes', 'The Corner That Held Them', 'The Flint Anchor'; short stories: 'Winter in the Air, and Other Stories', 'A Spirit Rises', 'Swans on an Autumn River'; also poems).

Warner Brothers, motion-picture company I-194
  motion pictures M-621

Warner Pacific College, Portland, Ore.; Church of God; founded 1937; liberal arts, education; graduate studies; quarter system.

Warner Robins, Ga., city located 17 mi (27 km) s. of Macon; agriculture, machine shop, aircraft parts; Robins Air Force Base; pop. 39,893.

War of 1812, war between United Kingdom and the United

Waterfield, Robert (or Bob Waterfield) (born 1920), U.S. football coach and quarterback, born in Elmira, N.Y.; quarterback Cleveland Rams and Los Angeles Rams 1945–52; head coach Los Angeles Rams 1960–62.

Water finders. *see in index* Divining rod

Water flea (or code-pod), fish diet, *picture* F-124
 crustaceans C-789, *pictures* C-791

Waterford, Conn., community on Thames River and Long Island Sound adjoining New London; incorporated 1801; pop. of township 17,227.

Waterford, county on coast of s.e. Ireland in Munster Province; area 710 sq mi (1,840 sq km); largely hilly; limestone, marble, slate; fisheries; pop. 73,080.

Waterford, Ireland, seaport, on estuary Waterford Harbor; stronghold of Danes; captured by Strongbow 1171; attacked by Oliver Cromwell 1649, taken by Henry Ireton 1650; pop. 29,842, *map* E-360

Waterfowl, hunting H-331

Water gap. *see in index* Gap

Watergate case, United States U-196b
 effects U-196b
 Ford F-302, 304
 impeachment I-58
 Nixon N-328

Water grass. *see in index* Dallis grass

Water gum. *see in index* Swamp tupelo

Water hazards, in golf G-188

Water hog. *see in index* Capybara

Water hemlock, genus of perennial plants *Cicuta* of the parsley family; one common wild flower is the musquash root *Cicuta maculata* often called wild parsnip, or spotted cowbane; flowers tiny, white, in small flat clusters H-127
 poisonous plants P-409

Water inch. *see in index* Miner's inch

Water injection, in turbojet jet propulsion J-109

Water-leaf family (or Hydrophyllaceae), family of plants including the water leaf, golden bells, ellisia, the phacelias, the nemophilas, and yerba santa.

Waterlettuce, weed *Pistia stratiotes* W-131

'Water Lilies', painting by Monet M-529

Water lily, freshwater plant of the Nymphaeceae family W-99
 yellow pond lily, *picture* P-360
 water plants W-101

Water lily family (or Nymphaeaceae), family of plants, including the fish grass, Carolina water shield, yellow water lily, or spatterdock, white pond lily, lotus W-99

Waterloo, Belgium, village 9 mi (15 km) s. of Brussels; scene of famous battle in which Wellington defeated Napoleon; pop. 11,846 G-122, N-17, *picture* N-15

Waterloo, Iowa, city on Cedar River about 50 mi (80 km) n.w. of Cedar Rapids; farm equipment, meat-packing, washing-machine parts; pop. 75,985
 Iowa, *map* I-302

Waterloo, Ont., city adjoining Kitchener in farming district; insurance center; distilling, flour milling; furniture, bedding, leather goods, farm machinery; University of Waterloo; pop. 49,428, *map* C-112

Waterloo, battle of (1815) W-99
 news gathering N-238
 strategy and tactics A-642
 warfare, *list* W-16
 Wellinton's victory W-148

Waterloo, University of, Waterloo, Ont.; private control; founded 1956, chartered 1959; arts, engineering, science; graduate studies; affiliated colleges O-552

Waterloo medal, in United Kingdom M-270

Waterman, Lewis Edson (1837–1901), U.S. inventor and manufacturer, born in Decatur, Otsego County, New York; improved ink-feeding device of fountain pen.

Watermarked paper
 postage stamps S-405

Water mass, in oceanography O-482

Watermelon, annual trailing vine and its fruit, *Citrullus lanatus* W-100
 fruitgrowing F-438
 melon comparison M-292

Water meter M-317

Water mite, species of the order Acarina S-387

Water moccasin, poisonous snake, *picture* S-226
 pit viper V-328

Water mold, aquatic fungus M-519

Water oak, tree *Quercus nigra* of beech family; grows to 80 ft (25 m); leaves, wedge-shaped, to 3 in. (8 cm) long; acorns, small, round; bark smooth, light brown
 wood, *table* W-283

Water oats. *see in index* Wild rice

Water opossum, marsupial *Chironectes minimus* M-154, 157

Water ouzel, popular name for the dipper, a perching bird. *see in index* Dipper

Water paspalum. *see in index* Dallis grass

Water pipes W-86, 90
 plumbing P-393

Water plants (or hydrophytes), plants that require great moisture, as contrasted with those that require only moderate moisture (mesophytes) and desert plants (xerophytes) W-101

Water polo W-102

Waterpower (or hydropower) W-103. *see also in index* Dam; Hydraulic machinery; Hydroelectric power
 Colorado River C-584
 Grand Coulee Dam G-213
 fuel F-442
 heating systems F-451
 Industrial Revolution I-79, *picture* I-77
 inventions, *table* I-279
 New York N-251
 nuclear energy N-423
 oceans O-460
 turbines T-315
 volcano power V-383
 water W-85
 waterfall W-98
 waterwheel. *see in index* Waterwheel

Waterproofing
 garments R-305
 textiles S-196, T-141

Water pump
 engine part A-849
 heating systems H-107

Water-repellant, treatment with a finish that is resistant but not impervious to penetration by water
 textiles T-141

Water retting, in hemp processing H-127

Waters, Ethel (1896–1977), U.S. actress and blues singer, born in Chester, Pa.; radio, television, and nightclub performer; appeared on stage and in films ('Cabin in the Sky', 'The Member of the Wedding'); memoirs: 'His Eye Is on the Sparrow', 'To Me It's Wonderful' B-302

Water scavenger beetles B-142

Water scorpion, insect of the family Nepidae W-94

Watershed (or drainage basin), area of land, of any size, from which all precipitation flows to a single stream or set of streams, *diagram* R-210. *see also in index* Continental Divide
 conservation C-672
 earth E-31
 forest erosion F-315
 United States, *map* U-32–3

Water shrew (or marsh shrew) S-186

Waterskiing, sport W-107
 kite flying K-253

Water snake S-226b, d, *pictures* S-224, 226d
 folktale, *picture* S-481d

Water softener, appliance H-213

Water softening, process W-91

Water-soluble, chemical property
 vitamins F-277

Water spider, spider that nests under water S-386

Water sports. *see in index* Sports, *subhead* water

Waterspout, generally short-lived tornado that occurs over a water surface; characterized by funnel-shaped columns of rotating clouds extending down from base of a thundercloud to disturbed sea surface beneath; most common in tropical oceans W-225

Water strider, insect of the family Gerridae W-94

Water supply and waterworks. *see in index* Water, *subhead* supply and waterworks

Water table W-89, 92
 conservation C-672
 forest erosion F-315
 oasis O-454

Water tank W-90

Waterton Lakes National Park, Alberta, *maps* A-250g, C-109
 Montana M-553

Water tower, tower in Chicago, Ill. C-317

Watertown, Conn., town 5 mi (8 km) n.w. of Waterbury; synthetic fibers, wire; incorporated 1780; pop. of township 19,489.

Watertown, Mass., town on Charles River about 7 mi (11 km) w. of Boston; Watertown United States Arsenal; rubber goods, machinery, paper products; pop. of township 39,307.

Watertown, N.Y., city on Black River about 65 mi (105 km) n. of Syracuse; dairying; air brakes, paper products; Thousand Islands resort area; pop. 27,861, *map* U-41

Watertown, S.D., city on Big Sioux River about 95 mi (150 km) n.w. of Sioux Falls; trade center for rich farming region; resort area; pop. 15,649 S-332d, *maps* S-335, 323, U-40–1

Watertown, Wis., city on Rock River 35 mi (55 km) n.e. of Madison; dairy-farming area; plastics, transformers, automatic cashiers and sorters, metal products, dairy products; pop. 18,113.

Water transportation. *see in index* Boat; Canals; Freighter; Galley; Inland waterways; Lake; Merchant marine; Motorboat; Navigation; Raft; River; Sailing craft; Ships; Steam craft; Tanker

Water-tube boiler S-439, 442

Water tupelo, tree *Nyssa aquatica* of the sour gum T-313

Water turbine (or hydraulic turbine) T-315
 waterpower W-103

Water turkey. *see in index* Darter

Water vapor I-5

Waterville, Me., city on Kennebec River, 18 mi (29 km) n.e. of Augusta; paper, textiles, iron products; railroad center; Colby College; Thomas College; pop. 17,779
 Maine M-62

Watervliet, N.Y., manufacturing city on Hudson River opposite Troy; steel products, abrasives, chemicals, textiles, wood products, brushes; U.S. government arsenal; pop. 12,404.

Waterway W-108. *see also in index* Canals; Great Lakes; Inland waterways; Intracoastal Waterway; Lake; River; St. Lawrence Seaway
 civilization influenced R-210
 North America N-343
 transportation T-254, *map* T-259

Water weed. *see in index* Elodea

Waterwheel W-103
 generator, *picture* P-166
 hydraulics H-339

Wathiq, al- (reigned 842–847), 'Abbasid caliph C-56

Watie, Stand (1806–71), Cherokee leader, born in Georgia; educated plantation owner and one of signers of treaty of New Echota, which provided for cession of Cherokee lands and for westward migration; appointed a Confederate general, he fought on borders of Indian Territory in Civil War and afterward ravaged property of Indian Union sympathizers.

Watkins, Franklin Chenault (1894–1972), U.S. painter, born in New York City; instructor in painting Pennsylvania Academy of Fine Arts, Philadelphia, Pa.; employed delicate colors and agitating forms; paintings sometimes symbolic; portraits.

Watkins Glen, N.Y., village on Seneca Lake; fruitgrowing area; resort; mineral springs; saltworks; Watkins Glen State Park adjoins village; pop. 2,716.

Watling Island, Bahamas. *see in index* San Salvador

Watling Street, England, a great old Roman road leading from Dover to London and past St. Albans to Wroxeter.

Watson, Arthur Kittredge (1919–74), U.S. executive and diplomat, born in Summit, N.J.; with IBM 1947–70, vice-chairman of board 1966–70; chairman of board IBM World Trade Corporation 1963–70; ambassador to France 1970–72.

Watson, Elkanah (1758–1842), U.S. merchant and agriculturist, born in Plymouth, Mass.; promoted the building of canals in U.S.

Watson, Homer Ransford (1855–1936), Canadian landscape painter, born in Doon, Ont.; paintings depict pioneer life in Ontario; two of his landscapes hang in Windsor Castle.

Watson, James Dewey (born 1928), U.S. biochemist, born in Chicago, Ill.; on staff Harvard University 1955–68; professor 1961–68. *see also in index* Nobel Prizewinners, *table*
 genetics G-54
 heredity H-140
 'The Double Helix' R-112f

Watson, John. *see in index* MacLaren, Ian

Watson, Dr. John, friend and confidant of Sherlock Holmes in Doyle's detective stories D-237

Watson, John Broadus (1878–1958), U.S. psychologist, born in Greenville, S.C.; professor of experimental and comparative psychology Johns Hopkins University 1908–20; chief exponent of behaviorist school of psychology ('Psychology from the Standpoint of a Behaviorist', 'Behaviorism') P-521
 habituation H-3

Watson, John Christian (1867–1941), Australian political leader, born in Valparaiso, Chile; Labor party leader 1901–4; prime minister 1904.

Watson, Thomas Edward (1856–1922), U.S. journalist and legislator, born in Columbia County, Georgia; leader in Populist party; candidate for president 1904, 1908; U.S. senator 1921–22; edited *The Weekly Jeffersonian.*

Watson, Tom (full name Thomas Sturges Watson) (born 1949), U.S. golfer, born in Kansas City, Mo.; professional since 1971; winner of Masters Tournament 1977 and the British Open 1975 and 1977
 golf G-189, 192, *picture* G-193

Watson, Sir William (1715–87), English physicist, born in London; theory of electricity similar to that of Benjamin Franklin
 electricity E-161

Watson, Sir William (1858–1935), English poet, born near Bradford, Yorkshire; known especially for brief, epigrammatic poems; work is thoughtful rather than emotional ('Wordsworth's Grave'; 'The Purple East'; 'The Man Who Saw').

'Watson and the Shark', painting by Copley C-710

Watsonville, Calif., city 15 mi (25 km) e. of Santa Cruz; packing and processing of apples and vegetables; frozen foods; pop. 23,543.

Watson-Watt, Sir Robert (1892–1973), physicist, born in Brechin, Scotland; in 1935 patented a radiolocator (British equivalent of radar) to detect airplanes; government adviser on telecommunications; autobiography, 'The Pulse of Radar'.

Watt, James (1736–1819), Scottish inventor and engineer W-108, *picture* S-57i
 flyball governor A-833
 horsepower first used P-483
 Industrial Revolution I-179
 invention, *picture* I-277
 steam engine S-442
 tachometer T-3

Watt, James Gaius (born 1938), U.S. executive and public official, born in Lusk, Wyo.; director U.S. Bureau of Outdoor Recreation 1972–75; member Federal Power Commission 1975–77; president and chief legal officer Mountain States Legal Foundation in Denver 1977–81; U.S. secretary of the interior 1981–83
environmental policies C-678

Watt, unit of measure, *table* W-140
electric power E-168
name P-483

Watteau, Antoine (in full Jean-Antoine Watteau) (1684–1721), French painter W-109
drawings D-254

Watterson, Henry (or Marse Henry Watterson) (1840–1921), U.S. journalist and orator, born in Washington, D.C.; served in Confederate Army; founder and editor of *Louisville Courier-Journal;* strong advocate of conciliation between North and South.

Watt-hour meter, measures electric flow I-230

Wattle, lobe of flesh, usually highly colored, that hangs from the throat or the chin of various fowls and reptiles
chicken, *picture* P-480

Wattle (or acacia), genus of shrubs and trees A-783

Wattle, woven network of branches B-103
wattle and daub S-158, 159

Wattmeter, instrument for measuring electric power in watts; watt-hour meter sometimes erroneously called wattmeter G-8. *see also in index* Watt

Watts, George Frederic (1817–1904), English painter and sculptor, famous for portraits and allegorical paintings
sculpture, *picture* R-195

Watts, Isaac (1674–1748), English clergyman, born in Southampton; remembered for hymns ('O God, Our Help in Ages Past', 'Joy to the World') and for phrases from his poems for children ("how doth the little busy bee", "let dogs delight to bark and bite").

Watts, Thomas Hill (1819–92), U.S. political leader, born near present Greenville, Ala.; attorney general Confederate States of America 1862–63; governor of Alabama 1863–65.

Watts-Dunton, Walter Theodore (1832–1914), English man of letters; art and literary critic; friend of Rossetti, Swinburne; wrote of gypsy life ('The Coming of Love', poems; 'Aylwin', prose romance)
Swinburne S-535

Watts riot U-196

Wat Tyler's Rebellion. *see in index* Peasants' Revolt

Watusi, an African people. *see in index* Tutsi

Wauconda Bog, Illinois
flower conservation F-240

Waugh, Alec (or Alexander Raban Waugh) (born 1898), English writer, born in Hampstead; brother of Evelyn Waugh ('Island in the Sun', novel; 'Sugar Islands; a Caribbean Travelogue'; 'A Family of Islands'; 'Lipton Story', life of Sir Thomas Lipton; 'The Early Years of Alec Waugh', autobiography).

Waugh, Evelyn Arthur (1903–66), English author, born in London; brother of Alec Waugh; novels 'A Handful of Dust', 'Vile Bodies', 'Decline and Fall' combine irony and fantastic humor; 'Brideshead Revisited' champions Roman Catholicism; 'The Loved One', a satire; 'Helena', a story of Constantine's mother; biographies include 'Edmund Campion'; 'Men at Arms', 'Officers and Gentlemen', and 'The End of the Battle', satirical novels about World War II; autobiography, 'A Little Learning' W-28

Waugh, Frederick Judd (1861–1940), U.S. painter, born in Bordentown, N.J.; fine marines ('The Roaring Forties'; 'The Surf Off Cape Ann').

Waukegan (incorporated as Little Fort 1841), Ill., city on Lake Michigan about 35 mi (55 km) n. of Chicago; pharmaceuticals and chemicals, marine and recreational motors, rare metals, automotive products; present name 1859; pop. 67,653
Illinois, *map* I-53

Waukesha, Wis., city 16 mi (26 km) w. of Milwaukee; mineral springs; dairying; aluminum, iron and steel products, machinery, air-conditioning equipment, furniture, dairy products, bottled mineral water; Carroll College; pop. 50,319.

Wausau, Wis., industrial city in central part of state, on Wisconsin River; paper products, metalworking, woodworking, granite products, dairy products; nearby is Rib Mountain State Park, known as a ski area; pop. 32,806, *map* U-41

Wauters, Emile (1846–1933), Belgian portrait and historical painter ('The Madness of Hugo van der Goes', 'Mary of Burgundy Before the Magistrates of Ghent').

Wauwatosa, Wis., residential city adjacent to w. Milwaukee; light industry; incorporated as village 1892, as city 1897; pop. 51,308.

Wave cyclone (or frontal cyclone), in meteorology W-118, *table* W-126, *diagram* W-119
climate control C-499

Wavelength, in physics
energy E-216
light L-200, 203, *diagram* L-202
ocean waves O-487, *diagram* O-488
television T-76

Wavell, Archibald Percival Wavell, first Earl (1883–1950), British field marshal, born in Essex, England; served in Boer War, World War I, Egypt 1917–20, Palestine and Transjordan 1937–38; commander in chief of British forces in Middle East 1939–41; commander in chief in India 1941–43; viceroy of India 1943–47; author of 'Soldiers and Soldiering'.

Wave mechanics (or quantum mechanics), in physics S-254h, P-308, R-37, R-67
Bohr theory modification B-332
matter M-227
mechanics M-263, 269
nuclear energy N-418
Wu's principle of parity conservation W-383

Wave motion, in magnetism M-45

'Waverley', name given to a series of novels by Scott S-73, 74
romanticism N-413

Waves
brain waves B-403, *diagram* B-200b
color C-558
compression S-259
electromagnetic length R-33, *diagram* R-35, *table* R-34. *see in index* Electromagnetic radiation
frequency. *see in index* Frequency
gamma. *see in index* Gamma rays
Hertzian R-56. *see also in index* Radio
laser beam L-54, *picture* L-55
light L-199, S-372, *pictures* L-200, 201
Huygens H-336
ocean. *see in index* Ocean waves
quantum mechanics R-37
radar R-29, *diagram* R-30
radio R-46, R-51
sound S-258, *diagram* S-259, *graph* S-260
sound interference S-262
speed R-33
supersonic S-260
ultrasonics A-22
ultraviolet U-3
X ray X-334

WAVES (Women Accepted for Volunteer Emergency Service), name given to the Women's Naval Reserve N-89
uniforms and insignia U-6, *picture* U-7

Wave soaring, method of flying gliders G-166, *diagram* G-168

Wavicle, in physics R-37

Wavy line (or undy), in heraldry H-136

Wavy top, snail shell *Astraea undosa*, *picture* S-151

Wax W-110
beeswax B-125
bronze casting S-81
candles C-136
doll, *picture* D-217
saddle soap S-231

Waxahachie, Tex., city 27 mi (43 km) s. of Dallas; cotton and other farming, livestock; fiber glass boats, refrigeration equipment, clothing; pecan-shelling plant; pop. 14,624.

Wax gourd (or Chinese watermelon), melon *Benincasa hispida* W-100

Waxing crescent moon, moon phase M-578

Wax myrtles, genus *Myrica* of aromatic woody shrubs or small trees grown chiefly as ornamental plants, also for edible fruit. Fruit of wax myrtle tree *Myrica cerifera* and of bayberry *Myrica carolinensis* yields a greenish wax called bayberry wax. Bark used for tanning and in medicine.

Waxwing, bird of the family Bombycillidae W-110

Waybill, document issued by the common carrier, describing goods in shipment, routing, and charges; a shipping guide to the carrier.

Waycross, Ga., city about 95 mi (150 km) s.w. of Savannah; tobacco market; railroad shops; pecans, naval stores; lumber products, footwear, cigars; pop. 19,371, *map* U-41

Wayfaring tree (or hobble bush), common shrub *Viburnum alnifolium* of the honeysuckle family; flowers white; autumn foliage deep red.

Wayland, Mass., 6 mi (10 km) s.w. of Waltham; electronic equipment, chemicals; incorporated 1780; pop. of township 12,170.

Wayland Baptist College, Plainview, Tex.; Southern Baptist; founded 1908; liberal arts and education.

Wayland the Smith, in English folklore, a clever smith who remained invisible to his customers; appears in various forms in Scandinavian, Anglo-Saxon, and German literature; in Sir Walter Scott's 'Kenilworth'.

Wayne, Anthony (nickname Mad Anthony) (1745–96), American Revolutionary War general W-110
battle of Fallen Timbers O-500, 505
Harrison H-49
Michigan M-361
Washington W-43

Wayne, David (originally David McMeekan) (born 1914), U.S. actor, born in Traverse City, Mich.; stage roles include Og in 'Finian's Rainbow', Ensign Pulver in 'Mister Roberts', Sakini in 'The Teahouse of the August Moon'; also appeared in motion pictures and on television; Tony award 1954.

Wayne, John (originally Marion Michael Morrison, nickname Duke) (1907–79), U.S. film actor, producer, and director; born in Winterset, Iowa; star of Western and adventure movies; 1970 Oscar for 'True Grit'; acted in 'Stagecoach', 'The Long Voyage Home', 'They Were Expendable', 'Fort Apache', 'The Sands of Iwo Jima'; produced 'Angel and the Badman', 'The Alamo', *picture* W-153

Wayne, Mich., city located 17 mi (27 km) w. of Detroit; airplane plants; steel products, wire cloth parts; pop. 21,159.

Wayne, N.J., urban township 6 mi (10 km) w. of Paterson; research laboratories; William Paterson College; pop. 46,474.

Waynesboro, Pa., borough 52 mi (84 km) s.w. of Harrisburg in agricultural and fruitgrowing section; tools, machinery, refrigerating equipment; pop. 9,726, *map* P-185

Waynesboro, Va., city 12 mi (19 km) s.e. of Staunton; textiles, furniture, lumber, rayon, stoves, near s. entrance to Shenandoah National Park; pop. 15,329, *map* V-348

Waynesburg College, Waynesburg, Pa.; United Presbyterian; opened 1849; arts and sciences, business administration, education, religion.

Wayne State College, Wayne, Neb.; founded 1889; arts and sciences, business, education, fine arts, music; graduate school.

Wayne State University, Detroit, Mich.; founded 1868; liberal arts, business administration, education, engineering, law, medicine, nursing, pharmacy, social work; Monteith College; graduate school; off-campus instructional centers D-122

'Way of All Flesh, The', novel by Butler B-519
English literature E-278
novel N-411

Way of the Cross. *see in index* Via Dolorosa

'Way of Zen, The', work by Watts Z-450

Wayside Inn, tavern at Sudbury, Mass.; celebrated by Longfellow in 'Tales of a Wayside Inn'; purchased by Henry Ford in 1923 for Longfellow Memorial.

'Ways of White Folks, The', work by Hughes H-316

Wazir, title for royal minister in 'Abbasid court, Iraq I-314

Waziristan, Pakistan; mountainous district on border of Afghanistan; scene of tribal troubles during period of British rule in India.

WBA. *see in index* World Boxing Association

WBC. *see in index* World Boxing Council

W.C.T.U. *see in index* Woman's Christian Temperance Union

'We', novel by Zamyatin S-62

Wea, American Indian tribe of Algonquian family; lived in Wisconsin, Indiana, Illinois, and Missouri; moved to Kansas 1832, to n.e. Oklahoma 1868.

Weakfish. *see in index* Squeteague

Weak interaction, in nuclear physics, the Fermi process in which a neutron emits and absorbs an electron and an antineutrino. *see also in index* Strong interaction

Weald, The, district of s.e. England between North and South Downs; formerly forested; populated by Saxons in 5th century E-230

Wealth E-205
economics E-60
estate and inheritance law D-307
money M-530

'Wealth of Nations, The' (full title 'Inquiry into the Nature and Causes of the Wealth of Nations'), work by Smith C-150, I-190, I-271, L-146, E-205, E-63

Weapon, implements of offense, defense, and hunting W-111. *see also in index* Artillery; Firearms; weapons listed below and other weapons by name
archery A-538
boomerang B-364
China, *picture* S-467
disarmament D-164
electronics E-180
explosives E-378
bombs B-337
nuclear N-422
torpedo and mine T-231
knights K-258
Krupp K-306
machine gun M-12
martial arts M-160
navy N-81, 84
nonproliferation treaties P-144
stone S-455
submarines S-499
Sumeria B-5
sword S-546
technology T-50
toys T-241
X rays X-406

Weapons systems W-111

'Wearing of the Green, The', famous song of Ireland, thought to have been written around end of 1700s; author unknown.

'Weary Blues, The', poetry by Hughes H-316

Weasel family, group of carnivorous mammals *Mustelidae;* subdivided into five groups: true weasels, honey badger, badgers, skunks, otters W-114
fur, *tables* F-464, 465

Weather W-117. *see also in index* Climate; Drought; Meteorology; Rainfall; Seasons; Wind
balloon B-41
barometric measurement B-81
earth's rotation E-28
farming F-29
geography G-63
hobby H-189
hygrometer H-342

1933, so called because the assembly that adopted its constitution met at Weimar, Germany W-142

Weinberg, Steven (born 1933), U.S. physicist, born in New York, N.Y.; on faculty of University of California, Berkeley, 1960–69, professor after 1965; at Massachusetts Institute of Technology 1969–73; professor Harvard University 1973–; developed theory concerning fundamental interactions between particles. *see also in index* Nobel Prizewinner, *table*
  electromagnetic theory A-757

Weinberger, Caspar Willard (nickname Cap) (born 1917), U.S. lawyer and government official, born in San Francisco, Calif.; member California legislature 1952–58; California state finance director 1968–69; chairman Federal Trade Commission 1970; deputy director Office of Management and Budget 1970–72, director 1972–73; secretary of health, education, and welfare 1973–75; secretary of defense 1981–
  Nixon N-327

Weinberger, Jaromir (1896–1967), U.S. composer, born in Prague, Bohemia; in U.S. teaching composition at Ithaca Conservatory, Ithaca, N.Y., 1922–26; returned to U.S. 1939, became citizen 1948; wrote operas ('Schwanda the Bagpiper').

Weiner, Leo (1885–1960), Hungarian composer of orchestral music, chamber pieces, and other music, in classical style.

Weingartner, Felix (1863–1942), Austrian musical conductor and composer, born in Dalmatia; conductor Berlin, Munich, Vienna; with Boston (Mass.) Opera Company 1912, 1913; composed operas ('Sakuntala'), orchestral and chamber music, piano pieces, songs; wrote 'On Conducting', 'The Symphony Since Beethoven'
  orchestra, *list* O-579

Weinman, Adolph Alexander (1870–1952), U.S. sculptor, born in Germany; came to U.S. at age of 10; noted for Lincoln memorials
  Pegasus, *picture* P-152

Weinsberg, West Germany, town 26 mi (42 km) n.e. of Stuttgart; victory of German king Conrad III over Count Welf of Bavaria 1140; once free imperial city; pop. 7,381, *map* G-134

Weir, Robert Walter (1803–89), U.S. portrait and historical painter, born in New Rochelle, N.Y.; for 42 years taught drawing at U.S. Military Academy ('The Embarkation of the Pilgrims', in U.S. Capitol; 'Landing of Hendrik Hudson').

Weir, Walter (born 1929), Canadian political leader, born in High Bluff, Man.; Progressive Conservative; premier of Manitoba 1967–69.

Weir
  dam D-15
  fish trap T-267

Weirton, W. Va., city in n. part of state, 26 mi (42 km) n. of Wheeling, on Ohio River; steel, tinplate, chemicals; restored iron furnace used to make cannonballs for War of 1812; pop. 24,736.

Weiser, Idaho, city at confluence of the Snake and Weiser rivers, about 60 mi (100 km) n.w. of Boise; trade center for farming and ranching region; pop. 4,771, *map* I-30

Weisgard, Leonard (born 1916), U.S. artist, illustrator, and author of children's books; born in New Haven, Conn.; received Caldecott Medal 1947 for his illustrations for 'The Little Island', by Margaret Wise Brown; also illustrated 'The Courage of Sarah Noble', by Alice Dalgliesh, and 'The Secret River', by Marjorie Rawlings; wrote and illustrated 'Pelican Here, Pelican There', 'Treasures to See', 'The Athenians in the Classical Period' R-111b, S-480

Weismann, August (1834–1914), German biologist; advanced theory that changes in the characteristics of a species are due to changes in germ plasm
  genetics G-53

Weiss, Albert Paul (1879–1931), U.S. psychologist, born in Steingrund, Silesia, Germany; to U.S. in infancy; professor of experimental psychology Ohio State University after 1918.

Weiss, George Martin (1894–1972), U.S. baseball executive, born in New Haven, Conn.; with New York Yankees 1932–60 when team won 19 pennants and 15 World Series; managed New York Mets 1961–66.

Weissmuller, Johnny (in full Peter John Weissmuller) (1904–84), U.S. swimmer and actor; born in Windber, Pa.; won five Olympic gold medals (1924 and 1928); starred in Jungle Jim series; most famous as Tarzan in several MGM films.

Weitz, Paul J. (born 1932), U.S. astronaut, born in Erie, Pa.; U.S. Navy officer selected for NASA 1966, *table* S-348

Weizmann, Chaim (1874–1952), president of Israel, Zionist leader, and chemist W-143
  Balfour Declaration P-80
  Israel I-372
  Weimar Republic W-143
  Zionism Z-455

Weizsäcker, Carl-Friedrich von (born 1912), German nuclear physicist and philosopher, born in Kiel; on staff Max Planck Institute for Physics 1945–57, director since 1970; professor of philosophy University of Hamburg 1957–69 P-355

Welch, Leo Dewey (1898–1978), U.S. business executive, born in Rochester, N.Y.; joined Standard Oil Company (New Jersey) 1944, board chairman 1960–63; board chairman and chief executive officer Communications Satellite Corporation (Comsat) 1963–65.

Welch, Michael Francis (nickname Smiling Mickey) (1859–1941), U.S. right-handed baseball pitcher, born in Brooklyn, N.Y.; with Troy, N.L., 1880–82, and New York, N.L., 1883–92; won 308 games, lost 209; won 44, lost 11, in best season, 1885.

Welch, William Henry (1850–1934), U.S. pathologist, born in Norfolk, Conn.; held first chair of pathology in U.S. 1879–84 at Bellevue Hospital Medical School, New York City; organized School of Hygiene and Public Health at Johns Hopkins University; fostered school hygiene.

Weld, Theodore Dwight (1803–95), U.S. abolitionist, born in Hampton, Conn.; lobbyist for abolitionists in Washington, D.C.; said to have influenced Harriet Beecher Stowe and John Q. Adams G-287

Welded pipe, iron and steel industry product I-348

Welding W-143
  blacksmithing B-308, *picture* B-217
   ships S-167, 171
  electron-beam machining T-226
  industrial robot, *picture* I-191
  vocations, *pictures* V-364, 374

Welding drafting M-262

Welensky, Sir Roy (born 1907), Rhodesian statesman, born in Salisbury; prime minister of former Federation of Rhodesia and Nyasaland 1956–63; white supremacist; author of 'Welensky's 4000 Days'.

Welf, House of (or House of Guelf), German ruling family G-301. *see also in index* Hanover, House of

Welfare, government system whereby money is taken from some segments of the population and given to other segments. *see also in index* Social legislation
  welfare state W-145
  women's rights W-273

Welfare Island, New York. *see in index* Roosevelt Island

Welfare measures. *see in index* Social legislation

Welfare state W-145
  health insurance H-95

Welfare work. *see in index* Social service

Welhaven, Johan Sebastian Cammermeyer (1807–73), Norwegian poet, critic; inspired by Old Norse subjects; conservative, opposed extravagances of Henrik Wergeland ('Norges Daemring', sonnet cycle)
  Norway N-391

Welk, Lawrence (born 1903), U.S. accordionist and orchestra leader, born in Strasburg, N.D.; orchestra first appeared throughout U.S. 1927; star of ABC-TV program The Lawrence Welk Show; won many awards and prizes.

Well. *see also in index* Pump
  desert, *picture* S-16a
  gas G-39
  oil. *see in index* Petroleum technology, *subhead* wells
  water W-89, 92

Welland, Ont., city on Welland Ship Canal 10 mi (16 km) s.w. of Niagara Falls; trading center for rich fruit belt; hydroelectric power; iron and steel products, rubber goods, electrical equipment, textiles, farm machinery; pop. 45,448, *map* C-112

Welland River, river in e.-central England, flows 70 mi (110 km) n.e. to The Wash.

Welland Ship Canal, canal in Canada, connecting Lake Erie with Lake Ontario C-129
  Ontario O-549, *picture* O-550

Welle River. *see in index* Uele River

Weller, Thomas Huckle (born 1915), U.S. physician, born in Ann Arbor, Mich.; on faculty Harvard school of public health after 1948, professor of tropical public health and head of department after 1954. *see also in index* Nobel Prizewinners, *table*

Welles, Gideon (1802–78), U.S. statesman, born in Glastonbury, Conn.; able secretary of Navy under Presidents Lincoln and A. Johnson; though ignorant of navigation and ship construction, he showed great executive ability
  Civil War C-478

Welles, Orson (in full George Orson Welles) (1915–85), U.S. actor, writer, and producer for radio, stage, and screen, born in Kenosha, Wis.; at age of 22 founded Mercury Theater, New York City, and directed and produced modernized version of Shakespeare's 'Julius Caesar'; wrote, directed, produced, and acted in 'Citizen Kane'; known for 1938 broadcast of Martian invasion
  directing D-155
  motion pictures M-622
  science fiction S-61

Welles, Sumner (1892–1961), U.S. diplomat, born in New York City; secretary of Tokyo embassy 1915–17, Buenos Aires 1917–19, Dominican Republic 1922; delegate to many conferences on Latin American affairs; opened way for good-neighbor policy; ambassador to Cuba 1933; undersecretary of state 1937–43.

Wellesley, Richard Colley Wellesley, marquis of (1760–1842), British statesman, one of greatest English colonial administrators; governor-general of India 1797–1805; found the (British) East India Co. a trading body, left it an imperial power; brother of duke of Wellington.

Wellesley, Mass., town 12 mi (19 km) w. of Boston, chiefly residential; Wellesley College; Babson College; settled 1660, incorporated 1881; pop. of township 27,209.

Wellesley College, Wellesley, Mass.; for women; chartered 1870; opened 1875; arts and sciences.

Wellington (in full Arthur Wellesley, first duke of Wellington, or Arthur Wesley) (1769–1852), British soldier and statesman W-148
  Battle of Waterloo W-100
  United Kingdom E-251

Wellington, New Zealand, port and capital, on s. coast of North Island; on Cook Strait; large trade; varied manufactures; Victoria College of University of New Zealand; pop. 133,200 W-148
  New Zealand N-282, *map* N-299, *pictures* N-284, 289
  Pacific Ocean, *map* P-6
  zoo Z-459

Wells, Carolyn (1869–1942), U.S. writer of mystery stories, parodies, and humorous verse, born in Rahway, N.J.; noted especially for the Fleming Stone detective stories.

Wells, Charles Jeremiah (1798–1879), English poet famous for Biblical drama 'Joseph and His Brethren'; written in 1823, it passed unnoticed for half a century until Dante G. Rossetti and Algernon C. Swinburne proclaimed its merit.

Wells, David Ames (1828–98), U.S. political economist, born in Springfield, Mass.; free trade advocate; influenced creation of Federal Bureau of Statistics in U.S. Treasury Department.

Wells, Henry (1805–78), U.S. pioneer expressman, born in Thetford, Vt.; president American Express Company 1850–68; founded Wells College 1868 E-382

Wells, H.G. (full name Herbert George Wells) (1866–1946), English author W-148
  literary contribution E-279
  science fiction S-61

Wells, Horace (1815–48), U.S. dentist, born in Hartford, Vt.; interested in painkilling effect of nitrous oxide
  medicine M-284

Wells, England, city 18 mi (29 km) s.w. of Bath; 13th-century cathedral; important Saxon town; made bishop's see in 905; pop. 8,190
  Cathedral, *picture* E-252

Wells College, Aurora, N.Y.; private control; for women; founded 1868; arts and sciences; graduate study N-255

Wells, Fargo & Company E-383
  stagecoach, *picture* T-262

'Well Tempered Clavier, The', work by Bach M-669

Well tube, pressure gauge O-464

Wels. *see in index* Danube sheatfish

Welsbach, Karl Auer von (1858–1929), Austrian chemist and inventor, discoverer of praseodymium and neodymium; inventor of Welsbach light and osmium incandescent electric light.

Welsh corgi (Cardigan), dog D-193, *picture* D-203

Welsh corgi (Pembroke), dog, *picture* D-203

Welsh language and literature (or Cymraeg language and literature)
  England E-232
  folktales S-472, *list* S-481b
  Wales W-6

Welsh Nationalist (or Plaid Cymru), political party, Wales W-7

Welsh pony, *picture* H-254

Welsh springer spaniel, dog, *picture* D-199

Welsh terrier, dog, *picture* D-204

Welt, strip of material or cord fastened to a seam to strengthen or decorate it
  shoemaking S-180

Welterweight, in boxing B-388

Welty, Eudora (born 1909), U.S. writer W-149
  American literature A-360

Wembley, large district in n.w. part of Greater London, England; Wembley Park was site of British Empire Exposition 1924–25.

Wenatchee, Wash., city near geographic center of state, on Columbia River, just s. of junction with Wenatchee River, about 95 mi (150 km) s.e. of Seattle; fruitgrowing and wheat area; shipping center for apples, lumber, aluminum and other metals; annual Washington State Apple Blossom Festival; incorporated 1892; pop. 17,257 U-40

Wenceslaus. *see in index* Wenzel

Wenchow, China, port in s.e. Chekiang Province; fishing center; exports timber, citrus fruit, tobacco, tea; pop. 250,000.

Wend, name given by Germans to a branch of Slavs occupying parts of Saxony and Prussia S-214

Wendell, Barrett (1855–1921), U.S. author and educator, born in Boston, Mass.; in English department, Harvard University 1880–1921; vitalized teaching of American literature

('Cotton Mather', 'William Shakespeare', 'A Literary History of America').
Wenham, Francis H. (1824–1908), British aeronautical engineer; developed high aspect ratio wing 1866 A-76
  wind tunnel W-235
Went, Frits Warmolt (born 1903), U.S. botanist, born in Utrecht, The Netherlands; professor California Institute of Technology 1933–58; director Missouri Botanical Garden 1958–63; professor Washington University 1963–65, University of Nevada 1965–75 P-375
Wen Ti (541–604), first emperor and founder of China's Sui Dynasty C-364
Wentletrap shell (or staircase shell), mollusk shell *Architectonica perspectiva*, *picture* S-152
Wentworth, Benning (1696–1770), New England colonial governor
  New Hampshire N-179
Wentworth, John (1815–88), U.S. journalist, born in Sandwich, N.H.; moved to Chicago, Ill., 1836 and was active in early development of city; editor of *Democrat* 25 years; elected mayor of Chicago 1857 and 1860.
Wentworth, Thomas, earl of Strafford. *see in index* Strafford
Wentworth, W.C. (full name William Charles Wentworth) (1793–1872), Australian statesman and author W-149
Wenzel (or Wenceslaus) (1361–1419), king of Bohemia and Holy Roman emperor; attempt to settle Great Schism antagonized archbishop of Mainz, who persuaded the imperial electors to depose him; succeeded by Sigismund.
Werewolf, person thought to be transformed into a wolf; belief in wer (or man) animals common in Middle Ages; popular subject for modern horror movies
  folklore F-262, *picture* F-264
  horror story H-245
Werfel, Franz V. (1890–1945), Austrian writer, born in Prague; came to U.S. 1940; his poetry ranks high; novels and dramas notable for strength and originality G-107
Wergeland, Henrik (1808–45), Norwegian poet; early erratic verse satirized by Welhaven; hailed by people as prophet of independence; popularity with masses waned after he became great lyric poet ('Jan van Huysums Blomerstykke', 'Svalen')
  Norway N-391
Werner, Alfred (1866–1919), Swiss chemist, born in Mulhouse, Upper Alsace, France; evolved coordination theory of valence in 1893 to explain how molecules having all valences satisfied could still unite chemically. *see also in index* Nobel Prizewinners, *table*
Werner, Zacharias (1768–1832), German romantic dramatist; 'Martin Luther' and 'Der 24 Februar' are typical of the lurid "fate tragedy"; in 1814 he became a Catholic priest and was famous for impassioned preaching.
Wertheimer, Max (1880–1943), psychologist, founder of Gestalt school of psychology; related Gestalt principles to theory of learning P-520
Werther, hero of Goethe's romance 'Die Leiden des jungen Werthers' who suffers intensely because of unrequited love and finally commits suicide.
Wescott, Glenway (born 1901), U.S. novelist and poet, born in Kewaskum, Wis.; known for earlier stories about his native Middle West, written while abroad; best-known work, 'The Grandmothers: a Family Portrait' ('Good-bye Wisconsin', 'The Pilgrim Hawk', 'Apartment in Athens', 'Images of Truth').
Weser, river of West Germany rising in s. Hanover; flows n. 280 mi (450 km) to North Sea; connected by canals with Rhine, Ems, and Elbe rivers, *maps* E-360, G-134
Weslaco, Tex., city 18 mi (31 km) s.w. of Harlingen; citrus fruit, cotton; oil and gas wells, food processing, insecticides and fertilizers; pop. 19,331.
Wesley, Arthur. *see in index* Wellington
Wesley, Charles (1707–88), English preacher and hymn writer W-149
  Methodism M-317
Wesley, John (1703–91), English preacher, founder of Methodism W-149
  holiness movement H-202
  Methodism M-317
  Oglethorpe O-496
Wesleyan church H-202
Wesleyan College, Macon, Ga.; Methodist; for women; founded 1836; liberal arts, fine arts G-89
Wesleyan Methodist church H-202
  Methodism M-318
Wesleyan Methodists, religious group, the original Methodist body, which was founded during the 18th century by John Wesley in Great Britain. *see also in index* Methodism
Wesleyan University, Middletown, Conn.; nonsectarian school; established 1831 by Methodist men; arts and sciences; graduate study.
Wessex, ancient kingdom of West Saxons in s. Britain; founded by Cedric and Cynric 519; Egbert became king 802 and later ruled all Britain
  Alfred the Great A-282
Wesson, Daniel Baird (1825–1906), U.S. inventor and manufacturer, born in Worcester, Mass.; in 1854 with Horace Smith patented repeating rifle (forerunner of Winchester) and revolver; formed partnership 1857 to manufacture Smith & Wesson revolvers and metal cartridges; Smith sold out to Wesson 1873.
West, Benjamin (1738–1820), U.S. painter W-150
  Fulton F-446
  painting P-50, *picture* P-49
  Stuart S-493
West, Jessamyn (1907–84), U.S. novelist, born in Indiana; works include: 'The Witch Diggers', 'Cress Delahanty', 'Except for Me and Thee'
  'The Friendly Persuasion' R-112b
West, Mae (1892?–1980), U.S. movie actress W-150
  motion pictures, *picture* M-624
West, Morris Langly (born 1916), Australian author, born in Melbourne; novice in monastery for a time ('Children of the Sun', 'The Devil's Advocate', 'Shoes of the Fisherman', 'The Ambassador') A-798
West, Nathanael (originally Nathan Weinstein) (1903–40), U.S. writer, born in New York, N.Y.; depicted degenerate 20th-century U.S. life; wrote screenplays.
West, Dame Rebecca (pen name of Cicily Fairfield, or Mrs. Henry M. Andrews) (1892–1983), English writer, born in County Kerry, Ireland ('The Fountain Overflows' and 'The Birds Fall Down', novels; 'Black Lamb and Grey Falcon: a Journey Through Yugoslavia'; 'The Meaning of Treason'; 'The New Meaning of Treason'; 'A Train of Powder', on guilt and punishment).
West, direction D-157
West, The, United States. *see also in index* Southwest, American; United States; *also* names of Western states
  literature A-351
  mythology M-695
  North America N-338
  Oñate O-544
  outlaws O-619
  War of 1812 W-32
Westall, Richard (1765–1836), English artist, born in Hertford; historical and rustic paintings, book illustrations, portraits.
West Allis, Wis., city just w. of Milwaukee; tractors, machinery, engines, motortrucks, auto accessories, steel products; pop. 63,982 W-260
West Baden Springs, Ind., town about 85 mi (140 km) s.w. of Indianapolis; health resort, mineral springs; pop. 796
  Indiana, *map* I-102
West Bend, Wis., city 28 mi. n.w. of Milwaukee; cookware, leather goods, farm machinery; incorporated 1885; pop. 21,484.
West Bengal, state in n.e. India, stretching n. from Bay of Bengal; 33,829 sq mi (87,617 sq km); cap. Calcutta; formed 1947 from part of former province Bengal and enlarged 1950, 1954, and 1956; coal, rice, tea, jute, textiles, metal products; pop. 44,440,095, *map* I-83. *see also in index* Bengal
West Berlin, city and state of West Germany; pop. 2,134,256 B-168, G-112, *maps* B-170. *see also in index* Berlin
  Airlift Memorial, *map* B-140
  blockade R-357
Westboro, Mass., town 12 mi (19 km) e. of Worcester; abrasives, shoes, weaving, tanning; birthplace of Eli Whitney; pop. of township 13,619.
West Bromwich, England, county borough 5 mi (8 km) n.w. of Birmingham; coal mines, metal manufactures, chemicals, paint; pop. 171,850.
Westbrook, Me., city located just w. of Portland and on Presumpscot River; paper, textiles, shoes, dowels, and cement blocks; pop. 14,976.
Westbrook College, Portland, Me.; private control; founded 1831 as Westbrook Seminary; liberal arts, medical technology.
Westbury, N.Y., village 7 mi (11 km) n.e. of Mineola; aircraft and aerospace industry; incorporated 1932; pop. 13,871.
Westbury, South Africa
  Johannesburg J-122
West Caldwell, N.Y., borough 9 mi (14 km) s.w. of Paterson; chiefly residential, light industry; pop. 11,887.
Westchester, Ill., residential village 15 mi (25 km) w. of Chicago; incorporated 1925; pop. 17,730
  Illinois, *map* I-53
West Chester, Pa., borough 22 mi (35 km) w. of Philadelphia; dairy region; mushroom cultivation; pharmaceuticals, dairy equipment, metal products, paper products; West Chester State College; pop. 17,435, *map* P-185
West Chester State College, West Chester, Pa.; established 1871; liberal arts, education; graduate study.
West coast hemlock. *see in index* Western hemlock
West coast rhododendron (or California rosebay), flowering plant *Rhododendron macrophyllum* R-196, *picture* F-237
  Washington state's flower, *pictures* S-427, W-56
West Covina, Calif., city 8 mi (13 km) w. of Pomona; citrus fruit and nut shipping, cold storage; pop. 80,094.
West Des Moines, Iowa, city just w. of Des Moines; name changed from Valley Junction 1938; pop. 21,894
  Iowa, *map* I-302
Westdeutscher Rundfunk, electronic music studio S-448
Westerly, R.I., town in s.w. on Pawcatuck River at Connecticut boundary; textiles, printing presses, elastic fabrics, felt, chemicals; pop. of township 18,580, *map* R-181
Westerly wind
  earth E-29
  rainfall R-89
  weather W-117
Westermarck, Edward Alexander (1862–1939), Finnish anthropologist and author; professor of sociology, University of London, in England, 1907–30; especially interested in history of marriage and ethical origins ('The History of Human Marriage', 'Origin and Development of the Moral Idea', 'Essays on Sex and Marriage', 'Memories of My Life').
Western, literature and film making W-151
  mythology M-695
  outlaws O-619
Western American mole, mammal of the genus *Scapanus* M-521
Western Australia, largest state of Australia, comprising w. third of continent; 975,000 sq mi (2,525,000 sq km); gold, copper, silver; farming; cap. Perth; pop. 1,382,600 W-153. *see also in index* Australia
  Australia A-767, *map* A-822
  Pacific Ocean, *map* P-6
Western Basins and Plateaus, United States. *see in index* United States, *subhead* geographic regions, Western Basins and Plateaus; *also* names of states in this region
Western Carolina University, Cullowhee, N.C.; state control; established 1889; arts and sciences, business, education and psychology; graduate school.
Western Coal Field, plateau in Kentucky K-209
Western College, Oxford, Ohio; founded 1853; absorbed by Miami University 1974.
Western Connecticut State College, Danbury, Conn.; founded 1904; liberal arts, education, music; graduate study.
Western Desert, part of the Sahara in Egypt E-115
Western Dvina River (or Dvina River), river about 630 mi (1,010 km) long, rises in Valday Hills, w. U.S.S.R., flows s.w. and then turns n.w. before crossing Latvian Soviet Socialist Republic to Gulf of Riga R-323, *maps* R-322, 344, 348
Western Empire, Roman history R-248, *table* R-247
Western European Union (WEU), seven-nation defense organization proposed by Britain in 1954; in effect with signing of Paris pacts May 5, 1955; includes Britain, France, West Germany, Belgium, Italy, Luxembourg, The Netherlands; secretariat in London E-355
Western fir F-92
Western Front, in World War I W-304, 310, *map* W-303
Western Ghats, mountains in India I-63, *map* I-86
Western Hemisphere H-126
Western hemlock (sometimes called west coast hemlock, or hemlock spruce, or hemlock fir, or Prince Albert fir, or gray fir, or Alaska pine), evergreen tree *Tsuga heterophylla* of the pine family; grows 130 ft to 150 ft (40 m to 45 m) high; may live to 500 years; bark thin; wood pale brown with pink tinge; used as core stock for plywood H-127
  rayon R-99
  Washington state tree, *picture* W-56
  wood, *table* W-282
Western Highlands, low hills in Florida F-195
Western Illinois University, Macomb, Ill.; state control; founded 1899; arts, sciences and education; graduate study.
Western Isles, islands off w. coast of Scotland. *see in index* Hebrides
Western juniper J-157
Western Kentucky University, Bowling Green, Ky.; founded 1906; arts and sciences, teacher training; graduate school.
Western larch, tree
  wood, *table* W-282
Western Maryland College, Westminster, Md.; Methodist; opened 1867; arts and sciences, education, music; graduate studies.
Western meadowlark, bird
  state bird
    Montana, *picture* M-556
    Nebraska, *picture* N-100
    North Dakota, *picture* N-378
    Oregon, *picture* O-588
    Wyoming, *picture* W-392
Western Michigan University, Kalamazoo, Mich.; state control; founded 1903; liberal arts and sciences, applied arts and sciences, business, education, library science; graduate schools.
Western Montana College, Dillon, Mont.; state control; established 1893; liberal arts, education; graduate study; quarter system.
Western New England College, Springfield, Mass.; private control; founded 1919; arts and sciences, business administration, engineering, law; graduate study.

Western New Mexico University, Silver City, N.M.; state control; founded 1893; liberal arts, education; graduate school
New Mexico N-217

Western Ontario, University of, London, Ont.; private control; founded 1878; arts and sciences, business administration, engineering science, law, medicine, nursing; graduate studies; affiliated colleges L-295, O-552

Western pine beetle, *picture* I-225

Western red cedar (or giant arborvitae), evergreen tree, often called simply cedar A-529
wood, *table* W-282

Western Reserve, part of Northwest Territory (now n.e. Ohio) reserved by Connecticut when latter ceded its claim to western lands C-654

Western saddle H-264, *diagram* H-265

Western Sahara (formerly Spanish Sahara), territory on coast of n.w. Africa; includes the regions Saguia el Hamra and Rio de Oro; formerly a province of Spain; ceded to Mauritania and Morocco 1976; claimed by Polisario Front; Mauritania's share annexed to Morocco 1979; total area 102,703 sq mi (266,000 sq km); cap. El Aaiun (pop. 23,708); pop. 150,000 W-154, *map* A-118
African political unit, *table* A-112
Mubarak M-643
Sahara S-14, *map* S-15, *pictures* S-15–16
Spain S-361

Western Samoa, island nation in s.-central Pacific Ocean; area 1,093 sq mi (2,831 sq km); capital and largest town Apia; pop. 160,000 W-154. *see also in index* Samoa
Commonwealth membership C-602
flag, *picture* F-172
Oceania O-468

Western sandpiper S-40

Western Springs, Ill., residential village 16 mi (26 km) s.w. of Chicago; incorporated 1886; pop. 12,876
Illinois, *map* I-53

Western State College of Colorado, Gunnison, Colo.; founded 1901; opened 1911; arts and sciences, business, education; graduate studies

Western Union Telegraph Company
Morse M-588
telecommunication T-56
telegraph T-58

Western Wall (or Wailing Wall), in Jerusalem J-101, *picture* J-100
Israel, *picture* I-370
Palestine P-81

Western Washington University (until 1978 Western Washington State College), Bellingham, Wash.; opened 1899; arts and sciences, education; graduate studies; quarter system.

Western white fir. *see in index* Giant fir

Western white pine (or evergreen tree), tree *Pinus monticola* of pine family; grows 90 ft to 150 ft (27 m to 45 m); branches short, forming narrow crown; leaves to 4 in. (10 cm) long, grow in clusters of 5, blue-green with white tinge; cones to 11 in. (28 cm) long; bark broken into square blocks, *table* W-282

Western yellow pine. *see in index* Ponderosa pine

Western yew (or Pacific yew), tree *Taxus brevifolia* of the Taxaceae family T-410

Westerville, Ohio, city 12 mi (19 km) n. of Columbus; metals, electrical products; dairying; incorporated 1858; pop. 23,414.

Westfalenhalle (or Westphalia Hall), exhibition hall, Dortmund, West Germany D-231

West Fargo, N.D., city 5 mi (8 km) s.w. of Fargo; in farming area; farm machinery, truck and trailer beds; meat processing; incorporated 1936; pop. 10,099 N-382

Westfield, Mass., city on Westfield River 9 mi (15 km) w. of Springfield; boilers and radiators, bicycles, textile machinery, paper products; Westfield State College; pop. 36,465.

Westfield, N.J., residential town 9 mi (15 km) s.w. of Newark; crushed stone, cinder and concrete products, paint, dairy products; incorporated 1903; pop. 30,447.

Westfield State College, Westfield, Mass., opened 1839; liberal arts, education; graduate studies; oldest coeducational teacher-training institution in U.S.

West Fjord, Norway. *see in index* Vestfjord

West Florida, name given by British in 1763 to that part of Florida between the Apalachicola River and the Mississippi River and as far north as 32°28′ N.

West Florida, University of, Pensacola, Fla.; state control; opened 1967; cluster colleges of liberal arts and professional departments; graduate study; off-campus centers at Eglin Air Force Base and Panama City.

West Ford, variation of the passive repeater communications satellite; made up of about 400 million tiny needlelike copper antennas spread like a ring around the Earth; reflected radio signals; first successful launch May 1963.

West Fork River, river in central West Virginia, 92 mi (148 km) long, rises in Upshur County and flows n.e. to Fairmont, where it joins the Tygart River to form the Monongahela.

West Frankfort, Ill., city in Franklin County in s. part of state, about 85 mi (140 km) s.e. of St. Louis, Mo.; coal mining; pop. 9,437
Illinois, *map* I-53

West Georgia College, Carrollton, Ga.; state control; opened 1933; liberal arts, education; graduate studies; quarter system.

West German Mark. *see in index* Mark

West Germany. *see in index* Germany, West

West Goths. *see in index* Visigoths

West Greenland Current, cold ocean current of the Atlantic along s.w. coast of Greenland; carries icebergs B-18

West Gulf Coastal Plain, in Louisiana L-309, *map* L-310

West Hartford, Conn., residential urban town, suburb of Hartford; machine tools and other metal products; St. Joseph College, University of Hartford; pop. 61,301.

West Haven, Conn., residential and industrial suburb of New Haven; rubber products, metal products; University of New Haven; pop. 53,401.

West Helena, Ark., city 3 mi (5 km) n.w. of Helena; farming, lumber, and wood products; founded 1909; pop. 11,367.

West Highland white terrier, dog, *picture* D-204

West Hollywood, Calif., residential community just e. of Beverly Hills; part of Los Angeles County; pop. 34,625.

West Indian mahogany, tree *Swietenia mahogani* of the Meliaceae family M-50

West Indies (or Caribbean), curved chain of islands dividing Caribbean Sea from Atlantic Ocean; total area is about 92,000 sq mi (238,000 sq km); pop. 33,000,000 W-155. *see also in index* names of islands and groups
American Colonies P-515
Barbados B-78
Columbus C-593, *picture* U-130
Commonwealth membership C-602
Cuba C-800
East Indian minority M-460
folktales S-477, *list* S-481d–2
Hispaniola H-169
Latin America L-57
monkey dinner bell S-106
North America N-334, *map* N-351
petroleum P-229
Puerto Rico P-257
slave trade S-214
Spanish exploration A-331
Trinidad and Tobago T-288
Virgin Islands V-351, *picture* V-352

Westinghouse, George (1846–1914), U.S. inventor and manufacturer W-162
air brake R-79
patent I-274, *table* I-273
electric power E-165
Hall of Fame, *table* H-16
Tesla T-114

West Irian. *see in index* Irian Jaya

West Kildonan, Man., city, suburb of Winnipeg; residential; site of Seven Oaks Monument; pop. 23,959.

West Lafayette, Ind., city on Wabash River opposite Lafayette; main campus of Purdue University; pop. 19,157
Indiana, *map* I-102

Westlake, Ohio, city 12 mi (19 km) s.w. of Cleveland; metal products, plastic tubing; formerly named Dover; pop. 19,483.

Westland, Mich., residential city 18 mi (29 km) w. of Detroit; spring festival; pop. 84,603.

West Liberty State College, West Liberty, W. Va.; chartered 1837; arts and sciences, business, dental hygiene, education, music and art; adult division at Wheeling
West Virginia W-168

West Locris, district of ancient Greece. *see in index* Locris

Westmacott, Sir Richard (1775–1856), English sculptor, born in London; studied with Canova (pediment figures of British Museum; 'Achilles', Hyde Park, London).

Westmar College, Le Mars, Iowa; United Methodist; founded 1890; liberal arts and teacher education.

Westmeath, inland county in Leinster Province, Ireland, on Shannon River; area 681 sq mi (1,764 sq km); limestone, cattle, potatoes; fishing resorts; pop. 52,900.

West Memphis, Ark., city in Crittenden County 8 mi (13 km) w. of Memphis, Tenn.; lumbering, cotton; pop. 26,070.

West Mifflin, Pa., borough 8 mi (13 km) s.e. of Pittsburgh; metal products; incorporated 1944; pop. 26,279, *map* P-184

Westminster, Calif., city 7 mi (11 km) w. of Santa Ana; carpet dyeing, machine shops; window coverings; pop. 71,133.

Westminster, Colo., city n.w. of Denver in Adams County; in an irrigated agricultural region; chiefly residential; pop. 50,211.

Westminster, England, central borough, Greater London; has royal palaces, Westminster Abbey, Houses of Parliament, cathedral, National and Tate galleries; pop. 240,360 L-286, *map* L-287

Westminster, Palace of, London, England L-292

Westminster, Statute of (1931), United Kingdom; gave equal status to Britain and the then dominions of Canada, Australia, New Zealand, South Africa, Ireland, and Newfoundland
New Zealand N-295

Westminster, Treaty of (1674) A-336

Westminster Abbey (official name Collegiate Church of St. Peter), church in London, England W-162
London L-286, 292, *map* L-288, *picture* L-291

Westminster Agreement (1107) A-467

Westminster Assembly (1643), English Reformation C-411

Westminster Cathedral, in London, England, designed by John Francis Bentley (1839–1902) L-292

Westminster College, Fulton, Mo.; Presbyterian; for men; established 1851; liberal arts.

Westminster College, New Wilmington, Pa.; United Presbyterian; founded and opened 1852; arts and sciences, business administration, education, music; graduate studies.

Westminster College, Salt Lake City, Utah; interdenominational; founded 1875; present name 1903; senior college 1944; liberal arts; graduate studies.

Westminster Hall, in London, England L-292

Westminster Massacre V-289

West Monroe, La., city just w. of Monroe; paper mills, bag and container factory; furniture; printing and publishing; pop. 14,868.

Westmont College, Santa Barbara, Calif.; private control; founded 1940; liberal arts and education.

Westmoreland, William Childs (born 1914), U.S. Army officer, born in Spartanburg County, South Carolina; served in World War II and Korean War; superintendent of West Point 1960–63; commander of all forces of U.S. in Vietnam 1964–68; Army chief of staff 1968–72, *picture* S-316

Westmoreland style, type of wrestling W-366

Westmorland, county of n. England; 789 sq mi (2,044 sq km); wooded, mountainous; w. part in Lake District; cattle and sheep raising; county town, Appleby; pop. 67,180.

Westmount, Que., city, a residential suburb of Montreal, situated on Montreal Island; pop. 23,606.

West New Guinea. *see in index* Irian Jaya

West New York, N.J., town on Hudson River opposite borough of Manhattan in New York City; embroidery, textiles; pop. 40,627.

West North Central States, name used by U.S. government for geographic division including Iowa, Kansas, Minnesota, Missouri, Nebraska, North Dakota, South Dakota.

Weston, Christine Goutiere (born 1904), U.S. author, born in United Provinces, India; to U.S. in 1923; 'Indigo', 'The World Is a Bridge'; for children, 'Bhimsa, the Dancing Bear', 'Ceylon', 'Afghanistan'.

Weston, Edward (1850–1936), British-born American electrical engineer and industrialist; founded the Weston Electrical Instrument Company N-150

Weston, Edward (1886–1958), U.S. photographer W-163

Weston-super-Mare, England, seaside resort town on Bristol Channel 18 mi (29 km) s.w. of Bristol; pop. 47,960.

West Orange, N.J., town 5 mi (8 km) n.w. of Newark; storage batteries, dictating machines, electrical products, ceramics, textiles, metal products; zoo; pop. 39,510
Edison E-76

West Pakistan. *see in index* Pakistan

West Palm Beach, Fla., city on w. shore of Lake Worth, opposite Palm Beach; trade and resort center; electronics and aeronautics, concrete products, metal products; pop. 62,530, *map* U-41
North America, *map* N-351

West Paterson, N.J., borough 3 mi (5 km) s.w. of Paterson; residential suburb; incorporated 1914; pop. 11,293.

Westphalia, former province in w. Germany; 7,807 sq mi (20,220 sq km); after World War II included in new state of North Rhine-Westphalia.

Westphalia, Kingdom of, created by Napoleon 1807 for his brother Jerome; included wide territory east of Rhine in addition to former province of Westphalia; about 15,000 mi (39,000 sq km); overthrown 1813.

Westphalia, Peace of (1648), ended Thirty Years' War A-829, T-170, *table* T-275
Alsace-Lorraine restored A-320
Germany G-121
Lutheranism L-339

West Point, N.Y., military post on Hudson River 52 mi (84 km) from New York City; U.S. Military Academy; U.S. government silver depository N-255, *pictures* N-244, 262
American Revolution R-168
MacArthur M-2
United States Mint C-538

Westport, Conn., residential town 4 mi (6 km) e. of Norwalk; chemical industry; incorporated 1835; pop. of township 25,290.

Westport Landing, Mo. *see in index* Kansas City

West Prussia, former district of e. Germany on Baltic, 9,862 sq mi (25,542 sq km); by Treaty of Versailles larger part went to Poland; remainder in e. border district (Grenzmark) of

Pomerania went to Poland in 1945.

West Quoddy Head, promontory on Atlantic coast of Maine, easternmost point of United States
  Maine M-51, *map* U-117

Westray, one of Orkney Islands, 10 mi (16 km) long; pop. 872.

West River, river about 50 mi (80 km) long, in s.e. corner of Vermont V-286, *map* V-301

West Saint Paul, Minn., city just s. of Saint Paul; on s. bank of Mississippi River; suburb of Saint Paul; pop. 18,799.

West Seneca, N.Y., town 10 mi (16 km) e. of Buffalo in Erie County; light industry; pop. 51,210.

'West Side Story', musical play composed by Bernstein M-686, *picture* M-625
  juvenile delinquency J-164
  opera O-560

West South Central States, name used by the U.S. government for the geographic division including the states of Arkansas, Louisiana, Oklahoma, and Texas.

West Springfield, Mass., town on Connecticut River opposite Springfield; machinery, paper products, gasoline and oil equipment; pop. of township 27,042.

West Texas State University, Canyon, Tex.; founded 1910; arts and sciences, education; graduate study.

West University Place, Tex., residential suburb of Houston; in 1948 absorbed by Houston; pop. 13,317.

West Virginia (nickname Mountain State), e.-central state of U.S.; 24,181 sq mi (62,628 sq km); cap. Charleston; pop. 1,949,644 W-164, *maps* U-41, 50, 59
  cities. *see also in index* cities listed below and other cities by name
    Harpers Ferry H-43
    Parkersburg P-124
  Civil War C-473
  geographic regions, *maps* U-50, 58–9
    Middle Atlantic U-49, *map* U-50, *pictures* U-52, *Reference-Outline* U-133
    the South U-56, *map* U-58, *picture* U-57
  name, *table* S-428
  North America, *map* N-351
  rivers
    Potomac P-468, *map* P-468
  state symbols
    flag, *picture* F-160
    flower, *picture* S-427
  Statuary Hall, *table* S-437b
    Pierpont, Francis, *picture* S-437b
  taxation, *tables* T-37, 39

West Virginia College of Graduate Studies, Institute in W. Va.; state control; established 1972; arts and sciences, education; graduate studies only
  West Virginia W-168

West Virginia Institute of Technology, in Montgomery, W. Va.; state control; founded 1895, senior college 1928; general studies, engineering, business administration and economics, education
  West Virginia W-168

West Virginia State College, Institute in W. Va.; founded 1891; arts and sciences, business administration, home economics, social work
  West Virginia W-168

West Virginia University, Morgantown, W. Va.; state control; founded 1867; arts and sciences, agriculture, commerce, dentistry, education, engineering, forestry, home economics, journalism, law, medicine, mines, music, pharmacy, physical education, and athletics; graduate school
  West Virginia W-168, *picture* W-173

West Virginia Wesleyan College, Buckhannon, W. Va.; United Methodist; founded 1890; arts and sciences, education; graduate studies
  West Virginia W-169

Westwall, German fortifications. *see in index* Siegfried Line

'Westward Ho!', novel by Kingsley K-247

Westward movement, in United States history, *map* U-176, *Reference-Outline* U-197b, c. *see also in index* Pioneer life in America; Southwest, American; United States history
  frontier F-419, *picture* F-20

West Warwick, R.I. *see in index* Warwick, R.I.

Westwego, La., industrial city 9 mi (15 km) s.w. of New Orleans; oil field nearby on w. bank of Mississippi River; pop. 12,663.

Westwood, Mass., town 4 mi (6 km) s.w. of Dedham; chiefly residential; separated from Dedham and incorporated 1897; pop. of township 12,750.

Westwood, N.J., borough 9 mi (15 km) n.e. of Paterson; trade center for surrounding area; light industry; pop. 10,714.

Westwood Lakes, Fla., residential community 11 mi (18 km) s.w. of Miami in Dade County; just s. of Tamiami Airport; pop. 12,811.

Wet-and-dry tropics (or tropical savanna climate)
  climate classification C-500

Wet-bulb thermometer H-343

Wet-collodion process, in early photography P-296

Wet fly, fly rod lure, *picture* F-142

Wethersfield, Conn., urban town 5 mi (8 km) s. of Hartford; tools, machinery, aircraft parts; pop. 26,013.

Wetmore, Alexander (1886–1978), U.S. biologist and ornithologist, born in North Freedom, Wis.; director U.S. National Museum, Washington, D.C., 1925–44; secretary Smithsonian Institution 1945–52, research associate after 1953; authority on bird migration.

Wet milling, corn C-722

Wet mustard (or prepared mustard), condiment M-694

Wet test, chemical analysis C-290

Wettin, German royal family; from 10th to 15th century acquired Thuringia and Saxony and divided possessions between Ernestine and Albertine branches; in 19th-century duchy of Saxe-Coburg-Gotha, of Ernestine branch, provided Leopold I of Belgium, Ferdinand, king consort of Maria II of Portugal, Albert, prince consort of Victoria of England, and Ferdinand, king of Bulgaria.

Wetting agents S-231–2

WEU. *see in index* Western European Union

Wexford, county on s.e. coast of Ireland in Leinster Province; area 908 sq mi (2,352 sq km); fisheries; granite, slate, marble; cattle, potatoes, grain; pop. 83,437.

Wexford, Ireland, seaport and county seat of Wexford County, in s.e. on Wexford Harbor; important Danish settlement; taken by Cromwell 1649; headquarters of rebels 1798; pop. 11,542.

Weyburn, Sask., city on Souris River, 65 mi (105 km) s.e. of Regina; oil, grain, dairying center; pop. 9,523 S-49h, *maps* C-112, S-49l

Weyden, Rogier van der (or Roger van der Weyden) (1400?–64), Flemish painter W-183
  Memling M-294
  painting P-31

Weygand, Maxime (1867–1965), French general, born in Brussels, Belgium; chief of staff under Foch 1914–23; commander in chief of French army 1931–35, of army in Near East 1939–40, of Allied armies May 1940; appointed delegate general to Africa Sept. 1940, later commander in chief of French in Africa; retired 1941; prisoner of Germans 1942–45; arrested in France 1945 for collaboration with Germans, exonerated 1948.

Weyl, Hermann (1885–1955), German mathematician, *table* M-218

Weyler y Nicolau, Valeriano, marquis of Teneriffe (1839–1930), Spanish colonial officer; captain general of Cuba 1896–97; nicknamed in U.S. "Butcher" Weyler for ruthless methods of repressing rebellion; recalled on demand of U.S.
  Spanish-American War S-364

Weyman, Stanley John (1855–1928), English novelist; many historical novels ('The House of the Wolf', 'A Gentleman of France', 'Under the Red Robe').

Weymouth, George, 17th-century English explorer; sailed as far as Labrador searching for northwest passage when mutiny of crew made him turn back (1602); returned 1605 and landed on Monhegan Island and traded with American Indians; explored coast and claimed territory for England A-332

Weymouth, Mass., industrial township 12 mi (19 km) s.e. of Boston; shoe factories and granite quarries; settled 1622; pop. 55,601.

Weymouth and Melcombe Regis, England, seaport and resort on English Channel; shipping and passenger trade; pop. 42,120.

Weyprecht, Karl (1838–81), German polar explorer; visited, in 1873, Franz Joseph Land (now Fridtjof Nansen Land); advocated scientific exploration of north by cooperation of various countries; under his general plan, United States sent out the Greely expedition 1882.

WFL (World Football League)
  football F-291

Whale W-183
  ambergris P-205
  animal A-432, *picture* A-436, *diagram* A-423
    life record, *table* E-24
  Antarctic regions A-473
  barnacle shell, *picture* S-149
  endangered species E-212
  flipper, *picture* H-26
  Melville's novel. *see in index* 'Moby-Dick'
  migration A-451
  money M-531
  oceanography O-485
  Persian manuscript P-67e
  vertebrate structure V-303

Whalebone. *see in index* Baleen whale

Whale oil W-186
  margarine M-134

Whales, Bay of, inlet off Ross Sea near Roosevelt Island in Antarctica; used as base by Byrd expedition 1928–30, 1933–35.

Whale shark S-144, F-124

Whaling W-186
  New Bedford, Mass. N-150
  scrimshaw H-183
  ships, *picture* S-165

Whalley, Edward (died 1675?), one of Oliver Cromwell's generals, signed death warrant of Charles I; later fled to North America and lived in New Haven and Hadley, Mass.

Wharf (or quay), part of a harbor H-35

Wharf of North America. *see in index* Nova Scotia

Wharton, Edith (formerly Edith Newbold Jones) (1862–1937), U.S. novelist W-186
  American literature A-358
  'Ethan Frome' R-112d

Wharton, John A. (1800?–38), U.S. soldier and statesman, born in Tennessee, brother of William H. Wharton; moved to Texas in 1829; prominent in revolt against Mexico; writer of declaration of Nov. 1835, which provided for a provisional government; adjutant general on Houston's staff and hero of San Jacinto; member of Texas congress 1837–38.

Wharton, William Harris (1802–39), U.S. lawyer, born in Virginia, brother of John A. Wharton; settled in Texas 1827 as owner by marriage of huge plantation in Brazoria County, which became meeting place of patriots; sent with Austin and Archer to ask help from U.S. (1835–36); as minister to U.S. (1836) conducted negotiations for recognition and annexation; state senator 1837–39.

Wharton School of Finance and Commerce, in Philadelphia, Pa.; part of University of Pennsylvania; oldest school of finance and commerce of university grade in U.S.; established 1881; graduate division.

Whately, Richard (1787–1863), English theologian; professor of political economy at Oxford University; appointed Protestant archbishop of Dublin, Ireland, 1831; promoted education in Ireland and relieved famine sufferers; liberal in politics and religion ('Elements of Logic', 'Elements of Rhetoric', and the widely used 'Christian Evidences').

'What Is Property?', work by Proudhon A-388

'What Is to Be Done?', work by Lenin C-619

'What's the Matter with Kansas?', work by White W-194

'What's up Tiger Lily?', film by Allen A-309

Wheat, Zachariah Davis (nickname Zack) (1888–1972), U.S. baseball outfielder, born in Hamilton, Mo.; with Brooklyn, N.L., 1909–26, Philadelphia, A.L., 1927; brilliant hitter and near-flawless outfielder; hit .375 in 1923 and 1924 and .359 in 1925; lifetime batting average of .317, fielding average of .966.

Wheat W-187
  bread and baking B-428
  farming F-27, *picture* F-26
  flour F-213
  grains G-207
  harvesting, *pictures* U-85, A-128
  producing regions
    Argentina A-579
    Australia A-808
    Canada, *picture* F-285
      Saskatchewan S-49d, *chart* S-491, *picture* S-49b
    East Germany G-119
    England E-235
    France F-352
    United States U-72
      Kansas K-173, *map* K-178, *picture* K-183
      Montana M-551, *picture* M-558
      Nebraska, *picture* N-103
      North Dakota, *pictures* N-372, 381
      Washington, *pictures* U-85, W-51
    Uruguay U-213
  rainfall R-89, U-72
  rusts and smuts R-363
  rye R-366b
  starch S-424
  straw utilized P-379

'Wheatfields', painting by Ruisdael P-45

Wheatland, home of James Buchanan from 1849 until his death; located near Lancaster, Pa.; restored and designated a national shrine 1962.

Wheatley, Phillis (1753?–84), U.S. poet, born in Africa; taken as slave to Boston, Mass., and became personal maid of wife of John Wheatley, tailor; wrote first poems at age of 13; visited London, England, 1773; married John Peters, a free man, 1778 ('Poems on Various Subjects, Religious and Moral').

Wheaton, Ill., city 24 mi (39 km) w. of Chicago; insurance, printing and publishing; residential; Wheaton College; pop. 43,043
  Illinois, *map* I-53

Wheaton, Md., community 10 mi (16 km) n. of Washington, D.C., a rolling, hilly area; pop. 48,598, *map* M-283

Wheaton College, Wheaton, Ill.; private control; founded 1860; arts and sciences, education; graduate school of theology; school of nursing in Oak Park.

Wheaton College, Norton, Mass.; private control; for women; founded 1834; present name 1912; arts and sciences.

Wheat Ridge, Colo., city w. of Denver in agricultural region; feed and fertilizer, confectionery; pop. 29,795.

Wheatstone, Sir Charles (1802–75), English physicist and inventor; with William Cooke devised an electric telegraph; also invented musical instruments, including the concertina
  stereoscope S-444

Wheat whiskey L-235

Wheel W-192
  airplane A-184
  bicycle B-187
  brake operation B-404
  Mesopotamia B-5
  potter's P-469, 478, *pictures* P-476–7

Wheel, water. *see in index* Waterwheel

Wheel bugs. *see in index* Assassin bugs

Wheelchair, *picture* S-348c

Wheel cipher, cipher device C-420, *picture* C-419

Wheeler, Benjamin Ide (1854–1927), U.S. scholar and educator, born in Randolph, Mass.; president of University of California 1899–1919 ('Introduction to the History of Language', 'Alexander the Great').

Wheeler, Burton Kendall (1882–1975), U.S. political leader, born in Hudson, Mass.; U.S. senator from Montana 1923–47; maintained isolationist policy during World War II; autobiography, 'Yankee from the West'.

Wheeler, Earle Gilmore (1908–75), U.S. Army officer, born in Washington, D.C.; started with U.S. Army, 1932, Army chief of staff 1962–64; chairman Joint Chiefs of Staff 1964–70.

Wheeler, Joseph (1836–1906), U.S. Civil War (Confederate) general, born in Augusta, Ga.; ranked next to Jeb Stuart as cavalry raider; service in Spanish-American War
  Statuary Hall, *table* S-437a

Wheeler, Schuyler Skaats (1860–1923), U.S. electrical engineer, inventor, and motor manufacturer, born in New York, N.Y.; member of Thomas A. Edison's engineering staff.

Wheeler, William Almon (1819–87), U.S. statesman, born in Malone, N.Y.; author of Wheeler Compromise for settling political dispute in Louisiana.

Wheeler, William Morton (1865–1937), U.S. zoologist, born in Milwaukee, Wis.; professor of economic entomology at Harvard University 1908–26, of entomology 1926–34; authority on ants and other insects ('Social Life Among the Insects').

Wheeler-Howard Act (or Indian Reorganization Act) I-150

Wheeler Peak, Taos County, n.e. New Mexico, in Sangre de Cristo Mts. n.e. of Santa Fe; highest point in state (13,160 ft; 4,010 m)
  Nevada N-133
  New Mexico N-214, *map* N-229

Wheeling, Ill., village 23 mi (37 km) n.w. of Chicago; television receivers, paint and paint shakers, insecticides, aluminum foil; pop. 23,266
  Illinois, *map* I-53

Wheeling, W. Va., city in n. panhandle, on Ohio River; industrial and shipping center for coal and steel; coal, iron and steel products, glass, tobacco products, tile, chemical products, textiles; site of Fort Henry (built 1774); state capital 1863–70, 1875–85; Wheeling College; pop. 43,070
  West Virginia W-167

Wheeling College, Wheeling, W. Va.; Roman Catholic; founded 1954; arts and sciences; junior year abroad program
  West Virginia W-169

Wheel lock, weapon F-96, *picture* F-97

Wheelmen of America R-216

Wheelock, John Hall (1886–1978), U.S. poet and editor, born in Far Rockaway, Long Island, N.Y.; lyric poetry ('The Beloved Adventure', 'The Black Panther', 'Poems, 1911–1936', 'Poems, Old and New').

Wheelock College, Boston, Mass.; private control; founded 1889; stress on early childhood education; graduate school; trimester system

Wheel of Fortune, game G-13

Wheel of life (or zoetrope), optical toy, forerunner of motion pictures M-615

Wheelwright, John (1592?–1679), English clergyman, born in Saleby, England; brother-in-law of Anne Hutchinson; emigrated to Boston, Mass., 1636 and preached at Quincy, Mass.; banished 1637 for religious views, retracted 1644; pastor at Salisbury, N.H. 1662–79
  founded Exeter, Mass. M-194
  Hutchinson H-336

Whelan, Edward (1824–67), Canadian journalist and political leader, born in County Mayo, Ireland
  Fathers of Canadian Confederation C-118, *picture* C-116

Whelk, marine mollusk S-222, *picture* A-433
  egg, *picture* E-111
  mollusk M-523
  wampum S-153

'When Johnny Comes Marching Home', American Civil War song by Louis Lambert, pen name of Patrick S. Gilmore.

Whewell, William (1794–1866), English scientist and philosopher ('History of the Inductive Sciences')
  sciences S-63

Whey, a milk by-product C-287

'Whidah', pirate ship that sank near Cape Cod in 1717
  treasure hunting T-272

Whidbey Island, part of Washington State, in northern part of Puget Sound, s.e. of the San Juan Islands; 40 mi (60 km) long; scene of American Indian uprising in 1857; blockhouse of early settlers preserved at town of Coupeville; farming district.

Whieldon, Thomas (1719–95), English potter, born in Stoke-on-Trent, England P-475

Whig party, England E-247, P-434
  American Revolution R-170
  Peel P-152
  Russell R-319
  Swift S-531

Whig party, Great Britain. *see in index* Liberal party

Whig party, United States P-433
  Clay P-438
  Fillmore F-84
  presidents elected, *table* P-495a

Whimbrel, European shorebird of family Scolopacidae; the whimbrel *Numenius phaeopus* resembles curlew but is smaller; total length 15 to 16 in. (38 to 41 cm), bill 3½ in. (9 cm); ranges from Iceland, British Isles, Scandinavia, Finland, and U.S.S.R. s. to Africa and India.

Whin. *see in index* Furze

Whip, member of the English Parliament whose duty it is to secure the attendance of all in his party when a vote is to be taken on important measures; term used in U.S. for similar party leader.

Whip, in cooking C-700

Whippet, dog, *picture* D-200

Whippet tank, lighter, shorter, and less clumsy type of war tank, designed for greater speed. *see also in index* Tank

Whipping cream, *list* D-6

Whipping post, traditional instrument of punishment to which lawbreakers were tied for flogging; now seldom used.

Whipping stitch (or hemming stitch), in sewing S-122

Whipple, Allen Oldfather (1881–1963), U.S. surgeon, born in present Rezaieh, Iran; professor of surgery Columbia University 1921–46; improved surgical methods in biliary tract and pancreas.

Whipple, Fred Lawrence (born 1906), U.S. astronomer, born in Red Oak, Iowa; on faculty Harvard University 1932–, professor 1950–; director Smithsonian Astrophysical Observatory 1955–73, senior scientist 1973–; contributions to space sciences.

Whipple, George Hoyt (1878–1976), U.S. pathologist, born in Ashland, N.H.; dean and professor of pathology University of Rochester 1921–55. *see also in index* Nobel Prizewinners, *table*

Whipple, Henry Benjamin (1822–1901), U.S. Episcopal bishop, born in Adams, N.Y.; elected bishop of Minnesota 1859; did notable work among American Indians.

Whipple, William (1730–85), signer of Declaration of Independence as New Hampshire delegate; born in Kittery, Me.; Revolutionary War general.

Whippoorwill, bird *Caprimulgus vociferus* W-194
  protective coloring P-509–10

Whipsnade Zoo, zoo in London, England Z-457

Whiptail wallaby, marsupial mammal *Macropus parryi* M-157

Whirligig, water beetle B-142

Whirling dervish. *see in index* Dervish

Whirlpool, rapid circular motion of water forming cone in center; caused by opposite tidal currents or irregular channel
  Charybdis S-192
  maelstrom. *see in index* Maelstrom

Whirlwind, tunnel-shaped column of air, nearly upright and rotating rapidly, moving over the Earth's surface; usually consists of small dust eddy in arid regions; larger forms are sand pillars of the desert, waterspouts of the tropics, and tornadoes
  wind W-225

Whirlybird. *see in index* Helicopter

Whiskers
  hair H-7
  squirrel A-430

Whiskey, alcoholic beverage A-275, L-234, *diagram* L-236

Whiskey Rebellion (1794), United States P-345b
  civil disobedience C-463
  Washington W-43

Whiskey Ring, popular term for a group of revenue officers and distillers who were convicted during President Grant's Administration of having defrauded the U.S. government of excise taxes amounting to nearly $2,000,000 in 1875 alone G-219

Whistle, instrument for making whistling sounds
  signaling S-194
  terra-cotta, *picture* S-78

Whistler, James Abbott McNeill (1834–1903), U.S. artist W-194, P-53
  Hall of Fame, *table* H-16
  'The White Girl: Symphony in White, No. 1', P-53, *picture* P-54

Whistler, duck. *see in index* Goldeneye

Whistling swan D-285

Whitby, England, seaport and resort of n. Yorkshire; Synod of Whitby (664) established time for Easter; pop. 12,130.

Whitcomb, Richard Travis (born 1921), U.S. aeronautical engineer, born in Evanston, Ill.; on National Advisory Committee for Aeronautics 1943–58; with National Aeronautics and Space Administration 1958–
  aerospace design A-79

White, Andrew (1579–1656), English Jesuit missionary, born in London, England; member of Gov. Leonard Calvert's colonizing party (1634); compiled American Indian grammar and dictionary; sent in irons to England by Puritan party, and exiled from British territory.

White, Andrew Dickson (1832–1918), U.S. diplomat and educator, born in Homer, N.Y.; first president of Cornell University 1867–85; minister 1879–81 and ambassador 1897–1902 to Germany; minister to Russia 1892–94.

White, Byron Raymond (nickname Whizzer) (born 1917), U.S. jurist, born in Fort Collins, Colo.; U.S. deputy attorney general 1961–62; justice U.S. Supreme Court 1962–.

White, Edward Douglass (1845–1921), U.S. associate justice of U.S. Supreme Court 1894–1910, chief justice 1910–21; born in Lafourche Parish, La.; appointed by William Howard Taft
  Statuary Hall, *table* S-437a

White, Edward Higgins, II (1930–67), U.S. astronaut, born in San Antonio, Tex.; U.S. Air Force officer; chosen for NASA program 1962; killed in launch-pad fire S-346f, *table* S-348
  NASA N-22

White, Elwyn Brooks (1899–1985), U.S. writer, born in Mount Vernon, N.Y.; writer for *The New Yorker* magazine; awarded Presidential Medal of Freedom 1963, Laura Ingalls Wilder Award 1970, National Medal for Literature 1971 ('Every Day Is Saturday', 'Quo Vadimus?', 'The Second Tree from the Corner', 'The Points of My Compass')
  'Charlotte's Web' R-111c
  essay E-306
  Thurber T-178

White, George Henry (1852–1918), U.S. lawyer and political leader, born in Rosindale, N.C.; elected to North Carolina House of Representatives 1880, to North Carolina Senate 1884; in U.S. Congress 1896–1901; born a slave, worked for civil and human rights for black Americans; introduced first antilynching bill in Congress.

White, Gilbert (1720–93), English country parson and naturalist; his 'Natural History and Antiquities of Selborne' has become a classic.

White, Hugh Lawson (1773–1840), U.S. jurist and political leader, born in Iredell County, North Carolina; U.S. senator from Tennessee 1825–40; candidate for U.S. presidency in 1836.

White, Israel Charles (1848–1927), U.S. geologist and teacher, born in Monongalia County, Virginia; state geologist of West Virginia 1897–1927.

White, James (1747–1821), U.S. officer K-265

White, John (1575–1648), English prelate, born in Oxfordshire, England; in 1628 helped found the Massachusetts Company; his 'Planters' Plea' first accurate account of the colony.

White, John (fl. 1585–93), governor of Lost Colony of Roanoke
  North Carolina N-359

White, Joshua Daniel (1908–69), U.S. folksinger and actor, born in Greenville, S.C.; noted for songs protesting injustice, *picture* S-316

White, Patrick (born 1912), Australian author of plays, novels, and short stories W-194. *see also in index* Nobel Prizewinners, *table*
  Australia, *table* A-798

White, Paul Dudley (1886–1973), U.S. heart specialist, born in Boston, Mass.; head of cardiac clinic Massachusetts General Hospital, Boston; professor Harvard Medical School; awarded Presidential Medal of Freedom 1964; author of 'Heart Disease'.

White, Peregrine (or Peregriene White) (1620–1704), first white child born in New England, born aboard the *Mayflower,* in Cape Cod harbor
  name's meaning N-8

White, Richard Grant (1821–85), U.S. writer and critic, born in New York; Shakespearean scholar and philologist.

White, Robert Mayer (born 1923), U.S. meteorologist, born in Boston, Mass.; chief U.S. Weather Bureau 1963–65; director Environmental Science Services Administration 1965–70; administrator, National Oceanic and Atmospheric Administration 1971–.

White, Robert Michael (born 1924), U.S. Air Force test pilot, born in New York, N.Y.; X-15 research pilot 1958–63; astronaut's wings 1962.

White, Stanford (1853–1906), U.S. architect, born in New York City; designed Madison Square Garden, where he was killed by Harry K. Thaw. *see also in index* McKim, Charles F., *profile* A-569
  Hall of Fame H-16

White, Stewart Edward (1873–1946), U.S. novelist, born in Grand Rapids, Mich. ('The Claim Jumpers', 'The Blazed Trail', 'The Silent Places', 'Conjuror's House').

White, Terence Hanbury (1906–64), English author, born in Bombay, India; social historian and satirist with great knowledge of medieval customs ('Book of Beasts', 'Mistress Masham's Repose'); best known for 'The Once and Future King', four volumes (including 'The Sword and the Stone') based on the Arthurian legend, basis for stage and motion picture musical 'Camelot' R-110d

White, Thomas Dresser (1901–65), U.S. Air Force officer, born in Walker, Minn.; Air Force deputy chief of staff for operations 1951–53, vice-chief of staff 1953–57,

Wieland, Christoph Martin (1733–1813), German epic poet ('The Golden Mirror', 'Agathon', 'Oberon') G-106
Wieland, Heinrich Otto (1877–1957), German chemist, born in Pforzheim, Baden; studied constitution of bile acids. *see also in index* Nobel Prizewinners, *table*
Wieliczka, Poland, town in Krakow Province 7 mi (11 km) s.e. of Cracow; a famous salt-mining and salt-processing center; pop. 13,600.
Wien, Wilhelm (1864–1928), German physicist; the two laws named for him concern the relations between wavelength as a measure of energy and temperature; lectured at Columbia University 1913. *see also in index* Nobel Prizewinners, *table*
Wien, Austria. *see in index* Vienna
Wiene, Robert (1881–1938), film actor and director, born in Saska, Sachsen, Germany; best known for his film 'The Cabinet of Dr. Caligari (1919) M-626, *picture* M-621
Wiener, Norbert (1894–1964), U.S. mathematician W-201
automation A-833
cybernetics C-808
Wiener. *see in index* Hot dog
Wieniawski, Henri (1835–80), Polish violinist and composer; taught at St. Petersburg (Leningrad), Russia, and Brussels, Belgium; toured U.S. with Anton Rubinstein ('Legende', 'Romance').
Wiesbaden, West Germany, city on Rhine River 20 mi (30 km) w. of Frankfurt; one of world's noted spas; metal products, chemicals; pop. 250,122, *maps* E-360, G-134
Wiese, Kurt (1887–1974), U.S. illustrator and writer of children's books, born in Minden, Germany; to U.S. 1926, became citizen 1938; wrote and illustrated 'The Chinese Ink Stick', 'You Can Write Chinese', 'Fish in the Air', 'Happy Easter', and 'The Dog, the Fox and the Fleas'; also illustrated many books by other authors including 'Young Fu of the Upper Yangtze' by Elizabeth Lewis R-107, 111b, S-481b
Wiesel, Elie (full name Eliezer Wiesel) (born 1928), U.S. writer W-202. *see also in index* Nobel Prizewinners, *table*
Wiesenthal, Simon (born 1908), Austrian Nazi hunter W-202
Wiesner, Jerome Bert (born 1915), U.S. communications engineer, born in Detroit, Mich.; professor of electrical engineering Massachusetts Institute of Technology 1950–, dean of science 1964–66, provost 1966–71, president 1971–; on leave as presidential special assistant for science and technology 1961–64.
'Wife of Bath', work by Chaucer C-287
Wig, covering of natural or synthetic hair for the head
dress D-264
hairdressing H-8
hats and caps H-53
Wigan, England, county borough in Lancashire, 17 mi (27 km) n.e. of Liverpool; collieries, iron and cotton industries; pop. 79,780.
Wiggin, Kate Douglas (or Mrs. George C. Riggs) (1856–1923), U.S. novelist and playwright, born in Philadelphia, Pa.; trained in kindergarten teaching in California; organized first free kindergartens on Pacific coast; won wide success among youthful readers with 'The Birds' Christmas Carol' and 'Rebecca of Sunnybrook Farm' ('Mother Carey's Chickens'; 'My Garden of Memory', autobiography)
'Arabian Nights' S-480
Wiggins, Carleton (1848–1932), U.S. artist, born in Turners, N.Y.; noted for landscapes and paintings of cattle and sheep ('A Holstein Bull'; 'Morning on the Hills').
Wiggins, James Russell (born 1903), U.S. journalist and public official, born in Luverne, Minn.; with *Washington Post* 1947–68, editor 1961–68; ambassador to United Nations 1968–69.
Wigglesworth, Michael (1631–1705), U.S. Puritan pastor; wrote 'The Day of Doom', a dismal Calvinistic poem that was popular in early New England A-342
Wight, Isle of, island off s. coast of England in English Channel; 147 sq mi (381 sq km); pop.120,900 W-202
double tide S-303
England E-230
Wightman Cup, awarded annually to nation winning women's tennis team championship; donated 1923 by **Hazel Hotchkiss Wightman** (1886–1974), outstanding woman tennis player for many years
tennis T-108
Wigman, Mary (1886–1973), modern dancer, born in Hanover, Germany; one of founders of modern German dancing; founded Wigman School in Dresden; first U.S. tour 1930 D-30
Wigner, Eugene Paul (born 1902), U.S. physicist, born in Budapest, Hungary; to U.S. 1930, citizen 1937; professor Princeton University 1938–; on leave at University of Chicago 1942–45 for work on first atomic reactor; won Enrico Fermi Award 1958, Atoms for Peace Award 1960, and National Science Medal 1969. *see also in index* Nobel Prizewinners, *table*
Wigwag signaling S-193, *pictures* S-194b, 195
Wigwam, shelter I-120
Wilberforce, Samuel (1805–73), British clergyman; bishop of Oxford 1845–69; prominent in House of Lords.
Wilberforce, William (1759–1833), British philanthropist and abolitionist W-202
abolitionist movement A-10
slavery S-214
Wilberforce University, Wilberforce, Ohio; African Methodist Episcopal; founded 1856; liberal arts; theological seminary.
Wilbur, Ray Lyman (1875–1949), U.S. educator, physician, and public official; born in Boonesboro, Iowa; president Stanford University 1916–43, chancellor 1943–49; secretary of interior under President Hoover.
Wilbur, Richard Purdy (born 1921), U.S. poet, born in New York, N.Y.; professor Wesleyan University 1957– ('The Beautiful Changes', 'Ceremony', 'Things of This World' awarded 1957 Pulitzer prize and National Book Award).
Wild, Jonathan (1682?–1725), English criminal who received stolen goods from a band of thieves and returned it to owner for a fee or sold it abroad; hanged at Tyburn; subject of stories, including Fielding's 'History of the Life of the Late Mr. Jonathan Wild the Great'.
Wild aster, plant
poisonous possibilities P-408
Wild blue phlox. *see in index* Sweet William
Wild boar. *see in index* Boar
Wild cabbage, plant C-2, *picture* C-3
Wild canary. *see in index* Goldfinch
Wild carrot. *see in index* Queen Anne's lace
Wildcat, name of many kinds of small, undomesticated cats; scientific name of European wildcat *Felis sylvestris;* usually in America applied to the lynx, particularly *Lynx rufus* or bobcat L-344
Wildcat oil well P-235
Wild celery. *see in index* Vallisneria
Wild columbine, plant, *picture* F-233
'Wild Duck, The', ironic play by Henrik Ibsen; the sincere but misguided reformer Werle, in his eagerness to tell the complete truth, brings disaster to the Ekdal family I-5
Wilde, Jane Francesca, Lady (or Speranze) (1826?–96), Irish poet I-327
Wilde, Oscar (1854–1900), British author W-203
drama D-246
Irish literature I-326
literary contribution E-278
'Wild Earth, The', work by Colum I-328
Wildebeest. *see in index* Gnu
Wilder, Laura Ingalls (1867–1957), U.S. author, born in Pepin, Wis.; her nine books for children are a saga of North American frontier life, moving westward from Wisconsin; they begin with 'The Little House in the Big Woods', when Laura was a little girl, and end with 'The First Four Years', the early years of Laura's marriage to Almanzo Wilder; Laura Ingalls Wilder Award of Children's Library Association first presented to her in 1954 R-111e, L-240
Wilder, Thornton Niven (1897–1975), U.S. novelist and playwright, born in Madison, Wis.; lecturer at University of Chicago 1930–36; Pulitzer prize for fiction (1928) for 'The Bridge of San Luis Rey'; for drama (1938) for 'Our Town' and (1943) for 'The Skin of Our Teeth'; also wrote 'The Ides of March', a novel; won Presidential Medal of Freedom 1963 and the first National Medal for Literature 1965 A-356
creative writing W-382
drama D-248
'The Bridge of San Luis Rey' R-112d
Wilderness, battle of the, indecisive Civil War battle fought in n. Virginia May 5–6, 1864 G-217
Wilderness Areas, United States
frontier F-418
Wilderness Road (first called Boone's Trace), in Kentucky K-211, R-221, B-365, *map* R-219
Wilderness Society L-276
Wildflower. *see in index* Flowers, Wild
Wild Flower Preservation Society, U.S. organization F-240
Wildgans, Anton (1881–1932), Austrian poet and dramatist; artistic manager Burg Theater, Vienna; poems show deep passion and human sympathy; plays combine realism with mysticism and symbolism ('Herbstfrühling', 'Armut', 'Kirbisch').
Wild geranium, flower G-103. *see also in index* Cranesbill
Wild ginger, genus *Asarum* of plants of the birthwort family having kidney- or heart-shaped fuzzy leaves on long stalks; purplish brown flower close to the ground; rootstock has gingerlike flavor.
Wild goat. *see in index* Goat
'Wild goose, The' (or 'Gan'), novel by Mori M-583
Wild hog. *see in index* Boar
Wild lemon M-237
Wildlife conservation. *see also in index* Animal; Birds
ecology E-56
endangered species E-209
preservation C-675
national parks N-26
Africa A-95
trapping legislation F-463
wild flowers F-231
zoo Z-457
Wild lupine, plant, *picture* F-234
Wild parsnip. *see in index* Water hemlock
Wild prairie rose. *see in index* wild rose
Wild rice (also called Indian rice, or water oats), genus *Zizania* of tall grasses that grows in marshes or open water; bears dark-colored grains or seeds that are gathered for food, especially by American Indians of n. U.S. and Canada; often planted in lakes to provide food for game birds R-201
Wild rose (also called wild prairie rose) R-294, 296, *picture* R-295, F-216
Cherokee rose, *picture* S-427
fruit comparison F-431
state flower, *picture* S-427
Iowa, *picture* I-296
North Dakota, *picture* N-378
swamp rose R-296
apple comparison, *picture* A-460
Wild rye. *see in index* Lyme grass
Wild sheep S-148
Wild strawberry, plant, *picture* F-234
Wild West shows
Buffalo Bill B-490
Hickok H-149
circus offshoot C-433
Wild yellow lily. *see in index* Canada lily
Wiley, Harvey Washington (1844–1930), U.S. chemist, born in Kent, Ind.; as chief of division of chemistry, U.S. Department of Agriculture, incurred great hostility for his vigorous enforcement of pure food and drug laws.
Wiley College, Marshall, Tex.; United Methodist; founded 1873; liberal arts and teacher education.
Wilfley table, machine used in copper refining C-712
Wilfred, Thomas (1889–1968), U.S. inventor, born in Nästved, Denmark; came to U.S. 1916; began experimenting in 1905 with use of light as an independent medium for aesthetic expression and produced the clavilux, or color organ, 1922; founded the Art Institute of Light, New York City, in 1930.
Wilhelm, rulers of Germany. *see in index* William
Wilhelmina (1880–1962), queen of the Netherlands 1890–1948
World War II W-324
'Wilhelm Meister's Apprenticeship', work by Goethe N-410
Wilhelmshaven, West Germany, seaport and health resort on North Sea 40 mi (60 km) n.w. of Bremen; naval base in World Wars I and II; pop. 102,732, *map* G-134
Wilkes, Charles (1798–1877), U.S. Navy officer and explorer, born in New York City
Antarctic exploration, A-474, *table* P-422
Samoa S-34
U.S. Navy N-91
Wilkes, John (1727–97), British political leader; lord mayor of London and member of Parliament; established right of constituency to elect whom it pleases to Parliament; advocated colonial rights during the American Revolution; Wilkes-Barre, Pa., named for him.
Wilkes-Barre, Pa., city 98 mi (158 km) n.w. of Philadelphia, on Susquehanna River; pop. 51,551 P-182b, *maps* P-185, 174, U-41
Wyoming Massacre P-166
Wilkes College, Wilkes-Barre, Pa.; private control; established 1933; chartered as Wilkes College 1947; arts and sciences, commerce and finance, education; graduate school.
Wilkes Land, Antarctica, large area facing Indian Ocean between Queen Mary Coast and George V Coast; named for Charles Wilkes, leader of U.S. expedition 1838–42 which discovered land.
Wilkins, Sir David (1785–1841), Scottish genre and historical painter, especially noted for scenes from village life ('Pitlessie Fair', 'Village Festival', 'Blind Man's Buff', 'John Knox Preaching').
Wilkins, Sir George Hubert (1888–1958), Australian polar explorer and aviator, born in South Australia ('Flying the Arctic', 'Under the North Pole') A-474, *table* P-422
Wilkins, Mary E. *see in index* Freeman, Mary Wilkins
Wilkins, Maurice Hugh Frederick (born 1916), British biochemist, born in Pongaroa, near Dannevirke, New Zealand; deputy director biophysics research unit Medical Research Council, King's College, University of London; 1955–74, director 1974–. *see also in index* Nobel Prizewinners, *table*
Wilkins, Roy (1901–81), U.S. civil and human rights leader, born in St. Louis, Mo.; on staff National Association for the Advancement of Colored People after 1931, executive director 1964–77, editor of *The Crisis,* NAACP magazines, 1934–49; won 1964 Spingarn Medal B-298, 302
Wilkinsburg, Pa., residential borough, suburb of Pittsburgh; light industry; pop. 23,669, *map* P-184

Wilkinson, Charles Bud, University of Oklahoma football coach 1947–63
football F-297

Wilkinson, Geoffrey (born 1921), British chemist, born in Todmorden; research into "sandwich compounds"; faculty member Harvard University 1951–56; professor University of London 1956–. *see also in index* Nobel Prizewinners, *table*

Wilkinson, James (1757–1825), American Revolutionary War general and adventurer involved in Conway Cabal, Aaron Burr conspiracy; founded Frankfort, Ky.

Wilkinson, Marguerite (1883–1928), U.S. poet and critic, born in Halifax, N.S.; came to U.S. as child; married James G. Wilkinson ('Citadels', poems; 'New Voices').

Will, U.S. author. *see in index* Lipkind, William

Will, legal document assigning property to survivors upon the death of the property owner W-203
estate and inheritance law E-307
law, *table* L-93
Shakespeare S-132

Willamette, river of w. Oregon, formed by union of McKenzie and Middleforks; flows n. 300 mi (480 km) to Columbia River, *map* U-90
forest, *picture* F-314
Oregon O-582, *picture* O-589, 590
Portland P-452, *picture* U-92
Salem S-26

Willamette University, Salem, Ore.; Methodist; founded 1842; liberal arts, law, music; graduate studies O-585

Willamette Valley, fertile trough between the Coast Ranges and the Cascade Mountains in n.w. U.S.
Oregon O-582

Willapa Hills, in Washington, s.w. corner of the state W-48, *map* W-49

Willard, Archibald M. (1836–1918), U.S. painter, works include 'Spirit of '76', *picture* M-194

Willard, Emma (formerly Emma Hart) (1787–1870), U.S. teacher W-204
educational contribution E-92
Hall of Fame, *table* H-16

Willard, Frances (full name Frances Elizabeth Caroline Willard) (1839–98), U.S. temperance leader W-204
Hall of Fame, *table* H-16
Statuary Hall, *table* S-437a
women's rights W-277

Willard, Jess (1883–1968), U.S. boxer, born in Pottawatomie County, Kansas
heavyweight champion B-391
Johnson J-128

Willemite, silicate ore of zinc; various colors; usually opaque; transparent variety cut as gem M-437

Willemstad, Netherlands Antilles, capital, on island of Curaçao; major seaport; petroleum refining; pop. 95,000, *map* S-298
West Indies, *map* W-159

Willet, shorebird of family Scolopacidae; the willet *Catoptrophorus semipalmatus* is a large 14–17 in. (36–43 cm) gray and white bird, showing flashy black and white wing pattern in flight; ranges from s. Canada to West Indies and South America.

Willett, William (1856–1915), British builder and advocate of daylight saving time; published pamphlet, 'The Waste of Daylight'.

William I (1797–1888), first German emperor W-204
Austria A-830
Bismarck B-285
Germany G-122
Versailles V-303
Washington state W-54

William II (or Wilhelm II) (1859–1941), German emperor W-205
Edward VII E-108
Germany G-122
Oakley O-453
Roosevelt, *picture* R-289
Weimar Republic W-142

William I (also called William the Conqueror) (1027?–87), king of England W-206
battle of Hastings H-52
Bayeux tapestry H-272
England E-239, E-264
Harold II H-43
Henry I H-131
London L-286
Tower of London T-237
naval power N-87
Norman conquest N-333
migration of people M-402
St. Anselm A-467

William II, Rufus (1056?–1100), king of England W-206
Anselm of Canterbury A-467
English history E-240

William III (1650–1702), king of England and stadholder of Holland W-207. *see also in index* Mary II
England E-247
Glorious Revolution G-168
King William's War K-247
religious controversies A-418
Stuart S-493
The Netherlands N-130

William IV (1765–1837), king of England W-207
Australia A-41
Reform Act R-319
United Kingdom E-252

William I (1772–1843), first king of The Netherlands, crowned in 1815 after revolt against France; harsh measures provoked revolt and loss of Belgian provinces 1830; abdicated 1840 N-130

William II (1792–1849), king of The Netherlands, came to throne 1840; gave The Netherlands constitution 1848 and averted revolution.

William III (1817–90), king of The Netherlands, came to throne 1849, after establishment of the Constitution of 1848; father of Queen Wilhelmina N-130

William I, the Lion (1143–1214), king of Scotland; succeeded his brother Malcolm IV 1165; invaded England 1174, was captured and forced to do homage to Henry II.

William I, the Silent, prince of Orange (1533–84) W-211
William III W-207

William II, prince of Orange (1626–50), grandson of William the Silent, married Mary, princess royal of England, daughter of Charles I J-20
The Netherlands N-129

William, prince of Sweden and duke of Södermanland (1884–1965), explorer and author; traveled through India, Thailand, Indochina, and e. Africa ('Among Pygmies and Gorillas: With Swedish Zoological Expedition to Central Africa', 'Roaring Bones', and 'Wild African Animals I Have Known').

William and Mary, rulers of England. *see in index* Mary II; William III

William and Mary, College of, Williamsburg, Va.; state control; founded 1693; granted coat of arms 1694; arts and sciences, education, law; graduate study; affiliated junior college at Petersburg V-334. *see also in index* Christopher Newport College
Williamsburg W-209

William Augustus, duke of Cumberland (1721–65), English military commander, born in London; 3rd son of George II of England; defeated Jacobites at Culloden Moor 1746.

William Carey College, Hattiesburg, Miss.; Baptist; founded 1906; arts and sciences, music, nursing; graduate study.

William Hayes Fogg Art Museum, in Cambridge, Mass. *see in index* Fogg Art Museum

William Jewell College, Liberty, Mo.; Baptist; founded 1849; opened 1850; arts and sciences, education.

William of Norwich, Saint (1132–44), tanner's apprentice of Norwich, England; crucified body found in Thorpe Wood; revered as "the innocent victim of hatred of the faith"; festival November 26.

William of Wied, Prince (1876–1945), king of Albania February to September 1914; distant cousin of William II of Germany.

William of Wykeham (1324–1404), English statesman and prelate, bishop of Winchester, twice chancellor of England; founded Winchester School (now Winchester College) and New College of Oxford University.

William Paterson College, Wayne, N.J.; state control; established 1855 as Paterson City Normal School; present name 1971; arts and sciences, education; graduate study.

William Penn College, Oskaloosa, Iowa; Quaker; founded 1873, liberal arts and education.

William Rockhill Nelson Gallery of Art, in Kansas City, Mo.; established 1926; noted for European and American paintings, American Indian art.

Williams, Ben Ames (1889–1953), U.S. writer, born in Macon, Miss. (novels: 'Leave Her to Heaven', 'House Divided', 'The Unconquered'; short stories of life in Maine: 'Fraternity Village').

Williams, Bert (or Egbert Austin Williams) (1876–1922), U.S. entertainer, born in New Providence, Bahamas: comedian archetype of black vaudeville; partner of George Walker; in Ziegfeld Follies B-302

Williams, Betty (born 1943), Irish housewife and peace movement leader; co-founder with Mairead Corrigan of The Community of Peace People, movement to end violence in Northern Ireland. *see also in index* Nobel Prizewinners, *table*

Williams, Charles Walter Stansby (1886–1945), British author, born in London; on staff of Oxford University Press 1908–45.

Williams, Daniel Hale (1858–1931), U.S. surgeon, born in Hollidaysburg, Pa.; pioneer in training blacks as interns and nurses; surgeon-in-chief Freedmen's Hospital, Washington, D.C., 1893–98; credited with first successful heart surgery, 1893; professor clinical surgery Meharry Medical College, Nashville, Tenn. 1899–1931.

Williams, Emlyn (in full George Emlyn Williams) (born 1905), Welsh playwright, actor, and dramatic reader; born in Mostyn, Flint, Wales; author ('Night Must Fall', psychological murder play; 'The Corn Is Green', set in Welsh mining village; 'George: an Early Autobiography').

Williams, Garth Montgomery (born 1912), U.S. illustrator, sculptor, cartoonist, and writer; born in New York City; educated abroad; won British Prix de Rome for sculpture 1936; returned to U.S. 1941 R-110a, 111c

Williams, Sir George (1821–1905), British merchant, founder (1844) of YMCA
Young Men's Christian Association Y-425

Williams, George Washington, author B-292, *list* B-299

Williams, Joe (born 1918), U.S. blues singer M-680

Williams, John Sharp (1854–1932), U.S. Democratic political leader, born in Memphis, Tenn.; U.S. representative from Mississippi 1893–1909; senator 1911–23; favored free silver and low tariff.

Williams, Mary Lou (1910–81), U.S. jazz pianist and composer, born in Atlanta, Ga.; wrote for many major bands; artist-in-residence at Duke University 1977–81; compositions include 'Walkin' and Swingin'', 'Froggy Bottom', 'Steppin' Pretty', 'Roll 'Em', 'Mary Lou's Mass'.

Williams, Paul Revere (1896–1980), U.S. architect, born in Los Angeles, Calif.; designer of office, government, and university buildings; won 1953 Spingarn medal.

Williams, Ralph Vaughan. *see in index* Vaughan Williams

Williams, Richard D'Alton (1821–62), Irish author I-327

Williams, Roger (1603?–83), founder of Rhode Island W-208
Baptist churches B-77
Hall of Fame, *table* H-16
Massachusetts M-194
Providence, *pictures* R-186, R-188
Rhode Island R-183, *picture* R-190
Statuary Hall, *table* S-437b

Williams, Spencer (1889–1965), U.S. jazz composer, born in New Orleans, La. ('Basin Street Blues', 'Mahogany Hall Stomp', 'I Ain't Got Nobody').

Williams, Ted (in full Theodore Samuel Williams) (born 1918), U.S. baseball player W-208
baseball B-93

Williams, Tennessee (born Thomas Lanier Williams) (1911–83), U.S. writer W-209
American literature A-357
drama D-248
'The Glass Menagerie' R-112b

Williams, William (1731–1811), signer of Declaration of Independence, born in Lebanon, Conn.

Williams, William Carlos (1883–1963), U.S. physician, poet, and novelist; born in Rutherford, N.J.; exponent of imagism in early poetry, later of objectivism ('Collected Poems', 'The Wedge', 'The Clouds', 'Paterson', 'Journey to Love', poetry; 'The White Mule', 'In the Money', novels; 'The Farmers' Daughters', stories; 'Selected Essays'; 'Autobiography'; 'Yes, Mrs. Williams', memoir of his mother); 1963 Pulitzer prize in poetry for 'Pictures from Brueghel'.

Williams, William Sherley (or Bill Williams) (1787–1849), U.S. trapper and guide; active on Yellowstone River and in Utah, Colorado, Arizona, and n. Texas (1826–43), sometimes living with Hopi and Ute Indians, occasionally acting as preacher; guide to Frémont's disastrous fourth expedition (1848) to headwaters of Rio Grande.

Williams, William Taylor Burwell (1866–1941), U.S. educator, born in Stone Bridge, Va., near Winchester; dean Tuskegee Institute 1927–36, vice-president 1936–41; won 1934 Spingarn Medal.

Williams Bay, Wis., resort village in s.e. part of state on Lake Geneva 45 mi (70 km) s.w. of Milwaukee; pop. 1,763.

Williamsburg (formerly called Middle Plantation), Va., city 45 mi (70 km) s.e. of Richmond; former capital of Virginia; pop. 10,800 W-209
Virginia, *map* V-349
'The Common Glory' P-20

Williamsburg Bridge, New York, N.Y., over East River B-446

Williams College, Williamstown, Mass.; formerly for men, women admitted 1970; opened 1793; arts and sciences; graduate studies
Institute of Politics. *see in index* Institute of Politics

William Smith College. *see in index* Hobart and William Smith Colleges

Williamson, Hugh (1735–1819), U.S. scientist and statesman, born in West Nottingham, Pa.; U.S. Army surgeon in Revolution; signed the United States Constitution for North Carolina; member of Congress from North Carolina (1789–93); ranked high in astronomy, mathematics, general science ('Observations on the Climate in Different Parts of North America').

Williamsport, Pa., city on w. branch of Susquehanna River 80 mi (130 km) n. of Harrisburg; airplane engines and parts, metal products, wire rope, photoflash lamps, textiles, wood and paper products; Lycoming College incorporated 1866; pop. 33,401, *maps* P-185, U-41
Little League, *picture* P-179

Williamstown, Mass., town in the Berkshires near n.w. corner of state; Williams College; pop. of township 8,741
Sterling and Francine Clark Art Institute, *picture* U-113

William the Jew (or Guglielmo Ebreo), medieval ballet pioneer D-26

William Woods College, Fulton, Mo.; private control; for women; founded 1870; liberal arts, music; cooperative program with Westminster College for men.

Willibrod, Saint (or Saint Willibrord) (657?–738?), Anglo-Saxon missionary to the Frisians (inhabitants of what is now The Netherlands)
Utrecht U-236

Willimantic, Conn., city 24 mi (39 km) e. of Hartford on Willimantic and Natchaug rivers; thread, yarn, radio parts, foundry products; Willimantic State College;

incorporated as city 1893; pop. 14,652.

Willimantic River, in Connecticut, a stream located in the n.e. part of the state that unites with the Natchaug River to form the Shetucket River.

Willingboro (formerly Levittown), N.J., urban township 12 mi (19 km) n.e. of Camden; steel products, food; pop. 39,912.

Willingdon, Freeman Freeman-Thomas, first **marquis of** (1866–1941), British statesman, member of Parliament until 1913, afterward serving in India 11 years; governor-general of Canada 1926–31; viceroy of India 1931–36.

Willington, Mount, mountain in Tasmania (4,167 ft; 1,270 m) H-179

Willis, Nathaniel Parker (1806–67), U.S. journalist and poet, born in Portland, Me.; as foreign correspondent wrote sketches of European fashionable society ('Pencillings by the Way').

Willis, William (nickname Bill) (born 1921), U.S. football player, born in Columbus, Ohio; guard; Cleveland Browns 1946–53.

Williston, Samuel Wendell (1852–1918), U.S. paleontologist, born in Boston, Mass.; professor at University of Chicago after 1902; noted for researches on prehistoric reptiles and amphibians.

Williston, N.D., city in n.w. on Missouri River, 20 mi (30 km) e. of Montana border; grain elevators, livestock markets, creameries, railroad shops, oil industries; lignite mines nearby; branch of University of North Dakota; pop. 13,336 N-382, *map* U-40
climatic region, *map* U-119

Williston Basin, in n.w. U.S.
Montana oil basin, *picture* M-553
North Dakota N-372, 376
petroleum P-233

Willkie, Wendell Lewis (1892–1944), U.S. lawyer and public utility executive, born in Elwood, Ind.; president Commonwealth and Southern Corp. 1933–40; Republican candidate for president 1940; author of 'One World' R-275

Willmar, Minn., city 92 mi (148 km) w. of Minneapolis; poultry processing, light industry, trading center; resort area; pop. 15,895.

Willmore City. *see in index* Long Beach, Calif.

Will-o'-the-wisp, patches of light sometimes visible above marshes and swamps; explained as phosphorescent gases from decaying plant and animal life.

Willoughby, Sir Hugh (died 1554), English navigator; led expedition to Arctic 1553–54; perished with crew on coast of Lapland; one of his ships, commanded by R. Chancellor, reached White Sea, *table* P-422

Willoughby, Ohio, a residential city located 8 mi (13 km) n.e. of Euclid; machine tools, clothing, automation equipment; pop. 19,329.

Willoughby Run, battle of Gettysburg G-136

Willow (or Salicaceae), family of shrubs and trees W-211

Willow goldfinch, bird
Washington state bird, *picture* W-56

Willow Grove, Pa., community 13 mi (21 km) n. of Philadelphia; naval air station; Six Gun Territory; pop. 16,494, *map* P-185

Willow herb, great. *see in index* Fireweed

Willowick, Ohio, city 14 mi (22 km) n.e. of Cleveland; situated on Lake Erie; residential and industrial suburb; incorporated 1922; pop. 17,834.

Willow oak, tree *Quercus phellos* of beech family, grows to 80 ft (25 m); crown narrow, branches short; leaves similar to those of willow, glossy, light green; acorns ripen in second year
wood, *table* W-283

Willow-pattern ware (or willoware china), popular blue-and-white chinaware named for its willow pattern that depicts old Chinese legend; shows garden of rich mandarin whose daughter is eloping with his secretary; just as mandarin overtakes them on bridge, the lovers are turned into birds and fly beyond his reach. Willow pattern (so called from willow tree in its design), early used in blue china of Nanking, was introduced in English earthenware about 1780 by Thomas Turner of Caughley, England S-467

Willow ptarmigan, type of snow grouse G-292

Willow Run, Mich., unincorporated area 4 mi (6 km) n.e. of Ypsilanti; Willow Run plant constructed here in 1941 by Ford Motor Co. for building heavy bombing planes during World War II; plant purchased 1953 by General Motors and used for manufacture of automotive parts, aeronautic research.

Willow thrush, bird *Hylocichla fuscescens* of the family Turdidae T-177

Wills, Bob (1905–75), U.S. country musician M-678

Wills, Helen (born 1906), U.S. tennis player W-212

Wills, William John (1834–61), British explorer, born in Totnes, England; to Australia 1852; died of starvation returning from first north-south crossing of Australia B-506

Will's Coffee House, coffee house, Covent Garden, England C-695

Willsie, Honoré. *see in index* Morrow, Honoré Willsie

Willstätter, Richard (1872–1942), German chemist, born in Karlsruhe, Baden. *see also in index* Nobel Prizewinners, *table*
chlorophyll research P-372

Willy, Colette. *see in index* Colette

Wilmette, Ill., residential village on Lake Michigan, 15 mi (25 km) n. of Chicago; named for Antoine Ouilmette, its first white settler, 1829; pop. 28,229
Illinois, *map* I-53

Wilmington, Del., largest city of state, on Delaware River; pop. 70,195 W-212, *map* U-41
Delaware D-72, *pictures* D-71, 74, *map* D-76
Delaware Memorial bridges, *picture* B-324
early colonization A-339

Wilmington, Mass., 4 mi (6 km) n. of Reading; machinery, truck and poultry farms; incorporated 1730; pop. of township 17,471.

Wilmington, N.C., seaport city on Cape Fear River about 28 mi (45 km) from ocean; cement, paper and pulp, chemicals, fertilizers, clothing, lumber, nuclear energy components; University of North Carolina at Wilmington; pop. 44,000 N-357, *picture* N-353, *map* U-41
North America, *map* N-351

Wilmington College, Wilmington, Ohio; opened 1863 as Franklin College; in 1870 bought by Society of Friends and renamed; arts and sciences; work-study program.

Wilmore City, Calif. *see in index* Long Beach

Wilmot, David (1814–68), U.S. jurist and political leader, born in Bethany, Pa.; in U.S. House of Representatives 1845–51, in Senate 1861–63; author of Wilmot Proviso.

Wilmot, Lemuel Allan (1809–78), Canadian political leader, born in New Brunswick; Reform member House of Assembly of New Brunswick 1836–51; attorney general in first "responsible government" in New Brunswick 1847–51; lieutenant governor 1868–73
Canada C-98

Wilmot, Robert Duncan (1809–91), Canadian political leader, born in Fredericton, N.B.
Fathers of Canada Confederation C-118, *picture* C-116

Wilmot Proviso (1846), amendment to an appropriation bill proposed by David Wilmot; provided that slavery should not be allowed in land acquired as a result of the Mexican War; passed the House of Representatives 1846 and 1847 but failed in the Senate; intensified the slavery issue.

Wilno, Lithuanian Soviet Socialist Republic. *see in index* Vilna

Wilson, Alexander (1766–1813), Scottish ornithologist, born in Paisley, Scotland; in U.S. 1794–1813; won fame as author of 'American Ornithology' (9 vols.); called Father of American Ornithology.

Wilson, Allen Benjamin (1824–88), U.S. cabinetmaker and inventor, born in New York, N.Y.
sewing machine improvements S-127

Wilson, Angus (born 1913), British writer
literary contribution E-283

Wilson, Bertha, (born 1923), Canadian jurist, appointed to Supreme Court 1982 W-276

Wilson, Charles Edward (1886–1972), U.S. industrialist and public official, born in New York, N.Y.; began career as office boy, General Electric Co., and was president of company 1940–42, 1944–50; on War Production Board 1942–44; director of Office of Defense Mobilization 1950–52.

Wilson, Charles Erwin (1890–1961), U.S. industrialist and electrical engineer, born in Minerva, Ohio; with Westinghouse Electric and Manufacturing Co. (now Westinghouse Electric Corporation) 1909–19; joined General Motors Corporation 1919, president 1941–52, also chief executive officer 1946–52, converted plants for intensive war production program, World War II; U.S. secretary of defense 1953–57.

Wilson, Charles Thomson Rees (1869–1959), Scottish physicist, born in Midlothian County, Scotland; professor of natural philosophy, Cambridge University, 1925–34. *see also in index* Nobel Prizewinners, *table*
Wilson cloud chamber R-65

Wilson, Sir Daniel (1816–92), Canadian educator and archaeologist; president University of Toronto and leader of successful fight for nondenominational university education.

Wilson, Edith Bolling Galt (1872–1961), 2nd wife of President Wilson W-217

Wilson, Edmund (1895–1972), U.S. writer, born in Red Bank, N.J.; associate editor *New Republic* 1926–31; book reviewer *The New Yorker* 1944–48; awarded Presidential Medal of Freedom 1963, National Medal for Literature 1966, and the Aspen Award 1968 ('Axel's Castle' and 'Shores of Light', literary criticism; 'Scrolls from the Dead Sea'; 'Red, Black, Blond and Olive; Studies in Four Civilizations: Zuñi, Haiti, Soviet Russia, Israel'; 'A Piece of My Mind'; 'Apologies to the Iroquois'; 'Night Thoughts'; 'Patriotic Gore'; 'O Canada'; 'The Bit Between My Teeth').

Wilson, Ellen Axson (1860–1914), first wife of President Wilson W-215

Wilson, Ethel Davis (1888–1980), Canadian writer and teacher, born in Port Elizabeth, South Africa.

Wilson, Halsey William (1868–1954), U.S. publisher, born in Wilmington, Vt.; originated cumulative indexing of periodicals and books 1898
H.W. Wilson Company R-128–9

Wilson, Harry Leon (1867–1939), U.S. author, born in Oregon, Ill.; won wide popularity with his humorous novels and plays ('Bunker Bean', 'Ruggles of Red Gap', 'The Wrong Twin', 'Merton of the Movies').

Wilson, Henry (1812–75), U.S. statesman, born in Farmington, N.H.; known as the "Natick Cobbler" from early occupation; opposed slavery; senator from Massachusetts 1855–73.

Wilson, Henry Maitland, first **baron of Libya and of Stowlangtoft** (1881–1964), British army officer after Boer War; field marshal; served in Africa 1939–41; led British in Greece and in Syria 1941; Iran-Iraq command 1942; commander in chief of British in Middle East Feb.-Dec. 1943, Allied Commander in Mediterranean theater Dec. 1943–Nov. 1944
World War II W-335

Wilson, James (1742–98), U.S. jurist, born in Scotland; signer of Declaration of Independence 1776, member Constitutional convention 1787; signed United States Constitution for Pennsylvania; associate justice of U.S. Supreme Court 1789–98
Declaration of Independence D-56

Wilson, James (1835–1920), U.S. agriculturist and Cabinet officer, born in Ayrshire, Scotland; secretary of agriculture under Presidents McKinley, T. Roosevelt, and Taft; developed department into a scientific organization.

Wilson, Sir James Harold (born 1916), British political leader W-212
Heath H-106
United Kingdom E-259

Wilson, John (1785–1854), Scottish author, the famous "Christopher North" of *Blackwood's Magazine* ('Noctes Ambrosianae').

Wilson, Laurence (or Larry Wilson) (born 1938), U.S. football player, born in Rigby, Idaho; free safety; St. Louis Cardinals 1960–72.

Wilson, Lewis Robert (nickname Hack) (1900–48), U.S. baseball player, born in Ellwood City, Pa.; outfielder for New York, N.L., 1923–25, Chicago, N.L., 1926–31, Brooklyn, N.L., 1932–34, and Philadelphia, N.L., 1934; career batting average .307.

Wilson, Richard (1714–82), British painter, called founder of English landscape painting; classic style ('Niobe', 'Hadrian's Villa').

Wilson, Robert Woodrow (born 1936), U.S. physicist and radio astronomer, born in Houston, Tex.; at Bell Telephone Laboratories since 1963, head of radio physics research department 1976–; research with Arno Penzias on electromagnetic radiation. *see also in index* Nobel Prizewinners, *table*

Wilson, Teddy (or Theodore Wilson) (1912–86), U.S. jazz pianist and arranger, born in Austin, Tex.; with Benny Goodman Trio in 1930s; his fine technique and warm feeling belonged to no particular school.

Wilson, William Lyne (1843–1900), U.S. political leader and educator, born in Middleway, Va. (now W. Va.); in Confederate army 1861–65; congressman from W. Va. (1883–95); tariff legislator (Wilson Act, 1894); postmaster general 1895–97.

Wilson, Woodrow (1856–1924), 28th president of the United States W-213. *see also in index* Nobel Prizewinners, *table*
Baruch B-86
Columbia, S.C. C-588
Hall of Fame, *table* H-16
history writing H-173
League of Nations L-103
New Jersey N-200
Panama Canal P-94
prohibition veto P-506
Roosevelt, F.D. R-262
Roosevelt, Theodore R-289
United States history U-184
World War I W-310, 319

Wilson, N.C., city 40 mi (60 km) e. of Raleigh; tobacco market; cotton, tobacco, and lumber products, fertilizer, school-bus bodies, clothing; Atlantic Christian College; pop. 34,424.

Wilson cloud chamber
nuclear energy N-419
radioactivity R-65

Wilson College, Chambersburg, Pa., Presbyterian; for women; opened 1870; liberal arts.

Wilson Dam, dam in Alabama, on Tennessee River
Tennessee Valley Authority T-100

Wilson-Gorman Act (or Wilson Act), Democratic measure for tariff reduction, framed chiefly by Representative W.L. Wilson and Senator A.P. Gorman (enacted 1894).

Wilson's Creek, small river near Springfield, Mo., where, Aug. 10, 1861, Confederates under General McCulloch defeated Federals under General Lyon, who was killed in the battle N-60

City; trading post here in 1850; city named for Paiute chief; sheep, cattle, and ore shipping; flagstone and rock products; pop. 4,140, *map* U-40

Winnemucca Lake, lake in w. Nevada near Pyramid Lake, 25 mi (40 km) long; area 180 sq mi (470 sq km); at 3,875 ft (1,180 m) above sea level.

Winnetka, Ill., residential village on Lake Michigan, 17 mi (27 km) n. of Chicago; incorporated 1869; North Shore Country Day School; pop. 12,772
- Illinois, *map* I-53

Winnipeg, capital of Manitoba, at junction of Red and Assiniboine rivers; pop. 612,100 (metropolitan area including St. James-Assiniboia, St. Boniface, St. Vital, East Kildonan, West Kildonan, and Transcona) W-240
- Canada, *map* C-109
- Manitoba M-98, 101, 104, *picture* M-103
- North America, *map* N-351
- Red River Rebellion R-120

Winnipeg, Lake, lake in Manitoba; 9,465 sq mi (24,514 sq km), length 260 mi (420 km); fed by Winnipeg River and drained by Nelson River into Hudson Bay W-240
- Canada, *map* C-109
- Manitoba M-100
- North America, *map* N-351

Winnipeg, University of, university located in Winnipeg, Man. M-102

Winnipegosis, Lake, lake in Manitoba, w. of Lake Winnipeg; 2,103 sq mi (5,447 sq km) M-100, *map* C-109
- North America, *map* N-351

Winnipeg River, river in Manitoba, flows 200 mi (320 km) from Lake of the Woods to Lake Winnipeg M-101, *map* C-109

Winnipesaukee, Lake, lake in New Hampshire N-176, *map* N-190

Winnowing, separating grain from chaff F-34, *picture* F-26

Winona, Minn., city on Mississippi River about 95 mi (150 km) s.e. of St. Paul; flour, textiles, clothing, patent medicines, wood and paper boxes, malt, automotive equipment; Winona State University, St. Mary's College, College of St. Teresa; pop. 25,075 M-442, *map* U-41

Winona State University (until 1975 Winona State College), Winona, Minn.; opened 1860; arts and sciences, education; graduate studies M-444

Winooski, Vt., city on Winooski River 2 mi (3 km) n.e. of Burlington; textiles, wood and metal products; St. Michael's College; pop. 6,318, *maps* V-286, 301

Winooski River, river in n. Vermont; cuts through Green Mts.; enters Lake Champlain near Burlington; about 100 mi (160 km) long, *map* V-301

Winslow, Edward (1595–1655), one of founders of Plymouth Colony; governor at intervals 1633–45; writings valuable to historians.

Winslow, Edward (1669–1753), North American silversmith, born in Boston, Mass.; examples of his work are in the Metropolitan Museum of Art, New York, N.Y.

Winslow, John Ancrum (1811–73), U.S. admiral, born in Wilmington, N.C.; commander of the U.S. cruiser *Kearsarge* when it sank the Confederate privateer *Alabama* (1864).

Winslow, Ariz., city in n.e. part of state, about 60 mi (100 km) s.e. of Flagstaff; stock-raising, railroad center, lumbering; incorporated 1900; pop. 7,921.

Winsor, Justin (1831–97), U.S. historian and librarian, born in Boston, Mass.; librarian Boston Public Library 1868–77, Harvard University 1877–97; president American Library Association 1876–85, 1897 ('Narrative and Critical History of America').

Winstanley, Gerrard (1609?–after 1660), English anarchist A-388

Winston-Salem, N.C., city in n.w., on Piedmont plateau; tobacco products, beer, textiles, electronic equipment, furniture; Salem College; Wake Forest University; Winston-Salem State University; formed 1913 (Winston founded 1849; Salem, 1766); pop. 145,468 W-240
- North America, *map* N-351
- North Carolina N-357, 366, *picture* N-365

Winston-Salem State University (founded 1892 as Slater Industrial Academy), Winston-Salem, N.C.; present name after 1925; education, nursing N-358
- Winston W-240

Winter, William (1836–1917), U.S. drama critic, born in Gloucester, Mass.; wrote many publications on U.S. theatrical history ('Other Days', stage chronicles; 'Shakespeare on the Stage', criticism).

Winter, season S-101. *see also in index* Seasons; Winter sports; subjects beginning with Winter
- Arctic A-572
- astronomical cause A-710
- plants P-363a
- sleep. *see in index* Hibernation

'Winter', woodcut by Kunihiro Amano, *picture* J-52

Winter aconite, bulb
- growing conditions G-25

Winterberry. *see in index* Inkberry

Winterberry (or black alder), shrub *Ilex verticillata* of the holly family having oval, pointed, deciduous leaves that turn black in autumn; flowers, small, greenish white; berries, scarlet red.

Winter cherry. *see in index* Chinese lantern plant

Winter flounder, fish *Pseudopleuronectes americanus* of the order Pleuronectiformes, *picture* F-174

Winter grape, grape *Vitis vulpina* of the family Vitaceae G-220

Wintergreen, plant of the Ericales order W-240

Winter Haven, Fla., city 15 mi (25 km) e.s.e. of Lakeland, in Polk County; citrus-fruit raising and packing; tourism; pop. 21,119.

Winter heliotrope (or sweet coltsfoot), woolly perennial garden herb *Petasites fragrans* of the family Compositae with heart-shaped leaves springing from the rootstock and fragrant purplish or whitish flower heads.

Winter melon, type of American melon *Cucumis melo indorus* M-292

Winter Park, Fla., city adjoining Orlando on n.e.; citrus fruit; trade center; Rollins College; area first settled in 1836; pop. 22,314.

Winters, Arthur Yvor (1900–68), U.S. poet, literary critic, and educator, born in Chicago, Ill.; became member of English department Stanford University 1928, professor 1949–68 ('Collected Poems', won 1960 Bollingen Prize in Poetry; criticism: 'Edwin Arlington Robinson').

Winter savory, herb *Satureia montana* H-138

'Winterset', play by Anderson A-357

Winter solstice. *see in index* Solstice

Winter sports W-241
- bobsledding S-216
- hockey. *see in index* Hockey, ice
- Norway N-391, S-210d
- Olympic Games O-541, S-210d, S-216, *picture* S-210a
- skating S-207–8, *pictures* V-295
- skiing. *see in index* Skiing
- sledding S-216
- Switzerland S-542, *picture* S-538
- tobogganing S-216
- Vermont V-288, *pictures* V-295

'Winter's Tale, The', comedy by Shakespeare
- Shakespeare S-133, S-139

Winterthur, Switzerland, town 12 mi (19 km) n.e. of Zürich; printed cotton, machinery; vineyards; pop. of greater city, 99,900, *map* S-537

Winterthur Museum. *see in index* Henry Francis du Pont Winterthur Museum

Winter wheat W-187, 191
- United States regions, *map* U-72

Winter wren (or common wren), bird *Troglodytes troglodytes* of the Troglodytidae family W-364

Winther, Christian (1796–1876), Danish poet ('The Stag's Flight', epic poem; 'In the Year of Grace', novel).

Winthrop, John (1588–1649), first governor of Massachusetts Bay Colony W-244
- American literature A-341
- Boston B-376
- Hutchinson H-336
- Massachusetts M-194
- Statuary Hall, *table* S-437a

Winthrop, John, Jr. (1606–76), son of John Winthrop, born in Suffolk, England; to colonies 1631; governor of Connecticut most of period 1657–76
- Connecticut charter C-654
- New London N-212

Winthrop, Mass., urban town on peninsula just n.e. of Boston; residential suburb and beach resort; pop. 19,294.

Winthrop College, Rock Hill, S.C.; state control since 1891; founded 1886; arts and sciences, business administration, communications, education, home economics, library science, music, physical education, secretarial science; graduate studies.

Winton, Alexander (1860–1932), U.S. inventor and pioneer automobile manufacturer, born in Grangemouth, Scotland; designed, built, and raced automobiles.

Winze, mine shaft M-427

Wipe, motion picture optical effect M-613

Wire W-245
- copper C-710
- electrical use
  - insulation I-232
  - iron and steel I-347
- pins P-327
- stringed instruments S-490
- telecommunication T-55
- telephone T-62

Wirehaired pointer, dog, *picture* D-199

Wireless telegraphy. *see also in index* Radio
- Marconi M-132
- pedal powered A-788

Wire-line, mining method M-426

Wire nail, hardware N-4

Wirephoto. *see in index* Telephotography

Wire sponge S-395

Wiretapping, electronic eavesdropping W-247

Wire walker, circus performer C-432, *picture* C-423

Wireworm, larva of click beetle B-140
- worms W-361

Wirt, William (1772–1834), U.S. lawyer, statesman, and author; assistant in prosecution of Aaron Burr; U.S. attorney general 1817–29 ('Life of Patrick Henry').

Wirt, William Albert (1874–1938), U.S. educator, born in Markle, Ind.; superintendent of schools, Bluffton, Ind., 1899–1907, at Gary, Ind., 1907–38; originated Gary school system (platoon plan), which he had first applied in Bluffton in 1900.

Wirtz, William Willard (born 1912), U.S. lawyer and public official, born in De Kalb, Ill.; on law staff Northwestern University 1939–42, professor 1946–54; on War Labor Board 1943–45; practiced law 1955–61 and 1970–; U.S. undersecretary of labor 1961–62, secretary 1962–69.

Wisby, Sweden. *see in index* Visby

Wisconsin, n.-central state of U.S.; 56,154 sq mi (145,438 sq km); cap. Madison; pop. 4,705,335 W-248, *maps* U-41, 70
- agriculture
  - farming, *picture* F-25
  - mural, *picture* U-139
- cities. *see also in index* cities listed below and other cities by name
  - Madison M-28
  - Milwaukee M-421
  - Racine R-28
- geographic region
  - North America, *map* N-351
  - North Central Plains U-68, *pictures* U-69, *map* U-70
- name, *table* S-428
- state symbols
  - bird R-223. *see also in index* Robin
  - flag, *picture* F-160
  - flower, *picture* S-427
- Statuary Hall, *table* S-437b
- taxation, *tables* T-37, 39

Wisconsin (or Würm), glacial phase M-83
- Newfoundland N-166

Wisconsin, University of, Madison, Wis.; state control; established 1848; opened 1849; letters and science, agriculture, commerce, education, engineering, home economics, journalism, law, library science, medicine, music, nursing, pharmacy, social work; graduate school; in 1973 the University of Wisconsin and the Wisconsin State Universities merged, and state universities are part of the University of Wisconsin (for example: Wisconsin State University—Eau Claire is officially University of Wisconsin—Eau Claire) W-251, *picture* W-257
- anthogens discovered P-369

Wisconsin, University of—Green Bay, Green Bay, Wis.; state control; established 1965; arts and sciences, education; graduate studies.

Wisconsin, University of—Milwaukee, Milwaukee, Wis.; state control; established 1955; arts and sciences, business administration, education, music; graduate studies
- Milwaukee M-421

Wisconsin, University of—Parkside, Kenosha, Wis.; state control; established 1965; arts and sciences, education; graduate studies.

Wisconsin, University of—Stout (originally called Stout State University), Menomonie, Wis.; founded 1893; home economics, industrial education, industrial technology; graduate study.

Wisconsin Conservatory of Music, in Milwaukee, Wis. M-421

Wisconsin Dells, recreational park, *picture* W-107

Wisconsin ice sheet, glacial formation I-7

Wisconsin Idea
- LaFollette L-21

Wisconsin Rapids, Wis., city on Wisconsin River about 70 mi (110 km) n.w. of Oshkosh; paper products, stoves and heaters, plastics; dairying, cranberry center; pop. 17,995.

Wisconsin River, flows s. about 400 mi (645 km) through center of Wisconsin into Mississippi River, *picture* W-252, *map* U-71

Wisconsin State University—Eau Claire, Eau Claire, Wis.; established 1916; arts and sciences, business administration, medical technology, speech pathology; graduate studies.

Wisconsin State University—La Crosse, La Crosse, Wis.; opened 1909; arts and sciences, education, graduate studies.

Wisconsin State University—Oshkosh, Oshkosh, Wis.; opened 1871; arts and sciences, education; graduate studies.

Wisconsin State University—Platteville, Platteville, Wis.; founded 1866; arts and sciences, education, engineering; graduate studies.

Wisconsin State University—River Falls, River Falls, Wis.; founded 1874; arts and sciences, education; graduate studies.

Wisconsin State University—Stevens Point, Stevens Point, Wis.; founded 1894; present name 1951; letters and science, applied arts and science, education, fine arts; graduate studies.

Wisconsin State University—Superior, Superior, Wis.; opened 1896; liberal arts, education; graduate studies.

Wisconsin State University—Whitewater, Whitewater, Wis.; opened 1868; arts and sciences, business administration, education; graduate studies.

'Wisdom of Solomon', apocryphal book of Bible's Old Testament B-184

Wise, Henry Alexander (1806–76), U.S. statesman, born in Drummondtown, Va.; governor of Virginia 1856–60; signed John Brown's death warrant

Wise, Isaac Mayer (1819–1900), U.S. rabbi and educator, born in Bohemia; leader of Reformed Judaism in U.S.; president of Hebrew Union College, Cincinnati, Ohio.

Wise, Robert (born 1914), U.S. movie director and producer, born in Winchester, Ind.; many award-winning movies ('Executive Suite', 'Run Silent Run Deep', 'Two for the Seesaw', 'The Andromeda Strain'), *picture* M-608

Wise, Stephen Samuel (1874–1949), U.S. rabbi, born in Budapest, Hungary; rabbi of Free Synagogue, New York City, 1907–49; an eloquent preacher of liberal views; known also as a leader in public affairs and social welfare.

Wiseman, Adele (born 1928), Canadian author, born in Winnipeg, *list* C-125

Wiseman, Nicholas, Cardinal (1802–65), English Roman Catholic prelate, archbishop of Westminster (1850), the first to hold title of cardinal after the restoration of the Roman Catholic hierarchy.

Wise Men of Gotham. *see in index* Gotham

Wise Men of the East. *see in index* Magi

Wisent. *see in index* European bison

'Wise old owl, A', nursery rhyme N-444

Wishart, George (1513?–46), Scottish religious reformer and martyr; converted John Knox; burned for heresy K-265

Wisla River, Poland. *see in index* Vistula

Wissembourg, France, town 40 mi (64 km) n.e. of Strasbourg; pop. 6,679, *picture* F-348, *map* F-372

Wissler, Clark (1870–1947), U.S. anthropologist, born in Wayne County, Ind.; professor of anthropology Yale University 1924–40.

Wistar, Caspar (1696–1752), North American colonial glassmaker, born near Heidelberg, Germany; grandfather of Caspar Wistar; first to manufacture flint glass in America
  glass manufacture G-162

Wistar, Caspar (1761–1818), U.S. physician and anatomist, born in Philadelphia, Pa.; grandson of Caspar Wistar; professor of anatomy University of Pennsylvania; wrote first book on anatomy published in U.S.; wistaria named for him.

Wistaria, flowering vine, *picture* F-227

Wister, Owen (1860–1938), U.S. novelist, born in Philadelphia, Pa.; well known for 'The Virginian', about Wyoming cowpunchers of 1870s and 1880s ('Lady Baltimore', 'Philosophy 4') W-152

Wister, Mount, peak near head of Avalanche Canyon, Grand Teton National Park, Wyoming; 11,480 ft (3,500 m) high; named for Owen Wister.

Wisteria, genus of twining, usually woody vines of pea family, Fabaceae; mostly native to Asia and North America; widely cultivated elsewhere for large drooping flower clusters of blue, purple, rose, or white

Wiswell, Ernie, U.S. clown C-107

Witan (also called Witenagemot), national or king's council, chiefly advisory, in Anglo-Saxon kingdoms in early England E-238
  democracy D-92

Witch W-266

Witchcraft W-266. *see also in index* Magic; Superstition
  American literature A-341, 357
  Bodin B-330
  folklore F-262

Witch doctor, Africa. *see also in index* Medicine man
  folk medicine F-270

Witch hazel, any of six species of shrubs and trees of the genus *Hamamelis* W-266

Witch of Endor. *see in index* Endor, Witch of

'Witch's Magic Cloth', work by Miyoko Matsutani

Witenagemot. *see in index* Witan

Withdrawal, process of breaking an addiction H-4

Wither, George (1588–1667), English lyric poet of Puritan age ('Shepherd's Hunting', 'Songs of the Old Testament', 'Psalms of David').

Withering, William (1741–99), British physician and botanist, born in Wellington, Shropshire; first to prescribe digitalis to treat edema (dropsy) caused by heart disease M-283
  drugs D-273

Withering, stage in the process of making black tea T-45, *picture* T-46

Witherspoon, John (1723–94), Scottish Presbyterian clergyman; came to American Colonies 1768 to become president of Princeton College, position he held until his death; member New Jersey constitutional convention 1776, signer Declaration of Independence and Articles of Confederation.

Witherspoon, Tim, U.S. boxer, heavyweight champion B-392

Witloof. *see in index* Endive

Witte, Sergei Yulievich, Count (1849–1915), Russian liberal statesman, chief Russian negotiator of peace with Japan 1905, and first constitutional prime minister 1905–6; struggled to free Russia from economic foreign bondage.

Wittekind (or Widukind) (died 807?), famous leader of the Saxons against Charlemagne; fought Franks for 8 years, but finally accepted Christianity in 785.

Wittelsbach, House of, family that ruled Bavaria from 1180–1918, first as counts and dukes, later as electors, finally, from 1806, as kings
  Munich M-653

Wittenberg, East Germany, city on Elbe River 58 mi (93 km) s.w. of Berlin; chemicals, machinery; home of Martin Luther; university incorporated with Halle 1817; tombs of Luther and Melanchthon; pop. 46,134, *map* G-134
  Luther L-338
  Saxony S-52e

Wittenberg University, Springfield, Ohio; Lutheran Church in America; founded 1845; arts and sciences, art, business administration, music, theology; graduate study.

Wittgenstein, Ludwig (1889–1951), British philosopher W-266
  philosophy P-266

Witticism. *see in index* Joke

Wittig, Georg (1897–1987), German chemist, born in Berlin; on faculty of University of Marburg 1926–32, Technical College of Braunschweig 1932–37, University of Freiburg 1937–44, University of Tübingen 1944–56, University of Heidelberg 1956–65; research in organic chemistry. *see also in index* Nobel Prizewinners, *table*

Witwatersrand (or Rand), gold-mining district in South Africa
  gold discovery S-267
  gold mining G-178
  Johannesburg J-122
  Kruger and Boer War K-306

Wizard of Oz. *see in index* Oz, Land of

Wladyslaw II Jagiello (1351–1434), king of Poland J-12

Wladyslaw III Warnenczyk (1424–44), king of Poland J-12

WMO, United Nations. *see in index* World Meteorological Organization

Woad, European herb of the mustard family; formerly grown for the blue dyestuff found in its leaves.

Woburn, Mass., city 10 mi (16 km) n.w. of Boston; electronic products, gelatins, leather processing, machinery; pop. 36,626.

Wodehouse, Pelham Grenville (1881–1975), U.S. writer of humorous stories and of song lyrics, born in Guildford, England; prisoner of war during German occupation of France 1940–44; became U.S. citizen 1955 ('Fish Preferred', 'The Inimitable Jeeves', 'Piccadilly Jim', 'Leave It to Psmith').

Woden. *see in index* Odin

Woestijne, Karel van de (1878–1928), Belgian poet; wrote verses of classic purity and simplicity ('The Father's House', 'Interludes').

Woffington, Peg (1714?–60), celebrated Irish comic and tragic actress, heroine of Charles Reade's romance 'Peg Woffington'.

Wofford College, Spartanburg, S.C.; United Methodist; chartered 1852; opened 1854; arts and sciences.

Wöhler, Friedrich (1800–82), German chemist; synthesized urea; isolated uric acid; developed process for isolating aluminum I-208, S-58
  aluminum research A-322
  organic chemistry O-601

Wohlgemuth, Michael (1434–1519), German painter, born in Nuremberg; directed workshop in which sacred paintings, altarpieces, retables were executed; teacher of Albrecht Dürer.

Wojciechowicz, Alexander (born 1915), U.S. football player, born in South River, N.J.; center-linebacker Detroit Lions 1938–46, Philadelphia Eagles 1946–50.

Wojciechowska, Maia (born 1927), U.S. author, born in Warsaw, Poland; became U.S. citizen 1951; awarded 1965 Newbery Medal for 'Shadow of a Bull' R-111c

Wolcott, Oliver (1726–97), signer of Declaration of Independence, born in Windsor, Conn.; governor Connecticut 1796–97
  Declaration of Independence D-56

Wolds, the, chalk hills in York and Lincoln counties, England, n. and s. of Humber River; rise to 800 ft (240 m).

Wolf, Christa (born 1929), German novelist
  German literature G-109

Wolf, Hugo (1860–1903), Austrian composer, great master of Kunstlied, or art song; composed more than 200 songs, chiefly in cycles based on lyrics by one poet; unusual skill in welding music and words; also wrote opera 'Der Corregidor' and symphonic poem 'Penthesilea'; died insane
  classical music M-675

Wolf W-267
  Arctic A-572
  average life expectancy, *chart* A-423
  dog's ancestor D-193
  domestication A-454
  fur, *table* F-465
  mythology M-696
  'Peter and the Wolf' P-507

'Wolf and Fox Hunt, The', painting by Rubens P-41, *picture* P-42

'Wolf and the Ass, The', fable F-4

Wolf comet, discovered 1884 by German astronomer Maximilian F.J.C. Wolf (1863–1932); orbit 8.4 years; in comet family of Jupiter.

Wolfe, Charles (1791–1823), Irish poet and clergyman, born in County Kildare; famed chiefly for poem 'Burial of Sir John Moore'.

Wolfe, James (1727–59), British soldier, hero of Quebec W-268
  Canada C-94
  Montcalm M-566
  monument at Quebec Q-14

Wolfe, Thomas (1900–38), U.S. novelist W-268
  American literature A-359
  creative writing W-380

Wolfe, Tom (born 1931), U.S. author and journalist W-268
  American literature A-361

Wolff, Kaspar Friedrich (1733–94), German embryologist, lived in St. Petersburg, Russia, after 1766; first to advance modern "cell theory" of embryology.

Wolf-Ferrari, Ermanno (1876–1948), Italian composer, born in Venice; operas combine German and Italian characteristics ('The Jewels of the Madonna', 'The Secret of Suzanne').

Wolffish, large carnivorous fish of coasts of Europe and North America; great interlocking front teeth give wolffish appearance.

Wolf 424, star S-413

Wolfhound, Irish, dog, *picture* P-243

Wolfram. *see in index* Tungsten

Wolframite, chief ore of the element tungsten T-307, *table* O-600
  minerals M-436

Wolfram von Eschenbach (1170–1220?), German minnesinger, greatest of Middle High German epic poets G-105
  Holy Grail H-207

Wolfsbane. *see in index* Monkshood

Wolf spider S-385, *picture* S-387

Wollaston, William Hyde (1766–1828), British chemist and physicist; the first to observe dark lines in the spectrum of the sun (later known as Fraunhofer lines); discovered palladium and rhodium
  light experiments L-201

Wollaston Lake, n.e. Saskatchewan; area 768 sq mi (1,989 sq km), *maps* C-112, S-49c, S-491
  North America, *map* N-351

Wollomombi Falls, formed by Wollomombi and Chandler rivers in n.e. New South Wales, Australia, *chart* W-98

Wollongong, Australia, municipality in coal-rich district on coast of New South Wales 42 mi (68 km) s.w. of Sydney; area 276 sq mi (715 sq km); includes number of towns, notably Wollongong and Port Kembla, the latter a seaport, iron and steel center; pop. 222,539, *maps* A-819, P-6

Wollstonecraft, Mary. *see in index* Godwin, Mary Wollstonecraft

Wolmyong (fl. 742–765), Korean writer K-292

Wolseley, Garnet Joseph, first viscount (1833–1913), British field marshal and commander in chief of British army 1895–99
  Red River expedition R-120, C-101

Wolsey, Cardinal (in full Thomas Cardinal Wolsey) (1475?–1530), English prelate and statesman W-269
  Cromwell C-782
  Henry VIII H-131

Wolverhampton, England, county borough of Staffordshire, 13 mi (21 km) n.w. of Birmingham; tinplate, japanned goods, enameled ware, iron products, machinery, tools, chemicals; pop. 264,520.

Wolverine, bearlike mammal *Gulo gulo* of the weasel family W-114
  fur, *table* F-465

Wolverine State. *see in index* Michigan

Woman. *see also in index* Women's rights; *also* notable women by name, as Cleopatra; Victoria
  Arab society A-523
  Bulgaria, *pictures* B-371, S-215
  careers and occupations V-364, *pictures* V-360, 365–71, *table* V-363
    Anglican ministry A-418
    astronaut S-346b
    Canadian Armed Forces, *picture* U-13
    medicine M-275, 280, R-330. *see also in index* Nursing; Physician
    military
      Coast Guard C-528
      navy N-89
    nun M-541. *see also in index* chief orders by name
    occupational therapist V-366, *picture* V-367
    police P-427, *picture* P-425
      Mounties R-300a, *picture* R-300b
    postal service P-458
    proportion of labor force, *chart* U-103
    uniforms, *picture* U-7
  China C-343, 375
  cosmetics C-728
  day care D-44
  education E-84, 92, 102
    China C-363, 366
    college U-207
  elections E-145, 148
  family F-20
  first lady W-199
  Fuller F-445

connected by canal with the Severn.

Wye Oak, white oak tree in Maryland, thought to be the oldest of its kind in U.S., *picture* M-176

Wyeth, Andrew (full name Andrew Newell Wyeth) (born 1917), U.S. painter and illustrator W-384
  painting P-62, *picture* P-64

Wyeth, Nathaniel Jarvis (1802–56), U.S. trader and Oregon pioneer, born in Cambridge, Mass.; projected great fur and salmon enterprise, and organized two expeditions (1832, 1834); efforts doomed by series of misfortunes and opposition of Hudson's Bay Co., but ventures furthered U.S. claims and aroused Eastern interest
  Fort Hall O-598

Wyeth, Newell Convers (or N.C. Wyeth) (1882–1945), U.S. artist, born in Needham, Mass.; father of Andrew Wyeth; well known for colorful and vivid illustrations for children's classics and for vigorous murals, among which are panels in Missouri State Capitol and in Hubbard Memorial Building, Washington, D.C. R-111e
  'The Black Arrow', *picture* E-278
  'The Last of the Mohicans', *picture* N-410

Wykeham, William of. *see in index* William of Wykeham

Wylie, Elinor (1885–1928), U.S. poet and novelist, born in Rosemont, Pa.; married William Rose Benét; praised for precise style, beautiful imagery ('Nets to Catch the Wind', 'Black Armour', 'Trivial Breath', 'Angels and Earthly Creatures', verse; 'Jennifer Lorn', 'The Venetian Glass Nephew', 'The Orphan Angel', novels of fantasy) A-356
  quoted P-404

Wylie, Ida Alexa Ross (1885–1959), British novelist, born in Melbourne, Australia; educated Belgium, England, and Germany ('Ho, the Fair Wind', 'Candles for Therese', 'The Undefeated').

Wylie, Philip Gordon (1902–71), U.S. author, newspaper columnist, born in Beverly, Mass.; wrote for motion pictures 1931–37 (on fishing: 'Crunch and Des', short stories, 'Denizens of the Deep', essays; satire on American behavior: 'Generation of Vipers'; novels: 'Night unto Night', 'Tomorrow!') R-112e

Wyman, Jeffries (1814–74), U.S. anatomist, born in Chelmsford, Mass.; professor of anatomy Harvard University 1847–74; helped establish anatomical museum there; curator, Peabody Museum, Harvard University, 1866–74.

Wynantskill, stream in s.e. New York, about 20 mi (30 km) long, flowing into Hudson River at Troy; furnishes waterpower.

Wynn, Early (born 1920), U.S. baseball pitcher, born in Hartford, Ala.; began career with Washington Senators 1939, finished with Chicago White Sox 1962; Cy Young Award 1959.

Wynn, Ed (1886–1966), U.S. actor
  'Requiem for a Heavyweight', *picture* T-71

Wynn, Keenan (1916–86), U.S. actor; son of Ed Wynn
  'Requiem for a Heavyweight', *picture* T-71

Wyoming, Rocky Mountain state of U.S.; 97,914 sq mi (253,596 sq km); cap. Cheyenne; pop. 470,816 W-385
  admission to Union S-429d
  agriculture, *picture* S-146
  mountains, *pictures* S-146
    Rockies R-234, *map* R-234a
  name, *table* S-428
  natural gas well, *picture* G-39
  North America, *map* N-351
  prehistoric life, *picture* P-489
  state symbols
    flag, *picture* F-160
    flower, *pictures* S-427, P-359
    tree P-446
  Statuary Hall, *table* S-437b
  taxation, *tables* T-37, 39
  United States U-75, U-78, *maps* U-36, U-40, 80, *pictures* U-76, U-79
  wild flowers, *picture* P-359

Wyoming, Mich., city just s.w. of Grand Rapids; truck farms; automobile and truck parts, metal products; pop. 59,616.

Wyoming, University of, Laramie, Wyo.; state control; founded 1887; liberal arts, agriculture, commerce and industry, education, engineering, law, music, nursing, pharmacy; graduate school W-389, *picture* W-393

Wyoming Massacre (or battle of Wyoming) (1778) P-166

Wyoming Valley, fertile valley of Luzerne County, Pennsylvania, along n. branch of Susquehanna River; defeat of Americans by Tories and American Indians July 3, 1778 P-175
  Connecticut ownership claims P-173
  massacre (1778) P-166

Wyspianski, Stanislaw (1869–1907), Polish painter and dramatist, born in Cracow; losing use of hand, turned to writing; voiced national aspirations ('The Wedding').

Wyss, Johann David (1743–1818), Swiss writer, born in Bern; father of Johann Rudolf Wyss; author of 'The Swiss Family Robinson'.

Wyss, Johann Rudolf (1781–1830), Swiss writer, educator, and editor; born in Bern; edited 'The Swiss Family Robinson' written by his father; author of Swiss national anthem, 'Rufst du, Mein Vaterland'.

Wythe, George (1726–1806), U.S. jurist, born near Hampton, Va.; as member of Virginia House of Burgesses drew up remonstrance to proposed Stamp Act (1764); signer Declaration of Independence, member Constitutional Convention
  Declaration of Independence D-56
  Jefferson J-90

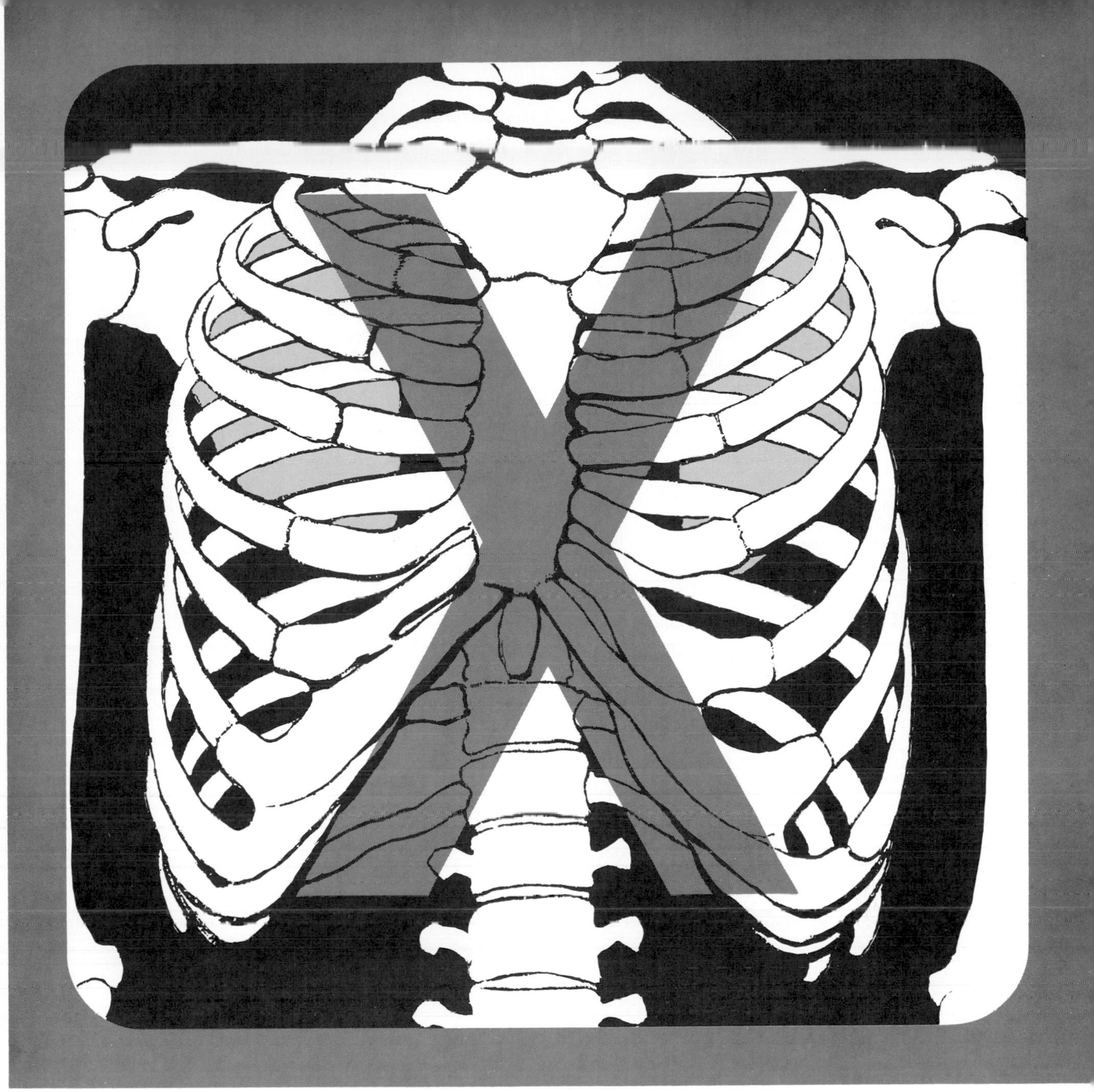

The letter X

probably started as a picture sign of a fish, such as is found in the Egyptian hieroglyphic writing (1) and in a very early Semitic writing which was used about 1500 B.C. on the Sinai Peninsula (2). About 1000 B.C., in Byblos and other Phoenician and Canaanite centers, the sign was given a linear form (3), the source of all later forms. The sign was called *samekh,* meaning "fish" in the Semitic languages.

The Greeks changed the Semitic name *samekh* to *sigma,* but they gave the name to their "s," as discussed at the beginning of the Fact-Index for Volume 21. At the same time the Greeks gave a new value to the *samekh* (which is pronounced as "s" in the Semitic languages)—namely "x." They renamed the sign *xi* (pronounced *ksee*). The early (4) and later (5) forms of the Greek sign passed on into Latin (6) in a form almost identical to the modern capital letter X.

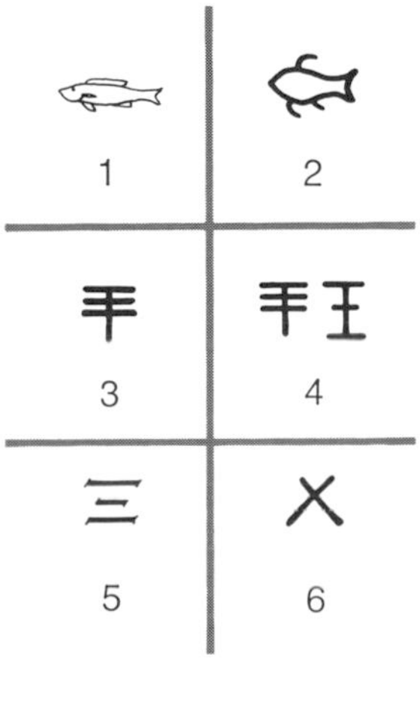

X

X-15, rocket plane S-346e

Xanadu, imaginary city in Samuel Taylor Coleridge's poem 'Kubla Khan'; named for a city mentioned in a book by Samuel Purchas. *see also in index* Purchas, Samuel

Xanthine, group of drugs that stimulate the central nervous system
  caffeine C-535

Xanthium, genus of coarse, annual herbs of the family Compositae; stems branching; leaves, toothed or lobed; fruit enclosed in spiny or hooked burs which cling to clothes and animals; cocklebur a typical species. *see also in index* Cocklebur
  seedling P-408

Xanthophyll, plant pigment L-102

Xantippe (or Xanthippe), Socrates' wife S-246

Xavier, Francis (or Saint Francis Xavier, known as the Apostle of the Indies) (1506–52), Spanish Jesuit missionary X-402

Xavier University, Cincinnati, Ohio; Roman Catholic; founded 1831; arts and sciences, business administration; graduate school, evening and summer study C-415

Xavier University of Louisiana, New Orleans, La.; Roman Catholic; founded 1915; arts and sciences, education, pharmacy; graduate school N-231

X chromosome, a sex chromosome G-56

Xenia, Ohio, city about 15 mi (25 km) s.e. of Dayton in rich farming and stock-raising region; rope, twine, furniture, shoes; state home for soldiers' and sailors' orphans; Central State College; pop. 24,653.

Xenobiology. *see in index* Exobiology

Xenocrates (396–314 BC), Greek philosopher, pupil and follower of Plato; emphasized ethics in his teaching and writings.

Xenograft (or heterograft), tissue transplantation from one species to another T-250

Xenon (Xe), chemical element
  air composition, *diagram* A-145
  noble gases N-330
  periodic table, *table* P-207, *list* P-208

Xenon flash lamp, light source
  eye repair B-312
  lighthouse use L-204

Xenophanes, Greek philosopher and poet of the 6th century BC; supposed founder of Eleatic school of philosophy, which taught that the law of the universe is fixed and unchanging.

Xenophobia, fear of foreigners W-301

Xenophon (430?–355? BC), Greek historian and general X-402
  exploration E-373
  Greek literature G-276
    steeplechase horse racing H-277

Xeranthemum, genus of annual plants, of the composite family, native to the Mediterranean region. One of the plants early used as immortelles of everlastings. Flowers solitary, long-stemmed, asterlike, white, lilac, rose, or purple; papery flower heads dry readily; similar to the strawflowers, or helichrysum.

Xeres, Spain. *see in index* Jerez

Xerography (or photocopying), duplicating process D-290. *see also in index* Photography
  ink I-206
  office equipment O-495
  printing P-503

Xerophthalmia, disease V-354

Xerophytes, plants, such as cactus, that are adapted structurally for growth with a limited supply of water.

Xerxes I (519?–465 BC), king of Persia; led expedition against Greece but returned to Persia after his navy's first defeat P-212
  Dardanelles D-35
  Persian Wars P-215
  relief portrait, *picture* P-213
  stairway, *picture* P-213
  Themistocles T-163
  Thermopylae T-168

Xerxes II (died 424 BC), king of Persia, son and successor of Artaxerxes I; assassinated by brother after a reign of 45 days.

Xhosa, a people of Africa
  frontier movement F-425
  Kaffir Wars K-166

Xiamen (or Amoy), China, port on Amoy Island, Fukien Province; sugar, tobacco, fruit, wine; food processing; became treaty port 1842; pop. 400,000 F-445, *map* A-697

Xi'an (or Sian), China, walled city, capital of Shaanxi province; commercial and educational center; famous Nestorian tablet; pop. 1,600,000 S-127, *map* A-700
  archaeological findings A-538

Ximenes de Cisneros, Francisco (or Francisco Jiménez de Cisneros) (1436–1517), Spanish prelate X-402
  Counter-Reformation influence C-744

Xingu River, large s. tributary of the Amazon, rising on Mato Grosso plateau of Brazil; about 1,200 mi (1,900 km) long, *maps* B-425, S-298

Xining (or Hsi-ning), provincial capital of Qinghai Province in western interior of China at strategic point on western frontier; pop. 873,000 Q-3, *map* A-700

Xinjiang Uygur (or Sinkiang Uighur, or Xinjiang, or Chinese Turkestan), in n.w. China; 635,900 sq mi (1,646,800 sq km); cap. Urumqi; pop. 13,440,000 X-402
  Turkestan T-317
  Uygur population C-345

Xochimilco, Lake, located near Mexico City in the residential suburb of Xochimilco; noted for floating vegetable and flower gardens M-346, *picture* M-347

'Xochitl', ballet
  Graham's performance G-205

X-ray diffraction photography
  Hodgkin's contributions H-198

X-ray fluorescence analysis, in chemical analysis C-292

X rays (or Roentgen rays) X-403
  alkaline earth metals A-308
  black hole B-306
  Compton effect C-624, R-40
  crystals studies C-798, S-374, S-254h
  diffraction B-237, B-166e
  fluoroscope F-241
  folk art F-250
  fracture study F-340
  Franklin F-385
  gamma rays comparison R-40
  hospital department H-282
  industrial uses, *pictures* S-331, 333
  light spectrum L-194, *diagram* L-202
  medicine and dentistry M-285, *picture* M-279
    cancer cause C-132
    diagnosis D-127
      heart H-99
    therapy T-165
  photography P-280
  Pupin P-535
  radioactivity's discovery B-123
  solar flares S-515
  spectrum S-374
  telescope T-67
  wavelengths and frequencies, *table* R-34

Xylem, plant tissue P-360
  tree T-277

Xylocaine, anesthetic A-413

Xylography, method of block printing B-351
  folk art F-250

Xylose (or wood sugar), sugarlike substance ($C_5H_{10}O_5$) S-508

XYZ affair X-406

The letter Y

is a descendant of the letter V, which is discussed in the Fact-Index for Volume 24. After the Romans had become the rulers of the Mediterranean world, they became acquainted with the Greek use of the letter called *upsilon*. Originally pronounced u (as in the English word "rude"), this letter gradually acquired the pronunciation ü (as in the German language) in some Greek dialects. From the sign used by the Phoenicians (1) the Greek form of the *upsilon* sign (2) was derived.

The Romans began to use the Greek sign as it occurred in Greek words taken over into the Latin language. The Romans could not place the new letter after T in their own alphabet, as the Greeks had done with *upsilon,* because in Latin the letter V had this place. The Romans thus placed it after X, which had ended their alphabet up to then. From Latin the capital letter Y came unchanged into English. The small handwritten "y" (3) is a quickly made variant of the capital.

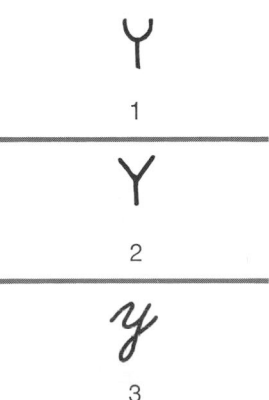

1

2

3

Y

Yablonovyy Range (or Yablonoi Range), range in s.e. Siberia; extends past Chita n.e. toward Stanovoy Range; watershed between rivers to Arctic and Pacific oceans, *maps* A-700, R-345

Yacht, sailing or motor craft with sharp, graceful lines, for racing or cruising
- Isle of Wight W-202
- model S-177, *picture* S-176b
- racing B-329
- yacht ensign F-158

Yadin, Yigael (born 1917), Israeli archaeologist and military leader noted for work on Dead Sea Scrolls D-46

Yadkin River (or Pee Dee River), river in North Carolina, rises in Blue Ridge Mts. and flows 300 mi (480 km) to South Carolina border.

Yafo, Israel. *see in index* Tel Aviv-Yafo

Yahoos, characters in Jonathan Swift's 'Gulliver's Travels'
- Swift S-532

Yahweh. *see in index* Jehovah

'Yajurveda', canon of Hinduism I-105

Yak, bovine animal *Bos grunniens* of the family Bovidae Y-408, *picture* C-341
- animal domestication A-455

Yakima, American Indians living in state of Washington, *table* I-139
- Oregon O-583
- Washington W-50

Yakima, Wash., city in s.-central part of state, on Yakima River; processing of fruits and vegetables, meat, poultry, dairy products; lumber products, farm machinery; pop. 49,826, *maps* N-351, U-40
- Washington W-50, 60

Yakutat, Alaska, city on Yakutat Bay, 200 mi (320 km) n.w. of Juneau; fishing; airfield nearby; pop. 449, *map* U-39

Yakutsk, U.S.S.R., city in e. Siberia on Lena River; shipyards; leather, bricks, lumber products; pop. 139,000 S-189, *maps* R-322, 345
- Asia, *map* A-700

Yale, Elihu (1648–1721), English philanthropist, born in Boston, Mass.; contributed large sum of money to Collegiate School of Connecticut, which was renamed Yale College, now Yale University, in his honor.

Yale, Linus (1821–68), U.S. inventor, born in Salisbury Center, N.Y.; improved structure of locks L-277

Yale University, chartered 1701 as **Collegiate School of Connecticut,** New Haven, Conn.; formerly for men, coeducational since 1969; 2nd oldest university in U.S.; name changed 1718 in honor of Elihu Yale; arts and sciences, divinity, engineering, fine arts, forestry, law, medicine, music, nursing; graduate school
- art gallery M-663
  - Trumbull's 'Battle of Bunker's Hill' P-49, *picture* P-48
- Connecticut C-653
- football F-297
- rowing R-300

Yalow, Rosalyn Sussman (born 1921), U.S. medical physicist, born in New York City; on staff of Bronx Veterans Administration Hospital 1950–; professor Mount Sinai School of Medicine, New York City, 1968–79; research on insulin resistance and antibody production in diabetics, nuclear medicine. *see also in index* Nobel Prizewinners, *table*

Yalta, U.S.S.R., seaport and resort city in the Crimea about 30 mi (50 km) s.e. of Sevastopol; a center of winemaking, orchards, and tobacco; pop. 43,994, *map* E-360
- Allied conference (1945) D-151, W-356
- U.S.S.R. R-356, *map* R-349

Yalu River, river flowing into Yellow Sea, forms part of boundary between China and North Korea; 491 mi (790 km) long Y-408
- Asia, *picture* A-700
- Korea K-282, 297, *map* K-290, *chart* K-299

Yam, vegetable S-530

Yam, Chinese. *see in index* Cinnamon vine

Yamaga, Soko (1622–85), Japanese military strategist and Confucian philosopher Y-408

Yamagata, Aritomo (1838–1922), first prime minister of Japan Y-408

Yamamoto, Isoroku (1884–1943), Japanese commander in chief Y-409
- World War II W-337

Yamani, Ahmed Zaki (born 1930), Saudi minister Y-409

Yamasaki, Minoru (1912–86), U.S. architect, born in Seattle, Wash.; commissioned to do World Trade Center, New York City.

Yamasee (or Yamacraw), former Muskhogean Indian tribe, originally of Georgia and Florida, later of South Carolina; driven into Florida, they were exterminated
- South Carolina S-309

Yamashita, Tomoyuki (1885–1946), Japanese army officer, strategist, and military aviation expert; commander in chief of Japanese forces in Malaya, World War II; conquered Singapore, later Philippines; after war, hanged as war criminal.

Yamato, Japanese farmhouse style J-31, *diagram* J-30

Yam bean, tuber L-121

Yamuna River (or Jumna River), tributary of the Ganges River, n. India; rises in Himalayas, flows 860 mi (1,385 km) s. and s.e. to Ganges River India I-63, *map* I-86

Yanam (or Yanaon), India, former French settlement, seaport in s.e. on Coromandel coast at n. mouth of Godavari River; 7 sq mi (18 sq km); became part of India in 1954; pop. 8,291.

Yancey, William Lowndes (1814–63), U.S. political leader, born in Warren County, Ga.; served as Democratic representative from Alabama 1844–46; strong states'-rights man and leader of radical secession from Democratic party which insured Lincoln's election.

Yang, Chen Ning (or Chen Ning-yang, or Frank Yang) (born 1922), Chinese physicist Y-409. *see in also index* Nobel Prizewinners, *table*
- Wu W-383

Yang and yin, in Chinese legend. *see in index* Yin and yang

Yangban, former Korean aristocracy K-284

Yang Hsien-chih (6th century AD), Chinese prose master C-388

Yang-min Shan, recreation area near Taipei, Taiwan T-11

Yang Ti (569–618), emperor during China's Sui Dynasty C-364

Yangtze Basin, basin, China Y-410

Yangtze River (or Yangtze Kiang, or Chang Jiang), most important river in China Y-409, *map* A-700
- basin C-352
- China C-338
  - Hubei province H-313
- flood, *table* F-181

Yankee, national nickname Y-410

Yankee clippers, U.S. clipper ships S-175, 165, 167

'Yankee Doodle', U.S. popular song N-65
- Connecticut state song C-656
- popular music M-683
- Yankee Y-410

'Yankee Doodle Dandy', song by and motion picture about George M. Cohan C-537

Yankton, American Indians, *table* I-138

Yankton, S.D., city in s.e., on Missouri River near Gavins Point Dam and Reservoir; nurseries; railroad center, cement products, electronics, industrial equipment; state hospital; Mount Marty College, Yankton College; pop. 12,011, *maps* S-335, U-40–1

Yanktonai, division of the Dakota Indians who themselves belong to the Sioux; live in South Dakota, North Dakota, and Montana, *table* I-138

Yankton College, Yankton, S.D.; United Church of Christ; founded 1881; arts and sciences, music.

Yao, Asian people
- Thailand T-147

Yaoundé, Cameroon, capital; railway terminus, educational and commercial center; pop. 435,892 Y-410
- Africa, *map* A-118

Yap, island group, w. Caroline Islands, in Pacific Ocean e. of Philippines; land area, about 39 sq mi (101 sq km); sold by Spain to Germany 1899; mandated to Japan 1919; occupied by U.S. 1945; cable station; naval base; pop. 5,140
- money M-532
- Pacific Ocean, *map* P-6, *picture* P-18

Yapurá River, tributary of the Amazon. *see in index* Japurá River

Yaqui, Piman Indians living in Sonora, Mexico; engaged in agriculture, weaving; much reduced in numbers by wars arising from rebellions against Mexico.

Yaqui River, river in state of Sonora in n.w. Mexico; flows 420 mi (675 km) to Gulf of California; part of course through deep canyons
- Mexico, *map* M-344
- North America, *map* N-351

Yard, unit of measurement W-138, *table* W-140, *diagram* W-139

Yareta (or llareta), woody moss *Laretia compocta* that forms large cushionlike clumps; found in treeless areas of w. South America.

Yarkand (Chinese Soche), China, town in oasis on Yarkand River in s.w. Sinkiang-Uigur Autonomous Region; serves as major trade center; silk, cotton, wool; pop. 80,000, *map* A-700

Yarmouth, England. *see in index* Great Yarmouth

Yarmouth, Mass., 4 mi (6 km) e. of Barnstable on Cape Cod; summer resort, cranberries; pop. of township 18,449.

Yarmouth, N.S., seaport town at s.w. extremity; exports lumber and fish; shipyards, textiles; pop. 8,516, *map* C-112

Yarmouth, interglacial period I-7

Yarmulke, skullcap, *picture* J-146

Yarn, strand of material used for fabrics
- braiding process B-395
- hosiery H-278
- synthetic fibers F-74
  - nylon N-450
  - rayon R-99
- wool W-289

Yaroslav I, the Wise (died 1054), grand duke of Kiev, Russia R-351

Yaroslav II Vsevolodovich, Russian Grand Prince of Vladimir A-278

Yaroslavl', U.S.S.R., port on Volga River, 160 mi (260 km) n.e. of Moscow; textiles, machinery; founded in 11th century; pop. 517,000, *maps* E-360, R-344, 348

Yarra River (or Yarra Yarra), river in Victoria, Australia, navigable, 150 mi (240 km) long; flows through Melbourne into Port Phillip Bay M-289, *map* A-822

Yarrow, Peter (born 1938), U.S. musician F-273

Yarrow, perennial herbs comprising the genus *Achillea* of the composite family with flower heads in flat-topped open clusters; among species cultivated as garden flowers are common yarrow or milfoil *Achillea millefolium* and sneezewort *Achillea ptarmica*.

Yasna, the chief ceremony of Zoroastrianism Z-471

Yassa, body of laws assembled by Genghis Khan G-58

Yasukuni Shinto Shrine, temple, Tokyo, Japan, *picture* T-209

Yataghan, Muslim sword with a pointed double-curved blade S-546

Yates, Alan Geoffrey (pen name Carter Brown) (1923–85), writer D-119

Yates, Elizabeth (or Mrs. William McGreal) (born 1905), author and editor, born in Buffalo, N.Y.; lived in England, 1929–39; books for children: 'Under the Little Fir', 'Mountain Born', 'Once in the Year, a Christmas Story', 'Amos Fortune, Free Man' (1951 Newbery Medal), 'Prudence Crandall'; novels for young readers: 'Patterns on the Wall', 'Nearby'; biography: 'Pebble in a Pool' (Dorothy Canfield Fisher), 'Howard Thurman'; autobiography: 'The Lighted Heart'. *see also in index* Tregarthen, Enys.

Yates, Richard (1818–73), U.S. statesman, born in Warsaw, Ky.; as governor of Illinois during Civil War, checked pro-Southern sentiment; in U.S. Senate 1865–71.

Yaukey, Grace Sydenstricker (pen name Cornelia Spencer) (born 1899), U.S. author, born near Chinkiang, China; sister of Pearl Buck; books for boys and girls: 'Made in China', 'Made in India', 'Understanding the Japanese', 'Nehru of India', 'More Hands for Man', 'Made in Japan', 'Ancient China'.

Yaupon (or yupon, or cassena), small tree or shrub *Ilex vomitoria* of the holly family with smooth leaves and clusters of small white flowers; fruit scarlet
- tea T-47

Yaw, movement of aircraft or space vehicle to the right or to the left around the vertical axis;

helped decipher text of Rosetta stone
  light experimentation L-200

Young, Whitney Moore, Jr (1921–71), U.S. civil rights leader, born in Lincoln Ridge, Ky.; dean of Atlanta University School of Social Work 1954–61; executive director National Urban League 1961–71; awarded Medal of Freedom 1969; author of 'To Be Equal' B-298

'Young America', painting by Wyeth P-62, 64

Young America Movement, political youth association Y-430

Young Annam League M-78

Youngberry, fruit-bearing vinelike shrub produced by crossing the loganberry and the dewberry; grown on Pacific coast; fruit thimble-shaped, deep purple.

Young Canada's Book Week, celebrated, usually in November, under the sponsorship of the Canadian Library Association; purpose is to encourage the reading of the best books by children at home, at school, and at the library, and to interest adults in the importance of good books for young people.

Young Citizens League, organization of children; founded in South Dakota in 1912 "to enable each boy and girl to love and serve his country better, and to become strong of body, alert of mind, and pure of soul."

Young Communist League (or Komsomol), organization of Communist youth in Soviet Union R-332a, 326, 334c, *picture* R-332a
  city S-188
  youth organization Y-431

Young Democrats, political youth organization Y-431

Younger, James (1850–1902), U.S. outlaw with his brothers, John (1846–74), Robert (1853–89), and Thomas Coleman (Cole)(1844–1916) Y-425
  outlaws O-619

Younger Edda (or Prose Edda), Scandinavian literature S-52g
  mythology M-704
  storytelling S-471

Young German Cinema, postwar West German motion picture group G-115

'Young Girl at an Open Half-Door', painting by Rembrandt P-43

Young-Helmholtz theory C-562

Younghusband, Sir Francis Edward (1863–1942), English soldier, author, and explorer; in youth made exploring trip across China; appointed political agent in India 1890; commissioner to Tibet 1902–04; British resident at Cashmere, India, 1906–09 ('India and Tibet', 'Wonders of the Himalaya', 'Epic of Mount Everest', 'Life in the Stars') E-376

Younghusband, Sir George John (1859–1944), English writer and major general, entered army, 1878; served in Afghan War, Sudan, S. Africa, World War I; keeper of Jewel House, Tower of London, after 1917 ('Tower of London', 'Crown Jewels of England', 'Forty Years a Soldier').

Young Ireland, Irish patriotic organization I-327

Young Italy, Italian secret revolutionary organization
  Mazzini M-240

Young Life Campaign, unaffiliated Christian youth organization; formed in 1940 by several young men just out of seminary; object is to reach teenagers who are not in touch with church life; has club and summer camp programs Y-430

Young Men's Christian Association (YMCA) Y-425
  library development L-177
  Young Women's Christian Association Y-426
  youth organizations Y-427

Young Pioneers, youth group in eastern Europe C-68

Young Plan, agreement for reparations to be paid by Germany to Allies G-123
  World War I W-321

Young Pretender. *see in index* Bonnie Prince Charlie

Young Republicans, political youth organization Y-431

Youngstown, Ohio, large steel center; pop. 108,042 Y-425
  Ohio O-512
  United States, *map* U-41

Youngstown Sheet & Tube Co. vs. Sawyer, case in U.S. constitutional law, *list* S-518b

Youngstown State University, Youngstown, Ohio; established 1908; arts and sciences, business administration, education, engineering, music; graduate studies.

Young Turks, revolutionary party in Turkey; originally, Turkish political exiles; after 1908, revolutionary leaders who ruled until World War I
  Iraqi history I-315

'Young Woman with a Water Jug', painting by Vermeer P-44

Young Women's Christian Association (YWCA) Y-426
  Young Men's Christian Association Y-425

Your Show of Shows, television program T-69

Youskevitch, Igor (born 1912), U.S. dancer, born in Russia; to U.S. 1938, became citizen 1944; participated in athletics with Yugoslavian Sokol before becoming dancer; *premier danseur* Ballet Russe de Monte Carlo 1938–44 and 1955–57 also artistic adviser 1955–57; in U.S. Navy 1944–45; *premier danseur* Ballet Theatre 1946–55; known for perfection of his classical technique.

Youth. *see in index* Adolescence

Youth, Isle of, Cuba. *see in index* Juventud, Isla de la

Youth Administration, National. *see in index* National Youth Administration

Youth Fitness Test, physical fitness battery for public schools H-92

Youth for Christ International (YFC International), religious association Y-430

Youth hostels. *see in index* Hostels

Youth International party. *see in index* Yippie

Youth organizations Y-427
  baseball leagues, *picture* V-239
  Boys' Clubs. *see in index* Boys' Clubs of America, Inc.
  Boy Scouts. *see in index* Boy Scouts of America
  Catholic Youth Organization. *see in index* Catholic Youth Organization
  De Molay. *see in index* De Molay, Order of
  4-H Clubs. *see in index* 4-H Clubs
  Future Homemakers. *see in index* Future Homemakers of America
  Future Teachers. *see in index* Future Teachers of America
  Girl Scouts. *see in index* Girl Scouts
  Girls' Friendly Society. *see in index* Girls' Friendly Society of the U.S.A.
  Girls State. *see in index* Girls State
  health and physical education H-93
  Junior Achievement. *see in index* Junior Achievement, Inc.
  Junior Story Leagues S-462
  Methodist Youth Fellowship. *see in index* Methodist Youth Fellowship
  National Association of Student Councils. *see in index* National Association of Student Councils
  National Honor Society. *see in index* National Honor Society of Secondary Schools
  parliamentary law P-132a, *table* P-132b
  Red Cross Youth R-119
  speech training P-526, *picture* P-526b
  Sunday schools S-516
  U.S.S.R. R-332, *picture* R-332a
  Young Citizens League. *see in index* Young Citizens League
  Young Life Campaign. *see in index* Young Life Campaign

'Youth's Companion', magazine M-33

Ypres, Belgium, town 35 mi (55 km) s. of Ostend; pop. 34,758 Y-431

Ypres, battles of (1914–15) W-305, 310
  warfare, *list* W-16
  chemical C-293

Ypsilanti, Alexander (1792–1828), Greek soldier, one of a family famous as leaders in Greek struggle for freedom; in 1821 led unsuccessful insurrection against Turks.

Ypsilanti, Mich., city on Huron River 30 mi (50 km) s.w. of Detroit; automobile and aircraft parts, paper, ladders, foundries and machine shops; Eastern Michigan University; Willow Run nearby; pop. 24,031.

Ysaye, Eugène (1858–1931), Belgian violinist, composer, and orchestra conductor; many concert tours in U.S.; conducted Cincinnati Symphony Orchestra.

Yser River, French and Belgian river rising 20 mi (30 km) s.e. of Calais, France, and flowing e. and n. to sea at Nieuport, Belgium; important in medieval trade; in World War I battle, Oct. 16–28, 1914, Belgians halted German advance by cutting dikes, creating flood.

Ysleta (or Isleta), Tex., village on Rio Grande, 10 mi (16 km) s.e. of El Paso; oldest settlement in Texas; former American Indian pueblo.

Y-Teens, YWCA club Y-426

Ytterbium (Yb), chemical element
  periodic table, *table* P-207, *list* P-208

Yttrium (Y), rare chemical element, discovered 1842; belongs to rare earth group
  periodic table, *table* P-207, *list* P-208

Yuan, after 1928 any one of the 4 departments (executive, legislative, judicial, control) in National, or Kuomintang, government of China.

Yüan Dynasty (or Mongol Dynasty), China (1279–1368) C-367, *map* C-371
  Kublai Khan K-308
  literature C-389
  Mongol Empire M-535
  Tibet T-181
  warfare W-20

Yüan Shih-kai (1859–1916), Chinese soldier and statesman, president of the Chinese republic from 1913 until his death; succeeded in holding China together after revolution of 1911
  China C-372
  Manchuria M-94

Yuba City, Calif., city 40 mi (60 km) n.w. of Sacramento; in farm area; food processing and shipping center; mobile homes, fiber glass, pop. 18,736.

Yucatán, Mexico, state in n. of Yucatán Peninsula, on Gulf of Mexico; 15,189 sq mi (39,339 sq km); cap. Mérida; pop. 903,773 A-532, *picture* A-537
  Mayas. *see in index* Maya
  Mexico, *map* M-344
  Yucatán Peninsula Y-432

Yucatán Channel, channel between Gulf of Mexico and Caribbean Sea C-800, *map* N-351. *see also in index* Ocean, *table*
  Gulf of Mexico M-345

Yucatán peninsula, peninsula between Gulf of Mexico and Caribbean Sea Y-432
  Gulf of Mexico M-345
  henequen S-206
  Latin America L-60
  Maya M-235, *picture* M-237
  Mexico M-325, 332, *pictures* M-333, 335, *map* M-344
  North America, *map* N-351
  West Indies W-155

Yucca, genus of about 40 species of succulent plants of family Agavaceae, native to southern North America; typically stemless, with stiff, long leaves and clusters of waxy flowers; some species cultivated as ornamentals
  New Mexico state flower, *pictures* N-220, S-427

Yucca Flat, desert basin in Nevada N-132

Yucca House National Monument, Colo. C-571, *map* C-583

Yucca palm. *see in index* Joshua tree

Yuchi, a North American Indian tribe and linguistic group that lived on Savannah River, Ga.; joined the Creeks 1729, later went with them to Indian Territory (Oklahoma) where they are now classed as Creeks.

Yudenich, Nikolai Nikolaevich (1862–1933), Russian general, leader of White Russian movement after World War I.

Yüeh Fu, Chinese Music Bureau; reactivated in 125 BC C-388

Yugoslavia (or Socialist Federal Republic of Yugoslavia, formerly Kingdom of the Serbs, Croats, and Slovenes), European nation formed after World War I; 98,766 sq mi (255,803 sq km); cap. Belgrade (Beograd); pop. 23,289,000 Y-434. *see also in index* Bosnia and Herzegovina; Croatia-Slavonia; Montenegro; Serbia; Slovenia
  cities. *see in index* cities listed below and other cities by name
    Belgrade B-151
    Dubrovnik, *picture* E-339
    Rijeka R-207
    Zagreb Z-442
  clothing, *picture* R-24, S-215
  Communist world, *map* C-619
  Croatia C-778
  [illegible]
  Europe, *map* E-360
  flag, *picture* F-172
  folktales S-470, *list* S-481
  history
    Balkan alliance B-25
    Fiume dispute R-207
    founding B-31
    World War II W-326
  Macedonia M-7
  national anthem, *table* N-64
  Slavs S-214, *picture* S-215
  Third World T-168
  transportation
    railroad mileage, *table* R-85

Yugoslavian Macedonia, political unit of Yugoslavia; area 9,928 sq mi (25,713 sq km); pop. 1,406,003 Y-436

Yukawa, Hideki (1907–81), Japanese physicist Y-439. *see also in index* Nobel Prizewinners, *table*
  atomic particles A-752
  nuclear physics N-432

'Yukiguni', novel by Kawabata. *see in index* 'Snow Country'

Yukon River, river of Canada and Alaska Y-439
  Alaska A-241, *maps* U-39, 94
  Canada, *map* C-112
  North America, *map* N-351
  Yukon Territory Y-440

Yukon Territory, most northwesterly political division of Canada; area 186,300 sq mi (482,500 sq km); cap. Whitehorse; goldfields; pop. 22,800 Y-439
  Mounties R-300a
  North America, *map* N-351
  Rockies R-234
  Selwyn Mountains, *picture* N-337
  telephone service S-195b

Yukon time T-189, *map* U-40

Yule, name of a winter month in Northern Europe; also means Christmas in some countries
  Christmas C-405

Yuma (son of the Captain), chief group of Yuman Indians of North America; lived originally at confluence of Gila and Colorado rivers.

Yuma, Ariz., city in s.w. on Colorado River at mouth of Gila; seed and farm products, clothing, photo-processing machines, paper plates; railroad center; Marine Air Corps Station nearby; pop. 42,433 A-598, *maps* A-547, 534, U-40, *picture* A-607
  North America, *map* N-310

Yuman, a linguistic group of North American Indians, living in California, Arizona, and lower California; agricultural rather than hunting people.

Yungas, forested regions in South America B-333

Yungay, Peru, city 32 mi (52 km) n.w. of Huarás; site of battle in which Chilean troops overthrew Peruvian-Bolivian Confederation in 1939; pop. 2,516.

Yunnan, province of s. China; 162,000 sq mi (419,600 sq km); cap. Kunming; pop. 33,190,000 Y-440

Yupon. *see in index* Yaupon

Yurok, a North American Indian tribe living on lower Klamath River and adjacent coast in California; originally occupied more than 50 villages
  mythology M-697

Yurt, type of tent S-156
  nomads N-332

Yusuf ibn Ayyub. *see in index* Saladin

YWCA. *see in index* Young Women's Christian Association

Y-Wives, YWCA club Y-426

The letter Z

is of uncertain origin. In a very early Semitic writing used about 1500 B.C. on the Sinai Peninsula, there often appeared a sign (1) believed by some scholars to mean the same as the sign (2) which was developed beginning about 1000 B.C. in Byblos and in other Phoenician and Canaanite centers. It is from the latter sign, called *zayin,* meaning "weapon" in the Semitic languages, that all later forms developed. The Greeks changed the Semitic name *zayin* to *zeta* and used the sign in several forms (3).

The early Romans did not use the "z" sound. After they conquered the Mediterranean world they used the Greek sign as it occurred in Greek words taken over into the Latin language. They added the new letter at the end of their alphabet. From one of the Greek forms the capital letter came into English unchanged.

1

2

3

Z

Zabrze (German Hindenburg), Poland, former German city in Silesia 95 mi (150 km) s.e. of Wrocław; coal mining; steel milling; machinery, glass, chemicals; in Poland 1945–; pop. 199,400, *map* E-360
Zacatecas, state in central Mexico; 28,973 sq mi (75,040 sq km); cap. Zacatecas; silver; pop. 1,096,993, *map* M-344
Zacatecas, Mexico, capital of state of Zacatecas, 320 mi (515 km) n.w. of Mexico City; pop. 31,701, *map* M-344
Zadar (Italian Zara), Yugoslavia, Adriatic port 90 mi (145 km) s.e. of Rijeka; assigned to Italy by Treaty of Rapallo 1920; ceded to Yugoslavia by treaty signed in Paris, 1947; pop. 95,300, *map* E-360
Zadkine, Ossip (1890–1967), Polish painter and sculptor; lived in England and France; noted work in abstract and geometric forms S-92
Zaehnsdorf, Joseph (1816–86), Austro-Hungarian-British bookbinder; one of foremost binders of his time.
Zagreb (or Agram), Yugoslavia, city 80 mi (130 km) n.e. of Rijeka; pop. 649,586 Z-442
  Croatia C-779
  Europe, *map* E-360
  Yugoslavia Y-435
Zagros Mountains, series of parallel ranges in w. Iran; highest elevation about 12,850 ft (3,920 m) I-304, *map* I-312
Zahal, Israel's military; combines army, navy, and air force M-413
Zaharias, Babe Didrikson (formerly Mildred Ella Didrikson) (1913–56), U.S. athlete Z-442
  athletics A-741
  golf, *picture* G-190
Zaharov, Sir Basil Zachariah (1850–1936), Turkish international financier, born in Phanaz; backer of European munition makers; influential in Balkan wars and World War I.
Zahir Shah. *see in index* Mohammad Zahir Shah
Zaïmis, Alexander (1855–1936), Greek statesman, six times premier; president 1929–35; left Greece 1935.
Zaire (formerly Democratic Republic of the Congo, formerly Belgian Congo), nation in central Africa; 905,365 sq mi (2,344,885 sq km); cap. Kinshasa; pop. 31,079,000 Z-443
  Africa, *map* A-118, *table* A-112
  cities. *see in index* Kinshasa and other cities by name
  flag, *picture* F-172
  history
    Baudouin I B-110
    Leopold II L-136
    Stanley S-410
  mountains
    Mount Margherita U-1
    Ruwenzori R-366a
  national parks N-26
  ores, *table* O-600
  Pygmies P-540, A-11
  railroad mileage, *table* R-85
  United Nations U-25, U-194
Zaire, National University of (formerly Lovanium University of Kinshasa) K-248
Zaire River, Africa. *see in index* Congo River
Zakat, contribution by Muslims to state or community I-360
Zakynthos. *see in index* Zante
Zaluski family, an influential family of Poland; **Andrew Chrysostom** (1650–1711), bishop and orator; **Joseph Andrew** (1702–74), bishop, collector of books and manuscripts.
Zaluzianskya, genus of annual and perennial plants of the figwort family, native to s. Africa; flat flower clusters; stems hairy; sometimes called lace verbena or night phlox.
Zama, battle of (202 BC), Carthage
  Hannibal H-31
  Scipio S-65
Zambezi River, river in s.e. Africa; 2,200 mi (3,540 km) long; rises in n.w. Zambia and empties in Mozambique into Indian Ocean; navigable for steamers upstream 400 mi; has Victoria Falls and Kariba Gorge Dam Z-446
  Africa, *map* A-118
  Livingstone L-263
  Mozambique M-641
  waterfalls W-96
    Victoria Falls V-311
  Zambia Z-447
Zambia (officially Republic of Zambia, formerly Northern Rhodesia), nation in s.-central Africa; 290,586 sq mi (752,614 sq km); cap. Lusaka; pop. 5,679,808 Z-447
  Africa A-99, *map* A-118, *table* A-112
  cities. *see in index* Lusaka and other cities by name
  Commonwealth membership, *table* C-602
  dance, *picture* D-31
  flag, *picture* F-172
  national parks N-26
  railroad mileage, *table* R-85
  Victoria Falls V-311
  Zambezi River Z-446
Zambo, a Latin American of American Indian and African ancestry S-282
Zamboanga, Philippines; city on Mindanao; port, market for timber, abaca, copra, hemp; settled by Spanish 1635; pop. 240,066 P-253c, 257a, *map* P-262, *table* P-259b
  Asia, *map* A-700
Zamenhof, Lazarus Ludwig (1859–1917), Russian philologist, inventor of language Esperanto L-39
Zamora y Torres, Niceto Alcalá. *see in index* Alcalá Zamora y Torres
Zamyatin, Yevgeny (1884–1937), Russian novelist S-62
Zamzam, Mecca M-254
Zancle. *see in index* Messina
Zande, African people
  Zaire Z-444
Zandeh. *see in index* Niam-Niam
Zandonai, Riccardo (1883–1944), Italian composer, chiefly of operas ('Francesca da Rimini', based on tragedy by D'Annunzio).
Zane, Ebenezer (1747–1812), U.S. pioneer; made first lasting settlement on Ohio River (now Wheeling, W. Va.), and helped found Zanesville.
Zanesville, Ohio, city 53 mi (85 km) e. of Columbus; coal region; railroad center; electrical equipment, steel products, ceramic tile, stoneware, glass products; National Road–Zane Grey Museum; pop. 28,655.
Zang. *see in index* Tibetans
Zangwill, Israel (1864–1926), British novelist and dramatist, leader in Zionist movement ('Children of the Ghetto'; 'The Melting Pot')
  Yiddish literature Y-418
Zante (or Zakynthos), Greece, one of Ionian Islands; 154 sq mi (399 sq km); wine, olives, citrus fruits.
ZANU (Zimbabwe African National Union)
  Mugabe M-645
Zanzibar, island of Tanzania, off e. coast of Africa; 640 sq mi (1,660 sq km); pop. 190,494
  Africa, *map* A-118
  Tanzania T-21
Zanzibar, Tanzania, city on island of Zanzibar; pop. 80,000, *map* A-118
Zapata, Emiliano (1879–1919), Mexican revolutionist Z-449
  Mexico M-337
  Orozco's 'Zapatistas' P-67a, *picture* P-67b
  Villa V-325
'Zapatistas', painting by Orozco P-67a, *picture* P-67b
Zaporozh'ye (or Zaporozhe), U.S.S.R., city in Ukrainian Soviet Socialist Republic, on Dnieper River; pop. 658,000 U-2, *maps* R-346, 350
  Europe, *map* E-360
Zapotec, people of s. Mexico; at time of Spanish conquest they formed a powerful nation occupying part of present state of Oaxaca
  Mexico M-325, 335
  pyramids P-543
ZAPU (Zimbabwe African People's Union)
  Nkomo N-329
Zara, Yugoslavia. *see in index* Zadar
Zaragoza, Spain. *see in index* Saragossa
Zarathustra. *see in index* Zoroaster
Zarzuela, Spanish opera
  Calderón's creations C-27
  Philippines P-258
Zauditu (1876–1930), empress of Ethiopia after 1916; daughter of Menelik II; shared rule with Ras Taffari, who became Emperor Haile Selassie I after her death
  Haile Selassie H-7
ZD (Zenith Distance) N-72
Zea, genus of American grasses encompassing the varieties of corn; plants of the genus are monoecious; staminate flowers in the tassels, pistillate in the ears. *see also in index* Corn
Zealand (Danish Själland), largest of the Danish islands; 2,709 sq mi (7,016 sq km); pop. 1,771,557 D-97, *map* D-100
Zeami, Motokiyo (1363?–1443), Japanese dramatist J-49, 81
  acting A-27
Zebra, animal Z-449
  hoof H-231
Zebra swallowtail butterfly, insect, *picture* B-522
Zebu (or Brahman), humped ox *Bos indicus* of India, used for pack transportation and milk; noted for hump of fat on shoulders; white bulls held sacred by Hindus; called Brahman cattle when imported into U.S.
  cattle C-224, 230, *picture* C-228
  rodeo riding R-236
Zebulun, Hebrew patriarch, tenth son of Jacob and sixth by his wife Leah; ancestor of the tribe of Zebulun.
Zechariah (6th–5th century BC), Hebrew minor prophet; returned to Palestine from captivity and promoted rebuilding the temple ('Book of Zechariah').
Zedekiah (6th century BC), last king of Judah; ruled under Nebuchadnezzar, who killed Zedekiah's sons and blinded Zedekiah when he attempted to revolt.
Zeeland, province of s.w. Netherlands; land area 653 sq mi (1,691 sq km); cap. Middelburg; has six islands connected by dams and bridges; pop. 283,465.
Zeeman, Pieter (1865–1943), Dutch physicist; professor physics and director Physical Institute, University of Amsterdam, 1900–35; discovered the Zeeman effect of magnetism on light. *see also in index* Nobel Prizewinners, *table*
  study of spectrum S-373
Zeeman effect, the influence of magnetism on light S-373
Zeisler, Fannie Bloomfield (1863–1927), U.S. concert pianist, born in Austrian Silesia; one of foremost women musicians.
Zeiss, Carl (1816–88), German manufacturer Z-449
Zeitlin, Aaron, British writer Y-418
Zelle, Margaretha. *see in index* Mata Hari
Zemach, Harve (pen name of Harvey Fischtrom) (1933–74), U.S. children's author; collaborated with his wife, **Margot Zemach** (born 1931), U.S. illustrator; ('A Small Boy Is Listening'; 'The Judge'; 'Duffy and the Devil', awarded 1974 Caldecott Medal).
Zen, Buddhist sect, originated in India in 6th century; taken to China soon after; active in Japan after 12th century, influenced culture; advocates rigid self-discipline, simple life, and spiritual enlightenment through personal meditation Z-450
  Buddhism B-482
  martial arts M-159
Zend-Avesta. *see in index* Avesta
Zenger, John Peter (1697–1746), U.S. publisher Z-450
  newspapers N-235
  New York history N-257
Zenith, in astronomy, the point in the heavens directly overhead, where a plumb line produced upward indefinitely at observation point would pierce celestial sphere
  navigation N-72
Zenith distance (ZD) N-72
Zenobia (3rd century), queen of Palmyra, Syria; ruled after her husband's death in 267; taken prisoner by Aurelian P-84
Zeno of Citium (335?–265? BC), Greek philosopher, born in Citium, Cyprus; founded Stoic school of philosophy P-265. *see also in index* Stoicism
  archaeological discovery A-538
Zeno of Elea (5th century BC), Greek philosopher, inventor of many ingenious paradoxes to discredit common beliefs about time, space, and motion; taught unity of all being.
Zeolite, mineral containing potassium and calcium silicates with water M-437
Zeolite process (or cation-exchange process), water softening W-91
Zephaniah (7th century BC), Hebrew minor prophet, prophesied punishment of Israel for its sins.
Zephyranthes, genus of perennial plants of the amaryllis family native to tropical America; roots bulbous; leaves grasslike; flowers funnel-shaped, white, red, or yellow; atamasco lily *Z. atamasco* is zephyr flower or fairy lily.
Zephyrus, in Greek mythology, the west wind.

ZODIAC SIGNS AND THEIR CORRESPONDING PERIODS

Note: *Dates supplied by American Federation of Astrologers.*

Aries (the Ram)	March 21–April 19
Taurus (the Bull)	April 20–May 20
Gemini (the Twins)	May 21–June 20
Cancer (the Crab)	June 21–July 22
Leo (the Lion)	July 23–Aug. 22
Virgo (the Virgin)	Aug. 23–Sept. 22
Libra (the Scales)	Sept. 23–Oct. 22
Scorpius (the Scorpion)	Oct. 23–Nov. 21
Sagittarius (the Archer)	Nov. 22–Dec. 21
Capricornus (the Goat)	Dec. 22–Jan. 19
Aquarius (the Water Bearer)	Jan. 20–Feb. 18
Pisces (the Fishes)	Feb. 19–March 20

PUBLISHERS' ACKNOWLEDGMENTS

The pictures in these volumes come from all parts of the world—from explorers and tourists and photojournalists, men and women of science and industry, official archives, specialists and generalists. In addition, whole series of photographs, drawings, graphs, and maps were specially prepared under the direct supervision of the Art and Editorial staffs of Compton's Encyclopedia. Special acknowledgments are listed below.

Volume 1—A-Anhui

231, 232 top left, center left, bottom, 233	Alabama Bureau of Publicity and Information
249, 250 top left, bottom left, 251 top, center left, bottom	Alaska State Department of Economic Development
250 right, 251 center right	Alaska State Department of Natural Resources
195 top right, center left, 196 center right, bottom	Bendix Corp.
341, 342, 343, 344, 346, 347, 349, 352, 353	Bettmann Archive
203 third row	British Information Services
35, 203 second row, fourth row, 204 third row, fourth row, 205 second row, third row	Brown Brothers
391	Chicago Wesley Memorial Hospital
390	Compton's Encyclopedia
33 bottom left	Culver Pictures
18	Doubleday & Co., Inc., Anchor Press
201 bottom left	Emhart Corp.
33 bottom right	Fogg Museum
354	Friedman-Abeles, Inc.
62	Ewing Galloway
188 bottom	Hamilton Standard Propellers
184 bottom right	Helio Aircraft Corp.
355 left	Houghton Mifflin Co.
195 top left	Kollsman Instrument Corp.
195 center right, 196 center left	Link Division of Singer Co.
32	National Gallery of Art
332	New Mexico State Tourist Bureau
239	Pan American World Airways, Inc.
201 bottom right, 202 center left, 204 top	Smithsonian Institution
331	State Historical Society of Wisconsin
203 bottom, 355 right	Wide World

Volume 2—Anima-Aztec

891, 892	American Museum of Natural History
605 center right	Arizona Office of Tourism Photo
607 bottom right	Arizona State Parks Board
619 top right, 620, 621	Arkansas Publicity and Parks Commission
662 right, 667 top	The Art Institute of Chicago
858 third row, 859 second row left, right, third row center	Automobile Manufacturers Association
524, 652, 830 bottom	Bettmann Archive
605 bottom right	Arthur H. Bilsten
537 right	Black Star
830 top, 859 first row left	Brown Brothers
537 left	Compton's Encyclopedia
532, 533	Field Museum of Natural History
859 second row center	Ford Motor Co.
858 second row center, 859 third row right	Ford News Bureau
667 bottom	Richard Garrison
858 second row right, 859 third row left	General Motors Corp.
536	Theresa Goell
422	Hal Harrison—Shostal
619 bottom	Little Rock Chamber of Commerce
605 bottom left	Lowell Observatory
629 top, 662 left, 663 bottom, 664 bottom	Metropolitan Museum of Art
663 top, 664 top, 665, 669 top	Museum of Modern Art
534 top	Ernest Nash
881	National Aviation Education Council
668	Portland Cement Association
606, 607 top left, top right, center, bottom left	Sante Fe Railway
858 first row, second row left, 859 first row center	Smithsonian Institution
666	Ezra Stoller Associates, Inc.
859 first row right	Studebaker Corp.
514–15	Three Lions, Inc.
605 top left	University of Arizona
619 top left	University of Arkansas
535	University of Chicago
534 bottom	UPI
654	Vermont Board of Historic Sites

Volume 3—B-Byzan

247, 254, 258 top, 260, 271	A.A. Allen
361	American Art Association, Anderson Galleries, Inc., New York
497 right	American Institute of Steel Construction
274	American Museum of Natural History
446 bottom	American-Swedish News Exchange
492	Armstrong Cork Co.
497 left	Bethlehem Steel Corp.
308	Black Star
92 right	F.N.M. Brown—University of Notre Dame
136	Brown Brothers
442 bottom	Canadian Consulate General
443 center	Cape Cod Chamber of Commerce
442 top	Chicago Burlington & Quincy Railroad Co.
325, 326 top	Compton's Encyclopedia
26 second row right	J. Cooke—Photo Researchers
255, 257 top, 269 top, bottom left	Allan D. Cruickshank—National Audubon Society
353 top, 354, 355	R.R. Donnelley & Sons Co.
26 second row left	D. Dumarie—Photo Researchers
270 bottom	H.E. Eckler
352 right	Encyclopædia Britannica, Inc.
440 bottom right	Fairchild Aerial Surveys, Inc.
138	Field Museum of Natural History
439 bottom	Ewing Galloway
26 first row left	Ralph Gerstle—Photo Researchers
240, 259 bottom, 269 bottom center, right, 270 top	Hal Harrison—National Audubon Society
26 fourth row left	Fritz Henle—Photo Researchers
12	Earl Hokens
526 bottom	James Press
272	Jasper-Pulaski State Game Reserve
253, 259 top	G. Blake Johnson—National Audubon Society
443 bottom	Keystone Press Agency, Inc.
140 top	Alexander B. Klots
476	Lancaster Chamber of Commerce
439 top	Mackinac Bridge Authority
475	Mercersburg Academy Press Club
26 first row right, third row left	Inge Morath—Magnum
347	Pierpont Morgan Library
140 bottom, 268	National Audubon Society
494 center, bottom	National Homes Corp.
494 top, 495 bottom	National Housing Center
348, 352 left, 353 bottom, 362	Newberry Library
446 top	New York City Department of Public Works
4 bottom, 5, 7, 8	Oriental Institute
26 third row right	Pix from Publix
256, 257 bottom, 258 bottom	Eliot F. Porter
440 center right	Port of New York Authority
521	Pearl Rice
345	Ken Short
444 top	D.B. Steinman
137, 141, 525	Edwin Way Teale
530 left	United States Department of Agriculture
440 top right, 445	United States Steel Corp.
6	University Museum (Philadelphia)
390	UPI
443 top center	Virginia Department of Highways
26 fourth row right	Sam Waagenaar—Pix from Publix
444 bottom	Wide World

Volume 4—C-Child

289	American Dairy Association
9 top right	American Telephone & Telegraph Co.
115 center right, 118 center right, 122 left, center right	Bettmann Archive
104	British Information Services
127 bottom	Dana Brown—FPG
301	Brown Brothers
46 first row left, center, 47 top right, bottom left	California Department of Parks and Recreation
91	Canadian Pacific Railway

171 top, 172 bottom	George Carlson
88, 92, 95, 102, 103	Confederation Life Collection
47 top left	Walt Disney Productions
269	EB Inc.
286	Ellesmere Manuscript of the Canterbury Tales
127 top	Ewing Galloway
285	Garnette's History of English Literature
170	Harris & Ewing
128	Fritz Henle—Monkmeyer Press
121	Hougen's Ltd.
93	Hudson's Bay Co.
113	Imperial Oil, Ltd. (Canada)
143, 284	James Press
171 bottom, 172 top	Harold M. Lambert Studios
283	W.A. Mansell &Co.
261	Metropolitan Museum of Art
233 left	Missouri State Park Board
233 right	Josef Muench
287	National Gallery
119	Newberry Library
118 left, center left, right	Ontario Archives
115 left, center left, right, 116, 122 center left, right	Public Archives of Canada
17	Publix Pictorial Service Corp.
47 bottom right	Redwood Empire Association
41 top	Sacramento Chamber of Commerce
41 bottom	Santa Barbara Chamber of Commerce
45 top left, bottom, 46 top left, first row right	Santa Fe Railway
35	United States Bureau of Reclamation
45 center	University of California
9 top left	Wide World

Volume 5—Chile-Czech

536 bottom	American Coffee Bureau
700	American Dairy Association
676	American Forest Institute
542, 543	American Numismatic Association
700 top right, third row right, fourth row left, right	Armour & Co.
427, 430 right	Authenticated News International
736 bottom right	Bell Helicopter Co.
700 second row right, third row left	Better Homes and Gardens
471, 593	Bettmann Archive
524 left	Bituminous Coal Institute
700 fifth row left, sixth row left, right	Wesley Bowman Studio, Inc.
601	British Information Services
470, 702, 703	Brown Brothers
541	George Carlson
416 right	Bill Cassin
697	Paul Child
576 top left, top right, bottom right, 577 top right, center, bottom	Colorado Department of Public Relations
570 top	Colorado State Advertising and Publicity Department
653, 657 top left, 658 top left, left center, 659	Connecticut Development Commission
522 bottom left	Consolidated Coal Co.
536 top left	Continental Coffee Co.
575 top left, bottom	Denver Chamber of Commerce
426 bottom, 430 left, 432	Leonard Farley Museum
424, 425, 426 top	FPG
700 top left	Frigidaire
472, 736 left center, 738 top	Ewing Galloway
658 bottom	General Dynamics Corp.
520 center	Goodman Manufacturing Co.
420	Historical Pictures Service, Chicago
630, 631, 633 left	IBM Corp.
719 second row center, right, 736 top right, center right, 738 bottom	International Harvester
536 top right	Jewel Tea Co.
521, 522 top	Joy Manufacturing Co.
657 bottom	Larry Kenny—Bridgeport office of Economic Development
522 bottom right	Lee-Norse Co.
751 top, 752, 753, 754 bottom	Frederick Lewis
584	Life © Time Inc.
524 right	Link-Belt Co.
520 top	Long Airdox Co.
652	Ray Mainwaring
477	Mariners' Museum
525	National Coal Association
735 top, bottom, 740 top left, top right, bottom right, 741	National Cotton Council of America
535	Pan American Coffee Bureau
699	Patterson Publishing Co.
700 second row left	Peoples Gas Light and Coke Co.
423, 431 top	Pix, Inc.
570 bottom	Pueblo Chamber of Commerce
431 bottom left, 435, 436, 437 bottom	Ringling Brothers and Barnum & Bailey
487	Taber & Prang
700 fifth row right	Taylor Instrument Companies
463 top left	United Airlines
519	United Electrical Coal Companies
576 bottom left	United States Air Force Academy
416 left, 419	United States Army
588	United States Bureau of Reclamation
658 top right	United States Coast Guard
735 center, 736 top left, bottom left, 739, 740 bottom left	United States Department of Agriculture
669, 670-1, 673, 674	United States Soil Conservation Service
516	United States Weather Service
575 top right	University of Colorado
657 top right	University of Connecticut
412, 428, 429, 431 bottom right, 437 top, 803	UPI
751 bottom, 754 bottom, 755 top, 756, 757	Western Ways
603, 703 bottom	Wide World
658 right center	Winchester-Western

Volume 6—D-Dys

244 top right	American National Theatre and Academy
251 bottom, 252 bottom	The Art Institute of Chicago
46	BBC Hulton Picture Library
238	Bettmann Archive
162 top	Boy Scouts of America
42, 217, 220 bottom	Brown Brothers
175	Chicago Wesley Memorial Hospital
116	Craft Horizons
70	Delaware River Port Authority
79 center left, 80 bottom, 81 bottom right	Delaware State Archives
71, 73 top right, bottom, 75, 79 left, 81 center left, bottom left	Delaware State Development Department
79 center right, 80 top left, center left, center right	Diamond State Telephone Co.
73 top left, 81 top	E.I. du Pont de Nemours & Co., Inc.
80 top right	Eleutherian Mills—Hagley Foundation, Inc.
53	J.L.G. Ferris
218, 219, 220 top right	Marshall Field & Co.
57	John Hancock Mutual Life Insurance Co.
114 top	Hedrich-Blessing
238 bottom, 239 bottom	James Press
115 top	Life © Time Inc.
38	W.A. Mansell & Co.
113 top	Metropolitan Museum of Art
115 bottom	Museum of Fine Arts (Boston)
110	Museum of Modern Art
94	Norwegian Information Service
14 bottom	Pacific Gas & Electric Co.
113 bottom	Phaidon Press Ltd.
108 bottom	Robert D. Sailors
129	Schwanke-Kasten Co.
14	Spence Art Photos
239 top	Edwin Way Teale
220 top left, center	Three Lions, Inc.
13 center, 16	United States Army Corps of Engineers
12, 13 top, 15	United States Bureau of Reclamation
161 bottom, 162 bottom	United States Geological Survey
79 bottom	University of Delaware
244 top left, 245 top, 246 right	Vandamm Studio
95	Frank Verticchio
66, 243 top, 246 left, center	Wide World
81 center right	Henry Francis du Pont Winterthur Museum, Inc.

Volume 7—E-Eye

182 top left	American Museum of Natural History
74 bottom, 75 right, 245, 247, 248, 254, 268, 275, 383 top right, bottom	Bettmann Archive
106 left	British Combine, Ltd.
240-41 bottom, 256 bottom	British Information Services
131 bottom, 250, 251, 253, 257 top	British Museum
240 top, 264, 266, 269, 270, 271, 272, 272	Brown Brothers
51 right	Carnegie Institute of Technology
243	Central Press—Pictorial Parade
123	Richard Davis—Photo Researchers
55 right	Earl E. Diemer
112	EB Inc.
183	Joan F. Falk
72, 73, 74 top, 75 left	Henry Ford Museum
252 right, 382	Ewing Galloway
50 left, 252 bottom	Philip D. Gendreau
280	Goodman Theatre
276, 277	Historical Pictures Service, Chicago
384	Earl Hokens
181 bottom	James Press
50 right	Kio—Camera Press
192	*Life* © Time Inc.
127	Metropolitan Museum of Art
55 left	National Park Service
373	National Screen Service Corp.
279	Newberry Library
128, 130 bottom, 131 top	Oriental Institute

244 top, 265	Pictorial Parade, Inc.
184	Publisher's Photo Service
[illegible] 354 top	Publix Pictorial Service Corp.
239, 246, 252 left, 256 top	Radio Times Hulton Picture Library
126, 130 top, 181 top	Rapho-Guillumette
51 left	Schall—Pix from Publix
278	Charles Scribner's Sons
383 top left	Smithsonian Institution
255, 267	Three Lions, Inc.
258	The Times (London)
111	United States Department of Agriculture
58	United States Department of the Interior
54	United States Forest Service
372	United States Navy
170	United States Steel Corp.
134 top, 136 top, bottom left, 140	UPI
163	Westinghouse Electric Corp.
136 bottom right, 138, 142 257 bottom, 374	Wide World

Volume 8—F-Furt

126 bottom right, 323	American Museum of Natural History
68, 85, 381 top, bottom, 382, 383 bottom, 394 right, 401, 402, 403	Bettmann Archive
232 top left, 233 top right, bottom right	Black Star
84 top, 394 left, center left, right, 395, 396	Brown Brothers
220 top	L.W. Brownell
232 center row right	Devereux Butcher—Camera Clix
50, 232 bottom, left, bottom right, 234 1st row left, right, third row left, right, 235 top right, bottom left, 237 bottom left	Camera Clix, Inc.
329 top left	Chicago Tribune
329 top right, bottom	Community Fund
257 bottom	Editorial Fischgrund (Mexico City)
324, 325	Mildred Adams Fenton
125 top	Field Museum of Natural History
203 top left, bottom, 204, 205	Florida Development Commission
256 top	Folk Arts Center, Inc.
381 center, 383 top, center, 384	Franklin Institute
362 top, 363 bottom, 364 bottom, 365	French Embassy
150, 466 bottom right	Ewing Galloway
471	Ginn & Co.
131	Fritz Goro, Life © Time Inc.
469 bottom	Great Northern Railway
222	Jackson & Perkins
242 top	James Press
237 bottom right	John Kabel—Publix
232 center row left, 233 top left, 236 bottom left, 237 top left, 238 top right, center right	Henry B. Kane
242 center, bottom	Leon Keinigsberg
219 top, 224 top right, bottom right, 225 top right, center right, bottom, 226 bottom right, 227 top right	J. Horace McFarland
127 right	Marine Biological Laboratory
239 bottom left	David Muench
228, 239 top, bottom center, bottom right	Josef Muench
244	National Audubon Society
469 top	National Gallery of Canada
234 second row left	National Park Service
126 bottom left, 127 left	New York Zoological Society
470	George F. Paul
232 first row center, right, third row center, 233 center left, bottom left, 234 first row center, second row right, third row center, 235 top left, center right, bottom right, 236 top left, right, bottom right, 237 top right, 238 top left, bottom left	Rutherford Platt
363 top	Radio Times Hulton Picture Library
255	G. Schirmer, Inc.
223 top left, 224 top left, 226 bottom left, 227 top left, center right, bottom left, bottom right	Shostal
223 top right, bottom left, bottom right, 224 bottom left, 225 top left, 257 top	Three Lions, Inc.
99, 364 top	United States Army
183, 184	United States Army Corps of Engineers
203 top right	University of Florida
466 top, bottom, left	Wide World
97, 98	Winchester Repeating Arms Co.

Volume 9—G-Gyro

86 right	American Forest Institute
105 left, 271, 273	The Art Institute of Chicago
93 bottom	Atlanta Chamber of Commerce
29, 30, 105 center, 106 right, 122 top, bottom left, 107 top, 216, 267 right	Bettmann Archive
106 center, 215, 217, 218	Brown Brothers
163 top	C.H. Cannings
56 top	Arnold Ryan Chalfant & Associates
156 bottom, 160, 161 left, 163 bottom	Corning Glass Works
272 bottom	EB Inc.
176 bottom	Federal Reserve Bank of New York
157	Fourco Glass Co.
266	FPG
122 bottom right	Ewing Galloway
55, 56 bottom	General Biological Supply House
23 bottom, 24, 25, 26	Paul E. Genereux
93 top right, 94 top left, center left, bottom right, 95 bottom left, right	Georgia Department of Industry and Trade
93 center left, 94 bottom left	Georgia Department of State Parks
86 left	Georgia Forestry Commission
95 top left	Georgia Poultry Federation
179	Guy Gillette
190 top right, bottom	Golfing Magazine
28, 270	Gramstorff Brothers
105 right, 106 left	Historical Pictures Service, Chicago
161 right	Earl Hokens
176 top	Homestake Mining Co.
52 top	Houghton Mifflin Co.
264, 269, 272	James Press
156 top, 158 bottom	Libbey-Owens-Ford Glass Co.
267 left, center, 268	Metropolitan Museum of Art
291	National Audubon Society
22	National Garden Bureau
20	Publix Pictorial Service Corp.
10	H. Armstrong Roberts
22 top	F.F. Rockwell
84	St. Simons Island Chamber of Commerce
95 top right	Savannah Port Authority
94 top right	United States Army
178b	United States Department of the Interior
93 top left	University of Georgia
127 bottom, 190 top left	UPI
34	Frank Verticchio
95 center left	James Waldrop Associates
307, 311	Wide World

Volume 10—H-Hypno

147	A.W. Amley—National Audubon Society
102 center	Argonne National Laboratory
232	The Art Institute of Chicago
118	Bell Helicopter Co.
38, 46	Bettmann Archive
39, 45, 176 second row left	Brown Brothers
102 right	Corning Glass Works
142	Allan D. Cruickshank—National Audubon Society
49 top	Charles Phelps Cushing
332 top, bottom	Byron Dairymple
69 bottom left	Dole Co.
148	Carroll Lane Fenton
48	Gramstorff Brothers
67 top right	Loye L. Guthrie
68 bottom right	Hawaiian Sugar Planter's Association
68 top right, 69 top right	Hawaii Division of State Parks
59 top, 63, 67 top left, bottom, 68 bottom left, 69 top left, center left, bottom right	Hawaii Visitors Bureau
76, 77	Hayes Memorial Library
129	Historical Pictures Service, Chicago
49 bottom	Indiana Historical Society
68 top left	National Park Service
177, 178	Oriental Institute
176 first row left	Press Associates
54, 55	John B. Stetson Co.
59 bottom	Werner Stoy—Camera Hawaii
176 first row center	Three Lions, Inc.
332 center	Union Pacific Railroad
67 center left	University of Hawaii
176 first row right, second row right, third row, fourth row, 233, 236	UPI
34 top	Verbelke Photo Aérienne
34 bottom	Wide World
102 left	Yerkes Observatory

Volume 11—I-Izmir

298 top left	Amana Society
9, 113, 119	American Museum of Natural History
98 center left	American Oil Co.
278 bottom left	Battelle Memorial Institute
274 left	Bausch & Lomb Optical Co.
278 bottom right	Bell Telephone Laboratories, Inc.
176, 177, 275 top, bottom right, 276 right	Bettmann Archive
396	Brown Brothers

297 top right	Cedar Rapids Chamber of Commerce
47 center right	Chicago Association of Commerce and Industry
46 bottom left	Commonwealth Edison Co.
41	Durant's Studio
273 top	Edison Electric Institute
114 bottom, 137	Field Museum of Natural History
181	Ford Motor Co.
38 bottom right, 93 left	Ewing Galloway
278 top	General Dynamics Corp.
275 bottom left	Goodyear Tire & Rubber Co.
26 top left, 27 top left	Greater Boise Chamber of Commerce
111, 124, 135	Great Northern Railway
179, 395	Historical Pictures Service, Chicago
221 top	Dr. Ross E. Hutchins
25 center, bottom, 26 top right, center, bottom, 27 top right	Idaho Department of Commerce and Development
27 center right, bottom	Idaho Department of Parks
47 top	Illinois Department of Agriculture
46 center left	Illinois Department of Business and Economic Development
46 top left, bottom right, 47 center left	Illinois Department of Conservation
93 right, 97 bottom right, 98 top left, top right, bottom, 99 center left, right, bottom left, center	Indiana Department of Commerce
97 bottom left, 99 bottom right	Indiana Department of Natural Resources
97 top left, top right	Indianapolis Chamber of Commerce
99 top	Indianapolis Motor Speedway Corp.
97 center left	Indiana University
274 right	International Harvester
299 top	Iowa State Conservation Commission
293 bottom, 297 top left, bottom, 298 top right, center left, bottom, 299 center, bottom left	Iowa State Development Commission
392	Italian State Tourist Office
212 right, 222	Alexander B. Klots
299 bottom right	Meredith Corp.
114 top, 115 left, 120,122, 131, 134, 142	Milwaukee Public Museum
117 bottom, 125	Museum of the American Indian, Heye Foundation
45 bottom left	Museum of Science and Industry
145	National Museum of Archaeology
180	New York Public Library
276 left	Parke, Davis & Co.
38 bottom left	Peabody Coal Co.
47 bottom	Peoria Association of Commerce
45 top right	Public Building Commission of Chicago
140 bottom	Sante Fe Railway
118	Mario Scacheri
293 top	Sioux City Chamber of Commerce
144	Smithsonian Institution
133 top	Southwest Museum
6	Bob and Ira Spring
45 top left, 46 top right	Springfield Association of Commerce & Industry
212 left	David Staeger
38 top	United States Army Corps of Engineers
121 top, 126 top, 128, 129 top, bottom right	United States Bureau of Indian Affairs
25 top	University of Idaho
45 bottom right	University of Illinois
117 top	Western Ways
273 bottom	Wide World

Volume 12—J-Kyoto

103	Art Extension Society
50 bottom, 51 bottom, 52, 104	The Art Institute of Chicago
2 top, 3, 5, 70 top right, 119, 126	Bettmann Archive
95 bottom	Black Star
112	British Museum
4, 89	Brown Brothers
57, 58	René Burri—Magnum
65	Camera Press—Miller Services, Ltd.
279 top right, center left, center right	Consulate General, Republic of Korea
28, 29, 32, 40 bottom, 41 top, 45, 46 top right, center right, bottom left, 47 top left, center left, 49, 50 top, 55 top, 56, 60 top, 64 bottom, 70 bottom right, 71 top left	Consulate General of Japan (Chicago)
67, 278 top, 298	Eastfoto
182 top left, center left, bottom left	Dwight D. Eisenhower Library
113 bottom	European Picture Service
8, 212 top right	Ewing Galloway
7	Philip D. Gendreau
42 center, 44 bottom, 47 top right, 55 bottom, 62	Bob Glaze—Artstreet
279 bottom left	John Holstein
46 bottom right, 63, 64 top, 70 top left, 71 bottom left	International Society for Educational Information, Tokyo, Inc.
258	James Press
38, 47 bottom right, 60 bottom	Japan National Tourist Organization
92, 93	Thomas Jefferson Memorial Foundation
114	Jewelry Industry Council
181 top right, left, 182 top right, bottom, 183 top right center, bottom left, bottom right	Kansas Department of Economic Development
183 top left	Kansas Forestry, Fish, and Game Commission
212 top left, bottom, 217 top left, right, bottom, 218, 219	Kentucky Department of Public Information
279 bottom right, 281	Klee—FPG
269	K.M. Lee
42 bottom	Nobuyuki Masaki
71 right	Masao Minagawa
70 bottom left	Museum of Fine Arts (Boston)
95 top	New York State Historical Association
129	George Reed
23, 47 bottom left	Bob and Ira Spring
33, 39 bottom, 51 top	Bob and Ira Spring—Publix
217 center left	University of Kentucky
131 top, 132, 200 top, 295	UPI
91	Virginia Conservation Commission
133	The White House
181 bottom left, right	Wichita Chamber of Commerce
66, 100 bottom, 131 bottom, 134, 197, 198, 199, 200 bottom, 201, 202, 203, 204, 205, 297 top	Wide World
113 top	Harry Winston, Inc.

Volume 13—L-Lyre

329, 330, 331, 332, 333, 334	American Forest Institute
281 second row right, third row right, 280 second row, third row, fourth row	Association of American Railroads
264 left	Ray Atkeson
52, 282 top right	Bettmann Archive
211	Brown Brothers
213, 216	Chicago Historical Society
282 center left	Chicago Public Library
214	Esquire, Inc.
224 top	FPG
224 bottom, 290, 292	Ewing Galloway
281 top right	Great Northern Railway
221	Eugene J. Hall
100 bottom	James Press
217, 220, 223	Library of Congress
282 top left, center right, bottom	Locomotive Association
317 center right	Louisiana State University
317 top, left, top right, bottom left, bottom right, 318, 319	Louisiana Tourist Development Commission
15, 16	Metropolitan Museum of Art
14	North American Lace Co.
281 top left	Santa Fe Railway
100 top	Ida Smith
13, 18, 287 top	Three Lions, Inc.
227	Underwood & Underwood
280 top	Union Pacific Railroad
212	Wide World

Volume 14—M-Meta

61 top left	American Telephone & Telegraph Co.
171 bottom	Baltimore Association of Commerce
177 bottom right	Bethlehem Steel Corp.
282, 283 left	Bettmann Archive
167	A. Aubrey Bodine
200 top left	Boston Chamber of Commerce
18, 19, 26, 293 top	Brown Brothers
87, 88	Field Museum of Natural History
30 top	Carl Frank—Photo Researchers
171 top, 192 top	Ewing Galloway
59 bottom left, 60 bottom left	Greater Portland Chamber of Commerce
192 bottom	Harvard University
17	Hayes Memorial Library
255 top	Hedrich-Blessing
283 right	Historical Pictures Service, Chicago
194 left	James Studio
59 top left, bottom right, 60 top left, top right, bottom, 61 top right, center left, bottom	Maine Department of Economic Development
177 top left, center right	Maryland Department of Economic Development
176 top, center left	Maryland Department of Forests and Parks
199 top left, right, 200 top right, center, bottom right, 201 top, center, bottom left	Massachusetts Department of Commerce and Development
199 bottom	Massachusetts Port Authority
82	Ralph Morse © 1959 Time Inc.
177 top right	National Park Service
195	Peabody Museum of Salem
30 bottom	C.A. Peterson—Rapho-Guillumette
176 center right, bottom, 177 center left	Potomac Edison Co.
201 bottom right	Raytheon Co.
256 bottom, 257, 258, 259	Frank Rowland—EB Inc.
194 right	Three Lions, Inc.
175 center left	United States Navy
59 top right	University of Maine
175 top right	University of Maryland

199 center right	University of Massachusetts
90	UPI
166, 175 top left, bottom	Bob Willis

Volume 15—Mete-Myth

428 top right	Anaconda Co.
672 top left, 673, 675	Bettmann Archive
476 bottom left	Biloxi Chamber of Commerce
429 top right	Black Star
620 bottom	Brown Brothers
665	L.W. Brownell
433, 434	Camera Clix, Inc.
430	Cleveland Cliffs Iron Co.
440 top	Duluth Convention and Visitation Bureau
420	Eclectic Magazine
366 top left, center left	Greater Detroit Board of Commerce
669, 672 bottom right, 674	Historical Pictures Service, Chicago
477 bottom left	International Paper Co.
475 top right, bottom left	Jackson Chamber of Commerce
574–5	Lick Observatory
365 bottom, 367 center left	Michigan Department of Conservation
365 top right, 366 first row center, right, second row center, right, bottom, 367 top, center right, bottom	Michigan Tourist Council
440 bottom	Minnesota Department of Business Research and Development
449, 450, 451	Minnesota Department of Economic Development
476 top left, 477 bottom right	Mississippi Agricultural and Industrial Board
489 bottom, 492, 497, 498 top left, right, center left, 499 center row, bottom	Missouri Division of Commerce and Industrial Development
498 bottom left, right, 499 top left, right	Missouri State Park Board
557 top left, bottom, 558, 559	Montana Highway Commission
476 center left, top right, bottom right, 477 center left, right	Natchez-Adams County Chamber of Commerce
475 bottom right	National Park Service
428 bottom	James S. Robbins & Associates, Inc.
577	Sovfoto
428 top left	Three Lions, Inc.
429 top left	United States Department of the Interior
365 top left	University of Michigan
475 top left	University of Mississippi
557 top right	University of Montana
576	Wide World
477 top	Yazoo County Chamber of Commerce

Volume 16—N-Nix

142 center right	Anaconda Co.
14, 15	Bettmann Archive
35	Fred Bond
12 top, 13 top, 16	Brown Brothers
77 top	John Crerar Library
221 bottom	Greater Albuquerque Chamber of Commerce
203 bottom	Greater Newark Chamber of Commerce
203 top left	Greater Trenton Chamber of Commerce
205 bottom right	Grant Heilman
137	Holiday Magazine
141 bottom left, right	Las Vegas Chamber of Commerce
262 top left	Long Island State Park Commission
61	National Park Service
101 top left, 102 top left, right, center left, bottom, 103	Nebraska Game, Forestation, and Parks Commission
132, 141 top left, 142 top left, center left, bottom, 143 top, bottom	Nevada Department of Economic Development
142 top right	Nevada State Park System
183 center, 184 top right, bottom right, 185 top left, center, bottom	New Hampshire Department of Resources and Economic Development
204, 205 top, center left, right, bottom left	New Jersey State Department of Conservation and Economic Development
221 top left, center left, 222, 223 top, center, bottom right	New Mexico Department of Development
223 bottom left	New Mexico State Park and Recreation Commission
256, 261 top right, bottom, 262 center left, center right, bottom right, 263 top right, bottom	New York State Department of Commerce
101 bottom, 102 bottom right	Omaha Chamber of Commerce
63	H.A. Ogden—T.D. Murphy Co.
185 top right	Portsmouth Naval Shipyard
136, 143 center	Reno Chamber of Commerce
203 top right	Rutgers University
183 bottom	Sanford Associates
263 top left	Sleepy Hollow Restorations
261 top left	State University of New York
184 left	Charles (Bud) Thompson
263 center left	Travel Literature Corp.
262 bottom left	United States Army
69 top	United States Navy
101 top right	University of Nebraska
141 top right	University of Nevada
183 top left	University of New Hampshire
221 top right	University of New Mexico
321 top, 322 top left, 324, 325	UPI
321 bottom, 322 top right, bottom, 323	Wide World
262 top right	Xerox Corp.

Volume 17—Nkomo-Ozark

529 top left, 531 top left	American Airlines
420 center right, 421 top	Brookhaven National Laboratory
363 bottom	Charlotte Chamber of Commerce
375	Greater North Dakota Association
379 top left	Russ Hanson—Hillstrom Stock Photo
491 top	James Press
478 center	National Geographic Society
419 top	National Institutes of Health
363 top right, 364, 365	North Carolina Department of Conservation and Development
380 top right, 381 top left, center left, right	North Dakota Economic Development Commission
379 bottom right	North Dakota School of Forestry
380 center right, bottom, 381 top right, bottom	North Dakota State Parks Board
379 top right, 380 top left, center left	North Dakota Travel Department
510 top left, top right, bottom left, bottom right, 511 center right, bottom	Ohio Department of Natural Resources
505, 509 top left, 511 top left, top right, center left	Ohio Development Department
509 top right	Ohio State University
510 center left	Ohio State University Cooperative Extension
531 top right	Oklahoma Department of Highways
530 top left, top right, center right, bottom left, 531 center, bottom left, bottom right	Oklahoma Industrial Development and Park Department
589 center left, top right, 590 top left, center left, top right, bottom left, 591 top left, top right, center right, bottom left	Oregon State Highway Commission
529 bottom	Philbrook Art Center
531 center right	Philips Petroleum Co.
509	Jim Pickerell—CLICK/Chicago
590 bottom right	Portland Chamber of Commerce
462–63	Rand McNally & Co.
473 bottom	Scripps Institution of Oceanography
475	Stenuit-Bruxelles
530 bottom right	United States Army
530 center left	United States Bureau of Indian Affairs
481	United States Coast Guard
473 top, 483	United States Navy
419 bottom, 420 center left	University of California
363 top	University of North Carolina
379 bottom left	University of North Dakota
529 center	University of Oklahoma
589 top left	University of Oregon
478 top, bottom	Westinghouse Electric Corp.
589 bottom, 591 bottom right	Weyerhaeuser Co.
491 bottom	Douglas P. Wilson, Marine Biological Laboratory
460–61	Woods Hole Oceanographic Institution

Volume 18—P-Phil

74 right	Adams Studio
245 top	All-Pets Magazine
106 top left	American Forest Institute
81	American Geographical Society
7 center left, 14, 108 bottom left	American Museum of Natural History
228	American Petroleum Institute
225	The Art Institute of Chicago
213 top right, bottom right	Asia Institute
131b, 132, 132a	Authenticated News International
9, 10, 11, 12	William J. Beecher
108 bottom right, 140, 162, 197b top right	Bettmann Archive
88 top, 122, 170 bottom, 173	Black Star
109a bottom	Boeing Co.
21, 133, 142b	Brown Brothers
82 bottom left, center, 83 top	Devereux Butcher
260 bottom	Camera Press—Miller Services, Ltd.
13 bottom, 75, 80 top, 88 center, bottom, 90, 91, 102, 103, 108 top, 109a top, 120, 147, 148 bottom left, 160, 165, 175, 197a top, 197b bottom, 200, 208 right, 212, 220, 224, 230, 235, 237, 239 bottom, 241a-b, 251a, 251b, 253a, 253b, 253c top, 255b, 255c top, 255d, 257 center, 257a, 257b top right, 259b, 261b	Compton's Encyclopedia
106 center right, bottom right	Crocker-Burbank Papers, Inc.
2	Charles Phelps Cushing

189 bottom	Dale Wild Sarcoxie Nurseries, Inc.
74 left	J.H. Day Co.
168 top	Delaware River Port Authority
158, 159 bottom left	Dixon Pencil Co.
72, 76, 248a	E.I. du Pont de Nemours & Co., Inc.
153, 154	Eastfoto
159 top, bottom right	Eberhard Faber Co.
82 bottom right	Field Museum of Natural History
180 top right, first row center left, second row right	Free Library of Philadelphia
203, 204 bottom	Fritzsche Brothers, Inc.
7 top right, bottom right, 8, 13, 82 top, 83 bottom right, 112, 169 bottom, 192 top, 194 top, 221	Ewing Galloway
178 top right	Gettysburg Travel Council, Inc.
260 top	Peter Gridley—FPG
210	Harris & Ewing
218	Harvard University Press
242	Grant Heilman
83 bottom left	Herbert Photos, Inc.
170 top	Holiday Magazine
239 top	Humble Oil & Refining Co.
180 second row left	Hurok Concerts, Inc.
104 top	Ingersoll-Rand Co. (Canada)
73	International Engineering
113, 214	James Press
106 bottom left	Kimberly-Clark Corp.
257b center left, 261c bottom right	Ewing Krainin
1	John La Due
255a	John Launois—Black Star
155 top left	Ralph E. Lawrence
197 bottom right	Bernard L. Lewis, Inc.
215	J. Horace McFarland
179 bottom right	McNally Pittsburgh Manufacturing Corp.
254, 255	Eddie Martinez
152 bottom	Metropolitan Museum of Art
180 bottom left	MGM Records
257b top right	Charles W. Miller & Sons (Manila)
146, 227 top	National Audubon Society
109 bottom left	National Aviation Education Council
116	National Congress of Parents and Teachers
152 top	New York Zoological Society
105, 106 top right, 107	Northern Paper Mills
232	Oil Well Supply Co.
213 top left, bottom left	Oriental Institute
87	Panama Canal Co.
234 top	Pan American Petroleum Corp.
156	Parker Pen Co.
168 bottom, 171 left, 177 bottom, 178 bottom right, 179 center right, bottom left	Pennsylvania Department of Commerce
179 center left	Pennsylvania Department of Forests and Waters
180 top left, first row right	Pennsylvania Historical and Museum Commission
178 bottom left, 179 top	Pennsylvania Power & Light Co.
257b bottom right, 258 bottom	C.A. Peterson—Publix
177 center, 178 top left, top center, 251d	Philadelphia Chamber of Commerce
256 bottom, 257b bottom left, 261c left	Philippine Air Lines, Inc.
253, 253d, 255c bottom, 257 top, 257d, 258 top, 259, 261c top right	Philippine Bureau of Travel and Tourist Information
253c bottom, 257b center right	Philippine Tourist & Travel Association
166 left, 169 top, 177 top left	Pittsburgh Chamber of Commerce
166 right	Pittsburgh Plate Glass Co.
7 center right	Pix, Inc.
161	Paul Popper—Globe Photos
129	Radio Times Hulton Picture Library
104 bottom	William M. Rittase
227 bottom, 244 top left, 251c bottom	H. Armstrong Roberts
257 bottom	Roberts—Miller Services, Ltd.
155 right, bottom left	Hugo H. Schroder
157	W.A. Sheaffer Pen Co.
231, 236 left, 238	Shell Oil Co.
134	Shostal
234 bottom	Sinclair Refining Co.
245 bottom	Ernest Sisto—New York Times
189 top	Social Security Administration
233	Standard Oil Co.
240	Texaco, Inc.
7 bottom left, 17, 148 top, bottom right, 149	Three Lions, Inc.
236 right	Leon Trice—Texaco Inc.
241d	Tuloma Gas Products Co.
180 first row center right	United States Army
115	United States Bureau of Entomology and Plant Quarantine
7 top left	United States Bureau of Indian Affairs
151, 197b top left	United States Department of Agriculture
177 top right	University of Pennsylvania
171 right	University of Pittsburgh
80 bottom, 141	UPI
180 second row center, bottom right	The White House Historical Association
15, 20 top, 89, 142, 142a, 180 first row left, 246 bottom, 259d	Wide World
256 top	Ace Williams—Black Star
101	Woltz Aerial Photo Service, Inc.

Volume 19—Phill-Pytho

264	Alinari
482	J.C. Allen & Sons
478 bottom	American House
513 bottom	American Museum of Natural History
325 first row center, right, third row	American Pigeon Journal
470 bottom, 471, 472, 474	The Art Institute of Chicago
463, 464 top	Australian News and Information Bureau
307	Bell Telephone Laboratories, Inc.
302, 303, 306, 308 center left, center right, right, 397, 401, 531 bottom left	Bettmann Archive
392 bottom	Bolens Products Division, Food Machinery & Chemical Corp.
455 bottom	Fred Bond
395, 396 bottom	Boston Photo News Co.
430a bottom right	British Information Service
369	Brookhaven National Laboratory
334, 341, 344 right, 436 top, 531 top	Brown Brothers
363b top left	L.W. Brownell
354	California Institute of Technology
505c top, 506	California Institution for Men
476	Chicago Park District
424, 425, 426, 427, 428 top, 429 bottom, 430	Chicago Police Department
346	A. Church—Commercial, Industrial Photographers, Inc.
528 top	Commonwealth of Puerto Rico
270 top, 271, 272, 274 bottom, 342a, 342b, 345b, 352, 358, 359, 360, 361, 363, 363a top, 363b top right, 363c, 363d, 364, 370, 371, 373, 374 center, right, 377, 378, 385, 398 top left, 399, 414, 417, 436 bottom, 439, 441d, 443, 447, 455 top, 457b, 463a, 466, 467 top left, 468, 497b top, 503, 515, 517, 530a, 530b, 533	Compton's Encyclopedia
511 bottom	Allan D. Cruickshank—National Audubon Society
276, 277, 278, 500, 501, 502	R.R. Donnelley and Sons Co.
441c	D.P.A. from Pictorial Parade
368	Du Pont Magazine
418 bottom	Eastman Kodak Co.
454, 456, 457 right	H.N. Elfenbaum—Artstreet
531 bottom right	Paul J. Fair
487, 488, 489, 490, 491	Carroll Lane Fenton
457 left	FPG
464 bottom left	French Embassy
363a bottom right, 437, 442, 527, 528 bottom, 530 bottom	Ewing Galloway
301	General Electric Co.
504	German Tourist Information Office
409 left	Gottscho-Schleisner, Inc.
479	Haeger Potteries, Inc.
537, 538	Sue Hastings
329	Hawaiian Pineapple Co.
441g, 465	Historical Pictures Service, Chicago
363a bottom center, 363b bottom left	Hendricks Hodge
328, 410	R.B. Hough
521, 522	Houghton Mifflin Co.
505, 505c bottom	Illinois State Penitentiary
429 top	Indiana State Police Department
467 bottom	International Harvester
400, 409 right, 411, 510 top	James Press
409 center	Henry B. Kane
420 bottom	Keystone Press Agency, Inc.
469, 470 top	Laurentz Knoff Collection
536	Kukla, Fran and Ollie
478 top	Homer Laughlin China Co.
523	Life © Time Inc.
356	J. Horace McFarland
513 top	Kenneth McVey
331	Mrs. Gari Melchers
475, 542	Metropolitan Museum of Art
274 top	Ronald Miller
441e	Masao Minagawa
332, 336, 337	Montpelier National Life Insurance Co.
340	John Morell & Co.
362	Josef Muench
440	Hans Namuth
344 bottom, 410 bottom	National Audubon Society
363f left	National Film Board of Canada
365	National Geographic Society
335a, 339	Nebraska State Historical Society
464 bottom right	New York Times
391, 392 top, center	Oliver Corp.
398 top center	Parker-Schwan Co.
441b	Photo Researchers, Inc.
363f right	Hustace H. Poor—National Audubon Society

477	Popular Science Monthly
497b bottom, 497c top	Prince Edward Island Travel Bureau
357, 512 center left	Publix Pictorial Service Corp.
343, 441a bottom	H. Armstrong Roberts
441a top	Martin Schneider—Life © Time Inc.
441h	Paul Schutt—Oak Brook Polo Club
372, 375 right	Science Service, Inc.
393	Small Homes Council—University of Illinois
507	Sovfoto
363a bottom left, 363b bottom right, 374 left, 408	Hugh Spencer
376	Standard Oil Co.
383	Tennessee Eastman Co.
430a top left, bottom left, 511 top, 512 top, bottom, 420	Three Lions, Inc.
335b	Union Pacific Railroad Historical Museum
325 second row	United States Army Signal Corps
366, 367, 375 left, 467 top right, 481	United States Department of Agriculture
505b bottom	United States Department of Justice
423 top	United States Navy
459, 460, 460a, 460c, 460d, 461, 462	United States Postal Service
348	University of Notre Dame
305, 308 left, 325 first row left, 347, 394, 423 bottom, 441, 505b top	UPI
333	A.R. Waud
526b	Rie Gaddis Wehrmann
342	Wichita City Library
273, 349, 396 top, 418 top, 526, 526c	Wide World

Volume 20—Q-Rye

311, 315 top	American Carpet Institute
96, 152, 158, 178, 245	American Museum of Natural History
117, 118, 119	American Red Cross
17 right, 143, 144, 148, 175, 237, 240, 243 top bottom left, bottom center, 298, 299b top	The Art Institute of Chicago
74, 75, 76 bottom, 79 top right, bottom, 80, 82 top, center, 83 top, 84, 86 top	Association of American Railroads
236 left	Ray Atkeson
328, 332b bottom, 332e top, 353, 354	Bernadine Bailey
90, 114, 134 top, 248, 289 bottom right, 366b left	Bettmann Archive
315 bottom	Bigelow-Sanford, inc.
208	Black Star
43, 202	British Information Services
115, 133 bottom, 134 bottom, 230, 236 right, 281 top, 283, 289 top bottom left, 299b bottom	Brown Brothers
310, 351	Camera Clix, Inc.
62 bottom	Central Scientific Co.
24 bottom	Lynwood M. Chace
288	Chicago Tribune
234, 235 bottom	Colorado State Advertising and Publicity Department
9a, 14, 26, 30, 31, 32 right, 33, 35, 37, 38, 39, 40, 41, 44 center, bottom, 45 bottom, 46 bottom, 47 bottom, 50, 51, 53, 56, 57, 58, 59, 60, 61, 62 top, 63 right, 65, 67, 68, 78, 89, 126, 136 top, 137, 140, 141, 142, 151d, 181, 185, 209, 210, 219, 220, 221, 229, 229a, 229b, 231, 232, 234a, 234b, 235 top, 242, 250–51, 266 top, 267, 281 bottom, 286, 287, 312, 313, 322, 323, 325, 333 left, bottom, 334, 334a, 334b, 334d, 334e, 334f, 335, 336, 337, 338, 339, 340, 362, 366b right	Compton's Encyclopedia
212	Conleurs du Monde
169	Cronhardt and Son
161 top, 319	Culver Pictures
170	Curtis & Cameron, Inc.
332c right	Charles Phelps Cushing
17 left, center	Edison Electric Institute
300, 332g bottom	European Picture Service
180	Fairchild Aerial Surveys, Inc.
154 bottom	Mildred Adams Fenton
153, 154 top, 155, 156, 157	Field Museum of Natural History
306 bottom, 307 top	Firestone Tire & Rubber Co.
190 top left	Giovanni Folcarelli
330 top, 332e bottom	FPG
86 bottom right	French National Railroads
24 top, 25, 249, 253 bottom right, 254 top, 258, 284	Ewing Galloway
303 left, center	Philip D. Gendreau
94, 95	John H. Gerard
163	Ginn & Co.
304, 305, 306 top, 307 bottom, 308 top, 309 bottom	Goodyear News Service
190 bottom right	Gorham Corp.
295 top, center, bottom left	Gottscho-Schleisner, Inc.
173, 241, 247	Gramstorff Brothers
188 bottom right	Greater Providence Chamber of Commerce
282	Harvard University Press
70 top, 113, 203	Historical Pictures Service, Chicago
331 bottom	Frank Holzman
332g top, 332h	House of Photography
72	Illinois Central Railroad Co.
98	Industrial Rayon Corp.
93, 253 top right	Italian State Tourist Office
22, 159, 164, 166, 167, 290, 364	James Press
49 bottom	Jensen Manufacturing Co.
314	James Lees and Sons Co.
116	Library of Congress
295 bottom, center, right	J. Horace McFarland
147, 243 center, bottom right	W.A. Mansell & Co.
190 third row left	Museum of Art, Rhode Island School of Design
161 bottom	National Archives
21, 71, 97, 176	National Audubon Society
302, 308 bottom	Natural Rubber Bureau
122	Newark Public Library
224	Newberry Library
214 right	New Jersey Turnpike Authority
360b top right	New York Times
190 third row right	Old Slater Mill Museum
83 center	Pennsylvania Railroad
277, 278, 279	Press Associates
253 top left	Publisher's Photo Service
294, 296	Publix Pictorial Service Corp.
9b, 9d	Quebec Department of Tourism
324 left	Ran Studio
187 top left, top right, 188 top left, top right, center left, bottom left, 189, 190 first row center, right, third row center, fourth row center	Rhode Island Development Council
190 second row right, fourth row left	Rhode Island Historical Society
200	H. Armstrong Roberts
300a	Royal Canadian Mounted Police
317	Rumanian Embassy
73 top, 136 bottom	Santa Fe Railway
42	Science Service, Inc.
151c	Dr. Landrum B. Shettles
320, 324 right, 329, 330 bottom, 332f, 334c, 355, 356, 359, 360, 360a, 360b top left, bottom	Sovfoto
228	Standard Oil Co. (N.J.)
123, 133 top	Three Lions, Inc.
162, 168, 171, 174	Underwood & Underwood
76 top, 82 bottom	Union Pacific Railroad
29 top right, 32 left	United States Air Force
46 top, 49 top, center left	United States Army
214 left, 218 top	United States Bureau of Public Roads
291, 363	United States Department of Agriculture
266 bottom	United States Housing Authority
29 top left, 52 top left, 172, 187 bottom, 269	United States Navy
309 top	United States Rubber Co.
187 center left	University of Rhode Island
70 bottom, 83 bottom, 253 bottom left, 271, 274, 276, 326 right, 365	UPI
52 bottom	Paul Weller
44 top, 49 center right, 55 left, 64, 252, 255 top, 268, 270, 272, 273, 275, 285, 303 right, 332b top, 332c left	Wide World
129	H.W. Wilson Co.

Volume 21—S-Sound

84 bottom right	American Artist Magazine
226a top	American Museum of Natural History
137, 138, 139	American National Theatre and Academy
58	Armour Research Foundation
79 top left, 83 left, 84 top, bottom left, 85, 86, 87, 88 left, 89 bottom, 90 top, 114, 201 top right, 246	The Art Institute of Chicago
69	Authenticated News International
210a	Berko Studio
150, 151	Ruth Bernhard
171 top	Bethlehem Steel Corp.
54 left, 56 left, 75, 108a left, 115 bottom right, 140 center right, 183, 184 top	Bettmann Archive
28 left, 98, 187 right	Black Star
177d	Boatmen's National Bank of St. Louis
196	Bradford-LaRiviere, Inc.
66, 79 bottom center, 132 top	British Information Services
45 bottom, 49, 52d left, 54 right, 55, 72 top, 108a top, 115 bottom left, 116, 117, 145, 184 bottom	Brown Brothers
25 bottom, 222 bottom	L.W. Brownell
96	Camera Clix, Inc.

31 right	Caterpillar Tractor Co.
226d bottom right	Lynwood M. Chace
72 bottom	Chicago Public Library
59a	Cities Service Oil Co.
15 top, 19 bottom, 20, 27, 30, 36, 41a, 41b, 49c, 57a, 57b, 57d, 57e, 57f, 57g, 57h, 57i, 57j, 58a, 58b, 58c, 58d, 67, 73, 103a, 103b, 106, 107, 153, 166, 170, 176, 194, 194a bottom, 194b, 195, 197 top, 206, 209, 211, 248, 252, 254, 254a left, 254b, 254c top right, 254d bottom, 259, 260, 261, 262	Compton's Encyclopedia
89 top	Corcoran Gallery of Art
226 second row left	Allan D. Cruickshank—National Audubon Society
177e top	Culver Pictures
210	Denoyer-Geppert Co.
226d top left	Jack Dermid—National Audubon Society
102	A. Devaney, Inc.
177b	Doremus & Co.
59d	E.I. du Pont de Nemours & Co., Inc.
226b bottom	Encyclopædia Britannica Films
52d right, 57c, 144, 226d top right	Field Museum of Natural History
134, 135, 136	Folger Shakespeare Library
16a top	France Actuelle
15 bottom, 79 top right, 83 right, 115 top, 198 top, 200 top left, 204	Ewing Galloway
74, 197 bottom center right	Philip D. Gendreau
223, 224 top, fourth row, 225 top, center left, bottom right, 226 first row, bottom left, 226c	John H. Gerard
220 right	Harris & Ewing
97	Lilo Hess—Globe Photos
177c	Historical Pictures Service, Chicago
104, 147 bottom right, 208 bottom, 222 top	James Press
177f	T.A. Jeffries
9 bottom right	Jones & Laughlin Steel Corp.
28 right, 199 bottom, 200 top right, bottom	Keystone Press Agency, Inc.
224 second row, third row left, 225 center right, bottom left, 226 second row right, third row	Cy La Tour
52	Lowell Observatory
224 third row right	John Markham
213	Metro-Goldwyn-Mayer, Inc.
79 bottom left, bottom right, 88 right, 201 top left, bottom	Metropolitan Museum of Art
187 top left	Miami Seaquarium
25 top	Charles Mohr
163	Moran Towing & Transportation Co., Inc.
31 left	Morton Salt Co.
195a	Motorola, Inc.
90 bottom	Museum of Modern Art
39, 186	National Audubon Society
140 center left, 141 bottom	National Broadcasting Co.
9 center left, bottom left, 10, 11	National Safety Council
140 right, 141 top	National Screen Service Corp.
9 top	National Society for Crippled Children and Adults
132 bottom	Newberry Library
46 bottom	New Mexico State Tourist Bureau
191	New York Times
100, 226b top, 226d bottom left	New York Zoological Society
59b	Parke, Davis & Co.
99 bottom	Clifford C. Pepper—FPG
217	Pickett & Eckel, Inc.
70 top	Pix, Inc.
192b	Publix Pictorial Service Corp.
70 bottom, 71 right, 177h	Radio Times Hulton Picture Library
112	Redwood Empire Association
249	Dr. George T. Renner—Teachers College, Columbia University
99 top	Revillon Frères
229	H. Armstrong Roberts
77	Rodin Museum
23	St. Paul Area Chamber of Commerce
41	San Francisco Chamber of Commerce
46 top left	Santa Claus (Ind.) Post Office
197 bottom left	James Sawders
197 bottom right	Science Service, Inc.
188 top, 189 bottom, 190	Sovfoto
228	Student Magazine
210b left	Sun Valley News Bureau
16a right, 68, 192	Three Lions, Inc.
164, 165	Edwin Tunis—World Publishing Co.
210b right	Union Pacific Railroad
193 bottom	United States Army
146 bottom, 147 top, bottom left, 151	United States Department of Agriculture
169	United States Lines, Inc.
174, 175	United States Maritime Commission
177g	United States Naval Academy Museum
193 top, 194a top	United States Navy
198 bottom, 199 top, center	United States Testing Co., Inc.
82	University Museum (Pennsylvania)
250	University of Nebraska
56 right, 140 left, 171 bottom, 197 bottom center left, 234	UPI
226a bottom	Walker Van Riper—Denver Museum of Natural History
57, 61h top, top center, bottom, 71 left, 218	Wide World

Volume 22—South-Syrin

438 top (inset)	Allis-Chalmers Manufacturing Co.
386 top, 390 bottom, 400 top right	American Museum of Natural History
379, 381 top	American Spice Trade Association
540 bottom	Toni Angermayer—Photo Researchers
438 top	Association of American Railroads
519	Australian Tourist Commission
549	Authenticated News International
359 top	Bernadine Bailey—Artstreet
416, 417, 418, 419, 420, 421, 422, 423	Robert H. Baker
409 right	Ralph Berry—New York Herald-Tribune
292	Bettmann Archive
353 top, 356, 360 bottom, 383 bottom right	Black Star
358 bottom	C.J. Brown
364, 365 top, 443, 511	Brown Brothers
383 bottom left	L.W. Brownell
393	Ralph Buchsbaum
538 top, 539, 544a bottom	Camera Press—Pix from Publix
355, 544	Henri Cartier-Bresson—Magnum
351, 352 top	J. Allan Cash—Rapho-Guillumette
316 bottom right	Leo Castelli
316 third row left	Charleston Library
313 top left, 314 left	Charleston Trident Chamber of Commerce
530	Chicago Public Library
264, 270, 271, 272, 274 top, 281d, 293, 294, 295, 296, 307, 311, 323, 327, 346d–e, 349, 350, 362, 371, 372, 374, 389, 391, 395 top, 396, 413, 414, 415, 429b, 429c, 438 bottom, 439, 440, 441, 442 top, 444, 454, 457, 458, 504, 524, 528, 533, 534, 537, 545, 546, 549a	Compton's Encyclopedia
399 bottom	Allan D. Cruickshank—National Audubon Society
485 top left, top right	Culver Pictures
365a right	E.P. Dutton & Co., Inc.
316 second row center right	Elektra Records
455	European Picture Service
427	Florists Transworld Delivery
304, 360 top, 394 bottom right, 509	Ewing Galloway
276 top, 277, 281b center, 281c, 284 bottom left, 289 left	Philip D. Gendreau
495b top, 497, 499 bottom, 500 top left, bottom	General Dynamics Corp.
341c right	Mrs. Robert H. Goddard
538 bottom	Louis Goldman—Rapho-Guillumette
407, 408, 409 bottom	Charles Hahn
412	Hale Observatories
406 right	H.R. Harmer, Inc.
348b	Hawker Siddeley Dynamics Ltd.
425 left	John Hendry, Jr.—National Audubon Society
354 bottom, 540 top	Fritz Henle—Photo Researchers
425 right	Robert C. Hermes
365 bottom, 365b	Hispanic Society of America
316 top left, first row left, center left, right, second row center left, third row center left, right, 341a bottom, 341c left	Historical Pictures Service, Chicago
331 center right	Homestake Mining Co.
521 bottom	Paul Hosmer
398	R.B. Hough
369, 381 bottom, 384, 385, 386 bottom, 390 top, 424, 483, 531, 532	James Press
352 bottom	Stig T. Karlsson—Black Star
406 left	E.H. Kehr
365a left	Alfred A. Knopf, Inc.
288 bottom	Lockwood Greene Engineers, Inc.
446	W.A. Mansell & Co.
303	Mart Studios, Inc.
331 top	John Morell & Co.
338, 339	Josef Muench
341, 341d, 342, 342a, 342c, 342d, 343, 343a, 346a right, 346c, 348a, 348c	NASA
368, 400 top left, bottom, 521 top	National Audubon Society
340 left	National Soybean Crop Improvement Council
451, 453	New York Stock Exchange
459	Pacific and Atlantic Photos, Inc.
268, 289 right	Panagra
274 bottom, 276 bottom, 284 bottom right, 290	Pan American Union
505	Pan-Pacific Press Bureau

359 bottom	Paul Pietzsch—Black Star
281b top	Pix, Inc.
399 top	Publix Pictorial Service Corp.
354 top, 358 top	Rapho-Guillumette
536, 543	H. Armstrong Roberts
383 top	Kosti Ruohornaa—Black Star
365a center	Charles Scribner's Sons
266	South Africa Government Information Office
267	South African Tourist Corp.
313 top right, bottom, 314 center right, top right, bottom, 315 top, center left, bottom	South Carolina Department of Parks, Recreation, and Tourism
324, 329 top left, bottom, 330, 331 center left, bottom	South Dakota Department of Highways
332 first row, second row, third row center	South Dakota State Historical Society
346	Sovfoto
452	Alfred Statler
315 center right	J.P. Stevens & Co., Inc.
380	William Strange Co.
506 top, 507, 508	Sugar Research Foundation, Inc.
523, 526	Swedish Information Center
544a top	Swiss National Tourist Office
382	Edwin Way Teale
280, 282 bottom, 283 bottom, 285, 287 bottom	United Nations
316 first row center right	United States Army
431	United States Bureau of the Census
340 right	United States Department of Agriculture
332 bottom right	United States Marine Corps
495b bottom, 498 bottom	United States Navy
316 second row left, right	United States Senate
332 bottom left	University of California
329 top right	University of South Dakota
406 center, 429a, 517, 518a center, center right	UPI
341a top	William Vandenvert
273 center	R. Van Nostrand—National Audubon Society
387, 388	Walker Van Riper
352 bottom	Michael Wagensinger
500 top right	Fred Ward—Black Star
269, 273 left, right, 275, 279, 281, 281a bottom, 282 top, 283 top, 286, 287 top, 288 top	Charles Perry Weimer
316 third row center right, 345, 346a left, 394 bottom left, 429d, 442 bottom, 484 top, 485 bottom, 518a left, top right, bottom right, 547	Wide World
394 top	Douglas P. Wilson, Marine Biological Laboratory

Volume 23—T-Tyrol

225 right	Aluminum Co. of America
120 right	Amarillo Chamber of Commerce
51, 52	American Dental Association
278 second row left, third row left, 279 second row center, third row left, center, 280 second row left, center, third row left, center, 281 second row center, right, third row center	American Forest Institute
142 top, bottom	The Art Institute of Chicago
7, 8 bottom, 156, 157 bottom, 158	Bettmann Archive
9, 42	Brown Brothers
278 first row left, right, 279 first row left, center, 280 first row, 281 first row center, right, second row left	L.W. Brownell
128 bottom	Dallas Chamber of Commerce
219 left, 220 left, 211 left, 222 left, 223, 224 left, bottom	DoALL Co.
120 left	Freeport Sulphur Co.
121 bottom	Ewing Galloway
142 center	Philip D. Gendreau
160 bottom	Graphic House, Inc.
144 left	Halliday Historic Photo Co.
6	Harris & Ewing
159 top	Squire Haskins
121 top	Fritz Henle
143 top, bottom center, 145	Historical Pictures Service, Chicago
129 top left, center, bottom left	Houston Chamber of Commerce
157 top	Italian State Tourist Office
91 bottom	Memphis Chamber of Commerce
26, 143 bottom left, right, 144 right	Metropolitan Museum of Art
159 bottom	Dr. Richard Moody—Indiana University
224 right, 225 top left	National Machine Tool Builders Association
282	Mrs. Walter E. Rogers
86, 91 top right, 92 top right, 93 right	Tennessee Department of Conservation
92 left, bottom right, 93 left	Tennessee Department of State Parks
128 top left, right, 129 top right, bottom right, 130 top right, center left, bottom right	Texas Highway Department
130 top left, bottom left	Texas Parks and Wildlife Department
278 first row center, second row center, right, third row center, right, 279 first row right, second row left, right, third row right, 280 second row right, third row right, 281 first row left, third row left, right	United States Forest Service
91 top left	University of Tennessee
295, 296, 299 top right, 334	UPI
155, 160 top	Vandamm Studio
195	Frederick Warne & Co., Inc.
298, 299 top left, bottom	Wide World

Volume 24—U-Vult

354, 356, 357	Abbott Laboratories
378, 379	American Museum of Natural History
341 top left	American Tobacco Co.
266, 271 right, 325 bottom	The Art Institute of Chicago
342 bottom left	Associated Publishers, Inc.
91, 97 bottom	Ray Atkeson—Publix
12 bottom	Australian News and Information Bureau
293 top left	Bennington Museum
15 left, 175, 178, 183, 186 left, 260, 282, 326, 385 right	Bettmann Archive
65 top, 107 top right, 280 top	Black Star
34, 77, 82, 92	Fred Bond
84 top	Jack Breed—FPG
17, 19	British Information Services
184 top	Brown Brothers
238 top	Esther Bubley
93 bottom right, 95 top, bottom left	Amos Burg
293 center left	Burlington-Lake Champlain Chamber of Commerce
13 bottom	Canadian Department of National Defence
16	Central Press Photos, Ltd.
262 first row center (inset)	Chase Manhattan Bank Money Museum
327 top	Chicago Symphony Orchestra
226 first row left	Church of Jesus Christ of Latter-Day Saints
296 first row left	Columbia University
52 bottom	Combustion Engineering, Inc.
8-9, 10, 11, 13 top, 21, 31 bottom, 36, 37, 43 top, 47 bottom, 49 top, 53 bottom, 54 bottom, 56 top, 60 bottom, 68 top, 72 top, 73 top, 75 top, 78 top, 83 top, 84 bottom, 86 top, 93 top, 97 top, 101, 104, 105, 106, 107 bottom, 115 top left, center, 116, 117, 119, 120, 122, 124, 125, 126, 127, 128, 130, 131, 167, 168, 176, 177, 180 top, 192 top, 214, 217, 221, 257, 258 top, 259 bottom, 262, 264, 265, 267, 269, 275, 286, 291, 321, 330, 331, 337, 377	Compton's Encyclopedia
47 top	Connecticut Development Commission
46 bottom	Crocker-Burbank Papers, Inc.
287 bottom	Curtis Publishing Co.
396 first row right	Deere & Co.
292 top left, third row left	Deseret News Publishing Co.
45 bottom	A. Devaney, Inc.
226 second row right	E.P. Dutton & Co.
270	Felici
43 bottom, 79 bottom, 89 bottom right, 145, 209 bottom, 245 right, 287 top, 327 bottom left	Ewing Galloway
45 top, 57 top	Globe Photos, Inc.
304	Gramstorff Brothers
288 bottom, 289	Greater Vermont Association
79 top	Great Northern Railway
109	Gulfgate Shopping City
98 bottom right	Hawaiian Pineapple Co.
99	Hawaii Visitors Bureau
296 second row right, third row right	Historical Pictures Service, Chicago
141	Historical Society of Pennsylvania
226 third row right	Houghton Mifflin Co.
318 left, 319	International Cooperation Administration
279, 325 top	Italian State Tourist Office
305	James Press
335 bottom	Jamestown Foundation
288 top	Jones & Lamson Machine Co.
89 bottom left	Kaiser Aluminum & Chemical Corp.
86 bottom	Kaiser Steel Corp.
327 bottom left, bottom right	Kay Musical Instrument Co.
280 bottom	Leon Keinigsberg
254	John Mather Lipton Co.
107 top left	Lukens Steel Co.
278 bottom	W.A. Mansell & Co.
73 bottom	Michigan Tourist Council
95 bottom right, 238 bottom, 239 bottom, 385 left	Monkmeyer Press

65 bottom	Monsanto Chemical Co.
31 top, 35, 218 bottom	Josef Muench
52 top	National Coal Association
340 right, 341 top right, center left, bottom left	National Park Service
61	New Orleans Times-Picayune
339 center left, bottom	Norfolk Tour Information Bureau
98 bottom left	Pan American World Airways, Inc.
353 right	Charles Pfizer & Co., Inc.
268, 271 left	Pix, Inc.
55	Power Authority of the State of New York
57 bottom, 66	Publix Pictorial Service Corp.
342 first row center left	Random House
69	William M. Rittase
12 top, 237	H. Armstrong Roberts
353 left	Dr. R.Q. Robinson
294 top left	Rock of Ages Corp.
327 top center	Scherl & Roth Inc.
295 top, center	Shelburne Museum
28 right, 93 bottom left	Shostal
241	Anne Shriber
3, 15 center, right, 383	Sovfoto
83 bottom	Standard Oil Co.
30, 75 right, 239 top	Standard Oil Co. (N.J.)
139	State Historical Society of Wisconsin
46 top	John Swenson Granite Co., Inc.
384	TASS
64	Tennessee Valley Authority
317, 318 bottom right, 381	Three Lions, Inc.
22, 23, 296 top left	United Nations
5 right, 6 bottom left	United States Air Force
5 left	United States Army
60 top	United States Army Corps of Engineers
75 bottom left	United States Bureau of Reclamation
226 first row right	United States Department of the Treasury
5 center, 6 top, bottom right	United States Navy
206 bottom	University of Chicago
206 top	University of Illinois at Chicago Circle
204	University of Montana
223 center	University of Utah
293 bottom right	University of Vermont
296 first row center	University of Vermont Extension Service
339 top left	University of Virginia
189 top, 192 bottom, 193, 259 top, 322, 323 bottom, 380	UPI
218 top, 219	Utah Department of Publicity and Industrial Development
226 first row center, second row left, center, third row center	Utah State Historical Society
223 top, bottom, 224, 225	Utah Travel Council
258 bottom	Vanadium Corp. of America
293 top right, 294 top right, center, bottom, 295 bottom	Vermont Development Department
296 second row left, center, third row left, center left	Vermont Historical Society
245 left	Frank Verticchio
333 top	Virginia State Chamber of Commerce
333 bottom, 335 top	Virginia Department of Conservation and Economic Development
342 top left, first row left, second row left, third row right, fourth row center left, center right, right	Virginia State Library
339 top right, 340 top left, bottom left, 341 bottom right	Virginia State Travel Service
38	Bradford Washburn
53 top	Todd Webb—Camera Clix
4 left	Westinghouse Electric Corp.
342 first row center right, right, second row center right, third row center left, center right	The White House Historical Association
4 right, 143, 186 right, 189 bottom, 278 top, 323 top	Wide World
296 third row center right	Yerkes Observatory

Volume 25—W-Zwor

87	Arizona Photographic Associates, Inc.
36 top, 38 left	The Art Institute of Chicago
39, 205, 207	Bettmann Archive
59 center left	Boeing Co.
325 bottom, 340 top	British Combine, Ltd.
327 bottom, 335 bottom, 339 left, 340 bottom	British Information Services
38 right, 41, 42, 213, 216 bottom	Brown Brothers
370 bottom	Carnegie Institution of Washington
313 top right, bottom	Chicago Public Library
464 top left	European Picture Service
46, 464 bottom	Ewing Galloway
241	Bob Glaze—Artstreet
259 bottom left	S.C. Johnson & Son, Inc.
313 top left	Keystone Press Agency, Inc.
461, 462 bottom, 464 top right	Lincoln Park Zoo
257 bottom right, 258 top left	Metropolitan Milwaukee Association of Commerce
257 bottom left	Buck Miller—Third Coast Stock Source
377, 378	Monkmeyer Press
37	National Park Service
457, 465 top	New York Zoological Society
96	Niagara Falls Convention & Visitors Service
324 left	Pix, Inc.
95, 97, 103	Publix Pictorial Service Corp.
459, 465 bottom	San Diego Zoo
57 center, bottom	Seattle Chamber of Commerce
98	Three Lions, Inc.
306, 308 top left, 312 top, 320 bottom, 321	Underwood & Underwood
329 bottom	United States Air Force
336 top	United States Army
309 bottom, 310	United States Army Signal Corps
104 right	United States Bureau of Reclamation
347 top	United States Coast Guard
308 top right, 309 top, 312 bottom, 319	United States Department of Defense
345 bottom	United States Marine Corps
328, 344 left, 354	United States Navy
332 bottom	United States Office for Emergency Management
57 top right	University of Washington
257 top left	University of Wisconsin
393 bottom left	University of Wyoming
216 top, 243, 324 right, 326 bottom, 334 bottom, 336 bottom, 338, 339 right, 341, 342, 343, 344 right, 345 top, 346, 347 bottom, 358, 359	UPI
59 top right	Washington Apple Commission
57 top left, 58 top left, top right, bottom right, 59 top left, bottom	Washington State Department of Commerce and Economic Development
58 center right, bottom left, 59 center right	Washington State Parks and Recreation Commission
168, 173 top right, bottom, 174, 175	West Virgina Department of Commerce
173 top left	West Virginia University
320 top, 325 top, 326 top, 283 top, 462 top	Wide World
257 top right, 258 top right, center left, bottom left, bottom right, 259 top, center, bottom right	Wisconsin Department of Natural Resources
393 top, center, bottom right, 394, 395	Wyoming Travel Commission

The publishers also wish to acknowledge the courtesy of those who have given special permission for the use of copyrighted text and picture matter, as follows.

A.S. Barnes and Co., Inc., for adaptation of drawings from 'The Outdoor Encyclopedia' T-110.

Doubleday & Co., Inc., for poem 'As toilsome I wandered Virginia's woods' from 'Leaves of Grass', by Walt Whitman P-407; for reproduction of color drawings from 'The Insect Guide', by Ralph B. Swain I-213–16.

Harcourt Brace Jovanovich, Inc., for poem 'The Song of the Jellicles' from 'Old Possum's Book of Practical Cats', by T.S. Eliot (© 1939 T.S. Eliot, © 1967 Esme Valerie Eliot) C-201.

Harper & Brothers, for basic material from chart page 89 of 'Oil for the World', by Schackne and Drake (© 1960) P-241.

Henry Holt & Co., Inc., for poem 'The Cherry Tree' from 'A Shropshire Lad', by A.E. Housman P-405.

Houghton Mifflin Co., for poem 'The Sonnet', by R.W. Gilder P-406.

Jeppesen & Co., for adaptations and reproductions of illustrations from 'Marine Navigation', by P.V.H. Weems and C.V. Lee (© 1958) N-69–71.

Macmillan Co., for reproduction of line drawing of a trip lever from 'Technical Drawing', by Henry C. Spencer (© 1952) M-261.

Parke-Davis & Co., for reproduction of painting by Robert A. Thom from 'A History of Pharmacy in Pictures', by George A. Bender P-248b.

Public Building Commission of Chicago (© 1967), for reproduction of photograph by Ezra Stoller Associates, Inc., of Picasso statue in Chicago Civic Center I-45.

Arthur H. Robinson, for Robinson Projection specially prepared by Donnelley Cartographic Services (© 1973 by Compton's Encyclopedia) C-498, 499, 501, 502, T-258–59, W-118.

Wolgensinger, Michael, © Europa Verlag Zürich, for reproduction of photograph of sheep grazing S-353.